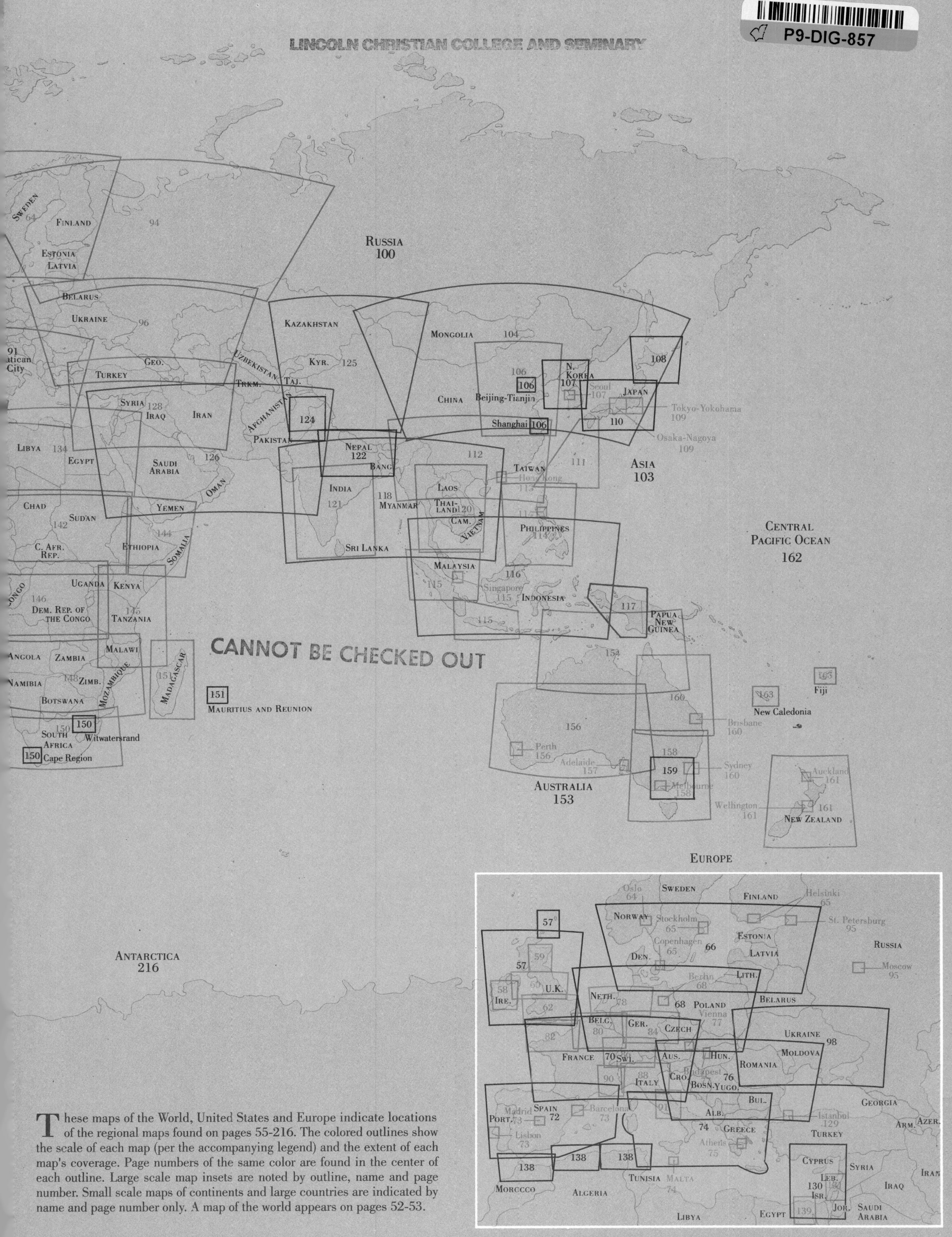

CANNOT BE CHECKED OUT

These maps of the World, United States and Europe indicate locations of the regional maps found on pages 55-216. The colored outlines show the scale of each map (per the accompanying legend) and the extent of each map's coverage. Page numbers of the same color are found in the center of each outline. Large scale map insets are noted by outline, name and page number. Small scale maps of continents and large countries are indicated by name and page number only. A map of the world appears on pages 52-53.

HAMMOND

World
Atlas

HAMMOND
World

Atlas

HAMMOND World Atlas Corporation
Mapmakers for the 21st Century

Hammond World Atlas

THIRD EDITION

LIBRARY OF CONGRESS
CATALOGING-IN-PUBLICATION DATA

Hammond World Atlas Corporation.
  Hammond world atlas. - 3rd ed.
    p. cm.
  Rev. ed. of:
  Hammond atlas of the world/Hammond Incorporated.
  Copyright 2000 by Hammond World Atlas Corporation.
Includes gazetteer and indexes.
  ISBN 0-8437-1352-6
  1. Atlases. I. Hammond Incorporated. Hammond
atlas of the world II. Title.
  G1021. H2665   1999 <G&M>
  912--dc21   99-28545
                                        CIP
                                        MAPS

Introduction

Four generations ago, Caleb Stillson Hammond believed he could produce a better map. So, in 1900, the visionary young man founded the company that still bears his name.

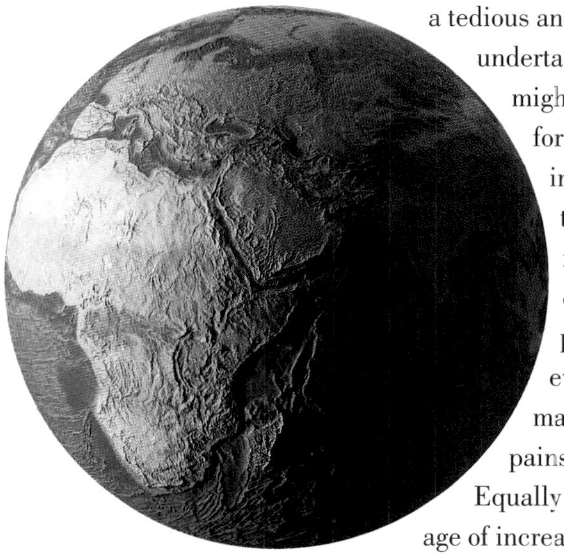

The world has changed dramatically since Caleb's time. But the mechanical process of making maps by hand has changed very little. Traditional map-making remains a tedious and expensive undertaking; a single map might require more than forty separate layers of information. And though maps must now be revised constantly to keep pace with world events, updating maps is still a painstaking effort. Equally important, in this age of increasing graphic sophistication, there is a renewed appreciation for maps as art, and a pressing need for a contemporary atlas design that presents geographic information in a more accessible, and dynamic fashion.

In 1992, the company saw an opportunity to create such an atlas and launched the *Hammond Atlas of the World*. But the world has not stood still, and advances in our own technology have put within our grasp the means of producing more informative and accurate mapping than ever before. In 1998, the *Hammond Atlas of the World, Second Edition*, featured for the first time dramatic satellite imaging and a comprehensive collection of digital mapping, incorporating shaded hypsometric tints for land elevations and bathymetric tints to depict ocean depths.

Now, in our third edition, revised for the year 2000, we have included a section of new digital shaded relief maps of the continents and major world regions. Computer simulation, using the best available digital elevation data, serve to create a dramatic, naturalistic portrait of land and the ocean floor.

At the heart of this superb new edition is a computerized geographic database, that enables maps to be created and changed at a moment's notice. This computerized format lends itself perfectly to the adaptation of this atlas to electronic media, and so we have launched a digital *Hammond World Atlas CD-ROM*. This electronic atlas utilizes state-of-the-art cartographic tools to enable the user to customize and visualize geographic information as never before.

We are particularly grateful for the support of our many contributors, whose efforts made this volume better. In particular, we wish to thank Mitchell Feigenbaum, a brilliant scientist and close collaborator, whose illumination of the world around him extends to the art — and science — of cartography. His genius is ever-present in this atlas, from his revolutionary map projection to his pioneering software, which was crucial to the success of our computer mapping system.

At last, a map-making system that moves as fast as the world is changing. As new technology continues to redefine what is possible, we will continue to push the envelope, to pioneer a better way. We are committed to maintaining the highest level of quality — in accuracy and timeliness, in design and printing, and in service to our customers. It is our goal to ensure that you can always turn to Hammond World Atlas Corporation for the very best in map and atlas design and geographic information.

As many ancient explorers and modern day armchair travellers have discovered, maps are powerful tools for achieving some control and understanding of their surroundings. Nearly one hundred years after Caleb Hammond started the company, we hope that we have come closer to realizing his simple and profound vision: to make the best maps in the world.

We think he would be proud.

The Publisher

Contents

Interpreting Maps

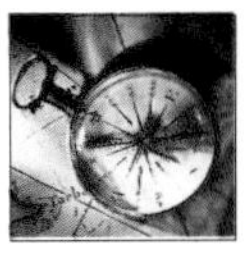

Designed to enhance your knowledge and enjoyment of maps, these pages explore map making throughout history, from ancient times to modern. They explain map scales and projections, describe how to locate information quickly, and show you how to weave together the sections of this atlas to gain a more dynamic world view.

Quick Reference Guide

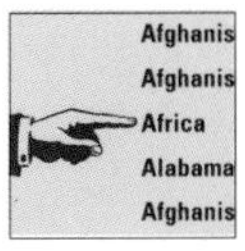

The world at your fingertips: a concise, completely current alphabetical listing of the world's continents, countries, states, provinces and territories, with the size, population and capital of each. Page numbers and reference keys for each entry are visible at a glance.

Global Relationships

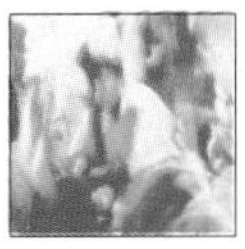

Maps, charts and graphs unveil the complex relationships between people and their environments. Coverage includes: demographic trends, population distribution and growth, and global energy production; assessing the consequences of pollution: acid rain, deforestation, ozone depletion and global warming; also revealing comparisons of GDP per capita and literacy and life expectancy around the globe.

The Physical World

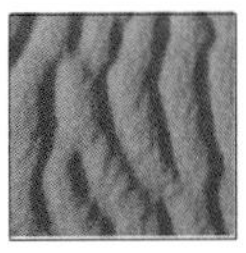

Using computer simulation and the best available digital elevation data, we created fifteen pages of TerraScape maps. These shaded relief maps depict the earth's surface and the ocean floors with stunning "three-dimensional" realism.

Maps of the World

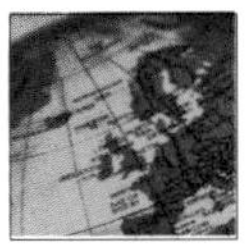

This collection of world maps is the first ever generated from a computer database structured by latitude and longitude. New maps artfully balance political and topographic detail while proprietary map projections present the most distortion-free views of the continents yet seen. Over 60 inset maps highlight metropolitan and special areas. Numbers following each entry indicate map scale (M= million, K= thousand).

Europe and Northern Asia

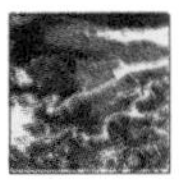

Asia

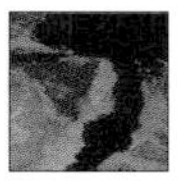

Africa

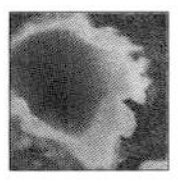

Australia, New Zealand and Pacific

North America

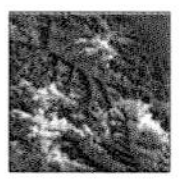

South America and Polar Regions

STATISTICAL TABLES AND INDEX

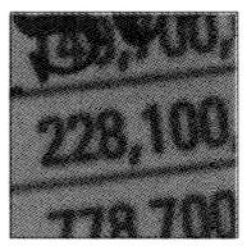

A superb reference section puts the world at your fingertips: World Statistics gives the dimensions of the earth's major mountain peaks, longest rivers and largest lakes and islands. Population offers the most up-to-date figures available for the world's major cities, and incorporates current U.S. Census estimates. A Master Index lists 110,000 places and features appearing in this atlas, complete with page numbers and easy-to-use alpha-numeric references.

Evolution of Cartography

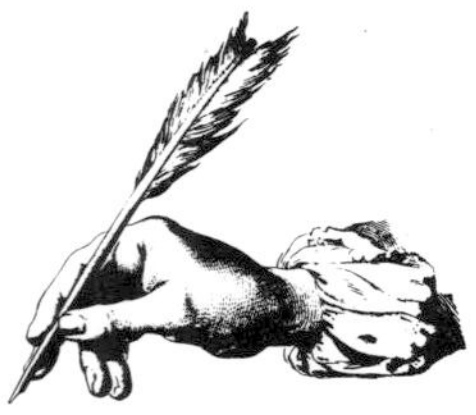

Land-based cartographers used increasingly sophisticated optical instruments and mathematical analysis to survey and measure distances on the ground. Map-making was slow and time consuming, though accuracy was impressive.

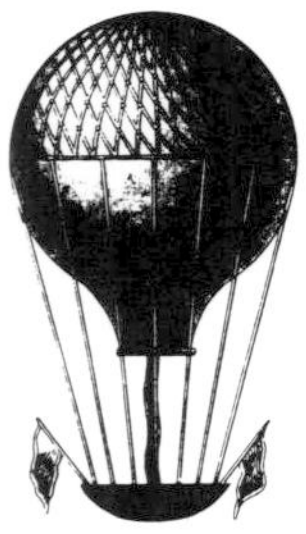

Hot air balloons were occasionally used by military observers to map battle areas not accessible by land. More importantly, the application of photography by cartographers early in the 20th century ushered in a new age of map-making.

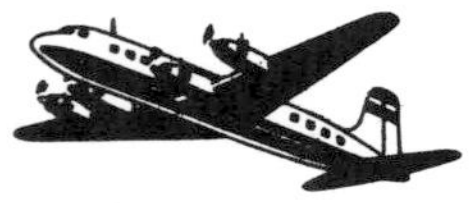

Airplanes permitted aerial reconnaissance at higher altitudes, greatly reducing surveying time. Meanwhile, advances in photography allowed sharp images of increasingly larger areas.

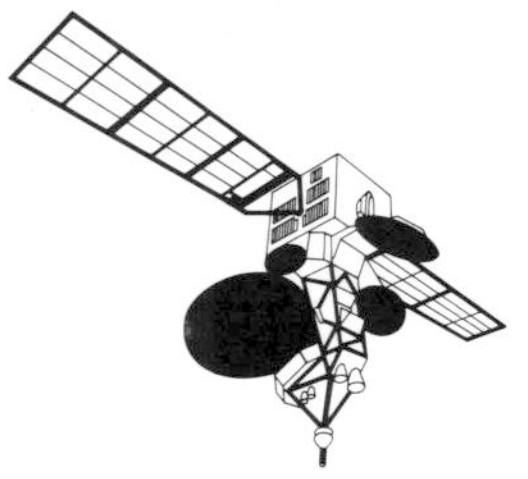

Satellites gave cartographers a global vantage point beyond the earth's atmosphere. Technological advances, many derived from military and aerospace research, permitted images to be systematically sent from space to sophisticated computers, where they were organized and enhanced.

Digital geographic databases are revolutionizing mapmaking in ways that the ancient Greeks never dreamed of. As this brief history of cartography reveals, maps can now be created and updated with greater accuracy and speed than ever before.

Maps extend our world, and our sense of place and direction within it. From mankind's earliest cave markings, people have drawn lines and sought to define their place within them. Indeed, maps have always been utilitarian tools. As far back as 2300 B.C., Babylonian officials used maps to aid in the collection of taxes.

The foundation of modern-day cartography was laid by the ancient Greeks, who recognized the spherical shape of the earth, developed our system of longitude and latitude, designed the first map projections and calculated the size of the earth — with surprising accuracy. Claudius Ptolemy's *Geographia*, produced in the 2nd century A.D., was the first bound collection of maps designed to serve both scholarship and administration.

During the Middle Ages, mapmakers made little attempt to show the world as it was. The typical medieval map represented a Christian ideal, usually placing Jerusalem in the center of the world. At the same time, however, Arab scholars were improving on Ptolemy's work, making significant advances in map presentation and accuracy.

At the end of the 13th century, the compass came into general use, and with it came a new kind of map, called a portolan chart, created by the Genovese fleet for navigational purposes. Based on compass surveys, these outline maps depicted the Mediterranean and Black seas with great accuracy. An elaborate system of lines indicating compass directions crisscrossed the maps' surfaces. In 1375, the Catalan Atlas used portolans to depict most of the world, following the text of Marco Polo.

Three key events contributed to the renaissance of cartography. First was the rediscovery of Ptolemy's *Geographia* in the West. Carefully preserved by devotees, the text

This map of Holland was reproduced from an original version of *Theatrum Orbis Terrarum*. (Courtesy of Federico Canobbio-Codelli)

eventually reached the Moorish rulers in Spain.

Second was the invention of printing, which greatly increased the number of available maps, and brought them within reach of the average person. In 1478, Ptolemy's *Geographia* became the first of the classical Greek works to be printed.

Third, and perhaps most important, was the age of the great discoveries, which was itself made possible by the development of new three-masted sailing vessels.

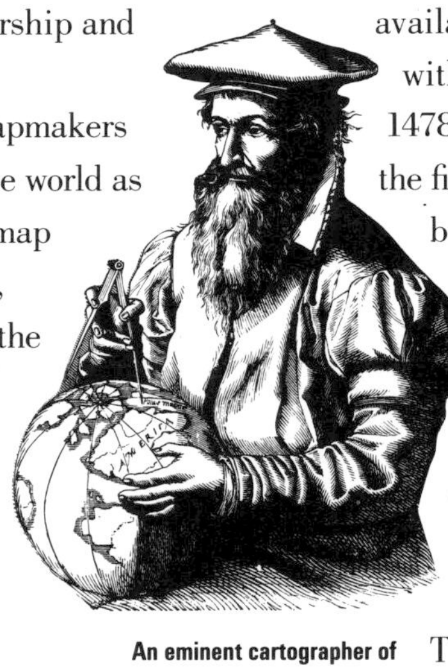

An eminent cartographer of the Age of Exploration, Gerardus Mercator, produced his first world map in 1538. As an aid to seamen, Mercator's map was unsurpassed, because all compass directions appeared as straight lines.

THE AGE OF EXPLORATION

European mariners set sail across the Atlantic beginning in the late 15th century. The great sea-going explorers of this era — Columbus, Cabot, Amerigo Vespucci, Magellan and Sir Francis Drake — all owed much to Ptolemy's ancient text, and to the refinements made at the navigational school founded by Prince Henry the Navigator. Ptolemy and others, however, considerably exaggerated the Eurasian landmass, showing it to occupy nearly half the globe. This error led Columbus to underestimate the distance to Asia; thus he failed to realize that he had reached the new world.

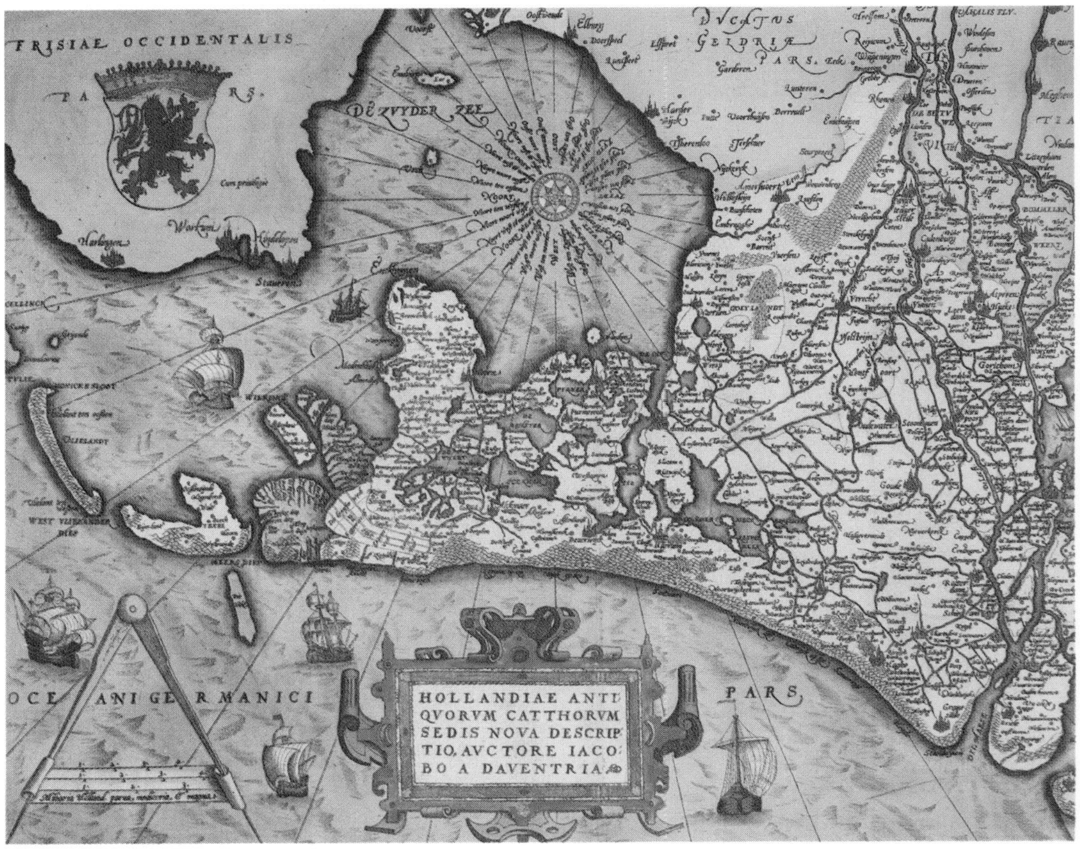

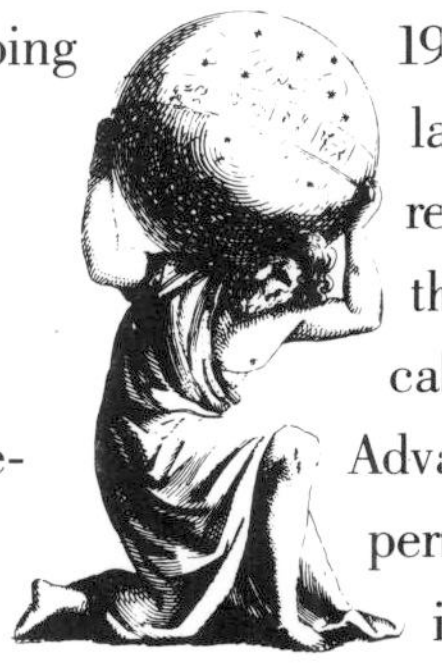

In 1572 a volume of maps published in Rome added the figure of Atlas holding up the world—hence the name "Atlas".

Gerardus Mercator, an important cartographer of his age, was the first to produce a true world navigational chart on a flat surface. It became the favored depiction among map publishers.

Many new maps followed as great explorers, and later traders, returned to correct and fill in the blank spaces of the expanding world. The first modern atlas, *Theatrum Orbis Terrarum*, was published in 1570.

The first successful marine chronometer, in use by 1761, offered a reliable means of measuring longitude. By the late 18th century, mapmakers were already producing a reasonable picture of the world as we know it today.

With the invention of photography in the 19th century, cartographers could at last record the landscape with photo-realistic precision and detail. Then, in the early 1900's, airplanes dramatically extended the scope of our view. Advances in photography kept pace, permitting crisp images of ever expanding areas. Aerial reconnaissance became the standard method for gathering cartographic data. Infrared and ultra-violet photography extended the range of perception beyond the visible spectrum, while radar penetrated visual obstacles such as clouds and fog.

A satellite view of the area shown on the map at left. Note the addition of Dutch "polders" or land reclaimed from the sea.

IMAGES FROM SPACE

But a quantum leap forward occurred in the 1970's, when remote sensing satellites launched a new age of cartography, giving us a vantage point beyond the earth's atmosphere. Satellites provided the first exact measurements of the earth's diameter and the distances between continents, and showed the earth to be flattened at the poles by precisely 26.6 miles (42.8 km.).

Today, satellites are mapping the globe. Landsat digital images of the earth are systematically broadcast from space to sophisticated computers, where the images are assembled and enhanced. This marriage of computers and satellites has given birth to radically new geographic information systems.

COMPUTER-ASSISTED MAPS

Computers were quickly employed in the everyday production of maps. In computer-assisted map-making systems, computers function as electronic versions of traditional drafting tools. Hand-drawn maps are scanned into a computer, where revisions such as name and color changes can be made quickly and easily. However, because these systems must use existing maps as their source material, their ability to output maps at various scales, projections or with different levels of detail is seriously limited.

CREATING A DIGITAL DATABASE

The Hammond World Atlas is the first world atlas created directly from a digital database, and its computer-generated maps represent a new phase in map-making technology.

To build the database capable of generating this world atlas, the latitude and longitude of every significant town, river, coastline, natural and political border, transportation network and peak elevation was researched and digitized. Engineering the complex data structure was critical to the success of the system, which relies on powerful computers and enormous data storage capacity. Hundreds of millions of data points describing nearly every important geographic feature on earth are organized into over 1,000 different map feature codes.

Cartographer Nadejda Naiman uses digital data and computer simulation to create shaded relief maps that depict the earth's surface with stunning "three-dimensional" realism.

Keeping the database current is a never-ending task. Every day, just as map-makers have done for centuries, researchers pore over government publications, maps, international journals and newspapers in search of geographic changes. They record renamed cities, new roads, revamped borders, diverted rivers, and hundreds of other constantly evolving political and topographic details.

HOW COMPUTER-GENERATED MAPS ARE MADE

There are no maps in this unique system. Rather, it consists entirely of coded points, lines and polygons. To create a map, cartographers determine what city, region or continent they want to show and select specific information to include, based on editorial considerations such as scale, town size, population density, and the relative importance of different features. How does a computer plot irregular rivers and mountains — at many different scales? Using fractal geometry to describe natural forms such as coastlines, mathematical physicist Mitchell Feigenbaum developed software capable of re-configuring coastlines, borders and mountain ranges to fit a multitude of map scales and projections.

Even map labeling has finally given way to new technology. Dr. Feigenbaum also created a new computerized type placement program which places thousands of map labels in minutes, a task which previously required days of tedious labor. The program insures that the type carefully follows the curve of the graticule, or map grid, for maximum legibility and aesthetic appeal. After these steps have been completed, the computer then draws the final map. The benefits of such a system go far beyond producing more timely and accurate maps. For the first time, geographers possess a uniquely creative map-making tool. Map projections can be changed at whim. Revisions that once took months can be completed in hours. Because the maps are digitally created, they can be utilized in a wide variety of electronic media.

The Hammond database is also the beginning of a unique historical record. Every new town, every redrawn political boundary and reshaped geographic feature will be permanently stored in the digital database, exceeding the predictable life span of printed maps or even archival films.

A traditionally-produced map may require ten to forty film overlays, each containing a portion of the final map. Updating city names and political boundaries in the conventional manner is a tedious manual effort requiring light tables, ink pens and opaquing brushes.

The computer-generated maps in this atlas represent a new phase in cartography. They are derived from a digital world database that contains the precise latitude and longitude coordinates for every significant point on the globe. A single change with the sweep of a mouse can alter the entire look of a map.

Once the map design is approved, a sophisticated laser plotter prints the final artwork onto film, producing a complete set of film positives for the standard four-color printing process in close to an hour — a savings of many days over conventional methods. Or, the image can be electronically transmitted anywhere in the world.

Map Projections

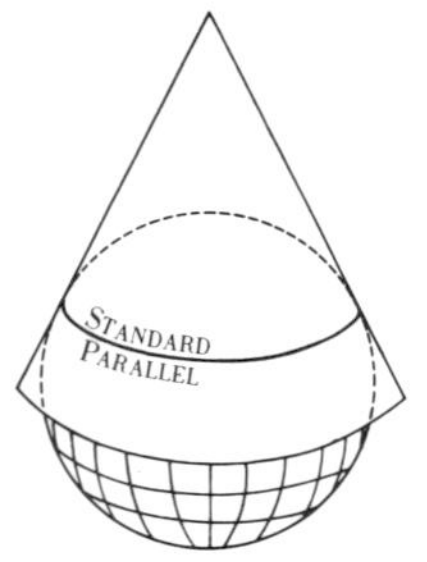

Simply stated, the map-maker's challenge is to project the earth's curved surface onto a flat plane. To achieve this elusive goal, cartographers have developed map projections — equations which govern this conversion of geographic data.

Since the Age of Exploration, literally hundreds of projections have been created, all attempting to present a view of the world which maintains true geographic relationships across the whole of the Earth. All have failed, for the goal is an impossible one. Yet some projections have achieved a remarkable degree of success.

This section explores some of the most widely used examples. It also introduces a new projection, the Hammond Optimal Conformal.

GENERAL PRINCIPLES AND TERMS

The earth rotates around its axis once a day. Its end points are the North and South poles; the line circling the earth midway between the poles is the equator. The arc from the equator to either pole is divided into 90 degrees of latitude. The equator represents 0° latitude. Circles of equal latitude, called parallels, are traditionally shown at every fifth or tenth degree.

The equator is divided into 360 degrees. Lines circling the globe from pole to pole through the degree points on the equator are called meridians, or great circles. All meridians are equal in length, but by international agreement the meridian passing through the Greenwich Observatory near London has been chosen as the prime meridian or 0° longitude. The distance in degrees from the prime meridian to any point east or west is its longitude.

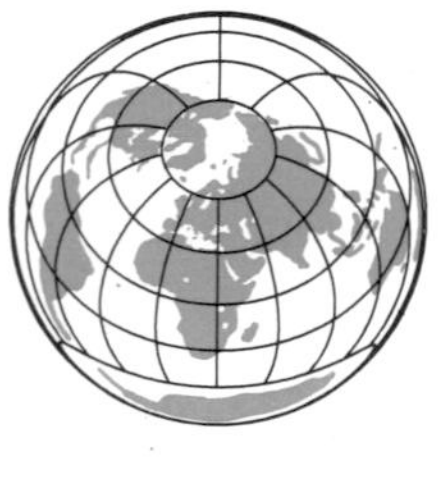

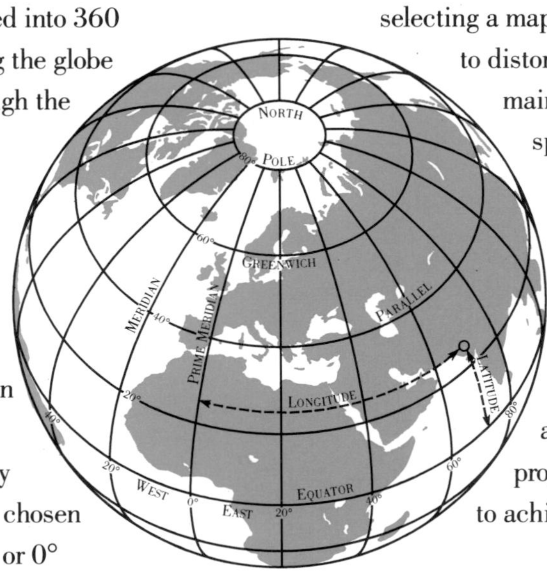

While meridians are all equal in length, parallels become shorter as they approach the poles. Whereas one degree of latitude represents approximately 69 miles (112 km.) anywhere on the globe, a degree of longitude varies from 69 miles (112 km.) at the equator to zero at the poles. Each degree of latitude and longitude is divided into 60

minutes. One minute of latitude equals one nautical mile (1.15 land miles or 1.85 km.).

HOW TO FLATTEN A SPHERE: THE ART OF CONTROLLING DISTORTION

There is only one way to represent a sphere with absolute precision: on a globe. All attempts to project our planet's surface onto a plane unevenly stretch or tear the sphere as it flattens, inevitably distorting shapes, distances, area (sizes appear larger or smaller than actual size), angles or direction.

Since representing a sphere on a flat plane always creates distortion, only the parallels or the meridians (or some other set of lines) can maintain the same length as on a globe of corresponding scale. All other lines must be either too long or too short. Accordingly, the scale on a flat map cannot be true everywhere; there will always be different scales in different parts of a map. On world maps or very large areas, variations in scale may be extreme. The cartographer's concern in creating or selecting a map projection is this: how to distort the map in order to maintain the accuracy of a specific kind of geographic information. Most maps seek to preserve either true area relationships (equal area projections) or true angles and shapes (conformal projections); some attempt to achieve overall balance.

PROJECTIONS: SELECTED EXAMPLES

Mercator (Fig. 1): This projection is especially useful because all compass directions appear as straight lines, making it a valuable navigational tool. Moreover, every small region conforms to its shape on a globe — hence the name conformal. But because its meridians are evenly-spaced vertical lines which never converge (unlike the globe), the horizontal parallels must be drawn farther and farther apart at higher

latitudes to maintain a correct relationship. Only the equator is true to scale, and the size of areas in the higher latitudes is dramatically distorted.

Robinson (Fig. 2): To create the thematic maps in Global Relationships and the two-page world map in the Maps of the World section, the Robinson projection was used. It combines elements of both conformal and equal area projections to show the whole earth with relatively true shapes and reasonably equal areas. Conic (Fig. 3): This projection has been used frequently for air navigation charts and to create most of the national and regional maps in this atlas. (See side bar).

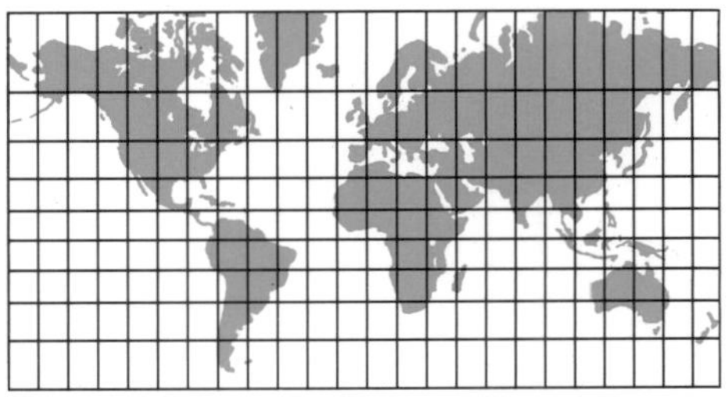

FIGURE 1 **Mercator Projection**

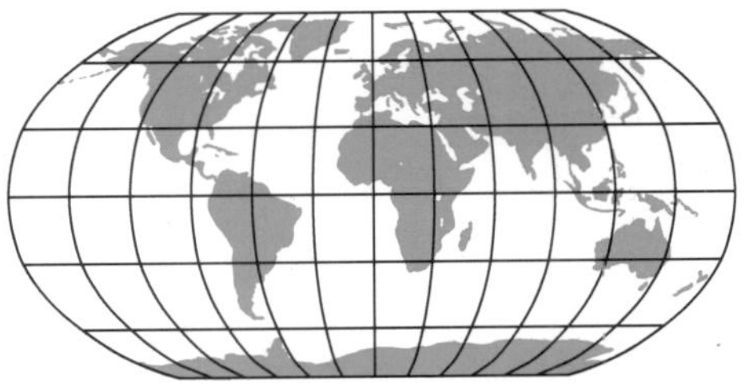

FIGURE 2 **Robinson Projection**

HAMMOND OPTIMAL CONFORMAL

As its name implies, this new conformal projection presents the optimal view of an area by reducing shifts in scale over an entire region to the minimum degree possible. While conformal maps generally preserve all small shapes, large shapes can become very distorted because of varying scales, causing considerable inaccuracy in distance measurements. The concept underlying the Optimal Conformal is that for any region on the globe, there is an ideal projection for which scale variation can be made as small as possible. Consequently, unlike other projections, the Optimal Conformal does not use one standard formula to construct a map. Each map is a unique projection — the optimal projection for that particular area.

In practice, the cartographer first defines the map subject, then, working on a computer, draws a band around the region to be mapped. Next, a sophisticated software program evaluates the size and shape of the region to determine the most accurate way to project it. The result is the most distortion-free conformal map possible, and the most accurate projections that have ever been made. All of the continents maps in this atlas (with the exception of Antarctica) have been drawn using this projection.

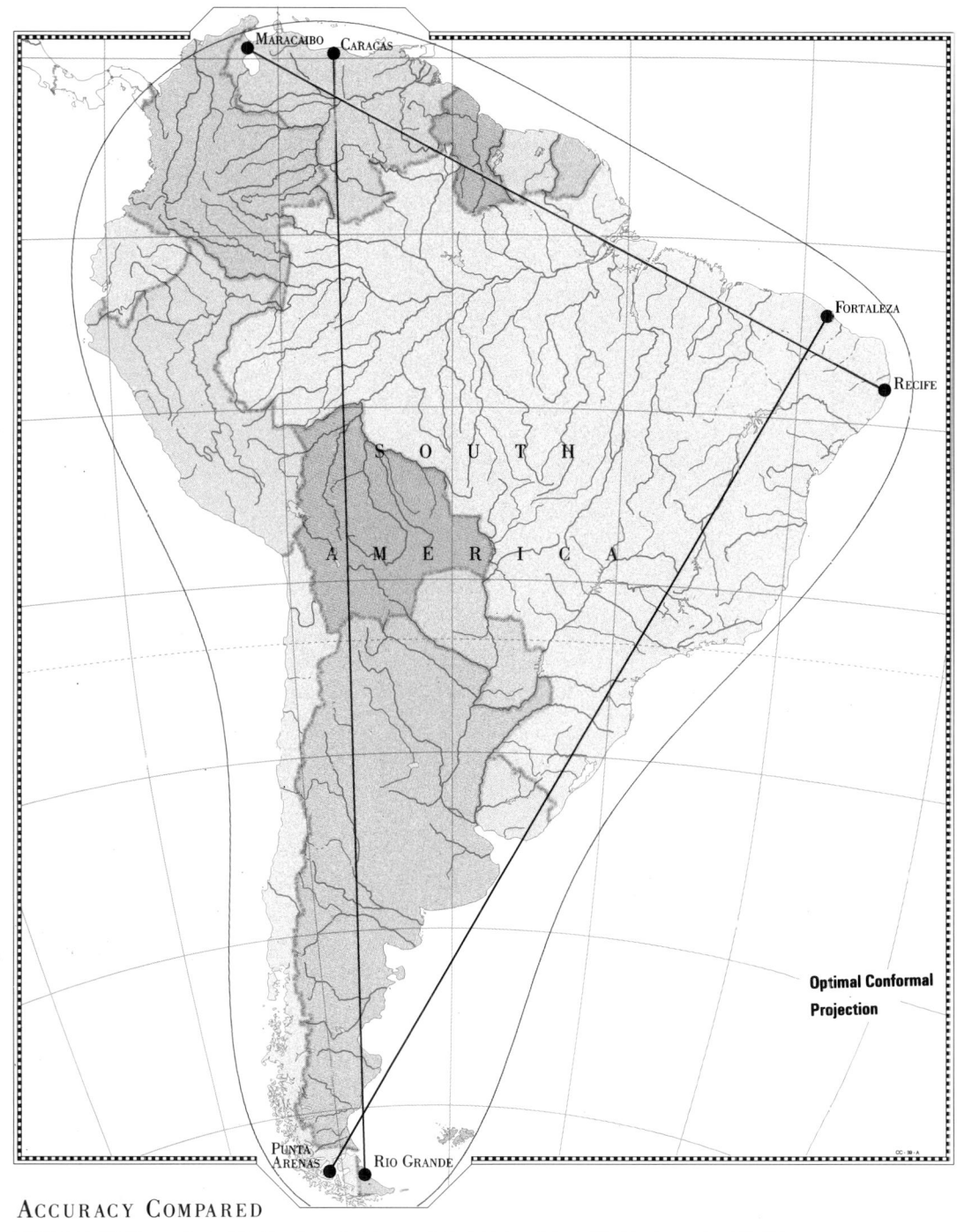

MARACAIBO CARACAS

FORTALEZA

RECIFE

S O U T H

A M E R I C A

**Optimal Conformal
Projection**

PUNTA
ARENAS   RIO GRANDE

ACCURACY COMPARED

CITIES	SPHERICAL (TRUE) DISTANCE	OPTIMAL DISTANCE	LAMBERT AZIMUTHAL DISTANCE
CARACAS TO RIO GRANDE	4,443 MI. (7,149 KM.)	4,429 MI. (7,126 KM.)	4,316 MI. (6,944 KM.)
MARACAIBO TO RECIFE	2,834 MI. (4,560 KM.)	2,845 MI. (4,578 KM.)	2,817 MI. (4,533 KM.)
FORTALEZA TO PUNTA ARENAS	3,882 MI. (6,246 KM.)	3,907 MI. (6,266 KM.)	3,843 MI. (6,163 KM.)

Continent maps drawn using the Lambert Azimuthal Equal Area projection (Fig. 4) contain distortions ranging from 2.3 percent for Europe up to 15 percent for Asia. The Optimal Conformal cuts that distortion in half, improving distance measurements on these continent maps. Less distortion means greater visual fidelity, so the shape of a continent on an Optimal projection more closely represents its True shape. The table above compares measurements on the Optimal projection to those of the Lambert Azimuthal Equal Area projection for selected cities.

PROJECTIONS COMPARED

Because the true shapes of earth's landforms are unfamiliar to most people, distinguishing between various projections can be difficult. The following diagrams reveal the distortions introduced by several commonly used projections. By using a simple face with familiar shapes as the starting point (The Plan), it is easy to see the benefits — and drawbacks — of each. Think of the facial features as continents. Note that distortion appears not only in the features themselves, but in the changing shapes, angles and areas of the background grid, or graticule.

Figure 6: The Plan
The Plan indicates that the continents are either perfect concentric circles or are true straight lines *on the earth*. They should appear that way on a "perfect" map.

Figure 7: Orthographic Projection
This view shows the continents on the earth as seen from space. The facial features occupy half of the earth, which is all that you can see from this perspective. As you move outward towards the edge, note how the eyes become elliptical, the nose appears larger and less straight, and the mouth is curved into a smile.

Figure 8: Mercator
This cylindrical projection preserves angles exactly, but the mouth is now smiling broadly, and shows extreme distortion at the map's outer edge. This rapid expansion as you move away from the map's center is typified by the extreme enlargement of Greenland found on Mercator world maps (also see Fig. 1).

Figure 9: Peters
The Peters projection is a square equal area projection elongated, or stretched vertically, by a factor of two. While representing areas in their correct proportions, it does not closely resemble the Plan, and angles, local shapes and global relations are significantly distorted.

Figure 10: Gnomonic
Neither conformal nor equal-area, this strange-looking projection is a "perspective" projection made by placing a plane tangent to the sphere at the center of the earth. Though its outer regions are badly distorted, the straight mouth and precise triangle of the nose indicate a key property of this map: all great circles appear as straight lines. This enables the user to find the shortest path between any two points on the map by simply connecting them with a straight line.

Figure 11: Hammond Optimal Conformal
As you can see, this projection minimizes inaccuracies between the angles and shapes of the Plan, yielding a near-perfect map of the given area, up to a complete hemisphere. Like all conformal maps, the Optimal projection preserves every angle exactly, but it is more successful than previous projections at spreading the inevitable curvature across the entire map. Note that the sides of the triangle appear almost straight while correctly containing more than 180°. And though the eyes are slightly too large, it is the only map with eyes which appear concentric. Both mathematically and visually, it offers the best conformal map that can be made of the ideal Plan.

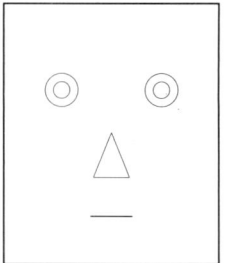

FIGURE 6
The Plan

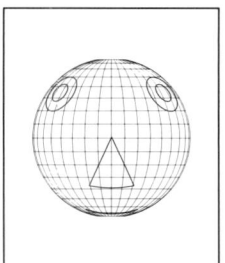

FIGURE 7
Orthographic Projection

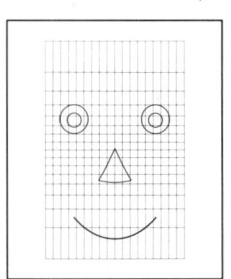

FIGURE 8
Mercator Projection

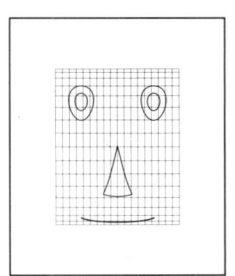

FIGURE 9
Peters Projection

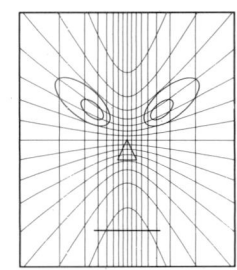

FIGURE 10
Gnomonic Projection

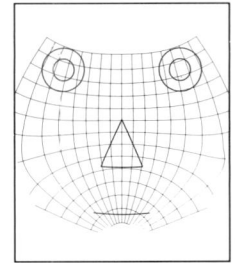

FIGURE 11
**Optimal Conformal
Projection**

Using This Atlas

How to Locate Information Quickly

For familiar locations such as continents, countries and major political divisions, the World Locator Map and Quick Reference Guide help you quickly pinpoint the map you need. For less familiar places, begin with the Master Index.

World Locator Map

This streamlined world map, conveniently located on the front end sheets, defines the coverage and page numbers of every political map in the atlas. Because it shows the overall arrangement of these maps, it's easy to locate maps of adjacent regions.

Quick Reference Guide

This concise guide lists continents, countries, states, provinces and territories in alphabetical order, complete with the size, population and capital of each. Red page numbers and alpha-numeric reference keys are visible at a glance.

, rt.		
(riv.), Ger.		6b,
₄a (riv.), Ger.		67/G.
Aabach (riv.), Swi.		81/E3
Aach, Ger.		81/E2
Aach (riv.), Ger.		81/F2
Aachen, Ger.		69/F2
Aaglet Tennuaca		
'well), WSah.		142/B⁵
⁻ᵈlet Yeraifia		
ᵞSah.		

Master Index of the World

When you're looking for an unfamiliar place or physical feature, your quickest route is the Master Index. This alphabetical index lists both the page number and alpha-numeric reference key for 110,000 places and features in Maps of the World.

The Hammond World Atlas has been thoughtfully designed to be easy and enjoyable to use, both as a general reference, and for armchair exploration of the globe. A short time spent familiarizing yourself with its organization will help you to benefit fully from its use.

GLOBAL RELATIONSHIPS

This section highlights key social, cultural, economic and geographic factors. Together, these eight succinct chapters — from Population to Standards of Living— provide a fresh perspective on the world today. In the case of complex and rapidly evolving topics such as Environment, data analysis is in a relatively early stage, and projected outcomes are sometimes controversial.

THE PHYSICAL WORLD

These relief maps of the continents and major regions of the world depict the topography of the earth's surface and ocean floor. Because the maps are created using actual digital elevation data and computer simulation, they represent the relationships of land and sea forms and the rugged contours of the terrain with startling realism.

MAPS OF THE WORLD

These detailed regional maps are arranged by continent, and introduced by a stunning satellite image and political map of that continent. The continent maps, which utilize Hammond Optimal Conformal projection, are distinguished by individual colors for each country to highlight political divisions.

On the regional maps, different line patterns and textures highlight distinctive features such as parks, forests, deserts and urban areas. These maps also provide considerable information concerning geographic features and political divisions. The realistic topography is achieved by combining the political map data with computer-generated hypsometric and bathymetric relief maps.

MASTER INDEX

This is an A-Z listing of 110,000 places and features found on the political maps. It also has its own abbreviation list which, along with other Index keys, appears on page 226.

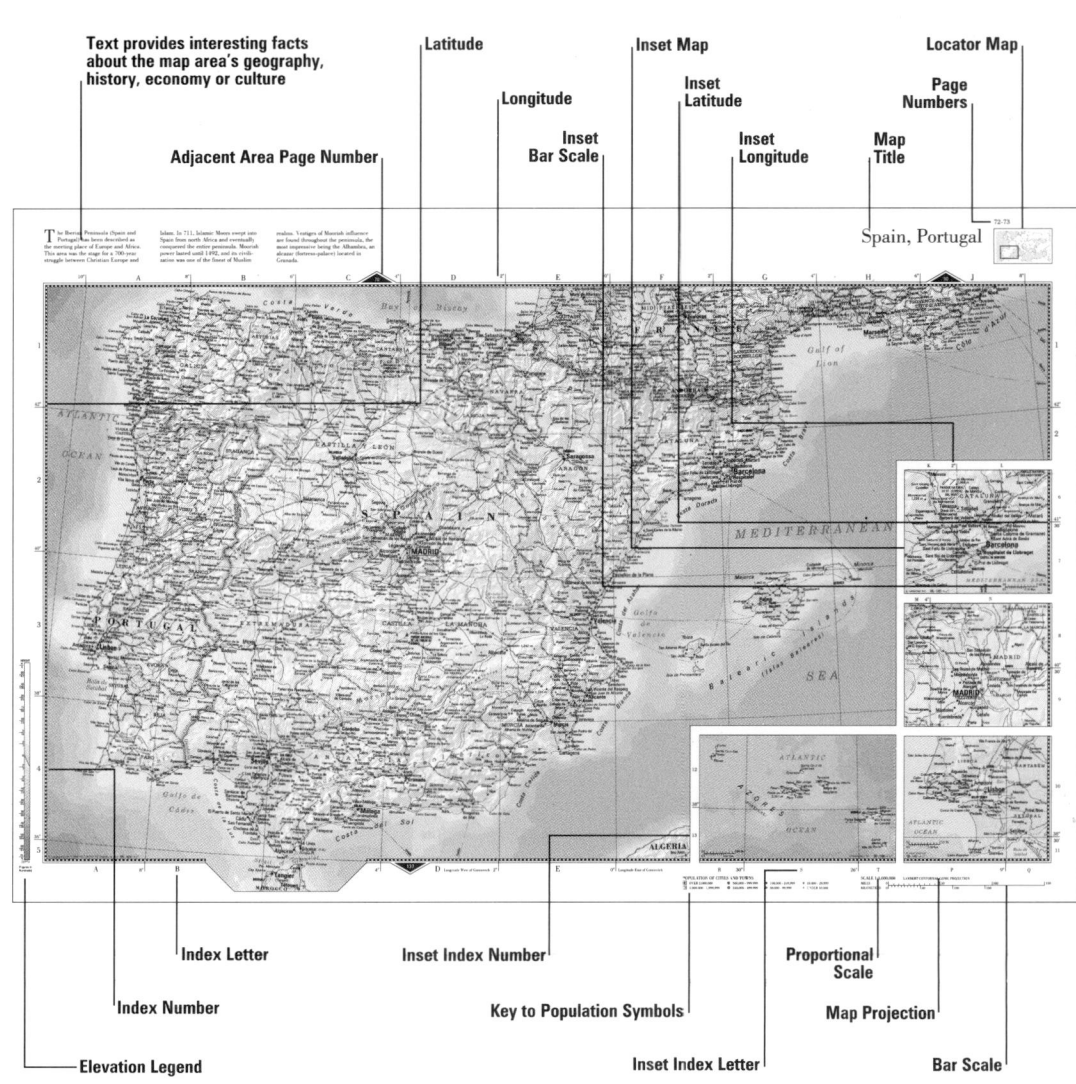

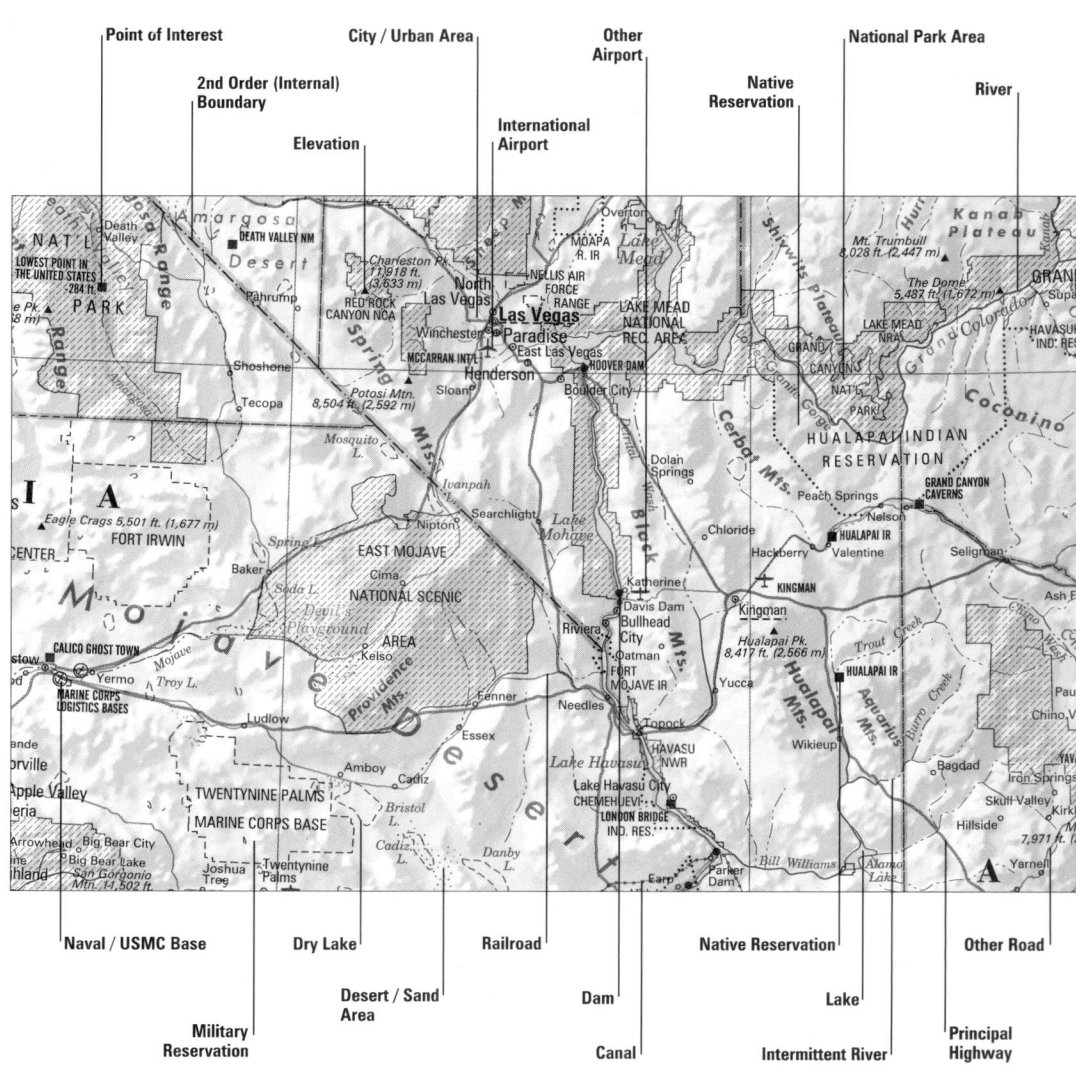

Symbols Used on Maps of the World

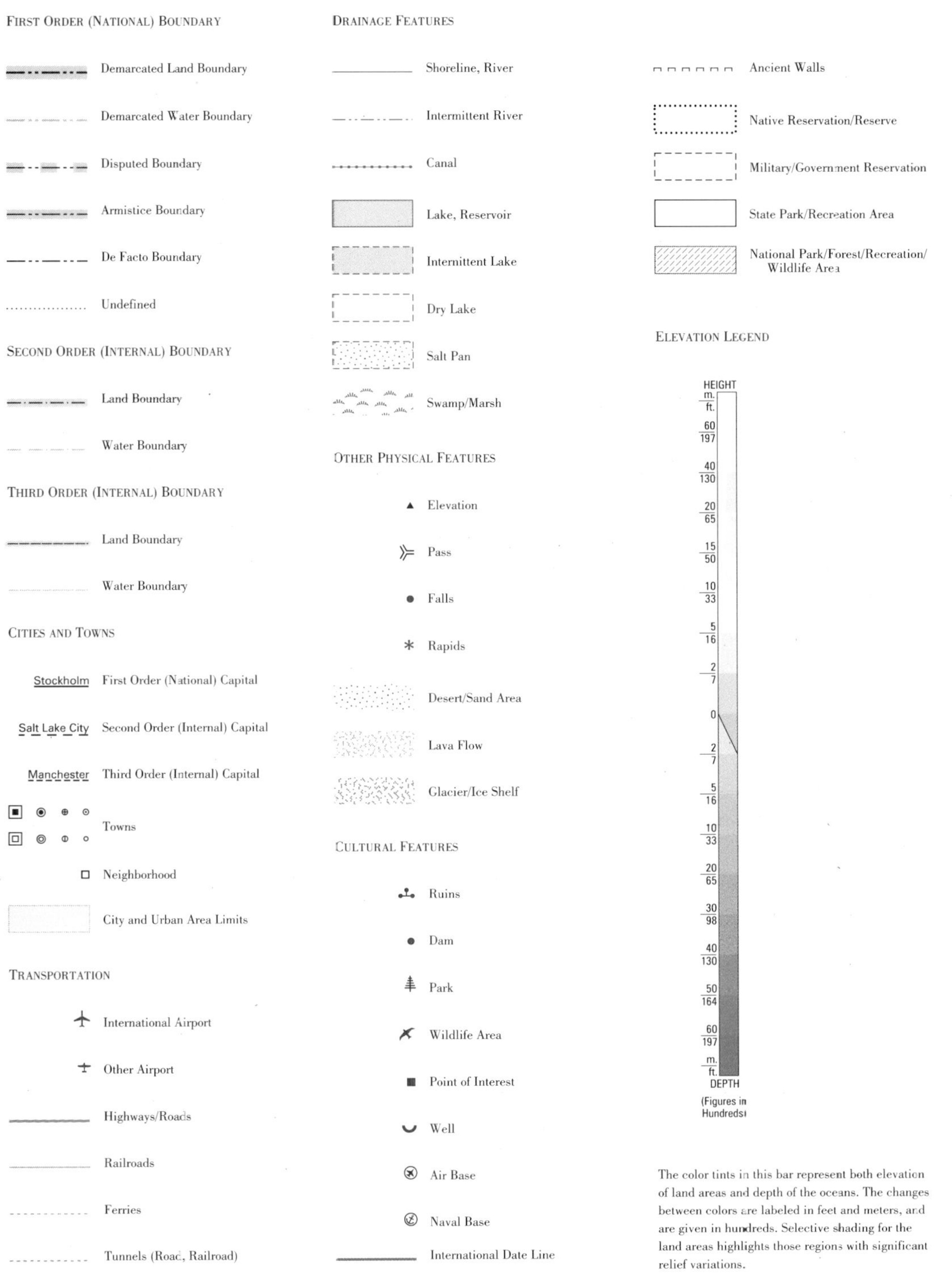

First Order (National) Boundary

- ┉┉┉ Demarcated Land Boundary
- ┉┉┉ Demarcated Water Boundary
- ┉┉┉ Disputed Boundary
- ┉┉┉ Armistice Boundary
- ┉┉┉ De Facto Boundary
- ··········· Undefined

Second Order (Internal) Boundary

- ┉┉┉ Land Boundary
- ──── Water Boundary

Third Order (Internal) Boundary

- ──── Land Boundary
- ──── Water Boundary

Cities and Towns

- Stockholm First Order (National) Capital
- Salt Lake City Second Order (Internal) Capital
- Manchester Third Order (Internal) Capital
- ■ ◉ ● ○ Towns
- ▢ ◎ ◌ ○
- ▫ Neighborhood
- ▭ City and Urban Area Limits

Transportation

- ✈ International Airport
- ✛ Other Airport
- ──── Highways/Roads
- ──── Railroads
- ········· Ferries
- ---------- Tunnels (Road, Railroad)

Drainage Features

- ──── Shoreline, River
- ─·─·─ Intermittent River
- ············ Canal
- ▭ Lake, Reservoir
- ▭ Intermittent Lake
- ▭ Dry Lake
- ▦ Salt Pan
- ✲✲✲ Swamp/Marsh

Other Physical Features

- ▲ Elevation
- ⟫ Pass
- ● Falls
- ✳ Rapids
- ⣿ Desert/Sand Area
- ▨ Lava Flow
- ▨ Glacier/Ice Shelf

Cultural Features

- ⚶ Ruins
- ● Dam
- ♣ Park
- ✗ Wildlife Area
- ■ Point of Interest
- ⌣ Well
- ⊗ Air Base
- ⊘ Naval Base
- ──── International Date Line

- ▭▭▭▭ Ancient Walls
- ⬚ Native Reservation/Reserve
- ⬚ Military/Government Reservation
- ▭ State Park/Recreation Area
- ▨ National Park/Forest/Recreation/ Wildlife Area

Elevation Legend

HEIGHT
m.
ft.
60 / 197
40 / 130
20 / 65
15 / 50
10 / 33
5 / 16
2 / 7
0
2 / 7
5 / 16
10 / 33
20 / 65
30 / 98
40 / 130
50 / 164
60 / 197
m.
ft.
DEPTH
(Figures in Hundreds)

The color tints in this bar represent both elevation of land areas and depth of the oceans. The changes between colors are labeled in feet and meters, and are given in hundreds. Selective shading for the land areas highlights those regions with significant relief variations.

Principal Map Abbreviations

Abor. Rsv.	Aboriginal Reserve	Ft.	Fort	NCA	National Conservation Area	Plat.	Plateau
Admin.	Administration	G.	Gulf			PN	Park National
AFB	Air Force Base	Govt.	Government	NHP	National Historical Park	Prom.	Promontory
Amm. Dep.	Ammunition Depot	Gd.	Grand			Prsv.	Preserve
Arch.	Archipelago	Gt.	Great	NHS	National Historic Site	Pt.	Point
Aut.	Autonomous	Har.	Harbor			R.	River
B.	Bay	Hist.	Historic(al)	NL	National Lakeshore	Rec.	Recreation(al)
Bfld.	Battlefield	Hts.	Heights	NM	National Monument	Ref.	Refuge
Bk.	Brook	I., Is.	Island(s)	NMEM	National Memorial	Reg.	Region
Br.	Branch	Ind. Res.	Indian Reservation	NMILP	National Military Park	Rep.	Republic
C.	Cape	Int'l	International			Res.	Reservoir, Reservation
Can.	Canal	IR	Indian Reservation	No.	Northern		
Cap.	Capital	Isth.	Isthmus	NP	National Park	Sa.	Sierra
C.G.	Coast Guard	Jct.	Junction	NPP	National Park and Preserve	Sd.	Sound
Chan.	Channel	L.	Lake			So.	Southern
Co.	County	Lag.	Lagoon	NPRSV	National Preserve	SP	State Park
Consv.	Conservation	Mem.	Memorial	NRA	National Recreation Area	Spr., Sprgs.	Spring, Springs
Cord.	Cordillera	Mil.	Military			St.	State
Cr.	Creek	Mon.	Monument	NRIV	National River	Sta.	Station
Ctr.	Center	Mt.	Mount	NRSV	National Reserve	Stm.	Stream
Dep.	Depot	Mtn.	Mountain	NS	National Seashore	Str.	Strait
Depr.	Depression	Mts.	Mountains	NWR	National Wildlife Refuge	Terr.	Territory
Des.	Desert	Nat.	Natural			Tun.	Tunnel
Dist.	District	Nat'l	National	Obl.	Oblast	Twp.	Township
DMZ	Demilitarized Zone	Nav.	Naval	Occ.	Occupied	UNDOF	United Nations Disengagement Observer Force
Est.	Estuary	NB	National Battlefield	Okr.	Okrug		
Fed.	Federal			Passg.	Passage		
Fk.	Fork	NBP	National Battlefield Park	Pen.	Peninsula	Val.	Valley
For.	Forest			Pk.	Peak	Vill.	Village

Statistics & Other Key Facts

World Statistics lists the dimensions of the earth's principal mountains, islands, rivers and lakes, along with other useful geographic information. Population of Countries and Major Cities contains the latest population figures for the world's largest cities, organized by country in alphabetical order. You'll find the size and population of major geographical areas, from states and territories to continents, in the Quick Reference Guide.

Map Scales

A map's scale is the relationship of any length on the map to an identical length on the earth's surface. A scale of 1:3,000,000 means that one inch on the map represents 3,000,000 inches (47 miles, 76 km.) on the earth's surface. Thus, a 1:1,000,000 scale is larger than 1:3,000,000, just as 1/1 is larger than 1/3.

The most densely populated areas are shown at a scale of 1:1,000,000, while selected metropolitan areas are covered at either 1:500,000 or 1:1,000,000. Other populous areas are presented at 1:3,000,000 and 1:6,000,000, allowing you to accurately compare areas and distances of similar regions. Remaining regions are scaled at 1:9,000,000. The continent maps, as well as the United States, Canada, Russia and the Pacific have smaller scales, in multiples of 3,000,000.

Boundary & Name Policies

This atlas observes the boundary policies of the U.S. Department of State. Boundary disputes, armistice and de facto boundaries are customarily handled with a special symbol treatment. The portrayal of independent nations in the atlas follows their recognition by the United Nations and/or the United States government.

Hammond uses accepted conventional names for certain major foreign place names. The U.S. Board of Geographic Names defines a conventional name as "a name approved for use in addition to, or in lieu of, an approved local official name or names". Usually, space permits the inclusion of the local form in parentheses. To make the maps more readily understandable to English-speaking readers, many foreign physical features are translated into more recognizable English forms.

Map Type Styles

Cartographers use a variety of type styles to differentiate between map features. The following styles are used in this Atlas.

Major Political Areas
LUXEMBOURG

Internal Political Divisions
SAXONY-ANHALT

Historical Regions
Polabská Nížina

Cities and Towns
Norfolk Sumter Smyrna

Neighborhoods
BIGGIN HILL

Points of Interest
MISSION SAN BUENAVENTURA

Water Features
L. Elsinore

Capes, Points, Peaks, Passes
Pt. La Jolla   Pacifico Mtn'

Islands, Peninsulas
Cape Breton I.

Mountain Ranges, Plateaus, Hills
Serra do Norte

Deserts, Plains, Valleys
San Fernando Valley

A Word About Names

Our source for all foreign names and physical names is the decision lists of the U.S. Board of Geographic Names, which contain hundreds of thousands of place names. If a place is not listed, Hammond follows the name form appearing on official foreign maps or in official gazetteers of the country concerned. For rendering domestic city, town and village names, this atlas follows the forms and spelling of the U.S. Postal Service.

Quick Reference Guide

This concise alphabetical reference lists continents, countries, states, territories, possessions and other major geographical areas, complete with the size, population and capital or chief town of each. Page numbers and red alpha-numeric reference keys (which refer to the grid squares of latitude and longitude on each map) are visible at a glance. The population figures are the latest and most reliable figures obtainable.

Place	Square Miles	Square Kilometers	Population	Capital or Chief Town	Page/ Index
A Afghanistan	250,000	647,500	23,738,085	Kabul	127/H 2
Africa	11,701,147	30,306,000	705,924,000	....	133
Alabama, U.S.	52,237	135,293	4,273,084	Montgomery	169/J 5
Alaska, U.S.	615,230	1,593,444	607,007	Juneau	168/W12
Albania	11,100	28,749	3,293,252	Tiranë	75/F 2
Alberta, Canada	255,285	661,185	2,545,553	Edmonton	166/E 3
Algeria	919,591	2,381,740	29,830,370	Algiers	137/F 3
American Samoa	77	199	61,819	Pago Pago	163/J 6
Andorra	174	450	74,839	Andorra la Vella	73/F 1
Angola	481,351	1,246,700	10,623,994	Luanda	133/D 6
Anguilla, U.K.	35	91	10,785	The Valley	197/N 7
Antarctica	5,500,000	14,245,000	....	....	216
Antigua and Barbuda	170	440	66,175	St. John's	197/N 7
Argentina	1,068,296	2,766,890	35,797,536	Buenos Aires	203/B 7
Arizona, U.S.	114,006	295,276	4,428,068	Phoenix	175/F 3
Arkansas, U.S.	53,182	137,742	2,509,793	Little Rock	169/H 4
Armenia	11,506	29,800	3,465,611	Yerevan	97/H 5
Aruba, Netherlands	75	193	68,031	Oranjestad	204/D 1
Ascension Island, St. Helena	34	88	719	Georgetown	52/J 6
Ashmore & Cartier Islands, Australia	2	5	....	....	154/A 3
Asia	17,159,867	44,444,100	3,407,967,000	....	103
Australia	2,967,893	7,686,850	18,438,824	Canberra	153
Australian Capital Territory	938	2,430	280,132	Canberra	158/D 2
Austria	32,375	83,851	8,054,078	Vienna	71/L 3
Azerbaijan	33,436	86,600	7,735,918	Baku	97/H 4
Azores, Portugal	902	2,335	237,000	Ponta Delgada	73/R12
B Bahamas, The	5,382	13,939	262,034	Nassau	197/F 2
Bahrain	240	622	603,318	Manama	126/F 3
Baker Island, U.S.	0.5	1.4	....	....	163/H 4
Balearic Islands, Spain	1,936	5,014	690,000	Palma	73/F 3
Bangladesh	55,598	144,000	125,340,261	Dhaka	123/G 4
Barbados	166	430	257,731	Bridgetown	197/P 8
Belarus	80,154	207,600	10,439,916	Minsk	55/G 3
Belgium	11,780	30,510	10,203,683	Brussels	68/C 3
Belize	8,865	22,960	224,663	Belmopan	200/D 2
Benin	43,483	112,620	5,902,178	Porto-Novo	141/F 4
Bermuda, U.K.	19	50	62,569	Hamilton	165/L 6
Bhutan	18,147	47,000	1,865,191	Thimphu	123/G 2
Bolivia	424,163	1,098,582	7,669,868	La Paz; Sucre	203/C 4
Bonaire, Neth. Antilles	111	288	10,187	Kralendijk	197/L 8
Bosnia & Herzegovina	19,781	51,233	2,607,734	Sarajevo	76/C 3
Botswana	231,803	600,370	1,500,765	Gaborone	133/E 7
Bouvet Island, Norway	22	57	....	....	53/K 8
Brazil	3,286,470	8,511,965	164,511,366	Brasília	203/D 3
British Columbia, Canada	365,946	947,800	3,282,061	Victoria	166/D 3
British Indian Ocean Terr., U.K.	23	60	....	....	103/G10
British Virgin Islands	59	153	13,368	Road Town	197/M7
Brunei	2,228	5,770	307,616	Bandar Seri Begawan	114/A 4
Bulgaria	42,823	110,912	8,652,745	Sofia	77/G 4
Burkina Faso	105,869	274,200	10,891,159	Ouagadougou	141/E 3
Burma, see Myanmar					
Burundi	10,745	27,830	6,052,614	Bujumbura	146/G 3
C California, U.S.	158,869	411,470	31,878,234	Sacramento	168/C 4
Cambodia	69,900	181,040	11,163,861	Phnom Penh	120/D 3
Cameroon	183,568	475,441	14,677,510	Yaoundé	133/D 4
Canada	3,851,787	9,976,139	29,123,194	Ottawa	166
Canary Islands, Spain	2,808	7,273	1,495,000	Las Palmas; Santa Cruz	136/A 3
Cape Verde	1,556	4,030	393,843	Praia	133/J 9
Cayman Islands, U.K.	100	259	36,153	George Town	201/F 2

Place	Square Miles	Square Kilometers	Population	Capital or Chief Town	Page/ Index
Celebes, Indonesia	72,986	189,034	12,520,711	Ujung Pandang	117/E 4
Central African Republic	240,533	622,980	3,342,051	Bangui	142/C 4
Chad	495,752	1,283,998	7,166,023	N'Djamena	133/D 3
Channel Islands, U.K.	75	194	133,000	St. Helier; St. Peter Port	82/C 2
Chile	292,258	756,950	14,508,168	Santiago	203/B 6
China, People's Rep. of	3,705,386	9,596,960	1,221,591,778	Beijing	103/J 6
Christmas Island, Australia	52	135	889	The Settlement	53/Q 6
Clipperton Island, France	2.7	7	....	....	52/D 5
Cocos (Keeling) Islands, Australia	5.4	14	604	West Island	53/P 6
Colombia	439,733	1,138,910	37,418,290	Bogotá	204/C 4
Colorado, U.S.	104,100	269,618	3,822,676	Denver	168/E 4
Comoros	838	2,170	589,797	Moroni	151/G 5
Congo, Dem. Rep. of the	905,563	2,345,410	47,440,362	Kinshasa	133/E 5
Congo, Rep. of the	132,046	342,000	2,583,198	Brazzaville	146/C 3
Connecticut, U.S.	5,544	14,358	3,274,238	Hartford	187/K 4
Cook Islands, New Zealand	93	240	19,776	Avarua	163/J 6
Coral Sea Islands, Australia	1.2	3	....	....	153/E 2
Corsica, France	3,352	8,682	249,737	Ajaccio	74/A 1
Costa Rica	19,730	51,100	3,534,174	San José	201/F 4
Côte d'Ivoire	124,502	322,460	14,986,218	Yamoussoukro	140/D 5
Croatia	22,050	56,538	5,026,995	Zagreb	76/C 3
Cuba	42,803	110,860	10,999,041	Havana	201/F 1
Curaçao, Neth. Antilles	172	445	144,097	Willemstad	197/H 5
Cyprus	3,571	9,250	752,808	Nicosia	130/C 2
Czech Republic	30,387	78,703	10,318,958	Prague	69/H 4
D Delaware, U.S.	2,396	6,206	724,842	Dover	169/L 4
Denmark	16,629	43,069	5,268,775	Copenhagen	66/C 4
District of Columbia, U.S.	68	177	543,213	Washington	194/B 6
Djibouti	8,494	22,000	434,116	Djibouti	144/B 2
Dominica	290	751	83,226	Roseau	197/N 8
Dominican Republic	18,815	48,730	8,228,151	Santo Domingo	197/H 4
E Eastern Cape, South Africa	65,858	170,616	6,665,400	Bisho	150/D 3
Ecuador	109,483	283,561	11,690,535	Quito	203/B 3
Egypt	386,659	1,001,447	64,791,891	Cairo	135/F 3
El Salvador	8,124	21,040	5,661,827	San Salvador	200/D 3
England, U.K.	50,356	130,423	48,068,400	London	57/K10
Equatorial Guinea	10,831	28,052	442,516	Malabo	146/B 2
Eritrea	46,842	121,320	3,589,687	Asmara	133/F 3
Estonia	17,413	45,100	1,444,721	Tallinn	67/L 2
Ethiopia	435,184	1,127,127	58,732,577	Addis Ababa	133/F 4
Europe	4,066,019	10,531,000	732,653,000	....	55
F Falkland Islands & Dependencies, U.K.	4,699	12,170	2,317	Stanley	215/M 8
Faroe Islands, Denmark	540	1,399	43,057	Tórshavn	55/D 2
Fiji	7,055	18,272	792,441	Suva	162/G 6
Finland	130,128	337,032	5,109,148	Helsinki	64/H 2
Florida, U.S.	59,928	155,214	14,399,985	Tallahassee	191/F 2
France	211,208	547,030	58,470,421	Paris	70/D 3
Free State, South Africa	49,963	129,437	2,804,600	Bloemfontein	150/D 3
French Guiana	35,135	91,000	156,946	Cayenne	206/C 2
French Polynesia	1,522	3,941	233,488	Papeete	163/L 6
G Gabon	103,347	267,670	1,190,159	Libreville	146/B 3
Gambia, The	4,363	11,300	1,248,085	Banjul	140/B 3
Gauteng, South Africa	7,241	18,760	6,847,000	Johannesburg	150/Q12
Gaza Strip	139	360	987,869	Gaza	130/C 4
Georgia	26,911	69,700	5,174,642	T'bilisi	97/G 4
Georgia, U.S.	58,977	152,750	7,353,225	Atlanta	169/K 5
Germany	137,803	356,910	84,068,216	Berlin	68/E 3
Ghana	92,100	238,540	18,100,703	Accra	141/E 4
Gibraltar, U.K.	2.5	6.5	28,913	Gibraltar	72/C 4

Sources: CIA Factbook; U.S. Bureau of the Census, International Data Base

Place	Square Miles	Square Kilometers	Population	Capital or Chief Town	Page/Index
Greece	50,942	131,940	10,583,126	Athens	75/G 3
Greenland, Denmark	840,000	2,175,600	58,768	Nuuk (Godthåb)	165/N 2
Grenada	131	340	95,537	St. George's	197/N 9
Guadeloupe & Dependencies, France	687	1,779	412,614	Basse-Terre	197/N 7
Guam, U.S.	209	541	160,595	Agaña	162/D 3
Guatemala	42,042	108,889	11,558,407	Guatemala	200/D 3
Guinea	94,927	245,860	7,405,375	Conakry	140/C 4
Guinea-Bissau	13,946	36,120	1,178,584	Bissau	140/B 3
Guyana	83,000	214,970	706,116	Georgetown	205/G 3
H Haiti	10,714	27,750	6,611,407	Port-au-Prince	201/H 2
Hawaii, U.S.	6,459	16,729	1,183,723	Honolulu	168/S 9
Heard & McDonald Islands, Australia	159	412	....	....	216b/E
Holland, see Netherlands					
Honduras	43,277	112,087	5,751,384	Tegucigalpa	200/E 3
Hong Kong, China	402	1,040	6,412,786	Victoria	113/G 4
Howland Island, U.S.	0.6	1.6	....	....	163/H 4
Hungary	35,919	93,030	9,935,774	Budapest	76/D 2
I Iceland	39,768	103,000	272,550	Reykjavík	64/N 7
Idaho, U.S.	83,574	216,456	1,189,251	Boise	168/C 3
Illinois, U.S.	57,918	150,007	11,846,544	Springfield	169/J 4
India	1,269,339	3,287,588	967,612,804	New Delhi	118/C 3
Indiana, U.S.	36,420	94,328	5,840,528	Indianapolis	169/J 4
Indonesia	741,096	1,919,440	209,774,138	Jakarta	117/E 4
Iowa, U.S.	56,275	145,752	2,851,792	Des Moines	181/G 2
Iran	636,293	1,648,000	67,540,002	Tehran	129/H 3
Iraq	168,753	437,072	22,219,289	Baghdad	128/E 3
Ireland	27,136	70,282	3,555,500	Dublin	57/G10
Isle of Man, U.K.	227	588	74,504	Douglas	60/D 3
Israel	8,019	20,770	5,534,672	Jerusalem	130/C 3
Italy	116,305	301,230	57,534,088	Rome	93/F 2
Ivory Coast, see Côte d'Ivoire					
J Jamaica	4,243	10,990	2,615,582	Kingston	201/G 2
Jan Mayen, Norway	144	373	....	....	55/D 1
Japan	145,882	377,835	125,716,637	Tōkyō	105/M 4
Jarvis Island, U.S.	1.7	4.5	....	....	163/J 5
Java, Indonesia	48,842	126,500	107,581,306	Jakarta	115/E 4
Johnston Atoll, U.S.	1	2.8	327	....	163/J 3
Jordan	34,445	89,213	4,324,638	Amman	130/D 4
K Kansas, U.S.	82,232	213,110	2,572,150	Topeka	169/G 4
Kazakhstan	1,049,150	2,717,300	16,898,572	Aqmola	100/G 5
Kentucky, U.S.	40,411	104,665	3,883,723	Frankfort	188/E 2
Kenya	224,960	582,646	28,803,085	Nairobi	133/F 4
Kermadec Islands, New Zealand	13	33	....	....	162/G 8
Kingman Reef, U.S.	0.4	1	....	....	163/J 4
Kiribati	277	717	82,449	Tarawa	162/H 5
Korea, North	46,540	120,539	24,317,004	P'yŏngyang	107/D 2
Korea, South	38,023	98,480	45,948,811	Seoul	107/D 4
Kuwait	6,830	17,820	2,076,805	Kuwait	129/F 4
KwaZulu Natal, South Africa	35,312	91,481	8,549,000	Pietermaritzburg	151/E 3
Kyrgyzstan	76,641	198,500	4,540,185	Bishkek	125/B 3
L Laos	91,428	236,800	5,116,959	Vientiane	120/C 2
Latvia	24,749	64,100	2,437,649	Riga	67/L 3
Lebanon	4,015	10,399	3,858,736	Beirut	130/D 3
Lesotho	11,718	30,350	2,007,814	Maseru	150/D 3
Liberia	43,000	111,370	2,602,068	Monrovia	140/C 5
Libya	679,358	1,759,537	5,648,359	Tripoli	134/C 2
Liechtenstein	62	160	31,461	Vaduz	87/F 3
Lithuania	25,174	65,200	3,635,932	Vilnius	67/K 4
Louisiana, U.S.	49,651	128,595	4,350,579	Baton Rouge	169/H 5
Luxembourg	999	2,587	422,474	Luxembourg	81/E 4
M Macau, Portugal	6	16	502,325	Macau	113/G 4
Macedonia (F.Y.R.O.M.)	9,781	25,333	2,113,866	Skopje	75/G 2
Madagascar	226,657	587,041	14,061,627	Antananarivo	151/H 8
Madeira Islands, Portugal	307	794	253,452	Funchal	136/A 2
Maine, U.S.	33,741	87,388	1,243,316	Augusta	184/B 3

Place	Square Miles	Square Kilometers	Population	Capital or Chief Town	Page/Index
Malawi	45,745	118,480	9,609,081	Lilongwe	133/F 6
Malaya, Malaysia	50,806	131,588	14,181,863	Kuala Lumpur	115/C 1
Malaysia	127,316	329,750	20,376,235	Kuala Lumpur	116/C 2
Maldives	116	300	280,391	Male	103/F 9
Mali	478,764	1,240,000	9,945,383	Bamako	133/B 3
Malta	124	320	379,365	Valletta	74/N 8
Manitoba, Canada	250,946	649,951	1,091,942	Winnipeg	166/F 3
Marquesas Islands, French Polynesia	405	1,049	7,538	Atuona	163/M 5
Marshall Islands	70	181	60,652	Majuro	162/G 3
Martinique, France	425	1,100	403,531	Fort-de-France	197/N 8
Maryland, U.S.	12,297	31,849	5,071,604	Annapolis	169/L 4
Massachusetts, U.S.	9,241	23,934	6,092,352	Boston	169/M 3
Mauritania	397,953	1,030,700	2,411,317	Nouakchott	133/A 3
Mauritius	718	1,860	1,154,272	Port Louis	151/S15
Mayotte, France	145	375	104,715	Mamoutzou	151/H 6
Mexico	761,601	1,972,546	97,563,374	Mexico	165/G 7
Michigan, U.S.	96,705	250,465	9,594,350	Lansing	169/J 2
Micronesia, Federated States of	271	702	122,950	Palikir	162/D 4
Midway Islands, U.S.	2	5.2	453	....	162/H 2
Minnesota, U.S.	86,943	225,182	4,657,758	St. Paul	169/G 2
Mississippi, U.S.	48,286	125,060	2,716,115	Jackson	169/H 5
Missouri, U.S.	69,709	180,546	5,358,692	Jefferson City	169/H 4
Moldova	13,012	33,700	4,475,232	Chişinău	98/E 4
Monaco	0.7	1.9	31,892		90/D 5
Mongolia	606,163	1,569,962	2,538,211	Ulaanbaatar	104/D 2
Montana, U.S.	147,046	380,849	879,372	Helena	168/D 2
Montserrat, U.K.	39	100	12,800	Plymouth	197/N 7
Morocco	172,414	446,550	30,391,423	Rabat	136/D 2
Mozambique	309,494	801,590	18,165,476	Maputo	149/G 3
Mpumalanga, South Africa	31,581	81,816	2,838,500	Nelspruit	151/E 2
Myanmar (Burma)	261,969	678,500	46,821,943	Yangon	119/G 2
N Namibia	318,694	825,418	1,727,183	Windhoek	133/D 7
Nauru	8	21	10,390	Yaren (district)	162/F 5
Navassa Island, U.S.	2	5	....	....	201/H 2
Nebraska, U.S.	77,358	200,358	1,652,093	Lincoln	180/D 3
Nepal	54,363	140,800	22,641,061	Kathmandu	122/D 1
Netherlands	14,413	37,330	15,653,091	The Hague; Amsterdam	78/B 5
Netherlands Antilles	371	960	211,093	Willemstad	204/D 1
Nevada, U.S.	110,567	286,367	1,603,163	Carson City	168/C 4
New Brunswick, Canada	28,355	73,440	723,900	Fredericton	184/D 2
New Caledonia & Dependencies, France	7,359	19,060	191,003	Nouméa	162/F 6
Newfoundland, Canada	156,649	405,721	568,474	St. John's	167/K 3
New Hampshire, U.S.	9,283	24,044	1,162,481	Concord	187/L 3
New Jersey, U.S.	8,215	21,277	7,987,933	Trenton	194/D 3
New Mexico, U.S.	121,598	314,939	1,713,407	Santa Fe	168/E 5
New South Wales, Australia	309,498	801,600	5,731,906	Sydney	158/C 1
New York, U.S.	53,989	139,833	18,184,774	Albany	187/J 3
New Zealand	103,736	268,676	3,587,275	Wellington	161
Nicaragua	49,998	129,494	4,386,399	Managua	201/E 3
Niger	489,189	1,267,000	9,388,859	Niamey	133/C 3
Nigeria	356,668	923,770	107,129,469	Abuja	133/C 4
Niue, New Zealand	100	259	1,837	Alofi	163/J 7
Norfolk Island, Australia	13.4	34.6	2,756	Kingston	162/F 7
North America	9,355,975	24,232,000	443,438,000	....	165
North Carolina, U.S.	52,672	136,421	7,322,870	Raleigh	189/G 3
North Dakota, U.S.	70,704	183,123	643,539	Bismarck	182/D 4
Northern Cape, South Africa	140,268	363,389	763,900	Kimberley	150/C 3
Northern Ireland, U.K.	5,459	14,138	1,610,000	Belfast	57/H 9
Northern Marianas, U.S.	184	477	53,552	Saipan	162/D 3
Northern Province, South Africa	46,168	119,606	5,120,600	Pietersburg	149/F 4
Northern Territory, Australia	519,784	1,346,241	175,876	Darwin	153/C 2
North Korea	46,540	120,539	23,486,550	P'yŏngyang	107/D 2
North-West, South Africa	45,347	117,450	3,506,800	Mmabatho	150/D 2
Northwest Territories, Canada	589,315	1,526,328	39,672	Yellowknife	166/E 2
Norway	125,181	324,220	4,404,456	Oslo	64/C 3

Place	Square Miles	Square Kilometers	Population	Capital or Chief Town	Page/Index
Nova Scotia, Canada	21,425	55,491	899,942	Halifax	184/E 3
Nunavut, Canada	733,590	1,900,000	24,730	Iqaluit	167/K 2
O Oceania	3,292,000	8,526,280	24,436,000	....	162
Ohio, U.S.	44,828	116,103	11,172,782	Columbus	169/K 3
Oklahoma, U.S.	69,903	181,048	3,300,902	Oklahoma City	179/E 3
Oman	82,031	212,460	2,264,590	Muscat	127/G 4
Ontario, Canada	412,580	1,068,582	10,084,885	Toronto	166/H 3
Oregon, U.S.	97,132	251,571	3,203,735	Salem	168/B 3
Orkney Islands, Scotland	376	974	19,700	Kirkwall	57/N13
P Pakistan	310,403	803,944	132,185,299	Islamabad	127/H 3
Palau	177	458	17,240	Koror	162/C 4
Palmyra Atoll, U.S.	5	12	....	....	163/J 4
Panama	30,193	78,200	2,693,417	Panamá	201/F 4
Papua New Guinea	178,259	461,690	4,496,221	Port Moresby	162/D 5
Paracel Islands	....	....			113/F 5
Paraguay	157,047	406,752	5,651,634	Asunción	212/D 2
Pennsylvania, U.S.	46,058	119,291	12,056,112	Harrisburg	187/G 4
Peru	496,223	1,285,220	24,949,512	Lima	208/C 3
Philippines	115,830	300,000	76,103,564	Manila	114
Pitcairn Islands, U.K.	18	47	73	Adamstown	163/N 7
Poland	120,725	312,678	38,700,291	Warsaw	69/K 2
Portugal	35,552	92,080	9,867,654	Lisbon	72/A 3
Prince Edward Island, Canada	2,184	5,657	129,765	Charlottetown	184/F 2
Puerto Rico, U.S.	3,508	9,085	3,817,833	San Juan	197/M7
Q Qatar	4,247	11,000	665,485	Doha	126/F 3
Québec, Canada	594,857	1,540,680	6,895,963	Québec	167/J 3
Queensland, Australia	666,872	1,727,200	2,977,813	Brisbane	160/A 3
R Réunion, France	969	2,510	692,204	St-Denis	151/R15
Rhode Island, U.S.	1,231	3,189	990,225	Providence	187/L 4
Romania	91,699	237,500	21,399,114	Bucharest	77/F 3
Russia	6,592,735	17,075,200	147,987,101	Moscow	100/H 3
Rwanda	10,169	26,337	7,737,537	Kigali	147/G 3
S Sabah, Malaysia	28,460	73,711	1,736,902	Kota Kinabalu	117/E 2
Saint Helena & Dependencies, U.K.	158	410	6,803	Jamestown	52/J 6
Saint Kitts and Nevis	104	269	41,803	Basseterre	197/N 7
Saint Lucia	239	620	159,639	Castries	197/N 8
Saint Pierre & Miquelon, France	93.5	242	6,862	Saint-Pierre	185/J 2
Saint Vincent & the Grenadines	131	340	119,092	Kingstown	197/N 8
Sakhalin, Russia	29,500	76,405	709,000	Yuzhno-Sakhalinsk	101/Q 4
Samoa	1,104	2,860	219,509	Apia	163/R 9
San Marino	23.4	60.6	24,714	San Marino	89/F 5
São Tomé and Príncipe	371	960	147,865	São Tomé	146/A 2
Sarawak, Malaysia	48,050	124,449	1,648,217	Kuching	116/D 3
Sardinia, Italy	9,301	24,090	1,650,000	Cagliari	74/A 2
Saskatchewan, Canada	251,865	652,330	988,928	Regina	166/F 3
Saudi Arabia	756,981	1,960,582	20,087,965	Riyadh	126/D 4
Scotland, U.K.	30,414	78,772	5,111,200	Edinburgh	57/J 8
Senegal	75,749	196,190	9,403,546	Dakar	140/B 3
Serbia and Montenegro, see Yugoslavia					
Seychelles	176	455	78,142	Victoria	53/M6
Shetland Islands, Scotland	552·	1,430	22,600	Lerwick	57/N12
Siam, see Thailand					
Sicily, Italy	9,926	25,708	4,966,000	Palermo	74/C 3
Sierra Leone	27,699	71,740	4,891,546	Freetown	140/B 4
Singapore	244	632.6	3,461,929	Singapore	115/H 6
Slovakia	18,859	48,845	5,393,016	Bratislava	69/K 4
Slovenia	7,836	20,296	1,945,998	Ljubljana	76/B 3
Society Islands, French Polynesia	677	1,753	117,703	Papeete	163/K 6
Solomon Islands	10,985	28,450	462,855	Honiara	162/E 6
Somalia	246,200	637,658	9,940,232	Mogadishu	133/G 4
South Africa	471,008	1,219,912	42,327,458	Cape Town; Pretoria	133/E 7
South America	6,879,916	17,819,000	314,335,000	....	203
South Australia, Australia	379,922	984,000	1,400,630	Adelaide	153/C 3
South Carolina, U.S.	31,189	80,779	3,698,746	Columbia	189/G 3
South Dakota, U.S.	77,121	199,744	732,405	Pierre	180/D 1

Place	Square Miles	Square Kilometers	Population	Capital or Chief Town	Page/Index
South Korea	38,023	98,480	45,553,882	Seoul	107/D 4
Spain	194,884	504,750	39,244,195	Madrid	72/C 2
Spratly Islands	....	....	....		116/D 2
Sri Lanka	25,332	65,610	18,762,075	Colombo	118/D 6
Sudan	967,494	2,505,809	32,594,128	Khartoum	133/E 3
Sumatra, Indonesia	182,811	473,481	36,505,703	Medan	115/D 3
Suriname	63,039	163,270	443,446	Paramaribo	206/B 1
Svalbard, Norway	23,957	62,049	2,914	Longyearbyen	100/C 2
Swaziland	6,703	17,360	1,031,600	Mbabane; Lomamba	151/E 2
Sweden	173,731	449,964	8,946,193	Stockholm	64/E 3
Switzerland	15,943	41,292	7,248,984	Bern	86/D 4
Syria	71,498	185,180	16,137,899	Damascus	128/D 3
T Tahiti, French Polynesia	402	1,041	115,820	Papeete	163/X15
Taiwan	13,892·	35,980	21,655,515	T'aipei	113/J 3
Tajikistan	55,251	143,100	6,013,855	Dushanbe	100/H 6
Tanzania	364,699	945,090	29,460,753	Dar es Salaam; Dodoma	133/F 5
Tasmania, Australia	26,178	67,800	452,851	Hobart	158/C 4
Tennessee, U.S.	42,146	109,158	5,319,654	Nashville	188/D 3
Texas, U.S.	267,277	692,248	19,128,261	Austin	168/G 5
Thailand	198,455	513,998	59,450,818	Bangkok	120/C 3
Tibet, China	471,428	1,221,000	2,196,029	Lhasa	125/D 5
Togo	21,927	56,790	4,735,610	Lomé	141/F 4
Tokelau, New Zealand	3.9	10	1,503	....	163/H 5
Tonga	289	748	107,335	Nuku'alofa	163/H 7
Trinidad and Tobago	1,980	5,128	1,273,141	Port-of-Spain	197/N 9
Tristan da Cunha, St. Helena	38	98	313	Edinburgh	52/J 7
Tuamotu Archipelago, French Polynesia	266	690	12,374	Apataki	163/L 6
Tunisia	63,170	163,610	9,183,097	Tunis	137/H 2
Turkey	301,382	780,580	63,528,225	Ankara	128/C 2
Turkmenistan	188,455	488,100	4,225,351	Ashgabat	100/F 6
Turks and Caicos Islands, U.K.	166	430	14,631	Grand Turk	201/H 1
Tuvalu	10	26	10,297	Funafuti	162/G 5
U Uganda	91,135	236,040	20,604,874	Kampala	133/F 4
Ukraine	233,089	603,700	50,684,635	Kiev	98/F 4
United Arab Emirates	29,182	75,581	2,262,309	Abu Dhabi	126/F 4
United Kingdom	94,525	244,820	58,610,182	London	57
United States	3,618,765	9,372,610	267,954,767	Washington, D.C.	168
Uruguay	68,039	176,220	3,261,707	Montevideo	203/D 6
Utah, U.S.	84,904	219,902	2,000,494	Salt Lake City	168/D 4
Uzbekistan	172,741	447,400	23,860,452	Tashkent	100/G 5
V Vanuatu	5,699	14,760	181,358	Port-Vila	162/F 6
Vatican City	0.17	0.44	830	....	91/E 7
Venezuela	352,143	912,050	22,396,407	Caracas	205/E 3
Vermont, U.S.	9,614	24,900	588,654	Montpelier	187/K 3
Victoria, Australia	87,876	227,600	4,244,282	Melbourne	158/C 3
Vietnam	127,243	329,560	75,123,880	Hanoi	120/D 2
Virginia, U.S.	42,326	109,625	6,675,451	Richmond	189/H 2
Virgin Islands, British	59	153	13,368	Road Town	197/M7
Virgin Islands, U.S.	136	352	97,240	Charlotte Amalie	197/M7
W Wake Island, U.S.	2.5	6.5	302	....	162/F 3
Wales, U.K.	8,017	20,764	2,886,400	Cardiff	57/J10
Wallis and Futuna, France	106	275	14,817	Mata Utu	162/G 6
Washington, U.S.	70,637	182,949	5,532,939	Olympia	170/D 4
West Bank	2,263	5,860	1,495,683	....	131/C 4
Western Australia, Australia	975,096	2,525,500	1,587,050	Perth	153/B 3
Western Cape, South Africa	49,943	129,386	3,620,200	Cape Town	150/C 4
Western Sahara	102,703	266,000	228,138	....	136/B 4
West Virginia, U.S.	24,231	62,758	1,825,754	Charleston	169/K 4
Wisconsin, U.S.	65,499	169,643	5,159,795	Madison	169/H 3
World	(land) 57,505,734	148,940,000	5,819,131,463		52
Wyoming, U.S.	97,818	253,349	481,400	Cheyenne	168/E 3
Y Yemen	203,849	527,970	13,972,477	Sanaa	126/E 5
Yugoslavia	39,517	102,350	10,655,317	Belgrade	76/E 3
Yukon Territory, Canada	186,660	483,450	27,797	Whitehorse	166/C 2
Z Zambia	290,583	752,610	9,349,975	Lusaka	133/E 6
Zimbabwe	150,803	390,530	11,423,175	Harare	149/F 3

Global Relationships

Population

 **I**n 6,000 B.C., earth's entire population stood between 5 and 20 million people. It took almost 8,000 years to reach the one billion mark, yet just 100 years more to reach two billion in 1930. Sixty years later, that figure had nearly tripled, to about 5.8 billion people. This massive expansion has been fueled not by an increasing birth rate, but by a gradual extension of life expectancy and a huge reduction in infant mortality. ❋ By 2025, the United Nations projects that our global population could exceed 8.3 billion. Ninety percent of this growth will be concentrated in the poorest countries. The most dramatic increases will take place in sub-Saharan Africa, where fertility rates have remained high. ❋ Population shifts are often driven by economic forces. In the late 15th and early 16th centuries, Europe's conquest of the sea spurred trade, exploration and settlements across the globe. The temperate zones of the Americas were especially well-suited to their crops and flocks. Between the 16th and mid-19th centuries, millions of black Africans were brought to the Americas by the Atlantic slave trade, victims of the New World's voracious need for labor. ❋ In the industrialized nations of Europe, Japan, Canada and the United States, the trend is towards zero growth. Birth rates have also fallen in India and China, yet 17 percent of the world's people live in India, and 20 percent — 1 of every 5 people — live in China. Aggressive educational programs are helping to change traditional beliefs, which held childbirth as a woman's duty, and viewed large families as proof of wealth, fortification against hardship and security for aging parents. Government-sponsored birth control programs are also showing positive results. ❋ Not all of the factors which could limit population growth are so well planned. In the end, the environmental pressures created by rapidly expanding population may deplete the very resources necessary for survival.

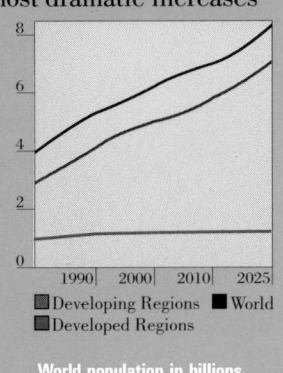

Developing Regions ■ ■ World
Developed Regions

World population in billions

CROWDED PLACES

THOUSANDS OF PERSONS PER SQUARE MILE (SQ. KM.)

Macau
81(31)
95(36)

Monaco
32(17)
34(18)

Hong Kong
16(6)
20(8)

Singapore
14(5)
18(7)

Gibraltar
9(4)
10(5)

Gaza Strip
7(3)
18(7)

□ 1997
□ 2020 (estimate)

Source: U.S. Bureau of the Census, International Database

WORLD'S LARGEST URBAN AREAS

MILLIONS OF INHABITANTS

Tokyo, Japan 26.5

New York, U.S. 18.0

São Paulo, Brazil 16.9

Osaka, Japan 16.9

Seoul, Korea 15.8

Mexico, Mexico 15.5

Shanghai, China 14.7

Mumbai, India 14.5

Los Angeles, U.S. 14.5

Moscow, Russia 13.1

Beijing, China 12.0

Calcutta, India 11.4

London, U.K. 11.1

Rio de Janeiro, Brazil 11.0

Jakarta, Indonesia 11.0

URBAN & RURAL POPULATION COMPONENTS

SELECTED COUNTRIES

□ URBAN   ■ RURAL

Uruguay 87% / 13%

Australia 85% / 15%

Japan 77% / 23%

United States 74% / 26%

Russia 73% / 27%

Hungary 62% / 38%

Iran 54% / 46%

Egypt 44% / 56%

Philippines 37% / 63%

Portugal 30% / 70%

China 26% / 74%

Maldives 20% / 80%

Bangladesh 15% / 85%

Nepal 6% / 94%

AGE DISTRIBUTION

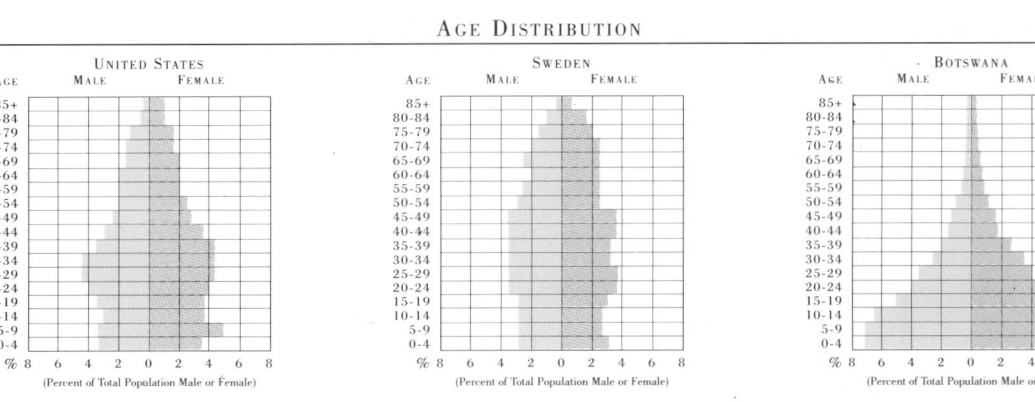

UNITED STATES — SWEDEN — BOTSWANA (Male / Female age pyramids, ages 0-4 through 85+, % 8 6 4 2 0 2 4 6 8, Percent of Total Population Male or Female)

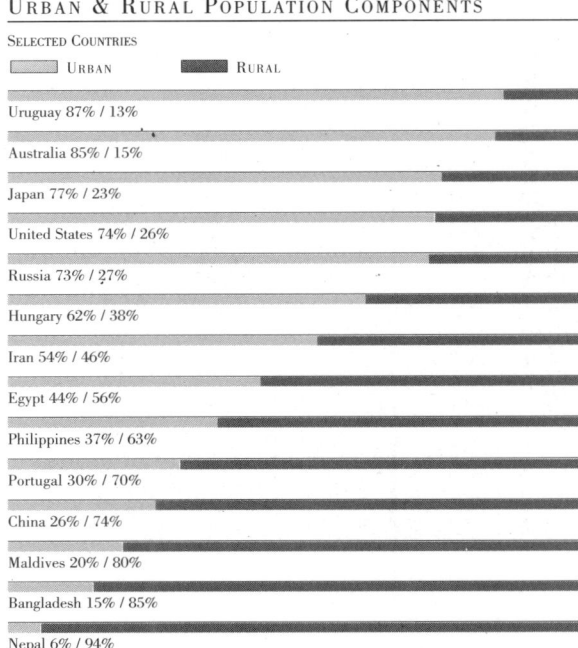

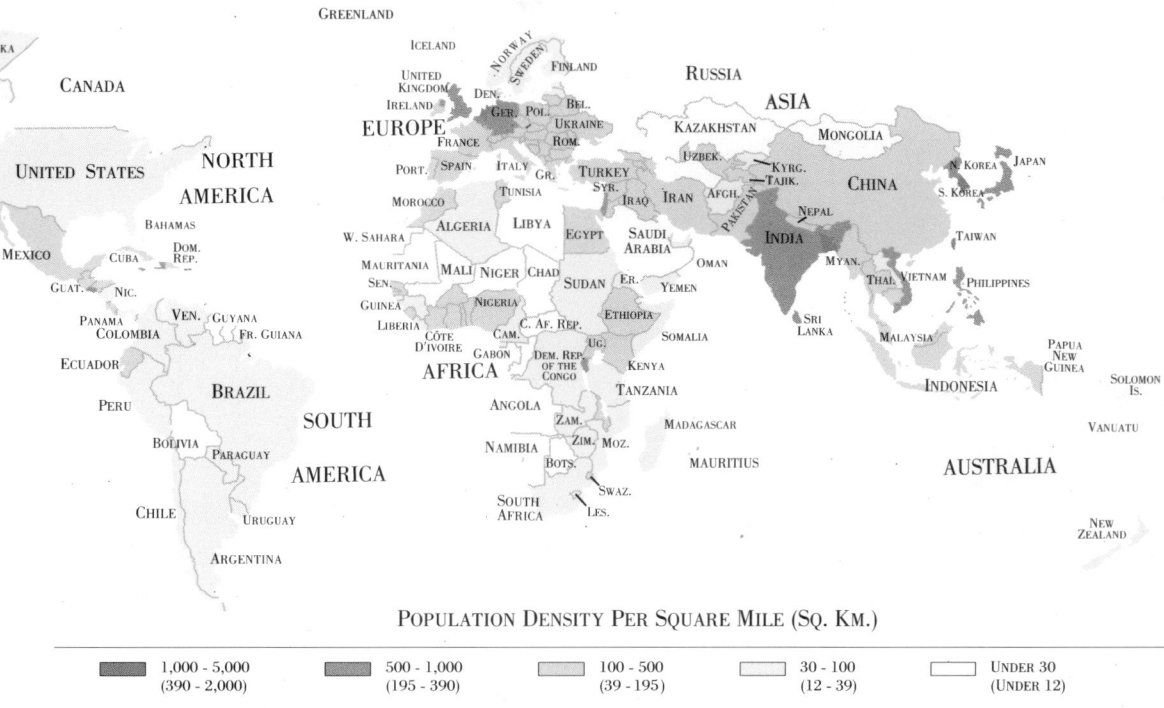

POPULATION DENSITY PER SQUARE MILE (SQ. KM.)

■ 1,000 - 5,000 (390 - 2,000)	■ 500 - 1,000 (195 - 390)	100 - 500 (39 - 195)	30 - 100 (12 - 39)	□ UNDER 30 (UNDER 12)

Source: U.S. Bureau of the Census, International Database

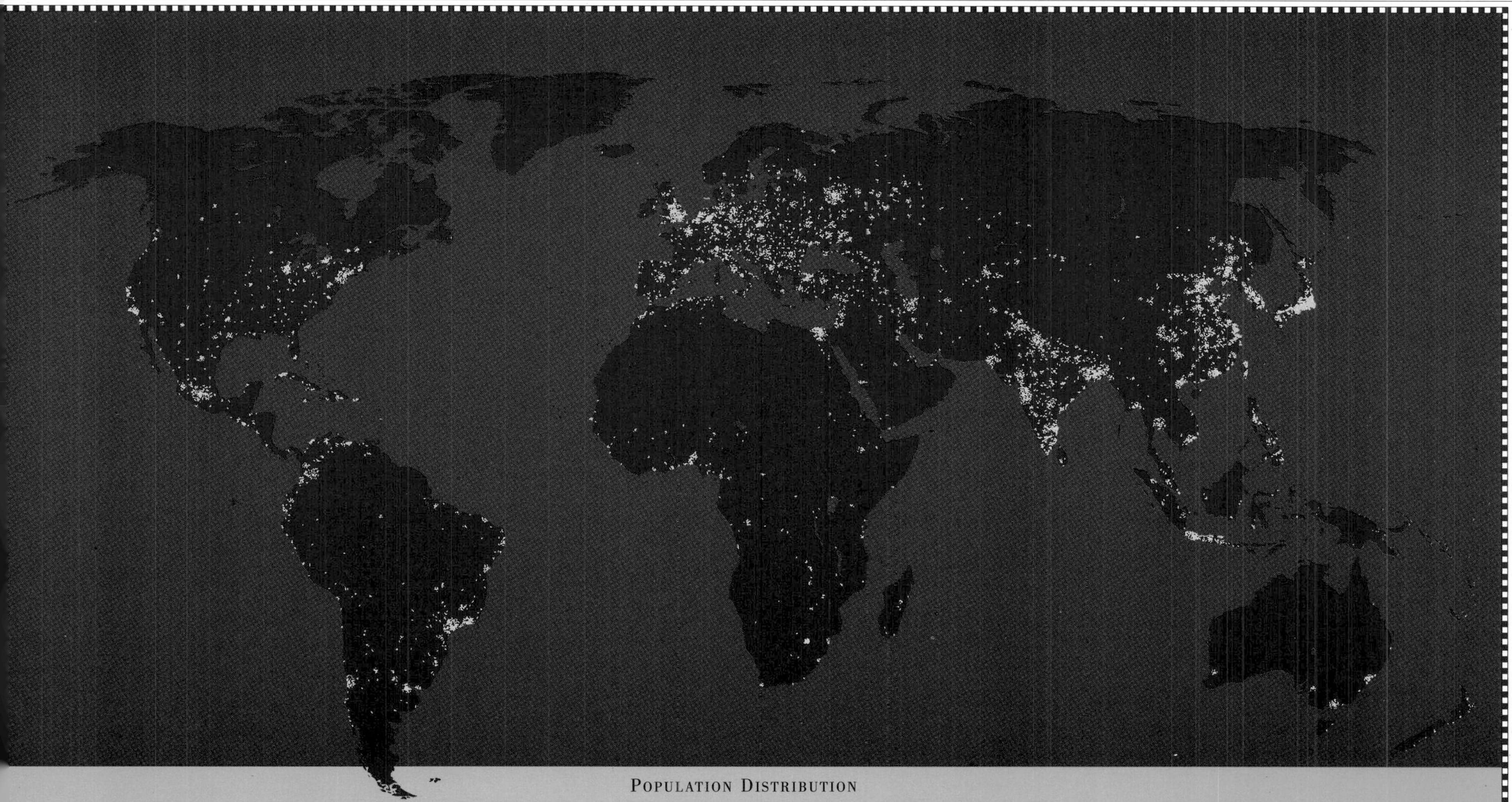

POPULATION DISTRIBUTION

This map provides a dramatic perspective by illuminating populated areas with one point of light per 50,000 residents. Over 675 million people live in cities with populations in excess of 500,000. According to the latest census data, there are 10,000 people per square mile (3,860 per sq km) in London. In New York, there are 11,000 (4,250). Hong Kong has over 16,000 people per square mile (6,200 per sq km), and the Tokyo-Yokohama agglomeration includes over 25,000 (9,650). During the last decade, the movement to the cities has accelerated dramatically, particularly in developing nations. In Lagos, Nigeria, where there are over 24,000 people per square mile (9,290 per sq km), most live in shantytowns. In São Paulo, Brazil, 2,000 buses arrive each day, bringing field hands, farm workers and their families in search of a better life. By the year 2000, the United Nations predicts that 17 of the world's 20 largest urban agglomerations will be in the third world. Tokyo-Yokohama, Mexico City and São Paulo will top the list.

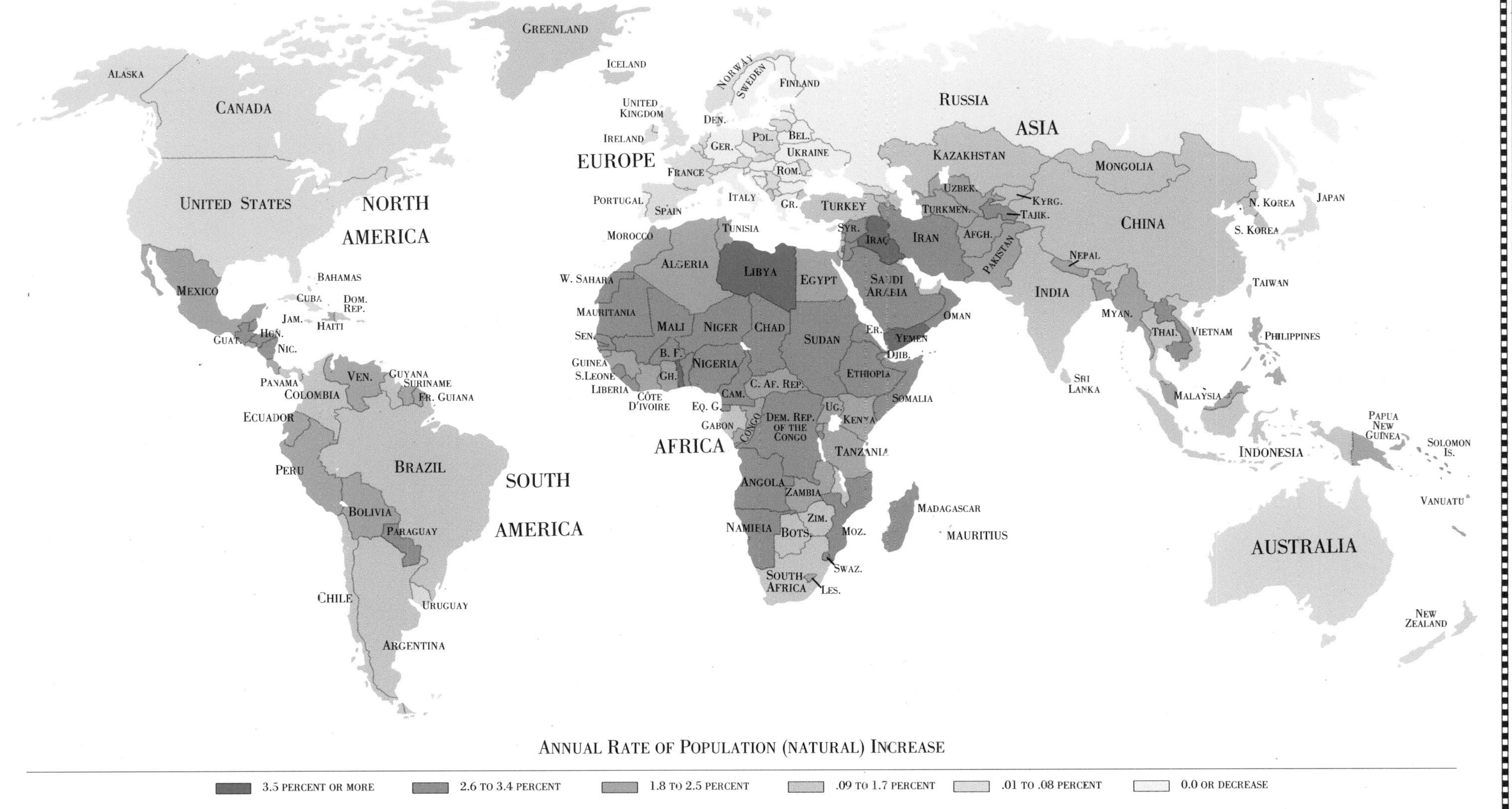

ANNUAL RATE OF POPULATION (NATURAL) INCREASE

3.5 PERCENT OR MORE	2.6 TO 3.4 PERCENT	1.8 TO 2.5 PERCENT	.09 TO 1.7 PERCENT	.01 TO .08 PERCENT	0.0 OR DECREASE

Source: U.S. Bureau of the Census, International Database

Over 4,000 languages are spoken in the world today. By searching for the roots of these languages, linguists have reconstructed their origins and charted the migrations of ancient peoples.◉ Indo-European, the ancestral tongue from which modern European languages are descended, may have originated 8,000 years ago in Anatolia, part of modern-day Turkey. By 1000 B.C., Indo-European was spoken over much of Europe, and in parts of southern and southwestern Asia.◉ Today, it is no longer migration, but rather global communications and the media which transport languages across continents. The emerging global business culture, in particular, has created a pressing need for a common tongue.◉ Language and culture are intimately bound and constantly evolving. Many religions are associated with a particular written language: Latin was the primary language of Christianity. For Judaism, it was Hebrew; for Islam, Arabic; and Chinese was the language of Confucianism.◉ Religion has been the chief inspiration for much of the world's greatest music, literature, architecture — and wars. The major religious influence on western civilization was Christianity; Islam and Judaism were also important. These same faiths, and particularly Islam, were also central to the development of Middle Eastern culture. Asian cultures were shaped by Buddhism, Hinduism, Taoism, Confucianism and the Shinto faith.◉ Today, almost one-third of the world's population is Christian; about 17 percent are Muslim; 13.5 percent are Hindus; and 6 percent are Buddhists.

More than 100 languages are spoken by a million or more people. Of these, 19 have over fifty million speakers each.

MAJOR LANGUAGES
NUMBER OF FIRST LANGUAGE SPEAKERS

Language	
Chinese (Mandarin) 885	
English 322	
Spanish 266	
Arabic 202	
Bengali 189	
Hindi 182	
Russian 170	
Portuguese 170	
Japanese 125	
German 98	
Javanese 76	
French 72	Millions of Speakers

Languages & Religions

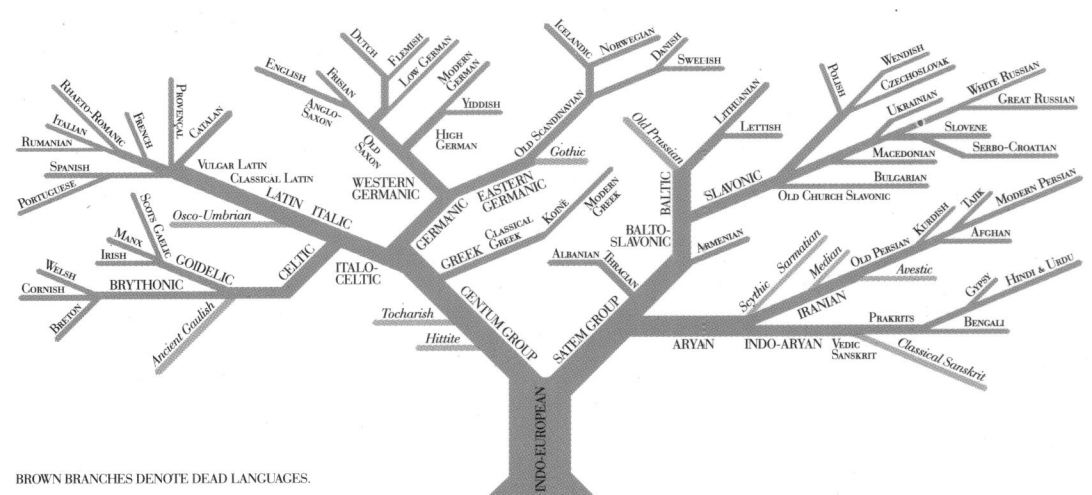

BROWN BRANCHES DENOTE DEAD LANGUAGES.

POSSIBLE CONNECTIONS WITH FINNIC-UGRIC, TURKIC AND SEMITIC FAMILIES

THE INDO-EUROPEAN LANGUAGE TREE

The most well-established family tree is Indo-European. Spoken by more than 2.5 billion people, it contains dozens of languages. Some linguists theorize that all people - and all languages - are descended from a tiny population that lived in Africa some 200,000 years ago.

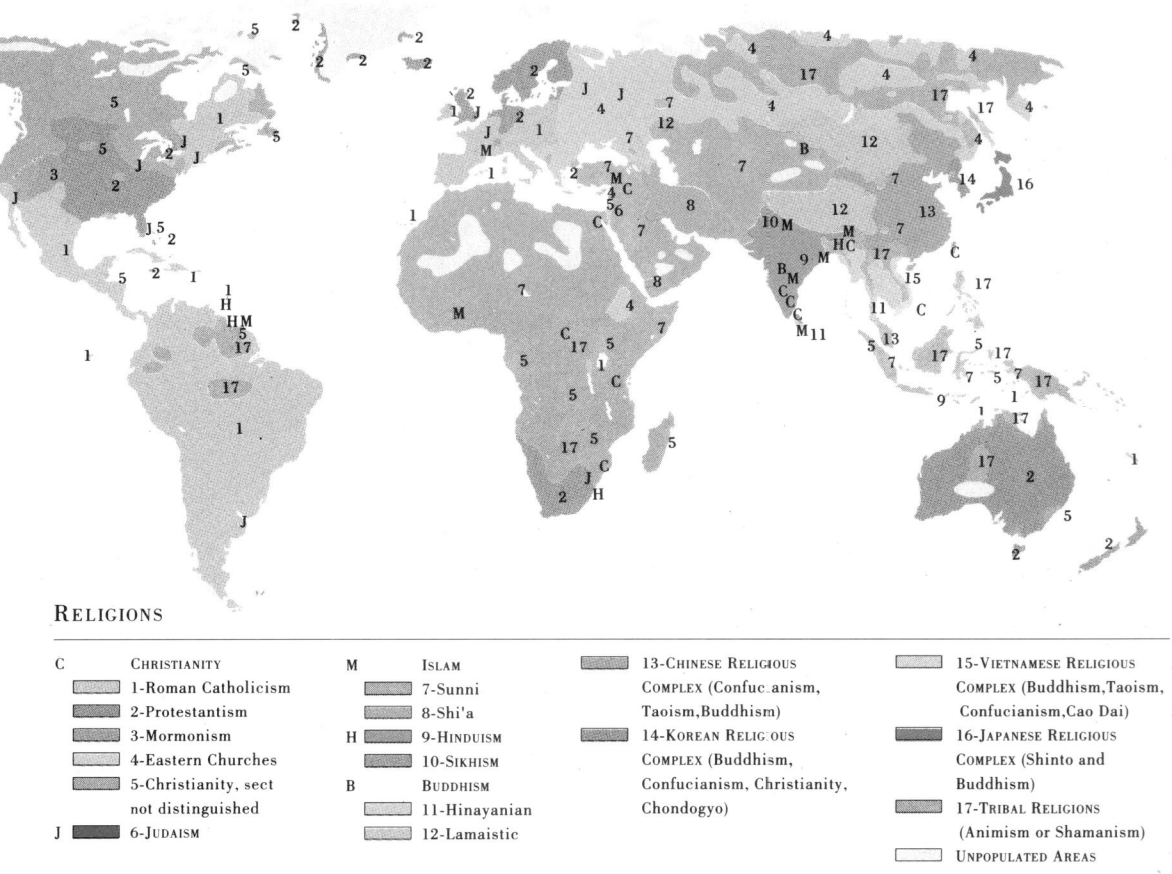

RELIGIONS

C	CHRISTIANITY	M	ISLAM		13-CHINESE RELIGIOUS COMPLEX (Confucianism, Taoism, Buddhism)		15-VIETNAMESE RELIGIOUS COMPLEX (Buddhism, Taoism, Confucianism, Cao Dai)	

- 1-Roman Catholicism
- 2-Protestantism
- 3-Mormonism
- 4-Eastern Churches
- 5-Christianity, sect not distinguished
- J 6-Judaism
- 7-Sunni
- 8-Shi'a
- H 9-Hinduism
- 10-Sikhism
- B Buddhism
- 11-Hinayanian
- 12-Lamaistic
- 14-Korean Religious Complex (Buddhism, Confucianism, Christianity, Chondogyo)
- 16-Japanese Religious Complex (Shinto and Buddhism)
- 17-Tribal Religions (Animism or Shamanism)
- Unpopulated Areas

Important Local Minorities are Indicated by Letter

Language Families

- 1-Indo-European
  - 1A-Germanic
  - 1B-Romance
  - 1C-Slavic
  - 1D-Baltic
  - 1E-Celtic
  - 1F-Albanian
  - 1G-Greek
  - 1H-Armenian
  - 1J-Iranian
  - 1K-Indo-Aryan
- 2-Basque
- 3-Caucasian Families
- 4-Burushaski
- 5-Afro-Asiatic (Hamitic-Semitic)
- 6-Nilo-Saharan
- 7-Niger-Congo
- 8-Khoisan
- 9-Uralic
- 10-Altaic
- 11-Paleo-Siberian Families
- 12-Sino-Tibetan
- 13-Thai-Kadai
- 14-Korean
- 15-Japanese
- 16-Dravidian
- 17-Vietnamese
- 18-Austro-Asiatic
- 19-Austronesian
- 20-Papuan
- 21-Australian
- 22-Eskimo-Aleut
- 23-American Indian Families
- Unpopulated Areas

Note: Names may vary, depending on source.

Languages of Europe

Indo-European Family
- Germanic Subfamily
- Romance Subfamily
- Celtic Subfamily
- Slavic Subfamily
- Baltic Subfamily
- Greek
- Albanian

Uralic Family
- Finnic Subfamily
- Ugric subfamily
- Samoyed

Altaic Family
- Turkic Subfamily

Afro-Asiatic Family
- Maltese

- Basque

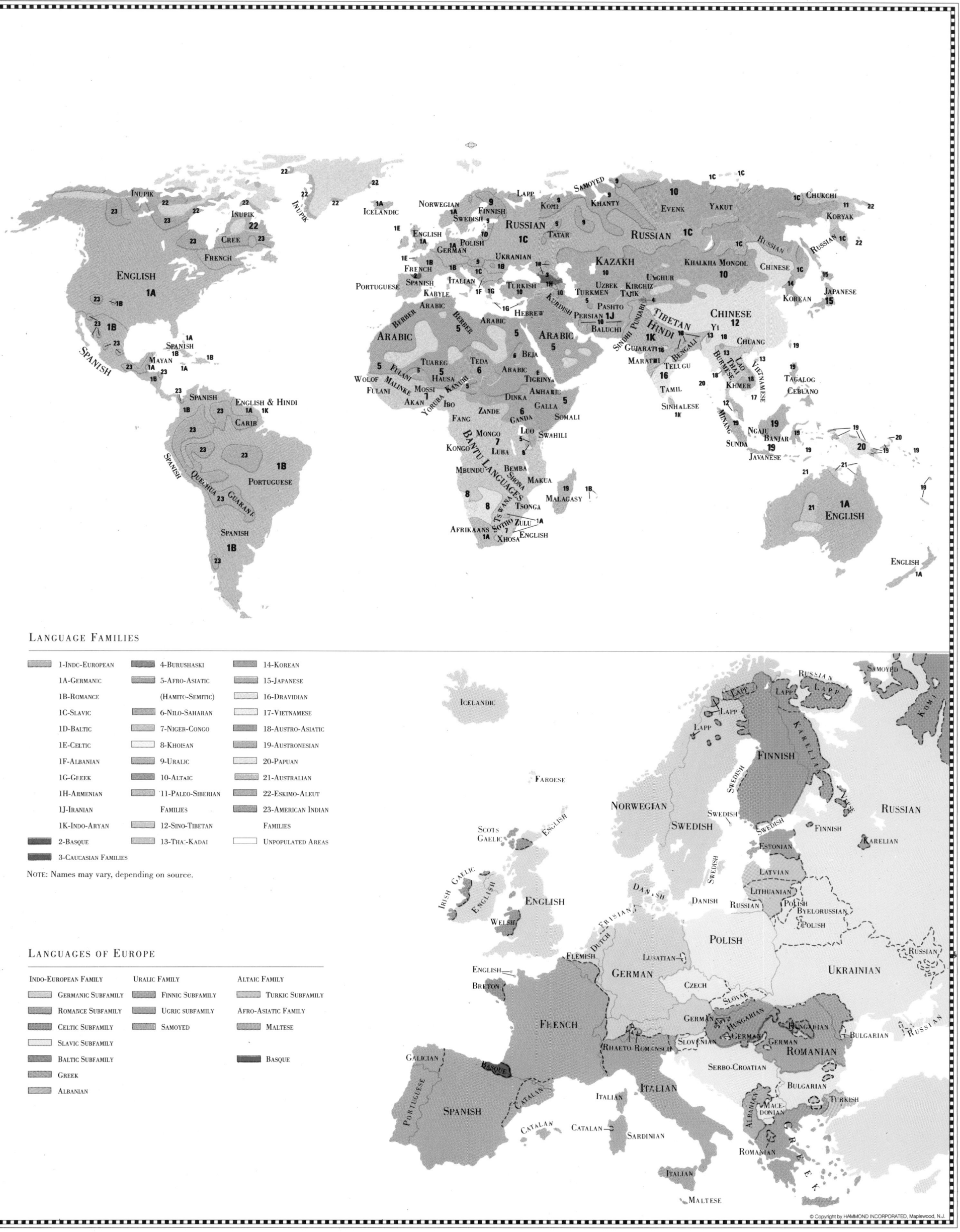

The living standards of less than two dozen highly industrialized nations stand in vivid contrast to conditions in the rest of the world. Though the developed countries represent only about a quarter of the earth's population, they create 80 percent of its wealth. The rest of the world must subsist on one-fifth of the total goods. ☻ Political instability, inadequate education and health care, and the lack or misuse of natural resources all contribute to this disparity. Most people in the developing world still live off the land, leaving them prey to natural disasters and market prices which no longer keep pace with rising costs. Drought, desertification, swelling populations and aggressive development further challenge traditional lifestyles. In third world nations from Mexico to Nigeria, the exodus from rural communities has resulted in intensely overcrowded cities where housing, jobs and clean water are inadequate. ☻ Despite these challenges, advances in education and health care have wrought stunning improvements in average life expectancy. In the developing world, it has risen from 46 years in 1960 to 62 years in 1993. Between 1962 and 1997, life expectancy in China jumped from 39 to 70 years. Antibiotics and immunizations have significantly reduced infant mortality levels in many third world countries. In North America, Western Europe and Japan, the average life expectancy is 71 years for men and 77 years for women. Elsewhere, in Afghanistan and sub-Saharan Africa, average life expectancy still hovers around 40. ☻ Literacy is the cornerstone of a healthy industrial nation. Yet by the year 2000, more than a billion people may be unable to read or write. Most of them will live in the 5 most populous Asian countries: China, India, Indonesia, Pakistan and Bangladesh. Ambitious literacy programs now underway in countries from Iraq to Chile and Mexico have reported significant reductions in their illiteracy rates. With each success comes new hope — for an individual, a family and a nation.

In the United States, the average person earns about $27,500 — the highest per capita Gross Domestic Product in the world. In Rwanda, the same person would earn about $400 in a year.

American workers typically get only 2 or 3 weeks of annual paid vacation, while western Europeans enjoy 4 to 6 weeks off.

Standards of

GREENLAND

ALASKA

CANADA

UNITED STATES

MEXICO

BAHAMAS

CUBA

JAM.   DOM. REP.

BEL.   HAITI
HON.
GUAT.   NIC.
EL SAL.

C.R.
PANAMA   VENEZUELA GUYANA
COLOMBIA   SURINAME
FR. GUIANA

ECUADOR

PERU   BRAZIL

BOLIVIA

PARAGUAY

CHILE

ARGENTINA   URUGUAY

UNITED STATES
The United States and other developed countries have committed greater resources to both public and private education. This has helped their populations develop the skills that are necessary in more complex, technical and competitive societies.

LATIN AMERICA
The gulf between rich and poor continues to widen, despite efforts to reform oppressive governments, increase literacy and relieve overburdened cities.

SOUTH AMERICA
Political unrest, rising inflation and slow economic growth continue to thwart efforts to bring unity and prosperity to the nations of South America.

EUROPE
The healthy, high-tech economies of many western European nations stand in sharp relief to the obsolete factories, high unemployment and ethnic rivalries of Eastern Europe.

ICELAND   NORWAY SWEDEN FINLAND
UNITED   E.
KINGDOM   DEN.   L.
IRELAND   N.   POLAND   BEL.
B.   GER. CZ.   UKRAINE
FRANCE   S.   A.   HUN. ROM.   M.
C.   BUL.
PORTUGAL   SPAIN   ITALY   A.
GR.   TURKEY

TUNISIA

MOROCCO
WESTERN   ALGERIA   LIBYA   EGYPT
SAHARA

MAURITANIA   MALI   NIGER   CHAD   SUDAN
SEN.
G.
G.B.   B. F.
GUINEA   NIGERIA
S.-LEONE   GH.
LIBERIA
CÔTE   C. AF. REP.
D'IVOIRE   CAM.
EQ. G.
GABON   DEM. REP.
CONGO   OF THE
CONGO
TANZ.

ANGOLA   ZAMBIA

NAMIBIA   ZIM.
BOTS.

SOUTH
AFRICA   LES.

AFRICA
Disastrous droughts, discriminatory government policies and ancient tribal rivalries, particularly in South Africa and the Sudan, have resulted in political instability and economic hardship.

WORKER COMPARISONS OF SELECTED COUNTRIES

COUNTRY	AVG. ACTUAL HOURS WORKED PER WEEK	YEARS OF FORMAL SCHOOLING	PERCENT WOMEN OF LABOR FORCE
AUSTRALIA	39	13.6	38
AUSTRIA	34	14.6	39
BELGIUM	33	14.4	33
CANADA	38	17.6	40
FRANCE	39	14.6	41
GERMANY	38	14.6	39
GREECE	41	13.2	27
HUNGARY	37	12.0	44
IRELAND	41	13.1	29
ISRAEL	42	NA	34
JAPAN	38	13.5	40
LUXEMBOURG	41	NA	32
NETHERLANDS	40	15.5	31
NEW ZEALAND	42	15.4	36
NORWAY	37	15.5	41
ROMANIA	38	10.8	45
SOUTH AFRICA	46	12.0	36
SOUTH KOREA	49	13.7	34
SPAIN	37	14.7	25
UNITED KINGDOM	43	14.9	39
UNITED STATES	42	16.0	41

NA=DATA NOT AVAILABLE   SOURCE: UNITED NATIONS

GROSS DOMESTIC PRODUCT GROWTH RATES

BEST GROWTH RATES		WORST GROWTH RATES	
LESOTHO	13.5	AZERBAIJAN	-17
CHINA	10.3	TAJIKISTAN	-12.4
EQUATORIAL GUINEA	10	GEORGIA	-11
ERITREA	10	BELARUS	-10
MALAWI	9.9	TURKMENISTAN	-10
MALAYSIA	9.5	KAZAKHSTAN	-8.9
VIETNAM	9.5	CONGO, DEM. REP. OF THE	-7.4
SOUTH KOREA	9	MEXICO	-6.9
SINGAPORE	8.9	MOROCCO	-6.5
THAILAND	8.6	KYRGYZSTAN	-6
CHILE	8.5	NORTH KOREA	-5
LAOS	8	ARGENTINA	-4.4
SOLOMON ISLANDS	8	RUSSIA	-4
INDONESIA	7.5	SIERRA LEONE	-4
ISRAEL	7.1	UKRAINE	-4
UGANDA	7.1	DJIBOUTI	-3
IRELAND	7	MOLDOVA	-3
MYANMAR	6.8	PAPUA NEW GUINEA	-3
PERU	6.8	RWANDA	-2.7
TURKEY	6.8	MOZAMBIQUE	-2.5

Source: CIA World Factbook

Living

STERN EUROPE AND RUSSIA
the former Soviet republics, population
wth is slowing because of rising mortality
e to a breakdown in health care services,
avy smoking, and heavy consumption of
ohol. Russia's life expectancy has dropped
dramatically that its population is shrinking
the fastest rate ever recorded
an industrial society.

RUSSIA

KAZAKHSTAN

MONGOLIA

UZBEK. KYRG.

TURKMEN. TAJIK.

AFGH.

IRAN

PAKISTAN NEPAL

INDIA

BANG.

MYAN.

LAOS

THAI. VIETNAM

CAM.

SRI
LANKA

BR.
MALAYSIA

N. KOREA

S. KOREA

JAPAN

TAIWAN

PHILIPPINES

INDONESIA

PAPUA
NEW
GUINEA

SOLOMON
IS.

VANUATU

NEW
CAL.

CHINA
The limited relaxation of Communist
dogma has encouraged growing indus-
trialization and exports, creating new
wealth in parts of China.

EAST ASIA
The economies of this region (excluding
China) have experienced annual per capita
growth of 7.6 percent between 1960 and 1993
with relatively low inequality in incomes.
This rare combination has been known to
achieve dramatic reductions in poverty.

MIDDLE EAST
Water has emerged as a significant
factor in Middle East politics.
Projected water shortages could lead
to economic hardship and regional
conflicts.

MADAGASCAR

MAURITIUS

AUSTRALIA
An influx of Japanese tourists and
investors is generating new capital and
development, escalating coastal real
estate prices and regional tensions.

AUSTRALIA

NEW
ZEALAND

SOMALIA

YEMEN

OMAN

AUDI
RABIA

U.A.E.

CHINA

GROSS DOMESTIC PRODUCT PER CAPITA IN DOLLARS (PER YEAR)

10,000 AND MORE	2,500-4,999	700-999	DATA NOT AVAILABLE
5,000-9,999	1,000-2,499	UNDER 700	

Source: CIA World Factbook

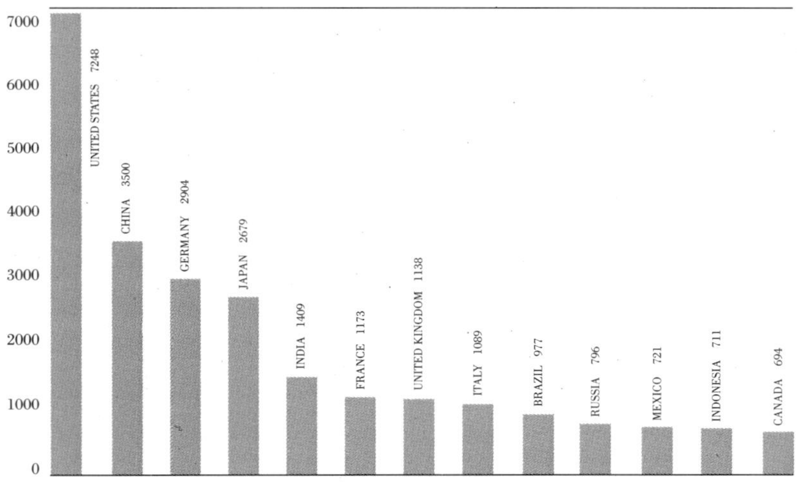

TOTAL GROSS DOMESTIC PRODUCT

UNITED STATES 7248
CHINA 3500
GERMANY 2904
JAPAN 2679
INDIA 1409
FRANCE 1173
UNITED KINGDOM 1138
ITALY 1089
BRAZIL 977
RUSSIA 796
MEXICO 721
INDONESIA 711
CANADA 694

BILLIONS OF DOLLARS

SOURCE: CIA WORLD FACTBOOK

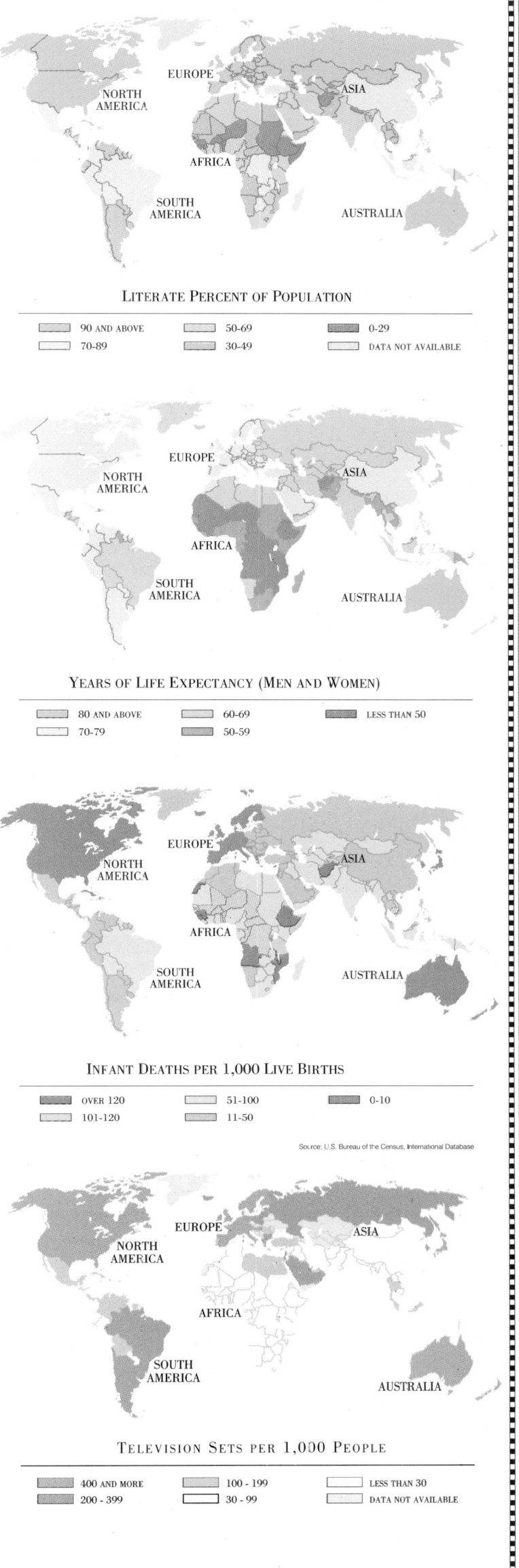

LITERATE PERCENT OF POPULATION

90 AND ABOVE	50-69	0-29
70-89	30-49	DATA NOT AVAILABLE

YEARS OF LIFE EXPECTANCY (MEN AND WOMEN)

80 AND ABOVE	60-69	LESS THAN 50
70-79	50-59	

INFANT DEATHS PER 1,000 LIVE BIRTHS

OVER 120	51-100	0-10
101-120	11-50	

Source: U.S. Bureau of the Census, International Database

TELEVISION SETS PER 1,000 PEOPLE

400 AND MORE	100 - 199	LESS THAN 30
200 - 399	30 - 99	DATA NOT AVAILABLE

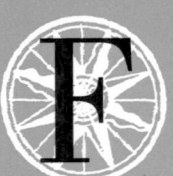

For thousands of years, the combustion of natural materials generated heat and light. Coal stoked the iron and steel furnaces of the Industrial Revolution, until eclipsed by oil in the late 19th century. Clean-burning natural gas, found directly above oil reserves, has also grown in popularity, aided by the ability to efficiently transport the gas in liquid form.✲ After World War II, booming cities and industries demanded cheap, abundant energy. In 1956, the first nuclear power station began operation in England, and France soon made nuclear fission its chief source of power. Recently, mounting safety concerns and the problems of disposing spent radioactive materials have slowed new plant construction.✲ Today, a new quest for renewable, environmentally-friendly energy has led to the efficient utilization of natural processes. Clean, inexpensive hydroelectric power currently supplies 4 percent of the world's energy needs — a figure expected to double by the year 2000 — though destruction of surrounding valleys remains an obstacle.✲ In 1981, the world's first solar power station opened in Sicily. Thermal energy from

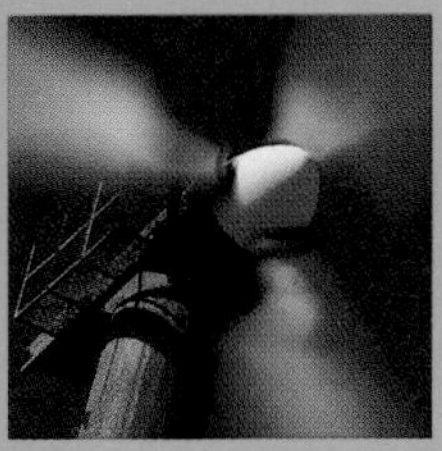

Wind power is now the fastest growing energy source, though it still produces less then 1 percent of the world's electricity.

hot springs and geysers is heating buildings and driving power stations from California to Japan. Power stations in Canada and France use tidal waters passing through narrow inlets to generate electricity. A worldwide research effort is now underway to develop a high temperature super conductor capable of transporting energy over vast distances so that these local energy sources can be utilized effectively on a global basis.✲ Technological advances have also expanded the number of elements used in manufacturing. Gold, silver and platinum are vital in the making of electrical components. Steel alloys now include chromium, nickel and cobalt for corrosion resistance; tungsten and vanadium for hardness; and molybdenum for elasticity. Aluminum and titanium are making cars and aircraft lighter and stronger.✲ Nonmetals also play key roles. Diamonds make cutting edges more durable. Potash and phosphates are used to enhance fertilizers. Sulphur is found in gunpowder, insecticides and pharmaceuticals. Perhaps the most important advance in recent years is the development of strong yet lightweight ceramics and carbon fibers. These materials, which can be produced cleanly and efficiently, are now being used to create the next generation of high-tech products.

Energy & Resources

TOP FIVE WORLD PRODUCERS OF SELECTED MINERAL COMMODITIES

MINERAL FUELS	1	2	3	4	5
CRUDE OIL	SAUDI ARABIA	UNITED STATES	RUSSIA	IRAN	CHINA
GASOLINE	UNITED STATES	RUSSIA	JAPAN	CHINA	UNITED KINGDOM
NATURAL GAS	RUSSIA	UNITED STATES	CANADA	NETHERLANDS	UNITED KINGDOM
HARD COAL	CHINA	UNITED STATES	INDIA	SOUTH AFRICA	AUSTRALIA
URANIUM-BEARING ORES	CANADA	NIGER	KAZAKHSTAN	RUSSIA	UZBEKISTAN

METALS					
CHROMITE	SOUTH AFRICA	KAZAKHSTAN	INDIA	TURKEY	FINLAND
IRON ORE	CHINA	BAZIL	RUSSIA	AUSTRALIA	UNITED STATES
MANGANESE ORE	SOUTH AFRICA	CHINA	UKRAINE	AUSTRALIA	BRAZIL
MINE NICKEL	RUSSIA	CANADA	NEW CALEDONIA	INDONESIA	AUSTRALIA
MINE SILVER	MEXICO	PERU	UNITED STATES	AUSTRALIA	CANADA
BAUXITE	AUSTRALIA	GUINEA	JAMAICA	BRAZIL	INDIA
ALUMINUM	UNITED STATES	RUSSIA	CANADA	AUSTRALIA	BRAZIL
MINE GOLD	SOUTH AFRICA	UNITED STATES	AUSTRALIA	CHINA	RUSSIA
MINE COPPER	CHILE	UNITED STATES	CANADA	RUSSIA	AUSTRALIA
MINE LEAD	AUSTRALIA	UNITED STATES	CHINA	PERU	CANADA
MINE TIN	CHINA	INDONESIA	BRAZIL	BOLIVIA	PERU
MINE ZINC	CANADA	AUSTRALIA	CHINA	PERU	UNITED STATES

NONMETALS					
NATURAL DIAMOND	AUSTRALIA	BOTSWANA	RUSSIA	SOUTH AFRICA	DEM. REP. OF THE CONGO
POTASH	CANADA	GERMANY	BELARUS	RUSSIA	UNITED STATES
PHOSPHATE ROCK	UNITED STATES	CHINA	MOROCCO	RUSSIA	TUNISIA
SULFUR (ALL FORMS)	UNITED STATES	CANADA	CHINA	MEXICO	JAPAN

Names in Black Indicate More Than 10% of Total World Production

Source: U.S. Geological Survey, Mineral Commodity Summary; Handbook of International Economic Statistics

COMMERCIAL ENERGY PRODUCTION/CONSUMPTION

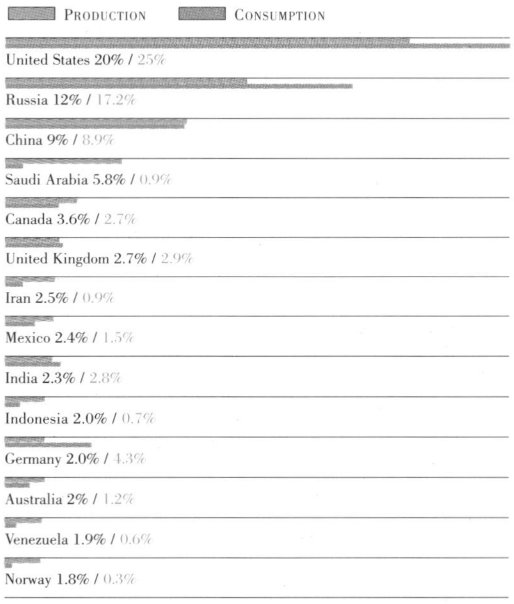

PERCENTAGE OF WORLD TOTAL

▇ PRODUCTION   ▇ CONSUMPTION

United States 20% / 25%

Russia 12% / 17.2%

China 9% / 8.9%

Saudi Arabia 5.8% / 0.9%

Canada 3.6% / 2.7%

United Kingdom 2.7% / 2.9%

Iran 2.5% / 0.9%

Mexico 2.4% / 1.5%

India 2.3% / 2.8%

Indonesia 2.0% / 0.7%

Germany 2.0% / 4.3%

Australia 2% / 1.2%

Venezuela 1.9% / 0.6%

Norway 1.8% / 0.3%

NATIONS WITH HIGHEST PERCENTAGE OF NUCLEAR POWER PRODUCTION

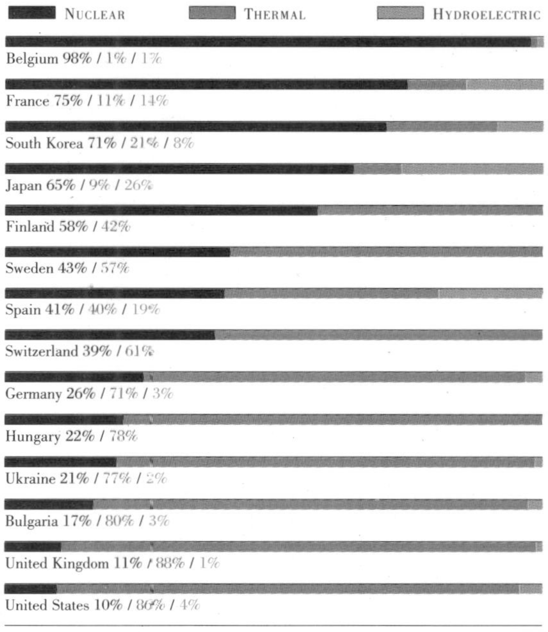

▇ NUCLEAR   ▇ THERMAL   ▇ HYDROELECTRIC

Belgium 98% / 1% / 1%

France 75% / 11% / 14%

South Korea 71% / 21% / 8%

Japan 65% / 9% / 26%

Finland 58% / 42%

Sweden 43% / 57%

Spain 41% / 40% / 19%

Switzerland 39% / 61%

Germany 26% / 71% / 3%

Hungary 22% / 78%

Ukraine 21% / 77% / 2%

Bulgaria 17% / 80% / 3%

United Kingdom 11% / 88% / 1%

United States 10% / 86% / 4%

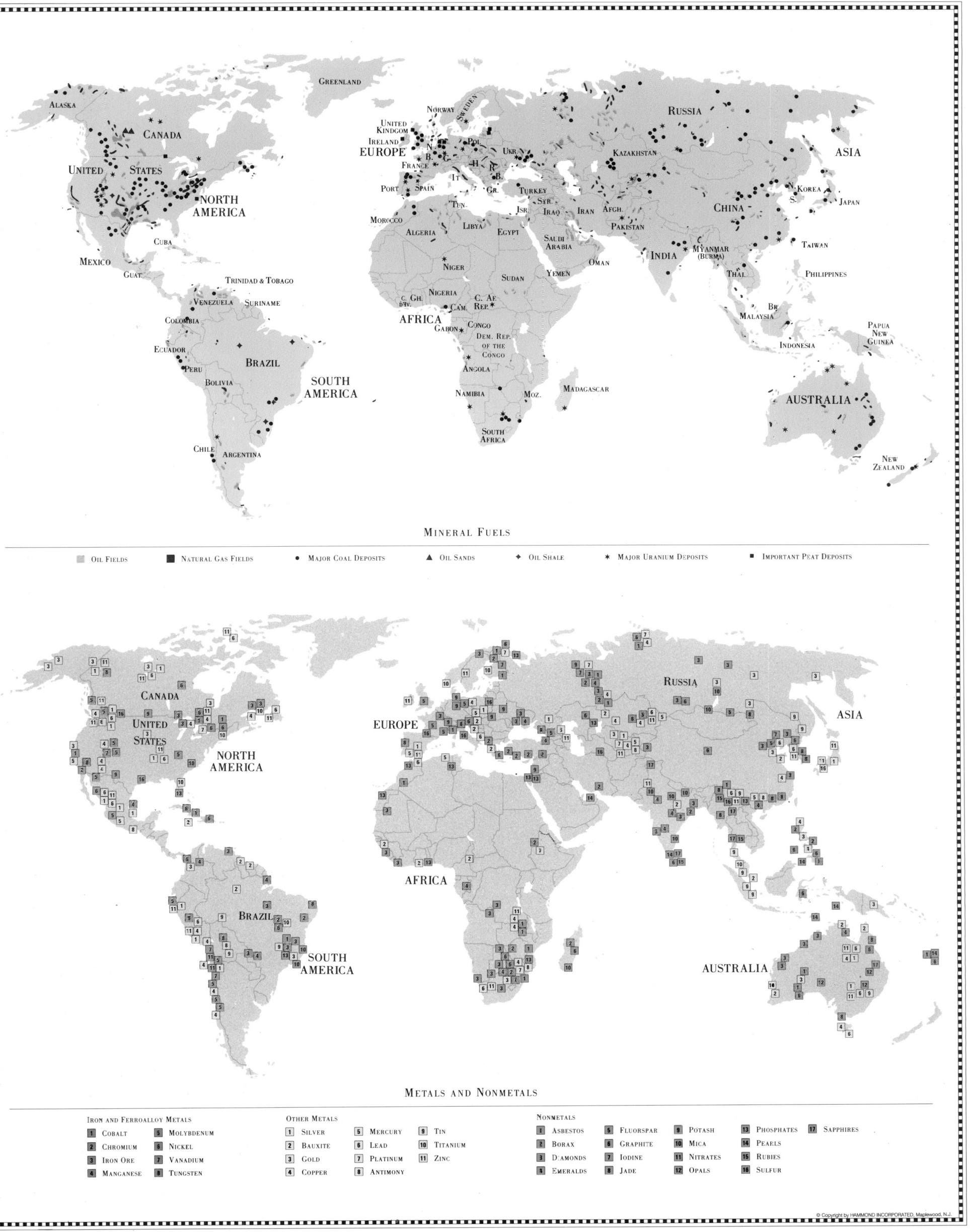

MINERAL FUELS

▨ OIL FIELDS	■ NATURAL GAS FIELDS	● MAJOR COAL DEPOSITS	▲ OIL SANDS	◆ OIL SHALE	✳ MAJOR URANIUM DEPOSITS	■ IMPORTANT PEAT DEPOSITS

METALS AND NONMETALS

IRON AND FERROALLOY METALS

1 COBALT	5 MOLYBDENUM
2 CHROMIUM	6 NICKEL
3 IRON ORE	7 VANADIUM
4 MANGANESE	8 TUNGSTEN

OTHER METALS

1 SILVER	5 MERCURY	9 TIN
2 BAUXITE	6 LEAD	10 TITANIUM
3 GOLD	7 PLATINUM	11 ZINC
4 COPPER	8 ANTIMONY	

NONMETALS

1 ASBESTOS	5 FLUORSPAR	9 POTASH	13 PHOSPHATES	17 SAPPHIRES
2 BORAX	6 GRAPHITE	10 MICA	14 PEARLS	
3 DIAMONDS	7 IODINE	11 NITRATES	15 RUBIES	
4 EMERALDS	8 JADE	12 OPALS	16 SULFUR	

oday, according to the World Bank, the combined Gross National Products of the United States, United Kingdom, France, Germany and Japan total about 14 trillion dollars. Agriculture and manufacturing are key elements in this total. In 1980, farmers harvested twice as much food as in 1950 — more than enough to feed the earth's population. A key factor has been the development of high-yielding strains of wheat, corn and rice. These three plants account for half of the world's harvest.❁ The sea, too, provides a rich annual harvest — nearly 80 million tons (72 million metric tons) of fish and algae. Deep sea fishing, supported by floating factories to process the catch, is now a major industry. Aquaculture, the breeding of fish and shellfish, contributes an ever-growing portion of the world's seafood.❁ With their adaptable diet and minimal space requirements, hogs are the world's main source of meat. China raises nearly 48 percent of the world's pork. Cattle can be raised in a broad temperate band, but their intensive consumption of grasses, grains and water make them an inefficient food source.❁

Our global food supply is grown on about 11 percent of the earth's total land area. Much of the remaining land lies in areas too dry, cold or mountainous to farm successfully.

Many African economies rely upon a single agricultural commodity for foreign exchange. But deforestation, drought and slash-and-burn farming have kept crop yields at below-subsistence levels. Meanwhile, in the traditional farming nations of China and southeastern Asia, manufacturing activity has increased dramatically, fostered by an educated, low-cost workforce and a global marketplace.❁ Advanced communications and transportation systems now permit companies to disperse production facilities and marketing forces across the globe, accelerating the shift from self-sufficient national economies to a worldwide production system. In the new, international labor market, routine manufacturing jobs, formerly plentiful in the U.S., have developed overseas, where labor is cheaper.❁ Eastern Europe and the former Soviet republics are struggling to learn the fundamentals of capitalism while confronting obsolete factories, ineffective distribution systems, inadequate capital, and serious and widespread ethnic conflicts which were suppressed by the previous communist governments. Despite such economic and political instability, the world's richest nations are offering financial support, hoping to avoid the dire prospects of failure and to enjoy the opportunities that success would bring.

Agriculture & Manufacturing

TOP FIVE WORLD PRODUCERS OF SELECTED AGRICULTURAL COMMODITIES

	1	2	3	4	5
WHEAT	CHINA	INDIA	UNITED STATES	FRANCE	RUSSIA
RICE	CHINA	INDIA	INDONESIA	BANGLADESH	VIETNAM
OATS	RUSSIA	CANADA	UNITED STATES	GERMANY	AUSTRALIA
CORN (MAIZE)	UNITED STATES	CHINA	BRAZIL	MEXICO	FRANCE
SOYBEANS	UNITED STATES	BRAZIL	CHINA	ARGENTINA	INDIA
POTATOES	CHINA	RUSSIA	UNITED STATES	POLAND	UKRAINE
COFFEE	BRAZIL	COLOMBIA	INDONESIA	MEXICO	UGANDA
TEA	INDIA	CHINA	KENYA	SRI LANKA	INDONESIA
TOBACCO	CHINA	UNITED STATES	INDIA	BRAZIL	TURKEY
COTTON	UNITED STATES	CHINA	INDIA	PAKISTAN	UZBEKISTAN
SUGAR	INDIA	BRAZIL	CHINA	UNITED STATES	THAILAND
CATTLE (STOCK)	BRAZIL	CHINA	UNITED STATES	ARGENTINA	RUSSIA
SHEEP (STOCK)	CHINA	AUSTRALIA	IRAN	NEW ZEALAND	INDIA
HOGS (STOCK)	CHINA	UNITED STATES	BRAZIL	GERMANY	RUSSIA
COW'S MILK	UNITED STATES	RUSSIA	INDIA	GERMANY	FRANCE
HEN'S EGGS	CHINA	UNITED STATES	JAPAN	RUSSIA	INDIA
WOOL	AUSTRALIA	CHINA	NEW ZEALAND	RUSSIA	URUGUAY
ROUNDWOOD	UNITED STATES	INDIA	CHINA	BRAZIL	CANADA
NATURAL RUBBER	THAILAND	INDONESIA	MALAYSIA	INDIA	CHINA
FISH CATCHES	CHINA	PERU	JAPAN	CHILE	UNITED STATES

Names in Black Indicate More Than 10% of Total World Production

Source: United Nations, Food and Agriculture Organization

PERCENT OF TOTAL EMPLOYMENT IN AGRICULTURE, MANUFACTURING AND OTHER INDUSTRIES

- AGRICULTURE (INCLUDES FORESTRY AND FISHING)
- MANUFACTURING
- CONSTRUCTION
- TRADE AND COMMERCE
- FINANCE, INSURANCE, REAL ESTATE
- SERVICES
- OTHER (INCLUDES MINING, UTILITIES, TRANSPORTATION)

| 0 | 20 | 40 | 60 | 80 | 100 |

India
China
Indonesia
Pakistan
Mexico
Brazil
Spain
Argentina
Italy
Japan
France
Canada
Australia
Germany
United States
United Kingdom

Finance, Insurance, Real Estate Data Included With "Other" for India, China, Indonesia and Pakistan

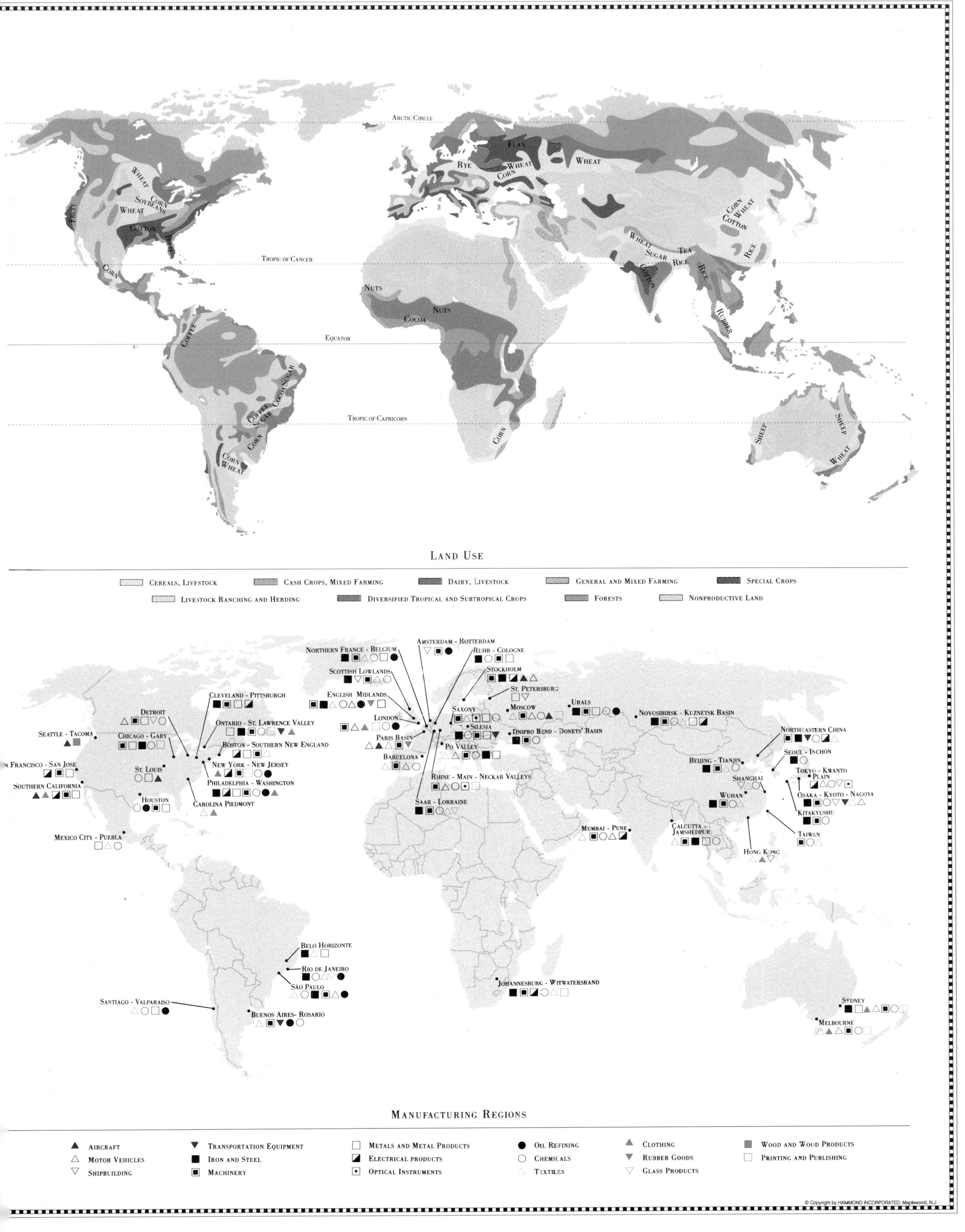

LAND USE

CEREALS, LIVESTOCK   CASH CROPS, MIXED FARMING   DAIRY, LIVESTOCK   GENERAL AND MIXED FARMING   SPECIAL CROPS

LIVESTOCK RANCHING AND HERDING   DIVERSIFIED TROPICAL AND SUBTROPICAL CROPS   FORESTS   NONPRODUCTIVE LAND

MANUFACTURING REGIONS

▲ AIRCRAFT   ▼ TRANSPORTATION EQUIPMENT   ☐ METALS AND METAL PRODUCTS   ● OIL REFINING   ▲ CLOTHING   ▨ WOOD AND WOOD PRODUCTS

△ MOTOR VEHICLES   ■ IRON AND STEEL   ◪ ELECTRICAL PRODUCTS   ○ CHEMICALS   ▽ RUBBER GOODS   ☐ PRINTING AND PUBLISHING

▽ SHIPBUILDING   ▣ MACHINERY   ⊡ OPTICAL INSTRUMENTS   △ TEXTILES   ▽ GLASS PRODUCTS

© Copyright by HAMMOND INCORPORATED, Maplewood, N.J.

The earth's human population, already 5.8 billion, is growing at a rate of 80 million people a year. This rapid rise is straining the global environment, devouring forests, fresh water and oil reserves while polluting the very resources necessary for survival.❁ Each year, the burning of fossil fuels releases more than 23 billion tons (21 billion metric tons) of carbon dioxide into the air. Man-made chlorofluoro-carbons are eating away at the layer of ozone which shields earth from harm-ful ultraviolet radiation. Highly acidic rains created by fossil fuel emissions are destroying lakes, forests and historic monuments from North America to Africa.❁ "Greenhouse gases" such as carbon diox-ide, sulphur and nitrogen oxides trap heat within our atmosphere and warm the planet by absorbing earth's infrared radiation. Tropical rainforests, with their capacity to consume carbon dioxide, generate fresh oxygen and regulate rain-fall, might offer an antidote. Yet from South America to Indonesia, they are being lev-elled for lumber and land at the rate of 44.5 million acres (18 million hectares) per year.❁ Some experts predict that "global warming" could raise the earth's temperature significantly in the next cen-tury, leading to unpredictable changes in climate. Soaring temperatures could bring severe recurring droughts, dust storms, forest fires and wildlife extinction. Melting glaciers and rising seas would flood coastal areas, drown wetlands, contaminate estuaries and pollute drinking water.❁ While indus-trialized nations can afford to invest in environmen-tal preservation, third world countries, home to most of the world's population and rainforests, must focus their limited resources on immediate economic survival. Feeding a nation takes prece-dence over saving a forest, even if the long-term cost could be incalculable.❁ The United Nations Conference on Environment and Development, held at Rio de Janeiro, set in motion initiatives which may help to repair our environment. It seems the solution requires nothing less than a unified global effort to transform the way we live, with nature conservation, population control and clean, efficient energy use as our goals.

In Mumbai (Bombay) India, as well as other cities around the world, smog is making it difficult to breathe.

Is a global warming trend under way? Containing the four warmest years in history, the 1990's are already the warmest decade ever recorded . Record droughts, floods and forest fires have become increasingly common throughout the world.

Environmental

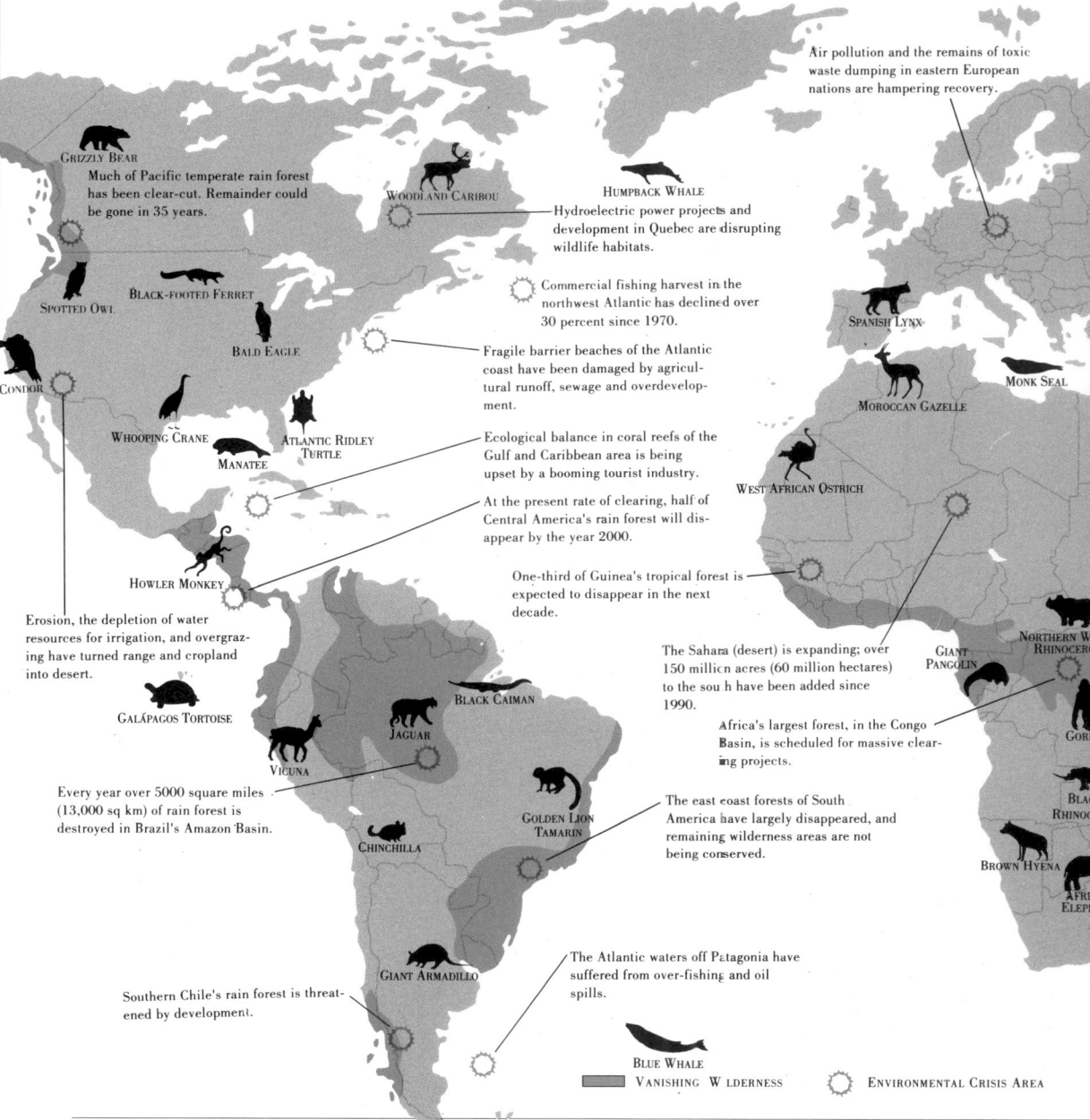

Air pollution and the remains of toxic waste dumping in eastern European nations are hampering recovery.

GRIZZLY BEAR
Much of Pacific temperate rain forest has been clear-cut. Remainder could be gone in 35 years.

WOODLAND CARIBOU

HUMPBACK WHALE
Hydroelectric power projects and development in Quebec are disrupting wildlife habitats.

SPANISH LYNX

SPOTTED OWL

BLACK-FOOTED FERRET

BALD EAGLE

CONDOR

WHOOPING CRANE

MANATEE

ATLANTIC RIDLEY TURTLE

HOWLER MONKEY

Commercial fishing harvest in the northwest Atlantic has declined over 30 percent since 1970.

Fragile barrier beaches of the Atlantic coast have been damaged by agricul-tural runoff, sewage and overdevelop-ment.

Ecological balance in coral reefs of the Gulf and Caribbean area is being upset by a booming tourist industry.

At the present rate of clearing, half of Central America's rain forest will dis-appear by the year 2000.

One-third of Guinea's tropical forest is expected to disappear in the next decade.

MONK SEAL

MOROCCAN GAZELLE

WEST AFRICAN OSTRICH

Erosion, the depletion of water resources for irrigation, and overgraz-ing have turned range and cropland into desert.

GALÁPAGOS TORTOISE

BLACK CAIMAN

JAGUAR

VICUÑA

CHINCHILLA

GOLDEN LION TAMARIN

The Sahara (desert) is expanding; over 150 million acres (60 million hectares) to the south have been added since 1990.

Africa's largest forest, in the Congo Basin, is scheduled for massive clear-ing projects.

The east coast forests of South America have largely disappeared, and remaining wilderness areas are not being conserved.

NORTHERN WHITE RHINOCEROS

GIANT PANGOLIN

GORILLA

BLACK RHINOCEROS

BROWN HYENA

AFRICAN ELEPHANT

Every year over 5000 square miles (13,000 sq km) of rain forest is destroyed in Brazil's Amazon Basin.

GIANT ARMADILLO

The Atlantic waters off Patagonia have suffered from over-fishing and oil spills.

Southern Chile's rain forest is threat-ened by development.

BLUE WHALE

▬ VANISHING WILDERNESS   ❁ ENVIRONMENTAL CRISIS AREA

Air Pollution
Billions of tons of industrial emissions and toxic pollu-tants — including carbon dioxide, sulphur, nitrogen oxide, lead, mercury and cadmium — are released into the air each year, depleting our ozone layer, killing our forests and lakes with acid rain and threaten-ing our health: in some parts of the world, lung cancer has become a lead-ing cause of death.

Water Pollution
Only 3 percent of the earth's water is fresh. Unfortunately, pollution from cities, farms and fac-tories has made much of it unfit to drink. In the devel-oping world, most sewage flows untreated into lakes and rivers; health officials estimate that 5 million peo-ple die each year from dis-eases caused by unclean water. Regional struggles to secure adequate water are becoming more intense.

Ozone Depletion
The layer of ozone in the stratosphere shields earth from harmful ultraviolet radiation. But man-made gases are destroying this vital barrier, increasing the risk of skin cancer and eye disease — with equally harmful effects for all plant and animal species. A hole in the ozone layer over Antarctica is now the size of the continental United States.

Concerns

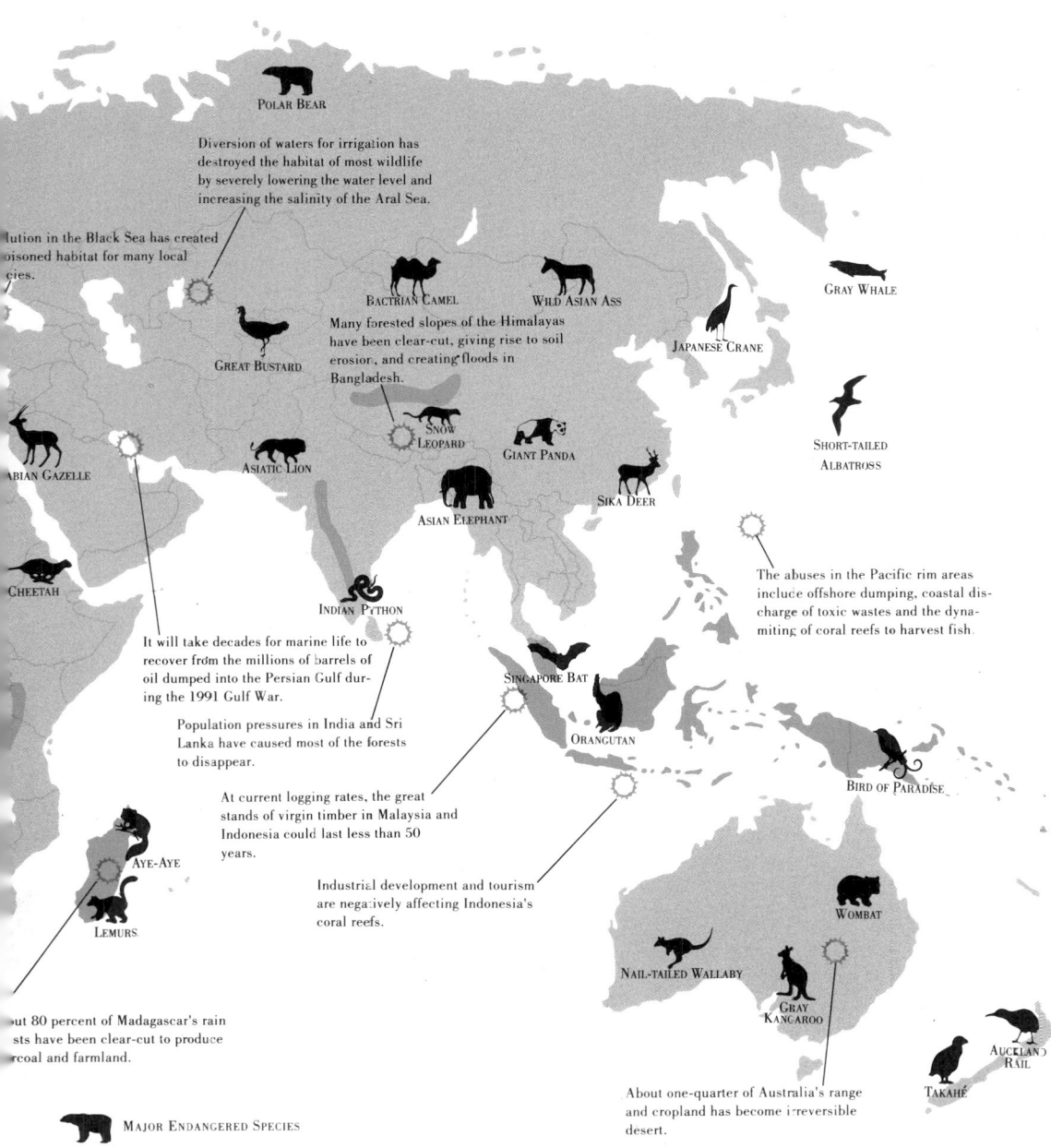

POLAR BEAR

Diversion of waters for irrigation has destroyed the habitat of most wildlife by severely lowering the water level and increasing the salinity of the Aral Sea.

...lution in the Black Sea has created ...oisoned habitat for many local ...cies.

GREAT BUSTARD

BACTRIAN CAMEL   WILD ASIAN ASS

Many forested slopes of the Himalayas have been clear-cut, giving rise to soil erosion, and creating floods in Bangladesh.

GRAY WHALE

JAPANESE CRANE

...ABIAN GAZELLE

ASIATIC LION

SNOW LEOPARD   GIANT PANDA

SIKA DEER

SHORT-TAILED ALBATROSS

CHEETAH

ASIAN ELEPHANT

INDIAN PYTHON

The abuses in the Pacific rim areas include offshore dumping, coastal discharge of toxic wastes and the dynamiting of coral reefs to harvest fish.

It will take decades for marine life to recover from the millions of barrels of oil dumped into the Persian Gulf during the 1991 Gulf War.

SINGAPORE BAT

Population pressures in India and Sri Lanka have caused most of the forests to disappear.

ORANGUTAN

AYE-AYE

At current logging rates, the great stands of virgin timber in Malaysia and Indonesia could last less than 50 years.

BIRD OF PARADISE

LEMURS

Industrial development and tourism are negatively affecting Indonesia's coral reefs.

WOMBAT

...out 80 percent of Madagascar's rain ...sts have been clear-cut to produce ...rcoal and farmland.

NAIL-TAILED WALLABY

GRAY KANGAROO

AUCKLAND RAIL

TAKAHÉ

About one-quarter of Australia's range and cropland has become irreversible desert.

Major Endangered Species

Acid Rain

Acid rain is created when fossil fuel emissions interact with sunlight and water vapor. The resulting clouds of nitric and sulfuric acids are carried thousands of miles. Acid rain has killed all life in thousands of lakes, and over 15 million acres (6 million hectares) of virgin forest in Europe and North America — and even some third world countries — are dead or dying.

Deforestation

Each year, 60 million acres (25 million hectares) of tropical rainforests are being felled by loggers — an area larger than Uruguay or Syria. Trees are vital to the prevention of both soil erosion and silting of rivers. They also remove heat-trapping carbon dioxide from the atmosphere.

Extinction

Biologists estimate that over 50,000 plant and animal species inhabiting the world's rain forests are disappearing each year due to pollution, unchecked hunting and the destruction of natural habitats. The loss of plant and animal species means fewer potential sources of new foods and medicines.

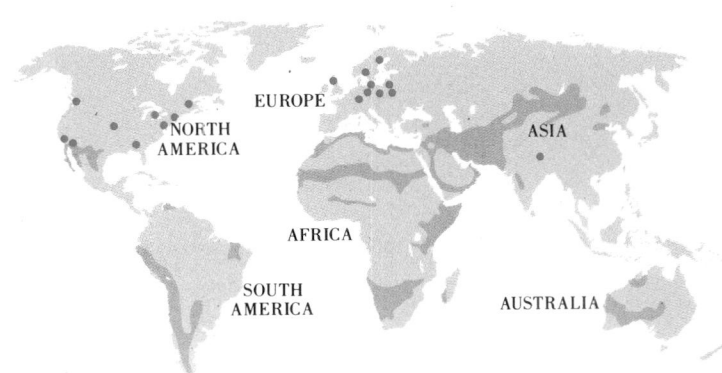

DESERTIFICATION AND ACID RAIN DAMAGE

AREAS OF PRODUCTIVE DRYLANDS DESERTIFIED BY EARLY 1980'S

AREAS OF DAMAGE FROM ACID RAIN AND OTHER AIRBORNE POLLUTANTS

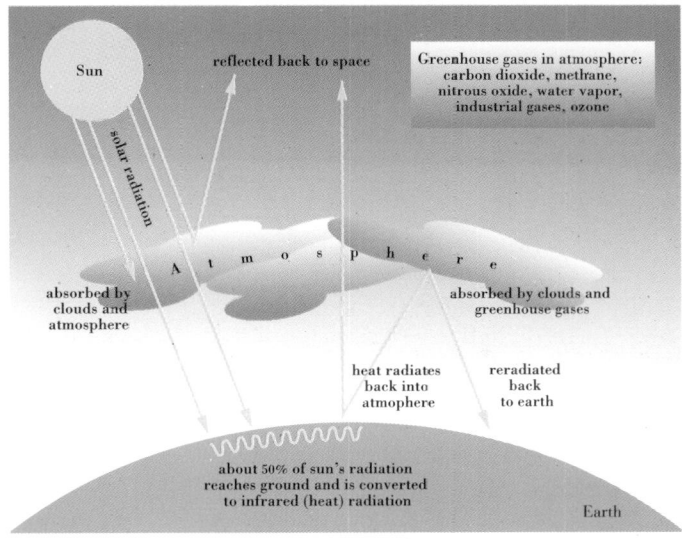

Sun   reflected back to space

Greenhouse gases in atmosphere: carbon dioxide, methane, nitrous oxide, water vapor, industrial gases, ozone

solar radiation

absorbed by clouds and atmosphere

absorbed by clouds and greenhouse gases

heat radiates back into atmophere

reradiated back to earth

about 50% of sun's radiation reaches ground and is converted to infrared (heat) radiation

Earth

GREENHOUSE EFFECT

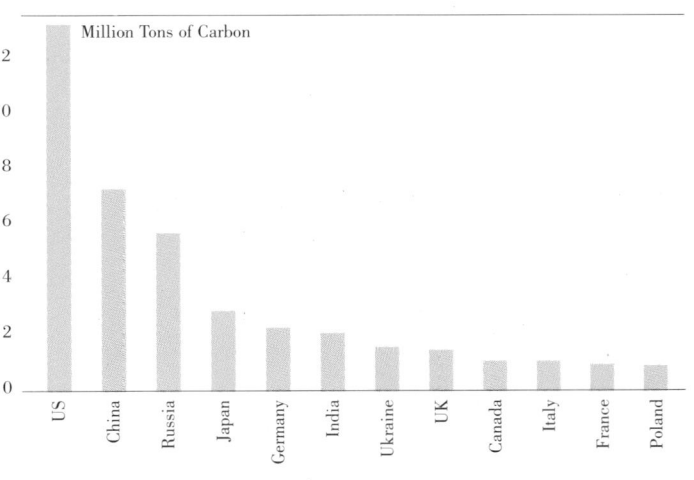

Million Tons of Carbon

US | China | Russia | Japan | Germany | India | Ukraine | UK | Canada | Italy | France | Poland

GREENHOUSE EMISSIONS

CARBON DIOXIDE EQUIVALENTS

SOURCE: HANDBOOK OF INTERNATIONAL ECONOMIC STATISTICS

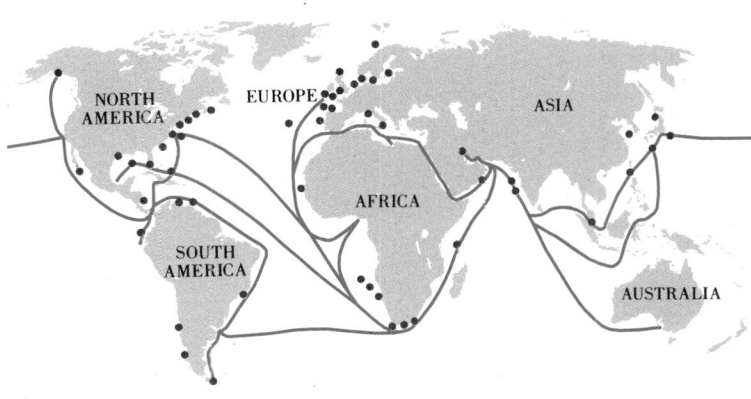

MAIN TANKER ROUTES AND MAJOR OIL SPILLS

ROUTES OF VERY LARGE CRUDE OIL CARRIERS   MAJOR OIL SPILLS

Climate

The earth is a living organism. It breathes ceaselessly, as the forces of convection circulate air in an endless stream around the globe. Warm air rises at the equator and flows north or south, while cold air moves down from the poles towards the equator. In this way, global air currents direct the weather. ❂ All weather occurs in the troposphere, the atmospheric level closest to the earth's surface. Chemical exchanges between air and sea help stabilize the oxygen and carbon dioxide content of both. Wind also whips up and carries along invisible droplets of salty water. Water condenses around the salt crystals to produce mists, clouds and rain. ❂ Climate, the average weather in an area as measured over many years, is determined by two key variables: temperature and precipitation. Humidity, sunshine, air pressure and wind play supporting roles. Since temperature depends upon the strength of the sun's rays, the earth's 14 climatic zones (see map) are related to latitude — though winds and elevation can modify these zones. ❂ Climates differ for many reasons, from variations in latitude, elevation and topography to changes in land and water temperatures. Every place on earth has its own climate and ecosystem which, in turn, influences the food, clothing, homes and culture of the local population. ❂ How do climates change? Climatologists point to several causes, from shifts in solar energy to volcanic ash in the atmosphere, which can severely reduce the amount of sunlight reaching the earth's surface — sometimes for years. ❂ Almost 3 billion pounds (1.36 million kg.) of chemicals are released into the air in the United States each year. The sky then transports the pollutants hundreds of miles. During the journey, the atmosphere functions as a complex chemical reactor where fossil fuel emissions interact with sunlight, water vapor and hundreds of man-made compounds. ❂ Our atmosphere, which rises 30 miles (48 km.) above the planet's surface and covers 260 billion cubic miles (1.08 trillion cubic km.), may seem too vast to pollute. But the ability of the atmosphere to warm and cool the earth, to shield us from ultraviolet rays and to enable life to flourish is diminishing. The changes we have wrought are altering our atmosphere, our climate and our lives.

Antarctica, the earth's coldest place, is also one of its driest. Its vast inland plateau is really a desert of ice and snow.

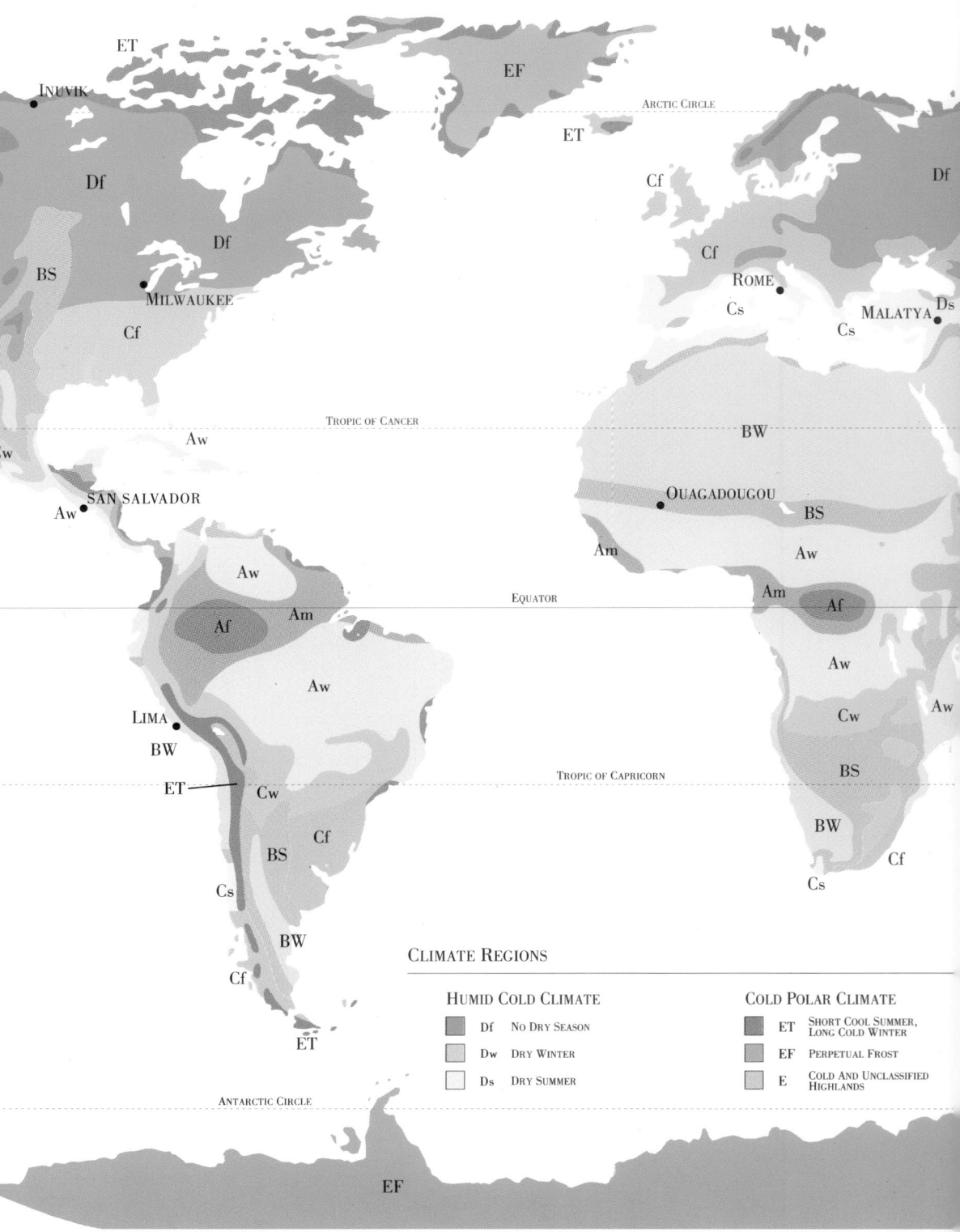

CLIMATE REGIONS

HUMID COLD CLIMATE

Df	No Dry Season	
Dw	Dry Winter	
Ds	Dry Summer	

COLD POLAR CLIMATE

ET	Short Cool Summer, Long Cold Winter	
EF	Perpetual Frost	
E	Cold And Unclassified Highlands	

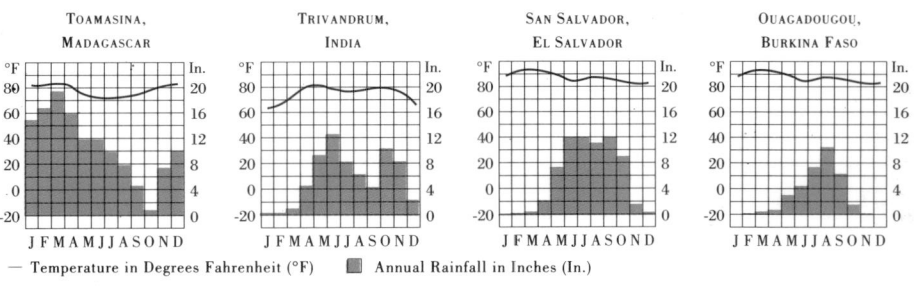

TOAMASINA, MADAGASCAR

TRIVANDRUM, INDIA

SAN SALVADOR, EL SALVADOR

OUAGADOUGOU, BURKINA FASO

— Temperature in Degrees Fahrenheit (°F)   ▪ Annual Rainfall in Inches (In.)

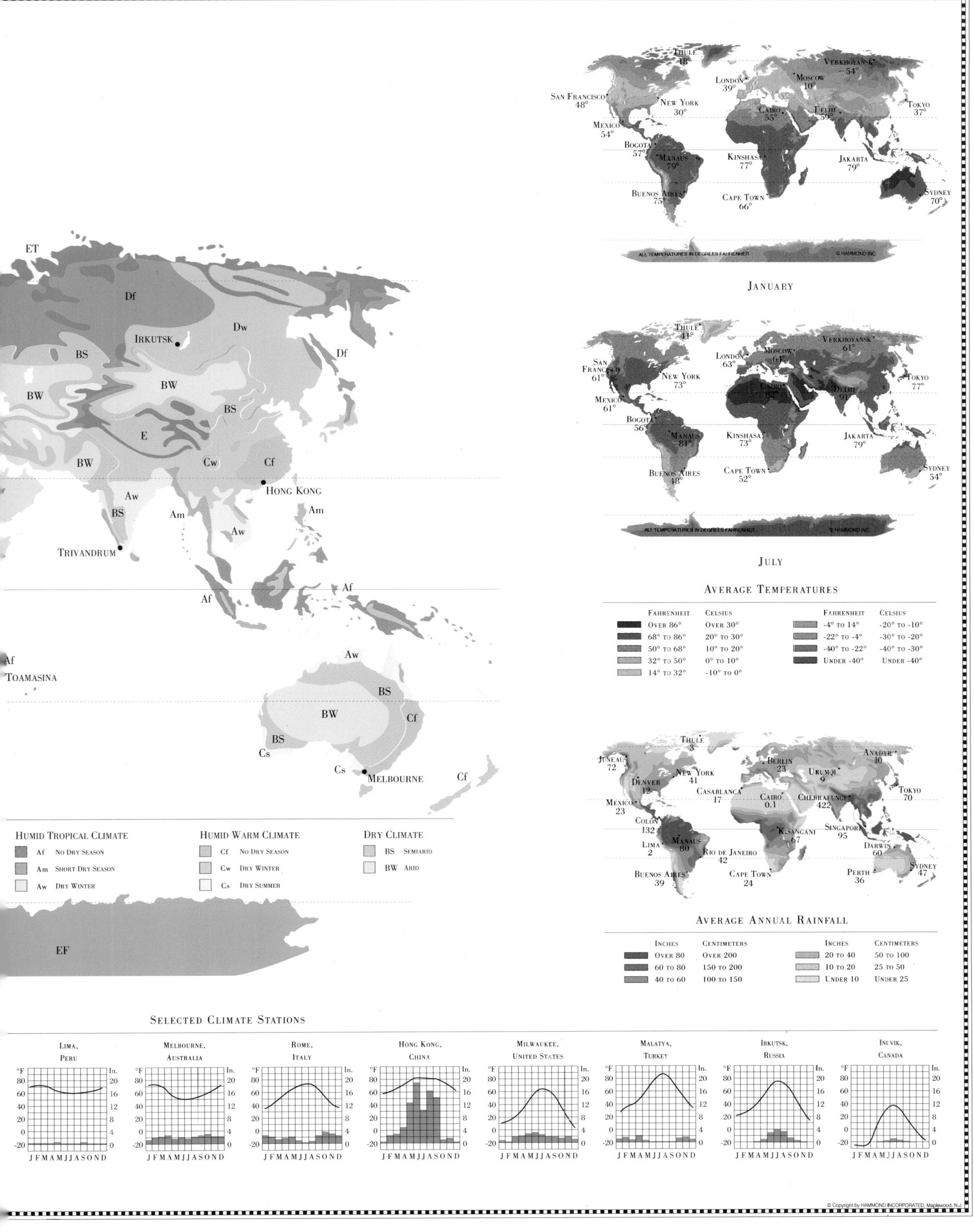

JANUARY

JULY

AVERAGE TEMPERATURES

FAHRENHEIT	CELSIUS	FAHRENHEIT	CELSIUS
OVER 86°	OVER 30°	-4° TO 14°	-20° TO -10°
68° TO 86°	20° TO 30°	-22° TO -4°	-30° TO -20°
50° TO 68°	10° TO 20°	-40° TO -22°	-40° TO -30°
32° TO 50°	0° TO 10°	UNDER -40°	UNDER -40°
14° TO 32°	-10° TO 0°		

AVERAGE ANNUAL RAINFALL

INCHES	CENTIMETERS	INCHES	CENTIMETERS
OVER 80	OVER 200	20 TO 40	50 TO 100
60 TO 80	150 TO 200	10 TO 20	25 TO 50
40 TO 60	100 TO 150	UNDER 10	UNDER 25

HUMID TROPICAL CLIMATE

Af NO DRY SEASON
Am SHORT DRY SEASON
Aw DRY WINTER

HUMID WARM CLIMATE

Cf NO DRY SEASON
Cw DRY WINTER
Cs DRY SUMMER

DRY CLIMATE

BS SEMIARID
BW ARID

SELECTED CLIMATE STATIONS

LIMA, PERU | MELBOURNE, AUSTRALIA | ROME, ITALY | HONG KONG, CHINA | MILWAUKEE, UNITED STATES | MALATYA, TURKEY | IRKUTSK, RUSSIA | INUVIK, CANADA

Fifty years ago, tropical rainforests covered twelve percent of the earth's land; today, half of those forests are gone. Yet rainforests play a crucial environmental role, absorbing the greenhouse gas carbon dioxide while releasing oxygen. The forests also serve as reservoirs for most of the non-glacial fresh water on earth, and are home to more than half of the world's plants, animals and insects. More than half of all prescriptions filled worldwide contain ingredients that can be traced to tropical plants. The northern hemisphere was once covered by vast stretches of broadleaf, deciduous woodlands. In the eastern and central United States, less than a tenth of the original forested areas remain. However, the older second-growth forests now closely approximate virgin forest conditions. In China, only vestiges of the great forests — and the wildlife that inhabited them — can be seen. At current rates of deforestation, 20-75 plant and animal species are lost every day. Wetlands, too, are quickly being filled in or drained off. These complex environments even out the flow rate of rivers and improve the sub-surface water supply.

The United Nations has designated over 325 Biosphere Reserves, from Australia's Great Barrier Reef to Yellowstone National Park (above), the world's first national park, created in 1872.

Attempts to turn wetlands into farmland usually result in very low crop yields. Before the colonization of the Americas, vast prairies stretched across the central plains. Today, most virgin prairie has been plowed for agricultural use, as in the United States, or transformed by domesticated plants, as in the Argentine Pampas. The African savannas are being burned off to make way for farming, though the poor soil is often spent in just a few years. Changes in vegetation usually occur gradually. As one passes from wet to dry regions, dense forests become lighter, trees become small and sparse, and lush undergrowth gives way to small shrubs, then grasslands, and finally desert. About one third of the earth's surface is arid. When the sparse vegetation is destroyed by overuse of the land, the soil is less able to spring back after a drought, and evaporation and rainfall decrease. An estimated 2,234,767 square miles (5,788,048 sq. km.) of land suffers from soil degradation caused by deforestation. When rains do occur, they often wash soil away, causing floods and droughts downstream.

Vegetation

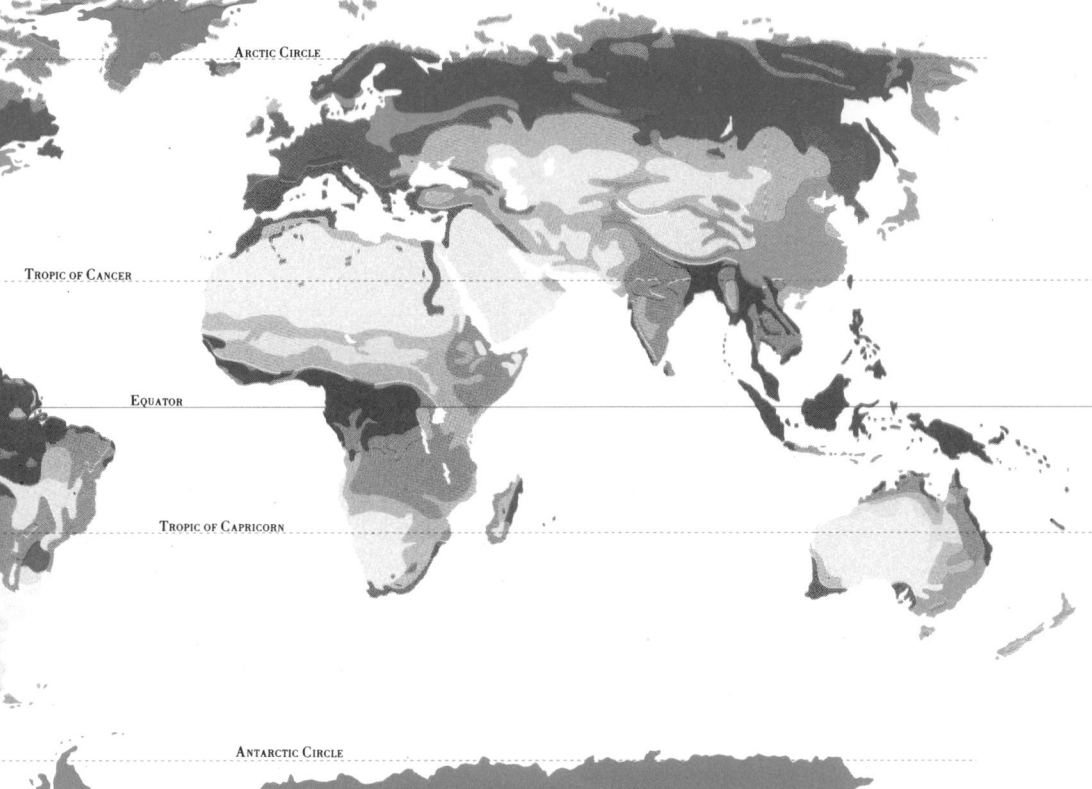

ARCTIC CIRCLE

TROPIC OF CANCER

EQUATOR

TROPIC OF CAPRICORN

ANTARCTIC CIRCLE

NATURAL VEGETATION

NEEDLELEAF FOREST
Found in higher latitudes with shorter growing seasons, and dominated by pure stands of softwood, evergreen conifers (cone-bearing trees) such as pine, fir and spruce. The light undergrowth consists of small shrubs, mosses, lichens and pine needles.

BROADLEAF FOREST
Found in the middle latitudes, this forest of deciduous (seasonal leaf-shedding) trees includes the hardwoods maple, hickory and oak. The forest floor is relatively barren, except for thick leaf cover during colder months.

MIXED NEEDLELEAF AND BROADLEAF FOREST
A transitional zone between northern softwoods and temperate hardwoods.

WOODLAND AND SHRUB (MEDITERRANEAN)
A mid-latitude area of broadleaf evergreens, dense growths of woody shrubs and open grassy woodland, characterized by pronounced dry summers and wet winters.

SHORT GRASS (STEPPE)
A mid-latitude, semi-arid area usually found on the fringe of desert regions, with continuous short-grass cover up to 8" (20cm.) tall, used chiefly to graze livestock.

TALL GRASS (PRAIRIE)
Mid-latitude, semi-moist areas with continuous tall-grass cover up to 24" (61cm.) in height, used for agricultural purposes. Rainfall is insufficient to support larger plants.

TROPICAL RAIN FOREST (SELVA)
A dense, evergreen forest of tall, varied hardwood trees with a thick broadleaf canopy and a dark, moist interior with minimal undergrowth.

LIGHT TROPICAL FOREST (TROPICAL SEMIDECIDUOUS OR MONSOON FOREST)
As above, with more widely spaced trees, heavier undergrowth, larger concentrations of single species. Dry season prevents most trees from remaining evergreen. Found in monsoon areas.

TROPICAL WOODLAND AND SHRUB (THORN FOREST)
Longer dry season results in low trees with thick bark and smaller leaves. Dense undergrowth of thorny plants, brambles and grasses. Transition belt between denser forests and grasslands.

TROPICAL GRASSLAND AND SHRUB (SAVANNA)
Stiff, sharp-edged grasses, from 2' to 12' (0.6m. to 3.7m.) high, with large areas of bare ground. Scattered shrubs and low trees in some areas.

WOODED SAVANNA
A transitional area where savanna joins a tropical or shrub forest, with low trees and shrubs dotting the grasslands.

DESERT AND DESERT SHRUB
Barren stretches of soft brown, yellow or red sand and rock wastes with isolated patches of short grass and stunted bushes, turning bright green when fed by infrequent precipitation.

RIVER VALLEY AND OASIS
River valleys are lush, fertile lands, with varied vegetation. An oasis is a fertile or verdant spot found in a desert near a natural spring or pool.

HEATH AND MOOR
A heath is open, uncultivated land covered with low, flowering evergreen shrubs such as heather. Moors are often high and poorly drained lands, with patches of heath and peat bogs.

TUNDRA AND ALPINE
An area of scarce moisture and short, cool summers where trees cannot survive. A permanently frozen subsoil supports low-growing lichens, mosses and stunted shrubs.

UNCLASSIFIED HIGHLANDS
Sequential bands or vertical zones of all vegetation types, which generally follow the warm-to-cold upward patterns found in corresponding areas of vegetation. (Map scale does not permit delineation of these areas.)

PERMANENT ICE COVER
Permanently ice and snow-covered terrain found in polar regions and atop high mountains.

The Physical World

World - Physical

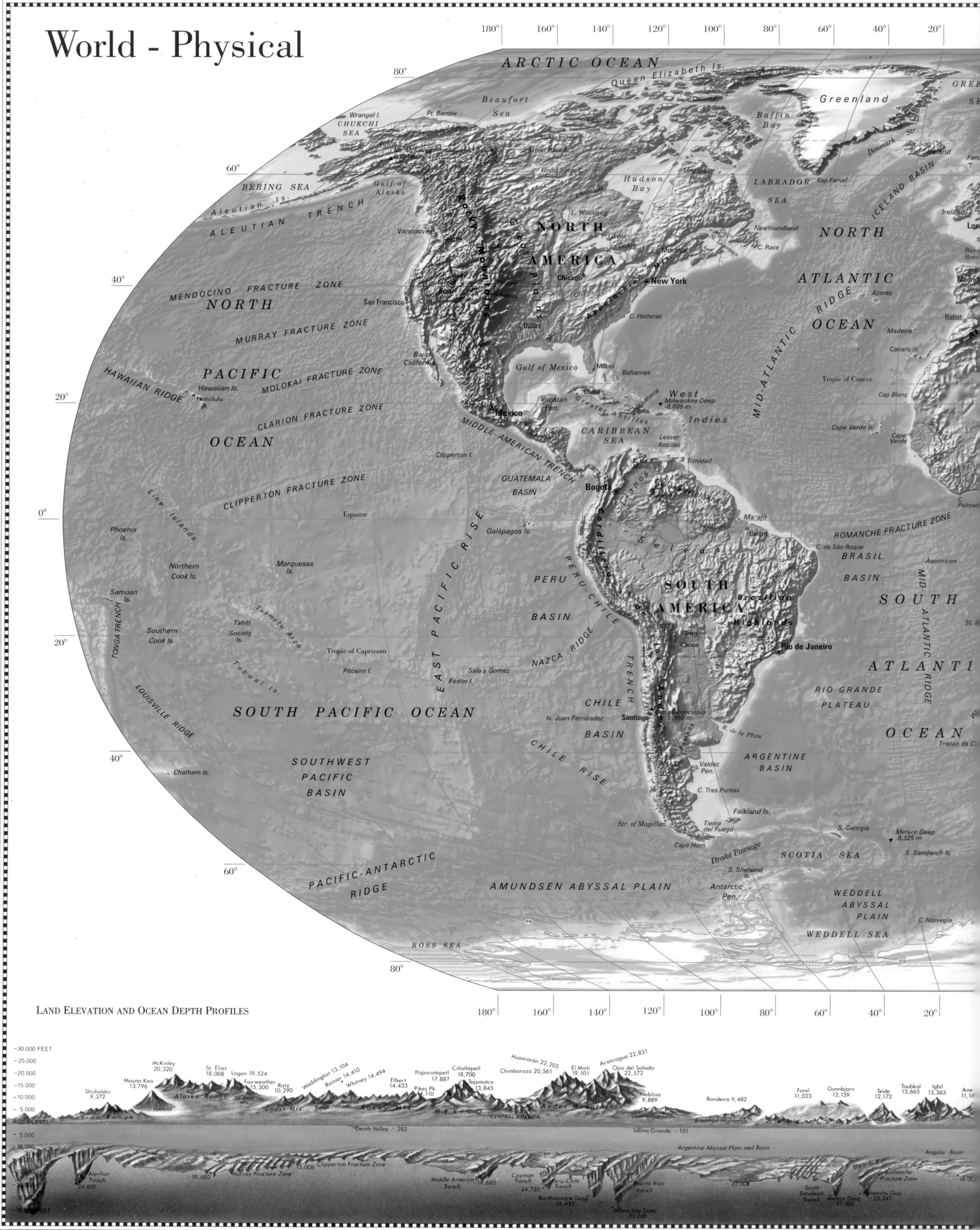

ARCTIC OCEAN

Queen Elizabeth Is.

Beaufort Sea

Wrangel I.
CHUKCHI SEA

Pt. Barrow

Greenland

GREE

Baffin Bay

Victoria I.

Devon I.

Mt. McKinley

BERING SEA

60°

80°

Gulf of Alaska

Great Bear L.

Hudson Bay

Great Slave L.

LABRADOR SEA

Denmark Str.

Iceland

Ireland

ICELAND BASIN

Lo

Aleutian Is.

ALEUTIAN TRENCH

Vancouver

ROCKY MOUNTAINS

NORTH AMERICA

L. Winnipeg

Great Lakes

St. Lawrence

Newfoundland

C. Race

NORTH

Kap Farvel

Bay Bisc

40°

MENDOCINO FRACTURE ZONE

NORTH

San Francisco

Missouri

Ohio

Chicago

Montreal

New York

ATLANTIC

MID-ATLANTIC RIDGE

Azores

Madrid

Iberia

MURRAY FRACTURE ZONE

PACIFIC

Dallas

APPALACHIANS

C. Hatteras

OCEAN

Madeira

Rabat

HAWAIIAN RIDGE

Hawaiian Is.

20°

Honolulu

MOLOKAI FRACTURE ZONE

Baja California

Gulf of Mexico

Miami

Bahamas

Cuba

Greater Antilles

West Indies

Tropic of Cancer

Cap Blanc

Canary Is.

Cape Verde Is.

Cap Vert

CLARION FRACTURE ZONE

S. Mexico

Yucatan Pen.

West Milwaukee Deep -8,605 m

CARIBBEAN SEA

Lesser Antilles

OCEAN

Trinidad

MIDDLE-AMERICAN TRENCH

P

Cape Verde

C. Palmas

Clipperton I.

GUATEMALA BASIN

Maracaibo

Bogotá

Llanos

Highlands

ROMANCHE FRACTURE ZONE

0°

Equator

Galápagos Is.

Cordillera

Marajó

Belém

BRASIL

Ascension

MID-ATLANTIC RIDGE

C. de São Roque

BASIN

Line Islands

Selvas

Phoenix Is.

Northern Cook Is.

Marquesas Is.

PERU BASIN

PERU-CHILE

SOUTH AMERICA

Brazilian Highlands

SOUTH

Samoan Is.

Tahiti Society Is.

Tuamotu Arch.

20°

Tropic of Capricorn

NAZCA RIDGE

Gran Chaco

Rio de Janeiro

ATLANTIC

Southern Cook Is.

Pitcairn I.

Sala y Gomez

Easter I.

TONGA TRENCH

EAST PACIFIC RISE

Tubuai Is.

CHILE

Andes

Cerro Aconcagua 6,959 m

RIO GRANDE PLATEAU

St.

OCEAN

LOUISVILLE RIDGE

SOUTH PACIFIC OCEAN

BASIN

Is. Juan Fernández

Santiago

R. de la Plata

Tristan da C

Chatham Is.

40°

SOUTHWEST PACIFIC BASIN

CHILE RISE

Valdez Pen.

C. Tres Puntas

ARGENTINE BASIN

Falkland Is.

Str. of Magellan

Tierra del Fuego

S. Georgia

Meteor Deep -8,325 m

S. Sandwich Is.

Cape Horn

Drake Passage

SCOTIA SEA

60°

PACIFIC-ANTARCTIC RIDGE

S. Shetland Is.

AMUNDSEN ABYSSAL PLAIN

Antarctic Pen.

WEDDELL ABYSSAL PLAIN

C. Norvegia

80°

ROSS SEA

WEDDELL SEA

LAND ELEVATION AND OCEAN DEPTH PROFILES

-30.000 FEET
-25.000
-20.000
-15.000
-10.000
-5.000
SEA LEVEL
-5.000
-10.000

McKinley 20,320

St. Elias 18,008

Logan 19,524

Waddington 13,104

Rainier 14,410

Whitney 14,494

Elbert 14,433

Huascarán 22,205

Chimborazo 20,561

El Misti 19,101

Aconcagua 22,831

Ojos del Salado 22,572

Forel 11,023

Gunnbjørn 12,139

Teide 12,172

Toubkal 13,665

Ighil 13,363

An 11,1

Shishaldin 9,372

Mauna Kea 13,796

Fairweather 15,300

Ratz 10,290

Popocatépetl 17,887

Citlaltépetl 18,700

Tajumulco 13,845

Pikes Pk. 14,110

Neblina 9,889

Bandeira 9,482

Atlas Mts.

Alaska Range

HAWAII

Coast Mts.

Rocky Mts.

MEXICO

CENTRAL AMERICA

Andes Mountains

Brazilian Highlands

Death Valley -282

Salina Grande -131

Argentine Abyssal Plain and Basin

Angola Basin

Aleutian Trench 24,600

Murray Fracture Zone

15,008

Clipperton Fracture Zone

Middle America Trench 19,680

Cayman Trench 24,720

Peru-Chile Trench

Puerto Rico Trench 28,000

Romanche Fracture Zone 25,347

18,00

19,680

Bartholomew Deep 26,453

Milwaukee Deep 30,246

South Sandwich Trench

Meteor Deep 27,000

180° 160° 140° 120° 100° 80° 60° 40° 20°

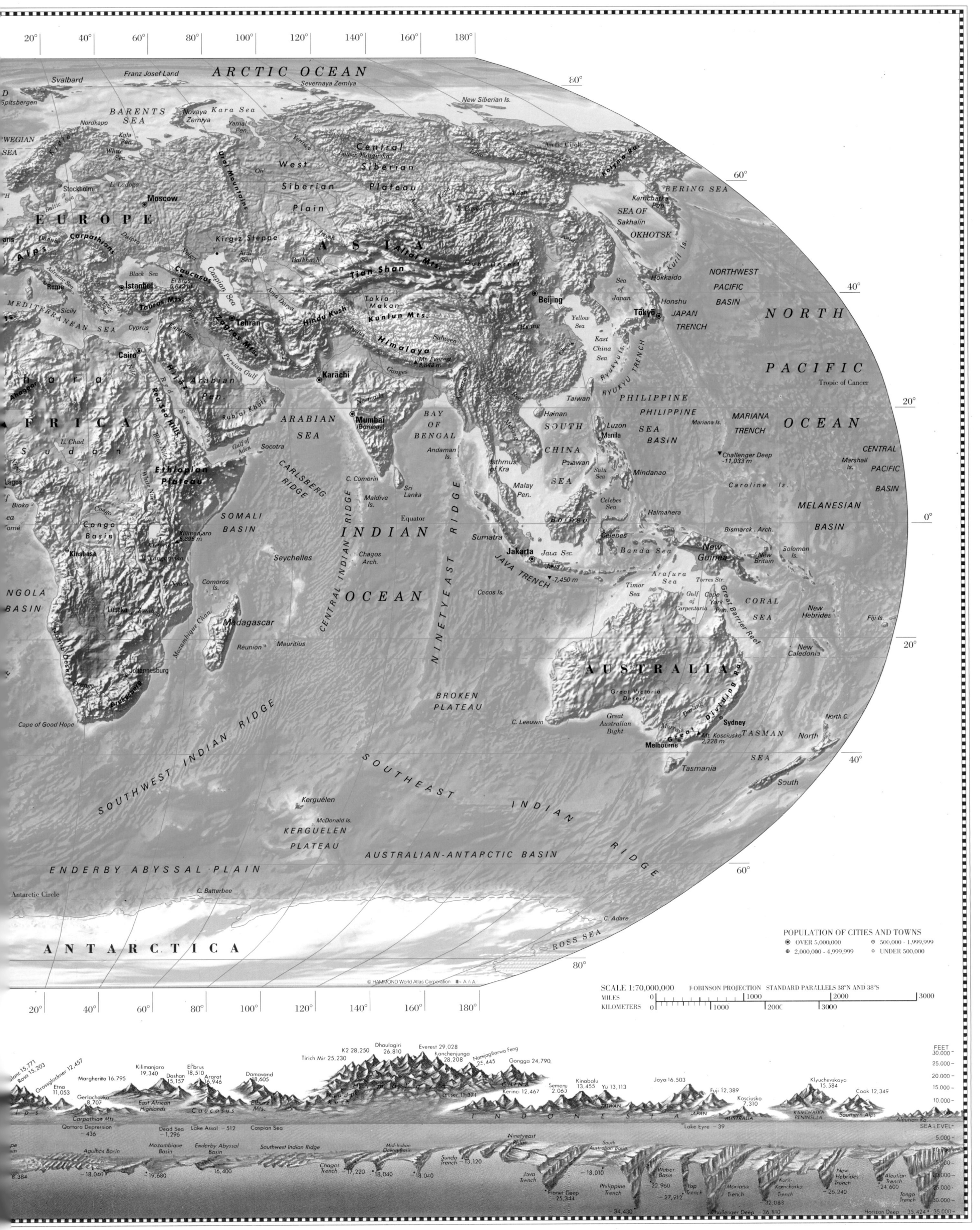

ARCTIC OCEAN

Svalbard
Franz Josef Land
Spitsbergen
Novaya Zemlya
Severnaya Zemlya
New Siberian Is.
BARENTS SEA
Kara Sea
Nordkapo
Kola Pen.
White Sea
Yamal Pen.
Ob
Yenisey
Lena
Arctic Circle
BERING SEA
Central Siberian Plateau
Kamchatka Pen.
60°
NORWEGIAN SEA
Stockholm
L. Ladoga
Moscow
Ural Mountains
West Siberian Plain
SEA OF OKHOTSK
Kolyma Ra.
80°

EUROPE
Alps
Carpathians
Dnieper
Kirgiz Steppe
ASIA
Altai Mts.
Caucasus
NORTHWEST PACIFIC BASIN
40°
Rome
Black Sea
Caspian Sea
Istanbul
Taurus Mts.
El'brus 5,642
Balkhash
Aral Sea
Tian Shan
Amu Darya
Takla Makan
Kunlun Mts.
Beijing
Hokkaido
Sea of Japan
Tokyo
Honshu
JAPAN TRENCH
MEDITERRANEAN SEA
Sicily
Cyprus
Zagros Mts.
Tehran
Hindu Kush
Himalaya
Mt. Everest 8,848 m
Huang
Yellow Sea
East China Sea
Taiwan
RYUKYU TRENCH
NORTH
Cairo
Persian Gulf
Arabian Pen.
Indus
Karachi
Ganges
SOUTH CHINA
Hainan
Luzon
Manila
PHILIPPINE SEA
Mariana Is.
MARIANA TRENCH
PACIFIC
Tropic of Cancer
20°
AFRICA
Sahara
Red Sea
Gulf of Aden
Rub' al Khali
ARABIAN SEA
Mumbai Bombay
BAY OF BENGAL
Andaman Is.
Isthmus of Kra
PHILIPPINE SEA BASIN
Challenger Deep -11,033 m
CENTRAL PACIFIC BASIN
OCEAN
Sudan
Red Sea Hills
Ethiopian Plateau
CARLSBERG RIDGE
C. Comorin
Maldive Is.
Sri Lanka
Malay Pen.
Palawan
Sulu Sea
Mindanao
Caroline Is.
Marshall Is.
Lagos
Bioko
São Tomé
Congo Basin
Kilimanjaro 5,895 m
Kinshasa
SOMALI BASIN
Seychelles
INDIAN
Chagos Arch.
Equator
Sumatra
Borneo
Celebes
Celebes Sea
Halmahera
Banda Sea
New Guinea
Bismarck Arch.
New Britain
Solomon Is.
MELANESIAN BASIN
0°
ANGOLA BASIN
Lusaka
Comoros Is.
Madagascar
Réunion
Mauritius
CENTRAL INDIAN RIDGE
OCEAN
NINETYEAST RIDGE
JAVA TRENCH
Jakarta
Java Sea
-7,450 m
Cocos Is.
Timor Sea
Arafura Sea
Gulf of Carpentaria
Cape York Pen.
Great Barrier Reef
CORAL SEA
New Hebrides
Fiji Is.
Johannesburg
Cape of Good Hope
BROKEN PLATEAU
C. Leeuwin
AUSTRALIA
Great Victoria Desert
Great Australian Bight
Murray
Great Dividing Ra.
Sydney
Mt. Kosciusko 2,228 m
Melbourne
New Caledonia
TASMAN SEA
North C.
North
20°
SOUTHWEST INDIAN RIDGE
SOUTHEAST
INDIAN
RIDGE
Tasmania
South
40°
Kerguélen
McDonald Is.
KERGUELEN PLATEAU
AUSTRALIAN-ANTARCTIC BASIN
ENDERBY ABYSSAL PLAIN
60°
Antarctic Circle
C. Batterbee
C. Adare
ROSS SEA
ANTARCTICA
80°

© HAMMOND World Atlas Corporation

POPULATION OF CITIES AND TOWNS
⊛ OVER 5,000,000   ⊙ 500,000 - 1,999,999
⊚ 2,000,000 - 4,999,999   ○ UNDER 500,000

SCALE 1:70,000,000   ROBINSON PROJECTION   STANDARD PARALLELS 38°N AND 38°S
MILES 0   1000   2000   3000
KILOMETERS 0   1000   2000   3000

Mont Blanc 15,771
Rosa 15,203
Grossglockner 12,457
Etna 11,053
Gerlachovka 8,707
Kilimanjaro 19,340
Margherita 16,795
Dashan 15,157
Ararat 16,946
El'brus 18,510
Damavand 18,605
Tirich Mir 25,230
K2 28,250
Dhaulagiri 26,810
Everest 29,028
Kanchenjunga 28,208
Namjagbarwa Feng 25,445
Gongga 24,790
Kinabalu 13,455
Jaya 16,503
Fuji 12,389
Klyuchevskaya 15,384
Cook 12,349
FEET 30,000
25,000
20,000
15,000
Semeru 2,063
Yü 13,113
Kosciusko 7,310
10,000
Alps
Sierra
Carpathian Mts.
East African Highlands
CAUCASUS
El'brus Mts.
Trolen 1h,871
Kerinci 12,467
TAIWAN
JAPAN
AUSTRALIA
KAMCHATKA PENINSULA
Southern Alps
Aleutian Ra.
Qattara Depression -436
Dead Sea -1,296
Lake Assol -512
Caspian Sea
Ninetyeast Ridge
South Australian Basin
Lake Eyre -39
SEA LEVEL
5,000
Agulhas Basin
Mozambique Basin
Enderby Abyssal Basin
Southwest Indian Ridge
Mid-Indian Ocean Basin
Sunda Trench -13,120
Java Trench
Weber Basin
Yap Trench
Kuril-Kamchatka Trench
New Hebrides Trench
Aleutian Trench
Chagos Trench -17,220
-18,040
-18,040
Philippine Trench
-22,960
-27,912
Mariana Trench -32,083
-26,240
24,600
Tonga Trench
-6,384
-18,040
-19,680
-16,400
-18,010
Planet Deep 25,344
-34,430
Challenger Deep 36,810
Horizon Deep 35,424
35,000

NORWEGIAN
BASIN

N O R W E G I A N

VORING
PLATEAU

Vesterålen
Lofoten

Arctic Circle

JAN MAYEN RIDGE

S E A

ICELAND BASIN

Reykjavik

ROCKALL
PLATEAU

Faroe Is.

HEBRIDIAN SHELF

Shetland
Is.

Rockall

Hebrides

Orkney Is.

Bergen

A T L A N T I C

Moray Firth

Lindesnes

Skagerrak

Göteborg

Väster
Stockholm

O C E A N

ROCKALL TROUGH

Aberdeen

NORTH

Vänern

Vättern

Gotl

50°

PORCUPINE
BANK

Glasgow

Great

SEA

Jutland

Kattegat

Öland

Belfast

I. of Man

Britain

Fyn

Copenhagen

Ireland

Dublin

Irish
Sea

Liverpool

Pennine Chain

Bornholm

BALT

C. Clear

PORCUPINE ABYSSAL PLAIN

St. George's Chan.

Birmingham

Frisian Is.

Hamburg

London

Amsterdam

Berlin

CELTIC
SHELF

Land's End

English Channel

Thames

The Hague

Rhine

Brussels

Cologne
Bonn

Leipzig

N

O

Channel
Is.

Le Havre
Seine

Paris

Stuttgart

Vienna

Bratislava

BISCAY ABYSSAL
PLAIN

Nantes

Loire

Munich

Bern

Graz

IBERIAN
ABYSSAL

Bay of
Biscay

Bordeaux

Central

Lyon

Mont Blanc

Zagreb

40°

PLAIN

Cabo Finisterre

Cordillera
Cantábrica

Bilbao

Massif

Rhône

Turin

Milan

Venice

Po

Dalmatian Is.

Pyrenees

Genoa

Adriatic

Lisbon

Tagus

Madrid

Marseille

Ligurian
Sea

Corsica

Rome

Se

Cabo de
São
Vicente

Sierra

Barcelona

G. of Lion

Naples

Cádiz

Valencia

Balearic Islands

Minorca

Sardinia

Tyrrhenian
Sea

Málaga

Mulhacén

Ibiza

Majorca

Capo Teulada

−3,630m

Palermo

ALGERIAN PLAINS

Str. of Gibraltar

Tangiers

M E D I T E R R A N E

Sicily

Capo Passero

Rabat

Algiers

Oran

A F R I C A

Pantelleria

Malta

30°

Europe

Europe is one large peninsula divided into many smaller peninsulas. The high peaks and glaciated ridges of the Alps form a continental divide across Central Europe from which major rivers flow to the North Sea, the Mediterranean Sea and the Black Sea. Europe's other significant highland area forms the backbone of Scandinavia, Scotland and the north of Ireland.

SCALE 1:11,250,000   OPTIMAL CONFORMAL PROJECTION

40° Longitude East of Greenwich

Asia

Asia and Europe make up the Eurasia plate, which is fringed by jagged peninsulas and island arcs. The ever-rising Himalayas, crowned by Mt. Everest, form the southern edge of an enormous plateau with numerous ranges. Asia is separated from Europe by the landlocked Caspian Sea and the Urals. Deep ocean trenches sear the boundaries of the Pacific and Indo-Australian plates.

SCALE 1:42,000,000 LAMBERT AZIMUTHAL EQUAL-AREA PROJECTION

East Asia

This region extends from the edge of Siberian permafrost to the tropical Philippines. The Plateau of Tibet, a cold rock desert, reaches east with extensive mountain ranges. The outlying islands rise near deep ocean trenches, and are dotted with active volcanoes. The Huang (Yellow) River, with its tributaries in the high plateaus, provides fertile soils to the lower plains.

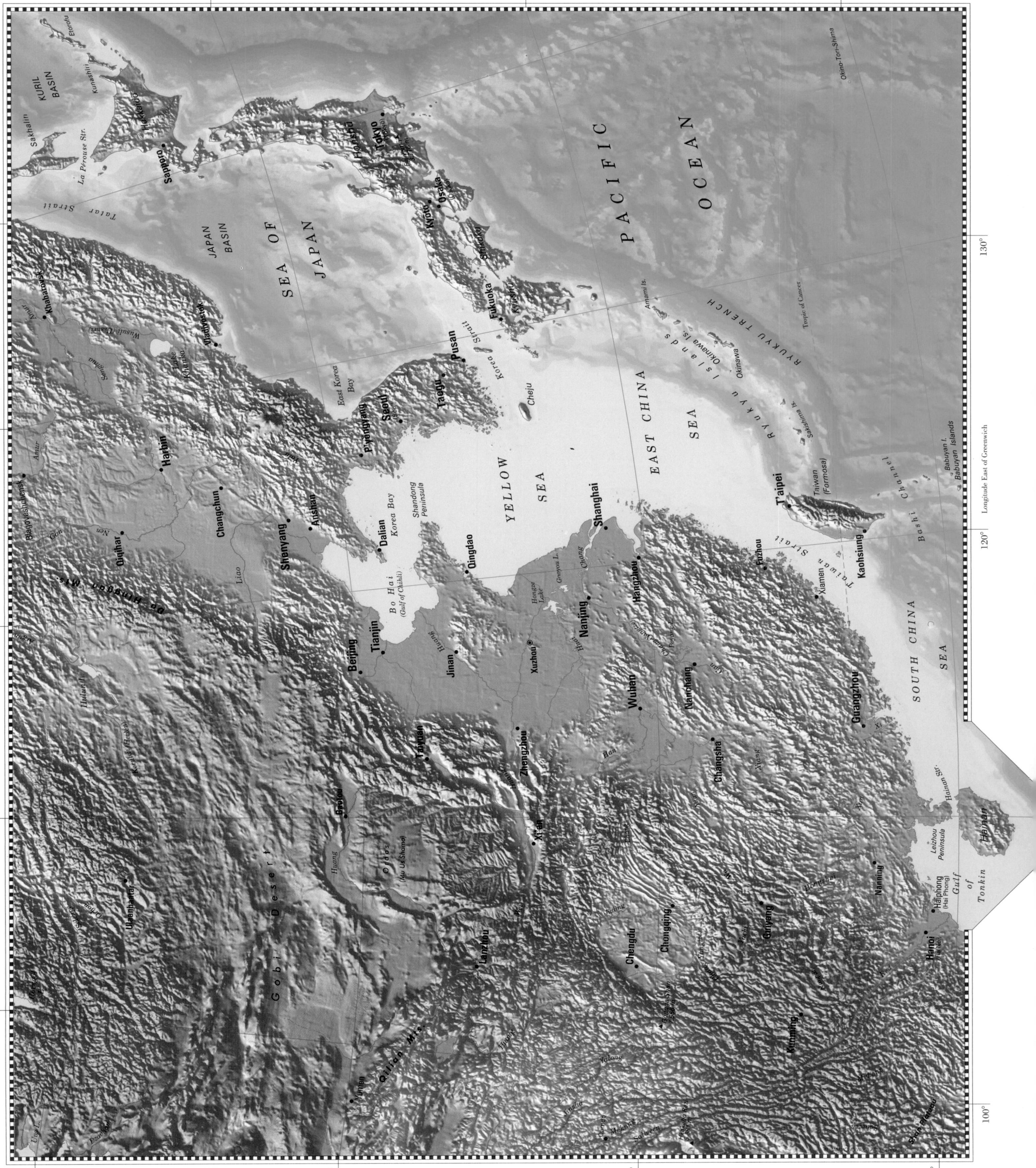

KURIL BASIN

Sakhalin

La Pérouse Str.

Tatar Strait

Hokkaido

Sapporo

JAPAN BASIN

SEA OF JAPAN

Tokyo

Honshu

Osaka

Kyoto

PACIFIC OCEAN

Khabarovsk

Wusuli (Ussuri)

Vladivostok

Fukuoka

Kyushu

East Korea Bay

Pusan

Korea Strait

Amami Is.

Tropic of Cancer

RYUKYU TRENCH

Ryukyu Islands

Okinawa Is.

Harbin

Pyongyang

Seoul

Taegu

Cheju

YELLOW SEA

EAST CHINA SEA

Longitude East of Greenwich

Blagoveshchensk

Qiqihar

Changchun

Anshan

Shenyang

Dalian

Shandong Peninsula

Korea Bay

Shanghai

Taipei

Taiwan (Formosa)

Bashi Channel

Babuyan Islands

Da Hinggan Mts.

Liao

Qingdao

Fuzhou

Kaohsiung

Xiamen

Taiwan Strait

Ulaanbaatar

Gobi Desert

Beijing

Tianjin

Bo Hai (Gulf of Chihli)

Jinan

Huang

Xuzhou

Hongze L.

Nanjing

Hangzhou

SOUTH CHINA SEA

Gan

Guangzhou

Ordos (Mu Us Shamo)

Huang

Taiyuan

Zhengzhou

Wuhan

Nanchang

Nanning

Hanoi (Ha Noi)

Gulf of Tonkin

Yinchuan

Xi'an

Han

Changsha

Leizhou Peninsula

Hainan Str.

Hainan

Lanzhou

Chengdu

Chongqing

Guiyang

Qilian Mts.

Kunming

Southeast Asia

Situated nearly astride the Equator, and on the shallow continental shelf, Southeast Asia is an oceanic realm of peninsulas and thousands of volcanic islands. The island arcs of Indonesia and the adjacent Java Trench are the result of the collision of oceanic crust against the continental plate. The tropical climate and the fertile volcanic soils nurture rain forests and agriculture.

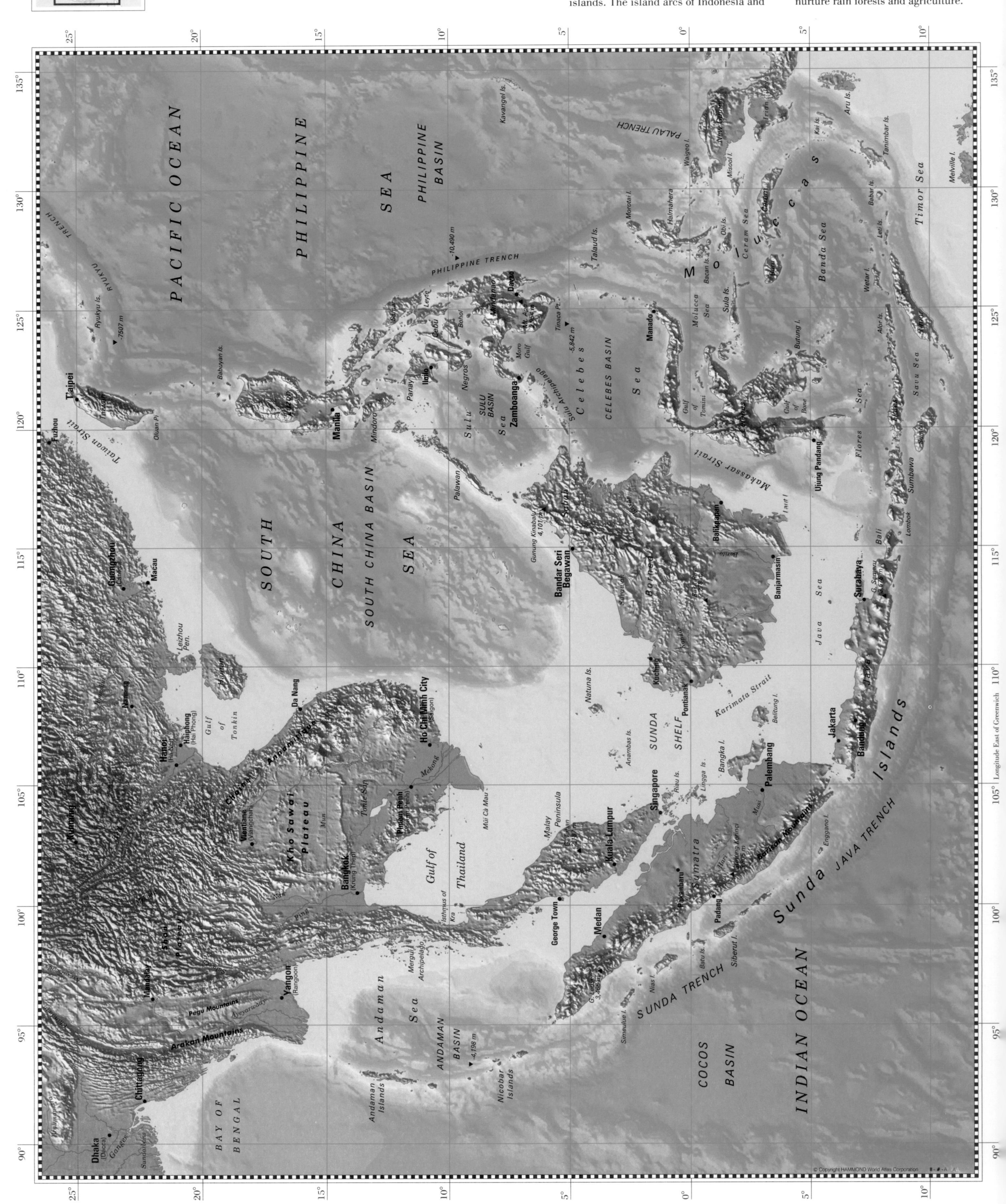

SCALE 1:17,700,000 MILLER CYLINDRICAL PROJECTION

MILES 0   200   400   600   800
KILOMETERS 0   200   400   600   800

© Copyright HAMMOND World Atlas Corporation

The Indian subcontinent is still moving north against Asia, pushing the Himalayas to even greater heights. The sparsely inhabited Plateau of Tibet, flanked by the Taklimakan desert, stretches 800 miles (1280 km.) east to west. The mighty Brahmaputra and Ganges rivers carry waters south from the Himalayas, creating an immense flood plain at the Ganes Delta.

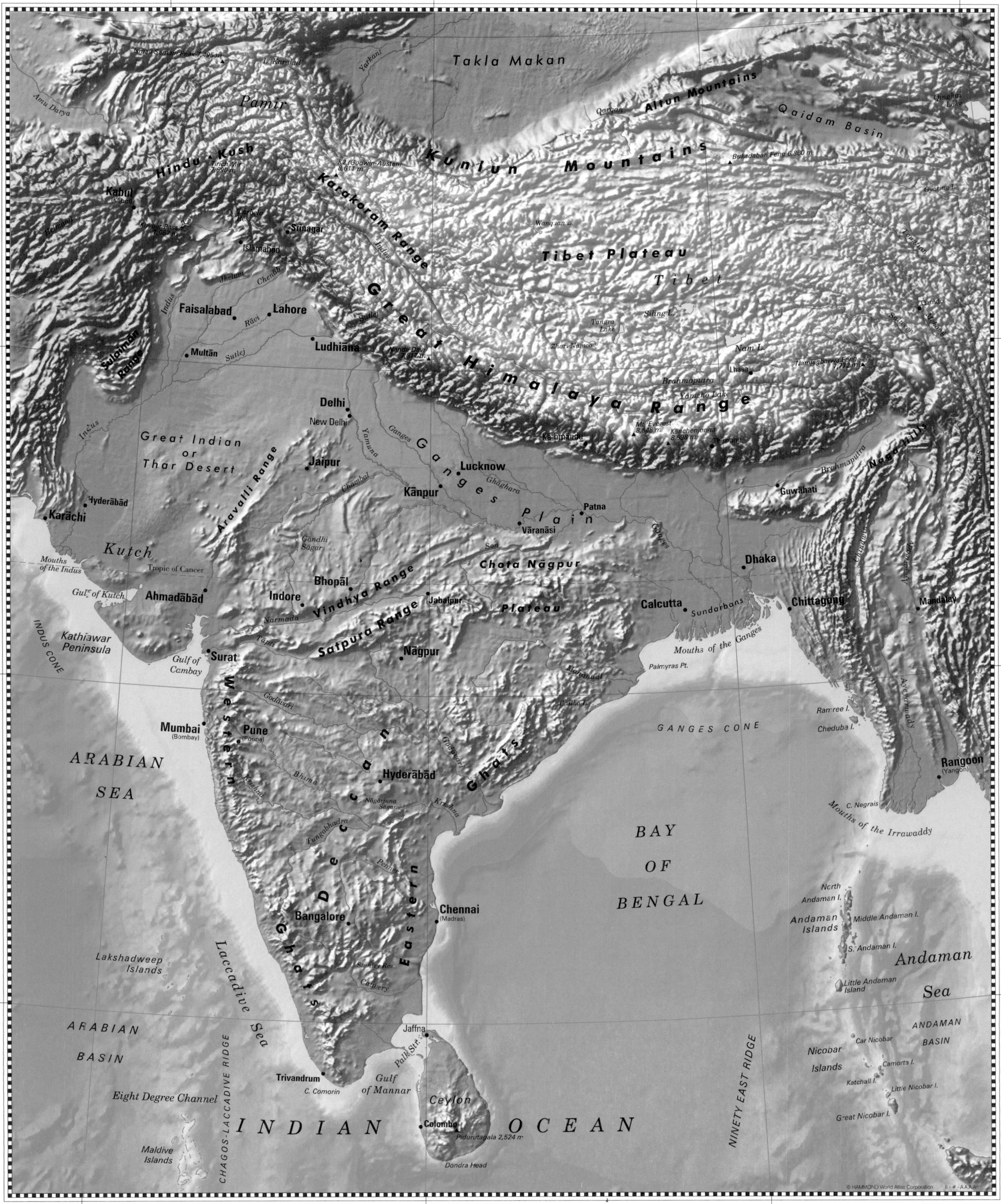

Takla Makan

Altun Mountains

Qaidam Basin

Pamir

Hindu Kush

Kunlun Mountains

Bukadaban Feng 6,860 m.

Kabul

Karakoram Range

K2 Godwin-Austen 8,611 m.

Tibet Plateau

Tibet

Srinagar

Islamabad

Faisalabad

Lahore

Great Himalaya Range

Nam L.

Ludhiāna

Lhasa

Multān

Sutlej

Brahmaputra

Delhi

New Delhi

Ganges

Mt. Everest 8,848 m.

Kanchenjunga 8,598 m.

Great Indian or Thar Desert

Jaipur

Aravalli Range

Yamuna

Lucknow

Ganges Plain

Ghāghara

Guwahati

Kānpur

Patna

Hyderābād

Karāchi

Vāranāsi

Son

Dhaka

Kutch

Gandhi Sāgar

Chota Nāgpur

Mouths of the Indus

Tropic of Cancer

Bhopāl

Plateau

Calcutta

Chittagong

Mandalay

Gulf of Kutch

Indore

Vindhya Range

Jabalpur

Sundarbans

Narmada

Ahmadābād

Satpura Range

Nāgpur

Mouths of the Ganges

Kathiawar Peninsula

Surat

Gulf of Cambay

Deccan

Palmyras Pt.

Western

GANGES CONE

Ram ree I.

Mumbai (Bombay)

Pune (Poona)

Hyderābād

Cheduba I.

ARABIAN SEA

Ghats

Eastern

Rangoon (Yangon)

Bhima

Krishna

Mouths of the Irrawaddy

C. Negrais

BAY OF BENGAL

Lakshadweep Islands

Bangalore

Ghats

Chennai (Madras)

North Andaman I.

Andaman Islands

Middle Andaman I.

ARABIAN BASIN

Laccadive Sea

S. Andaman I.

Andaman Sea

Little Andaman Island

Jaffna

Palk Str.

ANDAMAN BASIN

Trivandrum

Gulf of Mannar

Nicobar Islands

Car Nicobar

Camorta I.

C. Comorin

Ceylon

Katchall I.

Little Nicobar I.

Eight Degree Channel

Colombo

Pidurutagala 2,524 m.

Great Nicobar I.

CHAGOS-LACCADIVE RIDGE

Maldive Islands

INDIAN OCEAN

Dondra Head

NINETY EAST RIDGE

SCALE 1:13,100,000   LAMBERT CONFORMAL CONIC PROJECTION

MILES 0   200   400   600

KILOMETERS 0   200   400   600

© HAMMOND World Atlas Corporation

Near and Middle East

A continuous chain of mountain ranges meanders from Greece to the foothills of the Himalayas. Some 20 million years ago, the Arabian Peninsula pivoted at the Dead Sea and moved away from Africa, creating the Red Sea. Much of the region consists of either rock or sand desert. The Nile, Euphrates, Tigris and Indus river valleys are the most fertile areas.

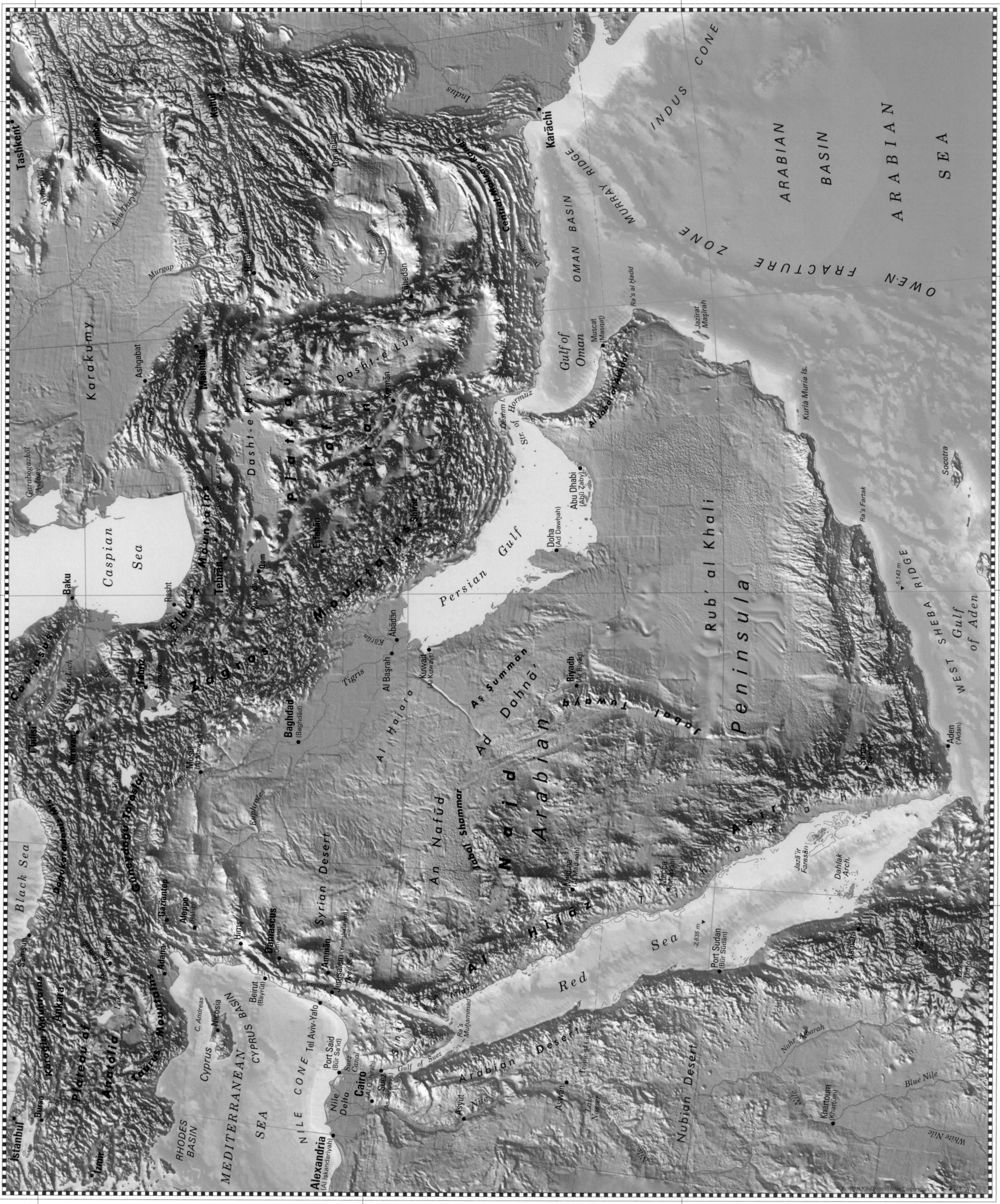

SCALE 1:13,700,000   LAMBERT CONFORMAL CONIC PROJECTION

MILES   0   200   400   600
KILOMETERS   0   200   400   600

Africa

P lanted squarely on the Equator, Africa is a vast plateau rising steeply from a narrow coast. Fractures in the continent's crust created the Great Rift Valley of East Africa. Africa's vegetation is densest in the Congo Basin, and decreases away from the Equator. The Sahara, an area of 3.5 million square miles (9.1 million sq. km.), is the largest desert in the world.

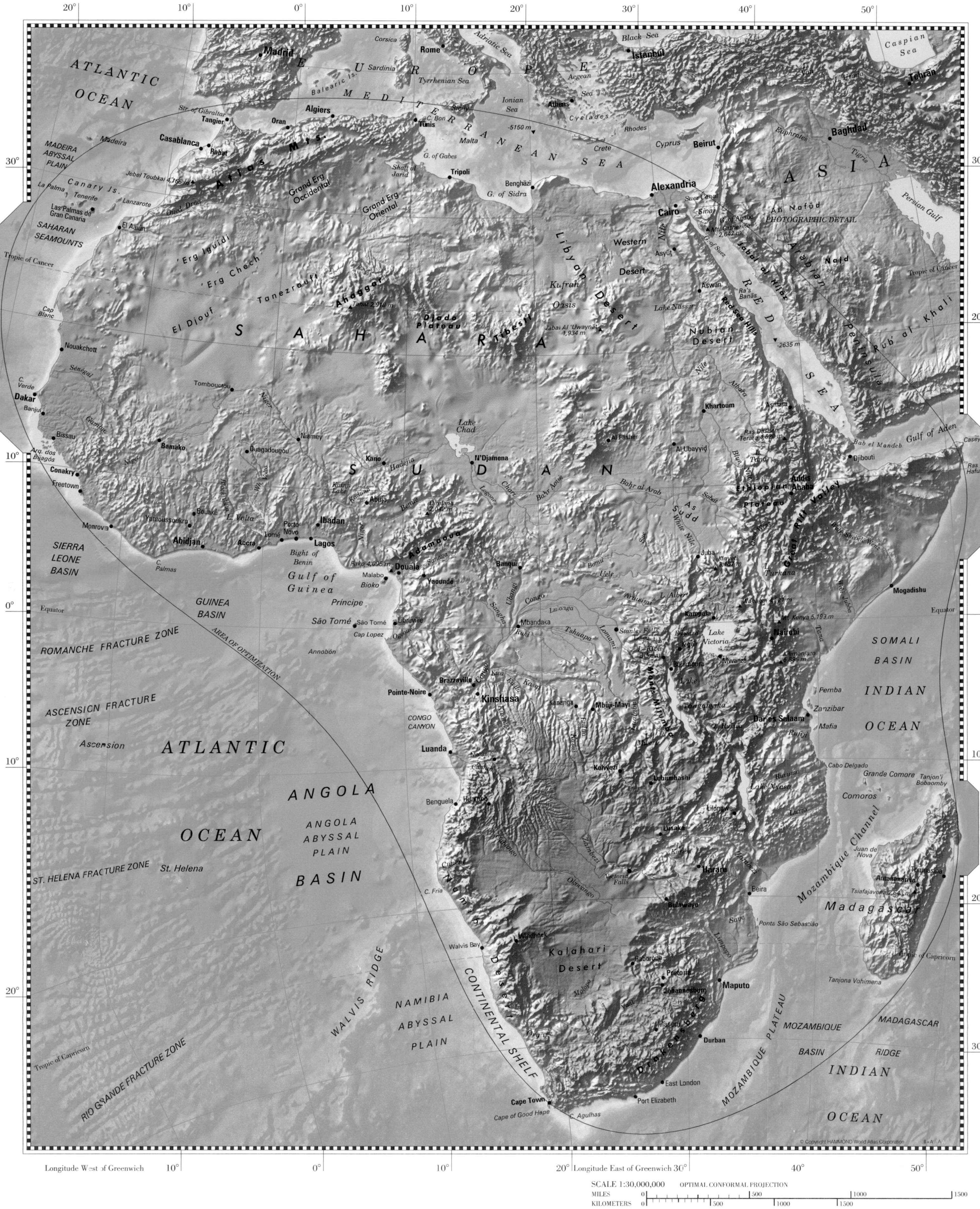

SCALE 1:30,000,000   OPTIMAL CONFORMAL PROJECTION

MILES 0 — 500 — 1000 — 1500

KILOMETERS 0 — 500 — 1000 — 1500

Australia and Pacific Ocean

Australia, the smallest continent, borders the Pacific Ocean as part of the Indo-Australian Plate. The Pacific is as large as the Indian, Atlantic and Arctic Oceans combined. It contains the ultimate abyss, the 35,000 foot-deep (10,500 m.) Mariana Trench, and numerous islands. It was named by its first European navigator, Magellan, because he experienced calm weather there.

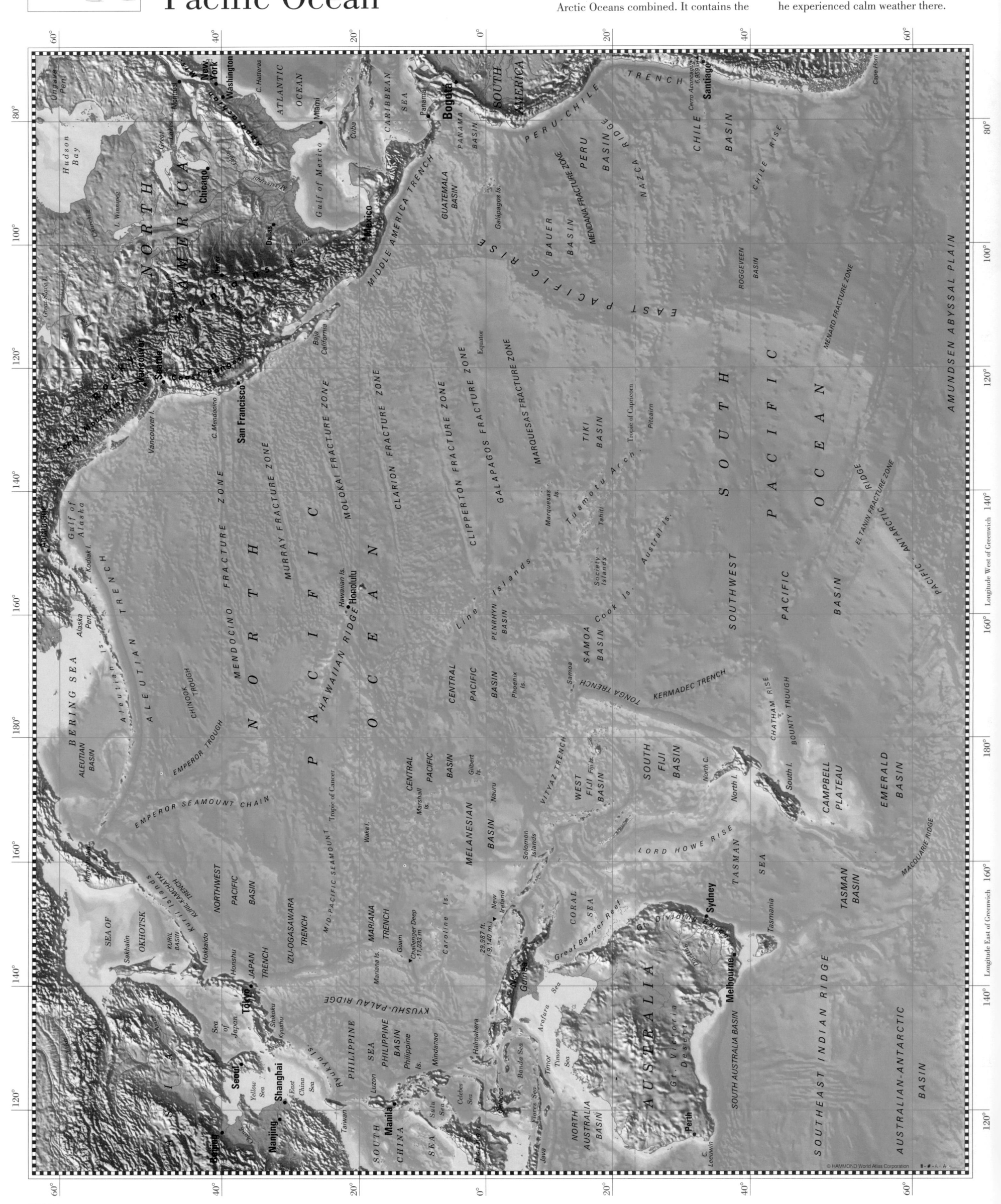

SCALE 1:68,000,000   MILLER CYLINDRICAL PROJECTION

MILES   0   1000   2000   3000

KILOMETERS   0   1000   2000   3000

© HAMMOND World Atlas Corporation

North America

North America extends over 3,900 miles (6240 km.) from the polar reaches of the Canadian north to the tropics of the Caribbean. Two mountain systems frame a vast interior plain. The younger western ranges, whose summits near 21,000 feet (6300 m.), were formed by the collision of continental plates and ocean crust. Erosion smoothed older eastern mountains into gently rolling hills.

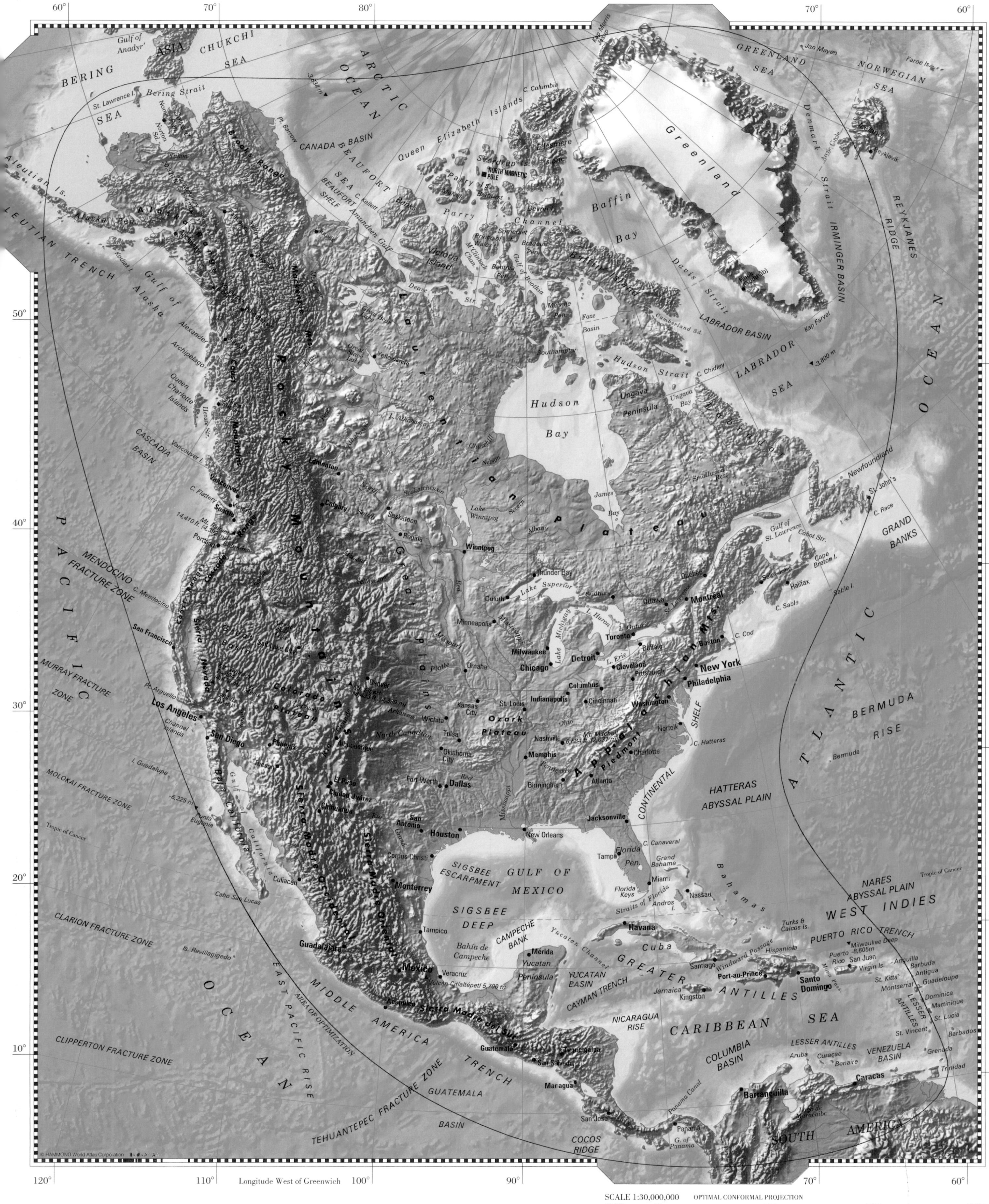

Middle America

The narrow isthmus between North and South America consists of a mountainous, volcanic spine, flanked by coastal lowlands. At its south end is the Panama Canal, connecting Atlantic and Pacific waters. The Antilles, where Columbus landed, are volcanic islands rising from the depths of the Caribbean Sea. The Puerto Rico Trench has an average depth of 20,000 feet (6000 m.).

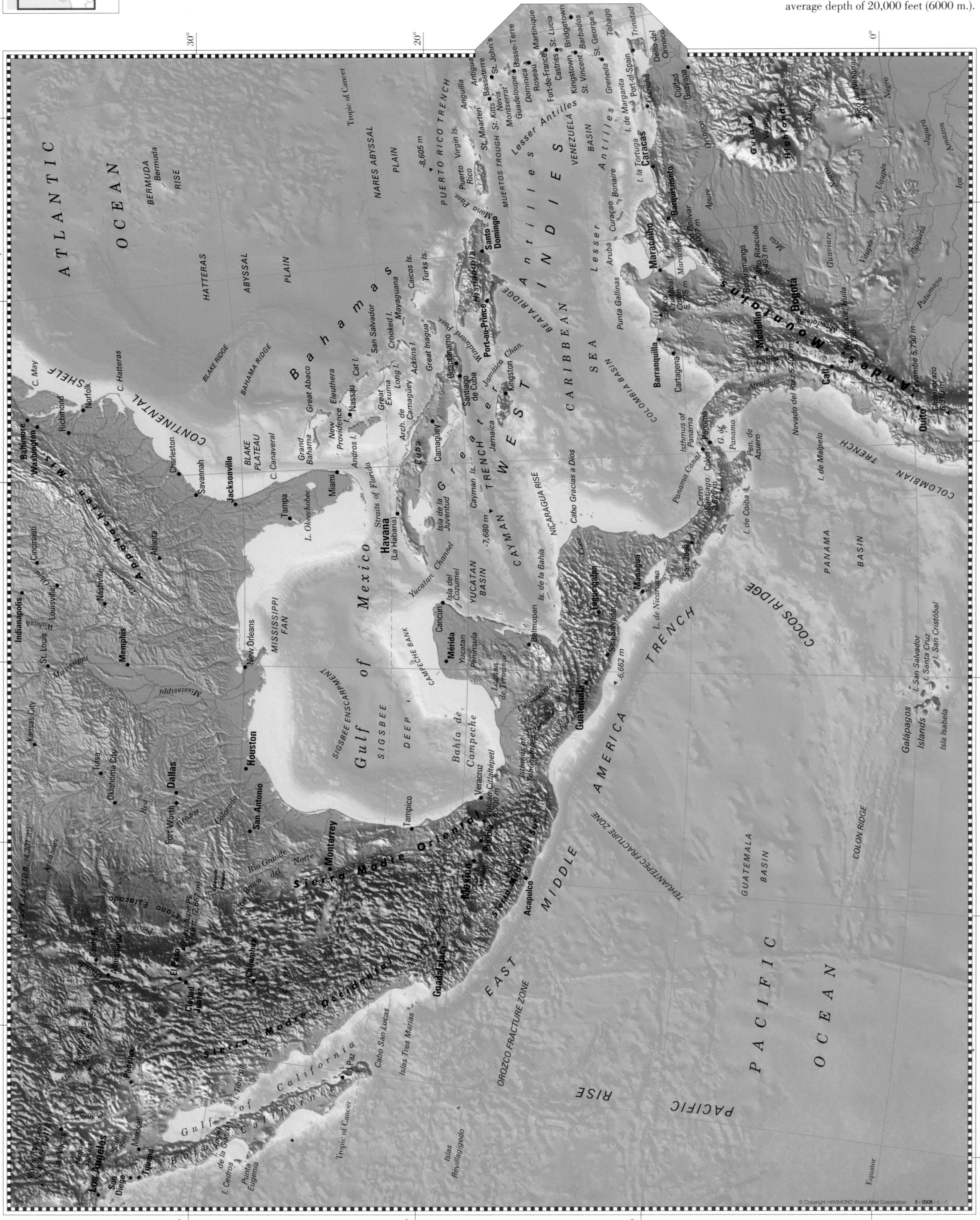

ATLANTIC OCEAN

PACIFIC OCEAN

CARIBBEAN SEA

Gulf of Mexico

WEST INDIES

Greater Antilles

Lesser Antilles

Bahamas

Cuba

Jamaica

Hispaniola

Puerto Rico

Virgin Is.

Sierra Madre Oriental

Sierra Madre Occidental

Sierra Madre del Sur

Gulf of California

Baja California

Andes Mountains

PUERTO RICO TRENCH

MIDDLE AMERICA TRENCH

CAYMAN TRENCH

COCOS RIDGE

BEATA RIDGE

NARES ABYSSAL PLAIN

HATTERAS ABYSSAL PLAIN

VENEZUELA BASIN

COLOMBIA BASIN

YUCATAN BASIN

GUATEMALA BASIN

PANAMA BASIN

SIGSBEE DEEP

CONTINENTAL SHELF

BAHAMA RIDGE

BLAKE PLATEAU

BLAKE RIDGE

BERMUDA RISE

MISSISSIPPI FAN

CAMPECHE BANK

NICARAGUA RISE

COLON RIDGE

PACIFIC RISE

EAST PACIFIC RISE

OROZCO FRACTURE ZONE

TEHUANTEPEC FRACTURE ZONE

Appalachian Mountains

Baltimore, Washington, Richmond, Norfolk, Charleston, Savannah, Jacksonville, Tampa, Miami, New Orleans, Houston, San Antonio, Dallas, Fort Worth, Oklahoma City, Tulsa, Kansas City, St. Louis, Memphis, Nashville, Atlanta, Louisville, Cincinnati, Indianapolis, El Paso, Ciudad Juárez, Chihuahua, Albuquerque, Phoenix, Las Vegas, Los Angeles, San Diego, Tijuana, Mexicali

Monterrey, Tampico, Veracruz, México, Guadalajara, Acapulco, Mérida, Cancún

Havana (La Habana), Nassau, Santiago de Cuba, Camagüey, Kingston, Port-au-Prince, Santo Domingo, San Juan

Guatemala, San Salvador, Tegucigalpa, Managua, San José, Panamá, Colón, Belmopan

Caracas, Maracaibo, Barquisimeto, Barranquilla, Cartagena, Medellín, Bogotá, Cali, Quito

Tropic of Cancer

Equator

Galápagos Islands

BERMUDA

Bermuda

© Copyright HAMMOND World Atlas Corporation

Continental United States

SCALE 1:14,500,000   LAMBERT CONFORMAL CONIC PROJECTION

MILES   0   200   400   600

KILOMETERS   0   200   400   600

South America

F rom a mere trickle in the high-lands of Peru, the Amazon swells mightily on its 4,000 mile (6400 km.) journey eastward to the Atlantic. The world's largest tropical rain forest lies in its basin. The towering, snow-capped Andes Mountains, second in height only to the Himalayas, form the earth's longest continental range, over 4,500 miles (7200 km.).

CARIBBEAN SEA

Punta Gallinas
Barranquilla
Willemstad
Maracaibo
Caracas
Port-of-Spain
Trinidad
G. of Venezuela
G. of Paria
Delta del Orinoco
San José
Panama Canal
Gulf of Panama
Cabo Corrientes
Pico Bolívar 5,007 m.
Bucaramanga
Ciudad Guayana
Georgetown
Medellín
Paramaribo
Alto Ritacuba 5,493 m.
PANAMA
Nevado de Ruiz 5,400 m.
Bogotá
Cayenne
Malpelo I.
BASIN
Cali
Salto Angostura
Guiana Highlands
Punta Galera
Equator
Quito
Chimborazo 6,267 m.
Salto Grande
Pico de la Neblina 3,014 m.
Guayaquil
Rep. de Balbina
Belém
G. of Guayaquil
Iquitos
Amazon
Manaus
São Luís
Punta Aguja
Selvas
Fortaleza
I. Fernando de Noronha
Trujillo
Cabo de São Roque
Natal
Callao
Recife
Serra dos Parecis
Meseta del
Brazilian
Maceió
Mato Grosso
Highlands
Salvador
PERU
Brasília
Goiânia
BASIN
Belo Horizonte
Pico da Bandeira 2,890 m.
PACIFIC
Campo Grande
Cabo de São Tomé
NAZCA
CHILE
Asunción
São Paulo
Rio de Janeiro
Tropic of Capricorn
Antofagasta
Cabo Frio
RIDGE
BASIN
Santos
I. de San Félix
I. San Ambrosio
Represa Itaipu
SANTOS PLATEAU
Córdoba
Pôrto Alegre
Mar Chiquita
RIO GRANDE PLATEAU
Santa Fe
OCEAN
Rosario
Valparaíso
Santiago
Buenos Aires
Montevideo
Juan Fernández Is.
La Plata
ATLANTIC
I. Alejandro Selkirk
I. Robinson Crusoe
Mendoza
CHALLENGER FRACTURE ZONE
Concepción
ARGENTINE
Bahía Blanca
Colorado
BASIN
Negro
Bahía Blanca
Golfo San Matías
OCEAN
Pen. Valdés
Puerto Montt
Isla de Chiloé
Chubut
G. Corcovado
Golfo San Jorge
Arch. de Los Chonos
Cabo Tres Puntas
FALKLAND ESCARPMENT
Pen. Taitao
Cabo Tres Montes
Bahía Grande
West Falkland
Falkland Is.
Isla Wellington
East Falkland
Strait of Magellan
Tierra del Fuego
Punta Arenas
Cape Horn

DEMERARA ABYSSAL PLAIN
ATLANTIC
PARA ABYSSAL PLAIN
OCEAN
CEARA ABYSSAL PLAIN
ROMANCHE FRACTURE ZONE
MID-ATLANTIC RIDGE
Equator
BRAZIL BASIN

PERU-CHILE TRENCH
Cordillera de los Andes
Llanos
Orinoco
Amazon
Cordillera
Altiplano
La Paz
Gran Chaco
Pampas
Patagonia
Cordillera de los Andes

PACIFIC BASIN
CHILE RISE

SCALE 1:24,000,000   LAMBERT AZIMUTHAL EQUAL-AREA PROJECTION
MILES   0   400   800   1200
KILOMETERS   0   400   800   1200

Longitude West of Greenwich

80° 60° 50° 40°
90° 80° 50° 40° 30° 20°

10° 0° 10° 20° 30° 40°

© HAMMOND World Atlas Corporation

Maps of the World

UNITED KINGDOM
IRELAND
DUBLIN
LONDON
NORTH SEA
DENMARK
POLAND
GERMANY
NETH.
BELG.
LUX.
PARIS
BREST
FRANCE
SWIT.
BAY OF BISCAY
BORDEAUX
MONACO
CORSICA
ROME
NAPLES
SARDINIA
ANDORRA
MADRID
BARCELONA
PALMA
SPAIN
CARTAGENA
ANNABA
PORTUGAL
LISBON
MALAGA
ALGIERS
ORAN
TANGIER
RABAT
CASABLANCA
MOROCCO
MARRAKECH
AZORES
MADEIRA
CANARY ISLANDS
EL AAIUN
WESTERN SAHARA
ALGERIA
TUNISIA
TUNIS
MALTA
SICILY
MEDITERRANEAN
ALB.
GREECE
BUL.
ROMANIA
BLACK
NORTH
ATLANTIC

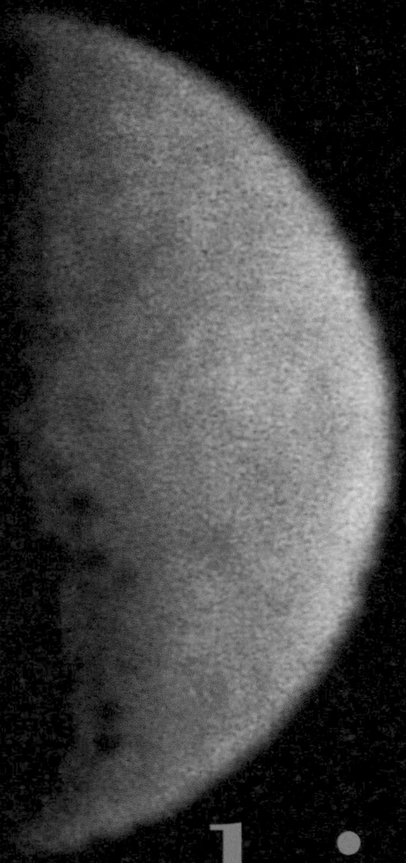

"Facts which at first se
stand forth in naked a

em improbable will . . .
nd simple beauty."

On December 16, 1992 the Galileo
spacecraft captured this remarkable
view of the Earth and Moon from
3.9 million miles away.

Of all the independent countries of the world, more than half have gained their independence since the end of World War II. Country sizes range from the city-states of Monaco and Vatican City to the vastness of Russia. But size often bears little correlation to a nation's population, or to its economic or political power. The world can be divided into three principal power centers: North America, Eastern Asia and Europe. The affects of a united Europe, and the industrial boom in southeast Asia, may significantly alter geopolitics in the next century.

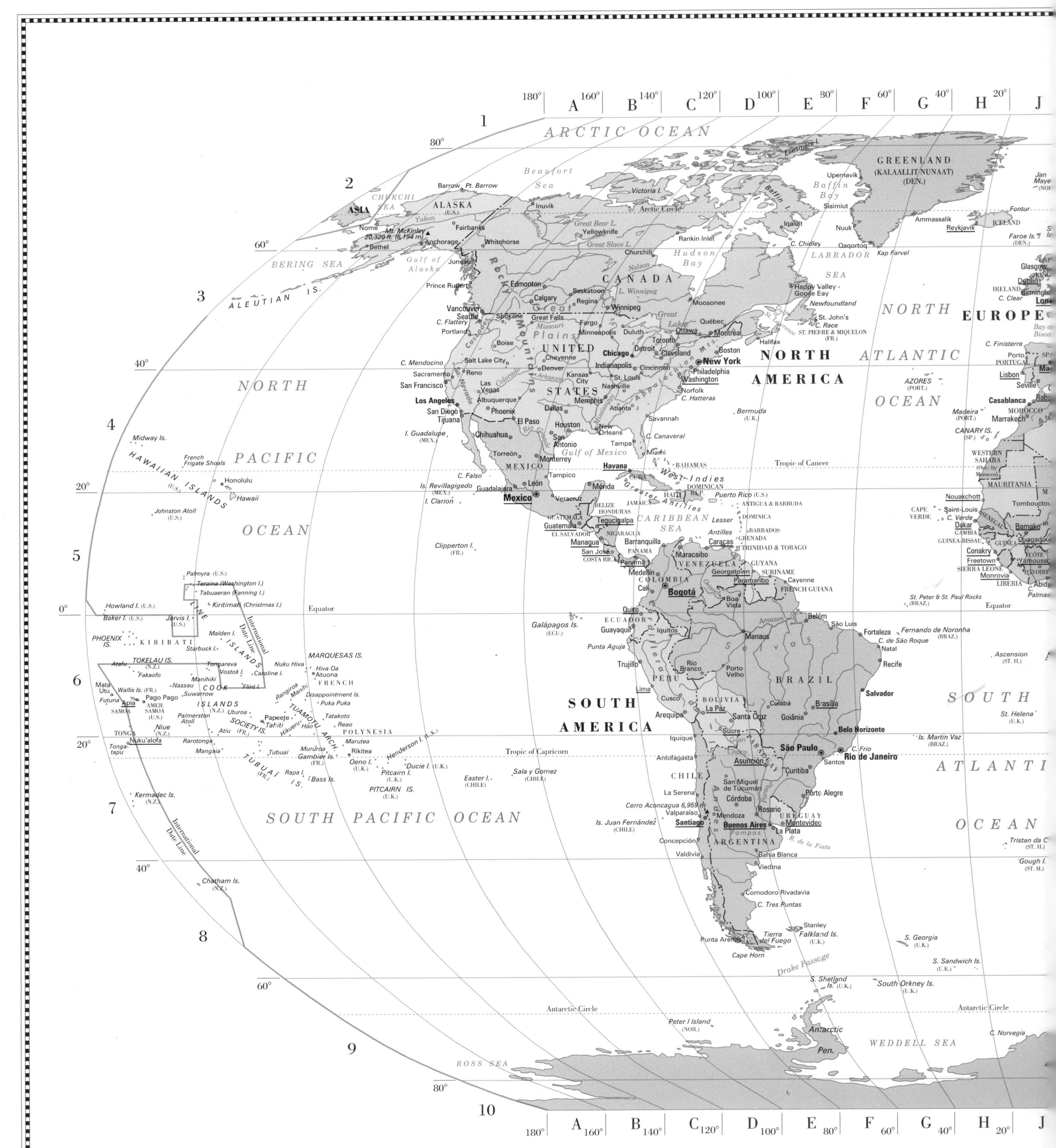

World

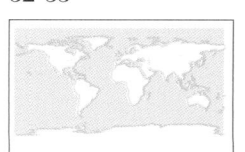

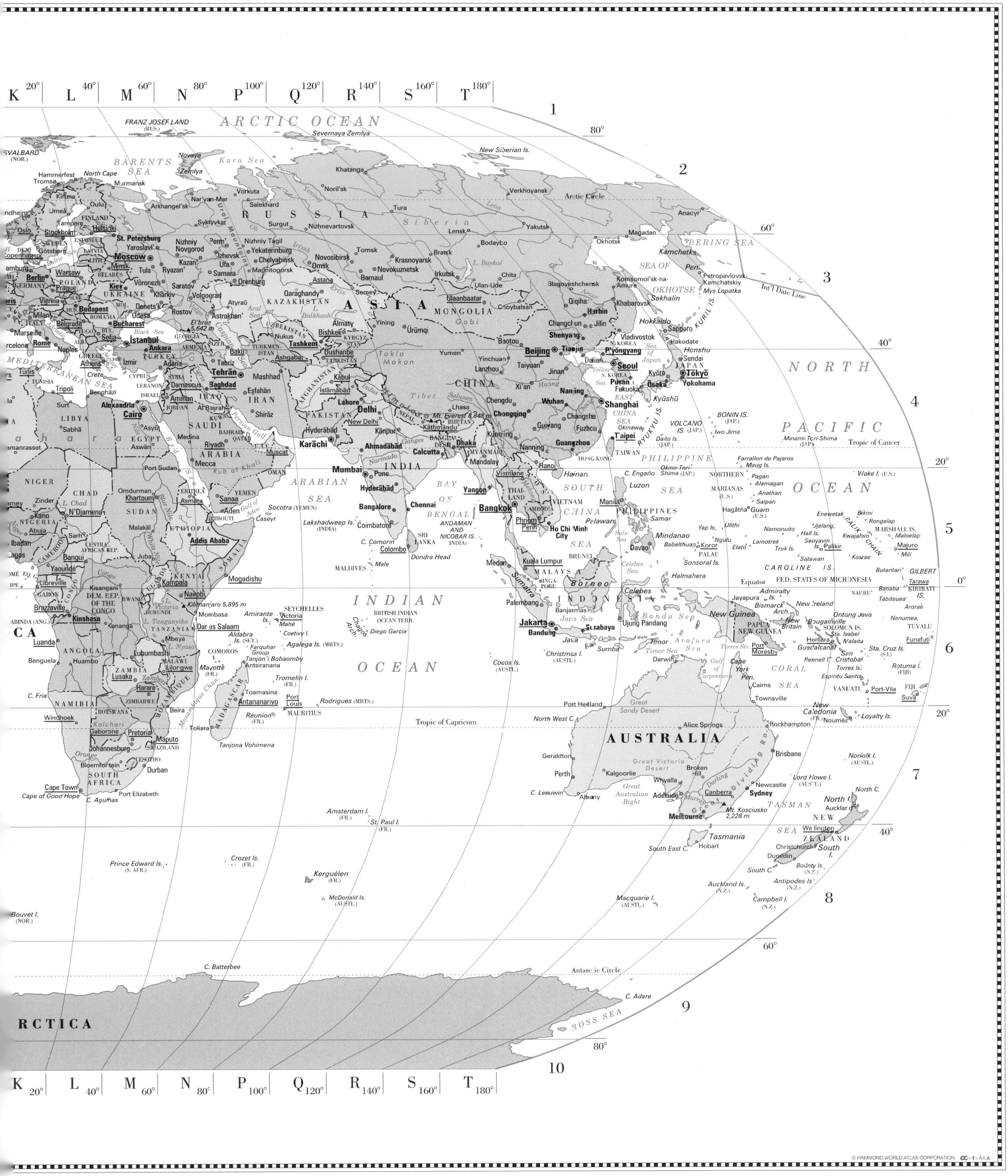

POPULATION OF CITIES AND TOWNS

⊚ OVER 5,000,000   ● 500,000 - 1,999,999
⊛ 2,000,000 - 4,999,999   ○ UNDER 500,000

SCALE 1:70,000,000   ROBINSON PROJECTION   STANDARD PARALLELS 38°N AND 38°S

MILES 0   1000   2000   3000   4000

KILOMETERS 0   1000   2000   3000   4000

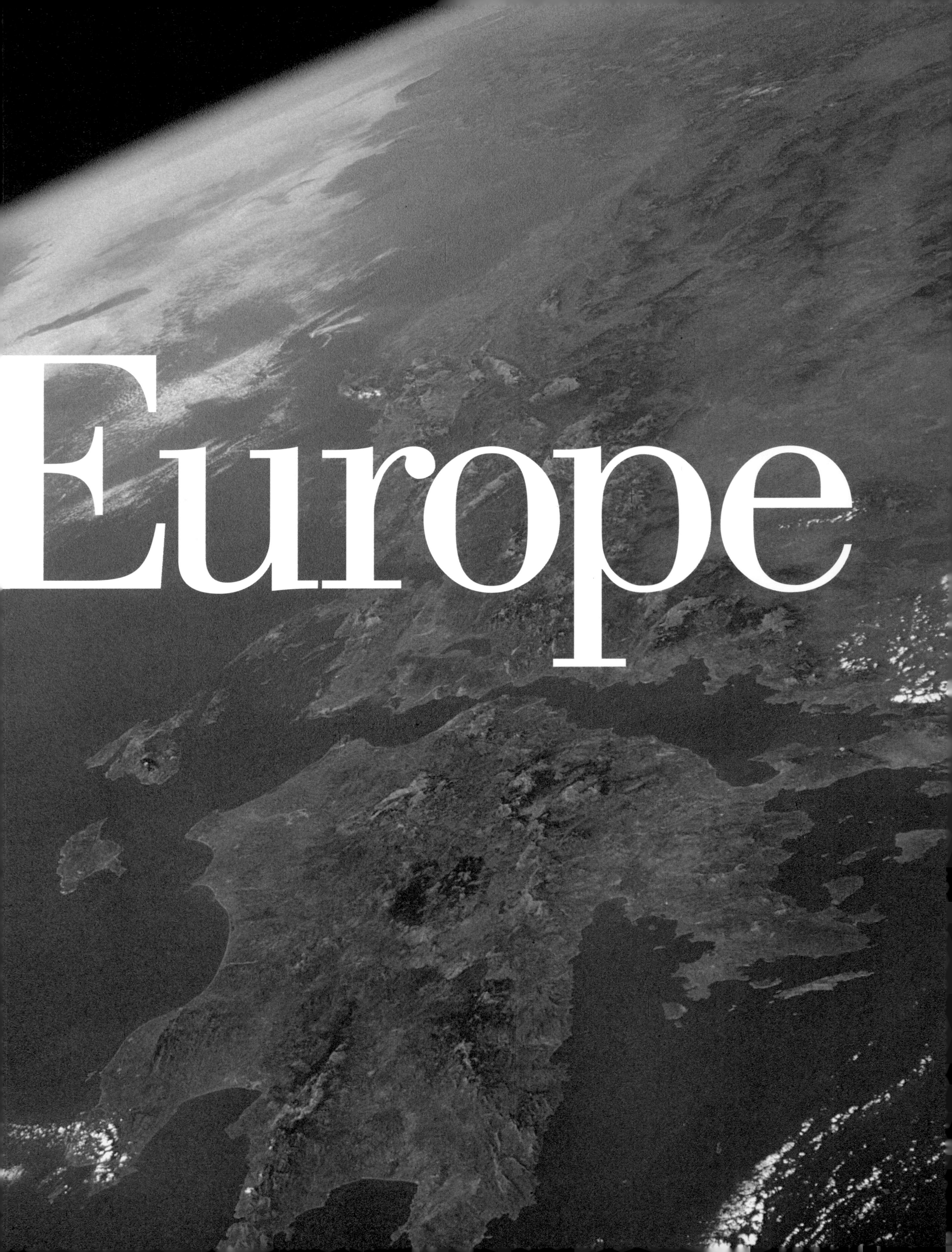

Europe

The terrain in this high-oblique, northwest-looking image, is indicative of the rugged, mountainous landscape characterizing most of Greece. Two major landform regions are captured in this image: the northwest to southeast-trending Mountains of Pindus in central Greece (north of the Gulf of Corinth), and the Peloponnisos Peninsula (south of the Gulf of Corinth). The Pindus, a massive continuation of the Dinaric Alps of Albania and the former Yugoslavia, make the land inhospitable and travel difficult. this rugged terrain caused the Greeks to become a seafaring people.

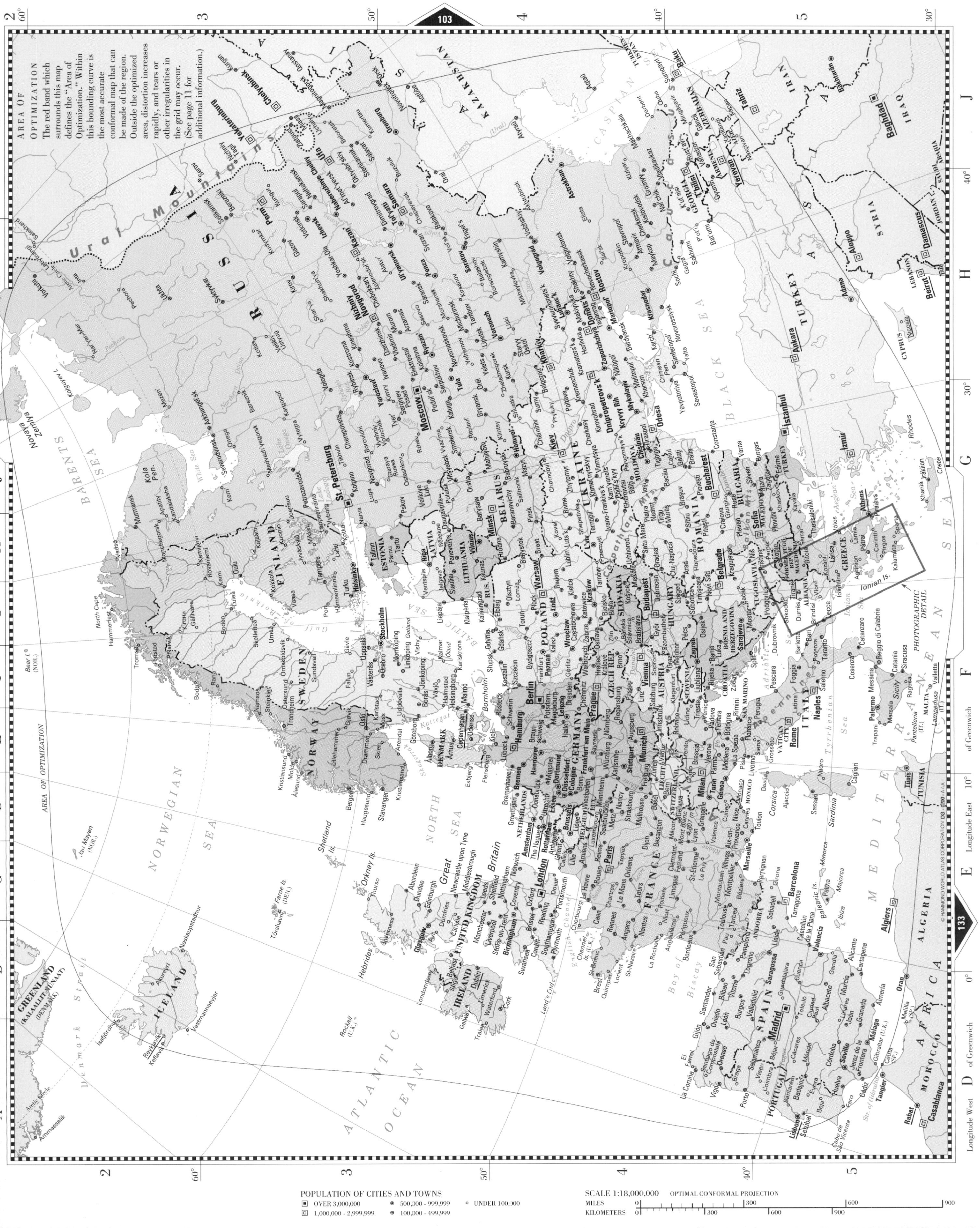

POPULATION OF CITIES AND TOWNS

■ OVER 3,000,000 ● 500,000 - 999,999 ○ UNDER 100,000
▣ 1,000,000 - 2,999,999 ● 100,000 - 499,999

SCALE 1:18,000,000 OPTIMAL CONFORMAL PROJECTION

MILES 0 300 600 900
KILOMETERS 0 300 600 900

London, Paris

London, United Kingdom, and Paris, France are situated on the banks of major rivers, the Thames and Seine. They are both national capitals as well as political and cultural centers.

Dating back to the Roman Empire, they have expanded over the centuries into their countries' largest metropolitan areas. Today, connected by the Channel Tunnel, these cities are only a few hours apart.

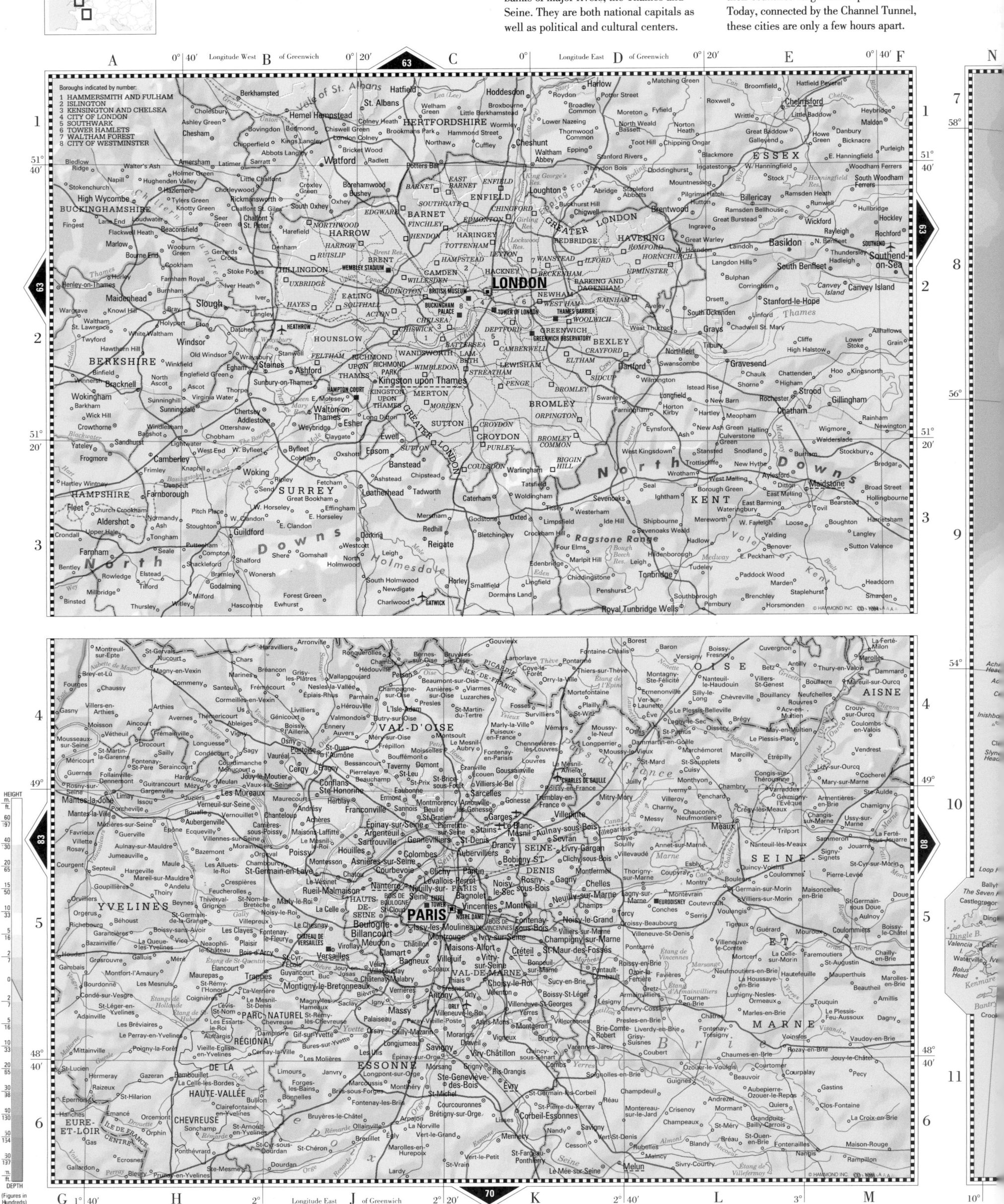

United Kingdom, Ireland

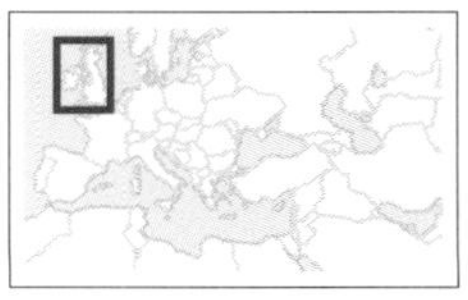

Over the centuries, these islands have been subject to many invasions and migrations. Modern political order began with the union of England and Wales in 1536. In 1707 a parliamentary union with Scotland gave rise to the name Great Britain. Union with Ireland was completed in 1801 under the name United Kingdom. In 1921 Ireland gained independence.

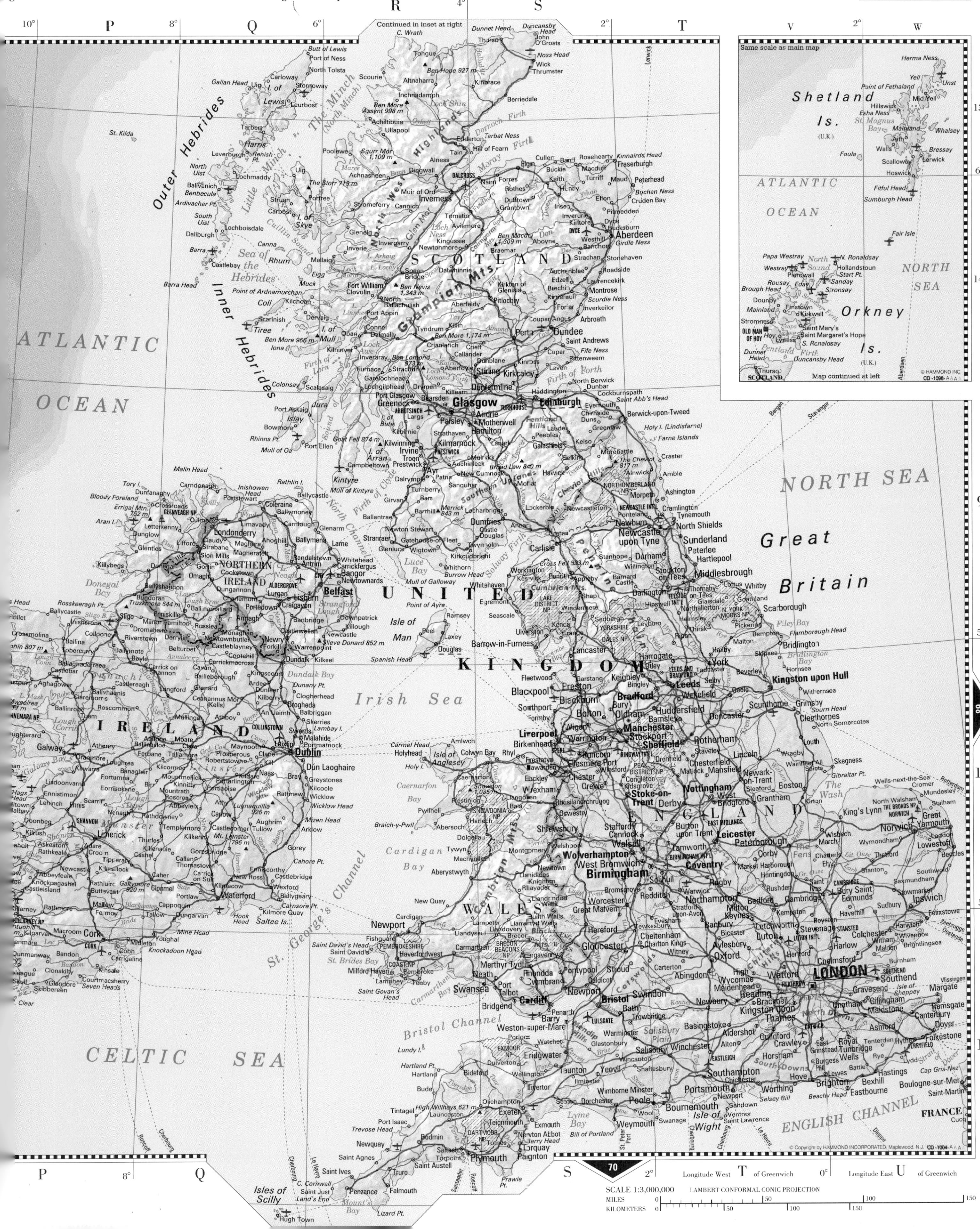

Same scale as main map

SCOTLAND

IRELAND

NORTHERN IRELAND

ENGLAND

WALES

UNITED KINGDOM

GREAT BRITAIN

ATLANTIC OCEAN

NORTH SEA

Irish Sea

CELTIC SEA

Bristol Channel

St. George's Channel

ENGLISH CHANNEL

Shetland Is. (U.K.)

Orkney Is. (U.K.)

Outer Hebrides

Inner Hebrides

Sea of the Hebrides

The Minch

Little Minch

LONDON

Dublin

Glasgow

Edinburgh

Belfast

Liverpool

Manchester

Birmingham

Leeds

Bradford

Sheffield

Nottingham

Cardiff

Bristol

Stoke-on-Trent

Coventry

Wolverhampton

Kingston upon Hull

Newcastle upon Tyne

Inverness

Aberdeen

Dundee

FRANCE

SCALE 1:3,000,000 — LAMBERT CONFORMAL CONIC PROJECTION

MILES

KILOMETERS

Longitude West of Greenwich 0° Longitude East of Greenwich

Central and Southern Ireland

The Celtic culture that once dominated Europe left its most vivid imprint upon Ireland. Though only a small minority claim Irish Gaelic as their mother tongue, the "Emerald Isle" retains its unique Celtic folkways in song, dance, literature and theater. Ireland, a member of the European Union is moving from its agrarian roots to a more industrial society.

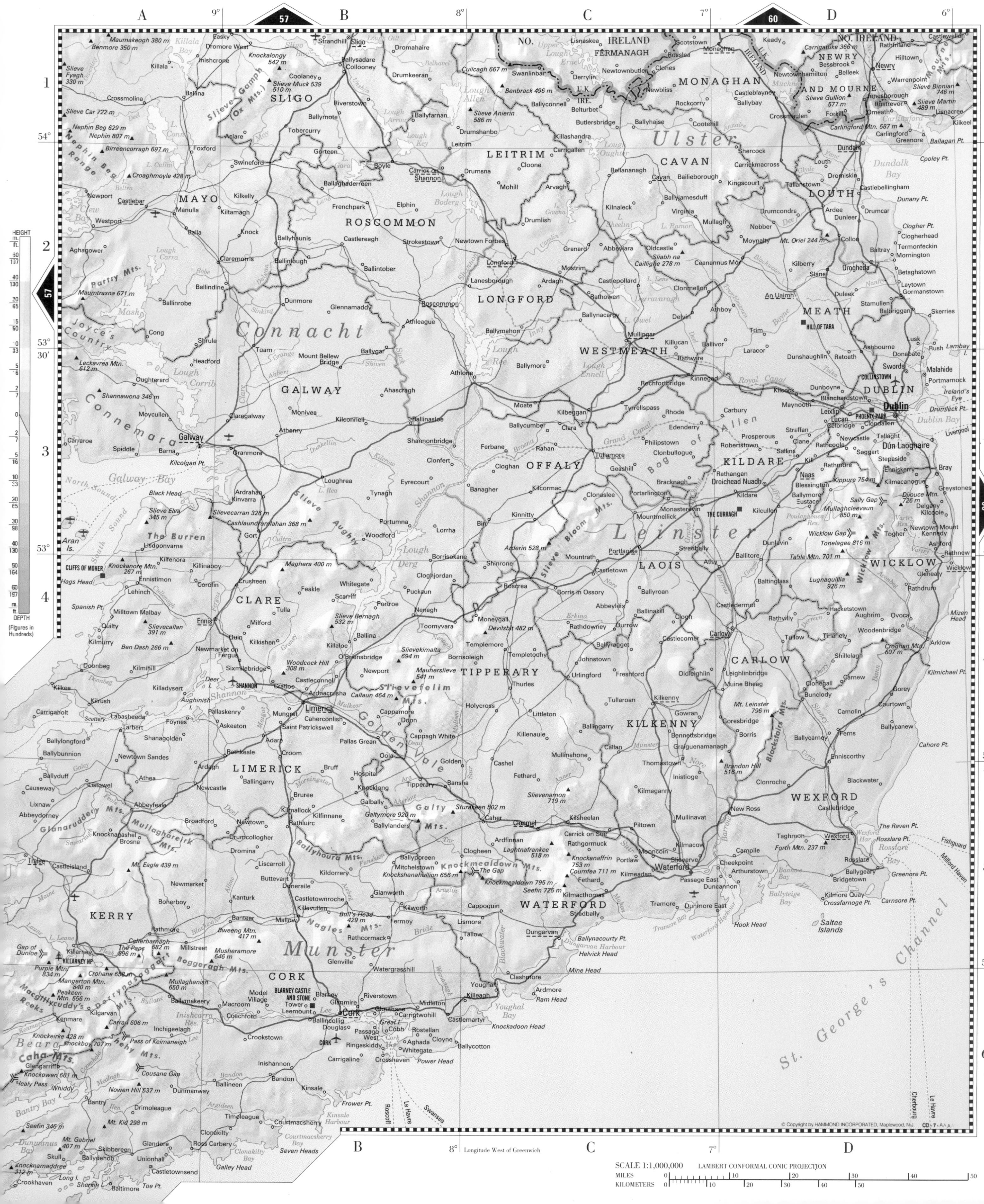

Provinces and Counties

Ulster — FERMANAGH, MONAGHAN, CAVAN, NEWRY AND MOURNE

Connacht — SLIGO, LEITRIM, MAYO, ROSCOMMON, GALWAY

Leinster — LONGFORD, WESTMEATH, MEATH, LOUTH, OFFALY, KILDARE, DUBLIN, LAOIS, CARLOW, KILKENNY, WEXFORD, WICKLOW

Munster — CLARE, LIMERICK, TIPPERARY, KERRY, CORK, WATERFORD

Selected places and features

Dublin, Dún Laoghaire, Cork, Limerick, Galway, Waterford, Newry, Dundalk, Drogheda, Naas, Bray, Athlone, Ennis, Tralee, Killarney, Kilkenny, Carlow, Wexford, Sligo, Castlebar, Westport, Cavan, Longford, Mullingar, Tullamore, Portlaoise, Thurles, Clonmel, Dungarvan, Youghal, Mallow, Kinsale, Bantry, Skibbereen

Lough Corrib, Lough Mask, Lough Derg, Lough Ree, Lough Allen, Lough Key, Lough Owel, Lough Ennell, Lough Neagh, Shannon, Galway Bay, Dublin Bay, Dundalk Bay, Bantry Bay, Dingle Bay, St. George's Channel, Youghal Bay, Dunmanus Bay, Kenmare River

Nephin Beg Range, Partry Mts., Joyce's Country, Connemara, The Burren, Slieve Aughty, Slieve Bloom Mts., Wicklow Mts., Galty Mts., Knockmealdown Mts., Comeragh Mts., Ballyhoura Mts., Mullaghareirk Mts., Boggeragh Mts., Nagles Mts., Caha Mts., MacGillycuddy's Reeks, Derrynasaggart Mts., Blackstairs Mts., Slievefelim Mts.

Carrantuohill 1041 m, Mt. Leinster 796 m, Lugnaquillia 926 m, Galtymore 920 m, Kippure 754 m, Mullaghcleevaun 850 m, Knockmealdown 795 m, Brandon Hill 518 m, Mt. Gabriel 407 m

HEIGHT / DEPTH (Figures in Hundreds)

Central Scotland

The northern Highlands were the rugged home of rival clans until the Highlanders were defeated by the English at the Battle of Culloden in 1746. Coal fields in the narrow waist between the River Clyde and the Firth of Forth brought Scotland into the Industrial Age. More recently, North Sea oil has fueled economic recovery and a resurgent nationalism.

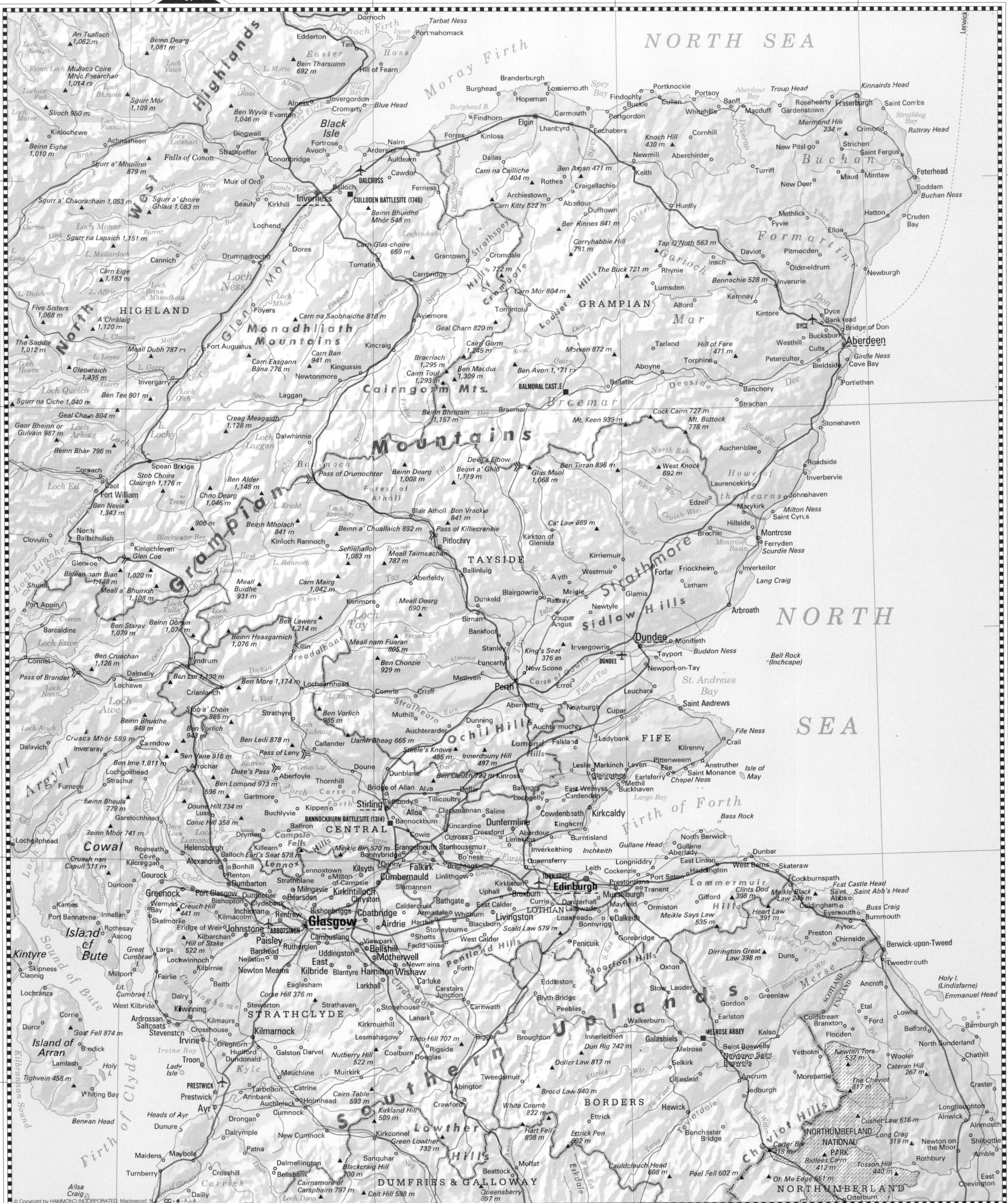

POPULATION OF CITIES AND TOWNS

| ■ OVER 2,000,000 | ● 500,000 - 999,999 | ⏺ 130,000 - 249,999 | ◦ 10,000 - 29,999 |
| □ 1,000,000 - 1,999,999 | ● 250,000 - 499,999 | ⊙ 33,000 - 99,999 | ○ UNDER 10,000 |

SCALE 1:1,000,000   LAMBERT CONFORMAL CONIC PROJECTION

© Copyright by HAMMOND INCORPORATED, Maplewood, N.J.

In the late 18th and early 19th centuries, the factory system arose in Lancashire and south Yorkshire, giving birth to the Industrial Age. The cotton and wool processing factories of Manchester and Leeds helped to change dramatically the culture and the economic base of the country. Population growth followed industrial development, and northern England soon became home to half the kingdom's people. Other important centers arose during this time— the shipyards of Belfast, the booming port of Liverpool, the metal shops of Sheffield, and the knitting mills of Nottingham.

Northeastern Ireland, Northern England and Wales

POPULATION OF CITIES AND TOWNS

- ■ OVER 2,000,000
- □ 1,000,000 - 1,999,999
- ● 500,000 - 999,999
- ◉ 250,000 - 499,999
- ⊙ 100,000 - 249,999
- ○ 30,000 - 99,999
- ○ 10,000 - 29,999
- · UNDER 10,000

SCALE 1:1,000,000   LAMBERT CONFORMAL CONIC PROJECTION

MILES 0 10 20 30 40 50
KILOMETERS 0 10 20 30 40 50

© Copyright by HAMMOND INCORPORATED, Maplewood, N.J.

Southern England and Wales

The major geographical aspect of this region is a dominance of peninsular forms: Cornwall in the southwest, Pembroke in the west and Kent bordering the Strait of Dover.

These landforms, together with the great estuaries of the Severn and Thames, place British people, products, ideas and culture within easy reach of seaports and the rest of the world. The area is anchored by two great metropolitan complexes: London, the center of government and commerce, and Birmingham, the industrial giant of the English Midlands.

POPULATION OF CITIES AND TOWNS

■ OVER 2,000,000	◉ 500,000 - 999,999	● 100,000 - 249,999	○ 10,000 - 29,999
◻ 1,000,000 - 1,999,999	◉ 250,000 - 499,999	● 30,000 - 99,999	○ UNDER 10,000

SCALE 1:1,000,000   LAMBERT CONFORMAL CONIC PROJECTION

MILES 0 .... 10 ...... 20 ...... 30 ...... 40 50

KILOMETERS 0 ...... 10 .... 20 .... 30 .... 40 50

Scandinavia and Finland, Iceland

The northern parts of Norway, Sweden and Finland extend beyond the Arctic Circle. The climates of this region, however, are influenced by the North Atlantic Drift, a warm ocean current that brings relatively warm, moist air across most of the peninsula. Iceland straddles the Mid-Atlantic Ridge and is of geologically-recent volcanic origin.

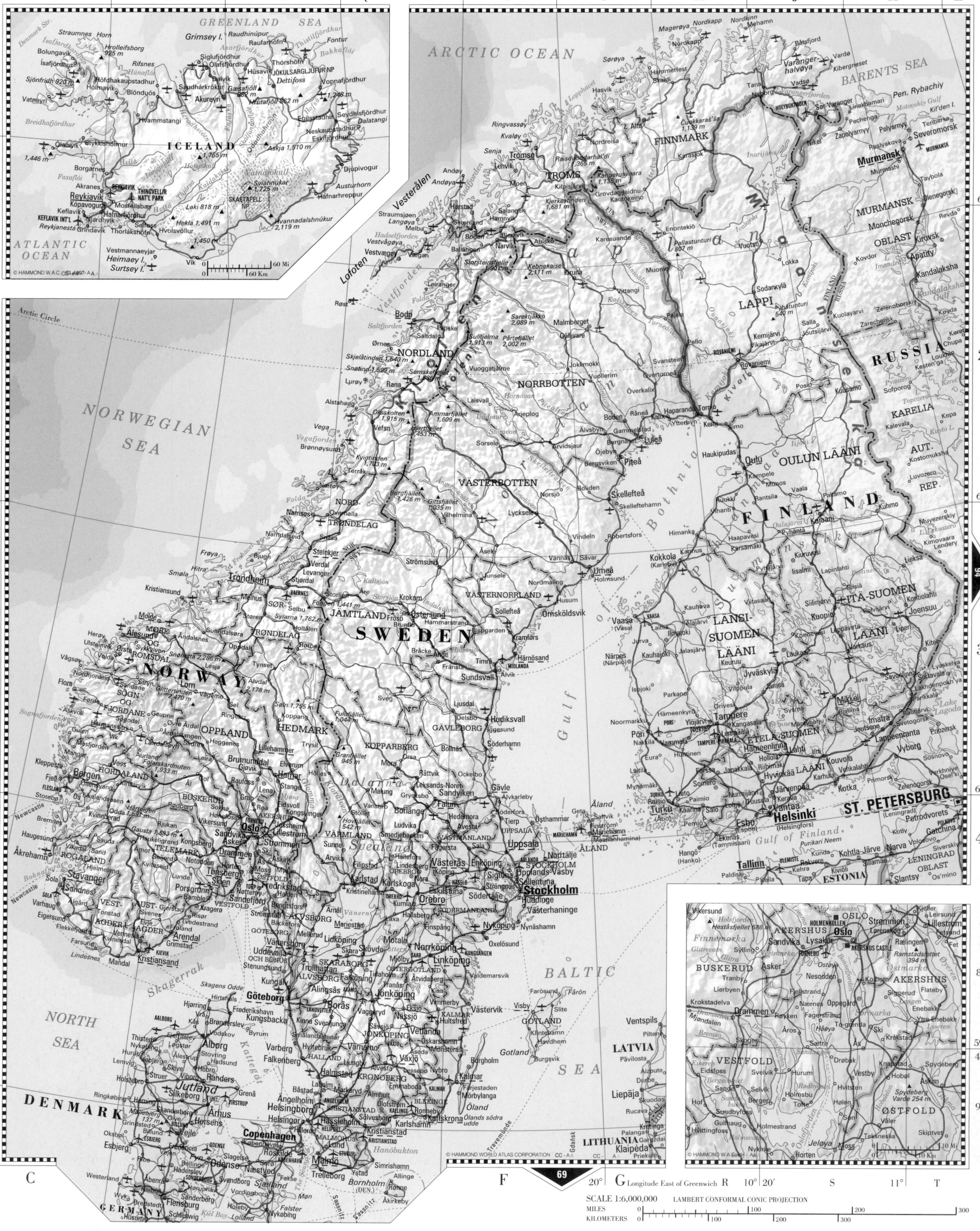

ICELAND

GREENLAND SEA
Denmark Str.
Straumnes Horn
Grimsey I.
Raufarhöfn
Fontur
Thistilfjördhur
Bakkafl.
ARCTIC OCEAN

NORWEGIAN SEA

ATLANTIC OCEAN

Hekla 1,491 m
Laki 818 m
Hvannadalshnúkur 2,119 m
Vatnajökull
Askja 1,510 m

REYKJAVIK
KEFLAVIK INT'L.
THINGVELLIR NAT'L PARK
Kópavogur

BARENTS SEA
ARCTIC OCEAN
Magerøya Nordkapp
Nordkinn

NORWAY
SWEDEN
FINLAND
RUSSIA
DENMARK
GERMANY
ESTONIA
LATVIA
LITHUANIA

NORTH SEA
BALTIC SEA
Gulf of Bothnia
Gulf of Finland
Skagerrak
Kattegat

FINNMARK
TROMS
NORDLAND
LAPPI
NORRBOTTEN
VÄSTERBOTTEN
OULUN LÄÄNI
NORD-TRØNDELAG
SØR-TRØNDELAG
JÄMTLAND
VÄSTERNORRLAND
ITÄ-SUOMEN LÄÄNI
LÄNSI-SUOMEN LÄÄNI
MØRE OG ROMSDAL
OPPLAND
HEDMARK
KOPPARBERG
GÄVLEBORG
SOGN OG FJORDANE
HORDALAND
BUSKERUD
VÄRMLAND
ÖREBRO
VÄSTMANLAND
UPPSALA
SVEALAND
ETELÄ-SUOMEN LÄÄNI
ROGALAND
TELEMARK
VESTFOLD
VEST-AGDER
AUST-AGDER
ÄLVSBORG
SKARABORG
ÖSTERGÖTLAND
SÖDERMANLAND
STOCKHOLM
GÖTEBORGS OCH BOHUS
HALLAND
KRONOBERG
JÖNKÖPING
KALMAR
BLEKINGE
MALMÖHUS
KRISTIANSTAD
GOTLAND
ÖLAND

Murmansk
St. Petersburg (Leningrad)
Helsinki
Stockholm
Oslo
Copenhagen
Göteborg
Bergen
Trondheim
Tallinn

OSLO (inset)

AKERSHUS
OSLO
BUSKERUD
VESTFOLD
ØSTFOLD
Drammen
Sandvika
Holmenkollen
Akershus Castle

© HAMMOND WORLD ATLAS CORPORATION

SCALE 1:6,000,000   LAMBERT CONFORMAL CONIC PROJECTION
MILES 0 100 200 300
KILOMETERS 0 100 200 300

Copenhagen, Denmark, traditionally known as København "merchant's harbor" is built along the Øresund, a narrow strait separating Denmark and Sweden. Stockholm, Sweden, located where Lake Mälaren joins the Baltic Sea, is sometimes called the "Venice of the North" for its many waterways. Helsinki, Finland's major seaport and commercial center, overlooks the Gulf of Finland.

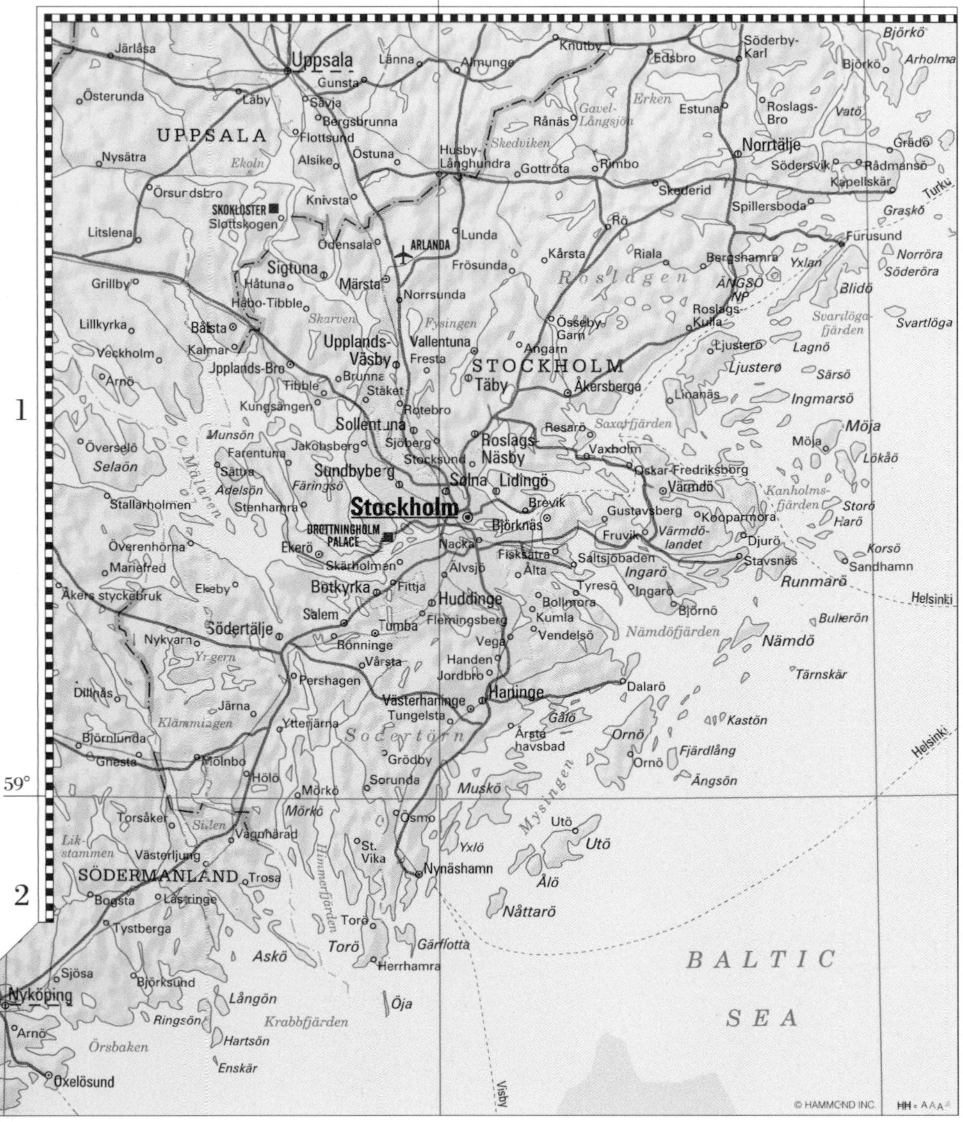

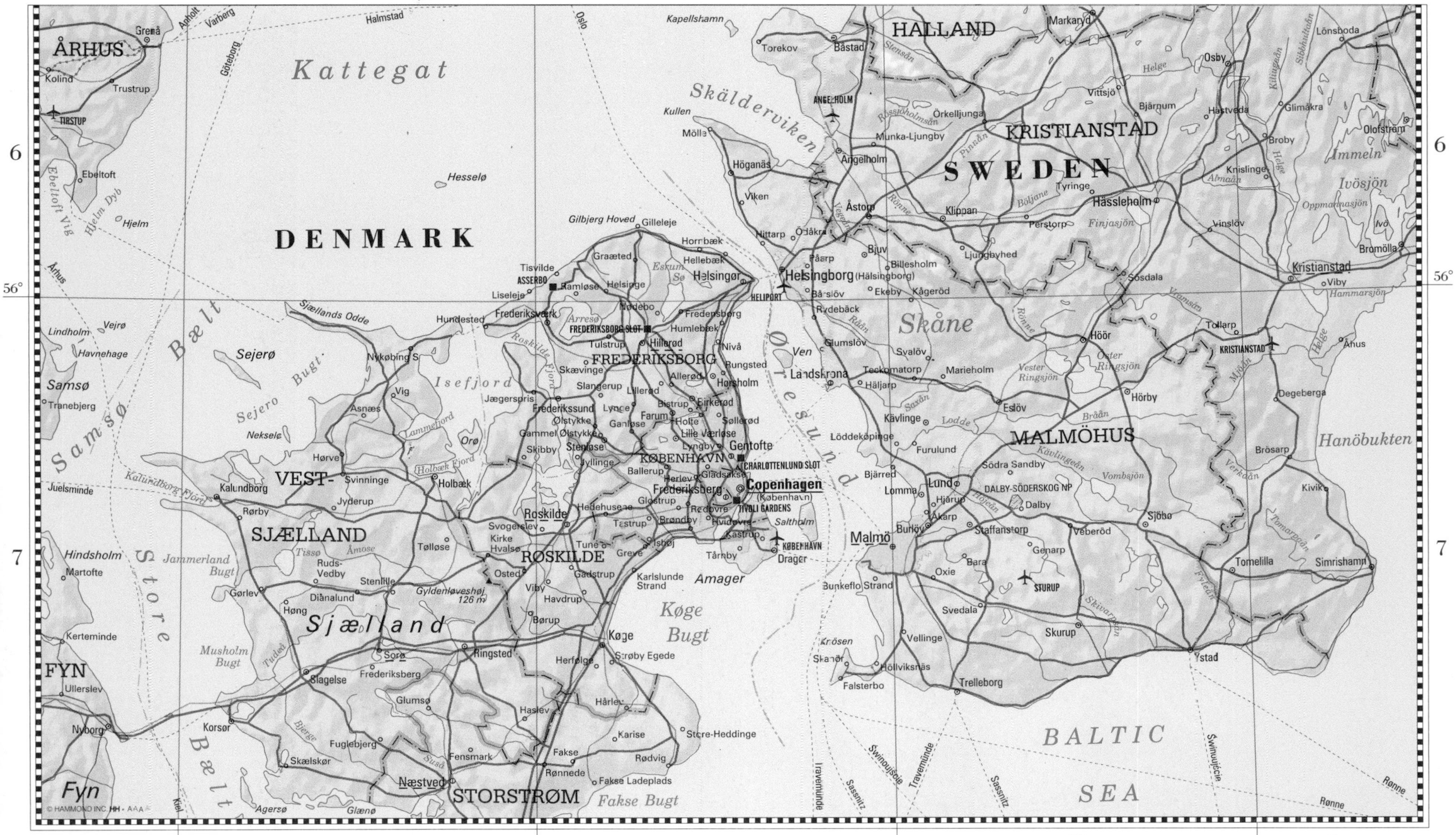

Stockholm, Helsinki, Copenhagen

© HAMMOND INC.

POPULATION OF CITIES AND TOWNS
- ■ OVER 2,000,000
- ◉ 500,000 - 999,999
- ● 100,000 - 249,999
- ⊙ 10,000 - 29,999
- ▢ 1,000,000 - 1,999,999
- ◍ 250,000 - 499,999
- ◐ 30,000 - 99,999
- ∘ UNDER 10,000

SCALE 1:1,000,000   LAMBERT CONFORMAL CONIC PROJECTION

MILES 0 10 20 30 40 50
KILOMETERS 0 10 20 30 40 50

HEIGHT
m. / ft.
60 / 197
40 / 130
20 / 65
15 / 53
10 / 33
5 / 16
2 / 7

DEPTH
2 / 7
5 / 16
10 / 33
20 / 65
40 / 164
(Figures in Hundreds)

The Baltic Sea is the remnant of an inland lake that received the outpoured meltwater of a glacier covering Scandinavia and Finland 10,000 years ago. With the general rise in sea level following the last Ice Age, the North Sea broke through at the Skagerrak and Kattegat between present day Denmark and Sweden. The Baltic then became a saltwater sea. However, drainage from northern Europe reduces its salinity to only one-third of that in the Atlantic Ocean. A major waterway, the Nord-Ostsee-Kanal, connects the Baltic and North seas.

Baltic Region

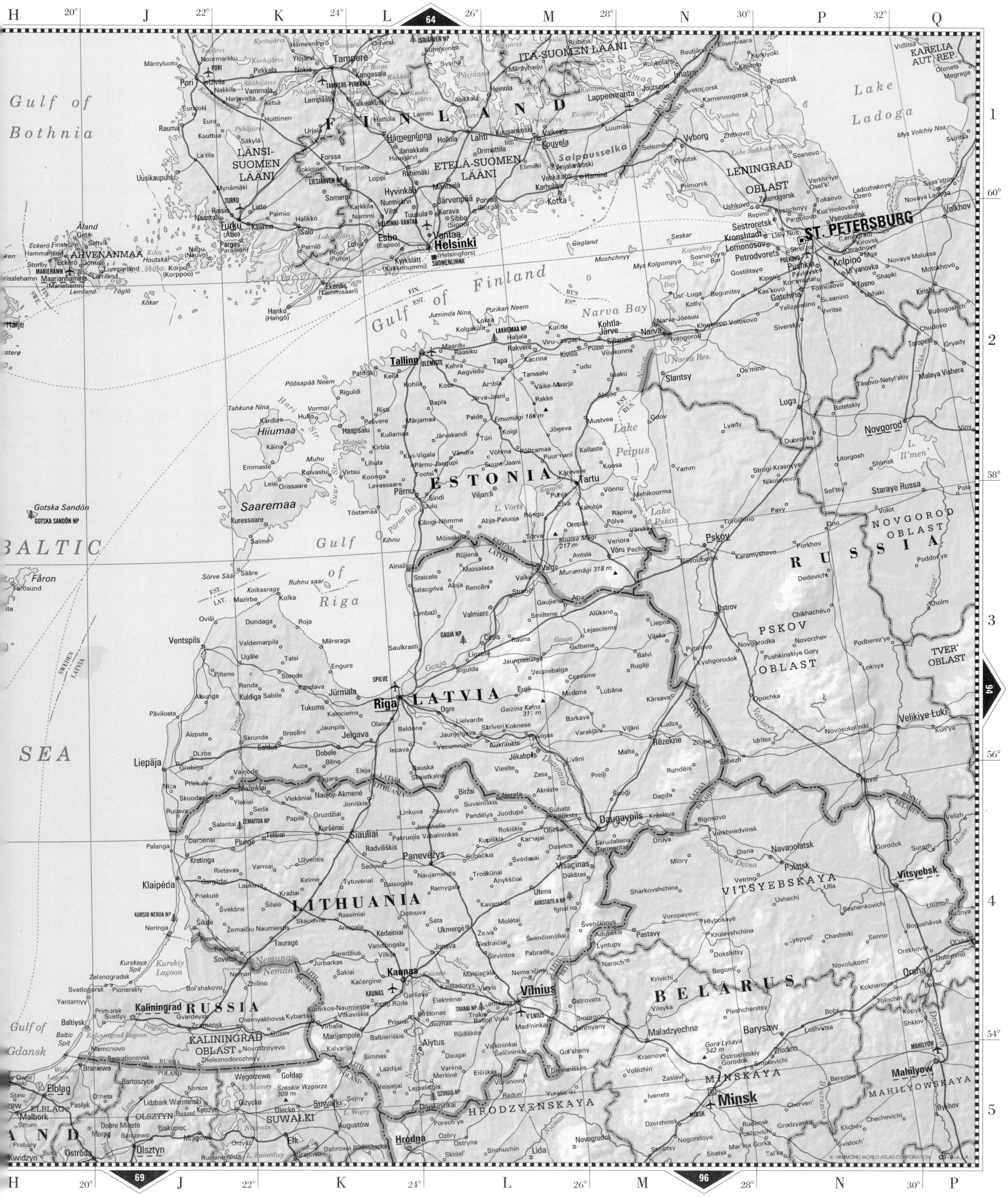

Since the Middle Ages, the great North European Plain has been the scene of numerous conflicts and the pathway for invasions. The lack of mountain barriers along the North Sea and Baltic Coasts has created a stage for marching armies and shifting boundaries well into the 20th century. Modern Germany, created in 1871, experienced major territorial losses in 1919 and, following World War II, was divided into two antagonistic states by the occupying powers. Not until 1990 were East and West Germany reunited as one nation, with Berlin becoming the capital again.

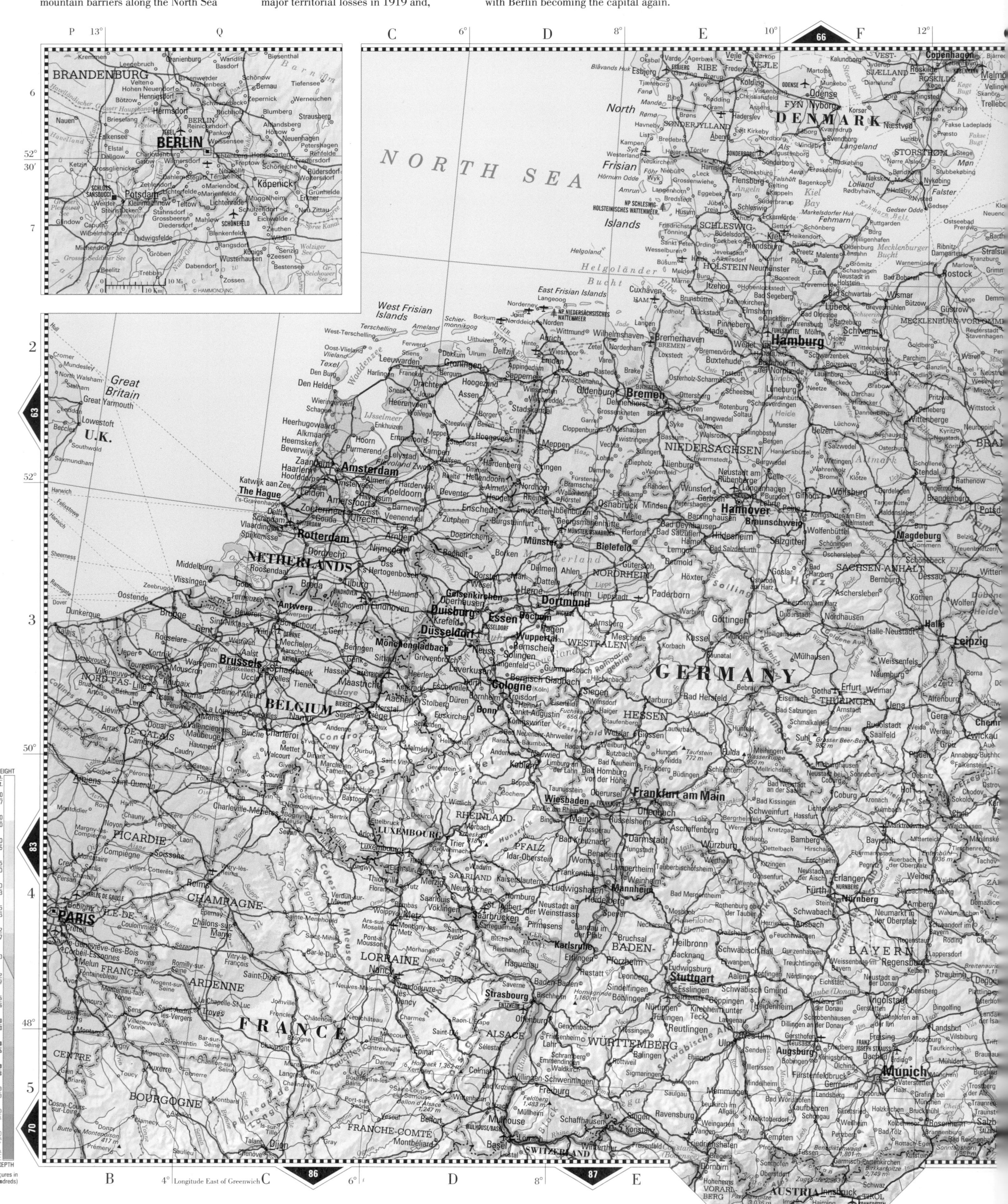

North Central Europe

POPULATION OF CITIES AND TOWNS

■ OVER 2,000,000   ● 500,000 – 999,999   ● 100,000 – 249,999   ○ 10,000 – 29,999
□ 1,000,000 – 1,999,999   ● 250,000 – 499,999   ○ 30,000 – 99,999   ○ UNDER 10,000

SCALE 1:3,000,000   LAMBERT CONFORMAL CONIC PROJECTION

MILES 0   50   100   150
KILOMETERS 0   50   100   150

Draw a line northward from central Italy, through the Rhineland and into Belgium. This is the geographical axis along which Western Civilization developed at the end of the Dark Ages.

Modern Germany, Italy and France flourished in the millennium following A.D. 1000. Unlike Germany, geography gave France secure boundaries on three sides – the English Channel on the northwest, the Atlantic on the west, and the Pyrenees, Mediterranean and Alps in the south and southeast. As a result, France has enjoyed relatively stable borders in these areas for the last 400 years.

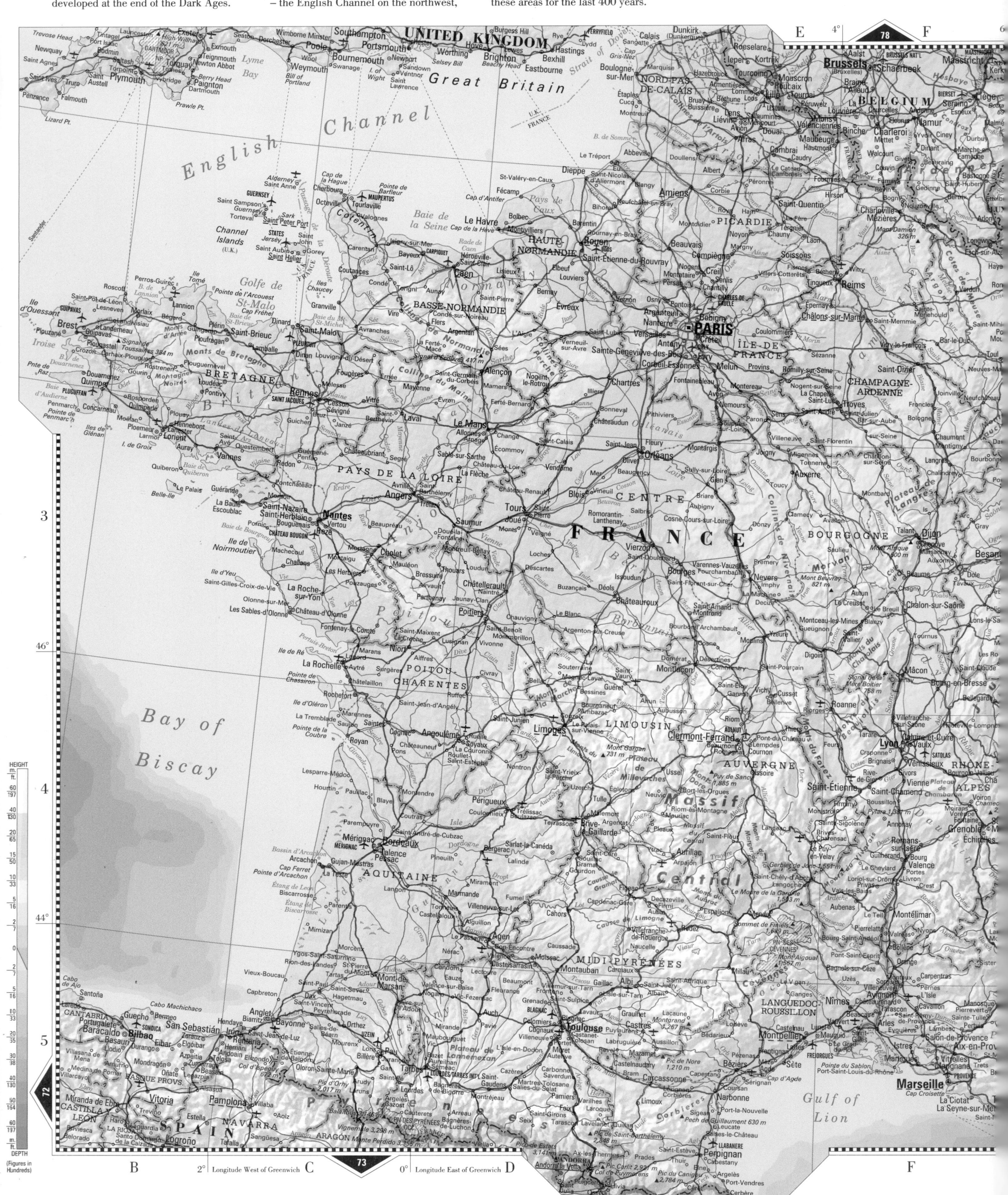

West Central Europe

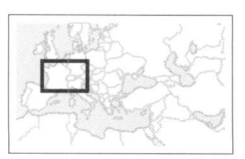

POPULATION OF CITIES AND TOWNS

- ■ OVER 2,000,000
- ▣ 1,000,000 - 1,999,999
- ● 500,000 - 999,999
- ◉ 250,000 - 499,999
- ● 100,000 - 249,999
- ◎ 30,000 - 99,999
- ◦ 10,000 - 29,999
- · UNDER 10,000

SCALE 1:3,000,000 LAMBERT CONFORMAL CONIC PROJECTION

MILES 0   50   100   150

KILOMETERS 0   50   100   150

© Copyright HAMMOND INCORPORATED, Maplewood, N.J. CC - 1015 - A A A

The Iberian Peninsula (Spain and Portugal) has been described as the meeting place of Europe and Africa. This area was the stage for a 700-year struggle between Christian Europe and Islam. In 711, Islamic Moors swept into Spain from north Africa and eventually conquered the entire peninsula. Moorish power lasted until 1492, and its civilization was one of the finest of Muslim realms. Vestiges of Moorish influence are found throughout the peninsula, the most impressive being the Alhambra, an alcázar (fortress-palace) located in Granada.

Spain, Portugal

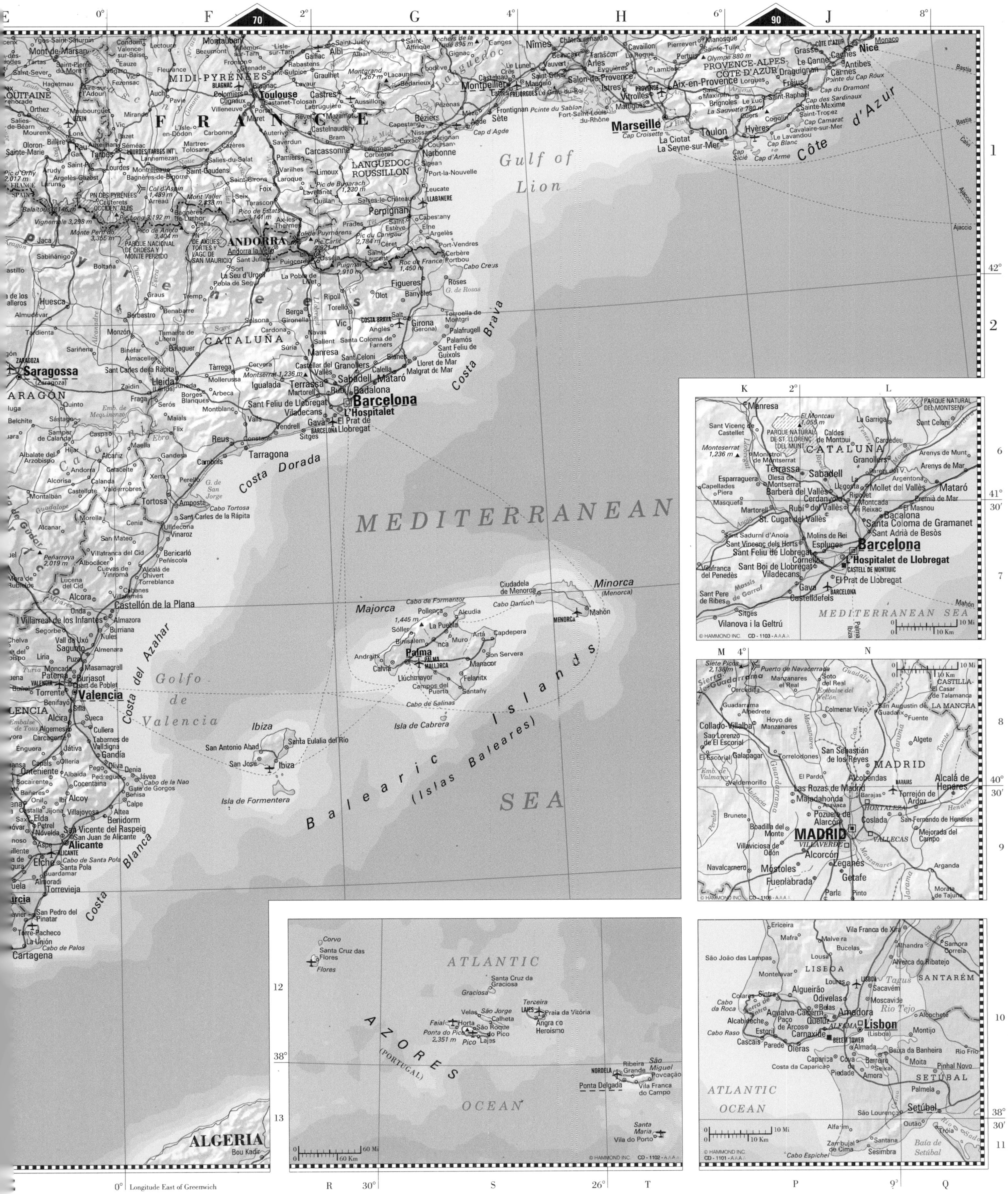

E 0° F 70 2° G 4° H 6° 90 J 8°

FRANCE

MIDI-PYRÉNÉES
Toulouse
LANGUEDOC-ROUSSILLON
Nîmes
PROVENCE-ALPES-CÔTE D'AZUR
Aix-en-Provence
Marseille
Toulon
Côte d'Azur
Nice
Monaco

Gulf of Lion

Perpignan
ANDORRA
Andorra la Vella
PARQUE NACIONAL DE ORDESA Y MONTE PERDIDO

Pyrenees

1

42°

2

CATALUÑA
Costa Brava
Girona (Gerona)
Figueres
Roses

Saragossa (Zaragoza)
ARAGÓN
Lleida
Manresa
Terrassa
Sabadell
Mataró
Badalona
Barcelona
L'Hospitalet
El Prat de Llobregat

6

Reus
Tarragona
Costa Dorada

MEDITERRANEAN

41° 30'

7

Tortosa
Castellón de la Plana

Majorca
Cabo de Formentor
Pollença
Alcudia
Palma
MALLORCA
Manacor
Felanitx

Minorca (Menorca)
Ciudadela de Menorca
Mahón
MENORCA

Golfo de Valencia
Costa del Azahar

Ibiza
San Antonio Abad
Ibiza
Isla de Formentera

Balearic Islands (Islas Baleares)

SEA

8

VALENCIA
Valencia
Costa Blanca
Alicante
Elche

Cabo de la Nao

40° 30'

9

Cartagena
Costa Blanca
ALGERIA

Cataluña inset

K 2° L

Manresa
El Montcau 1,055 m
PARQUE NATURAL DEL MONTSENY
PARQUE NATURAL DE ST. LLORENÇ DEL MUNT
Montserrat 1,236 m
CATALUÑA
Terrassa
Sabadell
Mollet del Vallès
Granollers
Arenys de Mar
Mataró
Premià de Mar
Santa Coloma de Gramanet
Sant Adrià de Besòs
Barcelona
L'Hospitalet de Llobregat
Viladecans
El Prat de Llobregat
Gavà
Castelldefels
Vilanova i la Geltrú
Mahón

6

41° 30'

7

MEDITERRANEAN SEA

0 10 Mi
0 10 Km
© HAMMOND INC. CD-1103-AAAA

Madrid inset

M 4° N

Sierra de Guadarrama
Puerto de Navacerrada
El Escorial
San Lorenzo de El Escorial
Galapagar
Torrelodones
San Sebastián de los Reyes
Alcobendas
Las Rozas de Madrid
Majadahonda
Pozuelo de Alarcón
Alcalá de Henares
Torrejón de Ardoz
MADRID
MADRID
Móstoles
Alcorcón
Leganés
Getafe
Fuenlabrada
Parla
Pinto

0 10 Mi
0 10 Km

8

40° 30'

9

© HAMMOND INC. CD-1106-AAAA

Azores inset

Corvo
Santa Cruz das Flores
Flores

ATLANTIC

Graciosa
Santa Cruz da Graciosa
São Jorge
Velas
Calheta
Terceira
Praia da Vitória
Angra do Heroísmo
Faial
Horta
São Roque do Pico
Pico
Lajes
2,351 m

12

AZORES (PORTUGAL)

38°

Ribeira Grande
São Miguel
Povoação
NORDELA
Ponta Delgada
Vila Franca do Campo

13

OCEAN

Santa Maria
Vila do Porto

0 60 Mi
0 60 Km
© HAMMOND INC. CD-1102-AAAA

Lisbon inset

Vila Franca de Xira
Mafra
Malveira
Bucelas
SANTARÉM
LISBOA
Algueirão
Sintra
Odivelas
Amadora
Cabo da Roca
Alcabideche
Lisbon (Lisboa)
BELEM TOWER
ALFAMA
Cabo Raso
Estoril
Cascais
Parede
Oeiras
Caparica
Costa da Caparica
Almada
SETÚBAL
Setúbal

ATLANTIC OCEAN

10

38° 30'

11

Cabo Espichel
Baía de Setúbal

0 10 Mi
0 10 Km
© HAMMOND INC. CD-1101-AAAA

R 30° S 26° T P 9° Q

0° Longitude East of Greenwich

POPULATION OF CITIES AND TOWNS

| ■ OVER 2,000,000 | ● 500,000 - 999,999 | ○ 100,000 - 249,999 | ○ 10,000 - 29,999 |
| □ 1,000,000 - 1,999,999 | ● 250,000 - 499,999 | ○ 30,000 - 99,999 | ○ UNDER 10,000 |

SCALE 1:3,000,000   LAMBERT CONFORMAL CONIC PROJECTION

MILES 0 50 100 150
KILOMETERS 0 50 100 150

Classical civilization was born on the northeastern shores of the Mediterranean. Here, in Greece and southern Italy, we find the intellectual and artistic roots of modern Europe. This intricate world of bays, gulfs, channels and lesser seas is crowded with storied places. Homer's Odyssey provides a geography of the area. Ulysses sails from Troy (on the Asian side of the Aegean Sea) and is swept out to sea near the isle of Kíthira. Finally, after many landfalls throughout the Mediterranean, he is able to return to his home – the isle of Ithaca (Itháki) on the Ionian Sea coast.

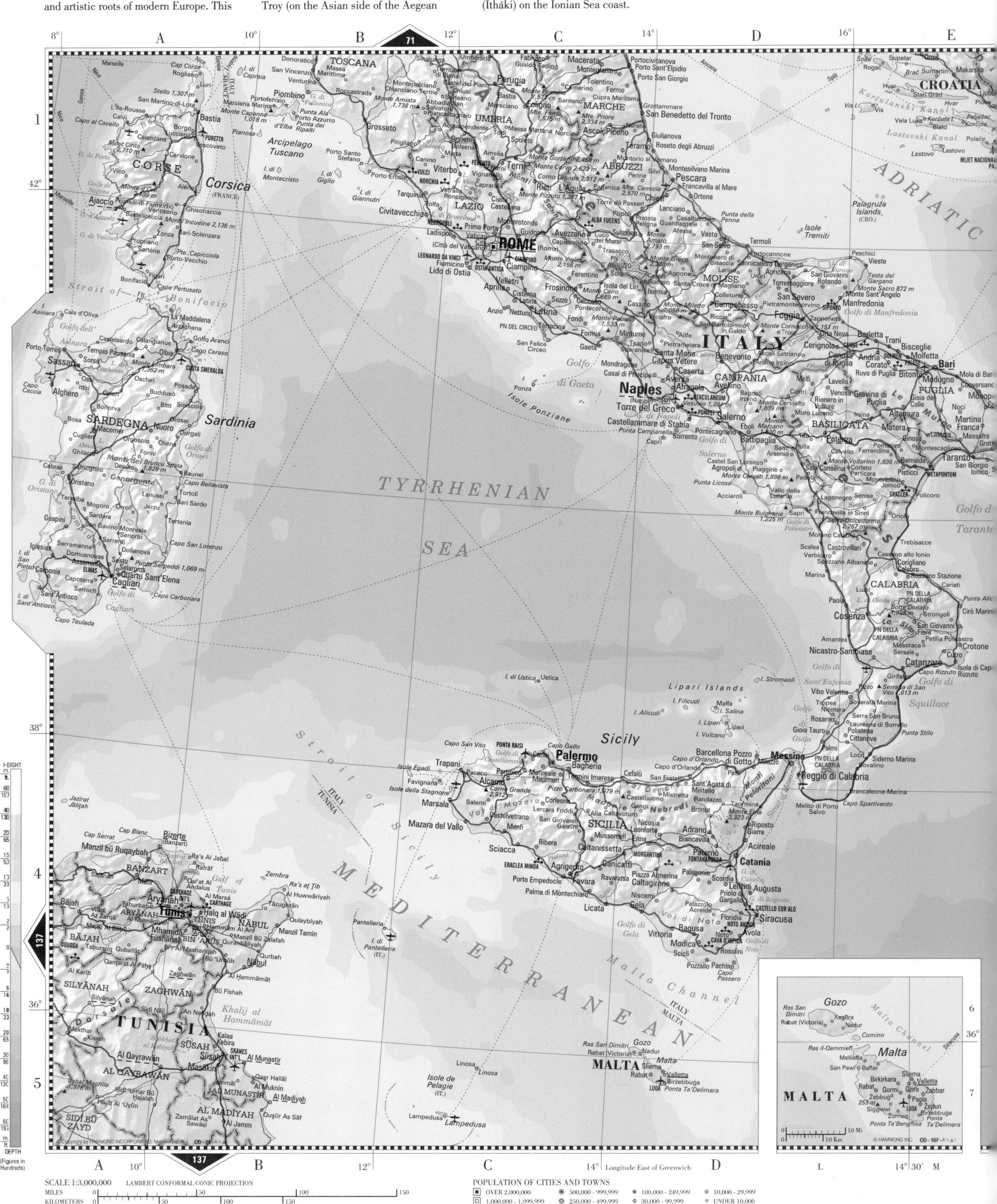

SCALE 1:3,000,000   LAMBERT CONFORMAL CONIC PROJECTION

MILES   0   50   100   150
KILOMETERS 0   50   100   150

POPULATION OF CITIES AND TOWNS
■ OVER 2,000,000   ● 500,000 - 999,999   ● 100,000 - 249,999   ● 10,000 - 29,999
□ 1,000,000 - 1,999,999   ● 250,000 - 499,999   ● 30,000 - 99,999   ○ UNDER 10,000

MALTA

Southern Italy, Albania, Greece

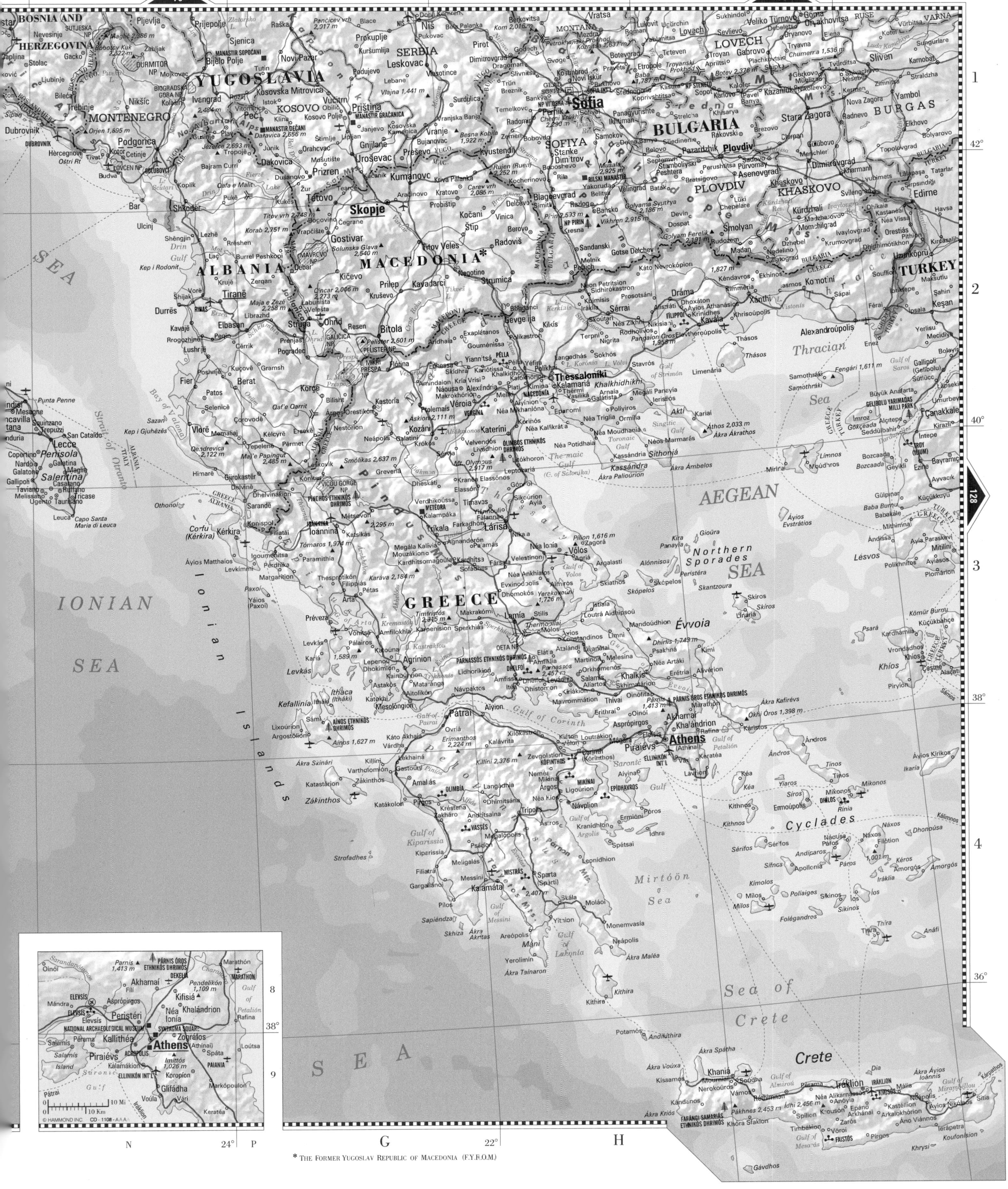

© HAMMOND INC.

The Balkan Peninsula's rugged mountains and occasional plains are home to a multitude of diverse ethnic groups. Divided by religious, historical and linguistic differences, Slovenes, Croats, Serbs, Bosnians, Montenegrins, Albanians, Macedonians and Turks have, more than once, erupted in conflict. World War I was triggered by the assassination of the Austrian archduke by a Serb at Sarajevo in 1914. The fragmented former republics of Yugoslavia are testament to the competition for territory and the desire for independent ethnic and religious homelands.

SCALE 1:3,000,000   LAMBERT CONFORMAL CONIC PROJECTION

MILES   0   50   100   150

KILOMETERS   0   50   100   150

POPULATION OF CITIES AND TOWNS
■ OVER 2,000,000   ● 500,000 - 999,999   ● 100,000 - 249,999   ● 10,000 - 29,999
□ 1,000,000 - 1,999,999   ◉ 250,000 - 499,999   ● 30,000 - 99,999   ○ UNDER 10,000

* THE FORMER YUGOSLAV REPUBLIC OF MACEDONIA (F.Y.R.O.M.)

76-77

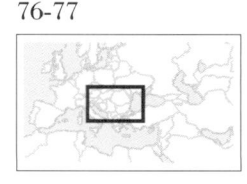

Hungary, Northern Balkan States

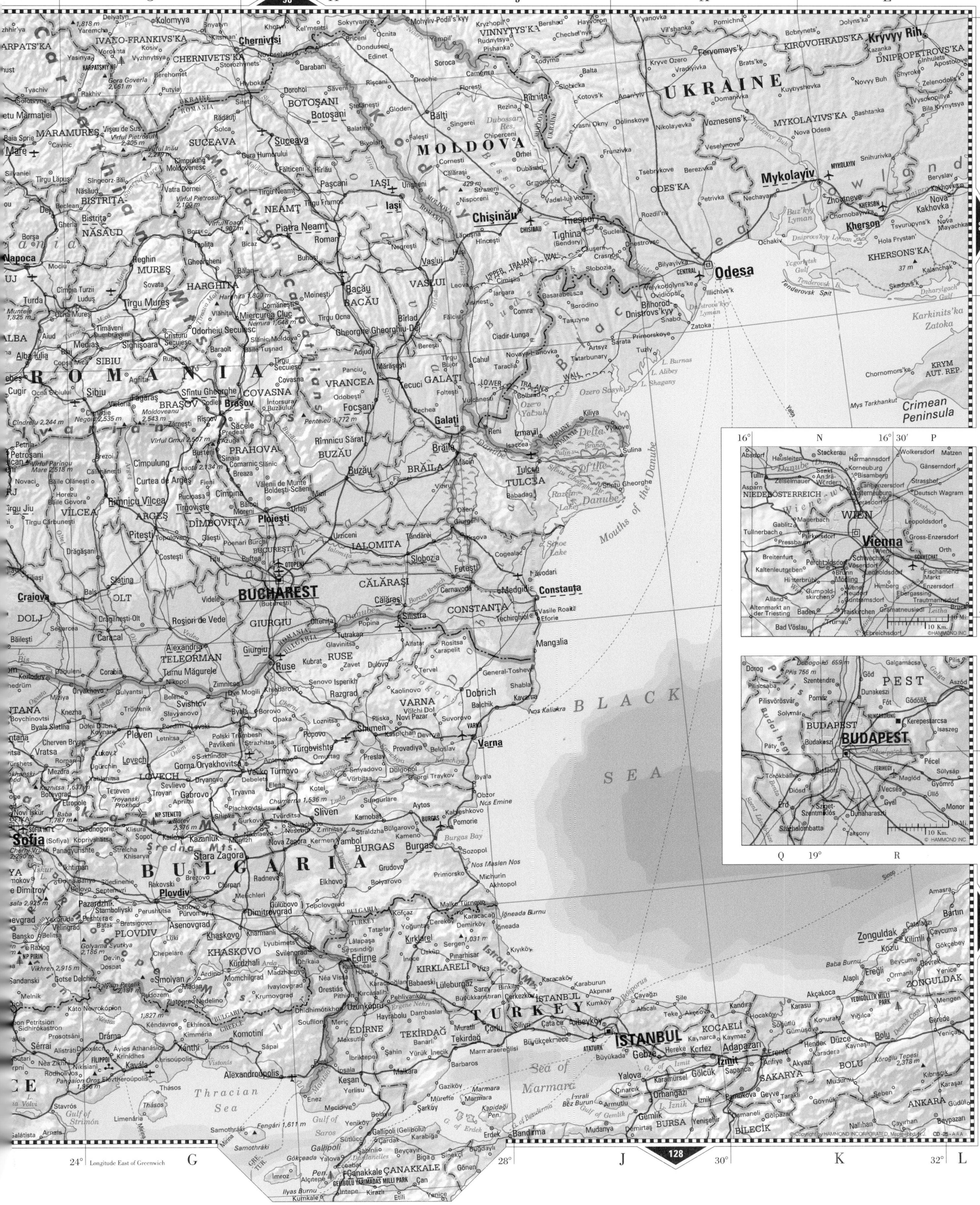

UKRAINE
MOLDOVA
ROMANIA
BULGARIA
TURKEY
BLACK SEA
Odesa
Chişinău
Mykolayiv
Kherson
Kryvyy Rih
Chernivtsi
Iaşi
Bacău
Braşov
Ploieşti
BUCHAREST
Constanţa
Galaţi
Brăila
Tulcea
Craiova
Piteşti
Sibiu
Ruse
Varna
Burgas
Pleven
Plovdiv
Sofia
Stara Zagora
Edirne
ISTANBUL
Izmit
Zonguldak
Crimean Peninsula
Thracian Sea
Sea of Marmara
Mouths of the Danube
Wien
Vienna
NIEDERÖSTERREICH
PEST
BUDAPEST
Budapest
© HAMMOND INC.
24°
G
26°
98
H
28°
J
30°
K
32°
L
48°
46°
2
3
5
128
Longitude East of Greenwich

Netherlands, Northwestern Germany

Since the 1400s the Dutch have drained and reclaimed great stretches of their below-sea level land, using a system of dikes. The vast Zuider Zee (now the "IJsselmeer") has been transformed into a freshwater lake; a massive dam separates it from the North Sea. Parts of the IJsselmeer have been drained to form new land called *polders*.

POPULATION OF CITIES AND TOWNS
- ■ OVER 2,000,000
- ◉ 500,000 - 999,999
- ● 100,000 - 249,999
- ◎ 10,000 - 29,999
- □ 1,000,000 - 1,999,999
- ◉ 250,000 - 499,999
- ● 30,000 - 99,999
- ○ UNDER 10,000

SCALE 1:1,000,000   LAMBERT CONFORMAL CONIC PROJECTION

MILES 0   10   20   30   40   50
KILOMETERS 0   10   20   30   40   50

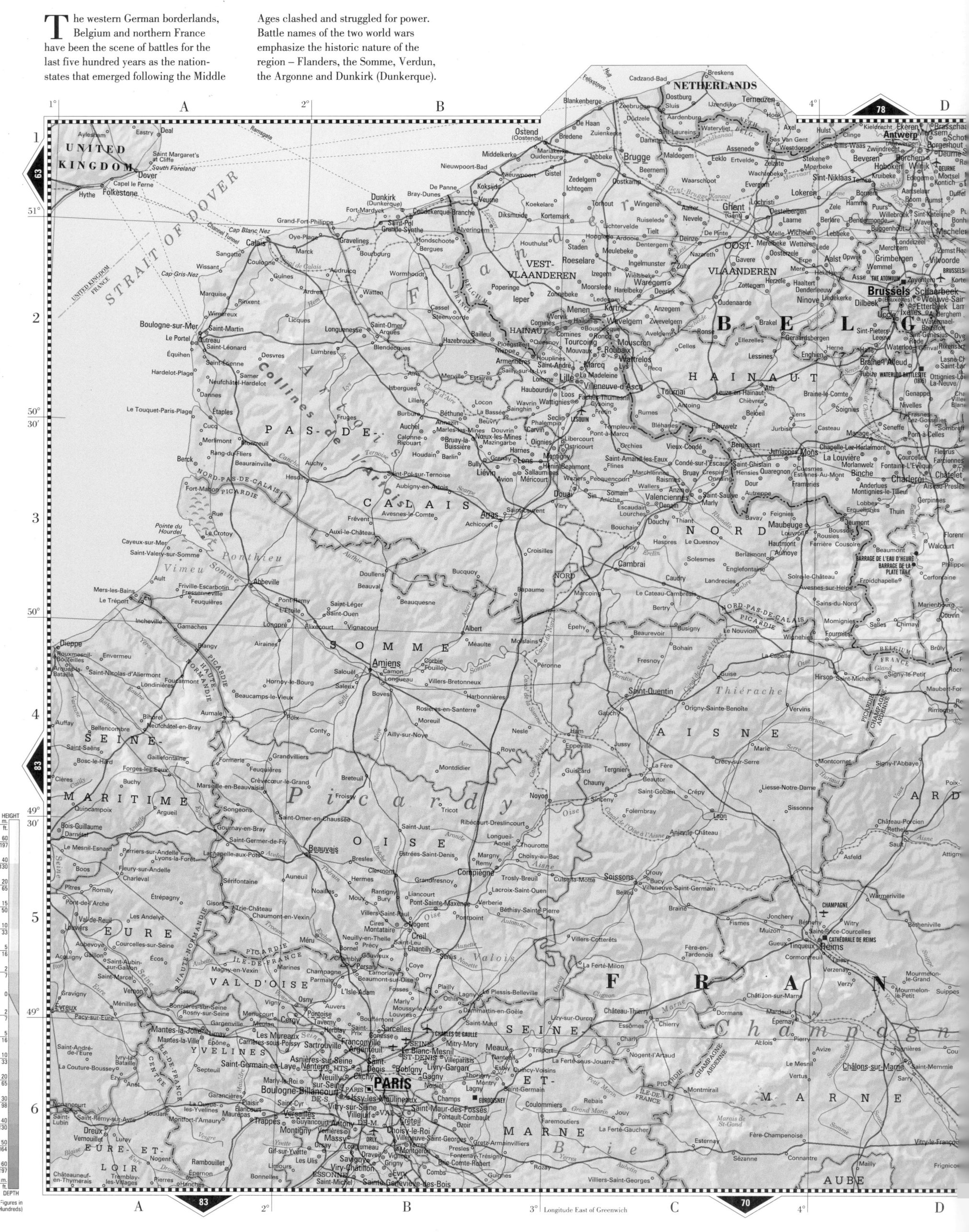

The western German borderlands, Belgium and northern France have been the scene of battles for the last five hundred years as the nation-states that emerged following the Middle Ages clashed and struggled for power. Battle names of the two world wars emphasize the historic nature of the region – Flanders, the Somme, Verdun, the Argonne and Dunkirk (Dunkerque).

Belgium, Northern France, Western Germany

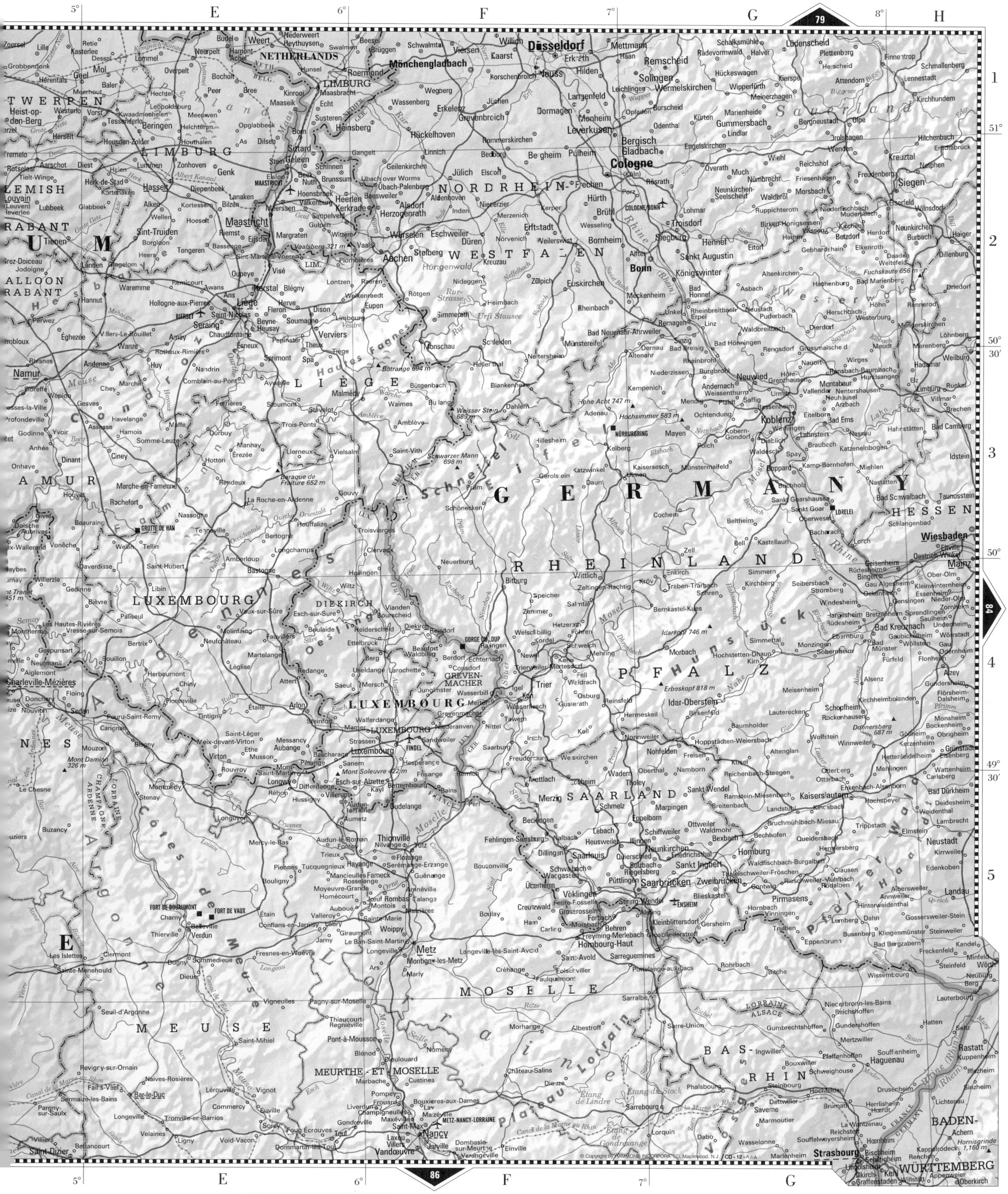

POPULATION OF CITIES AND TOWNS

■ OVER 2,000,000	● 500,000 - 999,999	● 100,000 - 249,999	● 10,000 - 24,999
▣ 1,000,000 - 1,999,999	● 250,000 - 499,999	● 50,000 - 99,999	○ UNDER 10,000

SCALE 1:1,000,000   LAMBERT CONFORMAL CONIC PROJECTION

MILES

KILOMETERS

© Copyright by HAMMOND INCORPORATED, Maplewood, N.J. CD-12-A-A

Northwestern France

Gentle climates make north-western France a prosperous agricultural region. Fields of grain thrive in the basins of the Seine and Loire. The valley of the Loire, the longest river in

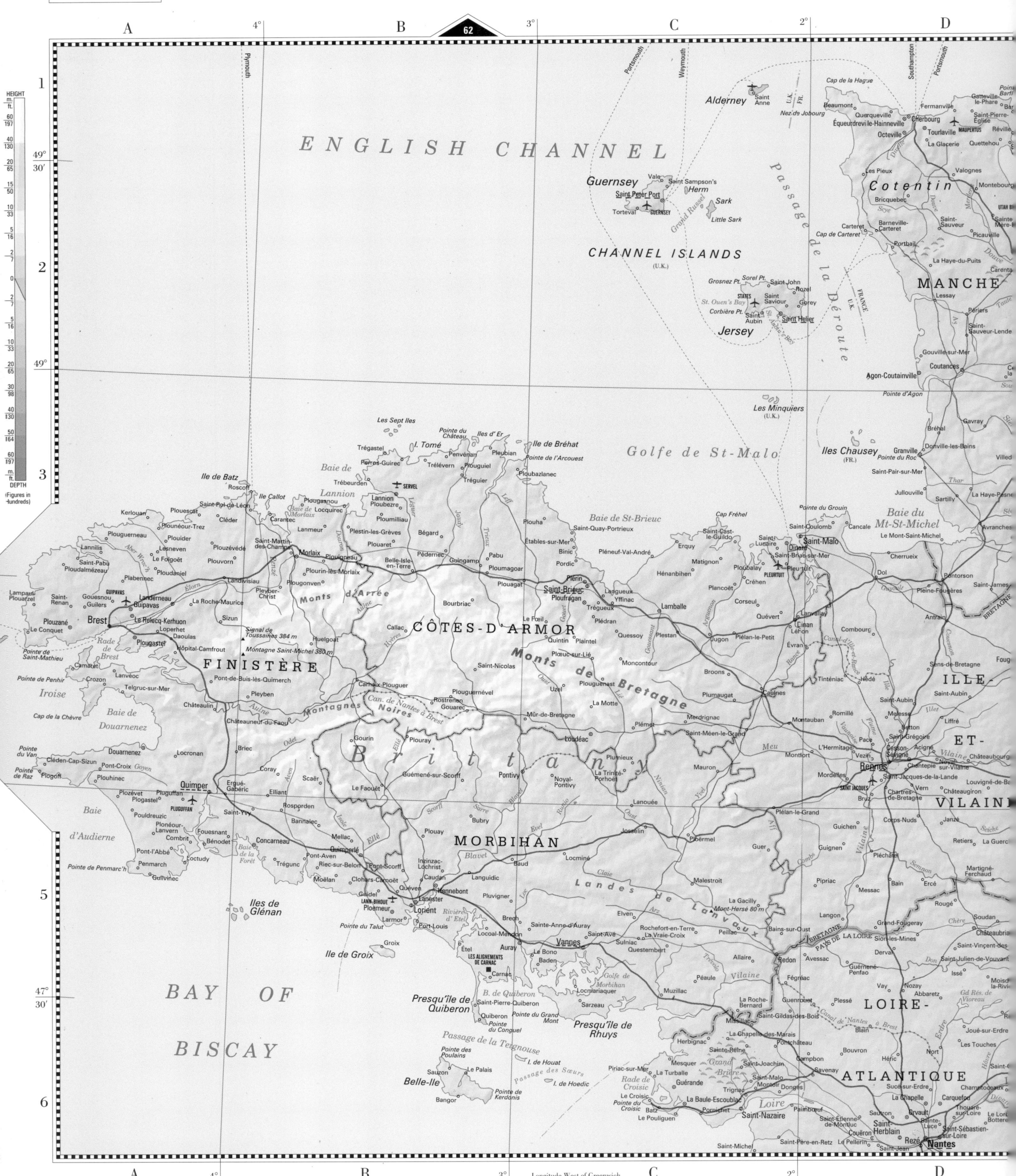

HEIGHT
m.
ft.
60 197
40 130
20 65
15 50
10 33
5 16
0
2 7
5 16
10 33
20 65
30 98
50 164
60 197
m.
ft.
DEPTH
(Figures in hundreds)

ENGLISH CHANNEL

CHANNEL ISLANDS
(U.K.)

Guernsey

Jersey

BAY OF

BISCAY

Golfe de St-Malo

Brittany

FINISTÈRE

CÔTES-D'ARMOR

MORBIHAN

ILLE-ET-VILAINE

MANCHE

Cotentin

LOIRE-ATLANTIQUE

Longitude West of Greenwich

France, is famous for its magnificent 15th and 16th century chateaux. Brittany, a prime example of French regionalism, dates from the Dark Ages, when Celtic refugees reached the peninsula from Saxon-overrun England. Normandy began with the Vikings, and traces historic connections to Britain. Normandy is renowned for its apples and *Calvados* (apple brandy).

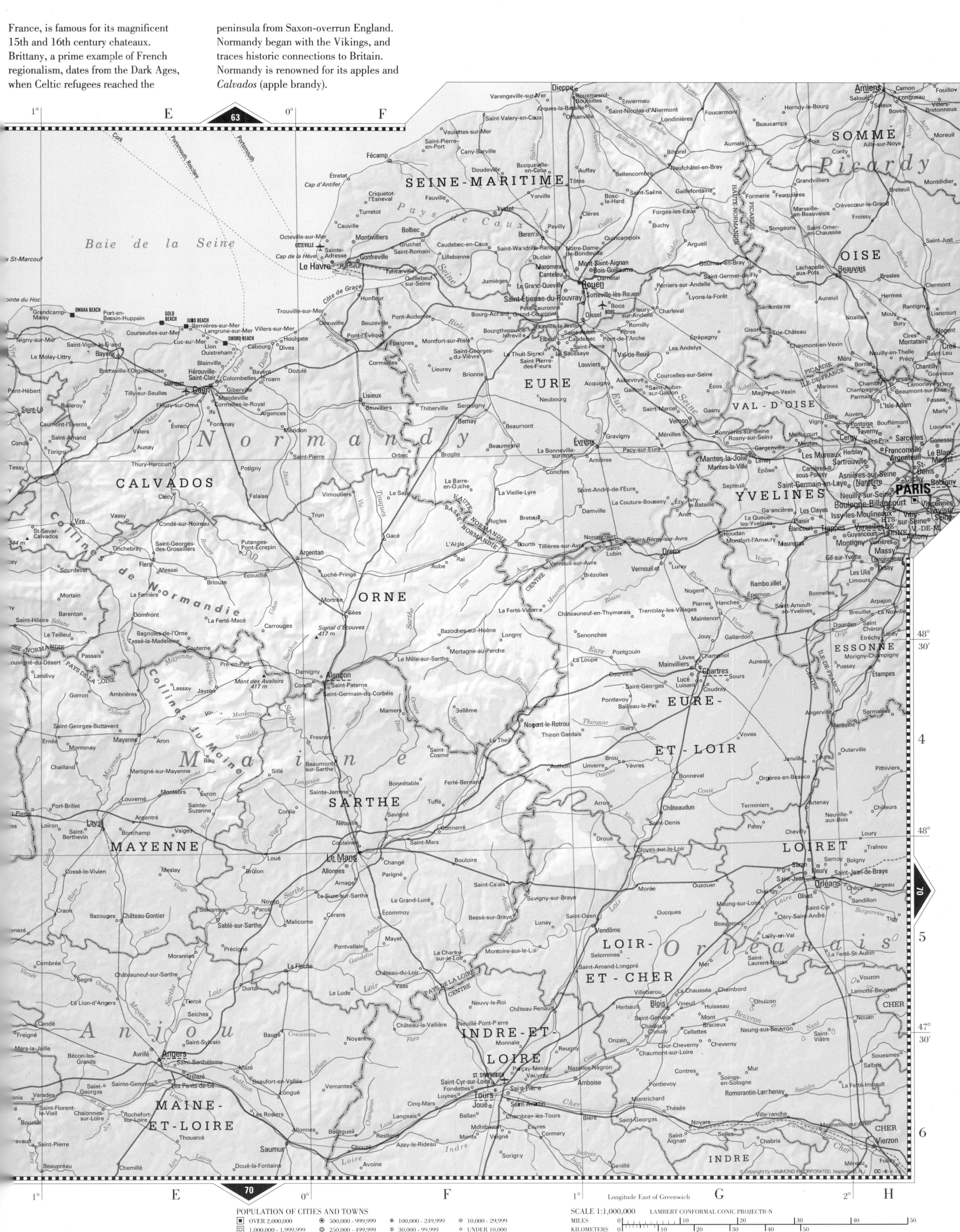

POPULATION OF CITIES AND TOWNS

■ OVER 2,000,000   ● 500,000 - 999,999   ● 100,000 - 249,999   ○ 10,000 - 29,999
□ 1,000,000 - 1,999,999   ◉ 250,000 - 499,999   ○ 30,000 - 99,999   · UNDER 10,000

SCALE 1:1,000,000   LAMBERT CONFORMAL CONIC PROJECTION

Longitude East of Greenwich

Medieval villages and castles flourished in this mountainous terrain; many survive to this day. On the Neckar River, near the Rhine, stands old Heidelberg. Its famous university dates back to 1386. To the east, a string of towns, from Würzburg to Augsburg, form the "Romantic Way," a picturesque route through a region rich in architecture from the Middle Ages. Munich, which grew from a Benedictine monastery, has numerous historic churches. Czech spas at Karlovy Vary (Karlsbad) and Mariánské Lázně (Marienbad) are world-renowned.

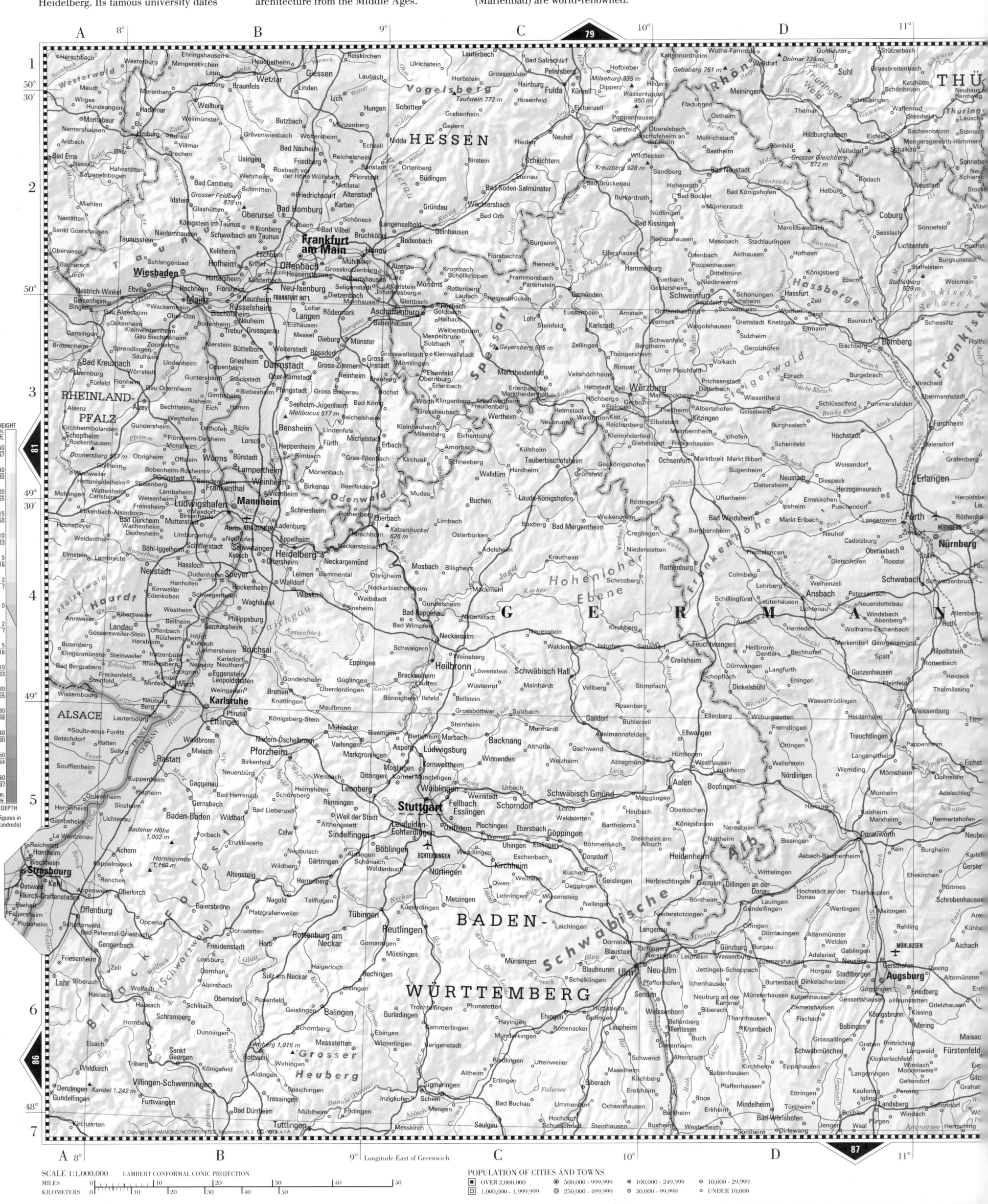

SCALE 1:1,000,000   LAMBERT CONFORMAL CONIC PROJECTION

MILES

KILOMETERS

POPULATION OF CITIES AND TOWNS

■ OVER 2,000,000   ● 500,000 - 999,999   ⊛ 100,000 - 249,999   ○ 10,000 - 29,999
□ 1,000,000 - 1,999,999   ⊙ 250,000 - 499,999   ◦ 30,000 - 99,999   · UNDER 10,000

© Copyright by HAMMOND INCORPORATED, Maplewood, N.J. CC-1013-AAA

Southern Germany, Czech Republic, Upper Austria

E
12°
F
13°
G
69
14°
H
CZECH REPUBLIC
SACHSEN
BAYERN
AUSTRIA
OBERÖSTERRICH
SEVEROČESKÝ
STŘEDOČESKÝ
ZÁPADOČESKÝ
JIHOČESKÝ
PRAHA
Prague
(Praha)
Plzeň
Regensburg
Munich
(München)
České Budějovice
Linz
Passau
Karlovy Vary
Cheb
Bayreuth
Hof
Plauen
Amberg
Landshut
Straubing
Deggendorf
Freising
Wels
Steyr
Chomutov
Most
Kladno
Příbram
Tábor
Písek
Klatovy
Erzgebirge
Krušné Hory
Fichtelgebirge
Oberpfälzer Wald
Český Les
Šumava
Bayerischer Wald
Böhmer Wald
Brdy
Středočeská Žulová Vrchovina
Doupovské Hory
Danube
Donau
Vltava
Ohře
Labe
Isar
Inn
Naab
Regen
Mühlviertel
Innviertel
NATIONALPARK BAYERISCHER WALD
Grosser Arber 1,456 m
Grosser Rachel 1,453 m
Fichtelberg 1,214 m
Klínovec 1,244 m
Schneeberg 1,051 m
WALHALLA
SCHLOSS HERRENCHIEMSEE
1
2
3
4
5
6
7
50° 30′
50°
49° 30′
49°
48° 30′
48°
76

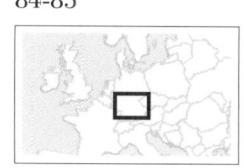

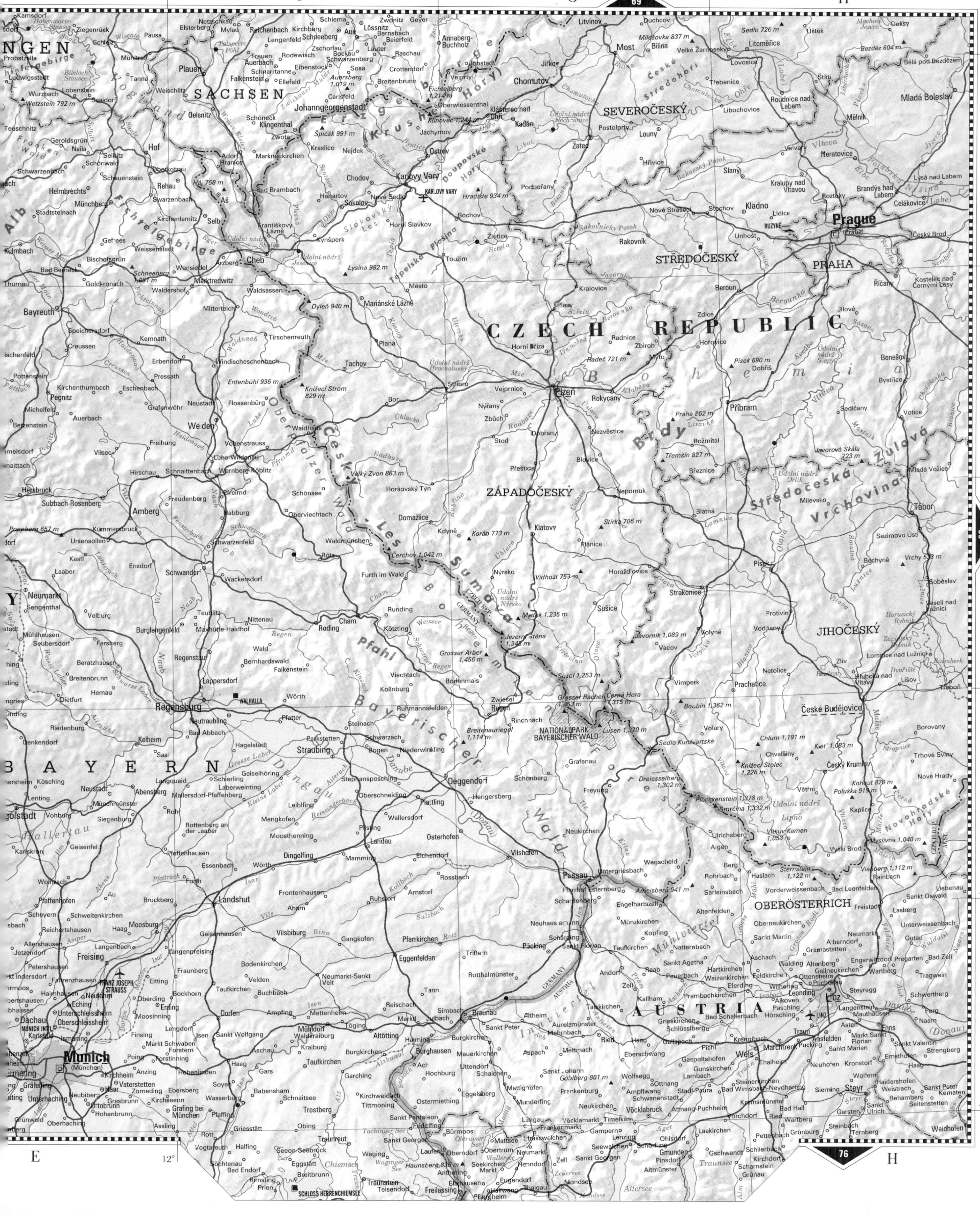

The great mountain system of the Alps includes the familiar peaks of Mont-Blanc, the Matterhorn, Jungfrau and Dufourspitze. It extends in a long semicircle from the Mediterranean seacoast in southeastern France to the outskirts of Vienna. The mountains' central region, which covers more than half of Switzerland, is home to some of the world's most visited glacial regions. These high-elevation "valley glaciers" are all that remain of the vast ice sheet that covered virtually all of the Alps and intervening valleys during the last ice age over 10,000 years ago.

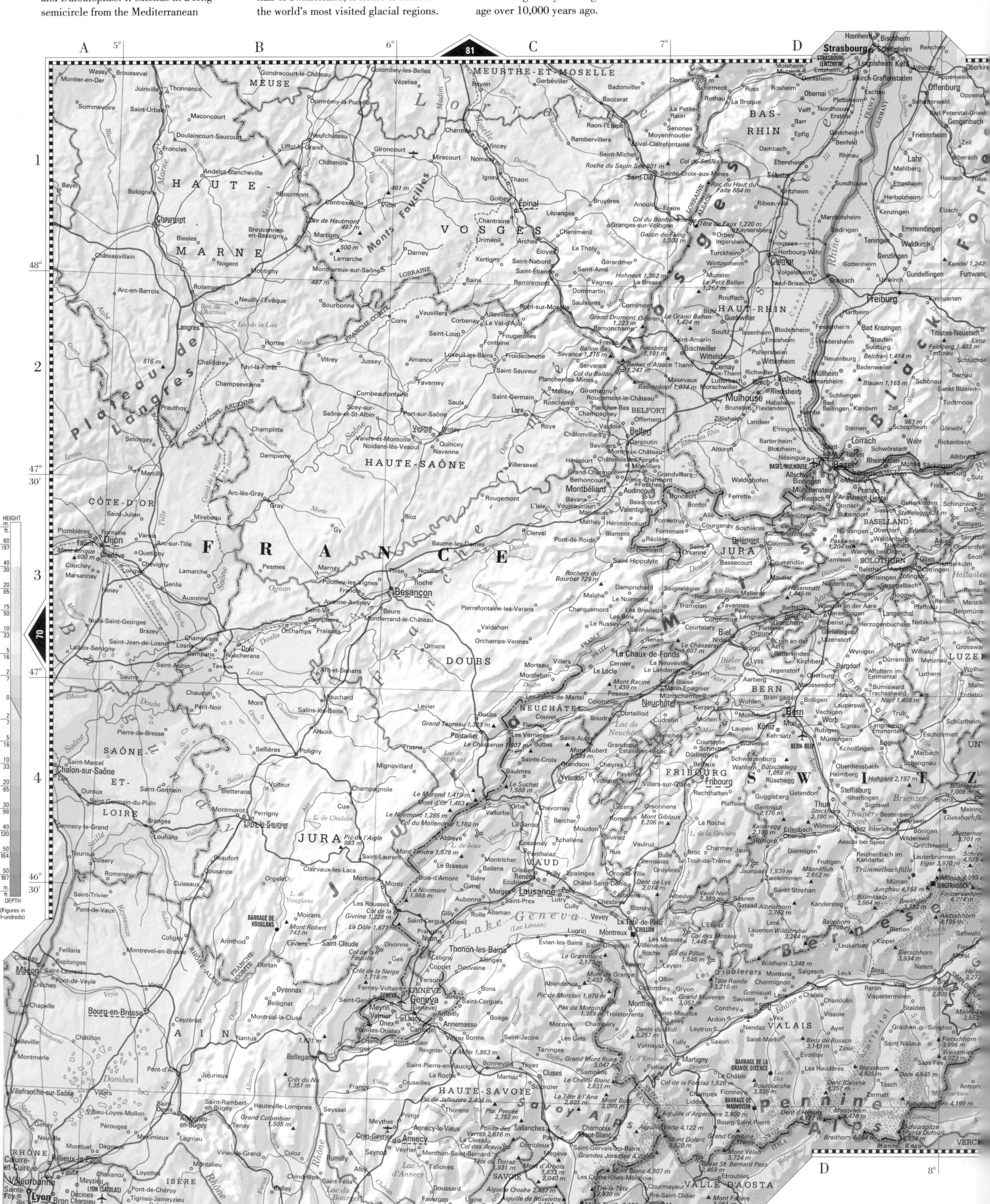

Central Alps Region

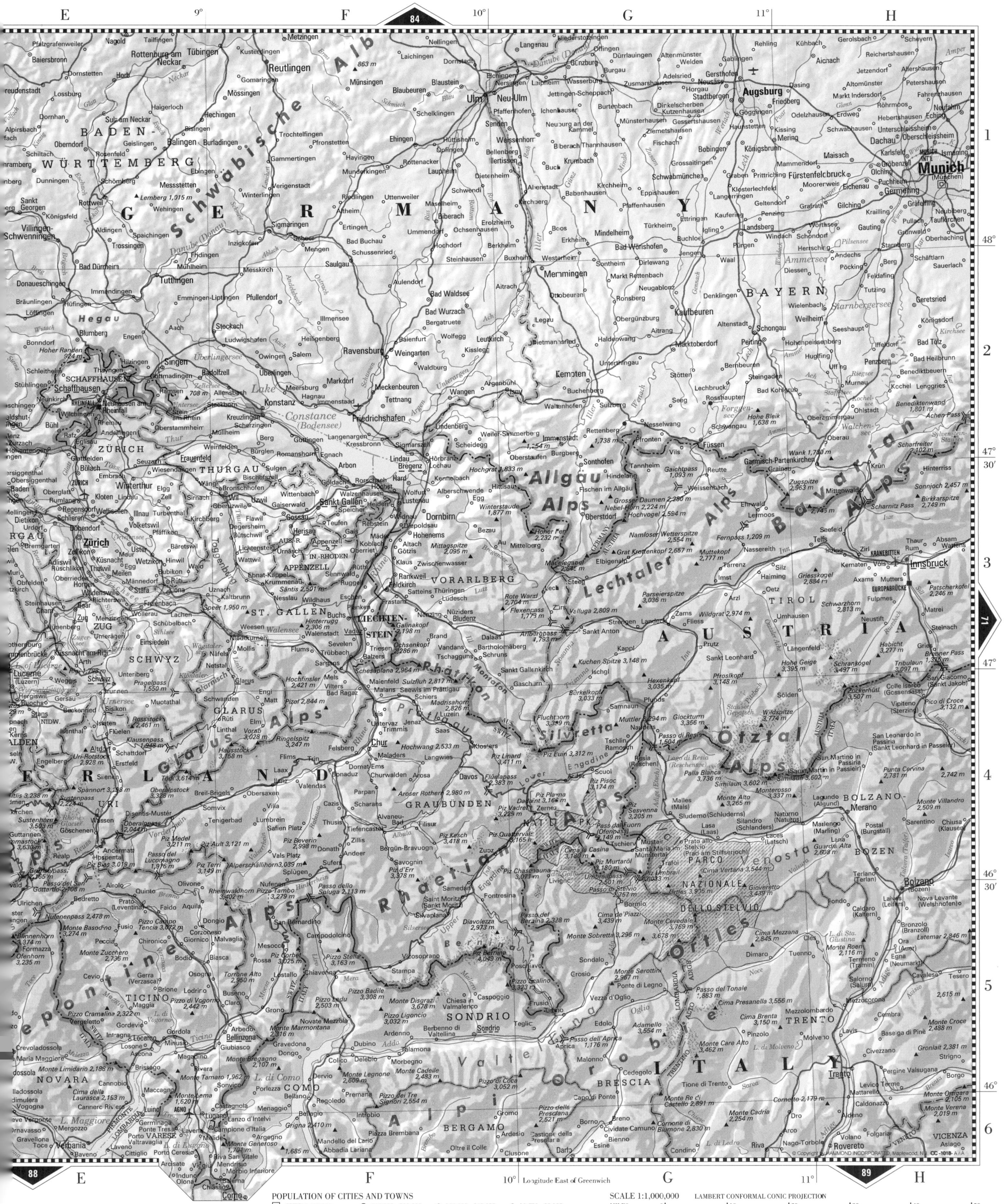

Northern Italy is the nation's industrial, agricultural and recreational heartland. Milan, Italy's primary financial and commercial center, has world-famous textile and machinery industries. Turin is noted for its car industry. The fertile Po Valley is the country's granary, and also leads in dairy farming and sugar beet production. Florence, Siena, Ravenna, Venice and Verona house some of the world's greatest art and architectural treasures. To the north, alpine foothills feature the beautiful glacier-fed lakes Maggiore, Como and Garda.

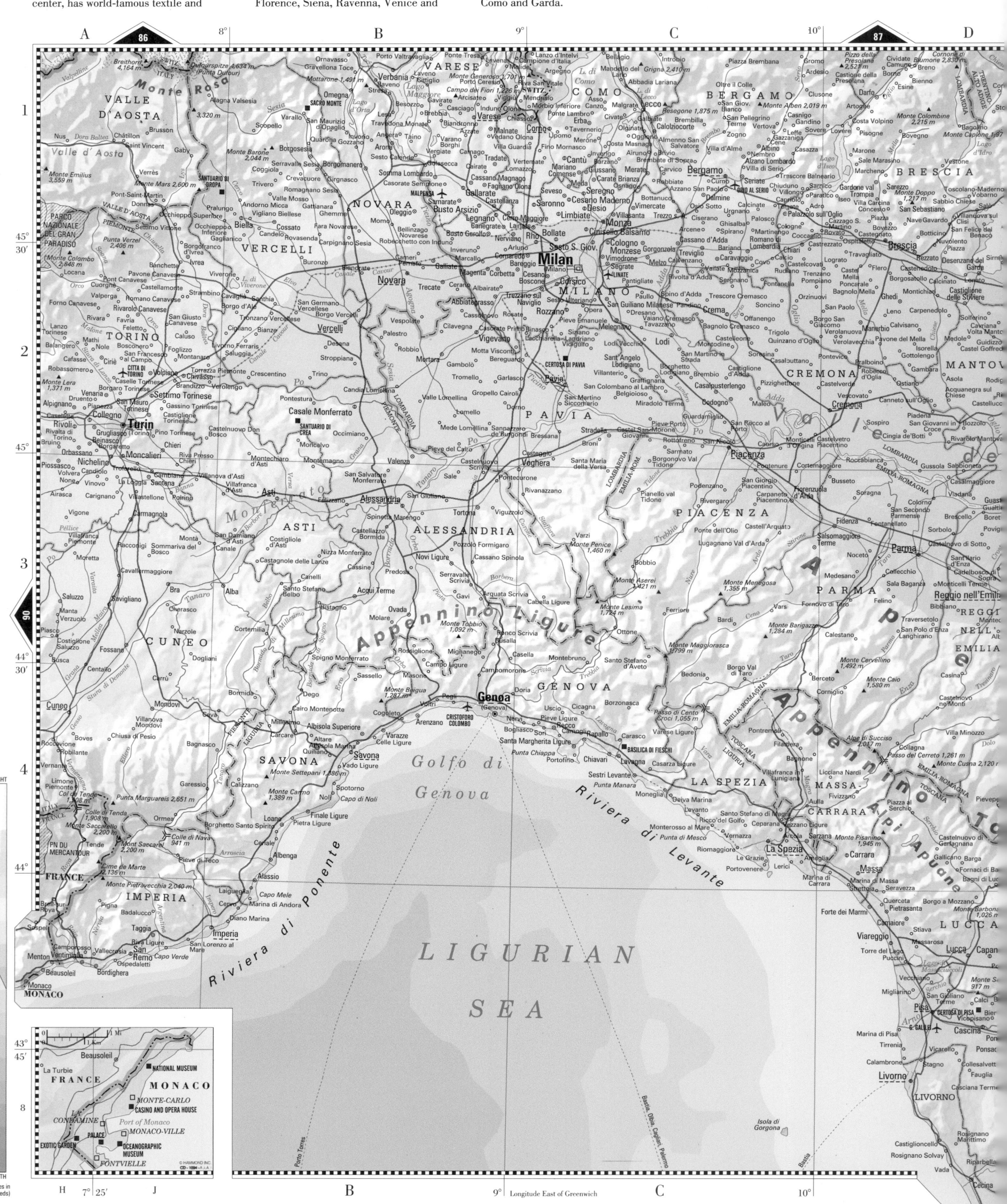

ADRIATIC SEA

Golfo di Venezia

Golfo di Trieste

SLOVENIA

CROATIA

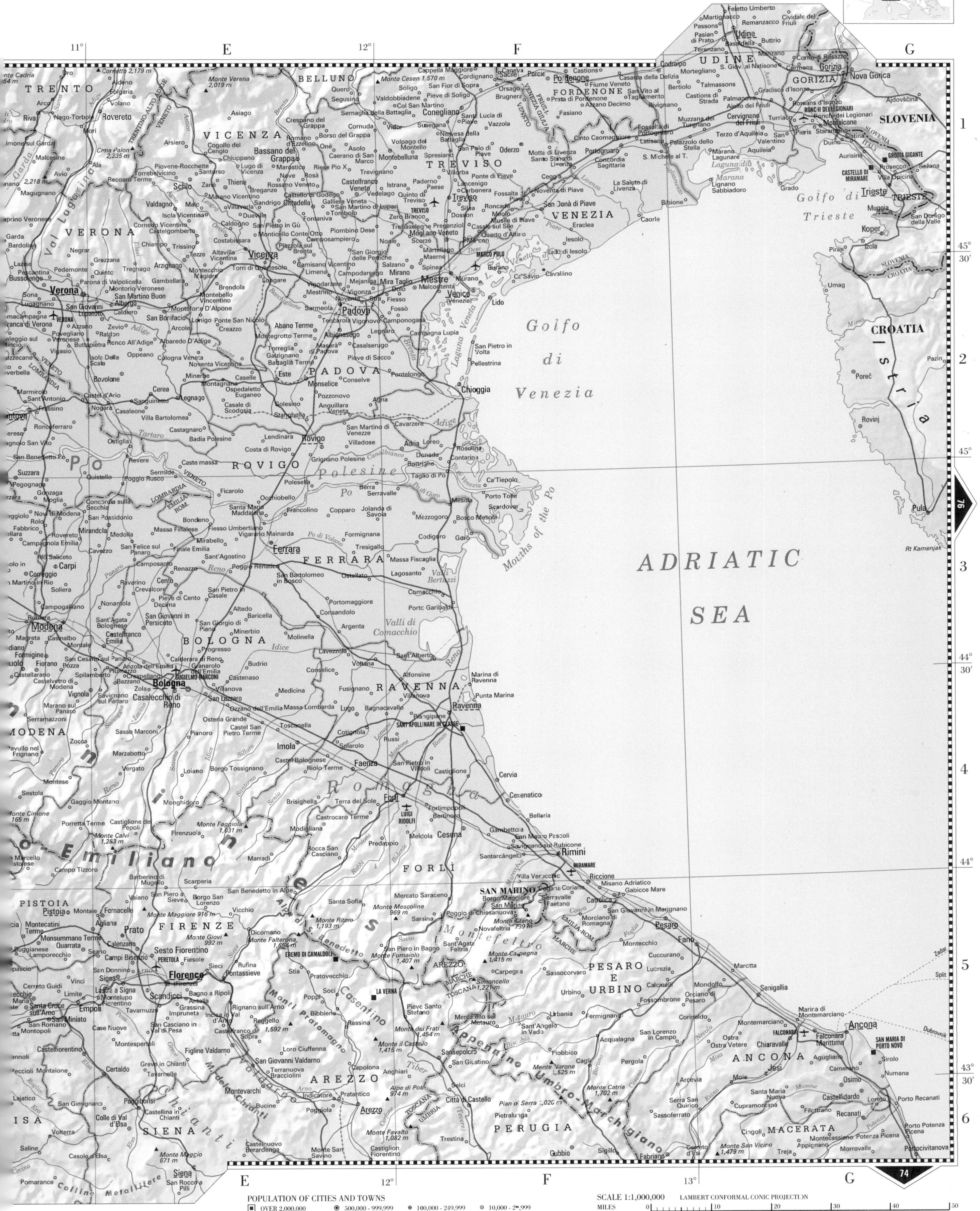

Istria

TRENTO

BELLUNO

VICENZA

TREVISO

VENEZIA

UDINE

GORIZIA

TRIESTE

VERONA

PADOVA

ROVIGO

Polesine

Po

FERRARA

BOLOGNA

MODENA

RAVENNA

Romagna

FORLÌ

SAN MARINO

PESARO E URBINO

MARCHE

ANCONA

MACERATA

PERUGIA

PISTOIA

FIRENZE

AREZZO

SIENA

Verona

Vicenza

Padova

Venice (Venezia)

Mestre

Treviso

Udine

Gorizia

Trieste

Rovigo

Ferrara

Bologna

Modena

Carpi

Ravenna

Faenza

Forlì

Cesena

Rimini

Riccione

Pesaro

Fano

Senigallia

Ancona

Florence (Firenze)

Prato

Arezzo

Nova Gorica

Koper

Pula

Rt Kamenjak

Monte Cornetto 2,179 m
Cima Cadria 54 m

Monte Verena 2,019 m

Monte Cesen 1,570 m

Cima Palon 2,235 m

Monte Maggiore 916 m

Monte Falterona 1,654 m

Monte Fumaiolo 1,407 m

Monte Catria 1,702 m

Monte San Vicino 1,479 m

Southeastern France

During the high Middle Ages, the Provence region was the home of the troubadours, who inspired a courtly culture based on chivalry and lyrical poetry. Today, the coast of Provence is known for the fashionable resorts, hotels and villas of the famed French Riviera (Côte d'Azur), which stretches from St-Tropez, through Cannes and Nice to the Italian border.

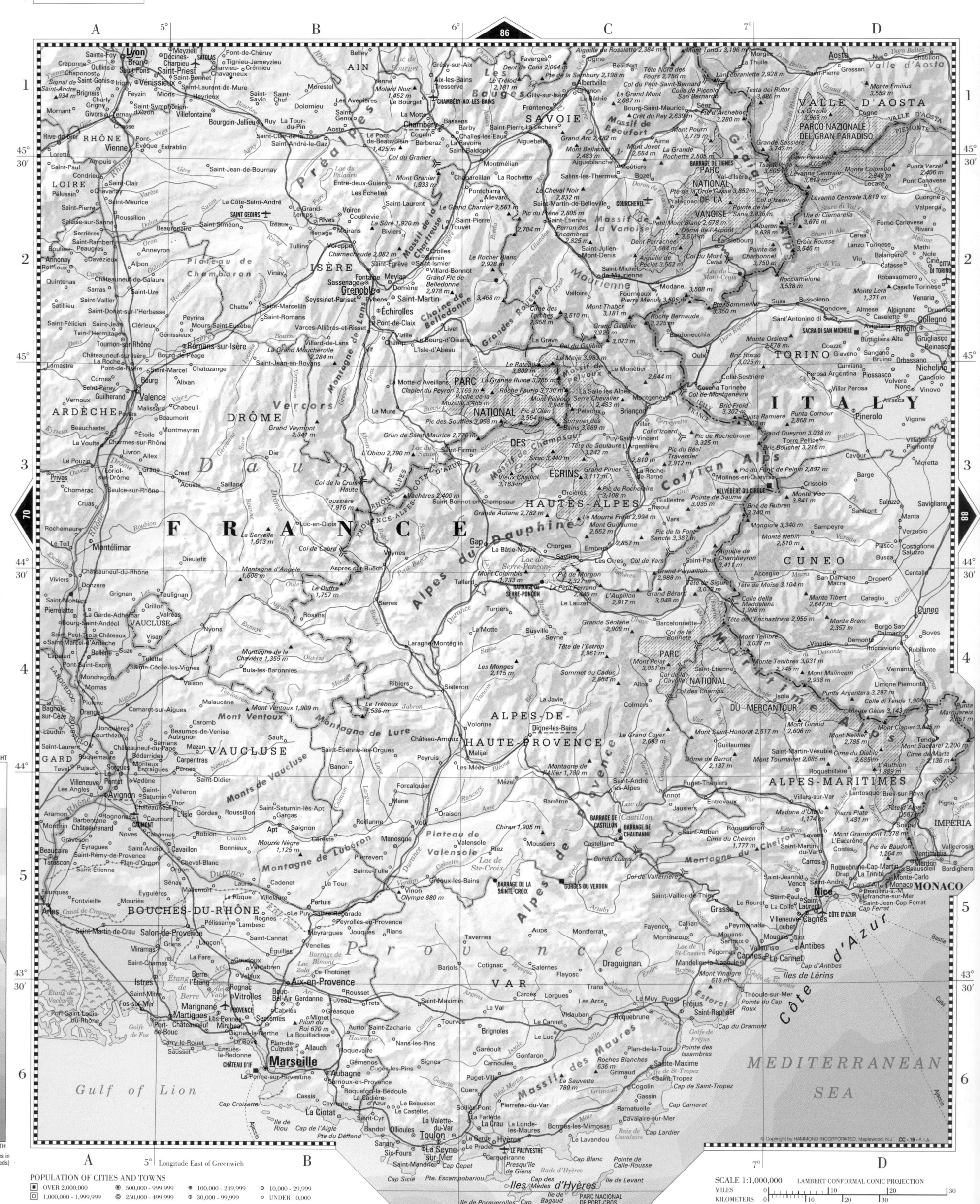

POPULATION OF CITIES AND TOWNS

■ OVER 2,000,000	● 500,000 - 999,999
□ 1,000,000 - 1,999,999	◉ 250,000 - 499,999
● 100,000 - 249,999	○ 30,000 - 99,999
○ 10,000 - 29,999	○ UNDER 10,000

SCALE 1:1,000,000   LAMBERT CONFORMAL CONIC PROJECTION

MILES 0 .... 10 .... 20 30
KILOMETERS 0 ... 10 ... 20 ... 30

Longitude East of Greenwich

Central Italy

This middle portion of the Italian peninsula was once the focus of the Roman Empire. Rome, the Eternal City, reflects a variety of historic influences, depending on the area one visits. Across the landscape of central Italy are found the artifacts of Roman civilization: great aqueducts, straight-as-an-arrow Roman roads, and well-preserved imperial villas.

POPULATION OF CITIES AND TOWNS

- ■ OVER 2,000,000
- ◻ 1,000,000 - 1,999,999
- ● 500,000 - 999,999
- ◉ 250,000 - 499,999
- ● 100,000 - 249,999
- ● 3C,000 - 99,999
- ● 10,000 - 25,999
- ○ UNDER 10,000

SCALE 1:1,000,000 LAMBERT CONFORMAL CONIC PROJECTION

MILES

KILOMETERS

HEIGHT
DEPTH
(Figures in Hundreds)

© Copyright by HAMMOND INCORPORATED, Maplewood, N.J.

Among the countries that border the Mediterranean are included some of the world's richest and poorest nations. Nearly 40 percent of the region's 350 million people live along the 30,000 mile (48,000 km.) coastline. In 30 years, population may double, with most growth occurring in the developing countries of North Africa. Bottled up behind the narrow Strait of Gibraltar, the sea cannot quickly disperse the pollution from human and industrial wastes. The Mediterranean Action Plan has brought disparate nations together to tackle the environmental problems.

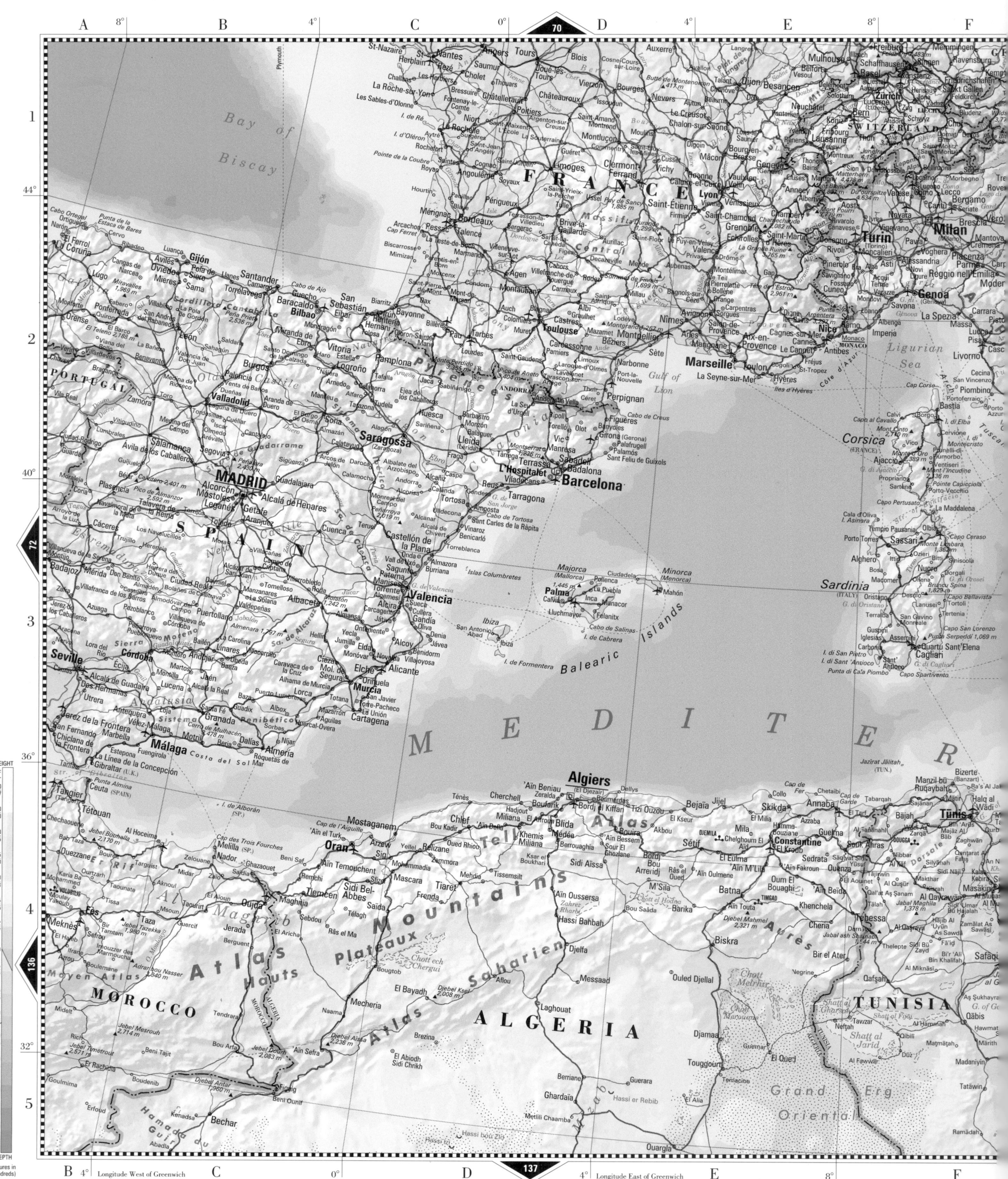

Mediterranean Region

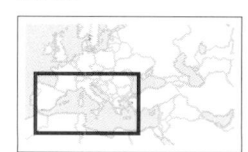

POPULATION OF CITIES AND TOWNS

SCALE 1:6,000,000   LAMBERT CONFORMAL CONIC PROJECTION

Rivers played a key role in Russian history. Peoples, armies and trade moved throughout Eastern Europe along Russia's famed waterways: the Volga, Don, Dnieper, Dniester, Oka, Kama and the two Dvinas. In·the Dark Ages, the Viking Varangians established a trade route from the Baltic to the Black Sea along the Volkhov and Dnieper rivers, and founded the first Russian State at Kiev, on the Dnieper. Even Moscow's ascendancy as the center of power can be attributed to its strategic location near the watershed from which the major rivers of European Russia arise.

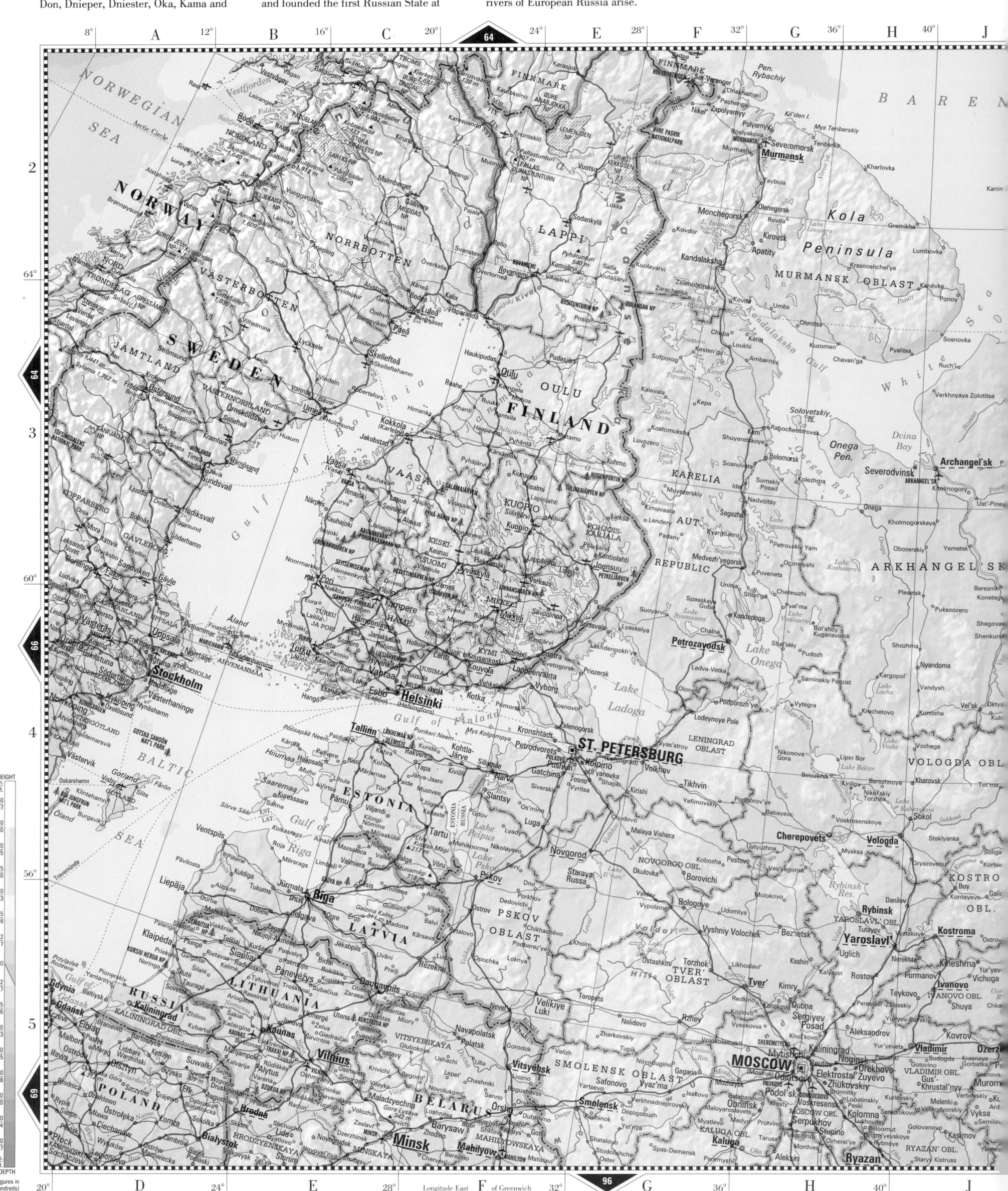

Northeastern Europe

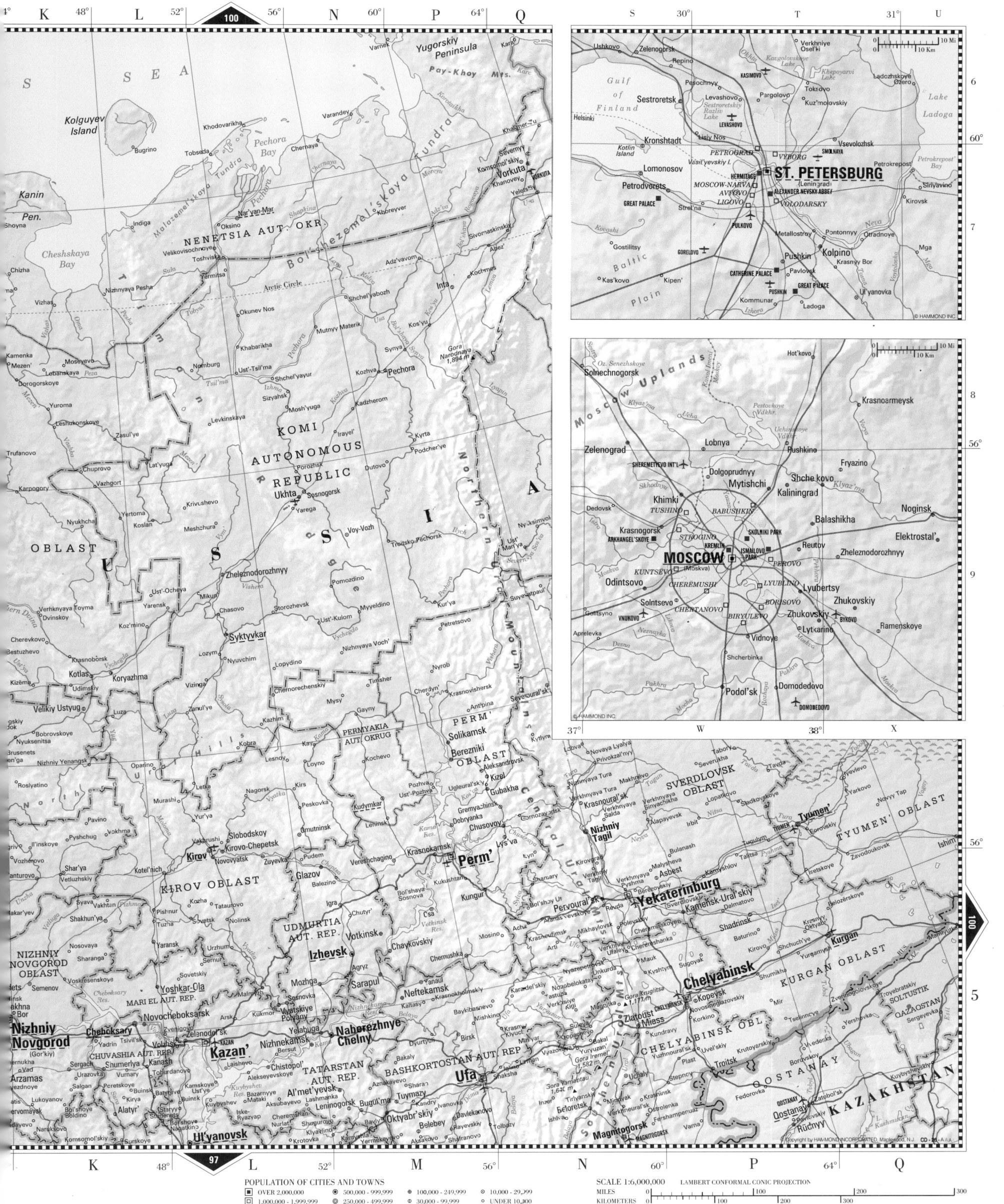

From the late 1400s Russian expansion moved in three main directions – east toward the Urals and Siberia, west and south toward the ice-free Baltic and Black Sea. On the west, tsarist Russia clashed with the Polish Kingdom. Farther south, Russian troops battled the Ottoman Empire of the Turks. By the late 1700s Russia had defeated both powers and was firmly established in the Ukraine and Crimea. During the 1800s, the tsars sought to dominate Constantinople (now Istanbul) and the strategic straits leading to the Mediterranean. They never realized their goal.

94
69
93
128

SCALE 1:6,000,000   LAMBERT CONFORMAL CONIC PROJECTION

MILES

KILOMETERS

POPULATION OF CITIES AND TOWNS

▫ OVER 2,000,000   ◉ 500,000 - 999,999   ⊕ 100,000 - 249,999   • 10,000 - 29,999
▢ 1,000,000 - 1,999,999   ◉ 250,000 - 499,999   ⊙ 30,000 - 99,999   ○ UNDER 10,000

96-97

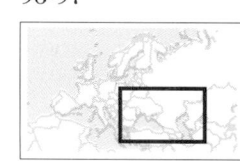

Southeastern Europe

RUSSIA
KAZAKHSTAN
GEORGIA
ARMENIA
AZERBAIJAN
TURKMENISTAN
UZBEKISTAN
IRAN
CASPIAN SEA
Aral Sea
BATYS QAZAQSTAN
ATYRAŪ
AQTÖBE
MANGGHYSTAU
QORAQALPOGHISTON AUT. REP.
QOSTANAY
QYZYLORDA
DASHHOWUZ
BALKAN
AHAL
KALMYKIA AUT. REP.
STAVROPOL' KRAY
VOLGOGRAD OBLAST
SARATOV OBLAST
SAMARA OBLAST
ORENBURG OBLAST
BASHKORTOSTAN AUT. REP.
CHELYABINSK OBLAST
PENZA OBLAST
ROSTOV OBLAST
ASTRAKHAN' OBL.
DAGESTAN AUT. REP.
CHECHNYA
Ustyurt Plateau
Mangyshlak Plateau
Mugodzharskoye Mts.
Greater Barsuki Desert
Ryn-Peski
Caucasus
Ul'yanovsk
Samara
Tol'yatti
Penza
Saratov
Volgograd
Orenburg
Aqtöbe
Oral
Atyraū
Astrakhan'
Aqtau
Makhachkala
Groznyy
Vladikavkaz
T'bilisi
Yerevan
Baku
Stavropol'
Elista
Magnitogorsk
Orsk
Türkmenbashi
Nebitdag
Ardabil
95
100
129
© Copyright by HAMMOND INCORPORATED, Maplewood, N.J.

The black soil (chernozem) of Ukraine's vast plains yields one of the world's most bountiful harvests of wheat, barley, sugar beets and sunflower seeds. Important coal deposits in the Donets River basin, and major iron ore resources at Krivoy Rog, proved vital to the economies of this region. As one of Europe's largest and most populous nations, Ukraine could claim to be the birthplace of both the Ukrainian and Russian culture, which was centered at Kiev in the 10th century. Yalta, located on the Crimean peninsula, is a popular Black Sea resort.

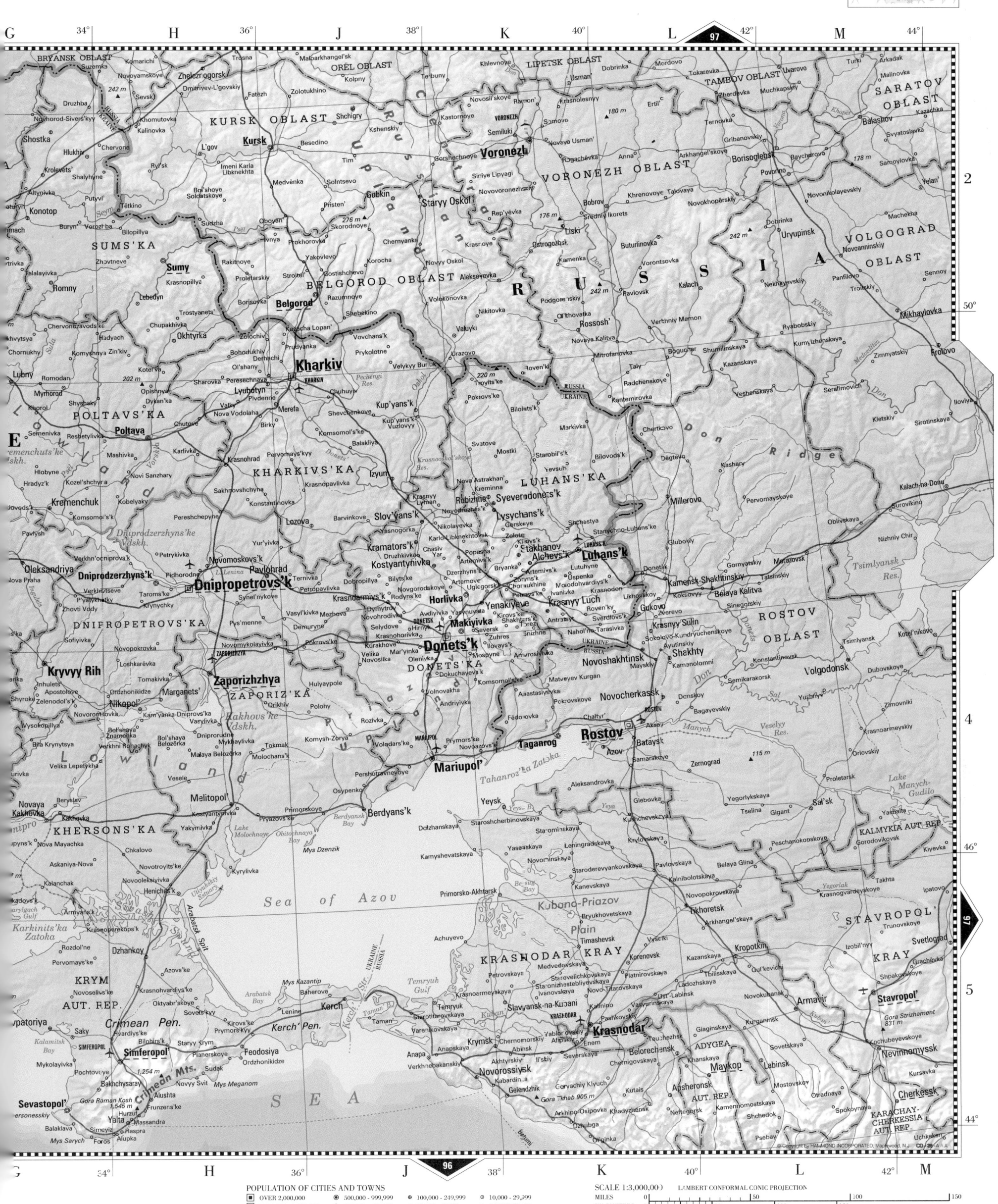

POPULATION OF CITIES AND TOWNS

| ■ OVER 2,000,000 | ● 500,000 - 999,999 | ◉ 100,000 - 249,999 | ○ 10,000 - 29,999 |
| □ 1,000,000 - 1,999,999 | ◎ 250,000 - 499,999 | ○ 30,000 - 99,999 | · UNDER 10,000 |

SCALE 1:3,000,000 LAMBERT CONFORMAL CONIC PROJECTION

MILES 0   50   100   150

KILOMETERS 0   50   100   150

Copyright © HAMMOND INCORPORATED, Maplewood, N.J.

The countries neighboring Russia stretch from the Polish border to the Bering Strait, spanning many time zones and 6000 miles (9600 km.). Their combined landmass - nearly 9 million square miles (23.4 mil. sq. km.) - wraps halfway around the globe. The vast Russian federation commands 76 percent of the region's land, over 60 percent of its population, most of its petroleum and natural gas, and over half of its iron and coal. Areas within this region have experienced much tension among the diverse ethnic groups in their struggle for greater autonomy.

Russia and Neighboring Countries

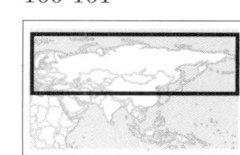

RUSSIA
(Administrative divisions are named only when they differ from their respective capitals.)

1. ADYGEA AUT. REP.
2. KARACHAY-CHERKESSIA AUT. REP.
3. KABARDINO-BALKARIA AUT. REP.
4. NORTH OSSETIA AUT. REP.
5. INGUSHETIA AUT. REP.
6. CHECHNYA AUT. REP.
7. DAGESTAN AUT. REP.
8. MORDOVIA AUT. REP.
9. CHUVASHIA AUT. REP.
10. MARI EL AUT. REP.
11. TATARSTAN AUT. REP.
12. BASHKORTOSTAN AUT. REP.
13. UDMURTIA AUT. REP.
14. PERMYAKIA AUT. OKRUG
15. KHAKASSIA AUT. OKRUG
16. UST-ORDA AUT. OKRUG
17. AGA AUT. OKRUG

POPULATION OF CITIES AND TOWNS

■ OVER 2,000,000
▣ 1,000,000 - 1,999,999
◼ 500,000 - 999,999
▫ 100,000 - 499,999
• 50,000 - 99,999
○ UNDER 50,000

SCALE 1:18,000,000   LAMBERT CONFORMAL CONIC PROJECTION

MILES 0 ___ 300 ___ 600 ___ 900

KILOMETERS 0 ___ 300 ___ 900

© Copyright by HAMMOND INCORPORATED, Maplewood, N.J.   CC-29-A-A

Occupied by Russia since 1945, claimed by Japan.

Asia

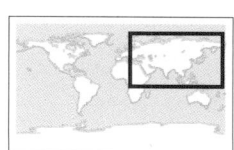

The delta of the Indus River, the longest river in southwest Asia, is the highlight of this southeast-looking, low-oblique image. Fed by snowmelt and glacial meltwater from the mountains of the Tibet Plateau, the Indus River flows nearly 1900 miles (3055 km.) before emptying into the Arabian Sea. After leaving the Tibet Plateau, the river flows onto the Punjab Plains of western Pakistan and through a vast alluvial lowland where it receives its major tributary, the Panjnad (five streams). In this severely arid landscape the rivers form precarious strips of fertile land.

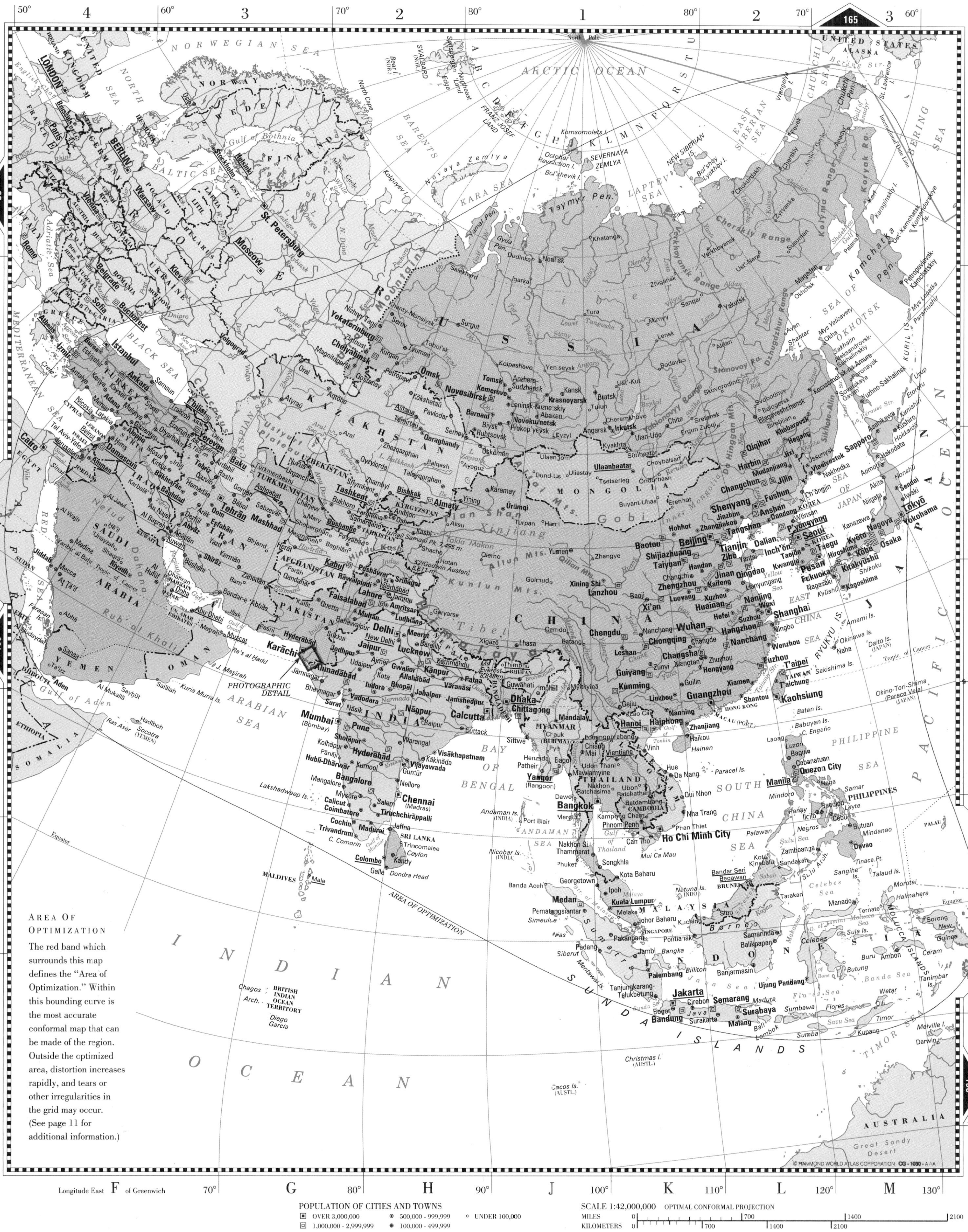

PHOTOGRAPHIC DETAIL

AREA OF OPTIMIZATION

The red band which surrounds this map defines the "Area of Optimization." Within this bounding curve is the most accurate conformal map that can be made of the region. Outside the optimized area, distortion increases rapidly, and tears or other irregularities in the grid may occur. (See page 11 for additional information.)

Longitude East F of Greenwich

POPULATION OF CITIES AND TOWNS

- OVER 3,000,000
- 1,000,000 - 2,999,999
- 500,000 - 999,999
- 100,000 - 499,999
- c UNDER 100,000

SCALE 1:42,000,000 OPTIMAL CONFORMAL PROJECTION

MILES 0   700   1400   2100
KILOMETERS 0   700   1400   2100

© HAMMOND WORLD ATLAS CORPORATION CG-1030-A-A-A

Marco Polo ventured through here on his trek from Venice to the palace of the Great Khan. Chinese, Japanese, Koreans and Russians have vied for strategic advantage and control over the valuable coal and mineral resources of Northern China for over a century. Today the region is one of the world's most productive industrial centers. While Japan successfully exports everything from cars to VCRs, emerging industrial powers such as Taiwan and Korea are joining a high-tech revolution. The Chinese have made Shenyang a center of heavy industry.

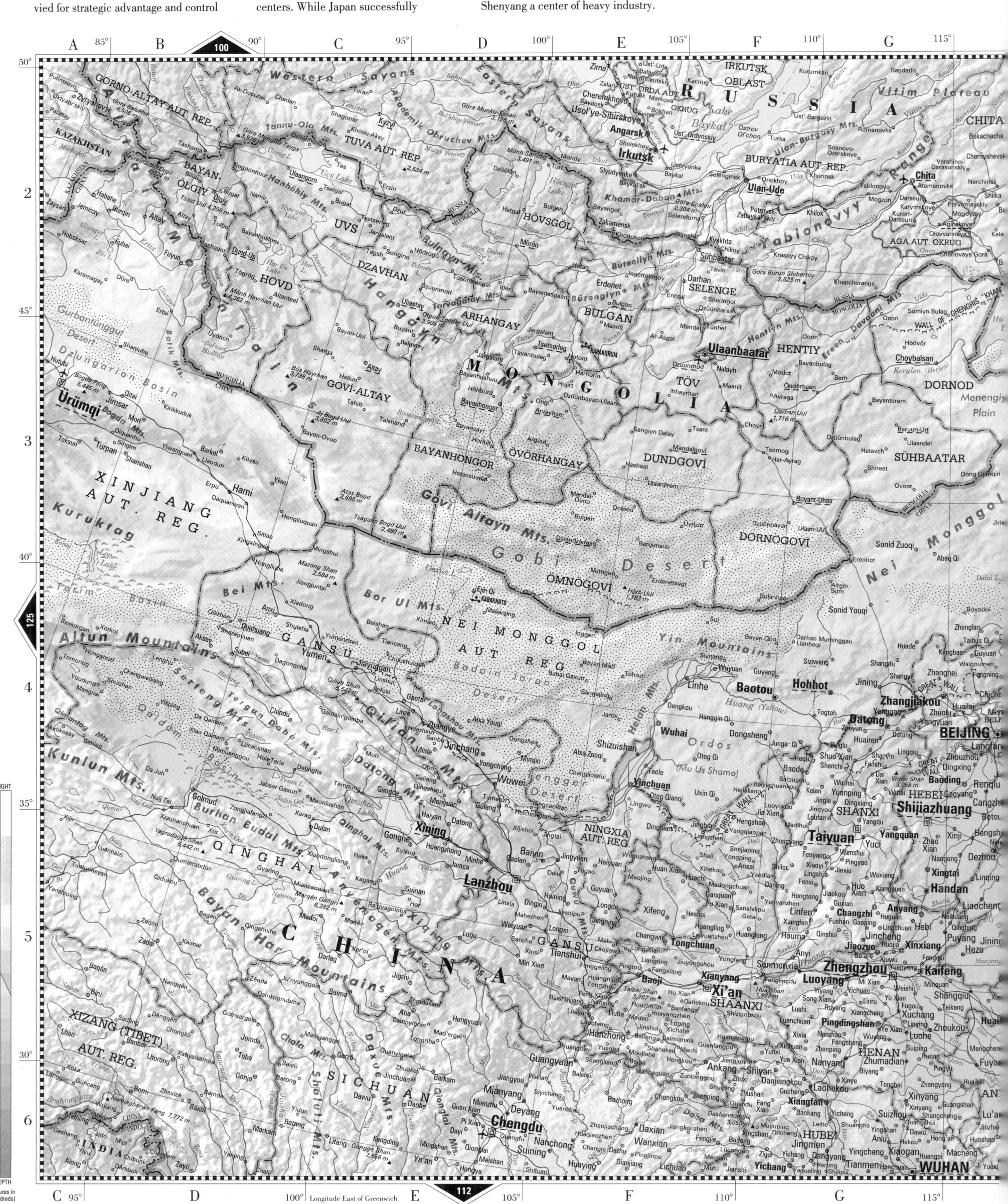

Eastern Asia

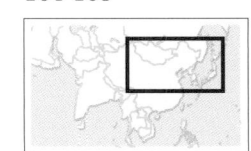

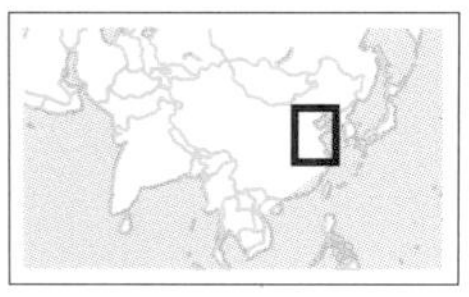

Northeastern China

Around 2200 B.C., in the lower Huang (Yellow) River valley, there emerged a high-level Chinese civilization, probably based on the fertile, easily worked soil. Shandong province, a leading center for heavy industry, was once the home of teacher-philosopher Confucius (551-479 B.C.). Shanghai is the leader in the manufacture of precision and consumer goods.

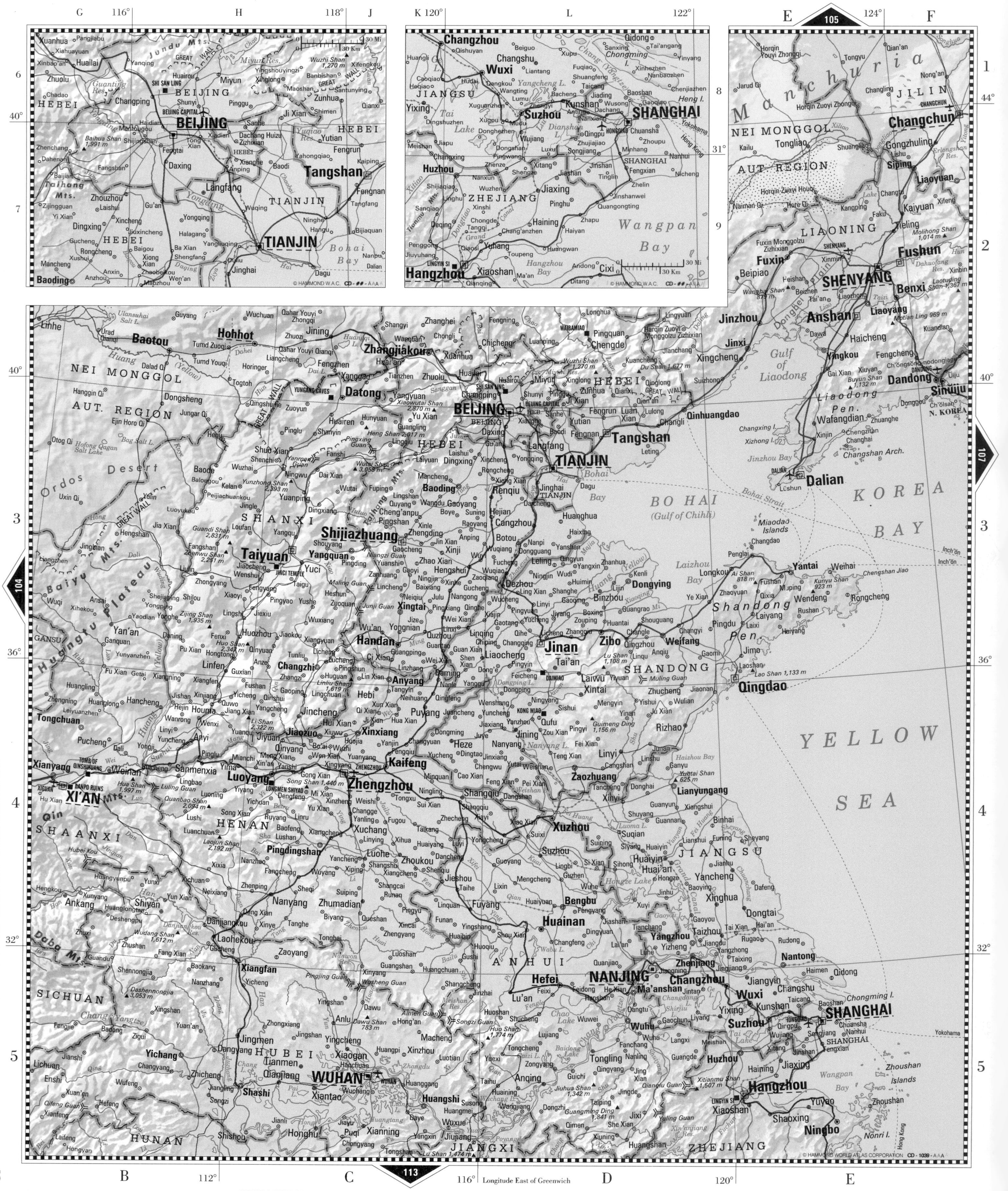

POPULATION OF CITIES AND TOWNS

- ■ OVER 2,000,000
- ■ 1,000,000 - 1,999,999
- ● 500,000 - 999,999
- ● 250,000 - 499,999
- ● 100,000 - 249,999
- ● 30,000 - 99,999
- ○ 10,000 - 29,999
- ○ UNDER 10,000

SCALE 1:6,000,000   LAMBERT CONFORMAL CONIC PROJECTION

MILES 0   100   200   300
KILOMETERS 0   100   200   300

HEIGHT
ft. / m.
60,197
40,130
20,65
15,50
10,33
7,20
5,16
0
5,16
30,98
40,130
m. / ft.
DEPTH
(Figures in Hundreds)

Korea

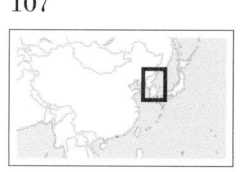

This peninsula has historically served as a bridge between three of the world's major cultures – Chinese, Russian and Japanese. In the early 20th century, Korea was annexed by Japan.

After 1945, it was divided into a communist north and a pro-western south. Although devastated by war in 1950, South Korea slowly became a major industrial power after a truce in 1953.

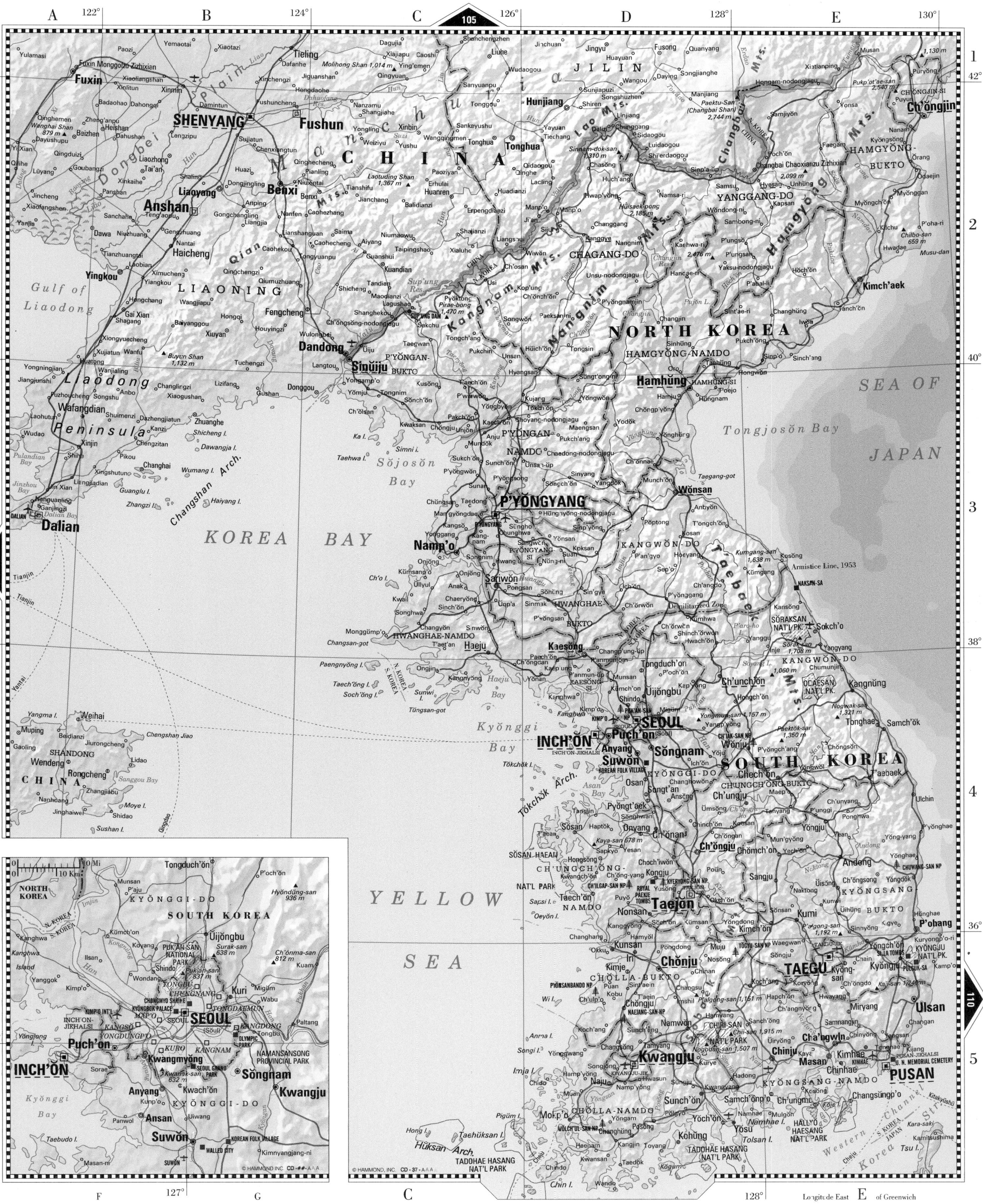

POPULATION OF CITIES AND TOWNS
■ OVER 2,000,000
□ 1,000,000 - 1,999,999
● 500,000 - 999,999
◉ 250,000 - 499,999
○ 100,000 - 249,999
● 30,000 - 99,999
○ 10,000 - 29,999
○ UNDER 10,000

SCALE 1:3,000,000   LAMBERT CONFORMAL CONIC PROJECTION
MILES 0   50   100   150
KILOMETERS 0   50   100   150

Northern Japan

Hokkaido, Japan's northernmost major island, is home to the Ainu, an aboriginal, possibly Caucasian people, unrelated to the Japanese. The Ainu gradually retreated to the island's fertile river valleys to hunt, fish and farm. Few traditional Ainu remain. In 1972, Hokkaido hosted the Winter Olympics in the city of Sapporo. The island also contains coal.

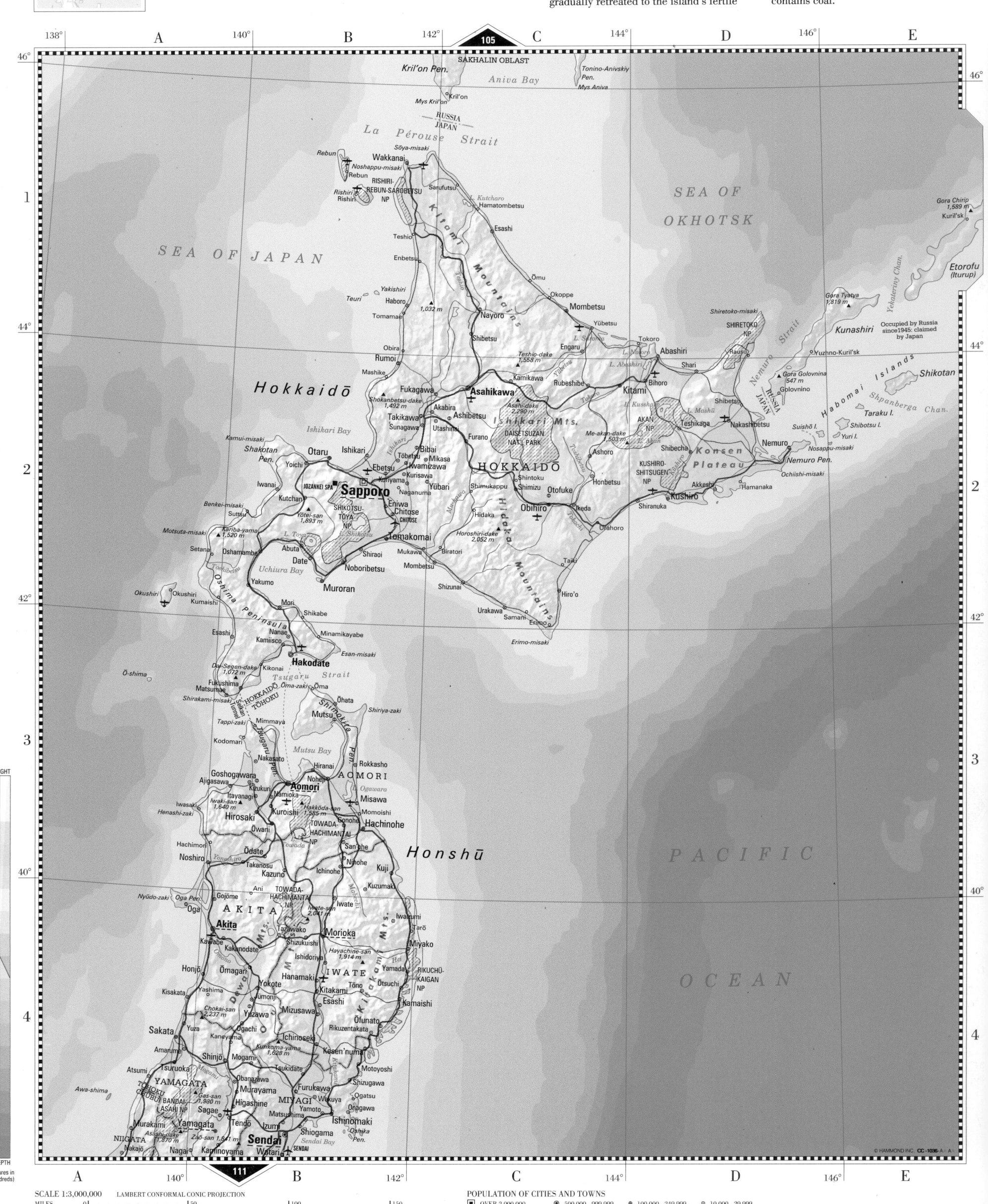

SCALE 1:3,000,000   LAMBERT CONFORMAL CONIC PROJECTION

MILES
KILOMETERS

POPULATION OF CITIES AND TOWNS

■ OVER 2,000,000	□ 500,000 - 999,999	● 100,000 - 249,999	● 10,000 - 29,999
□ 1,000,000 - 1,999,999	□ 250,000 - 499,999	● 30,000 - 99,999	○ UNDER 10,000

Although Tōkyō is one of the world's most densely populated cities, it is also considered one of the safest. This modern metropolis and capital of Japan is the financial, industrial and cultural hub of this country. Ōsaka has also developed into a modern industrial and commercial center. Because of its numerous canals and bridges, the city is sometimes called the "Venice of Japan."

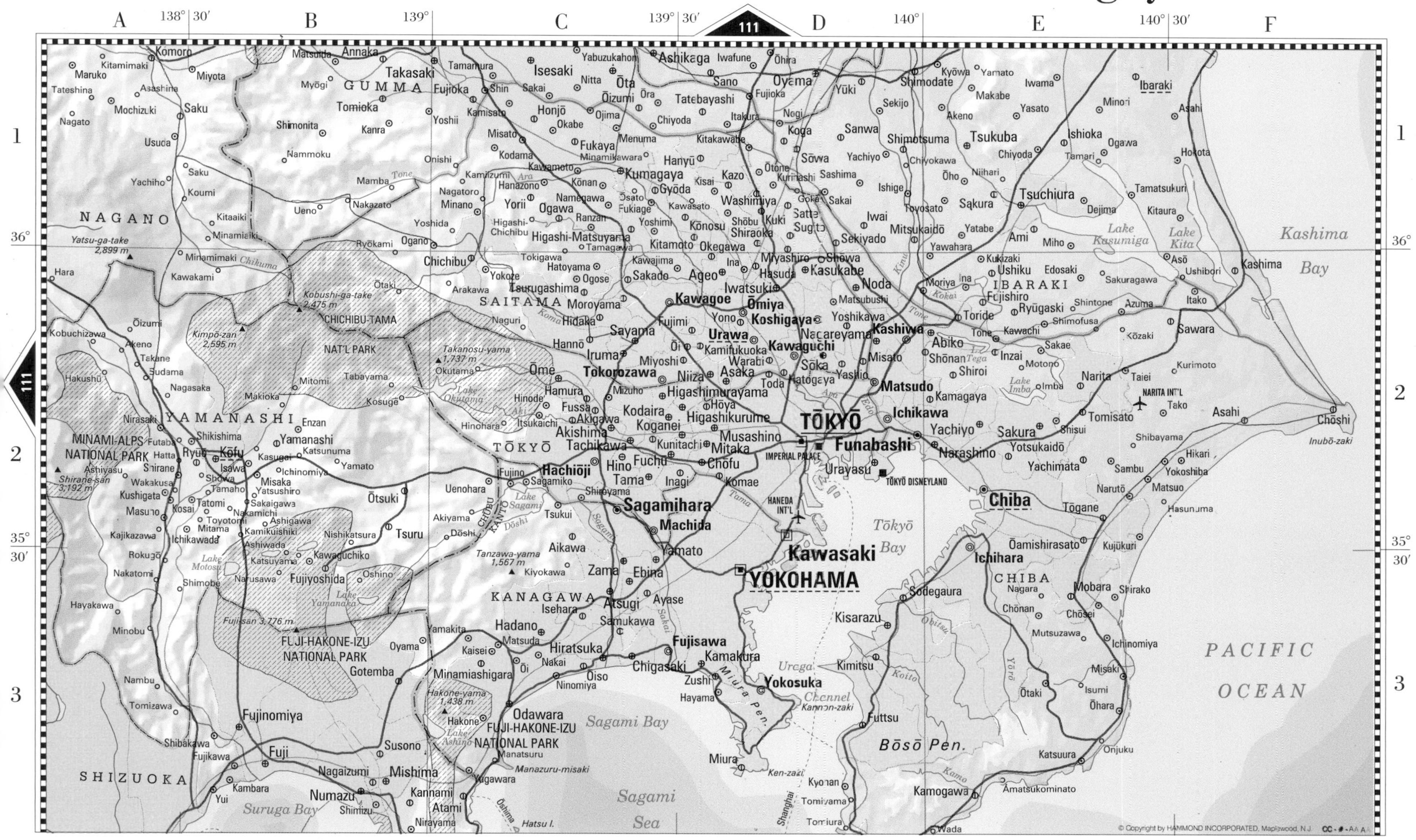

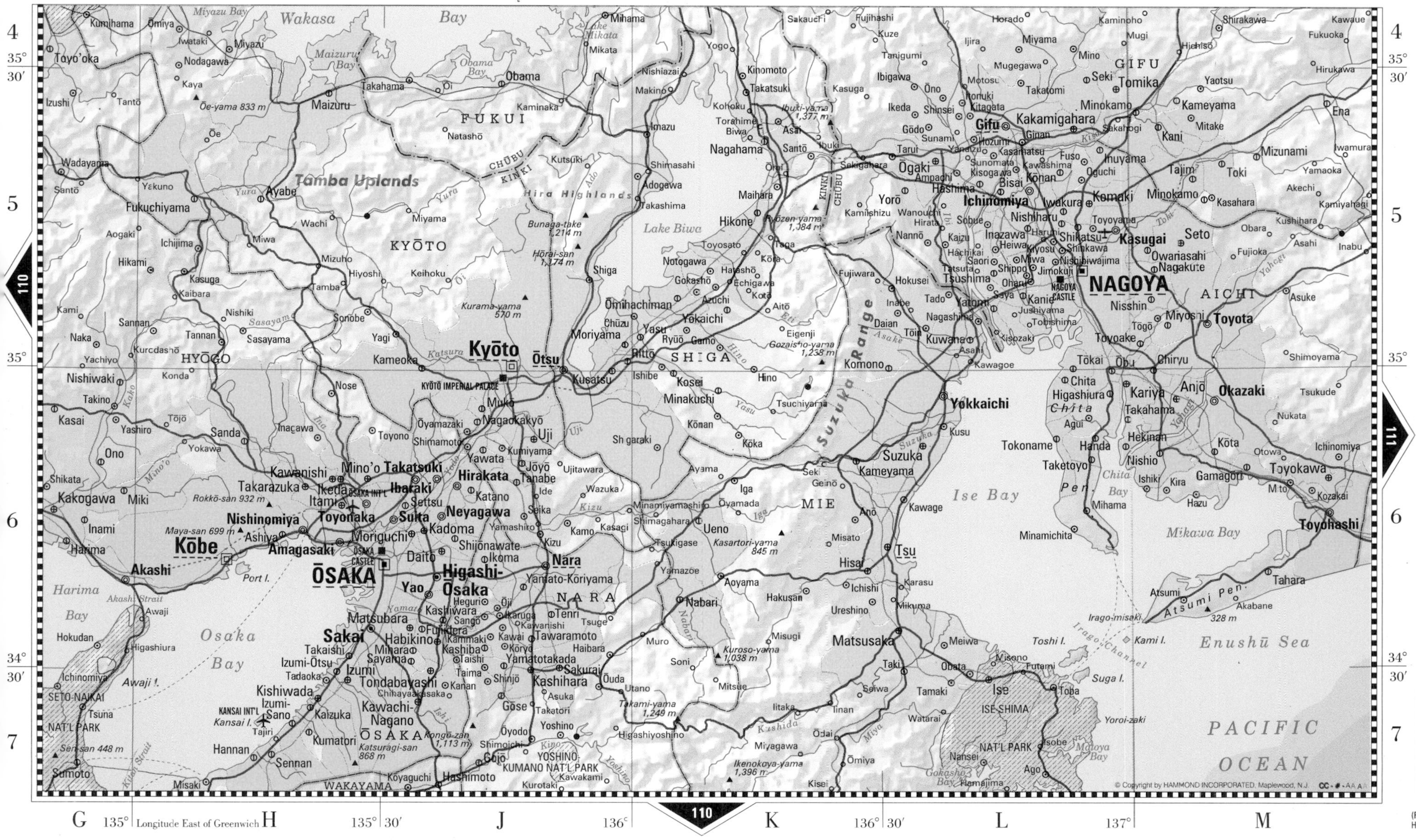

Tōkyō-Yokohama, Ōsaka-Nagoya

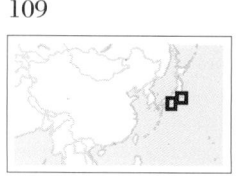

POPULATION OF CITIES AND TOWNS

SCALE 1:1,000,000   LAMPERT CONFORMAL CONIC PROJECTION

Longitude East of Greenwich
| OVER 2,000,000 | 500,000 - 999,999 | 100,000 - 249,999 | 10,000 - 29,999 |
| 1,000,000 - 1,999,999 | 250,000 - 499,999 | 30,000 - 99,999 | UNDER 10,000 |
SCALE 1:1,000,000 LAMBERT CONFORMAL CONIC PROJECTION
MILES 0 10 20 30
KILOMETERS 0 10 20 30 40 50
HEIGHT m. ft. 60 197; 40 130; 20 65; 15 50; 10 33; 5 16; 2 7; 0; 2 7; 5 16; 10 33; 20 65; 30 98; 40 130; 50 164; 60 197 m. ft. DEPTH (Figures in Hundreds)

The heart of Japan's industrial might lies in four highly urbanized clusters in southern Honshu and northern Kyushu. Rebuilt since World War II, Japan has become a major world power despite its lack of iron ore, coal or petroleum, and its limited arable land. It imports raw materials and uses its highly skilled work force to produce the cars, electronics, optical goods, textiles and other well-made products which supply the world market. Tokyo-Yokohama is the leading manufacturing center, followed by the Kobe-Osaka-Kyoto triangle, Nagoya and Kitakyushu.

Central and Southern Japan

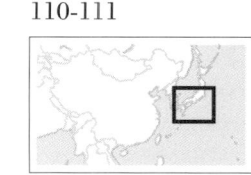

POPULATION OF CITIES AND TOWNS
- ■ OVER 2,000,000
- ▣ 1,000,000 - 1,999,999
- ● 500,000 - 999,999
- ◉ 250,000 - 499,999
- ● 100,000 - 249,999
- ◉ 10,000 - 29,999
- ◦ 30,000 - 99,999
- ◦ UNDER 10,000

SCALE 1:3,000,000   LAMBERT CONFORMAL CONIC PROJECTION

MILES 0 — 50 — 100 — 150
KILOMETERS 0 — 50 — 100 — 150

© Copyright by HAMMOND INCORPORATED, Maplewood, N.J.   CD · 1036 · A·A·A

© HAMMOND INC.   CC · 1116 · A·A·A

Southeastern China was once the backward, less developed part of the nation. In the last 20 years, growth has accelerated – particularly in Guangdong Province at Guangzhou (Canton) and nearby in the bustling city of Shenzhen. Both cities owe their progress to their proximity to Hong Kong, a special administrative region of the People's Republic of China. Taiwan, the island refuge of the Nationalist government since 1949, has developed into a major manufacturing power, with a per capita income many times higher than that of the mainland.

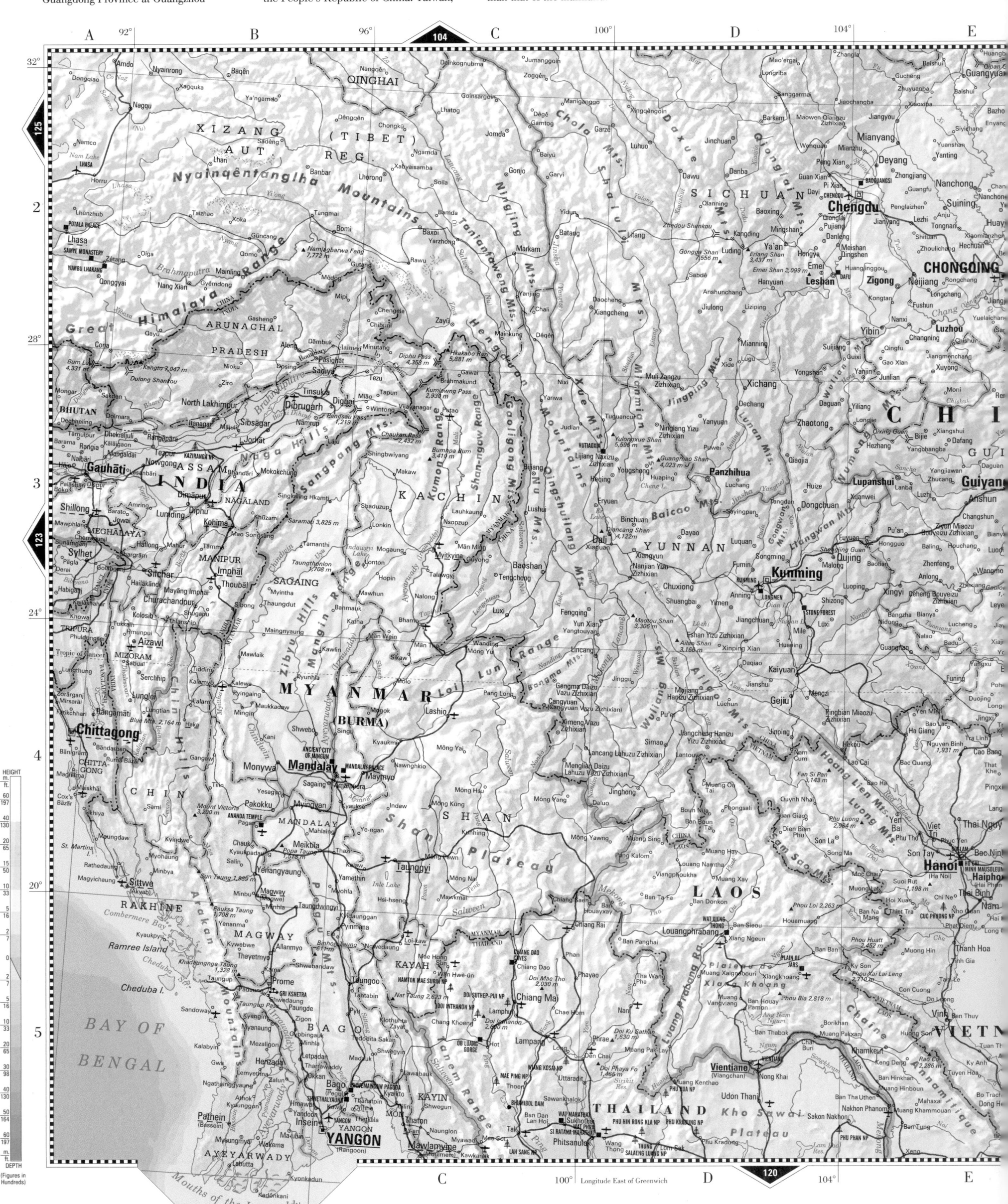

Southeastern China, Northern Indochina

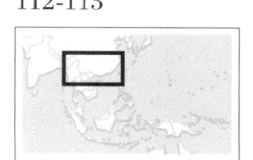

POPULATION OF CITIES AND TOWNS

■ OVER 2,000,000	● 500,000 - 999,999	● 100,000 - 249,999	⊙ 10,000 - 29,999
□ 1,000,000 - 1,999,999	● 250,000 - 499,999	⊙ 30,000 - 99,999	⊙ UNDER 10,000

SCALE 1:6,000,000   LAMBERT CONFORMAL CONIC PROJECTION

MILES 0   100   200   300

KILOMETERS 0   100   200   300

© HAMMOND W.A.C.

Philippines

Of the 7,000 islands which make up the Philippines, roughly one in ten are inhabited. The original residents were predominately of Malay stock. From 1565 to 1898, the Philippines were ruled by Spain, which made the Philippines a bastion of Roman Catholicism in East Asia. The following 48 years of United States rule left an equally Western imprint on the national character.

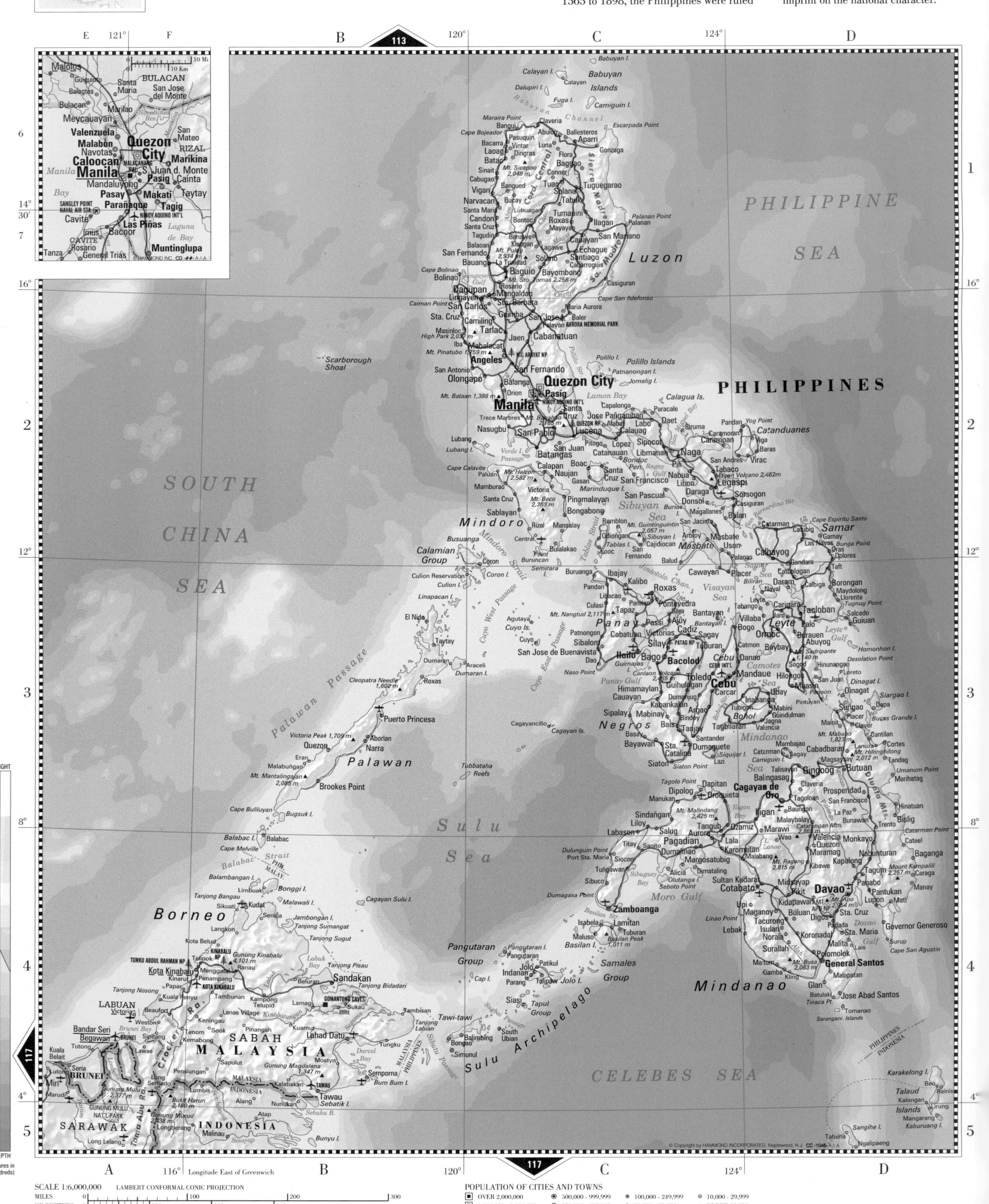

Western Indonesia and mainland Malaysia are the eastern outposts of Islam, which swept the region around A.D. 1100. Today, Indonesia is the most populous Islamic nation on earth; only

Bali retains the original Hindu faith of the medieval Indies. Malaysia's maritime location and rich harvests of fish, lumber, tin and rubber have produced one of the region's most successful economies.

Malaya, Sumatra, Java

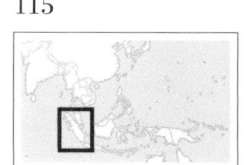

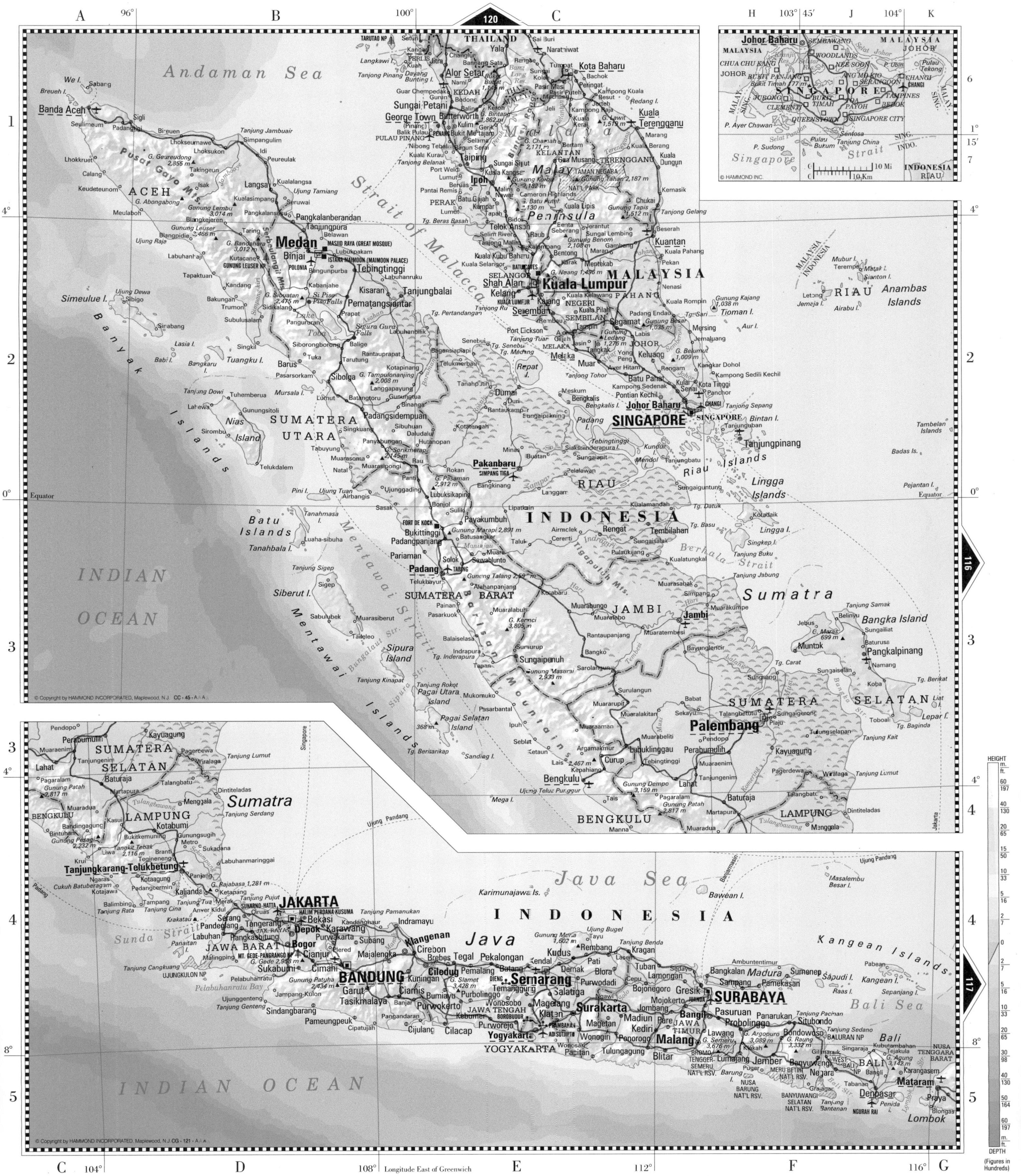

POPULATION OF CITIES AND TOWNS

SCALE 1:6,000,000 · LAMBERT CONFORMAL CONIC PROJECTION

From "stone age" New Guinea in the east, to mystical Bali, this region has been the inspiration for centuries of exotic island fantasies. Here are the Moluccas, the original Spice Islands coveted by European adventurers in the 16th century. Hindu culture that once flourished throughout the archipelago has declined. Java, with its volcano-enriched soils, supports a dense population. The nearby volcano Krakatoa erupted in 1883, taking thousands of lives. To the north, in Borneo, commercial loggers are stripping away what is left of the rain forest.

SCALE 1:9,000,000   LAMBERT CONFORMAL CONIC PROJECTION

MILES   0   150   300   450

KILOMETERS 0   150   300   450

POPULATION OF CITIES AND TOWNS

☐ OVER 2,000,000   ● 500,000 - 999,999   ● 100,000 - 249,999   ○ 10,000 - 29,999
☐ 1,000,000 - 1,999,999 ● 250,000 - 499,999   ○ 30,000 - 99,999   ○ UNDER 10,000

Indonesia, Malaysia

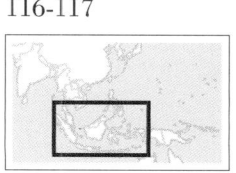

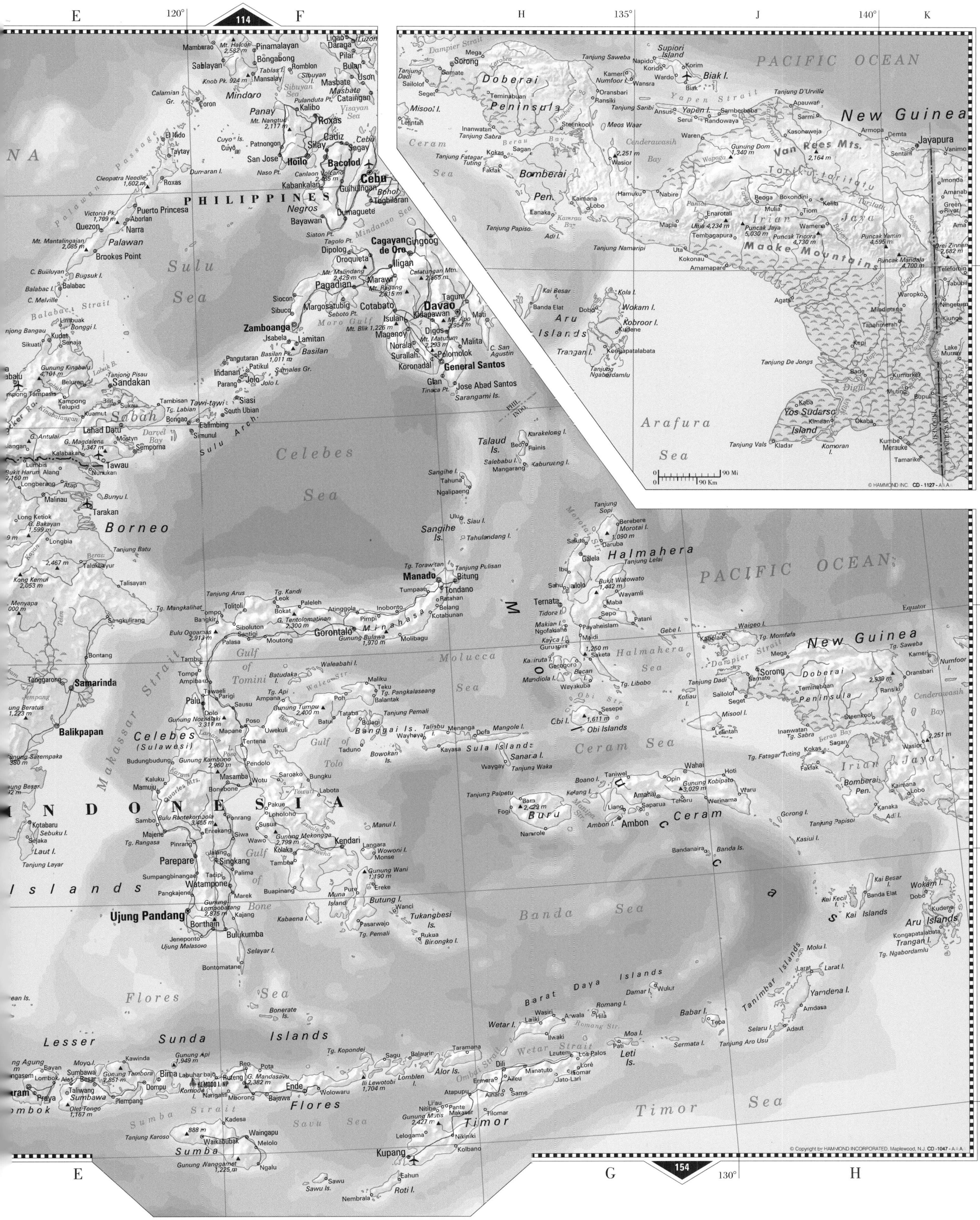

E
120°
114
F
H
135°
J
140°
K
PHILIPPINES
Mindoro
Panay
Negros
Palawan
Cebu
Bohol
Iloilo
Bacolod
Puerto Princesa
Brookes Point
Sulu Sea
Mindanao Sea
Cagayan de Oro
Iligan
Zamboanga
Davao
Cotabato
General Santos
Moro Gulf
Basilan
Jolo
Tawi-tawi
Sulu Arch.
Sabah
Sandakan
Tawau
Tarakan
Celebes Sea
Talaud Is.
Sangihe Is.
Borneo
Samarinda
Balikpapan
Makassar Strait
INDONESIA
Manado
Bitung
Gorontalo
Gulf of Tomini
Palu
Celebes (Sulawesi)
Gulf of Bone
Kendari
Parepare
Ujung Pandang
Watampone
Buton I.
Halmahera
Ternate
Molucca Sea
Halmahera Sea
Obi Islands
Sula Islands
Buru
Ambon
Ceram
Ceram Sea
Banda Sea
MOLUCCAS
Kai Islands
Aru Islands
Tanimbar Islands
Barat Daya Islands
Flores Sea
Lesser Sunda Islands
Lombok
Sumbawa
Bima
Flores
Ende
Sumba
Sumba Strait
Savu Sea
Timor
Kupang
Dili
Alor Is.
Wetar I.
Timor Sea
PACIFIC OCEAN
New Guinea
Sorong
Doberai Peninsula
Bomberai Pen.
Irian Jaya
Biak I.
Yapen Strait
Cenderawasih Bay
Jayapura
Van Rees Mts.
Maoke Mountains
Puncak Jaya 5,030 m
Arafura Sea
Yos Sudarso Island
Merauke
Equator
0°
5°
10°
130°
G
H
154
3
4
5
6
0 90 Mi
0 90 Km
© HAMMOND INC. CD - 1127
© Copyright by HAMMOND INCORPORATED, Maplewood, N.J. CD -1047

This is the vast monsoon region of Asia. These yearly rains (monsoon is derived from the Arabic "mausim" or season) bring life-bearing moisture to the rice crops of India, Bangladesh and the Andaman Sea coasts. However, when the monsoon fails, or materializes in the form of great storms, tragedy can come to the populace as famine or flood. About half of the world's population lives in regions affected by monsoons, and the scale of demographic problems exceeds those found anywhere else in the world. Most of the work force is employed in subsistence agriculture.

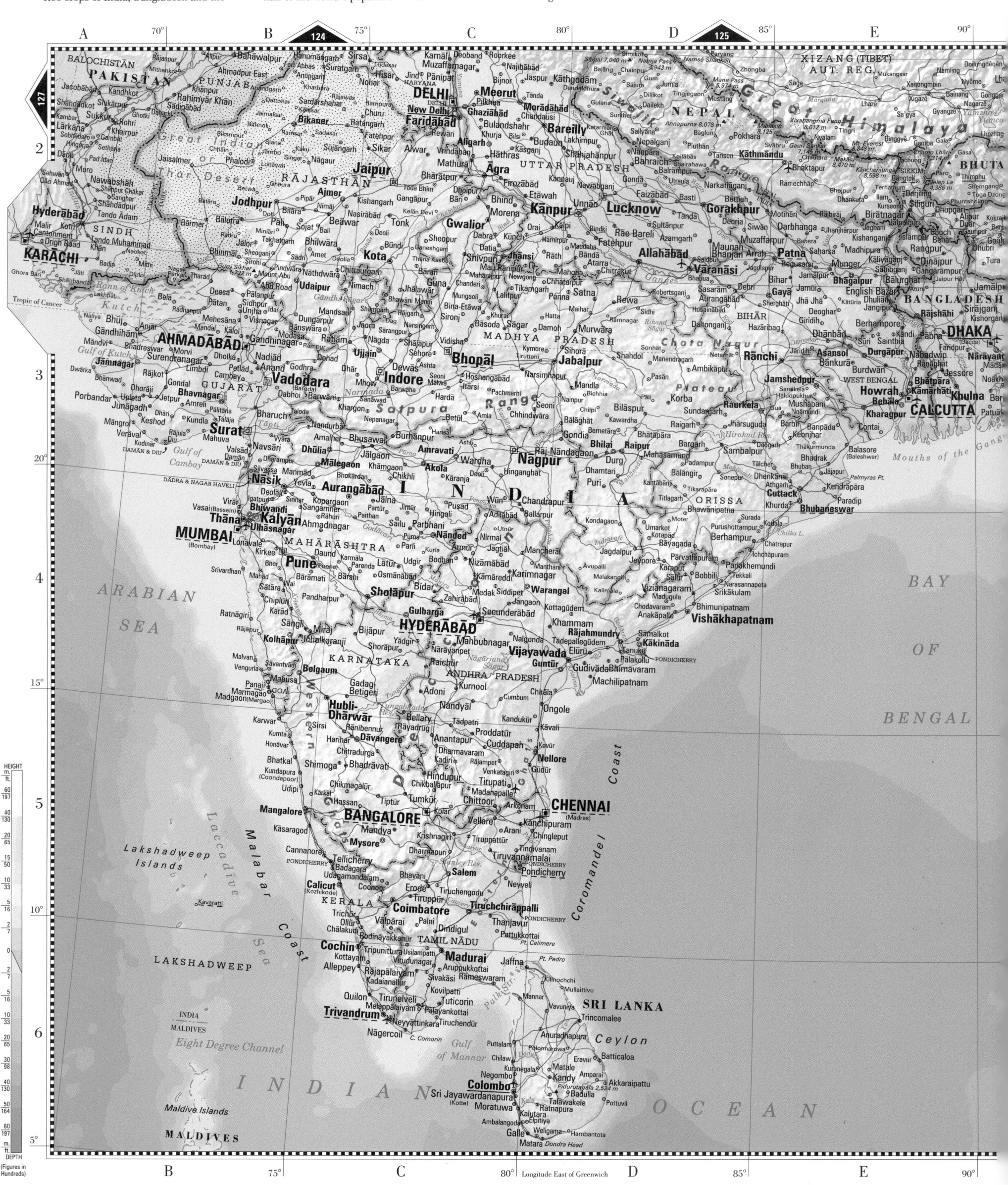

Southern Asia

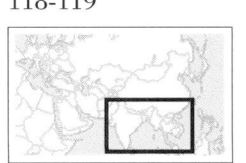

POPULATION OF CITIES AND TOWNS

- ■ OVER 2,000,000
- □ 1,000,000 - 1,999,999
- ● 500,000 - 999,999
- ◉ 250,000 - 499,999
- ● 100,000 - 249,999
- ◎ 30,000 - 99,999
- ● 10,000 - 29,999
- ○ UNDER 10,000

SCALE 1:9,000,000   LAMBERT CONFORMAL CONIC PROJECTION

MILES 0   150   300   450
KILOMETERS 0   150   300   450

© Copyright by HAMMOND INCORPORATED, Maplewood, N.J.

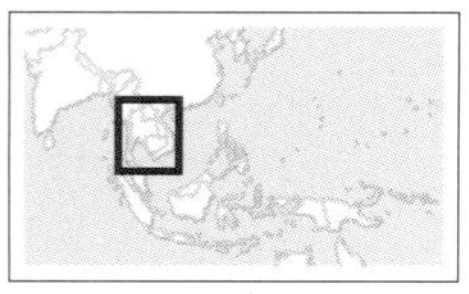

Indochina

Centuries of conflict have given this rugged yet fertile "shatterbelt" a unique history. Early expansion from India was followed by Thai and Burmese inroads and Vietnamese moves south of the Red River Valley. China also sought control of the region. Britain and France held sway in the 1800s. Intervention in Vietnam is seen in the many speakers of French, English and Chinese.

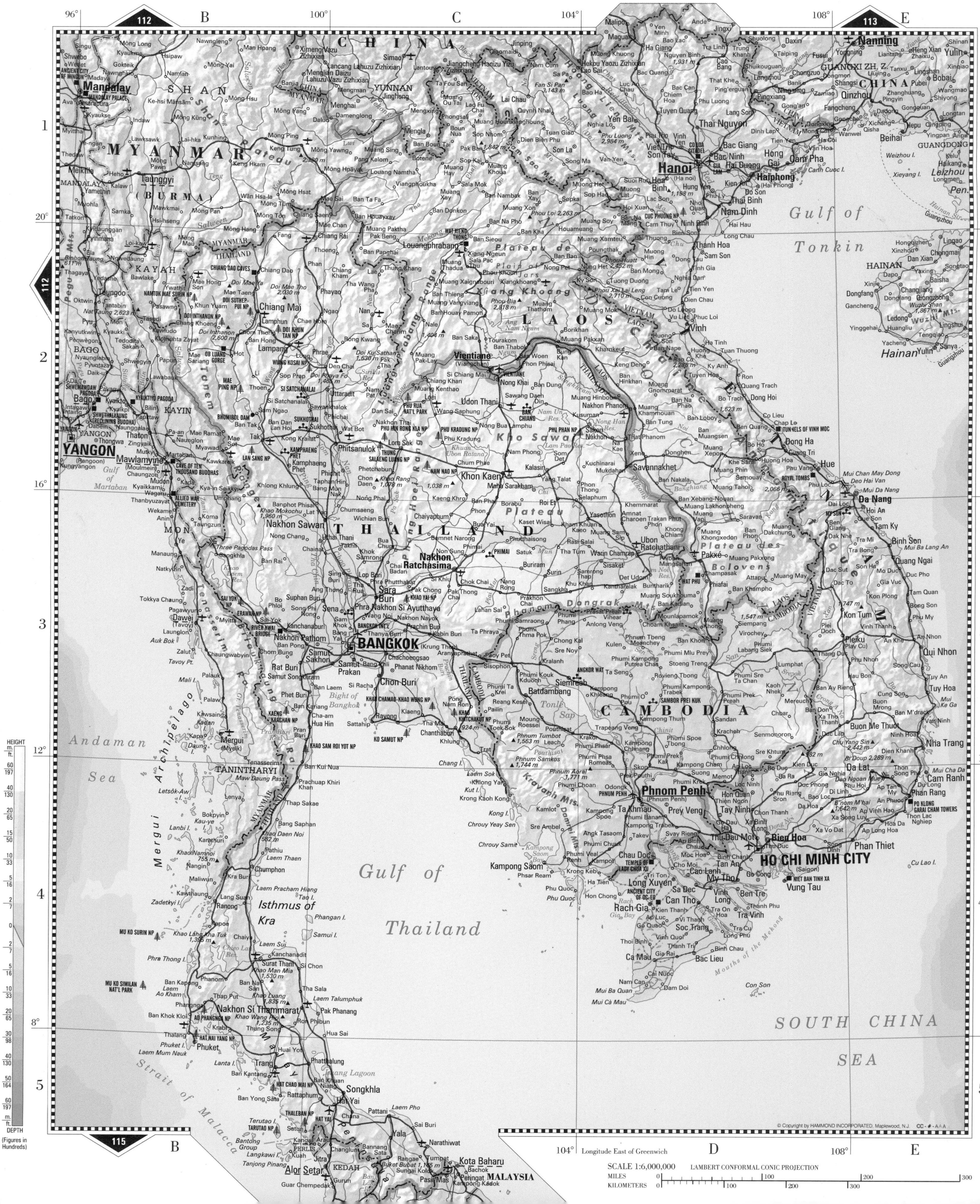

© Copyright by HAMMOND INCORPORATED, Maplewood, N.J.

SCALE 1:6,000,000 LAMBERT CONFORMAL CONIC PROJECTION

Longitude East of Greenwich

This region includes several of India's largest cities: Mumbai (Bombay), Hyderabad, Bangalore and Chennai (Madras). Cities continue to grow as a result of rural to urban migration. A major factor influencing India's relations with Sri Lanka has been the shared ethnicity of Tamils living in southern India and in northern and eastern Sri Lanka.

Southern India

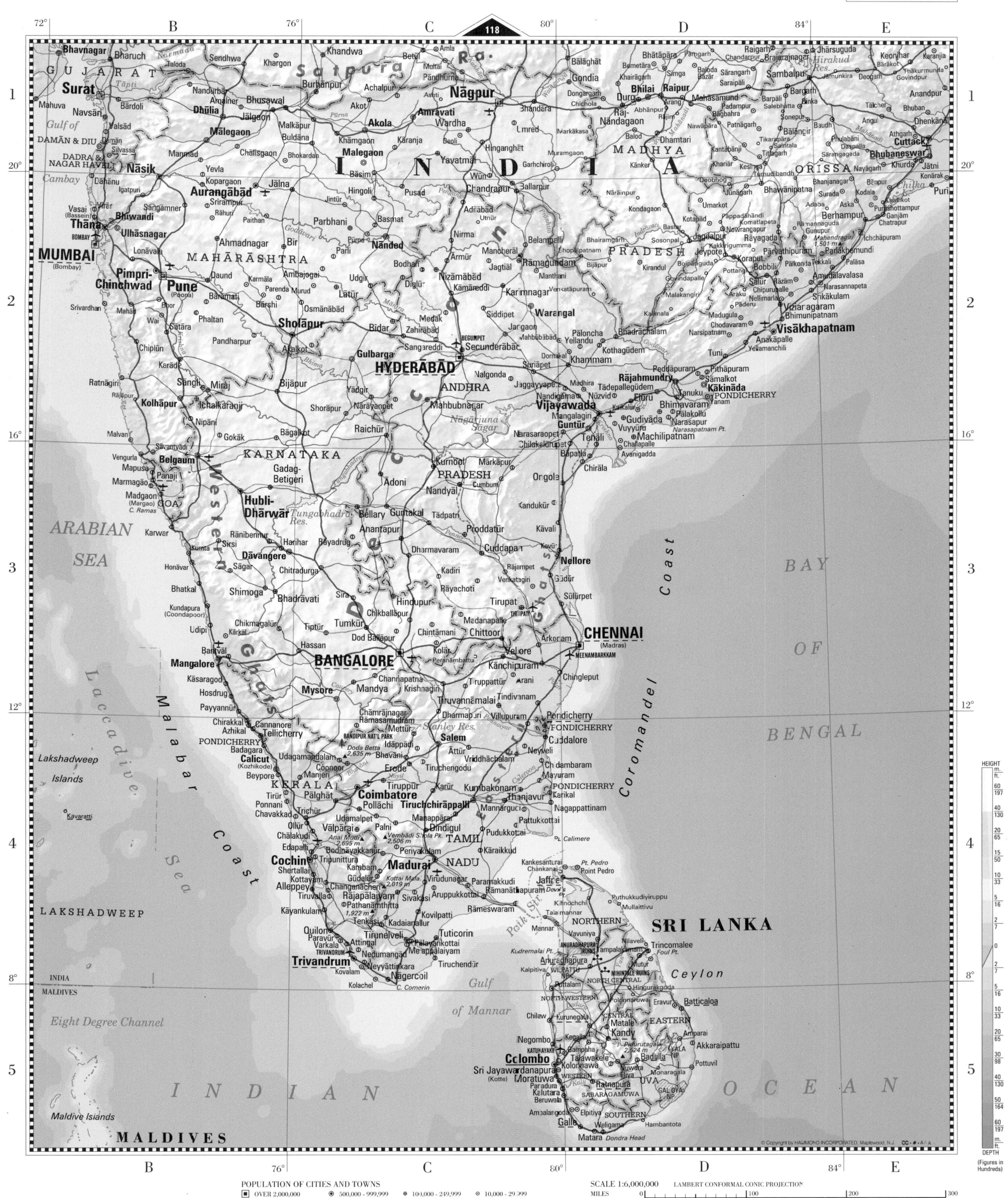

POPULATION OF CITIES AND TOWNS

| ■ OVER 2,000,000 | ● 500,000 - 999,999 | ⊙ 100,000 - 249,999 | ○ 10,000 - 29,999 |
| ▣ 1,000,000 - 1,999,999 | ⊙ 250,000 - 499,999 | ⊙ 30,000 - 99,999 | ○ UNDER 10,000 |

SCALE 1:6,000,000   LAMBERT CONFORMAL CONIC PROJECTION

MILES   0   50   100   200   300
KILOMETERS 0   50   100   200   300

This densely populated plain along the Ganges River is home to both peasant farmers and city dwellers. Two great Asian religions were born on this fertile soil. The holy city of Hinduism – Varanasi (Benares), sprouted on the banks of the sacred river. Buddha was born 150 miles (240 km.) to the north in Nepal, and attained enlightenment at the Bodh Gaya near Patna. The Ganges swings south, east of Patna, and works its way through the delta to the Bay of Bengal. To the north are the world's highest mountains, the Himalayas, including the great peak of Mt. Everest.

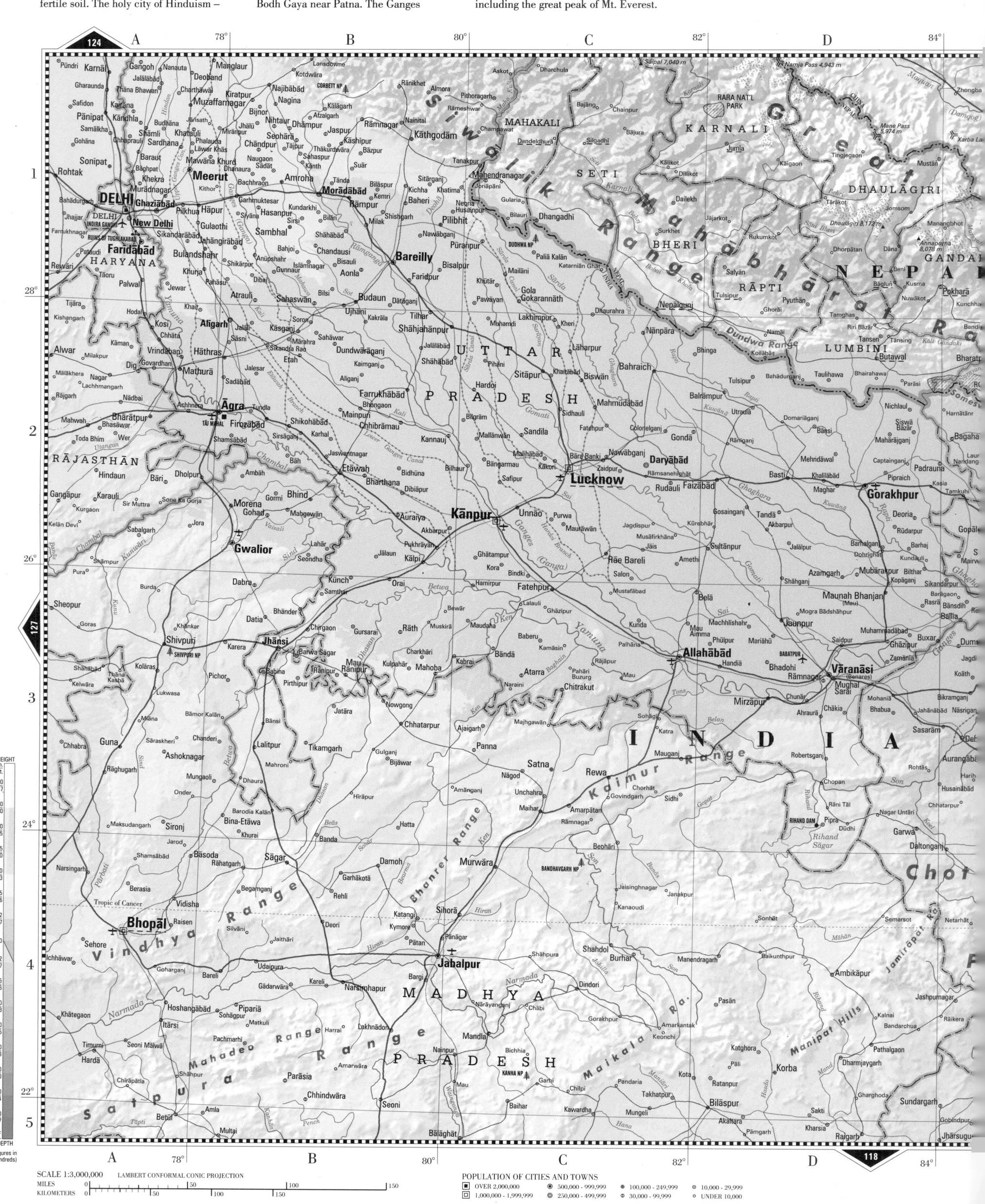

SCALE 1:3,000,000 LAMBERT CONFORMAL CONIC PROJECTION

MILES 0   50   100   150
KILOMETERS 0   50   100   150

POPULATION OF CITIES AND TOWNS
■ OVER 2,000,000
□ 1,000,000 - 1,999,999
◉ 500,000 - 999,999
◉ 250,000 - 499,999
● 100,000 - 249,999
◎ 30,000 - 99,999
○ 10,000 - 29,999
○ UNDER 10,000

122-123

Ganges Plain

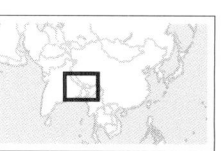

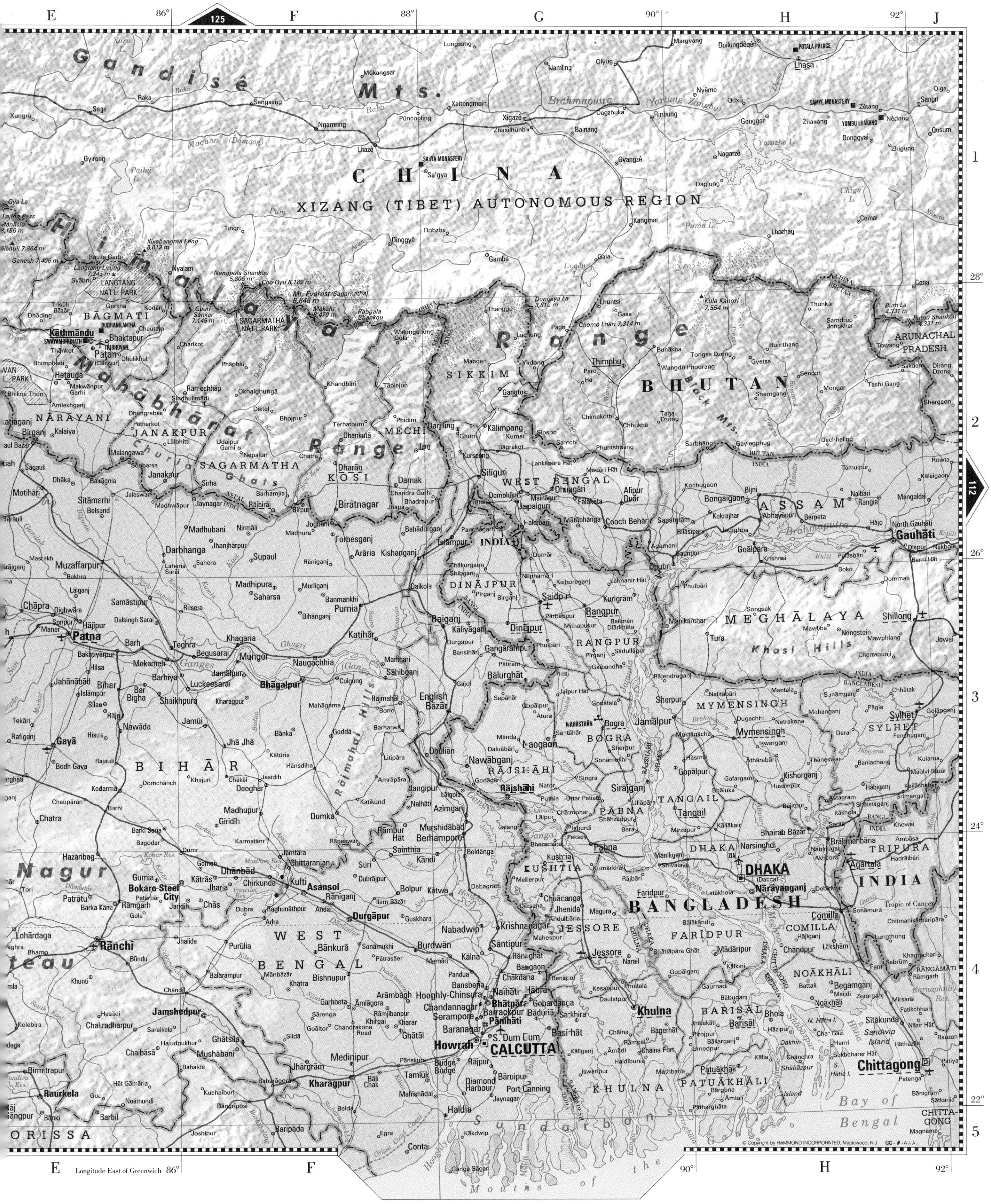

E
86°
125
F
88°
G
90°
H
92°
J
Gandisê Mts.
CHINA
XIZANG (TIBET) AUTONOMOUS REGION
Himalaya Range
Mahābhārat Range
Churia Ghats
BHUTAN
Black Mts.
SIKKIM
Lhasa
POTALA PALACE
Xigazê
Gyangzê
Kāthmāndu
Thimphu
Gangtok
Darjiling
Siliguri
WEST BENGAL
ASSAM
Gauhāti
Brahmaputra
MEGHĀLAYA
Shillong
Khasi Hills
ARUNACHAL PRADESH
BĀGMATI
NĀRĀYANI
JANAKPUR
SAGARMATHA
KOSI
MECHI
Biratnagar
Patna
Gayā
Ganges
BIHĀR
Bhāgalpur
Munger
Muzaffarpur
Darbhanga
Purnia
Rājmahal Hills
DINĀJPUR
RANGPUR
Rangpur
Dinājpur
BOGRA
Bogra
RĀJSHĀHI
Rājshāhi
PĀBNA
Pābna
TANGAIL
Tangail
MYMENSINGH
Mymensingh
SYLHET
Sylhet
DHAKA
Narāyanganj
KUSHTIA
JESSORE
Jessore
FARĪDPUR
Faridpur
BANGLADESH
COMILLA
Comilla
TRIPURA
Agartala
INDIA
Tropic of Cancer
NOĀKHĀLI
BARISĀL
Barisāl
Khulna
KHULNA
PATUĀKHĀLI
Chittagong
CHITTAGONG
Bay of Bengal
Sundarbans
Mouths of the Ganges
CALCUTTA
Howrah
Hooghly-Chinsura
Barrackpur
Haldia
Kharagpur
Medinipur
WEST BENGAL
Bānkurā
Burdwān
Durgāpur
Āsansol
Dhanbād
Bokaro Steel City
Rānchi
Jamshedpur
Raurkela
ORISSA
Nagur
teau
Mt. Everest (Sagarmatha) 8,848 m
Kānchenjunga
Makālu 8,470 m
Cho Oyu 8,189 m
Kula Kangri 7,554 m
Chomo Lhāri 7,314 m
Xixabangma Feng 8,012 m
SAGARMATHA NAT'L PARK
LANGTANG NAT'L PARK
Longitude East of Greenwich
28°
26°
24°
22°
1
2
3
4
5
112
© Copyright by HAMMOND INCORPORATED, Maplewood, N.J.

Punjab Plain

The fertile Punjab plain, formed by the Indus River and its tributaries, plays an important part in Indian history. It is also the focus of intense religious and political conflict between a Muslim Pakistan and a predominantly Hindu India. India's various separatist groups seeking greater communal or regional authority further compounds the tension in this region.

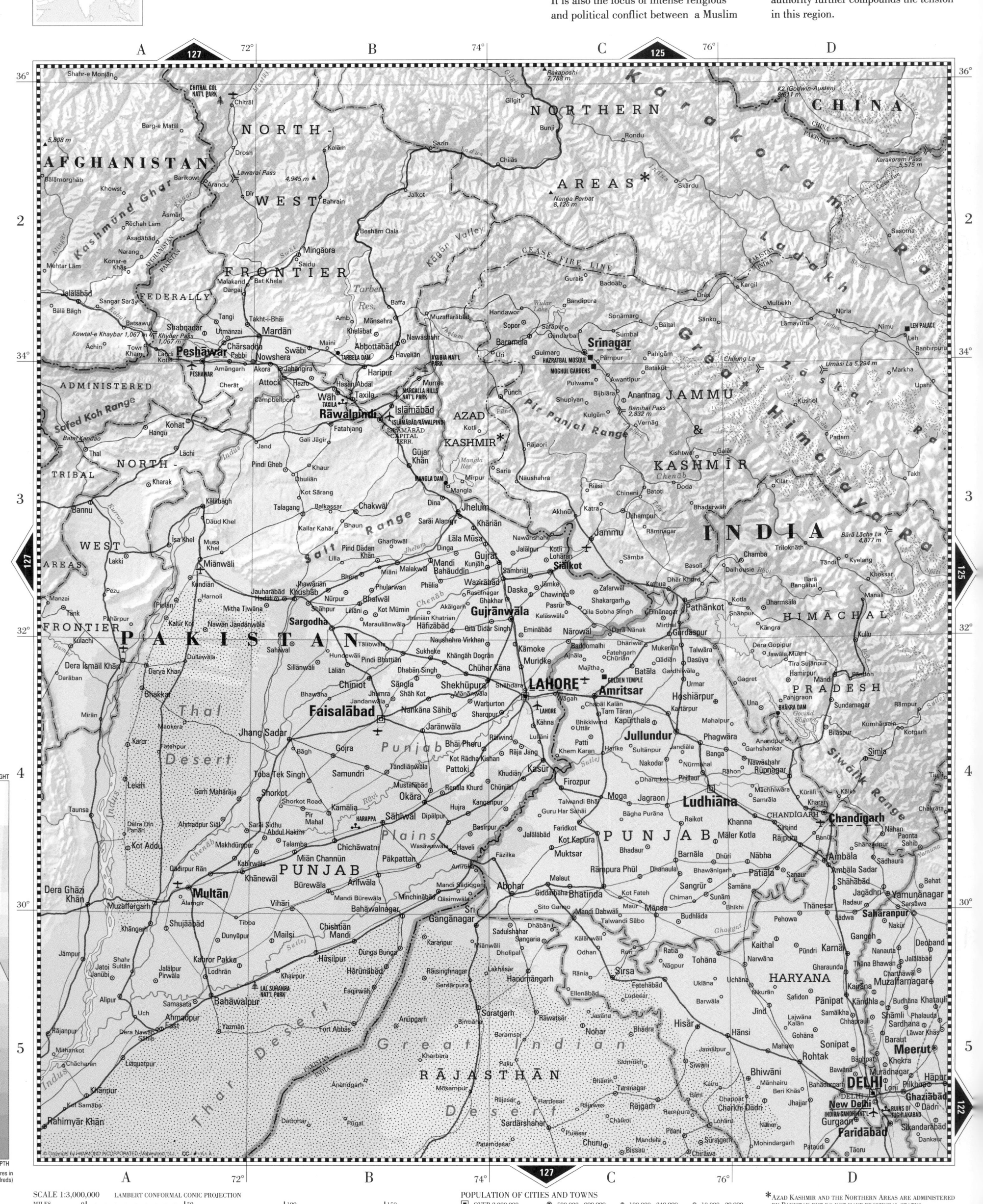

SCALE 1:3,000,000   LAMBERT CONFORMAL CONIC PROJECTION

MILES 0 ⊢⊣⊢⊣⊢⊣⊢⊣⊢⊣ 50 ⊢⊣⊢⊣ 100 ⊢⊣ 150

KILOMETERS 0 ⊢⊣⊢⊣⊢⊣ 50 ⊢⊣⊢⊣ 100 ⊢⊣ 150

POPULATION OF CITIES AND TOWNS

■ OVER 2,000,000   ● 500,000 - 999,999   ● 100,000 - 249,999   ○ 10,000 - 29,999
▢ 1,000,000 - 1,999,999   ● 250,000 - 499,999   ● 30,000 - 99,999   ○ UNDER 10,000

*AZAD KASHMIR AND THE NORTHERN AREAS ARE ADMINISTERED BY PAKISTAN BUT DO NOT HAVE PROVINCIAL STATUS.

Central Asia

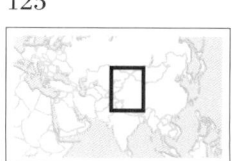

Known as the "Roof of the World," central Asia is dominated by the vast mountain systems of the Hindu Kush, the Pamir, the Tian Shan and the Himalayas, extending over 1600 miles (2400 km.) from Pakistan to Bhutan. Although isolated, great civilizations - Post-Alexandrian Greece, Imperial China, the Indian empires, the Turks and Mongols - first met in this region.

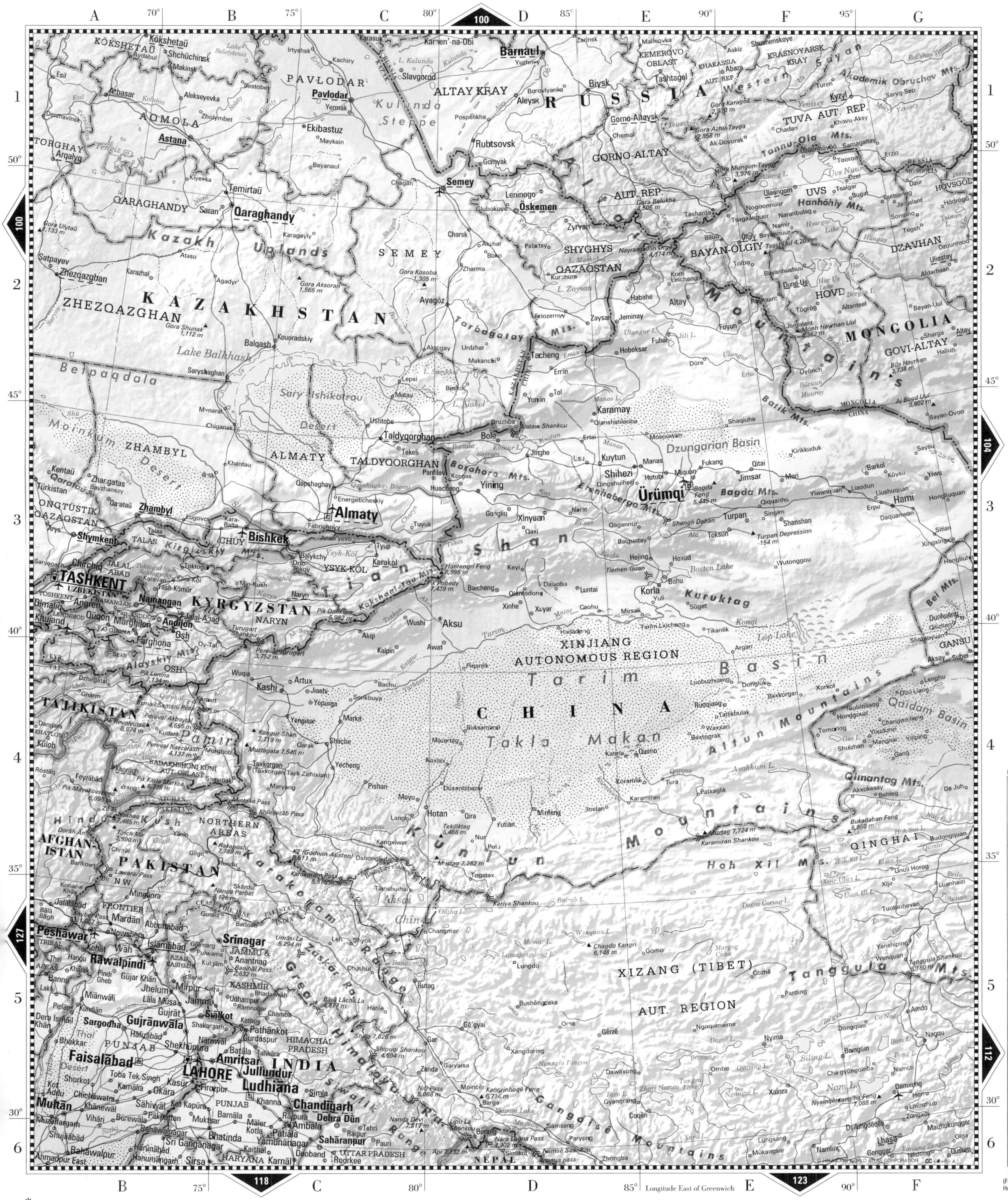

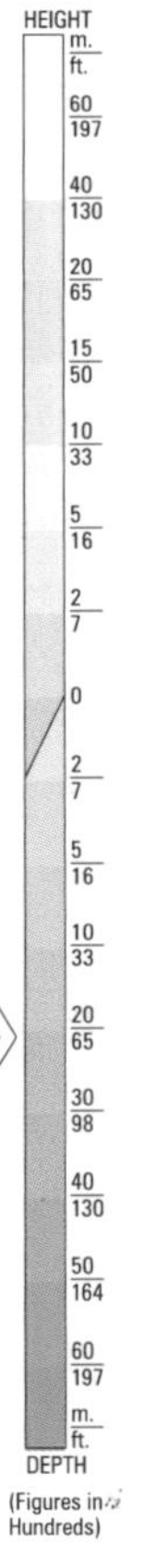

*AZAD KASHMIR AND THE NORTHERN AREAS ARE ADMINISTERED BY PAKISTAN BUT DO NOT HAVE PROVINCIAL STATUS.

POPULATION OF CITIES AND TOWNS

SCALE 1:9,000,000   LAMBERT CONFORMAL CONIC PROJECTION

Two great powers rule this parched land: Islam and oil. Barren desert stretches from the Arabian Peninsula to western Pakistan. Three productive river valleys: the Jordan, Tigris-Euphrates, and Indus provide relief. Mohammed, the founder of Islam, lived in Mecca. After his Hegira to Medina, Muslim horsemen swept out of Arabia to conquer the Middle East, North Africa, and beyond. The immense oil wealth of the Persian Gulf region, combined with rising oil demand, has extended the area's influence still further, transforming it into a center of global power.

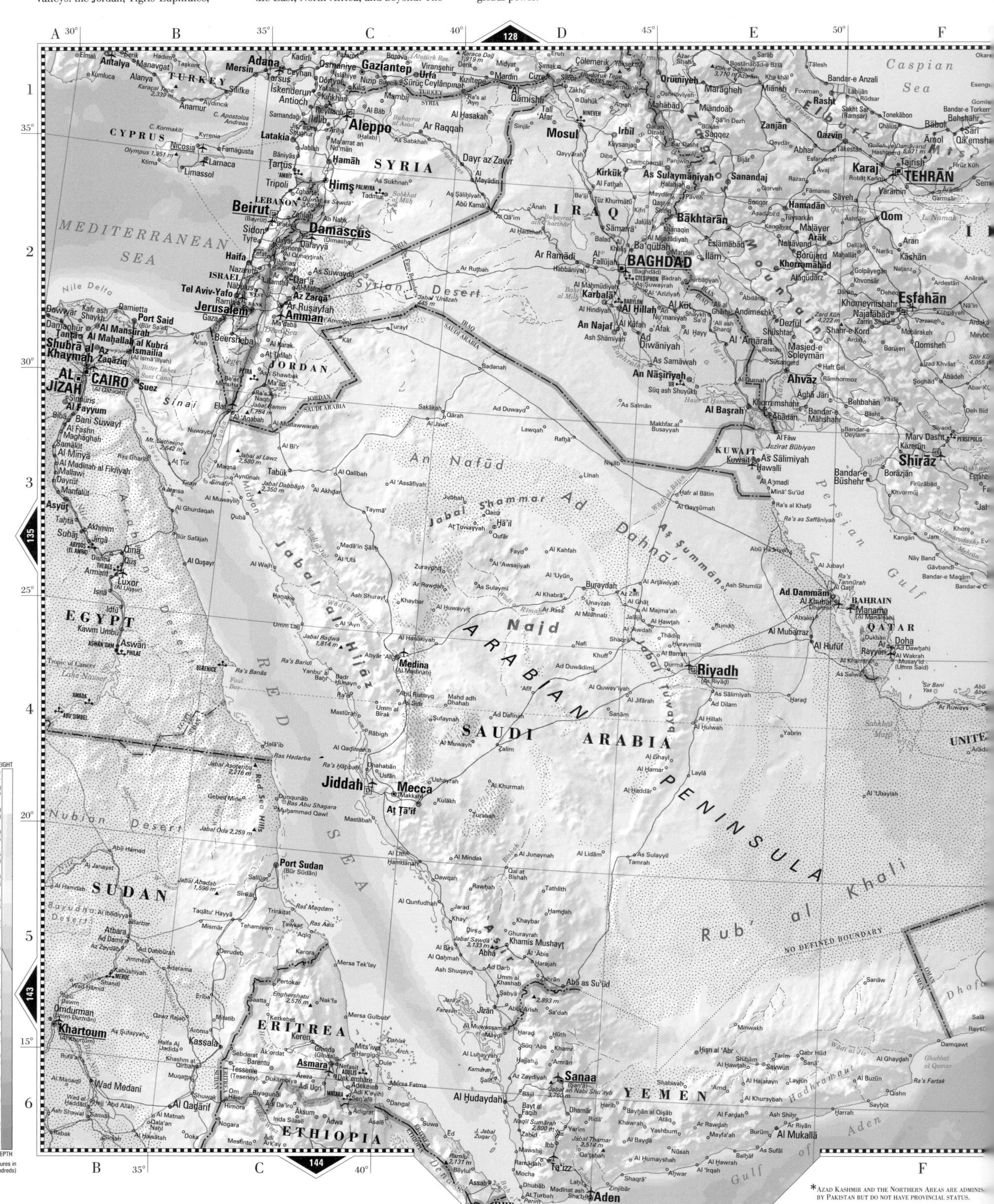

*AZAD KASHMIR AND THE NORTHERN AREAS ARE ADMINISTERED BY PAKISTAN BUT DO NOT HAVE PROVINCIAL STATUS.

Southwestern Asia

TURKMENISTAN

UZBEKISTAN

TAJIKISTAN

CHINA

AFGHANISTAN

Kabul (Kābol)

PAKISTAN

BALOCHISTAN

SINDH

PUNJAB

INDIA

RĀJASTHĀN

GUJARĀT

MADHYA PRADESH

MAHĀRĀSHTRA

KARNATAKA

HARYANA

HIMĀCHAL PRADESH

IRAN

OMAN

ARAB EMIRATES

Ashgabat

Mashhad

Herāt

Peshāwar

Rāwalpindi

Islāmābād

Srīnagar

LAHORE

Ludhiāna

Chandīgarh

DELHI

New Delhi

Faridābād

Meerut

Jaipur

KARACHI

Hyderābād

AHMADĀBĀD

Vadodara

Surat

MUMBAI (Bombay)

Pune

Pimpri-Chinchwad

Kalyān

Thāne

Ulhāsnagar

Sholāpur

Hubli-Dhārwār

Quetta

Multān

Faisalābād

Gujrānwāla

Amritsar

Jullundur

Muscat

Kermān

Zāhedān

Bandar-e 'Abbās

Gulf of Oman

ARABIAN SEA

Gulf of Masira

Makran Coast

Tropic of Cancer

Dasht-e Lūt

Dasht-e Margow

Dasht-e Kavīr

Thar Desert

Hindu Kush

Karakoram Ra.

Great Himālaya Range

Rann of Kutch

Gulf of Kutch

Gulf of Cambay

Kathiawar

Longitude East of Greenwich

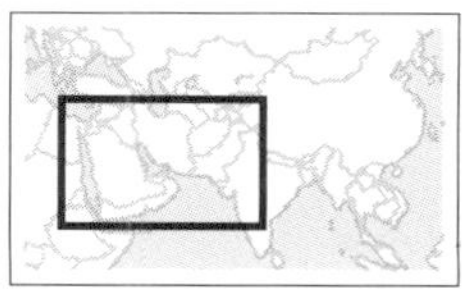

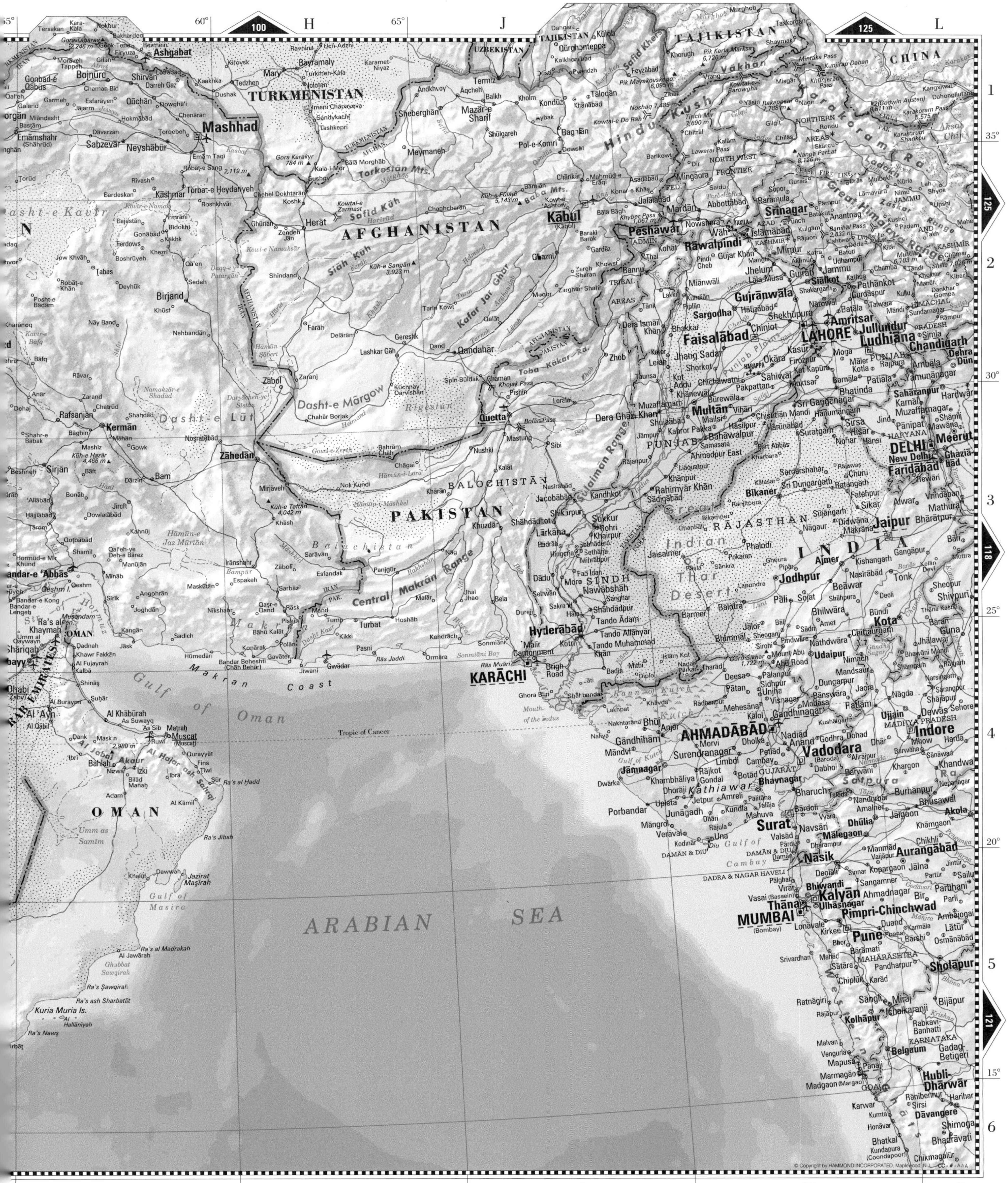

SCALE 1:9,000,000   LAMBERT CONFORMAL CONIC PROJECTION

POPULATION OF CITIES AND TOWNS

OVER 2,000,000
1,000,000 - 1,999,999
500,000 - 999,999
250,000 - 499,999
100,000 - 249,999
30,000 - 99,999
10,000 - 29,999
UNDER 10,000

MILES   0   150   300   450
KILOMETERS   0   150   300   450

© Copyright by HAMMOND INCORPORATED, Maplewood, N.J.

Recorded human history began here, on the fringes of the Fertile Crescent. Agriculture evolved along the Mediterranean coast and in the Tigris-Euphrates valleys, nurturing a sequence of great civilizations, from the Sumerian empire to the Babylonians, Egyptians, Hittites, Assyrians, Persians, Saracens and Turks. Today, Muslim fundamentalism is a powerful force throughout the area. Nationalistic aspirations among Armenians, Azerbaijani and Kurds transgress current political boundaries and keep parts of the region in a highly volatile state.

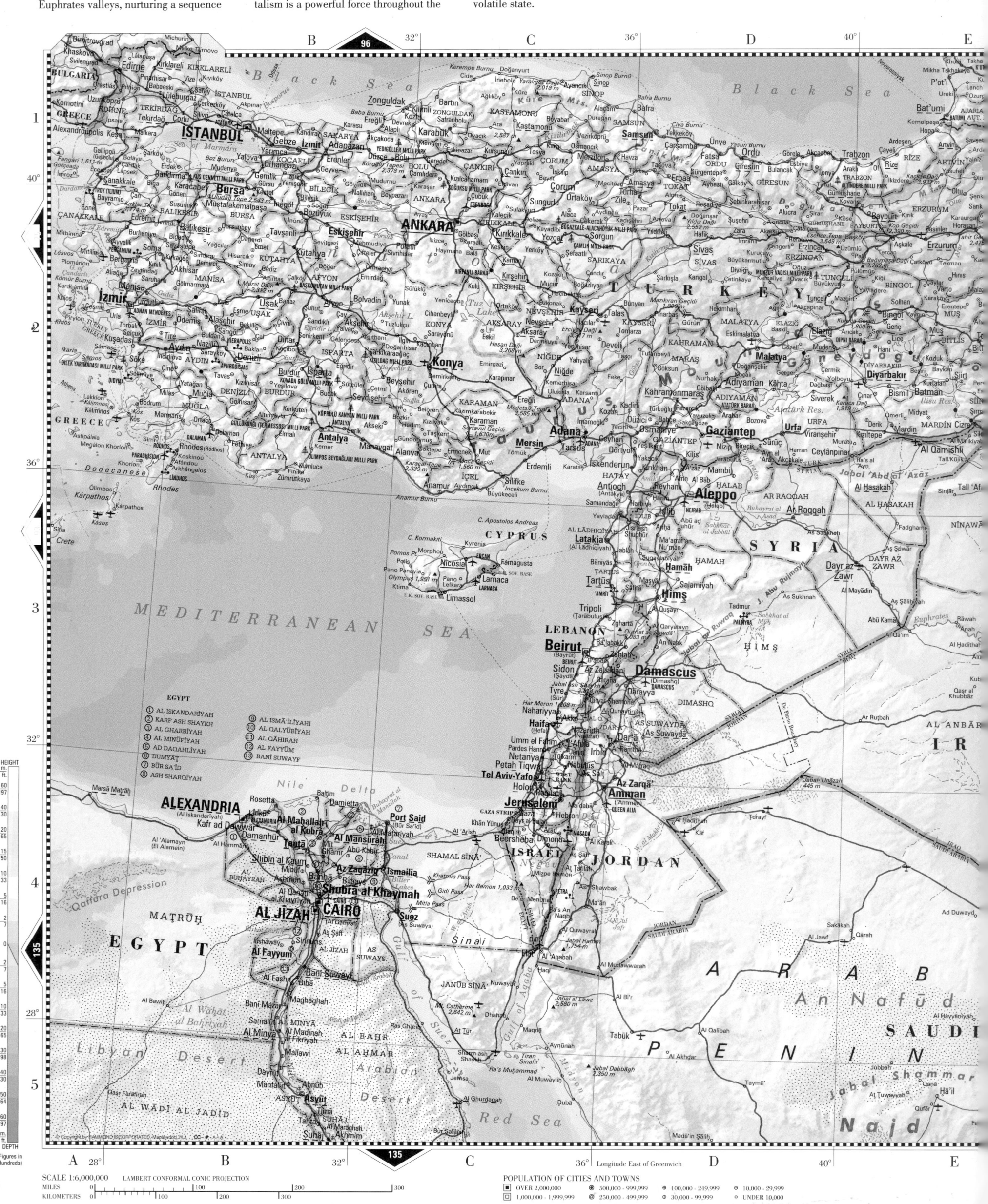

EGYPT
① AL ISKANDARĪYAH
② KARF ASH SHAYKH
③ AL GHARBĪYAH
④ AL MINŪFĪYAH
⑤ AD DAQAHLĪYAH
⑥ DUMYĀŢ
⑦ BŪR SAʿĪD
⑧ ASH SHARQĪYAH
⑨ AL ISMĀʿĪLĪYAH
⑩ AL QALYŪBĪYAH
⑪ AL QĀHIRAH
⑫ AL FAYYŪM
⑬ BANĪ SUWAYF

SCALE 1:6,000,000   LAMBERT CONFORMAL CONIC PROJECTION
MILES   0   100   200   300
KILOMETERS 0   100   200   300

POPULATION OF CITIES AND TOWNS
■ OVER 2,000,000   □ 500,000 - 999,999   ● 100,000 - 249,999   ⊙ 10,000 - 29,999
□ 1,000,000 - 1,999,999   ● 250,000 - 499,999   ⊙ 30,000 - 99,999   ○ UNDER 10,000

Northern Middle East

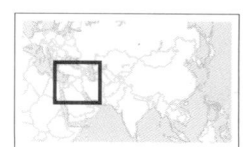

97
126
127
44°
48°
52°
29°
41°
36°
32°
28°
F
G
H
M
N
2
3
4
5
6
7
RUSSIA
GEORGIA
AZERBAIJAN
ARMENIA
AZER.
TURKMENISTAN
IRAN
KUWAIT
Caucasus
Lesser Caucasus
Elburz Mountains
Zagros Mountains
CASPIAN SEA
Persian Gulf
Strait of Hormuz
Black Sea
Sea of Marmara
Dasht-e Kavir
Dasht-e Lūt
T'bilisi
Yerevan
Baku
TEHRĀN
BAGHDAD
Tabrīz
Mosul
Kirkūk
Eşfahān
Shīrāz
Qom
Hamadān
Bakhtarān
Ahvāz
Al Başrah
Kuwait
Bandar-e 'Abbās
Kermān
Yazd
Ashgabat
Rasht
Sumqayıt
Gäncä
Gyumri
İSTANBUL
Kâğıthane
Bekoz
Pendik
Maltepe
Avcılar
Ardabīl
Orūmīyeh
Zanjān
Qazvīn
Karaj
Sanandaj
Arāk
Khorramābād
Dezfūl
An Najaf
Karbalā'
Al Ḩillah
An Nāşirīyah
Bandar-e Būshehr
Bushehr
Sabzevār
Neyshābūr
Gorgān
Sārī
Semnān
Kāshān
KHORĀSĀN
EŞFAHĀN
FĀRS
KERMĀN
HORMOZGĀN
Ra's al Khaymah
OMAN
© HAMMOND INC. CC-1113

Eastern Mediterranean Region

This is the traditional Holy Land of three of the world's great religions, Judaism, Christianity and Islam. Today, the Eastern Mediterranean, or Levant, region suffers from ethnic and religious struggles: Christians vs. Muslims in Lebanon, Greeks vs. Turks on the island of Cyprus, and continuing Arab-Israeli conflicts at the local settlement level in the West Bank.

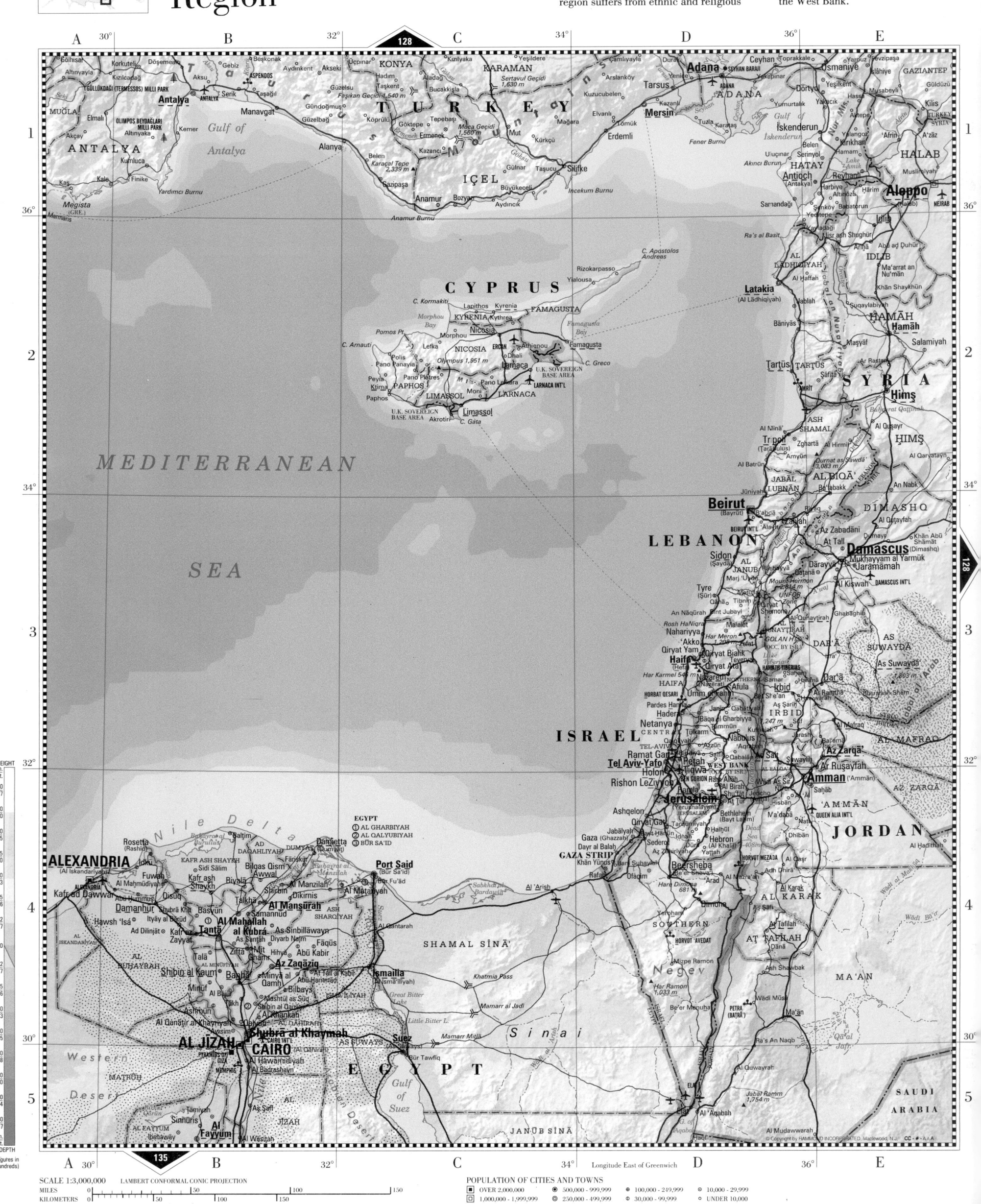

SCALE 1:3,000,000   LAMBERT CONFORMAL CONIC PROJECTION

MILES

KILOMETERS

Longitude East of Greenwich

POPULATION OF CITIES AND TOWNS

◼ OVER 2,000,000
◻ 1,000,000 - 1,999,999
⬛ 500,000 - 999,999
⬜ 250,000 - 499,999
● 100,000 - 249,999
◉ 30,000 - 99,999
◎ 10,000 - 29,999
○ UNDER 10,000

Jordan River Valley

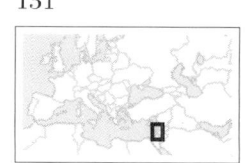

Much of Israel and the West Bank consist of highlands, which descend in the east into the Jordan River Valley and in the west into a narrow coastal plain bordering the Mediterranean Sea. The Dead Sea depression is the lowest land on earth. This region is home to people of various religions and ethnic divisions, as well as a multitude of historic and religious sites.

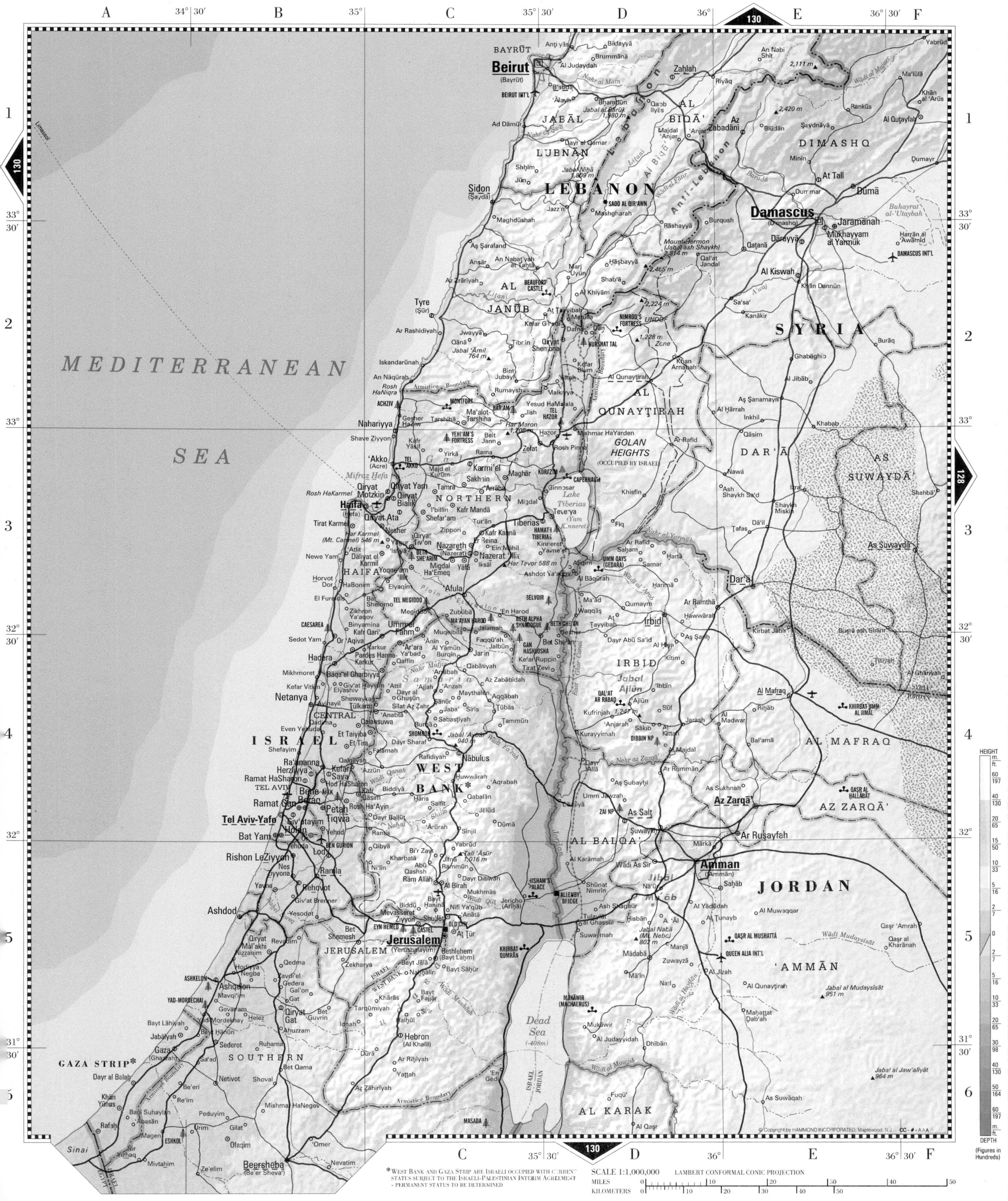

MEDITERRANEAN SEA

LEBANON

Beirut (Bayrūt)

Damascus (Dimashq)

SYRIA

GOLAN HEIGHTS (OCCUPIED BY ISRAEL)

ISRAEL

WEST BANK *

JORDAN

GAZA STRIP *

Jerusalem (Yerushalayim)

Tel Aviv-Yafo

Amman ('Ammān)

Dead Sea (-408m)

West Bank and Gaza Strip are Israeli occupied with current status subject to the Israeli-Palestinian Interim Agreement — permanent status to be determined

SCALE 1:1,000,000   LAMBERT CONFORMAL CONIC PROJECTION

MILES
KILOMETERS

HEIGHT
m. ft.

DEPTH
(Figures in Hundreds)

Copyright by HAMMOND INCORPORATED, Maplewood, N.J.

Africa

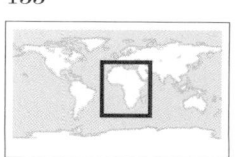

Several physiographic features are captured in this southeast-looking, high-oblique image. The Nile River Delta, the large, dark area at the bottom of the image, extends from the capital city of Cairo at the apex of the delta to the Suez Canal. The entire region is classified as desert (less than 10 inches [25 cm.] of rainfall per year). Desert-like areas are visible southwest of the delta and in the northwestern Sinai. Major rock outcrops (darker areas) are seen encircling the Red Sea. The two bodies of water flanking the southern end of the Sinai Peninsula are the Gulf of Suez and the Gulf of Aqaba.

Egypt is one of the most populous countries in Africa. The majority of its population lives within a dozen miles of the Nile River or one of its branches. The world's longest river (4,145 miles or 6632 km.), the Nile , through irrigation, supports almost all of the country's agriculture. Because of this, only a small percentage of Egypt's total land area is available for crops.

Oil has profoundly transformed life in this region. Libya, with a relatively small population, has significant oil reserves and has used them to exert political influence.

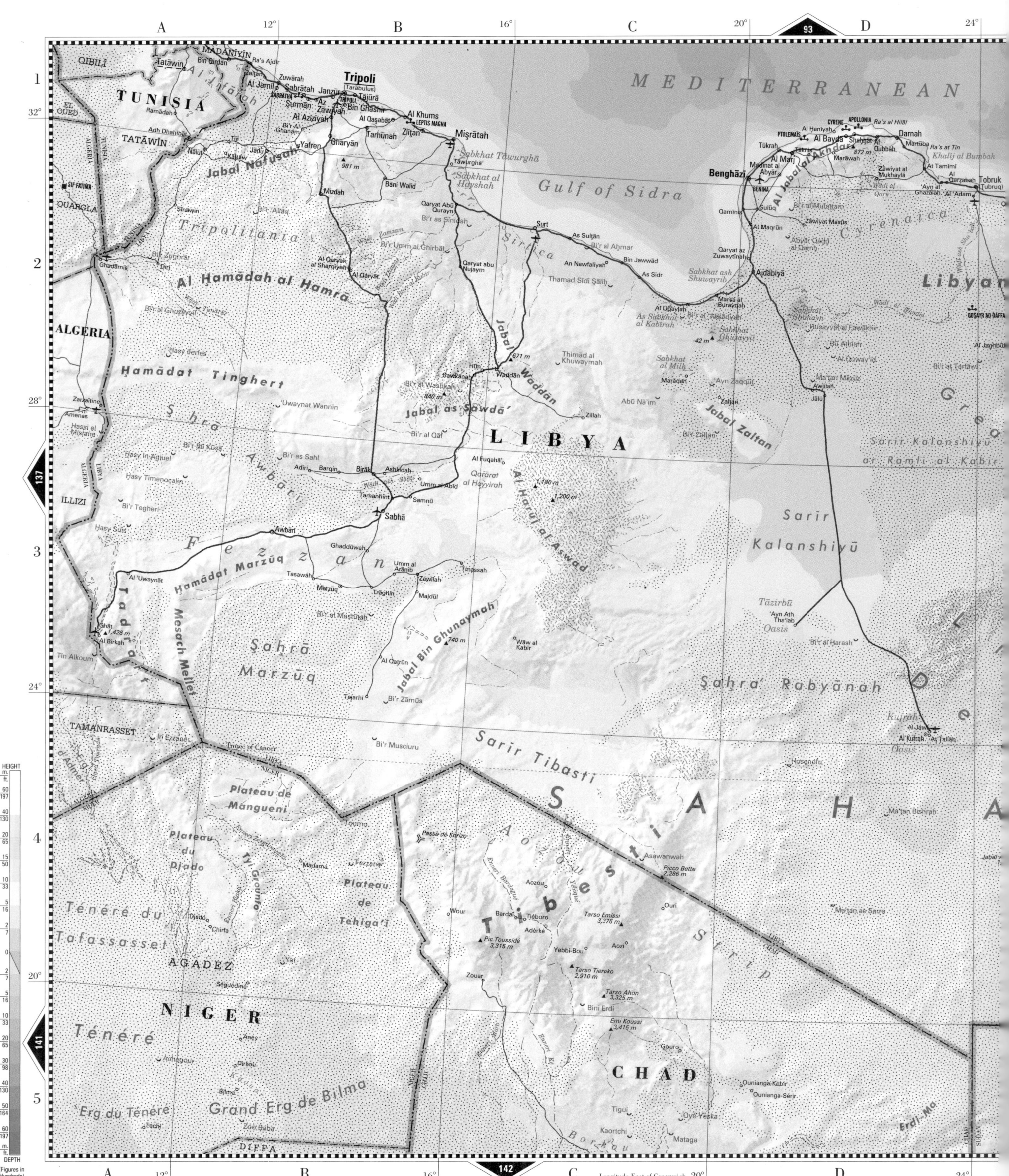

Northeastern Africa

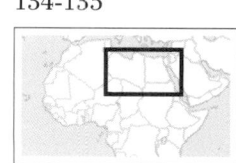

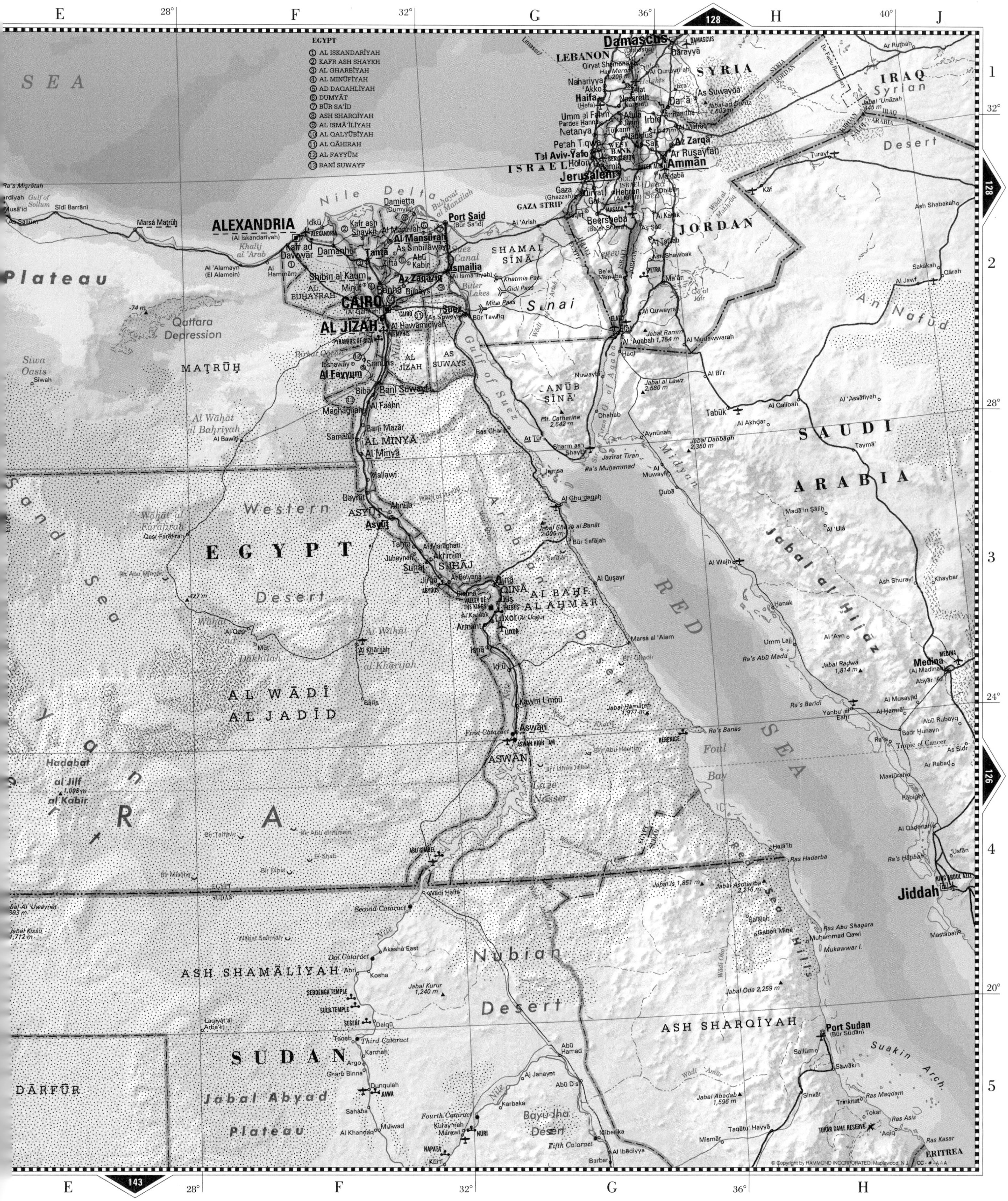

EGYPT
① AL ISKANDARÏYAH
② KAFR ASH SHAYKH
③ AL GHARBÏYAH
④ AL MINÜFÏYAH
⑤ AD DAQAHLÏYAH
⑥ DUMYÄT
⑦ BÜR SA'ÏD
⑧ ASH SHARQÏYAH
⑨ AL ISMÄ'ÏLIYAH
⑩ AL QALYÜBÏYAH
⑪ AL QÄHIRAH
⑫ AL FAYYÜM
⑬ BANÏ SUWAYF

SEA

Plateau

SAUDI ARABIA

EGYPT

Western Desert

Libyan Desert

AL WÄDÏ AL JADÏD

RED SEA

SUDAN

DÄRFÜR

ASH SHAMÄLÏYAH

Nubian Desert

ASH SHARQÏYAH

ERITREA

POPULATION OF CITIES AND TOWNS
■ OVER 2,000,000
□ 1,000,000 - 1,999,999
● 500,000 - 999,999
◎ 250,000 - 499,999
● 100,000 - 249,999
○ 30,000 - 99,999
• 10,000 - 29,999
· UNDER 10,000

SCALE 1:6,000,000   POLYCONIC PROJECTION
MILES 0   50   100   200   300
KILOMETERS 0 50 100   200   300

© Copyright by HAMMOND INCORPORATED, Maplewood, N. J.

The Sahara, the world's greatest desert, covers 3,500,000 square miles (9,100,000 sq. km.) and is 3100 miles (4960 km.) long and 1100 miles (1760 km.) wide. Extreme temperatures, as high as 136° Fahrenheit (58° C), have been recorded here. In addition, this region includes the Atlas Mountains, a structural extension of the Alpine system of Europe. These mountains trap needed moisture for the valleys in Algeria and Tunisia. Mali, Mauritania and Western Sahara are largely desert areas with subsistence-level agricultural economies.

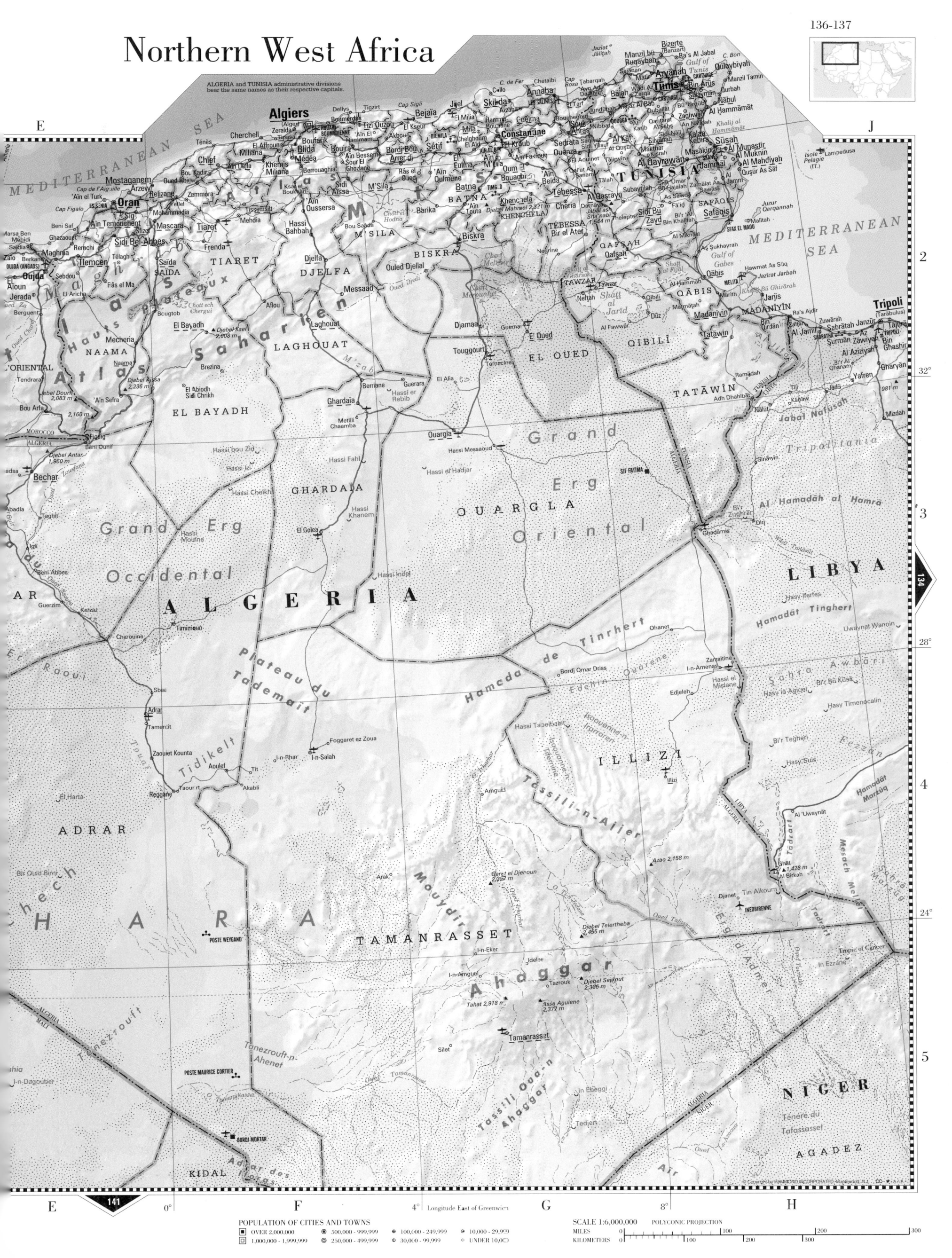

Northern West Africa

ALGERIA and TUNISIA administrative divisions
bear the same names as their respective capitals.

POPULATION OF CITIES AND TOWNS

■ OVER 2,000,000	● 500,000-999,999	● 100,000-249,999	● 10,000-29,999
▣ 1,000,000-1,999,999	● 250,000-499,999	● 30,000-99,999	○ UNDER 10,000

Longitude East of Greenwich

SCALE 1:6,000,000   POLYCONIC PROJECTION

MILES 0 ___ 100 ___ 200 ___ 300

KILOMETERS 0 ___ 100 ___ 200 ___ 300

© Copyright by RAND McNALLY INCORPORATED • Made in U.S.A.

Northern Morocco, Algeria, Tunisia

The Maghreb (the Arabic name for the northwest African countries of Morocco, Algeria and Tunisia), inhabited by Berbers and Arabs, has seen the rise and fall of Carthaginians, Romans, Byzantines, Moors and the Barbary pirates. Tunisia and Morocco gained their independence from France in 1956. Algeria won its independence from France in 1962 after an eight year war.

SCALE 1:3,000,000   LAMBERT CONFORMAL CONIC PROJECTION

MILES   0   50   100   150
KILOMETERS   0   50   100   150

HEIGHT
m. ft.
60 / 197
40 / 130
20 / 65
15 / 50
10 / 33
5 / 16
2 / 7
2 / 7
5 / 16
10 / 33
20 / 65
30 / 98
40 / 130
50 / 164
60 / 197
m. ft.
DEPTH
(Figures in Hundreds)

POPULATION OF CITIES AND TOWNS
- OVER 2,000,000
- 1,000,000 - 1,999,999
- 500,000 - 999,999
- 250,000 - 499,999
- 100,000 - 249,999
- 30,000 - 99,999
- 10,000 - 29,999
- UNDER 10,000

MOROCCO
① MOHAMMADIA-ZNATA
② BEN MSIK-SIDI OTHMANE
③ CASABLANCA-ANFA
④ AÏN CHOK-HAY MOHAMMADIA

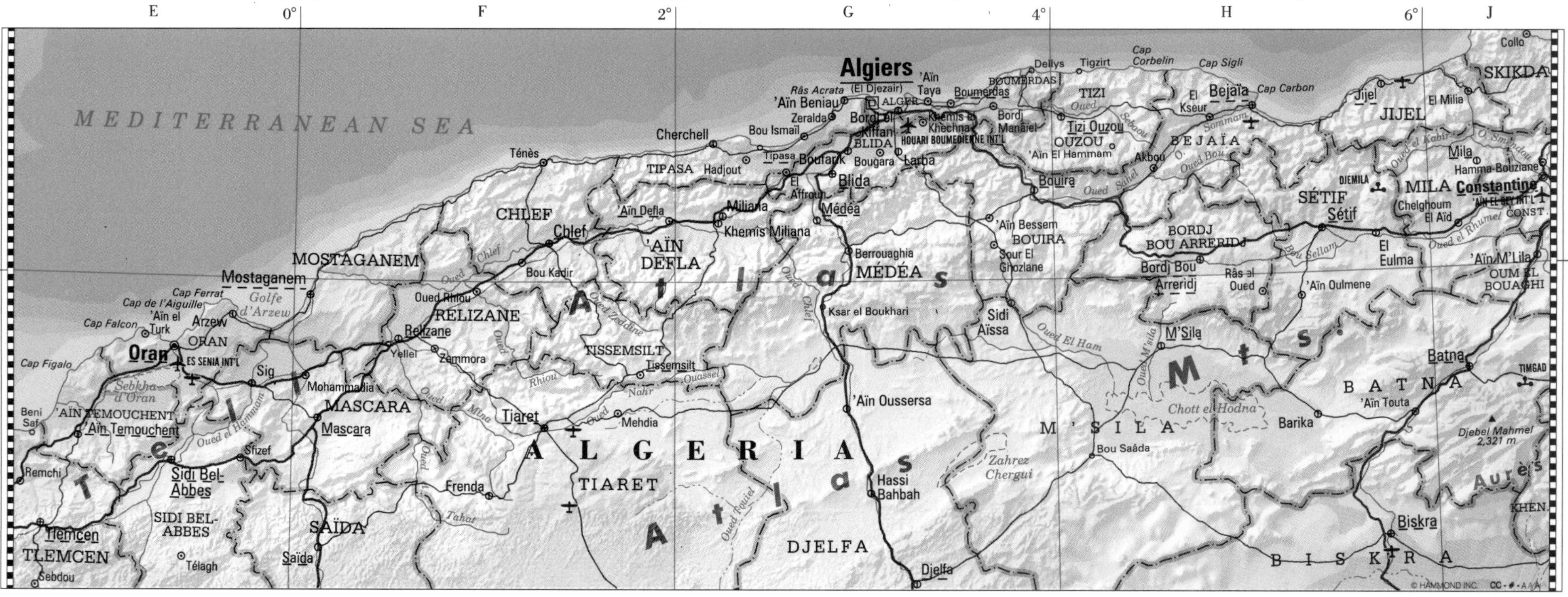

Nile River Delta

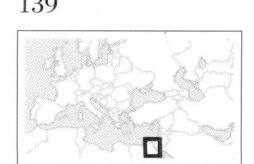

The valley and delta of the Nile River cut through the desert plateaus of Egypt. Canals criss-cross the fertile delta. This region also includes greater Cairo, with it's large urban population. Alexandria is a major industrial center and important harbor for exports and imports. The Suez Canal provides an important link between the Mediterranean and Red seas.

MEDITERRANEAN SEA

Rosetta Mouth (Massabb Rashid)

Damietta Mouth (Massabb Dumyāt)

ALEXANDRIA
(Al Iskandarīyah)

Port Said
(Būr Sa'īd)

AL BUHAYRAH

AL GHARBĪYAH

KAFR ASH SHAYKH

AD DAQAHLĪYAH

DUMYĀT

Al Manşūrah

Țalkhā

Ṭanṭā

ASH SHARQĪYAH

Az Zaqāzīg

Ismailia
(Al Ismā'īlīyah)

AL MINŪFĪYAH

Shibīn al Kawm

AL QALYŪBĪYAH

AL JĪZAH

Shubrā al Khaymah

CAIRO
(Al Qāhirah)

AL QĀHIRAH

AL JĪZAH

Western Desert

Arabian Desert

AL ISMĀ'ĪLĪYAH

AS SUWAYS

Great Bitter Lake

MAȚRŪḤ

Jabal Qaṭrāni

Birkat Qārūn (-45m)

Al Fayyūm

AL FAYYŪM

BANĪ SUWAYF

Banī Suwayf

AL BAḤR AL AḤMAR

Jabal al Jalālah al Baḥrīyah

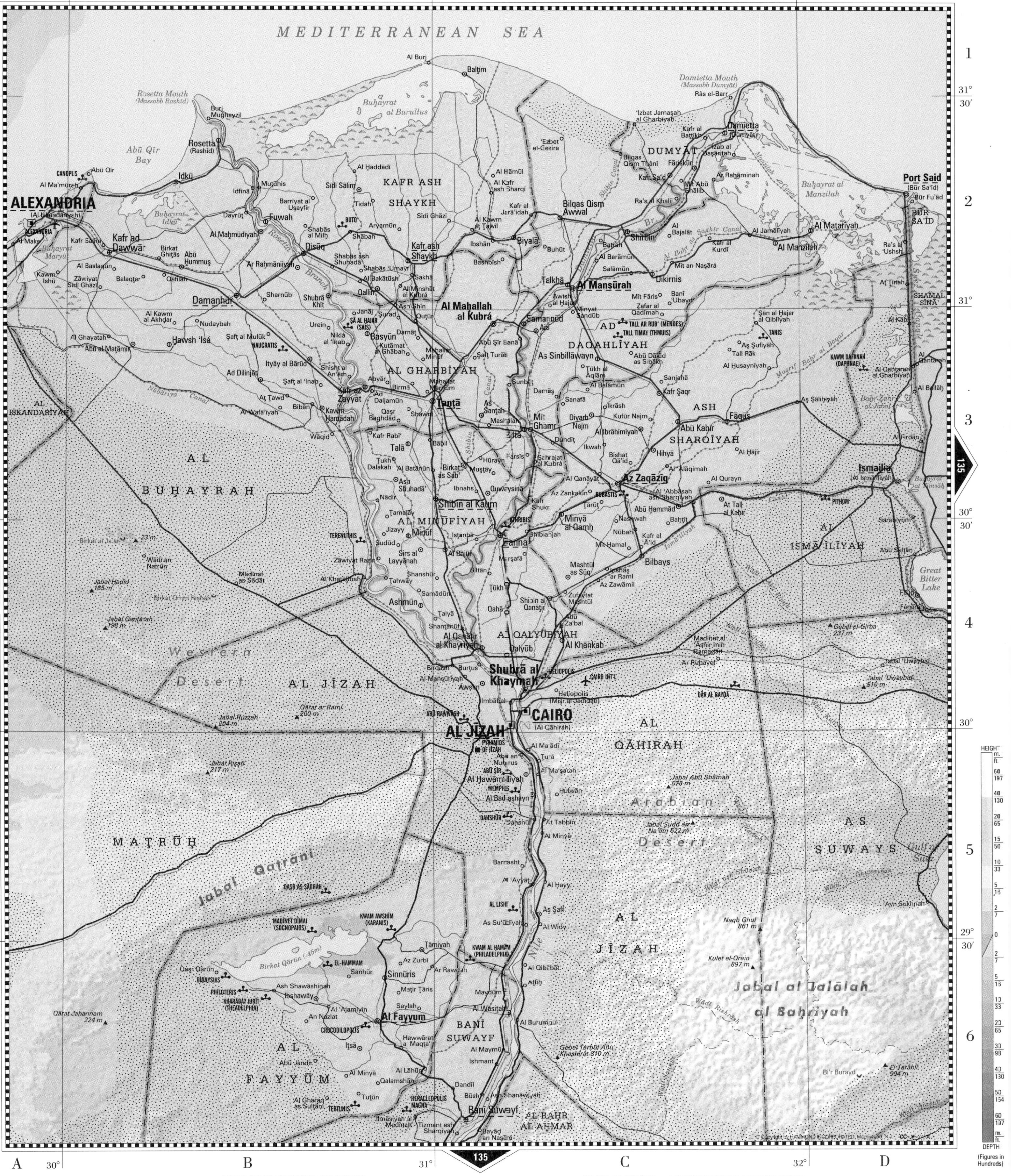

POPULATION OF CITIES AND TOWNS

■ OVER 2,000,000
□ 1,000,000 - 1,999,999
⊚ 500,000 - 999,999
◎ 250,000 - 499,999
● 100,000 - 249,999
◉ 30,000 - 99,999
◦ 10,000 - 29,999
○ UNDER 10,000

SCALE 1:1,000,000   LAMBERT CONFORMAL CONIC PROJECTION

MILES   0   10   20   30   40   50

KILOMETERS   0   10   20   30   40   50

HEIGHT
DEPTH
(Figures in Hundreds)

This region contains a significant diversity in environments, economies and life styles. It includes forests, savannas and deserts. A number of prosperous cities had evolved by the end of the 14th century. European activities in Black Africa began during the 15th century. Trade in slaves, gold, ivory and spices took firm hold in West Africa in part because this area was closest to European colonies in the Americas. African middlemen from coastal areas raided the interior for slaves, which weakened the interior savanna states and strengthened the coastal forest states.

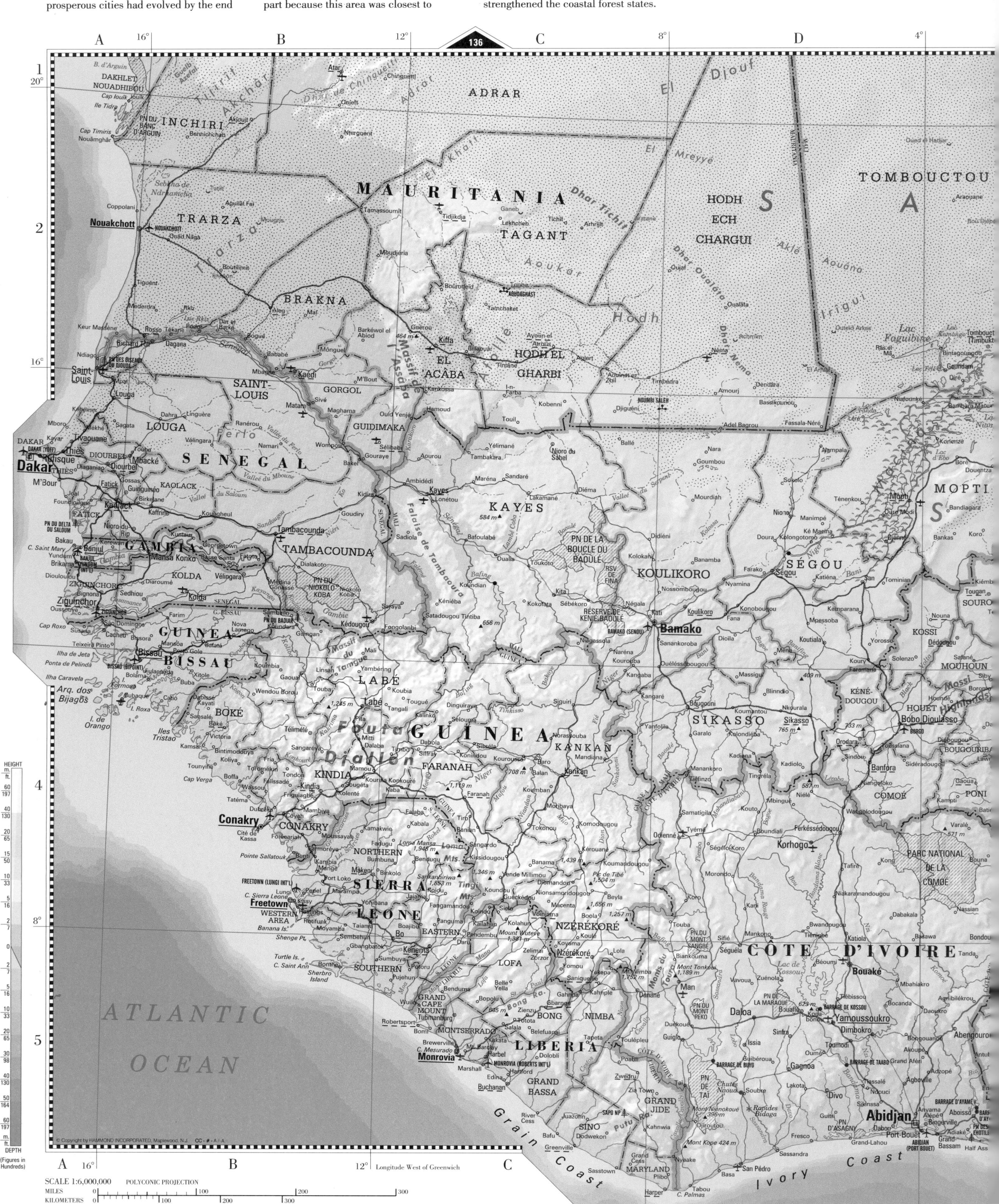

SCALE 1:6,000,000 POLYCONIC PROJECTION

MILES 0 100 200 300

KILOMETERS 0 100 200 300

Longitude West of Greenwich

Southern West Africa

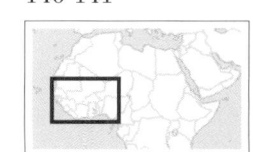

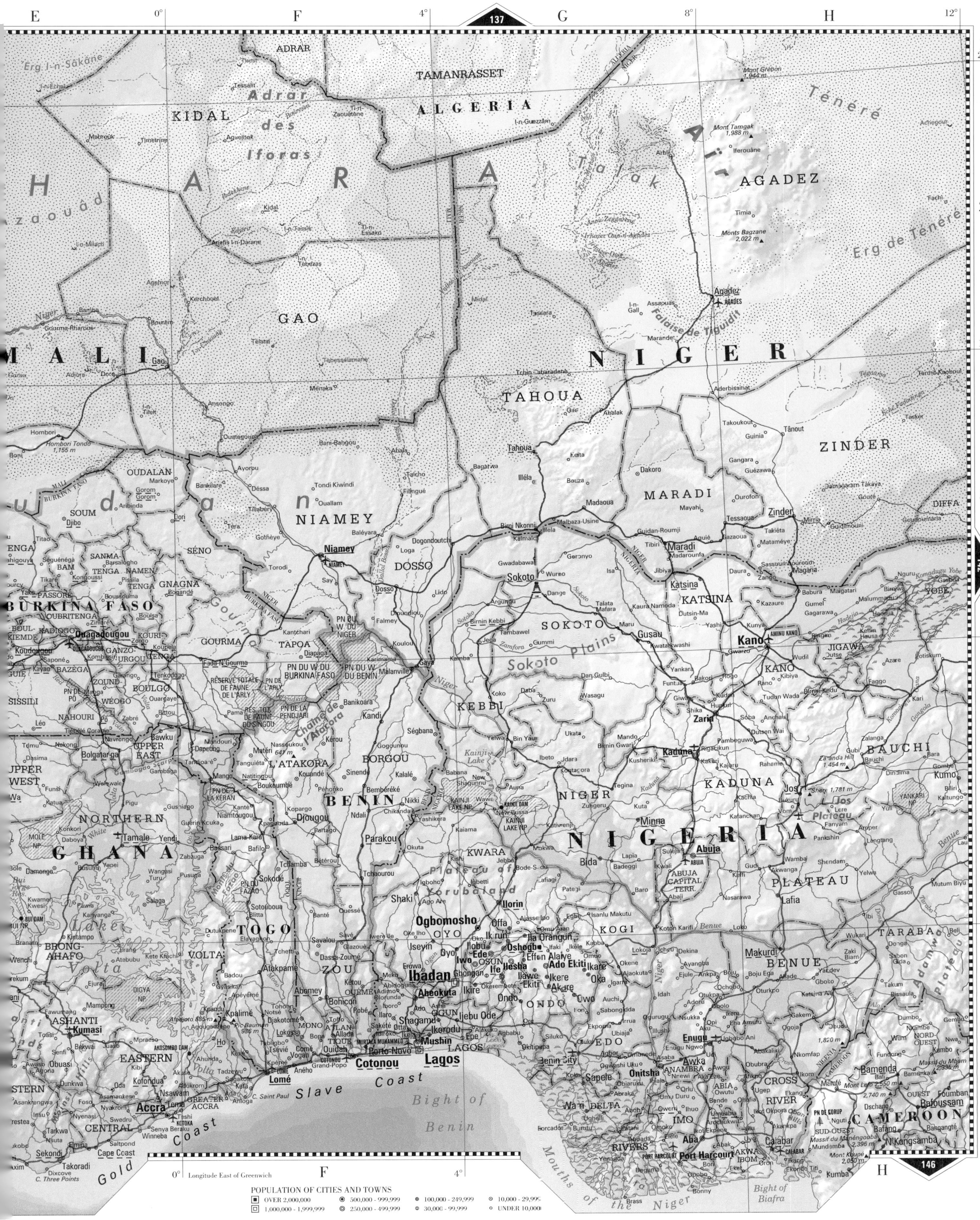

The great climatic band of savanna grassland and dry shrub country, stretching east to west north of the Congo Basin, is home to countless herds of cattle. Shifting rainfall patterns, and civil and ethnic wars, have cursed the region with famine, bringing periodic suffering to the peoples of Sudan and Chad. Cameroon and the Central African Republic contain more resources for agriculture, forestry and mining. This region is a transition zone where the cultures of Islam, traditions of Christianity and lifestyles of Black Africa both coexist and struggle with each other.

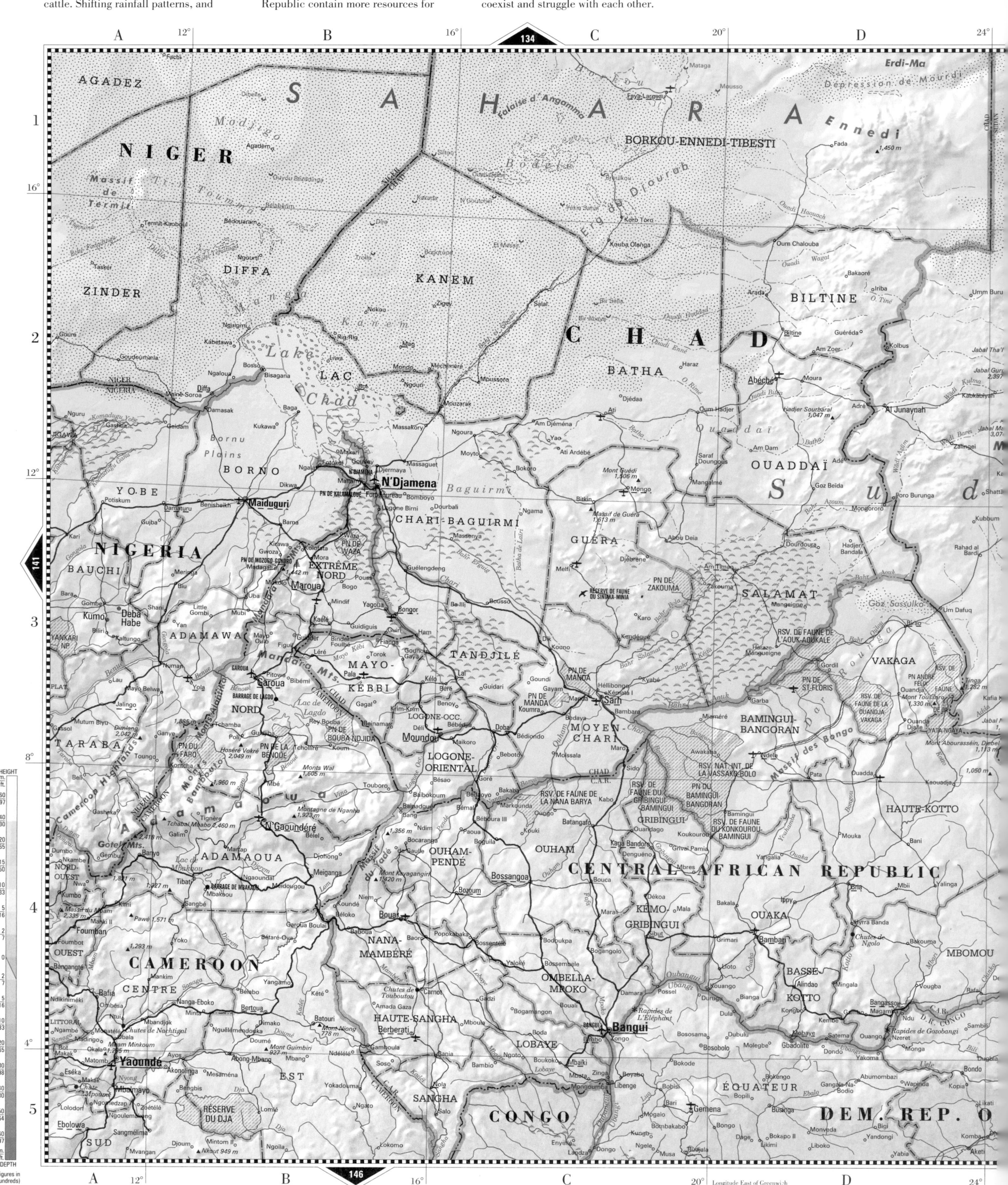

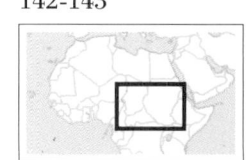

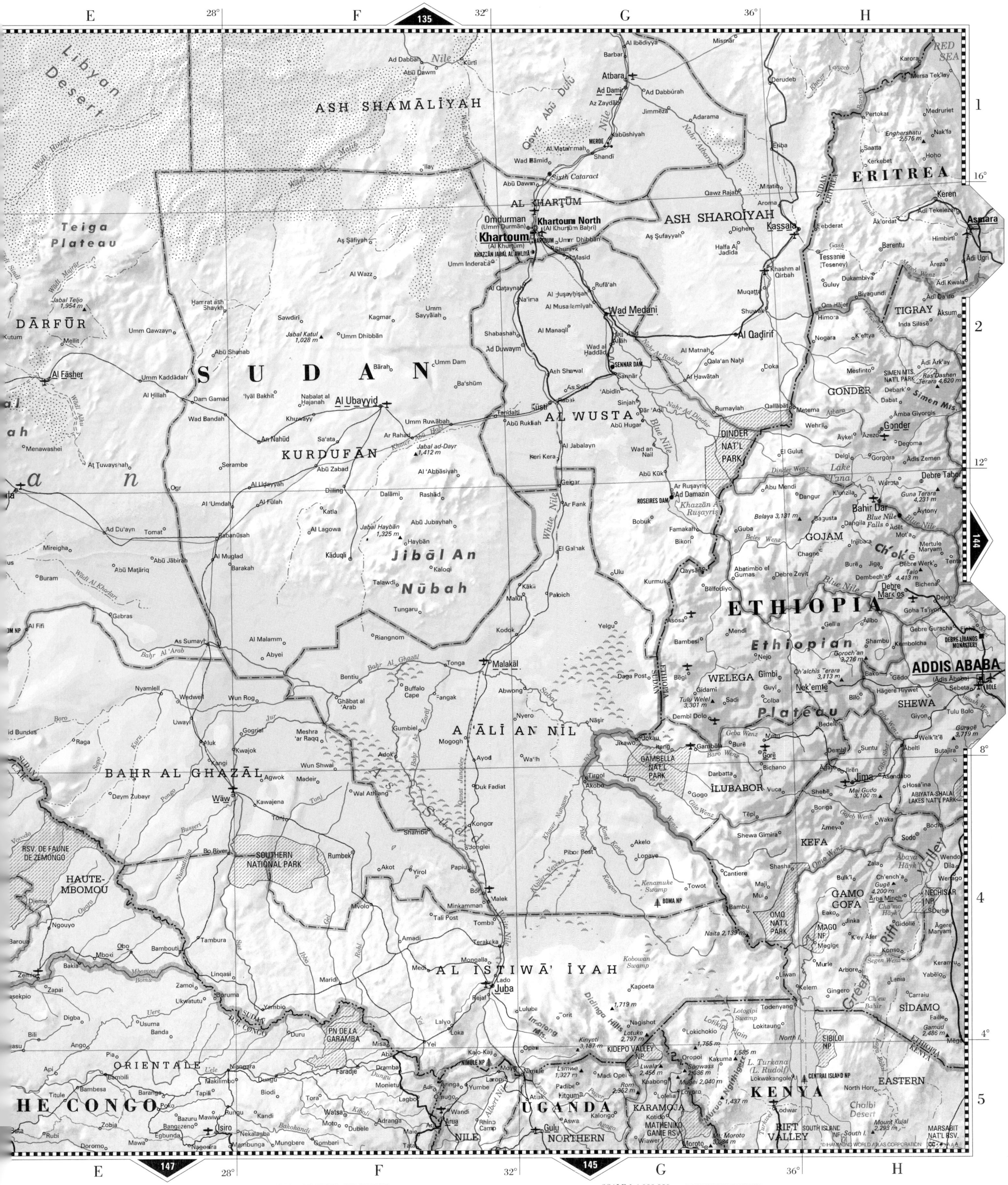

POPULATION OF CITIES AND TOWNS

■ OVER 2,000,000   ● 500,000 - 999,999   ◦ 100,000 - 249,999   ○ 10,000 - 29,999
□ 1,000,000 - 1,999,999   ◉ 250,000 - 499,999   ○ 30,000 - 99,999   · UNDER 10,000

SCALE 1:6,000,000   POLYCONIC PROJECTION

MILES   0   100   200   300
KILOMETERS   0   100   200   300

Ethiopia, Somalia

The historic isolation of Ethiopia by a high mountainous plateau, which protected its unique peoples from outside influences, enabled this country to retain its tradition of Christianity since the 4th century. Ethiopia and Somalia are two of the poorest countries in the world. Agriculture is mostly at subsistence level, and crop failures have resulted in widespread famines.

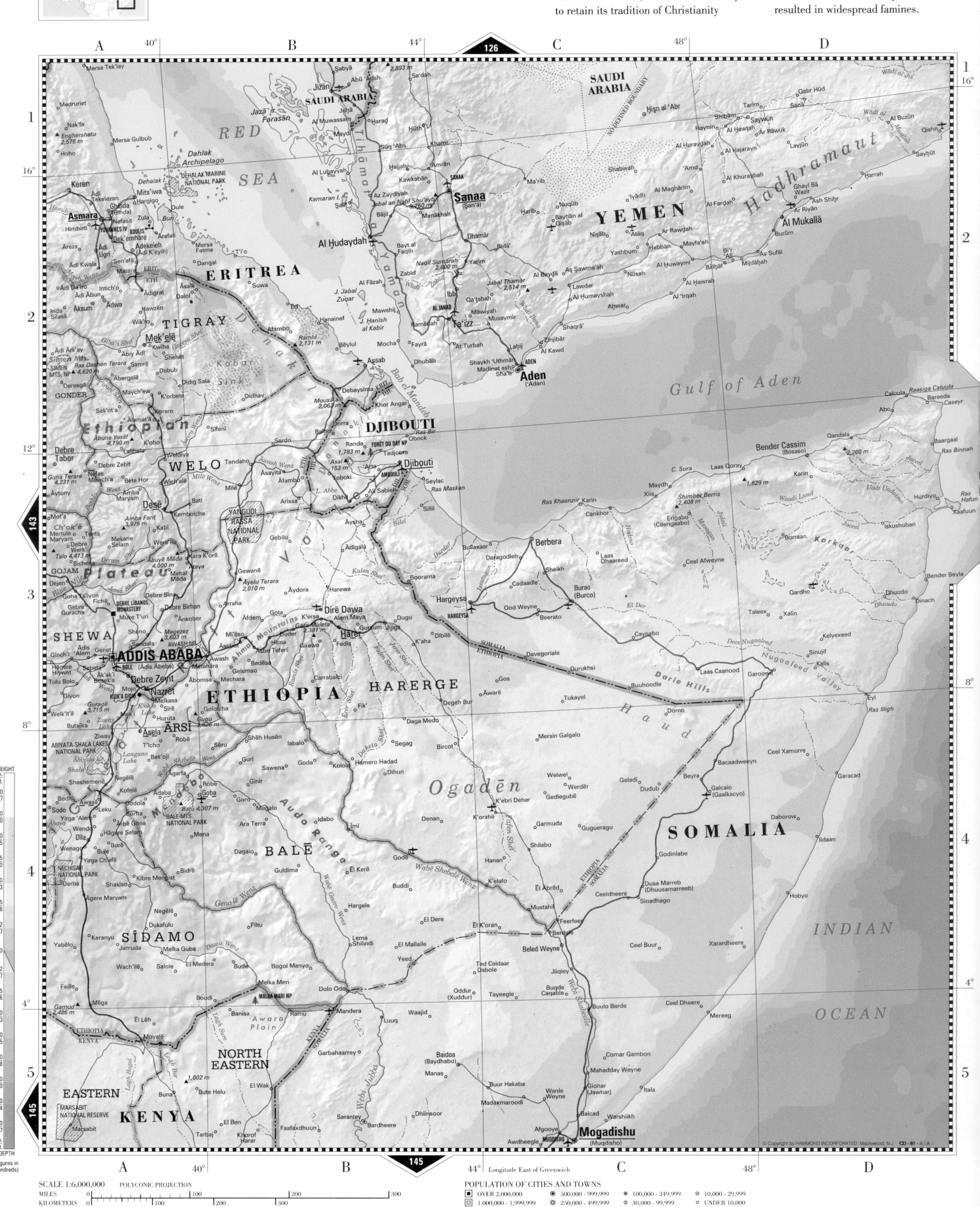

SCALE 1:6,000,000   POLYCONIC PROJECTION

MILES 0   100   200   300

KILOMETERS 0   100   200   300

POPULATION OF CITIES AND TOWNS

◉ OVER 2,000,000	◉ 500,000 - 999,999	⊕ 100,000 - 249,999	◎ 10,000 - 29,999
▣ 1,000,000 - 1,999,999	⊡ 250,000 - 499,999	⊕ 30,000 - 99,999	○ UNDER 10,000

Longitude East of Greenwich

© Copyright by HAMMOND INCORPORATED, Maplewood, N.J.

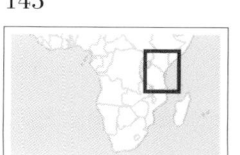

East Africa is the location of the Olduvai Gorge in Tanzania, now considered one of the original homelands of the human race. With limited mineral resources – diamonds in Tanzania and copper in Uganda – most people depend on agriculture and cattle for survival. Kenya has significant numbers of Asians, Europeans and Arabs. By contrast, Tanzania has very few minority groups.

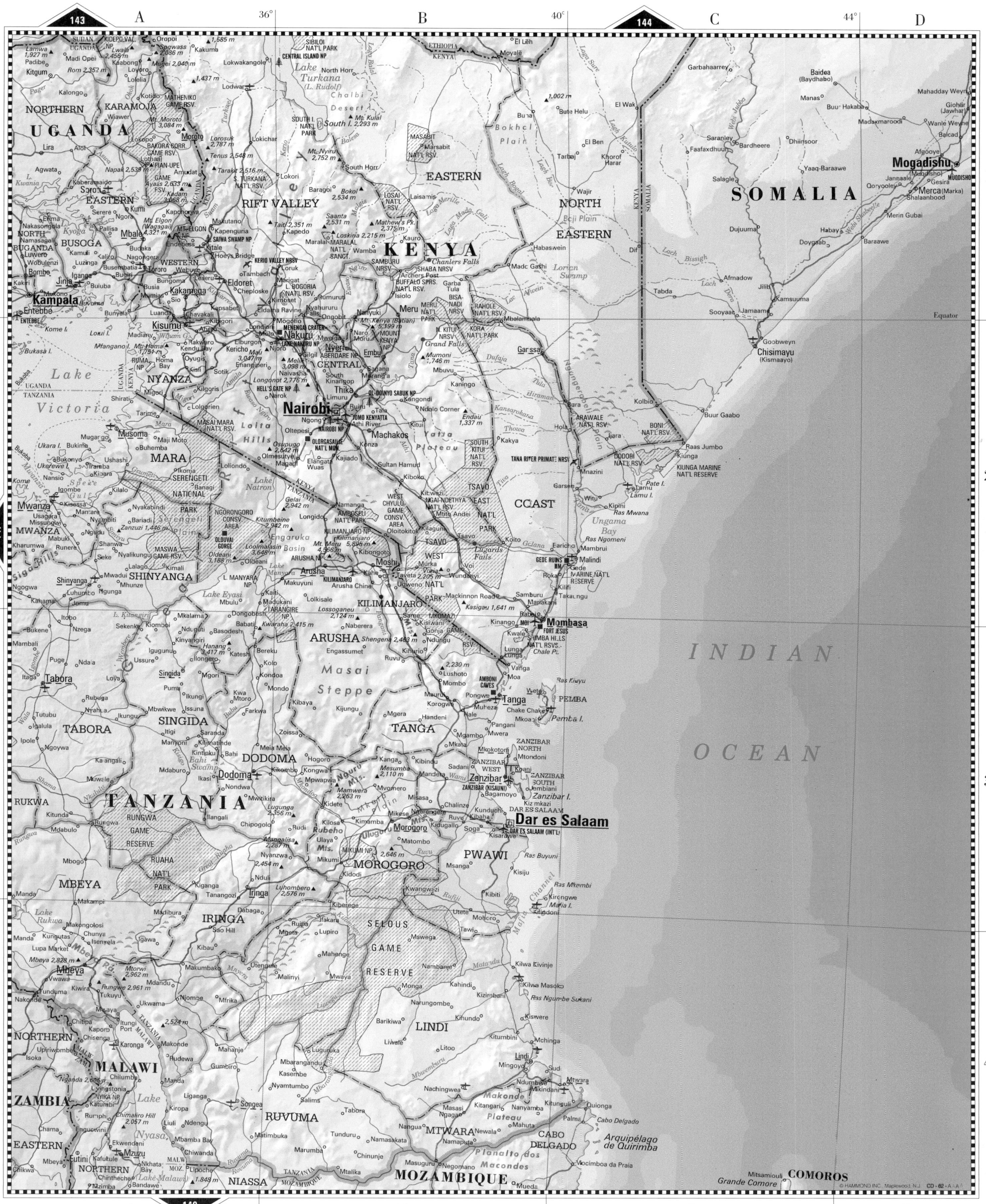

POPULATION OF CITIES AND TOWNS
- ■ OVER 2,000,000
- □ 1,000,000 – 1,999,999
- ● 500,000 – 999,999
- ◎ 250,000 – 499,999
- ● 100,000 – 249,999
- ◉ 30,000 – 99,999
- ○ 10,000 – 29,999
- ○ UNDER 10,000

SCALE 1:6,000,000 POLYCONIC PROJECTION

MILES 0   100   200   300
KILOMETERS 0   100   200   300

Longitude East of Greenwich

© HAMMOND INC., Maplewood, N.J.   CD - 62 - A - A

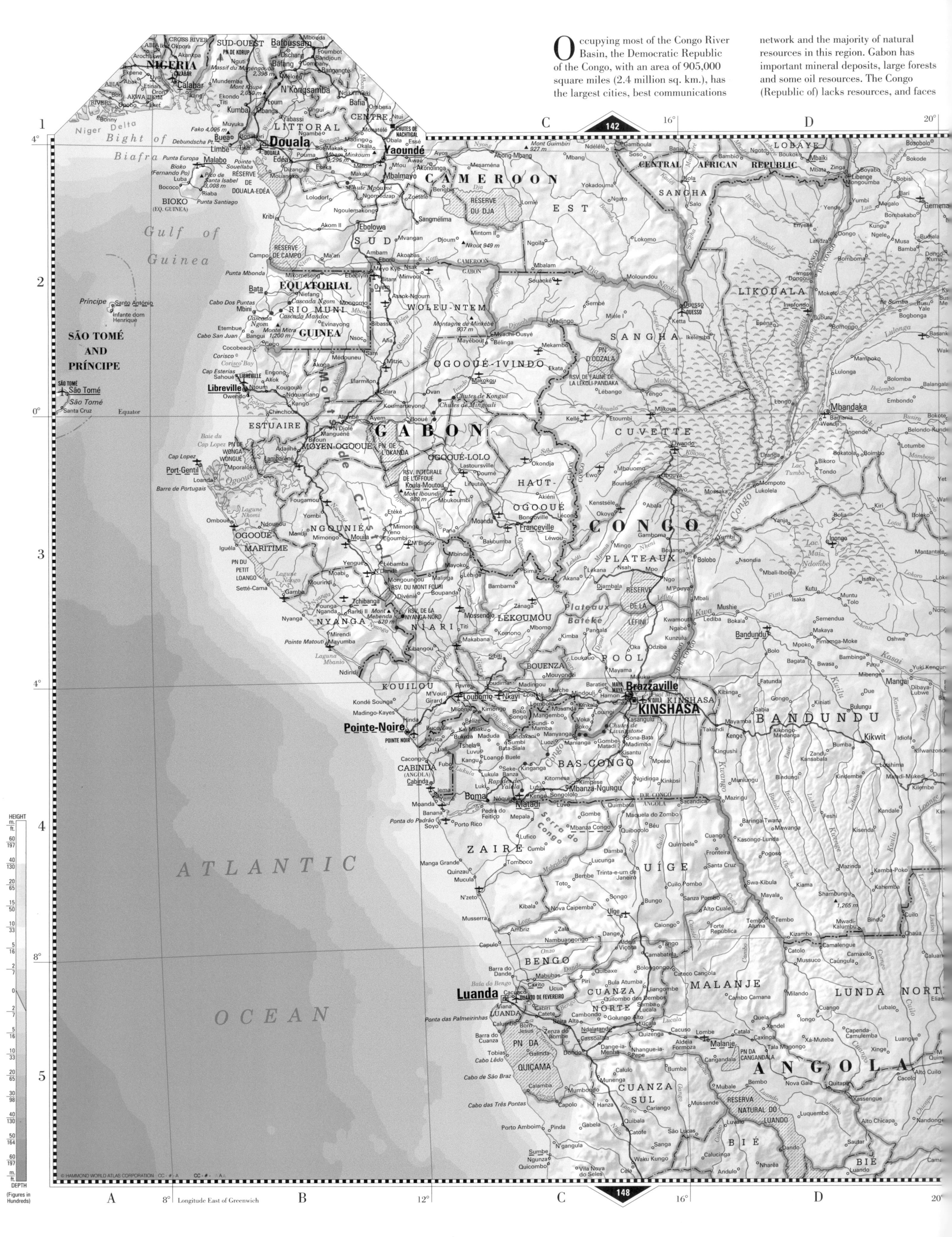

Occupying most of the Congo River Basin, the Democratic Republic of the Congo, with an area of 905,000 square miles (2.4 million sq. km.), has the largest cities, best communications network and the majority of natural resources in this region. Gabon has important mineral deposits, large forests and some oil resources. The Congo (Republic of) lacks resources, and faces

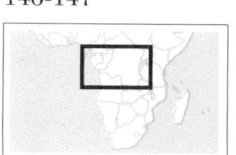

large expenses to move products to the coast. Angola has significant amounts of both diamonds and oil and its hydro-electric plants generate about three-quarters of the country's total power.

DEM. REP. OF THE CONGO

SUDAN

UGANDA

TANZANIA

ZAMBIA

MALAWI

BURUNDI

RWANDA

Kampala

Kisangani

Mbuji-Mayi

Kananga

Lubumbashi

Kolwezi

Likasi

Mbeya

Kigali

Bujumbura

Mwanza

POPULATION OF CITIES AND TOWNS
- ■ OVER 2,000,000
- ▣ 1,000,000 – 1,999,999
- ● 500,000 – 999,999
- ◉ 250,000 – 499,999
- ⊙ 100,000 – 249,999
- ⊕ 30,000 – 99,999
- ○ 10,000 – 29,999
- ○ UNDER 10,000

SCALE 1:6,000,000   POLYCONIC PROJECTION

MILES 0 · 100 · 200 · 300

KILOMETERS 0 · 100 · 200 · 300

The southern high country of Africa is a vast plateau, its elevation moderating not only temperatures, but rainfall as well. Semi-arid grassland and desert cover much of the region. The powerful Zambezi River cuts through the highlands of Zambia, Zimbabwe and Mozambique, and forms a wide delta as it empties into the ocean along a tropical coast. Rich deposits of diamonds, copper and nickel brought colonial interests here in the late 1800s. Exploitation of these resources provides an economic foundation for the countries within this region.

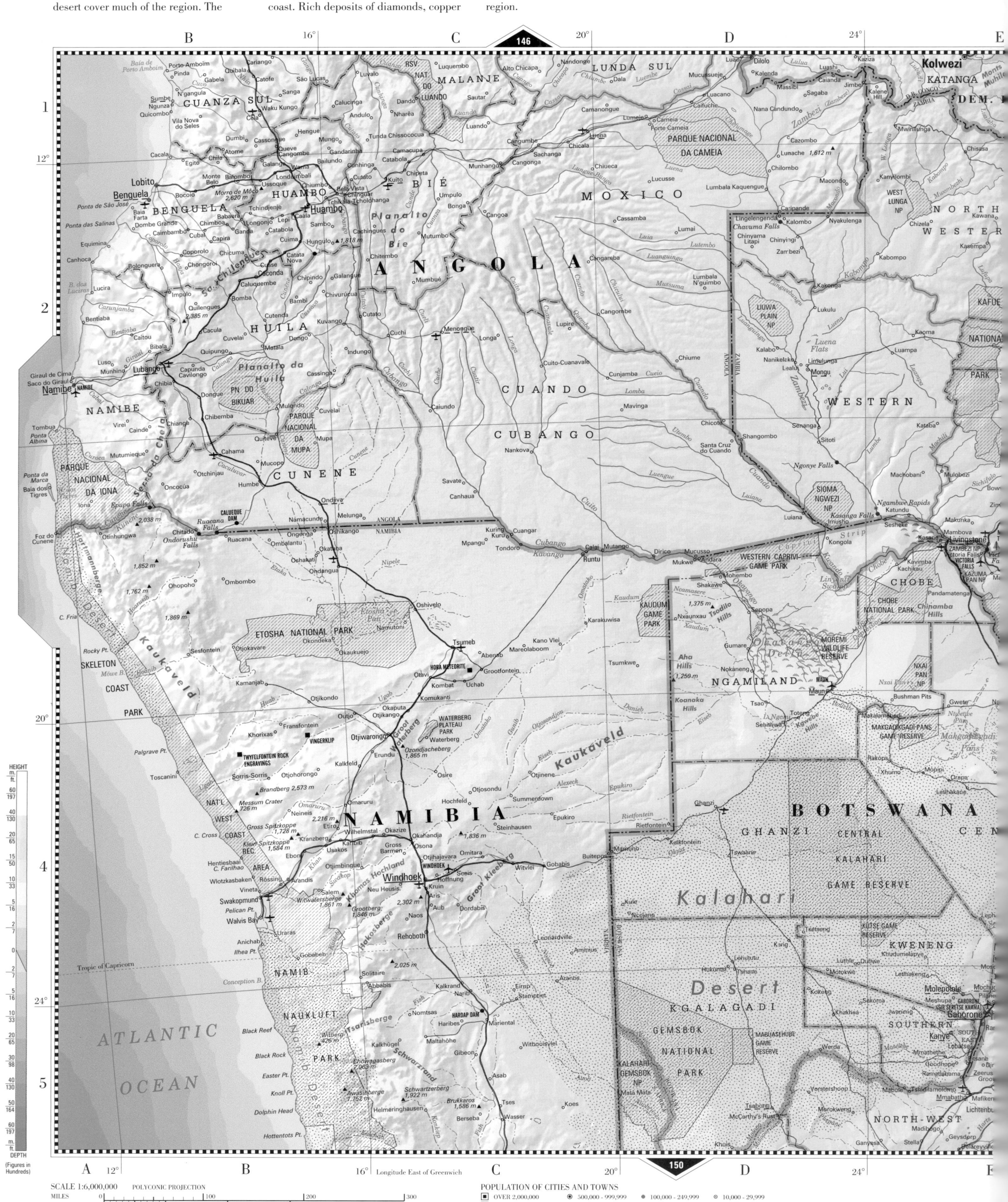

SCALE 1:6,000,000   POLYCONIC PROJECTION

MILES

KILOMETERS

Longitude East of Greenwich

POPULATION OF CITIES AND TOWNS

■ OVER 2,000,000
▣ 1,000,000 - 1,999,999
● 500,000 - 999,999
◉ 250,000 - 499,999
● 100,000 - 249,999
◉ 30,000 - 99,999
○ 10,000 - 29,999
○ UNDER 10,000

HEIGHT
m.
ft.

DEPTH
m.
ft.
(Figures in Hundreds)

South Central Africa

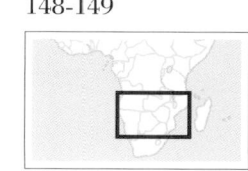

147
151
TANZANIA
ZAMBIA
MALAWI
MOZAMBIQUE
ZIMBABWE
SOUTH AFRICA
SWAZILAND
OF THE CONGO
RUVUMA
MTWARA
LINDI
NIASSA
CABO DELGADO
NAMPULA
ZAMBÉZIA
TETE
SOFALA
MANICA
INHAMBANE
GAZA
MAPUTO
NORTHERN
LUAPULA
COPPERBELT
CENTRAL
EASTERN
LUSAKA
SOUTHERN
MASHONALAND CENTRAL
MASHONALAND WEST
MASHONALAND EAST
MANICALAND
MIDLANDS
MASVINGO
MATABELELAND NORTH
MATABELELAND SOUTH
NORTHERN PROVINCE
MPUMALANGA
GAUTENG
Mozambique Channel
INDIAN OCEAN
Tropic of Capricorn
Lago de Cabora Bassa
Lake Nyasa (L. Malawi)
Lubumbashi
Lusaka
Ndola
Kitwe
Kabwe
Lilongwe
Blantyre
Zomba
Harare
Bulawayo
Gweru
Mutare
Masvingo
Beira
Maputo
Nampula
Quelimane
Tete
Pretoria
Johannesburg
Soweto
Mbabane
Francistown
Bassas da India (FRANCE)
Europa I. (FRANCE)
© HAMMOND WORLD ATLAS CORPORATION
28°
32°
36°
40°
20°
24°
F
G
H
J
3
4
5

This is Africa's richest region in terms of its natural resources. Gold, chromium, antimony, diamonds, platinum, vanadium and coal are mined in abundance. The favorable climate in South Africa produces a variety of tropical and temperate crops. However, this vast natural wealth is not distributed equally. Botswana, Namibia, Swaziland, Lesotho, and large parts of South Africa itself remain poor. The world's fourth-largest island, Madagascar, was settled by Malayo-Polynesian voyagers from the Sunda Islands of present-day Indonesia. Inhabitants speak the Malagasy language.

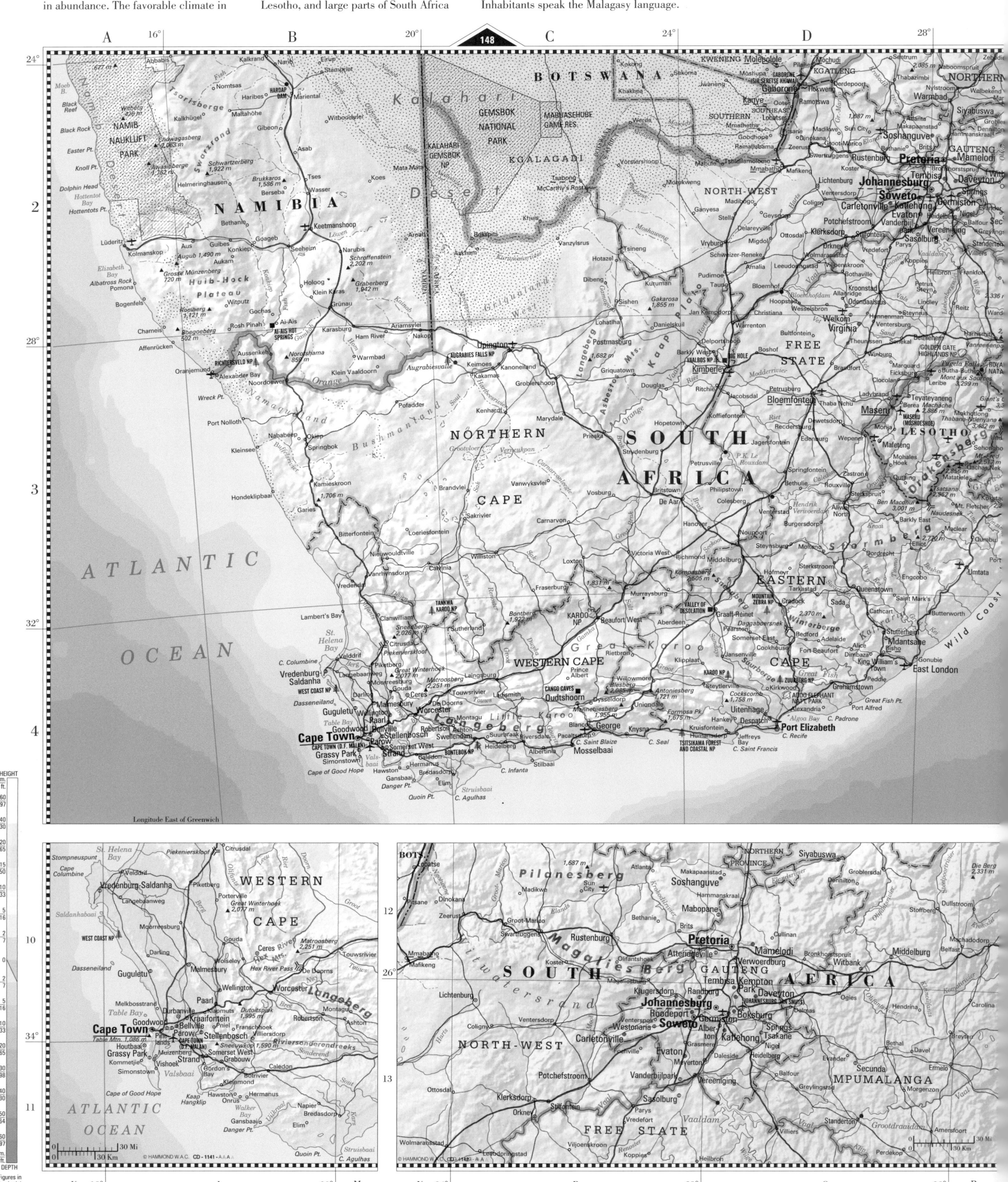

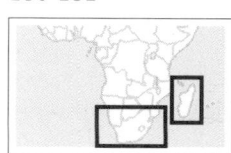

MOZAMBIQUE

INHAMBANE

GAZA

MAPUTO

Maputo (Internacional)

Maputo

Mbabane

SWAZILAND

MPUMALANGA

KWAZULU NATAL

Richard's Bay

Durban

DURBAN (LOUIS BOTHA)

KwaMashu

Pinetown

Port Shepstone

Margate

I N D I A N

O C E A N

COMOROS

Mitsamiouli
Hahaia *Grande*
Hahaia *Comore*
Moroni
Icono
Foumbouni

Oani Fomboni
Mohéli
Nioumachoua
MOHÉLI
Moya

MAYOTTE
(FRANCE)

Marroouzou Dzaoudzi
Dembeni
Sada **DZAOUDZI**
Bandeli

Iles Glorieuses
(FRANCE)

Geyser Reef

Tanjon' i Bobaomby

Antsiranana

PN MONTAGNE D'AMBRE

Ambilobe

ANTSIRANANA

Mozambique Channel

Tsaratanana Massif

Mahajanga

MAHAJANGA

Ikahavo Plateau

Analamaitso Plateau

Juan de Nova (FRANCE)

Nosy Chesterfield

Maintirano

Nosy Barren (Barren Is.)

ANTANANARIVO

Antananarivo

IVATO

TOAMASINA

Toamasina

Bongolava Plateau

Miandrivazo

Belo-Tsiribihina

Antsirabe

Antanifotsy

Fandriana

MADAGASCAR

Morondava

Fianarantsoa

FIANARANTSOA

Ifanadiana

Makay Massif

TOLIARA

Toliara

Betioky

Tropic of Capricorn

Ampanihy

Beloha
Amboasary
Ambondro
Ambovombe

I N D I A N OCEAN

INDIAN OCEAN

C. Malheureux

Triolet
Poudre d'Or
Port Louis
Beau Bassin
Quatre Bornes
Curepipe
Mahébourg
Rose Belle
827 m
MAURITIUS
Souillac
SIR SEEWOOSAGUR RAMGOOLAM

RÉUNION (FRANCE)

Le Port
Saint-Paul
Saint-Denis
GILLOT
Saint-André
Saint-Benoît
Piton des Neiges 3,069 m
Pointe des Cascades
Piton de la Fournaise 2,431 m
Saint-Leu
Le Tampon
Saint-Louis
Saint-Pierre
Saint-Joseph

Mascarene Islands

30 Mi
30 Km

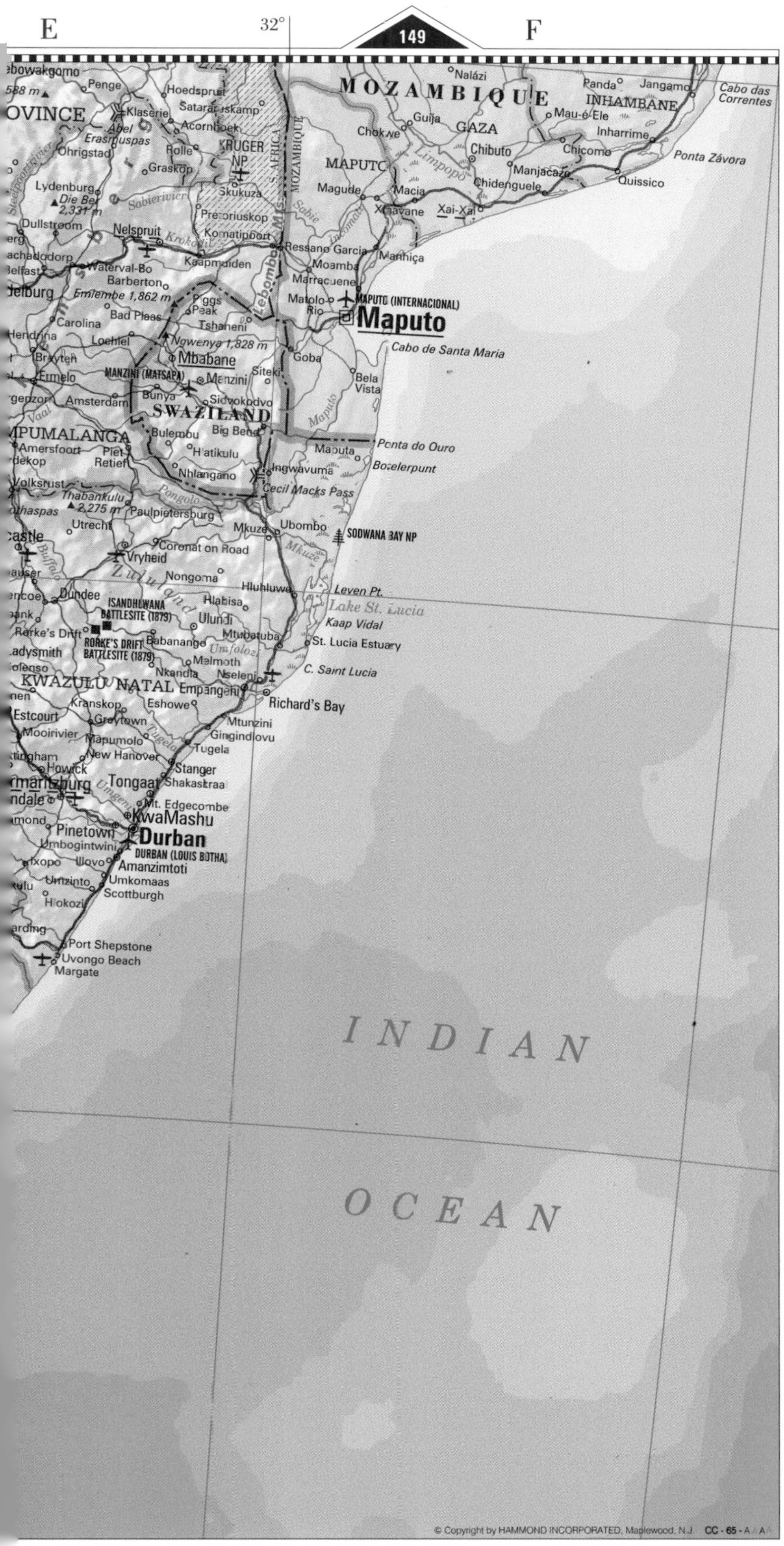

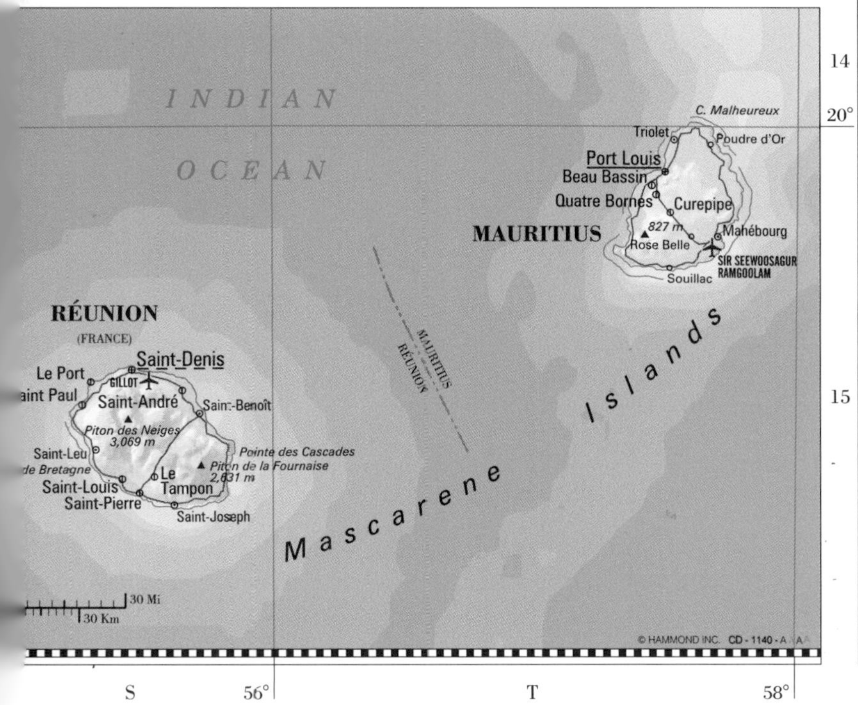

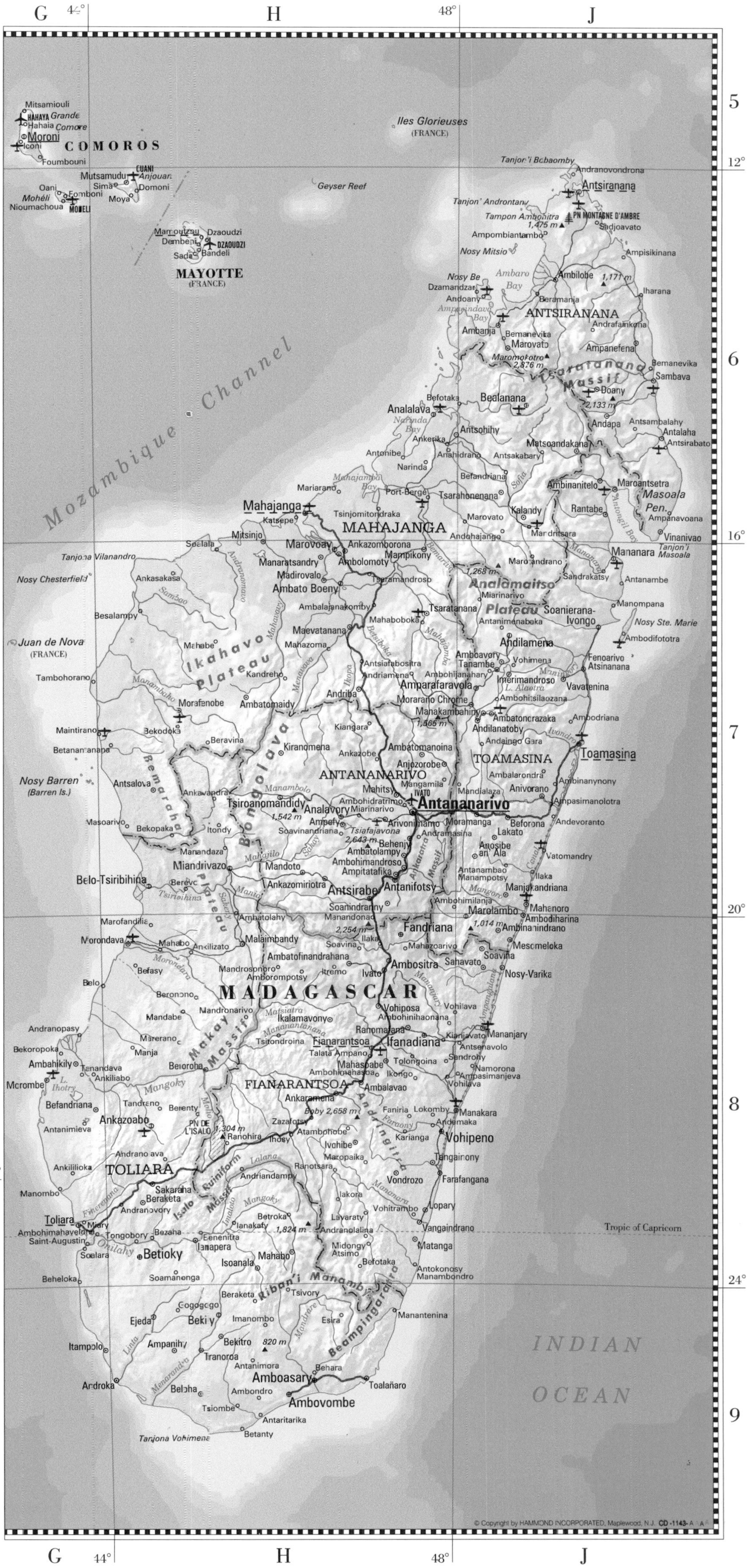

POPULATION OF CITIES AND TOWNS

| OVER 2,000,000 | 500,000 - 999,999 | 100,000 - 249,999 | 10,000 - 29,999 |
| 1,000,000 - 1,999,999 | 250,000 - 499,999 | 30,000 - 99,999 | UNDER 10,000 |

SCALE 1:6,000,000   LAMBERT CONFORMAL CONIC PROJECTION

MILES
KILOMETERS

© Copyright by HAMMOND INCORPORATED, Maplewood, N.J.

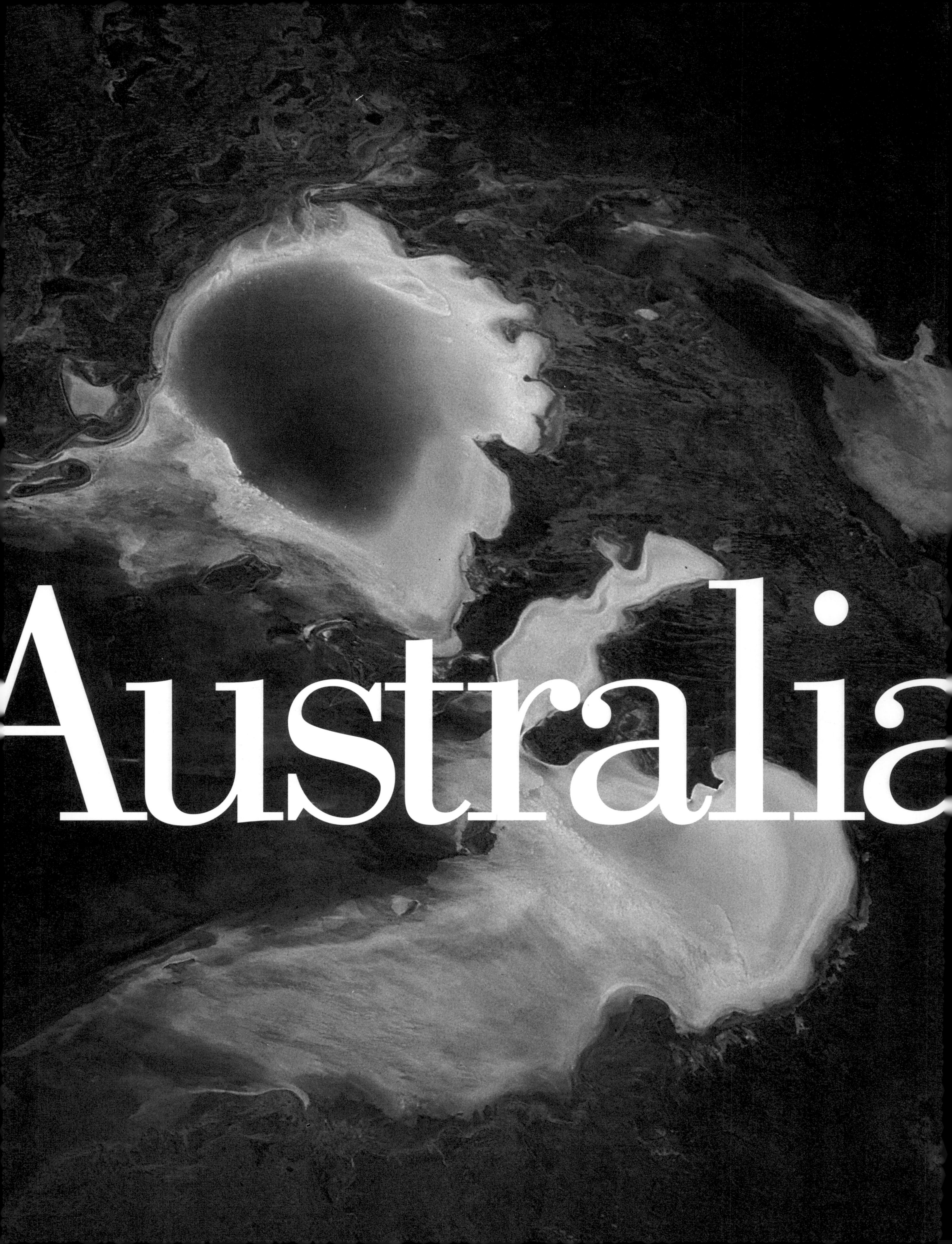

Australia

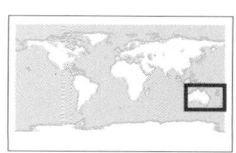

The Lake Eyre Basin is located in the arid interior of south central Australia. This basin is one of the largest areas of internal drainage in the world. It consists of two distinct, but interrelated basins: the north basin and the south basin. The much larger north basin shown here (the highly reflective areas) consists of two very large, normally dry lakebeds. The western lobe (bottom of the image) is Belt Bay, and the eastern lobe is Madigan Bay. The color change, especially in the Madigan Bay lobe, indicates that there was some water in this lobe at the time the image was taken.

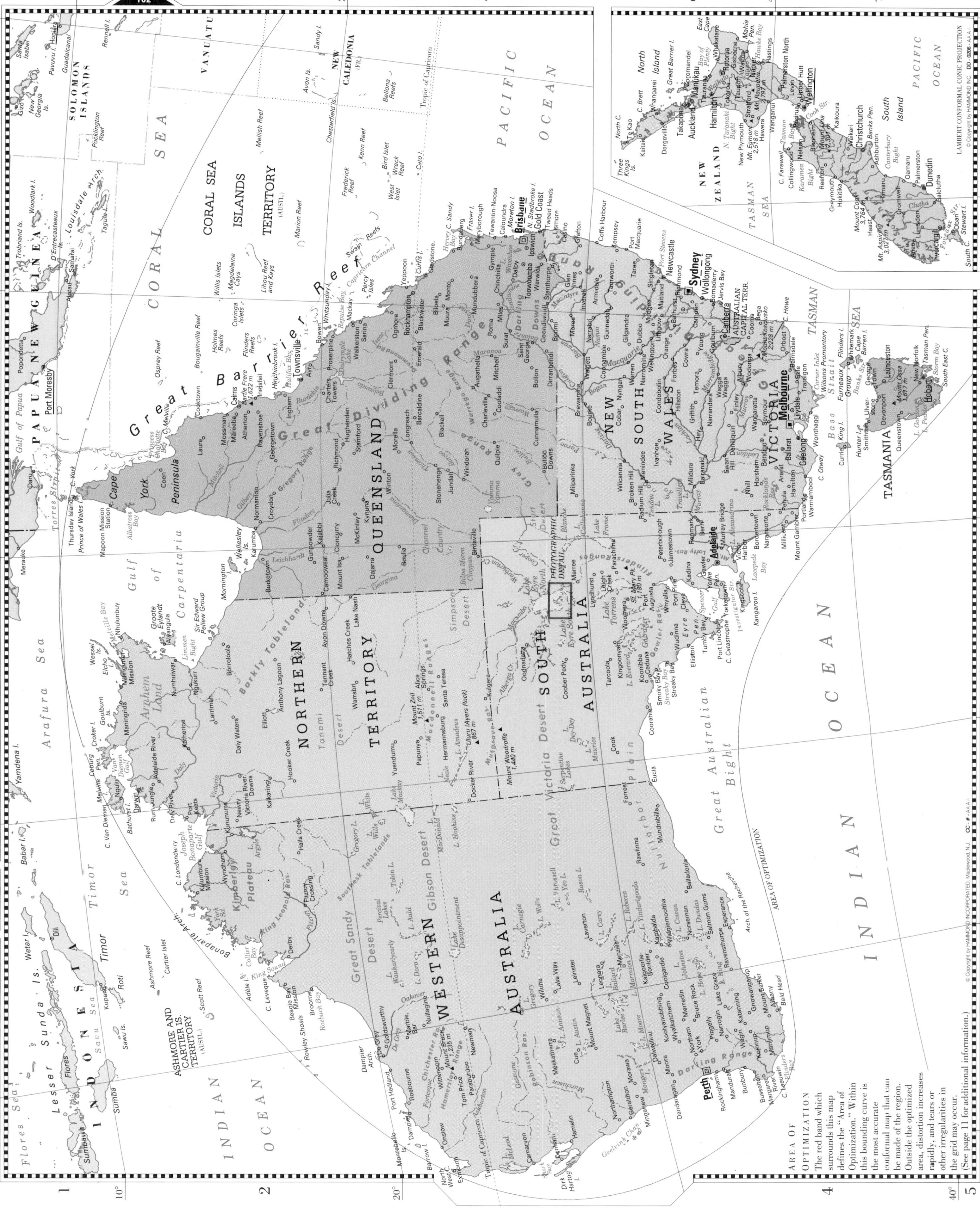

162

103

INDONESIA

Lesser Sunda Is.

Timor Sea

Arafura Sea

PAPUA NEW GUINEA

Gulf of Papua

Port Moresby

CORAL SEA

SOLOMON ISLANDS

VANUATU

NEW CALEDONIA (Fr.)

CORAL SEA ISLANDS TERRITORY (AUSTL.)

PACIFIC OCEAN

Great Barrier Reef

Gulf of Carpentaria

Cape York Peninsula

ASHMORE AND CARTIER IS. TERRITORY (AUSTL.)

INDIAN OCEAN

Kimberley Plateau

Great Sandy Desert

NORTHERN TERRITORY

Tanami Desert

Barkly Tableland

Arnhem Land

Darwin

Gibson Desert

Great Victoria Desert

WESTERN AUSTRALIA

QUEENSLAND

Great Dividing Range

Brisbane

SOUTH AUSTRALIA

Simpson Desert

Lake Eyre

Adelaide

NEW SOUTH WALES

Sydney
Wollongong

Canberra
AUSTRALIAN CAPITAL TERR.

VICTORIA

Melbourne

TASMANIA

Hobart

Great Australian Bight

Nullarbor Plain

INDIAN OCEAN

Perth

TASMAN SEA

NEW ZEALAND

North Island

South Island

Auckland

Wellington

Christchurch

Dunedin

PACIFIC OCEAN

TASMAN SEA

LAMBERT CONFORMAL CONIC PROJECTION

© Copyright by HAMMOND INCORPORATED, Maplewood, N.J.

AREA OF OPTIMIZATION
The red band which surrounds this map defines the "Area of Optimization." Within this bounding curve is the most accurate conformal map that can be made of the region. Outside the optimized area, distortion increases rapidly, and tears or other irregularities in the grid may occur. (See page 11 for additional information.)

POPULATION OF CITIES AND TOWNS

- OVER 2,000,000
- 1,000,000 - 1,999,999
- 500,000 - 999,999
- 100,000 - 499,999
- 50,000 - 99,999
- UNDER 50,000

SCALE 1:16,600,000   OPTIMAL CONFORMAL PROJECTION

MILES 0   250   500   750

KILOMETERS 0   250   500   750

New Guinea was probably first occupied at the same time as Australia, 50,000 to 70,000 years ago. A large population of Papuan highlanders were first encountered by Westerners as late as 1933. A number of intense battles occurred during World War II in New Guinea as the Japanese sought to isolate Australia. Australia's development began with the establishment of colonies in New South Wales in 1788. The native Aborigines were gradually displaced, and their numbers declined. Most now live in the Northern Territory and the Cape York area of Queensland.

Papua New Guinea, Northern Australia

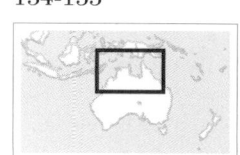

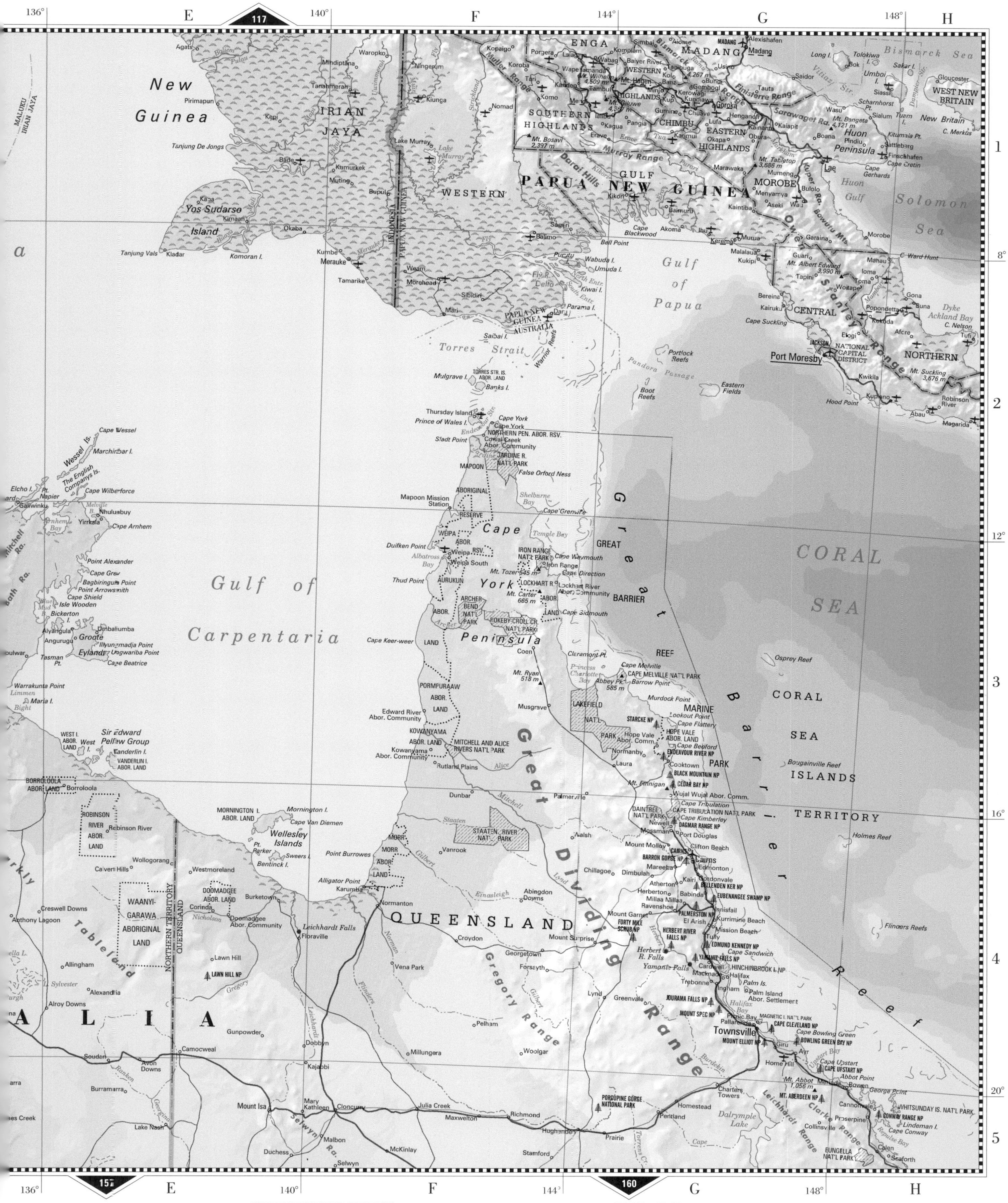

POPULATION OF CITIES AND TOWNS

■ OVER 2,000,000	◉ 500,000 - 999,999
▣ 1,000,000 - 1,999,999	◉ 250,000 - 499,999
● 100,000 - 249,999	⊙ 10,000 - 29,999
● 30,000 - 99,999	○ UNDER 10,000

SCALE 1:6,000,000   LAMBERT CONFORMAL CONIC PROJECTION

MILES 0   100   200   300

KILOMETERS 0   100   200   300

Australia is covered by more desert terrain for its size than any other inhabited continent, most of it in the "outback" region. Sheep and cattle graze along the fringes of the arid lands, but moist parts of coastal lowlands near Perth and Adelaide support cultivation. Major iron ore deposits are found in the Hamersley Range, while gold is mined near the southern town of Kalgoorlie-Boulder. The isolated scenic monolith, Ayers Rock within Uluru National Park, in the Northern Territory, has strange caves and ancient Aboriginal paintings and carvings.

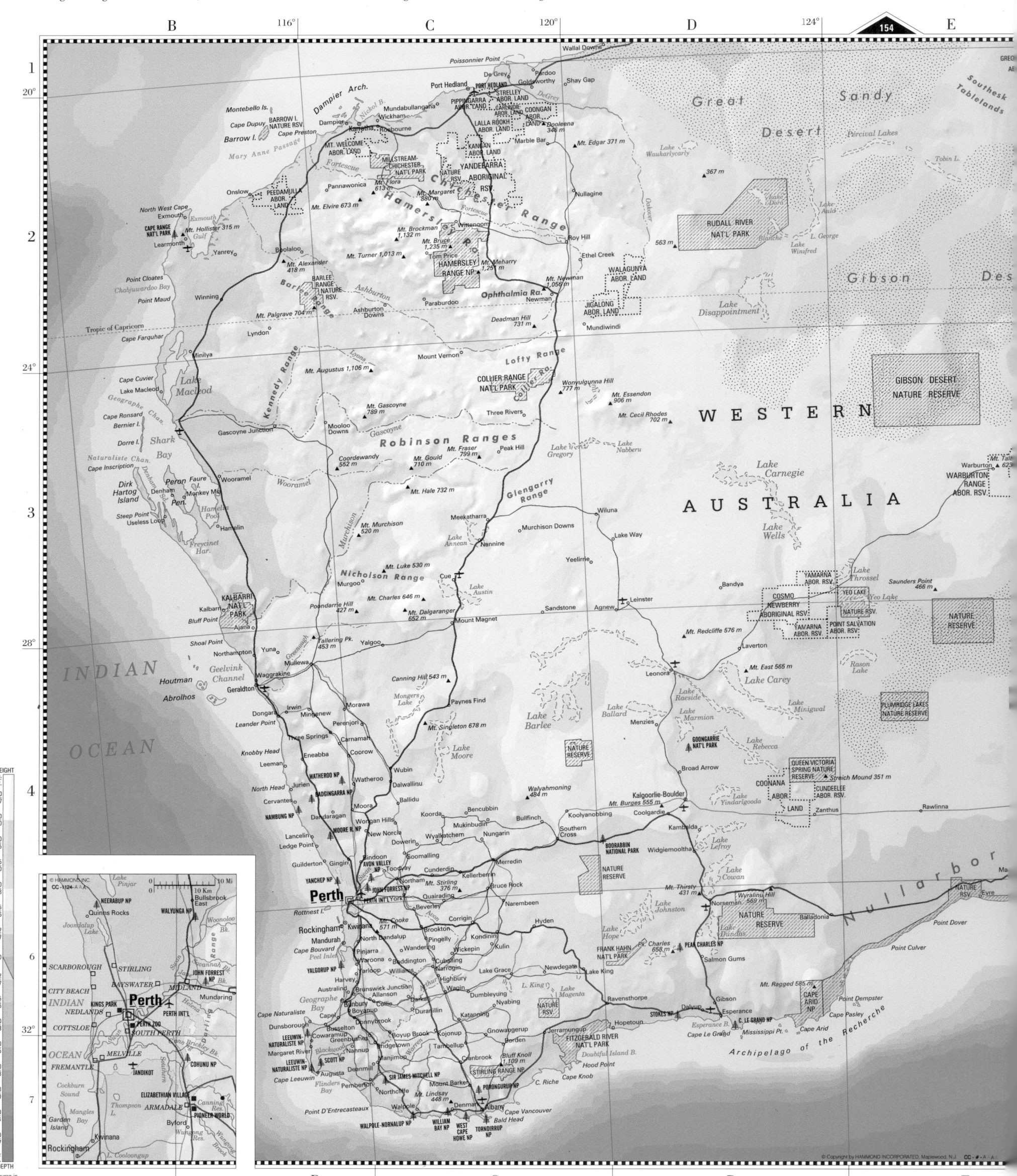

Western and Central Australia

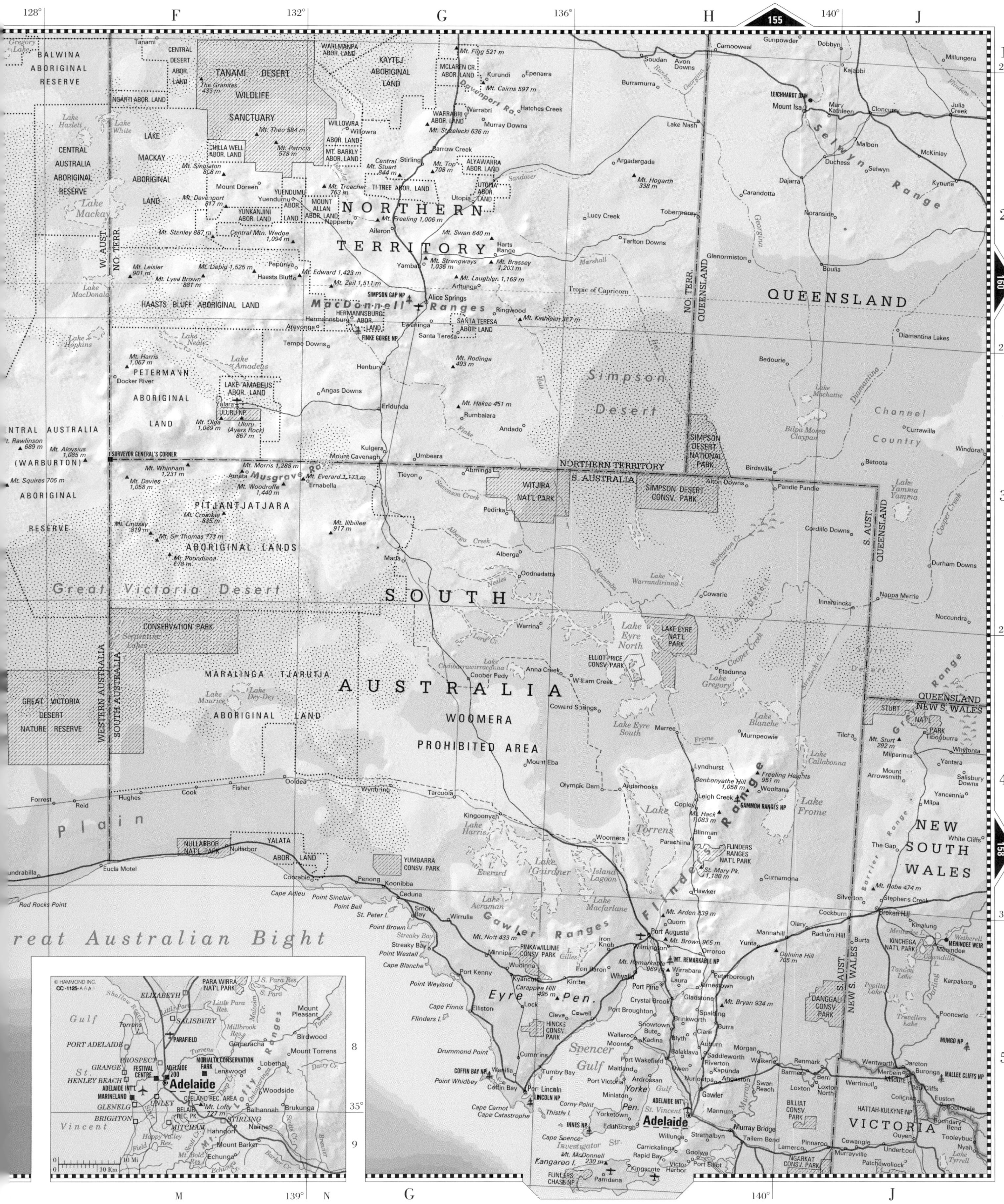

■ OVER 2,000,000 ▫ 500,000 - 999,999 ◉ 103,000 - 249,999 ◦ 10,000 - 29,999
▣ 1,000,000 - 1,999,999 ◎ 250,000 - 499,999 ● 30,000 - 99,999 ○ UNDER 10 000

MILES 0   100   200   300
KILOMETERS 0   100   200   300

© HAMMOND INC.
CC-1125-A A A

Southeastern Australia

With its relatively comfortable climate and reliable rainfall, this small portion of the continent is home to most Australians. Two hundred years ago, the first European settlement was established near what is now Sydney. Competition between Melbourne and Sydney to become the nation's capital was resolved when the Parliament was transferred in 1927 to Canberra.

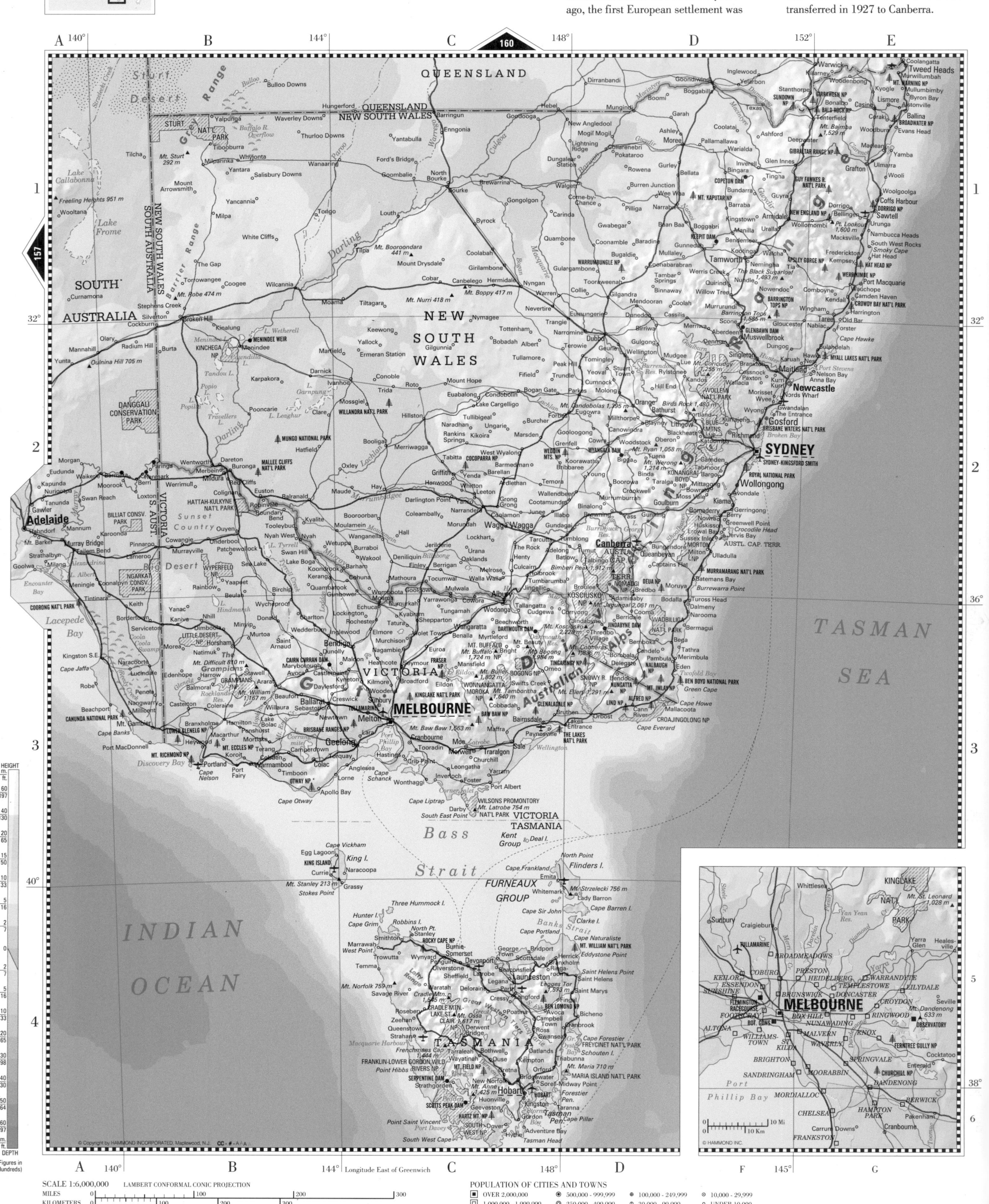

SCALE 1:6,000,000   LAMBERT CONFORMAL CONIC PROJECTION

POPULATION OF CITIES AND TOWNS

Sydney-Melbourne

Sydney, built around one of the world's most beautiful harbors, is Australia's oldest city, as well as host to the 2000 Olympics. Melbourne, one of Australia's largest cities, is considered the cultural capital. Between the two, Canberra, the nation's capital, is located in the Australian Capital Territory. The region is known for its beautiful beaches, quaint villages, and many national parks.

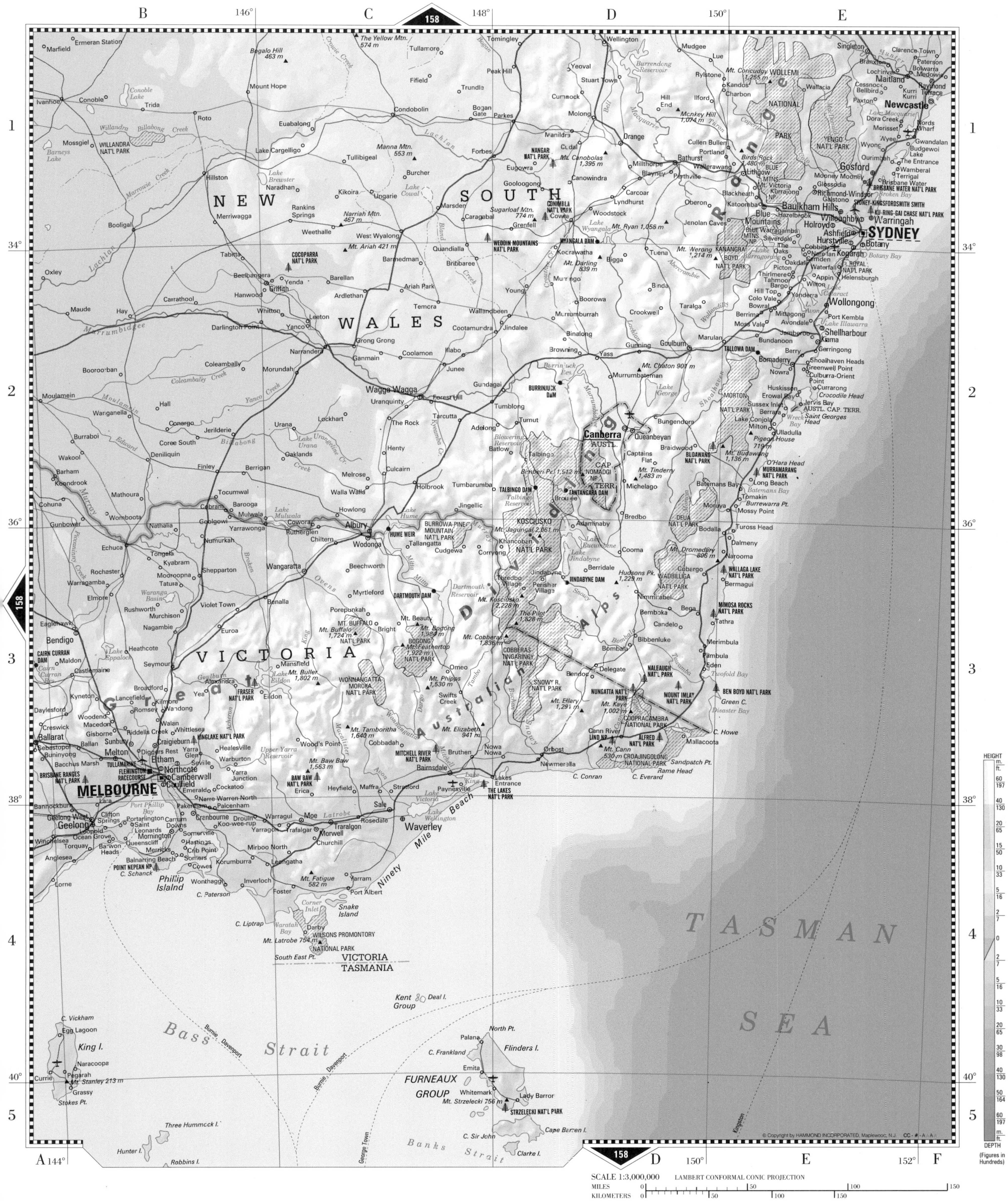

SCALE 1:3,000,000   LAMBERT CONFORMAL CONIC PROJECTION

Northeastern Australia

This is the Australian tropics, complete with rain forests and sugar cane plantations following the coastline as far south as Brisbane. The tropical rain forest thrives along the Queensland coast. Offshore, the Great Barrier Reef – the world's largest complex of coral islands, shoals and atolls, – extends for over 1200 miles (1920 km.), attracting tourists and naturalists.

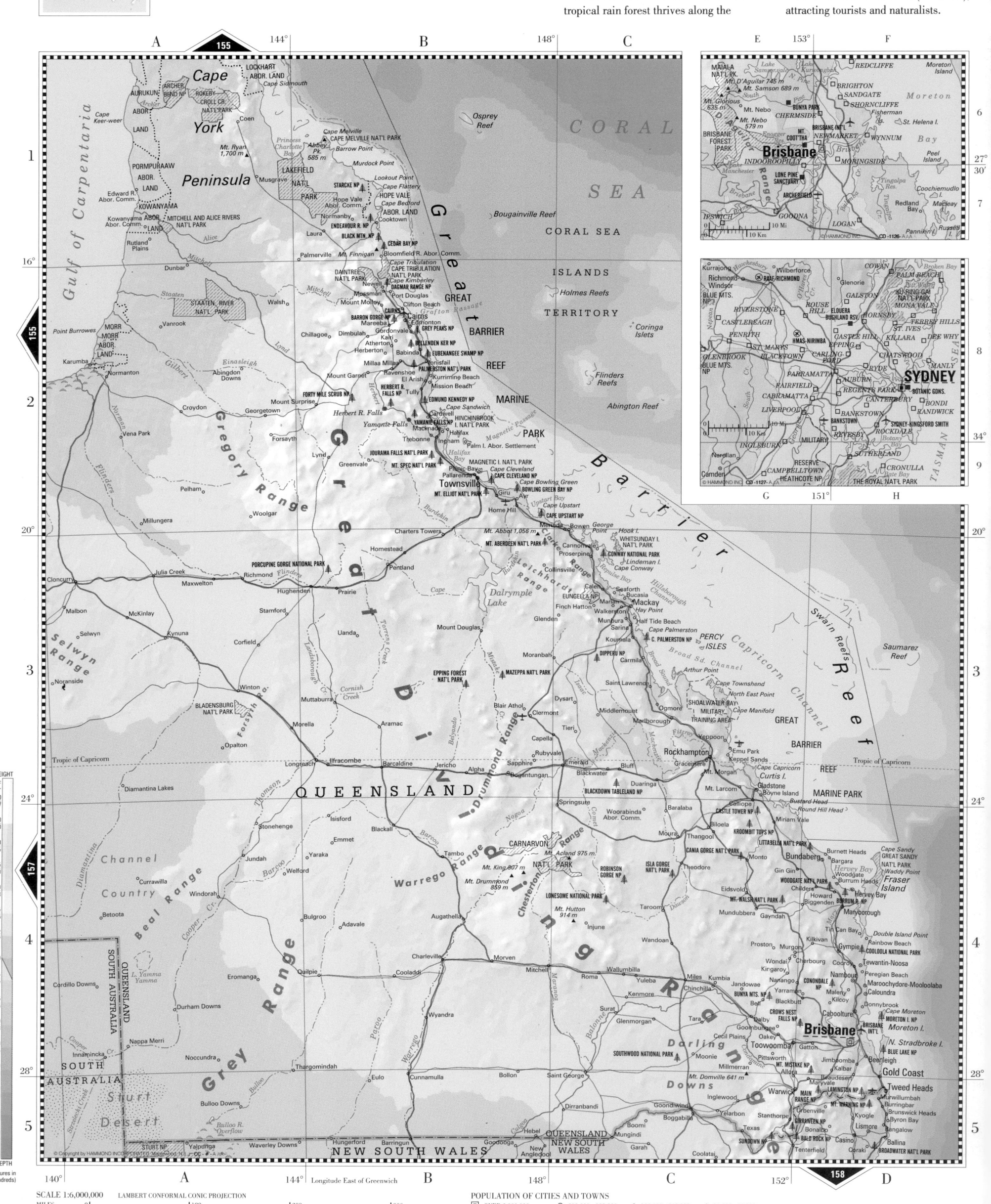

SCALE 1:6,000,000   LAMBERT CONFORMAL CONIC PROJECTION

MILES 0   100   200   300
KILOMETERS 0   100   200   300

POPULATION OF CITIES AND TOWNS
- OVER 2,000,000
- 1,000,000–1,999,999
- 500,000–999,999
- 250,000–499,999
- 100,000–249,999
- 30,000–99,999
- 10,000–29,999
- UNDER 10,000

T he sparsely populated South Island boasts magnificent fjords and Alpine scenery. Sheep and cattle are vital to the island's economy. North Island is less agricultural, with its larger cities and hot springs. Geysers have been harnessed to generate electricity. Most New Zealanders are of British descent. Maoris, earlier immigrants from across the Pacific form a small minority.

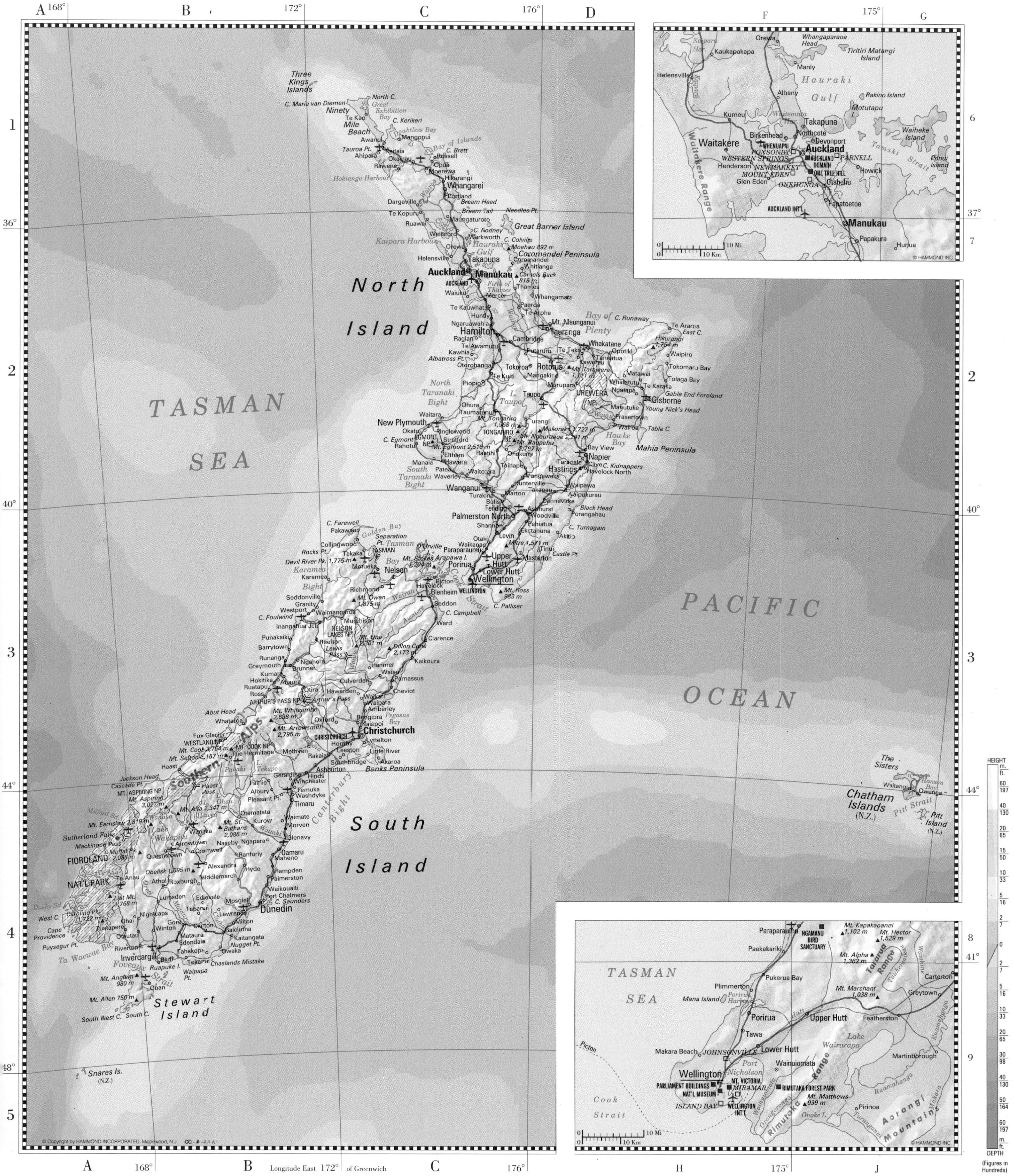

New Zealand

North Island

TASMAN SEA

Three Kings Islands

Ninety Mile Beach

C. Maria van Diemen
North C.
C. Kerikeri
Doubtless Bay
Te Kao
C. Brett
Awanui
Ahipara
Tauroa Pt.
Okaihau
Russell
Opua
Moerewa
Kawakawa
Hokianga Harbour
Whangarei
Dargaville
Bream Head
Te Kopuru
Bream Tail
Ruawai
Needles Pt.
Maungaturoto
C. Rodney
Wellsford
Warkworth
C. Colville
Orewa
Great Barrier Island
Helensville
Whitianga
Auckland Takapuna
Manukau
Waiuku
Firth of Thames
Mercer
Camels Back
Thames

North Taranaki Bight

Raglan
Hamilton
Cambridge
Te Awamutu
Kawhia
Albatross Pt.
Otorohanga
Te Kuiti
Piopio
Ohura

Bay of Plenty
C. Runaway
Te Puke
Mt. Maunganui
Tauranga
Whakatane
Opotiki
Te Araroa
East C.
Rotorua
Mt. Tarawera
Waipiro
Kawerau
Tokomaru Bay
Matawai
Te Karaka
Tolaga Bay
Gable End Foreland
Young Nick's Head
Gisborne
UREWERA NP

New Plymouth
Waitara
Inglewood
Stratford
Mt. Egmont 2,518 m
EGMONT NP
Eltham
Hawera
Manaia
Waverley
Patea
Mt. Tongariro 1,968 m
TONGARIRO NP
Mt. Ngauruhoe 2,291 m
Mt. Ruapehu 2,797 m

South Taranaki Bight

L. Taupo
Taupo
Taumarunui
Turangi
Ohakune
Raetihi
Taihape
Napier
Hastings
Havelock North
Hawke Bay
Mahia Peninsula
C. Kidnappers

Wanganui
Marton
Bulls
Feilding
Ashhurst
Palmerston North
Shannon
Woodville
Dannevirke
Pahiatua
Levin
Otaki
Waikanae
Paraparaumu
Porirua
Upper Hutt
Lower Hutt
Wellington

South Island

TASMAN SEA

C. Farewell
Pakawau
Collingwood
Takaka
Separation Pt.
Golden Bay
Rocks Pt.
Devil River Pk.
Motueka
TASMAN NP
Nelson
Richmond
Blenheim
Havelock
Picton
Seddon
Ward

Westport
Granity
Seddonville
Murchison
Reefton
Inangahua Jct.
C. Foulwind
Punakaiki
Barrytown
Runanga
Greymouth
Brunner
Hokitika
Ross

Kaikoura
Hanmer
Waiau
Culverden
Cheviot
Parnassus
Hawarden
Waipara
Amberley
Oxford
Rangiora
Kaiapoi
Pegasus Bay
Christchurch
Lyttelton
Hornby
Banks Peninsula
Akaroa
Little River
Leeston
Methven
Rakaia
Southbridge

Fox Glacier
WESTLAND NP
Mt. Cook 3,764 m
MT. COOK NP
The Hermitage
Mt. Sefton 3,157 m

Geraldine
Fairlie
Temuka
Pleasant Pt.
Timaru
Winchester
Hinds
Ashburton
Washdyke

Jackson Head
Cascade Pt.
MT. ASPIRING NP
Mt. Aspiring 3,027 m
Haast Pass
L. Hawea
Mt. Alta 2,347 m
Lake Wanaka
Pukaki
L. Tekapo
Mt. St. Bathans 2,086 m
Kurow
Waimate
Morven
Glenavy
Oamaru
Maheno

Sutherland Falls
Mackinnon Pass
Mt. Earnslaw 2,819 m
Lake Wakatipu
Queenstown
Arrowtown
Cromwell
Alexandra
Roxburgh
Middlemarch
Naseby
Ngapara
Palmerston
Hyde
Ranfurly
Waikouaiti
Port Chalmers
Dunedin
Mosgiel
C. Saunders

FIORDLAND NAT'L PARK
Te Anau
Lumsden
Edievale
Gore
Mataura
Tapanui
Lawrence
Milton
Balclutha
Kaitangata
Nugget Pt.

West C.
Carding Pk. 1,722 m
Cape Providence
Puysegur Pt.
Ta Waewae Bay
Flat Mt. 768 m
Nightcaps
Otautau
Ohai
Winton
Riverton
Otatara
Wrey's Bush
Invercargill
Bluff
Ruapuke I.
Tokanui
Waipapa Pt.
Chaslands Mistake

Stewart Island
Mt. Anglem 980 m
Oban
Mt. Allen 750 m
South West C. South C.

Snares Is. (N.Z.)

PACIFIC OCEAN

The Sisters
Chatham Islands (N.Z.)
Pitt Island (N.Z.)
Pitt Strait

Auckland inset

Kaipara Har.
Kaukapakapa
Orewa
Whangaparaoa Head
Helensville
Manly
Tiritiri Matangi Island
Kumeu
Takapuna
Rakino Island
Motutapu I.
Waitakere
Birkenhead
Northcote
Devonport
Auckland
WHENUAPAI
PONSONBY
WESTERN SPRINGS
NEWMARKET
PARNELL
Henderson
MOUNT EDEN
DOMAIN
ONE TREE HILL
Glen Eden
ONEHUNGA
Otahuhu
Howick
Hauraki Gulf
Waiheke Island
Ponui Island
Tamaki Strait
AUCKLAND INT'L
Papatoetoe
Manukau
Papakura
Hunua

Waitakere Range

Wellington inset

Paraparaumu
NGAMANJ BIRD SANCTUARY
Mt. Kapakapanei 1,102 m
Mt. Hector 1,529 m
Paekakariki
Mt. Alpha 1,362 m
TASMAN SEA
Plimmerton
Pukerua Bay
Mt. Marchant 1,038 m
Carterton
Mana Island
Porirua Harbour
Greytown
Porirua
Tawa
Upper Hutt
Featherston
Makara Beach
JOHNSONVILLE
Lower Hutt
Lake Wairarapa
Wellington
Port Nicholson
Wainuiomata
Martinborough
PARLIAMENT BUILDINGS
NAT'L MUSEUM
MT. VICTORIA
MIRAMAR
RIMUTAKA FOREST PARK
ISLAND BAY
Mt. Matthews 939 m
Pirinoa
WELLINGTON INT'L
Picton
Cook Strait
Onoke L.
Aorangi Mountains

Tararua Range
Rimutaka Range

HEIGHT
m. / ft.
60 / 197
40 / 130
20 / 65
15 / 50
10 / 33
5 / 16
2 / 7
0
2 / 7
5 / 16
10 / 33
20 / 65
30 / 98
40 / 130
50 / 164
60 / 197
m.
DEPTH
(Figures in Hundreds)

POPULATION OF CITIES AND TOWNS
■ OVER 2,000,000
■ 1,000,000 - 1,999,999
● 500,000 - 999,999
● 250,000 - 499,999
● 100,000 - 249,999
● 30,000 - 99,999
● 10,000 - 29,999
○ UNDER 10,000

SCALE 1:6,000,000   LAMBERT CONFORMAL CONIC PROJECTION
MILES 0 ... 100 ... 200 ... 300
KILOMETERS 0 ... 100 ... 200 ... 300

© HAMMOND INC

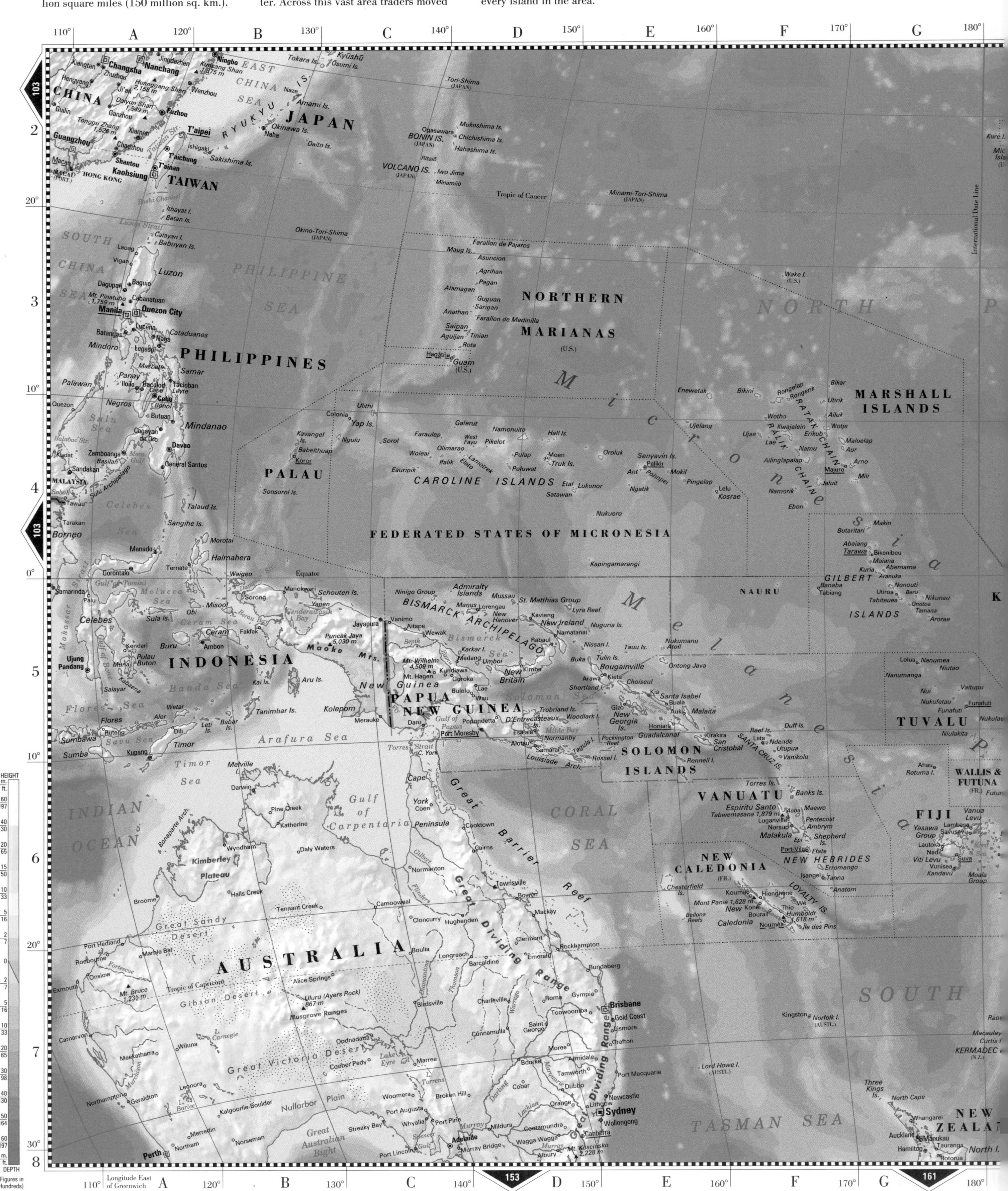

The Pacific Ocean is immense: its area covers about 64 million square miles (166 million sq. km.), while the world's land areas cover only 58 million square miles (150 million sq. km.).

It is more than twice the size of the next largest ocean, the Atlantic. It occupies about one-third of the world's surface, and holds 46 percent of the world's water. Across this vast area traders moved eastward, reaching Fiji by 1300 B.C., and shortly thereafter Tahiti. Between A.D. 400 and A.D. 1000 a distinct Polynesian culture reached virtually every island in the area.

Central Pacific Ocean

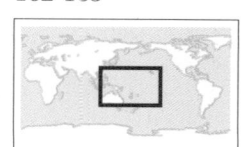

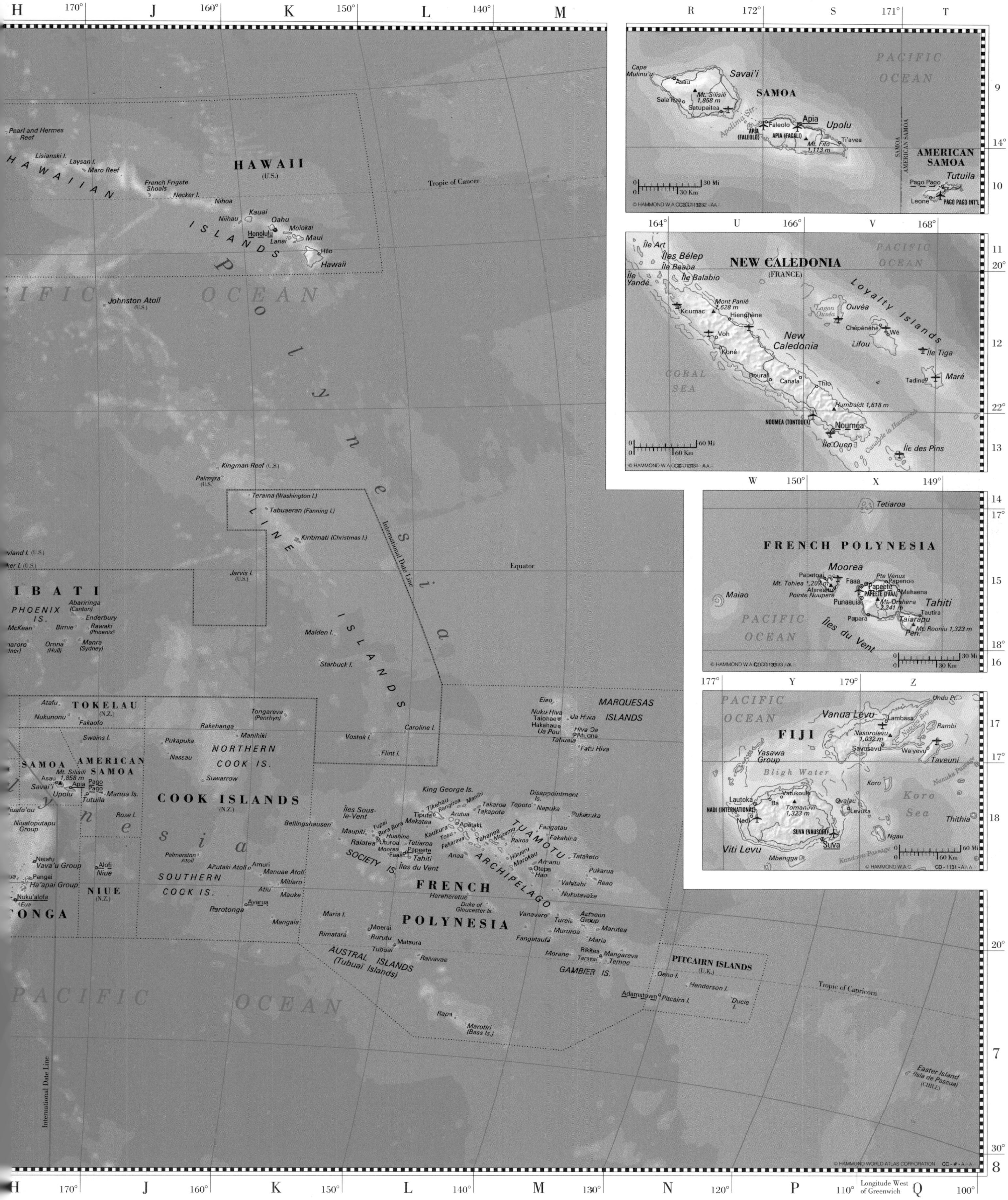

HAWAII (U.S.)

HAWAIIAN ISLANDS

Pearl and Hermes Reef
Lisianski I.
Laysan I.
Maro Reef
French Frigate Shoals
Necker I.
Nihoa
Niihau   Kauai
Oahu
Honolulu   Molokai
Lanai   Maui
Hilo
Hawaii

Johnston Atoll (U.S.)

P O L Y N E S I A

PACIFIC   OCEAN

Kingman Reef (U.S.)
Palmyra (U.S.)
Teraina (Washington I.)
Tabuaeran (Fanning I.)
Kiritimati (Christmas I.)

Jarvis I. (U.S.)

L I N E   I S L A N D S

International Date Line

Equator

Tropic of Cancer

IBATI
PHOENIX IS.
Abariringa (Canton)
McKean   Enderbury
Birnie   Rawaki (Phoenix)
Orona (Hull)   Manra (Sydney)

Malden I.

Starbuck I.

M I C R O N E S I A

TOKELAU (N.Z.)
Atafu
Nukunonu
Fakaofo
Swains I.

SAMOA
AMERICAN SAMOA
Asau   Mt. Silisili 1,858 m
Savai'i   Apia
Tutuila
Pago Pago

Rose I.

Niuafo'ou
Niuatoputapu Group
Neiafu   Vava'u Group
Pangai
Ha'apai Group
Nuku'alofa
'Eua

TONGA

Rakahanga
Manihiki
Pukapuka
Nassau
NORTHERN COOK IS.
Suwarrow
Palmerston Atoll

COOK ISLANDS (N.Z.)

SOUTHERN COOK IS.
Aputaki Atoll   Amuri
Manuae Atoll
Mitiaro
Atiu
Mauke
Avarua
Rarotonga
Mangaia

Tongareva (Penrhyn)
Caroline I.
Vostok I.
Flint I.

Maria I.
Moerai
Rimatara   Rurutu   Maria
Tubuai
Mataura
Raivavae

AUSTRAL ISLANDS (Tubuai Islands)

Rapa
Marotiri (Bass Is.)

SOCIETY IS.
Îles Sous-le-Vent
Maupiti   Bora Bora
Raiatea   Huahine
Tahaa   Moorea
Tupai   Tetiaroa
Faaa   Papeete
Tahiti
Îles du Vent

FRENCH POLYNESIA

Eiao
Nuku Hiva
Taiohae   Ua Huka
Hakahau   Ua Pou
Hiva Oa
Atuona
Tahuata   Fatu Hiva

MARQUESAS ISLANDS

King George Is.
Tikehau   Rangiroa   Manihi
Tiputa   Arutua   Takaroa   Takapoto
Makatea   Kaukura   Apataki
Fakarava   Toau
Tahanea   Makemo
Marokau   Raroia
Anaa   Amanu   Tatakoto
Hao   Reao
Otepa   Pukarua
Vahitahi   Reao
Nukutavake

Disappointment Is.
Napuka   Pukapuka
Tepoto
Fangatau
Fakahina

TUAMOTU ARCHIPELAGO

Hereheretue
Duke of Gloucester Is.
Vanavaro   Tureia   Actaeon Group
Maria   Mururoa   Marutea
Morane
Rikitea   Mangareva   Temoe

GAMBIER IS.

PITCAIRN ISLANDS (U.K.)
Oeno I.
Adamstown   Pitcairn I.   Henderson I.   Ducie I.

Tropic of Capricorn

Easter Island (Isla de Pascua) (CHILE)

PACIFIC   OCEAN

International Date Line

Longitude West of Greenwich

SAMOA (inset)

Cape Mulinu'u
Asau
Sala'ilua   Mt. Silisili 1,858 m
Satupaitea
Savai'i
Apolima Str.
APIA (FALEOLO)
APIA (FAGALI)   Faleolo
Upolu
Ti'avea
Mt. Fito 1,113 m
SAMOA

AMERICAN SAMOA
Tutuila
Pago Pago
Leone   PAGO PAGO INT'L

PACIFIC OCEAN

0   30 Mi
0   30 Km

© HAMMOND W.A. CORP. 1132 -AA

NEW CALEDONIA (FRANCE) (inset)

Île Art
Îles Bélep   Île Baaba
Île Yandé   Île Balabio
Koumac   Mont Panié 1,628 m
Hienghène
Voh
Koné
Bourail   Canala   Tho
NOUMEA (TONTOUTA)   Nouméa
Île Ouen   Humboldt 1,618 m
Île des Pins

Loyalty Islands
Lagon d'Ouvéa
Ouvéa
Chépénéhé   Wé
Lifou
Île Tiga
Tadine   Maré

New Caledonia

CORAL SEA

PACIFIC OCEAN

0   60 Mi
0   60 Km

© HAMMOND W.A. CORP. 1131 - AA

FRENCH POLYNESIA (inset)

Tetiaroa
Moorea
Papetoai   Pte Vénus   Papenoo
Mt. Tohiea 1,207 m   Faaa   Mahaena
Maiao   Afareaitu   PAPEETE (FAA)
Pointe Nuupere   Punaauia   Mt. Orohena 3,241 m
Papara   Tautira   Tahiti
Taiarapu Pen.
Maia   Pte Roonui 1,323 m
Îles du Vent

PACIFIC OCEAN

0   30 Mi
0   30 Km

© HAMMOND W.A. CORP. 1133 /AA

FIJI (inset)

Undu Pt.
Vanua Levu   Lambasa
Yasawa Group   Nasorolevu 1,032 m   Rambi
Savusavu
Wa'yevu   Taveuni

Lautoka   Vatukoula
NADI (INTERNATIONAL)   Ba   Tomaniivi 1,323 m
Nadi
Viti Levu   Ovalau   Levuka
SUVA (NAUSORI)   Ngau
Suva   Mbengga I.

Bligh Water
Koro
KORO SEA
Thithia

Mbenggga Passage   Kandavu Passage

PACIFIC OCEAN

0   60 Mi
0   60 Km

© HAMMOND W.A.C.   CD - 1131 - A A A

POPULATION OF CITIES AND TOWNS

▣ OVER 3,000,000	◉ 500,000 - 999,999	○ UNDER 100,000
▢ 1,000,000 - 2,999,999	◉ 100,000 - 499,999	

SCALE 1:27,000,000   LAMBERT AZIMUTHAL EQUAL-AREA PROJECTION

MILES   0   400   800   1200
KILOMETERS   0   400   800   1200

© HAMMOND WORLD ATLAS CORPORATION

North America

The Grand Canyon, one of the deepest canyons in the world, with a depth of 1 mile (1.6 km.), can be seen in this spectacular, west-looking, low-oblique image. The Colorado River cut through rocks billions of years old to create this canyon. The Grand Canyon is 277 miles (466 km.) long and averages nearly 10 miles (16 km.) in width. The snow-covered, forested Kaibab Plateau (north of the canyon) and the Coconino Plateau (south of the canyon) are visible. Western portions of the Painted Desert can be seen east of the canyon where the Little Colorado joins the Colorado River.

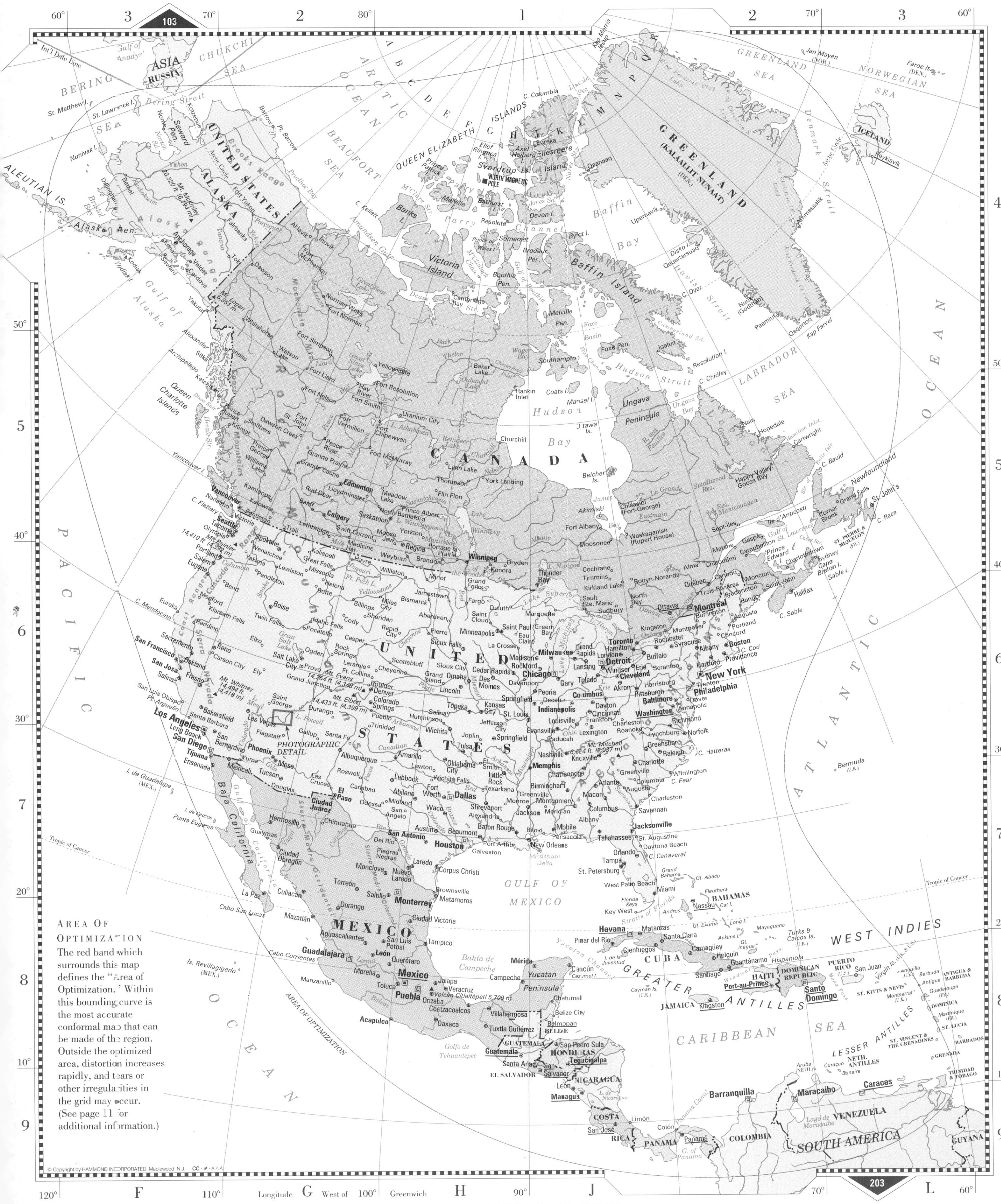

AREA OF OPTIMIZATION

The red band which surrounds this map defines the "Area of Optimization." Within this bounding curve is the most accurate conformal map that can be made of the region. Outside the optimized area, distortion increases rapidly, and tears or other irregularities in the grid may occur. (See page 11 for additional information.)

AREA OF OPTIMIZATION

PHOTOGRAPHIC DETAIL

© Copyright by HAMMOND INCORPORATED, Maplewood, N.J.   CC · · AAA

SCALE 1:30,000,000   OPTIMAL CONFORMAL PROJECTION

MILES 0   500   1000   1500
KILOMETERS 0   500   1000   1500

POPULATION OF CITIES AND TOWNS

■ OVER 3,000,000	● 500,000 - 999,999	○ UNDER 100,000
▣ 1,000,000 - 2,999,999	● 100,000 - 499,999	

ASIA
RUSSIA
UNITED STATES
ALASKA
CANADA
GREENLAND (KALAALLIT NUNAAT) (DEN.)
ICELAND
MEXICO
UNITED STATES
CUBA
BAHAMAS
WEST INDIES
GREATER ANTILLES
CARIBBEAN SEA
LESSER ANTILLES
SOUTH AMERICA
VENEZUELA
COLOMBIA
GUYANA

PACIFIC OCEAN
ATLANTIC OCEAN
ARCTIC OCEAN
BERING SEA
BEAUFORT SEA
HUDSON BAY
GULF OF MEXICO

Canada is larger, but its population is only one-tenth that of the U.S. A very short growing season north of 55° North Latitude, the extremely thin soils north of the St. Lawrence Valley, and the

Longitude West of Greenwich

Canada

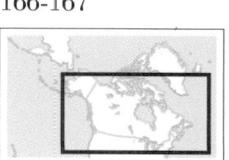

low precipitation of the northwestern coniferous forest and tundra region have discouraged widespread settlement throughout Canada. In fact, the vast majority of Canadians reside in the south, along a 100-mile-wide (161 km.) zone which stretches from Québec to Vancouver. English and French are both official languages, while Eskimo-Aleut is spoken in the far north.

POPULATION OF CITIES AND TOWNS
- ▣ OVER 2,000,000
- ▢ 1,000,000 - 1,999,999
- ◉ 500,000 - 999,999
- ◉ 100,000 - 499,999
- ◦ 50,000 - 99,999
- ◦ UNDER 50,000

SCALE 1:12,000,000   LAMBERT CONFORMAL CONIC PROJECTION

MILES 0   200   400   600

KILOMETERS 0   200   430   600

© HAMMOND WORLD ATLAS CORPORATION

Lying between the 24th and 49th parallels north of the equator (excluding Alaska and Hawaii), the U.S. has a wide range of climates. Although areas in the western states are very dry, the country, has many very productive agricultural regions. A rich natural storehouse of minerals and fuels provided the underpinning for industrial development. Americans continue to move more frequently than citizens of other countries. The geographic center of population is now located west of the Mississippi River, as the movement of people is to the west and to the south.

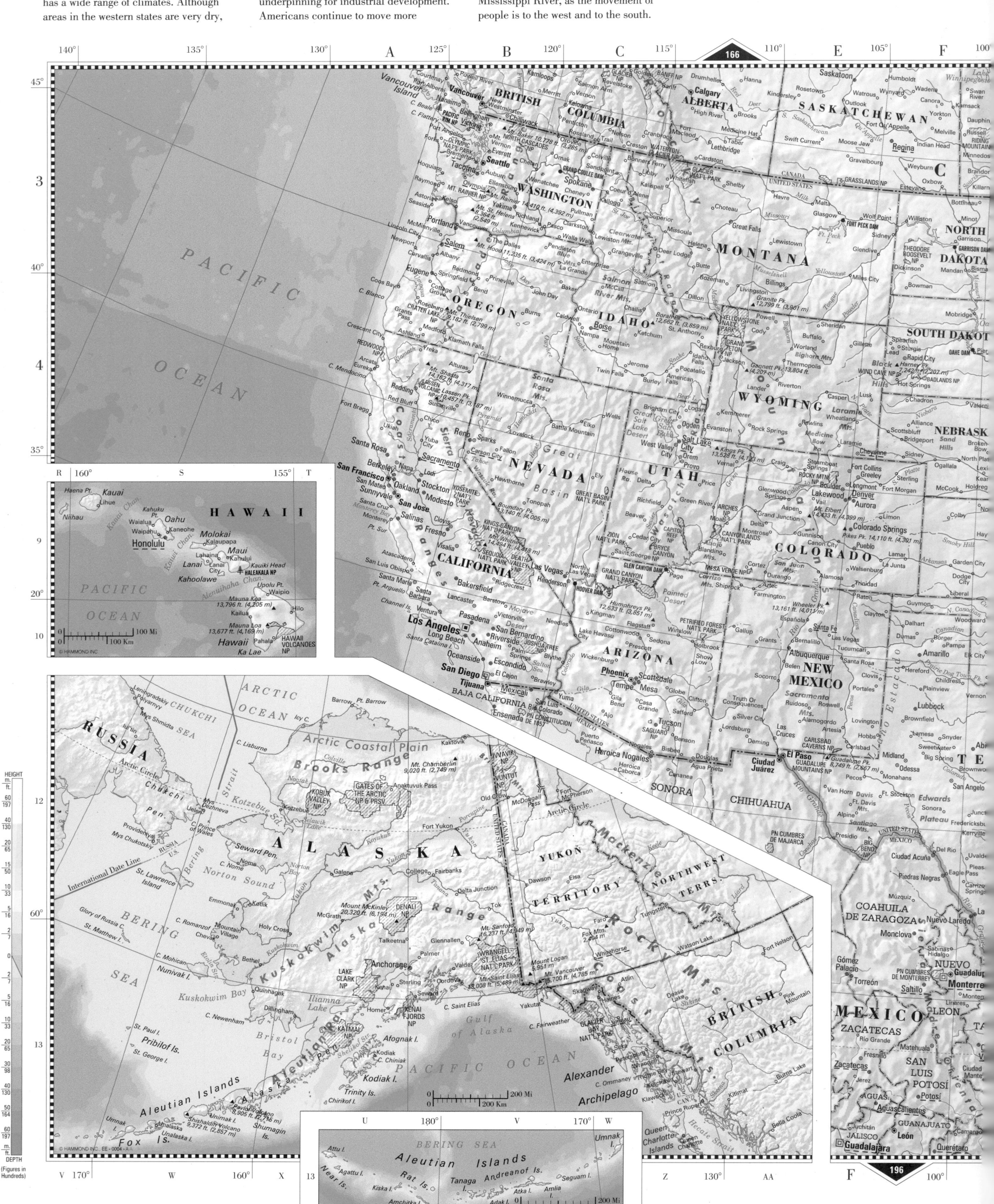

POPULATION OF CITIES AND TOWNS

■ OVER 2,000,000   ● 500,000 - 999,999   ○ 50,000 - 99,999
□ 1,000,000 - 1,999,999   ● 100,000 - 499,999   ○ UNDER 50,000

SCALE 1:12,000,000   LAMBERT CONFORMAL CONIC PROJECTION

MILES   0   200   400   600
KILOMETERS 0   200   400   600

The Rocky Mountains, Glacier and Olympic national parks and Puget Sound rank among the most beautiful areas of the United States. The Coast Ranges are part of the Pacific "Ring of Fire;" Mt. St. Helens erupted in 1980, and the possibility exists that Mount Rainier might erupt and threaten such metropolitan areas as Seattle and Tacoma. Canada's prairie provinces produce most of the country's grain and livestock. British Columbia has prospered due to its convenient strategic location for both transcontinental and transoceanic trade.

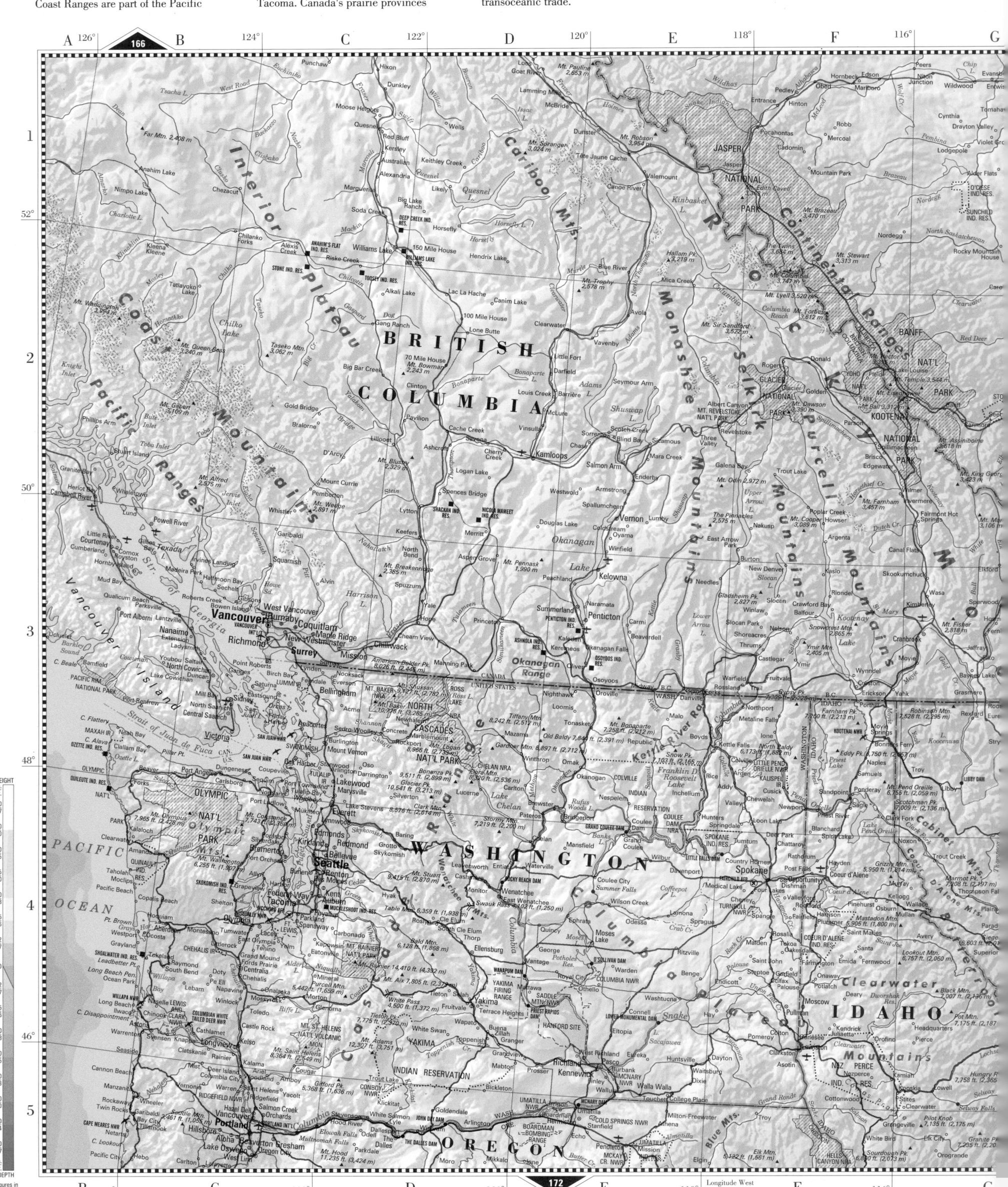

Southwestern Canada, Northwestern U.S.

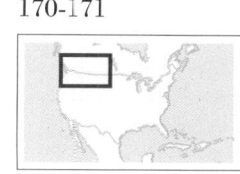

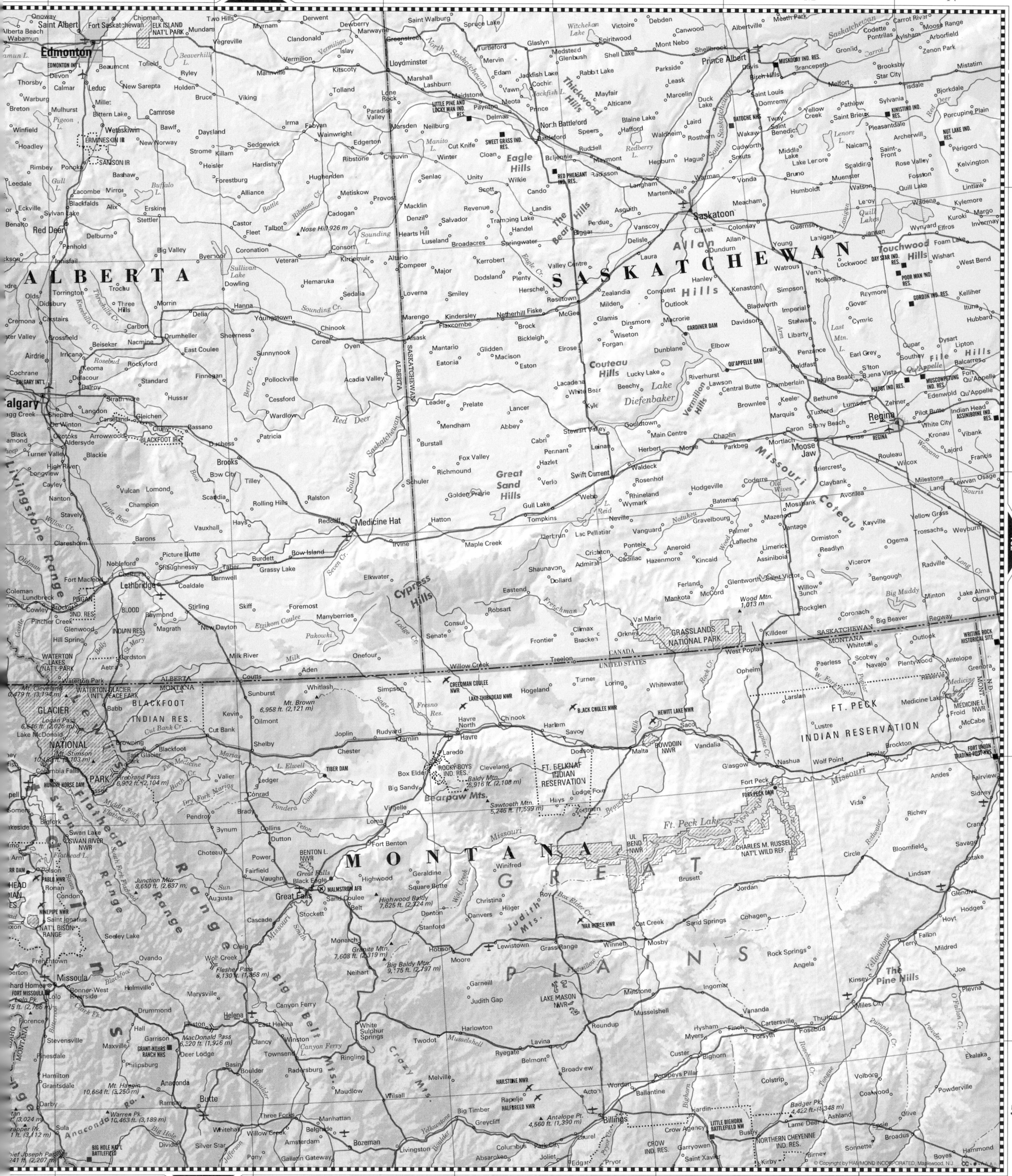

166

173

182

POPULATION OF CITIES AND TOWNS

- ■ OVER 2,000,000
- □ 1,000,000 - 1,999,999
- ● 500,000 - 999,999
- ◉ 250,000 - 499,999
- ● 100,000 - 249,999
- ◦ 30,000 - 99,999
- ◦ 10,000 - 29,999
- ◦ UNDER 10,000

SCALE 1:3,000,000   LAMBERT CONFORMAL CONIC PROJECTION

MILES 0   50   100   150

KILOMETERS 0   50   100   150

As in the Southwest, water is the driving human issue in much of this area. Large parts of Nevada and Utah receive, on the average, less than 10 inches (25 cm.) of rainfall a year.

Massive irrigation projects over the last hundred years have made Idaho's Snake River Valley fertile. Water from the headwaters of the Colorado River has been diverted by a system of tunnels to agricultural lands east of the Rockies north of Denver. Although production from copper mines in Montana and Utah has dropped drastically, coal and uranium extraction remain important.

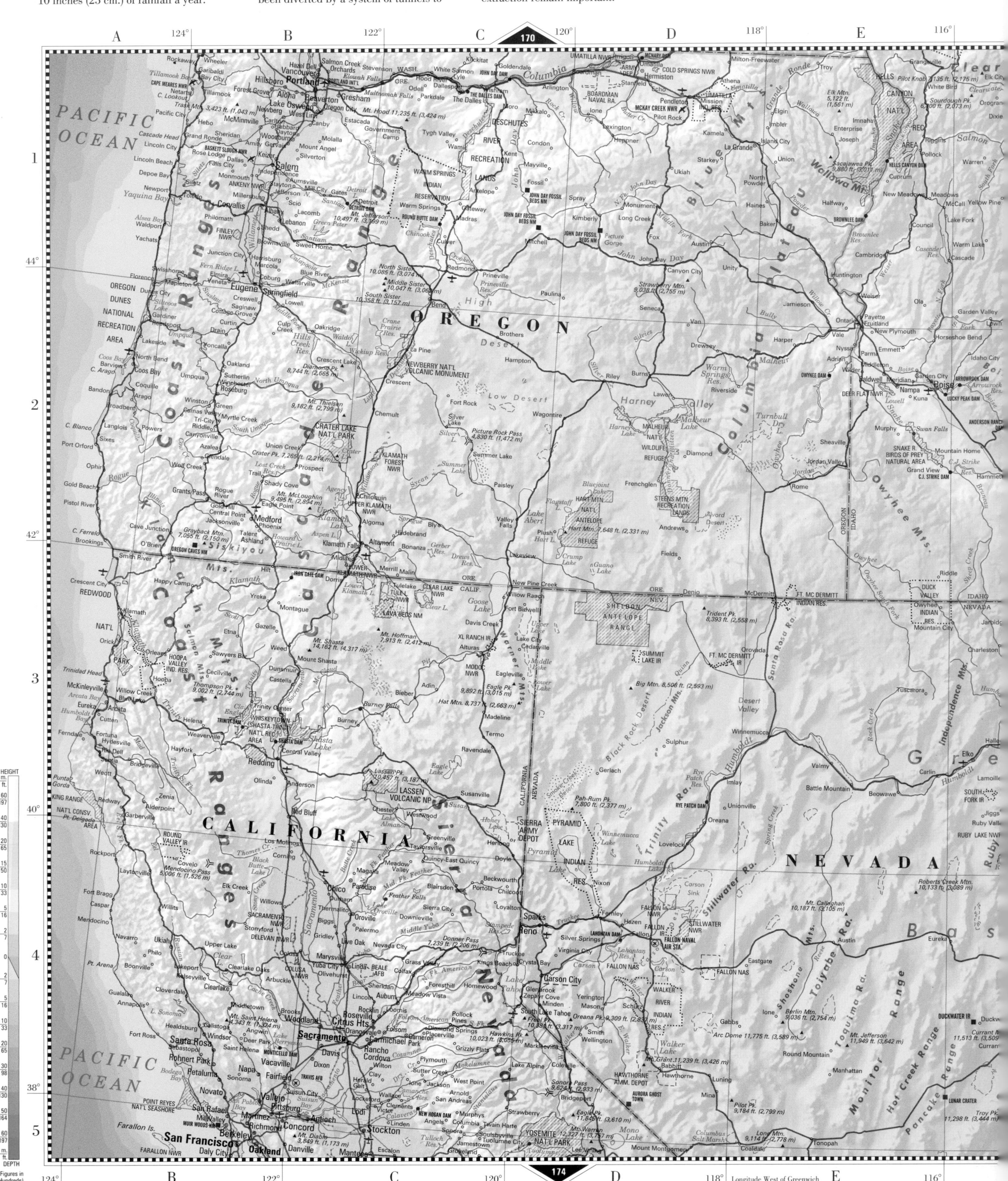

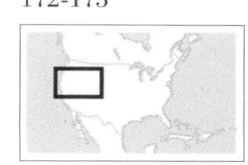

States and major features shown: MONTANA, IDAHO, WYOMING, UTAH, NEVADA, COLORADO.

Grid reference letters (top and bottom): F · G · H · J · K · L

Longitude marks (top): 114° · 112° · 110° · 108° · 106°
Latitude marks (right): 1 · 44° · 2 · 42° · 3 · 40° · 4 · 38° · 5

Selected labels: ROCKY Mts., Yellowstone, YELLOWSTONE NAT'L PARK, GRAND TETON NP, Wind River Range, Uinta Mts., Wasatch Range, Great Salt Lake, Salt Lake City, Idaho Falls, Pocatello, Twin Falls, Ogden, Provo, Green River, Casper, Billings, Bozeman, Great Divide Basin, Great Basin Nat'l Park, Sawtooth Nat'l Rec. Area, Craters of the Moon Nat'l Mon., Dinosaur Nat'l Monument, Flaming Gorge Nat'l Rec. Area, Arches Nat'l Park, Canyonlands National Park, Capitol Reef Nat'l Park, Glen Canyon Nat'l Rec. Area, Grand Staircase-Escalante NM, Black Canyon of the Gunnison NM, Grand Junction, San Juan Mts., Medicine Bow Mts., Bighorn Mts., Owl Creek Mts., Absaroka Ra., Beartooth Mts.

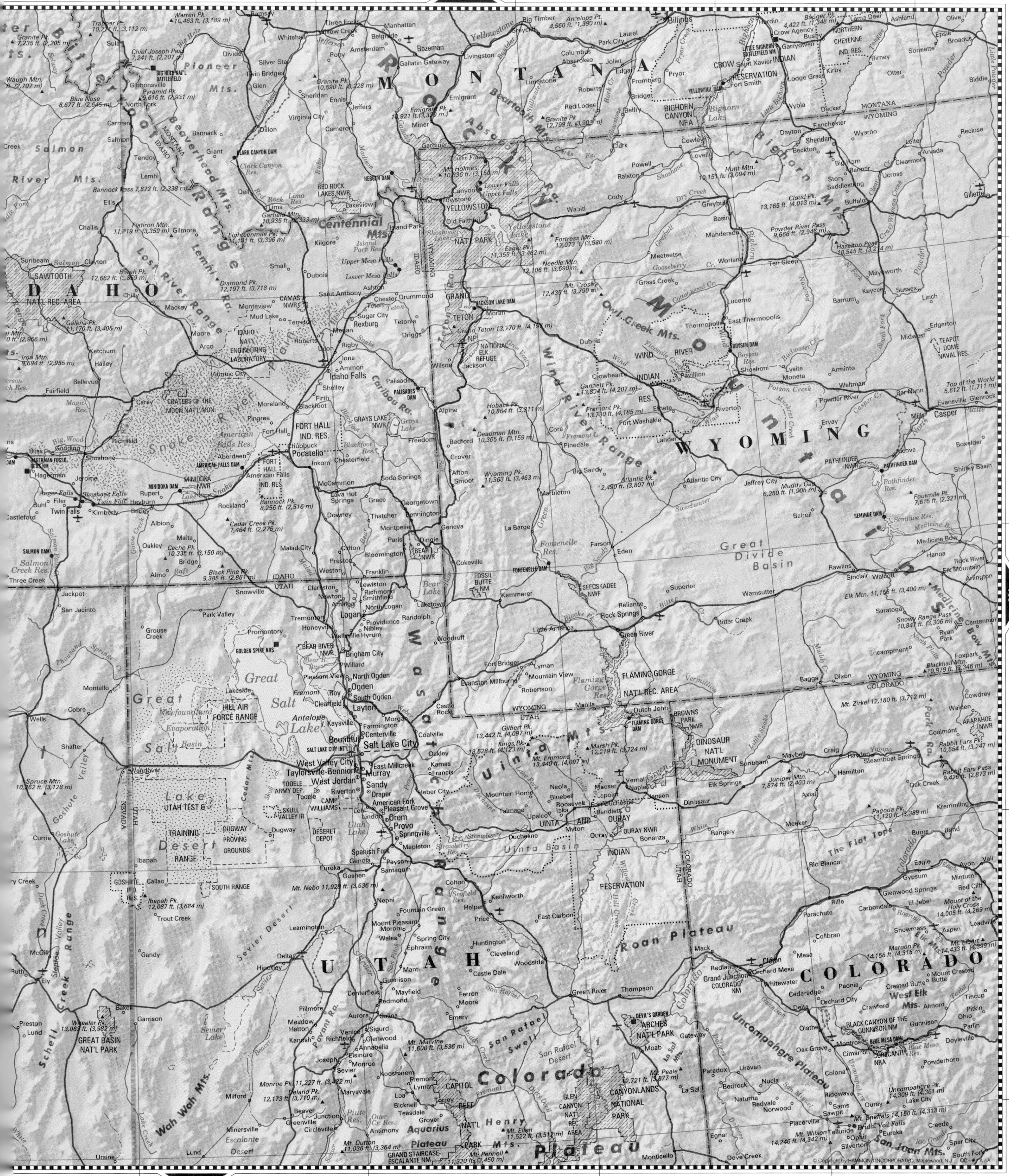

POPULATION OF CITIES AND TOWNS

Symbol	Population
■	OVER 2,000,000
●	500,000 – 999,999
□	1,000,000 – 1,999,999
◉	250,000 – 499,999
●	100,000 – 249,999
◉	10,000 – 29,999
●	30,000 – 99,999
○	UNDER 10,000

SCALE 1:3,000,000   LAMBERT CONFORMAL CONIC PROJECTION

MILES 0 · 50 · 100 · 150
KILOMETERS 0 · 50 · 100 · 150

Some of North America's earlier settlers – the Hopi, Navajo and Pueblo – flourished on the Colorado Plateau. Their ancient ruins echo the grandeur of the spires, arches and canyons nature has carved from the soft, bleached-red rock. The number and scale of national parks, monuments and recreation areas in the Southwest is unparalleled, from California's Sequoia, Death Valley and Yosemite to Arizona's Grand Canyon, Saguaro and Petrified Forest. Today, the overriding concern of this region is water, which is being depleted faster than nature can restore it.

Southwestern United States

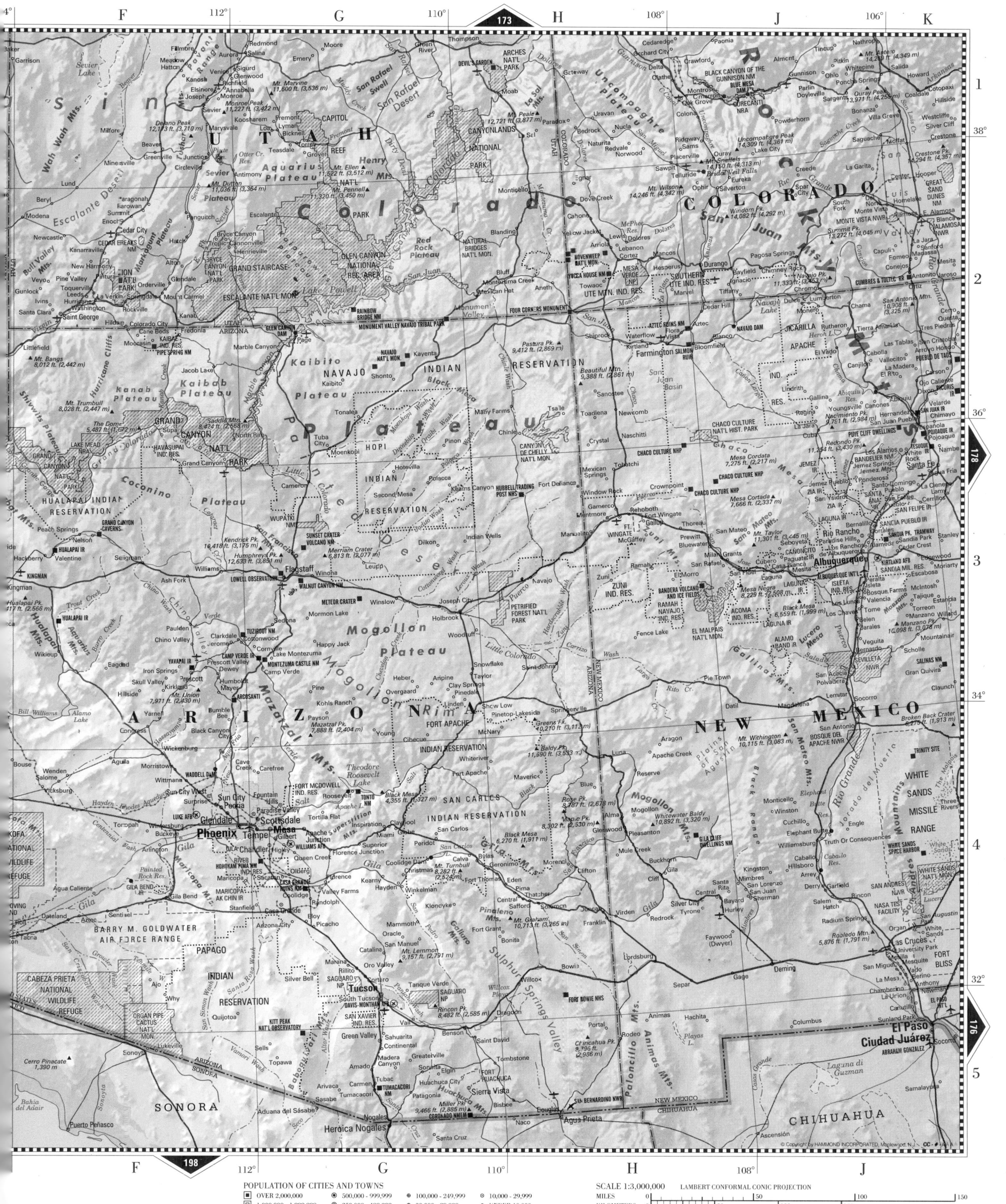

POPULATION OF CITIES AND TOWNS

■ OVER 2,000,000	● 500,000 - 999,999
□ 1,000,000 - 1,999,999	● 250,000 - 499,999

● 100,000 - 249,999   ◉ 10,000 - 29,999
● 30,000 - 99,999   ○ UNDER 10,000

SCALE 1:3,000,000   LAMBERT CONFORMAL CONIC PROJECTION

MILES
KILOMETERS

Like the state of Hawaii, Texas was an independent nation before it became a part of the United States. Thus Texans share a strong sense of state loyalty and pride. Texas entered the 20th century as a cattle and cotton kingdom. Then, following the discovery of the spectacular Spindletop oil field in 1901, the state became the nation's prime source of energy. Today, Texas is also the center of the U.S. chemical industry. With the possible future growth of U.S.-Mexican free trade, Texas occupies a strategic location for inter-American commerce.

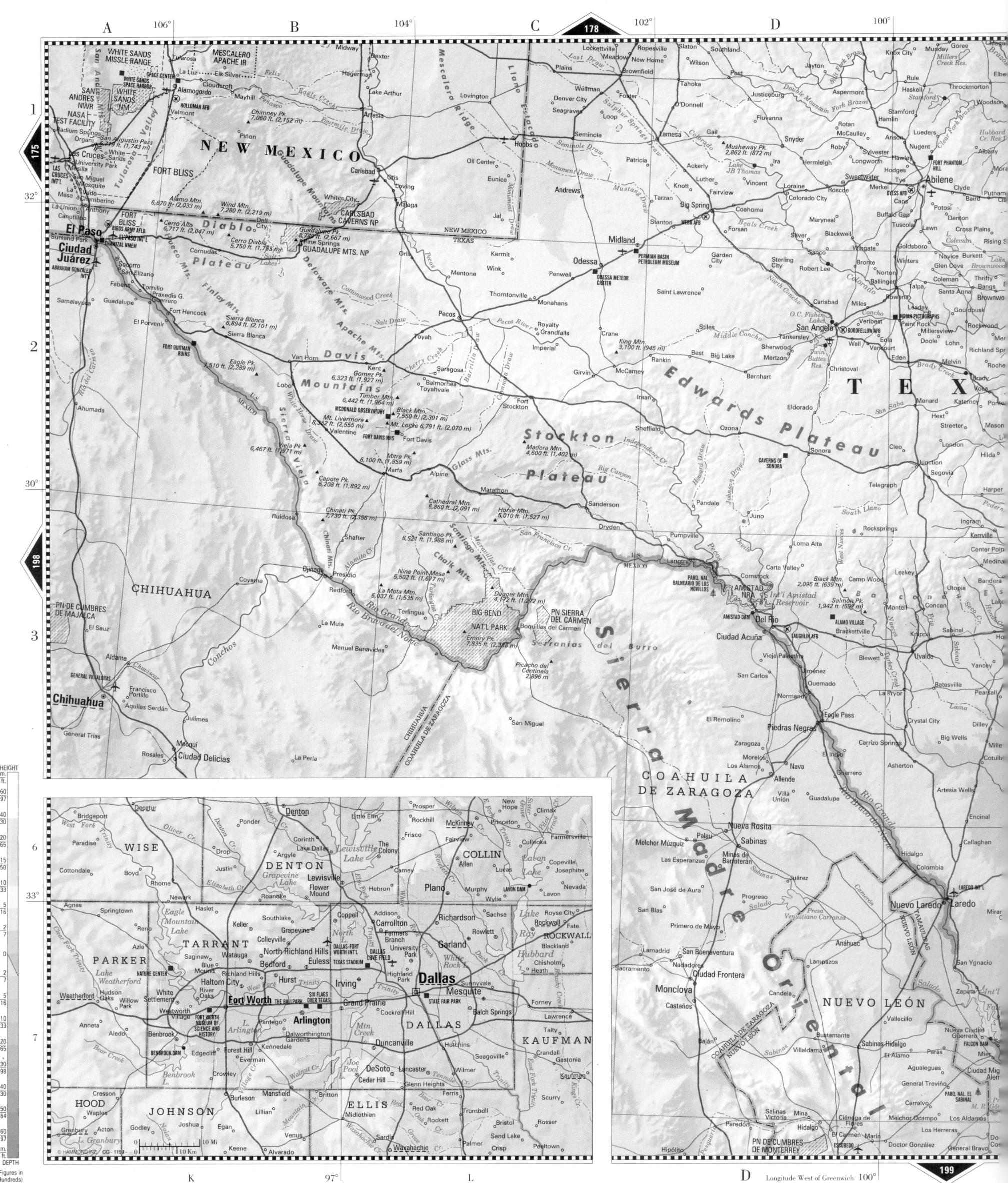

179

190

GULF OF MEXICO

© Copyright by HAMMOND INCORPORATED, Maplewood, N.J.

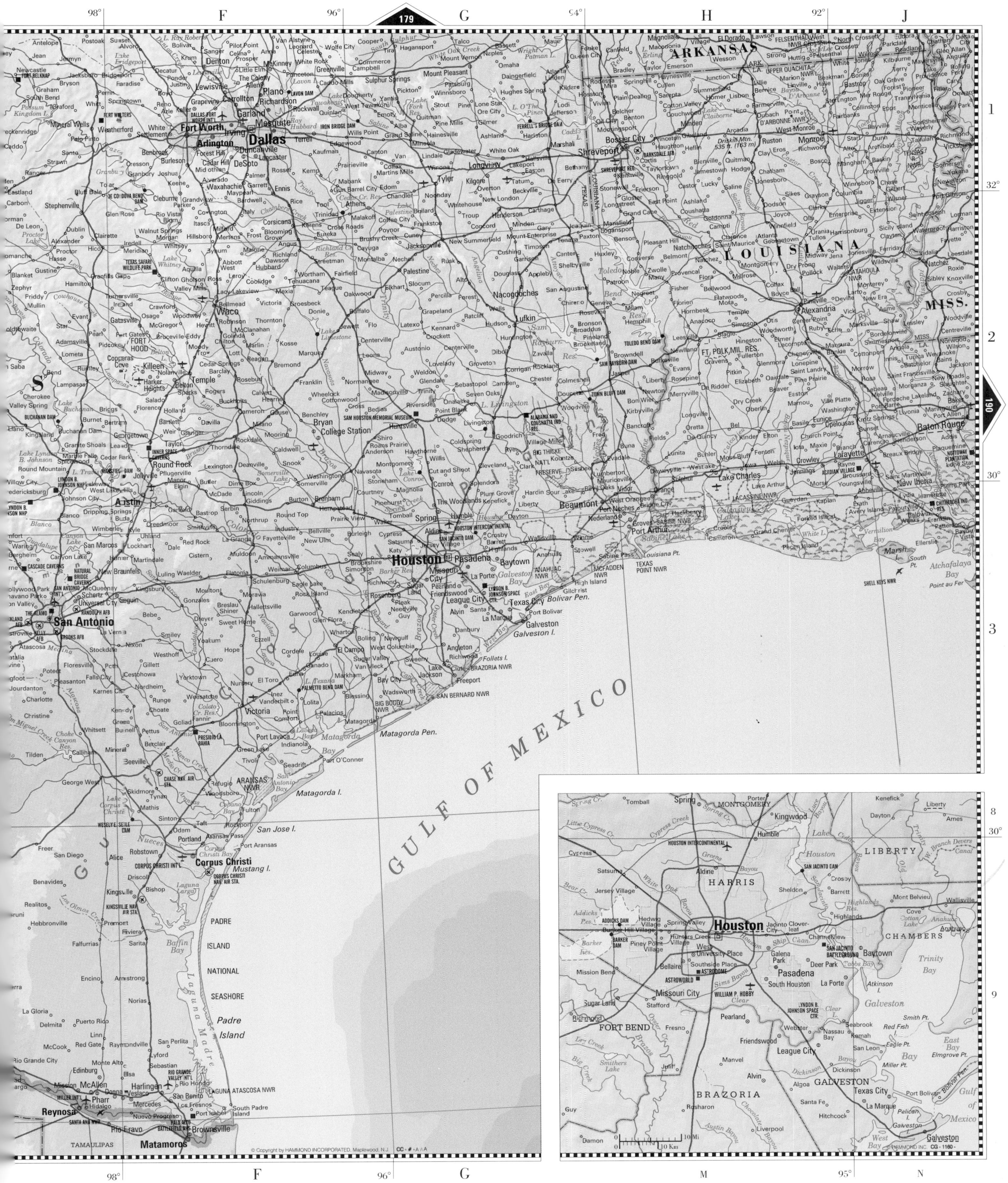

POPULATION OF CITIES AND TOWNS

| ■ OVER 2,000,000 | ■ 500,000 - 999,999 | ● 100,000 - 249,999 | ● 10,000 - 29,999 |
| □ 1,000,000 - 1,999,999 | ■ 250,000 - 499,999 | ● 30,000 - 99,999 | ○ UNDER 10,000 |

SCALE 1:3,000,000   LAMBERT CONFORMAL CONIC PROJECTION

MILES 0   50   100   150

KILOMETERS 0   50   100   150

CG - 1160 -

Originally, the endless grasslands of the Great Plains were home to the Plains Indians. After horses were introduced to the upper Rio Grande Valley in the 1600s, Native Americans of the region – Comanche, Cheyenne, Kiowa, Pawnee, etc. – adopted a totally new culture based on bison hunting from horseback. The end of the Civil War, brought the cattlemen, who dominated the region and created the legendary Cattle Kingdom of the 1870s and 80s. Eventually, homesteaders took over the Plains, producing an abundance of wheat and other grains.

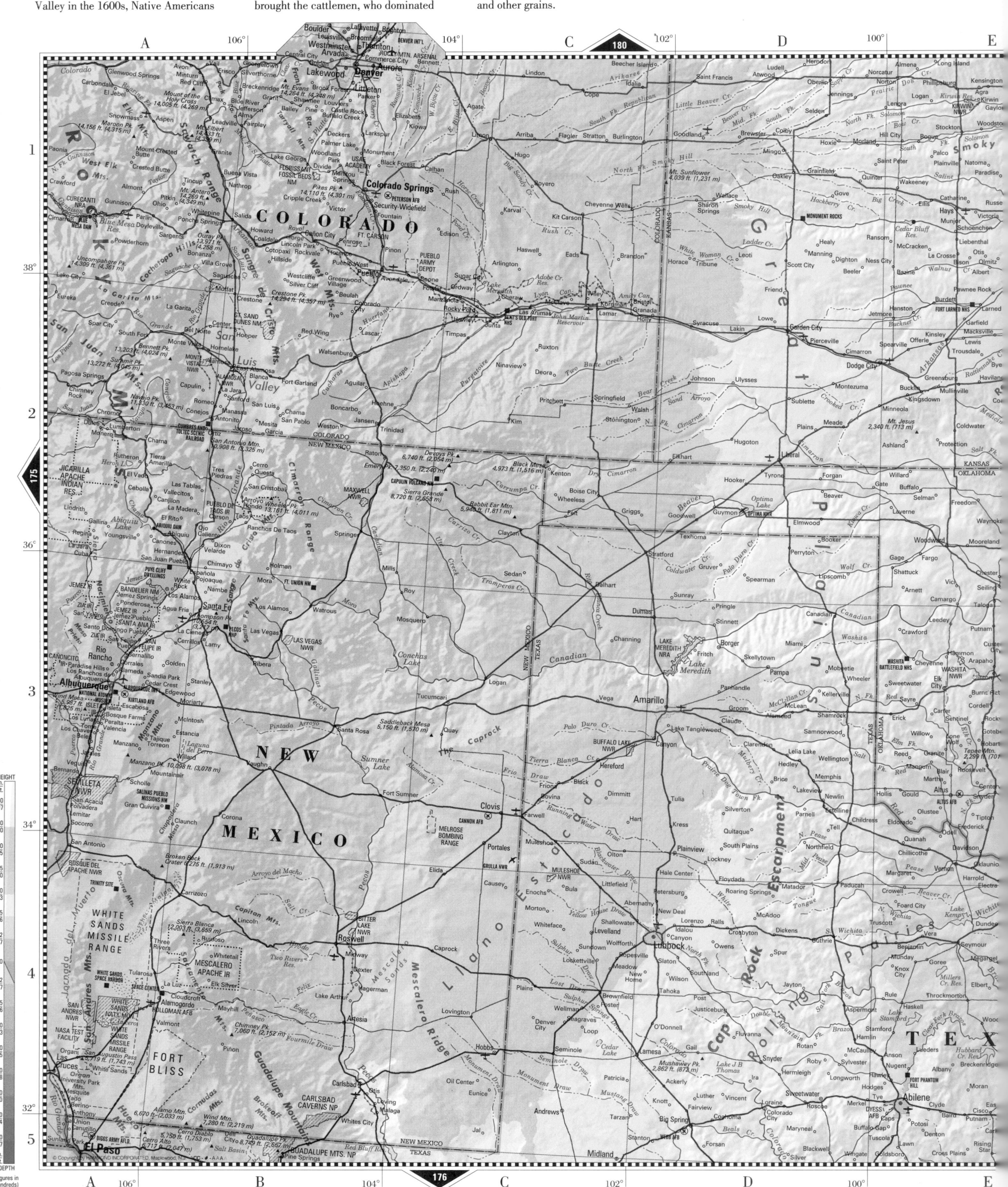

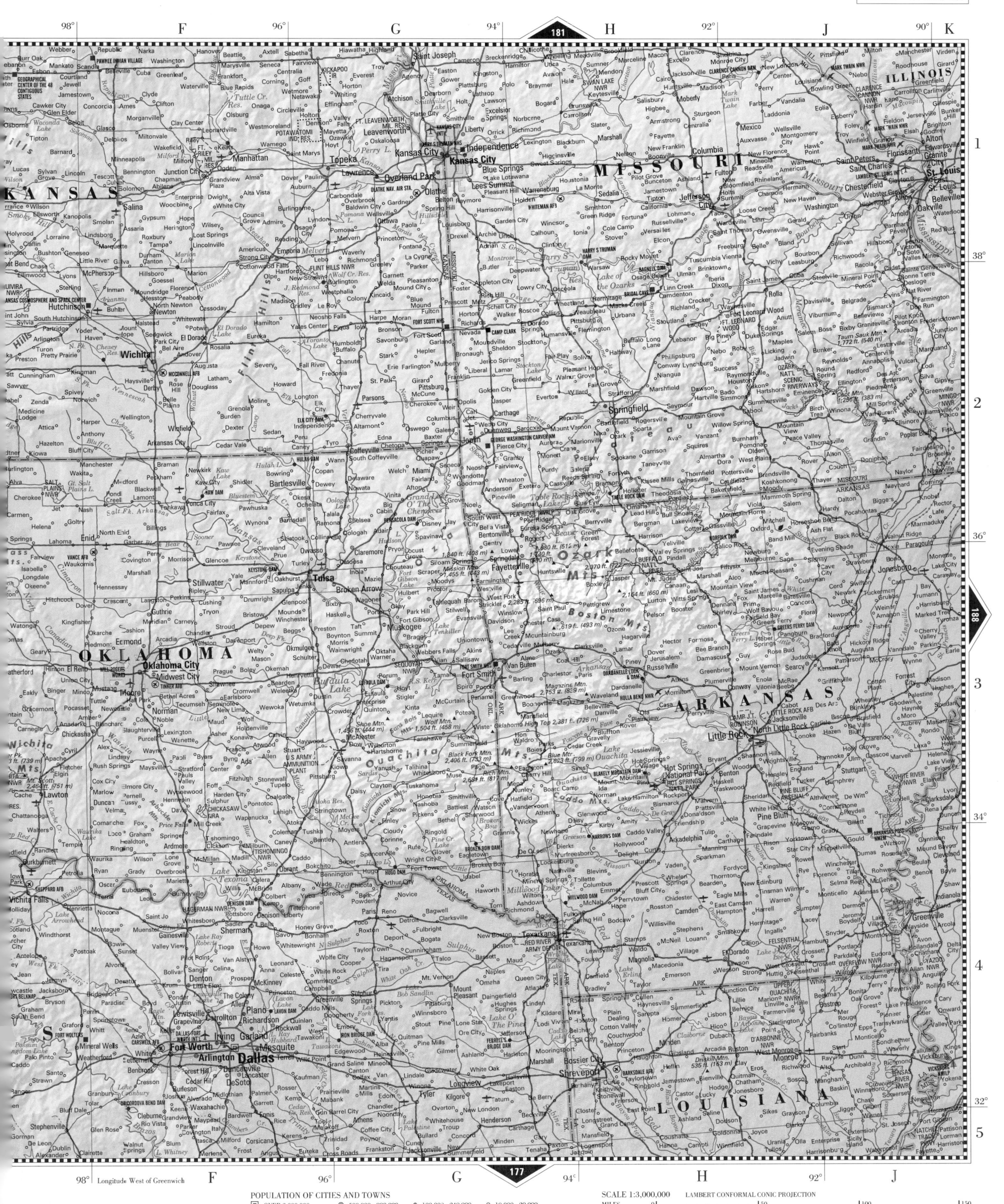

Longitudes West of Greenwich

POPULATION OF CITIES AND TOWNS

■ OVER 2,000,000	● 500,000 - 999,999	○ 100,000 - 249,999	○ 10,000 - 29,999
□ 1,000,000 - 1,999,999	◉ 250,000 - 499,999	◎ 30,000 - 99,999	○ UNDER 10,000

SCALE 1:3,000,000   LAMBERT CONFORMAL CONIC PROJECTION

MILES

KILOMETERS

The American heartland is the nation's breadbasket. The rich, dark soils, combined with advanced farming techniques, yield one of the world's richest harvests of wheat, oats, corn and soybeans. The great prairie cities - Minneapolis, St. Paul, Omaha and Kansas City - grew from feedlots and stockyards to major grain and meat processing centers, and major wholesale and distribution points for goods farmers needed. The mighty Mississippi and Missouri rivers played a major role in the settlement of the region, especially for transportation.

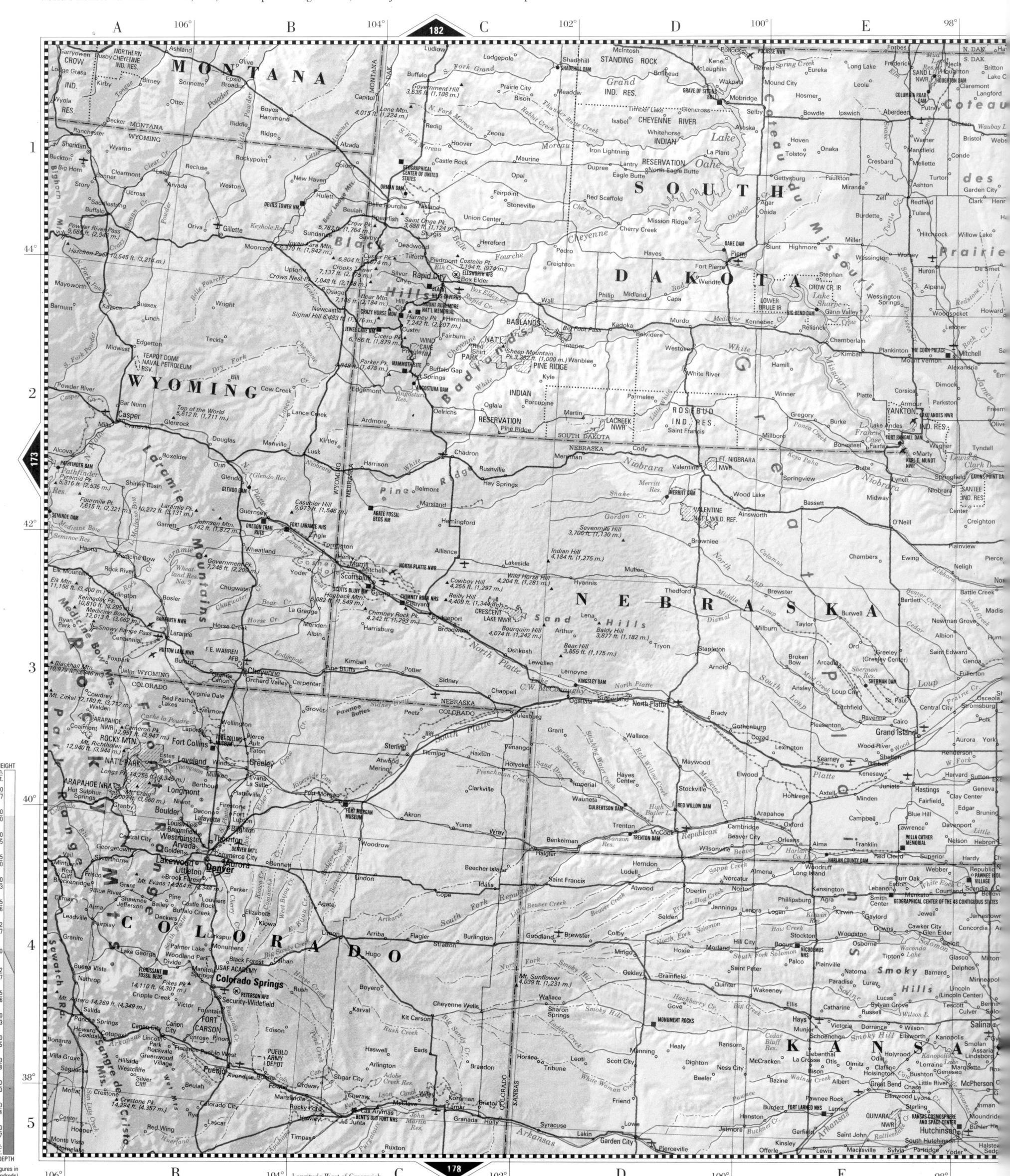

Central Great Plains

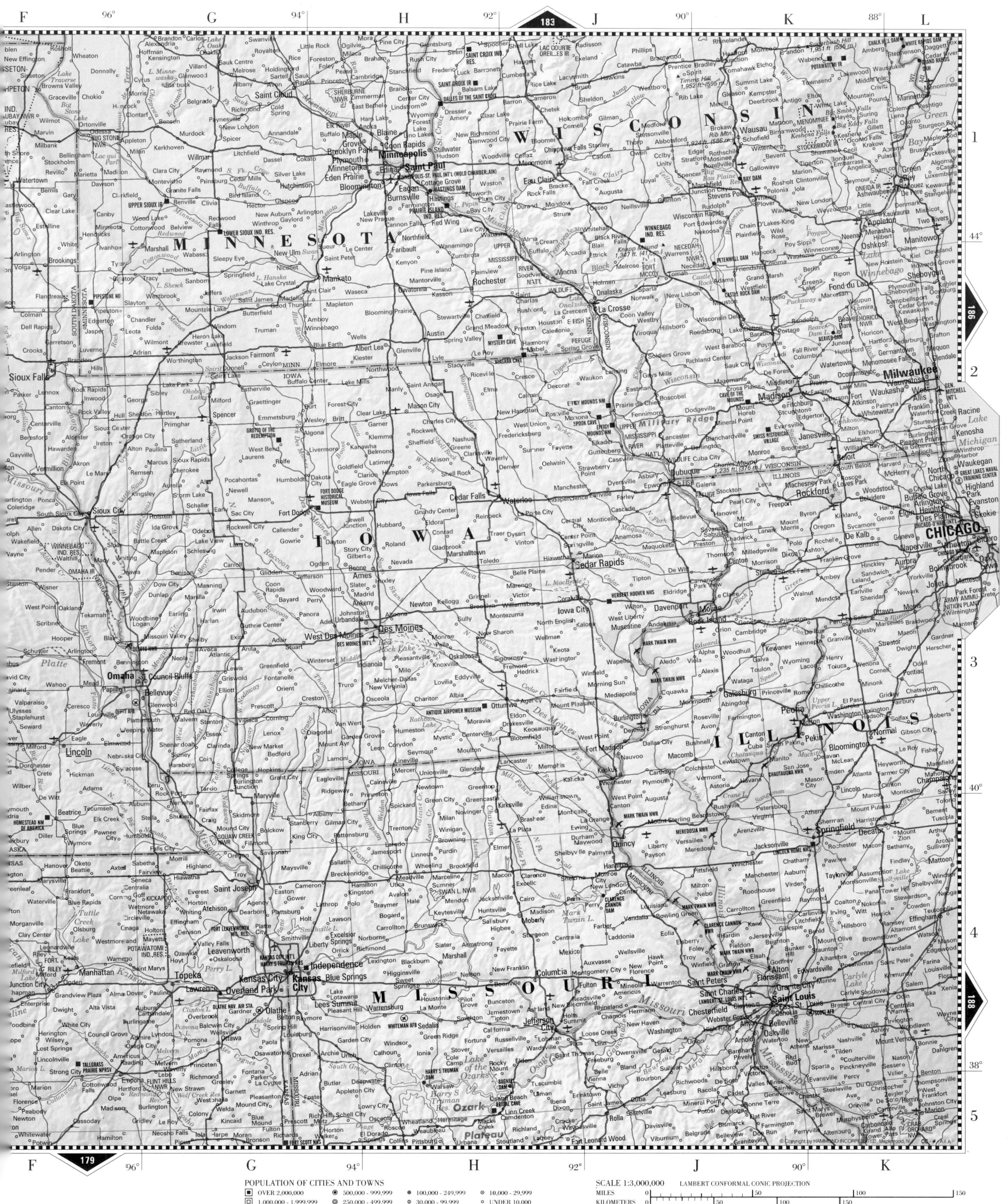

POPULATION OF CITIES AND TOWNS
- ■ OVER 2,000,000
- ▣ 1,000,000 - 1,999,999
- ● 500,000 - 999,999
- ◉ 250,000 - 499,999
- ● 100,000 - 249,999
- ⊕ 30,000 - 99,999
- ⊙ 10,000 - 29,999
- ○ UNDER 10,000

SCALE 1:3,000,000   LAMBERT CONFORMAL CONIC PROJECTION

MILES 0   50   100   150
KILOMETERS 0   50   100   150

© Copyright by HAMMOND INCORPORATED, Maplewood, N.J.

The northern Great Plains, which cover a vast expanse of both the American and Canadian landscape, are clothed in golden fields of spring wheat, barley and flax. In the second half of the 19th century, and in the early 20th century, Minnesota, the Dakotas and the Canadian prairie provinces became home to great numbers of immigrant farmers – Swedes, Norwegians, Volga Germans and Ukrainians. The thin-soiled uplands of northern Minnesota and western Ontario are forest covered and unpopulated except for occasional mining and lumbering communities.

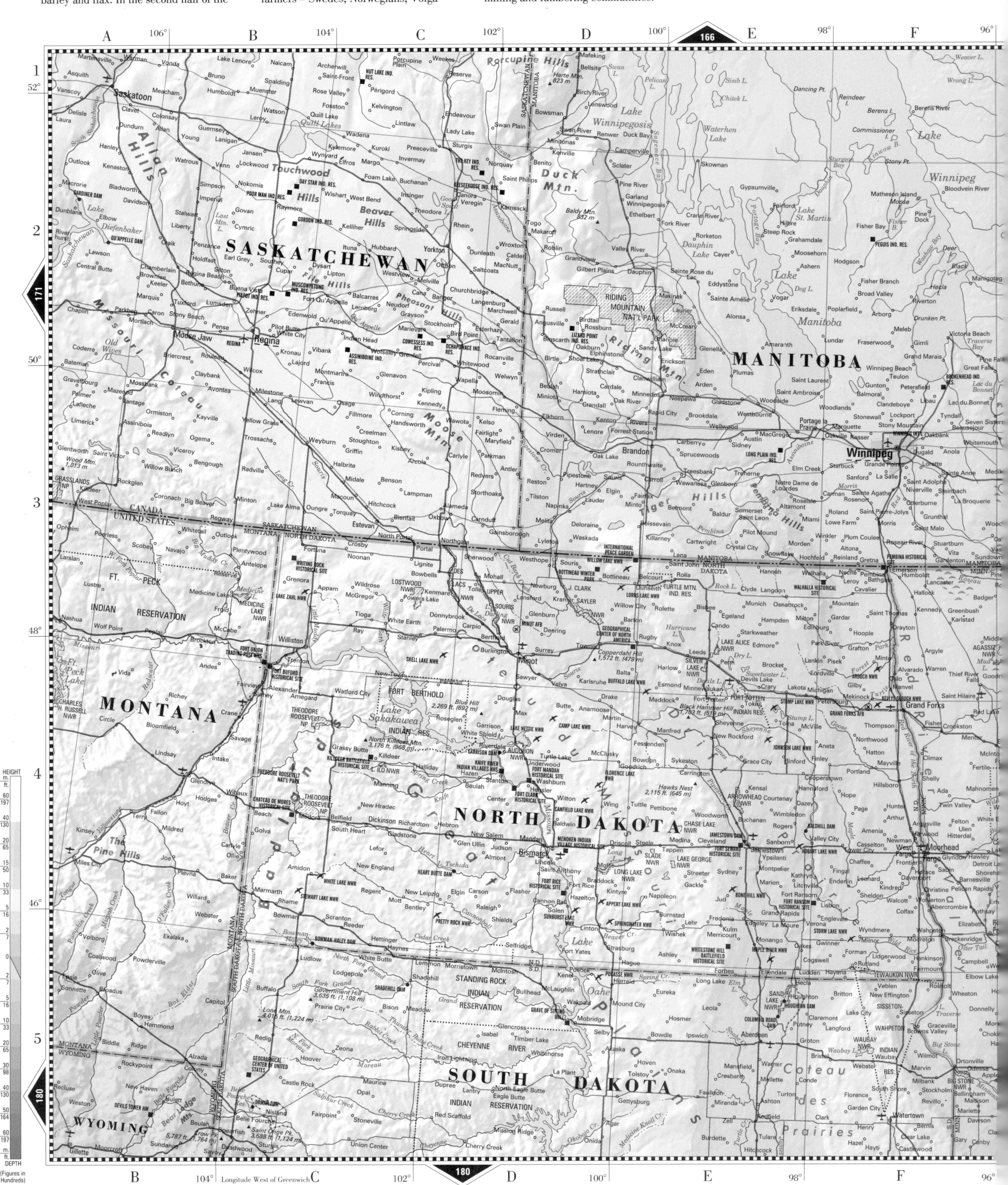

South Central Canada, North Central U.S.

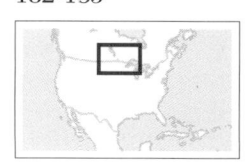

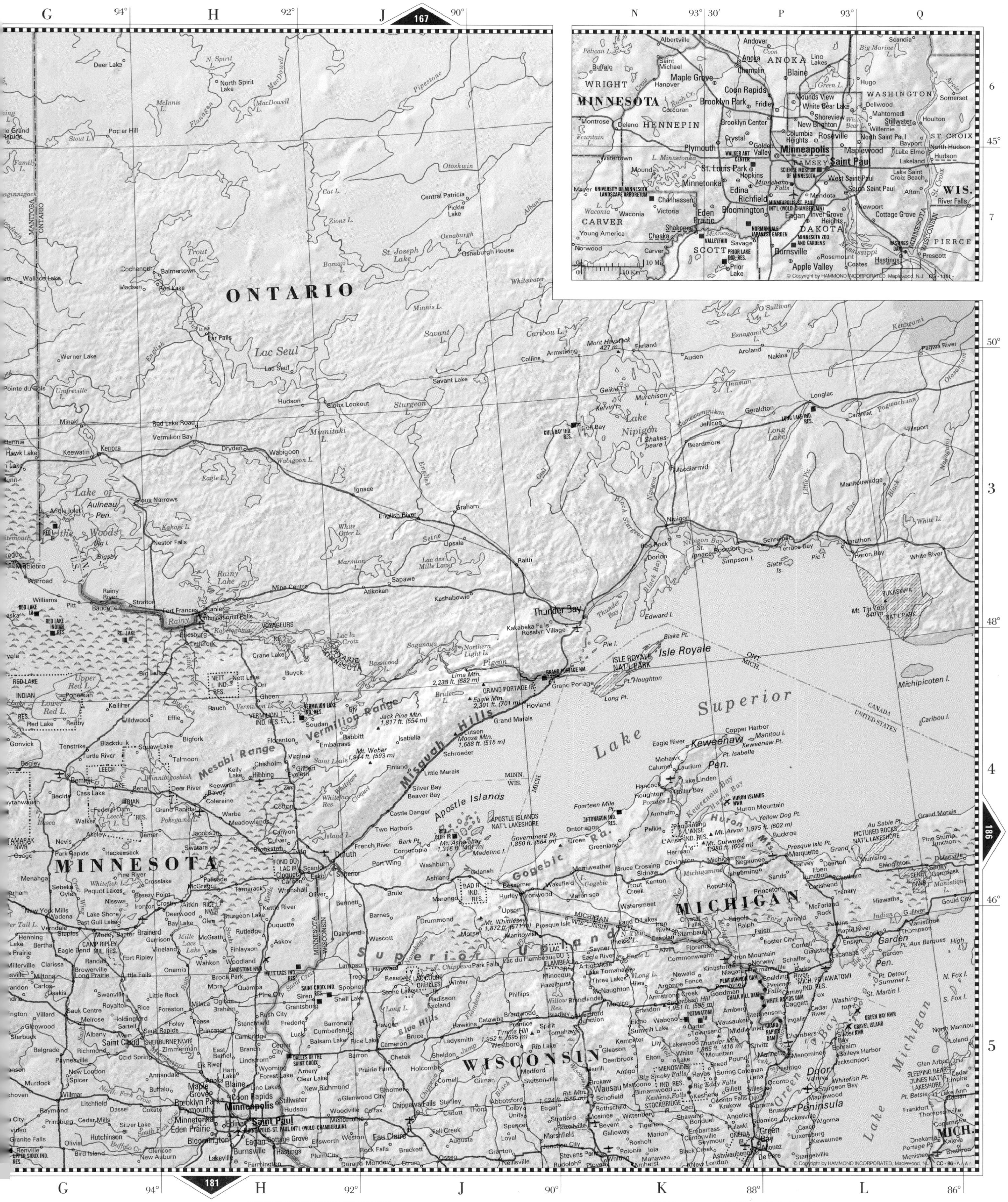

Maritime Canada and New England share a historic, economic and cultural identity that goes back to the first European settlements of the 17th century. The landscape on both sides of the border has remained rural except for the few larger central cities. Fishing, forestry in the uplands and farming in the more fertile valleys continue to be important; recreation and tourism add to the region's economy. French-speaking Quebec has vast amounts of hydro-electric power, minerals, and a growing manufacturing base, in addition to its agriculture and forestry.

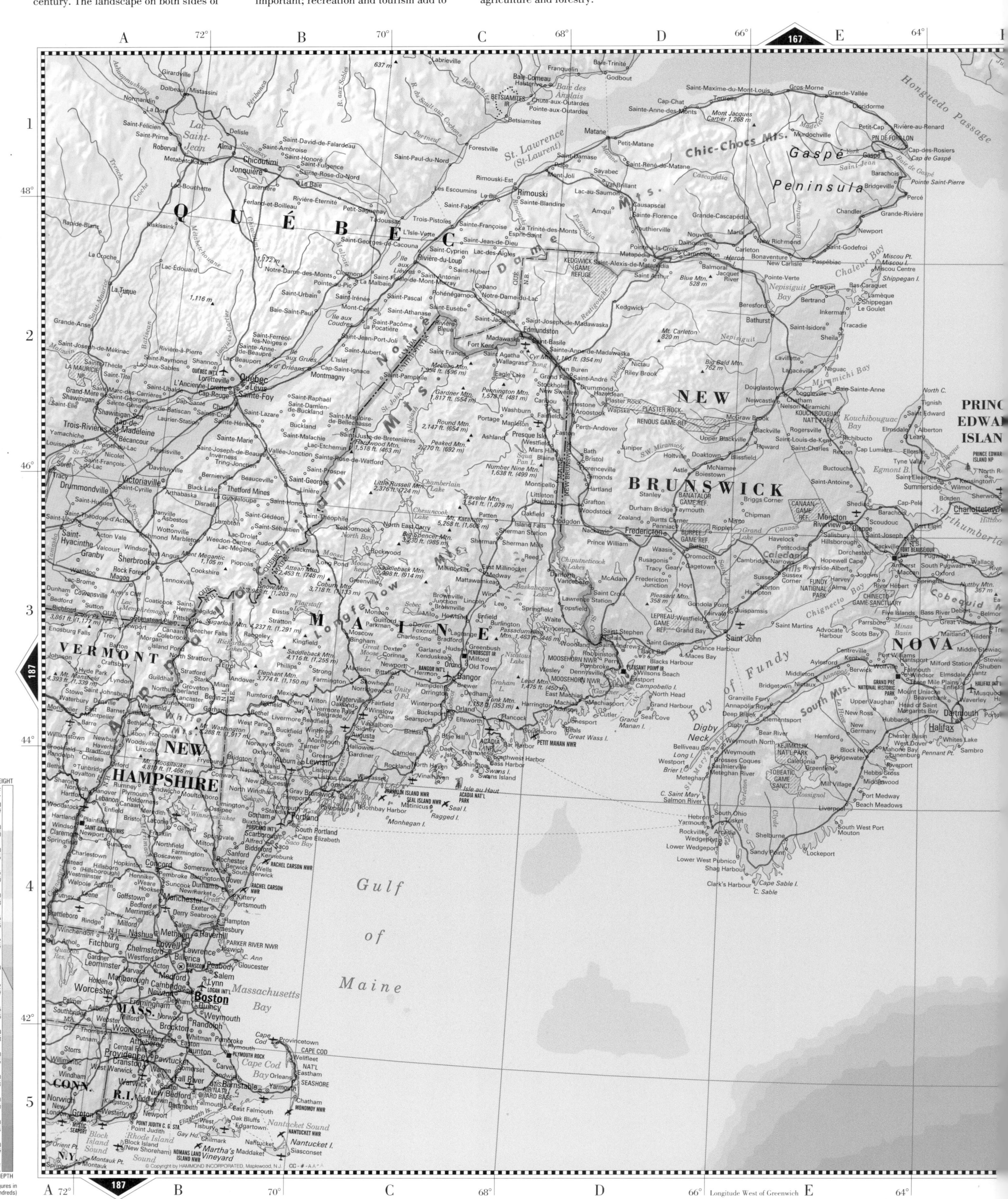

Southeastern Canada, Northeastern U.S.

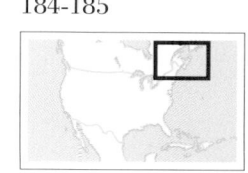

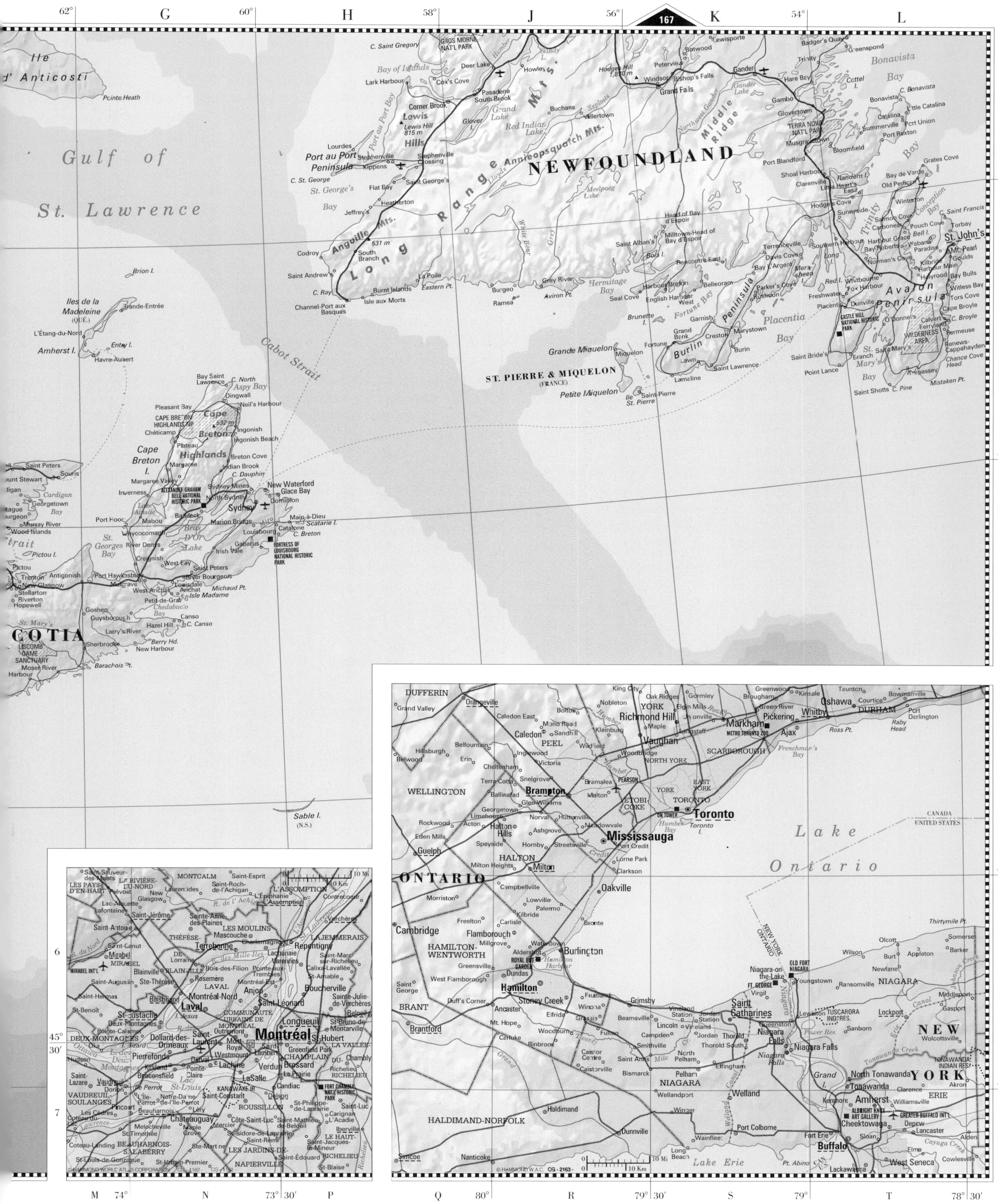

NEWFOUNDLAND

Gulf of St. Lawrence

Île d'Anticosti

Cabot Strait

St. Pierre & Miquelon (France)

Avalon Peninsula — St. John's

Cape Breton I. — Sydney

NOVA SCOTIA

Lake Ontario

ONTARIO — Toronto, Mississauga, Brampton, Hamilton, Buffalo, Niagara Falls

Montréal — Laval, Longueuil

Lake Erie

NEW YORK

As late as the 1960s, the broad region stretching from New England to the Mississippi was North America's Manufacturing Belt. The East Coast concentrated on textiles, apparel and other non-durables, while the Midwest churned out automobiles and heavy machinery. Appalachian coal fueled the blast furnaces of Pittsburgh, Youngstown, Cleveland, Buffalo and Gary, and ore boats brought iron ore and limestone. Aging plants, and foreign competition led to long term decline. Now, decades later, the "Rust Belt" cities are reviving with alternative industries.

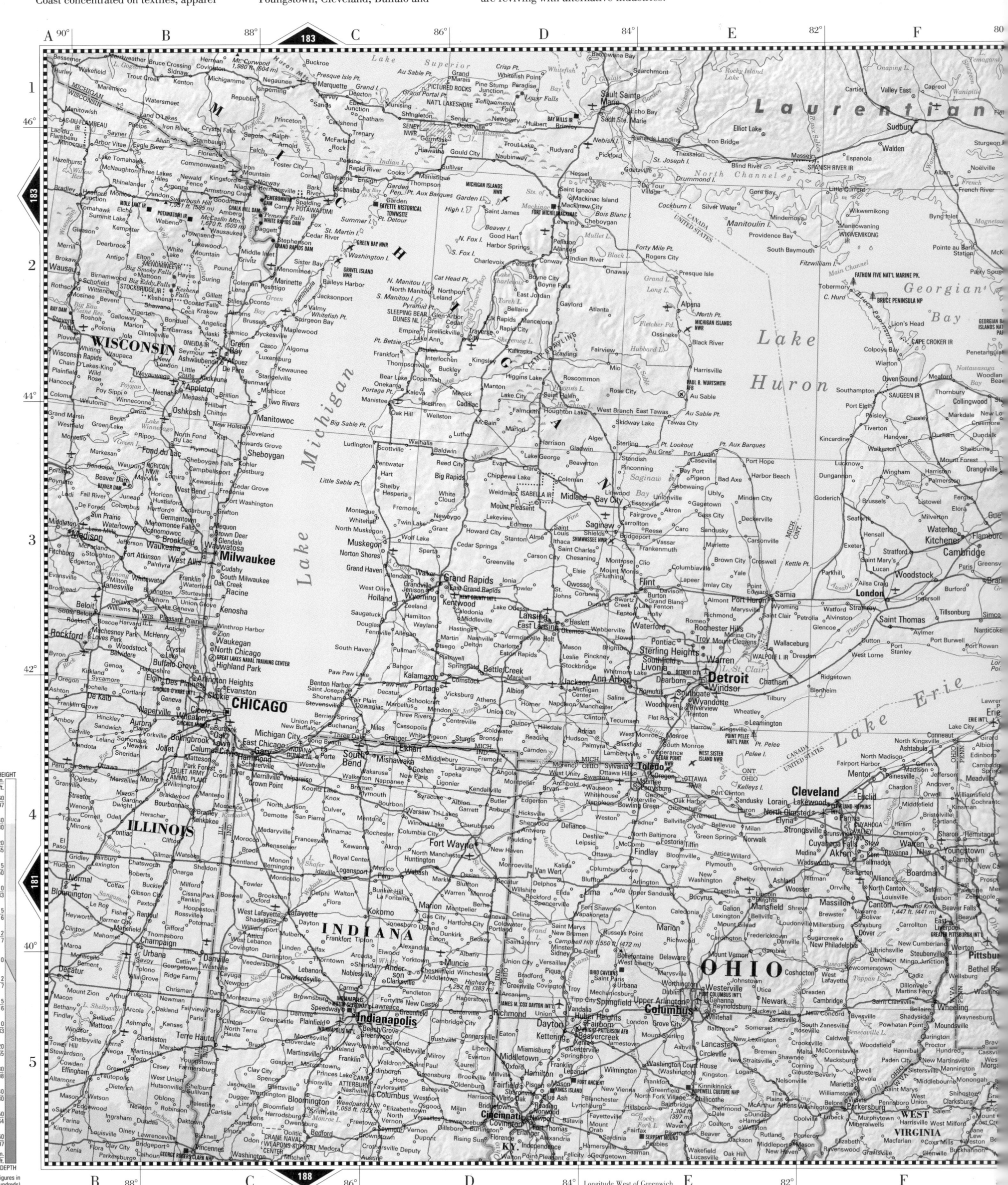

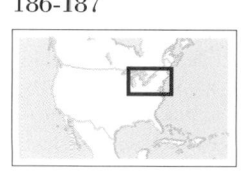

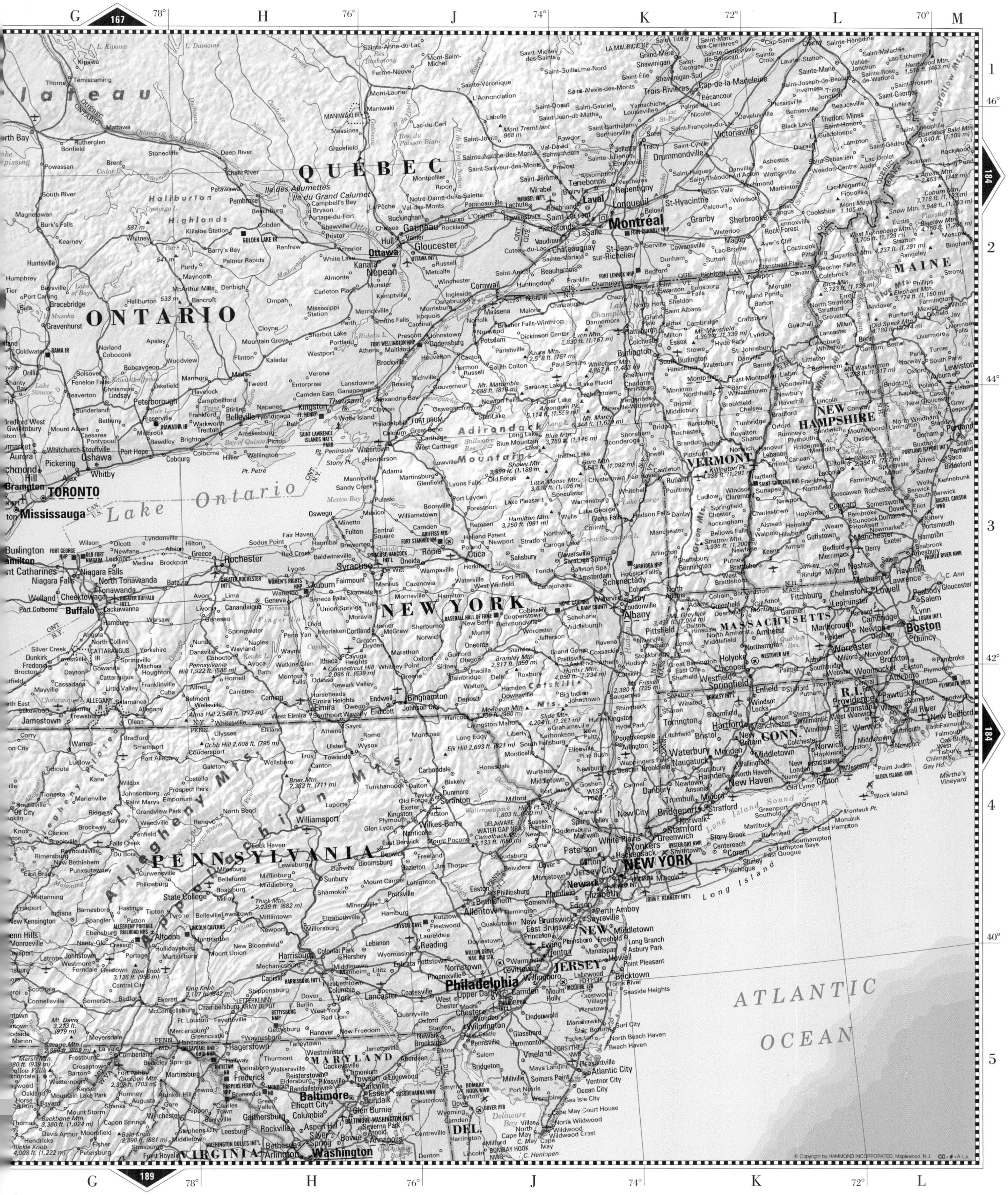

POPULATION OF CITIES AND TOWNS

■ OVER 2,000,000 ● 500,000 - 999,999 ● 100,000 - 249,999 ● 10,000 - 29,999
□ 1,000,000 - 1,999,999 ● 250,000 - 499,999 ● 30,000 - 99,999 ○ UNDER 10,000

SCALE 1:3,000,000 LAMBERT CONFORMAL CONIC PROJECTION

MILES 0   50   100   150
KILOMETERS 0   50   100   150

© Copyright by HAMMOND INCORPORATED, Maplewood, N.J.

Settlement by Europeans in this part of the eastern seaboard began at Jamestown in 1607. The first African-Americans arrived in 1619, brought as slaves to work the early tobacco planta-tions. Later the region became known as the "Cotton Kingdom," and it made up most of the Confederacy of 1861-1865. Long after the ruinous Civil War, this area suffered economic stagnation. The 1970s brought stunning economic growth as part of the Sun Belt phenomenon. People moved here, agriculture shifted to high-value commodities such as beef, and high-tech industry took root.

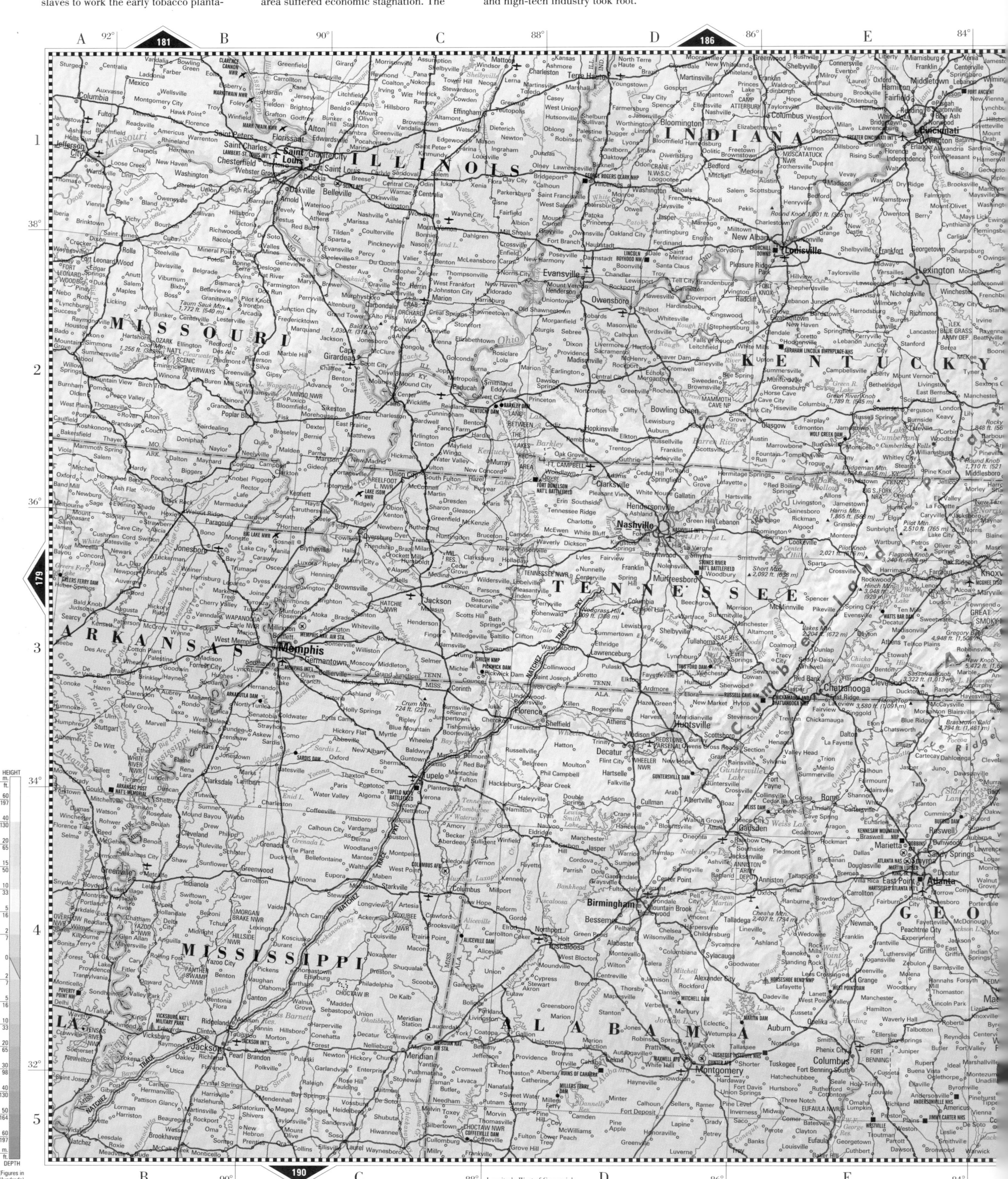

Longitude West of Greenwich

Mideastern United States

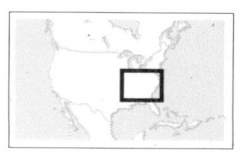

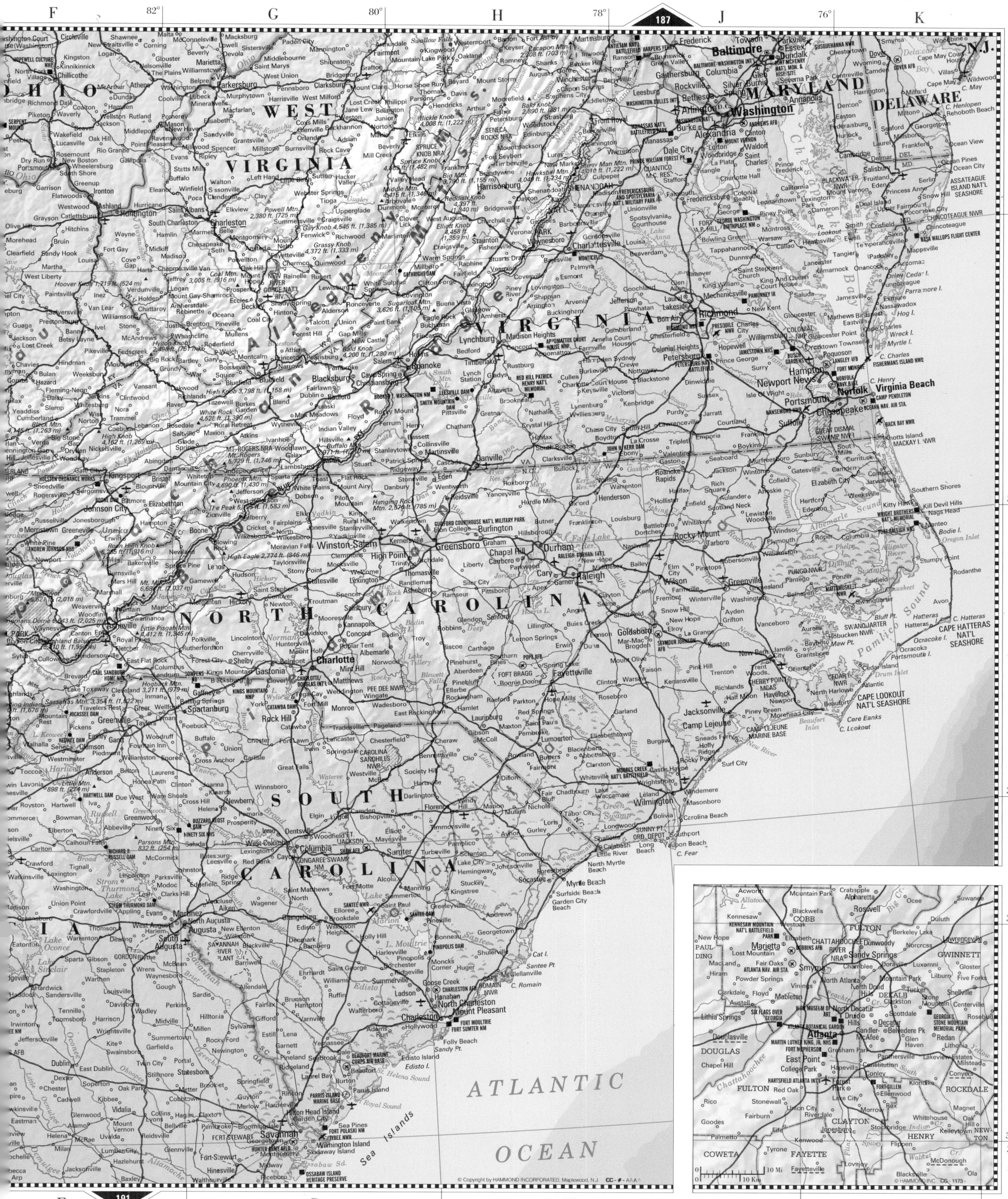

POPULATION OF CITIES AND TOWNS

- ⊛ OVER 2,000,000
- ▣ 1,000,000 – 1,999,999
- ⊛ 500,000 – 999,999
- ⊛ 250,000 – 499,999
- ⊕ 100,000 – 249,999
- ⊙ 30,000 – 99,999
- • 13,000 – 29,999
- ∘ UNDER 10,000

SCALE 1:3,000,000   LAMBERT CONFORMAL CONIC PROJECTION

MILES 0   50   100   150

KILOMETERS 0   50   100   150

ATLANTIC OCEAN

Since the 1950s, this lush and sunny region has boomed. Warm winter climate (with air conditioning to tame the humid summers) has drawn millions to the thriving Miami-Orlando-Tampa Bay triangle. Vacationers and retirees have flocked to the Atlantic and Gulf coasts, as well as the Orlando area, home of the famous Walt Disney World. Miami's Latin American commerce, and Cape Canaveral's space industry, have also spurred impressive growth. Rapid development and sugar farming have created many new challenges for the Everglades.

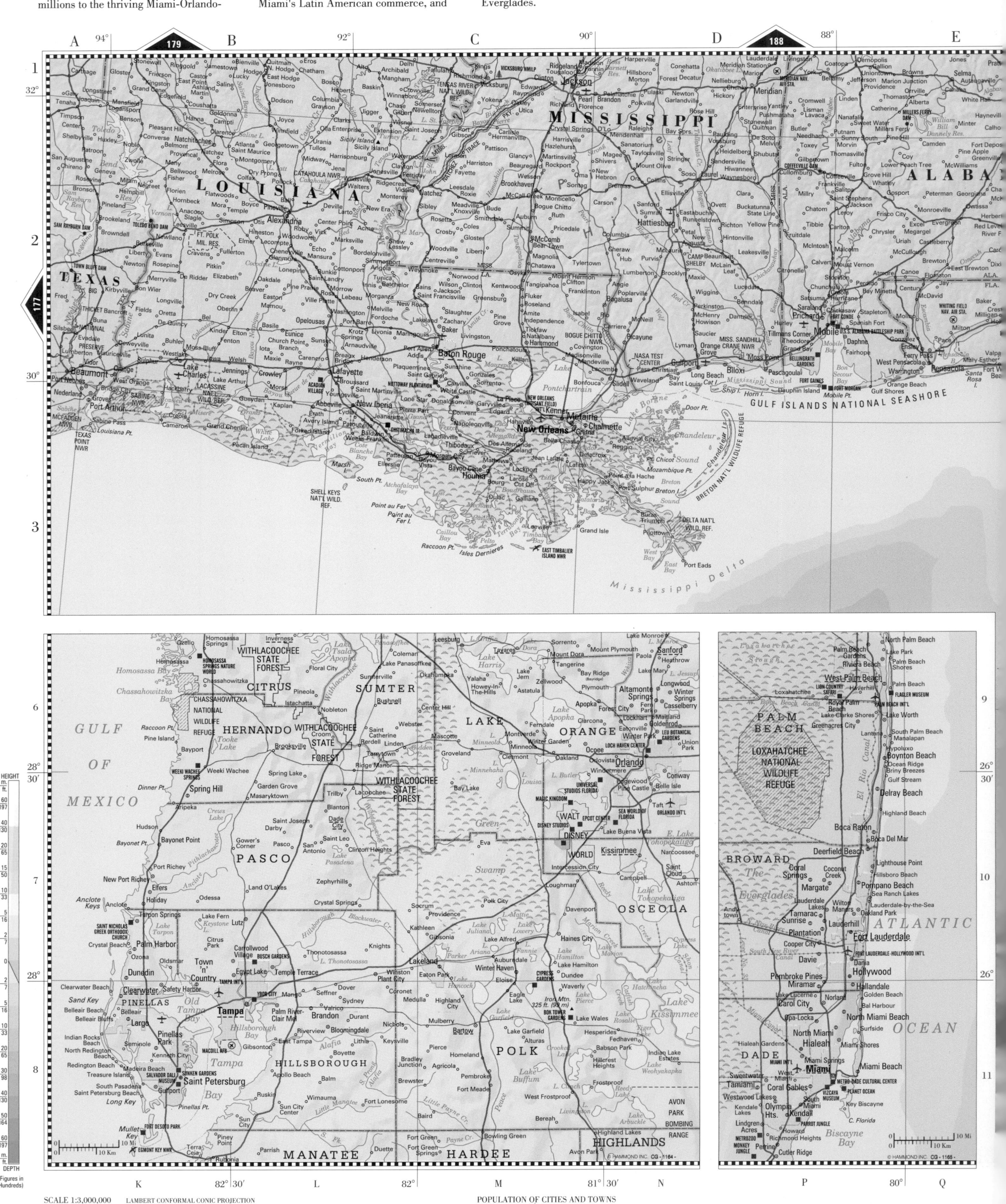

SCALE 1:3,000,000   LAMBERT CONFORMAL CONIC PROJECTION

POPULATION OF CITIES AND TOWNS

Northern Gulf Coast Region

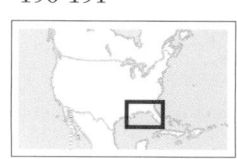

GEORGIA

ATLANTIC OCEAN

GULF OF MEXICO

FLORIDA

FLORIDA KEYS

Sea Islands

Montgomery · Columbus · Albany · Valdosta · Tallahassee · Panama City · Jacksonville · Gainesville · Ocala · Orlando · Tampa · Saint Petersburg · Sarasota · Fort Myers · Cape Coral · Naples · West Palm Beach · Fort Lauderdale · Hollywood · Hialeah · Miami · Miami Beach · Key West

Lake Okeechobee

EVERGLADES NATIONAL PARK

Florida Bay

Los Angeles-San Diego

Metropolitan Los Angeles stretches almost 115 miles (184 km.) from Ventura to San Bernardino. The movie industry, citrus orchards and oil fields fueled the region's early rapid growth.

Today, Los Angeles is the aircraft manufacturing capital of the United States, and along with New York and Chicago, leads in manufacturing, international banking and port trade.

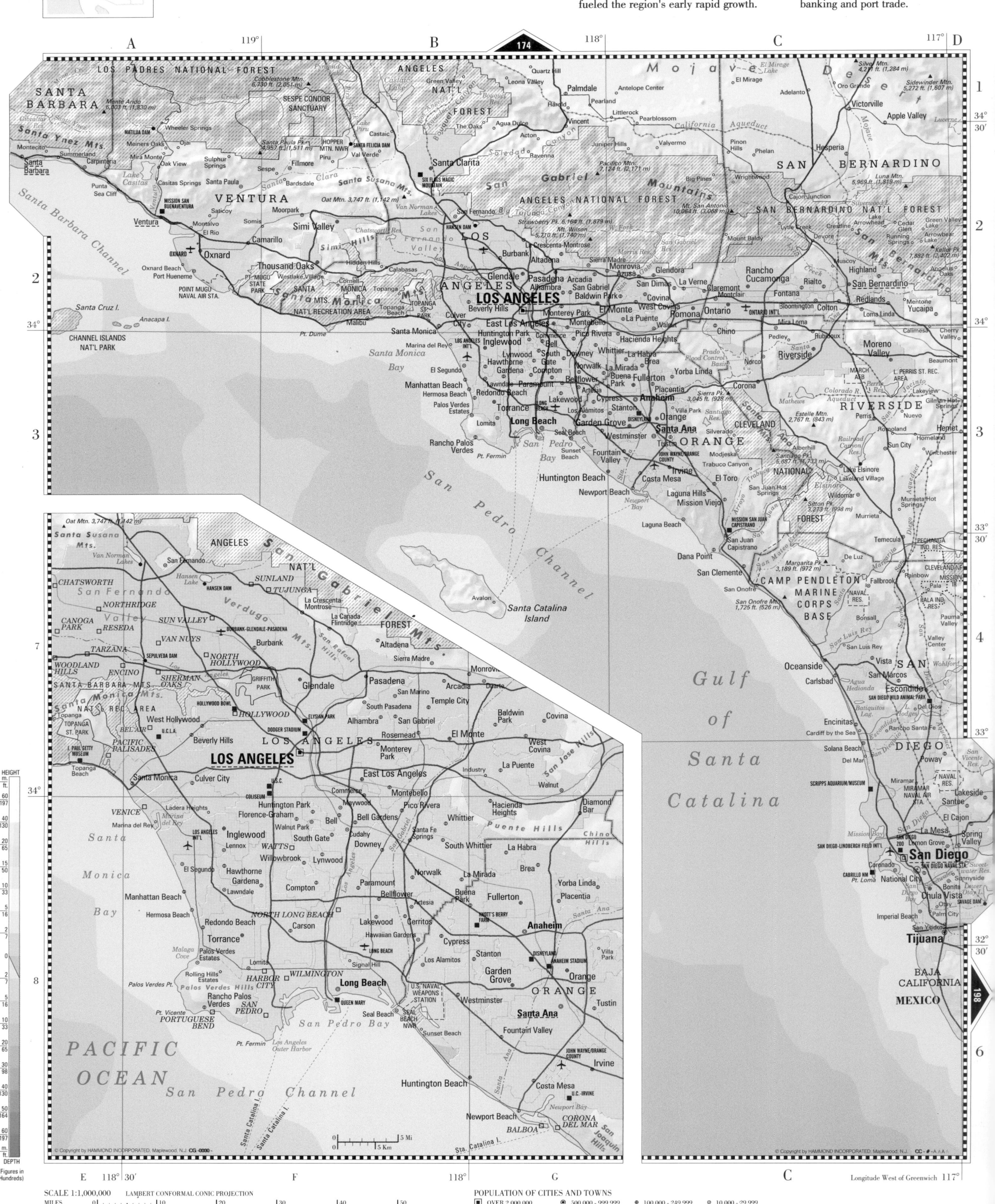

SCALE 1:1,000,000   LAMBERT CONFORMAL CONIC PROJECTION

POPULATION OF CITIES AND TOWNS

■ OVER 2,000,000	● 500,000 - 999,999	● 100,000 - 249,999	○ 10,000 - 29,999
□ 1,000,000 - 1,999,999	● 250,000 - 499,999	○ 30,000 - 99,999	○ UNDER 10,000

Longitude West of Greenwich 117°

Nestled between Puget Sound and Lake Washington, Seattle is the Northwest's largest city. San Francisco is the West Coast financial center; nearby San Jose is the heart of the "Silicon Valley" computer industry. Detroit is still the nation's automobile capital, while Chicago boasts one of the world's busiest airports, the largest commodities exchange and the Sears Tower.

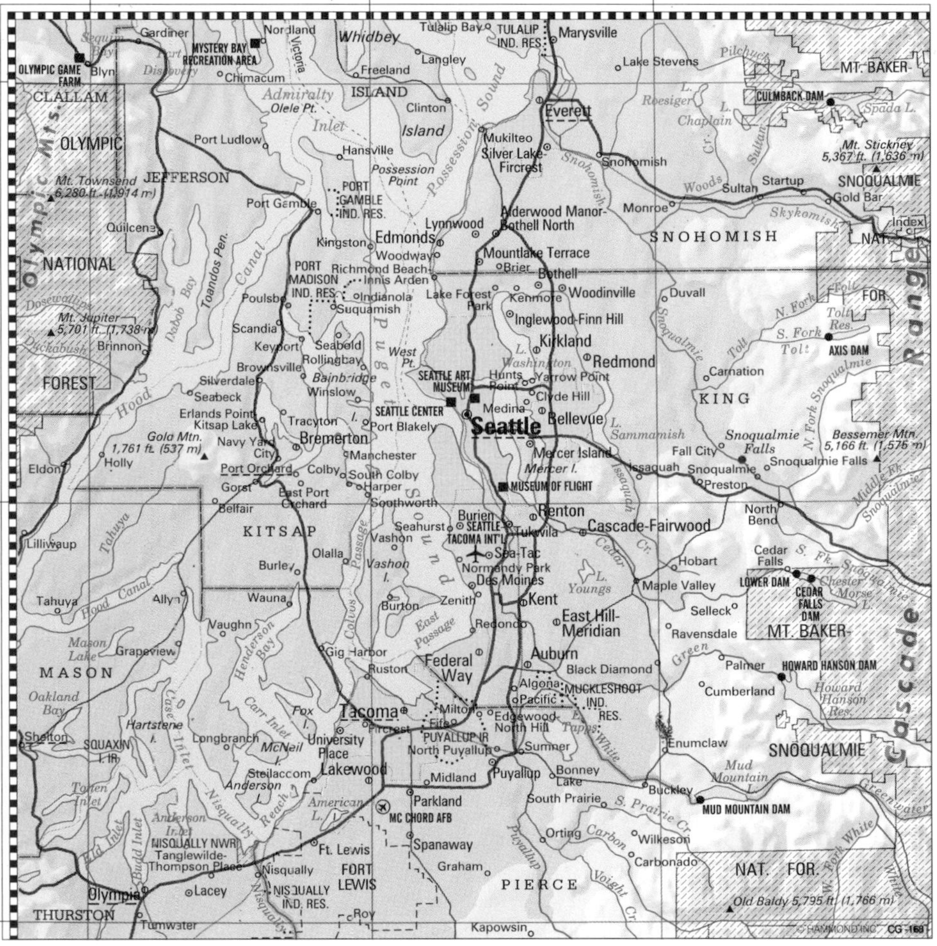

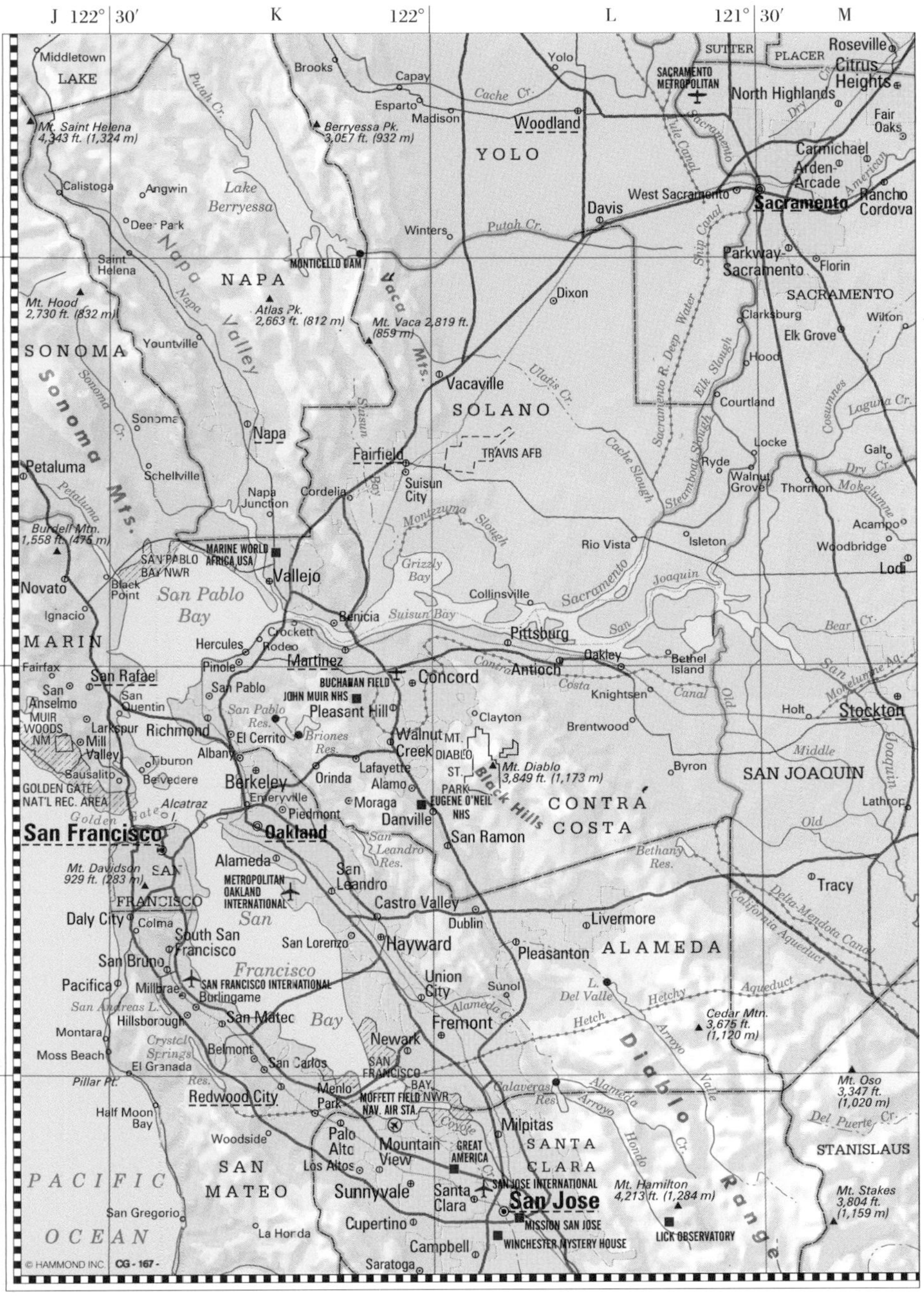

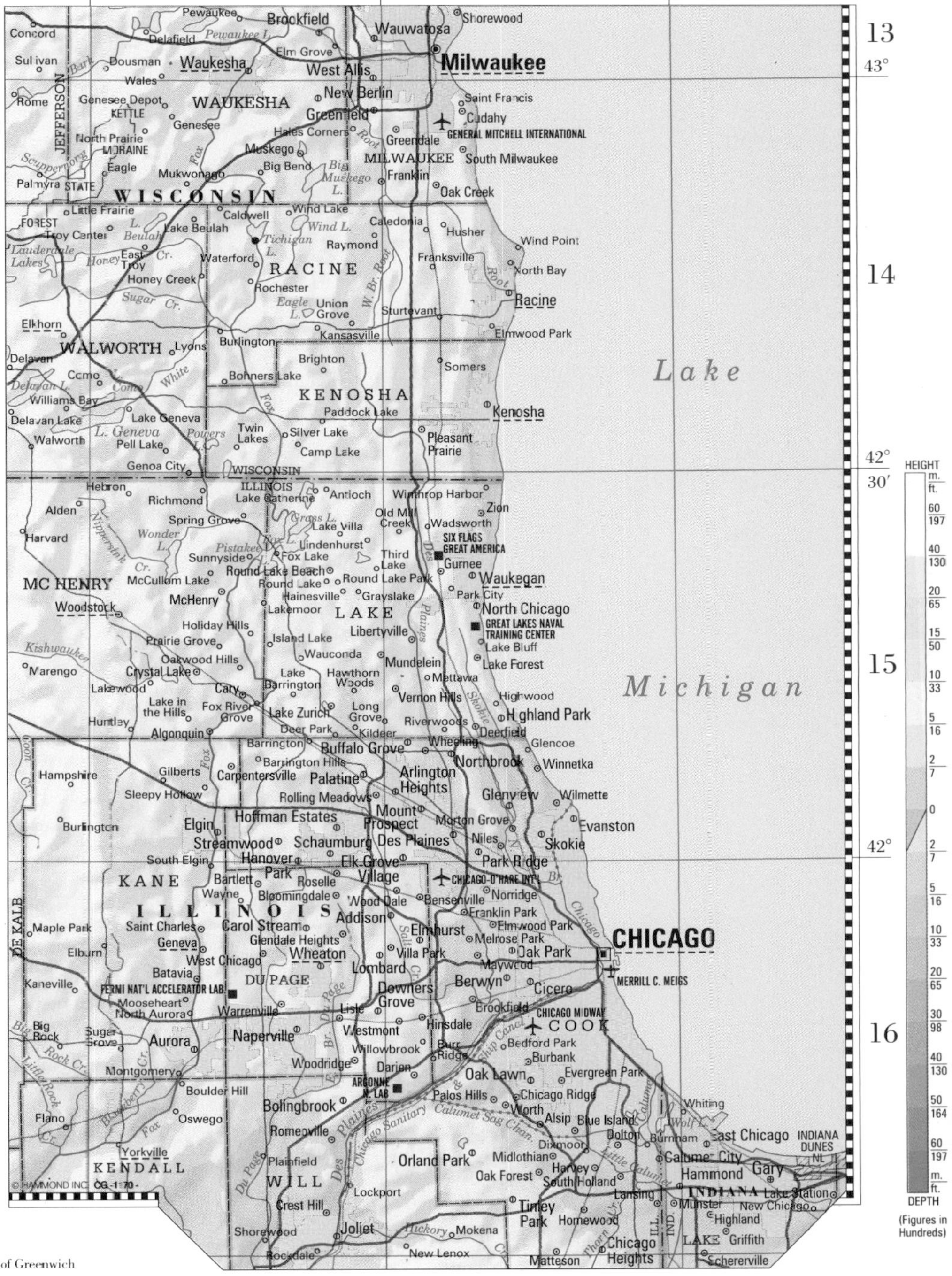

Seattle, San Francisco, Detroit, Chicago

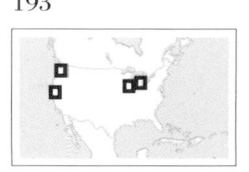

SCALE 1:1,000,000 LAMBERT CONFORMAL CONIC PROJECTION

MILES 0 | 10 | 20 | 30 | 40 | 50

KILOMETERS 0 | 10 | 20 | 30 | 40 | 50 | 60

Longitude West of Greenwich

HEIGHT
m.   ft.
60   197
40   130
20   65
15   49
10   33
7   23
2   7
0   0
16   53
40   164
50   164
100 328
164 538

DEPTH
ft.   (Figures in Hundreds)

The "Northeast Corridor" which links the nation's political capital with its financial and corporate center is the most densely urbanized megalopolis in North America. New York City, the core of a tri-state metropolitan area encompassing 18 million people, is also an international center for theater, the arts and publishing. Historic Philadelphia, a leader in medicine and pharmaceuticals, has one of the highest concentrations of colleges and universities in America. Baltimore's ambitious waterfront development project, including Harborplace, has given that city a new life.

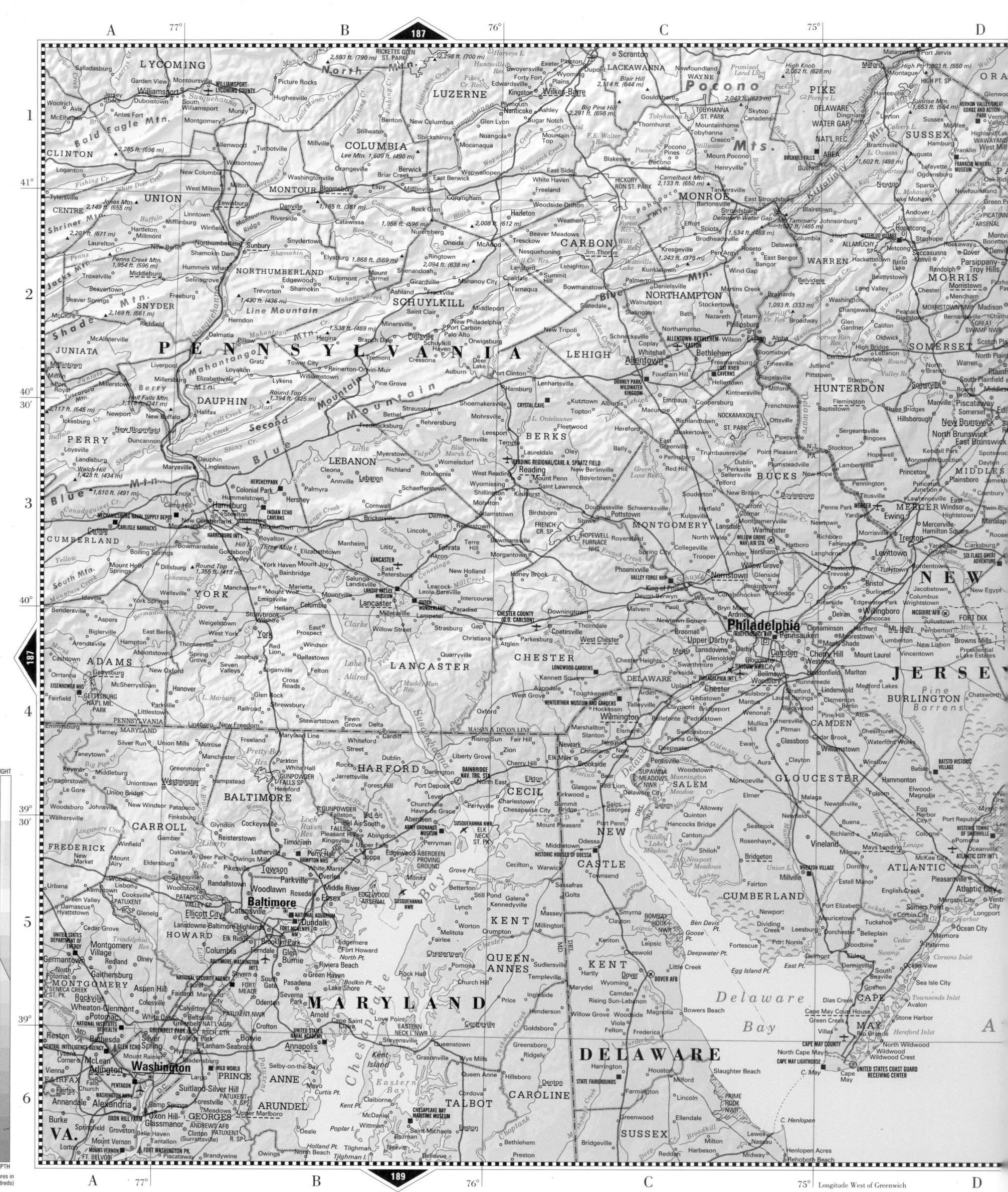

New York-Philadelphia-Washington

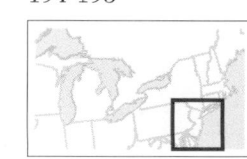

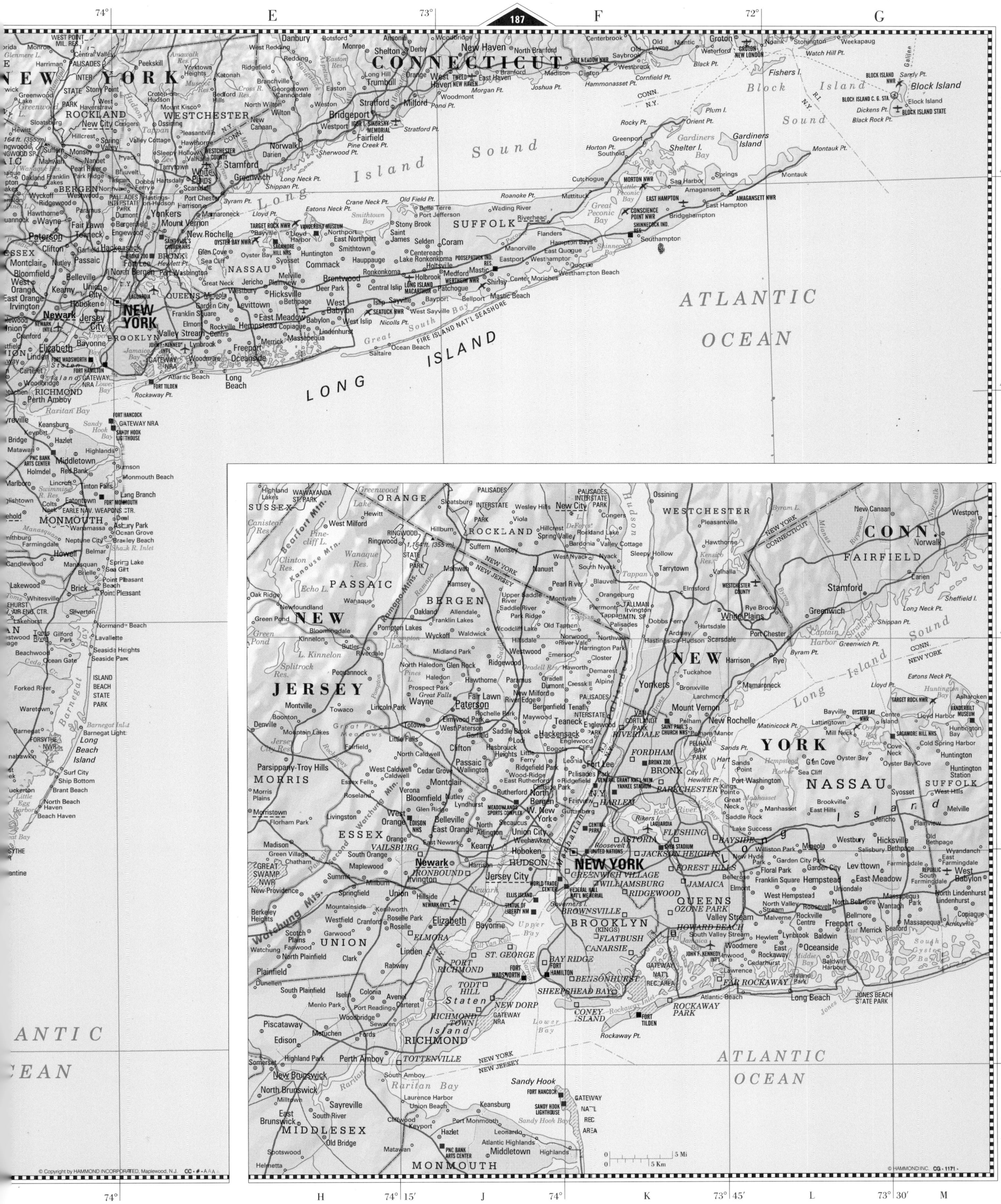

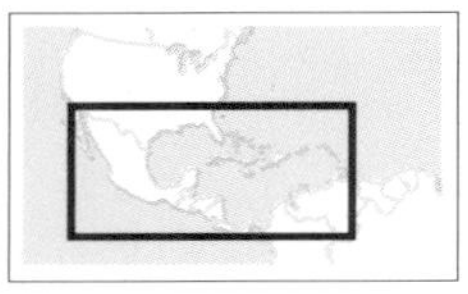

Middle America

This isthmian tract between the United States and Colombia marks the transition from North America to South America. The Mississippi, Rio Grande and other major rivers important to this region empty into the Gulf of Mexico. The Caribbean islands stretch from Florida to Venezuela. During the 16th–19th centuries European powers vied for possession of key islands in the

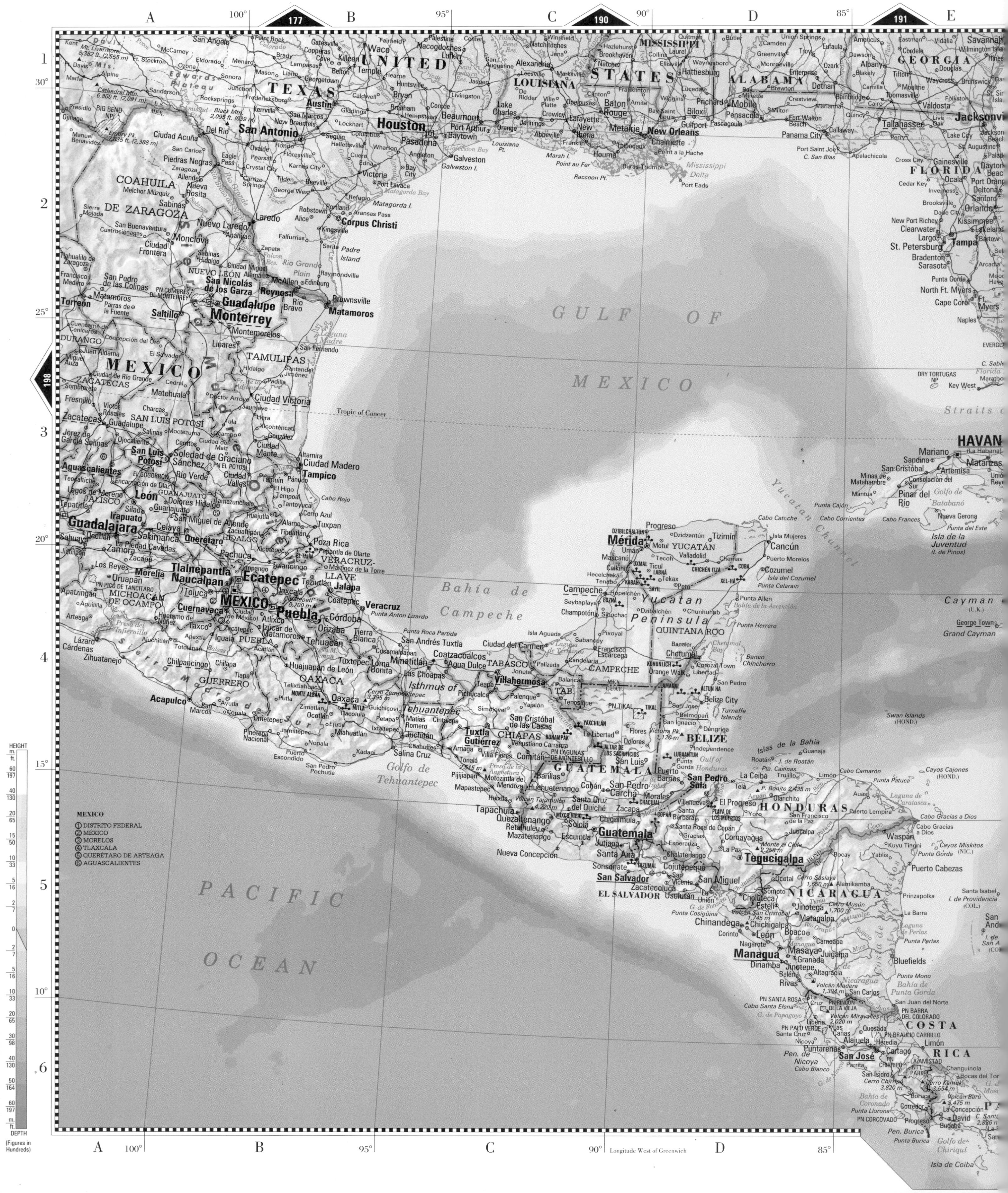

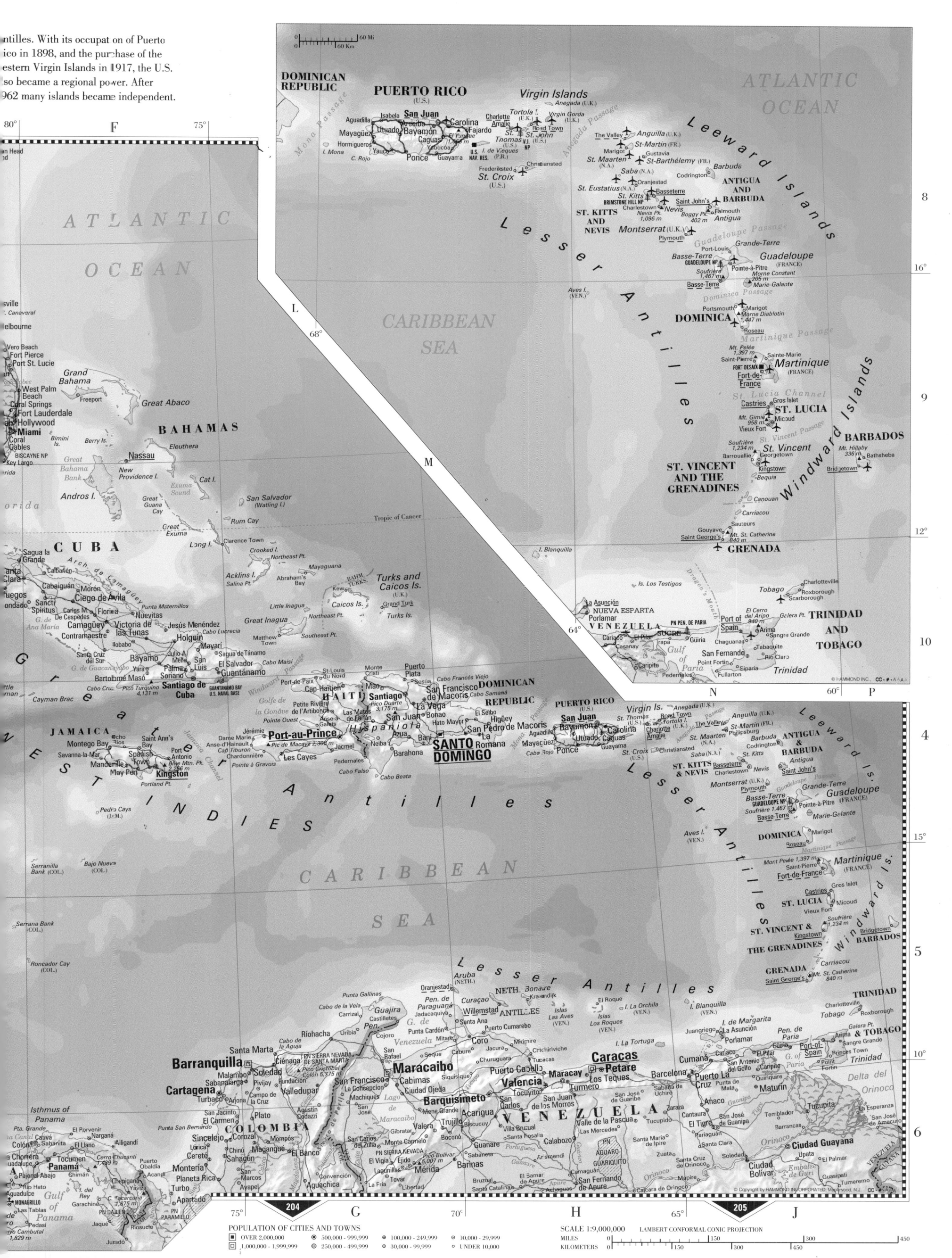

...ntiles. With its occupat on of Puerto
...ico in 1898, and the purchase of the
...estern Virgin Islands in 1917, the U.S.
...so became a regional power. After
...962 many islands became independent.

POPULATION OF CITIES AND TOWNS
■ OVER 2,000,000   ● 500,000 - 999,999   ⊙ 100,000 - 249,999   ⊕ 10,000 - 29,999
▣ 1,000,000 - 1,999,999   ◉ 250,000 - 499,999   ⊛ 30,000 - 99,999   ○ UNDER 10,000

SCALE 1:9,000,000   LAMBERT CONFORMAL CONIC PROJECTION
MILES   0   150   300   450
KILOMETERS   0   150   300   450

Mexico has a unique blend of Native American and Spanish cultural heritages. It forms the largest portion of the land bridge which joins North and South America, and played a role in the movement of animals and people. The vast Mexican plateau is bordered on the east and west by high mountain ranges of the Sierra Madres. Despite its size, a large part of Mexico's population is concentrated in a zone that centers on the city of Mexico and stretches from Veracruz to Guadalajara. The population of the metropolitan area alone is one of the largest in the world.

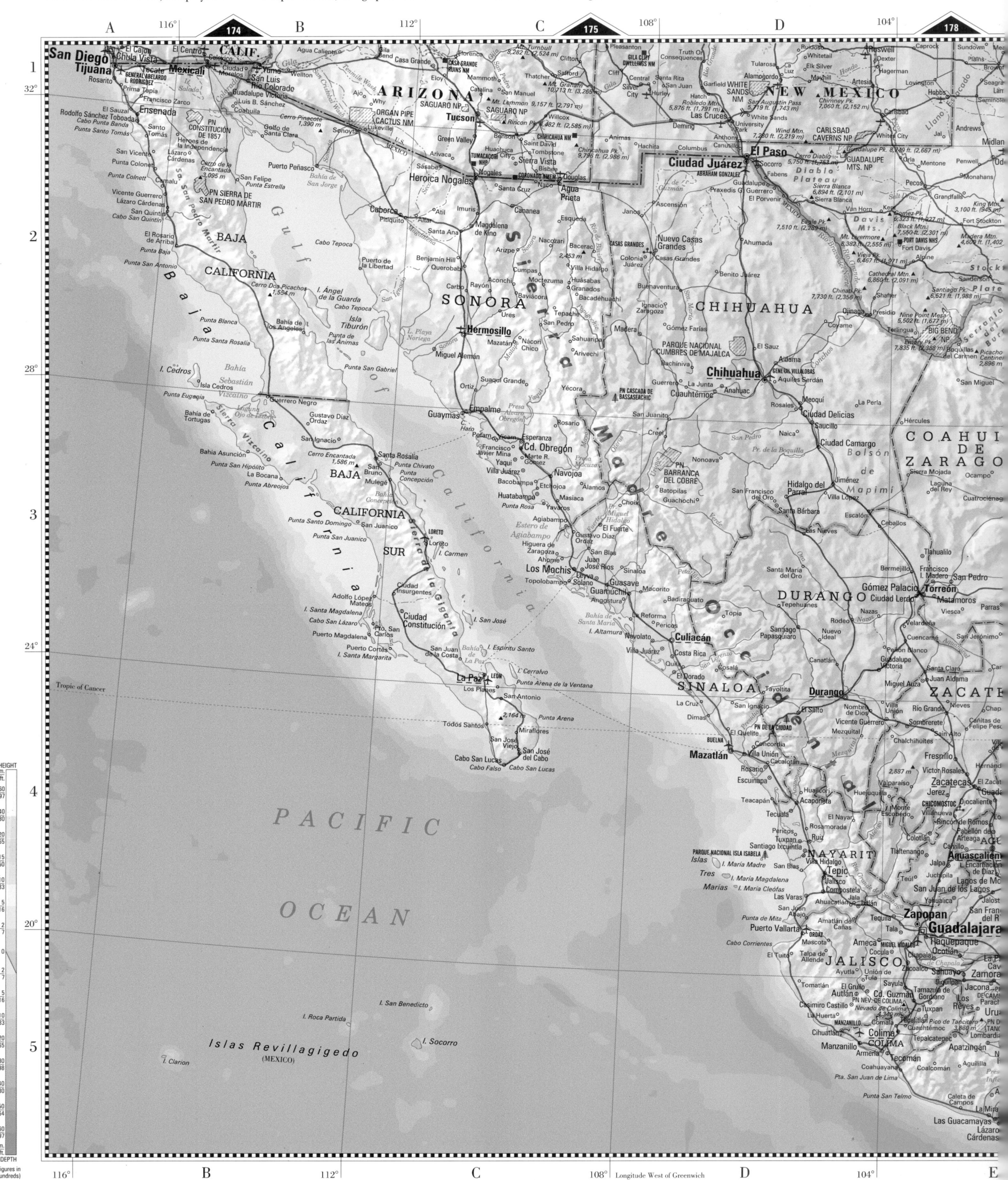

Northern and Central Mexico

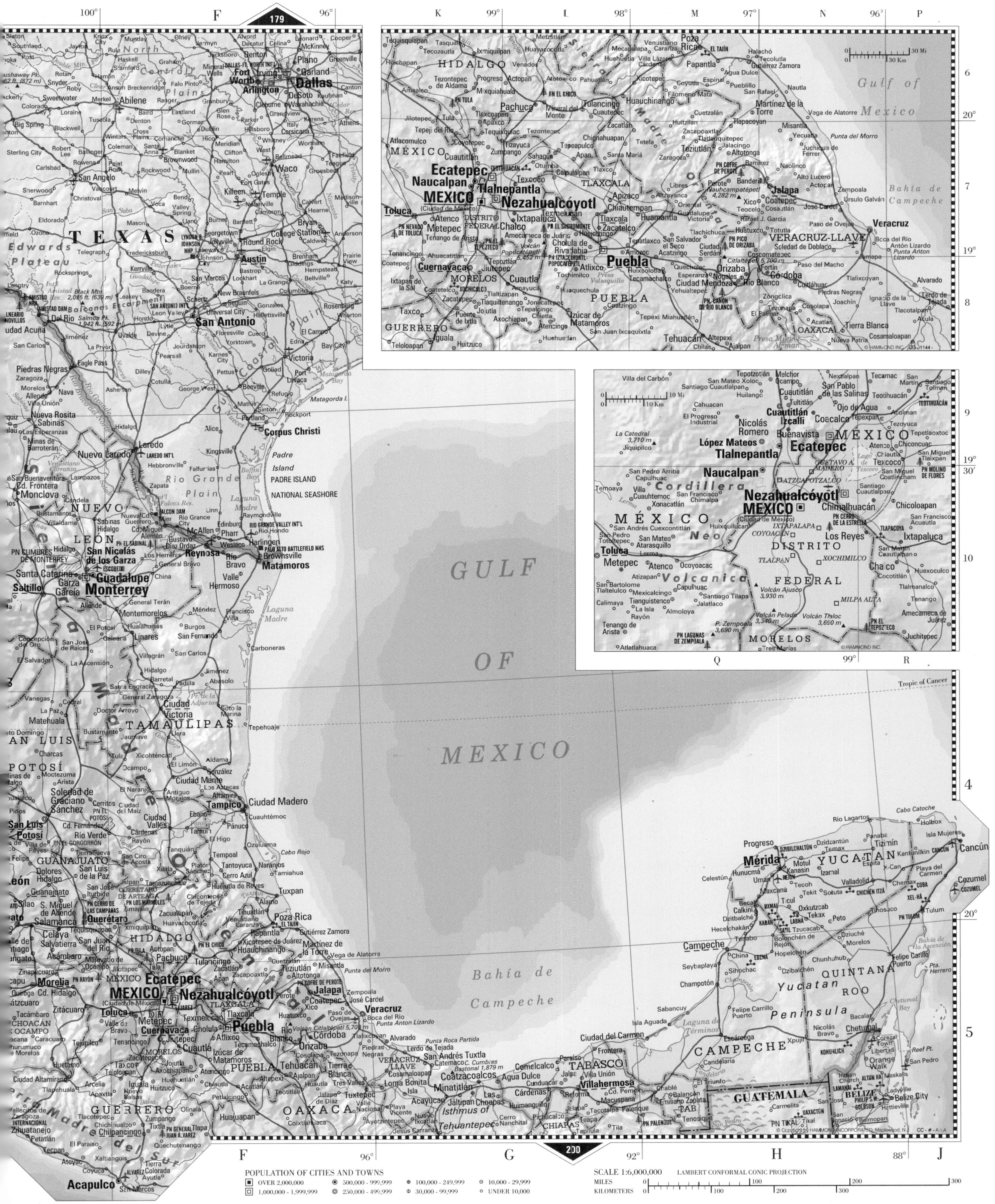

SCALE 1:6,000,000   LAMBERT CONFORMAL CONIC PROJECTION

POPULATION OF CITIES AND TOWNS

The history of southern Mexico and Central America can be traced back more than 12,000 years, when Paleo-Indian people migrated here. Their descendants created the great pre-Columbian cultures: the Olmec, Teotihuacan, Mayan, Toltec, Zapotec, Mixtec and highly advanced Aztec. Spanish involvement began shortly after Columbus reached the West Indies in 1492. Spanish rule in Mexico lasted until 1821. Guatemala, Costa Rica, Nicaragua, El Salvador and Honduras became independent in 1838. Belize gained its independence in 1981.

POPULATION OF CITIES AND TOWNS

| ■ OVER 2,000,000 | ● 500,000 - 999,999 | ⊕ 100,000 - 249,999 | ⊙ 10,000 - 29,999 |
| □ 1,000,000 - 1,999,999 | ◉ 250,000 - 499,999 | ⊕ 30,000 - 99,999 | ○ UNDER 10,000 |

© HAMMOND WORLD ATLAS CORPORATION CD-1067-A

Southern Mexico, Central America, Western Caribbean

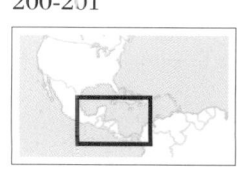

197
204

South America

The highest mountain peak in the Americas, Mount Aconcagua, at 22,831 feet (6959 m.) above sea level, is visible in this northeast-looking, low-oblique image. Several major snow-covered peaks with summits exceeding 20,000 feet (6100 m.) rise along the north-south axis of the cohesive and massive structure of the Andes Mountains through this area of Argentina and Chile. The narrow east-west valley immediately south of Mount Aconcagua contains a section of the American Highway that connects Mendoza, Argentina, with Santiago, Chile.

AREA OF OPTIMIZATION
The red band which surrounds this map defines the "Area of Optimization." Within this bounding curve is the most accurate conformal map that can be made of the region. Outside the optimized area, distortion increases rapidly, and tears or other irregularities in the grid may occur. (See page 11 for additional information.)

POPULATION OF CITIES AND TOWNS

SCALE 1:24,000,000   OPTIMAL CONFORMAL PROJECTION

© Copyright by HAMMOND INCORPORATED, Maplewood, N.J.

Coffee and cattle are the chief agricultural commodities of this often mountainous region, although the drug cocaine, made from the coca leaf, has become the most profitable export. Oil is vital to the economies of all three nations: largest reserves are near Lake Maracaibo and the Orinoco tar belt. High inland, the capital cities, Quito, Bogotá and Caracas enjoy cool climates and historic central plazas. The population of mixed Indian and Spanish ancestry is very different from the non-Hispanic Caribbean culture of the "three Guianas," home to a large African and Asian majority.

Longitude West of Greenwich

POPULATION OF CITIES AND TOWNS

☐ OVER 2,000,000   ⊙ 500,000 - 999,999   ⊕ 100,000 - 249,999   ○ 10,000 - 29,999
☐ 1,000,000 - 1,999,999   ◉ 250,000 - 499,999   ⊙ 30,000 - 99,999   · UNDER 10,000

SCALE 1:6,000,000   LAMBERT CONFORMAL CONIC PROJECTION

MILES 0   100   200   300
KILOMETERS 0   100   200   300

© Copyright by HAMMOND INCORPORATED, Maplewood, N.J.

Within the Amazon Basin of Brazil is the world's largest rain forest, home to over a million species of plants and animals. Indigenous people depend directly on the rain forest for food and shelter. The forest is also a nutrient and fresh-water reservoir. Many prescription drugs can be traced to rain forest plants. Thousands of other plants with life-saving properties have been identified, although many still remain. Every year, millions of hectares of this vital ecosystem are destroyed. National legislation and international protests are making limited progress in preserving the forest.

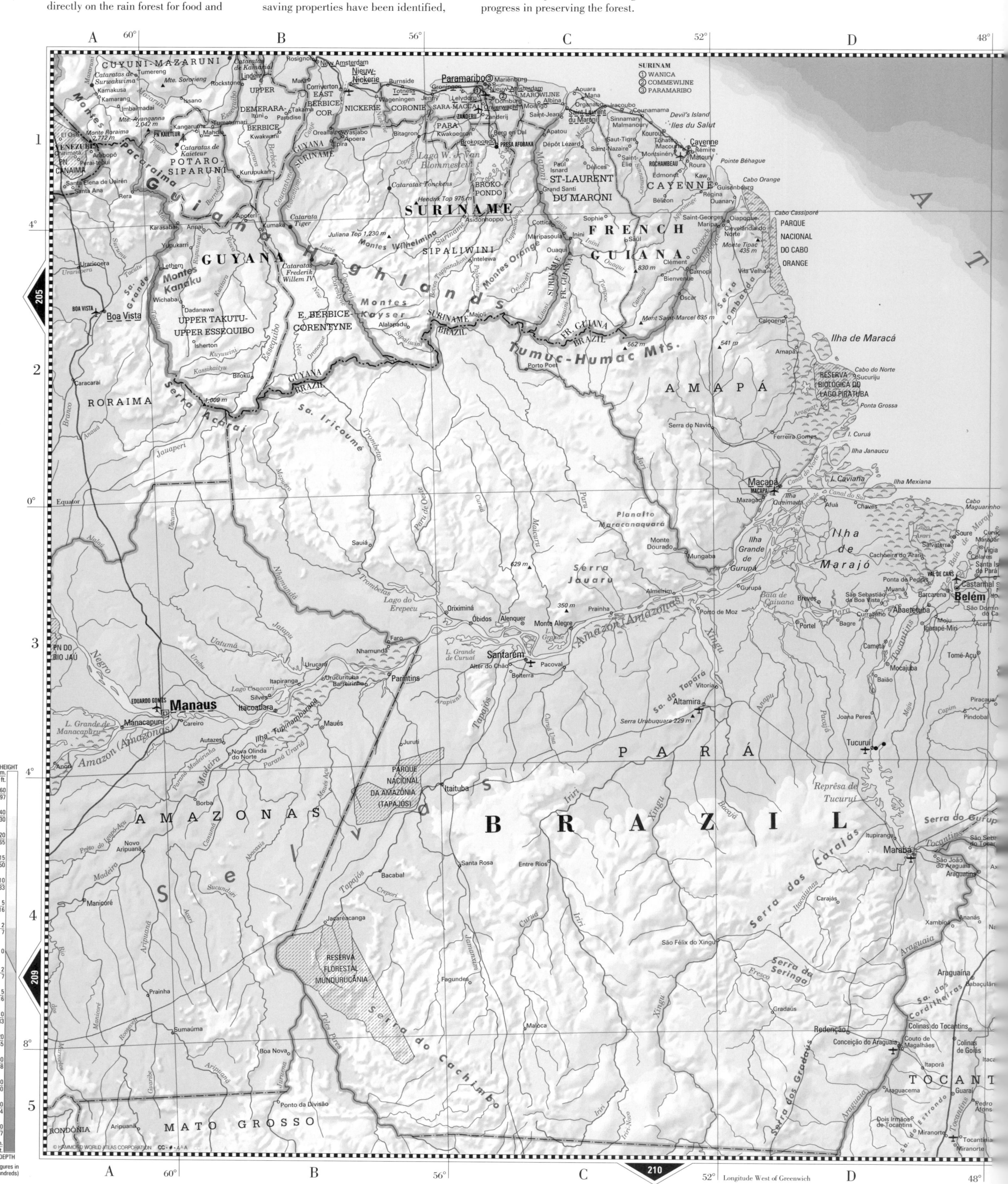

Guianas, Northern Brazil

CARIBBEAN SEA

A T L A N T I C   O C E A N

Inset 1 (Colombia):

SANTANDER · ANTIOQUIA · BOYACÁ · CALDAS · RISARALDA · CUNDINAMARCA · QUINDÍO · TOLIMA · VALLE DEL CAUCA · META · DISTRITO CAPITAL

Medellín · Bello · Envigado · Manizales · Pereira · Armenia · Ibagué · **BOGOTÁ**

Nevado del Ruiz 5,400 m · Nevado del Tolima 5,215 m · Parque Nacional Los Nevados

© HAMMOND INC.

Inset 2 (Venezuela):

CARABOBO · ARAGUA · MIRANDA · COJEDES · GUÁRICO

Caracas · Maracay · Valencia · Petare · Guarenas · Puerto Cabello · Los Teques

Cordillera de la Costa · PN El Ávila · PN Henri Pittier · PN Guácharo

© HAMMOND INC.

Main map (Brazil):

MARANHÃO · PIAUÍ · CEARÁ · RIO GRANDE DO NORTE · PARAÍBA · PERNAMBUCO · BAHIA · ALAGOAS

São Luís · Teresina · Fortaleza · Natal · João Pessoa · Campina Grande · Recife · Olinda · Parnaíba · Caxias · Timon · Mossoró · Juazeiro do Norte · Petrolina · Paulo Afonso · Imperatriz · Carolina

Parque Nacional dos Lençóis Maranhenses · Parque Nacional de Sete Cidades · Parque Nacional da Serra da Capivara

Serra do Tiracambu · Serra das Alpercatas · Represa de Sobradinho · Chapada do Araripe

POPULATION OF CITIES AND TOWNS

■ OVER 2,000,000 · ◉ 500,000 - 999,999 · ● 100,000 - 249,999 · ○ 10,000 - 29,995
□ 1,000,000 - 1,999,999 · ◉ 250,000 - 499,999 · ● 30,000 - 99,999 · ◦ UNDER 10,000

SCALE 1:6,000,000   LAMBERT CONFORMAL CONIC PROJECTION

MILES 0 · 100 · 200 · 300
KILOMETERS 0 · 100 · 200 · 300

Here are found the ancient ruins of the great native American pre-Columbian civilizations of Andean Peru and Bolivia - the Chavín, the Mochica, the Tiahuanaco, the Chimú and particularly the Inca. The highly developed Inca Empire had a centralized military-political system. It farmed intensively, and utilized domestic animals in economic and transport systems. Unlike major cultures in China and India, the pre-Columbian societies of the Americas fell quickly under the repeated assaults of the conquistadores well before the end of the 16th century.

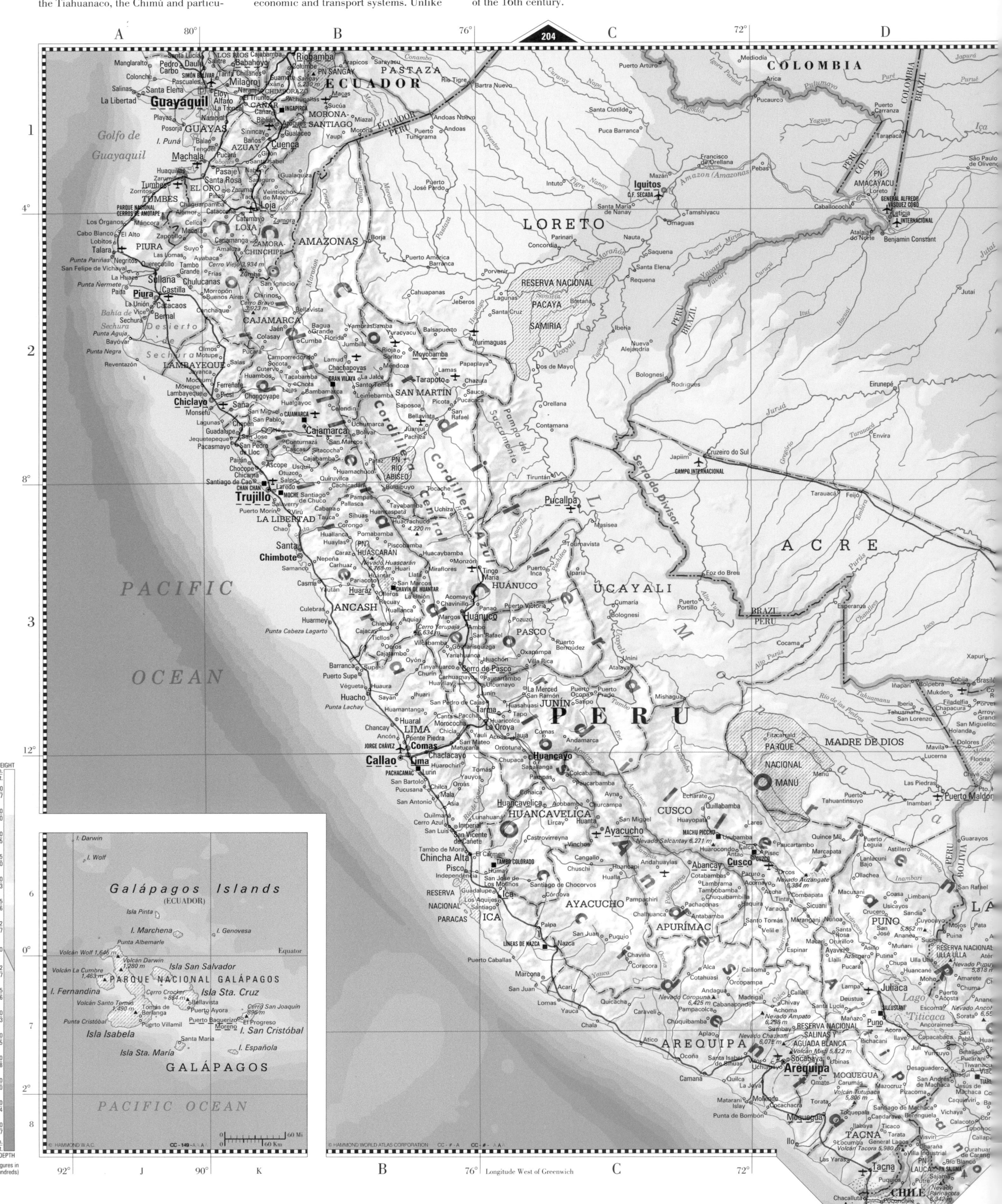

Peru, Northern Bolivia, Western Brazil

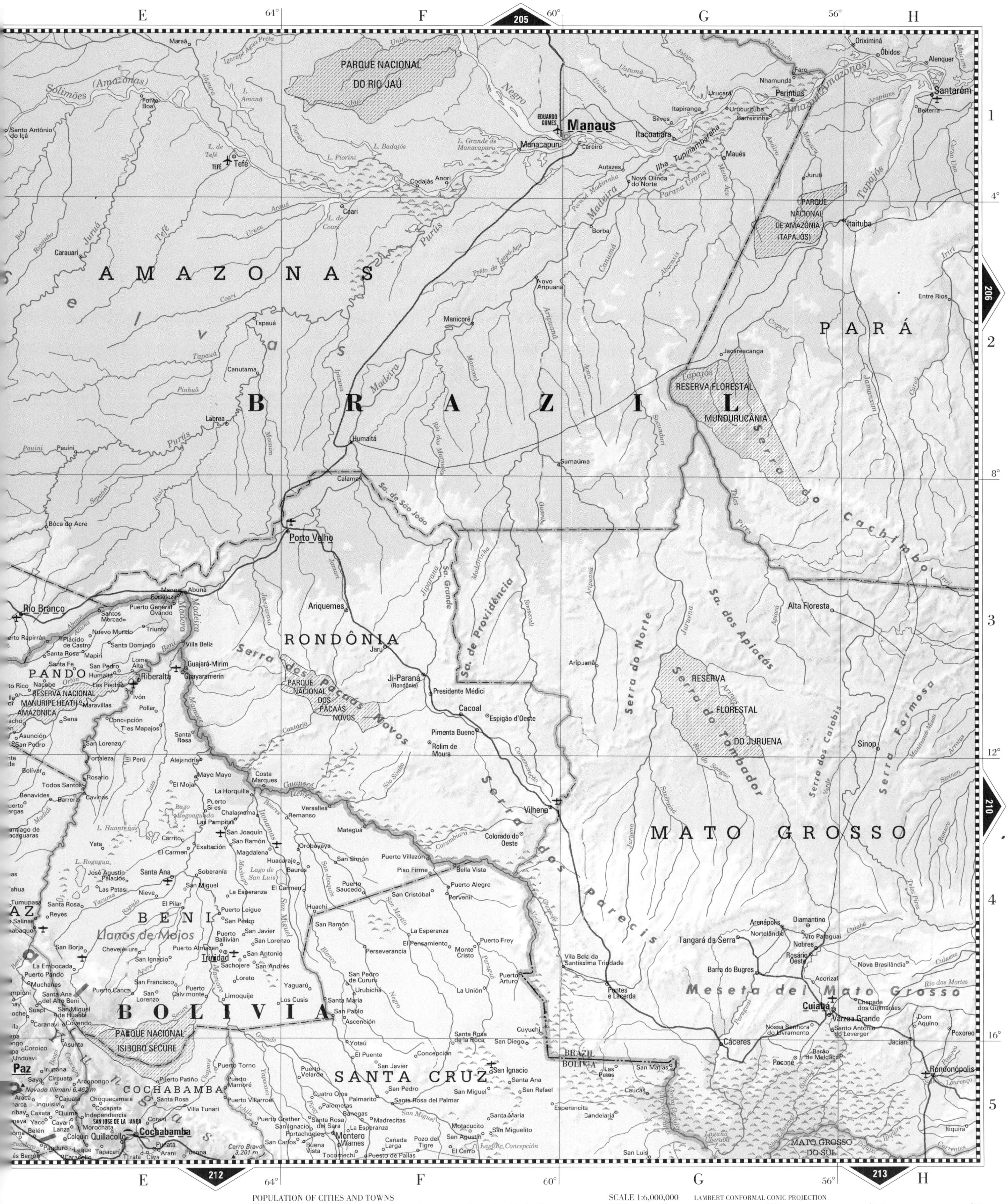

Parque Nacional do Rio Jaú

Manaus · Manacapuru · Careiro · Itacoatiara · Silves · Urucurituba · Parintins · Oriximiná · Óbidos · Alenquer · Santarém · Belterra

Eduardo Gomes · Codajás · Anori · Nova Olinda do Norte · Autazes · Ilha Tupinambarana · Maués · Juruti · Barreirinha · Nhamundá · Faro · Urucará · Itapiranga

Tefé · L. de Tefé · Coari · Borba · Parque Nacional de Amazônia (Tapajós) · Itaituba

Santo Antônio do Içá · Maraã · L. Amaná · Fonte Boa · L. Piorini · L. Badajós · L. Grande de Manacapuru

AMAZONAS · **PARÁ**

BRAZIL

Novo Aripuanã · Manicoré · Sumaúma · Jacareacanga · Entre Rios

Tapauá · Canutama · Lábrea · Humaitá · Calama · Reserva Florestal Mundurucânia · Serra do Cachimbo

Bôca do Acre · Porto Velho · Alta Floresta

RONDÔNIA · Ariquemes · Jaru · Ji-Paraná (Rondônia) · Presidente Médici · Cacoal · Espigão d'Oeste · Pimenta Bueno · Rolim de Moura · Reserva Florestal do Juruena · Sinop

Rio Branco · Abunã · Guajará-Mirim · Guayaramerín · Riberalta · Parque Nacional dos Pacaás Novos · Vilhena

PANDO · Reserva Nacional Manuripe Heath · Amazônica · Sena · Concepción · Tres Mapajos · Santa Rosa

BOLIVIA · **BENI** · Llanos de Mojos · Trinidad · Rurrenabaque · San Ignacio · San Borja

Paz · La Paz · Nevado Illimani 6,462 m · **COCHABAMBA** · Cochabamba · Punata

MATO GROSSO · Meseta del Mato Grosso · Cuiabá · Várzea Grande · Cáceres · Rondonópolis · Pocone · Tangará da Serra · Diamantino · Nortelândia · Nobres · Rosário Oeste · Nova Brasilândia

SANTA CRUZ · Concepción · San Ignacio · San Matías · San José · San Rafael · Robore

BRAZIL / BOLIVIA

MATO GROSSO DO SUL

POPULATION OF CITIES AND TOWNS

■ OVER 2,000,000 ● 500,000 - 999,999 ● 100,000 - 249,999 ○ 0,000 - 29,999
□ 1,000,000 - 1,999,999 ● 250,000 - 499,999 ● 30,000 - 99,999 · UNDER 10,000

SCALE 1:6,000,000   LAMBERT CONFORMAL CONIC PROJECTION

MILES 0 ____ 100 ____ 200 ____ 300
KILOMETERS 0 ____ 100 ____ 200 ____ 300

The largest and most populous South American country, Brazil is the only Portuguese-speaking nation in the Americas. Its tropical to semi-tropical climate and highland areas are ideal for coffee-growing, and Brazil is the world's leading producer. This economic dependence on one key crop – vulnerable to frosts, droughts, and market changes – has been mitigated by the rise of sugar, citrus, cotton, rice and tobacco exports. Brazil's dramatic industrial expansion has been matched by the explosive growth of its major cities.

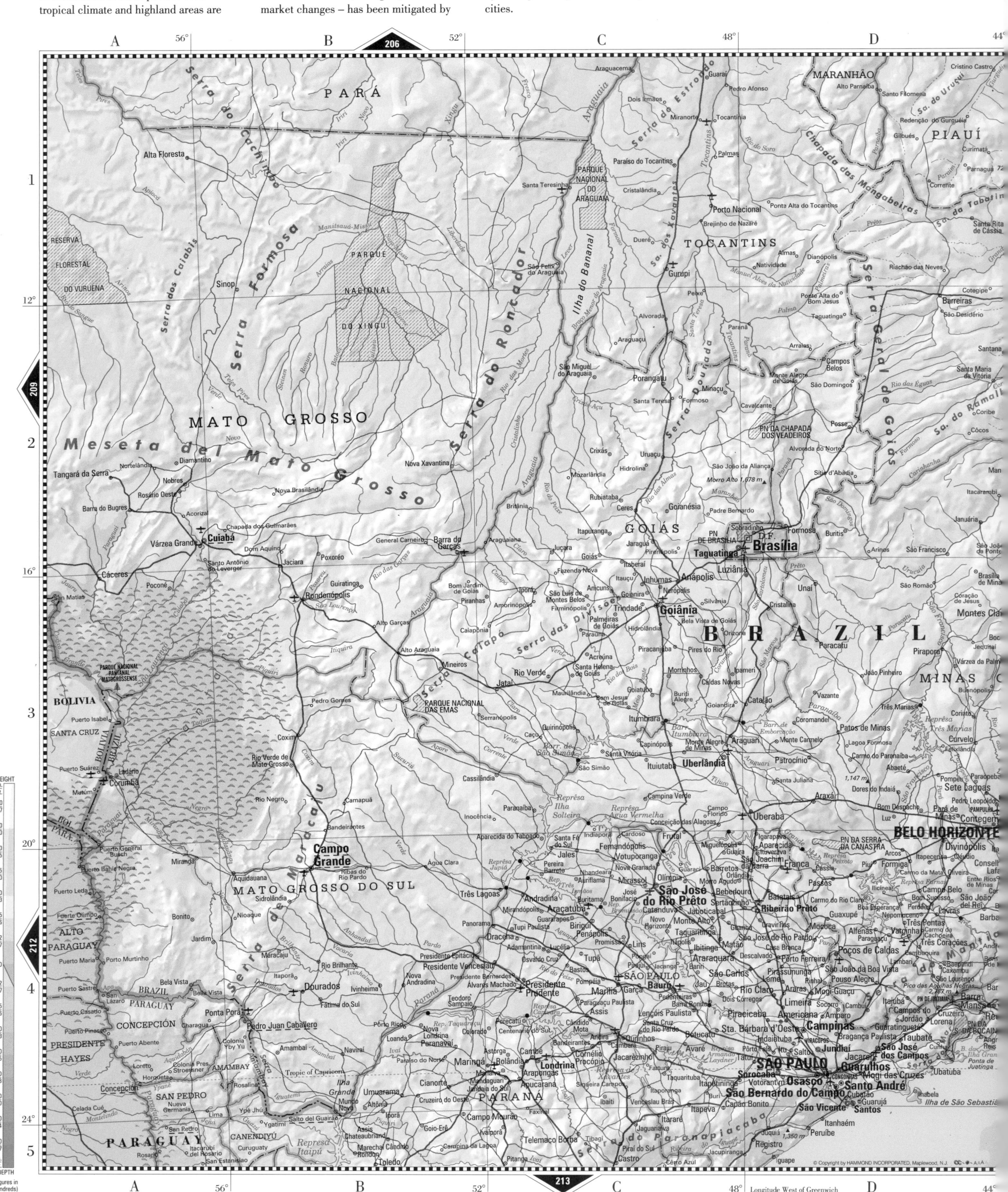

Eastern Brazil

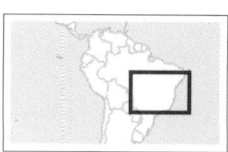

207

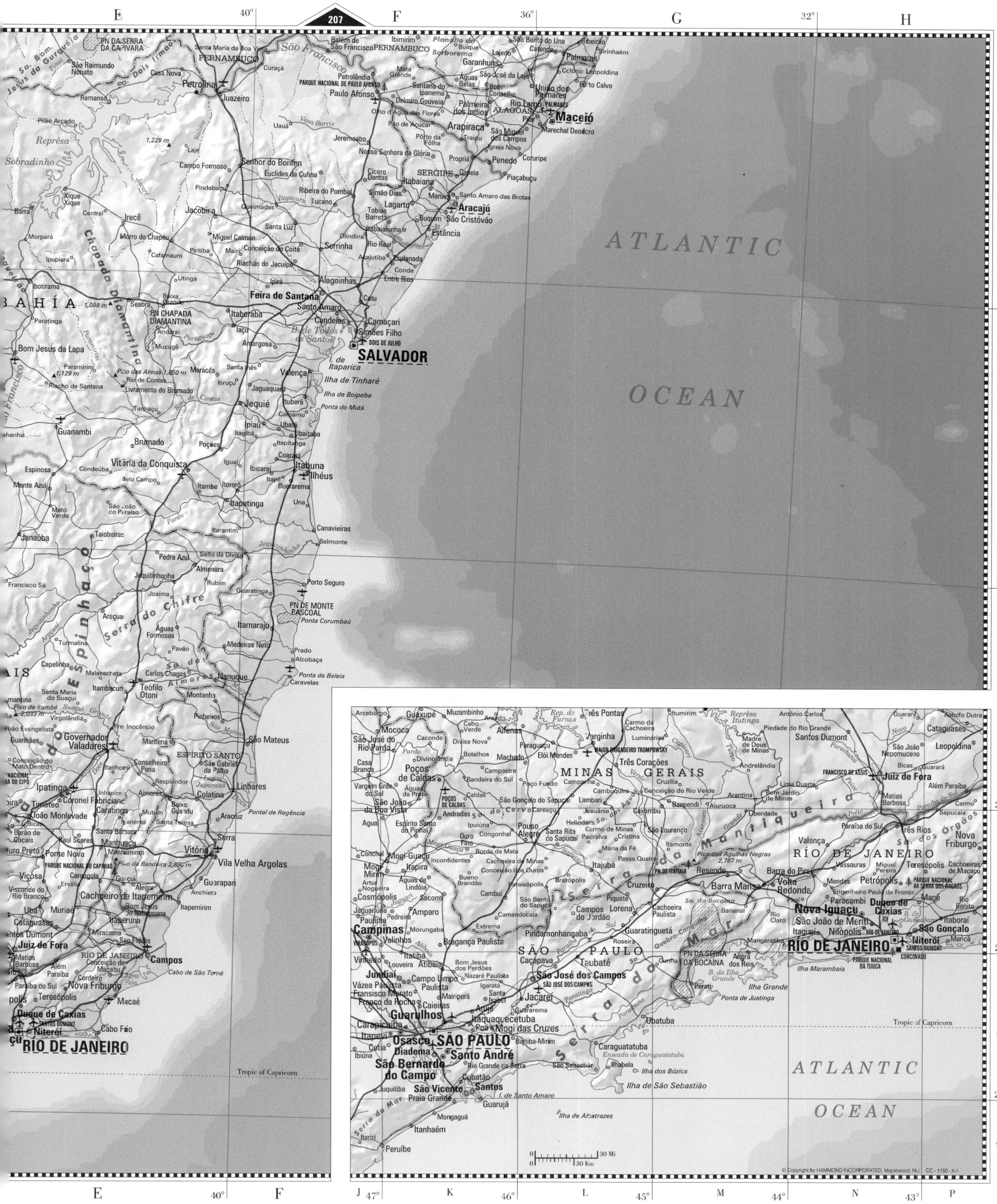

POPULATION OF CITIES AND TOWNS
- OVER 2,000,000
- 1,000,000 - 1,999,999
- 500,000 - 999,999
- 250,000 - 499,999
- 100,000 - 249,999
- 30,000 - 99,999
- 15,000 - 29,999
- UNDER 10,000

SCALE 1:6,000,000 LAMBERT CONFORMAL CONIC PROJECTION

MILES 0   100   200   300
KILOMETERS 0 100 200 300

© Copyright by HAMMOND INCORPORATED, Maplewood, N.J.   CC - 1150 - AA

SCALE 1:6,000,000
0   30 Mi
0   30 Km

Great mineral resources are buried within this wide band crossing the continent. Iron ore from the Brazilian state of Minas Gerais and the eastern Amazon basin feeds the growing Brazilian steel industry. Gold has also been discovered here, setting off a modern-day gold rush. Bolivia is one of the world's chief suppliers of tin, and an important supplier of tungsten and antimony. In Chile's northern desert region, copper ore is mined in great quantity. Vast dams on the Paraná and its tributaries supply Brazil and Paraguay with hydroelectric power.

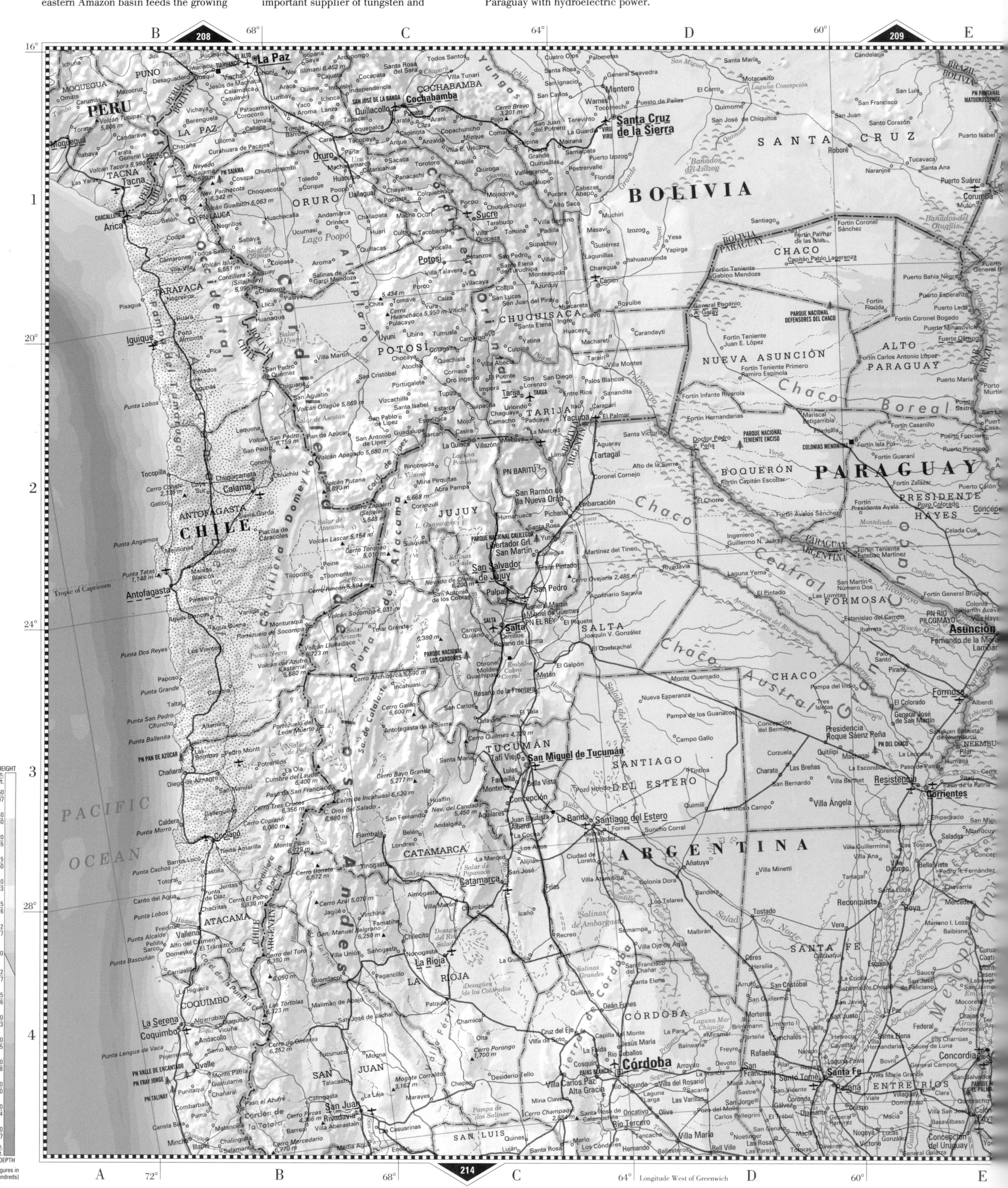

Central South America

SCALE 1:6,000,000   LAMBERT CONFORMAL CONIC PROJECTION

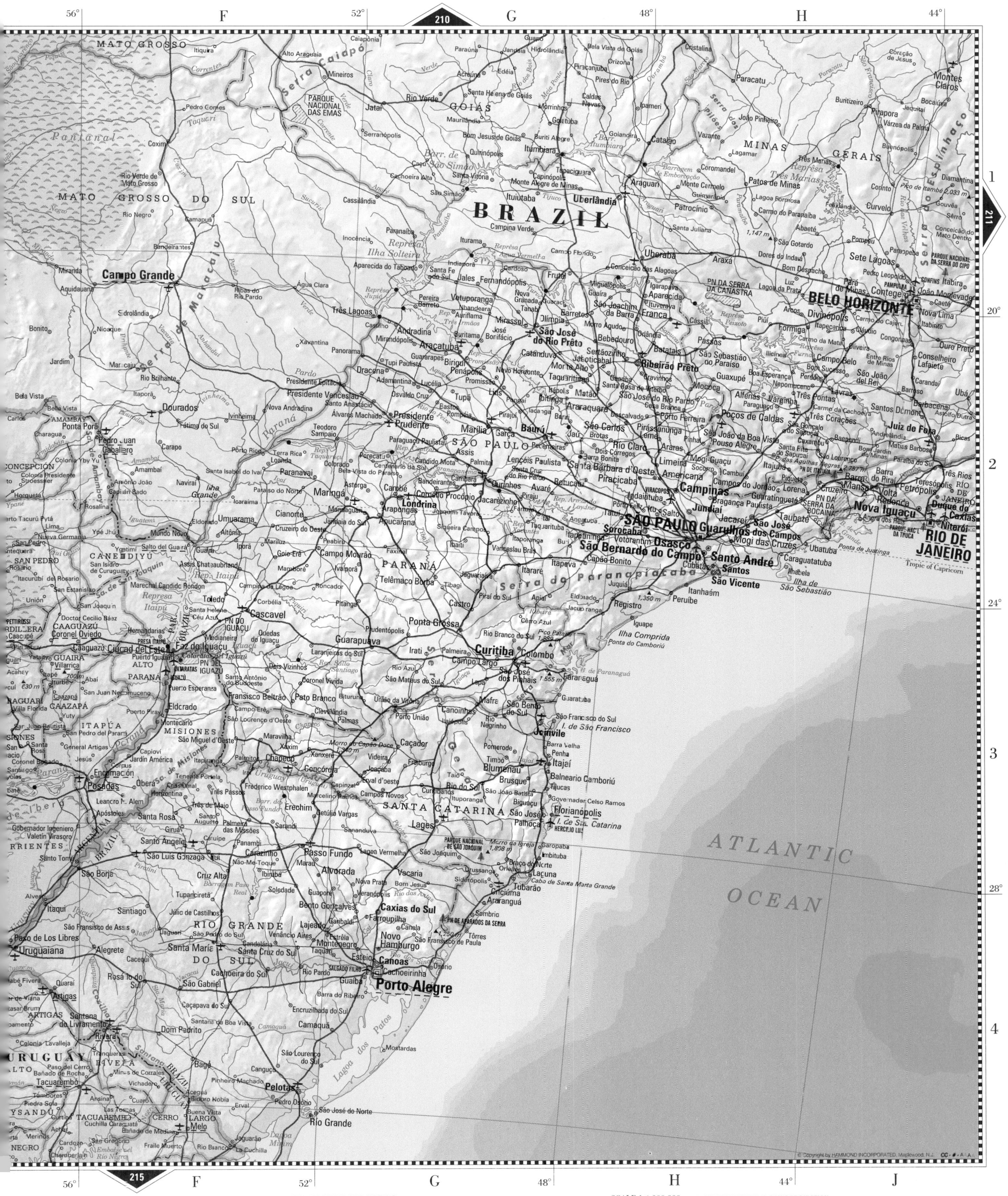

POPULATION OF CITIES AND TOWNS
■ OVER 2,000,000   ● 500,000 - 999,999   ● 100,000 - 249,999   ○ 10,000 - 29,999
□ 1,000,000 - 1,999,999   ● 250,000 - 499,999   ○ 30,000 - 99,999   ○ UNDER 10,000

MILES 0   100   200   300
KILOMETERS 0   100   200   300

© Copyright by HAMMOND INCORPORATED, Maplewood, N.J.

Agriculture is the hallmark of these two countries. The Argentine Pampas is famed for its cattle, corn, wheat and flax. Sheep graze in the dry scrub country of the southern Patagonian steppe. Despite the country's Indian heritage, most Argentines are of Spanish and Italian descent. Across the Andes, in Chile, the population is concentrated in a central valley. Chile's mountainous terrain and northern desert preclude farming. But the central region's Mediterranean-type climate yields bountiful fruit crops and fine red wines. The southern coast is heavily forested.

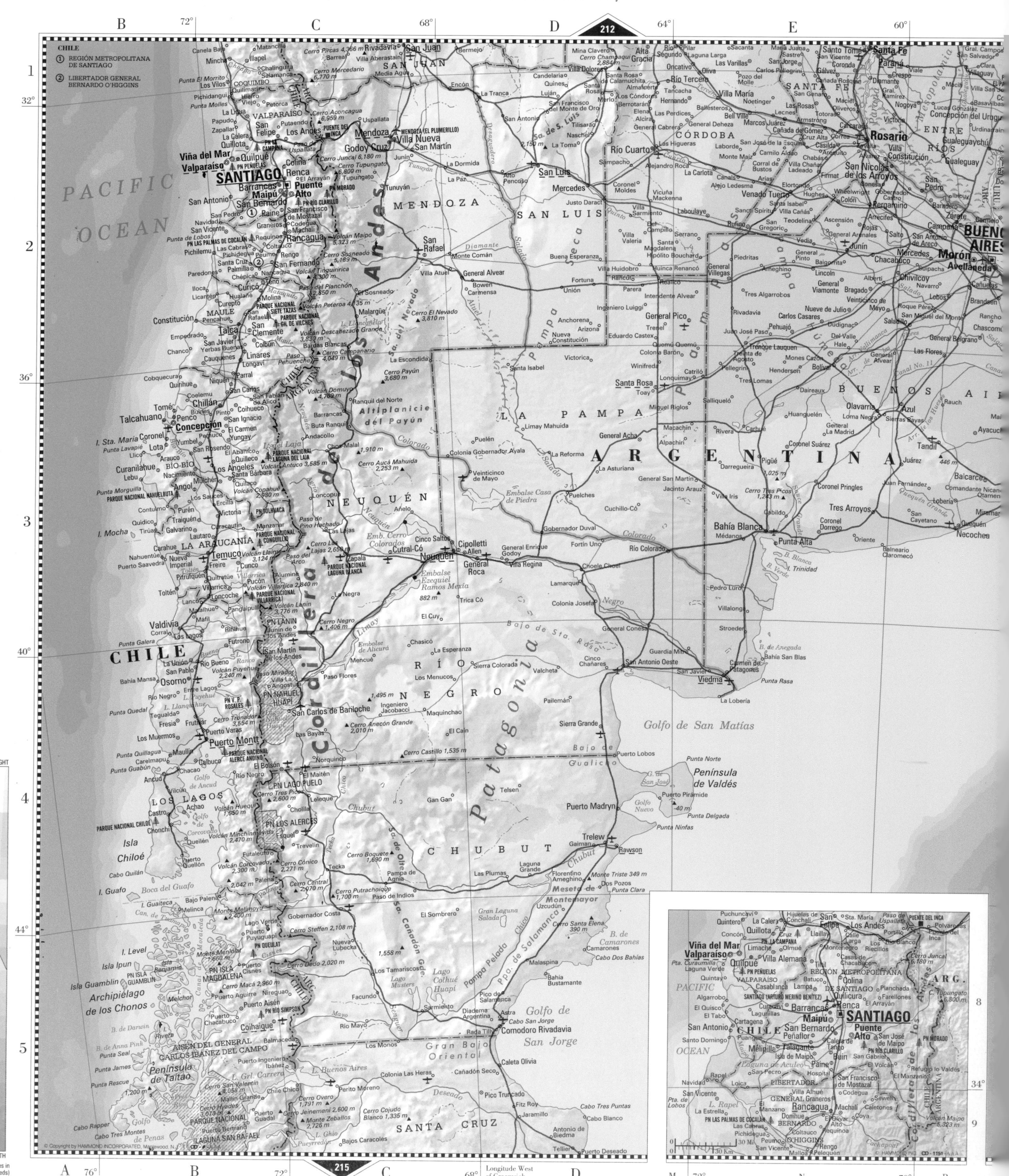

Southern Chile and Argentina

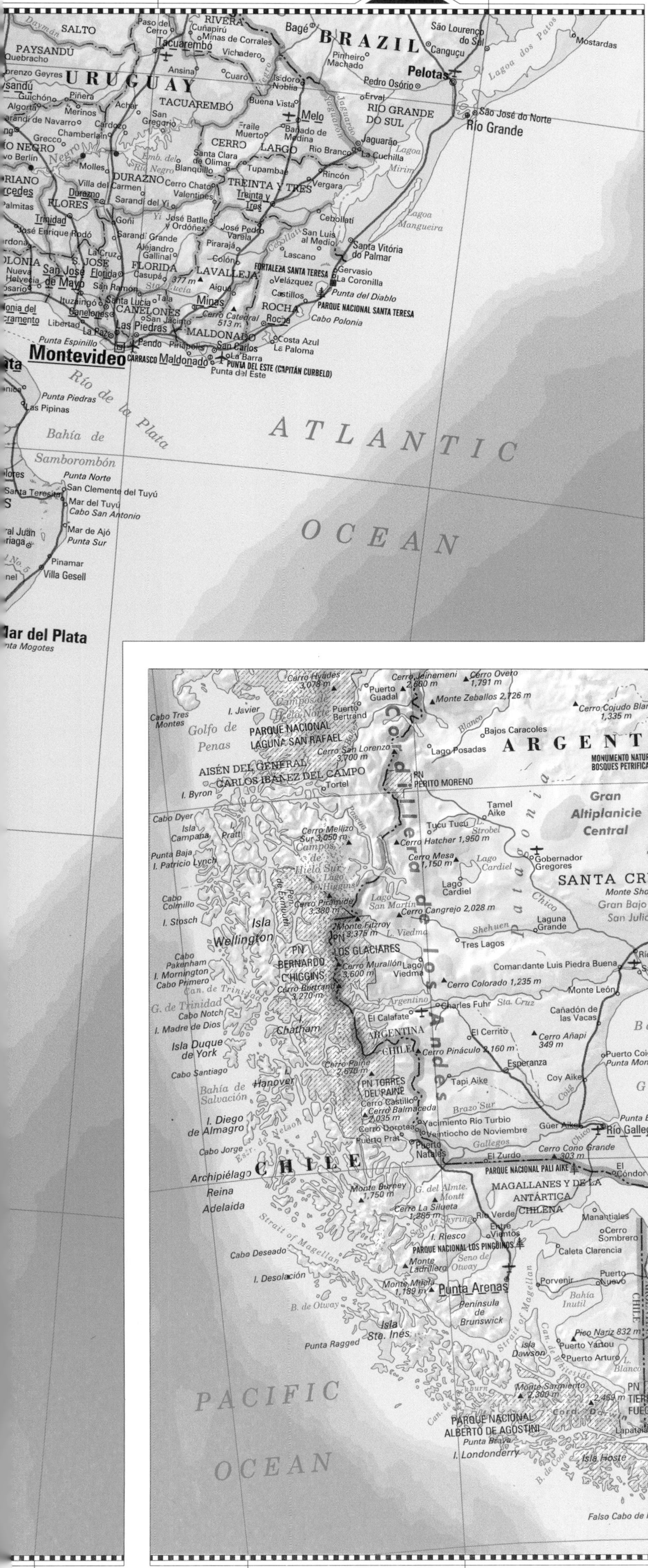

POPULATION OF CITIES AND TOWNS

■ OVER 2,000,000	◉ 500,000 - 999,999	◎ 100,000 - 249,999	⊙ 10,000 - 29,999
□ 1,000,000 - 1,999,999	◉ 250,000 - 499,999	○ 30,000 - 99,999	○ UNDER 10,000

SCALE 1:6,000,000   LAMBERT CONFORMAL CONIC PROJECTION

MILES   0   100   200   300

KILOMETERS   0   100   200   300

Arctic Regions, Antarctica

The Arctic Region, the northernmost area of the earth, is centered about the North Pole and the Arctic Ocean. The Arctic Circle is sometimes used as its arbitrary boundary. Centered about the South Pole, Antarctica, larger than Europe or Australia, covers over 5 million square miles (13 million sq. km.) and contains over 90 percent of the world's permanent ice and snow.

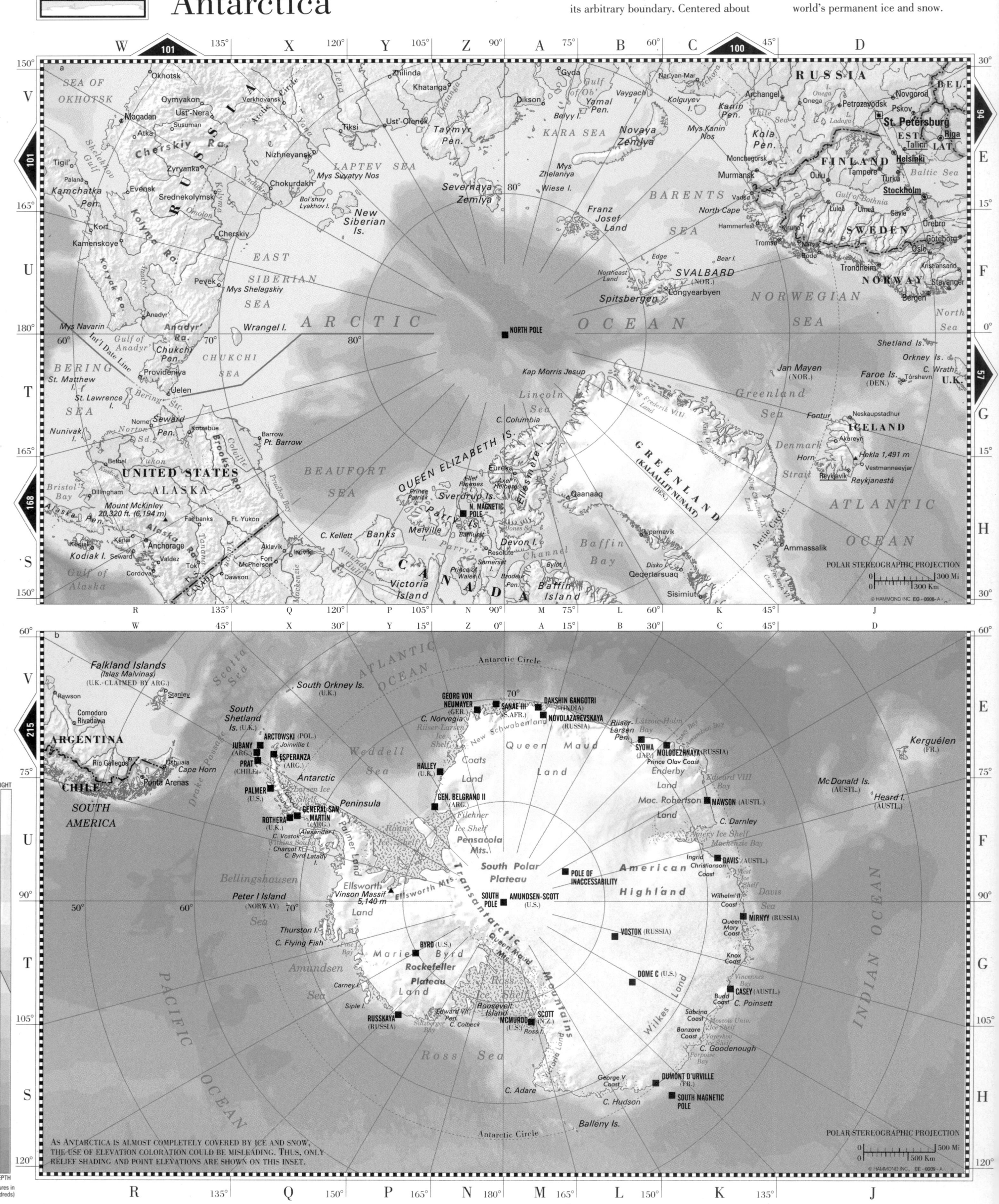

AS ANTARCTICA IS ALMOST COMPLETELY COVERED BY ICE AND SNOW, THE USE OF ELEVATION COLORATION COULD BE MISLEADING. THUS, ONLY RELIEF SHADING AND POINT ELEVATIONS ARE SHOWN ON THIS INSET.

POPULATION OF CITIES AND TOWNS
- OVER 2,000,000
- 1,000,000 - 1,999,999
- 500,000 - 999,999
- 100,000 - 499,999
- 50,000 - 99,999
- UNDER 50,000

Statistical Tables and Index

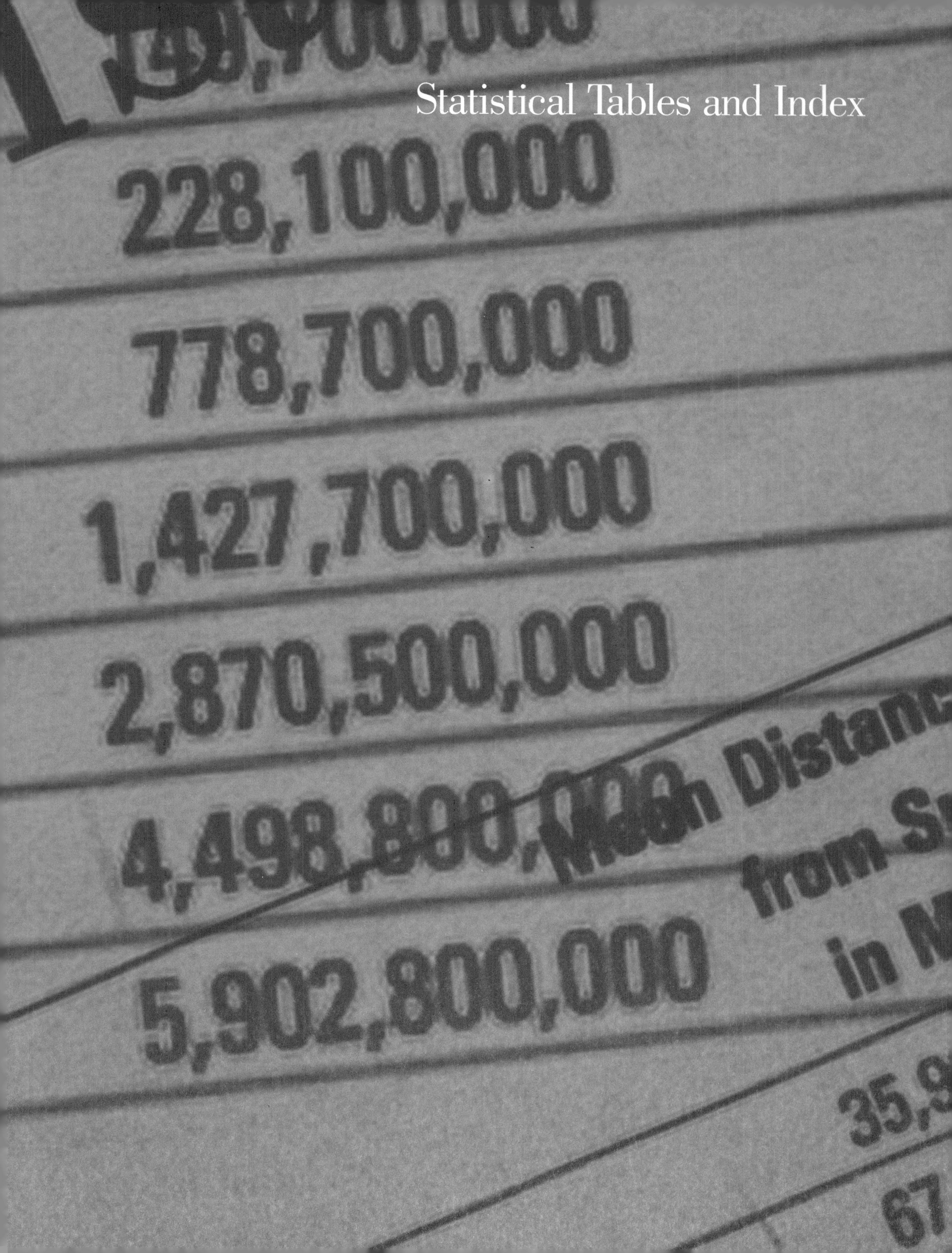
228,100,000
778,700,000
1,427,700,000
2,870,500,000
5,902,800,000

World Statistics

Elements of the Solar System

	Mean Distance from Sun: in Miles	in Kilometers	Period of Revolution around Sun	Period of Rotation on Axis	Equatorial Diameter in Miles	in Kilometers	Surface Gravity (Earth = 1)	Mass (Earth = 1)	Mean Density (Water = 1)	Number of Satellites
Mercury	35,990,000	57,900,000	87.97 days	58.7 days	3,032	4,880	0.38	0.055	5.4	0
Venus	67,240,000	108,200,000	224.70 days	243.7 days†	7,521	12,104	0.91	0.815	5.2	0
Earth	93,000,000	149,700,000	365.26 days	23h 56m	7,926	12,755	1.00	1.00	5.5	1
Mars	141,610,000	227,900,000	686.98 days	24h 37m	4,221	6,794	0.38	0.107	3.9	2
Jupiter	483,675,000	778,400,000	11.86 years	9h 55m	88,846	142,984	2.36	317.8	1.3	16
Saturn	886,572,000	1,426,800,000	29.46 years	10h 30m	74,898	120,536	0.92	95.2	0.7	18
Uranus	1,783,957,000	2,871,000,000	84.01 years	17h 14m†	31,763	51,118	0.89	14.5	1.3	15
Neptune	2,795,114,000	4,498,300,000	164.79 years	16h 6m	30,778	49,532	1.13	17.1	1.6	8
Pluto	3,670,000,000	5,906,400,000	247.70 years	6.4 days†	1,413	2,274	0.07	0.002	2.1	1

† Retrograde motion

Source: NASA, National Space Science Center

Dimensions of the Earth

	Area in: Sq. Miles	Sq. Kilometers
Superficial area	196,939,000	510,072,000
Land surface	57,506,000	148,940,000
Water surface	139,433,000	361,132,000

	Distance in: Miles	Kilometers
Equatorial circumference	24,902	40,075
Polar circumference	24,860	40,007
Equatorial diameter	7,926.4	12,756.4
Polar diameter	7,899.8	12,713.6
Equatorial radius	3,963.2	6,378.2
Polar radius	3,949.9	6,356.8

Volume of the Earth	2.6×10^{11} cubic miles	10.84×10^{11} cubic kilometers
Mass or weight	6.6×10^{21} short tons	6.0×10^{21} metric tons
Maximum distance from Sun	94,600,000 miles	152,000,000 kilometers
Minimum distance from Sun	91,300,000 miles	147,000,000 kilometers

Oceans and Major Seas

	Area in: Sq. Miles	Sq. Kms.	Greatest Depth in: Feet	Meters
Pacific Ocean	63,855,000	165,384,000	36,198	11,033
Atlantic Ocean	31,744,000	82,217,000	28,374	8,648
Indian Ocean	28,417,000	73,600,000	25,344	7,725
Arctic Ocean	5,427,000	14,056,000	17,880	5,450
Caribbean Sea	970,000	2,512,300	24,720	7,535
Mediterranean Sea	969,000	2,509,700	16,896	5,150
South China Sea	895,000	2,318,000	15,000	4,600
Bering Sea	875,000	2,266,250	15,800	4,800
Gulf of Mexico	600,000	1,554,000	12,300	3,750
Sea of Okhotsk	590,000	1,528,100	11,070	3,370
East China Sea	482,000	1,248,400	9,500	2,900
Yellow Sea	480,000	1,243,200	350	107
Sea of Japan	389,000	1,007,500	12,280	3,740
Hudson Bay	317,500	822,300	846	258
North Sea	222,000	575,000	2,200	670
Black Sea	185,000	479,150	7,365	2,245
Red Sea	169,000	437,700	7,200	2,195
Baltic Sea	163,000	422,170	1,506	459

The Continents

	Area in: Sq. Miles	Sq. Kms.	Percent of World's Land
Asia	17,128,500	44,362,815	29.5
Africa	11,707,000	30,321,130	20.2
North America	9,363,000	24,250,170	16.2
South America	6,879,725	17,818,505	11.9
Antarctica	5,405,000	14,000,000	9.4
Europe	4,057,000	10,507,630	7.0
Australia	2,967,893	7,686,850	5.1

Major Ship Canals

	Length in: Miles	Kms.	Minimum Depth in: Feet	Meters
Volga-Baltic, Russia	225	362	–	–
Baltic-White Sea, Russia	140	225	16	5
Suez, Egypt	100.76	162	42	13
Albert, Belgium	80	129	16.5	5
Moscow-Volga, Russia	80	129	18	6
Volga-Don, Russia	62	100	–	–
Göta, Sweden	54	87	10	3
Kiel (Nord-Ostsee), Germany	53.2	86	38	12
Panama Canal, Panama	50.72	82	41.6	13
Houston Ship, U.S.A.	50	81	36	11

Largest Islands

	Area in: Sq. Miles	Sq. Kms.
Greenland	840,000	2,175,600
New Guinea	305,000	789,950
Borneo	286,000	740,740
Madagascar	226,656	587,040
Baffin, Canada	195,928	507,454
Sumatra, Indonesia	164,000	424,760
Honshu, Japan	88,000	227,920
Great Britain	84,400	218,896
Victoria, Canada	83,896	217,290
Ellesmere, Canada	75,767	196,236
Celebes, Indonesia	72,986	189,034
South I., New Zealand	58,393	151,238
Java, Indonesia	48,842	126,501
North I., New Zealand	44,187	114,444
Cuba	42,803	110,860
Newfoundland, Canada	42,031	108,860
Luzon, Philippines	40,420	104,688
Iceland	39,768	103,000
Mindanao, Philippines	36,537	94,631
Ireland	32,589	84,406
Hokkaidō, Japan	30,436	78,829
Sakhalin, Russia	29,500	76,405

	Area in: Sq. Miles	Sq. Kms.
Hispaniola, Haiti & Dom. Rep.	29,399	76,143
Banks, Canada	27,038	70,028
Ceylon, Sri Lanka	25,332	65,610
Tasmania, Australia	24,600	63,710
Svalbard, Norway	23,957	62,049
Devon, Canada	21,331	55,247
Novaya Zemlya (north isl.), Russia	18,600	48,200
Marajó, Brazil	17,991	46,597
Tierra del Fuego, Chile & Argentina	17,900	46,360
Alexander, Antarctica	16,700	43,250
Axel Heiberg, Canada	16,671	43,178
Melville, Canada	16,274	42,150
Southampton, Canada	15,913	41,215
New Britain, Papua New Guinea	14,100	36,519
Taiwan	13,836	35,835
Kyushu, Japan	13,770	35,664
Hainan, China	13,127	33,999
Prince of Wales, Canada	12,872	33,338
Spitsbergen, Norway	12,355	31,999
Vancouver, Canada	12,079	31,285
Timor, Indonesia	11,527	29,855
Sicily, Italy	9,926	25,708

	Area in: Sq. Miles	Sq. Kms.
Somerset, Canada	9,570	24,786
Sardinia, Italy	9,301	24,090
Shikoku, Japan	6,860	17,767
New Caledonia, France	6,530	16,913
Nordaustlandet, Norway	6,409	16,599
Samar, Philippines	5,050	13,080
Negros, Philippines	4,906	12,707
Palawan, Philippines	4,550	11,785
Panay, Philippines	4,446	11,515
Jamaica	4,232	10,961
Hawaii, United States	4,038	10,458
Viti Levu, Fiji	4,010	10,386
Cape Breton, Canada	3,981	10,311
Mindoro, Philippines	3,759	9,736
Kodiak, Alaska, U.S.A.	3,670	9,505
Cyprus	3,572	9,251
Puerto Rico, U.S.A.	3,435	8,897
Corsica, France	3,352	8,682
New Ireland, Papua New Guinea	3,340	8,651
Crete, Greece	3,218	8,335
Anticosti, Canada	3,066	7,941
Wrangel, Russia	2,819	7,301

PRINCIPAL MOUNTAINS

	Height in : Feet	Meters
Everest, Nepal-China	29,028	8,848
K2 (Godwin Austen), Pakistan-China	28,250	8,611
Kánchenjunga, Nepal-India	28,208	8,598
Lhotse, Nepal-China	27,923	8,511
Makalu, Nepal-China	27,789	8,470
Dhaulagiri, Nepal	26,810	8,172
Nanga Parbat, Pakistan	26,660	8,126
Annapurna, Nepal	26,504	8,078
Nanda Devi, India	25,645	7,817
Rakaposhi, Pakistan	25,550	7,788
Kongur Shan, China	25,325	7,719
Tirich Mir, Pakistan	25,230	7,690
Gongga Shan, China	24,790	7,556
Ismail Samani Peak, Tajikistan	24,590	7,495
Pobedy Peak, Kyrgyzstan	24,406	7,439
Chomo Lhari, Bhutan-China	23,997	7,314
Muztag, China	23,891	7,282
Cerro Aconcagua, Argentina	22,831	6,959
Ojos del Salado, Chile-Argentina	22,572	6,880
Bonete, Chile-Argentina	22,546	6,872
Tupungato, Chile-Argentina	22,310	6,800
Pissis, Argentina	22,241	6,779
Mercedario, Argentina	22,211	6,770
Huascarán, Peru	22,205	6,763
Llullaillaco, Chile-Argentina	22,057	6,723
Nevada Ancohuma, Bolivia	21,489	6,550
Chimborazo, Ecuador	20,561	6,267
McKinley, Alaska	20,320	6,194
Logan, Yukon, Canada	19,524	5,951
Cotopaxi, Ecuador	19,347	5,897
Kilimanjaro, Tanzania	19,340	5,895
El Misti, Peru	19,101	5,822
Pico Cristóbal Colón, Colombia	18,947	5,775
Huila, Colombia	18,865	5,750
Citlaltépetl (Orizaba), Mexico	18,700	5,700
Damavand, Iran	18,605	5,671
El'brus, Russia	18,510	5,642
St. Elias, Alaska, U.S.A.-Yukon, Canada	18,008	5,489
Dykh-tau, Russia	17,070	5,203
Batian (Kenya), Kenya	17,058	5,199
Ararat, Turkey	16,946	5,165
Vinson Massif, Antarctica	16,864	5,140
Margherita (Ruwenzori), Africa	16,795	5,119
Kazbek, Georgia-Russia	16,558	5,047
Puncak Jaya, Indonesia	16,503	5,030
Blanc, France	15,771	4,807
Klyuchevskaya Sopka, Russia	15,584	4,750
Fairweather, Br. Col., Canada	15,300	4,663
Dufourspitze (Mte. Rosa), Italy-Switzerland	15,203	4,634
Ras Dashen, Ethiopia	15,157	4,620
Matterhorn, Switzerland	14,691	4,478
Whitney, California, U.S.A.	14,494	4,418
Elbert, Colorado, U.S.A.	14,433	4,399
Rainier, Washington, U.S.A.	14,410	4,392
Shasta, California, U.S.A.	14,162	4,317
Pikes Peak, Colorado, U.S.A.	14,110	4,301
Finsteraarhorn, Switzerland	14,022	4,274
Mauna Kea, Hawaii, U.S.A.	13,796	4,205
Mauna Loa, Hawaii, U.S.A.	13,677	4,169
Jungfrau, Switzerland	13,642	4,158
Grossglockner, Austria	12,457	3,797
Fujiyama, Japan	12,389	3,776
Cook, New Zealand	12,349	3,764

LONGEST RIVERS

	Length in: Miles	Kms.
Nile, Africa	4,145	6,671
Amazon, S. America	4,007	6,448
Mississippi-Missouri-Red Rock, U.S.A.	3,710	5,971
Chang Jiang (Yangtze), China	3,500	5,633
Ob'-Irtysh, Russia-Kazakhstan	3,362	5,411
Yenisey-Angara, Russia	3,100	4,989
Huang He (Yellow), China	2,950	4,747
Congo, Africa	2,780	4,474
Amur-Shilka-Onon, Asia	2,744	4,416
Lena, Russia	2,734	4,400
Mackenzie-Peace-Finlay, Canada	2,635	4,241
Paraná-La Plata, S. America	2,630	4,232
Mekong, Asia	2,610	4,200
Niger, Africa	2,580	4,152
Missouri-Red Rock, U.S.A.	2,564	4,125
Yenisey, Russia	2,500	4,028
Mississippi, U.S.A.	2,348	3,778
Murray-Darling, Australia	2,310	3,718
Volga, Russia	2,290	3,685
Madeira, S. America	2,013	3,240
Purus, S. America	1,995	3,211
Yukon, Alaska-Canada	1,979	3,185
Zambezi, Africa	1,950	3,138
São Francisco, Brazil	1,930	3,106
St. Lawrence, Canada-U.S.A.	1,900	3,058
Rio Grande, Mexico-U.S.A.	1,885	3,034
Syrdarïya-Naryn, Asia	1,859	2,992
Indus, Asia	1,800	2,897
Danube, Europe	1,775	2,857
Brahmaputra, Asia	1,700	2,736
Tocantins, Brazil	1,677	2,699
Salween, Asia	1,675	2,696
Euphrates, Asia	1,650	2,655
Xi (Si), China	1,650	2,655
Amu Darya, Asia	1,616	2,601
Nelson-Saskatchewan, Canada	1,600	2,575
Orinoco, S. America	1,600	2,575
Paraguay, S. America	1,584	2,543
Kolyma, Russia	1,562	2,514
Ganges, Asia	1,550	2,494
Zhayyq (Ural), Kazakhstan-Russia	1,509	2,428
Japurá, S. America	1,500	2,414
Arkansas, U.S.A.	1,450	2,334
Colorado, U.S.A.-Mexico	1,450	2,334
Negro, S. America	1,400	2,253
Dnepr (Dnyapro, Dnipro), Russia-Belarus-Ukraine	1,368	2,202
Orange, Africa	1,350	2,173
Ayeyarwady, Myanmar	1,325	2,132
Brazos, U.S.A.	1,309	2,107
Ohio-Allegheny, U.S.A.	1,306	2,102
Kama, Russia	1,252	2,031
Don, Russia	1,222	1,967
Red, U.S.A.	1,222	1,966
Columbia, U.S.A.-Canada	1,214	1,953
Tigris, Asia	1,181	1,901
Darling, Australia	1,160	1,867
Angara, Russia	1,135	1,827
Sungari, Asia	1,130	1,819
Pechora, Russia	1,124	1,809
Snake, U.S.A.	1,038	1,670
Churchill, Canada	1,000	1,609
Pilcomayo, S. America	1,000	1,609
Uruguay, S. America	994	1,600
Platte-N. Platte, U.S.A.	990	1,593
Ohio, U.S.A.	981	1,578
Magdalena, Colombia	956	1,538
Pecos, U.S.A.	926	1,490
Oka, Russia	918	1,477
Canadian, U.S.A.	906	1,458
Colorado, Texas, U.S.A.	894	1,439
Dnister (Nistru), Ukraine-Moldova	876	1,410
Fraser, Canada	850	1,369
Rhine, Europe	820	1,319
Northern Dvina, Russia	809	1,302
Ottawa, Canada	790	1,271

PRINCIPAL NATURAL LAKES

	Area in: Sq. Miles	Sq. Kms.	Max. Depth in: Feet	Meters
Caspian Sea, Asia	143,243	370,999	3,264	995
Lake Superior, U.S.A.-Canada	31,820	82,414	1,329	405
Lake Victoria, Africa	26,628	69,215	270	82
Lake Huron, U.S.A.-Canada	23,010	59,596	748	228
Lake Michigan, U.S.A.	22,400	58,016	923	281
Aral Sea, Kazakhstan-Uzbekistan	15,830	41,000	213	65
Lake Tanganyika, Africa	12,650	32,764	4,700	1,433
Lake Baykal, Russia	12,162	31,500	5,316	1,620
Great Bear Lake, Canada	12,096	31,328	1,356	413
Lake Nyasa (Malawi), Africa	11,555	29,928	2,320	707
Great Slave Lake, Canada	11,031	28,570	2,015	614
Lake Erie, U.S.A.-Canada	9,940	25,745	210	64
Lake Winnipeg, Canada	9,417	24,390	60	18
Lake Ontario, U.S.A.-Canada	7,540	19,529	775	244
Lake Balkhash, Kazakhstan	7,081	18,340	87	27
Lake Chad, Africa*	7,000	18,130	25	8
Lake Ladoga, Russia	6,900	17,871	738	225
Lake Maracaibo, Venezuela	5,120	13,261	100	31
Lake Onega, Russia	3,761	9,741	377	115
Lake Eyre, Australia*	3,500-0	9,065-0	–	–
Lake Titicaca, Peru-Bolivia	3,200	8,288	1,000	305
Lake Nicaragua, Nicaragua	3,100	8,029	230	70
Lake Athabasca, Canada	3,064	7,936	400	122
Reindeer Lake, Canada*	2,568	6,651	–	–
Lake Turkana (Rudolf), Africa	2,463	6,379	240	73
Ysyk-Köl, Kyrgyzstan	2,425	6,281	2,303	702
Lake Torrens, Australia*	2,230	5,776	–	–
Vänern, Sweden	2,156	5,584	328	100
Nettilling Lake, Canada*	2,140	5,543	–	–
Lake Winnipegosis, Canada	2,075	5,374	38	12
Lake Albert, Africa	2,075	5,374	160	49
Kariba Lake, Zambia-Zimbabwe	2,050	5,310	295	90
Lake Nipigon, Canada	1,872	4,848	540	165
Lake Mweru, Africa	1,800	4,662	60	18
Lake Manitoba, Canada	1,799	4,659	12	4
Lake Taymyr, Russia	1,737	4,499	85	26
Lake Khanka, China-Russia	1,700	4,403	33	10
Lake Kioga, Uganda	1,700	4,403	25	8
Lake of the Woods, U.S.A.-Canada	1,679	4,349	70	21

* Figures subject to great seasonal variations.

Population of Countries and Major Cities

The following pages include population figures for all countries, and cities with more than 100,000 inhabitants. All national capitals, regardless of size are also listed. Countries are listed alphabetically, and cities are grouped alphabetically within each country. Capitals are indicated with an asterisk (*). The population figures, given in thousands, represent the most current information available.

A

Country / City	Population in thousands
Afghanistan	**23,738**
Herāt	177
Kabul*	1,424
Mazār-e Sharīf	131
Qandahār	226
Albania	**3,293**
Tiranë*	244
Algeria	**29,830**
Algiers*	1,688
Annaba	228
Batna	185
Bechar	107
Bejaïa	118
Biskra	130
Blida	132
Chelif	130
Constantine	450
Mostaganem	115
Oran	599
Sétif	186
Sidi Bel-Abbes	155
Skikda	129
Tébessa	108
Tiaret	106
Tlemcen	108
Andorra	**75**
Andorra la Vella*	16
Angola	**10,624**
Luanda*	1,530
Antigua and Barbuda	**66**
Saint John's*	22
Argentina	**35,798**
Almirante Brown	449
Avellaneda	347
Bahía Blanca	240
Belén de Escobar	117
Berazateugi	245
Buenos Aires*	2,961
Catamaraca	110
Concordia	116
Córdoba	1,148
Corrientes	258
Florencio Varela	249
Formosa	154
General San Martín	408
General Sarmiento	647
Godoy Cruz	179
Guaymallén	201
Lanús	467
La Plata	520
La Rioja	104
Las Heras	146
Lomas de Zamora	573
Mar del Plata	512
Mariano Moreno	286
Mendoza	122
Merlo	386
Morón	642
Neuquén	167
Paraná	207
Pilar	113
Posadas	202
Quilmes	509
Resistencia	228
Río Cuarto	135
Rosario	895
Salta	367
San Fernando	141
San Isidro	249
San Juan	119
San Luis	110
San Miguel de Tucumán	471
San Nicolás de los Arroyes	115
San Salvador de Jujuy	181
Santa Fé	343
Santiago del Estero	189
Tigre	254
Vicente López	289
Villa Nueva	201
Armenia	**3,466**
Gyumri	120
Vanadzor	146
Yerevan*	1,199
Australia	**18,439**
Adelaide	957
Baulkham Hills	114
Brisbane	1146
Canberra*	276
Geelong	126
Gold Coast	226
Gosford	129
Hobart	127
Melbourne	2,762
Newcastle	262
Perth	1019
Salisbury	106
Stirling	173
Sydney	3,098
Townsville	101
Warringah	172
Waverley	118
Wollongong	211
Austria	**8,054**
Graz	238
Innsbruck	118
Linz	203
Salzburg	144
Vienna*	1,540
Azerbaijan	**7,736**
Baku*	1,149
Gäncä	281
Sumgayıt	235

B

Country / City	Population in thousands
Bahamas, The	**262**
Nassau*	172
Bahrain	**603**
Manama*	140
Bangladesh	**125,340**
Barisāl	180
Chittagong	1,560
Comilla	184
Dhaka*	3,638
Dinājpur	137
Jamālpur	108
Jessore	176
Khulna	601
Mymensingh	189
Naogaon	105
Nārāyanganj	285
Nawābganj	130
Pābna	110
Rājshāhi	302
Rangpur	221
Saidpur	108
Sirājganj	100
Sylhet	110
Tangail	108
Barbados	**258**
Bridgetown*	7
Belarus	**10,440**
Babruysk	226
Baranavichy	170
Barysaw	152
Brest	287
Homyel'	503
Hrodna	295
Mahilyow	363
Mazyr	105
Minsk*	1,655
Orsha	125
Pinsk	128
Vitsyebsk	365
Belgium	**10,204**
Antwerp	468
Brugge	117
Brussels*	954
Charleroi	206
Ghent	230
Liège	195
Namur	103
Schaerbeek	103
Belize	**225**
Belmopan*	4
Benin	**5,902**
Cotonou	537
Djougou	134
Parakou	104
Porto-Novo*	179
Bhutan	**1,865**
Thimphu*	30
Bolivia	**7,670**
Cochabamba	404
El Alto	404
La Paz*	711
Oruro	183
Potosí	112
Santa Cruz de la Sierra	695
Sucre*	131
Bosnia & Herzegovina	**2,608**
Banja Luka	196
Doboj	103
Mostar	127
Prijedor	113
Sarajevo*	529
Tuzla	132
Zenica	146
Botswana	**1,501**
Gaborone*	175
Brazil	**164,511**
Alvorada	133
Americana	154
Anápolis	222
Aracaju	402
Araçatuba	146
Arapiraca	125
Araraquara	101
Barra Mansa	145
Baurú	254
Belém	765
Belo Horizonte	2,206
Betim	153
Blumenau	185
Boa Vista	119
Brasília*	1,493
Cachoeiro de Itapemirim	112
Campina Grande	298
Campinas	748
Campo Grande	516
Campos	276
Canoas	269
Carapicuíba	207
Caruaru	181
Cascavel	175
Caxias do Sul	263
Colombo	105
Contegem	196
Cuiabá	253
Curitiba	842
Diadema	305
Divinópolis	142
Dourados	117
Duque du Caxias	326
Embu	156
Feira de Santana	340
Florianópolis	192
Fortaleza	1,027
Foz do Iguaçu	186
Franca	228
Goiânia	912
Governador Valadares	210
Gravataí	167
Guarapuava	107
Guarulhos	545
Ilhéus	135
Imperatriz	210
Ipatinga	120
Itabuna	170
Itajaí	115
Itapevi	108
Itaquaquecetuba	165
Jacarei	143
Jequié	115
João Pessoa	497
Joinvile	326
Juazeiro do Norte	164
Juiz de Fora	378
Jundiaí	253
Lages	137
Limeira	177
Londrina	355
Luziânia	194
Macapá	147
Maceió	555
Manaus	1,006
Marabá	102
Maracanau	133
Marília	145
Maringá	226
Mauá	295
Mogi das Cruzes	126
Montes Claros	233
Mossoró	177
Muribeca dos Guararapes	201
Natal	460
Nilópolis	105
Niterói	401
Nova Friburgo	111
Nova Iguaçu	562
Novo Hamburgo	199
Olinda	341
Osasco	567
Passo Fundo	135
Parnaíba	105
Pelotas	261
Petrolina	124
Petrópolis	165
Piracicaba	223
Poços de Caldas	105
Ponta Grossa	220
Porto Alegre	1,237
Porto Velho	226
Presidente Prudente	158
Recife	1,297
Ribeirão Prêto	416
Rio Branco	167
Rio Claro	130
Rio de Janeiro	5,474
Rio Grande	158
Salvador	2,070
Santa Bárbara d'Oeste	140
Santa Maria	193
Santarém	168
Santo André	518
Santos	416
São Bernardo do Campo	550
São Caetano do Sul	149
São Carlos	101
São Gonçalo	296
São João de Meriti	221
São José do Rio Preto	263
São José dos Campos	386
São Luís	164
São Leopoldo	160
São Paulo	9,394
São Vicente	268
Sapucia do Sul	105
Sete Lagoas	138
Sorocaba	349
Suzano	110
Taboão da Serra	160
Taubaté	186
Teresina	556
Uberaba	199
Uberlândia	355
Uruguaiana	103
Vitória	184
Vila Velha Argolas	114
Vitória da Conquista	180
Volta Redonda	220
Brunei	**308**
Bandar Seri Begawan*	46
Bulgaria	**8,653**
Burgas	196
Dobrich	104
Pleven	131
Plovdiv	341
Ruse	170
Sliven	106
Sofia*	1,114
Stara Zagora	150
Varna	309
Burkina Faso	**10,891**
Bobo Dioulasso	229
Ouagadougou*	442
Burundi	**6,053**
Bujumbura*	235

C

Country / City	Population in thousands
Cambodia	**11,164**
Phnom Penh*	620
Cameroon	**14,668**
Bafoussam	140
Bamenda	130
Douala	1,030
Garoua	170
Maroua	150
Ngaoundéré	100
N'Kongsamba	110
Yaoundé*	654
Canada	**29,123**
Abbotsford	105
Brampton	268
Burlington	137
Burnaby	179
Calgary	768
Cambridge	101
Coquitlam	102
Edmonton	616
Gatineau	101
Gloucester	104
Halifax	114
Hamilton	322
Kitchener	178
Laval	330
London	326
Longueuil	128
Markham	173
Mississauga	544
Montréal	1,016
Nepean	115
Oakville	128
Oshawa	134
Ottawa*	323
Québec	167
Regina	180
Richmond	149
Richmond Hill	102
Saint Catharines	131
Saint John's	102
Saskatoon	194
Surrey	304
Thunder Bay	114
Toronto	654
Vancouver	514
Vaughan	133
Windsor	198
Winnipeg	618
Cape Verde	**394**
Praia*	62
Central African Republic	**3,342**
Bangui*	597
Chad	**7,166**
Moundou	102
N'Djamena*	530
Sarh	113
Chile	**14,508**
Antofagasta	227
Arica	161
Barrancas	184
Calama	120
Chillán	146
Concepción	327
Coquimbo	115
Iquique	151
La Serena	109
Maipú	254
Osorno	114
Puente Alto	254
Puerto Montt	112
Punta Arenas	114
Quilpué	102
Rancagua	180
Renca	129
San Bernardo	191
Santiago*	4,298
Talca	161
Talcahuano	246
Temuco	211
Valdivia	114
Valparaíso	282
Viña del Mar	304
China	**1,221,592**
Acheng	193
Aksu	126
Anda	133
Ankang	129
Anqing	247
Anshan	1,215
Anshun	175
Anyang	395
Baicheng	214
Baiyin	199
Baoding	485
Baoji	325
Baotou	980
Bei'an	193
Beihai	116
Beijing*	5,715
Beipiao	190
Bengbu	441
Benxi	767
Binzhou	129
Cangzhou	222
Changchun	1,698
Changde	253
Changji	109
Changsha	1,077
Changshu	180
Changzhi	307
Changzhou	523
Chaoyang	218
Chaozhou	289
Chengde	243
Chengdu	1,719
Chenzhou	166
Chifeng	344
Chongqing	2,265
Chuzhou	120
Cixi	101
Da'an	124
Da Xian	185
Dali	134
Dalian	1,632
Dandong	525
Daqing	676
Datong	779
Deyang	171
Dezhou	183
Dongguan	271
Dongtai	131
Dongying	257
Dunhua	225
Duyun	130
Ezhou	137
Fengcheng	150
Foshan	291
Fuling	164
Fushun	1,210
Fuxin	623
Fuyang	161
Fuyu	174
Fuzhou	890
Ganzhou	219
Gejiu	212
Gongzhuling	218
Guangyuan	173
Guangzhou	2,892
Guigang	111
Guilin	371
Guiyang	1,009
Haicheng	196
Haikou	271
Hailar	176
Hailun	128
Hami	146
Handan	798
Hangzhou	1,119
Hanzhong	157
Harbin	2,468
Hebi	196
Hefei	733
Hegang	507
Hengyang	469
Heze	154
Hohhot	654
Honghu	130
Huadian	166
Huai'an	113
Huaibei	332
Huaihua	120
Huainan	674
Huaiyin	221
Huangshi	432
Huizhou	147
Hunjiang	475
Huzhou	398
Jiamusi	477
Ji'an	143
Jiangmen	219
Jiangyin	145
Jiaohe	172
Jiaozuo	386
Jiaxing	205
Jilin	1,038
Jinan	1,361
Jinchang	100
Jincheng	128
Jingdezhen	274
Jingmen	158
Jinhua	139
Jining (Nei Mong.)	248
Jining (Shandong)	190
Jinxi	349
Jinzhou	573
Jiujiang	284
Jiutai	173
Jixi	638
Kaifeng	503
Kaili	109
Kaiyuan	122
Karamay	194
Kashi	158
Korla	137
Kunming	1,108
Kunshan	100
Laiwu	186
Langfang	146
Lanzhou	1,205
Laohekou	108
Leiyang	129
Lengshuijiang	126
Leshan	333
Lianyuan	114
Lianyungang	352
Liaocheng	149
Liaoyang	485
Liaoyuan	341
Liling	107
Linchuan	161
Linfen	174
Linhe	131
Linyi	210
Liuzhou	602
Longyan	134
Loudi	121
Lu'an	137
Luohe	122
Luoyang	730
Lupanshui	342
Luzhou	262
Ma'anshan	297
Manzhouli	119
Maoming	162
Meihekou	205
Meizhou	120
Mianyang	250
Mudanjiang	562
Nanchang	1,026
Nanchong	179
Nanjing	2,114
Nanning	723
Nanping	188
Nantong	324
Nanyang	229
Neijiang	240
Ningbo	548
Panzhihua	407
Pingdingshan	442
Pingxiang	306
Puyang	120
Qingdao	1,317
Qingjiang	172
Qingyuan	134
Qinhuangdao	360
Qinzhou	105
Qiqihar	1,066
Qitaihe	218
Quanzhou	178
Qujing	163
Quzhou	105
Renqiu	128
Rizhao	109
Sanmenxia	114
Sanming	159
Shanghai	7,551
Shangqiu	159
Shangrao	127
Shangzhi	208
Shantou	558
Shaoguan	334
Shaoxing	180
Shaoyang	242
Shashi	277
Shenyang	3,588
Shenzhen	466
Sheung Shui-Fanling	201
Shihezi	160
Shijiazhuang	1,065
Shiyan	241
Shizuishan	245
Shuangyashan	392
Shuangcheng	131
Siping	310
Suihua	219
Suining	134
Suizhou	139
Suzhou (Anhui)	147
Suzhou (Jiangsu)	697
Tai'an	246
Taiyuan	1,514
Taizhou	151
Tangshan	1,042
Tianjin	4,521
Tianmen	138
Tianshui	238
Tieling	247
Tin Shui Wai	150
Tongchuan	259
Tonghua	321
Tongliao	247
Tongling	212
Tseung Kwan O	137
Ulanhot	152
Ürümqi	1071
Wafangdian	250
Wanxian	156
Weifang	359
Weinan	135
Wenzhou	204
Wuhai	261
Wuhan	3,177
Wuhu	419
Wuwei	125
Wuxi	806
Wuzhou	213
Xiamen	391
Xi'an	1,954
Xiangfan	390
Xiangtan	429
Xianning	110
Xiantao	124
Xianyang	328
Xiaogan	140
Xiaoshan	159
Xichang	133
Xingcheng	102
Xinghua	155
Xingtai	270
Xining	559
Xintai	209
Xinxiang	453
Xinyang	185
Xinyu	163
Xuchang	196
Xuzhou	795
Yan'an	106

Country / City	Population in thousands
Yancheng	239
Yangjiang	203
Yangquan	338
Yangzhou	306
Yanji	233
Yantai	400
Yibin	241
Yichang	364
Yichun (Heilonjiang)	787
Yichun (Jiangxi)	134
Yinchuan	350
Yingkou	423
Yining	172
Yixing	186
Yiyang	180
Yong'an	109
Yuci	189
Yueyang	296
Yulin	130
Yumen	112
Yuyao	103
Zaozhuang	309
Zhangjiakou	525
Zhangzhou	178
Zhanjiang	384
Zhaodong	164
Zhaoqing	173
Zhengzhou	1,139
Zhenjiang	355
Zhongshan	256
Zhoukou	136
Zhuhai	162
Zhumadian	121
Zhuzhou	383
Zibo	864
Zigong	385
Zixing	107
Zunyi	269
Colombia	**37,418**
Armenia	211
Barrancabermeja	136
Barranquilla	1,000
Bello	260
Bogotá*	5,699
Bucaramanga	403
Buenaventura	187
Cali	1,625
Cartagena	576
Cúcuta	462
Dos Quebradas	115
Envigado	110
Floridablanca	177
Ibagué	336
Itagüí	168
Manizales	341
Medellín	1,485
Montería	182
Neiva	223
Palmira	189
Pasto	244
Pereira	329
Popayán	175
Santa Marta	211
Sincelejo	120
Soacha	181
Soledad	236
Tuluá	104
Tunjá	102
Valledupar	209
Villavicencio	190
Comoros	**590**
Moroni*	30
Congo, Dem. Rep. of the	**47,440**
Boma	264
Bukavu	210
Kananga	372
Kikwit	183
Kinshasa*	3,800
Kisangani	373
Kolwezi	545
Lubumbashi	739
Matadi	173
Mbandaka	166
Mbuji-Mayi	613
Panda-Likasi	146
Tshikapa	110
Congo, Rep. of the	**2,583**
Brazzaville*	938
Pointe-Noire	576
Costa Rica	**3,534**
San José*	279
Côte d'Ivoire	**14,986**
Abidjan	1,929
Bouaké	330
Daloa	122
Korhogo	109
Yamoussoukro*	107
Croatia	**5,027**
Osijek	130
Rijeka	168
Split	200
Zagreb*	868
Cuba	**10,999**
Bayamo	138
Camagüey	249
Ciego de Ávila	101
Cienfuegos	130
Guantánamo	208
Havana*	2,176
Holguín	242
Las Tunas	127
Manzanillo	108
Marianao	128
Matanzas	123
Pinar del Río	129
Santa Clara	205
Santiago de Cuba	430
Victoria de las Tunas	115
Cyprus	**753**
Nicosia*	47
Czech Republic	**10,319**
Brno	390
Hradec Králové	101
Liberec	101
Olomouc	106
Ostrava	327
Plzeň	172
Prague*	1,217
Ústí nad Labem	100

D

Country / City	Population in thousands
Denmark	**5,269**
Ålborg	117
Århus	209
Copenhagen*	467
Odense	143
Djibouti	**434**
Djibouti*	200
Dominica	**83,226**
Roseau*	6
Dominican Republic	**8,228**
Santiago de los Caballeros	375
Santo Domingo*	2,135

E

Country / City	Population in thousands
Ecuador	**11,691**
Ambato	124
Cuenca	195
Esmeraldas	100
Guayaquil	1,513
Loja	111
Machala	146
Manta	130
Milagro	103
Portoviejo	153
Quito*	1,113
Riobamba	101
Santo Domingo de los Colorados	171
Egypt	**64,792**
Alexandria	3,380
Al Fayyum	250
Al Jīzah	2,144
Al Maḥallah al Kubrá	408
Al Manṣūra	371
Al Minyā	208
Aswān	220
Asyūt	321
Az Zaqāzīq	287
Banhā	136
Banī Suwayf	179
Cairo*	6,663
Damanhūr	222
Ismailia	255
Kafr ad Dawwār	226
Luxor	146
Port Said	460
Qinā	141
Shibīn al Kaum	158
Shubrā al Khaymah	834
Suez	376
Suhāj	156
Tantā	380
El Salvador	**5,662**
Mejicanos	132
San Miguel	128
San Salvador*	415
Santa Ana	139
Soyapango	261
Equatorial Guinea	**443**
Malabo*	30
Eritrea	**3,590**
Asmara*	435
Estonia	**1,445**
Tallinn*	482
Tartu	114
Ethiopia	**58,733**
Addis Ababa*	2,316
Bahir Dar	116
Debrezit	117
Dessi	195
Dirē Dawa	195
Gonder	167
Hārer	123
Jimma	120
Mekele	120
Nazerit	147

F

Country / City	Population in thousands
Fiji	**792**
Suva*	70
Finland	**5,109**
Esbo (Espoo)	191
Helsinki*	525
Oulu	109
Tampere	183
Turku	165
Vantaa	166
France	**58,470**
Aix-en-Provence	127
Amiens	136
Angers	146
Besançon	119
Bordeaux	213
Boulogne-Billancourt	102
Brest	153
Caen	116
Clermont-Ferrand	140
Dijon	152
Grenoble	154
Le Havre	197
Le Mans	148
Lille	178
Limoges	136
Lyon	422
Marseille	808
Metz	124
Montpellier	211
Mulhouse	110
Nancy	102
Nantes	252
Nice	346
Nîmes	134
Orléans	108
Paris*	2,175
Perpignan	108
Reims	185
Rennes	204
Rouen	105
Saint-Denis	122
Saint-Étienne	202
Strasbourg	256
Toulon	170
Toulouse	366
Tours	133
Villeurbanne	120

G

Country / City	Population in thousands
Gabon	**1,190**
Libreville*	362
Gambia, The	**1,248**
Banjul*	42
Georgia	**5,175**
Bat'umi	136
K'ut'aisi	235
Rust'avi	159
Sokhumi	121
T'bilisi*	1,260
Germany	**84,068**
Aachen	242
Augsburg	257
Bergisch Gladbach	104
Berlin*	3,434
Bielefeld	319
Bochum	396
Bonn	292
Bottrop	119
Braunschweig	259
Bremen	551
Bremerhaven	130
Chemnitz	294
Cologne	954
Cottbus	126
Darmstadt	139
Dortmund	599
Dresden	491
Duisburg	535
Düsseldorf	576
Erfurt	209
Erlangen	102
Essen	627
Frankfurt am Main	645
Freiburg	191
Fürth	103
Gelsenkirchen	294
Gera	129
Göttingen	122
Hagen	214
Halle	310
Hamburg	1,652
Hamm	180
Hannover	513
Heidelberg	137
Heilbronn	116
Herne	178
Hildesheim	105
Ingolstadt	105
Jena	103
Karlsruhe	275
Kassel	194
Kiel	246
Koblenz	109
Köpenick	118
Krefeld	244
Leipzig	511
Leverkusen	161
Lübeck	215
Ludwigshafen	162
Magdeburg	279
Mainz	179
Mannheim	310
Moers	105
Mönchengladbach	259
Mülheim an der Ruhr	178
Munich	1,229
Münster	259
Neuss	147
Nürnberg	494
Oberhausen	224
Offenbach	115
Oldenburg	143
Osnabrück	163
Paderborn	121
Pforzheim	113
Potsdam	140
Recklinghausen	125
Regensburg	122
Remscheid	123
Reutlingen	104
Rostock	237
Saarbrücken	191
Salzgitter	118
Schwerin	122
Siegen	112
Solingen	166
Stuttgart	594
Ulm	115
Wiesbaden	271
Witten	106
Wolfsburg	128
Wuppertal	387
Würzburg	129
Zwickau	108
Ghana	**18,101**
Accra*	954
Kumasi	399
Tamale	136
Tema	100
Greece	**10,583**
Athens*	772
Iráklion	115
Kallithéa	114
Lárisa	113
Pátrai	153
Peristérion	137
Piraiévs	183
Thessaloníki	384
Grenada	**96**
Saint George's*	5
Guatemala	**11,558**
Guatemala*	823
Mixco	305
Quezaltenango	109
San Pedro Carchá	103
Villa Nueva	192
Guinea	**7,405**
Conakry*	950
Labé	110
Guinea-Bissau	**1,179**
Bissau*	109
Guyana	**706**
Georgetown*	72
Pickersgill	249

H

Country / City	Population in thousands
Haiti	**6,611**
Port-au-Prince*	690
Honduras	**5,751**
San Pedro Sula	287
Tegucigalpa*	577
Hungary	**9,936**
Budapest*	2,017
Debrecen	212
Győr	129
Kecskemét	103
Miskolc	196
Nyíregyháza	114
Pécs	170
Szeged	175
Székesfehérvár	109

I

Country / City	Population in thousands
Iceland	**273**
Reykjavík*	96
India	**967,613**
Abohar	107
Ādoni	136
Āgra	892
Agartala	157
Ahmadābād	2,877
Ahmadnagar	131
Aizawl	155
Ajmer	403
Akola	328
Alīgarh	431
Allahābād	733
Alleppey	175
Alwar	205
Ambāla	119
Amravati	422
Amritsar	709
Amroha	137
Anand	110
Anantapur	175
Arrah	157
Asansol	262
Aurangābād	573
Bahraich	135
Bally	184
Bālurghāt	120
Bangalore	2,660
Bānkura	115
Baranagar	225
Bārāsat	170
Bareilly	587
Barrackpur	133
Basīrhāt	101
Beāwar	105
Belgaum	326
Bellary	245
Berhampore	115
Berhampur	210
Bhadrāvati	130
Bhāgalpur	253
Bharātpur	105
Bharuch	133
Bhatinda	159
Bhātpāra	305
Bhavnagar	402
Bhilai	386
Bhīlwāra	184
Bhīmavaram	121
Bhind	110
Bhiwandi	379
Bhiwāni	122
Bhopāl	1,063
Bhubaneswar	412
Bhūj	102
Bhusawal	145
Bīdar	108
Bihar	201
Bijāpur	187
Bīkaner	416
Bilāspur	180
Bīr	112
Bokaro Steel City	334
Budaun	117
Bulandshahr	127
Burdwān	245
Burhānpur	173
Calcutta	4,400
Calicut (Kozhikoda)	420
Champdāni	101
Chandannagar	120
Chandigarh	504
Chandrapur	226
Chāpra	137
Chennai (Madras)	3,841
Chittoor	133
Cochin	565
Coimbatore	816
Cuddalore	145
Cuddapah	121
Cuttack	403
Darbhanga	218
Daryābād	270
Dāvangere	266
Dehra Dūn	270
Delhi	7,207
Dewās	164
Dhānbād	152
Dhūlia	278
Dibrugarh	120
Dindigul	182
Dombivli	103
Durg	151
Durgāpur	426
Elūrū	213
English Bāzār	139
Erode	160
Etāwah	124
Faizābād	124
Farīdābād	618
Farrukhābād	195
Fatehpur	118
Fīrozābād	215
Gadag-Betigeri	134
Gāndhīdhām	105
Gandhinagar	123
Gayā	292
Ghaziābād	454
Gondia	109
Gorakhpur	506
Gudivāda	102
Gulbarga	304
Guna	100
Guntakal	108
Guntūr	471
Gurgaon	121
Guwāhati	584
Gwalior	691
Hābra	100
Haldīa	100
Hālisahar	114
Hāpur	146
Hardwār	147
Hāthras	113
Hindupur	105
Hisār	173
Hooghly-Chinsura	152
Hoshiārpur	123
Howrah	950
Hubli-Dhārwār	648
Hyderābād	3,044
Ichalkaranji	215
Imphāl	199
Indore	1,092
Jabalpur	742
Jaipur	1,458
Jālgaon	242
Jālna	175
Jammu	206
Jāmnagar	342
Jamshedpur	461
Jaunpur	136
Jhānsi	301
Jodhpur	666
Jullundur	510
Junāgadh	130
Kākināda	280
Kalyān	1,015
Kāmārhāti	267
Kānchīpuram	145
Kanchrāpāra	100
Kānpur	1,874
Karīmnagar	149
Karnāl	174
Kāthgodām	104
Katihār	135
Khammam	128
Khandwa	145
Kharagpur	262
Kolhāpur	406
Korba	125
Kota	537
Krishnanagar	121
Kulti	109
Kumbakonam	139
Kurnool	237
Lātūr	197
Lucknow	1,619
Ludhiāna	1,043
Machilipatnam	159
Madurai	941
Mahbubnagar	117
Mālegaon	343
Mandya	120
Mangalore	273
Mathurā	227
Maunath Bhanjan	137
Medinipur	125
Meerut	754
Mira-Bhayandar	176
Miraj	122
Mirzāpur	169
Morādābād	429
Morena	147
Mumbai (Bombay)	9,926
Munger	150
Murwāra	163
Muzaffarnagar	241
Muzaffarpur	241
Mysore	481
Nabadwīp	125
Nadiād	167
Nāgercoil	190
Nāgpur	1,625
Naihāti	133
Nānded	275
Nandyāl	120
Nāsik	657
Navsāri	126
Nellore	317
New Bombay	350
New Delhi*	301
Nizāmābād	241
North Barrackpore	101
Ongole	101
Pālghāt	123
Pāli	137
Pānīpat	191
Pānihāti	276
Parbhani	190
Pathānkot	124
Patiāla	238
Patna	917
Pīlībhīt	107
Pimpri-Chinchwad	517
Pollāchi	115
Pondicherry	203
Porbandar	117
Proddatūr	134
Pune (Poona)	1,567
Purī	125
Purnia	115
Quilon	140
Rāe Bareli	130
Raichūr	158
Raigarh	151
Raipur	439
Rājahmundry	325
Rājapālaiyam	114
Rāj-Nāndgaon	125
Rāmagundam	215
Rāmpur	244
Rānchī	599
Ratlām	183
Raurkela	356
Rewa	129
Rishra	103
Rohtak	216
Sāgar	195
Sahāranpur	375
Salem	367
Sambalpur	131
Sambhal	151
Sāngli	193
Sāntipur	107
Satna	157
Secunderābād	171
Serampore	137
Shāhjahānpur	238
Shillong	132
Shimoga	179
Shivpurī	108
Sholāpur	604
Sīkar	148
Silchar	115
Silīguri	217
Sirsa	113
Sītāpur	122
Sonīpat	144
South Dum Dum	233
Sri Gangānagar	161
Srīnagar	606
Surat	1,499
Surendranagar	106
Tellicherry	104
Tenāli	144
Thāna	803
Thanjavur	202
Tiruchchirāppalli	387
Tirunelveli	136
Tirupati	174
Tiruppūr	236
Tiruvannāmalai	109
Titāgarh	114
Tonk	100
Trivandrum	524
Tumkūr	139
Tuticorin	200
Udaipur	309
Ujjain	362
Ulbāria	155
Ulhāsnagar	369
Unnāo	107
Uttarpara-Kotrung	101
Vadodara (Baroda)	1,031
Vālpārai	106
Vārānasi	929
Vellore	175
Vijayawada	702
Visākhapatnam	752
Vizianagaram	160
Warangal	448
Wardha	103
Yamunānagar	144
Yavatmāl	109
Indonesia	**209,774**
Ambon	205
Balikpapan	309
Banda Aceh	143
Bandung	2,026
Bangil	386
Banjarmasin	443
Bekasi	146
Bengkulu	170
Binjai	127
Blitar	113
Bogor	271
Ciamis	105
Cianjur	109
Cibinong	264
Cilacap	142
Ciedug	293
Cimahi	197
Ciparay	135
Cirebon	225
Denpasar	210
Depok	382
Garut	146
Gorontalo	133
Gresik	102
Jakarta*	8,228
Jambi	301

Country City	Population in thousands
Jayapura	101
Jember	115
Karawang	143
Kediri	235
Klangenan	291
Klaten	120
Kudus	183
Kupang	111
Madiun	166
Magelang	123
Majalaya	177
Malang	650
Manado	321
Mataram	276
Medan	1,685
Padang	477
Pakanbaru	341
Palangkaraya	113
Palembang	1,084
Pangkalpinang	108
Parepare	109
Pasuran	134
Pekalongan	227
Pematangsiantar	203
Pontianak	397
Probolinggo	131
Purwokerto	158
Salatiga	103
Samarinda	335
Semarang	1,004
Sukabumi	120
Surabaya	2,410
Surakarta	504
Tanjungbalai	108
Tanjungkarang-Telukbetung	458
Tanjungpinang	106
Tasikmalaya	194
Tebingtinggi	117
Tegal	226
Ujung Pandang	913
Yogyakarta	412
Iran	**67,540**
Āmol	155
Ahvāz	828
Arāk	379
Ardabīl	330
Bābol	153
Bākhtarān	666
Bandar-e `Abbās	384
Bandar-e Mushehr	141
Bīrjand	115
Bojnūrd	126
Borūjerd	212
Būshehr	141
Dezfūl	202
Eşfahān	1,221
Eslāmshahr	240
Gorgān	178
Hamadān	406
Īlām	137
Karaj	588
Kāshān	166
Kermān	350
Khomeynīshahr	127
Khorramābād	277
Khvoy	153
Malāyer	150
Marāgheh	129
Mashhad	1,964
Masjed-e Soleymān	109
Najafābād	182
Neyshābūr	155
Orūmīyeh	396
Qā'emshahr	133
Qazvīn	299
Qom	780
Rasht	374
Sabzevār	161
Sanandaj	271
Sārī	186
Shīrāz	1,043
Sīrjān	120
Tabrīz	1,166
Tajrīsh	157
Tehrān*	6,750
Yazd	306
Zāhedān	420
Zanjān	281
Iraq	**22,219**
Ad Dīwānīyah	196
Al `Amārah	209
Al Başrah	406
Al Ḩillah	269
Al Karrādah	236
Al Kūt	183
An Najaf	309
An Nāşirīyah	266
Ar Ramādī	193
As Sulaymānīyah	364
Baghdad*	3,841
Ba`qūbah	115
Dīwānīyah	196
Irbīl	486
Karbalā'	297
Kirkūk	419
Mosul	664
Ireland	**3,556**
Cork	127
Dublin*	478
Israel	**5,535**
Ashdod	128
Bat Yam	142
Beersheba	153
Bene Beraq	129
Haifa	252
Holon	164
Jerusalem*	591
Netanya	148
Petah Tiqwa	153
Ramat Gan	122
Rishon LeZiyyon	165
Tel Aviv-Yafo	356
Italy	**57,534**
Ancona	103
Bari	341
Bergamo	116
Bologna	412
Bolzano	100
Brescia	197
Cagliari	212
Catania	330
Catanzaro	104
Cosenza	104
Ferrara	111
Florence	402
Foggia	155
Genoa	676
La Spezia	102
Lecce	102
Livorno	171
Messina	272
Mestre	182
Milan	1,371
Modena	176
Monza	121
Naples	1,025
Novara	103
Padova	215
Palermo	697
Parma	174
Perugia	110
Pescara	129
Piacenza	102
Prato	167
Reggio di Calabria	178
Reggio nell'Emilia	109
Rimini	115
Rome*	2,693
Salerno	153
Sassari	120
Siracusa	125
Taranto	232
Torre del Greco	101
Trieste	231
Turin	962
Verona	253
Vicenza	109

J

Country City	Population in thousands
Jamaica	**2,616**
Kingston*	104
Japan	**125,717**
Abiko	121
Ageo	195
Aizu-Wakamatsu	119
Akashi	271
Akishima	105
Akita	302
Amagasaki	499
Anjō	142
Aomori	288
Asahikawa	364
Asaka	104
Ashikaga	168
Atsugi	197
Beppu	130
Chiba	829
Chigasaki	202
Chofū	181
Daitō	126
Ebina	106
Fuchū	209
Fuji	222
Fujieda	120
Fujinomiya	117
Fujisawa	350
Fukui	253
Fukuoka	1,237
Fukushima	278
Fukuyama	366
Funabashi	533
Gifu	410
Habikino	115
Hachiōji	466
Hachinohe	241
Hadano	156
Hakodate	311
Hamakita	811
Hamamatsu	535
Higashikurume	114
Higashimurayama	134
Higashi-Ōsaka	518
Himeji	454
Hino	166
Hirakata	391
Hiratsuka	245
Hirosaki	174
Hiroshima	1,086
Hitachi	202
Hōfu	118
Ibaraki	254
Ichihara	258
Ichikawa	437
Ichinomiya	262
Ikeda	104
Imabari	123
Iruma	138
Ise	104
Isesaki	116
Ishinomaki	122
Itami	186
Iwaki	356
Iwakuni	110
Iwatsuki	106
Izumi	146
Jōetsu	130
Kadoma	142
Kagoshima	537
Kakamigahara	130
Kakogawa	240
Kamakura	174
Kanazawa	443
Kariya	120
Kashihara	116
Kashiwa	305
Kasugai	267
Kasukabe	189
Katsuta	110
Kawachi-Nagano	109
Kawagoe	305
Kawaguchi	439
Kawanishi	141
Kawasaki	1,174
Kiryū	126
Kisarazu	123
Kishiwada	189
Kitakyūshū	1,026
Kitami	107
Kōbe	1,477
Kōchi	317
Kōfu	201
Kōriyama	315
Kodaira	164
Koganei	106
Kokubunji	101
Komaki	124
Komatsu	106
Koshigaya	285
Kumagaya	152
Kumamoto	579
Kurashiki	415
Kure	217
Kurume	228
Kushiro	210
Kyōto	1,461
Machida	349
Maebashi	286
Matsubara	136
Matsudo	456
Matsue	142
Matsumoto	201
Matsusaka	119
Matsuyama	443
Mino'o	122
Misato	128
Mishima	105
Mitaka	166
Mito	235
Miyakonojō	130
Miyazaki	287
Moriguchi	157
Morioka	235
Muroran	126
Musashino	139
Nagano	347
Nagaoka	186
Nagareyama	140
Nagasaki	445
Nagoya	2,155
Naha	305
Nara	349
Narashino	151
Neyagawa	257
Niigata	486
Niihama	129
Niiza	139
Nishinomiya	427
Nobeoka	130
Noda	114
Numazu	212
Obihiro	168
Odawara	193
Ōgaki	148
Ōita	409
Okayama	594
Okazaki	307
Okinawa	106
Ōme	126
Ōmiya	404
Ōmuta	150
Ōsaka	2,624
Ota	140
Otaru	167
Ōtsu	260
Oyama	142
Saga	170
Sagamihara	532
Sakai	814
Sakata	101
Sakura	145
Sapporo	1,672
Sasebo	247
Sayama	157
Sendai	918
Seto	126
Shimizu	242
Shimonoseki	263
Shizuoka	472
Sōka	206
Suita	345
Suzuka	174
Tachikawa	153
Takamatsu	330
Takaoka	175
Takarazuka	202
Takasaki	236
Takatsuki	360
Tama	144
Tokorozawa	303
Tokushima	263
Tokuyama	111
Tōkyō*	8,164
Tomakomai	152
Tomika	109
Tondabayashi	110
Tottori	142
Toyama	321
Toyohashi	338
Toyokawa	112
Toyonaka	410
Toyota	332
Tsu	157
Tsuchiura	127
Tsukuba	143
Ube	175
Ueda	119
Uji	177
Urawa	418
Urayasu	116
Utsunomiya	427
Wakayama	397
Yachiyo	149
Yaizu	112
Yamagata	249
Yamaguchi	129
Yamato	192
Yao	278
Yatsushiro	108
Yokkaichi	274
Yokohama	3,220
Yokosuka	433
Yonago	133
Zama	112
Jordan	**4,325**
Amman*	965
Ar Ruşayfah	116
Az Zarqā'	359
Irbid	216

K

Country City	Population in thousands
Kazakhstan	**16,899**
Aqtöbe	264
Almaty	1,176
Atyraū	149
Aqmola*	287
Aqtaū	174
Atyraū	151
Ekibastuz	141
Kökshetaū	144
Oral	220
Öskemen	334
Pavlodar	349
Petropavl	248
Qaraghandy	596
Qostanay	234
Qyzylorda	164
Rudnyy	130
Semey	342
Shymkent	404
Taldyqorghan	125
Temirtaū	213
Zhambyl	317
Zhezqazghan	108
Kenya	**28,803**
Kisumu	185
Mombasa	465
Nairobi*	1,346
Nakuru	163
Kiribati	**82**
Tarawa*	2
Korea, North	**24,317**
Ch'ŏngjin	754
Haeju	131
Hamhŭng	775
Kaesŏng	346
Kimch'aek	281
Namp'o	691
P'yŏngyang*	2,639
Sariwŏn	130
Sinŭiju	500
Wŏnsan	350
Korea, South	**45,949**
Andong	117
Ansan	252
Anyang	481
Ch'angwŏn	323
Ch'ech'ŏn	102
Cheju	233
Chinhae	120
Chinju	256
Ch'ŏnan	211
Ch'ŏngju	478
Chŏnju	517
Ch'unch'ŏn	174
Ch'ungju	128
Inch'ŏn	2,203
Iri	203
Kangnŭng	153
Kimhae	106
Kohŭng	217
Kumi	206
Kunp'o	100
Kunsan	218
Kuri	109
Kwangju (Kwangju-Jikhalsi)	1,236
Kwangju (Kyŏnggi-Do)	906
Kwangmyŏng	329
Kyŏngju	142
Masan	494
Mokp'o	243
Nonsan	226
P'ohang	318
Puch'ŏn	668
Pusan	3,802
Seoul*	10,776
Sŏngnam	541
Sunch'ŏn	167
Suwŏn	665
Taegu	2,256
Taejŏn	1,183
Ŭijŏngbu	212
Ulsan	682
Wŏnju	173
Yŏsu	173
Kuwait	**2,077**
Al Jahrah	139
As Sālimīyah	116
Jalīb ash Shuyūkh	115
Kuwait*	31
Kyrgyzstan	**4,540**
Bishkek*	628
Osh	219

L

Country City	Population in thousands
Laos	**5,117**
Vientiane*	377
Latvia	**2,438**
Daugavpils	123
Liepāja	106
Riga*	865
Lebanon	**3,859**
Beirut*	1,000
Sidon	110
Tripoli	240
Lesotho	**2,008**
Maseru*	109
Liberia	**2,602**
Monrovia*	421
Libya	**5,648**
Benghāzī	446
Mişrātah	121
Tripoli*	590
Liechtenstein	**31**
Vaduz*	5
Lithuania	**3,636**
Kaunas	422
Klaipėda	204
Panevėžys	132
Šiauliai	148
Vilnius*	582
Luxembourg	**422**
Luxembourg*	75

M

Country City	Population in thousands
Macedonia	**2,114**
Gostivar	116
Skopje*	441
Madagascar	**14,062**
Amboasary	110
Ambovombe	144
Antananarivo*	676
Antsirabe	120
Betioky	140
Fandriana	135
Ifanadiana	102
Mahajanga	101
Toamasina	127
Vohipeno	106
Malawi	**9,609**
Blantyre	332
Lilongwe*	234
Malaysia	**20,376**
Alor Setar	125
George Town	219
Ipoh	383
Johor Baharu	329
Kelang	244
Kota Baharu	220
Kuala Lumpur*	1,145
Kuala Terengganu	229
Kuantan	198
Kuching	148
Petaling Jaya	255
Sandakan	126
Seremban	183
Shah Alam	102
Sibu	126
Sungai Petani	116
Taiping	183
Maldives	**280**
Male*	55
Mali	**9,945**
Bamako*	658
Malta	**379**
Valletta*	9
Marshall Islands	**61**
Majuro*	22
Mauritania	**2,411**
Nouakchott*	390
Mauritius	**1,154**
Port Louis*	144
Mexico	**97,563**
Acapulco de Juárez	515
Aguascalientes	440
Buenavista	115
Campeche	151
Cancún	168
Celaya	215
Chalco de Díaz Covarrubias	224
Chihuahua	516
Chimalhuacán	236
Ciudad Adolfo López Mateos	315
Ciudad Apodaca	113
Ciudad Juárez	790
Ciudad Madero	160
Ciudad Obregón	220
Ciudad Victoria	140
Coacalco de Berriozabal	151
Coatzacoalcos	199
Colima	107
Córdoba	137
Cuautitlán Izcalli	313
Cuautla Morelos	110
Cuernavaca	279
Culiacán Rosales	415
Durango de Victoria	348
Ecatepec de Morelos	1,218
Ensenada	169
Garza García	113
Gómez Palacio	164
Guadalajara	1,650
Guadalupe	535
Hermosillo	406
Heroica Matamoros	266
Heroica Nogales	106
Irapuato	265
Ixtapaluca	116
Jalapa Enríquez	279
La Paz	138
León	758
Los Mochis	163
Los Reyes Acaquilpan	135
Mazatlán	268
Mérida	529
Metepec	116
Mexicali	439
Mexico*	8,237
Minatitlán	145
Monclova	178
Monterrey	1,069
Morelia	428
Naucalpan de Juárez	846
Nezahualcóyotl	1,255
Nuevo Laredo	218
Oaxaca de Juárez	213
Orizaba	114
Pachuca de Soto	188
Poza Rica	164
Puebla de Zaragoza	1,007
Querétaro	387
Reynosa	266
Salamanca	123
Saltillo	421
San Luis Potosí	489
San Nicolás de los Garzas	437
Santa Catarina	163
Sánchez	124
Tampico	273
Tapachula	139
Tehuacán	139
Tepic	207
Tijuana	699
Tlalnepantla de Galeana	702
Tlaquepaque	151
Toluca de Lerdo	328
Tonalá	151
Torreón	439
Tuxtla Gutiérrez	290
Uruapan	188
Veracruz	439
Villahermosa	261
Villa Nicolás Romero	146
Zacatecas	100
Zamora de Hidalgo	110
Zapopan	668
Micronesia, Federated States of	**128**
Palikir*	6
Moldova	**4,475**
Bălți	159
Chișinău*	665
Tighina (Bendery)	130
Tiraspol	182
Monaco	**32**
Monaco*	27
Mongolia	**2,538**
Ulaanbaatar*	575
Morocco	**30,391**
Agadir	261
Beni Mallal	140
Casablanca	2,541
El Aaiún	137
El Jadida	119
Fès	508
Kénitra	293
Khouribga	152
Ksar el Kebir	107
Marrakech	521
Meknès	378
Mohammedia	169
Nador	208
Oujda	362
Rabat*	917
Safi	262
Salé	579
Témara	126
Tangier	519
Taza	121
Tétouan	278
Mozambique	**18,165**
Beira	264
Maputo*	1,007
Nampula	183
Myanmar (Burma)	**46,822**
Akyab	108
Bago (Pegu)	151
Insein	144
Mandalay	533
Mawlamyine (Moulmein)	220
Monywa	107
Pathein (Bassein)	144
Sittwe (Akyab)	108
Taunggyi	108
Yangon* (Rangoon)	2,513

N

Country City	Population in thousands
Namibia	**1,727**
Windhoek*	147
Nauru	**10**
Yaren (district)	0.4
Nepal	**22,641**
Birātnagar	129
Kāthmāndu*	421
Pāţan (Lalitpur)	116
Netherlands	**15,653**
Amersfoort	104
Amsterdam*	713
Apeldoorn	149
Arnhem	133
Breda	127
Dordrecht	112
Eindhoven	194
Enschede	147
Groningen	169
Haarlem	150
Leiden	113
Maastricht	118
Nijmegen	146
Rotterdam	590
The Hague*	445

Country City	Population in thousands
Tilburg	161
Utrecht	232
Zaandam	130
Zaanstad	131
Zoetermeer	101
New Zealand	**3,587**
Auckland	346
Christchurch	309
Dunedin	118
Hamilton	108
Manukau	254
North Shore	172
Waitakere	156
Wellington*	158
Nicaragua	**4,386**
Chinandega	118
León	160
Managua*	883
Masaya	121
Niger	**9,389**
Maradi	109
Niamey*	392
Zinder	120
Nigeria	**107,129**
Aba	271
Abeokuta	387
Abuja*	306
Ado Ekiti	325
Akure	147
Awka	101
Benin City	207
Bida	114
Calabar	158
Deba Habe	125
Ede	278
Effon Alaiye	139
Enugu	286
Gusau	143
Ibadan	1,295
Ife	269
Ijebu Ode	142
Ikare	128
Ikerre	221
Ikire	112
Ikirun	164
Ikorodu	167
Ila Orangun	239
Ilawe - Ekiti	167
Ilesha	342
Ilobu	180
Ilorin	431
Inisa	108
Iseyin	197
Iwo	335
Jos	185
Kaduna	310
Kano	700
Katsina	187
Kuma	134
Lafia	111
Lagos	1,347
Maiduguri	289
Makurdi	111
Minna	126
Mushin	302
Offa	178
Ogbomosho	660
Oka	130
Ondo	154
Onitsha	337
Oshogbo	441
Owo	166
Oyo	237
Port Harcourt	371
Sapele	126
Shagamu	106
Shaki	161
Shomolu	134
Sokoto	186
Warri	114
Zaria	345
Norway	**4,404**
Bergen	223
Oslo*	489
Stavanger	104
Trondheim	144

O

Oman	**2,265**
Muscat*	67

P

Pakistan	**132,185**
Bahāwalpur	180
Chiniot	106
Dera Ghāzi Khān	102
Faisalābād	1,104
Gujrānwāla	659
Gujrāt	155
Hyderābād	752
Islāmābād*	204
Jhang Sadar	196
Jhelum	106
Karāchi	5,076
Kasūr	156
Lahore	2,953
Lārkāna	124
Mardān	148
Mīrpur Khās	124
Multān	732
Nawābshāh	102
Okāra	127
Peshāwar	566
Quetta	286
Rahīmyār Khān	119
Rāwalpindi	795
Sāhīwāl	151
Sargodha	291
Shekhūpura	141
Siālkot	302
Sukkur	191

Country City	Population in thousands
Wāh	127
Palau	**17**
Koror*	9
Panama	**2,693**
Panamá*	456
San Miguelito	282
Papua New Guinea	**4,496**
Port Moresby*	193
Paraguay	**5,652**
Asunción*	547
Ciudad del Este	134
San Lorenzo	133
Peru	**24,950**
Arequipa	625
Ayacucho	106
Cajamarca	112
Callao	512
Chiclayo	412
Chimbote	269
Chincha Alta	110
Comas	287
Cusco	256
Huancayo	258
Huánuco	119
Ica	161
Iquitos	275
Juliaca	143
Lima*	376
Piura	278
Pucallpa	172
Santa	146
Sullana	147
Tacna	174
Trujillo	509
Philippines	**76,104**
Angeles	276
Bacolod	343
Bacoor	160
Bago	140
Baguio	170
Batangas	191
Biñan	135
Binangonan	128
Butuan	245
Cabanatuan	186
Cadiz	144
Cagayan de Oro	414
Cainta	127
Calbayog	130
Caloocan	643
Cavite	103
Cebu	688
Cotabato	113
Dagupan	117
Davao	961
General Santos	279
Gingoog	111
Iligan	210
Iloilo	302
Lapu-Lapu	141
Las Pinas	380
Legaspi	125
Lipa	160
Lucena	161
Makati	453
Malabon	280
Mandaue	213
Manila*	1,599
Marikina	310
Meycauayan	124
Muntinglupa	275
Naga	103
Navotas	187
Olongapo	209
Ormoc	142
Pagadian	114
Parañaque	209
Pasay	388
Pasig	398
Quezon City	1,677
Roxas	112
San Carlos (Negros Occ.)	106
San Carlos (Pangasinan)	123
San Fernando	158
San Juan del Monte	127
San Pablo	163
San Pedro	156
Silay	140
Tacloban	153
Taguig	267
Tarlac	208
Taytay	112
Toledo	126
Valenzuela	340
Zamboanga	464
Poland	**38,700**
Białystok	268
Bielsko-Biała	181
Bydgoszcz	380
Bytom	230
Chorzów	132
Częstochowa	257
Dąbrowa Górnicza	135
Elbląg	126
Gdańsk	462
Gdynia	251
Gliwice	212
Gorzów Wielkopolski	123
Grudziądz	102
Jastrzębie Zdroj	102
Kalisz	106
Katowice	366
Kielce	213
Koszalin	108
Kraków	746
Legnica	104
Łódź	849
Lublin	349
Olsztyn	161
Opole	127
Płock	121

Country City	Population in thousands
Poznań	587
Radom	226
Ruda Śląska	169
Rybnik	142
Rzeszów	151
Słupsk	100
Sosnowiec	259
Szczecin	411
Tarnów	121
Toruń	201
Tychy	190
Wałbrzych	142
Warsaw*	1,651
Włocławek	121
Wodzisław Śląski	111
Wrocław	641
Zabrze	203
Zielona Góra	113
Portugal	**9,868**
Lisbon*	818
Porto	330

Q

Qatar	**665**
Doha*	217

R

Romania	**21,399**
Arad	190
Bacău	205
Baia Mare	149
Botoşani	126
Brăila	234
Braşov	324
Bucharest*	2,068
Buzău	148
Cluj-Napoca	329
Constanţa	351
Craiova	304
Drobeta-Turnu Severin	115
Focşani	101
Galaţi	326
Iaşi	344
Oradea	223
Piatra Neamţ	123
Piteşti	179
Ploieşti	253
Reşiţa	106
Rîmnicu Vîlcea	114
Satu Mare	132
Sibiu	165
Suceava	114
Timisoara	334
Tîrgu Mures	164
Russia	**147,987**
Abakan	158
Achinsk	122
Al'met'yevsk	137
Angarsk	268
Anzhero-Sudzhensk	105
Arkhangel'sk	410
Armavir	161
Arzamas	111
Astrakhan'	508
Balakovo	207
Balashikha	136
Barnaul	595
Belgorod	314
Belovo	112
Berezniki	197
Biysk	233
Blagoveshchensk	212
Bratsk	260
Bryansk	456
Cheboksary	446
Chelyabinsk	1,130
Cherepovets	318
Cherkessk	118
Chita	365
Dimitrovgrad	131
Dzerzhinsk	286
Elektrostal'	152
Engel's	185
Glazov	107
Groznyy	354
Irkutsk	630
Ivanovo	474
Izhevsk	652
Kaliningrad (Kalin.)	413
Kaliningrad (Moscow)	136
Kaluga	344
Kamensk-Ural'skiy	206
Kamyshin	128
Kansk	111
Kazan'	1,086
Kemerovo	513
Khabarovsk	608
Khimki	136
Kineshma	103
Kirov	491
Kiselevsk	125
Kislovodsk	110
Kolomna	162
Kolpino	145
Komsomol'sk-na-Amure	314
Kostroma	281
Kovrov	162
Krasnodar	636
Krasnoyarsk	917
Kurgan	360
Kursk	434
Kuznetsk	102
Leninsk-Kuznetskiy	131
Lipetsk	466
Lyubertsy	164
Magadan	138
Magnitogorsk	439
Makhachkala	325
Maykop	162
Mezhdurechensk	108
Miass	170

Country City	Population in thousands
Michurinsk	106
Moscow*	8,527
Murmansk	454
Murom	125
Mytishchi	153
Naberezhnye Chelny	527
Nakhodka	164
Nal'chik	236
Neftekamsk	117
Nevinnomyssk	127
Nizhnekamsk	206
Nizhnevartovsk	245
Nizhniy Novgorod	1,425
Nizhniy Tagil	431
Noginsk	121
Noril'sk	170
Novgorod	233
Novocheboksarsk	123
Novocherkassk	187
Novokuybyshevsk	113
Novokuznetsk	597
Novomoskovsk	144
Novorossiysk	193
Novoshakhtinsk	106
Novosibirsk	1,424
Novotroitsk	108
Obninsk	106
Odintsovo	131
Oktyabr'skiy	108
Omsk	1,164
Orekhovo-Zuyevo	135
Orël	343
Orenburg	554
Orsk	275
Penza	548
Perm'	1,091
Pervoural'sk	143
Petropavlovsk-Kamchatskiy	265
Petrozavodsk	279
Podol'sk	204
Prokop'yevsk	265
Pskov	207
Pyatigorsk	128
Rostov	1,013
Rubtsovsk	171
Ryazan	524
Rybinsk	251
Saint Petersburg	4,329
Salavat	156
Samara	1,232
Saransk	321
Sarapul	110
Saratov	899
Sergiyev Posad	115
Serov	102
Serpukhov	140
Severodvinsk	249
Shakhty	227
Shchelkovo	108
Smolensk	349
Sochi	328
Solikamsk	109
Staryy Oskol'	190
Stavropol'	333
Sterlitamak	255
Surgut	261
Syktyvkar	226
Syzran'	175
Taganrog	290
Tambov	311
Tol'yatti	682
Tomsk	498
Tula	534
Tver'	449
Tyumen'	491
Ufa	1,092
Ukhta	112
Ulan-Ude	364
Ul'yanovsk	664
Usol'ye-Sibirskoye	107
Ussuriysk	161
Ust'-Ilimsk	113
Velikiye Luki	116
Vladikavkaz	308
Vladimir	335
Vladivostok	637
Volgodonsk	183
Volgograd	997
Vologda	290
Volzhskiy	282
Vorkuta	111
Voronezh	899
Votkinsk	105
Yakutsk	196
Yaroslavl'	628
Yekaterinburg	1,351
Yelets	118
Yoshkar-Ola	248
Yuzhno-Sakhalinsk	160
Zelenograd	179
Zhukovskiy	101
Zlatoust	207
Rwanda	**7,738**
Kigali*	233

S

Saint Kitts and Nevis	**42**
Basseterre*	13
Saint Lucia	**160**
Castries*	13
Saint Vincent and the Grenadines	**119**
Kingstown*	15
San Marino	**25**
San Marino*	3
Sao Tome and Principe	**148**
São Tomé*	43
Saudi Arabia	**20,088**
Ad Dammām	350
Al Hufūf	101

Country City	Population in thousands
Aţ Ţā'if	410
Jiddah	1,500
Mecca	630
Medina	400
Riyadh*	1,800
Senegal	**9,404**
Dakar*	1,641
Kaolack	193
Saint Louis	132
Thiès	216
Ziguinchor	162
Seychelles	**78**
Victoria*	24
Sierra Leone	**4,892**
Freetown*	470
Singapore	**3,462**
Singapore*	3,462
Slovakia	**5,393**
Bratislava*	442
Košice	235
Slovenia	**1,946**
Ljubljana*	287
Maribor	105
Solomon Islands	**427**
Honiara*	30
Somalia	**9,940**
Mogadishu*	600
South Africa	**42,327**
Alexandra	125
Benoni	114
Bloemfontein	127
Boksburg	120
Botshabelo	178
Cape Town*	855
Carletonville	119
Daveyton	152
Diepmeadow	241
Durban	716
East London	102
Evaton	201
Germiston	134
Johannesburg	714
Katlehong	202
Kempton Park	107
Khayelitsa	190
KwaMashu	157
Lekoa	218
Mamelodi	155
Ntuzuma	102
Pietermaritzburg	156
Port Elizabeth	303
Pretoria*	526
Roodeport	163
Sandton	101
Soshanguve	146
Soweto	597
Tembisa	209
Umlazi	299
Virginia	118
Spain	**39,244**
Albacete	141
Alcalá de Henares	166
Alcorcón	142
Algeciras	104
Alicante	275
Almería	167
Badajoz	130
Badalona	219
Baracaldo	104
Barcelona	1,631
Bilbao	372
Burgos	166
Cádiz	155
Cartagena	180
Castellón de la Plana	139
Córdoba	316
Elche	191
Fuenlabrada	158
Getafe	144
Gijón	270
Granada	271
Huelva	145
Jaén	113
Jerez de la Frontera	190
La Coruña	255
La Laguna	125
Las Palmas de Gran Canaria	372
Leganés	178
León	147
L'Hospitalet de Llobregat	266
Lleida	114
Logroño	125
Madrid*	3,041
Málaga	531
Mataró	102
Móstoles	199
Murcia	342
Orense	109
Oviedo	202
Palma	322
Pamplona	182
Sabadell	189
Salamanca	167
San Sebastián	178
Santa Coloma de Gramenet	132
Santa Cruz de Tenerife	204
Santander	195
Saragossa	607
Seville	714
Tarragona	115
Terrassa	161
Valencia	764
Valladolid	337
Vigo	289
Vitoria	214
Sri Lanka	**18,762**
Colombo*	615
Dehiwala-Mount Lavinia	196

Country City	Population in thousands
Galle	109
Jaffna	129
Kandy	104
Moratuwa	170
Sri Jayawardanapura (Kotte)	109
Sudan	**32,594**
Al Qaḑārif	189
Al Ubayyiḑ	228
Juba	115
Kassala	234
Khartoum*	925
Khartoum North	341
Nyala	112
Omdurman	229
Port Sudan	305
Wad Medanī	219
Suriname	**443**
Paramaribo*	180
Swaziland	**1,032**
Mbabane*	38
Sweden	**8,946**
Borås	102
Göteborg	433
Helsingborg	109
Jönköping	114
Linköping	122
Malmö	234
Norrköping	120
Örebro	121
Stockholm*	675
Uppsala	167
Västerås	120
Switzerland	**7,249**
Basel	174
Bern*	127
Geneva	174
Lausanne	116
Zürich	344
Syria	**16,138**
Aleppo	1,542
Al Mamishlī	113
Ar Raqqah	138
Damascus*	1,549
Dar'ā	180
Dayr az Zawr	133
Dūmā	131
Ḩamāh	273
Ḩimş	558
Idlib	113
Jaramānah	138
Latakia	303
Ţarţūs	137

T

Taiwan	**21,656**
Changhua	165
Chiai	262
Chungli	270
Chutung	105
Fengshan	291
Fengyüan	121
Hsinchu	340
Hsinchuang	299
Hsintien	226
Hualien	108
Kaohsiung	1,424
Keelung (Chilung)	368
P'ingchen	147
P'ingtung	172
Sanchung	376
Shulin	112
T'aichung	850
T'ainan	706
T'aipei*	2,639
T'aoyüan	241
Yungho	250
Tajikistan	**6,014**
Dushanbe*	602
Khujand	163
Tanzania	**29,461**
Dar es Salaam*	1,361
Dodoma*	204
Mbeya	194
Mwanza	223
Tabora	214
Tanga	188
Zanzibar	158
Thailand	**59,451**
Bangkok*	5,876
Chiang Mai	167
Chon Buri	187
Khon Kaen	206
Nakhon Ratchasima	278
Nakhon Sawan	152
Nakhon Si Thammarat	112
Nonthaburi	233
Sara Buri	107
Songkhla	243
Togo	**4,736**
Lomé*	450
Tonga	**107**
Nuku'alofa*	21
Trinidad and Tobago	**1,273**
Port-of-Spain*	51
Tunisia	**9,183**
Al Qayrawān	103
Aryānah	153
Ettadhamen Douarhicher	149
Sūsah	125
Safāqis	231
Tūnis*	674
Turkey	**63,528**
Adana	916
Adapazarı	171
Adıyaman	100
Ankara*	2,559
Antalya	378
Antioch	124
Aydın	107

Country / City	Population in thousands
Balıkesir	171
Batman	147
Bursa	835
Çorum	117
Denizli	204
Diyarbakır	381
Edirne	102
Elazığ	205
Erzurum	242
Eskişehir	413
Gaziantep	603
Gebze	159
İskenderun	155
Isparta	112
İstanbul	6,620
İzmir	1,757
İzmit	257
Kağıthane	269
Kahramanmaraş	228
Karabük	105
Kayseri	421
Kırıkkale	185
Konya	513
Kütahya	131
Malatya	282
Manisa	159
Mersin	422
Ordu	102
Osmaniye	122
Samsun	304
Sivas	222
Tarsus	188
Trabzon	144
Urfa	277
Uşak	105
Van	153
Zonguldak	117
Turkmenistan	4,225
Ashgabat*	407
Chärjew	164
Dashhowuz	114
Tuvalu	10
Funafuti*	2
U **Uganda**	20,605
Kampala*	774
Ukraine	50,685
Alchevs'k	127
Bila Tserkva	209
Berdyans'k	137
Cherkasy	308
Chernihiv	311
Chernivtsi	261
Dniprodzerzhyns'k	287
Dnipropetrovs'k	1,190
Donets'k	1,121
Horlivka	336
Ivano-Frankivs'k	230
Kam'yanets'-Podol's'kyy	106
Kerch	181
Kharkiv	1,622
Kherson	368
Khmel'nyts'kyy	250
Kirovohrad	280
Kiev*	2,643
Kostyantynivka	107
Kramators'k	203
Krasnyy Luch	114
Kremenchuk	245
Kryvyy Rih	729
Luhans'k	505
Luts'k	215
L'viv	807
Lysychans'k	127
Makiyivka	426
Mariupol'	523
Melitopol'	178
Mykolayiv	515
Nikopol'	160
Odesa	1,096
Oleksandriya	106
Pavlohrad	136

Country / City	Population in thousands
Poltava	324
Rivne	244
Sevastopol'	371
Simferopol'	357
Slov'yans'k	138
Stakhanov	113
Sumy	305
Syeverodonets'k	134
Ternopil'	225
Uzhhorod	125
Vinnytsya	384
Yenakiyeve	120
Yevpatoriya	108
Zaporizhzhya	898
Zhytomyr	299
United Arab Emirates	2,262
Abu Dhabi*	243
Al 'Ayn	102
Ash Shāriqah	125
Dubayy	266
United Kingdom	58,610
Aberdeen	219
Basildon	101
Belfast	295
Birmingham	966
Blackburn	106
Blackpool	146
Bolton	139
Bournemouth	155
Bradford	289
Brighton	125
Bristol	408
Cardiff	272
Coventry	299
Derby	224
Dudley	192
Dundee	151
Edinburgh	448
Glasgow	618
Gloucester	114
Hillingdon	231
Huddersfield	144
Ipswich	130
Kingston upon Hull	311
Kingston upon Thames	132
Leeds	424
Leicester	319
Liverpool	482
London*	6,680
Luton	172
Manchester	403
Middlesbrough	147
Newcastle upon Tyne	189
Newport	116
Northampton	180
Norwich	171
Nottingham	270
Oldham	104
Oxford	119
Peterborough	135
Plymouth	245
Poole	138
Portsmouth	175
Preston	178
Reading	213
Rotherham	121
Saint Helens	106
Sheffield	432
Slough	111
Southampton	210
Southend-on-Sea	159
Stockport	133
Stoke-on-Trent	267
Sunderland	183
Sutton Coldfield	106
Swansea	171
Swindon	145
Thanet	117
Walsall	175
Watford	113
West Bromwich	146
Wolverhampton	258
York	125

Country / City	Population in thousands
United States	267,955
Abilene	107
Akron	223
Albany	101
Albuquerque	385
Alexandria	111
Allentown	105
Amarillo	158
Amherst	112
Anaheim	266
Anchorage	226
Ann Arbor	110
Arlington (Tex.)	262
Arlington (Va.)	171
Atlanta	394
Aurora	222
Austin	466
Bakersfield	175
Baltimore	736
Baton Rouge	220
Beaumont	114
Berkeley	103
Birmingham	266
Boise	126
Boston	574
Bridgeport	142
Buffalo	328
Cedar Rapids	109
Charlotte	396
Chattanooga	152
Chesapeake	152
Chicago	2,784
Chula Vista	135
Cincinnati	364
Citrus Heights	107
Cleveland	506
Colorado Springs	281
Columbus (Ga.)	179
Columbus (Ohio)	633
Concord	111
Corpus Christi	257
Dallas	1,007
Dayton	182
Denver	468
Des Moines	193
Detroit	1,028
Durham	137
East Los Angeles	126
Elizabeth	110
El Monte	106
El Paso	515
Erie	109
Escondido	109
Eugene	113
Evansville	126
Flint	141
Fort Lauderdale	149
Fort Wayne	173
Fort Worth	448
Fremont	173
Fresno	354
Fullerton	114
Garden Grove	143
Garland	181
Gary	117
Glendale (Ariz.)	148
Glendale (Calif.)	180
Grand Rapids	189
Greensboro	184
Hampton	134
Hartford	140
Hayward	111
Hialeah	188
Hollywood	122
Honolulu	365
Houston	1,631
Huntington Beach	182
Huntsville	160
Independence	112
Indianapolis	742
Inglewood	110
Irvine	110
Irving	155
Jackson	197

Country / City	Population in thousands
Jacksonville	635
Jersey City	229
Kansas City (Kans.)	150
Kansas City (Mo.)	435
Knoxville	165
Lakewood	126
Lansing	127
Laredo	123
Las Vegas	258
Lexington	225
Lincoln	192
Little Rock	176
Livonia	101
Long Beach	429
Los Angeles	3,485
Louisville	269
Lowell	103
Lubbock	186
Macon	107
Madison	191
Memphis	610
Mesa	288
Mesquite	101
Metairie	149
Miami	359
Milwaukee	628
Minneapolis	368
Mobile	196
Modesto	165
Montgomery	187
Moreno Valley	119
Nashville	488
Newark	275
New Haven	130
New Orleans	497
Newport News	170
New York	7,323
Norfolk	261
Oakland	372
Oceanside	128
Oklahoma City	445
Omaha	336
Ontario	133
Orange	111
Orlando	165
Overland Park	112
Oxnard	142
Paradise	125
Pasadena (Calif.)	132
Pasadena (Tex.)	119
Paterson	141
Peoria	114
Philadelphia	1,586
Phoenix	983
Pittsburgh	370
Plano	129
Pomona	132
Portland	437
Portsmouth	104
Providence	161
Raleigh	208
Rancho Cucamonga (Cucamonga)	101
Reno	134
Richmond	203
Riverside	227
Rochester	232
Rockford	139
Sacramento	369
Saint Louis	397
Saint Paul	272
Saint Petersburg	239
Salem	108
Salinas	109
Salt Lake City	160
San Antonio	936
San Bernardino	164
San Diego	1,111
San Francisco	724
San Jose	782
Santa Ana	294
Santa Clarita	111
Santa Rosa	113
Savannah	138

Country / City	Population in thousands
Scottsdale	130
Seattle	516
Shreveport	199
Simi Valley	100
Sioux Falls	101
South Bend	106
Spokane	177
Springfield (Ill.)	105
Springfield (Mo.)	140
Springfield (Mass.)	157
Stamford	108
Sterling Heights	118
Stockton	211
Sunnyvale	117
Syracuse	164
Tacoma	177
Tallahassee	125
Tampa	280
Tempe	142
Thousand Oaks	104
Toledo	333
Topeka	120
Torrance	133
Tucson	405
Tulsa	367
Vallejo	109
Virginia Beach	393
Waco	104
Warren	145
Washington, D.C.*	607
Waterbury	109
Wichita	304
Winston-Salem	143
Worcester	170
Yonkers	188
Uruguay	3,262
Montevideo*	1,360
Uzbekistan	23,860
Andijon	297
Angren	133
Bukhoro	228
Chirchiq	159
Farghona	198
Jizzakh	108
Marghilon	125
Namangan	312
Nawoiy	110
Nukus	175
Olmaliq	116
Qarshi	163
Qŭqon	176
Samarqand	370
Tashkent*	2,094
Urganch	129
V **Vanuatu**	181
Port-Vila*	19
Vatican City	1
Vatican City*	1
Venezuela	22,396
Acarigua	117
Barcelona	222
Barinas	154
Barquisimeto	625
Baruta	183
Cabimas	166
Caracas*	1,822
Catia La Mar	100
Ciudad Bolívar	225
Ciudad Guayana	453
Coro	125
Cumaná	212
Guacara	101
Guarenas	134
Los Teques	141
Maracaibo	1,250
Maracay	354
Maturín	207
Mérida	171
Petare	338
Puerto Cabello	129
Puerto La Cruz	156

Country / City	Population in thousands
San Cristóbal	221
San Francisco	198
Turmero	174
Valencia	904
Vietnam	75,124
Bien Hoa	274
Cam Pha	105
Cam Ranh	118
Can Tho	208
Da Lat	103
Da Nang	370
Haiphong	450
Hanoi*	1,090
Ho Chi Minh City	2,900
Hong Gai	123
Hue	212
Long Xuyen	129
My Tho	105
Nam Dinh	166
Nha Trang	213
Phan Thiet	114
Qui Nhon	160
Rach Gia	138
Thai Nguyen	125
Vinh	111
Vung Tau	124
W **Western Samoa**	220
Apia*	32
Y **Yemen**	13,972
Al Ḥudaydah	155
Al Mukallā	154
Aden	562
Sanaa*	972
Ta'izz	178
Yugoslavia	10,655
Belgrade*	1,555
Kragujevac	147
Niš	176
Novi Sad	179
Podgorica	118
Priština	125
Subotica	100
Uroševac	114
Z **Zambia**	9,350
Chingola	168
Kabwe	167
Kitwe	247
Lusaka*	982
Ndola	376
Zimbabwe	11,423
Bulawayo	622
Chitungwiza	275
Gweru	125
Harare*	1,189
Mutare	132

Areas of Special Sovereignty

Country / City	Population in thousands
Hong Kong (China)	6,413
Kowloon	775
New Kowloon	1,527
Sha Tin	550
Tai Po	260
Tsuen Wan	700
Tuen Mun	432
Victoria*	1,251
Yuen Long	143
Macau (Port.)	502
Macau*	343
Puerto Rico (U.S.)	3,818
Bayamón	202
Carolina	162
Ponce	159
San Juan*	427

Foreign Geographic Terms

Foreign Term	Language	Geographic Term
A Adrar	Berber	Mountains
Aiguille	French	Peak
Ákra	Greek	Cape
Altos	Spanish	Mountains
Älv, Älven	Swedish	River
Anse	French	Cove
Archipiélago	Spanish	Archipelago
Arcipelago	Italian	Archipelago
Arquipélago	Portuguese	Archipelago
Arrecife	Spanish	Reef
Arroyo	Spanish	Stream
'Ayn	Arabic	Spring
B Baai	Dutch	Bay
Bab	Arabic	Strait
Bach	German	Stream
Bælt	Danish	Strait
Bahía	Spanish	Bay
Baḥr	Arabic	River, Sea
Baia	Portuguese	Bay
Baie	French	Bay
Ballon	French	Dome
Bana	Japanese	Cape
Bañados	Spanish	Marsh
Bandar	Persian	Harbor
Barrage	French	Dam, Reservoir
Bassin	French	Basin
Bāḡtlāq	Persian	Marsh
Be'er	Hebrew	Well
Belt	German	Strait
Ben, Beinn	Gaelic	Mountain
Berg	Afrikaans, German	Mountain
Bi'r	Arabic	Well
Birkat	Arabic	Lake
Boca	Spanish	River Mouth
Bogd	Mongolian	Range
Bolsón	Spanish	Depression
Botn	Norwegian	Bay
Brazo	Spanish	River Branch
Bucht	German	Bay
Bugt	Danish	Bay
Buhayrat	Arabic	Lake, Lagoon
Bukit	Malay	Mountain
Bukt, Bukten	Swedish	Bay
Bulu	Indonesian	Mountain
Burj	Arabic	Hill
Burnu, Burun	Turkish	Cape
Busen	German	Bay
C Cabo	Portuguese, Spanish	Cape
Cañada	Spanish	Stream
Canal	Portuguese, Spanish	Channel
Canale	Italian	Canal
Cap	French	Cape
Capo	Italian	Cape
Cataratas	Spanish	Waterfalls
Catena	Spanish	Range
Causse	French	Upland
Cayos	Spanish	Cays
Cerro(s)	Spanish	Hill(s)
Chaîne	French	Range
Chapada	Portuguese	Hills
Chott	Arabic	Intermittent Lakes, Marshes
Chroüy	Cambodian	Cape
Chute(s)	French	Waterfall(s)
Ciénaga	Spanish	Marsh
Cima	Italian, Spanish	Peak
Cime	French	Peak
Città	Italian	City
Ciudad	Spanish	City
Co	Tibetan	Lake
Col	French	Pass
Colina(s)	Spanish	Hill(s)
Colle	Italian	Pass
Colline	Italian	Hills
Collines	French	Hills
Cordillera	Spanish	Range
Corno	Italian	Peak
Costa	Portuguese, Spanish	Coast
Côte	French	Coast, Ridge
Coteau	French	Hills
Csatorna	Magyar	Canal
Cuchilla	Spanish	Hills
Cumbre	Spanish	Peak
D Dağ, Daği	Turkish	Mountain
Dake	Japanese	Mountain
Dal, Dalen	Swedish	Valley
Damāgheh	Persian	Cape
Daryācheh	Persian	Lake
Dasht	Persian	Desert
Desierto	Spanish	Desert
Détroit	French	Strait
Dhar	Arabic	Escarpment
Diep	Dutch	Channel
Dijk	Dutch	Dike
Ding	Chinese	Hill
Djebel	Arabic	Mountain(s)
Doi	Thai	Mountain
Dyb	Danish	Strait
E Eiland	Dutch	Island
Elv	Norwegian	River
Embalse	Spanish	Reservoir
Emi	Berber	Mountain
Enseada	Portuguese	Cove
Ensenada	Spanish	Cove
Erg	Arabic	Desert
Estrecho	Spanish	Strait
Étang	French	Lagoon
F Falaise	French	Cliff
Feld	German	Plain
Feng	Chinese	Mountain
Firth	Gaelic	Estuary
Fjärden	Swedish	Bay, Sound
Fjord, Fjorden	Norwegian	Inlet
Fjördhur	Icelandic	Bay
Fljót	Icelandic	River
Flói	Icelandic	Bay
Foci	Italian	River Mouths
G Gat	Danish, Dutch	Marine Channel
Gebirge	German	Range
Geçidi	Turkish	Pass
Gobi	Mongolian	Desert
Göl	Turkish	Lake
Golfe	French	Gulf
Golfo	Italian, Spanish	Gulf
Gora	Russian	Mountain
Got	Korean	Cape
Graben	German	Ditch
Guan	Chinese	Pass
Guelb	Arabic	Mountain
Gunung	Indonesian	Mountain
H Hai	Chinese	Sea
Hamada	Arabic	Desert
Ḥammādat	Arabic	Plateau
Ḥāmūn	Persian	Intermittent Salt Lake
Har	Hebrew	Mountain
Havet	Norwegian	Bay
Ḥawḍ	Arabic	Oasis
Hāyk'	Amharic (Ethiopia)	Lake
Hegy	Magyar	Mountain
Heide	Arabic	Heath
Hoek	Dutch	Point
Höhe	German	Height
Holm	Danish, Swedish	Island
Horn	German	Point
Hornatina	Czech, Slovak	Plateau
Hory	Czech, Slovak	Range
Hügel	German	Hill
I Île(s)	French	Island(s)
Ilha(s)	Portuguese	Island(s)
Insel(n)	German	Island(s)
Irmak	Turkish	River
Isla(s)	Spanish	Island(s)
Isola, Isole	Italian	Island, Islands
J Jabal	Arabic	Mountains
Järvi	Finnish	Lake
Jazīrat, Jazā'ir	Arabic	Island, Islands
Jbel	Arabic	Mountain(s)
Jezero	Czech, Slovak	Lake
Jezioro	Polish	Lake
Jiao	Chinese	Cape
Jibāl	Arabic	Mountain(s)
Joki	Finnish	River
Jökull	Icelandic	Glacier
Jolgeh	Persian	Plain
K Kaap	Dutch	Cape
Kabīr	Persian	Mountains
Kanaal	Dutch	Canal
Kanal	German, Serbo-Croatian	Canal
Kangri	Tibetan	Peak
Kap	German	Cape
Kapp	Norwegian	Cape
Kavīr	Persian	Desert
Kawlat	Arabic	Mountain
Kawm	Arabic	Hill
Kep	Albanian	Cape
Khalīj	Arabic	Gulf
Khao	Thai	Mountain
Khatt	Arabic	Intermittent River
Khawr	Arabic	Intermittent River
Khazzān	Arabic	Dam
Khuan	Thai	Lake
Kloof	Dutch	Gap
Kogel	German	Mountain
Kop	Dutch	Peak
Kopf	German	Peak
Kreb	Arabic	Dune
Küh	Persian	Mountain
L La	Tibetan	Pass
Lac(s)	French	Lake(s)
Laem	Thai	Cape
Laga, Lagh	Swahili	Intermittent River
Lago(s)	Italian, Portuguese, Spanish	Lake(s)
Lagoa	Portuguese	Lake
Laguna	Spanish	Lagoon
Les	Czech	Mountains
Ling	Chinese	Mountain
Llano(s)	Spanish	Plain(s)
Loch, Lough	Gaelic	Inlet, Lake
M Mägi	Estonian	Mountain
Mare	Italian	Sea
Marsá	Arabic	Bay
Maṣabb	Arabic	River Mouth
Maṣrif	Arabic	Canal
Massif	French	Upland
Meer	Afrikaans, Dutch, German	Lake, Sea
Meseta	Spanish	Plateau
Mifraz	Hebrew	Bay
Misaki	Japanese	Cape
Mont(s)	French	Mountain(s)
Montagna	Italian	Mountain
Montagne(s)	French	Mountain(s)
Montaña(s)	Spanish	Mountain(s)
Monte	Italian, Portuguese, Spanish	Mountain
Montes	Portuguese, Spanish	Mountains
Monti	Italian	Mountains
Morne	French	Mountain
Morro	Portuguèse, Spanish	Mountain
Mui	Vietnamese	Cape
Mys	Russian	Cape
N Nafūd	Arabic	Desert
Naḥal	Hebrew	River
Nahr	Arabic	River
Namakzār	Persian	Salt Flat
Neem	Estonian	Cape
Nek	Dutch	Pass
Nevado	Spanish	Snow-covered Peak
Nina	Estonian	Cape
Nos	Russian	Cape
Nosy	Malagasy	Island
O Ø, Øy	Norwegian	Island
Odde	Danish	Point
Óros	Greek	Mountain
Otok	Serbo-Croatian	Island
Ouadi, Oued	Arabic	Intermittent River
Ozero	Russian	Lake
P Pampa	Spanish	Plain
Pantanal	Portuguese, Spanish	Swamp
Pas	Dutch	Pass
Pas	French	Strait
Paso	Spanish	Pass
Passage	French	Marine Channel
Peña, Peñasco	Spanish	Peak
Pereval	Russian	Pass
Phnum	Cambodian	Mountain
Phou	Lao	Mountain
Pi	Chinese	Cape
Pic	French	Peak
Picacho	Spanish	Peak
Picco	Italian	Peak
Pico(s)	Portuguese, Spanish	Peak(s)
Pik	Russian	Peak
Pique	French	Peak
Piton	French	Mountain
Piz, Pizzo	Italian	Peak
Planalto	Portuguese	Plateau
Planina	Serbo-Croatian	Plain
Plato	Afrikaans	Plateau
Playa	Spanish	Beach
Plōsina	Czech	Plateau
Pointe	French	Point
Ponta	Portuguese	Point
Presa	Spanish	Dam, Reservoir
Presqu'île	French	Peninsula
Prokhod	Bulgarian	Pass
Promontorio	Italian	Promontory
Puncak	Indonesian	Mountain
Punt	Dutch	Point
Punta	Italian, Spanish	Point
Q Qanāt	Arabic	Canal
Qiryat	Hebrew	City
Qolleh	Persian	Mountain
R Rada	Spanish	Anchorage
Rade	French	Anchorage
Rann	Hindi	Marsh
Rapides	French	Rapids
Ras, Ra's	Arabic	Cape
Recifes	Portuguese	Reefs
Represa	Portuguese	Dam, Reservoir
Retto	Japanese	Islands
Rio	Portuguese	River
Río	Spanish	River
Rivier	Dutch	River
Rivière	French	River
Rosh	Hebrew	Cape
Rt	Serbo-Croatian	Cape
S Sabana	Spanish	Savanna
Sabkhat	Arabic	Lagoon, Salt Marsh
Sāgar	Hindi	Lake
Saguia	Arabic	Intermittent River
Ṣaḥrā'	Arabic	Desert
Saki	Japanese	Cape
Salar	Spanish	Salt Flat
Salina(s)	Spanish	Salt Flat(s)
Salto(s)	Portuguese, Spanish	Waterfall(s)
San	Japanese	Mountain
Sarīr	Arabic	Desert
Sebjet	Arabic	Dry Lake
Sebkha	Arabic	Salt Flat
See	German	Lake
Selkä	Finnish	Bay
Serra	Portuguese	Range
Serranía(s)	Spanish	Ridge(s)
Seto	Japanese	Strait
Sgurr	Gaelic	Mountain
Shan	Chinese	Mountain
Shankou	Chinese	Pass
Shaṭṭ	Arabic	Intermittent Lake
Shet'	Amharic (Ethiopia)	River
Shima	Japanese	Island
Shotō	Japanese	Islands
Sierra	Spanish	Range
Sistema	Spanish	Range
Sjö, Sjön	Swedish	Lake
Slieve	Gaelic	Mountain
Sø	Danish	Lake
Sommet	French	Peak
Sopka	Russian	Volcano
Spitze	German	Peak
Stausee	German	Reservoir
Stretto	Italian	Strait
Sund	Danish, Swedish	Sound
T Tal	German	Valley
Tall	Arabic	Mountain
Tanjona	Malagasy	Cape
Tanjong	Malay	Cape
Tanjung	Indonesian	Cape
Tassili	Berber	Plateau
Ténéré	Berber	Desert
Tepe	Turkish	Peak
Terara	Amharic (Ethiopia)	Mountain
Tō	Japanese	Island
Tó	Magyar	Lake
Tōge	Japanese	Pass
Tunturi	Finnish	Mountain
U Udde	Swedish	Point
Udolní	Czech	Reservoir
Uul	Mongolian	Mountain
Úval	Czech	Valley
V Val	French, Italian	Valley
Valle	Italian, Spanish	Valley
Vallée	French	Valley
Vallen	Dutch	Waterfall
Valli	Italian	Lagoon
Vatn	Norwegian	Lake
Veld	Dutch	Plain
Vig	Danish	Bay
Vik, Viken	Swedish	Bay
Vîrful	Romanian	Mountain
Vliet	Dutch	Channel
Vodoskhovyshche	Ukrainian	Reservoir
Volcán	Spanish	Volcano
Vrch	Serbo-Croatian	Mountain
Vrchy	Czech, Slovak	Range
Vysočina	Czech, Slovak	Plateau
W Wabē	Amharic (Ethiopia)	River
Wādī	Arabic	Intermittent River
Wāḩāt	Arabic	Oasis
Wald	German	Forest, Mountains
Webi	Somali	River
Wenz	Amharic (Ethiopia)	River
Y Yam	Hebrew	Lake, Sea
Yama	Japanese	Mountain
Z Zaki	Japanese	Point
Zatoka	Ukrainian	Gulf
Zee	Dutch	Lake, Sea
Zemlya	Russian	Land

Index of the World

This index is a comprehensive listing of the places and geographic features found in the atlas. Names are arranged in strict alphabetical order, without regard to hyphens or spaces. Every name is followed by the country or area to which it belongs. Except for cities, towns, countries and cultural areas, all entries include a reference to feature type, such as province, river, island, peak, and so on. The page number and alpha-numeric code appear in red to the right of each listing. The page number directs you to the largest scale map on which the name can be found. The code refers to the grid squares formed by the horizontal and vertical lines of latitude and longitude on each map. Following the letters from left to right and the numbers from top to bottom helps you to locate quickly the square containing the place or feature. Inset maps have their own alpha-numeric codes. Names that are accompanied by a point symbol are indexed to the symbol's location on the map. Other names are indexed to the initial letter of the name. When a map name contains a subordinate or alternate name, both names are listed in the index. To conserve space and provide room for more entries, many abbreviations are used in this index. The primary abbreviations are listed below.

Index Abbreviations

Abbr.	Meaning	Abbr.	Meaning
A Ab,Can	Alberta	Canl.	Canary Islands
Abor.	Aboriginal	Cap.	Capital
Acad.	Academy	Cap. Dist.	Capital District
ACT	Australian Capital Territory	Cap. Terr.	Capital Territory
A.F.B.	Air Force Base	Cay.	Cayman Islands
Afld.	Airfield	C.d'Iv.	Côte d'Ivoire
Afg.	Afghanistan	C.G.	Coast Guard
Afr.	Africa	Chan.	Channel
Ak,US	Alaska	Chl.	Channel Islands
Al,US	Alabama	Co.	County
Alb.	Albania	Co,US	Colorado
Alg.	Algeria	Col.	Colombia
Amm. Dep.	Ammunition Depot	Com.	Comoros
And.	Andorra	Cont.	Continent
Ang.	Angola	CpV.	Cape Verde Islands
Angu.	Anguilla	CR	Costa Rica
Ant.	Antarctica	Cr.	Creek
Anti.	Antigua and Barbuda	Cro.	Croatia
Ar,US	Arkansas	CSea.	Coral Sea Islands Territory
Arch.	Archipelago	Ct,US	Connecticut
Arg.	Argentina	Ctr.	Center
Arm.	Armenia	Ctry.	Country
Arpt.	Airport	Cyp.	Cyprus
Aru.	Aruba	Czh.	Czech Republic
ASam.	American Samoa	**D** DC,US	District of Columbia
Ash.	Ashmore and Cartier Islands	De,US	Delaware
Aus.	Austria	Den.	Denmark
Austl.	Australia	Depr.	Depression
Aut.	Autonomous	Dept.	Department
Az,US	Arizona	Des.	Desert
Azer.	Azerbaijan	DF	Distrito Federal
Azor.	Azores	Dist.	District
		Djib.	Djibouti
B Bahm.	Bahamas, The	Dom.	Dominica
Bahr.	Bahrain	Dpcy.	Dependency
Bang.	Bangladesh	D.R.Congo	Democratic Republic of the Congo
Bar.	Barbados	DRep.	Dominican Republic
BC,Can	British Columbia		
Bela.	Belarus	**E** Ecu.	Ecuador
Belg.	Belgium	Emb.	Embankment
Belz.	Belize	Eng.	Engineering
Ben.	Benin	Eng,UK	England
Berm.	Bermuda	EqG.	Equatorial Guinea
Bfld.	Battlefield	Erit.	Eritrea
Bhu.	Bhutan	ESal.	El Salvador
Bol.	Bolivia	Est.	Estonia
Bor.	Borough	Eth.	Ethiopia
Bosn.	Bosnia and Herzegovina	Eur.	Europe
Bots.	Botswana		
Braz.	Brazil	**F** Falk.	Falkland Islands
BrIn.	British Indian Ocean Territory	Far.	Faroe Islands
Bru.	Brunei	Fed. Dist.	Federal District
Bul.	Bulgaria	Fin.	Finland
Burk.	Burkina Faso	Fl,US	Florida
Buru.	Burundi	For.	Forest
BVI	British Virgin Islands	Fr.	France
		FrAnt.	French Southern and Antarctic Lands
C Ca,US	California	FrG.	French Guiana
CAfr.	Central African Republic	FrPol.	French Polynesia
Camb.	Cambodia	FYROM	Former Yugoslav Republic of Macedonia
Camr.	Cameroon		
Can.	Canada	**G** Ga,US	Georgia
Can.	Canal	Galp.	Galapagos Islands

Abbr.	Meaning	Abbr.	Meaning
G Gam.	Gambia, The	Mald.	Maldives
Gaza	Gaza Strip	Malw.	Malawi
GBis.	Guinea-Bissau	Mart.	Martinique
Geo.	Georgia	May.	Mayotte
Ger.	Germany	Mb,Can	Manitoba
Gha.	Ghana	Md,US	Maryland
Gib.	Gibraltar	Me,US	Maine
Glac.	Glacier	Mem.	Memorial
Gov.	Governorate	Mex.	Mexico
Govt.	Government	Mi,US	Michigan
Gre.	Greece	Micr.	Micronesia, Fed. States of
Grld.	Greenland	Mil.	Military
Gren.	Grenada	Mn,US	Minnesota
Grsld.	Grassland	Mo,US	Missouri
Guad.	Guadeloupe	Mol.	Moldova
Guat.	Guatemala	Mon.	Monument
Gui.	Guinea	Mona.	Monaco
Guy.	Guyana	Mong.	Mongolia
		Monts.	Montserrat
H Har.	Harbor	Mor.	Morocco
Hi,US	Hawaii	Moz.	Mozambique
Hist.	Historic(al)	Mrsh.	Marshall Islands
Hon.	Honduras	Mrta.	Mauritania
Hts.	Heights	Mrts.	Mauritius
Hun.	Hungary	Ms,US	Mississippi
		Mt.	Mount
I Ia,US	Iowa	Mt,US	Montana
Ice.	Iceland	Mtn., Mts.	Mountain, Mountains
Id,US	Idaho	Mun. Arpt.	Municipal Airport
Il,US	Illinois		
IM	Isle of Man	**N** NAm.	North America
In,US	Indiana	Namb.	Namibia
Ind. Res.	Indian Reservation	NAnt.	Netherlands Antilles
Indo.	Indonesia	Nat'l	National
Int'l	International	Nav.	Naval
Ire.	Ireland	NB,Can	New Brunswick
Isl., Isls.	Island, Islands	Nbrhd.	Neighborhood
Isr.	Israel	NC,US	North Carolina
Isth.	Isthmus	NCal.	New Caledonia
It.	Italy	ND,US	North Dakota
		Ne,US	Nebraska
J Jam.	Jamaica	Neth.	Netherlands
Jor.	Jordan	Nf,Can	Newfoundland
		Nga.	Nigeria
K Kaz.	Kazakhstan	NH,US	New Hampshire
Kiri.	Kiribati	NI,UK	Northern Ireland
Ks,US	Kansas	Nic.	Nicaragua
Kuw.	Kuwait	NJ,US	New Jersey
Ky,US	Kentucky	NKor.	North Korea
Kyr.	Kyrgyzstan	NM,US	New Mexico
		NMar.	Northern Mariana Isl.
L La,US	Louisiana	Nor.	Norway
Lab.	Laboratory	NP	National Park
Lag.	Lagoon	NS,Can	Nova Scotia
Lakesh.	Lakeshore	Nv,US	Nevada
Lat.	Latvia	Nun,Can	Nunavut
Lcht.	Liechtenstein	NW,Can	Northwest Territories
Ldg.	Landing	NWR	National Wildlife Refuge
Leb.	Lebanon	NY,US	New York
Les.	Lesotho	NZ	New Zealand
Libr.	Liberia		
Lith.	Lithuania	**O** Obl.	Oblast
Lux.	Luxembourg	Oh,US	Ohio
		Ok,US	Oklahoma
M Ma,US	Massachusetts	On,Can	Ontario
Madg.	Madagascar	Or,US	Oregon
Madr.	Madeira		
Malay.	Malaysia	**P** Pa,US	Pennsylvania

Abbr.	Meaning	Abbr.	Meaning
P PacUS	Pacific Islands, U.S.	StL.	Saint Lucia
Pak.	Pakistan	StP.	Saint Pierre and Miquelon
Pan.	Panama	StV.	Saint Vincent and the Grenadines
Par.	Paraguay	Sur.	Suriname
Par.	Parish	Sval.	Svalbard
PE,Can	Prince Edward Island	Swaz.	Swaziland
Pen.	Peninsula	Swe.	Sweden
Phil.	Philippines	Swi.	Switzerland
Phys. Reg.	Physical Region		
Pitc.	Pitcairn Islands	**T** Tah.	Tahiti
Plat.	Plateau	Tai.	Taiwan
PN	National Park	Taj.	Tajikistan
PNG	Papua New Guinea	Tanz.	Tanzania
Pol.	Poland	Ter.	Terrace
Port.	Portugal	Terr.	Territory
Poss.	Possession	Thai.	Thailand
Pkwy.	Parkway	Tn,US	Tennessee
PR	Puerto Rico	Tok.	Tokelau
Pref.	Prefecture	Trg.	Training
Prov.	Province	Trin.	Trinidad and Tobago
Prsv.	Preserve	Trkm.	Turkmenistan
Pt.	Point	Trks.	Turks and Caicos Islands
		Tun.	Tunisia
Q Qu,Can	Quebec	Tun.	Tunnel
		Turk.	Turkey
R Rec.	Recreation(al)	Tuv.	Tuvalu
Ref.	Refuge	Twp.	Township
Reg.	Region	Tx,US	Texas
Rep.	Republic		
Res.	Reservoir, Reservation	**U** UAE	United Arab Emirates
Reun.	Réunion	Ugan.	Uganda
RI,US	Rhode Island	UK	United Kingdom
Riv.	River	Ukr.	Ukraine
Rom.	Romania	Uru.	Uruguay
Rsv.	Reserve	US	United States
Rus.	Russia	USVI	U.S. Virgin Islands
Rvwy.	Riverway	Ut,US	Utah
Rwa.	Rwanda	Uzb.	Uzbekistan
S SAfr.	South Africa	**V** Va,US	Virginia
Sam.	Samoa	Val.	Valley
SAm.	South America	Van.	Vanuatu
SaoT.	São Tomé and Príncipe	VatC.	Vatican City
SAr.	Saudi Arabia	Ven.	Venezuela
Sc,UK	Scotland	Viet.	Vietnam
SC,US	South Carolina	Vill.	Village
SD,US	South Dakota	Vol.	Volcano
Seash.	Seashore	Vt,US	Vermont
Sen.	Senegal		
Sey.	Seychelles	**W** Wa,US	Washington
SGeo.	South Georgia and Sandwich Islands	Wal,UK	Wales
Sing.	Singapore	Wall.	Wallis and Futuna
Sk,Can	Saskatchewan	WBnk.	West Bank
SKor.	South Korea	Wi,US	Wisconsin
SLeo.	Sierra Leone	Wild.	Wildlife, Wilderness
Slov.	Slovenia	WSah.	Western Sahara
Slvk.	Slovakia	WV,US	West Virginia
SMar.	San Marino	Wy,US	Wyoming
Sol.	Solomon Islands		
Som.	Somalia	**Y** Yem.	Yemen
Sp.	Spain	Yk,Can	Yukon Territory
Spr., Sprs.	Spring, Springs	Yugo.	Yugoslavia
SrL.	Sri Lanka		
Sta.	Station	**Z** Zam.	Zambia
StH.	Saint Helena	Zim.	Zimbabwe
Str.	Strait		
StK.	Saint Kitts and Nevis		

228
Akör – Alstead

Akören, Turk. 128/C2
Akosombo (dam), Gha. 141/F5
Akot, Sudan 142/F4
Akot, India 121/C1
Akoupé, C.d'Iv. 140/E5
Akpatok (isl.), Qu, Can. 167/K2
Akpınar, Turk. 129/M6
Akqi, China 125/C3
Akrab, Kaz. 97/K2
Akranes, Ice. 64/M7
Ákrathos (cape), Gre. 75/J2
Åkrehamn, Nor. 66/A2
Akrítas (cape), Gre. 75/G4
Akron, Al, US 188/D4
Akron, Co, US 180/C3
Akron, In, US 186/C4
Akron, Ia, US 181/F2
Akron, Mi, US 186/E3
Akron, NY, US 186/W9
Akron, Oh, US 186/F4
Akron, Pa, US 194/B3
Akrotiri, Cyp. 130/C2
Aksai Chin (reg.), India 125/C4
Aksakovo, Rus. 95/M5
Aksaray, Turk. 128/C2
Aksaray (prov.), Turk. 128/C2
Aksay, Rus. 99/K4
Aksay Kazakzu Zizhixian, China 104/C4
Akşehir, Turk. 128/B2
Akşehir (lake), Turk. 128/B2
Akseki, Turk. 128/B2
Aksoran (peak), Kaz. 125/C2
Aksu, Turk. 130/B1
Aksu (riv.), Turk. 130/B1
Aksu, China 125/D3
Aksu (riv.), Kaz. 125/C2
Aksubayevo, Rus. 95/L5
Āksum, Eth. 144/A2
Aktash, Uzb. 100/G6
Aktau, Kaz. 100/H4
Aktepe, Turk. 130/E1
Aktí (pen.), Gre. 96/C4
Aktogay, Kaz. 125/C2
Aktumsyk, Kaz. 97/L3
Aku, Nga. 141/G5
Akula, D.R. Congo 146/E2
Akune, Japan 110/B4
Akure, Nga. 141/G5
Akureyri, Ice. 64/N6
Akuse, Gha. 141/F5
Akwa Ibom (state), Nga. 141/G5
Akwa Ibom (state), Nga. 146/A1
Akwanga, Nga. 141/H4
Akxokesay, China 104/C4
Akyab (Sittwe), Myan. 119/F3
Akyar, Rus. 97/L2
Akyazı, Turk. 77/K5
Akzhal, Kaz. 125/D2
Ål, Nor. 66/C1
Al 'Abbāsah ash Sharqīyah, Egypt 139/C3
Al 'Abbāsīyah, Sudan 142/F2
Āl 'Ābis, SAr. 126/D5
Al 'Adam, Libya 93/J5
Al Aḩmadī, Kuw. 129/G4
Al 'Ajamīyīn, Egypt 139/B6
Al Akhḑar, SAr. 135/H2
Al 'Āl, Jor. 131/D5
Al 'Alamayan (El Alamein), Egypt 135/F2
Al 'Alāqimah, Egypt 139/C3
Al 'Amārah, Iraq 129/F4
Al Anbār (gov.), Iraq 128/E3
Al 'Aqabah, Jor. 135/G2
Al 'Arīsh, Egypt 130/C4
Al Arţāwīyah, SAr. 126/E3
Al 'Assāfīyah, SAr. 135/H2
Al 'Awdah, SAr. 126/E3
Al 'Awsajīyah, SAr. 126/D3
Al 'Ayn, SAr. 135/H3
Al 'Ayn, UAE 127/G4
Al 'Ayyāţ, Egypt 139/C5
Al 'Azīzīyah, Iraq 129/F3
Al Azīzīyah, Libya 93/G4
Al Bāb, Syria 128/D2
Al Badrashayn, Egypt 139/C5
Al Baḩr Al Aḩmar (gov.), Egypt 135/G3
Al Bajalāt, Egypt 139/C2
Al Bājūr, Egypt 139/C4
Al Bakātūsh, Egypt 139/B2
Al Balāmūn, Egypt 139/C3
Al Ballāḩ, Egypt 139/D3
Al Balqā' (gov.), Jor. 130/D4
Al Balyanā, Egypt 135/G3
Al Bāqūrah, Jor. 131/D3
Al Barāmūn, Egypt 139/C2
Al Barrah, SAr. 126/E4
Al Baslaqūn, Egypt 139/B2
Al Başrah, Iraq 129/F4
Al Başrah (gov.), Iraq 129/F4
Al Batānūn, Egypt 139/C3
Al Batrūn, Leb. 130/D2
Al Bawīţi, Egypt 135/F2
Al Baydā, Libya 93/J4
Al Bayḑā, Yem. 144/C2
Al Biqā' (valley), Leb. 130/D3
Al Biqā (gov.), Leb. 131/D1
Al Bi'r, SAr. 135/H2
Al Bīrah, WBnk. 131/C5
Al Birk, SAr. 126/D5
Al Birkah, Libya 137/H4
Al Buḩayrah (gov.), Egypt 128/B4
Al Buraymī, Oman 127/G4
Al Burj, Egypt 139/B1
Al Burumbul, Egypt 139/C6
Al Buzūn, Yem. 144/D2
Al Fallūjah, Iraq 129/E3
Al Fanānahl, Tun. 138/L6
Al Farḑah, Yem. 144/D2
Al Fāsher, Sudan 142/E2
Al Fatḩah, Iraq 129/E3
Al Fāw, Iraq 129/G4
Al Fawwār, Tun. 137/H2
Al Fayyūm (gov.), Egypt 128/B3
Al Fayyum, Egypt 139/B6
Al Fāzah, Yem. 144/B2
Al Fifi, Sudan 142/E3
Al Firdān, Egypt 139/D3
Al Fuhūd, Iraq 129/F4
Al Fujayrah, UAE 127/G3
Al Fūlah, Sudan 142/F3
Al Fuqahā', Libya 134/C3
Al Gharaq as Sulţānī, Egypt 139/B6
Al Ghāriyah, Syria 131/F4
Al Ghāţ, SAr. 126/E3
Al Ghayatah, Egypt 139/B3
Al Ghayḑah, Yem. 126/F5
Al Ghayl, SAr. 126/E4
Al Ghurdaqah, Egypt 135/G3
Al Ḩaddādī, Egypt 139/B2
Al Ḩaddār, SAr. 126/E4
Al Ḩadīthah, SAr. 128/D4
Al Ḩadīthah, Iraq 128/E3
Al Ḩaḑr, Iraq 129/E3
Al Ḩaffah, Syria 130/E2
Al Ḩajar ash Sahrqī (mts.), Oman 127/G4
Al Hajarayn, Yem. 144/D2
Al Ḩājir, Egypt 139/C3
Al Ḩamādah al Ḩamrā (upland), Libya 134/A2
Al Ḩamar, SAr. 126/E4
Al Hamdab, Sudan 126/B5
Al Ḩammah, Tun. 92/F4
Al Hammām, Egypt 135/F2
Al Ḩammāmāt, Tun. 74/B4
Al Ḩamrā', SAr. 135/H4
Al Ḩāmūl, Egypt 139/C2
Al Hanākīyah, SAr. 126/D4
Al Ḩanīyah, Libya 93/J4
Al Hārithah, Iraq 129/F4
Al Ḩārrah, Syria 131/D2
Al Harūj al Aswad (hill), Libya 134/C3
Al Ḩasakah, Syria 128/E2
Al Ḩasakah (prov.), Syria 128/E2
Al Ḩawāmidīyah, Egypt 139/C5
Al Ḩawātah, Sudan 142/G2
Al Ḩawrah, Yem. 144/C2
Al Ḩawţah, SAr. 126/E3
Al Ḩawţah, Yem. 144/D2
Al Ḩayy, Iraq 129/F3
Al Ḩayy, Egypt 139/C5
Al Ḩayyānīyah, SAr. 128/E4
Al Ḩillah, Iraq 129/F3
Al Ḩillah, SAr. 126/E4
Al Ḩillah, Sudan 142/E2
Al Hindīyah, Iraq 129/F3
Al Hirmil, Leb. 130/E2
Al Ḩişn, Jor. 131/D4
Al Hoceima, Mor. 138/C2
Al Hoceima (prov.), Mor. 138/B2
Al Hoceima (Côte du Rif) (int'l arpt.), Mor. 138/C2
Al Ḩudaydah, Yem. 144/B2
Al Hufūf, SAr. 126/E3
Al Ḩulwah, SAr. 126/E4
Al Ḩumayshah, Yem. 144/C2
Al Ḩurayḑah, Yem. 144/D2
Al Ḩuşayḩişah, Sudan 142/G2
Al Ḩusaynīyah, Egypt 139/C3
Al Ḩuwaymī, Yem. 144/C2
Al Ḩuwayyiţ, SAr. 126/D3
Al Huwwārīyah, Tun. 74/B4
Al Ibēdiyya, Sudan 126/B5
Al Ibrāhīmīyah, Egypt 139/C3
Al 'Irqah, Yem. 144/C2
Al Iskandarīyah, Iraq 129/F3
Al Iskandarīyah (gov.), Egypt 128/B3
Al Iskandarīyah, Egypt 139/A2
Al Ismā'īlīyah (gov.), Egypt 130/C4
Al Ismā'īlīyah, Egypt 139/D3
Al Istiwā'īyah (pol. reg.), Sudan 142/F4
Al Jabal Akaur (mts.), Oman 127/G4
Al Jabal al Akhḑar (mts.), Libya 134/D2
Al Jabalayn, Sudan 142/G2
Al Jaghbūb, Libya 134/E2
Al Jamālīyah, Egypt 139/C2
Al Jamīl, Libya 93/G4
Al Jamm, Tun. 74/B5
Al Janad (int'l arpt.), Yem. 144/C2
Al Janūb (gov.), Leb. 131/C2
Al Jawārah, Oman 127/G5
Al Jawf, SAr. 128/D4
Al Jawf, Libya 134/D3
Al Jibāb, Syria 131/E2
Al Jifārah (plain), Libya 137/H2
Al Jifārah, SAr. 126/E4
Al Jifārah (plain), Tun. 92/F4
Al Jīzah, Egypt 139/C4
Al Jīzah, Jor. 131/D5
Al Jubayl, SAr. 129/G5
Al Judaydah, Leb. 131/D1
Al Judayyidah, Jor. 131/D5
Al Junaynah, Sudan 142/D2
Al Junaynah, SAr. 126/D4
Al Kāb, Egypt 139/D3
Al Kāf (gov.), Tun. 138/L6
Al Kāf, Tun. 138/L6
Al Kafr ash Sharqī, Egypt 139/C2
Al Kahfah, SAr. 129/E5
Al Kāmil, Oman 127/G4
Al Karak (gov.), Jor. 130/D4
Al Karak, Jor. 135/G2
Al Karāmah, Jor. 131/D5
Al Karīb, Tun. 138/L6
Al Karnak, Egypt 135/G3
Al Kawd, Yem. 144/C2
Al Kawm al Akhḑar, Egypt 139/B3
Al Kawm aţ Ţawīl, Egypt 139/C2
Al Khabrā', SAr. 126/D3
Al Khābūrah, Oman 127/G4
Al Khalīl (Hebron), WBnk. 131/C5
Al Khāliş, Iraq 129/F3
Al Khandaq, Sudan 135/F5
Al Khānkah, Egypt 139/C4
Al Khārijah, Egypt 135/F3
Al Kharrārah, Qatar 126/F4
Al Kharţūm (pol. reg.), Sudan 142/G2
Al Kharţūm Baḩrī (Khartoum North), Sudan 142/G2
Al Khaţāţibah, Egypt 139/B4
Al Khiḑr, Iraq 129/F4
Al Khiyām, Leb. 131/D2
Al Khubar, SAr. 126/F3
Al Khums, Libya 93/G4
Al Khuraybah, Yem. 144/D2
Al Khurmah, SAr. 126/D4
Al Khurtum (Khartoum) (cap.), Sudan 142/G2
Al Kiswah, Syria 131/E2
Al Kittah, Jor. 131/D4
Al Kūfah, Iraq 129/F3
Al Kufrah, Libya 134/D3
Al Kūt, Iraq 129/F3
Al Lādhiqīyah (Latakia), Syria 130/D2
Al Lādhiqīyah (prov.), Syria 128/C3
Al Lagowa, Sudan 142/F3
Al Lāhūn, Egypt 139/B6
Al Lidām, SAr. 126/D4
Al Lisht (ruin), Egypt 139/C5
Al Līth, SAr. 126/D4
Al Luḩayyah, Yem. 144/B2
Al Ma'ādī, Egypt 139/C5
Al Madīnah, SAr. 126/C4
Al Madīyah (prov.), Tun. 74/B5
Al Madīyah (gov.)., Alg. 138/M7
Al Madwar, Jor. 131/D4
Al Mafraq, Jor. 131/E4
Al Maghārīm, Yem. 144/C2
Al Maghrib (reg.), Alg. 136/E2
Al Maghrib (reg.), Alg.,Mor. 92/C4
Al Maḩallah al Kubrá, Egypt 139/C3
Al Mahdīyah, Tun. 74/B5
Al Maḩmūdīyah, Iraq 129/F3
Al Maḩmūdīyah, Egypt 139/B2
Al Majdal, Jor. 131/D4
Al Majma'ah, SAr. 126/E3
Al Maks, Egypt 139/A2
Al Malamm, Sudan 142/F3
Al Mālikīyah, Syria 128/E2
Al Ma'mūrah, Egypt 139/B2
Al Manāmah (Manama) (cap.), Bahr. 126/F3
Al Manaqīl, Sudan 142/G2
Al Mansūrah, Egypt 139/C2
Al Manşūrīyah, Egypt 139/C4
Al Manzilah, Egypt 139/C2
Al Maqrūn, Libya 134/D2
Al Marāghah, Egypt 135/F3
Al Marj, Libya 93/J4
Al Marsá, Tun. 74/B4
Al Ma'şarah, Egypt 139/C5
Al Masīd, Sudan 142/G2
Al Matammah, Sudan 142/G1
Al Maţarīyah, Egypt 139/D2
Al Matnah, Sudan 142/G2
Al Mawşil (Mosul), Iraq 129/E2
Al Mayādin, Syria 128/E3
Al Maymūn, Egypt 139/C6
Al Mazra'ah, Jor. 130/D4
Al Midhnab, SAr. 126/D3
Al Mīnā', Leb. 130/D2
Al Mindak, SAr. 126/D4
Al Minshāt el Kubrá, Egypt 139/B2
Al Minyā, Egypt 135/F2
Al Minyā, Egypt 139/C5
Al Minyā, Egypt 139/B6
Al Miqdādiyah, Iraq 129/F3
Al Mubarraz, SAr. 126/E4
Al Mudawwarah, Jor. 135/G2
Al Muglad, Sudan 142/E3
Al Mukallā, Yem. 144/D2
Al Muknīn, Tun. 74/B5
Al Munastīr, Tun. 74/B5
Al Munastīr (gov.), Alg. 138/M7
Al Murnāqīyah, Tun. 74/B4
Al Musallamīyah, Sudan 142/G2
Al Musayjīd, SAr. 135/H3
Al Musayyib, Iraq 129/F3
Al Muthanná (gov.), Iraq 129/F4
Al Muwaqqar, Jor. 131/E5
Al Muwassam, SAr. 144/B1
Al Muwayh, SAr. 126/D4
Al Muwayliḩ, SAr. 135/G3
Al Qābil, Oman 127/G4
Al Qaḑārif, Sudan 142/G2
Al Qaḑīmah, SAr. 126/C4
Al Qādisīyah (gov.), Iraq 129/F4
Al Qāhirah (Cairo) (cap.), Egypt 139/C4
Al Qāhirah (gov.), Egypt 128/B3
Al Qaḩmah, SAr. 126/D5
Al Qā'im, Iraq 128/E3
Al Qāmishlī, Syria 128/E2
Al Qanāţir al Khayrīyah, Egypt 139/C4
Al Qanāyāt, Egypt 139/C3
Al Qantarah, Egypt 139/D3
Al Qanţarah al Gharbīyah, Egypt 139/D3
Al Qaryah al Sharqīyah, Libya 134/B2
Al Qaryāt, Libya 134/B2
Al Qaryatayn, Syria 128/D3
Al Qarẓabah, Libya 93/J4
Al Qaşabāt, Libya 93/G4
Al Qaşr, Egypt 135/F3
Al Qaşr, Jor. 131/D6
Al Qaşrayn (gov.), Tun. 138/L7
Al Qaşrayn, Tun. 138/L7
Al Qaţaynah, Sudan 142/G2
Al Qaţīf, SAr. 126/F3
Al Qaţrūn, Libya 134/B3
Al Qayrawān, Tun. 74/B5
Al Qayrawān (gov.), Tun. 74/A5
Al Qayşūmah, SAr. 129/F4
Al Qibābāt, Egypt 139/C6
Al Qubbah, Libya 93/J4
Al Qunayţirah (prov.), Syria 131/D2
Al Qunayţirah, Jor. 131/E5
Al Qunayţirah, Syria 131/D2
Al Qunfudhah, SAr. 126/D5
Al Qurayn, Egypt 139/C3
Al Qurnah, Iraq 129/F4
Al Quşayr, Syria 130/E2
Al Quşayr, Egypt 135/G3
Al Quşūr, Tun. 138/L7
Al Quţayfah, Syria 131/F1
Al Quway'id (well), Libya 134/D2
Al Quway'īyah, SAr. 126/E4
Al Quwayrah, Jor. 130/D5
Al 'Ubaylah, SAr. 126/F4
Al Ubayyiḑ, Sudan 142/F2
Al Uḑayyah, Sudan 142/F2
Al 'Ulá, SAr. 135/H3
Al 'Umdah, Sudan 142/F3
Al Uqaylah, Libya 134/C2
Al Uqşur, Egypt 135/G3
Al 'Uwaynāt (peak), Sudan 134/E4
Al 'Uwaynāt, Libya 137/H4
Al 'Uyūn, SAr. 126/D3
Al 'Uzayr, Iraq 129/F4
Al Wādī al Jadīd (wadi), Egypt 128/B5
Al Wafā'īyah, Egypt 139/B3
Al Wāḩāt al Baḩrīyah (oasis), Egypt 135/F2
Al Wāḩāt al Baḩrtyah (reg.), Egypt 128/B4
Al Wāḩāt al Khārijah (oasis), Egypt 135/F3
Al Wajh, SAr. 135/H3
Al Wakrah, Qatar 126/F3
Al Wāsiţah, Egypt 139/C6
Al Wazz, Sudan 142/F2
Al Widy, Egypt 139/C5
Al Wusta (pol. reg.), Malw. 142/G2
Al Yādūdah, Jor. 131/D5
Al Yāmūn, WBnk. 131/C4
Ala (pt.), It. 74/B1
Ala, It. 89/E2
Ala (riv.), China 104/B3
Alabama (state), US 169/J5
Alabama (riv.), Al,Ga, US 169/J5
Alabama and Coushatta Ind. Res., Tx, US 177/G2
Alabaster, Al, US 188/D4
Alabat, Phil. 114/C2
Alaca, Turk. 128/C1
Alacalı, Turk. 77/J5
Alaçam, Turk. 96/E4
Alaçatı, Turk. 75/K3
Alachua, Fl, US 191/G3
Alacrán (reef), Mex. 200/D1
Alacranes (res.), Cuba 201/F1
Aladağ, Turk. 130/C1
Alaejos, Sp. 72/C2
Alafia (riv.), Fl, US 190/L8
Alagir, Rus. 97/H4
Alagna Valsesia, It. 88/A1
Alagnon (riv.), Fr. 70/E4
Alagoa Grande, Braz. 207/H4
Alagoas (state), Braz. 207/G5
Alagoinhas, Braz. 211/F2
Alagón, Sp. 73/E2
Alagón (riv.), Sp. 72/C2
Alah (riv.), Phil. 114/D4
Alahanpanjang, Indo. 115/C3
Alajärvi, Fin. 94/D3
Alajärvi (lake), Fin. 65/E4
Alajõe, Est. 67/M2
Alajuela, CR 201/E4
Alakol (lake), Kaz. 100/J5
Alakuko, Nga. 141/G5
Alalapadu, Sur. 206/B2
Alalaú (riv.), Braz. 205/F5
Alamaån (riv.), Swe. 65/K6
Alamagan (isl.), NMar. 162/D3
'Alāmarvdasht (riv.), Iran 129/H5
Ālamat'ā, Eth. 144/A2
Alameda, Sk, Can. 182/C3
Alameda (co.), Ca, US 193/L11
Alameda, Ca, US 193/K11
Alameda, NM, US 175/J3
Alameda (cr.), Ca, US 193/L11
Ālamgīr, Pak. 124/A4
Alamikamba, Nic. 201/E3
Alamito (cr.), Tx, US 177/B3
Alamo, Ca, US 193/K11
Alamo, Mex. 200/B1
Alamo, Ga, US 189/F4
Alamo, Nv, US 174/E2
Alamo, Tn, US 188/C3
Alamo (lake), Az, US 175/F3
Alamo (mtn.), NM, US 177/B1
Alamo Band Ind. Res., NM, US 175/J3
Alamo Village, Tx, US 177/D3
Alamor, Ecu. 208/A2
Álamos, Mex. 198/C3
Alamosa, Co, US 178/B2
Alamosa (cr.), NM, US 178/B3
Alamosa Nat'l Wild.Ref., Co, US 175/K2
Åland (isl.), Fin. 64/G3
Aland (riv.), Ger. 68/F2
Alang, Indo. 114/B4
Alanreed, Tx, US 178/D3
Alanson, Mi, US 186/D2
Alantika, Monts (mts.), Camr.,Nga. 142/B3
Alanya, Turk. 130/C1
Alaotra (lake), Madg. 152/J7
Alapaha, Ga, US 191/G2
Alapaha (riv.), Ga, US 191/G2
Alapayevsk, Rus. 95/P4
Alaplı, Turk. 77/K5
Alarcón (res.), Sp. 72/D3
Alarka, NC, US 189/F3
Alas, Indo. 117/E5
Alaşehir, Turk. 128/B2
Alaserjärvi (lake), Fin. 65/F3
Alashtar, Iran 129/G3
Alaska (pen.), Ak, US 168/W13
Alaska (range), Ak, US 168/X12
Alaska (gulf), Ak, US 168/Y13
Alaska (state), US 168/W12
Alassio, It. 88/B6
Ālāt, Azer. 129/G2
Alataw (pass), China 125/D2
Alatri, It. 92/C4
Alatyr', Rus. 95/K5
Alaverdi, Arm. 97/H4
Alavus, Fin. 94/D3
Alaw (riv.), Wal, UK 60/D5
Alawa Ngandi Abor. Land, Austl. 154/D3
'Ālayh, Leb. 131/D1
Alayor, Sp. 72/C3
Alayskiy (mts.), Kyr. 125/B4
Alazeya (riv.), Rus. 101/R3
Alb (riv.), Ger. 84/B5
Alba, Tx, US 179/G4
Alba (prov.), Rom. 77/F2
Alba Adriatica, It. 92/C2
Alba de Tormes, Sp. 72/C2
Alba Fucens (ruin), It. 92/C3
Alba Iulia, Rom. 77/F2
Albacete, Sp. 72/E3
Albaida, Sp. 73/E3
Albairate, It. 88/B3
Ålbæk, Den. 66/D3
Albalate del Arzobispo, Sp. 73/E2
Alban, On, Can. 186/F1
Alban, Fr. 70/E5
Albán, Col. 207/L8
Albania, Col. 207/M7
Albania(ctry.) 55/F4
Albanian Alps, North (mts.), Yugo. 75/F1
Albano (lake), It. 91/B4
Albano Laziale, It. 91/B4
Albany, Austl. 156/C5
Albany (riv.), Can. 165/J4
Albany (riv.), On, Can. 167/H3
Albany (riv.), On, Can. 166/H3
Albany, NZ 161/F6
Albany, Ca, US 193/K11
Albany, Ga, US 191/F2
Albany, In, US 186/D4
Albany, Ky, US 188/E2
Albany, Mn, US 183/G5
Albany, Mo, US 181/G3
Albany (cap.), NY, US 187/K3
Albany, Ok, US 179/F4
Albany, Or, US 172/B1
Albany, Tx, US 177/E1
Albaredo D'Adige, It. 89/E3
Albarine (riv.), Fr. 86/B5
Albarracín, Sp. 72/E2
Albatross (pt.), NZ 161/C2
Albatross (bay), Austl. 153/D2
Albatross Rock (pt.), Namb. 150/A2
Albbruck, Ger. 86/E2
Albemarle (pt.), Ecu. 208/J6
Albemarle, NC, US 189/G3
Albemarle (sound), NC, US 189/J3
Albenga, It. 88/B5
Alberche (riv.), Sp. 72/C2
Alberdi, Par. 212/E3
Alberga, Austl. 157/G3
Alberga (cr.), Austl. 153/C3
Alberhill, Ca, US 192/C3
Alberndorf in der Riedmark, Aus. 85/H6
Alberschwende, Aus. 87/F3
Albersdorf, Ger. 66/C4
Albersweiler, Ger. 84/B4
Albert, Ks, US 178/E1
Albert, Fr. 80/B3
Albert, Austl. 158/C2
Albert (lake), Austl. 158/A2
Albert (lake), Ugan., D.R.Cong 133/E4
Albert Canyon, BC, Can. 170/F2
Albert Edward (mt.), PNG 155/G2
Albert Kanaal (riv.), Belg. 81/E2
Albert Lea, Mn, US 181/H2
Albert Nile (riv.), Ugan. 142/F5
Alberta (prov.), Can. 166/E3
Alberta, Al, US 188/D4
Alberta Beach, Ab, Can. 170/G1
Alberti, Arg. 214/E2
Albertinia, SAfr. 150/C4
Albertirsa, Hun. 76/D2
Alberto de Agostini, PN, Chile 215/B7
Alberton, PE, Can. 184/E2
Alberton, SAfr. 150/Q13
Alberton, Mt, US 170/G4
Albertshofen, Ger. 84/D3
Albertville, Fr. 90/C1
Albertville, Al, US 188/D3
Albertville, Mn, US 183/N6
Albertville, Sk, Can. 171/M1
Albestroff, Fr. 81/F6
Albeuve, Swi. 86/D4
Albi, Fr. 70/E5
Albia, Ia, US 181/H3
Albignasego, It. 89/E3
Albin, Wy, US 180/B3
Albina (pt.), Ang. 148/A2
Albina, Sur. 206/C1
Albinea, It. 88/D4
Albino, It. 88/C2
Albion, Id, US 173/G2
Albion, Il, US 188/C1
Albion, In, US 186/D4
Albion, Mi, US 186/D3
Albion, Ne, US 180/E3
Albion, NY, US 187/G3
Albion, Pa, US 186/F4
Albisola Marina, It. 88/B5
Albisola Superiore, It. 88/B5
Alblasserdam, Neth. 78/B5
Albocácer, Sp. 73/E2
Albon, Fr. 90/A2
Alborán (isl.), Mor. 136/E2
Alborán (isl.), Sp. 92/C4
Ålborg, Den. 66/C3
Ålborg (bay), Den. 66/D3
Albox, Sp. 72/D4
Albright Knox Art Gallery, NY, US 186/V10
Albrighton, Eng, UK 62/D1
Albristhorn (peak), Swi. 86/D5
Albufeira, Port. 72/A4
Albula (riv.), Swi. 71/H3
Albuñol, Sp. 72/D4
Albuquerque (int'l arpt.), NM, US 175/J3
Albuquerque, NM, US 175/J3
Alburquerque, Sp. 72/B3
Alburtis, Pa, US 194/C3
Albury, NZ 161/B4
Albury, Austl. 159/C3
Alby-sur-Chéran, Fr. 86/C6
Alca, Peru 208/C4
Alcabideche, Port. 73/P10
Alcácer do Sal, Port. 72/A3
Alcalá, Col. 207/K8
Alcalá de Chivert, Sp. 73/F2
Alcalá de Guadaira, Sp. 72/C4
Alcalá de Henares, Sp. 73/N9
Alcalá de los Gazules, Sp. 72/C4
Alcalá la Real, Sp. 72/D4
Alcalde (pt.), Chile 212/B4
Alcamo, It. 74/C4
Alcanadre (riv.), Sp. 73/E2
Alcanar, Sp. 73/E2
Alcañices, Sp. 72/B2
Alcañiz, Sp. 73/E2
Alcántara, Sp. 72/B3
Alcántara (res.), Sp. 72/B3
Alcântara, Braz. 207/E3
Alcântaras, Braz. 207/F3
Alcantarilla, Sp. 72/E4
Alcaraz, Sp. 72/D3
Alcaraz (range), Sp. 72/D3
Alcaraz, Sierra de (mts.), Sp. 92/C3
Alcatraz (isl.), Ca, US 193/K11
Alcatrazes (isl.), Braz. 211/L9
Alcaudete, Sp. 72/C4
Alcázar de San Juan, Sp. 72/D3
Alcester, SD, US 181/F2
Alcester, Eng, UK 63/E2
Alchevs'k, Ukr. 99/K3
Alcira, Sp. 73/E3
Alcira, Arg. 214/D2
Alçıtepe, Turk. 75/K2
Alco, Ar, US 179/H3
Alcoa, Tn, US 188/F3
Alcobaça, Port. 72/A3
Alcobaça, Braz. 211/F3
Alcobendas, Sp. 73/N8
Alcoche, Bol. 209/E4
Alcochete, Port. 73/Q10
Alcolu, SC, US 189/G4
Alcora, Sp. 73/E2
Alcorcón, Sp. 73/N9
Alcorisa, Sp. 73/E2
Alcoutim, Port. 72/B4
Alcova, Wy, US 173/K2
Alcoy, Sp. 73/E3
Alcúdia, Sp. 73/G3
Aldabra (isls.), Sey. 133/G5
Aldama, Mex. 177/B3
Aldama, Mex. 199/F4
Aldan (plat.), Rus. 101/N4
Aldan (riv.), Rus. 103/N3
Aldan, Rus. 101/N4
Aldar, Mong. 125/G2
Aldbourne, Eng, UK 63/E4
Aldbrough, Eng, UK 61/H4
Alde (riv.), Eng, UK 63/H2
Aldeburgh, Eng, UK 63/H2
Aldeia Formoza, Ang. 146/C5
Aldeia Nova de São Bento, Port. 72/B4
Aldeia Viçosa, Ang. 146/C5
Alden, Il, US 193/N15
Alden, NY, US 186/W10
Aldenhoven, Ger. 81/F2
Aldeno, It. 87/H6
Alder (lake), Wa, US 170/C4
Alder Flats, Ab, Can. 170/G1
Aldergrove, NI, UK 60/B2
Aldergrove (int'l arpt.), NI, UK 60/B2
Alderley Edge, Eng, UK 61/F5
Aldermaston, Eng, UK 63/E4
Alderney (isl.), Chl, UK 70/B2
Alderney (The Blaye) (arpt.), Chl, UK 82/C1
Alderpoint, Ca, US 172/B3
Aldershot, Eng, UK 63/F4
Aldershot, On, Can. 186/T9
Alderson, WV, US 189/G2
Aldersyde, Ab, Can. 171/H2
Alderwood Manor-Bothell North, Wa, US 193/C2
Aldine, Tx, US 177/M9
Aldingen, Ger. 87/E1
Aldred (lake), Pa, US 194/B4
Aldridge, Eng, UK 63/E1
Ale Water (riv.), Sc, UK 59/D6
Aledo, Il, US 181/J3
Aledo, Tx, US 176/K7
Aleg, Mrta. 140/B2
Alegre, Braz. 211/E4
Alegrete, Braz. 213/F4
Alejandría, Bol. 209/E4
Alejandro Gallinal, Uru. 215/G2
Alejandro Roca, Arg. 214/E2
Alejandro Selkirk (isl.), Chile 203/A6
Alejo Ledesma, Arg. 214/E2
Aleksandro-Nevskiy, Rus. 96/G1
Aleksandrov, Rus. 94/H4
Aleksandrov Gay, Rus. 97/J2
Aleksandrovac, Yugo. 76/E4
Aleksandrovka, Rus. 99/K4
Aleksandrovsk, Rus. 95/N4
Aleksandrovsk-Sakhalinskiy, Rus. 105/N1
Aleksandrovskoye, Rus. 97/G3
Aleksandrów Kujawski, Pol. 69/K2
Aleksandrów Łódzki, Pol. 69/K3
Alekseyevka, Rus. 97/J1
Alekseyevka, Rus. 99/K2
Alekseyevka, Kaz. 125/B1
Alekseyevskoye, Rus. 95/L5
Aleksin, Rus. 94/H5
Aleksinac, Yugo. 76/E4
Alem Maya, Eth. 144/B3
Além Paraíba, Braz. 211/P6
Alembé, Gabon 146/B3
Alemdar, Turk. 129/N6
Alençon, Fr. 83/F4
Alenquer, Braz. 206/C3
Alento (riv.), It. 92/D3
Alenuihaha (chan.), Hi, US 168/S9
Alépé, C.d'Iv. 140/E5
Aleppo (Ḩalab), Syria 128/D2
Alerce Andino, PN, Chile 214/B4
Aléria, Fr. 74/A1
Alert (pt.), Nun, Can. 167/S6
Alert, Nun, Can. 167/T6
Aleşd, Rom. 76/F2
Alessandria (prov.), It. 88/B3
Alessandria, It. 88/B4
Ålestrup, Den. 66/C3
Ålesund, Nor. 64/C3
Aletschhorn (peak), Swi. 86/D5
Aleutian (isls.), Ak, US 165/A4
Aleutian (range), Ak, US 168/X13
Alex, Ok, US 179/F3
Alexander, ND, US 182/C4
Alexander (isl.), Ant. 216/V
Alexander (arch.), Ak, US 165/D4
Alexander (mt.), Austl. 156/B2
Alexander (pt.), Austl. 155/E3
Alexander, Tx, US 177/E1
Alexander Archipelago (isls.), Ak, US 168/Y13
Alexander Bay, SAfr. 150/B3
Alexander City, Al, US 188/E4
Alexander Graham Bell Nat'l Hist. Park, NS, Can. 185/G2
Alexander Hamilton (int'l arpt.), USVI 197/M8
Alexander Nevsky Abbey, Rus. 94/T7
Alexandra, NZ 161/B4
Alexandra, Austl. 159/B3
Alexándria, Gre. 75/H2
Alexandria, Austl. 155/E4
Alexandria, Braz. 207/G4
Alexandria (int'l arpt.), Egypt 139/A2
Alexandria, Rom. 77/G4
Alexandria, SAfr. 150/D4
Alexandria, BC, Can. 170/C1
Alexandria, In, US 186/D4
Alexandria, Ky, US 188/E1
Alexandria, La, US 190/B2
Alexandria, Mn, US 183/G5
Alexandria, Ne, US 181/F3
Alexandria, Sc, UK 59/B5
Alexandria, SD, US 180/F2
Alexandria, Va, US 194/A6
Alexandria Bay, NY, US 187/J2
Alexandrina (lake), Austl. 153/C4
Alexandroúpolis, Gre. 75/J2
Alexeck (riv.), Namb. 148/C4
Alexis, Il, US 181/J3
Alexis Creek, BC, Can. 170/C1
Alexishafen, PNG 155/G1
Aley (riv.), Rus. 125/D1
Aleysk, Rus. 125/D1
Alfama (nbrhd.), Port. 73/P10
Alfarim, Port. 73/P11
Alfaro, Sp. 72/E1
Alfatar, Bul. 77/H4
Alfbach (riv.), Ger. 81/F3
Alfeld, Ger. 79/G5
Alfenas, Braz. 211/L6
Alfhausen, Ger. 79/E3
Alfiós (riv.), Gre. 75/G4
Alfonsine, It. 89/F4
Alfonso Bonilla Aragón (int'l arpt.), Col. 204/B4
Alford, Eng, UK 61/J5
Alford, Sc, UK 59/D2
Alford, Fl, US 191/F2
Alfred, NY, US 187/H3
Alfred, Me, US 187/L3
Alfred (mt.), BC, Can. 170/B2
Alfred NP, Austl. 159/D3
Alfreton, Eng, UK 61/G5
Alfriston, Eng, UK 63/G5
Alfter, Ger. 81/G2
Alga, Kaz. 97/L2
Algabas, Kaz. 97/K2
Ålgård, Nor. 66/A2
Algarrobito, Chile 212/B4
Algarrobo, Chile 214/N8
Algarve (reg.), Port. 72/A4
Algeciras, Col. 204/C4
Algeciras, Sp. 72/C4
Algemesí, Sp. 73/E3
Alger, Mi, US 186/D2
Alger (wilaya), Alg. 138/G4
Algeria(ctry.) 133/B2
Algermissen, Ger. 79/G4
Algete, Sp. 73/N8
Alghero, It. 74/A2
Algiers (El Djezair) (cap.), Alg. 138/G4
Algoa, Tx, US 177/M9
Algoa (bay), SAfr. 150/D4
Algodonales, Sp. 72/C4
Algoma, Wi, US 186/C2
Algoma, Or, US 172/C2
Algoma, Ms, US 188/C3
Algona, Wa, US 193/C3
Algona, Ia, US 181/G2
Algonac, Mi, US 193/G6
Algonquin (peak), NY, US 187/K2
Algonquin, Il, US 193/P14
Algood, Tn, US 188/E2
Algorta, Uru. 215/K10
Algueirão, Port. 73/P10
Algund (Lagundo), It. 87/H4
Alhama de Granada, Sp. 72/D4
Alhama de Murcia, Sp. 72/E4
Alhambra, Ca, US 192/F7
Alhambra, Il, US 181/K4
Alhandra, Port. 73/P10
Alhandra, Braz. 207/H4
Alhaurín el Grande, Sp. 72/C4
'Alī al Gharbī, Iraq 129/F3
'Alī ash Sharqī, Iraq 129/F3
Āli Bayramlı, Azer. 129/G2
'Ali SabîehL, Djib. 144/B3
Alia, It. 74/C4
Alía, Sp. 72/C3
'Alīābād, Iran 129/H4
Aliade, Nga. 141/H5
Aliağa, Turk. 96/C5
Aliákmon (riv.), Gre. 75/G2
Aliákmonos (lake), Gre. 75/G2
Alíartos, Gre. 75/H3
Alibey (lake), Ukr. 98/F5
Alibey (riv.), Turk. 129/M6
Alibeyköy, Turk. 77/J5
Ālībo, Eth. 142/H3
Alicante (int'l arpt.), Sp. 73/E3
Alicante, Sp. 73/E3
Alice (pt.), It. 75/E3
Alice (riv.), Austl. 155/F3
Alice, SAfr. 150/D4
Alice, Tx, US 177/E4
Alice Springs, Austl. 157/G2
Aliceville, Al, US 188/C4
Aliceville (dam), Al, US 188/C4
Aliceville (lake), Al, US 188/C4
Alicia, Ar, US 188/B3
Alicia, Phil. 114/C4
Alicudi (isl.), It. 74/D3
Alicurá (res.), Arg. 214/C4
Alife, It. 92/D5
Alīganj, India 122/B2
Alīgarh, India 122/B2
Alijilán, Arg. 212/C4
Alijó, Port. 72/B2
Alīkadam, Bang. 119/F3
Alima (riv.), Congo 146/C3
Alindao, CAfr. 142/D4
Alingār (riv.), Afg. 124/A2
Alingsås, Swe. 66/E3
Alīpur, Pak. 124/A5
Alīpur Duār, India 123/G2
Alirājpur, India 127/K4
Aliskerovo, Rus. 101/S3
Alistráti, Gre. 75/H2
Alivérion, Gre. 75/J3
Aliwal North, SAfr. 150/D3
Alix, Ab, Can. 171/H1
Alixan, Fr. 90/B3
Aljezur, Port. 72/A4
Aljustrel, Port. 72/A4
Alkali Lake, BC, Can. 170/C2
Alken, Belg. 81/E2
Alkhan-Kala, Rus. 97/H4
Alkmaar, Neth. 78/B3
Alkoum (well), Alg. 137/H4
Alkoven, Aus. 85/H6
Alku (wadi), Sudan 142/E2
All American (canal), Ca, US 174/E4
Allada, Ben. 141/F5
Allagash (riv.), Me, US 184/C2
Allahābād, India 122/C3
Allaire, Fr. 82/C5
Allakh-Yun', Rus. 101/P3
Allaman, Swi. 86/C5
Allan, Sk, Can. 171/L2
Allan (hills), Sk, Can. 171/L2
Alland, Aus. 77/N7
Allanmyo, Myan. 112/B5
Allanridge, SAfr. 150/D2
Allanson, Austl. 156/C5
'Allāq (well), Libya 134/A2
`Allāqt (wadi), Egypt 126/B4
Allariz, Sp. 72/B1
Allatoona (lake), Ga, US 188/E3
Allauch, Fr. 90/B6
Alldays, SAfr. 149/F4
Alle, Swi. 86/D3
Allegan, Mi, US 186/D3
Allegany, NY, US 187/G3
Allegheny (plat.), Pa, US 187/G4
Allegheny (riv.), Pa, US 187/G4
Allegheny (mts.), US 169/K4
Allegheny Portage Railroad Nat'l Hist. Site, Pa, US 187/G4
Allemands (lake), La, US 190/C3
Allen, Ok, US 179/F3
Allen (mt.), NZ 161/A4
Allen, Arg. 214/D3
Allen, Ne, US 181/F2
Allen, Tx, US 176/L6
Allen (riv.), Eng, UK 62/B5
Allen Park, Mi, US 193/F7
Allenby Bridge, Jor.,WBnk. 131/D5
Allendale, Eng, UK 61/F2
Allendale, Mi, US 186/D3
Allendale, NJ, US 195/J7
Allendale, SC, US 189/G4
Allende, Mex. 177/D3
Allende, Mex. 199/E3
Allendorf, Ger. 79/F6
Allensbach, Ger. 87/F2
Allentown, Pa, US 194/C2
Allentown-Bethlehem-Easton (arpt.), Pa, US 194/C2
Allentsteig, Aus. 69/H4
Allenwood, Pa, US 194/B1
Aller (riv.), Ger. 79/H3
Allerkanal (canal), Ger. 79/H4
Allerød, Den. 65/J7
Allersberg, Ger. 84/E4
Allershausen, Ger. 85/E6
Allevard, Fr. 90/C2
Allex, Fr. 90/A3
Allgäu Alps (range), Aus.,Ger. 68/F5
Allhallows, Eng, UK 56/F2
Alliance, Oh, US 186/F4
Alliance, Ne, US 180/C2
Alliance, Ab, Can. 171/J1
Allied War Cemetery, Myan. 120/B2
Allier (riv.), Fr. 92/D1
Allier, Montagne de l' (peak), Fr. 90/C4
Alligator (lake), Fl, US 191/H3
Alligator (pt.), Austl. 155/F4
Alligator (riv.), NC, US 189/J3
Allingåbro, Den. 66/D3
Allinge, Den. 66/F4
Allinges, Fr. 86/C5
Allingham, Austl. 155/E4
Allison, Ia, US 181/H2
Alliston, On, Can. 187/G2
Alloa, Sc, UK 59/C4
Allonnes, Fr. 83/F6
Allonnes, Fr. 83/F5
Allons, Tn, US 188/E2
Allora, Austl. 160/C5
Allos, Fr. 90/C4
Allouez, Wi, US 186/B2
Allow (riv.), Ire. 58/B5
Alloway, NJ, US 194/C4
Alloway (cr.), NJ, US 194/C4
Allschwil, Swi. 86/D2
Allumettes (isl.), Qu, Can. 187/H2
Alluvial City, La, US 190/D3
Allyn, Wa, US 170/C4
Alm (riv.), Aus. 85/G7
Alma, Ar, US 179/G3
Alma, Ga, US 191/G2
Alma, Ks, US 179/F1
Alma, Mi, US 186/D3
Alma, NS, Can. 184/E3
Alma, Ne, US 180/E3
Alma, NM, US 175/H4
Alma (hill), NY, US 187/G3
Alma, Qu, Can. 184/B1
Alma, Wi, US 181/J1
Almacelles, Sp. 73/F2
Almacén, Ven. 205/F2
Almada, Port. 73/P10
Almadén, Sp. 72/C3
Almafuerte, Arg. 214/D2
Almagro, Sp. 72/D3
Almanor (lake), Ca, US 172/C3
Almansa, Sp. 73/E3
Almanza, Sp. 72/C1
Almanzor, Pico de (peak), Sp. 72/C2
Almanzora (riv.), Sp. 72/D4
Almartha, Mo, US 179/H2
Almas, Braz. 210/D1
Almas, Pico das (peak), Braz. 211/E2
Almas, Rio das (riv.), Braz. 210/C2
Almaty, Kaz. 125/C3
Almaty (int'l arpt.), Kaz. 125/C3
Almazán, Sp. 72/D2
Almaznyy, Rus. 101/M3
Almazora, Sp. 73/E3
Almeida, Port. 72/B2
Almeirim, Port. 72/A3
Almeirim, Braz. 206/C3
Almelo, Neth. 78/D4
Almena, Ks, US 180/E4
Almenara (peak), Sp. 72/D3
Almenara, Sp. 73/E3
Almenara, Braz. 211/E3
Almendra (res.), Sp. 72/B2
Almendralejo, Sp. 72/B3
Almenno San Salvatore, It. 88/C2
Almere, Neth. 78/C4
Almería, Sp. 72/D4
Almería (gulf), Sp. 72/D4
Almese, It. 90/D2
Al'met'yevsk, Rus. 95/M5
Älmhult, Swe. 66/F3
Almina (pt.), Sp. 138/B2
Almirós, Gre. 75/H3
Almiroú (gulf), Gre. 75/J5
Almo, Id, US 173/G2
Almodôvar, Port. 72/A4
Almodóvar del Campo, Sp. 72/C3
Almodóvar del Río, Sp. 72/C4
Almoharín, Sp. 72/B3
Almond (riv.), Sc, UK 59/C4
Almont, ND, US 182/D4
Almont, Mi, US 186/E3
Almont (riv.), Fr. 56/L6
Almont, Co, US 175/J1
Almonte, On, Can. 187/H2
Almonte, Sp. 72/B4
Almora, India 122/B1
Almoradi, Sp. 73/E3
Almorox, Sp. 72/C2
Almte. Montt (gulf), Chile 215/B7
Almudévar, Sp. 73/E1
Almuñécar, Sp. 72/D4
Almunge, Swe. 65/B1
Almus, Turk. 128/D1
Alness, Sc, UK 59/B1
Alness (riv.), Sc, UK 59/B1
Alnmouth, Eng, UK 59/E6
Alnwick, Eng, UK 59/E6
Ålö (isl.), Swe. 65/B2
Alofi, NZ 163/J6
Alofi (isl.), Wall. 162/H6
Aloha, Or, US 172/B1
Aloi, Ugan. 145/A1
Aloja, Lat. 67/L3
Along, India 112/B2
Alongshan, China 105/J1
Alónnisos (isl.), Gre. 75/H3
Alonsa, Mb, Can. 182/E2
Alor (isl.), Indo. 162/B5
Alor (isls.), Indo. 117/F5
Alor Gajah, Malay. 115/C2
Alor Setar, Malay. 115/C1
Álora, Sp. 72/C4
Alotau, PNG 162/E6
Aloysius (mt.), Austl. 157/F3
Alpachiri, Arg. 214/E3
Alpaugh, Ca, US 174/C3
Alpe di Poti (peak), It. 89/E7
Alpe di Succiso (peak), It. 88/D5
Alpedrete, Sp. 73/M8
Alpen, Ger. 78/D5
Alpena, Mi, US 186/E2
Alpena, SD, US 180/E1
Alpercatas, Serra das (mts.), Braz. 207/E4
Alperschällihorn (peak), Swi. 87/F4
Alpes de Provence (range), Fr. 71/G5
Alpes-de-Haute-Provence (dept.), Fr. 90/C4
Alpes-Maritimes (dept.), Fr. 90/D5
Alpha, Austl. 160/B3
Alpha, Il, US 181/J3
Alpha (mt.), NZ 161/J8
Alpha, NJ, US 194/C2
Alpharetta, Ga, US 189/M6
Alphen aan de Rijn, Neth. 78/B4
Alpi Apuane (range), It. 71/J4
Alpi Dolomitiche (range), It. 71/J4
Alpi Orobie (range), It. 71/J3
Alpiarça, Port. 72/A3
Alpignano, It. 90/D2
Alpine, NJ, US 195/K8
Alpine, Wy, US 173/H2
Alpine, Tx, US 176/C2
Alpirsbach, Ger. 87/E1
Alpnach, Swi. 87/E4
Alps (mts.), Eur. 55/E4
Alqōsh, Iraq 129/E2
Alrewas, Eng, UK 63/E1
Alroy Downs, Austl. 155/E4
Als (isl.), Den. 68/F1
Alsace (dept.), Fr. 84/A5
Alsace (pol. Reg.), Fr. 68/D4
Alsace (pol. reg.), Fr. 81/G6
Alsager, Eng, UK 61/F5
Alsask, Sk, Can. 171/K2
Alsasua, Sp. 70/B5
Alsdorf, Ger. 81/F2
Alsea (bay), Or, US 172/A1
Alsenz, Ger. 81/G4
Alsenz (riv.), Ger. 81/G4
Alsheim, Ger. 84/B3
Alsike, Swe. 65/A1
Alsip, Il, US 193/Q16
Alstahaug, Nor. 64/E2
Alstead, NH, US 187/K3

Alster (riv.), Ger. 79/H1
Alsting, Fr. 81/F5
Alston, Eng, UK 61/F2
Alstonville, Austl. 158/E1
Alsunga, Lat. 67/J3
Alt (riv.), Eng, UK 61/E4
Alta, Nor. 64/G1
Ålta, Swe. 65/B1
Alta (mt.), NZ 161/B4
Alta, Ia, US 181/G2
Alta Gracia, Arg. 212/C4
Alta Vista, Ks, US 179/F1
Altach, Aus. 87/F3
Altadena, Ca, US 192/F7
Altagracia, Nic. 200/E4
Altagracia de Orituco, Ven. 207/P8
Altai (mts.), Asia 103/H5
Altai (mts.), China 100/J5
Altamache (riv.), Ga, US 189/F5
Altamaha (riv.), Ga, US 196/E1
Altamira, Braz. 206/C3
Altamira, Chile 212/B3
Altamira, Mex. 200/B1
Altamira do Maranhão, Braz. 207/E4
Altamont, Il, US 188/C1
Altamont, Ks, US 179/G2
Altamont, Mb, Can. 182/E3
Altamont, Or, US 172/C2
Altamont, Tn, US 188/E3
Altamonte Springs, Fl, US 190/N6
Altamura, It. 74/E2
Altanteel, Mong. 104/C2
Altar (vol.), Ecu. 204/B5
Altar, Mex. 198/C2
Altar de los Sacrificios (ruin), Guat. 200/D2
Altar Wash (riv.), Az, US 175/G5
Altare, It. 88/B5
Altario, Ab, Can. 171/J2
Altavilla Irpina, It. 92/D6
Altavilla Vicentina, It. 89/E2
Altavista, Va, US 189/H2
Altay, China 125/E2
Altay, Mong. 104/D2
Altay, Mong. 104/B2
Altay Kray, Rus. 125/C1
Altdorf, Swi. 87/E4
Altdorf bei Nürnberg, Ger. 85/E4
Altea, Sp. 73/E3
Altedo, It. 89/E4
Altena, Ger. 79/E6
Altenahr, Ger. 81/G2
Altenau (riv.), Ger. 79/F5
Altenau, Ger. 79/H5
Altenbeken, Ger. 79/F5
Altenberg bei Linz, Aus. 85/H6
Altenburg, Ger. 68/G3
Altenburg, Mo, US 188/C2
Altenfelden, Aus. 85/G6
Altenglan, Ger. 81/G4
Altengottern, Ger. 79/H6
Altenkirchen, Ger. 81/G2
Altenmarkt an der Triesting, Aus. 77/N7
Altenmünster, Ger. 84/D6
Altenstadt, Ger. 87/G2
Altenstadt, Ger. 87/G1
Altenstadt, Ger. 84/B2
Altensteig, Ger. 84/B5
Altentreptow, Ger. 66/E5
Altepexi, Mex. 199/M8
Alter do Chão, Braz. 206/C3
Alter Rhein (riv.), Ger. 78/D5
Altes Land (phys. reg.), Ger. 79/G1
Altha, Fl, US 191/F2
Altheim, Aus. 85/G6
Altheim, Ger. 87/F1
Altheimer, Ar, US 179/J3
Althengstett, Ger. 84/B5
Althofen, Aus. 71/L3
Althorpe, Eng, UK 61/H4
Althütte, Ger. 84/C5
Alticane, Sk, Can. 171/L1
Altındere NP, Turk. 96/F4
Altınözü, Turk. 130/E1
Altıntaş, Turk. 128/B2
Altınyaka, Turk. 130/B1
Altınyayla, Turk. 128/B2
Altiplanicie del Payón (rocks), Arg. 214/C3
Altiplano (plat.), Bol.,Peru 203/C4
Altiplano (plat.), Peru 209/D4
Altkirch, Fr. 86/D2
Altlandsberg, Ger. 68/Q6
Altmark (phys. reg.), Ger. 68/F2
Altmühl (riv.), Ger. 71/J2
Altmünster, Aus. 85/G7
Altnaharra, Sc, UK 57/R7
Alto (peak), It. 87/G4
Alto, La, US 179/J4
Alto (peak), Braz. 210/D2
Alto, Tx, US 176/G2
Alto (mtn.), Tx, US 177/B2
Alto Araguaia, Braz. 210/B3
Alto Chicapa, Ang. 146/D5
Alto Cuale, Ang. 146/D4
Alto Cuilo, Ang. 146/D5
Alto de la Sierra, Arg. 212/D2
Alto de Tamar (peak), Col. 204/C3
Alto del Carmen, Chile 212/B4
Alto Garças, Braz. 210/B3
Alto Longá, Braz. 207/F4
Alto Lucero, Mex. 199/N7
Alto Molócuè, Moz. 149/H2
Alto Paraguai, Braz. 209/G4
Alto Paraguay (dept.), Par. 210/A4
Alto Paraná (dept.), Par. 213/F3
Alto Parnaíba, Braz. 207/E5
Alto Pass, Il, US 188/C2
Alto Pencoso, Arg. 214/D2
Alto Purús (riv.), Peru 208/D3
Alto Santo, Braz. 207/G4
Alto Seco, Bol. 212/C1
Alto Yuruá (riv.), Peru 208/C3
Altomünster, Ger. 84/E6
Alton, Eng, UK 63/F4
Alton, Il, US 181/J4
Alton, Ia, US 181/F2
Alton, Mo, US 179/J2
Alton, Ut, US 175/F2
Alton Downs, Austl. 157/H3
Altona, Mb, Can. 182/F3
Altona, Ger. 79/G1
Altona (nbrhd.), Austl. 158/F5
Altônia, Braz. 213/F2
Altoona, Ia, US 181/H3
Altoona, Pa, US 187/G4
Altopascio, It. 89/D6
Altos, Braz. 207/F4
Altos de Campana NP, Pan. 204/B2
Altotonga, Mex. 199/M7
Altötting, Ger. 85/F6
Altrincham, Eng, UK 61/F5
Altrip, Ger. 84/B4
Altukhovo, Rus. 96/E1
Altun (mts.), China 103/H6
Altun Ha (ruin), Belz. 200/D2
Alturas, Ca, US 172/C3
Alturas, Fl, US 190/M8
Altus (A.F.B.), Ok, US 178/E3
Altus, Ok, US 178/E3
Altykarasu, Kaz. 97/K2
Altynivka, Ukr. 99/G2
Altynkul', Uzb. 97/L4
Altzayanca, Mex. 199/M7
Alucra, Turk. 128/D1
Aluk, Sudan 142/E3
Alūksne, Lat. 67/M3
Alum Fork (riv.), Ar, US 179/H3
Aluminé, Arg. 214/C3
Alunda, Swe. 66/H1
Alupka, Ukr. 96/E3
Ālūs, Iraq 128/E3
Alushta, Ukr. 99/H5
Aluta, D.R. Congo 147/F3
Alva, Ok, US 179/E2
Alva, Sc, UK 59/C4
Alva, Fl, US 191/H4
Alvalade, Port. 72/A4
Alvaneu-Bad, Swi. 87/F4
Älvängen, Swe. 66/E3
Alvarado, Mn, US 182/F3
Alvarado, Col. 207/L8
Alvarado, Mex. 199/P8
Alvarado, Tx, US 176/K7
Álvares Machado, Braz. 213/G2
Álvarez, Arg. 214/E2
Alvaro Obregón, Presa (dam), Mex. 198/C2
Alvdal, Nor. 64/D3
Älvdalen, Swe. 66/F1
Alvear, Arg. 213/E4
Alvechurch, Eng, UK 63/E2
Alverca, Port. 73/P10
Alveringem, Belg. 80/B1
Alvesta, Swe. 66/F3
Alviano (lake), It. 91/B2
Alvignano, It. 92/D5
Ålvik, Nor. 66/B1
Alvin, BC, Can. 170/C3
Alvin, Tx, US 177/M9
Alvin, Wi, US 183/K5
Alvinston, On, Can. 186/F3
Alvito, Port. 72/B3
Älvkarleby, Swe. 66/G1
Alvorada, Braz. 213/F4
Alvorada, Braz. 210/C2
Alvorada do Norte, Braz. 210/D2
Alvord, Tx, US 179/F4
Alvord (des.), Or, US 172/D2
Älvsborg (co.), Swe. 64/E4
Älvsbyn, Swe. 64/G2
Älvsjö, Swe. 65/B1
Alwen (riv.), Wal, UK 60/E5
Alxa Youqi, China 104/E4
Alxa Zuoqi, China 104/F4
Alyangula, Austl. 155/E3
Alyawarra Abor. Land, Austl. 157/G2
Alyth, Sc, UK 59/C3
Alytus, Lith. 67/L4
Alz (riv.), Aus. 76/A1
Alz (riv.), Ger. 68/G4
Alzada, Mt, US 180/B1
Alzano Lombardo, It. 88/C2
Alzenau in Unterfranken, Ger. 84/C2
Alzette (riv.), Lux. 81/F4
Alzey, Ger. 84/B3
Am Dam, Chad 142/D2
Am Djéména, Chad 142/C2
Am Timan, Chad 142/D3
Am Zoer, Chad 142/D2
Ama, PNG 117/K4
Amacayacú NP, Col. 208/D1
Amacuro (delta), Ven. 205/F2
Amacuro (riv.), Ven. 205/F2
Amacuzac (riv.), Mex. 199/K8
Amada Gaza, CAfr. 142/B4
Amadeus (lake), Austl. 153/C3
Āmādi, Bang. 123/G4
Amadi, Sudan 142/F4
Amadjuak (lake), Nun, Can. 167/J2
Amado, Az, US 175/G5
Amadora, Port. 73/P10
Amagá, Col. 207/K6
Amagansett, NY, US 195/F2
Amagansett Nat'l Wild. Ref., NY, US 195/F2
Amagasaki, Japan 109/H6
Amager (isl.), Den. 65/J7
Amagi, Japan 110/B4
Amagi-san (peak), Japan 111/F3
Amagon, Ar, US 179/J3
Amaguaña, Ecu. 204/B5
Amahai, Indo. 117/G4
Amajac (riv.), Mex. 199/N7
Amakusa (sea), Japan 105/K5
Åmål, Swe. 66/E2
Amala (riv.), Kenya 145/A2
Amalat (riv.), Rus. 104/G1
Amalfi, It. 92/D6
Amalfi, Col. 204/C3
Amalga, Ut, US 173/H3
Amalia, SAfr. 150/D2
Amaliás, Gre. 75/G4
Amalner, India 121/B1
Amaluza, Ecu. 208/B2
Amamapare, Indo. 117/J4
Amambaí, Braz. 213/F2
Amambaí (riv.), Braz. 210/B4
Amambay (dept.), Par. 210/A4
Amambay (dept.), Braz. 213/F2
Amambay, Serra (mts.), Braz.,Par. 213/F2
Amami (isls.), Japan 103/M7
Amami-O-Shima (isl.), Japan 111/K6
Amamula, D.R. Congo 147/F3
Amanã (lake), Braz. 205/E5
Amanab, PNG 117/K4
Amanbidji Abor. Land, Austl. 154/C4
Amance, Fr. 86/C2
Amanda Park, Wa, US 170/C4
Amandola, It. 92/C2
Amānganj, India 122/C3
Amāngarh, Pak. 124/A2
Amantea, It. 74/E3
Amanu (isl.), FrPol. 163/L6
Amanzimtoti, SAfr. 151/E3
Amapá, Braz. 206/D2
Amapá (state), Braz. 205/H4
Amarante, Braz. 207/F4
Amarante, Port. 72/A2
Amarante do Marahão, Braz. 207/E4
Amaranth, Mb, Can. 182/E2
Amarapura, Myan. 112/C4
Amareleja, Port. 72/B3
Amarete, Bol. 208/D4
Amargosa (range), Ca, US 174/D2
Amargosa (riv.), Ca,Nv, US 174/D2
Amargosa (des.), Nv, US 174/D2
Amargosa, Braz. 211/F2
Amarillo, Tx, US 178/D3
Amarkantak, India 122/C4
Amaro (peak), It. 92/D3
Amarpātan, India 122/C3
Amarume, Japan 108/A4
Amarwāra, India 122/B4
Amaseno (riv.), It. 92/C5
Amasra, Turk. 77/L5
Amasya, Turk. 96/E4
Amasya (prov.), Turk. 96/E4
Amata, Austl. 157/F3
Amatlán de Cañas, Mex. 198/D4
Amatrice, It. 92/C2
Amatsukominato, Japan 109/E3
Amawalk (res.), NY, US 195/E1
Amay, Belg. 81/E2
Amayuca, Mex. 199/L8
Amazar, Rus. 105/J1
Amazon (riv.), Braz. 203/C3
Amazon (Amazonas) (riv.), Braz. 203/C3
Amazonas, Cuba 201/G1
Amazonas (state), Braz. 204/C5
Amazonas (state), Ven. 205/E3
Amazonas (Amazon) (riv.), Braz. 203/C3
Amazônia (Tapajós), PN de, Braz. 209/G2
Amb, Pak. 124/B2
Āmba Gīyorgīs, Eth. 142/H2
Āmba Maryam, Eth. 144/A3
Ambāh, India 122/B2
Ambahikily, Madg. 152/G8
Ambajogai, India 121/C2
Ambāla, India 124/D4
Ambāla Sadar, India 124/D4
Ambalajanakomby, Madg. 152/H7
Ambalangoda, SrL. 121/D5
Ambalarondra, Madg. 152/J7
Ambalavao, Madg. 152/H8
Ambalema, Col. 207/L8
Ambam, Camr. 146/B2
Ambanja, Madg. 152/J6
Ambarnyy, Rus. 94/G2
Ambaro (bay), Madg. 152/J6
Āmbāsa, India 123/H4
Ambato, Ecu. 204/B5
Ambato Boeny, Madg. 152/H7
Ambatofinandrahana, Madg. 152/H8
Ambatolahy, Madg. 152/H8
Ambatolampy, Madg. 152/H7
Ambatomaidy, Madg. 152/H7
Ambatomanoina, Madg. 152/H7
Ambatondrazaka, Madg. 152/J7
Ambazac, Fr. 70/D4
Ámbelos (cape), Gre. 75/H3
Amber, Ok, US 179/F3
Amberg, Wi, US 183/L5
Amberg, Ger. 85/E4
Ambergate, Eng, UK 61/G5
Ambergris Cay (isl.), Belz. 200/E2
Ambérieu-en-Bugey, Fr. 86/B6
Amberley, NZ 161/C3
Amberloup, Belg. 81/E3
Ambidédi, Mali 140/C3
Ambikāpur, India 122/D4
Ambilobe, Madg. 152/J6
Ambinanindrano, Madg. 152/J8
Ambinanitelo, Madg. 152/J6
Ambinanynony, Madg. 152/J7
Ambla, Est. 67/L2
Amble, Eng, UK 59/E6
Ambler, Pa, US 194/C3
Ambleside, Eng, UK 61/F3
Amblève, Belg. 81/F3
Amblève (riv.), Belg. 68/C3
Ambo, Peru 208/B3
Amboasary, Madg. 152/H9
Amboavory, Madg. 152/J7
Ambodifototra, Madg. 152/J7
Ambodiharina, Madg. 152/J8
Ambodriana, Madg. 152/J7
Ambohidratrimo, Madg. 152/H7
Ambohijanahary, Madg. 152/J7
Ambohimahasoa, Madg. 152/H8
Ambohimahavelona, Madg. 152/G8
Ambohimandroso, Madg. 152/H7
Ambohimilanja, Madg. 152/H7
Ambohinihaonana, Madg. 152/H8
Ambohitsilaozana, Madg. 152/J7
Amboise, Fr. 83/F6
Ambolomoty, Madg. 152/H7
Ambon (isl.), Indo. 117/G4
Ambondro, Madg. 152/H9
Amboni Caves, Tanz. 145/B3
Amborompotsy, Madg. 152/H8
Amboseli NP, Kenya 145/B2
Ambositra, Madg. 152/H8
Ambouli (int'l arpt.), Djib. 144/B3
Ambovombe, Madg. 152/H9
Amboy, Ca, US 174/E3
Amboy, Mn, US 181/G2
Amboy, Il, US 181/K3
Amboy, Wa, US 170/C5
Ambrières-le-Grand, Fr. 83/E4
Ambriz, Ang. 146/C4
Ambrolauri, Geo. 97/G4
Ambrose, Ga, US 191/G2
Ambrym (isl.), Van. 162/F6
Ambuntentimur, Indo. 115/F3
Amchitka (isl.), Ak, US 101/T4
'Amd, Yem. 144/C2
Amdasa, Indo. 154/C1
Amealco, Mex. 199/K6
Ameca, Mex. 198/D4
Amecameca de Juárez, Mex. 199/R10
Ameghino, Arg. 214/E2
Ameglia, It. 88/C5
Ameisberg (peak), Aus. 85/G5
Ameland (isl.), Neth. 78/C2
Amelia (isl.), Fl, US 191/H2
Amelia, It. 91/B2
Amelia City, Fl, US 191/H2
Amelia Court House, Va, US 189/J2
Ameliasburg, On, Can. 187/H2
Amelinghausen, Ger. 79/H2
Amenia, ND, US 182/F4
Amer (chan.), Neth. 78/B5
American (riv.), Ca, US 193/M9
American (lake), Wa, US 193/B3
American Bolder (peak), Wa, US 170/D3
American College, It. 91/G8
American Falls, Id, US 173/G2
American Falls (dam), Id, US 173/G2
American Falls (res.), Id, US 173/G2
American Fork, Ut, US 173/H3
American Highland (rocks), Ant. 216/F
American Samoa (terr.), US 163/H6
American, South Fork (riv.), Ca, US 172/C4
American, South Fork (riv.), Ca, US 175/J1
American, North Fork (riv.), Ca, US 172/C4
Americana, Braz. 213/H2
Americus, Ga, US 191/F1
Americus, Ks, US 179/F1
Americus, Mo, US 181/J4
Ameringkogel (peak), Aus. 71/L3
Amersfoort, Neth. 78/C4
Amersfoort, SAfr. 151/E2
Amersham, Eng, UK 63/F3
Amery, Wi, US 183/H5
Amery Ice Shelf, Ant. 216/E
Ames, Ks, US 180/F4
Ames, Ia, US 181/H2
Ames, Tx, US 177/N8
Amesbury, Eng, UK 63/E4
Amesbury, Ma, US 187/L3
Amet, India 118/B2
Amethi, India 122/C2
Āmeya, Eth. 142/H4
Amfíklia, Gre. 75/H3
Amfilokhía, Gre. 75/G3
Ámfissa, Gre. 75/H3
Amga (riv.), Rus. 101/N3
Amguema (riv.), Rus. 101/T3
Amguid, Alg. 137/G4
Amgun' (riv.), Rus. 101/P4
Amgun' (riv.), Rus. 105/M1
Amherst, NS, Can. 184/E3
Amherst, Wi, US 183/K5
Amherst (isl.), Qu, Can. 185/F2
Amherst, Ma, US 187/K3
Amherst, NY, US 186/V10
Amherst, Va, US 189/H2
Amherstburg, On, Can. 193/F7
Amherstdale-Robinette, WV, US 189/G2
Amhurst (mt.), Austl. 154/B4
Ami, Japan 109/E1
Amiata (peak), It. 74/B1
Amidon, ND, US 182/C4
Amiens, Fr. 80/B4
Amik (lake), Turk 128/D2
Amila (isl.), Ak, US 101/U4
Amilcar Cabral (int'l arpt.), CpV. 133/K10
Amillis, Fr. 56/M5
Amíndaion, Gre. 75/G2
Aminius, Namb. 148/C4
Aminu Kano (int'l arpt.), Nga. 141/H3
Amistad (res.), Mex.,US 196/A2
Amistad (dam), Tx, US 177/D3
Amistad (int'l. res), Tx, US 199/E2
Amistad Nat'l Rec. Area, Tx, US 199/E2
Amite, La, US 190/C2
Amite (cr.), La, US 190/C2
Amity (canal), Co, US 178/C1
Amity, Ar, US 179/H3
Amity, Or, US 172/B1
Amityville, NY, US 195/M9
Amla, India 122/B5
Āmlāgora, India 123/F4
Amlash, Iran 129/G2
Amlekhganj, Nepal 123/E2
Åmli, Nor. 66/C2
Amlia (isl.), Ak, US 168/V13
Amlwch, Wal, UK 60/D5
'Ammān (gov.), Jor. 130/E4
Amman (riv.), Wal, UK 62/C3
'Ammān (Amman) (cap.), Jor. 126/C2
Amman ('Ammān) (cap.), Jor. 131/D5
Ammanford, Wal, UK 62/C3
Ammannsville, Tx, US 177/F3
Ammarfjället (peak), Swe. 64/E2
Ammassalik, Grld 216/J
Ammer (riv.), Ger. 84/B5
Ammersee (lake), Ger. 71/J3
Ammon, Id, US 173/H2
Amnat Charoen, Thai. 120/D3
Amnéville, Fr. 81/F5
Amo (riv.), China 112/D4
Āmol, Iran 129/H2
Amora, Port. 73/P10
Amorbach, Ger. 84/C3
Amorgós, Gre. 75/J4
Amorgós (isl.), Gre. 93/K3
Amorinópolis, Braz. 210/C3
Amory, Ms, US 188/C4
Amos, Qu, Can. 167/J4
Åmose (riv.), Den. 65/H7
Åmot, Nor. 66/B2
Amotfors, Swe. 66/E2
Amourj, Mrta. 140/D2
Amozoc, Mex. 199/L7
Ampachi, Japan 109/L5
Ampana, Indo. 117/F4
Ampanavoana, Madg. 152/J6
Ampanefena, Madg. 152/J6
Ampangalana (canal), Madg. 152/J8
Ampanihy, Madg. 152/H9
Amparafaravola, Madg. 152/J7
Amparai, SrL. 121/D5
Amparo, Braz. 211/K7
Ampasimanjeva, Madg. 152/J8
Ampasimanolotra, Madg. 152/J7
Ampasindava (bay), Madg. 152/H6
Ampato (peak), Peru 208/D4
Ampefy, Madg. 152/H7
Amper, Nga. 141/H4
Amper (riv.), Ger. 85/E6
Ampfing, Ger. 85/F6
Ampflwang im Hausruckwald, Aus. 85/G6
Amphitrite Group (isls.), Asia 113/G5
Ampibako, Indo. 117/F4
Ampisikinana, Madg. 152/J6
Ampitatafika, Madg. 152/H7
Ampombiantambo, Madg. 152/J6
Amposta, Sp. 73/F2
Ampthill, Eng, UK 63/F2
Ampuis, Fr. 90/A2
Amqui, Qu, Can. 184/D1
'Amrān, Yem. 144/B2
Amrāpāra, India 123/F3
Amreli, India 127/K4
Amring, India 112/B3
'Amrīt (ruin), Syria 130/D2
Amritsar, India 124/C4
Amroha, India 122/B1
Amrūka, Pak. 124/B4
Amstel (riv.), Neth. 78/B4
Amstelveen, Neth. 78/B4
Amsterdam (isl.), Fr. 53/N7
Amsterdam, Ga, US 191/F2
Amsterdam, NY, US 187/J3
Amsterdam (cap.), Neth. 78/B4
Amsterdam, SAfr. 151/E2
Amsterdam (Schipol) (int'l arpt.), Neth. 78/B4
Amsterdam Rijnkan. (riv.), Neth. 78/C4
Amstetten, Aus. 71/L2
Āmtali, Bang. 123/H4
Amtkel, Geo. 97/G4
Amu Darya (riv.), Asia 103/F8
Amu Darya (riv.), Uzb. 97/L4
Amu Darya (riv.), Trkm. 100/G5
Amu-Dar'ya, Trkm. 100/G6
Amudālavalasa, India 121/D2
Amudar'ya (riv.), Trkm. 127/J1
Amudat, Ugan. 145/A1
Amuku (mts.), Guy. 205/G4
Amund Ringnes (isl.), Nun, Can. 167/S7
Amundsen (sea), Ant. 216/S
Amundsen (bay), Ant. 216/D
Amundsen (gulf), NW, Can. 166/D1
Amundsen-Scott, US, Ant. 216/A
Amunge (lake), Swe. 66/F1
Amur (riv.), Asia 103/M4
'Amūr (wadi), Sudan 135/G5
'Amur (wadi), Sudan 126/B5
Amur (Heilong) (riv.), China, Rus. 101/N4
Amur Oblast, Rus. 101/N4
Amur (Heilong) (riv.), China,Rus 105/J1
Amuri, NZ 163/K6
Amurrio, Sp. 70/B5
Amursk, Rus. 105/M1
Amvrosiyivka, Ukr. 99/K4
Amyūn, Leb. 130/D2
An Khe, Viet. 120/E3
An Nabaţīyah at Taḩtā, Leb. 131/C2
An Nabī Shīt, Leb. 131/E1
An Nafīdah, Tun. 74/B4
An Nafūd (des.), SAr. 135/H2
An Nahūd, Sudan 142/F2
An Najaf, Iraq 129/F4
An Najaf (gov.), Iraq 129/E4
An Nāqūrah, Leb. 131/C2
An Nāşirīyah, Iraq 129/F4
An Nawfalīyah, Libya 134/C2
An Nazlat, Egypt 139/B6
An Nhon, Viet. 120/E3
An Nu'manīyah, Iraq 129/F3
An Phuoc, Viet. 120/E4
An Teallach (peak), Sc, UK 59/A1
An Uaimh, Ire. 58/D2
Ana María (gulf), Cuba 197/F3
Anaa (isl.), FrPol. 163/L6
Anabar (riv.), Rus. 101/L3
'Anabtā, WBnk. 131/C4
Anacapa (isl.), Ca, US 174/C4
Anacapri, It. 92/D6
Anachucuna (mtn.), Pan. 204/B2
Anaco, Ven. 205/E2
Anacoco, La, US 190/B2
Anaconda (range), Mt, US 171/H5
Anaconda-Deer Lodge County, Mt, US 171/H4
Anacortes, Wa, US 170/C3
Anadarko, Ok, US 179/E3
Anadia, Port. 72/A2
Anadyr' (riv.), Rus. 103/S3
Anadyr', Rus. 101/T3
Anadyr' (gulf), Rus. 103/T3
Anadyr' (range), Rus. 216/U
Anáfi (isl.), Gre. 75/J4
Anafi (isl.), Gre. 93/K3
Anagni, It. 92/C4
'Ānah, Iraq 128/E3
Anaheim, Ca, US 192/G8
Anaheim Stadium, Ca, US 192/G8
Anahidrano, Madg. 152/H6
Anahim Lake, BC, Can. 170/B1
Anahim's Flat Ind. Res., BC, Can. 170/C1
Anáhuac, Mex. 177/D4
Anahuac, Tx, US 177/N9
Anahuac (lake), Tx, US 177/N9
Anahuac, Mex. 198/D2
Anahuac NWR, Tx, US 177/G3
Anai Mudi (peak), India 121/C4
Anajatuba, Braz. 207/E3
Anak, NKor. 107/C3
Anakāpalle, India 121/D2
Anaktuvuk Pass, Ak, US 168/X12
Analalava, Madg. 152/H6
Analamaitso (plat.), Madg. 152/J7
Analavory, Madg. 152/H7
Anambas (isls.), Indo. 116/C3
Anambra (state), Nga. 141/G5
Anamoose, ND, US 182/D4
Anamosa, Ia, US 181/J2
Anamur, Turk. 130/C1
Anamur (pt.), Turk. 130/C1
Anan, Japan 110/D4
Ananás, Braz. 206/D4
Anand, India 118/B3
Ananda Temple, Myan. 112/B4
Anandgarh, India 124/B5
Anandpur, India 124/D4
Anandpur, India 121/E1
Ananea, Bol. 208/D4
Ananea, Peru 208/D4
Anantapur, India 121/C3
Anantnag, India 124/C3
Anan'yevo, Kyr. 125/C3
Anan'yiv, Ukr. 98/E4
Anapa, Rus. 99/J5
Añapi (peak), Arg. 215/C6
Anápolis, Braz. 210/C3
Anapskaya, Rus. 99/J5
Anapu (riv.), Braz. 206/D3
Anār, Iran 129/H4
Anārak, Iran 129/H3
Anastasia (isl.), Fl, US 191/H3
Anastasiyevka, Rus. 99/K4
'Anātā, WBnk. 131/C5
Anathan (isl.), NMar. 162/D3
Anatolia (reg.), Turk. 96/D5
Añatuya, Arg. 212/D4
Anauá (riv.), Braz. 205/F4
Anbo, China 107/B3
Anbu, China 113/H4
Anbyŏn, NKor. 107/D3
Ancash (dept.), Peru 208/B3
Ancaster, On, Can. 186/T9
Ancenis, Fr. 83/D6
Anchangzhen, China 113/E2
Anchau, Nga. 141/H4
Anchieta, Braz. 211/E4
Anchor (bay), Mi, US 193/G6
Anchorage, Ak, US 168/Y12
Anchorena, Arg. 214/D2
Anchorville, Mi, US 193/G6
Anchovy, Jam. 201/G2
Ancient Bristlecone Pine Forest, Ca, US 174/C2
Ancient City of Oc-eo, Viet. 120/D4
Anclote (riv.), Fl, US 190/K7
Anclote, Fl, US 190/K7
Anclote Keys (isl.), Fl, US 190/K7
Ancoeur (riv.), Fr. 56/L6
Ancohuma (peak), Bol. 208/D4
Ancón, Peru 208/B3
Ancón de Sardinas (bay), Col. 204/B4
Ancona, It. 89/G6
Ancona (prov.), It. 89/G5
Ancoraimes, Bol. 208/D4
Ancre (riv.), Fr. 80/B3
Ancroft, Eng, UK 59/E5
Ancrum, Sc, UK 59/D5
Ancud, Chile 214/B4
Ancud (gulf), Chile 214/B4
Anda, China 105/K2
Andacollo, Arg. 214/C3
Andacollo, Chile 212/B4
Andado, Austl. 157/G3
Andagua, Peru 208/C4
Andahuaylas, Peru 208/C4
Andaingo Gara, Madg. 152/J7
Andāl, India 123/F4
Andalgalá, Arg. 212/C3
Åndalsnes, Nor. 64/C3
Andalusia, Al, US 191/E2
Andalusia (reg.), Sp. 92/B3
Andalusia, Il, US 181/J3
Andaman (sea), Asia 103/J8
Andaman (isls.), India 103/H8
Andaman and Nicobar (isls.), India 119/F5
Andaman, South (isl.), India 119/F5
Andamarca, Bol. 212/C1
Andamarca, Peru 208/C3
Andamooka, Austl. 157/H4
Andapa, Madg. 152/J6
Andara, Namb. 148/D3
Andaraí, Braz. 211/E2
Andau, Aus. 76/C2
Ande, China 120/D1
Andebu, Nor. 66/D2
Andechs, Ger. 87/H2
Andeer, Swi. 87/F4
Andelfingen, Swi. 87/E2
Andelle (riv.), Fr. 80/A5
Andelot-Blancheville, Fr. 86/B1
Andelsbach (riv.), Ger. 87/F2
Andelu, Fr. 56/H5
Andemaka, Madg. 152/H8
Andenne, Belg. 81/E3
Anderlues, Belg. 81/D3
Andermatt, Swi. 87/E4
Andernach, Ger. 81/G3
Anderson, Mo, US 179/G2
Anderson, In, US 186/D4
Anderson (isl.), Wa, US 193/B3
Anderson (inlet), Wa, US 193/B3
Anderson, Ca, US 172/B3
Anderson (riv.), NW, Can. 166/D2
Anderson, SC, US 189/F3
Anderson, Tx, US 177/G2
Anderson Ranch (res.), Id, US 173/F2
Anderson Ranch (dam), Id, US 172/F2
Andersonville, Ga, US 188/E4
Andersonville Nat'l Hist. Site, Ga, US 188/E4
Andes, Mt, US 182/B4
Andes (mts.), SAm. 203/C5
Andes, Col. 207/K7
Andevoranto, Madg. 152/J7
Andfjorden (chan.), Nor. 64/F1
Andhra Pradesh (state), India 118/C4
Andijk, Neth. 78/C3
Andijon, Uzb. 125/B3
Andikíthira (isl.), Gre. 93/J4
Andilamena, Madg. 152/J7
Andilanatoby, Madg. 152/J7
Andīmeshk, Iran 129/G3
Andíparos (isl.), Gre. 75/J4
Andira (riv.), Braz. 209/G1
Andira, Braz. 210/C4
Ándissa, Gre. 75/J3
Andoain, Sp. 70/B5
Andoany, Madg. 152/J6
Andoas, Peru 204/B5
Andohajango, Madg. 152/J6
Andong, SKor. 110/A2
Andong, China 106/L9
Andorf, Aus. 85/G6
Andorno Micca, It. 88/B2
Andorra, Sp. 73/E2
Andorra (ctry.) 55/E4
Andorra la Vella (cap.), And. 70/D5
Andover, Eng, UK 63/E4
Andover, Ks, US 179/F2
Andover, Me, US 187/L2
Andover, Mn, US 183/P6
Andover, NJ, US 194/D2
Andover, Oh, US 186/F4
Andøy, Nor. 64/F1
Andøya (isl.), Nor. 64/E1
Andradas, Braz. 211/K7
Andradina, Braz. 213/G2
Andrafainkona, Madg. 152/J6
Andraitx, Sp. 73/G3
Andramasina, Madg. 152/H7
Andranolalina, Madg. 152/H8
Andranolava, Madg. 152/H8
Andranomavo (riv.), Madg. 152/H7
Andranopasy, Madg. 152/G8
Andranovondrona, Madg. 152/J6
Andranovory, Madg. 152/H8
André Félix, PN, CAfr. 142/D3
Andreanof (isls.), Ak, US 168/V13
Andrelândia, Braz. 211/M6
Andrespol, Pol. 69/K3
Andrésy, Fr. 56/J5
Andrew Johnson Nat'l Hist. Site, Tn, US 189/F2
Andrews, NC, US 188/F3
Andrews, Or, US 172/D2
Andrews, Tx, US 176/C1
Andrews (A.F.B.), Md, US 194/B6
Andrews, SC, US 189/H4
Andreyevka, Rus. 97/K1
Andrezel, Fr. 56/L6
Andria, It. 74/E2
Andriamena, Madg. 152/H7
Andriandampy, Madg. 152/H8
Andriba, Madg. 152/H7
Andringitra (mts.), Madg. 152/H8
Andrítsaina, Gre. 75/G4
Andriyivka, Ukr. 99/J4
Androka, Madg. 152/H9
Androntany (cape), Madg. 152/J6
Ándros, Gre. 75/J4
Ándros (isl.), Gre. 93/K3
Andros (isl.), Bahm. 165/K7
Androscoggin (riv.), Me, US 184/B3
Androscoggin (riv.), NH, US 187/L2
Andrushivka, Ukr. 98/E2
Andújar, Sp. 72/C3
Āndulbāria, Bang. 123/G4
Andulo, Ang. 148/C1
Andytown, Fl, US 190/P10
Aneby, Swe. 66/F3
Anecón Grande (peak), Arg. 214/C4
Anefis I-n-Darane, Mali 141/F2
Anegada (isl.), UK 197/J4
Anegada (bay), Arg. 214/E4
Anegada Passage (chan), NAm. 197/J4
Anécho, Togo 141/F5
Aneityum (isl.), Van. 162/F7
Añelo, Arg. 214/C3
Aneroid, Sk, Can. 171/L3
Anet, Fr. 83/G3
Aneta, ND, US 182/F4
Aneth, Ut, US 175/H2
Aneto, Pico de (peak), Sp. 73/F1
Aney, Niger 134/B5
Anfu, China 119/K2
Ang Mo Kio (nbrhd.), Sing. 115/J6
Ang Nam Ngum (lake), Laos 119/H4
Ang Thong, Thai. 120/C3
Angads (Oujda) (int'l arpt.), Mor. 138/D2
Angamma, Falaise d' (cliff), Chad 142/C1
Angamos (pt.), Chile 212/B2
Angara (riv.), Rus. 103/J4
Angarn, Swe. 65/B1
Angarsk, Rus. 104/E1
Angas Downs, Austl. 157/G3
Angaston, Austl. 157/H5
Angatuba, Braz. 213/G2
Angel (riv.), Ger. 79/E5
Ángel (falls), Ven. 205/F3
Ángel de la Guarda (isl.), Mex. 198/B2
Angela, Mt, US 171/L4
Angèle, Montagne d' (peak), Fr. 90/B4
Angeles, Phil. 114/C2
Angeles National Forest, Ca, US 192/B1
Angeles Nat'l Forest, Ca, US 192/F7
Ängelholm, Swe. 66/E3
Ängelholm (int'l arpt.), Swe. 66/E3
Ängelholm, Den. 65/J6
Angelica, Wi, US 186/B2
Angelim, Braz. 207/G5
Angelina (riv.), Tx, US 177/G2
Angeln (reg.), Ger. 68/E1
Angelus (lake), Mi, US 193/F6
Angelus Oaks (Camp Angelus), Ca, US 192/D2
Angera, It. 88/B2
Ångermanalven (riv.), Swe. 64/E2
Angermünde, Ger. 69/H2
Angers, Fr. 83/E6
Angerville, Fr. 83/H4
Anghiari, It. 89/F6
Angical do Piauí, Braz. 207/F4
Angicos, Braz. 207/G4
Angie, La, US 190/D2
Angier, NC, US 189/H3
Angk Tasaom, Camb. 120/D4
Angkor (ruin), Camb. 120/C3
Anglais (bay), Qu, Can. 184/C1
Angle Inlet, Mn, US 183/G3
Angleine (riv.), Fr. 83/E4
Anglem (mt.), NZ 161/A4
Anglès, Sp. 73/G2
Anglesea, Austl. 159/B4
Anglesey (isl.), Wal, UK 60/D5
Anglet, Fr. 70/C5
Angleton, Tx, US 176/G3
Anglin (riv.), Fr. 70/D3
Ango, D.R. Congo 147/F1
Angoche, Moz. 149/H3
Angohrān, Iran 127/G3
Angol, Chile 214/B3
Angola, In, US 186/D4
Angola, NY, US 187/G3
Angola, La, US 190/C2
Angola (ctry.) 133/D6
Angostura (res.), Mex. 196/C4
Angostura (res.), SD, US 180/C2
Angostura (dam), SD, US 180/C2
Angostura, Mex. 198/C3
Angoulême, Fr. 70/D4
Angra do Heroísmo, Azor., Port. 73/S12
Angra dos Reis, Braz. 211/M7
Angren, Uzb. 125/B3
Angri, It. 92/D6
Ängsö NP, Swe. 65/B1
Ängsön (isl.), Swe. 65/B1
Angu, D.R. Congo 147/F2
Anguilla, Ms, US 188/B4
Anguilla (isl.), UK 197/N8
Anguillara Sabazia, It. 91/B3
Anguillara Veneta, It. 89/E3
Anguille (mts.), Nf, Can. 185/H2
Angul, India 121/E1
Angumu, D.R. Congo 147/F3
Angurugu, Austl. 155/E3
Angus, Tx, US 177/F1
Angusville, Mb, Can. 182/D2
Angwa (riv.), Zim. 149/F3
Angwin, Ca, US 172/B4
Anhanduí (riv.), Braz. 210/B4
Anhée, Belg. 81/D3
Anholt (isl.), Den. 66/D3
Anhua, China 113/F2
Anhui (prov.), China 104/H5
Ani, Japan 108/B4
Anichab, Namb. 148/B4
Aniche, Fr. 80/C3
Anicuns, Braz. 210/C3
Aniene (riv.), It. 91/B4
Anikhovka, Rus. 97/M2
Anille (riv.), Fr. 83/F5
Animas, NM, US 175/H5
Animas (riv.), Co,NM, US 175/J2
Animas (mts.), NM, US 175/H5
Anin, Myan. 120/B3
Ānīn, WBnk. 131/C3
Anina, Rom. 76/E3
Anita, Ia, US 181/G3
Aniva (bay), Rus. 108/C1
Aniva (sea), Rus. 105/N2
Anivorano, Madg. 152/J7
Anizy-le-Château, Fr. 80/C4
Anjalankoski, Fin. 67/M1
Anjār, India 127/K4
'Anjar, Leb. 131/D1
'Anjarah, Jor. 131/D4
Anjō, Japan 109/M6
Anjou (reg.), Fr. 92/C1
Anjou, Qu, Can. 185/N6
Anjouan (isl.), Com. 152/H6
Anjozorobe, Madg. 152/H7
Anju, NKor. 107/C3
Anju, China 112/E2
Anjum, Neth. 78/D2
Ankang, China 104/F5
Ankara (prov.), Turk. 96/E5
Ankara (cap.), Turk. 128/C2
Ankaramena, Madg. 152/H8
Ankaratra (mass.), Madg. 152/H7
Ankarsrum, Swe. 66/G3
Ankasakasa, Madg. 152/H7
Ankavandra, Madg. 152/H7
Ankazoabo, Madg. 152/H8
Ankazobe, Madg. 152/H7
Ankazomborona, Madg. 152/H7
Ankazomiriotra, Madg. 152/H7
Ankeny, Ia, US 181/H3
Ankeny NWR, Or, US 172/B1
Ankerika, Madg. 152/H6
Ankiliabo, Madg. 152/G8
Ankililioka, Madg. 152/G8
Ankilizato, Madg. 152/H8
Anklam, Ger. 66/E5
Ānkober, Eth. 144/A3
Ankoro, D.R. Congo 147/F4
Ankpa, Nga. 141/G5
Ankum, Ger. 79/E3
Anliu, China 113/G4
Anloga, Gha. 141/F5
Anlong, China 119/J2
Anlong Bouyeizu Miaozu Zizhixian, China 112/E3
Anlong Veng, Camb. 120/D3
Anloo, Neth. 78/D2
Anlu, China 106/C5
Anma (isl.), SKor. 107/D5
Ann Arbor, Mi, US 186/E3
Anna, Tx, US 179/F4
Anna, Rus. 99/L2
Anna, Il, US 188/C2
Anna (lake), Va, US 189/J1
Anna Bay, Austl. 158/E2
Anna Creek, Austl. 157/H4
Anna Maria, Fl, US 191/G4
Anna Pavlowna, Neth. 78/B3
Anna Pink (bay), Chile 214/B5
Anna Plains, Austl. 154/A4
Anna Regina, Guy. 205/G3
Annaba, Alg. 138/K6
Annaba (wilaya), Alg. 138/K6
Annabella, Ut, US 175/F1
Annaberg-Buchholz, Ger. 85/G1
Annaclone, NI, UK 60/B3
Annai, Guy. 205/G4
Annaka, Japan 109/B1
Annalong, NI, UK 60/C3
Annan, Sc, UK 61/E2
Annan (riv.), Sc, UK 59/C6
Annandale, Mn, US 181/G1
Annandale, NJ, US 194/D2
Annandale, Va, US 194/A6
Annapolis, Ca, US 172/B4
Annapolis, Mo, US 179/J2
Annapolis (riv.), NS, Can. 184/E3
Annapolis (cap.), Md, US 194/B6
Annapolis Royal, NS, Can. 184/E3
Annapurna (peak), Nepal 122/D1
Annbank Station, Sc, UK 59/B6
Anne (mt.), Austl. 158/C4
Anne Arundel (co.), Md, US 194/B6
Annean (lake), Austl. 153/A3
Annecy (lake), Fr. 86/C6
Annecy, Fr. 86/C6
Annecy (Meythet) (arpt.), Fr. 86/C6
Annecy-le-Vieux, Fr. 86/C6
Annemasse, Fr. 86/C5
Anner (riv.), Ire. 58/C5
Annet-sur-Marne, Fr. 56/L5
Anneta, Tx, US 176/K7
Anneyron, Fr. 90/A2
Annezin, Fr. 80/B2
Annieopsquatch (mts.), Nf, Can. 185/J1
Anning (riv.), China 112/D3
Anning, China 112/D3
Anniston, Al, US 188/E4
Anniston Army Depot, Al, US 188/D4
Annobón (isl.), EqG. 133/C5
Annonay, Fr. 90/A2
Annot, Fr. 90/C5
Annunziata, It. 92/D5
Annville, Pa, US 194/B3
Annweiler, Ger. 81/G5
Anō, Japan 109/K6
Año Nuevo (pt.), Ca, US 174/A2
Áno Viánnos, Gre. 75/J5
Anoia (riv.), Sp. 73/K7
Anoka, Mn, US 183/P6
Anoka (co.), Mn, US 183/P6
Anola, Mb, Can. 182/F3
Anolaima, Col. 207/L8
Anori, Braz. 209/F1
Anosibe An' Ala, Madg. 152/J7
Ânou-Zeggarene (riv.), Niger 141/G2
Anould, Fr. 86/C1
Anóyia, Gre. 75/J5
Anping, China 107/B2
Anping, China 106/C3
Anping, China 106/H7
Anpu, China 120/E1
Anqing, China 113/H2
Anqiu, China 106/D3
Anren, China 119/K2
Anrhomer (peak), Mor. 136/D3
Anröchte, Ger. 79/F5
Ans, Belg. 81/E2
Ansai, China 106/B3
Ansan, SKor. 107/F7
Anşār, Leb. 131/C2
Ansbach, Ger. 84/D4
Anse Rouge, Haiti 201/H2
Anse-à-Galets, Haiti 201/H2
Anse-d'Hainault, Haiti 201/H2
Anserma, Col. 207/K7
Ansfelden, Aus. 85/H6
Anshan, China 107/B2
Anshun, China 112/E3
Anshunchang, China 112/D2
Ansina, Uru. 213/F4
Ansley, Ne, US 180/E3
Anson (bay), Austl. 154/C3
Anson, Tx, US 177/E1
Ansŏng, SKor. 107/D4
Ansongo, Mali 141/F3
Ansonia, Ct, US 187/K4
Ansted, WV, US 189/G1
Anstruther, Sc, UK 59/D4
Ansus, Indo. 117/J4
Ant (isl.), Anti. 162/E4
Ant (riv.), Eng, UK 63/H1
Anta, Peru 208/C4
Antabamba, Peru 208/C4
Antakya, Turk. 130/E1
Antalaha, Madg. 152/J6
Antalya (gulf), Turk. 130/B1
Antalya (int'l arpt.), Turk. 128/B2
Antalya, Turk. 130/B1
Antalya (prov.), Turk. 128/B2
Antanambao Manampotsy, Madg. 152/J7
Antanambe, Madg. 152/J7
Antananarivo (cap.), Madg. 152/H7
Antananarivo (prov.), Madg. 152/H7
Antanifotsy, Madg. 152/H7
Antanimenabaka, Madg. 152/J7
Antanimieva, Madg. 152/G8
Antanimora, Madg. 152/H9
Antar (peak), Alg. 137/E3
Antarctic (pen.), Ant. 216/W
Antarctic Circle 216/Z
Antarctica (cont.) 216/*
Antaritarika, Madg. 152/H9
Antas, Rio das (riv.), Braz. 213/G4
Antella, It. 89/E6
Antelope, Tx, US 179/E4
Antelope, Mt, US 182/B3
Antelope, Or, US 172/C1
Antelope (isl.), Ut, US 173/G3
Antelope (peak), Mt, US 171/K5
Antelope Center, Ca, US 192/C1
Antelope Mine, Zim. 149/F4

230

Anten – Asaba

Antenor Navarro, Braz. 207/G4
Antequera, Sp. 72/C4
Antequera, Par. 213/E3
Antero (mt.), Co, US 175/J1
Antes Fort, Pa, US 194/A1
Anthering, Aus. 85/G7
Anthony, Ks, US 179/E2
Anthony, Fl, US 191/G3
Anthony, NM, US 176/A1
Anthony Lagoon, Austl. 155/D4
Anti-Atlas (mts.), Mor. 136/C3
Anti-Lebanon (mts.), Leb. 130/D3
Antibes, Fr. 90/D5
Anticosti, Ile d' (isl.), Qu, Can. 167/K4
Antiesen (riv.), Aus. 85/G6
Antietam Nat'l Bfld., Md, US 187/H5
Antifer (cape), Fr. 83/F1
Antigo, Wi, US 183/K5
Antigonish, NS, Can. 185/G3
Antigua, Sp. 136/B3
Antigua (isl.), Anti. 165/L8
Antigua and Barbuda (ctry.) 165/M8
Antigua Guatemala, Guat. 200/D3
Antiguo Cauce del Río Bermejo (riv.), Arg. 212/D3
Antiguo Morelos, Mex. 199/F4
Antilly, Fr. 56/L4
Anṭilyās, Leb. 131/D1
Antimony, Ut, US 175/G1
Anting, China 106/L8
Antioch, Ca, US 172/C4
Antioch, Il, US 186/B3
Antioquia, Col. 204/C3
Antioquia (dept.), Col. 201/H5
Antipina, Rus. 95/N3
Antipodes (isls.), NZ 53/T8
Antique Airpower Museum, Ia, US 181/H3
Antisana (vol.), Ecu. 204/B5
Antler, Sk, Can. 182/D3
Antlers, Ok, US 179/G3
Antofagasta, Chile 212/B2
Antofagasta (pol. reg.), Chile 212/B2
Antofagasta de la Sierra, Arg. 212/C3
Antoing, Belg. 80/C2
Antokonosy Manambondro, Madg. 152/H8
Antón, Pan. 204/A2
Anton Lizardo (pt.), Mex. 199/P7
Antón Lizardo, Mex. 199/P7
Antongil (bay), Madg. 152/J6
Antonibe, Madg. 152/H6
Antoniesberg (peak), SAfr. 150/C4
Antonina do Norte, Braz. 207/G4
Antônio Carlos, Braz. 211/N6
Antonio de Biedma, Arg. 215/D5
Antônio João, Braz. 213/F2
Antonito, Co, US 175/J2
Antonovo, Bul. 77/H4
Antony, Fr. 56/J5
Antrain, Fr. 82/D4
Antratsyt, Ukr. 99/K3
Antrim (dist.), NI, UK 60/B2
Antrim (mts.), NI, UK 60/B1
Antrim, NI, UK 60/B2
Antrim, NH, US 187/L3
Antrodoco, It. 92/C3
Antronapiana, It. 86/E5
Antsakabary, Madg. 152/J6
Antsalova, Madg. 152/H7
Antsambalahy, Madg. 152/J6
Antsenavolo, Madg. 152/J8
Antsiafabositra, Madg. 152/H7
Antsirabato, Madg. 152/J6
Antsirabe, Madg. 152/H7
Antsirañana (prov.), Madg. 152/J6
Antsirañana, Madg. 152/J6
Antsla, Est. 67/M3
Antsohihy, Madg. 152/H6
Antubia, Gha. 140/E5
Antuco (vol.), Chile 214/C3
Antulai (mtn.), Malay. 117/E3
Antwerp, Oh, US 186/D4
Antwerp (Deurne) (int'l arpt.), Belg. 78/B6
Antwerpen, Belg. 78/B6
Anūpgarh, India 124/B5
Anūpshahr, India 122/B1
Anuradhapura, SrL. 121/D4
Anuradhapura (ruin), SrL. 121/D4
Anutt, Mo, US 179/J2
Anxi, China 104/D3
Anxi, China 113/H3
Anxin, China 106/G7
Anyama, C.d'Iv. 140/D5
Anyang, SKor. 107/F7
Anyang (riv.), SKor. 107/F7
Anyang, China 106/C3
A'nyêmaqên (mts.), China 104/D4
Anyer Kidul, Indo. 115/D3
Anyi, China 106/B4
Anykščiai, Lith. 67/L4
Anyuan, China 113/H3
Anyuan, China 113/G3
Anyuy (riv.), Rus. 105/M2
Anza (riv.), It. 86/E6
Anzá, Col. 207/K6
'Anzah, WBnk. 131/C4
Anzaldo, Bol. 212/C1
Anze, China 106/C3
Anzegem, Belg. 80/C2
Anzhero-Sudzhensk, Rus. 100/J4
Anzhou, China 106/G7
Anzin, Fr. 80/C3
Anzing, Ger. 85/E6
Anzio, It. 91/B5
Anzoátegui (state), Ven. 205/E2
Anzoátegui, Ven. 204/D2
Anzoátegui (int'l arpt.), Ven. 205/E2
Anzoátegui, Col. 207/K8
Anzola dell'Emilia, It. 89/E4
Ao Kham (pt.), Thai. 120/B4
Ao Phangnga NP, Thai. 120/B4
Aoba (isl.), Van. 162/F6
Aoga (isl.), Japan 111/F4
Aogaki, Japan 109/H5
Aoiz, Sp. 70/C5
Aojiang, China 113/J3
Aomori, Japan 108/B3
Aomori (pref.), Japan 108/B3
Aonla, India 122/B1
Aoquanxu, China 113/G3
Aoral (peak), Camb. 120/D3
Aorangi (mts.), NZ 161/J9
Áos, Gre. 75/J4
Aosta, It. 90/D1
Aoste, Fr. 90/B1
Aouara, FrG. 206/C1
Aoudaghast (ruin), Mrta. 140/C2
'Aouînat ez Zbil, Mrta. 140/C2
Aouk-Aoukale, Rsv. de Faune de l', Chad 142/D3
Aoukar (phys. reg.), Mrta. 140/C2
Aoulef, Alg. 137/F4
Aourou, Mali 140/C3
Aouste-sur-Sye, Fr. 90/B3
Aoyama, Japan 109/K6
Aozi, Chad 134/C4
Aozou, Chad 134/C4
Aozou Strip (reg.), Chad 134/C4
Ap Binh Chau, Viet. 120/D4
Ap Loc Thanh, Viet. 120/D4
Ap Long Hoa, Viet. 120/E4
Ap Luc, Viet. 120/D4
Ap Tan My, Viet. 120/E4
Ap Vinh Hao, Viet. 120/E4
Apa (riv.), Braz.,Par. 210/A4
Apache, Ok, US 179/E3
Apache (mts.), Tx, US 177/B2
Apache (lake), Az, US 175/G4
Apache Creek, NM, US 175/H4
Apache Junction, Az, US 175/G4
Apagado (vol.), Bol.,Chile 212/C2
Apalachee (bay), Fl, US 191/F3
Apalachee (riv.), Ga, US 189/F4
Apalachicola, Fl, US 191/F3
Apalachicola (riv.), Fl, US 191/F2
Apan, Mex. 199/L7
Apanovka, Kaz. 97/M1
Apaporis (riv.), Col. 204/D5
Aparados da Serra, PN de, Braz. 213/G4
Aparecida, Braz. 213/H2
Aparecida do Taboado, Braz. 213/G2
Aparición, Ven. 204/D2
Aparri, Phil. 114/C1
Apartadó, Col. 204/B3
Aparurén, Ven. 205/F3
Apataki, FrPol. 163/L6
Apátfalva, Hun. 76/E2
Apatin, Yugo. 76/D3
Apatity, Rus. 94/G2
Apatou, FrG. 206/C1
Apatzingán de la Constitución, Mex. 198/E5
Apauwar, Indo. 117/J4
Apaxco, Mex. 199/K7
Apaxtla de Castrejon, Mex. 199/F5
Ape, Lat. 67/M3
Apeldoorn, Neth. 78/C4
Apelern, Ger. 79/G4
Apen, Ger. 79/E2
Apennines (mts.), It. 55/F4
Apensen, Ger. 79/G2
Apere (riv.), Bol. 209/E4
Apex, NC, US 189/H3
Apéyémé, Togo 141/F5
Aphrodisias (ruin), Turk. 128/B2
Api, D.R. Congo 147/F2
Api (riv.), D.R. Congo 147/F2
Api (cape), Indo. 117/F4
Api (cape), Indo. 116/C3
Api (peak), Indo. 117/E5
Api (peak), Nepal 125/D5
Apia (cap.), WSam. 163/S9
Apía, Col. 207/K7
Apia (Fagali) (int'l arpt.), WSam. 163/S9
Apia (Faleolo) (int'l arpt.), WSam. 163/S9
Apiacá (riv.), Braz. 209/G3
Apiacás, Serra dos (mts.), Braz. 209/G3
Apiaí, Braz. 213/G3
Apishapa (riv.), Co, US 180/B5
Apizaco, Mex. 199/L7
Aplao, Peru 208/C5
Apo (mt.), Phil. 114/D4
Apodi, Braz. 207/G4
Apoera, Sur. 205/G3
Apolima (str.), WSam. 163/R9
Apolinario Saravia, Arg. 212/C3
Apollo Bay, Austl. 158/B3
Apollo Beach, Fl, US 190/L8
Apollonía, Gre. 75/J4
Apollonia (ruin), Libya 93/J4
Apolo, Bol. 208/D4
Apopka (lake), Fl, US 191/H3
Apopka, Fl, US 190/M6
Aporé (riv.), Braz. 213/G1
Apore (riv.), Braz. 210/B3
Apostle (isls.), Wi, US 183/J4
Apostle Islands Nat'l Lakeshore, Wi, US 183/J4
Apóstoles, Arg. 213/F3
Apostolic Palace, VatC. 91/G7
Apostolos Andreas (cape), Cyp. 130/D2
Apostolove, Ukr. 99/G4
Apoteri, Guy. 205/G3
Appalachian (mts.), US 165/J6
Appam, ND, US 182/C3
Appelscha, Neth. 78/D3
Appen, Ger. 79/G1
Appennino Abruzzese (mts.), It. 92/C3
Appennino Ligure (mts.), It. 71/H4
Appennino Napoletano (mts.), It. 92/D4
Appennino Tosco-Emiliano (mts.), It. 71/J4
Appennino Umbro-Marchigiano (mts.), It. 71/K5
Appenweier, Ger. 86/D1
Appenzell, Swi. 87/F3
Appenzell (canton), Swi. 87/F3
Appert Lake Nat'l Wild. Ref., ND, US 182/D4
Appignano, It. 89/G7
Appin, Austl. 159/E2
Appingedam, Neth. 78/D2
Apple (riv.), Wi, US 183/Q6
Apple Valley, Ca, US 192/C1
Apple Valley, Mn, US 183/P7
Appleby, Eng, UK 61/F2
Appleby, Tx, US 177/G2
Appleby Magna, Eng, UK 63/E1
Appleton, Mn, US 181/F1
Appleton, NY, US 186/V9
Appleton, Wi, US 186/B2
Appleton City, Mo, US 179/G1
Appling, Ga, US 189/F4
Appomattox, Va, US 189/H2
Appomattox Court House Nat'l Hist. Park, Va, US 189/H2
Approuage (riv.), FrG. 206/C2
Aprelevka, Rus. 94/Y9
Aprica, It. 87/G5
Aprica, Passo dell' (pass), It. 87/G5
Apricena, It. 74/D2
Aprilia, It. 91/B4
Apriltsi, Bul. 77/G4
Apsheronsk, Rus. 99/K5
Apsley, On, Can. 187/G2
Apsley (str.), Austl. 154/C2
Apsley Gorge NP, Austl. 158/E1
Apt, Fr. 90/B5
Apucarana, Braz. 213/G2
Apuiarés, Braz. 207/G3
Apulia (reg.), It. 93/H2
Apulo, Col. 207/L8
Apure (riv.), Ven. 197/H6
Apure (prov.), Ven. 204/D3
Apurímac (riv.), Peru 203/B4
Apurímac (dept.), Peru 208/C4
Āq Qal'eh, Iran 129/H2
Aqaba (gulf), Asia 103/B7
'Aqdā, Iran 129/H3
'Aqīq, Sudan 126/C5
Aqmola (oblast), Kaz. 125/A1
'Aqqābah, WBnk. 131/C4
Aqqikkol (lake), China 125/E4
'Aqrabah, WBnk. 131/C4
'Aqrah, Iraq 129/E2
Aqsay, Kaz. 97/K2
Aqtaū, Kaz. 97/J4
Aqtöbe, Kaz. 97/L2
Aqtöbe (prov.), Kaz. 97/L3
Aqtöbe (int'l arpt.), Kaz. 97/L2
Aqua Fria (riv.), Az, US 175/F4
Aquanaval (riv.), Mex. 198/E3
Aquapei (riv.), Braz. 213/G2
Aquarius (plat.), Ut, US 173/H4
Aquarius (mts.), Az, US 175/F3
Aquia, Peru 208/B3
Aquidabán (riv.), Par. 210/A4
Aquidauana, Braz. 213/F2
Aquidauana (riv.), Braz. 210/B3
Aquila, Swi. 87/E5
Aquileia, It. 89/G2
Aquiles Serdán, Mex. 177/B3
Aquilla, Tx, US 177/F2
Aquin, Haiti 201/H2
Aquino, It. 92/C5
Aquiraz, Braz. 207/G3
Aquitaine (pol. reg.), Fr. 70/C4
Ar (riv.), China 104/D4
Ar Horqin Qi, China 106/E2
Ar Rabaḑ, SAr. 135/H4
Ar Rafīd, Jor. 131/D3
Ar Rafīd, Syria 131/D3
Ar Rahad, Sudan 142/F2
Ar Raḩāminah, Egypt 139/C2
Ar Raḩmānīyah, Egypt 139/B2
Ar Ramādī, Iraq 129/E3
Ar Ramthā, Jor. 131/D3
Ar Rank, Sudan 142/G3
Ar Raqqah, Syria 128/D3
Ar Raqqah (prov.), Syria 128/D2
Ar Rashīdīyah, Leb. 131/C2
Ar Rass, SAr. 126/D3
Ar Rastan, Syria 130/E2
Ar Rawḑah, SAr. 126/D3
Ar Rawḑah, Yem. 144/C2
Ar Rawḑah, Egypt 139/B6
Ar Rāwuk, Yem. 144/D2
Ar Rayyān, Qatar 126/F3
Ar Rifā'ī, Iraq 129/F4
Ar Rīḩīyah, WBnk. 131/C6
Ar Riyāḑ (Riyadh) (cap.), SAr. 126/E4
Ar Riyān, Yem. 144/D2
Ar Rubayqī, Egypt 139/C4
Ar Rumaythah, Iraq 129/F4
Ar Rummān, Jor. 131/D4
Ar Ruşayfah, Jor. 131/E4
Ar Ruşayriş, Sudan 142/G3
Ar Ruţbah, Iraq 128/E3
Ar Ruways, Qatar 126/F3
Ar-Asgat, Mong. 104/F2
Ara (riv.), Ire. 58/B5
Ara (riv.), Japan 111/F2
Ara Terra, Eth. 144/B4
'Arab (gulf), Egypt 135/F2
Arab, Al, US 188/D3
'Arab (wadi), Jor. 131/D3
'Arabah (wadi), Egypt 128/B4
Araban, Turk. 128/D2
Arabatsk (bay), Ukr. 99/H5
Arabatsk Spit (pen.), Ukr. 99/H4
Arabi, Ga, US 191/G2
Arabian (sea), Asia 103/F8
Arabian (des.), Egypt 126/B3
Arabian (pen.), Asia 128/D4
Arabopó, Ven. 205/F3
Araç (riv.), Turk. 96/E4
Araç, Turk. 96/E4
Araça (riv.), Braz. 205/F4
Araca, Bol. 212/C1
Aracaju, Braz. 211/F1
Aracataca, Col. 204/C2
Aracati, Braz. 207/G4
Araçatuba, Braz. 213/G2
Araceli, Phil. 114/B3
Aracena, Sp. 72/B4
Aračinovo, FYROM 75/G1
Aracoiaba, Braz. 207/G4
Aracruz, Braz. 211/E3
Araçuaí, Braz. 211/E3
Araçuaí (riv.), Braz. 211/E3
Arad (prov.), Rom. 76/E2
Arad, Rom. 76/E2
Arada, Chad 142/D2
'Arādah, UAE 126/F4
Ārādān, Iran 129/H3
Arafali, Erit. 144/A2
Arafura (sea), Austl.,Indo. 162/C5
Aragats (peak), Arm. 97/H4
Araglin (riv.), Ire. 58/B5
Arago, Or, US 172/A2
Arago (cape), Or, US 172/A2
Aragón (reg.), Sp. 92/C2
Aragón (riv.), Sp. 92/C2
Aragon, NM, US 175/H4
Aragon, Ga, US 188/E3
Aragua (state), Ven. 205/E2
Araguacema, Braz. 206/D5
Araguaçu, Braz. 210/C2
Araguaia (riv.), Braz. 203/D3
Araguaia, PN do, Braz. 210/C1
Araguaiana, Braz. 210/C2
Araguaína, Braz. 206/D4
Araguari, Braz. 210/C3
Araguari (riv.), Braz. 206/D2
Araguari (riv.), Braz. 213/H1
Araguatins, Braz. 206/D4
Arai, Japan 111/F2
Araioses, Braz. 207/F3
Arāk, Iran 129/G3
Arak, Alg. 137/F4
Arakan (mts.), Myan. 119/F3
Arakawa, Japan 109/C2
Árakhthos (riv.), Gre. 75/G3
Araklı, Turk. 96/G4
Araku, India 121/D2
Aral, Kaz. 100/G5
Aral (sea), Kaz. 103/E5
Aralık, Turk. 129/F2
Aralsor (lake), Kaz. 97/H2
Aramac, Austl. 160/B3
Arāmbāgh, India 123/F4
Aramon, Fr. 90/A5
Ārān, Iran 129/G3
Aran (isls.), Ire. 57/P10
Aran Fawddwy (peak), Wal, UK 60/E6
Aranda de Duero, Sp. 72/D2
Arandelovac, Yugo. 76/E3
Arandis, Namb. 148/B4
Arandu, Pak. 124/A2
Arang, India 121/D1
Arani, Bol. 212/C1
Arani, India 121/C3
Aranjuez, Sp. 72/D2
Aranos, Namb. 148/C5
Aransas (riv.), Tx, US 177/F3
Aransas NWR, Tx, US 177/F3
Aransas Pass, Tx, US 177/F4
Arantina, Braz. 211/M6
Aranuka (isl.), Kiri. 162/G5
Aranyaprathet, Thai. 120/C3
Araouane, Mali 140/E2
Arapaho, Ok, US 178/E3
Arapahoe, Ne, US 180/E3
Arapahoe Nat'l Rec. Area, Co, US 180/A3
Arapahoe NWR, Co, US 173/K3
Arapawa (isl.), NZ 161/C3
Arapicos, Ecu. 208/B1
Arapiraca, Braz. 211/F1
Arapiuns (riv.), Braz. 205/H5
Arapongas, Braz. 213/G2
'Ar'ara, WBnk. 131/C4
Araracuara, Col. 204/C5
Araranguá, Braz. 213/G4
Araraquara, Braz. 213/G2
Araras, Braz. 213/H2
Ararat, Austl. 158/B3
Ararat, Mount (Ağrı) (peak), Turk. 129/F2
Arari, Braz. 207/E3
Arari (lake), Braz. 206/D3
Arāria, India 123/F2
Araripe, Chapada do (uplands), Braz. 207/F4
Araripina, Braz. 207/F4
Araruna, Braz. 207/H4
Aras (riv.), Iran 100/E6
Aras (riv.), Turk. 128/E2
Aratane (well), Mrta. 140/C2
Aratoca, Col. 204/C3
Aratuba, Braz. 207/G4
Arau, Malay. 120/C5
Arauá (riv.), Braz. 209/E2
Arauca (riv.), Col. 204/D3
Arauca (riv.), Col.,Ven. 205/E3
Arauca (dept.), Col. 204/D3
Arauca, Col. 204/D3
Arauco, Chile 214/B3
Arauquita, Col. 204/D3
Araure, Ven. 204/D2
Aravaca, Sp. 73/N9
Arawa, PNG 162/E5
Arawale Nat'l Reserve, Kenya 145/C2
Araxá, Braz. 210/D3
Araya (pen.), Ven. 205/E2
Arazatí, Uru. 215/K11
Ārba Minch', Eth. 142/H4
Ārbē Gona, Eth. 144/A4
Arbeca, Sp. 73/F2
Arbedo, Swi. 87/F5
Arbeláez, Col. 207/L8
Arbīl (gov.), Iraq 129/E3
Arboga, Swe. 66/F2
Arbois, Fr. 86/B4
Arbois, Mont d' (peak), Fr. 86/C6
Arboletes, Col. 204/B2
Arbon, Swi. 87/F2
Arbor Vitae, Wi, US 183/K5
Arbore, Eth. 142/H4
Arborfield, Sk, Can. 171/N1
Arborg, Mb, Can. 182/F2
Arbovale, WV, US 189/H1
Arbrå, Swe. 66/G1
Arbroath, Sc, UK 59/D3
Arbuckle (mts.), Ok, US 179/F3
Arbuckle (lake), Fl, US 191/H4
Arbuckle, Ca, US 172/B4
Arc (riv.), Fr. 70/F5
Arc (mtn.), Nv, US 172/E4
Arc-en-Barrois, Fr. 86/B2
Arc-et-Senans, Fr. 86/B3
Arc-lès-Gray, Fr. 86/B3
Arc-sur-Tille, Fr. 86/B3
Arcachon, Fr. 70/C4
Arcadia, Ca, US 192/F7
Arcadia, Fl, US 191/H4
Arcadia, In, US 186/C4
Arcadia, La, US 179/H4
Arcadia, Mo, US 188/B2
Arcadia, Ne, US 180/E3
Arcadia, NS, Can. 184/D4
Arcadia, Ok, US 179/F3
Arcadia, Wi, US 181/J1
Arcanum, Oh, US 186/D5
Arcata, Ca, US 172/A3
Arcata (bay), Ca, US 172/A3
Arce, It. 92/C4
Arceburgo, Braz. 211/K6
Arcelia, Mex. 199/E5
Arcen, Neth. 78/D6
Arcene, It. 88/C2
Arceto, It. 89/D4
Arcevia, It. 89/F7
Archangel (Arkhangel'sk), Rus. 94/J2
Archbold, Oh, US 186/D4
Archdale, NC, US 189/H3
Archena, Sp. 72/E3
Archer, Fl, US 191/G3
Archer (riv.), Austl. 155/F3
Archer Bend NP, Austl. 155/F3
Archer City, Tx, US 179/E4
Archerfield (arpt.), Austl. 160/E7
Archers Post, Kenya 145/B1
Arches, Fr. 86/C1
Arches NP, Ut, US 173/J4
Archibald, La, US 179/J4
Archibarca (peak), Arg. 212/C3
Archidona, Sp. 72/C4
Archie, Mo, US 179/G1
Archiestown, Sc, UK 59/C2
Archman, Trkm. 97/L5
Archman, Trkm. 97/L5
Arcipelago Toscano (isl.), It. 71/H5
Arcisate, It. 87/E6
Arco, It. 87/G6
Arco, Id, US 173/G2
Arco, Paso del (pass), Arg. 214/C3
Arcola, Sk, Can. 182/C3
Arcola, It. 88/C5
Arcola, Ms, US 188/B4
Arcole, It. 89/E3
Arcopongo, Bol. 212/C1
Arcos, Braz. 210/D4
Arcos de Jalón, Sp. 72/D2
Arcos de la Frontera, Sp. 72/C4
Arcos de Valdevez, Port. 72/A2
Arcosanti, Az, US 175/F3
Arcoverde, Braz. 207/G5
Arctic (ocean) 52/A1
Arctic (ocean) 216/U
Arctic Bay, Nun, Can. 167/H1
Arctic Circle 216/J
Arctic Coastal (plain), Ak, US 168/W12
Arctowski, Pol., Ant. 216/W
Arda (riv.), Bul. 96/C4
Arda (riv.), It. 89/C3
Ardabīl, Iran 129/G2
Ardabīl (gov.), Iran 129/G2
Ardagh, Ire. 58/A4
Ardagh, Ire. 58/C2
Ardahan, Turk. 97/G4
Ardakān, Iran 129/H3
Ardal, Iran 129/G4
Årdalstangen, Nor. 66/B1
Ardanuç, Turk. 97/G4
Ardatov, Rus. 94/J5
Arddleen, Wal, UK 62/C1
Ardea, It. 91/B4
Ardèche (dept.), Fr. 90/A3
Ardèche (riv.), Fr. 70/F4
Ardee, Ire. 60/B4
Arden, Mb, Can. 182/E2
Arden, Den. 66/C3
Arden (mt.), Austl. 157/H5
Arden, De, US 194/C4
Arden, Wa, US 170/F3
Arden-Arcade, Ca, US 193/M9
Ardennes (for.), Fr. 68/C4
Ardennes (dept.), Fr. 81/D4
Ardennes (for.), Belg. 70/F1
Ardennes, Canal des (canal), Fr. 81/D4
Ardenno, It. 87/F5
Arderin (peak), Ire. 58/C3
Ardersier, Sc, UK 59/B1
Ardeşen, Turk. 97/G4
Ardesio, It. 87/F6
Ardestān, Iran 129/H3
Ardez, Swi. 87/G4
Ardfinnan, Ire. 58/C5
Ardglass, NI, UK 60/C3
Ardila (riv.), Sp. 72/B3
Ardino, Bul. 77/G5
Ardivachar (pt.), Sc, UK 57/Q8
Ardle (riv.), Sc, UK 59/C3
Ardlethan, Austl. 159/C2
Ardmore, Ire. 58/C6
Ardmore, Ok, US 179/F3
Ardmore, Pa, US 194/C4
Ardmore, SD, US 180/C2
Ardmore, Tn, US 188/D3
Ardnacrusha, Ire. 58/B4
Ardnamurchan (pt.), Sc, UK 57/Q8
Ardoch Nat'l Wild. Ref., ND, US 182/F3
Ardon, Swi. 86/D5
Ardooie, Belg. 80/C2
Ardrahan, Ire. 58/B3
Ardres, Fr. 80/A2
Ardrossan, Sc, UK 59/B5
Ardrossan, Austl. 157/H5
Ards (pen.), Sc, UK 60/C3
Ards (dist.), NI, UK 60/C2
Ardsley, NY, US 195/K7
Åre, Swe. 64/E3
Areado, Braz. 211/K6
Arecibo, PR 197/M8
Areia Branca, Braz. 207/G4
Arena (pt.), Ca, US 172/B4
Arena de la Ventana Punta (pt.), Mex. 198/C3
Arenal (vol.), CR 201/E4
Arenápolis, Braz. 209/G4
Arenas de San Pedro, Sp. 72/C2
Arenas, Punta de (pt.), Arg. 215/C7
Arendal, Nor. 66/C2
Arendonk, Belg. 78/C6
Arendtsville, Pa, US 194/A4
Arenig Fawr (peak), Wal, UK 60/E6
Arenys de Mar, Sp. 73/L6
Arenzano, It. 88/B5
Arenzville, Il, US 181/J4
Areo, Ven. 205/F2
Areópolis, Gre. 75/H4
Arequipa, Peru 208/D5
Arequipa (dept.), Peru 208/C5
Arequito, Arg. 214/E2
Aresing, Ger. 84/E5
Arévalo, Sp. 72/C2
Areyonga, Austl. 157/G3
Āreza, Erit. 144/A2
Arezzo, It. 89/E7
Arezzo (prov.), It. 89/E5
Arfa' Deh, Iran 129/H3
Arga (riv.), Sp. 70/C5
Argadargada, Austl. 157/H2
Argalastí, Gre. 75/H3
Argamakmur, Indo. 115/C3
Argamasilla de Alba, Sp. 72/D3
Argamasilla de Calatrava, Sp. 72/C3
Argan, China 125/E3
Arganda, Sp. 73/N9
Argao, Phil. 114/C3
Argatone (peak), It. 92/C4
Argegno, It. 87/F6
Argelès-Gazost, Fr. 70/C5
Argelès-sur-Mer, Fr. 70/E5
Argelia, Col. 207/K7
Argen (riv.), Ger. 87/F2
Argenbühl, Ger. 87/F2
Argences, Fr. 83/E2
Argens (riv.), Fr. 71/G5
Argenta, It. 89/E4
Argenta, BC, Can. 170/F2
Argentan, Fr. 83/E3
Argentat, Fr. 70/D4
Argentera (peak), It. 90/D4
Argenteuil, Fr. 56/J5
Argentina (riv.), It. 88/A5
Argentina (ctry.) 203/C6
Argentino (lake), Arg. 215/B6
Argenton-sur-Creuse, Fr. 70/D3
Argentona, Sp. 73/L6
Argentré, Fr. 83/E4
Argeş (riv.), Rom. 96/C3
Argeş (prov.), Rom. 77/G3
Arghandab (riv.), Afg. 127/J2
Argideen (riv.), Ire. 58/B6
Argıthanı, Turk. 128/B2
Argo, Sudan 135/F5
Argolis (gulf), Gre. 93/J3
Argonne, Wi, US 183/K5
Argonne (for.), Fr. 68/C4
Argonne Nat'l Lab., Il, US 193/P16
Argopuro (peak), Indo. 115/F3
Árgos, Gre. 75/H4
Árgos Orestikón, Gre. 75/G2
Argostólion, Gre. 75/G3
Argueil, Fr. 83/G1
Arguello (pt.), Ca, US 168/B5
Arguenon (riv.), Fr. 82/C4
Argun (riv.), Asia 103/L5
Argun' (riv.), Rus. 101/M4
Argun (riv.), China,Rus 105/J1
Argungu, Nga. 141/G3
Argusville, ND, US 182/F4
Argut (riv.), Rus. 104/B2
Arguut, Mong. 104/E2
Argyle, Mn, US 182/F3
Argyle (lake), Austl. 154/C4
Argyle, Tx, US 176/K6
Argyll (reg.), Sc, UK 59/A4
Arhangay (prov.), Mong. 104/D2
Arhli, Niger 141/G2
Arholma (isl.), Swe. 65/C1
Arhreijît (well), Mrta. 136/B5
Arhrîjît, Mrta. 140/C2
Århus, Den. 66/D3
Århus (co.), Den. 66/D3
Ariah (mtn.), Austl. 159/C2
Ariah Park, Austl. 159/C2
Ariamsvlei, Namb. 150/B3
Ariari (riv.), Col. 204/C4
Arias, Arg. 214/E2
Aribinda, Burk. 141/E3
Arica, Col. 204/D5
Arica, Chile 212/B1
Arica (Chacalluta) (int'l arpt.), Chile 212/B1
Arıcak, Turk. 128/E2
Ariccia, It. 91/B4
Arichat, NS, Can. 185/G3
Arid (cape), Austl. 156/D5
Arida, Japan 110/D3
Aridhaía, Gre. 75/H2
Arido (peak), Ca, US 192/A1
Aridol (lake), WSah. 136/B4
Ariège (riv.), Fr. 70/D5
Ariel, Wa, US 170/C5
Arienzo, It. 92/D5
Arifiye, Turk. 77/K5
Ārifwāla, Pak. 124/B4
Arīḩā, Syria 130/E2
Arīḩā (Jericho), WBnk. 131/C5
Arikaree (riv.), Co, US 180/C4
Arilje, Yugo. 76/E4
Arima, Trin. 205/F2
Aringa, Ugan. 147/G2
Arinos (riv.), Braz. 209/G3
Arinos, Braz. 210/D2
Arinthod, Fr. 86/B5
Ario de Rosales, Mex. 199/E5
Ariogala, Lith. 67/K4
Aripao, Ven. 205/E3
Aripeka, Fl, US 190/K7
Aripine, Az, US 175/G3
Aripuanã, Braz. 209/G3
Aripuanã (riv.), Braz. 203/C3
Ariquemes, Braz. 209/F3
Aris, Namb. 148/C4
Arish, Austl. 160/B2
`Arīsh (wadi), Egypt 135/G2
'Arīsh (wadi), Egypt 128/C4
Arismendi, Ven. 204/D2
Arissa, Eth. 144/B3
Ariton, Al, US 191/F2
Arivaca, Az, US 175/G5
Arivechi, Mex. 198/C2
Arivonimamo, Madg. 152/H7
Ariza, Sp. 72/D2
Arize (riv.), Fr. 73/F1
Arizona (state), US 168/D5
Arizona, Arg. 214/D2
Arizona City, Az, US 175/G4
Arizpe, Mex. 198/C2
Årjäng, Swe. 66/E2
Arjay, Ky, US 188/F2
Arjeplog, Swe. 64/F2
Arjona, Col. 204/C2
Arjona, Sp. 72/C4
Arkabutla (dam), Ms, US 188/B3
Arkadak, Rus. 97/G2
Arkadelphia, Ar, US 179/H3
Arkaig (lake), Sc, UK 59/A3
Arkalokhórion, Gre. 75/J5
Arkansas (riv.), US 165/G6
Arkansas (state), US 169/H4
Arkansas City, Ks, US 179/F2
Arkansas Post Nat'l Mem., Ar, US 179/J3
Arkansas, Salt Fork (riv.), Ok, US 179/F2
Arkanū (peak), Libya 134/E4
Arkhángelos, Gre. 128/B2
Arkhangel'sk (int'l arpt.), Rus. 94/J2
Arkhangel'sk (oblast), Rus. 94/H3
Arkhangel'sk (Archangel), Rus. 94/J2
Arkhangel'skaya, Rus. 99/L5
Arkhangel'skoye, Rus. 94/W9
Arkhangel'skoye, Rus. 99/L2
Arkhara, Rus. 105/L2
Arkhipo-Osipovka, Rus. 96/F3
Arkhyz, Rus. 97/G4
Arklow, Ire. 60/B6
Arkona (cape), Ger. 66/E4
Arksey, Eng, UK 61/G4
Arkticheskiy Institut (isls.), Rus. 100/H2
Årla, Swe. 66/G2
Arlanda (int'l arpt.), Swe. 66/G2
Arlanza (riv.), Sp. 72/C1
Arlazón (riv.), Sp. 72/D1
Arlbergpass (pass), Aus. 87/G3
Arles, Fr. 90/A5
Arlesheim, Swi. 86/D3
Arlington, Az, US 175/F4
Arlington, Co, US 178/C1
Arlington, Ga, US 191/F2
Arlington, Ks, US 179/E2
Arlington, Ky, US 188/C2
Arlington, Mn, US 181/G1
Arlington, Ne, US 181/F3
Arlington, NY, US 187/K4
Arlington, Oh, US 186/E4
Arlington, Or, US 170/D5
Arlington, SD, US 181/F1
Arlington, Tn, US 188/C3
Arlington, Tx, US 176/K7
Arlington (lake), Tx, US 176/K7
Arlington, Va, US 194/A6
Arlington, Vt, US 187/K3
Arlington, Wa, US 170/C3
Arlington Heights, Il, US 186/C3
Arló, Hun. 69/L4
Arlon, Belg. 81/E4
Arltunga, Austl. 157/G2
Arluno, It. 88/B2
Arly (riv.), Fr. 86/C6
Arm (riv.), Sk, Can. 171/M2
Armada, Mi, US 193/G6
Armadale, Sc, UK 59/C5
Armadale (nbrhd.), Austl. 156/L7
Armagh (dist.), NI, UK 60/B3
Armagh, NI, UK 60/B3
Armançon (riv.), Fr. 70/F3
Armando Laydner (res.), Braz. 210/C4
Armant, Egypt 135/G3
Armavir, Arm. 97/H4
Armavir, Rus. 99/L5
Armenia (ctry.) 103/D5
Armenia, Col. 207/K8
Armentières, Fr. 80/B2
Armentières-en-Brie, Fr. 56/M5
Armería, Mex. 198/E5
Armero, Col. 207/L8
Armidabán (riv.), Par. 213/E2
Armidale, Austl. 158/D1
Armilla, Sp. 72/D4
Arminto, Wy, US 173/K2
Armona, Ca, US 174/C2
Armopa, Indo. 117/J4
Armour, SD, US 180/E2
Armoy, NI, UK 60/B1
Armstrong, Arg. 214/E2
Armstrong, BC, Can. 170/E2
Armstrong, On, Can. 183/K2
Armstrong, Mo, US 181/H4
Armstrong, Tx, US 177/F4
Armstrong Creek, Wi, US 183/K5
Armthorpe, Eng, UK 61/G4
Ārmūr, India 121/C2
Armutlu, Turk. 77/J5
Army Ammunition Plant, Il, US 181/K3
Army Dep., Or, US 172/D1
Army Ordnance Museum, Md, US 194/B5
Armyans'k, Ukr. 99/G4
Arnage, Fr. 83/F5
Arnager (int'l arpt.), Den. 66/F4
Arnaía, Gre. 75/H2
Arnaud (riv.), Qu, Can. 167/J3
Arnaudville, La, US 190/C2
Arnauti (cape), Cyp. 130/C2
Arnavutköy, Turk. 129/M6
Arncott, Eng, UK 63/E3
Arnedo, Sp. 72/D1
Arnegard, ND, US 182/C4
Arneiroz, Braz. 207/F4
Arnett, Ok, US 178/E2
Arnheim, Mi, US 183/K4
Arnhem, Neth. 78/C5
Arnhem (cape), Austl. 155/E3
Arnhem (bay), Austl. 155/E3
Arnhem Land (reg.), Austl. 154/D3
Arnhem Land (reg.) 153/C2
Arnhem Land Abor. Land, Austl. 154/D3
Arnières-sur-Iton, Fr. 83/G3
Arno (riv.), It. 92/F2
Arnö, Swe. 65/A2
Arnö, Swe. 65/A1
Arno (isl.), Mrsh. 162/G4
Arnold, Eng, UK 61/G6
Arnold, Ca, US 172/C4
Arnold, Md, US 194/B5
Arnold, Mi, US 183/L4
Arnold, Mo, US 188/B1
Arnold, Ne, US 180/D3
Arnold (riv.), Austl. 154/D3
Arnoldstein, Aus. 71/K3
Arnon (riv.), Fr. 70/E3
Arnouville-lès-Gonesse, Fr. 56/K5
Arnprior, On, Can. 187/H2
Arnsberg, Ger. 79/F6
Arnside, Eng, UK 61/F3
Arnstein, Ger. 84/C3
Arnstorf, Ger. 85/F5
Aro Usu (cape), Indo. 154/C2
Aroab, Namb. 150/B2
Aroases, Braz. 207/F4
Aroche, Sp. 72/B4
Arochukwu, Nga. 141/G5
Aroland, On, Can. 183/L2
Arolsen, Ger. 79/G6
Aroma, Sudan 142/H2
Aroma, Bol. 212/C1
Aron, Fr. 83/E4
Aron (riv.), Fr. 70/E3
Arona, It. 88/B2
Aronde (riv.), Fr. 80/B5
Aroostook, NB, Can. 184/D2
Arorae (isl.), Kiri. 162/G5
Aroroy, Phil. 114/C2
Åros, Nor. 64/S8
Arosa, Swi. 87/F4
Aroser Rothern (peak), Swi. 87/F4
Ærøskøbing, Den. 66/D4
Arp, Ga, US 191/G2
Arpaçay, Turk. 97/G4
Arpajon, Fr. 56/J6
Arpajon-sur-Cère, Fr. 70/E4
Arqalyq, Kaz. 125/A1
Arquata Scrivia, It. 88/B4
Arque, Bol. 212/C1
Arques, Fr. 80/B2
Arques-la-Bataille, Fr. 83/G1
'Arrāba, Isr. 131/C3
'Arrābah, WBnk. 131/C4
Arrah, India 123/E3
Arraha, Eth. 144/B3
Arraias (riv.), Braz. 209/H3
Arraias, Braz. 210/D2
Arraiján, Pan. 204/B2
Arrais (riv.), Fr. 73/F1
Arram, Eng, UK 61/H4
Arran (isl.), Sc, UK 57/R8
Arrancabarba (peak), Nic. 201/E4
Arras, Fr. 80/B3
Arreau, Fr. 70/D5
Arrecifal, Col. 204/D4
Arrecife, Sp. 136/B3
Arrecifes, Arg. 214/E2
Arrée, Monts d' (mts.), Fr. 70/B2
Arresø (lake), Den. 65/J7
Arrey, NM, US 175/J4
Arriaga, Mex. 200/C2
Arriba, Co, US 180/C4
Arrington, Va, US 189/H2
Arriola, Co, US 175/H2
Arriondas, Sp. 72/C1
Arrochar, Sc, UK 59/B4
Arrone, It. 91/B2
Arrone (riv.), It. 91/B3
Arronville, Fr. 56/J4
Arroscia (riv.), It. 88/B4
Arrou, Fr. 83/G4
Arroux (riv.), Fr. 70/F3
Arrow (riv.), Eng, UK 62/C2
Arrowbear Lake, Ca, US 192/C2
Arrowhead (lake), Tx, US 179/E4
Arrowhead NWR, ND, US 182/E4
Arrowrock (res.), Id, US 172/F2
Arrowrock (dam), Id, US 172/F2
Arrowsmith (mt.), NZ 161/B3
Arrowsmith (pt.), Austl. 155/E3
Arrowtown, NZ 161/B4
Arrowwood, Ab, Can. 171/H2
Arroyito, Arg. 212/D4
Arroyo de la Luz, Sp. 72/B3
Arroyo del Macho (riv.), NM, US 178/B4
Arroyo Grande, Bol. 208/D3
Arroyo Grande, Ca, US 174/B3
Arroyo Hondo, NM, US 178/B2
Arroyo Hondo (riv.), Ca, US 193/L12
Arroyo Trabuco (riv.), Ca, US 192/C3
Arroyo Valle (brook), Ca, US 193/L11
Arrufó, Arg. 212/D4
Års, Den. 66/C3
Ars-sur-Moselle, Fr. 81/F5
Arsanjān, Iran 129/H4
Arsen'yev, Rus. 105/L3
Ārsī (prov.), Eth. 144/A4
Arsiero, It. 89/E2
Arsk, Rus. 95/L4
Arslanköy, Turk. 130/D1
Årsta havsbad, Swe. 65/B1
Árta, Gre. 75/G3
Arta (gulf), Gre. 75/G3
'Arta, Djib. 144/B3
Artá, Sp. 73/G3
Arteaga, Mex. 198/E5
Arteixo, Sp. 72/A1
Artem, Rus. 105/L3
Artemisa, Cuba 201/F1
Artemivs'k, Ukr. 99/K3
Artemove, Ukr. 99/J3
Artemovskiy, Rus. 101/M4
Artena, It. 91/B4
Artenay, Fr. 83/G4
Artesia, Ca, US 192/F8
Artesia, Ms, US 188/C4
Artesia, NM, US 178/B4
Artesia Wells, Tx, US 177/E3
Arth, Swi. 87/E3
Arthies, Fr. 56/H4
Arthur (riv.), Austl. 156/C5
Arthur (pt.), Austl. 160/C3
Arthur, ND, US 182/F4
Arthur, Ne, US 180/D3
Arthur, WV, US 189/H1
Arthur City, Tx, US 179/G4
Arthur Kill (riv.), US 195/J9
Arthur's Pass NP, NZ 161/B3
Arthurdale, WV, US 187/G5
Arthur's (pass), NZ 161/B3
Arthurstown, Ire. 58/D5
Arti, Rus. 95/N4
Artigas (dept.), Uru. 213/E4
Artigas, Uru. 213/E4
Art'ik, Arm. 129/E1
Artogne, It. 88/D2
Artois (reg.), Fr. 68/A3
Artova, Turk. 128/D1
Artsyz, Ukr. 77/J3
Artuby (riv.), Fr. 90/C5
Artur Nogueira, Braz. 211/J7
Arturo Merino Benitez (int'l arpt.), Chile 214/N8
Artux, China 125/C4
Artvin (prov.), Turk. 97/G4
Artvin, Turk. 97/G4
Artyom, Azer. 97/J4
Aru, D.R. Congo 147/G2
Aru (isls.), Indo. 162/C5
Arua, Ugan. 147/G2
Aruba (isl.), Aru., Neth. 203/B1
Arucas, Sp. 136/B3
Arudy, Fr. 70/C5
Arujá, Braz. 211/K8
Arun (riv.), China 123/F2
Arun (riv.), Eng, UK 63/F5
Arunāchal Pradesh (state), India 119/F2
Arundel, Eng, UK 63/F5
Aruppukkottai, India 121/C4
'Ārūrah, WBnk. 131/C4
Arus (cape), Indo. 117/F3
Arusha (prov.), Tanz. 145/B3
Arusha, Tanz. 145/B2
Arusha Chine, Tanz. 145/B2
Arusha NP, Tanz. 145/B2
Arutua (isl.), FrPol. 163/L6
Aruwimi (riv.), D.R. Congo 133/E4
Arvada, Co, US 180/B4
Arvada, Wy, US 180/A1
Arvagh, Ire. 58/C2
Arvan (riv.), Fr. 90/C2
Arvayheer, Mong. 104/E2
Arve (riv.), Fr. 86/C6
Arvidsjaur, Swe. 64/F2
Arviat, Nun, Can. 166/G2
Arvika, Swe. 66/E2
Arvin, Ca, US 174/C3
Arvon (mt.), Mi, US 183/K4
Arvonia, Va, US 189/H2
Arwala, Indo. 154/B1
Aryamūn, Egypt 139/B2
Aryānah, Tun. 74/B4
Aryānah (gov.), Tun. 74/A4
Arys', Kaz. 125/A3
Arz (riv.), Fr. 70/B3
Arzachena, It. 74/A2
Arzamas, Rus. 95/K5
Arzano, It. 92/D6
Arzbach, Ger. 81/G3
Arzberg, Ger. 85/F2
Ärzen, Ger. 79/G4
Arzew, Alg. 138/E5
Arzgir, Rus. 97/H3
Arzignano, It. 89/E2
Arzl im Pitztal, Aus. 87/G3
Arzúa, Sp. 72/A1
Ås, Nor. 66/D2
As, Belg. 81/E1
Aš, Czh. 85/F2
As Sabkhah, Syria 128/D3
As Sabkhat al Kabīrah (swamp), Libya 134/C2
Aş Şaff, Egypt 139/C5
Aş Şāfī, Jor. 130/D4
Aş Şāfiyah, Sudan 142/F2
Aş Şāliḩīyah, Syria 128/E3
Aş Şāliḩīyah, Egypt 139/C3
As Sālimīyah, Kuw. 129/G4
As Sallūm, Egypt 134/E2
As Salmān, Iraq 129/F4
As Salţ, Jor. 131/D4
As Salwá, SAr. 126/F4
As Samāwah, Iraq 129/F4
Aş Şanamayn, Syria 131/E2
As Sanţah, Egypt 139/C3
Aş Şarafand, Leb. 131/C2
Aş Şarīḩ, Jor. 131/D3
Aş Şawma'ah, Yem. 144/C2
As Sīb, Oman 127/G4
As Sidr, Libya 134/C2
As Sidr, SAr. 126/C4
As Sinbillāwayn, Egypt 139/C3
Aş Şubayḩī, Jor. 131/D4
As Sudd (reg.), Sudan 133/F4
As Sufāl, Yem. 144/D2
Aş Şufayyah, Sudan 142/G2
Aş Şufīyāh, Egypt 139/C3
As Sukhnah, Syria 128/D3
As Sukhnah, Jor. 131/E4
As Suki, Sudan 142/G2
As Sulaymānīyah, Iraq 129/F3
As Sulaymānīyah (gov.), Iraq 129/F3
As Sulaymī, SAr. 126/D3
As Sulayyil, SAr. 126/E4
As Sulţān, Libya 134/C2
As Sumayḩ, Sudan 142/E3
Aş Şummān (range), SAr. 129/F5
As Su'ūdīyah, Egypt 139/C5
As Suwāqah, Jor. 131/E6
Aş Şuwār, Syria 128/E3
As Suwaydā', Syria 131/F3
As Suwaydā' (gov.), Syria 131/E3
As Suwayq, Oman 127/G4
Aş Şuwayrah, Iraq 129/F3
As Suways (gov.), Egypt 128/C4
Asab, Namb. 148/C5
Asaba, Nga. 141/G5

Name	Ref	Name	Ref	Name	Ref	Name	Ref	Name	Ref	Name	Ref
Asad (lake), Syria	128/D2	Ashikaga, Japan	109/C1	Assaria, Ks, US	179/F1	Atchafalaya		Attalla, Al, US	188/D3	Affargis, Fr.	56/H5	Austria (ctry.)	55/F4	Awash NP, Eth.	144/A3
Asadābād, Afg.	124/A2	Ashino (lake), Japan	61/G1	Assateague Island Nat'l		(riv.), La, US	177/J2	Attapu, Laos	188/D3	Agathella, Fr.	83/G1	Aussturhorn (pt.), Ice.	64/P7	Āwash Wenz	142/H3		
Asadābād, Iran	129/G3	Ashino (lake), Japan	109/C3	Seashore, Md, US	189/K1	Atchafalaya		Attapulgus, Ga, US	191/F2	Agathella, Austl.	160/B4	Autaugaville, Al, US	188/D4	Ayutla, Mex.	198/D4
Asagny, PN d', C.d'Iv.	140/D5	Ashiwada, Japan	109/B3	Asse, Belg.	81/D2	(bay), La, US	177/J3	Auger (falls), Id, US	173/F2	Audazes, Braz.	206/B3	Awasibbergi		Ayutla de los Libres,	
Asahan (riv.), Indo.	116/A3	Ashiya, Japan	109/H6	Assegairivier		Atchison, Ks, US	181/G4	Aigher, NI, UK	60/A3	Auterive, Fr.	70/D5	(peak), Namb.	148/B5	Mex.	141/E5
Asahi (riv.), Japan	110/C3	Ashiyasu, Japan	149/F5	Roto, NJ, US	194/D4	(riv.), On, Can.	167/H3	Augher (falls), Id, US	58/A4	Authie (riv.), Fr.	68/B3	Awaso, Gha.	141/E5	Ayutthaya (ruin) Thai.	120/C3
Asahi, Japan	111/G3	Ashizuri-Misaki		Assemini, It.	74/A3	Atebubu, Gha.	141/E5	Aughnacloy, NI, UK	187/J2	Authion (riv.), Fr.	83/E4	Awat, China	125/D3	Ayvacık, Turk.	75/K3
Asahi, Japan	109/M5	(cape), Japan	110/C4	Assen, Neth.	78/D3	Ateca, Sp.	72/E2	Attel (riv.), Ger.	85/F7	Aughrim, Ire.	60/B6	Awatere (riv.), NZ	161/C3	Ayvacık, Turk.	75/K3
Asahi, Japan	109/L5	Ashkal (lake), Tun.	138/L6	Assenede, Belg.	80/C1	Ateelva (riv.), Nor.	64/G1	Attendorn, Ger.	79/E6	Auglaize (riv.), Oh, US	186/D4	Awbārī (des.), Libya	137/H4	Aywaille, Belg.	81/E3
Asahi, Japan	109/F1	Ashkelon NP, Isr.	131/B5	Assens, Den.	66/C4	Atén, Bol.	208/D4	Augrabies Falls NP,		Augrim, Ire.	80/B5	Awbārī, Libya	134/B3	Az Zabadānī, Syria	131/C1
(peak), Japan	108/C2	(int'l arpt.), Trkm.	127/G1	Assentoft, Den.	66/D3	Atencingo, Mex.	199/L8	SAfr.	71/Q3	Augrim, Ire.	92/C4	Awbeg (riv.), Ire.	58/B5	Az Zabdānī, Syria	131/E1
Asahikawa, Japan	108/C2	Ashki'dah, Libya	134/B3	Assesse, Belg.	81/E3	Atenco, Mex.	199/Q10	Attert, Belg.	81/E4	Augsburg, Ger.	84/D6	Awdeghle, Som.	144/C5	Az Zāhirī yah,	
Asai, Japan	109/K5	Ashland, Al, US	188/E4	Assiniboia, Sk, Can.	171/M3	Atengo (riv.), Mex.	198/D4	Attica, Ks, US	179/E2	Augsburg (Mühlhausen)		Awe (lake), Sc, UK	59/A4	WBnk.	131/B6
Asaka, Japan	109/D2	Ashland, Ks, US	178/E2	Assiniboine		Aterno (riv.), It.	92/C3	Attica, Oh, US	186/D4	Auvergne, Fr.	70/E4	Awira Wenz		Az Zaqāzīq, Egypt	139/C3
Asake, Japan	109/G4	Ashland, Ky, US	189/F1	(riv.), Sk, Can.	182/D2	Atessa, It.	92/D3	Attica, It.	186/C4	Auvergne (pol. reg.), Fr.	70/E4	Awbre Wenz	144/A2	Az Zarqā' (gov.), Jor.	130/E3
'Asal (depr.), Djib.	144/B3	Ashland, La, US	179/H4	Assiniboine		Atfīḥ, Egypt	139/C6	Attigliano, It.	91/B2	Auvers-sur-Oise, Fr.	56/J4	Awish al Ḥajar,		Az Zarqā' (riv.), Jor.	131/D3
Asalē, Eth.	144/B3	Ashland, Me, US	179/H1	(riv.), Mb, Can.	166/F4	Atglen, Pa, US	81/D5	Attigny, Fr.	81/D5	Auxerre, Fr.	70/D4	Egypt	139/C2	Az Zawāmil, Egypt	139/C4
'Asalūyeh, Iran	129/H5	Ashland, Ms, US	188/D3	Ath, Belg.	80/C2	Atri, WBnk.	131/C4	Augusta, Austl.	152/A4	Auxi-le-Château, Fr.	68/B3	Awjilah, Libya	134/D2	Az Zāwiyah, Libya	93/G4
Asama-yama (peak),		Ashland, Wi, US	171/L5	Athabasca	170/G2	Atholl, Belg.	121/C4	Augusta (gulf), It.	121/C4	Auxi-le-Château, Fr.	74/D4	Awlil (pt.), Mi, US	186/E2	Az Zawīyah, Yem.	141/G5
Japan	111/F3	Ashland, NY, US	187/J3	Assiniboine Ind. Res.,		Attleboro, Ma, US	187/L4	Augusta, Ar, US	179/J3	Auxois, Fr.	70/E3	Awsīm, Egypt	139/C4	Az Zaydī yah, Yem.	144/B2

[Remainder of this atlas index page consists of many further dense columns of place-name entries with grid references, continuing the alphabetical sequence from "Asad" to "Babar." Due to the extreme density and very small type, a complete line-by-line transcription of every entry cannot be rendered reliably.]

Babar – Bangg

Babar (isl.), Indo. 154/C1
Babat, Indo. 115/C3
Babati, Tanz. 145/A3
Babatorun, Turk. 130/E1
Babatpur (int'l arpt.), India 122/D3
Babayevo, Rus. 94/G4
Babb, Mt, US 171/H3
Babbacombe (bay), Eng, UK 62/C6
Babbitt, Mn, US 183/J4
Babbitt, Nv, US 172/D4
B'abdā, Leb. 131/D1
Babelthuap (isl.), Palau 162/C4
Babenhausen, Ger. 87/G1
Babenhausen, Ger. 84/B3
Babensham, Ger. 85/F6
Baberu, India 122/C3
Babi (isl.), Indo. 115/B2
Babia (peak), Pol. 96/A2
Babian (riv.), China 119/H3
Bābil (gov.), Iraq 129/F3
Bābil, Egypt 139/B3
Bābil (Babylon) (ruin), Iraq 129/F3
Babīna, India 122/B3
Babinda, Austl. 160/D2
Babine (riv.), BC, Can. 166/C3
Bābol, Iran 129/H2
Bābol Sar, Iran 129/H2
Baboquivari (mts.), Az, US 175/G5
Baboua, CAfr. 142/B4
Babson Park, Fl, US 190/M8
Bābuganj, Bang. 123/H4
Babura, Nga. 141/H3
Babushkin (nbrhd.), Rus. 94/W9
Babuyan (isl.), Phil. 103/M8
Babuyan (chan.), Phil. 114/C1
Babylon, NY, US 195/E2
Babylon (Bābil) (ruin), Iraq 129/F3
Bac Can, Viet. 120/D1
Bac Giang, Viet. 120/D1
Bac Lieu, Viet. 120/D4
Bac Ninh, Viet. 112/E4
Bac Quang, Viet. 112/E4
Bacaadweeyn, Som. 144/C4
Bacabal, Braz. 207/E4
Bacabal, Braz. 206/B4
Bacadéhuachi, Mex. 198/C2
Bacajá (riv.), Braz. 206/D4
Bacalar (lag.), Mex. 200/D2
Bacalar, Mex. 200/D2
Bacan (isl.), Indo. 117/G4
Bacarra, Phil. 114/C1
Bacău (prov.), Rom. 77/H2
Bacău, Rom. 98/D4
Baccarat, Fr. 82/E3
Bacchiglione (riv.), It. 89/E2
Bacchus Marsh, Austl. 159/B3
Bacerac, Mex. 198/C2
Bacharach, Ger. 81/G3
Bacheng, China 106/L8
Bachhraon, India 122/B1
Bachíniva, Mex. 198/D2
Bachok, Malay. 115/C1
Back (riv.), Nun, Can. 166/F2
Back (riv.), Can. 165/G3
Back (riv.), Md, US 194/B5
Back Bay, NB, Can. 184/D3
Back Bay Nat'l Wild. Ref., Va, US 189/K2
Bačka (reg.), Yugo. 93/H1
Bačka Palanka, Yugo. 76/D3
Bačka Topola, Yugo. 76/D3
Backbone (mtn.), Md, US 187/G5
Bäckefors, Swe. 66/E2
Backnang, Ger. 84/C5
Backwell, Eng, UK 62/D4
Baco (mt.), Phil. 114/C2
Bacobampa, Mex. 198/C3
Bacolod, Phil. 114/C3
Bacoor, Phil. 114/F2
Bacqueville-en-Caux, Fr. 83/F1
Bácsalmás, Hun. 76/D2
Bács-Kiskun (prov.), Hun. 76/D2
Bacup, Eng, UK 61/F4
Bacuri, Braz. 207/E3
Bād, Iran 129/H3
Bad (riv.), SD, US 180/D1
Bad Abbach, Ger. 85/F5
Bad Axe, Mi, US 186/E3
Bad Bellingen, Ger. 86/D2
Bad Bergzabern, Ger. 84/A4
Bad Berneck, Ger. 85/E2
Bad Bocklet, Ger. 84/D2
Bad Brambach, Ger. 85/F2
Bad Breisig, Ger. 81/G3
Bad Brückenau, Ger. 84/C2
Bad Buchau, Ger. 87/F1
Bad Camberg, Ger. 84/B2
Bad Doberan, Ger. 66/D4
Bad Driburg, Ger. 79/G5
Bad Dürrheim, Ger. 84/B4
Bad Dürrheim, Ger. 87/E1
Bad Ems, Ger. 81/G3
Bad Endorf, Ger. 85/F7
Bad Essen, Ger. 79/F4
Bad Freienwalde, Ger. 69/H2
Bad Gandersheim, Ger. 79/H5
Bad Grund, Ger. 79/H5
Bad Hall, Aus. 85/H6
Bad Harzburg, Ger. 79/H5
Bad Heilbrunn, Ger. 87/H2
Bad Herrenalb, Ger. 84/B5
Bad Hofgastein, Aus. 71/K3
Bad Homburg vor der Höhe, Ger. 84/B2
Bad Honnef, Ger. 81/G2
Bad Hönningen, Ger. 81/G2
Bad Karlshafen, Ger. 79/G5
Bad Kissingen, Ger. 84/D2
Bad Kohlgrub, Ger. 87/H2
Bad König, Ger. 84/C3
Bad Königshofen, Ger. 84/D2
Bad Kreuznach, Ger. 81/G4
Bad Krozingen, Ger. 86/D2
Bad Langensalza, Ger. 79/H6
Bad Lauterberg, Ger. 79/H5
Bad Leonfelden, Aus. 85/H5
Bad Liebenzell, Ger. 84/B5
Bad Lippspringe, Ger. 79/F3
Bad Marienberg, Ger. 81/G2
Bad Mergentheim, Ger. 84/C4

Bad Munder am Deister, Ger. 79/G4
Bad Münster am Stein, Ger. 81/G4
Bad Nauheim, Ger. 84/B2
Bad Nenndorf, Ger. 79/G4
Bad Neuenahr-Ahrweiler, Ger. 81/G2
Bad Neustadt an der Saale, Ger. 84/D2
Bad Oeynhausen, Ger. 79/F4
Bad Orb, Ger. 84/C2
Bad Peterstal-Griesbach, Ger. 86/E1
Bad Plaas, SAfr. 151/E2
Bad Pyrmont, Ger. 79/G5
Bad Ragaz, Swi. 87/F4
Bad Reichenhall, Ger. 71/K3
Bad River Ind. Res., Wi, US 183/J4
Bad Rothenfelde, Ger. 79/F4
Bad Sachsa, Ger. 79/H5
Bad Salzdetfurth, Ger. 79/G4
Bad Salzschlirf, Ger. 84/C1
Bad Salzuflen, Ger. 79/F4
Bad Salzungen, Ger. 68/F2
Bad Sankt-Leonhard im Lavanttal, Aus. 71/L3
Bad Sassendorf, Ger. 79/F5
Bad Schallerbach, Aus. 85/G6
Bad Schwalbach, Ger. 81/H3
Bad Schwartau, Ger. 66/D5
Bad Segeberg, Ger. 66/D5
Bad Soden-Salmünster, Ger. 84/C2
Bad Sooden-Allendorf, Ger. 79/G6
Bad Tölz, Ger. 87/H2
Bad Vilbel, Ger. 84/B2
Bad Waldsee, Ger. 87/F2
Bad Wildungen, Ger. 79/G6
Bad Wimpfen, Ger. 84/C4
Bad Wimsbach-Neydharting, Aus. 85/G6
Bad Windsheim, Ger. 84/D3
Bad Wörishofen, Ger. 87/G1
Bad Wurzach, Ger. 87/F2
Bad Zell, Aus. 85/H6
Bad Zwischenahn, Ger. 79/F2
Badaga Jaran, China 101/L5
Badajós (lake), Braz. 209/F1
Badajoz, Sp. 72/B3
Badalona, Sp. 73/L7
Badalucco, It. 88/A5
Badanah, SAr. 126/D2
Badaohao, China 107/A2
Badas (isls.), Indo. 115/D2
Baddeck, NS, Can. 185/G2
Baddomalhi, Pak. 124/C4
Bade, Indo. 155/E1
Badeggi, Nga. 141/G4
Bāgrākot, India 123/G2
Bagong, China 114/E5
Bagong, Swi. 87/E3
Bagration ovsk, Rus. 67/J4
Bagre, Braz. 206/D3
Bagshot, Eng, UK 56/A3
Bagua Grande, Peru 208/B2
Baguio, NY, US 187/J3
Baguio, Phil. 114/C1
Baguirmi (reg.), Chad 142/C2
Bagumbong, Phil. 115/C1
Bagusa, Eth. 142/H3
Bagwell, Tx, US 182/F3
Bagzane (peak), Niger 141/H2
Bahadurganj, Nepal 124/E2
Bahadurganj, India 124/D2
Bahamas (ctry.) 165/K7
Bahāragora, India 124/E3
Baharampur, India 124/D5
Bahāwalnagar, Pak. 124/B5
Bahāwalpur, Pak. 124/A5
Bahçe, Turk. 130/D2
Bahçesaray, Turk. 128/D2
Bahera, India 123/F2
Bahī, Tanz. 145/A3
Bahia (state), Braz. 207/G5
Bahía Asunción, Mex. 198/B3
Bahía Blanca, Arg. 214/E3
Bahía Bustamante, Arg. 214/D5
Bahía de Caráquez, Ecu. 208/A4
Bahía de los Ángeles, Mex. 198/B2
Bahia, Indo. 113/H2
Bahía Mansa, Chile 214/B4
Bahía San Blas, Arg. 214/E4
Bahía Solano, Col. 204/B3
Bahía Thetis, Arg. 215/D7
Bahía, Islas de la (isls.), Hon. 196/D4
Bahir Dar, Eth. 142/H3
Bahla, India 123/F2
Bahla, Oman 127/G4
Baixo Guandu, Braz. 211/E3
Bahraich, India 122/C1
Bahrain (ctry.) 127/F4
Bahrain 127/F4
Bahrain (int'l arpt.), Bahr. 126/F3
Bajina Bašta, Yugo. 76/D4
Bahrām Chāh, Afg. 127/H3

Bakhchysaray, Ukr. 99/G5
Bakhmach, Ukr. 99/G3
Bakhra, India 123/F2
Bakhshāyesh, Iran 129/F2
Bakhta, Rus. 100/J3
Bākhtarān, Iran 129/F3
Bakhteger (lake), Iran 129/H4
Bakhti'ārī (gov.), Iran 129/G4
Bakhuis (mts.), Sur. 205/G4
Bakia, CAfr. 142/D4
Bakkaflói (bay), Ice. 64/P6
Baklan, Turk. 128/B2
Bako, Eth. 142/H3
Bako, Eth. 142/H4
Bakokandi (riv.), D.R. Congo 142/F5
Bakony (mts.), Hun. 93/H1
Bakora Corr. Game Rsv., Ugan. 145/A2
Bakora Corridor Game Rsv., Ugan. 145/A2
Bakori, Nga. 141/G4
Bakouma, CAfr. 142/D4
Bakoumba, Gabon 146/C3
Bakovský Potok (riv.), Czh. 71/G3
Bakoye (riv.), Mali 140/C4
Baku (cap.), Azer. 129/G1
Baku (str.), Azer. 97/J4
Baku, D.R. Congo 146/D3
Bakungan, Indo. 115/B2
Bakwa-Kenge, D.R. Congo 146/D2
Bal Harbour, Fl, US 190/P11
Balā, Turk. 128/C2
Bala, Wal, UK 60/E6
Bala, On, Can. 187/G2
Bā'ir (wadi), Jor. 130/E4
Balabac (lake), China 117/F2
Balabac (str.), Phil. 162/A4
Balabac, Phil. 117/E2
Balabac 114/A4
Balabanovo, Rus. 94/H5
Balad, Iraq 129/F3
Balagansk, Rus. 101/J4
Bālāghāt, India 122/C5
Balagtas, Phil. 114/E6
Balaguer, Sp. 73/F2
Balaïnich, Sk, UK 57/G8
Bajennie, Sk, Can. 171/L1
Balaïtous (peak), Fr. 70/C5
Balk, Neth. 78/C3
Balaka, Malw. 149/G2
Balakān, Bang. 123/H4
Balakhna, Rus. 95/J4
Balakkassar, Pak. 124/B3
Balaklava, Austl. 157/H5
Balakliya, Ukr. 99/J3
Balakovo, Rus. 97/H1
Balla, Ire. 58/A2
Balambangan (isl.), Malay. 114/X
Balan, Gui. 140/C4
Balan, Rom. 98/D4
Balancán, Mex. 200/D2
Balanga, Phil. 114/C3
Balangala, D.R. Congo 146/D2
Bālāngīr, India 121/D1
Balārān, Nor. 98/C4
Balaka, Ecu. 208/B1
Ballé, Mali 140/C3
Balaqtar, Egypt 139/B2
Balarāmpur, India 123/F4
Balashikha, Rus. 94/W9
Balashov, Rus. 99/M2
Balasore (Baleshwar), India 118/D3
Balassagyarmat, Hun. 69/K4
Balaton (lake), Hun. 93/H1
Balatonfenyves, Hun. 73/G2
Balatonfüred, Hun. 76/D2
Balatonszabadi, Hun. 73/H2
Balatonszentgyörgy, Hun. 76/C2
Bājīl, Yem. 144/B2
Bajina Bašta, Yugo. 76/D4
Bājitpur, Bang. 123/H3

Bajmbat (mt.), Austl. 158/E1
Bajmok, Yugo. 76/D3
Bajo Boquete, Pan. 201/F4
Bajo de Gualicho (plain), Arg. 214/D4
Bajo de Sta. Rosa (plain), Arg. 214/D4
Bajo Nuevo (bank), Col. 197/F4
Bajo Palena, Chile 214/B4
Bajone (pt.), Moz. 149/J2
Bajos Caracoles, Arg. 215/C6
Bajram Curri, Alb. 105/E5
Bājura, Nepal 122/C1
Baka, Slvk. 76/C2
Bakaba, Chad 142/C4
Bakal, Rus. 95/N5
Bakala, CAfr. 142/D4
Bakali (riv.), D.R. Congo 146/D4
Bakaly, Rus. 95/M5
Bakanas (riv.), Kaz. 114/B5
Bakaoré, Chad 142/D2
Bakar, Cro. 71/L4
Bākārganj, Bang. 123/H4
Bakau, Gam. 140/A3
Bakayan (peak), Indo. 117/E3
Bakel, Sen. 140/B3
Bakel, Neth. 78/C5
Baker (beach), Ok, US 179/E3
Baker, Mt, US 182/B4
Baker, La, US 190/C2
Baker City, Ks, US 179/F2
Baker, Fl, US 190/E2
Baker (isl.), Pac., US 163/H4
Baker, Or, US 172/E1
Bakersville, NY, US 166/G2
Baker (riv.), Chile 215/B5
Baker (mt.), Can. 182/D2
Baker (riv.), Wa, US 170/D3
Baker Hill, Al, US 191/F2
Baker Lake, Nun, Can. 166/G2
Bakere, D.R. Congo 147/G2
Bakersfield, Ca, US 174/C3
Bakersville, NC, US 189/F2
Bakewell, Eng, UK 61/G5
Bakhchysaray, Ukr. 99/G5

Balba (res.), Braz. 203/D3
Balboa (nbrhd.), Ca, US 192/G8
Balboa, Pan. 201/G4
Balcarce, Arg. 214/F3
Balcarres, Sk, Can. 177/E2
Balcary (pt.), Sc, UK 60/E2
Balch Springs, Tx, US 176/L7
Balchik, Bul. 161/B4
Balclutha, NZ 161/B4
Balcombe, Eng, UK 63/F4
Bald (peak), Va, US 188/C2
Bald (pt.), Austl. 154/B5
Bald (mtn.), Wa, US 170/D4
Balcony, Or, US 189/H1
Bald Eagle Mtn., Pa, US 187/J3
Baldíssero, It. 88/A2
Bald Knob, Ar, US 179/J3
Bald Rock NP, Austl. 158/E1
Baldock, Eng, UK 63/F3
Baldhill (dam), ND, US 182/E4
Baldock, Eng, UK 63/F3
Baldoyle, Ire. 58/D3
Baldur, Mb, Can. 182/E3
Baldy, Pa, US 196/B2
Baldy (mtn.), Wa, US 170/D4
Baldwin, Fl, US 191/H2
Baldwin, La, US 190/C3
Baldwin, Mi, US 186/D3
Baldwin, ND, US 182/D3
Baldwin, NY, US 195/L9
Baldwin City, Ks, US 179/K9
Baldwin Harbour, Ct, US 195/L9
Baldwin Park, Ca, US 192/G7
Baldwinsville, NY, US 187/H3
Baldwyn, Ms, US 188/C3
Baldy (mtn.), Can. 182/D2
Baldy (peak), Az, US 175/H4
Baldy, easton, NJ, US 196/C2
Baldy (hill), Ne, US 180/D3
Baldy'farnan, Ire. 58/B1
Baldygar, Ire. 58/B2
Balearic (isls.), Sp. 73/G3
Balearic (isls.), Sp. 73/G3
Balbina (res.), Braz. 203/D3

Baltray, Ire. 60/B4
Baltrum (isl.), Ger. 79/E1
Bælum, Den. 66/D3
Bælum, Den. 66/D3
Balurghāt, India 123/G3
Balvard, Iran 129/H4
Balve, Ger. 79/F6
Balvi, Lat. 67/M3
Balvina Aboriginal Reserve, NB, Can. 184/D2
Balya, Turk. 96/C5
Balyamkari, Kyr. 100/H5
Balykshi, Kaz. 97/J3
Balzar, Ecu. 204/B5
Balzers, Lcht. 87/F3
Bam (prov.), Burk. 141/E3
Bam (leke), China 125/F5
Bama, Nga. 141/J3
Bamaji (lake), On, Can. 183/J2
Bamako (cap.), Mali 140/C3
Bamana, D.R. Congo 146/C3
Bamba, China 113/J2
Bamba, D.R. Congo 146/D2
Bambama, Congo 146/C3
Bambamarca, Peru 208/B2
Bamba (riv.), Nic. 201/E3
Bambara, Chad 142/C3
Bambara Maoundé, Mali 140/E3
Bambari, CAfr. 142/D4
Bamber Ridge, Eng, UK 84/D3
Bambesa, D.R. Congo 147/G2
Bambesi, Eth. 142/G3
Bambi, Ang. 148/B2
Bamenda, Camr. 141/H5
Bamforth Nat'l Wild. Ref., Wy, US 180/B4
Bamingui, CAfr. 142/C3
Bamingui-Bangoran, CAfr. 142/C3
Bamingui-Bangoran, PN de, CAfr. 142/C3
Bammental, Ger. 84/B4
Bamnet Narong, Thai. 120/C3
Bāmor Kalān, India 122/B3
Bampūr (riv.), Iran 127/H3
Bampūr, Iran 127/H3
Bamyili, Austl. 154/D3
Ban Ay Rieng, Laos 120/D3
Banaba (isl.), Kiri. 162/G5

233
Bangh – Beach

Banghiang (riv.), Laos 120/D2
Bangil, Indo. 115/F3
Bangka (isl.), Indo. 103/K10
Bangka (str.), Indo. 116/B4
Bangkalan, Indo. 115/F3
Bangkaru (isl.), Indo. 115/B2
Bangkinang, Indo. 115/C2
Bangkir, Indo. 117/F3
Bangko, Indo. 115/C3
Bangkok (int'l arpt.), Thai. 120/C3
Bangkok (Krung Thep) (cap.), Thai. 120/C3
Bangkok, Bight of (bay), Thai. 119/H5
Bangladesh(ctry.) 103/H7
Bangli, Indo. 115/F3
Bangma (mts.), China 112/C4
Bangor, Sk, Can. 182/C2
Bangor, NI, UK 60/C2
Bangor, Wal, UK 60/D5
Bangor, Mi, US 186/C3
Bangor, Fr. 82/B6
Bangor, Me, US 167/K4
Bangor, Pa, US 194/C2
Bangor-is-y-Coed, Wal, UK 61/F6
Bangoran (riv.), CAfr. 142/C3
Bāngriposi, India 123/F4
Bangs (mt.), Az, US 175/F2
Bangs, Tx, US 176/E2
Bangu, D.R. Congo 147/E5
Bangued, Phil. 114/C1
Bangui (cap.), CAfr. 142/C4
Bangui (int'l arpt.), CAfr. 142/C4
Bangui, EqG. 146/B2
Bangui, Phil. 114/C1
Bangunpurba, Indo. 115/B2
Bangzha, China 112/E3
Banhā, Egypt 139/C4
Banhine, PN de, Moz. 149/G4
Baní, DRep. 197/G4
Bani, CAfr. 142/D4
Bani (riv.), Mali 140/D3
Banī Mazār, Egypt 135/F2
Banī Suhaylah, Gaza 131/A6
Banī Suwayf (gov.), Egypt 128/B3
Banī Suwayf, Egypt 139/C6
Banī 'Ubayd, Egypt 139/C2
Bāni Walīd, Libya 134/B2
Bani-Bangou, Niger 141/F3
Bania, CAfr. 146/D2
Baniachang, Bang. 123/H3
Banian, Gui. 140/C4
Bánica, DRep. 201/J2
Banifing (riv.), Mali 140/D3
Banihāl (pass), India 124/C3
Banikoara, Ben. 141/F4
Banisa, Kenya 144/B5
Banister (riv.), Va, US 189/H2
Bāniyās, Syria 130/D2
Banja Koviljača, Yugo. 76/D3
Banja Luka, Bosn. 76/C3
Banjar, Indo. 115/E3
Banjarmasin, Indo. 116/D4
Banjia, China 120/B1
Banjiang, China 113/F3
Banjul (cap.), Gam. 140/A3
Banjul (Yundum) (int'l arpt.), Gam. 140/A3
Bankä, Azer. 129/G2
Bānka, India 123/F3
Banka Banka, Austl. 154/D4
Bankas, Mali 140/E3
Bankengting, China 113/H3
Bankeryd, Swe. 66/F3
Bankfoot, Sc, UK 59/C3
Bankhead, Sc, UK 59/D2
Bankhead (lake), Al, US 188/D4
Bānki, India 123/E4
Bankilare, Niger 141/F3
Banks, Al, US 191/F2
Banks (pen.), NZ 153/H7
Banks (cape), Austl. 158/B3
Banks (isls.), Van. 162/F6
Banks (isl.), NW, Can. 165/E2
Banks (isl.), Austl. 155/F2
Banks (lake), Wa, US 170/E4
Banks (str.), Austl. 153/D5
Bankstown (arpt.), Austl. 160/G8
Bankstown (nbrhd.), Austl. 160/H8
Bānkurā, India 123/F4
Bankya, Bul. 75/H1
Banmankhi, India 123/F3
Banmauk, Myan. 112/B3
Banmian, China 113/H3
Bann (riv.), NI, UK 60/B3
Bann (riv.), Ire. 58/D4
Banna (riv.), It. 88/A3
Bannack, Mt, US 172/G1
Bannalec, Fr. 82/B5
Bannang Sata, Thai. 115/C1
Banner, Wy, US 173/K1
Banner, Ky, US 188/F2
Banning, Ca, US 174/D4
Bannock (pass), Id, US 172/G1
Bannockburn, Sc, UK 59/C4
Bannockburn, Austl. 159/B4
Bannockburn Battlesite, Sc, UK 59/C4
Bannow (bay), Ire. 58/D5
Bannu, Pak. 124/A3
Banon, Fr. 90/B4
Baños, Ecu. 208/B1
Banphot Phisai, Thai. 120/B3
Banpo Ruins, China 106/B4
Bānpur, India 121/E2
Bansberia, India 123/G4
Bānsdīh, India 123/E3
Bansha, Ire. 58/B5
Banshi, China 113/G3
Bānsi, India 122/B3
Bānsi, India 122/D2
Bansihāri, India 123/G3
Bansin, Ger. 66/F5
Bansko, Bul. 75/H2
Banstead, Eng, UK 56/C3
Bānswāra, India 118/B3
Bantayan (isl.), Phil. 114/C3
Bantayan, Phil. 114/C3
Banté, Ben. 141/F4
Banteer, Ire. 58/B5
Bantenan (cape), Indo. 115/F3
Bantong Group (isls.), Thai. 120/B5
Bantry, Ire. 58/A6
Bantry (bay), Ire. 58/A6
Bantvāl, India 121/B3
Bañuelo (peak), Sp. 72/C3
Banūr, India 124/D4
Banxi, China 113/F2
Banyak (isls.), Indo. 116/A3
Banyo, Camr. 142/A4
Banyoles, Sp. 73/G1
Banyuwangi, Indo. 115/F3
Banz, PNG 155/G1
Banzare (coast), Ant. 216/J
Banzart (lake), Tun. 74/A4
Banzart (Bizerte), Tun. 74/A4
Bao Ha, Viet. 112/E4
Bao Lac, Viet. 112/E4
Bao Loc, Viet. 120/D4
Baode, China 106/B3
Baodi, China 106/H7
Baoding, China 106/G7
Baofeng, China 106/C4
Baoguangsi, China 112/E2
Baoji, China 104/F5
Baojing, China 119/J2
Baokang, China 106/B5
Baoro, CAfr. 142/B4
Baoruco (mts.), DRep. 201/J2
Baoshan, China 112/C3
Baoshan, China 106/L8
Baotian, China 112/E3
Baotou, China 106/B2
Baoulé (riv.), Mali 140/C3
Baoxing, China 112/D2
Baoxinji, China 113/G1
Baoying, China 106/D4
Bāpatla, India 121/D3
Bapaume, Fr. 80/B3
Baptistown, NJ, US 194/C2
Bāqa el Gharbiyya, Isr. 131/C4
Baqên, China 104/C5
Ba'qūbah, Iraq 129/F3
Baquedano, Chile 212/B2
Bar, Yugo. 75/F1
Bar (riv.), Fr 68/C4
Bar, Ukr. 98/D3
Bar Bigha, India 123/E3
Bar el Ksaïb (well), Mali 136/D5
Bar Harbor, Me, US 184/C3
Bar Hill, Eng, UK 63/G2
Bar-le-Duc, Fr. 81/E6
Bar-sur-Aube, Fr. 70/F2
Bar-sur-Seine, Fr. 70/F2
Bara, Swe. 66/E4
Bara, Indo. 117/G4
Barā Bangāhal, India 124/D3
Bāra Banki, India 122/C2
Bārā Lācha La (pass), India 124/D3
Baraawe, Som. 145/D1
Barabai, Indo. 116/E4
Barabinsk, Rus. 100/H4
Baraboo, Wi, US 181/K2
Baracaldo, Sp. 70/B5
Barachois, NB, Can. 184/E2
Barachois, Qu, Can. 184/E1
Barachois (pt.), NS, Can. 185/G3
Baracoa, Cuba 201/H1
Barada (riv.) Syria 130/E3
Baradero, Arg. 215/J10
Baradine, Austl. 158/D1
Barāgaon, India 123/E3
Baragoi, Kenya 145/B1
Baragua, Ven. 204/D2
Baraguá, Cuba 201/G1
Bārah, Sudan 142/F2
Barajas (int'l arpt.), Sp. 73/N9
Barajas, Sp. 73/N9
Barajevo, Yugo. 76/E3
Barāk (riv.), India 112/B3
Baraka, D.R. Congo 147/G4
Baraka (riv.), Sudan 142/H1
Barakah, Sudan 142/E3
Barākar (riv.), India 123/F3
Barakī Barak, Afg. 127/J2
Bārākot, India 121/E1
Baralaba, Austl. 160/C4
Baram (cape), Malay. 116/D3
Baram (riv.), Malay. 116/D3
Bar'am NP, Isr. 131/C2
Barama, India 123/H2
Barama (riv.), Guy. 205/G3
Baramanni, Guy. 205/G3
Baramita, Guy. 205/F3
Baramsar, India 124/C5
Baramula, India 124/C2
Baran', Bela. 67/P4
Bāran, India 118/C2
Baranagar, India 123/G4
Baranga, D.R. Congo 147/F2
Barani (well), Alg. 136/E4
Baranikha, Rus. 101/S3
Baranivka, Ukr. 98/D2
Barano d'Ischia, It. 92/C6
Baranoa, Col. 204/C2
Baranof (isl.), Ak, US 166/C3
Baranya (prov.), Hun. 76/C3
Barão de Cocais, Braz. 211/E3
Barão de Grajaú, Braz. 207/F4
Barão de Melgaço, Braz. 209/H5
Baraolt, Rom. 77/G2
Baraque de Fraiture (hill), Belg. 81/E3
Baras, Phil. 114/D2
Barat Daya (isls.), Indo. 117/G5
Barate, Indo. 154/A2
Baratier, Congo 146/C4
Barato, India 112/B3
Barauli, India 123/E2
Baraut, India 124/D5
Baraya, Col. 204/C4
Barbacena, Braz. 210/E4
Barbacoas, Col. 204/B4
Barbacoas, Ven. 207/P8
Barbados(ctry) 165/M8
Barbalha, Braz. 207/G4
Barbaros, Turk. 77/H5
Barbas (cape) Mor. 136/A5
Barbastro, Sp. 73/F1
Barbate de Franco, Sp. 72/C4
Barbeau (peak), Nun, Can. 167/T6
Barbentane, Fr. 90/A5
Barberà del Vallès, Sp. 73/L6
Barberaz, Fr. 90/B1
Barberino di Mugello, It. 89/E6
Barberton, Oh, US 186/F4
Barberton, SAfr. 151/E2
Barbil, India 123/E4
Barbon, Eng, UK 61/F3
Barbona (peak), It. 88/D6
Barbosa, Col. 204/C3
Barbosa, Col. 207/K6
Barboursville, Va, US 189/H1
Barbourville, Ky, US 188/F2
Barbuda (isl.), Anti. 165/L8
Barby, Fr. 90/B1
Barcaldine, Sc, UK 59/A3
Barcaldine, Austl. 160/B3
Barcarena, Braz. 206/D3
Barcarrota, Sp. 72/B3
Barcău (riv.), Rom. 93/J1
Barcellona Pozzo di Gotto, It. 74/D3
Barcelona, Ven. 205/E2
Barcelona (int'l arpt.), Sp. 73/L7
Barcelona, Sp. 73/L7
Barcelonnette, Fr. 90/C4
Barcelos, Braz. 205/F5
Barcelos, Port. 72/A2
Barcin, Pol. 69/J2
Barclay, Tx, US 177/F2
Barcoo (riv.), Austl. 153/D3
Barcs, Hun. 76/C3
Barczewo, Pol. 67/J5
Bard, Ca, US 174/E4
Bärdä, Azer. 129/F1
Bardaï, Chad 134/C4
Bardas Blancas, Arg. 214/C2
Bardejov, Slvk. 69/L4
Bardeskan, Iran 127/G1
Bardheere, Som. 145/C1
Bardi, It. 88/C4
Bardīyah, Libya 134/E2
Bardney, Eng, UK 61/H5
Bārdoli, India 121/B1
Bardolino, It. 89/D2
Bardonecchia, It. 90/C2
Bardonia, NY, US 195/K7
Bardsdale, Ca, US 192/B2
Bardsey (isl.), Wal, UK 60/D6
Bardstown, Ky, US 188/E2
Bardwell, Ky, US 188/C2
Bardwell, Tx, US 177/F1
Bareeda, Som. 144/D3
Bareggio, It. 88/B3
Barei (wadi), Sudan 142/D2
Bareilly, India 122/B1
Bareli, India 122/B4
Barellan, Austl. 159/C2
Barendrecht, Neth. 78/B5
Barentin, Fr. 83/F1
Barenton, Fr. 83/E3
Barents (sea), Eur. 55/H1
Barentu, Erit. 142/H2
Bäretswil, Swi. 87/E3
Barfleur, Fr. 82/D1
Barfleur (pt.), Fr. 82/D1
Barg-e Matāl, Afg. 124/A2
Barga, It. 88/D5
Barga, China 125/D5
Bargara, Austl. 160/D4
Bargarh, India 121/D1
Barge, It. 90/D3
Bargfeld-Stegen, Ger. 79/H1
Bargi, India 122/B4
Bargo, Austl. 159/E2
Bargoed, Wal, UK 62/C3
Bargteheide, Ger. 79/H1
Bārguna, Bang. 123/H4
Barguzin (riv.), Rus. 104/G1
Bārh, India 123/E3
Barhaj, India 122/D2
Barhalganj, India 122/D2
Barham, Austl. 159/B2
Barhamjia, Nepal 123/F2
Barharwā, India 123/F3
Barhi, India 123/E3
Barhiya, India 123/F3
Bari, It. 74/E2
Bāri, India 122/A2
Bari, D.R. Congo 146/D2
Bari Sardo, It. 74/A3
Bariadi, Tanz. 145/A2
Bariano, It. 88/C2
Baricella, It. 89/E4
Barichara, Col. 204/C3
Baricho, Kenya 145/B2
Barigazzo (peak), It. 88/C4
Barika, Alg. 138/H5
Barikiwa, Tanz. 145/B4
Barīkowt, Afg. 124/A2
Barillas, Guat. 200/D3
Barima (riv.), Guy. 205/G2
Barima-Waini (pol. reg.), Guy. 205/F3
Barinas (state), Ven. 204/D2
Barinas, Ven. 204/D2
Baring, Wa, US 170/D4
Baringa, D.R. Congo 147/E3
Baringa I, D.R. Congo 147/E2
Baringa-Twana, D.R. Congo 146/D4
Barinitas, Ven. 204/D2
Baripāda, India 123/F5
Bariri, Braz. 213/G2
Bārīs, Egypt 135/F3
Barisakho, Geo. 97/H4
Barisāl, Bang. 123/H4
Barisāl (pol. reg.), Bang. 123/H4
Barisan (mts.), Indo. 116/B4
Barisciano, It. 92/C3
Barito (riv.), Indo. 116/D4
Baritu, PN, Arg. 212/C2
Barjols, Fr. 90/C5
Bark (pt.), Wi, US 183/J4
Bark (lake), On, Can. 187/G2
Bark (riv.), Wi, US 193/N13
Bark River, Mi, US 186/C2
Barka Kāna, India 123/E4
Barkam, China 112/D2
Barkava, Lat. 67/M3
Barker (cr.), Austl. 157/M9
Barker (dam), Tx, US 177/M9
Barker, NY, US 186/V9
Barkéwol el Abiod, Mrta. 140/B2
Barkham, Eng, UK 56/A2
Barki Saria, India 123/E3
Barking and Dagenham (bor.), Eng, UK 56/D2
Barkley (dam), Ky, US 188/C2
Barkley (sound), BC, Can. 170/B3
Barkley (lake), Ky, US 188/D2
Barkly East, SAfr. 150/D3
Barkly Tableland (plat.), Austl. 153/C2
Barkly West, SAfr. 150/D3
Barkol (Barkol Kazak Zizhixian), China 104/C3
Barkol Kazak Zizhixian (Barkol), China 104/C3
Barksdale (A.F.B.), La, US 179/H4
Barlaston, Eng, UK 61/F6
Barlby, Eng, UK 61/G4
Barlee (range), Austl. 156/B2
Barlee (lake), Austl. 153/A3
Barlee Range Nature Reserve, Austl. 156/B2
Barletta, It. 74/E2
Barlin, Fr. 80/B3
Barlinek, Pol. 69/H2
Barling, Ar, US 179/G3
Barmedman, Austl. 159/C2
Bārmer, India 127/K3
Barmera, Austl. 157/J5
Barmouth, Wal, UK 62/B1
Barmstedt, Ger. 79/G1
Barna, Ire. 58/A3
Barnāla, India 124/C4
Barnard, Ks, US 180/E4
Barnard Castle, Eng, UK 61/G2
Barnasht, Egypt 139/C5
Barnaul, Rus. 125/D1
Bärnbach, Aus. 71/L3
Barnegat (bay), NJ, US 194/D4
Barnegat, NJ, US 194/D4
Barnegat (inlet), NJ, US 194/D4
Barnegat Light, NJ, US 194/D4
Barnes, Wi, US 183/J4
Barnesboro, Pa, US 187/G4
Barnesville, Mn, US 182/F4
Barnesville, Ga, US 188/E4
Barnet, Vt, US 187/K2
Barnet (nbrhd.), Eng, UK 56/C2
Barneveld, Neth. 78/C4
Barneville-Carteret, Fr. 82/D2
Barney, Ga, US 191/G2
Barneys (lake), Austl. 159/B1
Barnhart, Mo, US 188/B1
Barnhart, Tx, US 177/D2
Barni Hāt, India 123/H2
Barnoldswick, Eng, UK 61/F4
Barnsdall, Ok, US 179/F2
Barnsley, Eng, UK 61/G4
Barnstaple, Eng, UK 62/B4
Barnstaple (Bideford) (bay), Eng, UK 62/B4
Barnstorf, Ger. 79/F3
Barntrup, Ger. 79/G5
Barnum, Wy, US 173/K2
Barnwell, Ab, Can. 171/H3
Barnwell, SC, US 189/G4
Baro, Gui. 140/C4
Baro, Nga. 141/G4
Baro Wenz (riv.), Eth. 142/G3
Baroda (Vadodara), India 118/B3
Barodia Kalān, India 122/B3
Baron, Ok, US 179/G3
Baron, Fr. 56/L4
Barona Ranch Ind. Res., Ca, US 174/D4
Barone (peak), It. 88/B2
Barong, China 104/D5
Barons, Ab, Can. 171/H2
Barooga, Austl. 159/B2
Baroua, CAfr. 142/E4
Barow (riv.), Ire. 60/A5
Barowghīl (pass), Afg. 127/K1
Barpāli, India 121/D1
Barpeta, India 123/H2
Barqin, Libya 134/B3
Barquisimeto, Ven. 204/D2
Barquisimeto (int'l arpt.), Ven. 204/D2
Barr, Fr. 86/D1
Barr, Sc, UK 60/D1
Barra (isl.), Sc, UK 57/Q8
Barra, Braz. 211/E1
Barra Bonita, Braz. 213/G2
Barra del Colorado, PN, CR 196/E5
Barra do Bugres, Braz. 209/G4
Barra do Corda, Braz. 207/E4
Barra do Cuanza, Ang. 146/C5
Barra do Dande, Ang. 146/C5
Barra do Garças, Braz. 210/B2
Barra do Piraí, Braz. 211/N7
Barra do Ribeiro, Braz. 213/G4
Barra Head (pt.), Sc, UK 57/Q8
Barra Mansa, Braz. 211/M7
Barra Patuca, Hon. 201/E3
Barra Punta Gorda, Nic. 201/F4
Barra Velha, Braz. 213/G3
Barraba, Austl. 158/D1
Barrackpur, India 123/G4
Barrage d'Ayamé I (dam), C.d'Iv. 140/E5
Barrage d'Ayamé II (dam), C.d'Iv. 140/E5
Barrage de Bimont (res.), Fr. 90/B5
Barrage de Buyo (dam), C.d'Iv. 140/D5
Barrage de Castillon (dam), Fr. 90/C5
Barrage de Chaudanne (dam), Fr. 90/C5
Barrage de Kossou (dam), C.d'Iv. 140/D5
Barrage de la Grande Dixence (dam), Swi. 86/D5
Barrage de la Plate Taile (dam), Belg. 81/D3
Barrage de la Sainte-Croix (dam), Fr. 90/C5
Barrage de Lagdo (dam), Camr. 142/B3
Barrage de l'Eau d'Heure (dam), Belg. 81/D3
Barrage de Mauvoisin (dam), Swi. 86/D6
Barrage de Mbakaou (dam), Camr. 142/B4
Barrage de Serre-Ponçon (dam), Fr. 90/C4
Barrage de Taabo (dam), C.d'Iv. 140/D5
Barrage de Tignes (dam), Fr. 90/C1
Barrage de Vouglans (dam), Fr. 86/B5
Barrage Idriss I (res.), Mor. 138/B2
Barrage Mohamed V (res.), Mor. 138/C2
Barragem da Chicamba Real (dam), Moz. 149/G3
Barragem de Cabora Bassa (dam), Moz. 149/G2
Barragem Paso Real (res.), Braz. 213/F4
Barranca, Peru 208/B2
Barranca, Peru 208/B3
Barranca de Upía, Col. 204/C3
Barranca del Cobre PN, Mex. 198/D3
Barrancabermeja, Col. 204/C3
Barrancas, Col. 204/C2
Barrancas, Ven. 205/F2
Barrancas, Arg. 214/C3
Barrancas, Chile 214/N8
Barrancas, Arroyo (cr.), Arg. 212/E4
Barranco de Loba, Col. 204/C2
Barrancos, Port. 72/B3
Barranquilla, Col. 204/C2
Barras, Col. 204/C4
Barras, Braz. 207/F4
Barre, Vt, US 187/K2
Barre de Portugais (pt.), Gabon 146/B3
Barreal, Arg. 212/B4
Barreiras, Braz. 210/D2
Barreirinha, Braz. 206/B3
Barreirinhas, Braz. 207/F3
Barreiro, Port. 73/P10
Barreiros, Braz. 207/H5
Barrême, Fr. 90/C5
Barren (isl.), Madg. 152/G7
Barren (riv.), Ky, US 188/D2
Barren (Nosy Barren) (isls.), Madg. 152/G7
Barren River (lake), Ky, US 188/D2
Barrera, Bol. 209/E4
Barretal, Mex. 199/F3
Barretos, Braz. 213/G2
Barrett, Tx, US 177/M9
Barrhead, Sc, UK 59/B5
Barrhead, Ab, Can. 166/E3
Barrhill, Sc, UK 60/D1
Barrie, On, Can. 187/G2
Barrier (range), Austl. 157/J4
Barrière, BC, Can. 170/D2
Barrilla Draw (riv.), Tx, US 177/C2
Barrington, Il, US 193/P15
Barrington Hills, Il, US 193/P15
Barrington Tops (peak), Austl. 158/D1
Barrington Tops NP, Austl. 158/D1
Barringun, Austl. 158/C1
Barrīyat al Uşayfir, Egypt 139/B2
Barro Duro, Braz. 207/F4
Barron, Wi, US 183/J5
Barron Gorge NP, Austl. 160/B2
Barronett, Wi, US 183/J5
Barros Luco, Chile 212/B3
Barroso, Braz. 210/E4
Barrouallie, StV. 197/N9
Barrow (riv.), Ire. 58/D4
Barrow (pt.), Austl. 160/B1
Barrow (str.), Nun, Can. 166/G1
Barrow (pt.), Ak, US 168/X11
Barrow, Ak, US 168/X11
Barrow (isl.), Austl. 153/A3
Barrow Creek, Austl. 157/G2
Barrow Island, Austl. 156/B2
Barrow-in-Furness, Eng, UK 61/E3
Barrowby, Eng, UK 61/H6
Barrowford, Eng, UK 61/F4
Barruelo de Santullán, Sp. 72/C1
Barry, Wal, UK 62/C4
Barry M. Goldwater Air Force Range, Az, US 175/F4
Barry's Bay, On, Can. 187/H2
Barrytown, NZ 161/B3
Barsakel'mes (lake), Uzb. 97/L4
Barsalogho, Burk. 141/E3
Bārshi, India 121/B2
Barsinghausen, Ger. 79/G4
Bårslöv, Swe. 65/J6
Barssel, Ger. 79/E2
Barstow, Ca, US 174/D3
Bartang (riv.), Taj. 125/B4
Bartenheim, Fr. 86/D2
Barth, Ger. 66/E4
Bartholomä, Ger. 84/C5
Bartholomäberg, Aus. 87/F3
Bartica, Guy. 205/G3
Bartın, Turk. 96/E4
Bartle Frere (peak), Austl. 153/D2
Bartlesville, Ok, US 179/G2
Bartlett, Il, US 193/P16
Bartlett, Tn, US 188/C3
Bartlett, Ne, US 180/E3
Bartlett, Tx, US 177/F2
Bartley, WV, US 189/G2
Bartolomé Masó, Cuba 201/G1
Bartolomeu Dias, Moz. 149/G4
Barton, ND, US 182/D3
Barton, Vt, US 187/K2
Barton, Md, US 187/G5
Barton under Needwood, Eng, UK 63/E1
Barton-in-the-Clay, Eng, UK 63/F3
Barton-upon-Humber, Eng, UK 61/H4
Bartonsville, Pa, US 194/C2
Bartoszyce, Pol. 67/J4
Bartow, Ger. 66/E5
Bartow, Fl, US 190/M8
Barú (vol.), Pan. 201/F4
Bāruipur, India 123/G4
Baruman (riv.), Indo. 115/C2
Barumun (riv.), Indo. 116/B3
Barus, Indo. 115/B2
Baruta, Ven. 207/P7
Baruth, Ger. 69/G2
Baruun Huuray (phys. reg.), Mong. 104/C2
Baruun-Urt, Mong. 104/G2
Baruunsuu, Mong. 104/F3
Barview, Or, US 172/A2
Barvinkove, Ukr. 99/J3
Barwa Sāgar, India 122/B3
Barwāha, India 118/C3
Barwāla, India 124/C5
Barwāni, India 118/B3
Barwick, Ga, US 191/G2
Barwon (riv.), Austl. 153/D3
Barwon Heads, Austl. 159/B4
Barycz (riv.), Pol. 69/J3
Barysaw, Bela. 67/N4
Barysh, Rus. 97/H1
Baryshivka, Ukr. 98/F2
Barzanò, It. 88/C2
Bas-Caraquet, NB, Can. 184/E2
Bas-Congo (pol. reg.), D.R. Congo 146/A4
Bas-Rhin (dept.), Fr. 86/D1
Basa, C.d'Iv. 140/D5
Basaldella, It. 89/G1
Basankusu, D.R. Congo 146/D2
Basarabeasca, Mol. 98/E4
Basauri, Sp. 70/B5
Basavilbaso, Arg. 215/J10
Basawa, C.d'Iv. 140/D4
Basay, Phil. 114/C3
Bascharage, Lux. 81/E4
Baschurch, Eng, UK 62/D1
Bascom, Fl, US 191/F2
Bascuñán (pt.), Chile 212/B4
Basdorf, Ger. 68/Q6
Baseball Hall of Fame, NY, US 187/J3
Basekpio, D.R. Congo 142/E4
Basel, Swi. 86/D2
Basel/Mulhouse (int'l arpt.), Fr. 86/D2
Baselga di Pinè, It. 87/H5
Baselice, It. 92/D5
Baselland (canton), Swi. 86/D3
Bashaw, Ab, Can. 171/H1
Bashbīsh, Egypt 139/C2
Bashee (riv.), SAfr. 150/E3
Bashi (chan.), Phil.,Tai. 162/A2
Bashkaus (riv.), Rus. 104/B1
Bashkortostan Aut. Rep., Rus. 100/Q6
Bashmakovo, Rus. 97/G1
Bāsht, Iran 129/G4
Bashtanka, Ukr. 98/G4
Ba'shūm, Sudan 142/F2
Basilan (isl.), Phil. 162/B4
Basilan (str.), Phil. 114/C4
Basilan (peak), Phil. 114/C4
Basildon, Eng, UK 63/G3
Basile, La, US 190/B2
Basilica di Fieschi, It. 88/C5
Basilicata (reg.), It. 74/D2
Bāsim, India 121/C1
Basin, Wy, US 173/J1
Basin, Mt, US 171/H4
Basingstoke (canal), Eng, UK 56/A3
Basingstoke, Eng, UK 63/E4
Basīrhāt, India 123/G4
Basīrpur, Pak. 124/B4
Baška, Cro. 71/L4
Baskahegan (lake), Me, US 184/C3
Başkale, Turk. 129/F2
Baskatong (res.), Qu, Can. 187/J1
Baskerville (cape), Austl. 154/A4
Baskett Slough Nat'l Wild. Ref., Or, US 172/B1
Baskil, Turk. 128/D2
Baskin, La, US 179/J4
Başkomutan NP, Turk. 128/B2
Başköy, Turk. 128/D2
Basmat, India 121/C2
Bāsmenj, Iran 129/F2
Bāsoda, India 122/A4
Basodesh, Tanz. 145/A3
Basodino (peak), It. 87/E5
Basoko, D.R. Congo 147/E2
Basoli, India 124/C3
Basongo, D.R. Congo 147/E4
Basque Provinces (prov.), Sp. 70/B5
Bass (str.), Austl. 153/D4
Bass Is. (Marotiri) (isl.), FrPol. 163/L7
Bass River, NS, Can. 184/F3
Bass Rock (isl.), Sc, UK 59/D4
Bassae (Vassés) (ruin), Gre. 75/G4
Bassano, Ab, Can. 171/H2
Bassano del Grappa, It. 89/E2
Bassano Romano, It. 91/B3
Bassari, Togo 141/F4
Bassas da India (isl.), Reun., Fr. 149/H4
Basse Santa Su, Gam. 140/B3
Basse-Kotto (pref.), CAfr. 142/D4
Basse-Normandie (pol. reg.), Fr. 83/D3
Basse-Terre (isl.), Guad. 197/J4
Basse-Terre, Fr. 197/N8
Bassecourt, Swi. 86/D3
Bassein (riv.), Myan. 119/F4
Bassein (Pathein), Myan. 112/B5
Bassein (Vasai), India 127/K5
Bassenge, Belg. 81/E2
Bassenheim, Ger. 81/G3
Bassens, Fr. 90/B1
Bassenthwaite (lake), Eng, UK 61/E2
Basseterre (cap.), StK. 197/N8
Bassett, Tx, US 179/G4
Bassett, Ne, US 180/E2
Bassett, Va, US 189/H2
Bassikounou, Mrta. 140/D3
Bassum, Ger. 79/F3
Basswood (lake), Can.,US 183/J3
Båstad, Swe. 66/E3
Bastak, Iran 129/H5
Bastām, Iran 129/H2
Bastar, India 121/D2
Bastelicaccia, Fr. 74/A2
Bastheim, Ger. 84/D2
Bastī, India 122/D2
Bastia, Fr. 74/A1
Bastia, It. 91/B1
Bastogne, Belg. 81/E4
Bastos, Braz. 213/G2
Bastrop, La, US 179/J4
Bastrop, Tx, US 176/F2
Basu (cape), Indo. 115/C3
Basyūn, Egypt 139/B3
Bat Khela, Pak. 124/A2
Bat Shelomo, Isr. 131/B3
Bat Yam, Isr. 131/B4
Bata, EqG. 146/B2
Bata-Siala, D.R. Congo 146/C4
Bataan (mt.), Phil. 114/C2
Batabanó (gulf), Cuba 196/E3
Batac, Phil. 114/C1
Batagay, Rus. 101/P3
Batai (pass), Pak. 124/A3
Batak, Bul. 75/J2
Batakan, Indo. 115/F3
Batakūt, India 124/C3
Batāla, India 124/C4
Batalha, Port. 72/A3
Batalha, Braz. 207/F4
Batallas, Bol. 208/D5
Bataly, Kaz. 97/M1
Batama, D.R. Congo 147/F2
Batamshinskiy, Kaz. 97/L2
Batan (isls.), Phil. 103/M7
Batang, Indo. 115/E3
Batang, China 112/C2
Batangafo, CAfr. 142/C4
Batangas, Phil. 114/C2
Batangtoru, Indo. 115/B2
Bātāru, India 118/B2
Batatais, Braz. 213/H2
Batataria (bay), La, US 190/C3
Batavia, NY, US 187/G3
Batavia, Il, US 193/P16
Batavia, Oh, US 188/E1
Bataysk, Rus. 99/K4
Batchelor, La, US 190/C2
Batchelor, Austl. 154/C3
Batchwana Bay, On, Can. 186/D1
Bătdambang, Camb. 120/C3
Bate (bay), Austl. 160/H9
Bateman, Sk, Can. 171/L2
Batemans (bay), Austl. 159/E2
Batemans Bay, Austl. 159/E2
Batesburg-Leesville, SC, US 189/G4
Batesville, Ar, US 179/J3
Batesville, In, US 186/D5
Batesville, Al, US 191/F1
Batesville, Ms, US 188/C3
Batesville, Tx, US 177/E3
Batesville, Va, US 189/H2
Batetskiy, Rus. 67/P2
Bath, NS, Can. 184/D2
Bath, On, Can. 187/H2
Bath, NY, US 187/H3
Bath (range), Austl. 155/D3
Bath, Eng, UK 62/D4
Bath, Neth. 78/B6
Bath, Pa, US 194/C2
Bath (Berkeley Springs), WV, US 187/G5
Bath Springs, Tn, US 188/C3
Batha (pref.), Chad 142/C2
Batha (riv.), Chad 142/C2
Batha de Laïri (riv.), Chad 142/C3
Bathgate, ND, US 182/F3
Bathgate, Sc, UK 59/C5
Bathmen, Neth. 78/D4
Bathsheba, Bar. 197/P9
Bathurst, NB, Can. 184/E2
Bathurst (inlet), Nun, Can. 166/F2
Bathurst (isl.), Nun, Can. 165/G2
Bathurst (cape), NW, Can. 166/D1
Bathurst (isl.), Austl. 154/C2
Bathurst, Austl. 159/D1
Bathurst Abor. Land, Austl. 154/C2
Bathurst Inlet, Nun, Can. 166/F2
Batī, Eth. 144/B3
Batian (peak), Kenya 145/B2
Bāţiāq-e Gāv Khūnī (lake), Iran 129/H3
Batié, Burk. 140/E4
Batik (mts.), China 104/C2
Bāţin (wadi), SAr. 126/E3
Batiquitos (lag.), Ca, US 192/C4
Batiscan (riv.), Qu, Can. 184/A2
Batley, Eng, UK 61/G4
Batlow, Austl. 159/D2
Batman, Turk. 128/E2
Batman (dam), Turk. 128/E2
Batna (wilaya), Alg. 137/G2
Batna, Alg. 138/J5
Batoche Nat'l Hist. Site, Sk, Can. 171/L1
Batoka, Zam. 149/E3
Baton Rouge (cap.), La, US 190/C2
Batopilas, Mex. 198/D3
Batoti, India 124/C3
Batouri, Camr. 142/B4
Batovi (riv.), Braz. 210/B2
Baţrā' (ruin), Jor. 130/D4
Baţrah, Egypt 139/C2
Batsawul, Afg. 124/A2
Båtsfjord, Nor. 64/J1
Batsto, NJ, US 194/D4
Batsto (riv.), NJ, US 194/D4
Batsto Historic Village, NJ, US 194/D4
Battaglia Terme, It. 89/E3
Battali, Bang. 123/H4
Battenberg, Ger. 79/F6
Bätterkinden, Swi. 86/D3
Battersby, Eng, UK 61/G3
Battersea (nbrhd.), Eng, UK 56/C2
Battiest, Ok, US 179/G3
Battipaglia, It. 92/D6
Battle (riv.), Ab,Sk, Can. 166/E3
Battle, Eng, UK 63/G5
Battle (riv.), Ab, Can. 171/J1
Battle Creek, Mi, US 186/D3
Battle Creek, Ne, US 180/F3
Battle Creek, Ia, US 181/G2
Battle Lake, Mn, US 183/G4
Battle Mountain, Nv, US 172/E3
Battleboro, NC, US 189/J2
Battlefield, Mo, US 179/H2
Battleford, Sk, Can. 171/K1
Battock (mt.), Sc, UK 59/D3
Batu (peak), Eth. 144/A4
Batu (isls.), Indo. 116/A4
Batu (peak), Malay. 116/D3
Batu (bay), Malay. 116/D3
Batu (cape), Indo. 117/E3
Batu Caves, Malay. 115/C2
Batu Gajah, Malay. 115/C1
Batu Pahat, Malay. 115/C2
Batu Puteh (peak), Malay. 115/C1
Batuco, Chile 214/N8
Batudaka (isl.), Indo. 117/F4
Batuensambang (peak), Indo. 116/D3
Batui, Indo. 117/F4
Batulaki, Phil. 114/D4
Batumi (int'l arpt.), Geo. 97/G4
Bat'umi, Geo. 97/G4
Baturaja, Indo. 115/D3
Baturino, Rus. 95/P5
Baturité, Braz. 207/G4
Baturusa, Indo. 115/D3
Baturyn, Ukr. 99/G2
Batusangkar, Indo. 115/C3
Batyrevo, Rus. 95/K5
Batys Qazaqstan, Kaz. 100/E5
Batz-sur-Mer, Fr. 82/C6
Bauang, Phil. 114/C1
Baubau, Indo. 154/A1
Bauchi (state), Nga. 141/H4
Bauchi, Nga. 141/H4
Baud, Fr. 82/B5
Baudette, Mn, US 183/G3
Baudh, India 121/E1
Baudó (riv.), Col. 204/B3
Baudó (mts.), Col. 201/G5
Baudon, Pic de (peak), Fr. 90/D5
Baugé, Fr. 83/E5
Baukau, Indo. 154/B2
Bauld (cape), Nf, Can. 167/L3
Baulkham Hills, Austl. 159/E1
Baulmes, Swi. 86/C4
Bauman (peak), Togo 141/F5
Baume-les-Dames, Fr. 86/C3
Baumholder, Ger. 81/G4
Baunach, Ger. 84/D3
Baunach (riv.), Ger. 84/D2
Baunatal, Ger. 79/G6
Baunei, It. 74/A2
Baungon, Phil. 114/D3
Baures, Bol. 209/F4
Baures (riv.), Bol. 209/E4
Baurú, Braz. 213/G2
Bauska, Lat. 67/L3
Bautino, Kaz. 97/J3
Bautzen, Ger. 69/H3
Bavans, Fr. 86/C3
Bavarian Alps (mts.), Aus., Ger. 93/F1
Bavay, Fr. 80/C3
Båven (lake), Swe. 66/G2
Baveno, It. 87/E6
Bavent, Fr. 83/E2
Baviácora, Mex. 198/C2
Bavilliers, Fr. 86/C2
Bavly, Rus. 95/M5
Baw Baw (mt.), Austl. 159/C3
Baw Baw NP, Austl. 159/C3
Bawan, Indo. 116/D4
Bawāna, India 124/D5
Bawang (cape), Indo. 116/C4
Bawean (isl.), Indo. 116/D5
Bawku, Gha. 141/E4
Bawlake, Myan. 120/B2
Bawlf, Ab, Can. 171/H1
Baxian, China 113/F1
Baxkorgan, China 125/F4
Baxley, Ga, US 191/G2
Baxoi, China 112/C2
Baxter, Mn, US 183/G4
Baxter Springs, Ks, US 179/G2
Bay (dam), Wi, US 181/K1
Bay, Ar, US 188/B3
Bay Bulls, Nf, Can. 185/L2
Bay City, Tx, US 177/G3
Bay City, Mi, US 186/E3
Bay City, Wi, US 181/H1
Bay City, Or, US 170/C5
Bay de Verde, Nf, Can. 185/L1
Bay Lake, Mn, US 183/H4
Bay Lake, Fl, US 190/M7
Bay L'Argent, Nf, Can. 185/K2
Bay Mills Ind. Res., Mi, US 186/D1
Bay Minette, Al, US 190/E2
Bay Port, Mi, US 186/E3
Bay Ridge (nbrhd.), NY, US 195/J9
Bay Ridge (Bayridge), Fl, US 190/M6
Bay Roberts, Nf, Can. 185/L2
Bay Saint Lawrence, NS, Can. 185/G2
Bay Saint Louis, Ms, US 190/D2
Bay Springs, Ms, US 190/D2
Bay Springs (lake), Ms, US 188/C3
Bay View, NZ 161/D2
Bayāḑ an Naşārá, Egypt 139/C6
Bayamo, Cuba 201/G1
Bayamón, PR 197/M8
Bayan, Indo. 117/E5
Bayan, Mong. 104/D2
Bayan, China 105/K2
Bayan Har (mts.), China 104/D5
Bayan Mod, China 104/E3
Bayan Obo, China 104/F3
Bayan Qagan, China 105/J2
Bayan-Ölgiy (prov.), Mong. 104/B2
Bayan-Ovoo, Mong. 104/C3
Bayan-Ulaan, Mong. 104/E2
Bayanaul, Kaz. 125/C1
Bayanbulag, Mong. 104/F2
Bayangol, Rus. 104/E1
Bayanhongor, Mong. 104/E2
Bayanhongor (prov.), Mong. 104/D3
Bayanhushuu, Mong. 104/C2
Bayanhushuu, Mong. 104/E2
Bayannuur, Mong. 125/F2
Bayano (lake), Pan. 201/G4
Bayansayr, Mong. 104/D2
Bayanterem, Mong. 104/G2
Bayantsagaan, Mong. 104/E2
Bayard, WV, US 187/G5
Bayard, NM, US 175/H4
Bayard, Ne, US 180/C3
Bayard, Ia, US 181/G3
Bayat, Turk. 96/E4
Bayawan, Phil. 114/C3
Baybach (riv.), Ger. 81/G3
Baybay, Phil. 114/D3
Bayboro, NC, US 189/J3
Bayburt (prov.), Turk. 96/F4
Bayburt, Turk. 128/E1
Baychunas, Kaz. 97/K3
Baychurovo, Rus. 99/M2
Baydaratskaya (bay), Rus. 100/G2
Baydhabo (Baidoa), Som. 144/B5
Baydrog (riv.), Mong. 104/D2
Bayel, Fr. 86/A1
Bayerischer Wald (hills) Ger. 85/F4
Bayerischer Wald NP, Ger. 85/G5
Bayerischer Wald, NP, Ger. 71/K2
Bayern (state), Ger. 68/F4
Bayeux, Fr. 83/E2
Bayeux, Braz. 207/H4
Bayfield, Co, US 175/J2
Baygorria (res.), Uru. 215/K10
Bayḩān al Qişāb, Yem. 144/C2
Baykal (mts.), Rus. 101/L4
Baykal (lake), Rus. 103/L4
Baykal, Rus. 104/E1
Baykal'sk, Rus. 104/E1
Baykan, Turk. 128/E2
Baykibashevo, Rus. 95/N5
Baykit, Rus. 100/K3
Baykonyr, Kaz. 100/G5
Baymak, Rus. 97/L1
Baynes Lake, BC, Can. 170/G3
Bayo Grande (peak), Arg. 212/C3
Bayombong, Phil. 114/C1
Bayon, Fr. 86/C1
Bayona, Sp. 72/A1
Bayonet (pt.), Fl, US 190/K7
Bayonet Point, Fl, US 190/K7
Bayonne, NJ, US 195/J9
Bayonne, Fr. 70/C5
Bayonne-Anglet (Biarritz) (arpt.), Fr. 70/C5
Bayou Bartholomew (riv.), Ar, US 188/B4
Bayou Cane, La, US 190/C3
Bayou D'arbonne (lake), La, US 177/H1
Bayou de View (riv.), Ar, US 188/B3
Bayou Lafourche (riv.), La, US 190/C3
Bayou Macon (riv.), La, US 188/B4
Bayou Meto (riv.), Ar, US 188/B3
Bayou Nezpique (bayou), La, US 177/H2
Bayou Phalia (riv.), Ms, US 188/B4
Bayou Pierre (riv.), La, US 177/H1
Bayou Pierre (riv.), Ms, US 188/A4
Bayou Queue de Tortue (riv.), La, US 190/B2
Bayou Teche (riv.), La, US 177/H2
Bayou Vista, La, US 190/C3
Bayóvar, Peru 208/A2
Bayport, Mn, US 183/Q6
Bayport, Fl, US 190/K6
Bayport, NY, US 195/E2
Bayramaly, Trkm. 127/H1
Bayramiç, Turk. 75/K3
Bayreuth, Ger. 85/E3
Bayridge (Bay Ridge), Fl, US 190/M6
Bayrūt (gov.), Leb. 131/C1
Bayrūt (Beirut) (cap.), Leb. 131/C1
Bays (lake), On, Can. 187/G2
Bayse (riv.), Fr. 73/E1
Bayşehir (lake), Turk. 128/B2
Bayside (nbrhd.), NY, US 195/K8
Bayston Hill, Eng, UK 62/D1
Baysville, On, Can. 187/G2
Bayswater (nbrhd.), Austl. 156/K6
Bayt al Faqīh, Yem. 144/B2
Bayt Fajjār, WBnk. 131/C5
Bayt Ḩanīnā, WBnk. 131/C5
Bayt Ḩānūn, Gaza 131/B5
Bayt Jālā, WBnk. 131/C5
Bayt Lāhiyah, Gaza 131/B5
Bayt Laḩm (Bethlehem), WBnk. 131/C5
Bayt Sāḩūr, WBnk. 131/C5
Baytown, Tx, US 177/N9
Bayudha (des.), Sudan 135/G5
Bayunglencir, Indo. 115/C3
Bayville, NY, US 195/L8
Baywood-Los Osos, Ca, US 174/B3
Bayy al Kabīr (wadi), Libya 134/B2
Bayzhansay, Kaz. 125/A3
Baza, Sp. 72/D4
Bazainville, Fr. 56/G5
Bazardüzü (peak), Azer. 97/H4
Bāzargān, Iran 129/F2
Bazarnyye Mataki, Rus. 95/L5
Bazarshulan, Kaz. 97/J2
Bazèga (prov.), Burk. 141/E4
Bazemont, Fr. 56/H5
Bazet, Fr. 70/D5
Bazhong, China 113/E2
Bazine, Ks, US 178/E1
Bazoches-sur-Hoëne, Fr. 83/F3
Bazouges, Fr. 83/E5
Bāzpur, India 122/B1
Bazuru, D.R. Congo 147/F2
Bazzano, It. 89/E4
Beach, ND, US 182/B4
Beach Haven, NJ, US 194/D4

234

Beach – Bernh

Beach Meadows, NS, Can. 184/E3
Beachburg, On, Can. 187/H2
Beachport, Austl. 158/B3
Beachton, Ga, US 191/F2
Beachwood, NJ, US 194/D4
Beachy (pt.), Eng, UK 70/D1
Beachy (head), Eng, UK 63/G5
Beacon, NY, US 187/K4
Beacon, Tn, US 188/C3
Beacon (peak), Wal, UK 62/C2
Beacon Hill, Fl, US 191/F3
Beaconsfield, Austl. 158/C4
Beaconsfield, Qu, Can. 185/N7
Beaconsfield, Eng, UK 63/F3
Beagle (gulf), Austl. 154/C3
Beagle Bay Abor. Rsv., Austl. 154/A4
Beagle Bay Mission, Austl. 154/A4
Beal (range), Austl. 160/A4
Béal Traversier, Pic du (peak), Fr. 90/C3
Bealanana, Madg. 152/J6
Beale AFB, Ca, US 172/C4
Beals (cr.), Tx, US 177/D1
Beaminster, Eng, UK 62/D5
Beampingaratra (ridge), Madg. 152/H9
Beamsville, On, Can. 186/U9
Bear (riv.), Ca, US 172/C4
Bear (lake), Ut, US 168/D3
Bear (cr.), Wy, US 180/B3
Bear (mtn.), SD, US 180/C2
Bear (hill), Ne, US 180/D3
Bear (isl.), Nor. 216/E
Bear (hills), Sk, Can. 171/K1
Bear, De, US 194/C4
Bear Creek, Al, US 188/D3
Bear Lake, Mi, US 186/C2
Bear Lake NWR, Id, US 173/H2
Bear Lodge (mts.), Wy, US 180/B1
Bear River, NS, Can. 184/E3
Bear River (bay), Ut, US 173/G3
Bear River NWR, Ut, US 173/G3
Bear Town, Ms, US 190/C2
Beara (reg.), Ire. 58/A6
Bearden, Ar, US 179/H4
Bearden, Ok, US 179/F3
Beardmore, On, Can. 183/L3
Beardstown, Il, US 181/J3
Bearfort (mtn.), NJ, US 195/H7
Bearma (riv.), India 122/B4
Bearpaw (mts.), Mt, US 171/J3
Bearsden, Sc, UK 59/B5
Bearstead, Eng, UK 56/E3
Beartooth (mts.), Mt, US 173/H1
Beās (riv.), India 122/B3
Beas de Segura, Sp. 72/D3
Beasain, Sp. 70/B5
Beata (cape), DRep. 197/G4
Beata (pt.), DRep. 201/J2
Beata (isl.), Thai. 201/J2
Beatenberg, Swi. 86/D4
Beatrice, Zim. 149/F3
Beatrice, Ne, US 181/F3
Beatrice (cape), Austl. 155/E3
Beattie, Ks, US 181/F4
Beattock, Sc, UK 59/C6
Beatty, Nv, US 174/D2
Beattystown, NJ, US 194/D2
Beattyville, Ky, US 188/F2
Beau Bassin-Rose Hill, Mrts. 151/T15
Beaucaire, Fr. 90/A5
Beaucamps-le-Vieux, Fr. 80/A4
Beauceville, Qu, Can. 184/B2
Beauchamp, Fr. 56/J4
Beauchastel, Fr. 90/A3
Beaucourt, Fr. 86/C3
Beaudesert, Austl. 160/D4
Beaufort, Fr. 86/B4
Beaufort, Lux. 81/F4
Beaufort, Fr. 90/C1
Beaufort, Austl. 158/B3
Beaufort (sea), Can.,US 165/C2
Beaufort, Malay. 114/A4
Beaufort, SC, US 189/G4
Beaufort, NC, US 189/J3
Beaufort (inlet), NC, US 189/J3
Beaufort Castle (ruins), Leb. 131/D2
Beaufort Marine Corps Air Base, SC, US 189/G4
Beaufort West, SAfr. 150/C4
Beaufort-en-Vallée, Fr. 83/E6
Beaugency, Fr. 83/G5
Beauharnois, Qu, Can. 187/K2
Beauharnois (co.), Qu, Can. 185/M7
Beaujolais (mts.), Fr. 70/F4
Beaulieu, Eng, UK 63/E5
Beaulieu-sur-Mer, Fr. 90/D5
Beauly, Sc, UK 59/B2
Beauly (riv.), Sc, UK 59/B2
Beauly Firth (lake), Sc, UK 59/B2
Beaumaris, Wal, UK 60/D5
Beaumes-de-Venise, Fr. 90/B4
Beaumesnil, Fr. 83/F2
Beaumont, Fr. 82/D1
Beaumont, Belg. 81/D3
Beaumont, Ms, US 190/D2
Beaumont, Ca, US 192/D3
Beaumont, Fr. 70/E4
Beaumont, Ab, Can. 171/H1
Beaumont, Tx, US 177/G2
Beaumont-de-Lomagne, Fr. 70/D5
Beaumont-le-Roger, Fr. 83/F2
Beaumont-lès-Valence, Fr. 90/A3
Beaumont-sur-Oise, Fr. 56/J4
Beaumont-sur-Sarthe, Fr. 83/F4
Beaupréau, Fr. 83/E6
Beauquesne, Fr. 80/B3
Beauraing, Belg. 81/D3
Beaurainville, Fr. 80/A3
Beauregard, Ms, US 190/C2
Beaurepaire, Fr. 90/B2
Beaurevoir, Fr. 80/C4
Beausejour, Mb, Can. 182/F2
Beausoleil, Fr. 90/D5
Beautheil, Fr. 56/M5
Beautiful (mtn.), NM, US 175/H2
Beautor, Fr. 80/C4
Beauvais, Fr. 80/B5
Beauval, Fr. 80/B3
Beauvoir, Fr. 56/L6
Beaver, Ok, US 178/D2
Beaver (hills), Sk, Can. 182/C2
Beaver (lake), Ar, US 179/H2
Beaver, Pa, US 186/F4
Beaver (isl.), Mi, US 186/D2
Beaver, La, US 190/B2
Beaver (riv.), Yk, Can. 166/D2
Beaver (riv.), Ut, US 173/J4
Beaver, Ut, US 175/F1
Beaver (cr.), Ne, US 180/E3
Beaver, Oh, US 189/F1
Beaver (dam), Wi, US 181/K2
Beaver (cr.), Co,Ks, US 180/D4
Beaver (cr.), Co, US 180/C4
Beaver, Wa, US 170/B3
Beaver Bay, Mn, US 183/J4
Beaver City, Ne, US 180/E3
Beaver Creek, Yk, Can. 166/B2
Beaver Crossing, Ne, US 181/F3
Beaver Dam, Ky, US 188/D2
Beaver Dam, Wi, US 181/K2
Beaver Dam (lake), Wi, US 181/K2
Beaver Falls, Pa, US 186/F4
Beaver Meadows, Pa, US 194/C2
Beaver Springs, Pa, US 194/A2
Beaverbank, NS, Can. 184/F3
Beavercreek, Oh, US 186/D5
Beaverdam, Va, US 189/J2
Beaverdell, BC, Can. 170/E3
Beaverhead (mts.), Mt, US 173/G1
Beaverhead (riv.), Mt, US 173/G1
Beaverhill (lake), Ab, Can. 171/H1
Beaverton, On, Can. 187/G2
Beaverton, Mi, US 186/D3
Beaverton, Or, US 172/B1
Beavertown, Pa, US 194/A2
Beāwar, India 118/B2
Bebe, Tx, US 177/F3
Bébédjia, Chad 142/C3
Bebedouro, Braz. 213/G2
Beberibe, Braz. 207/G4
Bebington, Eng, UK 61/E5
Beboto, Chad 142/C3
Béboura Iii, CAfr. 142/C4
Bebra, Ger. 79/G7
Becal, Mex. 200/D1
Bécancour, Qu, Can. 187/K1
Beccles, Eng, UK 63/H2
Bečej, Yugo. 76/E3
Becerreá, Sp. 72/B1
Bechar, Alg. 137/E3
Bechar (wilaya), Alg. 136/E3
Bechhofen, Ger. 81/G5
Bechhofen, Ger. 84/D4
Bechtheim, Ger. 84/B3
Bechyně, Czh. 85/H4
Becida, Mn, US 183/G4
Beckdorf, Ger. 79/G2
Beckenham (nbrhd.), Eng, UK 56/D2
Beckenried, Swi. 87/E4
Becker, Ms, US 188/C4
Beckingen, Ger. 81/F5
Beckingham, Eng, UK 61/H5
Beckley, WV, US 189/G2
Beckton, Wy, US 173/K1
Beckum, Ger. 79/F5
Beckville, Tx, US 177/G1
Beckwourth, Ca, US 172/C4
Beclean, Rom. 77/G2
Bécon-les-Granits, Fr. 83/E5
Becs de Bosson (peak), Swi. 86/D5
Bedale, Eng, UK 61/G3
Bédaoyo, Chad 142/C4
Bédarieux, Fr. 70/E5
Bédarrides, Fr. 90/A4
Bedaya, Chad 142/C3
Bedburg, Ger. 81/F2
Bedburg-Hau, Ger. 78/D5
Beddau, Wal, UK 62/C3
Beddgelert, Wal, UK 60/D5
Bedelē, Eth. 142/H3
Beder, Den. 66/D3
Bederkesa, Ger. 79/G1
Bederkesa, Ger. 79/F1
Bedēsa, Eth. 144/B3
Bedford (cape), Austl. 160/B1
Bedford, Qu, Can. 187/K2
Bedford, SAfr. 150/D4
Bedford, Eng, UK 63/F2
Bedford, Ia, US 181/G3
Bedford, In, US 188/D1
Bedford, Ky, US 188/E1
Bedford, NH, US 187/L3
Bedford, Pa, US 187/G4
Bedford, Tx, US 176/K7
Bedford, Va, US 189/H2
Bedford, Wy, US 173/H2
Bedford Hills, NY, US 195/E1
Bedford Level (phys. reg.), Eng, UK 63/F2
Bedford Park, Il, US 193/Q16
Bedfordshire (co.), Eng, UK 63/F2
Bedias, Tx, US 177/G2
Bédiondo, Chad 142/C3
Bedlington, Eng, UK 61/G1
Bedmond, Eng, UK 56/B1
Bedok (nbrhd.), Sing. 115/J6
Bedong, Malay. 115/C1
Bedonia, It. 88/C4
Bédouaram, Niger 142/B2
Bedourie, Austl. 157/H3
Bedretto, Swi. 87/E5
Bedrock, Co, US 175/H1
Bedsted, Den. 66/C3
Bedum, Neth. 78/D2
Bedwas, Wal, UK 62/C3
Bedworth, Eng, UK 63/E2
Bee (cr.), Eng, UK 133/F6
Bee Branch, Ar, US 179/H3
Bee Spring, Ky, US 188/D2
Beebe, Ar, US 179/J3
Beech Grove, In, US 186/C5
Beecher Falls, Vt, US 187/L2
Beecher Island, Co, US 180/C4
Beechgrove, Tn, US 188/D3
Beechworth, Austl. 159/C3
Beechy, Sk, Can. 171/L2
Beef Island (int'l arpt.), UK 197/M8
Beek, Neth. 81/E2
Beek, Neth. 78/C5
Beekman, La, US 179/J4
Beelbangera, Austl. 159/C2
Beelen, Ger. 79/F5
Beeler, Ks, US 178/D1
Beelitz, Ger. 68/P7
Beenleigh, Austl. 160/D4
Beer, Eng, UK 62/C5
Beer (pt.), Eng, UK 62/C5
Be'er Menuḥa, Isr. 130/D4
Be'er Sheva' (Beersheba), Isr. 131/B6
Beerato, Som. 144/C3
Beerfelden, Ger. 84/B3
Be'eri, Isr. 131/A6
Beernem, Belg. 80/C1
Beersheba (Be'er Sheva'), Isr. 131/B6
Beerzel, Belg. 81/D1
Beesel, Neth. 78/D6
Beeville, Tx, US 176/F3
Befale, D.R. Congo 147/E2
Befandriana, Madg. 152/G8
Befandriana, Madg. 152/J6
Befasy, Madg. 152/H8
Befori, D.R. Congo 147/E2
Beforona, Madg. 152/J7
Befotaka, Madg. 152/H8
Befotaka, Madg. 152/J6
Beg (lake), NI, UK 60/B2
Bega (riv.), Ger. 79/F5
Bega, Austl. 159/D3
Bega Veche (riv.), Cro. 76/E3
Begamganj, India 122/B4
Begamganj, Bang. 123/H4
Bégard, Fr. 82/B3
Begarslan (peak), Trkm. 97/K4
Begejci, Yugo. 76/E3
Beggs, Ok, US 179/F3
Bēgī, Eth. 142/G3
Begichev (isl.), Rus. 101/M2
Begna (riv.), Nor. 64/D3
Begoml', Bela. 67/N4
Begumpet (int'l arpt.), India 121/C2
Begunitsy, Rus. 67/N2
Begusarai, India 123/F3
Béhague (pt.), FrG. 206/D1
Behāla, India 118/E3
Behala (str.), Indo. 116/B4
Behamberg, Aus. 85/H6
Behara, Madg. 152/H9
Behat, India 124/D4
Behbahān, Iran 129/G4
Beheloka, Madg. 152/G8
Behenjy-Afovany, Madg. 152/H7
Behleg, China 104/C4
Béhoust, Fr. 56/H5
Behren-lès-Forbach, Fr. 81/F5
Behri (riv.), Nepal 122/C1
Behshahr, Iran 129/H2
Bei (mts.), China 100/K5
Bei'an, China 105/K2
Beiba, China 104/F5
Beibei, China 113/E2
Beida (riv.), China 104/D4
Beidianzi, China 107/A4
Beierfeld, Ger. 85/F1
Beigantang (isl.), Tai. 113/J3
Beigua (peak), It. 88/B5
Beiguo, China 106/L8
Beihai, China 113/F4
Beijing (prov.), China 104/H3
Beijing (cap.), China 106/H7
Beijing Capital (int'l arpt.), China 106/H6
Beilen, Neth. 78/D3
Beiling, China 113/G3
Beiliu, China 113/F4
Beilngries, Ger. 85/E4
Beilstein, Ger. 84/C4
Beilu (riv.), China 104/C5
Beilun (pass), China 113/E4
Bein Tharsuinn (peak), Sc, UK 59/B1
Beinamar, Chad 142/B3
Beinasco, It. 90/D2
Beindersheim, Ger. 84/B3
Beinn a' Chuallaich (peak), Sc, UK 59/B3
Beinn a' Ghlò (peak), Sc, UK 59/C3
Beinn a' Mheadhoin (lake), Sc, UK 59/B2
Beinn Bhàn (peak), Sc, UK 59/A3
Beinn Bheula (peak), Sc, UK 59/B4
Beinn Bhrotain (peak), Sc, UK 59/C2
Beinn Bhuidhe (peak), Sc, UK 59/B4
Beinn Bhuidhe Mhór (peak), Sc, UK 59/B2
Beinn Dearg (peak), Sc, UK 59/B1
Beinn Dearg (peak), Sc, UK 59/C3
Beinn Dòrain (peak), Sc, UK 59/B4
Beinn Eighe (peak), Sc, UK 59/A1
Beinn Heasgarnich (peak), Sc, UK 59/B3
Beinn Mholach (peak), Sc, UK 59/B3
Beinn Mhór (peak), Sc, UK 59/A4
Beinwil am See, Swi. 86/E3
Beipiao, China 106/E2
Beira (int'l arpt.), Moz. 149/G3
Beira, Moz. 149/G3
Beira Alta, Ang. 146/C5
Beirong, China 113/F2
Beiru (riv.), China 106/C4
Beirut (int'l arpt.), Leb. 131/C1
Beirut (Bayrūt) (cap.), Leb. 131/C1
Beiseker, Ab, Can. 171/H2
Beishan, China 104/D3
Beishan, China 113/F3
Beit Jann, Isr. 131/C3
Beitbridge, Zim. 149/F4
Beith, Sc, UK 59/B5
Beiuş, Rom. 76/F2
Beizhen, China 107/A2
Beja, Port. 72/B3
Beja (dist.), Port. 72/A4
Bejaïa, Alg. 138/H4
Bejaïa (wilaya), Alg. 138/H4
Béjar, Sp. 72/C2
Bejhi (riv.), Pak. 127/J3
Bekasi, Indo. 115/D3
Bekdash, Trkm. 97/K4
Békés (prov.), Hun. 76/E2
Békés, Hun. 76/E2
Békéscsaba, Hun. 76/E2
Bekilli, Turk. 128/B2
Bekily, Madg. 152/H9
Bekitro, Madg. 152/H9
Bekodoka, Madg. 152/H7
Bek'ojī, Eth. 144/A4
Bekopaka, Madg. 152/H7
Bekoropoka, Madg. 152/G8
Bekwai, Gha. 141/E5
Bel, La, US 190/B2
Bel Air, Md, US 194/B4
Bel Air South, Md, US 194/B5
Bel Aire, Ks, US 179/F2
Belá, Slvk. 69/K4
Bela, Pak. 127/J3
Bela, D.R. Congo 147/G2
Belā, India 118/D2
Bela Crkva, Yugo. 76/E3
Bela Cruz, Braz. 207/F3
Bela Palanka, Yugo. 76/F4
Bělá pod Bezdězem, Czh. 85/H1
Belā Pratāpgarh, India 122/C3
Bela Vista, Ang. 148/C2
Bela Vista, Braz. 213/E2
Bela Vista, Moz. 151/F2
Bela Vista de Goiás, Braz. 210/C3
Bela Vista do Paraíso, Braz. 213/G2
Belabérim (well), Niger 142/B2
Bélabo, Camr. 142/B4
Belair Rec. Pk., Austl. 157/M9
Belampalli, India 121/C2
Belan (riv.), India 122/D3
Belanak (cape), Malay. 115/C1
Belang, Indo. 117/F3
Belarus(ctry.) 55/G3
Belas, Port. 73/P10
Belawan, Indo. 115/B2
Belaya (riv.), Rus. 100/F4
Belaya (peak), Eth. 142/H3
Belaya Glina, Rus. 99/L4
Belaya Kalitva, Rus. 99/L3
Belbo (riv.), It. 88/B3
Bełchatów, Pol. 69/K3
Belchen (peak), Ger. 86/D2
Belcher, La, US 179/H4
Belcher (isls.), Can. 165/J4
Belcher (isls.), On, Can. 167/H3
Belcher (chan.), Nun, Can. 167/S7
Belchite, Sp. 73/E2
Belcourt, ND, US 182/E3
Belda, India 123/F4
Beldānga, India 123/G4
Belebey, Rus. 95/M5
Beled Weyne, Som. 144/C4
Belefuanai, Libr. 140/C5
Bélel, Camr. 142/B4
Belém, Braz. 207/H4
Belém, Braz. 206/D3
Belém de São Francisco, Braz. 207/G5
Belem Tower, Port. 73/P10
Belen, Turk. 130/E1
Belen, Turk. 130/C1
Belén, Nic. 196/D5
Belen, NM, US 175/J3
Belén, Uru. 212/E4
Belén, Chile 212/B1
Belén, Arg. 212/C3
Belén, Bol. 209/E5
Belén de Escobar, Arg. 215/J11
Belén de Umbría, Col. 207/K7
Belene, Bul. 77/G4
Bélep (isls.), NCal. 163/T11
Beles Wenz (riv.), Eth. 142/G3
Belesar (res.), Sp. 72/B1
Belev, Rus. 96/F1
Belfair, Wa, US 193/B3
Belfast (dist.), NI, UK 60/B2
Belfast (cap.), NI, UK 60/C2
Belfast, SAfr. 151/E2
Belfast Lough (bay), NI, UK 60/C2
Belfaux, Swi. 86/D4
Belfield, ND, US 182/C4
Bēlfodiyo, Eth. 142/G3
Belford, Eng, UK 59/E5
Belfort (dept.), Fr. 86/C2
Belfort, Fr. 86/C2
Belfountain, On, Can. 186/S8
Belfry, Mt, US 173/J1
Belgioioso, It. 88/C3
Belgium(ctry.) 55/E3
Belgorod, Rus. 99/J2
Belgorod Oblast, Rus. 96/F2
Belgrade, Mn, US 183/G5
Belgrade, Mo, US 188/B2
Belgrade (Beograd) (cap.), Yugo. 76/E3
Belgreen, Al, US 188/D3
Belhavel (lake), Ire. 58/B1
Belhaven, NC, US 189/J3
Beli Drim (riv.), Yugo. 75/G1
Beli Drim (riv.), Alb. 76/E4
Beli Manastir, Cro. 76/D3
Beli Timok (riv.), Yugo. 76/F4
Belidzhi, Rus. 97/J4
Bélinga, Gabon 146/C2
Belington, WV, US 189/H1
Belinskiy, Rus. 97/G1
Belinyu, Indo. 115/D3
Belitsa, Bul. 75/H2
Belitung (isl.), Indo. 116/C4
Belize, Ang. 146/C4
Belize (riv.), Belz. 200/D2
Belize(ctry.) 165/J8
Belize City, Belz. 200/D2
Bélizon, FrG. 206/C1
Beljanica (peak), Yugo. 76/E3
Belk, Tx, US 179/G4
Belknap (mtn.), NH, US 187/L3
Bel'kovskiy (isl.), Rus. 101/N2
Bell, Ger. 81/G3
Bell (isl.), Nf, Can. 185/L2
Bell, Fl, US 191/G3
Bell, Ca, US 192/F8
Bell, Austl. 160/C4
Bell (riv.), Qu, Can. 167/J4
Bell (pen.), Nun, Can. 167/H2
Bell (pt.), PNG 155/F2
Bell (pt.), Austl. 157/G5
Bell (riv.), Austl. 159/D1
Bell Gardens, Ca, US 192/F8
Bell Rock (Inchcape) (isl.), Sc, UK 59/D4
Bell Ville, Arg. 212/D5
Bella Coola, BC, Can. 168/AA13
Bella Flor, Bol. 208/E3
Bella Vista, Ar, US 179/G2
Bella Vista, Bol. 209/F4
Bella Vista, Arg. 212/C3
Bella Vista, Par. 213/E2
Bella Vista, Arg. 212/E4
Bellac, Fr. 70/D3
Bellachat (peak), Fr. 90/C1
Bellaco, Uru. 215/K10
Bellaghy, NI, UK 60/B2
Bellagio, It. 87/F6
Bellaire, Oh, US 186/F4
Bellaire, Mi, US 186/D2
Bellaire, Tx, US 177/M9
Bellamy, Al, US 188/C4
Bellananagh, Ire. 58/C2
Bellano, It. 87/F5
Bellaria, It. 89/F5
Bellary, India 121/C3
Bellata, Austl. 158/D1
Bellavista (cape), It. 74/A3
Bellavista, Ecu. 208/J7
Bellavista, Peru 208/B2
Bellavista, Peru 208/B2
Bellbird, Austl. 159/E1
Belle, Mo, US 179/J1
Belle (riv.), On, Can. 193/G7
Belle, WV, US 189/G1
Belle Chasse, La, US 190/D3
Belle Fourche (res.), SD, US 182/C5
Belle Fourche, SD, US 180/C1
Belle Fourche (riv.), Wy,SD, US 180/B2
Belle Glade, Fl, US 191/H4
Belle Haven, Va, US 194/A6
Belle Isle, Fl, US 190/N7
Belle Isle (str.), NF, Can. 165/M4
Belle Plaine, Ks, US 179/F2
Belle Plaine, Ia, US 181/H3
Belle River, On, Can. 193/G7
Belle Terre, NY, US 195/E2
Belle Yella, Libr. 140/C5
Belle-Anse, Haiti 201/H2
Belle-Ile (isl.), Fr. 70/B3
Belle-isle-en-Terre, Fr. 82/B3
Belleair, Fl, US 190/K8
Belleair Beach, Fl, US 190/K8
Belleair Bluffs, Fl, US 190/K8
Belleek, NI, UK 60/B3
Bellefontaine, Oh, US 186/E4
Bellefontaine, Ms, US 188/C4
Bellefonte, Ar, US 179/H2
Bellefonte, Pa, US 187/H4
Bellefonte, De, US 194/C4
Bellegarde-sur-Valserine, Fr. 86/B5
Bellême, Fr. 83/F4
Bellenberg, Ger. 87/G1
Bellencombre, Fr. 83/G1
Bellenden Ker NP, Austl. 160/B2
Belleoram, Nf, Can. 185/K2
Belleplain, NJ, US 194/D5
Bellerive-sur-Allier, Fr. 70/E3
Bellerose, NY, US 195/L9
Belleu, Fr. 80/C5
Belleview, Fl, US 191/G3
Belleview, Mo, US 188/B2
Belleville, On, Can. 187/H2
Belleville, Fr. 86/A5
Belleville, Ar, US 179/H3
Belleville, Il, US 188/C1
Belleville, Ks, US 180/F4
Belleville, Mi, US 193/E7
Belleville, NJ, US 195/J8
Belleville, Pa, US 187/H4
Belleville-sur-Meuse, Fr. 81/E5
Bellevue, Id, US 173/F2
Bellevue, Ia, US 181/J2
Bellevue, Md, US 194/B6
Bellevue, Ne, US 181/G3
Bellevue, Oh, US 186/E4
Bellevue, Wa, US 170/C4
Belley, Fr. 86/B6
Bellflower, Ca, US 192/F8
Bellheim, Ger. 84/B4
Bellignat, Fr. 86/B5
Bellinge, Den. 66/D4
Bellingen, Austl. 158/E1
Bellingham, Eng, UK 61/F1
Bellingham, Mn, US 181/F1
Bellingham, Wa, US 170/C3
Bellingrath Gardens and Home, Al, US 190/D2
Bellingshausen (sea), Ant. 216/U
Bellingshausen (isl.), FrPol. 163/K6
Bellingwolde, Neth. 79/E2
Bellinzago Novarese, It. 88/B2
Bellinzona, Swi. 87/F5
Belliveau Cove, NS, Can. 184/D3
Bellizzi, It. 92/D6
Bellmawr, NJ, US 194/C4
Bellmead, Tx, US 177/F2
Bellmore, NY, US 195/L9
Bello, Col. 207/K6
Bellona, It. 92/D5
Bellona Reefs (reef), NCal. 162/E7
Bellot (str.), Nun, Can. 166/G1
Bellows Falls, Vt, US 187/K3
Bellport, NY, US 195/F2
Bells, Tx, US 179/F4
Bells, Tn, US 188/C3
Bellsbank, Sc, UK 59/B6
Bellshill, Sc, UK 59/B5
Bellsite, Mb, Can. 182/D1
Belluno (prov.), It. 89/E1
Belluno, It. 71/K3
Bellville, Oh, US 186/E4
Bellville, SAfr. 150/L10
Bellville, Tx, US 176/F3
Bellville, Ga, US 189/G4
Bellwald, Swi. 86/E5
Bellwood, La, US 190/B2
Belly (riv.), Ab, Can. 171/H3
Belm, Ger. 79/F4
Belmar, NJ, US 194/D3
Bélmez, Sp. 72/C3
Belmond, Ia, US 181/H2
Belmont, Mb, Can. 182/E3
Belmont, NS, Can. 184/F3
Belmont, Ca, US 193/K11
Belmont, La, US 190/B2
Belmont, Ms, US 188/C3
Belmont, Mt, US 171/K4
Belmont, NC, US 189/G3
Belmont, Ne, US 180/C2
Belmont, NY, US 187/G3
Belmonte, Port. 72/B2
Belmonte, Sp. 72/D3
Belmonte, Braz. 211/F2
Belmopan (cap.), Belz. 200/D2
Belmullet, Ire. 57/P9
Belo, Madg. 152/G8
Belo Campo, Braz. 211/E2
Belo Horizonte, Braz. 210/E3
Belo Jardim, Braz. 207/G5
Belo-Tsiribihina, Madg. 152/H7
Beloeil, Belg. 80/C2
Beloeil, Qu, Can. 185/P6
Belogorsk, Rus. 105/K1
Beloha, Madg. 152/H9
Beloit, Ks, US 180/E4
Beloit, Wi, US 181/K2
Belokany, Azer. 97/H4
Béloko, CAfr. 142/B4
Belomorsk, Rus. 94/G2
Belondo-Kundu, D.R. Congo 146/D3
Beloomut, Rus. 94/H5
Beloozërsk, Bela. 96/C1
Belorado, Sp. 70/B5
Belorechensk, Rus. 99/K5
Belören, Turk. 128/C2
Beloretsk, Rus. 95/N5
Beloslav, Bul. 77/H4
Belovo, Bul. 75/J1
Belovo, Rus. 100/J4
Beloye (lake), Rus. 100/D3
Belozersk, Rus. 94/H3
Belozërskoye, Rus. 95/Q5
Belper, Eng, UK 61/G5
Belpre, Oh, US 186/F5
Belsand, India 123/E2
Belsay, Eng, UK 61/G1
Belt, Mt, US 171/J4
Belterra, Braz. 206/C3
Belterwijde (lake), Neth. 78/D3
Beltheim, Ger. 81/G3
Belton (lake), Tx, US 177/F2
Belton, Mo, US 179/G1
Belton, SC, US 189/F3
Belton, Eng, UK 63/H1
Belton, Tx, US 176/F2
Beltra (lake), Ire. 58/A2
Beltrán, Arg. 212/C3
Beltsville, Md, US 194/B5
Belturbet, Ire. 58/C1
Beltzville (lake), Pa, US 194/C2
Belukha (peak), Rus. 125/E2
Belumut (peak), Malay. 115/C2
Beluran, Malay. 114/B4
Belvedere, Ca, US 193/K11
Belvédère du Cirque, Fr. 90/D3
Belvedere Park, Ga, US 189/M7
Belvidere, SD, US 180/D2
Belvidere, Il, US 181/K2
Belvidere, NJ, US 194/C2
Belview, Mn, US 181/G1
Belvoir NP, Isr. 131/D3
Belwood, On, Can. 186/S8
Belyando (riv.), Austl. 153/D3
Belyayevka, Rus. 97/L2
Belynkovichi, Bela. 96/E1
Belyy (isl.), Rus. 216/A
Belyy Yar, Rus. 100/J4
Belyye Berega, Rus. 96/E1
Belz, Ukr. 98/C2
Belzig, Ger. 68/G2
Belzoni, Ms, US 188/B4
Bełżyce, Pol. 69/M3
Bémal, CAfr. 142/C4
Bemanevika, Madg. 152/J6
Bemanevika, Madg. 152/J6
Bemaraha (plat.), Madg. 152/H7
Bemarivo (riv.), Madg. 152/H7
Bembe, Ang. 146/C4
Bembéréké, Ben. 141/F4
Bembezi (riv.), Zim. 149/F3
Bembibre, Sp. 72/B1
Bembo, Ang. 146/D5
Bemboka, Austl. 159/D3
Bembridge, Eng, UK 63/E5
Bemebesi, Zim. 149/F4
Bemetāra, India 121/D1
Bemidji, Mn, US 183/G4
Bemis, SD, US 181/F1
Bemmel, Neth. 78/C5
Bempton, Eng, UK 61/H3
Ben Aigan (hill), Sc, UK 59/C1
Ben Alder (peak), Sc, UK 59/B3
Ben Améra (well), Mrta. 136/B5
Ben Avon (peak), Sc, UK 59/C2
Ben Boyd NP, Austl. 159/E3
Ben Chonzie (peak), Sc, UK 59/C4
Ben Cleuch (peak), Sc, UK 59/C4
Ben Cruachan (peak), Sc, UK 59/A4
Ben Dash (peak), Ire. 58/A4
Ben Davis (pt.), NJ, US 194/C5
Ben Giang, Viet. 120/D3
Ben Gurion (int'l arpt.), Isr. 131/B4
Ben Hope (peak), Sc, UK 57/R7
Ben Ime (peak), Sc, UK 59/B4
Ben Lawers (peak), Sc, UK 59/B3
Ben Ledi (peak), Sc, UK 59/B4
Ben Lomond (peak), Sc, UK 59/B4
Ben Lomond, Ca, US 174/A2
Ben Lomond NP, Austl. 158/C4
Ben Lui (peak), Sc, UK 59/B4
Ben Macdui (peak), Sc, UK 59/C2
Ben More (peak), Sc, UK 57/Q8
Ben More (peak), Sc, UK 59/B4
Ben More Assynt (peak), Sc, UK 57/R7
Ben Msik-sidi Othmane (prov.), Mor. 138/A2
Ben Nevis (peak), Sc, UK 59/B3
Ben Quang, Viet. 120/D2
Ben Rinnes (peak), Sc, UK 59/C2
Ben Slimane, Mor. 136/D2
Ben Slimane (prov.), Mor. 138/A3
Ben Starav (peak), Sc, UK 59/A3
Ben Tee (peak), Sc, UK 59/B2
Ben Thuy, Viet. 112/E5
Ben Tirran (peak), Sc, UK 59/C3
Ben Tre, Viet. 120/D4
Ben Vane (peak), Sc, UK 59/B4
Ben Vorlich (peak), Sc, UK 59/B4
Ben Vrackie (peak), Sc, UK 59/C3
Ben Wyvis (peak), Sc, UK 59/B1
Ben Zohra (well), Alg. 136/E3
Bena, Mn, US 183/G4
Bena-Bendi, D.R. Congo 146/E4
Bena-Dibele, D.R. Congo 147/E4
Bena-Makima, D.R. Congo 147/E4
Benabarre, Sp. 73/F1
Benahmed, Mor. 136/D2
Benalla, Austl. 159/B3
Benalmádena, Sp. 72/C4
Benalto, Ab, Can. 170/G1
Benāpol, Bang. 123/G4
Benavente, Sp. 72/C1
Benavides, Bol. 209/E4
Benavides, Tx, US 177/E4
Benbane (pt.), NI, UK 60/B1
Benbecula (isl.), Sc, UK 57/Q8
Benbonyathe (peak), Austl. 157/H4
Benbrack (peak), Ire. 58/C1
Benbrook (lake), Tx, US 176/K7
Benbrook (dam), Tx, US 176/K7
Benbrook, Tx, US 176/K7
Benburb, NI, UK 60/B3
Benchley, Tx, US 177/F2
Bencubbin, Austl. 156/C4
Bend, Or, US 172/C1
Bend, Tx, US 177/E2
Benda (cape), Indo. 115/E3
Bende, Nga. 141/G5
Bendemeer, Austl. 158/D1
Bender Beyla, Som. 144/D3
Bender Cassim (Bosaaso), Som. 144/D3
Bendersville, Pa, US 194/A4
Bendery (Tighina), Mol. 98/E4
Bendigo, Austl. 159/B3
Bendoc, Austl. 159/D3
Bendorf, Ger. 66/C4
Bendugu, SLeo. 140/C4
Benduma, Libr. 140/C5
Bēne, Lat. 67/K3
Bene Beraq, Isr. 131/B4
Benedict (mt.), Nf, Can. 167/L3
Benediktbeuern, Ger. 87/H2
Benediktenwand (peak), Ger. 87/H2
Beneditinos, Braz. 207/F4
Benenitra, Madg. 152/H8
Benešov, Czh. 85/H3
Benevento (prov.), It. 92/D5
Benevento, It. 92/D5
Benfeld, Fr. 86/D1
Benga, Moz. 149/G3
Bengal (bay), Asia 103/H8
Bengal, Bay of (gulf), Asia 118/E4
Bengbis, Camr. 146/C2
Bengbu, China 106/D4
Benge, Wa, US 170/E4
Benghāzī, Libya 93/J4
Bengkalis, Indo. 115/C2
Bengkalis (isl.), Indo. 116/B3
Bengkayang, Indo. 116/C3
Bengkulu, Indo. 115/C3
Bengkulu (prov.), Indo. 115/C4
Bengo (riv.), Ang. 146/C5
Bengo (prov.), Ang. 146/C5
Bengo (bay), Ang. 146/C5
Bengough, Sk, Can. 182/B3
Bengtsby, Fin. 65/F4
Bengtsfors, Swe. 66/E2
Benguela, Ang. 148/B2
Benguela (prov.), Ang. 148/B2
Benguerir, Mor. 136/D2
Benguerua (isl.), Moz. 149/G4
Bengweulu (lake), Zam. 147/G5
Bengweulu (swamp), Zam. 147/G5
Beni, Nepal 122/D1
Beni, D.R. Congo 147/G2
Beni (riv.), Bol. 203/C4
Beni (dept.), Bol. 209/E4
Beni Abbes, Alg. 137/E3
Beni Bouayach, Mor. 138/C2
Beni Ensar, Mor. 138/B2
Beni Khiar, Tun. 138/M6
Beni Mellal, Mor. 136/D2
Beni Ounif, Alg. 137/E2
Beni Saf, Alg. 138/D2
Beni Tajit, Mor. 136/E2
Benicarló, Sp. 73/F2
Benicia, Ca, US 193/K10
Benidorm, Sp. 73/E3
Benifayó, Sp. 73/E3
Benin(ctry.) 133/C3
Benin City, Nga. 141/G5
Benina (int'l arpt.), Libya 93/J4
Benisa, Sp. 73/F3
Benisheikh, Nga. 142/B3
Benito, Mb, Can. 182/D2
Benito Juárez, Mex. 198/D2
Benjamin, Tx, US 178/E4
Benjamin Constant, Braz. 208/D2
Benjamín Hill, Mex. 198/C2
Benjamin, Isla (isl.), Chile 214/B5
Benkei-misaki (cape), Japan 108/B2
Benkelman, Ne, US 180/D3
Benld, Il, US 181/K4
Benllech, Wal, UK 60/D5
Benmore (peak), Ire. 58/A1
Bennachie (hill), Sc, UK 59/D2
Bennan (pt.), Sc, UK 59/A6
Benndale, Ms, US 190/D2
Benneckenstein, Ger. 79/H5
Bennett (isl.), Rus. 101/Q2
Bennett (peak), Co, US 178/A2
Bennett, Wi, US 183/J4
Bennett, Co, US 180/B4
Bennettsbridge, Ire. 58/C4
Bennettsville, SC, US 189/H3
Bennichchab, Mrta. 140/B2
Bennington, Id, US 173/H2
Bennington, Ks, US 179/F1
Bennington, Ne, US 181/F3
Bennington, Ok, US 179/F3
Bennington, Vt, US 187/K3
Bénodet, Fr. 82/A5
Benoit, Ms, US 188/B4
Benom (peak), Malay. 115/C2
Bénoué (riv.), Camr. 142/B3
Bénoue, PN de la, Camr. 142/B3
Benover, Eng, UK 56/E3
Benoy, Chad 142/C3
Bensenville, Il, US 193/Q16
Bensheim, Ger. 84/B3
Benson, Mn, US 183/G5
Benson, La, US 176/H2
Benson, Sk, Can. 182/C3
Benson, Az, US 175/G5
Benson, NC, US 189/H3
Bensonhurst (nbrhd.), NY, US 195/K9
Benta (riv.), Hun. 77/Q10
Benta Seberang, Malay. 115/C1
Bentham, Eng, UK 61/F3
Bentheim, Ger. 79/E4
Benti, Gui. 140/B4
Bentiaba, Ang. 148/B2
Bentiaba (riv.), Ang. 148/B2
Bentinck (isl.), Austl. 155/E4
Bentiu, Sudan 142/F3
Bentley, ND, US 182/C4
Bentley, Ok, US 179/F3
Bentley, Eng, UK 61/G4
Bentley, Eng, UK 56/A3
Bento Gonçalves, Braz. 213/G4
Benton, Ar, US 179/H3
Benton, La, US 179/H4
Benton, Il, US 188/C2
Benton, Ms, US 188/B4
Benton, Ky, US 188/C2
Benton, Mo, US 188/C2
Benton, Tn, US 188/E3
Benton, Pa, US 194/B1
Benton Harbor, Mi, US 186/C3
Benton Lake NWR, Mt, US 171/J4
Bentong, Malay. 115/C2
Bentonia, Ms, US 188/B4
Bentonville, Ar, US 179/G2
Bentonville, Va, US 189/H1
Bent's Old Fort Nat'l Hist. Site, Co, US 178/C1
Benua Martinus, Indo. 116/D3
Benue (state), Nga. 141/H5
Benue (riv.), Nga. 133/C4
Benxi, China 107/B2
Benxi, China 107/C2
Beo, Indo. 117/G3
Beočin, Yugo. 76/D3
Beoga, Indo. 117/J4
Beograd (int'l arpt.), Yugo. 76/E3
Beograd (Belgrade) (cap.), Yugo. 76/E3
Beohāri, India 122/C3
Béoumi, C.d'Iv. 140/D5
Béoux (riv.), Fr. 90/B3
Beowawe, Nv, US 172/E3
Beppu (bay), Japan 110/B4
Beppu, Japan 110/B4
Bequia (isl.), StV. 197/N9
Bequimão, Braz. 207/E3
Bera, Bang. 123/G3
Beragh, NI, UK 60/A2
Beraketa, Madg. 152/H8
Beraketa, Madg. 152/H9
Beramanja, Madg. 152/J6
Beras Basah (cape), Malay. 115/C2
Berasia, India 122/A4
Berat, Alb. 75/F2
Beratus (peak), Indo. 117/E4
Beratzhausen, Ger. 85/E4
Berau (bay), Indo. 162/C5
Berau (riv.), Indo. 117/E3
Beravina, Madg. 152/H7
Berbenno di Valtellina, It. 87/F5
Berbera, Som. 144/C3
Berbérati, CAfr. 142/B4
Berbice (riv.), Guy. 205/G3
Berceto, It. 88/C4
Berchem, Belg. 78/B6
Bercher, Swi. 86/C4
Berching, Ger. 85/E4
Berchogur, Kaz. 97/L2
Berchtesgaden, Ger. 71/K3
Berchtesgaden, NP Ger. 71/K3
Berck, Fr. 80/A3
Berclair, Tx, US 177/F3
Berdale, Som. 144/C4
Berdorf, Lux. 81/F4
Berdsk, Rus. 100/J4
Berdyans'k, Ukr. 99/J4
Berdyansk (bay), Ukr. 99/J4
Berdychiv, Ukr. 98/E3
Béré, Chad 142/C3
Bere Regis, Eng, UK 62/D5
Berea, Ky, US 188/E2
Berea, Les. 150/D3
Bereah, Fl, US 190/M8
Berebere, Indo. 117/G3
Bereguardo, It. 88/C3
Berehomet, Ukr. 98/C3
Berehove, Ukr. 69/M4
Bereina, PNG 155/G2
Bereku, Tanz. 145/A3
Berekum, Gha. 141/E5
Berenguela, Bol. 212/B1
Berenice (ruin), Egypt 135/G4
Berens (isl.), Mb, Can. 182/F1
Berens River, Mb, Can. 182/F1
Berenty, Madg. 152/H8
Beresford, NB, Can. 184/E2
Beresford, SD, US 181/F2
Bereşti, Rom. 77/H2
Berettyóújfalu, Hun. 76/E2
Berevo, Madg. 152/H7
Berezan', Ukr. 98/F2
Berezhany, Ukr. 98/C3
Berezhnoye, Rus. 94/H4
Berezino, Bela. 67/N5
Berezivka, Ukr. 98/F4
Bereznik, Rus. 94/J3
Berezniki, Rus. 95/N4
Berezovo, Rus. 100/G3
Berëzovskiy, Rus. 95/P4
Berezovyy, Rus. 105/L1
Berg, Ger. 87/H2
Berg, Swi. 87/F2
Berg, Lux. 81/F4
Berg, Ger. 84/B5
Berg (riv.), SAfr. 150/B4
Berg bei Rohrbach, Aus. 85/G5
Berg en Dal, Sur. 206/C1
Berga, Sp. 73/F1
Bergama, Turk. 96/C5
Bergamo (prov.), It. 87/F6
Bergamo, It. 88/C2
Bergara, Sp. 72/D1
Bergatruete, Ger. 87/F2
Bergedorf, Ger. 79/H2
Bergen, Nor. 66/A1
Bergen, Ger. 66/E4
Bergen, Ger. 79/G3
Bergen, Neth. 78/B3
Bergen (co.), NJ, US 194/D2
Bergen aan Zee, Neth. 78/B3
Bergen op Zoom, Neth. 78/B5
Bergenfield, NJ, US 195/K8
Berger, Nor. 64/S9
Bergerac, Fr. 70/D4
Bergeresse (riv.), Fr. 83/H5
Bergeyk, Neth. 78/C6
Bergheim, Ger. 81/F2
Bergheim, Aus. 85/G7
Bergheim, Tx, US 177/E3
Bergisch Gladbach, Ger. 81/G2
Bergkamen, Ger. 79/E5
Bergman, Ar, US 179/H2
Bergnäset, Swe. 94/D2
Bergneustadt, Ger. 81/G1
Bergrheinfeld, Ger. 68/F4
Bergsbrunna, Swe. 65/A1
Bergse Maas (riv.), Neth. 78/B5
Bergshamra, Swe. 66/H2
Bergsvatnet (lake), Nor. 64/R9
Bergsviken, Swe. 64/G2
Bergtheim, Ger. 84/D3
Berguent, Mor. 138/C2
Bergues, Fr. 80/B2
Bergum, Neth. 78/D2
Bergumermeer (lake), Neth. 78/D2
Bergün-Bravuogn, Swi. 87/F4
Bergviken (lake), Swe. 66/G1
Berh, Mong. 104/G2
Berhala (str.), Indo. 115/C3
Berhampore, India 123/G3
Berhampur, India 121/E2
Beri Khās, India 124/D5
Berikat (cape), Indo. 115/D3
Bering (str.), Rus.,US 103/U3
Bering (isl.), Rus. 101/S4
Bering (sea), Asia NAm. 101/U4
Beringen, Belg. 81/E1
Beringovskiy, Rus. 101/T3
Beritarikap (cape), Indo. 115/C3
Berja, Sp. 72/D4
Berkane, Mor. 138/C2
Berkel (riv.), Ger. 68/D2
Berkel, Neth. 78/B5
Berkeley, Eng, UK 62/D3
Berkeley Heights, NJ, US 195/H9
Berkeley Lake, Ga, US 189/M7
Berkeley Springs (Bath), WV, US 187/G5
Berkhamsted, Eng, UK 56/B1
Berkheim, Ger. 87/G1
Berkhout, Neth. 78/B3
Berkley, Mi, US 193/F6
Berkovitsa, Bul. 77/F4
Berks (co.), Pa, US 194/C3
Berkshire (co.), Eng, UK 63/E3
Berkshire Downs (hills), Eng, UK 63/E3
Berlaimont, Fr. 80/C3
Berlanga de Duero, Sp. 72/D2
Berlare, Belg. 80/D1
Berleburg, Ger. 79/F6
Berlicum, Neth. 78/C5
Berlin, Ga, US 191/G2
Berlin (cap.), Ger. 68/Q6
Berlin (state), Ger. 68/Q6
Berlin (mtn.), Nv, US 172/E4
Berlin, Wi, US 181/K2
Berlin, NJ, US 194/D4
Berlin, Md, US 189/K1
Bermagui, Austl. 159/E3
Bermejillo, Mex. 177/C5
Bermejo (riv.), Arg. 203/D5
Bermejo, Arg. 214/D1
Bermeo, Sp. 70/B5
Bermillo de Sayago, Sp. 72/B2
Bermuda (isl.), UK 165/L6
Bermudian (cr.), Pa, US 194/A4
Bern (canton), Swi. 86/D4
Bern (cap.), Swi. 86/D4
Bern-Belp (int'l arpt.), Swi. 86/D4
Bernabé Rivera, Uru. 213/E4
Bernal, Peru 208/A2
Bernalda, It. 74/E2
Bernalillo, NM, US 175/J3
Bernard (riv.), NW, Can. 166/D1
Bernardo, NM, US 175/J3
Bernardo O'Higgins, PN, Chile 215/B6
Bernardston, Ma, US 187/K3
Bernardsville, NJ, US 194/D2
Bernau, Ger. 86/E2
Bernau, Ger. 68/Q6
Bernay, Fr. 83/F2
Bernbeuren, Ger. 87/G2
Bernburg, Ger. 68/F3
Berne, In, US 186/D4
Berne (riv.), Ger. 79/F2
Bernes-sur-Oise, Fr. 56/J4
Bernese Alps (mtn.), Swi. 71/G3
Bernhardswald, Ger. 85/F4

Bernice, La, US 179/H4
Bernie, Mo, US 188/C2
Bernier (isl.), Austl. 156/B3
Bernier (bay), Nun, Can. 166/G1
Bernières-sur-Mer, Fr. 83/E2
Bernierville, Qu, Can. 184/B2
Bernin, Fr. 90/B2
Bernina (mtn.), Swi. 87/F5
Bernina (peak), Swi. 87/F5
Bernina, Passo del (pass), Swi. 87/G5
Bernissart, Belg. 80/C3
Bernkastel-Kues, Ger. 81/G4
Bernsbach, Ger. 85/F1
Bernville, Pa, US 194/B3
Beromünster, Swi. 86/E3
Béron (riv.), Fr. 83/E5
Berонono, Madg. 152/H8
Beroroha, Madg. 152/H8
Beroun, Czh. 85/H3
Berounka (riv.), Czh. 69/G4
Berovo, FYROM 75/H2
Berra, It. 89/E4
Berrara, Austl. 159/E2
Berre (lake), Fr. 70/F5
Berre-l'Étang, Fr. 90/B6
Berrechid, Mor. 36/D2
Berri, Austl. 157/J5
Berriane, Alg. 137/F2
Berridale, Austl. 59/D3
Berriedale, Sc, UK 57/S7
Berrien Springs, Mi, US 86/C4
Berriew, Wal, UK 62/C1
Berrigan, Austl. 59/B2
Berrima, Austl. 59/E2
Berriozábal, Mex. 200/C2
Berrondo, Uru. 2 5/K11
Berrotarán, Arg. 214/D2
Berrouaghia, Alg. 138/G4
Berry (canal), Fr. 83/G6
Berry (pt.), NS, Can. 185/G3
Berry (isls.), Bahm. 97/F2
Berry (reg.), Fr. 92/D1
Berry, Ky, US 88/E1
Berry (pt.), Eng, UK 62/C6
Berry (cr.), Ab, Can. 71/J2
Berry, Austl. 59/E2
Berry (mtn.), Pa, US 194/A2
Berryessa (peak), Ca, US 193/K9
Berryessa (lake), Ca, US 172/B4
Berryville, Ar, US 179/H2
Berryville, Va, US 189/J1
Berseba, Namb. 150/B2
Bersenbrück, Ger. 79/E3
Bershad', Ukr. 98/E3
Bersut, Rus. 95/L5
Bertam, Malay. 115/C1
Bertha, Mn, US 133/G4
Berthierville, Qu, Can. 137/K1
Berthold, ND, US 132/D3
Berthoud, Co, US 130/B3
Bertinoro, It. 89/F5
Bertiolo, It. 39/G2
Bertogne, Belg. 31/E3
Bertolínia, Braz. 207/F4
Bertoua, Camr. 142/B4
Bertram (mt.), Austl. 154/B4
Bertram, Tx, US 177/E2
Bertrand, NB, Can. 134/E2
Bertrand (peak), Arg. 2 5/B6
Bertrix, Belg. 31/E4
Bertry, Fr. 30/C3
Beru (isl.), Kiri. 162/G5
Beruas, Malay. 115/C1
Beruit (isl.), Malay. 116/D3
Beruwala, SrL. 121/C5
Bervie Water. (riv.), Sc, UK 59/D3
Berwa, India 118/B2
Berwick, Me, US 137/L3
Berwick, NS, Can. 134/E3
Berwick (nbrhd.), Austl. 158/G6
Berwick, Pa, US 194/B1
Berwick-Upon-Tweed, Eng, UK 59/D5
Berwyn (mts.), Wal, UK 60/E6
Berwyn, Il, US 193/Q16
Beryl, Ut, US 175/F2
Beryslav, Ukr. 99/G4
Berzence, Hun. 76/C2
Bès (riv.), Fr. 70/E2
Besalampy, Madg. 152/H7
Besançon, Fr. 86/C3
Bésao, Chad 142/B4
Besar (isl.), Indo. 154/A2
Besar (peak), Malay. 115/C2
Besar (peak), Indo. 117/E4
Besbre (riv.), Fr. 70/E3
Besedino, Rus. 99/J2
Beserah, Malay. 115/C2
Beshām Qala, Pak. 124/B2
Beshenkovichi, Bela. 67/N4
Beshlo Wenz (riv.), Eth. 144/A3
Beshneh, Iran 129/H4
Besikama, Indo. 154/B2
Beşiri, Turk. 128/E2
Beška, Yugo. 76/E3
Beskids (mts.), Pol. 69/L4
Beskol', Kaz. 125/D2
Beşkonak, Turk. 130/B1
Beslan, Rus. 97/H4
Besna Kobila (peak), Yugo. 76/F4
Besozzo, It. 88/B2
Bessacarr, Eng, UK 61/G5
Bessancourt, Fr. 56/J4
Bessarabia (reg.), Mol. 77/J2
Bessbrook, NI, UK 60/B3
Bessé-sur-Braye, Fr. 83/F5
Bessemer, Mi, US 183/J4
Bessemer (mtn.), Wa, US 193/D2
Bessemer, Al, US 188/D4
Bessines-sur-Gartempe, Fr. 70/D3
Best, Neth. 73/C5
Best, Tx, US 177/D2
Bestensee, Ger. 68/Q7
Bestobe, Kaz. 125/B1
Bestuzhevo, Rus. 95/K3
Bestwig, Ger. 79/F6
Beswick, Austl. 154/D3
Beswick Abor. Res., Austl. 154/D3
Bet Guvrin, Isr. 13 /B5
Bet Qama, Isr. 13 /B6
Bet She'an, Isr. 13 /D3
Bet Shemesh, Isr. 13 /B5
Betaghstown, Ire. 60/B4
Betanantanana, Madg. 152/H7
Betania, Col. 207/K7
Betanty, Madg. 152/H9
Betanzos, Sp. 72/A1
Betanzos, Bol. 212/C1
Bétaré-Oya, Camr. 142/B4
Bete Hor, Eth. 144/A3
Bétérou, Ben. 141/F4
Beth Alpha Synagogue (ruin), Isr. 131/C3
Beth She'an NP, Isr. 131/D3
Beth She'arim NP, Isr. 131/C3
Bethal, SAfr. 150/E2
Bethanie, SAfr. 149/E5
Bethanie, Namb. 150/B2
Bethany, On, Can. 187/G2
Bethany (res.), Ca, US 193/L11
Bethany, Mo, US 181/G3
Bethany, Il, US 181/K4
Bethany, La, US 176/G1
Bethel, Ak, US 168/W12
Bethel, Me, US 187/L2
Bethel, Ok, US 179/G3
Bethel, Pa, US 194/B3
Bethel, Vt, US 187/K3
Bethel Acres, Ok, US 179/F3
Bethel Island, Ca, US 193/L10
Bethel Park, Pa, US 186/F4
Bethelridge, Ky, US 188/E2
Bétheniville, Fr. 81/D5
Bétheny, Fr. 80/D5
Bethesda, Wal, UK 60/D5
Bethesda, Md, US 194/A6
Béthisy-Sainte-Pierre, Fr. 80/B5
Bethlehem, NH, US 187/L2
Bethlehem, SAfr. 150/E3
Bethlehem, Pa, US 194/C2
Bethlehem, Md, US 194/C6
Bethlehem (Bayt Laḩm), WBnk. 131/C5
Bethoncourt, Fr. 86/C2
Bethpage, NY, US 195/M9
Bethulie, SAfr. 150/D3
Béthune, Fr. 80/B2
Béthune (riv.), Fr. 70/D2
Bethune, Sk, Can. 171/M2
Betioky, Madg. 152/H8
Betoota, Austl. 160/A4
Betpak-Dala (des.), Kaz. 100/G5
Betroka, Madg. 152/H8
Betschdorf, Fr. 84/A5
Betsiamites, Qu, Can. 184/C1
Betsiamites (riv.), Qu, Can. 184/C1
Betsiamites (riv.), Qu, Can. 167/J3
Betsiamites Ind. Res., Qu, Can. 184/C1
Betsiboka (riv.), Madg. 152/H7
Betsie (pt.), Mi, US 186/C2
Betsy Layne, Ky, US 189/F2
Bettancourt-la-Ferrée, Fr. 81/D6
Bette (peak), Libya 134/C4
Bettembourg, Lux. 81/F4
Betteravia, Ca, US 174/B3
Betterton, Md, US 194/B5
Bettiah, India 123/E2
Bettlach, Swi. 86/D3
Betton, Fr. 82/D4
Betūl, India 122/A5
Betulia, Col 207/K6
Betuwe (phys. reg.), Neth. 78/C5
Betwa (riv.), India 122/B3
Betws-y-Coed, Wal, UK 60/E5
Betz, Fr. 56/L4
Betzdorf, Ger. 81/G2
Betzenstein, Ger. 85/E3
Béu, Ang. 146/C4
Beulah, ND, US 182/D4
Beulah, Mb, Can. 182/D2
Beulah, Co, US 178/B1
Beulah, Mi, US 186/C2
Beulah (lake), Wi, US 193/P14
Beulah, Austl. 158/B2
Beulah, Ms, US 188/B4
Beulah, Wy, US 180/B1
Beulakerwijde (lake), Neth. 78/C3
Beuningen, Neth. 78/C5
Beure, Fr. 86/C3
Beuvillers, Fr. 83/F2
Beuvray (peak), Fr. 70/F3
Beuvron (riv.), Fr. 70/D3
Beuvronne (riv.), Fr. 56/L5
Beuvry, Fr. 80/B2
Beuzeville, Fr. 83/F2
Bevagna, It. 91/B2
Bevensen, Ger. 79/H2
Bevent, Wi, US 181/K1
Bever (riv.), Ger. 79/E4
Bévera (riv.), Fr. 90/D5
Beveren, Belg. 78/B6
Beverin (peak), Swi. 87/F4
Beverley, Eng, UK 61/H4
Beverley, Austl. 156/C5
Beverly, Oh, US 186/F5
Beverly, WV, US 189/H1
Beverly Hills, Ca, US 192/F7
Beverly Hills, Mi, US 193/F6
Beverstedt, Ger. 79/F2
Beverungen, Ger. 79/G5
Beverwijk, Neth. 78/B4
Bevil Oaks, Tx, US 177/G2
Bewār, India 122/B3
Bewcastle, Eng, UK 61/F1
Bewdley, On, Can. 187/G2
Bewdley, Eng, UK 62/D2
Bewl Bridge (res.), Eng, UK 63/G4
Bex, Swi. 86/D5
Bexbach, Ger. 81/G5
Bexhill, Eng, UK 63/G5
Bexley (bor.), Eng, UK 56/D2
Bextograk, China 125/E4
Beyçayırı, Turk. 77/H5
Beycuma, Turk. 77/K5
Beykoz (nbrhd.), Turk. 129/N6
Beyla, Gui. 140/C4
Beylerbeyi Palace, Turk. 129/N6
Bēylul, Erit. 144/B2
Beyne-Heusay, Belg. 81/E2
Beynes, Fr. 56/H5
Beyneū, Kaz. 97/K3
Beyoglu (nbrhd.), Turk. 129/M6
Beyoneisu-Retsugan (isl.), Japan 111/F5
Beypazarı, Turk. 128/B1
Beypore, India 121/B4
Beyra, Som. 144/C4
Beyşehir, Turk. 128/B2
Beysug (bay), Rus. 99/K4
Bezaha, Madg. 152/H8
Bezau, Aus. 87/F3
Bezdan, Yugo. 76/D3
Bezděz (peak), Czh. 85/H1
Bezdrev (lake), Czh. 85/H4
Bezhetsk, Rus. 94/H4
Bezhta, Rus. 97/H4
Béziers, Fr. 70/E5
Bhabua, India 122/D3
Bhadarwāh, India 124/C3
Bhadaur, India 124/C4
Bhadohī, India 122/D3
Bhādra, India 124/C5
Bhadrāchalam, India 121/D2
Bhadrak, India 118/E3
Bhadrapur, Nepal 123/G2
Bhadreswar, India 118/A3
Bhāgalpur, India 123/F3
Bhāi Pheru, Pak. 124/B4
Bhairab (riv.), Bang. 123/G4
Bhairab Bāzār, Bang. 123/H3
Bhairahawa, Nepal 122/D2
Bhairamgarh, India 121/D2
Bhakkar, Pak. 124/A4
Bhākra (dam), India 124/D4
Bhaktapur, Nepal 123/E2
Bhāluka, Bang. 123/H3
Bhalwāl, Pak. 124/B3
Bḩamdūn, Leb. 131/D1
Bhamo, Myan. 112/C3
Bhandāra, India 121/C1
Bhandāri, India 112/B3
Bhānder, India 122/B3
Bhānin, India 124/C5
Bhanjanagar, India 121/E2
Bhānrer (range), India 122/B4
Bhānwad, India 118/A3
Bharatpur, Nepal 123/E2
Bhārātpur, India 122/A2
Bhareli (riv.), India 112/B3
Bharno, India 123/E4
Bharthana, India 122/B2
Bhasāwar, India 122/A2
Bhātiāpāra Ghāt, Bang. 123/G4
Bhatinda, India 124/C4
Bhatkal, India 121/B3
Bhātpāra, India 123/G4
Bhaun, Pak. 124/B3
Bhavāni (riv.), India 121/C4
Bhavāni, India 121/C4
Bhavnagar, India 121/B1
Bhawāna, Pak. 124/B4
Bhawāni Mandi, India 118/C3
Bhawānīgarh, India 124/D4
Bhera, Pak. 124/B3
Bheramara, Bang. 123/G3
Bheri (zone), Nepal 122/C1
Bhīkhi, India 124/C4
Bhikkīwind Uttār, India 124/C4
Bhikna Thorī, Nepal 123/E2
Bhīlwāra, India 118/B2
Bhīma (riv.), India 127/L5
Bhima (riv.), India 118/C4
Bhīmavaram, India 121/D2
Bhīmmāl, India 127/K4
Bhīmphedi, Nepal 123/E2
Bhind, India 122/B2
Bhinga, India 122/C2
Bhiwandi, India 121/B2
Bhiwāni, India 124/D5
Bhojpur, Nepal 123/F2
Bhokardan, India 121/B1
Bhola, Bang. 123/H4
Bhongaon, India 122/B2
Bhopāl, India 118/C3
Bhopālpatnam, India 121/D2
Bhor, India 121/B2
Bhraoin (lake), Sc, UK 59/A1
Bhuban, India 121/E1
Bhūj, India 127/J4
Bhumibol (dam), Thai. 120/B2
Bhutan (ctry.) 103/J7
Bi (riv.), China 104/C5
Bi Doup (peak), Viet. 120/E3
Bia (riv.), C.d'Iv. 140/E5
Biá (riv.), Braz. 208/E2
Biaboye, D.R. Congo 147/G2
Biak (isl.), Indo. 117/J4
Biak (int'l arpt.), Indo. 117/J4
Biak, Indo. 117/J4
Biakowieski NP, Pol. 69/M2
Biała Podlaska, Pol. 69/M2
Biała Podlaska (prov.), Pol. 69/M3
Białobrzegi, Pol. 69/L3
Białogard, Pol. 66/G4
Białowieski NP, Pol. 96/B1
Białowieski NP, Pol. 69/K4
Białystok (prov.), Pol. 69/M2
Białystok, Pol. 69/M2
Bianca (peak), It. 87/G4
Biancavilla, It. 74/D4
Bianco (peak), It. 92/C4
Biandrate, It. 88/B3
Biandronno, It. 88/B2
Bianga, CAfr. 142/D4
Biankouma, C.d'Iv. 140/D5
Bianya, China 112/E3
Bianyang, China 113/E3
Bianze, It. 88/B3
Biaro, D.R. Congo 147/F2
Biarritz, Fr. 70/C5
Biarvitz (Bayonne-Anglet) (arpt.), Fr. 70/C5
Biasca, Swi. 87/E5
Bibai, Japan 108/B2
Bibala, Ang. 148/B2
Bībān, Egypt 139/B3
Bibassé, Gabon 146/B2
Bibbenluke, Austl. 159/D3
Bibbiano, It. 88/D4
Bibbiena, It. 89/E6
Bibémi, Camr. 142/B3
Biberach, Ger. 86/E1
Biberach, Ger. 87/G1
Biberach an der Riss, Ger. 87/F1
Biberist, Swi. 86/D3
Bibione, It. 89/G2
Biblián, Ecu. 204/B5
Biblis, Ger. 84/B3
Bibrka, Ukr. 98/C3
Bicas, Braz. 211/N6
Bicas, Braz. 211/E3
Bicaz, Rom. 98/D4
Bicester, Eng, UK 63/E3
Bichano, Eth. 142/G4
Bicheno, Austl. 158/D4
Bichhia, India 122/C4
Bickerton (isl.), Austl. 155/E3
Bickle (peak), WV, US 189/H1
Bickleigh, Sk, Can. 171/K2
Bickleton, Wa, US 170/D5
Bicknacre, Eng, UK 56/E1
Bicknell, Ut, US 175/G1
Bicknell, In, US 188/D1
Bicske, Hun. 76/D2
Bīd Boland, Iran 129/G4
Bida, Nga. 141/G4
Bidadari (cape), Malay. 114/B4
Bidaga (rapids), C.d'Iv. 140/D5
Bīdar, India 121/C2
Biddeford, Me, US 187/L3
Biddinghuizen, Neth. 78/C4
Biddiyā, WBnk. 131/C4
Biddle, Mt, US 180/B1
Biddū, WBnk. 131/C5
Biddulph, Eng, UK 61/F5
Bidean nam Bian (peak), Sc, UK 59/A3
Bideford, Eng, UK 62/B4
Bideford (Barnstaple) (bay), Eng, UK 62/B4
Bidente (riv.), It. 89/F4
Bidford-on-Avon, Eng, UK 63/E2
Bidhūna, India 122/B2
Bīdokht, Iran 127/G2
Bidor, Malay. 115/C1
Bidouze (riv.), Fr. 73/E1
Bidrē, Eth. 144/A4
Bieber, Ca, US 172/C3
Biebesheim am Rhein, Ger. 84/B3
Biebzra (riv.), Pol. 69/M2
Biel, Swi. 86/D3
Bielawa, Pol. 69/J3
Bieldside, Sc, UK 59/D2
Bielefeld, Ger. 79/F4
Bieler (lake), Swi. 86/D3
Bieler (lake), Nun, Can. 167/J1
Biella, It. 88/B2
Bielsk Podlaski, Pol. 69/M2
Bielsko (prov.), Pol. 69/K4
Bielsko-Biała, Pol. 69/K4
Bien Hoa, Viet. 120/D4
Bien Son, Viet. 120/D1
Bienenbüttel, Ger. 79/H2
Bienfait, Sk, Can. 182/C3
Bienne (riv.), Fr. 86/B5
Bienno, It. 87/G6
Bientina, It. 88/D6
Bienvenue, FrG. 206/C2
Bienville, La, US 179/H4
Bienville (lake), Qu, Can. 167/J3
Bière, Swi. 86/C4
Bierset (int'l arpt.), Belg. 81/E2
Bierum, Neth. 78/D2
Bierutów, Pol. 69/J3
Biesbosch (reg.), Neth. 78/B5
Biesenthal, Ger. 68/Q6
Biesles, Fr. 86/B1
Biesme (riv.), Fr. 81/D5
Bieszczadzki NP, Pol. 96/B2
Bieszczadzkii NP, Pol. 69/M4
Bietigheim, Ger. 84/C5
Bietschhorn (peak), Swi. 86/D5
Bièvre, Belg. 81/E4
Bièvre (riv.), Fr. 56/J5
Bièvres, Fr. 56/J5
Biferno (riv.), It. 92/D4
Bifoun, Gabon 146/B3
Big (lake), Mi, US 193/E6
Big (des.), Austl. 158/B2
Big (isl.), On, Can. 166/G4
Big (mtn.), Nv, US 172/D3
Big (riv.), NW, Can. 166/D1
Big (cr.), Ks, US 180/D4
Big (riv.), Mo, US 180/J5
Big (cr.), Ga, US 189/M6
Big (cr.), BC, Can. 170/C2
Big (mtn.), WV, US 189/H1
Big Arm, Mt, US 170/G4
Big Bald (mtn.), NB, Can. 184/D2
Big Baldy (mtn.), Mt, US 171/J4
Big Bar Creek, BC, Can. 170/C2
Big Bear City, Ca, US 174/D3
Big Bear Lake, Ca, US 174/D3
Big Beaver, Sk, Can. 182/B3
Big Belt (mts.), Mt, US 171/J4
Big Bend, Wi, US 193/P14
Big Bend (dam), SD, US 180/E1
Big Bend, Swaz. 151/E2
Big Bend NP, Tx, US 196/A2
Big Black (riv.), Ms, US 188/B4
Big Blue (riv.), Ne, US 181/F3
Big Blue, West Fork (riv.), Ne, US 180/E3
Big Boggy NWR, Tx, US 177/G3
Big Cabin, Ok, US 179/G2
Big Canyon (riv.), Tx, US 177/C2
Big Creek, Ca, US 174/C2
Big Creek, Id, US 173/F1
Big Cypress (swamp), Fl, US 191/H4
Big Cypress National Preserve, Fl, US 191/H4
Big de Noc (bay), Mi, US 183/L5
Big Eau Plaine (res.), Wi, US 181/J1
Big Eddy (falls), Wi, US 181/K1
Big Falls, Mn, US 183/H3
Big Flat (brook), NJ, US 194/D1
Big Foot (pass), SD, US 180/C2
Big Fork (riv.), Mn, US 183/H4
Big Hole (riv.), Mt, US 173/G1
Big Hole, SAfr. 150/D3
Big Hole Nat'l Bfld., Mt, US 173/G1
Big Horn, Wy, US 173/K1
Big Indian, NY, US 187/J3
Big Lake, Tx, US 177/D2
Big Lake Nat'l Wild. Ref., Ar, US 188/B3
Big Lake Ranch, BC, Can. 170/D1
Big Lost (riv.), Id, US 173/G2
Big Marine (lake), Mn, US 183/Q6
Big Muddy (cr.), Mt, US 182/B3
Big Muddy (lake), Sk, Can. 171/M3
Big Muskego (lake), Wi, US 193/P14
Big Nemaha, North Fork (riv.), Ne, US 181/F3
Big Pine, Ca, US 174/C2
Big Pine (hill), Pa, US 194/C1
Big Pine Key, Fl, US 191/H5
Big Pines, Ca, US 192/C2
Big Piney, Mo, US 179/H2
Big Piney (riv.), Mo, US 188/B2
Big Pipe (cr.), Md, US 194/A4
Big Raccoon (riv.), In, US 186/C5
Big Rapids, Mi, US 186/D3
Big Rock (cr.), Il, US 193/N16
Big Rock, Il, US 193/N16
Big Rock, Va, US 189/F2
Big Sable (pt.), Mi, US 186/C2
Big Sandy (riv.), Wy, US 173/J3
Big Sandy, Wy, US 173/J2
Big Sandy (cr.), Co, US 180/C4
Big Sandy, Mt, US 171/J3
Big Satilla (cr.), Ga, US 191/G2
Big Sioux (riv.), Ia,SD, US 181/F2
Big Smoky (falls), Wi, US 183/K5
Big South Fork National River And Recreation Area, Tn, US 188/E2
Big Spring, Tx, US 177/D1
Big Stone (lake), Mn,SD, US 181/F1
Big Stone Gap, Va, US 189/F2
Big Stone NWR, Mn, US 181/F1
Big Sunflower (riv.), Ms, US 188/B4
Big Sur, Ca, US 174/B2
Big Thicket National Preserve, Tx, US 177/G2
Big Thicket National Preserve, Tx, US 190/A2
Big Thompson (riv.), Co, US 180/B3
Big Timber, Mt, US 171/K5
Big Trout (lake), On, Can. 166/H3
Big Tujunga Canyon (canyon), Ca, US 192/B2
Big Valley, Ab, Can. 171/H1
Big Wells, Tx, US 177/E3
Big Wood (riv.), Id, US 173/F2
Biga, Turk. 77/H5
Bigadiç, Turk. 96/D5
Bigbury (bay), Eng, UK 62/C6
Bigelow (mtn.), Me, US 187/L2
Bigfoot, Tx, US 177/E3
Bigfork, Mn, US 183/H4
Bigfork, Mt, US 171/G3
Bigga, Austl. 159/D2
Biggar, Sc, UK 59/C5
Biggar, Sk, Can. 171/L1
Bigge (riv.), Ger. 81/G1
Bigge (isl.), Austl. 154/B3
Biggenden, Austl. 160/D4
Biggers, Ar, US 188/B2
Biggin Hill (nbrhd.), Eng, UK 56/D3
Biggleswade, Eng, UK 63/F2
Biggs, Ca, US 172/C4
Biggs Army Afld., Tx, US 177/A2
Bighorn (mts.), Wy, US 168/E3
Bighorn (lake), Mt, US 173/J1
Bighorn (riv.), Wy, US 168/E2
Bighorn (riv.), Wy, US 166/F4
Bighorn, Mt, US 171/L4
Bighorn Canyon NRA, Mt, US 173/J1
Bight of Benin (bay), Afr. 133/C4
Bight of Biafra (bay), Afr. 146/A1
Bigi, D.R. Congo 147/E2
Biglerville, Pa, US 194/A4
Bignona, Sen. 140/A3
Bigosovo, Bela. 67/M4
Bigsby (isl.), On, Can. 183/G3
Biguaçu, Braz. 213/G3
Bihać, Bosn. 76/B3
Bīhar, India 123/E3
Bihār (state), India 118/D3
Biharamulo, Tanz. 147/G3
Biharamulo Game Rsv., Tanz. 147/G3
Bihārīganj, India 123/F3
Biharkeresztes, Hun. 76/E2
Bihor (co.), Rom. 69/M5
Bihorel, Fr. 83/G1
Bihoro, Japan 108/D2
Bijagós (arch.), GBis. 133/A3
Bijāpur, India 121/D2
Bījār, Iran 129/F3
Bijāwar, India 122/B3
Bijbiāra, India 124/C3
Bijeljina, Bosn. 76/D3
Bijelo Polje, Yugo. 76/D4
Bijiang, China 112/C3
Bijiaquan, China 106/J7
Bijie, China 112/E3
Bijni, India 123/H2
Bijnor, India 122/B1
Bikar (isl.), Mrsh. 162/G3
Bikenibeu, Kiri. 162/G4
Bikfayyā, Leb. 131/D1
Bikin (riv.), Rus. 105/M2
Bikin, Rus. 105/L2
Bikini (isl.), Mrsh. 162/F3
Bikita, Zim. 149/F4
Bikori, Sudan 142/G3
Bikoro, D.R. Congo 146/D3
Bikramganj, India 123/E3
Bikuar, PN do, Ang. 148/B2
Bila Krynytsya, Ukr. 99/G4
Bila Tserkva, Ukr. 98/F3
Bilād Manaḩ, Oman 127/G4
Bilāra, India 118/B2
Bilāri, India 122/B1
Bilāsipāra, India 123/H2
Bilāspur, India 124/D4
Bilāspur, India 122/B1
Bilāspur, India 122/D4
Biläsuvar, Azer. 129/G2
Bilauktaung (range), Myan.,Thai. 120/B3
Bilauri, Nepal 122/C1
Bilbao, Sp. 70/B5
Bilbays, Egypt 139/C4
Bileća, Bosn. 76/D4
Bilecik (prov.), Turk. 128/B1
Bīleh Savār, Iran 129/G2
Biłgoraj, Pol. 69/M3
Bilgrām, India 122/C2
Bilhaur, India 122/C2
Bilhorod-Dnistrovs'kyy, Ukr. 98/F4
Bili (riv.), D.R. Congo 142/D4
Bili, D.R. Congo 147/F1
Bilibino, Rus. 101/S3
Bilila, Malw. 149/G2
Bilin (riv.), Myan. 120/B2
Bilin, Myan. 112/C5
Bílina (riv.), Czh. 85/G2
Bílina, Czh. 85/G1
Biliran (isl.), Phil. 114/D3
Bilisht, Alb. 75/G2
Bilit, Malay. 114/B4
Biliu (riv.), China 107/B3
Bill, Wy, US 180/B2
Bill of Portland (pt.), Eng, UK 62/D5
Bill Williams (riv.), Az, US 175/F3
Billaouâr, Mrta. 140/C2
Bille (riv.), Ger. 79/H1
Billerbeck, Ger. 79/E5
Billère, Fr. 70/C5
Billericay, Eng, UK 56/E2
Billesholm, Swe. 65/K6
Billiat Consv. Park, Austl. 157/J5
Billiat Consv. Park, Austl. 158/B2
Billigheim, Ger. 84/C4
Billiluna Abor. Land, Austl. 154/B4
Billinge, Eng, UK 61/F4
Billingham, Eng, UK 61/G2
Billings, Ok, US 179/F2
Billings, Mt, US 171/K5
Billingsfors, Swe. 66/E2
Billingshurst, Eng, UK 63/F4
Billiton (isl.), Indo. 103/K10
Billund, Den. 66/C4
Billund (int'l arpt.), Den. 66/C4
Bilma, Niger 134/B5
Bīlo, Eth. 142/H3
Bilcela, Austl. 160/C4
Bilchirs'k, Ukr. 99/H5
Bilcku, Guy. 205/G4
Bilcluts'k, Ukr. 99/K3
Bilopillya, Ukr. 99/H2
Bilovods'k, Ukr. 99/K3
Biloxi, Ms, US 190/D2
Bilpa Morea Claypan (lake), Austl. 157/H3
Bilqas Qism Awwal, Egypt 139/C2
Bilqas Qism Thânî, Egypt 139/C2
Bilsi, India 122/B1
Biltān, Egypt 139/C4
Bilthar, India 122/D2
Bilthoven, Neth. 78/C4
Biltine, Chad 142/D2
Biltine (pref.), Chad 142/D2
Biltmore, Tn, US 189/F2
Bilüü, Mong. 125/E2
Bilyayivka, Ukr. 98/F4
Bilyts'ke, Ukr. 99/J3
Bilzen, Belg. 81/E2
Bima, Indo. 117/E5
Bimberi (peak), Austl. 159/D2
Bimbo, CAfr. 142/C4
Bimini (isls.), Bahm. 197/F2
Bin 'Arūs, Tun. 74/B4
Bin 'Arus (gov.), Tun. 74/B4
Bin Ghashīr, Libya 93/G4
Bin Jawwād, Libya 134/C2
Bin Qirdān, Tun. 93/F4
Bin Yauri, Nga. 141/G4
Bina (riv.), Ger. 85/F6
Bina-etāwa, India 122/B3
Binalong, Austl. 159/D2
Binanga, Indo. 115/B2
Binasco, It. 88/C3
Binatang, Malay. 116/D3
Binbrook, Eng, UK 61/H5
Binbrook, On, Can. 186/T9
Binche, Belg. 81/D3
Binchuan, China 112/D3
Binda, Austl. 159/D2
Binder Foulbé, Chad 142/B3
Bindki, India 122/C2
Bindoon, Austl. 156/C4
Bindoy, Phil. 114/C3
Bindu, D.R. Congo 146/D4
Bindungi, D.R. Congo 146/D4
Bindura, Zim. 149/F3
Binéfar, Sp. 73/F2
Binfield, Eng, UK 63/F4
Binford, ND, US 182/E4
Binga, Zim. 149/E3
Binga (mtn.), Moz. 149/G3
Bingara, Austl. 158/D1
Bingcaowan, China 104/E4
Bingen, Ger. 81/G4
Binger, Ok, US 179/E3
Bingerville, C.d'Iv. 140/E5
Bingham, Eng, UK 61/H6
Bingham, Me, US 187/M2
Binghamton, NY, US 187/J3
Bingley, Eng, UK 61/G4
Bingöl, Turk. 128/E2
Bingöl (prov.), Turk. 128/E2
Binh Chanh, Viet. 120/D4
Binh Chau, Viet. 120/D4
Binh Son, Viet. 120/E3
Binhai, China 106/D4
Binhon (peak), Myan. 112/B5
Binic, Fr. 82/C3
Binisalem, Sp. 73/G3
Binjai, Indo. 115/B2
Binka, India 121/D1
Binkılıç, Turk. 77/J5
Binkolo, SLeo. 140/C4
Binnah (cape), Som. 144/D3
Binnaway, Austl. 158/D1
Binningen, Swi. 86/D2
Binongko (isl.), Indo. 117/F5
Binscarth, Mb, Can. 182/D2
Binsted, Eng, UK 56/A3
Bint Jubayl, Leb. 131/C2
Bintagoungou, Mali 140/E2
Bintan (isl.), Indo. 115/D2
Bintang (peak), Malay. 115/C1
Bintang (range), Malay. 115/C1
Bintimodouya, Gui. 140/B4
Bintuhan, Indo. 115/C3
Binyamina, Isr. 131/B3
Binyang, China 113/F4
Binza, D.R. Congo 146/C4
Binzhou, China 106/D3
Bío-Bío (riv.), Chile 214/B3
Bío-Bío (pol. reg.), Chile 214/B3
Biodi, D.R. Congo 147/G2
Biograd, Cro. 76/B4
Biogradska Gora NP, Yugo. 75/F1
Biogradska NP, Yugo. 76/D4
Bioko (pol. reg.), EqG. 146/B2
Bioko (isl.), EqG. 133/C4
Bioko (Fernando Po) (isl.), EqG. 146/B2
Biola, Ca, US 174/B2
Biot, Fr. 90/D5
Biougra, Mor. 136/C3
Bipoint (Bissau) (int'l arpt.), GBis. 140/B4
Bippen, Ger. 79/E3
Bir (cape), Djib. 144/B3
Bīr, India 121/B2
Bîr Abu el-Husein (well), Egypt 135/F4
Bi'r Abu Hashim (well), Egypt 135/G4
Bîr Abu Minqâr (well), Egypt 135/E3
Bir Aïdiat (well), Mrta. 136/C4
Bi'r al Aḩmar (well), Libya 134/C2
Bi'r al 'Akkārīyah (well), Libya 134/C2
Bi'r Al Ghanam, Libya 134/B1
Bi'r al Ghuzayyil (well), Libya 134/A2
Bi'r al Ḩarash (well), Libya 134/D3
Bi'r Al Mashariqah, Tun. 138/L6
Bi'r al Mastūtah (well), Libya 134/B3
Bi'r al Mufaţţam (well), Libya 134/D2
Bi'r al Qāf (well), Libya 134/B2
Bi'r al Washkah (well), Libya 134/B2
Bi'r 'Alī, Yem. 144/D2
Bi'r as Sahl (well), Libya 134/B3
Bi'r as Sinidah (well), Libya 134/B2
Bi'r aţ Ţarfāwī (well), Libya 134/E2
Bir Bel Guerdâne (well), Mrta. 136/C4
Bi'r Burayd (well), Egypt 139/D6
Bîr Dibis (well), Egypt 135/F4
Bir el Ater, Alg. 92/F4
Bi'r Ghadir (well), Egypt 135/G3
Bîr Misâha (well), Egypt 135/E4
Bir Moghreïn, Mrta. 136/C4
Bîr Ounâne (well), Mali 136/E5
Bîr Safājah (well), Egypt 135/G3
Bir Tamtam, Mor. 138/B3
Bîr Tarfâwi (well), Egypt 135/F4
Bi'r Umm Hibal (well), Egypt 135/G4
Bi'r Zayt, WBnk. 131/C5
Bira, Rus. 105/L2
Birāk, Libya 134/B3
Birao, CAfr. 142/D3
Birātnagar, Nepal 123/F2
Biratori, Japan 108/C2
Birch (mts.), Ab, Can. 166/E3
Birch (cr.), Mt, US 171/H3
Birch Bay, Wa, US 170/C3
Birch Hills, Sk, Can. 171/M1
Birch River, Mb, Can. 182/D1
Birch Tree, Mo, US 179/J2
Birchenough Bridge, Zim. 149/G3
Birchip, Austl. 158/B2
Bircot, Eth. 144/B4
Bird (cr.), Ok, US 179/F2
Bird Island, Mn, US 181/G1
Bird Islet (isl.), Austl. 153/E3
Bird Point, Sk, Can. 182/C2
Birds Rock (peak), Austl. 159/E1
Birdsboro, Pa, US 194/C3
Birdsnest, Va, US 189/K2
Birdsville, Austl. 157/H3
Birdtail, Mb, Can. 182/D2
Birdum, Austl. 154/D3
Birdwood, Austl. 157/M8
Birecik, Turk. 128/D2
Bireuen, Indo. 115/B1
Bīrganj, Nepal 123/E2
Birganj, Bang. 123/G3
Birigui, Braz. 213/G2
Biritiba-mirim, Braz. 211/K8
Bīrjand, Iran 127/G2
Birkat al Ja'ār (well), Egypt 139/B4
Birkat as Sab', Egypt 139/C3
Birkat Ghiţās, Egypt 139/B2
Birkat Umm Rīshah (well), Egypt 139/B4
Birkelane, Sen. 140/B3
Birken-Honigsessen, Ger. 81/G2
Birkenau, Ger. 84/B3
Birkenfeld, Ger. 81/G4
Birkenfeld, Ger. 84/B5
Birkenhead, Eng, UK 61/E5
Birkenhead, NZ 161/F6
Birkenheide, Ger. 84/B4
Birkenwerder, Ger. 68/Q6
Birkerød, Den. 65/J7
Birkirkara, Malta 74/L7
Birkkarspitze (peak), Aus. 87/H3
Birky, Ukr. 99/J3
Bîrlad (riv.), Rom. 96/C3
Bîrlad, Rom. 77/H2
Birmā, Egypt 139/B3
Birmāna, India 124/B5
Birmingham, Mi, US 193/F6
Birmingham, Al, US 188/D4
Birmingham (int'l arpt.), Eng, UK 63/E2
Birmingham, Eng, UK 63/E2
Birmitrapur, India 123/E4
Birnam, Sc, UK 59/C3
Birnamwood, Wi, US 181/K1
Birney, Mt, US 173/K1
Birnhorn (peak), Aus. 71/K3
Birni Nkonni, Niger 141/G3
Birnie (isl.), Kiri. 163/H5
Birnin Gwari, Nga. 141/G4
Birnin Kebbi, Nga. 141/G3
Birnin Kudu, Nga. 141/H4
Birniwa, Nga. 141/H3
Birobijan (aut. obl.), Rus. 105/L2
Birobjian, Rus. 105/L2
Bīrpur, India 123/F2
Birqash, Egypt 139/C4
Birr, Ire. 58/C3
Birreencorragh (peak), Ire. 58/A2
Birrimbah, Austl. 154/D4
Birrindudu, Austl. 154/C4
Birriwa, Austl. 158/D2
Birs (riv.), Swi. 71/G3
Birsk, Rus. 95/M5
Birstein, Ger. 84/C2
Birštonas, Lith. 67/L4
Birtle, Mb, Can. 182/D2
Biru, China 104/C5
Biruaca, Ven. 205/E3
Biruni, Uzb. 100/G5
Biryulevo (nbrhd.), Rus. 94/W9
Biržai, Lith. 67/L3
Birżebbuġa, Malta 74/M7
Bis (lake), Hun. 77/F4
Bisa-Nadi Nat'l Rsv., Kenya 145/B1
Bisagana, Nga. 142/B2
Bisai, Japan 109/L5
Bīsalpur, India 122/B1
Bisamberg, Aus. 77/N7
Bisauli, India 122/B1
Bisbee, ND, US 182/E3
Bisbee, Az, US 175/H5
Bisbee Douglas (int'l arpt.), Az, US 198/C2
Biscarrosse (lake), Fr. 70/C4
Biscarrosse, Fr. 70/C4
Biscay (bay), Fr.,Sp. 55/D4
Biscayne (bay), Fl, US 190/P11
Biscayne NP, Fl, US 197/E2
Bisceglie, It. 74/E2
Bischberg, Ger. 84/D3
Bischheim, Fr. 81/G6
Bischofsgrün, Ger. 85/E2
Bischofsheim, Ger. 84/B3
Bischofsheim an der Rhön, Ger. 84/D2
Bischofshofen, Aus. 71/K3
Bischofszell, Swi. 87/F3
Bischwiller, Fr. 86/D2
Biscoe, NC, US 189/H3
Biscoe (Fredonia), Ar, US 179/J3
Biscubio (riv.), It. 89/F5
Biscucuy, Ven. 204/D2
Bisenge, D.R. Congo 147/E2
Bīshah (riv.), SAr. 126/D4
Bīshat Qā'id, Egypt 139/C3
Bishkek (cap.), Kyr. 125/B3
Bishnupur, India 123/F4
Bisho, SAfr. 150/D4
Bishop, Ca, US 174/C2
Bishop, Tx, US 177/F4
Bishop Auckland, Eng, UK 61/G2
Bishop Ind. Res., Ca, US 174/C2
Bishop International (arpt.), Mi, US 193/E6
Bishop Wilton, Eng, UK 61/H4
Bishopbriggs, Sc, UK 59/B5
Bishops Castle, Eng, UK 62/D1
Bishops Cleeve, Eng, UK 62/D3
Bishop's Falls, Nf, Can. 185/K1
Bishop's Stortford, Eng, UK 63/G3
Bishops Waltham, Eng, UK 63/E5
Bishopton, Sc, UK 59/B5
Bishopville, SC, US 189/G3
Bishrah (well), Libya 134/D4
Bisingen, Ger. 84/B6
Biskra, Alg. 138/H5
Biskupiec, Pol. 67/J5
Bislig, Phil. 114/D3
Bismarck, Ar, US 179/H3
Bismarck (cap.), ND, US 182/D4
Bismarck (sea), PNG 162/D5
Bismarck (arch.), PNG 162/D5
Bismarck, Mo, US 188/B2
Bismarck (range), PNG 155/G1
Bismarck, On, Can. 186/U9
Bismil, Turk. 128/E2
Bismuna (lag.), Nic. 201/F3
Biso, Ugan. 147/G2
Bison, SD, US 182/C5
Bison, Ks, US 178/E1
Bispgarden, Swe. 64/F3
Bispingen, Ger. 79/G2
Bissau, India 124/C5
Bissau (cap.), GBis. 140/B4
Bissau (Bipoint) (int'l arpt.), GBis. 140/B4
Bissaula, Nga. 141/H5
Bissendorf, Ger. 79/F4
Bissett, Mb, Can. 183/G2
Bissingen, Ger. 84/D5
Bissingen an der Enz, Ger. 84/C5
Bissora, GBis. 140/B3
Bistagno, It. 88/B4
Bistriţa, Rom. 77/G2
Bistriţa (riv.), Rom. 77/G2
Bistriţa-Năsăud (prov.), Rom. 77/G2
Bistrup, Den. 65/J7
Biswān, India 122/C2
Bita (riv.), Col. 204/D3
Bitagron, Sur. 206/B1
Bitale, Tanz. 147/G4
Bitam, Gabon 146/B2
Bitburg, Ger. 81/F4
Bitche, Fr. 81/G5
Bitéa, Ouadi (riv.), Chad 142/D2
Bithnok, India 118/B2
Bitkin, Chad 142/C3
Bitlis, Turk. 128/E2
Bitlis (prov.), Turk. 128/E2
Bitola, FYROM 75/G2
Bitonto, It. 74/E2
Bitter (cr.), Wy, US 173/J3
Bitter (lake), Egypt 128/C4
Bitter Creek, Wy, US 173/J3
Bitter Lake Nat'l Wildlife Reserve, NM, US 178/B4
Bitterfontein, SAfr. 150/B3
Bittern Lake, Ab, Can. 171/H1
Bitterroot (range), Id, US 173/F1
Bitterroot (riv.), Mt, US 171/G4
Bitti, It. 74/A2
Bittou, Burk. 141/E4
Bitung, Indo. 117/G3
Bituruna, Braz. 213/G3
Biu, Nga. 142/B3
Biviers, Fr. 90/B2
Bivolari, Rom. 98/D4
Biwa, Japan 109/K5
Bixby, Ok, US 179/G3
Bixby, Mo, US 188/B2
Biyagundi, Erit. 142/H2
Biyalā, Egypt 139/C2
Biyang, China 106/C4
Biysk, Rus. 125/E1
Bizard (isl.), Qu, Can. 185/M7
Bizerte (Banzart), Tun. 74/A4
Bjärnum, Swe. 65/K6
Bjärred, Swe. 66/E4
Bjelovar, Cro. 76/C3
Bjerge (riv.), Den. 65/H7
Bjerkvik, Nor. 64/F1
Bjerringbro, Den. 66/C3
Bjorkdale, Sk, Can. 171/N1
Bjørkelangen, Nor. 66/D2
Björklinge, Swe. 66/G1
Björknäs, Swe. 65/B1
Björkö, Swe. 65/C1
Björkö (isl.), Swe. 65/C1
Björksund, Swe. 65/A2
Bjørnafjorden (estu.), Nor. 66/A1
Bjorne (pen.), Nun, Can. 167/S7
Björnlunda, Swe. 65/A1
Björnö, Swe. 65/B1
Bjugn, Nor. 64/D3
Bjuv, Swe. 66/E3
Blå Jungfrun NP, Swe. 66/G3
Blaby, Eng, UK 63/E1
Blace, Yugo. 76/E4
Blachownia, Pol. 69/K3
Black (sea), Asia,Eur. 103/C5
Black (mesa), Ok, US 178/C2
Black (bay), On, Can. 183/K3
Black (isl.), Mb, Can. 182/F2
Black (riv.), On, Can. 183/M3
Black, Tx, US 178/C3
Black (isl.), Sc, UK 59/B1
Black (pt.), NI, UK 60/C2
Black (for.), Ger. 68/D5
Black (cr.), Ms, US 190/D2
Black (lake), Mi, US 186/D2
Black (mts.), Bhu. 123/H2
Black (pt.), Namb. 148/B5
Black (pt.), NZ 161/D3
Black (hills), SD, US 168/F3
Black (mesa), NM, US 175/J3
Black (mtn.), Ky, US 189/F2
Black (mts.), Az, US 174/E3
Black (range), NM, US 175/J4
Black (riv.), China,Vie 120/C1
Black (riv.), Viet. 119/H3
Black (mts.), Wal, UK 62/C3
Black (pt.), Eng, UK 62/A6
Black (mtn.), Wal, UK 62/C3
Black (mtn.), Tx, US 177/D3
Black (mtn.), Id, US 170/G4
Black (mtn.), Tx, US 177/C2
Black (pt.), Ct, US 195/F1
Black (cr.), Pa, US 194/B2
Black (Da) (riv.), Viet. 112/E4
Black Bear (cr.), Ok, US 179/F2
Black Bourton, Eng, UK 63/E3
Black Butte (lake), Ca, US 172/B4
Black Canyon City, Az, US 175/F3
Black Canyon Of The Gunnison Nat'l Mon., Co, US 173/K4
Black Coulee Nat'l Wild. Ref., Mt, US 171/K3
Black Creek, Wi, US 183/K5
Black Diamond, Wa, US 193/C3
Black Diamond, Ab, Can. 171/G2
Black Eagle, Mt, US 171/J4
Black Forest, Co, US 178/B1
Black Forest (Schwarzwald) (for.), Ger. 84/B6
Black Fork (mtn.), Ok, US 179/G3
Black Hammer (hill), ND, US 182/E4
Black Head (pt.), Ire. 58/A3
Black Hills Caverns, SD, US 180/C1
Black Lake, Qu, Can. 184/B2
Black Lake Bayou (riv.), La, US 179/H4
Black Mesa (int), Az, US 175/G4
Black Mesa (int.), Az, US 175/H4
Black Mesa (mesa), Az, US 175/G2
Black Mountain, NC, US 189/F3
Black Mountain NP, Austl. 160/B1
Black Mtn. (mtn.), Wal, UK 62/C3
Black Pine (peak), Id, US 173/G2
Black Point, Ca, US 193/K10
Black Reef (pt.), Namb. 148/B5
Black River, Mi, US 186/E2
Black River, Jam. 201/G2
Black River Falls, Wi, US 181/J1
Black Rock (des.), Nv, US 172/D3
Black Rock, Ar, US 188/B2
Black Rock (pt.), RI, US 195/G1
Black Sea Lowland (lowland), Ukr. 98/E4
Black Sea Lowlands (reg.), Ukr. 77/J3
Black Sturgeon (riv.), On, Can. 183/K3
Black Sugarloaf (peak), Austl. 158/D1
Black Volta (riv.), Burk. 133/B4

236

Black – Borku

Black Warrior (riv.), Al, US 188/D4
Black Warrior, Locust Fk. (riv.), Al, US 188/D4
Blackadder Water. (riv.), Sc, UK 59/D5
Blackall, Austl. 160/B4
Blackbeard Island NWR, Ga, US 191/H2
Blackberry (cr.), Il, US 193/P16
Blackburn, Sc, UK 59/C5
Blackburn, Eng, UK 61/F4
Blackburn, Mo, US 181/H4
Blackburne (int'l arpt.), UK 197/N8
Blackbutt, Austl. 160/D4
Blackcraig (peak), Sc, UK 59/B6
Blackdown (hills), Eng, UK 62/C5
Blackdown (hill), Eng, UK 63/F4
Blackdown Tableland NP, Austl. 160/C3
Blackduck, Mn, US 183/G4
Blackfalds, Ab, Can. 171/H1
Blackfoot (res.), Id, US 173/H2
Blackfoot, Id, US 173/G2
Blackfoot (riv.), Id, US 173/H2
Blackfoot, Mt, US 171/H3
Blackfoot Ind. Res., Mt, US 171/H3
Blackfoot Ind. Res., Ab, Can. 171/H2
Blackgum, Ok, US 179/G3
Blackhall Rocks, Eng, UK 61/G2
Blackheath, Austl. 159/E1
Blackie, Ab, Can. 171/H2
Blackland, Tx, US 176/L7
Blackmoor (upland), Eng, UK 62/B5
Blackmore, Eng, UK 56/D1
Blackpool, Eng, UK 61/E4
Blackpool (arpt.), Eng, UK 61/E4
Blackrod, Eng, UK 61/F4
Blacks Fk. (riv.), Wy, US 173/J3
Blacks Harbour, NB, Can. 184/D3
Blacksburg, Va, US 189/G2
Blacksburg, SC, US 189/G3
Blackshear, Ga, US 191/G2
Blackshear (lake), Ga, US 188/F5
Blackstairs (mts.), Ire. 58/D5
Blackstone, Va, US 189/H2
Blacksville, Ga, US 189/M8
Blacktown (nbrhd.), Austl. 160/G8
Blackville, NB, Can. 184/E2
Blackville, SC, US 189/G4
Blackwater (riv.), Mo, Ire. 179/H1
Blackwater (riv.), Ire. 60/B4
Blackwater (res.), Sc, UK 59/B3
Blackwater, Ire. 58/D5
Blackwater (cr.), Fl, US 190/L7
Blackwater (riv.), Eng, UK 56/A2
Blackwater, Austl. 160/C3
Blackwater (riv.), Mo, US 181/H4
Blackwater (inlet), Eng, UK 63/G3
Blackwater Draw (riv.), Tx, US 178/C3
Blackwater NWR, Md, US 189/J1
Blackwell, Ok, US 179/F2
Blackwell, Tx, US 177/D1
Blackwells, Ga, US 189/L6
Blackwood (riv.), Austl. 156/B5
Blackwood (cape), PNG 155/G1
Blackwood, Wal, UK 62/C3
Blackwood, NJ, US 194/C4
Bladel, Neth. 78/C6
Bladenboro, NC, US 189/H3
Bladensburg, Md, US 194/B6
Bladensburg NP, Austl. 160/A3
Bladnoch (riv.), Sc, UK 60/D2
Bladworth, Sk, Can. 171/L2
Blaenau-Ffestiniog, Wal, UK 60/E6
Blaenavon, Wal, UK 62/C3
Blagnac (int'l arpt.), Fr. 70/D5
Blagnac, Fr. 70/D5
Blagny, Fr. 81/E4
Blagodarniy, Rus. 97/G3
Blagoevgrad, Bul. 75/H1
Blagoveshchensk, Rus. 105/K1
Blain, Fr. 82/D6
Blaine, Tn, US 188/F2
Blaine, Mn, US 183/P6
Blaine Lake, Sk, Can. 171/L1
Blainville, Qu, Can. 185/N6
Blainville-sur-Orne, Fr. 83/E2
Blair, Ok, US 178/E3
Blair, Ne, US 181/F3
Blair, Wi, US 181/J1
Blair (hill), Pa, US 194/C1
Blair Athol, Austl. 160/B3
Blair Atholl, Sc, UK 59/C3
Blairgowrie, Sc, UK 59/C3
Blairmore, Ab, Can. 170/G3
Blairsden, Ca, US 172/C4
Blairstown, NJ, US 194/D2
Blairsville, Ga, US 188/F3
Blaise (riv.), Fr. 70/F2
Blaj, Rom. 77/F2
Blake (pt.), Mi, US 183/K3
Blakely, Pa, US 187/J4
Blakely, Ga, US 191/F2
Blakely Mountain (dam), Ar, US 179/H3
Blakeslee, Pa, US 194/C1
Blamont, Fr. 86/C3
Blanc (peak), Fr. 86/C6
Blanc (cape), Fr. 90/C6
Blanc Nez (cape), Fr. 80/A2
Blanca (peak), NM, US 178/B4
Blanca, Co, US 178/B2
Blanca (bay), Arg. 203/C6
Blanca (coast), Sp. 73/E4
Blanca (peak), Tx, US 177/B2
Blanca (pt.), Mex. 198/B2
Blanchard, Ok, US 179/F3
Blanchard, Id, US 170/F3
Blanchardstown, Ire. 60/B5
Blanchardville, Wi, US 181/K2
Blanche (peak), Swi. 86/D5
Blanche (riv.), Fr. 90/C4
Blanche (lake), Austl. 156/D2
Blanche (cape), Austl. 157/G5
Blanchester, Oh, US 186/E5
Blanchisseuse, Trin. 205/F2
Blanco (cr.), Tx, US 177/F3
Blanco (riv.), Tx, US 177/E2
Blanco (cape), Mor. 136/A5
Blanco (cape), CR 200/E4
Blanco, NM, US 175/J2
Blanco (cape), Or, US 168/A3
Blanco (lake), Chile 215/C7
Blanco (riv.), Arg. 212/B4
Blanco (riv.), Bol. 209/F4
Blanco, SAfr. 150/C4
Blanco, Tx, US 176/E2
Bland, Mo, US 179/J1
Bland, Va, US 189/G2
Bland (cr.), Austl. 159/C1
Blandford Forum, Eng, UK 62/D5
Blanding, Ut, US 175/H2
Blandy, Fr. 56/L6
Blanes, Sp. 73/G2
Blangkejeren, Indo. 115/B2
Blangpidie, Indo. 115/B2
Blangy-sur-Bresle, Fr. 80/A4
Blankenberge, Belg. 80/C1
Blankenese, Ger. 79/G1
Blankenfelde, Ger. 68/Q7
Blankenheim, Ger. 81/F3
Blanket, Tx, US 176/E2
Blanquilla (isl.), Ven. 197/J5
Blanquillo, Uru. 215/G2
Blansko, Czh. 69/J4
Blanton, Fl, US 190/L7
Blantyre, Sc, UK 59/B5
Blantyre, Malw. 149/G2
Blanzy, Fr. 70/F3
Blaricum, Neth. 78/C4
Blarney, Ire. 58/B6
Blarney Castle and Stone, Ire. 58/B6
Blas (peak), Swi. 87/E4
Blatná, Czh. 85/G4
Blato, Cro. 76/C4
Blatten, Swi. 86/D5
Blau (riv.), Ger. 84/C6
Blaubeuren, Ger. 84/C6
Blauen (peak), Ger. 86/D2
Blaustein, Ger. 84/C6
Blauvelt, NY, US 195/K7
Blåvands (pt.), Den. 66/C4
Blavet (riv.), Fr. 70/B3
Blaye, Fr. 70/C4
Blaye, The (Alderney) (arpt.), Chl, UK 82/C1
Blayney, Austl. 159/D1
Blaze (pt.), Austl. 154/C3
Bleckede, Ger. 79/H2
Bled, Slov. 71/L3
Bledlow Ridge, Eng, UK 56/A2
Blefjell (peak), Nor. 66/C2
Blégny, Belg. 81/E2
Bléharies, Belg. 80/C2
Bleiburg, Aus. 76/B2
Bleicherode, Ger. 79/H6
Bleik (peak), Ger. 87/G2
Bleiswijk, Neth. 78/B4
Blekinge (co.), Swe. 64/E4
Blendecques, Fr. 80/B2
Blender, Ger. 79/G3
Blenheim, On, Can. 186/F3
Blenheim, NZ 161/C3
Blénod-lès-Pont-à-Mousson, Fr. 81/F6
Bléone (riv.), Fr. 71/G4
Blera, It. 91/B3
Bléré, Fr. 83/G6
Blerick, Neth. 78/D6
Blesberg (peak), SAfr. 150/C4
Blessing, Tx, US 177/F3
Blessington, Ire. 60/B5
Bletchingley, Eng, UK 56/C3
Bletchley, Eng, UK 63/F3
Bletterans, Fr. 86/B4
Bleury, Fr. 56/H6
Bleus, Monts (mts.), D.R. Congo 147/G2
Blevins, Ar, US 179/H4
Blewbury, Eng, UK 63/E3
Blewett, Tx, US 177/D3
Blewett Falls (lake), NC, US 189/H3
Blida (wilaya), Alg. 138/G4
Blida, Alg. 138/G4
Blidö (isl.), Swe. 65/B1
Blidworth, Eng, UK 61/G5
Blies (riv.), Ger. 81/G5
Blieskastel, Ger. 81/G5
Bligh Water (bay), Fiji 163/Y18
Blik (mt.), Phil. 117/F2
Blind Bay, BC, Can. 170/E2
Blind River, On, Can. 186/E1
Blinman, Austl. 157/H4
Blinndio, Mali 140/D4
Blinnenhorn (peak), Swi. 87/E5
Bliss, Id, US 173/F2
Bliss (dam), Id, US 173/F2
Blissfield, NB, Can. 184/D2
Blissfield, Mi, US 186/E4
Blitar, Indo. 115/F3
Blithe (riv.), Eng, UK 61/F6
Blithfield (res.), Eng, UK 61/G6
Blitta, Togo 141/F4
Block (isl.), RI, US 195/F1
Block House, NS, Can. 184/E3
Block Island (sound), Ma, US 184/B5
Block Island (New Shoreham), RI, US 195/G1
Block Island C. G. Sta., RI, US 195/G1
Block Island Nat'l Wild. Ref., RI, US 195/G1
Block Island State (arpt.), RI, US 195/G1
Blodelsheim, Fr. 86/D2
Bloemendaal, Neth. 78/B4
Bloemfontein, SAfr. 150/D3
Bloemhof, SAfr. 150/D2
Bloemhofdam (res.), SAfr. 150/D2
Blois, Fr. 83/G5
Blokzijl, Neth. 78/C3
Blomberg, Ger. 79/G5
Blomberg, Ger. 79/E1
Blommestein (lake), Sur. 205/H3
Blomstermåla, Swe. 66/G3
Blonay, Swi. 86/C5
Blönduós, Ice. 64/N6
Blongas, Indo. 115/G3
Blood Indian Res., Ab, Can. 171/H2
Bloodvein (riv.), Mb,On, Can. 166/G3
Bloodvein River, Mb, Can. 182/F2
Bloody Foreland (pt.), Ire. 57/P9
Bloomer, Wi, US 181/J1
Bloomfield, Ct, US 187/K4
Bloomfield, Ia, US 181/H3
Bloomfield, In, US 188/D1
Bloomfield, Mo, US 188/C2
Bloomfield, Mt, US 182/B4
Bloomfield, Nf, Can. 185/L1
Bloomfield, NJ, US 195/J8
Bloomfield, NM, US 175/J2
Bloomfield Hills, Mi, US 193/F6
Blooming Grove, Tx, US 177/F1
Blooming Prairie, Mn, US 181/H2
Bloomingdale, Fl, US 190/L8
Bloomingdale, Il, US 193/P16
Bloomingdale, NJ, US 195/H7
Bloomingdale, Ga, US 189/G4
Bloomington, Ca, US 192/C2
Bloomington, Id, US 173/H2
Bloomington, Il, US 181/K3
Bloomington, In, US 186/C5
Bloomington, Mn, US 183/P7
Bloomington, Tx, US 177/F3
Bloomington Springs, Tn, US 188/E2
Bloomsburg, Pa, US 194/B2
Bloomsbury, NJ, US 194/C2
Bloomville, Oh, US 186/E4
Blora, Indo. 115/E3
Blotzheim, Fr. 86/D2
Blouberg (peak), SAfr. 149/F4
Blountstown, Fl, US 191/F2
Blountsville, Al, US 188/D3
Blountville, Tn, US 189/F2
Blovice, Czh. 85/G3
Blowering (res.), Austl. 159/D2
Blowing Rock, NC, US 189/G2
Bloxham, Eng, UK 63/E2
Bloxwich, Eng, UK 62/E1
Blšanka (riv.), Czh. 71/K1
Blūdān, Syria 131/E1
Bludenz, Aus. 87/F3
Blue (mtn.), Ar, US 179/G3
Blue (hills), Wi, US 183/J5
Blue (mtn.), NB, Can. 184/D2
Blue (hill), ND, US 182/D4
Blue (hill), Pa, US 187/G4
Blue (mtn.), NH, US 187/L2
Blue (mtn.), NY, US 187/J3
Blue, Az, US 175/H4
Blue (mts.), Or,Wa, US 168/C2
Blue (riv.), Co, US 180/A4
Blue (mtn.), India 112/B4
Blue and Gray Museum, Ga, US 191/G2
Blue Ash, Oh, US 188/E1
Blue Cypress (lake), Fl, US 191/H4
Blue Earth, Mn, US 181/G2
Blue Earth (riv.), Mn, US 181/G2
Blue Eye, Mo, US 179/H2
Blue Head (pt.), Sc, UK 59/C1
Blue Hill, Ne, US 180/E3
Blue Island, Il, US 193/Q16
Blue Lagoon NP, Zam. 149/E2
Blue Lake, Ca, US 172/B3
Blue Lake NP, Austl. 160/D4
Blue Marsh Lake (res.), Pa, US 194/B3
Blue Mesa (res.), Co, US 173/K4
Blue Mesa (dam), Co, US 175/J1
Blue Mound, Ks, US 179/G1
Blue Mound, Tx, US 176/K7
Blue Mountain (peak), Jam. 201/G2
Blue Mountain, Ms, US 188/C3
Blue Mountain (ridge), Pa, US 194/A3
Blue Mountain Lake, NY, US 187/J3
Blue Mountains, Austl. 159/E1
Blue Mud (bay), Austl. 155/D3
Blue Nile (riv.), Eth. 144/B3
Blue Nile (riv.), Eth.,Sudan 142/G2
Blue Nile (falls), Eth. 142/H3
Blue Nile (riv.), Sudan 133/F3
Blue Nose (peak), Mt, US 173/F1
Blue Rapids, Ks, US 181/F4
Blue Ridge, Ga, US 188/E3
Blue Ridge (mts.), Ga, US 188/G3
Blue Ridge Pky., US 189/G2
Blue River, Or, US 172/B1
Blue River, BC, Can. 170/E1
Blue Springs, Mo, US 181/G4
Blue Springs, Ne, US 181/F3
Bluebell, Ut, US 173/H3
Bluefield, WV, US 189/G2
Bluefield, Va, US 189/G2
Bluefields (bay), Nic. 201/F4
Bluefields, Nic. 201/F4
Bluejoint (lake), Or, US 172/D2
Bluenose (lake), Nun, Can. 166/E2
Bluestem (lake), Ok, US 179/F2
Bluestone (lake), WV, US 189/G2
Bluewater, NM, US 175/J3
Bluff (cr.), Ks,Ok, US 179/F2
Bluff, Austl. 160/C3
Bluff, NZ 161/B4
Bluff, Ut, US 175/H2
Bluff (peak), Austl. 156/C5
Bluff (pt.), Austl. 156/B3
Bluff (pt.), NC, US 189/J3
Bluff City, Ar, US 179/H4
Bluff City, Ks, US 179/F2
Bluff Dale, Tx, US 177/E1
Bluff Face (range), Austl. 154/B4
Bluffton, Ar, US 179/H3
Bluffton, In, US 186/D4
Bluffton, Oh, US 186/E4
Blum, Tx, US 177/F1
Blumberg, Ger. 87/E2
Blumberg, Ger. 68/Q6
Blumenau, Braz. 213/G3
Blumenthal, Ger. 79/G2
Blumenthal, Ger. 79/F2
Blümlisalp (peak), Swi. 86/D5
Blunt, SD, US 180/E1
Blustry (mt.), BC, Can. 170/D2
Bly, Or, US 172/C2
Blyn, Wa, US 193/B1
Blyth, Eng, UK 61/G5
Blyth, Eng, UK 61/G1
Blyth, Austl. 157/H5
Blyth Bridge, Sc, UK 59/C5
Blythe, Ca, US 174/E4
Blythe, Ga, US 189/F4
Blythe Bridge, Eng, UK 61/F6
Blytheswood, On, Can. 193/G7
Blytheville, Ar, US 188/C3
Bnom Mhai (peak), Viet. 120/D4
Bø, Nor. 66/C2
Bo, SLeo. 140/C5
Bo Duc, Viet. 120/D4
Bo Hai (Chihli) (gulf), China 101/M6
Bo Ho Su, Viet. 120/D2
Bo Phloi, Thai. 120/B3
Bo River, Sudan 142/E4
Bo Trach, Viet. 120/D2
Boa Esperança, Braz. 210/D4
Boa Esperança (res.), Braz. 207/E4
Boa Nova, Braz. 206/B5
Boa Viagem, Braz. 207/G4
Boa Vista (int'l arpt.), Braz. 205/F4
Boa Vista, Braz. 205/F4
Boa Vista (isl.), CpV. 133/K10
Boac, Phil. 114/C2
Boaco, Nic. 200/E3
Boadilla del Monte, Sp. 73/N9
Bo'ai, China 106/C4
Boajibu, SLeo. 140/C4
Boalsburg, Pa, US 187/H4
Boana, PNG 155/G1
Boano (isl.), Indo. 117/G4
Board Camp, Ar, US 179/G3
Boardman, Oh, US 186/F4
Boardman, Or, US 170/E5
Boardman Bombing Range, Or, US 170/E5
Boardman Naval Ra., Or, US 172/D1
Boas (riv.), Nun, Can. 167/H2
Boavita, Col. 204/C3
Boaz, Al, US 188/D3
Bob Sandlin (lake), Tx, US 179/G4
Boba, Hun. 76/C2
Bobadah, Austl. 158/C2
Bobai, China 113/F4
Bobaomby (cape), Madg. 152/J5
Bobbili, India 121/D2
Bobbio, It. 88/C4
Bobcaygeon, On, Can. 187/G2
Bobenge, D.R. Congo 147/F2
Bobenheim-Roxheim, Ger. 84/B3
Bobigny, Fr. 56/K5
Bobila, D.R. Congo 147/E2
Bobingen, Ger. 87/G1
Bobisi, D.R. Congo 146/D2
Böblingen, Ger. 84/C5
Bobo Dioulasso, Burk. 140/D4
Bobonong, Bots. 149/F4
Boboshevo, Bul. 75/H1
Bobotov Kuk (peak), Yugo. 76/D4
Bobovdol, Bul. 76/F4
Bobr, Bela. 67/N4
Bóbr (riv.), Pol. 69/H3
Bobrov, Rus. 99/L2
Bobrovskoye, Rus. 95/K3
Bobrovytsya, Ukr. 98/F2
Bobrynets', Ukr. 99/G3
Bobuk, Sudan 142/G3
Bobures, Ven. 204/D2
Boby (peak), Madg. 152/H8
Boca de Aroa, Ven. 204/D2
Boca de Pepé, Col. 204/B3
Boca del Grita, Ven. 204/C2
Boca del Guafo (chan.), Chile 214/B4
Boca del Mar, Fl, US 190/P10
Boca del Pao, Ven. 205/E2
Boca del Río, Mex. 199/N7
Bôca do Acre, Braz. 209/E3
Boca Grande, Fl, US 191/G4
Boca Raton, Fl, US 190/P10
Bocaina (mts.), Braz. 211/M7
Bocaina, Braz. 207/F4
Bocairente, Sp. 73/E3
Bocaiúva, Braz. 210/E3
Bocanda, C.d'Iv. 140/D5
Bocaranga, CAfr. 142/B4
Bocas del Toro, Pan. 201/F4
Bocay, Nic. 200/E3
Bocay (riv.), Nic. 200/E3
Bochil, Mex. 200/C2
Bochnia, Pol. 69/L4
Bocholt, Belg. 81/E1
Bocholt, Ger. 78/D5
Bochov, Czh. 85/G2
Bochum, SAfr. 149/F4
Bochum, Ger. 79/E6
Bockau, Ger. 85/F1
Bockenem, Ger. 79/H4
Bockenheim an der Weinstrasse, Ger. 81/H4
Bockhorn, Ger. 85/E6
Bockhorn, Ger. 79/F2
Bocking, Eng, UK 63/G3
Bococo, EqG. 146/B2
Bocoio, Ang. 148/B2
Boconó, Ven. 204/D2
Bocq (riv.), Belg. 81/D3
Boda, CAfr. 142/C4
Bodafors, Swe. 66/F3
Bodalla, Austl. 159/E3
Bodaybo, Rus. 101/M4
Bodcau (cr.), Ar, US 179/H4
Bodcaw, Ar, US 179/H4
Boddam, Sc, UK 59/E2
Boddington, Austl. 156/C5
Bode (riv.), Ger. 68/F3
Bode-Sadu, Nga. 141/G4
Bodega (bay), Ca, US 172/B4
Bodegraven, Neth. 78/B4
Bodélé (reg.), Chad 142/C1
Bodenheim, Ger. 84/B3
Bodenkirchen, Ger. 85/F6
Bodenmais, Ger. 85/G4
Bodensee (Constance) (lake), Swi.,Ger. 87/F2
Bodenteich, Ger. 79/H3
Bodfish, Ca, US 174/C3
Bodh Gaya, India 123/E3
Bodhan, India 121/C2
Bodie (isl.), NC, US 189/K3
Bodio, Swi. 87/E5
Bodkin (pt.), Md, US 194/B5
Bodmin, Eng, UK 62/B6
Bodmin Moor (upland), Eng, UK 62/B6
Bodø, Nor. 64/E2
Bodomijärvi (lake), Fin. 65/E4
Bodonchiyn (riv.), Mong. 104/C2
Bodoukpa, CAfr. 142/C4
Bodrog (riv.), Slvk.,Hun. 69/L4
Bodrum, Turk. 128/A2
Bódvaszilas, Hun. 69/L4
Boëge, Fr. 86/C5
Boegoeberg (peak), Namb. 150/A2
Boekel, Neth. 78/C5
Boende, D.R. Congo 147/E3
Boerne, Tx, US 177/E3
Boeuf (riv.), La, US 188/B4
Boffa, Gui. 140/B4
Bog of Allen (swamp), Ire. 60/A5
Boga, D.R. Congo 147/G2
Bogalo (mtn.), Austl. 159/C1
Bogalusa, La, US 190/D2
Bogamangon, CAfr. 142/C4
Bogan (riv.), Austl. 153/D4
Bogan Gate, Austl. 159/C1
Bogandé, Burk. 141/E3
Bogangolo, CAfr. 142/C4
Bogantungan, Austl. 160/B3
Bogard, Mo, US 181/H4
Bogata, Tx, US 179/G4
Bogatić, Yugo. 76/D3
Bogatoye, Rus. 97/J1
Bogatynia, Pol. 69/H3
Bogatyrëvo, Kaz. 97/J2
Boğazkale-Alacahöyük NP, Turk. 128/C1
Boğazlıyan, Turk. 128/C2
Bogbonga, D.R. Congo 146/D2
Bogcang (riv.), China 125/E5
Bogda (peak), China 125/E3
Bogda (mts.), China 104/B3
Bogdanci, FYROM 75/H2
Bogdanovka, Geo. 97/G4
Bogen, Nor. 64/F1
Bogen, Ger. 85/F5
Bogenfels, Namb. 150/A2
Bogenli, China 105/K2
Bogense, Den. 66/D4
Boggabilla, Austl. 160/C5
Boggabri, Austl. 158/D1
Boggeragh (mts.), Ire. 58/A5
Boggy (peak), Anti. 197/N8
Boglárlelle, Hun. 76/C2
Bogliasco, It. 88/C5
Bognor Regis, Eng, UK 63/F5
Bogny-sur-Meuse, Fr. 81/D4
Bogo, Camr. 142/B3
Bogo, Phil. 114/C3
Bogol Manyo, Eth. 144/B4
Bogong (mt.), Austl. 159/C3
Bogor, Indo. 115/D3
Bogoria Nat'l Rsv., Kenya 145/B1
Bogoro, D.R. Congo 147/G2
Bogoroud (well), Chad 142/B2
Bogota, NJ, US 195/J8
Bogotá (riv.), Col. 207/L8
Bogotá (cap.), Col. 207/L8
Bogovino, FYROM 75/G2
Bogra, Bang. 123/G3
Bogra (pol. reg.), Bang. 123/G3
Bogsta, Swe. 65/A2
Boguchar, Rus. 99/L3
Bogué, Mrta. 140/B2
Bogue, Ks, US 180/E4
Bogue Chitto (riv.), La, US 190/C2
Bogue Chitto, Ms, US 190/C2
Bogue Chitto NWR, La, US 190/C2
Bogue Homo (cr.), Ms, US 190/D2
Boguila Kota, CAfr. 142/C4
Bogushëvsk, Bela. 67/P4
Bohai (bay), China 106/D3
Bohain-en-Vermandois, Fr. 80/C4
Bohemia (reg.), Czh. 69/G4
Bohemian (for.), Czh.,Ger. 68/G4
Bohemian (for.), Ger.,Czh. 71/K2
Boherboy, Ire. 58/A5
Bohicon, Ben. 141/F5
Böhl-Iggelheim, Ger. 84/B4
Böhme (riv.), Ger. 79/G3
Böhmenkirch, Ger. 84/C5
Bohmte, Ger. 79/F4
Bohners Lake, Wi, US 193/P14
Bohodukhiv, Ukr. 99/H2
Bohol (isl.), Phil. 162/B4
Bohol (str.), Phil. 114/C3
Böhönye, Hun. 76/C2
Bohu, China 125/E3
Bohuslav, Ukr. 98/F3
Boiestown, NB, Can. 184/D2
Boigny-sur-Bionne, Fr. 83/H5
Boiling Springs, Pa, US 194/A3
Boiling Springs, SC, US 189/G3
Boimbo, D.R. Congo 146/D3
Boinu (riv.), Myan. 112/B4
Boipāriguda, India 121/D2
Boipeba (isl.), Braz. 211/F2
Boiro, Sp. 72/A1
Bois (isl.), Nf, Can. 185/K2
Bois Blanc (isl.), Mi, US 186/D2
Bois de Boulogne (dept.), Fr. 56/J5
Bois de Vincennes (dept.), Fr. 56/K5
Bois, Rio dos (riv.), Braz. 210/C3
Bois-d'Amont, Fr. 86/C4
Bois-d'Arcy, Fr. 56/J5
Bois-des-Filion, Qu, Can. 185/N6
Bois-Guillaume, Fr. 83/G2
Boisbriand, Qu, Can. 185/N6
Boise (riv.), Fr. 73/F1
Boise (mts.), Id, US 172/F2
Boise (riv.), Id, US 172/A3
Boise (cap.), Id, US 172/E2
Boise City, Ok, US 178/C2
Boissevain, Mb, Can. 182/D3
Boissevain, Va, US 189/G2
Boissy-Fresnoy, Fr. 56/L4
Boissy-L'Aillerie, Fr. 56/J4
Boissy-le-Châtel, Fr. 56/M5
Boissy-Saint-Léger, Fr. 56/K5
Boissy-Sans-Avoir, Fr. 56/H5
Boizenburg, Ger. 79/H2
Bojano, It. 92/D5
Bojeador (cape), Phil. 114/C1
Boji (plain), Kenya 145/B1
Bojkovice, Czh. 69/J4
Bojnūrd, Iran 129/J2
Bojonegoro, Indo. 115/E3
Boju, Nga. 141/G5
Boju Ega, Nga. 141/H5
Bok, PNG 155/G1
Bok Tower Gardens, Fl, US 190/M8
Bokala, D.R. Congo 146/D3
Bokapo Li, D.R. Congo 147/E2
Bokaro Steel City, India 123/F4
Bokat, Indo. 117/F3
Bokata, D.R. Congo 147/E2
Bokatola, D.R. Congo 146/D3
Bokchito, Ok, US 179/F3
Boké, Gui. 140/B4
Boké (pol. reg.), Gui. 140/B4
Bokele, D.R. Congo 147/E3
Bokengo, D.R. Congo 147/E2
Bokhan, Rus. 104/E1
Bokhol (plain), Kenya 145/B1
Boknafjorden (estu.), Nor. 64/C4
Boko, India 123/H3
Boko, Congo 146/C4
Boko, Kaz. 125/D2
Boko Songo, Congo 146/C4
Bokode, D.R. Congo 146/D2
Bokol (peak), Kenya 145/B1
Bokondini, Indo. 117/J4
Bokoro, Chad 142/C2
Bokote, D.R. Congo 146/E3
Bokpyin, Myan. 120/B4
Boksburg, SAfr. 150/Q13
Bokspits, Bots. 150/C2
Bokungu, D.R. Congo 147/E3
Bol, Chad 142/B2
Bol'shaya Khobda (riv.), Kaz. 97/K2
Bol'shaya Kinel' (riv.), Rus. 97/K1
Bol'shaya Ussurka (riv.), Rus. 105/L2
Bol'shoy Irgiz (riv.), Rus. 97/J1
Bol'shoy Uzen' (riv.), Rus. 97/J2
Bol'shoy Yenisey (riv.), Rus. 104/D1
Bolama, GBis. 140/B4
Bolama, D.R. Congo 147/E2
Bolān (pass), Pak. 127/J3
Bolaños de Calatrava, Sp. 72/D3
Bolayır, Turk. 77/H5
Bolbec, Fr. 83/F1
Bolckow, Mo, US 181/G3
Boldeşti-Scăeni, Rom. 77/H3
Boldon, Eng, UK 61/G2
Bole, Gha. 141/E4
Bole (int'l arpt.), Eth. 144/A3
Bole, China 125/D3
Bolekhiv, Ukr. 98/B3
Boleko, D.R. Congo 146/D3
Boleng (peak), Indo. 154/A2
Boles, Ar, US 179/G3
Bolesławiec, Pol. 69/H3
Boley, Ok, US 179/F3
Bolgatanga, Gha. 141/E4
Bolhrad, Ukr. 77/J3
Boli, China 105/L2
Bolia, D.R. Congo 146/D3
Boliden, Swe. 64/G2
Boligee, Al, US 188/C4
Bolinao (cape), Phil. 114/B1
Bolinao, Phil. 114/B1
Boling, Tx, US 177/G3
Bolingbrook, Il, US 186/B4
Bolivar (pen.), Tx, US 177/G3
Bolivar, Tx, US 179/F4
Bolivar, Mo, US 179/H2
Bolivar, Oh, US 186/F4
Bolívar (peak), Ven. 205/F3
Bolívar (state), Ven. 205/E3
Bolívar, Ecu. 204/A4
Bolívar, Col. 204/B3
Bolívar (dept.), Col. 204/C2
Bolívar (peak), Ven. 204/D2
Bolívar, Arg. 214/E3
Bolivar, Tn, US 188/C3
Bolívar, Bol. 209/E4
Bolívar, Peru 208/B2
Bolivia(ctry.) 203/C4
Bolivia, NC, US 189/H3
Böljane (riv.), Swe. 65/K6
Bolkhov, Rus. 96/F1
Bollate, It. 88/C2
Bollène, Fr. 90/A4
Bolligen, Swi. 86/D4
Bollin (riv.), Eng, UK 61/F5
Bollington, Eng, UK 61/F5
Bollmora, Swe. 65/B1
Bollnäs, Swe. 66/G1
Bollon, Austl. 160/B5
Bollullos Par del Condado, Sp. 72/B4
Bolmen (lake), Swe. 66/E3
Bolney, Eng, UK 63/F5
Bolnisi, Geo. 97/H4
Bolo, D.R. Congo 146/D3
Bolobo, D.R. Congo 146/D3
Bologna, It. 89/E5
Bologna (prov.), It. 89/E3
Bologne, Fr. 86/B1
Bolognesi, Peru 208/C3
Bolognesi, Peru 208/C2
Bologoye, Rus. 94/G4
Bolomba, D.R. Congo 146/D2
Bolombo (riv.), D.R. Congo 147/E2
Bolombo, D.R. Congo 147/E3
Bolon', Rus. 105/M2
Bolon' (lake), Rus. 105/M2
Bolonchén de Rejón, Mex. 200/D2
Bolongongo, Ang. 146/C5
Bolonguera, Ang. 148/B2
Bolpebra, Bol. 208/D3
Bolpur, India 123/F4
Bolsena (lake), It. 74/B1
Bolsena, It. 91/A2
Bol'shakovo, Rus. 67/J4
Bol'shaya Belozërka, Ukr. 99/H4
Bol'shaya Breëstovitsa, Bela. 69/N2
Bol'shaya Chernigovka, Rus. 97/J1
Bol'shaya Damba, Kaz. 97/J3
Bol'shaya Rogovaya (riv.), Rus. 95/P2
Bol'shaya Sosnova, Rus. 95/M4
Bol'shaya Synya (riv.), Rus. 95/N2
Bol'shaya Znamenka, Ukr. 99/H4
Bol'shevik (isl.), Rus. 103/H2
Bol'shevik, Bela. 96/D1
Bol'shezemel'skaya Tundra (tundra), Rus. 95/M2
Bol'shoy Bolvanskiy Nos (pt.), Rus. 100/F2
Bol'shoy Kuganavolok, Rus. 94/H3
Bol'shoy Lyakhov (isl.), Rus. 103/P2
Bol'shoy Lyakhovskiy (isl.), Rus. 101/Q2
Bol'shoy Ut, Rus. 95/N4
Bol'shoy Yenisey (riv.), Rus. 125/G1
Bol'shoye Boldino, Rus. 95/K5
Bol'shoye Nagatkino, Rus. 95/K5
Bol'shoye Soldatskoye, Rus. 99/H2
Bolsover, Eng, UK 61/G5
Bolsover, On, Can. 187/G2
Bolsward, Neth. 78/C2
Bolt (pt.), Eng, UK 62/C6
Boltaña, Sp. 73/F1
Boltigen, Swi. 86/D4
Bolton, Eng, UK 61/F4
Bolton, On, Can. 186/T8
Bolton Abbey, Eng, UK 61/G4
Bolu, Turk. 96/D4
Bolu (prov.), Turk. 96/D4
Bolungavík, Ice. 64/M6
Bolus Head (pt.), Ire. 56/N11
Bolvadin, Turk. 128/B2
Bolwarra, Austl. 159/E1
Bóly, Hun. 76/D3
Bolyarovo, Bul. 77/H4
Bolzano, It. 87/H5
Bolzano-Bozen (prov.), It. 87/H4
Bom Conselho, Braz. 207/G5
Bom Despacho, Braz. 210/D3
Bom Jardim de Goiás, Braz. 210/B3
Bom Jardin de Minas, Braz. 211/M6
Bom Jesus, Ang. 146/C5
Bom Jesus, Braz. 213/G4
Bom Jesus, Braz. 207/E5
Bom Jesus, Braz. 207/H4
Bom Jesus da Gurguéia, Serra (mts.), Braz. 211/E1
Bom Jesus da Lapa, Braz. 211/E2
Bom Jesus de Goiás, Braz. 210/C3
Bom Jesus do Gurgueia, Serra do (mts.), Braz. 207/F5
Bom Jesus do Itabapoana, Braz. 211/E4
Bom Jesus dos Perdões, Braz. 211/K8
Bom Sucesso, Braz. 210/D4
Boma, D.R. Congo 146/C4
Boma NP, Sudan 142/G4
Bomaderry, Austl. 159/E2
Bomaneh, D.R. Congo 147/E2
Bomba, Ang. 148/B2
Bombakabo, D.R. Congo 146/D2
Bombala, Austl. 159/D3
Bombala (riv.), Austl. 159/D3
Bombay (Mumbai), India 127/K5
Bombay Hook NWR, De, US 194/C5
Bomberai (pen.), Indo. 117/H4
Bombo, Ugan. 147/H2
Bomboma, D.R. Congo 146/D2
Bombombi, D.R. Congo 147/F2
Bomboyo, Chad 142/B2
Bomerano, It. 92/D6
Bomi, Libr. 140/C5
Bomi, China 112/B2
Bomili, D.R. Congo 147/F2
Bomlitz, Ger. 79/G3
Bømlo (isl.), Nor. 66/A2
Bomokandi (riv.), D.R. Congo 147/F2
Bomongo, D.R. Congo 146/D2
Bomu (riv.), D.R. Congo 133/E4
Bon Air, Va, US 189/J2
Bon Secour (bay), Al, US 190/E2
Bon Wier, Tx, US 177/H2
Bon, Cap (Ra's aṭ Ṭīb) (cape), Tun. 74/B4
Bon-Encontre, Fr. 70/D4
Bonāb, Iran 129/J4
Bonabéri, Camr. 146/B1
Bonaduz, Swi. 87/F4
Bonaire (isl.), NAnt. 165/L8
Bonalbo, Austl. 158/E1
Bonampak (ruin), Mex. 200/D2
Bonanza, Ut, US 173/J3
Bonanza, Or, US 172/C2
Bonanza, Co, US 175/J1
Bonanza (peak), Wa, US 170/D3
Bonao, DRep. 197/G4
Bonaparte (arch.), Austl. 162/B6
Bonaparte (riv.), BC, Can. 170/D2
Bonaparte (lake), BC, Can. 170/D2
Bonaparte (mt.), Wa, US 170/E3
Bonaparte (isls.), Austl. 153/B2
Bonaventure, Qu, Can. 184/E1
Bonaventure (riv.), Qu, Can. 184/E1
Bonavista, Nf, Can. 185/L1
Bonavista (cape), Nf, Can. 185/L1
Bonavista (bay), Nf, Can. 185/L1
Boncarbo, Co, US 178/B2
Bonchamp-lès-Laval, Fr. 83/E4
Bonchester Bridge, Sc, UK 59/D6
Boncourt, Swi. 86/D3
Bond, Co, US 173/K4
Bondari, Rus. 97/G1
Bondeno, It. 89/E4
Bondi (nbrhd.), Austl. 160/H8
Bondo, D.R. Congo 147/E2
Bondoc (pen.), Phil. 114/C2
Bondoukou, C.d'Iv. 140/E4
Bondowoso, Indo. 115/F3
Bonduel, Wi, US 181/K1
Bone (gulf), Indo. 103/M10
Bone Hill Nat'l Wild. Ref., ND, US 182/E4
Bonebone, Indo. 117/F4
Bonefro, It. 92/D4
Bönen, Ger. 79/E5
Bonerate (isls.), Indo. 117/F5
Bo'ness, Sc, UK 59/C4
Bonesteel, SD, US 180/E2
Bonete (peak), Arg. 212/B3
Bonfield, On, Can. 187/G1
Bonfol, Swi. 86/D3
Bonfouca, La, US 190/D2
Bong (co.), Libr. 140/C5
Bong (range), Libr. 140/C5
Bong (lake), China 125/F5
Bong Son, Viet. 120/E3
Bonga, Ang. 148/C2
Bonga, Eth. 142/H4
Bongabong, Phil. 114/C2
Bongaigaon, India 123/H2
Bongandanga, D.R. Congo 147/E2
Bongao, Phil. 114/B4
Bonggi (isl.), Malay. 117/E2
Bongka (riv.), Indo. 117/F4
Bongo, D.R. Congo 147/E4
Bongo, D.R. Congo 146/E2
Bongolava (uplands), Madg. 152/H7
Bongor, Chad 142/B3
Bongou (riv.), CAfr. 142/D4
Bongouanou, C.d'Iv. 140/D5
Bongoville, Gabon 146/C3
Bonham, Tx, US 179/F4
Bonheiden, Belg. 81/D1
Bonhill, Sc, UK 59/B5
Boni, Mali 141/E3
Boni Nat'l Rsv., Kenya 145/C2
Bonifacio, Fr. 74/A2
Bonifacio (str.), Fr.,It. 92/F2
Bonifay, Fl, US 191/F2
Bönigen, Swi. 86/D4
Bonin (isls.), Japan 162/C2
Bonita, La, US 179/J4
Bonita, Ca, US 192/C5
Bonita, Az, US 175/H4
Bonita Springs, Fl, US 191/H4
Bonito (peak), Hon. 200/E3
Bonito, Braz. 207/H5
Bonito, Braz. 213/E2
Bonito de Santa Fé, Braz. 207/G4
Bonjol, Indo. 115/C3
Bonn, Ger. 81/G2
Bonndorf im Schwarzwald, Ger. 87/E2
Bonne, Fr. 86/C5
Bonne (riv.), Fr. 90/B3
Bonne Terre, Mo, US 188/B2
Bonneau, SC, US 189/H4
Bonnefjorden (fd.), Nor. 64/S8
Bonnelles, Fr. 56/J6
Bonner-West Riverside, Mt, US 171/H4
Bonners Ferry, Id, US 170/F3
Bonnet (lake), Mb, Can. 182/F2
Bonnétable, Fr. 83/F4
Bonneuil-sur-Marne, Fr. 56/K5
Bonneval, Fr. 83/G4
Bonneville, Fr. 86/C5
Bonney Lake, Wa, US 193/C3
Bonnie, Il, US 188/C1
Bonnie Doone, NC, US 189/H3
Bonnières-sur-Seine, Fr. 83/G2
Bonnieux, Fr. 90/B5
Bönnigheim, Ger. 84/C4
Bonnybridge, Sc, UK 59/C5
Bonnyman, Ky, US 189/F2
Bonnyrigg, Sc, UK 59/C5
Bonnyville, Ab, Can. 166/E3
Bono, Ar, US 188/B3
Bonorva, It. 74/A2
Bons-en-Chablais, Fr. 86/C5
Bonsall, Ca, US 192/C4
Bontang, Indo. 117/E3
Bontberg (peak), SAfr. 150/C4
Bontebok NP, SAfr. 150/C4
Bonthain, Indo. 117/E5
Bonthe, SLeo. 140/B5
Bontoc, Phil. 114/C1
Bontomatane, Indo. 117/F5
Bonyeri, Gha. 140/E5
Bonyhád, Hun. 76/D2
Bonzart (lake), Tun. 138/L6
Booker, Tx, US 178/D2
Booker T. Washington Nat'l Mon., Va, US 189/H2
Boola, Gui. 140/C4
Boolaloo, Austl. 156/B2
Booligal, Austl. 159/B1
Boom, Belg. 81/D1
Boomi, Austl. 160/C5
Boone, Co, US 178/B1
Boone (riv.), Ia, US 181/H2
Boone, Ia, US 181/H2
Boone, NC, US 189/G2
Boone (dam), Tn, US 189/F2
Booneville, Ar, US 179/H3
Booneville, Ky, US 188/F2
Booneville, Ms, US 188/C3
Boonsboro, Md, US 187/H5
Boonton, NJ, US 195/H8
Bööntsagaan (lake), Mong. 104/D2
Boonville, NY, US 187/J3
Boonville, Ca, US 172/B4
Boonville, In, US 188/D1
Boonville, Mo, US 181/H4
Boopi (riv.), Bol. 209/E5
Boorabbin NP, Austl. 156/D4
Boorama, Som. 144/B3
Booroondara (mt.), Austl. 158/C1
Booroorban, Austl. 159/B2
Boorowa, Austl. 159/D2
Boos, Fr. 83/G2
Boos (int'l arpt.), Fr. 83/G2
Boos, Ger. 87/G1
Boostedt, Ger. 66/D4
Booster, Ar, US 179/H3
Boot Reefs (reef), PNG 155/G2
Boothia (pen.), Nun, Can. 166/G1
Boothia (gulf), Can. 165/H2
Bootjack, Ca, US 174/C2
Bootle, Eng, UK 61/E5
Booué, Gabon 146/B3
Bopa, Ben. 141/F5
Bopfingen, Ger. 84/D5
Bopili, D.R. Congo 147/E2
Bopolu, Libr. 140/C5
Boppard, Ger. 81/G3
Boppy (mt.), Austl. 158/C1
Boqueirão, Serra do (mts.), Braz. 211/E1
Boqueron (dept.), Par. 212/D2
Boquete (peak), Arg. 214/C4
Boquilla (res.), Mex. 198/D3
Boquillas del Carmen, Mex. 177/C3
Bor, Turk. 128/C2
Bor, Rus. 95/K4
Bor, Yugo. 76/F3
Bor, Sudan 142/F4
Bor, Czh. 85/F3
Bor Ul (mts.), China 100/K5
Bora Bora (isl.), FrPol. 163/K6
Borabu, Thai. 120/C2
Borah (peak), Id, US 173/G1
Borås, Swe. 66/E3
Borāzjān, Iran 129/G4
Borba, Port. 72/B3
Borba, Braz. 206/B4
Borbera (riv.), It. 88/B3
Borbona, It. 92/C2
Borbonnais (reg.), Fr. 70/D3
Borbore (riv.), It. 88/B3
Borča, Yugo. 76/E3
Borcea Branch (riv.), Rom. 77/H3
Borchen, Ger. 79/F5
Borçka, Turk. 97/G4
Borculo, Neth. 78/D4
Borda da Mata, Braz. 211/K7
Bordeaux, Fr. 70/C4
Bordelonville, La, US 190/C2
Borden, PE, Can. 184/F2
Borden (pen.), Nun, Can. 167/H1
Borden, Austl. 156/C5
Borden (isl.), NW, Can. 167/R7
Bordentown, NJ, US 194/D3
Bordertown, Austl. 158/B3
Bordighera, It. 90/D5
Bordj Bou Arreridj, Alg. 138/H4
Bordj Bou Arreridj (wilaya), Alg. 138/H4
Bordj el Kiffan, Alg. 138/G4
Bordj Manaïel, Alg. 138/G4
Bordj Moktar, Alg. 137/F5
Bordj Omar Driss, Alg. 137/G3
Bordj Sainte-Marie, Alg. 136/E4
Bordon, Eng, UK 63/F4
Boré, Mali 140/E3
Borē, Eth. 144/A4
Borehamwood, Eng, UK 56/C2
Borest, Fr. 56/L4
Boretto, It. 88/D4
Borgå (Porvoo), Fin. 67/L1
Borgaretto, It. 88/A2
Borgarnes, Ice. 64/N7
Borgaro Torinese, It. 88/A2
Børgefjell NP, Nor. 64/E2
Borgentreich, Ger. 79/G5
Borger, Tx, US 178/D3
Börger, Ger. 79/E3
Borger, Neth. 78/D3
Borgerhout, Belg. 78/B6
Borges Blanques, Sp. 73/F2
Borghetto Lodigiano, It. 88/C3
Borghetto Santo Spirito, It. 88/B5
Borgholm, Swe. 66/G3
Borgholzhausen, Ger. 79/F4
Borghorst, Ger. 79/E4
Borgloon, Belg. 81/E2
Borgnäs (Pornainen), Fin. 65/F4
Borgne (riv.), Swi. 86/D5
Borgne (lake), La, US 190/D3
Borgo, It. 87/H5
Borgo, Fr. 74/A1
Borgo (int'l arpt.), Burk. 140/D4
Borgo a Mozzano, It. 88/D6
Borgo Maggiore, SMar. 89/F6
Borgo Sabotino, It. 91/B5
Borgo San Dalmazzo, It. 90/D4
Borgo San Giacomo, It. 88/C3
Borgo San Lorenzo, It. 89/E6
Borgo Tossignano, It. 89/E5
Borgo Val di Taro, It. 88/C5
Borgo Vercelli, It. 88/B3
Borgofranco d'Ivrea, It. 88/A1
Borgomanero, It. 88/B2
Borgonovo Val Tidone, It. 88/C3
Borgosatollo, It. 88/D3
Borgosesia, It. 88/B2
Borgou (prov.), Ben. 141/F4
Borgund, Nor. 66/B1
Bori, Nga. 141/G5
Borikhan, Laos 120/C2
Borinskoye, Rus. 96/F1
Borio, India 123/F3
Borisoglebsk, Rus. 99/M2
Borisovka, Rus. 99/J2
Borisovo (nbrhd.), Rus. 94/W9
Borispol (int'l arpt.), Ukr. 98/F2
Borja, Sp. 72/E2
Borja, Peru 208/B2
Borken, Ger. 79/G6
Borken, Ger. 78/D5
Børkop, Den. 66/C4
Borkou (reg.), Chad 134/C5
Borkou-Ennedi-Tibesti (pref.), Chad 142/C1
Borkum (isl.), Ger. 78/D1
Borkum, Ger. 78/D1

237
Borku – Broni

Borkum (arpt.), Ger. 78/D1
Borlänge, Swe. 66/F1
Bormes-les-Mimosas, Fr. 90/C6
Bormida, It. 88/B5
Bormida (riv.), It. 71/H4
Bormida di Millesimo (riv.), It. 88/B4
Bormio, It. 87/G5
Born, Neth. 81/E1
Borna, Ger. 68/G3
Borndiep (chan.), Neth. 78/C2
Borne (riv.), Fr. 86/C6
Borne, Neth. 78/D4
Bornel, Fr. 80/B5
Bornem, Belg. 81/D1
Borneo (isl.), Indo.,Malay. 103/L9
Borneo (isl.), Indo. 117/E3
Bornheim, Ger. 81/G2
Bornholm (co.), Den. 66/F4
Bornholm (isl.), Swe.,Den. 55/F3
Bornholmsgat (chan.), Den.,Swi. 69/H1
Borno, It. 87/G6
Borno (state), Nga. 142/B2
Bornos, Sp. 72/C4
Börnsen, Ger. 79/H2
Bornus (plain), Nga. 142/B2
Boro (riv.), Sudan 142/E3
Borobudur (ruin), Indo. 115/E3
Borodino, Rus. 100/K4
Borodino, Ukr. 77/J2
Borodyanka, Ukr. 98/E2
Borohoro (mts.), China 125/D3
Boromo, Burk. 140/E4
Boron, Ca, US 174/D3
Borongan, Phil. 114/D3
Borough Green, Eng, UK 56/D3
Boroughbridge, Eng, UK 61/G3
Borovany, Czh. 85/H5
Borovichi, Rus. 94/G4
Borovlyanka, Rus. 125/D1
Borovo, Cro. 76/D3
Borovo, Bul. 77/G4
Borovsk, Rus. 96/F1
Borovskiy, Rus. 95/Q4
Borovskoy, Kaz. 95/Q5
Borraan, Som. 144/D3
Borre, Nor. 66/D2
Borrego Springs, Ca, US 174/D4
Borris, Ire. 58/D4
Borris in Ossory, Ire. 58/C4
Borrisokane, Ire. 58/B4
Borrisoleigh, Ire. 58/C4
Bornida (riv.), It. 88/B3
Borroloola, Austl. 155/E4
Borroloola Abor. Land, Austl. 155/D4
Borşa, Rom. 77/F2
Borsec, Rom. 98/C4
Borshchiv, Ukr. 98/D3
Borshchovochnyy (mts.), Rus. 105/H1
Borso del Grappa, It. 89/E2
Borsod-Abaúj-Zemplén (co.), Hun. 69/L4
Borssele, Neth. 78/A6
Borstel, Ger. 79/F3
Bort-les-Orgues, Fr. 70/E4
Bortala (riv.), China 125/D3
Borth, Wal, UK 62/B2
Boruca, CR 201/F4
Borūjen, Iran 129/G4
Borūjerd, Iran 129/G3
Børup, Den. 65/H7
Boryslav, Ukr. 69/M4
Boryspil', Ukr. 98/F2
Borzna, Ukr. 98/G2
Borzonasca, It. 88/C5
Borzya, Rus. 104/H1
Bosa, It. 74/A2
Bosaaso (Bender Cassim), Som. 144/D3
Bosanska Dubica, Bosn. 76/C3
Bosanska Gradiška, Bosn. 76/C3
Bosanska Kostajnica, Bosn. 76/C3
Bosanska Krupa, Bosn. 76/C3
Bosanski Brod, Bosn. 76/D3
Bosanski Petrovac, Bosn. 76/C3
Bosanski Šamac, Bosn. 76/D3
Bošany, Slvk. 69/K4
Bosavi (mt.), PNG 155/F1
Bosc-le-Hard, Fr. 83/G1
Boscawen, NH, US 187/L3
Bosco, La, US 179/H4
Bosco, It. 91/B1
Bosco Mesola, It. 89/F4
Boscobel, Wi, US 181/J2
Bosconero, It. 88/A2
Boscoreale, It. 92/D6
Bose, China 113/E4
Bosham, Eng, UK 63/F5
Boshnyakovo, Rus. 105/N2
Boshof, SAfr. 150/D3
Boshrūyeh, Iran 129/J3
Boskoop, Neth. 78/B4
Boskovice, Czh. 69/J4
Bosler, Wy, US 180/B3
Bosna (riv.), Bosn. 76/D3
Bosnia and Herzegovina (ctry.) 55/F4
Bošnjaci, Cro. 76/D3
Bōsō (pen.), Japan 111/G3
Bosobolo, D.R. Congo 142/C4
Bososama, D.R. Congo 142/D4
Bosporus (str.), Turk. 96/D4
Bosporus (riv.), Turk. 129/N6
Bosque del Apache Nat'l Wild Ref., NM, US 175/J4
Bosque Farms, NM, US 175/J3
Bosques Petrificados, Mon. Natural, Arg. 215/C5
Boss, Mo, US 188/B2
Bossangoa, CAfr. 142/C4
Bossembele, CAfr. 142/C4
Bossentélé, CAfr. 142/C4
Bossier City, La, US 179/H4
Bosso, Niger 142/B2
Bossut (cape), Austl. 154/A4
Bostān, Iran 129/G4
Bostan, China 125/D4
Bostānābād-e Bālā, Iran 129/F2
Bosten (lake), China 125/E3
Boston (mts.), Ar, US 179/H3
Boston, Tx, US 179/G4
Boston, Eng, UK 61/H6
Boston, Ga, US 191/G2
Boston (cap.), Ma, US 184/B4
Bostwick, Fl, US 191/H3
Bosut (riv.), Cro. 76/D3
Boswell, In, US 186/C4
Boswil, Swi. 87/E3
Bot Makak, Camr. 146/B2
Botād, India 127/K4
Botany, Austl. 159/E1
Botelerpunt (pt.), SAfr. 151/F2
Botelhos, Braz. 211/K6
Botene, Laos 120/C1
Botev (peak), Bul. 77/G4
Botevgrad, Bul. 77/F4
Bothaspas (pass), SAfr. 151/E2
Bothaville, SAfr. 150/D2
Bothel, Eng, UK 61/E2
Bothel, Ger. 79/G2
Bothell, Wa, US 193/C2
Bothenhampton, Eng, UK 62/D5
Bothnia (gulf), Swe.,Fin. 216/E
Bothwell, Austl. 158/C4
Botkyrka, Swe. 65/A1
Botletle (riv.), Bots. 148/D4
Botlikh, Rus. 97/H4
Botoşani, Rom. 98/D4
Botoşani (prov.), Rom. 77/H2
Botou, China 106/D3
Botrange (peak), Belg. 81/F3
Botrivier, SAfr. 150/L11
Botsford, Ct, US 195/E1
Botswana (ctry.) 133/E7
Bottanuco, It. 88/C2
Botte Donato (peak), It. 74/E3
Bottesford, Eng, UK 61/H6
Bottesford, Eng, UK 61/H4
Botticino, It. 88/D2
Bottineau, ND, US 182/D3
Bottineau Winter Park, ND, US 182/D3
Bottrighe, It. 89/F3
Bottrop, Ger. 78/D5
Botucatu, Braz. 213/G2
Botwood, Nf, Can. 185/K1
Bötzow, Ger. 68/Q6
Bou (riv.), C.d'Iv. 140/D4
Bou Arfa, Mor. 137/E2
Boû Djébéha (well), Mali 140/E2
Bou Hamdane, Oued (riv.), Alg. 138/K6
Bou Ismaïl, Alg. 138/G4
Bou Izakarn, Mor. 136/C3
Bou Kadir, Alg. 138/F4
Bou Laber (well), Alg. 136/D4
Boû Lanouâr, Mrta. 136/A5
Bou Naceur (peak), Mor 138/C3
Bou Regreg (riv.), Mor. 138/A3
Bou Saâda, Alg. 138/H5
Bou Salem, Tun. 138/L6
Bou Sellam, Oued (riv.), Alg. 138/H4
Bouaflé, C.d'Iv. 140/D5
Bouafle, Fr. 56/H5
Bouaké, C.d'Iv. 140/D5
Bouali, CAfr. 142/C4
Bouanga, Congo 146/D3
Bouar, CAfr. 142/B4
Bouba Ndjida, PN de, Camr. 142/B3
Boubín (peak), Czh. 85/G5
Bouc-Bel-Air, Fr. 90/B6
Bouca, CAfr. 142/C4
Bouchain, Fr. 80/C3
Bouchegouf, Alg. 138/K6
Boucherville, Qu, Can. 185/P6
Bouches-du-Rhône (dept.), Fr. 90/A5
Bouchet (mtn.), Fr. 90/D3
Boucle Du Baoulé, PN de la, Mali 140/C3
Boudenib, Mor. 136/E3
Boudi, Eth. 144/B4
Boudreaux (lake), La, US 190/C3
Boudry, Swi 86/C4
Bouenza (riv.), Congo 146/C3
Bouenza (pol. reg.), Congo 146/C3
Boufarik, Alg. 138/G4
Bouffémont, Fr. 56/J4
Bougainville (isl.), PNG 162/E5
Bougainville (cape), Austl. 154/B3
Bougainville (cape), UK 215/F6
Bougainville (reef), Austl. 153/D2
Bougainville Reef (reef), PNG 155/G3
Bougara, Alg. 138/G4
Bougar'oûn (cape), Alg. 138/K6
Bough Beech (res.), Eng, UK 56/D3
Boughton, Eng, UK 56/E3
Bougouni, Mali 140/D4
Bougouriba (prov.), Burk. 140/E4
Bougtob, Alg. 92/D4
Bouguenais, Fr. 70/C3
Bouhachem (peak), Mor. 138/B2
Bouhalla (peak), Mor. 138/B2
Bouillancy, Fr. 56/L4
Bouillon, Belg. 81/E4
Bouira, Alg. 138/G4
Bouira (wilaya), Alg. 138/G4
Boujad, Mor. 136/D2
Boukhalf (Tangier) (int'l arpt.), Mor. 138/B2
Boukoko, CAfr. 146/D2
Boukoumbé, Ben. 141/F4
Boulaide, Lux. 81/E4
Boulaouane, Mor. 136/C2
Boulay-Moselle, Fr. 81/F5
Boulazac, Fr. 70/D4
Boulder (riv.), Mt, US 173/H1
Boulder, Co, US 180/B3
Boulder, Mt, US 171/H4
Boulder City, Nv, US 174/E3
Boulder Creek, Ca, US 174/A2
Boulder Hill, Il, US 193/P16
Boulemane, Mor. 136/D2
Boulemane (prov.), Mor. 138/C3
Bouleurs, Fr. 56/L5
Boulgo (prov.), Burk. 141/E4
Boulia, Austl 157/H2
Boulieu-lès-Annonay, Fr. 90/A2
Bouligny, Fr. 81/E5
Boulkiemde (prov.), Burk. 141/E3
Boullarre, Fr. 56/M4
Boulogne (riv.), Fr. 70/C3
Boulogne-Billancourt, Fr. 56/J5
Boulogne-sur-Mer, Fr. 80/A2
Bouloire, Fr. 83/F5
Boulsa, Burk. 141/E3
Boulsworth (hill), Eng, UK 61/F4
Boumalne, Mor. 136/D3
Boumba (riv.), Camr. 146/C2
Boûmdeïd, Mrta. 140/C2
Boumerdas (wilaya), Alg. 138/G4
Boumerdas, Alg. 138/G4
Boun Nua, Laos 112/D4
Bouna, C.d'Iv. 140/E4
Bound Brook, NJ, US 194/D2
Boundary (peak), Nv, US 168/C4
Boundary Bald (mtn.), Me, US 187/L2
Boundary Bend, Austl. 158/B2
Boundiali, C.d'Iv. 140/D4
Boundji, Congo 146/C3
Bountiful, Ut, US 173/H3
Boupanda, Congo 146/C3
Bouquet (res.), Ca, US 192/B1
Bouquet (canyon), Ca, US 192/B2
Bourail, NCal. 163/U12
Bourbeuse (riv.), Mo, US 181/J4
Bourbon, Mo, US 179/J1
Bourbon, In, US 186/C4
Bourbon l'Archambault, Fr. 70/E3
Bourbonnais, Il, US 186/C4
Bourbonnais (reg.), Fr. 92/D1
Bourbonne-les-Bains, Fr. 86/B2
Bourbourg, Fr. 80/B2
Bourbre (riv.), Fr. 90/B1
Bourbriac, Fr. 82/B4
Bourdonné, Fr. 56/G5
Boureït, Mor. 138/B2
Bourem, Mali 141/E2
Bouressa (riv.), Mali 141/F2
Bourg, La, US 190/C3
Bourg-Achard, Fr. 83/F2
Bourg-de-Péage, Fr. 90/B2
Bourg-en-Bresse, Fr. 86/B5
Bourg-lès-Valence, Fr. 90/A3
Bourg-Saint-Andéol, Fr. 90/A4
Bourg-Saint-Maurice, Fr. 90/C1
Bourg-Saint-Pierre, Swi. 86/D6
Bourganeuf, Fr. 70/D4
Bourges, Fr. 70/E3
Bourget (lake), Fr. 86/B6
Bourgneuf (bay), Fr. 70/B3
Bourgogne (canal), Fr. 86/B3
Bourgogne (pol. reg.), Fr. 70/F3
Bourgoin-Jallieu, Fr. 90/B1
Bourgtheroulde-Infreville, Fr. 83/F2
Bourgueil, Fr. 83/F6
Bourke, Austl. 158/C1
Bourmont, Fr. 86/B1
Bourne (riv.), Fr. 90/B2
Bourne (riv.), Eng, UK 63/E4
Bourne, Eng, UK 63/F1
Bourne End, Eng, UK 63/F3
Bournemouth, Eng, UK 63/E5
Bournemouth (arpt.), Eng, UK 63/E5
Bournville, Eng, UK 63/E2
Bourquim (hill), Ne, US 180/D3
Bourscheid, Lux. 81/F4
Bourtanger Moor (reg.), Ger. 79/E3
Bourth, Fr. 83/F3
Bourton on the Water, Eng, UK 63/E3
Bousbecque, Fr. 80/C2
Bouse, Az, US 175/E4
Bousso, Chad 142/C3
Boussois, Fr. 80/D3
Boussouma, Burk. 141/E3
Boutilimit, Mrta. 140/B2
Bouvard (cape), Austl. 156/B5
Bouvet (isl.), Nor. 53/K8
Bouvron, Fr. 82/D6
Bouxières-aux-Dames, Fr. 81/F6
Bouxwiller, Fr. 81/G6
Bouza, Niger 141/G3
Bouzillé, Fr. 83/D6
Bouznika, Mor. 138/A3
Bouzonville, Fr. 81/F5
Bovalino, It. 74/E3
Bovegno, It. 88/D2
Boven Tapanahoni (riv.), Sur. 205/H4
Boven Tappanahoni (riv.), Sur. 206/C2
Boven-Hardinxveld, Neth. 78/B5
Bovenden, Ger. 79/G5
Bovenkarspel, Neth. 78/C3
Bovenwijde (lake), Neth. 78/D3
Boves, Fr. 80/B4
Boves, It. 90/D4
Bovey, Mn, US 183/H4
Bovey Tracey, Eng, UK 62/C5
Bovezzo, It. 88/D2
Bovina, Tx, US 178/C3
Bovingdon, Eng, UK 56/B1
Bovino, It. 76/B5
Bovolone, It. 89/E3
Bovril, Arg. 212/E4
Bow (riv.), Ab, Can. 166/E3
Bow (cr.), Ks, US 180/E4
Bow (riv.), Ab, Can. 171/H2
Bow City, Ab, Can. 171/H2
Bow Island, Ab, Can. 171/J3
Bow River Abor. Land, Austl. 154/B4
Bowbells, ND, US 182/C3
Bowdle, SD, US 182/E5
Bowdoin NWR, Mt, US 171/L3
Bowdon, ND, US 182/E4
Bowdon, Eng, UK 61/F5
Bowdon, Ga, US 188/E4
Bowen, Austl. 160/C3
Bowen, Arg. 214/D2
Bowen Island, BC, Can. 170/C3
Bowers Beach, De, US 194/C5
Bowes, Eng, UK 61/G3
Bowie, Tx, US 179/F4
Bowie, Az, US 175/H4
Bowie, Md, US 194/B6
Bowling Green, Oh, US 186/E4
Bowling Green, Fl, US 190/M8
Bowling Green (cape), Austl. 160/B2
Bowling Green, Ky, US 188/D2
Bowling Green, Mo, US 181/J4
Bowling Green, Va, US 189/J1
Bowling Green Bay NP, Austl. 160/B2
Bowman, ND, US 182/C4
Bowman (bay), Nun, Can. 167/J2
Bowman, Ga, US 189/F3
Bowman (mt.), BC, Can. 170/D2
Bowman-Haley (dam), ND, US 182/C5
Bowman-Haley (lake), ND, US 182/C4
Bowmansdale, Pa, US 194/B3
Bowmanstown, Pa, US 194/C2
Bowmansville, Pa, US 194/B3
Bowmanville, On, Can. 186/V8
Bowmore, Sc, UK 57/Q9
Bowness-on-Solway, Eng, UK 61/E2
Bowokan (isls.), Indo. 117/F4
Bowral, Austl. 159/E2
Bowring, Ok, US 179/F2
Bowron (riv.), BC, Can. 170/D1
Bowsman, Mb, Can. 182/D1
Bowutu (mts.), PNG 155/G1
Bowwood, Zam. 148/E3
Box Elder (riv.), Mt, US 182/B5
Box Elder (cr.), SD, US 180/C3
Box Elder (cr.), Co, US 180/B3
Box Elder, SD, US 180/C1
Box Elder, Mt, US 171/J3
Box Hill (nbrhd.), Austl. 158/G5
Box Springs, Ga, US 188/E4
Boxberg, Ger. 84/C4
Boxelder, Wy, US 180/B2
Boxholm, Swe. 66/F2
Boxing, China 106/D3
Boxley, Ar, US 179/H3
Boxmeer, Neth. 78/C5
Boxodoi, China 104/H3
Boxtel, Neth. 78/C5
Boxum, Neth. 78/C2
Boyabat, Turk. 96/E4
Boyabo, D.R. Congo 146/D2
Boyabo, D.R. Congo 142/C5
Boyaca (dept.), Col. 204/C3
Boyalık, Turk. 129/M6
Boyanup, Austl. 156/B5
Boyarka, Ukr. 98/F2
Boyce, La, US 190/B2
Boychinovtsi, Bul. 77/F4
Boyd, Tx, US 176/K6
Boydell, Ar, US 179/J4
Boyds, Wa, US 170/E3
Boydton, Va, US 189/H2
Boye, China 106/C3
Boyer (riv.), Ia, US 181/G2
Boyero, Co, US 180/C4
Boyertown, Pa, US 194/C3
Boyes, Mt, US 180/B1
Boyette, Fl, US 190/L8
Boykins, Va, US 189/J2
Boyle, Ire. 58/B2
Boyle, Ms, US 188/B4
Boyne (riv.), Ire. 60/B4
Boyne City, Mi, US 186/D2
Boyne Falls, Mi, US 186/D2
Boyne Island, Austl. 160/C3
Boynton, Ok, US 179/G3
Boynton Beach, Fl, US 190/P9
Boysen (res.), Wy, US 173/J2
Boysen (dam), Wy, US 173/J2
Boyuibe, Bol. 212/D2
Boyup Brook, Austl. 156/C5
Boz (pt.), Turk. 77/J5
Bozcaada, Turk. 75/K3
Bozcaada (isl.), Gre. 75/J3
Bozel, Fr. 90/C2
Bozeman, Mt, US 173/H1
Bozhai, China 113/F3
Bozkir, Turk. 128/C2
Bozkurt, Turk. 96/E4
Bozman, Md, US 194/B6
Bozoum, CAfr. 142/C4
Bozova, Turk. 128/D2
Bozüyük, Turk. 128/B2
Bozyazı, Turk. 130/C1
Bozzolo, It. 88/D3
Bra, It. 88/A3
Braan (riv.), Sc, UK 59/C3
Bråån (riv.), Swe. 65/K7
Brabourne Lees, Eng, UK 63/G4
Brač (isl.), Cro. 74/E1
Bracciano (lake), It. 74/B1
Bracciano, It. 91/B3
Bracebridge, On, Can. 187/G2
Bracieux, Fr. 83/G5
Bracigliano, It. 92/D6
Brackel, Ger. 79/H2
Bracken, Sk, Can. 171/K3
Brackenheim, Ger. 84/C4
Brackett, Wi, US 181/J1
Brackettville, Tx, US 177/D3
Brackley, Eng, UK 63/E2
Bracknagh, Ire. 58/C3
Bracknell, Eng, UK 63/F4
Brackwede, Ger. 79/F5
Braço do Norte, Braz. 213/G4
Braço Menor do Araguaia (riv.), Braz. 210/C2
Brad, Rom. 77/F2
Bradano (riv.), It. 76/B5
Bradda (pt.), IM, UK 60/D3
Braddock, ND, US 182/D4
Braden, Tn, US 188/C3
Bradenton, Fl, US 191/G4
Bradford, Eng, UK 61/G4
Bradford, Ar, US 179/J3
Bradford, Oh, US 186/D4
Bradford, Pa, US 187/G4
Bradford, Vt, US 187/K3
Bradford West Gwillimbury, On, Can. 187/G2
Bradford-on-Avon, Eng, UK 62/D4
Brading, Eng, UK 63/E5
Bradley, Wi, US 183/K5
Bradley, Ar, US 179/H4
Bradley (int'l arpt.), Ct, US 187/K4
Bradley, Il, US 186/C4
Bradley, Ca, US 174/B3
Bradley Beach, NJ, US 194/D3
Bradley Junction, Fl, US 190/M3
Bradner, Oh, US 186/E4
Brady (cr.), Tx, US 177/E2
Brady, Ne, US 180/D3
Brady, Mt, US 171/J3
Brady, Tx, US 177/E2
Braemar (reg.), Sc, UK 59/C2
Braemar, Sc, UK 59/C2
Braeriach (peak), Sc, UK 59/C2
Braga, Port. 72/A2
Braga (dist.), Port. 72/A2
Bragado, Arg. 214/E2
Bragança, Port. 72/B2
Bragança (dist.), Port. 72/B2
Bragança, Braz. 207/E3
Bragança Paulista, Braz. 211/K7
Bragg Creek, Ab, Can. 170/G2
Braggs, Ok, US 179/G3
Bragin, Bela. 98/F2
Braham, Mn, US 183/H5
Brahmakund, India 112/C3
Brāhmanbāria, Bang. 123/H4
Brahmaputra (riv.), Asia 103/J7
Braich-y-Pwll (pt.), Wal, UK 60/D6
Braid (riv.), NI, UK 60/B2
Braidwood, Il, US 186/B4
Braidwood, Austl. 159/D2
Brăila, Rom. 77/H3
Brăila (prov.), Rom. 77/H3
Brainard, Ne, US 181/F3
Brainards, NJ, US 194/C2
Braine, Fr. 80/C5
Braine-l'Alleud, Belg. 81/D2
Braine-le-Comte, Belg. 81/D2
Brainerd, Mn, US 183/G4
Braintree, Eng, UK 63/G3
Braithwaithe (pt.), Austl. 154/D2
Brajarajnagar, India 121/D1
Brak (riv.), SAfr. 150/C3
Brak (riv.), SAfr. 150/D3
Brake, Ger. 79/F2
Brakel, Belg. 80/C2
Brakel, Ger. 79/G5
Brakel, Neth. 78/C5
Brakna (pol. reg.), Mrta. 140/B2
Brålanda, Swe. 66/E2
Bralorne, BC, Can. 170/C2
Bram (peak), It. 90/D4
Bram, Fr. 70/E5
Bramalea, On, Can. 186/T8
Braman, Ok, US 179/F2
Bramdrupdam, Den. 66/C4
Bramhope, Eng, UK 61/G4
Bramley (mtn.), NY, US 187/J3
Bramley, Eng, UK 56/B3
Brampton, Eng, UK 61/F2
Brampton, On, Can. 186/T8
Bramsche, Ger. 79/F4
Bramstedt, Ger. 79/F2
Bran (riv.), Sc, UK 59/A1
Branam, Gha. 141/E5
Brancaleone-Marina, It. 74/E4
Brancepeth, Sk, Can. 171/M1
Branch, Mn, US 183/H5
Branch, Nf, Can. 185/L2
Branch, La, US 190/B2
Branch Dale, Pa, US 194/B2
Branch, North (riv.), Md, US 194/B5
Branch, South (riv.), WV, US 189/H1
Branchville, NJ, US 194/D1
Branchville, Ct, US 195/E1
Branco (riv.), Braz. 203/C2
Brand, Aus. 87/F3
Brandberg (peak), Namb. 148/B4
Brandbu, Nor. 66/D1
Brande, Den. 66/C4
Brandenburg, Ger. 68/G2
Brandenburg (state), Ger. 68/P6
Brandenburg, Ky, US 188/D2
Brander, Pass of (pass), Sc, UK 59/A4
Branderburgh, Sc, UK 59/C1
Brandesburton, Eng, UK 61/H4
Brandfort, SAfr. 150/D3
Brandizzo, It. 88/A2
Brandon, Mb, Can. 182/E3
Brandon (peak), Ire. 58/D5
Brandon, Eng, UK 61/G2
Brandon, Eng, UK 63/G2
Brandon, Co, US 178/C1
Brandon, Fl, US 190/L8
Brandon, Mn, US 183/G5
Brandon, Ms, US 188/C4
Brandon, SD, US 181/F2
Brandon, Vt, US 187/K3
Brandsen, Arg. 215/J11
Brandsville, Mo, US 179/J2
Brandvlei, SAfr. 150/C3
Brandýs nad Labem, Czh. 85/H2
Brandywine, Md, US 194/B6
Brandywine (riv.), Pa, US 194/C4
Brandywine, WV, US 189/H1
Branford, Fl, US 191/G3
Branford, Ct, US 195/F1
Branges, Fr. 86/B4
Braniewo, Pol. 67/H4
Brannenburg, Ger. 71/K3
Bransgore, Eng, UK 63/E5
Branson, Mo, US 179/H2
Brant (co.), On, Can. 186/S9
Brant Beach, NJ, US 194/D4
Brantford, On, Can. 186/S9
Branti, Indo. 115/D3
Brantley, Al, US 191/E2
Brantwood, Wi, US 183/J5
Branxholm, Austl. 158/C4
Branxholme, Austl. 158/B3
Branxton, Eng, UK 59/D5
Branxton, Austl. 159/E1
Branzoll (Bronzolo), It. 87/H4
Brasfield, Ar, US 179/J3
Brashear, Mo, US 181/H3
Brasher Falls-Winthrop, NY, US 187/J2
Brasiléia, Braz. 208/D3
Brasília (cap.), Braz. 210/D2
Brasília de Minas, Braz. 210/D3
Brasilia, PN de, Braz. 210/C2
Braşov, Rom. 77/G3
Braşov (prov.), Rom. 77/G3
Brass, Nga. 141/G5
Brasschaat, Belg. 78/B6
Brassey (mt.), Austl. 157/G2
Brasstown Bald (peak), Ga, US 188/F3
Brastad, Swe. 66/D2
Braswell, Ga, US 188/E4
Brat (isl.), Cro. 93/H2
Bratislava (pol. reg.), Slvk. 69/J4
Bratislava (cap.), Slvk. 76/C1
Bratislava (Ivanka) (int'l arpt.), Slvk. 76/C1
Bratsigovo, Bul. 75/J1
Bratsk, Rus. 101/L4
Brats'ke, Ukr. 98/F4
Bratslav, Ukr. 98/E3
Brattleboro, Vt, US 187/K3
Bratunac, Bosn. 76/D3
Braubach, Ger. 81/G3
Braulio Carrillo, PN, CR 196/E5
Braunau am Inn, Aus. 85/G6
Braunfels, Ger. 84/B1
Braunlage, Ger. 79/H5
Bräunlingen, Ger. 87/E2
Braunschweig, Ger. 79/H4
Braunschweig (arpt.), Ger. 79/H4
Braunton, Eng, UK 62/B4
Brava (coast), Sp. 73/G2
Brava (pt.), Chile 215/C7
Brava (isl.), CpV. 133/J11
Brava (pt.), Uru. 215/K11
Brave, Pa, US 186/F5
Bråviken (inlet), Swe. 66/G2
Bravo (peak), Bol. 212/C1
Bravo (peak), Peru 208/B2
Bravo del Norte (riv.), Mex. 196/A2
Brawley, Ca, US 174/E4
Bray (pt.), Ire. 60/B5
Bray, Ire. 60/B5
Bray, Eng, UK 56/A2
Bray (isl.), Nun, Can. 167/J2
Bray-Dunes, Fr. 80/B1
Braye (riv.), Fr. 70/D3
Braymer, Mo, US 181/H4
Brazeau (riv.), Ab, Can. 170/F1
Brazeau (mt.), Ab, Can. 170/F1
Brazey-en-Plaine, Fr. 86/B3
Brazil, In, US 186/C5
Brazil (ctry.) 203/D3
Brazil, Tn, US 188/C3
Brazilian Highlands (uplands), Braz. 203/E4
Brazo Casiquiare (riv.), Ven. 205/E4
Brazo Sur (riv.), Arg. 215/C6
Brazópolis, Braz. 211/L7
Brazoria (co.), Tx, US 177/M9
Brazoria NWR, Tx, US 177/G3
Brazos (riv.), US 165/H6
Brazos, Double Mountain Fork (riv.), Tx, US 178/D4
Brazos, Salt Fork (riv.), Tx, US 178/D4
Brazzaville (cap.), Congo 146/C4
Brčko, Bosn. 76/D3
Brda (riv.), Pol. 66/G5
Brdy (mts.), Czh. 69/G4
Brea, Ca, US 192/G8
Breadalbane (dist.), Sc, UK 59/B4
Breakenridge (mt.), BC, Can. 170/D3
Bream (pt.), NZ 161/C1
Bream, Eng, UK 62/D3
Bream Tail (pt.), NZ 161/C2
Breamish (riv.), Eng, UK 59/D6
Bréancon, Fr. 56/J4
Bréau, Fr. 56/L6
Breaux Bridge, La, US 190/C2
Breaza, Rom. 77/G3
Brebbia, It. 88/B2
Brebes, Indo. 115/E3
Brécey, Fr. 83/D3
Brech, Fr. 82/C5
Brêche (riv.), Fr. 80/B5
Brechen, Ger. 84/B2
Brechin, Sc, UK 59/D3
Brecht, Belg. 78/B6
Breckenridge, Mn, US 182/F4
Breckenridge, Mo, US 181/H4
Breckenridge, Tx, US 177/E1
Breckerfeld, Ger. 79/E6
Breckland (phys. reg.), Eng, UK 63/G2
Brecknock (pen.), Chile 215/C7
Brecon, Wal, UK 62/C3
Brecon Beacons (mts.), Wal, UK 62/C3
Bréda (riv.), Fr. 90/C2
Breda, Neth. 78/B5
Bredaryd, Swe. 66/E3
Bredasdorp, SAfr. 150/M11
Bredbo, Austl. 159/D2
Bredebro, Den. 66/C4
Bredene, Belg. 80/B1
Bredgar, Eng, UK 56/F3
Bredstedt, Ger. 66/C4
Bree, Belg. 81/E1
Breë (riv.), SAfr. 150/B4
Breeches (cr.), Pa, US 194/A3
Breed, Wi, US 183/K5
Breese, Il, US 188/C1
Breezand, Neth. 78/B3
Breezy Point, Mn, US 183/G4
Breg (riv.), Ger. 68/E5
Bregagno (peak), It. 87/F5
Bregalinca (riv.), FYROM 75/H2
Breganze, It. 89/E2
Bregenz, Aus. 87/F3
Bregenzer Ache (riv.), Aus. 87/F3
Bregovo, Bul. 76/F3
Brégy, Fr. 56/L4
Bréhal, Fr. 82/D3
Breidhafjördhur (bay), Ice. 64/M6
Breil-Brigels, Swi. 87/F4
Breil-sur-Roya, Fr. 90/D5
Breisach, Ger. 86/D1
Breitbrunn am Chiemsee, Ger. 85/F7
Breitenauriegel (peak), Ger. 85/G5
Breitenbach, Swi. 86/D3
Breitenbach, Ger. 81/G5
Breitenbrunn, Ger. 85/E4
Breitenbrunn, Ger. 85/F2
Breitenfurt bei Wien, Aus. 77/N7
Breitenworbis, Ger. 79/H6
Breithorn (peak), Swi. 86/D5
Breithorn (peak), Swi. 86/D6
Brejinho de Nazaré, Braz. 210/C1
Brejo, Braz. 207/F3
Brejo do Cruz, Braz. 207/G4
Brejo Santo, Braz. 207/G4
Brembate di Sopra, It. 88/C2
Brembilla, It. 88/C2
Brembio, It. 88/C3
Brembo (riv.), It. 87/F6
Bremen (state), Ger. 66/C5
Bremen, In, US 186/C4
Bremen, Oh, US 186/E5
Bremen, Ga, US 188/E4
Bremen (int'l arpt.), Ger. 79/F2
Bremen, Ger. 79/F2
Bremer (riv.), Austl. 160/E7
Bremerhaven (arpt.), Ger. 79/F1
Bremerhaven, Ger. 79/F1
Bremerton, Wa, US 170/C4
Bremervörde, Ger. 79/G2
Bremgarten, Swi. 87/E3
Bremgarten bei Bern, Swi. 86/D4
Bremnes, Nor. 66/A2
Bremond, Tx, US 177/F2
Bremsa (riv.), Nor. 64/R8
Brenchley, Eng, UK 56/E3
Brend (riv.), Ger. 84/D2
Brendel (lake), Mi, US 193/E7
Brendola, It. 89/E3
Brendon (hills), Eng, UK 62/C4
Brenham, Tx, US 177/F2
Brenne (riv.), Fr. 68/C5
Brenner (pass), Aus. 87/H4
Brenner (riv.), Austl. 157/N9
Brenno (riv.), Swi. 87/E5
Breno, It. 87/G6
Brent, On, Can. 187/G1
Brent (riv.), Eng, UK 56/B2
Brent (bor.), Eng, UK 56/C2
Brent (res.), Eng, UK 56/C2
Brent, Al, US 188/D4
Brenta (peak), It. 87/G5
Brenta (riv.), It. 71/J4
Brenton, WV, US 189/G2
Brentwood, Eng, UK 56/D2
Brentwood, Ca, US 193/L11
Brentwood, Tn, US 188/D2
Brentwood, NY, US 195/E2
Brenz (riv.), Ger. 84/D5
Brescello, It. 88/D4
Brescia (prov.), It. 87/G6
Brescia, It. 88/D2
Breskens, Neth. 80/C1
Breslau, Tx, US 177/F3
Bresle (riv.), Fr. 70/D1
Bresles, Fr. 80/B5
Bresque (riv.), Fr. 90/C5
Bressana, It. 88/C3
Bressanone, It. 71/J3
Bressay (isl.), Sc, UK 57/W13
Bressuire, Fr. 70/C3
Brest, Bela. 69/M2
Brest (int'l arpt.), Bela. 69/M2
Brest, Fr. 82/A4
Brestskaya (prov.), Bela. 96/C1
Bretagne (pt.), Fr. 151/T15
Bretagne (pol. reg.), Fr. 70/B2
Bretagne, Monts de (mts.), Fr. 70/B2
Bretaña, Peru 208/C2
Breteuil, Fr. 83/F3
Breteuil, Fr. 80/B4
Brethren, Mi, US 186/C2
Brétigny-sur-Orge, Fr. 56/J6
Breton (isls.), La, US 190/D3
Breton (cape), NS, Can. 185/H3
Breton (sound), La, US 190/D3
Breton, Ab, Can. 170/G1
Breton Cove, NS, Can. 185/G2
Breton Nat'l Wild. Ref., La, US 190/D3
Brett (cape), NZ 161/C1
Brett (riv.), Eng, UK 63/G2
Brettach (riv.), Ger. 84/C4
Bretten, Ger. 84/B4
Bretteville-L'Orgueilleuse, Fr. 83/E2
Bretzenheim, Ger. 81/G4
Breuberg, Ger. 84/C3
Breueh (isl.), Indo. 115/A1
Breugel, Neth. 78/C5
Breuillet, Fr. 56/J6
Breukelen, Neth. 78/B4
Breuna, Ger. 79/G6
Breuvannes-en-Bassigny, Fr. 86/B1
Brevard, NC, US 189/F3
Breves, Braz. 206/D3
Brevik, Nor. 66/C2
Brevik, Swe. 65/B1
Brevoort (isl.), Nun, Can. 167/K2
Brewarrina, Austl. 158/C1
Brewer, Mo, US 188/C2
Brewerton, NY, US 187/H3
Brewerville, Libr. 140/C5
Brewood, Eng, UK 62/D1
Brewster (cape), Austl. 154/B3
Brewster (lake), Austl. 159/C1
Brewster, Fl, US 190/M8
Brewster, Ks, US 180/D4
Brewster, Mn, US 181/G2
Brewster, Ne, US 180/E3
Brewster, Oh, US 186/F4
Brewster, Wa, US 170/E3
Brewton, Al, US 190/E2
Brey-et-lû, Fr. 56/G4
Breyten, SAfr. 151/E2
Brežice, Slov. 76/B3
Brezina, Alg. 137/F2
Březnice, Czh. 85/G3
Breznik, Bul. 76/F4
Brezoi, Rom. 77/G3
Brézolles, Fr. 83/G3
Brezovo, Bul. 77/G4
Bria, CAfr. 142/D4
Briançon, Fr. 90/C3
Briar Creek, Pa, US 194/B1
Briare, Fr. 70/E3
Bribbaree, Austl. 159/C2
Bric de Rubren (peak), Fr. 90/C3
Bric Rosso (peak), It. 90/D3
Brice, Tx, US 178/D3
Briceni, Mol. 98/D3
Brickerville, Pa, US 194/B3
Bricket Wood, Eng, UK 56/B1
Brickley (brook), Austl. 156/L7
Bricktown, NJ, US 194/D3
Bricquebec, Fr. 82/D2
Bridal Cave, Mo, US 179/H1
Bridal Veil (falls), Co, US 175/J2
Bride, IM, UK 60/D3
Bride (riv.), Ire. 58/B5
Bridge, Id, US 173/G2
Bridge (riv.), BC, Can. 170/C2
Bridge City, Tx, US 177/H2
Bridge of Allan, Sc, UK 59/C4
Bridge of Don, Sc, UK 59/D2
Bridge of Weir, Sc, UK 59/B5
Bridgehampton, NY, US 195/F2
Bridgeman (mtn.), Ky, US 188/E2
Bridgend, Wal, UK 62/C3
Bridgeport (lake), Tx, US 177/F1
Bridgeport, Mi, US 186/E3
Bridgeport, WV, US 186/F5
Bridgeport, Ca, US 172/D4
Bridgeport, Il, US 188/D1
Bridgeport, Ne, US 180/C3
Bridgeport, Tx, US 176/K6
Bridgeport, Wa, US 170/E3
Bridgeport, NJ, US 194/C4
Bridgeport, Ct, US 195/E1
Bridger, Mt, US 173/J1
Bridgeton, NJ, US 194/C5
Bridgetown, Ire. 58/D5
Bridgetown, NS, Can. 184/E3
Bridgetown, Oh, US 188/E1
Bridgetown, Austl. 156/C5
Bridgetown (cap.), Bar. 197/P9
Bridgeville, Qu, Can. 184/E1
Bridgeville, Ca, US 172/B3
Bridgeville, De, US 194/C6
Bridgewater, NS, Can. 184/E3
Bridgewater, Austl. 158/C4
Bridgewater, Va, US 189/H1
Bridgnorth, Eng, UK 62/D1
Bridgton, Me, US 187/L2
Bridgwater, Eng, UK 62/D4
Bridgwater (bay), Eng, UK 62/C4
Bridlington (bay), Eng, UK 61/H3
Bridlington, Eng, UK 61/H3
Bridport, Vt, US 187/K3
Bridport, Austl. 158/C4
Bridport, Eng, UK 62/D5
Brie (reg.), Fr. 68/B4
Brie-Comte-Robert, Fr. 56/K5
Briec, Fr. 82/A4
Brieg Brzeg, Pol. 69/J3
Brielle, Neth. 78/B5
Brielle, NJ, US 194/D3
Brienz, Swi. 86/E4
Brier (isl.), Ns., Can. 184/D3
Brier (mtn.), Pa, US 187/H4
Brier, Wa, US 193/C2
Brier (cr.), Ga, US 189/G4
Briercrest, Sk, Can. 171/M2
Brierfield, Eng, UK 61/F4
Brieselang, Ger. 68/Q6
Brig, Swi. 86/D5
Brigach (riv.), Ger. 84/B7
Brigantine, NJ, US 194/D5
Brigg, Eng, UK 61/H4
Briggs, Tx, US 176/F2
Briggs Corner, NB, Can. 184/E2
Brigham City, Ut, US 173/G3
Brighouse, Eng, UK 61/G4
Brighstone, Eng, UK 63/E5
Bright, Austl. 159/C3
Brightlingsea, Eng, UK 63/H3
Brighton, On, Can. 187/H2
Brighton, Mi, US 186/E3
Brighton, Wi, US 193/P14
Brighton, Co, US 180/B4
Brighton, Il, US 181/J4
Brighton, Tn, US 188/C3
Brighton (nbrhd.), Austl. 157/M9
Brighton (nbrhd.), Austl. 158/G5
Brighton (nbrhd.), Austl. 160/F6
Brighton, Eng, UK 63/F5
Brightons, Sc, UK 59/C5
Brignais, Fr. 90/A1
Brignoles, Fr. 90/C6
Brihante (riv.), Braz. 213/F2
Brihuega, Sp. 72/D2
Briis-sous-Forges, Fr. 56/J6
Brikama, Gam. 140/A3
Brilhante (riv.), Braz. 210/B4
Brill, Eng, UK 63/E3
Brillion, Wi, US 186/B2
Brilon, Ger. 79/F6
Brimington, Eng, UK 61/G5
Brimley, Mi, US 186/D1
Brimstone Hill NP, StK. 197/N8
Brindisi, It. 75/E2
Brinkley, Ar, US 179/J3
Brinkmann, Arg. 212/D4
Brinktown, Mo, US 179/H1
Brinkworth, Austl. 157/H5
Brinkworth, Eng, UK 62/E3
Brinnon, Wa, US 193/B2
Brinson, Ga, US 191/F2
Briny Breezes, Fl, US 190/P9
Brion (isl.), Qu, Can. 185/G2
Brión, Sp. 72/A1
Brione, Swi. 87/E5
Briones (res.), Ca, US 193/K11
Brionne, Fr. 83/F2
Briouze, Fr. 83/E3
Brisbane, Austl. 160/F6
Brisbane (int'l arpt.), Austl. 160/F6
Brisbane (riv.), Austl. 160/E7
Brisbane Forest Park, Austl. 160/E6
Brisbane Ranges NP, Austl. 159/B3
Brisbane Water, Austl. 159/E1
Brisbane Water NP, Austl. 159/E1
Brisco, BC, Can. 170/F2
Brisighella, It. 89/E5
Brissago, Swi. 87/E5
Bristol, NB, Can. 184/D2
Bristol, Qu, Can. 187/H2
Bristol, Eng, UK 62/D4
Bristol (chan.), Eng, Wal, UK 62/B4
Bristol (bay), Ak, US 165/A4
Bristol (lake), Ca, US 174/E3
Bristol, Co, US 178/C1
Bristol, Ct, US 187/K4
Bristol, Fl, US 191/F2
Bristol, Ga, US 191/G2
Bristol, NH, US 187/L3
Bristol, Pa, US 194/D3
Bristol, RI, US 187/L4
Bristol, SD, US 182/F5
Bristol, Tn, US 189/F2
Bristol, Tx, US 176/L7
Bristol, Vt, US 187/K2
Bristolville, Oh, US 186/F4
Bristow, Ok, US 179/F3
Britânia, Braz. 210/C2
British (mts.), Ak, US 168/Y12
British Columbia (prov.), Can. 166/D3
British Empire (range), Nun, Can. 167/S6
British Indian Ocean Terr. (terr.), UK 103/G10
British Museum, Eng, UK 56/C2
Brits, SAfr. 149/E5
Britstown, SAfr. 150/C3
Britt, Ia, US 181/H2
Brittany (reg.), Fr. 70/B3
Britton, SD, US 182/F5
Britton, Tx, US 176/K7
Brive-la-Gaillarde, Fr. 70/D4
Brives-Charensac, Fr. 70/E4
Briviesca, Sp. 70/B5
Brivio, It. 88/C2
Brixham, Eng, UK 62/C6
Brixworth, Eng, UK 63/F2
Brlik, Kaz. 125/B3
Brnik (int'l arpt.), Slov. 71/L3
Brno, Czh. 69/J4
Broa (bay), Cuba 201/F1
Broad (riv.), Ga, US 189/F4
Broad Arrow, Austl. 156/D4
Broad Law (peak), Sc, UK 59/C6
Broad Sound (isls.), Austl. 160/C2
Broad Street, Eng, UK 56/E3
Broad Valley, Mb, Can. 182/F2
Broadacres, Sk, Can. 171/K1
Broadbent, Or, US 172/A2
Broaddus, Tx, US 177/G2
Broadford, Ire. 58/B5
Broadford, Austl. 159/B3
Broadkill (riv.), De, US 194/C6
Broadley Common, Eng, UK 56/D1
Broadmeadows (nbrhd.), Austl. 158/F5
Broadstairs, Eng, UK 63/H4
Broadstone, Eng, UK 62/E5
Broadus, Mt, US 180/B1
Broadview, Mt, US 171/K4
Broadwater, Ne, US 180/C3
Broadwater NP, Austl. 158/E1
Broadway (hill), Eng, UK 63/E3
Broadway, NJ, US 194/C2
Broadwindsor, Eng, UK 62/D5
Broby, Swe. 65/L6
Broc, Swi. 86/D4
Brocēni, Lat. 67/K3
Brochet, Mb, Can. 166/F3
Brock (isl.), NW, Can. 167/R7
Brock, Sk, Can. 171/K2
Brocken (peak), Ger. 79/H5
Brockenhurst, Eng, UK 63/E5
Brocket, ND, US 182/E3
Brocket, Ab, Can. 171/H3
Brockman (mt.), Austl. 156/C2
Brockport, NY, US 187/H3
Brockton, Mt, US 182/B3
Brockton, Ma, US 187/L3
Brockville, On, Can. 187/J2
Brockway, Pa, US 187/G4
Brocton, NY, US 187/G3
Brodeur (pen.), Nun, Can. 166/G1
Brodhead, Wi, US 181/K2
Brodhead (cr.), Pa, US 194/C1
Brodheadsville, Pa, US 194/C2
Brodick, Sc, UK 59/A5
Brodnica, Pol. 69/K2
Brody, Ukr. 98/C2
Broek in Waterland, Neth. 78/B4
Broek Op Langedijk, Neth. 78/B3
Brogden, NC, US 189/H3
Broglie, Fr. 83/F2
Bröhn (peak), Ger. 79/G4
Brokaw, Wi, US 181/K1
Broken (bay), Austl. 158/D2
Broken (riv.), Austl. 159/B3
Broken Arrow, Ok, US 179/G2
Broken Back (crater), NM, US 175/J4
Broken Bow (dam), Ok, US 179/G3
Broken Bow, Ok, US 179/G3
Broken Bow (lake), Ok, US 179/G3
Broken Bow, Ne, US 180/E3
Broken Hill, Austl. 158/B1
Brokenhead Ind. Res., Mb, Can. 182/F2
Brokeoff (mts.), NM, US 178/B4
Brokopondo, Sur. 206/C1
Brokopondo (dist.), Sur. 205/H3
Brome, Ger. 68/F2
Bromley (nbrhd.), Eng, UK 56/D2
Bromley, Zim. 149/F3
Bromley Common (nbrhd.), Eng, UK 56/D3
Bromölla, Swe. 66/F3
Bromsgrove, Eng, UK 62/D2
Bromskirchen, Ger. 79/F6
Bromyard, Eng, UK 62/D2
Bron, Fr. 86/A6
Bronaugh, Mo, US 179/G2
Brøndby, Den. 65/J7
Brønderslev, Den. 66/C3
Brong-Ahafo (pol. reg.), Gha. 141/E5
Broni, It. 88/C3

Bronkhorstspruit, SAfr. 150/E2
Bronllys, Wal, UK 62/C2
Brønnøy, Nor. 64/E2
Brøns, Den. 66/C4
Bronschhofen, Swi. 87/F3
Bronson, Ks, US 179/G2
Bronson, Fl, US 191/G3
Bronson, Mi, US 186/D4
Bronson, Tx, US 177/G2
Bronte, It. 74/D4
Bronte, On, Can. 186/T9
Bronte, Tx, US 176/D2
Bronwood, Ga, US 191/F2
Bronx (bor.), NY, US 195/E2
Bronx Zoo, NY, US 195/K8
Bronxville, NY, US 195/K8
Bronzolo (Branzoll), It. 87/H5
Brook, In, US 186/C4
Brook Forest, Co, US 180/B4
Brook Park, Mn, US 183/H5
Brookdale, Mb, Can. 182/E2
Brookdale, SC, US 189/G4
Brookeland, Tx, US 177/H2
Brooker, Fl, US 191/G3
Brooke's Point, Phil. 114/B3
Brookfield, Ct, US 187/K4
Brookfield, Il, US 193/Q16
Brookfield, Mo, US 181/H4
Brookfield, Vt, US 187/K2
Brookfield, Wi, US 186/B3
Brookhaven, Ms, US 190/C2
Brookings, Or, US 172/A2
Brookings, SD, US 181/F1
Brooklet, Ga, US 189/G4
Brooklyn, Ms, US 190/D2
Brooklyn, Ia, US 181/H3
Brooklyn (bor.), NY, US 194/D2
Brooklyn Center, Mn, US 183/P6
Brooklyn Park, Mn, US 183/P6
Brooklyn Park, Md, US 194/B5
Brookmans Park, Eng, UK 56/C1
Brookneal, Va, US 189/H2
Brooks (range), Ak, US 165/B3
Brooks, Ca, US 172/B4
Brooks, Ab, Can. 171/J2
Brooks (A.F.B.), Tx, US 177/E3
Brooksby, Sk, Can. 171/M1
Brookshire, Tx, US 177/G3
Brookside, De, US 194/C4
Brookston, Mn, US 183/H4
Brookston, In, US 186/C4
Brooksville, Fl, US 190/L6
Brooksville, Ky, US 188/E1
Brooksville, Ms, US 188/C4
Brookton, Austl. 156/C5
Brookville, In, US 186/D5
Brookville, Pa, US 187/G4
Brookville, NY, US 195/L8
Brookville (lake), In, US 188/E1
Broomall, Pa, US 194/C4
Broome, Austl. 154/A4
Broomfield, Eng, UK 56/E1
Broomfield, Co, US 180/B4
Broons, Fr. 82/C4
Brørup, Den. 66/C4
Brösarp, Swe. 66/F4
Broseley, Mo, US 188/B2
Brosna, Ire. 58/A5
Brosna (riv.), Ire. 58/C3
Brossard, Qu, Can. 185/P7
Brotas, Braz. 213/G2
Brothers, Or, US 172/C2
Brotton, Eng, UK 61/H2
Brou, Fr. 83/G4
Brough, Eng, UK 61/F2
Brough (pt.), Sc, UK 57/V14
Brougham, On, Can. 186/U8
Broughshane, NI, UK 60/B2
Broughton, Sc, UK 59/C5
Broughton, Eng, UK 63/F2
Broughton in Furness, Eng, UK 61/E3
Broughton Street, Eng, UK 63/G4
Broulee, Austl. 159/D2
Broulkou (well), Chad 142/C1
Broussard, La, US 190/C2
Brousseval, Fr. 86/A1
Brouwersdam (dam), Neth. 78/A5
Brouwershaven, Neth. 78/A5
Brovary, Ukr. 98/F2
Brovst, Den. 66/C3
Broward (co.), Fl, US 190/P10
Browerville, Mn, US 183/G4
Brown (pt.), Austl. 157/G5
Brown (mt.), Austl. 157/H5
Brown (pt.), Wa, US 170/B4
Brown (mt.), Mt, US 171/J3
Brown City, Mi, US 186/E3
Brown Clee (hill), Eng, UK 62/D2
Brown Deer, Wi, US 186/C3
Browndell, Tx, US 177/H2
Brownfield, Tx, US 178/C4
Brownhills, Eng, UK 63/E1
Browning, Mo, US 181/H3
Browning, Mt, US 171/H3
Browning, Austl. 159/D2
Brownlee (dam), Id, US 172/E1
Brownlee (res.), Id, US 172/E1
Brownlee, Ne, US 180/D2
Brownlee, Sk, Can. 171/L2
Browns, Al, US 188/D4
Browns Mills, NJ, US 194/D4
Browns Park NWR, Co, US 173/J3
Browns Valley, Mn, US 182/F5
Brownsburg, In, US 186/C5
Brownsea (isl.), Eng, UK 63/E5
Brownstown, Il, US 188/C1
Brownstown, In, US 188/D1
Brownsville, Ky, US 188/D2
Brownsville (nbrhd.), NY, US 195/K9
Brownsville, Or, US 172/B1
Brownsville, Tn, US 188/C3
Brownsville, Tx, US 176/F5
Brownsville, Wa, US 193/B2
Brownwood (lake), Tx, US 177/E2
Brownwood, Tx, US 176/E2
Broxbourne, Eng, UK 56/C1
Broxburn, Sc, UK 59/C5
Broxton, Ga, US 191/G2
Broye (riv.), Swi. 86/C4
Broyle (cape), Nf, Can. 185/L2
Brozas, Sp. 72/B3
Bruay-la-Buissière, Fr. 80/B3
Bruay-sur-L'Escaut, Fr. 80/C3
Bruce, Wi, US 183/J5
Bruce (pen.), On, Can. 186/F2
Bruce (mt.), Austl. 156/C2
Bruce, Ab, Can. 171/H1
Bruce Crossing, Mi, US 183/K4
Bruce Peninsula NP, On, Can. 187/F2
Bruce Rock, Austl. 156/C4
Bruceton, Tn, US 188/C2
Bruceville-Eddy, Tx, US 177/F2
Bruchberg (peak), Ger. 79/H5
Bruche (riv.), Fr. 71/G2
Bruchhausen-Vilsen, Ger. 79/G3
Bruchköbel, Ger. 84/B2
Bruchmühlbach-Miesau, Ger. 81/G5
Bruchsal, Ger. 84/B4
Brucht (riv.), Ger. 79/G5
Bruck, Aus. 77/P7
Bruck an der Grossglocknerstrasse, Aus. 71/K3
Bruck an der Mur, Aus. 71/L3
Bruckberg, Ger. 85/F5
Brue (riv.), Eng, UK 62/D4
Bruff, Ire. 58/B5
Bruflat, Nor. 66/C1
Brügg, Swi. 86/D3
Brugg, Swi. 86/E3
Brugge, Belg. 80/C1
Brüggen, Ger. 78/D6
Brugnera, It. 89/F2
Brühl, Ger. 81/F2
Bruin, Ky, US 189/F1
Bruinisse, Neth. 78/B5
Bruino, It. 90/D2
Brukkaros (peak), Namb. 150/B2
Brukunga, Austl. 157/M8
Brule (lake), Mn, US 183/J4
Brule, Wi, US 183/J4
Brûlon, Fr. 83/E5
Brûly, Belg. 81/D4
Brumado, Braz. 211/E2
Brumath, Fr. 81/G6
Brummānā, Leb. 131/D1
Brummen, Neth. 78/D4
Brumunddal, Nor. 66/D1
Brundall, Eng, UK 63/H1
Brundidge, Al, US 191/F2
Brune (riv.), Fr. 80/C4
Bruneau (riv.), Id, US 172/F2
Brunei(ctry.) 103/L9
Brunei (bay), Bru. 114/A4
Brunei (int'l arpt.), Bru. 114/A4
Brunete, Sp. 73/M9
Brunette (isl.), Nf., Can. 185/J2
Brunflo, Swe. 64/E3
Bruni, Tx, US 177/E4
Brunico, It. 71/J3
Brünigpass (pass), Swi. 86/E4
Bruning, Ne, US 180/F3
Brunn am Gebirge, Aus. 77/N7
Brunna, Swe. 65/A1
Brunner, NZ 161/B3
Bruno, Sk, Can. 171/M1
Brunoy, Fr. 56/K5
Brunsbüttel, Ger. 79/G1
Brunson, SC, US 189/G4
Brunssum, Neth. 81/E2
Brunstatt, Fr. 86/D2
Brunswick (nbrhd.), Austl. 158/F5
Brunswick (pen.), Chile 215/C7
Brunswick, Ga, US 191/H2
Brunswick, Md, US 187/H5
Brunswick, Mo, US 181/H4
Brunswick, Oh, US 186/F4
Brunswick Heads, Austl. 160/D5
Brunswick Junction, Austl. 156/B5
Bruree, Ire. 58/B5
Brus (lake), Nic. 201/E3
Brusartsi, Bul. 76/F4
Brusenets, Rus. 95/K3
Brusett, Mt, US 171/L4
Brushy (cr.), Tx, US 177/F2
Brushy Creek, Tx, US 176/G2
Brusio, Swi. 87/G5
Brusque, Braz. 213/G3
Brussels (int'l arpt.), Belg. 81/D2
Brussels, Wi, US 186/C2
Brussels, On, Can. 186/F3
Brussels (Bruxelles) (cap.), Belg. 81/D2
Brusson, It. 88/A1
Bruthen, Austl. 159/C3
Bruton, Eng, UK 62/D4
Bruxelles (Brussels) (cap.), Belg. 81/D2
Bruyères, Fr. 86/C1
Bruyères-le-Châtel, Fr. 56/J6
Bruyères-sur-Oise, Fr. 56/J4
Bruz, Fr. 82/D4
Bruzual, Ven. 204/D2
Bryan, Oh, US 186/D4
Bryan (mt.), Austl. 157/H5
Bryan, Tx, US 176/F2
Bryanka, Ukr. 99/K3
Bryansk, Rus. 96/E1
Bryansk Oblast, Rus. 96/E1
Bryant, Ar, US 179/H3
Bryce Canyon, Ut, US 175/F2
Bryce Canyon NP, Ut, US 175/F2
Brymbo, Wal, UK 61/E5
Bryn Brawd (peak), Wal, UK 62/C2
Bryn Mawr, Pa, US 194/C3
Bryne, Nor. 66/A2
Brynithel, Wal, UK 62/C3
Brynmawr, Wal, UK 62/C3
Bryson, Tx, US 179/E4
Bryson, Qu, Can. 187/H2
Bryson City, NC, US 189/F3
Bryukhovetskaya, Rus. 99/K5
Brzeg Dolny, Pol. 69/J3
Brzesko, Pol. 69/L4
Brzozów, Pol. 69/M4
Bū Athlah (well), Libya 134/D2
Bu Craa, WSah. 136/B4
Bū Fīshah, Tun. 74/B4
Bū Kūsā (well), Libya 134/A3
Bū 'Urqūb, Tun. 74/B4
Bua, Swe. 66/E3
Bua (riv.), Malw. 149/G2
Bua Chum, Thai. 120/C3
Bua Yai, Thai. 120/C3
Buala, Sol. 162/E5
Buang, Indo. 116/D4
Buapinang, Indo. 117/F4
Buatan, Indo. 115/C2
Buaya (riv.), Indo. 155/E2
Buba, GBis. 140/B4
Bubanza, Buru. 147/G3
Bubaque, GBis. 140/B4
Bubastis (ruin), Egypt 139/C3
Bubendorf, Swi. 86/D3
Bubikon, Swi. 87/E3
Bubry, Fr. 82/B5
Bubu (riv.), Tanz. 145/A3
Buburu, D.R. Congo 146/D2
Bubye (riv.), Zim. 149/F4
Buc, Fr. 56/J5
Bucak, Turk. 128/B2
Bucakkişla, Turk. 130/C1
Bucaramanga, Col. 204/C3
Bucas Grande (isl.), Phil. 114/D3
Bucasia, Austl. 160/C3
Bucay, Phil. 114/C1
Buccaneer (arch.), Austl. 154/A4
Bucelas, Port. 73/P10
Buch, Ger. 87/G1
Bucha, Ukr. 98/F2
Buchach, Ukr. 98/C3
Buchan (reg.), Sc, UK 59/D1
Buchan (gulf), Nun, Can. 167/J1
Buchan (riv.), Austl. 159/D3
Buchan Ness (pt.), Sc, UK 59/E2
Buchanan, Sk, Can. 182/C2
Buchanan, ND, US 182/E4
Buchanan (lake), Tx, US 177/E2
Buchanan, Mi, US 186/C4
Buchanan, Libr. 140/C5
Buchanan, Ga, US 188/E4
Buchanan (dam), Tx, US 177/E2
Buchanan, Va, US 189/H2
Buchanan Dam, Tx, US 177/E2
Buchanan Field (arpt.), Ca, US 193/K11
Buchans, Nf, Can. 185/J1
Bucharest (Burcureşti) (cap.), Rom. 98/D5
Buchbach, Ger. 85/F6
Büchen, Ger. 79/H2
Buchen, Ger. 84/C3
Buchenberg, Ger. 87/G2
Buchenzi, Tanz. 147/H3
Buchholz, Ger. 81/G3
Buchholz, Ger. 68/Q6
Buchholz in der Nordheide, Ger. 79/G2
Buchloe, Ger. 87/G1
Buchlyvie, Sc, UK 59/B4
Buchon (pt.), Ca, US 174/B3
Buchs, Swi. 87/F3
Buchy, Fr. 83/G1
Bucine, It. 89/E7
Buckatunna, Ms, US 190/D2
Buckatunna (cr.), Ms, US 188/C4
Buckden Pike (peak), Eng, UK 61/F3
Bückeburg, Ger. 79/G4
Buckeye, Az, US 175/F4
Buckeye Lake, Oh, US 186/E5
Buckfastleigh, Eng, UK 62/C6
Buckhannon, WV, US 189/G1
Buckhaven, Sc, UK 59/C4
Buckholts, Tx, US 177/F2
Buckhorn, NM, US 175/H4
Buckhurst Hill, Eng, UK 56/D2
Buckie, Sc, UK 59/D1
Buckingham, Qu, Can. 187/J2
Buckingham, Eng, UK 63/F3
Buckingham, Va, US 189/H2
Buckingham Palace, Eng, UK 56/C2
Buckland, Qu, Can. 184/B2
Buckle (pt.), Austl. 154/B3
Buckley, Wal, UK 61/E5
Buckley, Il, US 186/B4
Buckley, Mi, US 186/D2
Buckley, Wa, US 193/C3
Bucklin, Ks, US 178/E2
Bucknell, Eng, UK 62/D2
Buckner (cr.), Ks, US 180/E4
Buckroe, Mi, US 183/L4
Bucks (co.), Pa, US 194/C3
Bucksburn, Sc, UK 59/D2
Buco-Zau, Ang. 146/C4
Bucquoy, Fr. 80/B3
Buctouche, NB, Can. 184/E2
Bucureşti (co.), Rom. 77/G3
Bucureşti (Bucharest) (cap.), Rom. 77/H3
Bucy-le-Long, Fr. 80/C5
Bucyrus, Oh, US 186/E4
Buda, Tx, US 177/F2
Buda-Koshelëvo, Bela. 96/D1
Budai hegy (hill), Hun. 77/Q9
Budaka, Ugan. 145/A1
Budakeszi, Hun. 77/Q9
Budaörs, Hun. 77/R10
Budapest (co.), Hun. 77/R9
Budapest (cap.), Hun. 77/R9
Budarino, Kaz. 97/J2
Budaun, India 122/B1
Budawang (mt.), Austl. 159/E2
Budawang NP, Austl. 159/D2
Budd (coast), Ant. 216/H
Budd (inlet), Wa, US 193/B3
Budd Lake, NJ, US 194/D2
Buddi, Eth. 144/B4
Buddon Ness (pt.), Sc, UK 59/D4
Buddusò, It. 74/A2
Bude, Ms, US 190/C2
Bude, Eth. 144/B4
Bude, Eng, UK 62/B5
Bude (bay), Eng, UK 62/B5
Budel, Neth. 78/C6
Büdelsdorf, Ger. 66/C4
Budge-Budge, India 123/G4
Budgewoi Lake, Austl. 159/E1
Budhāna, India 124/D5
Budhanilantha, Nepal 123/E2
Budhlāda, India 124/C5
Budia, Sp. 72/D2
Büdingen, Ger. 84/C2
Budjala, D.R. Congo 146/D2
Budleigh Salterton, Eng, UK 62/C5
Budogoshch', Rus. 67/Q2
Budongquan, China 125/F4
Budrio, It. 89/E4
Budungbudung, Indo. 117/E4
Budva, Yugo. 75/F1
Budzhak (reg.), Mol.,Ukr. 93/L1
Buea, Camr. 146/B1
Buellton, Ca, US 174/B3
Buelna (int'l arpt.), Mex. 198/D4
Buena, Wa, US 170/D4
Buena, NJ, US 194/D4
Buena Esperanza, Arg. 214/D2
Buena Fe, Ecu. 204/B5
Buena Park, Ca, US 192/G8
Buena Vista, Sk, Can. 182/B2
Buena Vista, Ven. 204/D3
Buena Vista, Ga, US 188/E4
Buena Vista, Bol. 209/F5
Buena Vista, Uru. 213/F5
Buena Vista, Va, US 189/H2
Buena Vista Lake Bed, Ca, US 174/C3
Buenaventura, Col. 204/B4
Buenaventura, Mex. 198/D2
Buenavista, Mex. 199/Q9
Bueno (riv.), Chile 214/B4
Bueno Brandão, Braz. 211/K7
Buenópolis, Braz. 210/D3
Buenos Aires, Col. 204/B4
Buenos Aires (lake), Arg.,Chile 203/B7
Buenos Aires, Col. 204/D4
Buenos Aires, Col. 204/C4
Buenos Aires, Ven. 205/E4
Buenos Aires (prov.), Arg. 214/E3
Buenos Aires (cap.), Arg. 215/J11
Buenos Aires, Peru 208/B2
Buenos Aires (Jorge Newbery) (int'l arpt.), Arg. 215/J11
Buenos Aires (Ministro Pistarini)(int'l arpt.), Arg. 215/J11
Buerarema, Braz. 211/F2
Buesaco, Col. 204/B4
Buet (peak), Fr. 86/C5
Bueu, Sp. 72/A1
Buffalo (mt.), Austl. 159/C3
Buffalo (lake), Ab, Can. 171/H1
Buffalo (riv.), SAfr. 151/E2
Buffalo, Ks, US 179/G2
Buffalo, Mo, US 179/H2
Buffalo (cr.), Mn, US 181/G1
Buffalo, Mn, US 183/N6
Buffalo, NY, US 186/V10
Buffalo, Ok, US 178/E2
Buffalo, SC, US 189/G3
Buffalo, SD, US 182/C5
Buffalo, Tx, US 177/F2
Buffalo (mtn.), Va, US 189/G2
Buffalo, Wi, US 181/J1
Buffalo, WV, US 189/G1
Buffalo, Wy, US 173/K1
Buffalo Cape, Sudan 142/F3
Buffalo Center, Ia, US 181/H2
Buffalo Creek, Co, US 178/B1
Buffalo Gap, SD, US 180/C2
Buffalo Gap, Tx, US 177/E1
Buffalo Grove, Il, US 186/C3
Buffalo Lake Nat'l Wildlife Res., Tx, US 178/C3
Buffalo Lake Nat'l Wild. Ref., ND, US 182/E3
Buffalo Nat'l River, Ar, US 179/H2
Buffalo River Overflow (swamp), Austl. 158/B1
Buffalo Sprs. Nat'l Rsv., Kenya 145/B1
Buffelsrivier (riv.), SAfr. 150/B3
Buffum (lake), Fl, US 190/M8
Buford, Ga, US 188/E3
Buford, Wy, US 180/B3
Buford (dam), Ga, US 188/E3
Buftea, Rom. 77/G3
Bug (riv.), Pol. 100/C4
Bug (riv.), Eur. 69/L2
Buga, Col. 204/B4
Bugaba, Pan. 201/F4
Bugac, Hun. 76/D2
Bugala (isl.), Ugan. 147/H3
Bugalagrande, Col. 204/B3
Bugaldie, Austl. 158/D1
Bugarach, Pic de (peak), Fr. 73/G1
Bugarama, Rwa. 147/G3
Bugat, Mong. 104/C2
Bugat, Mong. 104/C2
Bugaza, D.R. Congo 147/G3
Bugbrooke, Eng, UK 63/E2
Buğdaylı, Turk. 77/H5
Bugdayly, Trkm. 129/H2
Bugel (pt.), Indo. 115/E3
Bugene, Tanz. 147/G3
Buggenhout, Belg. 81/D1
Bugiri, Ugan. 145/A1
Bugojno, Bosn. 76/C3
Bugrino, Rus. 95/L1
Bugsuk (isl.), Phil. 117/E2
Bugul'ma, Rus. 95/M5
Buguruslan, Rus. 97/K1
Buh (riv.), Ukr. 69/M3
Buh (riv.), China 104/D4
Buḩayrat ath Tharthār (res.), Iraq 129/E3
Buhemba, Tanz. 145/A2
Buhera, Zim. 149/F3
Buhl, Fr. 86/D2
Bühl, Ger. 87/E2
Buhl, Id, US 173/F2
Buhler, Ks, US 179/F1
Buhler, La, US 190/B2
Bühler (riv.), Ger. 84/C4
Bühlerzell, Ger. 84/C5
Buhuşi, Rom. 98/D4
Buhūt, Egypt 139/C2
Bui (dam), Gha. 141/E4
Bui Gorge (res.), Gha. 141/E4
Bui NP, Gha. 141/E4
Buies Creek, NC, US 189/H3
Buiksloot, Neth. 78/B4
Builth Wells, Wal, UK 62/C2
Buin (peak), Swi. 87/G4
Buin, Chile 214/N8
Buinsk, Rus. 95/K5
Buinsk, Rus. 95/L5
Buíque, Braz. 207/G5
Buis-les-Baronnies, Fr. 90/B4
Buitepos, Namb. 148/C4
Bujalance, Sp. 72/C4
Bujanovac, Yugo. 76/E4
Bujumbura (cap.), Buru. 147/G3
Bujumbura (int'l arpt.), Buru. 147/G3
Buk, Pol. 69/J2
Buka (isl.), PNG 162/E5
Bukachacha, Rus. 104/H1
Bukadaban (peak), China 125/F4
Bukakata, Ugan. 147/H3
Bukama, D.R. Congo 147/F5
Būkān, Iran 129/F2
Bukasa (isl.), Ugan. 145/A2
Bukavu, D.R. Congo 147/G3
Bukene, Tanz. 147/H4
Buket Bubat (peak), Malay. 115/C1
Bukhoro, Uzb. 100/G6
Bukhovo, Bul. 75/H1
Bukhtarma (riv.), Kaz. 104/B2
Bukima, Tanz. 145/A2
Bukit Mertajam, Malay. 115/C1
Bukit Panjang, Sing. 115/J6
Bukit Timah (peak), Sing. 115/J6
Bukit Timah (nbrhd.), Sing. 115/J6
Bukitkemuning, Indo. 115/D3
Bukittinggi, Indo. 115/C3
Bükki NP, Hun. 96/B2
Bukoba, Tanz. 147/G3
Bukonyo, Tanz. 147/H3
Bukoza, Ang. 146/C4
Buksamaral, China 125/D4
Buku (cape), Indo. 115/D3
Bukuru, Nga. 141/H4
Bula, Tx, US 178/C4
Bula Atumba, Ang. 146/C5
Bulacan (prov.), Phil. 114/F6
Bulacan, Phil. 114/E6
Bülach, Swi. 87/E2
Bulagi, Indo. 117/F4
Bulahdelah, Austl. 158/E2
Bulalakao, Phil. 114/C2
Bulan, Ky, US 189/F2
Bulan, Phil. 114/C2
Bulanash, Rus. 95/P4
Bulancak, Turk. 96/F4
Bulandshahr, India 122/A1
Bulanık, Turk. 128/E2
Bulawa (peak), Indo. 117/F3
Bulawayo, Zim. 149/F4
Bulawayo (int'l arpt.), Zim. 149/F4
Bulayevo, Kaz. 100/H4
Buldan, Turk. 128/B2
Buldāna, India 121/C1
Buldibuyo, Peru 208/B3
Bule, Eth. 144/A4
Bulembu, Swaz. 151/E2
Bulgan, Mong. 104/E2
Bulgan (riv.), Mong. 104/C2
Bulgan, Mong. 104/E3
Bulgan (prov.), Mong. 104/E2
Bulgan, Mong. 104/E1
Bulgaria(ctry.) 55/G4
Bŭlgarovo, Bul. 77/H4
Bulgheria (peak), It. 74/D2
Bulgroo, Austl. 160/A4
Buliluyan (cape), Phil. 114/B3
Bulimba (cr.), Austl. 160/F7
Bulkī, Eth. 142/H4
Bulkington, Eng, UK 63/E2
Bull (pt.), NI, UK 60/B1
Bull (isl.), SC, US 191/H1
Bull (riv.), BC, Can. 170/G3
Bull Shoals, Ar, US 179/H2
Bull Shoals (lake), Ar, US 179/H2
Bull Valley (mts.), Ut, US 175/F2
Bullange, Belg. 81/F3
Bullard, Tx, US 177/G1
Bullas, Sp. 72/E3
Bullaxaar, Som. 144/C3
Bulle, Swi. 86/D4
Buller (mt.), Austl. 159/C3
Bullerön (isl.), Swe. 65/B1
Bullerup, Den. 66/D4
Bullfinch, Austl. 156/C4
Bullhead, SD, US 182/D5
Bullhead City, Az, US 174/E3
Bullion, Fr. 56/H6
Bullock, NC, US 189/H2
Bulloo (riv.), Austl. 153/D3
Bulloo Downs, Austl. 160/A5
Bulloo River Overflow (swamp), Austl. 160/A5
Bulls, NZ 161/C3
Bullsbrook East, Austl. 156/L6
Bully (riv.), Or, US 172/E1
Bully-les-Mines, Fr. 80/B3
Bulnayn (mts.), Mong. 104/D2
Bulnes, Chile 214/B3
Bulolo, PNG 155/G1
Bulongo, D.R. Congo 147/E4
Bulphan, Eng, UK 56/E2
Bultfontein, SAfr. 150/D3
Buluan, Phil. 114/D4
Buluba, Ugan. 145/A1
Bulukumba, Indo. 117/F5
Bulungu, D.R. Congo 147/E4
Bulungu, D.R. Congo 146/D4
Bulungwa, Tanz. 147/H4
Bum Bum (isl.), Malay. 114/B4
Bumba, D.R. Congo 147/E2
Bumba, Ang. 146/C5
Bumba, D.R. Congo 146/D4
Bumbah (gulf), Libya 93/J4
Bumble Bee, Az, US 175/F3
Bumbuna, SLeo. 140/C4
Bumhpa (peak), Myan. 112/C3
Bumiayu, Indo. 115/E3
Bumtang (riv.), Bhu. 123/H2
Bumthang, Bhu. 123/H2
Buna, Tx, US 177/H2
Buna, Kenya 145/B1
Buna, PNG 155/H2
Bunaga-take (peak), Japan 109/J5
Bunawan, Phil. 114/D3
Bunazi, Tanz. 147/G3
Bunbury, Austl. 156/B5
Bunceton, Mo, US 179/H1
Bunclody, Ire. 58/D4
Bundaberg, Austl. 160/D4
Bundanoon, Austl. 159/E2
Bundarra, Austl. 158/D1
Bunde, Ger. 79/E2
Bünde, Ger. 79/F4
Bunde, Ger. 79/F4
Būndi, India 118/C2
Bundi, PNG 155/G1
Bundoran, Ire. 57/P9
Būndu, India 123/E4
Bung Kan, Thai. 120/C2
Bunga (pt.), Phil. 114/D2
Bungalaut (str.), Indo. 115/B3
Bungay, Eng, UK 63/H2
Bungendore, Austl. 159/D2
Bungku, Indo. 117/F4
Bungo, Ang. 146/C4
Bungoma, Kenya 145/A1
Bunguran (isl.), Indo. 116/C3
Bunia, D.R. Congo 147/G2
Buninyong, Austl. 159/A3
Bunji, Pak. 124/C2
Bunkeflo Strand, Swe. 65/J7
Bunker, Mo, US 179/J2
Bunker Hill, In, US 186/C4
Bunker Hill, WV, US 187/G5
Bunker Hill, Il, US 181/K4
Bunker Hill Village, Tx, US 177/M9
Bunkeya, D.R. Congo 147/F5
Bunkie, La, US 190/B2
Bunnell, Fl, US 191/H3
Bunnik, Neth. 78/C4
Buñol, Sp. 73/E3
Bunschoten, Neth. 78/C4
Buntharik, Thai. 120/D3
Buntingford, Eng, UK 63/F3
Bunya, Austl. 160/E6
Bunya, Swaz. 151/E2
Bunya Mountains NP, Austl. 160/C4
Bunyala, Kenya 145/A1
Bünyan, Turk. 128/C2
Bunyu (isl.), Indo. 117/E3
Buochs, Swi. 87/E4
Buon Me Thuot, Viet. 120/E3
Buon Mrong, Viet. 120/E3
Buonconvento, It. 71/J5
Bupul, Indo. 155/F1
Buqayq, SAr. 126/E3
Buqde Caqable, Som. 144/C4
Buquim, Braz. 211/F1
Būr Fu'ād, Egypt 139/D2
Bur Sa`id (gov.), Egypt 130/C4
Būr Safājah, Egypt 135/G3
Būr Saʻīd (gov.), Egypt 135/F1
Būr Saʻīd (Port Said), Egypt 139/D2
Būr Sūdān (Port Sudan), Sudan 135/H5
Būr Tawfīq, Egypt 130/C5
Bura, Kenya 145/B2
Buram, Sudan 142/E3
Burang, China 125/D5
Burannoye, Rus. 97/K2
Burano, It. 89/F3
Burano (riv.), It. 89/F5
Burao (Burco), Som. 144/C3
Burāq, Syria 131/E2
Buras-Triumph, La, US 190/D3
Burauen, Phil. 114/D3
Buraydah, SAr. 126/D3
Burbach, Ger. 81/H2
Burbank, Il, US 186/C4
Burbank, Ca, US 192/F7
Burbank, Wa, US 170/E4
Burbank-Glendale-Pasadena (arpt.), Ca, US 192/F7
Burbure, Fr. 80/B2
Burcher, Austl. 159/C1
Burco (Burao), Som. 144/C3
Burda, India 122/A3
Burdekin (riv.), Austl. 153/D2
Burdell (mtn.), Ca, US 193/J10
Burden, Ks, US 179/F2
Burdett, Ks, US 178/E1
Burdett, Ab, Can. 171/J3
Burdette, SD, US 180/E1
Burdur, Turk. 128/B2
Burdur (lake), Turk. 128/B2
Burdur (prov.), Turk. 128/B2
Burdwān, India 123/F4
Burē, Eth. 142/H3
Burē, Eth. 142/G3
Bure (riv.), Eng, UK 63/H1
Büren, Ger. 79/F5
Buren, Neth. 78/C5
Buren, Neth. 78/C2
Büren an der Aare, Swi. 86/D3
Bürengiyn (mts.), Mong. 104/E2
Bures-sur-Yvette, Fr. 56/J5
Būrewāla, Pak. 124/B4
Bureya (riv.), Rus. 101/P4
Bureya (mts.), Rus. 105/L2
Burford, On, Can. 186/F3
Burford, Eng, UK 63/E3
Burg, Ger. 66/D4
Burg, Ger. 66/C4
Burg, Ger. 68/F2
Burgas (prov.), Bul. 75/K1
Burgas (bay), Bul. 93/K2
Burgas, Bul. 77/H4
Burgas (int'l arpt.), Bul. 77/H4
Burgau, Ger. 84/D6
Burgaw, NC, US 189/J3
Burgazada (riv.), Turk. 129/M7
Burgberg im Allgäu, Ger. 87/G2
Burgbernheim, Ger. 84/D4
Burgbrohl, Ger. 81/G3
Burgdorf, Swi. 86/D3
Burgdorf, Ger. 79/H4
Burgebrach, Ger. 84/D3
Burgenland (prov.), Aus. 69/J5
Burgeo, Nf, Can. 185/J2
Burgersdorp, SAfr. 150/D3
Burges (mt.), Austl. 156/D4
Burgess (mt.), Yk, Can. 166/C2
Burgess Hill, Eng, UK 63/F5
Burgfjället (peak), Swe. 64/E2
Burgh le Marsh, Eng, UK 61/J5
Burghaslach, Ger. 84/D3
Burghausen, Ger. 85/F6
Burghead (bay), Sc, UK 59/C1
Burghead, Sc, UK 59/C1
Burgheim, Ger. 84/E5
Burgin, Ky, US 188/E2
Burgkirchen, Aus. 85/G6
Burgkirchen an der Alz, Ger. 85/F6
Burgkunstadt, Ger. 84/E2
Bürglen, Swi. 87/F2
Burglengenfeld, Ger. 85/F4
Burglesum, Ger. 79/F2
Burgos, Sp. 72/D1
Burgos, Mex. 199/F3
Burgsinn, Ger. 84/C2
Burgstall (Postal), It. 87/H4
Burgsteinfurt, Ger. 79/E4
Burgsvik, Swe. 66/H3
Burgundy (reg.), Fr. 92/E1
Burgwedel, Ger. 79/G3
Burhābalang (riv.), India 123/F4
Burham, Eng, UK 56/E3
Burhan Budai (mts.), China 104/D4
Burhaniye, Turk. 96/C5
Burhānpur, India 121/C1
Burhar-dhanpuri, India 122/C4
Burhi Dihing (riv.), India 112/B3
Burhi Gandok (riv.), India 123/E2
Buri (pen.), Erit. 144/A2
Buri, Braz. 213/G2
Burias (isl.), Phil. 114/C2
Buribay, Rus. 97/L2
Burica (pen.), Pan. 196/E6
Burica (pt.), Pan. 201/F4
Burien, Wa, US 170/C4
Burin, Nf, Can. 185/K2
Burin (pen.), Nf, Can. 167/L4
Buriram, Thai. 120/C3
Buritama, Braz. 213/G2
Buriti, Braz. 207/F3
Buriti Alegre, Braz. 210/C3
Buriti Bravo, Braz. 207/F4
Buriti dos Lopes, Braz. 207/F3
Buritis, Braz. 210/D2
Buritizeiro, Braz. 213/H1
Burj Mughayzil, Egypt 139/B2
Burjasot, Sp. 73/E3
Burkardroth, Ger. 84/C2
Burkburnett, Tx, US 179/E3
Burke, SD, US 180/E2
Burke, Va, US 189/J1
Bürkelkopf (peak), Aus. 87/G4
Burkes Garden, Va, US 189/G2
Burkesville, Ky, US 188/E2
Burketown, Austl. 155/E4
Burkett, Tx, US 176/E2
Burkeville, Tx, US 177/H2
Burkeville, Va, US 189/H2
Burkina Faso(ctry.) 133/B3
Burk's Falls, On, Can. 187/G2
Burladingen, Ger. 87/F1
Burleigh, Tx, US 176/F3
Burleson, Tx, US 176/K7
Burley, Wa, US 193/B3
Burley, Id, US 173/G2
Burli, Kaz. 97/K2
Burlin (pen.), Nf, Can. 185/K2
Burlingame, Ks, US 179/G1
Burlingame, Ca, US 193/K11
Burlington, On, Can. 186/T9
Burlington, Co, US 180/C4
Burlington, Ia, US 181/J3
Burlington, Il, US 193/N15
Burlington, Ks, US 179/G1
Burlington, Ky, US 188/E1
Burlington, NC, US 189/H2
Burlington, ND, US 182/D3
Burlington (co.), NJ, US 194/D4
Burlington, NJ, US 194/D3
Burlington, Ok, US 179/E2
Burlington, Vt, US 187/K2
Burlington, Wi, US 186/B3
Burlington, Wa, US 170/C3
Burlington Junction, Mo, US 181/G3
Burlöv, Swe. 65/K7
Burma (Myanmar)(ctry.) 103/J7
Bürmoos, Aus. 85/F7
Burna, Ky, US 188/C2
Burnaby, BC, Can. 170/C3
Burnas (lake), Ukr. 77/K3
Burnell, Tx, US 177/F3
Burnet, Tx, US 176/E2
Burnett Heads, Austl. 160/D4
Burney, Ca, US 172/C3
Burney (falls), Ca, US 172/C3
Burney (peak), Chile 215/B7
Burneyville, Ok, US 179/F4
Burnham, Mo, US 179/J2
Burnham, Il, US 193/Q16
Burnham, Eng, UK 56/B2
Burnham-on-Crouch, Eng, UK 63/G3
Burnham-on-Sea, Eng, UK 62/D4
Burnie-Somerset, Austl. 158/C4
Burnley, Eng, UK 61/F4
Burnmouth, Sc, UK 59/D5
Burns, Or, US 172/D2
Burns, Co, US 173/K4
Burns Flat, Ok, US 178/E3
Burnside (riv.), Nun, Can. 166/E2
Burnside, Ky, US 188/E2
Burnside, Sur. 206/B1
Burnstad, ND, US 182/E4
Burnsville, NC, US 189/F3
Burnsville, WV, US 189/G1
Burnsville, Ms, US 188/C3
Burnsville, Mn, US 183/P7
Burnt Islands, Nf, Can. 185/H2
Burntisland, Sc, UK 59/C4
Burntwood (riv.), Mb, Can. 166/G3
Burntwood, Eng, UK 63/E1
Buronga, Austl. 158/B2
Buronzo, It. 88/B3
Burpee Game Ref., NB, Can. 184/D3
Burqā, WBnk. 131/C4
Burqin (riv.), China 104/B2
Burqin, China 104/B2
Burqīn, WBnk. 131/C4
Burqush, Syria 131/D2
Burr Oak, Ks, US 180/E4
Burr Ridge, Il, US 193/Q16
Burra, Austl. 157/H5
Burraboi, Austl. 159/B2
Burragorang (lake), Austl. 159/E2
Burramurra, Austl. 157/H2
Burrel, Alb. 75/G2
Burren Junction, Austl. 158/D1
Burrewarra (pt.), Austl. 159/E2
Burriana, Sp. 73/E3
Burringbar, Austl. 160/D5
Burrinjuck (dam), Austl. 159/D2
Burro (cr.), Az, US 175/F3
Burroburro (riv.), Guy. 206/B1
Burrow (pt.), Sc, UK 60/D2
Burrowa-Pine Mountain NP, Austl. 159/C3
Burrowes (pt.), Austl. 160/A2
Burrum Heads, Austl. 160/D4
Burrum River NP, Austl. 160/D4
Burry (inlet), Wal, UK 62/B3
Burry Port, Wal, UK 62/B3
Bursa (prov.), Turk. 96/D5
Burscheid, Ger. 81/G1
Burscough, Eng, UK 61/F4
Burshtyn, Ukr. 98/C3
Bürstadt, Ger. 84/B3
Burstall, Sk, Can. 171/K2
Burt, Ia, US 181/G2
Burt, NY, US 186/V9
Burta, Austl. 157/J5
Burtenbach, Ger. 84/D6
Burton, NS, Can. 184/D3
Burton, Mi, US 186/E3
Burton, Wa, US 193/C3
Burton, Eng, UK 63/E5
Burton, BC, Can. 170/F3
Burton, Tx, US 177/F2
Burton, SC, US 189/G4
Burton (lake), Ga, US 189/F3
Burton Latimer, Eng, UK 63/F2
Burton upon Trent, Eng, UK 63/E1
Burtts Corner, NB, Can. 184/D2
Burtus, Egypt 139/C4
Buru (isl.), Indo. 103/M10
Buruanga, Phil. 114/C3
Burullus (lake), Egypt 130/B4
Burūm, Yem. 144/D2
Burun Shibertuy (peak), Rus. 104/F2
Buruncan (pt.), Phil. 114/C2
Burundi(ctry.) 133/E5
Bururi, Buru. 147/G3
Burutu, Nga. 141/G5
Burwell, Ne, US 180/E3
Burwell, Eng, UK 63/G2
Bury, Eng, UK 61/F4
Bury, Fr. 80/B5
Bury, Eng, UK 63/F5
Bury Saint Edmunds, Eng, UK 63/G2
Buryatia (aut. rep.), Rus. 101/L4
Buryātia (aut. rep.), Rus. 104/F1
Buryn', Ukr. 99/G2
Burynshyk (pt.), Kaz. 97/J3
Büs Hayrhan (peak), Mong. 104/C2
Busa (mt.), Phil. 114/D4
Busalla, It. 88/B4
Busanga, D.R. Congo 147/F5
Busca, It. 90/D3
Busch Gardens, Fl, US 190/L7
Busch Gardens, Va, US 189/J2
Busembatia, Ugan. 145/A1
Busenberg, Ger. 81/G5
Buseno, Swi. 87/F5
Būsh, Egypt 139/C6
Bush (riv.), Md, US 194/B5
Bush Kill (riv.), Pa, US 194/C1
Būshehr (gov.), Iran 129/G4
Bushêngcaka, China 125/D5
Bushey, Eng, UK 56/B2
Bushimaie (riv.), D.R. Congo 147/E4
Bushkill, Pa, US 194/C1
Bushkill Falls, Pa, US 194/C1
Bushman Pits, Bots. 148/E4
Bushmanland (reg.), SAfr. 150/B3
Bushmills, NI, UK 60/B1
Bushnell, Fl, US 190/L6
Bushnell, Il, US 181/J3
Bushton, Ks, US 179/E1
Busia, Kenya 145/A1
Busigny, Fr. 80/C3
Businga, D.R. Congo 147/E2
Busira (riv.), D.R. Congo 146/D3
Bus'k, Ukr. 98/C3
Buskerud (co.), Nor. 64/D3
Busko-zdrój, Pol. 69/L3
Busoga (prov.), Ugan. 145/A1
Buşrá ash Shām, Syria 131/E3
Buss Craig (pt.), Sc, UK 59/D5
Busselton, Austl. 156/B5
Busseri (riv.), Sudan 142/E4
Busseto, It. 88/D4
Bussi sul Tirino, It. 92/C3
Bussolengo, It. 89/D3
Bussoleno, It. 90/D2
Bussum, Neth. 78/C4
Bustamante, Mex. 177/D4
Bustamante (pt.), Arg. 215/C6
Bustamante, Mex. 199/F4
Bustard (pt.), Austl. 160/C4
Buşteni, Rom. 77/G3
Busto Arsizio, It. 88/B2
Busto Garolfo, It. 88/B2
Busu Kwanga, D.R. Congo 146/E2
Busu Melo, D.R. Congo 146/E2
Busu Yale, D.R. Congo 146/D2
Busu-Djanoa, D.R. Congo 147/E2
Busuanga (isl.), Phil. 114/B2
Büsum, Ger. 66/C4
Busunu, Gha. 141/E4
Buta, D.R. Congo 147/F2
Buta Ranquil, Arg. 214/C3
Butajīra, Eth. 144/A3
Butare, Rwa. 147/G3
Butaritari (isl.), Kiri. 162/G4
Butawal, Nepal 122/D2
Bute (isl.), Sc, UK 59/A5
Bute, Austl. 157/H5
Bute (inlet), BC, Can. 170/B2
Bute Helu, Kenya 145/B1
Büteeliyn (mts.), Mong. 104/E2
Butembo, D.R. Congo 147/G2
Bütgenbach, Belg. 81/F3
Butha-Buthe, Les. 150/E3
Buti, It. 88/D6
Butiaba, Ugan. 147/G2
Butler, Al, US 190/D1
Butler (lake), Fl, US 190/M7
Butler, Ga, US 188/E4
Butler, In, US 186/D4
Butler, Mo, US 179/G1
Butler, NJ, US 195/H8
Butler, Pa, US 187/G4
Butler, Tx, US 176/F2
Butlersbridge, Ire. 58/C1
Butmir (int'l arpt.), Bosn. 76/D4
Butner, NC, US 189/H2
Buto (ruin), Egypt 139/B2
Butry-sur-Oise, Fr. 56/J4
Bütschelegg (peak), Swi. 86/D4
Bütschwil, Swi. 87/F3
Butt of Lewis (pt.), Sc, UK 57/Q7
Buttahatchee (riv.), Al,Ms, US 188/C4
Buttapietra, It. 89/D3
Butte, ND, US 182/D4
Butte (cr.), Ca, US 172/C4
Butte, Ne, US 180/E2
Butte-Silver Bow County, Mt, US 171/H4
Büttelborn, Ger. 84/B3
Butter (cr.), Or, US 172/D1
Butterfield, Mn, US 181/G2
Butters, NC, US 189/H3
Butterworth, Malay. 115/C1
Butterworth, SAfr. 150/E4
Buttes, Swi. 86/C4
Buttevant, Ire. 58/B5
Buttigliera Alta, It. 90/D2
Buttonwillow, Ca, US 174/C3
Buttrio, It. 89/G1
Butuan, Phil. 114/D3
Butung (isl.), Indo. 103/M10
Buturlinovka, Rus. 99/L2
Butzbach, Ger. 84/B2
Bützow, Ger. 66/D5
Buüech (riv.), Fr. 70/F4
Buuhoodle, Som. 144/C3
Buulo Berde, Som. 144/C5
Buur Gaabo, Som. 145/C2
Buur Hakaba, Som. 145/D1
Buvuma (isl.), Ugan. 145/A1
Buxar, India 122/D3
Buxheim, Ger. 87/G2
Buxtehude, Ger. 79/G2
Buxton, Eng, UK 61/G5
Buxton, Me, US 187/L3
Buy, Rus. 94/J4
Buyant, Mong. 104/D2
Buyant-uhaa, Mong. 104/G3
Buyck, Mn, US 183/H3
Buynaksk, Rus. 97/H4
Buyr (lake), Mong. 105/H2
Buyuan (riv.), China 112/D4
Büyük Anafarta, Turk. 75/K2
Büyükada, Turk. 77/J5
Büyükada (isl.), Turk. 129/N7
Büyükarmutlu, Turk. 128/D2
Büyükçekmece (lake), Turk. 129/M6
Büyükçekmece, Turk. 129/M6
Büyükeceli, Turk. 130/C1
Büyükkarıştıran, Turk. 77/H5
Buyukly, Rus. 105/N2
Büyükyurt, Turk. 128/D2
Buyun Shan (peak), China 107/B2
Buyuni (pt.), Tanz. 145/B3
Buz'kyy Lyman (estu.), Ukr. 98/F4
Buzachi (pen.), Kaz. 97/J3
Buzançais, Fr. 70/D3
Buzancy, Fr. 81/D5
Buzău (riv.), Rom. 96/C3
Buzău, Rom. 77/H3
Buzău (prov.), Rom. 77/H3
Búzi (riv.), Moz. 149/G3
Buziaş, Rom. 76/E3
Búzios (isl.), Braz. 211/L8
Buz'kyy Lyman (estu.), Ukr. 77/K2
Büzmeyin, Trkm. 127/G1
Buzsák, Hun. 76/C2
Buzuluk, Rus. 97/K1
Buzzard Roost (dam), SC, US 189/G3
Bwandougou, C.d'Iv. 140/D4
Bwasa, D.R. Congo 146/D3
Bweeng (mtn.), Ire. 58/B5
Bwindi Impenetrable Forest NP, Tanz. 147/G3
Byala, Bul. 77/G4
Byala, Bul. 77/H4
Byala Slatina, Bul. 77/F4
Byam Martin (isl.), Nun, Can. 167/R7
Byam Martin (chan.), Nun, Can. 167/R7
Byarezina (riv.), Bela. 94/E5
Byaroza, Bela. 96/C1
Byars, Ok, US 179/F3
Bydgoszcz, Pol. 69/J2
Bydgoszcz (prov.), Pol. 69/J2
Byemoor, Ab, Can. 171/H2
Byers, Ks, US 178/E2
Byesville, Oh, US 186/F5
Byfield, Eng, UK 63/E2
Byfleet, Eng, UK 56/B3
Byford, Austl. 156/L7
Bygland, Nor. 66/B2
Bykhov, Bela. 67/P5
Bykle, Nor. 66/B2
Bykovo, Rus. 97/H2
Bykovo (int'l arpt.), Rus. 94/X9
Bykovskiy, Rus. 101/N2
Bylas, Az, US 175/G4
Bylchau, Wal, UK 60/E5
Bylot (isl.), Can. 165/K2
Bylot (isl.), Nun, Can. 167/J1
Byng, Ok, US 179/F3
Byng Inlet, On, Can. 186/F2
Bynum, Tx, US 177/F2
Bynum, Mt, US 171/H4
Bynum Run (riv.), Md, US 194/B4
Byram (lake), NY, US 195/L7
Byram (pt.), Ct, US 195/L8
Byram (riv.), Ct, US 195/E1
Byrd (cape), Ant. 216/U
Byrd, US, Ant. 216/S
Byrdstown, Tn, US 188/E2
Byremo, Nor. 66/B2
Byrock, Austl. 158/C1
Byromville, Ga, US 188/F4
Byron, Ca, US 193/L11
Byron, Il, US 181/K2

Byron, Ga, US 188/F4
Byron (isl.), Chile 215/B5
Byron Bay, Austl. 160/D5
Byrranga (mts.), Rus. 100/K2
Byrum, Den. 66/D3
Bystice (riv.), Czh. 85/F2
Bystrá (peak), Slvk. 69/K4
Bystřice, Czh. 85/H3
Bytantay (riv.), Rus. 101/N3
Bytom, Pol. 69/K3
Bytów, Pol. 66/G4
Byumba, Rwa. 147/G3

C

C (canal), Co, US 175/H1
C.F. Secada (int'l arpt.), Peru 208/C1
C.J. Strike (res.), Id, US 172/E2
C.J. Strike (dam), Id, US 172/E2
C.W. McConaughy (lake), Ne, US 180/C3
Ca (riv.), Viet. 119/J4
Ca Mau (cape), Viet. 120/D4
Ca Mau, Viet. 120/D4
Caacupé, Par. 213/E3
Caaguazú (dept.), Par. 213/E3
Caaguazú, Par. 213/E3
Caála, Ang. 148/B2
Caatingas (phys. reg.), Braz. 203/E3
Caazapá, Par. 213/E3
Caazapá (dept.), Par. 213/E3
Cabadbaran, Phil. 114/D3
Cabaiguán, Cuba 201/G1
Caballo, NM, US 175/J4
Caballo (res.), NM, US 175/J4
Caballococha, Peru 208/D1
Caban-Coch (res.), Wal, UK 62/C2
Cabana, Peru 208/B3
Cabanaconde, Peru 208/D4
Cabañaquinta, Sp. 72/C1
Cabanatuan, Phil. 114/C2
Cabanes, Sp. 73/F2
Cabannes, Fr. 90/A5
Cabano, Qu, Can. 184/C2
Cabarroguis, Phil. 114/C1
Cabatuan, Phil. 114/C3
Cabedelo, Braz. 207/H4
Cabella Ligure, It. 88/C4
Cabestany, Fr. 70/E5
Cabeza del Buey, Sp. 72/C3
Cabeza Lagarto (pt.), Peru 208/B3
Cabeza Prieta Nat'l. Wild. Ref., Az, US 175/F4
Cabezas, Bol. 212/D1
Cabezón de la Sal, Sp. 72/C1
Cabildo, Arg. 214/E3
Cabimas, Ven. 204/D2
Cabinda, Ang. 146/C4
Cabinda (prov.), Ang. 146/B4
Cabinet (mts.), Mt, US 170/G3
Cabiri, Ang. 146/C5
Cabo, Braz. 207/H5
Cabo Blanco, Arg. 215/D5
Cabo Blanco, Peru 208/A2
Cabo Bojador, WSah. 136/B4
Cabo Corrientes, Cabo (cape), Mex. 198/D4
Cabo de Hornos, PN, Chile 215/D7
Cabo Delgado (prov.), Moz. 145/B4
Cabo Delgado (prov), Moz. 149/H2
Cabo do Norte (cape), Braz. 206/D2
Cabo Falso (bank), Hon. 201/F3
Cabo Frio, Braz. 211/E4
Cabo Gracias a Dios, Nic. 201/F3
Cabo Orange, PN do, Braz. 206/D2
Cabo San Lucas, Mex. 198/C4
Cabo Verde, Braz. 211/K6
Cabonga (res.), Qu, Can. 167/J4
Cabool, Mo, US 179/H2
Caboolture, Austl. 160/D4
Cabora Bassa (lake), Moz. 149/F2
Cabot, Ar, US 179/H3
Cabot (str.), NS,NF, Can. 167/K4
Cabourg, Fr. 83/E2
Cabra, Sp. 72/C4
Cabra Corral (res.), Arg. 212/C3
Cabra de Santo Cristo, Sp. 72/D4
Cabramatta (nbrhd.), Austl. 160/G8
Cabras, It. 74/A3
Cabrera, Isla de (isl.), Sp. 92/D3
Cabri, Sk, Can. 171/K2
Cabriel (riv.), Sp. 72/E3
Cabriès, Fr. 90/B6
Cabrillo Nat'l Mon., Ca, US 192/C5
Cabrobó, Braz. 207/G5
Cabruta, Ven. 205/E3
Cabudare, Ven. 204/D2
Cabugao, Phil. 114/C1
Cabure, Ven. 204/D2
Caçador, Braz. 213/G3
Čačak, Yugo. 76/E4
Cacala, Ang. 148/B1
Cacalotán, Mex. 198/D4
Caçapava, Braz. 211/L8
Caçapava do Sul, Braz. 213/F4
Cacapon (mtn.), WV, US 187/G5
Cacapon (riv.), WV, US 189/H1
Caccia (cape), It. 74/A2
Cacequi, Braz. 213/F4
Cáceres, Col. 204/C3
Cáceres, Sp. 72/B3
Cáceres, Braz. 209/G5
Cachapoal (riv.), Chile 214/N9
Cacharí, Arg. 215/J12
Cache, Ok, US 179/E3
Cache (cr.), Ca, US 172/B4
Cache (peak), Id, US 173/G2
Cache Creek, BC, Can. 170/D2
Cache la Poudre (riv.), Co, US 180/B3
Cache Slough (riv.), Ca, US 193/L10
Cacheu, GBis. 140/A3
Cachicadán, Peru 208/B3
Cachimbo, Serra do (mts.), Braz. 206/B4
Cachingues, Ang. 148/C2
Cachipo, Ven. 205/E2
Cachoeira Alta, Braz. 213/G1
Cachoeira de Minas, Braz. 211/L7
Cachoeira do Arari, Braz. 206/D3
Cachoeira do Sul, Braz. 213/F4
Cachoeira Paulista, Braz. 211/L7
Cachoeiras de Macacu, Braz. 211/P7
Cachoeirinha, Braz. 213/G4
Cachoeiro de Itapemirim, Braz. 211/E4
Cachorras, Col. 204/C4
Cachos (pt.), Chile 212/B3
Cacoal, Braz. 209/F3
Cacolo, Ang. 146/D5
Caconda, Ang. 148/B2
Caconde, Braz. 211/K6
Cacongo, Ang. 146/C4
Caçu, Braz. 210/C3
Cacuaco, Ang. 146/C5
Cacula, Ang. 148/B2
Caculuvar (riv.), Ang. 148/B3
Cacuri, Ven. 205/E3
Cacuso, Ang. 146/C5
Cadaadle, Som. 144/C3
Čadca, Slvk. 69/K4
Caddo (mts.), Ar, US 179/H3
Caddo (riv.), Ar, US 179/H3
Caddo, Ok, US 179/F3
Caddo, Tx, US 177/E1
Caddo Mills, Tx, US 179/F4
Caddo Valley, Ar, US 179/H3
Cadelbosco di Sopra, It. 88/D4
Cadelle (peak), It. 87/F5
Cadenberge, Ger. 79/G1
Cadenet, Fr. 90/B5
Cader Idris (peak), Wal, UK 62/C1
Cadet, Mo, US 188/B2
Cadibarrawirracanna (lake), Austl. 157/G4
Cadillac, Mi, US 186/D2
Cadillac, Sk, Can. 171/L3
Cadiz, Oh, US 186/F4
Cádiz, Sp. 72/B4
Cádiz (gulf), Port.,Sp. 72/B4
Cadiz, Ca, US 174/E3
Cadiz, Ky, US 188/D2
Cadiz (lake), Ca, US 174/E3
Cadiz, Phil. 114/C3
Cadnam, Eng, UK 63/E5
Cadogan, Ab, Can. 171/J1
Cadolzburg, Ger. 84/D4
Cadomin, Ab, Can. 170/F1
Cadott, W, US 181/J1
Cadria (peak), It. 87/G6
Cadwell, Ga, US 189/F4
Cadzand-Bad, Neth. 80/C1
Caen, Fr. 83/E2
Caen (bay), Fr. 70/C2
Caerano di San Marco, It. 89/F2
Caerleon, Wal, UK 62/D3
Caernarfon, Wal, UK 60/D5
Caernarfon (bay), Wal, UK 60/D5
Caernarfon Castle, Wal, UK 60/D5
Caerphilly, Wal, UK 62/C3
Caersws, Wal, UK 62/C1
Caesarea, On, Can. 187/G2
Caesarea NP, Isr. 131/B3
Caeté, Braz. 211/E3
Cafarnaum, Braz. 211/E1
Cafasse, It. 90/D2
Cafayate, Arg. 212/C3
Cagayan (isls.), Phil 114/C3
Cagayan de Oro, Phil. 114/D3
Cagayan Sulu (isl.), Phil. 114/B4
Cagayancillo, Phil. 114/C3
Cagli, It. 89/F6
Cagliari, It. 74/A3
Cagliari (gulf), It. 92/F3
Cagne (riv.), Fr. 90/D5
Cagnes-sur-Mer, Fr. 90/D5
Cagoyan (riv.), Phil. 114/C1
Cagua, Ven. 207/N7
Caguán (riv.), Col. 204/C4
Caguas, PR 197/M8
Caha (mts.), Ire. 58/A6
Cahaba, Al, US 188/D4
Cahaba (riv.), Al, US 188/D4
Cahama, Ang. 148/B3
Caher, Ire. 58/C5
Caherbarnagh (peak), Ire. 58/A5
Caherconlish, Ire. 58/B4
Cahirsiveen, Ire. 56/N11
Cahokia, Il, US 181/J4
Cahone, Co, US 175/H2
Cahore (pt.), Ire. 58/D4
Cahors, Fr. 70/D4
Cahuacan, Mex. 199/Q9
Cahuapanas, Peru 208/B2
Cahuilla Ind. Res., Ca, US 174/D4
Cahuinari (riv.), Col. 204/D5
Cahuita, PN, CR 201/F4
Cahul, Mol. 77/J3
Cai (riv.), Braz. 213/G4
Cai Nuoc, Viet. 120/D4
Caia, Moz. 149/G3
Caiabis, Serra dos (mts.), Braz. 209/G4
Caianda, Ang. 147/E5
Caiapó (riv.), Braz. 210/C3
Caiapó, Serra (mts.), Braz. 210/B3
Caiapônia, Braz. 210/C3
Caiazzo, It. 92/D5
Caibarién, Cuba 201/G1
Caicara, Ven. 205/F2
Caicara, Ven. 205/E3
Caiçara, Braz. 207/H4
Caicedo, Col. 207/K6
Caicedonia, Col. 207/K8
Caicó, Braz. 207/G4
Caicos (isls.), Uk 197/G3
Caicos Passage (chan.), Bahm. 201/H1
Caieiras, Braz. 211/K8
Caifuche, Ang. 148/D1
Cailloma, Peru 208/D4
Caillou (bay), La, US 190/C3
Caillou (lake), La, US 190/C3
Cailly (riv.), Fr. 80/A4
Caiman (pt.), Phil. 114/B2
Caimbambo, Ang. 148/B2
Cainde, Ang. 148/B2
Caine (riv.), Bol. 212/C1
Cainnyigoin, China 104/E5
Cainsville, Mo, US 181/H3
Cainta, Phil. 114/F6
Caio (peak), It. 88/D5
Caiongo, Ang. 146/C4
Cairate, It. 88/B2
Cairn Curran (res.), Austl. 159/A3
Cairn Curran (dam), Austl. 159/A3
Cairn Gorm (peak), Sc, UK 59/C2
Cairn Table (peak), Sc, UK 59/B6
Cairn Toul (peak), Sc, UK 59/C2
Cairndow, Sc, UK 59/B4
Cairngorm (mts.), Sc, UK 59/B2
Cairnryan, Sc, UK 60/C2
Cairns (int'l arpt.), Austl. 160/B2
Cairns, Austl. 160/B2
Cairns (mt.), Austl. 157/G2
Cairnsmore of Carsphairn (peak), Sc, UK 59/B6
Cairo, Ga, US 191/F2
Cairo (peak), It. 92/C4
Cairo, Mo, US 181/H4
Cairo, Ne, US 180/E3
Cairo, Il, US 188/C2
Cairo (int'l arpt.), Egypt 139/C4
Cairo (Al Qāhirah) (cap.), Egypt 139/C4
Cairo Montenotte, It. 88/B5
Caister-on-Sea, Eng, UK 63/H1
Caistor, Eng, UK 61/H5
Caistor Centre, On, Can. 186/T9
Caistorville, On, Can. 186/T9
Caitou, Ang. 148/B2
Caiuana (bay), Braz. 206/D3
Caiundo, Ang. 148/C2
Caixi, China 113/H3
Caiza, Bol. 212/C2
Caizi (lake), China 106/D5
Cajabamba, Ecu. 204/B5
Cajabamba, Peru 208/B2
Cajacay, Peru 208/B3
Cajamarca (ruin), Peru 208/B2
Cajamarca (dept.), Peru 208/B2
Cajamarca, Peru 208/B2
Cajapió, Braz. 207/E3
Cajari, Braz. 207/E3
Cajatambo, Peru 208/B3
Cajazeiras, Braz. 207/G4
Cajibío, Col. 204/B4
Cajidiocan, Phil. 114/C2
Cajón (pt.), Cuba 201/E1
Cajon Junction, Ca, US 192/C2
Cajones (isl.), Nic. 201/F2
Caju (isl.), Braz. 207/F3
Cajuapara (riv.), Braz. 207/E4
Cajuata, Bol. 212/C1
Çal, Turk. 128/B2
Cala d'Oliva, It. 74/A2
Cala, Piombo, Punta di (pt.), It. 92/F3
Calabar (int'l arpt.), Nga. 141/H5
Calabar, Nga. 141/H5
Calabasas, Ca, US 192/B2
Calabash, NC, US 189/H4
Calabozo, Ven. 205/E2
Calabria (pol. reg.), It. 93/H3
Calabria, Parco Nazionale della, It. 74/D3
Calaburras (pt.), Sp. 72/C4
Calaceite, Sp. 73/F2
Calacoto, Bol. 208/D5
Calafat, Rom. 76/F4
Calagua (isls.), Phil. 114/C2
Calahorra, Sp. 72/E1
Calaí, Ang. 148/C3
Calais, Fr. 80/A2
Calais, Me, US 167/K4
Calais, Canal de (canal), Fr. 80/A2
Calama, Braz. 209/F3
Calama, Chile 212/B2
Calamar, Col. 204/C4
Calamar, Col. 204/C2
Calamarca, Bol. 212/B1
Calamba, Ang. 146/C5
Calambrone, It. 88/D6
Calamian Gr. (isls.), Phil. 117/E1
Calamian Group (isls.), Phil. 114/B2
Calamocha, Sp. 72/E2
Calamonte, Sp. 72/B3
Calamus (riv.), Ne, US 180/E2
Călan, Rom. 76/F3
Calañas, Sp. 72/B4
Calanda, Sp. 73/E2
Calang, Indo. 115/A1
Calangianus, It. 74/A2
Calapan, Phil. 114/C2
Calapooia (riv.), Or, US 172/B1
Călăraşi (prov.), Rom. 77/H3
Călăraşi, Rom. 77/H3
Călăraşi, Mol. 98/E4
Calarcá, Col. 207/K8
Calasparra, Sp. 72/E3
Calatayud, Sp. 72/E2
Calatorao, Sp. 72/E2
Calauag, Phil. 114/C2
Calaveras (res.), Ca, US 193/L12
Calaveras (riv.), Ca, US 172/C4
Calavite (cape), Phil. 114/C2
Calavon (riv.), Fr. 90/B5
Calayan (isl.), Phil. 162/B3
Calbayog, Phil. 114/D2
Calberlah, Ger. 79/H4
Calbiga, Phil. 114/D3
Calbuco, Chile 214/B4
Calca, Peru 208/D4
Calcasieu (lake), La, US 177/H3
Calcasieu (riv.), La, US 177/H2
Calceta, Ecu. 204/A5
Calchaquí, Arg. 212/D4
Calchaquí (riv.), Arg. 212/C3
Calci, It. 88/D6
Calcinate, It. 88/C2
Calcinato, It. 88/D3
Calcinelli, It. 89/F6
Calcio, It. 88/C3
Calcium, NY, US 187/J2
Calçoene, Braz. 206/D2
Calcutta, India 123/G4
Calcutta (int'l arpt.), India 123/G4
Calcutta, Sur. 205/H3
Caldaro (Kaltern), It. 71/J3
Caldas (dept.), Col. 204/C3
Caldas, Col. 207/K6
Caldas, Braz. 211/K6
Caldas da Rainha, Port. 72/A3
Caldas Novas, Braz. 210/C3
Caldbeck, Eng, UK 61/E2
Calden, Ger. 79/G6
Calder, Sk, Can. 182/D2
Calder (riv.), Eng, UK 61/F4
Caldera, Chile 212/B3
Calderara di Reno, It. 89/E4
Calderas, Ven. 204/D2
Caldercruix, Sc, UK 59/C5
Caldes de Montbui, Sp. 73/L6
Caldew (riv.), Eng, UK 61/F2
Caldicot, Wal, UK 62/D3
Caldiero, It. 89/E3
Çaldıran, Turk. 129/E2
Caldogno, It. 89/E2
Caldonazzo, It. 87/H6
Caldono, Col. 204/B4
Caldwell, Id, US 172/E2
Caldwell, NJ, US 195/H8
Caldwell, Oh, US 186/F5
Caldwell, Tx, US 176/F2
Caldwell, Wi, US 193/P14
Caldy (isl.), Eng, UK 62/B3
Caledon, NI, UK 60/B3
Caledon, SAfr. 150/L11
Caledon, On, Can. 186/T8
Caledon (riv.), SAfr. 150/D3
Caledon East, On, Can. 186/T8
Caledonia (hills), NB, Can. 184/E3
Caledonia, Mi, US 186/D3
Caledonia, Mn, US 181/J2
Caledonia, Ms, US 188/C4
Caledonia, NS, Can. 184/E3
Caledonia, Oh, US 186/E4
Caledonia, Wi, US 193/P14
Caledonian (canal), Sc, UK 59/B2
Calella, Sp. 73/G2
Calen, Austl. 160/C3
Calenzana, Fr. 74/A1
Calenzano, It. 89/E6
Calera, Ok, US 179/F4
Calera, Al, US 188/D4
Calera de Tango, Chile 214/N8
Calestano, It. 88/D4
Caleta Clarencia, Chile 215/C7
Caleta de Campos, Mex. 198/E5
Caleta Olivia, Arg. 214/D5
Caletones, Chile 214/N9
Calf of Man (isl.), IM, UK 60/C3
Calgary (int'l arpt.), Ab, Can. 171/G2
Calgary, Ab, Can. 171/G2
Calhan, Co, US 180/B4
Calheta, Port. 136/A2
Calheta, Azor., Port. 73/S12
Calhoun, Al, US 190/E1
Calhoun, Ga, US 188/E3
Calhoun, Il, US 188/C1
Calhoun, Ky, US 188/D2
Calhoun, Mo, US 179/H1
Calhoun City, Ms, US 188/C4
Calhoun Falls, SC, US 189/F3
Cali, Col. 204/B4
Calico Ghost Town, Ca, US 174/D3
Calico Rock, Ar, US 179/H2
Calicut (Kozhikode), India 121/B4
Calida (coast), Sp. 72/E4
Caliente, Nv, US 174/E2
Califon, NJ, US 194/D2
California, Mo, US 179/H1
California (aqueduct), Ca, US 193/L11
California (gulf), Mex. 165/F6
California (state), US 168/C4
California (aqueduct), Ca, US 174/B2
California, Md, US 189/J1
California City, Ca, US 174/D3
Calilegua, Arg. 212/C2
Calilegua, PN, Arg. 212/C2
Călimăneşti, Rom. 77/G3
Calimaya, Mex. 199/Q10
Calimere (pt.), India 121/C4
Calimesa, Ca, US 192/C2
Calingasta, Arg. 212/B4
Calion, Ar, US 179/H4
Calipatria, Ca, US 174/E4
Calistoga, Ca, US 172/B4
Calitri, It. 74/D2
Calixa-Lavallée, Qu, Can. 185/P6
Calizzano, It. 88/B5
Calkiní, Mex. 200/D1
Çalköy, Turk. 128/B2
Callac, Fr. 82/B4
Callaghan (mt.), Nv, US 172/E4
Callaghan, Tx, US 177/E4
Callahan, Fl, US 191/H2
Callahonna (lake), Austl. 153/D3
Callalli, Peru 208/D4
Callan, Ire. 58/C4
Callander, Sc, UK 59/B4
Callantsoog, Neth. 78/B3
Callao, Ut, US 173/G4
Callao, Peru 208/B4
Callao, Va, US 189/J2
Callapa, Bol. 212/B1
Callaun (peak), Ire. 58/B4
Callaway, Mn, US 182/G4
Callaway, Fl, US 191/F2
Calle Larga, Chile 214/N8
Callender, Ia, US 181/G2
Callian, Fr. 90/C5
Calliham, Tx, US 177/E3
Callington, Eng, UK 62/B5
Calliope, Austl. 160/C4
Callosa de Segura, Sp. 73/E3
Calmar, Ia, US 181/J2
Calmar, Ab, Can. 171/H1
Calne, Eng, UK 62/E4
Calolziocorte, It. 88/C2
Calonga (riv.), Ang. 148/B2
Calonne (riv.), Fr. 83/F2
Calonne-Ricouart, Fr. 80/B3
Caloocan, Phil. 114/E6
Caloosahatchee (riv.), Fl, US 191/H4
Caloosahatchee Nat'l Wild. Ref., Fl, US 191/H4
Calore (riv.), It. 93/G2
Caloundra, Austl. 160/D4
Calpe, Sp. 73/F3
Calpulálpan, Mex. 199/L7
Calstock, Eng, UK 62/B6
Caltagirone, It. 74/D4
Caltanissetta, It. 74/D4
Caltavuturo, It. 74/C4
Caluango, Ang. 146/D5
Calucinga, Ang. 148/C1
Calueque (dam), Ang. 148/E3
Calulo, Ang. 146/C5
Calumbo, Ang. 146/C5
Calumet, Mi, US 183/K4
Calumet (riv.), Il, US 193/Q16
Calumet City, Il, US 186/C4
Calumet Sag (chan.), Il, US 193/Q16
Caluquembe, Ang. 148/B2
Caluso, It. 88/A2
Caluula (pt.), Som. 144/D3
Caluula, Som. 144/D3
Calva, Az, US 175/G4
Calvados (dept.), Fr. 83/E3
Calvary, Ga, US 191/F2
Calvello, It. 74/D2
Calvenzano, It. 88/C3
Calvert, Nf, Can. 185/L2
Calvert, Al, US 190/D2
Calvert, Tx, US 177/F2
Calvert City, Ky, US 188/C2
Calvert Hills, Austl. 155/E4
Calverton, Eng, UK 61/G5
Calverton, Md, US 194/B5
Calvi, Fr. 74/A1
Calvi (peak), It. 89/E5
Calvi Risorta, It. 92/D5
Calviá, Sp. 73/G3
Calvilli (peak), It. 92/C5
Calvillo, Mex. 198/E4
Calvin, Ok, US 179/F3
Calvinia, SAfr. 150/B3
Calvisano, It. 88/D3
Calvitero (peak), Sp. 72/C2
Calw, Ger. 84/B5
Calzada de Calatrava, Sp. 72/D3
Cam or Rhee (riv.), Eng, UK 63/F2
Cam Pha, Viet. 113/E4
Cam Ranh, Viet. 120/E4
Cam Thuy, Viet. 120/D1
Camabatela, Ang. 146/C5
Camaçari, Braz. 211/F2
Camacho, Bol. 212/C2
Camacho, Bol. 209/E3
Camacho, Mex. 198/E3
Camacupa, Ang. 148/C2
Camaguán, Ven. 205/E2
Camagüey (arch.), Cuba 197/F3
Camagüey, Cuba 201/G1
Camaiore, It. 88/D6
Camajuaní, Cuba 201/G1
Camalengue, Ang. 146/D5
Camalu, Mex. 198/A2
Camamu, Braz. 211/F2
Camaná, Peru 208/C5
Camanche (res.), Ca, US 172/C4
Camanche, Ia, US 181/J3
Camanducaia, Braz. 211/K7
Camanongue, Ang. 148/D1
Camapuã, Braz. 213/F1
Camaquã, Braz. 213/G4
Camaquã (riv.), Braz. 213/F4
Camarat (cape), Fr. 90/C6
Camaret-sur-Aigues, Fr. 90/A4
Camaret-sur-Mer, Fr. 82/A4
Camargo, Ok, US 178/E2
Camargo, Sp. 72/D1
Camargo, Bol. 212/C2
Camarillo, Ca, US 192/A2
Camariñas, Sp. 72/A1
Camarón (cape), Hon. 201/E3
Camarones (bay), Arg. 214/D5
Camarones, Arg. 214/D5
Camarones, Chile 212/B1
Camas, Sp. 72/B4
Camas NWR, Id, US 173/G2
Camas Prairie (grsld.), Id, US 170/F4
Camas Valley, Or, US 172/B2
Camatagua, Ven. 207/P8
Camaxilo, Ang. 146/D5
Cambados, Sp. 72/A1
Cambará, Braz. 213/G2
Cambay (gulf), India 118/B3
Cambé, Braz. 213/G2
Camberley, Eng, UK 56/A3
Camberwell (nbrhd.), Eng, UK 56/C2
Camberwell, Austl. 159/B3
Cambiano, It. 88/A3
Cambo (riv.), Ang. 146/D5
Cambo Camana, Ang. 146/D5
Cambodia (ctry.) 103/K8
Cambondo, Ang. 146/C5
Camborne, Eng, UK 62/A6
Cambrai, Fr. 80/C3
Cambria, Ca, US 174/B3
Cambrian (mts.), Wal, UK 60/E5
Cambridge (gulf), Austl. 154/C3
Cambridge, On, Can. 186/F3
Cambridge, NZ 161/C2
Cambridge (int'l arpt.), Eng, UK 63/G2
Cambridge, Eng, UK 63/G2
Cambridge, Id, US 172/E1
Cambridge, Il, US 181/J3
Cambridge, Ma, US 187/L3
Cambridge, Md, US 189/J1
Cambridge, Mn, US 183/H5
Cambridge, Ne, US 180/D3
Cambridge, Oh, US 186/F4
Cambridge, Vt, US 187/K2
Cambridge Bay, Nun, Can. 166/F2
Cambridge City, In, US 186/D5
Cambridge Springs, Pa, US 186/F4
Cambridge-Narrows, NB, Can. 184/E3
Cambridgeshire (co.), Eng, UK 63/F2
Cambrils, Sp. 73/F2
Cambuí, Braz. 211/K7
Cambulo, Ang. 147/E4
Cambuquira, Braz. 211/L6
Cambuslang, Sc, UK 59/B5
Cambutal (mtn.), Pan. 204/A3
Camden, Austl. 160/G9
Camden (sound), Austl. 154/A3
Camden (co.), Eng, UK 56/C2
Camden, Al, US 190/E2
Camden, Ar, US 179/H4
Camden, De, US 194/C5
Camden, Mi, US 186/D4
Camden, NC, US 189/J2
Camden, NJ, US 194/C4
Camden (co.), NJ, US 194/C4
Camden, NY, US 187/J3
Camden, SC, US 189/G3
Camden, Tn, US 188/C2
Camden, Tx, US 177/G2
Camden East, On, Can. 187/H2
Camden Haven, Austl. 158/E1
Camdenton, Mo, US 179/H1
Cameia, Ang. 148/D1
Cameia, PN da, Ang. 147/E5
Cameia, PN da, Ang. 148/D1
Camel (riv.), Eng, UK 62/B6
Camelback (mtn.), Pa, US 194/C1
Camelford, Eng, UK 62/B5
Camels Back (peak), NZ 161/C2
Camenca, Mol. 98/E3
Camerano, It. 89/G6
Cameri, It. 88/B3
Camerino, It. 92/C1
Camerón (riv.), Mex. 177/D4
Cameron (isl.), Nun, Can. 167/R7
Cameron, Az, US 175/G3
Cameron (peak), Co, US 180/B3
Cameron, La, US 190/B3
Cameron, Mo, US 181/G4
Cameron, Mt, US 173/H1
Cameron, Tx, US 177/F2
Cameron, Wi, US 183/J5
Cameron Highlands, Malay. 115/C1
Cameron Park, Ca, US 172/C4
Cameroon(ctry.) 133/D4
Cameroon Highlands (uplands), Nga. 142/A4
Cametá, Braz. 206/D3
Camey, Tx, US 176/L6
Camfield, Austl. 154/C4
Camicia (peak), It. 92/C3
Camiguin (isl.), Phil. 114/C1
Camiling, Phil. 114/C2
Camilla, Ga, US 191/F2
Camilo Aldao, Arg. 214/E2
Caminha, Port. 72/A2
Camiranga, Braz. 207/E3
Camiri, Bol. 212/D2
Camisano Vicentino, It. 89/E2
Camissombo, Ang. 147/E5
Çamlıdere, Turk. 96/E4
Çamlık NP, Turk. 128/C2
Camlin (riv.), Ire. 58/C2
Çamlıyayla, Turk. 130/D1
Camo-Camo, Moz. 149/G4
Camoapa, Nic. 200/E3
Camocim, Braz. 207/F3
Camogli, It. 88/C5
Camolin, Ire. 58/D4
Camon, Fr. 80/B4
Camooweal, Austl. 155/E4
Camopi, FrG. 206/C2
Camopi (riv.), FrG. 206/C2
Camorta (isl.), India 119/F6
Camoruco, Col. 204/D3
Camotes (sea), Phil. 114/D3
Camp Angelus (Angelus Oaks), Ca, US 192/D2
Camp Atterbury, In, US 188/D1
Camp Blanding Mil. Res., Fl, US 191/G3
Camp Grayling, Mi, US 186/D2
Camp Hill, Pa, US 194/B3
Camp J.T. Robinson, Ar, US 179/H3
Camp Lake, Wi, US 193/P14
Camp Lake Nat'l Wild. Ref., ND, US 182/D4
Camp Lejeune, NC, US 189/J3
Camp Lejeune Marine Base, NC, US 189/J3
Camp Pendleton, Ca, US 174/D4
Camp Ripley Mil. Res., Mn, US 183/G4
Camp Roberts, Ca, US 174/B3
Camp Shelby, Ms, US 190/D2
Camp Springs, Md, US 194/B6
Camp Verde, Az, US 175/G3
Camp Verde Ind. Res., Az, US 175/G3
Camp Williams, Ut, US 173/G3
Camp Wood, Tx, US 177/D3
Campagna di Roma (reg.), It. 91/B4
Campagna Lupia, It. 89/F3
Campagnano di Roma, It. 91/B3
Campagnola Emilia, It. 89/D4
Campamento, Uru. 213/E4
Campana (isl.), Chile 215/B6
Campana, Arg. 215/J11
Campanario, Sp. 72/C3
Campanario (peak), Arg. 214/C2
Campanella (cape), It. 92/D6
Campanha, Braz. 211/L6
Campania (prov.), It. 74/D2
Campbell (cape), NZ 161/C3
Campbell (isl.), NZ 53/T8
Campbell, Ca, US 193/L12
Campbell, Fl, US 190/N7
Campbell, Mn, US 182/F4
Campbell, Mo, US 188/B2
Campbell (hill), Oh, US 186/E4
Campbell, Oh, US 186/F4
Campbell, Ne, US 180/E3
Campbell, Tx, US 179/G4
Campbell Town, Austl. 158/C4
Campbellford, On, Can. 187/H2
Campbellpore, Pak. 124/B3
Campbell's Bay, Qu, Can. 187/H2
Campbellsport, Wi, US 186/B3
Campbellsville, Ky, US 188/E2
Campbellton, NB, Can. 184/D1
Campbellton, Fl, US 191/F2
Campbelltown (nbrhd.), Austl. 160/G9
Campbellville, On, Can. 186/T9
Campbeltown, Sc, UK 57/R9
Campbon, Fr. 82/D6
Campden, On, Can. 186/U9
Campeche (state), Mex. 196/C4
Campeche, Mex. 200/D2
Campeche (bay), Mex. 165/H7
Campello sul Clitunno, It. 91/B2
Camperdown, Austl. 158/B3
Camperville, Mb, Can. 182/D2
Campestre, Braz. 211/K6
Campi Bisenzio, It. 89/E6
Campidano (range), It. 74/A3
Campile, Ire. 58/D5
Campillo de Altobuey, Sp. 72/E3
Campillos, Sp. 72/C4
Campina da Lagoa, Braz. 213/F3
Campina Grande, Braz. 207/H4
Campina Verde, Braz. 210/C3
Campinas, Braz. 211/J7
Campione d'Italia, It. 87/E6
Campli, It. 92/C2
Camplong, Indo. 154/A2
Campo, Camr. 146/B2
Campo, Ca, US 174/D4
Campo (int'l arpt.), Braz. 208/C2
Campo Belo, Braz. 210/D4
Campo de Criptana, Sp. 72/D3
Campo de la Cruz, Col. 204/C2
Campo dei Fiori (peak), It 88/B2
Campo Erê, Braz. 213/F3
Campo Florido, Braz. 213/G1
Campo Formoso, Braz. 211/E1
Campo Gallo, Arg. 212/D3
Campo Grande, Braz. 213/F2
Campo Ind. Res., Ca, US 174/D4
Campo Largo, Braz. 213/G3
Campo Ligure, It. 88/B4
Campo Limpo Paulista, Braz. 211/K8
Campo Maior, Port. 72/B3
Campo Maior, Braz. 207/F4
Campo Mourão, Braz. 213/F3
Campo Quijano, Arg. 212/C3
Campo Redondo, Braz. 207/G4
Campo Tencia (peak), Swi. 87/E5
Campo Tizzoro, It. 89/D5
Campoalegre, Col. 204/C4
Campobasso (prov.), It. 92/D4
Campobasso, It. 92/D4
Campobello (isl.), Ns., Can. 184/D3
Campodarsego, It. 89/E3
Campodolcino, It. 87/F5
Campogalliano, It. 89/D4
Campomorone, It. 88/B4
Camponogara, It. 89/F3
Camporosso, It. 88/A5
Camporredondo (res.), Sp. 72/C1
Camporredondo, Peru 208/B2
Campos (phys. reg.), Braz. 203/D5
Campos Belos, Braz. 210/D2
Campos de Hielo Norte (glacier), Chile 215/B5
Campos de Hielo Sur (glacier), Chile 215/B6
Campos del Puerto, Sp. 73/G3
Campos do Jordão, Braz. 211/L7
Campos dos Goytacazes, Braz. 211/E4
Campos Novos, Braz. 213/G3
Campos Sales, Braz. 207/F4
Camposampiero, It. 89/E2
Camposanto, It. 89/E4
Camposauro (peak), It. 92/D5
Campotosto (lake), It. 92/C3
Campsie Fells (hills), Sc, UK 59/B4
Campti, La, US 190/B2
Campton, Ky, US 189/F2
Camrose, Ab, Can. 171/H1
Çan, Turk. 96/C4
Can (riv.), Eng, UK 56/E1
Can Tho, Viet. 120/D4
Cana, Sk, Can. 182/C2
Canaan, Ar, US 179/H3
Canaan, Vt, US 187/L2
Canaan (riv.), NB, Can. 184/E2
Canaan, NH, US 187/K3
Canaan Game Ref., NB, Can. 184/E2
Canaçari (lake), Braz. 205/G5
Canacari (lake), Braz. 206/B3
Canada(ctry.) 165/G4
Cañada de Gómez, Arg. 214/E2
Cañada Larga, Bol. 209/F5
Cañada Nieto, Uru. 215/J10
Cañada Rosquín, Arg. 214/E2
Canadensis, Pa, US 194/C1
Canadian, Tx, US 178/D3
Canadian (riv.), US 165/G6
Canadian, North (riv.), Ok, US 168/F4
Cañadón de las Vacas, Arg. 215/C6
Cañadon Grande (mts.), Arg. 214/C5
Cañadón Seco, Arg. 214/D5
Canaima, PN, Ven. 205/F3
Canajoharie, NY, US 187/J3
Çanakkale, Turk. 75/K2
Çanakkale (prov.), Turk. 96/C5
Canal Flats, BC, Can. 170/G2
Canal Point, Fl, US 191/H4
Canala, NCal. 163/U12
Canalbianco (riv.), It. 89/E2
Canale, It. 88/A3
Canale Cavour (canal), It. 88/B2
Canals, Sp. 73/E3
Canals, Arg. 214/E2
Canandaigua, NY, US 187/H3
Cananea, Mex. 198/C2
Canaos (riv.), Braz. 213/G3
Cañar (dept.), Ecu. 204/B5
Cañar, Ecu. 208/B1
Canard (riv.), On, Can. 193/G7
Canarsie (nbrhd.), NY, US 195/K9
Canary (isls.), Sp. 136/A3
Canary(isls.) 133/A2
Cañas, CR 200/E4
Cañasgordas, Col. 204/B3
Canatlán de las Manzanas, Mex. 198/D3
Canaveral (pen.), Fl, US 191/H3
Canaveral (cape), Fl, US 191/H3
Canaveral Nat'l Seashore, Fl., US 191/H3
Canavieiras, Braz. 211/F2
Canbelego, Austl. 158/C1
Canberra (cap.), Austl. 159/D2
Canby, Or, US 172/B1
Canby, Mn, US 181/F1
Cancale, Fr. 82/D3
Cance (riv.), Fr. 90/A2
Cancello-Arnone, It. 92/D5
Canchaque, Peru 208/B2
Canche (riv.), Fr. 70/E1
Cancun (int'l arpt.), Mex. 200/E1
Cancún, Mex. 200/E1
Candarave, Peru 212/B1
Çandarli (gulf), Gre. 128/A2
Candás, Sp. 72/C1
Candás, Sp. 72/B1
Candé, Fr. 83/D5
Candeias, Braz. 211/F2
Candela, Mex. 177/D4
Candelaria (riv.), Mex. 200/D2
Candelaria, Mex. 200/D2
Candelaria, Arg. 214/D2
Candelária, Braz. 213/F4
Candelaria, Bol. 212/E1
Candeleda, Sp. 72/C2
Candelo, It. 88/B2
Candelo, Austl. 159/D3
Candia Lomellina, It. 88/B3
Candiac, Qu, Can. 185/N7
Cândido Mendes, Braz. 207/E3
Cândido Mota, Braz. 213/G2
Canding (cape), Indo. 116/D5
Candiolo, It. 90/D3
Çandır, Turk. 128/C2
Candler-McAfee, Ga, US 189/M7
Candlewood, NJ, US 194/D3
Cando, ND, US 182/E3
Cando, Sk, Can. 171/K1
Candon, Phil. 114/C1
Cane (cr.), Ga, US 191/G2
Cane Beds, Az, US 175/F2
Cane Field (int'l arpt.), Dom. 197/N9
Canegrate, It. 88/B2
Canela, Braz. 213/G4
Canela Baja, Chile 212/B4
Canelli, It. 88/B4
Canelones (dept.), Uru. 215/F2
Canelones, Uru. 215/K11
Canepina, It. 91/B3
Cañete, Sp. 72/E2
Canete, Río de (riv.), Peru 208/B4
Caneva, It. 89/F2
Caney (cr.), Tx, US 177/G3
Caney, Ok, US 179/F3
Caney, Ks, US 179/G2
Caney (riv.), Ks,Ok, US 199/F2
Caneyville, Ky, US 188/D2
Canfield, Ar, US 179/H4
Canfield Lake Nat'l Wild. Ref., ND, US 182/D4
Cangallo, Peru 208/C4
Cangamba, Ang. 148/C2
Cangandala, Ang. 146/D5
Cangas, Sp. 72/A1
Cangas de Narcea, Sp. 72/B1
Cangas de Onís, Sp 72/C1
Cangkuang (cape), Indo. 115/D3
Cango Caves, SAfr. 150/C4
Cangoa, Ang. 148/C2
Cangombe, Ang. 148/D2
Cangonga, Ang. 148/C2
Cangqian, China 113/H3
Cangrejo (peak), Arg. 215/B6
Cangshan, China 106/D4
Cangshan, China 105/J1
Canguaretama, Braz. 207/H4
Canguçu, Braz. 213/F4
Cangumbe, Ang. 148/C1
Cangwu, China 119/K3
Cangyuan (Cangyuan Vazu Zizhixian), China 112/C4
Cangyuan Vazu Zizhixian (Cangyuan), China 112/C4
Cangzhou, China 106/D3
Canh Cuoc (isl.), Viet. 120/D1
Canhaua, Ang. 148/C3
Canhoca, Ang. 148/B2
Canhotinho, Braz. 207/G5
Cania Gorge NP, Austl. 160/C4
Caniapiscau (lake), Qu, Can. 167/K3
Caniapiskau (riv.), Qu, Can. 167/J3
Canicatti, It. 74/C4
Canigou, Pic du (peak), Fr. 70/E5
Canik (mts.), Turk. 128/C1
Caniles, Sp. 72/D4
Canim Lake, BC, Can. 170/D2
Canindé, Braz. 207/G4
Canindé (riv.), Braz. 207/F4
Canindeyú (dept.), Par. 210/B5
Canino, It. 74/B1
Canistear (res.), NJ, US 195/H7
Canisteo, NY, US 187/H3
Cañitas de Felipe Pescador, Mex. 198/E4
Canjáyar, Sp. 72/D4
Canje (riv.), Guy. 206/B1
Canjilon, NM, US 175/J2
Cankhor, Som. 144/C3
Çankırı, Turk. 96/E4
Çankırı (prov.), Turk. 96/E4
Canlaon (vol.), Phil. 114/C3
Canmore, Ab, Can. 170/G2
Cann (mtn.), Austl. 159/D3
Cann (riv.), Austl. 159/D3
Cann River, Austl. 159/D3
Canna (isl.), Sc, UK 57/Q8
Cannara, It. 91/B2
Canne (ruin), It. 74/E2
Cannel City, Ky, US 189/F2
Cannelton, In, US 188/D2
Canner (riv.), Fr. 81/F5
Cannero Riviera, It. 87/E5
Cannes, Fr. 90/D5
Canneto sull'Oglio, It. 88/D3
Cannich, Sc, UK 59/B2
Canning (peak), Austl. 156/C4
Canning (riv.), Austl. 156/K7
Canning (dam), Austl. 156/L7
Cannobio, It. 87/E5
Cannock, Eng, UK 62/D1
Cannon (A.F.B.), NM, US 178/C3
Cannon Ball, ND, US 182/D4
Cannon Beach, Or, US 170/C5
Cannon Falls, Mn, US 181/H1
Cannonball (riv.), ND, US 182/D4
Cannondale, Ct, US 195/E1
Cannonvale, Austl. 160/C3
Cannonville, Ut, US 175/F2
Caño Guaritico (riv.), Ven. 204/D3
Caño Negro Nat'l Wild. Ref., CR 201/E4
Canoas, Braz. 213/G4
Canobolas (mt.), Austl. 159/D1
Canoe, Al, US 190/E2
Canoe River, BC, Can. 170/E1
Canoga Park (nbrhd.), Ca, US 192/E7
Canoinhas, Braz. 213/G3
Canon City, Co, US 178/B1
Cañón de Río Blanco, PN, Mex. 199/M8
Cañón del Sumidero, PN, Mex. 200/C2
Cañon Largo (riv.), NM, US 175/J2
Canonbie, Sc, UK 61/F1
Cañoncito Ind. Res., NM, US 178/A3
Cañoncito Ind. Res., NM, US 175/J3
Canones, NM, US 175/J2
Canoochee (riv.), Ga, US 191/G1
Canopus (ruin), Egypt 139/B2
Canora, Sk, Can. 182/C2
Canosa di Puglia, It. 74/E2
Canouan (isl.), StV. 197/N9
Canowindra, Austl. 159/D1
Cansado, Mrta. 136/A5
Canso, NS, Can. 185/G3
Canso (cape), NS, Can. 185/G3
Canta, Peru 208/B3
Cantabria (prov.), Sp. 70/B5
Cantabria (dist.), Sp. 72/C1
Cantal (mass.), Fr. 70/E4
Cantalejo, Sp. 72/D2
Cantanhede, Port. 72/A2
Cantanhede, Braz. 207/E3
Cantaura, Ven. 205/E2
Canteleu, Fr. 83/G2
Canterbury (nbrhd.), Austl. 160/H8
Canterbury, Eng, UK 63/H4
Canterbury Bight (bay), NZ 153/H7
Canterbury Cathedral, Eng, UK 63/H4
Cantiere, Eth. 142/G4
Cantil, Ca, US 174/D3
Cantilan, Phil. 114/D3
Cantillana, Sp. 72/C4
Canto del Agua, Chile 212/B4
Canto do Buriti, Braz. 207/F5
Canton, Ga, US 188/E3
Canton, Il, US 181/J3
Canton, Ks, US 179/F1
Canton, Mi, US 193/E7
Canton, Mo, US 181/J3
Canton, Ms, US 188/B4
Canton, NC, US 189/F3
Canton, NJ, US 194/C5
Canton, NY, US 187/J2
Canton, Ok, US 179/E2
Canton, Oh, US 186/F4
Canton (lake), Ok, US 179/E2
Canton, Pa, US 187/H4
Canton, SD, US 181/F2
Canton, Tx, US 177/G1
Canton (Abariringa) (isl.), Kiri. 163/H5
Cantoria, Sp. 72/D4
Cantù, It. 88/C2
Cañuelas, Arg. 215/J11
Canumã (riv.), Braz. 206/B4
Canunda NP, Austl. 158/B3
Canutama, Braz. 209/E2
Canutillo, Tx, US 177/A2
Canvey (isl.), Eng, UK 56/E2
Canvey Island, Eng, UK 63/G3
Canwood, Sk, Can. 171/L1
Cany-Barville, Fr. 83/F1
Canyon, Mn, US 183/H4
Canyon (lake), Tx, US 177/E3
Canyon, Tx, US 178/D4
Canyon, Tx, US 178/D3
Canyon, Wy, US 173/H1
Canyon City, Or, US 172/D1
Canyon de Chelly Nat'l Mon., Az, US 175/H2
Canyon Ferry, Mt, US 171/J4
Canyon Lake, Tx, US 176/E3
Canyonlands NP, Ut, US 173/J4
Canyonville, Or, US 172/B2
Canzo, It. 88/C2
Cao (riv.), China 107/C2
Cao Bang, Viet. 113/E4
Cao Lanh, Viet. 120/D4
Cao Xian, China 106/C4
Cao'e (riv.), China 113/J2
Caodu (riv.), China 113/E3
Caohecheng, China 107/C2
Caohekou, China 107/B2
Caohezhang, China 107/C2
Caohu, China 125/D3
Caojiawan, China 104/F5
Caol, Sc, UK 59/A3
Caoqiao, China 106/K8
Caorle, It. 89/F2
Caorso, It. 88/C3
Caoshi, China 107/C1
Cap (isl.), Phil. 114/C4
Cap Blanc (cape), Tun. 74/A4
Cap d'Agde (cape), Fr. 70/E5
Cap d'Antibes (cape), Fr. 90/D5
Cap d'Arguin (cape), Mrta. 136/A5
Cap d'Arme (cape), Fr. 90/C7
Cap de Fer (cape), Alg. 138/K6

240

Cap de – Catta

Cap de Garde (cape), Alg. 138/K6
Cap de Gaspé (mtn.0, Qu, Can. 184/E1
Cap de l'Aigle (cape), Fr. 90/B6
Cap de l'Aiguille (cape), Alg. 138/E5
Cap de Saint-Tropez (cape), Fr. 90/C6
Cap des Mèdes (cape), Fr. 90/C6
Cap des Trois Fourches (cape), Mor. 138/C2
Cap du Dramont (cape), Fr. 90/C6
Cap Lopez (bay), Gabon 146/B3
Cap Lumière, NB, Can. 184/E2
Cap Rock Escarpment (cliff), Tx, US 178/D4
Cap-Chat, Qu, Can. 184/D1
Cap-D'Ail, Fr. 90/D5
Cap-de-la-Madeleine, Qu, Can. 187/K1
Cap-des-Rosiers, Qu, Can. 184/E1
Cap-Haïtien, Haiti 201/H2
Cap-Pelé, NB, Can. 184/E2
Cap-Rouge, Qu, Can. 184/B2
Cap-Saint-Ignace, Qu, Can. 184/B2
Cap-Santé, Qu, Can. 184/B2
Capa, SD, US 180/D1
Capac, Mi, US 193/G5
Capalonga, Phil. 114/C2
Capanaparo (riv.), Ven. 204/D3
Capanema, Braz. 207/E3
Capanne (peak), It. 74/B1
Capannoli, It. 89/D6
Capannori, It. 88/D6
Capão Bonito, Braz. 213/G3
Caparaó, PN do, Braz. 211/E4
Caparica, Port. 73/P10
Caparo (riv.), Ven. 204/D3
Caparrapí, Col. 207/L7
Capay, Ca, US 193/K9
Capbreton, Fr. 70/C5
Capdenac-Gare, Fr. 70/E4
Capdepera, Sp. 73/G3
Cape (riv.), Austl. 155/G5
Cape Alava (cape), Wa, US 170/B3
Cape Arid NP, Austl. 156/D5
Cape Barren (isl.), Austl. 153/D5
Cape Bougalinville Abor. Rsv., Austl. 154/B3
Cape Breton (isl.), NS, Can. 165/L5
Cape Breton Highlands (uplands), NS., Can. 185/G2
Cape Breton Highlands NP, Can. 185/G2
Cape Broyle, Nf, Can. 185/L2
Cape Canaveral (A.F.B.), Fl, US 191/H3
Cape Charles, Va, US 189/J2
Cape Cleveland NP, Austl. 160/B2
Cape Coast, Gha. 141/E5
Cape Cod (cape), Ma, US 184/B4
Cape Cod (bay), Ma, US 184/B5
Cape Cod Nat'l Seashore, Ma, US 184/C4
Cape Coral, Fl, US 191/H4
Cape Croker Ind. Res., On, Can. 186/F2
Cape Dorset, Nun, Can. 167/J2
Cape Fear (riv.), NC, US 189/H3
Cape Fear, Northeast (riv.), NC, US 189/J3
Cape Girardeau, Mo, US 188/C2
Cape Le Grand NP, Austl. 156/D5
Cape May, NJ, US 194/D6
Cape May (co.), NJ, US 194/D5
Cape May County (arpt.), NJ, US 194/D6
Cape May Court House, NJ, US 194/D5
Cape May Lighthouse, NJ, US 194/D6
Cape Meares Nat'l Wild. Ref., Or, US 170/C5
Cape Melville NP, Austl. 160/B1
Cape Melville NP, PNG 155/G3
Cape Palmerston NP, Austl. 160/C3
Cape Range NP, Austl. 156/B2
Cape Romain NWR, SC, US 189/H4
Cape Sable (isl.), NS, Can. 184/E4
Cape Sable (cape), Fl, US 191/H5
Cape Saint Claire, Md, US 194/B5
Cape Smith, Nun, Can. 167/J2
Cape Town (cap.), SAfr. 150/L10
Cape Town (D.F. Malan) (int'l arpt.), SAfr. 150/L10
Cape Tribulation NP, Austl. 160/B2
Cape Tribulation NP, Austl. 155/G4
Cape Upstart NP, Austl. 160/B2
Cape Verde(ctry.) 133/J9
Cape York, Austl. 155/F2
Cape York (pen.), Austl. 153/D2
Capel, Austl. 156/B5
Capel le Ferne, Eng, UK 63/H4
Capel Saint Mary, Eng, UK 63/H2
Capel-Curig, Wal, UK 60/E5
Capela, Braz. 211/F1
Capelinha, Braz. 211/E3
Capella, Austl. 160/C3
Capellades, Sp. 73/K6
Capena, It. 91/B3
Capenda-Camulemba, Ang. 146/D5
Capernaum (ruin), Isr. 131/D3
Capertree (riv.), Austl. 159/E1
Capestang, Fr. 70/E5
Capestrano, It. 92/C3
Capibara, Ven. 205/E4
Capicciola (pt.), Fr. 74/A2
Capilla del Monte, Arg. 212/C4
Capilla del Señor, Arg. 215/J11
Capim (riv.), Braz. 206/D3
Capinópolis, Braz. 210/C3
Capinota, Bol. 212/C1
Capinzal, Braz. 213/G3
Capioví, Arg. 213/F3
Capira, Ang. 148/B2
Capirara (res.), Braz. 213/G2
Capistrano, Braz. 207/G4
Capistrello, It. 92/C4
Capitan (mts.), NM, US 178/B4
Capitán Bado, Par. 213/F2
Capitán Curbelo (Punta del Este) (int'l arpt.), Uru. 215/G2
Capitán Pablo Lagerenza, Par. 212/D1
Capitão de Campos, Braz. 207/F4
Capitão Poço, Braz. 207/E3
Capitol, Mt, US 182/B5
Capitol Reef NP, Ut, US 173/H4
Capivara (res.), Braz. 210/C4
Capivari (riv.), Braz. 211/M6
Čapljina, Bosn. 76/C4
Caplone (peak), It. 88/D2
Capo di Ponte, It. 87/G5
Capo d'Orlando, It. 74/D3
Capoche (riv.), Moz. 149/G2
Capodichino (int'l arpt.), It. 92/D6
Capolo, Ang. 146/C5
Capolona, It. 89/E6
Capon Springs, WV, US 189/H1
Capote (peak), Tx, US 177/B2
Capoterra, It. 74/A3
Cappagh White, Ire. 58/B4
Cappamore, Ire. 58/B4
Cappella Maggiore, It. 89/F2
Cappoquin, Ire. 58/C5
Capracotta, It. 92/D4
Capraia (isl.), Fr. 74/A1
Capranica, It. 91/B3
Caprarola, It. 91/B3
Capreol, On, Can. 186/F1
Capri, It. 92/D6
Capri (isl.), It. 92/D6
Capricorn (cape), Austl. 160/C3
Capricorn(chan.) 153/E3
Caprino Veronese, It. 89/D2
Capriolo, It. 88/C2
Caprivi Strip (reg.), Namb. 148/D3
Caprock, NM, US 178/C4
Caprolace (lake), It. 92/B5
Caps, Tx, US 177/E1
Captain (har.), Ct, US 195/L7
Captainganj, India 122/D2
Captains Flat, Austl. 159/D2
Captiva, Fl, US 191/G4
Captiva (isl.), Fl, US 191/G4
Capua, It. 92/D5
Capulhuac, Mex. 199/Q10
Capulhuac, Mex. 199/Q10
Capulin, Co, US 175/J2
Capulin Volcano Nat'l Mon., NM, US 178/C2
Capulo, Ang. 146/C4
Capunda Cavilongo, Ang. 148/B2
Caputh, Ger. 68/Q7
Caquetá (dept.), Col. 204/C4
Caquetá (riv.), Col. 204/D5
Cáqueza, Col. 207/M8
Caquiaviri, Bol. 212/B1
Car Nicobar (isl.), India 119/F6
Carabobo (state), Ven. 204/D2
Carabobo, Ven. 205/F3
Caracal, Rom. 77/G3
Caracaraí, Braz. 205/F4
Caracas (cap.), Ven. 207/P7
Carache, Ven. 204/D2
Caracol, Braz. 207/F5
Caracolí, Col. 204/C3
Caracollo, Bol. 212/C1
Carácuaro de Morelos, Mex. 199/E5
Caradon (hill), Eng, UK 62/B5
Caraga, Phil. 114/D4
Caragabal, Austl. 159/C1
Caraglio, It. 90/D4
Caraguatatuba, Braz. 211/L8
Caraguatatuba (bay), Braz. 211/L8
Carahue, Chile 214/B3
Carajás, Braz. 206/D4
Carajás, Serra dos (mts.), Braz. 206/D4
Caramanico Terme, It. 92/D3
Caramanta, Col. 207/K7
Caramat, On, Can. 183/L3
Caramoan, Phil. 114/C2
Caramoran, Phil. 114/D2
Caranavi, Bol. 209/E4
Carandaí, Braz. 210/E4
Carandayti, Bol. 212/D2
Carandotta, Austl. 157/H2
Carangola, Braz. 211/E4
Caransebeş, Rom. 76/F3
Carantec, Fr. 82/B3
Caraparí, Bol. 212/D2
Carapicuíba, Braz. 211/K8
Carapó, Braz. 213/F2
Carappee Hill (peak), Austl. 157/H5
Caraquet, NB, Can. 184/E2
Carare (riv.), Col. 207/L6
Caraş-severin (prov.), Rom. 76/E3
Carasco, It. 88/C5
Carat (cape), Indo. 115/D3
Caratasca (lag.), Hon. 196/E4
Carate Brianza, It. 88/C2
Caratinga, Braz. 211/E3
Carauarí, Braz. 209/E2
Caraúbas, Braz. 207/G4
Caravaca de la Cruz, Sp. 72/E3
Caravaggio, It. 88/C3
Caravelas, Braz. 211/F3
Caravelí, Peru 208/C4
Caraway, Ar, US 188/B3
Carayaca, Ven. 207/N7
Caraz, Peru 208/B3
Carazinho, Braz. 213/F4
Carballino, Sp. 72/A1
Carballo, Sp. 72/A1
Carberry, Mb, Can. 182/E3
Carbo, Mex. 198/C2
Carbon (riv.), Wa, US 193/C3
Carbon (cape), Alg. 138/H4
Carbon, Tx, US 177/E1
Carbon, Ab, Can. 171/H2
Carbon (co.), Pa, US 194/C2
Carbon Hill, Al, US 188/D4
Carbonado, Wa, US 170/C4
Carbonara (peak), It. 74/D4
Carbonara (cape), It. 74/A3
Carbondale, Ks, US 179/G1
Carbondale, Pa, US 187/J4
Carbondale, Il, US 188/C2
Carbonear, Nf, Can. 185/L2
Carbonera, It. 89/F2
Carboneras, Mex. 199/F3
Carbonia, It. 74/A3
Carbonne, Fr. 70/D5
Carbost, Sc, UK 57/Q8
Carbury, Ire. 58/D3
Carcagente, Sp. 73/E3
Carcar, Phil. 114/C3
Carcarañá, Arg. 214/E2
Carcare, It. 88/B5
Carcassonne, Fr. 70/E5
Carcès, Fr. 90/C6
Carche (peak), Sp. 72/E3
Carchi (dept.), Ecu. 204/B4
Carcoar, Austl. 159/D1
Carcross, Yk, Can. 166/C2
Çardak, Turk. 77/H5
Cardal, Uru. 215/K11
Cardale, Mb, Can. 182/D2
Cardedeu, Sp. 73/L6
Cárdenas, Mex. 200/C2
Cárdenas, Cuba 201/F1
Cárdenas, Mex. 199/F4
Cardenden, Sc, UK 59/C4
Cardiel (lake), Arg. 215/C6
Cardiff (cap.), Wal, UK 62/C4
Cardiff, Md, US 194/B4
Cardiff by the Sea, Ca, US 192/C4
Cardiff-Wales (arpt.), Wal, UK 62/C4
Cardigan, PE, Can. 185/F2
Cardigan (bay), PE, Can. 185/F2
Cardigan, Wal, UK 62/B2
Cardinal, On, Can. 187/J2
Cardington, Oh, US 186/E4
Cardito, It. 92/D6
Cardona, Sp. 73/F2
Cardona, Uru. 215/K10
Cardoso, Braz. 213/G2
Cardozo, Uru. 215/K10
Cardston, Ab, Can. 171/H3
Cardwell, Austl. 160/B2
Cardwell, Mo, US 188/B2
Care Alto (peak), It. 87/G5
Careaçu, Braz. 211/L7
Carefree, Az, US 175/G4
Carei, Rom. 69/M5
Careiro, Braz. 206/B3
Carelmapu, Chile 214/B4
Carencro, La, US 190/B2
Carenero, Ven. 207/P7
Carentan, Fr. 82/D2
Carev vrh (peak), FYROM 75/H1
Carey, Oh, US 186/E4
Carey, Id, US 173/G2
Carey (lake), Austl. 153/B3
Carhaix-Plouguer, Fr. 82/B4
Carhuamayo, Peru 208/B3
Carhuaz, Peru 208/B3
Carhué, Arg. 214/E3
Cariaco, Ven. 205/F2
Cariamanga, Ecu. 208/B2
Cariango, Ang. 146/C5
Cariati, It. 74/E3
Caribbean (sea), NAm,SAm. 165/L8
Caribou (mts.), Ab, Can. 166/E3
Cariboo (mts.), BC, Can. 170/D1
Cariboo (riv.), BC, Can. 170/D1
Caribou (lake), On, Can. 183/K2
Caribou (isl.), On, Can. 183/M4
Caribou (range), Id, US 173/H2
Caribou, Me, US 167/K4
Caridade, Braz. 207/G4
Carigara, Phil. 114/D3
Carignan, Fr. 81/E4
Carignan, Qu, Can. 185/P7
Carignano, It. 88/A3
Carinda, Austl. 158/C1
Cariñena, Sp. 72/E2
Carinhanha, Braz. 210/E2
Carinhanha (riv.), Braz. 210/D2
Carini, It. 74/C3
Carinola, It. 92/C5
Caripande, Ang. 148/D2
Caripito, Ven. 205/F2
Cariré, Braz. 207/F3
Caririaçu, Braz. 207/G4
Cariris Novos, Serra dos (mts.), Braz. 207/F4
Cariús, Braz. 207/G4
Carl Junction, Mo, US 179/G2
Carl Sandburg Home Nat'l Hist. Site, NC, US 189/F3
Carleton (mt.), NB, Can. 184/D2
Carleton, Qu, Can. 184/D1
Carleton (riv.), NS, Can. 184/E3
Carleton, Mi, US 193/F7
Carleton Place, On, Can. 187/H2
Carletonville, SAfr. 150/D2
Carlin, Nv, US 172/E3
Carlindie Abor. Land, Austl. 156/C2
Carling, Fr. 81/F5
Carlingford (lake), Ire. 60/B3
Carlingford (mtn.), Ire. 60/B3
Carlingford, Ire. 60/B3
Carlingford (nbrhd.), Austl. 160/H8
Carlinville, Il, US 181/K4
Carlisle, On, Can. 186/T9
Carlisle, Eng, UK 61/F2
Carlisle, Ar, US 179/J3
Carlisle, In, US 188/D1
Carlisle, Ky, US 188/E1
Carlisle, Ms, US 190/C1
Carlisle, Pa, US 187/H4
Carlisle, SC, US 189/G3
Carlisle Barracks Mil. Res., Pa, US 194/A3
Carlit (peak), Fr. 70/D5
Carlos, Mn, US 183/G5
Carlos Casares, Arg. 214/E2
Carlos Chagas, Braz. 211/E3
Carlos M. de Cespedes, Cuba 201/G1
Carlos Pellegrini, Arg. 212/D5
Carlow (co.), Ire. 60/B6
Carlow, Ire. 58/D4
Carloway, Sc, UK 57/Q7
Carlsbad, Ca, US 192/C4
Carlsbad, Tx, US 176/D2
Carlsbad, NM, US 176/B1
Carlsbad Caverns NP, NM, US 198/D1
Carlsberg, Ger. 84/B3
Carlsborg, Wa, US 170/C3
Carlsfeld, Ger. 85/F2
Carlshend, Mi, US 183/L4
Carluke, On, Can. 186/T9
Carlton, Eng, UK 61/G6
Carlton, Al, US 190/E2
Carlton, Ga, US 189/F3
Carlton, Mn, US 183/H4
Carlton, Or, US 172/B1
Carlton, Wa, US 170/D3
Carluke, Sc, UK 59/C5
Carlyle, Sk, Can. 182/C3
Carlyle, Mt, US 182/B4
Carlyle, Il, US 188/C1
Carlyle (lake), Il, US 181/K4
Carmacks, Yk, Can. 166/C2
Carmagnola, It. 88/A3
Carman, Mb, Can. 182/F3
Carmarthen (bay), Wal, UK 62/B3
Carmarthen, Wal, UK 62/B3
Carmaux, Fr. 70/E4
Carmel (pt.), Wal, UK 60/D5
Carmel, NY, US 187/K4
Carmel, In, US 186/C5
Carmel (Carmel-by-the-Sea), Ca, US 174/B2
Carmel Valley, Ca, US 174/B2
Carmel-by-the-Sea (Carmel), Ca, US 174/B2
Carmelita, Guat. 200/D2
Carmelo, Uru. 215/J11
Carmen (isl.), Mex. 200/C2
Carmen, Az, US 175/G5
Carmen, Bol. 208/E3
Carmen, Id, US 173/G1
Carmen, Ok, US 179/E2
Carmen de Apicalá, Col. 207/L8
Carmen de Carupa, Col. 207/M7
Carmen de Cura, Ven. 207/P8
Carmen de Patagones, Arg. 214/E4
Carmen de Viboral, Col. 207/K6
Carmen, Río del (riv.), Mex. 177/A2
Carmensa, Arg. 214/D2
Carmi, Il, US 188/C1
Carmi, BC, Can. 170/E3
Carmichael, Ca, US 172/C4
Carmila, Austl. 160/C3
Carmo (peak), It. 88/B5
Carmo, Braz. 211/P6
Carmo da Cachoeira, Braz. 211/L6
Carmo da Mata, Braz. 210/D4
Carmo de Minas, Braz. 211/L7
Carmo do Cajuru, Braz. 213/H2
Carmo do Paranaíba, Braz. 210/D3
Carmo do Rio Claro, Braz. 210/D4
Carmona, Sp. 72/C4
Carn Ban (peak), Sc, UK 59/B2
Carn Easgann Bàna (peak), Sc, UK 59/B2
Càrn Eige (peak), Sc, UK 59/A2
Carn Glas-choire (peak), Sc, UK 59/C2
Carn Kitty (hill), Sc, UK 59/C2
Carn Mairg (peak), Sc, UK 59/B3
Carn Mór (peak), Sc, UK 59/C2
Carn na Cailliche (hill), Sc, UK 59/C1
Carn na Saobhaidhe (peak), Sc, UK 59/B2
Carnac, Fr. 82/B5
Carnago, It. 88/B2
Carnamah, Austl. 156/B4
Carnarvon, Austl. 162/A7
Carnarvon, SAfr. 150/C3
Carnarvon NP, Austl. 160/B4
Carnarvonleegte (riv.), SAfr. 150/C3
Carnation, Wa, US 193/D2
Carnaubais, Braz. 207/G4
Carnaubal, Braz. 207/F4
Carnaxide, Port. 73/P10
Carncastle, NI, UK 60/C2
Carndonagh, Ire. 60/A1
Carnduff, Sk, Can. 182/D3
Carnedd Llewelyn (peak), Wal, UK 60/E5
Carnegie, Ok, US 179/E3
Carnegie, Ga, US 191/F2
Carnegie (lake), Austl. 153/B3
Carnesville, Ga, US 189/F3
Carnew, Ire. 58/D4
Carney (isl.), Ant. 216/S
Carney, Mi, US 186/C2
Carney, Ok, US 179/F3
Carnforth, Eng, UK 61/F3
Carnlough, NI, UK 60/B2
Carnmore (Galway) (arpt.), Ire. 58/B3
Carnot, CAfr. 142/B4
Carnot (cape), Austl. 157/G5
Carnota, Sp. 72/A1
Carnoules, Fr. 90/C6
Carnoux-en-Provence, Fr. 90/B6
Carnsore (pt.), Ire. 58/D5
Carnwath, Sc, UK 59/C5
Carnwath (riv.), NW, Can. 166/D2
Caro, Mi, US 186/E3
Caroga Lake, NY, US 187/J3
Carol City, Fl, US 190/P11
Carol Stream, Il, US 193/P16
Carolina, Braz. 207/E4
Carolina, SAfr. 151/E2
Carolina, PR 197/M8
Carolina, Al, US 190/E2
Carolina Beach, NC, US 189/J3
Carolina Sandhills NWR, SC, US 189/G3
Caroline, Ab, Can. 170/G1
Caroline (isl.), Kiri. 163/K5
Caroline (isls), Micr. 162/D4
Caroline (peak), NZ 161/A4
Caroline (co.), Md, US 194/C6
Caromb, Fr. 90/B4
Caron, Sk, Can. 171/M2
Caroní (riv.), Ven. 203/C2
Carora, Ven. 204/D2
Carouge, Swi. 86/C5
Carovilli, It. 92/D4
Carp, Nv, US 174/E2
Carpaneto Piacentino, It. 88/C4
Carpathian (mts.), Eur. 55/G4
Carpegna, It. 89/F6
Carpegna (peak), It. 89/F6
Carpenedolo, It. 88/D3
Carpentaria (gulf), Austl. 153/C2
Carpenter, Wy, US 180/B3
Carpentersville, Il, US 193/P15
Carpentras, Fr. 90/B4
Carpi, It. 89/D4
Carpignano Sesia, It. 88/B2
Carpina, Braz. 207/H4
Carpineto Romano, It. 92/C4
Carpinone, It. 92/D4
Carpinteria, Ca, US 192/A2
Carpio, ND, US 182/D3
Carpiquet (int'l arpt.), Fr. 83/E2
Carquefou, Fr. 82/D6
Carqueiranne, Fr. 90/C6
Carr (inlet), Wa, US 193/B3
Carr Boyds (range), Austl. 154/C4
Carrabalci, Eth. 144/B3
Carrabelle, Fl, US 191/F3
Carraipía, Col. 204/C2
Carraiu, Eth. 142/H4
Carran (peak), Ire. 58/A6
Carrara, It. 88/D5
Carraroe, Ire. 58/A3
Carrasco (int'l arpt.), Uru. 215/K11
Carrasquero, Ven. 204/D2
Carrathool, Austl. 159/B2
Carrboro, NC, US 189/H3
Carrbridge, Sc, UK 59/C2
Carreg Ddu (pt.), Wal, UK 60/D6
Carriacou (isl.), Gren. 197/J5
Carrick, Mb, Can. 182/F3
Carrick (reg.), Sc, UK 59/B6
Carrick on Shannon, Ire. 58/B2
Carrick on Suir, Ire. 58/C5
Carrickalinga, Austl. 157/H5
Carrickfergus, NI, UK 60/C2
Carrickfergus (dist.), NI, UK 60/C2
Carrickmacross, Ire. 58/D2
Carrickmore, NI, UK 60/A2
Carriere, Ms, US 190/D2
Carrières-sous-Poissy, Fr. 56/J5
Carrigaholt, Ire. 58/A4
Carrigaline, Ire. 58/B6
Carrigallen, Ire. 58/C2
Carrigatuke (peak), NI, UK 58/D1
Carrigtwohill, Ire. 58/B6
Carrington, ND, US 182/E4
Carrión (riv.), Sp. 72/C1
Carrión de los Condes, Sp. 72/C1
Carrito, Bol. 209/E4
Carrizal, Col. 204/C1
Carrizalillo, Chile 212/B4
Carrizo (cr.), NM,Tx, US 178/C2
Carrizo (mts.), Az, US 168/D4
Carrizo Springs, Tx, US 177/E3
Carrizo Wash (riv.), Az, US 175/H3
Carrizozo, NM, US 178/B4
Carroll, Mb, Can. 182/D3
Carroll, Ia, US 181/G2
Carroll (co.), US 194/A5
Carrollton, Al, US 188/C4
Carrollton, Ga, US 188/E4
Carrollton, Il, US 181/J4
Carrollton, Ky, US 188/E1
Carrollton, Mi, US 186/E3
Carrollton, Ms, US 188/C4
Carrollton, Mo, US 181/H4
Carrollton, Oh, US 186/F4
Carrollton, Tx, US 176/L7
Carrollwood Village, Fl, US 190/K7
Carron (lake), Sc, UK 59/A2
Carron (riv.), Sc, UK 59/A2
Carros, Fr. 90/D5
Carrot (riv.), Sk, Can. 171/M1
Carrot River, Sk, Can. 171/N1
Carrouges, Fr. 83/E3
Carrowdore, NI, UK 60/C2
Carrowkeel, Ire. 60/A1
Carrù, It. 88/A4
Carrum Downs, Austl. 158/G6
Carrumpa (cr.), NM,Ok, US 178/C2
Carry-le-Rouet, Fr. 90/B6
Carryduff, NI, UK 60/C2
Çarşamba, Turk. 96/F4
Carse of Forth (plain), Sc, UK 59/B4
Carse of Gowrie (plain), Sc, UK 59/C4
Carseland, Ab, Can. 171/H2
Carsoli, It. 92/C3
Carson, Ca, US 192/F8
Carson, Ms, US 190/D2
Carson, ND, US 182/D4
Carson, NM, US 178/B2
Carson (lake), Nv, US 172/D4
Carson (des.), Nv, US 172/D4
Carson (riv.), Nv, US 172/D4
Carson City, Mi, US 186/D3
Carson City (cap.), Nv, US 172/D4
Carson River Abor. Land, Austl. 154/B3
Carson Sink (sink), Nv, US 172/D4
Carsonville, Mi, US 186/E3
Carsphairn, Sc, UK 60/D1
Carstairs, Ab, Can. 171/G2
Carstairs Junction, Sc, UK 59/C5
Carsulae (ruin), It. 91/B2
Carswell (A.F.B.), Tx, US 179/F4
Carta Valley, Tx, US 177/D3
Cartagena, Col. 204/C2
Cartagena, Sp. 73/E4
Cartagena, Chile 214/N8
Cartago, CR 201/F4
Cartago, Ca, US 174/C2
Cartago, Col. 207/K8
Cártama, Sp. 72/C4
Cartaya, Sp. 72/B4
Cartecay, Ga, US 188/E3
Carter, Ok, US 178/E3
Carter, Wi, US 183/K5
Carter (mt.), Austl. 155/F3
Carter Bar (hill), Eng, UK 59/D6
Carteret (cape), Fr. 82/D2
Carteret, Fr. 82/D2
Carteret, NJ, US 195/J9
Cartersville, Ga, US 188/E3
Cartersville, Mt, US 171/L4
Carterton, NZ 161/J9
Carterton, Eng, UK 63/E3
Carterville, Il, US 188/C2
Carthage (int'l arpt.), Tun. 74/B4
Carthage, Ar, US 179/H3
Carthage, Il, US 181/J3
Carthage, Mo, US 179/G2
Carthage, Ms, US 188/C4
Carthage, NC, US 189/H3
Carthage, NY, US 187/J3
Carthage, Tn, US 188/E2
Carthage, Tx, US 177/G1
Carthage (Qarţājannah) (ruin), Tun. 74/B4
Cartí (mtn.), Pan. 204/B2
Cartier, On, Can. 186/F1
Cartier Islet (isl.), Austl. 153/B2
Cartwright, Mb, Can. 182/E3
Cartwright, Nf, Can. 167/L3
Caruaru, Braz. 207/H5
Carumás, Peru 208/D5
Carunjamba (riv.), Ang. 148/B2
Carúpano, Ven. 205/F2
Carutapera, Braz. 207/E3
Caruthers, Ca, US 174/C2
Caruthersville, Mo, US 188/C2
Carver (co.), Mn, US 183/N7
Carver, Mn, US 183/N7
Carvico, It. 88/C2
Carville, La, US 190/C2
Carvin, Fr. 80/B3
Carvoeiro (cape), Port. 72/A3
Cary, Il, US 193/P15
Cary, Ms, US 188/B4
Cary, NC, US 189/H3
Caryville, Fl, US 191/F2
Caryville, Tn, US 188/E2
Casa, Ar, US 179/H3
Casa Agapito, Col. 204/C4
Casa Blanca, NM, US 175/J3
Casa Branca, Braz. 211/J6
Casa de Piedra (res.), Arg. 214/D3
Casa Grande, Az, US 175/G4
Casa Grande Ruins Nat'l Mon., Az, US 175/G4
Casa Nova, Braz. 207/F5
Casabianca, Col. 207/K7
Casablanca, Chile 214/N8
Casablanca (Dar-El-Beida), Mor. 136/D2
Casablanca (Mohamed V) (int'l arpt.), Mor. 136/D2
Casablanca-anfa (prov.), Mor. 138/A2
Casacalenda, It. 92/D4
Casagiove, It. 92/D5
Casal di Principe, It. 92/D5
Casalbordino, It. 92/D3
Casalbuttano, It. 88/C3
Casale di Scodosia, It. 89/E3
Casale Monferrato, It. 88/B3
Casale sul Sile, It. 89/F2
Casalecchio di Reno, It. 89/E5
Casaleone, It. 89/E3
Casalmaggiore, It. 88/D4
Casalpusterlengo, It. 88/C3
Casalserugo, It. 89/E3
Casamance (riv.), Sen. 140/A3
Casamicciola Terme, It. 92/C6
Casanare (dept.), Col. 204/D3
Casanare (riv.), Col. 204/D3
Casanay, Ven. 205/F2
Casapesenna, It. 92/D6
Casar de Cáceres, Sp. 72/B3
Casarano, It. 75/F2
Casarsa della Delizia, It. 89/F2
Casarza Ligure, It. 88/C5
Casas de Chacabuco, Chile 214/N8
Casas Grande (riv.), Mex. 175/J5
Casas Grandes (ruin), Mex. 198/C2
Casas Grandes, Mex. 198/D2
Casas-Ibáñez, Sp. 72/E3
Ca'Savio, It. 89/F3
Casazza, It. 88/C2
Cascada de Bassaseachic, PN, Mex. 198/C2
Cascade (pt.), NZ 161/B4
Cascade, Ia, US 181/J2
Cascade, Id, US 172/E1
Cascade (res.), Id, US 172/E1
Cascade, Mt, US 171/J4
Cascade (pt.), Or, US 172/A1
Cascade (range), Or,Wa, US 166/D4
Cascade, Va, US 189/H2
Cascade Caverns, Tx, US 177/E3
Cascade-Fairwood, Or, US 193/C3
Cascades (pt.), Fr. 151/S15
Cascais, Port. 73/P10
Cascapédia (riv.), Qu, Can. 184/D1
Cascas, Peru 208/B2
Cascavel, Braz. 213/F3
Cascia, It. 92/C2
Casciago, It. 88/B2
Casciana Terme, It. 88/D6
Cascina, It. 88/D6
Casco, Me, US 187/L2
Casco (bay), Me, US 184/B4
Casco, Wi, US 186/C2
Case (inlet), Wa, US 193/B3
Case Nuove, It. 89/E6
Casebier (hill), Wy, US 180/B2
Caselette, It. 90/D2
Casella, It. 88/B4
Caselle, It. 89/E3
Caselle Torinese, It. 90/D2
Caselton, Nv, US 174/E2
Casentino (valley), It. 89/E5
Caserta, It. 92/D5
Caserta (prov.), It. 92/D5
Caseville, Mi, US 186/E3
Casey, Austl., Ant. 216/H
Casey (bay), Ant. 216/D
Casey, Il, US 186/C5
Caseyr (cape), Som. 144/D3
Cash, Ar, US 179/J3
Cashel, Ire. 58/C4
Cashel, Zim. 149/G3
Cashion, Ok, US 179/F3
Cashlaundrumlahan (peak), Ire. 58/B3
Cashmere, Wa, US 170/D4
Cashtown, Pa, US 194/A4
Casigua, Ven. 204/C2
Casiguran, Phil. 114/C2
Casiguran, Phil. 114/C1
Casilda (pt.), Cuba 201/F1
Casilda, Arg. 214/E2
Casimiro Castillo, Mex. 198/D5
Casina, It. 88/D4
Casinalbo, It. 89/D4
Casino, Austl. 158/E1
Casino and Opera House, Mona. 88/J8
Casira, Bol. 212/C2
Casitas (lake), Ca, US 192/A2
Casitas Springs, Ca, US 192/A2
Casma, Peru 208/B3
Casmalia, Ca, US 174/B3
Casnigo, It. 88/C2
Casole d'Elsa, It. 89/E7
Casoli, It. 92/D3
Casorate Primo, It. 88/C3
Casorate Sempione, It. 88/B2
Casoria, It. 92/D6
Caspar, Ca, US 172/B4
Caspe, Sp. 73/E2
Casper (cr.), Wy, US 173/K2
Caspian (sea), Asia 103/E5
Caspian, Mi, US 183/K4
Caspoggio, It. 87/F5
Cass, Ar, US 179/H3
Cass (riv.), Mi, US 186/E3
Cass (lake), Mi, US 193/F6
Cass City, Mi, US 186/E3
Cass Lake, Mn, US 183/G4
Cassadaga, NY, US 187/G3
Cassai, Ang. 147/E5
Cassai (riv.), Ang. 147/E5
Cassamba, Ang. 148/D2
Cassanguidi, Ang. 147/E4
Cassano allo Ionio, It. 74/E3
Cassano d'Adda, It. 88/C2
Cassano Magnago, It. 88/B2
Cassano Spinola, It. 88/B4
Casscoe, Ar, US 179/J3
Cassel, Fr. 80/B2
Casselberry, Fl, US 190/N6
Casselton, ND, US 182/F4
Cássia, Braz. 213/H2
Cassiar, BC, Can. 166/D3
Cassiar (mts.), BC, Can. 166/C3
Cassilândia, Braz. 210/C3
Cassilis, Austl. 158/D1
Cassine, It. 88/B4
Cassinga, Ang. 148/C2
Cassino, It. 92/C5
Cassiporé (cape), Braz. 206/D2
Cassis, Fr. 90/B6
Cassoalala, Ang. 146/C5
Cassoday, Ks, US 179/F1
Cassolnovo, It. 88/B3
Cassongue, Ang. 148/B1
Cassopolis, Mi, US 186/C4
Cassville, Mo, US 179/H2
Cassville, WV, US 186/F5
Cassville, Wi, US 181/J2
Castagnaro, It. 89/E3
Castagneto Carducci, It. 71/J5
Castagnole delle Lanze, It. 88/B4
Castaic, Ca, US 192/B2
Castaic (lake), Ca, US 174/C3
Castalla, Sp. 73/E3
Castanet-Tolosan, Fr. 70/D5
Castanhal, Braz. 206/E3
Castaños, Mex. 177/D4
Casteau, Belg. 80/D2
Casteggio, It. 88/C3
Castegnato, It. 88/D2
Castel Bolognese, It. 89/E5
Castel d'Ario, It. 89/D3
Castel del Piano, It. 91/B1
Castel di Sangro, It. 92/D4
Castel Frentano, It. 92/D3
Castel Fusano, It. 91/B4
Castel Gandolfo, It. 91/B4
Castel Giorgio, It. 91/A2
Castel Goffredo, It. 88/D3
Castel Madama, It. 91/B4
Castel Mella, It. 88/D3
Castel NP, Isr. 131/C5
Castel San Giovanni, It. 88/C3
Castel San Lorenzo, It. 74/D2
Castel San Pietro Terme, It. 89/E5
Castel Viscardo, It. 91/B2
Castel Volturno, It. 92/C5
Castelbuono, It. 74/D4
Castelcovati, It. 88/C3
Castelfidardo, It. 89/G7
Castelfiorentino, It. 89/D6
Castelforte, It. 92/C5
Castelfranco di Sopra, It. 89/E6
Castelfranco Emilia, It. 89/E4
Castelfranco Veneto, It. 89/E2
Castelgomberto, It. 89/E2
Casteljaloux, Fr. 70/D4
Castell de Montjuic, Sp. 73/L7
Castella, Ca, US 172/B3
Castellammare (gulf), It. 74/C3
Castellammare di Stabia, It. 92/D6
Castellamonte, It. 88/A2
Castellane, Fr. 90/C5
Castellano (riv.), It. 92/C2
Castellanza, It. 88/B2
Castellar del Vallès, Sp. 73/G2
Castellarano, It. 89/D4
Castell'Arquato, It. 88/C4
Castellazzo Bormida, It. 88/B4
Castelldefels, Sp. 73/K7
Castelleone, It. 88/C3
Castelli, Arg. 215/K12
Castellina in Chianti, It. 89/E7
Castelliri, It. 92/C4
Castello di Godego, It. 89/E2
Castello di Miramare, It. 89/G2
Castello Eurialo (ruin), It. 74/D4
Castello, Monte il (peak), It. 89/E6
Castellón de la Plana, Sp. 73/E3
Castellote, Sp. 73/E2
Castellucchio, It. 88/D3
Castelmassa, It. 89/E3
Castelmauro, It. 92/D4
Castelnau-le-Lez, Fr. 70/E5
Castelnaudary, Fr. 70/D5
Castelnovo di Sotto, It. 88/D4
Castelnovo ne'Monti, It. 88/D5
Castelnuovo Berardenga, It. 89/E7
Castelnuovo di Garfagnana, It. 88/D5
Castelnuovo Don Bosco, It. 88/A2
Castelnuovo Scrivia, It. 88/B4
Castelo Branco (dist.), Port. 72/B2
Castelo Branco, Port. 72/B3
Castelo de Vide, Port. 72/B3
Castelo do Piauí, Braz. 207/F4
Castelraimondo, It. 92/C1
Castelsardo, It. 74/A2
Castelsarrasin, Fr. 70/D4
Castelvecchio Subequo, It. 92/C3
Castelverde, It. 88/C3
Castelvetere in Val Fortore, It. 92/D5
Castelvetrano, It. 74/C4
Castelvetro di Modena, It. 89/D4
Castelvetro Piacentino, It. 88/C3
Castenaso, It. 89/E4
Castenedolo, It. 88/D3
Casterton, Austl. 158/B3
Castiglioncello, It. 88/D7
Castiglione, It. 89/F5
Castiglione d'Adda, It. 88/C3
Castiglione dei Pepoli, It. 89/E5
Castiglione del Lago, It. 91/B1
Castiglione delle Stiviere, It. 88/D3
Castiglione in Teverina, It. 91/B2
Castiglione Messer Marino, It. 92/D4
Castiglione Torinese, It. 88/A2
Castilho, Braz. 213/G2
Castilla, Peru 208/A2
Castilla, Chile 212/B3
Castilla Y León (prov.), Sp. 70/B5
Castilla- La Mancha (pol. reg.), Sp. 73/N8
Castilla-La Mancha (dist.), Sp. 72/C3
Castilletes, Col. 204/D2
Castillo (peak), Arg. 214/C4
Castillo de San Marcos Nat'l Mon., Fl, US 191/H3
Castillon (lake), Fr. 90/C5
Castillos, Uru. 215/G2
Castione della Presolana, It. 87/G6
Castions, It. 89/F2
Castions di Strada, It. 89/G2
Castle (pt.), NZ 161/D3
Castle (riv.), Ab, Can. 170/G3
Castle Acre, Eng, UK 63/G1
Castle Cary, Eng, UK 62/D4
Castle Combe, Eng, UK 62/D4
Castle Dale, Ut, US 173/H4
Castle Danger, Mn, US 183/J4
Castle Donnington, Eng, UK 61/G6
Castle Douglas, Sc, UK 60/E2
Castle Hayne, NC, US 189/J3
Castle Hill (nbrhd.), Austl. 160/H8
Castle Hill Nat'l Hist. Park, Nf, Can. 185/K2
Castle Kennedy, Sc, UK 60/D2
Castle Rock, Ut, US 173/H3
Castle Rock (lake), Wi, US 181/J2
Castle Rock, Co, US 180/B4
Castle Rock, SD, US 180/C1
Castle Rock (dam), Wi, US 181/K2
Castle Rock, Wa, US 170/C4
Castle Tower NP, Austl. 160/C4
Castlebar, Ire. 58/A2
Castlebar (arpt.), Ire. 58/A2
Castlebay, Sc, UK 57/Q8
Castlebellingham, Ire. 60/B4
Castleberry, Al, US 190/E2
Castleblayney, Ire. 58/D1
Castlebridge, Ire. 58/D5
Castlecaufield, NI, UK 60/B3
Castlecomer, Ire. 58/C4
Castleconnell, Ire. 58/B4
Castledawson, NI, UK 60/B2
Castledermot, Ire. 58/D4
Castleford, Eng, UK 61/G4
Castleford, Id, US 173/F2
Castlegar, BC, Can. 170/F3
Castlegregory, Ire. 56/N10
Castleisland, Ire. 58/A5
Castlemaine, Austl. 159/B3
Castlemartyr, Ire. 58/B6
Castlepollard, Ire. 58/C2
Castlereagh, Ire. 58/B2
Castlereagh (nbrhd.), Austl. 160/G8
Castlerock, NI, UK 60/B1
Castleton, Vt, US 187/K3
Castletown, Ire. 58/C4
Castletown, IM, UK 60/D3
Castletownroche, Ire. 58/B5
Castletownsend, Ire. 58/A6
Castlewellan, NI, UK 60/C3
Castlewood, SD, US 181/F1
Castor (cr.), La, US 177/H1
Castor, La, US 179/H4
Castor, Ab, Can. 171/J1
Castor (riv.), Mo, US 188/B2
Castres, Fr. 70/E5
Castrezzato, It. 88/C2
Castricum, Neth. 78/B3
Castries (cap.), StL. 197/N9
Castro, Chile 214/B4
Castro, Braz. 213/G3
Castro Daire, Port. 72/B2
Castro de Rey, Sp. 72/B1
Castro del Río, Sp. 72/C4
Castro Verde, Port. 72/A4
Castro-Urdiales, Sp. 72/D1
Castrocaro Terme, It. 89/E5
Castrojeriz, Sp. 72/C1
Castrop-Rauxel, Ger. 79/E5
Castropol, Sp. 72/B1
Castrovillari, It. 74/E3
Castroville, Ca, US 174/B2
Castroville, Tx, US 177/E3
Castrovirreyna, Peru 208/C4
Castuera, Sp. 72/C3
Casupá, Uru. 215/G2
Çat, Turk. 128/E2
Cat (lake), On, Can. 183/J2
Cat (isl.), Bahm. 165/K7
Cat Ba (isl.), Viet. 113/E4
Cat Ba NP, Viet. 113/E4
Cat Creek, Mt, US 171/K4
Cat Head (pt.), Mi, US 186/D2
Cat Law (peak), Sc, UK 59/C3
Catabola, Ang. 148/C2
Catabola, Ang. 148/B2
Catacamas, Hon. 200/E3
Catacaos, Peru 208/A2
Catacocha, Ecu. 208/B2
Cataduanes (isl.), Phil. 162/B3
Cataguases, Braz. 211/P6
Catahoula (lake), La, US 190/B2
Catahoula NWR, La, US 177/H2
Cataiñgan, Phil. 117/F1
Çatak, Turk. 129/E2
Catala, Ang. 146/D5
Çatalağzı, Turk. 77/K5
Catalão, Braz. 210/D3
Çatalca, Turk. 129/M6
Çatalçam, Turk. 128/D2
Catalina, Nf, Can. 185/L1
Catalina, Az, US 175/G4
Catalina, Chile 212/B3
Catalone, NS, Can. 185/H3
Catalonia (reg.), Sp. 92/D2
Cataluña (prov.), Sp. 70/D5
Catamarca, Arg. 212/C4
Catamarca (prov.), Arg. 212/C3
Catamayo, Ecu. 208/B1
Catanauan, Phil. 114/C2
Catandica, Moz. 149/G3
Catanduanes (isl.), Phil. 114/D2
Catanduva, Braz. 213/G2
Catania, It. 74/D4
Catania (gulf), It. 74/D4
Catanzaro, It. 74/E3
Cataract (cr.), Az, US 175/F3
Cataract (lake), Austl. 159/E2
Cataratas (int'l arpt.), Braz. 213/F3
Cataratas del Iguazú (falls), Arg. 213/F3
Cataricahua, Bol. 212/C1
Catarina, Braz. 207/G4
Catarman, Phil. 114/D3
Catarman, Phil. 114/D2
Catarman (pt.), Phil. 114/D4
Catastrophe (cape), Austl. 157/G5
Catata Nova, Ang. 148/B2
Catatumbo (riv.), Col. 197/G6
Catatungan (mtn.), Phil. 114/D4
Catawba, Wi, US 183/J5
Catawba (dam), SC, US 189/G3
Catawba (riv.), NC, US 189/G3
Catawba, SC, US 189/G3
Catawba, South Fork (riv.), NC, US 189/G3
Catawissa, Pa, US 194/B2
Catbalogan, Phil. 114/D3
Cateco Cangola, Ang. 146/C5
Catedral (peak), Uru. 215/G2
Cateel, Phil. 114/D4
Catemaco (lake), Mex. 200/C2
Catemaco, Mex. 200/C2
Catende, Braz. 207/H5
Cateran (hill), Eng, UK 59/E5
Caterham, Eng, UK 56/C3
Caterham and Warlingham, Eng, UK 63/F4
Catete, Ang. 146/C5
Catfish (cr.), Fl, US 190/N8
Catharine, Ks, US 178/E1
Cathcart, SAfr. 150/D4
Cathedral (mtn.), Tx, US 177/C2
Cathedral City, Ca, US 174/D4
Cathédrale de Reims, Fr. 80/D5
Catherine (peak), Egypt 135/G2
Catherine, Al, US 188/D4
Catherine Palace, Rus. 94/T7
Cathlamet, Wa, US 170/C4
Ca'Tiepolo, It. 89/F4
Catierick, Eng, UK 61/G3
Catingueira, Braz. 207/G4
Catió, GBis. 140/B4
Cativá, Pan. 201/G4
Catlettsburg, Ky, US 189/F1
Catlin, Il, US 186/C4
Catmon, Phil. 114/D3
Cato (isl.), Aus. 153/E3
Catoche, Cabo (cape), Mex. 200/E1
Catofe, Ang. 146/C5
Catolé do Rocha, Braz. 207/G4
Catolo, Ang. 146/D5
Catonsville, Md, US 194/B5
Catoosa, Ok, US 179/G2
Catria (peak), It. 89/F7
Catriló, Arg. 214/E3
Catrimani, Braz. 205/F4
Catrimani (riv.), Braz. 205/F4
Catrine, Sc, UK 59/B6
Catshill, Eng, UK 62/D2
Catskill, NY, US 187/K3
Catskill (mts.), NY, US 187/J3
Cattaraugus, NY, US 187/G3
Cattaraugus Ind. Res., NY, US 187/G3

Cattawissa (cr.), Pa, US 194/B2
Cattolica, It. 89/F6
Catu, Braz. 211/F2
Catubig, Phil. 114/D2
Catuípe, Braz. 213/F4
Cauale (riv.), Ang. 146/D4
Cauayan, Phil. 114/C3
Cauayan, Phil. 114/C1
Cauca (riv.), Col. 204/C3
Cauca (riv.), Col. 203/B2
Cauca (dept.), Col. 204/B4
Caucagua, Ven. 204/D3
Caucagua, Ven. 207/P7
Caucaia, Braz. 207/G3
Caucas, Bol. 209/G5
Caucasia, Col. 204/C3
Caucasus (mts.), Geo.,Rus. 97/G4
Caucasus (mts.), Geo. 100/F6
Caucasus (mts.), Asia 128/E1
Caudan, Fr. 82/B5
Caudebec-en-Caux, Fr. 83/F1
Caudebec-lès-Elbeuf, Fr. 83/G2
Caudete, Sp. 73/E3
Caudry, Fr. 80/C3
Cauese, Montes (mts.), Moz. 149/F2
Cauldcleuch Head (peak), Sc, UK 59/D6
Caulfield, Mo, US 179/H2
Caulfield, Austl. 159/B3
Caulnes, Fr. 82/C4
Caumont (arpt.), Fr. 90/A5
Caumont-L'éventé, Fr. 83/E2
Caumont-sur-Durance, Fr. 90/A5
Caúngula, Ang. 146/D5
Cauquenes, Chile 214/B2
Caura (riv.), Ven. 205/E3
Cauresi (riv.), Moz. 149/G3
Cauron (riv.), Fr. 90/B6
Causapscal, Qu, Can. 184/D1
Căuşeni, Mol. 98/E4
Causeway, Ire. 58/A5
Causey, NM, US 178/C4
Caussade, Fr. 70/D4
Cautário (riv.), Braz. 209/F3
Cauterets, Fr. 70/C5
Cauto (riv.), Cuba 201/G1
Cauvery (riv.), India 118/C5
Cauville, Fr. 83/F1
Cava de'tirreni, It. 92/D6
Cava d'ispica (ruin), It. 74/D4
Cávado (riv.), Port. 72/A2
Cavaglià, It. 88/B3
Cavaillon, Fr. 90/B5
Cavalaire-sur-Mer, Fr. 90/C6
Cavalcante, Braz. 210/D2
Cavalese, It. 87/H5
Cavalier, ND, US 182/F3
Cavalla (Cavally) (riv.), Libr. 140/D5
Cavallermaggiore, It. 88/A3
Cavallino, It. 89/F3
Cavallo, Capo al (cape), Fr. 74/A1
Cavally (riv.), C.d'Iv. 140/C5
Cavally (Cavalla) (riv.), Libr. 140/D5
Cavan, Ire. 58/C2
Cavari, Bol. 209/E5
Cavarzere, It. 89/F3
Cave, It. 91/B4
Cave City, Ar, US 179/J3
Cave City, Ky, US 188/E2
Cave Creek, Az, US 175/G4
Cave Junction, Or, US 172/B2
Cave of Ten Thousand Buddhas, Myan. 120/B2
Cave Of The Mounds, Wi, US 181/K2
Cave Run (lake), Ky, US 189/F1
Cave Spring, Va, US 189/G2
Cave Spring, Ga, US 188/E3
Caverns of Sonora, Tx, US 177/D2
Cavezzo, It. 89/E4
Caviana (isl.), Braz. 206/D2
Cavinas, Bol. 209/E4
Cavite (co.), Phil. 114/E7
Cavite, Phil. 114/E7
Cavnic, Rom. 77/F2
Cavour, It. 90/D3
Cavriana, It. 88/D3
Cawayan, Phil. 114/C3
Cawdor, Sc, UK 59/C1
Cawker City, Ks, US 180/E4
Cawood, Eng, UK 61/G4
Cawston, Eng, UK 63/H1
Caxambu, Braz. 211/M6
Caxata, Bol. 209/E5
Caxias, Braz. 207/F4
Caxias do Sul, Braz. 213/G4
Caxinas (pt.), Hon. 200/E2
Caxinga, Ang. 146/D5
Caxito, Ang. 146/C5
Çay, Turk. 128/B2
Çayağzı, Turk. 129/N6
Çayağzi (riv.), Turk. 129/N6
Cayambe, Ecu. 204/B4
Cayambe (vol.), Ecu. 204/B4
Cayastá, Arg. 212/D4
Cayce, SC, US 189/G4
Çaycuma, Turk. 96/E4
Çayeli, Turk. 97/G4
Cayenne (cap.), FrG. 206/C1
Cayenne (dist.), FrG. 206/C1
Cayer, Mb, Can. 182/E2
Cayeux-sur-Mer, Fr. 80/A3
Çayırhan, Turk. 77/K5
Çaylar, Turk. 128/E2
Cayley, Ab, Can. 171/H2
Cayman (isls.), UK 165/J8
Cayman Brac (isl.), UK 197/F4
Caynabo, Som. 144/C3
Cayo Coco (isl.), Cuba 201/G1
Cayo Cocorocuma (isl.), Hon. 201/F3
Cayo Fragosa (isl.), Cuba 201/G1
Cayo Guayabo (isl.), Cuba 201/G1
Cayo Largo (isl.), Cuba 201/F1
Cayo Romano (isl.), Cuba 201/G1
Cayo Sabinal (isl.), Cuba 201/G1
Cayos Arcas (isl.), Mex. 200/D1
Cayos Cajones (isl.), Hon. 196/E4
Cayos de Albuquerque (isl.), Col. 201/F3
Cayos del Este Sudeste (isl.), Col. 201/F3
Cayos Miskitos (isl.), Nic. 196/E5
Cayucos, Ca, US 174/B3
Cayuga, In, US 186/C5
Cayuga (lake), NY, US 187/H3
Cayuga (cr.), NY, US 186/V10
Cayuga, Tx, US 176/G2
Cayuga Heights, NY, US 187/H3
Cazalla de la Sierra, Sp. 72/C4
Cazenovia, NY, US 187/J3
Cazères, Fr. 70/D5
Cazin, Bosn. 76/B3
Cazis, Swi. 87/F4
Cazombo, Ang. 148/D1
Cazones (riv.), Mex. 200/B1
Cazorla, Sp. 72/D4
Cazula, Moz. 149/G2
Cazzago San Martino, It. 88/D2
Cea (riv.), Sp. 72/C1
Ceanannus Mór (Kells), Ire. 58/D2
Ceará (state), Braz. 207/F4
Ceará-Mirim, Braz. 207/H4
Cébaco (isl.), Pan. 201/F5
Ceballos, Mex. 198/D3
Cebolla, NM, US 175/J2
Cebollatí, Uru. 215/G2
Cebollati (riv.), Uru. 215/G2
Cebreros, Sp. 72/C2
Cebu (isl.), Phil. 162/B3
Cebu, Phil. 114/C3
Cebu (int'l arpt.), Phil. 114/C3
Ceccano, It. 92/C4
Cecil, Wi, US 181/K1
Cecil (co.), Md, US 194/C4
Cecil Macks (pass), Swaz. 151/E2
Cecil Plains, Austl. 160/C4
Cecil Rhodes (mt.), Austl. 156/D3
Cecilia, Ky, US 188/E2
Cecilton, Md, US 194/C5
Cecilville, Ca, US 172/B3
Cecina (riv.), It. 89/D6
Cecina, It 71/J5
Cecita (lake), It. 74/E3
Ceclavín, Sp. 72/B3
Cedar (lake), Tx, US 178/C4
Cedar, Mi, US 186/D2
Cedar (lake), On, Can. 187/G1
Cedar (mtn.), Ca, US 193/L11
Cedar (lake), Sk, Mb, Can. 166/F3
Cedar (mts.), Ut, US 173/G3
Cedar (riv.), Ne, US 180/E3
Cedar (cr.), Ia, US 181/H3
Cedar (riv.), Mn, US 181/G1
Cedar (riv.), Ia, US 181/H2
Cedar (isl.), Md, US 189/K2
Cedar Bay NP, Austl. 160/B1
Cedar Bayou (riv.), Tx, US 177/M8
Cedar Bluff, Al, US 188/E3
Cedar Bluff (res.), Ks, US 180/E4
Cedar Breaks Nat'l Mon., Ut, US 175/F2
Cedar Brook, NJ, US 194/D4
Cedar City, Ut, US 175/F2
Cedar Creek, Ar, US 179/H3
Cedar Creek (peak), Id, US 173/G2
Cedar Creek (res.), Tx, US 199/F1
Cedar Crest, NM, US 175/J3
Cedar Falls (dam), Wa US 193/D3
Cedar Falls, Wa, US 193/D3
Cedar Falls, Ia, US 181/H2
Cedar Glen, Ca, US 192/C2
Cedar Grove, Wi, US 186/C3
Cedar Grove, NJ, US 195/J8
Cedar Grove, Tn, US 188/C3
Cedar Grove, Md, US 194/A5
Cedar Hill, NM, US 175/J2
Cedar Hill, Tn, US 188/D2
Cedar Hill, Tx, US 176/L7
Cedar Island, NC, US 189/J3
Cedar Island NWR, NC, US 189/J3
Cedar Key, Fl, US 191/G3
Cedar Mills, Mn, US 181/G1
Cedar Park, Tx, US 177/F2
Cedar Point Nat'l Wild. Ref., Oh, US 186/E4
Cedar Rapids, Ia, US 181/J3
Cedar River, Mi, US 186/C2
Cedar Springs, Mi, US 186/D3
Cedar Springs, Tx, US 177/F2
Cedar Vale, Ks, US 179/F2
Cedarburg, Wi, US 186/C3
Cedaredge, Co, US 175/J1
Cedarhurst, NY, US 195/L9
Cedartown, Ga, US 188/E3
Cedarville, Ar, US 179/G3
Cedarville, Ca, US 172/C3
Cedegolo, It. 87/G5
Cedeira, Sp. 72/A1
Cedral, Mex. 199/E4
Cedro, Braz. 207/G4
Cedros (isl.), Mex. 165/F7
Ceduna, Austl. 157/G5
Cee, Sp. 72/A1
Ceel Afweyne, Som. 144/C3
Ceel Buur, Som. 144/C4
Ceel Dheere, Som. 144/C5
Ceel Xamurre, Som. 144/D4
Ceeldheere, Som. 144/C4
Ceerigaabo (Erigabo), Som. 144/C3
Cefalù, It. 74/D3
Cefn-Mawr, Wal, UK 61/E6
Cefni (riv.), Wal, UK 60/D5
Cega (riv.), Sp. 72/C2
Ceggia, It. 89/F2
Cegléd, Hun. 76/D2
Čegrane, FYROM 75/G2
Cehegín, Sp. 72/E3
Ceheng Bouyeizu Zizhixian, China 112/E3
Cehu Silvaniei, Rom. 77/F2
Ceiriog (riv.), Wal, UK 61/E6
Çekerek (riv.), Turk. 96/F4
Çekerek, Turk. 128/C1
Cela, Ang. 148/B1
Celada Cué, Par. 212/E2
Celákovice, Czh. 85/H2
Celano, It. 92/C3
Celanova, Sp. 72/B1
Celaya, Mex. 199/E4
Celbridge, Ire. 58/D3
Celebes (isl.), Indo. 103/L10
Celebes (sea), Asia 103/M9
Celebes (Sulawesi) (isl.), Indo. 117/E4
Celendín, Peru 208/B2
Celenza Valfortore, It. 92/D4
Celeste, Tx, US 179/F4
Celestún, Mex. 200/D1
Celica, Ecu. 208/B2
Céligny, Swi. 86/C5
Celina, Tx, US 179/F4
Celina, Oh, US 186/D4
Celina, Tn, US 188/E2
Celje, Slov. 76/B2
Cella, Sp. 72/E2
Celldömölk, Hun. 76/C2
Celle (riv.), Fr. 68/B4
Celle, Ger. 79/H3
Celle Ligure, It. 88/B5
Celles, Belg. 80/C2
Cellettes, Fr. 83/G5
Cellole, It. 92/C5
Čelopek, FYROM 76/E5
Celorico da Beira, Port. 72/B2
Celtic (sea), Eur. 57/P11
Cemaes (pt.), Wal, UK 62/B2
Cemaru (peak), Indo. 116/D3
Cembra, It. 87/H5
Cenajo (res.), Sp. 72/E3
Cenderawasih (bay), Indo. 162/C5
Cene, It. 88/C2
Cenepa (riv.), Peru 208/B1
Çengerli, Turk. 128/D2
Cengong, China 119/J2
Cenia, Sp. 73/F2
Ceno (riv.), It. 88/C3
Centallo, It. 90/D3
Centenario do Sul, Braz. 213/G2
Centennial (mts.), Id, US 173/G1
Centennial Wash (riv.), Az, US 175/F4
Center, Ok, US 179/F3
Center, ND, US 182/D4
Center, Co, US 175/J2
Center, Mo, US 181/J4
Center, Ne, US 180/F2
Center, Tx, US 177/G2
Center City, Mn, US 183/H5
Center City, Mn, US 181/H1
Center Hill, Fl, US 190/M6
Center Hill (lake), Tn, US 188/E2
Center Moriches, NY, US 195/F2
Center Point, Al, US 188/D4
Center Point, Ia, US 181/J2
Center Point, La, US 190/B2
Center Point, Tx, US 177/E3
Centerbrook, Ct, US 195/F1
Centereach, NY, US 195/E2
Centerfield, Ut, US 173/H4
Centerville, Ga, US 188/F4
Centerville, Ga, US 189/M7
Centerville, In, US 186/D5
Centerville, Ia, US 181/H3
Centerville, Mo, US 188/B2
Centerville, Oh, US 186/D5
Centerville, Ok, US 178/E3
Centerville, SD, US 181/F2
Centerville, Tn, US 188/D3
Centerville, Tx, US 177/G2
Centerville, Tx, US 177/G2
Centerville, Ut, US 173/H3
Cento, It. 89/E4
Cento Croci, Passo di (pass), It. 88/C5
Central (peak), Arg. 214/C4
Central (dist), Bots. 148/E4
Central, Braz. 211/E1
Central (mass.), Fr. 70/E4
Central (pol. reg.), Gha. 141/E5
Central (dist.), Isr. 131/B4
Central (prov.), Kenya 145/B2
Central (dept.), Par. 212/E3
Central, Phil. 114/C2
Central (prov.), PNG 155/G2
Central (prov.), SrL. 121/D5
Central (co.), Sc, UK 59/B4
Central (int'l arpt.), Ukr. 98/F4
Central, Az, US 175/H4
Central, NM, US 175/H4
Central African Republic (ctry.) 133/D4
Central Australia (Warburton) Abor. Rsv., Austl. 157/E3
Central Australia Abor. Land, Austl. 157/F2
Central Butte, Sk, Can. 171/L2
Central City, Co, US 180/B4
Central City, Il, US 188/C1
Central City, Ky, US 188/D2
Central City, Ia, US 181/J2
Central City, Ne, US 180/F3
Central City, Pa, US 187/G4
Central Desert Abor. Rsv., Austl. 157/F2
Central Desert Aboriginal Land, Austl. 154/C4
Central Falls, RI, US 187/L4
Central Intelligence Agency Fed. Govt. Res., Va, US 194/A6
Central Island NP, Kenya 142/H5
Central Islip, NY, US 195/E2
Central Kalahari Game Reserve, Bots. 148/D4
Central Makrān (range), Pak. 127/H3
Central Mount Stuart (peak), Austl. 157/G2
Central Mount Wedge (peak), Austl. 157/F2
Central Park, NY, US 195/K8
Central Patricia, On, Can. 183/J2
Central Point, Or, US 172/B2
Central Russian Uplands (uplands), Rus. 99/J1
Central Saanich, BC, Can. 170/C3
Central Siberian (plat.), Rus. 101/L3
Central Square, NY, US 187/H3
Central Ural (mts.), Rus. 95/N4
Central Valley, Ca, US 172/B3
Central Valley, NY, US 194/D1
Centralia, Il, US 188/C1
Centralia, Ks, US 181/F4
Centralia, Mo, US 181/H4
Centralia, Wa, US 170/C4
Centre (prov.), Camr. 142/A4
Centre (pol. reg.), Fr. 70/D3
Centre (pol. reg.), Mor. 136/D2
Centre, Al, US 188/E3
Centre (co.), Pa, US 194/A2
Centre Island, NY, US 195/L8
Centre Nord (pol. reg.), Mor. 136/D2
Centre Sud (pol. reg.), Mor. 136/D3
Centre-Nord (pol. reg.), Mor. 138/B2
Centre-Sud (pol. reg.), Mor. 138/B2
Centreville, Al, US 188/D4
Centreville, Md, US 194/B5
Centreville, Mi, US 186/D4
Centreville, Ms, US 190/C2
Centreville, NS, Can. 184/E3
Century, Fl, US 190/E2
Cenxi, China 119/K3
Cepagatti, It. 92/D3
Ceparana, It. 88/C5
Cepet (cape), Fr. 90/B6
Čepin, Cro. 76/D3
Ceprano, It. 92/C4
Cepu, Indo. 115/E3
Ceram (isl.), Indo. 103/N10
Ceram (sea), Indo. 162/B5
Cerano, It. 88/B3
Cérans-Foulletourte, Fr. 83/F5
Ceraso (cape), It. 74/A2
Cerbat (mts.), Az, US 175/E3
Cerbère, Fr. 70/E5
Cercal, Port. 72/A4
Cercedilla, Sp. 73/M8
Cerchio, It. 92/C3
čerchov (peak), Czh. 85/F4
Cerdanyola del Vallès, Sp. 73/L7
Cère (riv.), Fr. 70/E4
Cerea, It. 89/E3
Cereal, Ab, Can. 171/J2
Cerenti, Indo. 115/C3
Ceres, It. 90/D2
Ceres, SAfr. 150/L10
Ceres, Ca, US 174/B2
Ceres, Arg. 212/D4
Ceres, Braz. 210/C2
Ceresco, Ne, US 181/F3
Cerese, It. 89/D3
Céreste, Fr. 90/B5
Céret, Fr. 70/E5
Cereté, Col. 204/C2
Cerfone (riv.), It. 89/E6
Cerfontaine, Belg. 81/D3
Cergy, Fr. 56/J4
Ceriale, It. 88/B5
Cerignola, It. 74/D2
Cerisy-la-Salle, Fr. 82/D2
Çerkeş, Turk. 96/E4
Çerkezköy, Turk. 77/J5
Çermik, Turk. 128/D2
Černá (riv.), Czh. 85/H5
Černá (peak), Czh. 85/G5
Cernavodă, Rom. 77/J3
Cernay, Fr. 86/D2
Cernay-la-Ville, Fr. 56/H5
Cerne Abbas, Eng, UK 62/D5
Cernier, Swi. 86/C3
Cérou (riv.), Fr. 70/D4
Cerralvo, Mex. 177/E4
Cerralvo (isl.), Mex. 198/C3
Cerreto di Spoleto, It. 91/B2
Cerreto Guidi, It. 89/D6
Cerreto Sannita, It. 92/D5
Cerreto, Passo del (pass), It. 88/D5
Cerrig-y-Druidion, Wal, UK 60/E5
Cërrik, Alb. 75/F2
Cerrillos, NM, US 175/J3
Cerrillos, Arg. 212/C3
Cerrito, Par. 212/E3
Cerritos, Ca, US 192/F8
Cerritos, Mex. 199/E4
Cerro, NM, US 178/B2
Cerro Azul, Mex. 200/B1
Cêrro Azul, Braz. 213/G3
Cerro Azul, Peru 208/B4
Cerro Castillo, Chile 215/B6
Cerro Chato, Uru. 215/G2
Cerro Colorados (res.), Arg. 214/C3
Cêrro Corá, Braz. 207/G4
Cerro de la Estrella, PN, Mex. 199/Q10
Cerro de las Armas, Uru. 215/K11
Cerro de las Campanas, PN, Mex. 199/E4
Cerro de Pasco, Peru 208/B3
Cerro de San Antonio, Col. 204/C2
Cerro Dorotea, Chile 215/B6
Cerro El Copey, PN, Ven. 205/F2
Cerro Largo (dept.), Uru. 213/F5
Cerro Maggiore, It. 88/B2
Cerro Nanchital, Mex. 200/C2
Cerro Sombrero, Chile 215/C7
Cerros de Amotape, PN, Peru 208/A2
Certaldo, It. 89/E6
Certosa di Pavia, It. 88/C3
Certosa di Pisa, It. 88/D6
Cervantes, Austl. 156/B4
Cervaro, It. 92/C5
Cervaro (riv.), It. 76/B5
Cervati (peak), It. 74/D2
Cervellino (peak), It. 88/D4
Cervera, Sp. 73/F2
Cervera de Pisuerga, Sp. 72/C1
Cervera del Río Alhama, Sp. 72/E1
Cerveteri, It. 91/B4
Cerveyrette (riv.), Fr. 90/C3
Cervia, It. 89/F5
Cervignano del Friuli, It. 89/G2
Cervina (peak), It. 87/H4
Cervinara, It. 92/D5
Cervione, Fr. 74/A1
Cervo (riv.), It. 88/B1
Cervo, It. 88/B6
Cervo, Sp. 92/B2
Cervo (hills), Braz. 211/K7
Cesana Torinese, It. 90/C3
Cesano, It. 91/B3
Cesano (riv.), It. 89/F6
Cesano Boscone, It. 88/C3
Cesano Maderno, It. 88/C2
César (riv.), Col. 197/G5
César (dept.), Col. 204/C2
Cesar (prov.), Col. 201/H4
Cesen (peak), It. 89/F2
Cesena, It. 89/F5
Cesenatico, It. 89/F5
Cēsis, Lat. 67/L3
České Budějovice, Czh. 85/H5
Ceské Středohoří (mts.), Czh. 85/G2
Českomoravská Vysočina (mts.), Czh. 69/H4
Český Brod, Czh. 85/H2
Český Krumlov, Czh. 85/H5
Český Les Sumava (mts.), Czh. 85/F3
Česma (riv.), Cro. 76/C3
Çeşme, Turk. 75/K3
Cessford, Ab, Can. 171/J2
Cessnock, Austl. 159/E1
Cesson, Fr. 56/K6
Cesson-Sévigné, Fr. 82/C4
Cestohowa, Tx, US 177/F3
Cestos (riv.), Libr. 140/C5
Cesvaine, Lat. 67/M3
Cetara, It. 92/D6
Cetina (riv.), Cro. 76/C4
Cetinje, Yugo. 76/D4
Çetinkaya, Turk. 128/C2
Çetmi, Turk. 128/B2
Céu Azul, Braz. 213/F3
Ceurda del Pozo (res.), Sp. 72/D2
Ceuta, Sp. 138/B2
Ceva, It. 88/B5
Cevedale (peak), It. 87/G5
Cévennes (mts.), Fr. 70/E4
Cevio, Swi. 87/E5
Ceyhan, Turk. 128/C2
Ceylânpınar, Turk. 128/E2
Ceylon (isl.), SrL. 103/H9
Ceylon, Mn, US 181/G2
Ceyreste, Fr. 90/B6
Ceyzériat, Fr. 86/B5
Cèze (riv.), Fr. 70/F4
Ch'o (isl.), NKor. 107/C3
Ch'ok'ē (mts.), Eth. 144/A3
Ch'ungman (riv.), NKor. 107/C2
Cha Da (cape), Viet. 120/E4
Cha-am, Thai. 120/B3
Cha'anpu, China 113/F2
Chabāl Kalān, India 124/C4
Chabás, Arg. 214/E2
Chabeuil, Fr. 90/B3
Chābi, India 122/C4
Chabjuwardoo (bay), Austl. 156/B2
Chablé, Mex. 200/D2
Chabris, Fr. 83/G3
Chacabuco, Arg. 214/E2
Chacalluta, Chile 208/D5
Chacalluta (Arica) (int'l arpt.), Chile 212/B1
Chacao, Chile 214/B4
Chachani (peak), Peru 208/D5
Chachapoyas, Peru 208/B2
Chācharān, Pak. 124/A5
Chachoengsao, Thai. 120/C3
Chaclacayo, Peru 208/B3
Chaco (riv.), NM, US 175/H2
Chaco (mesa), NM, US 175/J3
Chaco (dept.), Par. 212/D1
Chaco (dept.), Arg. 212/D3
Chaco Austral (plain), Arg. 212/D3
Chaco Boreal (plain), Par. 212/D2
Chaco Central (plain), Arg. 212/D2
Chaco Culture Nat'l Hist. Park, NM, US 175/J2
Chaco Culture Nat'l Hist. Park, NM, US 175/H3
Chaco Culture Nat'l Hist. Park, NM, US 175/J3
Chaco, PN del, Arg. 212/E3
Chacoma, Bol. 212/B1
Chacritas, Chile 212/B4
Chacujal (ruin), Guat. 200/D3
Chad (lake), Afr. 142/B2
Chad (lake), Niger 133/D3
Chad(ctry.) 133/D3
Chadan, Rus. 125/F1
Chadao, China 106/G6
Chadbourn, NC, US 189/H3
Chadiza, Zam. 149/G2
Chadlington, Eng, UK 63/E3
Chadong, China 113/F2
Chadron, Ne, US 180/C2
Chadwell Saint Mary, Eng, UK 56/E2
Chadwick, Il, US 181/K2
Chae Hom, Thai. 120/B2
Chaedong-nodongjagu, NKor. 107/D3
Chaeryŏng, NKor. 107/C3
Chafarinas (isl.), Sp. 138/C2
Chaffee, ND, US 182/F4
Chaffee, Mo, US 188/C2
Chafurray, Col. 204/C4
Chāgai, Pak. 127/H3
Chagan, Kaz. 125/C1
Chagang-do (prov.), NKor. 107/D2
Chagda, Rus. 101/P4
Chagdo Kangri (mtn.), China 125/D5
Chagne, Eth. 142/H3
Chagny, Fr 70/F3
Chagos (arch.), BIOT, UK 103/G10
Chaguanas, Trin. 205/F2
Chaguaramas, Ven. 207/P8
Chaguarpamba, Ecu. 208/B1
Chaguaya, Bol. 212/C2
Chagyl, Trkm. 97/K4
Cha'gyüngoinba, China 125/F5
Chahuites, Mex. 200/C2
Chai Badan, Thai. 120/C3
Chaibāsā, India 123/E4
Chailland, Fr. 83/E4
Chailles, Fr. 83/G5
Chailly-en-Brie, Fr. 56/M5
Chain, SKor. 107/E5
Chain O'Lakes-King, Wi, US 181/K1
Chainat, Thai. 120/C3
Chaîne Annamitique (mts.), Laos 119/H4
Chaîne Annamitique (mts.), Laos,Viet. 120/D2
Chaîne de Belledonne (range), Fr. 90/B2
Chaîne de l'atacora (mts.), Ben. 141/F4
Chaine de la Selle (peak), Haiti 201/J2
Chaingy, Fr. 83/G5
Chainpur, Nepal 122/C1
Chaiya, Thai. 120/B4
Chaiyaphum, Thai. 120/C3
Chajarí, Arg. 212/E4
Chākāi, India 123/F3
Chakari, Zim. 149/F3
Chākdaha, India 123/G4
Chake Chake, Tanz. 145/B3
Chākia, India 122/D3
Chakradharpur, India 123/E4
Chakrāta, India 124/D4
Chakwāl, Pak. 124/B3
Chala, Peru 208/C4
Chalain (lake), Fr. 86/B4
Chalais, Swi. 86/D5
Chālakudi, India 121/C4
Chalamama, Bol. 209/E4
Chalaronne (riv.), Fr. 86/A5
Chalatenango, ESal. 200/D3
Chalbi (des.), Kenya 142/H5
Chalchihuites, Mex. 198/E4
Ch'alchīs (peak), Eth. 142/H3
Chalchyn (riv.), Mong. 105/H2
Chalco, Mex. 199/R10
Chale (pt.), Kenya 145/B3
Chaleur (bay), NB,,Qu, Can. 184/D2
Chalfont, Pa, US 194/C3
Chalfont Saint Giles, Eng, UK 56/B2
Chalfont Saint Peter, Eng, UK 56/B2
Chalhuanca, Peru 208/C4
Chali, China 112/C2
Chalifert (canal), Fr. 56/L5
Chalindrey, Fr. 86/B2
Chaling, China 113/G3
Chalinguita, Chile 212/B4
Chalinze, Tanz. 145/B3
Chālisgaon, India 121/B1
Chalk (mts.), Tx, US 177/C3
Chalk Hill (dam), Mi, US 183/L5
Chalk River, On, Can. 187/H1
Chalkar, Kaz. 97/J2
Chalkoi, India 124/C5
Challana, Bol. 208/D4
Challans, Fr. 70/C3
Challapalle, India 121/D2
Challapata, Bol. 212/C1
Challenger (mts.), Nun, Can. 167/T6
Challes-les-Eaux, Fr. 90/B1
Challis, Id, US 173/F1
Challock, Eng, UK 63/G4
Chalmette, La, US 190/D3
Chalna, Rus. 94/G3
Chālna, Bang. 123/G4
Chālna Port, Bang. 123/G4
Chalon-sur-Saône, Fr. 86/A4
Chalonnes-sur-Loire, Fr. 83/E6
Châlons-sur-Marne, Fr. 81/D6
Châlonvillars, Fr. 86/C2
Chaltyr', Rus. 99/K4
Chālūs, Iran 129/G2
Cham, Swi. 87/E3
Cham, Ger. 85/F4
Cham (riv.), Ger. 85/F4
Chama, Co, US 178/B2
Chama, Zam. 145/A4
Chama, NM, US 175/J2
Chama (riv.), NM, US 175/J2
Chamah (peak), Malay. 115/C1
Chaman, Pak. 127/J2
Chaman Bīd, Iran 129/J2
Chamba, India 124/D3
Chambal (riv.), India 118/C2
Chambaran (plat.), Fr. 70/F4
Chambas, Cuba 201/G1
Chamberino, NM, US 176/A1
Chamberlain (lake), Me, US 184/C2
Chamberlain, SD, US 180/E2
Chamberlain, Uru. 215/K10
Chamberlain, Sk, Can. 171/M2
Chamberlin (mt.), Ak, US 168/Y12
Chambers (bay), Austl. 154/C3
Chambers (isl.), Mi, US 183/L5
Chambers, Ne, US 180/E2
Chambers (cr.), Tx, US 177/F1
Chambers (co.), Tx, US 177/N9
Chambersburg, Pa, US 187/H5
Chambéry, Fr. 90/B1
Chambéry-Aix-les-Bains (arpt.), Fr. 90/B1
Chambeshi, Zam. 147/G5
Chambeshi (riv.), Zam. 147/G5
Chambeyron, Aiguille de (peak), Fr. 90/C3
Chambishi, Zam. 149/F2
Chamblee, Ga, US 189/M7
Chambly, Fr. 56/J4
Chambly, Qu, Can. 185/P7
Chambord, Fr. 83/G5
Chambourcy, Fr. 56/J5
Chambray-lès-Tours, Fr. 83/F6
Chambry, Fr. 56/L5
Chamchamāl, Iraq 129/F3
Chamechaude (peak), Fr. 90/B2
Chameis, Namb. 150/A2
Chamical, Arg. 212/C4
Chamigny, Fr. 56/M5
Chamizal Nat'l Mem., Tx, US 177/A2
Chamizo, Uru. 215/L11
Cha'mo Hāyk' (lake), Eth. 142/H4
Chamois, Mo, US 179/J1
Chamonix-Mont-Blanc, Fr. 86/C6
Champ-sur-Drac, Fr. 90/B2
Champagne (reg.), Fr. 68/C4
Champagne (Reims) (arpt.), Fr. 80/D5
Champagne-Ardenne (pol.reg), Fr. 70/F2
Champagne-sur-Oise, Fr. 56/J4
Champagney, Fr. 86/C2
Champagnole, Fr. 86/B4
Champaign, Il, US 186/B4
Champaqui (peak), Arg. 212/C4
Champasak, Laos 120/D3
Champawat, India 122/C1
Champdeuil, Fr. 56/L6
Champeaux, Fr. 56/L6
Champéry, Swi. 86/C5
Champex, Swi. 86/D5
Champhol, Fr. 83/G4
Champigneulles, Fr. 81/F6
Champigny-sur-Marne, Fr. 56/K5
Champion, Oh, US 186/F4
Champion, Ab, Can. 171/H2
Champlain, NY, US 187/K2
Champlain (lake), NY,Vt, US 169/M3
Champlin, Mn, US 183/P6
Champlitte, Fr. 86/B2
Champotón, Mex. 200/D2
Champotón (riv.), Mex. 200/D2
Champs-sur-Marne, Fr. 56/K5
Champsevraine, Fr. 86/B2
Champtoceaux, Fr. 82/D6
Champvans, Fr. 86/B3
Chāmrājnagar-Rāmasamudram, India 121/C4
Chamusca, Port. 72/A3
Chan Chan (ruin), Peru 208/B3
Chan May Dong (cape), Viet. 120/E2
Chana, Thai. 120/C5
Chañaral, Chile 212/B4
Chañaral, Chile 212/B3
Chança (riv.), Port. 72/B4
Chancay, Peru 208/B3
Chance Cove (pt.), Nf, Can. 185/L2
Chance Harbour, NB, Can. 184/D3
Chānchra, Bang. 123/H4
Chanco, Chile 214/B2
Chancy, Swi. 86/B5
Chandannagar, India 123/G4
Chandarpur, India 121/D1
Chandausi, India 122/B1
Chandeleur (isls.), La, US 190/D3
Chandeleur (sound), La, US 190/D3
Chanderi, India 122/B3
Chandīgarh (state), India 124/D4
Chandīgarh, India 124/D4
Chāndil, India 123/F4
Chandlees (riv.), Braz. 208/D3
Chandler, Qu, Can. 184/E1
Chandler, Az, US 175/G4
Chandler, In, US 188/D1
Chandler, Mn, US 181/G2
Chandler, Ok, US 179/F3
Chandler, Tx, US 177/G1
Chandolin, Swi. 86/D5
Chāndpur, India 122/B1
Chāndpur, Bang. 123/H4
Chandra Garhi, Nepal 123/G2
Chandrakona Road, India 123/F4
Chanduy, Ecu. 204/A5
Chang (riv.), China 103/L6
Chang (isl.), Camb. 119/H5
Chang (lake), China 106/C5
Chang (Yangtze) (riv.), China 106/D5
Chang Khoeng, Thai. 112/C5
Changan, SKor. 107/E5
Changanācheri, India 121/C4
Changane (riv.), Moz. 149/G4
Chang'anzhen, China 106/L9
Changara, Moz. 149/G3
Changbai (peak), China 107/E2
Changbai (mts.), NKor. 105/K3
Changbai Chaoxianzu Zizhixian, China 107/E2
Changchun, China 105/K3
Changdang (lake), China 106/D5
Changdao, China 106/E3
Changde, China 113/F2
Ch'angdo, NKor. 107/D3
Changé, Fr. 83/F5
Changeon (riv.), Fr. 83/F6
Changewater, NJ, US 194/D2
Changfeng, China 106/D4
Changgang, NKor. 107/D2
Changge, China 106/C4
Changgi-ap (cape), SKor. 110/A2
Changhai, China 107/B3
Changhang, SKor. 107/D4
Changhowŏn, SKor. 107/D4
Changhua, Tai. 113/J3
Changhŭng, SKor. 107/D5
Changhŭng, NKor. 107/E2
Changi (nbrhd.), Sing. 115/J6
Changi (int'l arpt.), Sing. 115/J6
Changis-sur-Marne, Fr. 56/M5
Changjiang, China 113/F5
Changjiang Zhongxiayou (plain), China 113/G2
Changjin (lake), NKor. 107/D2
Changjin (res.), NKor. 107/D2
Changjin, NKor. 107/D2
Changle, China 113/J2
Changle, China 106/D3
Changle, China 113/E2
Changli, China 106/D3
Changling, China 106/E1
Changlingji, China 113/G1
Changlingzi, China 107/B3
Changlingzi, China 105/J4
Changlingzi, China 105/J4
Changliushui, China 104/F4
Changlun, Malay. 120/C5
Changmar, China 125/C5
Changning, China 119/G3
Changning, China 112/E2
Ch'angnyŏng, SKor. 107/E5
Changping, China 106/H6
Changp'ung-ŭp, NKor. 107/D3
Changqing, China 106/D3
Changsan-got (cape), NKor. 107/C3
Changsha, China 113/G2
Changshan, China 113/H4
Changshan (arch.), China 105/J4
Changsheng, China 113/G3
Changshoudian, China 113/G2
Changshu, China 106/L8
Changshun, China 113/E3
Changsŏng, SKor. 107/D5
Changsu, SKor. 107/D5
Changsŭngp'o, SKor. 107/E5
Changtu, China 106/F2
Changuinola, Pan. 201/F4
Changweiliang, China 104/C4
Ch'angwŏn, SKor. 107/E5
Changwu, China 104/F4
Changxing, China 106/K8
Changyang, China 113/F2
Changyi, China 106/D3
Changyŏn, NKor. 107/C3
Changyuan, China 106/C4
Changzhi, China 106/C3
Changzhou, China 106/K8
Chanhassen, Mn, US 183/N7
Chankanai, SrL. 121/C4
Chanlers (falls), Kenya 145/B1
Channapatna, India 121/C3
Channel (isls.), UK 55/D4
Channel Country (phys. reg.), Austl. 153/C3
Channel Islands NP, Ca, US 192/A3
Channel Islands NP, Ca, US 174/C3
Channel Tunnel (tun.), Eng, UK,Fr. 63/H5
Channel-Port aux Basques, Nf, Can. 185/H2
Channelview, Tx, US 177/M9
Channing, Tx, US 178/C3
Chantada, Sp. 72/B1
Chanteloup-les-Vignes, Fr. 56/J5
Chantepie, Fr. 82/D4
Chanthaburi, Thai. 120/C3
Chantilly, Fr. 80/B5
Chantraine, Fr. 86/C1
Chantrey (inlet), Nun, Can. 166/G2
Chanute, Ks, US 179/G2
Chao (riv.), China 104/H3
Chao (lake), China 106/D5
Chao, Peru 208/B3
Chao Phraya (riv.), Thai. 120/C3
Chaobai (riv.), China 105/H4
Chaor (riv.), China 105/J2
Chaoyang, China 113/H4
Chaoyang, China 106/E2
Chaozhou, China 113/H4
Chap Le, Viet. 120/D2
Chapacura, Bol. 208/D3
Chapada Diamantina, PN, Braz. 211/E2
Chapada dos Guimarães, Braz. 210/B2
Chapada dos Veadeiros, PN da, Braz. 210/D2
Chapadinha, Braz. 207/F3
Chapala (lake), Mex. 198/E4
Chapala, Mex. 198/E4
Chapará (riv.), Bol. 212/C1
Chaparé (riv.), Bol. 209/E5
Chapareillan, Fr. 90/B2
Chaparral, Col. 204/C4
Chaparrosa, Mex. 198/E4
Chapayev, Kaz. 97/J2
Chapayevsk, Rus. 97/J1
Chapecó, Braz. 213/F3
Chapecó (riv.), Braz. 213/F3
Chapel en le Frith, Eng, UK 61/G5
Chapel Hill, Tn, US 188/D3
Chapel Hill, Ga, US 189/L7
Chapel Hill, NC, US 189/H3
Chapel Ness (pt.), Sc, UK 59/D4
Chapel Saint Leonards, Eng, UK 61/J5
Chapelfell Top (peak), Eng, UK 61/F2
Chapelle-lez-herlaimont, Belg. 81/D3
Chapeltown, Eng, UK 61/G5
Chaplain (lake), Wa, US 193/D2
Chapleau, On, Can. 167/H4
Chaplin, Sk, Can. 171/L2
Chaplin (riv.), Ky, US 188/E2
Chaplygin, Rus. 96/F1
Chapman, Ks, US 179/F1
Chapman, Al, US 190/E2
Chapmanville, WV, US 189/F2
Chaponost, Fr. 90/A1
Chappār, India 124/D5
Chappell, Ne, US 180/C3
Chāpra, India 123/E3
Char (well), Mrta. 136/B5
Char Gāzi, Bang. 123/H4
Chara, Rus. 101/M4
Chara (riv.), Rus. 101/M4
Charagua, Bol. 212/D1
Charagua, Par. 213/E2
Charambirá (pt.), Col. 204/B3
Charaña, Bol. 212/B1
Charandra (riv.), Gre. 75/N8
Ch'arants'avan, Arm. 129/F1
Charata, Arg. 212/D3
Charbon, Austl. 159/D1
Charcas, Mex. 199/E4
Charcot (isl.), Ant. 216/U
Chard, Eng, UK 62/D5
Chardon, Oh, US 186/F4
Chardonnière, Haiti 201/H2
Charente (riv.), Fr. 92/C1
Chargrām, Bang. 119/F3
Chari (riv.), Chad 133/D3
Chari-Baguirmi (pref.), Chad 142/B3
Chārīkār, Afg. 127/J1
Charikot, Nepal 123/F2
Chariton (riv.), Mo,Ia, US 181/H3
Chariton, Ia, US 181/H3
Charity, Guy. 205/G3
Chārjew, Trkm. 100/G6
Charkhāri, India 122/B3
Charkhi Dādri, India 124/D5
Charlbury, Eng, UK 63/E3
Charlemagne, Qu, Can. 185/P6
Charlemont, NI, UK 60/B3
Charleroi, Belg. 81/D3
Charleroi, Pa, US 187/G4
Charleroi à Bruxelles, Canal de (canal), Belg. 81/D2
Charles (isl.), Qu, Can. 167/J2
Charles (hill), Il, US 181/J2
Charles (pt.), Austl. 154/C3
Charles (peak), Austl. 156/D5
Charles (mt.), Austl. 156/C3
Charles (cape), Va, US 189/K2
Charles City, Ia, US 181/H2
Charles City, Va, US 189/J2
Charles de Gaulle (int'l arpt.), Fr. 56/K4
Charles Fuhr, Arg. 215/C6
Charles H. Russell NWR, Mt, US 182/A4
Charles M. Russell Nat'l Wild Ref., Mt, US 171/L4
Charles Town, WV, US 187/H5
Charleston, Ar, US 179/G3
Charleston, Il, US 186/B5
Charleston, Mo, US 188/C2
Charleston, Ms, US 188/B3
Charleston, Nv, US 172/F3
Charleston (peak), Nv, US 174/E2
Charleston, SC, US 189/H4
Charleston (A.F.B.), SC, US 189/G4
Charleston (cap.), WV, US 189/G1
Charlestown, StK. 197/N8
Charlestown, NH, US 187/K3
Charlestown, In, US 188/E1
Charlestown, Md, US 194/C4
Charleval, Fr. 83/G2
Charleville, Austl. 160/B4
Charleville-Mézières, Fr. 81/D4
Charlevoix, Mi, US 186/D2
Charlevoix (lake), Mi, US 186/D2
Charlotte (lake), BC, Can. 170/B1
Charlotte (har.), Fl, US 191/G4
Charlotte, Mi, US 186/D3
Charlotte, Tn, US 188/D2
Charlotte, Vt, US 187/K2
Charlotte, NC, US 189/G3
Charlotte, Tx, US 176/E3
Charlotte Amalie, USVI 197/M8
Charlotte Court House, Va, US 189/H2
Charlotte Hall, Md, US 189/J1
Charlotte/douglas (int'l arpt.), NC, US 189/G3
Charlottenberg, Swe. 66/E2
Charlottenburg, Ger. 68/Q6
Charlottesville, Va, US 189/H1
Charlottetown (cap.), PE, Can. 184/F2
Charlotteville, Trin. 205/F2
Charlton, Austl. 158/B3
Charlton (isl.), On, Can. 167/H3
Charlton Kings, Eng, UK 62/D3
Charlwood, Eng, UK 56/C3
Charly, Fr. 80/C6
Charly, Fr. 90/A1
Charmco, WV, US 189/G1
Charmes (res.), Fr. 86/B2
Charmes, Fr. 86/C1
Charmes-sur-Rhône, Fr. 90/A3
Charmey, Swi. 86/D4
Charnay-lès-Mâcon, Fr. 70/F3
Charny, Qu, Can. 184/B2
Charny, Fr. 56/L5
Charny-sur-Meuse, Fr. 81/E5
Charolais, Monts du (mts.), Fr. 70/F3
Charouine, Alg. 137/E3
Charquemont, Fr. 86/C3
Chars, Fr. 56/H4
Chārsadda, Pak. 124/A2
Charsk, Kaz. 125/D2
Charters Towers, Austl. 160/B3
Charthāwāl, India 124/D5
Chartres, Fr. 83/G4
Chartres, UK 215/E6
Chartres-de-Bretagne, Fr. 82/D4
Charvieu-Chavagneux, Fr. 90/B1
Charyn (riv.), Kaz. 125/C3
Charysh (riv.), Rus. 125/D1
Chās, India 123/F4
Chaschauna (peak), Swi. 87/G4
Chascomús, Arg. 214/F2
Chase, BC, Can. 170/E2
Chase, Ks, US 179/E1
Chase, La, US 190/C1
Chase City, Va, US 189/H2
Chase Lake NWR, ND, US 182/E4
Chase Nav. Air Sta., Tx, US 177/F3
Chashniki, Bela. 67/N4
Chasicó, Arg. 214/C4
Chasiv Yar, Ukr. 99/J3
Chaska, Mn, US 183/N7
Chaslands Mistake (pt.), NZ 161/B4
Chasŏng, NKor. 107/D2
Chasovo, Rus. 95/L3
Chassahowitzka (bay), Fl, US 190/K6
Chassahowitzka, Fl, US 190/K6
Chassahowtzka Nat'l Wildlife Ref., Fl, US 191/G3
Chasse-sur-Rhône, Fr. 90/A1
Chassezac (riv.), Fr. 70/F4
Chastre-Villeroux-Blanmont, Belg. 81/D2
Chatauqua (lake), Il, US 181/J3
Chatawa, Ms, US 190/C2
Château (pt.), Fr. 82/B3
Chateau de Mores Historical Site, ND, US 182/C4
Chateau de Versailles, Fr. 56/J5
Château d'If, Fr. 90/B6
Château-Arnoux, Fr. 90/C4
Château-d'Olonne, Fr. 70/C3
Château-du-Loir, Fr. 83/F5

Château-Gontier, Fr. 83/E5
Château-la-Vallière, Fr. 83/F5
Château-Porcien, Fr. 81/D4
Château-Renault, Fr. 83/F5
Château-Salins, Fr. 81/F6
Château-Thierry, Fr. 80/C5
Châteaubourg, Fr. 82/D4
Châteaubriant, Fr. 82/D5
Châteaudun, Fr. 83/G4
Chateaugay, NY, US 187/J2
Châteaugiron, Fr. 82/D4
Châteauguay (co.), Qu, Can. 185/N7
Châteauguay, Qu, Can. 185/N7
Châteaulin, Fr. 82/A4
Châteauneuf-de-Gadagne, Fr. 90/A5
Châteauneuf-de-Galaure, Fr. 90/A2
Châteauneuf-du-Faou, Fr. 82/B4
Châteauneuf-du-Pape, Fr. 90/A4
Châteauneuf-du-Rhône, Fr. 90/A4
Châteauneuf-en-Thymerais, Fr. 83/G3
Châteauneuf-les-Martigues, Fr. 90/B6
Châteauneuf-sur-Charente, Fr. 70/C4
Châteauneuf-sur-Isère, Fr. 90/A2
Châteauneuf-sur-Sarthe, Fr. 83/E5
Châteaurenard, Fr. 90/A5
Châteauroux, Fr. 70/D3
Châteauvillain, Fr. 86/A1
Châtel-Saint-Denis, Swi. 86/C4
Châtelaillon-Page, Fr. 70/C3
Châtelet, Belg. 81/D3
Châtellerault, Fr. 70/D3
Châtenay-Malabry, Fr. 56/J5
Châtenois, Fr. 86/B1
Châtenois-les-Forges, Fr. 86/C2
Chatfield, Mn, US 181/H2
Chatham, NB, Can. 184/E2
Chatham, On, Can. 186/E3
Chatham (isls.), Chile 215/B6
Chatham (isls.), NZ 161/E4
Chatham, Eng, UK 63/G4
Chatham, Il, US 181/K4
Chatham, La, US 179/H4
Chatham, Mi, US 183/L4
Chatham, NJ, US 195/H9
Chatham, NY, US 187/K3
Chatham, Va, US 189/H2
Chathill, Eng, UK 59/E5
Châtillon, It. 90/D1
Châtillon, Fr. 56/J5
Châtillon-sur-Chalaronne, Fr. 86/A5
Châtillon-sur-Marne, Fr. 80/C5
Châtillon-sur-Seine, Fr. 70/F3
Chātmohar, Bang. 123/G3
Chatom, Al, US 190/D2
Chaton (mtn.), Austl. 159/D2
Chatou, Fr. 56/J5
Chatra, India 123/E3
Chatra, Nepal 123/F2
Châtres, Fr. 56/L5
Chatrūd, Iran 129/J4
Chatswood (nbrhd.), Austl. 160/H8
Chatsworth, Il, US 186/B4
Chatsworth (res.), Ca, US 192/B2
Chatsworth (nbrhd.), Ca, US 192/E7
Chatsworth, Ga, US 188/E3
Chatsworth, NJ, US 194/D4
Chatsworth, Zim. 149/F3
Chattahoochee, Fl, US 191/F2
Chattahoochee (riv.), Ga, US 196/D1
Chattahoochee (riv.), Ga, US 189/L7
Chattanooga, Ok, US 179/E3
Chattanooga, Tn, US 188/E3
Chattaroy, WV, US 189/F2
Chattaroy, Wa, US 170/F4
Chatte, Fr. 90/B2
Chattenden, Eng, UK 56/E2
Chatteris, Eng, UK 63/G2
Chattooga (riv.), Ga, US 189/F3
Chatuzange-le-Goubet, Fr. 90/B3
Chau Doc, Viet. 120/D4
Chaúa, Ang. 146/D5
Chaucey (isl.), Fr. 70/C2
Chauconin-Neufmontiers, Fr. 56/L5
Chaudfontaine, Belg. 81/E2
Chaudière (riv.), Qu, Can. 184/B2
Chauk, Myan. 112/B4
Chaukan (pass), India 112/C3
Chaulk, Eng, UK 56/E2
Chaumes-en-Brie, Fr. 56/L5
Chaumont, Fr. 86/B1
Chaumont-en-Vexin, Fr. 80/A5
Chaumont-sur-Lloire, Fr. 83/G6
Chaungwabyin, Myan. 120/B3
Chaungzon, Myan. 120/B2
Chaunskaya (bay), Rus. 101/T3
Chauny, Fr. 80/C4
Chaupāran, India 123/E3
Chaussin, Fr. 86/B4
Chaussy, Fr. 56/H4
Chausy, Bela. 96/D1
Chautara, Nepal 123/E2
Chautauqua (lake), NY, US 187/G3
Chautauqua Nat'l Wild. Ref., Il, US 181/J3
Chauvigny, Fr. 70/D3
Chauvin, Ab, Can. 171/J1
Chavakali, Kenya 145/A1
Chavakkad, India 121/C4
Chaval, Braz. 207/F3
Chavanay, Fr. 90/A2
Chavan'ga, Rus. 94/H2
Chavanoz, Fr. 86/B6
Chavarría, Arg. 212/E4
Chaves, Port. 72/B2
Chaves, Braz. 206/D3
Chavière, Montagne de la (peak), Fr. 90/B4
Chavies, Ky, US 189/F2
Chavín de Huantar (ruin), Peru 208/B3
Chaviña, Peru 208/C4
Chavinillo, Peru 208/B3
Chavornay, Swi. 86/C4
Chavuma (falls), Zam. 148/D2
Chawinda, Pak. 124/C3
Chay (riv.), Viet. 120/D1
Chayanta, Bol. 212/C1
Chayanta (riv.), Bol. 212/C1
Chaykovskiy, Rus. 95/M4
Chazuta, Peru 208/B2
Chazy, NY, US 187/K2
Chbar, Camb. 120/D3
Cheadle, Eng, UK 61/G6
Cheaha (mtn.), Al, US 188/E4
Cheam View, BC, Can. 170/D3
Cheat (riv.), WV, US 189/H1
Cheb, Czh. 85/F2
Cheben'ki, Rus. 97/K2
Cheboksary (res.), Rus. 95/K4
Cheboksary, Rus. 95/K4
Cheboygan, Mi, US 186/D2
Chechaouene (prov.), Mor. 138/B2
Chechaouene, Mor. 138/B2
Chechel'nyk, Ukr. 98/E3
Chechen' (isl.), Rus. 97/H3
Chechërsk, Bela. 96/D1
Chechevichi, Bela. 67/N5
Chechnya Aut. Rep., Rus. 100/Q6
Chech'ŏn, SKor. 107/E4
Checotah, Ok, US 179/G3
Chécy, Fr. 83/H5
Chedabucto (bay), NS, Can. 185/G3
Cheddar, Eng, UK 62/D4
Cheduba (isl.), Myan. 119/F4
Cheduba (str.), Myan. 112/B5
Cheekpoint, Ire. 58/D5
Cheektowaga, NY, US 186/V10
Chefumage (riv.), Ang. 148/D1
Chegdomyn, Rus. 105/L1
Chegutu, Zim. 149/F3
Chehalis (riv.), Wa, US 170/C4
Chehalis, Wa, US 170/C4
Chehalis Ind. Res., Wa, US 170/C4
Chehe, China 113/E3
Chehel Dokhtarān, Afg. 127/H1
Cheïkh (well), Alg. 137/F3
Cheiron, Montagne du (mts.), Fr. 90/C5
Cheju (str.), SKor. 105/K5
Cheju (isl.), SKor. 105/K5
Cheju (int'l arpt.), SKor. 105/K5
Cheju, SKor. 105/K5
Chekhov, Rus. 96/F1
Chekhov, Rus. 105/N2
Chelan (lake), Wa, US 170/D3
Chelan, Wa, US 170/D4
Chelan NRA, Wa, US 170/D3
Cheleken, Trkm. 129/H2
Chelford, Eng, UK 61/F5
Chelghoum El Aïd, Alg. 138/J4
Chelles, Fr. 56/K5
Chełm, Pol. 69/M3
Chełm (prov.), Pol. 69/M3
Chełmno, Pol. 69/K2
Chelmsford, Ma, US 187/L3
Chelmsford, Eng, UK 63/G3
Chelmuzhi, Rus. 94/G3
Chełmża, Pol. 69/K2
Chelsea (nbrhd.), Austl. 158/G6
Chelsea, Qu, Can. 187/J2
Chelsea (nbrhd.), Eng, UK 56/C2
Chelsea, Al, US 188/D4
Chelsea, Ok, US 179/G2
Chelsea, Vt, US 187/K3
Cheltenham, On, Can. 186/T8
Cheltenham, Eng, UK 62/D3
Chelva, Sp. 73/E3
Chelyabinsk, Rus. 95/P5
Chelyabinsk (oblast), Rus. 95/P5
Chelyabinsk (int'l arpt.), Rus. 95/P5
Chelyuskina (cape), Rus. 101/L2
Chemaïa, Mor. 136/C2
Chemal, Rus. 125/E1
Chemax, Mex. 200/E1
Chemba, Moz. 149/G3
Chembe, Zam. 149/F1
Chemehuevi Ind. Res., Ca, US 174/E3
Chemillé, Fr. 83/E6
Chemnitz, Ger. 68/G3
Chemult, Or, US 172/C2
Chen (riv.), China 113/F3
Chen Baraq Qi, China 105/H2
Chenāb (riv.), Pak. 127/K2
Chenachane (well), Alg. 136/D4
Chenango (riv.), NY, US 187/J3
Chenārān, Iran 127/G1
Ch'ench'a, Eth. 142/H4
Chencheng, China 113/H4
Cheney (res.), Ks, US 179/F2
Cheney, Wa, US 170/F4
Cheneyville, La, US 190/B2
Chenfang, China 113/H2
Cheng (lake), China 112/D3
Cheng'anpu, China 106/C3
Chengbu Miaozu Zizhixian, China 113/F3
Chengde, China 105/H3
Chengde, China 106/D2
Chengdu (int'l arpt.), China 112/D2
Chengdu, China 112/E2
Chengele, India 112/C2
Chengjiang, China 113/G3
Chengkou, China 113/H3
Chengkou, China 113/F2
Chengmai, China 113/F5
Chengshan Jiao (cape), China 107/B4
Chengwu, China 106/C4
Chengxiangzhen, China 113/H2
Chengzitan, China 107/B3
Cheniménil, Fr. 86/C1
Chenjiazhen, China 106/L8
Chennai (Madras), India 121/D3
Chennevières-lès-Louvres, Fr. 56/K4
Chenòve, Fr. 86/A3
Chenxi, China 113/F2
Chenxiangtun, China 107/B2
Chenzhou, China 113/G3
Chep Lak Kok (int'l arpt.), China 113/K7
Chepelare, Bul. 75/J2
Chepén, Peru 208/B2
Chépénéhé, NCal. 163/V12
Chepes, Arg. 212/C4
Chépica, Chile 214/C2
Chepigana, Pan. 204/B2
Cheploske, Kenya 145/A1
Chepo, Pan. 204/B2
Chepstow, Wal, UK 62/D3
Cheptsa (riv.), Rus. 95/M4
Cher (dept.), Fr. 83/H6
Cher (riv.), Fr. 92/D1
Chéran (riv.), Fr. 86/C6
Cherasco, It. 88/A3
Cherāt, Pak. 124/A3
Cheraw, Co, US 178/C1
Cheraw, Ms, US 190/D2
Cheraw, SC, US 189/H3
Cherbourg, Fr. 82/D1
Cherbourg, Austl. 160/C4
Cherchell, Alg. 138/G4
Cherdyn', Rus. 95/N3
Chère (riv.), Fr. 82/D5
Cheremisskoye, Rus. 95/P4
Cheremkhovo, Rus. 104/E1
Cheremshan, Rus. 95/L5
Cheremshanka, Rus. 95/P4
Cherëmushi (nbrhd.), Rus. 94/W9
Cherepovets, Rus. 94/H4
Cherevkovo, Rus. 95/K3
Cherf, Oued (riv.), Alg. 138/K6
Cheria, Alg. 138/K7
Cherikov, Bela. 96/D1
Cherkas'ka (prov.), Ukr. 96/D2
Cherkasy, Ukr. 98/G3
Cherkessk, Rus. 99/M5
Chermignon, Swi. 86/D5
Chermside (nbrhd.), Austl. 160/F6
Chern', Rus. 96/F1
Chernaya, Rus. 95/M1
Chernaya (riv.), Rus. 95/N1
Cherni Lom (riv.), Bul. 77/H4
Cherni Vrŭkh (peak), Bul. 77/F4
Chernigovskaya, Rus. 99/K5
Chernihiv, Ukr. 98/F2
Chernivets'ka (prov.), Ukr. 96/C2
Chernivtsi, Ukr. 98/C3
Chernomorskiy, Rus. 99/K5
Chernorechenskiy, Rus. 95/M3
Chernukha, Rus. 95/J5
Chernushka, Rus. 95/N4
Chernyakhiv, Ukr. 98/E2
Chernyakhovsk, Rus. 67/J4
Chernyanka, Rus. 99/J2
Chernyshevsk, Rus. 104/H1
Chernyshevskiy, Rus. 101/M3
Chernyy Otrog, Rus. 97/L2
Chernyy Yar, Rus. 97/H2
Cherokee, Al, US 188/D3
Cherokee, Ks, US 179/G2
Cherokee, Ia, US 181/G2
Cherokee, Ok, US 179/E2
Cherokee (lake), Tn, US 189/F2
Cherokee, Tx, US 177/E2
Cherrueix, Fr. 82/D3
Cherry (cr.), SD, US 180/D1
Cherry Creek, BC, Can. 170/D2
Cherry Creek, Nv, US 173/F4
Cherry Creek, SD, US 180/D1
Cherry Hill, Ar, US 179/H3
Cherry Hill, NJ, US 194/C4
Cherry Hill, Md, US 194/C4
Cherry Point MCAS, NC, US 189/J3
Cherry Valley, Ca, US 192/D3
Cherry Valley, Ar, US 188/B3
Cherryvale, Ks, US 179/G2
Cherryville, NC, US 189/G3
Cherski (range), Rus. 103/P3
Cherskiy, Rus. 101/R3
Chertanovo (nbrhd.), Rus. 94/W9
Chertkovo, Rus. 99/L3
Chertsey, Eng, UK 56/B2
Cherven', Bela. 67/N5
Cherven Bryag, Bul. 77/G4
Chervlënnaya, Rus. 97/H4
Chervone, Ukr. 99/H2
Chervonoarmiys'k, Ukr. 98/C2
Chervonohrad, Ukr. 98/C2
Chervonozavods'ke, Ukr. 99/G2
Cherwell (riv.), Eng, UK 63/E3
Chesaning, Mi, US 186/D3
Chesapeake (bay), US 169/L4
Chesapeake, WV, US 189/G1
Chesapeake, Va, US 189/J2
Chesapeake and Delaware (canal), De,Md, US 194/C4
Chesapeake and Ohio Nat'l Hist. Park, Md, US 187/H5
Chesapeake Bay Maritime Museum, Md, US 194/B6
Chesapeake City, Md, US 194/C4
Chesham, Eng, UK 63/F3
Cheshire (co.), Eng, UK 61/F5
Cheshire (plain), Eng, UK 61/F5
Cheshskaya (bay), Rus. 100/E3
Cheshunt, Eng, UK 56/C1
Chesilhurst, NJ, US 194/D4
Chesley, On, Can. 186/F2
Chester, Eng, UK 61/F5
Chester, Ar, US 179/G3
Chester, Ca, US 172/C3
Chester (riv.), De,Md, US 189/J1
Chester, Ga, US 189/F4
Chester, Id, US 173/H2
Chester, Il, US 188/C2
Chester (riv.), Md, US 194/B5
Chester, Mt, US 171/J3
Chester, Ne, US 180/F3
Chester, NJ, US 194/D2
Chester, Ok, US 178/E2
Chester, Pa, US 194/C4
Chester (cr.), Pa, US 194/C4
Chester (co.), Pa, US 194/C4
Chester, SC, US 189/G3
Chester, Tx, US 177/G2
Chester, Vt, US 187/K3
Chester Basin, NS, Can. 184/E3
Chester County G.O. Carlson (arpt.), Pa, US 194/C4
Chester Heights, Pa, US 194/C4
Chester Morse (lake), Wa, US 193/D3
Chester-le-Street, Eng, UK 61/G2
Chesterfield (inlet), Nun, Can. 165/H3
Chesterfield, Eng, UK 61/G5
Chesterfield (isls.), NCal. 162/E6
Chesterfield, Id, US 173/H2
Chesterfield, In, US 186/D4
Chesterfield, Mo, US 181/J4
Chesterfield, SC, US 189/G3
Chesterfield, Va, US 189/J2
Chesterfield Inlet, Nun, Can. 166/G2
Chesterton (range), Austl. 160/B4
Chestertown, NY, US 187/K3
Chestertown, Md, US 194/B5
Chesuncook (lake), Me, US 184/C2
Cheswold, De, US 194/C5
Chetaibi, Alg. 138/K6
Chetek, Wi, US 183/J5
Chéticamp, NS, Can. 185/G2
Chetopa, Ks, US 179/G2
Chetumal (bay), Mex. 196/D4
Chetumal, Mex. 200/D2
Chetwynd, BC, Can. 166/D3
Cheung Chau (isl.), China 113/K8
Chevak, Ak, US 168/W12
Cheval-Blanc, Fr. 90/B5
Chevejécure, Bol. 209/E4
Chevelon (cr.), Az, US 175/G3
Cheverny, Fr. 83/G5
Chevigny-Saint-Sauveur, Fr. 86/B3
Chevilly, Fr. 83/G4
Cheviot (hills), Sc, UK 59/D6
Cheviot, NZ 161/C3
Chèvre (cape), Fr. 82/A4
Chevreuse, Fr. 56/J5
Chèvreville, Fr. 56/L4
Chevry-Cossigny, Fr. 56/K5
Chew (riv.), Eng, UK 62/D4
Ch'ew Bahir (lake), Eth. 142/H4
Chew Valley (lake), Eng, UK 62/D4
Chewelah, Wa, US 170/F3
Chewore Game Rsv., Zim. 149/F2
Chexbres, Swi. 86/C5
Cheyenne, Ok, US 178/E3
Cheyenne (riv.), SD,Wy, US 180/D1
Cheyenne (cap.), Wy, US 180/B3
Cheyenne River Ind. Res., SD, US 180/E1
Cheyenne Wells, Co, US 178/C1
Cheyres, Swi. 86/C4
Chezacut, BC, Can. 170/B1
Chhabra, India 122/A3
Chhāin, India 118/B2
Chhaprauli, India 124/D5
Chhāta, India 122/A2
Chhātak, Bang. 123/H3
Chhatarpur, India 122/B3
Chhatarpur, India 123/E3
Chhibrāmau, India 122/B2
Chhindwāra, India 122/B4
Chhukha, Bhu. 123/G2
Chi (riv.), Thai. 119/H4
Chi Ne, Viet. 112/E4
Chía, Col. 207/L8
Chiafua, Ang. 147/E5
Chiai, Tai. 113/J4
Ch'iak-san NP, SKor. 107/E4
Chiali, Tai. 113/J4
Chiampo, It. 89/E2
Chianciano Terme, It. 74/B1
Chiang Dao, Thai. 112/C5
Chiang Dao Caves, Thai. 112/C5
Chiang Kai Shek (int'l arpt.), Tai. 113/J3
Chiang Kham, Thai. 120/C2
Chiang Khan, Thai. 120/C2
Chiang Mai, Thai. 112/C5
Chiang Rai, Thai. 112/C5
Chiang Saen, Thai. 112/D4
Chiange, Ang. 148/B2
Chiani (riv.), It. 91/B2
Chianti (reg.), It. 89/E5
Chianti (mts.), It. 89/E5
Chiapa de Corzo, Mex. 200/C2
Chiapas (state), Mex. 196/C4
Chiappa (pt.), It. 88/C5
Chiaravalle, It. 89/G6
Chiari, It. 88/C2
Chiascio (riv.), It. 91/B1
Chiasso, Swi. 87/F6
Chiat'ura, Geo. 97/G4
Chiautempan, Mex. 199/L7
Chiautla, Mex. 199/R9
Chiautla de Tapia, Mex. 200/B2
Chiavari, It. 88/C5
Chiavenna, It. 87/F5
Chiawa, Zam. 149/F2
Chiba, Japan 111/G3
Chibabava, Moz. 149/G4
Chibakou, China 113/G2
Chibemba, Ang. 148/B2
Chibi, Zim. 149/F4
Chibia, Ang. 148/B2
Chibougamau, Qu, Can. 167/J4
Chibuni, India 112/C2
Chibuto, Moz. 149/G5
Chibwe, Zam. 149/F2
Chic-Chocs (mts.), Qu, Can. 184/D1
Chicago, Il, US 186/C4
Chicago Heights, Il, US 193/Q16
Chicago Midway (int'l arpt.), Il, US 186/C4
Chicago Ridge, Il, US 193/Q16
Chicago Sanitary and Ship Canal, Il, US 193/P16
Chicago, North Branch (riv.), Il, US 193/Q15
Chicago-O'Hare (int'l arpt.), Il, US 186/C4
Chicala, Ang. 148/C1
Chicama, Peru 208/B2
Chicapa (riv.), Ang. 146/D5
Chichagof (isl.), Ak, US 166/C3
Chichaoua, Mor. 136/C3
Chīchāwatni, Pak. 124/B4
Chichén Itzá (ruin), Mex. 200/D1
Chicheng, China 104/H3
Chichester, Eng, UK 63/F5
Chichester (range), Austl. 153/A3
Chichibu, Japan 111/F3
Chichicastenango, Guat. 200/D3
Chichigalpa, Nic. 200/E3
Chichihualco, Mex. 199/F5
Chichiriviche, Ven. 204/D2
Chichishima (isls.), Japan 162/D2
Chichocane, Moz. 149/G4
Chichola, India 121/D1
Chickamauga, Ga, US 188/E3
Chickamauga (lake), Tn, US 188/E3
Chickamauga and Chattanooga Nat'l Mil. Park, Tn, US 188/E3
Chickasaw, Al, US 190/D2
Chickasaw Nat'l Rec. Area, Ok, US 179/F3
Chickasawhay (riv.), Ms, US 188/C5
Chickasha, Ok, US 179/F3
Chickerell, Eng, UK 62/D5
Chickies (cr.), Pa, US 194/B3
Chicla, Peru 208/B3
Chiclana de la Frontera, Sp. 72/B4
Chiclayo, Peru 208/B2
Chico (riv.), Arg. 203/B7
Chico, Ca, US 172/C4
Chico (riv.), Phil. 114/C1
Chicoloapan, Mex. 199/R10
Chicomo, Moz. 149/G5
Chicomostoc (ruin), Mex. 198/E4
Chicomuselo, Mex. 200/C3
Chiconcuac, Mex. 199/R9
Chicontepec de Tejeda, Mex. 200/B1
Chicopee, Ma, US 187/K3
Chicot (pt.), La, US 190/D3
Chicota, Tx, US 179/G4
Chicote, Ang. 148/D3
Chicoutimi, Qu, Can. 184/B1
Chicoutimi (riv.), Qu, Can. 184/B1
Chicualacuala, Moz. 149/F4
Chicului (riv.), Ang. 148/D2
Chicuma, Ang. 148/B2
Chidambaram, India 121/C4
Chiddingstone, Eng, UK 56/D3
Chidenguele, Moz. 149/G5
Chidester, Ar, US 179/H4
Chidley (cape), Nf, Can. 167/K2
Chido, SKor. 107/D5
Chief Joseph (pass), Mt, US 173/G1
Chiefland, Fl, US 191/G3
Chiem Hoa, Viet. 120/D1
Chiemsee (lake), Ger. 68/G5
Chieo Lan (res.), Thai. 119/G6
Chieri, It. 88/A2
Chierry, Fr. 80/C5
Chiers (riv.), Fr. 81/E5
Chiesa in Valmalenco, It. 87/F5
Chiese (riv.), It. 71/J3
Chieti (prov.), It. 92/D3
Chieti, It. 92/D3
Chietla, Mex. 199/L8
Chieueley, Eng, UK 63/E4
Chièvres, Belg. 80/C2
Chifre, Serra do (mts.), Braz. 211/E3
Chiganak, Kaz. 125/B2
Chigasaki, Japan 111/F3
Chignahuapan, Mex. 199/L7
Chignecto (bay), NB,NS, Can. 184/E3
Chigorodó, Col. 204/B3
Chigu (lake), China 123/H1
Chiguana, Bol. 212/C2
Chigubo, Moz. 149/G4
Chigwell, Eng, UK 56/D2
Chihayaakasaka, Japan 109/J7
Chihli (Bo Hai) (gulf), China 101/M6
Chihuahua, Mex. 177/A3
Chihuahua (state), Mex. 198/D2
Chiili, Kaz. 100/G5
Chiipperfield, Eng, UK 56/B2
Chijiang, China 113/G3
Chikanda, Nga. 141/F4
Chikaskia (riv.), Ks,Ok, US 179/F2
Chikhachëvo, Rus. 67/N3
Chikhli, India 118/C3
Chikmagalūr, India 121/B3
Chikoy (riv.), Rus. 101/L5
Chikoy, Rus. 104/F1
Chikugo (riv.), Japan 110/B4
Chikuma (riv.), Japan 111/F2
Chikwa, Zam. 149/G1
Chikwawa, Malw. 149/G3
Chila, Ang. 148/B2
Chilac, Mex. 199/M8
Chilakalūrupet, India 121/D2
Chilanga, Zam. 149/F2
Chilanko Forks, BC, Can. 170/B1
Chilās, Pak. 124/C2
Chilbo-san (peak), NKor. 107/E2
Chilca, Peru 208/B4
Chilcoot, Ca, US 172/C4
Chilcotin (riv.), BC, Can. 166/D3
Chilcotin (riv.), BC, Can. 170/C2
Childers, Austl. 160/D4
Childersburg, Al, US 188/D4
Childress, Tx, US 178/D3
Chile(ctry.) 203/B6
Chile Chico, Chile 214/C5
Chile, Monte el (peak), Hon. 200/E3
Chilecito, Arg. 212/C4
Chilembwe, Zam. 149/F2
Chilete, Peru 208/B2
Ch'ilgap-san NP, SKor. 107/D4
Chililabombwe, Zam. 149/E2
Chilka (lake), India 118/E4
Chilko (lake), BC, Can. 166/D3
Chilko (riv.), BC, Can. 170/B2
Chilla Well Abor. Land, Austl. 157/F2
Chillagoe, Austl. 160/B2
Chillán, Chile 214/B3
Chillanes, Ecu. 208/B1
Chilleurs-aux-Bois, Fr. 83/H4
Chillicothe, Tx, US 178/E3
Chillicothe, Oh, US 186/E5
Chillicothe, Mo, US 181/H4
Chillicothe, Il, US 181/K3
Chillisquaque (cr.), Pa, US 194/B2
Chilliwack, BC, Can. 170/D3
Chillon, Swi. 86/C5
Chilly, Id, US 173/G1
Chilly-Mazarin, Fr. 56/J5
Chiloé (isl.), Chile 203/B7
Chiloé, PN, Chile 214/B4
Chilombo, Ang. 148/D2
Chiloquin, Or, US 172/C2
Chilpancingo de los Bravos, Mex. 199/F5
Chilpi, India 122/C4
Chiltern (hills), Eng, UK 63/E3
Chiltern, Austl. 159/C3
Chiltern Hundreds (reg.), Eng, UK 56/A2
Chilton, Wi, US 186/B2
Chilton, Tx, US 177/F2
Chiluage, Ang. 147/E5
Chilumba, Malw. 145/A4
Chilung (Keelung), Tai. 113/J3
Chilung La (pass), India 124/D3
Chilwa (lake), Malw. 149/G2
Chimacum, Wa, US 193/B1
Chimakothi, Bhu. 123/G2
Chimalhuacán, Mex. 199/R10
Chimaliro (hill), Malw. 145/A4
Chimaltenango, Guat. 200/D3
Chiman, India 124/C4
Chimán, Pan. 204/B2
Chimanimani, Zim. 149/G3
Chimanimani NP, Moz. 149/G3
Chimantá-Tepuí (peak), Ven. 205/F3
Chimay, Belg. 81/D3
Chimayo, NM, US 175/K2
Chimbay, Uzb. 100/F5
Chimboa, Ang. 148/B2
Chimborazo (dept.), Ecu. 204/B5
Chimborazo (vol.), Ecu. 204/B5
Chimbote, Peru 208/B3
Chimbu (prov.), PNG 155/G1
Chimichaqua, Col. 204/C2
Chimney (peak), NM, US 178/B4
Chimney Rock, Co, US 175/J2
Chimney Rock (peak), Ne, US 180/C3
Chimney Rock Nat'l Hist. Site, Ne, US 180/C3
Chimoio, Moz. 149/G3
Chin (hills), Myan. 112/B4
Chin (state), Myan. 119/F3
Chin (isl.), SKor. 105/K5
China(ctry.) 103/J6
China, Mex. 200/D2
China (cape), Sing. 115/J7
China, Mex. 199/F3
China Lake Nav. Weapons Ctr., Ca, US 174/D3
Chinácota, Col. 204/C3
Chinamba (hills), Bots. 148/E3
Chinan, SKor. 107/D5
Chinandega, Nic. 200/E3
Chinati (mts.), Tx, US 177/B3
Chinati (peak), Tx, US 177/B3
Chincha Alta, Peru 208/B4
Chinchaga (riv.), Ab,BC, Can. 166/E3
Chinchilla, Austl. 160/C4
Chinchilla, Sp. 72/E3
Chinchiná, Col. 207/K8
Chinch'ŏn, SKor. 107/D4
Chinchón, Sp. 72/D2
Chinchoua, Gabon 146/B2
Chincoteague, Va, US 189/K2
Chincoteague NWR, Md, US 189/K1
Chinde, Moz. 149/H3
Chindo, SKor. 107/D5
Chindrieux, Fr. 86/B6
Chindu, China 104/D4
Chindwin (riv.), Myan. 119/F3
Chinecto Game Sanctuary, NS, Can. 184/E3
Chineni, India 124/C3
Chingaza, PN, Col. 204/C3
Chingford (nbrhd.), Eng, UK 56/D2
Chingirlau, Kaz. 97/K2
Chingleput, India 121/C3
Chingola, Zam. 149/E2
Chinguar, Ang. 148/C2
Chinhae, SKor. 107/E5
Chinhoyi, Zim. 149/F3
Chinhoyi Caves, Zim. 149/F3
Chiniak (cape), Ak, US 168/X13
Chiñijo, Bol. 208/D4
Chiniot, Pak. 124/B4
Chinit (riv.), Camb. 120/D3
Chinju, SKor. 107/E5
Chinko (riv.), CAfr. 142/E4
Chinle, Az, US 175/H2
Chinle Wash (riv.), Az, US 175/H2
Chinnor, Eng, UK 63/F3
Chino, Ca, US 192/C2
Chino, Japan 111/F3
Chino (hills), Ca, US 192/G8
Chino (valley), Az, US 175/F3
Chino Valley, Az, US 175/F3
Chino Wash (riv.), Az, US 175/F3
Chinook (lake), Or, US 172/C1
Chinook, Wa, US 170/C4
Chinook, Mt, US 171/K3
Chinook, Ab, Can. 171/J2
Chinsali, Zam. 147/H5
Chintāmani, India 121/C3
Chintheche, Malw. 149/G1
Chinú, Col. 204/C2
Chinunje, Tanz. 149/H1
Chiny, Belg. 81/E4
Chinyama Litapi, Zam. 148/D2
Chinyingi, Zam. 148/D2
Chinyŏng, SKor. 107/E5
Chioggia, It. 89/F3
Chip (lake), Ab, Can. 170/G1
Chipaque, Col. 207/L8
Chipasanse, Zam. 147/G5
Chipata, Zam. 149/G2
Chipatá, Col. 204/C3
Chiperceni, Mol. 98/E4
Chiperone (peak), Moz. 149/G3
Chipeta, Ang. 148/C2
Chipindo, Ang. 148/B2
Chiping, China 106/D3
Chipinge, Zim. 149/G4
Chipiona, Sp. 72/B4
Chipley, Fl, US 191/F2
Chipman, NB, Can. 184/E2
Chipman, Ab, Can. 171/H1
Chipogolo, Tanz. 145/B3
Chipoka, Malw. 149/G2
Chipola (riv.), Fl, US 191/F2
Chiponde, Malw. 149/G2
Chippenham, Eng, UK 62/D4
Chippewa (riv.), Mn, US 181/G1
Chippewa (riv.), Wi, US 181/H1
Chippewa (lake), Wi, US 183/J5
Chippewa Falls, Wi, US 181/J1
Chippewa Lake, Mi, US 186/D3
Chippewa, East Branch (riv.), Mn, US 181/G1
Chipping Campden, Eng, UK 63/E2
Chipping Norton, Eng, UK 63/E3
Chipping Ongar, Eng, UK 56/D1
Chiprovtsi, Bul. 76/F4
Chipstead, Eng, UK 56/C3
Chīpurupalle, India 121/D2
Chiputneticook Lakes, NB, Can. 184/D3
Chiquián, Peru 208/B3
Chiquimula, Guat. 200/D3
Chiquimulilla, Guat. 200/D3
Chiquinquirá, Col. 207/M7
Chiquita (sea), Arg. 203/C6
Chira, Gha. 141/E5
Chiradzulu, Malw. 149/G2
Chirakkal, India 121/B4
Chiran (peak), Fr. 90/C5
Chīrāpātla, India 122/A4
Chirāwa, India 124/C5
Chirchiq, Uzb. 125/A3
Chire (riv.), Moz. 149/G3
Chiredzi, Zim. 149/F4
Chireno, Tx, US 177/G2
Chirfa, Niger 134/B4
Chīrgaon, India 122/B3
Chiri-san (peak), SKor. 107/D5
Chiri-san NP, SKor. 107/D5
Chiricahua (peak), Az, US 175/H5
Chiricahua Nat'l Mon., Az, US 198/C1
Chiriguaná, Col. 204/C2
Chirikof (isl.), Ak, US 168/X13
Chirimatá, Ven. 206/A1
Chirimena, Ven. 207/P7
Chirinos, Peru 208/B2
Chirip (peak), Rus. 108/E1
Chiripa (peak), Nic. 201/E4
Chiriquí (gulf), Pan. 196/E6
Chiriquí (lag.), Pan. 201/F4
Chiriquí Grande, Pan. 201/F4
Chirk, Eng, UK 61/E6
Chirkunda, India 123/F4
Chirnside, Sc, UK 59/D5
Chiromo, Malw. 149/G3
Chironico, Swi. 87/E5
Chirpan, Bul. 77/G4
Chirripó (mtn.), CR 201/F4
Chirripó, PN, CR 196/E6
Chirundu, Zim. 149/F3
Chiryu, Japan 109/M6
Chisamba, Zam. 149/F2
Chisasa, Zam. 148/E2
Chisasibi (Fort-George), Qu, Can. 167/J3
Chiseldon, Eng, UK 63/E3
Chisenga, Malw. 145/A4
Chishi, China 113/H2
Chisholm, Mn, US 183/H4
Chisholm, Tx, US 176/L7
Chishtiān Mandi, Pak. 124/B5
Chishui, China 112/E2
Chishui (riv.), China 112/E3
Chisimayu (Kismaayo), Som. 145/C2
Chisimba (falls), Zam. 147/G5
Chişinău (int'l arpt.), Mol. 98/E4
Chişinău (cap.), Mol. 98/E4
Chişineu Criş, Rom. 76/E2
Chisomo, Zam. 149/F2
Chisone (riv.), It. 90/D3
Chistopol', Rus. 95/L5
Chiswell Green, Eng, UK 56/B1
Chiswick (nbrhd.), Eng, UK 56/C2
Chita, Bol. 212/C2
Chita, Col. 204/C3
Chita (pen.), Japan 109/L6
Chita (bay), Japan 109/L6
Chita, Japan 109/L6
Chita, Rus. 104/G1
Chita (int'l arpt.), Rus. 104/G1
Chitado, Ang. 148/B3
Chitato, Ang. 147/E4
Chitek (lake), Mb, Can. 182/E1
Chitembo, Ang. 148/C2
Chitimacha Ind. Res., La, US 190/C3
Chitipa, Malw. 145/A4
Chitmanikārbārīpāra, Bang. 123/J4
Chitobiço, Moz. 149/G4
Chitongo, Zam. 149/E3
Chitose, Japan 108/B2
Chitose (int'l arpt.), Japan 108/B2
Chitrakut, India 122/C3
Chitrāl, Pak. 124/A2
Chitral Gol NP, Pak. 124/A2
Chitré, Pan. 204/A3
Chittagong (pol. div.), Bang. 123/H4
Chittagong, Bang. 119/F3
Chittaranjan, India 123/F4
Chittaurgarh, India 118/B3
Chitungwiza, Zim. 149/F3
Chíuchíu, Chile 212/B2
Chiuduno, It. 88/C2
Chiueca, Ang. 148/C2
Chiumbe (riv.), Ang. 147/E5
Chiumbo, Ang. 148/C2
Chiume, Ang. 148/D2
Chiundaponde, Zam. 149/F2
Chiuppano, It. 89/E2
Chiusa (Klausen), It. 87/H4
Chiusa di Pesio, It. 88/A4
Chiusano di San Domenico, It. 92/D6
Chiusella (riv.), It. 88/A1
Chiusi, It. 91/A1
Chivacoa, Ven. 204/D2
Chivasso, It. 88/A2
Chivato (pt.), Mex. 198/C3
Chivay, Peru 208/D4
Chivé, Bol. 208/D4
Chivhu, Zim. 149/F3
Chivilcoy, Arg. 214/E2
Chivurúcua, Ang. 148/B2
Chiwanda, Tanz. 149/G1
Chixoy (riv.), Guat. 200/D3
Chiyoda, Japan 109/E1
Chiyoda, Japan 109/C1
Chiyokawa, Japan 109/D1
Chizarira (hills), Zim. 149/E3
Chizarira NP, Zim. 149/E3
Chizela, Zam. 148/E2
Chizha, Rus. 95/K2
Chkalovo, Ukr. 99/H4
Chkalovsk, Rus. 94/J4
Chlef (wilaya), Alg. 138/F4
Chlef (riv.), Alg. 138/F4
Chlef, Alg. 138/F4
Chloride, Az, US 175/E3
Chlum (peak), Czh. 85/H5
Chno Dearg (peak), Sc, UK 59/B3
Cho Moi, Viet. 120/D4
Cho Oyu (peak), Nepal 123/F1
Choachí, Col. 207/M8
Choam Khsant, Camb. 120/D3
Choapa (riv.), Chile 212/B4
Choate, Tx, US 177/F3
Chobe (riv.), Bots. 148/E3
Chobe (dist.), Bots. 148/E3
Chobe NP, Bots. 148/E3
Chobham, Eng, UK 56/B3
Chocaya, Bol. 212/C2
Choceň, Czh. 69/J4
Choch'iwŏn, SKor. 107/D4
Chocianów, Pol. 69/H3
Chocó (dept.), Col. 201/G5
Chocolate (mts.), Ca, US 174/E4
Chocolate Bayou (riv.), Tx, US 177/M9
Chocolate Mountains Aerial Gunnery Range, Ca, US 174/E4
Chocontá, Col. 204/C3
Chocope, Peru 208/B2
Choctaw Ind. Res., Ms, US 188/C4
Choctawhatchee (riv.), Fl, US 191/F2
Chodavaram, India 121/D2
Chodov, Czh. 85/F2
Chodzież, Pol. 69/J2
Choele Choel, Arg. 214/D3
Chōfu, Japan 111/F3
Ch'ŏgjin -si (prov.), NKor. 107/E2
Choiseul (isl.), Sol. 162/E5
Choisy-au-Bac, Fr. 80/B5
Choisy-le-Roi, Fr. 56/K5
Choix, Mex. 198/C3
Chojna, Pol. 69/H2
Chojnice, Pol. 66/G5
Chojnów, Pol. 69/H3
Chok Chai, Thai. 120/C3
Chokai-san (peak), Japan 108/B4
Ch'ok'ē (mts.), Eth. 142/H3
Choke Canyon (res.) Tx, US 177/E3
Chokio, Mn, US 182/F5
Chokoloskee, Fl, US 191/H5
Chokurdakh, Rus. 101/Q2
Chokwe, Moz. 149/G5
Chola (mts.), China 104/D5
Cholame, Ca, US 174/B3
Cholesbury, Eng, UK 56/B1
Cholila, Arg. 214/C4
Chŏlla-bukto (prov), SKor. 107/D5
Ch'ŏlla-namdo (prov), SKor. 107/D5
Ch'ŏlsan, NKor. 107/C3
Cholsey, Eng, UK 63/E3
Cholula de Rivadabia, Mex. 199/L7
Choluteca (riv.), Hon. 196/D5
Choluteca, Hon. 200/E3
Chom Bung, Thai. 120/B3
Chom Thong, Thai. 120/B2
Choma, Zam. 149/E3
Chŏmch'on, SKor. 107/E4
Chomérac, Fr. 90/A3
Chomo Lhāri (peak), Bhu. 123/G2
Chomutov, Czh. 85/G2
Chomutovka (riv.), Czh. 85/G2
Chon Buri, Thai. 120/C3
Chon Daen, Thai. 120/C2
Chon Thanh, Viet. 120/D4
Ch'ŏnan, SKor. 107/D4
Chōnan, Japan 109/E3
Chonchi, Chile 214/B4
Ch'ŏnch'ŏn, NKor. 107/D2
Chone, Ecu. 204/A5
Chong Kal, Camb. 120/C3
Ch'ŏng-yang, SKor. 107/D4
Ch'ŏngan, SKor. 107/D4
Ch'ŏngch'ŏn (riv.), NKor. 107/D2
Ch'ŏngdan, NKor. 107/C4
Chongde, China 106/L9
Ch'ŏngdo, SKor. 107/E5
Ch'ŏngjin, NKor. 107/E2
Chŏngju, SKor. 107/D5
Ch'ŏngju, SKor. 107/D4
Chŏngju, NKor. 107/C3
Chongkü, China 112/C2
Chongli, China 106/C2
Chongming (isl.), Asia 105/J5
Chongmyo Shrine, SKor. 107/G6
Chongo, Zam. 149/E3
Chongoroi, Ang. 148/B2
Chongoyape, Peru 208/B2
Chŏngp'yŏng, NKor. 107/D3
Chongqing, China 113/E2
Chongren, China 113/H3
Chŏngsŏn, SKor. 107/E4
Ch'ŏngsong, SKor. 110/A2
Ch'ŏngsŏng-Nodongjagu, NKor. 107/C2
Chongwe, Zam. 149/F2
Chongwu, China 113/H3
Chongyang, China 113/G2
Chongyi, China 119/K2
Chongzuo, China 113/E4
Chŏnju, SKor. 107/D5
Ch'ónma-san (peak), SKor. 107/G6
Ch'ŏnnae, NKor. 107/D3
Chonos, Archipiélago de los (arch.), Chile 214/B5
Chopan, India 122/D3
Choptank (riv.), Md, US 189/J1
Choquecamata, Bol. 209/E5
Choquecota, Bol. 212/C1
Chorcha (mtn.), Pan. 201/F4
Chorges, Fr. 90/C3
Chorhāt, India 122/C3
Chorley, Eng, UK 61/F4
Chorleywood, Eng, UK 56/B2
Chornobayivka, Ukr. 98/G4
Chornobyl', Ukr. 98/F2
Chornomors'ke, Ukr. 98/G5
Chornukhine, Ukr. 99/K3
Chornukhy, Ukr. 99/G2
Choroní, Ven. 207/N7
Choroszcz, Pol. 69/M2
Chortkiv, Ukr. 98/C3
Ch'ŏrwŏn, NKor. 107/D3
Ch'ŏrwŏn, SKor. 107/D3
Chorzele, Pol. 69/L2
Chorzów, Pol. 69/K3
Chos-Malal, Arg. 214/C3
Ch'osan, NKor. 107/C2
Chōsei, Japan 109/E3
Chōshi, Japan 111/G3
Choshui (riv.), Tai. 113/J4
Choszczno, Pol. 69/H2
Chota, Peru 208/B2
Chota Nagpur (plat.), India 118/D3
Choteau, Mt, US 171/H4
Chott el Rharbi (depr.), Alg. 138/D3
Chotýšanka (riv.), Czh. 85/H3
Choûm, Mrta. 136/B5
Choushuidun, China 104/D3
Chouteau, Ok, US 179/G2
Chouzé-sur-Loire, Fr. 83/F6
Chouzy-sur-Cisse, Fr. 83/G5
Chowagasberg (peak), Namb. 148/B5
Chowan (riv.), NC, US 189/J2
Chowchilla, Ca, US 174/B2
Chowchilla (riv.), Ca, US 174/B2
Choyang-nodongjagu, NKor. 107/D3
Choybalsan, Mong. 104/G2
Choyr, Mong. 104/F2
Chreïrik (well), Mrta. 136/B5
Chrisman, Il, US 186/C5
Christchurch (int'l arpt.), NZ 161/C3
Christchurch, Eng, UK 63/E5
Christchurch (bay), Eng, UK 63/E5
Christchurch, NZ 161/C3
Christiana, Jam. 201/G2
Christiana, SAfr. 150/D2
Christiana, Pa, US 194/C4
Christiana, De, US 194/C4
Christiansburg, Va, US 189/G2
Christiansfeld, Den. 66/C4
Christiansted, USVI 197/M8
Christina, Mt, US 171/K4
Christina (riv.), De, US 194/C5
Christine, ND, US 182/F4
Christine, Tx, US 176/E3
Christmas (isl.), Austl. 103/K11
Christmas (cr.), Austl. 154/B4
Christmas (isl.), Kiri. 163/K4
Christmas, Az, US 175/G4
Christopher, Il, US 188/C2
Christoval, Tx, US 177/D2
Chromo, Co, US 175/J2
Chrudim, Czh. 69/H4
Chrysler, Al, US 190/E2
Chryston, Sc, UK 59/B5
Chrzanów, Pol. 69/K3
Chu (riv.), Viet. 120/D2
Chu Yang Sin (peak), Viet. 120/E3
Chua Chu Kang (nbrhd.), Sing. 115/H6
Chuādanga, Bang. 123/G4
Chualar, Ca, US 174/B2
Chuanchang, China 113/H3
Chuansha, China 106/L8
Chuanshi, China 113/H3
Chuave, PNG 155/G1
Chubbuck, Id, US 173/G2
Chubut (riv.), Arg. 203/C7
Chubut (prov.), Arg. 214/C4
Chucanti (peak), Pan. 204/B2
Chuchkovo, Rus. 97/G1
Chudovo, Rus. 67/P2
Chūgoku (mts.), Japan 110/C3
Chūgoku (prov.), Japan 110/B4
Chugwater, Wy, US 180/B3
Chugwater (cr.), Wy, US 180/B3
Chūhar Kāna, Pak. 124/B4
Chuhuyiv, Ukr. 99/J3
Chukai, Malay. 115/C1
Chukch (sea), Asia, NAm. 101/U3
Chukchagirskoye (lake), Rus. 105/M1
Chukchi (sea), Rus. 103/T3
Chukchi (pen.), Rus. 103/T3
Chukotka Aut. Okrug, Rus. 101/S3
Chukou, China 113/G3
Chukuni (riv.), On, Can. 183/H2
Chula, Ga, US 191/G2
Chula Vista, Ca, US 192/C5
Chul'man, Rus. 101/N4
Ch'ulp'o, SKor. 107/D5
Chulucanas, Peru 208/A2
Chulym (riv.), Rus. 100/J4
Chulyshman (riv.), Rus. 104/B1
Chum Phae, Thai. 120/C2
Chuma, Bol. 208/D4
Chūmar, India 127/L2
Chumbicha, Arg. 212/C4
Chumerna (peak), Bul. 77/G4
Chumikan, Rus. 101/P4

243

Chump – Colón

Chumphon, Thai. 120/B4
Chumsaeng, Thai. 120/C3
Chumunjin, SKor. 107/E4
Chuna (riv.), Rus. 100/K4
Chunan, Tai. 113/J3
Chunār, India 122/D3
Chunchi, China 113/H3
Ch'unch'ŏn, SKor. 107/D4
Chunchula, Al, US 190/D2
Ch'ungch'ŏng-bukto (prov.), SKor. 107/D4
Ch'ungch'ŏng-namdo (prov.), SKor. 107/D4
Chunggang, NKor. 107/D2
Chunghsinghsintsun, Tai. 113/J4
Chunghwa, NKor. 107/C3
Ch'ungju, SKor. 107/D4
Ch'ungju (lake), SKor. 110/A2
Ch'ungmu, SKor. 107/E5
Chungnang (nbrhd.), SKor. 107/G6
Chŭngsan, NKor. 107/C3
Chungu, Zam. 147/G5
Chunheji, China 113/G1
Chunhuhub, Mex. 200/D2
Chūniān, Pak. 124/B4
Chunky, Ms, US 188/C4
Chunshui, China 113/G4
Chunya (riv.), Rus. 101/L3
Chunya, Tanz. 145/A4
Ch'unyang, SKor. 107/E4
Chupa, Rus. 94/G2
Chupa, Peru 208/D4
Chupaca, Peru 208/C4
Chupadera Mesa (mesa), NM, US 178/A3
Chupakhivka, Ukr. 99/H2
Chuprovo, Rus. 95/K2
Chuquibamba, Peru 208/C4
Chuquibambilla, Peru 208/C4
Chuquicamata, Chile 212/B2
Chuquichambi, Bol. 212/C1
Chuquichuqui, Bol. 212/C1
Chuquisaca (dept.), Bol. 212/C2
Chur, Swi. 87/F4
Churachandpur, India 112/B3
Churcampa, Peru 208/C4
Church, Eng, UK 61/F4
Church Crookham, Eng, UK 56/A3
Church Hill, Md, US 194/C5
Church Point, La, US 190/B2
Church Stretton, Eng, UK 62/D1
Churchbridge, Sk, Can. 182/D2
Churchill, Austl. 159/C4
Churchill (riv.), Can. 165/H4
Churchill (cape), Mb, Can. 166/G3
Churchill (riv.), Sk, Can. 166/F3
Churchill (lake), Sk, Can. 166/F3
Churchill, Mb, Can. 166/G3
Churchill (peak), BC, Can. 166/D3
Churchill Downs, Ky, US 188/E1
Churchill Falls, Nf, Can. 167/K3
Churchill NP, Austl. 158/G5
Churchville, Va, US 189/H1
Churchville, Md, US 194/B4
Churia Ghats (mts.), Nepal 123/E2
Churín, Peru 208/B3
Churnet (riv.), Eng, UK 61/G5
Churu, India 124/C5
Churubusco, In, US 186/D4
Churuguara, Ven. 204/D2
Churumuco de Morelos, Mex. 199/E5
Churwalden, Swi. 87/F4
Chuschi, Peru 208/C4
Chushul, India 125/C5
Chusovaya (riv.), Rus. 95/N4
Chusovoy, Rus. 95/N4
Chute-aux-Outardes, Qu, Can. 184/C1
Chutove, Ukr. 99/H3
Chutyr', Rus. 95/M4
Chuvashia Aut. Rep., Rus. 100/Q6
Chuviscar (riv.), Mex. 177/B3
Chuwang-san NP, SKor. 110/A2
Chuxiong, China 112/D3
Chuya (riv.), Rus. 104/B1
Chuzhou, China 113/H1
Chūzu, Japan 109/K5
Chvalšiny, Czh. 85/H5
Chyhyryn, Ukr. 98/G3
Ci Xian, China 106/C3
Ciadîr-lunga, Mol. 77/J2
Ciamis, Indo. 115/E3
Ciampino, It. 91/B4
Ciampino (int'l arpt.), It. 91/B4
Cianjur, Indo. 115/D3
Cianorte, Braz. 213/F2
Cibecue, Az, US 175/G3
Cibola Nat'l Wild Ref., Az,Ca, US 174/E4
Cicagna, It. 88/C5
Cicciano, It. 92/D6
Cicero, Il, US 186/C4
Cicero (peak), SD, US 180/C2
Cícero Dantas, Braz. 211/F1
Ćićevac, Yugo. 76/E4
Cide, Turk. 96/E4
Ciechanów, Pol. 69/L2
Ciechanow (prov.), Pol. 69/L2
Ciechocinek, Pol. 69/K2
Ciego de Ávila, Cuba 201/G1
Ciénaga, Col. 204/C2
Ciénaga de Oro, Col. 204/C2
Ciénega de Flores, Mex. 177/D5
Cienfuegos, Cuba 201/F1
Cieplice Śląskie Zdrój, Pol. 69/H3
Cieszyn, Pol. 69/K4
Cieza, Sp. 72/E3
Çifteler, Turk. 128/B2
Cifuentes, Cuba 201/F1
Cifuentes, Sp. 72/D2
Cifuncho, Chile 212/B3
Cigánd, Hun. 69/L4
Cigliano, It. 88/B3
Cigno (riv.), It. 92/D4
Cigüela (riv.), Sp. 72/D3
Cihanbeyli, Turk. 128/C2
Cihuatlán, Mex. 198/D5
Cijara (res.), Sp. 72/C3
Cijulang, Indo. 115/E3
Cilacap, Indo. 115/E3
Cilavegna, It. 88/B3
Çıldır (lake), Turk. 97/G4
Ciledug, Indo. 115/E3
Cilfaesty (peak), Wal, UK 62/C2
Cilleros, Sp. 72/B2
Cima, Ca, US 174/E3
Cima della Laurasca (peak), It. 87/E5
Cima de'Piazzi (peak), It. 87/G5
Cima la Casina (peak), It. 87/G4
Cimahi, Indo. 115/D3
Cimarron (range), NM, US 178/B2
Cimarron, Ks, US 178/D2
Cimarron (cr.), NM, US 178/B2
Cimarron (riv.), Ks,Ok, US 168/G4
Cimarron, Co, US 175/J1
Cimarron, North Fork (riv.), Co,Ks, US 178/C2
Cime de Gélas (peak), Fr. 90/D4
Cime de Marte (peak), Fr. 90/D4
Cime des Torches (peak), Fr. 90/C2
Cime du Cheiron (peak), Fr. 90/C5
Cime du Diable (peak), Fr. 90/D4
Cimino (peak), It. 91/B3
Cimişlia, Mol. 98/E4
Cimone (peak), It. 89/D5
Cîmpeni, Rom. 77/F2
Cîmpia Turzii, Rom. 77/F2
Cîmpina, Rom. 77/G3
Cîmpulung, Rom. 77/G3
Cîmpulung Moldovenesc, Rom. 98/C4
Cina (cape), Indo. 115/D3
Çınar, Turk. 128/E2
Çınarcık, Turk. 77/J5
Cinaruco (riv.), Ven. 204/D3
Cinca (riv.), Sp. 92/D2
Cincar (peak), Bosn. 76/C4
Cincinnati, Oh, US 188/E1
Cinco Chañares, Arg. 214/D4
Cinco Saltos, Arg. 214/C3
Cinderford, Eng, UK 62/D3
Cîndrelu (peak), Rom. 77/F3
Çine, Turk. 128/B2
Ciney, Belg. 81/E3
Cingia de'Botti, It. 88/D3
Cingoli, It. 89/G7
Cinisello Balsamo, It. 88/C2
Cinnaminson, NJ, US 194/D4
Cinq-mars-la-Pile, Fr. 83/F6
Cintalapa de Figueroa, Mex. 200/C2
Cinto (peak), Fr. 74/A1
Cinto Caomaggiore, It. 89/F2
Cintruénigo, Sp. 72/E1
Čiovo (isl.), Cro. 76/C4
Cipatujah, Indo. 115/D3
Cipolletti, Arg. 214/D3
Circeo (peak), It. 92/C5
Circeo Parco Nazionale del, It. 74/C2
Circle, Mt, US 171/M4
Circleville, Oh, US 186/E5
Circleville, Ut, US 175/F1
Circleville, Ks, US 181/G4
Circuata, Bol. 209/E5
Cirebon, Indo. 115/E3
Cirencester, Eng, UK 62/E3
Cires-lès-Mello, Fr. 80/B5
Ciriè, It. 90/D2
Cirò Marina, It. 75/E3
Ciron (riv.), Fr. 70/C4
Ciruas, Indo. 115/D3
Cisco, Tx, US 177/E1
Ciserano, It. 88/C2
Cisnădie, Rom. 77/G3
Cisne, Il, US 188/C1
Cisneros, Col. 204/C3
Cisnes (riv.), Chile 214/B5
Cisse (riv.), Fr. 70/D3
Cissna Park, Il, US 186/C4
Cistern, Tx, US 177/F3
Cisterna di Latina, It. 91/B4
Cistierna, Sp. 72/C1
Cité de Kassa, Gui. 140/B4
Citlaltépetl (vol.), Mex. 199/M7
Citra, Fl, US 191/G3
Citronelle, Al, US 190/D2
Citrus (co.), Fl, US 190/L6
Citrus Heights, Ca, US 172/C4
Citrus Park, Fl, US 190/K7
Citrusdal, SAfr. 150/L10
Città del Vaticano (cap.), VatC. 91/B4
Città della Pieve, It. 91/B2
Città di Castello, It. 89/F7
Citta di Torino (int'l arpt.), It. 90/D2
Cittadella, It. 89/E2
Cittaducale, It. 92/B3
Cittanova, It. 74/E3
Citta'sant'angelo, It. 92/D2
Cittiglio, It. 87/E6
City (int'l arpt.), NI, UK 60/C2
City (isl.), NY, US 195/K8
City Beach (nbrhd.), Austl. 156/K6
Ciudad Acuña, Mex. 177/D3
Ciudad Altamirano, Mex. 199/E5
Ciudad Bolívar, Ven. 205/F2
Ciudad Bolivia, Ven. 204/D2
Ciudad Camargo, Mex. 177/E4
Ciudad Camargo, Mex. 198/D3
Ciudad Constitución, Mex. 198/C3
Ciudad Cortés, CR 201/F4
Ciudad Cuauhtémoc, Mex. 200/B1
Ciudad de Dolores Hidalgo, Mex. 199/E4
Ciudad de Loreto, Arg. 212/C4
Ciudad de México (Mexico) (cap.), Mex. 199/Q10
Ciudad de Nutrias, Ven. 204/D2
Ciudad de Río Grande, Mex. 198/E4
Ciudad del Carmen, Mex. 200/D2
Ciudad del Este, Par. 213/F3
Ciudad del Maíz, Mex. 199/F4
Ciudad Delicias, Mex. 177/B3
Ciudad Fernández, Mex. 199/E4
Ciudad Frontera, Mex. 177/D4
Ciudad Guayana, Ven. 205/F2
Ciudad Guzmán, Mex. 198/E5
Ciudad Hidalgo, Mex. 200/C3
Ciudad Hidalgo, Mex. 199/E5
Ciudad Insurgentes, Mex. 198/C3
Ciudad Ixtepec, Mex. 200/C2
Ciudad Juárez, Mex. 177/A2
Ciudad Lerdo, Mex. 198/E3
Ciudad Madero, Mex. 200/B1
Ciudad Mante, Mex. 199/F4
Ciudad Mendoza, Mex. 199/M8
Ciudad Miguel Alemán, Mex. 177/E4
Ciudad Obregón, Mex. 198/C3
Ciudad Ojeda, Ven. 204/D2
Ciudad Pemex, Mex. 200/C2
Ciudad Piar, Ven. 205/F3
Ciudad Real, Sp. 72/D3
Ciudad Rodrigo, Sp. 72/B2
Ciudad Serdán, Mex. 199/M8
Ciudad Valles, Mex. 200/B1
Ciudad Victoria, Mex. 199/F4
Ciutadella de Menorca, Sp. 73/G3
Civa Burnu (pt.), Turk. 96/F4
Civate, It. 88/C2
Civezzano, It. 87/H5
Cividale del Friuli, It. 71/K3
Cividate Camuno, It. 87/G6
Civita Castellana, It. 91/B3
Civitavecchia, It. 74/B1
Civitella del Tronto, It. 92/C2
Civitella Roveto, It. 92/C4
Civray, Fr. 70/D3
Çivril, Turk. 128/B2
Cixi, China 106/L9
Cize, Fr. 86/B4
Cizre, Turk. 128/E2
Cizre (dam), Turk. 128/E2
Cizur, Sp. 72/E1
Clackamas (riv.), Or, US 172/B1
Clackmannan, Sc, UK 59/C4
Clacton-on-Sea, Eng, UK 63/H3
Claerwen (res.), Wal, UK 62/C2
Claflin, Ks, US 179/E1
Claiborne (lake), La, US 177/H1
Claiborne, Md, US 194/B6
Claie (riv.), Fr. 82/C5
Clain (riv.), Fr. 70/D3
Clair Engle (lake), Ca, US 172/B3
Claire (lake), Ab, Can. 166/E3
Clairefontaine-en-Yvelines, Fr. 56/H6
Clairette, Tx, US 177/E1
Clairton, Pa, US 187/G4
Clairvaux-les-Lacs, Fr. 86/B4
Claise (riv.), Fr. 70/D3
Clallam (co.), Wa, US 193/A2
Clallam Bay, Wa, US 170/B3
Clamart, Fr. 56/J5
Clamecy, Fr. 70/E3
Clancy, Mt, US 171/J4
Clandeboye, Mb, Can. 182/F2
Clandonald, Ab, Can. 171/J1
Clane, Ire. 58/D3
Clanfield, Eng, UK 63/F5
Clanton, Al, US 188/D4
Clanwilliam, Mb, Can. 182/E2
Clanwilliam, SAfr. 150/B4
Claonig, Sc, UK 59/A5
Clapier (peak), Fr. 90/D4
Clapier du Peyron (peak), Fr. 90/C3
Clara (pt.), Arg. 214/D4
Clara, Arg. 212/E4
Clara, Ire. 58/C3
Clara, Ms, US 190/D2
Clara City, Mn, US 181/G1
Claravale, Austl. 154/C3
Clarcona, Fl, US 190/N6
Clare (riv.), Ire. 58/B3
Clare (isl.), Ire. 56/N10
Clare (co.), Ire. 58/B4
Clare, Mi, US 186/D3
Clare, Austl. 158/B2
Clare, Austl. 157/H5
Clarée (riv.), Fr. 90/C2
Claregalway, Ire. 58/B3
Claremont (pt.), Austl. 155/F3
Claremont, Ca, US 192/C2
Claremont, SD, US 182/E5
Claremont, NH, US 187/K3
Claremore, Ok, US 179/G2
Claremorris, Ire. 58/A2
Clarence (riv.), Austl. 158/D4
Clarence, La, US 190/B2
Clarence, NZ 161/C3
Clarence, Mo, US 181/H4
Clarence (str.), Austl. 154/C3
Clarence, NY, US 186/V9
Clarence (pt.), Nun, Can. 167/T7
Clarence Cannon (dam), Mo, US 181/J4
Clarence Cannon Nat'l Wildlife Res., Mo, US 179/J1
Clarence Cannon Nat'l Wild. Ref., Mo, US 181/J4
Clarence Town, Bahm. 197/G3
Clarence Town, Austl. 159/E1
Clarendon, Tx, US 178/D3
Clarendon, Ar, US 179/J3
Clarenville, Nf, Can. 185/L1
Claresholm, Ab, Can. 171/H2
Clarinda, Ia, US 181/G3
Clarington, Oh, US 186/F5
Clarion, Pa, US 187/G4
Clarion, Ia, US 181/H2
Clarion (isl.), Mex. 198/B5
Clarissa, Mn, US 183/G4
Clark, NJ, US 195/H9
Clark, Wy, US 173/J1
Clark, SD, US 180/F1
Clark (mtn.), Wa, US 170/D3
Clark, Tx, US 177/G2
Clark (cr.), Pa, US 194/B3
Clark Canyon (dam), Mt, US 173/G1
Clark Canyon (res.), Mt, US 173/G1
Clark Fk. (riv.), Mt, US 171/H4
Clark Fork (riv.), Id, US 166/E4
Clark Fork, Id, US 170/F3
Clark Fork (riv.), Mt, US 170/G3
Clark Mil. Res., Mo, US 179/G2
Clarkdale, Az, US 175/F3
Clarkdale, Ga, US 189/L7
Clarke (range), Austl. 155/G5
Clarke (lake), Pa, US 194/B4
Clarkesville, Ga, US 189/F3
Clarkfield, Mn, US 181/G1
Clarks, La, US 190/B1
Clarks Fk. Yellowstone (riv.), Wy,Mt, US 173/J1
Clark's Harbour, NS, Can. 184/E4
Clarks Hill, SC, US 189/F4
Clarksburg, WV, US 186/F5
Clarksburg, Ca, US 193/L10
Clarksburg, Tn, US 188/C3
Clarksburg, NJ, US 194/D3
Clarksdale, Ms, US 188/B3
Clarkson, On, Can. 186/T8
Clarkston, Mi, US 193/F6
Clarkston, Ut, US 173/G3
Clarkston, Ga, US 189/M7
Clarkston, Wa, US 170/F4
Clarksville, Ar, US 179/H3
Clarksville, Ia, US 181/H2
Clarksville, In, US 186/D4
Clarksville, Tn, US 188/D2
Clarksville, Tx, US 179/G4
Clarksville, Va, US 189/H2
Clarkton, Mo, US 188/C2
Clarkton, NC, US 189/H3
Clarkville, Co, US 180/C3
Claro, Swi. 87/F5
Claro (riv.), Braz. 210/C3
Clashmore, Ire. 58/C6
Clatskanie, Or, US 170/C4
Clatteringshaws Loch (lake), Sc, UK 60/D1
Claude, Tx, US 178/D3
Cláudio, Braz. 210/D4
Claudy, NI, UK 60/A2
Claunch, NM, US 175/K3
Clausen, Ger. 81/G5
Clausthal-Zellerfeld, Ger. 79/H5
Claver, Phil. 114/D3
Claveria, Phil. 114/D3
Claveria, Phil. 114/C1
Clavet, Sk, Can. 171/L1
Clawson, Mi, US 193/F6
Claxton, Ga, US 189/G4
Clay, La, US 179/H4
Clay (pt.), IM, UK 60/D3
Clay, Ca, US 172/C4
Clay, Ky, US 188/D2
Clay, WV, US 189/G1
Clay Center, Ne, US 180/E3
Clay Center, Ks, US 181/F4
Clay City, In, US 186/C5
Clay City, Il, US 188/C1
Clay City, Ky, US 188/F2
Clay Cross-North Wingfield, Eng, UK 61/G5
Clay Springs, Az, US 175/G3
Claybank, Sk, Can. 171/M2
Claydon, Eng, UK 63/H2
Claye-Souilly, Fr. 56/L5
Claygate, Eng, UK 56/C2
Clayhatchee, Al, US 191/F2
Claymont, De, US 194/C4
Claypool, Az, US 175/G4
Clayton, Al, US 191/F2
Clayton, Ca, US 193/L11
Clayton, De, US 194/C5
Clayton (co.), Ga, US 189/M7
Clayton, Ga, US 189/F3
Clayton, Id, US 173/F1
Clayton, La, US 190/C2
Clayton, Mo, US 181/J4
Clayton, NJ, US 194/C4
Clayton, NC, US 189/H3
Clayton, NM, US 178/C2
Clayton, NY, US 187/H2
Clayton, Ok, US 179/G3
Clayton-le-Moors, Eng, UK 61/F4
Clé (stream), Arg. 215/J10
Cle Elum, Wa, US 170/D4
Clear (hills), Ab, Can. 166/E3
Clear (cape), Ire. 57/P11
Clear (lake), Ca, US 172/B3
Clear (riv.), Tx, US 177/M9
Clear (cr.), Wy, US 173/K1
Clear Fork (riv.), Tx, US 199/E1
Clear Fork Trinity (riv.), Tx, US 176/K7
Clear Lake, Ia, US 181/H2
Clear Lake, SD, US 181/F1
Clear Lake, Wi, US 183/H5
Clear Lake NWR, Ca, US 172/C3
Clearfield, Ut, US 173/G3
Clearfield, Ky, US 189/F1
Clearlake, Ca, US 172/B4
Clearlake Oaks, Ca, US 172/B4
Clearmont, Wy, US 173/K1
Clearwater (riv.), Id, US 172/F1
Clearwater (mts.), Id, US 168/C2
Clearwater, Fl, US 190/K8
Clearwater (riv.), BC, Can. 170/D2
Clearwater, Wa, US 170/B4
Clearwater, BC, Can. 170/D2
Clearwater, Id, US 170/G4
Clearwater (lake), Mo, US 188/B2
Clearwater Beach, Fl, US 190/K8
Cleator Moor, Eng, UK 60/E2
Cleburne, Tx, US 177/F1
Clécy, Fr. 83/E3
Cléden-Cap-Sizun, Fr. 82/A4
Cléder, Fr. 82/A3
Cleethorpes, Eng, UK 61/H4
Cleeve (hill), Eng, UK 62/D3
Cleland Rec. Area, Austl. 157/M8
Clément, FrG. 206/C2
Clementi (nbrhd.), Sing. 115/J6
Clementon, NJ, US 194/D4
Clements, Ca, US 172/C4
Clementsport, NS, Can. 184/E3
Clemmons, NC, US 189/G2
Clemson, SC, US 189/F3
Clendenin, WV, US 189/G1
Cleo, Tx, US 177/E2
Cleo (Cleo Springs), Ok, US 179/E2
Cleo Springs (Cleo), Ok, US 179/E2
Cleobury Mortimer, Eng, UK 62/D2
Cleona, Pa, US 194/E3
Cleopatra Needle (peak), Phil. 114/E3
Clères, Fr. 83/G1
Clérieux, Fr. 90/A2
Clermont, Qu, Can. 184/E2
Clermont, Fr. 80/E5
Clermont, Fl, US 190/M6
Clermont, Austl. 160/B3
Clermont-en-Argonne, Fr. 81/E5
Clermont-Ferrand, Fr. 70/E4
Clerval, Fr. 86/C3
Clervaux, Lux. 81/F3
Cléry-Saint-André, Fr. 83/G5
Cles, It. 87/H5
Cleve, Austl. 157/H5
Clevedon, Eng, UK 62/D4
Cleveland (cape), Austl. 160/B2
Cleveland (co.), Eng, UK 61/G2
Cleveland (hills), Eng, UK 61/G3
Cleveland, Fl, US 191/H4
Cleveland, Ga, US 188/F3
Cleveland, Ms, US 188/B4
Cleveland, Mt, US 171/K3
Cleveland (mt.), Mt, US 171/H3
Cleveland, ND, US 182/E4
Cleveland, Ok, US 179/F2
Cleveland, Oh, US 186/F4
Cleveland, SC, US 189/F3
Cleveland, Tn, US 188/E3
Cleveland, Tx, US 177/G2
Cleveland, Ut, US 173/H4
Cleveland, Wi, US 186/C3
Cleveland National Forest, Ca, US 192/C3
Cleveland-Hopkins (int'l arpt.), Oh, US 186/F4
Clevelândia, Braz. 213/F3
Clevelândia do Norte, Braz. 206/D2
Clew (bay), Ire. 58/A2
Clewiston, Fl, US 191/H4
Clichy, Fr. 56/J5
Clichy-sous-Bois, Fr. 56/K5
Clifden, Ire. 56/F10
Cliff, NM, US 175/H4
Cliffe, Eng, UK 56/E2
Cliffs of Moher, Ire. 58/A4
Cliffside Park, NJ, US 195/K8
Cliffwood, NJ, US 195/J10
Clifton, La, US 190/C2
Clifton, Il, US 186/C4
Clifton, NJ, US 195/J8
Clifton, Co, US 173/J4
Clifton, Az, US 175/H4
Clifton, Id, US 173/G2
Clifton, Ks, US 181/F4
Clifton, Tn, US 188/D3
Clifton, Eng, UK 62/D4
Clifton, Tx, US 176/F2
Clifton Beach, Austl. 160/B2
Clifton Forge, Va, US 189/H2
Clifton Springs, Austl. 159/B4
Clifton-on-Teme, Eng, UK 62/D2
Clifty, Ky, US 188/D2
Clignon (riv.), Fr. 80/C5
Climax, Sk, Can. 171/K3
Climax, Ga, US 191/F2
Climax, Mn, US 182/F4
Climax, Tx, US 176/L6
Clinch (lake), Fl, US 190/M8
Clinch (riv.), Va, US 189/F2
Clinge, Neth. 78/B6
Clingmans (mtn.), Tn, US 189/F3
Clinton, NZ 161/B4
Clinton, BC, Can. 170/D2
Clinton, Ar, US 179/H3
Clinton, Ct, US 195/F1
Clinton, Ia, US 181/J3
Clinton, Il, US 181/K3
Clinton, In, US 186/C5
Clinton (lake), Ks, US 181/G4
Clinton, Ky, US 188/C2
Clinton, La, US 190/C2
Clinton, NC, US 189/H3
Clinton, Mo, US 179/H1
Clinton, Mi, US 186/E3
Clinton (riv.), Mi, US 193/F6
Clinton, Mi, US 193/G6
Clinton, Ms, US 188/B4
Clinton (res.), NJ, US 194/D1
Clinton, NJ, US 194/D2
Clinton, Ok, US 178/E3
Clinton (co.), Pa, US 194/A1
Clinton, SC, US 189/G3
Clinton, Tn, US 188/E2
Clinton, Wa, US 193/C2
Clinton (Surrattsville), Md, US 189/J1
Clinton Creek, Yk, Can. 166/B2
Clinton Heights, Fl, US 190/L7
Clinton, Mid. Branch (riv.), Mi, US 193/G6
Clinton, North Branch (riv.), Mi, US 193/G6
Clinton-Colden (lake), NW, Can. 166/F2
Clintonville, Wi, US 181/K1
Clints Dod (hill), Sc, UK 59/D5
Clintwood, Va, US 189/F2
Clio, Al, US 191/F2
Clio, Mi, US 186/E3
Clio, SC, US 189/H3
Clipston, Eng, UK 63/F2
Clisbako (riv.), BC, Can. 170/C1
Clitheroe, Eng, UK 61/F4
Clitunno (riv.), It. 91/B2
Clive, NZ 161/D2
Cliza, Bol. 212/C1
Cloan, Sk, Can. 171/K1
Cloates (pt.), Austl. 156/B2
Clocolan, SAfr. 150/D3
Clogh, Ire. 58/C4
Cloghan, Ire. 58/C3
Clogheen, Ire. 58/B5
Clogher (pt.), Ire. 58/D2
Clogherhead, Ire. 60/B4
Cloghjordan, Ire. 58/B4
Cloghy, NI, UK 60/C3
Clohars-Carnoët, Fr. 82/B5
Clonakilty, Ire. 58/B6
Clonakilty (bay), Ire. 58/B6
Clonaslee, Ire. 58/C3
Clonbullogue, Ire. 58/C3
Cloncurry, Austl. 160/A3
Clondalkin, Ire. 60/B5
Clonegall, Ire. 58/D4
Clones, Ire. 58/C1
Clonfert, Ire. 58/B3
Clonmany, Ire. 60/A1
Clonmel, Ire. 58/C5
Clonmellon, Ire. 58/C2
Clonroche, Ire. 58/D5
Clontarf, Mn, US 181/G1
Cloone, Ire. 58/C2
Cloppenburg, Ger. 79/F3
Clopton, Al, US 191/F2
Cloquet (riv.), Mn, US 183/J4
Cloquet, Mn, US 183/H4
Cloridorme, Qu, Can. 184/E1
Clos-Fontaine, Fr. 56/M6
Closeburn, Sc, UK 60/E1
Closter, NJ, US 195/K8
Cloud (peak), Wy, US 173/K1
Cloudcroft, NM, US 178/B4
Cloudy, Ok, US 179/G3
Cloughmills, NI, UK 60/B2
Cloughton, Eng, UK 61/H3
Clover, SC, US 189/G3
Clover Lick, WV, US 189/H1
Cloverdale, In, US 186/C5
Cloverdale, Ca, US 172/B4
Cloverleaf, Tx, US 177/M9
Cloverport, Ky, US 188/D2
Clovis, NM, US 178/C3
Clovis, Ca, US 174/C2
Clovulin, Sc, UK 59/A3
Clowne, Eng, UK 61/G5
Cloyes-sur-le-Loir, Fr. 83/G4
Cloyne, Ire. 58/B6
Cloyne, On, Can. 187/H2
Cluanie (lake), Sc, UK 59/A2
Cluj (co.), Rom. 77/F2
Cluj-Napoca, Rom. 77/F2
Clun, Eng, UK 62/C2
Clunderwen, Wal, UK 62/B3
Cluny, Ab, Can. 171/H2
Cluses, Fr. 86/C5
Clusko (riv.), BC, Can. 170/B1
Clusone, It. 87/F6
Clute, Tx, US 176/G3
Clutha (riv.), NZ 153/G7
Clwyd (riv.), Wal, UK 61/E5
Clwyd (co.), Wal, UK 61/E5
Clwydian (range), Wal, UK 61/E5
Clydach, Wal, UK 62/C3
Clyde, Ks, US 179/F1
Clyde, ND, US 182/E3
Clyde (riv.), Sc, UK 59/B5
Clyde, Oh, US 186/E4
Clyde (riv.), NS, Can. 184/E4
Clyde, Ab, Can. 166/E3
Clyde, Tx, US 176/E1
Clyde Hill, Wa, US 193/C2
Clyde, Firth of (inlet), Sc, UK 57/R8
Clydebank, Sc, UK 59/B5
Clydesdale (valley), Sc, UK 59/C5
Clywedog (riv.), Wal, UK 62/C2
CN Tower, On, Can. 186/U8
Co Lieu, Viet. 120/D2
Co Loa Citadel, Viet. 120/D1
Co Nag (lake), China 125/F5
Côa (riv.), Port. 72/B2
Coacalco, Mex. 199/Q9
Coachella, Ca, US 174/D4
Coachella (canal), Ca, US 174/E4
Coachford, Ire. 58/B6
Coagh, NI, UK 60/B2
Coahoma, Tx, US 177/D1
Coahuayana de Hidalgo, Mex. 198/E5
Coahuila, Mex. 198/B1
Coahuila de Zaragoza (state), Mex. 177/D3
Coal (valley), Nv, US 174/E2
Coal (mtn.), WV, US 189/G2
Coal (riv.), WV, US 189/G1
Coal City, WV, US 189/G2
Coal Hill, Ar, US 179/H3
Coalburn, Sc, UK 59/C5
Coalcomán de Matamoros, Mex. 198/E5
Coaldale, Ab, Can. 171/H3
Coaldale, Co, US 178/B1
Coaldale, Pa, US 194/C2
Coalgate, Ok, US 179/F3
Coalhurst, Ab, Can. 171/H3
Coalinga, Ca, US 174/B2
Coalisland, NI, UK 60/B2
Coalmont, Tn, US 188/E3
Coalton, Oh, US 189/F1
Coalton, Il, US 181/K4
Coalville, Ut, US 173/H3
Coalville, Eng, UK 63/E1
Coalwood, Mt, US 171/M5
Coaraci, Braz. 211/F2
Coari (riv.), Braz. 209/E2
Coari, Braz. 209/F2
Coari (lake), Braz. 209/F2
Coarsegold, Ca, US 174/C2
Coasa, Peru 208/D4
Coast (prov.), Kenya 145/B2
Coast (mts.), Can.,US 165/D4
Coast (range), US 165/E6
Coast (mts.), BC,Yk, Can. 166/C2
Coastal (plain), US 189/G4
Coatbridge, Sc, UK 59/B5
Coatepec, Mex. 199/N7
Coatepec Harinas, Mex. 199/K8
Coates, Mn, US 183/P7
Coatesville, Pa, US 194/C4
Coatetelco, Mex. 199/K8
Coaticook, Qu, Can. 187/L2
Coatopa, Al, US 188/C4
Coats, Ks, US 178/E2
Coats (isl.), Nun, Can. 167/H2
Coats (isl.), Can. 165/J3
Coats Land (pol. reg.), Ant. 216/Y
Coatzacoalcos, Mex. 200/C2
Coatzingo, Mex. 199/L8
Coazze, It. 90/D2
Coba (ruin), Mex. 200/E1
Cobán, Guat. 200/D3
Cobar, Austl. 158/C1
Cobargo, Austl. 159/D3
Cobb (hill), Pa, US 187/H4
Cobb (co.), Ga, US 189/L6
Cobbadah, Austl. 159/C3
Cobberas (mt.), Austl. 159/D3
Cobberas-Tingaringy NP, Austl. 159/D3
Cobbitty, Austl. 159/E2
Cobblestone (mtn.), Ca, US 192/B1
Cobbtown, Ga, US 189/F4
Cobden, On, Can. 187/H2
Cobden, Austl. 158/B3
Cobden, Il, US 188/C2
Cobequid (mts.), NS, Can. 184/F3
Cóbh, Ire. 58/B6
Cobham, Eng, UK 56/B3
Cobija, Bol. 208/D3
Cobleskill, NY, US 187/J3
Coboconk, On, Can. 187/G2
Cobourg, On, Can. 187/G3
Cobourg (pen.), Austl. 154/D2
Cobquecura, Chile 214/B3
Cobram, Austl. 159/B2
Cobre, Nv, US 173/F3
Cóbuè, Moz. 149/G2
Coburg (nbrhd.), Austl. 158/F5
Coburg (pen.) Austl. 153/C2
Coburg (isl.), Nun, Can. 167/T7
Coburg, Ger. 84/D2
Coburg, Or, US 172/B1
Coburn (mtn.), Me, US 187/L2
Coca, Ecu. 204/B5
Coca (riv.), Ecu. 204/B5
Cocachacra, Peru 208/D5
Cocal, Braz. 207/F3
Cocalico (cr.), Pa, US 194/B3
Cocama, Peru 208/D3
Cocapata, Bol. 212/C1
Coccaglio, It. 88/C2
Cocentaina, Sp. 73/E3
Cochabamba, Bol. 212/C1
Cochabamba (dept.), Bol. 209/E5
Coche (isl.), Ven. 205/F2
Cochem, Ger. 81/G3
Cochenour, On, Can. 183/H2
Cocherel, Fr. 56/M4
Cochetopa (hills), Co, US 178/A1
Cochin, Sk, Can. 171/K1
Cochran, Ga, US 189/F4
Cochrane, On, Can. 167/H4
Cochrane, Ab, Can. 170/G2
Cochranton, Pa, US 186/F4
Cock Cairn (peak), Sc, UK 59/D3
Cockatoo, Austl. 158/G5
Cockburn, Austl. 157/J5
Cockburn (cape), Austl. 154/D2
Cockburn (sound), Austl. 156/K7
Cockburn (isl.), On, Can. 186/E2
Cockburn (chan.), Chile 215/B7
Cockburnspath, Sc, UK 59/D5
Cockenzie, Sc, UK 59/D5
Cockermouth, Eng, UK 61/E2
Cockeysville, Md, US 194/B5
Cockrell Hill, Tx, US 176/L7
Cockscomb (peak), SAfr. 150/D4
Coclé del Norte, Pan. 201/F4
Coco (riv.), Hon. 196/E5
Coco (riv.), Nic. 200/E3
Cocoa, Fl, US 191/H3
Cocobeach, Gabon 146/B2
Cocodrie (lake), La, US 190/B2
Coconino (plat.), Az, US 175/F3
Coconut Creek, Fl, US 190/P10
Cocopah Ind. Res., Az, US 174/E4
Cocoparra NP, Austl. 159/C2
Cocorná, Col. 207/K6
Cocos (isls.), Austl. 103/J11
Côcos, Braz. 210/D2
Cocotitlán, Mex. 199/R10
Cocula, Mex. 198/E4
Cod (isl.), Nf, Can. 167/K3
Codajás, Braz. 209/F1
Codegua, Chile 214/N9
Codera (cape), Ven. 207/P7
Coderre, Sk, Can. 171/L2
Codette, Sk, Can. 171/M1
Codigoro, It. 89/F4
Codlea, Rom. 77/G3
Codó, Braz. 207/F4
Codogno, It. 88/C3
Codorus (cr.), Pa, US 194/B4
Codpa, Chile 212/B1
Codrington, Anti. 197/N8
Codroy, Nf, Can. 185/H2
Codsall, Eng, UK 62/D1
Cody, Ne, US 180/D2
Cody, Wy, US 173/J1
Coeburn, Va, US 189/F2
Coelemu, Chile 214/B3
Coelho Neto, Braz. 207/F4
Coello, Col. 207/L8
Coen, Austl. 160/A1
Coeroeni (riv.), Sur. 206/B2
Coesfeld, Ger. 79/E5
Coeur d'Alene, Id, US 170/F4
Coeur D'Alene (mts.), Mt, US 170/G4
Coeur d'Alene (lake), Id, US 170/F4
Coeur d'Alene Ind. Res., Id, US 170/F4
Coevorden, Neth. 78/D3
Coffee City, Tx, US 177/G1
Coffeepot (lake), Wa, US 170/E4
Coffeeville (dam), Al, US 190/D2
Coffeeville, Al, US 190/D2
Coffeeville, Ms, US 188/C4
Coffeyville, Ks, US 179/G2
Coffin Bay, Austl. 157/G5
Coffin Bay NP, Austl. 157/G5
Coffs Harbour, Austl. 158/E1
Cofield, NC, US 189/J2
Cofre de Perote, PN, Mex. 199/M7
Cogealac, Rom. 77/J3
Coggeshall, Eng, UK 63/G3
Coggiola, It. 88/B2
Coghinas (lake), It. 74/A2
Cognac, Fr. 70/C4
Cogne, It. 90/D1
Cognin, Fr. 90/B1
Cogo, Gabon 146/B2
Cogoleto, It. 88/B5
Cogolin, Fr. 90/C6
Cogollo del Cengio, It. 89/E2
Cogolludo, Sp. 72/D2
Cogswell, ND, US 182/F4
Cohagen, Mt, US 171/L4
Cohansey (riv.), NJ, US 194/C5
Cohocton, NY, US 187/H3
Cohoes, NY, US 187/K3
Cohoni, Bol. 212/C1
Cohuna, Austl. 159/B2
Cohunu NP, Austl. 156/L7
Coiba, Isla de (isl.), Pan. 196/E6
Coig (riv.), Arg. 215/C6
Coignières, Fr. 56/H5
Coihaique, Chile 214/B5
Coihueco, Chile 214/C3
Coimbra, Port. 72/A2
Coimbra (dist.), Port. 72/A2
Coín, Sp. 72/C4
Coin, Ia, US 181/G3
Coina (riv.), Port. 73/P10
Coinjock, NC, US 189/K2
Coipasa, Bol. 212/B1
Coise (riv.), Fr. 70/F4
Cojedes (state), Ven. 204/D2
Cojimíes, Ecu. 204/A4
Cojoro, Ven. 204/D2
Cojudo Blanco (peak), Arg. 215/C5
Cojutepeque, ESal. 200/D3
Čoka, Yugo. 76/E3
Cokato, Mn, US 181/G1
Coker, Al, US 188/D4
Cokeville, Wy, US 173/H2
Col d'Aspin (pass), Fr. 73/F1
Col de Cabre (pass), Fr. 90/B3
Col de la Bonnete (pass), Fr. 90/C4
Col de la Cayolle (pass), Fr. 90/C4
Col de la Croix Haute (pass), Fr. 90/B3
Col de la Faucille (pass), Fr. 86/C5
Col de la Forclaz (pass), Swi. 86/D5
Col de la Givrine (pass), Swi. 86/C5
Col de Montgenèvre (pass), Fr. 90/C3
Col de Puymorens (pass), Fr. 70/D5
Col de Saales (pass), Fr. 86/D1
Col de Tende (pass), Fr. 88/A4
Col de Valferriére (pass), Fr. 90/C5
Col de Vars (pass), Fr. 90/C3
Col des Aravis (pass), Fr. 86/C6
Col des Champs (pass), Fr. 90/C4
Col des Mosses (pass), Swi. 86/D5
Col d'Iseran (pass), Fr. 90/D2
Col d'Ispéguy (pass), Fr. 70/C5
Col d'Izoard (pass), Fr. 90/C3
Col du Ballon (pass), Fr. 86/C2
Col du Bonhomme (pass), Fr. 86/D1
Col du Galibier (pass), Fr. 90/C2
Col du Grand Saint-Bernard (pass), Swi. 86/D6
Col du Granier (pass), Fr. 90/B2
Col du Luens (pass), Fr. 90/C5
Col du Mollendruz (pass), Swi. 86/C4
Col du Mont Cenis (pass), Fr. 90/C2
Col du Petit-Saint-Bernard (pass), Fr. 90/C1
Col du Pillon (pass), Swi. 86/D5
Col San Martino, It. 89/F2
Colac, Austl. 158/B3
Colares, Port. 73/P10
Colares, Braz. 206/D3
Colasay, Peru 208/B2
Colatina, Braz. 211/E3
Colba, Eth. 142/G3
Colbeck (cape), Ant. 216/P
Colbert, Ok, US 179/F4
Colborne, On, Can. 187/H3
Colbún, Chile 214/C2
Colby, Wa, US 193/B2
Colby, Wi, US 181/J1
Colby, Ks, US 180/D4
Colca (riv.), Peru 208/D4
Colcabamba, Peru 208/C4
Colchester, Ct, US 187/K4
Colchester, Vt, US 187/K2
Colchester, On, Can. 193/G8
Colchester, Il, US 181/J3
Colchester, Eng, UK 63/G3
Cold Fell (peak), Eng, UK 61/F2
Cold Spring, Mn, US 183/G5
Cold Spring Harbor, NY, US 195/M8
Cold Springs NWR, Or, US 172/D1
Coldingham, Sc, UK 59/D5
Coldspring, Tx, US 177/G2
Coldstream, BC, Can. 170/E2
Coldstream, Sc, UK 59/D5
Coldwater, Ks, US 178/E2
Coldwater, Mi, US 186/D4
Coldwater, Ms, US 188/C3
Coldwater (riv.), Ms, US 188/C3
Coldwater, Oh, US 186/D4
Coldwater, On, Can. 187/G2
Coldwater (cr.), Tx, US 178/D2
Cole, Ok, US 179/F3
Cole (riv.), Eng, UK 63/E3
Cole Camp, Mo, US 179/H1
Coleambally, Austl. 159/B2
Coleambally (cr.), Austl. 159/B2
Colebrook, NH, US 187/L2
Coleford, Eng, UK 62/D3
Coleman, Ab, Can. 170/G3
Coleman, Fl, US 190/L6
Coleman, Ga, US 191/F2
Coleman, Mi, US 186/D3
Coleman, Tx, US 176/E2
Coleman (lake), Tx, US 177/E1
Coleman, Ok, US 179/F3
Coleman, Wi, US 186/B2
Çölemerik, Turk. 129/E2
Colenso, SAfr. 151/E3
Coleraine, Mn, US 183/H4
Coleraine (dist.), NI, UK 60/B1
Coleraine, NI, UK 60/B1
Coleraine, Austl. 158/B3
Coleridge, Ne, US 181/F2
Coleroon (riv.), India 121/C4
Coles, Ms, US 190/C2
Colesberg, SAfr. 150/D3
Coleshill, Eng, UK 63/E1
Colesville, Md, US 194/A5
Coleto Cr. (res.), Tx, US 177/F3
Coleville, Ca, US 172/D4
Colfax, Ca, US 172/C4
Colfax, Il, US 181/K3
Colfax, In, US 186/C4
Colfax, La, US 190/B2
Colfax, ND, US 182/F4
Colfax, Tx, US 177/G1
Colfax, Wi, US 181/J1
Colfax, Wa, US 170/F4
Colfiorito, It. 91/B1
Colgate (cape), Nun, Can. 167/S6
Colgong, India 123/F3
Colhué Huapí (lake), Arg. 214/C5
Colico, It. 87/F5
Colignan, Austl. 158/B2
Coligny, Fr. 86/B5
Coligny, SAfr. 150/D2
Colijnsplaat, Neth. 78/A5
Colima, Mex. 198/E5
Colima (state), Mex. 198/D5
Colina, Chile 214/N8
Colinas, Braz. 207/E4
Colinas de Goiás, Braz. 206/D5
Colinas do Tocantins, Braz. 206/D5
Coliseum, Ca, US 192/F8
Coll (isl.), Sc, UK 57/Q8
Collado-villalba, Sp. 73/N8
Collagna, It. 88/D5
Collana, Bol. 208/D5
Collarenebri, Austl. 158/D1
Collbran, Co, US 173/K4
Colle de Piccolo San Bernardo (pass), It. 90/C1
Colle della Maddalena (pass), It. 90/C4
Colle di Nava (pass), It. 88/A4
Colle di Tenda (pass), It. 90/D4
Colle di Val d'Elsa, It. 89/E7
Colle Isarco (Gossensass), It. 87/H4
Colle Sannita, It. 92/D5
Colle Sestriere, It. 90/C3
Collecchio, It. 88/D4
Colleen Bawn, Zim. 149/F4
Colleferro, It. 92/C4
College, Ak, US 168/Y12
College Park, Ga, US 189/M7
College Park, Md, US 194/B6
College Place, Wa, US 170/E4
College Springs, Ia, US 181/G3
College Station, Tx, US 176/F2
Collegeville, Pa, US 194/C3
Collegno, It. 90/D2
Collelongo, It. 92/C4
Collesalvetti, It. 88/D6
Colletorto, It. 92/D4
Colleyville, Tx, US 176/K7
Colli a Volturno, It. 92/D4
Collie, Austl. 158/D1
Collie, Austl. 156/C5
Collier (range), Austl. 156/C3
Collier (bay), Austl. 153/B2
Collier Range NP, Austl. 156/C3
Collierville, Tn, US 188/C3
Colliford (res.), Eng, UK 62/B5
Collin (co.), Tx, US 176/L6
Collingham, Eng, UK 61/G4
Collingham, Eng, UK 61/H5
Collingwood, On, Can. 186/F2
Collingwood, NZ 161/C3
Collins, On, Can. 183/K2
Collins, Ga, US 189/F4
Collins, Mo, US 179/H2
Collins, Ms, US 190/D2
Collins, Mt, US 171/J4
Collins (riv.), Tn, US 188/E3
Collinston, La, US 179/J4
Collinstown (int'l arpt.), Ire. 60/B5
Collinsville, Austl. 160/B3
Collinsville, Al, US 188/E3
Collinsville, Ca, US 193/L10
Collinsville, Ms, US 188/C4
Collinsville, Ok, US 179/G2
Collinsville, Va, US 189/H2
Collinwood, Tn, US 188/D3
Collo, Alg. 138/K6
Collombey, Swi. 86/C5
Collon, Ire. 60/B4
Collonges, Fr. 86/B5
Collooney, Ire. 58/B1
Collpa, Bol. 212/C1
Colma, Ca, US 193/K11
Colman, SD, US 181/F2
Colmar, Fr. 86/D1
Colmar, Pa, US 194/C3
Colmars, Fr. 90/C4
Colmberg, Ger. 84/D4
Colmenar, Sp. 72/C4
Colmenar de Oreja, Sp. 72/D2
Colmenar Viejo, Sp. 73/N8
Colmesneil, Tx, US 177/G2
Colmillo (cape), Chile 215/B6
Colmonell, Sc, UK 60/D1
Colmont (riv.), Fr. 83/E4
Colne (riv.), Eng, UK 61/G4
Colne, Eng, UK 61/F4
Colne (riv.), Eng, UK 63/G3
Colney Heath, Eng, UK 56/C1
Colo (riv.), Austl. 159/E1
Colo Vale, Austl. 159/E2
Cologna Spiaggia, It. 92/C2
Cologna Veneta, It. 89/E3
Cologne, It. 88/C2
Cologne, NJ, US 194/D5
Cologne (Kölm), Ger. 71/G1
Cologne/Bonn (int'l arpt.), Ger. 81/G2
Cologno Monzese, It. 88/C2
Coloma, Wi, US 181/K1
Colombelles, Fr. 83/E2
Colombes, Fr. 56/J5
Colombey-les-Belles, Fr. 86/B1
Colombia (ctry.) 203/A2
Colombia, Col. 204/C4
Colombia, Mex. 177/E4
Colombier, Swi. 86/C4
Colombine (peak), It. 88/D2
Colombis (peak), Fr. 90/C3
Colombo (peak), It. 90/D2
Colombo, Braz. 213/G3
Colombo (cap.), SrL. 121/C5
Colomiers, Fr. 70/D5
Colomoncagua, Hon. 200/D3
Colón, Arg. 214/E2
Colón, Arg. 212/E5

244

Colón – Coven

Colón, Cuba 201/F1
Colón (mts.), Hon. 201/E3
Colón, Pan. 201/G4
Colón, Uru. 215/G2
Colon Koret, D.R. Congo 147/E2
Colona, Co, US 175/J1
Colonche, Ecu. 208/A1
Colonelganj, India 122/C2
Colonia, Micr. 162/C4
Colonia, NJ, US 195/H9
Colonia (dept.), Uru. 214/F2
Colonia Barón, Arg. 214/E3
Colonia Benjamín Aceval, Par. 212/E3
Colonia del Sacramento, Uru. 215/K11
Colonia Dora, Arg. 212/D4
Colonia Gobernador Ayala, Arg. 214/C3
Colonia Josefa, Arg. 214/D3
Colonia Juárez, Mex. 198/C2
Colonia Las Heras, Arg. 214/C5
Colonia Lavalleja, Uru. 213/E4
Colônia Leopoldina, Braz. 207/H5
Colonia Presidente Stroessner, Par. 213/E2
Colonia Yby Yu, Par. 213/F2
Colonial Beach, Va, US 189/J1
Colonial Heights, Va, US 189/J2
Colonial NHP, Va, US 189/J2
Colonial Park, Pa, US 194/B3
Colonna, It. 91/B4
Colonsay (isl.), Sc, UK 57/Q8
Colonsay, Sk, Can. 171/M2
Colony, Ks, US 179/G1
Colony, Wy, US 180/B1
Colorado, CR 201/F4
Colorado (peak), Arg. 215/C6
Colorado, Braz. 213/G2
Colorado (riv.), Mex. 199/B1
Colorado (riv.), US 165/H6
Colorado (riv.), Mex.,US 175/F2
Colorado (plat.), Ut, US 173/H4
Colorado (state), US 168/E4
Colorado (canal), Co, US 180/B4
Colorado City, Co, US 178/B2
Colorado City, Az, US 175/F2
Colorado City, Tx, US 177/D1
Colorado do Oeste, Braz. 209/F4
Colorado Nat'l Mon., Co, US 173/J4
Colorado River (aqueduct), Ca, US 174/E3
Colorado River Ind. Res., Az,Ca, US 174/E3
Colorado Springs, Co, US 178/B1
Colorno, It. 88/D4
Colostre (riv.), Fr. 90/B5
Colotlán, Mex. 198/E4
Colpoys Bay, On, Can. 186/F2
Colquechaca, Bol. 212/C1
Colquiri, Bol. 212/C1
Colquitt, Ga, US 191/F2
Colrain, Ma, US 187/K3
Colson (pt.), Belz. 200/D2
Colstrip, Mt, US 171/L5
Colt (hill), Sc, UK 59/B6
Coltauco, Chile 214/N9
Coltishall, Eng, UK 63/H1
Colton, Ca, US 192/C2
Colton, Ut, US 173/H4
Colton, Wa, US 170/F4
Colts Neck, NJ, US 194/D3
Coluene (riv.), Braz. 203/D4
Columbe, Ecu. 208/B1
Columbia (mt.), Ab, Can. 170/F1
Columbia (riv.), US 165/E5
Columbia, Al, US 191/F2
Columbia, Ky, US 188/E2
Columbia, La, US 179/H4
Columbia, Md, US 194/B5
Columbia, Mo, US 181/H4
Columbia, Ms, US 190/D2
Columbia, NC, US 189/J3
Columbia, NJ, US 194/C2
Columbia (co.), Pa, US 194/B1
Columbia, Pa, US 194/B3
Columbia (plat.), Or, US 166/E4
Columbia (plat.), Or, US 172/D2
Columbia (cap.), SC, US 189/G3
Columbia, Tn, US 188/D3
Columbia (riv.), Wa, US 168/B2
Columbia City, In, US 186/D4
Columbia City, Or, US 170/C5
Columbia Falls, Mt, US 171/G3
Columbia Heights, Mn, US 183/P6
Columbia NWR, Wa, US 170/E4
Columbia Reach (lake), BC, Can. 170/F2
Columbia Road (dam), SD, US 182/E5
Columbian White Tailed Deer Nat'l Wild. Ref., Or, US 170/C4
Columbiana, Al, US 188/D4
Columbiaville, Mi, US 186/E3
Columbine (cape), SAfr. 150/K10
Columbretes (isls.), Sp. 92/D3
Columbus, Ar, US 179/H4
Columbus, Ga, US 188/E4
Columbus, In, US 186/D5
Columbus, Ks, US 179/G2
Columbus, Ms, US 188/C4
Columbus (lake), Ms, US 188/C4
Columbus (A.F.B.), Ms, US 188/C4
Columbus, NC, US 189/F3
Columbus, Ne, US 181/F3
Columbus, NJ, US 194/D3
Columbus, NM, US 175/J5
Columbus (cap.), Oh, US 186/E5
Columbus, Wi, US 181/K2
Columbus, Tx, US 176/F3
Columbus Grove, Oh, US 186/D4
Columbus Salt Marsh (salt marsh), Nv, US 172/D4
Colunga, Sp. 72/C1
Colupo (peak), Chile 212/B2
Colusa, Ca, US 172/B4
Colusa NWR, Ca, US 172/B4
Colville (lake), NW, Can. 166/D2
Colville (cape), NZ 161/C2
Colville (riv.), Ak, US 216/S
Colville, Wa, US 170/F3
Colville Ind. Res., Wa, US 170/E3
Colvos (passg.), Wa, US 193/B3
Colwall, Eng, UK 62/D2
Colwinston, Wal, UK 62/C4
Colwyn Bay, Wal, UK 60/E5
Comacchio, It. 89/F4
Comacchio (lag.), It. 71/K4
Comai, China 123/H1
Comala, Mex. 198/E5
Comalcalco, Mex. 200/C2
Comanche, Ok, US 179/F3
Comanche (cr.), Co, US 180/B4
Comanche (res.), Ca, US 174/B1
Comanche, Tx, US 176/E2
Comandante Luis Piedra Buena, Arg. 215/C6
Comandante Nicanor Otamendi, Arg. 214/F3
Comănești, Rom. 98/D4
Comar Gambon, Som. 144/C5
Comarapa, Bol. 212/C1
Comarnic, Rom. 77/G3
Comas, Peru 208/B3
Comas, Peru 208/C3
Comayagua, Hon. 200/E3
Comayagua (mts.), Hon. 200/D3
Combahee (riv.), SC, US 189/G4
Combapata, Peru 208/D4
Combarbalá, Chile 212/B4
Combe Martin, Eng, UK 62/B4
Combeaufontaine, Fr. 86/B2
Comber, On, Can. 193/G7
Comber, NI, UK 60/C2
Combermere (bay), Myan. 112/B5
Comblain-au-Pont, Belg. 81/E3
Combloux, Fr. 86/C6
Combourg, Fr. 82/D4
Comboyne, Austl. 158/E1
Combrée, Fr. 83/D5
Combrit, Fr. 82/A5
Combs (riv.), Fr. 82/C5
Combs, Ky, US 189/F2
Combs-la-Ville, Fr. 56/K6
Comé, Ben. 141/F5
Come-By-Chance, Austl. 158/D1
Comemoração (riv.), Braz. 209/F3
Comendador, DRep. 201/J2
Comer, Al, US 191/F1
Comfort, Tx, US 177/E3
Comilla, Bang. 123/H4
Comilla (pol. reg.), Bang. 123/H4
Comines, Fr. 80/C2
Comines, Belg. 80/B2
Comino (isl.), Malta 74/L6
Comitán de Domínguez, Mex. 200/C2
Commack, NY, US 195/E2
Commentry, Fr. 70/E3
Commeny, Fr. 56/H4
Commerce, Tx, US 179/G4
Commerce, Ca, US 192/F7
Commerce, Ga, US 189/F3
Commerce City, Co, US 180/B4
Commercy, Fr. 81/E6
Commewijne (dist.), Sur. 205/H3
Commissioner (isl.), Mb, Can. 182/F1
Committee (bay), Nun, Can. 167/H2
Commonwealth, Wi, US 183/K5
Como, It. 87/F6
Como (lake), It. 92/F1
Como (lake), Wi, US 193/P14
Como, Wi, US 193/P14
Como, Ms, US 188/C3
Comodoro Rivadavia, Arg. 214/D5
Comoé (prov.), Burk. 140/D4
Comoé, PN de la, C.d'Iv. 140/D4
Comorin (cape), India 121/C4
Comoros(ctry.) 133/G6
Comox, BC, Can. 170/B3
Company, Camr. 146/B1
Compeer, Ab, Can. 171/J2
Compiègne, Fr. 80/B5
Compomarino, It. 92/E4
Compostela, Mex. 198/D4
Comprida (isl.), Braz. 213/H3
Compton, Ca, US 192/F8
Compton, Eng, UK 56/B3
Comrat, Mol. 77/J2
Comrie, Sc, UK 59/C4
Comstock, Mi, US 186/D3
Comstock, Tx, US 177/D3
Comunanza, It. 92/C2
Comunidad, Ven. 205/E4
Con Cuong, Viet. 120/D2
Con Son (isl.), Viet. 119/J6
Cona, China 119/F2
Conaica, Peru 208/C4
Conakry (cap.), Gui. 140/B4
Conakry (pol. reg.), Gui. 140/B4
Conakry (int'l arpt.), Gui. 140/B4
Conambo (riv.), Ecu. 204/B5
Conargo, Austl. 159/B2
Conay, Chile 212/B4
Conboy NWR, Wa, US 170/D5
Conca (riv.), It. 89/F5
Concan, Tx, US 177/E3
Concarneau, Fr. 82/B5
Conceição das Alagoas, Braz. 213/G1
Conceição de Macabu, Braz. 211/E4
Conceição do Araguaia, Braz. 206/D5
Conceição do Coité, Braz. 211/F1
Conceição do Mato Dentro, Braz. 211/E3
Conceição do Rio Verde, Braz. 211/L6
Conceição dos Ouros, Braz. 211/L7
Concepción, Arg. 212/E4
Concepción, Arg. 212/C3
Concepción, Bol. 209/E3
Concepción, Bol. 209/F5
Concepción (lake), Bol. 209/F5
Concepción (lag.), Bol. 212/D1
Concepción, Chile 214/B3
Concepción (pt.), Mex. 198/C3
Concepción (bay), Mex. 198/B3
Concepción, Par. 212/E2
Concepción (dept.), Par. 210/A4
Concepción de La Vega, DRep. 197/G4
Concepción del Bermejo, Arg. 212/D3
Concepción del Oro, Mex. 199/E3
Concepción del Uruguay, Arg. 215/J10
Conception (bay), Nf, Can. 185/L2
Conception (pt.), Ca, US 174/B3
Conception (bay), Namb. 148/B4
Concesio, It. 88/D2
Concession, Zim. 149/F3
Conchal, Braz. 211/J7
Conchas (lake), NM, US 178/B3
Conches, Fr. 56/L5
Conches-en-Ouche, Fr. 83/F3
Conchi, Chile 212/B2
Conchillas, Uru. 215/J11
Concho (riv.), Tx, US 177/D2
Conchos (riv.), Mex. 165/G7
Concón, Chile 214/N8
Concord, Ar, US 179/J3
Concord, Fl, US 191/F2
Concord, NC, US 189/G3
Concord (cap.), NH, US 187/L3
Concord, Tx, US 176/G1
Concord, Va, US 189/H2
Concord, Wi, US 193/N13
Concordia, Ks, US 180/F4
Concordia, Arg. 212/E4
Concórdia, Braz. 213/F3
Concordia, Col. 207/K6
Concordia, Mex. 198/D4
Concordia, Peru 208/C2
Concordia Sagittaria, It. 89/F2
Concordia sulla Secchia, It. 89/D4
Concrete, Wa, US 170/D3
Condado, Cuba 201/G1
Condamine, Austl. 160/C3
Condamine (riv.), Austl. 153/E3
Condar, Col. 204/C5
Conde, SD, US 180/E1
Conde, Braz. 211/F1
Condé-sur-L'Escaut, Fr. 80/C3
Condé-sur-Noireau, Fr. 83/E3
Condé-sur-Sarthe, Fr. 83/F4
Condé-sur-Vesgre, Fr. 56/G5
Condé-sur-Vire, Fr. 83/D2
Condécourt, Fr. 56/H4
Condeúba, Braz. 211/E2
Condino, It. 87/G6
Condobolin, Austl. 159/C1
Condom, Fr. 70/D5
Condon, Or, US 172/C1
Condon, Mt, US 171/H4
Condor, Ab, Can. 170/G1
Condove, It. 90/D2
Condrieu, Fr. 90/A2
Condroz (plat.), Belg. 68/C3
Conecuh (riv.), Al, US 190/E2
Conegliano, It. 89/F2
Conehatta, Ms, US 188/C4
Conejos, Co, US 175/J2
Conejos (riv.), Co, US 175/J2
Conequh (riv.), Al, US 188/E5
Conesa, Arg. 214/E2
Conestoga (riv.), Pa, US 194/B3
Conewago (lake), Pa, US 194/A3
Conewago (cr.), Pa, US 194/B4
Coney Island (nbrhd.), NY, US 195/K9
Confins (int'l arpt.), Braz. 210/E3
Conflans-en-Jarnisy, Fr. 81/E5
Conflans-Sainte-Honorine, Fr. 56/J5
Confuso (riv.), Par. 212/E3
Cong, Ire. 58/A2
Congaree Swamp Nat'l Mon., SC, US 189/G4
Congers, NY, US 195/K7
Conghua, China 113/G4
Congis-sur-Thérouanne, Fr. 56/L4
Congjiang, China 113/F3
Congleton, Eng, UK 61/F5
Congo (riv.), Afr. 146/C4
Congo, Braz. 207/G4
Congo(ctry.) 133/D5
Congo (riv.), D.R. Congo 133/D5
Congo (Zaire)(riv.) 133/D4
Congonhal, Braz. 211/K7
Congonhas (int'l arpt.), Braz. 211/K8
Congonhas, Braz. 213/J2
Congress, Az, US 175/F3
Conguel (pt.), Fr. 82/B6
Conguillío, PN, Chile 214/C3
Conic (hill), Sc, UK 59/B4
Cónico (peak), Arg. 214/C4
Conie (riv.), Fr. 83/G4
Conil de la Frontera, Sp. 72/B4
Conimbla NP, Austl. 159/D1
Coningsby, Eng, UK 61/H5
Conisbrough, Eng, UK 61/G5
Coniston, Eng, UK 61/E3
Conley, Ga, US 189/M7
Conlie, Fr. 83/E4
Conlig, NI, UK 60/C2
Conn (lake), Nun, Can. 167/J1
Conn (lake), Ire. 58/A1
Connacht (reg.), Ire. 58/B2
Connah's Quay, Wal, UK 61/E5
Connantre, Fr. 80/C6
Conneaut, Oh, US 186/F4
Connecticut (riv.), US 184/A4
Connecticut (state), US 169/M3
Connecticut (hill), NY, US 187/H3
Connel, Sc, UK 59/A4
Connell, Wa, US 170/E4
Connellsville, Pa, US 187/G4
Connemara (dist.), Ire. 58/A3
Connemara NP, Ire. 57/P10
Conner, Phil. 114/C1
Connerré, Fr. 83/F4
Connersville, In, US 186/D5
Cono Grande (peak), Arg. 215/C6
Conoble, Austl. 159/B1
Conoble (lake), Austl. 159/B1
Conocoto, Ecu. 204/B5
Conodoguinet (cr.), Pa, US 194/A3
Conon, Falls of (falls), Sc, UK 59/B1
Cononbridge, Sc, UK 59/B1
Conondale NP, Austl. 160/D4
Čonoplja, Yugo. 76/D3
Conover, NC, US 189/G3
Conquest, Sk, Can. 171/L2
Conrad, Ia, US 181/H2
Conrad, Mt, US 171/J3
Conran (cape), Austl. 159/D3
Conroe (lake), Tx, US 177/G2
Conroe, Tx, US 177/G2
Consandolo, It. 89/E4
Conscience Point Nat'l Wild. Ref., NY, US 195/F2
Consdorf, Lux. 81/F4
Conselheiro Lafaiete, Braz. 210/E4
Conselheiro Pena, Braz. 211/E3
Conselice, It. 89/E4
Conselve, It. 89/E3
Conservation Park, Austl. 157/F4
Consett, Eng, UK 61/G2
Conshohocken, Pa, US 194/C3
Consolación del Sur, Cuba 201/F1
Consort, Ab, Can. 171/J1
Constance (lake), Swi.,Ger. 87/F2
Constance (mt.), Wa, US 170/C4
Constance (Bodensee) (lake), Swi.,Ger. 87/F2
Constant (mtn.), Fr. 197/N9
Constanta (prov.), Rom. 77/H3
Constanța, Rom. 77/J3
Constantí, Sp. 73/F2
Constantina, Sp. 72/C4
Constantine, Alg. 138/K6
Constitución (res.), Uru. 215/K10
Constitución, Chile 214/B2
Constitución de 1857, PN, Mex. 198/B2
Constitution, Ga, US 189/M7
Constitution de 1857, PN, Mex. 174/E5
Consuegra, Sp. 72/D3
Consul, Sk, Can. 171/K3
Contai, India 123/F5
Contamana, Peru 208/C2
Contarina, It. 89/F3
Contas, Rio de (riv.), Braz. 211/E2
Contegem, Braz. 210/D3
Contes, Fr. 90/D5
Conthey, Swi. 86/D5
Contigliano, It. 91/B3
Continental, Az, US 175/G5
Continentals (range), Ab, Can. 170/F1
Contoy (isl.), Mex. 200/E1
Contra Costa (canal), Ca, US 193/L10
Contra Costa (co.), Ca, US 193/L11
Contramaestre, Cuba 201/G1
Contratación, Col. 204/C3
Contrecoeur, Qu, Can. 185/P6
Contreras (res.), Sp. 72/E3
Contres, Fr. 83/G6
Contrexéville, Fr. 86/B1
Contulmo, Chile 214/B3
Contumazá, Peru 208/B2
Contwig, Ger. 81/G5
Contwoyko (lake), Nun, Can. 166/F2
Conty, Fr. 80/B4
Convención, Col. 204/C2
Convent, La, US 190/C2
Convento San Francesco, It. 91/B3
Conversano, It. 75/E2
Converse, La, US 176/H2
Conway (cape), Austl. 160/C3
Conwy, Wal, UK 60/E5
Conwy (riv.), Wal, UK 60/E5
Conwy (bay), Wal, UK 60/D5
Conway, Ar, US 179/H3
Conway, Fl, US 190/N6
Conway, Mi, US 186/D2
Conway, Mo, US 179/H2
Conway, NH, US 187/L3
Conway, SC, US 189/H4
Conway NP, Austl. 160/C3
Conyers, Ga, US 189/M7
Conyngham, Pa, US 194/B2
Coober Pedy, Austl. 157/G4
Cooch Behār, India 123/G2
Coochiemudlo (isl.), Austl. 160/F7
Coogee, Austl. 158/B1
Cook, Austl. 157/F4
Cook (bay), Chile 215/C7
Cook (str.), NZ 153/H7
Cook (mt.), NZ 161/B3
Cook (inlet), Ak, US 166/A3
Cook (co.), Il, US 193/Q16
Cook Is. (terr.), CookIs. 163/J6
Cooke (mt.), Austl. 156/C5
Cookeville, Tn, US 188/E2
Cookham, Eng, UK 56/A2
Cookhouse, SAfr. 150/D4
Cooks, Mi, US 186/C2
Cookshire, Qu, Can. 187/L2
Cookstown, NI, UK 60/B2
Cookstown (dist.), NI, UK 60/B2
Cooksville, Md, US 194/A5
Cooktown, Austl. 160/B1
Coola Coola (swamp), Austl. 158/B3
Coolabah, Austl. 158/C1
Cooladdi, Austl. 160/B4
Coolah, Austl. 158/D1
Coolamon, Austl. 159/C2
Coolaney, Ire. 58/B1
Coolangatta, Austl. 158/E1
Coolatai, Austl. 158/D1
Cooley (pt.), Ire. 60/B4
Coolgardie, Austl. 156/D4
Coolibah, Austl. 154/C3
Coolidge, Ga, US 191/G2
Coolidge (dam), Az, US 175/G4
Coolidge, Tx, US 177/F2
Coolidge Dam, Az, US 175/G4
Cooloola NP, Austl. 160/D4
Cooloongup (lake), Austl. 156/K7
Coolville, Oh, US 189/G1
Cooma, Austl. 159/D3
Coon (cr.), Il, US 193/N15
Coon (riv.), Mn, US 183/P6
Coon Rapids, Ia, US 181/G3
Coon Rapids, Mn, US 183/P6
Coon Valley, Wi, US 181/J2
Coon, East Branch (cr.), Mi, US 193/G6
Coonabarabran, Austl. 158/D1
Coonalpyn, Austl. 158/A2
Coonamble, Austl. 158/D1
Coonana Abor. Land, Austl. 156/D4
Coondapoor (Kundapura), India 127/K6
Coongan Abor. Land, Austl. 156/C2
Cooper, Tx, US 179/G4
Cooper (cr.), Austl. 157/J3
Cooper (mt.), BC, Can. 170/F2
Cooper City, Fl, US 190/P10
Cooper (brook), Austl. 153/C3
Coopersburg, Pa, US 194/C2
Cooperstown, ND, US 182/E4
Cooperstown, NY, US 187/J3
Coopracambra NP, Austl. 159/D3
Coorabie, Austl. 157/G4
Coordewandy (peak), Austl. 156/C3
Coorong NP, Austl. 158/A3
Coorow, Austl. 156/C4
Cooroy, Austl. 160/D4
Coos (bay), Or, US 172/A2
Coos Bay, Or, US 172/A2
Coosa, Ga, US 188/E3
Coosa (riv.), Al, US 188/D4
Coosawattee (riv.), Ga, US 188/E3
Coot (mtn.), Mo, US 179/J2
Cootamundra, Austl. 159/D2
Cootehill, Ire. 58/C1
Coot'tha (mt.), Austl. 160/E6
Copacabana, Col. 207/K6
Copacabana, Bol. 208/D5
Copachuncho, Bol. 212/C1
Copahué (vol.), Chile 214/C3
Copainalá, Mex. 200/C2
Copala, Mex. 196/B4
Copalis Beach, Wa, US 170/B4
Copan, Ok, US 179/G2
Copán (ruin), Hon. 200/D3
Copano (bay), Tx, US 177/F3
Cope (cape), Sp. 72/E4
Cope, Co, US 180/C4
Copeland (isl.), NI, UK 60/C2
Copemish, Mi, US 186/D2
Copenhagen (København) (cap.), Den. 65/J7
Coper, Col. 207/L7
Copertino, It. 75/F2
Copeton (dam), Austl. 158/D1
Copeville, Tx, US 176/L6
Copiague, NY, US 195/M9
Copiapó (peak), Chile 212/B3
Copiapó (riv.), Chile 212/B3
Copiapó, Chile 212/B3
Coplay, Pa, US 194/C2
Copley, Austl. 157/H4
Coporolo, Ang. 148/B2
Coporolo (riv.), Ang. 148/B2
Copparo, It. 89/E4
Coppell, Tx, US 176/K7
Coppename (riv.), Sur. 205/H3
Coppenbrügge, Ger. 79/G4
Copper (riv.), Ak, US 166/B2
Copper Harbor, Mi, US 183/L4
Copperas Cove, Tx, US 176/F2
Copperbelt (prov.), Zam. 149/E2
Copperdahl (hill), ND, US 182/D3
Coppermine (riv.), NW,Nun, Can. 166/E2
Coppet, Swi. 86/C5
Coppolani, Mrta. 140/A2
Coppull, Eng, UK 61/F4
Copșa Mică, Rom. 77/G2
Coqên, China 125/E5
Coquet (riv.), Eng, UK 59/D6
Coquet Dale (valley), Eng, UK 61/G1
Coquille, Or, US 172/A2
Coquille (riv.), Or, US 172/A2
Coquimbo (pol. reg.), Chile 212/B4
Coquimbo, Chile 212/B4
Coquitlam, BC, Can. 170/C3
Cora, Wy, US 173/J2
Corabia, Rom. 77/G4
Coração de Jesus, Braz. 210/D3
Coracora, Peru 208/C4
Corail, Haiti 201/H2
Coraki, Austl. 158/E1
Coral(sea) 153/D2
Coral Gables, Fl, US 190/P11
Coral Harbour, Nun, Can. 167/H2
Coral Sea Islands Territory (terr.), Austl. 153/E2
Coral Springs, Fl, US 190/P10
Corales del Rosario, PN, Col. 204/C2
Coralville, Ia, US 181/J3
Coram, NY, US 195/E2
Corambá (riv.), Braz. 213/G1
Corani, Bol. 209/E5
Corantijne (riv.), Sur. 206/B1
Coranzulí, Arg. 212/C2
Corato, It. 74/E2
Coray, Fr. 82/B4
Corbara (lake), It. 91/B2
Corbeil-Essonnes, Fr. 56/K6
Corbélia, Braz. 213/F3
Corbelin (cape), Alg. 138/H4
Corbenay, Fr. 86/C2
Corbet (peak), Swi. 87/F5
Corbett NP, India 122/B1
Corbetta, It. 88/B3
Corbie, Fr. 80/B4
Corbière (pt.), Chl, UK 82/C2
Corbieres (mts.), Fr. 70/E5
Corbin, Ky, US 188/E2
Corbin City, NJ, US 194/D5
Corbridge, Eng, UK 61/F2
Corby, Eng, UK 63/F2
Corchiano, It. 91/B3
Corcoran, Ca, US 174/C2
Corcoran, Mn, US 183/N6
Corcovado, CR 201/E4
Corcovado (gulf), Chile 203/B7
Corcovado (vol.), Chile 214/B4
Corcovado, Braz. 211/N7
Corcovado, PN, CR 196/E6
Cord, Ar, US 179/J3
Cord. de la Punilla (mts.), Chile 212/B4
Cord. de Lipez (mts.), Bol. 212/C2
Cordata (mesa), NM, US 175/J3
Cordeiro, Braz. 211/E4
Cordele, Ga, US 191/G2
Cordele, Tx, US 177/F3
Cordelia, Ca, US 193/K10
Cordell (New Cordell), Ok, US 178/E3
Cordenons, It. 71/K4
Cordignano, It. 89/F2
Cordilheiras, Serra das (mts.), Braz. 206/D4
Cordillera (mts.), Sp. 92/B2
Cordillera (dept.), Par. 213/E3
Cordillera Central (mts.), Phil. 114/C1
Cordillera Darwin (mts.), Chile 212/B4
Cordillera de la Costa (mts.), Ven. 207/N8
Cordillera de los Andes (mts.), SAm. 212/B1
Cordillera de los Picachos, PN, Col. 204/C4
Cordillera Domeyko (mts.), Chile 212/B3
Cordillera Neo Volcanica (mts.), Mex. 199/Q10
Cordillera Occidental (mts.), Ecu. 204/B5
Cordillera Oriental (mts.), Col. 201/G7
Cordillera Oriental (mts.), SAm. 212/C1
Cordillera Real (mts.), Peru 208/C3
Cordillo Downs, Austl. 160/A4
Córdoba (dept.), Col. 201/H4
Córdoba, Sp. 72/C4
Córdoba (plain), SAm. 214/E2
Córdoba (prov.), Arg. 212/D4
Córdoba, Arg. 212/C4
Córdoba, Mex. 199/N8
Córdoba (Pajas Blancas) (int'l arpt.), Arg. 212/C4
Cordón. de la Totora (mts.), Arg. 212/B4
Cordova, Al, US 188/D4
Córdova, Peru 208/C4
Cordova, Ak, US 168/Y12
Cordova, Md, US 194/C6
Core Banks (isl.), NC, US 189/J3
Coreaú, Braz. 207/F3
Coree South, Austl. 159/B2
Corella, Sp. 72/E1
Coremas, Braz. 207/G4
Corentyne (riv.), Guy. 206/B2
Corfield, Austl. 160/A3
Corfu (Kérkira) (isl.), Gre. 93/H3
Corgémont, Swi. 86/D3
Corgo, Sp. 72/B1
Cori, It. 91/B4
Coria, Sp. 72/B3
Coria del Río, Sp. 72/B4
Coriano, It. 89/F6
Coribe, Braz. 210/D2
Coricudgy (mt.), Austl. 159/E1
Corigliano Calabro, It. 74/E3
Corinaldo, It. 89/G6
Corinda, Austl. 155/E4
Coringa Islets (isls.), Austl. 160/C2
Coringa Islets (isl.), Austl. 153/D2
Corinne, Ok, US 179/G3
Corinth, NY, US 187/K3
Corinth (gulf), Gre. 93/J3
Corinth, Ms, US 188/C3
Corinth, Tx, US 176/K6
Corinth (Kórinthos) (ruin), Gre. 75/H4
Corinto, Nic. 200/E3
Corinto, Braz. 210/D3
Corisco (bay), EqG. 146/B2
Corisco (isl.), EqG. 146/B2
Corixa Grande (riv.), Braz. 209/G5
Cork (int'l arpt.), Ire. 58/B6
Cork (har.), Ire. 58/B6
Cork, Ire. 58/B6
Corkscrew (swamp), Fl, US 191/H4
Corleone, It. 74/C4
Corleto Perticara, It. 74/E2
Çorlu, Turk. 77/H5
Cormeilles, Fr. 83/F2
Cormeilles-en-Vexin, Fr. 56/J4
Cormelles-le-Royal, Fr. 83/E2
Cormery, Fr. 83/F6
Cormons, It. 89/G2
Cormontreuil, Fr. 80/D5
Corn Palace, The, SD, US 180/E2
Cornaca, Bol. 212/C2
Cornacchia (peak), It. 92/C4
Cornaredo, It. 88/C3
Cornas, Fr. 90/A3
Cornberg, Ger. 79/G6
Corndon (peak), Wal, UK 62/C1
Cornedo Vicentino, It. 89/E2
Cornelia, Ga, US 189/F3
Cornélio Procópio, Braz. 213/G2
Cornelius Grinnel (bay), Nun, Can. 167/K2
Cornell, Ca, US 192/B2
Cornell, Mi, US 186/C2
Cornell, Wi, US 181/J1
Cornell, Il, US 181/K3
Cornella, Sp. 73/L7
Corner (inlet), Austl. 153/D4
Corner Brook, Nf, Can. 185/J1
Cornerstone, Ar, US 179/J3
Cornesti, Mol. 98/E4
Cornetto (peak), It. 87/H6
Cornfield (pt.), Ct, US 195/F1
Cornhill, Sc, UK 59/D1
Corniglio, It. 88/D5
Cornimont, Fr. 86/C2
Corning, Sk, Can. 182/C3
Corning, Ar, US 188/B2
Corning, Ca, US 172/B4
Corning, Ks, US 181/F4
Corning, Ia, US 181/G3
Corning, NY, US 187/H3
Corning, Oh, US 186/E5
Cornish (cr.), Austl. 160/B3
Corno (peak), It. 91/B2
Corno (riv.), It. 92/B2
Corno alle Scale (peak), It. 71/J4
Corno di Rosazzo, It. 89/G2
Cornone di Blumone (peak), It. 87/G6
Cornour (peak), It. 90/D3
Cornú (peak), Arg. 215/D7
Cornucopia, Wi, US 183/J4
Cornuda, It. 89/F2
Cornudas (mts.), NM, US 178/B4
Cornudas, Tx, US 177/B2
Cornville, Az, US 175/G3
Cornwall, On, Can. 187/J2
Cornwall (isl.), Nun, Can. 167/S7
Cornwall (co.), Eng, UK 62/A6
Cornwall (cape), Eng, UK 62/A6
Cornwall, Pa, US 194/B3
Cornwallis (isl.), Nun, Can. 167/S7
Cornwell, Fl, US 191/H4
Cornwerd, Neth. 78/C2
Corny (pt.), Austl. 157/H5
Coro, Ven. 204/D2
Coroatá, Braz. 207/E4
Corocoro, Bol. 212/B1
Corofin, Ire. 58/A4
Coroico, Bol. 208/E5
Coromandel, NZ 161/C2
Coromandel (pen.), NZ 161/C2
Coromandel (coast), India 118/D5
Coromandel, Braz. 210/D3
Coron (isl.), Phil. 114/C3
Coron, Phil. 114/C2
Corona, NM, US 178/B3
Corona, Ca, US 192/C3
Corona del Mar (nbrhd.), Ca, US 192/G8
Coronach, Sk, Can. 171/M3
Coronado, Ca, US 192/C5
Coronado (bay), CR 196/E6
Coronado Nat'l Mem., Az, US 175/G5
Coronation (gulf), Nun, Can. 166/E2
Coronation, Ab, Can. 171/J1
Coronation, SAfr. 151/E2
Coronda, Arg. 212/D4
Coronel, Chile 214/B3
Coronel Bogado, Par. 213/E3
Coronel Cornejo, Arg. 212/D2
Coronel Dorrego, Arg. 214/E3
Coronel Fabriciano, Braz. 211/E3
Coronel Moldes, Arg. 214/D2
Coronel Moldes, Arg. 212/C3
Coronel Oviedo, Par. 213/E3
Coronel Pringles, Arg. 214/E3
Coronel Suárez, Arg. 214/E3
Coronel Vidal, Arg. 214/F3
Coronel Vivida, Braz. 213/F3
Coronet, Fl, US 190/L8
Corongo, Peru 208/B3
Coronie (dist.), Sur. 205/G3
Coropuna (peak), Peru 208/C4
Çorovodë, Alb. 75/G2
Corozal, Belz. 200/D2
Corozal, Col. 204/C2
Corozo Pando, Ven. 205/E2
Corpach, Sc, UK 59/A3
Corps-Nuds, Fr. 82/D5
Corpus, Arg. 213/F3
Corpus Christi (lake), Tx, US 177/E3
Corpus Christi (bay), Tx, US 177/F4
Corpus Christi (int'l arpt.), Tx, US 199/F3
Corpus Christi, Tx, US 177/F4
Corpus Christi Nav. Air Sta., Tx, US 177/F4
Corque, Bol. 212/C1
Corral, Chile 214/B3
Corral de Almaguer, Sp. 72/D3
Corral de Bustos, Arg. 214/E2
Corrales, Col. 204/C3
Corrales, NM, US 175/J3
Corralillo, Cuba 201/F1
Corralitos (peak), Arg. 212/C4
Corre, Fr. 86/C2
Correa, Arg. 214/E2
Corredor, CR 201/F4
Correggio, It. 89/D4
Correlia (lake), Austl. 155/D4
Corrente (riv.), Braz. 210/C3
Corrente, Braz. 210/D1
Correntes (riv.), Braz. 209/H5
Correntes, Cabo das (cape), Moz. 149/G5
Corrib (lake), Ire. 58/A3
Corrie, Sc, UK 59/A5
Corrientes, Arg. 212/E3
Corrientes (prov.), Arg. 213/E4
Corrientes (pt.), Col. 204/B3
Corrientes (cape), Cuba 201/E1
Corrientes (riv.), Ecu. 204/B5
Corrientes (riv.), Peru 208/C1
Corrigan, Tx, US 177/G2
Corrigin, Austl. 156/C5
Corringham, Eng, UK 56/E2
Corris, Wal, UK 62/C1
Corriverton, Guy. 205/G3
Corry, Pa, US 187/G4
Corryhabbie (peak), Sc, UK 59/C2
Corryong, Austl. 159/C3
Corse (cape), Fr. 74/A1
Corse (hill), Sc, UK 59/B5
Corse (dept.), Fr. 71/H5
Corserine (peak), Sc, UK 60/D1
Corseul, Fr. 82/C4
Corsewall (pt.), NI, UK 60/C1
Corsham, Eng, UK 62/D4
Corsica, SD, US 180/E2
Corsica (isl.), Fr. 55/E4
Corsicana, Tx, US 177/F1
Corsico, It. 88/C3
Corsons (inlet), NJ, US 194/D5
Cortada (mesa), NM, US 175/J3
Cortaillod, Swi. 86/C4
Cortaro, Az, US 175/G4
Cortegana, Sp. 72/B4
Cortemaggiore, It. 88/C4
Cortemilia, It. 88/B4
Cortes, Phil. 114/D3
Cortez, Co, US 175/H2
Cortina d'Ampezzo, It. 71/K3
Cortines, Arg. 215/J11
Cortland, NY, US 187/H3
Cortland, Oh, US 186/F4
Cortland, Il, US 181/K3
Corubal (riv.), GBis. 140/B3
Coruche, Port. 72/A3
Çoruh (riv.), Turk. 97/G4
Çorum, Turk. 96/E4
Çorum (prov.), Turk. 96/E4
Corumbá, Braz. 212/E1
Corumbá (riv.), Braz. 210/C3
Corumbaú (pt.), Braz. 211/F3
Corumbiara (riv.), Braz. 209/F4
Corunna, Mi, US 186/D3
Corunna, On, Can. 193/H6
Coruripe, Braz. 211/F1
Corvallis, Or, US 172/B1
Corvaro, It. 92/C3
Corve (riv.), Eng, UK 62/D2
Corvo (peak), It. 92/C3
Corvo (isl.), Azor., Port. 73/R12
Corwen, Wal, UK 61/E6
Corydon, In, US 188/D1
Corydon, Ia, US 181/H3
Corzoneso, Swi. 87/E5
Corzuela, Arg. 212/D3
Cosalá, Mex. 198/D3
Cosamaloapan, Mex. 199/P8
Cosapa, Bol. 212/B1
Cosautlán, Mex. 199/N7
Coscapa, Bol. 208/D5
Coscerno (peak), It. 91/B2
Coscomatepec, Mex. 199/M7
Cosenza, It. 74/E3
Coshocton, Oh, US 186/F4
Cosigüina (pt.), Nic. 200/E3
Coslada, Sp. 73/N9
Cosmit Ind. Res., Ca, US 174/D4
Cosmo Newberry Aboriginal Rsv., Austl. 156/D3
Cosmópolis, Braz. 211/J7
Cosne d'Allier, Fr. 70/E3
Cosne-Cours-sur-Loire, Fr. 70/E3
Cosolapa, Mex. 199/N8
Cospeito, Sp. 72/B1
Cosquín, Arg. 212/C4
Cossa, Ang. 147/E4
Cossato, It. 88/B2
Cossé-le-Vivien, Fr. 83/E5
Cosson (riv.), Fr. 70/D3
Cossonay, Swi. 86/C4
Costa Azul, Uru. 215/G2
Costa Brava (int'l arpt.), Sp. 73/G2
Costa da Caparica, Port. 73/P10
Costa de Mosquitos (phys. reg.), Nic. 201/E4
Costa del Sol (coast), Sp. 92/B3
Costa di Rovigo, It. 89/E3
Costa Marques, Braz. 209/E4
Costa Masnaga, It. 88/C2
Costa Mesa, Ca, US 192/G8
Costa Rica(ctry.) 165/J8
Costa Rica, Bol. 208/D3
Costa Smeralda (int'l arpt.), It. 74/A2
Costa Volpino, It. 88/D2
Costabissara, It. 89/E2
Costello, Pa, US 187/G4
Costello (peak), SD, US 180/C1
Costessey, Eng, UK 63/H1
Costești, Rom. 77/G3
Costigliole d'Asti, It. 88/B4
Costiglione Saluzzo, It. 90/D3
Cosumnes (riv.), Ca, US 172/C4
Cotabambas, Peru 208/C4
Cotabato, Phil. 114/D4
Cotacachi (peak), Ecu. 204/B4
Cotacajes (riv.), Bol. 209/E5
Cotagaita, Bol. 212/C2
Cotahuasi, Peru 208/C4
Cotatumbo (riv.), Col. 201/H4
Cote Blanche (bay), La, US 190/C3
Côte d'Azur (coast), Fr. 73/J1
Côte d'Or (uplands), Fr. 70/F3
Côte d'Azur (int'l arpt.), Fr. 90/D5
Côte de Grace (coast), Fr. 83/F2
Côte de Hautmont (hill), Fr. 86/B1
Côte D'Ivoire(ctry.) 133/B4
Côte du Rif (Al Hoceima) (int'l arpt.), Mor. 138/C2
Côte-Saint-Luc, Qu, Can. 185/N7
Coteau des Prairies (plat.), SD, US 180/E1
Coteau du Missouri (plat.), SD, US 180/D1
Coteau-du-Lac, Qu, Can. 185/M7
Coteau-Landing, Qu, Can. 185/M7
Cotegipe, Braz. 210/D2
Cotentin (pen.), Fr. 70/C2
Cotento (peak), It. 92/C4
Côtes de Meuse (uplands), Fr. 68/C4
Côtes-D'Armor (dept.), Fr. 82/B4
Cothi (riv.), Wal, UK 62/B3
Cotia, Braz. 211/K8
Cotignac, Fr. 90/C5
Cotignola, It. 89/E5
Cotonou (int'l arpt.), Ben. 141/F5
Cotonou, Ben. 141/F5
Cotopaxi, Co, US 178/B1
Cotopaxi (vol.), Ecu. 204/B5
Cotopaxi (dept.), Ecu. 204/B5
Cotopaxi, PN, Ecu. 204/B5
Cotswolds (hills), Eng, UK 62/D3
Cottage Grove, Or, US 172/B2
Cottage Grove, Mn, US 183/Q7
Cottageville, SC, US 189/G4
Cottam, On, Can. 193/G7
Cottbus, Ger. 69/H3
Cottel (isl.), Nf, Can. 185/L1
Cottenham, Eng, UK 63/G2
Cotter, Ar, US 179/H2
Cottica, Sur. 206/C2
Cotton, Mn, US 183/H4
Cotton (lake), Tx, US 177/N9
Cotton Bowl (State Fair Park), Tx, US 176/L7
Cotton Plant, Ar, US 179/J3
Cotton Valley, La, US 179/H4
Cottondale, Fl, US 191/F2
Cottondale, Tx, US 176/K6
Cottonport, La, US 190/B2
Cottonton, Al, US 188/E4
Cottonwood, Al, US 191/F2
Cottonwood, Az, US 175/F3
Cottonwood, Id, US 170/F4
Cottonwood (riv.), Ks, US 181/F4
Cottonwood, Mn, US 181/G1
Cottonwood (riv.), Mn, US 181/G1
Cottonwood, Tx, US 177/F2
Cottonwood (cr.), Wy, US 173/J2
Cottonwood Falls, Ks, US 179/F1
Cottonwood Wash (riv.), Az, US 175/G3
Cottsloe (nbrhd.), Austl. 156/K6
Cotulla, Tx, US 177/E3
Couasnon (riv.), Fr. 83/E5
Coubert, Fr. 56/L6
Coublevie, Fr. 90/B2
Couch, Mo, US 179/J2
Couchey, Fr. 86/A3
Couchwood, La, US 179/H4
Coudekerque-Branche, Fr. 80/B1
Coudersport, Pa, US 187/G4
Coudoux, Fr. 90/B5
Couëron, Fr. 82/D6
Couesnon (riv.), Fr. 82/D4
Cougar, Wa, US 170/C4
Coulaines, Fr. 83/F4
Coulee City, Wa, US 170/E4
Coulee Dam, Wa, US 170/E4
Coulee Dam NRA, Wa, US 170/E3
Coulogne, Fr. 80/A2
Coulomb (pt.), Austl. 154/A4
Coulomb Pt. Nature Rsv., Austl. 154/A4
Coulombs-en-Valois, Fr. 56/M4
Coulommes, Fr. 56/L5
Coulommiers, Fr. 80/C6
Coulon (riv.), Fr. 90/B5
Coulonge (riv.), Qu, Can. 187/H1
Coulounieix-Chamiers, Fr. 70/D4
Coulsdon (nbrhd.), Eng, UK 56/C3
Coulterville, Ca, US 174/B2
Coulterville, Il, US 188/C1
Coumfea (peak), Ire. 58/C5
Counamama, FrG. 206/C1
Counce, Tn, US 188/C3
Council, Id, US 172/E1
Council Bluffs, Ia, US 181/G3
Council Grove, Ks, US 179/F1
Country Homes, Wa, US 170/F4
Coupar Angus, Sc, UK 59/C3
Coupeville, Wa, US 170/C3
Coupvray, Fr. 56/L5
Cour-Cheverny, Fr. 83/G5
Courantyne (riv.), Sur. 205/G3
Courantyne (riv.), Guy.,Sur. 203/D2
Courantyne (riv.), Guy. 206/B1
Courbevoie, Fr. 56/J5
Courcelles, Belg. 81/D3
Courcelles-sur-Seine, Fr. 83/G2
Courchevel (arpt.), Fr. 90/C2
Courcouronnes, Fr. 56/K6
Courdimanche, Fr. 56/H4
Courgenay, Swi. 86/D3
Courgent, Fr. 56/G5
Courmayeur, It. 86/C6
Cournon-d'Auvergne, Fr. 70/E4
Courpalay, Fr. 56/L6
Courrendlin, Swi. 86/D3
Courroux, Swi. 86/D3
Coursan, Fr. 70/E5
Courseulles-sur-Mer, Fr. 83/E2
Courtelary, Swi. 86/D3
Courtenay, ND, US 182/E4
Courtepin, Swi. 86/D4
Courthézon, Fr. 90/A4
Courtice, On, Can. 186/V8
Courtisols, Fr. 81/D6
Courtland, Ca, US 193/L10
Courtland, Ks, US 180/F4
Courtland, Va, US 189/J2
Courtmacsherry, Ire. 58/B6
Courtmacsherry (bay), Ire. 58/B6
Courtney, Tx, US 177/F2
Courtomer, Fr. 56/L6
Courtown, Ire. 58/D4
Courtright, On, Can. 193/H6
Courville-sur-Eure, Fr. 83/G4
Cousance, Fr. 86/B4
Cousane (pass), Ire. 58/A6
Coushatta, La, US 190/B1
Cousolre, Fr. 81/D3
Coutances, Fr. 82/D2
Couteau (hills), Sk, Can. 171/L2
Couterne, Fr. 83/E3
Coutevroult, Fr. 56/L5
Couto de Magalhães, Braz. 206/D5
Coutras, Fr. 70/C4
Coutts, Ab, Can. 171/J3
Couva, Trin. 205/F2
Couvet, Swi. 86/C4
Couvin, Belg. 81/D3
Couzeix, Fr. 70/D4
Covadonga, PN, Sp. 72/C1
Covasna (prov.), Rom. 77/G3
Covasna, Rom. 77/H3
Cove, Ar, US 179/G3
Cove, Sc, UK 59/B5
Cove, Tx, US 177/N9
Cove Bay, Sc, UK 59/D2
Cove Gap, WV, US 189/F1
Cove Neck, NY, US 195/L8
Covelo, Ca, US 172/B4
Covendo, Bol. 209/E4

245
Coven – Dalan

Coventry (canal), Eng, UK 63/E1
Coventry, Eng, UK 63/E2
Covered, Turk. 129/M6
Covesville, Va, US 189/H2
Covilhã, Port. 72/B2
Covina, Ca, US 192/G7
Covington, Ga, US 188/F4
Covington, In, US 186/C4
Covington, Ky, US 188/E1
Covington, La, US 190/C2
Covington, Mi, US 183/K4
Covington, Ok, US 179/F2
Covington, Oh, US 186/D4
Covington, Tn, US 188/C3
Covington, Tx, US 177/F1
Covington, Va, US 189/H2
Covo, It. 88/C3
Cow (cr.), Or, US 172/B2
Cow Creek, Wy, US 180/B2
Cow Green (res.), Eng, UK 61/F2
Cowal (reg.), Sc, UK 59/A4
Cowal (lake), Austl. 159/C1
Cowal Creek Aboriginal Community, Austl. 155/F2
Cowan, Tn, US 188/D3
Cowan (nbrhd.), Austl. 160/H8
Cowan (lake), Austl. 153/B4
Cowangie, Austl. 158/B2
Cowansville, Qu, Can. 187/K2
Cowaramup, Austl. 156/B5
Coward Springs, Austl. 157/H4
Cowarie, Austl. 157/H3
Cowboy (hill), Ne, US 180/C3
Cowbridge, Wal, UK 62/C4
Cowden, Il, US 181/K4
Cowdenbeath, Sc, UK 59/C4
Cowee (mts.), NC, US 189/F3
Cowell, Austl. 157/H5
Cowes, Eng, UK 63/E5
Cowes, Austl. 159/B4
Cowessess Ind. Res., Sk, Can. 182/C2
Coweta (co.), Ga, US 189/L8
Cowhouse (cr.), Tx, US 177/E2
Cowichan (lake), BC, Can. 170/B3
Cowie, Sc, UK 59/C4
Cowlesville, NY, US 136/W10
Cowley, Wy, US 173/J1
Cowley, Ab, Can. 171/G3
Cowlitz (riv.), Wa, US 170/D4
Cowora, Austl. 159/C3
Cowpens Nat'l Bfld., SC, US 189/G3
Cowra, Austl. 159/D1
Cox City, Ok, US 179/F3
Coxhoe, Eng, UK 61/G2
Coxilha de Santana (hills), Braz. 213/F4
Coxim, Braz. 213/F1
Coxim (riv.), Braz. 210/B3
Cox's Bāzār, Bang. 119/F3
Cox's Cove, Nf, Can. 185/H1
Coxs Mills, WV, US 189/G1
Coxsackie, NY, US 187/K3
Coy, Al, US 190/E2
Coy Aike, Arg. 215/C6
Coya, Chile 214/N9
Coya Sur, Chile 212/B2
Coyah, Gui. 140/B4
Coyame, Mex. 177/B3
Coyanosa Draw (riv.), Tx, US 177/C2
Coye-la-Forêt, Fr. 56/K4
Coyoacán (nbrhd.), Mex. 199/R10
Coyote (cr.), Ca, US 93/L12
Coyotepec, Mex. 199/K7
Coyuca de Benítez, Mex. 199/E5
Coyutla, Mex. 99/M6
Cozad, Ne, US 180/E3
Cozhê, China 125/E5
Cozumel, Mex. 200/E1
Cozumel (int'l arpt.), Mex. 200/E1
Cozumel (isl.), Mex. 165/J7
Crab (cr.), Wa, US 170/E4
Crab Orchard Nat'l Wild. Ref., Il, US 181/K5
Crab Orchard NWR, Il, US 188/C2
Crabapple, Ga, US 89/M6
Cradle (mtn.), Austl. 158/C4
Cradock, SAfr. 150/D4
Craftsbury, Vt, US 187/K2
Crag (peak), Eng, UK 61/F3
Craig, Co, US 173/K3
Craig (mt.), Co, US 180/B3
Craig, Mo, US 181/G3
Craig, Mt, US 171/J4
Craig (cr.), Va, US 189/G2
Craigavad, NI, UK 60/C2
Craigavon (dist.), NI, UK 60/B3
Craigavon, NI, UK 60/B3
Craigellachie, Sc, UK 59/C2
Craigieburn, Austl. 158/F5
Craigsville, WV, US 189/G1
Craigsville, Va, US 189/H1
Craik, Sk, Can. 71/M2
Crail, Sc, UK 59/D4
Crailsheim, Ger. 84/D4
Craiova, Rom. 77/F3
Cramalina (peak), Swi. 87/E5
Cramlington, Eng, UK 61/G1
Cran-Gevrier, Fr. 86/C6
Crana (riv.), Ire. 60/A1
Cranborne Chase (for.), Eng, UK 62/D5
Cranbourne, Austl. 158/G6
Cranbrook, Austl. 158/D4
Cranbrook, Austl. 156/C5
Cranbrook, BC, Can. 170/G3
Cranbury, NJ, US 194/D3
Crandall, Mb, Can. 182/D2
Crandall, Tx, US 176/L7
Crandon, Wi, US 183/K5
Crane, Mt, US 182/B4
Crane, Mo, US 179/H2
Crane (lake), Il, US 181/J3
Crane, Tx, US 176/C2
Crane Hill, Al, US 188/D3
Crane Lake, Mn, US 183/H3
Crane Naval Weapons Support Center, In, US 186/C5
Crane Neck (pt.), NY, US 195/E2
Crane NWSC, In, US 188/D1
Crane Prairie (res.), Or, US 172/C2
Crane River, Mb, Can. 182/E2
Cranfills Gap, Tx, US 176/F2
Cranford, NJ, US 195/H9
Cranleigh, Eng, UK 63/F4
Cranston, RI, US 187/L4
Craon, Fr. 83/E5
Craponne (canal), Fr. 90/A5
Craponne, Fr. 90/A1
Crary, ND, US 182/E3
Crasna (riv.), Rom. 76/F2
Crasnoe, Mol. 98/E4
Craster, Eng, UK 59/E6
Crater (peak), Or, US 172/B2
Crater (lake), Or, US 172/B2
Crater Lake NP, Or, US 172/B2
Craters Of The Moon Nat'l Mon., Id, US 173/G2
Crateús, Braz. 207/F4
Crati (riv.), It. 74/E3
Cratloe, Ire. 58/B4
Crato, Port. 72/B3
Crato, Braz. 207/G4
Cravens, La, US 190/B2
Cravinhos, Braz. 213/H2
Crawford, Co, US 175/J1
Crawford, Ga, US 189/F4
Crawford, Ms, US 188/C4
Crawford, Ok, US 178/E3
Crawford, Sc, UK 59/C6
Crawford, Tx, US 177/F2
Crawford Bay, BC, Can. 170/F3
Crawfordsville, In, US 186/C4
Crawfordville, Fl, US 191/F2
Crawfordville, Ga, US 189/F4
Crawley, Eng, UK 63/F4
Cray (riv.), Eng, UK 56/D2
Crayford (nbrhd.), Eng, UK 56/D2
Crazy (mts.), Mt, US 171/J4
Crazy Horse Monument, SD, US 180/C2
Crazy Woman (cr.), Wy, US 173/K1
Creag Meagaidh (peak), Sc, UK 59/B3
Creagerstown, Md, US 194/A4
Creal Springs, Il, US 188/C2
Cream, Wi, US 181/J1
Creasy (Mifflinville), Pa, US 194/B1
Creazzo, It. 89/E3
Crêches-sur-Saône, Fr. 86/A5
Crécy-sur-Serre, Fr. 80/C4
Credit (riv.), On, Can. 186/T8
Crediton, Eng, UK 62/C5
Cree (riv.), Sc, UK 60/D2
Cree (lake), Sk, Can. 166/F3
Cree (riv.), Sk, Can. 166/F3
Creede, Co, US 175/J2
Creedman Coulee Nat'l Wild. Ref., Mt, US 171/K3
Creedmoor, Tx, US 177/F2
Creek (Pryor), Ok, US 179/G2
Creel, Mex. 198/D3
Creelman, Sk, Can. 182/C3
Creemore, On, Can. 186/F2
Creetown, Sc, UK 60/D2
Creglingen, Ger. 84/D4
Crégy-lès-Meaux, Fr. 56/L5
Créhange, Fr. 81/F5
Créhen, Fr. 82/C3
Creighton, Sk, Can. 166/F3
Creighton, Ne, US 180/F2
Creighton, SD, US 180/C1
Creignish, NS, Can. 185/G3
Creil, Fr. 80/B5
Crema, It. 88/C3
Crémieu, Fr. 86/B6
Cremlingen, Ger. 79/H4
Cremona, It. 88/D3
Cremona (prov.), It. 88/C2
Cremona, Ab, Can. 170/G2
Crenshaw, Ms, US 188/B3
Creola, Al, US 190/D2
Creole, La, US 190/B3
Crepaja, Yugo. 76/E3
Crepori (riv.), Braz. 206/B4
Crépy, Fr. 80/C4
Creran (lake), Sc, UK 59/A3
Cres (isl.), Cro. 93/G1
Cres, Cro. 71/L4
Cresaptown, Md, US 187/G5
Cresbard, SD, US 180/E1
Crescent, Ok, US 179/F3
Crescent (lake), Fl, US 191/H3
Crescent, Or, US 172/C2
Crescent City, Fl, US 191/H3
Crescent City, Ca, US 172/A3
Crescent Group (isls.), Asia 113/F5
Crescent Lake, Or, US 172/C2
Crescent Lake Nat'l Wild. Ref., Ne, US 180/C3
Crescentino, It. 88/B3
Cresco, Ia, US 181/H2
Cresco, Pa, US 194/C1
Crespano del Grappa, It. 89/E2
Crespellano, It. 89/E4
Crespières, Fr. 56/H5
Crespin, Fr. 80/C3
Crespo, Arg. 212/D5
Cresskill, NJ, US 195/K8
Cresson, Pa, US 187/G4
Cresson, Tx, US 176/K7
Cressona, Pa, US 194/B2
Cressy, Austl. 158/C4
Crest, Fr. 90/B3
Crest Hill, Il, US 193/P16
Crestline, Ca, US 192/C2
Crestline, Oh, US 186/E4
Creston, Nf, Can. 185/K2
Creston, Ca, US 174/B3
Creston, Ia, US 181/G3
Creston, BC, Can. 170/F3
Crestone, Co, US 178/B2
Crestone (peak), Co, US 178/B2
Crestview, Fl, US 190/E2
Crestwood Village, NJ, US 194/D4
Creswell, Eng, UK 61/G5
Creswell, Or, US 172/B2
Creswell Downs, Austl. 155/D4
Creswick, Austl. 159/A3
Crêt de la Neige (peak), Fr. 86/B5
Crêt du Nu (peak), Fr. 86/B5
Crêt du Rey (peak), Fr. 90/C1
Crete, Il, US 186/C4
Crete (sea), Gre. 93/K3
Crete, Ne, US 181/F3
Crete (isl.), Gre. 55/G5
Créteil, Fr. 56/K5
Cretin (cape), PNG 155/G1
Creuch (hill), Sc, UK 59/B5
Creus (cape), Sp. 73/G1
Creuse (riv.), Fr. 92/D1
Creussen (riv.), Ger. 85/E3
Creussen, Ger. 85/E3
Creutzwald-la-Croix, Fr. 81/F5
Creuzburg, Ger. 79/H6
Crevacuore, It. 88/B2
Crevalcore, It. 89/E4
Crèvecœur-le-Grand, Fr. 80/B4
Crevillente, Sp. 73/E3
Crevoladossola, It. 87/E5
Crewe, Eng, UK 61/F5
Crewe, Va, US 189/H2
Crewkerne, Eng, UK 62/D5
Crews (lake), Fl, US 190/K7
Crianlarich, Sc, UK 59/B4
Crib Point, Austl. 159/B4
Criccieth, Wal, UK 60/D6
Crichton, Sk, Can. 171/L3
Criciúma, Braz. 213/G4
Cricket, NC, US 189/G2
Crickhowell, Wal, UK 62/C3
Cricklade, Eng, UK 63/E3
Crieff, Sc, UK 59/C4
Criffell (hill), Sc, UK 60/E2
Crikvenica, Cro. 71/L4
Crimean (pen.), Rom. 77/L3
Crimean (mts.), Ukr. 99/H5
Crimond, Sc, UK 59/E1
Cripple Creek, Co, US 178/B1
Criquetot-L'Esneval, Fr. 83/F1
Crisenoy, Fr. 56/L6
Crisfield, Md, US 189/K2
Crisp (pt.), Mi, US 186/D1
Crisp, Tx, US 176/L7
Crissier, Swi. 86/C4
Crissiumal, Braz. 213/F3
Crissolo, It. 90/D3
Cristal, Monts de (mts.), Gabon 146/B2
Cristalândia, Braz. 210/C1
Cristalina, Braz. 210/D3
Cristalinho (riv.), Braz. 210/C2
Cristina, Braz. 211/L7
Cristino Castro, Braz. 207/E5
Cristóbal (pt.), Ecu. 208/J7
Cristóbal Colón (peak), Col. 204/C2
Cristoforo Colombo (int'l arpt.), It. 88/B5
Cristuru Secuiesc, Rom. 77/G2
Crișul Negru (riv.), Rom. 76/E2
Crișul Repede (riv.), Rom. 98/B4
Crivitz, Wi, US 186/B2
Crixás, Braz. 210/C2
Crixás-Açu (riv.), Braz. 210/C2
Crna Reka (riv.), FYROM 75/G2
Črnomelj, Slov. 76/B3
Croaghmoyle (peak), Ire. 58/A2
Croatia(ctry.) 55/F4
Croce (peak), It. 87/H5
Croce, Pico di (peak), It. 87/H4
Croche (peak), Fr. 86/C6
Croche (riv.), Qu, Can. 184/A1
Crocker, Mo, US 179/H2
Crocker (range), Malay. 117/E3
Crocker (peak), Ecu. 208/J7
Crocketford, Sc, UK 60/E1
Crockett, Ca, US 193/K10
Crockett, Tx, US 177/G2
Crockett Mills, Tn, US 188/C3
Crockham Hill, Eng, UK 56/D3
Crocodile (pt.), Austl. 159/E2
Crocodilopolis (ruin), Egypt 139/B6
Crodo, It. 87/E5
Crofton, Ky, US 188/D2
Crofton, Md, US 194/B6
Crofty, Wal, UK 62/B3
Croghan (mtn.), Ire. 60/B6
Crohane (peak), Ire. 58/A6
Croisette (cape), Fr. 90/B6
Croisic (bay), Fr. 82/C6
Croisic (pt.), Fr. 82/C6
Croisilles, Fr. 80/B3
Croissy-Beaubourg, Fr. 56/K5
Croix (lake), On, Can. 183/J3
Croix Rousse (peak), Fr. 90/D2
Croker (cape), Austl. 154/D2
Croker (isl.), Austl. 153/C2
Crolles, Fr. 90/B2
Cromarty, Sc, UK 59/B1
Cromarty Firth (bay), Sc, UK 59/B1
Crombie (mt.), Austl. 157/F3
Cromdale, Sc, UK 59/C2
Cromdale (hills), Sc, UK 59/C2
Cromer, Mb, Can. 182/D3
Cromer, Eng, UK 63/H1
Cromwell, NZ 161/B4
Cromwell, Al, US 188/C4
Cromwell, Ky, US 188/D2
Cromwell, Ok, US 179/F3
Crondall, Eng, UK 56/A3
Crong A Na (riv.), Viet. 120/D3
Cronulla (nbrhd.), Austl. 160/H9
Crook, Eng, UK 61/G2
Crooked (cr.), Ks, US 178/D2
Crooked (isl.), Fl, US 191/F3
Crooked (lake), Fl, US 191/H4
Crooked (isl.), Bahm. 197/G3
Crooked (riv.), Or, US 172/C1
Crooked Island Passage (chan.), Bahm. 201/H1
Crookhaven, Ire. 58/A7
Crooks, SD, US 181/F2
Crooks Tower (peak), SD, US 180/C1
Crookston, Mn, US 182/F4
Crookstown, Ire. 58/B6
Crooksville, Oh, US 186/E5
Crookwell, Austl. 159/D2
Croom, Ire. 58/B4
Croom, Fl, US 190/L6
Crosby, Mn, US 183/H4
Crosby, ND, US 182/C3
Crosby, Eng, UK 61/E5
Crosby, Ms, US 190/C2
Crosby (mt.), Wy, US 173/J2
Crosby, Tx, US 177/M9
Crosbyton, Tx, US 178/D4
Cross (cape), Namb. 148/B4
Cross, Tx, US 177/F2
Cross Anchor, SC, US 189/G3
Cross City, Fl, US 191/G3
Cross Fell (peak), Eng, UK 61/F2
Cross Hill, SC, US 189/G3
Cross Plains, Wi, US 181/K2
Cross Plains, Tx, US 177/E1
Cross River (state), Nga. 141/H5
Cross River (res.), NY, US 195/E1
Cross Roads, Tx, US 177/G1
Cross Roads, Pa, US 194/B4
Crossett, Ar, US 179/J4
Crossfarnoge (pt.), Ire. 58/D5
Crossfield, Ab, Can. 171/G2
Crossford, Sc, UK 59/C4
Crossgar, NI, UK 60/C3
Crossgates, Wal, UK 62/C2
Crosshaven, Ire. 58/B6
Crosshill, Sc, UK 59/B6
Crosshouse, Sc, UK 59/B5
Crosskeys, Wal, UK 62/C3
Crosslake, Mn, US 183/G4
Crossmaglen, NI, UK 58/D1
Crossmichael, Sc, UK 60/E2
Crossmolina, Ire. 58/A1
Crossroads, Ire. 57/P9
Crossville, Il, US 188/C1
Crossville, Al, US 188/E3
Crossville, Tn, US 188/E3
Crosswicks (cr.), NJ, US 194/D3
Crostolo (riv.), It. 88/D3
Croston, Eng, UK 61/F4
Croswell, Mi, US 186/E3
Crothersville, In, US 188/E1
Croton-Harmon (Croton-On-Hudson), NY, US 195/E1
Croton-On-Hudson (Croton-Harmon), NY, US 195/E1
Crotone, It. 75/E3
Crottendorf, Ger. 85/F1
Croult (riv.), Fr. 56/K5
Crouy, Fr. 80/C5
Crouy-sur-Ourcq, Fr. 56/M4
Crow (cr.), Co, US 180/B3
Crow (riv.), Mn, US 183/N6
Crow (peak), SD, US 180/C1
Crow Creek Ind. Res., SD, US 180/E1
Crow Ind. Res., Mt, US 173/J1
Crow Ind. Res., Mt, US 171/K5
Crow Wing (riv.), Mn, US 183/G4
Crow, North Fork (riv.), Mn, US 183/G5
Crow, North Fork (riv.), Mn, US 181/G1
Crow, South Fork (riv.), Mn, US 183/G5
Crow, South Fork (riv.), Mn, US 181/G1
Crowborough, Eng, UK 63/G4
Crowder, Ok, US 179/G3
Crowdy Bay NP, Austl. 158/E1
Crowe (riv.), On, Can. 187/H2
Crowell, Tx, US 178/E4
Crowheart, Wy, US 173/J2
Crowie (cr.), Austl. 159/C1
Crowland, Eng, UK 63/F1
Crowle, Eng, UK 61/H4
Crowley (lake), Ca, US 174/C2
Crowley, La, US 190/B2
Crowley, Tx, US 176/K7
Crowley's (ridge), Ar, US 188/B3
Crown Point, In, US 186/C4
Crown Point (int'l arpt.), Trin. 205/F2
Crown Prince Frederik (isl.), Nun, Can. 167/H1
Crownpoint, NM, US 175/H3
Crows Nest (peak), SD, US 180/C1
Crows Nest Falls NP, Austl. 160/D4
Crowther (cr.), Austl. 159/D2
Crowthorne, Eng, UK 63/F4
Crowville, La, US 179/J4
Croxley Green, Eng, UK 56/B2
Croydon (bor.), Eng, UK 56/C2
Croydon (nbrhd.), Eng, UK 56/C2
Croydon, Austl. 160/A2
Croydon (nbrhd.), Austl. 158/G5
Croydon, Pa, US 194/D3
Crozet (isls.), Fr. 53/M8
Crozon, Fr. 82/A4
Cruach Mhór (peak), Sc, UK 59/A4
Cruach nan Capull (peak), Sc, UK 59/A5
Cruas, Fr. 90/A3
Crucero, Peru 208/D4
Cruden Bay, Sc, UK 59/E2
Cruger, Ms, US 188/B4
Cruick Water (riv.), Sc, UK 59/D3
Crum (mtn.), Ms, US 188/C3
Crumlin, NI, UK 60/B2
Crummock Water (lake), Eng, UK 61/E2
Crump (lake), Or, US 172/D2
Crump, Tn, US 188/C3
Crumpton, Md, US 194/C5
Cruseilles, Fr. 86/C5
Crusheen, Ire. 58/B4
Crusnes (riv.), Fr. 81/E5
Cruz (cape), Cuba 201/G2
Cruz Alta, Arg. 214/E2
Cruz Alta (peak), Port. 73/P10
Cruz Alta, Braz. 213/F4
Cruz del Eje, Arg. 212/C4
Cruz Grande, Mex. 200/B2
Cruzeiro, Braz. 211/M7
Cruzeiro do Oeste, Braz. 213/F2
Cruzeiro do Sul, Braz. 208/C2
Cruzeta, Braz. 207/G4
Cruzília, Braz. 211/M6
Crvenka, Yugo. 76/D3
Cryn-y-Brain (peak), Wal, UK 61/E5
Crystal, NM, US 175/H2
Crystal, Mn, US 183/P6
Crystal (lake), Pa, US 194/C1
Crystal Bay, Nv, US 172/D4
Crystal Beach, Fl, US 190/K7
Crystal Brook, Austl. 157/H5
Crystal Cave, Pa, US 194/C2
Crystal City, Mb, Can. 182/E3
Crystal City, Tx, US 177/E3
Crystal Falls, Mi, US 183/K4
Crystal Hill, Va, US 189/H2
Crystal Lake, Fl, US 191/F2
Crystal Lake, Il, US 186/B3
Crystal River, Fl, US 191/G3
Crystal Springs, Ms, US 190/C2
Crystal Springs, Fl, US 190/L7
Crystal Springs (res.), Ca, US 193/K11
Csenger, Hun. 69/M5
Csepreg, Hun. 76/C2
Csongrád, Hun. 76/E2
Csorna, Hun. 76/C2
Csorvás, Hun. 76/E2
Csóványos (peak), Hun. 76/D2
Csurgó, Hun. 76/C2
Ctesiphon (ruin), Iraq 129/F3
Cu Lao (isl.), Viet. 120/E4
Cuajinicuilapa, Mex. 200/B2
Cualedro, Sp. 72/B2
Cuamba, Moz. 149/H2
Cuanavale (riv.), Ang. 148/C2
Cuando (riv.), Ang. 148/D3
Cuangar, Ang. 148/C3
Cuango, Ang. 146/D5
Cuango, Ang. 146/D4
Cuango (riv.), Ang. 146/D5
Cuanza (riv.), Ang. 133/D6
Cuanza Norte (prov.), Ang. 146/C5
Cuanza Sul (prov.), Ang. 146/C5
Cuareim (riv.), Braz. 213/E4
Cuaró, Uru. 213/F4
Cuart de Poblet, Sp. 73/E3
Cuarto (riv.), Arg. 214/D2
Cuatir (riv.), Ang. 148/C2
Cuatro Ojos, Bol. 212/D1
Cuauhtémoc, Mex. 198/E5
Cuauhtémoc, Mex. 198/D2
Cuautepec, Mex. 199/L6
Cuautitlán, Mex. 199/Q9
Cuautitlán Izcalli, Mex. 199/Q9
Cuautla, Mex. 199/L8
Cuba(ctry.) 165/J7
Cuba, Il, US 181/J3
Cuba, Ks, US 180/F4
Cuba, Mo, US 179/J1
Cuba, NM, US 175/J2
Cuba, NY, US 187/G3
Cuba, Port. 72/B3
Cuba City, Wi, US 181/J2
Cubagua (isl.), Ven. 205/E2
Cubal, Ang. 148/B2
Cubal (riv.), Ang. 148/B2
Cuballing, Austl. 156/C5
Cubango (riv.), Ang. 133/D6
Cubatão, Braz. 211/K8
Cubati, Braz. 207/G4
Cubero, NM, US 175/J3
Çubuk, Turk. 128/C1
Cuc Phuong NP, Viet. 112/E4
Cucamonga (Rancho Cucamonga), Ca, US 192/C2
Cuccurano, It. 89/F6
Cucharas (riv.), Co, US 178/B2
Cuchi, Ang. 148/C2
Cuchi (riv.), Ang. 148/C2
Cuchilla Caraguatá, Uru. 213/F5
Cuchillo, NM, US 175/J4
Cuchillo-Có, Arg. 214/D3
Cuchivero (riv.), Ven. 205/E3
Cuchumatanes (mts.), Guat. 200/D3
Cuckfield, Eng, UK 63/F4
Cuckmere (riv.), Eng, UK 63/G5
Cucuí, Braz. 205/E4
Cúcuta, Col. 204/C3
Cucuyagua, Hon. 200/D3
Cudahy, Wi, US 186/C3
Cudahy, Ca, US 192/F8
Cudal, Austl. 159/D1
Cuddalore, India 121/C4
Cuddington, Eng, UK 61/F5
Cudgewa, Austl. 159/C3
Cudillero, Sp. 72/B1
Cudrefin, Swi. 86/D4
Cudworth, Eng, UK 61/G4
Cudworth, Sk, Can. 171/M1
Cue, Austl 156/C3
Cuebe (riv.), Ang. 148/C2
Cueio (riv.), Ang. 148/D2
Cueli (riv.), Ang. 148/C2
Cuéllar, Sp. 72/C2
Cuéllar-Baza, Sp. 72/D4
Cuenca, Ecu. 204/B5
Cuenca, Sp. 72/D2
Cuencamé de Ceniceros, Mex. 198/E3
Cuengo (riv.), Ang. 146/D5
Cuernavaca, Mex. 199/K8
Cuero, Tx, US 177/F3
Cuers, Fr. 90/C6
Cuesmes, Belg. 80/C3
Cueto, Cuba 201/H1
Cuetzalán, Mex. 199/M6
Cueva de la Quebrada del Toro, PN, Ven. 204/D2
Cuevas de Vinromá, Sp. 73/F2
Cuevas del Almanzora, Sp. 72/E4
Cuevo, Bol. 212/D2
Cuffley, Eng, UK 56/C1
Cufré, Uru. 215/K11
Cuges-les-Pins, Fr. 90/B6
Cugir, Rom. 77/F3
Cuglieri, It. 74/A2
Cugnaux, Fr. 70/D5
Cugo (riv.), Ang. 146/D4
Cuiabá, Braz. 210/A2
Cuiabá (riv.), Braz. 209/G5
Cuicas, Ven. 204/D2
Cuijk, Neth. 78/C5
Cuilapa, Guat. 200/D3
Cuilcagh (peak), NI, UK 58/C1
Cuilco (riv.), Guat. 200/C3
Cuillin (sound), Sc, UK 57/Q8
Cuilo, Ang 146/D4
Cuilo (riv.), Ang. 146/C4
Cuilo Pombo, Ang. 146/C4
Cuima, Ang. 148/B2
Cuisance (riv.), Fr. 86/B4
Cuise-la-Motte, Fr. 80/C5
Cuiseaux, Fr. 86/B5
Cuisery, Fr 86/A4
Cuisy, Fr. 56/L4
Cuité, Braz. 207/G4
Cuitláhuac, Mex. 199/N8
Cuito (riv.), Ang. 148/C2
Cuito-Cuanavale, Ang. 148/C2
Cuiuni (riv.), Braz. 205/E5
Cujmir, Rom. 76/F3
Cukuh Batuberagam (cape), Indo. 115/D3
Culasi, Phil. 114/C3
Culbertson (dam), Ne, US 180/D3
Culburra-Orient Point, Austl. 159/E2
Culcairn, Austl. 159/C2
Culdaff (riv.), Ire. 60/A1
Culdaff, Ire. 60/A1
Culebras, Peru 208/B3
Culemborg, Neth. 78/C5
Culfa, Azer. 129/F2
Culgoa (riv.), Austl. 153/D3
Culiacán Rosales, Mex. 198/D3
Culion (isl.), Phil. 114/B3
Culion Reservation, Phil. 114/C3
Culiseu (riv.), Braz. 210/B2
Cullen, Arg. 215/C7
Cullen, La, US 179/H4
Cullen, Sc, UK 59/D1
Cullen, Va, US 189/H2
Cullen Bullen, Austl. 159/E1
Cullenagh (riv.), Ire. 58/A4
Culleoka, Tx, US 176/L6
Cullera, Sp. 73/E3
Culleredo, Sp. 72/A1
Cullin (lake), Ire. 58/A2
Cullinan, SAfr. 149/F5
Cullman, Al, US 188/D3
Culloden Battlesite, Sc, UK 59/B2
Cullomburg, Al, US 190/D2
Cullompton, Eng, UK 62/C5
Cullowhee, NC, US 189/F3
Cully, Swi. 86/C5
Cullybackey, NI, UK 60/B2
Culmback (dam), Wa, US 193/D2
Culmore, NI, UK 60/A1
Culoz, Fr. 86/B6
Culp Creek, Or, US 172/B2
Culpeper, Va, US 189/J1
Culpina, Bol. 212/C2
Culross, Sc, UK 59/C4
Culta, Bol. 212/C1
Cultra (lake), Ire. 58/B3
Cults, Sc, UK 59/D2
Culuene (riv.), Braz. 209/H4
Culver (pt.), Austl. 156/E5
Culver, Ks, US 179/F1
Culver, In, US 186/C4
Culver, Mn, US 183/H4
Culver, Or, US 172/C1
Culver City, Ca, US 192/F7
Culverden, NZ 161/C3
Culvers (lake), NJ, US 194/D1
Culverstone Green, Eng, UK 56/E3
Cumã (bay), Braz. 207/E3
Cumaná, Ven. 205/E2
Cumane (riv.), Fr. 90/B2
Cumaría, Peru 208/C3
Cumba, Peru 208/B2
Cumbal, Col. 204/B4
Cumberland (isl.), Ga, US 191/H2
Cumberland, Md, US 187/G5
Cumberland, Wa, US 193/D3
Cumberland, Wi, US 183/H5
Cumberland (riv.), Ky,Tn, US 169/J4
Cumberland (pen.), Nun, Can. 167/K2
Cumberland (sound), Nun, Can. 167/K2
Cumberland (falls), Ky, US 188/E2
Cumberland, Ky, US 189/F2
Cumberland, BC, Can. 170/B3
Cumberland (co.), NJ, US 194/A3
Cumberland (plat.), US 188/D3
Cumberland (lake), Ky, US 188/E2
Cumberland, Va, US 189/H2
Cumberland Gap NHP, NC,Va, US 189/F2
Cumberland Island Nat'l Seashore, Ga, US 191/H2
Cumbernauld, Sc, UK 59/C5
Cumbi, Ang. 146/C4
Cumbre del Laudo (peak), Arg. 212/B3
Cumbre del Libertador General San Martín (peak), Arg. 212/C3
Cumbres and Toltec Railroad, Co, US 175/J2
Cumbres Bastonal, Cerro (peak), Mex. 200/C2
Cumbres de Majalca, PN, Mex. 198/D2
Cumbres de Monterrey, PN, Mex. 196/A2
Cumbres de Monterrey, PN, Mex. 198/E3
Cumbria (co.), Eng, UK 61/E2
Cumbrian (mts.), Eng, UK 61/E2
Cumbum, India 121/C3
Cumiana, It. 90/D3
Cumming, Ga, US 188/E3
Cummins, Austl. 157/G5
Cumnock, Sc, UK 59/B6
Cumnock, Austl. 159/D1
Cumpas, Mex. 198/C2
Çumra, Turk. 128/C2
Cuñapirú, Uru. 215/G1
Cuñaré, Col. 204/C4
Cunaviche, Ven. 205/E3
Cunco, Chile 214/B3
Cunde (riv.), Ang. 148/C2
Cundeelee Abor. Rsv., Austl. 156/D4
Cunderdin, Austl. 156/C4
Cundinamarca (dept.), Col. 204/C3
Cunduacán, Mex. 200/C2
Cunene (prov.), Ang. 148/B3
Cunene (riv.), Ang. 133/D6
Cuneo (prov.), It. 88/A3
Cuneo, It. 90/D4
Cuneo (prov.), Fr. 90/D3
Cuney, Tx, US 176/G1
Cung Son, Viet. 120/E3
Cunha, Braz. 211/M8
Cunhinga, Ang. 148/C2
Cunhinga (riv.), Ang. 148/C1
Cunjamba, Ang. 148/D2
Cunnamulla, Austl. 160/B5
Cunningham, Ks, US 179/E2
Cunningham, Ky, US 188/C2
Cunningham, Tx, US 179/G4
Cunninghame (reg.), Sc, UK 59/B5
Čuokkaraš'ša (peak), Nor. 64/H1
Cuorgnè, It. 90/D2
Cuozhen, China 113/H2
Cupar, Sk, Can. 182/B2
Cupar, Sc, UK 59/C4
Cupello, It. 92/D3
Cupertino, Ca, US 193/K12
Cupra Marittima, It. 92/C1
Cupramontana, It. 89/G7
Ćuprija, Yugo. 76/E4
Cuprija, Yugo. 76/E4
Cuprum, Id, US 172/E1
Cuquenán (riv.), Ven. 205/F3
Curaçá, Braz. 207/G5
Curaçao (isl.), Neth. 197/H5
Curacautín, Chile 214/C3
Curacaví, Chile 214/N8
Curahuara de Carangas, Bol. 208/D5
Curahuara de Pacajes, Bol. 212/B1
Curanilahue, Chile 214/B3
Curaray (riv.), Peru 204/C5
Curaray (riv.), Peru 204/B5
Curaray (riv.), Ecu.,Peru 208/C1
Curarén, Hon. 200/E3
Curaumilla (pt.), Chile 214/N8
Curcubăta (peak), Rom. 77/F2
Cure (riv.), Fr. 68/B5
Curecanti National Recreation Area, Co, US 173/K4
Curecanti Nat'l Rec. Area, Co, US 178/A1
Curepipe, Mrts. 151/T15
Curepto, Chile 214/B2
Curiche Grande (riv.), Bol. 209/G5
Curicó, Chile 214/C2
Curimatá, Braz. 210/D1
Curitiba, Braz. 213/G3
Curitibanos, Braz. 213/G3
Curnamona, Austl. 157/H4
Curno, It. 88/C2
Curoca (riv.), Ang. 148/B3
Curone (riv.), It. 88/C3
Currais Novos, Braz. 207/G4
Curral Velho, CpV. 133/K10
Curralinho, Braz. 206/D3
Currant (mtn.), Nv, US 172/F4
Currant, Nv, US 172/F4
Currarong, Austl. 159/E2
Currawilla, Austl. 160/A4
Current (riv.), Mo, US 188/B2
Currie, Austl. 159/A4
Currie, Sc, UK 59/C5
Currie, Nv, US 173/F3
Currituck, NC, US 189/J2
Currituck (sound), NC, US 189/K2
Curtea de Argeș, Rom. 77/G3
Curtici, Rom. 76/E2
Curtin, Or, US 172/B2
Curtina, Uru. 213/E5
Curtis (riv.), Austl. 160/D4
Curtis (isl.), NZ 162/G8
Curtis, Sp. 72/A1
Curtis, Ar, US 179/H4
Curtis, La, US 179/H4
Curtis (pt.), Md, US 194/B6
Curú Nat'l Wild. Ref., CR 201/E4
Curuá (riv.), Braz. 206/C4
Curuá (isl.), Braz. 206/D2
Curuá (riv.), Braz. 205/H5
Curuá Una (riv.), Braz. 205/H5
Curuçá, Braz. 206/E3
Curuçú (riv.), Braz. 208/D2
Curup, Indo. 115/C3
Cururupu, Braz. 207/E3
Curuzú Cuatiá, Arg. 212/E4
Curvelo, Braz. 210/D3
Curwensville, Pa, US 187/G4
Curwood (mt.), Mi, US 183/K4
Cusco, Peru 208/D4
Cusco (dept.), Peru 208/C4
Cushendall, NI, UK 60/B1
Cusher (riv.), NI, UK 60/B3
Cushet Law (peak), Eng, UK 59/D6
Cushing, Ok, US 179/F3
Cushing, Tx, US 177/G2
Cushman, Ar, US 179/J3
Cusick, Wa, US 170/F3
Cusna (peak), It. 88/D5
Cussava (riv.), Ang. 148/B2
Cusse, Ang. 148/B2
Cusset, Fr. 70/E3
Cusseta, Ga, US 188/E4
Cusseta, Al, US 188/E4
Custer (peak), SD, US 180/C1
Custer, SD, US 180/C2
Custer, Mt, US 171/L4
Custer City, Ok, US 178/E3
Custines, Fr. 81/F6
Custódia, Braz. 207/G5
Cut (hill), Eng, UK 62/C5
Cut and Shoot, Tx, US 177/G2
Cut Bank, Mt, US 171/H3
Cut Bank (cr.), Mt, US 171/H3
Cut Knife, Sk, Can. 171/K1
Cut Off, La, US 190/C3
Cutato, Ang. 148/C2
Cutato, Ang. 148/C2
Cutato (riv.), Ang. 146/D5
Cutchogue, NY, US 195/F2
Cutenda, Ang. 148/B2
Cutervo, Peru 208/B2
Cuthbert, Ga, US 191/F2
Cutler Ridge, Fl, US 191/H5
Cutral-Có, Arg. 214/C3
Cutro, It. 75/E3
Cuttack, India 121/E1
Cutten, Ca, US 172/A3
Cuvelai, Ang. 148/B2
Cuvergnon, Fr. 56/L4
Cuvette (pol. reg.), Congo 146/C3
Cuvier (cape), Austl. 156/B3
Cuvo (riv.), Ang. 148/B1
Cuxac, Fr. 73/G1
Cuxhaven, Ger. 79/F1
Cuyabeno, Ecu. 204/C5
Cuyahoga (riv.), Oh, US 186/F4
Cuyahoga Falls, Oh, US 186/F4
Cuyahoga Valley NRA, Oh, US 186/F4
Cuyama (riv.), Ca, US 174/B3
Cuyapaipe Ind. Res., Ca, US 174/D4
Cuyo (isls.), Phil. 117/F1
Cuyo, Phil. 114/C3
Cuyo East Passage (chan.), Phil. 114/C3
Cuyo West Passage (chan.), Phil. 114/C3
Cuyocuyo, Peru 208/D4
Cuyuchi, Bol. 209/F4
Cuyuni (riv.), Guy. 205/G3
Cuyuni (riv.), Ven. 205/F3
Cuyuni-Mazaruni (pol. reg.), Guy. 205/F3
Cuzco (ruin), Peru 208/D4
Cwm, Wal, UK 62/C3
Cwmafan, Wal, UK 62/C3
Cwmbran, Wal, UK 62/C3
Cyangugu, Rwa. 147/G3
Cyclades (isls.), Gre. 93/K3
Cymric, Sk, Can. 182/B2
Cynthia, Ab, Can. 170/G1
Cynthiana, Ky, US 188/E1
Cynwyl Elfed, Wal, UK 62/B3
Cypress (hills), Ab, Can. 171/J3
Cypress, Al, US 188/D4
Cypress, Ca, US 192/F8
Cypress (lake), Fl, US 190/N7
Cypress, Tx, US 177/M9
Cypress (cr.), Tx, US 177/M8
Cypress Gardens, Fl, US 190/M8
Cyprus(ctry.) 103/C6
Cyrenaica (reg.), Libya 93/J5
Cyrene (ruin), Libya 93/J4
Cyril, Ok, US 179/E3
Cyril E. King (int'l arpt.), USVI 197/M8
Cyrus, Mn, US 183/G5
Cysoing, Fr. 80/C2
Cywyn (riv.), Wal, UK 62/B3
Czaplinek, Pol. 69/J2
Czarna Białostocka, Pol. 69/M2
Czarnków, Pol. 69/J2
Czech Republic (ctry.) 55/F4
Częstochowa, Pol. 69/K3
Częstochowa (prov.), Pol. 69/K3
Człuchów, Pol. 66/G5

D

D'Aguilar (range), Austl. 160/E6
D'Arcachon, Bassin di (lag.), Fr. 70/C4
D'Arcy, BC, Can. 170/C2
D' Ouvéa (lag.), NCal. 163/V12
D'Urville (isl.), NZ 161/C3
D. F. Malan (Cape Town) (int'l arpt.), SAfr. 150/L10
D.C. (fed. dist.), US 189/J1
Da (riv.), China 104/D5
Da (Black) (riv.), Viet. 112/E4
Da Hinggan (mts.), China 103/M5
Da Hoa, Viet. 120/D4
Da Juh, China 104/C4
Da Lat, Viet. 120/E4
Da Nang, Viet. 120/E2
Da Nang (cape), Viet. 120/E2
Da Qaidam, China 104/D4
Da Te, Myan. 120/B2
Da Xian, China 113/E2
Daaden, Ger. 81/G2
Da'an, China 105/J2
Daba (mts.), China 104/F5
Dabaga, Tanz. 145/A4
Dabai, Nga. 141/G4
Dabajuro, Ven. 204/D2
Dabakala, C.d'Iv. 140/D4
Dabas, Hun. 76/D2
Dabat, Eth. 142/H2
Dabeiba, Col. 204/B3
Dabeibu, China 113/H2
Dabein, Myan. 120/B2
Dabendorf, Ger. 68/Q7
Dabhoi, India 118/B3
Dabie (mts.), China 113/G2
Dabissé Kayati, Gui. 140/B4
Dabo, Fr. 81/G6
Dabob (bay), Wa, US 193/B2
Daboji, China 105/K3
Dabola, Gui. 140/C4
Daborow, Som. 144/D4
Dabou, C.d'Iv. 140/D5
Daboya, Gha. 141/E4
Dabra, India 122/B3
Dąbrowa Białostocka, Pol. 67/K5
Dąbrowa Górnicza, Pol. 69/K3
Dabu, China 113/G3
Dăbuleni, Rom. 77/G4
Dac Sut, Viet. 120/D3
Dac To, Viet. 120/D3
Dacca (Dhaka) (cap.), Bang. 123/H4
Dachang, China 106/L8
Dachang Huizu Zizhixian, China 106/H7
Dachau, Ger. 85/E6
Dacheng, China 113/G2
Dacono, Co, US 180/B3
Dadanawa, Guy. 206/B2
Dade (co.), Fl, US 190/P11
Dade City, Fl, US 190/L7
Dades, Oued (riv.), Mor. 136/D3
Dadeville, Al, US 188/E4
Dadi (cape), Indo. 117/H4
Dadnah, UAE 127/G3
Dadong, China 120/E1
Dādra and Nagar Haveli (state), India 118/B4
Dādri, India 124/D5
Dādu, Pak. 127/J3
Dadu (riv.), China 104/E5
Daduru (riv.), SrL. 118/C6
Daen Noi (peak), Thai. 120/B4
Dăeni, Rom. 77/J3
Daet, Phil. 114/C2
Dafang, China 112/E3
Dafanhe, China 107/B1
Dafeng, China 106/E4
Dafna, Isr. 131/D2
Dafu, China 112/D2
Dafu, China 113/H2
Dag, India 118/C3
Daga Medo, Eth. 144/B4
Daga Post, Sudan 142/G3
Dagaio, Eth. 144/B4
Dagana, Sen. 140/B2
Dağardı, Turk. 128/B2
Dağbaşı, Turk. 128/D2
Dagda, Lat. 67/M3
Dage, D.R. Congo 147/E2
Dagestan Aut. Rep., Rus. 100/Q6
Dagestanskiye Ogni, Rus. 97/J4
Daggaboersnek (pass), SAfr. 150/D4
Dagger (mtn.), Tx, US 177/C3
Daggett, Mi, US 186/C2
Daglung, China 123/H1
Dagmar Range NP, Austl. 160/B2
Dagneux, Fr. 86/B6
Dagny, Fr. 56/M5
Dagongcha, China 104/D4
Dagu, China 106/H7
Daguan, China 113/E3
Daguan, China 112/D3
D'Aguilar (mt.), Austl. 160/E6
Dagujia, China 107/C1
Daguokui (peak), China 105/K2
Dagupan, Phil. 114/C1
Daguragu Abor. Land, Austl. 154/C4
Dagxoi, China 119/G2
Dagzê (lake), China 125/E5
Dagzhuka, China 123/G1
Dahana (des.), SAr. 103/D7
Dāhānu, India 121/B2
Daharki, Pak. 118/A2
Dahei (riv.), China 106/B2
Daheiding (peak), China 105/K2
Dahekou, China 104/F5
Dahenan, China 106/G7
Dahlak (arch.), Erit. 144/B1
Dahlem, Ger. 81/F3
Dahlem, Ger. 68/Q7
Dahlenburg, Ger. 79/H2
Dahlgren, Il, US 188/C1
Dahlonega, Ga, US 188/F3
Dahmani, Tun. 138/L7
Dahme (riv.), Ger. 69/G3
Dahn, Ger. 81/G5
Dahongliutan, China 125/C4
Dahongqi, China 107/B2
Dahra, Sen. 140/B3
Dahshūr, Egypt 139/C5
Dahshūr (ruin), Egypt 139/C5
Dahūk, Iraq 129/E2
Dahūk (gov.), Iraq 129/E2
Dahuofang (res.), China 106/D2
Dahushan, China 107/B2
Dai (isl.), Indo. 154/C1
Dai (isl.), China 113/J2
Dai (lake), China 106/C2
Dai Loc, Viet. 120/E3
Dai Xian, China 106/C3
Dai-segen-dake (peak), Japan 108/B3
Dai-sen (peak), Japan 110/C3
Daian, Japan 109/L5
Daicheng, China 106/D3
Daigo, Japan 111/G2
Daik-u, Myan. 120/B2
Dā'il, Syria 131/E3
Dailekh, Nepal 122/C1
Dailly, Sc, UK 59/B6
Daimiao, China 106/D3
Daimiel, Sp. 72/D3
Daingerfield, Tx, US 179/G4
Dainkognubma, China 104/D5
Daintree NP, Austl. 155/G4
Daiō-zaki (pt.), Japan 111/E3
Dāira Dīn Panāh, Pak. 124/A4
Daireaux, Arg. 214/E3
Dairy (cr.), Austl. 157/N8
Dairyland, Wi, US 183/H4
Daisen-Oki NP, Japan 110/C3
Daisetsuzan NP, Japan 108/C2
Daisy, Ok, US 179/G3
Daisy, Ar, US 179/H3
Daisy, Ky, US 189/F2
Daito (isl.), Japan 103/N7
Daitō, Japan 109/J6
Daiyun (peak), China 113/H3
Dajabón, DRep. 201/J2
Dajarra, Austl. 157/H2
Dajing, China 119/K3
Dak Nhe, Viet. 120/D3
Dakar (cap.), Sen. 140/A3
Dakar (pol. reg.), Sen. 140/A3
Dakar (Yoff) (int'l arpt.), Sen. 140/A3
Dakeng, China 113/G3
Daketa Shet' (riv.), Eth. 144/B4
Dakhin Shābāzpur (isl.), Bang. 123/H4
Dakhlet Nouadhibou (pol. reg.), Mrta. 136/A5
Dakoro, Niger 141/G3
Dakota (co.), Mn, US 183/P7
Dakota City, Ia, US 181/G2
Dakota City, Ne, US 181/F2
Dakovica, Yugo. 76/E4
Dakovo, Cro. 76/D3
Dakshin Gangotri, India, Ant. 216/A
Dal (riv.), Swe. 100/B3
Dal Cataract (falls) Sudan 135/F4
Dala, Ang. 146/E5
Dala-Järna, Swe. 66/F1
Dalaas, Aus. 87/F3
Dalaba, Gui. 140/B4
Dalad Qi, China 106/B2
Dalai (lake), China 104/H3
Dalaman, Turk. 128/B2
Dalaman (int'l arpt.), Turk. 128/B2
Dalāmī, Sudan 142/F3
Dalandzadgad, Mong. 101/L5
Dalandzadgad, Mong. 104/E3

246

Dalan – Des

Dalangwan, China 113/G4
Dalaoba, China 125/D3
Dalarna (reg.), Swe. 64/E3
Dalarö, Swe. 65/B1
Dalatangi (pt.), Ice. 64/Q6
Dalavich, Sc, UK 59/A4
Dalbeattie, Sc, UK 60/E2
Dalby, Austl. 160/C4
Dalby, Swe. 66/E4
Dalby, Swe. 65/K7
Dalby-Söderskog NP, Swe. 65/K7
Dalcross (int'l arpt.), Sc, UK 59/B1
Dale, Nor. 66/A1
Dale, In, US 188/D1
Dale, Tx, US 176/F3
Dale, SC, US 189/G4
Dale City, Va, US 189/J1
Dale Hollow (lake), Tn, US 188/E2
Dalen, Nor. 66/C2
Dalen, Neth. 78/D3
Daleside, SAfr. 150/Q13
Daletme, Myan. 119/F3
Daleville, Al, US 191/F2
Dalfsen, Neth. 78/D3
Dalgan (riv.), Ire. 58/B2
Dalgaranger (mt.), Austl. 156/C3
Dalhart, Tx, US 178/C2
Dalhousie, NB, Can. 184/D1
Dalhousie, India 124/C3
Dalhousie (cape), NW, Can. 166/D1
Dali, China 106/B4
Dali (riv.), China 104/F4
Dali, China 112/D3
Dalian (bay), China 107/A3
Dalian, China 107/A3
Dalian (int'l arpt.), China 106/E3
Daliang, China 104/E4
Dalías, Sp. 72/D4
Daliburgh, Sc, UK 57/Q8
Dalidag (peak), Azer. 129/F2
Daling (riv.), China 105/H3
Dāliyat el Karmil, Isr. 131/C3
Dalizi, China 107/D2
Dalj, Cro. 76/D3
Dalkeith, Sc, UK 59/C5
Dalkola, India 123/F3
Dall (isl.), Ak, US 166/C3
Dallas, Sc, UK 59/C1
Dallas, Ga, US 188/E4
Dallas, Or, US 172/B1
Dallas (co.), Tx, US 176/L7
Dallas, Tx, US 176/L7
Dallas City, Il, US 181/J3
Dallas Love Field (arpt.), Tx, US 176/L7
Dallas-Fort Worth (int'l arpt.), Tx, US 176/K7
Dallastown, Pa, US 194/B4
Dalles of the Saint Croix, Mn, US 183/H5
Dallesport, Wa, US 172/C1
Dallgow, Ger. 68/Q6
Dallol Bosso (riv.), Niger,Mali 141/F3
Dalmally, Sc, UK 59/B4
Dalmatia (reg.), Cro. 93/G1
Dalmatia, Pa, US 194/B2
Dalmatovo, Rus. 95/P4
Dalmellington, Sc, UK 59/B6
Dalmeny, Austl. 159/E3
Dalmine, It. 88/C2
Dal'negorsk, Rus. 105/M3
Dal'nerechensk, Rus. 105/L2
Daloa, C.d'Iv. 140/D5
Dalol, Eth. 144/B2
Dalqū, Sudan 135/F4
Dalroy, Ab, Can. 171/H2
Dalry, Sc, UK 59/B5
Dalrymple, Sc, UK 59/B6
Dalrymple (lake), Austl. 153/D3
Dals Långed, Swe. 66/E2
Dalsingh Sarai, India 123/E3
Dalsjöfors, Swe. 66/E3
Dalton, Ar, US 188/B2
Dalton, Ga, US 188/E3
Dalton, Mn, US 182/G4
Dalton, Ma, US 187/K3
Dalton, Pa, US 187/J4
Dalton-in-Furness, Eng, UK 61/E3
Daltonganj, India 123/E3
Dalu, China 104/E4
Daluābāri, Bang. 123/G3
Daludalu, Indo. 115/C2
Daluo (peak), China 113/G4
Dalupiri (isl.), Phil. 114/C1
Dalvík, Ice. 64/N6
Dalwallinu, Austl. 156/C4
Dalwhinnie, Sc, UK 59/B3
Dalworthington Gardens, Tx, US 176/K7
Daly (bay), Nun, Can. 166/G2
Daly (riv.), Austl. 154/C3
Daly(riv.) 153/C2
Daly R. Wild. Sanct., Austl. 154/C3
Daly River, Austl. 154/C3
Daly River Aboriginal Land, Austl. 154/C3
Daly Waters, Austl. 154/D4
Dalyup, Austl. 156/D5
Dam (riv.), China 125/F5
Dam Doi, Viet. 120/D4
Dam Gamad, Sudan 142/E2
Damagaram Takaya, Niger 141/H3
Damāgheh-ye Kūh (pt.), Iran 129/J5
Damak, Nepal 123/F2
Damān and Diu (state), India 118/B3
Damanhūr, Egypt 139/B2
Damara, CAfr. 142/C4
Damāş, Egypt 139/C3
Damasak, Nga. 142/B2
Damascus, Ar, US 179/H3
Damascus, Ga, US 191/F2
Damascus, Va, US 189/G2
Damascus (int'l arpt.), Syria 131/F2
Damascus, Md, US 194/A5
Damascus (Dimashq) (cap.), Syria 131/E1
Damāṭ, Egypt 139/B3
Damaturu, Nga. 142/A3
Damavānd (mtn.), Iran 129/H3
Damāvand, Iran 129/H3
Damaying, China 113/G3
Damba, Ang. 146/C4
Dambach-la-Ville, Fr. 86/D1
Dambaslar, Turk. 77/H5
Dāmbuk, India 112/B2
Dame Marie (cape), Haiti 201/H2
Dame Marie, Haiti 201/H2
Damenglong, China 120/C1
Damerham, Eng, UK 63/E5
Dameron, Md, US 189/J1
Dāmghān, Iran 129/H2
Damietta (Dumyāṭ) (mouth), Egypt 139/C1
Damietta Branch (riv.), Egypt 130/B4
Damigny, Fr. 83/F4
Daming (mtn.), China 113/F4
Daming, China 113/G3
Daming, China 106/C3
Damintun, China 107/B2
Damion (peak), Fr. 81/D4
Dāmiyā, Jor. 131/D4
Dammard, Fr. 56/M4
Dammartin-en-Goële, Fr. 56/L4
Dammastock (peak), Swi. 87/E4
Damme, Belg. 80/C1
Damme, Ger. 79/F3
Dāmodar (riv.), India 118/E3
Damoh, India 122/B4
Damon, Tx, US 177/M9
Damongo, Gha. 141/E4
Damparis, Fr. 86/B3
Dampier, Austl. 156/C2
Dampier (str.), Indo. 117/H4
Dampier (arch.), Austl. 153/A2
Dampier Downs, Austl. 154/A4
Dampierre, Fr. 86/B3
Dampierre, Fr. 56/H5
Dampierre-sur-Salon, Fr. 86/B2
Damprichard, Fr. 86/C3
Damqawt, Yem. 126/F5
Damqog (Maquan) (riv.), China 122/E1
Damrei (mts.), Camb. 120/C4
Damsterdiep (riv.), Neth. 78/D2
Damvant, Swi. 86/C3
Damville, Fr. 83/G3
Damwoude, Neth. 78/D2
Damxung, China 125/F5
Dan (riv.), China 104/G5
Dan, Isr. 131/D2
Dan (riv.), NC, US 188/H2
Dan Gulbi, Nga. 141/G4
Dan Sai, Thai. 120/C2
Dan Xian, China 113/F5
Ḑānā, Jor. 130/D4
Dana, In, US 186/C5
Dāna, Nepal 122/D1
Dana Point, Ca, US 192/C4
Danakil (reg.), Djib. 144/B3
Danané, C.d'Iv. 140/C5
Danao, Phil. 114/D3
Danba, China 112/D2
Danbury, Eng, UK 63/G3
Danbury, Ct, US 187/K4
Danbury, NC, US 189/G2
Danbury, Tx, US 176/G3
Danby, Vt, US 187/K3
Danby (lake), Ca, US 174/E3
Dancheng, China 106/C4
Dancing (pt.), Mb, Can. 182/E1
Dandaragan, Austl. 156/B4
Dande (riv.), Ang. 146/C5
Dandeldhurā, Nepal 122/C1
Dandenaong (cr.), Austl. 158/G5
Dandenong (nbrhd.), Austl. 158/G5
Dandenong (mt.), Austl. 158/G5
Danderhall, Sc, UK 59/C5
Dandīl, Egypt 139/C6
Dando, Ang. 148/C1
Dandong, China 107/C2
Dandridge, Tn, US 189/F2
Dane (riv.), Eng, UK 61/F5
Dang (riv.), China 104/D4
Dangal, Erit. 144/B2
Dangara, Taj. 125/A4
Dangayos (pt.), Phil. 113/J5
Dange, Nga. 141/G3
Dange, Ang. 146/C4
Dange-ia-Menha, Ang. 146/C5
Danger (pt.), SAfr. 150/L11
Danggali Conservation Park, Austl. 158/B2
Dangila, Eth. 142/H3
Dangkou, China 106/L8
Dangme (riv.), Bhu. 112/A3
Dangriga, Belz. 200/D2
Dangshan, China 106/D4
Dangtu, China 106/D5
Dangur, Eth. 142/H3
Dangyang, China 113/F2
Dania, Fl, US 190/P10
Danieb (riv.), Namb. 148/D4
Danielskuil, SAfr. 150/C3
Danielsville, Ga, US 189/F3
Danielsville, Pa, US 194/C2
Danilov, Rus. 94/J4
Daning, China 106/B3
Danjiangkou, China 106/B4
Danjiangkou (res.), China 104/G5
Danjoutin, Fr. 86/C2
Ḑank, Oman 127/G4
Dankaur, India 124/D5
Dankhar Gompa, India 127/L2
Dankov, Rus. 96/F1
Dankova (peak), Kyr. 125/C3
Danleng, China 112/D2
Danlí, Hon. 200/E3
Dannelly (res.), Al, US 188/D4
Dannemora, Swe. 66/G1
Dannemora, NY, US 187/K2
Dannenberg, Ger. 68/F2
Dannes, Fr. 80/A2
Dannevirke, NZ 161/D3
Dannhauser, SAfr. 151/E3
Dano, Burk. 140/E4
Dansville, NY, US 187/H3
Dantzler, Ms, US 190/D2
Danube (riv.), Yugo. 96/B3
Danube (riv.), Hun.,Rom. 98/D5
Danube (riv.), Eur. 93/K1
Danube (riv.), Aus. 55/F4
Danube (Donau) (riv.), Ger.,Aus. 71/H2
Danube, Delta of the (delta), Rom.,Ukr. 93/L1
Danube, Mouths of the (mouth), Rom.,Ukr. 96/D3
Danville, Qu, Can. 187/K2
Danville, Ar, US 179/H3
Danville, Il, US 186/C4
Danville, In, US 186/C5
Danville, Ky, US 188/E2
Danvers, Mt, US 171/K4
Danville, Oh, US 186/E4
Danville, Pa, US 194/B2
Danville, Va, US 189/H2
Danville, Vt, US 187/K2
Danville, Wa, US 170/E3
Dao, Phil. 114/C3
Dao Xian, China 113/F3
Daocheng, China 112/D2
Daodou'ao, China 113/J2
Daora, WSah. 136/B4
Daoshui, China 113/F4
D'Aosta (valley), It. 88/A1
Daotiandi, China 105/L2
Daoukro, C.d'Iv. 140/E5
Daoulas, Fr. 82/A4
Daoura, Oued ed (riv.), Alg. 136/D3
Daozhen, China 113/E2
Dapa, Phil. 114/D3
Dapaong, Togo 141/F4
Daphne, Al, US 190/E2
Dapingying, China 113/F2
Dapitan, Phil. 114/C3
Dapo, China 120/E2
Dapuzi, China 113/F3
Daqiao, China 112/D4
Daqiao, China 113/H3
Daqing, China 105/K2
Daqing (riv.), China 106/H7
Daqiu, China 113/H3
Daqu (isl.), China 113/J2
Daquanwan, China 104/C3
Dār al Bayḑā (ruin), Egypt 139/C4
Dār 'Aqīl, Sudan 142/G2
Dar Bel Hamri, Mor. 138/B2
Dar el Barka, Mrta. 140/B2
Dar es Salaam (prov.), Tanz. 145/B3
Dar es Salaam (int'l arpt.), Tanz. 145/B3
Dar es Salaam (cap.), Tanz. 145/B3
Dar Rounga (reg.), CAfr. 142/D3
Dar-e Rūd, Iran 129/J4
Dar-el-Beida (Casablanca), Mor. 136/D2
Dar'ā (prov.), Syria 130/E3
Dar'a (prov.), Syria 128/C3
Dar'ā, Syria 131/E3
Dar'ā (gov.), Syria 131/E3
Dārāb, Iran 129/H4
Dārāban, Pak. 124/A4
Darabani, Rom. 98/D3
Daraga, Phil. 114/C2
Daragodleh, Som. 144/C3
Darai (hills), PNG 155/F1
Daram, Phil. 114/D3
Dārān, Iran 129/G3
Darasun, Rus. 104/G1
Đaravica (peak), Yugo. 76/E4
Dārayyā, Syria 131/E2
Darbatta, Eth. 142/G4
Darbėnai, Lith. 67/J3
Darbhanga, India 123/E2
Darby, Fl, US 190/L7
Darby, Mt, US 171/G4
Darby, Austl. 159/C4
Darby, Pa, US 194/C4
Darda, Cro. 76/D3
Dardanelle, Ar, US 179/H3
Dardanelle (dam), Ar, US 179/H3
Dardanelles (str.), Turk. 96/C4
Darebin (cr.), Austl. 158/G5
Darent (riv.), Eng, UK 56/D3
Dareton, Austl. 158/B2
Darfield, BC, Can. 170/D2
Darfo, It. 87/G6
Dārfūr (pol. reg.), Sudan 135/E5
Dargai, Pak. 124/A2
Dargaville, NZ 161/C1
Argentière, Aiguille d' (peak), Swi. 86/D6
Dargle (riv.), Ire. 60/B5
Dargo (riv.), Austl. 159/C3
D'Arguin (bay), Mrta. 140/A1
Darhan (peak), Mong. 104/F2
Darhan, Mong. 104/F2
Darhan Muminggan Lianheqi, China 104/G3
Darie (hills), Som. 144/C3
Darien, Ga, US 191/H2
Darien, Il, US 193/P16
Darien, Ct, US 195/M7
Darién (mts.), Pan. 201/G4
Darién, PN, Pan. 197/F6
Darjazīn, Iran 129/G3
Darjiling, India 123/G2
Darkan, Austl. 156/C5
Darlag, China 104/D5
Darling (lake), ND, US 182/D3
Darling, SAfr. 150/L10
Darling (mtn.), Austl. 159/D2
Darling (range), Austl. 153/A4
Darling (riv.), Austl. 153/D4
Darling Downs (range), Austl. 160/C3
Darling Downs (reg.), Austl. 153/D3
Darling Nat'l Wild. Ref., Fl, US 191/G4
Darlington, Eng, UK 61/G2
Darlington, In, US 186/C4
Darlington, Wi, US 181/J2
Darlington, SC, US 189/H3
Darlington, Md, US 194/B4
Darlington Point, Austl. 159/C2
D'Armainvilliers (pond), Fr. 56/L5
Darmstadt, Ger. 84/B3
Darmstadt, In, US 188/D1
Darnah, Libya 93/J4
Darnāyah, Tun. 138/L7
Darnétal, Fr. 83/G2
Darney, Fr. 86/C1
Darnick, Austl. 158/B2
Darnley (cape), Ant. 216/E
Darnley (bay), NW, Can. 166/D2
Daroca, Sp. 72/E2
Darongjiang, China 113/F3
Darongtang, China 113/F2
Darras Hall, Eng, UK 61/G1
Darregueira, Arg. 214/E3
Darreh Gaz, Iran 127/G1
Darreh-ye Shahr, Iran 129/F3
Darrington, Wa, US 170/D3
Dārsana, Bang. 123/G4
Darsser (cape), Ger. 66/E4
Dart (riv.), Eng, UK 62/C6
Dart, West (riv.), Eng, UK 62/C6
Dartford, Eng, UK 56/D2
Dartington, Eng, UK 62/C6
Dartmoor (upland), Eng, UK 62/B5
Dartmoor NP, Eng, UK 70/A1
Dartmouth (dam), Austl. 159/C3
Dartmouth, NS, Can. 184/F3
Dartmouth, Eng, UK 62/C6
Dartmouth, Ma, US 187/L4
Darton, Eng, UK 61/G4
Dartowo, Pol. 66/G4
Dartuch (cape), Sp. 73/G3
Daru, SLeo. 140/C5
Daru, PNG 155/F2
Daruba, Indo. 117/G3
Daruvar, Cro. 76/C3
Darvel, Sc, UK 59/B5
Darvel (bay), Malay. 117/E3
Darwen, Eng, UK 61/F4
Darwendale, Zim. 149/F3
Darwin, Austl. 154/C3
Darwin (int'l arpt.), Austl. 154/C3
Darwin, Ca, US 174/D2
Darwin (bay), Chile 214/B5
Darwin (isl.), Ecu. 208/J6
Darwin (vol.), Ecu. 208/J7
Darya Khan, Pak. 124/A4
Daryābād, India 122/C2
Dārzīn, Iran 127/G3
Dashahe, China 105/K3
Dashanzui, China 105/K3
Dashengtang (peak), China 105/H3
Dashennongjia (peak), China 106/B5
Dasher, Ga, US 191/G2
Dashhowuz, Trkm. 100/F5
Dashi, China 113/H2
Dashowuz (prov.), Trkm. 97/L4
Dasht Kaur (riv.), Pak. 127/H3
Dasht-e Kavīr (des.), Iran 100/F6
Dasht-e Lūt (des.), Iran 100/F6
Dasht-e Mārgow (des.), Afg. 127/H2
Dasima, Gha. 141/E4
Dasing, Ger. 84/E6
Daska, Pak. 124/C3
Daspalla, India 121/E1
Dassa-Zoumé, Ben. 141/F5
Dassel, Ger. 79/G5
Dassel, Mn, US 181/G1
Dassendorf, Ger. 79/H1
Dasseneiland (isl.), SAfr. 150/B4
Dasūya, India 124/C4
Dat Do, Viet. 120/D4
Datadian, Indo. 116/E3
Dātāganj, India 122/B1
Datchet, Eng, UK 56/B2
Date, Japan 108/B2
Dateland, Az, US 175/F4
Datia, India 122/B3
Datian (peak), China 113/F4
Datil, NM, US 175/J3
Datong (riv.), China 104/D4
Datong, China 106/C2
Datong, China 104/E4
Datong (mts.), China 104/D4
Datong, China 104/G3
Datteln, Ger. 79/E5
Dattohar, India 124/B5
Datu(cape) 116/C3
Datuk (cape), Indo. 115/C2
Dāud Khel, Pak. 124/A3
Daugai, Lith. 67/L4
Daugava (riv.), Lat. 100/C4
Daugavpils, Lat. 67/M4
Daugherty Field (Long Beach) (arpt.), Ca, US 192/F8
Daulatpur, Bang. 123/G4
Daule (riv.), Ecu. 204/B5
Daule, Ecu. 204/B5
Daun, Ger. 81/F3
Daung (isl.), Myan. 120/B3
Dauphin, Mb, Can. 182/D2
Dauphin (riv.), Mb, Can. 182/E2
Dauphin (lake), Mb, Can. 182/E2
Dauphin (cape), NS, Can. 185/G2
Dauphin (co.), Pa, US 194/B3
Dauphin, Pa, US 194/B3
Dauphin Island, Al, US 190/D2
Dauphine (reg.), Fr. 92/E1
Dauphiné (range), Fr. 70/F4
Daura, Nga. 141/H3
Däväçi, Azer. 97/J4
Davao, Phil. 114/D4
Davao (gulf), Phil. 114/D4
Dāvarzan, Iran 129/J2
Davegoriale, Som. 144/C3
Davel, SAfr. 151/E2
Daveluyville, Qu, Can. 187/K1
Davenda, Rus. 105/H1
Davenport, ND, US 182/F4
Davenport, Ok, US 179/F3
Davenport, Fl, US 190/M7
Davenport, Ia, US 181/J3
Davenport, Ne, US 180/F3
Davenport (range), Austl. 154/D5
Davenport (mt.), Austl. 157/F2
Davenport, Wa, US 170/E4
Daventry, Eng, UK 63/E2
Daverdisse, Belg. 81/E3
Daveyton, SAfr. 150/E2
Davézieux, Fr. 90/A2
Davgaard-Jensen Land (phys. reg.), Grld. 167/T6
David, Pan. 201/F4
David City, Ne, US 181/F3
David-Gorodok, Bela. 98/D1
Davidson, Ar, US 179/G3
Davidson, Ok, US 178/E3
Davidson (mt.), Ca, US 193/J11
Davidson, Sk, Can. 171/M2
Davidson, NC, US 189/G3
Davie, Fl, US 190/P10
Davies (mt.), Austl. 157/F3
Davilla, Tx, US 177/F2
Daviot, Sc, UK 59/D2
Davis (sea), Ant. 216/F
Davis, Austl., Ant. 216/F
Davis (str.), Can.,Grld. 167/L2
Davis, Sk, Can. 171/M1
Davis (dam), Az, US 174/E3
Davis, Ca, US 172/C4
Davis (cr.), Mi, US 193/E7
Davis, Ok, US 179/F3
Davis (mt.), Pa, US 187/G5
Davis (mts.), Tx, US 168/F5
Davis, WV, US 189/H1
Davis Cove, Nf, Can. 185/K2
Davis Creek, Ca, US 172/C3
Davis Dam, Az, US 174/E3
Davis-Monthan (A.F.B.), Az, US 175/G4
Davisboro, Ga, US 189/F4
Davison, Mi, US 186/E3
Davisville, Mo, US 188/B2
Davlekanovo, Rus. 95/M5
Davo (riv.), C.d'Iv. 140/D5
Davos, Swi. 87/F4
Dawa, China 107/B2
Dawa Wenz (riv.), Eth. 144/B4
Dawan, China 113/F4
Dawangja (isl.), China 107/B3
Dawaxung, China 125/E5
Dawei (Tavoy), Myan. 120/B3
Dawen (riv.), China 104/H4
Dawlish, Eng, UK 62/C5
Dawqah, SAr. 126/D5
Dawson (riv.), Austl. 153/D3
Dawson (mt.), BC, Can. 170/F2
Dawson, Yk, Can. 168/Z12
Dawson (isl.), Chile 215/C7
Dawson, Ga, US 191/F2
Dawson, Mo, US 179/H2
Dawson, Mn, US 181/F1
Dawson, Tx, US 177/F2
Dawson Creek, BC, Can. 166/D3
Dawson Springs, Ky, US 188/D2
Dawsonville, Ga, US 188/E3
Dawu, China 112/D2
Dawu, China 106/C5
Dawu (mtn.), China 106/C5
Dawujiang, China 113/E3
Dax, Fr. 70/C5
Daxin, China 120/D1
Daxing, China 113/F3
Daxing, China 106/H7
Daxue (mts.), China 104/E5
Day Star Ind. Res., Sk, Can. 182/B2
Dayang (riv.), China 107/B2
Dayang, China 113/F4
Dayang Bunting (isl.), Thai. 115/B1
Dayao, China 112/D3
Daye, China 113/G2
Dayi, China 112/D2
Daying, China 107/D1
Daying (riv.), China 119/G3
Daylesford, Austl. 159/B3
Daylight (pass), Ca, US 174/D2
Daym Zubayr, Sudan 142/E4
Daymán (riv.), Uru. 213/E4
Dayong, China 113/F3
Dayong, China 113/F2
Dayr Abū Sa'īd, Jor. 131/D3
Dayr al Balaḩ, Gaza 131/A6
Dayr al Ghuşūn, WBnk. 131/C4
Dayr al Qamar, Leb. 131/D1
Dayr 'Allā, Jor. 131/D4
Dayr az Zawr, Syria 128/E3
Dayr Az Zawr (prov.), Syria 128/D3
Dayr Ballūţ, WBnk. 131/C4
Dayr Dibwān, WBnk. 131/C5
Dayr Sharaf, WBnk. 131/C4
Dayrūt, Egypt 135/F3
Dayrūţ, Egypt 139/B2
Daysland, Ab, Can. 171/H1
Dayton, Ia, US 181/G2
Dayton, In, US 186/C4
Dayton, NJ, US 194/D3
Dayton, NY, US 187/G3
Dayton, Oh, US 186/D5
Dayton, Or, US 172/B1
Dayton, Tn, US 188/E3
Dayton, Tx, US 177/N8
Dayton, Va, US 189/H1
Dayton, Wa, US 170/F4
Dayton, Wy, US 173/K1
Daytona Beach, Fl, US 191/H3
Dayu (isl.), China 113/J3
Dayu, China 113/G3
Dayuan, China 113/J2
Dayushupu, China 107/A2
Dazey, ND, US 182/E4
Dazhengjiatun, China 107/B3
Dazhizhu Dau (isl.), China 113/K8
Dazhu, China 113/E2
De Aar, SAfr. 150/D3
De Bary, Fl, US 191/H3
De Berry, Tx, US 177/G1
De Bilt, Neth. 78/C4
De Cocksdorp, Neth. 78/B2
De Cordova Bend (dam), Tx, US 177/F1
De Doorns, SAfr. 150/L10
De Forest, Wi, US 181/K2
De Funiak Springs, Fl, US 191/E2
De Gaulle, CAfr. 142/B4
De Graff, Oh, US 186/E4
De Gray (lake), Ar, US 179/H3
De Grey (riv.), Austl. 154/A5
De Grey, Austl. 156/C2
De Haan, Belg. 80/C1
De Hart (res.), Pa, US 194/B3
De Hoge Veluwe, NP, Neth. 78/C4
De Jongs (cape), Indo. 155/E1
De Kalb (co.), Il, US 193/N16
De Kalb, Il, US 181/K3
De Kalb, Ms, US 188/C4
De Koog, Neth. 78/B2
De La Vassako-Bolo, Rsv. Nat. Int., CAfr. 142/C3
De Lacs (riv.), ND, US 182/D3
De Land, Fl, US 191/H3
De Las Animas (pt.), Mex. 198/B2
De Leijen (lake), Neth. 78/D2
De Leon (lake), Fr. 70/C4
De Leon, Tx, US 176/E1
De Lier, Neth. 78/B5
Délįne, NW, Can. 166/D2
De Luz, Ca, US 192/C4
De Meern, Neth. 78/C4
De Motte (Demotte), In, US 186/C4
De Panne, Belg. 80/B1
De Peel (phys. reg.), Neth. 78/C6
De Pere, Wi, US 186/B2
De Pinte, Belg. 80/C2
De Pue, Il, US 181/K3
De Queen, Ar, US 179/G3
De Quincy, La, US 190/B2
De Ridder, La, US 190/B2
De Smet, SD, US 180/F1
De Soto, Ga, US 191/F2
De Soto, Il, US 188/C2
De Soto, Mo, US 188/B1
De Soto, Ms, US 190/D2
De Tour Village, Mi, US 186/E2
De Valls Bluff, Ar, US 179/J3
De Wijk, Neth. 78/D3
De Winton, Ab, Can. 171/G2
De Witt, Ar, US 179/J3
De Witt, NY, US 187/H3
De Witt, Ne, US 181/F3
De Witt, Ia, US 181/J3
Dead (riv.), Ire. 58/B4
Dead (lake), Fl, US 191/F2
Dead (sea), (Asia) 128/C4
Deadman (mtn.), Wy, US 173/H2
Deadman (peak), Austl. 156/C2
Deadwood, SD, US 180/C1
Deal (isl.), Austl. 158/C3
Deal, NJ, US 194/D3
Deal Island, Md, US 189/K1
Deale, Md, US 194/B6
Dean (for.), Eng, UK 62/D3
Dean (riv.), BC, Can. 170/B1
Deán Funes, Arg. 212/C4
Deanmill, Austl. 156/C5
Deanville, Tx, US 176/F2
Dearborn, Mi, US 186/E3
Dearborn, Mo, US 181/G4
Dearborn Heights, Mi, US 193/F7
Dearing, Ga, US 189/F4
Dearne, Eng, UK 61/G4
Deary, Id, US 170/F4
Dease (riv.), BC, Can. 166/D3
Dease (str.), Nun, Can. 165/F3
Dease Lake, BC, Can. 168/Z13
Death (valley), Ca, US 174/D2
Death Valley, Ca, US 174/D2
Death Valley NP, Ca,Nv, US 174/D2
Deauville, Fr. 83/F2
Deavgay (peak), Rus. 129/F1
Deba Habe, Nga. 142/A3
Debagrām, India 123/G4
Debar, FYROM 75/G2
Debark', Eth. 142/H2
Debaysīma, Erit. 144/B2
Debden, Sk, Can. 171/L1
Debelets, Bul. 77/G4
Deben (riv.), Eng, UK 63/H2
Debenham, Eng, UK 63/H2
Debert, NS, Can. 184/F3
Dębica, Pol. 69/L3
Debīdwār, Bang. 123/H4
Dęblin, Pol. 69/L3
Dębno, Pol. 69/H2
Debre Birhan, Eth. 144/A3
Debre Lībanos Monastery, Eth. 144/A3
Debre Mark'os, Eth. 142/H3
Debre Sīna, Eth. 144/A3
Debre Tabor, Eth. 142/H3
Debre Zebīt, Eth. 144/A3
Debre Zeyit, Eth. 144/A3
Debre Zeyit, Eth. 142/G3
Debrecen, Hun. 69/L5
Debub, Eth. 144/A2
Debundscha (pt.), Camr. 146/B1
DeBurgh (lake), Austl. 155/D4
Decatur, Al, US 188/D3
Decatur, Ga, US 189/M7
Decatur, Il, US 181/K4
Decatur, In, US 186/D4
Decatur, Mi, US 186/D3
Decatur, Ms, US 188/C4
Decatur, Tn, US 188/E3
Decatur, Tx, US 176/K6
Decaturville, Tn, US 188/C3
Decazeville, Fr. 70/E4
Deccan (plat.), India 118/C5
Dechang, China 112/D3
Dechheling, Bhu. 123/H2
Decima, It. 89/E4
Děčín, Czh. 69/H3
Décines-Charpieu, Fr. 86/A6
Decize, Fr. 70/E3
Decker, Mt, US 173/K1
Deckers, Co, US 178/B1
Deckerville, Mi, US 186/E3
Decorah, Ia, US 181/J2
Deddington, Eng, UK 63/E3
Dedemsvaart, Neth. 78/D3
Deder, Eth. 144/B3
Dedham, Ma, US 187/L3
Dedo (peak), Arg. 214/C5
Dédougou, Burk. 140/E3
Dedovichi, Rus. 67/N3
Dedovsk, Rus. 94/W9
Dedu, China 105/K2
Dedza, Malw. 149/G2
Dee (riv.), Sc, UK 59/C3
Dee Why (nbrhd.), Austl. 160/H8
Deel (riv.), Ire. 60/A4
Deep (cr.), Austl. 157/M8
Deep (cr.), De, US 194/C6
Deep (riv.), NC, US 189/H3
Deep Brook, NS, Can. 184/E3
Deep Creek Ind. Res., BC, Can. 170/C1
Deep Fork (riv.), Ok, US 179/F3
Deep Red (cr.), Ok, US 179/E3
Deep River, On, Can. 187/H1
Deep Springs, Ca, US 174/D2
Deepcut, Eng, UK 56/F3
Deeping Saint James, Eng, UK 63/F1
Deepwater, Mo, US 179/H1
Deepwater, Austl. 158/D1
Deepwater (pt.), De, US 194/C5
Deepwater, NJ, US 194/C4
Deer (isl.), Mb, Can. 182/F2
Deer (isl.), Ire. 58/A4
Deer (cr.), Ms, US 179/J4
Deer Flat NWR, Id, US 172/E2
Deer Island, Or, US 170/C5
Deer Lake, On, Can. 183/G1
Deer Lake, Nf, Can. 185/J1
Deer Lake, Pa, US 194/B2
Deer Lodge, Mt, US 171/H4
Deer Park, Ca, US 172/B4
Deer Park, Il, US 193/P15
Deer Park, Md, US 194/B5
Deer Park, NY, US 195/E2
Deer Park, Tx, US 177/M9
Deer Park, Wa, US 170/F4
Deer River, Mn, US 183/H4
Deerbrook, Wi, US 183/K5
Deerfield, Ma, US 187/K3
Deerfield, Il, US 193/P15
Deerfield Beach, Fl, US 190/P10
Deering, ND, US 182/D3
Deerlijk, Belg. 80/C2
Deerton, Mi, US 183/L4
Deerwood, Mn, US 183/H4
Deesa, India 127/K4
Deeside (valley), Sc, UK 59/D2
Deex Nugaaleed (riv.), Som. 144/C3
Defensores del Chaco, PN, Par. 212/D2
Defiance, Oh, US 186/D4
Deganwy, Wal, UK 60/E5
Dêgê, China 112/C2
Degeberga, Swe. 65/L7
Degeh Bur, Eth. 144/B3
Dégelis, Qu, Can. 184/C2
Degema, Nga. 141/G5
Degerfors, Swe. 66/F2
Degersheim, Swi. 87/F3
Deggendorf, Ger. 85/F5
Deggingen, Ger. 84/C5
Dego, It. 88/B5
Degoma, Eth. 142/H2
DeGrey (riv.), Austl. 156/C2
Dëgtevo, Rus. 99/L3
Deh Bīd, Iran 129/H4
Deh Dasht, Iran 129/G4
Deh-e Shīr, Iran 129/H4
Dehaj, Iran 129/H4
Dehalak (isl.), Erit. 144/A2
Dehalak Marine NP, Erit. 144/B2
Dehāqān, Iran 129/G4
Dehdez, Iran 129/G4
Deheq, Iran 129/G3
Dehlorān, Iran 129/F3
Dehri, India 123/E3
Dehua, China 113/H3
Dehui, China 105/K3
Deidesheim, Ger. 84/B4
Deil, Neth. 78/C5
Deinste, Ger. 79/G1
Deinze, Belg. 80/C2
Deister (mts.), Ger. 79/G4
Deiva Marina, It. 88/C5
Dej, Rom. 77/F2
Deje, Swe. 66/E2
Dejiang, China 113/F2
Dejima, Japan 109/E1
Dekalb (co.), Ga, US 189/M7
Dekelia (arpt.), Gre. 75/N8
Dekemhare (Dek'emhāre), Erit. 144/A2
Dek'emhāre (Dekemhare), Erit. 144/A2
Dekese, D.R. Congo 147/E3
Dekina, Nga. 141/G5
Dekle Beach, Fl, US 191/G3
Dékoa, CAfr. 142/C4
Del Campillo, Arg. 214/D2
Del Carril, Arg. 215/J11
Del Dios, Ca, US 192/C4
Del Gran Paradiso, It. 88/A2
Del Mar, Ca, US 192/C5
Del Norte, Co, US 175/J2
Del Puerte (cr.), Ca, US 193/M12
Del Rio, Tx, US 177/D3
Del Valle (lake), Ca, US 193/L11
Del Valle, Arg. 214/E2
Del Vallo Mazara (valley), It. 74/C4
Delacour, Ab, Can. 171/H2
Delacroix, La, US 190/D3
Delafield, Wi, US 193/P13
Delamar (lake), Nv, US 174/E2
Delano, Ca, US 174/C3
Delano (peak), Ut, US 175/F1
Delano, Mn, US 183/N6
Delareyville, SAfr. 150/D2
Delavan (lake), Wi, US 193/P14
Delavan, Il, US 181/K3
Delavan, Wi, US 181/K2
Delavan Lake, Wi, US 193/N14
Delaware (state), US 169/L4
Delaware (bay), US 189/K1
Delaware (riv.), US 187/J4
Delaware (riv.), Ks, US 181/G4
Delaware, NJ, US 194/C2
Delaware, Oh, US 186/E4
Delaware, Ok, US 179/G2
Delaware (co.), Pa, US 194/C4
Delaware (pass), Pa, US 194/C2
Delaware (mts.), Tx, US 177/B2
Delaware City, De, US 194/C4
Delaware Water Gap Nat'l Rec. Area, NJ,Pa, US 187/J4
Delbrück, Ger. 79/F5
Delburne, Ab, Can. 171/H1
Delčevo, FYROM 75/H2
Delcommune (lake), D.R. Congo 147/F5
Delden, Neth. 78/D4
Delebio, It. 87/F5
Delegate, Austl. 159/D3
Delémont, Swi. 86/D3
Delevan NWR, Ca, US 172/B4
Delft, Neth. 78/B4
Delfzijl, Neth. 78/D2
Delgada (pt.), Ca, US 172/A3
Delgada (pt.), Arg. 214/E4
Delgado (cape), Moz. 145/C4
Delgany, Ire. 60/B5
Delger (riv.), Mong. 104/D2
Delgī, Eth. 142/H2
Delhi, Ca, US 174/B2
Delhi, India 124/D5
Delhi, NY, US 187/J3
Delhi (state), India 118/C2
Déli, Chad 142/B3
Delia, Ab, Can. 171/H2
Delice, Turk. 128/C2
Delice (riv.), Turk. 96/E5
Délices, FrG. 206/C1
Delight, Ar, US 179/H3
Delījān, Iran 129/G3
Delingha, China 104/D4
Delisle, Qu, Can. 184/B1
Delisle, Sk, Can. 171/L2
Dell, Mt, US 173/G1
Dell City, Tx, US 177/B2
Dell Rapids, SD, US 181/F2
Delligsen, Ger. 79/G5
Dellwood, Mn, US 183/Q6
Dellys, Alg. 138/G4
Delmar, De, US 189/K1
Delmas, SAfr. 150/Q13
Delmas, Sk, Can. 171/K1
Delme (riv.), Ger. 79/F3
Delmenhorst, Ger. 79/F2
Delmiro Gouveia, Braz. 207/G5
Delmita, Tx, US 177/E4
Delmont, NJ, US 194/D5
Delnice, Cro. 71/L4
Deloraine, Mb, Can. 182/D3
Deloraine, Austl. 158/C4
Delphi, In, US 186/C4
Delphi (Dhelfoí) (ruin), Gre. 75/H3
Delphos, Oh, US 186/D4
Delphos, Ks, US 180/F4
Delportshoop, SAfr. 150/D3
Delran, NJ, US 194/D4
Delray Beach, Fl, US 190/P10
Delson, Qu, Can. 185/N7
Delta (state), Nga. 141/G5
Delta, Co, US 175/H1
Delta, Pa, US 194/B4
Delta, Ut, US 173/G4
Delta City, Ms, US 188/B4
Delta del Tigre, Uru. 215/K11
Delta du Saloum, PN du, Sen. 140/A3
Delta Junction, Ak, US 168/Y12
Delta Nat'l Wild. Ref., La, US 190/D3
Delta-Mendota (canal), Ca, US 193/M11
Delton, Mi, US 186/D3
Deltona, Fl, US 191/H3
Delvin, Ire. 58/C2
Delvinë, Alb. 75/G3
Delyatyn, Ukr. 98/C3
Dëma (riv.), Rus. 95/M5
Demak, Indo. 115/E3
Demanda (range), Sp. 72/D1
Demarest, NJ, US 195/K8
Demba, D.R. Congo 147/E4
Dembech'a, Eth. 142/H3
Dembeni, Fr. 152/H6
Dembī, Eth. 142/H3
Dembī Dolo, Eth. 142/G3
Dembia, CAfr. 142/E4
Demer (riv.), Belg. 68/C3
Demerara (riv.), Guy. 205/G3
Demerara-Mahaica (pol. reg.), Guy. 205/G3
Demerval Lobão, Braz. 207/F4
Deming, NM, US 175/J4
Demini (riv.), Braz. 205/F4
Demirci, Turk. 128/B2
Demirkent, Turk. 128/C2
Demirköprü (dam), Turk. 128/B2
Demirköy, Turk. 77/H5
Demirtaş, Turk. 77/J5
Demmin, Ger. 66/E5
Democratic Republic of the Congo (ctry.) 133/E5
Demone (valley), It. 74/D4
Demonte, It. 90/D4
Demopolis, Al, US 188/D4
Demotte (De Motte), In, US 186/C4
Dempo (peak), Indo. 115/C4
Dempster (pt.), Austl. 156/D5
Demta, Indo. 117/K4
Demuryne, Ukr. 99/J3
Den Burg, Neth. 78/B2
Den Chai, Thai. 120/C2
Den Ham, Neth. 78/D4
Den Helder, Neth. 78/B3
Den Oever, Neth. 78/C3
Denain, Fr. 80/C3
Denair, Ca, US 174/B2
Denakil (reg.), Eth. 126/D6
Denali NP, Ak, US 168/X12
Denan, Eth. 144/B4
Denbigh, Wal, UK 61/E5
Denbigh, On, Can. 187/H2
Denby Dale, Eng, UK 61/G4
Dendâra, Mrta. 140/D2
Dender (riv.), Belg. 68/b3
Denderleeuw, Belg. 81/D2
Dendermonde, Belg. 81/D1
Dendron, SAfr. 149/F4
Denekamp, Neth. 78/E4
Deng Xian, China 106/C4
Dengfeng, China 106/C4
Dengjiatang, China 113/G3
Dengkou, China 104/F3
Dêngqên, China 112/B2
Dengta, China 113/G3
Denguéno, CAfr. 142/C4
Denham, Eng, UK 56/B2
Denham (sound), Austl. 156/B3
Denham, Austl. 156/B3
Denholme, Eng, UK 61/G4
Denia, Sp. 73/F3
Deniliquin, Austl. 159/B2
Denio, Nv, US 172/D3
Denison (dam), Ok, US 179/F4
Denison, Ks, US 181/G4
Denison, Ia, US 181/G2
Denison, Tx, US 179/F4
Denizli, Turk. 128/B2
Denizli (prov.), Turk. 128/B2
Denkendorf, Ger. 85/E5
Denklingen, Ger. 87/G2
Denman, Austl. 158/D2
Denmark (str.), Grld.,Ice. 165/R3
Denmark, Ia, US 181/J3
Denmark, Austl. 156/C5
Denmark(ctry.) 55/E3
Denmark, SC, US 189/G4
Denmark, Wi, US 186/C2
Dennard, Ar, US 179/H3
Dennilton, SAfr. 149/F5
Dennison, Oh, US 186/F4
Dennisville, NJ, US 194/D5
Denny, Sc, UK 59/C4
Denpasar, Indo. 115/F3
Dent de Cons (peak), Fr. 90/C1
Dent de Lys (peak), Swi. 86/C4
Dent d'Hérens (peak), It. 86/D6
Dentergem, Belg. 80/C2
Dentlein am Forst, Ger. 84/D4
Denton, Eng, UK 61/F5
Denton, Eng, UK 63/G5
Denton, Ga, US 191/G2
Denton, Md, US 194/C6
Denton, Mt, US 171/K4
Denton, Tx, US 176/E1
Denton, Tx, US 176/K6
Denton (co.), Tx, US 176/K6
Denton (cr.), Tx, US 177/F1
D'Entrecasteaux (isls.), PNG 162/D5
D'Entrecasteaux (pt.), Austl. 156/B5
Dents du Midi (peak), Swi. 86/C5
Dentsville, SC, US 189/G3
Denver (cap.), Co, US 180/B4
Denver, Ia, US 181/H2
Denver, Pa, US 194/B3
Denver City, Tx, US 178/C4
Denver International (int'l arpt.), Co, US 178/B1
Denville, NJ, US 194/D2
Denzil, Sk, Can. 171/K1
Denzlingen, Ger. 86/D1
Deoband, India 124/D5
Deobhog, India 121/D2
Deoghar, India 123/F3
Deohā (riv.), India 122/B1
Deolāli, India 118/B4
Deoli, India 118/C2
Deoli, India 121/C1
Deolia, India 118/B2
Déols, Fr. 70/D3
Deora, Co, US 178/C2
Deorī, India 122/B4
Deoria, India 122/D2
Dependencias Federales (state), Ven. 205/E1
Depew, Ok, US 179/F3
Depew, NY, US 186/V10
Depoe Bay, Or, US 172/A1
Depok, Indo. 116/C5
Deport, Tx, US 179/G4
Deposit, NY, US 187/J3
Dépôt Lézard, FrG. 206/C1
Dépression de Mourdi (depr.), Chad 142/D1
Deptford (nbrhd.), Eng, UK 56/C2
Deputatskiy, Rus. 101/P3
Deputy, In, US 188/E1
Dêqên, China 112/C2
Deqing, China 106/L9
Dera, D.R. Congo 147/G2
Dera Ghāzi Khān, Pak. 124/A4
Dera Gopipur, India 124/D4
Dera Ismāīl Khān, Pak. 124/A4
Derā Nānak, India 124/C3
Dera Nawāb Sāhib, Pak. 124/A5
Derai, Bang. 123/H3
Deram Shet' (riv), Eth. 144/A3
Derazhnya, Ukr. 98/D3
Derbent, Rus. 97/J4
Derby, Austl. 154/A4
Derby, Eng, UK 61/G6
Derby, Ct, US 195/E1
Derby, Ks, US 179/F2
Derbyshire (co.), Eng, UK 61/G6
Derdap NP, Yugo. 76/F3
Derdara, Mor. 138/B2
Derdepoort, SAfr. 149/E5
Derecske, Hun. 76/E2
Dereköy, Turk. 77/H5
Dereköy (riv.), Turk. 129/M6
Derendingen, Swi. 86/D3
Deresgē, Eth. 144/A2
Dergachi, Rus. 97/J2
Derhachi, Ukr. 99/J2
Derik, Turk. 128/E2
Derinkuyu, Turk. 128/C2
Derkul, Kaz. 97/J2
Derma, Ms, US 188/C4
Dermott, Ar, US 179/J4
Dernau, Ger. 81/G2
Déroute, Passage de la (Chan), Fr., UK 70/B2
Derravaragh (lake), Ire. 58/C2
Derreen (riv.), Ire. 58/D4
Derrevaragh (lake), Ire. 60/A4
Derry, NH, US 187/L3
Derry, NM, US 175/J4
Derryboy, NI, UK 60/C3
Derrylin, NI, UK 58/C1
Derrynasaggart (mts.), Ire. 58/A6
Dersingham, Eng, UK 63/G1
Derudeb, Sudan 142/H1
Deruta, It. 91/B2
Dervaig, Sc, UK 57/Q8
Derval, Fr. 82/D5
Derventa, Bosn. 76/C3
Dervio, It. 87/F5
Dervock, NI, UK 60/B1
Derwent (riv.), Austl. 158/C4
Derwent, Ab, Can. 171/J1
Derwent (res.), Eng, UK 61/F2
Derwent (riv.), Eng, UK 61/E2
Derwent Bridge, Austl. 158/C4
Derwent Water (lake), Eng, UK 61/E2
Derzhavīnsk, Kaz. 125/A1
Des Allemands, La, US 190/C3
Des Arc, Ar, US 179/J3
Des Arc, Mo, US 188/B2
Des Lacs NWR, ND, US 182/C3
Des Moines (riv.), Ia, Mn, US 169/H3

247
Des – Dotnu

Des Moines (int'l arpt.), Ia, US 181/H3
Des Moines (cap.), Ia, US 181/H3
Des Moines, Wa, US 170/C4
Des Moines, East Fork (riv.), Ia, US 181/G2
Des Plaines, Il, US 186/C3
Desaguadero, Peru 212/B1
Desaguadero (riv.), Bol. 209/E9
Desagües de los Colorados, Arg. 212/C4
Desagües del Río Salvage, Arg. 212/C4
Desana, It. 88/B3
Desborough, Eng, UK 63/F2
Descabezado Grande (vol.), Chile 214/C2
Descalvado, Braz. 213/H2
Descartes, Fr. 70/D3
Deschutes (riv.), Or, US 172/C1
Deschutes River Recreation Lands, Or, US 172/C1
Desdunes, Haiti 201/H2
Dese (riv.), It. 89/F2
Desē, Eth. 144/A3
Deseado (riv.), Arg. 203/C7
Deseado (cape), Chile 215/B7
Desengaño (pt.), Arg. 215/D6
Desenzano del Garda, It. 88/D3
Deseret Depot, Ut, US 173/G3
Désert (riv.), Qu, Can. 187/H1
Desert (valley), Nv, US 172/D3
Desert (lake), Nv, US 174/E2
Desert Center, Ca, US 174/E4
Desert Hot Springs, Ca, US 174/D4
Désertines, Fr. 70/E3
Deshengpu, China 106/B4
Deshler, Oh, US 186/E4
Desiderio Tello, Arg. 212/C4
Desio, It. 88/C2
Desloge, Mo, US 188/B2
Desna (riv.), Ukr.,Rus. 94/W9
Desolación (isl.), Chile 215/B7
Desolation (pt.), Phil. 114/D3
Desoto, Tx, US 176/L7
Desoto Nat'l Wild.Ref., Ne, US 181/F3
Despatch, SAfr. 150/D4
Déssa, Niger 141/F3
Dessau, Ger. 68/G3
Dessel, Belg. 78/C6
Dessoubre (riv.), Fr. 86/C3
Destelbergen, Belg. 80/C1
Destêrro, Braz. 207/G4
Destin, Fl, US 190/E2
Desulo, It. 74/A2
Desvres, Fr. 80/A2
Det Udom, Thai. 120/D3
Deta, Rom. 76/E3
Dete, Zim. 149/E3
Detern, Ger. 79/E2
Detmold, Ger. 79/F5
Detour (pt.), Mi, US 186/C2
Detrital Wash (riv.), Az, US 174/E3
Detroit (riv.), Can.,US 193/F7
Detroit, Mi, US 186/E3
Detroit, Or, US 172/B1
Detroit (dam), Or, US 172/B1
Detroit (lake), Or, US 172/B1
Detroit, Tx, US 179/G4
Detroit City (arpt.), Mi, US 193/G7
Detroit Lakes, Mn, US 182/G4
Detroit Metropolitan Wayne County (int'l arpt.), Mi, US 186/E3
Dettelbach, Ger. 84/D3
Dettifoss (falls), Ice. 64/P6
Dettwiller, Fr. 81/G6
Deua NP, Austl. 159/D2
Deuil-la-Barre, Fr. 56/J5
Deûle (riv.), Fr. 80/B2
Deurne, Belg. 78/B6
Deurne, Neth. 78/C6
Deurne (Antwerp) (int'l arpt.), Belg. 78/B6
Deustua, Peru 208/D4
Deutsch Evern, Ger. 79/H2
Deutsch Wagram, Aus. 77/P7
Deutschkreutz, Aus. 76/C2
Deutschlandsberg, Aus. 76/B2
Deux-Montagnes, Qu, Can. 185/N6
Deux-Montagnes (lake), Qu, Can. 185/M7
Deux-Montagnes (co.), Qu, Can. 185/M6
Deva, Rom. 76/F3
Dévaványa, Hun. 76/E2
Develi, Turk. 128/C2
Deventer, Neth. 78/D4
Deveron (riv.), Sc, UK 59/D2
Devil River (peak), NZ 161/C3
Devil's Playground (des.), Ca, US 174/E3
Deville, Fr. 81/D4
Deville, La, US 190/B2
Devil's (isl.), FrG. 206/C1
Devils (riv.), Mex. 199/E2
Devil's (pt.), SrL. 121/D4
Devils (lake), ND, US 182/E3
Devils (riv.), Tx, US 177/D3
Devil's Elbow (pass), Sc, UK 59/C3
Devil's Garden, Ut, US 175/H1
Devils Lake, ND, US 182/E3
Devils Postpile Nat'l Mon., Ca, US 174/C2
Devils Tower Nat'l Mon., Wy, US 180/B1
Devilsbit (peak), Ire. 58/C4
Devin, Bul. 75/J2
Devine, Tx, US 177/E3
Devizes, Eng, UK 62/E4
Devnya, Bul. 77/H4
Devola, Oh, US 186/F5
Devoll (riv.), Alb. 93/J2
Devoll (riv.), Alb.,Gre. 76/E5
Devon, Ab, Can. 171/H1
Devon (isl.), Nun, Can. 167/H1
Devon (isl.), Can. 165/J2
Devon (riv.), Sc, UK 59/C4
Devon (co.), Eng, UK 62/C5
Devon-Berwyn, Pa, US 194/C3
Devonport, Austl. 158/C4
Devonport, NZ 161/F6
Devore, Ca, US 192/C2
Devoto, Arg. 212/D4
Devoys (peak), NM, US 178/C2
Devrek (riv.), Turk. 96/D4
Devrek, Turk. 96/D4
Devrez (riv.), Turk. 96/E4
Devure (riv.), Zim. 149/F3
Dewa (pt.), Indo. 115/A2
Dewa (mts.), Japan 108/B4
Dewar, Ok, US 179/G3
Dewās, India 118/C3
Dewberry, Ab, Can 171/J1
Dewetsdorp, SAfr. 150/D3
Dewey, Ok, US 179/G2
Dewey, Az, US 175/F3
Deweyville, Tx, US 177/H2
Dewsbury, Eng, UK 61/G4
Dexter, Ks, US 179/F2
Dexter, NM, US 178/B4
Dexter, Mo, US 188/C2
Dexter, Ga, US 189/F4
Dey-Dey (lake), Austl. 153/C3
Deyang, China 112/E2
Deyhūk, Iran 129/J3
Deyyer, Iran 129/G5
Dez (riv.), Iran 100/E6
Dezfūl, Iran 129/G3
Dezhneva (cape), Rus. 168/W12
Dezhou, China 106/D3
Dhābān, India 124/C5
Dhabān Singh, Pak. 124/B4
Dhāding, Nepal 123/E2
Dhahab, Egypt 135/G2
Dhahabān, SAr. 126/C4
Dhahran (int'l arpt.), SAr. 126/F3
Dhahran, SAr. 126/D5
Dhākā (pol. div.), Bang. 123/G4
Dhāka, India 123/E2
Dhākā (pol. reg.), Bang. 123/H4
Dhākā (Dacca) (cap.), Bang. 123/H4
Dhaleswari (riv.), Bang. 123/H4
Dhali, Cyp. 130/C2
Dhamār, Yem. 144/C2
Dhāmpur, India 122/B1
Dhamtari, India 121/D1
Dhanaula, India 124/C4
Dhanaura, India 122/B1
Dhānbād, India 123/F4
Dhangadhī, Nepal 122/C1
Dhankutā, Nepal 123/F2
Dhār, India 118/C3
Dhar de Chinguetti (cliff), Mrta. 136/B5
Dhār Khurd, India 124/C3
Dhar Néma (cliff), Mrta. 140/D2
Dhar Oualâta (cliff), Mrta. 140/D2
Dhar Tîchît (cliff), Mrta. 140/C2
Dharampur, India 118/B3
Dharān, Nepal 123/F2
Dharchula, Nepal 122/C1
Dhāri, India 127/K4
Dhāriwāl, India 124/C4
Dharmapuri, India 121/C3
Dharmavaram, India 121/C3
Dharmjaygarh, India 122/D4
Dharmkot, India 124/C4
Dharmsāla, India 124/D3
Dhasan (riv.), India 122/B3
Dhaulāgiri (zone), Nepal 122/D1
Dhaulāgiri (peak), Nepal 122/D1
Dhaura, India 122/B3
Dhaurahra, India 122/C1
Dhekialjuli, India 112/B3
Dhelfoí, Gre. 75/H3
Dhelfoí (Delphi) (ruin), Gre. 75/H3
Dhelvinákion, Gre. 75/G3
Dheskáti, Gre. 75/G3
Dheune (riv.), Fr. 86/A4
Dhī Qār (gov.), Iraq 129/F4
Dhībān, Jor. 131/D5
Dhidhimótikhon, Gre. 77/H5
Dhiinsoor, Som. 145/C1
Dhíkaia, Gre. 77/H5
Dhílos (ruin), Gre. 75/J4
Dhimitsána, Gre. 75/H4
Dhírfis (peak), Gre. 75/H3
Dhístomon, Gre. 75/H3
Dhlo Dhlo (ruin), Zim. 149/F3
Dhofar (reg.), Oman 126/F5
Dhokímion, Gre. 75/G3
Dholipal, India 124/C5
Dholka, India 127/K4
Dholpur, India 122/A2
Dhomokós, Gre. 75/H3
Dhonoúsa (isl.), Gre. 75/J4
Dhorāji, India 127/K4
Dhorpātan, Nepal 122/D1
Dhoxáton, Gre. 75/J2
Dhronbach (riv.), Ger. 81/F4
Dhubāb, Yem. 144/B2
Dhubri, India 123/G2
Dhuizon, Fr. 83/G5
Dhūlia, India 121/B1
Dhuliān, Pak. 124/B3
Dhuliān, India 123/F3
Dhulikhel, Nepal 123/E2
Dhungrebās, Nepal 123/E2
Dhupgāri, India 123/G2
Dhūri, India 124/C4
Dhuudo, Som. 144/D3
Dhuudo (riv.), Som. 144/D3
Dhuusamarreeb (Dusa Marreb), Som. 144/C4
Di Linh, Viet. 120/E4
Dia (isl.), Gre. 75/J5
Diablo (range), Ca, US 174/B2
Diablo (mtn.), Tx, US 177/B2
Diablo, Punta del (pt.), Uru. 215/G2
Diablotin (peak), Dom. 197/N9
Diadema, Braz. 211/K8
Diadema Argentina, Arg. 214/D5
Diaganiao, Sen. 140/A3
Diagonal, Ia, US 181/G3
Diaguitas, Chile 212/B4
Dialakoto, Sen. 140/B3
Diamante (riv.), Arg. 214/D2
Diamante, Arg. 212/D5
Diamantina, Braz. 211/E3
Diamantina (riv.), Austl. 153/D3
Diamantina Lakes, Austl. 160/A3
Diamantina, Chapada (hills), Braz. 211/E1
Diamantino, Braz. 209/G4
Diamond (cr.), Austl. 158/G5
Diamond (peak), Id, US 173/G1
Diamond, Or, US 172/D2
Diamond (peak), Or, US 172/B2
Diamond Bar, Ca, US 192/G8
Diamond Harbour, India 123/G4
Diamond Springs, Ca, US 172/C4
Dian (lake), China 112/D3
Dianalund, Den. 66/D4
Dianbai, China 113/F4
Diancang (mtn.), China 112/D3
Dianjiang, China 113/E2
Diano Marina, It. 88/B6
Dianópolis, Braz. 210/D1
Dianshan (lake), China 106/L8
Diapaga, Burk. 141/F3
Diaroumé, Sen. 140/B3
Dias Creek, NJ, US 194/D5
Diavolezza (peak), Swi. 87/F5
Diaz, Ar, US 179/J3
Dibai, India 122/B1
Dibaya, D.R. Congo 147/E4
Dibaya-Lubwe, D.R. Congo 146/D4
Dibbin NP, Jor. 131/D4
Dibella (well), Niger 142/B1
Dibeng, SAfr. 150/C2
Dibiāpur, India 122/B2
Dībīlē, Eth. 144/B3
Diboll, Tx, US 176/G2
Dibrugarh, India 112/B3
Dibs, Iraq 129/F3
Dickens, Tx, US 178/D4
Dickens (pt.), RI, US 195/G1
Dickinson, ND, US 182/C4
Dickinson, Tx, US 177/M9
Dickinson Bayou (riv.), Tx, US 177/M9
Dickinson Center, NY, US 187/J2
Dickson, Ab, Can. 170/G1
Dickson, Ok, US 179/F3
Dickson, Tn, US 188/D2
Dicle (dam), Turk. 128/E2
Dicomano, It. 89/E6
Didam, Neth. 78/D5
Didcot, Eng, UK 63/E3
Didhav, Eth. 144/B2
Didiéni, Mali 140/C3
Didig Sala, Eth. 144/A2
Didinga (hills), Sudan 142/G4
Didsbury, Ab, Can. 171/G2
Dīdwāna, India 127/K3
Didyma (ruin), Turk. 128/A2
Die, Fr. 90/B3
Die Berg (peak), SAfr. 149/F5
Dieblich, Ger. 81/G3
Diébougou, Burk. 140/E4
Dieburg, Ger. 84/B3
Diedersdorf, Ger. 68/Q7
Diefenbaker (lake), Sk, Can. 166/F3
Diefenbaker (lake), Sk, Can. 171/L2
Diego de Almagro (isl.), Chile 215/B6
Diego de Almagro, Chile 212/B3
Diego Garcia (isl.), UK 103/G10
Diekirch, Lux. 81/F4
Diekirch (dist.), Lux. 81/E4
Diéma, Mali 140/C3
Diemen, Neth. 78/B4
Diemtigen, Swi. 86/D4
Dien Bien, Viet. 112/D4
Dien Chau, Viet. 120/D2
Dien Khanh, Viet. 120/E3
Dieng (ruin), Indo. 115/E3
Diepenbeek, Belg. 81/E2
Diepenveen, Neth. 78/D4
Diepholz, Ger. 79/F3
Diepoldsau, Swi. 87/F3
Dieppe, Fr. 83/G1
Dieppe, NB, Can. 184/E2
Dierdorf, Ger. 81/G2
Dieren, Neth. 78/D4
Dierks, Ar, US 179/G3
Diespeck, Ger. 84/D3
Diessen am Ammersee, Ger. 87/H2
Diest, Belg. 81/E2
Dietenheim, Ger. 87/G1
Dietenhofen, Ger. 84/D4
Dieterich, Il, US 188/C1
Dietersheim, Ger. 84/D3
Dietfurt an der Altmühl, Ger. 85/E4
Dietikon, Swi. 87/E3
Dietmannsried, Ger. 87/G2
Dietzenbach, Ger. 84/B2
Dieue-sur-Meuse, Fr. 81/E5
Dieulefit, Fr. 90/B3
Dieulouard, Fr. 81/F6
Dieuze, Fr. 81/F6
Dieveniškės, Lith. 67/L4
Diever, Neth. 78/D3
Diez, Ger. 84/B2
Dif, Kenya 145/C1
Diffa, Niger 142/B2
Diffa (dept.), Niger 141/H3
Differdange, Lux. 81/E4
Difficult (mt.), Austl. 158/B3
Dīg, India 122/A2
Digba, D.R. Congo 142/E4
Digboi, India 112/B3
Digby, NS, Can. 184/E3
Digby Neck (pen), Ns, Can. 184/D3
Diggers Rest, Austl. 159/B3
Dighem, Sudan 142/G2
Dighton, Ks, US 178/D1
Dighwāra, India 123/E3
Dīglūr, India 121/C2
Digne-les-Bains, Fr. 90/C4
Digoin, Fr. 70/E3
Digor, Turk. 129/E1
Digos, Phil. 114/D4
Digul (riv.), Indo. 117/K4
Digya NP, Gha. 141/E5
Dihang (riv.), India 112/B2
Dihun, Eth. 144/B4
Dijon, Fr. 86/A3
Dik, Chad 142/C3
Dikhil, Djib. 144/B3
Dikirnis, Egypt 139/C2
Diklosmta (peak), Geo. 97/H4
Diksmuide, Belg. 80/B1
Dikson, Rus. 100/J2
Diktel, Nepal 123/F2
Dikwa, Nga. 142/B2
Dīla, Eth. 144/A4
Dilbeek, Belg. 81/D2
Dilek Yarımadası NP, Turk. 128/A2
Dili, Indo. 154/B2
Dilijan, Arm. 97/H4
Dilkon, Az, US 175/G3
Dillenburg, Ger. 81/H2
Diller, Ne, US 181/F3
Dilley, Tx, US 177/E3
Dillia (riv.), Niger 142/A2
Dillikot, Nepal 122/C1
Dilling, Sudan 142/F2
Dillingen, Ger. 81/F5
Dillingen an der Donau, Ger. 84/D5
Dillingham, Ak, US 168/X13
Dillnås, Swe. 65/A1
Dillon, Mt, US 173/G1
Dillon, SC, US 189/H3
Dillon Cone (peak), NZ 161/C3
Dillonvale, Oh, US 186/F4
Dillsboro, In, US 188/E1
Dillsburg, Pa, US 194/A3
Dilolo, D.R. Congo 147/E5
Dilsen, Belg. 81/E1
Dimako, Camr. 142/B4
Dimāpur, India 112/B3
Dimaro, It. 87/G5
Dimas, Mex. 198/D4
Dimashq (prov.), Syria 128/D3
Dimashq (gov.), Syria 131/E1
Dimashq (Damascus) (cap.), Syria 131/E1
Dimataling, Phil. 114/C4
Dimbaza, SAfr. 150/D4
Dimbelenge, D.R. Congo 147/E4
Dimbokro, C.d'Iv. 140/D5
Dimboola, Austl. 158/B3
Dîmbovița (prov.), Rom. 77/G3
Dîmbovița (riv.), Rom. 98/C5
Dimbulah, Austl. 160/B2
Dime Box, Tx, US 177/F2
Dimitriya Lapteva (str.), Rus. 101/P2
Dimitrovgrad, Rus. 97/J1
Dimitrovgrad, Yugo. 77/F4
Dimitrovgrad, Bul. 77/G4
Dimlang (peak), Nga. 142/A3
Dimmitt, Tx, US 178/C3
Dimock, SD, US 180/F2
Dimovo, Bul. 77/F4
Dina, Pak. 124/B3
Dinach, Som. 144/D3
Dinagat, Phil. 114/D3
Dinagat (isl.), Phil. 117/G1
Dinājpur (pol. reg.), Bang. 123/G3
Dinājpur, Bang. 123/G3
Dinan, Fr. 82/C4
Dīnānagar, India 124/C3
Dinant, Belg. 81/D3
Dinar, Turk. 128/B2
Dinard, Fr. 82/C3
Dinaric Alps (mts.), Cro. 76/C3
Dinas (pt.), Wal, UK 62/B2
Dinas Powys, Wal, UK 62/C4
Dinder NP, Sudan 142/G2
Dinder Wenz (riv.), Eth. 142/G2
Dindima, Nga. 141/H4
Dindori, India 122/C4
Dinga, Pak. 124/B3
Ding'an, China 113/F5
Dingbian, China 104/F4
Dingelstädt, Ger. 79/H6
Dinggyê, China 123/F1
Dingjiang, China 113/G3
Dingjiasuo, China 105/J5
Dingle, Ire. 56/F10
Dingle (bay), Ire. 56/N10
Dingle, Id, US 173/H2
Dingmans Ferry, Pa, US 194/D1
Dingolfing, Ger. 85/F5
Dingras, Phil. 114/C1
Dingshuzhen, China 106/K8
Dingtao, China 106/C4
Dinguiraye, Gui. 140/C4
Dingwall, Sc, UK 59/B1
Dingwall, NS, Can. 185/G2
Dingxi, China 104/E4
Dingxiang, China 106/C3
Dingxing, China 106/G7
Dingyuan, China 106/D4
Dinh Lap, Viet. 120/D1
Dinkel (riv.), Ger. 79/E4
Dinkelsbühl, Ger. 84/D4
Dinkelscherben, Ger. 84/D6
Dinklage, Ger. 79/F3
Dinnebito Wash (riv.), Az, US 175/G2
Dinner (pt.), Fl, US 190/K7
Dinnington, Eng, UK 61/G1
Dinokana, SAfr. 148/E5
Dinosaur, Co, US 173/J3
Dinosaur Nat'l Monument, Co, US 173/J3
Dinslaken, Ger. 78/D5
Dinsmore, Sk, Can. 171/L2
Dintel Mark (riv.), Neth. 78/B5
Dintenloord, Neth. 78/B5
Dintiteladas, Indo. 115/D3
Dinuba, Ca, US 174/C2
Dinwiddie, Va, US 189/J2
Dinxperlo, Neth. 78/D5
Dioïla, Mali 140/D3
Diomandou, Gui. 140/C4
Dion (riv.), Gui. 140/C4
Dionysias (ruin), Egypt 139/B6
Diósd, Hun. 77/Q10
Diouloulou, Sen. 140/A3
Dioundiou, Niger 141/F3
Diourbel (pol. reg.), Sen. 140/A3
Diourbel, Sen. 140/A3
Dīpālpur, Pak. 124/B4
Diphu, India 112/B3
Diphu (pass), India 112/C2
Diplo, Pak. 127/J4
Dipni (dam), Turk. 128/E2
Dipolog, Phil. 114/C3
Dipperu NP, Austl. 160/C3
Dipperz, Ger. 84/C1
Dique (canal), Col. 201/H4
Dīr, Pak. 124/A2
Dira (well), Chad 142/B2
Dirang Dzong, India 123/J2
Diré, Mali 140/E2
Dirē Dawa, Eth. 144/B3
Direct, Tx, US 179/G4
Direction (cape), Austl. 155/F3
Diriamba, Nic. 200/E4
Dirico, Ang. 148/D3
Dirj, Libya 137/H3
Dirk Hartog (isl.), Austl. 153/A3
Dirkou, Niger 134/B5
Dirksland, Neth. 78/B5
Dirlewang, Ger. 87/G2
Dirranbandi, Austl. 160/C5
Dirrington Great Law (hill), Sc, UK 59/D5
Dirs, SAr. 126/D5
Dirty Devil (riv.), Ut, US 173/H4
Disappointment (isls.), FrPol. 163/L6
Disappointment (cape), Wa, US 170/B4
Disappointment (lake), Austl. 153/B3
Disaster (bay), Austl. 159/D3
Discovery (bay), Austl. 158/E3
Discovery Bay, Jam. 201/G2
Disentis-Mustér, Swi. 87/E4
Disgrazi (peak), It. 87/F5
Dishman, Wa, US 170/F4
Dishnā, Egypt 135/G3
Disko (isl.), Grld. 165/M3
Disko (Qeqertarsuaq) (isl.), Grld. 167/L2
Disley, Eng, UK 61/F5
Dismal (riv.), Ne, US 180/C3
Disna, Bela. 67/N4
Disney, Ok, US 179/G2
Disney Studios, Fl, US 190/M7
Disneyland, Ca, US 192/G8
Dison, Belg. 81/E2
Dispur, India 119/F2
Disraëli, Qu, Can. 184/B3
Diss, Eng, UK 63/H2
Dissen am Teutoburger Wald, Ger. 79/F4
Distington, Eng, UK 60/E2
Distrito Especial (cap. dist.), Col. 207/L8
Distrito Federal (fed. dist.), Braz. 210/D2
Distrito Federal (fed. dist.), Col. 204/C3
Distrito Federal (fed. dist.), Mex. 196/A5
Distrito Federal (fed. dist.), Ven. 205/E2
Disūq, Egypt 139/B2
Ditang, China 106/L9
Ditchling Beacon (hill), Eng, UK 63/F5
Dittaino (riv.), It. 74/D4
Dittelbrunn, Ger. 84/D2
Ditton, Eng, UK 56/E3
Ditzingen, Ger. 84/C5
Diu, India 118/B3
Diuata (mts.), Phil. 114/D3
Diva (riv.). Yugo. 76/D4
Dīvān Darreh, Iran 129/F3
Divatte (riv.), Fr. 82/D6
Dive (riv.). Fr. 70/D3
Divénié, Congo 146/C3
Dives (riv.), Fr. 83/E2
Dives-sur-Mer, Fr. 83/E2
Divette (riv.), Fr. 82/D1
Divide, Co, US 178/B1
Divide, Mt, US 173/G1
Dividing Creek, NJ, US 194/C5
Divinolândia, Braz. 211/K6
Divinópolis, Braz. 210/D4
Divisa Nova, Braz. 211/K6
Divisões, Serra das (mts.), Braz. 210/C3
Divisor, Serra do (mts.), Braz.,Peru 208/C2
Divnogorsk, Rus. 100/K4
Divnoye, Rus. 97/G3
Divo, C.d'Iv. 140/D5
Divonne-les-Bains, Fr. 86/C5
Divriği, Turk. 128/D2
Divuma, D.R. Congo 147/E5
Dix (lake), Swi. 86/D5
Dixcove, Gha. 141/E5
Dixfield, Me, US 187/L2
Dixie, Ga, US 191/G2
Dixie, Al, US 190/E2
Dixie, Id, US 172/F1
Dixie, Wa, US 170/E4
Dixmoor, Il, US 193/Q16
Dixon, Ca, US 172/C4
Dixon, Ky, US 188/D2
Dixon, Il, US 181/K3
Dixon, Mt, US 170/G4
Dixon, NM, US 178/B2
Dixon, Mo, US 179/H2
Dixon, Wy, US 173/K3
Dixon Entrance (chan.), Can.,US 165/D4
Diyadin, Turk. 129/E2
Diyāla (gov.), Iraq 129/F3
Diyarb Najm, Egypt 139/C3
Diyarbakır, Turk. 128/E2
Diyarbakir (prov.), Turk. 128/E2
Dizangué, Camr. 146/B2
Dja (riv.), Camr. 142/B5
Djado, Niger 134/B4
Djado (plat.), Niger 133/D2
Djakotomé, Ben. 141/F5
Djamaa, Alg. 137/G2
Djamba, D.R. Congo 147/F2
Djambala, Congo 146/C3
Djamu, D.R. Congo 147/G2
Djanet, Alg. 137/H4
Djebel Tichka (peak), Mor. 136/C3
Djebel-Amrag (mtn.), Alg. 138/D3
Djébrène, Chad 142/C3
Djédaa, Chad 142/C2
Djedi, Oued (riv.), Alg. 137/G2
Djelfa, Alg. 92/D4
Djema, CAfr. 142/E4
Djemila (ruin), Alg. 138/H4
Djénné, Mali 140/D3
Djerem (riv.), Camr. 142/B4
Djermaya, Chad 142/B2
Djibo, Burk. 141/E3
Djibouti (cap.), Djib. 144/B3
Djibouti(ctry.) 133/G3
Djiguéni, Mrta. 140/C3
Djiouce (mtn.), Ire. 58/D3
Djiroutou, C.d'Iv. 140/D5
Djohong, Camr. 142/B4
Djouab (riv.), Congo 146/C2
Djoué (riv.), Congo 146/C3
Djougou, Ben. 141/F4
Djoum, Camr. 146/C2
Djugu, D.R. Congo 147/G2
Djúpivogur, Ice. 64/P7
Djurö, Swe. 65/B1
D'Lo, Ms, US 190/D2
Dmanisi, Geo. 97/H4
Dmitriyev-L'govskiy, Rus. 99/H1
Dmitriyevskiy, Kaz. 97/L2
Dmytrivka, Ukr. 99/G2
Dnepr (riv.), Rus. 100/D4
Dnestrovsc, Mol. 98/E4
Dnieper (lowland), Ukr. 98/F2
Dnieper (upland), Ukr. 98/E3
Dnipro (riv.), Ukr. 55/H3
Dniprodzerzhyns'ke Vodoskhovyshche (res.), Ukr. 99/H3
Dniprodzerzhyns'k, Ukr. 99/H3
Dnipropetrovs'k, Ukr. 99/H3
Dnipropetrovs'ka (prov.), Ukr. 96/E2
Dniprorudne, Ukr. 99/H4
Dniprovs'kyy Lyman (estu.), Ukr. 77/K2
Dnister (riv.), Eur. 100/C5
Dnister (riv.), Ukr. 68/M4
Dnistrovs'kyy Lyman (estu.), Ukr. 77/K2
Dno, Rus. 67/N3
Dnyapro (riv.), Bela. 67/P4
Do (lake), Mali 141/E3
Do (riv.), China 104/D5
Do Gonbadān, Iran 129/G4
Do Luong, Viet. 120/D2
Do Rāh (pass), Afg. 127/K1
Do Son, Viet. 120/D1
Doa, Moz. 149/G3
Doaktown, NB, Can. 184/D2
Doany, Madg. 152/J6
Doba, Chad 142/C3
Dobbins (A.F.B.), Ga, US 189/L7
Dobbs Ferry, NY, US 195/K7
Dobbyn, Austl. 155/F4
Dobele, Lat. 67/K3
Döbeln, Ger. 68/G3
Doberai (pen.), Indo. 117/H4
Dobiegniew, Pol. 69/H2
Dobo, Indo. 154/D1
Dobogo-kó (peak), Hun. 77/Q9
Doboj, Bosn. 76/D3
Dobřany, Czh. 85/G3
Dobre Miasto, Pol. 67/J5
Dobrich, Bul. 77/H4
Dobrinka, Rus. 97/G1
Dobrinka, Rus. 99/L1
Dobříš, Czh. 85/H3
Dobromyl', Ukr. 69/M4
Dobropillya, Ukr. 99/J3
Dobrovnik, Slov. 76/C2
Dobruja (reg.), Bul.,Rom. 93/K2
Dobrush, Bela. 96/D1
Dobryanka, Rus. 95/N4
Dobryanka, Ukr. 98/F1
Dobson, NC, US 189/G2
Dobzha, China 123/G1
Doce (riv.), Braz. 211/E3
Dochart (riv.), Sc, UK 59/B4
Dock Junction, Ga, US 191/H2
Docker River, Austl. 157/F3
Docking, Eng, UK 63/G1
Doctor Arroyo, Mex. 199/E4
Doctor Cecilio Báez, Par. 213/E3
Doctor Coss, Mex. 177/E5
Doctor González, Mex. 177/E5
Doctor Pedro P. Peña, Par. 212/D2
Doctor Petru Groza, Rom. 76/F2
Dod Ballāpur, India 121/C3
Doda (riv.), India 124/D3
Doda, India 124/C3
Doda Betta (peak), India 121/C4
Dodder (riv.), Ire. 60/B5
Doddinghurst, Eng, UK 56/D2
Dodge, Tx, US 177/G2
Dodge City, Ks, US 178/D2
Dodger Stadium, Ca, US 192/F7
Dodgeville, Wi, US 181/J2
Dodman (pt.), Eng, UK 62/B6
Dodola, Eth. 144/A4
Dodoma (prov.), Tanz. 145/A3
Dodoma, Tanz. 145/A3
Dodori Nat'l Rsv., Kenya 145/C2
Dodsland, Sk, Can. 171/K2
Dodson, La, US 190/B1
Dodson, Mt, US 171/K3
Dodwekon, Libr. 140/C5
Dodworth, Eng, UK 61/G4
Doe Run, Mo, US 188/B2
Doel, Belg. 78/B6
Doerun, Ga, US 191/G2
Doesburg, Neth. 78/D4
Doetinchem, Neth. 78/D5
Dofa, Indo. 117/G4
Dog (lake), Mb, Can. 182/E2
Dog (isl.), Fl, US 191/F3
Dog (riv.), BC, Can. 170/C2
Dogai Coring (lake), China 125/E5
Dogana, SMar. 89/F6
Doğanhisar, Turk. 128/B2
Doğankent (riv.), Turk. 96/F4
Doğanşar, Turk. 128/D1
Doğanşehir, Turk. 128/D2
Doğanyurt, Turk. 96/E4
Döğer, Turk. 128/B2
Dogliani, It. 88/A3
Dōgo (isl.), Japan 105/L4
Dogondoutchi, Niger 141/G3
Doğubayazıt, Turk. 129/F2
Doğukaradeniz (mts.), Turk. 128/D1
Doha (int'l arpt.), Qatar 126/F3
Doha (Ad Dawḩah) (cap.), Qatar 126/F3
Dohad, India 118/B3
Dohrīghāt, India 122/D2
Doi Inthanon NP, Thai. 112/C5
Doi Khun Tan NP, Thai. 120/B2
Doi Suthep-Pui NP, Thai. 112/C5
Doimara, India 112/B3
Doiras (res.), Sp. 72/B1
Dois Córregos, Braz. 213/G2
Dois de Julho (int'l arpt.), Braz. 211/F2
Dois Irmãos do Tocantins, Braz. 206/D5
Dois Irmãos, Serra (mts.), Braz. 207/F5
Dois Vizinhos, Braz. 213/F3
Doische, Belg. 81/D3
Doka, Sudan 142/G2
Dokka, Nor. 66/D1
Dokkum, Neth. 78/D2
Dokkumer Ee (riv.), Neth. 78/C2
Dokshitsy, Bela. 67/M4
Doksy, Czh. 85/H1
Dokuchayevs'k, Ukr. 99/J4
Dol-de-Bretagne, Fr. 82/D3
Dolan Springs, Az, US 174/E3
Dolbeau, Qu, Can. 184/A1
Dolcedorme (peak), It. 74/E3
Dole, Fr. 86/B3
Dolent (peak), Swi. 86/D6
Dolgellau, Wal, UK 62/C1
Dolgoprudnyy, Rus. 94/W9
Doli, India 118/B2
Dolianova, It. 74/A3
Dolinsk, Rus. 105/N2
Dolinskoye, Ukr. 98/E4
Dolj (prov.), Rom. 77/F3
Dollar, Sc, UK 59/C4
Dollar Bay, Mi, US 183/K4
Dollar Law (peak), Sc, UK 59/C5
Dollard, Sk, Can. 171/K3
Dollard (Dollart) (bay), Neth.,Ger. 79/E2
Dollard-des-Ormeaux, Qu, Can. 185/N7
Dollart (Dollard) (bay), Neth.,Ger. 79/E2
Dollarville, Mi, US 186/D1
Doller (riv.), Fr. 68/D5
Dollnstein, Ger. 84/E5
Dolmance Palace, Turk. 129/M6
Dolmar (peak), Ger. 84/D1
Dolmen (ruin), It. 74/E2
Dolna Banya, Bul. 77/F4
Dolni Dŭbnik, Bul. 77/G4
Dolní Kounice, Czh. 71/M2
Dolo (riv.), It. 88/D4
Dolo, It. 89/F3
Dolo, Eth. 144/B4
Dolo, Indo. 117/E4
Dolo Odo, Eth. 144/B4
Dolobli, Libr. 140/C5
Dolomieu, Fr. 90/B1
Dolomite Alps (mts.), It. 93/F1
Dolon (riv.), Fr. 90/A2
Doloon, Mong. 104/F3
Dolores, Arg. 214/F3
Dolores, Bol. 208/D3
Dolores, Guat. 200/D2
Dolores, Phil. 114/D2
Dolores, Uru. 215/J10
Dolores, Co, US 175/H2
Dolores (riv.), Co, US 173/J4
Dolores, Ven. 204/D2
Dolphin (pt.), Namb. 148/B5
Dolphin (cape), UK 215/F6
Dolphin and Union (str.), Nun, Can. 166/E2
Dolphinholme, Eng, UK 61/F4
Dölsach, Aus. 71/K3
Dolton, Il, US 193/Q16
Dolyna, Ukr. 98/C3
Dolyns'ka, Ukr. 99/G3
Dolzhanskaya, Rus. 99/J4
Dom (peak), Indo. 117/J4
Dom (peak), Swi. 86/D5
Dom Aquino, Braz. 210/B2
Dom Carlos (pt.), Moz. 149/G4
Dom Noi (res.), Thai. 120/D3
Dom Pedrito, Braz. 213/F4
Doma, Zim. 149/F3
Domanivka, Ukr. 98/F4
Domār, Bang. 123/G2
Domariāganj, India 122/D2
Domasi, Malw. 149/G2
Domat-Ems, Swi. 87/F4
Domažlice, Czh. 85/F4
Dombarovskiy, Rus. 97/L2
Dombasle-sur-Meurthe, Fr. 81/F6
Dombay-ul'gen (Gora peak), Geo. 97/G4
Dombe Grande, Ang. 148/B2
Dombes (lake), Fr. 86/B5
Dombey (cape), Austl. 154/C3
Domboshawa, Zim. 149/F3
Dombóvár, Hun. 76/D2
Dombrád, Hun. 76/E1
Domburg, Sur. 206/C1
Domburg, Neth. 78/A5
Domchānch, India 123/E3
Dome, Az, US 174/E4
Dome (peak), Az, US 175/F2
Dome C, US, Ant. 216/J
Dôme de Barrot (peak), Fr. 90/C4
Dôme de l'Arpont (peak), Fr. 90/C2
Domène, Fr. 90/B2
Domérat, Fr. 70/E3
Domeyko, Chile 212/B4
Domfront, Fr. 83/E3
Domínguez, Arg. 212/E4
Dominica (ctry.) 165/L8
Dominica Passage (chan.), Dom.,Guad. 197/N9
Dominican Republic (ctry.) 165/K8
Dominion, NS, Can. 185/G2
Domiongo, D.R. Congo 147/E4
Dommartin-lès-Remiremont, Fr. 86/C2
Dommartin-lès-Toul, Fr. 81/E6
Dommati, India 123/H3
Dommel (riv.), Belg. 81/E1
Domo, Eth. 144/C4
Domodedovo (int'l arpt.), Rus. 94/W9
Domodedovo, Rus. 94/W9
Domodossola, It. 87/E5
Domohāni, India 123/G2
Domoni, Com. 152/H6
Domont, Fr. 56/J4
Dompu, Indo. 117/E5
Domremy, Sk, Can. 171/M1
Domrémy-la-Pucelle, Fr. 86/B1
Dömsöd, Hun. 76/D2
Domusnovas, It. 74/A3
Domuyo (vol.), Arg. 214/C3
Domvilk (mt.), Austl. 160/C5
Domžale, Slov. 71/L3
Don (cape), Austl. 154/C2
Don (riv.), Eng, UK 61/G5
Don (riv.), Sc, UK 59/D2
Don (ridge), Rus. 100/E5
Don (riv.), Rus. 55/J4
Don Benito, Sp. 72/C3
Don Pedro (res.), Ca, US 174/B2
Dona Ana, Moz. 149/G3
Donabate, Ire. 60/B5
Donada, It. 89/F3
Donaghadee, NI, UK 60/C2
Donaghmore, NI, UK 60/B2
Donald, Austl. 158/B3
Donald, BC, Can. 170/F2
Donaldson, Ar, US 179/H3
Donaldsonville, La, US 190/C2
Donalsonville, Ga, US 191/F2
Doñana, PN, Sp. 72/B4
Donath, Swi. 87/F4
Donau (Danube) (riv.), Aus.,Ger. 71/H2
Donaueschingen, Ger. 87/E2
Donauwörth, Ger. 84/D5
Doncaster, Eng, UK 61/G4
Doncaster (nbrhd.), Austl. 158/G5
Donchery, Fr. 81/D4
Dondo, D.R. Congo 142/D4
Dondo, Moz. 149/G3
Dondo, Ang. 146/C5
Dondra Head (pt.), SrL. 121/D5
Donduseni, Mol. 98/D3
Donegal (bay), Ire. 57/P9
Donegal, Ire. 57/P9
Donegal (dist.), Ire. 60/A1
Doneraile, Ire. 58/B5
Donets (riv.), Rus. 97/G2
Donets' (riv.), Ukr. 99/J3
Donetsă (prov.), Ukr. 96/F3
Donetsk (int'l arpt.) Ukr. 99/J3
Donetsk, Rus. 99/L3
Donets'k, Ukr. 99/J3
Dong (riv.), China 104/E3
Dong, India 119/G2
Dong (riv.), Viet. 119/J5
Dong Dang, Viet. 119/J3
Dong Ha, Viet. 120/D2
Dong Hoi, Viet. 120/D2
Dong Noi (riv.), Viet. 120/D4
Dong Tau, Viet. 120/D2
Dong Ujimqin Qi, China 104/H2
Donga (riv.), Nga. 141/H4
Donga, Nga. 141/H5
Dongai (riv.), Camr. 142/A4
Dongar Parāsia, India 122/B4
Dongara, Austl. 156/B4
Dongargarh, India 121/D1
Dongbei (plain), China 106/E2
Dongchuan, China 112/D3
Dong'e, China 106/D3
Dongen, Neth. 78/B5
Donges, Fr. 82/C6
Dongfang, China 120/E2
Dongfang, China 113/F5
Donggou, China 107/C3
Dongguan, China 113/G4
Dongguang, China 106/D3
Donghai, China 106/D4
Donghen, Laos 120/D2
Donghezhen, China 106/L8
Dongio, Swi. 87/E5
Dongjia, China 113/G2
Dongjing (riv.), China 113/G2
Dongjingling, China 107/B2
Dongkeng, China 113/H3
Dongkya (pass), China 123/G2
Dongli, China 119/K3
Dongliao (riv.), China 106/F2
Donglük, China 125/E4
Dongmen, China 120/D1
Dongming, China 106/C4
Dongnan (plat.), China 113/F4
Dongo, It. 87/F5
Dongo, D.R. Congo 146/D2
Dongo, D.R. Congo 147/E2
Dongo, Ang. 148/B2
Dongo-Kuma, D.R. Congo 146/E2
Dongobesh, Tanz. 145/A3
Dongola, Il, US 188/C2
Dongou, Congo 146/D2
Dongping, China 106/D4
Dongqiao, China 125/F5
Dongsha (isl.), China 113/H4
Dongsha (Pratas) (isl.), China 113/H4
Dongshajiao, China 113/J2
Dongshan (isl.), China 113/H4
Dongshan, China 106/L8
Dongshao, China 113/G3
Dongsheng, China 106/B3
Dongtai, China 106/E4
Dongtiao (riv.), China 106/L9
Dongting (lake), China 113/G2
Dongtingxi, China 113/F2
Dongue, Ang. 148/B2
Dongxing, China 120/D1
Dongxing, China 113/F3
Dongying, China 106/D3
Dongzhen, China 104/E4
Dongzhi, China 113/H2
Donie, Tx, US 177/F2
Donihue, Chile 214/N9
Donington, Eng, UK 61/H6
Doniphan, Mo, US 188/B2
Donjek (riv.), Yk, Can. 166/C2
Donji Komren, Yugo. 76/E4
Donji Vakuf, Bosn. 76/C3
Donk, Neth. 78/C5
Donna, Tx, US 177/E4
Donnas, It. 88/A1
Donnelly, Mn, US 182/F5
Donner (pass), Ca, US 172/C4
Donner und Blitzen (riv.), Or, US 172/D2
Donnersberg (peak), Ger. 81/G4
Donnybrook, ND, US 182/D3
Donnybrook, Austl. 160/D4
Donnybrook, Austl. 156/B5
Donon (peak), Fr. 86/D1
Donora, Pa, US 187/G4
Donoratico, It. 71/J5
Donskoy, Rus. 99/L4
Donsol, Phil. 114/C2
Donville-les-Bains, Fr. 82/D3
Donyan (riv.), Myan. 112/B5
Donzdorf, Ger. 84/C5
Donzère, Fr. 90/A4
Donzy, Fr. 70/E3
Doole, Tx, US 177/E2
Dooleena (peak), Austl. 156/C2
Doomadgee Abor. Land, Austl. 155/E4
Doomadgee Aboriginal Community, Austl. 155/E4
Doon, Ire. 58/B4
Doon (lake), Sc, UK 59/B6
Doon (riv.), Sc, UK 59/B6
Doon Doon Abor. Land, Austl. 154/C4
Doonbeg (riv.), Ire. 58/A4
Doonbeg, Ire. 58/A4
Door (pen.), Wi, US 183/L5
Door (pt.), La, US 190/D2
Doorn, Neth. 78/C4
Doorn (riv.), SAfr. 150/B3
Doppo (peak), It. 88/D2
Doqên (lake), China 123/G1
Dora, Mo, US 179/H2
Dora (lake), Fl, US 190/M6
Dora, Al, US 188/D4
Dora (lake), Austl. 153/B3
Dora Baltea (riv.), It. 90/D1
Dora Creek, Austl. 159/E1
Dora di Rhêmes (riv.), It. 90/D1
Dora Riparia (riv.), It. 71/G4
Dorada (coast), Sp. 73/F2
Dorāh Ān (pass), Pak. 125/B4
Doraville, Ga, US 189/M7
Dorchester, NB, Can. 184/E3
Dorchester (cape), Nun, Can. 167/J2
Dorchester, Eng, UK 62/D5
Dorchester, Ne, US 181/F3
Dorchester, NJ, US 194/D5
Dorchester, SC, US 189/G4
Dordabis, Namb. 148/C4
Dordogne (riv.), Fr. 92/D1
Dordrecht, Neth. 78/B5
Dordrecht, SAfr. 150/D3
Dore (mts.), Fr. 70/E4
Dore (riv.), Fr. 70/E4
Dores, Sc, UK 59/B2
Dores do Indaiá, Braz. 210/D3
Dorfen (riv.), Ger. 85/E6
Dorfen, Ger. 85/F6
Dorgali, It. 74/A2
Dörgön (lake), Mong. 104/C2
Dori, Burk. 141/E3
Doria, It. 88/B5
Dorion, On, Can. 183/K3
Dorion, Qu, Can. 185/M7
Dorking, Eng, UK 56/C3
Dorlisheim, Fr. 86/D1
Dormagen, Ger. 81/F1
Dormans, Fr. 80/C5
Dormans Land, Eng, UK 56/D3
Dornach, Swi. 86/D3
Dornakal, India 121/D2
Dornbirn, Aus. 87/F3
Dorney Park/ Wildwater Kingdom, Pa, US 194/C2
Dornhan, Ger. 87/E1
Dorno, It. 88/B3
Dornoch, Sc, UK 59/B1
Dornoch Firth (inlet), Sc, UK 59/B1
Dornod (prov.), Mong. 104/G2
Dornogovĭ (prov.), Mong. 104/F3
Dornstadt, Ger. 84/C6
Dornstetten, Ger. 84/B6
Doro, Mali 141/E2
Dorog, Hun. 77/Q9
Dorogobuzh, Rus. 94/G5
Dorogorskoye, Rus. 95/K2
Dorohoi, Rom. 98/D4
Doromo, D.R. Congo 147/F2
Doron de Chavière (riv.), Fr. 90/C2
Dorothy, NJ, US 194/D5
Dorowa Mining Lease, Zim. 149/F3
Dörpen, Ger. 79/E3
Dorra, Djib. 144/B2
Dorrance, Ks, US 179/E1
Dorre (isl.), Austl. 156/B3
Dorridge, Eng, UK 63/E2
Dorrigo, Austl. 158/E1
Dorrigo NP, Austl. 158/E1
Dorrington, Eng, UK 62/D1
Dorris, Ca, US 172/C3
Dorsale (mts.), Tun. 92/F4
Dorsbach (riv.), Ger. 84/B2
Dorset (co.), Eng, UK 62/D5
Dorsten, Ger. 78/D5
Dortan, Fr. 86/B5
Dortches, NC, US 189/J2
Dortmund, Ger. 79/E5
Dortmund (Wickede) (int'l arpt.), Ger. 79/E5
Dortmund-Ems (canal), Ger. 79/E4
Dörtyol, Turk. 130/E1
Dorum, Ger. 79/F1
Doruma, D.R. Congo 142/E4
Dorval, Qu, Can. 185/N7
Dörverden, Ger. 79/G3
Dos Bahias (cape), Arg. 214/D5
Dos de Mayo, Peru 208/C2
Dos Hermanas, Sp. 72/C4
Dos Palos, Ca, US 174/B2
Dos Pozos, Arg. 214/D4
Dos Puntas (cape), EqG. 146/B2
Dos Quebradas, Col. 207/K8
Dos Reyes (pt.), Chile 212/B3
Döşemealtı, Turk. 130/B1
Dosewallips (riv.), Wa, US 193/A2
Dōshi (riv.), Japan 109/C2
Dōshi, Japan 109/C2
Dosing, India 112/B3
Dospat, Bul. 75/J2
Dosse (riv.), Ger. 68/G2
Dosso (dept.), Niger 141/F3
Dosso, Niger 141/F3
Dosson, It. 89/F2
Dossor, Kaz. 97/K3
Dothan, Al, US 191/F2
Dötlingen, Ger. 79/F3
Dotnuva, Lith. 67/K4

Döttingen, Swi. 87/E2
Doty, Wa, US 170/C4
Douai, Fr. 80/C3
Douala, Camr. 146/B1
Douala (int'l arpt.), Camr. 146/B1
Douar el Câïd el Gueddara, Mor. 138/A2
Douar Toulal, Mor. 138/B3
Douarnenez (bay), Fr. 70/A2
Douarnenez, Fr. 82/A4
Double Island (pt.), Austl. 160/D4
Double Mtn. Fork (riv.), Tx, US 199/E1
Double Springs, Al, US 188/D3
Doubs, Fr. 86/C4
Doubs (dept.), Fr. 86/C3
Doubs (riv.), Fr. 92/E1
Doubtful (bay), Austl. 154/B3
Doubtful Island (bay), Austl. 156/C5
Doubtless (bay), NZ 161/C1
Doucette, Tx, US 177/G2
Douchy-les-Mines, Fr. 80/C3
Doudeville, Fr. 83/F1
Doue, Fr. 56/M5
Doué-la-Fontaine, Fr. 83/E6
Douentza, Mali 140/E3
Dougga (ruin), Tun. 138/L6
Dougherty, Tx, US 179/G4
Douglas, Austl. 154/C3
Douglas (lake), BC, Can. 170/D2
Douglas, Ire. 58/B6
Douglas, SAfr. 150/C3
Douglas (cap.), IM, UK 60/D3
Douglas, Sc, UK 59/C5
Douglas, Az, US 175/H5
Douglas (co.), Ga, US 189/L7
Douglas, Ga, US 191/G2
Douglas, Mi, US 186/C3
Douglas, ND, US 182/D4
Douglas (lake), Tn, US 189/F3
Douglas, Wy, US 180/B2
Douglass, Ks, US 179/F2
Douglass, Tx, US 177/G2
Douglassville, Pa, US 194/C3
Douglastown, NB, Can. 184/E2
Douglasville, Ga, US 189/L7
Dougou, China 113/G1
Doujiang, China 113/F3
Doulaincourt-Saucourt, Fr. 86/B1
Doullens, Fr. 80/B3
Doumé, Camr. 142/B4
Doumé, Gabon 146/C3
Doumé (riv.), Camr. 142/B4
Dounby, Sc, UK 57/V14
Doune (peak), Sc, UK 59/B4
Doune, Sc, UK 59/B4
Doupovské Hory (mts.), Czh. 71/K1
Dour, Belg. 80/C3
Doura, Mali 140/D3
Dourada, Serra (mts.), Braz. 210/C2
Dourados, Braz. 213/F2
Dourados (riv.), Braz. 210/B4
Dourbali, Chad 142/B3
Dourdan, Fr. 56/J6
Dourdou (riv.), Fr. 70/E4
Dourdoura, Chad 142/D3
Dourh (peak), Mor. 137/E2
Douro (riv.), Port. 92/B2
Douron (riv.), Fr. 82/B3
Dousman, Wi, US 193/P13
Doussard, Fr. 86/C6
Douvaine, Fr. 86/C5
Douve (riv.), Fr. 82/D2
Douvrin, Fr. 80/B2
Doux (riv.), Fr. 70/F4
Douze (riv.), Fr. 70/C4
Dove Creek, Co, US 175/H2
Dover, Austl. 158/C4
Dover (pt.), Austl. 156/E5
Dover, Eng, UK 63/H4
Dover (str.), UK,Fr. 70/D1
Dover, Ar, US 179/H3
Dover (A.F.B.), De, US 194/C5
Dover (cap.), De, US 194/C5
Dover, Fl, US 190/L8
Dover, Ks, US 179/G1
Dover, NH, US 187/L3
Dover, NJ, US 194/D2
Dover, Oh, US 186/F4
Dover, Ok, US 179/F3
Dover, Pa, US 194/B4
Dover, Tn, US 188/D2
Dover Bluff, Ga, US 191/H2
Doveridge, Eng, UK 61/G6
Dovrefjell NP, Nor. 64/D3
Dovsk, Bela. 96/D1
Dow, Ok, US 179/G3
Dow City, Ia, US 181/G3
Dowagiac, Mi, US 186/C4
Dowerin, Austl. 156/C4
Dowghā'ī, Iran 127/G1
Dowi (cape), Indo. 115/B2
Dowlatābād, Iran 129/J4
Dowling, Ab, Can. 171/H2
Down (dist.), NI, UK 60/C3
Downers Grove, Il, US 193/P16
Downey, Ca, US 192/F8
Downey, Id, US 173/G2
Downham Market, Eng, UK 63/G1
Downieville, Ca, US 172/C4
Downingtown, Pa, US 194/C4
Downpatrick, NI, UK 60/C3
Downs, Ks, US 180/E4
Downsville, NY, US 187/J3
Downton, Eng, UK 63/E4
Dows, Ia, US 181/H2
Dowshī, Afg. 127/J1
Doygaab, Som. 145/C1
Doyle, Ca, US 172/C3
Doylestown, Pa, US 194/C3
Doyleville, Co, US 175/J1
Dōzen (isl.), Japan 110/C3
Dozier, Al, US 191/E2
Dozulé, Fr. 83/E2
Drâa (cape), Mor. 136/C3
Drâa, Oued (riv.), Mor. 133/B2
Drac (riv.), Fr. 70/F4
Dracena, Braz. 213/G2
Drachten, Neth. 78/D2
Drăgăneşti-olt, Rom. 77/G3
Drăgăşani, Rom. 77/G3
Dragoman, Bul. 77/F4
Dragon's Mouth (str.), Trin.,Ven. 205/F2
Dragoon, Az, US 175/G4
Dragør, Den. 65/J7
Draguignan, Fr. 90/C5
Drain, Or, US 172/B2
Drake, ND, US 182/D4
Drake(passg) 216/V
Drake (passg.), SAm. 215/D8
Drakensberg (mts.), SAfr. 133/E8
Drakesville, Ia, US 181/H3
Dráma, Gre. 75/J2
Dramba, D.R. Congo 147/G2
Drammen, Nor. 66/D2
Drammensfjorden (fd.), Nor. 64/R8
Dramselva (riv.), Nor. 64/R8
Drance (riv.), Swi. 86/D5
Drancy, Fr. 56/K5
Drangedal, Nor. 66/C2
Dranse (riv.), Fr. 86/C5
Dransfeld, Ger. 79/G5
Drap, Fr. 90/D5
Draper, Ut, US 173/H3
Draperstown, NI, UK 60/B2
Drās, India 124/C2
Drau (riv.), Aus. 71/K3
Drava (riv.), Cro. 76/C2
Dráva (riv.), Hun. 76/C3
Drava (riv.), Slov. 71/L3
Draveil, Fr. 56/K5
Drawa (riv.), Pol. 69/H2
Drawienski NP, Pol. 69/H2
Drawsko Pomorskie, Pol. 69/H2
Drayton, ND, US 182/F3
Drayton Valley, Ab, Can. 170/G1
Dreghorn, Sc, UK 59/B5
Drei Zinnen (peak), PNG 117/K4
Dreiesselberg (peak), Ger. 85/G5
Dreisam (riv.), Ger. 86/D2
Drensteinfurt, Ger. 79/E5
Drenthe (prov.), Neth. 78/D3
Drentse Hoofdvaart (riv.), Neth. 78/D3
Drentwede, Ger. 79/F3
Dresano, It. 88/C3
Dresden, Ger. 100/B4
Dresden, Oh, US 186/E4
Dresden, On, Can. 186/E3
Dresden, Tn, US 188/C2
Dresser, Wi, US 181/H1
Dreux, Fr. 83/G3
Drew, Ms, US 188/B4
Drews (res.), Or, US 172/C2
Drewsey, Or, US 172/D2
Drexel, Mo, US 179/G1
Dreyer, Tx, US 177/F3
Drezdenko, Pol. 69/H2
Driebergen, Neth. 78/C4
Driedorf, Ger. 81/H2
Driffield, Eng, UK 61/H4
Drift Prairie (grsld.), ND, US 182/E4
Driggs, Id, US 173/H2
Drigh Road, Pak. 127/J4
Drimoleague, Ire. 58/A6
Drin (gulf), Alb. 75/F2
Drin (riv.), Alb. 93/H2
Drina (riv.), Bosn.,Yugo 93/H2
Dripping Springs, Tx, US 177/E2
Driscoll, ND, US 182/D4
Driscoll, Tx, US 177/F4
Driskill (mtn.), La, US 179/H4
Drniš, Cro. 76/C4
Dro, It. 87/G6
Drøbak, Nor. 66/D2
Drobeta-Turnu Severin, Rom. 76/F3
Drochia, Mol. 98/D3
Drochtersen, Ger. 79/G1
Drocourt, Fr. 56/H4
Drogheda, Ire. 60/B4
Drogichin, Bela. 98/C1
Drohobych, Ukr. 98/B3
Droichead Nuadh, Ire. 58/D3
Droitwich, Eng, UK 62/D2
Drolshagen, Ger. 81/G1
Dromahaire, Ire. 58/B1
Drôme (riv.), Fr. 83/E2
Drôme (dept.), Fr. 90/B3
Dromedary (mt.), Austl. 159/E3
Dromina, Ire. 58/B5
Dromiskin, Ire. 60/B4
Dromore (riv.), Ire. 60/A3
Dromore, NI, UK 60/B3
Dromore West, Ire. 58/B1
Dronero, It. 90/D4
Dronfield, Eng, UK 61/G5
Drongan, Sc, UK 59/B6
Dronne (riv.), Fr. 70/D4
Dronten, Neth. 78/C3
Drop, Tx, US 176/K6
Dropt (riv.), Fr. 70/D4
Drosh, Pak. 124/A2
Droskovo, Rus. 96/F1
Drottningholm Palace, Swe. 65/A1
Droué, Fr. 83/G4
Drouette (riv.), Fr. 80/A6
Drouin, Austl. 159/B4
Druento, It. 90/D2
Druid Hills, Ga, US 189/M7
Drum (inlet), NC, US 189/J3
Drumaness, NI, UK 60/C3
Drumbeg, NI, UK 60/C2
Drumcar, Ire. 60/B4
Drumcollogher, Ire. 58/B5
Drumcondra, Ire. 58/D2
Drumheller, Ab, Can. 171/H2
Drumkeeran, Ire. 58/B1
Drumleck (pt.), Ire. 60/B5
Drumlish, Ire. 58/C2
Drummond (mt.), Austl. 160/B4
Drummond (pt.), Austl. 157/G5
Drummond (range), Austl. 153/D3
Drummond, NB, Can. 184/D2
Drummond, Id, US 173/H2
Drummond (isl.), MI, US 186/E1
Drummond, Mt, US 171/H4
Drummond, Wi, US 183/J4
Drummonds, Tn, US 188/C3
Drummondville, Qu, Can. 187/K2
Drummore, Sc, UK 60/D2
Drumnadrochit, Sc, UK 59/B2
Drumnakilly, NI, UK 60/A2
Drumochter, Pass of (pass), Sc, UK 59/B3
Drumright, Ok, US 179/F3
Drumshanbo, Ire. 58/B1
Drumsna, Ire. 58/B2
Drunen, Neth. 78/C5
Drunken (pt.), Mb, Can. 182/F2
Druridge (bay), Eng, UK 61/G1
Drusenheim, Fr. 81/G6
Druskininkai, Lith. 67/K4
Druten, Neth. 78/C5
Druya, Bela. 67/M4
Druzhba, Kaz. 125/D2
Druzhba, Ukr. 99/G1
Druzhkivka, Ukr. 99/J3
Drvar, Bosn. 76/C3
Drwęca (riv.), Pol. 69/K2
Dry (lake), ND, US 182/E3
Dry (cr.), Ca, US 172/C4
Dry Cimarron (riv.), Ok, US 178/C2
Dry Creek, La, US 190/B2
Dry Fork (riv.), Wy, US 180/B1
Dry Fork Marias (riv.), Mt, US 171/H3
Dry Prong, La, US 190/B2
Dry Ridge, Ky, US 188/E1
Dry Run, Oh, US 189/F1
Dry Tortugas (isl.), Fl, US 191/G5
Dry Tortugas Nat'l Pk., Fl, US 196/E3
Dryanovo, Bul. 77/G4
Dryden, On, Can. 183/H3
Dryden, Mi, US 193/F6
Dryden, NY, US 187/H3
Dryden, Tx, US 177/C2
Dryden, Va, US 189/F2
Drygarn Fawr (peak), Wal, UK 62/C2
Drymen, Sc, UK 59/B4
Drysdale (riv.), Austl. 154/B3
Drysdale River NP, Austl. 154/B3
Du (riv.), China 104/G5
Du Bois, Pa, US 187/G4
Du Dja, Réserve, Camr. 142/B5
Du Long, Viet. 120/E4
Du Page (co.), Il, US 193/P16
Du Page (riv.), Il, US 193/P16
Du Page, East Branch (riv.), Il, US 193/P16
Du Quoin, Il, US 188/C1
Duaringa, Austl. 160/C3
Duarte (peak), DRep. 197/G4
Duarte, Ca, US 192/G7
Ḑubā, SAr. 135/G3
Dubach, La, US 179/H4
Dubai (int'l arpt.), UAE 127/G3
Dubăsari, Mol. 98/E4
Dubawnt (riv.), NW, Can. 166/F2
Dubawnt (lake), Nun, Can. 166/F2
Dubawnt (lake), Can. 165/G3
Dubayy, UAE 127/G3
Dubele, D.R. Congo 147/G2
Dübendorf, Swi. 87/E3
Dübener Heide (phys. reg.), Ger. 68/G3
Dubino, It. 87/F5
Dublin (cap.), Ire. 60/B5
Dublin (co.), Ire. 60/B5
Dublin, Ca, US 193/L11
Dublin, Ga, US 189/F4
Dublin, Md, US 194/B4
Dublin, Oh, US 186/E4
Dublin, Pa, US 194/C3
Dublin, Tx, US 177/E1
Dublin, Va, US 189/G2
Dubna, Rus. 96/F1
Dubna, Rus. 94/H4
Dubnica nad Váhom, Slvk. 69/K4
Dubno, Ukr. 98/C2
Dubois, Wy, US 173/J2
Dubois, Id, US 173/G1
Duboistown, Pa, US 194/A1
Dubossary (res.), Mol. 77/J2
Dubovskiy, Rus. 97/G2
Dubovskoye, Rus. 99/M4
Dubovyy Umët, Rus. 97/J1
Dubra, India 123/F4
Dubrājpur, India 123/F4
Dubréka, Gui. 140/B4
Dubrovka, Rus. 96/E1
Dubrovka, Rus. 67/P2
Dubrovnik (int'l arpt.), Yugo. 76/D4
Dubrovnik, Cro. 76/D4
Dubrovno, Bela. 67/P4
Dubrovytsya, Ukr. 98/D2
Dubulu, D.R. Congo 142/D4
Dubuque, Ia, US 181/J2
Duc Lap, Viet. 120/D3
Duc Pho, Viet. 120/E3
Duc Phong, Viet. 120/D4
Duchcov, Czh. 85/G1
Duchesne, Ut, US 173/H3
Duchesne (riv.), Ut, US 173/H3
Duchess, Austl. 157/H2
Duchess, Ab, Can. 171/J2
Ducie (isl.), Pitc. 163/N7
Duck (lake), Mi, US 193/E7
Duck (cr.), Nv, US 173/F4
Duck (riv.), Tn, US 188/D3
Duck Bay, Mb, Can. 182/D1
Duck Hill, Ms, US 188/C4
Duck Lake, Sk, Can. 171/L1
Duck Mtn. (mtn.), Mb, Can. 182/D2
Duck Valley Ind. Res., Id, US 172/E2
Duckabush (riv.), Wa, US 193/A2
Ducktown, Tn, US 188/E3
Duckwater, Nv, US 172/F4
Duckwater Ind. Res., Nv, US 174/E1
Duclair, Fr. 83/F2
Duda (riv.), Col. 204/C4
Duddon (riv.), Eng, UK 61/E3
Dudelange, Lux. 81/F5
Dudenhofen, Ger. 84/B4
Duderstadt, Ger. 79/H5
Dudh Kosi (riv.), Nepal 123/F2
Dūdhi, India 122/D3
Dudhwa NP, India 122/C1
Dudignac, Arg. 214/E2
Düdingen, Swi. 86/D4
Dudinka, Rus. 100/J3
Dudley, Eng, UK 62/D1
Dudub, Eth. 144/C4
Dudzele, Belg. 80/C1
Due, D.R. Congo 146/D4
Due West, SC, US 189/F3
Duékoué, C.d'Iv. 140/D5
Dueñas, Sp. 72/C2
Duenweg, Mo, US 179/G2
Dueré, Braz. 210/C1
Duette, Fl, US 190/L8
Dueville, It. 89/E2
Dufaja (riv.), Kenya 145/B2
Duff (isls.), Sol. 162/F5
Duffel, Belg. 81/D1
Dufferin (co.), On, Can. 186/S8
Duffield, Eng, UK 61/G6
Duff's Corners, On, Can. 186/S9
Dufftown, Sc, UK 59/C2
Dufour (Dufourspitze) (peak), Swi. 88/A1
Dufourspitze (Dufour) (peak), Swi. 88/A1
Dugachhi, Bang. 123/H3
Dugald, Mb, Can. 182/F3
Dugbia, D.R. Congo 147/F2
Dugdemona (riv.), La, US 177/H1
Dugger, In, US 188/D1
Dugi (isl.), Cro. 71/L4
Dugi Otok (isl.), Cro. 93/G2
Dugny-sur-Meuse, Fr. 81/E5
Dugo Selo, Cro. 76/C3
Dugu, Eth. 144/B3
Dugway, Ut, US 173/G3
Dugway Proving Grounds, Ut, US 173/G3
Duich (lake), Sc, UK 59/A2
Duida (peak), Ven. 205/E4
Duida Marahuaca, PN, Ven. 205/E4
Duifken (pt.), Austl. 155/F3
Duingen, Ger. 79/G4
Duino, It. 89/G2
Duisburg, Ger. 78/D6
Duitama, Col. 204/C3
Duiven, Neth. 78/D5
Duivendrecht, Neth. 78/B4
Dujuuma, Som. 145/C1
Duk Fadiat, Sudan 142/F4
Dukafulu, Eth. 144/A4
Dukambīya, Erit. 142/H2
Duke, Mo, US 179/H2
Duke of Gloucester (isls.), FrPol. 163/L7
Duke's (pass), Sc, UK 59/B4
Dukhān, Qatar 126/F3
Dukielska (Dukla Pass) (pass), Pol. 69/L4
Dukla Pass (Dukielska) (pass), Pol. 69/L4
Dūkštas, Lith. 67/M4
Dula, D.R. Congo 142/D4
Dulac, La, US 190/C3
Dulan, China 104/D4
Dulce (riv.), Arg. 212/D4
Dulce, NM, US 175/J2
Dulce (gulf), Pan. 201/F4
Dulce Nombre de Culmí, Hon. 200/E3
Dule, Erit. 144/A2
Duleek, Ire. 60/B4
Dŭlgopol, Bul. 77/H4
Duliu (riv.), China 119/J2
Duliu, China 106/H7
Dullewāla, Pak. 124/A4
Dullstroom, SAfr. 149/F5
Dülmen, Ger. 79/E5
Dulnain (riv.), Sc, UK 59/C2
Dulong (pass), China 112/B3
Dulovo, Bul. 77/H4
Dulunguin (pt.), Phil. 114/C4
Duluth, Mn, US 183/H4
Duluth, Ga, US 189/M6
Dulverton, Eng, UK 62/C4
Dūmā, Syria 131/E1
Dūmā, WBnk. 131/C4
Dumagasa (pt.), Phil. 114/C4
Dumaguete, Phil. 114/C3
Dumai, Indo. 115/C2
Dumalinao, Phil. 114/C4
Dumanjug, Phil. 114/C3
Dumaran, Phil. 114/B3
Dumaran (isl.), Phil. 117/E1
Dumas, Tx, US 178/D3
Dumas, Ar, US 179/J4
Ḑumayr, Syria 130/E3
Ḑumayr, Syria 131/F1
Dumbarton, Sc, UK 59/B5
Dumbi, D.R. Congo 146/D4
Dumbi, Ang. 148/B1
Ďumbier (peak), Slvk. 69/K4
Dumbleyung, Austl. 156/C5
Dumbrăveni, Rom. 77/G2
Dume (pt.), Ca, US 192/B2
Dumei, China 113/H3
Dumfries, Sc, UK 60/E1
Dumfries and Galloway (co.), Sc, UK 59/C6
Duminichi, Rus. 96/E1
Dumka, India 123/F3
Dumlu, Turk. 97/G4
Dummar, Syria 131/E1
Dümmer (lake), Ger. 79/F3
Dumoine (riv.), Qu, Can. 187/H1
Dumoine (lake), Qu, Can. 167/J4
Dumont, NJ, US 195/K8
Dumont d'Urville, Fr., Ant. 216/K
Dumraon, India 123/E3
Dumri, India 123/F4
Dumyat (gov.), Egypt 128/B3
Dumyāţ (Damietta), Egypt 139/C2
Dumyāţ, Massabb (Damietta) (mouth), Egypt 139/C1
Dún Laoghaire, Ire. 60/B5
Dun Rig (peak), Sc, UK 59/C5
Dunaföldvár, Hun. 76/D2
Dunaharaszti, Hun. 77/R10
Dunajec (riv.), Pol. 69/L4
Dunakeszi, Hun. 77/R9
Dunany (pt.), Ire. 60/B4
Dunaszekcso, Hun. 76/D2
Dunaújváros, Hun. 76/D2
Dunavecse, Hun. 76/D2
Dunavtsi, Bul. 76/F4
Dunayivtsi, Ukr. 98/D3
Dunbar, Sc, UK 59/D5
Dunbar, Austl. 160/A2
Dunblane, Sk, Can. 171/L2
Dunblane, Sc, UK 59/C4
Dunboyne, Ire. 60/B5
Duncan, Ok, US 179/F3
Duncan, Az, US 175/H4
Duncan, Ms, US 188/B3
Duncan, BC, Can. 170/C3
Duncannon, Ire. 58/D5
Duncannon, Pa, US 194/A3
Duncansby Head (pt.), Sc, UK 57/V14
Duncanville, Tx, US 176/L7
Dund-Us, Mong. 104/C2
Dundaga, Lat. 67/K3
Dundalk (bay), Ire. 60/B4
Dundalk, Ire. 60/B4
Dundalk, On, Can. 186/F2
Dundalk, Md, US 194/B5
Dundas (lake), Austl. 156/D5
Dundas (str.), Austl. 154/C2
Dundas (pen.), NW, Can. 167/R7
Dundas, On, Can. 186/T9
Dundas, Oh, US 189/F1
Dundas, Il, US 188/C1
Dundee, Tx, US 178/E4
Dundee (arpt.), Sc, UK 59/C4
Dundee, Sc, UK 59/D4
Dundee, Fl, US 190/M7
Dundee, Ms, US 188/B3
Dundee, SAfr. 151/E3
Dundgovi (prov.), Mong. 104/F2
Dundīţ, Egypt 139/C3
Dundonald, Sc, UK 59/B5
Dundrum (bay), NI, UK 60/C3
Dundrum, NI, UK 60/C3
Dundurn, Sk, Can. 171/L2
Dundwa (range), Nepal 122/D2
Dundwārāganj, India 122/B2
Dunedin, NZ 161/B4
Dunedin, Fl, US 190/K7
Dunedoo, Austl. 158/D2
Dunellen, NJ, US 195/H9
Dunes City, Or, US 172/A2
Dunfanaghy, Ire. 57/Q9
Dunfermline, Sc, UK 59/C4
Dunga Bunga, Pak. 124/B5
Dungalear Station, Austl. 158/D1
Dungannon, NI, UK 60/B3
Dungannon (co.), NI, UK 60/B3
Dungannon, On, Can. 186/F3
Dungarpur, India 118/B3
Dungarvan, Ire. 58/C5
Dungarvan (har.), Ire. 58/C5
Dungau (reg.), Ger. 85/F5
Dungeness (pt.), Arg. 215/C7
Dungeness (pt.), Eng, UK 63/G5
Dungeness, Wa, US 170/C3
Dungiven, NI, UK 60/B2
Dunglow, Ire. 57/P9
Dungog, Austl. 158/D2
Dungu, D.R. Congo 147/G2
Dungu (riv.), D.R. Congo 142/F5
Dunham, Qu, Can. 187/K2
Dunhua, China 105/K3
Dunhuang, China 104/C3
Dunkeld, Sc, UK 59/C3
Dunkellin (riv.), Ire. 58/B3
Dunkerque (Dunkirk), Fr. 70/E1
Dunkery (hill), Eng, UK 62/C4
Dunkirk, NY, US 187/G3
Dunkirk, In, US 186/D4
Dunkirk (Dunkerque), Fr. 70/E1
Dunkley, BC, Can. 170/C1
Dunkwa, Gha. 141/E5
Dunlap, Tn, US 188/E3
Dunlap, Ia, US 181/G3
Dunlavin, Ire. 58/D3
Dunleath, Sk, Can. 182/C2
Dunleer, Ire. 60/B4
Dunloe, Gap of (pass), Ire. 58/A5
Dunloy, NI, UK 60/B2
Dunmanus (bay), Ire. 58/A6
Dunmanway, Ire. 58/A6
Dunmore, Ire. 58/B2
Dunmore, Pa, US 187/J4
Dunmore, WV, US 189/H1
Dunmore East, Ire. 58/C5
Dunmurry, NI, UK 60/B2
Dunn, La, US 179/J4
Dunn, NC, US 189/H3
Dunnamanagh, NI, UK 60/A2
Dunnamore, NI, UK 60/B2
Dunnell, Mn, US 181/G2
Dunnellon, Fl, US 191/G3
Dünnern (riv.), Swi. 86/D3
Dunnet Head (pt.), Sc, UK 57/V14
Dunning, Sc, UK 59/C4
Dunningen, Ger. 87/E1
Dunnington, Eng, UK 61/H4
Dunnsville, Va, US 189/J2
Dunnville, On, Can. 186/T10
Dunolly, Austl. 158/B3
Dunoon, Sc, UK 59/B5
Dunqulah, Sudan 135/F5
Dunqunāb, Sudan 126/C4
Dunragit, Sc, UK 60/D2
Duns, Sc, UK 59/D5
Dunsborough, Austl. 156/B5
Dunscore, Sc, UK 60/E1
Dunseith, ND, US 182/D3
Dunseverick, NI, UK 60/B1
Dunshaughlin, Ire. 60/B4
Dunsmuir, Ca, US 172/B3
Dunstable, Eng, UK 63/F3
Dunster, BC, Can. 170/E1
Duntocher, Sc, UK 59/B5
Dunure, Sc, UK 59/B6
Dunville, Nf, Can. 185/L2
Dunwoody, Ga, US 189/M7
Dunyāpur, Pak. 124/A5
Duobukur (riv.), China 105/J1
Duojing, China 113/E4
Duolun, China 104/H3
Dupont, In, US 188/E1
Dupont, Pa, US 194/C1
Dupree, SD, US 180/D1
Dupuy (cape), Austl. 156/B2
Duque Bacelar, Braz. 207/F4
Duque de Caxias, Braz. 211/N7
Duque de York (isl.), Chile 215/A6
Duquette, Mn, US 183/H4
Dūrā, WBnk. 131/C5
Durack (range), Austl. 154/B4
Durack (riv.), Austl. 154/B4
Durağan, Turk. 96/E4
Durak, Turk. 130/D1
Durand, Mi, US 186/E3
Durand, Wi, US 181/J1
Durango (state), Mex. 196/A3
Durango, Sp. 70/B5
Durango, Co, US 175/J2
Durango de Victoria, Mex. 198/D3
Duranillin, Austl. 156/C5
Durant, Ok, US 179/F4
Durant, Fl, US 190/L8
Durant, Ms, US 188/C4
Durazno (dept.), Uru. 215/F2
Durazno, Uru. 215/K10
Durban, SAfr. 151/E3
Durban (Louis Botha) (int'l arpt.), SAfr. 151/E3
Durbanville, SAfr. 150/L10
Durbe, Lat. 67/J3
Durbion (riv.), Fr. 86/C1
Durbuy, Belg. 81/E3
Dúrcal, Sp. 72/D4
Durdevac, Cro. 76/C2
Durdevo, Yugo. 76/E3
Durdur (riv.), Som. 144/B3
Düre, China 125/E2
Dureji, Pak. 127/J3
Düren, Ger. 81/F2
Durg, India 121/D1
Durgāpur, India 123/G3
Durgāpur, India 123/F4
Durgerdam, Neth. 78/B4
Durham, On, Can. 186/F2
Durham (co.), On, Can. 186/V8
Durham (co.), Eng, UK 61/F2
Durham, Eng, UK 61/G2
Durham, Ca, US 172/C4
Durham, Ks, US 179/F1
Durham, Mo, US 181/J4
Durham, NC, US 189/H3
Durham, NH, US 187/L3
Durham Bridge, NB, Can. 184/D2
Durham Downs, Austl. 160/A4
Duri, Indo. 115/C2
Durlston (pt.), Eng, UK 62/E5
Ḑurmā, SAr. 126/E4
Durmitor NP, Yugo. 75/F1
Durnford (pt.), WSah. 136/B5
Duror, Sc, UK 59/A5
Dürrenroth, Swi. 86/D3
Durrës, Alb. 75/F2
Durrington, Eng, UK 63/E4
Dürrlauingen, Ger. 84/D6
Durrow, Ire. 58/C4
Dürrwangen, Ger. 84/D4
Dursley, Eng, UK 62/D3
Dursunbey, Turk. 96/D5
Durtal, Fr. 83/E5
Duru, D.R. Congo 142/F4
Durugu, D.R. Congo 142/C4
Durukhsi, Eth. 144/C3
Durusu (lake), Turk. 129/M6
Durusu, Turk. 129/M6
Durūz (peak), Syria 135/H1
D'Urville (cape), Indo. 117/J4
Dusa Marreb (Dhuusamarreeb), Som. 144/C4
Dusanovo, Yugo. 75/G1
Dusetos, Lith. 67/L4
Dushak, Trkm. 127/H1
Dushan, China 113/E3
Dushanbe (cap.), Taj. 100/G6
Dusheti, Geo. 97/H4
Dushui (riv.), China 113/E3
Dusky (sound), NZ 161/A4
Düsseldorf (int'l arpt.), Ger. 78/D6
Düsseldorf, Ger. 78/D6
Dusti, Taj. 127/J1
Dustin, Ok, US 179/F3
Duszniki-Zdrój, Pol. 69/J3
Dutch (riv.), Eng, UK 61/H4
Dutch (cr.), BC, Can. 170/F2
Dutch John, Ut, US 173/J3
Dutch Wonderland, Pa, US 194/B3
Dutlwe, Bots. 148/D4
Dutoitspiek (peak), SAfr. 150/L10
Dutovo, Rus. 95/N3
Dutse, Nga. 141/H4
Dutsen Wai, Nga. 141/H4
Dutsin-Ma, Nga. 141/G3
Dutton, On, Can. 186/F3
Dutton (mt.), Ut, US 175/F1
Dutton, Mt, US 171/J4
Dutukpene, Gha. 141/F4
Duvall, Wa, US 193/D2
Duvno, Bosn. 76/C4
Düxanbibazar, China 125/D4
Duxun, China 113/H4
Duyang, China 113/E3
Duyun, China 113/E3
Dūz, Tun. 92/F4
Düzce, Turk. 77/K5
Düzici, Turk. 128/D2
Dve Mogili, Bul. 77/G4
Dvina (bay), Rus. 94/H2
Dvinskoy, Rus. 95/K3
Dvořiště (lake), Czh. 85/H4
Dvorníky, Slvk. 76/C1
Dwārka, India 127/J4
Dwārkeswar (riv.), India 123/F4
Dwight, Ks, US 179/F1
Dwight, Il, US 186/B4
Dworshak (res.), Id, US 170/F4
Dwyer (Faywood), NM, US 175/H4
Dwyfor (riv.), Wal, UK 60/D6
Dwyka (riv.), SAfr. 150/C4
Dyat'kovo, Rus. 96/E1
Dybvad, Den. 66/D3
Dyce, Sc, UK 59/D2
Dyce (int'l arpt.), Sc, UK 59/D2
Dyckesville, Wi, US 186/C2
Dyer, In, US 186/C4
Dyer (cape), Nun, Can. 167/K2
Dyer, Nv, US 174/C2
Dyer, Tn, US 188/C2
Dyer (cape), Chile 215/B6
Dyersburg, Tn, US 188/C2
Dyersville, Ia, US 181/J2
Dyess, Ar, US 188/B3
Dyess (A.F.B.), Tx, US 177/E1
Dyfed (co.), Wal, UK 62/B2
Dyffryn, Wal, UK 60/D6
Dyfi (riv.), Wal, UK 62/C1
Dyje (riv.), Czh. 69/J4
Dykan'ka, Ukr. 99/H3
Dyke Ackland(bay) 155/H2
Dykh-tau (peak), Rus. 97/G4
Dyle (riv.), Belg. 68/C3
Dyleň (peak), Czh. 85/F3
Dylewska (peak), Pol. 69/K2
Dymchurch, Eng, UK 63/G4
Dymer, Ukr. 98/F2
Dymytrov, Ukr. 99/J3
Dysart, Sk, Can. 182/B2
Dysart, Austl. 160/C3
Dysart, Ia, US 181/H2
Dysseldorp, SAfr. 150/C4
Dyul'tydag (peak), Rus. 97/H4
Dyurtyuli, Rus. 95/M5
Dzalanyama (range), Moz. 149/G2
Dzamandzar, Madg. 152/J6
Dzaoudzi (cap.), May. 152/H6
Dzaoudzi (int'l arpt.), Fr. 152/H6
Dzavhan (riv.), Mong. 104/C2
Dzavhan (prov.), Mong. 104/D2
Dzel, Mong. 125/F2
Dzenzik (pt.), Ukr. 99/J4
Dzerzhinsk, Rus. 94/J4
Dzerzhinsk, Bela. 67/M5
Dzerzhyns'k, Ukr. 99/J3
Dzerzhyns'k, Ukr. 98/D2
Dzhalinda, Rus. 105/J1
Dzhambeyty, Kaz. 97/K2
Dzhanga, Trkm. 129/H1
Dzhankoy, Ukr. 99/H5
Dzhanybek, Kaz. 97/H2
Dzharylgach (gulf), Ukr. 77/L2
Dzhebel, Bul. 75/J2
Dzhebrail, Azer. 129/F2
Dzhirgatal', Taj. 125/B4
Dzhubga, Rus. 96/F3
Dzhugdzhur (range), Rus. 103/N4
Dzhusaly, Kaz. 100/G5
Działdowo, Pol. 69/L2
Dzibalchén, Mex. 200/D2
Dzibilchaltún (ruin), Mex. 200/D1
Dzidzantún, Mex. 200/D1
Dzierżoniów, Pol. 69/J3
Dzitbalché, Mex. 200/D1
Dziuché, Mex. 200/D2
Dzöölön, Mong. 104/D1
Dzukija NP, Lith. 67/L4
Dzungarian (basin), China 100/J5
Dzur, Mong. 104/D2
Dzüünbayan, Mong. 104/G3
Dzüünbulag, Mong. 104/G2
Dzüünharaa, Mong. 104/F2
Dzüünhövöö, Mong. 125/F1
Dzuunmod, Mong. 104/F2

E

E.D.F. (canal), Fr. 90/B5
E.T. Joshua (int'l arpt.), StV. 197/N9
Eads, Co, US 178/C1
Eagan, Mn, US 183/P7
Eagle (riv.), Nf, Can. 167/L3
Eagle (cr.), Sk, Can. 171/K2
Eagle (hills), Sk, Can. 171/K1
Eagle (mt.), Ire. 58/A5
Eagle (lake), Ca, US 172/C3
Eagle (mts.), Ca, US 174/E4
Eagle (peak), Ca, US 172/C3
Eagle (peak), Ca, US 172/D4
Eagle, Co, US 173/K4
Eagle (riv.), Co, US 173/K4
Eagle, Id, US 172/E2
Eagle (cr.), Ky, US 188/E1
Eagle (mtn.), Mn, US 183/J4
Eagle, Ne, US 181/F3
Eagle (peak), Tx, US 177/B2
Eagle (pt.), Tx, US 177/N9
Eagle, Wi, US 193/P14
Eagle (peak), Wy, US 173/H1
Eagle Bend, Mn, US 183/G4
Eagle Butte, SD, US 180/D1
Eagle Crags (peak), Ca, US 174/D3
Eagle Grove, Ia, US 181/H2
Eagle Lake, Fl, US 190/M8
Eagle Lake, Tx, US 176/F3
Eagle Mills, Ar, US 179/H4
Eagle Mountain (lake), Tx, US 179/F4
Eagle Pass, Tx, US 177/D3
Eagle Point, Or, US 172/B2
Eagle River, Mi, US 183/K4
Eagle River, Wi, US 183/K5
Eagle Rock, Va, US 189/H2
Eaglehawk, Austl. 159/B3
Eaglesfield, Sc, UK 61/E1
Eaglesham, Sc, UK 59/B5
Eagleton, Ar, US 179/G3
Eagletown, Ok, US 179/G3
Eagleville, Ca, US 172/C3
Eagleville, Mo, US 181/H3
Eahun, Indo. 154/A2
Eakly, Ok, US 179/E3
Ealing (bor.), Eng, UK 56/B2
Ear Falls, On, Can. 183/H2
Earby, Eng, UK 61/F4
Earith, Eng, UK 63/G2
Earl Grey, Sk, Can. 182/B2
Earl Stonham, Eng, UK 63/H2
Earle, Ar, US 188/B3
Earle Nav. Weapons Ctr., NJ, US 194/D3
Earlimart, Ca, US 174/C3
Earling, Ia, US 181/G3
Earlington, Ky, US 188/D2
Earls Barton, Eng, UK 63/F2
Earls Colne, Eng, UK 63/G3
Earl's Seat (peak), Sc, UK 59/B4
Earlsboro, Ok, US 179/F3
Earlsferry, Sc, UK 59/D4
Earlston, Sc, UK 59/D5
Earltown, NS, Can. 184/F3
Earlville, Ia, US 181/J2
Earlville, Il, US 181/K3
Early, Ia, US 181/G2
Early, Tx, US 176/E2
Earn (riv.), Sc, UK 59/C4
Earn (lake), Sc, UK 59/B4
Earnslaw (mt.), NZ 161/B4
Earp, Ca, US 174/E3
Easington, Eng, UK 61/G2
Easingwold, Eng, UK 61/G3
Easky, Ire. 58/B1
Easley, SC, US 189/F3
East (mt.), Austl. 156/D4
East (cape), NZ 161/D2
East (cape), NZ 153/H6
East (mesa), Ca, US 174/E4
East (cape), Fl, US 191/H5
East (pt.), NJ, US 194/C5
East (riv.), NY, US 195/K8
East (bay), Tx, US 177/G3
East (passg.), Wa, US 193/C3
East Alamosa, Co, US 178/B2
East Alligator (riv.), Austl. 154/D3
East Anglia (reg.), Eng, UK 63/H2
East Angus, Qu, Can. 187/L2
East Arrow Park, BC, Can. 170/F2
East Baines (riv.), Austl. 154/C3
East Bangor, Pa, US 194/C2
East Barming, Eng, UK 56/E3
East Barnet (nbrhd.), Eng, UK 56/C2
East Berbice-Corentyne (pol. reg.), Guy. 205/G3
East Bergholt, Eng, UK 63/H3
East Berlin, Pa, US 194/B4
East Bernstadt, Ky, US 188/E2
East Berwick, Pa, US 194/B1
East Bethel, Mn, US 183/H5
East Bijou (cr.), Co, US 180/B4
East Brady, Pa, US 187/G4
East Brewton, Al, US 190/E2
East Brunswick, NJ, US 195/H10
East Cache (cr.), Ok, US 179/E3
East Caicos (isl.), UK 201/J1
East Calder, Sc, UK 59/C5
East Camden, Ar, US 179/H4
East Carbon, Ut, US 173/H4
East Chevington, Eng, UK 59/E6
East Chicago, In, US 186/C4
East China (sea), Asia 103/M6
East Clandon, Eng, UK 56/B3
East Coulee, Ab, Can. 171/H2
East Dart (riv.), Eng, UK 62/C5
East Dereham, Eng, UK 63/G1
East Detroit (East Pointe), Mi, US 193/G7
East Dismal (swamp), NC, US 189/J3
East Dublin, Ga, US 189/F4
East Falkland (isl.), UK 203/D8
East Falmouth, Ma, US 187/L4
East Farmingdale, NY, US 195/M9
East Flat Rock, NC, US 189/F3
East Fork (riv.), Tx, US 179/F4
East Fork Trinity (riv.), Tx, US 176/L6
East Frisian (isls.), Neth. 68/D2
East Frisian (isls.), Ger. 66/B5
East Ghor (canal), Jor. 131/D4
East Glacier Park, Mt, US 171/H3
East Glen (riv.), Eng, UK 61/H6
East Grand Rapids, Mi, US 186/D3
East Greenville, Pa, US 194/C3
East Griffin, Ga, US 188/E4
East Grinstead, Eng, UK 63/F4
East Gull Lake, Mn, US 183/G4
East Hampton, NY, US 195/F2
East Hampton (arpt.), NY, US 195/F2
East Hanningfield, Eng, UK 56/E2
East Haven, Ct, US 195/F1
East Helena, Mt, US 171/J4
East Hill-Meridian, Wa, US 193/C3
East Hills, NY, US 195/L8
East Hodge, La, US 190/B1
East Horseley, Eng, UK 56/B3
East Jordan, Mi, US 186/D2
East Kilbride, Sc, UK 59/B5
East Korea (bay), NKor. 105/K4
East Lamma (chan.), China 113/L8
East Lansing, Mi, US 186/D3
East Las Vegas, Nv, US 174/E2
East Leake, Eng, UK 61/G6
East Linton, Sc, UK 59/D5
East Liverpool, Oh, US 186/F4
East London, SAfr. 150/D4
East Los Angeles, Ca, US 192/F7
East Malling, Eng, UK 56/E3
East Meadow, NY, US 195/L9
East Midlands (int'l arpt.), Eng, UK 61/G6
East Millcreek, Ut, US 173/H3
East Mojave Nat'l Scenic Area, Ca, US 174/E3
East Molesey, Eng, UK 56/B2
East Montpelier, Vt, US 187/K2
East Naples, Fl, US 191/H4
East Newark, NJ, US 195/J9
East Nishnabotna (riv.), Ia, US 181/G3
East Nodaway (riv.), Ia, US 181/G3
East Northport, NY, US 195/E2
East Olympia, Wa, US 170/C4
East Orange, NJ, US 195/J8
East Otis, Ma, US 187/K3
East Palatka, Fl, US 191/H3
East Palestine, Oh, US 186/F4
East Peckham, Eng, UK 56/E3
East Petersburg, Pa, US 194/B3
East Point, La, US 176/H1
East Point, Ga, US 189/M7
East Pointe (East Detroit), Mi, US 193/G7
East Port Orchard, Wa, US 193/B2
East Prairie, Mo, US 188/C2
East Prospect, Pa, US 194/B4
East Quogue, NY, US 195/F2
East Retford, Eng, UK 61/H5
East Ridge, Tn, US 188/E3
East Rockaway, NY, US 195/L9
East Rockingham, NC, US 189/H3
East Rutherford, NJ, US 195/J8
East Saint Louis, Il, US 181/J4
East Siberian (sea), Rus. 101/S2
East Side, Pa, US 194/C1
East Stroudsburg, Pa, US 194/C2
East Sussex (co.), Eng, UK 63/G5
East Tampa, Fl, US 190/L8
East Tawas, Mi, US 186/E2
East Thermopolis, Wy, US 173/J2
East Timbalier Island Nat'l Wild. Ref., La, US 190/C3
East Troy, Wi, US 193/P14
East Walker (riv.), Ca, Nv, US 172/D4
East Walker (riv.), Ca,Nv, US 174/C1
East Wemyss, Sc, UK 59/C4
East Wenatchee, Wa, US 170/D4
East Windsor, NJ, US 194/D3
East Wittering, Eng, UK 63/F5
East York (city), On, Can. 186/U8
East-the-Water, Eng, UK 62/B4
Eastabuchie, Ms, US 190/D2
Eastbourne, Eng, UK 63/G5
Eastend, Sk, Can. 171/K3
Easter (pt.), Namb. 148/B5
Easter (Isla de Pascua) (isl.), Chile 163/Q7
Eastern (pt.), Nf, Can. 185/H2
Eastern (pol. reg.), Gha. 141/E5
Eastern (chan.), Japan 110/A4
Eastern (prov.), Kenya 144/A5
Eastern (prov.), Kenya 143/H5
Eastern (prov.), SLeo. 140/C4
Eastern (prov.), SrL. 121/D5
Eastern (prov.), Ugan. 147/H2
Eastern (prov.), Ugan. 145/A1
Eastern (plain), Eng, UK 61/H4
Eastern (bay), Md, US 194/B6
Eastern Fields (reef), PNG 155/G2
Eastern Ghats (mts.), India 118/C5
Eastern Highlands (prov.), PNG 155/G1
Eastern Neck Island NWR, Md, US 194/B5
Eastern Sayans (mts.), Rus. 100/K4
Eastfield, Eng, UK 61/H3
Eastgate, Nv, US 172/E4
Eastland, Tx, US 177/E1
Eastleigh, Eng, UK 63/E5
Eastleigh (int'l arpt.), Eng, UK 63/E5
Eastmain (riv.), Can. 165/K4
Eastmain (riv.), Qu, Can. 167/J3
Eastman, Ga, US 189/F4
Eastman, Wi, US 181/J2
Easton, Eng, UK 62/D5
Easton, Ca, US 174/C2
Easton, Ct, US 195/E1
Easton (res.), Ct, US 195/E1
Easton, Ma, US 187/L3
Easton, La, US 190/B2
Easton, Md, US 189/J1
Easton, Mo, US 181/G4
Easton, Pa, US 194/C2
Easton, Tx, US 177/G1
Eastport, NY, US 195/F2
Eastriggs, Sc, UK 61/E2
Eastry, Eng, UK 63/H4
Eastsound, Wa, US 170/C3
Eastville, Va, US 189/K2
Eastwood, Eng, UK 61/G6
Eatington, Eng, UK 63/E2
Eaton, Co, US 180/B3
Eaton, In, US 186/D4
Eaton, Oh, US 186/D5
Eaton Park, Fl, US 190/M7
Eaton Rapids, Mi, US 186/D3
Eaton Socon, Eng, UK 63/F2
Eatonia, Sk, Can. 171/K2
Eatons Neck (pt.), NY, US 195/M8
Eatonton, Ga, US 189/F4
Eatontown, NJ, US 194/D3
Eatonville, Fl, US 190/N6
Eatonville, Wa, US 170/C4
Eau (riv.), Eng, UK 61/H5
Eau Claire (lake), Qu, Can. 167/J3
Eau Claire (riv.), Wi, US 181/J1
Eau Claire, Wi, US 181/J1
Eau d'Heure (riv.), Belg. 81/D3
Eaubonne, Fr. 56/J5
Eaulne (riv.), Fr. 80/A4
Eauripik (isl.), Micr. 162/D4
Eauze, Fr. 70/D5
Ebalo (riv.), D.R. Congo 142/D5
Ebano, Mex. 200/B1
Ebble (riv.), Eng, UK 63/E4
Ebbw Vale, Wal, UK 62/C3
Ebebiyín, EqG. 146/B2
Ebeggi (well), Alg. 137/G5
Ebéjico, Col. 207/K6
Ebeleben, Ger. 79/H6
Ebeltoft, Den. 66/D3
Ebeltoft Vig (bay), Swe. 65/G6
Eben Junction, Mi, US 183/L4
Ebensburg, Pa, US 187/G4
Ebensee, Aus. 76/A2
Eberbach, Ger. 84/B4
Ebergassing, Aus. 77/P7
Ebergötzen, Ger. 79/H5
Ebermannstadt, Ger. 84/E3
Ebern, Ger. 84/D2
Ebernburg, Ger. 81/G4
Ebersbach an der Fils, Ger. 84/C5
Ebersberg, Ger. 85/E6
Eberschwang, Aus. 85/G6
Ebersheim, Fr. 86/D1
Eberswalde-Finow, Ger. 69/G2
Ebetsu, Japan 108/B2
Ebian, China 119/H2
Ebina, Japan 109/C3
Ebingen, Ger. 87/F1
Ebinur (lake), China 125/D3
Ebnat-Kappel, Swi. 87/F3
Ebo (lake), Mali 140/E3
Ebola (riv.), D.R. Congo 147/E2
Ebolowa, Camr. 146/B2
Ebon (isl.), Mrsh. 162/F4
Ebony, Namb. 148/B4
Ebony, Va, US 189/J2
Eboro, Gabon 146/B2
Ebrach, Ger. 84/D3
Ebreichsdorf, Aus. 77/N8
Ebro, Mn, US 183/G4

Ebro (riv.), Sp. 55/D4
Ebron (riv.), Fr. 90/B3
Ebstorf, Ger. 79/H2
Ecatepec, Mex. 199/Q9
Ecclefechan, Sc, UK 61/E1
Eccles, Eng, UK 61/F5
Eccles, WV, US 189/G2
Eccleshall, Eng, UK 61/F6
Echague, Phil. 114/C1
Echallens, Swi. 86/C4
Echarate, Peru 208/C4
Echaz (riv.), Ger. 84/C6
Éché Fadadinga (riv.), Niger 141/H3
Éché Téfidinga (riv.), Niger 142/B2
Echigawa, Japan 109/K5
Eching, Ger. 85/E6
Échirolles, Fr. 90/B2
Echo, La, US 190/B2
Echo (lake), NJ, US 194/D1
Echo Bay, On, Can. 186/D1
Echo Bay, NW, Can. 166/E2
Echols, Ky, US 188/D2
Echt, Neth. 81/E1
Echterdingen (int'l arpt.), Ger. 84/C5
Echternach, Lux. 81/F4
Echuca, Austl. 159/B3
Echunga, Austl. 157/M9
Echunga (cr.), Austl. 157/M9
Echzell, Ger. 84/B2
Écija, Sp. 72/C4
Ečka, Yugo. 76/E3
Eckernförde, Ger. 66/C4
Eckerö, Fin. 67/H1
Eckerö (isl.), Fin. 67/H1
Eckington, Eng, UK 61/G5
Eckington, Eng, UK 62/D2
Eckville, Ab, Can. 170/G1
Eclectic, Al, US 188/D4
Eclipse Sound (bay), Nun, Can. 167/H1
Écommoy, Fr. 83/F5
Ecorse, Mi, US 193/F7
Ecorse (riv.), Mi, US 193/F7
Écos, Fr. 83/G2
Écouché, Fr. 83/E3
Écouen, Fr. 56/K4
Ecquevilly, Fr. 56/H5
Ecrins, PN, Fr. 71/G4
Ecrosnes, Fr. 56/H6
Écrouves, Fr. 81/E6
Ecru, Ms, US 188/C3
Ecuador (ctry.) 203/A2
Ecublens, Swi. 86/C4
Ed, Swe. 66/D2
Ēd, Erit. 144/B2
Edam, Neth. 78/C3
Edam, Sk, Can. 171/K1
Edapalli, India 121/C4
Eday (isl.), Sc, UK 57/V14
Edchera, Mor. 136/B4
Edderton, Sc, UK 59/B1
Eddleston, Sc, UK 59/C5
Eddy (peak), Id, US 170/F3
Eddystone, Mb, Can. 182/E2
Eddystone (pt.), Austl. 158/D4
Eddystone Rocks (isls.), Eng, UK 62/B6
Eddyville, Ia, US 181/H3
Eddyville, Ky, US 188/C2
Ede, Nga. 141/G5
Ede, Neth. 78/C4
Edéa, Camr. 146/B2
Edegem, Belg. 81/D1
Edehin Ouarene (des.), Alg. 137/G4
Edéia, Braz. 213/G1
Edelény, Hun. 69/L4
Edemissen, Ger. 79/H4
Eden, Austl. 159/D3
Eden, Mb, Can. 182/E2
Eden (riv.), Sc, UK 59/D4
Eden, Az, US 175/H4
Eden, Md, US 189/K1
Eden, NC, US 189/H2
Eden, Tx, US 176/E2
Eden, Wy, US 173/J2
Eden Mills, On, Can. 186/S8
Eden Prairie, Mn, US 183/P7
Edenbridge, Eng, UK 56/D3
Edenburg, SAfr. 150/D3
Edendale, NZ 161/B4
Edendale, SAfr. 151/E3
Edenderry, Ire. 58/C3
Edenhope, Austl. 158/B3
Edenkoben, Ger. 84/B4
Edenside (valley), Eng, UK 61/F2
Edenton, NC, US 189/J2
Edenwold, Sk, Can. 182/B2
Eder (riv.), Ger. 68/E3
Eder-Stausee (lake), Ger. 79/F6
Edewecht, Ger. 79/E2
Edgar, Mt, US 173/J1
Edgar, Ne, US 180/F3
Edgar, Wi, US 181/K1
Edgar (mt.), Austl. 156/D2
Edgar Springs, Mo, US 179/J2
Edgard, La, US 190/C2
Edgartown, Ma, US 184/B5
Edgbaston, Eng, UK 63/E2
Edge (isl.), Sval. 216/E
Edgecliff, Tx, US 176/K7
Edgefield, La, US 190/B1
Edgefield, SC, US 189/G4
Edgeley, ND, US 182/E4
Edgell (isl.), Nun, Can. 167/K2
Edgemere, Md, US 194/B5
Edgemont, SD, US 180/C2
Edgerton, Ab, Can. 171/J1
Edgerton, Mn, US 181/F2
Edgerton, Oh, US 186/D4
Edgerton, Wi, US 181/K2
Edgerton, Wy, US 180/A2
Edgewater, BC, Can. 170/F2
Edgewater, Fl, US 191/H3
Edgewater Park, NJ, US 194/D3
Edgewood, Fl, US 190/N7
Edgewood, Il, US 188/C1
Edgewood, Md, US 194/B5
Edgewood, NM, US 175/J3
Edgewood, Pa, US 194/B2
Edgewood, Tx, US 177/G1
Edgewood Arsenal, Md, US 194/B5
Edgewood-North Hill, Wa, US 193/C3
Edgmond, Eng, UK 62/D1
Edgware (nbrhd.), Eng, UK 56/C2
Édhessa, Gre. 75/H2
Edievale, NZ 161/B4
Edina, Libr 140/C5
Edina, Mo, US 181/H3
Edina, Mn, US 183/P7
Edinboro, Pa, US 186/F4
Edinburg, ND, US 182/F3
Edinburg, Ms, US 188/C4
Edinburg, Tx, US 177/E4
Edinburg, Va, US 189/H1
Edinburgh (cap.), Sc, UK 59/C5
Edinburgh, In, US 186/D5
Edinet, Mol. 98/D3
Edingeni, Malw. 149/G2
Edirne (prov.), Turk. 96/C4
Edirne, Turk. 77/H5
Edison, Co, US 178/B1
Edison, Ga, US 191/F2
Edison, NJ, US 195/H9
Edison, Ca, US 174/C3
Edison Nat'l Hist. Site, NJ, US 195/J8
Edisto, SC, US 189/G4
Edisto (isl.), SC, US 189/G4
Edisto (riv.), SC, US 189/G4
Edisto Island, SC, US 189/G4
Edisto, South Fork (riv.), SC, US 189/G4
Edith Cavell (mt.), BC, Can. 170/E1
Edithburgh, Austl. 157/H5
Edjeleh, Alg. 137/H4
Édjérir (riv.), Mali 141/F2
Edmond, Ok, US 179/F3
Edmonds, Wa, US 170/C4
Edmondt, FrG. 206/C1
Edmonton (nbrhd.), Eng, UK 56/C2
Edmonton, Austl. 160/B2
Edmonton (cap.), Ab, Can. 171/H1
Edmonton, Ky, US 188/E2
Edmonton (int'l arpt.), Ab, Can. 171/H1
Edmore, ND, US 182/E3
Edmore, Mi, US 186/D3
Edmund Kennedy NP, Austl. 160/B2
Edmundston, NB, Can. 184/C2
Edna, Ks, US 179/G2
Edna, Tx, US 177/F3
Edo (state), Nga. 141/G5
Edo (riv.), Japan 109/D2
Edolo, It. 87/G5
Edom, Tx, US 177/G1
Edosaki, Japan 109/E2
Edremit (gulf), Gre., Turk. 96/C5
Edsbro, Swe. 65/B1
Edsbyn, Swe. 66/F1
Eduardo Castex, Arg. 214/D2
Eduardo Gomes (int'l arpt.), Braz. 206/A3
Edward (isl.), On, Can. 183/K3
Edward (mt.), Austl. 157/F2
Edward (riv.), Austl. 159/B2
Edward (lake), D.R. Congo, Ugan. 133/E5
Edward River Abor. Community, Austl. 160/A1
Edward VII (pen.), Ant. 216/P
Edward VIII (bay), Ant. 216/D
Edwards (plat.), Tx, US 168/F5
Edwards, Ms, US 188/B4
Edwards (riv.), Il, US 181/J3
Edwards (A.F.B.), Ca, US 174/C3
Edwardsville, Il, US 181/K4
Edwardsville, Pa, US 194/C1
Edwin, Al, US 191/F2
Edzell, Sc, UK 59/D3
Edzná (ruin), Mex. 200/D2
Eefde, Neth. 78/D4
Eeklo, Belg. 80/C1
Eel (riv.), Ca, US 172/B4
Eel, South Fork (riv.), Ca, US 172/B3
Eelde-Paterswolde, Neth. 78/D2
Eem (riv.), Neth. 78/C4
Eemenes, Neth. 78/C4
Eems (Ems) (riv.), Ger., Neth. 78/D2
Eemshaven (har.), Neth. 78/D2
Eemskanaal (riv.), Neth. 78/D2
Eersel, Neth. 78/C6
Efate (isl.), Van. 162/F6
Eferding, Aus. 85/H6
Effie, Mn, US 183/H4
Effigy Mounds Nat'l Mon., Ia, US 181/J2
Effingham, Eng, UK 56/B3
Effingham, Il, US 188/C1
Effingham, Ks, US 181/G4
Effingham, On, Can. 186/U9
Effon Alaiye, Nga. 141/G5
Effort, Pa, US 194/C2
Efogi, PNG 155/G2
Eforie, Rom. 77/J3
Efringen-Kirchen, Ger. 86/D2
Egadi (isls.), It. 93/G3
Egan (riv.), Ger. 84/D5
Egan, Tx, US 176/K7
Egaña, Uru. 215/K10
Egbe, Nga. 141/G4
Egbunda, D.R. Congo 147/F2
Egeland, ND, US 182/E3
Eger (riv.), Ger. 68/G3
Eger, Hun. 69/L5
Egeskov, Den. 66/D4
Egestorf, Ger. 79/H2
Egg, Aus. 87/F3
Egg, Swi. 87/E3
Egg Harbor City, NJ, US 194/D4
Egg Island (pt.), NJ, US 194/C5
Egg Lagoon, Austl. 159/A4
Eggebek, Ger. 66/C4
Eggegebirge (ridge), Ger. 79/F5
Eggelsberg, Aus. 85/F6
Eggenburg, Aus. 71/L2
Eggenfelden, Ger. 85/F6
Eggenstein-Leopoldshafen, Ger. 84/B4
Eggesin, Ger. 66/F5
Eggiwil, Swi. 86/D4
Egglescliffe, Eng, UK 61/G3
Eggleston, Eng, UK 61/G2
Eggstätt, Ger. 85/F7
Egham, Eng, UK 56/B2
Éghezée, Belg. 81/D2
Egilsstadhir, Ice. 64/P6
Egito, Ang. 148/B2
Egiyn (riv.), Mong. 104/E1
Égletons, Fr. 70/E4
Eglinton, NI, UK 60/A1
Eglinton (isl.), NW, Can. 167/Q7
Eglinton (Londonderry) (arpt.), UK 60/A1
Eglisau, Swi. 87/E2
Eglwys-Brewis, Wal, UK 62/C4
Égly, Fr. 56/J6
Egmond aan Zee, Neth. 78/B3
Egmont (bay), PE, Can. 184/E2
Egmont (mt.), NZ 161/C2
Egmont (cape), NZ 161/C2
Egmont Key Nat'l Wild. Ref., Fl, US 190/K8
Egmont NP, NZ 161/C2
Egna (Neumarkt), It. 87/H5
Egnach, Swi. 87/F2
Egnar, Co, US 175/H2
Egoumbi, Gabon 146/B3
Egra, India 123/F5
Egremont, Eng, UK 60/E3
Eğridir, Turk. 128/B2
Eğridir (lake), Turk. 128/B2
Éguas, Rio das (riv.), Braz. 210/D2
Éguilles, Fr. 90/B5
Egvekinot, Rus. 101/U3
Egypt (ctry.) 133/E2
Egypt Lake, Fl, US 190/L7
Eha Amufu, Nga. 141/G5
Ehebach (riv.), Ger. 84/D3
Ehekirchen, Ger. 84/D5
Ehime (pref.), Japan 110/C4
Ehingen, Ger. 87/F1
Ehingen, Ger. 84/D4
Ehrenberg, Az, US 174/E4
Ehrhardt, SC, US 189/G4
Ehringshausen, Ger. 84/B1
Ehrwald, Aus. 87/G3
Eiao (isl.), FrPol. 163/L5
Eibar, Sp. 70/B5
Eibelstadt, Ger. 84/C3
Eibenstock, Ger. 85/F1
Eibergen, Neth. 78/D4
Eich, Ger. 84/B3
Eichel (riv.), Fr. 81/G6
Eichenau, Ger. 84/E6
Eichenbühl, Ger. 84/C3
Eichendorf, Ger. 85/F5
Eichenzell, Ger. 84/C2
Eichstätt, Ger. 84/E5
Eichwalde, Ger. 68/Q7
Eicklingen, Ger. 79/H3
Eid, Nor. 64/C3
Eidelstedt, Ger. 79/G1
Eidfjord, Nor. 66/B1
Eidsfoss, Nor. 64/R9
Eidsvold, Austl. 160/C4
Eidsvoll, Nor. 66/D1
Eifel (plat.), Ger. 68/D3
Eiffel Flats, Zim. 149/F3
Eiffel Tower, Fr. 56/J5
Eigenji, Japan 109/K5
Eiger (peak), Swi. 86/D4
Eigersund, Nor. 66/A2
Eigg (isl.), Sc, UK 57/Q8
Eight Degree (chan.), India, Mald. 121/B5
Eighteenmile (peak), Id, US 173/G1
Eighty Mile Beach (beach), Austl. 154/A4
Eijerlandse Gat (chan.), Neth. 78/B2
Eijsden, Neth. 81/E2
Eikelandsosen, Nor. 66/A1
Eikeren (lake), Nor. 64/R9
Eil, Loch (inlet), Sc, UK 59/A3
Eildon, Austl. 159/B3
Eilerts de Haan (mts.), Sur. 205/G4
'Ein Māhil, Isr. 131/C3
Eina, Nor. 66/D1
Einbeck, Ger. 79/G5
Eindhoven (int'l arpt.), Neth. 78/C6
Eindhoven, Neth. 78/C6
Einsiedeln, Swi. 87/E3
Einville-au-Jard, Fr. 81/F6
Eirunepé, Braz. 208/D2
Eirup, Namb. 148/C5
Eisack (Isarco) (riv.), It. 87/H4
Eisch (riv.), Lux. 81/E4
Eiseb (riv.), Namb. 148/C4
Eisenach, Ger. 79/H7
Eisenberg, Ger. 84/B3
Eisenerz, Aus. 71/L3
Eisenhower (mt.), Ab, Can. 170/G2
Eisenhower Nat'l Hist. Site, Pa, US 194/A4
Eisenhüttenstadt, Ger. 69/H2
Eisenstadt, Aus. 76/C2
Eiserfeld, Ger. 81/G2
Eisfeld, Ger. 84/D2
Eisingen, Ger. 84/C3
Eišiškės, Lith. 67/L4
Eislingen, Ger. 84/C5
Eitelborn, Ger. 81/G3
Eiter (riv.), Ger. 79/F3
Eitorf, Ger. 81/G2
Eitting, Ger. 85/E6
Ejea de los Caballeros, Sp. 73/E1
Ejeda, Madg. 152/H9
Ejido, Ven. 204/D2
Ejin Horo Qi, China 106/B3
Ejin Qi, China 104/E3
Ejule, Nga. 141/G5
Ejura, Gha. 141/E5
Ejutla de Crespo, Mex. 200/B2
Ekalaka, Mt, US 182/B5
Ekang, Nga. 141/H5
Ekata, Gabon 146/C2
Ekeby, Swe. 66/E3
Ekeby, Swe. 65/A1
Ekenäs (Tammisaari), Fin. 67/K2
Ekeren, Belg. 78/B6
Ekerö, Swe. 65/A1
Eket, Nga. 146/A1
Eketahuna, NZ 161/C3
Ekhínos, Gre. 75/J2
Ekibastuz, Kaz. 125/C1
Ekimchan, Rus. 105/L1
Ekma, India 123/E3
Ekoko, D.R. Congo 147/E2
Ekoli, D.R. Congo 147/F3
Ekoln (lake), Swe. 65/A1
Ekondo Titi, Camr. 146/B1
Ekpoma, Nga. 141/G5
Eksjö, Swe. 66/F3
Ekuku, D.R. Congo 147/E3
Ekukula, D.R. Congo 147/E2
Ekwan (riv.), On, Can. 167/H3
Ekwendeni, Malw. 149/G1
El Aaiún, WSah. 136/B4
El Aaiún (Hassan) (int'l arpt.), WSah. 136/B4
El Aargub, WSah. 136/B5
El Aatf (reg.), WSah. 136/B5
El Abanico, Chile 214/C3
El Abiodh Sidi Chrikh, Alg. 137/F2
Ēl Ābrēd, Eth. 144/C4
El Affroun, Alg. 138/G4
El Aïoun, Mor. 138/C2
El Alamein (Al 'Alamayan), Egypt 135/F2
El Álamo, Mex. 177/E4
El Alia, Alg. 137/G2
El Alto, Peru 208/A2
El Alto (int'l arpt.), Bol. 212/B1
El Amparo de Apure, Ven. 204/D3
El Anegado, Ecu. 204/A5
El Aouinet, Alg. 138/K7
El Arahal, Sp. 72/C4
El Arhlaf (well), Mrta. 140/D2
El Aricha, Alg. 138/D2
El Arrayán, Chile 214/N8
El Astillero, Sp. 72/D1
El Avila, PN, Ven. 207/P7
El Bagre, Col. 204/C3
El Banco, Col. 204/C2
El Barco, Sp. 72/B1
El Barco de Ávila, Sp. 72/C2
El Baúl, Ven. 204/D2
El Bayadh (wilaya), Alg. 137/F2
El Bayadh, Alg. 137/F2
El Ben, Kenya 145/C1
El Bolsón, Arg. 214/C4
El Bonillo, Sp. 72/D3
El Borouj, Mor. 136/D2
El Burgo de Osma, Sp. 72/D2
El Caín, Arg. 214/C4
El Cajon, Ca, US 192/D5
El Cajón (res.), Hon. 200/E3
El Calafate, Arg. 215/B6
El Callao, Ven. 205/F3
El Campo, Tx, US 177/F3
El Capitan (peak), Mt, US 170/G4
El Carmen, Bol. 209/F4
El Carmen, Bol. 209/E4
El Carmen, Chile 214/B3
El Carmen, Col. 204/B3
El Carmen, Mex. 177/D5
El Carmen, Peru 208/B4
El Carmen, Ven. 205/E4
El Carmen de Bolívar, Col. 204/C2
El Casabe, Ven. 205/F3
El Casar de Talamanca, Sp. 73/N8
El Centro Nav. Air Facility, Ca, US 174/D4
El Cerrito, Ca, US 193/K11
El Cerrito, Col. 204/B4
El Cerrito, Arg. 215/C6
El Cerro, Bol. 212/D1
El Cerro del Aripo (peak), Trin. 205/F2
El Cerrón (peak), Ven. 204/D2
El Chico, PN, Mex. 199/L6
El Chorro, Arg. 212/D2
El Cocuy, Col. 204/C3
El Cocuy (dept.), Col. 204/C3
El Colegio, Col. 207/L8
El Colorado, Arg. 212/E3
El Cóndor, Arg. 215/C7
El Cuy, Arg. 214/C3
El Der (riv.), Som. 144/C3
El Dere, Eth. 144/B4
El Descanso, Mex. 174/D4
El Difícil, Col. 204/C2
El Djezair (Algiers) (cap.), Alg. 138/G4
El Djouf (des.), Alg. 136/D5
El Dorado, Ks, US 179/F2
El Dorado, Ar, US 179/H4
El Dorado (lake), Ks, US 179/F2
El Dorado, Ven. 205/F3
El Dorado, Mex. 198/D3
El Dorado Springs, Mo, US 179/G2
El Edén, Ecu. 204/B5
El Eglab (plat.), Alg. 136/D4
El Empedrado, Ven. 204/D2
El Escorial, Sp. 73/M8
El Espinar, Sp. 72/C2
El Eulma, Alg. 138/H4
El Fahs, Tun. 138/L6
El Ferrol, Sp. 72/A1
El Fuerte, Mex. 198/C3
El Fureidīs, Isr. 131/B3
El Galhak, Sudan 142/G3
El Galpón, Arg. 212/C3
El Gogorrón, PN, Mex. 196/A3
El Golea, Alg. 137/F3
El Golfete (lake), Guat. 200/D3
El Granada, Ca, US 193/K11
El Grullo, Mex. 198/D5
El Guachara, PN, Ven. 205/F2
El Guapo, Ven. 207/P7
El Gulut, Eth. 142/G2
El Had Harrara, Mor. 136/C2
El Hajeb, Mor. 138/B3
El Hank (cliff), Mali, 136/D4
El Harino, Pan. 204/A2
El Harta (well), Alg. 137/E4
El Higo, Mex. 200/B1
El Indio, Tx, US 177/D3
El Jadida, Mor. 136/C2
El Kbab, Mor. 136/D2
El Kelaâ des Srarhna, Mor. 136/D2
Ēl Kerē, Eth. 144/B4
El Khatt (depr.), Mrta. 140/C2
El Khnâchîch (cliff), Mali 136/E5
Ēl K'oran, Eth. 144/C4
El Kroub, Alg. 138/K6
El Kseur, Alg. 138/H4
Ēl Lēh, Eth. 144/A5
El Libertador General Bernardo O'Higgins (pol. reg.), Chile 214/N8
El Limón, Mex. 199/F4
El Mahia (phys. reg.), Mali 137/E5
El Maitén, Arg. 214/C4
El Mallaile, Eth. 144/B4
El Malpais Nat'l Mon., NM, US 175/H3
El Manteco, Ven. 205/F3
El Manzanito, Chile 214/N8
El Manzano, Chile 214/N9
El Medera, Eth. 144/B4
El Messir (well), Chad 142/C2
El Miamo, Ven. 205/F3
El Milia, Alg. 138/J4
El Mirage, Ca, US 192/C1
El Mirage (lake), Ca, US 174/D3
El Mojar, Bol. 209/E4
El Montcau (peak), Sp. 73/K6
El Monte, Ca, US 192/F7
El Morrito (pt.), Chile 214/C1
El Morro, NM, US 175/H3
El Mrâyer (well), Mrta. 136/C5
El Mreyyé (phys. reg.), Mrta. 140/C2
El Mzereb (well), Mali 136/D4
El Naranjo de Carlos Sarabia, Mex. 199/F4
El Nayar, Mex. 198/D4
El Nevado (peak), Arg. 214/C2
El Nido, Ca, US 174/B2
El Nido, Phil. 114/B3
El Olivar Alto, Chile 214/N9
El Oro (dept.), Ecu. 208/A1
El Oso, Ven. 206/A1
El Oued (wilaya), Alg. 137/G2
El Oued, Alg. 137/G2
El Palmar, Ven. 205/F3
El Palmar, Bol. 212/D2
El Palmar, Mex. 199/N8
El Palmar, PN, Arg. 212/E4
El Pao, Ven. 205/F2
El Pao, Ven. 205/E2
El Pao, Ven. 207/M8
El Paraíso, Hon. 200/E3
El Paraíso, Col. 204/C4
El Paraíso, Mex. 199/E5
El Pardo, Sp. 73/N8
El Paso, Il, US 181/K3
El Paso, Tx, US 177/A2
El Paso de Robles (Paso Robles), Ca, US 174/B3
El Paso International (int'l arpt.), Tx, US 177/A2
El Pato, Col. 204/C4
El Pensamiento, Bol. 209/F4
El Perú, Bol. 209/E4
El Pilar, Ven. 205/F2
El Pilar, Bol. 209/E4
El Pintado, Arg. 212/D3
El Piquete, Arg. 212/C3
El Plumerillo (Mendoza) (int'l arpt.), Arg. 214/C2
El Portal, Ca, US 174/C2
El Porvenir, Mex. 177/B2
El Porvenir, Pan. 204/B2
El Porvenir, Ven. 204/D3
El Porvenir, Mex. 174/D4
El Potosí, Mex. 199/E3
El Potosí, PN, Mex. 196/B3
El Prat de Llobregat, Sp. 73/L7
El Progreso, Guat. 200/D3
El Progreso, Hon. 200/E3
El Progreso, Ecu. 208/K7
El Progreso Industrial, Mex. 199/Q9
El Puente, Bol. 209/F5
El Puente, Bol. 212/C2
El Puerto de Santa María, Sp. 72/B4
El Pun, Ecu. 204/B4
El Quebrachal, Arg. 212/C3
El Quelite, Mex. 198/D4
El Quisco, Chile 214/N8
El Rama, Nic. 201/E3
El Rastro, Ven. 207/N8
El Remolino, Mex. 177/D3
El Reno, Ok, US 179/F3
El Rey, PN, Arg. 212/C3
El Rio, Ca, US 192/A2
El Rio (canal), Fl, US 190/P10
El Rito, NM, US 175/J2
El Roble, Pan. 204/A2
El Roque, Ven. 205/E2
El Rosario de Arriba, Mex. 198/B2
El Sabinal, PN, Mex. 177/E4
El Sacromonte, PN, Mex. 199/L7
El Salado, Col. 207/K8
El Salado, Arg. 215/D6
El Salto, Mex. 198/D4
El Salvador, Cuba 201/H1
El Salvador (int'l arpt.), ESal. 200/D3
El Salvador (ctry.) 165/H8
El Salvador, Mex. 199/E3
El Samán de Apure, Ven. 204/D3
El Sauz, Mex. 177/A3
El Sauzal, Mex. 198/A2
El Segundo, Ca, US 192/F8
El Shab (well), Egypt 135/F4
El Socorro, Col. 204/D3
El Sombrero, Arg. 214/C5
El Sombrero, Ven. 207/N8
El Sosneado, Arg. 214/C2
El Tabo, Chile 214/N8
El Tajín (ruin), Mex. 199/M6
El Tala, Arg. 212/C3
El Tama, PN, Ven. 204/C3
El Tambo, Ecu. 204/B5
El Tarf (wilaya), Alg. 138/K6
El Tarf, Alg 138/L6
El Teleno (peak), Sp. 72/B1
El Tepozteco, PN, Mex. 199/R10
El Tiemblo, Sp. 72/C2
El Tigre, Ven. 205/E2
El Tocuyo, Ven. 204/D2
El Toro, Ca, US 192/C3
El Toro, Ven. 205/F2
El Toro, Tx, US 177/F3
El Tránsito, Chile 212/B4
El Trébol, Arg. 212/D5
El Triunfo, Mex. 200/D2
El Triunfo, Ecu. 204/B5
El Tucuche (peak), Trin. 205/F2
El Tuito, Mex. 198/D4
El Tuparro, PN, Col. 204/D3
El Vado, NM, US 175/J2
El Valle, Pan. 204/A2
El Venado (isl.), Nic. 201/F4
El Viejo, Nic. 200/E3
El Viejo (peak), Col. 204/C3
El Vigía, Ven. 204/D2
El Vínculo, Ven. 204/D1
El Volcán, Chile 214/N8
El Wak, Kenya 145/C1
El Yagual, Ven. 204/D3
El Yunque (peak), PR 197/M8
El Zacatón, Mex. 198/E4
El Zurdo, Arg. 215/C6
El'ton (lake), Rus. 97/H2
El-Gezira, 'Erg, Egypt 139/C2
El-Girba (peak), Egypt 139/D4
El-Hammam (ruin), Egypt 139/B6
El-Kasdir, Alg. 138/D3
El-Menzel, Mor. 138/B3
El-Tarâbîl (peak), Egypt 139/D6
Ela, Myan. 112/C5
El'Acâba (pol. reg.), Mrta. 140/C2
Elaho (riv.), BC, Can. 170/C2
Elaine, Ar, US 188/B3
Elan (riv.), Wal, UK 62/C2
Élancourt, Fr. 56/H5
Elands (riv.), SAfr. 149/E5
Elandsrivier (riv.), SAfr. 150/Q12
Elangata Wuas, Kenya 145/B2
Elarmilon, Gabon 146/B2
Elassón, Gre. 75/H3
Elat (int'l arpt.), Isr. 130/D5
Elat, Isr. 135/G2
Elátia, Gre. 75/H3
Elato (isl.), Micr. 162/D4
Elavagnon, Togo 141/F5
Elazığ, Turk. 128/D2
Elazig (prov.), Turk. 128/D2
Elba, Al, US 191/E2
Elba (isl.), It. 92/F2
El'ban, Rus. 105/M1
Elbasan, Alb. 75/G2
Elbbach (riv.), Ger. 81/G2
Elbe (riv.), Ger. 55/F3
Elbe (Labe) (riv.), Czh., Ger. 69/H2
Elbe-Seitenkanaal (canal), Ger. 79/H2
Elbert, Tx, US 178/E4
Elberton, Ga, US 189/F3
Elbeuf, Fr. 83/G2
Elbigenalp, Aus. 87/G3
Elbląg, Pol. 67/H4
Elblag (prov.), Pol. 67/H4
Elbow (riv.), Ab, Can. 170/G2
Elbow, Sk, Can. 171/L2
Elbow Lake, Mn, US 182/G5
El'brus (peak), Rus. 97/G4
Elburg, Neth. 78/C4
Elburgon, Kenya 145/A2
Elburn, Il, US 193/N16
Elburz (mts.), Iran 100/E6
Elche, Sp. 73/E3
Elche de la Sierra, Sp. 72/D3
Elchingen, Ger. 84/D6
Elcho, Wi, US 183/K5
Elcho (isl.), Austl. 155/D2
Elcho (isl.) 153/C2
Eld (inlet), Wa, US 193/A3
Elda, Sp. 73/E3
Eldama Ravine, Kenya 145/A1
Elde (riv.), Ger. 68/G2
Eldersburg, Md, US 194/B5
El'dikan, Rus. 101/P3
Eldivan, Turk. 96/E4
Eldon, Mo, US 179/H1
Eldon, Wa, US 193/A2
Eldon, Ia, US 181/H3
Eldora, Ia, US 181/H2
Eldora, NJ, US 194/D5
Eldorado, Arg. 213/F3
Eldorado, Braz. 213/G3
Eldorado, Braz. 213/F2
Eldorado (int'l arpt.), Col. 207/L8
Eldorado, Il, US 188/C2
Eldorado, Ok, US 178/E3
Eldorado, Tx, US 177/D2
Eldoret, Kenya 145/A1
Eldridge, Al, US 188/D4
Eldridge, Ia, US 181/J3
Eleanor, WV, US 189/G1
Electra, Tx, US 178/E3
Eleja, Lat. 67/K3
Elek, Hun. 76/E2
Elèktrėnai, Lith. 67/L4
Elektrostal', Rus. 94/X9
Elele, Nga. 141/G5
Elena, Arg. 214/D2
Elena, Bul. 77/G4
Elephant (mtn.), Me, US 187/L2
Elephant Butte, NM, US 175/J4
Elephant Butte (res.), NM, US 175/J4
Elesbão Veloso, Braz. 207/F4
Eleşkirt, Turk. 129/E2
Eleuthera (isl.), Bahm. 165/K7
Eleven Point (riv.), Mo, Ar, US 179/J2
Elevsís (ruin), Gre. 75/N8
Elevsís, Gre. 75/N8
Elevsís (arpt.), Gre. 75/N8
Elevtheroúpolis, Gre. 75/J2
Elfers, Fl, US 190/K7
Elfershausen, Ger. 84/C2
Elfrida, On, Can. 186/T9
Elfros, Sk, Can. 182/C2
Elgg, Swi. 87/E3
Elgin, Mb, Can. 182/D3
Elgin, Sc, UK 59/C1
Elgin, Az, US 175/G5
Elgin, Il, US 186/B3
Elgin, Ks, US 179/F2
Elgin, ND, US 182/D4
Elgin, Nv, US 174/E2
Elgin, Ok, US 179/E3
Elgin, Or, US 172/E1
Elgin, SC, US 189/G3
Elgin, Tn, US 188/E2
Elgin, Tx, US 176/F2
Elgin Mills, On, Can. 186/U8
Elgóibar, Sp. 70/B5
Elgon (Wagagai) (peak), Ugan. 145/A1
Elias Garcia, Ang. 146/E5
Elida, NM, US 178/C4
Elida, Oh, US 186/D4
Elie, Sc, UK 59/D4
Elila (riv.), D.R. Congo 147/F3
Elila, D.R. Congo 147/F3
Elim, SAfr. 150/L11
Elimäki, Fin. 67/M1
Eling, Eng, UK 63/E5
Eliot, Me, US 187/L3
Elipa, D.R. Congo 147/E3
Elisenvaara, Rus. 67/N1
Eliseu Martins, Braz. 207/F5
Elista, Rus. 97/H3
Elixhausen, Aus. 85/G7
Elizabeth (mtn.), Austl. 159/C3
Elizabeth (nbrhd.), Austl. 157/M8
Elizabeth (bay), Namb. 150/A2
Elizabeth, Co, US 180/B4
Elizabeth, Ga, US 189/L7
Elizabeth, La, US 190/B2
Elizabeth (isls.), Ma, US 184/B5
Elizabeth, Mn, US 182/F4
Elizabeth, NJ, US 195/J9
Elizabeth (cr.), Tx, US 176/K6
Elizabeth, WV, US 189/G1
Elizabeth City, NC, US 189/J2
Elizabethan Village Hist. Site, Austl. 156/L7
Elizabethton, Tn, US 189/F2
Elizabethtown, Il, US 188/C2
Elizabethtown, In, US 188/E1
Elizabethtown, Ky, US 188/E2
Elizabethtown, NC, US 189/H3
Elizabethtown, Pa, US 194/B3
Elizabethtown, NY, US 187/K2
Elizabethville, Pa, US 194/B2
Elizondo, Sp. 70/C5
Ełk, Pol. 67/K5
Elk (riv.), BC, Can. 170/G2
Elk (riv.), Al, Tn, US 188/D3
Elk (mts.), Co, US 173/K4
Elk (mtn.), Or, US 172/E1
Elk (hill), Pa, US 187/J4
Elk (riv.), WV, US 189/G1
Elk City, Ks, US 179/G2
Elk City (dam), Ks, US 179/G2
Elk City, Ok, US 178/E3
Elk Creek, Ca, US 172/B4
Elk Creek, Ne, US 181/F3
Elk Grove, Ca, US 193/M10
Elk Grove Village, Il, US 193/P16
Elk Mills, Md, US 194/C4
Elk NP, Ab, Can. 171/H1
Elk Point, SD, US 181/F2
Elk Rapids, Mi, US 186/D2
Elk Ridge, Md, US 194/B5
Elk Ridge (ridge), Tn, US 188/D3
Elk River, Mn, US 183/H5
Elk Silver, NM, US 178/B4
Elk Slough (riv.), Ca, US 193/L10
Elk Springs, Co, US 173/J3
Elk Valley, Tn, US 188/E2
Elkader, Ia, US 181/J2
Elkenroth, Ger. 81/G2
Elkford, BC, Can. 170/G2
Elkhart, Ks, US 178/D2
Elkhart, In, US 186/D4
Elkhart, Tx, US 176/G2
Elkhorn, Mb, Can. 182/D3
Elkhorn (riv.), Ne, US 169/G3
Elkhorn, Wi, US 181/K2
Elkhovo, Bul. 77/H4
Elkin, NC, US 189/G2
Elkins, WV, US 189/H1
Elkland, Pa, US 187/H4
Elko, Nv, US 172/F3
Elko, BC, Can. 170/G3
Elkton, Ky, US 188/D2
Elkton, Md, US 194/C4
Elkton, Tn, US 188/D3
Elkton, Va, US 189/H1
Elkview, WV, US 189/G1
Elkwater, Ab, Can. 171/J3
Elland, Eng, UK 61/G4
Ellaville, Ga, US 188/E4
Ellé (riv.), Fr. 82/B5
Elle (riv.), Ger. 81/F2
Ellef Ringnes (isl.) 165/G2
Ellefeld, Ger. 85/F2
Ellen (riv.), Eng, UK 61/E2
Ellen (mt.), Ut, US 175/G1
Ellenābād, India 124/C5
Ellenberg, Ger. 84/D4
Ellendale, Austl. 154/B4
Ellendale, De, US 194/C6
Ellendale, ND, US 182/E4
Ellensburg, Wa, US 170/D4
Ellenton, Ga, US 191/G2
Ellenville, NY, US 187/J4
Ellenwood, Ga, US 189/M7
Eller (riv.), Ger. 79/H5
Ellerbach (riv.), Ger. 81/G4
Ellerbe, NC, US 189/H3
Ellero (riv.), It. 88/A4
Ellerslie, Ga, US 188/E4
Ellerslie, La, US 190/C3
Ellerslie, PE, Can. 184/F2
Ellery (mt.), Austl. 159/D3
Ellesmere (isl.), Can. 165/J2
Ellesmere Island NP, Nun, Can. 167/T6
Ellesmere Port, Eng, UK 61/F5
Ellettsville, In, US 186/C5
Ellezelles, Belg. 80/C2
Elliant, Fr. 82/B4
Ellice (riv.), Nun, Can. 166/F2
Ellicott City, Md, US 194/B5
Ellijay, Ga, US 188/E3
Ellington, Mo, US 188/B2
Ellinikón (int'l arpt.), Gre. 75/N9
Ellinwood, Ks, US 179/E1
Elliot, SAfr. 150/D3
Elliot Key (isl.), Fl, US 191/H5
Elliot Lake, On, Can. 186/E1
Elliot Price Consv. Park, Austl. 157/H4
Elliott, Ia, US 181/G3
Elliott, Austl. 154/D4
Elliott, SC, US 189/G3
Elliott (peak), Va, US 189/H1
Ellis, Id, US 173/F1
Ellis, Ks, US 178/E1
Ellis (co.), Tx, US 176/L7
Ellis Island, NJ, NY, US 195/J9
Ellisras, SAfr. 149/E4
Elliston, Austl. 157/G5
Elliston, Mt, US 171/H4
Ellisville, Ms, US 190/D2
Ellon, Sc, UK 59/D2
Elloree, SC, US 189/G4
Elloughton, Eng, UK 61/H4
Ellrich, Ger. 79/H5
Ellsinore, Mo, US 188/B2
Ellsworth, Ks, US 179/E1
Ellsworth (mts.), Ant. 216/U
Ellsworth (A.F.B.), SD, US 180/C1
Ellsworth, Wi, US 181/H1
Ellsworth Land (phys. reg.), Ant. 216/U
Ellwangen, Ger. 84/D5
Elm, Swi. 87/F4
Elm (lake), SD, US 182/E5
Elm (riv.), SD, US 180/E1
Elm City, NC, US 189/J3
Elm Creek, Mb, Can 182/F3
Elm Fork (riv.), Ok, US 178/E3
Elm Fork (riv.), Tx, US 176/L6
Elm Grove, Wi, US 193/P13
Elma, Ia, US 181/H2
Elma, NY, US 186/V10
Elmadağ, Turk. 96/E5
Elmalı, Turk. 130/A1
Elmas (int'l arpt.), It. 74/A3
Elmer, La, US 190/B2
Elmer, Mo, US 181/H4
Elmer, NJ, US 194/C4
Elmgrove (pt.), Tx, US 177/N9
Elmhurst, Il, US 193/Q16
Elmina, Gha. 141/E5
Elmira, NY, US 187/H3
Elmira, Or, US 172/B1
Elmira Heights, NY, US 187/H3
Elmo, Mt, US 170/G4
Elmont, NY, US 195/L9
Elmora (nbrhd.), NJ, US 195/J9
Elmore, Mn, US 181/G2
Elmore, Austl. 159/B3
Elmore City, Ok, US 179/F3
Elmsdale, PE, Can. 184/E2
Elmsdale, NS, Can. 184/F3
Elmsford, NY, US 195/K7
Elmshorn, Ger. 79/G1
Elmstein, Ger. 81/G5
Elmswell, Eng, UK 63/G2
Elmvale, On, Can. 187/G2
Elmwood, Ok, US 178/D2
Elmwood, Ne, US 181/F3
Elmwood Park, Il, US 193/Q16
Elmwood Park, NJ, US 195/J8
Elmwood Park, Wi, US 193/Q14
Elne, Fr. 70/E5
Elnora, In, US 188/D1
Elói Mendes, Braz. 211/L6
Eloise, Fl, US 190/M8
Elon College, NC, US 189/H2
Elora, On, Can. 186/F3
Elora, Tn, US 188/D3
Élorn (riv.), Fr. 70/A2
Elortondo, Arg. 214/E2
Elorza, Ven. 204/D3
Elouera Nat'l Rsv., Austl. 160/H8
Elowah (falls), Or, US 170/D5
Eloy, Az, US 175/G4
Eloy Alfaro, Ecu. 204/B5
Éloyes, Fr. 86/C1
Elphin, Ire. 58/B2
Elphinstone, Mb, Can. 182/D2
Elqui (riv.), Chile 212/B4
Elrod, Al, US 188/D4
Elrose, Sk, Can. 171/K2
Elroy, Wi, US 181/J2
Elroy, NC, US 189/J3
Elsa (riv.), Sp. 93/B2
Elsa (res.), Sp. 72/B2
Elsa, Yk, Can. 168/Z12
Elsa, Tx, US 177/F4
Elsah, Il, US 181/J4
Elsberry, Mo, US 181/J4
Elsdorf, Ger. 81/F2
Elsdorf, Ger. 79/G2
Else (riv.), Ger. 79/F4
Elsen (lake), China 125/F4
Elsenfeld, Ger. 84/C3
Elsenz (riv.), Ger. 84/B4
Elsey, Mo, US 179/H2
Elsfleth, Ger. 79/F2
Elsie, Mi, US 186/D3
Elsinore (lake), Ca, US 192/C3
Elsinore, Ut, US 175/F1
Elsloo, Neth. 81/E2
Elsmere, De, US 194/C4
Elst, Neth. 78/C5
Elstal, Ger. 68/Q6
Elstead, Eng, UK 63/F4
Elsterberg, Ger. 85/F1
Eltari (int'l arpt.), Indo. 154/A2
Eltham (nbrhd.), Eng, UK 56/D2
Eltham, NZ 161/C2
Eltham, Austl. 159/B3
Eltmann, Ger. 84/D3
Elton, Wi, US 183/K5
Elton, La, US 190/B2
Eltopia, Wa, US 170/E4
Eltville am Rhein, Ger. 84/B2
Elva, Est. 67/M2
Elvanlı, Turk. 130/D1
Elvas, Port. 72/B3
Elven, Fr. 82/C5
Elverum, Nor. 66/D1
Elvins, Mo, US 188/B2
Elvire (mt.), Austl. 156/C2
Elvo (riv.), It. 88/B2
Elwell (lake), Mt, US 171/J3
Elwood, In, US 186/D4
Elwood, Ne, US 180/E3
Elwood-Magnolia, NJ, US 194/D4
Elwy (riv.), Wal, UK 60/E5
Ely, Eng, UK 63/G2
Ely, Mn, US 183/J4
Ely, Nv, US 173/F4
Elyaqim, Isr. 131/C3
Elyashiv, Isr. 131/B4
Elyria, Oh, US 186/E4
Elysburg, Pa, US 194/B2
Elysian Park, Ca, US 192/F7
Elz, Ger. 84/B2
Elz (riv.), Ger. 84/B6
Elzach, Ger. 86/E1
Elzbach (riv.), Ger. 81/G3
Elze, Ger. 79/G4
Emajõgi (riv.), Est. 67/M2
Emām Taqī, Iran 127/G1
Emāmshahr, Iran 129/H2
Emån (riv.), Swe. 66/F3
Emancé, Fr. 56/H6
Emas, PN das, Braz. 210/B3
Emba (riv.), Kaz. 96/K3
Embarcación, Arg. 212/C2
Embarras (riv.), Il, US 188/C1
Embarrass, Mn, US 183/H4
Embarrass, Wi, US 181/K1
Embi, Kaz. 97/L2
Embi (riv.), Kaz. 100/F5
Embira (riv.), Braz. 208/D3
Embondo, D.R. Congo 146/D2
Emborcação (res.), Braz. 210/D3
Embrach, Swi. 87/E3
Embrun, Fr. 90/C3
Embsen, Ger. 79/H2
Embu, Kenya 145/B2
Emden, Il, US /K3
Emden, Ger. /E2
Emei (peak), China 112/D2
Emeishan, China 112/D2
Emerald, Austl. 160/C3
Emerald, Austl. 158/G5
Emeriau (pt.), Austl. 154/A4
Emerson, Mb, Can. 182/F3
Emerson, Ar, US 179/H4
Emerson, NJ, US 195/J8
Emery (peak), NM, US 178/C2
Emery, Ut, US 175/G1
Emery, SD, US 180/F2
Emeryville, On, Can. 193/G7
Emeryville, Ca, US 193/K11
Emet, Turk. 128/B2
Emida, Id, US 170/F4
Emigrant (peak), Mt, US 173/H1
Emigrant, Mt, US 173/H1
Emigsville, Pa, US 194/B3
Emilia-Romagna (pol. reg.), It. 71/J4
Emiliano Zapata, Mex. 200/D2
Emilius (peak), It. 90/D1
Emin, China 125/D2
Emin (riv.), China 125/D2
Eminābād, Pak. 124/C3
Eminence, Mo, US 179/J2
Emir Pasha (gulf), Tanz. 147/G3
Emirdağ, Turk. 128/B2
Emirgazi, Turk. 128/C2
Emissi, Tarso (peak), Chad 134/C4
Emita, Austl. 159/C4
Emlembe (peak), Swaz. 151/E2
Emlenton, Pa, US 187/G4
Emlichheim, Ger. 78/D3
Emma (riv.), Sur. 205/H4
Emmaboda, Swe. 66/F3
Emmanuel Head (pt.), Eng, UK 59/E5
Emmaste, Est. 67/K2
Emmaus, Pa, US 194/C2
Emme (riv.), Swi. 86/D4
Emmeloord, Neth. 78/C3
Emmen, Neth. 78/D3
Emmendingen, Ger. 86/D1
Emmental (valley), Swi. 86/D3
Emmer (riv.), Ger. 79/G4
Emmer-Compascuum, Neth. 78/E3
Emmerbach (riv.), Ger. 79/E5
Emmerich, Ger. 78/D5
Emmet, Ar, US 179/H4
Emmet, Austl. 160/B4
Emmetsburg, Ia, US 181/G2
Emmett, Mi, US 193/G6
Emmett, Id, US 172/E2
Emmingen-Liptingen, Ger. 87/E2
Emmitsburg, Md, US 194/A4
Emmonak, Ak, US 168/W12
Emmons (mt.), Ut, US 173/H3
Emneth, Eng, UK 63/G1
Emód, Hun. 76/E2
Emory, Tx, US 179/G4
Emory (peak), Tx, US 177/C3
Emosson (lake), Swi. 86/C5
Empalme, Mex. 198/C3
Empangeni, SAfr. 151/E3
Empedrado, Chile 214/B2
Empedrado, Arg. 212/E3
Empire, Mi, US 186/C2
Empire, Ga, US 189/F4
Empoli, It. 89/D6
Emporia, Ks, US 179/F1
Emporia, Va, US 189/J2
Emporium, Pa, US 187/G4
'Emrānī, Iran 127/G2
Ems (riv.), Ger. 68/D2
Ems (Eems) (riv.), Ger., Neth. 78/D2
Ems-Jade (canal), Ger. 79/E2
Emsbüren, Ger. 79/E4
Emsdetten, Ger. 79/E4
Emskirchen, Ger. 84/D3
Emsland (reg.), Ger. 68/D2
Emstek, Ger. 79/F3
Emu, China 105/K3
Emu Park, Austl. 160/C3
Emumägi (hill), Est. 67/M2
Emur (riv.), China 105/J1
Emyvale, Ire. 60/B3
'En Gedi, Isr. 131/C6
'En Harod, Isr. 131/C3
Ena, Japan 111/E3
Enangiperi, Kenya 145/A2
Enarotali, Indo. 117/J4
Enbetsu, Japan 108/B1
Encampment, Wy, US 173/K3
Encantada, Cerro (peak), Mex. 198/B3
Encantada, Cerro de la (peak), Mex. 198/B2
Encarnación, Par. 213/F3
Encarnación de Díaz, Mex. 198/E4
Enchi, Gha. 140/E5
Encinal, Tx, US 177/E3
Encinitas, Ca, US 192/C4
Encino (nbrhd.), Ca, US 192/E7
Encino, Tx, US 176/E4
Enciso, Col. 204/C3
Enciso, Col. 204/D4
Encón, Arg. 212/C5
Encontrados, Ven. 204/C2
Encounter (bay), Austl. 158/A2

Falcon Lake, Mb, Can. 183/G3
Falconara (arpt.), It. 89/G6
Falconara Marittima, It. 89/G6
Falconer, NY, US 187/G3
Falémé (riv.), Mali 140/C3
Faleolo, WSam. 163/S9
Faleolo (Apia) (int'l arpt.), WSam. 163/S9
Faleşti, Mol. 98/D4
Falfurrias, Tx, US 176/E4
Falissadé, Gui. 140/B4
Falkenberg, Swe. 66/E3
Falkensee, Ger. 68/Q6
Falkenstein, Ger. 85/F2
Falkenstein, Ger. 85/F4
Falkirk, Sc, UK 59/C5
Falkland, Sc, UK 59/C4
Falkland (isls.), UK 203/C8
Falkland Sound (str.), UK 215/E7
Falköping, Swe. 66/E2
Falkville, Al, US 188/D3
Fall (riv.), Ks, US 179/F2
Fall City, Wa, US 193/D2
Fall Creek, Wi, US 181/J1
Fall River, Ks, US 179/F2
Fall River, Ma, US 187/L4
Fall River, Wi, US 181/K2
Fallbrook, Ca, US 192/C4
Fallere (peak), It. 86/D6
Fallingbostel, Ger. 79/G3
Fallon, Mt, US 182/B4
Fallon, Nv, US 172/D4
Fallon Ind. Res., Nv, US 172/D4
Fallon Naval Air Station, Nv, US 172/D4
Falls Church, Va, US 194/A6
Falls City, Ne, US 181/G3
Falls City, Or, US 172/B1
Falls City, Tx, US 177/E3
Falls Creek, Pa, US 187/G4
Falls Lake (res.), NC, US 189/H2
Falls of Rough, Ky, US 188/D2
Fallston, Md, US 194/B4
Falmey, Niger 141/F3
Falmouth, Anti. 197/N8
Falmouth, Eng, UK 62/A6
Falmouth (bay), Eng, UK 62/A6
Falmouth, Ky, US 188/E1
Falmouth, Ma, US 187/L4
Falmouth, Mi, US 186/D2
Falmouth, NS, Can. 184/E3
Falmouth, Va, US 189/J1
False Cape Bossut (cape), Austl. 154/A4
False Orford Ness (cape), Austl. 155/F2
Falshöft (pt.), Ger. 66/C4
Falso (cape), Hon. 201/F3
Falso Cabo de Hornos (cape), Chile 215/C7
Falso, Cabo (cape), Mex. 198/C4
Falster (isl.), Den. 64/E5
Falsterbo, Den. 65/J7
Falterona (peak), It. 89/E6
Fălticeni, Rom. 98/D4
Falun, Swe. 66/F1
Famagusta (dist.), Cyp. 130/C2
Famagusta, Cyp. 130/C2
Famagusta (bay), Cyp. 130/C2
Famaillá, Arg. 212/C3
Famakah, Sudan 142/G3
Fāmanīn, Iran 126/E1
Famatina, Arg. 212/C4
Fameck, Fr. 81/F5
Famenne (reg.), Belg. 81/E3
Family (lake), Mb, Can. 183/G2
Famoso, Ca, US 174/C3
Fan Si Pan (peak), Viet. 112/D4
Fana, Nor. 66/A1
Fana, Mali 140/D3
Fanārah, Egypt 139/D4
Fanchang, China 106/D5
Fancy Farm, Ky, US 188/C2
Fandriana, Madg. 152/H8
Fane (riv.), Ire. 58/D2
Fang, Thai. 120/B2
Fang Xian, China 106/B4
Fangak, Sudan 142/F3
Fangamandou, Gui. 140/C4
Fangatau (isl.), FrPol. 163/L6
Fangataufa (isl.), FrPol. 163/L7
Fangcheng, China 106/C4
Fangcheng Gezu Zizhixian, China 113/F4
Fangcun, China 113/H3
Fangdao, China 113/H3
Fangdou (mts.), China 113/E2
Fangjiatun, China 105/J3
Fangliao, Tai. 113/J4
Fangshan, China 106/B3
Fangshan, China 106/G7
Fangxi, China 113/G2
Faniria, Madg. 152/H8
Fanjing (peak), China 113/F3
Fannich (lake), Sc, UK 59/A1
Fannie (lake), Fl, US 190/M7
Fannin, Ms, US 188/C4
Fannin, Tx, US 177/F3
Fanning (Tabuaeran) (isl.), Kiri. 163/K4
Fanø (isl.), Den. 66/C4
Fano, It. 89/G6
Fanshan, China 113/J3
Fanshawe, Ok, US 179/G3
Fanshi, China 106/C3
Fanwood, NJ, US 195/H9
Faqīrwāli, Pak. 124/B5
Faqqū'ah, WBnk. 131/C3
Fāqūs, Egypt 139/C3
Far (mtn.), BC, Can. 170/B1
Far Rockaway (nbrhd.), NY, US 195/K9
Fara in Sabina, It. 91/B3
Fara Novarese, It. 88/B2
Faradje, D.R. Congo 147/G2
Farafangana, Madg. 152/H8
Farāh, Afg. 100/G6
Farāh (riv.), Afg. 100/G6
Fa'rah (wadi), WBnk. 131/C4
Farako, Mali 140/D3
Farallon (isls.), Ca, US 172/B5
Farallón Centinela (isl.), Ven. 207/P7
Farallon de Medinilla (isl.), NMar. 162/D3
Farallon de Pajaros (isl.), NMar. 162/D2
Farallon NWR, Ca, US 172/B5
Farallones de Cali, PN, Col. 204/B4
Faramana, Burk. 140/D3
Faranah, Gui. 140/C4
Faranah (pol. reg.), Gui. 140/C4
Farángi Samariás NP, Gre. 75/H5
Faraony (riv.), Madg. 152/H8
Farasan (isls.), Sudan 144/B1
Faraulep (isl.), Micr. 162/D4
Farber, Mo, US 181/J4
Farciennes, Belg. 81/D3
Fare (riv.), Fr. 83/F5
Fareham, Eng, UK 63/E5
Farellones, Chile 214/N8
Faremoutiers, Fr. 80/C6
Farentuna, Swe. 65/A1
Farewell (cape), NZ 161/C3
Farfa (riv.), It. 91/B3
Färgelanda, Swe. 66/D2
Farghona, Uzb. 125/B3
Fargo, Ga, US 191/G2
Fargo, ND, US 182/F4
Fargo, Ok, US 178/E2
Faribault, Mn, US 181/H1
Farīdābād, India 124/D5
Farīdkot, India 124/C4
Farīdpur, India 122/B1
Farīdpur (pol. reg.), Bang. 123/G4
Farīdpur, Bang. 123/G4
Farilhao (cape), Namb. 148/B4
Farim, GBis. 140/B3
Farina, Il, US 188/C1
Farindale, Ar, US 179/H3
Färingsö (isl.), Swe. 65/A1
Fāriskūr, Egypt 139/C2
Farit (peak), Eth. 144/A3
Färjestaden, Swe. 66/G3
Farkadhón, Gre. 75/H3
Farkasgyepü, Hun. 76/C2
Farkwa, Tanz. 145/A3
Farley, Ia, US 181/J2
Farlington, Ks, US 179/G2
Farmer City, Il, US 181/K3
Farmers Branch, Tx, US 176/L7
Farmersburg, In, US 186/C5
Farmersville, Tx, US 176/L6
Farmerville, La, US 179/H4
Farmingdale, NJ, US 194/D3
Farmingdale, NY, US 195/M9
Farmington, Ar, US 179/G2
Farmington, De, US 194/C6
Farmington, Il, US 181/J3
Farmington, Me, US 187/L2
Farmington, Mi, US 193/F7
Farmington, Mn, US 181/H1
Farmington, Mo, US 188/B2
Farmington, NH, US 187/L3
Farmington, NM, US 175/H2
Farmington, Ut, US 173/H3
Farmington, Wa, US 170/F4
Farmington Hills, Mi, US 193/E6
Farmoréya, Gui. 140/B4
Farmville, NC, US 189/J3
Farmville, Va, US 189/H2
Farnborough, Eng, UK 63/F4
Farnham (mt.), BC, Can. 170/F2
Farnham, Eng, UK 63/F4
Farnham (peak), Id, US 170/F3
Farnham Royal, Eng, UK 56/B2
Farningham, Eng, UK 56/D2
Farnworth, Eng, UK 61/F4
Faro, Braz. 206/B3
Faro (riv.), Camr. 142/B4
Faro, Yk, Can. 168/Z12
Faro (int'l arpt.), Port. 72/B4
Faro, Port. 72/B4
Faro (dist.), Port. 72/A4
Faro, PN de, Camr. 142/B3
Faroe (isls.), Den. 216/G
Fåron (isl.), Swe. 67/H3
Farösund, Swe. 67/H3
Farquhar (cape), Austl. 156/B2
Farragut, Tn, US 188/E3
Farranfore (arpt.), Ire. 58/A5
Farrāshband, Iran 129/H4
Farrokh Shahr, Iran 129/G3
Farroupilha, Braz. 213/G4
Farrukhābād, India 122/B2
Farrukhnagar, India 122/A1
Fārs (gov.), Iran 129/H4
Fársala, Gre. 75/H3
Fārsān, Iran 129/G3
Farsīs, Egypt 139/C3
Farsø, Den. 66/C3
Farson, Wy, US 173/J2
Farsund, Nor. 66/B2
Fartura, Braz. 213/G2
Farum, Swe. 65/J7
Farwell, Tx, US 178/C3
Fasā, Iran 129/H4
Fasano, It. 75/E2
Faşıkan (pass), Turk. 130/C1
Fassala-Néré, Mrta. 140/D3
Fassberg, Ger. 79/H3
Fast Castle (pt.), Sc, UK 59/D5
Fastiv, Ukr. 98/E2
Fatagar Tuting (cape), Indo. 117/H4
Fatahjang, Pak. 124/B3
Fate, Tx, US 176/L7
Fate, Monte delle (peak), It. 92/C5
Fatehābād, India 124/C5
Fatehgarh Chūriān, India 124/C4
Fatehpur, Pak. 124/A4
Fatehpur, India 122/C3
Fatehpur, India 122/C2
Fatëzh, Rus. 99/H1
Fathom Five NP, On, Can. 187/F2
Fatick (pol. reg.), Sen. 140/A3
Fatick, Sen 140/A3
Fatigue (mt.), Austl. 159/C4
Fátima, Port. 72/A3
Fátima do Sul, Braz. 213/F2
Fātir (wadi), Leb. 131/D1
Fatoto, Gam. 140/B3
Fatsa, Turk. 96/F4
Fatu Hiva (isl.), FrPol. 163/M6
Fatunda, D.R. Congo 146/D4
Faucilles (mts.), Fr. 68/C4
Faughan(riv.) 60/A2
Fauglia, It. 88/D6
Fauldhouse, Sc, UK 59/C5
Faulkton, SD, US 180/E1
Faulquemont, Fr. 81/F5
Faure (isl.), Austl. 156/B3
Făurei, Rom. 77/H3
Fauske, Nor. 64/E2
Fauville-en-Caux, Fr. 83/F1
Fauvillers, Belg. 81/E4
Favalto (peak), It. 89/F7
Favara, It. 74/C4
Fave (riv.), Fr. 86/C1
Faverges, Fr. 86/C6
Faverney, Fr. 86/C2
Faversham, Eng, UK 63/G4
Favières, Fr. 56/L5
Favignana, It. 74/C4
Favria, It. 88/A2
Favrieux, Fr. 56/G5
Fawley, Eng, UK 63/E5
Fawn (riv.), On, Can. 166/H3
Fawn Grove, Pa, US 194/B4
Fawumang, Gha. 141/E5
Faxaflói (bay), Ice. 64/M7
Faxinal, Braz. 213/G2
Faya-Largeau, Chad 142/C1
Fayd, SAr. 128/E5
Fayence, Fr. 90/C5
Fayette, Al, US 188/D4
Fayette (co.), Ga, US 189/M8
Fayette, Ia, US 181/J2
Fayette, Mo, US 181/H4
Fayette, Ms, US 190/C2
Fayette Historical Townsite, Mi, US 186/C2
Fayetteville, Ar, US 179/G2
Fayetteville, Ga, US 189/M8
Fayetteville, NC, US 189/H3
Fayetteville, Oh, US 188/F1
Fayetteville, Pa, US 187/H5
Fayetteville, Tn, US 188/D3
Fayetteville, Tx, US 177/F3
Fayetteville, WV, US 189/G1
Fayl-la-Forêt, Fr. 86/B2
Fayrā, Yem. 144/B2
Faywood (Dwyer), NM, US 175/H4
Fazao, Monts du (mts.), Togo 141/F4
Fazao, PN du, Togo 141/F4
Fazenda Nova, Braz. 210/C3
Fāzilka, India 124/C4
Fdérik, Mrta. 136/B5
Feakle, Ire. 58/B4
Feale (riv.), Ire. 58/A5
Fear (cape), NC, US 189/J4
Feasterville-Trevose, Pa, US 194/D3
Feather (riv.), Ca, US 172/C4
Feather (falls), Ca, US 172/C4
Feather, Mid. Fk. (riv.), Ca, US 172/C4
Featherston, NZ 161/J9
Featherstone, Eng, UK 61/G4
Featherstone, Zim. 149/F3
Feathertop (mt.), Austl. 159/C3
Fécamp, Fr. 83/F1
Fecht (riv.), Fr. 86/D1
Federación, Arg. 212/E4
Federal, Arg. 212/E4
Federal Dam, Mn, US 183/G4
Federal Hall Nat'l Mem., NY, US 195/K9
Federal Way, Wa, US 170/C4
Federally Admin. Tribal Areas, Pak. 124/A2
Federalsburg, Md, US 189/K1
Federsee (lake), Ger. 84/C6
Fedhaven, Fl, US 190/N8
Fedīs, Eth. 144/B3
Fedje, Nor. 66/A1
Fedorovka, Kaz. 95/P5
Fëdorovka, Kaz. 97/J2
Fedorovka, Rus. 97/J1
Fëdorovka, Rus. 99/K4
Fedscreek, Ky, US 189/F2
Feeny, NI, UK 60/A2
Feerfeer, Som. 144/C4
Fegersheim, Fr. 84/A6
Fégréac, Fr. 82/C5
Fehérgyarmat, Hun. 76/F2
Fehmarn (isl.), Den. 66/D4
Fehmarn Belt (str.), Den. 68/F1
Fei Huang (riv.), China 106/D4
Fei Xian, China 106/D4
Feia (lake), Braz. 211/E4
Feicheng, China 106/D3
Feidong, China 106/D5
Feignies, Fr. 80/C3
Feijó, Braz. 208/D3
Feilding, NZ 161/C3
Feillans, Fr. 86/A5
Feira, Port. 72/A2
Feira de Santana, Braz. 211/F2
Feistritz (riv.), Aus. 71/L3
Feixi, China 106/D5
Fejér (co.), Hun. 76/D2
Fejø (isl.), Ger. 66/D4
Feke, Turk. 128/C2
Feketić, Yugo. 76/D3
Felanitx, Sp. 73/G3
Felch, Mi, US 183/L5
Feldafing, Ger. 87/H2
Feldaist (riv.), Aus. 85/H6
Feldberg (peak), Ger. 86/E2
Feldkirch, Aus. 87/F3
Feldkirchen an der Donau, Aus. 85/H6
Feldkirchen bei Graz, Aus. 76/B2
Feldkirchen in Kärnten, Aus. 71/L3
Feletto, It. 88/A2
Feletto Umberto, It. 89/G1
Feliciano, Arroyo (brook), Arg. 212/E4
Felicity, Oh, US 188/E1
Felino, It. 88/D4
Felipe Carrillo Puerto, Mex. 200/D2
Felix (riv.), NM, US 177/B1
Felixburg, Zim. 149/F3
Felixdorf, Aus. 76/C2
Felixlândia, Braz. 210/D3
Felixstowe, Eng, UK 63/H3
Felizzano, It. 88/B4
Fell, Ger. 81/F4
Fellbach, Ger. 84/C5
Felling, Eng, UK 61/G2
Fellows, Ca, US 174/C3
Fellsmere, Fl, US 191/H4
Felsberg, Ger. 79/G6
Felsberg, Swi. 87/F4
Felsenthal, Ar, US 179/H4
Felt, Ok, US 178/C2
Feltham (nbrhd.), Eng, UK 56/B2
Felton, Ca, US 174/A2
Felton, Ca, US 174/A2
Felton, De, US 194/C5
Felton, Mn, US 182/F4
Felton, Pa, US 194/B4
Feltwell, Eng, UK 63/G2
Fema (peak), It. 92/C2
Femø (isl.), Den. 66/D4
Femundsmarka NP, Nor. 64/D3
Fen (riv.), China 104/G5
Fénay, Fr. 86/B3
Fence, Wi, US 183/K5
Fence Lake, NM, US 175/H3
Fenchuganj, Bang. 123/H3
Fene, Sp. 72/A1
Fenelon Falls, On, Can. 187/G2
Fener (pt.), Turk. 130/D1
Feng Xian, China 106/D4
Feng Xian, China 104/F5
Fengári (peak), Gre. 75/J2
Fengcheng, China 107/C2
Fengchuihudie (peak), China 113/G3
Fenggeling, China 104/F5
Fenghuang, China 119/J2
Fenghuang, China 113/E3
Fengjie, China 113/F2
Fengkou, China 113/G2
Fengle (riv.), China 106/D5
Fengle, China 113/E2
Fengle, China 113/H3
Fenglin, Tai. 113/J4
Fenglingdu, China 104/G5
Fengnan, China 106/J7
Fengning, China 106/D2
Fengqing, China 112/C3
Fengqiu, China 106/C4
Fengrun, China 106/J7
Fengshan, China 119/J3
Fengshan, China 105/H3
Fengshan, China 113/F3
Fengshuba (res.), China 113/G3
Fengshui (peak), China 105/J1
Fengtai, China 106/H7
Fengtian, China 113/G3
Fengtian, China 113/G3
Fengxian, China 106/L9
Fengxiang, China 104/F5
Fengyang, China 106/D4
Fengyüan, Tai. 113/J3
Fengzhen, China 106/C2
Fengzhou, China 104/F5
Feni, Bang. 123/H4
Fenner, Ca, US 174/E3
Fennimore, Wi, US 181/J2
Fennville, Mi, US 186/C3
Fenoarivo Atsinanana, Madg. 152/J7
Fenshui (pass), China 113/H3
Fenshui Guan (pass), China 113/H4
Fenshuizhen, China 113/F2
Fensmark, Den. 66/D4
Fensterbach (riv.), Ger. 85/F4
Fenton, La, US 190/B2
Fenton, Mi, US 186/E3
Fenton (lake), Mi, US 193/E7
Fenwick, WV, US 189/G1
Fenxi, China 106/B3
Fenyang, China 106/B3
Feodosiya, Ukr. 99/H5
Férai, Gre. 77/H5
Ferbane, Ire. 58/C3
Ferdinand, In, US 188/D1
Ferdinandshof, Ger. 69/G2
Ferdows, Iran 127/G2
Fère-Champenoise, Fr. 80/C6
Fère-en-Tardenois, Fr. 80/C5
Ferentillo, It. 91/B2
Ferentino, It. 92/C4
Ferento (ruin), It. 91/B3
Fereydūn Shahr, Iran 129/G3
Fergus (riv.), Ire. 58/B4
Fergus, On, Can. 186/F3
Fergus Falls, Mn, US 182/F4
Ferguson (lake), Nun, Can. 166/F2
Ferguson, Ky, US 188/E2
Ferihegy (int'l arpt.), Hun. 76/D2
Ferkéssédougou, C.d'Iv. 140/D4
Ferlach, Aus. 71/L3
Ferland, On, Can. 183/K2
Ferland, Sk, Can. 171/L3
Ferland-et-Boilleau, Qu, Can. 184/B1
Ferlo (valley), Sen. 140/B3
Fermanagh (dist.), NI, UK 60/A3
Fermanville, Fr. 82/D1
Ferme-Neuve, Qu, Can. 187/J1
Fermeuse, Nf, Can. 185/L2
Fermi Nat'l Accelerator Lab., Il, US 193/P16
Fermignano, It. 89/F6
Fermin (pt.), Ca, US 192/F8
Fermo, It. 92/C1
Fermoselle, Sp. 72/B2
Fermoy, Ire. 58/B5
Fern Park, Fl, US 190/N6
Fern Ridge (lake), Or, US 172/B1
Fernán-Núñez, Sp. 72/C4
Fernández, Arg. 212/D3
Fernandina (isl.), Ecu. 208/J7
Fernandina Beach, Fl, US 191/H2
Fernando de la Mora, Par. 212/E3
Fernando de Noronha (isl.), Braz. 203/F3
Fernando Po (Bioko) (isl.), EqG. 146/B2
Fernandópolis, Braz. 213/G2
Ferndale, Ca, US 172/A3
Ferndale, Fl, US 190/M6
Ferndale, Md, US 194/B5
Ferndale, Mi, US 193/F7
Ferndale, Pa, US 187/G4
Ferndale, Wa, US 170/C3
Ferndown, Eng, UK 63/E5
Ferness, Sc, UK 59/C2
Ferney-Voltaire, Fr. 86/C5
Fernie, BC, Can. 170/G3
Fernley, Nv, US 172/D4
Fernpass (pass), Aus. 87/G3
Ferns, Ire. 58/D4
Ferntree Gully NP, Austl. 158/G5
Fernwood, Id, US 170/F4
Ferrandina, It. 74/E2
Ferrara, It. 89/E4
Ferrara (prov.), It. 89/E3
Ferrat (cape), Fr. 90/D5
Ferrat (cape), Alg. 138/E5
Ferreira do Alentejo, Port. 72/A3
Ferreira Gomes, Braz. 206/D2
Ferrell's Bridge (dam), Tx, US 179/G4
Ferrelo (cape), Or, US 172/A2
Ferreñafe, Peru 208/B2
Ferret (cape), Fr. 70/C4
Ferrette, Fr. 86/D3
Ferriday, La, US 190/C2
Ferriere, It. 88/C4
Ferrière-la-Grande, Fr. 80/D3
Ferrières, Belg. 81/E3
Ferris, Tx, US 176/L7
Ferrisburg, Vt, US 187/K2
Ferron, Ut, US 173/H4
Ferrum, Va, US 189/G2
Ferry Pass, Fl, US 190/E2
Ferryden, Sc, UK 59/D3
Ferryfield (int'l arpt.), Eng, UK 63/G5
Ferryhill, Eng, UK 61/G2
Ferryland, Nf, Can. 185/L2
Ferryside, Wal, UK 62/B3
Fershampenuaz, Rus. 95/N5
Ferté-Bernard, Fr. 83/F4
Fertile, Mn, US 182/F4
Fertő (Neusiedler) (lake), Aus. 71/M3
Ferwerd, Neth. 78/C2
Fès (prov.), Mor. 138/B3
Fès, Mor. 138/B2
Fesches-le-Châtel, Fr. 86/C2
Feshi, D.R. Congo 146/D4
Feshie (riv.), Sc, UK 59/C2
Fessenden, ND, US 182/E4
Fessenheim, Fr. 86/D2
Festival Centre, Austl. 157/M8
Festus, Mo, US 188/B1
Fet, Nor. 64/T8
Fetcham, Eng, UK 56/B3
Feteşti, Rom. 77/H3
Fethaland (pt.), Sc, UK 57/W13
Fethard, Ire. 58/C5
Fethard, Ire. 58/C5
Fethiye, Turk. 128/B2
Fetsund, Nor. 64/T8
Feucherolles, Fr. 56/H5
Feucht, Ger. 84/E4
Feuchtwangen, Ger. 84/D4
Feuilles (lake), Qu, Can. 167/J3
Feuilles, Rivière aux (riv.), Qu., Can. 165/K4
Feuquières, Fr. 80/A4
Feuquières-en-Vimeu, Fr. 80/A3
Feurs, Fr. 70/F4
Fevzipaşa, Turk. 130/E1
Feyzābād, Afg. 125/B4
Feyzin, Fr. 90/A1
Fez (Saiss) (int'l arpt.), Mor. 138/B3
Fezzane (well), Niger 134/B4
Ffestiniog, Wal, UK 60/E6
Fiambalá, Arg. 212/C3
Fianarantsoa, Madg. 152/H8
Fianarantsoa (prov.), Madg. 152/H8
Fianga, Chad 142/B3
Fiano Romano, It. 91/B3
Fiastrone (riv.), It. 92/C1
Ficarolo, It. 89/E4
Fichē, Eth. 144/A3
Fichtelberg (peak), Ger. 85/F2
Fichtelgebirge (mts.), Ger. 68/F3
Fichtelnaab (riv.), Ger. 85/E3
Ficksburg, SAfr. 150/D3
Ficulle, It. 91/B2
Fidenza, It. 88/D4
Fié (riv.), Gui. 140/C4
Field (isl.), Austl. 154/D3
Field (riv.), Austl. 157/M9
Field, Ab, Can. 170/F2
Field, On, Can. 186/F1
Fieldon, Il, US 181/J4
Fields, La, US 190/B2
Fields, Or, US 172/D2
Fieni, Rom. 77/G3
Fier, Alb. 75/F2
Fier (riv.), Fr. 86/B6
Fierzë (lake), Alb. 75/G1
Fiesch, Swi. 86/E5
Fiesole, It. 89/E6
Fiesso, It. 89/F3
Fiesso Umbertiano, It. 89/E4
Fife (co.), Sc, UK 59/D4
Fife, Wa, US 193/C3
Fife, Ga, US 189/L7
Fife Ness (pt.), Sc, UK 59/D4
Fifield, Austl. 159/C1
Fifth Cataract (falls), Sudan 135/G5
Fiftysix, Ar, US 179/H3
Figalo (cape), Alg. 138/D2
Figari, Fr. 74/A2
Figeac, Fr. 70/E4
Figg (mt.), Austl. 154/D5
Figline Valdarno, It. 89/E6
Figtree, Zim. 149/F4
Figueira da Foz, Port. 72/A2
Figueres, Sp. 73/G1
Figuig, Mor. 137/E2
Figuig (prov.), Mor. 138/C3
Figuil, Camr. 142/B3
Fiherenana (riv.), Madg. 152/G8
Fijāj (lake), Tun. 92/F4
Fiji(ctry.) 162/G6
Fik', Eth. 144/B3
Filabusi, Zim. 149/F4
Filadelfia, Col. 207/K7
Filadélfia, Braz. 207/E4
Filadelfia, Par. 212/D2
Filadelfia, Bol. 208/D3
Filandia, Col. 207/K8
Filattiera, It. 88/C5
Filchner Ice Shelf, Ant. 216/Y
File (hills), Sk, Can. 171/M2
Filer, Id, US 173/F2
Filey (bay), Eng, UK 61/H3
Filey, Eng, UK 61/H3
Filí, Gre. 75/N8
Filiaşi, Rom. 77/F3
Filiatái, Gre. 75/G3
Filiatrá, Gre. 75/G4
Filicudi (isl.), It. 74/D3
Filingué, Niger 141/F3
Filippiás, Gre. 75/G3
Filippoi (ruin), Gre. 75/J2
Filipstad, Swe. 66/F2
Filisur, Swi. 87/F4
Filière (riv.), Fr. 86/C6
Fillmore, Sk, Can. 182/C3
Fillmore, Ca, US 192/B2
Fillmore, Ut, US 175/F1
Fillmore, Mo, US 181/G3
Filo (mt.), WSam. 163/S9
Filomeno Mata, Mex. 199/M6
Filótion, Gre. 75/J4
Filottrano, It. 89/G7
Fils (riv.), Ger. 84/C5
Filsum, Ger. 79/E2
Filton, Eng, UK 62/D3
Filtu, Eth. 144/B4
Fimi (riv.), D.R. Congo 146/D3
Fina, Rsv. de, Mali 140/C3
Finale Emilia, It. 89/E4
Finale Ligure, It. 88/B5
Fiñana, Sp. 72/D4
Fincastle, Va, US 189/H2
Finch, Mt, US 171/L4
Finch Hatton, Austl. 160/C3
Finchley (nbrhd.), Eng, UK 56/C2
Findel (int'l arpt.), Lux. 81/F4
Findhorn, Sc, UK 59/C1
Findhorn (riv.), Sc, UK 59/B2
Findlay, Oh, US 186/E4
Findlay, Il, US 181/K4
Findochty, Sc, UK 59/D1
Finesville, NJ, US 194/C2
Fingal, ND, US 182/F4
Fingal, Austl. 158/C4
Finger, Tn, US 188/C3
Finger Lakes, NY, US 187/H3
Fingest, Eng, UK 56/A2
Fingoè, Moz. 149/F2
Finhaut, Swi. 86/C5
Finike, Turk. 130/B1
Finistère (dept.), Fr. 82/A4
Finisterre, Sp. 72/A1
Finisterre (cape), Sp. 72/A1
Finisterre (range), PNG 155/G1
Finjasjön (lake), Swe. 65/K6
Finke (riv.), Austl. 157/G3
Finke Gorge NP, Austl. 157/G3
Finkenwerder, Ger. 79/G1
Finksburg, Md, US 194/B5
Finland(ctry.) 55/G2
Finland (gulf), Eur. 100/C4
Finland, Mn, US 183/J4
Finlay (mts.), Tx, US 177/B2
Finlay (riv.), BC, Can. 166/D3
Finlayson, Mn, US 183/H4
Finley, Austl. 159/B2
Finley, ND, US 182/F4
Finley, Ok, US 179/G3
Finley, Tn, US 188/C2
Finley, Wa, US 170/E4
Finley NWR, Or, US 172/B1
Finn (riv.), Ire. 57/Q9
Finnegan, Ab, Can. 171/H2
Finnentrop, Ger. 79/E6
Finnigan (mt.), Austl. 160/B1
Finnis (cape), Austl. 157/G5
Finnmark (co.), Nor. 64/G1
Fino (riv.), It. 92/C2
Fino Mornasco, It. 88/C2
Fins, Oman 127/G4
Finschhafen, PNG 155/G1
Finsing, Ger. 85/E6
Finspång, Swe. 66/F2
Finsteraarhorn (peak), Swi. 86/E4
Finstown, Sc, UK 57/V14
Finström, Fin. 67/H1
Fintel, Ger. 79/G2
Fintona, NI, UK 60/A3
Fiolo (riv.), It. 92/C4
Fionn Loch (lake), Sc, UK 59/A1
Fionnay, Swi. 86/D5
Fiora (riv.), It. 71/J5
Fiorano, It. 89/D4
Fiordland NP, NZ 161/A4
Fiorenzuola d'Arda, It. 88/C4
Fiori, Monte de (peak), It. 92/C2
Fīq, Syria 131/D3
Fircrest, Wa, US 193/C3
Fire Island Nat'l Seashore, NY, US 195/E2
Firebaugh, Ca, US 174/B2
Firebrand (pass), Mt, US 171/H3
Firenze (prov.), It. 89/E5
Firenze (Florence), It. 89/E6
Firenzuola, It. 89/E5
Firesteel (cr.), SD, US 180/E1
Firestone, Co, US 180/B3
Firmat, Arg. 214/E2
Firmi, Fr. 70/E4
Firminópolis, Braz. 210/C3
Firminy, Fr. 70/F4
Fīrozābād, India 122/B2
Fīrozpur, India 124/C4
First Cataract (falls), Egypt 135/G3
Firth, Id, US 173/G2
Firth of Forth (inlet), Sc, UK 59/C4
Firth of Lorn (inlet), Sc, UK 57/Q8
Firth of Tay (inlet), Sc, UK 59/C4
Firth of Thames (inlet), NZ 161/C2
Fīrūz Kūh, Iran 129/H3
Fīrūzābād, Iran 129/H4
Firyuza, Trkm. 127/G1
Fischa (riv.), Aus. 77/P7
Fischach, Ger. 87/G1
Fischamend Markt, Aus. 77/P7
Fischbacher Alpen (mts.), Aus. 71/L3
Fischbek, Ger. 79/G2
Fischen im Allgäu, Ger. 87/G3
Fisenge, Zam. 149/F2
Fish (riv.), Namb. 148/C5
Fish Camp, Ca, US 174/C2
Fishburn, Eng, UK 61/G2
Fisher, Austl. 157/F4
Fisher (bay), Mb, Austl. 182/F2
Fisher (mt.), BC, Can. 170/G3
Fisher (str.), Nun, Can. 167/H2
Fisher, Ar, US 188/B3
Fisher, Il, US 186/B4
Fisher, La, US 190/B2
Fisher, Mn, US 182/F4
Fisher, WV, US 189/H1
Fisher Bay, Mb, Can. 182/F2
Fisher Branch, Mb, Can. 182/F2
Fisherman (isl.), Austl. 160/F6
Fishermans Island Nat'l Wild. Ref., Va, US 189/K2
Fishers (isl.), NY, US 195/G1
Fishersville, Va, US 189/H1
Fishguard, Wal, UK 62/B3
Fishing (lake), Mb, Can. 183/G1
Fishing (cr.), NC, US 189/J2
Fisht (peak), Rus. 96/F4
Fishtoft, Eng, UK 61/J6
Fisk, Mo, US 188/B2
Fiske, Sk, Can. 171/K2
Fisksätra, Swe. 65/B1
Fismes, Fr. 80/C5
Fitchburg, Ma, US 187/L3
Fitchburg, Wi, US 181/K2
Fitful Head (pt.), Sc, UK 57/W14
Fitjar, Nor. 66/A2
Fittja, Swe. 65/A1
Fitz Roy, Arg. 214/D5
Fitzcarrald, Peru 208/D3
Fitzgerald, Ga, US 191/G2
Fitzgerald River NP, Austl. 156/C5
Fitzhugh, Ok, US 179/F3
Fitzroy (peak), Arg. 215/B6
Fitzroy, UK 215/F6
Fitzroy (riv.), Austl. 153/B2
Fitzroy Crossing, Austl. 154/B4
Fitzwilliam (isl.), On, Can 186/E2
Fitzwilliam (str.), NW, Can. 167/R7
Fiuggi, It. 92/C4
Fiume Veneto, It. 89/F2
Fiumicino, It. 91/B4
Five Forks, Ga, US 189/M7
Five Islands, NS, Can. 184/E3
Five Sisters (peak), Sc, UK 59/A2
Fivemile (cr.), Wy, US 173/J2
Fivemiletown, NI, UK 60/A3
Fivizzano, It. 88/D5
Fizi, D.R. Congo 147/G4
Fizuli, Azer. 97/H5
Fjell, Nor. 66/A1
Fjellstrand, Nor. 64/S8
Fjerritslev, Den. 66/C3
Fjugesta, Swe. 66/F2
Flå, Nor. 66/C1
Flachslanden, Ger. 84/D4
Flackwell Heath, Eng, UK 56/A2
Fladungen, Ger. 84/D1
Flagler, Co, US 180/C4
Flagler Beach, Fl, US 191/H3
Flagler Museum, Fl, US 190/P9
Flagpole (peak), Tn, US 188/E2
Flagstaff, Az, US 175/G3
Flagstaff (lake), Or, US 172/D2
Flåm, Nor. 66/B1
Flambeau (riv.), Wi, US 183/J5
Flamborough Head (pt.), Eng, UK 61/H3
Flamborough, Eng, UK 61/H3
Flamborough, On, Can. 186/T9
Fläming (hills), Ger. 68/G2
Flaming Gorge (dam), Ut, US 173/J3
Flaming Gorge (res.), Ut.,Wy, US 173/J3
Flaming Gorge NRA, Wy, US 173/J3
Flamingo, Fl, US 191/H5
Flamingo Field (int'l arpt.), NAnt. 204/D1
Flanagan (riv.), On, Can. 183/H1
Flanders (reg.), Belg.,Fr. 80/B2
Flanders, NY, US 195/F2
Flandes, Col. 207/L8
Flandreau, SD, US 181/F1
Flärdlång (isl.), Swe. 65/B1
Flasher, ND, US 182/D4
Flat (mt.), NZ 161/A4
Flat Bay, Nf, Can. 185/H1
Flat Holm (isl.), Eng, UK 62/C4
Flat River, Mo, US 188/B2
Flat Rock, Mi, US 186/E3
Flat Rock, NC, US 189/G2
Flatbush (nbrhd.), NY, US 195/K9
Flateby, Nor. 64/T8
Flathead (lake), Mt, US 171/H4
Flathead (range), Mt, US 171/H3
Flathead (riv.), Mt, US 170/G4
Flathead Indian Res., Mt, US 170/G4
Flathead, South Fork (riv.), Mt, US 171/H4
Flatiron (mtn.), Id, US 173/G1
Flatonia, Tx, US 177/F3
Flattery (cape), Austl. 160/B1
Flattery (cape), Wa, US 168/A2
Flatwillow (cr.), Mt, US 171/K4
Flatwoods, La, US 190/B2
Flatwoods, Ky, US 189/F1
Flavio Alfaro, Ecu. 204/B5
Flawil, Swi. 87/F3
Flaxcombe, Sk, Can. 171/K2
Flaxlanden, Fr. 86/D2
Flayosc, Fr. 90/C5
Fleet, Eng, UK 63/F4
Fleet, Ab, Can. 171/J1
Fleetwood, Eng, UK 61/E4
Fleetwood, Pa, US 194/C3
Flekkefjord, Nor. 66/B2
Fleming, Sk, Can. 182/D2
Fleming, Co, US 180/C3
Fleming-Neon, Ky, US 189/F2
Flemingsberg, Swe. 65/A1
Flemingsburg, Ky, US 188/F1
Flemington, Mo, US 179/H2
Flemington, NJ, US 194/D2
Flemington Racecourse, Austl. 158/F5
Flemish Brabant (prov.), Belg. 81/D2
Flen, Swe. 66/G2
Flensburg, Ger. 66/C4
Flero, It. 88/D3
Fleron, Belg. 81/E2
Flers, Fr. 83/E3
Flesher (pass), Mt, US 171/H4
Flesk (riv.), Ire. 58/A5
Flesland (int'l arpt.), Nor. 66/A1
Fletcher, Ok, US 179/E3
Fletcher (pond), Mi, US 186/E2
Fletcher, NC, US 189/F3
Fletschhorn (peak), Swi. 86/D5
Fleurance, Fr. 70/D5
Fleurier, Swi. 86/C4
Fleurus, Belg. 81/D3
Fleury-les-Aubrais, Fr. 83/G5
Fleury-sur-Andelle, Fr. 83/G2
Fleury-sur-Orne, Fr. 83/E2
Flevoland (isl.), Neth. 68/C2
Flevoland (prov.), Neth. 78/C4
Flexenpass (pass), Aus. 87/G3
Flieden, Ger. 84/C2
Flieden (riv.), Ger. 84/C2
Fliess, Aus. 87/G3
Flimby, Eng, UK 60/E2
Flims, Swi. 87/F4
Flin Flon, Mb, Can. 166/F3
Flinders (range), Austl. 157/H5
Flinders (bay), Austl. 156/B5
Flinders (isl.), Austl. 153/D4
Flinders (riv.), Austl. 153/D2
Flinders Chase NP, Austl. 157/H5
Flinders Ranges (mts.), Austl. 153/C4
Flinders Ranges NP, Austl. 157/H4
Flinders Reefs (isls.), Austl. 160/C2
Flinders Reefs (reef), Austl. 155/H4
Flines-lez-Raches, Fr. 80/C3
Flint (hills), Ks, US 179/F2
Flint, Wal, UK 61/E5
Flint, Mi, US 186/E3
Flint (isl.), Kiri. 163/K6
Flint (lake), Nun, Can. 167/J2
Flint (riv.), Ga, US 189/M8
Flint City, Al, US 188/D3
Flint Hills Nat'l Wild. Ref., Ks, US 181/G4
Flint, South Branch (riv.), Mi, US 193/F5
Flintbek, Ger. 66/D4
Flinton, On, Can. 187/H2
Flippen, Ga, US 189/M8
Flisa, Nor. 66/E1
Flitwick, Eng, UK 63/F2
Flix, Sp. 73/F2
Flixecourt, Fr. 80/B3
Flize, Fr. 81/D4
Flo, Tx, US 177/G2
Floby, Swe. 66/E2
Floda, Swe. 66/E3
Flodden, Eng, UK 59/D5
Flögelner See (riv.), Ger. 79/F1
Flöha (riv.), Ger. 69/G3
Floing, Fr. 81/D4
Flomaton, Al, US 190/E2
Flonheim, Ger. 84/B3
Flora (mt.), Austl. 156/C2
Flora, Nor. 64/C3
Flora, Il, US 188/C1
Flora, In, US 186/C4
Flora, La, US 190/B2
Flora, Ms, US 188/B4
Flora, Phil. 114/C1
Flora (mtn.), Wa, US 170/D3
Flora Vista, NM, US 175/H2
Floral, Ar, US 179/J3
Floral City, Fl, US 190/L6
Floral Park, NY, US 195/L9
Florala, Al, US 191/E2
Florange, Fr. 81/F5
Florânia, Braz. 207/G4
Floraville, Austl 155/E4
Floreffe, Belg. 81/D3
Florence (Firenze), It. 89/E6
Florence, Al, US 188/D3
Florence, Ar, US 179/J4
Florence, Az, US 175/G4
Florence, Co, US 178/B1
Florence, Ks, US 179/F1
Florence, Ky, US 188/E1
Florence, Ms, US 188/B4
Florence, Mt, US 171/G4
Florence, Or, US 172/A2
Florence, SC, US 189/H3
Florence, SD, US 181/F1
Florence, Tx, US 177/F2
Florence, Wi, US 183/K5
Florence Junction, Az, US 175/G4
Florence Lake Nat'l Wild. Ref., ND, US 182/D4
Florence-Graham, Ca, US 192/F8
Florenceville, NB, Can. 184/D2
Florencia, Col. 204/C4
Florencia, Arg. 212/E4
Florennes, Belg. 81/D3
Florentino Ameghino, Arg. 214/D4
Florenton, Mn, US 183/H4
Florenville, Belg. 81/E4
Flores (isl.), Azor., Port. 73/R12
Flores, Braz. 207/G4
Flores, Guat. 200/D2
Flores (isl.), Indo. 103/M10
Flores (sea), Indo. 103/L10
Flores (dept.), Uru. 215/F2
Flores do Piauí, Braz. 207/F4
Flores, Arroyo de los (cr.), Arg. 214/E3
Floresta, Braz. 207/G5
Floreşti, Mol. 98/E4
Floresville, Tx, US 177/E3
Florham Park, NJ, US 195/H8
Floriano, Braz. 207/F4
Florianópolis, Braz. 213/G3
Florida, Bol. 208/D4
Florida, Bol. 212/D1
Florida, Col. 204/B4
Florida, Cuba 201/G1
Florida (str.), Cuba,US 169/K7
Florida, Hon. 200/D3
Florida, Peru 208/B2
Florida, Uru. 215/K11
Florida (dept.), Uru. 215/F2
Florida (state), US 169/K6
Florida (cape), Fl, US 190/P11
Florida, NY, US 194/D1
Florida City, Fl, US 191/H5
Florida Keys (isl.), Fl, US 191/H5
Florida Keys (isls.), Fl, US 165/J7
Florida Negra, Arg. 215/D6
Floridablanca, Col. 204/C3
Florida's Silver Springs, Fl, US 191/G3
Floridia, It. 74/D4
Florien, La, US 190/B2
Florin, Ca, US 193/M10
Flórina, Gre. 75/G2
Florissant, Mo, US 181/J4
Florissant Fossil Beds Nat'l Monument, Co, US 178/B1
Florissant Fossil Beds Nat'l Mon., Co, US 180/B4
Flörsbachtal, Ger. 84/C2
Flörsheim am Main, Ger. 84/B2
Flörsheim-Dalsheim, Ger. 84/B3
Florstadt, Ger. 84/B2
Flossenbürg, Ger. 85/F3
Flottsund, Swe. 65/A1
Flower Mound, Tx, US 176/K6
Floyd (riv.), Ia, US 181/F2
Floyd, Va, US 189/G2
Floyd, Ga, US 189/L7
Floydada, Tx, US 178/D4
Fluchthorn (peak), Aus. 87/G4
Flüelapass (pass), Swi. 87/F4
Flüelen, Swi. 87/E4
Fluessen (lake), Neth. 78/C3
Fluker, La, US 190/C2
Flume (riv.), Fr. 82/D4
Flums, Swi. 87/F3
Flushing, Mi, US 186/E3
Flushing (nbrhd.), NY, US 195/K8
Fluvanna, Tx, US 178/D4
Fly (riv.), PNG 162/D5
Fly River (delta), PNG 155/F2
Flying Fish (cape), Ant. 216/T
Fnjóská (riv.), Ice. 64/P6
Foam Lake, Sk, Can. 182/C2
Foard City, Tx, US 178/E4
Foča, Bosn. 76/D4
Fochabers, Sc, UK 59/C1
Fochville, SAfr. 150/P13
Fockbek, Ger. 66/C4
Focşani, Rom. 77/H3
Foëcy, Fr. 83/H6
Fog (bay), Austl. 154/C3
Fogang, China 119/K3
Foggaret ez Zoua, Alg. 137/F4
Foggia, It. 74/D2
Fogi, Indo. 117/G4
Foglia (riv.), It. 89/F5
Fogliano (lake), It. 91/B5
Foglizzo, It. 88/A2
Föglö (isl.), Fin. 67/J3
Fogo (isl.), CpV. 133/J10
Fohnsdorf, Aus. 71/L3
Föhren, Ger. 81/F4
Foix, Fr. 70/D5
Fokino, Rus. 96/E1
Folarskardnuten (peak), Nor. 66/B1
Folda (inlet), Nor. 64/E2
Földeák, Hun. 76/E2
Folégandros (isl.), Gre. 93/K3
Folembray, Fr. 80/C4
Foley, Mn, US 183/H5
Foley, Fl, US 191/G2
Foley (isl.), Nun, Can. 167/J2
Foley, Mo, US 181/J4
Folgaria, It. 87/H6
Foligno, It. 91/B2
Foligno, It. 91/B2
Folkestone, Eng, UK 63/H4
Folkston, Ga, US 191/G2
Follainville-Dennemont, Fr. 56/H4
Follets (isl.), Tx, US 177/G3
Follonica (gulf), It. 71/J5
Folly Beach, SC, US 189/H4
Folschviller, Fr. 81/F5
Folsom (dam), Ca, US 174/B1
Folsom (lake), Ca, US 172/C4
Folsom, Ca, US 172/C4
Folsom, NJ, US 194/D4
Foltesti, Rom. 77/J3
Fomboni, Com. 152/G6
Fómeque, Col. 207/M8
Fomin, Rus. 97/G3
Fond de Peinin, Pic du (peak), Fr. 90/C3
Fond du Lac, Sk, Can. 166/F3
Fond du Lac (riv.), Sk, Can. 166/F3
Fond du Lac, Wi, US 181/K2
Fond du Lac Ind. Res., Mn, US 183/H4
Fonda, NY, US 187/J3
Fondettes, Fr. 83/F6
Fondi (lake), It. 92/C5
Fondi, It. 92/C5
Fondo, It. 87/H5
Fongen (peak), Nor. 64/D3
Fongolanbi, Sen. 140/B3
Fonni, It. 74/A2
Fonsagrada, Sp. 72/B1
Fonseca (gulf), Nic. 196/D5
Fonseca, Col. 204/C2
Font Sancte, Pic de la (peak), Fr. 90/C3
Fontaine, Fr. 90/B2
Fontaine-Châalis, Fr. 56/L4
Fontaine-lès-Dijon, Fr. 86/A3
Fontaine-lès-Luxeuil, Fr. 86/C2
Fontaine-l'Evêque, Belg. 81/D3
Fontana, Ca, US 192/C2
Fontana, Ks, US 179/G1
Fontana (lake), NC, US 188/F3
Fontanarosa, It. 92/E5
Fontanarossa (int'l arpt.), It. 74/D4
Fontanella, It. 88/C3
Fontanellato, It. 88/D4
Fontanelle, Ia, US 181/G3
Fontaniva, It. 89/E2
Fonte Boa, Braz. 205/E5
Fontenailles, Fr. 56/L6
Fontenais, Swi. 86/D3
Fontenay-en-Parisis, Fr. 56/K4
Fontenay-le-Comte, Fr. 70/C3
Fontenay-le-Fleury, Fr. 56/J5
Fontenay-le-Marmion, Fr. 83/E2
Fontenay-les-Briis, Fr. 56/J6
Fontenay-Saint-Père, Fr. 56/H4
Fontenay-sous-Bois, Fr. 56/K5
Fontenay-Trésigny, Fr. 56/L5
Fontenelle (res.), Wy, US 173/H2

252

Fonte – Funaf

Fontenelle (dam), Wy, US 173/H2
Fontibón, Col. 207/L8
Fontoy, Fr. 81/F5
Fontur (pt.), Ice. 64/P6
Fontvieille, Fr. 90/A5
Fontvieille, Mona. 88/J8
Footscray (nbrhd.), Austl. 158/F5
Foping, China 104/F5
Forbach, Fr. 81/F5
Forbach, Ger. 84/B5
Forbes, ND, US 182/E5
Forbes (mt.), BC, Can. 170/F2
Forbes, Austl. 159/D1
Forbesganj, India 123/F2
Forcados, Nga. 141/G5
Forcalquier, Fr. 90/B5
Forcarey, Sp. 72/A1
Forchheim, Ger. 84/E3
Ford (riv.), Mi, US 183/L4
Ford, Eng, UK 59/D5
Ford (cape), Austl. 154/C3
Ford City, Ca, US 174/C3
Fordate (isl.), Indo. 154/D1
Førde, Nor. 64/C3
Fordham (nbrhd.), NY, US 195/K8
Fordingbridge, Eng, UK 63/E5
Fordoche, La, US 190/C2
Fords, NJ, US 195/H9
Ford's Bridge, Austl. 158/C1
Fords Prairie, Wa, US 170/C4
Fordsville, Ky, US 188/D2
Fordville, ND, US 182/F3
Fordyce, Ar, US 179/H4
Forécariah, Gui. 140/B4
Foreland (pt.), Eng, UK 62/C4
Foreland, The (pt.), Eng, UK 63/E5
Foremost, Ab, Can. 171/J3
Foreness (pt.), Eng, UK 63/H4
Forest, La, US 179/J4
Forest (riv.), ND, US 182/F3
Forest, Ms, US 188/C4
Forest, Tx, US 177/G2
Forest City, Fl, US 190/N6
Forest City, Ia, US 181/H2
Forest City, NC, US 189/G3
Forest Green, Eng, UK 56/B3
Forest Grove, Me, US 172/B1
Forest Hill, Austl. 159/C2
Forest Hill, Md, US 194/B4
Forest Hill, Tx, US 176/K7
Forest Hill, WV, US 189/G2
Forest Hills (nbrhd.), NY, US 195/K9
Forest Hills, Tn, US 188/D2
Forest Lake, Mn, US 183/H5
Forest Park, Ga, US 189/M7
Forestbrook, SC, US 189/H4
Forestburg, Ab, Can. 171/H1
Foresthill, Ca, US 172/C4
Forestier (cape), Austl. 158/D4
Forestier (pen.), Austl. 158/D4
Foreston, Mn, US 183/H5
Forestport, NY, US 187/J3
Forestville, Qu, Can. 184/C1
Forestville, NY, US 187/G3
Forestville, Md, US 194/B6
Forét (bay), Fr. 82/B5
Forêt du Day NP, Djib. 144/B3
Forez (mts.), Fr. 70/E4
Forfar, Sc, UK 59/D3
Forgan, Ok, US 178/D2
Forgan, Sk, Can. 171/L2
Forges-les-Bains, Fr. 56/J6
Forges-les-Eaux, Fr. 83/G1
Forggensee (lake), Ger. 87/G2
Forillon NP, Qu, Can. 184/E1
Forino, It. 92/D6
Forio, It. 92/C6
Fork Res. (lake), Tx, US 177/G1
Fork River, Mb, Can. 182/D2
Forked Deer, South Fork (riv.), Tn, US 188/C3
Forked Island, La, US 190/B3
Forked River, NJ, US 194/D4
Forkill, NI, UK 60/B3
Forkland, Al, US 188/D4
Forks, Wa, US 170/B4
Forlì, It. 89/F5
Forlì (prov.), It. 89/F4
Forlimpopoli, It. 89/F5
Forman, ND, US 182/F4
Formartine (reg.), Sc, UK 59/D2
Formazza, It. 87/E5
Formby, Eng, UK 61/E4
Formby (pt.), Eng, UK 61/E4
Formello, It. 91/B3
Formentera, Isla de (isl.), Sp. 92/D3
Formentor (cape), Sp. 73/G3
Former Yugoslav Republic of Macedonia (Macedonia) (ctry.) 55/G4
Formerie, Fr. 80/A4
Formia, It. 92/C5
Formiga, Braz. 210/D4
Formigine, It. 89/D4
Formignana, It. 89/E4
Formosa (prov.), Arg. 212/D3
Formosa, Arg. 212/E3
Formosa, Braz. 210/D2
Formosa (isl.), GBis. 140/B4
Formosa (peak), SAfr. 150/C4
Formosa, Ar, US 179/H3
Formosa, Serra (mts.), Braz. 209/H4
Formoso (riv.), Braz. 210/C1
Formoso, Braz. 210/C2
Fornacelle, It. 89/E6
Fornaci di Barga, It. 88/D5
Fornæs (cape), Den. 66/D3
Fornebu (int'l arpt.), Nor. 66/D2
Forney, Tx, US 176/L7
Forno Canavese, It. 90/D2
Fornosovo, Rus. 67/P2
Fornovo di Taro, It. 88/D4
Foro (riv.), It. 92/D3
Foro Burunga, Sudan 142/D2
Foros, Ukr. 96/E3
Forres, Sc, UK 59/C1
Forres, Arg. 212/D3
Forrest, Austl. 157/F4
Forrest City, Ar, US 188/B3
Forrest River Abor. Rsv., Austl. 154/B3
Forrest River Mission, Austl. 154/B3
Forrest Station, Mb, Can. 182/E3
Forsan, Tx, US 177/D1
Forsand, Nor. 66/B2
Forsayth, Austl. 160/A2
Forshaga, Swe. 66/E2
Forssa, Fin. 67/K1
Forster, Austl. 158/E2
Forstern, Ger. 85/E6
Forstinning, Ger. 85/E6
Forsyth, Mo, US 179/H2
Forsyth (range), Austl. 160/A3
Forsyth, Ga, US 188/F4
Forsyth, Mt, US 171/L4
Forsythe NWR, NJ, US 187/J5
Forsythe NWR, NJ, US 194/D5
Fort Polk Mil. Res., La, US 177/H2
Fort A.P. Hill, Va, US 189/J1
Fort Abbās, Pak. 124/B5
Fort Albany, On, Can. 167/H3
Fort Ancient, Oh, US 186/D5
Fort Apache, Az, US 175/H4
Fort Apache Ind. Res., Az, US 175/G3
Fort Ashby, WV, US 187/G5
Fort Atkinson, Wi, US 181/K2
Fort Augustus, Sc, UK 59/B2
Fort Beaufort, SAfr. 150/D4
Fort Beauséjour Nat'l Hist. Park, NB, Can. 184/E3
Fort Belknap, Tx, US 179/E4
Fort Belknap Ind. Res., Mt, US 171/K3
Fort Belvoir, Va, US 194/A6
Fort Bend (co.), Tx, US 177/M9
Fort Benning, Ga, US 188/E4
Fort Benning Mil. Res., Ga, US 191/F1
Fort Benning South, Ga, US 188/E4
Fort Benton, Mt, US 171/J4
Fort Berthold Ind. Res., ND, US 182/C4
Fort Bidwell, Ca, US 172/C3
Fort Bliss (mil. res.), NM, US 175/J4
Fort Bowie Nat'l Hist. Site, Az, US 175/H4
Fort Bragg, Ca, US 172/B4
Fort Bragg, NC, US 189/H3
Fort Branch, In, US 188/D1
Fort Bridger, Wy, US 173/H3
Fort Buford Historical Site, ND, US 182/C4
Fort Campbell, Tn,Ky, US 188/D2
Fort Carson, Co, US 178/B1
Fort Carson, Co, US 180/B4
Fort Chambly Nat'l Hist. Park, Qu, Can. 185/P7
Fort Chipewyan, Ab, Can. 166/E3
Fort Clark Historical Site, ND, US 182/D4
Fort Collins, Co, US 180/B3
Fort Collins Museum, Co, US 180/B3
Fort Conde, Al, US 190/D2
Fort Davis, Al, US 188/E4
Fort Davis, Tx, US 177/C2
Fort Davis Nat'l Hist. Site, Tx, US 177/C2
Fort de Douaumont, Fr. 81/E5
Fort de Kock, Indo. 115/C3
Fort de Vaux, Fr. 81/E5
Fort Defiance, Az, US 175/H3
Fort Deposit, Al, US 190/E2
Fort Desaix Mil. Res., Fr. 197/N9
Fort Desoto Park, Fl, US 190/K8
Fort Dix, NJ, US 187/J4
Fort Dodge, Ia, US 181/G2
Fort Dodge Historical Museum, Ia, US 181/G2
Fort Donelson Nat'l Bfld., Tn, US 188/D2
Fort Drum, NY, US 187/J2
Fort Duchesne, Ut, US 173/J3
Fort Erie, On, Can. 186/V10
Fort Frances, On, Can. 183/H3
Fort Frederica Nat'l Mon., Ga, US 191/H2
Fort Gaines, Al, US 190/D2
Fort Gaines, Ga, US 191/F2
Fort Garland, Co, US 178/B2
Fort Gates, Tx, US 176/F2
Fort Gay, WV, US 189/F1
Fort George Nat'l Hist. Park, On, Can. 186/U9
Fort Gibson, Ok, US 179/G3
Fort Gibson (lake), Ok, US 179/G2
Fort Good Hope, NW, Can. 166/D2
Fort Gordon, Ga, US 189/F4
Fort Grant, Az, US 175/H4
Fort Green, Fl, US 190/M8
Fort Green Springs, Fl, US 190/M8
Fort Hall, Id, US 173/G2
Fort Hall Ind. Res., Id, US 173/G2
Fort Hancock, NJ, US 195/J10
Fort Hancock, Tx, US 177/B2
Fort Hood, Tx, US 177/F2
Fort Howard, Md, US 194/B5
Fort Huachuca, Az, US 175/G5
Fort Hunter Liggett, Ca, US 174/B3
Fort Independence Ind. Res., Ca, US 174/C2
Fort Irwin (mil. res.), Ca, US 174/D3
Fort Jackson, SC, US 189/G3
Fort Jesus, Kenya 145/B3
Fort Knox, Ky, US 188/E2
Fort Laramie (canal), Wy, US 180/B2
Fort Laramie Nat'l Hist.Site, Wy, US 180/B2
Fort Larned Nat'l Hist. Site, Ks, US 178/E1
Fort Lauderdale, Fl, US 190/P10
Fort Lauderdale-Hollywood (int'l arpt.), Fl, US 190/P10
Fort Lawn, SC, US 189/G3
Fort Leavenworth Mil. Res., Ks, US 179/G1
Fort Lee, NJ, US 195/K8
Fort Lennox Nat'l Hist. Park, Qu, Can. 187/K2
Fort Leonard Wood, Mo, US 179/H2
Fort Lewis, Wa, US 193/B3
Fort Liard, NW, Can. 166/D2
Fort Liberté, Haiti 201/J2
Fort Lonesome, Fl, US 190/L8
Fort Loudon, Pa, US 187/H5
Fort Lupton, Co, US 180/B3
Fort Lyon (canal), Co, US 180/C4
Fort Macleod, Ab, Can. 171/H3
Fort Madison, Ia, US 181/J3
Fort Malden Nat'l Hist. Park, On, Can. 193/F7
Fort Mandan Historical Site, ND, US 182/D4
Fort Matanzas Nat'l Mon., Fl, US 191/H3
Fort Mc Dermitt Ind. Res., Nv, US 172/D3
Fort McCoy, Fl, US 191/H3
Fort McCoy (fort), Wi, US 181/J1
Fort McDowell Ind. Res., Az, US 175/G4
Fort McHenry Nat'l Mon., Md, US 194/B5
Fort McMurray, Ab, Can. 166/E3
Fort McPherson, NW, Can. 168/Z12
Fort Meade, Fl, US 190/M8
Fort Meade, Md, US 194/B5
Fort Michilimackinac, Mi, US 186/D2
Fort Mill, SC, US 189/G3
Fort Missoula, Mt, US 171/G4
Fort Mojave Ind. Res., Az,Ca, US 174/E3
Fort Morgan, Al, US 190/D2
Fort Morgan, Co, US 180/C3
Fort Morgan Museum, Co, US 180/C3
Fort Motte, SC, US 189/G4
Fort Moultrie, SC, US 189/H4
Fort Myers, Fl, US 191/H4
Fort Nelson (riv.), BC, Can. 166/D3
Fort Nelson, BC, Can. 168/AA13
Fort Niobrara NWR, Ne, US 180/D2
Fort Nottingham, SAfr. 151/E3
Fort Payne, Al, US 188/E3
Fort Peck (lake), Mt, US 165/G5
Fort Peck, Mt, US 171/L3
Fort Peck (dam), Mt, US 171/L4
Fort Peck Ind. Res., Mt, US 171/L3
Fort Phantom Hill, Tx, US 177/E1
Fort Pierce, Fl, US 191/H4
Fort Pierre, SD, US 180/D1
Fort Plain, NY, US 187/J3
Fort Portal, Ugan. 147/G2
Fort Providence, NW, Can. 166/E2
Fort Pulaski Nat'l Mon., Ga, US 189/G4
Fort Qu'Appelle, Sk, Can. 182/C2
Fort Quitman Ruins, Tx, US 177/B2
Fort Raleigh Nat'l Hist. Site, NC, US 189/K3
Fort Randall (dam), SD, US 180/E2
Fort Ransom, ND, US 182/F4
Fort Ransom Historical Site, ND, US 182/F4
Fort Resolution, NW, Can. 166/E2
Fort Rice, ND, US 182/D4
Fort Rice Historical Site, ND, US 182/D4
Fort Riley (fort), Ks, US 181/F4
Fort Riley Mil. Res., Ks, US 179/F1
Fort Ripley, Mn, US 183/G4
Fort Rixon, Zim. 149/F4
Fort Rock, Or, US 172/C2
Fort Ross, Ca, US 172/B4
Fort Rucker Military Res., Al, US 191/f2
Fort Saint James, BC, Can. 166/D3
Fort Saint John, BC, Can. 166/D3
Fort Scott, Ks, US 179/G2
Fort Scott Nat'l Hist. Site, Ks, US 179/G2
Fort Seward Historical Site, ND, US 182/E4
Fort Seybert, WV, US 189/H1
Fort Shawnee, Oh, US 186/D4
Fort Sill Mil. Res., Ok, US 179/E3
Fort Simpson, NW, Can. 166/D2
Fort Smith, Ar, US 179/G3
Fort Smith, NW, Can. 166/E2
Fort Smith, Mt, US 173/K1
Fort Smith Nat'l Hist. Site, Ar, US 179/G3
Fort Stanwix Nat'l Mon., NY, US 187/J3
Fort Stewart, Ga, US 191/H2
Fort Stockton, Tx, US 177/C2
Fort Sumner, NM, US 178/B3
Fort Sumter Nat'l Mon., SC, US 189/H4
Fort Thomas, Az, US 175/H4
Fort Thomas, Ky, US 186/D5
Fort Tilden, NY, US 195/K9
Fort Totten, ND, US 182/E4
Fort Totten Indian Res., ND, US 182/E4
Fort Towson, Ok, US 179/G3
Fort Union Nat'l Mon., NM, US 178/B3
Fort Union Trading Post Nat'l Hist. Site, Mt, US 182/B3
Fort Valley, Ga, US 188/F4
Fort Vermilion, Ab, Can. 166/E3
Fort Wadsworth, NY, US 195/J9
Fort Walton Beach, Fl, US 190/E2
Fort Washakie, Wy, US 173/J2
Fort Washington (park), Md, US 194/A6
Fort Wayne, In, US 186/D4
Fort Wellington Nat'l Hist. Park, On, Can. 187/J2
Fort White, Fl, US 191/G3
Fort William, Sc, UK 59/A3
Fort Wingate, NM, US 175/H3
Fort Wingate (mil. res.), NM, US 175/H3
Fort Worth, Tx, US 176/K7
Fort Worth Museum of Science and History, Tx, US 176/K7
Fort Yates, ND, US 182/D4
Fort Yukon, Ak, US 168/Y12
Fort Yuma Ind. Res., Ca, US 174/E4
Fort-de-France, Guad. 197/N9
Fort-Foureau, Camr. 142/B2
Fort-George (Chisasibi), Qu, Can. 167/J3
Fort-Mahon-Plage, Fr. 80/A3
Fort-Mardyck, Fr. 80/B1
Fort-Shevchenko, Kaz. 97/J3
Fortaleza, Bol. 209/E3
Fortaleza, Bol. 209/E4
Fortaleza, Braz. 207/G3
Fortaleza dos Nogueiras, Braz. 207/E4
Fortaleza Santa Teresa, Uru. 215/G2
Forte Cameia, Ang. 148/D1
Forte dei Marmi, It. 88/D6
Forte República, Ang. 146/D4
Fortescue (riv.), Austl. 162/A7
Fortescue, NJ, US 194/C5
Fortesque (riv.), Austl. 153/A3
Forth (mtn.), Ire. 58/D5
Forth (riv.), Sc, UK 59/B4
Forth, Sc, UK 59/C5
Fortín, Mex. 199/N8
Fortín Ávalos Sánchez, Par. 212/D2
Fortín Capitán Escobar, Par. 212/D2
Fortín Carlos Antonio López, Par. 212/E2
Fortín Casanillo, Par. 212/E2
Fortín Coronel Bogado, Par. 212/E2
Fortín Coronel Sánchez, Par. 212/E1
Fortín Florida, Par. 212/E2
Fortín General Bruguez, Par. 212/E3
Fortín Guaraní, Par. 212/E2
Fortín Hernandarias, Par. 212/D2
Fortín Infante Rivarola, Par. 212/D2
Fortín Isla Poi, Par. 212/E2
Fortín Palmar de las Islas, Par. 212/D1
Fortín Presidente Ayala, Par. 212/E2
Fortín Teniente Esteban Martínez, Par. 212/E3
Fortín Teniente Gabino Mendoza, Par. 212/D2
Fortín Teniente Juan E. López, Par. 212/D2
Fortín Teniente Primero Ramiro Espínola, Par. 212/D2
Fortín Uno, Arg. 214/D3
Fortín Zalazar, Par. 212/E2
Forton, Eng, UK 61/F4
Fortore (riv.), It. 74/D2
Fortress (mtn.), Wy, US 173/J1
Fortress of Louisbourg Nat'l Hist. Park, NS, Can. 185/G3
Fortrose, Sc, UK 59/B1
Fortuna, Arg. 214/D2
Fortuna, Braz. 207/E4
Fortuna, Ca, US 172/A3
Fortuna, Mo, US 179/H1
Fortuna, ND, US 182/C3
Fortune (bay), Nf, Can. 185/K2
Fortune, Nf, Can. 185/K2
Fortuneswell, Eng, UK 62/D5
Fortville, In, US 186/D5
Forty Fort, Pa, US 194/C1
Forty Mile (pt.), Mi, US 186/E2
Forty Mile Scrub NP, Austl. 160/B2
Fortymile Wash (riv.), Nv, US 174/D2
Forūr (isl.), Iran 129/H5
Fos (gulf), Fr. 90/A6
Fos-sur-Mer, Fr. 90/A6
Fosca, Col. 207/M8
Foshan, China 113/G4
Fosheim (pen.), Nun, Can. 167/S7
Foso, Gha. 141/E5
Foss (riv.), Eng, UK 61/G3
Fossacesia, It. 92/D3
Fossalta di Piave, It. 89/F2
Fossalta di Portogruaro, It. 89/F2
Fossano, It. 88/A3
Fosses, Fr. 56/K4
Fosses-la-Ville, Belg. 81/D3
Fossil, Or, US 172/C1
Fossil Butte Nat'l Mon., Wy, US 173/H3
Fossò, It. 89/F3
Fossombrone, It. 89/F6
Fosston, Sk, Can. 182/C1
Fosston, Mn, US 182/G4
Foster, Austl. 159/C4
Foster, Mo, US 179/G1
Foster, Tx, US 178/C4
Foster City, Mi, US 183/L5
Fostoria, Oh, US 186/E4
Fót, Hun. 77/R9
Fotan, China 113/H3
Fotokol, Camr. 142/B2
Foucarmont, Fr. 80/A4
Foucherans, Fr. 86/B3
Fouesnant, Fr. 82/A5
Foug, Fr. 81/E6
Fougamou, Gabon 146/B3
Fougères, Fr. 82/D4
Fougerolles, Fr. 86/C2
Fouilloy, Fr. 80/B4
Fouke, Ar, US 179/H4
Foul (pt.), SrL. 121/D4
Foula (isl.), Sc, UK 57/V13
Foulness (riv.), Eng, UK 61/H4
Foulness (pt.), Eng, UK 63/G3
Foulness (isl.), Eng, UK 63/G3
Foulsham, Eng, UK 63/H1
Foulwind (cape), NZ 161/B3
Foum el Hassane, Mor. 136/C3
Foum Zguid, Mor. 136/D3
Foumbouni, Com. 152/G5
Foundiougne, Sen. 140/A3
Fountain, Co, US 178/B1
Fountain, Fl, US 191/F2
Fountain (cr.), Co, US 180/B4
Fountain (lake), Mn, US 183/N6
Fountain Green, Ut, US 173/H4
Fountain Hill, Pa, US 194/C2
Fountain Hills, Az, US 175/G4
Fountain Inn, SC, US 189/F3
Fountain Run, Ky, US 188/E2
Fountain Valley, Ca, US 192/G8
Fountains Abbey, Eng, UK 61/G3
Four Corners Monument, US 175/H2
Four Elms, Eng, UK 56/D3
Four Lakes, Wa, US 170/F4
Fourchambault, Fr. 70/E3
Fourche La Fave (riv.), Ar, US 179/H3
Fourcroy (cape), Austl. 154/C2
Fourges, Fr. 56/G4
Fourmies, Fr. 80/D4
Fourmile (peak), Wy, US 173/K2
Fourmile Draw (riv.), NM, US 177/B1
Fourneaux, Fr. 90/C2
Fourques, Fr. 90/A5
Fourteen Mile (pt.), Mi, US 183/K4
Fourth Cataract (falls), Sudan 135/G5
Fouta Djallon (phys. reg.), Gui. 140/B4
Foveaux (str.), NZ 153/G7
Fowey (riv.), Eng, UK 62/B6
Fowey, Eng, UK 62/B6
Fowler, Ca, US 174/C2
Fowler, Co, US 178/B1
Fowler, In, US 186/C4
Fowler, Mi, US 186/D3
Fowlkes, Tn, US 188/C3
Fowman, Iran 129/G2
Fownhope, Wal, UK 62/D2
Fox (mtn.), Yk., Can. 168/Z12
Fox (isls.), Ak, US 168/W13
Fox, Ar, US 179/H3
Fox (lake), Il, US 181/K2
Fox, Mi, US 186/C2
Fox, Ok, US 179/F3
Fox, Or, US 172/D1
Fox (isl.), Wa, US 193/B3
Fox (riv.), Wi, US 183/K5
Fox (riv.), Wi,Il, US 181/"K2
Fox Glacier, NZ 161/B3
Fox Harbour, Nf, Can. 185/L2
Fox Lake, Il, US 193/P15
Fox River Grove, Il, US 193/P15
Fox Valley, Sk, Can. 171/K2
Foxe (pen.), Can. 165/K3
Foxe (chan.), Can. 165/K3
Foxe Basin (chan.), Can. 165/K3
Foxen (lake), Swe. 66/D2
Foxford, Ire. 58/A2
Foxton, Eng, UK 63/G2
Foyers, Sc, UK 59/B2
Foyle(riv.) 60/A2
Foynes, Ire. 58/A4
Foz, Sp. 72/B1
Foz do Breu, Braz. 208/C3
Foz do Cunene, Ang. 148/A3
Foz do Iguaçu, Braz. 213/F3
Frackville, Pa, US 194/B2
Fraga, Sp. 73/F2
Fraiburgo, Braz. 213/G3
Fraile Muerto, Uru. 213/F5
Fraile Pintado, Arg. 212/C2
Fraisans, Fr. 86/B3
Fraize, Fr. 86/D1
Frameries, Belg. 80/C3
Framlingham, Eng, UK 63/H2
Frammersbach, Ger. 84/C2
Franca, Braz. 213/H2
Francavilla al Mare, It. 92/D3
Francavilla Fontana, It. 75/E2
Francavilla in Sinni, It. 74/E2
France(ctry.) 55/E4
Frances (cape), Cuba 201/F1
Frances (lake), Yk, Can. 166/C2
Francés Viejo (cape), DRep. 197/H4
Francesville, In, US 186/C4
Franceville, Gabon 146/C3
Franche-Comté (pol. reg.), Fr. 86/B5
Francia, Uru. 215/K10
Francis, Sk, Can. 182/C2
Francis, Ok, US 179/F3
Francis, Ut, US 173/H3
Francis Case (lake), SD, US 180/E2
Francisco de Orellana, Peru 208/C1
Francisco Escárcega, Mex. 200/D2
Francisco I. Madero, Mex. 177/C5
Francisco Javier Mina, Mex. 198/C3
Francisco Portillo, Mex. 177/B3
Francisco Sá, Braz. 211/E3
Francisco Zarco, Mex. 198/A1
Francistown (int'l arpt.), Bots. 149/E4
Francistown, Bots. 149/E4
Franco da Rocha, Braz. 211/K8
Francolino, It. 89/E4
Franconville, Fr. 56/J5
Franeker, Neth. 78/C2
Frangy, Fr. 86/B5
Frank Hahn NP, Austl. 156/C5
Franken Wald (for.), Ger. 85/E2
Frankenau, Ger. 79/F6
Frankenberg-Eder, Ger. 79/F6
Frankenburg am Hausruck, Aus. 85/G6
Frankenhöhe (mts.), Ger. 68/F4
Frankenmarkt, Aus. 85/G7
Frankenmuth, Mi, US 186/E3
Frankenthal, Ger. 84/B3
Frankford, On, Can. 187/H2
Frankford, De, US 189/K1
Frankfort, SAfr. 150/E2
Frankfort, In, US 186/C4
Frankfort, Ks, US 181/F4
Frankfort (cap.), Ky, US 188/E1
Frankfort, Mi, US 186/C2
Frankfort, Oh, US 186/E5
Frankfurt (int'l arpt.), Ger. 84/B2
Frankfurt, Ger. 69/H2
Frankfurt am Main, Ger. 84/B2
Fränkische Alb (mts.), Ger. 68/F4
Fränkische Rezat (riv.), Ger. 84/D4
Fränkische Saale (riv.), Ger. 68/E3
Fränkische Schweiz (reg.), Ger. 68/F4
Fränkische Schweiz (reg.), Ger. 71/J2
Frankland (cape), Austl. 159/C4
Franklin (bay), NW, Can. 166/D2
Franklin (mts.), NW, Can. 166/D2
Franklin, Qu, Can. 187/K2
Franklin, Az, US 175/H4
Franklin, Ga, US 188/E4
Franklin, Id, US 173/H2
Franklin, In, US 186/C5
Franklin, Ks, US 179/G2
Franklin, Ky, US 188/D2
Franklin, La, US 190/C3
Franklin, Mi, US 193/F6
Franklin, NC, US 189/F3
Franklin, Ne, US 180/E3
Franklin, NH, US 187/L3
Franklin, NJ, US 194/D1
Franklin, Oh, US 186/D5
Franklin, Pa, US 187/G4
Franklin, Tn, US 188/D3
Franklin, Tx, US 177/F2
Franklin, Va, US 189/J2
Franklin, Wi, US 186/B3
Franklin, WV, US 189/H1
Franklin D. Roosevelt (lake), Wa, US 170/E3
Franklin Grove, Il, US 181/K3
Franklin Lakes, NJ, US 195/J7
Franklin Mineral Museum, NJ, US 194/D1
Franklin Park, Il, US 193/Q16
Franklin Square, NY, US 195/L9
Franklin-Lower Gordon Wild Rivers NP, Austl. 158/C4
Franklinton, La, US 190/C2
Franklinton, NC, US 189/H2
Franklinville, NY, US 187/G3
Frankston (nbrhd.), Austl. 158/G6
Frankston, Tx, US 176/G1
Franksville, Wi, US 193/Q14
Frankville, Al, US 190/D2
Franois, Fr. 86/B3
Franquelin, Qu, Can. 184/D1
Franschhoek, SAfr. 150/L10
Fransfontein, Namb. 148/B4
Fransisco Beltrão, Braz. 213/F3
Fransisco Morato, Braz. 211/K8
Františkovy Lázně, Czh. 85/F2
Franz Josef Land (isls.), Rus. 216/C
Franz Joseph Strauss (int'l arpt.), Ger. 85/E6
Franzburg, Ger. 66/E4
Frascati, It. 91/B4
Fraser (mt.), Austl. 156/C3
Fraser (isl.), Austl. 153/E3
Fraser (riv.), BC, Can. 170/D2
Fraser, Mi, US 193/G6
Fraser NP, Austl. 159/B3
Fraserburg, SAfr. 150/C3
Fraserburgh, Sc, UK 59/D1
Frasertown, NZ 161/D2
Fraserville, On, Can. 187/G2
Fraserwood, Mb, Can. 182/F2
Frasne, Fr. 86/C4
Frasnes-lez-Gosselies, Belg. 81/D2
Frassine (riv.), It. 89/E2
Frassino, It. 89/D3
Frasso Telesino, It. 92/D5
Frastanz, Aus. 87/F3
Frati, Monte dei (peak), It. 89/F6
Frauenfeld, Swi. 87/E2
Fraunberg, Ger. 85/F6
Fray Bentos, Uru. 215/J10
Fray Jorge, PN, Chile 212/B4
Fray Marcos, Uru. 215/L11
Frazier Downs Abor. Land, Austl. 154/A4
Frazier Park, Ca, US 174/C3
Frechen, Ger. 81/F2
Freckenfeld, Ger. 84/B4
Fred (mt.), Les. 150/E3
Fred, Tx, US 177/G2
Fredensborg, Den. 65/J7
Frederic, Wi, US 183/H5
Frederica, De, US 194/C6
Fredericia, Den. 66/C4
Frederick(reef), Austl. 153/E3
Frederick, Md, US 187/H5
Frederick (co.), Md, US 194/A5
Frederick, Ok, US 178/E3
Frederick, SD, US 180/E1
Fredericksburg, Ia, US 181/H2
Fredericksburg, Pa, US 194/B3
Fredericksburg, Tx, US 177/E2
Fredericksburg, Va, US 189/J1
Fredericksburg and Spotsylvania Nat'l Mil. Park, Va, US 189/J1
Frederickton, Austl. 158/E1
Fredericktown, Oh, US 186/E4
Fredericktown, Mo, US 188/B2
Frederico Westphalen, Braz. 213/F3
Fredericton (cap.), NB, Can. 184/D3
Fredericton Junction, NB, Can. 184/D3
Frederik Willem IV (falls), Sur. 205/G4
Frederiks, Den. 66/C3
Frederiksberg, Den. 65/H7
Frederiksberg, Den. 65/J7
Frederiksborg (co.), Den. 66/E4
Frederiksborg Castle (Frederiksborg Slot), Den. 66/E4
Frederiksborg Slot (Frederiksborg Castle), Den. 66/E4
Frederikshavn, Den. 66/D3
Frederikssund, Den. 65/J7
Frederiksted, USVI 197/M8
Frederiksværk, Den. 65/J7
Fredersdorf bei Berlin, Ger. 68/Q7
Fredonia, ND, US 182/E4
Fredonia, Ks, US 179/G2
Fredonia, Wi, US 186/C3
Fredonia, NY, US 187/G3
Fredonia, Az, US 175/F2
Fredonia, Col. 207/K7
Fredonia (Biscoe), Ar, US 179/J3
Fredriksberg, Swe. 66/F1
Fredrikstad, Nor. 66/D2
Free State (prov.), SAfr. 150/P13
Freeburg, Mo, US 179/J1
Freeburg, Pa, US 194/B2
Freedom, Ok, US 178/E2
Freedom, Wy, US 173/H2
Freehold, NJ, US 194/D3
Freel (peak), Ca, US 172/D4
Freeland, Md, US 194/B4
Freeland, Pa, US 194/C1
Freeland, Wa, US 193/B1
Freeling (mt.), Austl. 157/G2
Freeling Heights (peak), Austl. 157/H4
Freelton, On, Can. 186/S9
Freeman, SD, US 180/F2
Freemansburg, Pa, US 194/C2
Freeport, Bahm. 197/F2
Freeport, Fl, US 191/E2
Freeport, Il, US 181/K2
Freeport, Me, US 187/L3
Freeport, NY, US 195/L9
Freeport, Pa, US 187/G4
Freeport, Tx, US 176/G3
Freer, Tx, US 177/E4
Freetown (cap.), SLeo. 140/B4
Freetown, In, US 188/D1
Freetown (Lungi) (int'l arpt.), SLeo. 140/B4
Fregenal de la Sierra, Sp. 72/B3
Fregene, It. 91/B4
Fréhel (cape), Fr. 82/C3
Frei Inocêncio, Braz. 211/E3
Freib Mulde (riv.), Ger. 68/G3
Freiberg, Ger. 69/G3
Freiburg, Ger. 86/D2
Freiburg, Ger. 79/G1
Freienbach, Swi. 87/E3
Freigné, Fr. 83/D5
Freihung, Ger. 85/E3
Freilassing, Ger. 85/F7
Freinsheim, Ger. 84/B3
Freire, Chile 214/B3
Freirina, Chile 212/B4
Freisen, Ger. 81/G4
Freising, Ger. 85/E6
Freistadt, Aus. 85/H5
Freital, Ger. 69/G3
Freixo de Espada à Cinta, Port. 72/B2
Frejorgues (int'l arpt.), Fr. 70/E5
Fréjus, Fr. 90/C6
Frekhaug, Nor. 66/A1
Frémainfille, Fr. 56/H4
Fremantle (nbrhd.), Austl. 156/K7
Fremdingen, Ger. 84/D5
Frémécourt, Fr. 56/J4
Fremington, Eng, UK 62/B4
Fremont, Ia, US 181/H3
Fremont, In, US 186/D4
Fremont, Mi, US 186/D3
Fremont, NC, US 189/J3
Fremont, Ne, US 181/F3
Fremont, Oh, US 186/E4
Fremont (riv.), Ut, US 173/H4
Fremont (isl.), Ut, US 173/G3
Fremont, Ut, US 175/G1
Fremont (lake), Wy, US 173/J2
Fremont (peak), Wy, US 173/J2
French (riv.), On, Can. 186/F1
French (cr.), Pa, US 194/C3
French Broad (riv.), Tn, US 189/F3
French Camp, Ms, US 188/C4
French Cr. Sp, Pa, US 194/C3
French Frigate Shoals (bar), Hi, US 163/J2
French Guiana (dpcy.), FrG. 205/H3
French Lick, In, US 188/D1
French Polynesia (terr.), Fr. 163/L6
French River, On, Can. 186/F1
French River, Mn, US 183/J4
Frenchburg, Ky, US 188/F2
Frenchglen, Or, US 172/D2
Frenchman (riv.), Can.,US 166/F4
Frenchman (cr.), Co, US 180/C3
Frenchman (riv.), Sk, Can. 171/K3
Frenchman's (bay), On, Can. 186/U8
Frenchmans Cap (peak), Austl. 158/C4
Frenchpark, Ire. 58/B2
Frenchtown, Mt, US 170/G4
Frenchtown, NJ, US 194/C2
Frenda, Alg. 138/F5
Frêne, Pic du (peak), Fr. 90/C2
Frépillon, Fr. 56/J4
Freren, Ger. 79/E4
Fresco, C.d'Iv. 140/D5
Fresco (riv.), Braz. 206/D4
Freshford, Ire. 58/C4
Freshwater, Nf, Can. 185/L2
Freshwater, Eng, UK 63/E5
Fresia, Chile 214/B4
Fresnay-sur-Sarthe, Fr. 83/F4
Fresnes, Fr. 56/J5
Fresnes-en-Woëvre, Fr. 81/E5
Fresnillo, Mex. 198/E4
Fresno, Col. 207/K7
Fresno, Ca, US 174/C2
Fresno (riv.), Ca, US 174/B2
Fresno, Tx, US 177/M9
Fresno (res.), Mt, US 171/J3
Fresnoy-le-Grand, Fr. 80/C4
Fresse-sur-Moselle, Fr. 86/C2
Fressenneville, Fr. 80/A3
Fresta, Swe. 65/A1
Fretani (mts.), It. 92/D3
Fretin, Fr. 80/C2
Freuchie (lake), Sc, UK 59/C3
Freudenberg, Ger. 81/G2
Freudenberg, Ger. 85/E4
Freudenberg, Ger. 84/C3
Freudenburg, Ger. 81/F4
Freudenstadt, Ger. 87/E1
Frévent, Fr. 80/B3
Frewena, Austl. 155/D4
Frewsburg, NY, US 187/G3
Freycinet (har.), Austl. 156/B3
Freycinet NP, Austl. 158/D4
Freyming-Merlebach, Fr. 81/F5
Freyre, Arg. 212/D4
Freystadt, Ger. 85/E4
Freyung, Ger. 85/G5
Fria, Gui. 140/B4
Fria (cape), Namb. 148/B3
Friant, Ca, US 174/C2
Friant (dam), Ca, US 174/C2
Friant-Kern (canal), Ca, US 174/C3
Friars Point, Ms, US 188/B3
Frías, Peru 208/B2
Frías, Arg. 212/C4
Fribourg, Swi. 86/D4
Fribourg (canton), Swi. 86/D4
Frick, Swi. 86/E3
Frickenhausen am Main, Ger. 84/D3
Friday Harbor, Wa, US 170/C3
Fridingen an der Donau, Ger. 87/E1
Fridley, Mn, US 183/P6
Fridolfing, Ger. 85/F6
Friedberg, Ger. 84/B2
Friedberg, Ger. 84/D6
Friedeburg, Ger. 79/E2
Friedland, Ger. 79/G6
Friedrichsdorf, Ger. 84/B2
Friedrichshafen (arpt.), Ger. 87/F2
Friedrichshafen, Ger. 87/F2
Friedrichstadt, Ger. 66/C4
Friedrichsthal, Ger. 81/G5
Frielendorf, Ger. 79/G7
Friend, Ks, US 178/D1
Friend, Ne, US 181/F3
Friendship, Ar, US 179/H3
Friendship, Tn, US 188/C3
Friendship, Wi, US 181/K2
Friendswood, Tx, US 177/M9
Frierson, La, US 176/H1
Friesenhagen, Ger. 81/G2
Friesenheim, Ger. 86/D1
Friesland (prov.), Neth. 78/C2
Friesoythe, Ger. 79/E2
Friggesby, Fin. 65/E4
Frignano, It. 92/D6
Frignicourt, Fr. 81/D6
Friguiagbé, Gui. 140/B4
Frimley, Eng, UK 56/A3
Frinton, Eng, UK 63/H3
Frio (riv.), Tx, US 199/F2
Frio Draw (riv.), NM,Tx, US 178/C3
Friockheim, Sc, UK 59/D3
Friol, Sp. 72/B1
Friona, Tx, US 178/C3
Frisange, Lux. 81/F4
Frisco, Tx, US 176/L6
Frisco City, Al, US 190/E2
Frissell (mt.), Ct, US 187/K3
Fristad, Swe. 66/E3
Fritch, Tx, US 178/D3
Fritsla, Swe. 66/E3
Fritzlar, Ger. 79/G6
Friuli (reg.), It. 93/G1
Friuli-Venezia Giula (prov.), It. 71/K3
Friville-Escarbotin, Fr. 80/A3
Frizington, Eng, UK 60/E2
Frobisher (bay), Nun, Can. 167/K2
Frodsham, Eng, UK 61/F5
Frogmore, Eng, UK 56/A3
Frogue, Ky, US 188/E2
Frohavel (inlet), Nor. 64/D3
Frohnleiten, Aus. 71/L3
Froid, Mt, US 182/B3
Froid (mtn.), Fr. 90/C3
Froid-Chapelle, Belg. 81/D3
Froideconche, Fr. 86/C2
Froissy, Fr. 80/B4
Froland, Nor. 66/C2
Frolovo, Rus. 97/G2
Fromberg, Mt, US 173/J1
Frome (lake), Austl. 153/D4
Frome (riv.), Austl. 157/H4
Frome (riv.), Eng, UK 62/D2
Frome, Eng, UK 62/D4
Frome (riv.), Eng, UK 62/D5
Froncles, Fr. 86/B1
Front (range), Co, US 180/B3
Front Royal, Va, US 189/H1
Fronteira, Ang. 146/D4
Fronteira, Port. 72/B3
Frontenex, Fr. 90/C1
Frontenhausen, Ger. 85/F5
Frontera, Mex. 200/C2
Frontera Comalapa, Mex. 200/C3
Frontier, ND, US 182/F4
Frontier, Sk, Can. 171/K3
Frontignan, Fr. 70/E5
Fronton, Fr. 70/D5
Frosinone (prov.), It. 92/C4
Frosinone, It. 92/C4
Frösö, Swe. 64/E3
Frosolone, It. 92/D4
Frost, Tx, US 177/F1
Frostburg, Md, US 187/G5
Frostproof, Fl, US 190/M8
Frösunda, Swe. 65/B1
Frotey-lès-Vesoul, Fr. 86/C2
Frouard, Fr. 81/F6
Frövi, Swe. 66/F2
Frower (pt.), Ire. 58/B6
Frøya (isl.), Nor. 64/D3
Frozen (str.), Nun, Can. 167/H2
Fruges, Fr. 80/B2
Fruitdale, Al, US 190/D2
Fruitland, On, Can. 186/T9
Fruitland, Id, US 172/E1
Fruitland, Md, US 189/K1
Fruitvale, BC, Can. 170/F3
Fruitvale, Wa, US 170/D4
Frunze (int'l arpt.), Kyr. 125/B3
Frunzens'ke, Ukr. 99/H5
Frunzivka, Ukr. 98/E4
Fruška Gora (mts.), Cro.,Yugo. 93/H1
Fruška Gora NP, Cro. 76/D3
Frutal, Braz. 213/G1
Frutigen, Swi. 86/D4
Frutillar, Chile 214/B4
Fruvik, Swe. 65/B1
Fryazino, Rus. 94/X9
Frýdek-Místek, Czh. 69/K4
Fryeburg, Me, US 187/L2
Fu Xian, China 106/B4
Fu'an, China 113/H3
Fubo, Ang. 146/C4
Fucecchio, It. 89/D6
Fuch, WSah. 136/B5
Fucheng, China 106/D3
Fuchū, Japan 110/C3
Fuchū, Japan 109/C2
Fuchun, China 113/H2
Fuchun (riv.), China 106/D5
Fude, China 113/H3
Fuding, China 113/J3
Fuengirola, Sp. 72/C4
Fuenlabrada, Sp. 73/N9
Fuensalida, Sp. 72/C2
Fuente, Sp. 73/N8
Fuente de Cantos, Sp. 72/B3
Fuente del Maestre, Sp. 72/B3
Fuente Obejuna, Sp. 72/C3
Fuentelapeña, Sp. 72/C2
Fuentes de Oñoro, Sp. 72/B2
Fuentesaúco, Sp. 72/C2
Fuerte (riv.), Mex. 198/C3
Fuerte Olimpo, Par. 212/E2
Fuerteventura (isl.), Canl., Sp. 136/B3
Fufang, China 113/H3
Fuga (isl.), Phil. 114/C1
Fuglebjerg, Den. 66/D4
Fugong, China 119/G2
Fugou, China 106/C4
Fuhai, China 125/E2
Fuhlsbüttel (Hamburg) (int'l arpt.), Ger. 79/G1
Fuhne (riv.), Ger. 68/F3
Fuhse (riv.), Ger. 79/H4
Fuji, Japan 111/F3
Fuji (riv.), Japan 111/F3
Fuji-Hakone-Izu NP, Japan 111/F3
Fuji-san (peak), Japan 111/F3
Fujian (prov.), China 113/H3
Fujieda, Japan 111/F3
Fujihashi, Japan 109/K4
Fujiidera, Japan 109/J6
Fujikawa, Japan 109/B3
Fujimi, Japan 109/D2
Fujino, Japan 109/C2
Fujinomiya, Japan 109/B3
Fujioka, Japan 111/F2
Fujioka, Japan 109/M5
Fujioka, Japan 109/D1
Fujisawa, Japan 111/F3
Fujishiro, Japan 109/E2
Fujiwara, Japan 109/K5
Fujiyoshida, Japan 111/F3
Fukagawa, Japan 108/C2
Fukang, China 125/E3
Fukaya, Japan 109/C1
Fukiage, Japan 109/C1
Fukuchiyama, Japan 109/H5
Fukue, Japan 110/A4
Fukue (isl.), Japan 105/K5
Fukui, Japan 110/E2
Fukui (pref.), Japan 110/E3
Fukuoka (pref.), Japan 110/B4
Fukuoka, Japan 110/B4
Fukuoka (int'l arpt.), Japan 110/B4
Fukuoka, Japan 109/M4
Fukuroi, Japan 111/E3
Fukushima, Japan 111/G2
Fukushima (pref.), Japan 111/F2
Fukushima, Japan 108/B3
Fukuyama, Japan 110/C3
Fulacunda, GBis. 140/B4
Fūlādī (mtn.), Afg. 127/J2
Fulbourn, Eng, UK 63/G2
Fulbright, Tx, US 179/G4
Fulda (riv.), Ger. 68/E3
Fulda, Ger. 84/C1
Fulda, Mn, US 181/G2
Fulford, Eng, UK 61/G4
Fuling, China 113/E2
Fullarton, Trin. 205/F2
Fullerton, La, US 190/B2
Fullerton, Ca, US 192/G8
Fullerton, Ne, US 180/F3
Fullerton (Whitehall), Pa, US 194/C2
Fully, Swi. 86/D5
Fulpmes, Aus. 87/H3
Fulton, Al, US 190/E2
Fulton, Ar, US 179/H4
Fulton (co.), Ga, US 189/M7
Fulton, Ky, US 188/C2
Fulton, Ks, US 179/G1
Fulton, Mo, US 179/J1
Fulton, Ms, US 188/C3
Fulton, NY, US 187/H3
Fulton, On, Can. 186/T9
Fulton, Tx, US 176/F3
Fultondale, Al, US 188/D4
Fulufjället(peak) 66/E1
Fuluo, China 113/F3
Fulwood, Eng, UK 61/F4
Fumaiolo (peak), It. 89/F6
Fumay, Fr. 81/D4
Fumel, Fr. 70/D4
Fumin, China 112/D3
Funabashi, Japan 109/D2
Funafuti (cap.), Tuv. 162/G5

257
Hamād – Helen

Hamādat Marzūq (plat.), Libya 137/H4
Ḥamādat Tinghert (uplands), Libya 137/H3
Ḥamāh (prov.), Syria 130/E2
Ḥamāh, Syria 130/E2
Hamah (prov.), Syria 128/D3
Hamajima, Japan 109/L7
Hamakita, Japan 111/E3
Hamam, Turk. 130/E1
Hamamatsu, Japan 111/E3
Hamami (reg.), Mrta. 136/C5
Hamanaka, Japan 108/D2
Hamar, Nor. 66/D1
Ḥamāṭah (peak), Egypt 135/G3
Hamath Tiberias NP, Isr. 131/D3
Hamatombetsu, Japan 108/C1
Hambergen, Ger. 79/F2
Hamble, Eng, UK 63/E5
Hambleton (hills), Eng, UK 61/G3
Hambühren, Ger. 79/G3
Hamburg, Ar, US 179/J4
Hamburg (state), Ger. 66/D5
Hamburg, NY, US 187/G3
Hamburg, Ger. 79/G1
Hamburg, Ia, US 181/G3
Hamburg, Pa, US 194/C2
Hamburg, NJ, US 194/D1
Hamburg (Fuhlsbüttel) (int'l arpt.), Ger. 79/G1
Ḥamḍ (wadi), SAr. 126/C3
Ḥamḍah, SAr. 126/D5
Ḥamdānah, SAr. 126/D5
Hamden, Ct, US 187/K4
Hamden, NY, US 187/J3
Hamden, Oh, US 189/F1
Häme (prov.), Fin. 64/G3
Hämeenkyrö, Fin. 67/K1
Hämeenlinna, Fin. 67/L1
Hamelin, Austl. 156/B3
Hamelin Pool (bay), Austl. 156/B3
Hameln, Ger. 79/G4
Hamero Hadad, Eth. 144/B4
Hamersley (range), Austl. 153/A3
Hamersley Range NP, Austl. 156/C2
Hamersville, Oh, US 188/F1
Hamford Water (inlet), Eng, UK 63/H3
Hamgyŏng (mts.), NKor. 105/K3
Hamgyŏng-bukto (prov.), NKor. 107/E2
Hamgyŏng-namdo (prov.), NKor. 107/D2
Hamhŭ-si (prov.), NKor. 107/D3
Hamhŭng, NKor. 107/D3
Hami, China 104/C3
Ḥamīdīyeh, Iran 129/G4
Hamill, SD, US 180/E2
Hamilton, Austl. 158/B3
Hamilton, On, Can. 186/T9
Hamilton (har.), On, Can. 186/T9
Hamilton (inlet), Nf, Can. 165/M4
Hamilton, NZ 161/C2
Hamilton, Sc, UK 59/B5
Hamilton, Al, US 188/D3
Hamilton (mt.), Ca, US 193/L12
Hamilton, Co, US 173/K3
Hamilton (lake), Fl, US 190/M7
Hamilton, Ga, US 188/E4
Hamilton, Ks, US 179/F2
Hamilton, Mi, US 186/C3
Hamilton, Mo, US 181/H4
Hamilton, Mt, US 171/G4
Hamilton, NY, US 187/J3
Hamilton (mtn.), NY, US 187/J3
Hamilton, Oh, US 186/D5
Hamilton, Tx, US 177/E2
Hamilton Mil. Res., NY, US 195/J9
Hamilton-Wentworth (co.), On, Can. 186/S9
Ḥamīm (wadi), Libya 134/D2
Hamina, Fin. 67/M1
Hamiota, Mb, Can. 182/D2
Hamīrpur, India 124/D4
Hamīrpur, India 122/C3
Hamju, NKor. 107/D3
Hamlet, NC, US 189/H3
Hamlin, Tx, US 178/D4
Hamlin, WV, US 189/F1
Hamm, Ger. 81/G2
Hamm, Ger. 84/B3
Hamm, Ger. 79/E5
Hamma-Bouziane, Alg. 138/K6
Ḥammām Al Anf, Tun. 74/B4
Ḥammāmāt (gulf), Gabon 137/H1
Hammāmāt (gulf), Tun. 92/F3
Hammanskraal, SAfr. 149/F5
Hammarland, Fin. 67/H1
Hammarön (isl.), Swe. 66/E2
Hammarsjön (lake), Swe. 65/L7
Hammarstrand, Swe. 64/F3
Hamme, Belg. 81/D1
Hamme (riv.), Ger. 79/F2
Hammel, Den. 66/C3
Hammelburg, Ger. 84/C2
Hammer (cr.), Pa, US 194/B3
Hammerfest, Nor. 64/G1
Hammershus, Den. 66/F4
Hammersmith and Fulham (bor.), Eng, UK 56/A1
Hammett, Id, US 172/F2
Hamminkeln, Ger. 78/D5
Hammon, Ok, US 178/E3
Hammonasset (pt.), Ct, US 195/F1
Hammond, In, US 186/C4
Hammond, La, US 190/C2
Hammond, Mt, US 180/B1
Hammond Street, Eng, UK 56/C1
Hammonton, NJ, US 194/D4
Hamnvik, Nor. 64/F1
Hamois, Belg. 81/E3
Hamon, Congo 146/C4
Hamont-Achel, Belg. 78/C6
Hamoud, Mrta. 140/C3
Hampden, ND, US 182/E3
Hampden, NZ 161/B4
Hampden Sydney, Va, US 189/H2
Hampshire, Il, US 181/K2
Hampshire Downs (hills), Eng, UK 63/E4
Hampstead (nbrhd.), Eng, UK 56/C2
Hampstead, Md, US 194/B4
Hampton, Ar, US 179/H4
Hampton, Fl, US 191/G3
Hampton, Ia, US 181/H2
Hampton, NB, Can. 184/E3
Hampton, NH, US 187/L3
Hampton, Or, US 172/C2
Hampton, Pa, US 194/A4
Hampton, SC, US 189/G4
Hampton, Tn, US 189/F2
Hampton, Va, US 189/J2
Hampton Bays, NY, US 195/F2
Hampton Court, Eng, UK 56/C2
Hampton Nat'l Hist. Site, Md, US 194/B5
Hampton Park (nbrhd.), Austl. 158/G6
Hampton Roads (est.), Va, US 189/J2
Hamp'yŏng, SKor. 107/D5
Ḥamrat ash Shaykh, Sudan 142/E2
Hamtramck, Mi, US 193/F7
Hamuku, Indo. 117/J4
Hamura, Japan 109/C2
Hamyang, SKor. 107/D5
Hamyŏl, SKor. 107/D4
Han (riv.), China 103/M6
Hana (riv.), India 122/C5
Hanahan, SC, US 189/G4
Hanainef, Erit. 144/B2
Hanak, Turk. 97/G4
Ḥanak, SAr. 135/H3
Hanamaki, Japan 108/B4
Hanan, Eth. 144/C4
Hanang (peak), Tanz. 145/A3
Hanau, Ger. 84/B2
Hanazono, Japan 109/C1
Hanceville, Al, US 188/D3
Hancheng, China 106/B4
Hanches, Fr. 83/G3
Hancock (lake), Fl, US 190/M8
Hancock, Md, US 187/G5
Hancock, Mi, US 183/K4
Hancock, Mn, US 182/G5
Hancock, NY, US 187/J4
Hancock, Wi, US 181/K1
Hancocks Bridge, NJ, US 194/C5
Handa, Japan 109/L6
Handae-ri, NKor. 107/D2
Handan, China 106/C3
Handawor, India 124/C2
Handel, Sk, Can. 171/K1
Handeloh, Ger. 79/G2
Handen, Swe. 65/B1
Handeni, Tanz. 145/B3
Handiā, India 122/D3
Handsworth, Sk, Can. 182/C3
Handsworth, Eng, UK 63/E1
Hanford, Ca, US 174/C2
Hanford Site, Wa, US 170/E4
Hangayn (mts.), Mong. 100/K5
Hanggin Qi, China 106/B3
Hanging Rock (mtn.), NC, US 189/G2
Hangingstone (hill), Eng, UK 62/C5
Hangklip (cape), SAfr. 150/L11
Hangman (cr.), Wa, US 170/F4
Hangö (Hanko), Fin. 67/K2
Hangu, Pak. 124/A3
Hangu, China 106/H7
Hangzhou, China 106/L9
Hangzhou (bay), China 106/L9
Hanhofen, Ger. 84/B4
Hanhöhiy (mts.), Mong. 104/C2
Hani, Turk. 128/E2
Haninge, Swe. 66/H2
Hanja (riv.), Ang. 148/B2
Hanjalipan, Indo. 116/D4
Hanjiang, China 113/H3
Hankensbüttel, Ger. 79/H3
Hankey, SAfr. 150/D4
Hankinson, ND, US 182/F4
Hanko (Hangö), Fin. 67/K2
Hanle, India 125/C5
Hanley, Sk, Can. 171/L2
Hanmer, NZ 161/C3
Hann (mt.), Austl. 154/B3
Hanna, La, US 190/B2
Hanna, Ab, Can. 171/J2
Hannaford, ND, US 182/E4
Hannah, ND, US 182/E3
Hannahs Mill, Ga, US 188/E4
Hannan, Japan 109/H7
Hannibal, Oh, US 186/F5
Hannibal, NY, US 187/H3
Hannibal, Mo, US 181/J4
Hanningfield (res.), Eng, UK 56/E2
Hannō, Japan 109/C2
Hannover, Ger. 79/G4
Hannover (int'l arpt.), Ger. 79/G4
Hannut, Belg. 81/E2
Hanöbukten (bay), Swe. 64/E5
Hanoi (Ha Noi) (cap.), Viet. 112/E4
Hanover, On, Can. 186/F2
Hanover (isl.), Chile 215/B6
Hanover, SAfr. 150/D3
Hanover, Il, US 181/J2
Hanover, In, US 188/E1
Hanover, Ks, US 181/F4
Hanover, Mn, US 183/N6
Hanover, NH, US 187/K3
Hanover, Pa, US 194/B4
Hanover, Va, US 189/J2
Hanover Park, Il, US 193/P16
Hānsdiha, India 123/F3
Hansen (dam), Ca, US 192/F7
Hanshan, China 106/D5
Hānsi, India 124/C5
Hanska (lake), Mn, US 181/G1
Hanson (bay), NZ 161/E3
Hanstedt, Ger. 79/H2
Hanstholm, Den. 66/C3
Hanston, Ks, US 178/E1
Hansville, Wa, US 193/B2
Hantengri Feng (peak), China 125/D3
Hantsport, NS, Can. 184/E3
Hantzsch (riv.), Nun, Can. 167/J2
Hanumāngarh, India 124/C5
Hanuy (riv.), Mong. 104/E2
Hanwood, Austl. 159/C2
Hanyū, Japan 109/D1
Hanyuan, China 112/D2
Hanza, Ang. 146/C5
Hanzhong, China 104/F5
Hao (isl.), FrPol. 163/L6
Haoshan, China 113/G3
Haouach, Ouadi (riv.), Chad 142/D1
Håøya (isl.), Nor. 64/S8
Haparanda, Swe. 94/E2
Hapch'ŏn, SKor. 107/E5
Hapeville, Ga, US 189/M7
Happy Camp, Ca, US 172/B3
Happy Jack, La, US 190/D3
Happy Jack, Az, US 175/G3
Happy Valley (res.), Austl. 157/M9
Happy Valley-Goose Bay, Nf, Can. 167/K3
Haptŏk, SKor. 107/D4
Hāpur, India 122/A1
Ḥaql, SAr. 135/G2
Haquira, Peru 208/C4
Har (lake), Mong. 104/C2
Har Karmel (peak), Isr. 131/C3
Har Meron (peak), Isr. 131/C3
Har Nur, China 105/J2
Har Ramon (peak), Isr. 130/D4
Har Tavor (peak), Isr. 131/C3
Har Us (lake), Mong. 104/C2
Har-Ayrag, Mong. 104/F2
Har-Us (riv.), Mong. 104/D2
Hara, Japan 109/A2
Haraa (riv.), Mong. 104/F2
Ḥaraḍ, SAr. 126/E4
Ḥaraḍ, Yem. 144/B1
Ḥarajah, SAr. 126/D5
Haramachi, Japan 111/G2
Harappa (ruin), Pak. 124/B4
Harare (cap.), Zim. 149/F3
Harare (int'l arpt.), Zim. 149/F3
Haravilliers, Fr. 56/J4
Haraz, Chad 142/C2
Haraze-Mangueigne, Chad 142/D3
Harbel, Libr. 140/C5
Harbeson, De, US 194/C6
Harbin, China 105/K2
Harbiye, Turk. 130/E1
Harbonnières, Fr. 80/B4
Harboøre, Den. 66/C3
Harbor Beach, Mi, US 186/E3
Harbor City (nbrhd.), Ca, US 192/F8
Harbor Springs, Mi, US 186/D2
Harbour Breton, Nf, Can. 185/K2
Harbour Grace, Nf, Can. 185/L2
Harbour Main, Nf, Can. 185/L2
Harburg, Ger. 79/G2
Harburg, Ger. 84/D5
Harbury, Eng, UK 63/E2
Hårby, Den. 66/D4
Hard, Aus. 87/F3
Hardā, India 118/C3
Hardangervidda NP, Nor. 66/B1
Hardangervidda NP, Nor. 64/C3
Hardap (dam), Namb. 148/C5
Hardau (riv.), Ger. 79/H3
Hardaway, Al, US 188/E4
Hardee (co.), Fl, US 190/M8
Hardeeville, SC, US 189/G4
Hardegsen, Ger. 79/G5
Hardelot-Plage, Fr. 80/A2
Harden City, Ok, US 179/F3
Hardenberg, Neth. 78/D3
Harderwijk, Neth. 78/C4
Hardesar, India 124/C5
Hardheim, Ger. 84/C3
Hardin, Ky, US 188/C2
Hardin, Il, US 181/J4
Hardin, Mt, US 171/L5
Hardin, Tx, US 177/G2
Harding, SAfr. 151/E3
Harding (res.), Ga, US 188/E4
Hardinsburg, Ky, US 188/D2
Hardisty, Ab, Can. 171/J1
Hardoi, India 122/C2
Hardoi Branch (riv.), India 122/C2
Hardricourt, Fr. 56/H4
Hardscrabble Wash (riv.), Az, US 175/H3
Hardtner, Ks, US 179/E2
Hardwār, India 127/L3
Hardwick, Ga, US 189/F4
Hardwood (mtn.), Me, US 187/L1
Hardy, Ar, US 179/J2
Hardy, Ne, US 180/F3
Hardy (pen.), Chile 215/C7
Hare Bay, Nf, Can. 185/K1
Hare Dimona (peak), Isr. 130/D4
Harefield, Eng, UK 56/B2
Harelbeke, Belg. 80/C2
Haren, Neth. 78/D2
Haren, Ger. 79/E3
Hārer, Eth. 144/B3
Harerge (prov.), Eth. 144/B3
Harewa, Eth. 144/B3
Harfleur, Fr. 83/F1
Harford (co.), Md, US 194/B4
Hargele, Eth. 144/B4
Hargesheim, Ger. 81/G4
Hargeville, Fr. 56/H5
Hargeysa, Som. 144/C3
Hargeysa (int'l arpt.), Som. 144/C3
Harghita (prov.), Rom. 77/G2
Harghita (peak), Rom. 77/G2
Hargīgo, Erit. 144/A2
Harhorin, Mong. 104/E2
Hari (str.), Est. 67/K2
Hari (river), Indo. 115/C3
Hari (riv.), Indo. 116/B4
Ḥarīb, Yem. 144/C2
Haribes, Namb. 148/C5
Harihar, India 121/B3
Hariharganj, India 123/E3
Harīke, India 124/C4
Ḥārim, Syria 130/E1
Harima (sea), Japan 110/D3
Harima (bay), Japan 109/G6
Harima, Japan 109/G6
Ḥarīmā, Jor. 131/D3
Haringey (bor.), Eng, UK 56/C2
Haringhāta (riv.), Bang. 123/G4
Haringvliet (chan.), Neth. 78/B5
Haringvlietdam (dam), Neth. 78/B5
Harīpur, Pak. 124/B3
Harīrūd (riv.), Afg. 103/F6
Ḥāris, WBnk. 131/C4
Harisal, India 118/C3
Harjavalta, Fin. 67/K1
Harker Heights, Tx, US 177/F2
Harlan, Ky, US 189/F2
Harlan, Ia, US 181/G3
Harlan Co. (lake), Ne, US 180/E3
Harlan County (dam), Ne, US 180/E3
Harlech, Wal, UK 60/D6
Harlem (nbrhd.), NY, US 195/K8
Harlem, Ga, US 189/F4
Harlem, Mt, US 171/K3
Harleston, Eng, UK 63/H2
Harleton, Tx, US 177/G1
Hårlev, Den. 65/J7
Harleyville, SC, US 189/G4
Harlingen, Neth. 78/C2
Harlingen, Tx, US 176/F4
Harlington, Eng, UK 63/F3
Harlow, ND, US 182/E3
Harlow, Eng, UK 56/D1
Harlowton, Mt, US 171/K4
Harmannsdorf, Aus. 77/N7
Harmelen, Neth. 78/B4
Harmony, Mn, US 181/H2
Harnātānr, India 123/E2
Harnes, Fr. 80/B3
Harney (valley), Or, US 172/D2
Harney (lake), Or, US 172/D2
Harney (peak), SD, US 180/C2
Harney, Md, US 194/A4
Harni, Bang. 123/H4
Harnoli, Pak. 124/A3
Harö (isl.), Swe. 65/B1
Haro, Sp. 70/B5
Haro (cape), Mex. 198/C3
Harold, Ca, US 192/B1
Harpenden, Eng, UK 63/F3
Harper, Ks, US 179/E2
Harper, Libr. 140/D5
Harper, Wa, US 193/B2
Harper, Or, US 172/E2
Harper (lake), Ca, US 174/D3
Harper, Tx, US 177/E2
Harper Woods, Mi, US 193/F7
Harpers Ferry Nat'l Hist. Park, WV, US 187/H5
Harpersville, Al, US 188/D4
Harperville, Ms, US 188/C4
Harpeth (riv.), Tn, US 188/D2
Harpstedt, Ger. 79/F3
Harqin Qi, China 105/H3
Harqin Zuoyi Monggolzu Zizhixian, China 106/D2
Ḥarrah, Yem. 144/D2
Harrai, India 122/B4
Harran, Turk. 128/D2
Ḥarrān al 'Awāmīd, Syria 131/F2
Harrell, Ar, US 179/H4
Harricana (riv.), Qu, Can. 167/J4
Harrietsham, Eng, UK 56/F3
Harrietts Bluff, Ga, US 191/H2
Harriman, Tn, US 188/E3
Harriman, NY, US 194/D1
Harrington, Austl. 158/E1
Harrington, De, US 194/C6
Harrington Park, NJ, US 195/K8
Harris (isl.), Sc, UK 57/Q8
Harris (lake), Austl. 157/G4
Harris (mtn.), Tn, US 188/E2
Harris (mt.), Austl. 157/F3
Harris (co.), Tx, US 177/M9
Harrisburg, Or, US 172/B1
Harrisburg, Ne, US 180/C3
Harrisburg, Il, US 188/C2
Harrisburg, Ar, US 188/B3
Harrisburg (cap.), Pa, US 194/B3
Harrisburg (arpt.), Pa, US 194/B3
Harrislee, Ger. 66/C4
Harrismith, SAfr. 150/E3
Harrison (cape), Nf, Can. 167/L3
Harrison (lake), BC, Can. 170/C3
Harrison, Ar, US 179/H2
Harrison, Ga, US 189/F4
Harrison, Id, US 170/F4
Harrison, Mi, US 186/D2
Harrison, Ne, US 180/C2
Harrison, NJ, US 195/J9
Harrison, NY, US 195/L8
Harrison, Oh, US 186/D5
Harrison, Tn, US 188/E3
Harrisonburg, La, US 190/C2
Harrisonburg, Va, US 189/H1
Harrisonville, Mo, US 179/G1
Harriston, On, Can. 186/F3
Harriston, Ms, US 190/C2
Harristown, Il, US 181/K4
Harrisville, Ms, US 190/C2
Harrisville, Mi, US 186/E2
Harrisville, WV, US 189/G1
Harrodsburg, In, US 188/D1
Harrodsburg, Ky, US 188/E2
Harrogate, Eng, UK 61/G4
Harrogate-Shawnee, Tn, US 188/F2
Harrold, Tx, US 178/E3
Harrow, On, Can. 186/E3
Harrow (bor.), Eng, UK 56/B2
Harrow (nbrhd.), Eng, UK 56/C2
Harrow, Austl. 158/B3
Harry S Truman (dam), Mo, US 179/H1
Harry S Truman (res.), Mo, US 181/H4
Harry S Truman Nat'l Hist. Site, Mo, US 181/G4
Harsefeld, Ger. 79/G2
Harsewinkel, Ger. 79/F5
Harskamp, Neth. 78/C4
Harson's Island, Mi, US 193/G6
Hart, Tx, US 178/C3
Hart, Mi, US 186/C3
Hart (riv.), Eng, UK 56/A3
Hart (isl.), NY, US 195/K8
Hart (lake), Or, US 172/C2
Hart (riv.), Yk, Can. 166/C2
Hart (mtn.), Or, US 172/D2
Hart (mt.), Austl. 154/B4
Hart Fell (peak), Sc, UK 59/C6
Hart Mtn. Nat'l Antelope Refuge, Or, US 172/D2
Ḥartā, Jor. 131/D3
Hartbeesrivier (riv.), SAfr. 150/C3
Harte (mtn.), Can. 182/D1
Hårteigen (peak), Nor. 66/B1
Hartelkanaal (riv.), Neth. 78/B5
Hartford, Libr. 140/C5
Hartford, Al, US 191/F2
Hartford (cap.), Ct, US 187/K4
Hartford, Ks, US 179/G1
Hartford, Ky, US 188/D2
Hartford, NJ, US 194/D4
Hartford, Wi, US 186/B3
Hartford City, In, US 186/D4
Hartheim, Ger. 86/D2
Harthill, Sc, UK 59/C5
Hartington, Ne, US 181/F2
Hartkirchen, Aus. 85/H5
Hartland, NB, Can. 184/D2
Hartland, Vt, US 187/K3
Hartland, Mi, US 193/E6
Hartland (pt.), Eng, UK 62/B4
Hartland, Eng, UK 62/B4
Hartlebury, Eng, UK 62/D2
Hartlepool, Eng, UK 61/G2
Hartleton, Pa, US 194/A2
Hartley, Eng, UK 56/D2
Hartley, Ia, US 181/G2
Hartley Wintney, Eng, UK 56/A3
Hartly, De, US 194/C5
Hartmannberge (mts.), Namb. 148/B3
Hartney, Mb, Can. 182/D3
Harts, WV, US 189/F1
Harts (riv.), SAfr. 148/E5
Harts Range, Austl. 157/G2
Hartsdale, NY, US 195/K7
Hartselle, Al, US 188/D3
Hartsfield Atlanta Int'l (int'l arpt.), Ga, US 189/M7
Hartshill, Eng, UK 63/E1
Hartshorn, Mo, US 179/J2
Hartshorne, Ok, US 179/G3
Hartsön (isl.), Swe. 65/A2
Hartstene (isl.), Wa, US 193/B3
Hartsville, Tn, US 188/D2
Hartsville, SC, US 189/G3
Hartville, Mo, US 179/H2
Hartwell (dam), Ga, US 189/F3
Hartwell, Ga, US 189/F3
Hartwell (res.), SC, US 189/F3
Hartz Mountain NP, Austl. 158/C4
Haruhi, Japan 109/L5
Harun (peak), Indo. 114/A4
Hārūnābād, Pak. 124/B5
Hārūt (riv.), Afg. 127/H2
Harvard, Ma, US 187/L3
Harvard, Il, US 181/K2
Harvard, Ne, US 180/E3
Harvest, Al, US 188/D3
Harvey, ND, US 182/E4
Harvey, Mi, US 183/L4
Harvey, NB, Can. 184/E3
Harvey, Il, US 193/Q16
Harvey, Austl. 156/B5
Harveys (lake), Pa, US 194/B1
Harwich, Eng, UK 63/H3
Harwood, ND, US 182/F4
Harworth, Eng, UK 61/G5
Haryana (state), India 125/C6
Harz (mts.), Ger. 68/F3
Hasan (peak), Turk. 128/C2
Hasan Abdāl, Pak. 124/B3
Hasanpur, India 122/B1
Ḥāṣbayyā, Leb. 131/D2
Hasbrouck Heights, NJ, US 195/J8
Hascombe, Eng, UK 56/B3
Hasdo (riv.), India 122/D4
Hase (riv.), Ger. 68/D2
Hasel (riv.), Ger. 84/D1
Haselünne, Ger. 79/E3
Hasenmatt (peak), Swi. 86/D3
Hashaat, Mong. 104/E2
Hashima, Japan 109/L5
Hashimoto, Japan 110/D3
Hashtgerd, Iran 129/G3
Hasi el Farsía (well), WSah. 136/C4
Hāsilpur, Pak. 124/B5
Haskell, Ok, US 179/G3
Haskell, Tx, US 178/E4
Haskell, Ar, US 179/H3
Haslach an der Mühl, Aus. 85/H5
Haslach im Kinzigtal, Ger. 86/E1
Hasle bei Burgdorf, Swi. 86/D3
Haslemere, Eng, UK 63/F4
Hasler (cr.), Mi, US 193/F6
Haslet, Tx, US 176/K7
Haslett, Mi, US 186/D3
Haslev, Den. 65/H7
Haslingden, Eng, UK 61/F4
Haslington, Eng, UK 61/F5
Hasloh, Ger. 79/G1
Hāsmāi, Bang. 123/G3
Haspra, Ukr. 99/H5
Haspres, Fr. 80/C3
Hassa, Turk. 130/E1
Hassan (El Aaiún) (int'l arpt.), WSah. 136/B4
Hassayampa (riv.), Az, US 175/F3
Hassberge (hills), Ger. 84/D2
Hasse, Tx, US 176/E2
Hassel, Ger. 79/G3
Hassel Sound (str.), Nun, Can. 167/S7
Hasselt, Belg. 81/E2
Hasselt, Neth. 78/D3
Hassfurt, Ger. 84/D2
Hassi Bahbah, Alg. 138/G5
Hassi bou Zid (well), Alg. 137/F3
Hassi el Hadjar (well), Alg. 137/G3
Hassi el Mislane (well), Alg. 137/H4
Hassi er Rebib (well), Alg. 137/G2
Hassi Messaoud, Alg. 137/G3
Hässleholm, Swe. 66/E3
Hasslo (int'l arpt.), Swe. 66/G2
Hassloch, Ger. 84/B4
Haste, Ger. 79/G4
Hastings, Fl, US 191/H3
Hastings, Mi, US 186/D3
Hastings, Pa, US 187/G4
Hastings, SLeo. 140/B4
Hastings, NZ 161/D2
Hastings, Ne, US 180/E3
Hastings, Mn, US 183/Q7
Hastings (dam), Mn, US 183/Q7
Hastings, Eng, UK 63/G5
Hastings, Austl. 159/B4
Hastings Battlesite, Eng, UK 63/G5
Hastings-On-Hudson, NY, US 195/K7
Hästveda, Swe. 65/K6
Hasuda, Japan 109/D2
Hasunuma, Japan 109/E2
Hasvik, Nor. 64/G1
Haswell, Co, US 178/C1
Hat (mtn.), Ca, US 172/C3
Hat Chao Mai NP, Thai. 120/B5
Hāt Gāmāria, India 123/E4
Hat Head, Austl. 158/E1
Hat Head NP, Austl. 158/E1
Hat Nai Yang NP, Thai. 120/B5
Hat Yai, Thai. 120/C5
Hat Yai (int'l arpt.), Thai. 120/C5
Hatansuudal, Mong. 104/E3
Hatashō, Japan 109/K5
Hatavch, Mong. 104/G2
Hatay (prov.), Turk. 128/C2
Hatboro, Pa, US 194/C3
Hatch, Ut, US 175/F2
Hatch, NM, US 175/J4
Hatchechubbee, Al, US 188/E4
Hatcher (peak), Arg. 215/B6
Hatches Creek, Austl. 157/G2
Hatchie (riv.), Tn, US 188/C3
Hatchie NWR, Tn, US 188/C3
Hatchineha (lake), Fl, US 191/H3
Haţeg, Rom. 76/F3
Hatfield, Ar, US 179/G3
Hatfield, Eng, UK 56/C1
Hatfield, Austl. 158/B2
Hatfield, Pa, US 194/C3
Hatfield Peverel, Eng, UK 56/E1
Hatgal, Mong. 104/E1
Hāthazāri, Bang. 123/H4
Hathersage, Eng, UK 61/G5
Hāthras, India 122/B2
Hātia (riv.), Bang. 123/H4
Hātia, North (isl.), Bang. 123/H4
Hātia, South (isl.), Bang. 123/H4
Hato (int'l arpt.), NAnt. 204/D1
Hato Corozal, Col. 204/D3
Hato Mayor, DRep. 197/H4
Hatogaya, Japan 109/D2
Hatoyama, Japan 109/C2
Hatsu (isl.), Japan 109/C3
Hatta, India 122/B3
Hatta, Japan 109/A2
Hattah-Kulkyne NP, Austl. 157/J5
Hattelmala, Fin. 65/E4
Hattem, Neth. 78/D4
Hatten, Fr. 81/G6
Hatten, Ger. 79/F2
Hatteras, NC, US 189/K3
Hatteras (isl.), NC, US 189/K3
Hattersheim am Mein, Ger. 84/B2
Hattiesburg, Ms, US 190/D2
Hattieville, Belz. 200/D2
Hattingen, Ger. 79/E6
Hatton, ND, US 182/F4
Hatton, Sc, UK 59/E2
Hatton, Eng, UK 61/G6
Hatton, Ut, US 175/F1
Hatton, Al, US 188/D3
Hatton, Sk, Can. 171/K2
Hattula, Fin. 67/L1
Håtuna, Swe. 65/A1
Hatvan, Hun. 76/D2
Hatzenbühl, Ger. 84/B4
Hatzfeld, Ger. 79/F6
Hau Bon, Viet. 120/E3
Hau Giang (riv.), Viet. 120/D4
Haubourdin, Fr. 80/B2
Haubstadt, In, US 188/D1
Haud (reg.), Eth. 144/C4
Hauge, Nor. 66/B2
Haugen, Wi, US 183/J5
Haugesund, Nor. 66/A2
Haughton, La, US 179/H4
Haubo, Fin. 65/E3
Haukeligrend, Nor. 66/B2
Haukipudas, Fin. 94/E2
Haune (riv.), Ger. 68/E3
Haunsberg (peak), Aus. 85/F7
Haunstetten, Ger. 84/D6
Hauonselkä (lake), Fin. 65/E3
Hauppauge, NY, US 195/E2
Hauraki (gulf), NZ 161/C2
Haus, Nor. 66/A1
Hausach, Ger. 86/E1
Hausjärvi, Fin. 67/L1
Hausleiten, Aus. 77/N7
Hausstock (peak), Swi. 87/F4
Haut Atlas (mts.), Mor. 136/D3
Haut-Ogooue (prov.), Gabon 146/C3
Haut-Rhin (dept.), Fr. 86/D2
Haut-Zaïre, D.R. Congo 147/F2
Haute-Kotto (pref.), CAfr. 142/D4
Haute-Normandie (pol. reg.), Fr. 70/D2
Haute-Sangha (pref.), CAfr. 142/B4
Haute-Saône (dept.), Fr. 86/B2
Haute-Savoie (dept.), Fr. 86/C5
Hautefeuille, Fr. 56/L5
Hautes Fagnes (uplands), Belg. 81/E3
Hautes-Alpes (dept.), Fr. 90/C3
Hauteurs de Gâtine (uplands), Fr. 70/C3
Hauteville-Lompnes, Fr. 86/B6
Hautmont, Fr. 80/C3
Hautsx (plat.), Alg. 137/E2
Hautsx (plat.), Alg.,Mor. 92/C4
Havana, ND, US 182/F5
Havana, Fl, US 191/F2
Havana, Il, US 181/J3
Havannah, Canal de la (chan.), NCal. 163/V13
Havant, Eng, UK 63/F5
Havasu (lake), Az, Ca, US 174/E3
Havasu Nat'l Wild Ref., Az, US 174/E3
Havasupai Ind. Res., Az, US 175/F2
Havdhem, Swe. 66/H3
Havdrup, Den. 66/E4
Havel (riv.), Ger. 69/G2
Havel (canal), Ger. 68/P6
Havelange, Belg. 81/E3
Haveli, Pak. 124/B4
Haveliān, Pak. 124/B2
Havelländischer Grosser Hauptkanal (canal), Ger. 68/P6
Havelock, NB, Can. 184/E2
Havelock, On, Can. 187/H2
Havelock, NZ 161/C3
Havelock, NC, US 189/J3
Havelock North, NZ 161/D2
Havelte, Neth. 78/D3
Haven, Ks, US 179/F2
Havencore (isl.), Eng, UK 63/G3
Haverfordwest, Wal, UK 62/B3
Haverhill, NH, US 187/K2
Haverhill, Ma, US 187/L3
Haverhill, Fl, US 190/P9
Haverhill, Eng, UK 63/G2
Havering (bor.), Eng, UK 56/D2
Haviland, Ks, US 178/E2
Ḥavīq, Iran 129/G2
Havířov, Czh. 69/K4
Havixbeck, Ger. 79/E5
Havlíčkuv Brod, Czh. 69/H4
Havneby, Den. 66/C4
Havnehage (isl.), Den. 65/G7
Hâvre (riv.), Fr. 82/D6
Havre, Mt, US 171/K3
Havre de Grace, Md, US 194/B4
Havre North, Mt, US 171/K3
Havre-Aubert, Qu, Can. 185/G2
Havre-Saint-Pierre, Qu, Can. 167/K3
Havsa, Turk. 77/H5
Havza, Turk. 96/E4
Haw (peak), NC, US 188/E3
Haw (riv.), NC, US 189/H2
Hawaii (state), US 168/S9
Hawaii (isl.), Hi, US 163/K3
Hawaii Volcanoes Nat'l Pk., Hi, US 168/S10
Hawaiian (isls.), US 163/H2
Hawaiian Gardens, Ca, US 192/F8
Ḥawallī, Kuw. 129/G4
Hawarden, Wal, UK 61/E5
Hawarden, NZ 161/C3
Hawarden, Ia, US 181/F2
Hawea (lake), NZ 161/B4
Hawera, NZ 161/C2
Hawes, Eng, UK 61/F3
Hawesville, Ky, US 188/D2
Haweswater (res.), Eng, UK 61/F2
Hawick, Sc, UK 59/D6
Hawk Point, Mo, US 181/J4
Hawke (bay), NZ 153/H6
Hawke (cape), Austl. 158/E2
Hawker, Austl. 157/H4
Hawkesbury, On, Can. 187/J2
Hawkesbury (pt.), Austl. 154/D2
Hawkesbury (riv.), Austl. 160/G8
Hawkins, Wi, US 183/J5
Hawkins (peak), Ca, US 172/D4
Hawkinsville, Ga, US 189/F4
Hawks Nest (peak), ND, US 182/E4
Hawks Nest, Austl. 158/E2
Hawksbill (mtn.), Va, US 189/H1
Hawley, Mn, US 182/F4
Hawley, Co, US 178/C2
Hawley, Tx, US 177/E1
Haworth, Ok, US 179/G4
Haworth, NJ, US 195/K8
Hawr al Ḥammār (lake), Iraq 129/F4
Ḥawsh 'Isá, Egypt 139/B3
Hawston, SAfr. 150/L11
Hawthorn Hill, Eng, UK 56/A2
Hawthorn Woods, Il, US 193/P15
Hawthorne, Ca, US 192/F8
Hawthorne, Fl, US 191/G3
Hawthorne, NJ, US 195/J8
Hawthorne, NY, US 195/K8
Hawthorne, Nv, US 172/D4
Hawthorne, Tx, US 177/G2
Hawthorne Ammunition Depot, Nv, US 172/D4
Ḥawwārah, Jor. 131/D3
Hawwārat al Maqṭa', Egypt 139/B6
Hawzēn, Eth. 144/A2
Haxby, Eng, UK 61/G3
Haxtun, Co, US 180/C3
Hay, Austl. 159/B2
Hay (cape), Austl. 154/C3
Hay (pt.), Austl. 160/C3
Hay (riv.), Austl. 157/A1
Hay (riv.), Can. 165/F4
Hay (riv.), Ab, BC, Can. 166/E3
Hay, Wal, UK 62/C2
Hay, Wa, US 170/F4
Hay River, NW, Can. 166/E2
Hay Springs, Ne, US 180/C2
Hayachine-san (peak), Japan 108/B4
Hayakawa, Japan 109/A3
Hayama, Japan 109/D3
Hayange, Fr. 81/F5
Haybān (peak), Sudan 142/F3
Haybān, Sudan 142/F3
Haybes, Fr. 81/D4
Haydān (wadi), Jor. 131/D5
Hayden, Az, US 175/G4
Hayden, Co, US 173/K3
Hayden, Id, US 170/F4
Hayden-Rhodes (aqueduct), Az, US 175/F4
Haydock, Eng, UK 61/F5
Haydon Bridge, Eng, UK 61/F2
Hayes, Wi, US 186/B2
Hayes (nbrhd.), Eng, UK 56/B2
Hayes (mt.), Ak, US 166/B2
Hayes (riv.), Mb, Can. 166/G3
Hayes, SD, US 180/D1
Hayes (pen.), Grld. 167/T7
Hayes Center, Ne, US 180/D3
Hayesville, NC, US 188/F3
Hayfork, Ca, US 172/B3
Hayingen, Ger. 87/F1
Hāyk' (lake), Eth. 142/H4
Haylaastay, Mong. 101/M5
Hayle (riv.), Eng, UK 62/A6
Hayle, Eng, UK 62/A6
Hayling (isl.), Eng, UK 63/F5
Haylow, Ga, US 191/G2
Haymana, Turk. 128/C2
Haynes, ND, US 182/C5
Haynes, Ar, US 188/B3
Haynesville, La, US 179/H4
Hayneville, Al, US 188/D4
Haynin, Yem. 144/D2
Hayrabolu, Turk. 77/H5
Hays, Ks, US 178/E1
Hays, Ab, Can. 171/J2
Hays, Mt, US 171/K4
Haystack (peak), On, Can. 183/K2
Haysville, Ks, US 179/F2
Haysville, In, US 188/D1
Haysyn, Ukr. 98/E3
Hayti, Mo, US 188/C2
Hayti, SD, US 181/F1
Hayvoron, Ukr. 98/E3
Hayward, Wi, US 183/J4
Haywards Heath, Eng, UK 63/F5
Haywood, Ok, US 179/G3
Hazār (mtn.), Iran 129/J4
Hazard, Ky, US 189/F2
Hazāribag, India 123/E4
Hazebrouck, Fr. 80/B2
Hazel, SD, US 180/F1
Hazel, Ky, US 188/C2
Hazel Dell, Wa, US 170/C5
Hazel Green, Al, US 188/D3
Hazel Grove, Eng, UK 61/F5
Hazel Hill, NS, Can. 185/G3
Hazel Park, Mi, US 193/F7
Hazelbrook, Austl. 159/E1
Hazeldean, NB, Can. 184/D2
Hazelhurst, Wi, US 183/K5
Hazelton, ND, US 182/D4
Hazelton, Ks, US 179/E2
Hazelton (peak), Wy, US 173/K1
Hazen, ND, US 182/D4
Hazen, Ar, US 179/J3
Hazen, Nv, US 172/D4
Hazen (str.), NW,Nun, Can. 167/R7
Hazenmore, Sk, Can. 171/L3
Hāzipur, Bang. 123/H4
Hazlehurst, Ga, US 191/G2
Hazlehurst, Ms, US 190/C2
Hazlemere, Eng, UK 56/A2
Hazlet, NJ, US 195/J10
Hazlet, Sk, Can. 171/K2
Hazleton, Pa, US 194/C2
Hazlett (lake), Austl. 157/F2
Hazor, Isr. 131/D3
Hazratbal Mosque, India 124/C2
Hazro, Pak. 124/B3
Hazu, Japan 109/M6
He (riv.), China 119/K2
He Xian, China 113/F3
He Xian, China 106/D5
Heacham, Eng, UK 63/G1
Head of Bay d'Espoir, Nf, Can. 185/K2
Head of Saint Margarets Bay, NS, Can. 184/F3
Headcorn, Eng, UK 63/G4
Headford, Ire. 58/A3
Headingley, Eng, UK 61/G4
Headland, Al, US 191/F2
Headlands, Zim. 149/G3
Headquarters, Id, US 170/G4
Heads of Ayr (pt.), Sc, UK 59/B6
Heafford Junction, Wi, US 183/K5
Healdsburg, Ca, US 172/B4
Healdton, Ok, US 179/F3
Healesville, Austl. 158/G5
Healy, Ks, US 178/D1
Healy (pass), Ire. 58/A6
Heanor, Eng, UK 61/G6
Heany Junction, Zim. 149/F4
Heard (isl.), Austl. 216/E
Hearne, Tx, US 177/F2
Hearst, On, Can. 167/H4
Heart (riv.), ND, US 182/C4
Heart Butte (dam), ND, US 182/D4
Heart Law (hill), Sc, UK 59/D5
Hearts Hill, Sk, Can. 171/K1
Heath (pt.), QU, Can. 185/G1
Heath, Tx, US 176/L7
Heathcote, Austl. 159/B3
Heathcote NP, Austl. 160/G9
Heatherton, Nf, Can. 185/H1
Heathfield, Eng, UK 63/G5
Heathrow, Fl, US 190/N6
Heathrow (int'l arpt.), Eng, UK 56/B2
Heathsville, Va, US 189/J2
Hebbronville, Tx, US 177/E4
Hebbs Cross, NS, Can. 184/E3
Hebden Bridge, Eng, UK 61/F4
Hebei (prov.), China 104/G4
Hebel, Austl. 158/C1
Heber, Az, US 175/G3
Heber, Ca, US 174/E4
Heber City, Ut, US 173/H3
Heber Springs, Ar, US 179/H3
Hebert, La, US 190/C1
Hebertshausen, Ger. 85/E6
Hebgen (lake), Mt, US 173/H1
Hebgen (dam), Mt, US 173/H1
Hebi, China 106/C4
Hebo, Or, US 172/B1
Hebrides (sea), Sc, UK 57/Q8
Hebrides (isls.), UK 55/D3
Hebron, NS, Can. 184/D4
Hebron, ND, US 182/C4
Hebron, Il, US 193/P15
Hebron, Ne, US 180/F3
Hebron, Tx, US 176/L6
Hebron (Al Khalīl), WBnk. 131/C5
Heby, Swe. 66/G2
Hecate (str.), BC, Can. 165/D4
Hecelchakán, Mex. 200/D1
Hechi, China 113/F3
Hechingen, Ger. 84/B6
Hechtel, Belg. 81/E1
Hechthausen, Ger. 79/G1
Hechuan, China 113/E2
Heckington, Eng, UK 61/H6
Hecla, SD, US 182/E5
Hecla (isl.), Mb, Can. 182/F2
Hecla and Griper (bay), NW, Can. 167/R7
Hector, Ar, US 179/H3
Hector, Mn, US 181/G1
Hector (mt.), NZ 161/J8
Hector (mt.), Ab, Can. 170/F2
Hecun, China 113/H2
Heddal, Nor. 66/C2
Hédé, Fr. 82/D4
Hedehusene, Den. 65/J7
Hedel, Neth. 78/C5
Hedemora, Swe. 66/F1
Hedensted, Den. 66/C4
Hedi (res.), China 113/F4
Hedley, Tx, US 178/D3
Hedmark (co.), Nor. 64/D3
Hedo-misaki (cape), Japan 111/K7
Hedon, Eng, UK 61/H4
Hédouville, Fr. 56/J4
Hedrick, Ia, US 181/H3
Hedwig Village, Tx, US 177/M9
Heede, Ger. 79/E3
Heek, Ger. 79/E4
Heemskerk, Neth. 78/B3
Heemstede, Neth. 78/B4
Heerde, Neth. 78/D4
Heerenveen, Neth. 78/C3
Heerhugowaard, Neth. 78/B3
Heerlen, Neth. 81/E2
Heers, Belg. 81/E2
Heesch, Neth. 78/C5
Heeslingen, Ger. 79/G2
Heeze, Neth. 78/C6
Hefa (Haifa), Isr. 131/B3
Hefei, China 106/D5
Hefeng Tujiazu Zizhixian, China 113/F2
Heflin, La, US 179/H4
Heflin, Al, US 188/E4
Hegang, China 105/L2
Hegau (reg.), Ger. 68/E5
Hegau (mts.), Ger. 71/H3
Heggenes, Nor. 66/C1
Hegins, Pa, US 194/B2
Heguri, Japan 109/J6
Heho, Myan. 120/B1
Hei (riv.), Japan 108/B4
Hei (riv.), China 104/D4
Heichongtan, China 104/E4
Heide, Ger. 66/C4
Heideck, Ger. 84/E4
Heidelberg, Ger. 84/B4
Heidelberg, Ms, US 190/D2
Heidelberg (nbrhd.), Austl. 158/G5
Heidelberg, SAfr. 150/E2
Heidelberg, SAfr. 150/C4
Heiden, Swi. 87/F3
Heiden, Ger. 78/D5
Heidenheim, Ger. 84/D4
Heidenheim, Ger. 84/D5
Heidenreichstein, Aus. 69/H4
Heiderscheid, Lux. 81/E4
Heigenbrücken, Ger. 84/C2
Heihe, China 105/K1
Heikendorf, Ger. 66/D4
Heilbron, SAfr. 150/D2
Heilbronn, Ger. 84/C4
Heilbronn, Ger. 84/D4
Heiligenberg, Ger. 87/F2
Heiligenblut, Aus. 71/K3
Heiligenhafen, Ger. 66/D4
Heiligenhaus, Ger. 78/D6
Heiligenstadt, Ger. 79/H6
Heilong (Amur) (riv.), China, Rus. 101/N5
Heilongjiang (prov.), China 105/K2
Heiloo, Neth. 78/B3
Heimaey (isl.), Ice. 64/N7
Heimbach, Ger. 81/F2
Heimberg, Swi. 86/D4
Heimsheim, Ger. 84/B5
Heino, Neth. 78/D4
Heinola, Fin. 67/M1
Heinsberg, Ger. 81/F1
Heishan, China 107/B2
Heisler, Ab, Can. 171/H1
Heist-op-den-Berg, Belg. 81/D1
Heitersheim, Ger. 86/D2
Heiwa, Japan 109/L5
Hejialiang, China 104/F4
Hejian, China 106/D3
Hejiang, China 113/F4
Hejin, China 106/B4
Hejing, China 125/E3
Heka, China 104/D4
Hekelgem, Belg. 81/D2
Hekimhan, Turk. 128/D2
Hekinan, Japan 109/L6
Hekla (vol.), Ice. 64/N7
Hekou, China 112/D4
Hekou, China 104/G5
Hel, Pol. 67/H4
Helan (mts.), China 104/F4
Helbe (riv.), Ger. 79/H6
Helburg, Ger. 84/D2
Helchteren, Belg. 81/E1
Helden, Neth. 78/D6
Helen, Ga, US 188/F3
Helen Springs, Austl. 154/D4
Helena (riv.), Austl. 156/L6
Helena, Ar, US 188/B3
Helena, Ca, US 172/B3
Helena, Ga, US 191/G1

Helena (cap.), Mt, US 171/H4
Helena, Ok, US 179/E2
Helena, SC, US 189/G3
Helensburgh, Sc, UK 59/B4
Helensburgh, Austl. 159/E2
Helensville, NZ 161/F6
Helez, Isr. 131/B5
Helgasjön (lake), Swe. 66/F3
Helge (riv.), Swe. 65/K6
Helgoland (isl.), Ger. 66/B4
Helgoländer (bay), Ger. 66/C5
Helgoländer (bay), Wa, US 193/B3
Heliodora, Braz. 211/L7
Heliopolis (ruin), Egypt 139/C4
Heliport (int'l arpt.), Swe. 66/E3
Helixi, China 113/H2
Hellam (Hallam), Pa, US 194/B4
Hellas see Greece */*
Hellebæk, Den. 65/J6
Helleh (riv.), Iran 126/F3
Hellendoorn, Neth. 78/D4
Hellenthal, Ger. 81/F3
Hellertown, Pa, US 194/C2
Hellevoetsluis, Neth. 78/B5
Héllibongo, Chad 142/C3
Hellín, Sp. 72/E3
Hells Canyon (canyon), Or, Id, US 172/E1
Hells Canyon (dam), Id, US 172/E1
Hells Canyon Nat'l Rec. Area, Or, Id, US 172/E1
Hells Canyon NRA, Or, US 170/F5
Hell's Gate NP, Kenya 145/B2
Helmand (riv.), Afg. 103/F6
Helmbrechts, Ger. 85/E2
Helmeringhausen, Namb. 150/B2
Helmetta, NJ, US 195/H10
Helmond, Neth. 78/C6
Helmsley, Eng, UK 61/G3
Helmstadt, Ger. 84/C3
Helmstedt, Ger. 68/F2
Helmville, Mt, US 171/H4
Helong, China 105/K3
Helper, Ut, US 173/H4
Helsby, Eng, UK 61/F5
Helsenhorn (peak), Swi. 86/E5
Helsingborg (Hälsingborg), Swe. 66/E3
Helsinge, Den. 65/J6
Helsingfors (Helsinki) (cap.), Fin. 65/E4
Helsingør, Den. 66/E3
Helsinki (Helsingfors) (cap.), Fin. 65/E4
Helsinki-Vantaa (int'l arpt.), Fin. 67/L1
Helston, Eng, UK 62/A6
Helukou, China 113/F3
Helvecia, Arg. 212/D4
Helvick Head (pt.), Ire. 58/C5
Hem (riv.), Fr. 80/B2
Hemaruka, Ab, Can. 171/J2
Hemau, Ger. 85/E4
Hemel Hempstead, Eng, UK 56/B1
Hemelingen, Ger. 79/F2
Hemer, Ger. 79/E6
Hemet, Ca, US 192/D3
Hemford, NS, Can. 184/E3
Hemingford, Ne, US 180/C2
Hemingway, SC, US 189/H4
Hemmingen, Ger. 79/G4
Hemmoor, Ger. 79/G1
Hemp Top (peak), Ga, US 188/E3
Hemphill, Tx, US 177/H2
Hempstead, NY, US 195/L9
Hempstead (har.), NY, US 195/L8
Hempstead, Tx, US 177/F2
Hemse, Swe. 66/H3
Hemsedal, Nor. 66/C1
Hemsworth, Eng, UK 61/G4
Henagar, Al, US 188/E3
Henån, Swe. 66/D2
Henan (prov.), China 104/G5
Hénanbihen, Fr. 82/C3
Henares (riv.), Sp. 72/D2
Henashi-zaki (pt.), Japan 108/A3
Henbury, Austl. 157/G3
Hendaye, Fr. 70/C5
Hendek, Turk. 77/K5
Henderson, Arg. 214/E3
Henderson, NZ 161/F6
Henderson (isl.), Pitc. 163/N7
Henderson, Ky, US 188/D2
Henderson, La, US 190/C2
Henderson, Md, US 194/C5
Henderson, NC, US 189/H2
Henderson, Ne, US 180/F3
Henderson, Nv, US 174/E2
Henderson, NY, US 187/H3
Henderson, Tn, US 188/C3
Henderson, Tx, US 177/G1
Hendersonville, NC, US 189/F3
Hendersonville, Tn, US 188/D2
Hendon (nbrhd.), Eng, UK 56/C2
Hendricks, Mn, US 181/F1
Hendricks, WV, US 189/H1
Hendrik Top (peak), Sur. 206/B1
Hendrik Verwoerdam (res.), SAfr. 150/D3
Hendrik-Ido-Ambacht, Neth. 78/B5
Hendrina, SAfr. 151/E2
Hendrix Lake, BC, Can. 170/D1
Henfield, Eng, UK 63/F5
Heng (mtn.), China 106/C3
Heng (riv.), China 112/D2
Heng (peak), China 113/G3
Heng (isl.), China 106/L8
Heng Xian, China 113/F4
Henganofi, PNG 155/G1
Hengdaohe, China 107/B1
Hengelo, Neth. 78/D4
Hengersberg, Ger. 85/G5
Hengkou, China 104/F5
Hengshan, China 106/B3
Hengshui, China 106/C3
Hengue, Ang. 148/B1
Hengxi, China 113/J2
Hengyang, China 113/G3
Heniches'k, Ukr. 99/H4
Hénin-Beaumont, Fr. 80/B3
Henley Beach (nbrhd.), Austl. 157/M8
Henley-in-Arden, Eng, UK 63/E2
Henley-on-Thames, Eng, UK 63/F3
Henlopen (cape), De, US 194/C6
Henlopen Acres, De, US 194/C6
Henndorf am Wallersee, Aus. 85/G7
Henne, Den. 66/C4
Hennebont, Fr. 82/B5
Hennef, Ger. 81/G2
Hennenman, SAfr. 150/D2
Hennepin, Ok, US 179/F3
Hennepin (canal), Il, US 181/K3
Hennepin, Il, US 181/K3
Hennepin (co.), Mn, US 183/N6
Hennessey, Ok, US 179/F2
Hennigsdorf, Ger. 68/Q6
Henniker, NH, US 187/L3
Henning, Mn, US 183/G4
Henning, Tn, US 188/C3
Henri Pittier, PN, Ven. 207/N7
Henrietta, Tx, US 179/E4
Henrietta Maria (cape), On, Can. 167/H3
Henrieville, Ut, US 175/G2
Henry (mts.), Ut, US 173/H4
Henry, SD, US 180/F1
Henry, Ne, US 180/B3
Henry, Il, US 181/K3
Henry (co.), Ga, US 189/M7
Henry (cape), Va, US 189/J2
Henry, Va, US 189/H2
Henry Ford Museum and Greenfield Village Historical Site, Mi, US 193/E7
Henryetta, Ok, US 179/G3
Henrys Fork (riv.), Id, US 173/H2
Henryville, In, US 188/E1
Henryville, Pa, US 194/C1
Hensall, On, Can. 186/F3
Hensies, Belg. 80/C3
Hensler, ND, US 182/D4
Hensley, Ar, US 179/H3
Hentiesbaai, Namb. 148/B4
Hentiy (prov.), Mong. 104/F2
Hentiyn (mts.), Mong. 104/F2
Henty, Austl. 159/C2
Henzada, Myan. 112/B5
Hepburn, Sk, Can. 171/L1
Heping, China 113/H4
Hepler, Ks, US 179/G2
Heppenheim an der Bergstrasse, Ger. 84/B3
Heppner, Or, US 172/D1
Hepu, China 113/F4
Heqiao, China 106/K8
Heqing, China 112/D3
Hequ, China 106/B3
Heracleopolis Magna (ruin), Egypt 139/B6
Heradhsvötn (riv.), Ice. 64/N6
Herald, Ca, US 172/C4
Herāt, Afg. 127/H2
Herbasse (riv.), Fr. 90/B2
Herbault, Fr. 83/G5
Herbert, Al, US 190/E2
Herbert (riv.), Austl. 155/G4
Herbert (mt.), PNG 155/G1
Herbert, Sk, Can. 171/L2
Herbert Hoover Nat'l Hist. Site, Ia, US 181/J3
Herbert River (falls), Austl. 160/B2
Herbert River Falls NP, Austl. 160/B2
Herberton, Austl. 160/B2
Herbeumont, Belg. 81/E4
Herbignac, Fr. 82/C6
Herblay, Fr. 56/J5
Herbolzheim, Ger. 86/D1
Herbrechtingen, Ger. 84/D5
Herbstein, Ger. 84/C1
Hercegnovi, Yugo. 76/D4
Hercílio Luz (int'l arpt.), Braz. 213/G3
Herculaneum (ruin), It. 92/D6
Hércules, Mex. 177/C3
Hercules, Ca, US 193/K10
Herdecke, Ger. 79/E6
Herdorf, Ger. 81/G2
Heredia, CR 201/E4
Hereford, Tx, US 178/C3
Hereford, SD, US 180/C1
Hereford, Eng, UK 62/D2
Hereford, Pa, US 194/C3
Hereford (inlet), NJ, US 194/D5
Hereford, Md, US 194/B4
Hereford and Worcester (co.), Eng, UK 62/D2
Hereheretue (isl.), FrPol. 163/L7
Hereke, Turk. 77/J5
Herencia, Sp. 72/C3
Herentals, Belg. 78/B6
Herfølge, Den. 65/J7
Herford, Ger. 79/F4
Hergiswil, Swi. 87/E4
Héric, Fr. 82/D6
Héricourt, Fr. 86/C2
Hérimoncourt, Fr. 86/C3
Herington, Ks, US 179/F1
Heriot Bay, BC, Can. 170/B2
Herīs, Iran 129/F2
Herisau, Swi. 87/F3
Herk (riv.), Belg. 81/E2
Herk-de-Stad, Belg. 81/E2
Herkimer, NY, US 187/J3
Herlen (Kerulen) (riv.), Mong. 104/G2
Herleshausen, Ger. 79/H6
Herlev, Den. 65/J7
Herlong, Ca, US 172/C3
Herm (isl.), UK 82/C2
Herma Ness (cape), Sc, UK 57/W13
Herman, Mi, US 183/K4
Hermann, Mo, US 181/J4
Hermannsburg, Ger. 79/H3
Hermannsburg, Austl. 157/G2
Hermannsburg Abor. Land, Austl. 157/G2
Hermannsdenkmal (arpt.), Ger. 79/F5
Hermansverk, Nor. 66/B1
Hermansville, Mi, US 183/L5
Hermanus, SAfr. 150/L11
Hermanville, Ms, US 190/C2
Hermeray, Fr. 56/G6
Hermersberg, Ger. 81/G5
Hermes, Fr. 80/B5
Hermeskeil, Ger. 81/F4
Hermidale, Austl. 158/C1
Hermiston, Or, US 170/E5
Hermitage, Ar, US 179/H4
Hermitage, Mo, US 179/H2
Hermitage, Rus. 94/T7
Hermitage (bay), Nf, Can. 185/J2
Hermitage, Pa, US 186/F4
Hermitage Springs, Tn, US 188/E2
Hermleigh, Tx, US 177/D1
Hermon, NY, US 187/J2
Hermosa, SD, US 180/C2
Hermosa Beach, Ca, US 192/F8
Hermosillo, Mex. 198/C2
Hermoso Campo, Arg. 212/D3
Hermsdorf, Ger. 68/Q6
Hernandarias, Par. 213/F3
Hernandez, NM, US 175/J2
Hernández, Mex. 198/E4
Hernando (co.), Fl, US 190/K6
Hernando, Ms, US 188/C3
Hernando, Arg. 212/D5
Hernani, Sp. 70/C5
Herndon, Ks, US 180/D4
Herndon, Pa, US 194/B2
Herne, Belg. 80/D2
Herne, Ger. 79/E5
Herne Bay, Eng, UK 63/H4
Herning, Den. 66/C3
Heroes de la Independencia, Mex. 198/B2
Heroica Caborca, Mex. 198/B2
Heroica Ciudad de Tlaxiaco, Mex. 200/B2
Heroica Matamoros, Mex. 177/F5
Heroica Nogales, Mex. 175/G5
Heroldsberg, Ger. 84/E3
Heron (isl.), Nb, Can. 184/D2
Heron (lake), NM, US 175/J2
Heron Bay, On, Can. 183/L3
Heron Lake, Mn, US 181/G2
Herong, China 113/F2
Hérouville, Fr. 56/J4
Hérouville-Saint-Clair, Fr. 83/E2
Herøy, Nor. 64/C3
Herpf (riv.), Ger. 84/D1
Herre, Nor. 66/C2
Herreid, SD, US 182/D5
Herrenberg, Ger. 84/B5
Herrera, Sp. 72/C4
Herrera de Pisuerga, Sp. 72/C1
Herrera del Duque, Sp. 72/C3
Herrero (pt.), Mex. 200/E2
Herrestad, Swe. 66/D2
Herrhamra, Swe. 65/A2
Herrick, Austl. 158/C4
Herrick, Il, US 181/K4
Herrieden, Ger. 84/D4
Herrin, Il, US 188/C2
Herrlisheim, Fr. 81/G6
Herrljunga, Swe. 66/E2
Herrsching am Ammersee, Ger. 87/H2
Hers (riv.), Fr. 70/D5
Hersbruck, Ger. 85/E3
Herschbach, Ger. 81/G2
Herscheid, Ger. 79/E6
Herschel, Sk, Can. 171/K2
Herscher, Il, US 186/B4
Hersé (peak), Fr. 82/C5
Herselt, Belg. 81/D1
Hershey, Pa, US 194/B3
Hersheypark, Pa, US 194/B3
Hersilia, Arg. 212/D4
Herstal, Belg. 81/E2
Herstmonceux, Eng, UK 63/G5
Herten, Ger. 79/E5
Hertford, Eng, UK 63/F3
Hertford, NC, US 189/J2
Herval d'Oeste, Braz. 213/G3
Hervás, Sp. 72/C2
Herve, Belg. 81/E2
Herveo, Col. 207/K7
Hervey Bay, Austl. 160/D4
Hervey Bay (reef), Austl. 160/D3
Herwen, Neth. 78/D5
Herxheim bei Landau, Ger. 84/B4
Herzberg am Harz, Ger. 79/H5
Herzebrock-Clarholz, Ger. 79/F5
Herzele, Belg. 80/C2
Herzlake, Ger. 79/E3
Herzliyya, Isr. 131/B4
Herzogenaurach, Ger. 84/D3
Herzogenbuchsee, Swi. 86/D3
Herzogenburg, Aus. 76/B1
Herzogenrath, Ger. 81/F2
Hesādi, India 123/E4
Hesbaye (plat.), Belg. 68/C3
Hesdin, Fr. 80/B3
Hesel, Ger. 79/E2
Heshan, China 113/F4
Heshengqiao, China 113/G2
Heshui Qi, China 104/F4
Heshun, China 106/C3
Hésingue, Fr. 86/D2
Hesperange, Lux. 81/F4
Hesperia, Ca, US 192/C2
Hesperia, Mi, US 186/C3
Hesperides, Fl, US 190/N8
Hesperus, Co, US 175/H2
Hess (riv.), Yk, Can. 166/C2
Hessel, Mi, US 186/D1
Hessel (riv.), Ger. 79/F5
Hesselø (isl.), Den. 66/D3
Hessen, Ger. 79/H4
Hessen (state), Ger. 71/H1
Hessisch Lichtenau, Ger. 79/G6
Hessisch Oldendorf, Ger. 79/G4
Hessle, Eng, UK 61/H4
Hesston, Ks, US 179/F1
Heståsfjellet (peak), Nor. 64/R8
Heswall, Eng, UK 61/E5
Heṭaūḍā, Nepal 123/E2
Hetch Hetchy (aqueduct), Ca, US 174/B2
Heteren, Neth. 78/C5
Hettenleidelheim, Ger. 84/B3
Hettinger, ND, US 182/C4
Hetton-le-Hole, Eng, UK 61/G2
Hettstadt, Ger. 84/C3
Hetzerath, Ger. 81/F4
Heubach (riv.), Ger. 79/E5
Heubach, Ger. 84/C5
Heuchelheim, Ger. 84/B1
Heukuppe (peak), Aus. 69/H5
Heusden, Neth. 78/C5
Heusden-Zolder, Belg. 81/E1
Heusenstamm, Ger. 84/B2
Heusweiler, Ger. 81/F5
Heuvelton, NY, US 187/J2
Hève (cape), Fr. 83/F1
Heverlee, Belg. 81/D2
Heves (co.), Hun. 69/L5
Heves, Hun. 76/E2
Hewanorra (int'l arpt.), StL. 197/N9
Hewitt, NJ, US 195/H7
Hewitt, Tx, US 177/F2
Hewitt Lake Nat'l Wild. Ref., Mt, US 171/L3
Hewlett, NY, US 195/L9
Hewlett (pt.), NY, US 195/L8
Hex River (mts.), SAfr. 150/L10
Hex River (pass), SAfr. 150/L10
Hexenkopf (peak), Aus. 87/G3
Hexham, Eng, UK 61/F2
Hexi, China 113/F2
Hexigten, China 105/H3
Hext, Tx, US 177/E2
Heybeli (isl.), Turk. 129/N7
Heybridge, Eng, UK 56/F1
Heyburn, Id, US 173/G2
Heyerode, Ger. 79/H6
Heyfield, Austl. 159/C3
Heyrieux, Fr. 90/B1
Heysham, Eng, UK 61/F3
Heythuysen, Neth. 78/C6
Heyuan, China 113/G4
Heywood, Eng, UK 61/F4
Heywood, Austl. 158/B3
Heyworth, Il, US 181/K3
Heze, China 106/C4
Hezhang, China 112/E3
Hialeah, Fl, US 190/P11
Hialeah Gardens, Fl, US 190/P11
Hiawassee, Ga, US 188/F3
Hiawatha, Mi, US 186/C1
Hiawatha, Ia, US 181/J2
Hiawatha, Ks, US 181/G4
Hiawatha Ind. Res., On, Can. 187/G2
Hibbing, Mn, US 183/H4
Hibbs (pt.), Austl. 158/C4
Hicacos (pt.), Cuba 201/F1
Hichisō, Japan 109/M4
Hickman, Ky, US 188/C2
Hickman, Ne, US 181/F3
Hickory (cr.), Il, US 193/Q16
Hickory, Ms, US 188/C4
Hickory, NC, US 189/G3
Hickory (lake), NC, US 189/G3
Hickory Flat, Ms, US 188/C3
Hickory Ridge, Ar, US 188/B3
Hickory Run St. Park, Pa, US 194/C1
Hicksville, Oh, US 186/D4
Hicksville, NY, US 195/L8
Hico, La, US 179/H4
Hico, Tx, US 177/E2
Hida (riv.), Japan 111/E3
Hīdaj, Iran 129/G2
Hidaka (riv.), Japan 110/D4
Hidaka (mts.), Japan 108/C2
Hidaka, Japan 108/C2
Hidaka, Japan 109/C2
Hidalgo, Mex. 177/E4
Hidalgo (state), Mex. 196/B3
Hidalgo, Mex. 199/F3
Hidalgo, Tx, US 177/E4
Hidalgo del Parral, Mex. 198/D3
Hidden Hills, Ca, US 192/B2
Hiddenhausen, Ger. 79/F4
Hidrolândia, Braz. 210/C3
Hidrolândia, Braz. 207/F4
Hidrolina, Braz. 210/C2
Hienghene, NCal. 163/U12
Hierapolis (ruin), Turk. 128/B2
Hière (riv.), Fr. 83/E5
Hierro (isl.), Sp. 136/A4
Hierro Viejo, Chile 214/C2
Hieve (lake), Ger. 79/E2
Higashi-Chichibu, Japan 109/C1
Higashi-Matsuyama, Japan 109/C1
Higashi-Ōsaka, Japan 109/J6
Higashikurume, Japan 109/D2
Higashimurayama, Japan 109/C2
Higashine, Japan 108/B4
Higashiura, Japan 109/L6
Higashiura, Japan 109/G6
Higashiyoshino, Japan 109/J7
Higbee, Mo, US 181/H4
Higgins (lake), Mi, US 186/D2
Higgins Lake, Mi, US 186/D2
Higginsville, Mo, US 181/H4
High (isl.), China 113/M7
High (isl.), Mi, US 183/M5
High (peak), NJ, US 187/J4
High (des.), Or, US 172/C1
High (hill), Pa, US 194/C1
High (peak), Va, US 189/G2
High (peak), Va, US 189/F2
High Bridge, NJ, US 194/D2
High Butler (lake), Ne, US 180/D3
High Eagle (peak), NC, US 189/G2
High Halstow, Eng, UK 56/E2
High Island, Tx, US 177/G3
High Level, Ab, Can. 166/E3
High Park (peak), Phil. 114/C2
High Point, NC, US 189/G3
High Prairie, Ab, Can. 166/E3
High Ridge, Mo, US 188/B1
High River, Ab, Can. 171/H2
High Rock (lake), NC, US 189/G3
High Springs, Fl, US 191/G3
High Street (peak), Eng, UK 61/F3
High Willhays (hill), Eng, UK 62/B5
High Wycombe, Eng, UK 63/F3
Higham, Eng, UK 56/E2
Higham Ferrers, Eng, UK 63/F2
Highbridge, Eng, UK 62/D4
Highbury, Austl. 156/C5
Highest (peak), In, US 186/D4
Highland (co.), Sc, US 59/A2
Highland, Ca, US 192/C2
Highland, In, US 193/R16
Highland (peak), Nv, US 174/E2
Highland, Ks, US 181/G4
Highland Beach, Fl, US 190/P10
Highland City, Fl, US 190/M8
Highland Lakes, Fl, US 190/M8
Highland Lakes, NJ, US 194/D1
Highland Park, Il, US 186/C3
Highland Park, NJ, US 195/H10
Highland Park, Mi, US 193/F7
Highland Park, Tx, US 176/L7
Highlands (co.), Fl, US 190/M8
Highlands, NJ, US 195/K10
Highlands, NC, US 189/F3
Highlands, Tx, US 177/M9
Highlands (res.), Tx, US 177/M9
Highley, Eng, UK 62/D2
Highmore, SD, US 180/E1
Highspire, Pa, US 194/B3
Hightown, Eng, UK 61/E4
Hightstown, NJ, US 194/D3
Highwood, Il, US 193/Q15
Highwood, Mt, US 171/J4
Highwood Baldy (peak), Mt, US 171/J4
Highworth, Eng, UK 63/E3
Higley, Az, US 175/G4
Higuera de Zaragoza, Mex. 198/C3
Higuerote, Ven. 207/P7
Hihyā, Egypt 139/C3
Hiidenportin NP, Fin. 94/F3
Hiidenvesi (lake), Fin. 65/E4
Hiiumaa (isl.), Est. 94/D4
Híjar, Sp. 73/E2
Hijāz, Jabal al (mts.), SAr. 126/C3
Hiji, Japan 110/B4
Hijuelas de Conchali, Chile 214/N8
Hikami, Japan 109/H5
Hikari, Japan 109/F2
Hiko, Nv, US 174/E2
Hikone, Japan 109/K5
Hikueru (isl.), FrPol. 163/L6
Hikurangi (peak), NZ 161/D2
Hikurangi, NZ 161/C1
Hila, Indo. 154/B1
Hilāl, Ral's al (pt.), Libya 93/J4
Hilbert, Wi, US 186/B2
Hilbre, Mb, Can. 182/E2
Hilda, Tx, US 177/E2
Hildale, Ut, US 175/F2
Hildburghausen, Ger. 84/D2
Hildebrand, Or, US 172/C2
Hilden, Ger. 81/F1
Hilden, NS, Can. 184/F3
Hildenborough, Eng, UK 56/D3
Hilders, Ger. 84/C1
Hildesheim, Ger. 79/G4
Hiles, Wi, US 183/K5
Hilger, Mt, US 171/K4
Hilgermissen, Ger. 79/G3
Hill (cr.), Ut, US 173/J4
Hill (isl.), Pa, US 194/B3
Hill Air Force Range, Ut, US 173/G3
Hill City, Ks, US 180/E4
Hill City, SD, US 180/C2
Hill End, Austl. 159/D1
Hill of Fare (hill), Sc, UK 59/D2
Hill of Fearn, Sc, UK 59/C1
Hill of Stake (hill), Sc, UK 59/B5
Hill of Tara, Ire. 58/D2
Hill Spring, Ab, Can. 171/H3
Hill Top, Austl. 159/E2
Hillaby (mt.), Bar. 197/P9
Hillburn, NY, US 195/J7
Hillcrest, NY, US 195/J7
Hillcrest Heights, Fl, US 190/M8
Hille, Ger. 79/F4
Hillegom, Neth. 78/B4
Hillerød, Den. 66/E4
Hillesheim, Ger. 81/F3
Hillhall, NI, UK 60/B3
Hilli, Bang. 123/G3
Hilliard, Fl, US 191/H2
Hillier, On, Can. 187/H3
Hillingdon (bor.), Eng, UK 56/B2
Hills, Mn, US 181/F2
Hills Creek (res.), Or, US 172/B2
Hillsboro (canal), Fl, US 191/H4
Hillsboro, Il, US 181/K4
Hillsboro, Ks, US 179/F1
Hillsboro, Md, US 194/C6
Hillsboro, Mo, US 188/B1
Hillsboro, Ms, US 188/C4
Hillsboro, ND, US 182/F4
Hillsboro, NM, US 175/J4
Hillsboro, Oh, US 188/F1
Hillsboro, Or, US 170/C5
Hillsboro, Tx, US 177/F1
Hillsboro, Wi, US 181/J2
Hillsboro (Hillsborough), NH, US 187/L3
Hillsboro Beach, Fl, US 190/P10
Hillsborough, NI, UK 60/B3
Hillsborough, NB, Can. 184/E3
Hillsborough (bay), Pe, Can. 184/F2
Hillsborough, Ca, US 193/K11
Hillsborough (riv.), Fl, US 190/L7
Hillsborough (co.), Fl, US 190/L8
Hillsborough (bay), Fl, US 190/L8
Hillsborough (chan.), Austl. 160/C3
Hillsborough, NJ, US 194/D3
Hillsborough, NC, US 189/H2
Hillsborough (Hillsboro), NH, US 187/L3
Hillsburgh, On, Can. 186/S8
Hillsdale, Mi, US 186/D4
Hillsdale, NJ, US 195/J7
Hillsdale (lake), Ks, US 181/G4
Hillside, Co, US 178/B1
Hillside, Sc, UK 59/D3
Hillside, NJ, US 195/J9
Hillside, Az, US 175/F3
Hillside NWR, Ms, US 188/B4
Hillsport, On, Can. 183/M3
Hillston, Austl. 159/B1
Hillsville, Va, US 189/G2
Hillswick, Sc, UK 57/W13
Hilltonia, Ga, US 189/G4
Hilltown, NI, UK 60/B3
Hillview, Ky, US 188/E1
Hilmar-Irwin, Ca, US 174/B2
Hilo, Hi, US 168/S10
Hilonghilong (mt.), Phil. 114/D3
Hilongos, Phil. 114/D3
Hilpoltstein, Ger. 84/E4
Hilpsford (pt.), Eng, UK 61/E3
Hilsa, India 123/E3
Hilt, Ca, US 172/B3
Hilterfingen, Swi. 86/D4
Hilton, Ga, US 191/F2
Hilton, NY, US 187/H3
Hilton Head (isl.), SC, US 191/H1
Hilton Head Island, SC, US 189/G4
Hilvarenbeek, Neth. 78/C6
Hilversum, Neth. 78/C4
Hilzingen, Ger. 87/E2
Hima, Ky, US 188/F2
Himachal Pradesh (state), India 125/C5
Himalaya (range), Asia 103/G6
Himālchuli (peak), Nepal 123/E1
Himamaylan, Phil. 114/C3
Himanka, Fin. 94/D2
Himarë, Alb. 75/F2
Himberg, Aus. 77/N7
Himbirtī, Erit. 144/A2
Himeji, Japan 110/D3
Himeji Castle, Japan 110/D3
Himi, Japan 111/E2
Himmelpforten, Ger. 79/G1
Himmerfjärden (bay), Swe. 65/A2
Himora, Eth. 142/H2
Ḥimş, Syria 130/E2
Ḥimş (prov.), Syria 128/D3
Hinatuan, Phil. 114/D3
Hînceşti, Mol. 98/E4
Hinch (mtn.), Tn, US 188/E3
Hinche, Haiti 201/H2
Hinchinbrook (isl.), Austl. 153/D2
Hinchinbrook Island, Austl. 160/B2
Hinchinbrook Island NP, Austl. 155/G4
Hinckley, Ut, US 173/G4
Hinckley, Il, US 181/K3
Hinckley, Eng, UK 63/E1
Hincks Consv. Park, Austl. 157/H5
Hinda, Congo 146/C4
Hindan (riv.), India 122/A1
Hindaun, India 122/A2
Hindelang, Ger. 87/G3
Hindeloopen, Neth. 78/C3
Hinderwell, Eng, UK 61/H2
Hindhår (Hinthaara), Fin. 65/F4
Hindley, Eng, UK 61/F4
Hindman, Ky, US 189/F2
Hindmarsh (lake), Austl. 158/B3
Hinds, NZ 161/B3
Hindsholm (isl.), Den. 65/G7
Hindu Kush (mts.), Asia 103/F6
Hindupur, India 121/C3
Hinesburg, Vt, US 187/K2
Hineston, La, US 190/B2
Hinesville, Ga, US 191/H2
Hinganghāt, India 121/C1
Hingol (riv.), Pak. 127/J3
Hingoli, India 121/C2
Hingorja, Pak. 127/J3
Hingurakgoda, SrL. 121/D4
Hınıs, Turk. 128/E2
Hino, Japan 109/C2
Hino, Japan 109/K5
Hino (riv.), Japan 109/K5
Hino-misaki (cape), Japan 110/C3
Hinode, Japan 109/C2
Hinohara, Japan 109/C2
Hinojosa del Duque, Sp. 72/C3
Hinsdale, Ma, US 187/K3
Hinsdale, Il, US 193/Q16
Hinstock, Eng, UK 61/F6
Hinte, Ger. 79/E2
Hinterbrühl, Aus. 77/N7
Hinterrhein (riv.), Swi. 87/F4
Hinterriss, Aus. 87/H3
Hinterrugg (peak), Swi. 87/F3
Hinterweidenthal, Ger. 81/G5
Hinthaara (Hindhår), Fin. 65/F4
Hinton, Ok, US 179/E3
Hinton, WV, US 189/G2
Hinton, Ab, Can. 170/F1
Hintonville, Ms, US 190/D2
Hinunangan, Phil. 114/D3
Hinwil, Swi. 87/E3
Hipólito, Mex. 177/D5
Hipólito Bouchard, Arg. 214/E2
Hippolytushoef, Neth. 78/B3
Hipswell, Eng, UK 61/G3
Hira Highlands (uplands), Japan 109/J5
Hirado, Japan 110/A4
Hirakata, Japan 109/J6
Hirakud (res.), India 118/D3
Hiram, Oh, US 186/F4
Hiram, Ga, US 189/L7
Hiraman (riv.), Kenya 145/B2
Hiran (riv.), India 122/B4
Hiranai, Japan 108/B3
Hīrāpur, India 122/B3
Hirara, Japan 111/H8
Hirata, Japan 110/C3
Hirata, Japan 109/L5
Hiratsuka, Japan 109/C3
Hirfanlı (dam), Turk. 128/C2
Hîrlău, Rom. 98/D4
Hīrna, Eth. 144/B3
Hirnyk, Ukr. 99/J3
Hiro'o, Japan 108/C2
Hirosaki, Japan 108/B3
Hiroshima (pref.), Japan 110/C3
Hiroshima, Japan 110/C3
Hirschaid, Ger. 84/D3
Hirschau, Ger. 85/E3
Hirschhorn, Ger. 84/B4
Hirson, Fr. 81/D4
Hîrşova, Rom. 77/H3
Hirtshals, Den. 66/C3
Hirukawa, Japan 109/M4
Hirvijärvi (lake), Fin. 65/E4
Hirwaun, Wal, UK 62/C3
Hisai, Japan 109/K6
Hisār, India 124/C5
Hisarcık, Turk. 128/B2
Ḥisbān, Jor. 131/D5
Hiseville, Ky, US 188/E2
Hisham's Palace (ruin), WBnk. 131/C5
Ḥişn al 'Abr, Yem. 144/C1
Hispaniola (isl.), DRep., Haiti 165/K7
Historic Houses of Odessa, De, US 194/C5
Historic Towne of Smithville, NJ, US 194/D5
Hisua, India 123/E3
Hīt, Iraq 129/E3
Hitachi, Japan 111/G2
Hitachi-Ōta, Japan 111/G2
Hitchcock, Sk, Can. 182/C3
Hitchcock, Ok, US 179/E3
Hitchcock, SD, US 180/E1
Hitchcock, Tx, US 177/M9
Hitchin, Eng, UK 63/F3
Hitchins, Ky, US 189/F1
Hitoyoshi, Japan 110/B4
Hitra (isl.), Nor. 64/C3
Hittarp, Swe. 65/J6
Hitterdal, Mn, US 182/F4
Hittisau, Aus. 87/F3
Hitzacker, Ger. 68/F2
Hitzkirch, Swi. 87/E3
Hiva Oa (isl.), FrPol. 163/M5
Hiwannee, Ms, US 190/D2
Hiwassee (lake), NC, US 188/E3
Hiwassee (riv.), Tn, US 188/E3
Hixon, BC, Can. 170/C1
Hiyoshi, Japan 109/J5
Hizan, Turk. 128/E2
Hjälmaren (lake), Swe. 66/G2
Hjartfjellet (peak), Nor. 64/E2
Hjärup, Swe. 65/K7
Hjellestad, Nor. 66/A1
Hjelm (str.), Den. 65/G6
Hjelm (isl.), Den. 65/G6
Hjelmeland, Nor. 66/B2
Hjerm, Den. 66/C3
Hjo, Swe. 66/F2
Hjørring, Den. 66/C3
Hka (riv.), Myan. 120/B1
Hkakabo (peak), Myan. 112/C2
Hlabisa, SAfr. 151/E3
Hlatikulu, Swaz. 151/E2
Hlegu, Myan. 120/B2
Hlobyne, Ukr. 99/G3
Hlokozi, SAfr. 151/E3
Hluboká nad Vltava, Czh. 85/H4
Hluhluwe, SAfr. 151/F3
Hlukhiv, Ukr. 99/G2
Hlyboka, Ukr. 98/C3
Hlybokaye, Bela. 67/M4
Hmawbi, Myan. 112/C5
Hmunpui, India 112/B4
Hnivan', Ukr. 98/E3
Ho, Gha. 141/F5
Ho Chi Minh Mausoleum, Viet. 112/E4
Hoa Binh, Viet. 120/D1
Hoa Da, Viet. 120/E4
Hoadley, Ab, Can. 170/G1
Hoang Lien (mts.), Viet. 112/D4
Hoanib (riv.), Namb. 148/B3
Hoare (bay), Nun, Can. 167/K2
Hoarusib (riv.), Namb. 148/B3
Hoba Meteorite, Namb. 148/C3
Hoback (peak), Wy, US 173/H2
Hobara, Japan 111/G2
Hobart, Ok, US 178/E3
Hobart, Wa, US 193/D3
Hobart (int'l arpt.), Austl. 158/C4
Hobart, Austl. 158/C4
Hobart Lake Nat'l Wild. Ref., ND, US 182/E4
Hobbs, NM, US 176/C1
Hobe Sound Nat'l Wild. Ref., Fl, US 191/H4
Hoboken, NJ, US 195/J9
Hoboken, Belg. 78/B6
Hoboksar Monggol Zizhixian, China 125/E2
Hobøl, Nor. 64/S9
Hobølelva (riv.), Nor. 64/S9
Hobro, Den. 66/C3
Hobson, Mt, US 171/K4
Hobucken, NC, US 189/J3
Hobyo, Som. 144/D4
Hoc (pt.), Fr. 83/D2
Hocaköy, Turk. 77/K5
Hochalmspitze (peak), Aus. 71/K3
Höchberg, Ger. 84/C3
Hochburg, Aus. 85/F6
Hochdorf, Ger. 87/F1
Hochfeld, Mb, Can. 182/F3
Hochfeld, Namb. 148/C4
Hochfelden, Fr. 81/G6
Hochfinsler (peak), Swi. 87/F3
Hochgrat (peak), Ger. 87/G3
Hochheim am Main, Ger. 84/B2
Hochkönig (peak), Aus. 71/K3
Hŏch'ŏn (riv.), NKor. 107/D2
Hŏch'ŏn, NKor. 107/E2
Hochschwab (peak), Aus. 71/L3
Hochsimmer (peak), Ger. 81/G3
Hochspeyer, Ger. 81/G5
Höchst, Aus. 87/F3
Höchst im Odenwald, Ger. 84/B3
Hochstadt am Main, Ger. 84/E2
Höchstadt an der Aisch, Ger. 84/D3
Hochstädt an der Donau, Ger. 84/D5
Hochstetten-Dhaun, Ger. 81/G4
Hochvogel (peak), Aus. 87/G3
Hochwang (peak), Swi. 87/F4
Hockenheim, Ger. 84/B4
Hockessin, De, US 194/C4
Hocking (riv.), Oh, US 189/F1
Hockley, Eng, UK 56/F2
Hod Ha Sharon, Isr. 131/B4
Hodal, India 122/A2
Hodder (riv.), Eng, UK 61/F4
Hoddesdon, Eng, UK 56/D1
Hodenhagen, Ger. 79/G3
Hodge, La, US 179/H4
Hodgenville, Ky, US 188/E2
Hodges, Mt, US 182/B4
Hodges (hill), Nf, Can. 185/K1
Hodges (lake), Ca, US 192/C4
Hodges, Tx, US 177/E1
Hodge's Cove, Nf, Can. 185/L1
Hodgeville, Sk, Can. 171/L2
Hodgson, Mb, Can. 182/F2
Hodgson (riv.), Austl. 154/D3
Hodh (phys. reg.), Mrta. 140/C2
Hodh El Gharbi (pol. reg.), Mrta. 140/C2
Hodiyya, Isr. 131/B5
Hódmezóvśáhely, Hun. 76/E2
Hodmo (riv.), Som. 144/C3
Hodna (lake), Alg. 92/E4
Hodnet, Eng, UK 61/F6
Hodonín, Czh. 69/J4
Hödrögö, Mong. 104/D2
Hoedic (isl.), Fr. 82/C6
Hoedspruit, SAfr. 149/F5
Hoehne, Co, US 178/B2
Hoek, Neth. 80/C1
Hoek van Holland, Neth. 78/B5
Hoekse Waard (isl.), Neth. 78/B5
Hoensbroek, Neth. 81/E2
Hoeselt, Belg. 81/E2
Hoevelaken, Neth. 78/C4
Hoeven, Neth. 78/B5
Hoeyang, NKor. 107/D3
Hoeybuktmoen (int'l arpt.), Nor. 64/J1
Hoeys Bridge, Kenya 145/A1
Hof, Nor. 64/R9
Hof, Ger. 85/E2
Hofbieber, Ger. 84/C1
Höfdhakaupstadhur, Ice. 64/N6
Hoffman, Mn, US 182/G5
Hoffman (mt.), Ca, US 172/C3
Hoffman Estates, Il, US 193/P15
Hoffnung, Namb. 148/C4
Hofgeismar, Ger. 79/G6
Hofheim am Taunus, Ger. 84/B2
Hofheim in Unterfranken, Ger. 84/D2
Hofmeyr, SAfr. 150/D3
Hofong Qagan Salt (lake), China 106/B3
Hofors, Swe. 66/G1
Hofsá (riv.), Ice. 64/P6
Hofsjökull (glacier), Ice. 64/N7
Hōfu, Japan 110/B3
Hog (isl.), US 189/K2
Höganäs, Swe. 65/J6
Hogansville, Ga, US 188/E4
Hogarth (mt.), Austl. 157/H2
Hogback (mtn.), SC, US 189/F3
Hogback (mtn.), Ne, US 180/C3
Hogeland, Mt, US 171/K3
Hogoro, Tanz. 145/B3
Hogyész, Hun. 76/D2
Hoh Sai (lake), China 125/F4
Hoh Xil (mts.), China 125/E4
Hoh Xil (lake), China 125/F4
Höhbürd, Mong. 104/E2
Hohe Acht (peak), Ger. 81/G3
Hohe Geige (peak), Aus. 87/G4
Hohe Tauern (mts.), Aus. 93/G1
Hohe Tauern NP (nat'l park), Aus. 71/K3
Hohegrass (peak), Ger. 79/G6
Hohen Neuendorf, Ger. 68/Q6
Hohenbrunn, Ger. 85/E6
Hohenems, Aus. 87/F3
Hohenhameln, Ger. 79/H4
Hohenlinden, Ger. 85/F6
Hohenlockstedt, Ger. 68/E2
Hohenloher Ebene (plain), Ger. 68/E4
Hohenpeissenberg, Ger. 87/G2
Hohenroth, Ger. 84/D2
Hohentengen, Ger. 87/E2
Hohenwald, Tn, US 188/D3
Hoher Dachstein (peak), Aus. 71/K3
Hoher Ifen (peak), Ger. 87/G3
Hoher Randen (peak), Ger. 87/E2
Hohgant (peak), Swi. 86/D4
Höhn, Ger. 81/G2
Hohneck (peak), Fr. 86/D1
Hohnstorf, Ger. 79/H2
Hohokam Pima Nat'l Mon., Az, US 175/G4
Höhr-Grenzhausen, Ger. 81/G3
Hoi An, Viet. 120/E3
Hoi Xuan, Viet. 112/E4
Hoima, Ugan. 147/G2
Hoisington, Ks, US 179/E1
Hoit Taria, China 104/D4
Højby, Den. 66/D4
Höjeån (riv.), Swe. 65/K7
Højer, Den. 66/C4
Hōjō, Japan 110/C4
Hokianga (har.), NZ 161/C1
Hokitika, NZ 161/B3
Hokkaidō (isl.), Japan 103/P5
Hokksund, Nor. 66/C2
Ḥokmābād, Iran 129/J2
Hokota, Japan 111/G2
Hokudan, Japan 109/G6
Hokusei, Japan 109/L5
Hol, Nor. 66/C1
Hola, Kenya 145/C2
Hola Prystan', Ukr. 98/G4
Holanda, Bol. 208/D3
Holbæk, Den. 65/H7
Holbæk (inlet), Den. 65/H7
Holbeach, Eng, UK 61/J6
Holbox, Mex. 200/E1
Holbrook, Az, US 175/G3
Holbrook, Eng, UK 63/H3
Holbrook, Austl. 159/C2
Holbrook, NY, US 195/E2
Holcombe, Wi, US 183/J5
Holden, Mo, US 179/H1
Holden, Ma, US 187/L3
Holden, WV, US 189/F2
Holden, Ab, Can. 171/H1
Holdenville, Ok, US 179/F3
Holderness (pen.), Eng, UK 61/H4
Holderness, NH, US 187/L3
Holdfast, Sk, Can. 171/M2
Holdingford, Mn, US 183/G5
Holdorf, Ger. 79/F3
Holdrege, Ne, US 180/E3
Holeby, Den. 66/D4
Hølen, Nor. 64/S9
Holguín, Cuba 201/G1
Holiday, Fl, US 190/K7
Holiday Hills, Il, US 193/P15
Höljes, Swe. 66/E1
Holla Bend Nat'l Wild. Ref., Ar, US 179/H3
Holladay, Tn, US 188/C3
Holland, Mi, US 186/C3
Holland, Tx, US 176/F2
Holland (pt.), Md, US 194/B6
Holland Patent, NY, US 187/J3
Hollandale, Ms, US 188/B4
Hollande (pond), Fr. 56/H5
Hollandse Ijssel (riv.), Neth. 78/B5
Hollandstoun, Sc, UK 57/V14
Hollenstedt, Ger. 79/G2
Hollesley, Eng, UK 63/H2
Hollfeld, Ger. 84/E3
Holliday, Tx, US 179/E4
Hollidaysburg, Pa, US 187/G4
Hollingbourne, Eng, UK 56/F3
Hollins, Va, US 189/H2
Hollis, Ok, US 178/E3
Hollister, Mo, US 179/H2
Hollister, Ca, US 174/B2
Hollister (mt.), Austl. 156/B2
Hollister, NC, US 189/J2
Hollogne-aux-Pierres, Belg. 81/E2
Hollola, Fin. 67/L1
Holloman (A.F.B.), NM, US 178/A4
Holloman (A.F.B.), NM, US 177/B1
Hollum, Neth. 78/C2
Höllviksnäs, Swe. 66/E4
Holly, Co, US 178/C1
Holly, Mi, US 186/E3
Holly, Wa, US 193/B2
Holly Grove, Ar, US 179/J3
Holly Hill, Fl, US 191/H3
Holly Hill, SC, US 189/G4
Holly Ridge, NC, US 189/J3
Holly Springs, Ms, US 188/C3
Hollysloot, Neth. 78/C4
Hollywood, Ar, US 179/H3
Hollywood (nbrhd.), Ca, US 192/F7
Hollywood, Fl, US 190/P10
Hollywood, SC, US 189/G4
Hollywood Bowl, Ca, US 192/F7
Hollywood Park, Tx, US 176/E3
Holm, Ger. 79/G1
Holman, NM, US 178/B2
Holman, NW, Can. 166/E1
Hólmavík, Ice. 64/N6
Holmdel, NJ, US 194/D3
Holme upon Spalding Moor, Eng, UK 61/H4
Holmen, Wi, US 181/J2
Holmenkollen, Nor. 64/S8
Holmer Green, Eng, UK 56/A2
Holmes (mt.), Wy, US 173/H1
Holmes (riv.), BC, Can. 170/E1
Holmes Chapel, Eng, UK 61/F5
Holmes Reef (reef), Austl. 155/H4
Holmes Reefs (isl.), Austl. 153/D2
Holmesdale (valley), Eng, UK 56/C3
Holmestrand, Nor. 66/D2
Holmfirth, Eng, UK 61/G4
Holmhead, Sc, UK 59/B6
Holmsbu, Nor. 64/S9
Holmsjön (lake), Swe. 64/F3
Holmsund, Swe. 64/G3
Holmsvatnet (lake), Nor. 64/R9
Hölö, Swe. 65/A1
Holoby, Ukr. 98/C2
Holon, Isr. 131/B4
Holoog, Namb. 150/B2
Holroyd, Austl. 159/E1
Holsfjorden (lake), Nor. 64/R8
Holstebro, Den. 66/C3
Holstein, Ia, US 181/G2
Holston (riv.), Tn, US 188/F3
Holston Ordnance Works Fed. Govt. Res., Tn, US 189/F2
Holston, North Fork (riv.), Va, US 189/F2
Holsworthy, Eng, UK 62/B5
Holt, Fl, US 190/E2
Holt, Mi, US 186/D3
Holt, Ca, US 193/M11
Holt, Al, US 188/D4
Holt, Mo, US 181/G4
Holt, Eng, UK 63/H1
Holtålen, Nor. 64/D3
Holte, Den. 65/J7
Holten, Neth. 78/D4
Holtland, Ger. 79/E2
Holton, Ks, US 181/G4
Holts Summit, Mo, US 179/H1
Holtsville, NY, US 195/E2
Holtville, NB, Can. 184/D2
Holtville, Ca, US 174/E4
Holwerd, Neth. 78/C2
Holy (isl.), Sc, UK 59/A5
Holy Cross, Ak, US 168/X12
Holy Trinity, Al, US 188/E4
Holycross, Ire. 58/C4
Holyhead, Wal, UK 60/D5
Holyoke, Ma, US 187/K3
Holyoke, Co, US 180/C3
Holyport, Eng, UK 56/A2
Holyrood, Ks, US 179/E1
Holyrood, Nf, Can. 185/L2
Holywell, Wal, UK 61/E5
Holywood, NI, UK 60/C2
Holzminden, Ger. 79/G5
Holzwickede, Ger. 79/E5
Hom (riv.), Namb. 150/B3
Homa (mt.), Kenya 145/A2
Homa Bay, Kenya 145/A2
Homathko (riv.), BC, Can. 170/B2
Homberg, Ger. 79/G6
Homberg, Ger. 78/D6
Hombori, Mali 141/E3

Hombori Tondo (peak), Mali 141/E3
Hombourg-Haut, Fr. 81/F5
Homburg, Ger. 81/G5
Home (bay), Nun, Can. 167/K2
Home Hill, Austl. 160/B2
Homécourt, Fr. 81/E5
Homelake, Co, US 175/J2
Homeland, Ga, US 191/G2
Homeland, Ca, US 192/C3
Homeland, Fl, US 190/M8
Homer, La, US 179/H4
Homer, Mi, US 186/D3
Homer, NY, US 187/H3
Homer, Ga, US 189/F3
Homer, Ak, US 168/X13
Homerville, Ga, US 191/G2
Homestead, Fl, US 191/H5
Homestead, Austl. 160/B3
Homestead of America Nat'l Mon., Ne, US 181/F3
Homewood, Il, US 193/Q16
Homewood, Ca, US 172/C4
Homewood, Al, US 188/D4
Homib (riv.), Erit. 126/C5
Hommersåk, Nor. 66/A2
Homochitto (riv.), Ms, US 188/B5
Homoíne, Moz. 149/G4
Homonhon (isl.), Phil. 114/D3
Homosassa (bay), Fl, US 190/K6
Homosassa, Fl, US 190/K6
Homosassa Springs, Fl, US 190/K6
Homosassa Springs Nature World, Fl, US 190/K6
Homyel', Bela. 96/D1
Homyel'skaya (prov.), Bela. 96/D1
Hon, Ar, US 179/G3
Hon Chong, Viet. 120/D4
Hon Quan, Viet. 120/D4
Honbetsu, Japan 108/C2
Honda, Col. 207/L7
Honddu (riv.), Wal, UK 62/C2
Hondeklipbaai, SAfr. 150/B3
Hondo, Japan 110/B4
Hondo (riv.), Belz. 200/D2
Hondo, Tx, US 177/E3
Hondo Creek (res.), Tx, US 177/E3
Hondschoote, Fr. 80/B2
Hondsrug (hills), Neth. 68/D2
Hondsrug (reg.), Neth 78/D3
Honduras (gulf), NAm 196/D4
Honduras(ctry.) 165/J8
Honea Path, SC, US 189/F3
Hønefoss, Nor. 66/D1
Honesdale, Pa, US 187/J4
Honey (cr.), Wi, US 193/N14
Honey (lake), Ca, US 172/C3
Honey Brook, Pa, US 194/C3
Honey Creek, Wi, US 193/P14
Honey Grove, Tx, US 179/G4
Honeybourne, Eng, UK 63/E2
Honeyville, Ut, US 173/G3
Honfleur, Fr. 83/F2
Hong (isl.), SKor. 107/C5
Høng, Den. 65/H7
Hong (lake), China 106/C5
Hong (riv.), China 106/C4
Hong (Red) (riv.), Viet. 112/E4
Hong Gai, Viet. 113/E4
Hong Kong (dpcy.), China 103/L7
Hong Kong (int'l arpt.), China 113/G4
Hong Kong (isl.), China 113/L7
Hongam-nodongjagu, NKor. 107/E1
Hong'an, China 106/C5
Hongchang, China 107/B2
Hongch'ŏn, SKor. 107/D4
Hongdu (riv.), China 119/J2
Hongdu, China 113/F4
Honggouzi, China 104/C4
Hongguo, China 112/E3
Honghu, China 113/G2
Hongjiang, China 113/F3
Honglai, China 113/H3
Hongliu (riv.), China 104/F4
Hongliuhe, China 104/C3
Hongliuquan, China 104/D3
Honglu, China 113/H3
Hongqi, China 107/B2
Hongqiao, China 113/J2
Hongqiao (int'l arpt.), China 106/L8
Hongqizhen, China 120/E2
Hongshui (riv.), China 119/J3
Hongsŏng, SKor. 107/D4
Hongtian, China 113/H3
Hongtong, China 106/B3
Honguedo Passage, (chan.), Qu, Can. 167/K4
Honguedo Passage, Qu, Can. 184/E1
Hongwŏn, NKor. 107/D2
Hongya, China 112/D2
Hongyan, China 113/F2
Hongyang, China 113/H4
Hongyuan, China 104/E5
Hongze (lake), China 105/H5
Hongze, China 106/D4
Hœnheim, Fr. 81/G6
Honiara (cap.), Sol. 162/E5
Honiton, Eng, UK 62/C5
Honjō, Japan 108/B4
Honjō, Japan 109/C1
Honobia, Ok, US 179/G3
Honolulu (cap.), Hi, US 168/S9
Honoraville, Al, US 191/E2
Hönow, Ger. 68/Q6
Honshu (isl.), Japan 101/Q6
Honshū (isl.), Japan 103/P6
Hontianske Nemce, Slvk. 76/D1
Hoo, Eng, UK 56/E2
Hood (mt.), Ca, US 193/J10
Hood (canal), Wa, US 193/B2
Hood, Ca, US 193/L10
Hood (mt.), Or, US 172/C1
Hood (pt.), Austl. 156/C5
Hood (pt.), PNG 155/G2
Hood (co.), Tx, US 176/K7
Hood River, Or, US 170/D5
Hoofddorp, Neth. 78/B4
Hoogeloon, Neth. 78/C6
Hoogeveen, Neth. 78/D3
Hoogeveense Vaart (canal), Neth. 78/D3
Hoogezand, Neth. 78/D2
Hooghly (riv.), India 123/F5
Hooghly-Chinsura, India 123/G4
Hoogkarspel, Neth 78/C3
Hooglede, Belg. 80/C2
Hoogstraten, Belg. 78/B6
Hook (sound), Austl. 160/C3
Hook, Eng, UK 63/F4
Hook Head (pt.), Ire. 58/D5
Hooker, Ok, US 178/D2
Hooker Creek, Austl. 154/C4
Hooker Creek Abor. Land, Austl. 154/C4
Hooksett, NH, US 187/L3
Hoonah, Ak, US 166/C3
Hoopa, Ca, US 172/B3
Hoopa Valley Ind. Res., Ca, US 172/B3
Hooper, Co, US 178/B2
Hooper, Ne, US 181/F3
Hooper (Endwell), NY, US 187/H3
Hoopeston, Il, US 186/C4
Hoople, ND, US 182/F3
Hoopstad, SAfr. 150/D2
Höör, Swe. 66/E4
Hoorn, Neth. 78/C3
Hoornse Hop (bay), Neth. 78/C3
Hoosick Falls, NY, US 187/K3
Hoover (dam), Az, US 168/D4
Hoover (peak), WV, US 189/F2
Hoover, SD, US 180/C1
Höövör, Mong. 104/G2
Hopa, Turk. 97/G4
Hopatcong, NJ, US 194/D2
Hopatcong (lake), NJ, US 194/D2
Hope (lake), Austl. 153/A4
Hope, BC, Can. 170/D3
Hope, Wal, UK 61/E5
Hope, Ar, US 179/H4
Hope, In, US 186/D5
Hope, Ks, US 179/F1
Hope, ND, US 182/F4
Hope, NJ, US 194/D2
Hope, Tx, US 177/F3
Hope Mills, NC, US 189/H3
Hope Vale Abor. Land, Austl. 155/G3
Hope Vale Aboriginal Community, Austl. 160/B1
Hope-under-Dinmore, Eng, UK 62/D2
Hopedale, Nf, Can. 167/K3
Hopelchén, Mex. 200/D2
Hopeman, Sc, UK 59/C1
Hopes Advance (cape), Qu, Can. 167/K2
Hope's Nose (pt.), Eng, UK 62/C6
Hopetoun, Austl. 156/D5
Hopetown, SAfr. 150/D3
Hopewell, NS, Can. 185/F3
Hopewell, NJ, US 194/D3
Hopewell, Va, US 189/J2
Hopewell Cape, NB, Can. 184/E3
Hopewell Culture Nat'l Mon., Oh, US 186/E5
Hopewell Furnace NHS, Pa, US 194/C3
Hopi Ind. Res., Az, US 175/G2
Hopin, Myan. 112/C3
Hôpital-Camfrout, Fr. 82/A4
Hopkins (lake), Austl. 157/F3
Hopkins (riv.), Austl. 158/B3
Hopkins, Mo, US 181/G3
Hopkins, Mn, US 183/P7
Hopkinsville, Ky, US 188/D2
Hopkinton, RI, US 187/L4
Hopkinton, NH, US 187/L3
Hoppecke (riv.), Ger. 79/F6
Hoppegarten, Ger. 68/Q6
Hopper Mtn. NWR, Ca, US 192/B2
Hoppstädten-Weiersbach, Ger. 81/G4
Hopsten, Ger. 79/E4
Hoquiam, Wa, US 170/C4
Hor, China 104/E4
Horace, Ks, US 178/D1
Horace, ND, US 182/F4
Horadiz, Azer. 129/F2
Horado, Japan 109/L4
Hōrai-san (peak), Japan 109/J5
Horasan, Turk. 128/E1
Horatio, Ar, US 179/G4
Horažďovice, Czh. 85/G4
Horb am Neckar, Ger. 84/B6
Horbat Qesari (ruin), Isr. 130/D3
Horbourg-Wihr, Fr. 86/D1
Hörbranz, Aus. 87/F2
Horbury, Eng, UK 61/G4
Hörby, Swe. 65/K7
Horche, Sp. 72/D2
Horconcitos, Pan. 201/F4
Horcones (riv.), Arg. 212/C3
Hordaland (co.), Nor. 64/C3
Horden, Eng, UK 61/G2
Hœrdt, Fr. 81/G6
Hördt, Ger. 84/B4
Horezu, Rom. 77/G3
Horgau, Ger. 84/D6
Horgen, Swi. 87/E3
Hörh (peak), Mong. 104/F3
Horicon, Wi, US 181/K2
Horicon NWR, Wi, US 181/K2
Horinger, China 106/B2
Horiult, Mong. 104/E2
Horizontina, Braz. 213/F3
Horley, Eng, UK 56/C3
Horlivka, Ukr. 99/K3
Hormigüeros, PR 197/M8
Hormozgān (gov.), Iran 129/J5
Hormūd-e Mīr Khūnd, Iran 129/H5
Hormuz (str.), Oman 127/G3
Horn (isl.), Ms, US 190/D2
Horn (pt.), Ice. 216/H
Horn Lake, Ms, US 188/B3
Horn-Bad Meinberg, Ger. 79/F5
Hornachuelos, Sp. 72/C4
Hornád (riv.), Slvk. 69/L4
Hornavan (lake), Swe 64/F2
Hornbach, Ger. 81/G5
Hornbæk, Den. 65/J6
Hornbeck, La, US 190/B2
Hornbeck, Ab, Can. 170/F1
Hornberg, Ger. 87/E1
Hornburg, Ger. 79/H4
Hornby, NZ 161/C3
Hornby, On, Can. 186/T8
Hornby Island, BC, Can. 170/B3
Horncastle, Eng, UK 61/H5
Hornchurch (nbrhd.), Eng, UK 56/D2
Horndal, Swe. 66/G1
Horné Saliby, Slvk. 76/C1
Horneburg, Ger. 79/G1
Hornell, NY, US 187/H3
Hornersville, Mo, US 188/B2
Horní Bříza, Czh. 85/G3
Horní Slavkov, Czh. 85/F2
Hornisgrinde (peak), Ger. 84/B5
Hornitos, Ca, US 174/B2
Hornos, (cape), Chile 215/D7
Hornoy-le-Bourg, Fr. 80/A4
Hornsby (nbrhd.), Austl. 160/H8
Hornsea, Eng, UK 61/H4
Hornslet, Den. 66/D3
Hörnum (cape), Ger. 66/C4
Horodenka, Ukr. 98/C3
Horodnya, Ukr. 98/F2
Horodok, Ukr. 98/D3
Horodok, Ukr. 98/B3
Horodyshche, Ukr. 98/F3
Horokhiv, Ukr. 98/C2
Horoshiri-dake (peak), Japan 108/C2
Hořovice, Czh. 85/G3
Horqin Youyi Zhongqi, China 105/J2
Horqin Zuoyi Houqi, China 106/E2
Horqin Zuoyi Zhongqi, China 106/E1
Horqueta, Par. 213/E2
Horrabridge, Eng, UK 62/B5
Hörsching, Aus. 85/H6
Horse (cr.), Co, US 180/B4
Horse (mtn.), Tx, US 177/C2
Horse Cave, Ky, US 188/E2
Horse Creek, Wy, US 180/B3
Horse Shoe Run, WV, US 187/G5
Horsefly, BC, Can. 170/D1
Horsefly (riv.), BC, Can. 170/D1
Horsefly (lake), BC, Can. 170/D1
Horseheads, NY, US 187/H3
Horsens, Den. 66/C4
Horseshoe Beach, Fl, US 191/G3
Horseshoe Bend, Ar, US 179/J2
Horseshoe Bend, Id, US 172/E2
Horseshoe Bend Nat'l Mil. Park, Al, US 188/E4
Horsethief (cr.), BC, Can. 170/F2
Horsey (isl.), Eng, UK 63/H3
Horsforth, Eng, UK 61/G4
Horsham, Austl. 158/B3
Horsham, Eng, UK 63/F4
Horsham, Pa, US 194/C3
Hørsholm, Den. 65/J7
Horsmonden, Eng, UK 56/E3
Horšovský Týn, Czh. 85/F3
Horst, Ger. 79/H2
Horst, Neth. 78/D6
Hörstel, Ger. 79/E4
Horstmar, Ger. 79/E4
Horta, Azor., Port. 73/S12
Hortaleza (nbrhd.), Sp. 73/N9
Horten, Nor. 66/D2
Hortense, Ga, US 191/H2
Hortes, Fr. 86/B2
Hortobágyi NP, Hun. 96/B3
Horton, Mo, US 179/G2
Horton (riv.), NW, Can. 166/D2
Horton, Ks, US 181/G4
Horton (pt.), NY, US 195/F1
Horton Kirby, Eng, UK 56/D2
Høruphav, Den. 66/C4
Horusický Rybník (lake), Czh. 85/H4
Hørve, Den. 66/D4
Hørve, Den. 65/H7
Horvot 'Avedat (ruin), Isr. 130/D4
Horvot Dor, Isr. 131/B3
Horw, Swi. 87/E3
Horwich, Eng, UK 61/F4
Hosa'ina, Eth. 142/H4
Hösbach, Ger. 84/C2
Hosdrug, India 121/B3
Hosenfeld, Ger. 84/C1
Hosenofu (well), Libya 134/D4
Hoséré Vokré (peak), Camr. 142/B3
Hosford, Fl, US 191/F2
Hoshāb, Pak. 127/H3
Hoshangābād, India 122/A4
Hoshcha, Ukr. 98/D2
Hoshiārpur, India 124/C4
Hosingen, Lux. 81/F3
Hosmer, SD, US 182/E5
Hosmer, BC, Can. 170/G3
Hospental, Swi. 87/E4
Hospital, Ire. 58/B5
Hospital, Chile 214/N8
Hosston, La, US 179/H4
Hosszúpereszteg, Hun. 76/C2
Hoste (isl.), Chile 215/C7
Hostomel', Ukr. 98/F2
Hoswick, Sc, UK 57/W13
Hot, Thai. 120/B2
Hot Creek (range), Nv, US 172/E4
Hot Springs, SD, US 180/C2
Hot Springs NP, Ar, US 179/H3
Hot Springs Village, Ar, US 179/H3
Hot Sulphur Springs, Co, US 180/A3
Hotaka, Japan 111/E2
Hotaka-dake (peak), Japan 111/E2
Hotan (riv.), China 125/D4
Hotan, China 125/C4
Hotazel, SAfr. 150/C2
Hotevilla, Az, US 175/G3
Hotham (cape), Austl. 154/C3
Hoti, Indo. 117/H4
Hot'Kovo, Rus. 94/X9
Hotont, Mong. 104/E2
Hottah (lake), NW, Can. 166/E2
Hottentot (bay), Namb. 150/A2
Hottentots (pt.), Namb. 148/B5
Hotton, Belg. 81/E3
Hou (riv.), China 104/F5
Houamuang, Laos 112/D4
Houari Boumedienne (int'l arpt.), Alg. 138/G4
Houat (isl.), Fr. 82/C6
Houchang, China 113/E3
Houdain, Fr. 80/B3
Houdan, Fr. 83/G3
Houdan, Fr. 56/G5
Houet (prov.), Burk. 140/D4
Houffalize, Belg. 81/E3
Houghton, SD, US 182/E5
Houghton (pt.), Mi, US 183/K4
Houghton (dam), SD, US 182/E5
Houghton, Mi, US 183/K4
Houghton, NY, US 187/G3
Houghton (lake), Mi, US 186/D2
Houghton Lake, Mi, US 186/D2
Houghton-le-Spring, Eng, UK 61/G2
Houilles, Fr. 56/J5
Houlgate, Fr. 83/E2
Houlton, Me, US 167/K4
Houlton, Wi, US 183/Q6
Houma, La, US 190/C3
Houma, China 106/B4
Houndé, Burk. 140/E4
Houplines, Fr. 80/B2
Hourn, Loch (inlet), Sc, UK 59/A2
Hourtin, Fr. 70/C4
Housatonic (riv.), Ct, US 195/E1
House (range), Ut, US 168/D4
Housesteads Roman Fort, Eng, UK 61/F1
Houssen, Fr. 86/D1
Houston, De, US 194/C6
Houston, Fl, US 191/G2
Houston, Mn, US 181/J2
Houston, Mo, US 179/J2
Houston, Ms, US 188/C4
Houston, Tx, US 177/M9
Houston (lake), Tx, US 177/G2
Houston Intercontinental (int'l arpt.), Tx, US 177/M9
Houston Ship (chan.), Tx, US 177/M9
Houstonia, Mo, US 179/H1
Houtbaai, SAfr. 150/L11
Houten, Neth. 78/C4
Houthalen, Belg. 81/E1
Houthulst, Belg. 80/B2
Houtman Abrolhos (isl.), Austl. 156/B4
Houtribdijk (dam), Neth. 78/C3
Houtskär (isl.), Fin. 67/J1
Houyet, Belg. 81/E3
Houyingzi, China 107/B2
Houzhenzi, China 104/F5
Hov, Nor. 66/D1
Hova, Swe. 66/F2
Hovd (prov.), Mong. 104/C2
Hove, Eng, UK 63/F5
Hövelhof, Ger. 79/F5
Hoven, SD, US 180/E1
Hovenweep Nat'l Mon., Co, US 175/H2
Hoveton, Eng, UK 63/H1
Hovfjället (peak), Swe. 66/E1
Hovingham, Eng, UK 61/H3
Hovland, Mn, US 183/K4
Hovmantorp, Swe. 66/F3
Hövsgöl (prov.), Mong. 125/G2
Hövsgöl (lake), Mong. 104/E1
Hovsta, Swe. 66/F2
Howa, Oued (riv.), Chad 142/D2
Howar (wadi), Sudan 142/E1
Howard, Austl. 160/D4
Howard (isl.), Austl. 155/D2
Howard, NB, Can. 184/E2
Howard, Co, US 178/B1
Howard, Fl, US 190/P11
Howard, Ks, US 179/F2
Howard (co.), Md, US 194/B5
Howard, SD, US 180/F1
Howard Beach (nbrhd.), NY, US 195/K9
Howard City, Mi, US 186/D3
Howard Draw (riv.), Tx, US 177/D2
Howard Hanson (res.), Wa, US 193/D3
Howard Hanson (dam), Wa, US 193/D3
Howard Prairie (lake), Or, US 172/B2
Howards Grove, Wi, US 186/C3
Howden, Eng, UK 61/H4
Howe, Ok, US 179/G3
Howe, Tx, US 179/F4
Howe (sound), BC, Can. 170/C3
Howe (cape), Austl. 159/D3
Howe Caverns, NY, US 187/J3
Howe Green, Eng, UK 56/E1
Howe of the Mearns (reg.), Sc, UK 59/D3
Howell, Mi, US 186/E3
Howell, NJ, US 194/D3
Howey-in-the-Hills, Fl, US 190/M6
Howick, NZ 161/F6
Howick, SAfr. 151/E3
Howison, Ms, US 190/D2
Howland (isl.), Pac., US 163/H4
Howley, Nf, Can. 185/J1
Howlong, Austl. 159/C2
Howrah, India 123/G4
Howser, BC, Can. 170/F2
Hoxie, Ks, US 180/D4
Hoxie, Ar, US 188/B2
Höxter, Ger. 79/G5
Hoxud, China 125/E3
Hoy (isl.), Sc, UK 57/V14
Hoya, Ger. 79/G3
Hōya, Japan 109/D2
Høyanger, Nor. 66/B1
Hoyerswerda, Ger. 69/H3
Hoylake, Eng, UK 61/E5
Hoyland Nether, Eng, UK 61/G4
Hoyo de Manzanares, Sp. 73/N8
Hoyos, Sp. 72/B2
Hoyoux (riv.), Belg. 81/E3
Hoyt, NB, Can. 184/D3
Hoyt, Mt, US 182/B4
Hoyt, Ok, US 179/G3
Hoyt, Ks, US 181/G4
Hoyt Tamir (riv.), Mong. 104/E2
Hozumi, Japan 109/L5
Hracholusky (res.), Czh. 85/F3
Hradec Králové, Czh. 69/H3
Hradište (peak), Czh. 85/G2
Hradyz'k, Ukr. 99/G3
Hranice, Czh. 85/F2
Hrasnica, Bosn. 76/D4
Hrastnik, Slov. 76/B2
Hrazdan, Arm. 129/F1
Hrebinka, Ukr. 99/G1
Hrebinky, Ukr. 98/F3
Hřivice, Czh. 85/G2
Hrodna, Bela. 67/K5
Hrodzyenskaya (prov.), Bela. 94/E5
Hrolleifsborg (peak), Ice. 64/M6
Hron (riv.), Slvk. 96/A2
Hronov, Czh. 69/J3
Hrubieszów, Pol. 98/B2
Hrubý Jeseník (mts.), Czh.,Pol. 69/J3
Hrútafjöll (peak), Ice. 64/P6
Hrymayliv, Ukr. 98/D3
Hsenwi, Myan. 119/G3
Hsi-hseng, Myan. 112/C4
Hsinchu, Tai. 113/J3
Hsipaw, Myan. 120/B1
Hsüeh (peak), Tai. 113/J3
Htawgaw, Myan. 119/G2
Hts-de-Seine (dept.), Fr. 83/H3
Hu Xian, China 104/F5
Hua (peak), China 106/B4
Hua Hin, Thai. 120/B3
Hua Sai, Thai. 120/C4
Hua Xian, China 106/C4
Huab (riv.), Namb. 148/B3
Huacaraje, Bol. 209/F4
Huacareta, Bol. 212/D2
Huacaya, Bol. 212/D2
Huacaybamba, Peru 208/B3
Huachacalla, Bol. 212/B1
Huacheng, China 113/G3
Huachi, China 104/F4
Huachi, Bol. 209/F4
Huacho, Peru 208/B3
Huachón, Peru 208/C3
Huachuan, China 105/L2
Huachuca (mts.), Az, US 175/G5
Huachuca City, Az, US 175/G5
Huacrachuco, Peru 208/B3
Huade, China 104/G3
Huadian, China 105/K3
Huadianzi, China 107/C2
Huahine (isl.), FrPol. 163/K6
Huai (riv.), China 106/C4
Huai Yot, Thai. 120/B5
Huai'an, China 106/C2
Huai'an, China 106/D4
Huaibei, China 104/H5
Huaibin, China 106/C4
Huaihua, China 113/F3
Huaiji, China 113/G4
Huailai, China 106/G6
Huainan, China 106/D4
Huaining, China 113/H2
Huairen, China 106/C3
Huairou, China 106/H6
Huaiyang, China 106/C4
Huaiyin, China 106/D4
Huaiyin, China 106/D4
Huaiyuan, China 106/D4
Huajicori, Mex. 198/D4
Huajuapan de León, Mex. 200/B2
Hualahuises, Mex. 199/F3
Hualañé, Chile 214/C2
Hualapai (peak), Az, US 175/F3
Hualapai (mts.), Az, US 175/F3
Hualapai Ind. Res., Az, US 175/F3
Hualfín, Arg. 212/C3
Hualgayoc, Peru 208/B2
Hualien, Tai. 113/J4
Hualla, Peru 208/C4
Huallaga (riv.), Peru 203/B3
Huallanca, Peru 208/B3
Huamachuco, Peru 208/B2
Huamantanga, Peru 208/B3
Huamantla, Mex. 199/M7
Huambo, Ang. 148/B2
Huambo (dist.), Ang. 148/B2
Huambos, Peru 208/B2
Huan (riv.), China 106/C5
Huan Xian, China 104/F4
Huanan, China 105/L2
Huanaque, Bol. 212/B2
Huancané, Peru 208/D4
Huancapi, Peru 208/C4
Huancaspata, Peru 208/B3
Huancavelica, Peru 208/C4
Huancavelica (dept.), Peru 208/C4
Huancayo, Peru 208/C4
Huanchaca (peak), Bol. 212/C2
Huang (riv.), China 103/L6
Huang (Yellow) (riv.), China 104/G4
Huangbayi, China 104/F5
Huangbei, China 113/H3
Huangchuan, China 106/C4
Huangcun, China 113/F3
Huanggang (peak), China 113/H3
Huanggang, China 113/G2
Huanghua, China 106/D3
Huangjinbu, China 113/H2
Huangjinggou, China 112/E2
Huangli, China 106/K8
Huangling, China 106/B4
Huangliu, China 113/F5
Huanglong, China 106/B4
Huanglong, China 113/G3
Huanglongtan, China 106/B4
Huangmao (peak), China 113/H3
Huangmei, China 113/G2
Huangniupu, China 104/F5
Huangpi, China 113/G2
Huangping, China 119/J2
Huangqi (lake), China 106/C2
Huangshan, China 113/H2
Huangshi, China 113/G2
Huangshidu, China 113/H3
Huangtang (lake), China 106/C5
Huangtianpu, China 113/F3
Huangtu (plat.), China 106/B4
Huangtudian, China 113/F2
Huanguelén, Arg. 214/E3
Huangwan, China 106/L9
Huangyunpu, China 106/B4
Huangzhai, China 113/H2
Huangzhan, China 113/G2
Huangzhong, China 104/E4
Huaning, China 112/D3
Huanjiang, China 119/J3
Huanren, China 107/C2
Huanta, Peru 208/C4
Huantai, China 106/D3
Huántar, Peru 208/B3
Huantunas (lake), Bol. 209/E4
Huánuco, Peru 208/B3
Huánuco (dept.), Peru 208/C3
Huanuni, Bol. 212/C1
Huanxi, China 113/G3
Huapi (mts.), Nic. 200/E3
Huaping, China 112/D3
Huaqiaozhen, China 104/F5
Huaquechula, Mex. 199/L8
Huaquillas, Ecu. 208/A1
Huara, Chile 212/B1
Huaral, Peru 208/B3
Huaraz, Peru 208/B3
Huari, Bol. 212/C1
Huari, Peru 208/B3
Huaricolca, Peru 208/C3
Huarina, Bol. 208/D5
Huarmey, Peru 208/B3
Huarochirí, Peru 208/B4
Huarocondo, Peru 208/C4
Huásabas, Mex. 198/C2
Huasahuasi, Peru 208/C3
Huascarán (peak), Peru 208/B3
Huascaran, PN, Peru 208/B3
Huasco (riv.), Chile 212/B4
Huashi (mts.), China 113/G3
Huashi, China 113/G3
Huatabampo, Mex. 198/C3
Huatong, China 107/A2
Huatuxco, Mex. 199/N7
Huauchinango, Mex. 199/L6
Huaura, Peru 208/B3
Huautla de Jiménez, Mex. 200/B2
Huayacocotla, Mex. 199/L6
Huayang, China 113/J2
Huayangzhen, China 104/F5
Huaying, China 113/E2
Huaylas, Peru 208/B3
Huayllay, Peru 208/B3
Huayopata, Peru 208/C4
Huayuan, China 107/D1
Huayuan, China 119/J2
Huayuan, China 113/G2
Huazhaizi, China 104/E4
Huazhou, China 119/K3
Huazi, China 107/B2
Hub, Ms, US 190/D2
Hubbard, Sk, Can. 182/C2
Hubbard (lake), Mi, US 186/E2
Hubbard, Or, US 172/B1
Hubbard, Ia, US 181/H2
Hubbard, Tx, US 177/F2
Hubbard Creek (res.), Tx, US 177/E1
Hubbards, NS, Can. 184/E3
Hubbell Trading Post Nat'l Hist. Site, Az, US 175/H3
Hubei (pass), China 106/B4
Huber Heights, Oh, US 186/D5
Hubli-Dhārwār, India 121/B3
Huch'ang, NKor. 107/D2
Hückelhoven, Ger. 81/F1
Hückeswagen, Ger. 81/G1
Hucknall, Eng, UK 61/G5
Hudai, China 106/L8
Huddersfield, Eng, UK 61/G4
Huddinge, Swe. 66/G2
Hude, Ger. 79/F2
Hudiksvall, Swe. 66/G1
Hudson (cape), Ant. 216/L
Hudson (bay), Can. 165/J3
Hudson, On, Can. 183/H2
Hudson, Qu, Can. 185/M7
Hudson (str.), Nun,Qu, Can. 167/J2
Hudson, Fl, US 190/K7
Hudson, Il, US 181/K3
Hudson, Mi, US 186/D4
Hudson, NC, US 189/G3
Hudson (co.), NJ, US 195/J9
Hudson, NY, US 187/K3
Hudson (riv.), NJ, NY, US 187/K3
Hudson (lake), Ok, US 179/G2
Hudson, Tx, US 177/G2
Hudson, Wi, US 183/Q7
Hudson Bay, Sk, Can. 166/F3
Hudson Falls, NY, US 187/K3
Hudson Oaks, Tx, US 176/K7
Hudsons (peak), Austl. 159/D3
Hudson's Hope, BC, Can. 166/D3
Hue, Viet. 120/D2
Hueco (mts.), Tx, US 177/B2
Huedin, Rom. 77/F2
Huehuetenango, Guat. 200/D3
Huehuetla, Mex. 199/L6
Huehuetlán, Mex. 199/L8
Huejotzingo, Mex. 199/L7
Huejuquilla el Alto, Mex. 198/E4
Huejutla de Reyes, Mex. 200/B1
Huelgoat, Fr. 82/B4
Huelma, Sp. 72/D4
Huelva (riv.), Sp. 72/B4
Huelva, Sp. 72/B4
Huequi (vol.), Chile 214/B4
Huercal-Overa, Sp. 72/E4
Huerfano (riv.), Co, US 180/B5
Huesca, Sp. 73/E1
Huéscar, Sp. 72/D4
Huesos (stream), Arg. 214/F3
Huetamo de Nuñez, Mex. 199/E5
Huete, Sp. 72/D2
Huexoculco, Mex. 199/R10
Hüfingen, Ger. 87/E2
Huger, SC, US 189/H4
Hugh Town, Eng, UK 57/Q12
Hughenden, Austl. 160/B3
Hughenden, Ab, Can. 171/J1
Hughenden Valley, Eng, UK 56/A2
Hughes, Arg. 214/E2
Hughes, Ar, US 188/B3
Hughes, Austl. 157/F4
Hughes Springs, Tx, US 179/G4
Hughesville, Pa, US 194/B1
Hughson, Ca, US 174/B2
Huglfing, Ger. 87/H2
Hugli (riv.), India 118/E3
Hugo, Ok, US 179/G3
Hugo (lake), Ok, US 179/G3
Hugo (dam), Ok, US 179/G3
Hugo, Co, US 180/C4
Hugo, Mn, US 183/Q6
Hugoton, Ks, US 178/D2
Huguan, China 106/C3
Hui (riv.), China 105/H2
Hui Xian, China 106/C4
Huib-Hoch (plat.), Namb. 150/B2
Huichapan, Mex. 199/K6
Hŭich'ŏn, NKor. 107/D2
Huila (dept.), Col. 204/C4
Huila (dept.), Ang. 148/B2
Huilango, Mex. 199/Q9
Huili, China 119/H2
Huimanguillo, Mex. 200/C2
Huimin, China 106/D3
Huinan, China 105/K3
Huinca Renancó, Arg. 214/D2
Huining, China 104/F4
Hŭisaek-pong (peak), NKor. 107/D2
Huishui, China 119/J2
Huisne (riv.), Fr. 70/D2
Huisseau-sur-Cosson, Fr. 83/G5
Huissen, Neth. 78/C5
Huitong, China 119/J2
Huittinen, Fin. 67/K1
Huitzilan, Mex. 199/M7
Huitzuco, Mex. 199/K8
Huixcolotla, Mex. 199/M8
Huixquilucan, Mex. 199/Q10
Huixtla, Mex. 200/C3
Huize, China 112/D3
Huizen, Neth. 78/C4
Huizhou, China 113/G4
Hujirt, Mong. 104/E2
Hujra, Pak. 124/B4
Hŭksan (arch.), SKor. 105/J5
Hukuntsi, Bots. 148/D4
Hulah (dam), Ok, US 179/F2
Hulah (lake), Ok, US 179/F2
Hulan, China 105/K2
Hulan (riv.), China 105/K2
Hulbert, Ok, US 179/G3
Hulbert, Mi, US 186/D1
Hulett, Wy, US 180/B1
Hull (riv.), Eng, UK 61/H4
Hull, Qu, Can. 187/J2
Hull, Ia, US 181/F2
Hull (Orona) (isl.), Kiri. 163/H5
Hullbridge, Eng, UK 56/E2
Hüllhorst, Ger. 79/F4
Hullo, Est. 67/K2
Hulst, Neth. 78/B6
Hultsfred, Swe. 66/F3
Hulu (riv.), China 104/F4
Hulun (lake), China 104/H2
Ḥulwān, Egypt 139/C5
Hulyaypole, Ukr. 99/J4
Huma (riv.), China 101/N4
Huma, China 105/K1
Humahuaca, Arg. 212/C2
Humaitá, Par. 212/E3
Humaitá, Braz. 209/F2
Humaitá, Bol. 209/E3
Humaljärvi (lake), Fin. 65/E4
Humansdorp, SAfr. 150/D4
Humansville, Mo, US 179/H2
Humay, Peru 208/C4
Humbe, Ang. 148/B3
Humber (riv.), Eng, UK 61/H4
Humber (riv.), Nf, Can. 184/J1
Humber (bay), On, Can. 186/U8
Humber, West (riv.), On, Can. 186/T8
Humberside (arpt.), Eng, UK 61/H4
Humberside (co.), Eng, UK 61/H4
Humberston, Eng, UK 61/H4
Humberto de Campos, Braz. 207/F3
Humble, Tx, US 177/M9
Humboldt, Sk, Can. 171/M1
Humboldt (bay), Col. 201/G5
Humboldt (peak), NCal. 163/V12
Humboldt, Az, US 175/F3
Humboldt (bay), Ca, US 172/A3
Humboldt, Ks, US 179/G2
Humboldt, Ia, US 181/G2
Humboldt, Mn, US 182/F3
Humboldt, Ne, US 181/G3
Humboldt (lake), Nv, US 172/D3
Humboldt (riv.), Nv, US 168/C3
Humboldt, Tn, US 188/C3
Humboldt, North Fork (riv.), Nv, US 172/F3
Hume (dam), Austl. 159/C3
Hūmedān, Iran 127/G3
Humenné, Slvk. 69/L4
Humeston, Ia, US 181/H3
Humlebæk, Den. 65/J7
Humlum, Den. 66/C3
Hummels Wharf, Pa, US 194/B2
Hummelstown, Pa, US 194/B3
Humnoke, Ar, US 179/J3
Humphrey, Ar, US 179/J3
Humphrey, On, Can. 187/G2
Humphrey, Ne, US 180/F3
Humphreys (peak), Az, US 175/G3
Humphreys (mt.), Ca, US 174/C2
Humpty Doo, Austl. 154/C3
Humshaugh, Eng, UK 61/F1
Hūn, Libya 134/B2
Hun (riv.), China 105/J3
Húnaflói (bay), Ice. 64/N6
Hunan (prov.), China 119/K2
Hunchun, China 105/L3
Hundested, Den. 65/H7
Hundewāli, Pak. 124/B4
Hundred, WV, US 186/F5
Hundred Fifty Mile House, BC, Can. 170/D1
Hundred Mile House, BC, Can. 170/D2
Hundsangen, Ger. 81/G3
Hunedoara (prov.), Rom. 76/F3
Hunedoara, Rom. 76/F3
Hünenberg, Swi. 87/E3
Hung Yen, Viet. 120/D1
Hungaroring, Hun. 77/R9
Hungary(ctry.) 55/F4
Hungen, Ger. 84/B2
Hungerford, Austl. 158/C1
Hungerford, Eng, UK 63/E4
Hŭnghae, SKor. 107/E4
Hŭngnam, NKor. 107/D3
Hŭngnyŏng-nodongjagu, NKor. 107/D3
Hungry (peak), Id, US 170/G4
Hungry Horse (dam), Mt, US 171/G3
Hungulo, Ang. 148/C2
Hüngüy (riv.), Mong. 104/C2
Hunjiang, China 107/D2
Hunkui, Nga. 141/G4
Hunmanby, Eng, UK 61/H3
Hunnebostrand, Swe. 66/D2
Hunsel, Neth. 78/C6
Hunsrück (mts.), Ger. 68/D4
Hunstanton, Eng, UK 63/G1
Hunt (mtn.), Wy, US 173/K1
Hunte (riv.), Ger. 68/E2
Hunter, ND, US 182/F4
Hunter (mtn.), NY, US 187/J3
Hunter (riv.), Austl. 158/D2
Hunter, Tx, US 176/E3
Hunter (isl.), Austl. 153/D5
Hunter Army Afld., Ga, US 191/H1
Hunterdon (co.), NJ, US 194/C2
Hunters, Wa, US 170/E3
Hunters Creek Village, Tx, US 177/M9
Huntersville, NC, US 189/G3
Hunterville, NZ 161/C2
Huntingburg, In, US 188/D1
Huntingdon, Qu, Can. 187/J2
Huntingdon, Eng, UK 63/F2
Huntingdon, Tn, US 188/C2
Huntingdon, Pa, US 187/G4
Huntington, Eng, UK 61/G4
Huntington, In, US 186/D4
Huntington, NY, US 195/M8
Huntington (bay), NY, US 195/M8
Huntington, Or, US 172/E1
Huntington (cr.), Pa, US 194/B1
Huntington, Tx, US 176/G2
Huntington, Ut, US 173/H4
Huntington, WV, US 189/F1
Huntington Bay, NY, US 195/M8
Huntington Beach, Ca, US 192/G8
Huntington Park, Ca, US 192/F8
Huntington Station, NY, US 195/M8
Huntington Woods, Mi, US 193/F7
Huntland, Tn, US 188/D3
Huntley, Il, US 193/P15
Huntly, Sc, UK 59/D2
Huntly, NZ 161/C2
Hunts Point, Wa, US 193/C2
Huntsville, On, Can. 187/G2
Huntsville, Al, US 188/D3
Huntsville, Ar, US 179/H2
Huntsville, Mo, US 181/H4
Huntsville (res.), Pa, US 194/B1
Huntsville, Tn, US 188/E2
Huntsville, Tx, US 177/G2
Huntsville, Wa, US 170/E4
Hunua, NZ 161/G7
Hunucmá, Mex. 200/D1
Hünxe, Ger. 78/D5
Hunyuan, China 106/C3
Huo (mtn.), China 106/B3
Huo (mtn.), China 106/D5
Huocheng, China 125/D3
Huojia, China 106/C4
Huolin Gol, China 105/H2
Huolongmen, China 105/K2
Huolupu, China 113/E2
Huon (gulf), PNG 155/G1
Huon (pen.), PNG 155/G1
Huong Hoa, Viet. 120/D2
Huong Khe, Viet. 120/D2
Huong Son, Viet. 120/D2
Huong Thuy, Viet. 119/J4
Huonville, Austl. 158/C4
Huoqiu, China 106/D4
Huoshan, China 106/D5
Huotong, China 113/H3
Huozhou, China 106/B3
Huraymilā, SAr. 126/E3
Hūraya, Egypt 139/B3
Hurd (cape), On, Can. 186/F2
Hurdal, Nor. 66/D1
Hurdiyo, Som. 144/D3
Hurdle Mills, NC, US 189/H2
Hure Qi, China 106/E2
Hurepoix (reg.), Fr. 56/H6
Hurley, Wi, US 183/J4
Hurley (riv.), Ire. 60/B4
Hurley, Ms, US 190/D2
Hurley, NY, US 187/J4
Hurley, Eng, UK 56/A2
Hurley, NM, US 175/H4
Hurlford, Sc, UK 59/B5
Hurlock, Md, US 189/K1
Huron (bay), Mi, US 183/K4
Huron (mts.), Mi, US 183/K4
Huron, Oh, US 186/E4
Huron (pt.), Mi, US 193/G6
Huron (riv.), Mi, US 193/E7
Huron, Ca, US 174/B2
Huron (lake), Can.,US 165/J5
Huron, SD, US 180/E1
Huron Islands Nat'l Wild. Ref., Mi, US 183/K4
Huron Mountain, Mi, US 183/L4
Hurricane (lake), ND, US 182/E3
Hurricane, Al, US 190/E2
Hurricane, Ut, US 175/F2
Hurricane, WV, US 189/F1
Hurricane (cliffs), Az, US 175/F2
Hurshat Tal NP, Isr. 131/D2
Hurst, Tx, US 176/K7
Hurstville, Austl. 159/E1
Hurtaut (riv.), Fr. 80/D4
Hürtgenwald (reg.), Ger. 81/F2
Hürth, Ger. 81/F2
Hurtsboro, Al, US 188/E4
Hurum, Nor. 64/S9
Hurup, Den. 66/C3
Huruta, Eth. 144/A3
Hurworth, Eng, UK 61/G3
Husainābād, India 123/E3
Husainpur, Bang. 123/H3
Húsavík, Ice. 64/P6
Ḥusayyāt al Fawākhir (well), Libya 134/D2
Husbands Bosworth, Eng, UK 63/E2
Husby-långhundra, Swe. 65/B1
Hushan, China 113/H2
Husher, Wi, US 193/Q14
Hushi, China 113/H3
Huşi, Rom. 98/E4
Huskisson, Austl. 159/E2
Husnes, Nor. 66/A2
Hussar, Ab, Can. 171/H2
Hussigny-Godbrange, Fr. 81/E5
Hustisford, Wi, US 181/K2
Husum, Ger. 66/C4
Husum, Swe. 64/F3
Husyatyn, Ukr. 98/D3
Hutag, Mong. 104/E2
Hutanopan, Indo. 115/C2
Hutchins, Tx, US 176/L7
Hutchinson, Ks, US 179/F1
Hutchinson (isl.), Fl, US 191/H4
Hutchinson, Mn, US 181/G1
Ḥūth, Yem. 144/B1
Hutiaoxia, China 112/D3
Hutsonville, Il, US 186/C5
Hutt (riv.), NZ 161/J9
Huttig, Ar, US 179/H4
Hüttisheim, Ger. 87/F1
Hüttlingen, Ger. 84/D5
Huttoft, Eng, UK 61/J5
Hutton, Eng, UK 56/E2
Hutton (mt.), Austl. 160/C4
Hutton Cranswick, Eng, UK 61/H4
Hutton Lake Nat'l Wild. Ref., Wy, US 180/B3
Hutton Rudby, Eng, UK 61/G3
Huttonville, On, Can. 186/T8
Huttwil, Swi. 86/D3
Hutubi, China 125/E3
Hutuo (riv.), China 106/C3
Huveane (riv.), Fr. 73/H1
Huveaune (riv.), Fr. 90/B6
Huwan, China 113/G2
Ḥuwwārah, WBnk. 131/C4
Huxi, China 113/G3
Huxley, Tx, US 177/H2
Huxley, Ia, US 181/H3
Huy, Belg. 81/E2
Huyton-with-Roby, Eng, UK 61/F5
Hūzgān, Iran 129/G4
Huzhou, China 106/L9
Hvammstangi, Ice. 64/N6
Hvannadalshnúkur (peak), Ice. 64/P7
Hvar, Cro. 76/C4
Hvar (isl.), Cro. 93/H2
Hvardiys'ke, Ukr. 99/H5
Hvide Sande, Den. 66/C4
Hvidovre, Den. 65/J7
Hvítá (riv.), Ice. 64/N7
Hvitsten, Nor. 64/S9
Hvittingfoss, Nor. 64/R9
Hvolsvöllur, Ice. 64/N7
Hwach'ŏn, SKor. 107/D3
Hwadae, NKor. 107/E2
Hwange, Zim. 149/E3
Hwange (Wankie) NP, Zim. 149/E3
Hwanghae-bukto (prov.), NKor. 107/D3
Hwanghae-namdo (prov.), NKor. 107/C3
Hwangju (riv.), NKor. 107/C3
Hwangju, NKor. 107/C3
Hwap'yŏng, NKor. 107/D2
Hwasun, SKor. 107/D5
Hyades (peak), Chile 214/B5
Hyak, Wa, US 170/D4
Hyangsan, NKor. 107/D2
Hyannis, Ne, US 180/D2
Hyargas (lake), Mong. 104/C2
Hyattstown, Md, US 194/A5
Hyattsville, Md, US 194/B6
Hyco (res.), NC, US 189/H2
Hyde, Eng, UK 61/F5
Hyde, NZ 161/B4
Hyde Park, Vt, US 187/K2
Hyde Park, NY, US 187/K4
Hyden, Ky, US 189/F2
Hyden, Austl. 156/C5
Hyderābād, Pak. 127/J3
Hyderābād, India 121/C2
Hydesville, Ca, US 172/A3
Hyères (riv.), Fr. 82/B4
Hyères (bay), Fr. 90/C6
Hyères, Fr. 90/C6
Hyères, Iles d' (isls.), Fr. 92/E2
Hyesan, NKor. 107/E2
Hyland (riv.), Yk, Can. 166/D2
Hyllestad, Nor. 66/A1
Hyltebruk, Swe. 66/E3
Hylton (hill), Ky, US 189/F2
Hyō-no-sen (peak), Japan 110/D3
Hyōgo (pref.), Japan 110/D3
Hyŏndŭng-san (peak), SKor. 107/G6
Hypoluxo, Fl, US 190/P9
Hyrra Banda, CAfr. 142/D4
Hyrum, Ut, US 173/H3
Hyrylä (Skavaböle), Fin. 65/F4
Hysham, Mt, US 171/L4
Hythe, Austl. 158/C4
Hythe, Eng, UK 63/E5
Hythe, Eng, UK 63/H4
Hytop, Al, US 188/D3
Hyūga, Japan 110/B4
Hyvinkää, Fin. 67/L1

I

I-n-Amenas, Alg. 137/H3
I-n-Amguel, Alg. 137/G5
I-n-Azaoua, Oued (riv.), Niger 137/H5
I-n-Chaouâg (wadi), Mali 141/F2
I-n-Dagouber (well), Mali 137/E5
I-n-Échaï (well), Mali 141/E1
I-n-Eker, Alg. 137/G4
I-n-Farba, Mrta. 140/C3
I-n-Gall, Niger 141/G2

I-n – Isacc

Isachsen (cape), Nun, Can. 167/R7
Isachsen, Nun, Can. 167/R7
Ísafjardhardjúp (inlet), Ice. 64/M6
Ísafjördhur, Ice. 64/M6
Isahaya, Japan 110/B4
Isak, Indo. 115/B1
Isaka, D.R. Congo 146/D3
Isaka, D.R. Congo 146/D3
Isakovo, Rus. 94/G5
Isalo Ruiniform (mass.), Madg. 152/H8
Isalo, PN de l', Madg. 152/H8
Isana (riv.), Col. 204/D4
Isandhlwana Battlesite, SAfr. 151/E3
Isangano NP, Zam. 147/G5
Isangel, Van. 162/F6
Isangi, D.R. Congo 147/F2
Isango-Isoro, D.R. Congo 147/G3
Isanlu Makutu, Nga. 141/G4
Isaouanne-n-Irarraren (des.), Alg. 137/G4
Isaouanne-n-Tifernine (des.), Alg. 137/G4
Isar (riv.), Aus. 87/H3
Isarco (riv.), It. 71/J3
Isarco (Eisack) (riv.), It. 87/H4
Isaszeg, Hun. 77/R9
Isawa, Japan 109/B2
Isbergues, Fr. 80/B2
Iscar, Sp. 72/C2
Ischgl, Aus. 87/G3
Ischia, It. 92/C6
Ischia (isl.), It. 92/C6
Isclero (riv.), It. 92/D5
Ise (riv.), Ger. 79/H3
Ise (bay), Japan 111/E3
Ise, Japan 109/L7
Ise (riv.), Eng, UK 63/F2
Ise-Shima NP, Japan 111/E3
Isehara, Japan 111/F3
Isel (riv.), Aus. 93/G1
Iselin, NJ, US 195/H9
Isen (riv.), Ger. 68/G4
Isen, Ger. 85/F6
Isenthal, Swi. 87/E4
Isenyela, Tanz. 145/A4
'Iseo (lake), It. 88/C1
Iseo, It. 88/D2
Iseo (lake), It. 71/J4
Iseramagazi, Tanz. 147/H4
Isère (dept.), Fr. 86/B6
Isère (riv.), Fr. 70/F4
Iserlohn, Ger. 79/E6
Isernia, It. 92/D4
Isernia (prov.), It. 92/D4
Isesaki, Japan 111/F2
Iset' (riv.), Rus. 95/Q4
Isetskoye, Rus. 95/Q4
Iseyin, Nga. 141/F5
Isfahan (int'l arpt.), Iran 129/G3
'Isfiyā, Isr. 131/C3
Ishenga Oswe, D.R. Congo 147/E3
Isherton, Guy. 205/G4
Ishi (riv.), Japan 109/J7
Ishibashi, Japan 111/F2
Ishibe, Japan 109/K5
Ishidoriya, Japan 108/B4
Ishigaki (isl.), Japan 111/G8
Ishige, Japan 111/F2
Ishikari, Japan 108/B2
Ishikari (riv.), Japan 108/B2
Ishikari (bay), Japan 108/B2
Ishikari (mts.), Japan 108/C2
Ishikawa, Japan 111/G2
Ishikawa (pref.), Japan 111/E2
Ishiki, Japan 109/M6
Ishim, Rus. 95/R4
Ishim (riv.), Rus. 100/H4
Ishimbay, Rus. 97/L1
Ishinomaki, Japan 108/B4
Ishioka, Japan 111/G2
Ishizuchi-san (peak), Japan 110/C4
Ishlya, Rus. 95/N5
Ishmant, Egypt 139/C6
Ishøj, Den. 65/J7
Ishpeming, Mi, US 183/L4
Ishurdi, Bang. 123/G3
Isiboro Secure, PN (riv.), Bol. 209/E4
Isidoro Noblía, Uru. 213/F4
Isigny-le-Buat, Fr. 83/D3
Isigny-sur-Mer, Fr. 83/D2
Isil'kul', Rus. 100/H4
Isiolo, Kenya 145/B1
Isiro, D.R. Congo 147/F2
Isisford, Austl. 160/B4
Iskandarūnah, Leb. 131/C2
Iske-Ryazyap, Rus. 95/L5
İskenderun (gulf), Turk. 130/D1
İskenderun, Turk. 130/E1
İskilip, Turk. 96/E4
Iskininskiy, Kaz. 97/K3
Iskitim, Rus. 100/J4
Iskŭr (res.), Bul. 75/H1
Iskŭr (riv.), Bul. 75/H1
Iskŭr (riv.), Aus. 77/G4
Iskŭr (riv.), Bul. 93/K2
Iskur (lake), Hun. 77/F4
Iskushuban, Som. 144/D3
Isla (riv.), Sc, UK 59/C3
Isla, Mex. 200/C2
Isla Aguada, Mex. 200/D2
Isla Cabritos, PN, DRep. 201/J2
Isla Cedros, Mex. 198/B2
Isla Cristina, Sp. 72/B4
Isla de Maipo, Chile 214/N8
Isla de Salamanca, PN, Col. 204/C2
Isla de San Andrés (int'l arpt.), Col. 201/F3
Isla Gorge NP, Austl. 160/C4
Isla Guamblin, PN, Chile 214/B5
Isla Isabela, PN, Mex. 198/D4
Isla Magdalena, PN, Chile 214/B5
Isla Mujeres, Mex. 200/E1
Islām Kot, Pak. 127/K4
Islāmābād (cap.), Pak. 124/B3
Islāmābād (cap. terr.), Pak. 124/B3
Islāmābād/Rāwalpindi (int'l arpt.), Pak. 124/B3
Islāmnagar, India 122/B1
Islamorada, Fl, US 191/H5
Islāmpur, India 123/G2
Islāmpur, India 123/E3
Island (lake), Mn, US 183/H4
Island (co.), Wa, US 193/B2
Island (lake), Mb, Can. 166/G3
Island Bay (nbrhd.), NZ 161/H9
Island Bay Nat'l Wild. Ref., Fl, US 191/G4
Island Beach State Park, NJ, US 194/D4
Island City, Or, US 172/D1
Island Lagoon (lake), Austl. 157/H4
Island Lake, Il, US 193/P15
Island Park, NY, US 195/L9
Island Park, Id, US 173/H1
Island Park (res.), Id, US 173/H1
Island Pond, Vt, US 187/L2
Islands (bay), NF, Can. 184/H1
Islands (bay), NZ 161/C1
Islay (isl.), Sc, UK 57/Q9
Islay, Peru 208/C5
Islay, Ab, Can. 171/J1
Isle, Mn, US 183/H4
Isle au Haut (isl.), Me, US 184/C3
Isle aux Morts, Nf, Can. 185/H2
Isle Madame (isl.), Ns., Can. 185/G3
Isle of Ely (phys. reg.), Eng, UK 63/G2
Isle of Man (Ronaldsway) (arpt.), IM, UK 60/D3
Isle of Portland (pen.), Eng, UK 62/D5
Isle of Thanet (phys. reg.), Eng, UK 63/H4
Isle of Whithorn, Sc, UK 60/D2
Isle of Wight (co.), Eng, UK 63/E5
Isle of Wight, Va, US 189/J2
Isle Royale (isl.), Mi, US 183/K3
Isle Royale NP, Mi, US 183/K3
Isle Wooden (isl.), Austl. 155/E3
Isleham, Eng, UK 63/G2
Isles Dernieres (isls.), La, US 190/C3
Isleta, NM, US 175/J3
Isleta Ind. Res., NM, US 175/J3
Isleten, Swi. 87/E4
Isleton, Ca, US 193/L10
Islington (bor.), Eng, UK 56/A1
Islip, NY, US 195/E2
Isluga (vol.), Chile 212/B1
Ismā'īlīyah (canal), Egypt 139/C4
Ismailovo Park, Rus 94/W9
Ismail Samani (peak), Taj. 125/B4
Ismaning, Ger. 85/E6
Ismayıllı, Azer. 97/J4
Isnā, Egypt 135/G3
Isny, Ger. 87/G2
Iso-Evo, Fin. 65/F3
Iso-Roine (lake), Fin. 65/E3
Isoanala, Madg. 152/H8
Isobe, Japan 109/L7
Isojärven NP, Fin. 67/L1
Isojärvi (lake), Fin. 67/J1
Isoka, Zam 147/H5
Isola, Fr. 90/D4
Isola, Ms, US 188/B4
Isola del Gran Sasso d'Italia, It. 91/C3
Isola del Liri, It. 92/C4
Isola della Scala, It. 89/D3
Isola di Capo Rizzuto, It. 75/E3
Isola Vicentina, It. 89/E2
Isole (riv.), Fr. 82/B5
Isonzo (riv.), It. 89/G1
Isorella, It. 88/D3
Isparta, Turk. 128/B2
Isparta (prov.), Turk. 128/B2
Isperikh, Bul. 77/H4
Ispir, Turk. 97/G4
Israel(ctry.) 103/C6
Issac (lake), BC, Can. 170/D1
Issac (riv.), Austl. 153/D3
Issano, Guy. 206/B1
Issaquah, Wa, US 193/C2
Issaquah (cr.), Wa, US 193/C2
Issé, Fr. 82/D5
Issel (riv.), Ger. 78/D5
Isselburg, Ger. 78/D5
Issenheim, Fr. 86/D2
Issia, C.d'Iv. 140/D5
Issoire, Fr. 70/E4
Issou, Fr. 56/H5
Issum, Ger. 78/D5
Issuna, Tanz. 145/A3
Issutugan (riv.), Som. 144/C3
Issy-les-Moulineaux, Fr. 56/J5
Istachatta, Fl, US 190/L6
Istállós-Kő (peak), Hun. 76/E1
Istana Maimoon (Maimoon Palace), Indo. 115/B2
İstanbul (prov.), Turk. 96/D4
İstanbul, Turk. 129/M6
Işţanhā, Egypt 139/C4
Istead Rise, Eng, UK 56/E2
Istiaía, Gre. 75/H3
Istmina, Col. 204/B3
Istok, Yugo. 76/E4
Istokpaga (lake), Fl, US 191/H4
Istra (riv.), Rus. 94/W9
Istrana, It. 89/F2
Istranca (mts.), Turk. 93/K2
Istres, Fr. 90/A5
Istria (reg.), Cro. 93/G1
Istria (pen.), Cro. 71/K4
Isulan, Phil. 114/D4
Isumi, Japan 109/E3
Iswarganj, Bang. 123/H3
Iswarīpur, Bang. 123/G4
Isyangulovo, Rus. 97/L1
Itá Ibaté, Arg. 213/E3
Itabaiana, Braz. 211/F1
Itabaiana, Braz. 207/H4
Itabaianinha, Braz. 211/F1
Itaberaba, Braz. 211/E2
Itaberaí, Braz. 210/C3
Itabira, Braz. 211/E3
Itabirito, Braz. 210/E4
Itaboraí, Braz. 211/P7
Itabuna, Braz. 211/F2
Itacaiunas (riv.), Braz. 206/D4
Itacajá, Braz. 206/E5
Itacarambi, Braz. 210/D2
Itacoatiara, Braz. 206/B3
Itacuaí (riv.), Braz. 208/D2
Itacuruba, Braz. 207/G5
Itacurubí del Rosario, Par. 213/E3
Itaga, Tanz. 147/H4
Itagibá, Braz. 211/F2
Itaguaí, Braz. 211/N7
Itaguatins, Braz. 207/E4
Itagüí, Col. 207/K6
Itahuazurenda, Bol. 212/D1
Itaí, Braz. 213/G2
Itaíba, Braz. 207/G5
Itaiçaba, Braz. 207/G4
Itainópolis, Braz. 207/F4
Itaiópolis, Braz. 213/G3
Itaipu (res.), Braz.,Par. 203/D5
Itaipú (dam), Par. 213/F3
Itaituba, Braz. 206/C4
Itajaí, Braz. 213/G3
Itajaí (riv.), Braz. 213/G3
Itajubá, Braz. 211/L7
Itākhola, Bang. 123/H3
Itako, Japan 111/G3
Itakura, Japan 109/D1
Itala, Som. 144/C5
Italy, Tx, US 177/F1
Italy(ctry.) 55/F4
Itamaraju, Braz. 211/F3
Itambacuri, Braz. 211/E3
Itambé, Braz. 207/H4
Itambé, Braz. 211/E2
Itambé, Pico de (peak), Braz. 211/E3
Itami, Japan 109/H6
Itamonte, Braz. 211/M7
Itampolo, Madg. 152/G9
Itanagar, India 112/B3
Itang, Eth. 142/G3
Itanhaém, Braz. 211/K9
Itanhomi, Braz. 211/E3
Itapagé, Braz. 207/G3
Itaparica (isl.), Braz. 211/F2
Itapé, Braz. 211/F2
Itapé, Par. 213/E3
Itapecerica, Braz. 210/D4
Itapecuru-Mirim, Braz. 207/E3
Itapemirim, Braz. 211/E4
Itaperuna, Braz. 211/E4
Itapetim, Braz. 207/G4
Itapetinga, Braz. 211/E2
Itapetininga, Braz. 213/G2
Itapeva, Braz. 213/G2
Itapevi, Braz. 211/K8
Itapicuru (riv.), Braz. 207/F4
Itapipoca, Braz. 207/G3
Itapira, Braz. 211/K7
Itapiranga, Braz. 206/B3
Itapiranga, Braz. 213/F3
Itapitanga, Braz. 211/F2
Itapiúna, Braz. 207/G4
Itápolis, Braz. 213/G2
Itaporã, Braz. 213/F2
Itaporã do Tocantins, Braz. 206/D5
Itaporanga, Braz. 213/G2
Itapúa (dept.), Par. 213/F3
Itapuranga, Braz. 210/C2
Itaquaquecetuba, Braz. 211/K8
Itaqui, Braz. 213/E4
Itarantim, Braz. 211/E2
Itararé, Braz. 213/G3
Itariri, Braz. 211/J9
Itārsi, India 122/A4
Itasca (lake), Mn, US 183/G4
Itasca, Tx, US 177/F1
Itatí, Arg. 212/E3
Itatiaia, PN de, Braz. 211/M7
Itatiba, Braz. 211/K7
Itaú, Bol. 212/D2
Itauçu, Braz. 210/C3
Itaueira, Braz. 207/F4
Itaueira (riv.), Braz. 207/F5
Itayanagi, Japan 108/B3
Itbayat (isl.), Phil. 162/B2
Itbayat, Phil. 113/J4
Itchen (riv.), Eng, UK 63/E4
Itéa, Gre. 75/H3
Itembiri (riv.), D.R. Congo 147/E2
Iténez (riv.), Bol. 203/C4
Ith (hills), Ger. 79/G4
Ithaca, Mi, US 186/D3
Ithaca, NY, US 187/H3
Ithaca (Itháki) (isl.), Gre. 75/G3
Itháki, Gre. 75/G3
Itháki (isl.), Gre. 93/J3
Itháki (Ithaca) (isl.), Gre. 75/G3
Ithon (riv.), Wal, UK 62/C2
Itigi, Tanz. 145/A3
Itiquira (riv.), Braz. 209/H5
Itiruçu, Braz. 211/E2
Itō, Japan 111/F3
Itobo, Tanz. 145/A3
Itoigawa, Japan 111/E2
Itoko, D.R. Congo 147/E3
Itoman, Japan 111/J7
Iton (riv.), Fr. 70/D2
Itonamas (riv.), Bol. 209/E4
Itondy, Madg. 152/H7
Itonuki, Japan 109/L5
Itororó, Braz. 211/E2
Itremo, Madg. 152/H8
Itri, It. 92/C5
Iţsā, Egypt 139/B6
Itsukaichi, Japan 109/C2
Itter (riv.), Ger. 79/F6
Itterbeck, Ger. 78/D3
Ittiri, It. 74/A2
Itu, Nga. 141/G5
Itu, Braz. 213/H2
Ituango, Col. 204/C3
Ituberá, Braz. 211/F2
Ituí (riv.), Braz. 208/D2
Ituiutaba, Braz. 210/C3
Itumbiara (res.), Braz. 210/C3
Itumbiara, Braz. 210/C3
Itumirim, Braz. 211/M6
Ituna, Sk, Can. 182/C2
Itungi Port, Tanz. 145/A4
Ituni, Guy. 205/G3
Itupiranga, Braz. 206/D4
Ituporanga, Braz. 213/G3
Iturama, Braz. 213/G1
Iturbe, Par. 213/E3
Ituri (riv.), D.R. Congo 147/F2
Ituri Forest (for.), D.R. Congo 147/F2
Itutinga (res.), Braz. 211/M6
Ituverava, Braz. 213/H2
Ituxi (riv.), Braz. 209/E3
Ituzaingó, Uru. 215/K11
Ityāy al Bārūd, Egypt 139/B3
Iuka, Ks, US 179/E2
Iuka, Il, US 188/C1
Iuka, Ms, US 188/C3
Iul'tin, Rus. 168/V12
Iva, SC, US 189/F3
Ivaí (riv.), Braz. 210/B4
Ivaiporã, Braz. 213/G3
Ivalojoki (riv.), Fin. 64/H1
Ivančice, Czh. 71/M2
Ivanec, Cro. 76/C2
Ivangorod, Rus. 67/N2
Ivangrad, Yugo. 76/D4
Ivanhoe, Mn, US 181/F1
Ivanhoe, Va, US 189/G2
Ivanhoe, Austl. 154/C3
Ivanhoe, Austl. 159/B1
Ivanivka, Ukr. 99/K3
Ivanjica, Yugo. 76/E4
Ivanjska, Bosn. 76/C3
Ivanka (Bratislava) (int'l arpt.), Slvk. 76/C1
Ivankiv, Ukr. 98/E2
Ivankovo, Cro. 76/D3
Ivano-Frankivs'k, Ukr. 98/C3
Ivano-Frankivs'k (int'l arpt.), Ukr. 98/C3
Ivano-Frankivs'ka (prov.), Ukr. 96/C2
Ivanov, Ukr. 98/E3
Ivanovka, Rus. 95/M5
Ivanovo, Bela. 96/C1
Ivanovo, Rus. 94/J4
Ivanovo (dist.), Rus. 94/J4
Ivanovskaya, Rus. 99/K5
Ivanpah (lake), Nv, US 174/E3
Ivato (int'l arpt.), Madg. 152/H7
Ivato, Madg. 152/H8
Ivatsevichi, Bela. 96/C1
Ivaylovgrad (res.), Bul. 75/J2
Ivaylovgrad, Bul. 77/H5
Ivdel, Rus. 100/G3
Ivel, Ky, US 189/F2
Ivenets, Bela. 67/M5
Iver, Eng, UK 56/B2
Iver Heath, Eng, UK 56/B2
Iveragh (pen.), Ire. 56/P11
Iverny, Fr. 56/L5
Ivey, Ga, US 189/F4
Ivindo (riv.), Gabon 146/C2
Ivinheima (riv.), Braz. 210/B4
Ivinheima, Braz. 213/F2
Ivins, Ut, US 175/F2
Ivnya, Rus. 99/J2
Ivö (isl.), Swe. 65/L6
Ivohibe, Madg. 152/H8
Ivón, Bol. 209/E3
Ivondro (riv.), Madg. 152/J7
Ivösjön (lake), Swe. 66/F3
Ivrea, It. 88/A2
İvrindi, Turk. 96/C5
Ivry-la-Bataille, Fr. 83/G3
Ivry-sur-Seine, Fr. 56/K5
Ivujivik, Qu, Can. 167/J2
Ivvavik NP, Yk, Can. 166/B2
Ivybridge, Eng, UK 62/C6
Iwafune, Japan 109/D1
Iwai, Japan 111/F2
Iwaizumi, Japan 108/B4
Iwaki, Japan 111/G2
Iwaki-san (peak), Japan 108/B3
Iwakuni, Japan 110/C3
Iwakura, Japan 109/L5
Iwama, Japan 109/E1
Iwami, Japan 110/D3
Iwamizawa, Japan 108/B2
Iwamura, Japan 109/M5
Iwanai, Japan 108/B2
Iwanuma, Japan 111/G1
Iwasaki, Japan 108/A3
Iwata, Japan 111/E3
Iwataki, Japan 109/H4
Iwate, Japan 108/B4
Iwate (pref.), Japan 108/B4
Iwate-san (peak), Japan 108/B4
Iwatsuki, Japan 109/D2
Iwere Ile, Nga. 141/F5
Iwo, Nga. 141/G5
Iwo Jima (isl.), Japan 162/D2
Iwŏn, NKor. 107/E2
Iwuy, Fr. 80/C3
Ixcán (riv.), Guat. 200/D3
Ixelles, Belg. 81/D2
Ixiamas, Bol. 208/D4
Ixmiquilpan, Mex. 199/K6
Ixopo, SAfr. 151/E3
Ixtapalapa (nbrhd.), Mex. 199/Q10
Ixtapaluca, Mex. 199/L7
Ixtapan de la Sal, Mex. 199/K8
Ixtlán del Río, Mex. 198/D4
Ixworth, Eng, UK 63/G2
Iya (riv.), Rus. 104/D1
'Iyādh, Yem. 144/C2
'Iyāl Bakhīt, Sudan 142/F2
Iyevlevo, Rus. 95/Q4
Iyo, Japan 110/C4
Iyo (sea), Japan 110/B4
'Izab al Başāriţah, Egypt 139/C2
Izabal (lake), Guat. 196/D4
Īzad Khvāst, Iran 129/H4
Izamal, Mex. 200/D1
'Izbat Jamaşah al Gharbīyah, Egypt 139/C2
Izberbash, Rus. 97/H4
Izeaux, Fr. 90/B2
Izegem, Belg. 80/C2
Izhevsk, Rus. 95/M4
Izhma (riv.), Rus. 95/M2
Izhora (riv.), Rus. 94/T7
Izi (well), Alg. 137/F3
Izkī, Oman 127/G4
Izmayil, Ukr. 77/J3
Izmir (prov.), Turk. 96/C5
Izmit, Turk. 77/J5
Izmit (gulf), Turk. 77/J5
Iznájar, Sp. 72/C4
Iznik, Turk. 77/J5
Iznik (lake), Turk. 77/J5
Izobil'noye, Rus. 97/K2
Izobil'nyy, Rus. 99/L5
Izola, Slov. 89/G2
Izozog, Bol. 212/D1
Izra', Syria 131/E3
Izsák, Hun. 76/D2
Iztaccíhuatl-Popocatépetl, PN, Mex. 199/L7
Izu (isls.), Japan 101/P6
Izu (pen.), Japan 111/F3
Izúcar de Matamoros, Mex. 199/L8
Izuhara, Japan 110/A3
Izumi, Japan 110/B4
Izumi, Japan 108/B4
Izumi, Japan 109/H7
Izumi-Ōtsu, Japan 109/H7
Izumi-Sano, Japan 109/H7
Izumo, Japan 110/C3
Izunagaoka, Japan 109/B3
Izushi, Japan 109/G5
Izvestkovyy, Rus. 105/L2
Izyaslav, Ukr. 98/D2
Izyum, Ukr. 99/J3

J

J. B. Thomas (lake), Tx, US 178/D4
J. Clark Sayler NWR, ND, US 182/D3
J. Ḩanīsh al Kabīr (isl.), Yem. 144/B2
J. Jabal Zuqar (isl.), Yem. 144/B2
J. Lee (lake), Ar, US 179/H4
J. P. Priest (lake), Tn, US 188/D2
J. Paul Getty Museum, Ca, US 192/E7
Jääsjärvi (lake), Fin. 67/M1
Jaba', WBnk. 131/C4
Jabal Abu Rujmayn (mts.), Syria 128/D3
Jabal Abyad (plat.), Sudan 135/F5
Jabal ad-Dayr (peak), Sudan 142/F2
Jabal Ajlūn (mts.), Jor. 131/D4
Jabal al 'Arab (mts.), Syria 130/E3
Jabal al Bārūk (peak), Leb. 131/D1
Jabal al Jaw'alīyāt (peak), Jor. 131/E6
Jabal al Lawz (peak), SAr. 135/G2
Jabal al Mudaysīsāt (peak), Jor. 131/E5
Jabal an Nabī Shu'ayb (peak), Yem. 144/B2
Jabal an Nusayriyab (mts.), Syria 130/E2
Jabal ar Ruwaq (mts.), Syria 128/D3
Jabal as Sawdā' (mts.), Libya 134/B2
Jabal ash Shām (peak), Oman 127/G4
Jabal ash Sha'nabī (peak), Tun. 138/L7
Jabal ash Shaykh (peak), Leb. 131/D2
Jabal 'Aybāl (peak), WBnk. 131/C4
Jabal Bin Ghunaymah (mts.), Libya 134/B3
Jabal Dabbāgh (peak), SAr. 135/G3
Jabāl Lubnan (gov.), Leb. 131/D1
Jabal Marrah (mts.), Sudan 142/E2
Jabal Nafūsah (mts.), Libya 137/H3
Jabal Qaţrānī (mts.), Egypt 139/B5
Jabal Raḑwá (peak), SAr. 135/H3
Jabal Ramm (peak), Jor. 130/D5
Jabal Thamar (peak), Yem. 144/C2
Jabal 'Unāzah (peak), SAr. 128/D3
Jabal 'Uwaybid, Egypt 139/D4
Jabal Waddān (mts.), Libya 134/C2
Jabal Zaltan (mts.), Libya 134/C2
Jabal'āmil (peak), Leb. 131/C2
Jabalí (pt.), Pan. 201/F5
Jabalón (riv.), Sp. 92/C3
Jabalpur, India 122/B4
Jabalyāh, Gaza 131/B5
Jabālyah, Gaza 131/A5
Jabbeke, Belg. 80/C1
Jabbūl (lake), Syria 128/D3
Jabiru, Austl. 154/D3
Jabjabah (wadi), Sudan 126/B4
Jablah, Syria 130/D2
Jablanica (mts.), Alb. 75/G2
Jablanica, Bosn. 76/C4
Jablonec nad Nisou, Czh. 69/H3
Jaboatão dos Guararapes, Braz. 207/H5
Jaboticabal, Braz. 213/G2
Jabron (riv.), Fr. 90/B4
Jabsar Gaxun, China 104/D4
Jabuka, Yugo. 76/E3
Jabung (cape), Indo. 115/D3
Jaca, Sp. 73/E1
Jacaré (riv.), Braz. 211/E1
Jacareacanga, Braz. 206/B4
Jacareí, Braz. 211/L8
Jacarèzinho, Braz. 213/G2
Jaceel (riv.), Som. 144/D3
Jáchal (riv.), Arg. 212/B4
Jáchymov, Czh. 85/F2
Jaciara, Braz. 210/B2
Jacinto Arauz, Arg. 214/E3
Jacinto City, Tx, US 177/M9
Jaciparaná (riv.), Braz. 209/E3
Jack, Al, US 191/E2
Jack Lee (lake), Ar, US 177/H1
Jack Pine (mtn.), Mn, US 183/J4
Jackfish (lake), Sk, Can. 171/K1
Jackfish Lake, Sk, Can. 171/K1
Jackman, Me, US 187/L2
Jackpot, Nv, US 173/F3
Jacks Fk. (riv.), Mo, US 188/B2
Jacks Mtn. (range), Pa, US 194/A2
Jacksboro, Tx, US 179/E4
Jacksboro, Tn, US 188/E2
Jackson (int'l arpt.), PNG 155/G2
Jackson, Al, US 190/E2
Jackson, Ca, US 172/C4
Jackson, Ga, US 188/F4
Jackson (lake), Ga, US 188/E4
Jackson, Ky, US 189/F2
Jackson, La, US 190/C2
Jackson, Mi, US 186/D3
Jackson, Mn, US 181/G2
Jackson, Mo, US 188/C2
Jackson (cap.), Ms, US 188/B4
Jackson, NC, US 189/J2
Jackson (mts.), Nv, US 172/D3
Jackson, Oh, US 189/F1
Jackson, Tn, US 188/C3
Jackson, Wy, US 173/H2
Jackson Head (pt.), NZ 161/B3
Jackson Heights (nbrhd.), NY, US 195/K9
Jackson Lake (dam), Wy, US 173/H2
Jacksonport, Wi, US 186/C2
Jacksonville, Al, US 188/E4
Jacksonville, Ar, US 179/H3
Jacksonville, Fl, US 191/H2
Jacksonville (int'l arpt.), Fl, US 191/H2
Jacksonville, Ga, US 191/G2
Jacksonville, Il, US 181/J4
Jacksonville, Or, US 172/B2
Jacksonville, Mo, US 181/H4
Jacksonville, NC, US 189/J3
Jacksonville, Tx, US 176/G2
Jacksonville Beach, Fl, US 191/H2
Jacksonville Nav. Air Sta., Fl, US 191/H2
Jacmel, Haiti 201/H2
Jacob Lake, Az, US 175/F2
Jacobābād, Pak. 127/J3
Jacobina, Braz. 211/E1
Jacobsdal, SAfr. 150/D3
Jacobson, Mn, US 183/H4
Jacobstown, NJ, US 194/D3
Jacobus, Pa, US 194/B4
Jácome, Ven. 207/P8
Jacona de Plancarte, Mex. 198/E5
Jacques Cartier (peak), Qu, Can. 184/E1
Jacques-Cartier (riv.), Qu, Can. 184/B2
Jacquet River, NB, Can. 184/D2
Jacuí (riv.), Braz. 213/F4
Jacuípe (riv.), Braz. 211/F1
Jacupiranga, Braz. 213/H3
Jacura, Ven. 204/D2
Jadacaquiva, Ven. 204/D2
Jaddi (pt.), Pak. 127/H3
Jade (bay), Ger. 68/E2
Jade (riv.), Ger. 79/F1
Jade, Ger. 79/F2
Jadebusen (bay), Ger. 79/F2
Jadito Wash (riv.), Az, US 175/G3
Jādū, Libya 134/B2
Jadwin, Mo, US 179/J2
Jaén, Sp. 72/D4
Jaen, Phil. 114/C2
Jaén, Peru 208/B2
Jaffa (cape), Austl. 158/A3
Jaffna, SrL. 121/C4
Jaffray, BC, Can. 170/G3
Jaffrey, NH, US 187/K3
Jagādhri, India 124/D4
Jagdīspur, India 122/C2
Jagdīspur, India 123/E3
Jagersfontein, SAfr. 150/D3
Jægerspris, Den. 66/D4
Jægerspris, Den. 65/H7
Jaggayyapeta, India 121/D2
Jagna, Phil. 114/D3
Jagraon, India 124/C4
Jagst (riv.), Ger. 71/J2
Jaguaquara, Braz. 211/F2
Jaguarão (riv.), Braz. 215/G2
Jaguarão, Braz. 213/F5
Jaguaretama, Braz. 207/G4
Jaguari, Braz. 213/F4
Jaguari (riv.), Braz. 213/F4
Jaguariaíva, Braz. 213/G3
Jaguaribara, Braz. 207/G4
Jaguaribe, Braz. 207/G4
Jaguaribe (riv.), Braz. 207/G4
Jaguariúna, Braz. 211/K7
Jaguaruana, Braz. 207/G4
Jagüé, Arg. 212/B4
Jagungal (mt.), Austl. 159/D3
Jahānābād, India 122/D3
Jahānābād, India 123/E3
Jahāngīra, Pak. 124/B3
Jahāngīrābād, India 122/B1
Jahleel (pt.), Austl. 154/C2
Jahrom, Iran 129/H4
Jai (brook), Sur. 205/H4
Jaiama, SLeo. 140/C4
Jaicós, Braz. 207/F4
Jailolo, Indo. 117/G3
Jaile (riv.), China 106/C4
Jaimalsar, India 118/B2
Jainca, China 104/E4
Jaipur, India 118/C2
Jaipur Hāt, Bang. 123/G3
Jāis, India 122/C2
Jaisalmer, India 127/K3
Jaisinghnagar, India 122/C4
Jaitbāri, India 122/B4
Jājapur, India 118/E3
Jājarkot, Nepal 122/D1
Jājarm, Iran 129/J2
Jajce, Bosn. 76/C3
Jakarta (cap.), Indo. 115/D3
Jakes (mtn.), Tn, US 188/E3
Jakin, Ga, US 191/F2
Jakobsberg, Swe. 65/A1
Jakobstad (Pietarsaari), Fin. 94/D3
Jal, NM, US 176/C1
Jala, Mex. 198/D4
Jalacingo, Mex. 199/M7
Jalaid Qi, China 105/J2
Jalājil, SAr. 126/E3
Jalal-abad, Kyr. 125/B3
Jalālābād, India 124/C4
Jalālābād, Afg. 124/A2
Jalālābād, India 124/D5
Jalālābād, India 122/B2
Jalāli, India 122/B2
Jalālpur, Pak. 124/C3
Jalālpur, India 122/D2
Jalālpur Pīrwāla, Pak. 124/A5
Jalamah, Isr. 131/C3
Jalang, Indo. 117/F4
Jalangi (riv.), India 123/G3
Jalangi, India 123/G3
Jålanti (lake), Fin. 65/D3
Jalapa, Mex. 200/C2
Jalapa, Guat. 200/D3
Jalapa, Mex. 199/N7
Jalatlaco, Mex. 199/Q10
Jālaun, India 122/B2
Jalbūn, WBnk. 131/C4
Jaldhāka (riv.), India 123/G2
Jales, Braz. 213/G2
Jalesar, India 122/B2
Jaleswar, Nepal 123/E2
Jalīb ash Shuyūkh, Kuw. 129/F4
Jalingo, Nga. 142/A3
Jalisco, Mex. 198/D4
Jāliţah, Jazīrat (isl.), Tun. 92/F3
Jalkot, Pak. 124/B2
Jallouvre, Pic de (peak), Fr. 86/C6
Jalon (riv.), Sp. 72/E2
Jālor, India 127/K3
Jalostotitlán, Mex. 198/E4
Jalpa, Mex. 198/E4
Jalpa de Méndez, Mex. 200/C2
Jalpaiguri, India 123/G2
Jalpan de Serra, Mex. 199/F4
Jaltenango de la Paz, Mex. 200/C3
Jaltepec (riv.), Mex. 200/C2
Jáltipan de Morelos, Mex. 200/C2
Jālū, Libya 134/D2
Jālūd, WBnk. 131/C4
Jaluit (isl.), Mrsh. 162/F4
Jalūlā', Iraq 129/F3
Jām, Iran 129/H5
Jamaame, Som. 145/C1
Jamaare (riv.), Nga. 141/H3
Jamaica (chan.), Jam. 197/F4
Jamaica (nbrhd.), NY, US 195/K9
Jamaica(ctry.) 165/K8
Jamaica (bay), NY, US 194/K9
Jamālpur, India 124/C5
Jamālpur, Bang. 123/G3
Jamālpur, India 123/F3
Jamanxim (riv.), Braz. 206/C4
Jamapa, Mex. 199/N7
Jamari (riv.), Braz. 209/F3
Jamberoo, Austl. 159/E2
Jambi (prov.), Indo. 115/C3
Jambi, Indo. 115/C3
Jāmbo, India 118/B2
Jamboaye (riv.), Indo. 115/B1
Jambongan (isl.), Malay. 114/B4
Jambuair (cape), Indo. 115/B1
James (bay), Qu, Can. 165/J4
James (pt.), Chile 214/B5
James (riv.), SD, US 180/E1
James (lake), NC, US 189/F3
James City, NC, US 189/J3
James M. Cox Dayton (int'l arpt.), Oh, US 186/D5
James Ross (str.), Nun, Can. 166/G1
Jamesburg, NJ, US 194/D3
Jamesport, Mo, US 181/H4
Jamestown, Austl. 157/H5
Jamestown, Ks, US 180/F4
Jamestown, Ky, US 188/E2
Jamestown, La, US 179/H4
Jamestown, Mo, US 179/H1
Jamestown (dam), ND, US 182/E4
Jamestown, ND, US 182/E4
Jamestown, NY, US 187/G3
Jamestown, Oh, US 186/E5
Jamestown, Tn, US 188/E2
Jamestown Nat'l Hist. Site, Va, US 189/J2
Jamesville, Va, US 189/K2
Jamieson, Or, US 172/E1
Jamīrāpāt (range), India 122/D4
Jāmke, Pak. 124/C3
Jammāl, Tun. 74/B5
Jammerbugt (bay), Den. 66/C3
Jammerland (bay), Den. 65/G7
Jammu, India 124/C3
Jammu and Kashmīr (state), India 125/C5
Jāmnagar, India 127/K4
Jampang-Kulon, Indo. 115/D3
Jāmpur, Pak. 124/A5
Jamshedpur, India 123/F4
Jāmtāra, India 123/F4
Jämtland (co.), Swe. 64/E3
Jamuda, Eth. 144/A4
Jamūi, India 123/F3
Jamuna (riv.), Bang. 123/G3
Jāmunkira, India 121/E1
Jan Kempdorp, SAfr. 150/D2
Jan Mayen (isl.), Nor. 216/G
Jan Smuts (Johannesburg) (int'l arpt.), SAfr. 150/E2
Janāj, Egypt 139/B3
Janakkala, Fin. 67/L1
Janakpur, India 122/C4
Janakpur (zone), Nepal 123/E2
Janakpur, Nepal 123/E2
Janaúba, Braz. 211/E2
Janaucu (isl.), Braz. 206/D2
Jand, Pak. 124/B3
Jandaia, Braz. 213/G1
Jandaia do Sul, Braz. 213/G2
Jandanwāla, Pak. 124/B4
Jandaq, Iran 129/H3
Jandiāla, India 124/C4
Jandikot (arpt.), Austl. 156/K7
Jandowae, Austl. 160/C4
Jándula (riv.), Sp. 72/C4
Jane (brook), Austl. 156/L6
Jane Lew, WV, US 189/G1
Janesville, Wi, US 181/K2
Jangamo, Moz. 149/G5
Jangaon, India 121/C2
Jangipur, India 123/G3
Janikowo, Pol. 69/K2
Janīn, WBnk. 131/C4
Janja, Bosn. 76/D3
Janjevo, Yugo. 76/E4
Jannaale, Som. 145/D1
Janos, Mex. 198/C2
Jánoshalma, Hun. 76/D2
Jánosháza, Hun. 76/C2
Janów Lubelski, Pol. 69/M3
Jānsath, India 122/A1
Jansen, Sk, Can. 182/B2
Jansen, Co, US 178/B2
Jansenville, SAfr. 150/D4
Januária, Braz. 210/D2
Janville, Fr. 83/G4
Janvry, Fr. 56/J6
Janzé, Fr. 82/D5
Janzūr, Libya 93/G4
Jaora, India 118/C3
Japan (sea), Asia 103/N5
Japan(ctry.) 103/N6
Japanese Alps NP, Japan 111/E2
Japiim, Braz. 208/C2
Japurá (riv.), Braz. 203/C3
Jaqué, Pan. 204/B3
Jarābulus, Syria 128/D2
Jarad, SAr. 126/D5
Jaraguá, Braz. 210/C2
Jaraíz de la Vera, Sp. 72/C2
Jarales, NM, US 175/J3
Jarama (riv.), Sp. 72/D2
Jaramānah, Syria 131/E2
Jaramillo, Arg. 215/D5
Jarandilla de la Vera, Sp. 72/C2
Jarānwāla, Pak. 124/B4
Jarash, Jor. 131/D4
Jarbah, Jazīrat (isl.), Tun. 93/F4
Jarbidge, Nv, US 172/F3
Järbo, Swe. 66/G1
Jarby (pt.), IM, UK 60/D3
Jardas al 'Abīd, Libya 93/J4
Jardim, Braz. 213/E2
Jardim, Braz. 207/G4
Jardim do Seridó, Braz. 207/G4
Jardín, Col. 207/K7
Jardín América, Arg. 213/F3
Jardine (riv.), Austl. 155/F2
Jardine R. Nat'l Park, Austl. 155/F2
Jardines de la Reina (arch.), Cuba 201/G1
Jargalant, Mong. 104/E2
Jargalant, Mong. 125/F2
Jargalant, Mong. 104/D2
Jargeau, Fr. 83/H5
Jari (riv.), Braz. 203/D2
Jaridih, India 123/F4
Jarjīs, Tun. 93/F4
Järlåsa, Swe. 65/A1
Jarmen, Ger. 66/E5
Järna, Swe. 66/G2
Jarny, Fr. 81/E5
Jaro, Phil. 114/D3
Jarocin, Pol. 69/J3
Jarod, India 122/A4
Jaroměř, Czh. 69/H3
Jarosław, Pol. 69/M3
Jaroso, Co, US 178/B2
Jarratt, Va, US 189/J2
Jarrettsville, Md, US 194/B4
Jarrow, Eng, UK 61/G2
Jars (plain), Laos 120/C2
Jartai, China 104/F4
Jaru, Braz. 209/F3
Jarud Qi, China 106/E1
Järva-Jaani, Est 67/L2
Järvakandi, Est. 67/L2
Järvelä, Fin. 65/F4
Järvenpää, Fin. 67/L1
Jarville-la-Malgrange, Fr. 81/F6
Jarvis (isl.), Pac., US 163/J5
Jarvisburg, NC, US 189/K2
Järvsö, Swe. 66/G1
Jás-Nagykun-Szonok (co.), Hun. 69/L5
Jasāna, India 124/C5
Jasenagykun-Seolnok (prov.), Hun. 76/E2
Jashpurnagar, India 123/E4
Jasidih, India 123/F3
Jasin, Malay. 115/C2
Jāsk, Iran 127/G3
Jasło, Pol. 69/L4
Jason (isl.), Mald. 215/E6
Jasonville, In, US 186/C5
Jasper, Ab, Can. 170/E1
Jasper, Al, US 188/D4
Jasper, Ar, US 179/H2
Jasper, Fl, US 191/G2
Jasper, Ga, US 188/E3
Jasper, In, US 188/D1
Jasper, Mn, US 181/F2
Jasper, Mo, US 179/G2
Jasper, Tn, US 188/E3
Jasper, Tx, US 177/H2
Jasper NP, Ab, Can. 166/E3
Jasper NP, Ab, Can. 170/E1
Jaspur, India 122/B1
Jastrebarsko, Cro. 76/B3
Jastrowie, Pol. 69/J2
Jastrzębie Zdroj, Pol. 69/K4
Jaswantnagar, India 122/B2
Jászapáti, Hun. 69/L5
Jászárokszállás, Hun. 76/D2
Jászberény, Hun. 69/K5
Jataí, Braz. 210/C3
Jatapu (riv.), Braz. 205/G5
Jatāra, India 122/B3
Jataté (riv.), Mex. 200/D2
Jāti, Pak. 127/J4
Jati, Braz. 207/G4
Jatibonico, Cuba 201/G1
Játiva, Sp. 73/E3
Jātni, India 121/E1
Jatoi Janūbi, Pak. 124/A5
Jaú (riv.), Braz. 205/F5
Jaú, Braz. 213/G2
Jaua Sarisarinama, PN, Ven. 205/E3
Jauaperi (riv.), Braz. 205/F5
Jauaperi (riv.), Braz. 205/E5
Jauaru (mts.), Braz. 205/H5
Jaubert (cape), Austl. 154/A4
Jaudy (riv.), Fr. 82/B3
Jauharābād, Pak. 124/B3
Jauja, Peru 208/C3
Jaumave, Mex. 199/F4
Jaun, Swi. 86/D4
Jaunay-Clan, Fr. 70/D3
Jaunjelgava, Lat. 67/L3
Jaunpass (pass), Swi. 86/D4
Jaunpiebalga, Lat. 67/M3
Jaunpils, Lat. 67/K3
Jaunpur, India 122/D3
Jauru (riv.), Braz. 210/A3
Jausiers, Fr. 90/C5
Java (isl.), Indo. 103/K10
Java (sea), Indo. 103/K10
Javari (riv.), Braz. 208/C2
Jávea, Sp. 73/F3
Javier (isl.), Chile 215/B5
Javier de Viana, Uru. 213/E4
Javorie (peak), Slvk. 76/D1
Javornice (riv.), Czh. 85/G2
Javorník (peak), Czh. 85/G4
Javorová Skála (peak), Czh. 85/H3
Javron-les-Chapelles, Fr. 83/E4
Jawāla Mukhi, India 124/D4
Jawhar, Som. 144/C5
Jawi, Indo. 116/C4
Jawor, Pol. 69/J3
Jay, Ok, US 179/G2
Jay, Me, US 187/L2
Jay, Fl, US 190/E2
Jayanca, Peru 208/B2
Jayapura, Indo. 162/D5
Jaynagar, India 123/G4
Jaynagar, India 123/F2
Jayton, Tx, US 178/D4
Jaywick, Eng, UK 63/H3
Jazīrat Būbiyan (isl.), Kuw. 129/G4
Jazīrat Maşirah (isl.), Oman 103/F5
Jazzīn, Leb. 131/D1
JB Thomas (lake), Tx, US 177/D1
Jbel Bani (mts.), Mor. 136/D3
Jean, Tx, US 179/E4
Jean Lafitte, La, US 190/C3
Jeanerette, La, US 190/C3
Jebba, Nga. 141/G4
Jeberos, Peru 208/B2
Jebjerg, Den. 66/C3
Jebus, Indo. 115/D3
Jed Water (riv.), Sc, UK 59/D6
Jedburgh, Sc, UK 59/D6
Jedlicze, Pol. 69/L4
Jędrzejów, Pol. 69/L3
Jeetze (riv.), Ger. 68/F2
Jeffers, Mn, US 181/G1
Jeffers, Mt, US 173/H1
Jefferson, Al, US 188/D4
Jefferson, Ga, US 189/F3
Jefferson, Oh, US 186/F4
Jefferson, Ia, US 181/G2
Jefferson (riv.), Mt, US 173/H1
Jefferson, NC, US 189/G2
Jefferson (mt.), Nv, US 172/E4
Jefferson, NY, US 187/J3
Jefferson, Or, US 172/B1
Jefferson (mt.), Or, US 172/C1
Jefferson, Tx, US 179/G4
Jefferson (co.), Wi, US 193/N14
Jefferson, Wi, US 181/K2
Jefferson, Va, US 189/J2
Jefferson City (cap.), Mo, US 179/H1
Jefferson City, Tn, US 189/F2
Jeffersonville, In, US 188/E1
Jeffersonville, Ky, US 188/F2
Jeffersonville, Ga, US 189/F4
Jeffrey, WV, US 189/G2
Jeffrey City, Wy, US 173/K2
Jeffrey's, Nf, Can. 185/H1
Jeffreys Bay, SAfr. 150/D4
Jega, Nga. 141/G3
Jegenstorf, Swi. 86/D3
Jeinemeni (peak), Chile 214/B5
Jejui Guazú (riv.), Par. 210/A5
Jēkabpils, Lat. 67/L3
Jekyll (isl.), Ga, US 191/H2
Jelcz-Laskowice, Pol. 69/J3
Jelenec, Slvk. 76/D1
Jelenia Gora (prov.), Czh.,Ger. 69/E2
Jelenia Góra, Pol. 69/H3
Jelep (pass), China 118/E2
Jelgava, Lat. 67/K3
Jeli, Malay. 115/C1
Jelka, Slvk. 76/C1
Jellico, Tn, US 188/E2
Jellicoe, On, Can. 183/L3
Jelm, Wy, US 180/A3
Jelow Gīr, Iran 129/F3
Jeløya (isl.), Nor. 64/S9
Jelsi, It. 92/D4
Jema Shet' (riv.), Eth. 142/H3
Jemaa Sahim, Mor. 136/C2
Jemaja (isl.), Indo. 115/D2
Jemaluang, Malay. 115/C2
Jemappes, Belg. 80/C3
Jember, Indo. 115/F3
Jembiani, Tanz. 145/B3
Jemez (mts.), NM, US 175/J3
Jemez (riv.), NM, US 175/J3
Jemez Ind. Res., NM, US 175/J3
Jemez Pueblo, NM, US 175/J3
Jemez Springs, NM, US 175/J3
Jeminay, China 125/E2
Jemison, Al, US 188/D4
Jempang (lake), Indo. 117/E4
Jemsa, Egypt 135/G3
Jena, Ger. 68/F3
Jena, La, US 190/B2
Jenaz, Swi. 87/F4
Jenbach, Aus. 71/J3
Jendouba, Tun. 138/L6

Jendouba (gov.), Tun. 138/L6
Jeneponto, Indo. 117/E5
Jengen, Ger. 87/G2
Jenison, Mi, US 186/D3
Jenkins, Ky, US 189/F2
Jenkintown, Pa, US 194/C3
Jenks, Ok, US 179/G2
Jennersdorf, Aus. 76/C2
Jennings, La, US 190/B2
Jennings, Fl, US 191/G2
Jennings, Ks, US 180/D4
Jenny, Sur. 206/C1
Jenny Lind (isl.), Nun, Can. 166/F2
Jenolan Caves, Austl. 159/E1
Jens Muck (isl.), Nun, Can. 167/H2
Jensen, Ut, US 173/J3
Jensen Beach, Fl, US 191/H4
Jeppener, Arg. 215/J11
Jequetepeque, Peru 208/B2
Jequié, Braz. 211/E2
Jequitaí, Braz. 210/D3
Jequitinhonha (riv.), Braz. 203/E4
Jequitinhonha, Braz. 211/E3
Jerada, Mor. 138/C2
Jerantut, Malay. 115/C2
Jerdera, Indo. 154/D1
Jérémie, Haiti 201/H2
Jeremoabo, Braz. 211/F1
Jerer Shet' (riv.), Eth. 144/B3
Jerez de García Salinas, Mex. 198/E4
Jerez de la Frontera, Sp. 72/B4
Jerez de los Caballeros, Sp. 72/B3
Jericho, NY, US 195/L8
Jericho, Austl. 160/B3
Jericho (Arīḩā), WBnk. 131/C5
Jericó, Col. 207/K7
Jericó, Braz. 207/G4
Jerico Springs, Mo, US 179/G2
Jerilderie, Austl. 159/B2
Jerissa, Tun. 138/L7
Jermyn, Tx, US 179/E4
Jerome, Ar, US 179/J4
Jerome, Id, US 173/F2
Jerome, Az, US 175/F3
Jerramungup, Austl. 156/C5
Jersey (isl.), Chl, UK 70/B2
Jersey City, NJ, US 195/J9
Jersey City (res.), NJ, US 195/H8
Jersey Shore, Pa, US 194/A1
Jersey Village, Tx, US 177/M9
Jerseyville, Il, US 181/J4
Jerteh, Malay. 115/C1
Jerumenha, Braz. 207/F4
Jerusalem (dist.), Isr. 130/D4
Jerusalem, Ar, US 179/H3
Jerusalem (arpt.), WBnk. 131/C5
Jerusalem (Yerushalayim) (cap.), Isr. 131/C5
Jervis (inlet), BC, Can. 170/C2
Jervis Bay, Austl. 159/E2
Jerzu, It. 74/A3
Jesberg, Ger. 79/G6
Jesenice (res.), Czh. 85/F2
Jesenice, Slov. 71/L3
Jesi, It. 89/G6
Jessheim, Nor. 66/D1
Jessieville, Ar, US 179/H3
Jessore, Bang. 123/G4
Jessore (pol. reg.), Bang. 123/G4
Jessup (lake), Fl, US 191/H3
Jesuânia, Braz. 211/L6
Jesup, Ga, US 191/H2
Jesus (mt.), Ks, US 178/E2
Jésus (isl.), Qu, Can. 185/N6
Jesús, Par. 213/F3
Jesús Carranza, Mex. 200/C2
Jesús de Machaca, Bol. 212/B1
Jesús María, Col. 207/M7
Jesús María, Arg. 212/C4
Jesús Menéndez, Cuba 201/G1
Jet, Ok, US 179/E2
Jetmore, Ks, US 178/E1
Jetpur, India 127/K4
Jettingen-Scheppach, Ger. 84/D6
Jetzendorf, Ger. 85/E6
Jeu (riv.), Fr. 83/E6
Jeumont, Fr. 81/D3
Jevenstedt, Ger. 68/E1
Jever, Ger. 79/E1
Jevnaker, Nor. 66/D1
Jewar, India 122/A1
Jewel Cave Nat'l Mon., SD, US 180/C2
Jewell, Ks, US 180/E4
Jewell Junction, Ia, US 181/H2
Jewett, Tx, US 177/F2
Jezerce (peak), Alb. 76/D4
Jezerní Stěna (peak), Czh. 85/G4
Jeziorak (lake), Pol. 69/K2
Jhā Jhā, India 123/F3
Jhajjar, India 124/D5
Jhal Jhao, Pak. 127/J3
Jhālakāti, Bang. 123/H4
Jhālawār, India 118/C3
Jhalida, India 123/E4
Jhālū, India 122/B1
Jhang Sadar, Pak. 124/B4
Jhaniān Khatrian, Pak. 124/B3
Jhanjhārpur, India 123/F2
Jhānsi, India 122/B3
Jhāpa, Nepal 123/F2
Jhārgrām, India 123/F4
Jharia, India 123/F4
Jhārsuguda, India 123/E5
Jhawāriān, Pak. 124/B3
Jhelum, Pak. 124/B3
Jhelum (riv.), Pak. 124/B3
Jhelum (riv.), India 125/B5
Jhenida, Bang. 123/G4
Jhumra, Pak. 124/B4
Ji (riv.), China 104/D5
Ji Xian, China 106/C4
Ji Xian, China 106/H6
Ji-Paraná, Braz. 209/F3
Jia Xian, China 106/B3
Jiading, China 106/L8
Jiahe, China 119/K2
Jialing (riv.), China 103/K6
Jialu (riv.), China 104/G5
Jiamusi, China 105/L2
Ji'an, China 107/D2
Jian (riv.), China 113/H3
Ji'an, China 113/G3
Jianchang, China 107/C2
Jianchang, China 106/D2
Jiancheng, China 113/F4
Jiang (riv.), China 120/E1
Jiang Xian, China 106/B4
Jiang'an, China 119/J2
Jiangcheng Hanizu Yizu Zizhixian, China 112/D4
Jiangchuan, China 112/D3
Jiangdu, China 106/D4
Jianghua Yaozu Zizhixian, China 113/F3
Jiangjiadian, China 105/H3
Jiangjin, China 113/E2
Jiangjunhe, China 104/G5
Jiangjunshi, China 107/A3
Jiangjuntai, China 104/D3
Jiangkou, China 113/J2
Jiangkou, China 113/F2
Jiangkou, China 113/G3
Jiangkouzhen, China 113/F2
Jiangling, China 113/G2
Jiangmen, China 113/G4
Jiangmenchang, China 112/E2
Jiangning, China 106/D5
Jiangsu (prov.), China 105/H5
Jiangwan, China 113/G3
Jiangxi (prov.), China 106/C5
Jiangxiang, China 113/H1
Jiangya, China 113/F2
Jiangyin, China 106/E5
Jiangyong, China 113/F3
Jiangyou, China 112/E2
Jianhe, China 119/J2
Jianhu, China 106/D4
Jianli, China 113/G2
Jian'ou, China 113/H3
Jianping, China 105/H3
Jianshi, China 113/F2
Jianshui, China 112/D4
Jianyang, China 112/E2
Jianyang, China 113/H3
Jiaochangba, China 112/D1
Jiaocheng, China 106/C3
Jiaohe, China 105/K3
Jiaojiang, China 113/J2
Jiaokou, China 106/C3
Jiaolai (riv.), China 105/J3
Jiaonan, China 106/D4
Jiaotou, China 113/J2
Jiaozuo, China 106/C4
Jiapu, China 106/K8
Jiashan, China 106/D4
Jiashan, China 106/L9
Jiashi, China 125/C4
Jiaxiang, China 106/D4
Jiaxing, China 106/L9
Jiaya, China 113/F3
Jiayin, China 105/L2
Jiayou, China 113/E3
Jiayu, China 113/G2
Jiayuguan, China 104/D4
Jiazi, China 113/H4
Jibāl An Nūbah (mts.), Sudan 142/F3
Jibāl Múāb (mts.), Jor. 131/D5
Jibiya, Nga. 141/G3
Jibóia, Braz. 204/D4
Jibou, Rom. 77/F2
Jicarilla Apache Ind. Res., NM, US 175/J2
Jicarón (isl.), Pan. 201/F5
Jičín, Czh. 69/H3
Jidali (riv.), Som. 144/C3
Jiddah, SAr. 126/C4
Jidong, China 105/L2
Jiehualong, China 113/G3
Jieshi, China 113/G4
Jieshipu, China 104/F4
Jieshou, China 106/C4
Jiexiu, China 106/B3
Jieyang, China 113/H4
Jieznas, Lith. 67/L4
Jifnā, WBnk. 131/C5
Jiga, Eth. 142/H3
Jigalong Abor. Land, Austl. 156/D2
Jigawa (prov.), Nga. 141/H4
Jigger, La, US 190/C1
Jiggs, Nv, US 172/F3
Jiguaní, Cuba 201/G1
Jiguanshan, China 107/C1
Jigzhi, China 104/E5
Jihlava, Czh. 69/H4
Jihlava (riv.), Czh. 71/L2
Jihocesky (pol. reg.), Czh. 71/K2
Jihomoravsky (pol. reg.), Czh. 69/J4
Jiiqley, Som. 144/C4
Jijel (wilaya), Alg. 138/H4
Jijel, Alg. 138/H4
Jijia (riv.), Rom. 96/C3
Jijiga, Eth. 144/B3
Jijona, Sp. 73/E3
Jikawo, Eth. 142/G3
Jilhava (riv.), Czh. 69/H4
Jili (lake), China 104/B2
Jilib, Som. 145/C1
Jilin (prov.), China 105/K3
Jilin, China 105/K3
Jiliu (riv.), China 105/J1
Jiloca (riv.), Sp. 72/E2
Jilotepec, Mex. 199/K7
Jílové u Prahy, Czh. 85/H3
Jim Thorpe, Pa, US 194/C2
Jim Woodruff (dam), Fl, US 191/F2
Jīma, Eth. 142/H4
Jimaní, DRep. 201/J2
Jimbe, Ang. 147/E5
Jimbolia, Rom. 76/E3
Jimboomba, Austl. 160/D4
Jimei, China 113/H3
Jimena de la Frontera, Sp. 72/C4
Jiménez, Mex. 177/D3
Jiménez, Mex. 198/D3
Jimingsi, China 113/F2
Jimmēza, Sudan 142/G1
Jimmy Carter Nat'l Hist. Site, Ga, US 191/F1
Jimo, China 106/E3
Jimokuji, Japan 109/L5
Jimsar, China 125/E3
Jin (riv.), China 119/K2
Jin Xian, China 107/A3
Jin Xian, China 106/C3
Jinan, China 106/D3
Jin'an, China 113/H2
Jinchang, China 104/E4
Jincheng, China 107/A2
Jincheng, China 106/C4
Jinchuan, China 112/D2
Jinchuan, China 105/K3
Jinci Temple, China 106/C3
Jīnd, India 124/D5
Jindabyne (lake), Austl. 159/D3
Jindabyne (dam), Austl. 159/D3
Jindabyne, Austl. 159/D3
Jindalee, Austl. 159/D2
Jindřichuv Hradec, Czh. 69/H4
Jinfosi, China 104/D4
Jing (riv.), China 104/F5
Jing Xian, China 113/H2
Jing Xian, China 113/F3
Jingbian, China 106/B3
Jingde, China 113/H2
Jingdezhen, China 113/H2
Jingdong, China 119/H3
Jingellic, Austl. 159/C2
Jinggangshan, China 113/G3
Jinggu, China 112/D4
Jinghai, China 113/H4
Jinghai, China 106/H7
Jinghaiwei, China 107/B4
Jinghe, China 125/D3
Jinghong, China 112/D4
Jingjiang, China 106/E4
Jingle, China 106/B3
Jingmen, China 106/C5
Jingning, China 104/F4
Jingping (mts.), China 112/D3
Jingshan, China 106/C5
Jingtai, China 104/E4
Jingxi, China 113/E4
Jingyou, China 104/G4
Jingyu, China 105/K3
Jingyuan, China 104/E4
Jinhu, China 106/D4
Jinhua, China 113/H2
Jining, China 106/D4
Jining, China 106/C2
Jinja, Ugan. 145/A1
Jinjie, China 113/E4
Jinka, Eth. 142/H4
Jinkouhe, China 119/H2
Jinlansi, China 113/G3
Jinmen (isl.), Tai. 113/H3
Jinotega, Nic. 200/E3
Jinotepe, Nic. 200/E4
Jinping, China 112/D4
Jinping, China 113/F3
Jinqian (riv.), China 104/F5
Jinsha (riv.), China 103/J7
Jinsha, China 119/J2
Jinsha, China 113/H2
Jinshan, China 106/L9
Jinshanwei, China 106/L9
Jinshi, China 113/F2
Jinshui, China 104/F5
Jintan, China 106/D5
Jintang, China 113/G2
Jintotolo (chan.), Phil. 114/C3
Jintūr, India 121/C2
Jinxi, China 113/H3
Jinxi, China 106/E2
Jinxiang, China 106/D4
Jinxiu Yaozu Zizhixian, China 119/K3
Jinyun, China 113/J2
Jinzhai, China 106/C5
Jinzhou (bay), China 107/A3
Jinzhou, China 106/E2
Jiparana (riv.), Braz. 209/F3
Jipijapa, Ecu. 204/A5
Jiquilpan de Juárez, Mex. 198/E5
Jiquipilco, Mex. 199/Q9
Jīrēn, Eth. 142/H4
Jirgā, Egypt 135/F3
Jirin Gol, China 105/H3
Jiřkov, Czh. 85/G1
Jīroft, Iran 127/G3
Jīsh, Isr. 131/C2
Jishan, China 106/B4
Jishou, China 113/F2
Jisr ash Shughūr, Syria 130/E2
Jitan, China 113/G3
Jitra, Malay. 115/C1
Jiu (riv.), Rom. 96/B3
Jiucheng, China 113/E2
Jiudongshan, China 113/H4
Jiufeng, China 113/H3
Jiugong (mtn.), China 113/G2
Jiuhua (mtn.), China 113/H2
Jiujiang, China 113/G2
Jiulianshan, China 113/G3
Jiuling (mts.), China 113/G2
Jiulong, China 112/D2
Jiun (riv.), China 113/F4
Jiurongcheng, China 107/B4
Jiutai, China 105/K3
Jiutang, China 113/F4
Jiutepec, Mex. 199/K8
Jiuwan (mts.), China 113/E3
Jiuxincheng, China 106/G7
Jiuyongshou, China 104/F5
Jiuyuhang, China 106/K9
Jiuzhan, China 105/K1
Jīwani, Pak. 127/H3
Jixi, China 105/L2
Jixi, China 113/H2
Jixian, China 105/L2
Jiyang, China 106/D3
Jiyuan, China 106/C4
Jiz' (wadi), Yem. 126/F5
Jīzān, SAr. 126/D5
Jizayy, Egypt 139/B4
Jize, China 106/C3
Jizera (riv.), Czh. 69/H3
Jizl (wadi), SAr. 126/C3
Jizō-zaki (pt.), Japan 110/C3
Jizzakh, Uzb. 100/G5
Jmijin (riv.), SKor. 107/F6
Joaçaba, Braz. 213/G3
Joachín, Mex. 199/N8
Joaíma, Braz. 211/E3
Joal, Sen. 140/A3
Joana Peres, Braz. 206/D3
Joanna, SC, US 189/G3
João Câmara, Braz. 207/H4
João Lisboa, Braz. 207/E4
João Monlevade, Braz. 211/E3
João Pessoa, Braz. 207/H4
João Pinheiro, Braz. 210/D3
Joaquim Távora, Braz. 213/G2
Joaquin, Tx, US 177/G2
Joaquín V. González, Arg. 212/C3
Jobabo, Cuba 201/G1
Jocassee (dam), SC, US 189/F3
Jockgrim, Ger. 84/B4
Jocón, Hon. 200/E3
Jódar, Sp. 72/D4
Jodhpur, India 118/B2
Jodoigne, Belg. 81/D2
Joe, Mt, US 182/B4
Joe Pool (lake), Tx, US 176/L7
Joensuu, Fin. 94/F3
Jōetsu, Japan 111/F2
Jogbani, India 123/F2
Jõgeva, Est. 67/M2
Joggins, NS, Can. 184/E3
Joghdān, Iran 127/G3
Jogighpa, India 123/H2
Johannesberg, Ger. 84/C2
Johannesburg, Ca, US 174/D3
Johannesburg, SAfr. 150/E2
Johannesburg (Jan Smuts) (int'l arpt.), SAfr. 150/E2
Johanngeorgenstadt, Ger. 85/F2
Johilla (riv.), India 122/C4
John Day (riv.), Or, US 168/B2
John Day, Or, US 172/D1
John Day (dam), Or, US 170/D5
John Day Fossil Beds Nat'l Mon., Or, US 172/C1
John Day Fossil Beds Nat'l Mon., Or, US 172/D1
John Day,North Fork (riv.), Or, US 172/D1
John F. Kennedy (int'l arpt.), NY, US 195/K9
John Forrest NP, Austl. 156/L6
John H. Kerr (dam), Va, US 189/H2
John Martin (res.), Co, US 180/C4
John O'Groats, Sc, UK 57/S7
John Wayne/Orange County (int'l arpt.), Ca, US 192/G8
Johnshaven, Sc, UK 59/D3
Johnson (mtn.), Wy, US 180/B2
Johnson (co.), Tx, US 176/K7
Johnson (cr.), NY, US 186/V9
Johnson (Johnson City), Ks, US 178/D2
Johnson City, NY, US 187/J3
Johnson City, Tn, US 189/F2
Johnson City, Tx, US 176/E2
Johnson City (Johnson), Ks, US 178/D2
Johnson Draw (riv.), Tx, US 177/D2
Johnson Lake Nat'l Wild. Ref., ND, US 182/E4
Johnsonburg, Pa, US 187/G4
Johnsonburg, NJ, US 194/D2
Johnsonville (nbrhd.), NZ 161/H9
Johnsonville, SC, US 189/H4
Johnston (falls), Zam. 147/G5
Johnston, Ia, US 181/H3
Johnston, Wal, UK 62/B3
Johnston (lake), Austl. 153/B4
Johnston, SC, US 189/G4
Johnston Atoll (isl.), Pac., US 163/J3
Johnston City, Il, US 188/C2
Johnstone, Sc, UK 59/B5
Johnstown, Ire. 58/C4
Johnstown, Oh, US 186/E4
Johnstown, NY, US 187/J3
Johnstown, On, Can. 187/J2
Johnstown, Pa, US 187/G4
Johnsville, Md, US 194/A4
Johor (state), Malay. 115/C2
Johor (river), Malay. 115/C2
Johor (str.), Malay.,Sing. 115/J6
Johor Baharu, Malay. 115/J6
Jöhstadt, Ger. 85/G1
Joigny, Fr. 70/E3
Joiner, Ar, US 188/B3
Joinvile, Braz. 213/G3
Joinville, Fr. 86/B1
Joinville (isl.), Can. 216/Ant.
Jojutla, Mex. 199/K8
Jokau, Sudan 142/G3
Jokela, Fin. 65/E4
Jokioinen, Fin. 67/K1
Jokkmokk, Swe. 64/F2
Jökulsargljufur NP, Ice. 64/P6
Jolanda di Savoia, It. 89/E4
Jolfā, Iran 129/F2
Jolgeh-ye Khūzestan (plain), Iran 129/G4
Joliet, Il, US 186/B4
Joliet, Mt, US 173/J1
Joliet Army Ammo. Plant, Il, US 186/B4
Joliette, Qu, Can. 187/K1
Jollyville, Tx, US 177/F2
Jolo (isl.), Phil. 117/F2
Jolo, Phil. 114/C4
Jomala, Fin. 67/H1
Jomalig (isl.), Phil. 114/C2
Jombang, Indo. 115/F3
Jombo (riv.), Ang. 146/D5
Jomda, China 112/C2
Jomo Kenyatta (int'l arpt.), Kenya 145/B2
Jomsom, Nepal 122/D1
Jomu, Tanz. 145/A2
Jona, Swi. 87/E3
Jonacatepec, Mex. 199/L8
Jonava, Lith. 67/L4
Jonchery-sur-Vesle, Fr. 80/C5
Jones, La, US 179/J4
Jones (inlet), NY, US 195/L9
Jones (sound), Can. 165/J2
Jones, Al, US 188/D4
Jones (mtn.), Pa, US 194/A2
Jones Beach State Park, NY, US 195/L9
Jonesboro, La, US 179/H4
Jonesboro, In, US 186/D4
Jonesboro, Il, US 188/C2
Jonesboro, Ar, US 188/B3
Jonesboro, Ga, US 189/M7
Jonesborough, NI, UK 60/B3
Jonesborough, Tn, US 189/F2
Jonestown, Ms, US 188/B3
Jonesville, La, US 190/C2
Jonesville, Va, US 189/F2
Jonesville, NC, US 189/G2
Jonglei, Sudan 142/F4
Joniškelis, Lith. 67/L3
Joniškis, Lith. 67/K3
Jönköping (co.), Swe. 64/E4
Jönköping, Swe. 66/F3
Jonquière, Qu, Can. 184/B1
Jonquières, Fr. 90/A4
Jonuta, Mex. 196/C4
Joondalup (lake), Austl. 156/K6
Joplin, Mo, US 179/G2
Joplin, Mt, US 171/J3
Joppa, Il, US 188/C2
Joppa (Joppatowne), Md, US 194/B5
Joppatowne (Joppa), Md, US 194/B5
Jora, India 122/A2
Jordan (riv.), Isr.,Jor. 130/D4
Jordan(ctry.) 103/C6
Jordan (riv.), Or, US 173/E2
Jordan (riv.), Jor. 131/D4
Jordan, On, Can. 186/U9
Jordan, Mt, US 171/L4
Jordan (cr.), Pa, US 194/C2
Jordan (lake), Al, US 188/D4
Jordan Station, On, Can. 186/U9
Jordan Valley, Or, US 172/E2
Jordbro, Swe. 65/B1
Jorge (cape), Chile 215/B6
Jorge Chavez (int'l arpt.), Peru 208/B4
Jorge Newbury (Buenos Aires) (int'l arpt.), Arg. 215/J11
Jorhāt, India 112/B3
Joriāpāni, Nepal 122/C1
Jork, Ger. 79/G1
Jornada del Muerto (val.), NM, US 178/A4
Jørpeland, Nor. 66/B2
Jos, Nga. 141/H4
Jos (plat.), Nga. 141/H4
Jose Abad Santos, Phil. 114/D4
José Agustín Palacios, Bol. 209/E4
José Batlle y Ordóñez, Uru. 215/G2
José Bonifácio, Braz. 213/G2
José Cardel, Mex. 199/N7
José de Freitas, Braz. 207/F4
José Enrique Rodó, Uru. 215/K10
José María Córdova (int'l arpt.), Col. 207/K6
José María Morelos, Mex. 200/D2
Jose Marti (int'l arpt.), Cuba 201/F1
Jose Panganiban, Phil. 114/C2
José Pedro Varela, Uru. 215/G2
José, South (dept.), Uru. 215/F2
Josefa Camejo (int'l arpt.), Ven. 204/D2
Joseph, Or, US 172/E1
Joseph, Ut, US 175/F1
Joseph Bonaparte (gulf), Austl. 153/B2
Joseph City, Az, US 175/G3
Josephine, Tx, US 176/L6
Joshin-Etsu Kogen NP, Japan 111/F2
Joshipur, India 123/F5
Joshua, Tx, US 176/K7
Joshua (pt.), Ct, US 195/F1
Joshua Tree, Ca, US 174/D3
Joshua Tree NP, Ca, US 174/D4
Jossa (riv.), Ger. 84/C2
Josselin, Fr. 82/C5
Jotunheimen NP, Nor. 66/C1
Jouanne (riv.), Fr. 70/C2
Jouarre, Fr. 56/M5
Joué-lès-Tours, Fr. 83/F6
Joué-sur-Erdre, Fr. 82/D6
Jœuf, Fr. 81/F5
Jouques, Fr. 90/B5
Jourama Falls NP, Austl. 160/B2
Jourdanton, Tx, US 176/E3
Joure, Neth. 78/C3
Joutseno, Fin. 67/N1
Joutsijärvi, Fin. 94/E2
Joux (lake), Swi. 86/C4
Jouy, Fr. 83/G3
Jouy-en-Josas, Fr. 56/J5
Jouy-le-Châtel, Fr. 56/M6
Jouy-le-Moutier, Fr. 56/J4
Jouy-sur-Morin, Fr. 80/C6
Jovellanos, Cuba 201/F1
Jovet (peak), Fr. 90/C2
Joveyn (riv.), Iran 127/G1
Jow Khvāh, Iran 129/J3
Jowai, India 119/F2
Jowsheqān-e Qālī, Iran 129/G3
Joyce, La, US 190/B2
Joyce's Country (dist.), Ire. 58/A2
Jōyō, Japan 109/J6
Jozankei Spa, Japan 108/B2
Ju (riv.), China 104/G5
Ju Xian, China 106/D4
Juan Aldama, Mex. 198/E3
Juan Bautista Alberdi, Arg. 212/C3
Juan de Fuca (str.), BC, Can.,US 166/D4
Juan de Nova (isl.), Fr. 133/G6
Juan Fernández (isls.), Chile 203/A6
Juan Fernández, Arg. 214/F3
Juan Jackson, Uru. 215/K10
Juan José Paso, Arg. 214/E2
Juan L. Lacaze, Uru. 215/K11
Juan Santamaria (int'l arpt.), CR 201/E4
Juancheng, China 106/C4
Juancho Yrausquin (int'l arpt.), Neth. 197/N8
Juanda (int'l arpt.), Indo. 115/F3
Juangriego, Ven. 205/F2
Juanjuí, Peru 208/B2
Juárez, Mex. 177/D4
Juárez, Arg. 214/F3
Juarez (arpt.), Mex. 199/Q10
Juaso, Gha. 141/E5
Juazeirinho, Braz. 207/G4
Juazeiro, Braz. 207/F5
Juazeiro do Norte, Braz. 207/G4
Juazohn, Libr. 140/C5
Juba, Sudan 142/F4
Jubany, Arg., Ant. 216/W
Jubbah, SAr. 128/E4
Jübek, Ger. 68/E1
Jubones (riv.), Ecu. 208/B1
Juby (cape), Mor. 136/B4
Júcar (riv.), Sp. 92/C3
Juçara, Braz. 210/C2
Jucás, Braz. 207/G4
Jüchen, Ger. 81/F1
Juchipila, Mex. 198/E4
Juchique de Ferrer, Mex. 199/N7
Juchitán de Zaragoza, Mex. 200/C2
Juchitepec, Mex. 199/R10
Jucurutu, Braz. 207/G4
Jud, ND, US 182/E4
Judaberg, Nor. 66/A2
Judenburg, Aus. 71/L3
Judian, China 112/C3
Judith (mts.), Mt, US 171/K4
Judith Gap, Mt, US 171/K4
Judson, ND, US 182/D4
Judsonia, Ar, US 179/J3
Juelsminde, Den. 66/D4
Jufrah (wadi), Egypt 139/C4
Jugon-les-Lacs, Fr. 82/C4
Juḩā, SAr. 144/B1
Juhaynah, Egypt 135/F3
Juicai (mtn.), China 113/F3
Juigalpa, Nic. 200/E3
Juilly, Fr. 56/L4
Juine (riv.), Fr. 70/E2
Juishui, Tai. 113/J4
Juist (isl.), Ger. 78/D1
Juist, Ger. 78/E1
Juist (arpt.), Ger. 78/E1
Juiz de Fora, Braz. 211/N6
Juizhen, China 113/H3
Jujurieux, Fr. 86/B5
Jujuy (prov.), Arg. 212/C2
Julbach, Ger. 85/F6
Julesburg, Co, US 180/C3
Juli, Peru 208/D5
Julia Creek, Austl. 160/A3
Juliaca, Peru 208/D4
Juliaetta, Id, US 170/F4
Julian, Ca, US 174/D4
Julian Alps (mts.), It. 71/K3
Juliana (lake), Fl, US 190/M7
Juliana Top (peak), Sur. 206/B2
Jülich, Ger. 81/F2
Juliff, Tx, US 177/M9
Julimes, Mex. 177/B3
Julio A. Mella, Cuba 201/H1
Júlio de Castilhos, Braz. 213/F4
Juliustown, NJ, US 194/D3
Jullouville, Fr. 82/D3
Jullundur, India 124/C4
Julu, China 106/C3
Juma (riv.), China 104/H4
Jumanggoin, China 112/C1
Jumbilla, Peru 208/B2
Jumbo, Zim. 149/F3
Jumeauville, Fr. 56/H5
Jumièges, Fr. 83/F2
Jumilla, Sp. 72/E3
Jūmīn (wadi), Tun. 138/L6
Juminda (pt.), Est. 67/L2
Jumla, Nepal 122/D1
Jümme (riv.), Ger. 79/E2
Jūmonji, Japan 108/B4
Jump (riv.), Wi, US 181/J1
Jumpertown, Ms, US 188/C3
Jūn, Leb. 131/C1
Junāgadh, India 127/K4
Jūnāgarh, India 121/D2
Junan, China 106/D4
Juncal (peak), Chile 214/N8
Junction, Ut, US 175/F1
Junction (mtn.), Mt, US 171/H4
Junction, Tx, US 177/E2
Junction City, Ar, US 179/H4
Junction City, Ks, US 179/F1
Junction City, Ky, US 188/E2
Junction City, La, US 176/H1
Junction City, Mo, US 188/B2
Junction City, Or, US 172/B1
Junction City, Wi, US 181/K1
Jundah, Austl. 160/A4
Jundiaí, Braz. 211/K8
Jundu (mts.), China 106/H6
June Lake, Ca, US 174/C2
Juneau, Wi, US 181/K2
Juneau (cap.), Ak, US 168/Z13
Juneda, Sp. 73/F2
Junee, Austl. 159/C2
Jungar Qi, China 106/B3
Jungfrau (peak), Swi. 86/D4
Jungfraujoch, Swi. 86/D4
Jungkat, Indo. 116/C3
Junglinster, Lux. 81/F4
Juniata (riv.), Pa, US 187/H4
Juniata, Ne, US 180/E3
Juniata (co.), Pa, US 194/A2
Junik, Yugo. 76/E4
Junín, Ecu. 204/A5
Junín, Col. 204/B4
Junín, Arg. 214/E2
Junín, Arg. 214/C2
Junín, Peru 208/B3
Junín (dept.), Peru 208/C3
Junín de los Andes, Arg. 214/C3
Junior, WV, US 189/H1
Juniper, NB, Can. 184/D2
Juniper (mtn.), Co, US 173/J3
Juniper, Ga, US 188/E4
Juniper Hills, Ca, US 192/C2
Junipero Serra (peak), Ca, US 174/B2
Jūniyah, Leb. 130/D3
Junji (pass), China 106/C3
Junkou, China 113/H3
Junlian, China 112/E2
Juno, Ga, US 188/E3
Juno, Tx, US 177/D2
Juno Beach, Fr. 83/E2
Juno Beach, Fl, US 191/H4
Junpu, China 113/H2
Junsele, Swe. 64/F3
Juntas, Chile 212/B4
Ju'nyunggoin, China 104/D5
Juodupė, Lith. 67/L3
Juparanã (lake), Braz. 211/E3
Jupiá (res.), Braz. 210/C4
Jupiter, Fl, US 191/H4
Jupiter (riv.), Qu, Can. 184/F1
Jupiter (mt.), Wa, US 193/A2
Juquiá, Braz. 213/H3
Juquitiba, Braz. 211/J8
Jur (riv.), Sudan 142/F3
Jur pri Bratislave, Slvk. 76/C1
Jura (dept.), Fr. 86/B4
Jura (canton), Swi. 86/D3
Jura (isl.), Sc, UK 57/Q9
Jura (pen.), Sc, UK 57/R8
Jura (mts.), Fr. 92/E1
Juradó, Col. 204/B3
Jurançon, Fr. 70/C5
Jurbarkas, Lith. 67/K4
Jurbise, Belg. 80/C2
Jurien, Austl. 156/B4
Jūrmala, Lat. 67/K3
Jurong (nbrhd.), Sing. 115/H6
Juruá (riv.), Braz. 203/C3
Juruena (riv.), Braz. 203/D4
Juruena, Res. Florestal do, Braz. 209/G3
Juruti, Braz. 206/B3
Jushi, China 113/F4
Jushiyama, Japan 109/L5
Jushui, China 113/H3
Jussey, Fr. 86/B2
Jussy, Swi. 86/C5
Jussy, Fr. 80/C4
Justice, WV, US 189/G2
Justiceburg, Tx, US 178/D4
Justin, Tx, US 176/K6
Justo Daract, Arg. 214/D2
Jutaí (riv.), Braz. 205/E5
Jutaí, Braz. 208/D2
Jutiapa, Guat. 200/D3
Juticalpa, Hon. 200/E3
Jutland (pen.), Den. 64/D4
Jutland, NJ, US 194/D2
Juventud, Isla de la (Isla de Pinos) (isl.), Cuba 196/E3
Juye, China 106/D4
Jūyom, Iran 129/H4
Juzhang (riv.), China 106/C5
Juziers, Fr. 56/H4
Južna Morava (riv.), Yugo. 76/E4
Juzur Qarqannah (isl.), Congo 137/H2
Jwaneng, Bots. 148/E5
Jwayyā, Leb. 131/C2
Jyderup, Den. 66/D4
Jylisjärvi (lake), Fin. 65/E3
Jyllinge, Den. 65/J7

K

K'ok'a (lake), Eth. 144/A3
K2 (Godwin Austen) (peak), Pak. 124/D2
Ka (isl.), NKor. 107/C3
Ka Lae (cape), Hi, US 168/S10
Kaabong, Ugan. 142/G5
Kaakhka, Trkm. 127/G1
Kaap Plato (plat.), SAfr. 150/C3
Kaapmuiden, SAfr. 149/F5
Kaarina, Fin. 67/K1
Kaarst, Ger. 78/D6
Kaartjärvi (lake), Fin. 65/E4
Kaba, Gui. 140/C4
Kaba, Hun. 76/E2
Kaba, Indo. 155/E1
Kaba (riv.), China 125/E2
Kabadak (riv.), Bang. 123/G4
Kabaena (isl.), Indo. 162/B5
Kabah (ruin), Mex. 200/D1
Kabala, SLeo. 140/C4
Kabale, Ugan. 147/G3
Kabalega (falls), Ugan. 147/G2
Kabalega NP, Ugan. 147/G2
Kabalo, D.R. Congo 147/F4
Kabamba (lake), D.R. Congo 147/F5
Kabambare, D.R. Congo 147/F4
Kabango, D.R. Congo 147/F4
Kabanjahe, Indo. 115/B2
Kabankalan, Phil. 114/C3
Kabardinka, Rus. 99/J5
Kabardino-Balkaria Aut. Rep., Rus. 101/Q6
Kabare, D.R. Congo 147/G3
Kābāw, Libya 134/A2
Kabba, Nga. 141/G5
Kabeke, D.R. Congo 147/G4
Kabelekese, D.R. Congo 147/E4
Kaberamaido, Ugan. 145/A1
Kabeta, D.R. Congo 147/F3
Kabetawa, Niger 142/B2
Kabetogama (lake), Mn, US 183/H3
Kabeya Maji, D.R. Congo 147/F4
Kabī, Eth. 144/A3
Kabin Buri, Thai. 120/C3
Kabinda, D.R. Congo 147/F4
Kabīr Kūh (mts.), Iran 129/F3
Kabîr, Oued el (riv.), Alg. 138/H4
Kabīrwāla, Pak. 124/A4
Kabkābīyah, Sudan 142/E2
Kableshkovo, Bul. 77/H4
Kabo, CAfr. 142/C4
Kabobo, D.R. Congo 147/G4
Kābol (Kābul) (cap.), Afg. 127/J2
Kabolaa, Indo. 117/H4
Kabompo, Zam. 148/E2
Kabompo (riv.), Zam. 148/D2
Kabong, Malay. 116/D3
Kabongo, D.R. Congo 147/F4
Kabrai, India 122/C3
Kābul (riv.), Afg. 127/J2
Kābul (Kābol) (cap.), Afg. 127/J2
Kabunda, D.R. Congo 149/F2
Kaburuang (isl.), Indo. 117/G3
Kabūshīyah, Sudan 142/G1
Kabwe, Zam. 149/F2
Kačanik, Yugo. 75/G1
Kačergine, Lith. 67/K4
Kachalola, Zam. 149/F2
Kachia, Nga. 141/G4
Kachikau, Bots. 148/E3
Kachin (state), Myan. 119/G2
Kachiry, Kaz. 125/C1
Kachug, Rus. 104/F1
Kaçkar Daği (peak), Turk. 97/G4
Kada, Myan. 120/B2
Kadam (peak), Ugan. 145/A1
Kadam (isl.), Myan. 119/G5
Kadaň, Czh. 85/G2
Kadan (isl.), Myan. 120/B3
Kadavu (isl.), Fiji 162/G6
Kadaya, Rus. 105/H1
Kadéï (riv.), CAfr. 142/B4
Kadesa, Indo. 117/F5
Kadiana, Mali 140/D4
Kadiköy (nbrhd.), Turk. 129/N7
Kadina, Austl. 157/H5
Kadınhanı, Turk. 128/C2
Kadiogo (prov.), Burk. 141/E3
Kadiolo, Mali 140/D4
Kadirli, Turk. 128/D2
Kadışehri, Turk. 128/C1
Kadoka, SD, US 180/D2
Kadoma, Zim. 149/F3
Kadoma, Japan 109/J6
Kadônkani, Myan. 119/G4
Kadoshkino, Rus. 97/H1
Kadrina, Est. 67/M2
Kaduna (state), Nga. 141/G4
Kaduna, Nga. 141/G4
Kaduna (riv.), Nga. 133/C4
Kāduqli, Sudan 142/F3
Kadzharan, Arm. 97/H5
Kadzherom, Rus. 95/M2
Kaech'ŏn, NKor. 107/C3
Kaédi, Mrta. 140/B2
Kaehwa-ri, NKor. 107/D2
Kaélé, Camr. 142/B3
Kaeng Khro, Thai. 120/C2
Kaeng Krachan NP, Thai. 120/B3
Kaep'ung, NKor. 107/D4
Kaesŏng, NKor. 107/D3
Kaesŏng-si (prov.), NKor. 107/D4
Kafakumba, D.R. Congo 147/E5
Kafanchan, Nga. 141/H4
Kafar Jar Ghar (mts.), Afg. 127/J2
Kaffraria (reg.), SAfr. 150/D4
Kaffrine, Sen. 140/B3
Kafia Kingi, Sudan 142/E3
Kafirevs (cape), Gre. 75/J3
Kafr ad Dawwār, Egypt 139/B2
Kafr al 'ā'id, Egypt 139/C4
Kafr al Baţţīkh, Egypt 139/C2
Kafr al Jarā'idah, Egypt 139/C2
Kafr al Kurdī, Egypt 139/C2
Kafr Ash Shaykh (gov.), Egypt 135/F1
Kafr ash Shaykh, Egypt 139/B2
Kafr az Zayyāt, Egypt 139/B3
Kafr Kannā, Isr. 131/C3
Kafr Mandā, Isr. 131/C3
Kafr Qari', Isr. 131/C3
Kafr Qāsim, Isr. 131/B4
Kafr Rabī', Egypt 139/B3
Kafr Sa'd, Egypt 139/C2
Kafr Salīm, Egypt 139/B2
Kafr Şaqr, Egypt 139/C3
Kafr Shukr, Egypt 139/C3
Kafr Yāsīf, Isr. 131/C3
Kafu (riv.), Ugan. 147/G2
Kafubu (riv.), D.R. Congo 149/E1
Kafue (dam), Zam. 149/F2
Kafue, Zam. 149/F2
Kafue (riv.), Zam. 148/E2
Kafue Flats (swamp), Zam. 149/E2
Kafue Gorge (res.), Zam. 149/E2
Kafue NP, Zam. 148/E2
Kafukule, Malw. 149/G1
Kafulwe, Zam. 147/G5
Kaga, Japan 110/E2
Kaga Bandoro, CAfr. 142/C4
Kagan, Uzb. 100/G6
Kāgān (valley), Pak. 124/B2
Kagang, China 104/E4
Kagawa (pref.), Japan 110/D3
Kagera (riv.), Tanz. 147/G3
Kågeröd, Swe. 65/K7
Kağıthane, Turk. 129/M6
Kâğıthane (riv.), Turk. 129/M6
Kağızman, Turk. 129/E1
Kagmar, Sudan 142/F2
Kagoshima (int'l arpt.), Japan 110/B5
Kagoshima (bay), Japan 110/B5
Kagoshima, Japan 110/B5
Kagoshima (dept.), Japan 111/L5
Kagua, PNG 155/F1
K'aha, Eth. 144/B3
Kahama, Tanz. 147/H3
Kaharlyk, Ukr. 98/F3
Kahayan (riv.), Indo. 116/D4
Kahe, Tanz. 145/B2
Kahemba, D.R. Congo 146/D4
Kahindi, Tanz. 145/B4
Kahl am Main, Ger. 84/C2
Kahmsara (riv.), Rus. 104/D1
Kāhna, Pak. 124/C4
Kahnple, Libr. 140/C5
Kahnūj, Iran 127/G3
Kahnwia, Libr. 140/C5
Kahoka, Mo, US 181/J3
Kahoolawe (isl.), Hi, US 168/S9
Kahperusvaara (peak), Fin. 64/G1
Kahramanmaraş, Turk 128/D2
Kahramanmaraş (prov.), Turk. 128/D2
Kahror Pakka, Pak. 124/A5
Kâhta, Turk. 128/D2
Kahuku (pt.), Hi, US 168/S9
Kahului, Hi, US 168/S9
Kahuzi-Biega, PN de, D.R. Congo 147/F3
Kai (isls.), Indo. 162/C5
Kai Besar (isl.), Indo. 117/H5
Kai Kecil (isl.), Indo. 117/H5
Kai Mbaku, D.R. Congo 146/C4
Kaiama, Nga. 141/F4
Kaiapit, PNG 155/G1
Kaiapoi, NZ 161/C3
Kaibab (plat.), Az, US 175/F2
Kaibab Ind. Res., Az, US 175/F2
Kaibara, Japan 109/H5
Kaibito, Az, US 175/G2
Kaibito (plat.), Az, US 175/G2
Kaidu (riv.), China 125/D3
Kaieteur (falls), Guy. 205/G3
Kaieteur NP, Guy. 205/G3
Kaifeng, China 106/C4
Kāigaon, Nepal 122/D1
Kaijiang, China 113/E2
Kaikalūr, India 121/D2
Kaikoura, NZ 161/C3
Kailahun, SLeo. 140/C4
Kaili, China 113/E3
Kailu, China 106/E2
Kailua, Hi, US 168/S10
Kaimar, China 104/D5
Kaimganj, India 122/B2
Kaimur (range), India 122/C3
Käina, Est. 67/K2
Kainab (riv.), Namb. 150/B2
Kainach (riv.), Aus. 76/B2
Kainan, Japan 110/D3
Kainantu, PNG 155/G1
Kaindu, Zam. 149/E2
Kainji (dam), Nga. 141/G4
Kainji (lake), Nga. 133/C3
Kainji Lake NP, Nga. 141/F4
Kainoúryion, Gre. 75/G3
Kaintiba, PNG 155/G1
Kaipara (riv.), NZ 161/F6
Kaiparowits (plat.), Ut, US 175/G2
Kaiping, China 106/J7
Kairāna, India 124/D5
Kairi, Austl. 160/B2
Kairu, India 124/C5
Kairuku, PNG 155/G2
Kaisei, Japan 109/C3
Kaiseregg (peak), Swi. 86/D4
Kaisersesch, Ger. 81/G3
Kaiserslautern, Ger. 81/G5
Kaisheim, Ger. 84/D5
Kaišiadorys, Lith. 67/L4
Kait (cape), Indo. 115/D3
Kaitaia, NZ 161/C1
Kaitangata, NZ 161/B4
Kaithal, India 124/D5
Kaiti, Tanz. 145/A2
Kaiwi (chan.), Hi, US 168/S9
Kaiyang, China 119/J2
Kaiyuan, China 106/F2
Kaiyuan, China 112/D4
Kaizu, Japan 109/L5
Kaizuka, Japan 109/H7
Kajaani, Fin. 100/C3
Kajabbi, Austl. 155/F5
Kajang (peak), Malay. 115/D2
Kajang, Malay. 115/C2
Kajang, Indo. 117/F5
Kaji-san (peak), SKor. 110/A3
Kajiado, Kenya 145/B2
Kajikazawa, Japan 109/A2
Kajo-Kaji, Sudan 147/G2
Kajuru, Nga. 141/G4
Kākā, Sudan 142/G3
Kakabeka Falls, On, Can. 183/K3
Kakada (well), Chad 142/B1
Kakadu NP, Austl. 154/D3
Kakagi (lake), On, Can. 183/H3
Kakamas, SAfr. 150/C3
Kakamega, Kenya 145/A1
Kakamigahara, Japan 109/L5
Kakanj, Bosn. 76/D3
Kakata, Libr. 140/C5
Kākdwīp, India 123/G5
Kākhk, Iran 127/G2
Kakhovka, Ukr. 98/G4
Kakhovs'ke Vodoskhovyshche (res.), Ukr. 96/E3
Kakielo, D.R. Congo 149/F2
Kākināda, India 121/D2
Kakiri, Ugan. 147/H2
Kakkirigumma, India 121/D2
Kako (riv.), Japan 109/G6
Kakogawa, Japan 109/G6
Kakonga, Zam. 148/D2
Kakonko, Tanz. 147/G3
Kākori, India 122/C2
Kakrāla, India 122/B2
Kakrima (riv.), Gui. 140/B4
Kaktovik, Ak, US 168/Y11
Kaku, India 118/B2
Kakuda, Japan 111/G2
Kakuma, Kenya 142/G5
Kakumbi, Zam. 149/F2
Kakuna, D.R. Congo 147/E4
Kakunodate, Japan 108/B4
Kakuri, Nga. 141/G4
Kakuto, Ugan. 147/G3
Kakya, Kenya 145/B2
Kāl-e Shūr (riv.), Iran 129/J2
Kalā Chāy, Iran 129/G2
Kala-i-Mor, Trkm. 127/H1
Kalaa Kebira, Tun. 74/B5
Kalaallit Nunaat (Greenland) (dpcy.), Den. 165/N2
Kālābāgh, Pak. 124/A3
Kalabahi, Indo. 154/B2
Kalabakan, Malay. 114/B4
Kalabo, Zam. 148/D2
Kalabyin, Myan. 112/B5
Kalach, Rus. 99/L2
Kalach-na-Donu, Rus. 97/G2
Kalachinsk, Rus. 100/H4
Kaladan (riv.), Myan. 119/F3
Kaladar, On, Can. 187/H2
Kālāgarh, India 122/B1
Kalahari (des.), Namb. 133/D7
Kalahari-Gemsbok NP, SAfr. 150/C2
Kalaiya, Nepal 123/E2
Kalakan, Rus. 101/M4
Kalalé, Ben. 141/F4
Kalāleh, Iran 129/H2
Kalaloch, Wa, US 170/B4
Kalām, Pak. 124/B2
Kalama, Wa, US 170/C4
Kalamákion, Gre. 75/N8
Kalamaloué, PN de, Camr. 142/B2

263

Kalam – Keady

Kalamare, Bots. 149/E4
Kalamariá, Gre. 75/H2
Kalamáta, Gre. 75/H4
Kalamazoo (riv.), Mi, US 186/D3
Kalamazoo, Mi, US 186/D3
Kalamitsk (bay), Ukr. 99/G5
Kalampáka, Gre. 75/G3
Kalanchak, Ukr. 99/G4
Kalandy, Madg. 152/J6
Kalangali, Tanz. 145/A3
Kalanguy, Rus. 104/H1
Kālānwāli, India 124/C5
Kalaotoa (isl.), Indo. 154/A1
Kalasin, Thai. 120/C2
Kalāswāla, Pak. 124/C3
Kalāt, Pak. 127/J3
Kalaupapa, Hi, US 168/S9
Kalávrita, Gre. 75/H3
Kalaw, Myan. 112/C4
Kalbā, UAE 127/G3
Kälbäcär, Azer. 129/F1
Kalbach, Ger. 84/B2
Kalbar, Austl. 160/D4
Kalbarri, Austl. 156/B3
Kalbarri NP, Austl. 156/B3
Kaldakvísl (riv.), Ice. 64/N7
Kale, Turk. 130/A1
Kale, Turk. 128/D1
Kalecik, Turk. 128/C1
Kaleden, BC, Can. 170/E3
Kaledupa (isl.), Indo. 154/A1
Kalefeld, Ger. 79/H5
Kalehe, D.R. Congo 147/G3
Kalema, D.R. Congo 147/F4
Kalemie (int'l arpt.), D.R. Congo 147/G4
Kalemie, D.R. Congo 147/G4
Kalemyo, Myan. 112/B4
Kalenda, D.R. Congo 147/E5
Kalety, Pol. 69/K3
Kaleva, Mi, US 186/C2
Kalevala, Rus. 94/F2
Kalewa, Myan. 112/B4
Kaleya, Zam. 149/E2
Kalgoorlie-Boulder, Austl. 156/D4
Kāli (riv.), India 122/B1
Kali (riv.), India 122/B2
Kāli (riv.), Nepal 122/D2
Kālia, Bang. 123/H4
Kāliākair, Bang. 123/H3
Kalianda, Indo. 115/D3
Kalibo, Phil. 114/C3
Kalida, Oh, US 186/D4
Kālīganj, Bang. 123/G4
Kālikot, Nepal 122/C1
Kalima, D.R. Congo 147/F3
Kalimala, India 121/D2
Kalimantan (reg.), Indo. 116/D4
Kálimnos, Gre. 93/K3
Kālimpong, India 123/G2
Kaliningrad (oblast), Rus. 94/D5
Kaliningrad, Rus. 94/W9
Kaliningrad, Rus. 67/J4
Kalinino, Rus. 99/K5
Kalininsk, Rus. 97/H2
Kalinkavichy, Bela. 98/E1
Kalinko, Gui. 140/C4
Kalinovka, Rus. 99/H2
Kaliro, Ugan. 145/A1
Kalis, Som. 144/D3
Kalisizo, Ugan. 147/G3
Kalispel Ind. Res., Wa, US 170/F3
Kalispell, Mt, US 170/G3
Kalisz, Pol. 69/K3
Kaliua, Tanz. 147/G4
Kalix, Swe. 94/D2
Kalixälven (riv.), Swe. 64/G2
Kāliyāganj, India 123/G3
Kālka, India 124/D4
Kalkaringi, Austl. 154/C4
Kalkaska, Mi, US 186/D2
Kalkbruk, Fin. 65/F4
Kalkfeld, Namb. 148/C4
Kalkfontein, Bots. 148/D4
Kalkhügel, Namb. 148/C5
Kālkini, Bang. 123/H4
Kalkrand, Namb. 148/C5
Kallar Kahār, Pak. 124/B3
Kallaste, Est. 67/M2
Kallham, Aus. 85/G6
Kallinge, Swe. 66/F3
Kallinge (int'l arpt.), Swe. 66/F3
Kalliola, Fin. 65/F4
Kallithéa, Gre. 75/N9
Kallsjön (lake), Swe. 64/E3
Kalmalo, Nga. 141/G3
Kalmar (co.), Swe. 64/F4
Kalmar (int'l arpt.), Swe. 66/G3
Kalmar, Swe. 66/G3
Kalmar, Swe. 65/A1
Kalmarsund (sound), Swe. 66/G3
Kalmthout, Belg. 78/B6
Kalmykia Aut. Rep., Rus. 100/E5
Kalmykovo, Kaz. 97/J2
Kālna, India 123/G4
Kalnai, India 122/D4
Kalnciems, Lat. 67/K3
Kalni (riv.), Bang. 123/H3
Kalnibolotskaya, Rus. 99/L4
Kalocsa, Hun. 76/D2
Kalofer, Bul. 75/J1
Kalokhórion, Gre. 75/H2
Kaloko, D.R. Congo 147/F4
Kālol, India 127/K4
Kalole, D.R. Congo 147/F3
Kalombo, Zam. 148/D2
Kalomo, Zam. 149/E3
Kalona, Ia, US 181/J3
Kalongan, Indo. 114/D4
Kalongo, Ugan. 145/A1
Kaloqi, Sudan 142/F3
Kālpi, India 122/B2
Kalpin, China 125/C3
Kalpitiya, SrL. 121/C4
Kalsdorf bei Graz, Aus. 76/B2
Kaltasy, Rus. 95/M5
Kaltbrunn, Swi. 87/F3
Kaltenleutgeben, Aus. 77/N7
Kaltennordheim, Ger. 84/D1
Kaltern (Caldaro), It. 71/J3
Kalu (riv.), SrL. 118/D6
Kaluga (oblast), Rus. 94/G5
Kaluga, Rus. 94/H5
Kaluku, Indo. 117/E4
Kalulushi, Zam. 149/F2
Kalumburu Abor. Rsv., Austl. 154/B3
Kalumburu Mission, Austl. 154/B3
Kalumpang, Malay. 115/C2
Kalundborg, Den. 66/D4
Kalundborg (inlet), Den. 65/G7
Kalungu, Ugan. 147/G3
Kalungwishi (riv.), Zam. 147/G5
Kalūr Kot, Pak. 124/A3
Kalush, Ukr. 98/C3
Kalvarija, Lith. 67/K4
Kalwelwe, Zam. 149/F2
Kalyān, India 118/B4
Kalyazin, Rus. 94/H4
Kalynivka, Ukr. 98/E3
Kama (res.), Rus. 95/M4
Kama, D.R. Congo 147/F3
Kama, Myan. 112/B5
Kama (riv.), Rus. 55/K3
Kamachumu, Tanz. 147/G3
Kamagaya, Japan 109/E2
Kamaishi, Japan 108/B4
Kamajai, Lith. 67/L4
Kamakura, Japan 109/D3
Kamakusa, Guy. 206/A1
Kamakwie, SLeo. 140/B4
Kamalampaka, Tanz. 147/G4
Kamālia, Pak. 124/B4
Kaman, Turk. 128/C2
Kāman, India 122/A2
Kamande, D.R. Congo 147/G3
Kamango (lake), Mali 140/E2
Kamango, D.R. Congo 147/G2
Kamanjab, Namb. 148/B3
Kamanyola, D.R. Congo 147/G3
Kamaran (isl.), Yem. 144/B2
Kamarang, Guy. 205/F3
Kāmāreddi, India 121/C2
Kāmārhāti, India 118/E3
Kamaria (falls), Guy 205/G3
Kamas, Ut, US 173/H3
Kamāsin, India 122/C3
Kamativi, Zim. 149/E3
Kamba, Nga. 141/G3
Kamba-Poko, D.R. Congo 146/D4
Kambalda, Austl. 156/D4
Kambam, India 121/C4
Kambar, Pak. 118/A2
Kambara, Japan 109/B3
Kambaswana, D.R. Congo 147/E4
Kambia, SLeo. 140/B4
Kambja, Est. 67/M2
Kambove, D.R. Congo 147/F5
Kambuno (peak), Indo. 117/F4
Kamchatka (pen.), Rus. 103/Q4
Kamchatka Oblast, Rus. 101/R4
Kamchiya (riv.), Bul. 96/C4
Kamela, Or, US 172/D1
Kamen, Ger. 79/E5
Kamen'-na-Obi, Rus. 125/D1
Kamena, D.R. Congo 147/F4
Kamende, D.R. Congo 147/F4
Kamenets, Bela. 69/M2
Kamenična, Slvk. 76/D2
Kamenjak, Rt (cape), Cro. 71/K4
Kamenka, Kaz. 97/J2
Kamenka, Rus. 97/H1
Kamenka, Rus. 95/K2
Kamenka, Rus. 99/K2
Kamenka, Rus. 105/M3
Kamennogorsk, Rus. 67/N1
Kamennomostskaya, Rus. 99/L5
Kameno, Bul. 77/H4
Kamenolomni, Rus. 99/L4
Kamensk-Shakhtinskiy, Rus. 99/L3
Kamensk-Ural'skiy, Rus. 95/P4
Kamenskoye, Rus. 101/S3
Kameoka, Japan 109/J5
Kameri, Indo. 117/H4
Kames, Sc, UK 59/A5
Kameyama, Japan 109/K6
Kami, Japan 109/G5
Kami (isl.), Japan 109/M6
Kami-koshiki (isl.), Japan 110/A5
Kamiah, Id, US 170/F4
Kamień Pomorski, Pol. 66/F5
Kamieskroon, SAfr. 150/B3
Kamifukuoka, Japan 109/D2
Kamiisco, Japan 108/B3
Kamiishizu, Japan 109/K5
Kamiizumi, Japan 109/C1
Kamiji, D.R. Congo 147/E4
Kamikawa, Japan 108/C2
Kamikuishiki, Japan 109/B2
Kamin'-Kashyrs'kyy, Ukr. 98/C2
Kamina, D.R. Congo 147/F5
Kaminaka, Japan 109/J5
Kaminoho, Japan 109/M4
Kaminoyama, Japan 111/G1
Kamisato, Japan 109/C1
Kamiyahagi, Japan 109/M5
Kamiyaku, Japan 111/L5
Kamla (riv.), India 123/F3
Kamloops, BC, Can. 170/D2
Kamlot, Camb. 120/C4
Kammaki, Japan 109/J6
Kamnik, Slov. 71/L3
Kamo, Arm 129/F1
Kamo, Japan 111/F2
Kamo (riv.), Japan 109/E3
Kamo, Japan 109/J6
Kamogawa, Japan 111/G3
Kamojima, Japan 110/D3
Kāmoke, Pak. 124/C4
Kamonia, D.R. Congo 147/E4
Kamp (riv.), Aus. 69/H4
Kamp-Bornhofen, Ger. 81/G3
Kamp-Lintfort, Ger. 78/D5
Kampala (cap.), Ugan. 147/H2
Kampalili (mt.), Phil. 114/D4
Kampar, Malay. 115/C1
Kampar (riv.), Indo. 116/B3
Kampar (river), Indo. 115/C2
Kampen, Ger. 66/C4
Kampen, Neth. 78/C3
Kampene, D.R. Congo 147/F3
Kamphaeng Phet, Thai. 120/C5
Kamphaeng Phet (ruin), Thai. 120/B2
Kamp'o, SKor. 107/E5
Kampong Cham, Camb. 120/D4
Kampong Chhnang, Camb. 120/D3
Kampong Kadok, Malay. 120/C5
Kampong Khleang, Camb. 120/D3
Kampong Kuala Besut, Malay. 115/C1
Kampong Raja, Malay. 115/C1
Kampong Saom (bay), Camb. 116/B1
Kampóng Saom, Camb. 120/C4
Kampong Sedenak, Malay. 115/C2
Kampong Sedili Kechil, Malay. 115/D2
Kampong Spoe, Camb. 120/D4
Kampong Tampasis, Malay. 117/E2
Kampong Telupid, Malay. 114/B4
Kampong Thum, Camb. 120/D3
Kampong Trabek, Camb. 120/D4
Kampot, Camb. 120/D4
Kampti, Burk. 140/E4
Kamrau (bay), Indo. 117/H4
Kamsack, Sk, Can. 182/D2
Kamsar, Gui. 140/B4
Kamsdorf, Ger. 85/E1
Kamskoye Ust'ye, Rus. 95/L5
Kamsuuma, Som. 145/C1
Kamtsha (riv.), D.R. Congo 146/D4
Kamui-misaki (cape), Japan 108/B2
Kámuk (mtn.), CR 201/F4
Kamuli, Ugan. 145/A1
Kamuzu (Lilongwe) (int'l arpt.), Malw. 149/G2
Kamwandu, D.R. Congo 147/E4
Kam'yanets'-Podil's'kyy, Ukr. 98/D3
Kam'yanka, Ukr. 99/G3
Kam'yanka-Buz'ka, Ukr. 98/C2
Kam'yanka-Dniprovs'ka, Ukr. 99/H4
Kāmyārān, Iran 129/F3
Kamyshevatskaya, Rus. 99/J4
Kamyshin, Rus. 97/H2
Kamyshla, Rus. 95/M5
Kamyshlov, Rus. 95/P4
Kamyzyak, Rus. 97/J3
Kanaaupscow (riv.), Qu, Can. 167/J3
Kanab, Ut, US 175/F2
Kanab (plat.), Az, US 175/F2
Kanab (cr.), Az, US 175/F2
Kanairiktok (riv.), Nf, Can. 167/K3
Kanākir, Syria 131/E2
Kanan, Japan 109/J7
Kananga, D.R. Congo 147/E4
Kanaoudi, India 122/C4
Kanarraville, Ut, US 175/F2
Kanash, Rus. 95/K5
Kanasin, Mex. 200/D1
Kanata, On, Can. 187/J2
Kanawake Ind. Res., Qu, Can. 185/N7
Kanawha, Ia, US 181/H2
Kanawha (riv.), WV, US 189/F1
Kanazawa, Japan 111/E2
Kanazi, Tanz. 147/G3
Kanchanaburi, Thai. 120/B3
Kanchanadit, Thai. 120/B4
Kānchenjunga (peak), Nepal 118/E2
Kānchīpuram, India 121/C3
Kanda-Kanda, D.R. Congo 147/E4
Kandalaksha, Rus. 94/G2
Kandalaksha (gulf), Rus. 64/K2
Kandale, D.R. Congo 146/D4
Kandang, Indo. 115/B2
Kandanghaur, Indo. 115/E3
Kándanos, Gre. 75/H5
Kandava, Lat. 67/K3
Kandavu Passage, Fiji 163/Y18
Kandé, Togo 141/F4
Kandel (peak), Ger. 86/E1
Kandel, Ger. 84/B4
Kandep, PNG 155/F1
Kander (riv.), Swi. 86/D4
Kandern, Ger. 86/D2
Kandersteg, Swi. 86/D5
Kandhkot, Pak. 127/J3
Kāndhla, India 124/D5
Kandi, Ben. 141/F4
Kāndi, India 123/G4
Kandi, D.R. Congo 147/G2
Kandi (cape), Indo. 117/F3
Kandıra, Turk. 77/K5
Kandos, Austl. 159/D1
Kandrāch, Pak. 127/J3
Kandreho, Madg. 152/H7
Kandry, Rus. 95/M5
Kandukūr, India 121/C3
Kandy, SrL. 121/D5
Kane, Pa, US 187/G4
Kane (co.), Il, US 193/P16
Kane, Il, US 181/J4
Kane (basin), Grld. 167/T7
Kanem (reg.), Chad 142/B2
Kanem (pref.), Chad 142/B2
Kaneohe, Hi, US 168/S9
Kaneville, Il, US 193/N16
Kanëvka, Rus. 94/H2
Kanevskaya, Rus. 99/K4
Kaneyama, Japan 108/B4
Kang, Bots. 148/D4
Kanga (riv.), Bang. 123/G5
Kanga, D.R. Congo 147/G2
Kanga, Tanz. 145/B3
Kangaba, Mali 140/C4
Kangal, Turk. 128/D2
Kangān, Iran 129/H5
Kangān, Iran 127/G3
Kangan Abor. Land, Austl. 156/C2
Kanganpur, Pak. 124/C4
Kangar, Malay. 120/C5
Kangaré, Mali 140/C4
Kangaroo (isl.), Austl. 153/C4
Kangaruma, Guy. 205/G3
Kangasala, Fin. 67/L1
Kangāvar, Iran 129/F3
Kangbao, China 104/G3
Kangding, China 112/D2
Kangdong (nbrhd.), SKor. 107/G6
Kangean (isl.), Indo. 115/F3
Kangean (isls.), Indo. 117/E5
Kangen (riv.), Sudan 142/G4
Kangendala, PN da, Ang. 146/D5
Kanggye, NKor. 107/D2
Kanggyŏng, SKor. 107/D4
Kanghwa, SKor. 107/F6
Kangi, Sudan 142/E3
Kangiqcliniq (Rankin Inlet), Nun, Can. 166/G2
Kangiqsualujjuaq, Qu, Can. 167/K3
Kangiqsujuaq, Qu, Can. 167/J2
Kangirsuk, Qu, Can. 167/J2
Kangjin, SKor. 107/D5
Kangkar Dohol, Malay. 115/C2
Kangmar, China 123/G1
Kangnam (mts.), NKor. 107/C2
Kangnam, NKor. 107/C3
Kangnam (nbrhd.), SKor. 107/G6
Kangnŭng, SKor. 110/A2
Kangnyŏng, NKor. 107/C4
Kango, Gabon 146/B2
Kangondi, Kenya 145/B2
Kangping, China 106/E2
Kāngra, India 124/D3
Kangrinboqê (peak), China 125/D5
Kangsŏ, NKor. 107/C3
Kangsŏ (nbrhd.), SKor. 107/F6
Kangto (peak), China 112/B3
Kangu, D.R. Congo 146/C4
Kangwŏn-do (prov.), NKor. 107/D3
Kangwŏn-do (prov.), SKor. 110/A2
Kangxiwar, China 125/C4
Kanha NP, India 122/C4
Kanhān (riv.), India 118/C3
Kanholmsfjärden (sound), Swe. 65/B1
Kani, C.d'Iv. 140/D4
Kani, Myan. 112/B4
Kani, Japan 109/M5
Kaniama, D.R. Congo 147/F4
Kanie, Japan 109/L5
Kanin (pen.), Rus. 216/C
Kanin Nos, Rus. 94/J1
Kanin Nos (pt.), Rus. 100/E3
Kaningo, Kenya 145/B2
Kaniv, Ukr. 98/F3
Kaniva, Austl. 158/B3
Kanivs'ke Vodoskhovyshche (res.), Ukr. 98/F2
Kanjiža, Yugo. 76/E2
Kankakee, Il, US 186/C4
Kankakee (riv.), Il, US 186/C4
Kankan (pol. reg.), Gui. 140/C4
Kankan, Gui. 140/C4
Kānker, India 121/D1
Kankesanturai, SrL. 121/D4
Kankossa, Mrta. 140/C3
Kanmen, China 113/J2
Kanmuri-yama (peak), Japan 110/C3
Kannami, Japan 109/B3
Kannapolis, NC, US 189/G3
Kannauj, India 122/B2
Kannon-zaki (pt.), Japan 109/D3
Kannus, Fin. 94/D3
Kano (state), Nga. 141/H4
Kano, Nga. 141/H4
Kano Vlei, Namb. 148/C3
Kanona, Zam. 149/F2
Kanoneiland, SAfr. 150/C3
Kan'onji, Japan 110/C3
Kanopolis, Ks, US 179/E1
Kanopolis (lake), Ks, US 180/E4
Kanosh, Ut, US 175/F1
Kanouse (mtn.), NJ, US 195/H7
Kanowit, Malay. 116/D3
Kanoya, Japan 110/B5
Kānpur, India 122/C2
Kanra, Japan 109/B1
Kansai (int'l arpt.), Japan 109/H7
Kansai (isl.), Japan 109/H7
Kansarokana (riv.), Kenya 145/B2
Kansas, Il, US 186/C5
Kansas (state), US 169/G4
Kansas (riv.), US 169/G4
Kansas, Al, US 188/D4
Kansas City, Ks, US 181/G4
Kansas City (int'l arpt.), Mo, US 181/G4
Kansas City, Mo, US 181/G4
Kansas Cosmosphere and Space Center, Ks, US 179/F1
Kansasville, Wi, US 193/P14
Kansenia, D.R. Congo 147/F5
Kansk, Rus. 100/K4
Kansŏng, SKor. 107/E3
Kantābānji, India 121/D1
Kantchari, Burk. 141/F3
Kantemirovka, Rus. 99/K3
Kānth, India 122/B1
Kantharalak, Thai. 120/D3
Kantō (prov.), Japan 111/F2
Kantunilkin, Mex. 200/E1
Kanturk, Ire. 58/B5
Kantvik, Fin. 65/E4
Kanuku (mts.), Guy. 205/G4
Kanuma, Japan 111/F2
Kanyanga, Gha. 141/E4
Kanye, Bots. 148/E5
Kanyilombi, Zam. 148/E2
Kanyutkwin, Myan. 120/B2
Kanzenze, D.R. Congo 147/F5
Kanzi, China 107/B3
Kaoh Nhek, Camb. 120/D3
Kaohsiung (int'l arpt.), Tai. 113/J4
Kaohsiung, Tai. 113/J4
Kaolack (pol. reg.), Sen. 140/B3
Kaolack, Sen. 140/A3
Kaolinovo, Bul. 77/H4
Kaoma, Zam. 148/E2
Kaongweshi (riv.), D.R. Congo 147/E5
Kaortchi (well), Chad 134/C5
Kaouadja, CAfr. 142/D4
Kaouar (reg.), Niger 134/B5
Kapa, Myan. 120/B3
Kapakapanui (mt.), NZ 161/J8
Kapalala, Zam. 149/F2
Kapalong, Phil. 114/D4
Kapambwe, D.R. Congo 147/E4
Kapan, Arm. 129/F2
Kapanga, D.R. Congo 147/E5
Kapaonik (mts.), Yugo. 75/G1
Kapchorwa, Ugan. 145/A1
Kapedo, Kenya 145/B1
Kapellen, Belg. 78/B6
Kapellshamn (isl.), Swe. 65/J6
Kapellskär, Swe. 65/C1
Kapenguria, Kenya 145/A1
Kapengwe, Zam. 149/F2
Kapfenberg, Aus. 71/L3
Kapidaği (pen.), Turk. 77/H5
Kapingamarangi (isl.), Micr. 162/E4
Kapiri Mposhi, Zam. 149/F2
Kapiskau (riv.), On, Can. 167/H3
Kaplan, La, US 190/B3
Kaplice, Czh. 85/H5
Kapoe, Thai. 120/B4
Kapoeta, Sudan 142/G4
Kapona, D.R. Congo 147/G4
Kaporo, Malw. 145/A4
Kapos (riv.), Hun. 76/C2
Kaposvár, Hun. 76/C2
Kapowsin, Wa, US 170/C4
Kapp, Nor. 66/D1
Kappeln, Ger. 66/C4
Kappl, Aus. 87/G3
Kapsabet, Kenya 145/A1
Kapsan, NKor. 107/E2
Kapuas (riv.), Indo. 116/C4
Kapuas Hulu (mts.), Indo.,Malay. 116/D3
Kapunda, Austl. 157/H5
Kapūrthala, India 124/C4
Kapuskasing, On, Can. 167/H4
Kaputa, Zam. 147/G5
Kapuvár, Hun. 76/C2
Kapydzhik (peak), Azer. 129/F2
Kap'yŏng, SKor. 107/D4
Kara (riv.), Rus. 95/Q1
Kara, Rus 95/Q1
Kara, Togo 141/F4
Kara (sea), Rus. 216/A
Kara K'orē, Eth. 144/A3
Kara-Balta, Kyr. 125/B3
Kara-Kala, Trkm. 129/J2
Kara-Köl, Kyr. 125/B3
Kara-Saki (pt.), Japan 110/A3
Karaali, Turk. 128/C2
Karaart, Taj. 125/B4
Karabau, Kaz. 97/K2
Karabiğa, Turk. 77/H5
Karabra (riv.), Indo. 117/H4
Karabudakhkent, Rus. 97/H4
Karabük, Turk. 96/E4
Karabula, Rus. 100/K4
Karabulak, Rus. 97/H4
Karaburun, Turk. 77/J5
Karaca (peak), Turk. 128/D2
Karacadağ, Turk. 77/H5
Karacaköy, Turk. 77/J5
Karaçal (peak), Turk. 130/C1
Karacaoğlan, Turk. 77/H5
Karachala, Azer. 97/J5
Karachay-Cherkessia Aut. Rep., Rus. 101/Q6
Karachev, Rus. 96/E1
Karachi (int'l arpt.), Pak. 127/J4
Karāchi, Pak. 127/J4
Karād, India 121/B2
Karadere, Turk. 77/K5
Karagayly, Kaz. 125/C2
Karaginskiy (isl.), Rus. 103/R4
Karagoš (peak), Rus. 125/E1
Karaidel'skiy, Rus. 95/N5
Kāraikkudi, India 121/C4
Karaj, Iran 129/G3
Karak, Malay. 115/C2
Karakax (riv.), China 125/C4
Karakaya (dam), Turk. 128/D2
Karakelong (isl.), Indo. 117/G3
Karakhoto (ruin), China 104/E3
Karakol, Kyr. 125/C3
Karakoram (pass), India 124/D2
Karakoram (range), India 125/C4
Karakoro (riv.), Mali 140/C3
Karakorum (pass), China 127/L1
Karakorum (ruin), Mong 104/E2
Karaköse, Turk. 129/E2
Karaköy, Turk. 128/E2
Karakul', Uzb. 100/G6
Karakul' (lake), Taj. 125/B4
Karakumy (des.), Trkm. 100/F5
Karakuwisa, Namb. 148/C3
Karakyon (peak), Trkm. 129/H1
Karakyr (peak), Trkm. 127/H1
Karam (riv.), Indo. 117/E4
Karamagay, China 104/B2
Karaman, Turk. 128/C2
Karaman (prov.), Turk. 128/C2
Karamay, China 125/D2
Karambi, Tanz. 147/G3
Karamea, NZ 161/C3
Karamea Bight (bay), NZ 153/H7
Karamet-Niyaz, Trkm. 127/H1
Karamiran, China 125/E4
Karamiran (pass), China 125/E4
Karamiran (riv.), China 125/D4
Karamoja (prov.), Ugan. 142/G5
Karamürsel, Turk. 77/J5
Karamyshevo, Rus. 67/N3
Karangasem, Indo. 115/F3
Karanginskiy (isl.), Rus. 101/S4
Karanginskiy (bay), Rus. 101/S4
Karanjia, India 121/E1
Karanpur, India 124/B5
Karapelit, Bul. 77/H4
Karapınar, Turk. 128/C2
Karasabai, Guy. 205/G3
Karaşar, Turk. 96/E4
Karasburg, Namb. 150/B3
Karasjohka-Karasjok, Nor. 64/H1
Karasu, Turk. 77/K5
Karasu, Japan 109/L6
Karasuk, Rus. 125/C1
Karatá (lag.), Nic. 201/F3
Karatal (riv.), Kaz. 125/C2
Karataş, Turk. 130/D1
Karatau (mts.), Kaz. 125/A3
Karathuri, Myan. 120/B4
Karatobe, Kaz. 97/K2
Karaton, Kaz. 97/K3
Karatoya (riv.), Bang. 123/G3
Karatsu, Japan 110/A4
Karauli, India 122/A2
Karaurgan, Turk. 128/E1
Karáva (peak), Gre. 75/G3
Karavan, Kyr. 125/B3
Karawang, Indo. 115/D3
Karayaka, Turk. 96/F4
Karayazı, Turk. 128/E2
Karazhal, Kaz. 125/B2
Karbaka, Sudan 135/G5
Karbalā', Iraq 129/F3
Karbalā (gov.), Iraq 129/E3
Karben, Ger. 84/B2
Karcag, Hun. 76/E2
Kardhámila, Gre. 75/K3
Kardhítsa, Gre. 75/G3
Kardhitsomagoúla, Gre. 75/G3
Kärdla, Est. 67/K2
Kareha (riv.), India 123/E3
Karelī, India 122/B4
Karelia (reg.), Rus. 64/J2
Karelia Aut. Rep., Rus. 100/D3
Karema, Tanz. 147/G4
Karenga (riv.), Rus. 104/H1
Karera, India 122/B3
Karesuando, Swe. 64/G1
Karêt (reg.), Mrta. 136/D4
Kärevere, Est. 67/M2
Kargala, Rus. 97/K2
Kargasok, Rus. 100/J4
Kargı, Turk. 96/E4
Kargil, India 124/D2
Kargopol', Rus. 94/H3
Karhal, India 122/B2
Karhijärvi (lake), Fin. 67/K1
Karhula, Fin. 67/M1
Kariá, Gre. 75/G3
Karia Ba Mohammed, Mor. 138/B2
Kariaí, Gre. 75/J2
Karianga, Madg. 152/H8
Kariba, Zam.,Zim. 149/F3
Kariba (dam), Zim. 149/F3
Kariba (lake), Zim. 133/E6
Kariba-yama (peak), Japan 108/A2
Karibib, Namb. 148/B4
Karibumba, D.R. Congo 147/G2
Karikal, India 121/C4
Karimama, Ben. 141/F3
Karimata (str.), Indo. 116/C4
Karimata (isl.), Indo. 116/D4
Karīmnagar, India 121/C2
Karimui, PNG 155/G1
Karimunjawa Islands (isls.), Indo. 116/D5
Karin, Som. 144/C3
Karin, Som. 144/D3
Kariótissa, Gre. 75/H2
Karis (Karjaa), Fin. 65/D4
Karise, Den. 66/E4
Karisimbi (vol.), D.R. Congo 147/G3
Karislojo (Karjalohja), Fin 65/D4
Káristos, Gre. 75/J3
Kariya, Japan 109/L6
Karjaa (Karis), Fin. 65/D4
Karjalohja (Karislojo), Fin. 65/D4
Karkaar (mts.), Som. 144/D3
Karkar (isl.), PNG 162/D5
Karkinits'ka Zatoka (gulf), Ukr. 96/D3
Karkkila, Fin. 67/L1
Kärkölä, Fin. 65/F4
Karkonski NP, Pol. 69/H3
Karkur, Isr. 131/B4
Karl E. Mundt NWR, SD, US 180/E2
Karla Marksa (peak), Taj. 125/B4
Karleby (Kokkola), Fin. 94/D3
Karlholmsbruk, Swe. 66/G1
Karlino, Pol. 66/F4
Karlivka, Ukr. 99/H3
Karlo-Libknekhtovsk, Ukr 99/K3
Karlovac, Cro. 76/B3
Karlovo, Bul. 77/G4
Karlovy Vary (arpt.), Czh. 85/F2
Karlovy Vary, Czh. 85/F2
Karlsdorf-Neuthard, Ger. 84/B4
Karlsfeld, Ger. 85/E6
Karlshamn, Swe. 66/F3
Karlshuld, Ger. 84/E5
Karlskoga, Swe. 66/F2
Karlskron, Ger. 85/E5
Karlskrona, Swe. 66/F3
Karlslunde Strand, Den. 65/J7
Karlsruhe, ND, US 182/D3
Karlsruhe, Ger. 84/B4
Karlstad, Mn, US 182/F3
Karlstad, Swe. 66/E2
Karlstadt, Ger. 84/C3
Karlstein am Main, Ger. 84/C2
Karmah, Sudan 135/F5
Karmāla, India 121/B2
Karmatānr, India 123/F3
Karmi'el, Isr. 131/C3
Karnāl, India 124/D5
Karnali (zone), Nepal 122/C1
Karnali (riv.), Nepal 122/C1
Karnaphuli (res.), Bang. 123/H4
Karnataka (state), India 118/C4
Karnes City, Tx, US 177/F3
Karnobat, Bul. 77/H4
Kärnten (prov.), Aus. 71/K3
Karo, Chad 142/C3
Karoi, Zim. 149/F3
Karomatan, Phil. 114/C4
Karonga, Malw. 145/A4
Karoo NP, SAfr. 150/D4
Karoo NP, SAfr. 150/C4
Karoonda, Austl. 158/A2
Karor, Pak. 124/A4
Karora, Sudan 126/C5
Karoso (cape), Indo. 117/E5
Karpakora, Austl. 158/B2
Kárpathos, Gre. 93/K4
Kárpathos (isl.), Gre. 128/A3
Karpatskiy NP, Ukr. 98/C3
Karpenísion, Gre. 75/G3
Karpogory, Rus. 95/K3
Karratha, Austl. 156/C2
Kars (riv.), Turk. 97/G4
Kars, Turk. 129/E1
Kars (prov.), Turk. 97/G4
Kars (riv.), SAfr. 150/M11
Kars (prov.), Geo. 129/E1
Kärsämäki, Fin. 94/E3
Karsantı, Turk. 128/C2
Kārsava, Lat. 67/M3
Kårsta, Swe. 65/B1
Kartaly, Rus. 97/M1
Kartārpur, India 124/C4
Kartushi, D.R. Congo 147/F4
Kartuzy, Pol. 66/H4
Karuah, Austl. 158/D2
Karuma (falls), Ugan. 147/H2
Karumba, Austl. 160/A2
Karūn (riv.), Iran 100/E6
Karunjie, Austl. 154/B4
Karup, Den. 66/C3
Karūr, India 121/C4
Karushe, D.R. Congo 147/F3
Karval, Co, US 178/C1
Karviná, Czh. 69/K4
Karwar, India 121/B3
Karymskoye, Rus. 104/G1
Kaş, Turk. 128/B2
Kås, Den. 66/C3
Kas, Sudan 142/E2
Kasagi, Japan 109/J6
Kasahara, Japan 109/M5
Kāsai (riv.), India 123/F4
Kasai, Japan 110/D3
Kasai (riv.), D.R. Congo 133/D5
Kasai Occidental (pol. reg.), D.R. Congo 147/E4
Kasai Oriental (pol. reg.), D.R. Congo 147/E3
Kasaji, D.R. Congo 147/E5
Kasakalawe, Zam. 147/G5
Kasalu, Zam. 149/E2
Kasama, Japan 111/G2
Kasama, Zam. 147/G5
Kasamatsu, Japan 109/L5
Kasane, Bots. 148/E3
Kasanga (falls), Zam. 148/E3
Kasanga, Tanz. 147/G5
Kasangulu, D.R. Congo 146/C4
Kasanka NP, Zam. 149/F2
Kasaoka, Japan 110/C3
Kasar (cape), Sudan 135/H5
Kasartori-yama (peak), Japan 109/K6
Kasba (lake), NW,Nun, Can. 166/F2
Kasba Tadla, Mor. 136/D2
Kaseda, Japan 110/B5
Kaseke, D.R. Congo 149/E1
Kasembe, Tanz. 145/B4
Kasempa, Zam. 148/E2
Kasenga, D.R. Congo 147/G5
Kasenyi, D.R. Congo 147/G2
Kasese, Ugan. 147/G2
Kasese, D.R. Congo 147/F3
Kaset Wisai, Thai. 120/C3
Kāsganj, India 122/B2
Kashabowie, On, Can. 183/J3
Kashaf (riv.), Iran 127/H1
Kāshān, Iran 129/G3
Kashary, Rus. 99/L3
Kashi, China 125/C4
Kashiba, Zam. 147/G5
Kashiba, Japan 109/J6
Kashihara, Japan 109/J6
Kashima, Japan 111/G3
Kashima, Japan 110/B4
Kashima (bay), Japan 109/F1
Kashin, Rus. 94/H4
Kāshīpur, India 122/B1
Kashiwa, Japan 109/D2
Kashiwara, Japan 109/J6
Kashiwazaki, Japan 111/F2
Kāshmar, Iran 127/G1
Kashmūnd Ghar (range), Afg. 124/A2
Kashof (riv.), Iran 129/J2
Kashofu, D.R. Congo 147/G3
Kasia, India 122/D2
Kasidiji (riv.), D.R. Congo 147/E5
Kasigau (peak), Kenya 145/B2
Kasimov, Rus. 94/J5
Kasimovo (arpt.), Rus. 94/T6
Kasindi, D.R. Congo 147/G2
Kasinge, D.R. Congo 147/F4
Kasiruta (isl.), Indo. 117/G4
Kasiui (isl.), Indo. 117/H4
Kasiya, Malw. 149/G2
Kaskaskia (riv.), Il, US 181/K4
Kas'kovo, Rus. 67/N2
Kaslo, BC, Can. 170/F3
Kasonaweja, Indo. 117/J4
Kasongan, Indo. 116/D4
Kasongo, D.R. Congo 147/F4
Kasongo-Lunda, D.R. Congo 146/D4
Kasonguele, D.R. Congo 147/F4
Kásos (isl.), Gre. 128/A3
Kaspi, Geo. 97/H4
Kaspichan, Bul. 77/H4
Kaspiysk, Rus. 97/H4
Kaspiyskiy, Rus. 97/H3
Kassala, Sudan 142/H2
Kassándra (pen.), Gre. 96/B5
Kassándria, Gre. 75/H2
Kassel, Ger. 79/G6
Kassikaityu (riv.), Guy. 205/G4
Kasson, Mn, US 181/H1
Kastamonu (prov.), Turk. 96/E4
Kastamonu, Turk. 96/E4
Kastanéai, Gre. 77/H5
Kaštel Stari, Cro. 76/C4
Kaštel Sućurac, Cro. 76/C4
Kastellaun, Ger. 81/G3
Kastéllion, Gre. 75/J5
Kasterlee, Belg. 78/B6
Kastl, Ger. 85/E4
Kastön (isl.), Swe. 65/B1
Kastoría, Gre. 75/G2
Kastornoye, Rus. 99/K2
Kastrakíou (lake), Gre. 75/G3
Kastrup, Den. 65/J7
Kasuga, Japan 109/K5
Kasuga, Japan 109/H5
Kasugai, Japan 109/B2
Kasugai, Japan 109/L5
Kasui, Indo. 115/D3
Kasukabe, Japan 111/F3
Kasuku (riv.), D.R. Congo 147/F3
Kasulu, Tanz. 147/G4
Kasumiga (lake), Japan 111/G2
Kasungu, Malw. 149/G2
Kasungu NP, Malw. 149/G2
Kasupe, Malw. 149/G2
Kasūr, Pak. 124/C4
Kat O Chau (isl.), China 113/M6
Kataba, Zam. 148/E3
Katagum (riv.), Nga. 142/A2
Katako-Kombe, D.R. Congo 147/F3
Katákolon, Gre. 75/G4
Katale, D.R. Congo 147/G3
Kataloinen, Fin. 65/E4
Katana, D.R. Congo 147/G3
Katanda, D.R. Congo 147/E4
Katanda, D.R. Congo 147/G3
Katanga (pol. reg.), D.R. Congo 147/F5
Katangi, India 122/B4
Katanning, Austl. 156/C5
Katano, Japan 109/J6
Katanti, D.R. Congo 147/F3
Katarniān Ghāt, India 122/C1
Katastárion, Gre. 75/G4
Katavi NP, Tanz. 147/G4
Katchall (isl.), India 119/F6
Katea, D.R. Congo 147/F4
Katea, D.R. Congo 147/E4
Katebo, Ugan. 147/H3
Katemcy, Tx, US 177/E2
Katenga, D.R. Congo 147/G4
Kateríni, Gre. 75/H2
Katesh, Tanz. 145/A3
Katete, Malw. 149/G2
Katete, Zam. 149/G2
Katghora, India 122/D4
Katha, Myan. 112/C3
Katherine, Az, US 174/E3
Katherine, Austl. 154/D3
Katherine (riv.), Austl. 154/D3
Katherine Gorge NP, Austl. 154/D3
Kāthgodām, India 122/B1
Kathiawar (pen.), India 127/K4
Kathleen, Ga, US 191/G1
Kathleen, Fl, US 190/L7
Kathleen (mt.), Austl. 157/G2
Kāthmāndu (cap.), Nepal 123/E2
Kathryn, ND, US 182/F4
Kathua, India 124/C3
Kati, Mali 140/C3
Katiéna, Mali 140/D3
Katihār, India 123/F3
Kātikund, India 123/F3
Katiola, C.d'Iv. 140/D4
Katla, Sudan 142/F3
Katlehong, SAfr 150/E2
Katlenburg-Lindau, Ger. 79/H5
Katma, China 125/E4
Katmai NP, Ak, US 168/X13
Káto Akhaía, Gre. 75/G3
Káto Nevrokópion, Gre. 75/H2
Katoba, Tanz. 147/G4
Katokhí, Gre. 75/G3
Katombe, D.R. Congo 147/E4
Katonah, NY, US 195/E1
Katonga (riv.), Ugan. 147/G2
Katoomba, Austl. 159/E1
Katoúna, Gre. 75/G3
Katowice, Pol. 69/K3
Katra, India 124/C3
Katra, India 122/C3
Kātrās, India 123/F4
Katrichev, Rus. 97/H2
Katrine (lake), Sc, UK 59/B4
Katrineholm, Swe. 66/G2
Katsepe, Madg. 152/H6
Katshi, D.R. Congo 147/F4
Katsikás, Gre. 75/G3
Katsina (state), Nga 141/G3
Katsina, Nga. 141/G3
Katsina Ala (riv.), Nga. 141/H5
Katsina Ala, Nga. 141/H5
Katsunuma, Japan 109/B2
Katsura (riv.), Japan 109/J5
Katsuragi, Japan 110/D3
Katsuragi-san (peak), Japan 109/H7
Katsuta, Japan 111/G2
Katsuura, Japan 111/G3
Katsuyama, Japan 110/E2
Katsuyama, Japan 109/B3
Kattegat (str.), Den. 55/F3
Katua, Gha. 141/E4
Katul (mtn.), Sudan 142/F2
Katumajävi (lake), Fin. 65/E4
Katumbi, Malw. 145/A4
Katun' (riv.), Rus. 104/B1
Katunayake (int'l arpt.), SrL. 121/C5
Katun'chuya (riv.), Rus. 125/E1
Katundu, Zam. 148/E3
Kātūria, India 123/F3
Katuta Kampemba, Zam. 147/G5
Kātwa, India 123/G4
Katwa, D.R. Congo 147/G2
Katwe-Kabatooro, Ugan. 147/G3
Katwijk aan Zee, Neth. 78/B4
Katy, Tx, US 177/G3
Katzenbach (riv.), Ger. 84/B4
Katzenbuckel (peak), Ger. 84/C4
Katzenelnbogen, Ger. 81/G3
Katzhütte, Ger. 84/D1
Katzwinkel, Ger. 81/F3
Kau-ye (isl.), Myan. 120/B4
Kauai (isl.), HI, US 163/K2
Kauai (chan.), Hi, US 168/S9
Kaudum (riv.), Namb 148/D3
Kaudum Game Park, Namb. 148/D3
Kaufbeuren, Ger 87/G2
Kaufering, Ger. 87/G1
Kaufman (co.), Tx, US 176/L7
Kaufman, Tx, US 177/F1
Kaufungen, Ger. 79/G6
Kauhava, Fin. 94/D3
Kauiki (pt.), Hi, US 168/S9
Kaukapakapa, NZ 161/F6
Kaukauna, Wi, US 186/B2
Kaukaveld (uplands), Namb. 148/B3
Kaukura (isl.), FrPol. 163/L6
Kaulashishi (hill), Zam. 149/F2
Kaulsdorf, Ger. 85/E1
Kaumba, D.R. Congo 147/F5
Kaunas (res.), Lith. 67/L4
Kaunas, Lith. 67/K4
Kaunas (int'l arpt.), Lith. 67/K4
Kauniainen (Grankulla), Fin. 65/E4
Kaupanger, Nor. 66/B1
Kaura Namoda, Nga. 141/G3
Kauro, Kenya 145/B1
Kauttua, Fin. 67/K1
Kavadarci, FYROM 75/H2
Kavajë, Alb. 75/F2
Kavála, Gre. 75/J2
Kavalerovo, Rus. 105/M3
Kāvali, India 121/C3
Kavangel (isls.), Indo. 162/C4
Kavango (riv.), Namb. 148/C3
Kavār, Iran 129/H4
Kavarna, Bul. 77/J4
Kavarskas, Lith. 67/L4
Kavgolovskoye (lake), Rus. 94/T6
Kavieng, PNG 162/E5
Kavimba, Bots. 148/E3
Kavīr-e Bāfq (Salt pan), Iran 129/H4
Kavīr-e Namak (Salt pan), Iran 129/J3
Kävlinge, Swe. 66/E4
Kävlingeån (riv.), Swe. 65/K7
Kaw (lake), Ok, US 179/F2
Kaw (dam), Ok, US 179/F2
Kaw, FrG. 206/C1
Kaw City, Ok, US 179/F2
Kawa (ruin), Sudan 135/F5
Kawa, Myan. 112/C5
Kawabe, Japan 108/B4
Kawachi, Japan 109/E2
Kawachi-nagano, Japan 109/J7
Kawage, Japan 109/L6
Kawagoe, Japan 111/F3
Kawagoe, Japan 109/L5
Kawaguchi, Japan 111/F3
Kawaguchiko, Japan 109/B3
Kawai, Japan 109/J6
Kawajena, Sudan 142/F4
Kawajima, Japan 109/C2
Kawakami, Japan 109/B2
Kawakami, Japan 109/J7
Kawamata, Japan 111/G2
Kawambwa, Zam. 147/G5
Kawamoto, Japan 109/C1
Kawana, Zam. 148/E2
Kawanishi, Japan 109/J6
Kawanishi, Japan 109/H6
Kawardha, India 122/C4
Kawartha Lakes, On, Can. 187/G2
Kawasaki, Japan 111/F3
Kawasato, Japan 109/D1
Kawashima, Japan 109/L5
Kawaue, Japan 109/M4
Kawerau, NZ 161/D2
Kawhia, NZ 161/C2
Kawich (peak), Nv, US 174/D2
Kawinda, Indo. 117/E5
Kawkabān, Yem. 144/B2
Kawkareik, Myan. 120/B2
Kawlin, Myan. 112/B4
Kawludo, Myan. 120/B2
Kawm Dafanah (ruin), Egypt 139/D3
Kawm Ḩamādah, Egypt 139/B3
Kawm Ishū, Egypt 139/A2
Kawm Umbū, Egypt 135/G3
Kawsaing, Myan. 120/B3
Kawthaung, Myan. 120/B4
Kax (riv.), China 100/J5
Kay, Rus. 95/M4
Kaya, SKor. 107/E5
Kaya, Burk. 141/E3
Kaya, Japan 109/H5
Kaya-san (peak), SKor. 107/D4
Kayadibi, Turk. 128/C2
Kayagangiri (peak), CAfr. 142/B4
Kayah (state), Myan. 119/G4
Kayamba (hills), Zam. 149/E2
Kayan (riv.), Indo. 103/L9
Kayanga (riv.), Sen. 140/B3
Kāyankulam, India 121/C4
Kayar, Sen. 140/A3
Kayasa, Indo. 117/F4
Kaycee, Wy, US 173/K2
Kaye (mtn.), Austl. 159/D3
Kayembe-Mukulu, D.R. Congo 147/E5
Kayenta, Az, US 175/G2
Kayes, Mali 140/C3
Kayes (pol. reg.), Mali 140/C3
Kayin (state), Myan. 119/G4
Kayl, Lux. 81/F5
Kaymaz, Turk. 77/K5
Kaynarca, Turk. 77/J5
Kaynaşlı, Turk. 77/K5
Kayoa (isl.), Indo. 117/G3
Kaysatskoye, Rus. 97/H2
Kayser (mts.), Sur. 205/G4
Kayseri, Turk. 128/C2
Kayseri (prov.), Turk. 128/C2
Kaysersberg, Fr. 86/D1
Kaysville, Ut, US 173/H3
Kaytej Aboriginal Land, Austl. 154/D5
Kayuagung, Indo. 115/D3
Kayville, Sk, Can. 182/B3
Kayyerkan, Rus. 100/J3
Kazachka, Rus. 99/M2
Kazakh (uplands), Kaz. 100/H5
Kazakhstan(ctry.) 103/E4
Kazan', Rus. 95/L5
Kazan (int'l arpt.), Rus. 95/L5
Kazan (riv.), Nun, Can. 166/F2
Kazancı, Turk. 130/C1
Kazanka, Ukr. 99/G4
Kazanlı, Turk. 130/D1
Kazanlŭk, Bul. 77/G4
Kazanskaya, Rus. 99/L3
Kazanskaya, Rus. 99/L5
Kazantip (cape), Ukr. 99/H5
Kazaure, Nga. 141/H3
Kazbegi, Geo. 97/H4
Kazbek (peak), Geo. 97/H4
Kāzerūn, Iran 129/G4
Kazgar (riv.), China 125/C3
Kazhim, Rus. 95/L3
Kazimierza Wielka, Pol. 69/L3
Kâzımkarabekir, Turk. 128/C2
Kazincbarcika, Hun. 69/L4
Kaziranga NP, India 112/B3
Kaziza, D.R. Congo 147/E5
Kazlų Rūda, Lith. 67/K4
Kazo, Japan 109/D1
Kaztalovka, Kaz. 97/J2
Kazuma Pan NP, Zim. 148/E3
Kazumba, D.R. Congo 147/E4
Kazuno, Japan 108/B3
Kazy, Trkm. 97/L5
Kdyně, Czh. 85/G4
Ke Ga (cape), Viet. 120/E3
Ké Macina, Mali 140/D3
Ke-hsi Mānsām, Myan. 120/B1
Kéa, Gre. 75/J4
Keady, NI, UK 60/B3

Keams – Kings

Kelvedon, Eng., UK 63/G3
Kelvington (isl.), On, Can. 183/K3
Kelvington, Sk, Can. 182/C1
Kelwära, India 122/A3
Keansburg, NJ, US 195/J10
Kearney, On, Can. 187/G2
Kearney, Ne, US 180/E3
Kearny, NJ, US 195/J8
Kearny, NJ, US 175/G4
Kearsley (cr.), Mi, US 193/E5
Keats, Ks, US 181/F4
Keavy, Ky, US 188/E2
Keban (dam), Turk. 128/D2
Kebbi (state), Nga. 141/G4
Kébémer, Sen. 140/A3
Kebnekaise (peak), Swe. 64/F2
K'ebri Dehar, Eth. 144/C4
Kebumen, Indo. 115/C3
Kecel, Hun. 76/D2
Keçiborlu, Turk. 128/B2
Kecskemét, Hun. 76/D2
Kedah (state), Malay. 120/C5
Kédainiai, Lith. 67/K4
Kedgwick, NB, Can. 184/D2
Kedgwick Game Refuge, NB, Can. 184/D2
Kediri, Indo. 115/F3
Kedong, China 105/K2
Kédougou, Sen. 140/A3
Kędzierzyn-Koźle, Pol. 69/K3
Keefers, BC, Can. 170/D2
Keego Harbor, Mi, US 193/F6
Keele (peak), Yk, Can. 166/C2
Keele (riv.), NW, Can. 166/D2
Keeler, Ca, US 174/D3
Keeler, Sk, Can. 171/M2
Keelung, Japan 111/G8
Keelung (Chilung), Tai. 113/J3
Keen (mt.), Sc, UK 59/D3
Keene, Ca, US 187/K3
Keene, Ca, US 174/C3
Keene, Tx, US 176/K7
Keep River NP, Austl. 154/C3
Keepit (dam), Austl. 158/D1
Keer-Weer (cape), Austl. 160/A1
Keeseekoose Ind. Res., Sk, Can. 182/D2
Keetmanshoop, Namb. 150/B2
Keewatin, On, Can. 183/G3
Keewatin, Mn, US 183/H4
Keewong, Austl. 158/C2
Kefa (pol. reg.), Eth. 142/H4
Kefallinía (isl.), Gre. 93/J3
Kefamenanu, Indo. 154/B2
Kefar Blum, Isr. 131/D2
Kefar Gil'adi, Isr. 131/D2
Kefar Ruppin, Isr. 131/D4
Kefar Sava, Isr. 131/B4
Kefar Vitkin, Isr. 131/B4
Keffi, Nga. 141/G4
Keffin Hausa, Nga. 141/H3
Keflavík, Ice. 64/M7
Keflavík, Ice. 64/M7
K'eftya, Eth. 142/H2
Kegalla, SrL. 121/D5
Kegworth, Eng., UK 61/G6
Kehl, Ger. 86/D1
Kehra, Est. 67/L2
Kehrsatz, Swi. 86/D4
Keighley, Eng., UK 61/G4
Keihoku, Japan 109/J5
Keila, Est. 67/L2
Keilor (nbrhd.), Austl. 158/F5
Keimaneigh (pass), Ire. 58/A6
Keimoes, SAfr. 150/C3
Keisha, D.R. Congo 147/F3
Keïta, Niger 141/G3
Keith, Sc, UK 59/D1
Keith, Austl. 158/B3
Keith (cape), Austl. 154/C2
Keithley Creek, BC, Can. 170/D1
Keithville, La, US 176/H1
Keizer, Or, US 172/B3
Kejimkujik NP, NS, Can. 184/D3
Kékes (peak), Hun. 69/K5
K'elafo, Eth. 144/C4
Kelan, China 106/B3
Kelän Devi', India 118/C2
Kelang (isl.), Indo. 117/G4
Kelang, Malay. 115/C2
Kelantan (state), Malay. 115/C1
Kelantan (riv.), Malay. 115/C1
Kelberg, Ger. 81/F3
Kelčyrë, Alb. 75/G2
Kelem, Eth. 142/G4
Keles, Turk. 96/D5
Kelheim, Ger. 85/E3
Kelila, Indo. 117/J4
Kelkheim, Ger. 84/B2
Kelkit, Turk. 96/F4
Kelkit (riv.), Turk. 128/D1
Kell, Ger. 81/F4
Kellé, Congo 146/C3
Kellen, Ger. 78/D5
Kellenhusen, Ger. 66/D4
Keller (peak), Ca, US 192/C2
Keller, NW, Can. 166/D2
Keller, Tx, US 176/K7
Kellerberrin, Austl. 156/C4
Kellerville, Tx, US 178/D3
Kelleys (isl.), On, US 186/E4
Kelleytown, Ga, US 189/M7
Kelliher, Mn, US 183/G4
Kelliher, Sk, Can. 182/C2
Kellogg, Ia, US 181/H3
Kellogg, Id, US 170/D4
Kellokoski, Fin. 65/F4
Kells, NI, UK 60/B2
Kells (Ceannannus Mór), Ire. 58/D2
Kelly (A.F.B.), Tx, US 177/E3
Kelly Lake, BC, Can. 183/H4
Kellys Slough Nat'l Wild. Ref., ND, US 182/C4
Kelmė, Lith. 67/K4
Kel'mentsi, Ukr. 98/D3
Kélo, Chad 142/B3
Kelowna, BC, Can. 170/E3
Kelsall, Eng., UK 61/F5
Kelsey (pt.), Mb, US 62/A6
Kelseyville, Ca, US 172/B4
Kelso, Sk, Can. 182/D3
Kelso, Sc, UK 59/D5
Kelso, Wa, US 174/C3
Kelsterbach, Ger. 84/B2
Kelu, China 113/H4
Keluang, Malay. 115/C2

Kennesaw, Ga, US 189/L6
Kennesaw Mountain Nat'l Bfld.
Kennett and Avon
Kennett City, FI, US
Kennett Square, Pa, US
Kennewick, Wa, US
Kenogami (riv.), On, US
Kenogami
Kenora, On, Can.
Kenosha, Wi, US
Kenosha (co.), Wi, US
Kensal, ND, US
Kensett, Ar, US
Kensico (res.), NY, US
Kensington, Mn, US
Kensington, PE, Can.
Kensington, Ks, US
Kensington and Chelsea
Kenstsále, Congo
Kenton, Ger.
Kent (pen.), Nun, Can.
Kent (co.), On, Can.
Kent, Eng., UK
Kent, Oh, US
Kent, Or, US
Kent, Tx, US
Kent, Wa, US
Kent County
Keski-Suomi (prov.), Fin.
Keskin, Turk.
Kesselbach (riv.), Ger.
Kessingland, Eng., UK
Kesten'ga, Rus.
Kesteren, Neth.
Keszthely, Hun.
Ket (riv.), Rus.
Keta (riv.), Rus.
Keta, Gha.
Ketama, Mor.
Ketapang, Indo.
Ketaun, Indo.
Ketchikan, Ak, US
Ketchum, Id, US
Kete Krachi, Gha.
Ketelmeer (lake), Neth.
Kétou, Ben.
Kętrzyn, Pol.
Ketsch, Ger.
Ketta, Congo
Kettering, Oh, US
Kettering, Eng., UK
Kettle (pt.), On, Can.
Kettle (riv.), Wa, US
Kettle Falls, Wa, US
Kettle River
Kettleman City, Ca, US
Kettlewell, Eng., UK
Ketzin, Ger.
Keudeteunom, Indo.
Keuka (lake), NY, US
Keukenhof, Neth.
Keur Massène, Mrta.
Kevé, Togo
Kevelaer, Ger.
Kevin, Mt, US
Keweenaw (pt.), Mi, US
Kew, UK
Kewanee, Il, US
Kewanna, In, US
Kewaskum, Wi, US
Kewaunee, Wi, US
Keweenaw (pen.), Mi,
Keweenaw (bay), Mi, US
Keweenaw (co.), Mi, US
Key' Afer, Eth.
Key Biscayne, Fl, US
Key Largo, Fl, US
Key Largo (isl.), Fl, US
Key West
Key West, Fl, US
Key West Nat'l Wildlife Refuge, Fl, US
Key West Nav. Air Sta.,
Keya Paha
Keyenberg, Ger.
Keyhole (res.), Wy, US
Keyi, China
Keyishami, Eng, UK
Keymar, Md, US
Keynsham, Eng, UK
Keyport, NJ, US
Keyport, Wa, US
Keyser, WV, US
Keystone (lake), Ok, US
Keystone, SD, US
Keystone Heights,
Keysville, Fl, US
Keysville, Va, US
Keytesville, Mo, US
Keytü, Iran
Kezhma, Rus.
Kezi, Zim.

Kings Island, Oh, US 186/D5
Kings Langley, Eng, UK 56/B1
King's Lynn, Eng, UK 63/G1
Kings Mountain, NC, US 189/G3
Kings Mountain Nat'l Mil. Park, SC, US 189/G3
Kings Park, Austl. 156/K6
Kings Point, NY, US 195/L8
King's Seat (hill), Sc, UK 59/C4
Kings Sutton, Eng, UK 63/E2
Kingsbridge, Eng, UK 62/C6
Kingsburg, Ca, US 174/C2
Kingsbury, Tx, US 177/F3
Kingsclere, Eng, UK 63/E4
Kingscote, Austl. 157/H5
Kingscourt, Ire. 58/D2
Kingsdown, Ks, US 178/E2
Kingsford, Mi, US 183/K5
Kingsland, Eng, UK 62/D2
Kingsland, Ar, US 179/H4
Kingsland, Ga, US 191/H2
Kingsland, Tx, US 177/E2
Kingsley, Mi, US 186/D2
Kingsley (dam), Ne, US 180/D3
Kingsley, Ia, US 181/G2
Kingsnorth, Eng, UK 56/E2
Kingsport, Tn, US 189/F2
Kingston, Austl. 158/C4
Kingston, Austl. 162/F7
Kingston, On, Can. 187/H2
Kingston (cap.), Jam. 201/G2
Kingston, La, US 190/B1
Kingston, Mo, US 181/G4
Kingston, NM, US 175/J4
Kingston, NY, US 187/K4
Kingston, Oh, US 186/E5
Kingston, Ok, US 179/F4
Kingston, Pa, US 194/C1
Kingston, RI, US 187/L4
Kingston, Tn, US 188/E3
Kingston, Wa, US 193/B2
Kingston S.E., Austl. 158/A3
Kingston Springs, Tn, US 188/D2
Kingston upon Hull, Eng, UK 61/H4
Kingston Upon Thames (bor.), Eng, UK 56/C2
Kingston upon Thames, Eng, UK 56/C2
Kingstown, Austl. 158/D1
Kingstown (cap.), StV. 197/N9
Kingstree, SC, US 189/H4
Kingsville, On, Can. 186/E3
Kingsville, Tx, US 177/F4
Kingsville, Md, US 194/B5
Kingsville Nav. Air Sta., Tx, US 177/F4
Kingswear, Eng, UK 62/C6
Kingswood, Ky, US 188/D2
Kingswood, Eng, UK 62/D4
Kington, Eng, UK 62/D2
Kingushi, D.R. Congo 146/D4
Kingussie, Sc, UK 59/B2
Kingwood, WV, US 187/G5
Kingwood, Tx, US 177/M8
Kiniama, D.R. Congo 149/F1
Kiniati, D.R. Congo 146/D4
Kınık, Turk. 96/C5
Kinistino Ind. Res., Sk, Can. 171/M1
Kinkaid (lake), Il, US 188/C2
Kinkala, Congo 146/C4
Kinki (prov.), Japan 110/D3
Kinkosi, D.R. Congo 146/C4
Kinloch Rannoch, Sc, UK 59/B3
Kinlochewe, Sc, UK 59/A1
Kinlochleven, Sc, UK 59/B3
Kinloss, Sc, UK 59/C1
Kinmel, Wal, UK 60/E5
Kinmundy, Il, US 188/C1
Kinna, Swe. 66/E3
Kinnairds (pt.), Sc, UK 59/D1
Kinnegad, Ire. 58/C3
Kinnelon, NJ, US 195/H8
Kinnelon (lake), NJ, US 195/H8
Kinneret, Isr. 131/D3
Kinnikinnick, Oh, US 186/E5
Kinnitty, Ire. 58/C3
Kino (riv.), Japan 110/D3
Kinomoto, Japan 109/K5
Kinrooi, Belg. 81/E1
Kinross, Sc, UK 59/C4
Kinsach (riv.), Ger. 85/F4
Kinsale (har.), Ire. 58/B6
Kinsale, Ire. 58/B6
Kinsale, On, Can. 186/U8
Kinsarvik, Nor. 66/B1
Kinsey, Mt, US 171/M4
Kinshasa (pol. reg), D.R. Congo 146/C4
Kinshasa (cap.), D.R. Congo 146/C4
Kinsley, Ks, US 178/E2
Kinsman, Oh, US 186/F4
Kinston, Al, US 191/E2
Kinston, NC, US 189/J3
Kinta, Ok, US 179/G3
Kintampo, Gha. 141/E4
Kintinku, Tanz. 145/A3
Kintnersville, Pa, US 194/C2
Kintore, Sc, UK 59/D2
Kintyre, ND, US 182/E4
Kintyre (isl.), Sc, UK 57/R8
Kintzheim, Fr. 86/D1
Kinu (riv.), Japan 111/F2
Kinvarra, Ire. 58/B3
Kinwow (bay), Mb, Can. 182/F2
Kinyangiri, Tanz. 145/A3
Kinyeti (peak), Sudan 142/G5
Kinzig (riv.), Ger. 68/E4
Kiomboi, Tanz. 145/A3
Kiowa, Ok, US 179/G3
Kiowa, Ks, US 179/E2
Kiowa (cr.), Co, US 180/B4
Kiowa, Co, US 180/B4
Kipange, D.R. Congo 147/F4
Kiparissía, Gre. 75/G4
Kiparissía (gulf), Gre. 93/J3
Kipawa (lake), Qu, Can. 187/G1
Kipawa, Qu, Can. 187/G1
Kipen', Rus. 94/S7
Kipili, Tanz. 147/G4
Kipilingu, D.R. Congo 149/F2
Kipini, Kenya 145/C2
Kipkarren (riv.), Kenya 145/A1
Kipling, Sk, Can. 182/C2
Kippel, Swi. 86/D5
Kippen, Sc, UK 59/B4
Kippens, Nf, Can. 185/H1
Kippure (peak), Ire. 60/B5
Kipti, Ukr. 98/F2
Kipushi, D.R. Congo 149/E1
Kira, Japan 109/M6
Kira Panayía (isl.), Gre. 75/H3
Kirakira, Sol. 162/F6
Kirandul, India 121/D2
Kiranomena, Madg. 152/H7
Kīratpur, India 122/B1
Kirawa, Nga. 142/B3
Kirazlı, Turk. 75/K2
Kirbla, Est. 67/K2
Kirby, Ar, US 179/H3
Kirby, Mt, US 173/K1
Kirbyville, Tx, US 177/H2
Kırcasalih, Turk. 77/H5
Kirchberg, Swi. 86/D3
Kirchberg, Swi. 87/F3
Kirchberg, Ger. 81/G4
Kirchberg, Ger. 85/F1
Kirchberg an der Iller, Ger. 87/G1
Kirchberg an der Jagst, Ger. 84/C4
Kirchdorf, Ger. 79/F3
Kirchdorf an der Krems, Aus. 85/H7
Kirchen, Ger. 81/G2
Kirchenlamitz, Ger. 85/E2
Kirchenthumbach, Ger. 85/E3
Kirchheim, Ger. 87/G1
Kirchheim bei München, Ger. 85/E6
Kirchheim unter Teck, Ger. 84/C5
Kirchheimbolanden, Ger. 84/B3
Kirchhundem, Ger. 79/F6
Kirchlengern, Ger. 79/F4
Kirchlinteln, Ger. 79/G3
Kirchsee (lake), Ger. 87/H2
Kirchseeon, Ger. 85/E6
Kirchweidach, Ger. 85/F6
Kirchzarten, Ger. 86/D2
Kirchzell, Ger. 84/C3
Kircubbin, NI, UK 60/C3
Kircudbright (bay), Sc, UK 60/D2
Kirensk, Rus. 101/L4
Kirgiz Steppe (upland), Kaz. 100/F5
Kirgizskiy (mts.), Kyr 125/B3
Kiri, D.R. Congo 146/D3
Kiriákion, Gre. 75/H3
Kiribati (ctry.) 162/H5
Kırık, Turk. 128/E1
Kırıkhan, Turk. 130/E1
Kırıkkale, Turk. 128/C2
Kirikkuduk, China 104/C3
Kirillov, Rus. 94/H4
Kirishi, Rus. 67/Q2
Kirishima-Yaku NP, Japan 110/B5
Kirishima-yama (peak), Japan 110/B5
Kiritimati (Christmas) (isl.), Kiri. 163/K4
Kirk kale (prov.), Turk. 128/C2
Kırkağaç, Turk. 96/C5
Kirkburton, Eng, UK 61/G4
Kirkby, Eng, UK 61/F5
Kirkby in Ashfield, Eng, UK 61/G5
Kirkby Lonsdale, Eng, UK 61/F3
Kirkby Stephen, Eng, UK 61/F3
Kirkbymoorside, Eng, UK 61/H3
Kirkcaldy, Sc, UK 59/C4
Kirkcolm, Sc, UK 60/C2
Kirkconnel, Sc, UK 59/C6
Kirkcowan, Sc, UK 60/D2
Kirkcudbright, Sc, UK 60/D2
Kirke Hvalsø, Den. 65/H7
Kirkee, India 118/B4
Kirkenær, Nor. 66/E1
Kirkham, Eng, UK 61/F4
Kirkhill, Sc, UK 59/B2
Kirkinner, Sc, UK 60/D2
Kirkintilloch, Sc, UK 59/B5
Kirkkonummi (Kyrkslätt), Fin. 67/L1
Kirkland (hill), Sc, UK 59/C6
Kirkland, Az, US 175/F3
Kirkland, Il, US 181/K2
Kirkland, Qu, Can. 185/N7
Kirkland, Wa, US 170/C4
Kirkland Lake, On, Can. 167/H4
Kırklar (peak), Turk. 96/C5
Kırklareli (prov.), Turk. 128/A1
Kırklareli (prov.), Turk. 96/C4
Kirklareli (prov.), Turk. 77/H5
Kırklareli, Turk. 77/H5
Kirkliston, Sc, UK 59/C5
Kirkmichael, IM, UK 60/D3
Kirkmuirhill, Sc, UK 59/C5
Kirkstone (pass), Eng, UK 61/F3
Kirksville, Mo, US 181/H3
Kirkton of Glenisla, Sc, UK 59/C3
Kirkūk, Iraq 129/F3
Kirkwall, Sc, UK 57/V14
Kirkwood, SAfr. 150/D4
Kirkwood, De, US 194/C4
Kirn, Ger. 81/G4
Kirongwe, Tanz. 145/B3
Kiropa, Tanz. 145/A4
Kirov, Rus. 95/L4
Kirov, Rus. 96/E1
Kirov (oblast), Rus. 95/L4
Kirovo, Rus. 95/P5
Kirovo-Chepetsk, Rus. 95/L4
Kirovohrad, Ukr. 99/G3
Kirovohrads'ka (prov.), Ukr. 96/D2
Kirovsk, Bela. 96/D1
Kirovsk, Rus. 94/G2
Kirovsk, Rus. 94/U7
Kirovs'k, Ukr. 99/K3
Kirovs'ke, Ukr. 99/H5
Kirovs'ke, Ukr. 99/K3
Kirovskiy, Rus. 97/J3
Kirovskiy, Kaz. 100/H5
Kirovskiy, Rus. 105/L2
Kirriemuir, Sc, UK 59/D3
Kirriemuir, Ab, Can. 171/J2
Kirrweiler, Ger. 84/B4
Kirs, Rus. 95/M4
Kirsanov, Rus. 97/G1
Kırşehir, Turk. 128/C2
Kirsehir (prov.), Turk. 128/C2
Kirtland, NM, US 175/H2
Kirtland (A.F.B.), NM, US 175/J3
Kirtley, Wy, US 180/B2
Kirton, Eng, UK 61/H6
Kirton in Lindsey, Eng, UK 61/H5
Kiruna, Swe. 64/G2
Kirundu, D.R. Congo 147/F3
Kirwin (res.), Ks, US 180/E4
Kirwin, Ks, US 180/E4
Kirwin Nat'l Wildlife Res., Ks, US 178/E1
Kirya, Rus. 95/K5
Kiryū, Japan 111/F2
Kisa, Swe. 66/F3
Kisai, Japan 109/D1
Kisakata, Japan 108/A4
Kisangani, D.R. Congo 147/F2
Kisangani (int'l arpt.), D.R. Congo 147/F2
Kisantu, D.R. Congo 146/C4
Kisar (isl.), Indo. 154/B1
Kisaran, Indo. 115/B2
Kisarawe, Tanz. 145/B3
Kisarazu, Japan 111/F3
Kisauni (Zanzibar) (int'l arpt.), Tanz. 145/B3
Kisber, Hun. 69/K5
Kisbey, Sk, Can. 182/C3
Kisei, Japan 109/K7
Kiselevsk, Rus. 100/J4
Kisenda, D.R. Congo 146/D4
Kisenge, D.R. Congo 147/E5
Kisessa, Tanz. 145/A2
Kīsh, Iran 129/H5
Kīsh (isl.), Iran 129/H5
Kishanda, Tanz. 147/G3
Kishanganj, India 123/F2
Kishangarh, India 122/A2
Kishangarh, India 118/B2
Kishi, Nga. 141/F4
Kishiwada, Japan 109/H7
Kishoreganj, Bang. 123/G3
Kishorganj, Bang. 123/H3
Kishtwar, India 124/C3
Kishwaukee (riv.), Il, US 193/N15
Kisi, D.R. Congo 147/G3
Kisigo (riv.), Tanz. 145/A3
Kisii, Kenya 145/A2
Kisiju, Tanz. 145/B3
Kisiwani, Tanz. 145/B3
Kiska (isl.), Ak, US 101/T4
Kiskissink, Qu, Can. 184/A2
Kiskórös, Hun. 76/D2
Kiskunfélegyháza, Hun. 76/D2
Kiskunhalas, Hun. 76/D2
Kiskunmajsa, Hun. 76/D2
Kiskunsági Nemzeti NP, Hun. 76/D2
Kislovodsk, Rus. 97/G4
Kismaayo, Som. 145/C2
Kismaayo (Chisimayu), Som. 145/C2
Kiso (riv.), Japan 111/E3
Kisogawa, Japan 109/L5
Kisoro, Ugan. 147/G3
Kisozaki, Japan 109/L5
Kisrah, Tun. 138/L7
Kíssamos, Gre. 75/H5
Kissee Mills, Mo, US 179/H2
Kissidougou, Gui. 140/C4
Kissimmee (riv.), Fl, US 191/H4
Kissimmee (lake), Fl, US 191/H4
Kissimmee, Fl, US 190/N7
Kissing, Ger. 84/D6
Kisslegg, Ger. 87/F2
Kissū (peak), Sudan 134/E4
Kissy, SLeo. 140/B4
Kist, Ger. 84/C3
Kisújszállás, Hun. 76/E2
Kisumu, Kenya 145/A2
Kisvárda, Hun. 69/M4
Kiswere, Tanz. 145/B4
Kit Carson, Co, US 178/C1
Kita, Mali 140/C3
Kita (lake), Japan 111/G2
Kita-ibaraki, Japan 111/G2
Kitaaiki, Japan 109/B1
Kitab, Uzb. 100/G6
Kitadaitō (isl.), Japan 111/L8
Kitagata, Japan 109/L5
Kitakami, Japan 108/B4
Kitakami (mts.), Japan 108/B4
Kitakami (riv.), Japan 108/B4
Kitakata, Japan 111/F2
Kitakawabe, Japan 109/D1
Kitakyūshū, Japan 110/B4
Kitale, Kenya 145/A1
Kitami, Japan 108/C2
Kitami (mts.), Japan 105/N2
Kitamimaki, Japan 109/A1
Kitamoto, Japan 109/D1
Kitan (str.), Japan 109/G7
Kitangari, Tanz. 145/B4
Kitangiri (lake), Tanz. 145/A3
Kitaura, Japan 109/F1
Kitchener, On, Can. 186/F3
Kite, Ga, US 189/F4
Kitendwe, D.R. Congo 147/G4
Kitengo, D.R. Congo 147/F4
Kitgum, Ugan. 147/H2
Kíthira, Gre. 75/H4
Kíthira (isl.), Gre. 93/J3
Kíthnos, Gre. 75/J4
Kíthnos (isl.), Gre. 93/K3
Kithor, India 122/A1
Kitim, Jor. 131/D4
Kitimat, BC, Can. 168/AA13
Kitomesa, D.R. Congo 146/C4
Kitsap (co.), Wa, US 193/B3
Kitscoty, Ab, Can. 171/J1
Kitsman', Ukr. 98/C3
Kitt Peak National Observatory, Az, US 175/G5
Kittanning, Pa, US 187/G4
Kittatinny (mts.), NJ, US 194/C1
Kittery, Me, US 187/L3
Kitty Hawk, NC, US 189/K2
Kitu, D.R. Congo 147/F4
Kitui, Kenya 145/B2
Kitui Nat'l Rsv., Kenya 145/B2
Kitumala (pt.), PNG 155/G1
Kitumbeine (peak), Tanz. 145/B2
Kitumbini, Tanz. 145/B4
Kitunda, Tanz. 145/A3
Kitunguli, Tanz. 145/C4
Kitwe, Zam. 149/F2
Kitzbühel, Aus. 71/K3
Kitzingen, Ger. 84/D3
Kiunga, Kenya 145/C2
Kiunga, PNG 155/F1
Kiunga Marine Nat'l Res., Kenya 145/C2
Kiuruvesi, Fin. 94/E3
Kiuyu (pt.), Tanz. 145/B3
Kivalo (mts.), Fin. 64/H2
Kivertsi, Ukr. 98/C2
Kivi-Vigala, Est. 67/L2
Kivijärvi (lake), Fin. 67/M1
Kivik, Swe. 65/L7
Kiviõli, Est. 67/M2
Kivu (lake), D.R. Congo 133/E5
Kiwai (isl.), PNG 155/F2
Kiwela, D.R. Congo 147/F4
Kiwira, Tanz. 145/A4
Kiyevka, Rus. 97/G3
Kiyevka, Kaz. 125/B1
Kıyıköy, Turk. 77/J5
Kiyokawa, Japan 109/C3
Kiyosu, Japan 109/L5
Kizamba, D.R. Congo 146/D5
Kizel, Rus. 95/N4
Kizëma, Rus. 95/K3
Kizhaba, Azer. 129/G2
Kizil (riv.), China 100/H6
Kızılcadağ, Turk. 130/A1
Kızılcahamam, Turk. 96/E4
Kızıldag NP, Turk. 128/B2
Kızılhisar, Turk. 128/B2
Kızılırmak (riv.), Turk. 96/E4
Kizil'skoye, Rus. 97/L1
Kızıltepe, Turk. 128/E2
Kızılyaka, Turk. 128/C2
Kizimbani, Tanz. 145/B4
Kizimkazi, Tanz. 145/B3
Kizlyar, Rus. 97/H4
Kizu (riv.), Japan 110/E3
Kizu, Japan 109/J6
Kizukuri, Japan 108/B3
Kizyl-Aatrek, Trkm. 129/H2
Kizyl-Su, Trkm. 129/H2
Kjeller, Nor. 64/T8
Kjerkestinden (peak), Nor. 64/F1
Kjevik (int'l arpt.), Nor. 66/C2
Kjølen (mts.), Nor. 64/E2
Klabava (riv.), Czh. 85/G3
Kladanj, Bosn. 76/D3
Kladar, Indo. 155/E2
Kladno, Czh. 85/H2
Kladovo, Yugo. 76/F3
Klaeng, Thai. 120/C3
Klagenfurt, Aus. 71/L3
Klaipėda, Lith. 67/J4
Klakah, Indo. 115/F3
Klamath (riv.), Ca, US 168/B3
Klamath, Ca, US 172/A3
Klamath (mts.), Ca,Or, US 172/B2
Klamath Falls, Or, US 172/C2
Klamath Forest NWR, Or, US 172/C2
Klåmmingen (lake), Swe. 65/A1
Klangenan, Indo. 115/E3
Klapmuts, SAfr. 150/L10
Klar (riv.), Swe. 100/B4
Klarälven (riv.), Swe. 64/E3
Klarup, Den. 66/D3
Klaserie, SAfr. 149/F5
Klášterec nad Ohří, Czh. 85/G2
Klaten, Indo. 115/E3
Klatovy, Czh. 85/G4
Klaukkala, Fin. 65/E4
Klaus, Aus. 87/F3
Klausen (Chiusa), It. 87/H4
Klausenpass (pass), Swi. 87/E4
Klawock, Ak, US 168/Z13
Klazienaveen, Neth. 78/E3
Kleena Kleene, BC, Can. 170/B2
Klein Karas, Namb. 150/B2
Klein Spitzkoppe (peak), Namb. 148/B4
Klein Vaaldoorn, Namb. 150/B3
Klein-Letabarivier (riv.), SAfr. 149/F4
Kleinblittersdorf, Ger. 81/G5
Kleinburg, On, Can. 186/T8
Kleine Elster (riv.), Ger. 69/G3
Kleine Emme (riv.), Swi. 86/E4
Kleine Gete (riv.), Belg. 81/D2
Kleine Laber (riv.), Ger. 85/F5
Kleine Nete (riv.), Belg. 81/D1
Kleinheubach, Ger. 84/C3
Kleinlützel, Swi. 86/D3
Kleinmachnow, Ger. 68/Q7
Kleinmond, SAfr. 150/L11
Kleinolifants (riv.), SAfr. 150/Q12
Kleinrinderfeld, Ger. 84/C3
Kleinsee, SAfr. 150/B3
Kleinwallstadt, Ger. 84/C3
Kleinwinternheim, Ger. 84/B3
Klemme, Ia, US 181/H2
Kleppe, Nor. 66/A2
Kleppestø, Nor. 66/A1
Klerksdorp, SAfr. 150/D2
Klesiv, Ukr. 98/D2
Klet' (peak), Czh. 85/H5
Kletnya, Rus. 96/E1
Kletskiy, Rus. 99/M3
Kleve, Ger. 78/D5
Klichev, Bela. 67/N5
Klichka, Rus. 105/H1
Klickitat (riv.), Wa, US 170/D4
Klickitat, Wa, US 170/D5
Klimovichi, Bela. 96/D1
Klimovo, Rus. 96/E1
Klina, Yugo. 76/E4
Klinaklini (riv.), BC, Can. 170/B2
Kling, Phil. 114/D4
Klingenberg am Main, Ger. 84/C3
Klingenmünster, Ger. 84/B4
Klingenthal, Ger. 85/F2
Klínovec (peak), Czh. 85/F2
Klintehamn, Swe. 66/H3
Klintsy, Rus. 96/E1
Klip (riv.), SAfr. 150/E2
Klippan, Swe. 66/E3
Klipplaat, SAfr. 150/D4
Klisura, Bul. 77/G4
Klitmøller, Den. 66/C3
Kljajićevo, Yugo. 76/D3
Ključ, Bosn. 76/C3
Kłodawa, Pol. 69/K2
Kłodzko, Pol. 69/J3
Klondike, Ga, US 189/M7
Klondyke, Az, US 175/G4
Klöntaler-See (lake), Swi. 87/E3
Kloosterzande, Neth. 78/B6
Kloster, Ger. 66/E4
Klosterbach (riv.), Ger. 79/F3
Klosterlechfeld, Ger. 87/G1
Klosterneuburg, Aus. 77/N7
Klosters, Swi. 87/F4
Klosterwappen (peak), Aus. 69/H5
Kloten, Swi. 87/E3
Klothuhta Zayat, Myan. 112/C5
Klötze, Ger. 68/F2
Kluane, Yk, Can. 166/C2
Kluane NP, Yk, Can. 166/C2
Kluczbork, Pol. 69/K3
Klundert, Neth. 78/B5
Klyavlino, Rus. 95/M5
Klyaz'ma (riv.), Rus. 94/J4
Klyuchevskaya (peak), Rus. 101/S4
Klyuchi, Rus. 101/R4
Knaphill, Eng, UK 56/B3
Knapp (hill), Wi, US 181/J1
Knappa, Or, US 170/C4
Knapstad, Nor. 64/T9
Knäred, Swe. 66/E3
Knaresborough, Eng, UK 61/G3
Knebworth, Eng, UK 63/F3
Kneehills (cr.), Ab, Can. 171/H2
Knetzgau, Ger. 84/D3
Knezha, Bul. 77/G4
Knife (riv.), ND, US 182/C4
Knife River Indian Villages Nat'l Hist. Site, ND, US 182/D4
Knight (inlet), BC, Can. 170/B2
Knighton, Wal, UK 62/C2
Knights, Fl, US 190/L7
Knightsen, Ca, US 193/L11
Knin, Cro. 76/C3
Knippa, Tx, US 177/E3
Knislinge, Swe. 65/L6
Knittelfeld, Aus. 71/L3
Knittlingen, Ger. 84/B4
Knivsta, Swe. 66/G2
Knížecí Stolec (peak), Czh. 85/H5
Knížecí Strom (peak), Czh. 85/F3
Knjaževac, Yugo. 76/F4
Knob (peak), Phil. 117/F1
Knob (cape), Austl. 156/C5
Knobby (pt.), Austl. 156/B4
Knobel, Ar, US 188/B2
Knoch (hill), Sc, UK 59/D1
Knock, Ire. 58/B2
Knockadoon Head (pt.), Ire. 58/C6
Knockalongy (peak), Ire. 58/B1
Knockanaffrin (peak), Ire. 58/C5
Knockanore (mtn.), Ire. 58/A4
Knockboy (peak), Ire. 58/A6
Knockcloghrim, NI, UK 60/B2
Knockeirke (peak), Ire. 58/A6
Knocklong, Ire. 58/B5
Knockmealdown (peak), Ire. 58/C5
Knockmealdown (mts.), Ire. 58/B5
Knocknagashel, Ire. 58/A5
Knocknamaddree (peak), Ire. 58/A7
Knockowen (peak), Ire. 58/A6
Knockshanahullion (peak), Ire. 58/B5
Knoll (pt.), Namb. 148/B5
Knøsen (peak), Den. 66/D3
Knösen (pt.), Swe. 66/E4
Knosós (Knossos) (ruin), Gre. 75/J5
Knossos (Knosós) (ruin), Gre. 75/J5
Knott, Tx, US 177/D1
Knott End, Eng, UK 61/F4
Knottingley, Eng, UK 61/G4
Knott's Berry Farm, Ca, US 192/G8
Knotts Island, NC, US 189/K2
Knotty Green, Eng, UK 56/B2
Knowl Hill, Eng, UK 56/A2
Knox, ND, US 182/E3
Knox, Pa, US 187/G4
Knox, In, US 186/C4
Knox (coast), Ant. 216/G
Knox (cape), BC, Can. 166/C3
Knox (nbrhd.), Austl. 158/G5
Knox City, Tx, US 178/E4
Knoxville, Ms, US 190/C2
Knoxville, Ia, US 181/H3
Knoxville, Tn, US 188/F3
Knoxville, Ga, US 188/F4
Knutby, Swe. 65/B1
Knutsford, Eng, UK 61/F5
Knysna, SAfr. 150/C4
Ko (riv.), Sen. 140/B3
Ko (peak), Rus. 105/M2
Ko Samut NP, Thai. 120/C3
Ko-saki (pt.), Japan 110/A3
Koanaka (hills), Bots. 148/D4
Koani, Tanz. 145/B3
Koāth, India 123/E3
Koba, Indo. 115/D3
Kobar Sink (depr.), Eth. 144/B2
Kobayashi, Japan 110/B5
Kōbe, Japan 109/H6
Kobelyaky, Ukr. 99/H3
København (int'l arpt.), Den. 66/E4
København (co.), Den. 65/J7
København (Copenhagen) (cap.), Den. 65/J7
Kobenni, Mrta. 140/C3
Kobern-Gondorf, Ger. 81/G3
Kobipato (peak), Indo. 117/G4
Koblach, Aus. 87/F3
Koblenz, Swi. 87/E2
Koblenz, Ger. 81/G3
K'obo, Eth. 144/A2
Kobowan (swamp), Sudan 142/G4
Kobozha, Rus. 94/G4
Kobra, Rus. 95/L3
Kobroor (isl.), Indo. 117/H5
Kobryn, Bela. 96/C1
Kobu, SKor. 107/D5
Kobuchizawa, Japan 109/A2
Kobuk Valley NP, Ak, US 168/X12
K'obulet'i, Geo. 97/G4
Kobushi-ga-take (peak), Japan 111/F3
Kocába (riv.), Czh. 85/H3
Kocaeli (prov.), Turk. 96/D4
Koçalı, Turk. 128/D2
Kočani, FYROM 75/H2
Kocapınar, Turk. 129/E2
Kočevje, Slov. 71/L4
Koch (isl.), Nun, Can. 167/J2
Koch'ang, SKor. 107/D5
Koch'ang, SKor. 107/D5
Kochel am See, Ger. 87/H2
Kochelsee (lake), Ger. 87/H2
Kochen'ga, Rus. 95/J3
Kocher (riv.), Ger. 71/H2
Kocherinovo, Bul. 75/H1
Kochetovka, Rus. 97/G1
Kochevo, Rus. 95/M4
Kōchi (pref.), Japan 110/C4
Kōchi, Japan 110/C4
Kochmes, Rus. 95/P2
Kochubey, Rus. 97/H3
Kochubeyevskoye, Rus. 99/L5
Kochugaon, India 123/H2
Kodaira, Japan 109/C2
Kodala, India 121/E2
Kodama, Japan 109/C1
Kodāri, Nepal 123/E2
Kodarmā, India 123/E3
Kodiak (isl.), Ak, US 165/B4
Kodiak, Ak, US 168/X13
Kodinār, India 127/K4
Kodomari, Japan 108/B3
Kodry (hills), Mol. 77/H2
Kodyma, Ukr. 98/E3
Koekelare, Belg. 80/B1
Koel (riv.), India 118/D3
Koes, Namb. 150/B2
Koesan, SKor. 107/D4
Koetari (riv.), Sur. 205/G4
Kofa (mts.), Az, US 175/E4
Kofa NWR, Az, US 175/E4
Kofçaz, Turk. 77/H5
Kofelē, Eth. 144/A4
Koffiefontein, SAfr. 150/D3
Kofiau (isl.), Indo. 117/G4
Koforidua, Gha. 141/E5
Kōfu, Japan 111/F3
Koga, Japan 111/F2
Koga, Tanz. 147/H4
Koganei, Japan 109/D2
Kogarah, Austl. 159/E1
Køge (bay), Den. 66/E4
Kogi, Nga. 141/G4
Kogon (riv.), Gui. 140/B4
Kōgum (isl.), SKor. 107/D5
Kohāt, Pak. 124/A3
Kohila, Est. 67/L2
Kohīma, India 112/B3
Kohkīlūyeh and Bovīr Aḩmadi (gov.), Iran 129/G4
Kohler, Wi, US 186/C3
Kohls Ranch, Az, US 175/G3
Kohoku, Japan 109/K5
Kohout (peak), Czh. 85/H5
Kohtla-Järve, Est. 67/M2
Kohung, SKor. 107/D5
Kohunlich (ruin), Mex. 200/D2
Koichab (riv.), Namb. 148/B5
Koidu, SLeo. 140/C4
Koigi, Est. 67/L2
Koihoa, India 119/F6
Koilābās, Nepal 122/D2
Koímisis, Gre. 75/H2
Koindu, SLeo. 140/C4
Koito, Kenya 145/B2
Koito (riv.), Japan 109/D3
Koiva (riv.), Lat. 67/M3
Köje (isl.), SKor. 110/A3
Kojonup, Austl. 156/C5
Kojšovská (peak), Slvk. 69/L4
Kok (riv.), Myan. 120/B1
Kōka, Japan 109/K6
K'ok'a Gidib (dam), Eth. 144/A3
Kokai (riv.), Japan 109/E2
Kökar (isl.), Fin. 67/J3
Kokas, Indo. 117/H4
Kokemäenjoki (riv.), Fin. 67/J1
Kokhanovo, Bela. 67/N4
Kokkola (Karleby), Fin. 94/D3
Koknese, Lat. 67/L3
Koko, Nga. 141/G5
Koko, Nga. 141/G4
Kokoda, PNG 155/G2
Kokofata, Mali 140/C3
Kokola, D.R. Congo 147/G2
Kokomo, In, US 186/C4
Kokonau, Indo. 117/J4
Kokong, Bots. 148/D5
Kokonjärvi (lake), Fin. 65/D3
Kokrajhar, India 123/H2
Koksan, NKor. 107/D3
Kokshaal-Tau (mts.), Kyr. 125/C3
Kökshetaū, Kaz. 125/A1
Kökshetaū (oblast), Kaz. 125/A1
Koksijde, Belg. 80/B1
Koksoak (riv.), Qu, Can. 167/K3
Koksovyy, Rus. 99/L3
Kokstad, SAfr. 150/E3
Kokubu, Japan 110/B5
Kokuy, Rus. 105/H1
Kol, PNG 155/G1
Kola (riv.), Rus. 94/G1
Kola (isl.), Indo. 117/H5
Kola (pen.), Rus. 216/D
Kolachel, India 121/C4
Kolahun, Libr. 140/C4
Kolaka, Indo. 117/F4
Kolāras, India 122/A3
Kolašin, Yugo. 76/D4
Kolbäck, Swe. 66/G2
Kolbano, Indo. 154/B2
Kolbio, Kenya 145/C2
Kolbotn, Nor. 64/S8
Kolbus, Sudan 142/D2
Kolbuszowa, Pol. 69/L3
Kolda, Sen. 140/B3
Kolda (pol. reg.), Sen. 140/B3
Kolding, Den. 66/C4
Kole, D.R. Congo 147/F2
Kolebira, India 123/E4
Kölen (mts.), Swe. 64/E2
Kolenté, Gui. 140/B4
Kolepom (isl.), Indo. 162/C5
Kolezhma, Rus. 94/G2
Kolgaküla, Est. 67/L2
Kolgompya (cape), Rus. 67/N2
Kolguyev (isl.), Rus. 216/C
Koliba (riv.), Gui. 140/B3
Kolín, Czh. 69/H3
Kolind, Den. 65/G6
Koliya, Gui. 140/B4
Kolka, Lat. 67/K3
Kolkasrags (pt.), Lat. 67/K3
Kolkhozabad, Taj. 127/J1
Kollbach (riv.), Ger. 85/F5
Kollnburg, Ger. 85/F4
Kollum, Neth. 78/D2
Kolmanskop, Namb. 150/A2
Köln (Cologne), Ger. 81/F2
Kolno, Pol. 69/L2
Koło, Pol. 96/A1
Kolo, Tanz. 145/A3
Kołobrzeg, Pol. 66/F4
Kolofata, Camr. 142/B3
Kologriv, Rus. 95/K4
Kolokani, Mali 140/C3
Kololo, Eth. 144/B4
Kolomna, Rus. 94/H5
Kolomyya, Ukr. 98/C3
Kolondiéba, Mali 140/D4
Kolongotomo, Mali 140/D3
Kolonnawa, SrL. 121/C5
Kolosib, India 112/B3
Kolossa (riv.), Mali 140/D3
Kolpashevo, Rus. 100/J4
Kolpino, Rus. 94/T7
Kolpny, Rus. 96/F1
Kolpyta, Ukr. 98/F2
Kolsva, Swe. 66/F2
Kolubara (riv.), Yugo. 76/D3
Koluszki, Pol. 69/K3
Koluton (riv.), Kaz. 125/A1
Kolva (riv.), Rus. 95/N2
Kolwezi, D.R. Congo 147/F5
Kolyma (riv.), Rus. 103/Q3
Kolyma (range), Rus. 103/Q3
Kolyma Lowland (plain), Rus. 101/R2
Kolyshley, Rus. 97/H1
Kom (peak), Bul. 77/F4
Kom (riv.), Gabon 146/C2
Koma, Myan. 120/B3
Koma (riv.), Japan 109/C2
Komádi, Hun. 76/E2
Komadugu Gana (riv.), Nga. 141/H4
Komadugu Yobe (riv.), Nga. 141/H3
Komae, Japan 109/D2
Komagane, Japan 111/E3
Komaki, Japan 109/L5
Komaki (arpt.), Japan 109/L5
Komanda, D.R. Congo 147/G2
Komandorskiye (isls.), Rus. 103/R4
Komarichi, Rus. 99/H1
Komarin, Bela. 98/F2
Komárno, Slvk. 76/D2
Komárom, Hun. 76/D2
Komárom-Esztergom (prov.), Hun. 76/D2
Komatipoort, SAfr. 149/F5
Komatirivier (riv.), SAfr. 150/Q13
Komatlapeta, India 121/D2
Komatsu, Japan 110/E2
Komatsu (int'l arpt.), Japan 110/E2
Komatsushima, Japan 110/D3
Komba, D.R. Congo 147/E2
Kombat, Namb. 148/C3
Kombe, D.R. Congo 147/F4
Kombissiri, Burk. 141/E3
Kome (isl.), Ugan. 145/A2
Komering (riv.), Indo. 115/D4
Komi (aut. rep.), Rus. 95/M2
Komjatice, Slvk. 69/K4
Komló, Hun. 76/D2
Kommetjie, SAfr. 150/L11
Kommunar, Rus. 67/P2
Komo, PNG 155/F1
Komodo (isl.), Indo. 117/E5
Komodo Island NP, Indo. 117/E5
Komodougou, Gui. 140/C4
Komoé (riv.), C.d'Iv. 140/E5
Komono, Congo 146/C3
Komono, Japan 109/L5
Komoran (isl.), Indo. 117/J5
Komoro, Japan 109/A1
Komotiní, Gre. 75/J2
Kompasberg (peak), SAfr 150/D3
Kompiam, PNG 155/F1
Komsomolets (isl.), Rus. 103/J1
Komsomol's'k, Ukr. 99/G3
Komsomol'sk-na-Amure, Rus. 105/M1
Komsomol's'ke, Ukr. 99/J3
Komsomol's'ke, Ukr. 99/K4
Komsomol'skiy, Rus. 95/P2
Komsomol'skiy, Rus. 95/K5
Komsomol'skiy, Kaz. 97/K3
Komsomol'skiy, Rus. 100/G3
Komsomol'skiy, Rus. 97/H3
Komsomol'skoye, Rus. 97/H2
Komukanti, Namb. 148/C3
Kömür (pt.), Turk. 75/K3
Komysh-Zorya, Ukr. 99/J4
Komyshnya, Ukr. 99/G2
Kon (riv.), Kaz. 125/A2
Kon Plong, Viet. 120/E3
Kon Tum, Viet. 120/D3
Konabonou, C.d'Iv. 140/D5
Konakovo, Rus. 94/H4
Kōnan, Japan 109/K6
Kōnan, Japan 109/L5
Kōnan, Japan 109/C1
Konar (riv.), Afg. 124/A2
Konār (riv.), India 123/E4
Konār (res.), India 123/E4
Konar-e Khāş, Afg. 124/A2
Konārak, Iran 127/H3
Konārak, India 121/E2
Konawa, Ok, US 179/F3
Konaweha (riv.), Indo. 117/F4
Konda (riv.), Rus. 104/G1
Konda, Japan 109/H6
Kondagaon, India 121/D2
Kondé Sounga, Congo 146/B4
Kondinin, Austl. 156/C5
Kondoa, Tanz. 145/A3
Kondopoga, Rus. 94/G3
Kondūz, Afg. 100/G6
Koné, NCal. 163/U12
Konetsgor'ye, Rus. 94/J3
Kong, C.d'Iv. 140/D4
Kong (isl.), Camb. 120/C4
Kong (riv.), Laos 120/D3
Kong Kong (riv.), Sudan 142/G4
Kong Krailat, Thai. 120/B2
Kong Miao, China 106/D4
Kongapatalabata, Indo. 154/D1
Kongbo, CAfr. 142/D4
Kongju, SKor. 107/D4
Kongnŭg (riv.), SKor. 107/F6
Kongō-zan (peak), Japan 109/J7
Kongola, Namb. 148/D3
Kongolo, D.R. Congo 147/F4
Kongor, Sudan 142/F4
Kongoussi, Burk. 141/E3
Kongsberg, Nor. 66/C2
Kongsvinger, Nor. 66/E1
Kongtan, China 112/E2
Kongué, Chutes de (falls), Gabon 146/C2
Kongur (peak), China 125/C4
Kongwa, Tanz. 145/B3
Koniecpol, Pol. 69/K3
Königs Wusterhausen, Ger. 68/Q7
Königsberg in Bayern, Ger. 84/D2
Königsberg-Stein, Ger. 84/B5
Königsbronn, Ger. 84/D5
Königsbrunn, Ger. 87/G1
Königsdorf, Ger. 87/H2
Königsfeld im Schwarzwald, Ger. 87/E1
Königslutter am Elm, Ger. 79/H4
Königstein im Taunus, Ger. 84/B2
Königswinter, Ger. 81/G2
Konin, Pol. 69/K2
Konindou, Gui. 140/C4
Konispol, Alb. 75/G3
Kónitsa, Gre. 75/G2
Köniz, Swi. 86/D4
Konjic, Bosn. 76/C4
Könkämäeno (riv.), Fin. 94/D1
Konkiep (riv.), Namb. 148/C5
Konkiep, Namb. 150/B2
Konkola, Zam. 149/E2
Konkori, Gha. 141/E4
Konkouré (riv.), Gui. 140/B4
Konkourou-Bamingui, Rsv. de Faune du, CAfr. 142/D4
Konnevesi, Fin. 94/E3
Konobougou, Mali 140/D3
Konolfingen, Swi. 86/D4
Konosha, Rus. 94/J3
Kōnosu, Japan 109/D1
Konotop, Ukr. 99/G2
Konqi (riv.), China 100/J5
Konsen (plat.), Japan 108/D2
Końskie, Pol. 69/L3
Konso, Eth. 142/H4
Konstancin-Jeziorna, Pol. 69/L2
Konstantinovka, Ukr. 99/H3
Konstantinovsk, Rus. 99/L4
Konstantynówłódzki, Pol. 69/K3
Konstanz, Ger. 87/F2
Kontagora, Nga. 141/G4
Kontcha, Camr. 142/B4
Konteyevo, Rus. 94/J4
Kontich, Belg. 81/D1
Kontiolahti, Fin. 94/F3
Konuralp, Turk. 77/K5
Kóny, Hun. 76/C2
Konya, Turk. 128/C2
Konya (prov.), Turk. 128/C2
Konz, Ger. 81/F4
Konza, Kenya 145/B2
Koo-wee-rup, Austl. 159/B4
Koocanusa (lake), Mt, US 170/G3
Koog aan de Zaan, Neth. 78/B4
Koolpinyah, Austl. 154/C3
Koolyanobbing, Austl 156/C4
Koondrook, Austl. 159/B2
Koonga, Est. 67/L2
Koonibba, Austl. 157/G4
Koontz Lake, In, US 186/C4
Kooparmora, Swe. 65/B1
Koorawatha, Austl. 159/D2
Koorda, Austl. 156/C4
Koosa, Est. 67/M2
Koosharem, Ut, US 175/G1
Kooskia, Id, US 170/G4
Kootenai Nat'l Wild. Ref., Id, US 170/F3
Kootenay (lake), BC, Can. 166/E3
Kootenay (riv.), BC, Can. 170/G2
Kootenay NP, BC, Can. 170/F2
Kootingal, Austl. 158/D1
Kop (pass), Turk. 128/E1
Kopāganj, India 122/D2
Kopaigo, PNG 155/F1
Kopargaon, India 121/B2
Kopargo, Ben. 141/F4
Kópavogur, Ice. 64/N7
Kope (peak), C.d'Iv. 140/D5
Köpenick, Ger. 68/Q7
Koper, Slov. 71/K4
Kopervik, Nor. 66/A2
Kopeysk, Rus. 95/P5
Kopfing im Innkreis, Aus. 85/G6
Kopia, D.R. Congo 147/E2
Kopili (riv.), India 112/B3
Köping, Swe. 66/G2
Koplik, Alb. 75/F1
Kopondei (cape), Indo 154/A2
Koporskiy (bay), Rus. 67/N2
Koppang, Nor. 66/D1
Kopparberg (co.), Swe. 64/E3
Kopparberg, Swe. 66/F2
Koppi (riv.), Rus. 105/M2
Koppies, SAfr. 150/D2
Koprivnica, Cro. 76/C2
Koprivshtitsa, Bul. 77/G4
Kopru (riv.), Turk. 130/B1
Köprülü, Turk. 130/C1
Köprülü Kanyon NP, Turk 128/B2
Kop'ung, NKor. 107/C2
Kopyl', Bela. 96/C1
Kopys', Bela. 67/P4
Kor (riv.), Iran 126/F2
Kora, India 122/C2
Kōra, Japan 109/K5
Kora NP, Kenya 145/B2
Korab (peak), Alb. 75/G2
Koráb (peak), Czh. 85/G4
Korablino, Rus. 96/G1
K'orahē, Eth. 144/C4
Korakuen Garden, Japan 110/C3
Koraluk (riv.), Nf, Can. 167/K3
Koramlik, China 125/E4
Korana (riv.), Cro. 71/L4
Korazim NP, Isr. 131/D3
Korba, India 122/D4
Korbach, Ger. 79/F6
K'orbeta, Eth. 144/A2
Korbu (peak), Malay. 115/C1
Korçë, Alb. 75/G2
Korčula (isl.), Cro. 93/H2
Korčula, Cro. 76/C4
Korčulanski Kanal (chan.), It. 74/E1
Korčulanski Kanal (chan.), Cro. 76/C4
Kord Kūy, Iran 129/H2
Kordel, Ger. 81/F4
Kordestān (gov.), Iran 129/F3
Korea (bay), China,NKor. 101/N6
Korea (str.), Japan,Skor. 101/P6
Korean Folk Village, SKor. 107/G7
Korem, Eth. 144/A2
Korenovsk, Rus. 99/K5
Korets', Ukr. 98/D2
Korf, Rus. 101/S3
Korgas, China 125/D3
Korhogo, C.d'Iv. 140/D4
Korido, Indo. 117/J4
Korienzé, Mali 140/E3
Korim, Indo. 117/J4
Korinós, Gre. 75/H2
Kórinthos (Corinth), Gre. 75/H4
Kórinthos (Corinth) (ruin), Gre. 75/H4
Kóris-Hegy (peak), Hun. 76/C2
Köritz, Ger. 68/G2
Kōriyama, Japan 111/G2
Korizo, Passe de (pass), Chad 134/B4
Korkino, Rus. 95/P5
Korkodon (riv.), Rus. 101/R3
Korkuteli, Turk. 128/B2
Korla, China 125/E3
Kormakiti (cape), Cyp. 130/C2
Körmend, Hun. 76/C2
Kornat (isl.), Cro. 71/L5
Körner, Ger. 79/H6
Korneuburg, Aus. 77/N7
Kornman, Co, US 178/C1
Korntal-Münchingen, Ger. 84/C5
Kornwestheim, Ger. 84/C5
Koro, C.d'Iv. 140/D4
Koro, Mali 140/E3
Koro (sea), Fiji 162/G6
Koro Toro, Chad 142/C1
Koroba, PNG 155/F1
Korocha, Rus. 99/J2
Köroğlu (peak), Turk. 96/D4
Korogwe, Tanz. 145/B3
Koroit, Austl. 158/B3
Koronadal, Phil. 114/D4
Korónia (lake), Gre. 75/H2
Koronowo, Pol. 69/J2
Koropion, Gre. 75/N9
Koror (cap.), Palau 162/C4
Körös (riv.), Hun. 76/E2
Korosten', Ukr. 98/E2
Korostyshiv, Ukr. 98/E2
Korotaikha (riv.), Rus. 95/P1
Korovino, Rus. 97/K1
Korpo (Korppoo), Fin. 67/J1
Korppoo (Korpo), Fin. 67/J1
Korsakov, Rus. 105/N2
Korschenbroich, Ger. 78/D6
Korsö (isl.), Swe. 65/B1
Korsør, Den. 66/D4
Korsun'-Shevchenkivs'kyy, Ukr. 98/F3
Korsze, Pol. 67/J4
Kortemark, Belg. 80/C1
Kortenaken, Belg. 81/E2
Kortenberg, Belg. 81/D2
Kortessem, Belg. 81/E2
Korti Linchang, China 125/E2
Kortrijk, Belg. 80/C2
Kortsevo, Rus. 94/J4
Korumburra, Austl. 159/B4
Korup, PN de, Camr. 141/H5
Koryak (range), Rus. 103/R3
Koryakia Aut. Okrug, Rus. 101/S3
Koryazhma, Rus. 95/K3
Kōryō, Japan 109/J6
Koryŏng, SKor. 107/E5
Koryukivka, Ukr. 98/G2
Kós, Gre. 128/A2
Kós (isl.), Gre. 128/A2
Kosai, Japan 111/E3
Kosai, Japan 109/A2
Kosan, NKor. 107/D3
Kosaya Gora, Rus. 96/F1
Koschagyl, Kaz. 97/K3
Kösching, Ger. 85/E5
Kościan, Pol. 69/J2
Kościerzyna, Pol. 66/G4
Kosciusko, Ms, US 188/C4
Kosciusko (mt.), Austl. 159/D3
Köse, Turk. 128/D1
Kose, Est. 67/L2
Kosei, Japan 109/K6
Kosha, Sudan 135/F4
Koshigaya, Japan 111/F3
Koshiki (isls.), Japan 111/K5
Koshkar, Kaz. 97/K3
Koshkonong, Mo, US 179/J2

266
Kosh – La Con

Koshkonong (lake), Wi, US 181/K2
Kosi (zone), Nepal 123/F2
Kosi, India 122/A2
Kosi (riv.), India 118/E2
Košice, Slvk. 69/L4
Kosiv, Ukr. 98/C3
Koski, Fin. 65/F3
Koskinoú, Gre. 128/B2
Koslan, Rus. 95/L3
Kosoba (peak), Kaz. 125/C2
Kosŏng, SKor. 107/E5
Kosŏng, NKor. 107/E3
Kosovo (reg.), Yugo. 75/G1
Kosovo (prov.), Yugo. 76/E4
Kosovo Polje, Yugo. 76/E4
Kosovska Kamenica, Yugo. 76/E4
Kosovska Mitrovica, Yugo. 76/E4
Kosový (riv.), Czh. 85/F3
Kosrae (isl.), Micr. 162/F4
Kosse, Tx, US 177/F2
Kossi (prov.), Burk. 140/D3
Kossou (lake), C.d'Iv. 140/D5
Kosta, Swe. 66/F3
Kostelec nad Černými Lesy, Czh. 85/H3
Koster, SAfr. 150/D2
Kostinbrod, Bul. 77/F4
Kostomuksha, Rus. 94/F2
Kostopil', Ukr. 98/D2
Kostroma (oblast), Rus. 94/J4
Kostroma (riv.), Rus. 94/J4
Kostroma, Rus. 94/J4
Kostrzyn, Pol. 69/H2
Kostrzyn, Pol. 69/J2
Kostyantynivka, Ukr. 99/J3
Kostyantynivka, Ukr. 99/H4
Kostyukovichi, Bela. 96/E1
Kosuge, Japan 109/B2
Kos'va (riv.), Rus. 95/N4
Kos'yu (riv.), Rus. 95/N2
Kos'yu, Rus. 95/N2
Koszalin, Pol. 66/G4
Koszalin (prov.), Pol. 66/F5
Kőszeg, Hun. 76/C2
Kot Addu, Pak. 124/A4
Kot Fateh, India 124/C4
Kot Kapūra, India 124/C4
Kot Mūmin, Pak. 124/B3
Kot Rādha Kishan, Pak. 124/C4
Kot Samāba, Pak. 124/A5
Kot Sārang, Pak. 124/B3
Kota, India 122/D4
Kota, India 118/C2
Kōta, Japan 109/M6
Kota Baharu, Malay. 115/C1
Kota Belud, Malay. 114/B4
Kota Kinabalu (int'l arpt.), Malay. 114/B4
Kota Kinabalu, Malay. 114/B4
Kota Tinggi, Malay. 115/C2
Kotaagung, Indo. 115/D3
Kotabaru, Indo. 117/E4
Kotabaru, Indo. 115/C3
Kotabesi, Indo. 116/D4
Kotabumi, Indo. 115/D3
Kotabunan, Indo. 117/F3
Kotadaik, Indo. 115/D3
Kotajawa, Indo. 115/D3
Kotapād, India 121/D2
Kotapinang, Indo. 115/C2
Kotatengah, Indo. 115/C2
Kotdwāra, India 122/B1
Kotel, Bul. 77/H4
Kotel'nich, Rus. 95/L4
Kotel'nikovo, Rus. 97/G3
Kotel'nyy (isl.), Rus. 101/P2
Kotel'va, Ukr. 99/H2
Kotgarh, India 124/D4
Kothagūdem, India 121/D2
Köthen, Ger. 68/F3
Kotido, Ugan. 145/A1
Kotka, Fin. 67/M1
Kotla, India 124/D3
Kotlas, Rus. 95/K3
Kotli, Pak. 124/B3
Kotli Lohārān, Pak. 124/C3
Kotlik, Ak, US 168/W12
Kotlin (isl.), Rus. 94/S7
Kotly, Rus. 67/N2
Kotō, Japan 109/K5
Kotoka (int'l arpt.), Gha. 141/E5
Koton Karifi, Nga. 141/G4
Kotor, Yugo. 76/D4
Kotor Varoš, Bosn. 76/C3
Kotovo, Rus. 97/H2
Kotovsk, Rus. 97/G1
Kotovs'k, Ukr. 98/E4
Kotri, Pak. 127/J3
Kottai Malai (peak), India 121/C4
Kottayam, India 121/C4
Kotte (Sri Jayawardanapura), SrL. 121/C5
Kotto (riv.), CAfr. 142/D4
Kotuy (riv.), Rus. 103/K3
Kotzebue, Ak, US 168/W12
Kotzebue (sound), Ak, US 168/W12
Kötzting, Ger. 85/F4
Kouandé, Ben. 141/F4
Kouango, CAfr. 142/C4
Kouba Olanga, Chad 142/C2
Koubia, Gui. 140/C4
Kouchibouguac (bay), Nb, Can. 184/E2
Kouchibouguac NP, NB, Can. 184/E2
Koudougou, Burk. 141/E3
Koufonision (isl.), Gre. 75/J5
Kougoulé, Gabon 146/B2
Kouhu, Tai. 113/J4
Kouilou, Congo 146/B4
Kouilou (riv.), Congo 146/C3
Koukdjuak (riv.), Nun, Can. 167/J2
Kouki, CAfr. 142/C4
Koukourou, CAfr. 142/D4
Koula-Moutou, Gabon 146/C3
Koulé, Gui. 140/C4
Koulikoro (pol. reg.), Mali 140/C3
Koulikoro, Mali 140/D3
Koulou, Niger 141/F3
Kouloutou (riv.), Sen. 140/B3
Koum, Camr. 142/B3
Koumac, NCal. 163/U12
Koumala, Austl. 160/C3
Koumameyong, Gabon 146/B2
Koumandougou, Gui. 140/D4
Koumantou, Mali 140/D4
Koumban, Gui. 140/C4
Koumbi Saleh (ruin), Mrta. 140/D3
Koumbia, Gui. 140/B4
Koumi, Japan 109/A1
Koumra, Chad 142/C3
Koundara, Gui. 140/B3
Koundé, CAfr. 142/B4
Koundian, Mali 140/C3
Koundou, Gui. 140/C4
Koungheul, Sen. 140/B3
Kouno, Chad 142/C3
Kounradskiy, Kaz. 125/C2
Kountze, Tx, US 177/G2
Koupé (peak), Camr. 146/B1
Koupela, Burk. 141/E3
Kouraïa Konkouré, Gui. 140/B4
Kouritenga (prov.), Burk. 141/E3
Kourou, FrG. 206/C1
Kourouba, Mali 140/C3
Kouroussa, Gui. 140/C4
Koury, Mali 140/D3
Koussi (peak), Chad 134/C5
Koutiala, Mali 140/D3
Kouto, C.d'Iv. 140/D4
Kouvola, Fin. 67/M1
Kouyou (riv.), Congo 146/C3
Kovačica, Yugo. 76/E3
Kovada Gölü NP, Turk. 128/B2
Kovalam, India 121/C4
Kovashi (riv.), Rus. 94/S7
Kovda, Rus. 94/G2
Kovdor, Rus. 94/F2
Kovdozero (lake), Rus. 64/J2
Kovel', Ukr. 98/C2
Kovilj, Yugo. 76/E3
Kovilpatti, India 121/C4
Kovrov, Rus. 94/J4
Kovūr, India 121/C3
Kovylkino, Rus. 97/G1
Kowanyama Abor. Land, Austl. 155/F3
Kowanyama Aboriginal Community, Austl. 160/A1
Kowe, D.R. Congo 147/F3
Kowkcheh (riv.), Afg. 125/A4
Kowloon, China 113/G4
Kowŏn, NKor. 105/K4
Kowt-e 'Ashrow, Afg. 127/J2
Koxlax, China 125/D4
Kōyaguchi, Japan 109/J7
Koyama, Gui. 140/C5
Kōyama, Japan 110/B5
Koyang, SKor. 107/F6
Koynare, Bul. 77/G4
Koyukuk (riv.), Ak, US 168/X12
Kozacha Lopan', Ukr. 99/J2
Kozakai, Japan 109/M6
Kōzaki, Japan 109/E2
Kozaklı, Turk. 128/C2
Kozan, Turk. 128/C2
Kozáni, Gre. 75/G2
Kozara NP, Aus. 76/C3
Kozel'shchyna, Ukr. 99/G3
Kozel'sk, Rus. 96/E1
Kozha, Rus. 95/L4
Kozhikode (Calicut), India 121/B4
Kozhozero (lake), Rus. 94/H3
Kozhva, Rus. 95/N2
Kozhva (riv.), Rus. 95/M2
Kozienice, Pol. 69/L3
Kozloduy, Bul. 77/F4
Kozlovo, Rus. 94/H4
Kozlu, Turk. 96/D4
Kozluk, Turk. 128/E2
Koźmin, Pol. 69/J3
Koz'mino, Rus. 95/L3
Koznitsa (peak), Bul. 77/F4
Kozova, Ukr. 98/C3
Kōzu (isl.), Japan 111/F3
Kożuchów, Pol. 69/H3
Kozyatyn, Ukr. 98/E3
Kpagouda, Togo 141/F4
Kpalimé, Togo 141/F5
Kpandu, Gha. 141/F5
Kpémé, Togo 141/F5
Kra (isth.), Myan. 119/G6
Kra Buri, Thai. 120/B4
Kraai (riv.), SAfr. 150/D3
Kraaifontein, SAfr. 150/L10
Krabbendijke, Neth. 78/B6
Krabbfjärden (sound), Swe. 65/A2
Krabi, Thai. 120/B4
Kracheh, Camb. 120/D3
Kragan, Indo. 115/E3
Kragerø, Nor. 66/C2
Kragujevac, Yugo. 76/E3
Kraiburg am Inn, Ger. 85/F6
Kraichbach (riv.), Ger. 84/B4
Kraichgau (reg.), Ger. 71/H2
Krailling, Ger. 85/E6
Krakatau (vol.), Indo. 115/D3
Krakor, Camb. 120/D3
Kraków (prov.), Pol. 69/K3
Kraków, Pol. 69/K3
Krakow, Wi, US 186/B2
Kråkstad, Nor. 64/S8
Kralanh, Camb. 120/C3
Kralendijk, NAnt. 204/D1
Kraljevo, Yugo. 76/E4
Kralkızı (dam), Turk. 128/E2
Kralovice, Czh. 85/G3
Kralupy nad Vltavou, Czh. 85/H2
Kramators'k, Ukr. 99/J3
Kramer, ND, US 182/D3
Kramfors, Swe. 64/F3
Krammer (chan.), Neth. 78/B5
Kranéa Elassónos, Gre. 75/G3
Kranebitten (int'l arpt.), Aus. 87/H3
Kranenburg, Ger. 78/D5
Kranídhion, Gre. 75/H4
Kranj, Slov. 71/L3
Kranji (res.), Sing. 115/H6
Kranskop, SAfr. 151/E3
Kranzberg, Namb. 148/B4
Krapkowice, Pol. 69/J3
Krāslava, Lat. 67/M4
Kraslice, Czh. 85/F2
Krasnaya Gorbatka, Rus. 94/J5
Krasnaya Sloboda, Bela. 96/C1
Krasne, Ukr. 98/C3
Krasni Okny, Ukr. 98/E4
Kraśnik, Pol. 69/M3
Kraśnik Fabryczny, Pol. 69/M3
Krasninsk, Rus. 95/N5
Krasnoarmeysk, Rus. 97/H2
Krasnoarmeysk, Rus. 94/X9
Krasnoarmeyskaya, Rus. 99/K5
Krasnoarmeyskiy, Rus. 99/M4
Krasnoarmiys'k, Ukr. 99/J3
Krasnoborsk, Rus. 95/K3
Krasnodar (int'l arpt.), Rus. 99/K5
Krasnodar, Rus. 99/K5
Krasnodar Kray, Rus. 100/D5
Krasnodon, Ukr. 99/K3
Krasnogorsk, Rus. 94/W9
Krasnogvardeyskoye, Rus. 99/L5
Krasnohorivka, Ukr. 99/J3
Krasnohrad, Ukr. 99/H3
Krasnohvardiys'ke, Ukr. 99/H5
Krasnokamensk, Rus. 105/H1
Krasnokamsk, Rus. 95/M4
Krasnokholmskiy, Rus. 95/M5
Krasnolesnyy, Rus. 99/K2
Krasnooskol'skoye (res.), Ukr. 99/J3
Krasnopavlivka, Ukr. 99/J3
Krasnoperekops'k, Ukr. 99/G5
Krasnopillya, Ukr. 99/H2
Krasnoshchel'ye, Rus. 94/H2
Krasnoslobodsk, Rus. 97/G1
Krasnoslobodsk, Rus. 97/H2
Krasnotur'insk, Rus. 100/G4
Krasnoufimsk, Rus. 95/N4
Krasnoural'sk, Rus. 95/P4
Krasnovishersk, Rus. 95/N3
Krasnowodsk (int'l arpt.), Trkm. 129/H1
Krasnowodsk (Türkmenbashi), Trkm. 129/H2
Krasnoyarsk, Rus. 100/K4
Krasnoyarskiy, Rus. 97/L2
Krasnoye, Bela. 67/M4
Krasnoye, Rus. 99/K2
Krasnyy Bor, Rus. 94/T7
Krasnyy Chikoy, Rus. 104/F1
Krasnyy Gulyay, Rus. 97/J1
Krasnyy Kholm, Rus. 97/K2
Krasnyy Klyuch, Rus. 95/N5
Krasnyy Kut, Rus. 97/H2
Krasnyy Luch, Ukr. 99/K3
Krasnyy Lyman, Ukr. 96/F2
Krasnyy Oktyabr', Rus. 95/Q5
Krasnyy Sulin, Rus. 99/L4
Krasnyy Yar, Rus. 97/J3
Krasnyy Yar, Rus. 97/J1
Krasnyy Yar, Rus. 97/H2
Krasyliv, Ukr. 98/D3
Kratovo, FYROM 75/H1
Krautheim, Ger. 84/C4
Kravanh (mts.), Camb. 119/H5
Kraynovka, Rus. 97/H4
Kražiai, Lith. 67/K4
Kreb en Nâga (cliff), Mali 136/D5
Krechetovo, Rus. 94/H3
Kreck (riv.), Ger. 84/D2
Krefeld, Ger. 78/D6
Kreiensen, Ger. 79/G5
Kremastón (lake), Gre. 75/G3
Křemelna (riv.), Czh. 85/G4
Kremenchuk, Ukr. 99/G3
Kremenchuts'ke Vdskh. (res.), Ukr. 96/E2
Kremenets', Ukr. 98/C2
Kreminna, Ukr. 99/K3
Kremlin, Rus. 94/W9
Kremlin, Mt, US 171/J3
Kremmen, Ger. 68/Q6
Kremmling, Co, US 173/K3
Krempe, Ger. 79/G1
Krems an der Donau, Aus. 69/H4
Kremsmünster, Aus. 85/H6
Krenglbach, Aus. 85/G6
Kresgeville, Pa, US 194/C2
Kresna, Bul. 75/H2
Kress, Tx, US 178/D3
Kressbronn am Bodensee, Ger. 87/F2
Kresta (gulf), Rus. 101/T3
Kréstena, Gre. 75/G4
Kresty, Rus. 94/H5
Kretinga, Lith. 67/J4
Kreuzau, Ger. 81/F2
Kreuzberg (peak), Ger. 84/C2
Kreuzlingen, Swi. 87/F2
Kreuztal, Ger. 81/G2
Kreuzwertheim, Ger. 84/C3
Kría Vrísi, Gre. 75/H2
Kribi, Camr. 146/B2
Krieglach, Aus. 71/L3
Kriens, Swi. 87/E3
Kriftel, Ger. 84/B2
Kril'on (pen.), Rus. 108/B1
Kril'on (cape), Rus. 108/C1
Kril'on, Rus. 108/C1
Krim-Krim, Chad 142/B3
Krimpen aan de Ijssel, Neth. 78/B5
Krinídhes, Gre. 75/J2
Kriós (cape), Gre. 75/H5
Krishna (riv.), India 103/G8
Krishnagiri, India 121/C3
Krishnai, India 123/H2
Krishnanagar, India 123/G4
Kristdala, Swe. 66/G3
Kristiansand, Nor. 66/B2
Kristianstad (co.), Swe. 64/E4
Kristianstad (int'l arpt.), Swe. 66/F4
Kristianstad, Swe. 66/F3
Kristiansund, Nor. 64/C3
Kristinehamn, Swe. 66/F2
Kriva Palanka, FYROM 75/H1
Krivichi, Bela. 67/M4
Krivushevo, Rus. 95/L3
Krk (isl.), Cro. 93/G1
Krk, Cro. 71/L4
Krnov, Czh. 69/J3
Krokodil (riv.), SAfr. 149/F5
Krokodilrivier (riv.), SAfr. 149/E5
Krokom, Swe. 64/E3
Krókos, Gre. 75/G2
Krokstadelva, Nor. 64/R8
Krolevets', Ukr. 99/G2
Krombach, Ger. 84/C2
Kroměříž, Czh. 69/J4
Kromy, Rus. 96/E1
Kronach, Ger. 85/E2
Kronau, Sk, Can. 182/B2
Kronberg im Taunus, Ger. 84/B2
Krong Kaoh Kong, Camb. 120/C4
Krong Keb, Camb. 120/D4
Kronoberg (co.), Swe. 64/E4
Kronshtadt, Rus. 94/S6
Kronstorf, Aus. 85/H6
Kroombit Tops NP, Austl. 160/C4
Kroonstad, SAfr. 150/D2
Kropachevo, Rus. 95/N5
Kropotkin, Rus. 99/L5
Kropp, Ger. 66/C4
Krosno, Pol. 69/L4
Krosno (prov.), Pol. 98/B3
Krosno Odrzańskie, Pol. 69/H2
Krotoszyn, Pol. 69/J3
Krotovka, Rus. 95/L5
Krottenkopf (peak), Aus. 87/G3
Krotz Springs, La, US 190/C2
Krousón, Gre. 75/J5
Kröv, Ger. 81/G4
Krško, Slov. 76/B3
Kruckau (riv.), Ger. 79/G1
Kruger NP, SAfr. 149/F4
Krugersdorp, SAfr. 150/P13
Kruglitsa (peak), Rus. 95/N5
Krui, Indo. 115/C3
Kruibeke, Belg. 78/B6
Kruin, Namb. 148/C4
Kruiningen, Neth. 78/B6
Kruisfontein, SAfr. 150/D4
Krujë, Alb. 75/F2
Krulevshchina, Bela. 67/M4
Krum, Tx, US 179/F4
Krumbach, Ger. 87/G1
Krummenau, Swi. 87/F3
Krumovgrad, Bul. 77/G5
Krün, Ger. 87/H3
Krung Thep (Bangkok) (cap.), Thai. 120/C3
Kruså, Den. 66/C4
Kruševac, Yugo. 76/E4
Kruševo, FYROM 75/G2
Krušné Hory (Erzgebirge) (mts.), Czh.,Ger. 71/K1
Kruszwica, Pol. 69/K2
Krutoyarskiy, Rus. 95/P5
Krychaw, Bela. 96/D1
Krylovskaya, Rus. 99/K4
Krym Aut. Rep., Ukr. 99/G5
Krymsk, Rus. 99/K5
Krynica, Pol. 69/L4
Krynychky, Ukr. 99/H3
Kryve Ozero, Ukr. 98/F4
Kryvyy Rih, Ukr. 99/G4
Kryzhopil', Ukr. 98/E3
Krzna (riv.), Pol. 69/M3
Krzyż, Pol. 69/J2
Ksar el Boukhari, Alg. 138/G5
Ksar el Kebir, Mor. 138/B2
Ksel (peak), Alg. 137/F2
Ksen'yevka, Rus. 105/H1
Kshenskiy, Rus. 99/J2
Ktima, Cyp. 130/C2
Ku Sathan (peak), Thai. 120/C2
Ku-Ring-Gai Chase NP, Austl. 159/E1
Ku-Ring-Gai NP, Austl. 160/H8
Kuah, Malay. 120/B5
Kuai (riv.), China 104/H5
Kuala Belait, Bru. 116/D3
Kuala Berang, Malay. 115/C1
Kuala Dungun, Malay. 115/C1
Kuala Kangsar, Malay. 115/C1
Kuala Kelawang, Malay. 115/C2
Kuala Kerai, Malay. 115/C1
Kuala Kubu Baharu, Malay. 115/C2
Kuala Kurau, Malay. 115/C1
Kuala Lipis, Malay. 115/C1
Kuala Lumpur (int'l arpt.), Malay. 115/C2
Kuala Lumpur (cap.), Malay. 115/C2
Kuala Pahang, Malay. 115/C2
Kuala Penyu, Malay. 114/A4
Kuala Pilah, Malay. 115/C2
Kuala Rompin, Malay. 115/C2
Kuala Selangor, Malay. 115/C2
Kuala Terengganu, Malay. 115/C1
Kualalangsa, Indo. 115/B1
Kualamandah, Indo. 115/C3
Kualasimpang, Indo. 115/B1
Kualatungkal, Indo. 115/C3
Kuam, SKor. 107/G6
Kuamut, Malay. 114/B4
Kuancheng, China 106/D2
Kuandian, China 107/C2
Kuantan, Malay. 115/C2
Kuban' (riv.), Rus. 100/D5
Kubano-Priazov (plain), Rus. 99/K5
Kubaysah, Iraq 128/E3
Kubbum, Sudan 142/D3
Kubenskoye (lake), Rus. 94/H4
Kubokawa, Japan 110/C4
Kubrat, Bul. 77/H4
Kubumesaai, Indo. 116/E3
Kubutambahan, Indo. 115/F3
Kučevo, Yugo. 76/E3
Kuchaiburi, India 123/F4
Kuchen (peak), Aus. 87/G3
Kuchen, Ger. 84/C5
Kuchinarai, Thai. 120/D2
Kuching, Malay. 116/D3
Kuchino (isl.), Japan 111/K6
Kuchinoerabu (isl.), Japan 110/A5
Kuchl, Aus. 71/K3
Kūchnay Darvīshān, Afg. 127/H2
Kuçovë, Alb. 75/F2
Küçükbahçe, Turk. 75/K3
Küçükcekmece (lake), Turk. 129/M6
Küçükkuyu, Turk. 75/K3
Kuda, Indo. 116/D3
Kudamatsu, Japan 110/B3
Kudan, Nga. 141/G4
Kudara, Taj. 125/B4
Kudat, Malay. 114/B4
Kudene, Indo. 154/D1
Kudirkos-Naumiestis, Lith. 67/K4
Kudremalai (pt.), SrL. 121/C4
Kudus, Indo. 115/E3
Kudymkar, Rus. 95/M4
Kufrah (oasis), Libya 134/D3
Kufrinjah, Jor. 131/D4
Kufstein, Aus. 71/K3
Kufūr Najm, Egypt 139/C3
Kugarchi, Rus. 97/L1
Kugluktuk, Nun, Can. 166/E2
Kuhardt, Ger. 84/B4
Kühbach, Ger. 84/E6
Kūhdasht, Iran 129/F3
Kūhestak, Iran 129/J5
Kuhmo, Fin. 94/F2
Kuhmoinen, Fin. 67/L1
Kūhpāyeh, Iran 129/H3
Kuikuina, Nic. 201/E3
Kuinder of Tjonger (riv.), Neth. 78/C3
Kuiseb (riv.), NAmb. 148/B4
Kuishan (mtn.), China 113/F4
Kuitan, China 113/G4
Kuito, Ang. 148/C2
Kuiu (isl.), Ak, US 166/C3
Kuivajärvi (lake), Fin. 65/D4
Kuivastu, Est. 67/K2
Kujang, NKor. 107/D3
Kujawy (reg.), Pol. 69/K2
Kuji, Japan 108/B3
Kujū-san (peak), Japan 110/B4
Kujūkuri, Japan 109/E2
Kukalaya (riv.), Nic. 201/E3
Kukawa, Nga. 142/B2
Kuke (riv.), China 112/C3
Kukës, Alb. 75/G1
Kuki, Japan 111/F2
Kukipi, PNG 155/G2
Kukizaki, Japan 109/E2
Kukkia (lake), Fin. 67/L1
Kukmor, Rus. 95/L4
Kukushtan, Rus. 95/N4
Kūl (riv.), Iran 126/C3
Kula, Turk. 128/B2
Kula, Bul. 76/F4
Kula, Yugo. 76/D3
Kula Kangri (peak), Bhu. 123/H1
Kulachi, Pak. 124/A4
Kulagino, Kaz. 97/J2
Kulai, Malay. 115/C2
Kulākh, SAr. 126/D4
Kulal (mt.), Kenya 145/B1
Kulaly (isl.), Kaz. 97/J3
Kulandag (mts.), Trkm. 97/K4
Kularua, Bang. 123/J3
Kulashi, Geo. 97/G4
Kuldīga, Lat. 67/J3
Kule, Bots. 148/D4
Kulebaki, Rus. 94/J5
Kulen, Camb. 120/D3
Kulen Shet' (riv.), Eth. 144/B3
Kulet el-Qrein (peak), Egypt 139/C6
Kulgām, India 124/C3
Kulgera, Austl. 157/G3
Kulgunino, Rus. 97/L1
Kulim, Malay. 115/C1
Kulin, Austl. 156/C5
Kullamaa, Est. 67/L2
Kullen (cape), Swe. 66/E3
Kullu, India 124/D4
Kulm, ND, US 182/E4
Kulma (wadi), Sudan 142/D2
Kulmbach, Ger. 85/E2
Kŭlob, Taj. 125/A4
Kuloy (riv.), Rus. 95/J2
Kuloy, Rus. 94/J3
Kuloy, Rus. 95/J2
Kulpahār, India 122/B3
Kulpmont, Pa, US 194/B2
Kulpsville, Pa, US 194/C3
Kul'sary, Kaz. 97/K3
Külsheim, Ger. 84/C3
Kulsi (riv.), India 123/H2
Kulti, India 123/F4
Kulu, Turk. 128/C2
Kulunda, Rus. 100/H4
Kulunda (lake), Rus. 125/C1
Kulunda (riv.), Rus. 125/D1
Kulunda Steppe (plain), Kaz. 125/C1
Kulykivka, Ukr. 98/F2
Kŭm (riv.), SKor. 107/D4
Kuma (riv.), Rus. 100/E5
Kumagaya, Japan 111/F2
Kumai, India 123/G2
Kumaishi, Japan 108/A2
Kumak, Rus. 97/M2
Kumaka, Guy. 205/G4
Kumamoto (int'l arpt.), Japan 110/B4
Kumamoto (pref.), Japan 110/B4
Kumamoto, Japan 110/B4
Kumano (riv.), Japan 110/D4
Kumano, Japan 110/E4
Kumanovo, FYROM 75/G1
Kumār (riv.), Bang. 123/G4
Kumara, NZ 161/B3
Kumārkhāli, Bang. 123/G4
Kumasi, Gha. 141/E5
Kumatori, Japan 109/H7
Kumba, Camr. 146/B1
Kumbakonam, India 121/C4
Kumbe, Indo. 155/F2
Kumbia, Austl. 160/C4
Kŭmch'on, SKor. 107/F6
Kumé (isl.), Japan 111/J7
Kumertau, Rus. 97/K1
Kumeu, NZ 161/F6
Kŭmgang, NKor. 107/D3
Kŭmgang-san (peak), NKor. 107/E3
Kumhārsain, India 124/D4
Kŭmho (riv.), SKor. 107/E5
Kŭmhwa, SKor. 107/D3
Kumi, SKor. 107/E4
Kumi, Ugan. 145/A1
Kumihama, Japan 109/G4
Kumiyama, Japan 109/J6
Kumjawng (pass), India 112/C3
Kumköy, Turk. 129/N6
Kumla, Swe. 66/F2
Kumla, Swe. 65/B1
Kumluca, Turk. 130/B1
Kümmersbruck, Ger. 85/E4
Kumon (range), Myan. 119/G2
Kŭmsan, SKor. 107/D4
Kŭmsanp'o, NKor. 107/C3
Kumsenga, Tanz. 147/G3
Kumta, India 121/B3
Kumurkek, Indo. 155/F1
Kumylzhenskaya, Rus. 99/M3
Kuna, Id, US 172/E2
Kunashiri (isl.), Rus. 101/Q5
Kūnch, India 122/B3
Kunchha, Nepal 123/E1
Kunda, Est. 67/M2
Kunda, India 122/C3
Kundapura (Coondapoor), India 127/K6
Kundarkhi, India 122/B1
Kundauli, India 122/D2
Kundelungu, Monts (mts.), D.R. Congo 147/F5
Kundelungu, PN de, D.R. Congo 147/F5
Kundiān, Pak. 124/A3
Kundiawa, PNG 155/G1
Kundla, India 127/K4
Kundravy, Rus. 95/P5
Kunduchi, Tanz. 145/B3
Kundur (isl.), Indo. 115/C2
Kunene (riv.), Namb. 148/B3
Kungälv, Swe. 66/D3
Kungsangen (int'l arpt.), Swe. 66/G2
Kungsängen, Swe. 65/A1
Kungsbacka, Swe. 66/E3
Kungshamn, Swe. 66/D2
Kungu, D.R. Congo 146/D2
Kungu, Zam. 147/G5
Kungur, Rus. 95/N4
Kungutas, Tanz. 145/A4
Kungyangon, Myan. 120/B2
Kunhegyes, Hun. 76/E2
Kunhing, Myan. 112/C4
Kunimi-dake (peak), Japan 110/B4
Kuningan, Indo. 115/E3
Kunishiri (isl.), Rus. 103/P5
Kunitachi, Japan 109/C2
Kunjāh, Pak. 124/B3
Kunjirap (pass), China 127/L1
Kunkletown, Pa, US 194/C2
Kunlong, Myan. 119/G3
Kunlun (mts.), China 103/H6
Kunlun (pass), China 113/F4
Kunmadaras, Hun. 69/L5
Kunming (int'l arpt.), China 112/D3
Kunming, China 112/D3
Kunmunya Abor. Rsv., Austl. 154/B3
Kunp'o, SKor. 107/F7
Kunsan, SKor. 107/D5
Kunshan, China 106/L8
Kunszentmárton, Hun. 76/E2
Kuntaur, Gam. 140/B3
Kuntsëvo (nbrhd.), Rus. 94/W9
Kuntshankoie, D.R. Congo 147/E3
Kunu (riv.), India 127/L3
Kununurra, Austl. 154/C3
Kunwāri (riv.), India 122/A2
Kunwi, SKor. 107/E4
Kun'ya, Rus. 67/P3
Kunya, Nga. 141/H3
Kunyu (mtn.), China 106/E3
Künzell, Ger. 84/C1
K'unzila, Eth. 142/H3
Kunzulu, D.R. Congo 146/D3
Kunžvartské (pass), Czh. 85/G5
Kuocang (peak), China 113/J2
Kuohijärvi (lake), Fin. 67/L1
Kuolayarvi, Rus. 94/F2
Kuolimo (lake), Fin. 67/M1
Kuopio, Fin. 94/E3
Kuopio (prov.), Fin. 64/H3
Kup, PNG 155/G1
Kupa (riv.), Cro. 71/L4
Kupang, Indo. 154/A2
Kuper (range), PNG 155/G1
Kupiano, PNG 155/H2
Kupino, Rus. 100/H4
Kupiškis, Lith. 67/L4
Kuppenheim, Ger. 84/B5
Kupreanof (isl.), Ak, US 166/C3
Kup'yans'k, Ukr. 99/J3
Kup'yans'k-Vuzlovyy, Ukr. 99/J3
Kuqa, China 101/M5
Kür (riv.), Azer. 100/E6
Kur (riv.), Rus. 105/M1
Kurakh, Rus. 97/H4
Kurakhove, Ukr. 99/J4
Kurakino, Rus. 97/H1
Kūrālī, India 124/D4
Kurama-yama (peak), Japan 109/J5
Kurashiki, Japan 110/C3
Kuraymah, Sudan 135/F5
Kurayoshi, Japan 110/C3
Kurayyimah, Jor. 131/D4
Kurchum, Kaz. 125/D2
Kürdämir, Azer. 129/G1
Kurdistan (reg.), Asia 100/E6
Kurdufān (pol. reg.), Sudan 142/F2
Kŭrdzhali (res.), Bul. 75/J2
Kŭrdzhali, Bul. 77/G5
Küre, Turk. 96/E4
Kure, Japan 110/C3
Kure (isl.), Hi, US 162/H2
Küre (mts.), Turk 128/C1
Kūrebhār, India 122/D2
Kuressaare, Est. 67/K2
Kureyka (riv.), Rus. 100/K3
Kurgan, Rus. 95/Q5
Kurgan Oblast, Rus. 95/P5
Kurganinsk, Rus. 99/L5
Kurgaon, India 122/A2
Kuri, SKor. 107/G6
Kuria (isl.), Kiri. 162/G4
Kuria Muria (isls.), Oman 103/F5
Kurīgrām, Bang. 123/G3
Kurihashi, Japan 109/D1
Kurikoma-yama (peak), Japan 108/B4
Kuril (isls.), Rus. 103/Q5
Kurilovka, Rus. 97/J2
Kuril'sk, Rus. 108/E1
Kurimoto, Japan 109/F2
Kuring Kuru, Namb. 148/C3
Kurinwas (riv.), Nic. 201/E3
Kurisawa, Japan 108/B2
Kuriyama, Japan 108/B2
Kürkçü, Turk. 130/C1
Kurkiyoki, Rus. 67/N1
Kurlovskiy, Rus. 94/J5
Kurmuk, Eth. 142/G3
Kurnool, India 121/C3
Kuro (nbrhd.), SKor. 107/F7
Kuro-shima (isl.), Japan 110/A5
Kurodashō, Japan 109/G5
Kuroishi, Japan 108/B3
Kuroiso, Japan 111/G2
Kuroki, Sk, Can. 182/C2
Kurort-Darasun, Rus. 104/G1
Kuroso-yama (peak), Japan 109/K6
Kurotaki, Japan 109/J7
Kurow, NZ 161/B4
Kurrajong, Austl. 160/G8
Kurram (riv.), Pak. 127/K2
Kurri Kurri, Austl. 159/E1
Kurrimine Beach, Austl. 160/B2
Kursavka, Rus. 99/M5
Kuršėnai, Lith. 67/K3
Kurseong, India 123/G2
Kursiu Nerija NP, Lith. 67/J4
Kursk, Rus. 99/J2
Kursk Oblast, Rus. 96/E2
Kurskaya Spit (bar), Lith.,Rus. 67/J4
Kurskiy (lag.), Lith.,Rus. 69/L1
Kurskiy (lag.), Lith. 67/J4
Kuršumlija, Yugo. 76/E4
Kurşunlu, Turk. 96/E4
Kurtalan, Turk. 128/E2
Kürten, Ger. 81/G1
Kurtköy, Turk. 129/N7
Kuru (riv.), Bhu. 123/H2
Kuru (riv.), Sudan 142/E1
Kuruca (pass), Turk. 128/E2
Kuruçay (riv.), Turk. 97/G4
Kuruçay, Turk. 128/D2
Kuruktag (mts.), China 104/B3
Kuruman, SAfr. 150/C2
Kurumansrivier (riv.), SAfr. 150/C2
Kurume, Japan 110/B4
Kurumkan, Rus. 104/G1
Kurundi, Austl. 157/G2
Kurupukari, Guy. 205/G3
Kurur (peak), Sudan 135/F4
Kurwongbah (lake), Austl. 160/E6
Kur'ya, Rus. 95/N3
Kurye, SKor. 107/D5
Kuryong (riv.), NKor. 107/C3
Kuryongp'o-ri, SKor. 107/E5
Kuşadası, Turk. 128/A2
Kusakan, Kaz. 97/M1
Kusatsu, Japan 109/J5
Kusel, Ger. 81/G4
Kushālgarh, India 127/K4
Kushchevskaya, Rus. 99/K4
Kusheriki, Nga. 141/G4
Kushida (riv.), Japan 109/K7
Kushigata, Japan 109/A2
Kushihara, Japan 109/M5
Kushikino, Japan 110/B5
Kushima, Japan 110/B5
Kushimoto, Japan 110/D4
Kushiro (riv.), Japan 108/D2
Kushiro, Japan 108/D2
Kushiro-Shitsugen NP, Japan 108/D2
Kushmurun (lake), Kaz. 95/Q5
Kushol, India 124/D3
Kushtia, Bang. 123/G4
Kushtia (pol. reg.), Bang. 123/G4
Kushui (riv.), China 104/F4
Kushum (riv.), Kaz. 97/J2
Kusiyana (riv.), Bang. 123/H3
Kuskokwim (riv.), Ak, US 165/A3
Kuskokwim (mts.), Ak, US 168/W12
Kuskokwim (bay), Ak, US 168/W13
Kusma, Nepal 122/D1
Küsnacht, Swi. 87/E3
Kusŏng, NKor. 107/C3
Kussharo (lake), Japan 108/C2
Küssnacht am Rigi, Swi. 87/E3
Kustarevka, Rus. 97/G1
Küstenkanal (canal), Ger. 79/E3
Kusterdingen, Ger. 84/C5
Kūstī, Sudan 142/G2
Kusu, Japan 109/L6
Kusuman, Thai. 120/D2
Kut (isl.), Camb. 119/H5
Kuta, Nga. 141/G4
Kutacane, Indo. 115/B2
Kütahya (prov.), Turk. 96/D5
Kütahya, Turk. 128/B2
Kutais, Rus. 99/K5
K'ut'aisi (int'l arpt.), Geo. 97/G4
K'ut'aisi, Geo. 97/G4
Kutāmat al Ghābah, Egypt 139/B3
Kutch (gulf), India 118/A3
Kutch (reg.), India 118/A3
Kutchan, Japan 108/B1
Kutcharo (lake), Japan 108/C1
Kutenholz, Ger. 79/G2
Kutiwenji, Nga. 141/G4
Kutná Hora, Czh. 69/H4
Kutno, Pol. 69/K2
Kutse Game Reserve, Bots. 148/D4
Kutsuki, Japan 109/J5
Küttigen, Swi. 86/E3
Kutu, D.R. Congo 146/D3
Kutu-Owanga, D.R. Congo 147/E3
Kutulik, Rus. 104/E1
Kutum, Sudan 142/E2
Kutzenhausen, Ger. 84/D6
Kutztown, Pa, US 194/C2
Kuujjua (riv.), NW, Can. 166/E1
Kuujjuaq, Qu, Can. 167/K3
Kuujjuarapik, Qu, Can. 167/J3
Kuuli-Mayak, Trkm. 129/H1
Kuurila, Fin. 65/E3
Kuusamo, Fin. 64/J2
Kuusankoski, Fin. 67/M1
Kuutse (hill), Est. 67/M2
Kuvandyk, Rus. 97/L2
Kuvango, Ang. 148/C2
Kuwait (cap.), Kuw. 129/F4
Kuwait(ctry.) 103/D7
Kuwait (int'l arpt.), Kuw. 129/F4
Kuwānā (riv.), India 118/D2
Kuwana, Japan 109/L5
Kuybyshev, Rus. 95/L5
Kuybyshev (res.), Rus. 100/E4
Kuybyshevka, Ukr. 98/F4
Kuybyshevskiy, Kaz. 95/Q5
Kuye (riv.), China 104/G4
Kūysanjaq, Iraq 129/F2
Küysu, China 104/C3
Kuyto (lake), Rus. 64/J2
Kuytun, China 125/E3
Kuytun (riv.), China 125/D3
Kuyu Tingni, Nic. 201/F3
Kuyuwini (riv.), Guy. 205/G4
Kuze, Japan 109/K4
Kuz'molovskiy, Rus. 94/T6
Kuznetsk, Rus. 97/H1
Kuzomen', Rus. 94/H2
Kuzovatovo, Rus. 97/H1
Kuzucubelen, Turk. 130/D1
Kuzumaki, Japan 108/B3
Kvaløy (isl.), Nor. 64/F1
Kværndrup, Den. 66/D4
Kvarner (gulf), Cro. 93/G1
Kvarneric (chan.), Cro. 76/B3
Kvigtinden (peak), Nor. 64/E2
Kvinesdal, Nor. 66/B2
Kvinnherad, Nor. 66/B2
Kviteseid, Nor. 66/C2
Kwa (riv.), D.R. Congo 133/D5
Kwa Mtoro, Tanz. 145/A3
Kwaadmechelen, Belg. 81/E1
Kwach'ŏn, SKor. 107/F7
Kwail, NKor. 107/C3
Kwajalein (isl.), Mrsh. 162/F4
Kwajok, Sudan 142/F3
Kwakoegron, Sur. 206/C1
Kwaksan, NKor. 107/C3
Kwakwani, Guy. 205/G3
Kwale, Kenya 145/B3
Kwali, Nga. 141/G4
Kwam al Ḥamām (ruin), Egypt 139/C6
Kwam Awshīm (ruin), Egypt 139/B5
Kwamashu, SAfr. 151/E3
Kwamen Kwesi, Gha. 141/E4
Kwamouth, D.R. Congo 146/D3
Kwanak-san (peak), SKor. 107/F7
Kwando (riv.), Namb. 148/D3
Kwangch'ŏn, SKor. 107/D4
Kwangju, SKor. 107/D5
Kwangju, SKor. 107/G7
Kwangju-jikhalsi (prov.), SKor. 107/D5
Kwangmyŏng, SKor. 107/F7
Kwango (riv.), D.R. Congo 133/D5
Kwangwazi, Tanz. 145/B3
Kwangyang, SKor. 107/D5
Kwania (lake), Ugan. 145/A1
Kwansan, SKor. 107/D5
Kwara (state), Nga. 141/G4
Kwaraha (peak), Tanz. 145/A3
Kwatarkwashi, Nga. 141/G3
Kwazulu Natal (prov.), SAfr. 151/E3
Kwekwe, Zim. 149/F3
Kweneng (dist.), Bots. 148/E4
Kwenge (riv.), D.R. Congo 146/D4
Kwidzyn, Pol. 67/H5
Kwīha, Eth. 144/A2
Kwikila, PNG 155/G2
Kwilu (riv.), D.R. Congo 133/D5
Kwinana, Austl. 156/K7
Kwitara (riv.), Guy. 206/B2
Ky Anh, Viet. 120/D2
Ky Son, Viet. 120/D2
Kya-in Seikkyi, Myan. 120/B2
Kyabé, Chad 142/C3
Kyabram, Austl. 159/B3
Kyaikkami, Myan. 120/B2
Kyaikpi, Myan. 120/B2
Kyaiktiyo Pagoda, Myan. 120/B2
Kyaikto, Myan. 112/C5
Kyaka, Tanz. 147/G3
Kyakhta, Rus. 104/F1
Kyalite, Austl. 158/B2
Kyan-zaki (cape), Japan 111/J7
Kyancutta, Austl. 157/G5
Kyangin, Myan. 112/B5
Kyargozero, Rus. 94/G3
Kyaukki, Myan. 120/B2
Kyaukme, Myan. 112/C4
Kyaukpadaung, Myan. 112/B4
Kyaukpyu, Myan. 112/B5
Kyaukse, Myan. 112/C4
Kyaunggon, Myan. 112/B5
Kybartai, Lith. 67/K4
Kyeamba (cr.), Austl. 159/C2
Kyegegwa, Ugan. 147/G2
Kyelang, India 124/D3
Kyenjojo, Ugan. 147/G2
Kyeryong-san NP, SKor. 107/D4
Kyidaunggan, Myan. 112/C5
Kyikug, China 104/E4
Kyindwe, Myan. 112/B4
Kyjov, Czh. 69/J4
Kyle (reg.), Sc, UK 59/B5
Kyle, SD, US 180/C2
Kyle, Sk, Can. 171/K2
Kyle, Tx, US 177/F3
Kylemore, Sk, Can. 182/C2
Kyll (riv.), Ger. 68/D3
Kylmäkoski, Fin. 65/D3
Kym (riv.), Eng, UK 63/F2
Kymi (prov.), Fin. 64/H3
Kymijärvi (lake), Fin. 65/F4
Kymijoki (riv.), Fin. 67/M1
Kymore, India 122/B4
Kyn, Rus. 95/N4
Kyneton, Austl. 159/B3
Kynšperk nad Ohří, Czh. 85/F2
Kynuna, Austl. 160/A3
Kyoga (lake), Ugan. 145/A1
Kyōga-misaki (cape), Japan 110/D3
Kyogle, Austl. 160/D5
Kyonan, Japan 111/F3
Kyŏngan (riv.), SKor. 107/G7
Kyŏngbok Palace, SKor. 107/F6
Kyŏnggi (bay), SKor. 107/C4
Kyŏnggi-Do (prov.), SKor. 107/D4
Kyŏngju, SKor. 110/A3
Kyŏngju NP, SKor. 107/E5
Kyŏngju NP, SKor. 110/A3
Kyŏngsan, SKor. 110/A3
Kyŏngsang-bukto (prov.), SKor. 107/E4
Kyŏngsang-namdo (prov.), SKor. 107/E5
Kyŏngsŏng, NKor. 107/E2
Kyônkadun, Myan. 112/B5
Kyōto (pref.), Japan 110/D3
Kyōto, Japan 109/J5
Kyōtō Imperial Palace, Japan 109/J6
Kyōwa, Japan 109/E1
Kyrenia, Cyp. 130/C2
Kyrenia (dist.), Cyp. 130/C2
Kyrgyzstan(ctry.) 103/G5
Kyritz, Ger. 68/G2
Kyrkslätt (Kirkkonummi), Fin. 67/L1
Kyrösjärvi (lake), Fin. 67/K1
Kyrta, Rus. 95/N2
Kyrykuduk, Kaz. 97/J2
Kyrylivka, Ukr. 99/H4
Kyshtym, Rus. 95/P5
Kythrea, Cyp. 130/C2
Kytlym, Rus. 95/N4
Kytätä, Fin. 65/E4
Kyunhla, Myan. 112/B4
Kyūshū (isl.), Japan 103/M6
Kyūshū Highlands (uplands), Japan 110/B4
Kyustendil, Bul. 75/H1
Kyusyur, Rus. 101/N2
Kywebwe, Myan. 112/B5
Kyyiv (Kiev) (cap.), Ukr. 98/F2
Kyyivs'ka (prov.), Ukr. 96/D2
Kyyivs'ke Vodoskhovyshche (res.), Ukr. 96/D2
Kyzyl, Rus. 104/C1
Kyzylkum (des.), Kaz. 100/G5
Kzyltu, Kaz. 100/H4

L

L Ariana (lake), Fl, US 190/M7
L' Achigan (riv.), Qu, Can. 185/N6
L'Anguille (riv.), Ar, US 188/B3
L'Anse, Mi, US 183/K4
L'Aquila (prov.), It. 92/C3
L'Artois, Collines de (hills), Fr. 68/A3
L'Assomption (riv.), Qu, Can. 185/P6
L'Assomption (co.), Qu, Can. 185/N6
L'Hongrin (lake), Swi. 86/D5
L'Oriental (pol. reg.), Mor. 137/E2
La Algaba, Sp. 72/B4
La Almunia de Doña Godina, Sp. 72/E2
La Amistad Int'l Park, CR 196/E6
La Araucanía (pol. reg.), Chile 214/B3
La Ascensión, Mex. 199/F3
La Asturiana, Arg. 214/D3
La Asunción, Ven. 205/F2
La Aurora (int'l arpt.), Guat. 200/D3
La Baie, Qu, Can. 184/B1
La Banda, Arg. 212/C3
La Bañeza, Sp. 72/C1
La Barge, Wy, US 173/H2
La Barra, Nic. 201/F3
La Barra, Uru. 215/G2
La Barre-en-Ouche, Fr. 83/F3
La Bassée, Fr. 80/B2
La Bâthie, Fr. 90/C1
La Bâtie-Neuve, Fr. 90/C3
La Baule-Escoublac, Fr. 82/C6
La Belle, Fl, US 191/H4
La Birse (riv.), Swi. 86/D3
La Blanquilla (isl.), Ven. 205/E2
La Bocana, Mex. 198/B3
La Bonneville-sur-Iton, Fr. 83/G3
La Bouilladisse, Fr. 90/B6
La Bresse, Fr. 86/C2
La Broque, Fr. 86/D1
La Broquerie, Mb, Can. 182/F3
La Cadière-d'Azur, Fr. 90/B6
La Caldera de Taburiente, PN, Sp. 136/A3
La Calera, Col. 207/M8
La Calera, Chile 214/N8
La Campana, Sp. 72/C4
La Campana, PN, Chile 214/N8
La Cañada (peak), Cuba 201/F1
La Canada-Flintridge, Ca, US 192/F7
La Canoa, Ven. 205/F2
La Capelle, Fr. 80/C4
La Carlota, Sp. 72/C4
La Carlota, Arg. 214/E2
La Carolina, Sp. 72/D3
La Catedral (peak), Mex. 199/Q9
La Ceiba, Ven. 204/D3
La Ceiba (int'l arpt.), Hon. 200/E3
La Ceiba, Hon. 200/E3
La Ceja, Col. 207/K6
La Celle-les-Bordes, Fr. 56/H6
La Celle-Saint-Cloud, Fr. 56/J5
La Celle-sur-Morin, Fr. 56/L5
La Center, Ky, US 188/C2
La Chapelle-de-Guinchay, Fr. 86/A5
La Chapelle-des-Marais, Fr. 82/C6
La Chapelle-Saint-Luc, Fr. 70/F2
La Chapelle-sur-Erdre, Fr. 82/D6
La Chartre-sur-le-Loir, Fr. 83/F5
La Chaussée-Saint-Victor, Fr. 83/G5
La Chaux-de-Bonds, Swi. 86/C3
La Chinita (int'l arpt.), Ven. 204/D2
La Chorrera, Col. 204/C5
La Cienega, NM, US 175/J3
La Ciotat, Fr. 90/B6
La Ciudad, PN, Mex. 198/D4
La Clusaz, Fr. 86/C6
La Cocha, Arg. 212/C3
La Colle-sur-Loup, Fr. 90/D5
La Concepción, Pan. 201/F4
La Concepción, Nic. 200/E4
La Concepcíon, Ven. 204/D2
La Condamine (nbrhd.), Mona. 88/J8

La Coronilla, Uru. 215/G2
La Coruña, Sp. 72/A1
La Côte-Saint-André, Fr. 90/B2
La Couronne, Fr. 70/D4
La Couture-Boussey, Fr. 83/G3
La Crau, Fr. 90/C6
La Crèche, Fr. 70/C3
La Crescent, Mn, US 181/J2
La Crescenta-Montrose, Ca, US 192/F7
La Criolla, Arg. 212/D4
La Croche, Qu, Can. 184/A2
La Croix-en-Brie, Fr. 56/M6
La Crosse, Ks, US 178/E1
La Crosse, Wi, US 181/J2
La Crosse, Va, US 189/H2
La Cruz, Col. 204/B4
La Cruz, CR 200/E4
La Cruz, Uru. 215/K10
La Cruz, Chile 214/N8
La Cruz, Mex. 198/D4
La Cuchilla, Uru. 213/F5
La Cumbre (vol.), Ecu. 208/J7
La Cygne, Ks, US 179/G1
La Dôle (peak), Swi. 86/C5
La Dorada, Col. 207/L7
La Doré, Qu, Can. 184/A1
La Dormida, Arg. 214/D2
La Durande (peak), Fr. 92/D1
La Embocada, Bol. 209/E4
La Escondida, Arg. 214/C3
La Escondida, Arg. 212/E3
La Esmeralda, Ven. 205/E4
La Esperanza, Arg. 214/C4
La Esperanza, Bol. 209/F4
La Esperanza, Bol. 209/F5
La Esperanza, Bol. 209/E4
La Esperanza, Hon. 200/D3
La Esperanza, Ven. 205/F2
La Estanzuela, Uru. 215/K11
La Estrada, Sp. 72/A1
La Estrella, Chile 214/N9
La Falda, Arg. 212/C4
La Fare-les-Oliviers, Fr. 90/B5
La Farlède, Fr. 90/C6
La Fayette, Ga, US 188/E3
La Fère, Fr. 80/C4
La Ferrière-aux-étangs, Fr. 83/E3
La Ferté-Gaucher, Fr. 80/C6
La Ferté-Imbault, Fr. 83/G6
La Ferté-Macé, Fr. 83/E3
La Ferté-Milon, Fr. 56/M7
La Ferté-Sous-Jouarre, Fr. 80/C6
La Ferté-St-Aubin, Fr. 83/G5
La Ferté-Vidame, Fr. 83/F3
La Flèche, Fr. 83/E5
La Follette, Tn, US 188/E2
La Fontaine, In, US 186/D4
La Francia, Arg. 212/D4
La Fria, Ven. 204/C2
La Gacilly, Fr. 82/C5
La Garde, Fr. 90/C6
La Garde-Adhémar, Fr. 90/A4
La Garita (mts.), Co, US 178/A2
La Garita, Co, US 175/J2
La Garriga, Sp. 73/L6
La Gineta, Sp. 72/E3
La Glacerie, Fr. 82/D1
La Gloria, Col. 204/C2
La Gloria, Tx, US 187/E4
La Gran Sabana (plain), Ven. 205/F3
La Grand Moucherolle (peak), Fr. 90/B2
La Grande (riv.), Qu, Can. 167/J3
La Grande (riv.), Can. 65/K4
La Grande, Or, US 172/D1
La Grande Rochette (peak), Fr. 90/C2
La Grande Ruine (peak), Fr. 90/C3
La Grange, Austl. 154/A4
La Grange, Ga, US 188/E4
La Grange, Ky, US 188/E1
La Grange, Mo, US 181/J3
La Grange, NC, US 189/J3
La Grange, Tx, US 177/F3
La Grange, Wy, US 180/B3
La Grave, Fr. 90/C2
La Grita, Ven. 201/J4
La Grivola (peak), It. 90/D1
La Grue Bayou (riv.), Ar, US 188/B3
La Gruyère (lake), Swi. 86/D4
La Guadeloupe, Qu, Can. 184/B3
La Guaira, Ven. 207/P7
La Guajira (pen.), Col. 201/H4
La Guajira (dept.), Col. 201/H4
La Guardia, Sp. 72/A2
La Guardia, Arg. 212/C4
La Guardia, Bol. 212/D1
La Guardia (int'l arpt.), NY, US 195/K8
La Guerche-de-Bretagne, Fr. 82/D5
La Habana (Havana) (cap.), Cuba 196/E3
La Habra, Ca, US 192/G8
La Harpe, Ks, US 179/G2
La Have (riv.), NS, Can. 184/E3
La Haye-du-Puits, Fr. 82/D2
La Haye-Pesnel, Fr. 82/D3
La Higuera, Chile 212/B4
La Honda, Ca, US 193/K12
La Horqueta, Ven. 205/F3
La Horqueta, Ven. 205/F2
La Horquilla, Bol. 209/E4
La Houssaye-en-Brie, Fr. 56/L5
La Huaca, Peru 208/A2
La Huacana, Mex. 199/E5
La Huerta, Mex. 198/D5
La Isla, Mex. 199/Q10
La Jalca, Peru 208/B2
La Jara, NM, US 175/J2
La Jara, Co, US 175/K2
La Javie, Fr. 90/C4
La Jolla Ind. Res., Ca, US 174/D4
La Joya, Bol. 212/C1
La Joya, Peru 208/D5
La Joya de los Sachas, Ecu. 204/B5
La Junta, Co, US 178/C2
La Junta, Mex. 198/D2
La Juventud (isl.), Cuba 195/J7
La Laguna, Sp. 136/A3
La Laja, Arg. 212/B4
La Léchère, Fr. 90/C1
La Leonesa, Arg. 212/E3
La Libertad, Guat. 200/D2
La Libertad, Hon. 200/E3
La Libertad, Ecu. 204/A5
La Libertad (dept.), Peru 208/B3
La Ligua, Chile 214/C2
La Línea de la Concepción, Sp. 72/C4
La Llagosta, Sp. 73/L6
La Lobería, Arg. 214/E4
La Loche, Sk, Can. 166/F3
La Loggia, It. 88/A3
La Londe-les-Maures, Fr. 90/C6
La Loupe, Fr. 83/G4
La Louvière, Belg. 81/D3
La Luisiana, Sp. 72/C4
La Machine, Fr. 70/E3
La Maddalena, It. 74/A2
La Madeleine, Fr. 80/C2
La Madera, NM, US 175/J2
La Magdalena, Col. 207/L6
La Malbaie, Qu, Can. 184/B2
La Mancha (reg.), Sp. 92/C3
La Margarita, Ven. 205/F2
La Marque, Tx, US 177/N9
La Martre (lake), NW, Can. 166/E2
La Masica, Hon. 200/E3
La Maurice NP, Qu, Can. 184/A2
La Media Luna (isls.), Hon. 201/F3
La Meije (peak), Fr. 90/C2
La Mensura (peak), Col. 204/C4
La Merca, Sp. 72/B1
La Merced, Bol. 212/C2
La Merced, Peru 208/C3
La Merced, Arg. 212/C4
La Mesa, Ca, US 192/C5
La Mesa (int'l arpt.) Hon. 200/E3
La Mesa, Ven. 204/D2
La Mesa, Col. 207/L8
La Mesa, NM, US 176/A1
La Mira, Mex. 198/E5
La Mirada, Ca, US 192/F8
La Moine (riv.), Il, US 181/J3
La Monna (peak), It. 92/C4
La Montaña (phys. reg.), Peru 203/B3
La Monte, Mo, US 179/H1
La Mota (mtn.), Tx, US 177/C3
La Motte, Fr. 82/C4
La Motte-d'Aveillans, Fr. 90/B3
La Motte-du-Caire, Fr. 90/C4
La Motte-Servolex, Fr. 90/B1
La Moure, ND, US 182/E4
La Mula, Mex. 177/B3
La Mure, Fr. 90/B3
La Negra, Arg. 214/C3
La Neuveville, Swi. 86/D3
La Nouvelle, Fr. 56/J6
La Ola, Chile 212/B3
La Orchila (isl.), Ven. 197/H5
La Orotava, Sp. 136/A3
La Oroya, Peru 208/C3
La Palma, Pan. 201/G4
La Palma, Col. 207/L7
La Palma (isl.), Sp. 133/A2
La Paloma, Uru. 215/G2
La Pampa (prov.), Arg. 214/D3
La Para, Arg. 212/D4
La Paragua, Ven. 205/F3
La Paz, Arg. 214/D2
La Paz, Arg. 212/E4
La Paz (cap.), Bol. 212/B1
La Paz (dept.), Bol. 208/D4
La Paz, Col. 204/C3
La Paz, Col. 204/C2
La Paz, Hon. 200/E3
La Paz, Mex. 198/C3
La Paz (bay), Mex. 198/C3
La Paz, Phil. 114/D3
La Paz, Uru. 215/K11
La Paz, Uru. 215/K11
La Pêche, Qu, Can. 187/H2
La Pedrera, Col. 204/D5
La Peña, Pan. 196/E6
La Peña, Col. 207/L7
La Penne-sur-Huveaune, Fr. 90/B6
La Perla, Mex. 177/B3
La Perouse (str.), Japan, Rus. 103/P5
La Petite-Raon, Fr. 86/C1
La Piedad Cavadas, Mex. 198/E4
La Pine, Or, US 172/C2
La Place, La, US 190/C2
La Plant, SD, US 180/D1
La Plata, Arg. 215/K11
La Plata, Col. 204/C4
La Plata (riv.), Co, US 175/H2
La Plata, Md, US 189/J1
La Plata, Mo, US 181/H3
La Pobla de Lillet, Sp. 73/F1
La Pocatière, Qu, Can. 184/B2
La Poile, Nf, Can. 185/H2
La Pola de Gordón, Sp. 72/C1
La Porte, In, US 186/C4
La Porte, Tx, US 177/M9
La Porte City, Ia, US 181/H2
La Posta Ind. Res., Ca, US 174/D4
La Prairie (co.), Qu, Can. 185/N7
La Prairie, Qu, Can. 185/P7
La Pryor, Tx, US 177/E3
La Puebla, Sp. 73/G3
La Puebla de Almoradiel, Sp. 72/D3
La Puebla de Cazalla, Sp. 72/C4
La Puebla de Montalbán, Sp. 72/C3
La Puente, Ca, US 192/G7
La Puntilla (pt.), Ecu. 204/A5
La Quebrada, Ven. 204/D2
La Queue-les-Yvelines, Fr. 80/A6
La Quiaca, Arg. 212/C2
La Rambla, Sp. 72/C4
La Ravoire, Fr. 90/B1
La Reforma, Arg. 214/D3
La Reforma, Mex. 198/C3
La Rinconada, Sp. 72/C4
La Rioja (dist.), Sp. 72/C3
La Rioja (prov.), Arg. 212/C4
La Rioja, Arg. 212/C4
La Robla, Sp. 72/C1
La Roche, Swi. 86/D4
La Roche-Bernard, Fr. 82/C5
La Roche-de-Glun, Fr. 90/A3
La Roche-de-Rame, Fr. 90/C3
La Roche-en-ardenne, Belg. 81/E3
La Roche-Maurice, Fr. 82/A4
La Roche-sur-Foron, Fr. 86/C5
La Roche-sur-Yon, Fr. 70/C3
La Rochelle, Fr. 70/C3
La Rochette, Fr. 90/C2
La Roda, Sp. 72/D3
La Romana, DRep. 197/H4
La Ronge, Sk, Can. 166/F3
La Roque-d'Anthéron, Fr. 90/B5
La Rotta, It. 89/D6
La Rúa, Sp. 72/B1
La Rumorosa, Mex. 174/D4
La Sabana, Ven. 207/P7
La Sal, Ut, US 175/H1
La Sal (mts.), Ut, US 173/J4
La Salle, Mb, Can. 182/F3
La Salle, Co, US 180/B3
La Salle, Il, US 181/K3
La Salle les Alpes, Fr. 90/C3
La Salute di Livenza, It. 89/F2
La Sara, Arg. 215/C7
La Sarraz, Swi. 86/C4
La Sarre, Qu, Can. 167/J4
La Saussaye, Fr. 83/F2
La Sauvette (peak), Fr. 90/C6
La Serena, Chile 212/B4
La Servelle (peak), Fr. 90/B3
La Seu d'Urgell, Sp. 73/F1
La Seyne-sur-Mer, Fr. 90/B6
La Sierpe, Cuba 201/G1
La Sila (mts.), It. 74/E3
La Silueta (peak), Chile 215/B7
La Solana, Sp. 72/D3
La Souterraine, Fr. 70/D3
La Spezia, It. 88/C5
La Spezia (prov.), It. 88/C4
La Sûre (peak), Fr. 90/B2
La Suze-sur-Sarthe, Fr. 83/F5
La Tabatière, Qu, Can. 167/L3
La Tebaida, Col. 207/K8
La Teste, Fr. 70/C4
La Tête à l'Ane (peak), Fr. 86/C6
La Thuile, It. 90/C1
La Tigra, PN, Hon. 200/E3
La Toma, Arg. 214/D2
La Tortue (isl.), Haiti 201/H1
La Tortuga (isl.), Ven. 205/E2
La Tour-d'Aigues, Fr. 90/B5
La Tour-de-Peilz, Swi. 86/C5
La Tour-de-Trême, Swi. 86/D4
La Tour-du-Pin, Fr. 90/B1
La Tranca, Arg. 214/D2
La Tremblade, Fr. 70/C4
La Trinidad, Phil. 114/C1
La Trinitaria, Mex. 200/C2
La Trinité, Fr. 90/D5
La Trinité-des-Monts, Qu, Can. 184/C1
La Trinité-Porhoët, Fr. 82/C4
La Troncal, Ecu. 204/B5
La Troya (riv.), Arg. 212/B4
La Turballe, Fr. 82/C6
La Turbie, Fr. 88/H8
La Uníon, Ven. 204/E2
La Unión, ESal. 200/E3
La Unión, Col. 204/B4
La Unión, Sp. 73/E4
La Unión, Chile 214/B4
La Unión, Col. 207/K7
La Unión, Bol. 209/F4
La Unión, Peru 208/A2
La Unión, Peru 208/B3
La Union, NM, US 176/A2
La Unión, Mex. 199/E5
La Urbana, Ven. 205/E3
La Vale, Md, US 187/G5
La Valette-du-Var, Fr. 90/B6
La Vecilla, Sp. 72/C1
La Vega, Col. 207/L8
La Vergne, Tn, US 188/D2
La Verkin, Ut, US 175/F2
La Verna, It. 89/E6
La Verne, Ca, US 192/C2
La Vernia, Tx, US 177/E3
La Verrière, Fr. 56/H5
La Victoria, Col. 204/B4
La Victoria, Ven. 204/D3
La Victoria, Col. 207/J8
La Victoria, Ven. 207/N7
La Vieille-Lyre, Fr. 83/F3
La Vieja (riv.), Col. 207/K8
La Virginia, Col. 207/K8
La Voulte-sur-Rhône, Fr. 90/A3
La Vraie-Croix, Fr. 82/C5
La Wantzenau, Fr. 81/G6
Laa an der Thaya, Aus. 71/M2
Laaber, Ger. 85/E4
Laage, Ger. 66/E5
Laakirchen, Aus. 85/G7
Laarne, Belg. 80/C1
Laas (Lasa), It. 87/G4
Laas Caanood, Som. 144/C3
Laas Dhaareed, Som. 144/C3
Laas Qoray, Som. 144/D3
Laatzen, Ger. 79/G4
Laax, Swi. 87/F4
Labadieville, La, US 190/C3
Labang, Malay. 116/D3
Labasheeda, Ire. 58/A4
Labason, Phil. 114/C3
L'Abbaye, Swi. 86/C4
Labdah (Leptis Magna) (ruin), Libya 71/G3
Labé (pol. reg.), Gui. 140/B4
Labé, Gui. 140/B4
Labe (Elbe) (riv.), Czh., Ger. 69/H2
Labelle, Qu, Can. 187/J1
Laberweinting, Ger. 85/F5
Labian (cape), Malay. 114/B4
Labin, Cro. 71/L4
Labinsk, Rus. 99/L5
Labis, Malay. 115/C2
Labná (ruin), Mex. 200/D1
Labo, Phil. 114/C2
Laborde, Arg. 214/E2
Laborec (riv.), Slvk. 69/L4
Labota, Indo. 117/F4
Labouglé, Arg. 212/E4
Laboulaye, Arg. 214/E2
Labrador (reg.), Can. 165/L4
Labrador (sea), Can., NAm 165/M4
Labrador City, Nf, Can. 167/K3
Lábrea, Braz. 209/E2
Labrieville, Qu, Can. 184/C1
Labruguière, Fr. 70/E5
Labry, Fr. 81/E5
Labuan (terr.), Bru. 114/A4
Labuhan, Indo. 115/D3
Labuhanbajo, Indo. 117/E5
Labuhanbilik, Indo. 115/C2
Labuhanhaji, Indo. 115/B2
Labuhanmaringgai, Indo. 115/D3
Labuhanruku, Indo. 115/B2
Labuk (riv.), Malay. 117/E2
Labuk (bay), Malay. 117/E2
Labuništa, FYROM 75/G2
Labutta, Myan. 112/B5
Läby, Swe. 65/A1
Labytnangi, Rus. 100/G3
Laç, Alb. 75/F2
Lac (pref.), Chad 142/B2
Lac Afwein (riv.), Kenya 145/B1
Lac Court Oreilles Ind. Res., Wi, US 183/J5
Lac du Bonnet, Mb, Can. 182/F2
Lac du Flambeau, Wi, US 183/K5
Lac du Flambeau Ind. Res., Wi, US 183/K4
Lac La Biche, Ab, Can. 166/E3
Lac La Hache, BC, Can. 170/D2
Lac la Martre, NW, Can. 166/E2
Lac Pelletier, Sk, Can. 171/L3
Lac Seul, On, Can. 183/H2
Lac Son, Viet. 120/D1
Lac Thien, Viet. 116/C1
Lac-Alouette, Qu, Can. 185/N6
Lac-au-Saumon, Qu, Can. 184/D1
Lac-aux-Sables, Qu, Can. 184/A2
Lac-Beauport, Qu, Can. 184/B2
Lac-Bouchette, Qu, Can. 184/A1
Lac-Brome, Qu, Can. 187/K2
Lac-des-Aigles, Qu, Can. 184/C2
Lac-Drolet, Qu, Can. 184/B3
Lac-du-Cerf, Qu, Can. 187/J1
Lac-Édouard, Qu, Can. 184/A2
Lac-Etchemin, Qu, Can. 184/B2
Lac-Mégantic, Qu, Can. 184/B3
Lacadena, Sk, Can. 171/K2
L'Acadie, Qu, Can. 185/P7
Lacantum (riv.), Mex. 200/D2
Lacassine Nat'l Wild. Ref., La, US 177/H2
Lacaune, Fr. 70/E5
Laccadive (sea), Asia 118/B5
Lacchiarella, It. 88/C3
Lacco Ameno, It. 92/C6
Lacepede (bay), Austl. 153/C4
Lacerdónia, Moz. 149/G3
Laces (Latsch), It. 87/G4
Lacey, Ar, US 179/J4
Lacey, Wa, US 170/C4
Lach Bissigh (riv.), Som. 145/C1
Lach Dera (riv.), Som. 145/C1
Lacha (lake), Rus. 94/H3
Lachapelle-aux-Pots, Fr. 80/A5
Lachay (pt.), Peru 208/B3
Lachen, Swi. 87/E3
Lachenaie, Qu, Can. 185/N6
Lachendorf, Ger. 79/H3
Lachhmangarh, India 122/A2
Lāchi, Pak. 124/A3
Lachine, Qu, Can. 185/N7
Lachlan (riv.), Austl. 153/D4
Lachte (riv.), Ger. 79/H3
Lachung, India 123/G2
Lachute, Qu, Can. 187/J2
Laçin, Azer. 129/F2
Lackawanna, NY, US 186/V10
Lackawanna (co.), Pa, US 194/C1
Lackland (A.F.B.), Tx, US 177/E3
Läckö, Swe. 66/E2
Laclubar, Indo. 154/B2
Lacob ti-Duyong (mt.), Phil. 113/J5
Lacock, Eng, UK 62/D4
Lacomb, Or, US 172/B1
Lacombe, La, US 190/D2
Lacombe, Ab, Can. 171/H1
Lacon, Il, US 181/K3
Laconia, NH, US 187/L3
Lacoochee, Fl, US 190/L7
Lacreek Nat'l Wild. Ref., SD, US 180/D2
Lacroix-Saint-Ouen, Fr. 80/B5
Lacross (isl.), Austl. 154/C3
Lacy-Lakeview, Tx, US 177/F2
Ladakh (mts.), India 127/L2
Ladário, Braz. 212/E1
Ladbergen, Ger. 79/E4
Ladder (hills), Sc, UK 59/C2
Ladder (cr.), Ks, Co, US 180/D4
Laddonia, Mo, US 181/J4
Lądek-Zdrój, Pol. 69/J3
Ladenburg, Ger. 84/B4
Ladera Heights, Ca, US 192/F8
Ladismith, SAfr. 150/C4
Ladispoli, It. 91/B4
Lado, Sudan 142/F4
Ladoga, Rus. 94/T7
Ladoga (lake), Rus. 216/D
Ladoix-Serrigny, Fr. 86/A3
Ladozhskaya, Rus. 99/K5
Ladozhskoye Ozero, Rus. 94/T6
Ladrillero (mtn.), Chile 215/B7
Ladson, SC, US 189/G4
Ladva-Vetka, Rus. 94/G3
Lādwa, India 124/D5
Lady Barron, Austl. 159/D5
Lady Isle (isl.), Sc, UK 59/B5
Lady Lake, Sk, Can. 182/C1
Lady Lake, Fl, US 191/H3
Ladybank, Sc, UK 59/C4
Ladybower (res.), Eng, UK 61/G5
Ladybrand, SAfr. 150/D3
Ladysmith, Wi, US 183/J5
Ladysmith, BC, Can. 170/C3
Ladysmith, SAfr. 151/E3
Ladyville, Belz. 199/H5
Ladyzhyn, Ukr. 98/E3
Lae (isl.), Mrsh. 162/F4
Lae, Thai. 120/C2
Laer, Ger. 79/E4
Lafayette, Al, US 188/E4
Lafayette, Ca, US 193/K11
Lafayette, Co, US 180/B4
Lafayette, In, US 186/C4
Lafayette, La, US 190/B2
Lafayette, NJ, US 194/D1
Lafayette, Or, US 170/C5
Lafayette, Tn, US 188/D2
Lafe, Ar, US 188/B2
Lafia, Nga. 141/H4
Lafiagi, Nga. 141/G4
Lafitte, La, US 190/C3
Lafleche, Sk, Can. 171/L3
Lafnitz (riv.), Aus. 71/L3
Lafontaine, Qu, Can. 185/M6
Lāfūl, India 119/F6
Laga (mts.), It. 92/C2
Laga Balal (riv.), Kenya 142/H5
Laga Mado Gali (riv.), Kenya 145/B1
Laga Merille (riv.), Kenya 145/B1
Lagacéville, NB, Can. 184/E2
Lagamar, Braz. 213/H1
Lagan, Swe. 66/E3
Lagan (riv.), NI, UK 60/B3
Lagan (riv.), Swe. 66/E3
Lagarto, Braz. 211/F1
Lagawe, Phil. 114/C1
Lagbo, D.R. Congo 147/G2
Lagdo (lake), Camr. 142/B3
Lage, Ger. 79/F5
Lage Vaart (canal), Neth. 78/C4
Lågen (riv.), Nor. 66/C1
Lages, Braz. 213/G3
Laggan, Sc, UK 59/B2
Laggan (lake), Sc, UK 59/B3
Lagh Bogal (riv.), Kenya 144/A5
Lagh Bor (riv.), Kenya 144/A5
Lagh Kutulo (riv.), Kenya 145/C1
Laghouat (wilaya), Alg. 137/F2
Laghouat, Alg. 137/F2
Laghtnafrankee (peak), Ire. 58/C5
Lagnieu, Fr. 86/B6
Lagnö (isl.), Swe. 65/B1
Lagny-le-Sec, Fr. 56/L4
Lagny-sur-Marne, Fr. 56/L5
Lago Cardiel, Arg. 215/C6
Lago da Pedra, Braz. 207/E4
Lago de Atitlán, PN, Guat. 200/D3
Lago Piratuba, Reserva Biológica do, Bol. 206/B4
Lago Posadas, Arg. 215/C5
Lago Puelo, PN, Arg. 214/C4
Lago Verde, Chile 214/C5
Lago Viedma, Arg. 215/B6
Lagoa, Port. 72/A4
Lagoa da Prata, Braz. 213/H2
Lagoa Formosa, Braz. 210/D3
Lagoa Vermelha, Braz. 213/G4
Lagoda (lake), Rus. 64/J3
Lagodekhi, Geo. 97/H4
Lagonegro, It. 74/D2
Lagord, Fr. 70/C3
Lagos, Nga. 141/F5
Lagos (state), Nga. 141/F5
Lagos, Port. 72/A4
Lagos de Moreno, Mex. 198/E4
Lagosanto, It. 89/F4
Lagrange, In, US 186/D4
Laguardia, Sp. 70/B5
Laguna (cr.), Ca, US 193/M10
Laguna, NM, US 175/J3
Laguna (dam), Az, US 174/E4
Laguna (mts.), Ca, US 174/D4
Laguna (bay), Phil. 114/F7
Laguna, Braz. 213/G4
Laguna Atascosa NWR, Tx, US 177/F4
Laguna Beach, Fl, US 191/F2
Laguna Beach, Ca, US 192/C3
Laguna Blanca, PN, Arg 214/C3
Laguna de Duero, Sp. 72/C2
Laguna de la Restinga, PN, Ven. 205/E2
Laguna del Laja, PN, Chile 214/C3
Laguna del Rey, Mex. 198/E3
Laguna Grande, Arg. 214/D4
Laguna Grande, Arg. 215/C6
Laguna Hills, Ca, US 192/C3
Laguna Ind. Res., NM, US 175/J3
Laguna Larga, Arg. 212/D4
Laguna Paiva, Arg. 212/D4
Laguna San Rafael, PN, Chile 214/B5
Laguna Verde, Chile 214/N8
Laguna Yema, Arg. 212/D3
Lagunas, Chile 212/B2
Lagunas, Peru 208/B2
Lagunas, Peru 208/C2
Lagunas de Chacahua, PN, Mex. 200/B2
Lagunas de Montebello, Mex. 196/C4
Lagunas de Zempoala, PN, Mex. 199/Q10
Lagundo (Algund), It. 87/H4
Lagunetas, Ven. 204/D2
Lagunillas, Ven. 204/D2
Lagunillas, Chile 214/N8
Lagunillas, Bol. 212/D1
Laguntara (lag.), Hon. 201/E3
Lagushao, China 107/C2
Lahad Datu, Malay. 114/B4
Lahaina, Hi, US 168/S9
Lahan Sai, Thai. 120/C3
Lahār, India 122/B2
Lāharpur, India 122/C2
Lahat, Indo. 115/C3
Laheria Sarāi, India 123/E2
Lahewa, Indo. 115/B2
Laḩij, Yem. 144/C2
Lāhījān, Iran 129/G2
Lahn (riv.), Ger. 68/E3
Lahnstein, Ger. 81/G3
Laholm, Swe. 66/E3
Laholms (bay), Den. 66/F3
Lahoma, Ok, US 179/E2
Lahontan (res.), Nv, US 172/D4
Lahontan (dam), Nv, US 172/D4
Lahore, Pak. 124/C4
Lahore (int'l arpt.), Pak. 124/C4
Lahr, Ger. 86/D1
Lāhrūd, Iran 129/F2
Lahti, Fin. 67/L1
Laï, Chad 142/C3
Lai Chau, Viet. 120/C1
Lai-hka, Myan. 120/B1
Laiagam, PNG 155/F1
Lai'an, China 106/D4
Laichingen, Ger. 84/C5
Laidon (lake), Sc, UK 59/B3
Laifeng Tujiazu Zizhixian, China 113/F2
L'Aigle, Fr. 83/F3
Laigueglia, It. 88/B6
Laihia, Fin. 64/G3
Lailly-en-Val, Fr. 83/G5
Lainate, It. 88/C2
Laindon, Eng, UK 56/E2
Laingsburg, SAfr. 150/C4
Lainioälven (riv.), Swe. 64/G1
Laird, Sk, Can. 171/L1
Lais, Indo. 115/C3
Lais, Phil. 114/D4
Laisamis, Kenya 145/B1
Laishevo, Rus. 95/L5
Laishui, China 106/G7
Laisvall, Swe. 64/F2
Laitila, Fin. 67/J1
Laives (Leifers), It. 87/H5
Laiwu, China 106/D3
Laixi, China 106/E3
Laiyang, China 106/E3
Laiyuan, China 106/C3
Laizhou (bay), China 106/D3
Laja (lake), Chile 214/C3
Lajas, Peru 208/B2
Lajatico, It. 89/D7
Laje, Braz. 211/E1
Lajeado, Braz. 213/G4
Lajedo, Braz. 207/G5
Lajes, Azor., Port. 73/S12
Lajes (int'l arpt.), Azor., Port. 73/S12
Lajes, Braz. 207/G4
Lajing (pass), Nepal 123/E1
Lajord, Sk, Can. 182/B2
Lajosmizse, Hun. 76/D2
Lāju, India 112/B3
Lajwāna Kalān, India 124/D5
Lakamané, Mali 140/C3
Lakato, Madg. 152/J7
Lake (co.), Fl, US 190/M6
Lake (co.), Il, US 193/P15
Lake Mason NWR, Mt, US 171/K4
Lake Woodruff Nat'l Wild. Ref., Fl, US 191/H3
Lake Alfred, Fl, US 190/M7
Lake Alice NWR, ND, US 182/E3
Lake Alma, Sk, Can. 182/B3
Lake Alpine, Ca, US 172/C4
Lake Amadeus Abor. Land, Austl. 157/F3
Lake Andes, SD, US 180/E2
Lake Andes Nat'l Wild. Ref., SD, US 180/E2
Lake Ann, Mi, US 186/D2
Lake Arrowhead, Ca, US 192/C2
Lake Arthur, NM, US 178/B4
Lake Arthur, La, US 190/B2
Lake Barrington, Il, US 193/P15
Lake Beulah, Wi, US 193/P14
Lake Bluff, Il, US 193/Q15
Lake Boga, Austl. 158/B2
Lake Bolac, Austl. 158/B3
Lake Buena Vista, Fl, US 190/M7
Lake Butler, Fl, US 191/G2
Lake Cargelligo, Austl. 159/C1
Lake Catherine, Il, US 193/P15
Lake Charles, La, US 190/B2
Lake City, Ar, US 188/B3
Lake City, Ca, US 172/C3
Lake City, Co, US 175/J1
Lake City, Fl, US 191/G2
Lake City, Ga, US 189/M7
Lake City, Ia, US 181/G2
Lake City, Mi, US 186/D2
Lake City, Mn, US 181/H1
Lake City, Pa, US 186/F3
Lake City, SC, US 189/H4
Lake City, SD, US 182/F5
Lake City, Tn, US 188/E2
Lake Clark NP, Ak, US 168/X12
Lake Clarke Shores, Fl, US 190/P9
Lake Conjola, Austl. 159/E2
Lake Cowichan, BC, Can. 170/B3
Lake Creek (riv.), Ut, US 173/G4
Lake Crystal, Mn, US 181/G1
Lake Dallas, Tx, US 176/K6
Lake Delton, Wi, US 181/K2
Lake District NP, Eng, UK 61/E2
Lake Elmo, Mn, US 183/Q7
Lake Elsinore, Ca, US 192/C3
Lake Fenton, Mi, US 186/E3
Lake Fern, Fl, US 190/K7
Lake Forest, Il, US 193/Q15
Lake Forest Park, Wa, US 193/C2
Lake Fork (riv.), Ut, US 173/H3
Lake Fork, Id, US 172/E1
Lake Garfield, Fl, US 190/M8
Lake Geneva, Wi, US 186/B3
Lake George, Co, US 178/B1
Lake George, NY, US 187/K3
Lake George, Mi, US 186/D3
Lake George NWR, ND, US 182/E4
Lake Grace, Austl. 156/C5
Lake Hamilton, Ar, US 179/H3
Lake Hamilton, Fl, US 190/M7
Lake Havasu City, Az, US 174/E3
Lake Helen, Fl, US 191/H3
Lake Hughes, Ca, US 174/C3
Lake Ilo NWR, ND, US 182/C4
Lake in the Hills, Il, US 193/P15
Lake Isom Nat'l Wild. Ref., Tn, US 188/C2
Lake Jackson, Tx, US 176/G3
Lake Jem, Fl, US 190/M6
Lake King, Austl. 156/C5
Lake Lenore, Sk, Can. 171/M1
Lake Linden, Mi, US 183/K4
Lake Lotawana, Mo, US 179/G1
Lake Louise, Ab, Can. 170/F2
Lake Lucerne, Fl, US 190/P11
Lake Macleod, Austl. 156/B3
Lake Malawi NP, Malw. 149/G2
Lake Mary, Fl, US 190/N6
Lake Mburo NP, Ugan. 147/G3
Lake McDonald, Mt, US 171/H3
Lake Mead Nat'l Rec. Area, Az, Nv, US 174/E2
Lake Meredith Nat'l Rec. Area, Tx, US 178/D3
Lake Mills, Ia, US 181/H2
Lake Mills, Wi, US 181/K2
Lake Mohawk, NJ, US 194/D1
Lake Monroe, Fl, US 190/N6
Lake Montezuma, Az, US 175/G3
Lake Murray, PNG 155/F1
Lake Nakuru NP, Kenya 145/B2
Lake Nash, Austl. 157/H2
Lake Nettie Nat'l Wild. Ref., ND, US 182/D4
Lake Odessa, Mi, US 186/D3
Lake Orion, Mi, US 193/F6
Lake Oswego, Or, US 172/B1
Lake Panasoffkee, Fl, US 190/L6
Lake Park, Mn, US 182/F4
Lake Park, Ga, US 191/G2
Lake Park, Ia, US 181/G2
Lake Park, Fl, US 190/P9
Lake Placid, NY, US 187/K2
Lake Placid, Fl, US 191/H4
Lake Pleasant, NY, US 187/J3
Lake Preston, SD, US 181/F1
Lake Ronkonkoma, NY, US 195/E2
Lake Saint Croix Beach, Mn, US 183/Q7
Lake Shore, Mn, US 183/G4
Lake Shore, Md, US 194/B5
Lake Station, In, US 193/R16
Lake Stevens, Wa, US 170/C3
Lake Success, NY, US 195/L8
Lake Tanglewood, Tx, US 178/D3
Lake Thibadeau Nat'l Wild. Ref., Mt, US 171/K3
Lake Tomahawk, Wi, US 183/K5
Lake Toxaway, NC, US 189/F3
Lake View, Ar, US 179/J3
Lake View, Ia, US 181/G2
Lake Villa, Il, US 193/P15
Lake Waccamaw, NC, US 189/H3
Lake Wales, Fl, US 190/M8
Lake Way, Austl. 156/D3
Lake Worth, Fl, US 190/P9
Lake Zahl Nat'l Wild. Ref., ND, US 182/C3
Lake Zurich, Il, US 193/P15
Lakefield, On, Can. 187/G2
Lakefield, Mn, US 181/G2
Lakefield NP, Austl. 155/F3
Lakehills, Tx, US 176/E3
Lakehurst, NJ, US 194/D3
Lakehurst Nav. Air Eng. Ctr., NJ, US 194/D3
Lakeland, Ga, US 191/G2
Lakeland, La, US 190/C2
Lakeland, Fl, US 190/M7
Lakeland, Mn, US 183/Q7
Lakeland Village, Ca, US 192/C3
Lakemoor, Il, US 193/P15
Lakenheath, Eng, UK 63/G2
Lakeport, Ca, US 172/B4
Lakeport, Tx, US 177/G1
Lakes Entrance, Austl. 159/D3
Lakesfjorden (inlet), Nor. 64/H1
Lakeside, Ca, US 192/D5
Lakeside, Mt, US 170/G3
Lakeside, Ne, US 180/C2
Lakeside, Or, US 172/A2
Lakeside, Ut, US 173/G3
Lakeside, Va, US 189/J2
Laketown, Ut, US 173/H3
Lakeview, Ar, US 179/H2
Lakeview, Ca, US 192/C3
Lakeview, Ga, US 188/E3
Lakeview, Mi, US 186/D3
Lakeview, Mt, US 173/H1
Lakeview, Or, US 172/C2
Lakeview, Tx, US 178/D3
Lakeview Estates, Ga, US 189/M7
Lakeville (lake), Mi, US 193/F6
Lakeville, Mn, US 181/H1
Lakeway, Tx, US 177/F2
Lakewood, Ca, US 192/F8
Lakewood, Co, US 180/B4
Lakewood, Il, US 193/P15
Lakewood, NJ, US 194/D3
Lakewood, NY, US 187/G3
Lakewood, Oh, US 186/F4
Lakewood, Wa, US 170/C3
Lakewood, Wi, US 183/K5
Lakhāsar, India 124/B5
Lakhemaa NP, Est. 67/L2
Lakhīmpur, India 122/C2
Lakhnādon, India 122/B4
Lakhpat, India 127/J4
Lakhva, Bela. 98/D1
Laki (vol.), Ice. 64/N7
Lakin, Ks, US 178/D2
Lakki, Pak 124/A3
Lakkíon, Gre. 93/K3
Lakonía (gulf), Gre. 93/J3
Lakor (isl.), Indo. 154/C2
Lakota, ND, US 182/E3
Lakota, C.d'Iv. 140/D5
Lakshadweep (isls.), India 103/F8
Lakshadweep (terr.), India 118/B6
Lākshām, Bang. 123/H4
Lal Suhanra NP, Pak. 124/B5
Lala, Phil. 114/C4
Lāla Mūsa, Pak. 124/B3
Lalago, Tanz. 145/A2
Lālajīn, Iran 129/G3
Lalana (riv.), Madg. 152/H8
Lalang (riv.), Indo. 116/B4
Lâlapaşa, Turk. 77/H5
Lalara, Gabon 146/B2
Lalauli, India 122/C3
L'Albaron (peak), Fr. 90/D2
Lālbhitti, Nepal 123/E2
Lālganj, India 123/E3
Lālgola, India 123/G3
Lālī, Iran 129/G3
Lāliān, Pak. 124/B4
Lalībela, Eth. 144/A2
Laliki, Indo. 154/B1
Lalín, Sp. 72/A1
Lalin (riv.), China 105/K3
Lalinde, Fr. 70/D4
Lalitpur, India 122/B3
Lalitpur (Pāṭan), Nepal 123/E2
Lalla Rookh Abor. Land, Austl. 156/C2
Lālmanir Hāt, Bang. 123/G3
Lālpur, Bang. 123/G3
Lalyo, Sudan 142/F4
Lam Pao (res.), Thai. 112/D5
Lāma, Bang. 119/F3
Lamachan (peak), Sc, UK 60/D1
Lamadi, China 119/G2
Lamadrid, Mex. 177/D4
Lamag, Malay. 114/B4
Lamakera, Indo. 154/A2
Lamaline, Nf, Can. 185/K2
Lamanai (ruin), Belz. 200/D2
Lamandau (riv.), Indo. 116/D4
Lamar, Ar, US 179/H3
Lamar, Mo, US 179/G2
Lamar, Co, US 178/C1
Lamar, SC, US 189/G3
Lamarche, Fr. 86/B1
Lamarche-sur-Saône, Fr. 86/B3
Lamarque, Arg. 214/D3
Lamas, Peru 208/B2
Lamastre, Fr. 90/A3
Lāmayūrū, India 124/D2
Lambach, Aus. 85/G6
Lamballe, Fr. 82/C4
Lambaré, Par. 212/E3
Lambaréné, Gabon 146/B3
Lambari, Braz. 211/L6
Lambasa, Fiji 163/Z17
Lambay (isl.), Ire. 60/B5
Lambayeque (dept.), Peru 208/A2
Lambayeque, Peru 208/B2
Lambé Coba (riv.), Mali 140/C3
Lambeg, NI, UK 60/B3
Lambert, Ms, US 188/B3
Lambert-St. Louis (int'l arpt.), Mo, US 181/J4
Lamberton, Mn, US 181/G1
Lambert's Bay, SAfr. 150/B4
Lambertville, Mi, US 186/E4
Lambertville, NJ, US 194/D3
Lambesc, Fr. 90/B5
Lambeth (bor.), Eng, UK 56/C2
Lambourn, Eng, UK 63/E3
Lambrama, Peru 208/C4
Lambrecht, Ger. 84/B4
Lambro (riv.), It. 88/C2
Lambsburg, Va, US 189/G2
Lambsheim, Ger. 84/B3
Lambton, Qu, Can. 184/B3
Lambton (co.), On, Can. 193/H6
Lame Deer, Mt, US 171/L5
Lamego, Port. 72/B2
Lamentin (int'l arpt.), Fr. 197/N9
Lamèque, NB, Can. 184/E2
Lameroo, Austl. 157/J5
Lamesa, Tx, US 176/D1
Lamía, Gre. 75/H3
Lamine (riv.), Mo, US 179/H1
Lamington (riv.), NJ, US 194/D2
Lamington NP, Austl. 160/D5
Lamitan, Phil. 114/C4
Lamlash, Sc, UK 59/A5
Lamma (isl.), China 113/L8
Lammefjord (inlet), Den. 65/H7
Lammermuir (hills), Sc, UK 59/D5
Lammhult, Swe. 66/F3
Lammi, Fin. 67/L1
Lamming Mills, BC, Can. 170/D1
Lamoille, Nv, US 172/F3
Lamon (bay), Phil. 114/C2
Lamona, Wa, US 170/E4
Lamone (riv.), It. 71/J4
Lamongan, Indo. 115/F3
Lamoni, Ia, US 181/H3
Lamont, Ok, US 179/F2
Lamont, Fl, US 191/G2
Lamont, Ca, US 174/C3
Lamorlaye, Fr. 56/K4
Lamotrek (isl.), Micr. 162/D4
Lamotte-Beuvron, Fr. 83/H5
Lampa, Chile 214/N8
Lampa, Peru 208/D4
Lampang, Thai. 120/B2
Lampasas, Tx, US 177/E2
Lampasas (riv.), Tx, US 199/F2
Lampaul-Plouarzel, Fr. 82/A4
Lampazos de Naranjo, Mex. 177/D4
Lampe, Mo, US 179/H2
Lampedusa, It. 74/C5
Lampedusa (isl.), It. 55/F5
Lampertheim, Ger. 84/B3
Lampeter, Wal, UK 62/B2
Lampeter, Pa, US 194/B4
Lamphey, Wal, UK 62/B3
Lamphun, Thai. 120/B2
Lampman, Sk, Can. 182/C3
Lamporecchio, It. 89/D6
Lampson, Wi, US 183/J5
Lampung (prov.), Indo. 115/D4
Lamstedt, Ger. 79/G1
Lamu, Kenya 145/C2
Lamu (isl.), Kenya 145/C2
Lamud, Peru 208/B2
Lamwa (peak), Ugan. 142/G5
Lamy, NM, US 178/B3
Lan (isl.), Tai. 113/J4
Lan Sang NP, Thai. 120/B2
Lana, It. 87/H4
Lana, Río de la (riv.), Mex. 200/C2
Lanai (isl.), Hi, US 163/K2
Lanai City, Hi, US 168/S9
Lanaken, Belg. 81/E2
Lanao (lake), Phil. 114/D4
Lanark, Sc, UK 59/C5
Lanark, Il, US 181/K2
Lanas Village, Malay. 114/B4
Lanba, China 112/E3
Lanbi (isl.), Myan. 119/G5
Lancang (riv.), China 112/C2
Lancang (Mekong) (riv.), China 104/D5
Lancashire (plain), Eng, UK 61/E4
Lancashire (co.), Eng, UK 61/F4
Lancaster (sound), Nun, Can. 167/H1
Lancaster, Eng, UK 61/F3
Lancaster, Ca, US 174/C3
Lancaster, Ky, US 188/E2
Lancaster, Mn, US 182/F3
Lancaster, Mo, US 181/H3
Lancaster, NH, US 187/L2
Lancaster, NY, US 186/V10
Lancaster, Oh, US 186/E5
Lancaster (arpt.), Pa, US 194/B3
Lancaster (co.), Pa, US 194/B4
Lancaster, Pa, US 194/B3
Lancaster, SC, US 189/G3
Lancaster, Tx, US 176/L7
Lancaster, Va, US 189/J2
Lancaster, Wi, US 181/J2
Lance (cr.), Wy, US 180/B2
Lance Creek, Wy, US 180/B2
Lancebranlette (peak), Fr. 90/C1
Lancefield, Austl. 159/B3
Lancelin, Austl. 156/B4
Lancenigo, It. 89/F2
Lancer, Sk, Can. 171/K2
Lanchester, Eng, UK 61/G2
Lanch'khut'i, Geo. 97/G4
Lanciano, It. 92/D3
L'Ancienne-Lorette, Qu, Can. 184/B2
Lanco, Chile 214/B3
Lançon-Provence, Fr. 90/B5
Łańcut, Pol. 69/M3
Lancy, Swi. 86/C5
Land Between The Lakes Recreation Area, Ky, US 188/C2
Land Kehdingen (reg.), Ger. 79/G1
Land O'Lakes, Fl, US 190/L7
Land O'Lakes, Wi, US 183/K4
Landau an der Isar, Ger. 85/F5
Landau in der Pfalz, Ger. 84/B4
Landeck, Aus. 87/G3
Landen, Belg. 81/E2
Lander, Wy, US 173/J2
Landerneau, Fr. 82/A4
Landes (reg.), Fr. 70/C4
Landes de Lanvaux (mts.), Fr. 70/B3
Landesbergen, Ger. 79/G3
Landi Kotal, Pak. 124/A2
Landis, Sk, Can. 171/K1
Landis Valley Museum, Pa, US 194/B3
Landisburg, Pa, US 194/A3
Landivisiau, Fr. 82/A3
Landivy, Fr. 83/D4
Landrecies, Fr. 80/C3
Landri Sales, Braz. 207/F4
Landriano, It. 88/C3
Landrum, SC, US 189/F3
Land's End (pt.), Eng, UK 62/A6
Landsberg, Ger. 87/G1
Landsborough (cr.), Austl. 160/B3
Landser, Fr. 86/D2
Landshut, Ger. 85/F5
Landskrona, Swe. 66/E4
Landsmeer, Neth. 78/B4
Landstuhl, Ger. 81/G5
Landvetter (int'l arpt.), Swe. 66/E3
Landza, Congo 146/D2
Lane (riv.), Fr. 83/F6
Lane End, Eng, UK 56/A2
Lanercost, Eng, UK 61/F2
Lanesborough, Ire. 58/C2
Lanester, Fr. 82/B5
Lanett, Al, US 188/E4
Lang, Sk, Can. 182/B3
Lang Craig (pt.), Sc, UK 59/D3
Lang Kha Tuk (peak), Thai. 120/B4
Lang Son, Viet. 113/E4
Lang Suan, Thai. 120/B4
Langadhás, Gre. 75/H2
Langádhia, Gre. 75/H4
Langano (lake), Eth. 144/A4
Langara, Indo. 117/F4
Langdon, ND, US 182/E3
Langdon, Ab, Can. 171/H2
Langdon Hills, Eng, UK 56/E2
Langeac, Fr. 70/E4
Langeais, Fr. 83/F6
Langebaanweg, SAfr. 150/L10
Langeberg (mts.), SAfr. 150/L10
Langeland (isl.), Ger. 66/D4
Langelsheim, Ger. 79/H5
Langen (lake), Nor. 64/S8
Langen, Ger. 84/B3
Langen, Ger. 79/F1
Langenaltheim, Ger. 84/D5
Langenargen, Ger. 87/F2
Langenau, Ger. 84/D5
Langenbach, Ger. 85/E6
Langenberg, Ger. 79/E6
Langenburg, Sk, Can. 182/D2
Längenfeld, Aus. 87/G3
Langenfeld, Ger. 81/F1
Langenhagen, Ger. 79/G4
Langenhorn, Ger. 66/C4
Langenlois, Aus. 69/H4
Langenpreising, Ger. 85/E6
Langenselbold, Ger. 84/C2
Langenstein, Aus. 85/H6
Langenthal, Swi. 86/D3
Langenwang, Aus. 71/L3
Langenzenn, Ger. 84/D3
Langenzersdorf, Aus. 77/N7
Langeoog (isl.), Ger. 79/E1
Langeoog, Ger. 79/E1
Langepas, Rus. 100/H3
Langerringen, Ger. 87/G1
Langeskov, Den. 66/D4
Langesund, Nor. 66/C2
Langeten (riv.), Swi. 86/D3
Langfang, China 106/H7
Langford, SD, US 182/F5
Langfurth, Ger. 84/D4
Langgam, Indo. 115/C2
Langgapayung, Indo. 115/B2
Langgar, China 104/C6
Langham, Eng, UK 63/F1
Langham, Sk, Can. 171/L1
Langhirano, It. 88/D4
Langholm, Sc, UK 61/F1
Langhorne, Pa, US 194/D3
Langjökull (glacier), Ice. 64/N7
Langkawi (isl.), Thai. 119/G6
Langkon, Malay. 114/B4
Langley, Eng, UK 56/E3
Langley, Eng, UK 56/B2
Langley, Wa, US 193/C1
Langley (A.F.B.), Va, US 189/J2
Langlois, Or, US 172/A2
Langnau im Emmental, Swi. 86/D4
Langney (pt.), Eng, UK 63/G5
Langogne, Fr. 70/E4
Langon, Fr. 82/D5
Långön (isl.), Swe. 65/A2
Langon, Fr. 70/C4
Langøya (isl.), Nor. 64/E1
Langqên (riv.), China 125/C5
Langquaid, Ger. 85/F5
Langres, Fr. 86/B2
Langres, de (plat.), Fr. 92/E1

Langru – Les

Name	Ref
Langru, China	125/C4
Langrune-sur-Mer, Fr.	83/E2
Langsa, Indo.	115/B1
Langshyttan, Swe.	66/G1
Langstaff, On, Can.	186/U8
Langston, Ok, US	179/F3
Langtang, Nga.	141/H4
Langtang, China	113/F2
Langtang Lirung (peak), Nepal	123/E1
Langtang NP, Nepal	123/E1
Langtou, China	107/C2
Langtry, Tx, US	177/D3
Languedoc (reg.), Fr.	92/D2
Languedoc-Roussillon (pol. reg.), Fr.	70/E5
Langueux, Fr.	82/C3
Languidic, Fr.	82/B5
Langwedel, Ger.	79/G3
Langweid an Lech, Ger.	84/E6
Langwies, Swi.	87/F4
Langxi, China	106/D5
Lanham-Seabrook, Md, US	194/B6
Lanigan (riv.), Sk, Can.	171/M2
Lanigan, Sk, Can.	171/M2
Lanin (vol.), Arg.	214/C3
Lanin, PN, Arg.	214/C3
Lankäpära Hät, India	123/G2
Länkäran, Azer.	129/G2
Lankin, ND, US	182/F3
Lankou, China	113/G4
Lanlacuni Bajo, Peru	208/D4
Lanmeur, Fr.	82/B3
Länna, Swe.	65/A1
Lannemezan (plat.), Fr.	70/D5
Lannemezan, Fr.	73/F1
Lanner, Eng, UK	62/A6
Lannilis, Fr.	82/A3
Lannion, Fr.	82/B3
Lannion (bay), Fr.	70/B2
Lannion (Servel) (arpt.), Fr.	82/B3
L'Annonciation, Qu, Can.	187/J1
Lanouée, Fr.	82/C4
Lans, Montagne de (mts.), Fr.	90/B3
Lansdale, Pa, US	194/C3
Lansdowne, On, Can.	187/H2
Lansdowne, India	122/B1
Lansdowne, Pa, US	194/C4
Lansdowne-Baltimore Highlands, Md, US	194/B6
L'Anse Ind. Res., Mi, US	183/K4
Lansford, ND, US	182/D3
Lansford, Pa, US	194/C2
Lanshan, China	113/G3
Lansing (cap.), Mi, US	186/D3
Lansing, Il, US	193/Q16
Lansing, Ia, US	181/J2
Lanslebourg-Mont-Cenis, Fr.	90/C2
Lanta (isl.), Thai.	119/G6
Lantana, Fl, US	190/P9
Lantau (isl.), China	113/K7
Lantau (peak), China	113/K8
Lantau (chan.), China	113/K8
Lanterne (riv.), Fr.	86/C2
Lantosque, Fr.	90/D5
Lantry, SD, US	180/D1
Lantz, NS, Can.	184/F3
Lantzville, BC, Can.	184/C3
Lanús, Arg.	215/J11
Lanusei, It.	74/A3
Lanuvio, It.	91/B4
Lanuza, Phil.	114/D3
Lanvallay, Fr.	82/C4
Lanvéoc, Fr.	82/A4
Lanxi, China	105/K2
Lanxi, China	113/H2
Lanza, Bol.	212/C1
Lanzara, It.	92/D6
Lanzarote (int'l arpt.), Sp.	136/B3
Lanzarote (isl.), Canl., Sp.	133/A2
Lanzhot, Czh.	69/J4
Lanzhou, China	104/E4
Lanzo d'Intelvi, It.	87/F6
Lanzo Torinese, It.	90/D2
Lao (mts.), China	107/D2
Lao (riv.), China	113/G2
Lao (isl.), Laos	106/E3
Lao (isl.), China	113/G2
Lao Cai, Viet.	112/D4
Lao Fu Chai, Laos	120/C1
Laoag, Phil.	114/C1
Laobian, China	107/B2
Laocheng, China	104/F5
Laodao (riv.), China	113/G2
Laodaodian, China	105/K1
Laoguanzui, China	113/G2
Laoha (riv.), China	105/H3
Laohekou, China	106/B4
Laohutun, China	107/A3
Laojun (mtn.), China	106/B4
Laoling, China	107/D2
Laon, Fr.	80/C4
Laos (ctry.)	103/K8
Laoshan, China	107/C2
Laotuding (peak), China	107/C2
Laou (riv.), Mor.	138/B2
Lapa, Braz.	213/G3
Lapalud, Fr.	90/A4
Lapataia, Arg.	215/C7
Lapeer, Mi, US	186/E3
Lapeer (co.), Mi, US	193/F6
Lapia, Nga.	141/G4
Lapinlahti, Fin.	94/E3
Lapithos, Cyp.	130/C2
Lapland (reg.), Eur.	100/B3
Lapland (reg.), Swe.	216/D
Lapoint, Ut, US	173/J3
Laporte, Pa, US	187/H4
Laporte, Co, US	180/B3
Lappeenranta, Fin.	67/N1
Lappersdorf, Ger.	85/F4
Lappi (prov.), Fin.	64/H2
Läpsehi, Iran	75/K2
Laptev (sea), Rus.	103/M2
Lapua, Fin.	94/D3
Lapundra, India	127/K3
Läpuşna, Mol.	98/E4
Lapy, Pol.	69/M2
Laqī yat al Arbaīn, Sudan	135/F4
Laquey, Mo, US	179/H2
L'Aquila, It.	92/C3
Lār, Iran	129/H5
Lara (state), Ven.	204/D2
Lara, Austl.	159/B4
Laracha, Sp.	72/A1
Larache (prov.), Mor.	138/B2
Laracor, Ire.	58/D2
Laragne-Montéglin, Fr.	90/B4
Larak (isl.), Iran	129/J5
Laramie, Wy, US	180/B3
Laramie (mts.), Wy, US	168/E3
Laramie (peak), Wy, US	180/B2
Laramie (riv.), Wy, US	180/B3
Laranjeiras do Sul, Braz.	213/F3
Larantuka, Indo.	154/A2
Larat (isl.), Indo.	117/H5
Larat, Indo.	117/H5
Larchmont, NY, US	195/K8
L'Arcouest (pt.), Fr.	82/B3
Lærdalsøyri, Nor.	66/B1
Lardier (cape), Fr.	90/C6
Lærø (isl.), Den.	66/D3
Laredo, Sp.	70/B5
Laredo, Mo, US	181/H3
Laredo, Peru	208/B3
Laredo, Tx, US	177/E4
Laredo (int'l arpt.), Tx, US	177/E4
Laredo, Sp.	78/C4
Lares, Peru	208/C4
Lares (lag.), Tx, US	177/F4
L'Argentière-la-Bessée, Fr.	90/C3
Lārkāna, Pak.	127/J3
Larkhall, Sc, UK	53/...
Larkspur, Ca, US	193/J11
Larkspur, Ca, US	187/H2
L'Arly, PN de, Burk.	141/F4
Larmor-Plage, Fr.	82/B5
Larnaca, Cyp.	130/C3
Larnaca (int'l arpt.), Cyp.	130/C3
Larnaca (dist.), Cyp.	130/C2
Larne, NI, UK	60/C2
Larne (dist.), NI, UK	60/C2
Larne Lough (inlet), NI, UK	60/C2
Larned, Ks, US	178/E1
Larochette, Lux.	81/F4
Laroque-d'Olmes, Fr.	70/D5
Larose, La, US	190/C5
Larreynaga, Nic.	203/E3
Larrimah, Austl.	154/D3
Larroque, Arg.	215/J10
Larrys (cr.), Pa, US	194/A1
Larry's River, NS, Can.	185/G3
Larsen Ice Shelf, Ant.	216/V
Larsen Sound	

Name	Ref
Las Trincheras, Ven.	205/E3
Las Varas, Mex.	198/D4
Las Varillas, Arg.	212/D4
Las Vegas, NM, US	179/F5
Las Vegas, Nv, US	174/E2
Las Vegas Nat'l Wildlife Reserve, NM, US	179/F5
Laurel Hill, Fl, US	191/E2
Layon (riv.), Fr.	70/C3
Le Rove, Fr.	90/B6
Lee Creek, Ar, US	179/G3
Leiyuanzhen, China	106/B4
Lens, Fr.	80/B3
Les Clayes-sous-Bois, Fr.	56/H5

Les Contamines-Montjoie, Fr. 86/C6
Les Diablerets (range), Swi. 86/D5
Les Échelles, Fr. 90/B2
Les Escoumins, Qu, Can. 184/C1
Les Essarts-le-Roi, Fr. 56/H5
Les Gets, Fr. 86/C5
Les Haudères, Swi. 86/D5
Les Hautes-Rivières, Fr. 81/D4
Les Herbiers, Fr. 70/C3
Les Islettes, Fr. 81/E5
Les Mées, Fr. 90/B4
Les Mesnuls, Fr. 56/H5
Les Minquier (isl.), UK 82/C3
Les Molières, Fr. 56/J6
Les Monges (peak), Fr. 90/C4
Les Mosses, Swi. 86/D5
Les Mureaux, Fr. 80/A6
Les Orres, Fr. 90/C3
Les Pennes-Mirabeau, Fr. 90/B6
Les Pieux, Fr. 82/D2
Les Ponts-de-Cé, Fr. 83/E6
Les Ponts-de-Martel, Swi. 86/C4
Les Rosiers, Fr. 83/E6
Les Rousses, Fr. 86/C5
Les Sables-d'Olonne, Fr. 70/C3
Les Salines (int'l arpt.), Alg. 138/K6
Les Sept Iles (isl.), Fr. 82/B3
Les Touches, Fr. 82/D6
Les Ulis, Fr. 56/J5
Les Verrières, Swi. 86/C4
Lesa, It. 88/B2
L'Escarène, Fr. 90/D5
Leselidze, Geo. 96/G4
Leseru, Kenya 145/A1
Leshan, China 112/D2
Leshukonskoye, Rus. 95/K2
Lésigny, Fr. 56/K5
Lesima (peak), It. 88/C4
Lesja, Nor. 64/D3
Lesjöfors, Swe. 66/F2
Lesko, Pol. 69/M4
Leskovac, Yugo. 76/E4
Leskovik, Alb. 75/G2
Leslie, Ar, US 179/H3
Leslie, Sc, UK 59/C4
Leslie, Ga, US 191/F2
Leslie, Mi, US 186/D3
Lesmahagow, Sc, UK 59/C5
Lesneven, Fr. 82/A3
Lešnica, Yugo. 76/D3
Lesnoy, Rus. 95/M4
Lesogorsk, Rus. 105/N2
Lesopil'noye, Rus. 105/L2
Lesosibirsk, Rus. 100/K4
Lesotho (ctry.) 133/E7
Lesozavodsk, Rus. 105/L2
Lesparre-Médoc, Fr. 70/C4
Lesquin (int'l arpt.), Fr. 80/C2
Lessay, Fr. 82/D2
Lesse (riv.), Belg. 68/C3
Lessebo, Swe. 66/F3
Lesser Antilles (isls.), NAm. 165/L8
Lesser Caucasus (mts.), Asia 97/G4
Lesser Slave (lake), Ab, Can. 166/E3
Lesser Sunda (isls.), Indo. 117/E5
Lessines, Belg. 80/C2
Lessley, Ms, US 190/C2
Lesterville, Mo, US 188/B2
Lesung (peak), Indo. 116/D3
Lésvos (isl.), Gre. 96/C5
Leswalt, Sc, UK 60/C2
Leszno, Pol. 69/J3
Letaba, SAfr. 149/F4
L'étang-du-Nord, Qu, Can. 185/G2
Létavértes, Hun. 76/E2
Letcher, SD, US 180/E2
Letchworth, Eng, UK 63/F3
Lete (riv.), It. 92/D5
Letegge (peak), It. 92/C1
Letham, Sc, UK 59/D3
Lethbridge, Ab, Can. 171/H3
Lethe (riv.), Ger. 79/F2
Lethem, Guy. 205/G4
Leti (isls.), Indo. 162/B5
Leti (isl.), Indo. 154/B2
Leticia, Col. 208/D2
Leting, China 106/D3
L'Etivaz, Swi. 86/D5
Letka, Rus. 95/L4
Letlhakane, Bots. 148/E4
Letlhakeng, Bots. 148/E5
Letnitsa, Bul. 77/G4
L'étoile, Fr. 80/B3
Letong, Indo. 115/D2
Letpadan, Myan. 112/B5
Letschin, Ger. 69/H2
Letsôk-Aw (isl.), Myan. 116/A1
Letterkenny, Ire. 57/Q9
Letterkenny Army Depot, Pa, US 187/H4
Lettomanoppello, It. 92/D3
Letychiv, Ukr. 98/D3
Leu Botanical Gardens, Fl, US 190/N6
Leuca, It. 75/F3
Leucate, Fr. 70/E5
Leuchars, Sc, UK 59/D4
Leuk, Swi. 86/D5
Leukerbad, Swi. 86/D5
Leun, Ger. 84/B1
Leupp, Az, US 175/G3
Leurbost, Sc, UK 57/Q7
Leusden-Zuid, Neth. 78/C4
Leuser (peak), Indo. 115/B2
Leuterhausen, Ger. 84/D4
Leutkirch im Allgäu, Ger. 87/G2
Leuven (Louvain), Belg. 81/D2
Leuze-en-Hainaut, Belg. 80/C2
Levádhia, Gre. 75/H3
Levallois-Perret, Fr. 56/J5
Levanger, Nor. 64/D3
Levanna Centrale (peak), Fr. 90/D2
Levante, Riviera di (coast), Fr. 88/C4
Levanto, It. 88/C5
Levashovo (arpt.), Rus. 94/T6
Levashovo, Rus. 94/T6
Levee No. 33 (canal), Fl, US 190/P10
Level (isl.), Chile 214/B5
Level, Md, US 194/B4
Levelland, Tx, US 178/C4
Leven, Sc, UK 59/D4
Leven, Eng, UK 61/H4
Leven (lake), Sc, UK 59/A3
Leven (riv.), Sc, UK 59/C4
Leven (lake), Sc, UK 59/C4
Leven (pt.), SAfr. 151/F2
Levens, Fr. 90/D5
Leventina (Prato), Swi. 87/E5
Leveque (cape), Austl. 154/A4
Lever (riv.), Braz. 210/C1
Leverburgh, Sc, UK 57/Q8
Levering, Mi, US 186/D2
Leverkusen, Ger. 81/F1
Lèves, Fr. 83/G4
Levice, Slvk. 76/D1
Levico Terme, It. 87/H5
Levier, Fr. 86/C4
Levin, NZ 161/C3
Lévis, Qu, Can. 184/B2
Lévis-Saint-Nom, Fr. 56/H5
Levittown, NY, US 195/L9
Levittown, Pa, US 194/D3
Levkás, Gre. 75/G3
Levkás (isl.), Gre. 93/J3
Levkímmi, Gre. 75/G3
Levkinskaya, Rus. 95/L2
Levoča, Slvk. 69/L4
Levrier (bay), Mrta. 136/A5
Levski, Bul. 77/G4
Levuka, Fiji 163/Y18
Levy (lake), Fl, US 191/G3
Lewellen, Ne, US 180/C3
Lewes, Eng, UK 63/G5
Lewin Brzeski, Pol. 69/J3
Lewis (hill), Nf, Can. 185/H1
Lewis (hills), Nf, Can. 185/H1
Lewis (isl.), Sc, UK 57/Q7
Lewis, Ks, US 178/E2
Lewis (pass), NZ 161/C3
Lewis, Co, US 175/H2
Lewis, Ia, US 181/G3
Lewis (riv.), Wa, US 170/D4
Lewis and Clark (lake), SD,Ne, US 180/E2
Lewis and Clark NWR, Wa, US 170/C4
Lewis Smith (lake), Al, US 188/D3
Lewisburg, Ky, US 188/D2
Lewisburg, WV, US 189/G2
Lewisburg, Tn, US 188/D3
Lewisburg, Pa, US 194/B2
Lewisham (bor.), Eng, UK 56/C2
Lewisport, Ky, US 188/D2
Lewisporte, Nf, Can. 185/K1
Lewiston, Me, US 184/B3
Lewiston, Ut, US 173/H3
Lewiston, NY, US 186/U9
Lewiston, Id, US 170/F4
Lewiston Woodville, NC, US 189/J2
Lewistown, Pa, US 187/H4
Lewistown, Il, US 181/J3
Lewistown, Mt, US 171/K4
Lewisville, Ar, US 179/H4
Lewisville (lake), Tx, US 177/F1
Lewisville, Tx, US 176/L6
Lewotobi (peak), Indo. 154/A2
Léwou, Gabon 146/C3
Lewvan, Sk, Can. 182/B2
Lex (riv.), Fr. 73/F1
Lexa, Ar, US 188/B3
Lexington, Ga, US 189/F4
Lexington, Il, US 181/K3
Lexington, Ky, US 188/E1
Lexington, Oh, US 186/E4
Lexington, Ok, US 179/F3
Lexington, Or, US 172/D1
Lexington, Mo, US 181/H4
Lexington, Ms, US 188/B4
Lexington, Ne, US 180/E3
Lexington, NC, US 189/G3
Lexington, SC, US 189/G4
Lexington, Tn, US 188/C3
Lexington, Tx, US 177/F2
Lexington, Va, US 189/H2
Lexington Blue Grass Army Depot, Ky, US 188/E2
Lexington Park, Md, US 189/J1
Leyburn, Eng, UK 61/G3
Leye, China 113/E3
Leyland, Eng, UK 61/F4
Leysdown, Eng, UK 63/G4
Leysin, Swi. 86/D5
Leyte (isl.), Phil. 103/M8
Leyte (gulf), Phil. 114/D3
Leyte, Phil. 114/D3
Leyton (nbrhd.), Eng, UK 56/C2
Leytron, Swi. 86/D5
Lez (riv.), Fr. 70/F4
Leżajsk, Pol. 69/M3
Lezama, Ven. 207/P8
Lèze (riv.), Fr. 90/B5
Lezhë, Alb. 75/F2
Lezhi, China 112/E2
Lézignan-Corbières, Fr. 70/E5
Lezuza, Sp. 72/D3
L'gov, Rus. 99/H2
Lhanbyrd, Sc, UK 59/C1
Lhari, China 112/B2
Lhasa (riv.), China 125/F6
Lhasa (int'l arpt.), China 125/F5
Lhatog, China 112/C2
Lhazê, China 123/F1
L'Hermitage, Fr. 82/D4
Lhokkruet, Indo. 115/A1
Lhokseumawe, Indo. 115/B1
Lhoksukon, Indo. 115/B1
Lhorong, China 112/C2
L'Hospitalet de Llobregat, Sp. 73/L7
Lhozhag, China 123/H1
Lhuntsi, Bhu. 123/G2
Lhünzê, China 119/G2
Li, Thai. 120/B2
Li (riv.), China 119/K2
Li (mtn.), China 106/B4
Li ani (riv.), Leb. 131/C2
Li Xian, China 113/F2
Lian (riv.), China 113/E3
Lian Xian, China 113/G3
Liancheng, China 113/H3
Liancourt, Fr. 80/B5
Liancourt Rocks (isl.), Asia 110/B2
Liang, Indo. 117/G4
Liangcheng, China 106/C2
Liangcun, China 113/G3
Liangdong, China 113/F4
Lianghekou, China 113/F2
Liangjia, China 107/B2
Liangjiadian, China 107/A3
Liangpran (peak), Indo. 116/D3
Liangshui, China 107/C2
Liangting, China 104/F5
Liangwan (mts.), China 112/D3
Liangzhen, China 104/F4
Liangzi (lake), China 106/C5
Lianhua (mts.), China 113/G4
Lianhua, China 119/K2
Lianjiang, China 119/K3
Lianjiang, China 113/H3
Lianjiangkou, China 113/G3
Liannan Yaozu Zizhixian, China 113/G3
Lianping, China 113/G3
Lianpu, China 113/H3
Lianshanguan, China 107/B2
Lianshui, China 106/D4
Liantang, China 120/E1
Liantang, China 113/F3
Liantang, China 106/L8
Lianyun (peak), China 113/G2
Lianyungang, China 106/D4
Liao (riv.), China 103/M5
Liaocheng, China 106/C3
Liaodong (pen.), China 107/A3
Liaodong (isls.), China 106/E3
Liaodong (gulf), China 105/J3
Liaodun, China 104/C3
Liaoning (prov.), China 105/J3
Liaoyang, China 107/B2
Liaoyuan, China 105/K3
Liaozhong, China 107/B2
Liāquatpur, Pak. 124/A5
Liard (riv.), Can. 165/E3
Liat (isl.), Indo. 115/D3
Libacao, Phil. 114/C3
Líbano, Col. 207/K8
Libau, Mb, Can. 182/F2
Libby (dam), Mt, US 170/G3
Libby, Mt, US 170/G3
Liběchovka (riv.), Czh. 85/H2
Libenge, D.R. Congo 146/D2
Liberal, Ks, US 178/D2
Liberal, Mo, US 179/G2
Libercourt, Fr. 80/C3
Liberdade, Braz. 211/M7
Liberdade (riv.), Braz. 210/B1
Liberec, Czh. 69/H3
Liberi (arpt.), It. 92/D3
Liberia, CR 200/E4
Liberia (ctry.) 133/B4
Libertad, Ven. 204/D2
Libertad, Belz. 200/D2
Libertad, Ven. 204/D2
Libertad, Uru. 215/K11
Libertad de Orituco, Ven. 207/P8
Libertador General San Martín, Arg. 212/C2
Liberty, Il, US 181/J4
Liberty, In, US 186/D5
Liberty, Ky, US 188/E2
Liberty (res.), Md, US 194/B5
Liberty, Mo, US 181/G4
Liberty, Ms, US 190/C2
Liberty, NC, US 189/H3
Liberty, NY, US 187/J4
Liberty, Ok, US 179/F4
Liberty, Sk, Can. 171/M2
Liberty, Tx, US 177/H2
Liberty, Tx, US 177/N8
Liberty (co.), Tx, US 177/N9
Liberty Grove, Md, US 194/B4
Libertyville, Al, US 191/E2
Libertyville, Il, US 193/P15
Libin, Belg. 81/E4
Libmanan, Phil. 114/C2
Libo, China 113/E3
Libobo (cape), Indo. 117/G4
Liboc (riv.), Czh. 69/G3
Libochovice, Czh. 85/H2
Liboko, D.R. Congo 147/E2
Libon, Phil. 114/C2
Librazhd, Alb. 75/G2
Libres, Mex. 199/M7
Libreville (cap.), Gabon 146/B2
Libreville (int'l arpt.), Gabon 146/B2
Libu, China 113/F4
Libya (ctry.) 133/D2
Libyan (plat.), Egypt,Libya 134/D2
Libyan (des.), Egypt,Libya 133/E2
Licantén, Chile 214/B2
Licata, It. 74/C4
Licciana Nardi, It. 88/D5
Lice, Turk. 128/E2
Lich, Ger. 84/B1
Licheng, China 106/D3
Licheng, China 106/C3
Lichfield, Eng, UK 63/E1
Lichinga, Moz. 149/G2
Lichtenau, Ger. 79/F5
Lichtenau, Ger. 84/B5
Lichtenau, Ger. 84/D4
Lichtenberg, Ger. 68/Q6
Lichtenburg, SAfr. 150/D2
Lichtenfels, Ger. 84/D2
Lichtenrade, Ger. 68/Q7
Lichtensteig, Swi. 87/F3
Lichtenvoorde, Neth. 78/D5
Lichterfelde, Ger. 68/Q7
Lichtervelde, Belg. 80/C1
Lichuan, China 113/F2
Lichuan, China 113/H3
Lick Observatory, Ca, US 193/L12
Licking, Mo, US 179/J2
Licking (riv.), Ky, US 188/E1
Licques, Fr. 80/A2
Licun, China 113/F4
Licungo (riv.), Moz. 149/H2
Lida, Bela. 67/L5
Lidao, China 107/B4
Liddell Water (riv.), Sc, UK 61/F1
Liddes, Swi. 86/D6
Liddon (gulf), NW, Can. 167/R7
Lidgerwood, ND, US 182/F4
Lidhorikion, Gre. 75/H3
Lidice, Czh. 85/H2
Lidingö, Swe. 66/H2
Lidköping, Swe. 66/E2
Lidlington, Eng, UK 63/F2
Lido, Niger 141/F3
Lido, It. 89/F3
Lido di Iesolo, It. 89/F2
Lido di Ostia, It. 91/B4
Lidzbark, Pol. 69/K2
Lidzbark Warmiński, Pol. 67/J4
Lié (riv.), Fr. 82/C4
Liebenau, Ger. 79/G6
Liebenau, Aus. 85/H5
Liebenbergsvlei (riv.), SAfr. 150/E2
Liebenthal, Ks, US 178/E1
Liebig (mt.), Austl. 157/F2
Liechtenstein (ctry.) 55/E4
Liedekerke, Belg. 81/D2
Liège, Belg. 81/E2
Liège (prov.), Belg. 81/E3
Lieksa, Fin. 94/F3
Lielvarde, Lat. 67/L3
Lienden, Neth. 78/C5
Lienen, Ger. 79/E4
Lienz, Aus. 71/K3
Liepāja, Lat. 67/J3
Liepna, Lat. 67/M3
Lier, Belg. 81/D1
Lierbyen, Nor. 64/R8
Lierneux, Belg. 81/E3
Lies (riv.), Belg. 70/E1
Lieser (riv.), Ger. 81/F3
Liesjärven NP, Fin. 67/K1
Liesjärven NP, Fin. 65/D4
Liesse-Notre-Dame, Fr. 80/C4
Liestal, Swi. 86/D3
Lieto, Fin. 67/K1
Lieurey, Fr. 83/F2
Liévin, Fr. 80/B3
Lievio, Fin. 65/E4
Lièvre (riv.), Qu, Can. 187/J1
Liez (lake), Fr. 86/B2
Liezen, Aus. 71/L3
Lifake, D.R. Congo 147/E2
Lifau, Indo. 154/B2
Liffey (riv.), Ire. 60/B5
Liffol-le-Grand, Fr. 86/B1
Lifford, Ire. 57/Q9
Liffré, Fr. 82/D4
Lifou (isl.), NCal. 163/V12
Lifouta, Gabon 146/C3
Lifton, Eng, UK 62/B5
Liganga, Tanz. 145/A4
Ligao, Phil. 117/F1
Līgatne, Lat. 67/L3
Lighthouse (pt.), Fl, US 191/F3
Lighthouse Point, Fl, US 190/P10
Lightning Ridge, Austl. 158/C1
Lightwater, Eng, UK 56/B3
Lignano Sabbiadoro, It. 89/G2
Lignite, ND, US 182/C3
Ligny-en-Barrois, Fr. 81/E6
Ligoncio (peak), It. 87/F5
Ligonha (riv.), Moz. 149/H2
Ligonier, In, US 186/D4
Ligoúrion, Gre. 75/H4
Ligovo (nbrhd.), Rus. 94/T7
Liguria (pol. reg.), It. 88/B4
Ligurian (sea), Eur. 92/F2
Lihou Reef and Kays (isl.), Austl. 153/E2
Lihue, Hi, US 168/S9
Lihula, Est. 67/K2
Lijiang Naxizu Zizhixian, China 112/D3
Lijin, China 106/D3
Likasi, D.R. Congo 147/F5
Likati, D.R. Congo 147/E2
Likely, BC, Can. 170/D1
Likhoslavl', Rus. 94/G4
Likhovskoy, Rus. 99/L3
Likimi, D.R. Congo 147/E2
Likoma (isl.), Malw. 149/G2
Likoto, D.R. Congo 147/E3
Likouala (pol. reg.), Congo 146/D2
Likouala (riv.), Congo 146/C2
Likouala aux Herbes (riv.), Congo 146/D2
Likouala Mossaka (riv.), Congo 146/D3
Likova (riv.), Rus. 94/W9
Likstammen (lake), Swe. 65/A2
Liku, Indo. 116/C3
Lilanga, D.R. Congo 147/E3
Lilbourn, Mo, US 188/C2
Lilburn, Ga, US 189/M7
L'Île-Perrot, Qu, Can. 185/N7
L'Île-Rousse, Fr. 74/A1
Liliāni, Pak. 124/B3
Lilienthal, Ger. 79/F2
Liling, China 119/K2
Lilla, Pak. 124/B3
Lilla Edet, Swe. 66/E2
Lille, Fr. 80/C2
Lille, Belg. 78/B6
Lille Bælt (chan.), Ger. 66/C4
Lille Værløse, Den. 65/J7
Lillebonne, Fr. 83/F1
Lillehammer, Nor. 66/D1
Lillerød, Den. 65/J7
Lillers, Fr. 80/B2
Lillesand, Nor. 66/C2
Lillestrøm, Nor. 66/D2
Lillian, Tx, US 176/K7
Lillie, La, US 179/H4
Lilliesleaf, Sc, UK 59/D5
Lillington, NC, US 189/H3
Lilliwaup, Wa, US 193/A3
Lillkyrka, Swe. 65/A1
Lillo, Sp. 72/D3
Lillooet (riv.), BC, Can. 170/C2
Lillooet, BC, Can. 170/D2
Lilongwe (cap.), Malw. 149/G2
Lilongwe (Kamuzu) (int'l arpt.), Malw. 149/G2
Liloy, Phil. 114/C3
Lily, Wi, US 183/K5
Lily, Ky, US 188/E2
Lilydale (nbrhd.), Austl. 158/G5
Lim (riv.), Yugo. 75/F1
Lima, Arg. 215/J11
Lima (riv.), It. 89/D4
Lima, Par. 213/E2
Lima (cap.), Peru 208/B4
Lima (dept.), Peru 208/B3
Lima (riv.), Port. 73/A2
Lima (mtn.), Mn, US 183/J3
Lima, Mt, US 173/G1
Lima (res.), Mt, US 173/G1
Lima, NY, US 187/H3
Lima, Oh, US 186/D4
Lima Duarte, Braz. 211/N6
Limache, Chile 214/N8
Limal, Bol. 212/C2
Liman, Rus. 97/H3
Limanowa, Pol. 69/L4
Limassol (dist.), Cyp. 130/C2
Limassol, Cyp. 130/C2
Limavady (dist.) 60/A2
Limavady, NI, UK 60/B1
Limay, Fr. 83/G3
Limay (riv.), Arg. 203/C7
Limay Mahuida, Arg. 214/D3
Limbach, Ger. 84/C4
Limbang (riv.), Malay. 114/A4
Limbani, Peru 208/D4
Limbara (peak), It. 74/A2
Limbaži, Lat. 67/L3
Limbdi, India 127/K4
Limbe, Camr. 146/B1
Limbe, Malw. 149/G2
Limbé, Haiti 201/H2
Limbiate, It. 88/C2
Limbourg, Belg. 81/E2
Limbuak, Malay. 114/B4
Limbunya, Austl. 154/C4
Limburg (prov.), Belg. 81/E1
Limburg an der Lahn, Ger. 84/B2
Limburgerhof, Ger. 84/B4
Limedsforsen, Swe. 66/E1
Limehouse, On, Can. 186/T8
Limeira, Braz. 213/H2
Limekilns, Sc, UK 59/C4
Limena, It. 89/E3
Limenária, Gre. 75/J2
Limerick (co.), Ire. 58/B5
Limerick, Ire. 58/B4
Limerick, Sk, Can. 171/L3
Limestone, Ar, US 179/H3
Limestone (lake), Tx, US 177/F2
Limestone, Mt, US 173/J1
Limfjorden (chan.), Den. 66/C3
Limidario (peak), It. 87/E5
Limington, Me, US 187/L3
Limite, It. 89/D5
Limmat (riv.), Swi. 87/E3
Limmen Bight (riv.), Austl. 155/D3
Limmen Bight (bay), Austl. 153/C2
Límni, Gre. 75/H3
Límnos (isl.), Gre. 96/C5
Limoeiro, Braz. 207/H4
Limoeiro do Norte, Braz. 207/G4
Limoges, Fr. 70/D4
Limogne (plat.), Fr. 70/D4
Limón, Hon. 200/E3
Limón, CR 201/F4
Limon, Co, US 180/C4
Limone Piemonte, It. 90/D4
Limone sul Garda, It. 89/D2
Limoquije, Bol. 209/E4
Limours, Fr. 56/J6
Limousin (mts.), Fr. 70/D4
Limousin (pol. reg.), Fr. 70/D4
Limoux, Fr. 70/E5
Limpopo (riv.), Afr. 149/G5
Limpopo (riv.), Moz. 133/F7
Limpsfield, Eng, UK 56/D3
Limu (mtn.), China 113/F5
Limu, China 113/F3
Limulunga, Zam. 148/D2
Limuru, Kenya 145/B2
Lin Xian, China 106/C3
Līnah, SAr. 129/E4
Linakhamari, Rus. 94/F1
Linanäs, Swe. 65/B1
Linao (pt.), Phil. 114/C4
Linapacan (isl.), Phil. 114/B3
Linard (peak), Swi. 87/G4
Linares, Sp. 72/D3
Linares, Chile 214/C2
Linares, Mex. 199/F3
Linariá, Gre. 75/J3
Linate (int'l arpt.), It. 88/C3
Lincang, China 112/D4
Linch, Wy, US 180/A2
Lincheng, China 106/C3
Linchuan, China 113/H3
Lincoln, Arg. 214/E2
Lincoln (sea), Can. 165/L1
Lincoln, On, Can. 186/U9
Lincoln, Eng, UK 61/H5
Lincoln, Ca, US 172/C4
Lincoln, De, US 194/C6
Lincoln, Il, US 181/K3
Lincoln, ND, US 182/D4
Lincoln (cap.), Ne, US 181/F3
Lincoln, NH, US 187/L2
Lincoln, NM, US 178/B4
Lincoln, Tx, US 177/F2
Lincoln, Pa, US 194/B3
Lincoln (Lincoln Center), Ks, US 179/E1
Lincoln Beach, Or, US 172/A1
Lincoln Boyhood Nat'l Mem., In, US 188/D1
Lincoln Caverns, Pa, US 187/G4
Lincoln Center (Lincoln), Ks, US 179/E1
Lincoln City, Or, US 172/A1
Lincoln Heath (woodld.), Eng, UK 61/H5
Lincoln Heights, Oh, US 186/E4
Lincoln Home Nat'l Hist. Site, Il, US 181/K4
Lincoln NP, Austl. 157/G5
Lincoln Park, Co, US 178/B1
Lincoln Park, NJ, US 195/H8
Lincoln Park, Mi, US 193/F7
Lincoln Park, Ga, US 188/E4
Lincolnshire (co.), Eng, UK 61/H5
Lincolnshire Wolds (grsld.), Eng, UK 61/H4
Lincolnton, Ga, US 189/F4
Lincolnton, NC, US 189/G3
Lincolnville, Ks, US 179/F1
Lincroft, NJ, US 194/D3
Lind, Den. 66/C3
Lind NP, Austl. 159/D3
Linda, Ca, US 172/C4
Lindale, Ga, US 188/E3
Lindale, Tx, US 177/G1
Lindau, Swi. 87/E3
Lindau, Ger. 87/F2
Linde (riv.), Neth. 78/C3
Lindeman (chan.), Austl. 160/C3
Lindeman (isl.), Austl. 155/H5
Linden, Ger. 84/E1
Linden, Guy. 205/G3
Linden, Al, US 188/C4
Linden, Az, US 175/G3
Linden, Fl, US 190/L6
Linden, In, US 186/C4
Linden, Mi, US 193/E6
Linden, NJ, US 195/J9
Linden, Tn, US 188/D3
Linden, Tx, US 179/G4
Linden Beach, On, Can. 193/G7
Lindenberg im Allgäu, Ger. 87/F2
Lindenfels, Ger. 84/B3
Lindenhurst, Il, US 193/P15
Lindenhurst, NY, US 195/E2
Lindenwold, NJ, US 194/D4
Lindern, Ger. 79/E3
Lindesberg, Swe. 66/F2
Lindesnes (cape), Nor. 66/B3
Lindesnes, Nor. 66/B2
Lindewitt, Ger. 66/C4
Lindgren Acres, Fl, US 190/P11
Lindholm (isl.), Den. 65/G7
Lindhorst, Ger. 79/E5
Líndhos (ruin), Gre. 128/B2
Lindi (riv.), D.R. Congo 147/F2
Lindi (prov.), Tanz. 145/B4
Lindi, Tanz. 145/B4
Lindian, China 105/J2
Lindlar, Ger. 81/G1
Lindley, SAfr. 150/D2
Lindome, Swe. 66/E3
Lindon, Ut, US 173/H3
Lindon, Co, US 180/C4
Lindre (lake), Fr. 81/F6
Lindrith, NM, US 175/J2
Lindsay (mt.), Austl. 156/C5
Lindsay (mt.), Austl. 157/F3
Lindsay, On, Can. 187/G2
Lindsay, Ca, US 174/C2
Lindsay, Mt, US 182/B4
Lindsay, Ok, US 179/F3
Lindsborg, Ks, US 179/F1
Lindsdal, Swe. 66/G3
Lindstrom, Mn, US 183/H5
Line (isls.), Kiri. 163/J4
Line Mountain (mtn.), Pa, US 194/B2
Líneas de Nazca, Peru 208/C4
Lineboro, Md, US 194/B4
Lineville, Al, US 188/E4
Lineville, Ia, US 181/H3
Linfen, China 106/B3
Linford, Eng, UK 56/E2
Ling (riv.), Sc, UK 59/A2
Ling Xian, China 119/K2
Ling Xian, China 106/D3
Linganore (cr.), Md, US 194/A5
Lingao, China 113/F5
Lingayen, Phil. 114/C1
Lingayen (gulf), Phil. 114/B1
Lingbao, China 106/B4
Lingbi, China 106/D4
Lingchuan, China 119/K2
Lingchuan, China 106/C4
Linge (riv.), Neth. 78/C5
Lingelengenda, Zam. 148/D2
Lingen, Ger. 79/E3
Lingfield, Eng, UK 56/C3
Lingga (isls.), Indo. 116/B3
Lingga (isl.), Indo. 115/D3
Linghu, China 106/L9
Lingle, Wy, US 180/B2
Linglestown, Pa, US 194/B3
Lingma, China 113/E4
Lingolsheim, Fr. 86/D1
Lingomo, D.R. Congo 147/E2
Lingqiu, China 106/C3
Lingshan, China 106/C3
Lingshan, China 113/F4
Lingshi, China 106/B3
Lingshui, China 113/F5
Lingtou, China 113/H3
Linguère, Sen. 140/B3
Lingunda, D.R. Congo 147/E2
Lingwu, China 104/F4
Lingxi, China 113/J3
Lingyin Si, China 106/L9
Lingyuan, China 106/D2
Lingyun, China 119/J3
Linhai, China 105/J1
Linhai, China 113/J2
Linhares, Braz. 211/E3
Linhe, China 104/F3
Linière, Qu, Can. 184/B2
Linjiang, China 107/D2
Linköping, Swe. 66/F2
Linkuva, Lith. 67/K3
Linlithgow, Sc, UK 59/C5
Linliu (mtn.), China 106/C3
Linn, Mo, US 179/J1
Linn, Tx, US 177/E4
Linn Creek, Mo, US 179/H1
Linneus, Mo, US 181/H4
Linney (pt.), Wal, UK 62/A3
Linnhe (lake), Sc, UK 59/A3
Linnich, Ger. 81/F2
Linntown, Pa, US 194/B2
Lino Lakes, Mn, US 183/P6
Linosa, It. 74/C5
Linosa (isl.), It, 74/C5
Linosa (isl.), It. 138/N7
Linqasi, Sudan 142/E4
Linqing, China 106/C3
Linqu, China 106/D3
Linquan, China 106/C4
Linru, China 106/C4
Lins, Braz. 213/G2
Linsan, Gui. 140/B4
Linschoten, Neth. 78/B4
Linshu, China 106/D4
Linshui, China 104/D4
Linta (riv.), Madg. 152/H9
Linth (riv.), Swi. 87/F3
Linthal, Swi. 87/F4
Lintlaw, Sk, Can. 182/C1
Linton, ND, US 182/D4
Linton, In, US 188/D1
Linton, Eng, UK 63/G2
Linville, La, US 179/H4
Linwood, Eng, UK 61/H5
Linwood, Mi, US 186/E3
Linwu, China 119/K2
Linxi, China 106/C3
Linxia, China 104/E4
Linyanti (swamp), Bots. 148/D3
Linyi, China 106/D4
Linyi, China 106/D3
Linyi, China 106/B4
Linying, China 106/C4
Linz (int'l arpt.), Aus. 85/H6
Linz, Aus. 85/H6
Linz am Rhein, Ger. 81/G2
Linze, China 104/E4
Linzhang, China 106/C3
Lioma, Moz. 149/H2
Lion (gulf), Fr.,Sp. 92/E2
Lion Country Safari, Fl, US 190/P9
Lion-sur-Mer, Fr. 83/E2
Lions Den, Zim. 149/F3
Lion's Head, On, Can. 186/F2
Lioppa, Indo. 154/B1
Lioto, CAfr. 142/D4
Liozno, Bela. 67/P4
Lipari, It. 74/D3
Lipari (isl.), It. 93/G3
Lipari (isls.), It. 93/G3
Lipatkain, Indo. 115/C3
Lipcani, Mol. 98/D3
Liperi, Fin. 94/F3
Lipetsk (int'l arpt.), Rus. 96/F1
Lipetsk, Rus. 96/F1
Lipetsk Oblast, Rus. 96/F1
Lipez (riv.), Bol. 212/C2
Liphook, Eng, UK 63/F4
Lipin Bor, Rus. 94/H3
Liping, China 113/F3
Lipljan, Yugo. 76/E4
Lipno, Pol. 69/K2
Lipno (res.), Czh. 85/H5
Lipno, UN (lake), Czh. 71/L2
Lipobane (pt.), Moz. 149/H3
Lipoche, Moz. 149/G1
Lipomo, It. 88/C2
Lipova, Rom. 76/E2
Lippe (riv.), Ger. 68/D3
Lippstadt, Ger. 79/F5
Lipscomb, Tx, US 178/D2
Lipsko, Pol. 98/A2
Lipton, Sk, Can. 182/C2
Liptovská Lúžna, Slvk. 69/K4
Liptovský Svätý Mikuláš, Slvk. 69/K4
Liptrap (cape), Austl. 159/B4
Lipu, China 113/F3
Lipu La (pass), India 125/D5
Lira, Ugan. 147/H2
Liranga, Congo 146/D3
Lirangwe, Malw. 149/G2
Lircay, Peru 208/C4
Liré, Fr. 83/D6
Liri (riv.), It. 74/C2
Liria, Sp. 73/E3
Liro (riv.), It. 87/F5
Lirung, Indo. 114/D5
Lisala, D.R. Congo 147/E2
Lisboa (dist.), Port. 72/A3
Lisboa (int'l arpt.), Port. 73/P10
Lisboa (Lisbon) (cap.), Port. 73/P10
Lisbon, La, US 179/H4
Lisbon, Md, US 194/A5
Lisbon, Me, US 187/L2
Lisbon, ND, US 182/F4
Lisbon, NH, US 187/L2
Lisbon, Oh, US 186/F4
Lisbon (Lisboa) (cap.), Port. 73/P10
Lisburn (dist.), NI, UK 60/B3
Lisburn, NI, UK 60/B2
Lisburne (cape), Ak, US 168/W12
Liscarroll, Ire. 58/B5
Liscomb Game Sanctuary, NS, Can. 185/F3
Lisdoonvarna, Ire. 58/A3
Liseleje, Den. 66/D3
Lisha (riv.), China 119/H2
Lishe (riv.), China 112/D3
Lishu, China 106/F2
Lishui, China 113/H2
Lisianski (isl.), HI, US 163/H2
Lisieux, Fr. 83/F2
Lisiy Nos, Rus. 94/T6
Liskeard, Eng, UK 62/B6
Liski, Rus. 99/K2
Lisle, Il, US 193/P16
L'Isle-Adam, Fr. 56/J4
L'Isle-d'Abeau, Fr. 90/B2
L'Isle-en-Dodon, Fr. 70/D5
L'Isle-sur-la-Sorgue, Fr. 90/B5
L'Isle-sur-le-Doubs, Fr. 86/C3
Lisle-sur-Tarn, Fr. 70/D5
L'Isle-Verte, Qu, Can. 184/C1
L'Islet, Qu, Can. 184/B2
Lisman, Al, US 188/C4
Lismore, Ire. 58/C5
Lismore, Austl. 158/E1
Lisnacree, NI, UK 60/B3
Lisnaskea, NI, UK 58/C1
Lišov, Czh. 85/H4
Lispeszentadorján, Hun. 76/C2
Liss, Eng, UK 63/F4
Lisse, Neth. 78/B4
Lisses, Fr. 56/K6
List, Ger. 66/C4
Lister (riv.), Ger. 79/E6
Listowel, Ire. 58/A5
Listowel, On, Can. 186/F3
Listvyanka, Rus. 104/E1
Lit. Scarcies (riv.), SLeo. 140/B4
Litang (riv.), China 119/H2
Litang, China 112/D2
Līṭānī (riv.), Leb. 130/D3
Litani (riv.), Sur.,FrG. 206/C2
Litavka (riv.), Czh. 85/G3
Litchfield, Austl. 154/C3
Litchfield, Ct, US 187/K4
Litchfield, Il, US 181/K4
Litchfield, Mn, US 181/G1
Litchfield, Ne, US 180/E3
Litchville, ND, US 182/E4
Liteta, Zam. 149/F2
Lith, Neth. 78/C5
Litherland, Eng, UK 61/F5
Lithgow, Austl. 159/E1
Lithia, Fl, US 190/L8
Lithia Springs, Ga, US 189/L7
Lithonia, Ga, US 189/M7
Lithuania (ctry.) 55/G3
Litija, Slov. 71/L3
Litipāra, India 123/F3
Lititz, Pa, US 194/B3
Litókhoron, Gre. 75/H2
Litoměřice, Czh. 85/H1
Litoo, Tanz. 145/B4
Litovko, Rus. 105/M2
Litslena, Swe. 65/A1
Littabella NP, Austl. 160/D4
Littau, Swi. 87/E3
Little (lake), La, US 190/C3
Little (mtn.), SC, US 189/F3
Little (riv.), Ga, US 188/B5
Little America, Wy, US 173/J3
Little Andaman (isl.), India 119/F5
Little Arkansas (riv.), Ks, US 179/F1
Little Arkansas (riv.), Ks, US 180/E4
Little Baddow, Eng, UK 56/E1
Little Beaver (cr.), Co, US 180/D4
Little Berkhamstead, Eng, UK 56/C1
Little Bighorn (riv.), Mt, Wy, US 173/K1
Little Birch, WV, US 189/G1
Little Bitter (lake), Egypt 130/C4
Little Blue (riv.), Ne, US 180/F3
Little Bow (riv.), Ab, Can. 171/H2
Little Calumet (riv.), Il, US 193/Q16
Little Catalina, Nf, Can. 185/L1
Little Cayman (isl.), Cay. 197/E4
Little Chalfont, Eng, UK 56/B2
Little Chute, Wi, US 186/B2
Little Colorado (riv.), Az, US 175/H3
Little Creek, De, US 194/C5
Little Cumbrae (isl.), Sc, UK 59/A5
Little Current, On, Can. 186/F2
Little Cypress (cr.), Tx, US 177/M8
Little Deschutes (riv.), Or, US 172/C2
Little Desert NP, Austl. 158/B3
Little Egg (har.), NJ, US 194/D4
Little Elm, Tx, US 176/L6
Little Falls, Mn, US 183/G5
Little Falls, NJ, US 195/J8
Little Falls (dam), Wa, US 170/F4
Little Ferry, NJ, US 195/J8
Little Fishing (cr.), Pa, US 194/B1
Little Fork (riv.), Mn, US 183/H3
Little Fort, BC, Can. 170/D2
Little Gombi, Nga. 142/B3
Little Grand Rapids, Mb, Can. 183/G1
Little Heart's Ease, Nf, Can. 185/L1
Little Inagua (isl.), Bahm. 197/G3
Little Kanawha (riv.), WV, US 189/G1
Little Karoo (valley), SAfr. 150/C4
Little Lake, Ca, US 174/D3
Little Lehigh (riv.), Pa, US 194/C3
Little Manatee (riv.), Fl, US 190/L8
Little Manatee, South Fork (riv.), Fl, US 190/L8
Little Marais, Mn, US 183/J4
Little Minch (str.), Sc, UK 57/Q8
Little Missouri (riv.), Ar, US 179/H3
Little Missouri (riv.), Mt, Wy, US 180/B1
Little Moose (mtn.), NY, US 187/J3
Little Muddy (riv.), ND, US 182/C3
Little Muncy (cr.), Pa, US 194/B1
Little Neck (bay), NY, US 195/K8
Little Nemaha (riv.), Ne, US 181/F3
Little Nicobar (isl.), India 119/F6
Little Ocmulgee (riv.), Ga, US 189/F4
Little Para (res.), Austl. 157/M8
Little Para (riv.), Austl. 157/M8
Little Patuxent (riv.), Md, US 194/B5
Little Payne (cr.), Fl, US 190/M8
Little Peconic (bay), NY, US 195/F2
Little Pee Dee (riv.), SC, US 189/H3
Little Pend Orielle NWR, Wa, US 170/F3
Little Pic (riv.), On, Can. 183/L3
Little Pine and Lucky Man Ind. Res., Sk, Can. 171/K1
Little Pisgah (mtn.), NC, US 189/F3
Little Powder (riv.), Mt, US 173/L1
Little Prairie, Wi, US 193/N14
Little Red (riv.), Ar, US 179/J3
Little River, Ks, US 179/E1
Little River, NZ 161/C3
Little River, BC, Can. 170/B3
Little River, SC, US 189/H4
Little Rock, Mn, US 183/G5
Little Rock (cap.), Ar, US 179/H3
Little Rock (A.F.B.), Ar, US 179/H3
Little Rock (cr.), Il, US 193/N16
Little Sable (pt.), Mi, US 186/C3
Little Sark (isl.), UK 82/C2
Little Schuylkill (riv.), Pa, US 194/B2
Little Sioux (riv.), Ia, US 169/G3
Little Sioux, West Fork (riv.), Ia, US 181/F2
Little Snake (riv.), Co, US 173/J3
Little St. George (isl.), Fl, US 191/F3
Little Stour (riv.), Eng, UK 63/H4
Little Stukeley, Eng, UK 63/F2
Little Swatara (cr.), Pa, US 194/B3
Little Tallapoosa (riv.), Al, US 188/E4
Little Valley, NY, US 187/G3
Little Wabash (riv.), Il, US 188/C1
Little White (riv.), SD, US 180/D2
Little Wichita (riv.), Tx,Ok, US 179/E4
Little Wind (riv.), Wy, US 173/J2
Little Wood (riv.), Id, US 173/F2
Little Zab (riv.), Iraq 129/E3
Littleborough, Eng, UK 61/F4
Littlefield, Tx, US 178/C4
Littlefield, Az, US 175/F2
Littlefork, Mn, US 183/H3
Littlehampton, Eng, UK 63/F5
Littleport, Eng, UK 63/G2
Littlerock, Ca, US 192/C1
Littlerock, Wa, US 170/C4
Littlestown, Pa, US 194/A4
Littleton, Ire. 58/C4
Littleton, NH, US 187/L2
Littleton, Co, US 180/B4
Littoral (prov.), Camr. 142/A4
Litvinov, Czh. 85/G1
Lityn, Ukr. 98/E3
Liu (riv.), China 101/N6
Liuba, China 104/F5
Liuche, China 113/G3
Liuchen, China 113/F4
Liucheng, China 119/J3
Liudongqiao, China 113/H2
Liuduo, China 105/J5
Liuhe, China 105/K3
Liuheng (isl.), China 113/J2
Liujing, China 120/E1
Liukou, China 113/H2
Liukuei, Tai. 113/J4
Liuli, Tanz. 145/A4
Liulin, China 106/B3
Liushi, China 113/G3
Liushuquan, China 125/F3
Liuwa Plain NP, Zam. 148/D2
Liuxi (riv.), China 113/G4
Liuyang, China 119/K2
Liuyang (riv.), China 113/G2
Liuzhou, China 113/F3
Liuzigang, China 113/G2
Livádhion, Gre. 75/H2
Livanátai, Gre. 75/H3
Līvāni, Lat. 67/M3
Live Oak, Fl, US 191/G2
Live Oak, Ca, US 172/C4
Livenza (riv.), It. 89/F2
Liverdun, Fr. 81/F6
Liverdy-en-Brie, Fr. 56/L5
Livermore, Me, US 187/L2
Livermore, Ky, US 188/D2
Livermore, Ia, US 181/G2
Livermore, Co, US 180/B3
Livermore (mt.), Tx, US 177/B2
Livermore Falls, Me, US 187/L2
Liverpool (bay), Wal, UK 61/E5
Liverpool, Eng, UK 61/F5
Liverpool, NS, Can. 184/E3
Liverpool (bay), NW, Can. 166/C1
Liverpool (cape), Nun, Can. 167/J1
Liverpool (nbrhd.), Austl. 160/G8
Liverpool, Tx, US 177/M9
Liverpool, Pa, US 194/B2
Liverton, Eng, UK 61/H2
Livet-et-Gavet, Fr. 90/B2
Livigno, It. 87/G4
Livilliers, Fr. 56/J4
Lívingston, Guat. 200/D3
Livingston, Sc, UK 59/C5
Livingston, Al, US 188/C4
Livingston, Ca, US 174/B2
Livingston (lake), Fl, US 190/M8
Livingston, Ky, US 188/E2
Livingston, La, US 190/C2
Livingston (co.), Mi, US 193/E6
Livingston, Mt, US 173/H1
Livingston, NJ, US 195/H8
Livingston, Tn, US 188/E2
Livingston, Tx, US 177/G2
Livingston (lake), Tx, US 177/G2
Livingston Manor, NY, US 187/J4
Livingstone, Zam. 148/E3
Livingstone (range), Ab, Can. 170/G2
Livingstone Memorial, Zam. 149/F2
Livingstone, Chutes de (falls), Congo 146/C4
Livingstonia, Malw. 145/A4
Livno, Bosn. 76/C4
Livny, Rus. 96/F1
Livojoki (riv.), Fin. 64/H2
Livonia, Mi, US 186/E3
Livonia, La, US 190/C2
Livonia, NY, US 187/H3
Livorno, It. 88/D6
Livorno (prov.), It. 88/D6
Livorno Ferraris, It. 88/B3
Livramento do Brumado, Braz. 211/E2
Livron-sur-Drôme, Fr. 90/A3
Livry-Gargan, Fr. 56/K5
L'ivs'ka (prov.), Ukr. 69/M4
Liwa, Chad 142/B2
Liwa, Indo. 115/D3
Liwale, Tanz. 145/B4
Liwan, Sudan 142/G4
Liwonde, Malw. 149/G2
Liwonde NP, Malw. 149/G2
Lixin, China 113/H3
Lixin, China 106/D4
Lixnaw, Ire. 58/A5
Lixoúrion, Gre. 75/G3
Lixus (ruin), Mor. 138/A2
Liyang, China 106/D5
Liyong, China 113/F3
Lizard, Eng, UK 62/A7
Lizard (pt.), Eng, UK 62/A7
Lizard Point Ind. Res., Sk, Can. 182/D2
Lizella, Ga, US 188/F4
Lizifang, China 107/B3
Liziping, China 112/D2
Lizy-sur-Ourcq, Fr. 80/C5
Ljubic, Yugo. 76/E4
Ljubija, Bosn. 76/C3
Ljubinje, Bosn. 76/D4
Ljubljana (cap.), Slov. 71/L3
Ljubuški, Bosn. 76/C4
Ljungan (riv.), Swe. 64/F3
Ljungby, Swe. 66/E3
Ljungbyhed, Swe. 65/K6
Ljungsbro, Swe. 66/F2
Ljungskile, Swe. 66/D2
Ljusnan (riv.), Swe. 64/E3
Ljusne, Swe. 66/G1
Ljusterø (isl.), Swe. 67/H2
Ljusterö, Swe. 65/B1
Lkst (peak), Mor. 136/C3
Llabanere (int'l arpt.), Fr. 70/E5
Llaillay, Chile 214/N8
Llaima (vol.), Chile 214/C3
Llallagua, Bol. 212/C1
Llalli, Peru 208/D4
Llanberis, Wal, UK 60/D5
Llanberis, Pass of (pass), Wal, UK 60/D5
Llancañelo (lake), Arg. 214/C2
Llandeilo, Wal, UK 62/C3
Llandogo, Wal, UK 62/D3
Llandovery, Wal, UK 62/C3
Llandrillo, Wal, UK 60/E6

270

Llan – Luche

Llandrindod Wells, Wal, UK 62/C2
Llandudno, Wal, UK 60/E5
Llandyssul, Wal, UK 62/B2
Llanelltyd, Wal, UK 62/C1
Llanenddwyn, Wal, UK 60/D6
Llanerchymedd, Wal, UK 60/D5
Llanes, Sp. 72/C1
Llanfair-Pwllgwyngyll, Wal, UK 60/D5
Llanfairfechan, Wal, UK 60/E5
Llanfyllin, Wal, UK 62/C1
Llangammarch Wells, Wal, UK 62/C2
Llangattock, Wal, UK 62/C3
Llangollen, Wal, UK 61/E6
Llangurig, Wal, UK 62/C2
Llanidloes, Wal, UK 62/C2
Llanllyfni, Wal, UK 60/D5
Llano (riv.), Tx, US 177/E2
Llano, Tx, US 177/E2
Llano Estacado (plain), US 168/F5
Llanos (plain), Col.,Ven. 203/B2
Llanquihue (lake), Chile 214/B4
Llanrhaeadr, Wal, UK 61/E5
Llanrian, Wal, UK 62/A3
Llanrwst, Wal, UK 60/E5
Llanthony, Wal, UK 62/C3
Llanuwchllyn, Wal, UK 60/E6
Llata, Peru 208/B3
Llay, Wal, UK 61/F5
Lledrod, Wal, UK 62/C2
Lleida, Sp. 73/F2
Llera de Canales, Mex. 199/F4
Llerena, Sp. 72/B3
Lleyn (pen.), Wal, UK 60/D6
Llica, Bol. 212/B1
Llico, Chile 214/B3
Llivia, Sp. 70/D5
Llobregat (riv.), Sp. 73/F1
Llodio, Sp. 70/B5
Llorente, Phil. 114/D3
Lloret de Mar, Sp. 73/G2
Llorona (pt.), CR 196/E6
Lloyd (pt.), NY, US 195/M8
Lloyd Harbor, NY, US 195/M8
Lloydminster, Sk, Can. 171/K1
Lloyds (riv.), Nf, Can. 185/J1
Lluchmayor, Sp. 73/G3
Llullaillaco (vol.), Arg.,Chile 212/B3
Llwchwr (riv.), Wal, UK 62/B3
Llyn Alaw (lake), Wal, UK 60/D5
Llyn Brenig (lake), Wal, UK 60/E5
Llyn Brianne (res.), Wal, UK 62/C2
Llyn Efyrnwy (lake), Wal, UK 60/E6
Llyn Tegid (lake), Wal, UK 60/E6
Llyn Trawsfynydd (lake), Wal, UK 60/D6
Llynfi (riv.), Wal, UK 62/C3
Lo Wu, China 113/L6
Loa (riv.), Chile 203/C5
Loa, Ut, US 175/G1
Loanda, Gabon 146/B3
Loanda, Braz. 213/F2
Loange (riv.), D.R. Congo 146/D4
Loango Buele, D.R. Congo 146/C4
Loanhead, Sc, UK 59/C5
Loano, It. 88/B5
Loaoya (canal), Sp. 73/N8
Loashi, D.R. Congo 147/G3
Lobanskaya, Rus. 95/K2
Lobatse, Bots. 148/E5
Lobbes, Belg. 81/D3
Lobelville, Tn, US 188/D3
Lobenstein, Ger. 85/E2
Lobería, Arg. 214/F3
Lobethal, Austl. 157/M8
Łobez, Pol. 69/H2
L'Obiou (peak), Fr. 90/B3
Lobito, Ang. 148/B2
Lobitos, Peru 208/A2
Lobnya, Rus. 94/Y9
Lobo (riv.), C.d'Iv. 140/D5
Lobo, Tx, US 176/B2
Lobos, Arg. 215/J11
Lobos (pt.), Chile 212/B2
Lobos (pt.), Chile 212/B4
Lobos, Punta de (pt.), Chile 214/M9
Lobva, Rus. 95/P4
Loc (riv.), Fr. 82/C5
Loc Ninh, Viet. 120/D4
Locana, It. 90/D2
Locarno, Swi. 87/E5
Loch Haven Center, Fl, US 190/N6
Loch na Sealga (sea), Sc, UK 59/A1
Loch Raven (res.), Md, US 194/B5
Lochaber (reg.), Sc, UK 59/A3
Lochans, Sc, UK 60/D2
Locharbriggs, Sc, UK 60/E1
Lochau, Aus. 87/F2
Lochawe, Sc, UK 59/A4
Lochboisdale, Sc, UK 57/Q8
Lochearnhead, Sc, UK 59/B4
Lochem, Neth. 78/D4
Lochend, Sc, UK 59/B2
Loches, Fr. 70/D3
Lochgelly, Sc, UK 59/C4
Lochgilphead, Sc, UK 59/A4
Lochgoilhead, Sc, UK 59/B4
Lochiel, SAfr. 151/E2
Lochindorb (lake), Sc, UK 59/C2
Lochinvar, Austl. 159/E1
Lochinvar NP, Zam. 149/E2
Lochmaben, Sc, UK 60/E1
Lochmaddy, Sc, UK 57/Q8
Łochów, Pol. 69/L2
Lochranza, Sc, UK 59/A5
Lochristi, Belg. 80/C1
Lochsa (riv.), Id, US 170/G4
Lochwinnoch, Sc, UK 59/B5
Lochy (lake), Sc, UK 59/B3
Lochy (riv.), Sc, UK 59/B3
Lock, Austl. 157/G5
Lock Haven, Pa, US 187/H4
Locke, Ca, US 193/L10
Locke (mt.), Tx, US 177/B2
Lockeford, Ca, US 172/C4
Lockeport, NS, Can. 184/E4
Lockerbie, Sc, UK 61/E1
Lockesburg, Ar, US 179/G4
Lockettville, Tx, US 178/C4
Lockhart, Fl, US 190/N6
Lockhart, Tx, US 176/F3
Lockhart, Austl. 159/C2
Lockhart Abor. Land, Austl. 155/F3
Lockhart Abor. Rsv., Austl. 160/A1
Lockhart River Aboriginal Community, Austl. 155/F3
Lockington, Austl. 158/C3
Lockney, Tx, US 178/D3
Locknitz (riv.), Ger. 68/F2
Lockport, Mb, Can. 182/F2
Lockport, La, US 190/C3
Lockport, Il, US 193/P16
Lockport, NY, US 186/V9
Lockwood, Sk, Can. 182/B2
Lockwood (res.), Eng, UK 56/C2
Locmariaquer, Fr. 82/C5
Locminé, Fr. 82/C5
Loco, Ok, US 179/F3
Locoal-Mendon, Fr. 82/B5
Locon, Fr. 80/B2
Locquirec, Fr. 82/B3
Locri, It. 74/E3
Locronan, Fr. 82/A4
Loctudy, Fr. 82/A5
Locumba, Peru 208/D5
Locust (cr.), Mo, Ia, US 181/H3
Locust Grove, Ok, US 179/G2
Lod, Isr. 131/B5
Lodan (cr.), Ne, US 181/F2
Lodde (riv.), Swe. 65/K7
Löddeköpinge, Swe. 65/K7
Loddon (riv.), Austl. 158/B3
Loddon (riv.), Eng, UK 63/E4
Loddon, Eng, UK 63/H1
Lodenice (riv.), Czh. 85/H2
Lodève, Fr. 70/E5
Lodeynoye Pole, Rus. 94/G3
Lodge (cr.), Ab, Can. 171/J3
Lodge Grass, Mt, US 173/K1
Lodge Pole, Mt, US 171/K3
Lodgepole, SD, US 182/C5
Lodgepole (cr.), Wy, Ne, US 180/B3
Lodgepole, Ab, Can. 170/G1
Lodhrān, Pak. 124/A5
Lodi, Tx, US 179/G4
Lodi, It. 88/C3
Lodi, NJ, US 195/J8
Lodi, D.R. Congo 147/E4
Lodi, Ca, US 172/C4
Lodi, Wi, US 181/K2
Lodi, Mo, US 188/B2
Lodi Vecchio, It. 88/C3
Lodja, D.R. Congo 147/E3
Lodosa, Sp. 72/D1
Lodrino, Swi. 87/E5
Lodwar, Kenya 145/A1
Lodz (prov.), Pol. 69/K3
Łódź, Pol. 69/K3
Loei, Thai. 120/C2
Loenen, Neth. 78/C4
Loengo, D.R. Congo 147/F4
Loeriesfontein, SAfr. 150/B3
Lofa (riv.), Libr. 140/C5
Lofa (co.), Libr. 140/C5
Löffingen, Ger. 87/E2
Lofonda, D.R. Congo 147/E2
Lofoten (isle.), Nor. 64/D2
Loftus, Eng, UK 61/H2
Lofty (range), Austl. 156/C3
Lofty (mt.), Austl. 157/M8
Loga, Niger 141/F3
Logan (nbrhd.), Austl. 160/F7
Logan (mt.), Yt., Can. 168/Y12
Logan, Ia, US 181/G3
Logan, Ks, US 180/E4
Logan (pass), Mt, US 171/H3
Logan, NM, US 178/C3
Logan, Oh, US 186/E5
Logan, Ut, US 173/H3
Logan (mt.), Wa, US 170/D3
Logan, WV, US 189/G2
Logan Int'l (General Edward Lawrence Logan) (int'l arpt.), Ma, US 187/L3
Logan Lake, BC, Can. 170/D2
Logan Martin (lake), Al, US 188/D4
Logansport, La, US 176/H2
Logansport, In, US 186/C4
Loganton, Pa, US 194/A1
Loganville, Ga, US 188/F4
Loganville, Pa, US 194/B4
Logatec, Slov. 71/L4
Loge (riv.), Ang. 146/C4
Loggieville, NB, Can. 184/E2
Logone (riv.), Chad 133/D3
Logone Birni, Camr. 142/B3
Logone Occ. (riv.), Chad 142/B4
Logone Oriental (riv.), Chad 142/C3
Logone-Occidental (pref.), Chad 142/B3
Logone-Oriental (pref.), Chad 142/B3
Lograto, It. 88/D3
Logroño, Sp. 70/B5
Logrosán, Sp. 72/C3
Løgstør, Den. 66/C3
Løgten, Den. 66/D3
Lohals, Den. 66/D4
Lohārdaga, India 123/E4
Lohāru, India 124/C5
Lohatlha, SAfr. 150/C3
Lohāwat, India 118/B2
Lohfelden, Ger. 79/G6
Lohja, Fin. 67/L1
Lohjanjärvi (lake), Fin. 67/K1
Lohman, Mo, US 179/H1
Lohmar, Ger. 81/G2
Lohn, Tx, US 177/E2
Löhnberg, Ger. 84/B1
Löhne, Ger. 79/F4
Lohne, Ger. 79/F3
Loholoho, Indo. 117/F4
Lohr, Ger. 84/C3
Loi-kaw, Myan. 112/C5
Loiano, It. 89/E5
Loica, Chile 214/N9
Loile (riv.), D.R. Congo 147/E3
Loing (riv.), Fr. 68/B5
Loir (riv.), Fr. 70/D3
Loir-et-Cher (dept.), Fr. 83/G5
Loire (dept.), Fr. 90/A2
Loire (riv.), Fr. 55/E4
Loire-Atlantique (dept.), Fr. 82/D6
Loiret (dept.), Fr. 83/G5
Loiron, Fr. 83/E4
Loisin (riv.), Fr. 81/E5
Loita (hills), Kenya 145/A2
Loja, Sp. 72/C4
Loja, Ecu. 208/B2
Loja (prov.), Ecu. 208/B2
Løjt Kirkeby, Den. 66/C4
Loka, Sudan 142/F4
Lokandu, D.R. Congo 147/F3
Lökåö (isl.), Swe. 65/B1
Lökbatan, Azer. 129/G1
Lokeren, Belg. 80/D1
Lokhvytsya, Ukr. 99/G2
Lokichar, Kenya 145/A1
Lokichokio, Kenya 142/G4
Lokitaung, Kenya 142/G4
Lokka, Fin. 94/E2
Løkken, Den. 66/C3
Loknya, Rus. 67/P3
Loko, Nga. 141/G5
Lokofe, D.R. Congo 147/E3
Lokoja, Nga. 141/G5
Lokolama, D.R. Congo 146/D3
Lokolia, D.R. Congo 147/E3
Lokolo (riv.), D.R. Congo 146/D3
Lokomby, Madg. 152/H8
Lokomo, Camr. 146/C2
Lokopo, Ugan. 145/A1
Lokori, Kenya 145/B1
Lokoro (riv.), D.R. Congo 146/D3
Lökösháza, Hun. 76/E2
Lokossa, Ben. 141/F5
Lokot', Rus. 96/E1
Loks (isl.), Nun, Can. 167/K2
Loksa, Est. 67/L2
Lokwakangole, Kenya 142/G5
Lola, Gui. 140/C5
Lola, Ky, US 188/C2
Lolelia, Ugan. 142/G5
Lolgorien, Kenya 145/A2
Lolingo, D.R. Congo 147/E2
Loliondo, Tanz. 145/A2
Lolita, Tx, US 177/F3
Lolkisale, Tanz. 145/B2
Lolland (isl.), Den. 64/D5
Lollar, Ger. 84/B3
Lolo, D.R. Congo 147/E2
Lolo (riv.), Gabon 146/C3
Lolo, D.R. Congo 147/F3
Lolo, Mt, US 171/G4
Lolo (peak), Mt, US 170/G4
Lolodorf, Camr. 146/B2
Lolua, Tuv. 162/G5
Lolui (isl.), Ugan. 145/A2
Lom, Nor. 64/D3
Lom, Bul. 77/F4
Lom (riv.), Camr. 142/B4
Lom Sak, Thai. 120/C2
Loma (pt.), Ca, US 192/C5
Loma (mts.), SLeo. 140/C4
Loma, Mt, US 171/J4
Loma Alta, Bol. 209/E3
Loma Alta, Tx, US 177/D3
Loma Bonita, Mex. 200/C2
Loma Linda, Ca, US 192/C2
Loma Mansa (peak), SLeo. 140/C4
Loma Negra, Arg. 214/E3
Lomami (riv.), D.R. Congo 133/E5
Lomas, Peru 208/C4
Lomas de Zamora, Arg. 215/J11
Lomazzo, It. 88/C2
Lomba (riv.), Ang. 148/D2
Lombard, Il, US 193/P16
Lombarda, Serra (mts.), Braz. 206/D2
Lombardia (pol.reg.), It. 87/E6
Lombardia (pol. reg.), It. 71/H4
Lombardia, Mex. 198/E5
Lombe, Ang. 146/D5
Lombe, Indo. 154/A1
Lomblen (isl.), Indo. 117/F5
Lombok (isl.), Indo. 103/L10
Lombok (str.), Indo. 115/F3
Lombok, Indo. 117/E5
Lombolo, Congo 146/C4
Lomé (cap.), Togo 141/F5
Lomé (int'l arpt.), Togo 141/F5
Lomela (riv.), D.R. Congo 147/E3
Lomela, D.R. Congo 147/E3
Lomello, It. 88/B3
Lometa, Tx, US 177/E2
Lomié, Camr. 146/C2
Lomira, Wi, US 186/B3
Lomita, Ca, US 192/F8
Lomma (riv.), Nor. 64/S8
Lomma, Swe. 66/E4
Lomme, Fr. 80/B2
Lommel, Belg. 78/C6
Lomnice (riv.), Czh. 85/G4
Lomnice nad Lužnicí, Czh. 85/H4
Lomond (lake), Sc, UK 59/B4
Lomond (hills), Sc, UK 59/C4
Lomond, Ab, Can. 171/H2
Lomone (riv.), It. 89/E4
Lomonosov, Rus. 94/S7
Lompobatang (peak), Indo. 117/E5
Lompoc, Ca, US 174/B3
Łomża, Pol. 69/M2
Lonato, It. 88/D3
Lonāvale, India 121/B2
Loncoche, Chile 214/B3
Loncopué, Arg. 214/C3
Londerzeel, Belg. 81/D2
Londiani, Kenya 145/A2
Londinières, Fr. 83/G1
London, On, Can. 186/F3
London (cap.), UK 56/C2
London, Ky, US 188/E2
London, Oh, US 186/E5
London, Tx, US 177/E2
London Bridge, Az, US 174/E3
London Colney, Eng, UK 56/C1
London Reef (reef), Nic. 201/F3
London, City of (bor.), Eng, UK 56/A1
Londonderry(dist.) 60/A2
Londonderry, NI, UK 60/A2
Londonderry (cape), Austl. 154/B3
Londonderry (isl.), Chile 215/C7
Londonderry (Eglinton) (arpt.), UK 60/A1
Londres, Arg. 212/C3
Londrina, Braz. 213/G2
Londuimbali, Ang. 148/B2
Lone (mtn.), SD, US 182/C5
Lone (riv.), Ger. 84/C5
Lone Butte, BC, Can. 170/D2
Lone Grove, Ok, US 179/F3
Lone Pine, Ca, US 174/C2
Lone Pine Ind. Res., Ca, US 174/C2
Lone Pine Sanct., Austl. 160/E7
Lone Rock, Sk, Can. 171/K1
Lone Star, Tx, US 179/G4
Lone Star, La, US 190/C2
Lone Wolf, Ok, US 178/E3
Lonepine, La, US 190/B2
Lonesome NP, Austl. 160/C4
Lonétou, Mali 140/C3
Long (isl.), Bahm. 165/K7
Long (isl.), Nf., Can. 184/K2
Long (pt.), On, Can. 186/F3
Long (cr.), Sk, Can. 171/M3
Long (riv.), China 113/F3
Long (peak), Fr. 73/F1
Long (isl.), Ire. 58/A7
Long (isl.), PNG 155/G1
Long (str.), Rus. 101/T2
Long, Thai. 120/B2
Long (lake), Sc, UK 59/A2
Long (mtn.), Wal, UK 62/C1
Long (pt.), Mi, US 183/K4
Long (lake), ND, US 182/D4
Long (isl.), NY, US 195/K9
Long Beach, In, US 186/C4
Long Beach, Ms, US 190/D2
Long Beach, Ca, US 192/F8
Long Beach, NY, US 195/L9
Long Beach, On, Can. 186/U10
Long Beach (pen.), Wa, US 170/B4
Long Beach, Wa, US 170/B4
Long Beach (isl.), NJ, US 194/D4
Long Beach, Austl. 159/E2
Long Beach, NC, US 189/H4
Long Beach (Daugherty Field) (arpt.), Ca, US 192/F8
Long Branch, NJ, US 194/E3
Long Buckby, Eng, UK 63/E2
Long Cay (isl.), India 201/H1
Long Chau, Viet. 113/E4
Long Crag (hill), Eng, UK 59/E6
Long Creek, Or, US 172/D1
Long Crendon, Eng, UK 63/F3
Long Ditton, Eng, UK 56/C2
Long Eaton, Eng, UK 61/G6
Long Eddy, NY, US 187/J4
Long Grove, Il, US 193/P15
Long Hill, Ct, US 195/E1
Long Island, Ks, US 180/E4
Long Island MacArthur (arpt.), NY, US 195/E2
Long Ketiok, Indo. 117/E3
Long Key (isl.), Fl, US 191/H5
Long Lake, SD, US 182/E5
Long Lake, NY, US 187/J3
Long Lake Ind. Res., On, Can. 183/L3
Long Lake NWR, ND, US 182/D4
Long Lane, Mo, US 179/H2
Long Lelang, Malay. 114/A5
Long Mynd, The (hill), Eng, UK 62/D1
Long Neck (pt.), Ct, US 195/M7
Long Phu, Viet. 120/D4
Long Plain Ind. Res., Mb, Can. 182/E3
Long Pond, Me, US 187/L2
Long Prairie, Mn, US 183/G5
Long Range (mts.), Nf, Can. 185/H2
Long Semado, Malay. 114/A4
Long Sutton, Eng, UK 61/J6
Long Valley, NJ, US 194/D2
Long Xian, China 104/F5
Long Xuyen, Viet. 120/D4
Long, Loch (inlet), Sc, UK 59/B4
Longa, Ang. 148/C2
Longa (riv.), Ang. 146/C5
Longá (riv.), Braz. 207/F3
Long'an, China 119/J3
Longare, It. 89/E3
Longaví, Chile 214/C2
Longberang, Indo. 117/E3
Longbia, Indo. 117/E3
Longboat Key, Fl, US 191/G4
Longboh, Indo. 116/E3
Longbranch, Wa, US 193/B3
Longchamps, Belg. 81/E3
Longchang, China 112/E2
Longchuan, China 119/G3
Longchuan (riv.), China 112/C3
Longchuan, China 113/G3
Longdale, Ok, US 179/E2
Longde, China 104/F4
Longdongping, China 113/F2
Longeau (riv.), Fr. 81/E5
Longeuve (riv.), Fr. 83/E4
Longeville-en-Barrois, Fr. 81/E6
Longeville-lès-Metz, Fr. 81/F5
Longeville-lès-Saint-Avold, Fr. 81/F5
Longfellow (mts.), Me, US 184/B3
Longfield, Eng, UK 56/D2
Longford (co.), Ire. 58/C2
Longford, Ire. 58/C2
Longford, Austl. 158/C4
Longgang, China 113/H3
Longguang, China 113/E4
Longgun, China 113/F5
Longhoughton, Eng, UK 59/E6
Longhua (pass), China 113/F3
Longhua, China 106/D2
Longhui, China 113/F3
Longido, Tanz. 145/B2
Longjiang, China 105/J2
Longjie, China 112/E3
Longjumeau, Fr. 56/J5
Longkou, China 106/E3
Longlac, On, Can. 183/L3
Longli, China 119/J2
Longmen, China 120/E1
Longmen, China 112/D3
Longmen Shiyao, China 106/C4
Longmont, Co, US 180/B3
Longnan, China 113/G3
Longniddry, Sc, UK 59/D5
Longnor, Eng, UK 61/G5
Longny-au-Perche, Fr. 83/F3
Longo, Congo 146/D2
Longonjo, Ang. 148/B2
Longonot (peak), Kenya 145/B2
Longperrier, Fr. 56/K4
Longpont-sur-Orge, Fr. 56/J6
Longport, NJ, US 194/D5
Longpré-les-Corps-Saints, Fr. 80/A3
Longquan, China 113/H2
Longreach, Austl. 160/B3
Longriba, China 104/E5
Longridge, Eng, UK 61/F4
Longs (peak), Co, US 180/B3
Longshan, China 113/F2
Longshou (mts.), China 104/E4
Longstreet, La, US 176/H1
Longtan, China 113/F4
Longton, Ks, US 179/F2
Longtown, Eng, UK 61/F2
Longué-Jumelles, Fr. 83/E6
Longueau, Fr. 80/B4
Longueil-Annel, Fr. 80/B5
Longuenesse, Fr. 80/B2
Longuesse, Fr. 56/H4
Longueuil, Qu, Can. 185/P6
Longuyon, Fr. 81/E5
Longvic, Fr. 86/B3
Longview, Ms, US 188/C4
Longview, Tx, US 177/G1
Longview, Wa, US 170/C4
Longview, Ab, Can. 171/G2
Longville, La, US 190/B2
Longwo, China 113/G4
Longwood, Fl, US 190/N6
Longwood, NC, US 189/H3
Longwood Gardens, Pa, US 194/C4
Longworth, Tx, US 177/D1
Longwy, Fr. 81/E4
Longxi, China 104/E4
Longxingshi, China 113/G3
Longyan, China 113/H3
Longyearbyen, Nor. 100/B2
Longyou, China 113/H2
Longzhou, China 120/D1
Loni, India 124/D5
Lonigo, It. 89/E3
Löningen, Ger. 79/E3
Lonkin, Myan. 112/C3
Lonneker, Neth. 78/D4
Lonoke, Ar, US 179/J3
Lonquimay, Arg. 214/E3
Lons, Fr. 70/C5
Lons-le-Saunier, Fr. 86/B4
Lönsboda, Swe. 66/F3
Lonton, Myan. 112/C3
Lontzen, Belg. 81/F2
Lonza (riv.), Swi. 86/D5
Looc, Phil. 114/C2
Looe (isl.), Eng, UK 62/B6
Loogootee, In, US 188/D1
Lookout (pt.), Mi, US 186/E2
Lookout (pt.), Austl. 160/B1
Lookout (cape), Or, US 172/B1
Lookout (mtn.), Id, US 170/G4
Lookout (pt.), Md, US 189/J1
Lookout (cape), NC, US 189/J3
Loolmalasin (peak), Tanz. 145/A2
Looma, Austl. 154/B4
Loomis, Ca, US 172/C4
Loomis, Wa, US 170/E3
Loon Lake, Wa, US 170/F3
Loon op Zand, Neth. 78/C5
Loop, Tx, US 178/C4
Loop Head (pt.), Ire. 56/P10
Loos, Fr. 80/C2
Loos, BC, Can. 170/D1
Loose, Eng, UK 56/E3
Loose Creek, Mo, US 179/J1
Lop (lake), China 104/C3
Lop Buri, Thai. 120/C3
Lopary, Madg. 152/H8
Lopatin, Rus. 97/H4
Lopatinskiy, Rus. 94/H5
Lopatkovo, Rus. 95/P4
Lopaye, Sudan 142/G4
Lopeno, Tx, US 177/E4
Loperhet, Fr. 82/A4
Lopez (cape), Gabon 146/B3
Lopez (pt.), Ca, US 174/B2
Lopez, Phil. 114/C2
López Mateos, Mex. 199/Q9
Lopik, Neth. 78/B5
Lopori (riv.), D.R. Congo 147/E2
Lopphavet (bay), Nor. 64/G1
Loppi, Fin. 67/L1
Loppijärvi (lake), Fin. 65/E4
Lopukhovka, Rus. 97/H2
Lopydino, Rus. 95/M3
Lora (cr.), Austl. 157/G4
Lora del Río, Sp. 72/C4
Lorain, Oh, US 186/E4
Loraine, Tx, US 177/D1
Loralai, Pak. 127/J2
Lorca, Sp. 72/E4
Lorch, Ger. 81/G3
Lorch, Ger. 84/C5
Lord Howe (isl.), Austl. 162/E8
Lordegān, Iran 129/G4
Lords Lake Nat'l Wild. Ref., ND, US 182/D3
Lordsburg, NM, US 175/H4
Loré, Indo. 154/B2
Lorelei, Ger. 81/G3
Lorena, Braz. 211/L7
Lorengau, PNG 162/D5
Lørenskog, Nor. 66/D2
Lorentz (riv.), Indo. 117/J5
Lorentzsluizen (dam), Neth. 78/C2
Lorenzo, Tx, US 178/D4
Lorenzo Geyres, Uru. 214/F2
Loreo, It. 89/F3
Lorestān (gov.), Iran 129/G3
Loreto, It. 89/G7
Loreto, Ecu. 204/B5
Loreto (state), Peru 204/C5
Loreto, Phil. 114/D3
Loreto, Braz. 207/E4
Loreto, Col. 208/D1
Loreto, Bol. 209/E4
Loreto, Par. 213/E2
Loreto, Mex. 198/C3
Loreto (int'l arpt.), Mex. 198/C3
Loreto, Mex. 198/E4
Loreto Aprutino, It. 92/C3
Lorette, Mb, Can. 182/F3
Lorette, Fr. 90/A1
Loretteville, Qu, Can. 184/B2
Loretto, Tn, US 188/D3
Loretto, Ky, US 188/E2
Lorgues, Fr. 90/C6
Lorian (swamp), Kenya 145/B1
Lorica, Col. 204/C2
Lorient, Fr. 82/B5
Lorient (Lann-Bihoue) (arpt.), Fr. 82/B5
L'Oriental (pol. reg.), Mor. 138/C3
L'Orignal, On, Can. 187/J2
Lorillard (riv.), Nun, Can. 166/G2
Lorinci, Hun. 69/K5
Loring, Mt, US 171/L3
Loriol-sur-Drôme, Fr. 90/A3
Loris, SC, US 189/H3
Lorman, Ms, US 190/C2
Lorne, Austl. 159/A4
Lorne Park, On, Can. 186/T8
Loro Ciuffenna, It. 89/E6
Lorosuk (peak), Kenya 145/A1
Lorquin, Fr. 81/G6
Lörrach, Ger. 86/D2
Lorrain (plat.), Fr. 68/D4
Lorraine (pol. reg.), Fr. 86/C1
Lorraine, Ks, US 179/E1
Lorraine (reg.), Fr. 81/E5
Lorraine (pol.reg.), Fr. 70/G2
Lorraine, Qu, Can. 185/N6
Lorrha, Ire. 58/B3
Lorsch, Ger. 84/B3
Lorton, Eng, UK 61/E2
Lorton, Va, US 189/J1
Loruk, Kenya 145/B1
Lorup, Ger. 79/E3
Los Alamitos, Ca, US 192/F8
Los Alamos, NM, US 178/B3
Los Álamos, Mex. 177/D3
Los Alamos, NM, US 175/J3
Los Alamos, Ca, US 174/B3
Los Aldamas, Mex. 177/E4
Los Alerces, PN, Arg. 214/C4
Los Altos, Ca, US 193/K12
Los Altos, Arg. 212/C4
Los Amates, Guat. 200/D3
Los Andes, Col. 204/B4
Los Andes, Chile 214/N8
Los Angeles (co.), Ca, US 192/B2
Los Angeles (riv.), Ca, US 192/B2
Los Angeles (int'l arpt.), Ca, US 192/F8
Los Angeles, Ca, US 192/F7
Los Ángeles, Chile 214/B3
Los Angeles (aqueduct), Ca, US 174/C3
Los Angeles Outer (har.), Ca, US 192/F8
Los Aquijes, Peru 208/C4
Los Aztecas, Mex. 199/F4
Los Banos, Ca, US 174/B2
Los Barrios, Sp. 72/C4
Los Canarreos (arch.), Cuba 201/F1
Los Cardales, Arg. 215/J11
Los Cardoñes, PN, Arg. 212/C3
Los Castillos, Ven. 205/F2
Los Cerrillos, Uru. 215/K11
Los Charrúas, Arg. 212/E4
Los Chaves, NM, US 175/J3
Los Chonos (arch.), Chile 203/B7
Los Cóndores, Arg. 212/C5
Los Corrales de Buelna, Sp. 72/C1
Los Coyotes Ind. Res., Ca, US 174/D4
Los Cusis, Bol. 209/E4
Los Estados (isl.), Arg. 215/D7
Los Fresnos, Tx, US 176/F4
Los Glaciares, PN, Arg. 215/B6
Los Herreras, Mex. 177/E5
Los Katios, PN, Col. 204/B3
Los Lagos, Chile 214/B3
Los Lagos (pol. reg.), Chile 214/B4
Los Llanos de Aridane, Sp. 136/A3
Los Lunas, NM, US 175/J3
Los Mármoles, PN, Mex. 200/B1
Los Menucos, Arg. 214/C4
Los Mochis, Mex. 198/C3
Los Molinos, Ca, US 172/B3
Los Monos, Arg. 214/C5
Los Mosquitos (gulf), Pan. 201/F4
Los Muermos, Chile 214/B4
Los Navalmorales, Sp. 72/C3
Los Navalucillos, Sp. 72/C3
Los Nevados, PN, Col. 207/K8
Los Olmos (cr.), Tx, US 177/E4
Los Órganos, Peru 208/A2
Los Padres National Forest, Ca, US 192/A1
Los Palacios y Villafranca, Sp. 72/C4
Los Palos, Indo. 154/B2
Los Pingüinos, PN, Chile 215/C7
Los Pinos (riv.), Co, US 178/A2
Los Planes, Mex. 198/C3
Los Ranchos de Albuquerque, NM, US 175/J3
Los Reyes, Mex. 199/R10
Los Reyes de Salgado, Mex. 198/E5
Los Riecillos, Chile 214/N8
Los Ríos (prov.), Ecu. 208/B1
Los Roques (isls.), Ven. 197/H5
Los Santos, Pan. 204/A3
Los Santos de Maimona, Sp. 72/B3
Los Sauces, Chile 214/B3
Los Tamariscos, Arg. 214/C5
Los Taques, Ven. 204/D2
Los Telares, Arg. 212/D4
Los Teques, Ven. 207/N7
Los Testigos (isls.), Ven. 205/F2
Los Vientos, Chile 212/B3
Los Vilos, Chile 214/C1
Los Yébenes, Sp. 72/D3
Losai Nat'l Rsv., Kenya 145/B1
Losheim, Ger. 81/F4
Loshkarëvka, Ukr. 99/H4
Loshnitsa, Bela. 67/N4
Łosice, Pol. 69/M2
Losinj (isl.), Cro. 93/G1
Lošinj (isl.), Cro. 71/L4
Loskiria (peak), Kenya 145/B1
Losne, Fr. 86/B3
Losone, Swi. 87/E5
Lossburg, Ger. 87/E1
Losser, Neth. 78/E4
Lossie (riv.), Sc, UK 59/C1
Lossiemouth, Sc, UK 59/C1
Lössnitz, Ger. 85/F1
Lossoganeu (hill), Tanz. 145/B3
Lost (lake), La, US 190/C3
Lost (riv.), Or, US 172/C2
Lost Creek (res.), Or, US 172/B2
Lost Creek, WV, US 189/G1
Lost Creek, Ky, US 189/F2
Lost Draw (riv.), Tx, US 177/C1
Lost Hills, Ca, US 174/C3
Lost Mountain, Ga, US 189/L7
Lost River (range), Id, US 173/G1
Lost River Caverns, Pa, US 194/C2
Lost Springs, Ks, US 179/F1
Lostallo, Swi. 87/F5
Lostwithiel, Eng, UK 62/B6
Lostwood NWR, ND, US 182/C3
Losynivka, Ukr. 98/F2
Lot (riv.), Fr. 92/D1
Lota, Chile 214/B3
Løten, Nor. 66/D1
Lotfābād, Iran 127/G1
Lothaa, Ugan. 145/A1
Lothian (pol. reg.), Sc, UK 59/C5
Lotikipi (plain), Kenya 142/G4
Loto, D.R. Congo 147/E3
Lotogipi (swamp), Kenya 142/G4
Lotoi (riv.), D.R. Congo 146/D3
Lotsane (riv.), Bots. 149/E4
Lott, Tx, US 177/F2
Lotte, Ger. 79/E4
Lotuke (peak), Sudan 142/G4
Lotumbe, D.R. Congo 146/D3
Lou (riv.), China 106/B5
Louang Namtha, Laos 112/D4
Louangphrabang, Laos 112/D5
Louann, Ar, US 179/H4
Loubomo, Congo 146/C4
Loudéac, Fr. 82/C4
Loudi, China 113/F3
Loudima, Congo 146/C4
Loudon, Tn, US 188/E3
Loudonville, NY, US 187/K3
Loudonville, Oh, US 186/E4
Loudun, Fr. 70/D3
Loudwater, Eng, UK 56/A2
Loué, Fr. 83/E4
Loue (riv.), Fr. 70/F3
Louessé (riv.), Congo 146/C3
Louet (riv.), Fr. 83/E6
Loufan, China 106/B3
Louga, Sen. 140/A3
Louga (pol.reg.), Sen. 140/B3
Lough Foyle (lake), UK 60/A1
Loughborough, Eng, UK 63/E1
Loughbrickland, NI, UK 60/B3
Lougheed (isl.), Nun, Can. 167/R7
Loughgall, NI, UK 60/B3
Loughman, Fl, US 190/M7
Loughrea, Ire. 58/B3
Loughton, Eng, UK 56/D2
Louhans, Fr. 86/B4
Louingi, Congo 146/C4
Louis Botha (Durban) (int'l arpt.), SAfr. 151/E3
Louis Creek, BC, Can. 170/D2
Louis Trichardt, SAfr. 149/F4
Louisa (lake), Fl, US 190/M7
Louisa, Ky, US 189/F1
Louisa, Va, US 189/H1
Louisbourg, NS, Can. 185/H3
Louisburg, Ks, US 179/G1
Louisburg, NC, US 189/H2
Louisdale, NS, Can. 185/G3
Louise, Tx, US 177/F3
Louiseville, Qu, Can. 187/K1
Louisiade (arch.), PNG 162/E6
Louisiana (pt.), La, US 177/H3
Louisiana (state), US 169/H5
Louisiana, Mo, US 181/J4
Louisville, Al, US 191/F2
Louisville, Co, US 180/B4
Louisville, Ga, US 189/F4
Louisville, Il, US 188/C1
Louisville, Ky, US 188/E1
Louisville, Ms, US 188/C4
Louisville, Ne, US 181/F3
Louisville, Oh, US 186/F4
Loukhi, Rus. 94/G2
Loukkos (riv.), Mor. 138/A2
Loukouo, Congo 146/C3
Loulé, Port. 72/A4
Loum, Camr. 146/B1
Louny, Czh. 85/G2
Loup (riv.), Fr. 90/C5
Loup (riv.), Ne, US 180/E3
Loup City, Ne, US 180/E3
Lourches, Fr. 80/C3
Lourdes, Nf, Can. 185/H1
Lourdes, Fr. 70/C5
Lourdes/Tarbes (int'l arpt.), Fr. 70/D5
Loures, Port. 73/P10
Louriçal, Port. 72/A2
Lourinhã, Port. 72/A3
Loury, Fr. 83/H4
Lousã, Port. 72/A2
Lousa, Port. 73/Q10
Loushan (pass), China 113/E2
Loutété, Congo 146/C4
Louth, Ire. 60/B4
Louth, Eng, UK 61/H5
Louth (co.), Ire. 60/B4
Louth, Austl. 158/C1
Loutrá Aidhipsoú, Gre. 75/H3
Loutrákion, Gre. 75/H4
Louts (riv.), Fr. 73/E1
Loútsa, Gre. 75/P9
Louvain (Leuven), Belg. 81/D2
Louvale, Ga, US 188/E4
Louveira, Braz. 211/K8
Louverné, Fr. 83/E4
Louviers, Fr. 83/G2
Louviers, Co, US 180/B4
Louvigné-de-Bais, Fr. 82/D4
Louvigné-du-Désert, Fr. 83/D4
Louvres, Fr. 56/K4
Louvroil, Fr. 80/C3
Lovaart (riv.), Belg. 80/B1
Lovat' (riv.), Rus. 94/F4
Lovat' (riv.), Bela.,Rus. 67/P3
Lovćen NP, Yugo. 75/F1
Lovćenac, Yugo. 76/D3
Love Point, Md, US 194/B5
Lovech (prov.), Bul. 75/J1
Lovech, Bul. 77/G4
Lovejoy, Ga, US 189/M8
Lovelady, Tx, US 177/G2
Loveland, Co, US 180/B3
Lovell, Wy, US 173/J1
Lovelock, Nv, US 172/D3
Lovere, It. 88/D2
Loverna, Sk, Can. 171/K2
Loves Park, Il, US 181/K2
Lovilia, Ia, US 181/H3
Loving, NM, US 176/B1
Lovingston, Va, US 189/H2
Lovington, NM, US 178/C4
Lovios, Sp. 72/A2
Lövó, Hun. 76/C2
Lovosice, Czh. 85/H1
Lovozero (lake), Rus. 94/G2
Lóvua, Ang. 146/E4
Low (des.), Or, US 172/C2
Low (cape), Nun, Can. 167/H2
Lowa (riv.), D.R. Congo 133/E5
Lowdham, Eng, UK 61/H6
Lowe, Ks, US 178/D1
Lowe Farm, Mb, Can. 182/F3
Lowell, Ar, US 179/G2
Lowell, In, US 186/C4
Lowell, Oh, US 186/F5
Lowell (lake), Id, US 172/E2
Lowell, Or, US 172/B2
Lowell, Id, US 170/G4
Lowell Observatory, Az, US 175/G3
Löwen (riv.), Namb. 150/B2
Löwenstein, Ger. 84/C4
Lower (falls), Mi, US 186/D1
Lower (dam), Wa, US 193/D3
Lower (lake), Ca, US 172/C3
Lower (falls), Wy, US 173/H1
Lower (bay), NJ, US 194/D2
Lower Arrow (lake), BC, Can. 170/E3
Lower Brailes, Eng, UK 63/E2
Lower Brule Ind. Res., SD, US 180/D1
Lower Engadine (valley), Swi. 87/G4
Lower Ganges (canal), India 122/B2
Lower Glenelg NP, Austl. 158/B3
Lower Granite (gorge), Az, US 175/E2
Lower Heyford, Eng, UK 63/E3
Lower Hutt, NZ 161/H9
Lower Klamath (lake), Ca, US 172/C3
Lower Klamath NWR, Or, US 172/C2
Lower Mesa (falls), Id, US 173/H1
Lower Monumental (dam) Wa, US 170/E4
Lower Nazeing, Eng, UK 56/D1
Lower Otay (lake), Ca, US 192/D5
Lower Peach Tree, Al, US 190/E2
Lower Red (lake), Mn, US 183/G4
Lower Rhine (riv.), Neth. 78/C5
Lower Rouge (riv.), Mi, US 193/E7
Lower Sioux Ind. Res., Mn, US 181/G1
Lower Stoke, Eng, UK 56/E2
Lower Suwannee Nat'l Wild. Ref., Fl, US 191/G3
Lower Trajan's Wall (wall), Mol.,Ukr 96/D3
Lower Trajan's Wall (wall), Mol.,Ukr. 98/E5
Lower Trajan's Wall (wall), Mol. 77/J3
Lower Trajan's (wall), Mol.,Ukr. 93/L1
Lower Tunguska (riv.), Rus. 103/J3
Lower Wedgeport, NS, Can. 184/E4
Lower West Pubnico, NS, Can. 184/E4
Lower Zambezi NP, Zam. 149/F2
Lowery (lake), Fl, US 190/M7
Lowestoft, Eng, UK 63/H2
Lowick, Eng, UK 59/E5
Łowicz, Pol. 69/K2
Lowman, Id, US 172/F1
Lowry City, Mo, US 179/H1
Lowther (hills), Sc, UK 59/C6
Lowville, NY, US 187/J3
Lowville, On, Can. 186/T9
Loxahatchee, Fl, US 190/P9
Loxahatchee National Wildlife Refuge, Fl, US 191/H4
Loxahatchee Slough (swamp), Fl, US 190/P9
Loxstedt, Ger. 79/F2
Loxton, Austl. 157/J5
Loxton, SAfr. 150/C3
Loxton North, Austl. 157/J5
Loya, Tanz. 145/A3
Loyal, Wi, US 181/J1
Loyall, Ky, US 189/F2
Loyalton, Ca, US 172/C4
Loyalton, Pa, US 194/B2
Loyalty (isls.), NCal. 162/F7
Loyettes, Fr. 86/B6
Loyev, Bela. 98/F2
Loyne (lake), Sc, UK 59/A2
Loyno, Rus. 95/M4
Loyoro, Ugan. 142/G5
Loysville, Pa, US 194/A3
Loznica, Yugo. 76/D3
Loznitsa, Bul. 77/H4
Lozova, Ukr. 99/J3
Lozovik, Yugo. 76/E3
Lozym, Rus. 95/L3
Itz (riv.), Ger. 68/F3
Lü (isl.), Tai. 113/J4
Lu (riv.), China 106/C5
Lu (mtn.), China 106/D3
Lu (peak), China 113/G2
Lu Xian, China 119/J2
Lua (riv.), Congo 142/C5
Lua (riv.), D.R. Congo 146/D2
Lua Dekere (riv.), D.R. Congo 146/D2
Luabo, Moz. 149/H3
Luacano, Ang. 148/D1
Luachimo, Ang. 147/E4
Luachimo (riv.), Ang. 147/E5
Luaco, Ang. 147/E4
Luaha-Sibuha, Indo. 115/B3
Luala (riv.), Moz. 149/H3
Lualaba (riv.), D.R. Congo 133/E5
Luale, D.R. Congo 147/E2
Luali, D.R. Congo 146/C4
Luama (riv.), D.R. Congo 147/F4
Luambe NP, Zam. 149/G2
Luampa, Zam. 148/E2
Luampa (riv.), Zam. 148/E2
Luan (riv.), China 101/M5
Lu'an, China 106/D5
Luan Xian, China 106/D3
Luancheng, China 113/F4
Luanchuan, China 106/B4
Luanco, Sp. 72/C1
Luanda (prov.), Ang. 146/C5
Luanda, Kenya 145/A1
Luanda (cap.), Ang. 146/C5
Luando (riv.), Ang. 146/D5
Luando, Ang. 148/C1
Luando, Rsv. Nat. do, Ang. 146/D5
Luang (peak), Thai. 120/B4
Luang (lag.), Malay. 119/H6
Luangue (riv.), Ang. 146/D4
Luangue, Ang. 146/D5
Luanguinga (riv.), Ang. 148/D2
Luangwa (riv.), Zam. 147/G5
Luanhaizi, China 104/C5
Luano (int'l arpt.), D.R. Congo 149/E1
Luanping, China 106/D2
Luanshya, Zam. 149/F2
Luao (riv.), D.R. Congo 147/E5
Luao, Ang. 147/E5
Luapula (riv.), Zam. 147/G5
Luapula (prov.), Zam. 147/G5
Luarca, Sp. 72/B1
Luashi, D.R. Congo 147/E5
Luatize (riv.), Moz. 149/F2
Luau (riv.), Ang. 147/E5
Luba, EqG. 146/B2
Lubaantun (ruin), Belz. 200/D2
Lubaczów, Pol. 69/M3
Lubalo, Ang. 146/D5
Lubań, Pol. 69/H3
Lubāna, Lat. 67/M3
Lubang (isl.), Phil. 114/B2
Lubang, Phil. 114/C2
Lubango, D.R. Congo 147/F3
Lubango, Ang. 148/B2
Lubansenshi (riv.), Zam. 147/G5
Lubao, D.R. Congo 147/F4
Lubartów, Pol. 69/M3
Lubawa, Pol. 69/K2
Lübbecke, Ger. 79/F4
Lubbeek, Belg. 81/D2
Lubbock, Tx, US 178/D4
Lubeck, WV, US 189/G1
Lubefu (riv.), D.R. Congo 147/E4
Lubefu, D.R. Congo 147/F4
Lubelska (uplands), Pol. 69/M3
Lubenka, Kaz. 97/K2
Lubero, D.R. Congo 147/G3
Lubero (riv.), D.R. Congo 147/G3
Lubéron, Montagne de (mts.), Fr. 90/B5
Lubi (riv.), D.R. Congo 147/E4
Lubień Kujawski, Pol. 69/K2
Lubika, D.R. Congo 147/G4
Lubilash (riv.), D.R. Congo 147/E5
Lubin, Pol. 69/J3
Lublin, Pol. 69/M3
Lublin (prov.), Pol. 98/B2
Lubliniec, Pol. 69/K3
Lubmin, Ger. 66/E4
Lubnaig (lake), Sc, UK 59/B4
Lubny, Ukr. 99/G2
Luboń, Pol. 69/J2
Lubongola, D.R. Congo 147/F3
Lubrín, Sp. 72/D4
Lubsko, Pol. 69/H3
Lubuagan, Phil. 114/C1
Lububu, D.R. Congo 147/F4
Lubudi (riv.), D.R. Congo 147/E4
Lubudi, D.R. Congo 147/F5
Lubue (riv.), D.R. Congo 146/D4
Lubuklinggau, Indo. 115/C3
Lubukpakam, Indo. 115/B2
Lubuksikaping, Indo. 115/C2
Lubumbashi, D.R. Congo 149/E1
Lubunda, D.R. Congo 147/F4
Lubunza, D.R. Congo 147/E4
Lubutu, D.R. Congo 147/F3
Lubwe, Zam. 147/G5
Luc An Chau, Viet. 120/D1
Luc-en-Diois, Fr. 90/B3
Luc-sur-Mer, Fr. 83/E2
Lucala, Ang. 146/C5
Lucala (riv.), Ang. 146/C5
Lucan, Ire. 60/B5
Lucan, On, Can. 186/F3
Lücaoshan, China 104/D4
Lucapa, Ang. 147/E5
Lucas, Ks, US 179/E1
Lucas, Tx, US 176/L6
Lucas González, Arg. 215/J10
Lucasville, Oh, US 189/F1
Lucca (prov.), It. 88/D5
Lucca, It. 88/D6
Lucciana, Fr. 74/A1
Lucé, Fr. 83/G4
Luce (bay), Sc, UK 60/D2
Luce Bayou (riv.), Tx, US 177/M8
Lucedale, Ms, US 190/D2
Lucélia, Braz. 213/G2
Lucena, Sp. 72/C4
Lucena, Phil. 114/C2
Lucena del Cid, Sp. 73/E2
Lučenec, Slvk. 69/K4
Lucens, Swi. 86/C4
Lucerna, Peru 208/D4
Lucerne (lake), Ca, US 192/C1
Lucerne, Wy, US 173/J2
Lucerne, Wa, US 170/D3
Lucerne (Luzern), Swi. 71/H3
Lucerne (Vierwaldstättersee) (lake), Swi. 87/E3
Lucero (lake), NM, US 178/A4
Lucero (mesa), NM, US 175/J3
Luchang, China 112/D3
Luché-Pringé, Fr. 83/F3
Luchegorsk, Rus. 105/L2
Lucheng, China 106/C3
Lucheng, China 113/E3

Mahl – Marat

Majd el Kurŭm, Isr. 131/C3
Majdal 'Anjar, Leb. 131/D1
Majdanpek, Yugo. 76/E3
Mahlberg, Ger. 86/D1
Mahlow, Ger. 68/Q7
Mahmel (peak), Alg. 92/E4
Mahmŭd-e 'Erāqĭ, Afg. 127/J1
Mahmūdābād, India 122/C2
Mahmudiye, Turk. 128/B2
Mahnomen, Mn, US 182/G4
Mahoba, India 122/B3
Mahon (riv.), Ire. 58/C5
Mahón, Sp. 73/H3
Mahone Bay, NS, Can. 184/F3
Mahoning (riv.), Oh, US 188/E2
Mahroni, India 122/B3
Mahtomedi, Mn, US 183/Q6
Mahuanggou, China 104/D4
Mahur, India 112/B3
Mahusekwa, Zim. 149/F3
Mahuta, Tanz. 145/B4
Mahuva, India 121/A1
Mahwah, India 122/A2
Mahwah, NJ, US 195/J7
Mai-Ndombe
(lake), D.R. Congo 146/D3
Maia, Port. 72/A2
Maiala Nat'l Pk., Austl. 160/E6
Maials, Sp. 73/F2
Maiana (isl.), Kiri. 162/G4
Maiao (isl.), FrPol. 163/W15
Maicao, Col. 204/C2
Maiche, Fr. 86/C3
Maicuru (riv.), Braz. 205/H5
Maiden (cr.), Pa, US 194/C2
Maiden Newton, Eng, UK 62/D5
Maidenhead, Eng, UK 63/F3
Maidens, Sc, UK 59/B6
Maidi, Indo. 117/G3
Maidstone, On, Can. 193/G7
Maidstone, Eng, UK 63/G4
Maidstone, Sk, Can. 171/K1
Maiduguri, Nga. 142/B3
Maie, D.R. Congo 147/G2
Maienfeld, Swi. 87/F4
Maigatari, Nga. 141/H3
Maigue (riv.), Ire. 58/B4
Maihar, India 122/C3
Maihara, Japan 109/K5
Maijdi, Bang. 123/H4
Maikala (range), India 122/C4
Maiko (riv.), D.R. Congo 147/F3
Maikoor (riv.), Indo. 154/D1
Maikoro, Chad 142/C3
Mailāni, India 122/C1
Mailly-le-Camp, Fr. 81/D6
Mailsi, Pak. 124/B5
Maimoon Palace (Istana
Maimoon), Indo. 115/B2
Maimon, D.R. Congo 147/G2
Main (riv.), NI, UK 60/B2
Main (riv.), Ger. 68/C4
Main (chan.), On, Can. 186/F2
Māʾīn, Jor. 131/D5
Main Centre, Sk, Can. 171/L2
Main Range NP, Austl. 160/D5
Main-à-Dieu, NS, Can. 185/H2
Main-Donau (canal), Ger. 84/D3
Maināguri, India 123/G2
Mainbernheim, Ger. 84/D3
Maincy, Fr. 56/D4
Maine (riv.), Ire. 58/A5
Maine (reg.), Fr. 70/C2
Maine (gulf), US 185/G4
Maine (state), US 169/N2
Maine, Collines du
(hill), Fr. 83/E6
Maine-et-Loire (dept.), Fr. 83/E6
Maïné-Soroa, Niger 142/B2
Maingkwan, Myan. 119/G2
Maingnyaung, Myan. 112/B4
Mainhardt, Ger. 84/C4
Mainhausen, Ger. 84/B2
Maini, Pak. 124/B2
Mainit, Phil. 114/D3
Mainkung, China 112/C2
Mainland (isl.), Sc, UK 57/V14
Mainling, China 112/B2
Mainoru, Austl. 154/D3
Mainpuri, India 122/B2
Mainstockheim, Ger. 84/D3
Maintenon, Fr. 81/G3
Maintirano, Madg. 152/H7
Mainvilliers, Fr. 83/G4
Mainz, Ger. 81/H4
Maio (isl.), CpV. 133/K10
Maiori, It. 92/D6
Maipo (riv.), Chile 214/N8
Maipo (vol.), Chile 214/P9
Maipú, Arg. 214/E4
Maipú, Chile 214/N8
Maiquetía, Ven. 207/P7
Maira (riv.), It. 71/G4
Mairana, Bol. 212/D1
Maire (str.), Arg. 215/D7
Mairi, Braz. 211/E1
Mairiporã, Braz. 211/K8
Mairwa, India 123/E2
Mais Gate
(int'l arpt.), Haiti 201/H2
Maisach, Ger. 84/E6
Maisi (cape), Cuba 197/C3
Maišiagala, Lith. 67/L4
Maiskhāl, Bang. 112/A4
Maisome (isl.), Tanz. 147/G3
Maison-Rouge, Fr. 56/M5
Maisoncelles-en-Brie,
Fr. 56/M5
Maisons-Alfort, Fr. 56/K5
Maisons-Laffitte, Fr. 56/J5
Maitengwe, Bots. 149/E4
Maithon (res.), India 123/F4
Maitland, On, Can. 187/J2
Maitland (riv.), On, Can. 186/F4
Maitland, NS, Can. 184/F3
Maitland, Fl, US 190/N6
Maitland, Austl. 157/H5
Maitland, Austl. 159/E1
Maitum, Phil. 114/D4
Maizières-lès-Metz, Fr. 81/F5
Maizuru (bay), Japan 109/H4
Maizuru, Japan 109/H5
Maja e Zezë (peak), Alb. 105/G3
Majadahonda, Sp. 73/N9
Majagual, Col. 204/C2
Majalengka, Indo. 115/G4
Majardah (riv.), Alg. 138/K6
Majarr (wadi), Syria 131/E3
Majāz Al Bāb, Tun. 138/L6

Malākhera, India 122/A2
Malakoff, Tx, US 177/F1
Malakwāl, PNG 124/B3
Malalaua, PNG 134/B3
Malalhue, Chile 214/B3
Malambo, Col. 204/C2
Malang, Indo. 115/F3
Malangawa, Nepal 123/E2
Malanje, Ang. 146/D5
Malanje (prov.), Ang. 146/D5
Malanville, Ben. 141/F4
Malapatan, Phil. 114/D4
Malār, Pak. 127/J4
Malārgüe, Arg. 214/C2
Malāsoro (pt.), Indo. 117/E5
Malaspina, Arg. 214/C4
Malatya, Turk. 128/D2
Malatya (prov.), Turk. 128/D2
Malaucène, Fr. 90/B4
Malaut, India 124/C4
Malawali (isl.), Malay. 109/E1
Malawi (ctry.) 133/F6
Malay (pen.), India 148/D4
Malay (pen.), Thai. 123/F2
Malaya (reg.), Malay. 119/G3
Malaya Belozërka, Ukr. 99/H4
Malaya Vishera, Rus. 125/D2
Malaybalay, Phil. 114/D3
Malo, It. 89/E2
Malo, Wa, US 170/E3
Maloarkhangel'sk, Rus. 99/K3
Maloca (riv.), Braz. 95/J2
Malolos, Phil. 114/E6
Malombe (lake), Malw. 149/G2
Malone, NY, US 157/J2
Malone, Fl, US 191/F2
Malone, Tx, US 177/F2
Malong, China 112/D3
Malonga, D.R. Congo 146/E4
Malonje (peak), Tanz. 147/G5
Malpas, Eng, UK 61/F5
Malpelo (isl.), Col. 103/C9
Malpensa (int'l arpt.), It. 88/B2
Malpica, Sp. 72/A1
Mals (Malles), It. 87/G6
Malsch, Ger. 84/B5
Malschwitz, Ger. 85/H5
Mältö, Swe. 64/F2
Malters, Swi. 88/D2
Malton, Eng, UK 61/G1
Malton, On, Can. 186/T8
Maltorne (riv.), Fr. 56/G6
Malu, China 104/D5
Maluku, D.R. Congo 146/C4
Maluku (prov.), Indo. 154/D1
Malu'ū, Sol. 131/F1
Malumba, D.R. Congo 147/F3
Malumi, Japan 109/B7
Malung, Swe. 66/E1
Maluso, Phil. 114/C4
Malūt, Sudan 133/B3
Malvaglia, Swi. 87/E5
Malvan, Port. 73/P10
Malvern, Ar, US 179/H4
Malvern, Ia, US 181/G3
Malvern (nbrhd.), Austl. 158/G5
Malvern, Eng, UK 61/E4
Malvern, NY, US 195/L8
Malvern, NY, US 195/L9
Malvinas (Falkland
(isls.)), UK 117/E4
Mancha Real, Sp. 216/W

Marau, Braz. 213/F4
Maraulīānwāla, Pak. 124/B3
Maravatío de Ocampo, Mex. 199/E5
Maravilha, Braz. 213/F3
Maravillas (cr.), Tx, US 177/C3
Maravillas, Bol. 209/E3
Marāwah, Libya 93/J4
Marawaka, PNG 155/G1
Marawī, Sudan 135/F5
Marawi, Phil. 114/D3
Marayes, Arg. 212/C4
Marazion, Eng, UK 62/A6
Marbach, Swi. 86/D4
Marbach am Neckar, Ger. 84/C5
Marbache, Fr. 81/F6
Marbella, Sp. 72/C4
Marble (canyon), Az, US 175/G2
Marble, NC, US 188/F3
Marble Bar, Austl. 156/C2
Marble Canyon, Az, US 175/G2
Marble Falls, Tx, US 176/E2
Marble Hall, SAfr. 149/F5
Marble Hill, Mo, US 188/C2
Marblemount, Wa, US 170/D3
Marbleton, Qu, Can. 187/L2
Marbleton, Wy, US 173/H2
Marburg (lake), Pa, US 194/B4
Marbury, Al, US 188/D4
Marcali, Hun. 76/C2
Marcallo, It. 88/B3
Marcapata, Peru 208/D4
Marcelin, Sk, Can. 171/L1
Marceline, Mo, US 181/H4
Marcelino Ramos, Braz. 213/G3
Marcella, Ar, US 179/J3
Marcellina, It. 91/B3
Marcellus, Mi, US 186/D3
March (A.F.B.), Ca, US 192/C3
March, Eng, UK 63/G1
Marchant (mt.), NZ 161/J9
Marche (pol. reg.), It. 92/C2
Marche, Congo 146/C4
Marche (mts.), Fr. 70/d3
Marche-en-Famenne, Belg. 81/E3
Marchémoret, Fr. 56/L4
Marchena, Sp. 72/C4
Marchena (isl.), Ecu. 208/J6
Marcheno, It. 88/D2
Marches (reg.), It. 93/G2
Marchiennes, Fr. 80/C3
Marchin, Belg. 81/E3
Marchinbar (isl.), Austl. 155/E2
Marchtrenk, Aus. 85/H6
Marchwell, Sk, Can. 182/D2
Marciana Marina, It. 74/B1
Marcianise, It. 92/D5
Marcilly, Fr. 56/L4
Marcilly-sur-Tille, Fr. 86/B2
Marck, Fr. 80/A2
Marckolsheim, Fr. 86/D1
Marco, Fl, US 191/H5
Marco (isl.), Fl, US 191/H5
Marco, Braz. 207/F3
Marco Polo (int'l arpt.), It. 89/F3
Marcoing, Fr. 80/C3
Marcola, Or, US 172/B1
Marcon, It. 89/F2
Marcona, Peru 208/C4
Marconi (mt.), BC, Can. 170/G2
Marcos Juárez, Arg. 214/E2
Marcosli (riv.), BC, Can. 170/C1
Marcoussis, Fr. 56/J6
Marcovia, Hon. 200/E3
Marcq-en-Barœul, Fr. 80/C2
Marcus, Ia, US 181/G2
Marcy (mt.), NY, US 187/K2
Mardān, Pak. 124/B2
Marden, Eng, UK 56/E3
Mardeuil, Fr. 80/C5
Mardin, Turk. 128/E2
Mardin (prov.), Turk. 128/E2
Maré (isl.), NCal. 163/W12
Marecchia (riv.), It. 89/F5
Marechal Cândido Rondon, Braz. 213/F3
Marechal Deodoro, Braz. 211/G1
Maree (lake), Sc, UK 57/R8
Mareeba, Austl. 160/B2
Mareham le Fen, Eng, UK 61/H5
Mareil-sur-Mauldre, Fr. 56/H5
Marek, Indo. 117/F4
Maréna, Mali 140/C3
Marengo, Wi, US 183/J4
Marengo, Il, US 193/N15
Marengo, Ia, US 181/H3
Marengo, In, US 188/D1
Marengo, Sk, Can. 171/K2
Marenisco, Mi, US 183/K4
Marennes, Fr. 70/C4
Mareolaboom, Namb. 148/C3
Marerano, Madg. 152/H8
Maresfield, Eng, UK 63/G5
Mareuil-sur-Ourcq, Fr. 56/M4
Marfa, Tx, US 177/B2
Marfield, Austl. 159/B1
Marfino, Rus. 97/J3
Margalla Hills NP, Pak. 124/B3
Margam, Wal, UK 62/C3
Marganets', Ukr. 99/H4
Margao (Madgaon), India 121/B3
Margaree, NS, Can. 185/G2
Margaree Valley, NS, Can. 185/G2
Margaret, Tx, US 178/E3
Margaret (riv.), Austl. 154/B4
Margaret (mt.), Austl. 156/C2
Margaret River, Austl. 156/B5
Margarita (peak), Ca, US 192/C4
Margarita (isl.), Ven. 205/F2
Margarita, Isla de (isl.), Trin. 197/J5
Margarítion, Gre. 75/G3
Margate, Eng, UK 63/H4
Margate, Fl, US 190/P10
Margate, SAfr. 151/E3
Margate City, NJ, US 194/D5
Margeride (mts.), Fr. 70/E4
Margeta (cape), Indo. 154/B2
Margherita (peak), Ugan. 147/G2
Marghilon, Uzb. 125/B3
Marghita, Rom. 76/F2
Margny-lès-Compiègne Fr. 80/B5
Margo, Sk, Can. 182/C2
Margog Caka (lake), China 125/E5
Margos, Peru 208/B3
Margosatubig, Phil. 114/C4
Margraten, Neth. 81/E2
Marguareis (peak), It. 90/D4
Marguerite, BC, Can. 170/C1
Margyang, China 123/H1
Mari, PNG 155/F2
Mari, Braz. 207/H4
Mari El Aut. Rep., Rus. 100/Q6
Maria, Qu, Can. 184/E1
Maria (mt.), Austl. 158/D4
Maria (isl.), Austl. 155/D3
Maria Aurora, Phil. 114/C2
María Cleófas (isl.), Mex. 198/D4
Maria da Fé, Braz. 211/L7
Maria Island NP, Austl. 158/D4
Maria Juana, Arg. 212/D4
María Madre (isl.), Mex. 198/D4
María Magdalena (isl.), Mex. 198/D4
Maria van Diemen (cape), NZ 161/C1
Mariāhū, India 122/D3
Mariakani, Kenya 145/B2
Mariakerke, Belg. 80/B1
Marialva, Braz. 210/C4
Marian, Austl. 160/C3
Marianao, Cuba 201/F1
Marianna, Fl, US 191/F2
Marianna, Ar, US 188/B3
Mariano Comense, It. 88/C2
Mariano I. Loza, Arg. 212/E4
Mariánské Lázně, Czh. 85/F3
Mariarano, Madg. 152/H6
Marias (riv.), Mt, US 171/H3
Mariato (pt.), Pan. 204/A3
Ma'rib, Yem. 144/C2
Maribo, Den. 66/D4
Maribor, Slov. 76/B2
Maricá, Braz. 211/P7
Maricopa, Ca, US 174/C3
Maricopa, Az, US 175/F4
Maricopa (mts.), Az, US 175/F4
Maricopa Ak Chin Ind. Res., Az, US 175/F4
Maridalsvatn (lake), Nor. 64/S8
Marīdī, Sudan 142/F4
Marié (riv.), Braz. 205/E5
Marie Byrd Land (phys. reg.), Ant. 216/S
Marie-Galante (isl.), Dom. 197/J4
Mariefred, Swe. 65/A1
Mariehamn (int'l arpt.), Fin. 67/H1
Mariehamn (Maarianhamina), Fin. 67/H1
Marieholm, Swe. 65/K7
Mariel, Cuba 201/F1
Marienbourg, Belg. 81/D3
Mariënburg, Sur. 206/C1
Mariendorf, Ger. 68/Q7
Marienfelde, Ger. 68/Q7
Marienhafe, Ger. 79/E1
Marienheide, Ger. 81/G1
Mariental, Namb. 148/C5
Marienville, Pa, US 187/G4
Mariestad, Swe. 66/E2
Marietta, Ga, US 189/L7
Marietta, Mn, US 181/F1
Marietta, Ms, US 188/C3
Marietta, Oh, US 186/F5
Marietta, Ok, US 179/F4
Marietta, Pa, US 194/B3
Marieval, Sk, Can. 182/C2
Marigat, Kenya 145/A1
Marigliano, It. 92/D6
Marignane, Fr. 90/B6
Marigot, Fr. 197/N8
Marigot, Dom. 197/N9
Marihatag, Phil. 114/D3
Marijampolė, Lith. 67/K4
Marikina, Phil. 114/F6
Marikina (riv.), Phil. 114/F6
Marilao, Phil. 114/E6
Marília, Braz. 213/G2
Mariluz, Braz. 213/F3
Marín, Mex. 177/D5
Marin (co.), Ca, US 193/J10
Marín, Sp. 72/A1
Marin-Epagnier, Swi. 86/D3
Marina, It. 74/D3
Marina, Ca, US 174/B2
Marina del Rey (harbor), Ca, US 192/F8
Marina del Rey, Ca, US 192/F8
Marina di Andora, It. 88/B6
Marina di Carrara, It. 88/D5
Marina di Massa, It. 88/D5
Marina di Montemarciano, It. 89/G6
Marina di Pisa, It. 88/D6
Marina di Ravenna, It. 89/F5
Marina di Vasto, It 92/D3
Mar'ina Gorka, Bela. 67/N5
Marinduque (isl.), Phil. 114/C2
Marine, Il, US 181/K4
Marine City, Mi, US 186/E3
Marine Nat'l Res., Kenya 145/C2
Marine World Africa USA, Ca, US 193/K10
Marineland, Austl. 157/M8
Marineland of Florida, Fl, US 191/H3
Marines, Fr. 56/H4
Marinette, Wi, US 186/C2
Maringa (riv.), D.R. Congo 147/E2
Maringá, Braz. 213/G2
Maringouin, La, US 190/C2
Marínguè, Moz. 149/G3
Marinha Grande, Port. 72/A3
Marinhas, Port. 72/A2
Marino, It. 91/B4
Marion (reef), Austl. 153/E2
Marion, Al, US 188/D4
Marion, Ar, US 188/B3
Marion (cr.), Fl, US 190/M7
Marion (lake), Fl, US 190/M7
Marion, Ia, US 181/J2
Marion, Il, US 188/C2
Marion, In, US 186/D4
Marion, Ks, US 179/F1
Marion, Ky, US 188/C2
Marion, La, US 179/H4
Marion, Mi, US 186/D2
Marion, Ms, US 188/C4
Marion, NC, US 189/F3
Marion, ND, US 182/E4
Marion, Oh, US 186/E4
Marion, SC, US 189/H3
Marion (lake), SC, US 169/K5
Marion, SD, US 181/F2
Marion, Va, US 189/G2
Marion, Wi, US 181/K1
Marion Bridge, NS, Can. 185/G3
Marion Junction, Al, US 188/D4
Marionville, Mo, US 179/H2
Maripa, Ven. 205/E3
Maripa, FrG. 206/D2
Maripasoula, FrG. 206/C2
Mariposa, Ca, US 174/C2
Mariposa Grove, Ca, US 174/C2
Mariquita, Col. 207/L7
Mariscal Estigarribia, Par. 212/D2
Mariscal Sucre (int'l arpt.), Ecu. 204/B5
Marissa, Il, US 188/C1
Mārith, Tun. 92/F4
Maritime Alps (mts.), Fr. 92/E1
Maritsa (riv.), Bul. 96/C4
Maritsa (riv.), Turk. 77/H5
Mariupol', Ukr. 99/J4
Mariupol (int'l arpt.), Ukr. 99/J4
Marj 'Uyūn, Leb. 131/D2
Märjamaa, Est. 67/L2
Mark (riv.), Belg. 78/B6
Mark Twain (lake), Mo, US 181/H4
Mark Twain Nat'l Wild. Ref., Il, Ia, US 181/J3
Mark Twain Nat'l Wild. Ref., Il, Mo, US 181/J4
Marka (riv.), Ger. 79/E3
Marka, Som. 145/D1
Mārkā, Jor. 131/D5
Markagunt (plat.), Ut, US 175/F2
Markākasa, India 121/D1
Markakol (lake), Kaz. 104/D4
Markam, China 112/C2
Mārkāpur, India 121/C3
Markaryd, Swe. 66/E3
Markazī (gov.), Iran 129/G3
Markdale, On, Can. 186/F2
Markdorf, Ger. 87/F2
Marked Tree, Ar, US 188/B3
Markelsdorfer (pt.), Ger. 66/D4
Marken (isl.), Neth. 78/C4
Markerwaard (polder), Neth. 78/C3
Markesan, Wi, US 181/K2
Market Bosworth, Eng, UK 63/E1
Market Deeping, Eng, UK 63/F1
Market Drayton, Eng, UK 61/F6
Market Harborough, Eng, UK 63/F2
Market Rasen, Eng, UK 61/H5
Market Weighton, Eng, UK 61/H4
Markethill, NI, UK 60/B3
Markgroningen, Ger. 84/C5
Markha, India 124/D3
Markham, On, Can. 185/S8
Markham (bay), Nun, Can. 167/J2
Markham (riv.), PNG 155/G1
Markham, Tx, US 177/F3
Marki, Pol. 69/L2
Markinch, Sc, UK 59/C4
Markit, China 125/C4
Markivka, Ukr. 99/K3
Markle, In, US 186/D4
Markleeville, Ca, US 172/D4
Marknesse, Neth. 78/C3
Markneukirchen, Ger. 85/F2
Markópoulon, Gre. 75/N9
Markounda, CAfr. 142/C4
Markova, Rus. 104/E1
Markovac, Yugo. 76/E3
Markovo, Rus. 101/S3
Markoye, Burk. 141/F3
Marks, Rus. 97/H2
Marks, Ms, US 188/B3
Marksville, La, US 190/B2
Markt Bibart, Ger. 84/D3
Markt Erlbach, Ger. 84/D4
Markt Indersdorf, Ger. 85/E6
Markt Rettenbach, Ger. 87/G2
Markt Sankt Florian, Aus. 85/H6
Markt Schwaben, Ger. 85/E6
Marktbreit, Ger. 84/D3
Marktheidenfeld, Ger. 84/C3
Marktl, Ger. 85/F6
Marktoberdorf, Ger. 87/G2
Marktredwitz, Ger. 85/F3
Marl, Ger. 79/E5
Marla, Austl. 157/G3
Marlboro, Ab, Can. 170/F1
Marlboro, NJ, US 194/D3
Marlboro (Upper Marlboro), Md, US 194/B6
Marlborough, Ma, US 187/L3
Marlborough, Austl. 160/C3
Marlborough, Eng, UK 63/E4
Marle, Fr. 80/C4
Marlengo (Marling), It. 87/H4
Marlenheim, Fr. 81/G6
Marles-en-Brie, Fr. 56/L5
Marles-les-Mines, Fr. 80/B3
Marlette, Mi, US 186/E3
Marlin, Tx, US 177/F2
Marling (Marlengo), It. 87/H4
Marlinton, WV, US 189/G1
Marlow, Ok, US 179/F3
Marlow, Ger. 66/E4
Marlow, Eng, UK 63/F3
Marlow, Ga, US 189/G4
Marlpit Hill, Eng, UK 56/D3
Marlton, NJ, US 194/D4
Marly, Fr. 80/C3
Marly, Fr. 81/F5
Marly-la-Ville, Fr. 56/K4
Marly-le-Roi, Fr. 56/J5
Marmaduke, Ar, US 188/B2
Marmagão, India 121/B3
Marmande, Fr. 70/D4
Marmara (sea), Turk. 96/D4
Marmara (isl.), Turk. 93/K2
Marmara, Turk. 77/H5
Marmaraereğlisi, Turk. 77/H5
Marmaris, Turk. 128/B2
Marmarth, ND, US 182/C4
Marmelos, Rio dos (riv.), Braz. 206/A4
Marmet, WV, US 189/G1
Marmion (lake), On, Can. 183/J3
Marmion (lake), Austl. 156/D4
Marmirolo, It. 89/D3
Marmolada (peak), It. 71/J3
Marmolejo, Sp. 72/C3
Marmontana (peak), It. 87/F5
Marmora, On, Can. 187/H2
Marmora, NJ, US 194/D5
Marmot (peak), Mt, US 170/G4
Marmoutier, Fr. 81/G6
Marnay, Fr. 86/B3
Marnaz, Fr. 86/C5
Marne, Ger. 66/C5
Marne (dept.), Fr. 80/C6
Marne (riv.), Fr. 68/C4
Marne au Rhin, Canal de la (canal), Fr. 81/D6
Marneuli, Geo. 97/H4
Marnhull, Eng, UK 62/D5
Maro, Chad 142/C3
Maro Reef (reef), Hi, US 163/H2
Maroa, Ven. 205/E4
Maroa, Il, US 181/K3
Maroantsetra, Madg. 152/J6
Marofandilia, Madg. 152/H8
Marokau (isl.), FrPol. 163/L6
Marolambo, Madg. 152/J8
Maroldsweisach, Ger. 84/D2
Marolles, Fr. 56/M4
Marolles-en-Brie, Fr. 56/M5
Marolles-en-Hurepoix, Fr. 56/J6
Maromme, Fr. 83/G2
Maromokotro (peak), Madg. 152/J6
Marondera, Zim. 149/F3
Marone, It. 88/D2
Maroni (riv.), FrG.,Sur. 203/D2
Maroni (riv.), Sur.,FrG. 206/C1
Maroni (riv.), Sur. 205/H3
Maroochydore-Mooloolaba, Austl. 160/D4
Maroon Town, Jam. 201/G2
Maropaika, Madg. 152/H8
Marostica, It. 89/E2
Marotandrano, Madg. 152/J7
Marotiri (Bass Is.) (isl.), FrPol. 163/L7
Marotta, It. 89/G6
Maroua, Camr. 142/B3
Marouini (riv.), FrG. 205/H4
Marovato, Madg. 152/J6
Marovato, Madg. 152/J6
Marovoay, Madg. 152/H7
Marowijne (dist.), Sur. 205/H3
Marpingen, Ger. 81/G5
Marple, Eng, UK 61/F5
Marqên Gangri (peak), China 104/D5
Marquan (riv.), China 118/E2
Marquand, Mo, US 188/B2
Marquard, SAfr. 150/D3
Marquarie (riv.), Austl. 162/D8
Marquesas (isls.), FrPol. 163/M5
Marquesas Keys (isls.), Fl, US 191/G5
Marquetalia, Col. 207/K7
Marquette, Mi, US 183/L4
Marquette, Ks, US 179/F1
Marquette, Mb, Can. 182/F2
Marquez, Tx, US 177/F2
Marquis, Sk, Can. 171/M2
Marquise, Fr. 80/A2
Marracuene, Moz. 151/F2
Marradi, It. 89/E5
Marrah (peak), Sudan 142/E2
Marrakech, Mor. 136/D3
Marrakech (Menara) (int'l arpt.), Mor. 136/C3
Marrawah, Austl. 158/C4
Marree, Austl. 157/H4
Marromeu, Moz. 149/G3
Marrowbone, Ky, US 188/E2
Marrowie (cr.), Austl. 159/B1
Marrupa, Moz. 149/H2
Mars, Pa, US 186/F4
Mars (peak), It. 88/A1
Mars Hill, NC, US 189/F3
Marsá al 'Alam, Egypt 135/G3
Marsá al Burayqah, Libya 134/C2
Marsa Ben Mehidi, Alg. 138/C2
Marsá Matrūh, Egypt 135/E2
Marsabit, Kenya 145/B1
Marsabit Nat'l Rsv., Kenya 143/H5
Marsabit National Reserve, Kenya 144/A5
Marşafā, Egypt 139/C4
Marsala, It. 74/C4
Marsange (riv.), Fr. 56/L5
Marsannay, Fr. 86/A3
Marsberg, Ger. 79/F6
Marsciano, It. 91/B2
Marsden, Eng, UK 61/G4
Marsden, Sk, Can. 171/K1
Marsden, Austl. 159/C1
Marsdiep Texelstroom (chan.), Neth. 78/B3
Marseille, Fr. 90/B6
Marseille au Rhône (canal), Fr. 90/A5
Marseille-en-Beauvaisis, Fr. 80/A4
Marseilles, Il, US 181/K3
Marsella, Col. 207/K8
Marsh (mtn.), Md, US 187/G5
Marsh (isl.), La, US 196/C2
Marsh (peak), Ut, US 173/J3
Marsh (cr.), Pa, US 194/F1
Marsh Gibbon, Eng, UK 63/E3
Marshall, Ok, US 179/F2
Marshall, Ar, US 179/H3
Marshall, Il, US 186/C5
Marshall, Mi, US 186/D3
Marshall, Libr. 140/C5
Marshall (riv.), Austl. 157/H2
Marshall, Mo, US 181/H4
Marshall, NC, US 189/F3
Marshall, Mn, US 181/G1
Marshall, Sk, Can. 171/K1
Marshall, Tx, US 177/G1
Marshall Islands(ctry.) 162/G3
Marshallton, De, US 194/C4
Marshalltown, Ia, US 181/H2
Marshallville, Ga, US 188/F4
Marshfield, Mo, US 179/H2
Marshfield, Wi, US 181/J1
Marshyhope (cr.), Md, US 194/C6
Marske-by-the-Sea, Eng, UK 61/G2
Marsland, Ne, US 180/C2
Märsta, Swe. 66/G2
Marston, Mo, US 188/C2
Marsyandi (riv.), Nepal 123/E1
Marta, It. 74/B1
Marta (mts.), Col. 201/H4
Martaban, Myan. 120/B2
Martaban (gulf), Myan. 120/B2
Martano (peak), It. 91/B2
Martap, Camr. 142/B4
Martapura, Indo. 115/D3
Martapura, Indo. 116/D4
Marte R. Gomez, Mex. 198/C3
Martelange, Belg. 81/E4
Martellago, It. 89/F2
Martensville, Sk, Can. 171/L1
Martfeld, Ger. 79/G3
Martha, Ok, US 178/E3
Martha, Ky, US 189/F1
Martha's Vineyard (isl.), Ma, US 184/B5
Martignacco, It. 89/G1
Martigné-Ferchaud, Fr. 82/D5
Martigné-sur-Mayenne, Fr. 83/E4
Martigny, Swi. 86/D5
Martigny-les-Bains, Fr. 86/B1
Martigues, Fr. 90/B6
Martil, Mor. 138/B2
Martilla, Fin. 65/F4
Martin, ND, US 182/D4
Martin, La, US 190/B1
Martin, Mi, US 186/D3
Martin, SD, US 180/D2
Martin (dam), Al, US 188/E4
Martin, Tn, US 188/C2
Martin (lake), Al, US 188/E4
Martín Chico, Uru. 215/J11
Martin Luther King, Jr. Nat'l Hist. Site, Ga, US 189/M7
Martina Franca, It. 75/E2
Martinborough, NZ 161/J9
Martindale, Tx, US 176/F3
Martinengo, It. 88/C2
Martinez, Ca, US 172/B4
Martinez, Ga, US 189/F4
Martínez de la Torre, Mex. 199/M6
Martínez del Tineo, Arg. 212/C2
Martinique (isl.), Fr. 165/L8
Martinique Passage (chan.), Dom.,Mart. 197/N9
Martínon, Gre. 75/H3
Martinópole, Braz. 207/F3
Martins, Braz. 207/G4
Martins Creek, Pa, US 194/C2
Martins Ferry, Oh, US 186/F4
Martins Mills, Tx, US 177/G1
Martinsburg, WV, US 187/H5
Martinsburg, Pa, US 187/G4
Martinsburg, NY, US 187/J3
Martinsicuro, It. 92/C2
Martinsville, Il, US 186/C5
Martinsville, Ms, US 190/C2
Martinsville, In, US 186/C5
Martinsville, Va, US 189/H2
Martock, Eng, UK 62/D5
Martofte, Den. 66/D4
Marton, NZ 161/C3
Martorell, Sp. 73/K7
Martos, Sp. 72/D4
Martovce, Slvk. 76/D2
Martres-Tolosane, Fr. 70/D5
Martūba, Libya 93/J4
Martuk, Kaz. 97/L2
Martuni, Arm. 97/H4
Marty, SD, US 180/E2
Martynovo, Kaz. 97/J2
Maru, Nga. 141/G3
Marudi, Malay. 114/A4
Marugame, Japan 110/C3
Maruim, Braz. 211/F1
Maruko, Japan 111/F2
Marulan, Austl. 159/E2
Marulanda, Col. 207/K7
Marum, Neth. 78/D2
Marumba, Tanz. 149/H1
Marungu (mts.), D.R. Congo 147/G5
Maruoka, Japan 110/E2
Marutea (isl.), FrPol. 163/M7
Marv Dasht, Iran 129/H4
Marvel, Co, US 175/H2
Marvell, Ar, US 188/B3
Marvin, SD, US 181/F1
Marvine (mt.), Ut, US 175/G1
Marwayne, Ab, Can. 171/J1
Marxheim, Ger. 84/D5
Mary (lake), Ms, US 190/C2
Mary, Trkm. 127/H1
Mary Anne Passage, Austl. 156/B2
Mary Esther, Fl, US 190/E2
Mary Kathleen, Austl. 157/H2
Mary-sur-Marne, Fr. 56/M4
Maryānaj, Iran 129/G3
Maryang, China 125/C4
Maryborough, Austl. 160/D4
Maryborough, Austl. 158/B3
Marydale, SAfr. 150/C3
Marydel, Md, US 194/C5
Maryfield, Sk, Can. 182/D3
Mar'yinka, Ukr. 99/J4
Marykirk, Sc, UK 59/D3
Maryland (co.), Libr. 140/C5
Maryland (state), US 169/L4
Maryland City, Md, US 194/B5
Maryland Junction, Zim. 149/F3
Maryland Line, Md, US 194/B4
Maryneal, Tx, US 177/D1
Maryport, Eng, UK 60/E2
Marystown, Nf, Can. 185/K2
Marysvale, Ut, US 175/F1
Marysville, Mi, US 186/E3
Marysville, Oh, US 186/E4
Marysville, Ca, US 172/C4
Marysville, Ks, US 181/F4
Marysville, Wa, US 170/C3
Marysville, Mt, US 171/H4
Marysville, Pa, US 194/B3
Maryūt (lake), Egypt 139/A2
Maryvale, Austl. 160/D5
Maryville, Tn, US 188/F3
Maryville, Mo, US 181/G3
Marzabotto, It. 89/E5
Marzano (peak), It. 74/D2
Marzo (pt.), Col. 204/B3
Marzūq, Libya 134/B3
Marzūq (des.), Libya 134/B3
Masabit Nat'l Rsv., Kenya 145/B1
Masada (ruin), Isr. 135/G2
Masada NP, Isr. 131/C6
Masagan (riv.), Som. 144/C3
Masai Mara Nat'l Rsv., Kenya 145/A2
Masai Steppe (crsld.), Tanz. 145/B3
Masaka, Ugan. 147/G3
Masākin, Tun. 74/B5
Masalembu Besar (isl.), Indo. 115/F3
Masallı, Azer. 129/G2
Masamagrell, Sp. 73/E3
Masamba, Indo. 117/F4
Masan, SKor. 107/E5
Masan-ni, SKor. 107/F7
Masanga, D.R. Congo 147/E3
Masangwe (hill), Tanz. 147/G4
Masaryktown, Fl, US 190/L7
Masasi, Tanz. 145/B4
Masavi, Bol. 212/D1
Masaya, Nic. 200/E4
Masbate (isl.), Phil. 162/B3
Masbate, Phil. 114/C2
Mascara, Alg. 138/F5
Mascarene (isls.), Mrts 151/T15
Mascot, Tn, US 188/F2
Mascota, Mex. 198/D4
Mascotte, Fl, US 190/M6
Mascouche, Qu, Can. 185/N6
Mase, D.R. Congo 147/F4
Masela (isl.), Indo. 154/C2
Maselheim, Ger. 87/F1
Maserà di Padova, It. 89/E3
Masereka, D.R. Congo 147/G3
Maseru (cap.), Les. 150/D3
Maseru (Moshoeshoe) (int'l arpt.), Les. 150/D3
Masevaux, Fr. 86/D2
Masfjorden, Nor. 66/A1
Masha, China 113/H3
Mashaba, Zim. 149/F4
Mashad (int'l arpt.), Iran 127/G1
Mashala, D.R. Congo 147/E4
Mashalah, Egypt 139/C3
Masham, Eng, UK 61/G3
Mashhad, Iran 127/G1
Mashike, Japan 108/B2
Mashivka, Ukr. 99/H3
Mashīz, Iran 129/J4
Māshkīd (riv.), Iran 127/H3
Mashonaland Central (prov.), Zim. 149/F3
Mashonaland East (prov.), Zim. 149/F3
Mashonaland West (prov.), Zim. 149/F3
Mashqharah, Leb. 131/D1
Mashtūl as Sūq, Egypt 139/C4
Mashū (lake), Japan 108/D2
Masiaca, Mex. 198/C3
Maside, Sp. 72/A1
Masīlah (wadi), Yem. 144/D2
Masim (peak), Rus. 97/L1
Masindi, Ugan. 147/G2
Masindi Port, Ugan. 147/H2
Masinloc, Phil. 114/B2
Masis, Arm. 129/F1
Masisea, Peru 208/C3
Masisi, D.R. Congo 147/G3
Masjed-e Soleymān, Iran 129/G4
Masjid Raya (Great Mosque), Indo. 115/B2
Mask (lake), Ire. 58/A2
Maskall, Belz. 200/D2
Maskan (cape), Som. 144/B3
Masker (peak), Mor. 136/D2
Maskin, Oman 127/G4
Maskūtān, Iran 127/G3
Masnou, Sp. 73/L7
Masoala (pen.), Madg. 152/J6
Masoala (cape), Madg. 152/J6
Masoarivo, Madg. 152/H7
Mason, Il, US 188/C1
Mason, Mi, US 186/D3
Mason, Nv, US 172/D4
Mason, Oh, US 186/D5
Mason, Ok, US 179/F3
Mason, Tx, US 177/E2
Mason (co.), Wa, US 193/A3
Mason (lake), Wa, US 193/B3
Mason, WV, US 189/F1
Mason and Dixon Line, Pa, US 194/B4
Mason City, Il, US 181/K3
Mason City, Ia, US 181/H2
Masonboro, NC, US 189/J3
Masone, It. 88/B5
Masontown, Pa, US 187/G5
Masonville, Ky, US 188/D2
Masquefa, Sp. 73/K6
Masrakh, India 123/E2
Maşrif Bahr al Baqar (canal), Egypt 139/C3
Massa, It. 88/D5
Massa Finalese, It. 89/E4
Massa Fiscaglia, It. 89/F4
Massa Lombarda, It. 89/E5
Massa Lubrense, It. 92/D6
Massa Marittima, It. 74/B1
Massa Martana, It. 91/B2
Massa-Carrara (prov.), It. 88/C4
Massachusetts (bay), Ma, US 184/B4
Massachusetts (state), US 169/M3
Massaciuccoli (lake), It. 88/D5
Massafra, It. 75/E2
Massaguet, Chad 142/B2
Massakory, Chad 142/B2
Massandra, Ukr. 99/H5
Massangena, Moz. 149/G4
Massapê, Braz. 207/F3
Massapequa, NY, US 195/M9
Massapequa Park, NY, US 195/M9
Massarosa, It. 88/D6
Massbach, Ger. 84/D2
Massena, NY, US 187/J2
Massenya, Chad 142/C3
Masset, BC, Can. 166/C3
Massey, On, Can. 186/E1
Massey (sound), Nun, Can. 167/S7
Massey, Md, US 194/C5
Massibi, Ang. 147/E5
Massif Central (upland), Fr. 92/D1
Massif de Beaufort (mass.), Fr. 90/C1
Massif de Champsaur (mass.), Fr. 90/C3
Massif de Guéra (peak), Chad 142/C3
Massif de la Chartreuse (mass.), Fr. 90/B2
Massif de la Vanoise (mass.), Fr. 90/C2
Massif de l''Assâba (mass.), Mrta. 140/C2
Massif de Pelvoux (mass.), Fr. 90/C3
Massif de Termit (mass.), Niger 142/A1
Massif des Bongos (uplands), CAfr. 142/D3
Massif des Maures (mass.), Fr. 90/C6
Massif du Manéngouba (peak), Camr. 141/H5
Massif du Tamgue (mass.), Gui. 140/B3
Massigui, Mali 140/D4
Massillon, Oh, US 186/F4
Massinga, Moz. 149/G4
Massingir, Moz. 149/G4
Massy, Fr. 56/J5
Mastābah, SAr. 126/C4
Mastadon (mtn.), Id, US 170/G4
Maştağa, Azer. 97/J4
Masterton, NZ 161/C3
Mastgat (chan.), Neth. 78/B5
Mastic, NY, US 195/F2
Mastic Beach, NY, US 195/F2
Mastník (riv.), Czh. 85/H3
Mastūj (riv.), Pak. 124/A2
Mastung, Pak. 127/J3
Mastūrah, SAr. 126/C4
Masuda, Japan 110/B3
Masuguru, Tanz. 149/H1
Masuho, Japan 109/A2
Masurai (peak), Indo. 115/C3
Masvingo, Zim. 149/F4
Masvingo (prov.), Zim. 149/F4
Maswa Game Rsv., Tanz. 145/A2
Maşyāf, Syria 130/E2
Mat (riv.), Alb. 75/F2
Mata, D.R. Congo 147/E4
Mata Bia (peak), Indo. 154/B2
Mata de Guanábano, Ven. 204/D3
Mata Grande, Braz. 207/G5
Mata Mata, SAfr. 150/C2
Mata Utu, Fr. 163/H6
Matabeleland North (prov.), Zim. 149/E3
Matabeleland South (prov.), Zim. 149/F4
Mātābhānga, India 123/G2
Matadi, D.R. Congo 146/C4
Matador, Tx, US 178/D3
Matagalpa, Nic. 200/E3
Matagorda, Tx, US 177/G3
Matagorda (pen.), Tx, US 177/G3
Matagorda (bay), Tx, US 196/B2
Matagorda (isl.), Tx, US 196/B2
Matak (isl.), Indo. 115/D2
Matala, Ang. 148/B2
Matam, Sen. 140/B3
Matamba, D.R. Congo 147/E4
Mataméye, Niger 141/H3
Matamoras, Pa, US 194/D1
Matamoros, Mex. 198/E3
Ma'ţan as Sarra (well), Libya 134/D4
Matancilla, Chile 212/B4
Matanda, Zam. 149/F1
Matandu (riv.), Tanz. 145/B4
Matane, Qu, Can. 184/D1
Matane (riv.), Qu, Can. 184/D1
Matanga, Madg. 152/H8
Matanzas, Cuba 196/E3
Matão, Braz. 213/G2
Matape (riv.), Mex. 198/C2
Matapédia, Qu, Can. 184/D2
Mataquito (riv.), Chile 214/C2
Matara (ruin), Erit. 126/C6
Matara, Erit. 144/A2
Mataram, Indo. 117/E5
Matarānga, Gre. 75/G3
Matarani, Peru 208/C5
Mataranka, Austl. 154/D3
Mataró, Sp. 73/L6
Matatiele, SAfr. 150/E3
Mataura, FrPol. 163/L7
Mataura, NZ 161/B4
Mataura (riv.), NZ 161/B4
Matawai, NZ 161/D2
Matawan, NJ, US 195/J10
Matawin (riv.), Qu, Can. 184/A2
Matay, Kaz. 97/L3
Matay, Kaz. 125/C2
Matching Green, Eng, UK 56/D1
Matecaña (int'l arpt.), Col. 207/K8
Mateguá, Bol. 209/F4
Matehuala, Mex. 199/E4
Mateke (hills), Zim. 149/F4
Matelica, It. 92/C1
Matera, It. 74/E2
Matéri, Ben. 141/F4
Maternillos (pt.), Cuba 197/F3
Matese (lake), It. 92/D5
Matese (mts.), It. 92/D5
Mátészalka, Hun. 69/M5
Matetsi, Zim. 148/E3
Mathay, Fr. 86/C3
Mathbaria, Bang. 123/G4
Matheniko Game Rsv., Ugan. 142/G5
Matheson Island, Mb, Can. 182/F2
Mathews, La, US 190/C3
Mathews (lake), Ca, US 192/C3
Mathew's (peak), Kenya 145/B1
Mathews, Va, US 189/J2
Mathi, It. 90/D2
Mathis, Tx, US 177/F3
Mathiston, Ms, US 188/C4
Mathoura, Austl. 159/B2
Mathurā, India 122/A2
Mati, Phil. 114/D4
Matias Barbosa, Braz. 211/N6
Matias Olímpio, Braz. 207/F3
Matías Romero, Mex. 200/C2
Matignon, Fr. 82/C3
Matíguas, Nic. 200/E3
Matilija (dam), Ca, US 192/A2
Matimbuka, Tanz. 145/A4
Matinha, Braz. 207/E4
Matinicock (pt.), NY, US 195/L8
Mātir, Tun. 74/A4
Maţir Ţāris, Egypt 139/B6
Matiyuri (riv.), Ven. 204/D3
Matkuli, India 122/B4
Mātla (riv.), India 123/G5
Matlock, Eng, UK 61/G5
Maţmāţah, Tun. 92/F4
Matn (riv.), Leb. 131/D1
Mato Grosso (plat.), Braz. 203/D4
Mato Grosso (state), Braz. 206/A5
Mato Grosso do Sul (state), Braz. 209/G5
Mato Grosso, Meseta do (plat.), Braz. 209/G4
Mato Verde, Braz. 211/E2
Matobo (Matopos) NP, Zim. 149/F4
Matões, Braz. 207/F4
Matolo-Rio, Moz. 151/F2
Matomb, Camr. 146/B2
Matombo, Tanz. 145/B3
Matopos, Zim. 149/F4
Matopos (Matobo) NP, Zim. 149/F4
Matosinhos, Port. 72/A2
Matoury, FrG. 206/C1
Matouti (pt.), Gabon 146/B3
Matoya (bay), Japan 109/L7
Maţraḩ, Oman 127/G4
Matrei am Brenner, Aus. 87/H3
Matrei in Osttirol, Aus. 71/K3
Matriz de Camaragibe, Braz. 207/H5
Matroosberg (peak), SAfr. 150/L10
Matsalu (gulf), Est. 67/K2
Matsapa (Manzini) (int'l arpt.), Swaz. 151/E2
Matsiatra (riv.), Madg. 152/H8
Matsoandakana, Madg. 152/J6
Matsubara, Japan 109/J6
Matsubushi, Japan 109/D2
Matsuda, Japan 109/C3
Matsudo, Japan 109/D2
Matsue, Japan 110/C3
Matsuida, Japan 109/B1
Matsumae, Japan 108/B3
Matsumoto, Japan 111/E2
Matsuo, Japan 109/E2
Matsusaka, Japan 109/L6
Matsushima, Japan 108/B4
Matsutō, Japan 110/E2
Matsuyama, Japan 110/C4
Matt, Swi. 87/F4
Mattamuskeet (lake), NC, US 189/J3
Mattamuskeet Nat'l Wild. Ref., NC, US 189/J3
Mattaponi (riv.), Va, US 189/J2
Mattarello, It. 87/H6
Mattawa, On, Can. 187/G1
Mattawa, Wa, US 170/E4
Matterhorn (peak), It.,Swi. 86/D6
Mattertal (valley), Swi. 86/D5
Matteson, Il, US 186/C4
Matthew Town, Bahm. 201/H1
Matthews, Mo, US 188/C2
Matthews (mt.), NZ 161/J9
Matthews, NC, US 189/G3
Mattie (lake), Fl, US 190/M7
Mattig (riv.), Aus. 85/G6
Mattighofen, Aus. 85/G6
Mattituck, NY, US 195/F2
Mattmarksee (lake), Swi. 86/D5
Mattō, Japan 110/E2
Mattock (riv.), Ire. 60/B4
Mattoon, Wi, US 181/K1
Mattsee, Aus. 85/G7
Matucana, Peru 208/B3
Matumbla (mt.), NY, US 187/J2
Matundwe (range), Malw.,Moz. 149/G3
Maturín, Ven. 205/F2
Matusadona NP, Zim. 149/F3
Matutum (mt.), Phil. 117/G2
Matveyev Kurgan, Rus. 99/K4
Matzen, Aus. 77/P7
Mau, India 122/C3
Mau, India 122/C4
Mau (peak), Kenya 145/A2
Maú (riv.), Guy. 205/G3
Maú (riv.), Guy.,Ven. 206/B1
Mau Aimma, India 122/C3
Mau Rānīpur, India 122/B3
Mau-é-Ele, Moz. 149/G5
Maúa, Moz. 149/H2
Maubert-Fontaine, Fr. 81/D4
Maubeuge, Fr. 80/C3
Maubourguet, Fr. 70/D5
Mauchline, Sc, UK 59/B5
Maud, Ok, US 179/F3
Maud, Tx, US 179/G4
Maud, Sc, UK 59/D1
Maud (pt.), Austl. 156/B2
Maudaha, India 122/C3
Maude, Austl. 159/B2
Maudlow, Mt, US 171/J4
Mauerbach, Aus. 77/N7
Mauerkirchen, Aus. 85/G6
Maués, Braz. 206/B3
Maués Açu (riv.), Braz. 206/B4
Maug (isls.), NMar. 162/D2
Mauganj, India 122/C3
Maughold, IM, UK 60/D3
Maughold (pt.), IM, UK 60/D3
Mauguio, Fr. 70/F5
Mauherslieve (peak), Ire. 58/B4
Maui (isl.), Hi, US 163/K2
Mauk, Rus. 95/P5
Mauke (isl.), CookIs. 163/K7
Maukkadaw, Myan. 112/B4
Maulbronn, Ger. 84/B5
Mauldre (riv.), Fr. 80/A6
Maule, Fr. 56/H5
Maule (riv.), Chile 214/C2
Maule (pol. reg.), Chile 214/B2
Mauléon, Fr. 70/C3
Maullín, Chile 214/B4
Maulvi Bāzār, Bang. 123/H3
Maumakeogh (peak), Ire. 58/A1
Maumee, Oh, US 186/E4
Maumere, Indo. 154/A2
Maumtrasna (peak), Ire. 58/A2
Maun, Bots. 148/D3
Maun (int'l arpt.), Bots. 148/D3
Mauna Kea (peak), Hi, US 168/S10
Mauna Loa (peak), Hi, US 168/S10
Maunath Bhanjan, India 122/D3
Maunatlala, Bots. 149/E4
Maungaturoto, NZ 161/C2
Maungdaw, Myan. 119/F3
Mauperthuis, Fr. 56/M5
Maupertus (int'l arpt.), Fr. 82/D1
Maupiti (isl.), FrPol. 163/K6
Maur, Swi. 87/E3
Maur, India 124/C4
Maurāwān, India 122/C2
Maurecourt, Fr. 56/J5
Maurepas, Fr. 80/A6
Maurepas (lake), La, US 190/C2
Mauriac, Fr. 70/E4
Maurice (riv.), NJ, US 194/C5
Maurice (lake), Austl. 153/C3
Mauricetown, NJ, US 194/D5
Mauriceville, Tx, US 177/H2
Mauricie, PN de la, Qu, Can. 187/K1
Maurienne (valley), Fr. 71/G4
Maurilândia, Braz. 210/C3
Maurine, SD, US 180/C1
Mauritania(ctry.) 133/A3
Mauriti, Braz. 207/G4
Mauritius(ctry.) 151/T15
Mauro (peak), It. 92/D4
Mauron, Fr. 82/C4
Maurui, Tanz. 145/B3
Maury City, Tn, US 188/C3
Mauston, Wi, US 181/J2
Mauthausen, Aus. 85/H6
Maverick, Az, US 175/H4
Mavila, Peru 208/D3
Mavinga, Ang. 148/D2
Mavis (reef), Austl. 154/A3
Mavqi'im, Isr. 131/B5
Mavrommátion, Gre. 75/H3
Mavrovo NP, FYROM 75/G2
Mavuradonha (mts.), Zim. 149/F3
Maw (pt.), NC, US 189/J3
Maw Daung (pass), Thai. 120/B4
Mawa, D.R. Congo 147/F2
Mawāna, India 122/A1
Mawanga, D.R. Congo 146/D4
Mawasangka, Indo. 154/A1
Mawei, China 113/E3
Mawhun, Myan. 112/C3
Mawiwi, D.R. Congo 147/F2
Māwiyah, Yem. 144/C2
Mawjib (wadi), Jor. 131/D6
Mawkmai, Myan. 112/C4
Mawlaik, Myan. 112/B4
Mawlamyine (Moulmein), Myan. 120/B2
Mawliba, India 123/H3
Mawshij, Yem. 144/B2
Mawson, Austl., Ant. 216/E
Max, ND, US 182/D4
Max Meadows, Va, US 189/G2
Maxah Ind. Res., Wa, US 170/B3
Maxaranguape, Braz. 207/H4
Maxcanú, Mex. 200/D1
Maxdorf, Ger. 84/B4
Maxéville, Fr. 81/F6
Maxhütte-Haidhof, Ger. 85/F4
Maxie, Ms, US 190/D2
Maxie, La, US 190/B2
Maxixe, Moz. 149/G4
Maxton, NC, US 189/H3
Maxville, Mt, US 171/H4
Maxwell (A.F.B.), Al, US 188/D4
Maxwell Nat'l Wildlife Reserve, NM, US 178/B2
Maxwelton, Austl. 160/A3
May, Tx, US 176/E2
May (cape), NJ, US 194/D5
May Pen, Jam. 201/G2
May, Isle of (isl.), Sc, UK 59/D4
May-en-Multien, Fr. 56/M4
Maya (riv.), Rus. 103/N4
Maya (mts.), Guat. 200/D2
Maya (isl.), Indo. 116/C4
Maya Beach, Belz. 200/D2
Maya Maya (int'l arpt.), Congo 146/C4
Maya-san (peak), Japan 109/H6
Mayaguana (isl.), Bahm. 165/K7
Mayaguana Passage (chan.), Bahm. 201/H1
Mayagüez, PR 197/M8
Mayahi, Niger 141/G3
Mayakovskogo (peak), Taj. 125/B4
Mayala, D.R. Congo 146/D4
Mayama, Congo 146/C3
Mayamba, D.R. Congo 146/D4
Mayāmey, Iran 129/H2
Mayan, China 104/F5
Mayang, China 119/J2
Mayāng Imphāl, India 112/B3
Mayaoyao, Phil. 114/C1
Mayarí, Cuba 201/H1
Maybee, Mi, US 193/E8
Maybell, Co, US 173/J3
Maybole, Sc, UK 59/B6
Maych'ew, Eth. 144/A2
Maydān, Iraq 129/F3
Maydh, Som. 144/C3
Maydī, Yem. 144/B1
Maydolong, Phil. 114/D3
Maydūm, Egypt 139/C6
Mayébout, Gabon 146/C2
Mayen, Ger. 81/G3
Mayenne (dept.), Fr. 83/E4
Mayenne, Fr. 83/E4
Mayenne (riv.), Fr. 70/C3
Mayer, Az, US 175/F3
Mayer, Mn, US 183/N7
Mayesville, SC, US 189/G4
Mayet, Fr. 83/F5
Mayetta, Ks, US 181/G4
Mayfa'ah, Yem. 144/C2
Mayfair, Sk, Can. 171/L1
Mayfield, Sc, UK 59/C5
Mayfield, Ut, US 173/H4
Mayfield, Ky, US 188/C2
Mayhill, NM, US 178/B4

Maykain, Kaz. 125/C1
Maykop, Rus. 99/L5
Mayland, Eng, UK 63/G3
Maymont, Sk, Can. 171/L1
Maymyo, Myan. 112/C4
Mayna, Rus. 97/H1
Maynard, Ar, US 188/B2
Maynardville, Tn, US 188/F2
Maynooth, Ire. 58/D3
Maynooth, On, Can. 187/H2
Mayo (co.), Ire. 58/A2
Mayo, Fl, US 191/G2
Mayo, Yk, Can. 166/C2
Mayo (riv.), Arg. 214/C5
Mayo (riv.), Mex. 199/C3
Mayo (res.), NC, US 189/H2
Mayo, Md, US 194/B6
Mayo Belwa, Nga. 142/B3
Mayo Kébi (riv.), Chad 142/B3
Mayo Mayo, Bol. 209/E4
Mayo Oulo, Camr. 142/B3
Mayo-Kébbi (pref.), Chad 142/B3
Mayoko, Congo 146/C3
Mayon (vol.), Phil. 114/C2
Mayotte (dpcy.), Fr. 152/H6
Mayotte (isl.), Fr. 133/G6
Mayoworth, Wy, US 173/K2
Maypearl, Tx, US 177/F1
Mayport Nav. Air Sta., Fl, US 191/H2
Mays Landing, NJ, US 194/D5
Mays Lick, Ky, US 188/F1
Maysān (gov.), Iraq 129/F4
Mayskiy, Rus. 97/H4
Mayskiy, Rus. 99/L4
Mayskiy, Rus. 105/K1
Maysville, Ok, US 179/F3
Maysville, Mo, US 181/G4
Maysville, Ky, US 188/F1
Maythalūn, WBnk. 131/C4
Mayuka, Zam. 149/F1
Mayumba, Gabon 146/B3
Mayuram, India 121/C4
Mayville, ND, US 182/F4
Mayville, NY, US 187/G3
Mayville, Wi, US 186/B3
Mayville, Or, US 172/C1
Maywood, Ca, US 192/F8
Maywood, Il, US 193/Q16
Maywood, Mo, US 181/J4
Maywood, Ne, US 180/D3
Maywood, NJ, US 195/J8
Mazabuka, Zam. 149/E2
Mazagão, Braz. 206/D3
Mazama, Wa, US 170/D3
Mazamet, Fr. 70/E5
Mazan, Fr. 90/B4
Mazán, Peru 208/C1
Mazandaran (gov.), Iran 129/H2
Mazār-e Sharīf, Afg. 127/J1
Mazara del Vallo, It. 74/C4
Mazarrón, Sp. 72/E4
Mazartag, China 125/D4
Mazaruni (riv.), Guy. 205/G3
Mazatán, Mex. 198/C2
Mazatenango, Guat. 200/D3
Mazatlán, Mex. 198/D4
Mazatzal (peak), Az, US 175/G3
Mazatzal (mts.), Az, US 175/G3
Mazé, Fr. 83/E6
Mažeikiai, Lith. 67/K3
Mazenod, Sk, Can. 171/L3
Mazeppa NP, Austl. 160/B3
Mazetown, NI, UK 60/B3
Mazgirt, Turk. 128/D2
Mazie, Ok, US 179/G2
Mazıkıran (pass), Turk. 128/D2
Mazinda, D.R. Congo 146/D4
Mazingarbe, Fr. 80/B3
Mazingu, D.R. Congo 146/D4
Mazirbe, Lat. 67/K3
Mazocruz, Peru 212/B1
Mazoe, Zim. 149/F3
Mazoe (riv.), Moz. 149/G3
Mazomanie, Wi, US 181/K2
Mazomeno, D.R. Congo 147/F4
Mazon, Il, US 186/B4
Mazong (peak), China 104/D3
Mazowe (riv.), Zim. 149/F3
Mazsalaca, Lat. 67/L3
Mazunga, Zim. 149/F4
Mazury (reg.), Pol. 69/L2
Māzūz (well), Libya 134/D2
Mazyr, Bela. 98/E1
Mbabala (isl.), Zam. 147/G5
Mbabala, Zam. 149/E3
Mbabane (cap.), Swaz. 151/E2
Mbabo (peak), Camr. 142/B4
Mbacké, Sen. 140/B3
Mbagne, Mrta. 140/B2
Mbahiakro, C.d'Iv. 140/D5
Mbaïki, CAfr. 146/D2
Mbakaou, Camr. 142/B4
Mbakaou (lake), Camr. 142/B4
Mbala, Zam. 147/G5
Mbalabala, Zim. 149/F4
Mbalam, Camr. 146/C2
Mbalambala, Kenya 145/B2
Mbale, Ugan. 145/A1
Mbali, D.R. Congo 146/D3
Mbali-Iboma, D.R. Congo 146/D3
Mbalmayo, Camr. 146/B2
Mbam (riv.), Camr. 142/A4
Mbam Minkoum (peak), Camr. 146/B2
Mbamba Bay, Tanz. 149/G1
Mban (riv.), Camr. 146/B1
Mbandaka, D.R. Congo 146/D2
Mbandjok, Camr. 142/A4
Mbang, Camr. 146/C2
Mbanga, Camr. 146/B1
Mbanio (lag.), Gabon 146/B3
Mbanza Congo, Ang. 146/C4
Mbanza-Ngungu, D.R. Congo 146/D2
Mbaranganda (riv.), Tanz. 145/B4
Mbarangandu, Tanz. 145/B4
Mbarara, Ugan. 147/G3
Mbari (riv.), CAfr. 142/D4
Mbata, CAfr. 146/D2
Mbé, Camr. 142/B4
Mbengga (isl.), Fiji 163/Y18
Mberengwa, Zim. 149/F4
Mbereshi Mission, Zam. 147/G5
Mbeya, Tanz. 145/A4
Mbeya, Zam. 149/G1
Mbeya (prov.), Tanz. 145/A3
Mbeya (range), Tanz. 145/A4
Mbeya (peak), Tanz. 145/A4
M'Bigou, Gabon 146/B3
Mbii, CAfr. 142/D4
Mbinda, Congo 146/C3
Mbingué, C.d'Iv. 140/D4
Mbini (riv.), EqG. 146/B2
Mbini, EqG. 146/B2
Mbirira, Tanz. 147/G4
Mbirizi, Ugan. 147/G3
Mbizi, Zim. 149/F4
Mbogo, Tanz. 145/A3
Mboki, CAfr. 142/E4
Mboko, D.R. Congo 147/G3
Mboloma, Zam. 149/F2
Mbomo, Congo 146/C3
Mbomou (pref.), CAfr. 142/D4
Mbomou (riv.), CAfr. 142/E4
Mbonda (pt.), EqG. 146/B2
Mboro, Sen. 140/A3
Mborong, Indo. 117/F5
Mbouda, Camr. 146/B1
Mboula, CAfr. 142/C4
Mbouomo, Congo 146/C3
M'Bour, Sen. 140/A3
M'Bout, Mrta. 140/B2
Mbres, CAfr. 142/C4
Mbuji-Mayi, D.R. Congo 147/E4
Mbulu, Tanz. 145/A2
Mburucuya, Arg. 212/E4
Mbuvu, Kenya 145/B2
Mbuzi, Zam. 149/G2
Mbwemburu (riv.), Tanz. 145/B4
Mbwikwe, Tanz. 145/A3
McAdam, NB, Can. 184/D3
McAdoo, Tx, US 178/D4
McAdoo, Pa, US 194/C2
McAfee, NJ, US 194/D1
McAlester, Ok, US 179/G3
McAlisterville, Pa, US 194/A2
McAllen, Tx, US 177/E4
McAndrews, Ky, US 189/F2
McArthur, Oh, US 189/F1
McArthur Mills, On, Can. 187/H2
McBain, Mi, US 186/D2
McBean, Ga, US 189/G4
McBee, SC, US 189/G3
McBride, Ok, US 179/F4
McBride, BC, Can. 170/D1
McCabe, Mt, US 182/B3
McCall, Id, US 172/E1
McCall Creek, Ms, US 190/C2
McCamey, Tx, US 177/C2
McCammon, Id, US 173/G2
McCarran (int'l arpt.), Nv, US 174/E2
McCarthy's Rust, Bots. 150/C2
McCaslin (mtn.), Wi, US 186/B2
McCaulley, Tx, US 177/D1
McCaysville, Ga, US 188/E3
McChord (A.F.B.), Wa, US 170/C4
McClanahan, Tx, US 177/F2
McClave, Co, US 178/C1
McClellan (cr.), Tx, US 178/D3
McClellanville, SC, US 189/H4
McCloud (riv.), Ca, US 172/B3
McClure, Il, US 188/C2
McClure, Pa, US 194/A2
McClusky, ND, US 182/D4
McColl, SC, US 189/H3
McComb, Ms, US 190/C2
McComb, Oh, US 186/E4
McConnell (A.F.B.), Ks, US 179/F2
McConnell, Tn, US 188/C2
McConnellsburg, Pa, US 187/H5
McConnelsville, Oh, US 186/F5
McCook, Ne, US 180/D3
McCook, Tx, US 177/E4
McCord, Sk, Can. 171/L3
McCormick, SC, US 189/F4
McCracken, Ks, US 178/E1
McCreary, Mb, Can. 182/E2
McCrory, Ar, US 179/J3
McCullom Lake, Il, US 193/P15
McCullough, Al, US 190/E2
McCune, Ks, US 179/G2
McCurtain, Ok, US 179/G3
McDade, Tx, US 176/F2
McDaniel, Md, US 194/B6
McDavid, Fl, US 190/E2
McDermitt, Nv, US 172/E3
McDonald (isls.), Austl. 53/N8
McDonald (isls.), Austl. 216/E
McDonald Observatory, Tx, US 177/B2
McDonnell (mt.), Austl. 157/H5
McDonough, Ga, US 189/M8
McDougall (pass), Nw, Yt., Can. 168/Z12
McElhattan, Pa, US 194/A1
McEwen, Tn, US 188/D2
McFadden NWR, Tx, US 177/G3
McFarland, Mi, US 183/L4
McFarland, Ca, US 174/C3
McFarland, Wi, US 181/K2
McGaffey, NM, US 175/H3
McGee, Sk, Can. 171/K2
McGee Creek (lake), Ok, US 179/G3
McGehee, Ar, US 179/J4
McGhee Tyson (int'l arpt.), Tn, US 188/F3
McGill, Nv, US 173/F4
McGrath, Mn, US 183/H4
McGrath, Ak, US 168/X12
McGraw, NY, US 187/H3
McGraw Brook, NB, Can. 184/D2
McGregor, Mn, US 183/H4
McGregor, ND, US 182/C3
McGregor, On, Can. 193/G7
McGregor, Tx, US 177/F2
McGuire (A.F.B.), NJ, US 194/D3
McHenry, Il, US 186/B3
McHenry (co.), Il, US 193/N15
McHenry, Ky, US 188/D2
McHenry, Ms, US 190/D2
McHinga, Tanz. 145/B4
McHinji, Malw. 149/G2
McInnis (lake), On, Can. 183/H1
McIntosh, Mn, US 182/G4
McIntosh, SD, US 182/D5
McIntosh, Al, US 190/D2
McIntosh, NM, US 175/J3
McKay Creek Nat'l Wild. Ref., Or, US 172/D1
McKay Creek NWR, Or, US 170/E5
McKean (isl.), Kiri. 163/H5
McKeand (riv.), Nun, Can. 167/K2
McKee, Ky, US 188/F2
McKee City, NJ, US 194/D5
McKeesport, Pa, US 187/G4
McKellar, On, Can. 186/G2
McKenzie, Al, US 190/E2
McKenzie (riv.), Or, US 172/B1
McKenzie, Tn, US 188/C2
McKinlay, Austl. 160/A3
McKinley (mt.), Ak, US 168/X12
McKinleyville, Ca, US 172/A3
McKinney, Tx, US 176/L6
McKinney Bayou (riv.), Tx,Ar, US 179/G4
McKittrick, Ca, US 174/C3
McLain, Ms, US 190/D2
McLaren Creek Abor. Land, Austl. 154/D5
McLaughlin, SD, US 182/D5
McLaurin, Ms, US 190/D2
McLean, Tx, US 178/D3
McLean, Il, US 181/K3
McLean, Va, US 194/A6
McLeansboro, Il, US 188/C1
McLeod (bay), NW, Can. 166/E2
McLeod (riv.), Ab, Can. 170/F1
McLeod(lake) 153/A3
McLoughlin (mt.), Or, US 172/B2
M'Clure (str.), NW, Can. 166/E2
McLure, BC, Can. 170/D2
McMillan, Ok, US 179/F3
McMinnville, Or, US 172/B1
McMinnville, Tn, US 188/E3
McMunn, Mb, Can. 183/G3
McMurdo, US, Ant. 216/M
McNab, Ar, US 179/H4
McNamee, NB, Can. 184/D2
McNary, Az, US 175/H3
McNary (dam), Or, US 170/E5
McNary NWR, Wa, US 170/E4
McNaughton, Wi, US 183/K5
McNeil, Ar, US 179/H4
McNeil (isl.), Wa, US 193/B3
McNeill, Ms, US 190/D2
McOcha, Malw. 149/G2
McPhee (res.), Co, US 175/H2
McPherson, Ks, US 179/F1
McQueeney, Tx, US 177/E3
McRae, Ar, US 179/J3
McRae, Ga, US 191/G1
McVille, ND, US 182/E4
McWilliams, Al, US 190/E2
Mdabulo, Tanz. 145/A3
Mdaburo, Tanz. 145/A3
Mdandu, Tanz. 145/A4
Mdantsane, SAfr. 150/D4
M'diq, Mor. 138/B2
Mê (riv.), China 104/E5
Me-akan-dake (peak), Japan 108/C2
Meacham, Sk, Can. 171/M1
Mead (lake), Az,Nv, US 165/F6
Mead, Ne, US 181/F3
Meade, Ks, US 178/D2
Meadow, Tx, US 178/C4
Meadow, SD, US 182/C5
Meadow, Ut, US 175/F1
Meadow Lake, Sk, Can. 166/F3
Meadow Valley, Ca, US 172/C4
Meadow Valley Wash (riv.), Nv, US 174/E2
Meadow Vista, Ca, US 172/C4
Meadowlands, Mn, US 183/H4
Meadowlands Sports Complex, NJ, US 195/J8
Meadows, Id, US 172/E1
Meadows, Md, US 194/B6
Meadowvale, On, Can. 186/T8
Meadville, Ms, US 190/C2
Meadville, Pa, US 186/F4
Meadville, Mo, US 181/H4
Meaford, On, Can. 186/F2
Mealhada, Port. 72/A2
Meall a' Bhuiridh (peak), Sc, UK 59/B3
Meall Buidhe (peak), Sc, UK 59/B3
Meall Dearg (peak), Sc, UK 59/C3
Meall Dubh (peak), Sc, UK 59/B2
Meall nam Fuaran (peak), Sc, UK 59/C4
Meall Tairneachan (peak), Sc, UK 59/C3
Mearim (riv.), Braz. 207/E4
Measham, Eng, UK 63/E1
Meath (co.), Ire. 60/B4
Meath Park, Sk, Can. 171/M1
Méaulte, Fr. 80/B4
Meaux, Fr. 56/L5
Mebenda (peak), Gabon 146/B3
Mebridege (riv.), Ang. 146/C4
Mecapalapa, Mex. 199/M6
Mècatina,Rivière du Petit (riv.), Nf,Qu, Can. 167/K3
Mecca, Ca, US 174/D4
Mechanicsburg, Oh, US 186/E4
Mechanicsburg, Pa, US 194/A3
Mechanicsburg Nav. Res., Pa, US 194/B3
Mechanicsville, Va, US 189/J2
Mechant (lake), La, US 190/C3
Mechara, Eth. 144/B3
Mechelen, Belg. 81/D1
Mecheria, Alg. 137/E2
Mechi (zone), Nepal 123/F2
Méchiméré, Chad 142/B2
Mechra-Bel-Ksiri, Mor. 138/B2
Mechrâ-Saf-Saf, Mor. 138/C2
Mecidiye, Turk. 77/H5
Mecitözü, Turk. 128/C1
Meckenbeuren, Ger. 87/F2
Meckenheim, Ger. 81/G2
Mecklenburg-Vorpommern (state), Ger. 66/E5
Mecklenburger (bay), Ger. 68/F1
Meconta, Moz. 149/H2
Mecoya, Bol. 212/C2
Mecsek (mts.), Hun. 93/H1
Mecuburi (riv.), Moz. 149/H2
Mecúfi, Moz. 149/J2
Mecuia (peak), Moz. 149/G2
Mecula, Moz. 149/H2
Meda, It. 88/C2
Medak, India 121/C2
Medan, Indo. 115/B2
Medang (cape), Indo. 115/C2
Médanos, Arg. 214/E3
Medanos de Coro, PN, Ven. 204/D2
Medanosa (pt.), Arg. 215/D6
Medaryville, In, US 186/C4
Medbourne, Eng, UK 63/F1
Mede Lomellina, It. 88/B3
Médéa (wilaya), Alg. 138/G4
Médéa, Alg. 138/G4
Medebach, Ger. 79/F6
Medeiros Neto, Braz. 211/E3
Medel (peak), Swi. 87/E4
Medellín, Col. 207/K6
Medemblik, Neth. 78/C3
Meden (riv.), Eng, UK 61/G5
Mederdra, Mrta. 140/B2
Medesano, It. 88/D4
Medetsiz (peak), Turk. 128/C2
Medford, Ok, US 179/F2
Medford, Wi, US 183/J5
Medford, Or, US 172/B2
Medford, NY, US 195/E2
Medford Lakes, NJ, US 194/D4
Medgidia, Rom. 77/J3
Medi, Sudan 142/F4
Media, Pa, US 194/C4
Media Agua, Arg. 212/B4
Medianeira, Braz. 213/F3
Mediapolis, Ia, US 181/J3
Mediaş, Rom. 77/G2
Medical Lake, Wa, US 170/F4
Medicina, It. 89/E5
Medicine (cr.), Mo, US 181/H3
Medicine (cr.), Ne, US 180/D3
Medicine (lake), Mt, US 171/M3
Medicine (riv.), Ab, Can. 170/G1
Medicine Bow (mts.), Wy, US 168/E3
Medicine Bow (riv.), Wy, US 173/K2
Medicine Bow (peak), Wy, US 180/A3
Medicine Hat, Ab, Can. 171/J2
Medicine Knoll (cr.), SD, US 182/E5
Medicine Lake, Mt, US 182/B3
Medicine Lake NWR, Mt, US 182/B3
Medicine Lodge, Ks, US 179/E2
Medicine Lodge (riv.), Ks,Ok, US 178/E2
Medika, Mb, Can. 182/G3
Medina (riv.), Tx, US 177/E3
Medina, ND, US 182/E4
Medina, Oh, US 186/F4
Medina, NY, US 187/G3
Medina (int'l arpt.), SAr. 135/H3
Medina, Wa, US 193/C2
Medina, Col. 204/C3
Medina, Tn, US 188/C3
Medina (riv.), Eng, UK 63/E5
Medina, Tx, US 176/E3
Medina de Pomar, Sp. 70/B5
Medina de Rioseco, Sp. 72/C2
Medina del Campo, Sp. 72/C2
Médina Gonassé, Sen. 140/B3
Medina-Sidonia, Sp. 72/C4
Medinaceli, Sp. 72/D2
Medininkai, Lith. 67/L4
Medinipur, India 123/F4
Medio (cr.), Tx, US 177/F3
Mediodía, Col. 204/C5
Mediouna, Mor. 136/D2
Mediterranean(sea) 55/E5
Medje, D.R. Congo 147/F2
Mednogorsk, Rus. 97/L2
Mêdog, China 112/B2
Medole, It. 88/D3
Medolla, It. 89/E4
Medora, ND, US 182/C4
Medora, In, US 188/D1
Médouneu, Gabon 146/B2
Medowie, Austl. 159/E1
Medstead, Sk, Can. 171/K1
Medulla, Fl, US 190/M8
Medveditsa (riv.), Rus. 100/E5
Medvedovskaya, Rus. 99/K5
Medvënka, Rus. 99/J2
Medvezh'i (isls.), Rus. 101/S2
Medvezh'yegorsk, Rus. 94/G3
Medvode, Slov. 71/L3
Medyn', Rus. 94/G5
Medzilaborce, Slvk. 98/A3
Meekatharra, Austl. 156/C3
Meeker, Co, US 173/K3
Meelpaeg (lake), Nf, Can. 185/J1
Meenambarkkam (int'l arpt.), India 121/D3
Meer, Belg. 78/B6
Meerbusch, Ger. 78/D6
Meerhout, Belg. 81/E1
Meersburg, Ger. 87/F2
Meerssen, Neth. 81/E2
Meerut, India 122/A1
Meeteetse, Wy, US 173/J1
Meeuwen, Belg. 81/E1
Mēga, Eth. 144/A4
Mega (isl.), Indo. 115/C4
Mega, Indo. 117/H4
Megála Kalívia, Gre. 75/G3
Megáli Panayía, Gre. 75/H2
Megalo, Eth. 144/B4
Megálon Khoríon, Gre. 128/A2
Megalópolis, Gre. 75/H4
Meganom (cape), Ukr. 99/H5
Megantic (peak), Qu, Can. 184/B3
Mégara, Gre. 75/H3
Megargel, Tx, US 178/E4
Megargel, Al, US 190/E2
Megève, Fr. 86/C6
Megezez (peak), Eth. 144/A3
Meghalaya (state), India 119/F2
Meghna (riv.), Bang. 123/H4
Megiddo, Isr. 131/C3
Megista (isl.), Gre. 130/A1
Megrega, Rus. 67/Q1
Megri, Arm. 129/F2
Meguzalala, Moz. 149/F4
Mehaigne (riv.), Belg. 81/E2
Mehal Mēda, Eth. 144/A3
Mehamn, Nor. 64/H1
Meharry (mt.), Austl. 156/C2
Mehdia, Alg. 138/F5
Mehdīshahr, Iran 129/H3
Mehdiya-Plage, Mor. 138/A2
Mehe (riv.), Ger. 79/G1
Mehedinti (co.), Rom. 98/B5
Meherpur, Bang. 123/G4
Meherrin (riv.), Va, US 189/H2
Mehikoorma, Est. 67/M2
Mehlingen, Ger. 81/G4
Mehndāwal, India 122/D2
Mehrabad (int'l arpt.), Iran 129/G3
Mehrabān, Iran 129/F2
Mehrān (riv.), Iran 127/F3
Mehring, Ger. 81/F4
Mehrīz, Iran 129/H4
Mehrnbach, Aus. 85/G6
Mehtar Lām, Afg. 124/A2
Mei (riv.), China 113/G3
Meia Meia, Tanz. 145/A3
Meia Ponte (riv.), Braz. 210/C3
Meidougou, Camr. 142/B4
Meiganga, Camr. 142/B4
Meighen (isl.), Nun, Can. 167/R7
Meigle, Sc, UK 59/C3
Meigs, Ga, US 191/F2
Meigu, China 119/H2
Meihekou, China 105/K3
Meikle Bin (peak), Sc, UK 59/B4
Meikle Black Law (hill), Sc, UK 59/D5
Meikle Says Law (peak), Sc, UK 59/D5
Meikou, China 113/H3
Meiktila, Myan. 112/B4
Meilen, Swi. 87/E3
Meine, Ger. 79/H4
Meiners Oaks, Ca, US 192/A2
Meinersen, Ger. 79/H4
Meinerzhagen, Ger. 81/G1
Meiningen, Ger. 84/D1
Meiringen, Swi. 86/E4
Meisenheim, Ger. 81/G4
Meishan, China 112/D2
Meishan, China 113/H3
Meishan (res.), China 106/C5
Meishan, China 113/H3
Meishan, China 106/K8
Meishuikeng, China 113/H3
Meissen, Ger. 69/G3
Meissner (peak), Ger. 79/G6
Meitian, China 113/G3
Meitingen, Ger. 84/D5
Meiwa, Japan 109/L6
Meix-devant-Virton, Belg. 81/E4
Meizhou, China 113/H3
Mejaniga, It. 89/E3
Mejaouda (well), Mrta. 136/D5
Mejillones, Chile 212/B2
Mejorada del Campo, Sp. 73/N9
Mekambo, Gabon 146/C2
Mekane Selam, Eth. 144/A3
Mek'elē, Eth. 144/A2
Mékhé, Sen. 140/A3
Mek'ī, Eth. 144/A3
Mekinock, ND, US 182/F3
Meknès, Mor. 138/B3
Meknès (prov.), Mor. 138/B3
Meko, Nga. 141/F5
Mekong (riv.), Asia 120/C1
Mekongga (peak), Indo. 117/F4
Melaka, Malay. 115/C2
Melaka (state), Malay. 115/C2
Melanesia(reg.) 162/E5
Melappālaiyam, India 121/C4
Melawi (riv.), Indo. 116/D4
Melbeck, Ger. 79/H2
Melbourn, Eng, UK 63/G2
Melbourne, Ar, US 179/J2
Melbourne, Eng, UK 61/G6
Melbourne, Fl, US 191/H3
Melbourne (isl.), Nun, Can. 166/F2
Melbourne, Austl. 158/G5
Melbu, Nor. 64/E1
Melcher-Dallas, Ia, US 181/H3
Melchor (isl.), Chile 214/B5
Melchor Múzquiz, Mex. 177/D4
Melchor Ocampo, Mex. 177/E4
Melchor Ocampo, Mex. 199/Q9
Melcombe Regis, Eng, UK 62/D5
Meldola, It. 89/F5
Meldorf, Ger. 66/C4
Mele (cape), It. 88/B6
Meleb, Mb, Can. 182/F2
Melegnano, It. 88/C3
Melenci, Yugo. 76/E3
Melenki, Rus. 94/J5
Melesse, Fr. 82/D4
Meleuz, Rus. 97/K1
Mélèzes (riv.), Qu, Can. 167/J3
Melezza (riv.), It. 87/E5
Melfa (riv.), It. 92/C4
Melfi, It. 74/D2
Melfi, Chad 142/C3
Melfort, Sk, Can. 171/M1
Melgaço, Port. 72/A1
Melgar, Col. 207/L8
Melgar de Fernamental, Sp. 72/C1
Melhus, Nor. 64/D3
Melibocus (peak), Ger. 84/B3
Melide, Swi. 87/E6
Meligalás, Gre. 75/G4
Melíki, Gre. 75/H2
Melili (peak), Kenya 145/B2
Melilla, Sp. 138/C2
Melimoyu (peak), Chile 214/B5
Melinca, Chile 214/B4
Melipilla, Chile 214/N8
Mélisey, Fr. 86/C2
Melissano, It. 75/F3
Melita, Mb, Can. 182/D3
Melita (int'l arpt.), Tun. 93/F4
Melito di Porto Salvo, It. 74/D4
Melitopol', Ukr. 99/H4
Melitota, Md, US 194/B5
Melka Guba, Eth. 144/A4
Melka Meri, Eth. 144/B4
Melkasa, Eth. 144/A3
Melkbosstrand, SAfr. 150/L10
Melksham, Eng, UK 62/D4
Mella (riv.), It. 88/D2
Mellac, Fr. 82/B5
Mellan Fryken (lake), Swe. 66/E2
Melle, Belg. 80/C2
Melle, Ger. 79/F4
Mellea (riv.), It. 88/A3
Mellègue, Oued (riv.), Alg. 138/K7
Mellerud, Swe. 66/E2
Mellette, SD, US 180/E1
Mellid, Sp. 72/A1
Mellieħa, Malta 74/L7
Melling, Eng, UK 61/F3
Mellingen, Swi. 87/E3
Mellit, Sudan 142/E2
Mellizo Sur (peak), Chile 215/B6
Mellrichstadt, Ger. 84/D2
Mellum (isl.), Ger. 79/F1
Melmoth, SAfr. 151/E3
Melnik, Bul. 75/H2
Mělník, Czh. 85/H2
Mel'nytsya-Podil's'ka, Ukr. 98/D3
Melo, Uru. 213/F5
Melocheville, Qu, Can. 185/N7
Melolo, Indo. 117/F5
Mélong, Camr. 146/B1
Melrose, Mn, US 183/G5
Melrose, Sc, UK 59/D5
Melrose, La, US 190/B2
Melrose, Wi, US 181/J1
Melrose, Md, US 194/B4
Melrose, Austl. 159/C2
Melrose Abbey, Sc, UK 59/D5
Melrose Bombing Range, NM, US 178/C3
Melrose Park, Il, US 193/Q16
Mels, Swi. 87/F3
Melstone, Mt, US 171/L4
Melsungen, Ger. 79/G6
Meltham, Eng, UK 61/G4
Melton, Austl. 159/B3
Melton Mowbray, Eng, UK 63/F1
Melúli (riv.), Moz. 149/H2
Melun, Fr. 56/K6
Melunga, Ang. 148/C3
Melvern, Ks, US 179/G1
Melvern (lake), Ks, US 181/G4
Melville, Sk, Can. 182/C2
Melville, La, US 190/C2
Melville, NY, US 195/M8
Melville (cape), Austl. 160/B1
Melville (pen.), Can. 165/J3
Melville (lake), Nf, Can. 167/L3
Melville (cape), Phil. 114/B4
Melville (nbrhd.), Austl. 156/K7
Melville, Mt, US 171/K4
Melville (isl.), Can. 153/C2
Melville (bay), Austl. 153/C2
Melville Abor. Land, Austl. 154/C2
Melville Hall (int'l arpt.), Dom. 197/N9
Melvin, Al, US 190/D2
Melvin, Tx, US 177/E2
Melvindale, Mi, US 193/F7
Mélykút, Hun. 76/D2
Melzo, It. 88/C3
Memaliaj, Alb. 75/F2
Memar (lake), China 125/D5
Memāri, India 123/G4
Memba, Moz. 149/J2
Membalong, Indo. 116/C4
Même (riv.), Fr. 83/F4
Memmert (isl.), Ger. 78/D1
Memmingen, Ger. 87/G2
Memot, Camb. 120/D4
Memphis, Tx, US 178/D3
Memphis, Mi, US 193/G6
Memphis, Mo, US 181/H3
Memphis, Tn, US 188/B3
Memphis (int'l arpt.), Tn, US 188/C3
Memphis (ruin), Egypt 139/C5
Memphis Nav. Air Sta., Tn, US 188/C3
Memphrémagog (lake), Qu, Can. 184/A3
Mena, Ar, US 179/G3
Mèna, Mali 140/D3
Mena, Ukr. 98/G2
Mena, Eth. 144/A4
Mena, Indo. 154/B2
Menafra, Uru. 215/K10
Menaggio, It. 87/F5
Menahga, Mn, US 183/G4
Menai (str.), Wal, UK 60/D5
Menai Bridge, Wal, UK 60/D5
Ménaka, Mali 141/F3
Menaldum, Neth. 78/C2
Menan, Id, US 173/H2
Menanga, Indo. 117/F4
Menara (Marrakech) (int'l arpt.), Mor. 136/C3
Menarandra (riv.), Madg. 152/H9
Menard, Tx, US 177/E2
Menasalbas, Sp. 72/C3
Menasha, Wi, US 181/K1
Menavava (riv.), Madg. 152/H7
Menawashei, Sudan 142/E2
Mencué, Arg. 214/C4
Mendawai (riv.), Indo. 116/D4
Mende, Fr. 70/E4
Mendebo (mts.), Eth. 144/A4
Menden, Ger. 79/E6
Mendenhall, Ms, US 190/D2
Mendes, Braz. 211/N7
Méndez, Mex. 199/F3
Mendham, Sk, Can. 171/K2
Mendham, NJ, US 194/D2
Mendī, Eth. 142/G3
Mendi, PNG 155/F1
Mendig, Ger. 81/G3
Mendip (hills), Eng, UK 62/D4
Mendocino, Ca, US 172/B4
Mendocino (pass), Ca, US 172/B4
Mendocino (cape), Ca, US 168/A3
Mendol (isl.), Indo. 115/C2
Mendon, Mi, US 186/D3
Mendon, Mo, US 181/H4
Mendooran, Austl. 158/D1
Mendota, Ca, US 174/B2
Mendota, Il, US 181/K3
Mendota, Mn, US 183/P7
Mendoza, Cuba 201/E1
Mendoza (prov.), Arg. 214/C2
Mendoza, Arg. 214/C2
Mendoza, Uru. 215/K11
Mendoza, Peru 208/B2
Mendoza (El Plumerillo) (int'l arpt.), Arg. 214/C2
Mendrisio, Swi. 87/E6
Mene Grande, Ven. 204/D2
Menegosa (peak), It. 88/C4
Menemen, Turk. 96/C5
Menen, Belg. 80/C2
Menengai Crater, Kenya 145/B2
Menengiyn (plain), Mong. 101/M5
Menfi, It. 74/C4
Meng Xian, China 106/C4
Mengcheng, China 106/D4
Mengen, Ger. 87/F1
Mengen, Turk. 96/E4
Mengersgereuth-Hämmern, Ger. 84/D2
Mengerskirchen, Ger. 84/B1
Mengeš, Slov. 71/L3
Menggala, Indo. 115/D3
Menggatal, Malay. 114/B4
Menghai, China 120/C1
Mengibar, Sp. 72/D4
Mengjian, China 113/F4
Mengkofen, Ger. 85/F5
Mengla, China 120/C1
Menglian Daizu Lahuzu Vazu Zizhixian, China 112/C4
Mengman, China 120/C1
Mengshan, China 113/F3
Mengxing, China 120/C1
Mengyin, China 106/D4
Mengzi, China 112/D4
Ménilles, Fr. 83/G2
Menindee (dam), Austl. 158/B2
Menindee, Austl. 158/B2
Menindee (lake), Austl. 157/J5
Meningie, Austl. 158/A2
Menlo, Ga, US 188/E3
Menlo Park, Ca, US 193/K12
Menlo Park, NJ, US 195/H9
Menlolat (peak), Chile 214/B5
Mennecy, Fr. 56/K6
Mennetou-sur-Cher, Fr. 83/G6
Menoken Indian Village Historical Site, ND, US 182/D4
Menominee (riv.), Mi, Wi, US 183/L5
Menominee, Mi, US 186/C2
Menominee Ind. Res., Wi, US 181/K1
Menomonee Falls, Wi, US 186/B3
Menomonie, Wi, US 181/J1
Menongue, Ang. 148/C2
Menonitas Colonias, Par. 212/E2
Menorca (int'l arpt.), Sp. 73/H3
Menorca (Minorca) (isl.), Sp. 73/H2
Mentana, It. 91/B3
Mentawai (isls.), Indo. 103/J10
Mentawai (str.), Indo. 116/A4
Mentekab, Malay. 115/C2
Menteroda, Ger. 79/H6
Menthon-Saint-Bernard, Fr. 86/C6
Mentmore, NM, US 175/H3
Menton, Fr. 90/D5
Mentone, Ca, US 192/C2
Mentone, In, US 186/C4
Mentone, Tx, US 177/C2
Mentor, Mn, US 182/F4
Mentor, Oh, US 186/F4
Mentougou, China 106/H7
Mentue (riv.), Swi. 86/C4
Menucourt, Fr. 56/H4
Menuma, Japan 109/C1
Menyamya, PNG 155/G1
Menyapa (peak), Indo. 117/E3
Menyuan Huizu Zizhixian, China 104/E4
Menzel Bourguiba, Tun. 74/A4
Menzies, Austl. 156/D4
Menziken, Swi. 86/E3
Menzingen, Swi. 87/E3
Menznau, Swi. 86/E3
Meolo, It. 89/F2
Meon (riv.), Eng, UK 63/E5
Meopham, Eng, UK 56/E2
Meoquí, Mex. 177/B3
Meos Waar (isl.), Indo. 117/H4
Meota, Sk, Can. 171/K1
Méouge (riv.), Fr. 90/B4
Mepala, Ang. 146/C4
Mepistskaro (peak), Geo. 97/G4
Meppel, Neth. 78/D3
Meppen, Ger. 79/E3
Mequinenzo (res.), Sp. 73/E2
Mequon, Wi, US 186/C3
Mer, Fr. 83/G5
Mer Rouge, La, US 179/J4
Mera (riv.), It. 87/F5
Merak, Indo. 115/D3
Meramec (riv.), Mo, US 181/J5
Merano, It. 87/H4
Merasheen (isl.), Nf, Can. 185/K2
Merate, It. 88/C2
Meratus (mts.), Indo. 116/D4
Merauke (riv.), Indo. 155/F2
Merauke, Indo. 155/F2
Merbein, Austl. 158/B2
Mercaderes, Col. 204/B4
Mercantour, PN, Fr. 71/G4
Mercatello sul Metauro, It. 89/F6
Mercato, It. 92/D6
Mercato San Severino, It. 92/D6
Mercato Saraceno, It. 89/F6
Merced, Ca, US 174/B2
Merced (peak), Ca, US 174/C2
Merced (riv.), Ca, US 174/B2
Merced Grove, Ca, US 174/C2
Mercedario (peak), Arg. 212/B4
Mercedes, Arg. 214/D2
Mercedes, Uru. 215/J10
Mercedes, Arg. 215/J11
Mercedes, Arg. 212/E4
Mercedes, Tx, US 177/F4
Mercer, Pa, US 186/F4
Mercer (isl.), Wa, US 193/C2
Mercer, NZ 161/C2
Mercer, Mo, US 181/H3
Mercer (co.), NJ, US 194/D3
Mercer County (arpt.), NJ, US 194/D3
Mercer Island, Wa, US 193/C2
Mercersburg, Pa, US 187/H5
Mercerville-Hamilton Square, NJ, US 194/D3
Merchtem, Belg. 81/D2
Mercier, Qu, Can. 185/N7
Mercoal, Ab, Can. 170/F1
Mercogliano, It. 92/D6
Mercury, Nv, US 174/E2
Mercury, Tx, US 177/E2
Mercy (cape), Nun, Can. 167/K2
Mercy-le-Bas, Fr. 81/E5
Merdereau (riv.), Fr. 83/E4
Merderet (riv.), Fr. 82/D2
Merdrignac, Fr. 82/C4
Mere, Belg. 80/C2
Méré, Fr. 56/H5
Mere, Eng, UK 62/D4
Méreau, Fr. 83/H6
Mereb Wenz (riv.), Erit. 142/H2
Meredith (lake), Co, US 178/C1
Meredith, NH, US 187/L3
Meredith (cape), UK 215/E7
Meredosia, Il, US 181/J4
Meredosia Nat'l Wild. Ref., Il, US 181/J4
Mereeg, Som. 144/C5
Merefa, Ukr. 99/J3
Merelbeke, Belg. 80/C2
Merenberg, Ger. 84/B1
Mereuch, Camb. 120/D3
Méréville, Fr. 83/H4
Mereworth, Eng, UK 56/E3
Mergel (riv.), China 105/J2
Mergozzo, It. 87/E6
Mergui (arch.), Myan. 119/G5
Mergui (Myeik), Myan. 120/B3
Meriç, Turk. 77/H5
Meriç (riv.), Turk. 93/K2
Merichleri, Bul. 77/G4
Méricourt, Fr. 80/B3
Méricourt, Fr. 56/G4
Mérida, Mex. 200/D1
Mérida, Ven. 204/D2
Mérida (state), Ven. 204/D2
Mérida, Sp. 72/B3
Mérida, Cordillera de (mts.), Ven. 204/D3
Meriden, Ct, US 187/K4
Meriden, Wy, US 180/B3
Meridian, Ok, US 179/F3
Meridian, Pa, US 186/G4
Meridian, Ga, US 191/H2
Meridian, Id, US 172/E2
Meridian, Ms, US 188/C4
Meridian, Tx, US 176/F2
Meridian Nav. Air Sta., Ms, US 188/C4
Meridian Station, Ms, US 188/C4
Meridianville, Al, US 188/D3
Mérignac, Fr. 70/C4
Merignac (int'l arpt.), Fr. 70/C4
Merimbula, Austl. 159/D3
Merin Gubai, Som. 145/D1
Merinda, Austl. 160/C3
Mering, Ger. 84/D6
Meringa, Nga. 142/B3
Merino, Co, US 180/C3
Merinos, Uru. 215/K10
Merja Zerga (lake), Mor. 138/A2
Mérk, Hun. 76/F2
Merkel, Tx, US 177/D1
Merkendorf, Ger. 84/D4
Merkinė, Lith. 67/L4
Merksem, Belg. 78/B6
Merksplas, Belg. 78/B6
Merkus (cape), PNG 155/H1
Merlimont, Fr. 80/A3
Merlo, Arg. 215/J11
Merlo, Arg. 212/C5
Meroe (ruin), Sudan 142/G1
Merone, It. 88/C2
Merouane, Chott (lake), Alg. 92/E4
Merredin, Austl. 156/C4
Merri (cr.), Austl. 158/F5
Merriam (crater), Az, US 175/G3
Merrick (peak), Sc, UK 60/D1
Merrick, NY, US 195/L9
Merricks, Austl. 159/B4
Merrickville, On, Can. 187/J2
Merricourt, ND, US 182/E4
Merrill, Wi, US 183/K5
Merrill, Or, US 172/C2
Merrill C. Meigs (arpt.), Il, US 193/Q16
Merrill Creek (res.), NJ, US 194/C2
Merrillville, In, US 186/C4
Merrimack, NH, US 187/L3
Merrimack (riv.), NH, US 184/B4
Merriman, Ne, US 180/D2
Merriott, Eng, UK 62/D5
Merritt (isl.), Fl, US 191/H3
Merritt (dam), Ne, US 180/D2
Merritt (res.), Ne, US 180/D2
Merritt, BC, Can. 170/D2
Merritt Island, Fl, US 191/H3
Merritt Island Nat'l Wild. Ref., Fl, US 191/H3
Merriwa, Austl. 158/D2
Merriwagga, Austl. 159/B1
Merriweather, Mi, US 183/K4
Merryville, La, US 190/B2
Mers-les-Bains, Fr. 80/A3
Mersa Fatma, Erit. 144/B2
Mersa Gulbub, Erit. 144/A1
Mersa Tek'lay, Erit. 126/C5
Mersch, Lux. 81/F4
Merse (reg.), Sc, UK 59/D5
Mersey (riv.), Eng, UK 61/F5
Merseyside (co.), Eng, UK 61/F5
Mershon, Ga, US 191/G2
Mersin, Turk. 130/D1
Mersin Galgalo, Eth. 144/C4
Mersing, Malay. 115/C2
Mērsrags, Lat. 67/K3
Merstham, Eng, UK 56/C3
Mertens, Tx, US 177/F1
Mertert, Lux. 81/F4
Mertesdorf, Ger. 81/F4
Merthyr Tydfil, Wal, UK 62/C3
Mértola, Port. 72/B4
Merton (bor.), Eng, UK 56/C2
Mertzon, Tx, US 177/D2
Mertzwiller, Fr. 81/G6
Méru, Fr. 80/B5
Meru, Kenya 145/B1
Meru (mt.), Tanz. 145/B2
Meru NP, Kenya 145/B1
Meruoca, Braz. 207/F3
Merville, Fr. 80/B2
Mervin, Sk, Can. 171/K1
Merwedekanaal (riv.), Neth. 78/C5
Méry-sur-Oise, Fr. 56/J4
Merzen, Ger. 79/E4
Merzenich, Ger. 81/F2
Merzifon, Turk. 96/E4
Merzig, Ger. 81/F5
Mesa, Az, US 175/G4
Mesa, Co, US 173/J4
Mesa (peak), Arg. 215/C6
Mesa Prieta (mesa), NM, US 178/A3
Mesa Verde NP, Co, US 175/H2
Mesabi (range), Mn, US 183/H4
Mesach Mellet (hills), Libya 137/H4
Mesagne, It. 75/E2
Mesaména, Camr. 146/C2
Mesarás (gulf), Gre. 75/J5
Mescalero (ridge), NM, US 178/C4
Mescalero Sands (des.), NM, US 178/B4
Meschede, Ger. 79/F6
Mesco, Punta di (pt.), It. 88/C5
Mescolino (peak), It. 89/F6
Meseta de Montemayor (plat.), Arg. 214/D5
Mesfinto, Eth. 142/H2
Meshchura, Rus. 95/L3
Meshgīn Shahr, Iran 129/F2
Meshra'ar Raqq, Sudan 142/F3
Mesick, Mi, US 186/D2
Mesilla, NM, US 175/J4
Mesita, Co, US 178/B2
Mesita, NM, US 175/J3
Meskum, Indo. 115/C2
Meslay-du-Maine, Fr. 83/E5
Mesola, It. 89/F4
Mesolóngion, Gre. 75/G3
Mesomeloka, Madg. 152/J8
Mesopotamia (reg.), Iraq 126/D2
Mesopotamia (reg.), Arg 212/E4
Mesoraca, It. 74/E3
Mespelbrunn, Ger. 84/C3
Mesquer, Fr. 82/C6
Mesquite, NM, US 175/J4
Mesquite, Tx, US 176/L7
Mesrouh (peak), Mor. 136/E2
Messaad, Alg. 92/D4
Messac, Fr. 82/D5
Messalo (riv.), Moz. 149/H2
Messancy, Belg. 81/E4
Messei, Fr. 83/E3
Messel, Ger. 84/B3
Messina, It. 74/D3
Messina (str.), It. 93/G3
Messina, SAfr. 149/F4
Messines, Qu, Can. 187/H1
Messinge (riv.), Moz. 149/G2
Messíni, Gre. 75/H4
Messini (gulf), Gre. 93/J3
Messkirch, Ger. 87/F2
Messstetten, Ger. 87/E1
Messum Crater (peak), Namb. 148/B4
Messy, Fr. 56/L5
Mesta (riv.), Bul. 77/F5
Mestia, Geo. 97/G4
Město, Czh. 85/F3
Mestre, It. 89/F3
Mestrino, It. 89/E3
Mesudiye, Turk. 96/F4
Mesumba (peak), Tanz. 145/B3
Mesurado (cape), Libr. 140/C5
Meta, It. 92/D6
Meta (dept.), Col. 204/C4
Meta (riv.), Col.,Ven. 203/C2
Meta Incognita (pen.), Nun, Can. 167/K2
Metabetchouan, Qu, Can. 184/B1
Métabetchouane (riv.), Qu, Can. 184/B2
Metacáua (pt.), Moz. 149/J2
Metahāra, Eth. 144/A3
Metairie, La, US 190/C3
Metaline Falls, Wa, US 170/F3
Metallifere, Colline (mts.), It. 89/D6
Metallostroy, Rus. 94/T7
Metamora, Mi, US 193/F6
Metán, Arg. 212/C3
Metangula, Moz. 149/G2
Metapontum (ruin), It. 74/E2
Metauro (riv.), It. 71/K5
Metcalfe, On, Can. 187/J2
Metcalfe, Ms, US 188/B4
Meteghan, NS, Can. 184/D3
Meteghan River, NS, Can. 184/D3
Metelen, Ger. 79/E4
Metema, Eth. 142/H2
Meteor Crater, Az, US 175/G3
Metéora, Gre. 75/G3
Metepec, Mex. 199/Q10
Metheringham, Eng, UK 61/H5
Methil, Sc, UK 59/C4
Methlick, Sc, UK 59/D2
Methow (riv.), Wa, US 170/D3
Methuen, Ma, US 187/L3
Methuen (mt.), Austl. 154/B3
Methven, Sc, UK 59/C4
Methven, NZ 161/B3
Metica (riv.), Col. 204/C4
Metiskow, Ab, Can. 171/J1
Metković, Cro. 76/C4
Metlakatla, Ak, US 166/C3
Metlatonoc, Mex. 200/B2
Metlili Chaamba, Alg. 137/F2
Metoro, Moz. 149/H2
Metro, Indo. 115/D3
Metro Toronto Zoo, On, Can. 186/U8
Metro-Dade Cultural Center, Fl, US 190/P11
Metropolis, Il, US 188/C2
Metropolitana de Santiago (pol. reg.), Chile 214/N8
Metrozoo, Fl, US 190/P11
Métsovon, Gre. 75/G3
Mettawa, Il, US 193/Q15
Mettenheim, Ger. 85/F6
Metter, Ga, US 189/F4
Mettet, Belg. 81/D3
Mettingen, Ger. 79/E4
Mettlach, Ger. 81/F4
Mettler, Ca, US 174/C3
Mettmach, Aus. 85/G6
Mettmann, Ger. 78/D6

Mettür, India 121/C4
Metu, Eth. 142/G3
Metuchen, NJ, US 195/H9
Metulla, Isr. 131/D2
Metz, Mo, US 179/G2
Metz, Fr. 81/F5
Metz-Nancy-Lorraine (int'l arpt.), Fr. 81/F6
Metzingen, Ger. 84/C5
Metztitlán, Mex. 199/L6
Meu (riv.), Fr. 82/C4
Meudon, Fr. 56/J5
Meudt, Ger. 81/G3
Meulaboh, Indo. 115/B1
Meulan, Fr. 56/H4
Meulebeke, Belg. 80/C2
Meung-sur-Loire, Fr. 83/G5
Meurthe (riv.), Fr. 86/C1
Meurthe-et-Moselle (dept.), Fr. 81/E6
Meuse (riv.), Fr. 68/C4
Meuse (dept.), Fr. 81/E6
Meuvette (riv.), Fr. 83/F3
Meuzin (riv.), Fr. 86/A3
Mevasseret Ziyyon, Isr. 131/C5
Mexborough, Eng, UK 61/F5
Mexia, Tx, US 177/F2
Mexiana (isl.), Braz. 206/D2
Mexicalcingo, Mex. 199/Q10
Mexican Hat, Ut, US 175/H2
Mexican Springs, NM, US 175/H3
Mexico (bay), NY, US 187/H3
Mexico, Me, US 187/L2
Mexico, NY, US 187/H3
Mexico, In, US 186/C4
México (state), Mex. 196/A5
Mexico(ctry.) 165/G7
Mexico, Mo, US 181/J4
Mexico (Ciudad de México) (cap.), Mex. 199/Q10
Mexico Beach, Fl, US 191/F3
Meximieux, Fr. 86/B6
Meybod, Iran 129/H4
Meycauayan, Phil. 114/E6
Meydān-e Gel (lake), Iran 129/H4
Meyers Chuck, Ak, US 168/Z13
Meyersdale, Pa, US 187/G5
Meyerton, SAfr. 150/Q13
Meylan, Fr. 90/B2
Mid Yell, Sc, UK 57/W13
Meymaneh, Afg. 127/H1
Méyo Kyé, Gabon 146/B2
Meyrargues, Fr. 90/B5
Meyrin, Swi. 86/C6
Meythet (Annecy) (arpt.), Fr. 86/C6
Meyzieu, Fr. 86/A6
Mezalingon, Myan. 112/B5
Mezdra, Bul. 77/F4
Mèze, Fr. 70/E5
Mézel, Fr. 90/C5
Mezen', Rus. 95/K2
Mezen (bay), Rus. 95/J2
Mezen' (riv.), Rus. 100/E3
Mezha (riv.), Bela. 67/F4
Mezhdurechensk, Rus. 100/U4
Mezhdurechenskiy, Rus. 100/G4
Mezhdusharskiy (isl.), Rus. 100/E2
Mezhova, Ukr. 99/J3
Mézidon-Canon, Fr. 83/E2
Mézières-sur-Seine, Fr. 56/H5
Mezőberény, Hun. 76/E2
Mezőkovácsháza, Hun. 76/E2
Mezőkövesd, Hun. 69/L5
Mezőtúr, Hun. 76/E2
Mezquital (riv.), Mex. 198/D4
Mézy, Fr. 56/H5
Mezzana (peak), It. 87/G5
Mezzocorona, It. 87/H5
Mezzogoro, It. 89/F4
Mezzolombardo, It. 87/H5
Mfangano (isl.), Kenya 145/A2
Mfou, Cam. 146/B2
Mfrika, Tanz. 145/A4
Mga (riv.), Rus. 94/U7
Mga, Rus. 94/U7
Mgachi, Rus. 105/N1
Mgambo, Tanz. 145/B3
Mgera, Tanz. 145/B3
Mgeta, Tanz. 145/B4
Mglin, Rus. 96/F1
Mgori, Tanz. 145/A3
M'goun (peak), Mor. 156/D3
Mhamdia Fūshānah, Tun. 74/B4
Mhòr (lake), Sc, UK 59/B2
Mhow, India 118/C3
Mhunze, Tanz. 145/A2
Mi (riv.), China 106/D3
Mi Xian, China 106/C3
Mi-shima (isl.), Japan 110/B3
Miahuatlán de Porfirio Díaz, Mex. 200/B2
Miajadas, Sp. 72/C3
Miamére, CAfr. 142/C3
Miami, Tx, US 178/D3
Miami, Mb, Can. 182/E3
Miami, Ok, US 175/N5
Miami (canal), Fl, US 191/H4
Miami, Az, US 176/D3
Miami, Fl, US 190/P11
Miami (int'l arpt.), Fl, US 190/P11
Miami, Oh, US 188/E1
Miami Beach, Fl, US 190/P11
Miami Shores, Fl, US 190/P11
Miami Springs, Fl, US 190/P11
Miamisburg, Oh, US 186/D5
Miān Channūn, Pak. 124/B4
Miāna, India 122/A3
Miancuang, China 104/D4
Mianchi, China 106/B4
Mīāndoāb, Iran 129/J2
Mīāndrivazo, Madg. 152/H7
Mīaneh, Iran 129/F2
Miani, China 113/H4
Miani, Pak. 124/B3
Mianmian (mts.), China 112/D2
Mianning, China 112/D2
Mianus (riv.), Ct, US 195/E1
Miānwāli, Pak. 124/A3
Mianyang, China 112/E2
Mianzhu, China 112/E2
Miao, India 112/C3
Miao'er (peak), China 113/F3
Miaoshi, China 113/F2

Miarinarivo, Madg. 152/H7
Miarinarivo, Madg. 152/J7
Miary, Madg. 152/G8
Miass (riv.), Rus. 95/P5
Miass, Rus. 95/P5
Miastko, Pol. 65/G4
Miazal, Ecu. 208/B1
Mibenge, D.R. Congo 146/D3
Miberika, Sudan 135/G5
Mica Creek, BC, Can. 199/L4
Micanopy, Fl, US 191/G3
Micay, Col. 204/B4
Micco, Fl, US 191/H4
Miccosukee, Fl, US 191/F2
Miccosukee Ind. Fes., 191/H4
Michalovce, Slvk. 69/L4
Michelago, Austl. 159/D2
Michel (bay), Fr. 70/C2
Michelfeld, Ger. 85/E3
Michelstadt, Ger. 84/C3
Michendorf, Ger. 68/Q7
Michigamme 183/K4
Michigame, Mi, US 183/K4
Michigan, ND, US 182/C3
Michigan (lake), US 165/J5
Michigan (state), US 169/J2
Michigan Center, Mi, US 186/D3
Michigan City, In, US 186/C4
Michigan City, Ms, US 188/C4
Michigan Islands Nat'l Wild., 187/J2
Michigan Ref., Mi, US 187/H3
Michipicoten 186/C4
Michipiceten 183/M4
Michoacán de Ocampo 165/G7
Midzor (peak), Yugo. 77/F4
Michurinsk, Rus. 97/J4
Mickle Fell 61/F2
Międzychód, Pol. 96/B2
Międzylesie, Pol. 69/J3
Mickleton, Eng, UK 69/J3
Międzyrzec Podlaski, Pol. 65/M2
Międzyrzecz, Pol. 69/H2
Międzyzdroje, Pol. 66/F5
Miehlen, Ger. 81/G3
Miéle I, Congo 146/C2
Mielec, Pol. 69/L3
Mielno, Pol. 62/C3
Miercurea Cluc, Rom. 77/G2
Mieres, Sp. 141/G2
Miesbach, Ger. 71/J3
Mi'eso, Eth. 144/B3
Mifflin, Pa, US 194/A2
Mifflinburg, Pa, US 150/D3
Mifflintown, Pa, US 187/H4
Mifflinville (Creasy), Pa, US 194/B1
Mifraz Hefa (bay), Isr. 131/B3
Miłki, Mrsh. 131/D3
Migdal Ha'emeq, Isr. 131/C3
Migdol, SAfr. 150/D2
Migennes, Fr. 70/E3
Miglarino, It. 119/F5
Mignano Monte Lungo, It. 92/C5
Mignovillard, Fr. 86/C4
Migori (riv.), Kenya 145/A2
Migori, Kenya 145/A2
Migrim, Neth. 78/C5
Miguel Alemán, Mex. 198/C2
Miguel Aleman, Presa (dam), Mex. 199/M8
Miguel Alves, Braz. 207/F4
Miguel Auza, Mex. 198/D4
Miguel Calmon, Braz. 211/E1
Miguel Hidalgo 196/A7
Miguel Hidalgo (int'l arpt.), Mex. 198/E4
Miguel Pereira, Braz. 211/N7
Miguel Riglos, Arg. 214/E3
Miguelete, Uru. 215/K11
Miguelópolis, Braz. 213/G2
Miguelturra, Sp. 72/D3
Migūm, SKor. 107/G6
Mihama, Japan 110/D3
Mihara, Japan 109/L6
Mihara, Japan 110/D3
Mihara, Japan 109/J6
Mihintale (ruin), SrL. 121/D4
Mihla, Ger. 80/D2
Miho, Japan 109/G2
Mihrāb Pur, Pak. 127/J3
Mijares (riv.), Sp. 73/E2
Mijas, Sp. 72/C4
Mijdaḥah, Yem. 144/D2
Mijdrecht, Neth. 160/C3
Mikasa, Japan 108/B2
Mikashevichi, Bela. 186/W9
Mikata (lake), Japan 175/G5
Mikawa (bay), Japan 109/M6
Mikenge, D.R. Congo 63/F4
Mikese, Tanz. 145/B3
Mikhaylov, Rus. 96/F1
Mikhaylovka, Rus. 61/F4
Mikhaylovka, Rus. 99/M2
Mikhaylovsk, NS, Can. 95/N4
Mikhmoret, Isr. 131/B4
Miki, Japan 109/G6
Mikinai, Gre. 75/H4
Mikinai (Mycenae) 75/H4
Mikindani, Tanz. 145/C3
Mikkeli (prov.), Fin. 60/B3
Mikkeli, Fin. 60/D3
Mikołajki, Pol. 65/L2
Mikomeseng, EqG. 146/B2
Mikonos, It. 187/K4
Mikonos (isl.), Gre. 75/J4
Mikope, D.R. Congo 146/C2
Mikri Prespa NP, Gre. 75/G2
Mikromeri, Nf, Can. 187/H3
Mikumi, Japan 195/J10
Mikumi, Tanz. 145/B3
Mikun', Rus. 172/M1
Mikuni NP, Tanz. 189/H1
Mikuni, Japan 109/H1
Mikun' (riv.), Sc, UK 95/L3
Mikuni-tōge 109/H2
Mikura (isl.), Japan 111/F4
Mila (wilaya), Alg. 138/H4
Milaca, Mn, US 183/H5
Milagres, Braz. 207/G4
Milagro, Ecu. 204/B5
Milak, India 122/B1
Milano Marittima 119/F4
Milas, Tur. 126/A2
Milat, It. 165/G5
Milazzo, It. 74/D3
Milan, Tx, US 177/H2

Midland, Wa, US 152/H7
Midland 152/J7
Midland, SD, US 152/G8
Midland, Tx, US 180/D1
Midland (nbrhd.), Austl. 156/L6
Midland
Midland, Mi, US 66/G4
Midland City, Al, US 146/D3
Midland Park, NJ, US 195/J8
Midlands (prov.), Zim. 170/E1
Midleton, Ire. 58/B6
Midlothian, Il, US 193/Q16
Midlothian (co.), UK 176/L7
Midlothian, Tx, US 191/F2
Midnight, Ms, US 188/B4
Midongy Atsimo, Madg. 152/H8
Midsomer Norton, Eng, UK 70/C5
Midu, China 119/H2
Midway, Ga, US 189/F4
Midway (isls.) 178/B4
Midway, NM, US 190/B2
Midway, La, US 188/C3
Midway, Al, US 191/F2
Midway, Fl, US 191/F1
Midway (isls.), Pac., US 162/H7
Midway, Ne, US 180/E2
Midway, Ga, US 177/G2
Midway, Tx, US 177/G2
Midway, BC, Can. 170/E3
Midway (peak), Czh. 194/C6
Midway City, Ca, US 194/C6
Midway, Ia, US 181/G2
Midwest, Wy, US 180/A2
Midwest City, Ok, US 179/F3
Midyat, Turk. 128/E2
Midževsko, It. 126/C3
Mie (pref.), Japan 110/D4
Mie, Japan 77/F4
Miechów, Pol. 96/B2
Mickle Fell, Eng, UK 61/F2
Międzychód, Pol. 69/J3
Mildhurst, Eng, UK 63/F5
Midi-Pyrénées (reg.), Fr. 70/D4
Milaca, Mn, US 183/H5
Milam, Tx, US 177/H2
Midland, On, Can. 186/E2
Milford, Ga, US 189/F4
Milford, Ok, US 179/F3
Milford, Ne, US 180/D5
Milford, Il, US 189/F4
Milford, De, US 187/K2
Milford, Pa, US 187/J4
Milford, Ut, US 175/F1
Milford, NH, US 181/F1
Milford, Ma, US 181/K1
Milford, Eng, UK 59/H5
Milford, Ia, US 181/F2
Milford, Ct, US 195/E1
Milford, Tx, US 177/F1
Milford, Wa, US
Milford, Ne, US 181/B4
Milford, Ia, US 181/J4
Milford, Wi, US
Milford (inlet), Wal, UK 62/A3
Milford Haven 62/A3
Milford Haven, Wal, UK 62/A3
Milford Station, NS, Can. 184/F3
Milford-on-Sea, Eng, UK 63/E5
Mili (isl.), Mrsh. 162/G4
Miliana, Alg. 138/G4
Milicz, Pol. 69/J3
Milikapiti, Austl. 131/C2
Milingimbi Mission, Sc, UK
Milton-Freewater, Myan. 155/D3
Milk (riv.), Mt, Can., US 166/F4
Milk River, Ab, Can. 171/H3
Milan Monte Lungo, It. 92/C5
Milbank, SD, US 182/D4
Milborne Port, Eng, UK 62/D4
Milbourne, WV, US 186/F5
Milbridge, Eng, UK 58/C4
Milledgeville, Ga, US 189/F4
Milledgeville, Il, US 62/D5
Mile, China 181/K3
Minami Alps NP, Japan 111/F3
Millau, Fr. 70/E4
Millville (vol.), Chile 214/B4
Millen, Ga, US 189/G3
Miller (peak), Az, US 175/G5
Miller, SD, US 180/D4
Miller (pt.), Tx, US 177/N9
Miller, SD, US 177/N9
Miller, On, Can. 194/E2
Miller Peak, Tx, US 176/E2
Millers Creek, 99/N3
Millers Ferry, Al, US 190/E1
Millers Ferry (dam), Al, US 201/G1
Millersburg, Oh, US 190/E1
Millersburg, Pa, US 172/E2
Millerston, Pa, US 194/E2
Millersview, Tx, US 176/E2
Millersville, Pa, US 194/E2
Millerton (lake), Ca, US 174/C2
Millerville, Pa, US 183/G4
Millet, Ab, Can. 171/H1
Millett NP, Tanz. 177/E3
Milleur (pt.), Sc, UK 59/L3
Millfield, Eng, UK 60/C1
Millgrove, On, Can. 70/T9
Milligan, Fl, US 191/F5
Milligan, Ne, US 180/E3
Millinocket, Me, US 182/D2
Millingen aan de Rijn,
Neth. 214/B4
Million, Tn, US 188/C3
Millis, Ma, US 189/G3
Millport, Sc, UK 59/35
Millport, Al, US 188/B3
Millroy, NJ, US 194/D3

Milan, NH, US 193/C3
Milan, Oh, US 172/C2
Milan, Ga, US 180/D1
Milan, NM, US 19/G1
Milan, Tn, US
Milan, Mn, US 188/C3
Milan, Mo, US 198/E2
Milan City, Al, US 177/H3
Milan (Milano), It. 71/H4
Milando, Ang. 146/D5
Milange, Moz. 149/G3
Milangthorpe, Austl. 88/C2
Milano (prov.), It. 159/D1
Milano (Milan), It. 71/H4
Milas, Turk. 126/A2
Milazzo, It. 74/D3
Milbank, SD, US 182/D4
Milborne Port, Eng, UK 62/D5
Milburn, Ok, US 179/F3
Milburn, Ne, US 180/D5
Milburn, NJ, US 194/C5
Mildenhall, Eng, UK 63/G2
Mildmay, On, Can. 186/D2
Mildura, Austl. 191/H2
Mile, China 191/F1
Milē Wenz (riv.), Eth. 112/D3
Milepa, Tanz. 147/G5
Miles, Austl. 160/C4
Miles, Tx, US 177/G2
Miles City, Mt, US 171/M4
Milesburg, Pa, US 194/C6
Milešovka (peak), Czh. 85/G1
Miletto (peak), It. 92/D5
Milevsko, Cz. 85/H4
Milford, NJ, US 187/L3
Milford, Ut, US 175/J3
Milford, Il, US 186/C4
Milford, NI, UK
Milford, Pa, US 187/J4
Milford (sound), NZ
Milford, Ut, US 175/F1
Milford, NH, US 181/F1
Milford, Ma, US 181/K1
Milford, Eng, UK 59/H5
Milford, Ia, US 181/F2
Milford, De, US 187/K2
Milford, Ct, US 195/E1
Milford, Tx, US 177/F1
Milford, Wa, US
Milford, Ne, US 181/B4
Milford, Ia, US 181/J4
Milford, Wi, US
Milford (inlet), Wal, UK 62/A3
Milford Haven 62/A3
Milford Haven, Wal, UK 62/A3
Milford Station, NS, Can. 184/F3
Milford-on-Sea, Eng, UK 63/E5
Mili (isl.), Mrsh. 162/G4
Miliana, Alg. 138/G4
Milicz, Pol. 69/J3
Milikapiti, Austl. 131/C2
Milin, China 112/B2
Milford Station, NS, Can. 184/E3

Millmont, Pa, US 187/L2
Millbrook, Al, US 185/E4
Millbrook, On, Can. 187/G2
Millerton, NY, US 195/E1
Millry, Al, US 188/C3
Mills, NM, US 175/K1
Millsap, Tx, US 188/C3
Millstone, De, US 180/E3
Millstone, WV, US 189/G1
Millstone (riv.), NJ, US 194/D3
Millstream-Chichester NP, 146/D5
Millthorpe, Austl. 158/A2
Millthrop, Eng, UK 88/C2
Milltown, NJ, US 195/H10
Milltown Malbay, Ire. 58/A4
Milltown-Head of Bay d'Espoir,
Mineiros, Braz. 210/B3
Millungera, Austl. 160/A2
Millville, NY, US 195/L8
Millville, Mo, US 186/D5
Millville, NJ, US 194/C5
Millville, Tx, US 177/G1
Millwood (dam), Ar, US 182/B4
Millwood (lake), Ar, US 179/G4
Millwood, Wa, US 171/G2
Milly, NJ, US 181/G2
Milmay, NJ, US 194/D5
Milnathort, Wal, UK 60/C4
Milne (bay), PNG 161/H5
Milne Point, Wi, US 181/J2
Milngavie, UK 59/B5
Milo, India 121/H4
Milo, Ia, US 181/H2
Milos, Gre. 175/F1
Milos (isl.), Gre. 89/J3
Miluo (riv.), Gui. 140/C4
Milpa Alta 60/B3
Milpa (riv.), Austl. 158/E1
Milpitas, Ca, US 187/L3
Milroy, Pa, US 187/L3
Milroy, In, US 186/C5
Milrow, NY, US 194/A2
Milsburg (peak), Ger. 84/C1
Milstead, Ga, US 193/E6
Miltenberg, Ger. 84/C3
Milton, ND, US 175/F1
Milton, Eng, UK
Milton, NH, US 187/L3
Milton, Vt, US 181/G2
Milton, Ct, US 195/E1
Milton, Wa, US 177/F1
Milton, Ia, US 181/B4
Milton, Wi, US
Milton, Ks, US 180/D4
Milton, On, Can. 186/F4
Milton, Eng, UK 63/G4
Milton, Pa, US 194/B1
Milton Heights, On, Can. 186/T8
Milton Keynes, Eng, UK 63/F2
Milton Ness (pt.), Sc, UK 59/D3
Milton of Campsie, Sc, UK 59/B5
Milton-Freewater,
Myan.
Miltona, Mn, US 166/F4
Miltonvale, Ks, US 180/F4
Milu, Japan 167/J2
Miluo, China 113/G2
Milverton, On, Can. 186/F3
Milverton, Eng, UK 62/C4
Milwaukee (co.), Wi, US 195/E1
Milwaukee, Wi, US 173/P14
Milz (riv.), Ger. 84/D2
Mim, Gha.
Mimel (riv.), Ger. 84/D2
Mimizan, Fr.
Mimmaya, Japan 108/B3
Mimongo, Gabon 146/B3
Mimoň, PNG
Mimosa Rocks NP, Austl.
Mimuro, Japan
Min Xian, China 104/E5
Min (riv.), China 104/E5
Min-Kush, Kyr. 125/B3
Mina, Mex. 177/M8
Mina, Nv, US 186/A3
Mina (riv.), Alg. 138/F5
Minā Su'ūd, Kuw. 129/J5
Minā al Qamḥ, Egypt 138/F5
Minaki, On, Can. 183/G1
Minakuchi, Japan 109/K6
Minamata, Japan 110/B4
Minami Alps NP, Japan 111/F3
Minami-tori-shima 162/E2
Minami-Izu, Japan 111/LE
Minami-Daitō (isl.), Japan 111/LE
Minas, Cuba 201/G1
Minas, Uru. 215/G2
Minas, Pres., Ecu. 204/B5
Minas de Barroterán, Mex. 177/D4
Minas de Corrales, Uru. 176/D2
Minas de Matahambre, 201/F1
Minas de Riotinto, Sp. 72/B4
Minas Gerais 210/D3
Minatitlán, Mex. 171/H1
Minbu, Myan. 112/B4
Minbya, Myan. 112/B4
Minch, The (North Minch), 70/T9
Mincha, Chile 214/B4
Minchinābād, Pak. 124/B4
Minchinhampton, Eng, UK 62/D3

Mindelheim, Ger. 194/A2
Mindelo, CpV. 61/E3
Mindemoya, On, Can. 186/E2
Minden, Eng, UK 63/H4
Minden, Al, US 188/C3
Minden, La, US 179/H4
Minden, Ger. 190/J2
Minden, Nv, US 172/D4
Minden, Ne, US 180/E3
Minden City, Mi, US 186/E4
Mindif, Camr. 142/B3
Mindiptana, Indo. 155/F7
Mindoro (isl.), Phil. 103/L8
Mindoro (str.), Phil. 114/C2
Mindouli, Congo 146/C4
Mine Centre, On, Can. 183/H3
Mine Head (pt.), Ire. 58/C6
Minehead, Eng, UK 62/C4
Mineiros, Braz. 210/B3
Mineola, NY, US 195/L8
Mineola, Tx, US 179/F3
Mineola, Ks, US 180/D5
Mineola (lake), Fl, US 190/M6
Mineral, Tx, US 177/E1
Mineral, Wa, US 199/L6
Mineral del Monte, Mex. 199/L6
Mineral Point, Mo, US 181/J2
Mineral Point, Wi, US
Mineral Springs,
Mineral Wells, WV, US 177/E1
Mineral Wells, Tx, US 177/E1
Mineralnyye Vody, Rus. 97/G3
Mineralwells, WV, US 75/J4
Minerbio, It. 89/E4
Minersville, Ut, US 175/F1
Minersville, Pa, US 194/B2
Minetto, NY, US 186/C5
Mineville-Witherbee, 187/K2
Minfeld, Ger. 84/C1
Minfeng, China 125/D4
Mingala, CAfr. 142/D4
Mingāora, Pak. 124/B3
Mingenew, Austl. 156/B4
Mingin, Myan. 112/B4
Minglanilla, Sp. 181/J4
Mingo, D.R. Congo 146/C2
Mingo Junction, Oh, US 186/F4
Mingo NWR, Mo, US 188/B2
Mingoyo, Tanz. 145/B4
Mingui, Chutes de
Mingshui, China 104/D3
Mingun, Ancient City of,
Myan.
Minhang, China 106/L8
Minhe, China 104/E5
Minho, Myan.
Minho (riv.), Port. 72/A1
Miniāri, India 118/B2
Minidoka (dam), Id, US 173/G2
Minidoka NWR, Id, US 173/G2
Minigwal (lake), Austl. 156/D4
Minilya (riv.), Austl. 156/A3
Minimata, SD, US 180/E1
Minimoto, Japan 189/G1
Minisink (isl.), Japan 111/LE
Minisink Hills, On, Can. 182/E2
Minitonas, Mb, Can. 182/E2
Minjilang, Austl. 156/F2
Minkamman, Sudan 142/G4
Minlaton, Austl. 159/G2
Minne Xian, China 104/E5
Mina, China 104/E5
Mina, Mex. 177/M8
Minna, Nga. 141/G4
Minneapolis, Ks, US 180/D4
Minneapolis-St. Paul (Wold-Chamberlain)
(int'l arpt.), Mn, US 183/P7
Mineral Wells, Mn, US 183/P7
Minnedosa, Mb, Can. 182/E2
Minnehaha
Minnehaha
Minnie, On, Can. 183/P7
Minnenqua
Minnesota (state), US 169/G2
Minnesota (riv.), US 183/G1
Minnesota Zoo and Gardens,
Mn, US 183/P7
Minnetonka, Mn, US 183/P7
Minnewaska
Minnewaukan, ND, US 182/D3
Minne, Cuba 201/G1
Minas, Uru. 204/B5
Minas, Ecu. 215/G2
Minerva, Ven. 204/D3
Mines, Uru.
Minas de Barroterán, Mex. 177/D4
Minas de Matahambre, 201/F1
Minta, Camr. 146/B2
Minho, Eng, UK 181/G1
Minsen, Ger. 67/E4
Minsk (cap.), Bela. 67/M5
Minsk (int'l arpt.), Bela. 67/M5

Mińsk Mazowiecki, Pol. 87/G1
Minster, Eng, UK 63/H4
Mint Hill, NC, US 189/G3
Mintlaw, Sc, UK 59/E1
Minto Li, Camr. 146/C2
Minton, Sk, Can. 182/B3
Minto, NB, Can. 184/D2
Minto, ND, US 182/D3
Minto, Mb, Can. 182/D3
Minto (inlet), NW, Can. 166/D1
Minturno, It. 92/C5
Minturn, Co, US 175/K1
Minusinsk, Rus. 100/K4
Minvoul, Gabon 146/C2
Minwakh, Yem. 126/F5
Minxian, China 113/F3
Min'yar, Rus. 95/N5
Minya al Qamḥ, Egypt 139/C3
Minyat Sandūb, Egypt 139/C3
Minyip, Austl. 158/B3
Mio, Mi, US 186/D2
Mions, Fr. 90/A1
Miory, Bela. 67/M4
Mipi, India 112/B2
Miping, China 125/E3
Mira (riv.), NS, Can. 184/G3
Mira (riv.), Col. 204/B4
Mira (riv.), Port. 72/A4
Mira, Port. 89/E4
Mira (riv.), It. 89/E4
Mira Loma, Ca, US 175/F1
Mira Monte, Ca, US 194/B2
Mira Taglio, It. 89/F3
Mirabel
Mirabella Eclano, It. 92/D5
Miramar (pass), Chile 214/C4
Mirador, Braz. 207/E4
Miraflores, Col. 204/C4
Miraflores, Col. 204/D4
Miraflores, Peru 208/B3
Miraflores, Mex. 198/C4
Miragoâne, Haiti 201/H2
Mirai, India 121/B2
Miraj, India 121/B2
Miramar, Ca, US 192/C5
Miramar, Arg. 214/F3
Miramar (nbrhd.), NZ 161/H9
Miramar, Fl, US 190/P11
Miramar Naval Air Station,
Miramare (arpt.), It. 89/F5
Miramas, Fr. 90/A5
Miramichi (riv.), Nf, Can. 184/E2
Miramichi, South West (lake), Can. 184/E2
Miramont-de-Guyenne, Fr. 70/D4
Miranda, It. 118/B2
Miranda (riv.), Gre. 75/H4
Miranda, SD, US 180/E1
Miranda, Braz. 213/A3
Miranda (state), Ven. 214/D4
Miranda de Ebro, Sp. 70/B5
Miranda do Corvo, Port. 72/A2
Miranda do Douro, Port. 72/D5
Mirande, Fr. 70/D5
Mirandela, Port. 72/B2
Mirandiba, Braz. 207/G5
Mirando City, Tx, US 177/E4
Mirandópolis, Braz. 213/B2
Miranorte, Braz.
Mirassol, Braz. 89/F3
Mirassol (vol.), CR 200/E4
Miravalles (peak), Sp. 72/B1
Miravalles, CR 156/B4
Mirbāt, Oman 127/F5
Mirboo North, Austl. 156/F6
Mirebalais, Haiti 201/H2
Mirebeau, Fr. 86/B3
Mirecourt (Épinal), Fr.
Mireigha, Sudan 142/E3
Mirepoix, Fr. 70/D5
Mirfield, Eng, UK 61/G4
Miri, Malay. 116/D3
Miriam Vale, Austl. 160/D3
Minnie (riv.), Col. 204/C4
Mirim (lake), Braz. 215/G2
Minas de Corrales, Uru. 215/F2
Mirnaya, It. 87/G5
Mirna, Cro. 89/F2
Mirny, Rus., Ant. 216/G8
Mirny, Rus. 101/M3
Mirow, Ger. 67/G2
Mirpur, Pak. 124/B3
Mirpur Khās, Pak. 127/J3
Mirpur Sakro 127/J4
Mirria, Niger 141/H3
Mirror, Ab, Can. 171/H1
Mirny, Sc, UK 60/D2
Mirnis (lake), On, Can. 183/J2
Mirsali, Rus. 177/D4
Mirtóön, Gre. 75/H4
Miro (riv.), Sp. 72/A1
Miro, Japan 109/L6
Miro'o (riv.), Japan
Mirzāni, Geo. 97/H3
Mirzāpur, India 122/D3
Misa, D.R. Congo 147/G1
Misaki, Japan 109/J6
Misano Adriatico, It. 89/F6
Misantla, Mex. 92/D6
Misawa, Japan 108/B3
Miscou Centre, NB, Can. 69/L2
Miscou (pt.), Nf, Can. 185/L2
Miscou (isl.), NB, Can. 184/E1

Misere (lake), La, US 186/D4
Misgär, Pak. 190/B3
Mishan, China 105/L2
Mishawaka, In, US 186/C4
Mishima, Japan 111/F3
Mishkino, Rus. 95/M5
Mishmar Hayarden, Isr. 131/D3
Mishmar Hanegev, Isr. 131/B6
Misiones (dept.), Arg. 213/E3
Miskina, Col.
Miskolc, Hun. 69/L4
Mismār, Sudan 126/C5
Misool (isl.), Indo. 162/B5
Misrātah, Libya 139/C4
Mişrātah, Libya 139/C4
Mişr al Jadīdah, Egypt 139/C4
Missão Velha, Braz. 207/G4
Missillac, Fr. 82/C6
Missinaibi, On, Can. 167/H3
Mission (pen.), Japan 109/D3
Mission (mtn.), Ok, US 179/G2
Mission, Mi, US
Mission (bay), Ca, US 192/C5
Mission, BC, Can. 170/C3
Mission, SD, US 180/D1
Mission, Tx, US 177/M9
Mission Beach, Austl. 160/B2
Mission Bend, Tx, US 177/M9
Mission Ind. Res., Ca, US 192/C4
Mission Ridge, SD, US 180/D1
Mission San Buenaventura,
Mission San Jose,
Mission San Juan Capistrano,
Mission San Luis Obispo de Tolosa,
Mission San Miguel Arcangel,
Mission Viejo, Ca, US 192/C3
Missisa (riv.), On, Can. 186/T8
Mississagi (riv.), On, Can. 186/C3
Mississippi
Mississippi (sound), Al, Ms, US 190/D2
Mississippi (delta), US 165/J7
Mississippi (state), US 169/G4
Mississippi (riv.), US 165/J6
Mississippi Sandhill Crane NWR, Ms, US 190/D2
Mississippi Valley, Ia, US 181/G3
Missoula, Mt, US 165/H6
Missouri (state), US 169/H4
Missouri (riv.), US 165/F5
Missouri Valley, Ia, US 181/G3
Missungwi, Tanz. 145/A2
Mist, Or, US 170/C5
Mistake (cr.), Austl. 160/B3
Mistassini, Qu, Can. 184/A1
Mistassini (lake), Qu, Can. 167/J3
Mistelbach, Sk, Can. 171/N1
Misti (vol.), Peru 208/B5
Mistretta, It. 74/D4
Misumi, Tanz. 145/A3
Miswa, Tanz. 145/B3
Mit Abū Ghālib, Egypt 139/C2
Mit an Naşārā, Egypt 139/C2
Mit Fāris, Egypt 139/C2
Mit Ghamr, Egypt 139/C2
Mit Ḩamal, Egypt 139/C3
Mita, Punta de 198/C4
Mitaka, Japan 111/F3
Mitama, Japan 109/M5
Mitana, Uga. 145/A2
Mitara, Japan 109/K6
Mitatib, Sudan 142/H1
Mitchel (riv.), Zam. 145/A3
Mitcham, Austl. 156/B2
Mitchell, Austl. 160/D4
Mitchell, SD, US 180/E1
Mitchell, Ne, US 180/C2
Mitchell (peak), Tx, US 177/C2
Mitchell, NE, US 180/C2
Mitchell and Alice Rivers NP, Austl. 160/B2
Mitchell Bay, On, Can. 186/C3
Mitchell River NP, Austl. 156/F2
Mitchellville, Ar, US 179/J4
Mithankot, Pak. 124/A5
Mithi, Pak. 127/J4
Mithapukur, Bang. 122/F3
Miti, On, Can.
Mitla (ruin), Mex. 200/B2
Mito, Japan 111/G2
Mitole, Tanz. 145/B3
Mitomi, Japan 109/M5
Mitre (peak), NZ 161/C3
Mitre (peak), Tx, US 177/C2
Mitre Bay, On, Can. 187/H2
Mitrovica, Yugo. 77/E4
Mitsamiouli, Com. 152/H4
Mits'iwa, Erit. 144/A2
Mitsinjo, Madg. 152/H6
Mitsukaidō, Japan 111/G2
Mitsuke, Japan 108/B4
Mitsu, Japan 110/C3
Mitta Mitta (riv.), Austl. 159/C3
Mittagong, Austl. 159/D2
Mittagspitze (peak), Aus. 87/F3
Mittberg, Aus. 87/G3
Mittelberg (canal), Ger. 79/F4
Mittelberg (canal), Ger. 79/F4
Mittelradde (riv.), Ger. 79/E3
Mittersill, Aus. 71/K3
Mittenwald, Ger. 87/H3
Mittersill, Aus. 71/K3
Mitterteich, Ger. 85/F3
Miura, Japan 111/G3
Miwa, Japan 140/B4
Miwani, Kenya 145/A2
Miwa, Japan 109/L5
Miwa, Japan 109/H5
Mixco, Guat. 200/C2
Mixco Viejo (ruin), Guat. 200/D3
Mixquiahuala, Mex. 199/K6
Mixteco (riv.), Mex. 200/B2
Miyagi (pref.), Japan 109/K7
Miyagawa, Japan 109/K7
Miyagi (pref.), Japan 108/B4
Miyake (isl.), Japan 108/B4
Miyake, Japan 111/F3
Miyako (isls.), Japan 111/H8
Miyako, Japan 111/H8
Miyakonojō, Japan 110/B5
Miyama, Japan 109/L4
Miyama, Japan 110/B5
Miyanojō, Japan 110/B5
Miyazaki, Japan 110/B5
Miyazaki (pref.), Japan 110/B4
Miyazu, Japan 109/H4
Miyazu (bay), Japan 109/H4
Miyi, China 119/H2
Miyoshi, Japan 110/C3
Miyoshi, Japan 109/M5
Miyoshi, Japan 109/M5
Miyun (res.), China 106/H6
Mizdah, Libya 134/B2
Mizen (pt.), Ire. 60/B6
Mizhhir'ya, Ukr. 98/B3
Mizil, Rom. 77/H3
Miziya, Bul. 77/F4
Mizoram (state), India 119/F3
Mizpah (cr.), Mt, US 182/B5
Mizpe Ramon, Isr. 130/D4
Mizque, Bol. 212/C1
Mizuho, Japan 109/C2
Mizuho, Japan 109/E1
Miziwari, Japan 108/B4
Miznami, Japan 109/L6
Mizunami, Japan 109/M5
Mizusawa, Japan 108/B4
Mjölby, Swe. 65/K7
Mjösa (lake), Nor. 66/F2
Mjøndalen, Nor. 66/D2
Mjöm (lake), Swe. 64/D3
Mkalama, Tanz. 145/A3
Mka'a (plain), Tanz. 145/A3
Mkandwe (mt.), Tanz.
Mkata, Tanz. 145/A3
Mka'ra, Tanz. 145/A3
Mkokotoni, Tanz. 145/B3
Mkomazi Game Rsv.,
Tanz. 145/B3
Mkombo (riv.), Tanz. 147/G4
Mkondoa (riv.), Tanz. 145/B3
Mkuka (riv.), Tanz. 145/B3
Mkumbi (pt.), Tanz.
Mkuze, Zam. 151/F2
Mkushi (riv.), Zam. 151/F2
Mkushi, SAfr. 151/F2
Mkuze, SAfr. 151/F2
Mladá Boleslav, Czh. 85/H2
Mladá Vožice, Czh. 85/H3
Mladenovac, Yugo. 76/E3
Mlala (hills), Tanz. 147/G4
Mława, Pol. 69/L2
Mljet (isl.), Cro. 93/H2
Mljet NP, Cro. 76/C4
Mliba, Swaz. 149/G2
Mliwe, Tanz. 149/G2
Mmabatho, SAfr. 150/D2
Mmadinare, Bots. 149/E4
Mmamabula, Bots. 149/E4
Mmathethe, Bots. 148/D5
Mnazini, Kenya 145/C2
Mnyera (riv.), Tanz. 145/A4
Mo, W, US 174/E2
Mo Duc, Viet. 120/D3
Moa (riv.), SLeo. 140/C4
Moa, Cuba 201/H1
Moa, Indo. 117/G5
Moab, Ut, US 175/H1
Moala (isl.), Fiji 162/G6
Moala Group (isl.), Fiji 162/G6
Moamba, Moz. 151/F2
Moapa, Nv, US 72/A1
Moardda, Gabon 146/C3
Moba, D.R. Congo 147/E2
Moatatize, Moz. 149/G2
Mobaye, CAfr. 142/D4
Mobayi-Mbongo,
D.R. Congo 147/E2
Moberly, Mo, US 181/H4
Mobile (bay), Al, US 190/D2
Mobile, Al, US 190/D2
Mobridge, SD, US 182/D5
Mitry-Mory, Fr.
Moc Hoa, Viet. 120/D4
Mocache, Ecu. 204/B5

Morpeth, Eng, UK 61/G1
Morphou (bay), Cyp. 130/C2
Morphou, Cyp. 130/C2
Morra (lake), Neth. 78/C3
Morrill, Ne, US 180/C3
Morrill, Ks, US 181/G4
Morrilton, Ar, US 179/H3
Morrin, Ab, Can. 171/H2
Morrinhos, Braz. 210/C3
Morrinhos, Braz. 207/F3
Morris (riv.), Mb, Can. 182/F3
Morris, Mn, US 182/G5
Morris, Mb, Can. 182/F3
Morris, Ok, US 179/G3
Morris, NY, US 187/J3
Morris, Il, US 186/B4
Morris (res.), Ca, US 192/C2
Morris (mt.), Austl. 157/F3
Morris (co.), NJ, US 194/D2
Morris Jesup (cape), Grld 216/J
Morris Plains, NJ, US 195/H8
Morrisburg, On, Can. 187/J2
Morrison, Ok, US 179/F2
Morrison, Il, US 181/K3
Morrison, Tn, US 188/E3
Morrisonville, Il, US 181/K4
Morriston, On, Can. 186/S9
Morriston, Wal, UK 62/C3
Morristown, SD, US 182/D5
Morristown, Az, US 175/F4
Morristown, Tn, US 189/F2
Morristown, NJ, US 194/D2
Morristown NHP, NJ, US 194/D2
Morrisville, NY, US 187/J3
Morrisville, Pa, US 194/D3
Morro (pt.), Chile 212/B3
Morro Agudo, Braz. 213/G2
Morro Bay, Ca, US 174/B3
Morro da Igreja (peak), Braz. 213/G4
Morro de Môco (peak), Ang. 148/B2
Morro de Puercos (pt.), Pan. 201/F5
Morro do Capão Doce (hill), Braz. 213/G3
Morro do Chapéu, Braz. 211/E1
Morro, Punta del (pt.), Mex. 199/N7
Morrocoy, PN, Ven. 204/D2
Morrocoyes, Ven. 207/N8
Morrone (peak), It. 92/C3
Mórrope, Peru 208/A2
Morropón, Peru 208/B2
Morros, Braz. 207/E3
Morrosquillo (gulf), Col. 201/G4
Morrow, La, US 190/B2
Morrow, Ga, US 189/M7
Morrow Point (dam), Co, US 175/J1
Mörrum, Swe. 66/F3
Morrumbala, Moz. 149/G3
Morrumbene, Moz. 149/G4
Mørs (isl.), Den. 66/C3
Morsang-sur-Orge, Fr. 56/K6
Morsbach, Fr. 81/F5
Morsbach, Ger. 81/G2
Morschwiller-le-Bas, Fr 86/D2
Morse, Wi, US 183/J4
Morse, La, US 190/B2
Morse, Sk, Can. 171/L2
Morshansk, Rus. 97/G1
Morskoy (isl.), Kaz. 97/J3
Morsum, Ger. 79/G3
Mortagne (riv.), Fr. 86/C1
Mortagne-au-Perche, Fr 83/F3
Mortagne-sur-Sèvre, Fr. 70/C3
Mortain, Fr. 83/E3
Mortara, It. 88/B3
Mortcerf, Fr. 56/L5
Morte (riv.), Fr. 86/B3
Morte (pt.), Eng, UK 62/B4
Morteau, Fr. 86/C3
Mortefontaine, Fr. 56/K4
Mortegliano, It. 89/G2
Morteros, Arg. 212/D4
Mortes, Rio das (riv.), Braz. 209/H4
Mortimer, Eng, UK 63/E4
Mortlach, Sk, Can. 171/L2
Mortlake, Austl. 158/B3
Morton, Tx, US 178/C4
Morton, Ms, US 188/C4
Morton, Il, US 181/K3
Morton, Wa, US 170/C4
Morton Grove, Il, US 193/Q15
Morton Nat'l Wild. Ref., NY, US 195/F2
Morton NP, Austl. 158/D2
Mortrée, Fr. 83/F3
Mortsel, Belg. 78/B6
Morundah, Austl. 159/C2
Morungaba, Braz. 211/K7
Moruya, Austl. 159/E2
Moruya (riv.), Austl. 159/D2
Morvan (plat.), Fr. 70/E3
Morven (peak), Sc, UK 59/C2
Morven, Ga, US 191/G2
Morven, Austl. 160/B4
Morven, NZ 161/B4
Morvi, India 127/K4
Morvillars, Fr. 86/C2
Morvin, Al, US 190/E2
Morwell, Austl. 159/C4
Morzine, Fr. 86/C5
Mos, Sp. 72/A1
Mosbach, Ger. 84/C4
Mosby, Mt, US 171/L4
Moscavide, Port. 73/P10
Mosciano Sant'Angelo, It. 92/C2
Moscow (oblast), Rus. 94/H5
Moscow, Ar, US 179/J3
Moscow, Me, US 187/M2
Moscow, Tn, US 188/C3
Moscow, Id, US 170/F4
Moscow (Moskva) (cap.), Rus. 94/H5
Moscow U. Ice Shelf, Ant. 216/J
Moscow Upland (upland), Rus. 94/F5
Moscow-Narva (nbrhd.), Rus. 94/T7
Mosel (riv.), Ger. 68/D3
Moselebe (riv.), Bots. 148/E5
Moselle (dept.), Fr. 81/F5
Moselotte (riv.), Fr. 86/C2
Moser River, NS, Can. 185/F3
Moses (lake), Wa, US 170/E4
Moses Lake, Wa, US 170/E4
Mosetse, Bots. 149/E4
Moseyevo, Rus. 95/K2
Mosfellsbær, Ice. 64/N7
Mosgiel, NZ 161/B4
Moshaweng (riv.), SAfr. 150/C2
Moshchnyy (isl.), Rus. 67/M2
Moshi, Tanz. 145/B2
Moshi, China 113/F2
Moshoeshoe (Maseru) (int'l arpt.) Les. 150/D3
Moshupa, Bots. 148/E5
Mosh'yuga, Rus. 95/M2
Mosi-oa-Tunya NP, Zam. 148/E3
Mosina, Pol. 69/J2
Mosinee, Wi, US 181/K1
Mosino, Rus. 95/N4
Mosite, D.R. Congo 147/E2
Moskalëvka, Kaz. 97/M1
Moskva (riv.), Rus. 94/G5
Moskva (Moscow) (cap.), Rus. 94/H5
Mosley (riv.), BC, Can. 170/B2
Mosolovo, Rus. 97/G1
Mosomane, Bots. 148/E5
Mosonmagyaróvár, Hun. 76/C2
Mosouwan, China 125/E3
Mospyne, Ukr. 99/K4
Mosquera, Col. 204/B4
Mosquero, NM, US 178/C3
Mosquitia (phys. reg.), Hon. 201/E3
Mosquito (pt.), Pan. 201/G4
Mosquito (cr.), Ia, US 181/G3
Mosquito (lake), Ca, US 174/E3
Mosquitos (gulf), Pan. 196/E6
Moss, Nor. 66/D2
Moss Beach, Ca, US 193/J11
Moss Bluff, La, US 190/B2
Moss Point, Ms, US 190/D2
Moss Vale, Austl. 159/E2
Moss-Side, NI, UK 60/B1
Mossaka, Congo 146/D3
Mossbank, Sk, Can 171/M3
Mosselbaai, SAfr. 150/C4
Mossendjo, Congo 146/C3
Mossgiel, Austl. 159/B1
Mossi Highlands (uplands), Burk. 140/E4
Mössingen, Ger. 84/C6
Mossley, NI, UK 60/C2
Mossman, Austl. 160/B2
Mossoró, Braz. 207/G4
Mossuril, Moz. 149/J2
Mossy Head, Fl, US 191/E2
Mossy Point, Austl. 159/E2
Mossyrock, Wa, US 170/C4
Most, Czh 85/G1
Mostaganem, Alg. 138/F5
Mostaganem (wilaya), Alg. 138/F4
Mostar, Bosn. 76/C4
Mostardas, Braz. 213/G4
Mostki, Ukr. 99/K3
Móstoles, Sp. 73/N9
Mostovskoy, Rus. 99/L5
Mostrim, Ire. 58/C2
Mostyn, Wal, UK 61/E5
Mostyn, Malay. 114/B4
Mostys'ka, Ukr. 69/M4
Mosu, Bots. 148/E4
Mosul (Al Mawşil), Iraq 129/E2
Mot'a, Eth. 142/H3
Mota del Cuervo, Sp. 72/D3
Motacucito, Bol. 212/D1
Motagua (riv.), Guat. 196/D4
Motala, Swe. 66/F2
Moter, India 118/D4
Motherwell, Sc, UK 59/C5
Motian (mtn.), China 106/E2
Motīhāri, India 123/E2
Motilla del Palancar, Sp. 72/E3
Motley, Mn, US 183/G4
Motloutse, Bots. 149/E4
Motloutse (riv.), Bots. 149/E4
Moto, D.R. Congo 147/G2
Motobu, Japan 111/J7
Motokhovo, Rus. 67/Q2
Motokwe, Bots. 148/D5
Motol', Bela. 96/C1
Motomiya, Japan 111/G2
Motono, Japan 109/E2
Motosu (lake), Japan 109/B3
Motosu, Japan 109/L5
Motovskiy (gulf), Rus. 64/K1
Motoyoshi, Japan 108/B4
Motozintla de Mendoza, Mex. 200/C3
Motril, Sp. 72/D4
Motsuta-misaki (cape), Japan 108/A2
Mott, ND, US 182/C4
Motta di Livenza, It. 89/F2
Motta Visconti, It. 88/B3
Mottarone (peak), It. 88/B2
Motueka, NZ 161/C3
Motul de Carrillo Puerto, Mex. 200/D1
Motupe, Peru 208/B2
Motutapu (isl.), NZ 161/F6
Motygino, Rus. 100/K4
Mouangko, Camr. 146/B2
Mouans-Sartoux, Fr. 90/C5
Mouchard, Fr. 86/B4
Mouchoir Passage (chan.), UK 201/J1
Moúdhros, Gre. 75/J3
Moudjéria, Mrta. 140/B2
Moudon, Swi. 86/C4
Mougins, Fr. 90/D5
Mougris (well), Mrta. 140/B2
Mouhoun (prov.), Burk. 140/E3
Mouila, Gabon 146/B3
Mouïna (well), Alg 137/F3
Moujiaba, China 104/F5
Mouka, CAfr. 142/D4
Moukoumbi, Gabon 146/C3
Moulamein, Austl. 159/B2
Moulay Idriss, Mor. 138/B2
Moulay Yakoub, Mor. 138/B2
Mould Bay, NW, Can. 167/R7
Mouldsworth, Eng, UK 61/F5
Moulins, Fr. 70/E3
Moulmein (Mawlamyine), Myan. 120/B2
Moulouya (riv.), Mor. 138/C2
Moulouya, Oued (riv.), Mor. 92/C4
Moulton, Ia, US 181/H3
Moulton, Al, US 188/D3
Moulton, Eng, UK 63/G2
Moulton, Tx, US 177/F3
Moultonboro, NH, US 187/L3
Moultrie, Ga, US 191/G2
Moultrie (lake), SC, US 189/G4
Mound, Mn, US 183/N7
Mound Bayou, Ms, US 188/B4
Mound City, SD, US 182/D5
Mound City, Ks, US 179/G1
Mound City, Il, US 188/C2
Mound City, Mo, US 181/G3
Moundou, Chad 142/C3
Moundridge, Ks, US 179/F1
Mounds, Ok, US 179/F3
Mounds, Il, US 188/C2
Mounds View, Mn, US 183/P6
Moundsville, WV, US 186/F5
Moundville, Mo, US 179/G2
Moundville, Al, US 188/D4
Moung Roessei, Camb. 120/C3
Mounlapamok, Laos 120/D3
Mount Aberdeen NP, Austl. 160/B3
Mount Abu, India 127/K4
Mount Airy, NC, US 189/G2
Mount Airy, Md, US 194/A5
Mount Albert, On, Can. 187/G2
Mount Allan Abor. Land, Austl. 157/G2
Mount Angel, Or, US 172/B1
Mount Arayat NP, Phil. 114/C2
Mount Arrowsmith, Austl. 158/B1
Mount Ayliff, SAfr. 150/E3
Mount Ayr, Ia, US 181/G3
Mount Baker-Snoqualmie Nat'l. For., Wa, US 193/D3
Mount Baldy, Ca, US 192/C2
Mount Barclay, Libr. 140/C5
Mount Barker, Austl. 156/C5
Mount Barker, Austl. 157/M9
Mount Barkly Abor. Land, Austl. 157/G2
Mount Beauty, Austl. 159/C3
Mount Bellew Bridge, Ire. 58/B3
Mount Bold (res.), Austl. 157/M9
Mount Carmel, Ut, US 175/F2
Mount Carmel, Il, US 188/D1
Mount Carmel, Pa, US 194/B2
Mount Carroll, Il, US 181/K2
Mount Cavenagh, Austl. 157/G3
Mount Clare, WV, US 189/G1
Mount Clemens, Mi, US 186/E3
Mount Currie, BC, Can. 170/C2
Mount Dora, Fl, US 190/M6
Mount Doreen, Austl. 157/F2
Mount Douglas, Austl. 160/B3
Mount Drysdale, Austl. 158/C1
Mount Eba, Austl. 157/G4
Mount Eccles NP, Austl. 158/B3
Mount Eden (nbrhd.), NZ 161/F6
Mount Edgecombe, SAfr. 151/E3
Mount Elliot NP, Austl. 160/B2
Mount Emu (cr.), Austl. 158/B3
Mount Enterprise, Tx, US 177/G2
Mount Etna (Monte Etna) (vol.), It. 74/D4
Mount Everard, Guy. 205/G3
Mount Field NP, Austl. 158/C4
Mount Fletcher, SAfr. 150/E3
Mount Forest, On, Can. 186/F3
Mount Gambier, Austl. 158/B3
Mount Garnet, Austl. 160/B2
Mount Gay-Shamrock, WV, US 189/F2
Mount Gilead, Oh, US 186/E4
Mount Hagen, PNG 155/G1
Mount Hermon, La, US 190/C2
Mount Holly, NC, US 189/G3
Mount Holly, NJ, US 194/D4
Mount Holly Springs, Pa, US 194/A3
Mount Hope, Ks, US 179/F2
Mount Hope, WV, US 189/G2
Mount Hope, On, Can. 186/T9
Mount Hope, Austl. 159/B1
Mount Horeb, Wi, US 181/K2
Mount Ida, Ar, US 179/H3
Mount Imlay NP, Austl. 159/D3
Mount Isa, Austl. 157/H2
Mount Jackson, Va, US 189/H1
Mount Joy, Pa, US 194/B3
Mount Judea, Ar, US 179/H3
Mount Kaputar NP, Austl. 158/D1
Mount Kenya NP, Kenya 145/B2
Mount Kisco, NY, US 195/E1
Mount Larcom, Austl. 160/C3
Mount Laurel, NJ, US 194/D4
Mount Magnet, Austl. 156/C4
Mount Maunganui, NZ 161/D2
Mount Mistake NP, Austl. 160/D4
Mount Molloy, Austl. 160/B2
Mount Morgan, Austl. 160/C3
Mount Morris, Mi, US 186/E3
Mount Morris, Il, US 181/K2
Mount Nebo, WV, US 189/G1
Mount Nebo, Austl. 160/E6
Mount Olive, Ms, US 190/D2
Mount Olive, Il, US 181/K4
Mount Olive, NC, US 189/H3
Mount Olivet, Ky, US 188/E1
Mount Orab, Oh, US 188/F1
Mount Pearl, Nf, Can. 185/L2
Mount Penn, Pa, US 194/C3
Mount Pleasant, Ar, US 179/J3
Mount Pleasant, Tx, US 179/G4
Mount Pleasant, Mi, US 186/D3
Mount Pleasant, Ut, US 173/H4
Mount Pleasant, Ia, US 181/J3
Mount Pleasant, Austl. 157/N8
Mount Pleasant (int'l arpt.), UK 215/F6
Mount Pleasant, SC, US 189/H4
Mount Pleasant, De, US 194/C4
Mount Plymouth, Fl, US 190/M6
Mount Pocono, Pa, US 194/C1
Mount Prospect, Il, US 193/P15
Mount Pulaski, Il, US 181/K3
Mount Rainier, Md, US 194/B6
Mount Remarkable NP, Austl. 157/H5
Mount Richmond NP, Austl. 158/B3
Mount Rushmore Nat'l Mem., SD, US 180/C2
Mount Selinda, Zim. 149/G4
Mount Shasta, Ca, US 172/B3
Mount Spec NP, Austl. 160/B2
Mount Sterling, Oh, US 186/E5
Mount Sterling, Il, US 181/J4
Mount Sterling, Ky, US 188/F1
Mount Stewart, PE, Can. 185/F2
Mount Storm, WV, US 187/G5
Mount Surprise, Austl. 160/B2
Mount Torrens, Austl. 157/M8
Mount Uniacke, NS, Can. 184/F3
Mount Union, Pa, US 187/H4
Mount Vernon, Ar, US 179/H3
Mount Vernon, Mo, US 179/H2
Mount Vernon, Tx, US 179/G4
Mount Vernon, Oh, US 186/E4
Mount Vernon, Al, US 190/D2
Mount Vernon, NY, US 195/K8
Mount Vernon, Il, US 188/C1
Mount Vernon, Ga, US 189/F4
Mount Vernon, SD, US 180/E2
Mount Vernon, In, US 188/D2
Mount Vernon, Ky, US 188/E2
Mount Vernon, Austl. 156/C3
Mount Vernon, Wa, US 170/C3
Mount Vernon, Va, US 194/A6
Mount Vernon, Md, US 189/K1
Mount Victoria, Austl. 159/E1
Mount Walsh NP, Austl. 160/C4
Mount Warning NP, Austl. 160/D5
Mount William NP, Austl. 158/D4
Mount Wolf, Pa, US 194/B3
Mount Zion, Il, US 181/K4
Mount's (bay), Eng, UK 62/A6
Mountain, Wi, US 183/K5
Mountain, ND, US 182/F3
Mountain (riv.), NW, Can. 166/D2
Mountain (cr.), Tx, US 176/K7
Mountain (cr.), Pa, US 194/A3
Mountain Ash, Wal, UK 62/C3
Mountain Brook, Al, US 188/D4
Mountain City, Nv, US 172/F3
Mountain City, Tn, US 189/G2
Mountain Creek (lake), Tx, US 176/L7
Mountain Grove, Mo, US 179/H2
Mountain Grove, On, Can. 187/H2
Mountain Home, Ar, US 179/H2
Mountain Home, Ut, US 173/H3
Mountain Home, Id, US 172/F2
Mountain Lake, Mn, US 181/G2
Mountain Lake Park, Md, US 187/G5
Mountain Lakes, NJ, US 195/H8
Mountain Park, Ga, US 189/M7
Mountain Park, Ab, Can. 170/F1
Mountain Pine, Ar, US 179/H3
Mountain Rest, SC, US 189/F3
Mountain Top, Pa, US 194/C1
Mountain View, Ar, US 179/H3
Mountain View, Ok, US 179/E3
Mountain View, Mo, US 179/J2
Mountain View, Ca, US 193/K12
Mountain View, Wy, US 173/H3
Mountain Village, Ak, US 168/W12
Mountain Zebra NP, SAfr. 150/D4
Mountainair, NM, US 175/J3
Mountainburg, Ar, US 179/G3
Mountainhome, Pa, US 194/C1
Mountainside, NJ, US 195/H9
Mountlake Terrace, Wa, US 193/C2
Mountmellick, Ire. 58/C3
Mountnessing, Eng, UK 56/E2
Mountnorris (bay), Austl. 154/D2
Mountrath, Ire. 58/C4
Mountville, Pa, US 194/B3
Moura, Chad 142/D2
Moura, Austl. 160/C4
Moura, Port. 72/B3
Mourão, Port. 72/B3
Mourdiah, Mali 140/D3
Mourenx, Fr. 70/C5
Mouriès, Fr. 90/A5
Mourindi, Gabon 146/B3
Mourmelon-le-Grand, Fr. 81/D5
Mourmelon-le-Petit, Fr. 81/D5
Mourne (mts.), NI, UK 60/B3
Mourniaí, Gre. 75/J5
Mouroux, Fr. 56/M5
Mourre Nègre (peak), Fr. 90/B5
Mours-Saint-Eusèbe, Fr. 90/B2
Mousâ'alli (peak), Djib. 144/B2
Mouscron, Belg. 80/C2
Moussayah, Gui. 140/B4
Mousseaux-sur-Seine, Fr. 56/G4
Mousso (well), Chad 142/C1
Moussoro, Chad 142/C2
Moussy-le-Neuf, Fr. 56/K4
Moussy-le-Vieux, Fr. 56/K4
Moustiers-Sainte-Marie, Fr. 90/C5
Mouth of the Severn (mouth), Wal, UK 62/C4
Mouthcard, Ky, US 189/F2
Mouths of the Irrawaddy (delta), Myan. 119/F4
Mouths of the Mekong (delta), Viet. 119/J6
Moutier, Swi. 86/D3
Moûtiers, Fr. 90/C2
Moutong, Indo. 117/F3
Mouvaux, Fr. 80/C2
Mouy, Fr. 80/B5
Mouydir (plat.), Alg. 137/G4
Mouyondzi, Congo 146/C3
Mouzákion, Gre. 75/G3
Mouzarak, Chad 142/B2
Mouzon (riv.), Fr. 86/B1
Mouzon, Fr. 81/E4
Moville, Ire. 60/A1
Mowanjum Mission, Austl. 154/A4
Möwe (bay), Namb. 148/B3
Moxico (prov.), Ang. 147/E5
Moy, NI, UK 60/B3
Moy (riv.), Ire. 58/B1
Moya, Com. 152/H6
Moyale, Kenya 144/A5
Moyalē, Eth. 144/A5
Moyamba, SLeo. 140/B4
Moycullen, Ire. 58/A3
Moye (isl.), China 107/B4
Moyen Atlas (mts.), Mor. 92/B4
Moyen-Chari (pref.), Chad 142/C3
Moyen-Ogooué (prov.), Gabon 146/B3
Moyenmoutier, Fr. 86/C1
Moyenne-Sido, CAfr. 142/C3
Moyers, Ok, US 179/G3
Moyeuvre-Grande, Fr. 81/F5
Moygashel, NI, UK 60/B3
Moyie (riv.), Id, US 170/F3
Moyie, BC, Can. 170/G3
Moyie Springs, Id, US 170/F3
Moyle (dist.), NI, UK 60/B1
Moynalty, Ire. 58/D2
Moyo, Ugan. 147/G2
Moyo (isl.), Indo. 117/E5
Moyobamba, Peru 208/B2
Moyowosi (riv.), Tanz. 147/G3
Moyto, Chad 142/C2
Moyu, China 125/C4
Moyuta, Guat. 200/D3
Mozambique (pt.), La, US 190/D3
Mozambique (chan.), Afr. 133/F7
Mozambique(ctry.) 133/F5
Mozarlândia, Braz. 210/C2
Mozdok, Rus. 97/H4
Mozhaysk, Rus. 94/H5
Mozhga, Rus. 95/M4
Mozogo-Gokoro, PN de, Camr. 142/B3
Mozzanica, It. 88/C3
Mozzecane, It. 89/D3
Mpal, Sen. 140/A3
Mpalapata, Zam. 147/G5
Mpama (riv.), Congo 146/C3
Mpanda, Tanz. 147/G4
Mpangu, Namb. 148/C3
Mpese, D.R. Congo 146/C4
Mpessoba, Mali 140/D3
Mphoengs, Zim. 149/E4
Mpigi, Ugan. 147/H2
Mpika, Zam. 149/F1
Mpo, Congo 146/C3
Mpoko, D.R. Congo 146/D3
Mpoko (riv.), CAfr. 142/C4
Mporaloko, Gabon 146/B3
Mporokoso, Zam. 147/G5
Mpoumé (falls), Camr. 146/B2
M'pouya, Congo 146/D3
Mpraeso, Gha. 141/E5
Mpulungu, Zam. 147/G5
Mpumalanga (prov.), SAfr. 151/E2
Mpwapwa, Tanz. 145/B3
Mrągowo, Pol. 67/J5
Mrkonjić Grad, Bosn. 76/C3
Msanga, Tanz. 145/B3
M'sila (riv.), Alg. 138/H5
M'sila, Alg. 138/H5
Msoro, Zam. 149/F2
Msoun, Mor. 138/C2
Msoun (riv.), Mor. 138/C2
Msta (riv.), Rus. 94/G4
Mstislavl', Bela. 94/F5
Mswega, Tanz. 145/B4
Mszana Dolna, Pol. 69/L4
Mt-St-Michel (bay), Fr. 82/D3
Mt. Apo NP, Phil. 114/D4
Mt. Aspiring NP, NZ 161/A4
Mt. Baker-Snoqualmie, Wa, US 193/D1
Mt. Buffalo NP, Austl. 158/C3
Mt. Cook NP, NZ 161/B3
Mt. Diablo St. Park, Ca, US 193/L11
Mt. Elgon NP, Ugan. 145/A1
Mt. Lofty (range), Austl. 157/M9
Mt. Rainier NP, Wa, US 170/D4
Mt. Revelstoke NP, BC, Can. 170/E2
Mt. Rogers, Va, US 189/G2
Mt. St. Helens, Wa, US 170/C4
Mt. Victoria, NZ 161/H9
Mt. Welcome Abor. Land, Austl. 156/C2
Mtakuja, Tanz. 147/G4
Mtalika, Tanz. 149/H1
Mtarazi (falls), Zim. 149/G3
Mtarazi Falls NP, Zim. 149/G3
Mtito Andei, Kenya 145/E2
Mtondoni, Tanz. 145/E3
Mtorwi (peak), Tanz. 145/A4
Mtsensk, Rus. 96/F1
Mtubatuba, SAfr. 151/F3
Mtunzini, SAfr. 151/E3
Mtwara (prov.), Tanz. 145/E4
Mtwara, Tanz. 145/C4
Mu Ko Similan NP, Thai. 120/E4
Mu Ko Surin NP, Thai. 120/E4
Mu Us Shamo (Ordos) (des.), China 104/F4
Mu-kawa (riv.), Japan 108/C2
Muadiala, D.R. Congo 147/E4
Mualama, Moz. 149/H3
Muan, SKor. 107/D5
Muaná, Braz. 206/D3
Muang Dakchung, Laos 120/D3
Muang Gnommarat, Laos 120/D2
Muang Hay, Laos 112/D4
Muang Hinboun, Laos 120/D2
Muang Hounxianghoung, Laos 120/C1
Muang Kenthao, Laos 120/C2
Muang Khammouan, Laos 120/D2
Muang Khong, Laos 120/D3
Muang Khongxedon, Laos 120/D3
Muang Khoua, Laos 120/C1
Muang Lakhonpheng, Laos 120/D3
Muang May, Laos 120/D3
Muang Mok, Laos 120/D2
Muang Ou Tai, Laos 112/D4
Muang Pak-lay, Laos 120/C2
Muang Paktha, Laos 120/C1
Muang Pakxan, Laos 120/C2
Muang Pakxong, Laos 120/D3
Muang Phin, Laos 120/D2
Muang Sam Sip, Thai. 120/D3
Muang Sing, Laos 112/D4
Muang Soukhouma, Laos 120/D3
Muang Soy, Laos 120/D1
Muang Tahoi, Laos 120/D2
Muang Thadua, Laos 120/C2
Muang Thathom, Laos 120/C2
Muang Vangviang, Laos 120/C2
Muang Vapi, Laos 120/D3
Muang Xaignabouri, Laos 120/C2
Muang Xamteu, Laos 120/D2
Muang Xay, Laos 112/D4
Muang Xepon, Laos 120/D2
Muang Xon, Laos 120/C1
Muar (river), Malay. 115/C2
Muar, Malay. 115/C2
Muara, Indo. 115/C3
Muaraaman, Indo. 115/C3
Muarabeliti, Indo. 115/C3
Muarabenangin, Indo. 116/E4
Muarabungo, Indo. 115/C3
Muaradua, Indo. 115/D3
Muaraenim, Indo. 115/C3
Muarakumpe, Indo. 115/D3
Muaralabuh, Indo. 115/C3
Muaralakitan, Indo. 115/C3
Muararupit, Indo. 115/C3
Muarasabak, Indo. 115/C3
Muarasiberut, Indo. 115/B3
Muarasipongi, Indo. 115/B2
Muarasoma, Indo. 115/B2
Muaratebo, Indo. 115/C3
Muaratembesi, Indo. 115/C3
Muāri (pt.), Pak. 127/J4
Muatechissengue, Ang. 147/E5
Mubale, Ang. 146/D5
Mubārakpur, India 122/D2
Mubayira, Zim. 149/F3
Mubende, Ugan. 147/G2
Mubi, Nga. 142/B3
Mubur (isl.), Indo. 115/D2
Mucajaí (riv.), Braz. 205/F4
Mucambo, Braz. 207/F3
Muccia, It. 92/C1
Much, Ger. 81/G2
Much Wenlock, Eng, UK 62/D1
Muchanes, Bol. 209/E4
Muchinga (mts.), Zam. 147/G5
Muchinga Escarpment (cliff), Zam. 149/F2
Muchiri, Bol. 212/D1
Muchkapskiy, Rus. 97/G2
Muck (isl.), Sc, UK 57/Q8
Muckamore Abbey, NI, UK 60/B2
Muckleshoot Ind. Res., Wa, US 193/C3
Muckleshoot Ind. Res., Wa, US 170/C4
Muckno (lake), Ire. 58/D1
Mucojo, Moz. 149/J2
Mucope, Ang. 148/B3
Mucugê, Braz. 211/E2
Mucula, Ang. 146/C4
Mucupina (mtn.), Hon. 200/E3
Mucur, Turk. 128/C2
Mucuri (riv.), Braz. 211/E3
Mucusso, Ang. 148/D3
Mucussueje, Ang. 147/E5
Mud (lake), Mn, US 182/F3
Mud (cr.), Ne, US 180/E3
Mud Bay, BC, Can. 170/B3
Mud Lake, Id, US 173/G2
Mud Lake (res.), SD, US 180/E1
Mud Mountain (dam), Wa, US 193/D3
Mud Mountain (lake), Wa, US 193/D3
Mudanjiang, China 105/K3
Mudanya, Turk. 77/J5
Mudau, Ger. 84/C3
Mudaysīsāt (wadi), Jor. 131/E5
Mudbach (riv.), Ger. 84/C3
Muddan (riv.), China 101/N5
Muddas NP, Swe. 64/G2
Muddy (cr.), Ut, US 173/H4
Muddy Gap (pass), Wy, US 173/K2
Muddy (riv.), Nv, US 174/E2
Muddy Boggy (cr.), Ok, US 179/F3
Muddy Run (res.), Pa, US 194/B4
Müden, Ger. 79/H3
Mudersbach, Ger. 81/G2
Mudgee, Austl. 159/D1
Mudjatik (riv.), Sk, Can. 166/F3
Mudon, Myan. 120/B2
Mudu, China 106/L8
Mudurnu, Turk. 77/K5
Muecate, Moz. 149/H2
Mueda, Moz. 149/H1
Muela (peak), Chile 215/B7
Mueller (range), Austl. 154/B4
Muenster, Tx, US 179/F4
Muenster, Sk, Can. 171/M1
Muerte, Cerro de la (peak), CR 201/F4
Muff, Ire. 60/A1
Mufjir (wadi), Isr. 131/C4
Mufu (peak), China 113/G2
Mufu, China 113/F2
Mufulira, Zam. 149/F2
Mufulwe (hills), Zam. 149/F2
Mugango, Tanz. 145/A2
Mugardos, Sp. 72/A1
Mugegawa, Japan 109/L4
Mugei (peak), Ugan. 142/G5
Muggelheim, Ger. 68/Q7
Muggia, It. 71/K4
Mughal Sarai, India 122/D3
Mugi, Japan 109/L4
Mugia, Sp. 72/A1
Muğla, Turk. 128/B2
Muğla (prov.), Turk. 130/A1
Mugla (prov.), Turk. 128/B2
Mŭglizh, Bul. 77/G4
Mugodzharskoye (mts.), Kaz. 97/L2
Mugombazi, Tanz. 147/G4
Mūḩ (lake), Syria 128/D3
Muhala, D.R. Congo 147/G4
Muhamdi, India 122/C2
Muḩammad Qawl, Sudan 135/H4
Muhammadābad, India 122/D3
Muhavura (vol.), Rwa. 147/G3
Muheza, Tanz. 145/B3
Muhila, Monts (mts.), D.R. Congo 147/F5
Mühlacker, Ger. 84/B5
Mühlbach (riv.), Ger. 84/A2
Mühldorf, Ger. 85/F6
Mühleberg, Swi. 86/D4
Mühlenbeck, Ger. 68/Q6
Mühlhausen, Ger. 85/E4
Mühlhausen (Augsburg) (arpt.), Ger. 84/D6
Mühlheim am Main, Ger. 84/B2
Mühlheim an der Donau, Ger. 87/E1
Mühltroff, Ger. 85/E1
Mühlviertel (reg.), Aus. 69/G4
Muhos, Fin. 94/E2
Muhu (isl.), Est. 94/D4
Muhulu, D.R. Congo 147/F3
Muhutwe, Tanz. 147/G3
Mui, Eth. 142/G4
Muiden, Neth. 78/C4
Muine Bheag, Ire. 58/D4
Muir of Ord, Sc, UK 59/B1
Muir Woods Nat'l Mon., Ca, US 193/J11
Muirkirk, Sc, UK 59/B5
Muizenberg, SAfr. 150/L11
Muizon, Fr. 80/C5
Muju, SKor. 107/D4
Mukacheve, Ukr. 69/M4
Mükangsar, China 123/F1
Mukawa, Japan 108/B2
Mukāwir, Jor. 131/D5
Mukāwir (Machaerus) (ruin), Jor. 131/D5
Mukawwar (isl.), Sudan 135/H4
Mukdahan, Thai. 120/D2
Mukden, Bol. 208/D3
Muke T'urī, Eth. 144/A3
Mukeriān, India 124/C4
Mukhayyam al Yarmūk, Syria 131/E2
Mukhmās, WBnk. 131/C5
Mukilteo, Wa, US 170/C4
Mukinbudin, Austl. 156/C4
Mukishi, D.R. Congo 147/E4
Muko, Ugan. 147/G3
Mukō, Japan 109/J6
Mukomuko, Indo. 115/C3
Mukono, Ugan. 145/A1
Mukope (riv.), Ang. 148/B2
Mukoshima (isls.), Japan 162/D2
Muktāgācha, Bang. 123/H3
Muktsar, India 124/C4
Mukuku, Zam. 149/F2
Mukunsa, Zam. 147/G5
Mukwakwa, Zam. 147/G5
Mukwe, Namb. 148/D3
Mukwikile, Zam. 149/F1
Mukwonago, Wi, US 193/P14
Mula, Sp. 72/E3
Mulan, China 105/K2
Mulanje, Malw. 149/G3
Mulbekh, India 124/D2
Mulberry (cr.), Tx, US 178/D3
Mulberry, Ar, US 179/G3
Mulberry, Ks, US 179/G2
Mulberry, In, US 186/C4
Mulberry, Fl, US 190/M8
Mulberry, NC, US 189/G2
Mulberry Fk. (riv.), Al, US 188/D4
Mulchén, Chile 214/B3
Mulde (riv.), Ger. 68/G3
Muldoon, Tx, US 177/F3
Mule Creek, NM, US 175/H4
Mulegé, Mex. 198/C3
Muleshoe, Tx, US 178/C3
Muleshoe Nat'l Wildlife Res., Tx, US 178/C3
Muleta (peak), Eth. 144/B3
Mulgŏn, SKor. 107/E5
Mulgrave, NS, Can. 185/G3
Mulgrave (isl.), Austl. 155/F2
Mulhacén, Cerro de (peak), Sp. 72/D4
Mülhausen, Ger. 79/H6
Mülheim an der Ruhr, Ger. 78/D6
Mulhouse, Fr. 86/D2
Mulhurst, Ab, Can. 171/H1
Muli (riv.), Indo. 117/J5
Muli Zangzu Zizhixian, China 112/D3
Mulia, Indo. 117/J4
Mulilansolo Mission, Zam. 147/H5
Mulima, D.R. Congo 147/G4
Muling (riv.), China 105/L2
Muling (pass), China 106/D3
Mulinu'u (cape), WSam. 163/R9
Mulkear (riv.), Ire. 58/B4
Mull (isl.), Sc, UK 57/R8
Mull of Galloway (pt.), Sc, UK 60/D2
Mull of Kintyre (pt.), Sc, UK 60/C1
Mull of Logan (pt.), Sc, UK 60/D2
Mullach Coire Mhic Fhearchair (peak), Sc, UK 59/A1
Mullagh, Ire. 58/D2
Mullaghanish (peak), Ire. 58/A6
Mullaghareirk (mts.), Ire. 58/A5
Mullaghcleevaun (peak), Ire. 60/B5
Mullaghmore (peak), NI, UK 60/B2
Mullaley, Austl. 158/D1
Mullan, Id, US 170/G4
Mullardoch (lake), Sc, UK 59/A2
Mullen, Ne, US 180/D2
Mullens, WV, US 189/G2
Muller (mts.), Indo. 116/D4
Muller (range), PNG 155/F1
Mullet (lake), Mi, US 186/D2
Mullet Key (isl.), Fl, US 190/K8
Mullewa, Austl. 156/B4
Müllheim, Ger. 86/D2
Müllheim, Swi. 87/F2
Mullica (riv.), NJ, US 194/D4
Mullica Hill, NJ, US 194/C4
Mullin, Tx, US 177/E2
Mullinahone, Ire. 58/C4
Mullinavat, Ire. 58/C5
Mullingar, Ire. 58/C2
Mullins, SC, US 189/H3
Mullinville, Ks, US 178/E2
Mullion, Eng, UK 62/A6
Mullumbimby, Austl. 158/E1
Mulobezi, Zam. 148/E3
Mulondo, Ang. 148/B2
Mulongo, D.R. Congo 147/F4
Multai, India 122/B5
Multān, Pak. 124/A4
Multeen (riv.), Ire. 58/B4
Mulu (peak), Malay. 114/A4
Mulumba, D.R. Congo 147/E4
Mulungu, Braz. 207/G4
Mulungushi, Zam. 149/F2
Mulungwishi, D.R. Congo 147/F5
Mulwad, Sudan 135/F5
Mulwala, Austl. 159/C2
Mulwala (lake), Austl. 159/C2
Mum Nauk (pt.), Thai. 120/B5
Mumbai (Bombay), India 127/K5
Mumbondo, Ang. 146/C5
Mumbotuta (falls), Zam. 149/F2
Mumbué, Ang. 148/C2
Mumbwa, Zam. 149/E2
Mumena, D.R. Congo 149/E1
Mumeng, PNG 155/G1
Mumias, Kenya 145/A1
Mümling (riv.), Ger. 84/B3
Mumoni (peak), Kenya 145/B2
Mumra, Rus. 97/H3
Mun (riv.), Thai. 119/H4
Muna (isl.), Indo. 162/B5
Muna, Mex. 200/D1
Munamägi (hill), Est. 67/M3
Muñani, Peru 208/D4
Munayly, Kaz. 97/K3
Munbura, Austl. 160/C3
Muncar, Indo. 116/D5
Münchberg, Ger. 85/E2
München (Munich), Ger. 85/E6
Münchenstein, Swi. 86/D2
Munchique (peak), Col. 204/B4
Munchique, PN, Col. 204/B4
Münchmünster, Ger. 85/E5
Munch'ŏn, NKor. 107/D3
Muncie, In, US 186/D4
Muncy (cr.), Pa, US 194/B1
Muncy, Pa, US 194/B1
Mundabullangana, Austl. 156/C2
Mundare, Ab, Can. 171/H1
Mundaring, Austl. 156/L6
Munday, Tx, US 178/E4
Mundelein, Il, US 193/Q15
Mundemba, Camr. 141/H5
Münden, Ger. 79/G6
Munderfing, Aus. 85/G6
Munderkingen, Ger. 87/F1
Mundesley, Eng, UK 63/H1
Mundford, Eng, UK 63/G1
Mundiwindi, Austl. 156/D2
Mundo Novo, Braz. 213/F2
Mundŏk, NKor. 107/C3
Mundrabilla, Austl. 157/E4
Mundubbera, Austl. 160/C4
Mundurucânia, Res. Florestal, Braz. 209/G2
Munenga, Ang. 146/C5
Munera, Sp. 72/D3
Munford, Tn, US 188/C3
Munfordville, Ky, US 188/E2
Mungaba, Braz. 206/C3
Mungaolī, India 122/B3
Mungbere, D.R. Congo 147/G2
Mungeli, India 122/C4
Munger, India 123/F3
Mungindi, Austl. 158/D1
Mungo, Ang. 148/C1
Mungo NP, Austl. 158/B2
Mungret, Ire. 58/B4
Mungun-Tayga (peak), Rus. 125/F1
Mun'gyŏng, SKor. 107/E4
Munhango, Ang. 148/C2
Munhino, Ang. 148/B2
Munich, ND, US 182/E3
Munich (München), Ger. 85/E6
Munising, Mi, US 183/L4
Muniungu, D.R. Congo 146/D4
Munjor, Ks, US 178/E1
Munka-Ljungby, Swe. 65/J6
Munkebo, Den. 66/D4
Munkedal, Swe. 66/D2
Munkfors, Swe. 66/E2
Munku-Sardyk (peak), Rus. 101/L4
Munku-Sasan (peak), Rus. 104/D1
Münnerstadt, Ger. 84/D2
Muñoz Gamero (pen.), Chile 215/B7
Munsan, SKor. 107/F6
Münsingen, Swi. 86/D4
Münsingen, Ger. 84/C6
Munsön (isl.), Swe 65/A1
Munster, Fr. 86/D1
Münster, Swi. 87/E5
Munster (riv.), Ire. 58/C4
Munster (reg.), Ire. 58/B5
Münster, Ger. 84/B3
Munster, On, Can. 187/J2
Munster, Ger. 79/H3
Munster, In, US 193/R16
Münster, Ger. 79/E5
Münster/Osnabrück (int'l arpt.), Ger. 79/E4
Münstereifel, Ger. 81/F2
Münsterhausen, Ger. 84/D6
Münsterland (reg.), Ger. 68/D2
Münstermaifeld, Ger. 81/G3
Muntele Mare (peak), Rom. 77/F2
Muntendam, Neth. 78/D2
Muntinglupa, Phil. 114/F7
Muntok, Indo. 115/D3
Müntschemier, Swi. 86/D4
Muntu, D.R. Congo 146/D3
Münzenberg, Ger. 84/B2
Münzkirchen, Aus 85/G6
Munzur Vadisi NP, Turk. 128/D2
Muong Het, Laos 120/D1
Muong Hin, Viet. 112/E5
Muong Khuong, Viet. 120/D1
Muong Lat, Viet. 112/E4
Muonio, Fin. 64/G2
Muonioälven (riv.), Swe. 64/G1
Muotathal, Swi. 87/E4
Mupa, Ang. 148/B3
Mupa, PN da, Ang. 148/B2
Muping, China 106/E3
Muqaddan (wadi), Sudan 142/F1
Muqatta', Sudan 142/G2
Muqeibila, Isr. 131/C3
Müqtädir, Azer. 97/J4
Mur (riv.), Aus. 93/G1
Mûr-de-Bretagne, Fr. 82/C4
Mur-de-Sologne, Fr. 83/G6
Mura (riv.), Slov.,Hun. 76/C2
Muradiye, Turk. 129/E2
Murādnagar, India 124/D5
Murakami, Japan 111/F1
Murallón (peak), Chile 215/B6
Muramgaon, India 121/D1
Muramvya, Buru. 147/G3
Murang'a, Kenya 145/B2
Murano, It. 89/F3
Murashi, Rus. 95/L4
Murat (peak), Turk. 128/B2
Muratlı, Turk. 128/E2
Muratlı, Turk. 77/H5
Murayama, Japan 108/B4
Mūrcheh Khvort, Iran 129/G3
Murchison (isl.), On, Can. 183/K3
Murchison, NZ 161/C3
Murchison (mt.), Austl. 156/C3
Murchison (riv.), Austl. 153/A3
Murchison, Austl. 159/B3
Murchison Downs, Austl. 156/C3
Murcia (pol. reg.), Sp. 72/E4
Murcia, Sp. 73/E4
Murderkill (riv.), De, US 194/C6
Murdo, SD, US 180/D2
Murdochville, Qu, Can. 184/E1
Murdock (pt.), Austl. 160/B1
Murdock, Mn, US 181/G1
Mürefte, Turk. 77/H5
Mureş (riv.), Rom. 96/B3
Mureş (prov.), Rom. 77/G2
Muret, Fr. 70/D5
Murewa, Zim. 149/F3
Murfreesboro, Ar, US 179/H3
Murfreesboro, Tn, US 188/D3
Murfreesboro, NC, US 189/J2
Murg (riv.), Ger. 81/H6
Murgap (riv.), Trkm. 100/G6
Murgenella Wildlife Sanctuary, Austl. 154/D2
Murghob, Taj. 125/B4
Murgon, Austl. 160/C4
Murgoo, Austl. 156/C3
Muri, Swi. 87/E3
Muri, China 104/D4
Muri bei Bern, Swi. 86/D4
Muria (peak), Indo. 115/E3
Muriaé, Braz. 211/E4
Murias de Paredes, Sp. 72/B1
Murici, Braz. 207/H5
Murīdke, Pak. 124/C4
Muriege, Ang. 147/E5
Müritz (lake), Ger. 68/G2
Murka, Kenya 145/B2
Murle, Eth. 142/H4
Murlīganj, India 123/F3
Murmansk (int'l arpt.), Rus. 94/G1
Murmansk, Rus. 94/G1
Murmansk Oblast (reg.), Rus. 64/J1
Murmashi, Rus. 94/G1
Murnau, Ger. 87/H2
Murnpeowie, Austl. 157/H4
Muro, Sp. 73/G3
Muro, Japan 109/K6
Muro Lucano, It. 74/D2
Murom, Rus. 94/J5
Murongo, Tanz. 147/G3
Muroran, Japan 108/B2
Muros, Sp. 72/A1
Muroto, Japan 110/D4
Muroto-zaki (pt.), Japan 110/D4
Murowana Goślina, Pol. 69/J2
Murphy, Id, US 172/E2
Murphy, NC, US 188/E3
Murphy, Tx, US 176/L6
Murphys, Ca, US 172/C4
Murphysboro, Il, US 188/C2
Murphytown, WV, US 189/G1
Murr (riv.), Ger. 84/C5
Murra, Nic. 200/E3
Murramarang NP, Austl. 159/E2
Murray, Ut, US 173/H3
Murray, Ky, US 188/C2
Murray (lake), PNG 155/F1
Murray (range), PNG 155/F1
Murray, Id, US 170/G4
Murray (riv.), Austl. 153/D4
Murray Bridge, Austl. 157/H5
Murray Downs, Austl. 157/G2
Murray River, PE, Can. 185/F2
Murraysburg, SAfr. 150/C3
Murrayville, Austl. 158/B2
Murrayville, Ga, US 188/F3
Murree, Pak. 124/B3
Mürren, Swi. 86/D4
Murrhardt, Ger. 84/C5
Murrieta, Ca, US 192/C3
Murrieta Hot Springs, Ca, US 192/C3
Murringo, Austl. 159/D2
Murrumbateman, Austl. 159/D2
Murrumbidgee (riv.), Austl. 153/D4
Murrumburrah, Austl. 159/D2
Murrupula, Moz. 149/H2
Murrurundi, Austl. 158/D1
Mursala (isl.), Indo. 115/B2
Murshidābād, India 123/G3
Murska Sobota, Slov. 76/C2
Murtala Muhammed (int'l arpt.), Nga. 141/F5
Murtaröl (peak), Swi. 87/G4
Murten, Swi. 86/D4
Murtle (riv.), BC, Can. 170/D1
Murtoa, Austl. 158/B3
Murton, Eng, UK 61/G2
Murua, PNG 155/G1
Murua Ngithigerr (mts.), Kenya 142/G5
Murud (peak), Malay. 114/A5
Murud, India 121/C2
Murupara, NZ 161/D2
Mururoa (isl.), FrPol. 163/M7
Murwāra, India 122/C4
Murwillumbah, Austl. 160/D5
Mürz (riv.), Aus. 69/H5
Mürzzuschlag, Aus. 69/H5
Muş, Turk. 128/E2
Muş (prov.), Turk. 128/E2
Musa, D.R. Congo 146/D2
Musa Khel, Pak. 124/A3
Musabeyli, Turk. 130/E1
Musāfirkhāna, India 122/C2

Musā'id, Libya 134/E2
Musala (peak), Bul. 75/H1
Musan, NKor. 107/E1
Musanda, D.R. Congo 146/C4
Musandam (pen.), Oman 129/H5
Musasa, Tanz. 147/G3
Musashino, Japan 109/D2
Musayʻīd, Qatar 126/F4
Musaymir, Yem. 144/C2
Muscat (cap.), Oman 127/G4
Muscatatuck NWR, In, US 188/E1
Muscatine, Ia, US 181/J3
Musciuru (well), Libya 134/B4
Musconetcong (riv.), NJ, US 194/C2
Muscoot (res.), NY, US 195/E1
Muscowpetung Ind. Res., Sk, Can. 182/B2
Muscoy, Ca, US 192/C2
Muse, Ok, US 179/G3
Muse, Tanz. 147/G4
Museum of Flight, Wa, US 193/C2
Musgrave (range), Austl. 162/B7
Musgrave, Austl. 160/A1
Musgravetown, Nf, Can. 185/L1
Mushābani, India 123/F4
Mushāsh (wadi), Isr. 131/C5
Mushaway (peak), Tx, US 177/D1
Musheramore (peak), Ire. 58/B5
Mushie, D.R. Congo 146/D3
Mushin, Nga. 141/F5
Musholm (bay), Den. 65/H7
Musi (river), Indo. 115/C3
Musi (riv.), Indo. 116/B4
Musile di Piave, It. 89/F2
Musinga (peak), Col. 204/B3
Muskego, Wi, US 193/P14
Muskegon, Mi, US 186/C3
Muskegon (riv.), Mi, US 186/D3
Muskingum (riv.), Oh, US 186/E4
Muskirā, India 122/B3
Muskö (isl.), Swe. 65/B1
Muskoday Ind. Res., Sk, Can. 171/M1
Muskogee, Ok, US 179/G3
Muskrat (cr.), Wy, US 173/K2
Muslimīyah, Syria 130/E1
Musofu, Zam. 149/F2
Musoka (lake), On, Can. 187/G2
Musoma, Tanz. 145/A2
Musone (riv.), It. 89/G6
Musquodoboit Harbour, NS, Can. 184/F3
Mussau (isl.), PNG 162/D5
Mussel Fk. (riv.), Mo, US 181/H3
Musselburgh, Sc, UK 59/C5
Musselshell (riv.), Mt, US 168/E2
Musselshell, Mt, US 171/K4
Mussende, Ang. 146/D5
Musserra, Ang. 146/C4
Mussomeli, It. 74/C4
Musson, Belg. 81/E4
Mussuco, Ang. 146/D5
Mussuma (riv.), Ang. 148/D2
Mustafābād, Pak. 124/B4
Mustafābad, India 122/C3
Mustafakemalpaşa, Turk. 96/D4
Mustahīl, Eth. 144/C4
Müstair, Swi. 87/G4
Mustān, Nepal 122/D1
Mustang, Ok, US 179/F3
Mustang (isl.), Tx, US 177/F4
Muşţāy, Egypt 139/C3
Mustayevo, Rus. 97/K2
Musters (lake), Arg. 214/C5
Mustio (Svartå), Fin. 65/D4
Mustvee, Est. 67/M2
Musu-dan (pt.), NKor. 107/E2
Musún (mtn.), Nic. 200/E3
Müsüslü, Azer. 129/F1
Mušutište, Yugo. 75/G1
Muswellbrook, Austl. 158/D2
Mut, Turk. 130/C1
Mūt, Egypt 135/F3
Mutá, Ponta do (pt.), Braz. 211/F2
Mutambara, Zim. 149/G3
Mutango, Ang. 148/D3
Mutare, Zim. 149/G3
Mutenge, Zam. 149/F2
Mutepatepa, Zim. 149/F3
Muthill, Sc, UK 59/C4
Muting, Indo. 155/F1
Mutis (peak), Indo. 154/B2
Mutkyi, Myan. 120/B2
Mutnyy Materik, Rus. 95/M2
Mutoko, Zim. 149/G3
Mutombo, D.R. Congo 147/E4
Mutombo-Dibwe, D.R. Congo 147/E4
Mutombo-Mukulu, D.R. Congo 147/F4
Mutria (peak), It. 92/D5
Mutsamudu, Com. 152/H6
Mutshatsha, D.R. Congo 147/F5
Mutsu, Japan 108/B3
Mutsu (bay), Japan 108/B3
Mutsuzawa, Japan 109/E3
Muttaburra, Austl. 160/B3
Muttekopf (peak), Aus. 87/G3
Muttenz, Swi. 86/D2
Mutters, Aus. 87/H3
Mutterstadt, Ger. 84/B4
Muttler (peak), Swi. 87/G4
Muttonville, Mi, US 193/G6
Mutu (mtn.), Indo. 154/A2
Muţūhis, Egypt 139/B2
Mutum, Braz. 211/E3
Mutumbo, Ang. 148/C2
Mutumieque, Ang. 148/B3
Mutún, Bol. 212/E1
Mutur, SrL. 121/D4
Mutwanga, D.R. Congo 147/G2
Mutzig, Fr. 86/D1
Muwale, Tanz. 145/A3
Muyezerskiy, Rus. 94/F3
Muyinga, Buru. 147/G3
Müynoq, Uzb. 100/F5
Muyuka, Camr. 146/B1
Muyumba, D.R. Congo 147/F4
Muyuya, D.R. Congo 147/F5
Muzaffarābād, Pak. 124/B2
Muzaffargarh, Pak. 124/A4
Muzaffarnagar, India 124/D5
Muzaffarpur, India 123/E2
Muzambinho, Braz. 211/K6
Muzat (riv.), China 125/D3
Muzillac, Fr. 82/C5
Muzo, Col. 207/L7
Muzoka, Zam. 149/E3
Muztag (peak), China 125/D4
Muztagata (peak), China 125/C4
Muzzana del Turgnano, It. 89/G2
Mvadhi-Ousyé, Gabon 146/C2
Mvangane, Camr. 146/B2
Mvolo, Sudan 142/F4
Mvomero, Tanz. 145/B3
Mvoung (riv.), Gabon 146/C2
M'vouti, Congo 146/C4
Mvuma, Zim. 149/F3
Mwadi-Kalumbu, D.R. Congo 146/D4
Mwadingusha, D.R. Congo 147/F5
Mwadui, Tanz. 145/A2
Mwami, Zim. 149/F3
Mwana (cape), Kenya 145/C2
Mwana-Ndeke, D.R. Congo 147/F4
Mwanza (gulf), Tanz. 145/A2
Mwanza, Malw. 149/G2
Mwanza (prov.), Tanz. 145/A2
Mwanza, Tanz. 147/H3
Mwanza, D.R. Congo 147/F4
Mwase Lundaz, Zam. 149/G2
Mwaya, Tanz. 145/B4
Mwaya, Tanz. 145/A4
Mweelrea (peak), Ire. 57/P10
Mweiga, Kenya 145/B2
Mweka, D.R. Congo 147/E4
Mwenda, Zam. 147/G5
Mwene-Ditu, D.R. Congo 147/E4
Mwenezi, Zim. 149/F4
Mwenezi (riv.), Zim. 149/F4
Mwenga, D.R. Congo 147/G3
Mwense, Zam. 147/G5
Mwenzo Mission, Zam. 147/H5
Mwera, Tanz. 145/B3
Mweru (lake), D.R. Congo 133/E5
Mweru-Wantipa (lake), D.R. Congo 147/G5
Mweru-Wantipa NP, Zam. 147/G5
Mwesi (mtn.), Tanz. 147/G4
Mwesi, Tanz. 147/G4
Mwimba, Tanz. 147/G5
Mwimba, D.R. Congo 147/E5
Mwinilunga, Zam. 148/E1
Mwitikira, Tanz. 145/A3
Mwombezhi (riv.), Zam. 148/E2
My Son Temples (ruin), Viet. 120/E3
My Tho, Viet. 120/D4
Myaksa, Rus. 94/H4
Myall Lakes NP, Austl. 158/E2
Myanaung, Myan. 112/B5
Myanmar (Burma)(ctry.) 103/J7
Myatlevo, Rus. 94/G5
Myaungmya, Myan. 112/B5
Myawadi, Myan. 120/B2
Mycenae (Mikínai) (ruin), Gre. 75/H4
Myebon, Myan. 119/F3
Myeik (Mergui), Myan. 120/B3
Myers, Mt, US 171/L4
Myerstown, Pa, US 194/B3
Myggenäs, Swe. 66/D2
Myingyan, Myan. 112/B4
Myintha, Myan. 112/B3
Myitinge (riv.), Myan. 112/C4
Myitkyinā, Myan. 112/C3
Myitta, Myan. 120/B3
Myittha, Myan. 120/B1
Myittha (riv.), Myan. 112/B4
Myjava, Slvk. 69/J4
Mykhaylivka, Ukr. 99/H4
Mykolayiv, Ukr. 98/B3
Mykolayiv, Ukr. 99/G4
Mykolayiv (int'l arpt.), Ukr. 98/G4
Mykolayivka, Ukr. 99/G5
Mykolayivs'ka (prov.), Ukr. 96/D3
Mykulyntsi, Ukr. 98/C3
Mylau, Ger. 85/F1
Mymensingh, Bang. 123/H3
Mymensingh (pol. reg.), Bang. 123/H3
Mynämäki, Fin. 67/J1
Mynaral, Kaz. 125/B2
Mynydd Eppynt (mts.), Wal, UK 62/C2
Mynydd Pencarreg (peak), Wal, UK 62/B2
Mynydd Preseli (mtn.), Wal, UK 62/B3
Myōgi, Japan 109/B1
Myohaung, Myan. 112/B4
Myohla, Myan. 112/C4
Myōkō-san (peak), Japan 111/F2
Myŏngch'ŏn, NKor. 107/E2
Myŏnggan, NKor. 107/E2
Myrhorod, Ukr. 99/G3
Myrnam, Ab, Can. 171/J1
Myronivka, Ukr. 98/F3
Myrtle, Ms, US 188/C3
Myrtle (isl.), Md, US 189/K2
Myrtle Beach, SC, US 189/H4
Myrtle Creek, Or, US 172/B2
Myrtleford, Austl. 159/C3
Mys Shmidta, Rus. 168/V12
Mysen, Nor. 66/D2
Mysingen (bay), Swe. 65/B2
Myślenice, Pol. 69/K4
Myślibórz, Pol. 69/H2
Myslivna (peak), Czh. 85/H5
Mysore, India 121/C3
Mystery Bay Rec. Area, Wa, US 193/B1
Mystery Cave, Mn, US 181/H2
Mystic, Ga, US 191/G2
Mystic, Ia, US 181/H3
Mystic Island, NJ, US 194/D4
Mystic Seaport, Ct, US 187/L4
Mysy, Rus. 95/M3
Myszków, Pol. 69/K3
Mytishchi, Rus. 94/W9
Mýto, Czh. 85/G3
Myton, Ut, US 173/H3
Myyeldino, Rus. 95/M3
M'zab (reg.), Alg. 92/D4
Mže (riv.), Czh. 68/G4
Mzimba, Malw. 149/G1
Mzuzu, Malw. 149/G1

N

N'Djamena (cap.), Chad 142/B2
Na (riv.), Viet. 120/C1
Na Kae, Thai. 120/D2
Naaldwijk, Neth. 78/B4
Naama, Alg. 137/E2
Naantali, Fin. 67/K1
Naarden, Neth. 78/C4
Naarn im Machlande, Aus. 85/H6
Naas, Ire. 58/D3
Nabā (peak), Jor. 131/D5
Nababeep, SAfr. 150/B3
Nabadwīp, India 123/G4
Nabalat al Ḩajanah, Sudan 142/F2
Nabari, Japan 109/K6
Nabari (riv.), Japan 109/K6
Nabberu (lake), Austl. 156/D3
Nabburg, Ger. 85/F4
Naberera, Tanz. 145/B3
Naberezhnye Chelny, Rus. 95/M5
Nābha, India 124/D4
Nabiac, Austl. 158/E2
Nabīnagar, Bang. 123/H4
Nabire, Indo. 117/J4
Nabón, Ecu. 208/B1
Naboomspruit, SAfr. 149/F5
Nabua, Phil. 114/C2
Nābul, Tun. 74/B4
Nābul (gov.), Tun. 74/B4
Nābulus, WBnk. 131/C4
Nabunturan, Phil. 114/D4
Nacala, Moz. 149/J2
Nacaome, Hon. 200/E3
Nacebe, Bol. 209/E3
Nachi-katsuura, Japan 110/D4
Nachingwea, Tanz. 145/B4
Náchod, Czh. 69/J3
Nachrodt-Wiblingwerde, Ger. 79/E6
Nachtigal, Chutes de (falls), Camr. 146/B1
Nachuge, India 119/F5
Nacimiento, Chile 214/B3
Nacimiento (peak), NM, US 175/J2
Nacimiento (res.), Ca, US 174/B3
Nacka, Swe. 65/B1
Nackawic, NB, Can. 184/D2
Nacmine, Ab, Can. 171/H2
Naco, Mex. 175/H5
Nacogdoches, Tx, US 177/G2
Nácori Chico, Mex. 198/C2
Nacozari de García, Mex. 198/C2
Nadadores, Mex. 177/D4
Nādbai, India 122/A2
Nadder (riv.), Eng, UK 62/D4
Nadi (int'l arpt.), Fiji 163/Y18
Nadi, Fiji 163/Y18
Nadiād, India 118/B3
Nādir, Egypt 139/B3
Nădlac, Rom. 76/E2
Nador, Mor. 138/C2
Nador (prov.), Mor. 138/C2
Nadur, Malta 74/L6
Nadvirna, Ukr. 98/C3
Nadvoitsy, Rus. 94/G3
Nadym, Rus. 100/H3
Naejang-san NP, SKor. 107/D5
Näfels, Swi. 87/F3
Nafferton, Eng, UK 61/H4
Nafī, SAr. 126/D3
Naftalan, Azer. 129/F1
Naga, Phil. 114/C2
Naga (hills), India 112/B3
Nagagami (riv.), On, Can. 183/M3
Nagahama, Japan 110/C4
Nagahama, Japan 109/K5
Nagai, Japan 111/G1
Nagaizumi, Japan 109/B3
Nagakute, Japan 109/M5
Nāgāland (state), India 119/F2
Nagambie, Austl. 159/B3
Nagano, Japan 111/F2
Nagano (pref.), Japan 111/E3
Naganuma, Japan 108/B2
Nagaoka, Japan 111/F2
Nagaokakyō, Japan 109/J6
Nagaon (Nowgong), India 112/B3
Nagappattinam, India 121/C4
Nagar, India 122/A2
Nagar Pārkar, Pak. 127/K4
Nagar Untāri, India 122/D3
Nagara (riv.), Japan 111/E3
Nagara, Japan 109/E3
Nagareyama, Japan 109/D2
Nāgārjuna Sāgar (res.), India 118/C4
Nagarote, Nic. 196/D5
Nagarzê, China 123/H1
Nagasaka, Japan 109/A2
Nagasaki, Japan 110/A4
Nagasaki (int'l arpt.), Japan 110/A4
Nagasaki (pref.), Japan 110/A4
Nagasaki Peace, Japan 110/A4
Nagashima, Japan 109/L5
Nagato, Japan 110/B3
Nagato, Japan 109/A1
Nagatoro, Japan 109/C1
Nāgaur, India 118/B2
Nāgda, India 118/C3
Nagele, Neth. 78/C3
Nāgercoil, India 121/C4
Nagīna, India 122/B1
Nagir, Pak. 127/K1
Nagishot, Sudan 142/G4
Nagles (mts.), Ire. 58/B5
Nago, Japan 111/J7
Nago-Torbole, It. 87/G6
Nāgod, India 122/C3
Nagold, Ger. 84/B5
Nagold (riv.), Ger. 84/B5
Nagongera, Ugan. 145/A1
Nagorno-Karabakh (prov.), Arm. 97/H5
Nagornyy, Rus. 101/N4
Nagorsk, Rus. 95/L4
Nagosira, D.R. Congo 147/F2
Nagoya, Japan 109/L5
Nagoya Castle, Japan 109/L5
Nagpula (pass), China 123/F1
Nāgpur, India 124/C5
Nāgpur, India 121/C1
Nagqu (riv.), China 104/C5
Nagqu, China 112/B2
Nags Head, NC, US 189/K3
Nagu (Nauvo), Fin. 67/J1
Naguri, Japan 109/C2
Nagy-Milic (peak), Hun. 69/L4
Nagyatád, Hun. 76/C2
Nagybatony, Hun. 76/D2
Nagyecsed, Hun. 69/M5
Nagyhalász, Hun. 76/E1
Nagykanizsa, Hun. 76/C2
Nagykáta, Hun. 76/D2
Nagykőrös, Hun. 76/D2
Naha, Japan 111/J7
Nahabuan, Indo. 116/D3
Nahal Shillo (wadi), Isr. 131/C4
Nāhan, India 124/D4
Nahanni NP, NW, Can. 166/D2
Nāhar, India 124/D5
Nahariyya, Isr. 131/C3
Nahatlatch (riv.), BC, Can. 170/C3
Nahāvand, Iran 129/G3
Nahel Soreq (riv.), Isr. 131/B5
Naḩḩālīn, WBnk. 131/C5
Nahol'no-Tarasivka, Ukr. 99/K3
Nahouri (prov.), Burk. 141/E4
Nahr Ad Dindar (riv.), Sudan 142/G2
Nahr Ar Rahad (riv.), Sudan 142/G2
Nahr aş Şafā (riv.), Leb. 131/C1
Nahr Ouassel (riv.), Alg. 138/F5
Nahuel Huapi (lake), Arg. 203/B7
Nahuel Huapí, PN, Arg. 214/C4
Nahuelbuta, PN, Chile 214/B3
Nahuentúe, Chile 214/B3
Nahunta, Ga, US 191/H2
Naica, Mex. 198/D3
Naicam, Sk, Can. 171/M1
Naiguatá, Ven. 207/P7
Naihāti, India 123/G4
Naij Gol (riv.), China 104/C4
Naij Tal, China 104/C4
Naikliu, Indo. 154/A2
Naila, Ger. 85/E2
Nailsea, Eng, UK 62/D4
Nailsworth, Eng, UK 62/D3
Nā'im (well), Libya 134/C2
Na'ima, Sudan 142/G2
Naiman Qi, China 106/E2
Nā'īn, Iran 129/H3
Nain, Nf, Can. 167/K3
Nainital, India 122/B1
Nainpur, India 122/C4
Naintré, Fr. 70/D3
Nairn (riv.), Sc, UK 59/B2
Nairn, Sc, UK 59/C1
Nairne, Austl. 157/M9
Nairobi (cap.), Kenya 145/B2
Nairobi NP, Kenya 145/B2
Naita (peak), Eth. 142/G4
Naivasha, Kenya 145/B2
Naives-Rosières, Fr. 81/E6
Najafābād, Iran 129/G3
Najd (des.), SAr. 128/E5
Nájera, Sp. 72/D1
Naju, SKor. 107/D5
Naka (riv.), Japan 110/D4
Naka, Japan 109/G5
Nakadōri (isl.), Japan 110/A4
Nakai, Japan 109/C3
Nakajō, Japan 111/F1
Nakamichi, Japan 109/B2
Nakaminato, Japan 111/G2
Nakamura, Japan 110/C4
Nakano, Japan 111/F2
Nakano (lag.), Japan 110/C3
Nakasato, Japan 108/B3
Nakashibetsu, Japan 108/D2
Nakasongola, Ugan. 147/H2
Nakatane, Japan 111/L5
Nakatomi, Japan 109/A3
Nakatsu, Japan 110/B4
Nakatsugawa, Japan 111/E3
Nakazato, Japan 109/B1
Nak'fa, Erit. 126/C5
Nakhodka, Rus. 105/L3
Nakhola, India 123/J2
Nakhon Nayok, Thai. 120/C3
Nakhon Pathom, Thai. 120/C3
Nakhon Phanom, Thai. 120/D2
Nakhon Ratchasima, Thai. 120/C3
Nakhon Sawan, Thai. 120/C3
Nakhon Si Thammarat, Thai. 120/B4
Nakhon Thai, Thai. 120/C2
Nakhtarāna, India 127/J4
Nakifuma, Ugan. 147/H2
Nakina, On, Can. 183/L2
Nakkila, Fin. 67/J1
Nakło nad Notecią, Pol. 69/J2
Nakodar, India 124/C4
Nakonde, Zam. 147/H5
Nakong, Gha. 141/E4
Nakop, Namb. 150/B3
Naksan-sa, SKor. 107/E3
Nakskov, Den. 66/D4
Naktong, SKor. 107/E4
Naktong (riv.), SKor. 110/A3
Nakūr, India 124/D5
Nakuru, Kenya 145/B2
Nakusp, BC, Can. 170/F2
Nāl (riv.), Pak. 127/J3
Nalao, China 112/E3
Nalayh, Mong. 104/F2
Nalázi, Moz. 149/G5
Nalbach, Ger. 81/F5
Nalbāri, India 123/H2
Nalbaugh NP, Austl. 159/D3
Nal'chik, Rus. 97/G4
Nalchik (int'l arpt.), Rus. 97/G4
Nale, Laos 120/C2
Nalgonda, India 121/C2
Nalhāti, India 123/F3
Nalitābāri, Bang. 123/H3
Naliya, India 127/J4
Nallıhan, Turk. 77/K5
Nalón (riv.), Sp. 72/B1
Nalong, Myan. 112/C3
Nālūt, Libya 137/H3
Nam (riv.), SKor. 107/D5
Nam (riv.), NKor. 107/D3
Nam (lake), China 125/E5
Nam Can, Viet. 120/D4
Nam Cum, Viet. 112/D4
Nam Dinh, Viet. 113/E4
Nam Nao NP, Thai. 120/C2
Nam Pat, Thai. 120/C2
Nam Phong, Thai. 120/C2
Nam Un (res.), Thai. 120/C2
Namacunde, Ang. 148/B3
Namacurra, Moz. 149/H3
Namadzi, Malw. 149/G2
Namāi, Nepal 122/D2
Namak (lake), Iran 129/G3
Namakzār-e Shahdād (salt pan), Iran 129/J4
Namang, Indo. 115/D3
Namanga, Kenya 145/B2
Namangan, Uzb. 125/B3
Namansansong Provicial Park, SKor. 107/G7
Namanyere, Tanz. 147/G4
Namapa, Moz. 149/H2
Namaputa, Tanz. 145/B4
Namaqualand (reg.), SAfr. 150/B3
Namari, Sen. 140/B3
Namaripi (cape), Indo. 117/J4
Namarrói, Moz. 149/H2
Namasagali, Ugan. 145/A1
Namasakata, Tanz. 149/H1
Namatanai, PNG 162/E5
Nambanje, Tanz. 145/B4
Nambe, NM, US 175/K3
Namborn, Ger. 81/G4
Nambour, Austl. 160/D4
Nambu, Japan 109/A3
Nambuangongo, Ang. 146/C5
Nambucca Heads, Austl. 158/E1
Nambung NP, Austl. 156/B4
Namco, China 125/F5
Namdae (riv.), NKor. 107/E2
Namdalseid, Nor. 64/D2
Nämdö (isl.), Swe. 65/B1
Nämdöfjärden (sound), Swe. 65/B1
Namegawa, Japan 109/C1
Namekagon (riv.), Wi, US 183/J4
Namentenga (prov.), Burk. 141/E3
Namerikawa, Japan 111/E2
Nametil, Moz. 149/H2
Namewaminikan (riv.), On, Can. 183/L3
Namhae (isl.), SKor. 107/D5
Namhae, SKor. 107/D5
Nami, Malay. 115/C1
Namib (des.), Namb. 133/D6
Namib-Naukluft Park, Namb. 148/B4
Namibe (int'l arpt.), Ang. 148/B2
Namibe, Ang. 148/B2
Namibe (dist.), Ang. 148/B2
Namibia(ctry.) 133/D7
Namie, Japan 111/G2
Namioka, Japan 108/B3
Namir, Mong. 104/C2
Namitete, Malw. 149/G2
Namja (pass), Nepal 125/D6
Namjagbarwa (peak), China 112/B2
Namlan, Myan. 120/B1
Namling, China 125/E6
Namloser Wetterspitze (peak), Aus. 87/G3
Nammoku, Japan 109/B1
Namnoi (peak), Myan. 120/B4
Namoi (riv.), Austl. 153/D4
Namonuito (isl.), Micr. 162/D4
Namorik (isl.), Mrsh. 162/F4
Namorona, Madg. 152/J8
Nampa, Id, US 172/E2
Nampala, Mali 140/D3
Namp'o, NKor. 107/C3
Nampula, Moz. 149/H2
Nampula (prov.), Moz. 149/H2
Namp'yŏng, SKor. 107/D5
Namrole, Indo. 117/G4
Nāmrup, India 112/B3
Namsa-ri, NKor. 107/D2
Namsang, Myan. 120/B1
Namsê (pass), China 125/D6
Namsos, Nor. 64/D2
Namtok Mae Surin NP, Thai. 112/C5
Namu (isl.), Mrsh. 162/F4
Namúli (mts.), Moz. 149/H2
Namuno, Moz. 149/H2
Namur (prov.), Belg. 81/D3
Namur, Belg. 81/D3
Namutoni, Namb. 148/C3
Namwala, Zam. 149/E2
Namwŏn, SKor. 107/D5
Namysłów, Pol. 69/J3
Nan, Thai. 120/C2
Nan (mts.), China 113/G3
Nan (riv.), China 104/F5
Nan (riv.), Thai. 113/F4
Nan'ao (isl.), China 113/H4
Nana Barya (riv.), Chad 142/C4
Nana Barya, Rsv. de Faune, CAfr. 142/C4
Nana Candundo, Ang. 148/D1
Nana-Mambéré (pref.), CAfr. 142/B4
Nanae, Japan 108/B3
Nanafalia, Al, US 188/D4
Nanaimo, BC, Can. 170/C3
Nanam, NKor. 107/E2
Nanango, Austl. 160/D4
Nanao, Japan 111/E2
Nanauta, India 124/D5
Nanay (riv.), Peru 208/C1
Nanbaozhen, China 106/L8
Nancagua, Chile 214/C2
Nancha, China 105/K2
Nanchang, China 113/G2
Nancheng, China 113/H3
Nanchong, China 112/E2
Nanchong, China 113/E2
Nanchuan, China 113/E2
Nancy, Fr. 81/F6
Nanda Devi (peak), India 125/C5
Nandan, China 119/J3
Nandashan, China 113/G2
Nānded, India 121/C2
Nandi Mill, Zim. 149/F4
Nandigāma, India 121/D2
Nanding (riv.), China 119/G3
Nandonge, Ang. 146/D5
Nandrin, Belg. 81/E3
Nandu, China 113/F4
Nandu (riv.), China 113/F5
Nandy, Fr. 56/K6
Nandyāl, India 121/C3
Nanfen, China 107/B2
Nanfeng, China 113/H3
Nang (isl.), Phil. 113/J4
Nang Rong, Thai. 120/C3
Nang Xian, China 112/B2
Nanga Parbat (peak), Pak. 124/C2
Nanga-Eboko, Camr. 142/B4
Nangalili, Indo. 117/F5
Nangamahap, Indo. 116/D4
Nangamentebah, Indo. 116/D3
Nangapinoh, Indo. 116/D4
Nangar NP, Austl. 159/D1
Nangata (pt.), Moz. 149/J2
Nangin, Myan. 120/B4
Nangis, Fr. 56/M6
Nangnim (mts.), NKor. 107/D2
Nangnim, NKor. 107/D2
Nangong, China 106/C3
Nangqên, China 104/D5
Nangtud (mt.), Phil. 114/C3
Nangua, Tanz. 145/B4
Nanguanling, China 107/A3
Nangwarry, Austl. 158/B3
Nanhsi, Tai. 113/J4
Nanhuang, China 107/A4
Nanhui, China 106/L8
Nanikelako, Zam. 148/D2
Nanjian Yizu Zizhixian, China 112/D3
Nanjiangkou, China 113/F4
Nanjing, China 106/D4
Nanka (riv.), Myan. 112/C4
Nankāna Sāhib, Pak. 124/B4
Nankoku, Japan 110/C4
Nankou, China 113/H3
Nankova, Ang. 148/C3
Nanlan (riv.), China 112/D4
Nanle, China 106/C3
Nanling, China 113/H2
Nanlinqiao, China 113/G2
Nanliu (riv.), China 119/J3
Nanlou (peak), China 105/K3
Nannestad, Nor. 66/D1
Nannine, Austl. 156/C3
Nanning, China 113/F4
Nannō, Japan 109/L5
Nannup, Austl. 156/B5
Nanny (riv.), Ire. 60/B4
Nanpan (riv.), China 112/E3
Nānpāra, India 122/C2
Nanpi, China 106/D3
Nanping, China 113/H3
Nanpu, China 106/J7
Nans-les-Pins, Fr. 90/B6
Nansei, Japan 109/L7
Nansemond Nat'l Wild. Ref., Va, US 189/J2
Nansen (sound), Nun, Can. 167/S6
Nansheng, China 113/H3
Nansio, Tanz. 145/A2
Nant (riv.), Fr. 83/G5
Nant (lake), Sc, UK 59/A4
Nantai, China 107/B2
Nantai-san (peak), Japan 111/F2
Nanterre, Fr. 56/J5
Nantes, Fr. 82/D6
Nantes à Brest (canal), Fr. 82/B4
Nanteuil-le-Haudouin, Fr. 56/L4
Nanteuil-lès-Meaux, Fr. 80/B6
Nantian, China 113/H3
Nantian, China 113/J2
Nanticoke, On, Can. 186/F3
Nanticoke, Pa, US 194/B1
Nanton, Ab, Can. 171/H2
Nantong, China 106/E4
Nantong, China 113/J1
Nantou, China 113/K6
Nantua, Fr. 86/B5
Nantucket, Ma, US 184/B5
Nantucket (isl.), Ma, US 184/C5
Nantucket (sound), Ma, US 184/B5
Nantucket Nat'l Wild. Ref., Ma, US 184/B5
Nantúpi, Moz. 149/H2
Nantwich, Eng, UK 61/F5
Nanty-Glo, Pa, US 187/G4
Nanuet, NY, US 195/J7
Nanuku Passage (chan.), Fiji 163/Y18
Nanumanga (isl.), Tuv. 162/G5
Nanumea (isl.), Tuv. 162/G5
Nanuque, Braz. 211/E3
Nanwon (res.), China 106/C4
Nanxi, China 112/E2
Nanxiang, China 106/L8
Nanxing, China 104/F5
Nanxun, China 106/L9
Nanyamba, Tanz. 145/B4
Nanyang, China 106/D4
Nanyang (lake), China 104/H4
Nanyang, China 106/C4
Nanyue, China 113/G3
Nanyuki, Kenya 145/B1
Nanzamu, China 107/C2
Nanzhang, China 106/B5
Nanzhao, China 106/C4
Nao, Cabo de la (cape), Sp. 73/F3
Não-Me-Toque, Braz. 213/F4
Naococane (lake), Qu, Can. 167/J3
Naogaon, Bang. 123/G3
Naokot, Pak. 118/A3
Naoli (riv.), China 105/L2
Naolinco, Mex. 199/N7
Naos, Namb. 148/C4
Naoua (falls), C.d'Iv. 140/D5
Náousa, Gre. 75/J4
Náousa, Gre. 75/H2
Naozhou (isl.), China 113/F4
Napa (riv.), Ca, US 193/K10
Napa (valley), Ca, US 193/K9
Napa (co.), Ca, US 193/K10
Napa, Ca, US 172/B4
Napa Junction, Ca, US 193/K10
Napak (peak), Ugan. 145/A1
Napanee, On, Can. 187/H2
Napata (ruin), Sudan 135/F5
Napavine, Wa, US 170/C4
Nape, Laos 120/D2
Naperville, Il, US 186/B4
Napf (peak), Swi. 86/D4
Napido, Indo. 117/J4
Napier, SAfr. 150/L11
Napier, NZ 161/D2
Napier (pt.), Austl. 155/D2
Napier (mt.), Austl. 154/C4
Napier Broome (bay), Austl. 154/B3
Napierville (co.), Qu, Can. 185/N7
Napill, Eng, UK 56/A2
Napinka, Mb, Can. 182/D3
Naples, Tx, US 179/G4
Naples, NY, US 187/H3
Naples, Me, US 187/L3
Naples, Fl, US 191/H4
Naples, Ut, US 173/J3
Naples, Id, US 170/F3
Naples Park, Fl, US 191/H4
Napo (riv.), Peru 204/C5
Napo (riv.), Ecu. 204/B5
Napo (riv.), Ecu.,Peru 203/B3
Napo (prov.), Ecu. 204/B5
Napo, China 119/J3
Napoleon, ND, US 182/E4
Napoleon, Oh, US 186/D4
Napoleon, Mi, US 186/D3
Napoleonville, La, US 190/C3
Napoli (gulf), It. 74/C2
Napoli (prov.), It. 92/D6
Napoli, It. 92/D6
Napoule (gulf), Fr. 90/C5
Nappa Merrie, Austl. 160/A4
Nappanee, In, US 186/C4
Napperby, Austl. 157/G2
Napton-on-the-Hill, Eng, UK 63/E2
Napuka (isl.), FrPol. 163/L6
Naqb Ghul (peak), Egypt 139/C5
Naqīl Sumārah (pass), Yem. 144/C2
Nara, Mali 140/D3
Nāra (riv.), Pak. 127/J4
Nara, Japan 109/J6
Nara Logna (pass), Nepal 125/D5
Naracoopa, Austl. 159/B4
Naracoorte, Austl. 158/B3
Naradhan, Austl. 159/C1
Narail, Bang. 123/G4
Naraini, India 122/C3
Nārāinpur, India 121/D2
Naramata, BC, Can. 170/E3
Naranbulag, Mong. 125/F2
Narang, Afg. 124/A2
Naranjal, Ecu. 204/B5
Naranjito, Ecu. 208/B1
Naranjos, Mex. 200/B1
Naranjos, Bol. 212/E1
Narāq, Iran 129/G3
Narasannapeta, India 121/E2
Narasapatnam (pt.), India 121/D2
Narasapur, India 121/D2
Narasaraopet, India 121/D2
Narashino, Japan 109/E2
Narat, China 125/D3
Narathiwat, Thai. 120/C5
Nārāyanganj, India 122/C4
Nārāyanganj, Bang. 123/H4
Nārāyani (zone), Nepal 123/E2
Narayani (riv.), Nepal 123/E2
Narbonne, Fr. 70/E5
Narceo (riv.), Sp. 72/B1
Narcoossee, Fl, US 190/N7
Nardò, It. 75/F2
Nare (pt.), Eng, UK 62/B6
Narellan, Austl. 160/G9
Narembeen, Austl. 156/C5
Naréna, Mali 140/C3
Nares (str.), Can.,Grld. 165/K2
Narew (riv.), Pol. 94/D5
Narganá, Pan. 204/B2
Narib, Namb. 148/C5
Narinda, Madg. 152/H6
Narinda (bay), Madg. 152/H6
Nariño (dept.), Col. 204/B4
Nariño, Col. 207/K7
Narita (int'l arpt.), Japan 111/G3
Narita, Japan 109/E2
Nariz (peak), Chile 215/C7
Narka, Ks, US 180/F4
Narkatiāganj, India 123/E2
Narmada (riv.), India 103/G7
Narman, Turk. 97/G4
Nærnes, Nor. 64/S8
Narni, It. 91/B2
Naro Moru, Kenya 145/B2
Naroch', Bela. 67/M4
Narodnaya (peak), Rus. 95/P2
Narok, Kenya 145/A2
Narón, Sp. 72/A1
Narooma, Austl. 159/E3
Narovlya, Bela. 98/E2
Nārowāl, Pak. 124/C3
Nærøy, Nor. 64/D2
Närpes (Närpiö), Fin. 94/D3
Närpiö (Närpes), Fin. 94/D3
Narra, Phil. 114/B3
Narrabri, Austl. 158/D1
Narrandera, Austl. 159/C2
Narre Warren North, Austl. 159/B3
Narriah (mtn.), Austl. 159/C1
Narrogin, Austl. 156/C5
Narromine, Austl. 158/D2
Narrows (dam), Ar, US 179/H3
Narrows (riv.), NY, US 195/J9
Narrows, Va, US 189/G2
Narsimhapur, India 122/B4
Narsingarh, India 118/C3
Narsinghdi, Bang. 123/H4
Narsī Patnam, India 121/D2
Nartuby (riv.), Fr. 90/C5
Narubis, Namb. 150/B2
Naruksovo, Rus. 95/K5
Narungombe, Tanz. 145/B4
Narusawa, Japan 109/B3
Naruto, Japan 110/D3
Narutō, Japan 109/E2
Narva (riv.), Est.,Rus. 94/E4
Narva (res.), Rus. 94/F4
Narva (bay), Rus.,Est. 67/M2
Narva, Est. 67/N2
Narva (riv.), Rus. 67/M2
Narva-Jõesuu, Est. 67/N2
Narvacan, Phil. 114/C1
Narvik, Nor. 64/F1
Narwāna, India 124/D5
Nar'yan-Mar, Rus. 95/M2
Naryn (riv.), Kyr. 100/H5
Naryn, Kyr. 125/C3
Naryn Khuduk, Rus. 97/H3
Narzole, It. 88/A3
NASA Test Center, Ms, US 190/D2
NASA Test Facility, NM, US 178/A4
NASA Wallops Space Ctr., Va, US 189/K2
Nasarawa, Nga. 141/G4
Năsăud, Rom. 77/G2
Naschel, Arg. 214/D2
Naschitti, NM, US 175/H2
Naseby, NZ 161/B4
Naselle, Wa, US 170/C4
Nash, Ok, US 179/E2
Nash, Eng, UK 63/F3
Nash (pt.), Wal, UK 62/C4
Nashoba, Ok, US 179/G3
Nashua, NH, US 187/L3
Nashua, Ia, US 181/H2
Nashua, Mt, US 171/L3
Nashville, Ar, US 179/H4
Nashville, Ga, US 191/G2
Nashville, In, US 186/C5
Nashville, Mi, US 186/D3
Nashville (int'l arpt.), Tn, US 188/D2
Nashville (cap.), Tn, US 188/D2
Nashville, Il, US 188/C1
Nashville, NC, US 189/J3
Nashwah, Egypt 139/C3
Našice, Cro. 76/D3
Nasielsk, Pol. 69/L2
Nasijärvi (lake), Fin. 67/K1
Nasikonis (cape), Indo. 154/A2
Nāşir, Sudan 142/G3
Nasīrābād, India 118/B2
Naso (pt.), Phil. 114/C3
Nason, Il, US 188/C1
Nasori (Suva) (int'l arpt.), Fiji 163/Y18
Nasorolevu (peak), Fiji 163/Z17
Nasosnyy, Azer. 97/J4
Nāsriganj, India 123/E3
Nassach (riv.), Ger. 84/D2
Nassau, Ger. 81/G3
Nassau (sound), Fl, US 191/H2
Nassau (cap.), Bahm. 197/F2
Nassau (isl.), Cookls. 163/J6
Nassau (bay), Chile 215/D7
Nassau, De, US 194/C6
Nassau (co.), NY, US 195/E2
Nassau Bay, Tx, US 177/M9
Nassawadox, Va, US 189/K2
Nasser (lake), Egypt 133/E2
Nassereith, Aus. 87/G3
Nassian, C.d'Iv. 140/E4
Nässjö, Swe. 66/F3
Nassogne, Belg. 81/E3
Nassoukou, Ben. 141/F4
Nastapoka (isls.), Qu, Can. 167/J3
Nastätten, Ger. 81/G3
Næstved, Den. 66/D4
Nasu-dake (peak), Japan 111/F2
Nasugbu, Phil. 114/C2
Nat (peak), Myan. 112/C5
Nat'l West Coast Rec. Area, Namb. 148/B4
Nata, Bots. 148/E4
Natá, Pan. 204/A2
Natagaima, Col. 204/C4
Natal, Indo. 115/B2
Natal, Braz. 207/H4
Natalbany, La, US 190/C2
Natalia, Tx, US 177/E3
Naţanz, Iran 129/G3
Natashō, Japan 109/J5
Natashquan (riv.), Qu, Can. 167/K3
Natchez, La, US 190/B2
Natchez, Ms, US 190/C2
Natchez Trace (pkwy), Ms, US 179/J5
Natchez Trace, US 188/C4
Natchitoches, La, US 190/B2
Naters, Swi. 86/D5
Natewa (bay), Fiji 163/Z17
Nathalia, Austl. 159/B3
Nathalie, Va, US 189/H2
Nāthdwāra, India 118/B3
Nathenje, Malw. 149/G2
Nathrop, Co, US 175/J1
Natimuk, Austl. 158/B3
National Agriculture Rsch. Ctr., Md, US 194/B6
National Aquarium, Md, US 194/B5
National Archaeological Museum, Gre. 75/N8
National Atomic Musuem, NM, US 178/A3
National Capital District (cap. dist.), PNG 155/G2
National City, Ca, US 192/C5
National Elk (refuge), Wy, US 173/H2
National Exhibition Centre, Eng, UK 63/E2
National Institutes of Health, Md, US 194/A6
National Mine, Mi, US 183/L4
National Museum, Mona. 88/J8
National Security Agency, Md, US 194/B5
Natitingou, Ben. 141/F4
Natividade, Braz. 210/D1
Natkyizin, Myan. 120/B3
Natl, Jor. 131/D5
Nat'l Bison Range, Mt, US 171/G4
Nat'l Key Deer Refuge Nat'l Wild. Ref., Fl, US 191/H5
Nat'l Museum, NZ 161/H9
Natoma, Ks, US 180/E4
Nator, Bang. 123/G3
Natron (lake), Tanz. 145/A2
Nåttarö (isl.), Swe. 65/B2
Natternbach, Aus. 85/G6
Nattheim, Ger. 84/D5
Nättraby, Swe. 66/F3
Natuna (isls.), Indo. 103/K9
Natural Bridge Caverns, Tx, US 177/E3
Natural Bridges Nat'l Mon., Ut, US 175/H2
Naturaliste (chan.), Austl. 156/B3
Naturaliste (cape), Austl. 158/D4
Naturaliste (cape), Austl. 156/B5
Nature Center, Tx, US 176/K7
Nature Reserve, Austl. 156/C2
Nature Reserve, Austl. 156/C4
Nature Reserve, Austl. 156/C5
Nature Reserve, Austl. 156/E5
Naturita, Co, US 175/H1
Naturno (Naturns), It. 87/G4
Naturns (Naturno), It. 87/G4
Naubinway, Mi, US 186/D1
Naucalpan, Mex. 199/Q10
Naucelle, Fr. 70/E4
Naucratis (ruin), Egypt 139/B3
Nauders, Aus. 87/G4
Naudesnek (pass), SAfr. 150/E3
Nauen, Ger. 68/P6
Naugachhia, India 123/F3
Naugaon Sādāt, India 122/B1
Naugatuck, Ct, US 187/K4
Nauhcampatépetl (vol.), Mex. 199/M7
Nauheim, Ger. 84/B3
Naujamiestis, Lith. 67/L4
Naujan, Phil. 114/C2
Naujoji-Akmenė, Lith. 67/K3
Naumburg, Ger. 68/F3
Naumburg, Ger. 79/G6
Naunggala, Myan. 120/B2
Naunglon, Myan. 120/B2
Nauort, Ger. 81/G3
Nā'ūr, Jor. 131/D5
Nauru(ctry.) 162/F5
Nāushahra, India 124/C3
Naushahra Virkhan, Pak. 124/B4
Naushki, Rus. 104/F1
Nauta, Peru 208/C2
Nautla, Mex. 199/N6
Nauvo (Nagu), Fin. 67/J1
Nauvoo, Il, US 181/J3
Nauvoo, Al, US 188/D4
Nava, Mex. 177/D3
Nava del Rey, Sp. 72/C2
Navajo, Mt, US 182/B3
Navajo (riv.), NM,Co, US 178/A2
Navajo (dam), NM, US 175/J2
Navajo, Az, US 175/H3
Navajo (peak), Co, US 175/J2
Navajo (lake), NM, US 175/J2
Navajo Ind. Res., Az,NM, US 175/G2
Navajo Nat'l Mon., Az, US 175/G2
Naval, Phil. 114/D3
Naval Res., Ca, US 192/C4
Navalcarnero, Sp. 73/M9
Navalmoral de la Mata, Sp. 72/C3
Navalvillar de Pela, Sp. 72/C3
Navapolatsk, Bela. 67/N4
Navarin (cape), Rus. 101/T3
Navarino (isl.), Chile 215/C7
Navarra (reg.), Sp. 72/D1
Navarre, Oh, US 186/F4
Navarro, Ca, US 172/B4
Navarro, Arg. 215/J11
Navàs, Sp. 73/F2
Navas de San Juan, Sp. 72/D3
Navasota, Tx, US 177/F2
Navasota (riv.), Tx, US 199/F2
Navassa (isl.), Myan. 201/H2
Navax (pt.), Eng, UK 62/A6
Nave, It. 88/D2
Navenne, Fr. 86/C2
Navia (riv.), Sp. 72/B1
Navia, Sp. 72/B1
Navidad (riv.), Tx, US 177/F3
Navidad, Chile 214/N8
Naviraí, Braz. 213/F2
Navlya, Rus. 96/E1
Năvodari, Rom. 77/J3
Navojoa, Mex. 198/C3
Navolato, Mex. 198/D3
Navotas, Phil. 114/E6
Návpaktos, Gre. 75/G3
Návplion, Gre. 75/H4
Navrongo, Gha. 141/E4
Navy Board (inlet), Nun, Can. 167/H1
Navy Yard City, Wa, US 193/B2
Nawā, Syria 131/E3
Nawābganj, India 122/B1
Nawābganj, India 122/C2
Nawābganj, Bang. 123/G3
Nawābshāh, Pak. 127/J3
Nawāda, India 123/E3
Nawān Jandānwāla, Pak. 124/A3
Nawānshahr, India 124/C3
Nawāpāra, India 121/D1
Nawāshahr, India 124/D4
Nawāshahr, Pak. 124/B2
Nawnghkio, Myan. 112/C4
Nawngleng, Myan. 120/B1
Nawoiy, Uzb. 100/G5
Naxçıvan, Azer. 129/F2
Naxçivan Aut. Rep., Azer. 129/F2
Naxi, China 119/J2
Náxos, Gre. 75/J4
Náxos (isl.), Gre. 93/K3
Nāy Band, Iran 129/H5
Nāy Band, Iran 129/J3
Naya, Col. 204/B4
Nayāgarh, India 121/E1
Nayarit (state), Mex. 198/D4
Nayland, Eng, UK 63/G3
Naylor, Mo, US 188/B2
Nayong, China 119/J2
Nayoro, Japan 108/C1
Nayramadlïn (peak), Mong. 125/E2
Naytahwaush, Mn, US 183/G4
Nayuci, Malw. 149/G2
Nayzatash (pass), Taj. 125/B4
Nazaré, Port. 72/A3
Nazaré, Braz. 206/E4
Nazaré da Mata, Braz. 207/H4
Nazaré do Piauí, Braz. 207/F4
Nazaré Paulista, Braz. 211/K8
Nazareth, Belg. 80/C2

279

Nazar – Niede

Nazareth, Pa, US 194/C2
Nazas, Mex. 198/D3
Nazas (riv.), Mex. 198/D3
Nazca, Peru 208/C4
Naze, Japan 111/K6
Nazelles-Négron, Fr. 83/F6
Naẕerat, Isr. 131/C3
Naẕerat 'Illit, Isr. 131/C3
Nazilli, Turk. 128/B2
Nāzir Hāt, Bang. 123/H4
Nazko (riv.), BC, Can. 170/C1
Nazran', Rus. 97/H4
Nazrēt, Eth. 144/A3
Nazyvayevsk, Rus. 100/H4
Ncamasere (riv.), Bots. 148/D3
Nchanga, Zam. 149/E2
Nchelenge, Zam. 147/G5
Ncheu, Malw. 149/G2
Nchisi, Malw. 149/G2
Ncojane, Bots. 148/D4
Ndabala, Zam. 149/F2
Ndala, Tanz. 145/A3
Ndalatando, Ang. 146/C5
Ndali, Ben. 141/F4
Ndele, CAfr. 142/D3
Ndélélé, Camr. 146/C1
N'Dendé, Gabon 146/B3
Ndende (isl.), Sol. 162/F6
Ndengu, Tanz. 145/A4
Ndiago, Mrta. 140/A2
Ndikiniméki, Camr. 146/B1
Ndim, CAfr. 142/B4
Ndindi, Gabon 146/B3
N'Djamena (int'l arpt.), Chad 142/B2
N'Djili (int'l arpt.), D.R. Congo 146/C4
N'Djolé, Gabon 146/B3
Ndogo (lag.), Gabon 146/B3
Ndola, Zam. 149/F2
Ndolo Corner, Kenya 145/B2
Ndombi, D.R. Congo 147/E4
Ndouaniang, Gabon 146/B2
Ndouci, C.d'Iv. 140/D5
Ndougou, Gabon 146/B3
Ndrhamcha (lake), Mrta. 140/B2
Ndu, D.R. Congo 142/D4
Nduguti, Tanz. 145/A3
Nduli, Tanz. 145/A3
Ndumbwe, Tanz. 145/B4
Ndungu, Tanz. 145/B3
Né (riv.), Fr. 70/C4
Néa Alikarnassós, Gre. 75/J5
Néa Ankhíalos, Gre. 75/H3
Néa Artáki, Gre. 75/H3
Néa Ionía, Gre. 75/H3
Néa Ionía, Gre. 75/N8
Néa Kallikrátia, Gre. 75/H2
Néa Kíos, Gre. 75/H4
Néa Mikhanióna, Gre. 75/H2
Néa Moudhaniá, Gre. 75/H2
Néa Potídhaia, Gre. 75/H2
Néa Tríglia, Gre. 75/H2
Néa Víssa, Gre. 77/H5
Néa Zíkhni, Gre. 75/H2
Neagh (lake), NI, UK 60/B2
Neah Bay, Wa, US 170/B3
Neale (lake), Austl. 157/F3
Neale(lake) 153/C3
Neales (riv.), Austl. 157/G3
Neamţ (prov.), Rom. 77/H2
Neaophli-le-Château, Fr. 56/H5
Neápolis, Gre. 75/J5
Neápolis, Gre. 75/H4
Neápolis, Gre. 75/G2
Near Islands (isls.), Rus. 68/U13
Neath, Wal, UK 62/C3
Neath (riv.), Wal, UK 62/C3
Neavitt, Md, US 194/B6
Nebbi, Ugan. 147/G2
Nebel-Horn (peak), Ger. 87/G3
Nebikon, Swi. 86/D3
Nebin (peak), It. 90/D3
Nebish (isl.), Mi, US 186/D1
Nebitdag, Trkm. 129/H2
Neblina (peak), Braz. 205/E4
Nebo, Mo, US 179/H2
Nebo, SAfr. 149/F5
Nebo (mt.), Ut, US 173/H4
Nebo, Il, US 181/J4
Nebo (mt.), Austl. 160/E6
Nebraska (state), US 168/F3
Nebraska City, Ne, US 181/G3
Nebrodi (mts.), It. 74/C4
Necedah, Wi, US 181/J1
Necedah Nat'l Wild. Ref., Wi, US 181/J1
Nechako (riv.), BC, Can. 166/D3
Nechayane, Ukr. 98/F4
Neche, ND, US 182/F3
Neches (riv.), Tx, US 169/G5
Neches, Tx, US 176/G2
Nechī sar NP, Eth. 142/H4
Nechranice (res.), Czh. 85/G2
Neckar (riv.), Ger. 68/D4
Neckarbischofsheim, Ger. 84/B4
Neckargemünd, Ger. 84/B4
Neckarsteinach, Ger. 84/B4
Neckarsulm, Ger. 84/C4
Necker (isl.), Hi, US 163/J2
Necochea, Arg. 214/F3
Necoclí, Col. 204/B2
Necropoli (ruin), It. 91/B3
Neda, Sp. 72/A1
Nedelino, Bul. 75/J2
Nedelišće, Cro. 76/C2
Nederland, Tx, US 177/H3
Nederweert, Neth. 78/C6
Nedlands (nbrhd.), Aust. 156/K6
Nedumangād, India 121/C4
Nee Soon (nbrhd.), Sing 115/J6
Neede, Neth. 78/D4
Needham, Al, US 190/D2
Needham Market, Eng, UK 63/H2
Needingworth, Eng, UK 63/F2
Needle (mtn.), Wy, US 173/J1
Needles (pt.), NZ 161/C2
Needles, Ca, US 174/E3
Needles, BC, Can. 170/E3
Needles, The, Eng, UK 63/E5
Needville, Tx, US 177/G3
Neely Henry (lake), Al, US 188/D4
Neelyville, Mo, US 188/B2
Neembucú (dept.), Par. 212/E3
Neenah, Wi, US 181/K1
Neepawa, Mb, Can. 182/E2
Neerabup NP, Austl 156/K6
Neerpelt, Belg. 78/C6
Neetze, Ger. 79/H2
Neetze (riv.), Ger. 79/H2
Nefas Mewch'a, Eth. 144/A3
Nefasīt, Erit. 144/A2
Neffelbach (riv.), Ger. 81/F2
Nefṭah, Tun. 92/E4
Neftçala, Azer. 129/G2
Neftegorsk, Rus. 97/J1
Neftegorsk, Rus. 99/K5
Neftekamsk, Rus. 95/M4
Neftekumsk, Rus. 97/H3
Nefud (des.), SAr. 103/B7
Nefyn, Wal, UK 60/D6
Nega Nega, Zam. 149/F2
Négala, Mali 140/C3
Negara, Indo. 115/F3
Negara, Indo. 116/E4
Negaunee, Mi, US 183/L4
Negba, Isr. 131/B5
Negēlē, Eth. 144/A4
Negēlē, Eth. 144/A4
Negeri Sembilan (state), Malay. 115/C2
Negev (reg.), Isr. 128/C4
Negoiu (peak), Rom. 77/G3
Negomano, Moz. 149/H1
Negoreloye, Bela. 67/M5
Negotin, Yugo. 76/F3
Negotino, FYROM 75/H2
Negra (pt.), Belz. 200/D2
Negra (mesa), NM, US 175/J3
Negra (pt.), Peru 208/A2
Negrais (cape), Myan. 119/F4
Negrar, It. 89/D2
Negreet, La, US 190/B2
Negreira, Sp. 72/A1
Negreiros, Chile 212/B1
Negreşti, Rom. 98/D4
Negril, Jam. 201/G2
Negrillos, Bol. 212/B1
Negrine, Alg. 92/E4
Negritos, Peru 208/A2
Negro (peak), Arg. 214/C3
Negro (riv.), Uru. 215/J11
Negro (brook), Uru. 215/K10
Negro (riv.), Bol. 209/F4
Negro (riv.), Braz. 206/A3
Negro (riv.), Par. 212/E3
Negros (isl.), Phil. 103/M9
Neguac, NB, Can. 184/E2
Nehalem (riv.), Or, US 170/C5
Nehbandān, Iran 127/H2
Neheim-Hüsten, Ger. 79/E6
Nei Monggol (plat.), China 104/G3
Nei Monggol (aut. reg.), China 104/E3
Neiafu, Tonga 163/H6
Neiba, DRep. 197/G4
Neiba (mts.), DRep. 201/J2
Neiderösterreich (prov.), Aus. 71/L2
Neihart, Mt, US 171/J4
Neihuang, China 106/C4
Neijiang, China 112/E2
Neilburg, Sk, Can. 171/K1
Neillier (peak), Fr. 90/D4
Neillsville, Wi, US 181/J1
Neil's Harbour, NS, Can. 185/G2
Neilston, Sc, UK 59/B5
Neineis, Namb. 148/B4
Neiqiu, China 106/C3
Neira, Col. 207/K7
Neisse (riv.), Ger. 69/H3
Neiva, Col. 204/C4
Neixiang, China 106/B4
Nejanilini (lake), Mb, Can. 166/G3
Nejdek, Czh. 85/F2
Nejo, Eth. 142/G3
Nejrab (int'l arpt.), Syria 128/D2
Nekā, Iran 129/H2
Nekalagba, D.R. Congo 147/G2
Nek'emtē, Eth. 142/H3
Nekhayevskiy, Rus 99/L2
Nekoosa, Wi, US 181/K1
Nekrasovo, Rus. 97/H2
Nekselø (isl.), Den. 65/H7
Neksø, Den. 66/F4
Nelas, Port. 72/B2
Nelidovo, Rus. 94/G4
Neligh, Ne, US 180/E2
Nellieburg, Ms, US 188/C4
Nellimarla, India 121/D2
Nellingen, Ger. 84/C5
Nellis Air Force Range, Nv, US 174/D2
Nellore, India 121/C3
Nelson, Eng, UK 61/F4
Nelson (cape), Austl. 158/B3
Nelson, NZ 161/C3
Nelson, Az, US 175/F3
Nelson (riv.), Mb, Can. 166/G3
Nelson (riv.), Can. 165/H4
Nelson, Mo, US 181/H4
Nelson, Ne, US 180/E3
Nelson (cape), PNG 155/H2
Nelson (str.), Chile 215/B6
Nelson, Arg. 212/D4
Nelson, Wal, UK 62/C3
Nelson, BC, Can. 170/F3
Nelson Bay, Austl. 158/E2
Nelson Forks, BC, Can. 166/D3
Nelson Lakes NP, NZ 161/C3
Nelson-Miramichi, NB, Can. 184/E2
Nelsonville, Oh, US 186/E5
Nelspruit, SAfr. 149/F5
Néma, Mrta. 140/D2
Nemaha, Ne, US 181/G3
Neman, Rus. 67/K4
Neman (riv.), Rus. 69/M1
Neman (Nemunas) (riv.), Eur. 67/K4
Nembrala, Indo. 154/A2
Nembro, It. 88/C2
Neméa, Gre. 75/H4
Nemenčinė, Lith. 67/L4
Nemi, It. 91/B4
Nemingha, Austl. 158/D1
Nemira (peak), Rom. 77/H2
Nemocón, Col. 207/M7
Nemor (riv.), China 105/K2
Nemours, Fr. 70/E2
Nemunas (riv.), Lith. 94/D5
Nemunas (Neman) (riv.), Eur. 67/K4
Nemuro (str.), Japan,Rus. 105/P3
Nemuro (pen.), Japan 108/D2
Nemuro, Japan 108/D2
Nemyriv, Ukr. 98/B2
Nemyriv, Ukr. 98/E3
Nen (riv.), China 103/M5
Nenagh (riv.), Ire. 58/B4
Nenagh, Ire. 58/B4
Nenasi, Malay. 115/C2
Nendaz, Swi. 86/D5
Nene (riv.), Eng, UK 61/J6
Nenetsia (aut. okrug), Rus. 95/M2
Nenetsia Aut. Okrug, Rus. 100/F3
Nenjiang, China 105/K2
Nentershausen, Ger. 81/G3
Nentershausen, Ger. 79/G6
Nenzing, Aus. 87/F3
Neola, Ut, US 173/H3
Neola, Ia, US 181/G3
Néon Petrítsion, Gre. 75/H2
Neoria Husainpur, India 122/B1
Néos Marmarás, Gre. 75/H2
Neosho, Mo, US 179/G2
Neosho (riv.), US 169/G4
Neosho Falls, Ks, US 179/G1
Nepal(ctry.) 103/H7
Nepālganj, Nepal 122/C1
Nepāltār, Nepal 123/F2
Nepanagar, India 118/C3
Nepean, On, Can. 187/J2
Nepean (riv.), Austl. 160/G8
Nepeña, Peru 208/B3
Nepessina (lake), Mi, US 193/F6
Nephi, Ut, US 173/H4
Nephin (peak), Ire. 58/A1
Nephin Beg (range), Ire. 58/A1
Nephin Beg (peak), Ire. 58/A1
Nepi, It. 91/B3
Nepisiguit (bay), NB, Can. 184/E2
Nepisiguit (riv.), NB, Can. 184/D2
Nepoko (riv.), D.R. Congo 147/G2
Nepomuceno, Braz. 210/D4
Nepomuk, Czh. 85/G4
Neptune City, NJ, US 194/D3
Nera (riv.), It. 71/K5
Nérac, Fr. 70/D4
Neratovice, Czh. 85/H2
Nercha (riv.), Rus. 104/H1
Nerchinsk, Rus. 104/H1
Nerekhta, Rus. 94/J4
Neresheim, Ger. 84/D5
Nereta, Lat. 67/L3
Nereto, It. 92/C2
Neretva (riv.), Bosn.,Cro. 93/H2
Neretva (riv.), Bosn. 76/D4
Neringa, Lith. 67/J4
Neris (riv.), Lith. 94/E5
Nerja, Sp. 72/D4
Ñermete (pt.), Peru 208/A2
Nerokoúros, Gre. 75/J5
Nerone (peak), It. 89/F6
Nerópolis, Braz. 210/C3
Nerpio, Sp. 72/D3
Nersingen, Ger. 84/D6
Nerva, Sp. 72/B4
Nervesa della Battaglia, It. 89/F2
Nervi, It. 88/C5
Nerviano, It. 88/B2
Neryungri, Rus. 101/N4
Nes, Nor. 66/C1
Nes, Nor. 66/D1
Nes, Neth. 78/C2
Nes Ẕiyyona, Isr. 131/B5
Nesbyen, Nor. 66/C1
Nescopeck (cr.), Pa, US 194/C1
Nesebŭr, Bul. 77/H4
Neshaminy (cr.), Pa, US 194/C3
Nesher, Isr. 131/C3
Neskaupstadhur, Ice. 64/Q6
Nesle, Fr. 80/B4
Nesles-la-Vallée, Fr. 56/J4
Nesodden, Nor. 64/S8
Nespelem, Wa, US 170/E3
Nesque (riv.), Fr. 90/B4
Nesquehoning, Pa, US 194/C2
Ness (riv.), Sc, UK 59/B2
Ness (lake), Sc, UK 59/B2
Ness City, Ks, US 178/E1
Nesselwang, Ger. 87/G2
Nesslau, Swi. 87/F3
Nesterovka, Rus. 97/K1
Neston, Eng, UK 61/E5
Nestor Falls, On, Can. 183/H3
Nestore (riv.), It. 91/B1
Nestórion, Gre. 75/G2
Néstos (riv.), Gre. 93/K2
Nesvizh, Bela. 96/C1
Net (riv.), Mi, US 183/K4
Netanya, Isr. 131/B4
Netarhāt, India 123/E4
Netarts, Or, US 170/C5
Netawaka, Ks, US 181/G4
Netcong, NJ, US 194/D2
Nethe (riv.), Ger. 79/G5
Netherend, Eng, UK 62/D3
Netherhill, Sk, Can. 171/K2
Netherlands(ctry.) 55/E2
Netherlands Antilles (isls.), StL. 165/L8
Netishyn, Ukr. 98/D2
Netivot, Isr. 131/B6
Netley, Eng, UK 63/E5
Netolice, Czh. 85/H4
Netphen, Ger. 81/H2
Netrakona, Bang. 123/H3
Netstal, Swi. 87/F3
Nett Lake, Mn, US 183/H3
Nett Lake Ind. Res. (lake), Mn, US 183/H3
Nette (riv.), Ger. 78/D6
Nettebach (riv.), Ger. 81/G3
Nettersheim, Ger. 81/F3
Nettetal, Ger. 78/D6
Nettilling (lake), Nun, Can. 167/J2
Nettleham, Eng, UK 61/H5
Nettleton, Ms, US 188/C3
Nettuno, It. 91/B5
Netzschkau, Ger. 85/F1
Neu Darchau, Ger. 79/H2
Neu Heusis, Namb. 148/C4
Neu Zittau, Ger. 68/Q7
Neu-Isenburg, Ger. 84/B2
Neu-Ostheim (Mannheim) (arpt.), Ger. 84/B4
Neu-Ulm, Ger. 84/D6
Neubiberg, Ger. 85/E6
Neubourg, Fr. 83/F2
Neubrandenburg, Ger. 69/G2
Neubrunn, Ger. 84/C3
Neubulach, Ger. 84/B5
Neuburg, Ger. 84/B5
Neuburg an der Donau, Ger. 84/E5
Neuburg an der Kammel, Ger. 87/G1
Neuchâtel (canton), Swi. 86/C4
Neuchâtel, Swi. 86/C4
Neuchâtel, de (lake), Fr. 92/E1
Neudorf, Sk, Can. 182/C2
Neuenbürg, Ger. 84/B5
Neuenburg am Rhein, Ger. 86/D2
Neuendettelsau, Ger. 84/D4
Neuendorf, Ger. 66/E4
Neuenhagen, Ger. 68/Q6
Neuenhaus, Ger. 78/D3
Neuenkirchen, Ger. 79/F3
Neuenkirchen, Ger. 79/F3
Neuenkirchen, Ger. 79/E4
Neuenrade, Ger. 79/E6
Neuenstadt am Kocher, Ger. 84/C4
Neuenstein, Ger. 84/C4
Neuerburg, Ger. 81/F3
Neuf-Brisach, Fr. 86/D1
Neufahrn bei Freising, Ger. 85/E6
Neufchâteau, Fr. 86/B1
Neufchâteau, Belg. 81/E4
Neufchâtel-en-Bray, Fr. 83/G1
Neufchâtel-Hardelot, Fr. 80/A2
Neufchelles, Fr. 56/M4
Neufmanil, Fr. 81/D4
Neufmoutiers-en-Brie, Fr. 56/L5
Neugablonz, Ger. 87/G2
Neuhaus am Inn, Ger. 85/G6
Neuhaus am Rennweg, Ger. 84/E1
Neuhaus-Schierschnitz, Ger. 84/E2
Neuhäusel, Ger. 81/G3
Neuhausen am Rheinfall, Swi. 87/E2
Neuhof, Ger. 84/C2
Neuhof an der Zenn, Ger. 84/D4
Neuhofen, Ger. 84/B4
Neuhofen an der Krems, Aus. 85/H6
Neuillé-Pont-Pierre, Fr. 83/F5
Neuilly-en-Thelle, Fr. 80/B5
Neuilly-L'Évêque, Fr. 86/B2
Neuilly-sur-Marne, Fr. 56/K5
Neuilly-sur-Seine, Fr. 56/J5
Neukirchen, Ger. 66/C4
Neukirchen an der Vöckla, Aus. 85/G6
Neukirchen vorm Wald, Ger. 85/G5
Neukölln, Ger. 68/Q7
Neumarkt (Enga), It. 87/H5
Neumarkt am Wallersee, Aus. 85/G7
Neumarkt im Mühlkreis, Aus. 85/H6
Neumarkt in der Oberpfalz, Ger. 85/E4
Neumarkt-Sankt Veit, Ger. 85/F6
Neumünster, Ger. 66/C4
Neung-sur-Beuvron, Fr. 83/G5
Neunkirch, Swi. 87/E2
Neunkirchen, Ger. 81/H2
Neunkirchen, Ger. 81/G5
Neunkirchen, Aus. 71/M3
Neunkirchen-Seelscheid, Ger. 81/G2
Neupotz, Ger. 84/B4
Neuquén, Arg. 214/C3
Neuquén (riv.), Arg. 214/C3
Neuquén (prov.), Arg. 214/C3
Neuruppin, Ger. 68/G2
Neusäss, Ger. 84/D6
Neuse (riv.), NC, US 189/J3
Neusiedl am See, Aus. 71/M3
Neusiedler (lake), Aus. 69/J5
Neusiedler (Fertő) (lake), Aus. 71/M3
Neuss, Ger. 78/D6
Neustadt, Ger. 68/G2
Neustadt, Ger. 81/G2
Neustadt am Rübenberge, Ger. 79/G3
Neustadt an der Aisch, Ger. 84/D3
Neustadt an der Donau, Ger. 85/E5
Neustadt an der Waldnaab, Ger. 85/F3
Neustadt an der Weinstrasse, Ger. 84/B4
Neustadt bei Coburg, Ger. 84/E2
Neustadt in Holstein, Ger. 66/D4
Neustift im Stubaital, Aus. 87/H3
Neustrelitz, Ger. 68/G2
Neutraubling, Ger. 85/F5
Neuvic, Fr. 70/E4
Neuville-aux-Bois, Fr. 83/H4
Neuville-sur-Saône, Fr. 86/A6
Neuville-sur-Sarthe, Fr. 83/F4
Neuvy-le-Roi, Fr. 83/F5
Neuwied, Ger. 81/G3
Neuzelle, Ger. 69/H2
Neva (riv.), Rus. 67/P2
Nevada, Mo, US 179/G2
Nevada (mts.), Col. 201/H4
Nevada (state), US 168/C4
Nevada, Ia, US 181/H2
Nevada, Tx, US 176/L6
Nevada City, Ca, US 172/C4
Nevada del Huila, PN, Col. 204/C4
Nevada Test Site, Nv, US 174/D2
Nevada, PN, Ven. 204/D2
Nevado de Chañi (peak), Arg. 212/C3
Nevado de Colima (peak), Mex. 198/E5
Nevado de Colima PN, Mex. 198/D5
Nevado de Cumbal (peak), Col. 204/B4
Nevado de Toluca, PN, Mex. 199/K7
Nevado del Candado (peak), Arg. 212/C3
Nevado del Huila (peak), Col. 204/C4
Nevado del Ruiz (peak), Col. 207/K8
Nevado del Tolima (peak), Col. 207/K8
Nevatim, Isr. 131/B6
Nevel', Rus. 67/N3
Nevele, Belg. 80/C1
Nevel'sk, Rus. 105/N2
Never, Rus. 105/J1
Nevers, Fr. 70/E3
Nevertire, Austl. 158/C1
Nevesinje, Bosn. 76/D4
Neville, Sk, Can. 171/L3
Nevinnomyssk, Rus. 99/L5
Nevis, Mn, US 183/G4
Nevis (isl.), UK 197/J4
Nevis (int'l arpt.), StK. 197/N8
Nevis (peak), StK. 197/N8
Nevola (riv.), It. 89/G5
Nevşehir, Turk. 128/C2
Nevsehir (prov.), Turk. 128/C2
New (riv.), Guy. 205/G4
New (riv.), NC, US 189/J3
New Abbey, Sc, UK 60/E2
New Albany, Ms, US 188/C3
New Albany, In, US 188/E1
New Alfresford, Eng, UK 63/E4
New Amsterdam, Guy. 205/G3
New Ancholme (riv.), Eng, UK 61/H4
New Angledool, Austl. 158/C1
New Ash Green, Eng, UK 56/D2
New Athens, Il, US 188/C1
New Auburn, Mn, US 181/G1
New Augusta, Ms, US 190/D2
New Baltimore, Mi, US 193/G6
New Barn, Eng, UK 56/E2
New Bedford, Ma, US 187/L4
New Berlin, NY, US 187/J3
New Berlin, Wi, US 193/P14
New Berlin, Pa, US 194/B2
New Berlinville, Pa, US 194/C3
New Bern, NC, US 189/J3
New Bethlehem, Pa, US 187/G4
New Bloomfield, Mo, US 179/H1
New Bloomfield, Pa, US 187/H4
New Boston, Tx, US 179/G4
New Boston, Oh, US 189/F1
New Braunfels, Tx, US 176/E3
New Bremen, Oh, US 186/D4
New Brighton, Mn, US 183/P6
New Britain, Ct, US 187/K4
New Britain (isl.), PNG 162/D5
New Britain, Pa, US 194/C3
New Brunswick, NJ, US 195/H10
New Brunswick (prov.), Can. 167/K4
New Buffalo, Mi, US 186/C4
New Buffalo, Pa, US 194/B3
New Buildings, NI, UK 60/A2
New Bussa, Nga. 141/G4
New Caledonia (terr.), Fr. 162/F6
New Caledonia (isl.), NCal. 162/F7
New Canaan, Ct, US 195/M7
New Carlisle, Qu, Can. 184/E1
New Castile (reg.), Sp. 92/C3
New Castle, In, US 186/D5
New Castle, Pa, US 186/F4
New Castle, Ky, US 188/E1
New Castle, Va, US 189/G2
New Castle, De, US 194/C4
New Castle (co.), De, US 194/C5
New Chicago, In, US 193/R16
New City, NY, US 195/K7
New Columbia, Pa, US 194/B1
New Columbus, Pa, US 194/B1
New Concord, Oh, US 186/F5
New Concord, Ky, US 188/C2
New Cordell (Cordell), Ok, US 178/E3
New Cumberland, WV, US 186/F4
New Cumberland, Pa, US 194/B3
New Cumnock, Sc, UK 59/B6
New Dayton, Ab, Can. 171/H3
New Deal, Tx, US 178/D4
New Deer, Sc, UK 59/D1
New Delhi (cap.), India 124/D5
New Denver, BC, Can. 170/F3
New Dorp (nbrhd.), NY, US 195/J9
New Edinburg, Ar, US 179/H4
New Effington, SD, US 182/F5
New Egypt, NJ, US 194/D3
New Ellenton, SC, US 189/G4
New England, ND, US 182/C4
New England NP, Austl. 158/E1
New Era, La, US 190/C2
New Exchequer (dam), Ca, US 174/B2
New Florence, Mo, US 181/J4
New Franklin, Mo, US 181/H4
New Freedom, Pa, US 194/B4
New Galloway, Sc, UK 60/D1
New Georgia (isls.), Sol. 162/E5
New Georgia (sound), Sol. 162/E5
New Germany, NS, Can. 184/E3
New Glasgow, NS, Can. 185/F3
New Glasgow, Qu, Can. 185/N6
New Gloucester, Me, US 187/L3
New Gretna, NJ, US 194/D4
New Guinea (isl.), Indo.,PNG 103/N10
New Hampshire (state), US 169/M3
New Hampton, Ia, US 181/H2
New Hanover (isl.), PNG 162/D5
New Hanover, SAfr. 151/E3
New Harbour, NS, Can. 185/G3
New Harmony, Ut, US 175/F2
New Harmony, In, US 188/C1
New Haven, Ct, US 187/K4
New Haven, In, US 186/C4
New Haven, Mi, US 193/G6
New Haven, WV, US 189/E1
New Haven, Il, US 188/C2
New Haven, Mo, US 181/J4
New Haven, Ky, US 188/E2
New Haven, Wy, US 180/B1
New Hebrides (isls.), Van. 162/F6
New Hebron, Ms, US 190/D2
New Hogan (dam), Ca, US 172/C4
New Holland, Pa, US 194/B3
New Holstein, Wi, US 186/B3
New Home, Tx, US 178/D4
New Hope, Ms, US 188/C4
New Hope, Al, US 188/D3
New Hope, Ga, US 189/L7
New Hope, Tx, US 176/L6
New Hope, NC, US 189/H3
New Hope, NC, US 189/J3
New Hope, Pa, US 194/D3
New Hradec, ND, US 182/C4
New Hyde Park, NY, US 195/L9
New Hythe, Eng, UK 56/E3
New Iberia, La, US 190/C2
New Ireland (isl.), PNG 162/E5
New Jersey (state), US 169/M3
New Johnsonville, Tn, US 188/D2
New Kensington, Pa, US 187/G4
New Kent, Va, US 189/J2
New Kowloon, China 113/L7
New Leipzig, ND, US 182/D4
New Lenox, Il, US 193/Q16
New Lexington, Oh, US 186/E5
New Lima, Ok, US 179/F3
New Lisbon, Wi, US 181/J2
New Lisbon, NJ, US 194/D4
New Liskeard, On, Can. 167/J4
New London, Ct, US 187/K4
New London, Wi, US 181/K1
New London, Mn, US 181/G1
New London, Mo, US 181/J4
New London, Tx, US 177/G1
New Lowell, On, Can. 186/G2
New Madrid, Mo, US 188/C2
New Market, Ia, US 181/G3
New Market, Al, US 188/D3
New Market, Va, US 189/H1
New Market, Md, US 194/A5
New Martinsville, WV, US 186/F5
New Meadows, Id, US 172/E1
New Mexico (state), US 168/E5
New Milford, NJ, US 195/J8
New Mills, Eng, UK 61/F5
New Norcia, Austl. 156/C4
New Norfolk, Austl. 158/C4
New Norway, Ab, Can. 171/H1
New Orleans, La, US 190/C3
New Orleans (Moisant Field) (int'l arpt.), La, US 190/C3
New Oxford, Pa, US 194/A4
New Paltz, NY, US 187/J4
New Paris, In, US 186/D4
New Pekin (Pekin), In, US 188/D1
New Philadelphia, Oh, US 186/F4
New Philadelphia, Pa, US 194/B2
New Pine Creek, Or, US 172/C3
New Pitsligo, Sc, UK 59/D1
New Plymouth, NZ 161/C2
New Plymouth, Id, US 172/E2
New Port Richey, Fl, US 190/K7
New Prague, Mn, US 181/H1
New Providence (isl.), Bahm. 197/F3
New Providence, NJ, US 195/H9
New Quay, Wal, UK 62/B2
New Radnor, Wal, UK 62/C2
New Richmond, Qu, Can. 184/E1
New Richmond, Wi, US 181/H1
New River Gorge Nat'l Riv., WV, US 189/G2
New Roads, La, US 190/C2
New Rochelle, NY, US 195/K8
New Rockford, ND, US 182/E4
New Romney, Eng, UK 63/G5
New Ross, Ire. 58/D5
New Ross, NS, Can. 184/E3
New Rossington, Eng, UK 61/G5
New Salem, ND, US 182/D4
New Sarepta, Ab, Can. 171/H1
New Schwabenland (phys. reg.), Ant. 216/Z
New Scone, Sc, UK 59/C4
New Shagunnu, Nga. 141/G4
New Sharon, Ia, US 181/H3
New Shoreham (Block Island), RI, US 195/G1
New Shrewsbury (Tinton Falls), NJ, US 194/D3
New Siberian (isls.), Rus. 103/N2
New Smyrna Beach, Fl, US 191/H3
New South Wales (state), Austl. 153/D4
New Straitsville, Oh, US 186/E5
New Strawn (Strawn), Ks, US 179/G1
New Summerfield, Tx, US 176/G2
New Tazewell, Tn, US 188/F2
New Town, ND, US 182/C4
New Tredegar, Wal, UK 62/C3
New Tripoli, Pa, US 194/C2
New Ulm, Mn, US 181/G1
New Ulm, Tx, US 176/F3
New Vienna, Oh, US 186/E5
New Virginia, Ia, US 181/H3
New Washington, Oh, US 186/E4
New Waterford, NS, Can. 185/G2
New Westminster, BC, Can. 170/C3
New Whiteland, In, US 186/C5
New Windsor, Md, US 194/A4
New York, NY, US 195/K9
New York (state), US 169/L3
New York Mills, Mn, US 183/G4
New Zealand(ctry.) 153/H6
Newala, Tanz. 145/B4
Newald, Wi, US 183/K5
Newark, Ar, US 179/J3
Newark, Oh, US 186/E4
Newark, NJ, US 195/J9
Newark (int'l arpt.), NJ, US 195/J9
Newark, Ca, US 193/K11
Newark (bay), NJ, US 195/J9
Newark, Il, US 181/K3
Newark, Tx, US 176/K6
Newark, De, US 194/C4
Newark Valley, NY, US 187/H3
Newark-on-Trent, Eng, UK 61/H5
Newaygo, Mi, US 186/D3
Newberg, Or, US 172/B1
Newbern, Tn, US 188/C2
Newberry, Fl, US 191/G3
Newberry, Mi, US 186/D1
Newberry, SC, US 189/G3
Newberry Nat'l Volcanic Mon., Or, US 172/C2
Newbiggin-by-the-Sea, Eng, UK 61/G1
Newbliss, Ire. 58/C1
Newbridge-on-Wye, Wal, UK 62/C2
Newburg, ND, US 182/D3
Newburg, Ar, US 179/J2
Newburgh, Sc, UK 59/E2
Newburgh, Sc, UK 59/C4
Newburgh, NY, US 187/J4
Newburn, Eng, UK 61/G2
Newbury, Vt, US 187/K2
Newbury, Eng, UK 63/E4
Newby Bridge, Eng, UK 61/F3
Newcastle, Ok, US 179/F3
Newcastle, Tx, US 179/E4
Newcastle, NB, Can. 184/E2
Newcastle (int'l arpt.), Eng, UK 61/G1
Newcastle, NI, UK 60/C3
Newcastle, Ire. 60/B5
Newcastle, Ire. 58/A5
Newcastle, Ut, US 175/F2
Newcastle, Wy, US 180/B2
Newcastle, SAfr. 151/E2
Newcastle, Austl. 159/E1
Newcastle upon Tyne, Eng, UK 61/G2
Newcastle Waters, Austl. 154/D4
Newcastle-under-Lyme, Eng, UK 61/F6
Newcastleton, Sc, UK 61/F1
Newcomb, NM, US 175/H2
Newcomerstown, Oh, US 186/F4
Newdegate, Austl. 156/C5
Newdigate, Eng, UK 56/C3
Newe Yam, Isr. 131/B3
Newel, Ger. 81/F4
Newell, Austl. 160/B2
Newell, Ia, US 181/G2
Newellton, La, US 190/C1
Newenham (cape), Ak, US 168/W13
Newent, Eng, UK 62/D3
Newfane, Vt, US 187/K3
Newfane, NY, US 186/V9
Newfield, NJ, US 194/C4
Newfoundland, NJ, US 195/H7
Newfoundland (isl.), Can. 165/M5
Newfoundland (prov.), Can. 167/K3
Newfoundland, Pa, US 194/C1
Newfoundland Evaporation (basin), Ut, US 173/G3
Newgulf, Tx, US 177/G3
Newhalem, Wa, US 170/D3
Newham (bor.), Eng, UK 56/D2
Newhaven, Eng, UK 63/F5
Newhope, Ar, US 179/H3
Newick, Eng, UK 63/G5
Newington, Eng, UK 56/F3
Newington, Ga, US 189/G4
Newkirk, Ok, US 179/F2
Newland, NC, US 189/G2
Newlin, Tx, US 178/D3
Newllano, La, US 190/B2
Newlyn, Eng, UK 62/A6
Newmains, Sc, UK 59/C5
Newman, ND, US 182/F4
Newman, Il, US 186/C5
Newman, NM, US 175/J4
Newman (mt.), Austl. 156/C2
Newman, Austl. 156/C2
Newman Grove, Ne, US 180/F3
Newmarket, Ire. 58/A5
Newmarket, NH, US 187/L3
Newmarket, On, Can. 187/G2
Newmarket (nbrhd.), Austl. 160/F6
Newmarket (nbrhd.), NZ 161/F6
Newmarket, Eng, UK 63/G2
Newmarket on Fergus, Ire. 58/B4
Newmerella, Austl. 159/D3
Newmill, Sc, UK 59/D1
Newnan, Ga, US 188/E4
Newnans (lake), Fl, US 191/G3
Newnham, Eng, UK 62/D3
Newport, Qu, Can. 184/E1
Newport, Ar, US 179/J3
Newport, Ire. 58/B4
Newport, Ire. 58/A2
Newport, In, US 186/C5
Newport, Vt, US 187/K2
Newport, NH, US 187/K3
Newport, NY, US 187/J3
Newport, RI, US 187/L4
Newport, Ky, US 186/D5
Newport, Or, US 172/A1
Newport, Tn, US 189/F3
Newport, Mn, US 183/P7
Newport, Wal, UK 62/D3
Newport, Eng, UK 62/D1
Newport, Eng, UK 63/E5
Newport, Wal, UK 62/B2
Newport, Wa, US 170/F3
Newport, De, US 194/C4
Newport, NC, US 189/J3
Newport, NJ, US 194/C5
Newport, Pa, US 194/A3
Newport (bay), Ca, US 192/C3
Newport Beach, Ca, US 192/G8
Newport Meadows (lake), NJ, US 194/C5
Newport News, Va, US 189/J2
Newport Pagnell, Eng, UK 63/F2
Newport-On-Tay, Sc, UK 59/D4
Newquay, Eng, UK 62/A6
Newquay Civil (arpt.), Eng, UK 62/A6
Newry (dist.), NI, UK 60/B3
Newry, NI, UK 60/B3
Newry (canal), NI, UK 60/B3
Newry, Austl. 154/C4
Newton, Tx, US 177/H2
Newton, Ks, US 179/F1
Newton, Sc, UK 61/E1
Newton, Ga, US 191/F2
Newton, Ma, US 187/L3
Newton, Ut, US 173/H3
Newton, Il, US 188/C1
Newton, Ms, US 188/C4
Newton, Ia, US 181/H3
Newton, Eng, UK 62/D2
Newton, NC, US 189/G3
Newton, NJ, US 194/D1
Newton (co.), Ga, US 189/M7
Newton Abbot, Eng, UK 62/C5
Newton Aycliffe, Eng, UK 61/G2
Newton Falls, NY, US 187/J2
Newton Mearns, Sc, UK 59/B5
Newton on the Moor, Eng, UK 59/E6
Newton Stewart, Sc, UK 60/D2
Newton Tors (hill), Eng, UK 59/D5
Newton-le-Willows, Eng, UK 61/F5
Newtonmore, Sc, UK 59/B2
Newtonville, NJ, US 194/D4
Newtown, Ire. 58/B5
Newtown, Ct, US 187/K4
Newtown, Austl. 158/B3
Newtown, Mo, US 181/H3
Newtown, Wal, UK 62/C1
Newtown, Pa, US 194/D3
Newtown Forbes, Ire. 58/C2
Newtown Mount Kennedy, Ire. 60/B5
Newtown Saint Boswells, Sc, UK 59/D5
Newtown Sandes, Ire. 58/A4
Newtown Square, Pa, US 194/C4
Newtownabbey, NI, UK 60/C2
Newtownards, NI, UK 60/C2
Newtownbutler, NI, UK 58/C1
Newtownhamilton, NI, UK 60/B3
Newtownstewart, NI, UK 60/A2
Newtyle, Sc, UK 59/C3
Newville, Al, US 191/F2
Nextlalpan, Mex. 199/Q9
Neyagawa, Japan 109/J6
Neyrīz, Iran 129/H4
Neyshābūr, Iran 127/G1
Neyva (riv.), Rus. 95/P4
Neyveli, India 121/C4
Neyyāttinkara, India 121/C4
Nez de Jobourg (pt.), Fr. 82/D1
Nez Perce Ind. Res., Id, US 170/F4
Nezahualcóyotl, Mex. 199/Q10
Nezlobnaya, Rus. 97/G3
Neznayka (riv.), Rus. 94/W9
Nezperce, Id, US 170/F4
Nezvěstice, Czh. 85/G3
Ngabang, Indo. 116/C3
Ngabé, Congo 146/D3
Ngabordamlu (cape), Indo. 154/D1
Ngabu, Malw. 149/G3
Ngabwe, Zam. 149/E2
Ngaga, Tanz. 145/B4
Ngahere, NZ 161/B3
Ngai-Ndethya Nat'l Rsv., Kenya 145/B2
Ngalipaeng, Indo. 117/G3
Ngaloua, Niger 142/B2
Ngalu, Indo. 117/F6
Ngama, Chad 142/C3
Ngamanu Bird Sanct., NZ 161/J8
Ngambé, Camr. 146/B1
Ngambwe (falls), Zam. 148/E3
Ngamda, China 112/C2
Ngami (lake), Bots. 148/D4
Ngamiland (dist.), Bots. 148/D3
Ngamring, China 123/F1
Nganda (peak), Malw. 145/A4
Ngangerabeli (plain), Kenya 145/B2
Ngangla Ringco (lake), China 125/D5
Ngangzê (lake), China 125/E5
Nganha, Montagne de (peak), Camr. 142/B4
Ngao, Thai. 120/B2
Ngaoundal, Camr. 142/B4
Ngaoundéré, Camr. 142/B4
Ngapara, NZ 161/B4
Ngara, Tanz. 147/G3
Ngaras, Indo. 115/D3
Ngarkat Consv. Park, Austl. 157/J5
Ngaruawahia, NZ 161/C2
Ngatapa, NZ 161/D2
Ngathainggyaung, Myan. 112/B5
Ngatik (isl.), Micr. 162/E4
Ngato, Camr. 146/C2
Ngau (isl.), Fiji 163/Y18
Ngauruhoe (vol.), NZ 161/C2
Ngawi, Indo. 115/E3
Ngele, D.R. Congo 146/D2
Ngerengere, Tanz. 145/B3
Nghia Dan, Viet. 120/D2
Nghia Lo, Viet. 120/D1
Ngidinga, D.R. Congo 146/C4
Ngiva, Ang. 148/B3
Ngo, Congo 146/C3
Ngoan Muc (pass), Viet. 120/E4
Ngoc Linh (peak), Viet. 119/J4
Ngofakiaha, Indo. 117/G3
Ngogwa, Tanz. 147/H3
Ngoïla, Camr. 146/C2
Ngoko (riv.), Camr. 146/C2
Ngolo, Chutes de (falls), CAfr. 142/D4
Ngom (falls), EqG. 146/B2
Ngom (falls), EqG. 146/B2
Ngomahuru, Zim. 149/F4
Ngomedzap, Camr. 146/B2
Ngomeni (cape), Kenya 145/C2
Ngong, Kenya 145/B2
Ngonye (falls), Zam. 148/D3
Ngoqumaima, China 125/E5
Ngora, Ugan. 145/A1
Ngoring (lake), China 104/D5
Ngorongoro Consv. Area, Tanz. 145/A2
Ngoto, CAfr. 146/D2
Ngotwane (riv.), Bots. 149/E5
Ngoulemakong, Camr. 146/B2
Ngounié (riv.), Gabon 146/B3
Ngounié (prov.), Gabon 146/B3
Ngoura, Chad 142/C2
Ngouri, Chad 142/B2
Ngourti, Niger 142/B2
N'Gcutcheï (well), Chad 142/C1
Ngouyo, CAfr. 142/E4
Ngowwa, Tanz. 147/H4
Ngozi, Buru. 147/G3
Ngudu, Tanz. 145/A2
Nguelémendouka, Camr. 142/B4
Nguigmi, Niger 142/B2
Nguiu, Austl. 154/C2
Ngukurr, Austl. 155/D3
Ngulu (isl.), Micr. 162/C4
Ngumbe Sukani (pt.), Tanz. 145/B4
Ngundu Halt, Zim. 149/F4
Ngunga, Tanz. 145/A2
Nguza, Ang. 148/B1
Ngurah Rai (int'l arpt.), Indo. 115/F3
Nguru (mts.), Tanz. 145/B3
Nguti, Camr. 141/H5
Nguyen Binh, Viet. 112/E4
Ngwedaung, Myan. 112/C5
Ngwenya (peak), Swaz. 151/E2
Ngwerere, Zam. 149/F2
Nha Trang, Viet. 120/E3
Nhamunda (riv.), Braz. 203/D3
Nhamundá, Braz. 206/B3
Nhandeara, Braz. 213/G2
Nhandugue (riv.), Moz. 149/G3
Nhangue-ia-Pepe, Ang. 146/C5
Nharêa, Ang. 148/C1
Nhia (riv.), Ang. 146/C5
Nhill, Austl. 158/B3
Nhlangano, Swaz. 151/E2
Nho Quan, Viet. 112/E4
Nhulunbuy, Austl. 155/E3
Nia-Nia, D.R. Congo 147/F2
Niabembe, D.R. Congo 147/F3
Niafounké, Mali 140/E3
Niagara, Wi, US 183/L5
Niagara (falls), Can.,US 186/U9
Niagara (co.), On, Can. 186/U9
Niagara (riv.), On, Can. 186/U9
Niagara Cave, Mn, US 181/H2
Niagara Falls, On, Can. 186/U9
Niagara Falls, NY, US 186/U9
Niagara-on-the-Lake, On, Can. 186/U9
Niagassola, Gui. 140/C3
Niakaramandougou, C.d'Iv. 140/D4
Niamey (int'l arpt.), Niger 141/F3
Niamey (cap.), Niger 141/F3
Niamey (dept.), Niger 141/F3
Niamtougou, Togo 141/F4
Niandan (riv.), Afr. 141/G5
Niangara, D.R. Congo 147/F2
Niangay (lake), Mali 140/E3
Niangoloko, Burk. 140/D4
Niangua (riv.), Mo, US 179/H2
Niangua, Mo, US 179/H2
Niangzi (pass), China 106/C3
Niantic, Ct, US 187/K4
Niari (pol. reg.), Congo 146/B3
Niari (riv.), Congo 146/C3
Nias (isl.), Indo. 103/J9
Niassa (prov.), Moz. 145/A4
Nibbar, Tun. 138/L6
Nibley, Ut, US 173/H3
Nibong Tebal, Malay. 115/C1
Nīca, Lat. 67/J3
Nicaragua (lake), Nic. 165/J8
Nicaragua(ctry.) 165/J8
Nicastro-Sambiase, It. 74/E3
Nicatous (lake), Me, US 184/C3
Nice, Fr. 90/D5
Niceville, Fl, US 191/E2
Nichelino, It. 90/D3
Nicheng, China 106/L9
Nichinan, Japan 110/B5
Nichlaul, India 122/D2
Nicholas (chan.), Bang. 201/F1
Nicholasville, Ky, US 188/E2
Nicholls, Ga, US 191/G2
Nichols, Fl, US 190/L8
Nichols, SC, US 189/H3
Nicholson (range), Austl. 156/C3
Nicholson, Austl. 154/C4
Nicholson (riv.), Austl. 155/E4
Nickby (Nikkilä), Fin. 65/F4
Nickelsville, Va, US 189/F2
Nickerie (dist.), Sur. 205/G3
Nickerie (riv.), Sur. 205/G3
Nickol (bay), Austl. 156/C2
Nicobar (isls.), India 103/J9
Nicodemus Nat'l Hist. Site, Ks, US 180/E4
Nicola Mameet Ind. Res., BC, Can. 170/D2
Nicolás Bravo, Mex. 200/D2
Nicolás Romero, Mex. 199/Q9
Nicolet, Qu, Can. 187/K1
Nicollet, Mn, US 181/G1
Nicolls (pt.), NY, US 195/E2
Nicosia, It. 74/D4
Nicosia (dist.), Cyp. 130/C2
Nicosia (cap.), Cyp. 130/C2
Nicotera, It. 74/D3
Nicoya (pen.), CR 196/D6
Nicoya (gulf), CR 196/D6
Nicoya, CR 200/E4
Nictau, NB, Can. 184/D2
Nictaux, NS, Can. 184/E3
Nidau, Swi. 86/D3
Nidd (riv.), Eng, UK 61/G3
Nidd (riv.), Eng, UK 61/G4
Nidda, Ger. 84/B2
Nidda (riv.), Ger. 68/E3
Niddatal, Ger. 84/B2
Nidder (riv.), Ger. 84/C2
Nideggen, Ger. 81/F2
Nidge (prov.), Turk. 128/C2
Nidong, China 112/E3
Nidwalden (canton), Swi. 87/E4
Nidzica, Pol. 69/L2
Niebüll, Ger. 66/C4
Nied (riv.), Fr. 71/G2
Niedenstein, Ger. 79/G6
Nieder-Olm, Ger. 81/H4
Niederanven, Lux. 81/F4
Niederbipp, Swi. 86/D3

Niederbronn-les-Bains, Fr. 81/G6	Ni'Tīn, WBnk. 131/C5	Nissan, Fr. 73/G1	Nogent-l'Artaud, Fr. 80/C6
Niedere Tauern (mts.), Aus. 93/G1	Nilo, Col. 207/L8	Nisser (lake), Nor. 66/C2	Nogent-le-Roi, Fr. 83/G3
Niederfischbach, Ger. 81/G2	Nilópolis, Braz. 211/N7	Nisshin, Japan 109/M5	Nogent-le-Rotrou, Fr. 83/F4
Niederlausitz (reg.), Ger. 69/G3	Nilphāmāri, Bang. 123/G3	Nissum (bay), Den. 66/C2	Nogent-sur-Oise, Fr. 80/B5
Niederhausen, Ger. 84/B2	Nilsiä, Fin. 94/F3	Nisswa, Mn, US 188/G3	Nogoa (riv.), Austl. 160/B4
Niederösterreich (prov.), Aus. 76/B2	Nīmach, India 118/B3	Nistru (riv.), Mol.,Ukr. 98/D3	Nogodan-san 107/D5
Niedersachsen (state), Ger. 66/C5	Nīmāj, India 118/B2	Nistru (riv.), Mol. 101/Q4	Nogoonnuur, Mong. 125/F2
Niedersächsisches Wattenmeer NP, Ger. 79/E1	Niman (riv.), Rus. 105/L1	Nitelva (riv.), Nor. 64/S8	Nográd (co.), Hun. 69/K5
Niedersachswerfen, Ger. 79/H5	Nimba (co.), Libr. 140/C5	Niterói, Braz. 211/N7	Nogwak-san 107/C2
Niederstetten, Ger. 84/C4	Nimba (peak), C.d'Iv. 140/C5	Nith (riv.), Sc, UK 59/C6	Nordborg, Den. 66/C4
Niederstotzingen, Ger. 84/D5	Nîmes, Fr. 70/F5	Nithsdale (valley), Sc, UK 60/E1	Norddeich, Ger. 79/E1
Niederurnen, Swi. 87/F3	Nimitabel, Austl. 159/D4	Niti (pass), India 125/C5	Nordegg (riv.), Ab, Can. 170/G1
Niederwerrn, Ger. 84/D2	Nimmo Lake, BC, Can. 170/B1	Nitibe, Indo. 154/B2	Nordegg, Ab, Can. 170/G1
Niederwinkling, Ger. 85/F5	Nimrod's Fortress 131/D2	Nitra, Slvk. 69/K4	Nordela 124/C5
Niederzier, Ger. 81/F2	Nimsbach (riv.), Ger. 81/F4	Nitsa (riv.), Rus. 95/P4	Nohejli, Japan 108/B3
Niederzissen, Ger. 81/G3	Nīnawā (gov.), Iraq 128/E3	Nitta, Japan 109/C1	Nohfelden, Ger. 81/G4
Niefang, EqG. 146/B2	Nīnawā (ruin), Iraq 129/E2	Nittedal, Nor. 66/C1	Nohku (pt.), Mex. 200/E2
Niefern-Öschelbronn, Ger. 84/B5	Nine Point 113/M8	Nittel, Ger. 81/F4	Nohwa, SKor. 105/K5
Niegocin (lake), Pol. 67/J5	Ninepin Group 79/G5	Nittenau, Ger. 85/F4	Noi (riv.), Viet. 119/J5
Niehem, Ger. 79/G5	Niélé, C.d'Iv. 140/D4	Niuafo'ou (isl.), Tonga 163/H6	Noirtable, Fr. 80/D6
Niélé, C.d'Iv. 140/D4	Niem, CAfr. 142/B4	Niuatoputapu Group (isls.), Tonga 163/H6	Noirmoutier (isl.), Fr. 70/B3
Niemba, D.R. Congo 147/G4	Niemodlin, Pol. 69/J3	Niubiziliang, China 125/F4	Noisiel, Fr. 83/F3

281
Novay – Olfen

Novaya Maluksa, Rus. 67/P2
Novaya Sibir' (isl.), Rus. 101/R2
Novaya Usman', Rus. 99/K2
Novaya Zemlya (isl.), Rus. 216/C
Nove, It. 89/E2
Nové Hrady, Czh. 85/H5
Nové Město nad Váhom, Slvk. 69/J4
Nové Sedlo, Czh. 85/F2
Nové Strašecí, Czh. 85/G2
Nové Zámky, Slvk. 76/D2
Novelda, Sp. 73/E3
Novellara, It. 89/D4
Noventa, It. 89/E3
Noventa di Piave, It. 89/F2
Noventa Vicentina, It. 89/E3
Noves, Fr. 90/A5
Novgorod (oblast), Rus. 94/G4
Novgorod, Rus. 67/P2
Novgorod Obalst, Rus. 67/P3
Novgorodka, Rus. 67/N3
Novgorodskoye, Ukr. 99/J3
Novhorod-Sivers'kyy, Ukr. 99/G2
Novhorodka, Ukr. 98/G3
Novi, Mi, US 193/E7
Novi Bečej, Yugo. 76/E3
Novi di Modena, It. 89/D4
Novi Iskŭr, Bul. 77/F4
Novi Pazar, Yugo. 76/E4
Novi Pazar, Bul. 77/H4
Novi Sad, Yugo. 76/D3
Novi Sanzhary, Ukr. 99/H3
Novi Vinodolski, Cro. 71/L4
Novice, Tx, US 179/G4
Novice, Tx, US 176/E2
Novikovo, Rus. 105/N2
Novillars, Fr. 86/C3
Novinger, Mo, US 181/H3
Nóvita, Col. 204/B3
Novo (riv.), Braz. 211/N6
Novo Alexeyevka (int'l arpt.), Geo. 97/H4
Novo Aripuanã, Braz. 209/F2
Novo Hamburgo, Braz. 213/G4
Novo Horizonte, Braz. 213/G2
Novo Mesto, Slov. 76/B3
Novo Miloševo, Yugo. 76/E3
Novo Oriente, Braz. 207/F4
Novo-titarovskaya, Rus. 99/K5
Novoalekseyevka, Kaz. 97/K2
Novoaltaysk, Rus. 100/J4
Novoanninskiy, Rus. 99/M2
Novoazovs'k, Ukr. 99/K4
Novobelokatay, Rus. 95/N5
Novobogatinskoye, Kaz. 97/J3
Novocheboksarsk, Rus. 95/K4
Novocherkassk, Rus. 99/L4
Novodevich'ye, Rus. 97/J1
Novodruzhes'k, Ukr. 99/K3
Novodugino, Rus. 94/G5
Novogrudok, Bela. 67/L5
Novohrad-Volyns'kyy, Ukr. 98/D2
Novohradské Hory (mts.), Czh. 85/H5
Novohrodivka, Ukr. 99/J3
Novoizborsk, Rus. 67/M3
Novokhopërskiy, Rus. 99/L2
Novokubansk, Rus. 99/L5
Novokuybyshevsk, Rus. 97/J1
Novokuznetsk, Rus. 100/J4
Novolazarevskaya, Rus., Ant. 216/A
Novolukoml', Bela. 67/N4
Novominskaya, Rus. 99/K4
Novomoskovsk, Rus. 96/F1
Novomoskovs'k, Ukr. 99/H3
Novomykolayivka, Ukr. 99/H4
Novomyrhorod, Ukr. 98/F3
Novonikolayevskiy, Rus. 99/M2
Novonukutskiy, Rus. 104/E1
Novooleksiyivka, Ukr. 99/H4
Novopokrovka, Ukr. 99/H3
Novopokrovskaya, Rus. 99/L5
Novorontsovka, Ukr. 99/G4
Novorossiysk, Rus. 99/J5
Novorossiyskoye, Kaz. 97/L2
Novorzhev, Rus. 67/N3
Novoselivs'ke, Ukr. 99/G5
Novoselytsya, Ukr. 98/D3
Novosergiyevka, Rus. 97/K1
Novoshakhtinsk, Rus. 99/K4
Novosibirsk, Rus. 100/J4
Novosil', Rus. 96/F1
Novosil'skoye, Rus. 99/K2
Novosineglazovskiy, Rus. 95/P5
Novosokol'niki, Rus. 67/P3
Novostroyevo, Rus. 67/J4
Novotroitsk, Rus. 97/L2
Novotroyits'ke, Ukr. 99/H4
Novoukrayinka, Ukr. 98/F3
Novoul'yanovsk, Rus. 97/J1
Novouzensk, Rus. 97/J2
Novovolyns'k, Ukr. 98/C2
Novovoronezhskiy, Rus. 99/K2
Novovyatsk, Rus. 95/L4
Novoyamskoye, Rus. 96/E1
Novozybkov, Rus. 96/D1
Novska, Cro. 76/C3
Novy (int'l arpt.), Rus. 105/M2
Nový Jičín, Czh. 69/K4
Novyy Buh, Ukr. 99/G4
Novyy Oskol, Rus. 99/J2
Novyy Port, Rus. 100/H3
Novyy Rozdol, Ukr. 98/C3
Novyy Svit, Ukr. 99/H5
Novyy Urengoy, Rus. 100/H3
Nowa Dęba, Pol. 69/L3
Nowa Nowa, Austl. 159/D3
Nowa Ruda, Pol. 69/J3
Nowa Sarzyna, Pol. 69/M3
Nowa Sól, Pol. 69/H3
Nowata, Ok, US 179/G2
Nowe, Pol. 69/K2
Nowe Miasto Lubawskie, Pol. 69/K2
Nowen (peak), Ire. 58/A6
Nowendoc, Austl. 158/D1
Nowgong, India 122/B3
Nowgong (Nagaon), India 112/B3
Nowogard, Pol. 66/F5
Nowood (riv.), Wy, US 173/K2
Nowra, Austl. 159/E2
Nowrangapur, India 121/D2
Nowshera, Pak. 124/A2
Nowy Dwór Gdański, Pol. 67/H4
Nowy Sącz (prov.), Pol. 69/L4
Nowy Sącz, Pol. 69/L4
Nowy Staw, Pol. 67/H4
Nowy Targ, Pol. 69/L4
Nowy Tomyśl, Pol. 69/J2
Noxapater, Ms, US 188/C4
Noxon, Mt, US 170/G4
Noxubee NWR, Ms, US 188/C4
Noya, Sp. 72/A1
Noyabr'sk, Rus. 100/H3
Noyal-Pontivy, Fr. 82/C4
Noyal-sur-Vilaine, Fr. 82/D4
Noyant, Fr. 83/F5
Noye (riv.), Fr. 80/B4
Noyen-sur-Sarthe, Fr. 83/E5
Noyers-sur-Cher, Fr. 83/G6
Noyil (riv.), India 121/C4
Noyon, Fr. 80/C4
Nozay, Fr. 82/D5
Nsah, Congo 146/C3
Nsak, Gabon 146/C2
Nsanje, Malw. 149/G3
Nsawam, Gha. 141/E5
Nsoc, EqG. 146/B2
Nsondia, D.R. Congo 146/D3
Nsopzup, Myan. 112/C3
Nsukka, Nga. 141/G5
Nsumbu NP, Zam. 147/G5
Nsuta, Gha. 141/E5
Ntem (riv.), Camr. 146/B2
Nterguent, Mrta. 140/B2
Ntoroko, Ugan. 147/G2
Ntoum, Gabon 146/B2
Ntui, Camr 146/B1
Ntulume, D.R. Congo 147/E4
Ntungamo, Ugan. 147/G3
Ntusi, Ugan. 147/G2
Ntwetwe Pan (salt pan), Bots. 148/E4
Nu (riv.), China 119/G2
Nu (mts.), China 112/C3
Nu (Salween) (riv.), China 104/D5
Nuang (peak), Malay. 115/C2
Nuangola, Pa, US 194/C1
Nuanshui, China 113/H2
Nūbah, Egypt 139/C4
Nūbāriya (canal), Egypt 139/B3
Nubian (des.), Sudan 133/F2
Nucet, Rom. 76/F2
Nucla, Co, US 175/H1
Nucourt, Fr. 56/H4
Nudaybah, Egypt 139/B3
Nüdlingen, Ger. 84/D2
Nueces (riv.), Tx, US 196/B2
Nueltin (lake), Nun, Can. 166/G2
Nuenen, Neth. 78/C6
Nueva Alejandría, Peru 208/C2
Nueva Asunción (dept.), Par. 212/D2
Nueva Ciudad Guerrero, Mex. 177/E4
Nueva Concepción, Guat. 200/D3
Nueva Constitución, Arg 214/D2
Nueva Esparta (state), Ven. 205/E2
Nueva Esperanza, Arg. 212/D3
Nueva Florida, Ven. 204/D2
Nueva Germania, Par. 213/E2
Nueva Gerona, Cuba 201/F1
Nueva Helvecia, Uru. 215/K11
Nueva Imperial, Chile 214/B3
Nueva Italia de Ruiz, Mex. 198/E5
Nueva Loja, Ecu. 204/B4
Nueva Lubecka, Arg. 214/C5
Nueva Ocotepéque, Hon. 200/D3
Nueva Palmira, Uru. 215/J10
Nueva Patria, Mex. 199/N8
Nueva Rosita, Mex. 177/D4
Nueva Villa de Padilla, Mex. 199/F3
Nueve de Julio, Arg. 214/E2
Nuevitas, Cuba 201/G1
Nuevo, Ca, US 192/C3
Nuevo (gulf), Arg. 214/D4
Nuevo Andoas, Peru 208/B1
Nuevo Balsas, Mex. 199/F5
Nuevo Berlín, Uru. 215/J10
Nuevo Casas Grandes, Mex. 198/D2
Nuevo Chagres, Pan. 201/F4
Nuevo Ideal, Mex. 198/D3
Nuevo Ixcatlán, Mex. 200/C2
Nuevo Laredo, Mex. 177/E4
Nuevo Leon (state), Mex. 196/A2
Nuevo León, Mex. 174/E4
Nuevo Mundo, Bol. 209/E3
Nuevo Progreso, Mex. 177/F4
Nuevo Rocafuerte, Ecu. 204/C5
Nufenen, Swi. 87/F4
Nufenenpass (pass), Swi. 87/E5
Nugaaleed (valley), Som. 144/D3
Nugent, Tx, US 177/E1
Nugget (pt.), NZ 161/B4
Nuguria (isls.), PNG 162/E5
Nuhne (riv.), Ger. 79/F6
Nui (isl.), Tuv. 162/G5
Nuits-Saint-Georges, Fr. 86/A3
Nukata, Japan 109/M6
Nuku Hiva (isl.), FrPol. 163/L5
Nuku'alofa (cap.), Tonga 163/H7
Nukufetau (isl.), Tuv. 162/G5
Nukulaelae (isl.), Tuv. 162/H5
Nukumanu Atoll (atoll), PNG 162/E5
Nukunonu (isl.), Tok. 163/H5
Nukuoro (isl.), Micr. 162/E4
Nukus, Uzb. 100/F5
Nukutavake (isl.), FrPol. 163/M6
Nules, Sp 73/E3
Nullagine, Austl. 156/D2
Nullarbor, Austl. 157/F4
Nullarbor (plain), Austl. 153/B4
Nullarbor NP, Austl. 157/F4
Numan, Nga. 142/B3
Numana, It. 89/G6
Numansdorp, Neth 78/B5
Numata, Japan 111/F2
Numatinna (riv.), Sudan 142/E4
Numazu, Japan 111/F3
Numbi, D.R. Congo 147/G3
Nümbrecht, Ger. 81/G2
Numbulwar, Austl. 155/D3
Numfoor (isl.), Indo. 117/H4
Nummela, Fin. 65/E4
Nummi, Fin. 67/K1
Numurkah, Austl. 159/B3
Nunawading (nbrhd.), Austl. 158/G5
Nunchía, Col. 204/C3
Nunda, NY, US 187/H3
Nundle, Austl. 158/D1
Nuneaton, Eng, UK 63/E1
Nŭng-ni, NKor. 107/D3
Nungarin, Austl. 156/C4
Nungatta NP, Austl. 159/D3
Nungo, Moz. 149/H2
Nungwe, Tanz. 147/H3
Nunivak (isl.), Ak, US 165/A4
Nunley, Ar, US 179/G3
Nunnelly, Tn, US 188/D3
Nunningen, Swi. 86/D3
Nuñoa, Peru 208/D4
Nunspeet, Neth. 78/C4
Nunthorpe, Eng, UK 61/G2
Nunukan, Indo. 114/B4
Nuomin (riv.), China 105/J1
Nuon (riv.), Libr. 140/C5
Nuoro, It. 74/A2
Nupurbölе (Nupurila), Fin. 65/E4
Nupurila (Nupurböle), Fin. 65/E4
Nuqūb, Yem. 144/C2
Nuquí, Col. 204/B3
Nur (mts.), Turk. 130/E1
Nur, China 125/D4
Nura (riv.), Kaz. 125/B2
Nūrābād, Iran 129/G4
Nurata, Uzb. 100/G5
Nürburgring, Ger. 81/F3
Nure (riv.), It. 88/C3
Nuremberg, Pa, US 194/B2
Nurhak, Turk. 128/D2
Nuri (ruin), Sudan 135/F5
Nuria (peak), It. 92/C3
Nuriootpa, Austl. 157/H5
Nūrla, India 124/D2
Nurlat, Rus. 95/L5
Nūrmahal, India 124/C4
Nurmijärvi, Fin. 67/L1
Nürnberg (int'l arpt.), Ger. 84/E3
Nürnberg, Ger. 84/E4
Nūrpur, Pak. 124/B3
Nurri (mt.), Austl. 158/C1
Nursery, Tx, US 177/F3
Nürtingen, Ger. 84/C5
Nus, It. 90/D1
Nusa Tenggara Timur (prov.), Indo. 154/A2
Nūsah, Yem. 144/C2
Nūshābād, Iran 129/G3
Nushki, Pak. 127/J3
Nutberry (hill), Sc, UK 59/C5
Nuth, Neth. 81/E2
Nuthe-Graben (riv.), Ger. 68/Q7
Nutley, NJ, US 195/J8
Nuttby (mtn.), NS, Can. 184/F3
Nutwood Downs, Austl. 154/D3
Nuuk (Godthåb), Grld. 165/M3
Nuuksion NP, Fin. 65/E4
Nuupere (pt.), FrPol. 163/X15
Nuvolento, It. 88/D2
Nuwākot, Nepal 122/D1
Nuwara Eliya, SrL. 121/D5
Nuwaybi', Egypt 135/G2
Nuy (riv.), SAfr. 150/L10
Nuza (mt.), Zim. 149/G3
Nüziders, Aus. 87/F3
Nūzvīd, India 121/D2
Nxai Pan (salt pan), Bots. 148/E3
Nxai Pan NP, Bots. 148/E3
Nxaunxau, Bots. 148/D3
Nya-ghezi, D.R. Congo 147/G3
Nyaake, Libr. 140/D5
Nyabing, Austl. 156/C5
Nyabisindu, Rwa. 147/G3
Nyack, NY, US 195/K7
Nyah, Austl. 158/B2
Nyah West, Austl. 158/B2
Nyahua, Tanz. 145/A3
Nyahururu Falls, Kenya 145/B1
Nyainqêntanglha (peak), China 125/F5
Nyainqêntanglha (mts.), China 112/B2
Nyainrong, China 112/B1
Nyakabindi, Tanz. 145/A2
Nyakanyasi, Tanz. 147/G3
Nyaki NP, Malw. 145/A4
Nyaki NPP, Malw. 149/G1
Nyakrom, Gha. 141/E5
Nyaksimvol', Rus. 95/P3
Nyakulenga, Zam. 148/D2
Nyala, Sudan 142/E2
Nyalam, China 123/E1
Nyalikungu, Tanz. 145/A2
Nyamandhlovu, Zim. 149/F3
Nyamapande, Zim. 149/G3
Nyambiti, Tanz. 145/A2
Nyamina, Mali 140/D3
Nyamlell, Sudan 142/E3
Nyamtumbo, Tanz. 145/B4
Nyandoma, Rus. 94/J3
Nyanga (riv.), Gabon 146/B3
Nyanga (prov.), Gabon 146/B3
Nyanga, Gabon 146/B3
Nyanga NP, Zim. 149/G3
Nyanga-Nord, Rsv. de la, Gabon,Congo 146/B3
Nyangui (peak), Zim. 149/G3
Nyanyadzi, Zim. 149/G3
Nyanza (prov.), Kenya 145/A2
Nyanza-Lac, Buru. 147/G4
Nyanzwa, Tanz. 145/B3
Nyaruonga, Tanz. 147/G3
Nyasa (lake), Malw. 133/F6
Nyaunglebin, Myan. 120/B2
Nyazepetrovsk, Rus. 95/N4
Nyazura, Zim. 149/G3
Nybergsund, Nor. 66/E1
Nybro, Swe. 66/F3
Nyêmo, China 123/H1
Nyenasi, Gha. 141/E5
Nyeri, Kenya 145/B2
Nyerol, Sudan 142/G3
Nyikog (riv.), China 104/E5
Nyima, China 125/E5
Nyimba, Zam. 149/F2
Nyírábrány, Hun. 76/F2
Nyíradony, Hun. 69/L5
Nyírbátor, Hun. 69/M5
Nyíregyháza, Hun. 69/L5
Nyírmada, Hun. 69/M4
Nyiru (mt.), Kenya 145/B1
Nykirke, Nor. 64/S9
Nykøbing, Den. 66/D4
Nykøbing, Den. 66/C3
Nykøbing S, Den. 65/H7
Nyköping, Swe. 66/G2
Nykvarn, Swe. 65/A1
Nylrivier (riv.), SAfr. 149/F5
Nylstroom, SAfr. 149/F5
Nymagee, Austl. 158/C2
Nynäshamn, Swe. 66/G2
Nyngan, Austl. 158/C1
Nyoman (riv.), Bela. 94/E5
Nyon, Swi. 86/C5
Nyong (riv.), Camr. 142/A5
Nyons, Fr. 90/B4
Nýřany, Czh. 85/G3
Nyrob, Rus. 95/N3
Nýrsko (res.), Czh. 85/G4
Nýrsko, Czh. 85/G4
Nysa, Pol. 69/J3
Nysätra, Swe. 65/A1
Nyssa, Or, US 172/E2
Nysted, Den. 66/D4
Nyūdo-zaki (pt.), Japan 108/A4
Nyuk (lake), Rus. 94/F2
Nyukhcha, Rus. 95/K3
Nyuksenitsa, Rus. 95/K3
Nyúl, Hun. 76/C2
Nyunzu, D.R. Congo 147/G4
Nyurba, Rus. 101/M3
Nyuvchim, Rus. 95/L3
Nyūzen, Japan 111/E2
Nzega, Tanz. 145/A3
Nzérékoré (pol. reg.), Gui. 140/C4
Nzérékoré, Gui. 140/C5
Nzeret, D.R. Congo 142/D4
N'Zeto, Ang. 146/C4
Nzi (riv.), C.d'Iv. 140/D5

O

O'Ciese Ind. Res., Ab, Can. 170/G1
O'The Pines (lake), Tx, US 177/G1
O' The Pines (lake), Tx, US 179/G4
O'Fallon (cr.), Mt, US 182/B4
O'Hares (cr.), Austl. 160/G8
O'Higgins (lake), Chile 215/B6
O'Sullivan (lake), On, Can. 183/L2
O-shima (isl.), Japan 108/A3
O. T. Downs, Austl. 155/D4
O.C. Fisher (lake), Tx, US 177/D2
Oa, Mull of (pt.), Sc, UK 57/Q9
Oadby, Eng, UK 63/E1
Oahe (lake), ND,SD, US 168/F2
Oahe (dam), SD, US 180/D1
Oahu (isl.), Hi, US 163/K2
Oak Bluffs, Ma, US 184/B5
Oak Creek, Co, US 173/K3
Oak Creek, Wi, US 186/C3
Oak Forest, Il, US 193/Q16
Oak Grove, La, US 179/J4
Oak Grove, Ar, US 179/H2
Oak Grove, Co, US 175/J1
Oak Grove, Tn, US 188/D2
Oak Grove, Ky, US 188/D2
Oak Harbor, Oh, US 186/E4
Oak Harbor, Wa, US 170/C3
Oak Hill, Mi, US 186/C2
Oak Hill, Fl, US 191/H3
Oak Hill, Tn, US 188/D2
Oak Hill, Oh, US 189/F1
Oak Hill, WV, US 189/G2
Oak Hill, Ga, US 189/M7
Oak Lake, Mb, Can. 182/D3
Oak Lawn, Il, US 186/C4
Oak Park, Il, US 193/Q16
Oak Park, Mi, US 193/F7
Oak Park, Ga, US 189/F4
Oak Ridge, Tn, US 188/E2
Oak Ridge, NJ, US 194/D1
Oak Ridges, On, Can. 186/U8
Oak River, Mb, Can. 182/D2
Oak View, Ca, US 192/A2
Oakbank, Mb, Can. 182/F3
Oakburn, Mb, Can. 182/D2
Oakdale, La, US 190/B2
Oakdale, Ca, US 174/B2
Oakdale, Austl. 159/E2
Oakes, ND, US 182/E4
Oakesdale, Wa, US 170/F4
Oakey, Austl. 160/C4
Oakham, Eng, UK 63/F1
Oakhurst, Ok, US 179/F2
Oakhurst, Ca, US 174/C2
Oakland, Fl, US 190/M6
Oakland, Il, US 186/B5
Oakland, Md, US 187/G5
Oakland, NJ, US 195/J7
Oakland (lake), Mi, US 193/F6
Oakland (co.), Mi, US 193/E6
Oakland, Or, US 172/B2
Oakland, Ne, US 181/F3
Oakland, Md, US 194/B5
Oakland (bay), Wa, US 193/A3
Oakland City, In, US 188/D1
Oakland Park, Fl, US 190/P10
Oaklands, Austl. 159/C2
Oakley, Ca, US 193/L10
Oakley, Ut, US 173/H3
Oakley, Id, US 173/G2
Oakley, Ks, US 180/D4
Oakley, Ms, US 188/B4
Oakley, Eng, UK 63/F2
Oakover (riv.), Austl. 153/B3
Oakridge, Or, US 172/B2
Oaktown, In, US 188/D1
Oakville, Mb, Can. 182/F3
Oakville, Mo, US 188/B1
Oakville, On, Can. 185/R9
Oakwood, Ga, US 188/F3
Oakwood, Va, US 189/F2
Oakwood, Tx, US 177/G2
Oakwood Hills, Il, US 193/P15
Oamaru, NZ 161/B4
Ōamishirasato, Japan 109/E2
Oani, Com. 152/G6
Oat (mtn.), Ca, US 192/B2
Oatlands, Austl. 158/C4
Oatman, Az, US 174/E3
Oaxaca (state), Mex. 196/B4
Oaxaca de Juárez, Mex. 200/B2
Ob' (riv.), Rus. 103/F3
Ob' (gulf), Rus. 103/G3
Ob Luang Gorge, Thai. 120/B2
Obala, Camr. 146/B1
Obama (bay), Japan 109/J4
Obama, Japan 109/J5
Oban, Sc, UK 57/R8
Oban (hills), Nga. 141/H5
Oban, NZ 161/B4
Obanazawa, Japan 108/B4
Obando, Col. 207/K8
Obara, Japan 109/M5
Obata, Japan 109/L7
Obaya, D.R. Congo 147/F3
Obbnäs (Upinniemi), Fin. 65/E4
Obed, Ab, Can. 170/F1
Obeliai, Lith. 67/L4
Obelisk (peak), NZ 161/B4
Ober Ramstadt, Ger. 84/B3
Ober-Olm, Ger. 84/B3
Oberá, Arg. 213/F3
Oberalppass (pass), Swi. 87/E4
Oberalpstock (peak), Swi. 87/E4
Oberammergau, Ger. 87/H2
Oberasbach, Ger. 84/D4
Oberau, Ger. 87/H2
Oberburg, Swi. 86/D3
Oberderdingen, Ger. 84/B4
Oberdiessbach, Swi. 86/D4
Oberding, Ger. 85/E6
Oberdorf, Swi. 86/D3
Oberdorla, Ger. 79/H6
Oberelsbach, Ger. 84/D2
Oberentfelden, Swi. 86/E3
Oberglatt, Swi. 87/E3
Obergünzburg, Ger. 87/G2
Oberhaching, Ger. 85/E6
Oberhausen, Ger. 78/D6
Oberkirch, Ger. 86/E1
Oberkochen, Ger. 84/D5
Oberkotzau, Ger. 85/E2
Oberlausitz (reg.), Ger. 69/H3
Oberlin, La, US 190/B2
Oberlin, Ks, US 180/D4
Obernai, Fr. 86/D1
Obernburg am Main, Ger. 84/C3
Oberndorf am Neckar, Ger. 87/E1
Oberndorf bei Salzburg, Aus. 85/F7
Oberneukirchen, Aus. 85/H6
Obernkirchen, Ger. 79/G4
Oberon, Austl. 159/D1
Oberösterreich (prov.), Aus. 69/G4
Oberpfälzer Wald (for.), Ger. 85/F3
Oberrieden, Swi. 87/E3
Oberriet, Swi. 87/F3
Obersaxen, Swi. 87/F4
Oberschleissheim, Ger. 85/E6
Oberschneiding, Ger. 85/F5
Obersiggenthal, Swi. 87/E3
Oberstammheim, Swi. 87/E2
Oberstaufen, Ger. 87/G2
Oberstdorf, Ger. 87/G3
Oberthal, Ger. 81/G4
Obertrum am See, Aus. 85/G7
Obertshausen, Ger. 84/B2
Oberursel, Ger. 84/B2
Oberuzwil, Swi. 87/F3
Oberviechtach, Ger. 85/F4
Oberwald, Swi. 87/E4
Oberwart, Aus. 76/C2
Oberwesel, Ger. 81/G3
Oberwiessenthal, Ger. 85/F2
Oberwil, Swi. 86/D4
Oberwölz, Aus. 71/L3
Obfelden, Swi. 87/E3
Obi (isl.), Indo. 162/B5
Obi (isls.), Indo. 117/G4
Obi (str.), Indo. 117/G4
Obiaruku, Nga. 141/G5
Óbidos, Port. 72/A3
Óbidos, Braz. 206/C3
Obihiro, Japan 108/C2
Obilić, Yugo. 76/E4
Obing, Ger. 85/F6
Obion, Tn, US 188/C2
Obion (riv.), Tn, US 188/C2
Obion, North Fork (riv.), Tn, US 188/C2
Obion, South Fork (riv.), Tn, US 188/C2
Obira, Japan 108/B1
Obitochnaya (bay), Ukr. 99/H4
Obitsu (riv.), Japan 109/D3
Oblivskaya, Rus. 99/M3
Oblong, Il, US 188/D1
Obluch'ye, Rus. 105/L2
Obninsk, Rus. 94/H5
Obo, CAfr. 142/E4
Obo, China 104/E4
Obo Liang, China 125/F4
Obock, Djib. 144/B3
Obokote, D.R. Congo 147/F3
Obolo, Nga. 141/G5
Oborniki, Pol. 69/J2
Oborniki Śląskie, Pol. 69/J3
Obouya, Congo 146/C3
Oboyan', Rus. 99/J2
Obozerskiy, Rus. 94/J3
Obra (riv.), Pol. 69/J2
Obrenovac, Yugo. 76/E3
Obrež, Yugo. 76/E4
O'Brien, Or, US 172/B2
O'Briensbridge, Ire. 58/B4
Obrigheim, Ger. 84/B3
Obrigheim, Ger. 84/C4
Observatory, Austl. 158/G5
Obsharovka, Rus. 97/J1
Obtrumer (lake), Aus. 85/F7
Ōbu, Japan 109/L6
Obuasi, Gha. 141/E5
Obubra, Nga. 141/H5
Obudu, Nga. 141/H5
Obukhiv, Ukr. 98/F2
Obura, PNG 155/G1
Obw. (canton), Swi. 87/E4
Obzor, Bul. 77/H4
Ocala, Fl, US 191/G3
Ocampo, Mex. 198/E3
Ocaña, Col. 204/C2
Ocaña, Sp. 72/D3
Occhieppo Inferiore, It. 88/B2
Occhieppo Superiore, It. 88/A1
Occhiobello, It. 89/E4
Occhito (lake), It. 92/D4
Occidental, Cordillera (mts.), SAm. 208/B2
Occimiano, It. 88/B3
Ocean (co.), NJ, US 194/D4
Ocean Beach, NY, US 195/E2
Ocean City, Md, US 189/K1
Ocean City, NJ, US 194/D5
Ocean Falls, BC, Can. 166/D3
Ocean Gate, NJ, US 194/D4
Ocean Grove, NJ, US 194/D3
Ocean Grove, Austl. 159/B4
Ocean Park, Wa, US 170/B4
Ocean Pines, Md, US 189/K1
Ocean Ridge, Fl, US 190/P9
Ocean View, De, US 189/K1
Ocean View, NJ, US 194/D5
Oceana, WV, US 189/G2
Oceana Nav. Air Sta., Va, US 189/J2
Oceano, Ca, US 174/B3
Oceanographic Museum, Mona. 88/J8
Oceanside, Ca, US 192/C4
Oceanside, NY, US 195/L9
Oceanville, NJ, US 194/D5
Ocee, Ga, US 189/M6
Ochakiv, Ukr. 98/F4
Och'amch'ire, Geo. 97/G4
Ochapowace Ind. Res., Sk, Can. 182/C2
Ochelata, Ok, US 179/G2
Ochiishi-misaki (cape), Japan 108/D2
Ochil (hills), Sc, UK 59/C4
Ochlocknee, Ga, US 191/F2
Ochlockonee (riv.), Fl, US 191/F2
Ocho Rios, Jam. 201/G2
Ochobo, Nga. 141/G5
Ochopee, Fl, US 191/H5
Ochsenfurt, Ger. 84/D3
Ochsenhausen, Ger. 87/F1
Ochsenkopf (peak), Aus. 87/F3
Ochtendung, Ger. 81/G3
Ochtrup, Ger. 79/E4
Ochtum (riv.), Ger. 79/F2
Ocilla, Ga, US 191/G2
Ockelbo, Swe. 66/G1
Ockenheim, Ger. 81/G4
Ocklawaha, Fl, US 191/H3
Ocmulgee (riv.), Ga, US 188/F4
Ocmulgee Nat'l Mon., Ga, US 188/F4
Ocna Mureş, Rom. 77/F2
Ocna Sibiului, Rom. 77/G3
Ocnele Mari, Rom. 98/C5
Ocnita, Mol. 98/D3
Ocoee, Fl, US 190/M6
Ocoña, Peru 208/C5
Ocoña (riv.), Peru 208/C4
Oconee (res.), Ga, US 189/F4
Oconee (riv.), Ga, US 189/F4
Oconomowoc, Wi, US 181/K2
Oconto (riv.), Wi, US 183/K5
Oconto, Wi, US 186/C2
Oconto Falls, Wi, US 186/B2
Ocosingo, Mex. 200/C2
Ocosta, Wa, US 170/B4
Ocotal, Nic. 200/E3
Ocotlán, Mex. 198/E4
Ocotlán de Morelos, Mex. 200/B2
Ocoyoacac, Mex. 199/Q10
Ocozocoautla de Espinosa, Mex. 200/C2
Ocracoke (isl.), NC, US 189/K3
Ocracoke, NC, US 189/K3
Ocros, Peru 208/B3
Octararo (cr.), Pa, US 194/B4
Octeville, Fr. 82/D1
Octeville-sur-Mer, Fr. 83/F1
October Revolution (isl.), Rus. 103/H2
Ocumare de la Costa, Ven. 207/N7
Ocumare del Tuy, Ven. 207/P7
Ocurí, Bol. 212/C1
Oda, Gha. 141/E5
Oda (peak), Sudan 135/H4
Oda, Japan 110/C3
Ódádhahraun (lava flow), Ice. 64/P7
Ŏdaejin, NKor. 107/E2
Odaesan NP, SKor. 110/A2
Ōdai, Japan 109/K7
Ōdaigahara-san (peak), Japan 110/E3
Ödåkra, Swe. 65/J6
Odanah, Wi, US 183/J4
Ōdate, Japan 108/B3
Odawara, Japan 111/F3
Odda, Nor. 66/B1
Odder, Den. 66/D4
Oddur (Xuddur), Som. 144/B4
Odebolt, Ia, US 181/G2
Odeborn (riv.), Ger. 79/F6
Odell, Tx, US 178/E3
Odell, Il, US 181/K3
Odell, Or, US 170/D5
Odelzhausen, Ger. 84/E6
Odem, Tx, US 177/F4
Odemira, Port. 72/A4
Ödemiş, Turk. 128/A2
Odendaalsrus, SAfr. 150/D2
Odensala, Swe. 65/A1
Odense, Den. 66/D4
Odense (int'l arpt.), Den. 66/D4
Odenthal, Ger. 81/G1
Odenton, Md, US 194/B5
Odenwald (reg.), Ger. 84/B3
Oder (Odra) (riv.), Ger.,Pol. 69/H2
Oder-Spree Kanal (canal), Ger. 68/Q7
Oderen, Fr. 86/C2
Oderhaff (lag.), Ger. 69/H2
Oderzo, It. 89/F2
Odesa, Ukr. 98/F4
Odes'ka (prov.), Ukr. 96/D3
Odessa, De, US 194/C5
Odessa, Fl, US 190/K7
Odessa, Mn, US 181/F1
Odessa, NY, US 187/H3
Odessa, Tx, US 177/C2
Odessa, Wa, US 170/E4
Odessa Meteor Crater, Tx, US 177/C2
Odet (riv.), Fr. 70/B2
Odhan, India 124/C5
Odienné, C.d'Iv. 140/D4
Odin, Ks, US 179/E1
Odin, Il, US 188/C1
Odin (mt.), BC, Can. 170/E2
Odintsovo, Rus. 94/W9
Odiongan, Phil. 114/C2
Odivelas, Port. 73/P10
Odobeşti, Rom. 77/H3
Odon (riv.), Fr. 70/C2
Odon, In, US 188/D1
Odongk, Camb. 120/D4
O'Donnell, Tx, US 178/D4
O'Donnells, Nf, Can. 185/L2
Odoorn, Neth. 78/D3
Odorheiu Secuiesc, Rom. 77/G2
Odra (Oder) (riv.), Ger.,Pol. 69/H2
Odum, Ga, US 191/G2
Odžaci, Yugo. 76/D3
Odzala, PN d', Congo 146/C2
Odzi, Zim. 149/G3
Odzi (riv.), Zim. 149/G3
Odziba, Congo 146/C3
Ōe, Japan 109/H5
Ōe-yama (peak), Japan 109/H5
Oegstgeest, Neth. 78/B4
Oeiras, Braz. 207/F4
Oelde, Ger. 79/F5
Oelemari (riv.), Sur. 206/C2
Oelrichs, SD, US 180/C2
Oelsnitz, Ger. 85/F2
Oelwein, Ia, US 181/J2
Oeno (isl.), Pitc. 163/M7
Oenpelli, Austl. 154/D3
Oensingen, Swi. 86/D3
Oer-Erkenschwick, Ger. 79/E5
Oesling (mts.), Lux. 81/E4
Oesterdam (dam), Neth. 78/B6
Oestrich-Winkel, Ger. 84/B3
Oeta NP, Gre. 75/H3
Oetz, Aus. 87/G3
Oey'ŏn (isl.), SKor. 107/D3
Of, Turk. 96/G4
Ofahoma, Ms, US 188/C4
Ofaqim, Isr. 131/B6
Ofenhorn (peak), Swi. 87/E5
Ofenpass (Pass dal Fuorn) (pass), Swi. 87/G4
Offa, Nga. 141/G4
Offaly (co.), Ire. 60/A5
Offanengo, It. 88/C3
Offement, Fr. 86/C2
Offenbach, Ger. 84/B2
Offenbach an der Queich, Ger. 84/B4
Offenburg, Ger. 86/D1
Offerle, Ks, US 178/E2
Offerman, Ga, US 191/G2
Offida, It. 92/C2
Offingen, Ger. 84/D6
Offoué (riv.), Gabon 146/B3
Offoué, Rsv. Integrale de l', Gabon 146/B3
Offranville, Fr. 83/G1
Offstein, Ger. 84/B3
Offut (A.F.B.), Ne, US 181/G3
Oftersheim, Ger. 84/B4
Oftringen, Swi. 86/D3
Ōfunato, Japan 108/B4
Oga (pen.), Japan 108/A4
Oga, Japan 108/A4
Ogachi, Japan 108/B4
Ogadēn (reg.), Eth. 144/B4
Ōgaki, Japan 109/L5
Ogallala, Ne, US 180/D3
Ogano, Japan 109/C2
Ogasawara, Japan 162/D2
Ogatsu, Japan 108/B4
Ogawa, Japan 109/E1
Ogawa, Japan 109/C1
Ogawara (lake), Japan 108/B3
Ogbomosho, Nga. 141/G4
Ogden, Ar, US 179/G4
Ogden, Ut, US 173/H3
Ogden, Ks, US 181/F4
Ogden, Ia, US 181/G2
Ogdensburg, NY, US 187/J2
Ogdensburg, NJ, US 194/D1
Ogeechee (riv.), Ga, US 189/G4
Ogema, Sk, Can. 182/B3
Oggiono, It. 88/C2
Ogi, Japan 111/F2
Ogidaki (mtn.), On, Can. 167/H4
Ogies, SAfr. 150/E2
Ogilvie, Mn, US 183/H5
Ogilvie (riv.), Yk, Can. 166/C2
Ogilvie (mts.), Yk, Can. 166/C2
Oglala, SD, US 180/C2
Oglanly, Trkm. 97/K5
Oglanly, Trkm. 129/H2
Oglesby, Il, US 181/K3
Oglesby, Tx, US 199/F2
Oglethorpe, Ga, US 188/E4
Oglio (riv.), It. 71/J4
Ogmore, Austl. 160/C3
Ogmore-by-Sea, Wal, UK 62/C4
Ognon (riv.), Fr. 68/C5
Ogoamas (peak), Indo. 117/F3
Ogodzha, Rus. 105/L1
Ogoja, Nga. 141/H5
Ogooué (riv.), Gabon 133/C5
Ogooué-Ivindo (prov.), Gabon 146/C2
Ogooué-Lolo (prov.), Gabon 146/C3
Ogooue-Maritime (prov.), Gabon 146/B3
Ogorelyshi, Rus. 94/G3
Ogose, Japan 109/C2
Ogosta (riv.), Bul. 77/F4
Ogr, Sudan 142/E2
Ogre, Lat. 67/L3
Oguchi, Japan 109/L5
Ogulin, Cro. 76/B3
Ogun (riv.), Nga. 141/F5
Ogun (state), Nga. 141/F5
Ogurchinskiy (isl.), Trkm. 97/K5
Ogurugu, Nga. 141/G5
Oğuz, Turk. 128/D2
Ogwashi Uku, Nga. 141/G5
Oh Me Edge (hill), Eng, UK 59/D6
Ohafia, Nga. 141/G5
Ohai, NZ 161/A4
Ohakune, NZ 161/C2
Ohanet, Alg. 137/H3
Ōhara, Japan 109/E3
O'Hara Head (cape), Austl. 159/E2
Oharu, Japan 109/L5
Ōhata, Japan 108/B3
Ohau (lake), NZ 161/B4
Ohey, Belg. 81/E3
O'Higgins (pol. reg.), Chile 214/B1
Ohio, Co, US 175/J1
Ohio (riv.), US 165/J6
Ohio (state), US 169/K3
Ohio Caverns, Oh, US 186/E4
Ōhira, Japan 109/D1
Ohlsdorf, Aus. 85/G7
Ohlstadt, Ger. 87/H2
Ohm (riv.), Ger. 84/C1
Ōho, Japan 109/E1
Ohoopee (riv.), Ga, US 189/F4
Ohopoho, Namb. 148/B3
Ohre (riv.), Ger. 68/F2
Ohře (riv.), Czh. 68/H3
Ohrid, FYROM 75/G2
Ohrid (lake), FYROM,Alb. 76/E5
Ohrigstad, SAfr. 149/F5
Ohura, NZ 161/C2
Ōi (riv.), Japan 105/M4
Oi (riv.), China 104/D6
Ōi, Japan 109/C3
Ōi, Japan 109/D2
Ōi, Japan 109/J5
Oiapoque (riv.), Braz. 206/C2
Oiapoque, Braz. 206/D2
Oich (lake), Sc, UK 59/B2
Oieras, Port. 73/P10
Oiga, China 112/B2
Oignies, Fr. 80/B3
Oignin (riv.), Fr. 86/B5
Oil Center, NM, US 176/C1
Oil City, La, US 179/H4
Oil City, Pa, US 187/G4
Oildale, Ca, US 174/C3
Oilmont, Mt, US 171/J3
Oinasjärvi, Fin. 65/E4
Oinófita, Gre. 75/H3
Oinóï, Gre. 75/N8
Oir (riv.), Fr. 82/D3
Oirschot, Neth. 78/C5
Oise (riv.), Fr. 68/B4
Oise (dept.), Fr. 80/B5
Oise à l'Aisne, Canal de l' (canal), Fr. 80/C4
Oiseaux du Djoudj, PN des, Sen. 140/A2
Ōiso, Japan 109/C3
Oissel, Fr. 83/G2
Oissery, Fr. 56/L4
Oisterwijk, Neth. 78/C5
Ōita, Japan 110/B4
Ōita (pref.), Japan 110/B4
Ōita (riv.), Japan 110/B4
Oitti, Fin. 65/F4
Oiyug, China 123/G1
Ōizumi, Japan 109/A2
Ōizumi, Japan 109/C1
Öja (isl.), Swe. 65/A2
Ojai, Ca, US 192/A2
Ojajärvi (lake), Fin. 65/E4
Ojakkala, Fin. 65/E4
Ojcowski NP, Pol. 69/K3
Öjebyn, Swe. 64/G2
Ōji, Japan 109/J6
Ojima, Japan 109/C1
Ojinaga, Mex. 177/B3
Ojiya, Japan 111/F2
Ojo Caliente, NM, US 175/J2
Ojo de Agua, Mex. 199/Q9
Ojo de Liebre (lag.), Mex. 198/B3
Ojocaliente, Mex. 198/E4
Ojos del Salado (peak), Arg.,Chile 212/B3
Ojos Negros, Sp. 72/E2
Ojuelos de Jalisco, Mex. 199/E4
Oka (riv.), Rus. 101/L4
Oka, Nga. 141/G5
Oka, Congo 146/C3
Oka, Qu, Can. 185/M7
Okaba, Indo. 155/E2
Okabe, Japan 109/C1
Okahandja, Namb. 148/C4
Okahumpka, Fl, US 190/M6
Okaihau, NZ 161/C1
Okak (isl.), Nf, Can. 167/K3
Okala, Camr. 146/B1
Okanagan (lake), BC, Can. 166/D4
Okanagan (range), BC, Can. 170/D3
Okanagan Falls, BC, Can. 170/E3
Okanda, PN de l', Gabon 146/B3
Okano (riv.), Gabon 146/B2
Okanogan (riv.), Wa, US 170/E3
Okanogan, Wa, US 170/E3
Okapa, PNG 155/G1
Okaputa, Namb. 148/C4
Okāra, Pak. 124/B4
Okarche, Ok, US 179/F3
Okarem, Trkm. 129/H2
Okatana, Namb. 148/B3
Okatibbee (res.), Ms, US 188/C4
Okato, NZ 161/C2
Okaukuejo, Namb. 148/B3
Okavango (delta), Bots. 148/D3
Okavango (riv.), Bots. 148/D3
Ōkawa, Japan 110/B4
Okawville, Il, US 188/C1
Okay, Ok, US 179/G3
Okaya, Japan 111/F2
Okayama, Japan 110/C3
Okayama (pref.), Japan 110/C3
Okazaki, Japan 109/M6
Okazize, Namb. 148/C4
Okch'ŏn, SKor. 107/D4
Oke Iho, Nga. 141/F4
Okęcie (int'l arpt.), Pol. 69/L2
Okeechobee, Fl, US 191/H4
Okeechobee (lake), Fl, US 169/K6
Okeene, Ok, US 179/E2
Okefenokee (swamp), Ga, US 191/G2
Okefenokee Heritage Center, Ga, US 191/G2
Okefenokee Nat'l Wildlife Refuge, Ga, US 191/G2
Okegawa, Japan 109/D2
Okehampton, Eng, UK 62/C5
Okemah, Ok, US 179/F3
Okement (riv.), Eng, UK 62/B5
Okemos, Mi, US 186/D3
Okene, Nga. 141/G5
Okerembete, Nga. 141/G5
Okesa, Ok, US 179/F2
Oketo, Ks, US 181/F4
Okha, Rus. 101/Q4
Okhaldhungā, Nepal 123/F2
Ókhi, Óros (peak), Gre. 75/J3
Okhotsk (sea), Rus 103/P4
Okhotsk, Rus. 101/Q4
Okhta (riv.), Rus. 94/T6
Okhtyrka, Ukr. 99/H2
Oki (isls.), Japan 101/P6
Okidaitō (isl.), Japan 111/L8
Okiep, SAfr. 150/B3
Okinawa (isl.), Japan 103/M7
Okinawa (pref.), Japan 111/J8
Okino-shima (isl.), Japan 110/C4
Okino-Tori-Shima (Parece Vela) (isl.), Japan 103/N7
Okinoerabu (isl.), Japan 111/K7
Okitipupa, Nga. 141/G5
Okkan, Myan. 112/B5
Okku, SKor. 107/D5
Oklahoma (state), US 169/G4
Oklahoma City (cap.), Ok, US 179/F3
Oklahoma High Top (peak), Ok, US 179/G3
Oklaunion, Tx, US 178/E3
Oklawaha (riv.), Fl, US 191/H3
Okmulgee, Ok, US 179/G3
Oko, Nga. 141/G5
Okobaji (lakes), Ia, US 181/G2
Okobojo (cr.), SD, US 180/D1
Okok (riv.), Ugan. 145/A1
Okolona, Ms, US 188/C3
Okondeka, Namb. 148/B3
Okondja, Gabon 146/C3
Okoppe, Japan 108/C1
Okotoks, Ab, Can. 171/H2
Okovango (riv.), Namb. 133/E6
Okoyo, Congo 146/C3
Oksbøl, Den. 66/C4
Oksino, Rus. 95/M2
Oksjärvi (lake), Fin. 65/D4
Oksskolten (peak), Nor. 64/E2
Oktaha, Ok, US 179/G3
Oktwin, Myan. 120/B2
Oktyabr', Kaz. 97/L2
Oktyabr'sk, Rus. 97/J1
Oktyabr'skiy, Rus. 95/M5
Oktyabr'skiy, Rus. 97/G3
Oktyabr'skiy, Rus. 94/J3
Oktyabr'skiy, Rus. 101/R4
Oktyabr'skiy, Rus. 105/K1
Oktyabr'skiy, Kaz. 104/A2
Oktyabr'skoye, Rus. 97/K1
Oktyabr'skoye, Ukr. 99/H5
Ōkuchi, Japan 110/B4
Okulovka, Rus. 94/G4
Okunev Nos, Rus. 95/M2
Okushiri, Japan 108/A2
Okushiri (isl.), Japan 105/M3
Okuta, Nga. 141/F4
Okutama (lake), Japan 109/C2
Okutama, Japan 109/C2
Okwa (riv.), Bots. 148/D4
Ol Doinyo Sabuk NP, Kenya 145/B2
Ola, Rus. 101/R4
Ola, Ar, US 179/H3
Ola, Id, US 172/E1
Ola, Ga, US 189/M8
Ólafsfjördhur, Ice. 64/N6
Ólafsvík, Ice. 64/M7
Olaine, Lat. 67/K3
Olalla, Wa, US 193/B3
Olan, Pic d' (peak), Fr. 90/C3
Olancha, Ca, US 174/C2
Olancha (peak), Ca, US 174/C2
Olanchito, Hon. 200/E3
Öland (isl.), Swe. 64/F4
Ölands södra udde (pt.), Swe. 66/G3
Olary, Austl. 157/J5
Olathe, Ks, US 179/G1
Olathe, Co, US 175/J1
Olathe Nav. Air Sta., Ks, US 179/G1
Olavarría, Arg. 214/E3
Oľawa, Pol. 69/J3
Ölbach (riv.), Ger. 79/F5
Olberg, Az, US 175/G4
Olbia, It. 74/A2
Olching, Ger. 85/E6
Ol'chon (isl.), Rus. 104/F1
Olcott, NY, US 186/V9
Old (riv.), Ca, US 193/L11
Old Bahama (chan.), Cuba 201/G1
Old Baldy (peak), Wa, US 170/E3
Old Bar, Austl. 158/E1
Old Bedford (canal), Eng, UK 63/G2
Old Bethpage, NY, US 195/M9
Old Bridge, NJ, US 195/H10
Old Castile (reg.), Sp. 92/B2
Old City, WBnk. 131/C5
Old Crow, Yk, Can. 168/Z12
Old Faithful, Wy, US 173/H1
Old Field (pt.), NY, US 195/E2
Old Forge, NY, US 187/J3
Old Forge, Pa, US 187/J4
Old Fort Niagara, NY, US 186/U9
Old Hickory (lake), Tn, US 188/D2
Old Lyme, Ct, US 187/K4
Old Man of Hoy, Sc, UK 57/V14
Old Mill Creek, Il, US 193/Q15
Old Nene (riv.), Eng, UK 63/F2
Old Perlican, Nf, Can. 185/L1
Old Rhine (riv.), Neth. 78/B4
Old Saybrook, Ct, US 195/F1
Old Shawneetown, Il, US 188/C2
Old Speck (mtn.), Me, US 187/L2
Old Tampa (bay), Fl, US 190/K8
Old Tappan, NJ, US 195/K8
Old Town, Fl, US 191/G3
Old Windsor, Eng, UK 56/B2
Old Wives (lake), Sk, Can. 171/L2
Oldcastle, Ire. 58/C2
Oldeani (peak), Tanz. 145/A2
Oldeani, Tanz. 145/A2
Oldebroek, Neth. 78/C4
Oldemarkt, Neth. 78/C3
Olden, Mo, US 179/J2
Olden, Tx, US 177/E1
Oldenburg, Ger. 66/D4
Oldenburg, In, US 186/D5
Oldenburg, Ger. 79/F2
Oldenzaal, Neth. 78/D4
Oldham, Eng, UK 61/F4
Oldleighlin, Ire. 58/C4
Oldman (riv.), Ab, Can. 170/G3
Oldmans (cr.), NJ, US 194/C4
Oldmeldrum, Sc, UK 59/D2
Oldoog (isl.), Ger. 79/E1
Olds, Ab, Can. 171/G2
Oldsmar, Fl, US 190/K7
Olduvai Gorge, Tanz. 145/A2
Oldwick, NJ, US 194/D2
Olean, NY, US 187/G3
O'Leary, PE, Can. 184/E2
Olecko, Pol. 67/K4
Oleggio, It. 88/B2
Oleiros, Port. 72/B3
Oleiros, Sp. 72/A1
Olekma (riv.), Rus. 101/N4
Olëkminsk, Rus. 101/N3
Oleksandrivka, Ukr. 99/G3
Oleksandriya, Ukr. 98/G3
Olele (pt.), Wa, US 193/B2
Olemari (riv.), Sur. 205/H4
Ølen, Nor. 66/A2
Olenegorsk, Rus. 94/G1
Olenëk (riv.), Rus. 103/L3
Olënek, Rus. 101/M3
Olenek (bay), Rus. 101/M2
Olenitsa, Rus. 94/G2
Olenivka, Ukr. 99/J4
Olentangy (riv.), Oh, US 186/E4
Olenty (riv.), Kaz. 125/B1
Oléron (isl.), Fr. 92/C1
Olesa de Montserrat, Sp. 73/K6
Oles'ko, Ukr. 98/C3
Oleśnica, Pol. 69/J3
Olesno, Pol. 69/K3
Olevano Romano, It. 92/C4
Olevs'k, Ukr. 98/D2
Oley, Pa, US 194/C3
Olfen, Ger. 79/E5

Olga – Ouled

283
Oulje – Paria

Ouljet es Soltane, Mor. 138/B3
Oullins, Fr. 90/A1
Oulnina (peak), Austl. 157/H5
Oulu, Fin. 94/E2
Oulu (prov.), Fin. 64/H2
Oulujärvi (lake), Fin. 64/H2
Oulx, It. 90/C2
Oum Chalouba, Chad 142/D2
Oum El Bouaghi, Alg. 138/K7
Oum er Rbia, Oued (riv.), Mor. 136/D2
Oum Hadjer, Chad 142/C2
Oumé, C.d'Iv. 140/D5
Ounara, Mor. 136/C3
Ounasjoki (riv.), Fin. 64/H2
Oundle, Eng, UK 63/F2
Oungre, Sk, Can. 182/C3
Ounianga Sérir, Chad 134/D5
Ounianga-Kébir, Chad 134/D5
Ouogo, CAfr. 142/C4
Oupeye, Belg. 81/E2
Our (riv.), Eur. 81/E4
Ouray, Co, US 175/J1
Ouray (peak), Co, US 175/J1
Ouray, Ut, US 173/J3
Ouray NWR, Ut, US 173/J3
Ource (riv.), Fr. 68/C5
Ourcq (riv.), Fr. 68/B4
Ourcq, Canal de l' (canal), Fr. 56/K5
Øure Anarjokka NP, Nor. 64/H1
Øure Dividal NP, Nor. 64/F1
Ourém, Braz. 207/E3
Ouri, Chad 134/C4
Ouricuri, Braz. 207/F4
Ourimbah, Austl. 159/E1
Ourinhos, Braz. 213/G2
Ourique, Port. 72/A4
Ouro Branco, Braz. 207/G5
Ouro Fino, Braz. 211/K7
Ouro Modi, Mali 140/D3
Ouro Preto, Braz. 211/E4
Ourofon, Niger 141/H3
Ouroux-sur-Saône, Fr. 86/A4
Ourthe Occidentale (riv.), Belg. 81/E3
Ourthe Orientale (riv.), Belg. 81/E3
Ourtzarh, Mor. 138/B2
Ouse (riv.), Eng, UK 61/H4
Ouse, Austl. 158/C4
Ousley, Ga, US 191/G2
Oussouye, Sen. 140/A3
Oust (riv.), Fr. 70/B3
Outão, Port. 73/Q11
Outaouais (Ottawa) (riv.), Qu, Can. 187/G1
Outarville, Fr. 83/H4
Outeïd Arkas (well), Mali 140/D2
Outer Hebrides (isls.), Sc, UK 57/P8
Outer Santa Barbara Passage (chan.), Ca, US 174/C4
Outes, Sp. 72/A1
Outjo, Namb. 148/C4
Outlook, Mt, US 182/B3
Outlook, Sk, Can. 171/L2
Outreau, Fr. 80/A2
Outremont, Qu, Can. 185/N6
Ouvéa (isl.), NCal. 163/V12
Ouvéze (riv.), Fr. 70/F4
Ouyen, Austl. 158/B2
Ouyou Bézédinga (well), Niger 142/B1
Ouzouer-le-Marché, Fr. 83/G5
Ovacık, Turk. 128/D2
Ovacık, Turk. 96/E4
Ovada, It. 88/B4
Ovalau (isl.), Fiji 163/Y18
Ovalle, Chile 212/B4
Ovan, Gabon 146/C2
Ovana (peak), Ven. 205/E3
Ovando, Mt, US 171/H4
Ovar, Port. 72/A2
Ovejaria (peak), Arg 212/C3
Ovens (riv.), Austl. 159/C3
Overath, Ger. 81/G2
Overbrook, Ks, US 179/G1
Overbrook, Ok, US 179/F3
Överenhörna, Swe. 65/A1
Overflakkee (isl.), Neth. 78/B5
Overflow NWR, Ar, US 188/B4
Overgaard, Az, US 175/G3
Overhalla, Nor. 64/D2
Overijse, Belg. 81/D2
Overijssel (prov.), Neth. 78/D3
Overijssels (riv.), Neth. 78/D4
Överkalix, Swe. 64/G2
Overland Park, Ks, US 179/G1
Overlea, Md, US 194/B5
Overloon, Neth. 78/C5
Overo (peak), Arg. 214/C5
Overpelt, Belg. 78/C6
Overseal, Eng, UK 63/E1
Överselö, Swe. 65/A1
Overstrand, Eng, UK 63/H1
Overton, Eng, UK 63/E4
Overton, Wal, UK 61/F6
Overton, Nv, US 174/E2
Overton, Tx, US 177/G1
Övertorneå, Swe. 94/D2
Överum, Swe. 66/G3
Ovett, Ms, US 190/D2
Ovid, NY, US 187/H3
Ovidiopol', Ukr. 98/F4
Oviedo, Sp. 72/C1
Oviši, Lat. 67/J3
Ovoca, Ire. 60/B6
Ovoot, Mong. 104/G2
Övörhangay (prov.), Mong. 104/E2
Øvre Årdal, Nor. 66/B1
Övre Fryken (lake), Swe. 66/E1
Øvre Pasvik NP, Nor. 64/J1
Øvre Sirdal, Nor. 66/B2
Ovriá, Gre. 75/G3
Ovruch, Ukr. 98/E2
Owaka, NZ 161/B4
Owama, D.R. Congo 147/E3
Owando, Congo 146/C3
Ōwani, Japan 108/B3
Owariasahi, Japan 109/M5
Owase, Japan 110/E3
Owassa, Al, US 190/E2
Owassa (lake), NJ, US 194/D1
Owasso, Ok, US 179/G2
Owatonna, Mn, US 181/H1
Owego, NY, US 187/H3
Owel (lake), Ire. 58/C2
Owen (mt.), NZ 161/C3
Owen, Ger. 84/C5
Owen, Wi, US 181/J1
Owen, Austl. 157/H5
Owen Falls (dam), Ugan. 147/H2
Owen Roberts (int'l arpt.), UK 201/F2
Owen Sound, On, Can. 186/F2
Owen Stanley (range), PNG 155/G1
Owendo, Gabon 146/B2
Owenga, NZ 161/E4
Oweniny (riv.), Ire. 58/A1
Owenkillew(riv.) 60/A2
Owens, Tx, US 178/D4
Owens (peak), Ca, US 174/D3
Owens (riv.), Ca, US 174/C2
Owens (lake), Ca, US 174/D2
Owens Cross Roads, Al, US 188/D3
Owensboro, Ky, US 188/D2
Owensburg, In, US 188/D1
Owensville, Mo, US 179/J1
Owensville, In, US 188/D1
Owenton, Ky, US 188/E1
Owerri, Nga. 141/G5
Owingen, Ger. 87/F2
Owings, Md, US 194/B6
Owings Mills, Md, US 194/B5
Owingsville, Ky, US 188/F1
Owl Creek (mts.), Wy, US 173/J2
Owo, Nga. 141/G5
Owosso, Mi, US 186/D3
Owrāmān, Iran 129/F3
Owutu, Nga. 141/G5
Owyhee (mts.), Id, US 172/E2
Owyhee, Nv, US 172/E3
Owyhee (riv.), Id, US 168/C3
Owyhee (dam), Or, US 172/E2
Owyhee, South Fork (riv.), Id,Nv, US 172/E2
Ox (Slieve Gamph) (mts.), Ire. 58/A1
Oxapampa, Peru 208/C3
Oxbow, Sk, Can. 182/C3
Oxbow (lake), Mi, US 193/F6
Oxelösund, Swe. 66/G2
Oxford, NS, Can. 184/F3
Oxford (canal), Eng, UK 63/E3
Oxford, Eng, UK 63/E3
Oxford, NZ 161/C3
Oxford, Al, US 188/E4
Oxford, Ar, US 179/J2
Oxford, In, US 186/C4
Oxford, Me, US 187/L2
Oxford, Mi, US 193/F6
Oxford, Ms, US 188/C3
Oxford, NC, US 189/H2
Oxford, Ne, US 180/E3
Oxford, NY, US 187/J3
Oxford, Oh, US 186/D5
Oxford, Pa, US 194/C4
Oxfordshire (co.), Eng, UK 63/E3
Oxhey, Eng, UK 56/B2
Oxie, Swe. 66/E4
Oxkutzcab, Mex. 200/D1
Oxley (cr.), Austl. 160/E7
Oxley, Austl. 159/B2
Oxnard (arpt.), Ca, US 192/A2
Oxnard, Ca, US 192/A2
Oxnard Beach, Ca, US 192/A2
Oxon Hill (farm), Md, US 194/A6
Oxon Hill-Glassmanor, Md, US 194/B6
Oxshott, Eng, UK 56/B3
Oxted, Eng, UK 56/D3
Oxton, Sc, UK 59/D5
Oy-Tal, Kyr. 125/B3
Oya, Malay. 116/D3
Oyabe, Japan 111/E2
Oyama, Japan 111/F2
Oyama, Japan 109/B3
Oyama, BC, Can. 170/E2
Ōyamada, Japan 109/K6
Ōyamazaki, Japan 109/J6
Oyapock (riv.), FrG.,Braz 203/D2
Oyé Yeska (well), Chad 134/C5
Oye-Plage, Fr. 80/B2
Oyem, Gabon 146/B2
Oyen, Ab, Can. 171/J2
Øyer, Nor 66/D1
Øyeren (lake), Nor. 64/T8
Oykell (riv.), Sc, UK 57/R8
Oylen, Mn, US 183/G4
Oymyakon, Rus. 101/Q3
Oyo, Nga 141/F5
Oyo (state), Nga. 141/F4
Oyo, Congo 146/C3
Ōyodo (riv.), Japan 110/B5
Ōyodo, Japan 109/J7
Oyón, Peru 208/B3
Oyonnax, Fr. 86/B5
Oyster (cr.), Tx, US 177/G3
Oyster Bay, NY, US 195/L8
Oyster Bay (har.), NY, US 195/L8
Oyster Bay Cove, NY, US 195/L8
Oyster Bay Nat'l Wild. Ref., NY, US 195/L8
Oyten, Ger. 79/G2
Oyugis, Kenya 145/A2
Ozamiz, Phil. 114/C3
Ozanne (riv.), Fr. 70/D2
Ozarichi, Bela. 96/D1
Ozark, Al, US 191/F2
Ozark (mts.), Ar,Mo, US 169/H4
Ozark, Ar, US 179/H3
Ozark, Mo, US 179/H2
Ozark (plat.), Mo, US 181/H4
Ozark Nat'l Scenic Riverways, Mo, US 188/B2
Ozarks (lake), Mo, US 169/H4
Ożarów, Pol. 98/A2
Ozawkie, Ks, US 181/G4
Ózd, Hun. 69/L4
Ozello, Fl, US 190/K6
Ozernovskiy, Rus. 101/R4
Ozernoy (cape), Rus. 101/S4
Ozernoye, Rus. 97/J2
Ozërnyy, Rus. 97/M2
Ozero Sasyk (lake), Ukr. 77/J3
Ozero Yalpuh (lake), Urk. 98/E5
Ozerskiy, Rus. 105/N2
Ozëry, Bela. 67/L5
Ozette (lake), Wa, US 170/B3
Ozette Ind. Res., Wa, US 170/B3
Ozherel'ye, Rus. 94/H5
Ozieri, It. 74/A2
Ozimek, Pol. 69/K3
Özkonak, Turk. 128/C2
Ozoir-la-Ferrière, Fr. 56/L5
Ozona, Fl, US 190/K7
Ozona, Tx, US 176/D2
Ozondjacheberg (peak), Namb. 148/C4
Ozone, Ar, US 179/H3
Ozone Park (nbrhd.), NY, US 195/K9
Ozora, Hun. 76/D2
Ozorków, Pol. 69/K3
Ozouer-le-Voulgis, Fr. 56/L6
Ōzu, Japan 110/C4
Ozuluama de Mascareñas, Mex. 200/B1
Ozurget'i, Geo. 97/G4
Ozzano dell'Emilia, It. 89/E5

P

P'abal-li, NKor. 107/E2
P'aju, SKor. 107/F6
P'aro-ho (lake), SKor. 107/D3
P'yŏngan-bukto (prov.), NKor. 107/C2
P. K. Le Rouxdam (res.), SAfr. 150/D3
Pa Sak (riv.), Thai. 119/H4
Pääjärvi (lake), Fin. 65/F3
Pa-an, Myan. 120/B2
Paar (riv.), Ger. 68/F4
Paarl, SAfr. 150/L10
Påarp, Swe. 65/J6
Pabbi, Pak. 124/A2
Pabean, Indo. 115/F3
Pabellón de Arteaga, Mex. 198/E4
Pabianice, Pol. 69/K3
Pablo Nat'l Wild. Ref., Mt, US 171/G4
Pābna (pol. reg.), Bang. 123/G3
Pābna, Bang. 123/G3
Pabradė, Lith. 67/L4
Pabu, Fr. 82/B3
Pacaás Novos, PN dos, Braz. 209/F3
Pacaás Novos, Serra dos (mts.), Braz. 209/E3
Pacajá (riv.), Braz. 206/D3
Pacajus, Braz. 207/G4
Pacaltsdorp, SAfr. 150/C4
Pacaraimã, Sierra (mts.), SAm. 206/A2
Pacasmayo, Peru 208/B2
Pacatuba, Braz. 207/G3
Pacaya Samiria, Res. Nacional, Peru 208/C2
Paccha, Peru 208/C3
Pacé, Fr. 82/D4
Pace, Fl, US 190/E2
Paceco, It. 74/C4
Pachacamac (ruin), Peru 208/B4
Pachaconas, Peru 208/C4
Pachamarca (riv.), Peru 208/C4
Pacheco (pass), Ca, US 174/B2
Pachelma, Rus. 97/G1
Pachino, It. 74/D4
Pachitea (riv.), Peru 208/C3
Pachiza, Peru 208/B2
Pachmarhī, India 122/B4
Pacho, Col. 207/L7
Pachuca, Mex. 199/L6
Pachwa, Ugan. 147/G2
Pacific (Ocean) 162/*
Pacific (range), BC, Can. 170/B2
Pacific, Wa, US 193/C3
Pacific Beach, Wa, US 170/B4
Pacific City, Or, US 172/B1
Pacific Palisades (nbrhd.), Ca, US 192/E7
Pacific Rim NP, BC, Can. 170/B3
Pacifico (mtn.), Ca, US 192/B2
Pacinan (cape), Indo. 115/F3
Pacitan, Indo. 115/E3
Paço de Arcos, Port. 73/P10
Pacolet (riv.), SC, US 189/G3
Pácora, Col. 207/K7
Pacoval, Braz. 206/C3
Pacy-sur-Eure, Fr. 83/G2
Pad Idan, Pak. 127/J3
Padada, Phil. 114/D4
Padam, India 124/D3
Padampur, India 121/D1
Padang (isl.), Indo. 115/C2
Padang, Indo. 115/C3
Padang Endau, Malay. 115/C2
Padangcermin, Indo. 115/D3
Padangpanjang, Indo. 115/C3
Padangsidempuan, Indo. 115/B2
Padangtigi, Indo. 115/A1
Padany, Rus. 94/G3
Padas (riv.), Malay. 114/A4
Padaung, Myan. 112/B5
Padcaya, Bol. 212/C2
Paddington (nbrhd.), Eng, UK 56/C2
Paddock Lake, Wi, US 193/P14
Paddock Wood, Eng, UK 56/E3
Paden City, WV, US 186/F5
Paderborn (arpt.), Ger. 79/F5
Paderborn, Ger. 79/F5
Paderno, It. 89/F2
Pāderu, India 121/D2
Padibe, Ugan. 142/G5
Padiham, Eng, UK 61/F4
Padilla, Bol. 212/C1
Padina, Yugo. 76/E3
Padjelanta NP (nat'l park), Nor. 94/B2
Padova, It. 89/E3
Padova (prov.), It. 89/E2
Padrauna, India 122/D2
Padre (isl.), Tx, US 169/G6
Padre Bernardo, Braz. 210/C2
Padre Island National Seashore, Tx, US 199/F3
Padrón, Sp. 72/A1
Pādru, India 118/B2
Padstow, Eng, UK 62/B5
Paducah, Tx, US 178/D3
Paducah, Ky, US 188/C2
Padul, Sp. 72/D4
Padula, It. 74/D2
Paduli, It. 92/D5
Paech'ŏn, NKor. 107/D4
Paegam, NKor. 107/E2
Paekakariki, NZ 161/H8
Paeksan-ni, NKor. 107/D2
Paektŏk-san (peak), SKor. 107/E4
Paektu-san (peak), NKor. 107/E2
Paengnyŏng (isl.), NKor. 105/J4
Paeroa, NZ 161/C2
Paese, It. 89/F2
Páez, Col. 204/C3
Páez, Col. 204/C4
Pafúri, Moz. 149/F4
Pag, Cro. 76/B3
Pag (isl.), Cro. 93/G1
Pagadian, Phil. 114/C4
Pagai Selatan (isl.), Indo. 116/B4
Pagai Utara (isl.), Indo. 116/B4
Pagan (isl.), NMar. 162/D3
Pagan, Myan. 112/B4
Pagancillo, Arg. 212/B4
Pagani, It. 92/D6
Paganica, It. 92/C3
Pagaralam, Indo. 115/C4
Pagatan, Indo. 116/D4
Pagawyun, Myan. 120/B3
Page, ND, US 182/F4
Page, Ok, US 179/G3
Page, Az, US 175/G2
Pagégiai, Lith. 67/J4
Pageland, SC, US 189/G3
Pager (riv.), Ugan. 142/G5
Pagerdewa, Indo. 115/D3
Pāgla, Bang. 123/H3
Paglieta, It. 92/D3
Pagny-sur-Moselle, Fr. 81/F6
Pago Pago (int'l arpt.), ASam. 163/T10
Pago Pago (cap.), ASam. 163/T10
Pagoda (peak), Co, US 173/K3
Pagosa Springs, Co, US 175/J2
Pagri, China 123/G2
Paguate, NM, US 175/J3
Pagwa River, On, Can. 183/M2
Pagwachuan (riv.), On, Can. 183/M3
Pah-Rum (peak), Nv, US 172/D3
Pahala, Hi, US 168/S10
Pahang (state), Malay. 115/C2
Pahang (riv.), Malay. 116/B3
Páhara (lag.), Nic. 201/F3
Pahāri Buzurg, India 122/C3
Pahārpur, Pak. 124/A3
Pahāsu, India 122/B1
Pahiatua, NZ 161/C3
Pahlgām, India 124/C2
Pahokee, Fl, US 191/H4
Pahranagat Nat'l Wild. Ref., Nv, US 174/E2
Pahrump, Nv, US 174/E2
Pahuatlán, Mex. 199/L6
Pahute (mesa), Nv, US 174/D2
Pai (lake), China 106/C5
Paiania (arpt.), Gre. 75/N9
Paicines, Ca, US 174/B2
Paide, Est. 67/L2
Paignton, Eng, UK 62/C6
Paiján, Peru 208/B2
Päijänne (lake), Fin. 64/H3
Paikü (lake), China 123/E1
Pailemán, Arg. 214/D4
Pailin, Camb. 120/C3
Paimbœuf, Fr. 82/C6
Paime, Col. 207/L7
Paimio, Fin. 67/K1
Painan, Indo. 115/B3
Paine (peak), Chile 215/B6
Paine, Chile 214/N8
Painesville, Oh, US 186/F4
Painio (lake), Fin. 65/D4
Painscastle, Wal, UK 62/C2
Paint (riv.), Mi, US 183/K4
Paint Bank, Va, US 189/G2
Paint Rock, Tx, US 176/E2
Painted (des.), Az, US 168/D4
Painted Rock (res.), Az, US 175/F4
Painted Rocks (dam), Az, US 175/F4
Paintsville, Ky, US 189/F2
Paipa, Col. 204/C3
Paisley, Sc, UK 59/B5
Paisley, On, Can. 186/F2
Paisley, Or, US 172/C2
Paita, Peru 208/A2
Paithan, India 121/B2
Pajala, Swe. 64/G2
Paján, Ecu. 204/A5
Pajas Blancas (Córdoba) (int'l arpt.), Arg. 212/C4
Pajęczno, Pol. 69/K3
Pak Ban, Laos 120/C1
Pak Beng, Laos 120/C2
Pak Chong, Thai. 120/C3
Pak Thong Chai, Thai. 120/C3
Pakanbaru, Indo. 115/C2
Pakawau, NZ 161/C3
Pakch'ŏn, NKor. 107/C3
Pakenham (cape), Chile 215/B6
Pakenham, Austl. 158/G6
Pákhnes (peak), Gre. 75/J5
Pakhra (riv.), Rus. 94/W9
Pakistan(ctry.) 103/F7
Paklenica NP (nat'l park), Cro. 71/L4
Pakokku, Myan. 112/B4
Pakowki (lake), Ab, Can. 171/J3
Pākpattan, Pak. 124/B4
Pakrac, Cro. 76/C3
Pakruojis, Lith. 67/K4
Paks, Hun. 76/D2
Paksey, Bang. 123/G3
Pakue, Indo. 117/F4
Pakwach, Ugan. 147/G2
Pakxe, Laos 120/D3
Pala, Ca, US 192/C4
Pala, Chad 142/B3
Pala Ind. Res., Ca, US 192/C4
Palace, Mona. 88/J8
Palacios, Tx, US 177/F3
Paladru (lake), Fr. 90/B2
Palafrugell, Sp. 73/G2
Palagonia, It. 74/D4
Palagruža (isls.), Cro. 93/H2
Pálairos, Gre. 75/G3
Palais (riv.), Fr. 83/E4
Palaiseau, Fr. 56/J5
Pālakollu, India 121/D2
Palalarivier (riv.), SAfr. 149/F4
Palamás, Gre. 75/H3
Palamós, Sp. 73/G2
Palana, Rus. 101/R4
Palana, Austl. 159/C4
Palanan, Phil. 114/C1
Palanan (pt.), Phil. 114/C1
Palanas, Phil. 114/C2
Palanga, Lith. 67/J4
Palangkaraya, Indo. 116/D4
Pālanpur, India 127/K4
Palapye, Bots. 149/E4
Palar (riv.), India 118/C5
Palas de Rey, Sp. 72/B1
Palasa, Indo. 117/F3
Palāsa, India 121/E2
Palāsbāri, India 123/H2
Palata, It. 92/D4
Palatine, Il, US 193/P15
Palatka, Rus. 101/R3
Palatka, Fl, US 191/H3
Palattsy, Kaz. 125/D2
Palau, Mex. 177/D4
Palau(ctry.) 162/C4
Palau We (isl.), Indo. 119/G6
Palauk, Myan. 120/B3
Palaw, Myan. 120/B3
Palawan (isl.), Phil. 103/L9
Palawan Passage (chan.), Phil. 117/E2
Palaya, Bol. 212/B1
Palayan, Phil. 114/C2
Palazzo dei Penitenzieri, It. 91/G7
Palazzo del Sant'Uffizio, VatC. 91/G7
Palazzo Salviati, It. 91/G6
Palazzo Torlonia, It. 91/G7
Palazzolo Acreide, It. 74/D4
Palazzolo dello Stella, It. 89/G2
Palazzolo sull'Oglio, It. 88/C2
Palca, Bol. 208/E5
Palcenham, Austl. 159/B4
Palco, Ks, US 180/E4
Paldiski, Est. 67/L2
Pale, Bosn. 76/D4
Paleleh, Indo. 117/F3
Palembang, Indo. 115/D3
Palen (lake), Ca, US 174/E4
Palena, It. 92/D4
Palena, Chile 214/C4
Palena (riv.), Chile 214/B4
Palencia, Sp. 72/C1
Palenque, Mex. 200/D2
Palenque, PN, Mex. 200/C2
Palermo, It. 74/C3
Palermo, Ca, US 172/C4
Palermo, ND, US 182/C3
Palermo, On, Can. 186/T9
Palermo, NJ, US 194/D5
Palese (int'l arpt.), It. 74/E2
Palestina, Col. 207/K7
Palestina, Chile 212/B2
Palestine, Ar, US 188/B3
Palestine, Il, US 188/D1
Palestine, Tx, US 176/G2
Palestine (lake), Tx, US 177/G1
Palestrina, It. 91/B4
Palestro, It. 88/B3
Pālghar, India 127/K5
Pālghāt, India 121/C4
P'algong-san (peak), SKor. 107/D5
P'algong-san (peak), SKor. 110/A2
Palgrave (pt.), Namb. 148/B4
Palgrave (mt.), Austl. 156/B2
Palhāna, India 122/C3
Palhano, Braz. 207/G4
Palhoça, Braz. 213/G3
Pāli, India 122/D4
Pāli, India 118/B2
Pali-Aike, PN, Chile 215/C7
Paliā Kalān, India 122/C1
Paliano, It. 92/C4
Palić, Yugo. 76/D2
Palidoro, It. 91/B4
Palikir (cap.), Micr. 162/E4
Palima, Indo. 117/F4
Palioúrion (cape), Gre. 75/H3
Palisade, Mn, US 183/H4
Palisades, NY, US 195/K8
Palisades (cliff), NJ,NY 195/K8
Palisades, Id, US 173/H2
Palisades (dam), Id, US 173/H2
Palisades Interstate Park, NJ, US 194/D1
Palisades Park, NJ, US 195/K8
Paliseul, Belg. 81/E4
Pālitāna, India 127/K4
Palivere, Est. 67/K2
Palizada, Mex. 196/C4
Paljenik (peak), Bosn. 76/C3
Palk (str.), India, SrL. 118/C6
Pālkonda, India 121/E2
Pallamallawa, Austl. 158/C1
Pallano (peak), It. 92/C3
Pallarenda, Austl. 160/E2
Pallas Green, Ire. 58/E4
Pallas-Ounastunturin NP, Fin. 64/H1
Pallasca, Peru 208/B3
Pallaskenry, Ire. 58/B4
Pallasovka, Rus. 97/H2
Pallastunturi (peak), Fin. 64/H1
Pallisa, Ugan. 145/A1
Palliser (cape), NZ 161/C3
Pallu, India 124/C5
Palm (isls.), Austl. 155/G4
Palm Bay, Fl, US 191/H3
Palm Beach (nbrhd.), Austl. 160/H8
Palm Beach, Fl, US 190/P9
Palm Beach (int'l arpt.), Fl, US 190/P9
Palm Beach (co.), Fl, US 190/P9
Palm Beach Gardens, Fl, US 190/P9
Palm Beach Shores, Fl, US 190/P9
Palm City, Ca, US 192/C5
Palm City, Fl, US 191/H4
Palm Desert, Ca, US 174/D4
Palm Harbor, Fl, US 190/K7
Palm Island Aboriginal Settlement, Austl. 160/B2
Palm River-Clair Mel, Fl, US 190/L8
Palm Springs, Ca, US 174/D4
Palma, Moz. 145/C4
Palma, Sp. 73/G3
Palma (riv.), Braz. 210/D2
Palma Campania, It. 92/D6
Palma del Río, Sp. 72/C4
Palma di Montechiaro, It. 74/C4
Palma Mallorca (int'l arpt.), Sp. 73/G3
Palma Soriano, Cuba 201/H1
Palmácia, Braz. 207/G4
Palmanova, It. 89/G2
Palmar (riv.), Ven. 201/H4
Palmares, Braz. 207/H5
Palmarito, Ven. 204/D3
Palmarito, Bol. 209/F5
Palmas (cape), Libr. 140/D5
Palmas, Braz. 213/G3
Palmas, Braz. 210/C1
Palmdale, Ca, US 192/B1
Palmeira, CpV. 133/K10
Palmeira, Braz. 213/G3
Palmeira das Missões, Braz. 213/F3
Palmeira dos Índios, Braz. 207/G5
Palmeirais, Braz. 207/F4
Palmeiras (riv.), Braz. 210/D2
Palmeiras de Goiás, Braz. 210/C3
Palmeirina, Braz. 207/G5
Palmela, Port. 73/Q10
Palmer, Sk, Can. 171/L3
Palmer, US, Ant. 216/V
Palmer, Ak, US 168/Y12
Palmer, Ma, US 187/K3
Palmer, Tx, US 176/L7
Palmer, Wa, US 193/D3
Palmer Lake, Co, US 178/B1
Palmer Land (phys. reg.), Ant. 216/V
Palmer Rapids, On, Can. 187/H2
Palmerston, On, Can. 186/F3
Palmerston, NZ 161/B4
Palmerston (cape), Austl. 160/C3
Palmerston Atoll (atoll), Cookls. 163/J6
Palmerston North, NZ 161/C3
Palmerston NP, Austl. 160/B2
Palmerton, Pa, US 194/C2
Palmerville, Austl. 160/B1
Palmetto, Fl, US 191/G4
Palmetto, Ga, US 189/L7
Palmetto Bend (dam), Tx, US 177/F3
Palmi, It. 74/D3
Palmilla, Chile 214/C2
Palmillas (pt.), Cuba 201/F1
Palmira, Col. 204/B4
Palmital, Braz. 213/G2
Palmitas, Uru. 215/K10
Palmitos, Braz. 213/F3
Palmyra, Mi, US 186/E4
Palmyra (isl.), PacUS 163/J4
Palmyra, In, US 188/D1
Palmyra, Mo, US 181/J4
Palmyra, Pa, US 194/B3
Palmyra, Va, US 189/H2
Palmyra, Wi, US 181/K2
Palmyra (Tadmur) (ruin), Syria 128/D3
Palmyras (pt.), India 118/E3
Palnackie, Sc, UK 60/E2
Palo, Phil. 114/D3
Palo Alto, Pa, US 194/B2
Palo Alto Battlefield Nat'l Hist. Site, Tx, US 177/F4
Palo Duro (cr.), Tx, US 178/C3
Palo Pinto, Tx, US 177/E1
Palo Santo, Arg. 212/E3
Palo Verde, Ca, US 174/E4
Palo Verde, PN, CR 196/D5
Paloemeu (riv.), Sur. 206/C2
Paloh, Indo. 116/C3
Paloich, Sudan 142/G3
Palombara Sabina, It. 91/B3
Palometas, Bol. 212/D1
Palomeu (riv.), Sur. 205/H4
Palon (peak), It. 89/E2
Paloncha, India 121/D2
Paloncillo (mts.), NM, US 175/H5
Palos (cape), Sp. 73/E4
Palos Blancos, Bol. 212/D2
Palos de la Frontera, Sp. 72/B4
Palos Hills, Il, US 193/Q16
Palos Verdes (pt.), Ca, US 192/F8
Palos Verdes (hills), Ca, US 192/F8
Palos Verdes Estates, Ca, US 192/F8
Palosco, It. 88/C2
Palouse (riv.), Wa, US 170/F4
Palouse, Wa, US 170/F4
Palpa, Peru 208/C4
Palpalá, Arg. 212/C3
Palpetu (cape), Indo. 117/G4
Paltamo, Fin. 94/E2
Paltang, SKor. 107/G6
Palu, Indo. 117/E4
Palu (isl.), Indo. 154/A2
Palu, Turk. 128/D2
Paluan, Phil. 114/C2
Palwal, India 122/A1
Pama, Burk. 141/F4
Pama, Chile 212/B4
Pamangkat, Indo. 116/C3
Pamanukan (cape), Indo. 115/D3
Pamar, Col. 204/D5
Pambeguwa, Nga. 141/H4
Pambula, Austl. 159/D3
Pamekasan, Indo. 115/F3
Pameungpeuk, Indo. 115/D3
Pāmgarh, India 122/D5
Pamiers, Fr. 70/D5
Pamir (reg.), Taj.,China 100/H6
Pamir (riv.), Afg.,Taj. 100/H6
Pamlico (riv.), NC, US 189/J3
Pamlico (sound), NC, US 189/J3
Pamoni, Ven. 205/E4
Pampa, Tx, US 178/D3
Pampa de Agnia, Arg. 214/C4
Pampa de los Guanacos, Arg. 212/D3
Pampa de los Salinas, Arg. 212/C4
Pampa del Indio, Arg. 212/E3
Pampa del Sacramento (plain), Peru 208/C2
Pampa del Tamarugal (plain), Chile 212/B1
Pampa Grande, Bol. 212/C1
Pampa Húmeda (plain), Arg. 214/E2
Pampa Pelada (plain), Arg. 214/C5
Pampa Seca (plain), Arg. 214/D3
Pampachiri, Peru 208/C4
Pampacolca, Peru 208/C4
Pampas (plain), Arg. 203/C6
Pampas (riv.), Peru 208/C4
Pampas, Peru 208/C4
Pampas, Peru 208/B3
Pampilhosa da Serra, Port. 72/B2
Pamplico, SC, US 189/H4
Pamplona, Col. 204/C3
Pamplona, Sp. 70/C5
Pampulha (int'l arpt.), Braz. 210/E3
Pāmpur, India 124/C2
Pamukova, Turk. 77/K5
Pamunkey Ind. Res., Va, US 189/J2
Pan de Azúcar, Bol. 212/C2
Pan de Azúcar, PN, Chile 212/B3
Pana, Gabon 146/C3
Pana, Il, US 181/K4
Panaba, Mex. 200/D1
Panabo, Phil. 114/D4
Panaca, Nv, US 174/E2
Panacachi, Bol. 212/C1
Panacea, Fl, US 191/F2
Panadura, SrL. 121/C5
Pānāgar, India 122/B4
Panagyurishte, Bul. 77/G4
Panaitan (isl.), Indo. 116/B5
Panaji, India 121/B3
Panama(ctry.) 165/J9
Panamá (isth.), Pan. 197/F5
Panamá (cap.), Pan. 204/B2
Panamá (bay), Pan. 201/G4
Panama (gulf), Pan. 165/K9
Panama (canal), Pan. 165/K9
Panama City, Fl, US 191/F2
Panama, Ok, US 179/G3
Panamá Viejo (ruin), Pan. 204/B2
Panambi, Braz. 213/F4
Panamint (range), Ca, US 174/D2
Panao, Peru 208/B3
Panaon (isl.), Phil. 114/D3
Panaro (riv.), It. 71/J4
Panarukan, Indo. 115/F3
Panasoffkee (lake), Fl, US 190/L6
Panay (isl.), Phil. 103/M8
Panay (gulf), Phil. 114/C3
Pancake (range), Nv, US 172/E4
Pančevo, Yugo. 76/E3
Panchagarh, Bang. 123/G2
Panchor, Malay. 115/D2
Pančicev vrh (peak), Yugo. 76/E4
Pancilet (res.), India 123/F4
Panciu, Rom. 77/H3
Panda, D.R. Congo 147/F5
Panda, Moz. 149/G5
Pandale, Tx, US 177/D2
Pandamatenga, Bots. 148/E3
Pandan, Phil. 114/D2
Pandan, Phil. 114/C3
Pandan (str.), Sing. 115/H7
Pandaria, India 122/C4
Pandeglang, Indo. 115/D3
Pandėlys, Lith. 67/L3
Pāndhurna, India 121/C1
Pandie Pandie, Austl. 157/H3
Pandino, It. 88/C3
Pando, Uru. 215/L11
Pando (state), Bol. 209/E3
Pāndoh, India 124/D4
Pandora (passage), PNG 155/G2
Pandrup, Den. 66/C3
Pandua, India 123/G4
Panduro, Bol. 209/E5
Panelas, Braz. 207/G5
Panevėžys, Lith. 67/L4
Panfilov, Kaz. 125/D3
Panfilovo, Rus. 99/M2
Pang (riv.), Myan. 112/C4
Pang Kalom, Laos 112/D4
Pang Long, Myan. 112/C4
Pangai, Tonga 163/H6
Pangaion (peak), Gre. 75/J2
Pangala, Congo 146/C3
Pangandaran, Indo. 115/E3
Pangani (riv.), Tanz. 145/B2
Pangani, Tanz. 145/B3
Pangbourne, Eng, UK 63/E4
Pangburn, Ar, US 179/J3
Pangi, D.R. Congo 147/F3
Pangia, PNG 155/G1
Pangjiabu, China 106/G6
Pangkajene, Indo. 117/E4
Pangkalanberandan, Indo. 115/B1
Pangkalanpembuang, Indo. 116/D4
Pangkalansusu, Indo. 115/B1
Pangkalaseang (cape), Indo. 117/F4
Pangkalpinang, Indo. 115/D3
Pangnirtung, Nun, Can. 167/K2
Pangsau (pass), India 112/C3
Panguipulli, Chile 214/B3
Panguitch, Ut, US 175/F2
Panguma, SLeo. 140/C4
Panguruan, Indo. 115/B2
Pangutaran, Phil. 114/C4
Pangutaran (isl.), Phil. 114/C4
Pangutaran Group (isls.), Malay. 114/B4
P'an'gyo, NKor. 107/D3
Panhandle, Tx, US 178/D3
Pania-Mutombo, D.R. Congo 147/E4
Paniai (lake), Indo. 117/J4
Panicale, It. 91/B1
Panié (peak), NCal. 163/U12
Pānihāti, India 123/G4
Pānīpat, India 124/D5
Panitan, Phil. 114/C3
Panj (riv.), Afg.,Taj. 100/G6
Panj (riv.), Afg. 127/K1
Panj (Pyandzh) (riv.), Afg.,Taj. 125/B4
Panjakent, Taj. 100/G6
Panjang, Indo. 115/D3
Panjgraon, India 124/D4
Panjgūr, Pak. 127/H3
Panjwīn, Iraq 129/F3
Panke (riv.), Ger. 68/Q6
Pankow, Ger. 68/Q6
Pankshin, Nga. 141/H4
P'anmun-üp, NKor. 107/D4
P'anmunjŏm, NKor. 107/D4
Panna, India 122/C3
Pannawonica, Austl. 156/C2
Pannikin (isl.), Austl. 160/F7
Pano Lefkara, Cyp. 130/C2
Pano Panayia, Cyp. 130/C2
Pano Platres, Cyp. 130/C2
Panora, Ia, US 181/G3
Panorama, Braz. 213/G2
Panshan, China 107/B2
Panshi, China 105/K3
Panshizhen, China 113/F2
Pānskura, India 123/F4
Pant, Eng, UK 62/C1
Pantai Remis, Malay. 115/C1
Pantanal (reg.), Braz. 213/E1
Pantanal (reg.), Braz. 210/A3
Pantanal Matogrossense PN, Braz. 212/E1
Pantano Wash (riv.), Az, US 175/G4
Pantar (isl.), Indo. 154/A2
Pante Makasar, Indo. 154/B2
Pantego, Tx, US 176/K7
Pantego, NC, US 189/J3
Pantelleria, It. 74/B4
Pantelleria (isl.), It. 55/F5
Pantha, Myan. 119/F3
Panther Swamp NWR, Ms, US 188/B4
Panthersville, Ga, US 189/M7
Panti, Indo. 115/C2
Pantigliate, It. 88/C3
Pantijan Abor. Land, Austl. 154/B4
Pantin, Fr. 56/K5
Pantoja, Peru 204/C5
Pantón, Sp. 72/B1
Pantukan, Phil. 114/D4
Panu, D.R. Congo 146/D3
Pánuco (riv.), Mex. 196/B3
Pánuco, Mex. 200/B1
Panwol, SKor. 107/F7
Panyabungan, Indo. 115/B2
Panyam, Nga. 141/H4
Panzhihua, China 112/D3
Panzós, Guat. 200/D3
Pao (riv.), Ven. 207/M8
Pão de Açúcar, Braz. 211/F1
Paola, It. 74/E3
Paola, Ks, US 179/G1
Paola, Fl, US 190/N6
Paola, Malta 74/M7
Paoli, In, US 188/D1
Paoli, Ok, US 179/F3
Paoli, Pa, US 194/C3
Paonia, Co, US 175/J1
Paonta Sahib, India 124/D4
Paoua, CAfr. 142/C4
Paoy Pet, Camb. 120/C3
Paozi, China 107/B1
Paoziyan, China 107/C2
Pap, Uzb. 125/B3
Pápa, Hun. 76/C2
Papa Westray (isl.), Sc, UK 57/V14
Papagayo (gulf), CR 196/D5
Papago Ind. Res., Az, US 175/F4
Papakura, NZ 161/F7
Papantla, Mex. 199/M6
Papaplaya, Peru 208/C2
Papar, Malay. 114/A4
Papara, FrPol. 163/X15
Papatoetoe, NZ 161/F6
Papeete (cap.), FrPol. 163/X15
Papeete (Faaa) (int'l arpt.), FrPol. 163/X15
Papenburg, Ger. 79/E2
Papendrecht, Neth. 78/B5
Papenoo, FrPol. 163/X15
Papetoai, FrPol. 163/X15
Paphos, Cyp. 130/C2
Paphos (dist.), Cyp. 130/C2
Papilė, Lith. 67/K3
Papillion, Ne, US 181/F3
Papineauville, Qu, Can. 187/J2
Papingut (peak), Alb. 75/G2
Papiu, Sudan 142/F4
Paposo, Chile 212/B3
Pāppadāhāndi, India 121/D2
Pappenheim, Ger. 84/D5
Papua (gulf), PNG 162/D5
Papua New Guinea(ctry.) 162/D5
Papudo, Chile 214/C2
Papun, Myan. 120/B2
Papunya, Austl. 157/F2
Paquera, CR 201/E4
Pará (state), Braz. 205/G5
Pará (riv.), Braz. 210/D3
Pará (falls), Ven. 205/E3
Para (riv.), Braz. 206/D3
Para (dist.), Sur. 205/H3
Pará de Minas, Braz. 210/D3
Para de Oeste (riv.), Braz. 205/H4
Para Wirra NP, Austl. 157/M8
Para, South (riv.), Austl. 157/M8
Paraburdoo, Austl. 156/C2
Paracale, Phil. 114/C2
Paracambi, Braz. 211/N7
Paracas (pen.), Peru 208/B4
Paracas, Res. Nacional, Peru 208/B4
Paracatu, Braz. 210/D3
Paracatu (riv.), Braz. 210/D3
Paracel (isls.), Asia 112/F5
Parachilna, Austl. 157/H4
Paracho de Verduzco, Mex. 198/E5
Parachute, Co, US 173/J4
Paraćin, Yugo. 76/E4
Paracuru, Braz. 207/G3
Paradhision (int'l arpt.), Gre. 128/B2
Paradip, India 118/E3
Paradise, Nf, Can 185/L2
Paradise, Guy. 206/B1
Paradise, Ca, US 172/C4
Paradise, Ks, US 180/E4
Paradise, Mi, US 186/D1
Paradise, Mt, US 170/G4
Paradise, Nv, US 174/E2
Paradise, Pa, US 194/B4
Paradise, Tx, US 176/K6
Paradise Hills, NM, US 175/J3
Paradise Valley, Az, US 175/G4
Paradise Valley, Ab, Can. 171/J1
Paradox, Co, US 175/H1
Parafield (arpt.), Austl. 157/M8
Parafiyivka, Ukr. 99/G1
Paragominas, Braz. 207/E3
Paragonah, Ut, US 175/F2
Paragould, Ar, US 188/B2
Paragua (riv.), Ven. 205/F3
Paraguá (riv.), Bol. 209/F4
Paraguaçu (riv.), Braz. 203/E4
Paraguaçu, Braz. 211/L6
Paraguaçu Paulista, Braz 213/G2
Paraguai (riv.), SAm. 203/D5
Paraguaipoa, Ven. 204/D2
Paraguaná (pen.), Ven. 197/G5
Paraguarí (dept.), Par. 213/E3
Paraguarí, Par. 213/E3
Paraguay(ctry.) 203/C5
Paraguay (riv.), Par. 210/A4
Paraíba (riv.), Braz. 213/J2
Paraíba (state), Braz. 207/G4
Paraíba do Sul (riv.), Braz. 203/E5
Paraíba do Sul, Braz. 211/N7
Paraibano, Braz. 207/F4
Paraibuna (riv.), Braz. 211/L8
Paraim (riv.), Braz. 210/D1
Parainen (Pargas), Fin. 67/K1
Paraíso, CR 201/F4
Paraíso, Mex. 200/C2
Paraíso do Norte, Braz. 213/F2
Paraíso do Tocantins, Braz. 210/C1
Paraisópolis, Braz. 211/L7
Parakou, Ben. 141/F4
Parama (isl.), PNG 155/F2
Paramakkudi, India 121/C4
Paramaribo (dist.), Sur. 205/H3
Paramaribo (cap.), Sur. 206/C1
Parambu, Braz. 207/F4
Paramillo (peak), Col. 204/C3
Paramillo, PN, Col. 197/F6
Paramirim (riv.), Braz. 211/E2
Paramirim, Braz. 211/E2
Paramithía, Gre. 75/G3
Paramoti, Braz. 207/G4
Paramount, Ca, US 192/F8
Paramus, NJ, US 195/J8
Paramushir (isl.), Rus. 103/Q5
Paraná (riv.), SAm. 203/D5
Paraná (riv.), Braz. 210/D2
Paraná (state), Braz. 210/C4
Paraná, Arg. 212/D4
Paraná, Braz. 210/D2
Paraná Ibicuy (riv.), Arg. 215/J10
Paraná Madeirinha (riv.), Braz. 206/B4
Paraná Urariá (riv.), Braz. 205/G5
Paranaguá (bay), Braz. 213/G3
Paranaguá, Braz. 213/G3
Paranaíba, Braz. 213/G1
Paranaíba (riv.), Braz. 210/D3
Paranapanema (riv.), Braz. 213/G2
Paranapiacaba, Serra do (mts.), Braz. 210/C5
Parañaque, Phil. 114/E6
Paranatinga (riv.), Braz. 203/D4
Paranavaí, Braz. 213/F2
Parang, Phil. 114/C4
Paraopeba, Braz. 210/D3
Paraopeba (riv.), Braz. 210/D3
Parapara, Ven. 207/N8
Paraparaumu (arpt.), NZ 161/H8
Paraparaumu, NZ 161/J8
Parapetí (riv.), Bol. 212/D1
Parás, Mex. 177/E4
Parāsi, Nepal 122/D2
Parati, Braz. 211/M8
Paratico, It. 88/C2
Paratinga (riv.), Braz. 211/L8
Paratinga, Braz. 211/E2
Paraúna, Braz. 210/C3
Paravūr, India 121/C4
Paray-Vieille-Poste, Fr. 56/K5
Parazinho, Braz. 207/H4
Pārbati (riv.), India 127/L4
Pārbatipur, Bang. 123/G3
Parçay-Meslay, Fr. 83/F6
Parcé-sur-Sarthe, Fr. 83/E5
Parchim, Ger. 68/F2
Parczew, Pol. 69/M3
Pardes Hanna-Karkur, Isr. 131/B4
Pārdi, India 127/K4
Parding, China 125/E5
Pardo (riv.), Braz. 213/H2
Pardo (riv.), Braz. 210/B4
Pardone (cape), SAfr. 150/D4
Pardoo, Austl. 156/C2
Pardubice, Czh. 69/H3
Pare, Indo. 115/F3
Pare (mts.), Tanz. 145/B2
Parece Vela (Okino-Tori-Shima) (isl.), Japan 103/N7
Parecis (mts.), Braz. 203/C4
Parede, Port. 73/P10
Paredes de Nava, Sp. 72/C1
Paredón, Mex. 177/D5
Paredón, Mex. 200/C2
Paredones, Chile 214/C2
Parelhas, Braz. 207/G5
Parempuyre, Fr. 70/C4
Parenda, India 121/B2
Parentis-en-Born, Fr. 70/C4
Parepare, Indo. 117/E4
Parera, Arg. 214/D2
Parets del Valles, Sp. 73/L6
Pargas (Parainen), Fin. 67/K1
Pargny-sur-Saulx, Fr. 81/D6
Pargolovo, Rus. 94/T6
Paria (pen.), Ven. 197/J5

Paria (gulf) 203/C1
Paria (riv.), Ut, US 175/G2
Paria, Bol. 212/C1
Pariacoto, Peru 208/B3
Pariaguán, Ven. 205/E2
Pariaman, Indo. 115/C3
Parichi, Bela. 96/D1
Parigi, Indo. 117/F4
Parigné-L'Évêque, Fr. 83/F5
Parikkala, Fin. 64/J3
Parima (mts.), Braz. 205/E4
Parima (riv.), Braz. 205/F4
Parinacota (peak), Bol. 208/D5
Parinacota (peak), Bol.,Chile 212/B1
Parinari, Peru 208/C2
Pariñas (pt.), Peru 208/A2
Paringa, Austl. 158/B2
Parîngu Mare (peak), Rom. 77/F3
Parintins, Braz. 206/B3
Paris, Tx, US 179/G4
Paris, Ar, US 179/H3
Paris (dept.), Fr. 80/B6
Paris, On, Can. 186/F3
Paris, Me, US 187/L2
Paris, Il, US 186/C5
Paris (cap.), Fr. 56/K5
Paris, Id, US 173/H2
Paris, Tn, US 188/C2
Paris, Ky, US 188/E1
Paris, Ms, US 188/C3
Paris, Mo, US 181/H4
Paris (Le Bourget) (arpt.), Fr. 56/K5
Parishville, NY, US 187/J2
Parita (bay), Pan. 201/F4
Park (riv.), ND, US 182/F3
Park (range), Co, US 173/K3
Park (pt.), Eng, UK 62/A5
Park City, Ks, US 179/F2
Park City, Il, US 193/Q15
Park City, Ky, US 188/D2
Park Falls, Wi, US 183/J5
Park Forest, Il, US 186/C4
Park Hill, Ok, US 179/G3
Park Rapids, Mn, US 183/G4
Park Ridge, Il, US 193/Q16
Park Ridge, NJ, US 195/J7
Park River, ND, US 182/F3
Park Valley, Ut, US 173/G3
Park View, Ia, US 181/J3
Parkano, Fin. 64/G3
Parkbeg, Sk, Can. 171/L2
Parkchester (nbrhd.), NY, US 195/K8
Parkdale, Ar, US 179/J4
Parkdale, Or, US 172/C1
Parker, Ks, US 179/G1
Parker, Pa, US 187/G4
Parker (lake), Fl, US 190/M7
Parker, Az, US 174/E3
Parker, SD, US 181/F2
Parker, Co, US 180/B4
Parker (peak), SD, US 180/C2
Parker (pt.), Austl. 155/E4
Parker (co.), Tx, US 176/K7
Parker, Tx, US 177/F1
Parker Dam, Az, Ca, US 175/E3
Parker River Nat'l Wild. Ref., Ma, US 187/L3
Parker's Cove, Nf, Can. 185/K2
Parkers Prairie, Mn, US 183/G4
Parkersburg, Ia, US 181/H2
Parkersburg, WV, US 189/G1
Parkersburg, Il, US 188/C1
Parkes, Austl. 159/D1
Parkesburg, Pa, US 194/C4
Parkeston, Eng, UK 63/H3
Parkgate, NI, UK 60/B2
Parkhill, On, Can. 186/F3
Parkhurst, Eng, UK 63/E5
Parkin, Ar, US 188/B3
Parkland, Wa, US 170/C4
Parkman, Sk, Can. 182/D3
Parks, Ar, US 179/H3
Parkside, Sk, Can. 171/L1
Parkside, Pa, US 194/C4
Parksley, Va, US 189/K2
Parkstetten, Ger. 85/F5
Parkston, SD, US 180/F2
Parksville, SC, US 189/F4
Parksville, BC, Can. 170/B3
Parkton, Md, US 194/B4
Parkton, NC, US 189/H3
Parkville, Md, US 194/B5
Parkville, Pa, US 194/B4
Parkway-Sacramento, Ca, US 193/L9
Parkwood, NC, US 189/H3
Parla, Sp. 73/N9
Parliament Buildings, NZ 161/H9
Parlier, Ca, US 174/C2
Parlin, Co, US 175/J1
Parma, Oh, US 186/F4
Parma (prov.), It. 88/C3
Parma, It. 88/D4
Parma (riv.), It. 88/D3
Parma, Id, US 172/E2
Parma, Mo, US 188/C2
Parmain, Fr. 56/J4
Parmelee, SD, US 180/D2
Parnaguá, Braz. 210/D1
Parnaíba (riv.), Braz. 203/E3
Parnaíba, Braz. 207/F3
Parnamirim, Braz. 207/G5
Parnarama, Braz. 207/F4
Parnassós (peak), Gre. 75/H3
Parnassós NP, Gre. 75/H3
Parnassus, NZ 161/C3
Parndana, Austl. 157/H5
Parnell, Tx, US 178/D3
Parnell (nbrhd.), NZ 161/F6
Párnis (peak), Gre. 75/N8
Párnis Óros NP, Gre. 75/N8
Párnon (mts.), Gre. 75/H4
Pärnu, Est. 67/L2
Pärnu (bay), Est. 67/L2
Pärnu-Jaagupi, Est. 67/L2
Paro, Bhu. 123/G2
Paron, Fr. 70/E2
Parona di Valpolicella, It. 89/D3
Paroo (riv.), Austl. 153/D3
Páros, Gre. 75/J4
Páros (isl.), Gre. 93/K3
Parow, SAfr. 150/L10
Parowan, Ut, US 175/F2
Parpan, Swi. 87/F4
Parrachée (mtn.), Fr. 90/C2
Parral, Chile 214/C3
Parramatta (nbrhd.), Austl. 160/H8
Parramore (isl.), Md, US 189/K2
Parras de la Fuente, Mex. 198/E3
Parrett (riv.), Eng, UK 62/D4
Parris Island, SC, US 189/G4
Parris Island Marine Base, SC, US 189/G4
Parrish, Fl, US 190/L8
Parrish, Al, US 188/D4
Parrita, CR 201/E4
Parrot Jungle, Fl, US 190/P11
Parrott, Ga, US 191/F2
Parr's Halt, Bots. 149/E4
Parrsboro, NS, Can. 184/E3
Parry (chan.), Can. 165/F2
Parry (isls.), Can. 165/F2
Parry (bay), Nun, Can. 167/H2
Parry Sound, On, Can. 186/F2
Parsberg, Ger. 85/E4
Parseierspitze (peak), Aus. 87/G3
Parshall, ND, US 182/C4
Parsippany-Troy Hills, NJ, US 195/H8
Parson, BC, Can. 170/F2
Parsons, Ks, US 179/G2
Parsons (mtn.), SC, US 189/F3
Parsons, Tn, US 188/C3
Parsons (mt.), Austl. 155/D3
Parsons (range), Austl. 155/D3
Parsons, WV, US 189/H1
Partago, Ben. 141/F4
Pårtefjället (peak), Swe. 64/F2
Partenstein, Ger. 84/C2
Parthenay, Fr. 70/C3
Partille, Swe. 66/E3
Partinico, It. 74/C3
Partizansk, Rus. 105/L3
Partizánske, Slvk. 69/K4
Partridge, Ks, US 179/E2
Partry (mts.), Ire. 58/A2
Partūr, India 118/C4
Paru (riv.), Braz. 205/H4
Paru de Oeste (riv.), Braz. 203/D2
Paruro, Peru 208/D4
Pārvathīpuram, India 121/D2
Parwich, Eng, UK 61/G5
Paryang, China 125/D5
Parys, SAfr. 150/D2
Pas de Morgins (pass), Fr. 86/C5
Pas-de-Calais (dept.), Fr. 80/A3
Pasadena, Nf, Can. 185/J1
Pasadena (lake), Fl, US 190/L7
Pasadena, Ca, US 192/F7
Pasadena, Tx, US 177/M9
Pasadena, Md, US 194/B5
Pasado (cape), Ecu. 204/A5
Pasaje, Ecu. 208/B1
Pasaman (peak), Indo. 115/C2
Pasān, India 122/D4
Pasanauri, Geo. 97/H4
Pasarbantal, Indo. 115/C3
Pasarkuok, Indo. 115/C3
Pasarsorkam, Indo. 115/B2
Pasarwajo, Indo. 154/A1
Pasawng, Myan. 120/B2
Pasay, Phil. 114/F6
Pascagoula (riv.), Ms, US 190/D2
Pascagoula, Ms, US 190/D2
Paşcani, Rom. 98/D4
Pasching, Aus. 85/H6
Pasco (co.), Fl, US 190/L7
Pasco, Fl, US 190/L7
Pasco (dept.), Peru 208/C3
Pasco, Wa, US 170/E4
Pascua (riv.), Chile 215/B6
Pascua, Isla de (Easter) (isl.), Chile 163/Q7
Pascuales, Ecu. 208/B1
Pasewalk, Ger. 66/E5
Pashkovo, Rus. 97/G1
Pashkovskiy, Rus. 99/K5
Pasian di Prato, It. 89/G1
Pasiano, It. 89/F2
Pasig, Phil. 114/F6
Pāsighāt, India 112/B2
Pasinler, Turk. 128/E2
Pasión, Río de la (riv.), Guat. 200/D2
Pasir Mas, Malay. 115/C1
Pasir Puteh, Malay. 115/C1
Pasłęk, Pol. 67/H4
Pasłęka (riv.), Pol. 69/L2
Pasley (cape), Austl. 156/D5
Pašman (isl.), Cro. 71/L5
Pasni, Pak. 127/H3
Paso de Indios, Arg. 214/C4
Paso de la Patria, Arg. 212/E3
Paso de los Libres, Arg. 213/E4
Paso de los Toros, Uru. 215/K10
Paso de Ovejas, Mex. 199/N7
Paso de Patria, Par. 212/E3
Paso del Cerro, Uru. 213/F4
Paso del Macho, Mex. 199/N8
Paso del Planchón (peak), Chile 214/C2
Paso Flores, Arg. 214/C4
Paso Real, Ven. 207/P8
Paso Robles (El Paso de Robles), Ca, US 174/B3
Paspébiac, Qu, Can. 184/E1
Pasrūr, Pak. 124/C3
Pass Christian, Ms, US 190/D2
Passa Quatro, Braz. 211/M7
Passage East, Ire. 58/D5
Passage Key Nat'l Wild. Ref., Fl, US 191/G4
Passage West, Ire. 58/B6
Passagem Franca, Braz. 207/F4
Passaic, NJ, US 195/J8
Passaic (riv.), NJ, US 194/D2
Passais, Fr. 83/E3
Passau, Ger. 85/G5
Passero (pt.), It. 74/D4
Passi, Phil. 114/C3
Passignano sul Trasimeno, It. 91/B1
Passo Corese, It. 91/B3
Passo Fundo, Braz. 213/F4
Passo Fundo, Barragem do (res.), Braz. 213/F3
Passons, It. 89/G1
Passoré (prov.), Burk. 141/E3
Passos, Braz. 213/H2
Passwang (peak), Swi. 86/D3
Passy, Fr. 86/C6
Pastavy, Bela. 67/M4
Pastaza (riv.), Peru 204/B5
Pastaza (dept.), Ecu. 204/B5
Pastaza (riv.), Ecu.,Peru 203/B3
Pastek (riv.), Pol. 67/J5
Pasto, Col. 204/B4
Pastoriza, Sp. 72/B1
Pastos Bons, Braz. 207/E4
Pastura (peak), Az, US 175/H2
Pasuquin, Phil. 114/C1
Pasuruan, Indo. 115/F3
Pasvalys, Lith. 67/L3
Pásztó, Hun. 69/K5
Pata, CAfr. 142/D3
Pata, Bol. 208/D4
Patacamaya, Bol. 212/C1
Patag NP, Phil. 114/C3
Patagonia (phys. reg.), Arg. 203/B8
Patagonia, Az, US 175/G5
Patah (peak), Indo. 116/B4
Patamdesar, India 124/C5
Pātan, India 122/B4
Pātan, India 127/K4
Pāṭan (Lalitpur), Nepal 123/E2
Pataná (peak), Braz. 213/G3
Patani, Nga. 141/G5
Patani, Indo. 117/G3
Patapédia (riv.), Qu, Can. 184/D1
Patapsco, Md, US 194/B4
Patapsco (riv.), Md, US 194/A5
Pataudi, India 124/D5
Patay, Fr. 83/G4
Pataz, Peru 208/B2
Patchewollock, Austl. 158/B2
Patchogue, NY, US 195/E2
Patchway, Eng, UK 62/D3
Pate (isl.), Kenya 145/C2
Patea, NZ 161/C2
Pategi, Nga. 141/G4
Pateley Bridge, Eng, UK 61/G3
Patenga, Bang. 123/H4
Paterna, Sp. 73/E3
Paternion, Aus. 71/K3
Paternò, It. 74/D4
Paterno, It. 92/C3
Pateros, Wa, US 170/E3
Paterson, NJ, US 195/J8
Paterson, Austl. 159/E1
Paterson (cape), Austl. 159/B4
Pathalgaon, India 122/D4
Pathanāmthitta, India 121/C4
Pathānkot, India 124/C3
Pātharghāta, Bang. 123/G4
Patharkot, Nepal 123/E2
Pathein (Bassein), Myan. 112/B5
Pathfinder (dam), Wy, US 173/K2
Pathfinder (res.), Wy, US 173/K2
Pathfinder NWR, Wy, US 173/K2
Pathiu, Thai. 120/B4
Pathlow, Sk, Can. 171/M1
Pati, Indo. 115/E3
Pati, Indo. 154/B2
Patía (riv.), Col. 204/B4
Patía, Col. 204/B4
Patiāla, India 124/D4
Patikul, Phil. 114/C4
Pātiram, India 123/G3
Patiya, Bang. 123/H4
Patkaglik, China 125/E4
Patna, Sc, UK 59/B6
Patna, India 123/E3
Patnāgarh, India 121/D1
Patnanongan (isl.), Phil. 114/C2
Patnongon, Phil. 114/C3
Patnos, Turk. 129/E2
Pato Branco, Braz. 213/F3
Patoka, In, US 188/D1
Patoka (riv.), In, US 188/D1
Patoka (lake), In, US 188/D1
Patos, Alb. 75/F2
Patos, Braz. 207/G4
Patos de Minas, Braz. 210/D3
Patos, dos (lake), Braz. 213/G4
Patoutville, La, US 190/C3
Patquía, Arg. 212/C4
Pátrai, Gre. 75/G3
Patrai (gulf), Gre. 75/G3
Pātrasāer, India 123/F4
Patrātu, India 123/E4
Patricia (mt.), Austl. 157/F2
Patricia, Ab, Can. 171/J2
Patricia, Tx, US 177/C1
Patricio Lynch (isl.), Chile 215/A6
Patrick (A.F.B.), Fl, US 191/H3
Patrick Springs, Va, US 189/G2
Patrington, Eng, UK 61/H4
Patrocínio, Braz. 210/D3
Patroon, Tx, US 177/H2
Patsaliga (cr.), Al, US 191/E2
Patscherkofel (peak), Aus. 87/H3
Pattani, Thai. 120/C5
Pattensen, Ger. 79/G4
Patterson, Ar, US 179/J3
Patterson, Ga, US 191/G2
Patterson, La, US 190/C3
Patterson, Mo, US 188/B2
Patti, It. 74/D3
Patti, India 124/C4
Pattingham, Eng, UK 62/D1
Pattison, Ms, US 190/C2
Pattoki, Pak. 124/B4
Patton, Pa, US 187/G4
Pattonsburg, Mo, US 181/G3
Pattukkottai, India 121/C4
Patu, Braz. 207/G4
Patuākhāli, Bang. 123/H4
Patuākhāli (pol. reg.), Bang. 123/G4
Patuca (riv.), Hon. 196/D5
Patuca (pt.), Hon. 201/E3
Patuca (mts.), Hon. 200/E3
Patuha (peak), Indo. 115/D3
Pătulele, Rom. 76/F3
Patuxent (riv.), Md, US 194/B5
Patuxent NWR, Md, US 194/B5
Patuxent R. Sp, Md, US 194/B5
Páty, Hun. 77/Q9
Pátzcuaro, Mex. 199/E5
Pau, Fr. 70/C5
Pau dos Ferros, Braz. 207/G4
Paucarbamba, Peru 208/C4
Paucartambo, Peru 208/D4
Paucartambo, Peru 208/C3
Pauillac, Fr. 70/C4
Pauini (riv.), Braz. 209/E2
Pauini, Braz. 209/E2
Pauksa (peak), Myan. 112/B5
Pauktaw, Myan. 120/B2
Paul B. Wurtsmith (A.F.B.), Mi, US 186/E2
Paul Isnard, FrG. 206/C1
Paul Smiths, NY, US 187/J2
Paulaya (riv.), Hon. 200/E3
Paulden, Az, US 175/F3
Paulding, Oh, US 186/D4
Paulding, Ms, US 190/D1
Paulding (co.), Ga, US 189/L7
Paulina, Or, US 172/D1
Pauline, Ks, US 179/G1
Pauline (mt.), BC, Can. 170/E1
Paulínia, Braz. 211/J7
Paulins Kill (riv.), NJ, US 194/D2
Paulista, Braz. 207/H4
Paulistana, Braz. 207/F5
Paullina, Ia, US 181/G2
Paullo, It. 88/C3
Paulo Afonso, Braz. 207/G5
Paulo Afonso, PN de, Braz. 207/G5
Paulo Ramos, Braz. 207/E4
Paulpietersburg, SAfr. 151/E2
Pauls Valley, Ok, US 179/F3
Paulsboro, NJ, US 194/C4
Paulton, Eng, UK 62/D4
Pauma Valley, Ca, US 192/D4
Pauna, Col. 207/M7
Paungde, Myan. 112/B5
Pauri, India 125/C5
Pausa, Ger. 85/E1
Pavant (range), Ut, US 173/G4
Pavão, Braz. 211/E3
Pāveh, Iran 129/F3
Pavel Banya, Bul. 75/J1
Pavia, It. 88/C3
Pavia (prov.), It. 88/C2
Pavie, Fr. 70/D5
Pavilion, BC, Can. 170/D2
Pavillion, Wy, US 173/J2
Pavilly, Fr. 83/F1
Pāvilosta, Lat. 67/J3
Pavino, Rus. 95/K4
Pavlikeni, Bul. 77/G4
Pavlodar (oblast), Kaz. 125/B1
Pavlodar, Kaz. 125/C1
Pavlof (vol.), Ak, US 168/W13
Pavlohrad, Ukr. 99/H3
Pavlovo, Rus. 94/J5
Pavlovsk, Rus. 94/T7
Pavlovsk, Rus. 99/L2
Pavlovskaya, Rus. 99/K4
Pavlovskiy, Kaz. 95/P5
Pavlysh, Ukr. 99/G3
Pavo, Ga, US 191/G2
Pavón, Col. 204/C4
Pavone Canavese, It. 88/A2
Pavone del Mella, It. 88/D3
Pavullo nel Frignano, It. 89/D5
Pavy, Rus. 67/N2
Paw Paw, Mi, US 186/D3
Paw Paw Lake, Mi, US 186/C3
Pawa, D.R. Congo 147/F2
Pawan (riv.), Indo. 116/D4
Pawāyan, India 122/C1
Pawé (peak), Camr. 142/A4
Pawhuska, Ok, US 179/F2
Pawia, Gha. 141/E4
Pawn (riv.), Myan. 112/C4
Pawnee, Ok, US 179/F2
Pawnee (riv.), Ks, US 180/E4
Pawnee, Il, US 181/K4
Pawnee Buttes (butte), Co, US 180/C3
Pawnee City, Ne, US 181/F3
Pawnee Indian Village, Ks, US 180/F4
Pawnee Rock, Ks, US 178/E1
Pawtucket, RI, US 187/L4
Paxoí (isl.), Gre. 93/H3
Paxoí (Yáios), Gre. 75/G3
Paxton, Tx, US 177/G2
Paxton, Il, US 186/B4
Paxton, Austl. 159/E1
Pay, Rus. 94/G3
Pay-Khoy (mts.), Rus. 100/G3
Payagyi, Myan. 120/B2
Payaheislam, Indo. 117/G3
Payakumbuh, Indo. 115/C3
Payerne, Swi. 86/C4
Payette, Id, US 172/E1
Payette (riv.), Id, US 172/E2
Payette, North Fork (riv.), Id, US 172/E1
Payette, South Fork (riv.), Id, US 172/E1
Payne (cr.), Fl, US 190/M8
Payne (lake), Qu, Can. 167/J3
Paynes Find, Austl. 156/C4
Paynesville, Mn, US 183/G5
Paynesville, Austl. 159/C3
Paynton, Sk, Can. 171/K1
Pays de Caux (reg.), Fr. 70/D2
Pays de France (reg.), Fr. 56/K4
Pays de la Loire (pol. reg.), Fr. 82/D5
Pays de la Loire (reg.), Fr. 70/C3
Paysandú, Uru. 215/J10
Paysandú (dept.), Uru. 213/E5
Payson, Ut, US 173/H3
Payson, Az, US 175/G3
Payson, Il, US 181/J4
Payún (peak), Arg. 214/C3
Payyannūr, India 121/B3
Paz (riv.), Guat. 200/D3
Paz de Ariporo, Col. 204/D3
Paz de Río, Col. 204/C3
Pāzanān, Iran 129/G4
Pazar, Turk. 128/D1
Pazar, Turk. 97/G4
Pazarcık, Turk. 128/D2
Pazardzhik, Bul. 75/J1
Pazaryeri, Turk. 96/D5
Pazin, Cro. 71/K4
Pe Ell, Wa, US 170/C4
Pea (riv.), Al, US 191/F2
Pea Ridge, Ar, US 179/G2
Peabiru, Braz. 213/F2
Peabody, Ks, US 179/F1
Peabody, Ma, US 187/L3
Peace (riv.), BC, Can. 166/D3
Peace (riv.), Can. 165/F4
Peace Memorial Park, Japan 110/C3
Peace River, Ab, Can. 166/E3
Peace Valley, Mo, US 179/J2
Peach Springs, Az, US 175/F3
Peachland, BC, Can. 170/E3
Peachtree (cr.), Ga, US 189/M7
Peachtree City, Ga, US 188/E4
Peak Charles NP, Austl. 156/D5
Peak District NP, Eng, UK 61/G5
Peak Hill, Austl. 156/C3
Peak Hill, Austl. 159/D1
Peakeen (mtn.), Ire. 58/A6
Peal de Becerro, Sp. 72/D4
Peale (mt.), Ut, US 175/H1
Peapack-Gladstone, NJ, US 194/D2
Pearblossom, Ca, US 192/C1
Pearce (pt.), Austl. 154/C3
Pearisburg, Va, US 189/G2
Pearl (riv.), La,Ms, US 169/J5
Pearl, Ms, US 188/B4
Pearl, Tx, US 176/E2
Pearl and Hermes (reef), Hi, US 163/H2
Pearl Beach, Mi, US 193/G6
Pearl City, Il, US 181/K2
Pearl River, NY, US 195/J7
Pearl River (est.), China 113/G4
Pearland, Ca, US 192/B1
Pearland, Tx, US 177/M9
Pearsall, Tx, US 177/E3
Pearson, Ga, US 191/G2
Pearson (int'l arpt.), On, Can. 186/T8
Pearston, SAfr. 150/D4
Peary (chan.), Nun, Can. 167/R7
Pease (riv.), Tx, US 178/E3
Pease, Mn, US 183/H5
Peaugres, Fr. 90/A2
Péaule, Fr. 82/C5
Pebane, Moz. 149/H3
Pebas, Peru 208/D1
Pebble (isl.), Mald. 215/E6
Pebworth, Eng, UK 63/E2
Peć, Yugo. 76/E4
Pecan Bayou (bayou), Tx, US 177/E2
Pecan Island, La, US 190/B3
Peccia, Swi. 87/E5
Peccioli, It. 89/D6
Pécel, Hun. 77/R10
Pech de Guillaument (peak), Fr. 70/E5
Pechanga Ind. Res., Ca, US 192/C4
Pechanga Ind. Res., Ca, US 174/D4
Pechea, Rom. 77/H3
Pechenga, Rus. 94/F1
Pechengi (res.), Ukr. 99/J3
Pechora, Rus. 95/N2
Pechora (bay), Rus. 95/M1
Pechora (riv.), Rus. 103/C3
Pechory, Rus. 67/M3
Pecica, Rom. 76/E2
Peckham, Ok, US 179/F2
Pecks Pond (pond), Pa, US 194/C1
Peclet, Aiguille de (peak), Fr. 90/C2
Peconic (riv.), NY, US 195/F2
Pecos (riv.), US 165/G6
Pecos, Tx, US 177/C2
Pecos Nat'l Hist. Park, NM, US 178/B3
Pecq, Belg. 80/C2
Pecquencourt, Fr. 80/C3
Pécs, Hun. 76/D2
Pecy, Fr. 56/M6
Pedasí, Pan. 204/A3
Pedaso, It. 92/C1
Peddāpuram, India 121/D2
Pedder (lake), Austl. 153/D5
Peddie, SAfr. 150/D4
Pedemonte, It. 89/D3
Pedernales, Ven. 205/F2
Pedernales (riv.), Tx, US 199/F2
Pédernec, Fr. 82/B3
Pederneiras, Braz. 213/G2
Pedirka, Austl. 157/G3
Pedley, Ca, US 192/C3
Pedley, Ab, Can. 170/F1
Pedra Azul, Braz. 211/E3
Pedra do Feitiço, Ang. 146/C4
Pedra Lume, CpV. 133/K10
Pedralva, Braz. 211/L7
Pedregal, Ven. 204/D2
Pedreguer, Sp. 73/F3
Pedreira, Braz. 211/K7
Pedreiras, Braz. 207/E4
Pedricktown, NJ, US 194/C4
Pedro (pt.), SrL. 121/D4
Pedro, SD, US 180/C1
Pedro Afonso, Braz. 206/D5
Pedro Avelino, Braz. 207/G4
Pedro Betancourt, Cuba 201/F1
Pedro Carbo, Ecu. 204/A5
Pedro Cays (isl.), Jam. 197/F4
Pedro Chico, Col. 204/D4
Pedro Gomes, Braz. 213/F1
Pedro II Braz. 207/F4
Pedro IV (isl.), Braz. 205/E4
Pedro Juan Caballero, Par. 213/F2
Pedro Leopoldo, Braz. 210/D3
Pedro Luro, Arg. 214/E3
Pedro Montt, Chile 212/B3
Pedro Osório, Braz. 213/F4
Pedro R. Fernández, Arg. 212/E4
Peduyim, Isr. 131/B6
Pee Dee (riv.), NC, US 189/G3
Pee Dee NWR, NC, US 189/G3
Peebles, Sc, UK 59/C5
Peebles, Oh, US 189/F1
Peedamulla Abor. Land, Austl. 156/B2
Peekskill, NY, US 194/E1
Peel (isl.), Austl. 160/F6
Peel (inlet), Austl. 156/B5
Peel (sound), Nun, Can. 166/G1
Peel (co.), On, Can. 186/T8
Peel (riv.), Yk, Can. 166/C2
Peel, IM, UK 60/D3
Peel Fell (peak), Eng, UK 59/D6
Peeltown, Tx, US 176/L7
Peene (riv.), Ger. 66/E5
Peer, Belg. 81/E1
Peerless, Mt, US 171/M3
Peers, Ab, Can. 170/F1
Peetz, Co, US 180/C3
Pegarah, Austl. 159/B4
Pegasus (bay), NZ 161/C3
Pegli, It. 88/B5
Peglia (peak), It. 91/B2
Pegnitz (riv.), Ger. 68/F4
Pegnitz, Ger. 85/E3
Pego, Sp. 73/E3
Pego do Altar (res.), Port. 72/A3
Pegognaga, It. 89/D4
Pégomas, Fr. 90/C5
Pegswood, Eng, UK 61/G1
Pegu (Bago), Myan. 112/C5
Peguis Ind. Res., Mb, Can. 182/F2
Pegwell (bay), Eng, UK 63/H4
Pehlivanköy, Turk. 77/H5
Péhonko, Ben. 141/F4
Pehowa, India 124/D5
Pehuajó, Arg. 214/E2
Pehuenche (pass), Chile 214/C2
Pei Xian, China 106/D4
Peigan Ind. Res., Ab, Can. 171/H3
Peijiachuankou, China 106/B3
Peikang, Tai. 113/J4
Peillac, Fr. 82/C5
Peine, Chile 212/B2
Peine, Ger. 79/H4
Peipus (lake), Est.,Rus. 100/C4
Peitawu (peak), Tai. 113/J4
Peiting, Ger. 87/G2
Peixe, Braz. 210/C2
Peixe, Rio do (riv.), Braz. 210/C2
Peixoto (res.), Braz. 210/D4
Pejantan (isl.), Indo. 115/D2
Pejerreyes, Chile 212/B4
Pekalongan, Indo. 115/E3
Pekan, Malay. 115/C2
Pekan Nanas, Malay. 116/B3
Pekhora (riv.), Rus. 94/W9
Pekin, Il, US 181/K3
Pekin (New Pekin), In, US 188/D1
Pelabuhanratu, Indo. 115/D3
Pelabuhanratu (bay), Indo. 115/D3
Pelado (vol.), Mex. 199/Q10
Pelagie (isls.), It. 93/G4
Pelahatchie, Ms, US 188/C4
Pelaihari, Indo. 116/D4
Pelalawan, Indo. 115/C2
Pelat (peak), Fr. 90/C4
Peleaga (peak), Rom. 76/F3
Peleduy, Rus. 101/M4
Pelee (pt.), On, Can. 186/E4
Pelee (isl.), On, Can. 186/E4
Pelée (peak), Fr. 197/N9
Pelequén, Chile 214/N9
Pelham, Austl. 160/A2
Pelham, Al, US 188/D4
Pelham, Ga, US 191/F2
Pelham, NY, US 195/K8
Pelham, On, Can. 186/U9
Pelham Bay Park, NY, US 195/K8
Pelham Manor, NY, US 195/K8
Pelhřimov, Czh. 69/H4
Pelican (lake), Mn, US 183/N6
Pelican (pt.), Namb. 148/B4
Pelican (isl.), Tx, US 177/N9
Pelican Island Nat'l Wild. Ref., Fl, US 191/H4
Pelican Rapids, Mn, US 182/F4
Pélissanne, Fr. 90/B5
Pelister (peak), FYROM 75/G2
Pelister NP, FYROM 75/G2
Peljekaise NP, Swe. 64/F2
Pelješac (pen.), Cro. 75/E1
Pelkie, Mi, US 183/K4
Pell City, Al, US 188/D4
Pell Lake, Wi, US 193/P14
Pélla, Gre. 75/H2
Pélla (ruin), Gre. 75/H2
Pella, Ia, US 181/H3
Pellegrini, Arg. 214/E3
Pellestrina, It. 89/F3
Péllice (riv.), It. 90/D3
Pello, Fin. 94/E2
Pellston, Mi, US 186/D2
Pelly (bay), Nun, Can. 166/H2
Pelly (riv.), Yk, Can. 166/C2
Pelly Bay, Nun, Can. 166/H2
Pelly Crossing, Yk, Can. 166/C2
Peloponnesus (reg.), Gre. 93/J3
Peloritani (mts.), It. 74/D4
Pelotas (riv.), Braz. 213/G3
Pelotas, Braz. 213/F4
Pelplin, Pol. 67/H5
Pelsor, Ar, US 179/H3
Pelto (lake), La, US 190/C3
Pélussin, Fr. 90/A2
Pelvoux (peak), Fr. 90/C3
Pelvoux, Fr. 90/C3
Pemalang, Indo. 115/E3
Pemali (cape), Indo. 117/F4
Pematangsiantar, Indo. 115/B2
Pemba, Moz. 149/J2
Pemba (prov.), Tanz. 145/B3
Pemba (isl.), Tanz. 145/B3
Pemba, Zam. 149/E3
Pemba (isl.), Afr. 133/G5
Pemberton, Austl. 156/C5
Pemberton, BC, Can. 170/C2
Pemberton, NJ, US 194/D4
Pembina, ND, US 182/F3
Pembina (hills), Mb, Can. 182/E3
Pembina (riv.), Can.,US 182/E3
Pembina Historical Site, ND, US 182/F3
Pembine, Wi, US 183/L5
Pembroke, Wal, UK 62/B3
Pembroke, Fl, US 190/M8
Pembroke, Ga, US 189/G4
Pembroke, Ky, US 188/D2
Pembroke, Ma, US 187/L3
Pembroke, NC, US 189/H3
Pembroke, NH, US 187/L3
Pembroke, On, Can. 187/H2
Pembroke, Va, US 189/G2
Pembroke Dock, Wal, UK 62/B3
Pembroke Pines, Fl, US 190/P11
Pembrokeshire Coast NP, Wal, UK 62/A3
Pembury, Eng, UK 63/G4
Pemebonwon (dam), Mi, US 183/L5
Pemenee (falls), Wi, US 183/L5
Pemuco, Chile 214/B3
Pen Argyl, Pa, US 194/C2
Pen y Gurnos (peak), Wal, UK 62/C2
Pen-y-Cae, Wal, UK 61/E6
Pen-y-Ghent (peak), Eng, UK 61/F3
Pen-y-Gogarth (pt.), Wal, UK 60/E5
Peña Blanca (mtn.), Pan. 201/F4
Peña de Cerredo (mtn.), Sp. 72/C1
Pena Forte, Braz. 207/G4
Penafiel, Port. 72/A2
Peñafiel, Sp. 72/C2
Peñaflor, Chile 214/N8
Peñalara (peak), Sp. 92/C2
Penalva, Braz. 207/E3
Penamacor, Port. 72/B2
Penambulai (isl.), Indo. 155/D1
Penampang, Malay. 114/B4
Penang (int'l arpt.), Malay. 115/C1
Penápolis, Braz. 213/G2
Peñaranda de Bracamonte, Sp. 72/C2
Peñarroya (peak), Sp. 73/E2
Peñarroya-Pueblonuevo, Sp. 72/C3
Penarth, Wal, UK 62/C4
Penas (gulf), Arg. 214/B5
Peñas (cape), Arg. 215/D7
Peñas, Bol. 208/D5
Peñas (cape), Sp. 72/C1
Peñasco (riv.), NM, US 177/B1
Pencahue, Chile 214/C2
Pench (riv.), India 122/B5
Penchard, Fr. 56/L5
Penco, Chile 214/B3
Peñd (res.), Col. 207/K6
Pend Oreille (mt.), Id, US 170/F3
Pend Oreille (lake), Id, US 170/F3
Pend Orielle (riv.), Wa, US 170/F3
Pendé (riv.), CAfr. 142/C4
Pendelikón (peak), Gre. 75/N8
Pendembu, SLeo. 140/C4
Pendências, Braz. 207/G4
Pender, Ne, US 181/F2
Pender (bay), Austl. 154/A4
Pender Bay Abor. Land, Austl. 154/A4
Pendik (nbrhd.), Turk. 129/N7
Pendjar (riv.), Burk. 141/F4
Pendjari, PN de la, Ben. 141/F4
Pendle (hill), Eng, UK 61/F4
Pendleton, In, US 186/D5
Pendleton, Or, US 172/D1
Pendleton Mil. Res., Va, US 189/K2
Pendolo, Indo. 117/F4
Pendopo, Indo. 115/C3
Pendroy, Mt, US 171/H3
Pene-Mende, D.R. Congo 147/G4
Peneda-Gerês, PN, Port. 72/A2
Penedo, Braz. 211/F1
Penegoes, Wal, UK 62/C1
Penetanguishene, On, Can. 186/G2
Penfield, Pa, US 187/G4
Peng Xian, China 112/D2
Penganga (riv.), India 118/C4
Penge (nbrhd.), Eng, UK 56/C2
Penge, SAfr. 149/F5
Penge, D.R. Congo 147/F4
Penggong, China 106/K9
Penghu (isls.), Tai. 113/H4
Penghu, China 113/H3
Penghu (Pescadores) (isls.), China 113/H4
Penglai, China 106/E3
Penglaizhen, China 112/E2
Penguin, Austl. 158/C4
Penha, Braz. 213/G3
Penhalonga, Zim. 149/G3
Penhir (pt.), Fr. 82/A4
Penhold, Ab, Can. 171/H1
Penibético (mts.), Sp. 72/D4
Penice (peak), It. 88/C4
Peniche, Port. 72/A3
Penicuik, Sc, UK 59/C5
Peninsula (pt.), NY, US 187/H3
Península de Paria, PN, Ven. 205/F2
Peñíscola, Sp. 73/F2
Peñita, Chile 212/B4
Penitente, Serra do (mts.), Braz. 207/E5
Penkridge, Eng, UK 62/D1
Penmaenmawr, Wal, UK 60/E5
Penmarc'h (pt.), Fr. 82/A5
Penmarch, Fr. 82/A5
Penn, ND, US 182/E3
Penn Forest (res.), Pa, US 194/C2
Penn Hills, Pa, US 187/G4
Penn Yan, NY, US 187/H3
Penna (peak), It. 91/B1
Penna, Punta della (cape), It. 92/D3
Pennant (pt.), NS, Can. 184/F3
Pennant, Sk, Can. 171/K2
Pennask (mt.), BC, Can. 170/D3
Penne (pt.), It. 75/E2
Penne, It. 92/C3
Pennell (mt.), Ut, US 175/G2
Penner (riv.), India 118/C5
Penney Farms, Fl, US 191/H3
Penniac, NB, Can. 184/D2
Pennine Alps (mts.), Swi. 71/G4
Pennine Chain (mts.), Eng, UK 61/F2
Pennington, NJ, US 194/D3
Pennington Gap, Va, US 189/F2
Pennino (peak), It. 91/B1
Penns (cr.), Pa, US 194/A2
Penns Creek (mtn.), Pa, US 194/A2
Penns Grove, NJ, US 194/C4
Penns Park, Pa, US 194/D3
Pennsauken, NJ, US 194/C4
Pennsboro, WV, US 186/F5
Pennsburg, Pa, US 194/C3
Pennsville, NJ, US 194/C4
Pennsylvania (hill), NY, US 187/H3
Pennsylvania (state), US 169/L3
Penny (str.), Nun, Can. 167/S7
Pennypack (cr.), Pa, US 194/C3
Penobscot (bay), Me, US 184/C3
Penobscot (riv.), Me, US 184/C3
Peñol, Col. 207/K6
Penola, Austl. 158/B3
Peñón Blanco, Mex. 198/D3
Penon de Al Hoceima (isl.), Sp. 138/C2
Penong, Austl. 157/G4
Penonomé, Pan. 204/A2
Penpont, Sc, UK 60/E1
Penrhyn (Tongareva) (isl.), CookIs. 163/J5
Penrhyn Mawr (pt.), IM, UK 60/D5
Penrhyn Mawr (pt.), Wal, UK 60/D6
Penrith, Eng, UK 61/F2
Penrith (nbrhd.), Austl. 160/G8
Penrose, Co, US 178/B1
Penryn, Eng, UK 62/A6
Pensacola (mts.), Ant. 216/X
Pensacola, Fl, US 190/E2
Pensacola (bay), Fl, US 190/E2
Pensacola (dam), Ok, US 179/G2
Pense, Sk, Can. 182/B2
Penshurst, Eng, UK 56/D3
Penshurst, Austl. 158/B3
Pensiangan, Malay. 114/B4
Pensilva, Eng, UK 62/B5
Pensilvania, Col. 207/K7
Pentagon Fed. Govt. Res., Va, US 194/A6
Pentecost (isl.), Van. 162/F6
Pentecoste, Braz. 207/G3
Penteleu (peak), Rom. 77/H3
Penthalaz, Swi. 86/C4
Penticton, BC, Can. 170/E3
Penticton Ind. Res., BC, Can. 170/E3
Pentire (pt.), Eng, UK 62/B5
Pentland (hills), Sc, UK 59/C5
Pentland, Austl. 160/B3
Pentland Firth (inlet), Sc, UK 57/V14
Pentwater, Mi, US 186/C3
Pentyrch, Wal, UK 62/C3
Peñuelas, PN, Chile 214/N8
Penvénan, Fr. 82/B3
Pènwègon, Myan. 120/B2
Penwell, Tx, US 177/C2
Penwith (pen.), Eng, UK 62/A6
Penza, Rus. 97/H1
Penza Oblast, Rus. 97/G1
Penzance, Eng, UK 62/A6
Penzance, Sk, Can. 171/M2
Penzberg, Ger. 87/H2
Penzé (riv.), Fr. 82/B3
Penzhina (riv.), Rus. 101/S3
Penzhina (bay), Rus. 101/S3
Penzing, Ger. 87/G1
Penzlin, Ger. 68/G2
Peoria, Az, US 175/F4
Peoria, Il, US 181/K3
Pepe (cape), Cuba 201/F1
Pepel, SLeo. 140/B4
Pepin (lake), Mn,Wi, US 181/H1
Pepinster, Belg. 81/E2
Peqin, Alb. 75/F2
Pequaming, Mi, US 183/K4
Pequannock, NJ, US 195/H8
Pequea (cr.), Pa, US 194/B4
Pequeña Isla del Maíz (isl.), Nic. 201/F3
Pequest (riv.), NJ, US 194/D2
Pequot Lakes, Mn, US 183/G4
Perabumulih, Indo. 115/D3
Perai-Tepuí, Ven. 205/F3
Perak (riv.), Malay. 115/C1
Perak (state), Malay. 115/C1
Perales (riv.), Sp. 73/M9
Peralta, Sp. 72/E1
Peralta, Uru. 215/K10
Peralta, NM, US 175/J3
Pérama, Gre. 75/J5
Pérama, Gre. 75/N9
Peranāmbattu, India 121/C3
Percé, Qu, Can. 184/E1
Percée (peak), Fr. 86/C6
Percha (dam), NM, US 175/J4
Perche, Collines du (hills), Fr. 70/D2
Perchtoldsdorf, Aus. 77/N7
Percilla, Tx, US 177/G2
Percival, Sk, Can. 182/C2
Percival (lakes), Austl. 156/E2
Percy, Fr. 83/D3
Percy, Il, US 188/C1
Percy (isls.), Austl. 153/E3
Percy Isles (chan.), Austl. 160/C3
Perdekop, SAfr. 151/E2
Pérdhika, Gre. 75/G3
Perdido, Al, US 190/E2
Perdido (mtn.), Sp. 70/D5
Perdões, Braz. 210/D4
Perdue, Sk, Can. 171/L1
Perechyn, Ukr. 69/M4
Peregian Beach, Austl. 160/D4
Perehins'ke, Ukr. 98/C3
Pereira, Col. 207/K8
Pereira Barreto, Braz. 213/G2
Pereiro, Braz. 207/G4
Perelló, Sp. 73/F2
Peremëtnoye, Kaz. 97/J2
Peremyshl', Rus. 94/H5
Peremyshlyany, Ukr. 98/C3
Perenjori, Austl. 156/C4
Peresechnaya, Ukr. 99/H2
Pereshchepyne, Ukr. 99/H3
Pereslavl'-Zalesskiy, Rus. 94/H4
Peretola (int'l arpt.), It. 89/E6
Perevolotskiy, Rus. 97/K2
Pereyaslav-Khmel'nyts'kyy, Ukr. 98/F2
Pereyaslavka, Rus. 105/M2
Perg, Aus. 85/H6
Pergamino, Arg. 214/E2
Pergamum (ruin), Turk. 96/C5
Pergine Valsugana, It. 87/H5
Perham, Mn, US 183/G4
Peri-Mirim, Braz. 207/E3
Periam, Rom. 76/E2
Péribonca (riv.), Qu, Can. 184/B1
Perico, Cuba 201/F1
Perico, Arg. 212/C3
Pericos, Mex. 198/D3
Pericos, Mex. 198/D4
Peridot, Az, US 175/G4
Périers, Fr. 82/D2
Périgueux, Fr. 70/D4
Perijá (mts.), Ven. 201/H4
Peringat, Malay. 115/C1
Perisher Village, Austl. 159/D3
Peristéra (isl.), Gre. 75/H3
Peristéri, Gre. 75/N8
Perito Moreno, Arg. 214/C5
Perito Moreno, PN, Arg. 215/B5
Periyakulam, India 121/C4
Perkasie, Pa, US 194/C3
Perkins, Ok, US 179/F3
Perkins, Mi, US 186/C2
Perkins, Ga, US 189/G4
Perkinston, Ms, US 190/D2
Perkiomen (cr.), Pa, US 194/C3
Perl, Ger. 81/F5
Perlas (lag.), Nic. 196/E5
Perlas, (pt.), Nic. 201/F3
Perleberg, Ger. 68/F2
Perlez, Yugo. 76/E3
Perlis (state), Malay. 120/B5
Perm' (oblast), Rus. 95/N4
Perm', Rus. 95/N4
Përmet, Alb. 75/G2
Permian Basin Petroleum Museum, Tx, US 177/C2
Permyakia (aut. okrug), Rus. 95/M3
Pernambuco (state), Braz. 207/G5
Pernate, It. 88/B3
Pernell, Ok, US 179/F3
Pernes-les-Fontaines, Fr. 90/B4
Pernik, Bul. 76/F4
Perniö, Fin. 67/K1
Peron (pen.), Austl. 156/B3
Peron, North (isl.), Austl. 154/C3
Péronne, Fr. 80/B4
Perosa Argentina, It. 90/D3
Perote, Al, US 191/F2
Perote, Mex. 199/M7
Pérouges, Fr. 86/B6
Perovo (nbrhd.), Rus. 94/W9
Perranporth, Eng, UK 62/A6
Perray (riv.), Fr. 56/H6
Perriers-sur-Andelle, Fr. 83/G2
Perrigny, Fr. 86/B4
Perrin, Tx, US 179/E4
Perrine, Fl, US 190/P11
Perris (res.), Ca, US 192/C3
Perris, Ca, US 192/C3
Perris St. Rec. Area, Ca, US 192/C3
Perro (lag.), NM, US 178/B3
Perron des Encombres (peak), Fr. 90/C2
Perros-Guirec, Fr. 82/B3
Perry (riv.), Nun, Can. 166/F2
Perry, Fl, US 191/G2
Perry (lake), Ks, US 181/G4
Perry, Ga, US 188/F4
Perry, Ia, US 181/G3
Perry, Mo, US 181/J4
Perry, Ok, US 179/F2
Perry (co.), Pa, US 194/A3
Perry Hall, Md, US 194/B5
Perryman, Md, US 194/B5
Perrysburg, Oh, US 186/E4
Perryton, Tx, US 178/D2
Perrytown, Ar, US 179/H4
Perryville, Ar, US 179/H3
Perryville, Ky, US 188/E2
Perryville, Tn, US 188/C3
Perryville, Mo, US 188/C2
Perryville, Md, US 194/B4
Persan, Fr. 56/J4
Persepolis (ruin), Iran 129/H4
Perseverancia, Bol. 209/F4
Pershagen, Swe. 65/A1
Pershore, Eng, UK 62/D2
Pershotravens'k, Ukr. 98/D2
Pershotravnevoye, Ukr. 99/J4
Pershotravnevoye, Ukr. 98/D2
Persian (gulf), Asia 103/D7
Perstorp, Swe. 66/E3
Pertandangan (cape), Indo. 115/C2
Perth, Austl. 158/C4
Perth, Austl. 156/K6
Perth (int'l arpt.), Austl. 156/K6
Perth, On, Can. 187/H2
Perth, Sc, UK 59/C4
Perth Amboy, NJ, US 195/H9
Perth Zoo, Austl. 156/K6
Perth-Andover, NB, Can. 184/D2
Perthville, Austl. 159/D1
Pertokar, Erit. 142/H1
Pertuis, Fr. 90/B5
Pertuis Breton (inlet), Fr. 70/C3
Pertusato (cape), Fr. 74/A2
Peru(ctry.) 203/B3
Peru, Ks, US 179/F2
Peru, In, US 186/C4
Peru, Ne, US 181/G3
Peru, Il, US 181/K3
Perućačko (lake), Bosn. 76/D4
Perugia, It. 91/B1
Perugia (prov.), It. 91/B1
Peruíbe, Braz. 211/K9
Perushtitsa, Bul. 75/J1
Péruwelz, Belg. 80/C2
Pervari, Turk. 128/E2
Pervomaysk, Rus. 95/J5
Pervomays'k, Ukr. 98/F3
Pervomays'ke, Ukr. 99/G5
Pervomayskiy, Rus. 97/G1
Pervomayskiy, Rus. 97/J2
Pervomayskiy, Rus. 104/H1
Pervomayskoye, Rus. 97/H2
Pervomayskoye, Rus. 99/L3
Pervomays'kyy, Ukr. 99/J3
Pervoural'sk, Rus. 95/N4
Perwez, Belg. 81/D2
Péry, Swi. 86/D3
Pesa (riv.), It. 89/E5
Pesagi (peak), Indo. 115/D3

285

Pesaro – Plano

Pesaro, It. 89/F6
Pesaro E Urbino (prov.), It. 89/F5
Pescadero (pt.), Ca, US 174/A2
Pescadero, Ca, US 174/A2
Pescadore (chan.), Tai. 113/H4
Pescadores (Penghu) (isls.), China 113/H4
Pescantina, It. 89/D3
Pescara (riv.), It. 92/D3
Pescara (prov.), It. 92/C3
Pescara, It. 92/D3
Pescasseroli, It. 92/C4
Peschanokopskoye, Rus. 99/L4
Peschanyy (cape), Kaz. 97/J4
Peschici, It. 74/E2
Pescia, It. 89/D6
Pescina, It. 92/C3
Pescocostanzo, It. 92/D4
Peseux, Swi. 86/C4
Pesha (riv.), Rus. 95/L2
Peshawar (int'l arpt.), Pak. 124/A2
Peshāwar, Pak. 124/A2
Peshkopi, Alb. 75/G2
Peshtera, Bul. 75/J1
Peshtigo (riv.), Wi, US 183/L5
Peshtigo, Wi, US 186/C2
Peski, Rus. 94/H5
Peskovka, Rus. 95/M4
Pesmes, Fr. 86/B3
Peso da Régua, Port. 72/B2
Pesochnyy, Rus. 94/S6
Pesqueira, Braz. 207/G5
Pesquería (riv.), Mex. 177/D5
Pessac, Fr. 70/C4
Pest (co.), Hun. 69/K5
Pest (prov.), Hun. 76/D2
Pestovkoye (lake), Rus. 94/W9
Pestovo, Rus. 94/G4
Petacciato, It. 92/D4
Petah Tiqwa, Isr. 131/B4
Petal, Ms, US 190/D2
Petalión (gulf), Gre. 93/K3
Petaluma (riv.), Ca, US 193/J10
Petaluma, Ca, US 172/B4
Pétange, Lux. 81/E4
Petārbār, India 123/E4
Petare, Ven. 207/P7
Pétas, Gre. 75/G3
Petatlán, Mex. 199/E5
Petatlán (riv.), Mex. 198/D3
Petauke, Zam. 149/F2
Petawawa, On, Can. 187/H2
Petawawa (riv.), On, Can. 187/G2
Peten Itzá (lake), Guat. 200/D2
Petenwell (dam), Wi, US 181/J1
Peter (isl.), Nor. 216/U
Peter (pond), Sk, Can. 166/F3
Peterborough, On, Can. 187/G2
Peterborough, Austl. 157/H5
Peterborough, Eng, UK 63/F1
Peterculter, Sc, UK 59/D2
Peterhead, Sc, UK 59/E1
Peterlee, Eng, UK 61/G2
Peterman, Al, US 190/E2
Petermann Aboriginal Land, Austl. 157/F3
Peteroa (vol.), Chile 214/C2
Petersaurach, Ger. 84/D4
Petersberg, Ger. 84/C1
Petersburg, Ak, US 168/Z13
Petersburg, Tx, US 178/D4
Petersburg, In, US 188/D1
Petersburg, Il, US 181/K3
Petersburg, ND, US 182/E3
Petersburg, Va, US 189/J2
Petersburg, WV, US 189/H1
Petersburg Nat'l Bfld., Va, US 189/J2
Petersfield, Mb, Can. 182/F2
Petersfield, Eng, UK 63/F4
Petershagen, Ger. 79/F4
Petershagen, Ger. 68/Q6
Petershausen, Ger. 85/E6
Peterson (A.F.B.), Co, US 178/B1
Pétervására, Hun. 69/L4
Peterview, Nf, Can. 185/K1
Petilia Policastro, It. 74/E3
Pétionville, Haiti 201/H2
Petit Buëch (riv.), Fr. 90/B4
Petit Goâve, Haiti 201/H2
Petit Loango, PN du, Gabon 146/B3
Petit Mont Blanc (peak), Fr. 90/C2
Petit Rosne (riv.), Fr. 56/J4
Petit-Cap, Qu, Can. 184/E1
Petit-Couronne, Fr. 83/G2
Petit-de-Grat, NS, Can. 185/G3
Petit-Matane, Qu, Can. 184/D1
Petit-Noir, Fr. 86/B4
Petit-Saguenay, Qu, Can. 184/B1
Petitcodiac, NB, Can. 184/E3
Petite Miquelon (isl.), Nf, Can. 185/J2
Petite Nation (riv.), Qu, Can. 187/J1
Petite Rivière de l'Artibonite, Haiti 201/H2
Petite Rivière Noire (peak), Mrts. 151/T15
Petite-Rosselle, Fr. 81/F5
Petkeljärven NP, Fin. 94/F3
Petlād, India 127/K4
Petlalcingo, Mex. 200/B2
Peto, Mex. 200/D1
Petorca, Chile 214/C2
Petoskey, Mi, US 186/D2
Petra (isls.), Rus. 101/M2
Petre (pt.), On, Can. 187/H3
Petrel, Sp. 73/E3
Petrella (peak), It. 92/C5
Petrella Tifernina, It. 92/D4
Petretsovo, Rus. 95/N3
Petrey, Al, US 191/E2
Petrich, Bul. 75/H2
Petrified Forest NP, Az, US 175/H3
Petrikov, Bela. 96/D1
Petrila, Rom. 77/F3
Petritoli, It. 92/C1
Petrivka, Ukr. 98/F4
Petrodvorets, Rus. 94/S7
Petrograd (nbrhd.), Rus. 94/T7
Petrokhanski Prokhod (pass), Bul. 77/F4
Petrokrepost' (bay), Rus. 94/U7
Petrokrepost', Rus. 94/T7
Petrolândia, Braz. 207/G5
Petrolia, Tx, US 179/E3
Petrolia, On, Can. 186/E3
Petrolina, Braz. 207/F5
Petropavl, Kaz. 100/G4
Petropavlivka, Ukr. 99/J3
Petropavlovsk-Kamchatskiy, Rus. 101/R4
Petropavlovskoye, Rus. 97/H3
Petrópolis, Braz. 211/N7
Petros, Tn, US 188/E2
Petroșani, Rom. 77/F3
Petroso (peak), It. 92/C4
Petrovaradin, Yugo 76/D3
Petrovsk, Rus. 97/H1
Petrovsk-Zabaykal'skiy, Rus. 104/F1
Petrovskaya, Rus. 99/J5
Petrovs'ke, Ukr. 99/K3
Petrovskiy Yam, Rus. 94/G3
Petrovskoye, Rus. 97/L1
Petrozavodsk, Rus. 94/G3
Petrus Steyn, SAfr. 150/E2
Petrusburg, SAfr. 150/D3
Petrusville, SAfr. 150/D3
Petrykivka, Ukr. 99/H3
Pettenbach, Aus. 85/H7
Petteril (riv.), Eng, UK 61/F2
Pettibone, ND, US 182/E4
Pettigrew, Ar, US 179/H3
Pettus, Tx, US 176/F3
Petushki, Rus. 94/H5
Petworth, Eng, UK 63/F5
Petzeck (peak), Aus. 71/K3
Peuerbach, Aus. 85/G6
Peumo, Chile 214/N9
Peureulak, Indo. 115/B1
Pevek, Rus. 101/T3
Pevely, Mo, US 188/B1
Pevensey, Eng, UK 63/G5
Pewaukee, Wi, US 193/P13
Pewaukee (lake), Wi, US 193/X13
Pewsey, Eng, UK 63/E4
Peyia, Cyp. 130/C2
Peyk, Iran 129/G3
Peymeinade, Fr. 90/C5
Peyrehorade, Fr. 70/C5
Peyrins, Fr. 90/B2
Peyrolles-en-Provence, Fr. 90/B5
Peyruis, Fr. 90/B4
Peza (riv.), Rus. 95/K2
Pézenas, Fr. 70/E5
Pezu, Pak. 124/A3
Pfaffenhausen, Ger. 87/G1
Pfaffenhofen an der Ilm, Ger. 84/D6
Pfaffenhofen an der Ilm, Ger. 85/E5
Pfaffenhoffen, Fr. 81/G6
Pfäffikon, Swi. 87/E3
Pfaffing, Ger. 85/F6
Pfaffnau, Swi. 86/D3
Pfahl (ridge), Ger. 85/F4
Pfälzer Wald (mts.), Ger. 81/G5
Pfälzerwald (mts.), Ger. 84/A4
Pfalzgrafenweiler, Ger. 84/B5
Pfarrhof Esternberg, Aus. 85/G5
Pfarrkirchen, Ger. 85/F6
Pfatter, Ger. 85/F5
Pfeffenhausen, Ger. 85/E5
Pfettrach (riv.), Ger. 85/E5
Pfieffe (riv.), Ger. 79/G6
Pfinztal, Ger. 84/B5
Pflugerville, Tx, US 177/F2
Pforzheim, Ger. 84/B5
Pfreimd (riv.), Ger. 85/F3
Pfreimd, Ger. 85/F3
Pfronstetten, Ger. 87/F1
Pfronten, Ger. 87/G2
Pfroslkopf (peak), Aus. 87/G4
Pfullendorf, Ger. 87/F2
Pfunds, Aus. 87/G4
Pfungstadt, Ger. 84/B3
Phagwāra, India 124/C4
Phalaborwa, SAfr. 149/F4
Phalauda, India 124/D5
Phalempin, Fr. 80/C2
Phālia, Pak. 124/B3
Phalodi, India 127/K3
Phalombe, Malw. 149/G2
Phalsbourg, Fr. 81/G6
Phaltan, India 121/B2
Phan, Thai. 120/B2
Phan Rang Viet. 120/E4
Phan Thiet, Viet. 120/E4
Phanat Nikhom, Thai. 120/C3
Phang Hoei (range), Thai. 120/C3
Phangan (isl.), Thai. 119/H6
Phangnga, Thai. 120/B4
Phanom, Thai. 120/B4
Phanom Dongrak (mts.), Thai. 119/H5
Phāphlu, Nepal 123/F2
Pharr, Tx, US 177/E4
Phat Diem, Viet. 113/E4
Phatthalung, Thai. 120/C5
Phaya Fo (peak), Thai. 120/C2
Phayao, Thai. 120/B2
Pheasant (hills), Sk, Can. 182/C2
Phelan, Ca, US 192/C2
Phelps, Wi, US 183/K4
Phelps (lake), NC, US 189/J3
Phenix City, Al, US 188/E4
Phepane (riv.), SAfr. 148/D5
Phet Buri, Thai. 120/B3
Phetchabun, Thai. 120/C2
Phiafai, Laos 120/D3
Phibun Mangsahan, Thai. 120/D3
Phichai, Thai. 120/C2
Phichit, Thai. 120/C2
Phidim, Nepal 123/F2
Phil Campbell, Al, US 188/D3
Philadelphia, NY, US 187/J2
Philadelphia, Ms, US 188/C4
Philadelphia (int'l arpt.), Pa, US 194/C4
Philadelphia, Pa, US 194/C4
Philip, SD, US 180/D1
Philip S.W. Goldson (int'l arpt.), Belz. 200/D2
Philipp, Ms, US 188/B4
Philippeville, Belg. 81/D3
Philippi, WV, US 189/G1
Philippine (sea), Asia 103/M8
Philippines(ctry.) 103/M8
Philippsburg, Ger. 84/B4
Philipsburg, Pa, US 187/G4
Philipsburg, Neth. 197/J4
Philipsburg, Mt, US 171/H4
Philipsdam (dam), Neth. 78/B5
Philipstown, Ire. 58/C3
Philipstown, SAfr. 150/D3
Phillaur, India 124/C4
Phillip (isl.), Austl. 159/B4
Phillips, Wi, US 183/J5
Phillips, Me, US 187/L2
Phillips Arm, BC, Can. 170/B2
Phillipsburg, Mo, US 179/H2
Phillipsburg, Ga, US 191/G2
Phillipsburg, Ks, US 180/E4
Phillipsburg, NJ, US 194/C2
Philo, Ca, US 172/B4
Philomath, Or, US 172/B1
Philoteris (ruin), Egypt 139/B6
Philpot, Ky, US 188/D2
Phimai, Thai. 120/C3
Phimai (ruin), Thai. 120/C3
Phipps (mtn.), Austl. 159/C3
Phitsanulok, Thai. 120/C2
Phnom Penh (Phnum Pénh) (cap.), Camb. 120/D4
Phnum Penh (int'l arpt.), Camb. 120/D4
Phnum Pénh (Phnom Penh) (cap.), Camb. 120/D4
Phnum Tbeng Meanchey, Camb. 120/D3
Pho (pt.), Thai. 120/C5
Phoenix (isls.), Kiri. 163/H5
Phoenix, Or, US 172/B2
Phoenix (cap.), Az, US 175/F4
Phoenix (mtn.), NC, US 189/G2
Phoenix (Rawaki) (isl.), Kiri. 163/H5
Phoenix Park, Ire. 60/B5
Phoenix Sky Harbor (int'l arpt.), Az, US 175/F4
Phoenixville, Pa, US 194/C3
Phon, Thai. 120/C3
Phon Phisai, Thai. 120/C2
Phon Thong, Thai. 120/C2
Phongsali, Laos 112/D4
Phou Bia (peak), Laos 120/C2
Phou Huatt (peak), Viet. 112/E5
Phou Khoun, Laos 120/C2
Phou Loi (peak), Laos 112/D4
Phou Xai Lai Leng (peak), Laos 120/D2
Phra Nakhon Si Ayutthaya, Thai. 120/C3
Phra Phutthabat, Thai. 120/C3
Phra Thong (isl.), Thai. 120/B4
Phrae, Thai. 120/C2
Phsar Ream, Camb. 120/C4
Phu Hin Rong Kla NP, Thai. 120/C2
Phu Hoi, Viet. 120/E4
Phu Kradung, Thai. 120/C2
Phu Kradung NP, Thai. 120/C2
Phu Loc, Viet. 120/D2
Phu Luong, Viet. 120/D1
Phu Luong (peak), Viet. 112/E4
Phu Ly, Viet. 120/D1
Phu My, Viet. 120/E3
Phu Nhon, Viet. 120/E3
Phu Phan NP, Thai. 120/D2
Phu Quoc (isl.), Camb. 119/H5
Phu Quoc (isl.), Viet. 120/C4
Phu Quoc, Viet. 120/C4
Phu Rieng Sron, Viet. 120/D4
Phu Rua NP, Thai. 120/C2
Phu Tho, Viet. 112/E4
Phu Vang, Viet. 120/D2
Phuc Loi, Viet. 120/D2
Phuc Yen, Viet. 112/E4
Phuket (isl.), Thai. 119/G6
Phuket, Thai. 120/B5
Phulabāni, India 121/E1
Phularwan, Pak. 124/B3
Phulbāri, Bang. 123/G3
Phulbāri, India 123/H3
Phuldungsei, India 112/B4
Phūlpur, India 122/D3
Phultala, Bang. 123/G4
Phumi Banam, Camb. 120/D4
Phumi Chhlong, Camb. 120/D3
Phumi Choan, Camb. 120/C4
Phumi Chuuk, Camb. 120/D4
Phumi Kampong Putrea Chas, Camb. 120/D3
Phumi Kampong Trabek, Camb. 120/D3
Phumi Kouk Kduoch, Camb. 120/C3
Phumi Krek, Camb. 120/D4
Phumi Labang Siek, Camb. 120/D3
Phumi Mlu Prey, Camb. 120/D3
Phumi O Pou, Camb. 120/D3
Phumi Phang, Camb. 120/C3
Phumi Phsa Romeas, Camb. 120/D3
Phumi Phsar, Camb. 120/D3
Phumi Prek Kak, Camb. 120/D3
Phumi Prek Preah, Camb. 120/D3
Phumi Samraong, Camb. 120/C3
Phumi Spoe Tbong, Camb. 120/D3
Phumi Sre Ta Chan, Camb. 120/D3
Phumi Ta Krei, Camb. 120/C3
Phumi Thma Pok, Camb. 120/C3
Phumi Toek Sok, Camb. 120/C3
Phumi Veal Renh, Camb. 120/C4
Phuntsholing, Bhu. 123/G2
Phutthaisong, Thai. 120/C3
Pi (riv.), China 104/H5
Pi Xian, China 112/D2
Pia, D.R. Congo 147/F2
Piaçabuçu, Braz. 211/F1
Piacenza, It. 88/C3
Piacenza (prov.), It. 88/C3
Piacoa, Ven. 205/F2
Piadena, It. 88/D3
Piaggine, It. 74/D2
Pian di Serra (peak), It. 89/F7
Pian-Upe Game Rsv., Ugan. 145/A1
Piancastagnaio, It. 74/B1
Pianella, It. 92/D3
Pianello val Tidone, It. 88/C4
Pianezza, It. 88/A2
Piangipane, It. 89/F5
Pianling, China 107/B2
Piano di Sorrento, It. 92/D6
Pianoro, It. 89/E5
Pianosa (isl.), It. 74/A1
Piaoli, China 113/F3
Piapot Ind. Res., Sk, Can. 182/B2
Piarco (int'l arpt.), Trin. 205/F2
Piasco, It. 90/D3
Piaseczno, Pol. 69/L2
Piatra Neamț, Rom. 98/D4
Piauí (riv.), Braz. 207/F5
Piauí (state), Braz. 207/F4
Piave (riv.), It. 71/K3
Piazza, It. 88/D2
Piazza, It. 88/D2
Piazza al Serchio, It. 88/D5
Piazza Armerina, It. 74/D4
Piazza Brembana, It. 87/F6
Piazzola sul Brenta, It. 89/E2
Pibor (riv.), Sudan 142/G4
Pibor Post, Sudan 142/G4
Pic (isl.), On, Can. 183/L3
Pic (riv.), On, Can. 183/L3
Pica, Chile 212/B2
Picacho, Az, US 175/G4
Picacho del Centinela (peak), Mex. 177/C3
Picahos, Cerro Dos (peak), Mex. 198/B2
Picardie (pol. reg.), Fr. 70/E2
Picardy (reg.), Fr. 80/B4
Picatinny Arsenal, NJ, US 194/D2
Picauville, Fr. 82/D2
Picayune, Ms, US 190/D2
Piccaninny (cr.), Austl. 159/B3
Piccolo (lag.), It. 75/E2
Picentino (riv.), It. 92/D6
Pichacani, Peru 208/D5
Pichanal, Arg. 212/C2
Picher, Ok, US 179/G2
Pichidangui, Chile 214/C2
Pichidegua, Chile 214/N9
Pichilemu, Chile 214/B2
Pichincha (dept.), Ecu. 204/B4
Pichincha, Ecu. 204/B5
Pichkiryayevo, Rus. 97/G1
Pichl bei Wels, Aus. 85/G6
Pichor, India 122/B3
Pichucalco, Mex. 200/C2
Pickens, Ok, US 179/G3
Pickens, SC, US 189/F3
Pickens, Ms, US 188/C4
Pickering, Eng, UK 61/H3
Pickering, On, Can. 186/U8
Pickford, Mi, US 186/D1
Pickle Lake, On, Can. 183/J2
Pickton, Tx, US 179/G4
Pickwick (dam), Tn, US 188/C3
Pickwick (lake), Al,Ms, US 188/C3
Pickwick Dam, Tn, US 188/C3
Picnic Bay, Austl. 160/B2
Pico (isl.), Azor., Port. 73/S12
Pico da Neblina, PN do, Braz. 205/E4
Pico de Orizaba, PN, Mex. 199/M7
Pico de Salamanca, Arg 214/D5
Pico Rivera, Ca, US 192/F8
Pico Truncado, Arg. 214/D5
Picos, Braz. 207/F4
Picota, Peru 208/B2
Picsi, Peru 208/B2
Picton, On, Can. 187/H3
Picton, NZ 161/C3
Picton, Austl. 159/E2
Pictou (isl.), NS, Can. 185/F3
Pictou, NS, Can. 185/F3
Picture Butte, Ab, Can. 171/H3
Picture Gorge (gorge), Or, US 172/D1
Picture Rock (pass), Or, US 172/C2
Picture Rocks, Pa, US 194/B1
Pictured Rocks Nat'l Lakeshore, Mi, US 183/L4
Picuí, Braz. 207/G4
Picuris Ind. Res., NM, US 175/K2
Pidcoke, Tx, US 176/F2
Piddle (riv.), Eng, UK 62/D5
Pidhorodne, Ukr. 99/H3
Pidi, D.R. Congo 147/F4
Pidurutagala (peak), SrL. 121/D5
Pidvolochys'k, Ukr. 98/D3
Pie (isl.), On, Can. 183/K3
Pie Town, NM, US 175/H3
Piedade, Port. 73/P10
Piedade do Rio Grande, Braz. 211/M6
Piedecuesta, Col. 204/C3
Piediluco (lake), It. 91/B2
Piedimulera, It. 87/E5
Piedmont, Al, US 188/E4
Piedmont, Ca, US 193/K11
Piedmont, Mo, US 188/B2
Piedmont, Ok, US 179/F3
Piedmont, SD, US 180/C1
Piedmont, SC, US 189/F3
Piedmont (upland), SC, US 189/G3
Piedmont NWR, Ga, US 188/F4
Piedra, Ca, US 174/C2
Piedra Grande, Ven. 204/D2
Piedra Sola, Uru. 213/E5
Piedrabuena, Sp. 72/C3
Piedrahita, Sp. 72/C2
Piedras (pt.), Arg. 215/K11
Piedras, Col. 207/L8
Piedras Coloradas, Uru 215/K10
Piedras Negras, Mex. 199/N8
Piedras, Río de las (riv.), Peru 208/D3
Piedritas, Arg. 214/E2
Piekary Śląskie, Pol. 69/K3
Piekenierskloof (pass), SAfr. 150/L10
Pieksämäki, Fin. 94/E3
Pielinen (lake), Fin. 64/J3
Piemonte (pol.reg.), It. 71/G4
Pieniński NP, Pol. 69/L4
Piennes, Fr. 81/E5
Pieńsk, Pol. 69/H3
Piera, Sp. 73/K6
Pierce, Co, US 180/B3
Pierce (lake), Fl, US 190/M8
Pierce, Fl, US 190/M8
Pierce, Id, US 170/G4
Pierce, Ne, US 180/F2
Pierce (co.), Wi, US 183/Q7
Pierce City, Mo, US 179/G2
Pierceville, Ks, US 178/D2
Pieris, It. 89/G2
Piermont, NY, US 195/K7
Pierowall, Sc, UK 57/V14
Pierre (cap.), SD, US 180/D1
Pierre Menue (peak), It. 90/C2
Pierre Part, La, US 190/C3
Pierre Plate (peak), Fr. 90/D5
Pierre-de-Bresse, Fr. 86/B4
Pierre-Levée, Fr. 56/M5
Pierrefeu-du-Var, Fr. 90/C6
Pierrefitte-sur-Seine, Fr. 56/K5
Pierrefonds, Qu, Can. 185/N7
Pierrefontaine-les-Varans, Fr. 86/C3
Pierrelatte, Fr. 90/A4
Pierrelaye, Fr. 56/J4
Pierres, Fr. 83/G3
Pierrevert, Fr. 90/B5
Pierry, Fr. 80/C5
Pierson, Fl, US 191/H3
Piešťany, Slvk. 69/J4
Piesting (riv.), Aus. 77/P7
Piet Retief, SAfr. 151/E2
Pietarsaari (Jakobstad), Fin. 94/D3
Pieterlen, Swi. 86/D3
Pietermaritzburg, SAfr. 151/E3
Pietersburg, SAfr. 149/F4
Pietra Ligure, It. 88/B5
Pietracatella, It. 92/D4
Pietralunga, It. 89/F7
Pietramelara, It. 92/D5
Pietrasanta, It. 88/D6
Pietravairano, It. 92/D5
Pietravecchia (peak), It. 88/A5
Pietrosul (peak), Rom. 77/G2
Pieve del Cairo, It. 88/B3
Pieve di Cento, It. 89/E4
Pieve di Soligo, It. 89/F2
Pieve di Teco, It. 88/A4
Pieve Emanuele, It. 88/C3
Pieve Ligure, It. 88/C5
Pieve Porto Morone, It. 88/C3
Pieve Santo Stefano, It. 89/F6
Pieve Vergonte, It. 87/E5
Pievepelago, It. 88/D5
Pigum (isl.), SKor. 107/C5
Pigeon (riv.), Can.,US 183/J3
Pigeon, Mi, US 186/E3
Pigeon (riv.), On, Can. 166/G4
Pigeon (lake), Ab, Can. 171/H1
Pigeon House (mtn.), Austl. 159/E2
Piggott, Ar, US 188/B2
Piggs Peak, Swaz. 151/E2
Piglio, It. 92/C4
Pigna, It. 90/D5
Pignataro Maggiore, It. 92/D5
Pigs (bay), Cuba 196/E3
Pigu, Gha. 141/E4
Pigüé, Arg. 214/E3
Pihāni, India 122/C2
Pijáo, Col. 207/K3
Pijijiapan, Mex. 200/C3
Pijnacker, Neth. 78/B4
Pijol (peak), Hon. 200/E3
Pike (co.), Pa, US 194/C1
Pikelot (isl.), Micr. 162/D4
Pikes (peak), Co, US 178/B1
Pikes Creek (res.), Pa, US 194/B1
Pikesville, Md, US 194/B5
Piketberg, SAfr. 150/L10
Piketon, Oh, US 189/F1
Pikeville, Ky, US 189/F2
Pikeville, Tn, US 188/E3
Pikit, Phil. 114/D4
Pikou, China 107/B3
Piła, Pol. 69/J2
Pila, Arg. 215/J12
Pilane, Bots. 148/E5
Pilanesberg (range), SAfr. 150/P12
Pilani, India 124/C5
Pilão Arcado, Braz. 211/E1
Pilar, Arg. 214/E1
Pilar, Arg. 212/D4
Pilar, Braz. 211/G1
Pilar, Par. 212/E3
Pilar, Phil. 117/F1
Pilatus (peak), Swi. 87/E4
Pilaya (riv.), Bol. 212/C2
Pilchuck (riv.), Wa, US 193/D1
Pilcomayo (riv.), SAm. 203/C5
Pilgrims Hatch, Eng, UK 56/D2
Pili, Phil. 114/C2
Pīlībhīt, India 122/B1
Pilica (riv.), Pol. 96/B2
Pílion (peak), Gre. 75/H3
Pilis (mts.), Hun. 77/R9
Pilis (peak), Hun. 77/Q9
Pilis, Hun. 76/D2
Piliscsaba, Hun. 77/Q9
Pilisvörösvár, Hun. 77/Q9
Pilkhua, India 124/D5
Pillar (cape), Austl. 158/C4
Pillar (peak), Eng, UK 61/E3
Pillar (pt.), Ca, US 193/J12
Pillar (pt.), Wa, US 170/B3
Pilliga, Austl. 158/D1
Pillow, Pa, US 194/B2
Pilões, Serra dos (mtn.), Braz. 213/H1
Pilon du Roi (peak), Fr. 90/B6
Pílos, Gre. 75/G4
Pilot (peak), Id, US 170/G5
Pilot (peak), Nv, US 172/E4
Pilot (mtn.), Tn, US 188/E2
Pilot (peak), Tn, US 188/E2
Pilot Butte, Sk, Can. 182/B2
Pilot Grove, Mo, US 179/H1
Pilot Grove (cr.), Tx, US 176/L6
Pilot Knob, Mo, US 188/B2
Pilot Mound, Mb, Can. 182/E3
Pilot Mountain, NC, US 189/G2
Pilot Point, Tx, US 179/F4
Pilot Rock, Or, US 172/D1
Pilottown, La, US 190/D3
Pilsting, Ger. 85/F5
Piltene, Lat. 67/J3
Piltown, Ire. 58/C5
Pilyugino, Rus. 97/K1
Pima, Az, US 175/H4
Pimamga-Moke, D.R. Congo 146/D3
Pimenta Bueno, Braz. 209/F3
Pimpi, Indo. 117/F3
Pimpri-Chinchwad, India 121/B2
Piña (pt.), Pan. 201/G5
Pinacate, Cerro (peak), Mex. 175/F5
Pináculo (peak), Arg. 215/B6
Pinaleno (mts.), Az, US 175/G4
Pinamalayan, Phil. 114/C2
Pinamar, Arg. 215/F3
Pinang (isl.), Malay. 116/A2
Pinang (cape), Malay. 115/B1
Pinangah, Malay. 114/B4
Pinar del Río, Cuba 201/F1
Pınarbaşı, Turk. 128/D2
Pınarhisar, Turk. 77/H5
Piñas, Ecu. 208/B1
Pinatubo (mt.), Phil. 114/C2
Pinawa, Mb, Can. 182/G2
Pinchbeck, Eng, UK 61/H6
Pincher Creek, Ab, Can. 171/H3
Pinckney, Mi, US 186/E3
Pinckneyville, Il, US 188/C1
Pinconning, Mi, US 186/E3
Pîncota, Rom. 76/E2
Pincourt, Qu, Can. 185/N7
Pińczów, Pol. 69/L3
Pind Dādan Khān, Pak. 124/B3
Pinda, Ang. 146/C5
Pindall, Ar, US 179/H2
Pindamonhangaba, Braz. 211/L7
Pindaré (riv.), Braz. 207/E4
Pindaré-Mirim, Braz. 207/E3
Píndhos NP, Gre. 75/G3
Pindi Bhattiān, Pak. 124/B4
Pindi Gheb, Pak. 124/B3
Pindiu, PNG 155/G1
Pindobaçu, Braz. 211/E1
Pindobal, Braz. 206/D3
Pindus (mts.), Gre. 93/J2
Pindwāra, India 118/B3
Pine (cape), Nf, Can. 185/L2
Pine, Az, US 175/G3
Pine, Co, US 178/B1
Pine (isl.), Fl, US 191/G4
Pine (pt.), Fl, US 191/G3
Pine, Id, US 173/F2
Pine (riv.), Mi, US 186/D3
Pine (hills), Ms, US 190/C2
Pine (ridge), Ne, US 180/C2
Pine (cr.), Pa, US 194/A1
Pine, Tx, US 179/G4
Pine Apple, Al, US 190/E2
Pine Barrens (phys. reg.), NJ, US 194/D4
Pine Bluff, Ar, US 179/H3
Pine Bluff Arsenal, Ar, US 179/H3
Pine Bluffs, Wy, US 180/B3
Pine Bush, NY, US 187/J4
Pine Castle, Fl, US 190/N7
Pine City, Mn, US 183/H5
Pine Creek (lake), Ok, US 179/G3
Pine Creek, Austl. 154/C3
Pine Creek (pt.), Ct, US 195/E1
Pine Dock, Mb, Can. 182/F2
Pine Falls, Mb, Can. 182/F2
Pine Flat (res.), Ca, US 174/C2
Pine Grove, La, US 190/C2
Pine Grove, Pa, US 194/B2
Pine Hill, Al, US 190/E2
Pine Hill, NJ, US 194/D4
Pine Island, Fl, US 190/K6
Pine Island, Mn, US 181/H1
Pine Island Bay (flat), Ant. 216/S
Pine Island Nat'l Wild. Ref., Fl, US 191/G4
Pine Knot, Ky, US 188/E2
Pine Level, Al, US 191/E1
Pine Mills, Tx, US 177/G1
Pine Point, NW, Can. 166/E2
Pine Prairie, La, US 190/B2
Pine Ridge, SD, US 180/C2
Pine Ridge Ind. Res., SD, US 180/C2
Pine River, Mn, US 183/G4
Pine River, Mb, Can. 182/D2
Pine Springs, Tx, US 176/B2
Pine Stump Junction, Mi, US 186/D1
Pine Valley, Ut, US 175/F2
Pine Valley, Ca, US 174/D4
Pine, South Branch (riv.), Mi, US 193/G6
Pinebluff, NC, US 189/H3
Pinecliff (lake), NJ, US 195/H7
Pinecreek, Mn, US 182/G3
Pinedale, Wy, US 173/J2
Pinedale, Ca, US 174/C2
Pinedale, Az, US 175/G3
Pinega (riv.), Rus. 100/E3
Pinega, Rus. 94/J2
Pinehurst, Ga, US 188/F4
Pinehurst, Id, US 170/F4
Pinehurst, NC, US 189/H3
Pinehurst, Tx, US 177/G2
Pineland, Fl, US 191/G4
Pineland, SC, US 189/G4
Pineland, Tx, US 177/H2
Pinelands, SAfr. 150/L10
Pinellas (co.), Fl, US 190/K8
Pinellas (pt.), Fl, US 190/K8
Pinellas Park, Fl, US 190/K8
Pineola, Fl, US 190/L6
Piñera, Uru. 215/K10
Pinerolo, It. 90/D3
Pinesdale, Mt, US 171/G4
Pineto, It. 92/D2
Pinetop-Lakeside, Az, US 175/H3
Pinetops, NC, US 189/J3
Pinetown, SAfr. 151/E3
Pinetta, Fl, US 191/G2
Pineuilh, Fr. 70/D4
Pineview, Ga, US 191/G1
Pineville, Ky, US 188/F2
Pineville, La, US 190/B2
Pineville, Mo, US 179/G2
Pineville, SC, US 189/G4
Pineville, WV, US 189/G2
Piney, Ar, US 179/H3
Piney (isl.), Fl, US 191/F2
Piney Green, NC, US 189/J3
Piney Point, Fl, US 190/K8
Piney Point, Md, US 189/J1
Piney Point Village, Tx, US 177/M9
Piney River, Va, US 189/H2
Ping (riv.), Thai. 119/G4
Ping (riv.), Myan. 120/B2
Ping Chau (isl.), China 113/M6
Pingbian Miaozu Zizhixian, China 112/D4
Pingchang, China 113/E2
Pingchao, China 113/J1
Pingding, China 106/C3
Pingdingshan, China 106/C4
Pingdu, China 106/D3
Pingelap (isl.), Micr. 162/F4
Pingelly, Austl. 156/C5
Ping'erguan, China 120/D1
Pingfa, China 113/E3
Pinggu, China 106/H6
Pingguo, China 119/J3
Pinghai, China 113/H3
Pinghai, China 113/G4
Pinghu, China 106/L9
Pingjing (pass), China 106/C5
Pingjinpu, China 113/E2
Pingle, China 113/F3
Pinglu, China 106/C3
Pinglu, China 106/B4
Pingquan, China 106/D2
Pingree, Id, US 173/G2
Pingsha, China 113/G4
Pingshan, China 106/C3
Pingshi, China 113/G3
Pingshun, China 106/C3
Pingtang, China 119/J2
Pingtou, China 104/F5
P'ingtung, Tai. 113/J4
Pingwang, China 106/L9
Pingxiang, China 113/E4
Pingxiang, China 113/G3
Pingxiang, China 106/C3
Pingxing Guan (pass), China 106/C3
Pingyang, China 105/J4
Pingyao, China 106/C3
Pingyi, China 106/D4
Pingyin, China 120/E1
Pingyin, China 106/D3
Pingyong, China 113/F3
Pingyu, China 106/C4
Pingyuan, China 106/D3
Pinhal, Braz. 211/K7
Pinhal Novo, Port. 73/Q10
Pinheiro, Braz. 207/E3
Pinheiro Machado, Braz. 213/F4
Pinheiros, Braz. 211/E3
Pinhel, Port. 72/B2
Pinhook (swamp), Fl, US 191/G2
Pinhuã (riv.), Braz. 209/E2
Pini (isl.), Indo. 115/B2
Pinjar (lake), Austl. 156/K6
Pinjarra, Austl. 156/B5
Pink Hill, NC, US 189/J3
Pink Mountain, BC, Can. 168/AA13
Pinkafeld, Aus. 76/C2
Pinkawillinie Consv. Park, Austl. 157/G5
Pinkegat (chan.), Neth. 78/C2
Pinlebu, Myan. 119/G3
Pinnacles Nat'l Mon., Ca, US 174/B2
Pinnån (riv.), Swe. 65/K6
Pinnaroo, Austl. 157/J5
Pinnau (riv.), Ger. 79/G1
Pinneberg, Ger. 79/G1
Pino Hachado, (pass), Arg. 214/C3
Pino Torinese, It. 88/A2
Pinole, Ca, US 193/K10
Pinon, Co, US 178/B1
Piñon, NM, US 178/B4
Pinon, Az, US 175/G2
Pinon Hills, Ca, US 192/C2
Pinopolis, SC, US 189/G4
Pinopolis (dam), SC, US 189/H4
Pinos (mt.), Ca, US 174/C3
Pinos, Mex. 199/E4
Pinos, Isla de (Isla de la Juventud) (isl.), Cuba 196/E3
Pinos-Puente, Sp. 72/D4
Pinoso, Sp. 73/E3
Pinrang, Indo. 117/E4
Pinsdorf, Aus. 85/G7
Pinsk, Bela. 96/C1
Pinta, Isla (isl.), Ecu. 208/J6
Pintada Arroyo (cr.), NM, US 178/B3
Pintado, Uru. 215/K10
Pintados, Chile 212/B2
Pinto, Chile 214/C3
Pinto, Sp. 73/N9
Pintura, Ut, US 175/F2
Pintuyan, Phil. 114/D3
Pinzolo, It. 87/G5
Pio Xii, Braz. 207/E3
Piobbico, It. 89/F6
Pioche, Nv, US 174/E2
Piolenc, Fr. 90/A4
Piomba (riv.), It. 92/C2
Piombino, It. 74/B1
Piombino Dese, It. 89/F2
Pioneer, La, US 179/J4
Pioneer (mts.), Mt, US 173/G1
Pioneer World, Austl. 156/L7
Pioner (isl.), Rus. 100/J2
Pionerskiy, Rus. 67/J4
Pionki, Pol. 69/L3
Piopio, NZ 161/C2
Piopolis, Qu, Can. 184/B3
Piorini (lake), Braz. 205/F5
Piorini (riv.), Braz. 209/F1
Piossasco, It. 90/D3
Piota (riv.), It. 88/B3
Piotrków Trybunalski, Pol. 69/K3
Piove di Sacco, It. 89/F3
Piovene-Rocchette, It. 89/E2
Pīpār, India 118/B2
Pipariā, India 122/B4
Pipe Spring Nat'l Mon., Az, US 175/F2
Pipersville, Pa, US 194/C3
Pipestem (cr.), ND, US 182/E4
Pipestone (cr.), Sk, Can. 182/D3
Pipestone, Mb, Can. 182/D3
Pipestone (riv.), On, Can. 166/G3
Pipestone, Mn, US 181/F1
Pipestone Nat'l Mon., Mn, US 181/F1
Piplān, Pak. 124/A3
Pipmuacan (res.), Qu, Can. 167/J4
Pippingarra Abor. Land, Austl. 156/C2
Pipra, India 122/D3
Pipraich, India 122/D2
Pipriac, Fr. 82/D5
Piqanlik, China 125/D3
Piqua, Ks, US 179/G2
Piqua, Oh, US 186/D4
Piquet Carneiro, Braz. 207/G4
Piquete, Braz. 211/L7
Piquiri (riv.), Braz. 213/F3
Pīr Mahal, Pak. 124/B4
Pir Panjal (range), India 124/C3
Piracanjuba, Braz. 210/C3
Piracaua, Braz. 206/E3
Piracicaba, Braz. 213/H2
Piracuruca, Braz. 207/F3
Pirae-bong (peak), NKor. 107/C2
Piraí, Braz. 211/N7
Piraí do Sul, Braz. 213/G3
Piraiévs, Gre. 75/N9
Piraju, Braz. 213/G2
Pirajuí, Braz. 213/G2
Pirámide (peak), Chile 215/B6
Piran, Slov. 89/G2
Pirané, Arg. 212/E3
Piranga (riv.), Braz. 211/E4
Piranhas (riv.), Braz. 207/G4
Piranhas, Braz. 210/C3
Pirapemas, Braz. 207/E3
Pirapora, Braz. 210/D3
Pirarajá, Uru. 215/G2
Pirássununga, Braz. 213/H2
Piratini (riv.), Braz. 213/F4
Piray (riv.), Bol. 209/F5
Pircas (peak), Arg. 212/B4
Pirenópolis, Braz. 210/C2
Pires do Rio, Braz. 210/C3
Pīrganj, Bang. 123/G3
Pírgos, Gre. 75/J5
Pírgos, Gre. 75/G4
Piri, Ang. 146/C5
Piriac-sur-Mer, Fr. 82/C6
Piriápolis, Uru 215/G2
Piribebuy, Par. 213/E3
Pirimapun, Indo. 155/E1
Pirin (peak), Bul. 75/H2
Pirin (mts.), Bul. 75/H2
Pirin NP, Bul. 75/H2
Pirinoa, NZ 161/J9
Piripiri, Braz. 207/F4
Piritiba, Braz. 211/E1
Píritu, Ven. 204/D2
Pirkkala, Fin. 67/K1
Pirmasens, Ger. 81/G5
Pirna, Ger. 69/G3
Piro, India 123/E3
Pirojpur, Bang. 123/G4
Pirot, Yugo. 76/F4
Pirpirituba, Braz. 207/H4
Pirre (mtn.), Pan. 204/B3
Pirthīpur, India 122/B3
Pirttikoski, Fin. 65/D3
Pirttsaari (isl.), Fin. 65/F4
Piru, Ca, US 192/B2
Piru (cr.), Ca, US 192/B1
Piru (lake), Ca, US 192/B1
Piryion, Gre. 75/J3
Pisa, It. 88/D6
Pisa (prov.), It. 89/D6
Pisac, Peru 208/D4
Pisagua, Chile 212/B1
Pisanino (peak), It. 88/D5
Pisau (cape), Malay. 114/B4
Pisba, PN, Col. 204/C3
Piscataway, NJ, US 194/D2
Piscataway, Md, US 194/B6
Pisco, Peru 208/B4
Pisco (riv.), Peru 208/C4
Piscobamba, Peru 208/B3
Pisek, ND, US 182/F3
Písek, Czh. 85/H4
Písek (peak), Czh. 85/H3
Pisgah, Oh, US 186/D5
Pishan, China 125/C4
Pishanka, Ukr. 98/E3
Pishīn, Pak. 127/J2
Pīshīn, Iran 127/H3
Pishnur, Rus. 95/K4
Pīshvā, Iran 129/G3
Piskavica, Bosn. 76/C3
Piskivka, Ukr. 98/E2
Piso Firme, Bol. 209/F4
Pisoc (peak), Swi. 87/G4
Pisogne, It. 88/D2
Pisoniano, It. 92/B4
Pissila, Burk. 141/E3
Pissis (peak), Arg. 212/B3
Pistakee (lake), Il, US 193/P15
Pisticci, It. 74/E2
Pistoia, It. 89/D6
Pistoia (prov.), It. 89/D5
Pistol River, Or, US 172/A2
Pisuerga (riv.), Sp. 72/C1
Pisz, Pol. 69/L2
Pit (riv.), Ca, US 172/C3
Pita (prov.), Pol. 69/J2
Pita, Gui. 140/B4
Pitalito, Col. 204/B4
Pitanga, Braz. 213/G3
Pitcairn (isl.), Pitc. 163/N7
Pitcairn Islands (dpcy.), UK 163/N7
Pitch Place, Eng, UK 56/B3
Piteå, Swe. 64/G2
Piteälven (riv.), Swe. 64/F2
Pitești, Rom. 77/G3
Pithāpuram, India 121/D2
Píthion, Gre. 77/H5
Pithiviers, Fr. 83/H4
Pithlachascotee (riv.), Fl, US 190/K7
Pithom (ruin), Egypt 139/D3
Pithoragarh, India 122/C1
Pitigliano, It. 74/B1
Pitimbu, Braz. 207/H4
Pitiquito, Mex. 198/B2
Pitjantjatjara Aboriginal Lands, Austl. 157/F3
Pitkin, La, US 190/B2
Pitkin, Co, US 175/J1
Pitlochry, Sc, UK 59/C3
Pitman, NJ, US 194/C4
Pitmedden, Sc, UK 59/D2
Pitogo, Phil. 114/C2
Pitomača, Cro. 76/C3
Piton de la Fournaise (peak), Fr. 151/S15
Piton des Neiges (peak), Fr. 151/S15
Pitowa, Camr. 142/B3
Pîtres, Fr. 83/G2
Pitrufquén, Chile 214/B3
Pitsane, Bots. 148/E5
Pitsunda, Geo. 96/G4
Pitt, Mn, US 183/G3
Pitt (str.), NZ 161/E4
Pitt (isl.), NZ 161/E4
Pitt (riv.), BC, Can. 170/C3
Pitt Water (bay), Austl. 160/H8
Pittenweem, Sc, UK 59/D4
Pitts, Ga, US 191/G2
Pittsboro, Ms, US 188/C4
Pittsboro, NC, US 189/H3
Pittsburg, Ca, US 172/C4
Pittsburg, Ks, US 179/G2
Pittsburg, Mo, US 179/H2
Pittsburg, NH, US 187/L2
Pittsburg, Ok, US 179/G3
Pittsburgh, Pa, US 186/G4
Pittsburg, Tx, US 179/G4
Pittsfield, Ma, US 187/K3
Pittsfield, Il, US 181/J4
Pittsford, Vt, US 187/K3
Pittston, Pa, US 187/J4
Pittstown, NJ, US 194/D2
Pittsville, Va, US 189/H2
Pittsworth, Austl. 160/C4
Pitzbach (riv.), Aus. 87/G4
Piuí, Braz. 210/D4
Piumazzo, It. 89/E4
Piura (dept.), Peru 208/A2
Piura, Peru 208/A2
Piute (res.), Ut, US 173/G4
Pivan', Rus. 105/M1
Pivdenne, Ukr. 99/J3
Pivdenny Buh (riv.), Ukr. 100/C5
Pivijay, Col. 204/C2
Pivsko (lake), Yugo. 75/F1
Pixoyal, Mex. 196/C4
Piz d'Err (peak), Swi. 87/F4
Pizacoma, Peru 208/D5
Pizarra, Sp. 72/C4
Pizhma (riv.), Rus. 95/K4
Pizol (peak), Swi. 87/F4
Pizzighettone, It. 88/C3
Pizzo, It. 74/E3
Pizzo dei Tre Signori (peak), It. 87/F6
Pizzo della Presolana (peak), It. 87/G6
Pizzo di Coca (peak), It. 87/G5
Pizzo di Vogorno (peak), Swi. 87/E5
Pizzoli, It. 92/C3
Pizzuto (peak), It. 91/B3
Plabennec, Fr. 82/A3
Placentia, Nf, Can. 185/L2
Placentia (bay), Nf, Can. 185/K2
Placentia, Ca, US 192/G8
Placer (co.), Ca, US 193/M9
Placer, Phil. 114/C3
Placer, Phil. 114/D3
Placerville, Co, US 175/H1
Placerville, Ca, US 172/C4
Placetas, Cuba 201/G1
Plachkovtsi, Bul. 77/G4
Plácido de Castro, Braz. 209/E3
Placilla de Caracoles, Chile 212/B2
Plaffeien, Swi. 86/D4
Plai Mat (riv.), Thai. 120/C3
Plaidt, Ger. 81/G3
Plailly, Fr. 56/K4
Plain Dealing, La, US 179/H4
Plain of Jars, Laos 112/D5
Plaine (riv.), Fr. 86/C1
Plainfield, In, US 186/C5
Plainfield, Il, US 193/P16
Plainfield, NJ, US 195/H9
Plainfield, Wi, US 181/K1
Plains, Tx, US 178/C4
Plains, Ga, US 191/F1
Plains, Mt, US 170/G4
Plains, Pa, US 194/C1
Plains (West Plains), Ks, US 178/D2
Plainsboro, NJ, US 194/D3
Plaintel, Fr. 82/C4
Plainview, Ar, US 179/H3
Plainview, Mn, US 181/H1
Plainview, Ne, US 180/F2
Plainview, NY, US 195/M8
Plainview, Tx, US 178/D3
Plainville, Ks, US 180/E4
Plainwell, Mi, US 186/D3
Plaisir, Fr. 56/H5
Plaju, Indo. 115/D3
Plampang, Indo. 117/E5
Plan-de-Cuques, Fr. 90/B6
Plan-de-la-Tour, Fr. 90/C6
Plan-d'Orgon, Fr. 90/A5
Plan-les-Ouates, Swi. 86/C5
Planá, Czh. 85/F3
Plana Cays (isls.), Bahm. 201/H1
Planada, Ca, US 174/B2
Planalto da Borborema (plat.), Braz. 207/G4
Planalto da Huíla (plat.), Ang. 148/B2
Planalto da Lichinga (plat.), Moz. 149/G2
Planalto do Bíe (plat.), Ang. 148/C2
Planalto do Chimoio (plat.), Moz. 149/G3
Planalto dos Macondes (plat.), Moz. 145/B4
Planchada, Chile 214/N8
Plancher-Bas, Fr. 86/C2
Plancher-les-Mines, Fr. 86/C2
Plancoët, Fr. 82/C3
Plandište, Yugo. 76/E3
Planerskoye, Ukr. 99/H5
Planet Ocean, Fl, US 190/P11
Planeta Rica, Col. 204/C2
Plánice, Czh. 85/G4
Planken, Lcht. 87/F3
Plankinton, SD, US 180/E2
Plano, Il, US 181/K3

287
Posor – Puula

Posorja, Ecu. 204/A5
Pospelikha, Rus. 125/D1
Posse, Braz. 210/D2
Possel, CAfr. 142/C4
Possession (pt.), Wa, US 193/C2
Possession (sound), Wa, US 193/C2
Possum Kingdom (lake), Tx, US 177/E1
Post, Tx, US 178/D4
Post Falls, Id, US 170/F4
Post Office, VatC. 91/G7
Postal (Burgstall), It. 87/H4
Poste Maurice Cortier (ruin), Alg. 137/F5
Postmasburg, SAfr. 150/C3
Postoak, Tx, US 179/E4
Postojna, Slov. 71/L4
Postolprty, Czh. 85/G2
Poston, Az, US 174/E4
Postrervalle, Bol. 212/D1
Postville, Ia, US 181/J2
Pot (mtn.), Id, US 170/G4
Pota, Indo. 117/F5
Potam, Mex. 198/C3
Potamós, Gre. 75/H5
Potaro (riv.), Guy. 206/B1
Potaro-Siparuni (pol. reg.), Guy. 205/G3
Potawatomi Ind. Res., Mi, US 183/L5
Potawatomi Ind. Res., Wi, US 183/K5
Potawatomi Ind. Res., Mi, US 186/C2
Potawatomi Ind. Res., Wi, US 181/K1
Potawatomi Ind. Res., Ks, US 181/F4
Potchefstroom, SAfr. 150/D2
Poteau, Ok, US 179/G3
Poteet, Tx, US 176/E3
Potengi, Braz. 207/G4
Potenza, It. 74/D2
Potenza (riv.), It. 74/C1
Potenza Picena, It. 89/G7
Potes, Sp. 72/C1
Potgietersrus, SAfr. 149/F5
Poth, Tx, US 177/E3
Potholes (res.), Wa, US 170/E4
P'ot'i, Geo. 97/G4
Poti (riv.), Braz. 207/F4
Potigny, Fr. 83/E3
Potlatch, Id, US 170/F4
Potomac, Il, US 186/C4
Potomac, Md, US 194/A5
Potomac (riv.), Md, US 189/J1
Potoru, SLeo. 140/C5
Potosi (mtn.), Nv, US 174/E3
Potosi, Mo, US 188/B2
Potosí (dept.), Bol. 212/C2
Potosí, Bol. 212/C1
Potosi, Tx, US 177/E1
Potrerillos, Chile 212/B3
Potrero, Ca, US 174/D4
Potro, Cerro del (peak), Arg.,Chile 212/B4
Potsdam, NY, US 187/J2
Potsdam, Ger. 68/Q7
Pottangi, India 121/D2
Pottenstein, Ger. 85/E3
Potter, Ne, US 180/C3
Potter Street, Eng, UK 56/D1
Potters Bar, Eng, UK 56/C1
Potterspury, Eng, UK 63/F2
Pottersville, Mo, US 179/H2
Pöttmes, Ger. 84/E5
Potton, Eng, UK 63/F2
Potts Camp, Ms, US 188/C3
Pottsboro, Tx, US 179/F4
Pottstown, Pa, US 194/C3
Pottsville, Pa, US 194/B2
Potwin, Ks, US 179/F2
Pouch Cove, Nf, Can. 185/L2
Poudre d'or, Mrts. 151/T15
Poughkeepsie, NY, US 187/K4
Pouilley-les-Vignes, Fr. 86/B3
Poulains (pt.), Fr. 82/B6
Poulan, Ga, US 191/G2
Poulaphouca (res.), Ire. 58/D3
Poulaphoucha (res.), Ire. 60/B5
Pouldreuzic, Fr. 82/A5
Poulsbo, Wa, US 170/C4
Poulter (riv.), Eng, UK 61/G5
Poultney, Vt, US 187/K3
Poulton-le-Fylde, Eng, UK 61/F4
Pouma, Camr. 146/B2
Poŭn, SKor. 107/D4
Pound, Wi, US 186/B2
Pounga-Nganda, Gabon 146/B3
Poungthak, Laos 120/D2
Poura, Burk. 140/E4
Pourri (peak), Fr. 90/C1
Pouru-Saint-Remy, Fr. 81/E4
Pouso Alegre, Braz. 211/L7
Pouss, Camr. 142/B3
Pouthisat, Camb. 120/C3
Pouthisat (riv.), Camb. 119/H5
Pouzauges, Fr. 70/C3
Považská Bystrica, Slvk. 69/K4
Povegliano Veronese, It. 89/D3
Povenets, Rus. 94/G3
Poverty Point Nat'l Mon., La, US 188/B4
Poviglio, It. 88/D4
Póvoa de Varzim, Port. 72/A2
Povoação, Azor., Port. 73/T13
Povorino, Rus. 99/M2
Povorotnyy, Mys (pt.), Rus. 105/L3
Povungnituk (riv.), Qu, Can. 167/J2
Povungnituk, Qu, Can. 167/J2
Powassan, On, Can. 187/G1
Poway, Ca, US 192/C5
Powder (riv.), Mt,Wy, US 168/E2
Powder River (pass), Wy, US 173/K1
Powder River, Wy, US 173/K2
Powder Springs, Ga, US 189/L7
Powder, North Fork (riv.), Wy, US 80/A2
Powder, South Fork (riv.), Wy, US 80/A2
Powderhorn, Co, US 175/J1
Powderly, Tx, US 79/G4
Powderville, Mt, US 82/B5
Powell (lake), Az,Ut, US 165/F6
Powell (cr.), Pa, US 194/B3
Powell, Tn, US 188/E2
Powell (riv.), Va, US 189/F2
Powell (mtn.), WV, US 189/G1
Powell, Wy, US 173/J1
Powell River, BC, Can. 170/B3
Powellton, WV, US 189/G1
Power (res.), NY, US 186/U9
Power, Mt, US 171/J4
Power Head (pt.), Ire. 58/B6
Powers (lake), Wi, US 193/P14
Powers, Or, US 172/A2
Powers Lake, ND, US 182/C3
Powhatan, Va, US 189/J2
Powhatan Point, Oh, US 186/F5
Powys (co.), Wal, UK 61/E6
Poxoreo, Braz. 210/B2
Poxoreu (riv.), Braz. 209/H5
Poy Sippi, Wi, US 181/K1
Poyang (lake), China 106/D5
Poygan (lake), Wi, US 181/K1
Poynette, Wi, US 181/K2
Poynor, Tx, US 177/G1
Poynton, Eng, UK 61/F5
Poyo, Sp. 72/A1
Poysdorf, Aus. 69/J4
Poza Rica, Mex. 199/M6
Požarevac, Yugo. 76/E3
Požega, Yugo. 76/E4
Pozhva, Rus. 95/N4
Poznań, Pol. 69/J2
Poznan (prov.), Pol. 69/J2
Pozo Alcón, Sp. 72/D4
Pozo Almonte, Chile 212/B2
Pozo Colorado, Par. 212/E2
Pozo del Molle, Arg. 212/D5
Pozo del Tigre, Bol. 209/F5
Pozo Hondo, Arg. 212/C3
Pozoblanco, Sp. 72/C3
Pozohondo, Sp. 72/E3
Pozuelo de Alarcón, Sp. 73/N9
Pozuelos, Ven. 205/E2
Pozuelos (lag.), Arg. 212/C2
Pozuzo, Peru 208/C3
Pozza, It. 89/D4
Pozzallo, It. 74/D4
Pozzilli, It. 92/D4
Pozzolo Formigaro, It. 88/B4
Pozzoni (peak), It. 92/C2
Pozzonovo, It. 89/E3
Pozzuoli, It. 92/D6
Pozzuolo, It. 91/A1
Ppa. de Salamanca (plain), Arg. 214/F1
Prabuty, Pol. 67/H5
Pracham Hiang (pt.), Thai. 120/B4
Prachatice, Czh. 85/H4
Prachin Buri, Thai. 120/C3
Prachin Buri (riv.), Thai. 120/C3
Prachuap Khiri Khan, Thai. 120/B4
Prad am Stilfserjoch (Prato allo Stelvio), It. 87/G4
Praděd (peak), Czh. 69/J3
Pradera, Col. 204/B4
Prado (dam), Ca, US 174/D4
Prado, Braz. 211/F3
Prado del Rey, Sp. 72/C4
Prado Flood Control (basin), Ca, US 192/C3
Pragelpass (pass), Swi. 87/E4
Prague, Ok, US 179/F3
Prague (Praha) (cap.), Czh. 85/H2
Praha (pol. reg.), Czh. 69/H3
Praha (peak), Czh. 85/G3
Praha (Prague) (cap.), Czh. 85/H2
Prahova (prov.), Rom. 77/G3
Praia (int'l arpt.), CpV. 133/K11
Praia (cap.), CpV. 133/K11
Praia da Vitória, Azor., Port. 73/S12
Praia Grande, Braz. 211/K9
Prainha, Braz. 206/A4
Prainha, Braz. 206/C3
Prairie, Austl. 160/B3
Prairie (cr.), Ne, US 180/E3
Prairie City, SD, US 182/C5
Prairie Dog (cr.), Ks, US 180/D4
Prairie Dog Town Fk. (riv.), Tx, US 168/F4
Prairie du Chien, Wi, US 181/J2
Prairie Farm, Wi, US 183/J5
Prairie Grove, Il, US 193/P15
Prairie Island Ind. Res., Mn, US 181/H1
Prairie Point, Ms, US 188/C4
Prairie View, Tx, US 177/G2
Prairie, South (cr.), Wa, US 193/C3
Prairies (riv.), Qu, Can. 185/N6
Prairieville, Tx, US 177/F1
Prakhon Chai, Thai. 120/C3
Pralboino, It. 88/D3
Pralognan-la-Vanoise, Fr. 90/C2
Pralungo, It. 88/B2
Pram (riv.), Aus. 85/G6
Prambachkirchen, Aus. 85/G6
Prambanan (ruin), Indo. 115/E3
Pramort, Ger. 66/E4
Pran Buri (res.), Thai. 119/G5
Pran Buri, Thai. 120/B3
Prang, Gha. 141/E5
Prangins, Swi. 86/C5
Prānhita (riv.), India 118/C4
Prapat, Indo. 115/B2
Prasat Preah Vihear, Camb. 120/D3
Praskoveya, Rus. 97/H3
Præstø, Den. 66/E4
Praszka, Pol. 69/K3
Prat, Chile, Ant. 216/W
Prata, Braz. 207/G4
Prata di Pordenone, It. 89/F2
Prata di Principato Ultra, It. 92/D6
Prata do Piauí, Braz. 207/F4
Pratantico, It. 89/E7
Pratas (Dongsha) (isl.), China 113/H4
Pratas Reef (reef), China 113/H4
Prätlgau (valley), Swi. 87/F4
Prato, It. 89/E6
Prato (Leventina), Swi. 87/E5
Prato allo Stelvio (Prad am Stilfserjoch), It. 87/G4
Pratola Peligna, It. 92/C3
Pratomagno (mts.), It. 89/E4
Pratovecchio, It. 89/E6
Pratt, Ks, US 179/E2
Pratt (isl.), Chile 215/B6
Pratteln, Swi. 86/D2
Prattsville, Ar, US 179/H3
Prattsville, NY, US 187/J3
Prattville, Al, US 188/D4
Prauthoy, Fr. 86/B2
Pravdinsk, Rus. 95/J4
Pravets, Bul. 75/H1
Pravia, Sp. 72/B1
Prawle (pt.), Eng, UK 62/C6
Praxedis G. Guerrero, Mex. 177/B2
Praya, Indo. 117/E5
Pré-en-Pail, Fr. 83/E4
Pré-Saint-Didier, It. 86/C6
Preah Vihear (ruin), Camb. 120/D3
Préalpes (upland), Fr. 90/B2
Précigné, Fr. 83/E5
Précy-sur-Oise, Fr. 80/B5
Predappio, It. 89/E5
Predazzo, It. 71/J3
Predeal, Rom. 77/G3
Predosa, It. 88/B4
Preeceville, Sk, Can. 182/C2
Prees, Eng, UK 61/F6
Preesall, Eng, UK 61/F4
Preetz, Ger. 66/D4
Preganziol, It. 89/F2
Pregarten, Aus. 85/H6
Pregolya (riv.), Pol. 67/J4
Pregolya (riv.), Rus. 69/L1
Pregonero, Ven. 204/D2
Preiļi, Lat. 67/M3
Prek Pouthi, Camb. 120/D4
Prelate, Sk, Can. 171/K2
Premana, It. 87/F5
Prémery, Fr. 70/E3
Premià de Mar, Sp. 73/L7
Premont, Tx, US 177/E4
Prenjas, Alb. 75/G2
Prentice, Wi, US 183/J5
Prentiss, Ms, US 190/D2
Prenzlau, Ger. 69/G2
Preobrazheniye, Rus. 105/L3
Přerov, Czh. 69/J4
Presanella (peak), It. 87/G5
Prescot, Eng, UK 61/F5
Prescott, On, Can. 187/J2
Prescott, Ar, US 179/H4
Prescott, Az, US 175/F3
Prescott, Ks, US 179/G1
Prescott, Ia, US 181/G3
Prescott, Wi, US 183/Q7
Prescott Valley, Az, US 175/F3
Preševo, Yugo. 75/G1
Presidencia Roque Sáenz Peña, Arg. 212/D3
Presidente Bernardes, Braz. 210/C4
Presidente Dutra, Braz. 207/E4
Presidente Epitácio, Braz. 213/F2
Presidente Hayes (dept.), Par. 210/A4
Presidente Médici, Braz. 209/F3
Presidente Prudente, Braz. 213/G2
Presidente Venceslau, Braz. 213/G2
Presidential Lake Estates, NJ, US 194/D4
Presidio, Tx, US 177/B3
Presidio (riv.), Mex. 198/D4
Presidio La Bahia, Tx, US 177/F3
Preslav, Bul. 77/H4
Presles, Fr. 56/J4
Presles-en-Brie, Fr. 56/L5
Prešov, Slvk. 69/L4
Prespa (lake), Alb. 76/E5
Presqu'Île de Giens (pen.), Fr. 90/C6
Presque Isle, Wi, US 183/K4
Presque Isle (pt.), Mi, US 183/L4
Presque Isle, Mi, US 186/E2
Presque Isle, Me, US 167/K4
Presquile Nat'l Wild. Ref., Va, US 189/J2
Pressath, Ger. 85/E3
Pressbaum, Aus. 77/N7
Prestatyn, Wal, UK 61/E5
Prestea, Gha. 141/E5
Prestfoss, Nor. 66/C1
Přeštice, Czh. 85/G3
Preston (cape), Austl. 156/C2
Preston (nbrhd.), Austl. 158/G5
Preston, Eng, UK 62/D5
Preston, Eng, UK 61/F4
Preston, Ga, US 191/F1
Preston, Ia, US 181/J2
Preston, Id, US 173/H2
Preston, Ks, US 179/E2
Preston, Md, US 194/C6
Preston, Mn, US 181/H2
Preston, Ms, US 188/C4
Preston, Nv, US 173/F4
Preston, Ok, US 179/G3
Preston, Sc, UK 59/D5
Preston, Wa, US 193/D2
Prestonpans, Sc, UK 59/D5
Prestonsburg, Ky, US 189/F2
Prestwich, Eng, UK 61/F4
Prestwick, Sc, UK 59/B6
Prestwick (int'l arpt.), Sc, UK 59/B5
Prêto (riv.), Braz. 210/D3
Prêto do Igapó-Açu (riv.), Braz. 206/A4
Pretoria (cap.), SAfr. 150/E2
Pretoriuskop, SAfr. 149/F5
Pretty Boy (res.), Md, US 194/B4
Pretty Prairie, Ks, US 179/E2
Pretty Rock Nat'l Wild. Ref., ND, US 182/D4
Preussisch Olendorf, Ger. 79/F4
Prevalje, Slov. 71/L3
Préveza, Gre. 75/G3
Prévost, Qu, Can. 185/M6
Prewitt, NM, US 175/H3
Prey Veng, Camb. 120/D4
Priargunsk, Rus. 105/H1
Priazov Upland (upland), Ukr. 99/J4
Pribilof (isls.), Ak, US 168/W13
Priboj, Yugo. 76/D4
Příbram, Czh. 85/H3
Price, Qu, Can. 184/C1
Price (falls), Ok, US 179/F3
Price (riv.), Ut, US 173/H4
Price, Ut, US 173/H4
Price, Md, US 194/C5
Pricedale, Ms, US 190/C2
Prichard, Al, US 190/D2
Prichsenstadt, Ger. 84/D3
Priddy, Tx, US 177/E2
Pridgen, Ga, US 191/G2
Priego, Sp. 72/D2
Priego de Córdoba, Sp. 72/C4
Priekulė, Lith. 67/J4
Priekule, Lat. 67/J3
Prien am Chiemsee, Ger. 85/F7
Prienai, Lith. 67/K4
Prieska, SAfr. 150/C3
Priest (riv.), Id, US 170/F3
Priest Rapids (dam), Wa, US 170/E4
Priest River, Id, US 170/F3
Prieta (mtn.), Sp. 72/C1
Prievidza, Slvk. 69/K4
Prignitz (reg.), Ger. 68/F2
Prijedor, Bosn. 76/C3
Prijepolje, Yugo. 76/D4
Prikaspian (plain), Kaz.,Rus. 100/E5
Prikumsk, Rus. 97/H3
Prikumskiy, Rus. 97/H3
Prilep, FYROM 75/G2
Prilly, Swi. 86/C4
Prim, Ar, US 179/H3
Prima Porta, It. 91/B4
Primavera, Braz. 207/E3
Prime Hook NWR, De, US 194/C6
Primeira Cruz, Braz. 207/F3
Primero (cape), Chile 215/B6
Primero (riv.), Arg. 212/D4
Primero de Mayo, Mex. 177/D4
Primethorpe, Eng, UK 63/E1
Primghar, Ia, US 181/G2
Primorsk, Azer. 129/G1
Primorsk, Rus. 97/H2
Primorsk, Rus. 67/N1
Primorsk, Rus. 67/J4
Primorskiy Kray, Rus. 101/P5
Primorsko, Bul. 77/H4
Primorsko-Akhtarsk, Rus. 99/K4
Primorskoye, Ukr. 99/J4
Primorskoye, Ukr. 77/K3
Prims (riv.), Ger. 81/F4
Prince, Sk, Can. 171/K1
Prince Albert (sound), NW, Can. 166/E1
Prince Albert (pen.), NW, Can. 166/E1
Prince Albert, SAfr. 150/C4
Prince Albert NP, Sk, Can. 166/F3
Prince Alfred (cape), NW, Can. 167/Q7
Prince Charles (isl.), Nun, Can. 167/J2
Prince Edward (isls.), S.Afr. 53/L7
Prince Edward (isl.), Can. 165/L5
Prince Edward Island (prov.), Can. 167/K4
Prince Edward Island NP, PE, Can. 184/F2
Prince Frederick, Md, US 189/J1
Prince George, BC, Can. 166/D3
Prince George, Va, US 189/J2
Prince Georges (co.), Md, US 194/B6
Prince Gustav Adolf (sea), Nun, Can. 167/R7
Prince Leopold (isl.), Nun, Can. 166/G1
Prince of Wales (isl.), Austl. 155/F2
Prince of Wales (isl.), Nun, Can. 165/G2
Prince of Wales (str.), NW, Can. 166/E1
Prince of Wales (isl.), Ak, US 166/C3
Prince of Wales (cape), Ak, US 168/W12
Prince Olav (coast), Ant. 216/D
Prince Patrick (isl.), Can. 165/E2
Prince Regent (inlet), Nun, Can. 166/G1
Prince Regent Nature Rsv., Austl. 154/B3
Prince Rupert, BC, Can. 168/Z13
Prince William, NB, Can. 184/D3
Prince William (sound), Ak, US 166/B2
Prince William Forest Park NP, Va, US 189/J1
Princenhof (lake), Neth. 78/C2
Princes Lake, In, US 186/C5
Princes Risborough, Eng, UK 63/F3
Princes Town, Trin. 197/J5
Princesa Isabel, Braz. 207/G4
Princess Anne, Md, US 189/K1
Princess Charlotte (bay), Austl. 153/D2
Princess Juliana (int'l arpt.), Neth. 197/N8
Princess Margaret (range), Nun, Can. 167/S6
Princess Royal (isl.), BC, Can. 166/C3
Princeton, BC, Can. 170/D3
Princeton, Il, US 181/K3
Princeton, In, US 188/D1
Princeton, Ks, US 179/G1
Princeton, Ky, US 188/D2
Princeton, La, US 179/H4
Princeton, Mi, US 183/L4
Princeton, Mn, US 183/H5
Princeton, Mo, US 181/H3
Princeton, NJ, US 194/D3
Princeton, Tx, US 176/L6
Princeton, WV, US 189/G2
Princeton Junction, NJ, US 194/D3
Princeville, Il, US 181/K3
Príncipe (isl.), SaoT. 146/A2
Prineville, Or, US 172/C1
Prineville (res.), Or, US 172/C1
Pringle, Tx, US 178/D3
Pringle, SD, US 180/C2
Pringsewu, Indo. 116/B5
Pringy, Fr. 86/C5
Prinsburg, Mn, US 181/G1
Prinsenbeek, Neth. 78/B5
Prinses Margriet (canal), Neth. 78/C3
Prinzapolka (riv.), Nic. 201/E3
Prinzapolka, Nic. 201/F3
Priolo di Gargallo, It. 74/D4
Prior (cape), Sp. 72/A1
Prior Lake, Mn, US 183/P7
Prior Lake Ind. Res., Mn, US 183/P7
Priore (peak), It. 92/C2
Priozernyy, Kaz. 125/D2
Priozersk, Rus. 67/P1
Pripet Marshes (swamp), Bela.,Ukr. 96/C1
Pripyat' (riv.), Ukr. 96/C2
Prisdorf, Ger. 79/G1
Pristen', Rus. 99/J2
Priština, Yugo. 76/E4
Pritchett, Co, US 178/C2
Prittriching, Ger. 87/G1
Pritzwalk, Ger. 68/G2
Privas, Fr. 90/A3
Priverno, It. 92/C5
Privokzal'nyy, Rus. 95/P4
Privolzhskiy, Rus. 97/H2
Privolzh'ye, Rus. 97/J1
Priyutnoye, Rus. 97/G3
Priyutovo, Rus. 97/K1
Prizren, Yugo. 75/G1
Prnjavor, Yugo. 76/D3
Prnjavor, Bosn. 76/C3
Probištip, FYROM 75/H1
Probolinggo, Indo. 115/F3
Probstzella, Ger. 85/E1
Procida, It. 92/D6
Proctor (lake), Tx, US 177/E1
Proctor, Ok, US 179/G3
Proctor, WV, US 186/F5
Proctor, Tx, US 176/E2
Proddatūr, India 121/C3
Proença-a-nova, Port. 72/B3
Profondeville, Belg. 81/D3
Progreso, Mex. 177/D4
Progreso, Mex. 200/D1
Progreso, Mex. 199/K6
Progreso, Pan. 201/F4
Progreso, Uru. 215/K11
Progress, Rus. 105/K2
Progresso, It. 89/E4
Prokhladnyy, Rus. 97/G4
Prokhorovka, Rus. 99/J2
Prokop'yevsk, Rus. 125/E1
Prokuplje, Yugo. 76/E4
Proletarsk, Rus. 99/L4
Proletarskiy, Rus. 99/H2
Promised Land (lake), Pa, US 194/C1
Promissão, Braz. 213/G2
Promissão (res.), Braz. 210/C4
Promontory, Ut, US 173/G3
Promyslovoye, Rus. 97/H3
Propriá, Braz. 211/F1
Propriano, Fr. 74/A2
Prorva, Kaz. 97/K3
Prosecco, It. 89/G2
Proserpine, Austl. 160/C3
Prosna (riv.), Pol. 69/J2
Prosotsáni, Gre. 75/H2
Prospect, Pa, US 186/F4
Prospect, Or, US 172/B2
Prospect (nbrhd.), Austl. 157/M8
Prospect Park, Pa, US 187/G4
Prospect Park, NJ, US 195/J8
Prosper, Tx, US 176/L6
Prosperidad, Phil. 114/D3
Prosperity, WV, US 189/G2
Prosperity, SC, US 189/G3
Prosperous, Ire. 58/D3
Prosser, Wa, US 170/E4
Prostějov, Czh. 69/J4
Proston, Austl. 160/C4
Proszowice, Pol. 69/L3
Protection, Ks, US 178/E2
Protivín, Czh. 85/H4
Protvino, Rus. 94/H5
Provadiya, Bul. 77/H4
Provencal, La, US 190/B2
Provence (int'l arpt.), Fr. 90/B6
Provence (reg.), Fr. 92/E2
Provence-Alpes-Côte D'Azur (pol. reg.), Fr. 73/H1
Provence-Alpes-Côte-D'Azur, Fr. 71/G4
Providence, Fl, US 190/M7
Providence (cape), NZ 161/A4
Providence, Ut, US 173/H3
Providence (mts.), Ca, US 174/E3
Providence, Ky, US 188/D2
Providence, Al, US 188/D4
Providence (cap.), RI, US 184/B5
Providence Bay, On, Can. 186/E2
Providencia, Isla de (isl.), Col. 196/E5
Providência, Serra de (mts.), Braz. 209/F3
Providenciales (isl.), Bahm. 201/H1
Provideniya, Rus. 168/V12
Provo, Ut, US 173/H3
Provo (riv.), Ut, US 173/H3
Provost, Ab, Can. 171/J1
Prozor, Bosn. 76/C4
Prudentópolis, Braz. 213/G3
Prudhoe, Eng, UK 61/G2
Prudhoe (bay), Ak, US 165/C2
Prudnik, Pol. 69/J3
Prudyanka, Ukr. 99/J2
Prue, Ok, US 179/F2
Prüm, Ger. 81/F3
Prüm (riv.), Ger. 68/D4
Prunay-en-Yvelines, Fr. 56/H6
Prunedale, Ca, US 174/B2
Prunelli-di-Fiumorbo, Fr. 74/A1
Pruszcz Gdański, Pol. 66/H4
Pruszków, Pol. 69/L2
Prut (riv.), Eur. 100/C5
Prut (riv.), Rom. 93/K1
Prut (riv.), Ukr. 98/C3
Prutz, Aus. 87/G3
Pruzhany, Bela. 69/N2
Pryazovs'ke, Ukr. 99/H4
Prykolotne, Ukr. 99/J2
Pryluky, Ukr. 99/G1
Prymors'ke, Ukr. 99/J4
Prymors'kyy, Ukr. 99/H5
Pryor, Mt, US 173/J1
Pryor (cr.), Mt, US 173/J1
Pryor (Creek), Ok, US 179/G2
Prypyat', Ukr. 98/F2
Prypyats' (riv.), Bela. 100/C4
Przasnysz, Pol. 69/L2
Przemków, Pol. 69/H3
Przemyś (prov.), Pol. 69/M4
Przemyśl, Pol. 69/M4
Przeworsk, Pol. 69/M3
Przylądek Rozewie (cape), Pol. 66/H4
Przysucha, Pol. 69/L3
Psakhná, Gre. 75/H3
Psará (isl.), Gre. 75/J3
Psárion, Gre. 75/G4
Psebay, Rus. 97/G3
Psël (riv.), Ukr.,Rus. 96/E2
Psël (riv.), Ukr. 99/G3
Pskov (oblast), Rus. 94/F4
Pskov (lake), Rus. 94/E5
Pskov, Rus. 67/N3
Pšovka (riv.), Czh. 85/H2
Pszczyna, Pol. 69/K4
Pt Morin (riv.), Fr. 70/E2
Pt. Reyes Nat'l Seashore, Ca, US 174/A1
Ptolemaís, Gre. 75/G2
Ptolemaïs (ruin), Libya 134/D1
Ptuj, Slov. 76/B2
Pu Xian, China 106/B3
Puan, SKor. 107/D5
Pu'an, China 112/E3
Puangue, Chile 214/N8
Puca Barranca, Peru 204/C5
Pucacaca, Peru 208/B2
Pucallpa, Peru 208/C3
Pucara, Bol. 212/C1
Pucará, Ecu. 208/B1
Pucará, Peru 208/D4
Pucará, Peru 208/B2
Pucarani, Bol. 212/B1
Pucaurco, Peru 204/D5
Puce, On, Can. 193/G7
Puchenau, Aus. 85/H6
Pucheng, China 106/B4
Puchheim, Ger. 85/E6
Puch'on, SKor. 107/F7
Puchuncaví, Chile 214/N8
Pucioasa, Rom. 77/G3
Puck, Pol. 66/H4
Puckaun, Ire. 58/B4
Puckaway (lake), Wi, US 181/K2
Puckeridge, Eng, UK 63/G3
Pucking, Aus. 85/H6
Pucón, Chile 214/C3
Pucusana, Peru 208/B4
Pudasjärvi, Fin. 94/E2
Puddletown, Eng, UK 62/D5
Pudem, Rus. 95/M4
Puderbach, Ger. 81/G2
Pudimoe, SAfr. 150/D2
Pudozh, Rus. 94/H3
Pudsey, Eng, UK 61/G4
Pudukkottai, India 121/C4
Puebla (state), Mex. 196/B4
Puebla, Mex. 199/L7
Puebla de Alcocer, Sp. 72/C3
Puebla de Don Fadrique, Sp. 72/D4
Puebla de la Calzada, Sp. 72/B3
Puebla de Sanabria, Sp. 72/B1
Puebla de Trives, Sp. 72/B1
Puebla del Caramiñal, Sp. 72/A1
Pueblillo, Mex. 199/M6
Pueblito, Col. 204/C2
Pueblo, Co, US 178/B1
Pueblo Army Depot, Co, US 180/B4
Pueblo de Taos Ind. Res., NM, US 178/B2
Pueblo de Taos Ind. Res., NM, US 175/K2
Pueblo Nuevo, Nic. 200/E3
Pueblo Nuevo, Ven. 204/D2
Pueblo West, Co, US 178/B1
Pueblo Yaqui, Mex. 198/C3
Puelches, Arg. 214/D3
Puelén, Arg. 214/D3
Puente (hills), Ca, US 192/G8
Puente Alto, Chile 214/N8
Puente Caldelas, Sp. 72/A1
Puente de Ixtla, Mex. 199/K8
Puente del Inca, Arg. 214/C2
Puente del Inca, Arg. 214/P8
Puente Nacional, Col. 204/C3
Puente Piedra, Peru 208/B3
Puente-Ceso, Sp. 72/A1
Puente-Genil, Sp. 72/C4
Puenteareas, Sp. 72/A1
Puentedeume, Sp. 72/A1
Puentes de García Rodríguez, Sp. 72/B1
Pu'er, China 112/D4
Puerco (riv.), Az,NM, US 175/H3
Puerto Abente, Par. 212/E2
Puerto Acosta, Bol. 208/D4
Puerto Aguirre, Chile 214/B5
Puerto Aisén, Chile 214/B5
Puerto Alegre, Bol. 209/F4
Puerto Almacen, Bol. 209/E4
Puerto América, Peru 208/B2
Puerto Ángel, Mex. 200/B3
Puerto Argentina, Col. 204/C4
Puerto Armuelles, Pan. 201/F4
Puerto Arturo, Chile 215/C7
Puerto Arturo, Bol. 209/F4
Puerto Arturo, Peru 204/C5
Puerto Asís, Col. 204/B4
Puerto Ayacucho, Ven. 205/E3
Puerto Ayora, Ecu. 208/J7
Puerto Bahía Negra, Par. 212/E2
Puerto Ballivián, Bol. 209/E4
Puerto Baquerizo Moreno, Ecu. 208/K7
Puerto Barrios, Guat. 200/D3
Puerto Bermúdez, Peru 208/C3
Puerto Berrío, Col. 204/C3
Puerto Bertrand, Chile 215/B5
Puerto Caballas, Peru 208/C4
Puerto Cabello, Ven. 204/D2
Puerto Cabezas, Nic. 201/F3
Puerto Calvimonte, Bol. 209/E4
Puerto Canoa, Bol. 209/E4
Puerto Carranza, Col. 204/D5
Puerto Carreño, Col. 205/E3
Puerto Casado, Par. 212/E2
Puerto Chacabuco, Chile 214/B5
Puerto Cisnes, Chile 214/B5
Puerto Coig, Arg. 215/C6
Puerto Colón, Par. 212/E2
Puerto Cortés, Hon. 200/E3
Puerto Cortés, Mex. 198/C3
Puerto Cumarebo, Ven. 204/D2
Puerto de la Cruz, Sp. 136/A3
Puerto de la Libertad, Mex. 198/B2
Puerto de Navacerrada (pass), Sp. 73/M8
Puerto del Rosario, Sp. 136/B3
Puerto del Son, Sp. 72/A1
Puerto Deseado, Arg. 215/D5
Puerto El Carmen, Ecu. 204/C4
Puerto Escondido, Col. 204/B2
Puerto Escondido, Mex. 200/B3
Puerto Esperanza, Arg. 213/F3
Puerto Esperanza, Par. 212/E2
Puerto Fonciere, Par. 212/E2
Puerto Frey, Bol. 209/F4
Puerto General Busch, Bol. 212/E1
Puerto General Ovando, Bol. 209/E3
Puerto Grether, Bol. 209/E5
Puerto Guadal, Chile 214/B5
Puerto Harberton, Arg. 215/D7
Puerto Heath, Bol. 208/D4
Puerto Huitoto, Col. 204/C4
Puerto Iguazú, Arg. 213/F3
Puerto Inca, Peru 208/C3
Puerto Ingeniero Ibáñez, Chile 214/C5
Puerto Inírida, Col. 204/E4
Puerto Isabel, Bol. 212/E1
Puerto Izozog, Bol. 212/D1
Puerto José Pardo, Peru 208/B1
Puerto La Cruz, Ven. 205/E2
Puerto Leda, Par. 212/E2
Puerto Leguía, Peru 208/D4
Puerto Leguízamo, Col. 204/C5
Puerto Leigue, Bol. 209/E4
Puerto Lempira, Hon. 201/F3
Puerto Lobos, Arg. 214/D4
Puerto López, Col. 204/C3
Puerto López, Col. 204/D2
Puerto Lumbreras, Sp. 72/E4
Puerto Madero, Mex. 200/C3
Puerto Madryn, Arg. 214/D4
Puerto Magdalena, Mex. 198/B3
Puerto Maldonado, Peru 208/D4
Puerto Mamoré, Bol. 209/E5
Puerto María, Par. 212/E2
Puerto Mercedes, Col. 204/C4
Puerto Mihanovich, Par. 212/E2
Puerto Montt, Chile 214/B4
Puerto Morazán, Nic. 200/E3
Puerto Morelos, Mex. 196/D3
Puerto Morín, Peru 208/B3
Puerto Napo, Ecu. 204/B5
Puerto Natales, Chile 215/B6
Puerto Niño, Col. 207/L7
Puerto Nuevo, Col. 204/D3
Puerto Nuevo, Chile 215/C7
Puerto Obaldía, Pan. 204/B2
Puerto Ocopa, Peru 208/C3
Puerto Olaya, Col. 207/L6
Puerto Padre, Cuba 201/G1
Puerto Páez, Ven. 205/E3
Puerto Pando, Bol. 208/E4
Puerto Patiño, Bol. 209/E5
Puerto Peñasco, Mex. 175/F5
Puerto Pinasco, Par. 212/E2
Puerto Pirámides, Arg. 214/D4
Puerto Piray, Arg. 213/F3
Puerto Píritu, Ven. 205/E2
Puerto Pizarro, Col. 204/C4
Puerto Portillo, Peru 208/C3
Puerto Prado, Peru 208/C3
Puerto Prat, Chile 215/B6
Puerto Princesa, Phil. 114/B3
Puerto Puyuguapi, Chile 214/B5
Puerto Quellón, Chile 214/B4
Puerto Real, Sp. 72/B4
Puerto Rico, Col. 204/C4
Puerto Rico, Col. 204/C4
Puerto Rico, Bol. 209/E3
Puerto Rico (dpcy.), US 165/L8
Puerto Rico, Tx, US 177/E4
Puerto Rondón, Col. 204/D3
Puerto Ruiz, Arg. 215/J10
Puerto Saavedra, Chile 214/B3
Puerto Saíz, Col. 204/C4
Puerto Salgar, Col. 207/L7
Puerto Salinas, Bol. 209/E4
Puerto San Carlos, Mex. 198/B3
Puerto San Julián, Arg. 215/D6
Puerto Santa Cruz, Arg. 215/C6
Puerto Santa Maria, Phil. 114/C4
Puerto Sastre, Par. 212/E2
Puerto Saucedo, Bol. 209/F4
Puerto Serrano, Sp. 72/C4
Puerto Siles, Bol. 209/E4
Puerto Suárez, Bol. 212/E1
Puerto Supe, Peru 208/B3
Puerto Tacurú Pytá, Par. 213/E2
Puerto Tahuantinsuyo, Peru 208/D4
Puerto Tejada, Col. 204/B4
Puerto Toledo, Col. 204/C5
Puerto Torno, Bol. 209/E5
Puerto Tunigrama, Peru 204/B5
Puerto Vallarta, Mex. 198/D4
Puerto Varas, Chile 214/B4
Puerto Vargas, Bol. 209/E4
Puerto Velarde, Bol. 209/F5
Puerto Victoria, Peru 208/C3
Puerto Viejo, CR 201/E4
Puerto Villamil, Ecu. 208/J7
Puerto Villarroel, Bol. 209/E5
Puerto Villazón, Bol. 209/F4
Puerto Wilches, Col. 204/C3
Puerto Williams, Chile 215/D7
Puerto Yartou, Chile 215/C7
Puertollano, Sp. 72/C3
Puesto Cunambo, Peru 208/B1
Puesto de Pailas, Bol. 212/D1
Pueyrredón (lake), Arg. 214/C5
Puffin (isl.), Wal, UK 60/D5
Pugachev, Rus. 97/J1
Pūgal, India 124/B5
Puge, Tanz. 145/A3
Puger, Indo. 115/F3
Puget (sound), Wa, US 168/B2
Puget-sur-Argens, Fr. 90/C6
Puget-Théniers, Fr. 90/C5
Puget-Ville, Fr. 90/C6
Puglia (pol. reg.), It. 74/E2
Puglia (prov.), It. 76/C5
Pugwash, NS, Can. 184/F3
Puhja, Est. 67/M2
Puigcerdà, Sp. 70/D5
Puigmal (peak), Fr. 73/G1
Puina, Bol. 208/D4
Puiseux-en-France, Fr. 56/K4
Pujaut, Fr. 90/A5
Pujehun, SLeo. 140/C5
Pujiang, China 112/D2
Pujilí, Ecu. 204/B5
Pujŏn (lake), NKor. 107/D2
Pujut (cape), Indo. 115/D3
Pukaki (lake), NZ 161/B3
Puk'an-san (peak), SKor. 107/F6
Puk'an-san NP, SKor. 107/D4
Pukapuka (isl.), CookIs. 163/J6
Pukarua (isl.), FrPol. 163/M6
Pukaskwa NP, On, Can. 183/L3
Pukch'ang, NKor. 107/D3
Pukchin, NKor. 107/C2
Pukch'ŏng, NKor. 107/E2
Pukdae (riv.), NKor. 107/E2
Pukë, Alb. 75/F1
Pukerua Bay, NZ 161/H9
Pukhan (riv.), NKor.,SKor. 107/D3
Pukhan (riv.), SKor. 107/G6
Pukhovichi, Bela. 67/N5
Pukhrāyān, India 122/B2
Pukkila, Fin. 65/F4
Pukŕi-san, SKor. 107/F6
Pukou, China 113/H3
Pukovac, Yugo. 76/E4
Pukp'ot'ae-san (peak), NKor. 107/E2
Puksoozero, Rus. 94/J3
Pukuatu (cape), Indo. 154/A2
Pula, Cro. 71/K4
Pulacayo, Bol. 212/C2
Pulandian (bay), China 107/A3
Puladuta (pt.), Phil. 117/F1
Pulangi (riv.), Phil. 114/D3
Pulap (isl.), Micr. 162/D4
Pulāsar, India 124/C5
Pulaski, Ms, US 188/C4
Pulaski, NY, US 187/H3
Pulaski, Tn, US 188/D3
Pulaski, Wi, US 186/B2
Pulaski, Va, US 189/G2
Pulau (riv.), Indo. 117/J5
Pulau Ayer Chawan (isl.), Sing. 115/H6
Pulau Bukum (isl.), Sing. 115/J7
Pulau Pinang (state), Malay. 115/B1
Pulau Sudong (isl.), Sing. 115/H7
Pulau Tekong (isl.), Sing. 115/K6
Pulau Ubin (isl.), Sing. 115/J6
Pulaukijang, Indo. 115/C3
Puławy, Pol. 69/L3
Pulborough, Eng, UK 63/F5
Pulguk-sa, SKor. 110/A3
Pulheim, Ger. 81/F2
Pulí, Col. 207/L8
Pulisan (cape), Indo. 117/G3
Pulkovo (int'l arpt.), Rus. 94/T7
Pullach im Isartal, Ger. 87/H1
Pullman, Mi, US 186/C3
Pullman, Wa, US 170/F4
Pully, Swi. 86/C5
Pulog (mt.), Phil. 114/C1
Pulsnitz (riv.), Ger. 69/G3
Pułtusk, Pol. 69/L2
Pulu, China 125/D4
Pülümür, Turk. 128/D2
Puluwat (isl.), Micr. 162/D4
Pulversheim, Fr. 86/D2
Pulwama, India 124/C3
Pum (riv.), China 123/F1
Puma (lake), China 123/H1
Puma, Tanz. 145/A3
Pumpkin (cr.), Mt, US 171/M4
Pumpsaint, Wal, UK 62/C2
Pumpville, Tx, US 177/D3
Pumu (pass), China 119/F2
Puna de Atacama (plat.), Arg. 212/C3
Punaauia, FrPol. 163/X15
Punakaiki, NZ 161/B3
Punākha, Bhu. 123/G2
Punata, Bol. 212/C1
Pūnch, India 124/C3
Pūnch (riv.), India 124/C3
Punchaw, BC, Can. 170/C1
Püncogling, China 123/F1
Punda Maria, SAfr. 149/F4
Pūndri, India 124/D5
Pune (Poona), India 127/K5
Punelia (lake), Fin. 65/E4
Punggai (cape), Malay. 116/B3
P'unggi, SKor. 107/E4
Pungo (riv.), NC, US 189/J3
Pungo NWR, NC, US 189/J3
Púngoè (riv.), Moz. 149/G3
Pungoteague, Va, US 189/K2
P'ungsan, NKor. 107/E2
P'ungsŏ, NKor. 107/E2
Pungwe (falls), Zim. 149/G3
Punia, D.R. Congo 147/F3
Punitaqui, Chile 212/B4
Punjab (plain), Pak. 127/K2
Punjab (state), India 125/B5
Puno (dept.), Peru 212/B1
Puno, Peru 208/D4
Pūnpūn (riv.), India 123/E3
Punta, Ca, US 192/A2
Punta Allen, Mex. 196/D4
Punta Alta, Arg. 214/E3
Punta Arena, (pt.), Mex. 198/C4
Punta Arenas, Chile 215/C7
Punta Banda, (cape), Mex. 198/A2
Punta Cardón, Ven. 204/D2
Punta Celarain, (pt.), Mex. 200/E1
Punta Colnett, (pt.), Mex. 198/A2
Punta Colonet, Mex. 198/A2
Punta de Bombón, Peru 208/D5
Punta de Díaz, Chile 212/B4
Punta de Mata, Ven. 205/F2
Punta de Pietra (res.), Ven. 207/Q8
Punta del Este, Uru. 215/G2
Punta del Este (Capitán Curbelo) (int'l arpt.), Uru. 215/G2
Punta Gorda, Fl, US 191/G4
Punta Gorda (bay), Nic. 196/E5
Punta Gorda, Belz. 200/D2
Punta Marina, It. 89/F5
Punta Raisi (int'l arpt.), It. 74/C3
Punta Umbría, Sp. 72/B4
Puntarenas, CR 201/E4
Puntas de Maciel, Uru. 215/K10
Punxsutawney, Pa, US 187/G4
Pupiales, Col. 204/B4
Pupuya (peak), Bol. 208/D4
Puqi, China 113/G2
Puqian, China 119/K3
Puquio, Peru 208/C4
Puquios, Chile 208/D5
Pur (riv.), Rus. 100/H3
Pura, India 122/A3
Puracé (vol.), Col. 204/B4
Puracé, PN, Col. 204/B4
Pūranpur, India 122/C1
Purari (riv.), PNG 155/G1
Purbeck (isl.), Eng, UK 62/D5
Purbolinggo, Indo. 115/E3
Purcell, Ok, US 179/F3
Purcell (mts.), BC, Can. 170/F2
Purcell (mtn.), Wa, US 170/D4
Purdin, Mo, US 181/H4
Purdy, Mo, US 179/H2
Purdy, On, Can. 187/H2
Purdy, Va, US 189/J2
Puré (riv.), Col. 204/D5
Pure, Indo. 154/A1
Purén, Chile 214/B3
Purgatoire (riv.), Co, US 180/C5
Pürgen, Ger. 87/G1
Purgstall an der Erlauf, Aus. 71/L2
Purificación, Col. 204/C4
Purikari (pt.), Est. 67/L2
Purkersdorf, Aus. 77/N7
Purleigh, Eng, UK 56/F1
Purley (nbrhd.), Eng, UK 56/C3
Purmerend, Neth. 78/B3
Pūrna (riv.), India 118/C3
Pūrna, India 121/C2
Purnia, India 123/F3
Purple (mtn.), Ire. 58/A6
Purton, Eng, UK 63/E3
Puruê (riv.), Braz. 204/D5
Puruey, Ven. 205/E3
Purūlia, India 123/F4
Puruname, Ven. 205/E4
Puruni (riv.), Guy. 205/G3
Purús (riv.), Braz. 203/C3
Purushottampur, India 121/E2
Purutu (isl.), PNG 155/F2
Purvis, Ms, US 190/D2
Pŭrvomay, Bul. 77/G4
Purwa, India 122/C2
Purwakarta, Indo. 115/D3
Purwodadi, Indo. 115/E3
Purwokerto, Indo. 115/E3
Purworejo, Indo. 115/E3
Puryear, Tn, US 188/C2
Puryŏng, NKor. 105/K3
Pusad, India 121/C2
Pusan-jikhalsi (prov.), SKor. 110/A3
Pusat Gayo (mts.), Indo. 116/A3
Puschendorf, Ger. 84/D3
Pushchino, Rus. 94/H5
Pushkin, Rus. 94/T7
Pushkin (arpt.), Rus. 94/T7
Pushkino, Rus. 97/H2
Pushkino, Rus. 94/Y9
Pushkinskiye Gory, Rus. 67/N3
Pushmataha, Al, US 188/C4
Püspökladány, Hun. 76/E2
Pussay, Fr. 83/H4
Püssi, Est. 67/M2
Pustomyty, Ukr. 98/B3
Pustoshka, Bela. 98/E1
Pusuga, Gha. 141/E4
Pusula, Fin. 65/D4
Pusur (riv.), Bang. 123/G4
Puta, Zam. 147/G5
Putaendo, Chile 214/C2
Putah (cr.), Ca, US 174/A1
Putai, Tai. 113/J4
Putana (vol.), Chile 212/C2
Putanges-Pont-Écrepin, Fr. 83/E3
Putao, Myan. 112/C3
Putaoxu, China 113/F3
Putaruru, NZ 161/C2
Puthia, Bang. 123/G3
Puthukkudiyiruppu, SrL. 121/D4
Putian, China 113/G2
Putina, Peru 208/D4
Puting (cape), Indo. 116/D4
Putintsevo, Kaz. 104/A2
Putla de Guerrero, Mex. 200/B2
Putnam, Al, US 190/D1
Putnam, Ct, US 187/L4
Putnam, Ok, US 178/E3
Putnam, Tx, US 176/E1
Putney, SD, US 182/E5
Putney, Ga, US 191/F2
Putney, Vt, US 187/K3
Putomayo (dept.), Col. 204/C4
Putorana (mts.), Rus. 100/K3
Putrachoique (peak), Arg. 214/C4
Putre, Chile 212/B1
Putte, Belg. 81/D1
Puttelange-aux-Lacs, Fr. 81/F5
Putten (isl.), Neth. 78/B5
Putten, Neth. 78/C4
Puttenham, Eng, UK 56/B3
Puttgarden, Ger. 66/D4
Püttlach (riv.), Ger. 85/E3
Püttlingen, Ger. 81/F5
Putu (range), Libr. 140/C5
Putula, Fin. 65/F4
Putumayo (riv.), Ecu. 204/B4
Putumayo (riv.), SAm. 203/B3
Putumayo (riv.), SAm. 204/C5
Putumayo (riv.), Col.,Peru 208/D1
Putussibau, Indo. 116/D3
Putyla, Ukr. 98/C3
Putyvl', Ukr. 99/G2
Puula (lake), Fin. 67/M1

289

Rapide – Ring

Rapides de Gozobangi (rapids), CAfr. 142/D4
Rapides de L'ELéphant (rapids), CAfr. 142/C4
Rapides de Yalala (falls), D.R. Congo 146/C4
Rapido (riv.), It. 92/C4
Räpina, Est. 67/M2
Rapirrán, Bol. 209/E3
Rapla, Est. 67/L2
Rappahannock (riv.), Va, US 189/J2
Rapper (cape), Chile 214/B5
Rāpti (zone), Nepal 122/D1
Rapti (riv.), India 118/D2
Rápulo (riv.), Bol. 209/E4
Rara NP, Nepal 122/D1
Raritan (bay), NJ, US 194/D3
Raritan (riv.), NJ, US 194/D2
Raritan, South Branch (riv.), NJ, US 194/D2
Raron, Swi. 86/D5
Rarotonga (isl.), CookIs. 163/J7
Ra's Abū Madd (pt.), SAr 135/H3
Ra's Ajdīr, Libya 93/F4
Ra's al 'Ayn, Syria 128/E2
Ra's al Basīt (pt.), Syria 130/D2
Ra's al Ḥadd (pt.), Oman 127/G4
Ra's Al Jabal, Tun. 74/B4
Ra's al Khafjī, SAr. 129/G4
Ra's al Khalīj, Egypt 139/C2
Ra's al Khaymah, UAE 127/G3
Ra's al Madrakah (pt.), Oman 127/G5
Ra's al Mish'āb (pt.), SAr. 129/G4
Ra's al 'Ushsh, Egypt 139/D2
Ra's An Naqb, Jor. 130/D5
Ra's as Saffānīyah (pt.), SAr. 126/E3
Ra's ash Sharbatāt (pt.), Oman 127/G5
Ra's aţ Ţīb (Cape Bon) (cape), Tun. 74/B4
Ra's at Tín (pt.), Libya 93/J4
Ra's Banās (pt.), Egypt 135/G4
Ra's Barīdī (pt.), SAr. 135/H3
Râs el Mâ, Mali 140/D2
Râs el Ma, Alg. 138/D2
Râs el Oued, Alg. 138/H5
Râs el-Barr, Egypt 139/C1
Ra's Fartak (pt.), Yem. 126/F5
Ras Gharib, Egypt 135/G2
Ra's Ḥāţibah (pt.), SAr. 126/C4
Ras il-Qammieħ (pt.), Malta 74/L7
Ra's Jibsh (pt.), Oman 127/G4
Ra's Muḥammad (pt.), Egypt 135/G3
Ra's Nawş (pt.), Oman 127/G5
Ras San Dimitri (pt.), Malta 74/L6
Ra's Şawqirah (pt.), Oman 127/G5
Rasa (pt.), Arg. 214/E4
Raschau, Ger. 85/F1
Raseiniai, Lith. 67/K4
Rashaant, Mong. 104/C2
Rashād, Sudan 142/F3
Rasharkin, NI, UK 60/B2
Rāshayyā, Leb. 131/D1
Rashīd, Egypt 139/B2
Rashīd, Massabb (Rosetta) (mouth), Egypt 139/B1
Rasht, Iran 129/G2
Rasi Salai, Thai. 120/D3
Rāsk, Iran 127/H3
Raška, Yugo. 76/E4
Rāsla, India 127/K3
Rasmussen (basin), Nun, Can. 166/G2
Raso (cape), Port. 73/P10
Rason (lake), Austl. 153/B3
Rasrā, India 122/D3
Rassina, It. 89/E6
Rasskazovo, Rus. 97/G1
Rassypnaya, Rus. 97/K2
Rastatt, Ger. 84/B5
Rastede, Ger. 79/F2
Rasūlnagar, Pak. 124/B3
Rat (isls.), Ak, US 68/U13
Rat Buri, Thai. 120/B3
Rata (cape), Indo. 115/D3
Ratahan, Indo. 117/F3
Ratak Chain (isls.), Mrsh. 162/F3
Ratanpur, India 122/D4
Ratcliff, Tx, US 177/G2
Rāth, India 122/B3
Rathangan, Ire. 58/C3
Rathbun (lake), Ia, US 181/H3
Rathcoole, Ire. 60/B5
Rathcormack, Ire. 58/B5
Rathdowney, Ire. 58/C4
Rathdrum, Ire. 60/B6
Rathdrum, Id, US 170/F4
Rathedaung, Myan. 119/F3
Rathenow, Ger. 68/G2
Rathfriland, NI, UK 60/B3
Rathgormuck, Ire. 58/C5
Rathkeale, Ire. 58/B4
Rathlin (isl.), NI, UK 60/B1
Rathlin (sound), NI, UK 60/B1
Rathluirc, Ire. 58/B5
Rathmore, Ire. 58/A5
Rathmore, Ire. 58/D3
Rathnew, Ire. 60/B6
Rathowen, Ire. 58/C2
Rathvilly, Ire. 58/D4
Rathwire, Ire. 58/C2
Ratia, India 124/C5
Ratingen, Ger. 78/D6
Ratlām, India 118/C3
Ratnapura, SrL. 121/D5
Ratne, Ukr. 98/C2
Ratoath, Ire. 60/B4
Raton, NM, US 178/B2
Rattaphum, Thai. 120/C5
Rattlesnake (cr.), Ks, US 180/E4
Rattray, Sc, UK 59/C3
Rattray (pt.), Sc, UK 59/E1
Rättvik, Swe. 66/F1
Rau, Indo. 115/C2
Raub, Malay. 115/C2
Rauch, Mn, US 183/H4
Rauch, Arg. 214/F3
Raudales Malpaso, Mex. 200/C2
Raudhinúpur (pt.), Ice. 64/P6
Raufarhöfn, Ice. 64/P6
Raufoss, Nor. 66/D1
Rauhe Ebrach (riv.), Ger. 84/D3
Raul Soares, Braz. 211/E4
Rauma, Fin. 67/J1
Rauna, Lat. 67/L3
Raunds, Eng, UK 63/F2
Raung (peak), Indo. 115/F3
Raunheim, Ger. 84/B2
Raupehu (vol.), NZ 161/C2
Raurkela, India 123/E4
Rausa Garhi, Nepal 123/E1
Rausu, Japan 108/D1
Rautjärvi, Fin. 67/N1
Rauzan, Bang. 123/H4
Rava-Rus'ka, Ukr. 98/B2
Ravanusa, It. 74/C4
Rāvar, Iran 129/J4
Ravarino, It. 89/E4
Ravels, Belg. 78/B6
Raven, Va, US 189/G2
Ravena, NY, US 187/K3
Ravendale, Ca, US 172/C3
Ravenglass, Eng, UK 61/E3
Ravenna, Oh, US 186/F4
Ravenna, Ca, US 192/B2
Ravenna, It. 89/F5
Ravenna (prov.), It. 89/E4
Ravenna, Ky, US 188/F2
Ravenna, Ne, US 180/E3
Ravensburg, Ger. 87/F2
Ravensdale, Wa, US 193/D3
Ravenshead, Eng, UK 61/G5
Ravenshoe, Austl. 160/B2
Ravensthorpe, Austl. 156/D5
Ravenswood, WV, US 189/G1
Rāvi (riv.), India 125/C5
Ravne na Koroškem, Slov. 71/L3
Ravnina, Trkm. 127/H1
Rawa Mazowiecka, Pol. 69/L3
Rāwah, Iraq 128/E3
Rawaki (Phoenix) (isl.), Kiri. 163/H5
Rāwalpindi, Pak. 124/B3
Rāwatsār, India 124/C5
Rawdon, Qu, Can. 187/K1
Rawene, NZ 161/C1
Rawḥah, SAr. 126/D5
Rawicz, Pol. 69/J3
Rawlinna, Austl. 156/E4
Rawlins, Wy, US 173/K3
Rawlinson (mt.), Austl. 157/E3
Rawmarsh, Eng, UK 61/G5
Rawson, Arg. 214/D4
Rawtenstall, Eng, UK 61/F4
Rawu, China 112/C2
Raxaul Bazar, India 123/E2
Ray, ND, US 182/C3
Ray (cape), Nf, Can. 185/H2
Ray Hubbard (lake), Tx, US 176/L7
Ray Roberts (lake), Tx, US 177/F1
Raya (peak), Indo. 116/D4
Rāyachoti, India 121/C3
Rāyadrug, India 121/C3
Raybon, Ga, US 191/H2
Raychikhinsk, Rus. 105/K2
Rāyen, Iran 129/J4
Rayevskiy, Rus. 95/M5
Rayleigh, Eng, UK 63/G3
Raymond, Wi, US 193/P14
Raymond, Ca, US 174/C2
Raymond, Ms, US 188/B4
Raymond, Mn, US 181/G1
Raymond, Il, US 181/K4
Raymond, Wa, US 170/C4
Raymond, Ab, Can. 171/H3
Raymond Terrace, Austl. 159/E1
Raymondville, Mo, US 179/J2
Raymondville, Tx, US 177/F4
Raymore, Sk, Can. 182/B2
Raymore, Mo, US 179/G1
Rayne, La, US 190/B2
Rayón, Mex. 199/Q10
Rayón, Mex. 198/C2
Rayón, Mex. 199/F4
Rayón, PN, Mex. 199/E5
Rayong, Thai. 120/C3
Raysūt, Oman 126/F5
Rayville, La, US 179/J4
Rāzām, India 121/D2
Razan, Iran 129/G3
Razelm (lake), Rom. 93/L1
Razgrad, Bul. 77/H4
Razlog, Bul. 75/H2
Razumnoye, Rus. 99/J2
Ré (isl.), Fr. 92/C1
Re di Castello (peak), It. 87/G5
Rea (lake), Ire. 58/B3
Rea (riv.), Eng, UK 62/D1
Reading, Ks, US 179/G1
Reading, Mi, US 186/D4
Reading, Oh, US 188/E1
Reading, Eng, UK 63/F4
Reading, Pa, US 194/C3
Reading Regional/Carl A. Spaatz Field (arpt.), Pa, US 194/C3
Readlyn, Sk, Can. 171/M3
Readsville, Mo, US 179/J1
Reagan, Tx, US 177/F2
Real de San Carlos, Uru. 215/K11
Réal Martin (riv.), Fr. 90/C6
Realicó, Arg. 214/D2
Realitos, Tx, US 177/E4
Realp, Swi. 87/E4
Reamstown, Pa, US 194/B3
Reang Kesei, Camb. 120/C3
Reao (isl.), FrPol. 163/M6
Réau, Fr. 56/K6
Rebais, Fr. 80/C6
Rebecca, Ga, US 191/G2
Rebecca (lake), Austl. 153/B4
Rębiechowo (int'l arpt.), Pol. 66/H4
Rebstein, Swi. 87/F3
Rebun, Japan 108/B1
Rebun (isl.), Japan 105/N2
Recanati, It. 89/G7
Recco, It. 88/C5
Rēchah Lām, Afg. 124/A2
Recherche (arch.), Austl. 153/B4
Rechnitz, Aus. 71/M3
Rechthalten, Swi. 86/D4
Rechytsa, Bela. 96/D1
Recife, Braz. 207/H5
Recife (cape), SAfr. 150/D4
Recke, Ger. 79/E4
Reckingen, Swi. 87/E5
Recklinghausen, Ger. 79/E5
Recknitz (riv.), Ger. 68/G2
Réclère, Swi. 86/C3
Reclining Buddha (Shwethalyaung), Myan. 112/C5
Recluse, Wy, US 180/B1
Recoaro Terme, It. 89/E2
Reconquista, Arg. 212/E4
Reconvilier, Swi. 86/D3
Recreo, Arg. 212/C4
Recreo, Arg. 212/D4
Rector, Ar, US 188/B2
Recuay, Peru 208/B3
Red (lakes), China 103/H7
Red (sea), Afr.,Asia 103/C7
Red (riv.), Mb, Can. 182/F3
Red (bay), NI, UK 60/B1
Red (isl.), Nf, Can. 185/K2
Red (cr.), Ms, US 190/D2
Red (riv.), La, US 196/C1
Red (riv.), Mn, US 169/G2
Red (lake), Mn, US 169/H2
Red (riv.), Viet. 120/D1
Red (Yuan) (riv.), China 112/D4
Red Bank, Tn, US 188/E3
Red Bank, NJ, US 194/D3
Red Bank, SC, US 189/G4
Red Bay, Fl, US 191/F2
Red Bay, Al, US 188/C3
Red Bluff (res.), Tx, US 178/B5
Red Bluff, Ca, US 172/B3
Red Bluff, BC, Can. 170/C1
Red Boiling Springs, Tn, US 188/E2
Red Bud, Il, US 188/C1
Red Cliff Ind. Res., Wi, US 183/J4
Red Cliffs, Austl. 158/B2
Red Cloud, Ne, US 180/E3
Red Creek, NY, US 187/H3
Red Deer (riv.), Sk, Can. 166/E3
Red Deer, Ab, Can. 171/H1
Red Feather Lakes, Co, US 180/B3
Red Fish (isl.), Tx, US 177/N9
Red Gate, Tx, US 177/E4
Red Hill, Pa, US 194/C3
Red Hill Patrick Henry Nat'l Mem., Va, US 189/H2
Red Indian (lake), Nf, Can. 185/J1
Red Lake, On, Can. 183/H2
Red Lake, Mn, US 183/G4
Red Lake Falls, Mn, US 182/F4
Red Lake Ind. Res., Mn, US 183/G3
Red Lake Road, On, Can. 183/H3
Red Level, Al, US 190/E2
Red Lion, Pa, US 194/B4
Red Lion, De, US 194/C4
Red Lodge, Mt, US 173/J1
Red Mountain, Ca, US 174/D3
Red Oak, Ia, US 181/G3
Red Oak, Ga, US 189/M7
Red Oak (cr.), Tx, US 176/L7
Red Oak, Tx, US 176/L7
Red River of the North (riv.), ND,Mn, US 182/F4
Red Pheasant Ind. Res., Sk, Can. 171/K1
Red River (valley), Mn, US 182/F3
Red River Army Depot, Tx, US 179/G4
Red Rock, On, Can. 183/K3
Red Rock (riv.), Mt, US 173/G1
Red Rock (plat.), Ut, US 175/G2
Red Rock (lake), Ia, US 181/H3
Red Rock, Tx, US 176/F3
Red Rock Lakes NWR, Mt, US 173/G1
Red Rocks (pt.), Austl. 157/E5
Red Scaffold, SD, US 180/D1
Red Sea (hills), Sudan 133/F2
Red Shirt, SD, US 180/C2
Red Springs, NC, US 189/H3
Red Volta (riv.), Burk. 141/E4
Red Willow (dam), Ne, US 180/D3
Red Willow (cr.), Ne, US 180/D3
Red Wing, Co, US 178/B2
Red Wing, Mn, US 181/H1
Red, North Fork (riv.), Tx,Ok, US 178/D3
Red, Salt Fork (riv.), Tx,Ok, US 178/D3
Reda, Pol. 66/H4
Redan, Ga, US 189/M7
Redang (isl.), Malay. 115/C1
Redange-sur-Attert, Lux. 81/E4
Redberry (lake), Sk, Can. 171/L1
Redbourn, Eng, UK 63/F3
Redbridge (bor.), Eng, UK 56/D2
Redby, Mn, US 183/G4
Redcar, Eng, UK 61/G2
Redcliff, Zim. 149/F3
Redcliff, Ab, Can. 171/J2
Redcliffe (mt.), Austl. 156/D4
Redcliffe (nbrhd.), Austl. 160/F6
Redden, De, US 194/C6
Reddersburg, SAfr. 150/D3
Reddick, Fl, US 191/G3
Redding, Ca, US 172/B3
Redding, Ct, US 195/E1
Reddish (peak), WV, US 189/H1
Redditch, Eng, UK 63/E2
Rede (riv.), Eng, UK 61/F1
Redenção, Braz. 206/D5
Redenção do Gurguéia, Braz. 207/E5
Redfield, Ar, US 179/H3
Redfield, SD, US 180/E1
Redford, Mi, US 193/F7
Redford, Mo, US 188/B2
Redford, Tx, US 177/B3
Redhill, Eng, UK 56/C3
Rédics, Hun. 76/C2
Redig, SD, US 182/C5
Redington Beach, Fl, US 190/K8
Redkey, In, US 186/D4
Redkino, Rus. 94/H4
Redland, Md, US 194/A5
Redland Bay, Austl. 160/F7
Redlands, Ca, US 192/C2
Redlands, Co, US 173/J4
Redlin, Ger. 68/G2
Redmond, Ut, US 175/G1
Redmond, Or, US 172/C1
Redmond (res.), Ks, US 181/F4
Redmond, Wa, US 170/C4
Rednitz (riv.), Ger. 84/D4
Redon, Fr. 82/C5
Redondela, Sp. 72/A1
Redondo, Wa, US 193/C3
Redondo, Port. 72/B3
Redondo (peak), NM, US 175/J3
Redondo Beach, Ca, US 192/F8
Redrock, NM, US 175/H4
Redruth, Eng, UK 62/A6
Redstone (riv.), NW, Can. 166/D2
Redstone (cr.), SD, US 180/F1
Redstone Arsenal, Al, US 188/D3
Redvale, Co, US 175/H1
Redvers, Sk, Can. 182/D3
Redwater (riv.), Mt, US 171/M4
Redway, Ca, US 172/B3
Redwood (riv.), Mn, US 181/G1
Redwood Falls, Mn, US 181/G1
Redwood NP, Ca, US 172/A3
Ree, Lough (lake), Ire. 58/C3
Reece City, Al, US 188/D3
Reed, Ar, US 179/J4
Reed, Ok, US 178/E3
Reed City, Mi, US 186/D3
Reeder, ND, US 182/C4
Reedham, Eng, UK 63/H1
Reedley, Ca, US 174/C2
Reeds (bay), NJ, US 194/D5
Reeds Spring, Mo, US 179/H2
Reedsburg, Wi, US 181/J2
Reedsport, Or, US 172/A2
Reedy (cr.), Fl, US 190/N7
Reedy (lake), Fl, US 190/N8
Reedy (cr.), Austl. 158/B3
Reef (isls.), Sol. 162/F6
Reef (pt.), Belz. 199/J5
Reefton, NZ 161/B3
Reelfoot Lake NWR, Tn, US 188/C2
Reepham, Eng, UK 63/H1
Rees, Ger. 78/D5
Reese, Mi, US 186/E3
Reese (riv.), Nv, US 168/C4
Reessum, Ger. 79/G2
Reest (riv.), Neth. 78/D3
Reeth, Eng, UK 61/G3
Reeuwijk, Neth. 78/B4
Refahiye, Turk. 128/D2
Reform, Al, US 188/C4
Reforma, Mex. 200/C2
Refugio, Tx, US 177/F3
Refugio lo Valdés, Chile 214/N8
Rega (riv.), Pol. 66/F5
Regen, Ger. 85/G5
Regen (riv.), Ger. 85/F4
Regência, Pontal da (pt.), Braz. 211/F3
Regeneração, Braz. 207/F4
Regensburg, Ger. 85/F4
Regensdorf, Swi. 87/E3
Regenstauf, Ger. 85/F4
Regent, ND, US 182/C4
Regents Park (nbrhd.), Austl. 160/H8
Reggane, Alg. 137/F4
Regge (riv.), Neth. 78/D4
Reggello, It. 89/E6
Reggio, La, US 190/D3
Reggio di Calabria, It. 74/D3
Reggio di Calabria (prov.), It. 74/D3
Reggio nell' Emilia (prov.), It. 88/D3
Reggio nell'Emilia, It. 88/D4
Reggiolo, It. 89/D4
Reghin, Rom. 77/G2
Regina (cap.), Sk, Can. 182/B2
Regina, NM, US 175/J2
Régina, FrG. 206/C1
Regina Beach, Sk, Can. 182/B2
Región Metropolitana Santiago (pol. reg.), Chile 214/B1
Registro, Braz. 213/H3
Regnitz (riv.), Ger. 71/J2
Regoledo, It. 87/F5
Reguengos de Monsaraz, Port. 72/B3
Regway, Sk, Can. 182/B3
Rehau, Ger. 85/F2
Rehburg-Loccum, Ger. 79/G4
Rehfelde, Ger. 68/Q6
Rehlī, India 122/B4
Rehling, Ger. 84/D6
Rehlingen-Siersburg, Ger. 81/F5
Rehoboth, Namb. 148/C4
Rehoboth, NM, US 175/H3
Réhon, Fr. 81/E4
Rehovot, Isr. 131/B5
Rehrersburg, Pa, US 194/B3
Reichelsheim, Ger. 84/B3
Reichelsheim, Ger. 84/B2
Reichenbach, Ger. 85/F1
Reichenbach im Kandertal, Swi. 86/D4
Reichenbach-Steegen, Ger. 81/G4
Reichenberg, Ger. 84/C3
Reichertshausen, Ger. 85/E6
Reichshof, Ger. 81/G2
Reichshoffen, Fr. 81/G6
Reichstett, Fr. 81/G6
Reid, Austl. 157/F4
Reid (lake), Sk, Can. 171/L2
Reiden, Swi. 86/D3
Reidland, Ky, US 188/C2
Reidsville, Ga, US 189/F4
Reidsville, NC, US 189/H2
Reigate, Eng, UK 56/C3
Reignier, Fr. 86/C5
Reillanne, Fr. 90/B5
Reilly (hill), Ne, US 180/C3
Re'im, Isr. 131/A6
Reims, Fr. 80/D5
Reims (Champagne) (arpt.), Fr. 80/D5
Reina Adelaida (arch.), Chile 215/A6
Reina Beatrix (int'l arpt.), NAnt. 204/D1
Reinach, Swi. 86/D3
Reinach, Swi. 86/E3
Reinbeck, Ia, US 181/H2
Reinbek, Ger. 79/H1
Reindeer (isl.), Mb, Can. 182/F1
Reindeer (lake), Sk, Can. 165/G4
Reinerton-Orwin-Muir, Pa, US 194/B2
Reinheim, Ger. 84/B3
Reinickendorf, Ger. 68/Q6
Reinland, Mb, Can. 182/F3
Reinosa, Sp. 72/C1
Reinsfeld, Ger. 81/F4
Reischach, Ger. 85/F6
Reisdorf, Lux. 81/F4
Reisduoddarhal'di (peak), Nor. 64/G1
Reiskirchen, Ger. 84/B1
Reisterstown, Md, US 194/B5
Reitdiep (riv.), Neth. 78/D2
Reitz, SAfr. 150/E2
Rejaf, Sudan 142/F4
Rejón (int'l arpt.), Mex. 200/D1
Rekkam (plat.), Mor. 138/C2
Reliance, NW, Can. 166/F2
Reliance, Wy, US 173/J3
Reliance, SD, US 180/E2
Relizane (wilaya), Alg. 138/F5
Relizane, Alg. 138/F5
Rellingen, Ger. 79/G1
Remagen, Ger. 81/G2
Remanso, Bol. 209/F4
Remanso, Braz. 207/F5
Remanzacco, It. 89/G1
Remarde (riv.), Fr. 56/H6
Remarkable (mt.), Austl. 157/H5
Rembang, Indo. 115/E3
Rembau, Malay. 115/C2
Remchi, Alg. 138/D2
Remedios, Pan. 201/F4
Remer, Mn, US 183/H4
Remerton, Ga, US 191/G2
Remich, Lux. 81/F4
Remicourt, Belg. 81/E2
Remington, In, US 186/C4
Rémire, FrG. 206/C1
Remiremont, Fr. 86/C1
Remlap, Al, US 188/D4
Remlingen, Ger. 79/H4
Remontnoye, Rus. 97/G3
Rems (riv.), Ger. 71/H2
Remscheid, Ger. 79/E6
Remsen, NY, US 187/J3
Remsen, Ia, US 181/G2
Remy, Fr. 80/B5
Ren (riv.), China 104/F5
Rena, Nor. 66/D1
Rena Lara, Ms, US 188/B3
Renage, Fr. 90/B2
Renāla Khurd, Pak. 124/B4
Renan, Swi. 86/C3
Renarde (riv.), Fr. 56/J6
Renazé, Fr. 83/D5
Renazzo, It. 89/E4
Renca, Chile 214/N8
Rencēni, Lat. 67/L3
Rench (riv.), Ger. 84/A5
Renchen, Ger. 86/E1
Rencontre East, Nf, Can. 185/K2
Rend (lake), Il, US 188/C1
Renda, Lat. 67/K3
Rendeux, Belg. 81/E3
Rendsburg, Ger. 66/C4
Renens, Swi. 86/C4
Renews-Cappahayden, Nf, Can. 185/L2
Renfrew, Sc, UK 59/B5
Renfrew, On, Can. 187/H2
Rengam, Malay. 115/C2
Rengat, Indo. 115/C3
Rengo, Chile 214/N9
Rengsdorf, Ger. 81/G3
Renhua, China 119/K2
Renhuai, China 113/E3
Reni, Ukr. 77/J3
Renish (pt.), Sc, UK 57/Q8
Renkajärvi (lake), Fin. 65/E4
Renko, Fin. 65/E4
Renkomäki, Fin. 65/F4
Renkum, Neth. 78/C5
Renmark, Austl. 157/J5
Rennell (isl.), Sol. 162/F6
Rennerod, Ger. 81/H2
Rennertshofen, Ger. 84/E5
Rennes, Fr. 82/D4
Rennie, Mb, Can. 183/G3
Renningen, Ger. 84/B5
Reno, Tx, US 179/G4
Reno (riv.), It. 93/F1
Reno, Nv, US 172/D4
Reno, Tx, US 176/K7
Renoster (riv.), SAfr. 150/C3
Renovo, Pa, US 187/H4
Renqiu, China 106/D3
Renshizhen, China 113/E2
Renshou, China 113/H3
Rensselaer, In, US 186/C4
Rentería, Sp. 70/C5
Renton, Sc, UK 59/B5
Renton, Wa, US 170/C4
Rentz, Ga, US 191/G1
Renville, Mn, US 181/G1
Renwer, Mb, Can. 182/D1
Renwez, Fr. 81/D4
Réo, Burk. 141/E3
Reo, Indo. 117/F5
Reoti, India 123/E3
Répcelak, Hun. 76/C2
Repelón, Col. 201/H4
Repentigny, Qu, Can. 185/P6
Repino, Rus. 94/S6
Replonges, Fr. 86/A5
Repton, Eng, UK 61/G6
Republic, Mi, US 183/L4
Republic, Mo, US 179/H2
Republic (arpt.), NY, US 195/M9
Republic, Ks, US 180/F4
Republic, Wa, US 170/E3
Republican (riv.), Ks,Ne, US 169/G3
Republican, South Fork (riv.), Co,Ks, US 178/C1
Republican, South Fork (riv.), Co, US 180/C4
Repulse (bay), Ausrl. 153/D3
Repulse Bay (isl.), Austl. 160/C3
Repulse Bay, Nun, Can. 167/H2
Rep'yëvka, Rus. 99/K2
Requena, Sp. 73/E3
Requena, Peru 208/C2
Requínoa, Chile 214/N9
Rera, Braz. 205/F3
Rerdell, Fl, US 190/L6
Reriutaba, Braz. 207/F4
Reşadiye, Turk. 128/D1
Resaro, Swe. 65/B1
Reschen (Resia), It. 87/G4
Reschensee (Resia) (lake), It. 87/G4
Rescue (pt.), Chile 214/B5
Reseda (nbrhd.), Ca, US 192/E7
Resegone (peak), It. 88/C2
Resen, FYROM 75/G2
Resende, Port. 72/B2
Resende, Braz. 211/M7
Reserve, Sk, Can. 182/C1
Reserve, Mt, US 182/B3
Reserve, Wi, US 183/J5
Reserve, NM, US 175/H4
Réserve de Campo, Camr. 146/B2
Réserve de Douala-Edéa, Camr. 146/B2
Réserve de Faune du Siniaka-minia, Chad 142/C3
Réserve de Kenié-baoulé, Mali 140/C3
Réserve de La Léfini, Congo 146/C3
Réserve Totale de Faune de l'Arly, Burk. 141/F4
Reshetylivka, Ukr. 99/H3
Resia (Reschen), It. 87/G4
Resia (Reschensee) (lake), It. 87/G4
Resia, Passo di (pass), It. 87/G4
Resistencia, Arg. 212/E3
Reşiţa, Rom. 76/E3
Resolution (is.), Nun, Can. 167/K2
Resolven, Wal, UK 62/C3
Respenda de la Peña, Sp. 72/C1
Resplendor, Braz. 211/E3
Ressano Garcia, Moz. 149/G5
Restigné, Fr. 83/F6
Restigouche (riv.), NB, Can. 184/D2
Reston, Mb, Can. 182/D3
Reston, Va, US 194/A6
Reszel, Pol. 67/J4
Retalhuleu, Guat. 200/D3
Rethel, Fr. 81/D4
Rethem, Ger. 79/G3
Réthimnon, Gre. 75/J5
Retie, Belg. 78/C6
Retiers, Fr. 82/D5
Retrezap NP, Rom. 96/B3
Rétság, Hun. 76/D2
Rettenberg, Ger. 87/G2
Retz, Aus. 69/H4
Reugny, Fr. 83/F6
Réunion (dpcy.), Fr. 151/S15
Reus, Sp. 73/F2
Reusel, Neth. 78/C6
Reuss (riv.), Swi. 87/E3
Reuterstadt Stavenhagen, Ger. 66/E5
Reutlingen, Ger. 84/C6
Reutov, Rus. 94/W9
Reutte, Aus. 87/G3
Revadim, Isr. 131/B5
Revda, Rus. 94/G2
Revda, Rus. 95/N4
Reveille (peak), Nv, US 174/D2
Réveillon (riv.), Fr. 56/K5
Revel, Fr. 70/D5
Revelstoke, BC, Can. 170/E2
Reventazón, Peru 208/A2
Revenue, Sk, Can. 171/K1
Revere, It. 89/E3
Revesby (nbrhd.), Austl. 160/H8
Revfülöp, Hun. 76/C2
Revigny-sur-Ornain, Fr. 81/D6
Revillagigedo (is s.), Mex. 165/F8
Réville, Fr. 82/D1
Revillo, SD, US 181/F1
Revin, Fr. 81/D4
Revolyutsii (peak), Taj. 125/B4
Revsbotn (inlet), Nor. 64/G1
Revúboè (riv.), Moz. 149/G2
Revuè (riv.), Moz. 149/G3
Rewa, India 122/C3
Rewa (riv.), Guy. 205/G4
Rex, Ga, US 189/M7
Rexburg, Id, US 173/H2
Rexford, Mt, US 170/G3
Rexton, NB, Can. 184/E2
Rey (isl.), Pan. 197/F6
Rey Bouba, Camr. 142/B3
Reydell, Ar, US 179/J3
Reydon, Eng, UK 63/H2
Reyes, Bol. 209/E4
Reyhanlı, Turk. 130/E1
Reykjanestá (cape), Ice. 64/M7
Reykjavík (cap.), Ice. 64/N7
Reykjavik (int'l arpt.), Ice. 64/N7
Reynolds, Mo, US 179/J2
Reynolds, Ga, US 188/E4
Reynoldsburg, Oh, US 186/E5
Reynoldsville, Pa, US 187/G4
Reynosa, Mex. 177/E4
Reyran (riv.), Fr. 90/C5
Reyssouze (riv.), Fr. 86/B5
Rezé, Fr. 82/D6
Rēzekne, Lat. 67/M3
Rezina, Mol. 98/E4
Rezzato, It. 88/D2
Rhaetian Alps (mts.), Swi., Aus. 71/H3
Rhallamane (lake), Mrta. 136/C4
Rhallamane (reg.), Mrta. 136/C5
Rhame, ND, US 182/C4
Rhart (peak), Mor. 136/D3
Rhat (peak), Mor. 136/D3
Rhätikon (mts.), Swi.,Aus. 87/F3
Rhayader, Wal, UK 62/C2
Rheda-Wiedenbrück, Ger. 79/F5
Rhede, Ger. 78/D5
Rhede, Ger. 79/E2
Rheden, Neth. 78/D4
Rheidol (riv.), Wal, UK 62/C2
Rhein, Sk, Can. 182/C2
Rhein (Rhine) (riv.), Aus.,Ger. 68/D3
Rheinau, Swi. 87/E2
Rheinbach, Ger. 81/F2
Rheinberg, Ger. 78/D5
Rheinbreitbach, Ger. 81/G2
Rheinbrohl, Ger. 81/G3
Rheine, Ger. 79/E4
Rheinfall, Swi. 87/E2
Rheinfelden, Ger. 86/D2
Rheinland-Pfalz (state), Ger. 84/A3
Rheinwaldhorn (peak), Swi. 87/F5
Rheinzabern, Ger. 84/B4
Rhemiles (well), Alg. 136/D3
Rhenen, Neth. 78/C5
Rheris, Oued (riv.), Mor. 136/D3
Rhin (Rhine) (riv.), Fr. 81/H6
Rhinau, Fr. 86/D1
Rhine (riv.), Eur. 92/F1
Rhine-Herne (canal), Ger. 79/E5
Rhinebeck, NY, US 187/K4
Rhineland, Mo, US 181/J4
Rhineland, Sk, Can. 171/L2
Rhinelander, Wi, US 183/K5
Rhinns (pt.), Sc, UK 57/Q9
Rhino Camp, Ugan. 147/G2
Rhiou (riv.), Alg. 138/F5
Rhiou (riv.), Alg. 138/F5
Rhir (cape), Mor. 136/C3
Rhisnes, Belg. 81/D3
Rhiw (riv.), Wal, UK 62/C1
Rho, It. 88/C2
Rhode, Ire. 58/C3
Rhode Island (sound), RI, US 184/B5
Rhode Island (state), US 169/M3
Rhodes (isl.), Gre. 55/G5
Rhodes (Pódhos), Gre. 128/B2
Rhodope (mts.), Bul.,Gre. 93/J2
Rhome, Tx, US 176/K6
Rhön (mts.), Ger. 84/D1
Rhondda, Wal, UK 62/C3
Rhône (dept.), Fr. 86/A6
Rhone (glacier), Swi. 87/E4
Rhône (riv.), Fr. 55/E4
Rhône au Rhin (canal), Fr. 86/B3
Rhône-Alpes (pol. reg.), Fr. 86/B5
Rhonelle (riv.), Fr. 80/C3
Rhosllanerchrugog, Wal, UK 61/E6
Rhossili, Wal, UK 62/B3
Rhuddlan, Wal, UK 60/E5
Rhum (isl.), Sc, UK 57/Q8
Rhume (riv.), Ger. 79/H5
Rhumel, Oued el (riv.), Alg. 138/J4
Rhuys (pen.), Fr. 82/C6
Rhyddhywel (peak), Wal, UK 62/C2
Rhydowen, Wal, UK 62/B2
Rhyl, Wal, UK 60/E5
Rhynie, Sc, UK 59/D2
Rhyolite, Nv, US 174/D2
Riaba, EqG. 146/B2
Riachão, Braz. 207/E4
Riachão das Neves, Braz. 210/D1
Riachão do Jacuípe, Braz. 211/F1
Riacho de Santana, Braz. 211/E2
Riacho Monte Lindo (riv.), Arg. 212/E3
Riacho Pilagá (riv.), Arg. 212/E3
Riachuelo, Uru. 215/K11
Riachuelo, Braz. 207/H4
Riaillé, Fr. 82/D5
Riala, Swe. 65/B1
Rialto, Ca, US 192/C2
Riangnom, Sudan 142/F3
Rianjo, Sp. 72/A1
Riano, It. 91/B3
Riaño, Sp. 72/C1
Rians, Fr. 90/B5
Riāsi, India 124/C3
Riau (isls.), Indo. 116/B3
Riau (prov.), Indo. 115/C2
Riaza, Sp. 72/D2
Rib (mtn.), Wi, US 181/K1
Rib Lake, Wi, US 183/J5
Ribadeo, Sp. 72/B1
Ribadesella, Sp. 72/C1
Riban'i Manamby (mts.), Madg. 152/H9
Ribas do Rio Pardo, Braz. 213/F2
Ribauè, Moz. 149/H2
Ribble (riv.), Eng, UK 61/F4
Ribblesdale (valley), Eng, UK 61/F3
Ribe, Den. 66/C4
Ribe (co.), Den. 66/C4
Ribeauvillé, Fr. 86/D1
Ribécourt-Dreslincourt, Fr. 80/B4
Ribeira (riv.), Braz. 213/G3
Ribeira Brava, Port. 136/A2
Ribeira Brava, CpV. 133/J10
Ribeira de Pena, Port. 72/B2
Ribeira do Pombal, Braz. 211/F1
Ribeira Grande, CpV. 133/J9
Ribeira Grande, Azor., Port. 73/T13
Ribeirão, Braz. 207/H5
Ribeirão Preto, Braz. 213/H2
Ribeiro Gonçalves, Braz. 207/E4
Ribera, It. 74/C4
Ribera, NM, US 178/B3
Riberalta, Bol. 209/E3
Ribiers, Fr. 90/B4
Ribniţa, Mol. 98/E4
Ribnitz-Damgarten, Ger. 66/E4
Ribstone, Ab, Can. 171/J1
Ribstone (cr.), Ab, Can. 171/J1
Říčany u Prahy, Czh. 85/H3
Ricaurte, Col. 204/B4
Riccia, It. 92/D5
Riccione, It. 89/F6
Ricco'del Golfo, It. 88/C5
Rice, Mn, US 183/G5
Rice (lake), On, Can. 187/G2
Rice, Ca, US 174/E3
Rice, Wa, US 170/E3
Rice, Tx, US 177/F1
Rice Lake, Wi, US 183/J5
Rice Lake NWR, Mn, US 183/H4
Riceboro, Ga, US 191/H2
Riceville, Ia, US 181/H2
Rich (mtn.), Ar, US 179/G3
Rich, Mor. 136/D2
Rich Hill, Mo, US 179/G1
Rich Square, NC, US 189/J2
Richard B. Russell (dam), SC, US 189/F3
Richard Toll, Sen. 140/B2
Richards, Mo, US 179/G2
Richards (isl.), NW, Can. 166/C2
Richard's Bay, SAfr. 151/F3
Richards Landing, On, Can. 186/D1
Richardson, Tx, US 176/L7
Richardson Lakes (lakes), NH, US 184/B3
Richardton, ND, US 182/C4
Richboro, Pa, US 194/C3
Riche (cape), Austl. 156/C5
Richebourg, Fr. 56/G5
Richel (isl.), Neth. 78/C2
Richelieu (riv.), Qu, Can. 187/K2
Richelieu, Qu, Can. 185/P7
Richey, Mt, US 182/B4
Richfield, Ut, US 175/F1
Richfield, Id, US 173/F2
Richfield, Mn, US 183/P7
Richfield, Pa, US 194/A2
Richford, Vt, US 187/K2
Richhill, NI, UK 60/B3
Richibucto, NB, Can. 184/E2
Richland, Mo, US 179/H2
Richland, Ga, US 191/F1
Richland, Ms, US 188/B4
Richland, Tx, US 177/F2
Richland, Wa, US 170/E4
Richland, Pa, US 194/B3
Richland, NJ, US 194/D5
Richland Balsam (peak), NC, US 189/F3
Richland Center, Wi, US 181/J2
Richland Creek (res.), Tx, US 177/F2
Richland Hills, Tx, US 176/K7
Richland Springs, Tx, US 177/E2
Richlands, Va, US 189/G2
Richlands, NC, US 189/J3
Richlandtown, Pa, US 194/C3
Richmond, Austl. 160/A3
Richmond, BC, Can. 170/C3
Richmond, Qu, Can. 187/K2
Richmond, NZ 161/C3
Richmond, SAfr. 150/C3
Richmond, SAfr. 151/E3
Richmond, Eng, UK 61/G3
Richmond, Ar, US 179/G4
Richmond, Ks, US 179/G1
Richmond, Mn, US 183/G5
Richmond, In, US 186/D5
Richmond, Mi, US 186/E3
Richmond, Il, US 193/P15
Richmond, Ut, US 173/H3
Richmond, Ky, US 188/E2
Richmond, Mo, US 181/H4
Richmond, Tx, US 177/M9
Richmond (cap.), Va, US 189/J2
Richmond (co.), NY, US 194/D2
Richmond Beach-Innis Arden, Wa, US 193/B2
Richmond Dale, Oh, US 189/F1
Richmond Heights, Fl, US 190/P11
Richmond Hill, On, Can. 186/U8
Richmond Nat'l Bfld. Park, Va, US 189/J2
Richmond Park (bor.), Eng, UK 56/C2
Richmond Town (nbrhd.), NY, US 195/J9
Richmond Upon Thames (bor.), Eng, UK 56/B2
Richmond-Windsor, Austl. 160/G8
Richmondville, NY, US 187/J3
Richmound, Sk, Can. 171/K2
Richtersveld NP, SAfr. 150/B3
Richterswil, Swi. 87/E3
Richthofen (mt.), Co, US 180/B3
Richton, Ms, US 190/D2
Richville, NY, US 187/J2
Richwiller, Fr. 86/D2
Richwood, Tx, US 176/G3
Richwood, La, US 179/H4
Richwood, Oh, US 186/E4
Richwood, WV, US 189/G1
Richwoods, Mo, US 188/B1
Rickenbach, Ger. 86/D2
Ricketts Glen St. Park, Pa, US 194/B1
Rickman, Tn, US 188/E2
Rickmansworth, Eng, UK 56/B2
Ricla, Sp. 72/E2
Rico, Ga, US 189/L7
Ricse, Hun. 69/L4
Ridā', Yem. 144/C2
Riddells Creek, Austl. 159/B3
Ridderkerk, Neth. 78/B5
Riddle, Id, US 172/E2
Riddle, Or, US 172/B2
Rideau (riv.), On, Can. 187/J2
Rideau (lake), On, Can. 187/H2
Ridge, Mt, US 180/B1
Ridge Farm, Il, US 186/C5
Ridge Manor, Fl, US 190/L6
Ridge Spring, SC, US 189/G4
Ridgecrest, La, US 190/C2
Ridgecrest, Ca, US 174/D3
Ridgefield, NJ, US 195/K8
Ridgefield, Wa, US 170/C5
Ridgefield, Ct, US 195/E1
Ridgefield NWR, Or, US 170/C5
Ridgefield Park, NJ, US 195/J8
Ridgeland, Ms, US 188/B4
Ridgeland, SC, US 189/G4
Ridgely, Tn, US 188/C2
Ridgely, Md, US 194/C6
Ridgetown, On, Can. 186/F3
Ridgeville, SC, US 189/G4
Ridgeway, Mo, US 181/H3
Ridgeway, Va, US 189/H2
Ridgewood (nbrhd.), NY, US 195/K9
Ridgewood, NJ, US 195/J8
Ridgewood State Park, NJ, US 194/D2
Ridgway, Pa, US 187/G4
Ridgway, Co, US 175/J1
Riding Mill, Eng, UK 61/G2
Riding Mountain NP, Mb, Can. 182/D2
Riding Mtn. (mtn.), Mb, Can. 182/D2
Ridlees Cairn (hill), Eng, UK 59/D6
Ridley (cr.), Pa, US 194/C4
Riec-sur-Belon, Fr. 82/B5
Riecito (riv.), Col. 204/D3
Ried im Innkreis, Aus. 85/G6
Ried im Traunkreis, Aus. 85/H6
Riede, Ger. 79/F3
Riedenburg, Ger. 85/E5
Riedisheim, Fr. 86/D2
Riedlingen, Ger. 87/F1
Riegelsberg, Ger. 81/F5
Riegelsville, Pa, US 194/C2
Riegsee (lake), Ger. 87/H2
Riehen, Swi. 86/D2
Riemst, Belg. 81/E2
Rieneck, Ger. 84/C2
Rienzi, Ms, US 188/C3
Riesa, Ger. 69/G3
Rieschweiler-Mühlbach, Ger. 81/G5
Riesco (isl.), Chile 215/B7
Riese Pio X, It. 89/E2
Riet (riv.), SAfr. 150/D3
Rietavas, Lith. 67/J4
Rietberg, Ger. 79/F5
Rietbron, SAfr. 150/C4
Rietfontein, Namb. 148/D4
Rietfontein (riv.), Namb. 148/D4
Rieti, It. 91/B3
Rieti (prov.), It. 91/B3
Rievaulx, Eng, UK 61/G3
Riez, Fr. 90/C5
Riffe (lake), Wa, US 170/C4
Rifle, Co, US 173/K4
Rifsnes (pt.), Ice. 64/N6
Rift Valley (prov.), Kenya 142/G5
Rig-Rig, Chad 142/B2
Riga (gulf), Eur. 100/C4
Riga (Rīga) (cap.), Lat. 67/L3
Rīga (Riga) (cap.), Lat. 67/L3
Rigacikun, Nga. 141/G4
Rigby, Id, US 173/H2
Rīgestan (pol. reg.), Afg. 127/H2
Riggins, Id, US 172/E1
Rigi (peak), Swi. 87/E3
Rignano Flaminio, It. 91/B3
Rignano sull'Arno, It. 89/E6
Rigolet, Nf, Can. 167/L3
Rigside, Sc, UK 59/C5
Riguldi, Est. 67/K2
Rihāb, Jor. 131/E4
Rihand (riv.), India 122/D3
Rihand (dam), India 122/D3
Rihand Sāgar (res.), India 118/D3
Riihimäki, Fin. 67/L1
Riiser-Larsen (pen.), Ant. 216/C
Riiser-Larsen Ice Shelf, Ant. 216/Y
Riisitunturin NP, Fin. 94/F2
Rijeka, Cro. 71/L4
Rijen, Neth. 78/B5
Rijksmuseum Kröller Müller, Neth. 78/C4
Rijnsburg, Neth. 78/B4
Rijsbergen, Neth. 78/B5
Rijssen, Neth. 78/D4
Rijswijk, Neth. 78/B4
Rikers (isl.), NY, US 195/K8
Rikitea, FrPol. 163/M7
Rikuchū-Kaigan NP, Japan 108/C4
Rikuzentakata, Japan 108/B4
Rila, Bul. 75/H1
Rila (mts.), Bul. 75/H1
Riley, Or, US 172/D2
Riley, Ks, US 181/F4
Riley Brook, NB, Can. 184/D2
Rillieux-la-Pape, Fr. 86/A6
Rillito, Az, US 175/G4
Rilski Manastir, Bul. 75/H1
Rīmah (wadi), SAr. 126/D3
Rimatara (isl.), FrPol. 163/K7
Rimavská Sobota, Slvk. 69/L4
Rimbach, Ger. 84/B3
Rimbey, Ab, Can. 171/G1
Rimbo, Swe. 65/B1
Rimé (riv.), Chad 142/C2
Rimersburg, Pa, US 187/G4
Rimforsa, Swe. 66/F2
Rimini, It. 89/F5
Rîmnicu Sărat, Rom. 77/H3
Rîmnicu Vîlcea, Rom. 77/G3
Rimogne, Fr. 81/D4
Rimouski, Qu, Can. 184/C1
Rimouski (riv.), Qu, Can. 184/C1
Rimouski-Est, Qu, Can. 184/C1
Rimpar, Ger. 84/C3
Rimpfischhorn (peak), Swi. 86/D5
Rimsting, Ger. 85/F7
Rimutaka (range), NZ 161/H9
Rimutaka Forrest Park, NZ 161/H9
Rinas (int'l arpt.), Alb. 75/F2
Rinbung, China 123/G1
Rinchnach, Ger. 85/G5
Rincon (peak), Az, US 175/G4
Rincón, Uru. 215/G2
Rincon, NM, US 175/J4
Rincón (peak), Arg.,Chile 212/C3
Rincon, Ga, US 189/G4
Rincón de la Vieja, PN, CR 196/D5
Rincón de Romos, Mex. 198/E4
Rinconada, Arg. 212/C2
Rindge, NH, US 187/K3
Ringarooma, Austl. 158/C4
Ringaskiddy, Ire. 58/B6
Ringboy (pt.), NI, UK 60/C3
Ringebu, Nor. 66/D1
Ringelspitz (peak), Swi. 87/F4
Ringgold, La, US 179/H4
Ringgold, Ga, US 188/E3
Ringim, Nga. 141/H3
Ringkøbing, Den. 66/C3
Ringkøbing (co.), Den. 66/B3
Ringkøbing (fjord), Den. 66/B3
Ringling, Ok, US 179/F3
Ringling, Mt, US 171/J4
Ringling Museum of Art, Fl, US 191/G4
Ringmer, Eng, UK 63/G5
Ringoes, NJ, US 194/D3
Ringold, Ok, US 179/G3
Ringsend, NI, UK 60/B1
Ringsön (isl.), Swe. 65/A2
Ringsted, Den. 66/D4
Ringtown, Pa, US 194/B2

Ring – Rover

Ringvaart (riv.), Neth. 78/B4
Ringvassøy (isl.), Nor. 64/F1
Ringway (Manchester) (int'l arpt.), Eng, UK 61/F5
Ringwood, NJ, US 195/H7
Ringwood, Austl. 157/G2
Ringwood (nbrhd.), Austl. 158/G5
Ringwood, Eng, UK 63/E5
Ringwood State Park, NJ, US 194/D1
Rínia (isl.), Gre. 75/J4
Riñihue, Chile 214/B3
Rinteln, Ger. 79/G4
Rinxent, Fr. 80/A2
Rio, La, US 190/D2
Río Abiseo, PN, Peru 208/B2
Rio Azul, Braz. 213/G3
Rio Blanco, Co, US 173/K4
Río Blanco, Chile 214/N8
Río Blanco, Bol. 208/D5
Río Blanco, Mex. 199/M8
Rio Bonito, Braz. 211/P7
Rio Branco, Braz. 208/E3
Rio Branco, Uru. 213/F5
Rio Branco do Sul, Braz. 213/G3
Río Bravo, Mex. 177/E5
Rio Brilhante, Braz. 213/F2
Río Bueno, Chile 214/B4
Río Cauto, Cuba 201/G1
Río Ceballos, Arg. 212/C4
Río Chico, Arg. 215/C6
Río Clarillo, PN, Chile 214/N8
Rio Claro, Trin. 205/F2
Rio Claro, Braz. 211/M7
Rio Claro, Braz. 213/H2
Río Colorado, Arg. 214/D3
Río Cuarto, Arg. 214/D2
Río de Bavispe (riv.), Mex. 198/C2
Rio de Contas, Braz. 211/E2
Rio de Janeiro (int'l arpt.), Braz. 211/N7
Rio de Janeiro, Braz. 211/N7
Rio de Janeiro (state), Braz. 211/E4
Rio Dell, Ca, US 172/A3
Rio do Sul, Braz. 213/G3
Rio Frio, Port. 73/Q10
Río Gallegos, Arg. 215/C6
Rio Grande (riv.), Mex. 177/B3
Rio Grande (canal), Co, US 178/A2
Rio Grande (riv.), US 196/A2
Rio Grande (plain), Tx, US 196/B2
Rio Grande, Oh, US 189/F1
Río Grande, Arg. 215/D7
Rio Grande, Braz. 213/F5
Rio Grande, NJ, US 194/D5
Rio Grande City, Tx, US 177/E4
Rio Grande da Serra, Braz. 211/K8
Río Grande de Matagalpa (riv.), Nic. 196/D5
Río Grande de Santiago (riv.), Mex. 198/D4
Rio Grande do Norte (state), Braz. 207/G4
Rio Grande do Piauí, Braz. 207/F4
Rio Grande do Sul (state), Braz. 213/F4
Rio Grande Valley (int'l arpt.), Tx, US 177/F4
Rio Hondo, Tx, US 176/F4
Rio Jaú, PN do, Braz. 205/F5
Río Lagartos, Mex. 200/D1
Rio Largo, Braz. 207/H5
Rio Maior, Port. 72/A3
Río Mayo, Arg. 214/C5
Rio Muni (pol. reg.), EqG. 146/B2
Rio Negrinho, Braz. 213/G3
Río Negro, Chile 214/B4
Río Negro (prov.), Arg. 214/E3
Río Negro, Chile 214/B4
Río Negro (res.), Uru. 213/F5
Rio Negro, Braz. 213/F1
Rio Negro (dept.), Uru. 213/F5
Rio Pardo, Braz. 213/F4
Rio Rancho, NM, US 175/J3
Rio Real, Braz. 211/F1
Rio Saliceto, It. 89/D4
Río Segundo, Arg. 212/D4
Río Simpson, PN, Chile 214/B5
Río Tala, Arg. 215/J10
Río Tercero, Arg. 212/C5
Río Tigre, Ecu. 204/B5
Rio Tinto, Braz. 207/H4
Río Verde, Chile 215/C7
Rio Verde, Braz. 210/C3
Río Verde, Mex. 199/F4
Rio Verde de Mato Grosso, Braz. 213/F1
Rio Vista, Ca, US 193/L10
Rio Vista, Tx, US 177/F1
Riobamba, Ecu. 204/B5
Ríohacha, Col. 204/C2
Rioja, Peru 208/B2
Riolo Terme, It. 89/E5
Riom, Fr. 70/E4
Riom-ès-Montagne, Fr. 70/E4
Riomaggiore, It. 88/C5
Rion-des-Landes, Fr. 70/C5
Riondel, BC, Can. 170/F3
Rionegro, Col. 204/C3
Rionegro, Col. 207/K6
Rionero in Vulture, It. 74/D2
Rionero Sannitico, It. 92/D4
Riorges, Fr. 70/F3
Ríos, Sp. 72/B2
Ríos (lake), Chile 214/B5
Ríosucio, Col. 204/B3
Ríosucio, Col. 207/K7
Rioz, Fr. 86/C3
Riozinho (riv.), Braz. 209/E2
Ripa Sottile (lake), It. 91/B3
Ripalimosano, It. 92/D4
Ripalti, Punta dei (pt.), It. 74/B1
Ripanj, Yugo. 76/E3
Riparbella, It. 88/D7
Ripatransone, It. 92/C2
Ripky, Ukr. 98/F2
Ripley, Eng, UK 61/G5
Ripley, Eng, UK 56/B3
Ripley, Ca, US 174/E4
Ripley, Ms, US 188/C3
Ripley, Ok, US 179/F2
Ripley, WV, US 189/G1
Ripley, Tn, US 188/C3
Ripley, Oh, US 188/F1
Ripoll, Sp. 73/G1
Ripoll (riv.), Sp. 73/L6
Ripollet, Sp. 73/L6
Ripon, Eng, UK 61/G3
Ripon, Qu, Can. 187/J2
Ripon, Ca, US 174/B2
Ripon, Wi, US 181/K2
Riposto, It. 74/D4
Ripples, NB, Can. 184/D2
Rippon, WV, US 187/H5
Ripponden, Eng, UK 61/G4
Rippowam (riv.), Ct, US 195/L7
Riri Bāzār, Nepal 122/D2
Ris-Orangis, Fr. 56/K6
Risaralda (dept.), Col. 204/A4
Risaralda, Col. 207/K7
Risasi, D.R. Congo 147/F3
Rîşcani, Mol. 98/D4
Rishiri, Japan 108/B1
Rishiri (isl.), Japan 105/N2
Rishiri-Rebun-Sarobetsu NP, Japan 108/B1
Rishon Leẕiyyon, Isr. 131/B5
Rishrāsh (wadi), Egypt 139/C6
Rising Star, Tx, US 177/E1
Rising Sun, In, US 188/E1
Rising Sun, Md, US 194/B4
Rising Sun-Lebanon, De, US 194/C5
Riske Creek, BC, Can. 170/C2
Risle (riv.), Fr. 70/D2
Risley (Estell Manor), NJ, US 194/D5
Risnjak (peak), Cro. 71/L4
Risnjak NP, Cro. 76/B3
Rîşnov, Rom. 77/G3
Rison, Ar, US 179/H4
Risør, Nor. 66/C2
Risoul, Fr. 90/C3
Riss (riv.), Ger. 87/F1
Risse (riv.), Fr. 86/C5
Rişşū (peak), Egypt 139/B5
Risti, Est. 67/L2
Ristiina, Fin. 67/M1
Rita Blanca (cr.), Tx, US 178/C2
Ritacuba (peak), Col. 204/C3
Ritaiō (isl.), Japan 162/D2
Rito (cr.), NM, US 175/H3
Ritoio (peak), It. 89/E6
Ritterhude, Ger. 79/F2
Rittman, Oh, US 186/F4
Rittō, Japan 109/J5
Ritzville, Wa, US 170/E4
Riva, It. 87/G6
Riva Ligure, It. 88/A5
Riva Presso Chieri, It. 88/A3
Riva San Vitale, Swi. 87/E6
Rivadavia, Arg. 214/E2
Rivadavia, Arg. 212/D3
Rivadavia, Arg. 212/B4
Rival (riv.), Fr. 90/B2
Rivalta, It. 88/D3
Rivalta di Torino, It. 88/A2
Rivanazzano, It. 88/C4
Rivanna (riv.), Va, US 189/H2
Rivara, It. 90/D2
Rivarolo Canavese, It. 88/A2
Rivarolo Mantovano, It. 88/D3
Rivas, Nic. 200/E4
Rīvash, Iran 127/G1
Rive-de-Gier, Fr. 90/A1
River Bourgeois, NS, Can. 185/G3
River Cess, Libr. 140/C5
River Denys, NS, Can. 185/G3
River Edge, NJ, US 195/J8
River Falls, Al, US 190/E2
River Falls, Wi, US 183/Q7
River Hébert, NS, Can. 184/E3
River John, NS, Can. 184/F3
River Kwai Bridge, Thai. 120/B3
River Oaks, Tx, US 176/K7
River Rouge, Mi, US 193/F7
River Vale, NJ, US 195/J8
Rivera, Swi. 87/E5
Rivera (isl.), Chile 214/B5
Rivera, Arg. 214/E3
Rivera (dept.), Uru. 213/F4
Rivera, Uru. 213/F4
Riverdale, ND, US 182/D4
Riverdale, NJ, US 195/H8
Riverdale (nbrhd.), NY, US 195/K8
Riverdale, Ca, US 174/C2
Riverdale, Ga, US 189/M7
Rivergaro, It. 88/C4
Riverhead, NY, US 195/F2
Riverhurst, Sk, Can. 171/L2
Riverport, NS, Can. 184/E3
Rivers, Mb, Can. 182/D2
Rivers (state), Nga. 141/G5
Riversdale, SAfr. 150/C4
Riverside, Tx, US 177/G2
Riverside (co.), Ca, US 192/C3
Riverside, Ca, US 192/C3
Riverside, Or, US 172/D2
Riverside (canal), Co, US 180/B3
Riverside, Pa, US 194/B2
Riverside, NJ, US 194/D3
Riverside-Albert, NB, Can. 184/E3
Riverstone (nbrhd.), Austl. 160/G8
Riverstown, Ire. 58/B6
Riverstown, Ire. 58/B1
Riverton, Mb, Can. 182/F2
Riverton, NS, Can. 185/F3
Riverton, Austl. 157/H5
Riverton, NZ 161/B4
Riverton, Wy, US 173/J2
Riverton, Ut, US 173/H3
Riverview, NB, Can. 184/E2
Riverview, Mi, US 186/E3
Riverview, Fl, US 190/L8
Riverwoods, Il, US 193/Q15
Rîves, Fr. 90/B2
Riviera, Az, US 174/E3
Riviera, Tx, US 177/F4
Riviera Beach, Fl, US 190/P9
Riviera Beach, Md, US 194/B5
Rivière-à-Pierre, Qu, Can. 184/A2
Rivière-au-Renard, Qu, Can. 184/E1
Rivière-Bleue, Qu, Can. 184/C2
Rivière-du-Loup, Qu, Can. 184/C2
Rivière-Éternité, Qu, Can. 184/B1
Riviersonderendreeks (mts.), SAfr. 150/L11
Rivignano, It. 89/G2
Rivne, Ukr. 98/D2
Rivnens'ka (prov.), Ukr. 96/C2
Rivoli, It. 90/D2
Rivolta d'Adda, It. 88/C3
Rixensart, Belg. 81/D2
Rixheim, Fr. 86/D2
Riyadh (Ar Riyāḑ) (cap.), SAr. 126/E4
Rīyāq, Leb. 131/D1
Rizal, Phil. 114/C2
Rizal (prov.), Phil. 114/F6
Rize, Turk. 97/G4
Rizhao, China 106/D4
Rizokarpasso, Cyp. 130/D2
Rizzuto (cape), It. 75/E3
Rjukan, Nor. 66/C2
Rkîz, Mrta. 140/B2
Rkîz (lake), Mrta. 140/B2
Rö, Swe. 65/B1
Roa, Nor. 66/D1
Roa, Sp. 72/D2
Road Town (cap.), BVI 197/M8
Roade, Eng, UK 63/F2
Roadside, Sc, UK 59/D3
Roan (plat.), Ut, US 173/J4
Roan Fell (hill), Sc, UK 61/F1
Roan High (peak), NC, US 189/F2
Roanne (riv.), Fr. 90/B3
Roanne, Fr. 70/F3
Roanoke, Al, US 188/E4
Roanoke, Tx, US 176/K6
Roanoke (riv.), Va, US 189/H2
Roanoke (pt.), NY, US 195/F2
Roanoke, Va, US 189/H2
Roanoke Rapids, NC, US 189/J2
Roans Prairie, Tx, US 177/G2
Roaring (cr.), Pa, US 194/B2
Roaring Fk. (riv.), Co, US 173/K4
Roaring Springs, Tx, US 178/D4
Roatán (isl.), Hon. 196/D4
Roatán, Hon. 200/E2
Robards, Ky, US 188/D2
Robassomero, It. 90/D2
Robāţ Karīm, Iran 129/G3
Robāţ-e Khān, Iran 129/J3
Robāţ-e Sang, Iran 127/G1
Robb, Ab, Can. 170/F1
Robbiate, It. 88/C2
Robbins (isl.), Austl. 158/C4
Robbins, NC, US 189/H3
Robbinsville, NC, US 188/F3
Robbio, It. 88/B3
Robe (riv.), Ire. 58/A2
Robē, Eth. 144/A4
Robe (mt.), Austl. 158/B1
Robe, Austl. 158/A3
Robecchetto con Induno, It. 88/B2
Röbel, Ger. 66/E4
Röbel, Ger. 68/G2
Robersonville, NC, US 189/J3
Robert (peak), Fr. 86/B5
Robert Lee, Tx, US 176/D2
Roberta, Ga, US 188/E4
Roberts, Il, US 186/B4
Roberts, Mt, US 173/J1
Roberts, Id, US 173/G2
Roberts (Monrovia) (int'l arpt.), Libr. 140/C5
Roberts Creek (mtn.), Nv, US 172/E4
Roberts Creek, BC, Can. 170/C3
Robertsbridge, Eng, UK 63/G5
Robertsfors, Swe. 64/G2
Robertsganj, India 122/D3
Robertson, SAfr. 150/L10
Robertson, Wy, US 173/H3
Robertsport, Libr. 140/C5
Robertstown, Ire. 58/D3
Roberval, Qu, Can. 184/A1
Robesonia, Pa, US 194/B3
Robilante, It. 90/D4
Robin Hood's Bay, Eng, UK 61/H3
Robins (A.F.B.), Ga, US 189/F4
Robinson, Il, US 188/D1
Robinson, Tx, US 177/F2
Robinson (mtn.), Mt, US 170/G3
Robinson . (range), Austl. 153/A3
Robinson Crusoe (isl.), Chile 203/B6
Robinson Gorge NP, Austl. 160/C4
Robinson River, Austl. 155/E4
Robinson River, PNG 155/H2
Robinson River Abor. Land, Austl. 155/E4
Robinson Springs, Al, US 188/D4
Robinvale, Austl. 158/B2
Robion, Fr. 90/B5
Robledo (mtn.), NM, US 175/J4
Roblin, Mb, Can. 182/D2
Roboré, Bol. 212/E1
Robsart, Sk, Can. 171/K3
Robson (mt.), BC, Can. 170/E1
Robstown, Tx, US 177/F4
Roby, Mo, US 179/H2
Roby, Tx, US 177/D1
Roc (pt.), Fr. 82/D3
Roc de France (peak), Fr. 73/G1
Roc du Haut du Faite (peak), Fr. 86/D1
Roca Partida (isl.), Mex. 198/B5
Roca Partida, Punta (pt.), Mex. 200/C2
Roca, Cabo da (cape), Port. 73/P10
Rocafuerte, Ecu. 204/A5
Rocanville, Sk, Can. 182/D2
Rocas (isl.), Braz. 207/H3
Rocca di Mezzo, It. 92/C3
Rocca di Papa, It. 91/B4
Rocca San Casciano, It. 89/E5
Roccabianca, It. 88/D3
Roccagorga, It. 92/C4
Roccamandolfi, It. 92/D5
Roccamonfina, It. 92/C5
Roccarainola, It. 92/D6
Roccasecca, It. 92/C4
Roccastrada, It. 74/B1
Roccavione, It. 90/D4
Rocciamelone (peak), It. 90/D2
Rocha, Uru. 215/G2
Rocha (dept.), Uru. 215/G2
Rochambeau (int'l arpt.), FrG. 206/C1
Rochdale, Eng, UK 61/F4
Roche, Swi. 86/C5
Roche, Eng, UK 62/B6
Roche Bernaude (peak), Fr. 90/C2
Roche de la Muzelle (peak), Fr. 90/C3
Roche du Sapin Sec (peak), Fr. 86/C1
Roche Faurio (peak), Fr. 90/C3
Roche-lez-Beaupré, Fr. 86/C3
Rochebrune, Pic de (peak), Fr. 90/C3
Rochefort, Belg. 81/E3
Rochefort, Fr. 70/C4
Rochefort-en-Terre, Fr. 82/C5
Rochefort-sur-Loire, Fr. 83/E6
Rochelaire, Pic de (peak), Fr. 90/C3
Rochelle, Ga, US 191/G2
Rochelle, Il, US 181/K3
Rochelle, Tx, US 177/E2
Rochelle Park, NJ, US 195/J8
Rochemaure, Fr. 90/A3
Rochers de la Tude (peak), Fr. 73/G1
Rochers du Bourbet (peak), Fr. 86/C3
Roches Blanches (peak), Fr. 90/C6
Rochester, Austl. 159/B3
Rochester, Eng, UK 63/G4
Rochester, NY, US 187/H3
Rochester, In, US 186/C4
Rochester, NH, US 187/L3
Rochester, Vt, US 187/K3
Rochester, Wi, US 193/P14
Rochester, Mi, US 193/F6
Rochester, Mn, US 181/H1
Rochester, Ky, US 188/D2
Rochester, Il, US 181/K4
Rochester Hills, Mi, US 186/E3
Rochford, Eng, UK 56/F2
Rochfortbridge, Ire. 58/C3
Rock (lake), ND, US 182/E3
Rock, Mi, US 183/L4
Rock (riv.), Il, US 169/J3
Rock (cr.), Mt, US 173/J1
Rock (riv.), Ia,Mn, US 181/F2
Rock Bluff, Fl, US 191/F2
Rock Cave, WV, US 189/G1
Rock Falls, Wi, US 181/J1
Rock Falls, Il, US 181/K3
Rock Forest, Qu, Can. 187/L2
Rock Glen, Pa, US 194/B2
Rock Hall, Md, US 194/B5
Rock Hill, SC, US 189/G3
Rock Island, Il, US 181/J3
Rock Island, Tx, US 176/F3
Rock Mills, Al, US 188/E4
Rock Port, Mo, US 181/G3
Rock Rapids, Ia, US 181/F2
Rock River, Wy, US 180/B3
Rock Springs, Wy, US 173/J3
Rock Springs, Mt, US 171/L4
Rock Valley, Ia, US 181/F2
Rockall (isl.), UK 55/C3
Rockaway (pt.), NY, US 195/K9
Rockaway (inlet), NY, US 195/K9
Rockaway (riv.), NJ, US 194/D2
Rockaway, NJ, US 194/D2
Rockaway (Rockaway Beach), Or, US 170/C5
Rockaway Beach (Rockaway), Or, US 170/C5
Rockaway Park (nbrhd.), NY, US 195/K9
Rockcorry, Ire. 58/C1
Rockdale, Il, US 193/P17
Rockdale (nbrhd.), Austl. 160/H8
Rockdale (co.), Ga, US 189/M7
Rockdale, Tx, US 177/F2
Rockefeller (plat.), Ant. 216/R
Rockenhausen, Ger. 81/G4
Rockett, Tx, US 176/L7
Rockfield, Ky, US 188/D2
Rockford, Oh, US 186/D4
Rockford, Il, US 181/K2
Rockford, Al, US 188/D4
Rockford, Wa, US 170/F4
Rockglen, Sk, Can. 171/M3
Rockhampton, Austl. 160/C3
Rockhampton Downs, Austl. 155/D4
Rockhill, Tx, US 176/L6
Rockingham, Vt, US 187/K3
Rockingham, Austl. 156/K7
Rockingham, NC, US 189/H3
Rockland, Tx, US 177/G2
Rockland, On, Can. 187/J2
Rockland, Id, US 173/G2
Rockland (co.), NY, US 194/D1
Rockland Lake, NY, US 195/K7
Rocklands (res.), Austl. 158/B3
Rockledge, Fl, US 191/H3
Rockledge, Pa, US 194/C3
Rocklin, Ca, US 172/C4
Rockmart, Ga, US 188/E3
Rockport, Ar, US 179/H3
Rockport, Ms, US 190/C2
Rockport, Ca, US 172/B4
Rockport, Ky, US 188/D2
Rockport, In, US 188/D2
Rockport, Wa, US 170/D3
Rockport, Tx, US 176/F3
Rocks (pt.), NZ 161/C3
Rocks, Md, US 194/B4
Rocksprings, Tx, US 177/D2
Rockstone, Guy. 205/G3
Rockton, Il, US 186/B3
Rockvale, Co, US 178/B1
Rockville, NS, Can. 184/D4
Rockville, In, US 186/C5
Rockville, Ut, US 175/F2
Rockville, Md, US 189/J1
Rockville Centre, NY, US 195/L9
Rockwall, Tx, US 176/L7
Rockwall (co.), Tx, US 176/L7
Rockwell, Ia, US 181/H2
Rockwell City, Ia, US 181/G2
Rockwood, Me, US 187/M2
Rockwood, Tn, US 188/E3
Rockwood, On, Can. 186/S8
Rockwood, Tx, US 176/E2
Rocky, Ok, US 178/E3
Rocky (pt.), Namb. 148/B3
Rocky (mts.), Can.,US 165/E4
Rocky (mtn.), Ky, US 188/F2
Rocky (pt.), Austl. 154/C2
Rocky (pt.), NY, US 195/F1
Rocky (riv.), NC, US 189/G3
Rocky Boys Ind. Res., Mt, US 171/K3
Rocky Cape NP, Austl. 158/C4
Rocky Ford, Co, US 178/C1
Rocky Ford, Ga, US 189/G4
Rocky Fork (lake), Oh, US 186/E5
Rocky Island (lake), On, Can. 186/E1
Rocky Mount, Mo, US 179/H1
Rocky Mount, NC, US 189/J3
Rocky Mount, Va, US 189/H2
Rocky Mountain Arsenal, Co, US 178/B1
Rocky Mountain House, Ab, Can. 170/G1
Rocky Mountain NP, Co, US 180/A3
Rocky Point, NC, US 189/J3
Rocky Reach (dam), Wa, US 170/D4
Rockyford, Ab, Can. 171/H2
Rockypoint, Wy, US 180/B1
Rocroi, Fr. 81/D4
Roda, Sp. 92/C3
Rodach (riv.), Ger. 85/E2
Rodach bei Coburg, Ger. 84/D2
Rodalben, Ger. 81/G5
Rodanthe, NC, US 189/K3
Rødberg, Nor. 66/C1
Rødbyhavn, Den. 66/D4
Rødbyvatn (lake), Nor. 64/S9
Rødding, Den. 66/C4
Roden (riv.), Eng, UK 61/F6
Rodenbach, Ger. 84/C2
Rodeo, Ca, US 193/K10
Rodeo, NM, US 175/H5
Rodeo, Mex. 198/D3
Roderfield, WV, US 189/G2
Rödermark, Ger. 84/B3
Rodessa, La, US 179/H4
Rodewisch, Ger. 85/F1
Rodez, Fr. 70/E4
Rodholívos, Gre. 75/H2
Ródhos (ruin), Gre. 128/B2
Ródhos (Rhodes), Gre. 128/B2
Rodigo, It. 88/D3
Roding (riv.), Eng, UK 56/D2
Roding, Ger. 85/F4
Rodinga (mt.), Austl. 157/G3
Rödinghausen, Ger. 79/F4
Rodney (cape), NZ 161/C2
Rodoč, Bosn. 76/C4
Rodolfo Sánchez Toboada, Mex. 198/A2
Rødovre, Den. 65/J7
Rodrigues, Braz. 208/C2
Rodríguez, Uru. 215/K11
Rødvig, Den. 65/J7
Rodyns'ke, Ukr. 99/J3
Roe (riv.), NI, UK 60/B2
Roebourne, Austl. 156/C2
Roebuck (bay), Austl. 153/B2
Roebuck, SC, US 189/G3
Roebuck Plains, Austl. 154/A4
Roedtan, SAfr. 149/F5
Roen (peak), It. 87/H5
Roer (riv.), Neth. 78/D6
Roermond, Neth. 78/C6
Roes Welcome Sound (str.), Nun, Can. 167/H2
Roeselare, Belg. 80/C2
Roesiger (lake), Wa, US 193/D2
Roff, Ok, US 179/F3
Rogač, Cro. 76/C4
Rogachev, Bela. 96/D1
Rogachëvka, Rus. 99/K2
Rogagua (lake), Bol. 209/E4
Rogaland (co.), Nor. 64/C4
Rogaška Slatina, Slov. 71/L3
Rogatica, Bosn. 76/D4
Rogers, ND, US 182/E4
Rogers, Ar, US 179/G2
Rogers (mt.), Va, US 189/G2
Rogers, BC, Can. 170/F2
Rogers, Tx, US 176/F2
Rogers City, Mi, US 186/E2
Rogersville, NB, Can. 184/E2
Rogersville, Mo, US 179/H2
Rogersville, Tn, US 189/F2
Rogersville, Al, US 188/D3
Roggwil, Swi. 86/D3
Rogliano, Fr. 74/A1
Roglio (riv.), It. 89/D5
Rognac, Fr. 90/B6
Rognes, Fr. 90/B5
Rognon (riv.), Fr. 70/F2
Rognonas, Fr. 90/A5
Rogo, Nga. 141/G4
Rogoaguado (lake), Bol. 209/E4
Rogoźno, Pol. 69/J2
Rogue (riv.), Or, US 172/A2
Rogue River, Or, US 172/B2
Rohatyn, Ukr. 98/C3
Rohl (riv.), Sudan 142/F4
Rohnert Park, Ca, US 172/B4
Rohr, Ger. 85/E5
Rohrbach bei Mattersburg, Aus. 76/C2
Rohrbach in Oberösterreich, Aus. 85/G5
Rohrbach-lès-Bitche, Fr. 81/G5
Rohri, Pak. 127/J3
Röhrmoos, Ger. 85/E6
Rohtak, India 124/D5
Rohtās, India 122/D3
Rohwer, Ar, US 179/J4
Roi Et, Thai. 120/C2
Roia (riv.), It. 90/D5
Roiffieux, Fr. 90/A2
Roine (lake), Fin. 67/L1
Roissy, Fr. 56/K5
Roissy-en-France, Fr. 56/K4
Roja, Lat. 67/K3
Rojas, Arg. 214/E2
Rojo (cape), PR 197/M8
Rojo, Cabo (cape), Mex. 200/B1
Roka, Kenya 145/B2
Rokan, Indo. 115/C2
Rokan (river), Indo. 115/C2
Rokan (riv.), Indo. 116/B3
Rokeby Croll Creek NP, Austl. 160/A1
Rokel (riv.), SLeo. 140/C4
Rokiškis, Lith. 67/L4
Rokkasho, Japan 108/B3
Rokkō-san (peak), Japan 109/H6
Rokot (cape), Indo. 115/B3
Rokugō, Japan 109/A3
Rokycany, Czh. 85/G3
Rokytka (riv.), Czh. 85/H2
Rokytne, Ukr. 98/D2
Rokytne, Ukr. 98/F3
Rolampont, Fr. 86/B2
Roland, Mb, Can. 182/F3
Roland, Ia, US 181/H2
Rolândia, Braz. 210/C4
Rolava (riv.), Czh. 85/F2
Røldal, Nor. 66/B2
Rolde, Neth. 78/D3
Rolette, ND, US 182/E3
Rolfe, Ia, US 181/G2
Rolim de Moura, Braz. 209/F3
Roll, Az, US 175/F4
Rolla, ND, US 182/E3
Rolla, Mo, US 179/J2
Rolle, Swi. 86/C5
Rolle, SAfr. 149/F5
Rolling Fork, Ms, US 188/B4
Rolling Hills, Ab, Can. 171/J2
Rolling Hills Estates, Ca, US 192/F8
Rolling Meadows, Il, US 193/P15
Rolling Prairies (plain), Tx, US 178/D4
Rollingbay, Wa, US 193/B2
Rolo, It. 89/D4
Rom (peak), Ugan. 142/G5
Roma, Swe. 66/H3
Roma (prov.), It. 91/B4
Roma, Austl. 160/C4
Roma, Tx, US 177/E4
Roma (Rome) (cap.), It. 91/B4
Romagna (reg.), It. 93/F1
Romagnano Sesia, It. 88/B2
Romagnat, Fr. 70/E4
Romain (cape), SC, US 189/H4
Romaine (riv.), Fr. 86/B2
Romaine (riv.), Qu, Can. 167/K3
Roman, Rom. 98/D4
Roman, Bul. 77/F4
Roman Kosh (peak), Ukr. 99/H5
Romanche (riv.), Fr. 90/C2
Romang (str.), Indo. 117/G5
Romang (isl.), Indo. 117/G5
Romania(ctry.) 55/G4
Romano (cape), Fl, US 191/H5
Romano Canavese, It. 88/A2
Romano d'Ezzelino, It. 89/E2
Romano di Lombardia, It. 88/C2
Romanovka, Rus. 97/H2
Romanovka, Rus. 104/G1
Romans d'Isonzo, It. 89/G2
Romans-sur-Isère, Fr. 90/B2
Romanshorn, Swi. 87/F2
Romanzof (cape), Ak, US 168/W12
Romashki, Rus. 97/H2
Rombas, Fr. 81/F5
Romblon, Phil. 114/C2
Rome (Roma) (cap.), It. 91/B4
Rome, NY, US 187/J3
Rome, Pa, US 187/H4
Rome, Wi, US 193/N14
Rome, Or, US 172/E2
Rome, Il, US 181/K3
Rome, Ga, US 188/E3
Romenay, Fr. 86/B4
Romeo, Mi, US 186/E3
Romeo, Co, US 175/K2
Romeoville, Il, US 193/P16
Romford (nbrhd.), Eng, UK 56/D2
Römhild, Ger. 84/D2
Romillé, Fr. 82/D4
Romilly-sur-Andelle, Fr. 83/G2
Rommani, Mor. 136/D2
Rommerskirchen, Ger. 81/F1
Romney, WV, US 187/G5
Romney Marsh (phys. reg.), Eng, UK 63/G4
Romny, Ukr. 99/G2
Rømø (isl.), Den. 68/E1
Romodan, Ukr. 99/G3
Romodanovo, Rus. 97/H1
Romoland, Ca, US 192/C3
Romont, Swi. 86/C4
Romorantin-Lanthenay, Fr. 83/G6
Romsey, Eng, UK 63/E5
Romsey, Austl. 159/B3
Rømskog, Nor. 66/D2
Romulus, Mi, US 186/E3
Ron, Viet. 120/D2
Ron (cape), Viet. 113/E5
Ron Phibun, Thai. 120/B4
Ronaldsway (Isle of Man) (arpt.), IM, UK 60/D3
Ronan, Mt, US 171/G4
Roncade, It. 89/F2
Roncador, Braz. 213/F3
Roncador Cay (isl.), Col. 197/F5
Roncador, Serra do (mts.), Braz. 210/B2
Ronceverte, WV, US 189/G2
Ronchamp, Fr. 86/C2
Ronchi dei Legionari (int'l arpt.), It. 89/G2
Ronchi dei Legionari, It. 89/G2
Ronciglione, It. 91/B3
Ronco (riv.), It. 89/F5
Ronco All'Adige, It. 89/E3
Ronco Scrivia, It. 88/B4
Roncoferraro, It. 89/D3
Roncq, Fr. 80/C2
Ronda, Sp. 72/C4
Rondane NP, Nor. 64/D3
Rondo, Ar, US 188/B3
Rondônia (state), Braz. 206/A5
Rondonópolis, Braz. 210/B3
Rondu, Pak. 124/C2
Rong (riv.), China 119/J2
Rong Kwang, Thai. 120/C2
Rong Xian, China 119/K3
Rong'an, China 113/F3
Rongchang, China 112/E2
Rongcheng, China 107/B4
Rongcheng, China 106/G7
Ronge (lake), Sk, Can. 166/F3
Rongelap (isl.), Mrsh. 162/F3
Rongerik (isl.), Mrsh. 162/F3
Rongjiang, China 113/F3
Rongjiawan, China 113/G2
Rongkou, China 113/H2
Rongshui Miaozu Zizhixian, China 119/J2
Rõngu, Est. 67/M2
Roniu (peak), FrPol. 163/X15
Ronkonkoma, NY, US 195/E2
Rønne, Den. 66/F4
Rönne (riv.), Swe. 65/K6
Ronne Ice Shelf, Ant. 216/W
Ronneby, Swe. 66/F3
Rønnede, Den. 65/J7
Ronnenberg, Ger. 79/G4
Rönninge, Swe. 65/A1
Ronquerolles, Fr. 56/J4
Ronsard (cape), Austl. 156/B3
Ronsberg, Ger. 87/G2
Ronse, Belg. 80/C2
Ronuro (plat.), Braz. 209/H4
Roodeport, SAfr. 150/P13
Roodhouse, Il, US 181/J4
Rooiberg (peak), Namb. 150/B2
Roosendaal, Neth. 78/B5
Roosevelt (isl.), Ant. 216/N
Roosevelt (riv.), Braz. 203/C4
Roosevelt (mt.), BC, Can. 166/D3
Roosevelt, Ok, US 178/E3
Roosevelt, NY, US 195/L9
Roosevelt (isl.), NY, US 195/K8
Roosevelt, Az, US 175/G4
Roosevelt, Ut, US 173/J3
Roosevelt, NJ, US 194/D3
Roosville, BC, Can. 170/G3
Root (riv.), Wi, US 193/P14
Root, West Branch (riv.), Wi, US 193/P14
Roper (riv.), Austl. 154/D3
Roper, NC, US 189/J3
Roper Valley, Austl. 154/D3
Ropesville, Tx, US 178/C4
Roque Pérez, Arg. 215/J11
Roquebillière, Fr. 90/D4
Roquebrune-Cap-Martin, Fr. 90/D5
Roquebrune-sur-Argens, Fr. 90/C6
Roquefort-la-Bédoule, Fr. 90/B6
Roquemaure, Fr. 90/A4
Roquesteron, Fr. 90/D5
Roquetas de Mar, Sp. 72/D4
Roquevaire, Fr. 90/B6
Roraima (peak), Ven. 205/F3
Roraima (state), Braz. 205/F4
Rørby, Den. 65/H7
Rori, India 124/C5
Rorke's Drift, SAfr. 151/E3
Rorke's Drift Battlesite, SAfr. 151/E3
Rorketon, Mb, Can. 182/E2
Røros, Nor. 64/D3
Rorschach, Swi. 87/F3
Rosa, La, US 190/B2
Rosà, It. 89/E2
Rosa (lake), Bahm. 201/H1
Rosa (cape), Alg. 138/L6
Rosa Punta (pt.), Mex. 198/C3
Rosa Zárate, Ecu. 204/B4
Rosablanche (peak), Swi. 86/D5
Rosal, Sp. 72/A2
Rosales, Mex. 177/B3
Rosalia, Ks, US 179/F2
Rosalia, Wa, US 170/F4
Rosalie (lake), Fl, US 190/N8
Rosalina, Par. 213/F2
Rosamond, Ca, US 174/C3
Rosamorada, Mex. 198/D4
Rosanna (riv.), Aus. 87/G3
Rosans, Fr. 90/B4
Rosario, Arg. 214/E2
Rosario, Phil. 114/C1
Rosario, Uru. 215/K11
Rosario, Phil. 114/E7
Rosario (riv.), Arg. 212/C3
Rosario, Par. 213/E3
Rosario, Bol. 209/E4
Rosário, Braz. 207/E3
Rosario, Mex. 198/D4
Rosario, Mex. 198/C3
Rosario de la Frontera, Arg. 212/C3
Rosario de Lerma, Arg. 212/C3
Rosario del Tala, Arg. 215/J10
Rosário do Sul, Braz. 213/F4
Rosário Oeste, Braz. 209/G4
Rosarno, It. 74/D3
Rosas, Col. 204/B4
Rosas (gulf), Sp. 73/G1
Rosate, It. 88/C3
Rosay, Fr. 56/G5
Rosbach vor der Höhe, Ger. 84/B2
Rosche, Ger. 79/H3
Roscoe, Mo, US 179/H2
Roscoe, Il, US 181/K2
Roscoe, Tx, US 177/D1
Roscoff, Fr. 82/B3
Roscommon, Ire. 58/B2
Roscommon (co.), Ire. 58/B2
Roscommon, Mi, US 186/D2
Roscrea, Ire. 58/C4
Rosdorf, Ger. 79/G5
Rose (isl.), ASam. 163/J6
Rose (peak), Az, US 175/H4
Rose Belle, Mrts. 151/T15
Rose Bud, Ar, US 179/H3
Rose City, Mi, US 186/D2
Rose Hill, Ks, US 179/F2
Rose Hill, Ms, US 188/C4
Rose Hill, Va, US 189/F2
Rose Lodge, Or, US 172/B1
Rose Valley, Sk, Can. 182/C1
Roseau, Mn, US 182/G3
Roseau (riv.), Mn, US 182/F3
Roseau (cap.), Dom. 197/N9
Roseau River, Mb, Can. 182/F3
Roseaux, Haiti 201/H2
Rosebery, Austl. 158/C4
Roseboro, NC, US 189/H3
Rosebud, Ga, US 189/N7
Rosebud, Tx, US 177/F2
Rosebud (riv.), Ab, Can. 171/H2
Rosebud, Mt, US 171/L4
Rosebud (cr.), Mt, US 171/L4
Rosebud Ind. Res., SD, US 180/D2
Roseburg, Or, US 172/B2
Rosedale, Ca, US 174/C3
Rosedale, Ms, US 188/B4
Rosedale, Va, US 189/G2
Rosedale, Austl. 159/C4
Rosedale, Md, US 194/B5
Roseglen, ND, US 182/D4
Rosehearty, Sc, UK 59/D1
Roseira, Braz. 211/L7
Roseires (dam), Sudan 142/G3
Roseisle, Mb, Can. 182/E3
Roseland, La, US 190/C2
Roseland, NJ, US 195/H8
Roselette, Aiguille de (peak), Fr. 86/C6
Roselle, NJ, US 195/H9
Roselle, Il, US 193/P16
Roselle Park, NJ, US 195/H9
Rosemark, Tn, US 188/C3
Rosemead, Ca, US 192/F7
Rosemère, Qu, Can. 185/N6
Rosemount, Oh, US 189/F1
Rosemount, Mn, US 183/P7
Rosenberg, Tx, US 177/G3
Rosenberg, Ger. 84/D4
Rosenfeld, Ger. 87/E1
Rosenhayn, NJ, US 194/C5
Rosenhof, Sk, Can. 171/L2
Rosenort, Mb, Can. 182/F3
Rosepine, La, US 190/B2
Roses, Sp. 73/G1
Roseto, Pa, US 194/C2
Roseto degli Abruzzi, It. 92/D2
Rosetown, Sk, Can. 171/L2
Rosetta, Ms, US 190/C2
Rosetta (Massabb Rashīd) (mouth), Egypt 139/B1
Rosetta Branch (riv.), Egypt 130/B4
Roseville, Oh, US 186/E5
Roseville, Mi, US 193/G6
Roseville, Ca, US 172/C4
Roseville, Il, US 181/J3
Roseville, Mn, US 183/P6
Rosevine, Tx, US 177/H2
Rosewood, Austl. 154/C4
Rosh Ha'ayin, Isr. 131/B4
Rosh Hakarmel (pt.), Isr. 131/B3
Rosh Haniqra (pt.), Isr. 131/C2
Rosh Pina (arpt.), Isr. 131/D3
Rosh Pinah, Namb. 150/B2
Rosh Pinna, Isr. 131/D3
Rosharon, Tx, US 177/M9
Rosheim, Fr. 86/D1
Roshkhvār, Iran 127/G2
Rosholt, SD, US 182/F5
Rosholt, Wi, US 181/K1
Rosiclare, Il, US 188/C2
Rosières-en-Santerre, Fr. 80/B4
Rosignano Marittimo, It. 88/D7
Rosignano Solvay, It. 88/D7
Rosignol, Guy. 206/B1
Roşiori de Vede, Rom. 77/G3
Rositsa, Bul. 77/H4
Roskilde, Den. 66/E4
Roskilde (co.), Den. 66/D4
Roskilde (inlet), Den. 65/H7
Roslags-Bro, Swe. 65/B1
Roslags-Kulla, Swe. 65/B1
Roslags-Näsby, Swe. 65/B1
Roslavl', Rus. 96/E1
Roslev, Den. 66/C3
Roslyakova, Rus. 94/G1
Roslyatino, Rus. 95/K4
Roslyn, Wa, US 170/D4
Rosmalen, Neth. 78/C5
Rosmaninhal, Port. 72/B3
Rosneath, Sc, UK 59/B4
Rosny-sous-Bois, Fr. 56/K5
Rosny-sur-Seine, Fr. 83/G2
Rosolina, It. 89/F3
Rosolini, It. 74/D4
Rosporden, Fr. 82/B5
Rösrath, Ger. 81/G2
Ross (dist.), Sc, UK 59/C1
Ross (isl.), Ant. 216/M
Ross (sea), Ant. 216/P
Ross, Austl. 158/C4
Ross (mt.), NZ 161/C3
Ross, NZ 161/B3
Ross (pt.), On, Can. 186/V8
Ross, Tx, US 177/F2
Ross (lake), Wa, US 170/D3
Ross Barnett (res.), Ms, US 188/C4
Ross Carbery, Ire. 58/A6
Ross Ice Shelf, Ant. 216/N
Ross Lake NRA, Wa, US 170/D3
Ross River, Yk, Can. 166/C2
Ross-on-Wye, Eng, UK 62/D3
Rossa, Swi. 87/F5
Rossa (peak), It. 71/K3
Rossall (pt.), Eng, UK 61/E4
Rossano Stazione, It. 74/E3
Rossano Veneto, It. 89/E2
Rossbach, Ger. 85/F5
Rossberg (peak), Fr. 86/D2
Rossburn, Mb, Can. 182/D2
Rossdorf, Ger. 84/B3
Rossel (isl.), PNG 162/E6
Rosselange, Fr. 81/F5
Rosser, Mb, Can. 182/F3
Rosser, Tx, US 176/L7
Rosshaupten, Ger. 87/G2
Rossie, NY, US 187/J2
Rossiglione, It. 88/B4
Rossignol (lake), NS, Can. 184/E3
Rössing, Namb. 148/B4
Rössjöholmsån (riv.), Swe. 65/J6
Rosskeeragh (pt.), Ire. 57/P9
Rossland, BC, Can. 170/F3
Rosslare (bay), Ire. 58/D5
Rosslare (pt.), Ire. 58/D5
Rosslare, Ire. 58/D5
Rosslea, NI, UK 58/C1
Rosslyn Village, On, Can. 183/K3
Rosso, Mrta. 140/B2
Rossosh', Rus. 99/K2
Rossport, On, Can. 183/L3
Rossstock (peak), Swi. 87/E4
Rosstal, Ger. 84/D4
Rosston, Ar, US 179/H4
Rossville, Il, US 186/C4
Røst, Nor. 64/E2
Rostāq, Iran 129/H5
Rostāq, Afg. 125/A4
Rostellan, Ire. 58/B6
Rosthern, Sk, Can. 171/L1
Rostock, Ger. 66/E4
Rostov, Rus. 94/H4
Rostov (int'l arpt.), Rus. 99/K4
Rostov, Rus. 99/K4
Rostov Oblast, Rus. 97/G2
Rostrenen, Fr. 82/B4
Rostrevor, NI, UK 60/B3
Roswell, NM, US 178/B4
Roswell, Ga, US 189/M6
Rot (riv.), Ger. 68/E4
Rota (isl.), NMar. 162/D3
Rota, Sp. 72/B4
Rotan, Tx, US 178/D4
Rote Wand (peak), Aus. 87/F3
Rotebro, Swe. 65/A1
Rotenburg, Ger. 79/G2
Rotenburg an der Fulda, Ger. 79/G7
Roter Main (riv.), Ger. 68/F3
Rötgen, Ger. 81/F2
Roth (riv.), Ger. 87/G1
Roth bei Nürnberg, Ger. 84/E4
Rothaargebirge (mts.), Ger. 79/F6
Rothau, Fr. 86/D1
Rothbury, Eng, UK 59/E6
Röthenbach an der Pegnitz, Ger. 84/E4
Rothenberg, Ger. 84/B3
Rothenburg, Swi. 87/E3
Rothenburg ob der Tauber, Ger. 84/D4
Rothera, UK, Ant. 216/V
Rotherham, Eng, UK 61/G5
Rothes, Sc, UK 59/C1
Rothesay, Sc, UK 59/A5
Rotheux-Rimière, Belg. 81/E2
Rothsay, Mn, US 182/F4
Rothschild, Wi, US 181/K1
Rothwell, Eng, UK 61/G4
Rothwell, Eng, UK 63/F2
Roti (isl.), Indo. 117/F6
Rotifunk, SLeo. 140/B4
Roto, Austl. 159/B1
Rotonda, Fl, US 191/G4
Rotondo (peak), It. 92/C2
Rotorua, NZ 161/D2
Rotselaar, Belg. 81/D2
Rott (riv.), Ger. 68/G4
Rott am Inn, Ger. 85/F7
Rottach-Egern, Ger. 68/F5
Rotte (riv.), Fr. 81/F6
Rotten (riv.), Swi. 86/E5
Rottenacker, Ger. 87/F1
Röttenbach, Ger. 84/E4
Rottenberg, Ger. 84/C2
Rottenburg am Neckar, Ger. 84/B6
Rottenburg an der Laaber, Ger. 85/F5
Rotterdam, Neth. 78/B5
Rotterdam (int'l arpt.), Neth. 78/B5
Rottershausen, Ger. 84/D2
Rotthalmünster, Ger. 85/G6
Rottingdean, Eng, UK 63/F5
Röttingen, Ger. 84/C3
Rottne, Swe. 66/F3
Rottnest (isl.), Austl. 156/B5
Rottofreno, It. 88/C3
Rottum (riv.), Ger. 87/F1
Rottumeroog (isl.), Neth. 78/D1
Rottumerplaat (isl.), Neth. 78/D1
Rottweil, Ger. 87/E1
Rotuma (isl.), Fiji 162/G6
Rötz, Ger. 85/F4
Roubaix, Fr. 80/C2
Roubion (riv.), Fr. 70/F4
Roudnice nad Labem, Czh. 85/H2
Rouen, Fr. 83/G2
Rouffach, Fr. 86/D2
Rougé, Fr. 82/D5
Rouge (riv.), Qu, Can. 167/J4
Rouge, Middle (riv.), Mi, US 193/F7
Rougemont, Fr. 86/C3
Rougemont-le-Château, Fr. 86/C2
Rough (riv.), Ky, US 188/D2
Rough River (lake), Ky, US 188/D2
Rouleau, Sk, Can. 182/B2
Roullet-Saint-Estèphe, Fr. 70/D4
Round (hill), Oh, US 186/F4
Round (hill), In, US 188/E1
Round (hill), Ky, US 188/E2
Round (hill), Pa, US 194/B3
Round Butte (dam), Or, US 172/C1
Round Hill (pt.), Austl. 160/C4
Round Lake, Il, US 193/P15
Round Lake Beach, Il, US 193/P15
Round Lake Park, Il, US 193/P15
Round Mountain, Nv, US 172/E4
Round Mountain, Tx, US 176/E2
Round Rock, Tx, US 177/F2
Round Spring, Mo, US 179/J2
Round Top, Tx, US 177/F2
Round Valley (res.), NJ, US 194/D2
Round Valley Ind. Res., Ca, US 172/B4
Roundup, Mt, US 171/K4
Roundway (hill), Eng, UK 62/E4
Rounthwaite, Mb, Can. 182/E3
Roura, FrG. 206/C1
Rousay (isl.), Sc, UK 57/V14
Rouse Hill (nbrhd.), Austl. 160/G8
Rouses Point, NY, US 187/K2
Rouseville, Pa, US 187/G4
Rousies, Fr. 80/D3
Rousínov, Czh. 69/J4
Rousset, Fr. 90/B6
Roussillon, Fr. 90/B5
Roussillon, Fr. 90/A2
Routhierville, Qu, Can. 184/D1
Rouvre (riv.), Fr. 83/E3
Rouvres, Fr. 56/M4
Rouvroy, Belg. 81/E4
Rouxmesnil-Bouteilles, Fr. 83/G1
Rouxville, SAfr. 150/D3
Rouyn-Noranda, Qu, Can. 167/J4
Rovaniemi (int'l arpt.), Fin. 94/E2
Rovaniemi, Fin. 94/E2
Rovasenda, It. 88/B2
Rovato, It. 88/C2
Roven'ki, Rus. 99/K3
Roven'ky, Ukr. 99/K3
Rover, Mo, US 179/J2

291
Rover – Saint

Rover, Ar, US 179/H3
Roverbella, It. 89/D3
Rovereto, It. 87/H6
Rovereto, It. 89/D4
Roviano, It. 92/C3
Rovieng Tbong, Camb. 120/D3
Rovigo, It. 89/E3
Rovigo (prov.), It. 89/E2
Rovinj, Cro. 89/G3
Rovira, Col. 207/K8
Rovnoye, Rus. 97/H2
Rovuma (riv.), Moz. 145/A4
Rowell, Ar, US 179/H4
Rowena, Austl. 158/D1
Rowena, Tx, US 177/D2
Rowland, NC, US 189/H3
Rowledge, Eng, UK 56/A3
Rowlett (cr.), Tx, US 176/L6
Rowlett, Tx, US 176/L7
Rowley (isl.), Nun, Can. 167/J2
Rowley Shoals(isl.) 153/A2
Rowta, India 123/J2
Roxa (isl.), GBis. 140/B4
Roxas, Phil. 114/C3
Roxas, Phil. 114/C1
Roxas, Phil. 114/B3
Roxboro, NC, US 189/H2
Roxborough, Trin. 205/F2
Roxburgh, NZ 161/B4
Roxbury, Ks, US 179/F1
Roxbury, NY, US 187/J3
Roxen (lake), Swe. 66/F2
Roxie, Ms, US 190/C2
Roxo (cape), Sen. 140/A3
Roxton, Tx, US 179/G4
Roxwell, Eng, UK 56/E1
Roy, NM, US 178/B3
Roy, Wa, US 193/B3
Roy, Ut, US 173/G3
Roy, Mt, US 171/K4
Roy Hill, Austl. 156/C2
Roya (riv.), Fr. 71/G5
Royal (canal), Ire. 61/B3
Royal Botanical Garden, On, Can. 186/T9
Royal Center, In, US 186/C4
Royal Chitwan NP, Nepal 123/E2
Royal City, Wa, US 170/E4
Royal (gorge), Co, US 178/B1
Royal Natal NP, SAfr. 150/E3
Royal NP, Austl. 158/D2
Royal Oak, Mi, US 193/F7
Royal Paekje Tombs, SKor. 107/D4
Royal Palm Beach, Fl, US 190/P9
Royal Pines, NC, US 189/F3
Royal Tombs, Viet. 120/D2
Royal Tunbridge Wells, Eng, UK 63/G4
Royalton, Mn, US 183/G5
Royalton, Vt, US 187/K3
Royalton, Pa, US 194/B3
Royalty, Tx, US 177/C2
Royan, Fr. 70/C4
Roydon, Eng, UK 56/D1
Roye, Fr. 86/C2
Roye, Fr. 80/B4
Royersford, Pa, US 194/C3
Røyken, Nor. 66/D2
Royse City, Tx, US 176/L7
Royston, Eng, UK 61/G4
Royston, Ga, US 189/F3
Royston, Eng, UK 63/F2
Royston, BC, Can. 170/B3
Royton, Eng, UK 61/F4
Rožaj, Yugo. 76/E4
Rozay-en-Brie, Fr. 80/B6
Rozdil'na, Ukr. 98/F4
Rozdol'ne, Ukr. 99/G5
Rozel, Chl, UK 82/C2
Rozellville, Wi, US 181/J1
Rozenburg, Neth. 78/B5
Rozendo, Moz. 149/H3
Rozhaya (riv.), Rus. 94/W9
Rozhyshche, Ukr. 98/C2
Rozivka, Ukr. 99/J4
Rožmberk (lake), Czh. 85/H4
Rožmital pod Třemšínem Czh. 85/G3
Rožňava, Slvk. 69/L4
Roztoczański PN, Pol. 98/B2
Roztoky, Czh. 85/H2
Rozzano, It. 88/C3
Rrëshen, Alb. 75/F2
Rrogozhinë, Alb. 75/F2
Rtishchevo, Rus. 97/G1
Ru (cape), Malay. 115/C2
Ruabon, Wal, UK 61/E6
Ruacana (falls), Ang. 148/B3
Ruacana, Namb. 148/B3
Ruaha NP, Tanz. 145/A3
Ruamahanga (riv.), NZ 161/J9
Ruapuke (isl.), NZ 161/B4
Ruatapu, NZ 161/B3
Ruawai, NZ 161/C2
Rub' al Khali (des.), SAr. 103/D7
Rubeho (mts.), Tanz. 145/B3
Rubelles, Fr. 56/L6
Rubeshibe, Japan 108/C2
Rubi (riv.), D.R. Congo 147/F2
Rubi, D.R. Congo 147/F2
Rubí, Sp. 73/L7
Rubiataba, Braz. 210/C2
Rubidoux, Ca, US 192/C3
Rubiera, It. 89/D4
Rubigen, Swi. 86/D4
Rubim, Braz. 211/E3
Rubizhne, Ukr. 99/K3
Rubondo NP, Tanz. 147/G3
Rubonia, Fl, US 190/K8
Rubottom, Ok, US 179/F4
Řubřina (riv.), Czh. 85/G4
Rubtsovsk, Rus. 125/D1
Rubuga, Tanz. 145/A3
Ruby, La, US 190/B2
Ruby (lake), Nv, US 172/F3
Ruby (mts.), Nv, US 172/F3
Ruby (riv.), Mt, US 173/G1
Ruby Lake NWR, Nv, US 172/F3
Ruby Valley, Nv, US 172/F3
Rubyvale, Austl. 160/B3
Rucava, Lat. 67/J3
Ruch'i, Rus. 94/J2
Rucphen, Neth. 78/B5
Ruda Woda (lake), Pol. 69/K2
Rudall River NP, Austl. 156/D2
Rūdarpur, India 122/D2
Rudauli, India 122/C2
Ruddell, Sk, Can. 171/L1
Ruddington, Eng, UK 61/G6
Rudensk, Bela. 67/M5
Rüdersdorf, Ger. 68/Q7
Rüdesheim, Ger. 81/G4
Rüdesheim, Ger. 81/G4
Rudewa, Tanz. 145/A4
Rudi, Tanz 145/B3
Rudiano, It. 88/C3
Rūdiškės, Lith. 67/L4
Rudkøbing, Den. 66/D4
Rudky, Ukr. 98/B3
Rudnaya Pristan', Rus. 105/M3
Rudnik, Pol. 69/M3
Rudnya, Rus. 67/P4
Rudnytsya Ukr. 98/E3
Rūdnyy, Kaz. 95/P5
Rudolf (isl.), Rus. 100/F1
Rudolf (Turkana) (lake), Kenya 133/F4
Rudolph, Wi, US 181/K1
Rudong, China 106/E4
Rudozem, Bul. 75/J2
Ruds-Vedby, Den. 65/H7
Rūdsar, Iran 129/G2
Rudston, Eng, UK 61/H3
Rudyard, Mi, US 186/D1
Rudyard, Mt, US 171/J3
Rue, Swi. 86/C4
Rue (pt.), NI, UK 60/B1
Rue, Fr. 80/A3
Rueda, Sp. 72/C2
Rueil-Malmaison, Fr. 56/J5
Ruell (riv.), Sc, UK 59/A4
Ruelle-sur-Touvre, Fr. 70/D4
Ruen (peak), Bul. 76/F4
Ruenya (riv.), Zim. 149/G3
Ruetzbach (riv.), Aus. 87/H3
Rufā'ah, Sudan 142/G2
Rufe, Ok, US 179/G3
Ruffano, It. 75/F3
Ruffec, Fr. 70/D3
Ruffin, SC, US 189/G4
Rufiji (riv.), Tanz. 133/F5
Rufina, It. 89/E6
Rufino, Arg. 214/E2
Rufisque, Sen. 140/A3
Rufunsa, Zam. 149/F2
Rufus Woods (lake), Wa, US 170/E3
Rugāji, Lat. 67/M3
Rugao, China 106/E4
Rugby, ND US 182/E3
Rugby, Eng, UK 63/E2
Rugeley, Eng, UK 63/E1
Rügen (isl.), Ger. 66/E4
Ruggell, Lcht. 87/F3
Rugles, Fr. 83/F3
Ruḩama, Isr. 131/B5
Ruhmannsfelden, Ger. 85/F5
Ruhnu saar (isl.), Lat. 67/K3
Ruhr (reg.) Ger. 68/E3
Ruhr (riv.), Ger. 68/D3
Ruhrgebiet (phys. reg.), Ger. 78/D6
Ruhstorf an der Rott, Ger. 85/F5
Ruicheng, China 106/B4
Ruidosa, Tx, US 177/B3
Ruidoso, NM, US 178/B4
Ruihong, China 113/H2
Ruinen, Neth. 78/D3
Ruins of Cahabra, Al, US 188/D4
Ruipa, Tanz. 145/B4
Ruiru, Kenya 145/B2
Ruiselede, Belg. 80/C1
Ruislip (nbrhd.), Eng, UK 56/B2
Ruiz, Mex. 198/D4
Rujen (peak), FYROM 75/H1
Rūjiena, Lat. 67/L3
Ruki (riv.), D.R. Congo 133/D5
Rukua, Indo. 154/B1
Rukumkot, Nepal 122/D1
Rukuru, South (riv.), Tanz. 149/G1
Rukwa (prov.), Tanz. 145/A3
Rukwa (lake), Tanz. 133/F5
Rule, Tx, US 178/E4
Ruleville, Ms, US 188/B4
Rulhieres (cape), Austl. 154/B3
Rulles (riv.), Belg. 81/E4
Rülzheim, Ger. 84/B4
Rum, Aus. 87/H3
Rum (riv.), Mn, US 183/H5
Rum Cay (isl.), Bahm. 197/G3
Rum Jungle, Austl. 154/C3
Ruma, Yugo. 76/D3
Ruma Bāzār, Bang. 112/B4
Ruma NP, Kenya 145/A2
Rumāḩ, SAr. 126/E3
Rumán, Ven. 205/F3
Rumaylah, Sudan 142/G2
Rumaysh, Leb. 131/C2
Rumbalara, Austl. 157/G3
Rumbek, Sudan 142/F4
Rumeli Hisar, Turk. 129/N6
Rumelifeneri, Turk. 129/N6
Rumes, Belg. 80/C2
Rumia, Pol. 66/H4
Rumilly, Fr 86/B6
Rümlang, Swi. 87/E3
Rumley, Tx, US 177/E2
Rumney, NH, US 187/L3
Rumney, Wal, UK 62/C3
Rumoi, Japan 108/B2
Rumphi, Malw. 145/A4
Rumson, NJ, US 194/E3
Rumst, Belg. 81/D1
Rumuruti, Kenya 145/B1
Run (riv.), Mn, US 181/H1
Runabay (pt.), NI, UK 60/B1
Runan, China 106/C4
Runanga, NZ 161/B3
Runaway (cape), NZ 161/D2
Runcorn, Eng, UK 61/F5
Rundēni, Lat. 67/M3
Runding, Ger. 85/F4
Rundu, Namb. 148/C3
Runere, Tanz. 145/A2
Runge, Tx, US 177/F3
Rungsted, Den. 65/J7
Rungu, D.R. Congo 147/F2
Rungwa (riv.), Tanz. 145/A3
Rungwa, Tanz. 145/A3
Rungwa, Tanz. 147/G4
Rungwa Game Reserve, Tanz. 145/A3
Rungwe (peak), Tanz. 145/A4
Runio (riv.), Fr. 82/C5
Runkel, Ger. 84/B2
Runmarö (isl.), Swe. 65/B1
Runn (lake), Swe. 66/F1
Runnelstown, Ms, US 190/D2
Runnemede, NJ, US 194/C4
Running (cr.), Co, US 178/B1
Running Springs, Ca, US 192/C2
Running Water Draw (riv.), Tx,NM, US 178/C3
Runwell, Eng, UK 56/E2
Ruo (riv.), China 101/K5
Ruokolahti, Fin. 67/N1
Ruoqiang, China 125/E4
Rupat (isl.), Indo. 116/B3
Rupea, Rom. 77/G2
Rupel (riv.), Belg. 81/D1
Rupert, Id, US 173/G2
Rupert (riv.), Qu, Can. 167/J3
Rupert, Ga, US 188/E4
Rupert, WV, US 189/G2
Rupert House (Waskaganish), Qu, Can. 167/J3
Rūpnagar, India 124/D4
Ruppichteroth, Ger. 81/G2
Rupt-sur-Moselle, Fr. 86/C2
Rupununi (riv.), Guy. 205/G4
Rur (riv.), Ger. 68/D3
Rur-Strasse (lake), Ger. 81/F2
Rural Hall, NC, US 189/G2
Rural Retreat, Va, US 189/G2
Rurrenabaque, Bol. 209/E4
Rurutu (isl.), FrPol. 163/K7
Rusagonis, NB, Can. 184/D3
Rusape, Zim. 149/G3
Rüschegg, Swi. 86/D4
Rüschlikon, Swi. 87/E3
Ruscom (riv.), On, Can. 193/G7
Ruse (pol. reg.), Bul. 75/K1
Ruse, Bul. 77/G4
Rusera, India 123/F3
Rush, Co, US 178/B1
Rush, Ire. 60/B4
Rush (cr.), Co, US 180/C4
Rush City, Mn, US 183/H5
Rush Springs, Ok, US 179/F3
Rushall, Eng, UK 63/E4
Rushan, China 106/E3
Rushden, Eng, UK 63/F2
Rushford, Mn, US 181/J2
Rushoon, Nf, Can. 185/K2
Rushville, In, US 186/D5
Rushville, Il, US 181/J3
Rushville, Ne, US 180/C2
Rushworth, Austl. 159/B3
Rusk, Tx, US 176/G2
Ruskin, Fl, US 190/L8
Ruskington, Eng, UK 61/H5
Ruskovce, Slvk. 76/C1
Rusnė, Lith. 67/J4
Russ, Fr. 86/D1
Russas, Braz. 207/G4
Russbach (riv.), Aus. 77/N7
Russell, Ks, US 178/E1
Russell, Mb, Can. 182/D2
Russell, On, Can. 187/J2
Russell, NY, US 187/J2
Russell, NZ 161/C1
Russell (isls.), Austl. 160/F7
Russell (isl.), Nun, Can. 167/R7
Russell (res.), SC, US 189/F3
Russell Cave Nat'l Mon., Al, US 188/E3
Russell Springs, Ky, US 188/E2
Russells Point, Oh, US 186/E4
Russellville, Mo, US 179/H1
Russellville, Ar, US 179/H3
Russellville, Ky, US 188/D2
Russellville, Tn, US 189/F2
Russellville, Al, US 188/D3
Rüsselsheim, Ger. 84/B3
Russi, It. 89/F5
Russia(ctry.) 100/H3
Russian (riv.), Ca, US 172/B4
Russkaya, Rus., Ant. 216/Q
Russkiy Brod, Rus. 96/F1
Rust'avi, Geo. 97/H4
Rustburg, Va, US 189/H2
Rustenburg, SAfr. 149/E5
Ruston, La, US 179/H4
Ruston, Wa, US 193/C3
Rusutjärvi, Fin. 65/E4
Rutana, Buru. 147/G3
Rute, Sp. 72/C4
Rutenga, Zim. 149/F4
Ruth, Ms, US 190/C2
Ruth, Nv, US 173/F4
Rüthen, Ger. 79/F6
Rutherford, NJ, US 195/J8
Rutherford, Tn, US 188/C2
Rutherford, Al, US 188/E4
Rutherfordton, NC, US 189/G3
Rutherglen, Sc, UK 59/B5
Rutherglen, On, Can. 187/G1
Rutherglen, Austl. 159/C3
Rutheron, NM, US 175/J2
Rüthi, Swi. 87/F3
Ruthin, Wal, UK 61/E5
Ruthven, On, Can. 193/G7
Rüti, Swi. 87/F4
Rüti, Swi. 87/E3
Rutland, ND, US 182/F4
Rutland, Vt, US 187/K3
Rutland, Oh, US 189/F1
Rutland Plains, Austl. 160/A1
Rutland Water (res.), Eng, UK 63/F1
Rutledge, Mn, US 183/H4
Rutledge, Tn, US 189/F2
Rutog, China 125/C5
Rutshuru (riv.), D.R. Congo 147/G3
Rutshuru, D.R. Congo 147/G3
Rutten, Neth. 78/C3
Ruukki, Fin. 94/E2
Ruurlo, Neth. 78/D4
Ruvo di Puglia, It. 74/E2
Ruvu (riv.), Tanz. 145/B3
Ruvu, Tanz. 145/B3
Ruvu, Tanz. 145/B3
Ruvubu (riv.), Buru. 147/G3
Ruvuma (prov.), Tanz. 145/B4
Ruvuma (riv.), Tanz. 133/F6
Ruwa, Zim. 149/F3
Ruwāndūz, Iraq 129/F2
Ruwenzori (range), Ugan. 147/G2
Ruwī, Oman 127/G4
Ruxton, Co, US 178/C2
Ruy, Fr. 90/B1
Ruya (riv.), Zim. 149/F3
Ruyang, China 106/C4
Ruyigi, Buru. 147/G3
Ruyuan Yaozu Zizhixian, China 113/G3
Ruzayevka, Rus. 97/H1
Ruzhany, Bela. 69/N2
Ruzhyn, Ukr. 98/E3
Ruzizi (riv.), D.R. Congo 147/G3
Ružomberok, Slvk. 69/K4
Ruzyně (int'l arpt.), Czh. 85/H2
Ruzzah (peak), Egypt 139/B4
Rwanda(ctry.) 133/F5
Rwenjaza, Ugan. 147/G2
Rwenzori NP, Ugan. 147/G3
Ryabobskiy, Rus. 99/L2
Ryan, Ok, US 179/F3
Ryan (inlet), Sc, UK 60/C2
Ryan (mt.), Austl. 160/A1
Ryan (mt.), Austl. 159/D1
Ryazan', Rus. 94/H5
Ryazhsk, Rus. 96/G1
Rybachiy (pen.), Rus. 64/K1
Rybinsk, Rus. 94/H4
Rybinsk (res.), Rus. 55/J2
Rybnik, Pol. 69/K3
Rybnoye, Rus. 94/H5
Ryd, Swe. 66/F3
Rydaholm, Swe. 66/F3
Ryde, Ca, US 193/L10
Ryde (nbrhd.), Austl. 160/H8
Ryde, Eng, UK 63/E5
Rydebäck, Swe. 65/J7
Rydet, Swe. 66/D3
Rye, Co, US 178/B2
Rye, Tx, US 177/G2
Rye, Ar, US 179/J4
Rye (riv.), Eng, UK 61/H3
Rye, NY, US 195/L8
Rye (bay), Eng, UK 63/G5
Rye, Eng, UK 63/G5
Rye Brook, NY, US 195/L7
Rye Patch (dam), Nv, US 172/D3
Rye Patch (res.), Nv, US 172/D3
Ryegate, Mt, US 171/K4
Rygge, Nor. 66/D2
Ryki, Pol. 69/L3
Ryley, Ab, Can. 171/H1
Ryl'sk, Rus. 99/H2
Rylstone, Austl. 159/D1
Ryn-peski (plain), Kaz. 97/J2
Ryōkami, Japan 109/B2
Ryökkä, Fin. 65/E4
Ryōtsu, Japan 111/F1
Ryōzen-yama (peak), Japan 109/K5
Rypin, Pol. 69/K2
Rysy (peak), Pol. 69/L4
Ryton, Eng, UK 61/G2
Ryton-on-Dunsmore, Eng, UK 63/E2
Rytterknægten (peak), Den. 66/F4
Ryttylä, Fin. 65/E4
Ryūgasaki, Japan 111/G3
Ryukyu (isls.), Japan 103/M7
Ryūō, Japan 109/K5
Ryūō, Japan 109/B2
Rzeszów (prov.), Pol. 69/M3
Rzeszów, Pol. 69/M3
Rzhev, Rus. 94/G4
Rzhyshchiv, Ukr. 98/F3

S

's-Graveland, Neth. 78/C4
's Gravendeel, Neth. 78/B5
's-Gravenhage (The Hague) (cap.), Neth. 78/B4
's Heerenberg, Neth. 78/D5
's Hertogenbosch, Neth. 78/C5
S'ør-Trøndelag (co.), Nor. 64/D3
Sa, Thai. 120/C2
Şā al Ḩajar (ruin), Egypt 139/B3
Sa Dec, Viet. 120/D4
Sa Pa, Viet. 120/C1
Saab (int'l arpt.), Swe. 66/F2
Sa'ad, Isr. 131/B6
Sääksjärvi (lake), Fin. 67/K1
Saal an der Donau, Ger. 85/E5
Saalbach (riv.), Ger. 84/B4
Saaldorf, Ger. 85/E2
Saale (riv.), Ger. 68/F3
Saalfelden am Steinernen Meer, Aus. 71/K3
Saâne (riv.), Fr. 83/F1
Saane (riv.), Swi. 86/D5
Saanen, Swi. 86/D5
Saanta (peak), Kenya 145/B1
Saar (riv.), Ger. 81/F5
Saarbrücken, Ger. 81/F5
Saarbrücken (Ensheim) (arpt.), Ger. 81/G5
Saarburg, Ger. 81/F4
Sääre, Est. 67/K3
Saaremaa (isl.), Est. 94/D4
Saarland (state), Ger. 71/G2
Saarlouis, Ger. 81/F5
Saas, Swi. 87/F4
Saas Fee, Swi. 86/D5
Saastal (valley), Swi. 86/D5
Sa'ata, Sudan 142/F2
Saatlı, Azer. 129/G2
Saatta, Erit. 142/H1
Sab (riv.), Camb. 120/D3
Saba (isl.), NAm. 197/J4
Saba (isl.), NAnt. 197/N8
Šabac, Yugo. 76/D3
Sabadell, Sp. 73/L6
Sabae, Japan 110/E3
Sabah (reg.), Malay. 103/L9
Sabalgarh, India 122/A2
Sabana, Cuba 201/H1
Sabana (arch.), Bang. 201/F1
Sabana de Uchire, Ven. 205/E2
Sabanalarga, Col. 204/C2
Sabanalarga, Col. 204/C3
Sabancuy, Mex. 200/D2
Sabaneta, Ven. 204/D2
Sabang, Indo. 115/A1
Sabanita, Pan. 201/G4
Sabará, Braz. 210/E3
Sabaragamuwa (prov.), SrL. 121/D5
Sabasţīyah, WBnk. 131/C4
Sabat (riv.), Sudan 133/F4
Sabato (riv.), It. 92/D5
Sabaudia, It. 92/C5
Sabaudia (lake), It. 92/C5
Sabaya, Bol. 212/B1
Sabbio Chiese, It. 88/D2
Sabbioneta, It. 88/D4
Sabdê, China 112/D2
Sabetha, Ks, US 181/G4
Sabhā, Libya 134/B3
Sabie (riv.), Moz. 151/F2
Sabierivier (riv.), SAfr. 149/F5
Sabile, Lat. 67/K3
Sabin, Mn, US 182/F4
Sabinal (riv.), Tx, US 177/E3
Sabinal, Tx, US 177/E3
Sabiñánigo, Sp. 73/E1
Sabinas, Mex. 177/D4
Sabinas (riv.), Mex. 196/A2
Sabinas Hidalgo, Mex. 177/D4
Sabine (lake), La, US 177/H3
Sabine (riv.), La, US 196/C
Sabine NWR, La, US 177/H3
Sabine Pass, Tx, US 177/H3
Sabini, Monti (mts.), It. 74/C
Sabirabad, Azer. 129/G
Sabkhat al Bardawīl (lag.), Egypt 130/C4
Sabkhat al Hayshah (swamp), Libya 134/B2
Sabkhat al Kabīyah (swamp), Tun. 74/A5
Sabkhat al Milḩ (swamp), Libya 134/C2
Sabkhat ash Shuwayrib (swamp), Libya 134/C2
Sabkhat Ghuzayyil (swamp), Libya 134/C2
Sabkhat Shunayn (swamp), Libya 134/D2
Sablayan, Phil. 114/C2
Sable (cape), NS, Can. 184/E4
Sable (cape), Fl, US 196/E2
Sable (isl.), NS, Can. 167/L4
Sable (isl.), Can. 165/M5
Sablé-sur-Sarthe, Fr. 83/E5
Sables (riv.), Qu, Can. 184/B
Saboeiro, Braz. 207/G4
Sabon Gida, Nga. 141/H5
Sabongidda, Nga. 141/G5
Sabor (riv.), Port. 72/B2
Sabou, Burk. 141/E3
Saboyá, Col. 207/M7
Sabra (cape), Indo. 117/H4
Şabrātah, Libya 93/G4
Sabratha (ruin), Libya 93/G4
Sabrina (coast), Ant. 216/J
Sabrūm, India 123/H4
Sabual, India 112/B4
Sabugal, Port. 72/B2
Sabula, Ia, US 181/J2
Sabulubek, Indo. 115/B3
Şabyā, SAr. 126/D5
Sabzevār, Iran 129/J2
Sac City, Ia, US 181/G2
Sacaca, Bol. 212/C1
Sacajawea (peak), Or, US 172/E1
Sacajawea (lake), Wa, US 170/E4
Sácama, Col. 204/C3
Sacandica, Ang. 146/C4
Sacanta, Arg. 212/D4
Sacarnoochee (riv.), Ms, US 188/C4
Sacaton, Az, US 175/G4
Sacavém, Port. 73/P10
Saccarel (peak), Fr. 90/D4
Saccarello (peak), It. 88/A4
Sacco (riv.), It. 74/C2
Sacedón, Sp. 72/D2
Săcele, Rom. 77/G3
Sachanga, Ang. 148/C2
Sachigo (riv.), On, Can. 166/G3
Sachojere, Bol. 209/E4
Sachs Harbour, NW, Can. 166/D1
Sachse, Tx, US 176/L7
Sachseln, Swi. 87/E4
Sachsen (state), Ger. 68/G3
Sachsen-Anhalt (state), Ger. 68/F3
Sachsenbrunn, Ger. 84/D2
Sachsenhagen, Ger. 79/G4
Sacile, It. 89/F2
Säckingen, Ger. 86/D2
Sackville, NB, Can. 184/E3
Saclay, Fr 56/J5
Saco, Me, US 187/L3
Saco, Al, US 191/F2
Saco (bay), Me, US 184/B4
Saco (riv.), Me, US 187/L3
Saco, Mt, US 171/L3
Saco do Giraul, Ang. 148/B2
Sacra di San Michele, It. 90/D2
Sacramento, Mex. 177/D4
Sacramento (co.), Ca, US 193/M10
Sacramento (riv.), Ca, US 168/B4
Sacramento (mts.), NM, US 168/E5
Sacramento (cap.), Ca, US 172/C4
Sacramento, Ky, US 188/D2
Sacramento Metropolitan (arpt.), Ca, US 193/L9
Sacramento NWR, Ca, US 172/B4
Sacramento River Deep Water Ship Canal, Ca, US 193/L10
Sacratif (cape), Sp. 72/D4
Sacriston, Eng, UK 61/G2
Sacristy, VatC. 91/F7
Sacro (peak), It. 74/E2
Sacro Monte, It. 88/B2
Sada, Fr. 152/H6
Sada, SAfr. 150/D4
Sádaba, Sp. 72/E
Sadābād, India 122/B2
Sa'dah, Yem. 126/D5
Sadani, Tanz. 145/B3
Sadasar, India 118/B2
Sādāt Maḩalleh, Iran 129/G2
Sadd al Qir'awn (dam), Leb. 131/D
Saddam (int'l arpt.), Iraq 129/F3
Saddle (mtn.), Az, US 175/G2
Saddle (riv.), NJ, US 195/J8
Saddle (mtn.), Or, US 170/C5
Saddle Brook, NJ, US 195/J8
Saddle Mtn. NWR, Wa, US 170/E4
Saddle River, NJ, US 195/J7
Saddle Rock, NY, US 195/K8
Saddleback (mesa), NM, US 178/C3
Saddlestring, Wy, US 173/K1
Saddleworth, Eng, UK 61/G4
Saddleworth, Austl. 157/H5
Sadêng, China 112/B2
Sādhaura, India 124/D4
Sadi, Eth. 142/G3
Sadīch, Iran 127/G3
Sadiola, Mali 140/C3
Sadiya, India 112/B3
Sadjoavato, Madg. 152/J6
Sadler, Tx, US 179/F4
Sado (riv.), Port. 72/A3
Sado (isl.), Japan 105/M4
Sadovo, Bul. 77/G4
Sadovoye, Rus. 97/H3
Sadowara, Japan 110/B4
Sādri, India 118/B2
Sadripante (mt.), Phil. 114/D3
Sādullāpur, Bang. 123/G3
Sadulshahar, India 124/C5
Saerbeck, Ger. 79/E4
Saeul, Lux. 81/E4
Safané, Burk. 140/E3
Safāpur, India 124/C2
Safāqis (gov.), Tun. 137/H2
Safed Koh (range), Pak. 124/A3
Safety Harbor, Fl, US 190/K8
Saffig, Ger. 81/G3
Säffle, Swe. 66/E2
Safford, Az, US 175/H4
Saffron Walden, Eng, UK 63/G2
Safi, Mor. 136/C2
Safi (cape), Mor. 136/C2
Safīd (riv.), Afg. 127/J1
Safid Khers (mts.), Afg. 127/K1
Safid Kūh (mts.), Afg. 127/H2
Safidon, India 124/D5
Safien, Swi. 87/F4
Safīpur, India 122/C2
Şāfītā, Syria 130/E2
Safonovo, Rus. 94/G5
Safranbolu, Turk. 96/E4
Şaft al 'Inab, Egypt 139/B3
Şaft al Mulūk, Egypt 139/B3
Şaft Turāb, Egypt 139/C3
Sag Harbor, NY, US 195/F2
Saga, China 123/E1
Saga, Japan 110/B4
Saga (pref.), Japan 110/A4
Sagaba, Ang. 148/D1
Sagae, Japan 108/B4
Sagaing (state), Myan. 119/F3
Sagaing, Myan. 112/B4
Sagami (sea), Japan 111/F3
Sagami (riv.), Japan 109/C2
Sagami (lake), Japan 109/C2
Sagami (bay), Japan 109/C3
Sagamihara, Japan 111/F3
Sagamiko, Japan 109/C2
Sagamore Hill Nat'l Hist. Site, NY, US 195/M8
Sagan, Indo. 117/H4
Sagana, Kenya 145/B2
Saganaga (lake), Can.,US 183/J3
Sāgar, India 122/B4
Sāgar, India 121/B3
Sagard, Ger. 66/E4
Sagarejo, Geo. 97/H4
Sagarmatha (zone), Nepal 123/F2
Sagarmatha (Everest) (mtn.), China, Nepal 123/F2
Sagarmatha NP, Nepal 123/F2
Sagata, Sen. 140/A3
Sagauli, India 123/E2
Sagay, Phil. 114/C3
Sagay, Phil. 114/D3
Sage, Ar, US 179/J2
Sage (cr.), Mt, US 171/J3
Sagemace (bay), Mb, Can. 182/D1
Saggart, Ire. 60/B5
Şaghīr (canal), Egypt 139/C2
Saginaw, Mi, US 186/E3
Saginaw (bay), Mi, US 186/E3
Saginaw, Or, US 172/B2
Saginaw, Tx, US 176/K7
Sagittario (riv.), It. 92/C4
Sagiz, Kaz. 97/K2
Sagle, Id, US 170/F3
Saglek (bay), Nf, Can. 167/K3
Sagola, Mi, US 183/K4
Sagone (gulf), Fr. 74/A1
Sagsay (riv.), Mong. 125/E2
Sagter Ems (riv.), Ger. 79/E2
Sagu, Indo. 154/A2
Sagua de Tánamo, Cuba 201/H1
Sagua la Grande, Cuba 201/F1
Saguache, Co, US 175/J1
Saguache (cr.), Co, US 175/J1
Saguaro NP, Az, US 175/G4
Saguia el Hamra (riv.), WSah. 136/C4
Sagunto, Sp. 73/E3
Sagy, Fr. 56/H4
Sa'gya, China 123/G1
Sagyz (riv.), Kaz. 97/K2
Saḩāb, Jor. 131/D5
Sahaba, Sudan 135/F5
Sahagún, Col. 204/C2
Sahagún, Sp. 72/C1
Sahagún, Mex. 199/L7
Saḩam, Jor. 131/D3
Sahand (mtn.), Iran 129/F2
Sahara (des.), Afr. 133/B2
Sahāranpur, India 124/D5
Saharsa, India 123/F3
Sahaspur, India 122/B1
Sahaswān, India 122/B1
Sahavato, Madg. 152/J8
Sahāwar, India 122/B2
Sahel (riv.), Alg. 138/H4
Sāhibganj, India 123/F3
Şahin, Turk. 77/H5
Şahinli, Turk. 77/H5
Sāhīwāl, Pak. 124/B4
Sahiwal, Pak. 124/B4
Şaḩneh, Iran 129/F3
Sahoué, Gabon 146/B2
Şahrajat al Kubrá, Egypt 139/C3
Sahrho, Jebel (mts.), Mor. 136/D3
Sahu, Indo. 117/G3
Sahuaripa, Mex. 198/C2
Sahuarita, Az, US 175/G5
Sahuayo de Morelos, Mex. 198/E4
Šahy, Slvk. 69/K4
Sai (riv.), India 122/C2
Sai (chan.), India 118/D2
Sai (riv.), Japan 110/E2
Sai Buri, Thai. 120/C5
Sai Kung, China 113/M7
Sai Yok, Thai. 120/B3
Sai Yok NP, Thai. 120/B3
Saibai (isl.), Austl. 155/F2
Sa'id Bundas, Sudan 142/E3
Saïda, Alg. 138/F5
Saïdia, Mor. 138/C2
Saidor, PNG 155/G1
Saidpur, India 122/D3
Saidpur, Bang. 123/G3
Saidu, Pak. 124/B2
Saignelégier, Swi. 86/D3
Saignon, Fr. 90/B5
Saigō, Japan 110/C2
Saigon, Viet. 120/D4
Saijō, Japan 110/C4
Saikai NP, Japan 110/A4
Saiki, Japan 110/B4
Saillans, Fr. 90/B3
Sailly, Fr. 56/H4
Sailly-sur-la-Lys, Fr. 80/B2
Sailolof, Indo. 117/H4
Sailu, India 118/C4
Saima, China 107/C2
Saimaa (lake), Fin. 64/J3
Sain Alto, Mex. 198/E4
Şā'īn Dezh, Iran 129/F2
Sainghin-en-Weppes, Fr. 80/B2
Sains-du-Nord, Fr. 80/D3
Saint (swamp), Fl, US 191/H3
Saint Mary's (riv.), NS, Can. 185/F3
Saint Abb's (pt.), Sc, UK 59/D5
Saint Abbs, Sc, UK 59/D5
Saint Adolphe, Mb, Can. 182/F3
Saint Agnes (pt.), Eng, UK 62/A6
Saint Agnes, Eng, UK 62/A6
Saint Alban's, Nf, Can. 185/K2
Saint Albans, Eng, UK 56/C1
Saint Albans, Vt, US 187/K2
Saint Albans, WV, US 189/G1
Saint Albert, Ab, Can. 171/H1
Saint Ambroise, Mb, Can. 182/E2
Saint Andrews (bay), Sc, UK 59/D4
Saint Andrews, NB, Can. 184/D3
Saint Andrews, Sc, UK 59/D4
Saint Andrew's, Nf, Can. 185/H2
Saint Ann (cape), SLeo. 140/B5
Saint Anne, Chl, UK 82/C1
Saint Ann's (pt.), Wal, UK 62/A3
Saint Anns, On, Can. 186/U9
Saint Ann's Bay, Jam. 197/F4
Saint Ansgar, Ia, US 181/H2
Saint Anthony, Id, US 173/H2
Saint Anthony, ND, US 182/D4
Saint Anthony, Nf, Can. 167/L3
Saint Arnaud, Austl. 158/B3
Saint Arthur, NB, Can. 184/D2
Saint Asaph, Wal, UK 60/E5
Saint Athan, Wal, UK 62/C4
Saint Aubin, Chl, UK 82/C2
Saint Aubin's (bay), UK 82/C2
Saint Augustine, Fl, US 191/H3
Saint Augustine Beach, Fl, US 191/H3
Saint Austell (bay), Eng, UK 62/B6
Saint Austell, Eng, UK 62/B6
Saint Barthélemy (int'l arpt.), Neth. 197/N8
Saint Bathans (mt.), NZ 161/B4
Saint Bees, Eng, UK 60/E3
Saint Bees (pt.), Eng, UK 60/E2
Saint Benedict, Sk, Can. 171/M1
Saint Blaize (cape), SAfr. 150/C4
Saint Boswells, Sc, UK 59/D5
Saint Briavels, Eng, UK 62/D3
Saint Bride's (bay), Wal, UK 62/A3
Saint Bride's, Nf, Can. 185/K2
Saint Brieux, Sk, Can. 171/M1
Saint Catharines, On, Can. 186/U9
Saint Catherine, Fl, US 190/L6
Saint Catherine (mt.), Gren. 205/F1
Saint Catherines (isl.), Ga, US 191/H2
Saint Catherine's (hill), Eng, UK 63/E5
Saint Catherine's (pt.), Eng, UK 63/E5
Saint Charles, Il, US 193/P16
Saint Charles, Mi, US 186/D3
Saint Charles, Mo, US 181/J4
Saint Charles, Mn, US 181/H2
Saint Charles, Md, US 189/J1
Saint Christoffel (peak), NAnt. 204/D1
Saint Clair (riv.), On, Can. 186/E3
Saint Clair (lake), Can.,US 193/G7
Saint Clair (co.), Mi, US 193/G6
Saint Clair, Mi, US 186/E3
Saint Clair, Mn, US 181/H1
Saint Clair, Pa, US 194/B2
Saint Clair Beach, On, Can. 193/G7
Saint Clair Shores, Mi, US 193/G6
Saint Clairsville, Oh, US 186/F4
Saint Cloud, Fl, US 190/N7
Saint Cloud, Mn, US 183/G5
Saint Columb Major, Eng, UK 62/B6
Saint Combs, Sc, UK 59/E1
Saint Croix, NB, Can. 184/D3
Saint Croix (riv.), Wi, US 183/H5
Saint Croix (riv.), Mn,Wi, US 181/H1
Saint Croix (co.), Wi, US 183/Q6
Saint Croix (isl.), USVI 197/M8
Saint Croix Ind. Res., Wi, US 183/H5
Saint Cyrus, Sc, UK 59/D3
Saint David, Az, US 175/G5
Saint David's, Wal, UK 62/A3
Saint David's (pt.), Wal, UK 62/A3
Saint Edward, PE, Can. 184/E2
Saint Edward, Ne, US 180/F3
Saint Eleanors, PE, Can. 184/F2
Saint Elias (mts.), Ak, US 166/B2
Saint Elias (mt.), Ak, US 168/Y12
Saint Elias (cape), Ak, US 168/Y13
Saint Eustatius (isl.), NAnt. 197/N8
Saint Fergus, Sc, UK 59/E1
Saint Francis (cape), SAfr. 150/D4
Saint Francis (riv.), Ar,Mo, US 188/B2
Saint Francis, Ks, US 180/D4
Saint Francis, SD, US 180/D2
Saint Francis, Wi, US 193/Q14
Saint Francisville, La, US 190/C2
Saint Francisville, Il, US 188/D1
Saint Francois (mts.), Mo, US 179/J2
Saint François (riv.), Qu, Can. 187/L2
Saint Gabriel, La, US 190/C2
Saint Gallen (canton), Swi. 87/F3
Saint Geoirs (arpt.), Fr. 90/B2
Saint George, Austl 160/C5
Saint George, NB, Can. 184/D3
Saint George (cape), Nf, Can. 185/H1
Saint George, On, Can. 186/S9
Saint George (isl.), Ak, US 168/W13
Saint George (cape), Fl, US 191/F3
Saint George, Ga, US 191/G2
Saint George (nbrhd.), NY, US 195/J9
Saint George, SC, US 189/G4
Saint George, Ut, US 175/F2
Saint George's(chan.) 60/C6
Saint George's (bay), Nf, Can. 185/H1
Saint George's, Nf, Can. 185/H1
Saint George's (cap.), Gren. 205/F1
Saint Georges, De, US 194/C4
Saint Georges Head (pt.), Austl. 159/E2
Saint Govan's (pt.), Wal, UK 62/B3
Saint Gregory (cape), Nf, Can. 185/H1
Saint Helen, Mi, US 186/D2
Saint Helena (isl.), Austl. 160/F6
Saint Helena (isl.), UK 52/J6
Saint Helena (bay), SAfr. 150/B4
Saint Helena (mt.), Ca, US 172/B4
Saint Helena, Ca, US 172/B4
Saint Helena (sound), SC, US 189/G4
Saint Helens, Austl. 158/D4
Saint Helens (pt.), Austl. 158/D4
Saint Helens, Eng, UK 61/F5
Saint Helens, Or, US 170/C5
Saint Helens (mt.), Wa, US 170/C4
Saint Helier, Chl, UK 82/C2
Saint Henry, Oh, US 186/D4
Saint Hilaire, Mn, US 182/F3
Saint Ignace (isl.), On, Can. 183/L3
Saint Ignace, Mi, US 186/D2
Saint Ignatius, Mt, US 171/G4
Saint Ives (nbrhd.), Austl. 160/H8
Saint Ives, Eng, UK 63/F2
Saint Ives (bay), Eng, UK 62/A6
Saint Ives, Eng, UK 62/A6
Saint Jacques (int'l arpt.), Fr. 82/D4
Saint James, Mo, US 179/J2
Saint James, Ar, US 179/J3
Saint James, Mi, US 186/D2
Saint James (cape), BC, Can. 166/C3
Saint James, Mn, US 181/G2
Saint James, NY, US 195/E2
Saint James City, Fl, US 191/G4
Saint Jo, Tx, US 179/F4
Saint Joe, Ar, US 179/H2
Saint Joe (riv.), Id,Wa, US 168/C2
Saint John, Chl, UK 82/C2
Saint John, Ks, US 179/E1
Saint John, NB, Can. 184/D3
Saint John, ND, US 182/E3
Saint John (riv.), NB, Can. 184/D3
Saint John (lake), La, US 190/C2
Saint John (riv.), Me, US 167/K4
Saint John (isl.), USVI 197/M8
Saint John, Wa, US 170/F4
Saint John's (cap.), Anti. 197/N8
Saint John's (cap.), Nf, Can. 185/L2
Saint John's (pt.), NI, UK 60/C3
Saint Johns, Az, US 175/H3
Saint Johns (riv.), Fl, US 191/H3
Saint Johns, Mi, US 186/D3
Saint Johnsbury, Vt US 187/K2
Saint Jones (riv.), De, US 194/C5
Saint Joseph (pen.), Fl, US 191/F3
Saint Joseph (lake), La, US 190/C1
Saint Joseph (isl.), On, Can. 186/E1
Saint Joseph, Mi, US 186/C3
Saint Joseph (riv.), Mi, US 186/D3
Saint Joseph (lake), On, Can. 166/G3
Saint Joseph (pt.), Fl, US 191/F3
Saint Joseph, Fl, US 190/L7
Saint Joseph, La, US 190/C2
Saint Joseph, Mo, US 181/G4
Saint Joseph, Tn, US 188/D3
Saint Just, Eng, UK 62/A6
Saint Just-in-Roseland, Eng, UK 62/A6
Saint Kilda (isl.), UK 57/P8
Saint Kilda (nbrhd.), Austl. 158/F5
Saint Kitts (isl.), StK. 197/J4
Saint Kitts and Nevis (ctry) 165/L8
Saint Landry, La, US 190/B2
Saint Laurent, Mb, Can. 182/F2
Saint Lawrence, Nf, Can. 185/K2
Saint Lawrence (riv.), NAm. 187/J2
Saint Lawrence, Austl. 160/C3
Saint Lawrence, Eng, UK 63/E5
Saint Lawrence (riv.), Can.,US 165/K5
Saint Lawrence (gulf), Can. 165/L5
Saint Lawrence (isl.), Ak, US 165/A3
Saint Lawrence, Tx, US 177/D2
Saint Lawrence, Pa, US 194/C3
Saint Lawrence Islands NP, On, Can. 187/H2
Saint Leo, Fl, US 190/L7
Saint Leon, Mb, Can. 182/E3
Saint Leonard (mt.), Austl. 158/G5
Saint Leonards, Austl. 159/B4
Saint Llorenc del Munt, PN, Sp. 73/K6
Saint Louis (lake), Qu, Can. 185/N7
Saint Louis, Sk, Can. 171/M1
Saint Louis (riv.), Mn, US 183/H4
Saint Louis, Mi, US 186/D3
Saint Louis, Mo, US 181/J4
Saint Louis Park, Mn, US 183/P7
Saint Lucia(ctry.) 165/L8
Saint Lucia (cape), SAfr. 151/F3
Saint Lucia (lake), SAfr. 151/F3
Saint Lucia (chan.), Mart.,StL. 197/N9
Saint Lucia Estuary, SAfr. 151/F3
Saint Lucie, Fl, US 191/H4
Saint Lucie (canal), Fl, US 191/H4
Saint Lucie (inlet), Fl, US 191/H4
Saint Maarten (isl.), NAnt. 197/N8
Saint Magnus (bay), Sc, UK 57/W13
Saint Malo, Mb, Can. 182/F3
Saint Margaret's at Cliffe, Eng, UK 80/A1
Saint Margaret's Hope, Sc, UK 57/V14
Saint Maries, Id, US 170/F4
Saint Marks, Fl, US 191/F2
Saint Marks, SAfr. 150/D4
Saint Marks NWR, Fl, US 191/F2
Saint Martin (lake), Mb, Can. 182/E2
Saint Martin (isl.), Mi, US 183/L5
Saint Martins, NB, Can. 184/E3
Saint Martins (isl.), Bang. 112/A4
Saint Martinville, La, US 190/C2
Saint Mary (peak), Austl. 157/H4
Saint Mary (riv.), BC, Can. 170/F3
Saint Mary (cape), NS, Can. 184/D3
Saint Mary (cape), Gam. 140/A3
Saint Mary's (bay), Ns., Can. 184/D3
Saint Mary's, Nf, Can. 185/L2
Saint Mary's, On, Can. 186/F3
Saint Mary's, Sc, UK 57/V14
Saint Mary's, Zam. 149/E2
Saint Marys, Austl. 158/D4
Saint Marys (nbrhd.), Austl. 160/G8
Saint Marys, Ga, US 191/H2
Saint Marys (riv.), In, US 186/D4
Saint Marys, Ks, US 181/F4
Saint Marys, Mo, US 188/C2
Saint Marys, Oh, US 186/D4
Saint Marys, Pa, US 187/G4
Saint Marys, WV, US 186/F5
Saint Mary's Entrance (inlet), Ga,Fl, US 191/H2
Saint Matthew (isl.), Ak, US 165/A4
Saint Matthews, SC, US 189/G4
Saint Matthias Group (isls.), PNG 162/E5
Saint Maurice, La, US 190/B2
Saint Mawes, Eng, UK 62/A6
Saint Meinrad, In, US 188/D1
Saint Mellons, Wal, UK 62/C3
Saint Michael, Mn, US 183/N6
Saint Michaels, Md, US 194/B6
Saint Monance, Sc, UK 59/D4
Saint Moritz (Sankt Moritz), Swi. 71/H3
Saint Neots, Eng, UK 63/F2
Saint Nicholas Greek Orthodox Church, Fl, US 190/K7
Saint Niklaus, Swi. 86/D5
Saint Onge (peak), SD, US 180/C1
Saint Ouen's (bay), Chi., UK 82/C2
Saint Paris, Oh, US 186/E4
Saint Patrickswell, Ire. 58/B4
Saint Paul, Ab, Can. 166/E3
Saint Paul (isl.), Fr. 53/N7
Saint Paul (cape), Gha. 141/F5
Saint Paul (riv.), Libr. 140/C5
Saint Paul, Ar, US 179/H3
Saint Paul, Ks, US 179/G2
Saint Paul, In, US 186/D5
Saint Paul, Fr. 151/S15
Saint Paul, Ne, US 180/E3
Saint Paul (cap.), Mn, US 183/P7
Saint Paul (isl.), Ak, US 168/W13
Saint Paul, SC, US 189/G4

292

Saint – Sam

Saint Pauls, NC, US 189/H3
Saint Paul's Church Nat'l Hist. Site, NY, US 195/K8
Saint Peter (isl.), Austl. 157/G5
Saint Peter, Il, US 188/C1
Saint Peter, Ks, US 180/D4
Saint Peter, Mn, US 181/H1
Saint Peter and Saint Paul Rocks, (isl.), Braz. 52/H5
Saint Peter Port, Chl, UK 82/C2
Saint Peters, PE, Can. 185/F2
Saint Peters, NS, Can. 185/G3
Saint Peter's, Eng, UK 63/H4
Saint Peters, Mo, US 181/J4
Saint Peter's, VatC. 91/G7
Saint Peter's Basilica, VatC. 91/G7
Saint Petersburg, Rus. 94/T7
Saint Petersburg, Fl, US 190/K8
Saint Petersburg Beach, Fl, US 190/K8
Saint Petersburg-Clearwater International (arpt.), Fl, US 190/K8
Saint Philips, Sk, Can. 182/D2
Saint Pierre and Miquelon (dpcy.), Fr. 165/M5
Saint Pierre-Jolys, Mb, Can. 182/F3
Saint Regis Ind. Res., NY, US 187/J2
Saint Sampson's, Chl, UK 82/C2
Saint Saviour, Chl, UK 82/C2
Saint Shotts, Nf, Can. 185/L2
Saint Simons (isl.), Ga, US 191/H2
Saint Simons Island, Ga, US 191/H2
Saint Stephen, NB, Can. 184/D3
Saint Stephen-in-Brannel, Eng, UK 62/B6
Saint Stephens, Al, US 190/D2
Saint Stephens, NC, US 189/G3
Saint Stephens Church, Va, US 189/J2
Saint Thomas, Mo, US 179/H1
Saint Thomas, ND, US 182/F3
Saint Thomas, On, Can. 186/F3
Saint Thomas (isl.), USVI 197/H4
Saint Victor, Sk, Can. 171/M3
Saint Vika, Swe. 65/A2
Saint Vincent (pt.), Austl. 158/C4
Saint Vincent, It. 88/A1
Saint Vincent (isl.), StV. 197/N9
Saint Vincent and the Grenadines (ctry.) 165/L8
Saint Vincent Nat'l Wild. Ref., Fl, US 191/F3
Saint Vincent Passage (chan.), StL.,StV. 197/N9
Saint Walburg, Sk, Can. 171/K1
Saint Xavier, Mt, US 173/K1
Saint-Affrique, Fr. 70/E5
Saint-Aignan, Fr. 83/G6
Saint-Alexis-de-Matapédia, Qu, Can. 184/D2
Saint-Alexis-des-Monts, Qu, Can. 187/K1
Saint-Amable, Qu, Can. 185/P6
Saint-Amand, Fr. 83/E2
Saint-Amand-les-Eaux, Fr. 80/C3
Saint-Amand-Longpré, Fr. 83/G5
Saint-Amand-Montrond, Fr. 70/E3
Saint-Amarin, Fr. 86/D2
Saint-Ambroise, Qu, Can. 184/B1
Saint-Amé, Fr. 86/C1
Saint-Andiol, Fr. 90/A5
Saint-André, NB, Can. 184/D2
Saint-André, Fr. 80/C2
Saint-André, Fr. 90/D5
Saint-André, Fr. 151/S15
Saint-André-de-Cubzac, Fr. 70/C4
Saint-André-de-l'Eure, Fr. 83/G3
Saint-André-le-Gaz, Fr. 90/B1
Saint-André-les-Alpes, Fr. 90/C5
Saint-André-les-Vergers, Fr. 70/F2
Saint-Anicet, Qu, Can. 187/J2
Saint-Antoine, NB, Can. 184/E2
Saint-Antoine, Qu, Can. 185/N6
Saint-Antonin, Qu, Can. 184/C2
Saint-Arnoult-en-Yvelines, Fr. 56/H6
Saint-Athanase, Qu, Can. 184/C2
Saint-Auban, Fr. 90/C5
Saint-Aubert, Qu, Can. 184/B2
Saint-Aubin, Fr. 86/B3
Saint-Aubin, Swi. 86/C4
Saint-Aubin-d'Aubigné, Fr. 82/D4
Saint-Aubin-du-Cormier, Fr. 82/D4
Saint-Aubin-lès-Elbeuf, Fr. 83/G2
Saint-Aubin-sur-Gaillon, Fr. 83/G2
Saint-Augustin, Madg. 152/G8
Saint-Augustin, Fr. 56/M5
Saint-Augustin, Qu, Can. 185/N6
Saint-Avé, Fr. 82/C5
Saint-Avertin, Fr. 83/F6
Saint-Avold, Fr. 81/F5
Saint-Baldoph, Fr. 90/B1
Saint-Barthélemy, Qu, Can. 187/K1
Saint-Barthélemy (isl.), Fr. 197/N8
Saint-Barthélemy, Pic de (peak), Fr. 70/D5
Saint-Barthélemy-d'Anjou, Fr. 83/E6
Saint-Basile, NB, Can. 184/C2
Saint-Benoît, Fr. 151/S15
Saint-Benoît, Fr. 70/D3
Saint-Benoît, Qu, Can. 185/M6
Saint-Berthevin, Fr. 83/E4
Saint-Blaise, Swi. 86/C3
Saint-Blaise, Qu, Can. 185/P7
Saint-Bonnet-de-Mure, Fr. 90/B1
Saint-Bonnet-en-Champsaur, Fr. 90/C3
Saint-Briac-sur-Mer, Fr. 82/C3
Saint-Brice-Courcelles, Fr. 80/C5
Saint-Brice-sous-Forêt, Fr. 56/K5
Saint-Brieuc, Fr. 82/C3
Saint-Brieuc (bay), Fr. 70/B2
Saint-Bruno (co.), Qu, Can. 185/P6
Saint-Bruno-de-Montarville, Qu, Can. 185/P6
Saint-Calais, Fr. 83/F5
Saint-Cannat, Fr. 90/B5
Saint-Canut, Qu, Can. 185/M6
Saint-Cassien (lake), Fr. 90/C5
Saint-Cast-le-Guildo, Fr. 82/C3
Saint-Céré, Fr. 70/D4
Saint-Cergue, Swi. 86/C5
Saint-Cergues, Fr. 86/C5
Saint-Chamas, Fr. 90/B5
Saint-Charles, NB, Can. 184/E2
Saint-Chef, Fr. 90/B1
Saint-Chély-d'Apcher, Fr. 70/E4
Saint-Chéron, Fr. 56/J6
Saint-Clair-de-la-Tour, Fr. 90/B1
Saint-Clair-du-Rhône, Fr. 90/A2
Saint-Claude, Fr. 86/B5
Saint-Cloud, Fr. 56/J5
Saint-Constant, Qu, Can. 185/N7
Saint-Cosme-de-Vair, Fr. 83/F4
Saint-Coulomb, Fr. 82/D3
Saint-Croix (lake), Fr. 90/C5
Saint-Cyprien, Qu, Can. 184/C2
Saint-Cyr-en-Val, Fr. 83/G5
Saint-Cyr-l'École, Fr. 56/J5
Saint-Cyr-sous-Dourdan, Fr. 56/J6
Saint-Cyr-sur-Loire, Fr. 83/F6
Saint-Cyr-sur-Mer, Fr. 90/B6
Saint-Cyr-sur-Morin, Fr. 56/M5
Saint-Cyrille, Qu, Can. 187/K2
Saint-Damase, Qu, Can. 184/D1
Saint-Damien-de-Buckland, Qu, Can. 184/B2
Saint-David-de-Falardeau, Qu, Can. 184/B1
Saint-Denis, Fr. 151/S15
Saint-Denis, Fr. 56/K5
Saint-Denis-en-Bugey, Fr. 86/B6
Saint-Denis-les-Ponts, Fr. 83/G4
Saint-Didier, Fr. 90/B5
Saint-Dié, Fr. 86/C1
Saint-Dizier, Fr. 81/D6
Saint-Donat, Qu, Can. 187/J1
Saint-Donat-sur-L'Herbasse, Fr. 90/A2
Saint-Doulchard, Fr. 70/E3
Saint-Édouard, Qu, Can. 185/N7
Saint-Égrève, Fr. 90/B2
Saint-Élie, FrG. 206/C1
Saint-Éloy-les-Mines, Fr. 70/E3
Saint-Esprit, Qu, Can. 185/N6
Saint-Estève, Fr. 70/E5
Saint-Étienne-au-Mont, Fr. 80/A2
Saint-Étienne-de-Baïgorry, Fr. 70/C5
Saint-Étienne-de-Cuines, Fr. 90/C2
Saint-Étienne-de-Montluc, Fr. 82/D6
Saint-Étienne-de-Tinée, Fr. 90/C4
Saint-Étienne-du-Grès, Fr. 90/A5
Saint-Étienne-du-Rouvray, Fr. 83/G2
Saint-Étienne-les-Orgues, Fr. 90/B4
Saint-Étienne-lès-Remiremont, Fr. 86/C1
Saint-Eusèbe, Qu, Can. 184/C2
Saint-Eustache, Qu, Can. 185/N6
Saint-Fabien, Qu, Can. 184/C1
Saint-Fargeau-Ponthierry, Fr. 56/K6
Saint-Félicien, Qu, Can. 184/A1
Saint-Félicien, Fr. 90/A2
Saint-Félix, Fr. 86/B6
Saint-Ferréol-les-Neiges, Qu, Can. 184/B2
Saint-Fidèle-de-Mont-Murray, Qu, Can. 184/C2
Saint-Firmin, Fr. 90/C3
Saint-Florent-le-Vieil, Fr. 83/D6
Saint-Florent-sur-Cher, Fr. 70/E3
Saint-Florentin, Fr. 70/E2
Saint-Fons, Fr. 90/A1
Saint-Four, Fr. 70/E4
Saint-François (riv.), Qu, Can. 184/A3
Saint-François-du-Lac, Qu, Can. 187/K1
Saint-Front, Sk, Can. 171/M1
Saint-Fulgence, Qu, Can. 184/B1
Saint-Gabriel, Qu, Can. 187/K1
Saint-Gaudens, Fr. 70/D5
Saint-Gaudens Nat'l Hist. Site, NH, US 187/K3
Saint-Gédéon, Qu, Can. 184/B3
Saint-Genis-Laval, Fr. 90/A1
Saint-Genis-Pouilly, Fr. 86/C5
Saint-Genix-sur-Guiers, Fr. 90/B1
Saint-Georges, Qu, Can. 184/B2
Saint-Georges, FrG. 206/D2
Saint-Georges-Buttavent, Fr. 83/E4
Saint-Georges-de-Cacouna, Qu, Can. 184/C2
Saint-Georges-des-Groseillers, Fr. 83/E3
Saint-Georges-du-Vièvre, Fr. 83/F2
Saint-Georges-sur-Cher, Fr. 83/G6
Saint-Georges-sur-Eure, Fr. 83/G4
Saint-Georges-sur-Loire, Fr. 83/E6
Saint-Géréon, Fr. 82/D6
Saint-Germain, Fr. 86/C2
Saint-Germain-de-la-Grange, Fr. 56/H5
Saint-Germain-du-Bois, Fr. 86/B4
Saint-Germain-du-Corbéis, Fr. 83/F4
Saint-Germain-du-Plain, Fr. 86/A4
Saint-Germain-en-Laye, Fr. 56/J5
Saint-Germain-lès-Corbeil, Fr. 56/K6
Saint-Germain-sous Doue, Fr. 56/M5
Saint-Germain-sur-Morin, Fr. 56/L5
Saint-Germer-de-Fly, Fr. 80/A5
Saint-Gervais, Fr. 56/H4
Saint-Gervais-la-Forêt, Fr. 83/G5
Saint-Gervais-les-Bains, Fr. 86/C6
Saint-Ghislain, Belg. 80/C3
Saint-Gildas-des-Bois, Fr. 82/C5
Saint-Gilles-Croix-de-Vie, Fr. 70/C3
Saint-Gingolph, Swi. 86/C5
Saint-Girons, Fr. 70/D5
Saint-Gobain, Fr. 80/C4
Saint-Godefroi, Qu, Can. 184/E1
Saint-Gratien, Fr. 56/J5
Saint-Grégoire, Fr. 82/D4
Saint-Guillaume-Nord, Qu, Can. 187/J1
Saint-Herblain, Fr. 82/D6
Saint-Hermas, Qu, Can. 185/M6
Saint-Herménégilde, Qu, Can. 184/B3
Saint-Hilaire-du-Harcouët, Fr. 83/D3
Saint-Hilarion, Fr. 56/H6
Saint-Hippolyte, Fr. 86/C3
Saint-Honorat (peak), Fr. 90/C4
Saint-Honoré, Qu, Can. 184/B3
Saint-Honoré, Qu, Can. 184/B1
Saint-Hubert, Qu, Can. 184/C2
Saint-Hubert, Belg. 81/E3
Saint-Hubert (pond), Fr. 56/H5
Saint-Hubert, Qu, Can. 185/P6
Saint-Hugues, Qu, Can. 187/K2
Saint-Hyacinthe, Qu, Can. 187/K2
Saint-Imier, Swi. 86/D3
Saint-Irénée, Qu, Can. 184/B2
Saint-Isidore, NB, Can. 184/E2
Saint-Isidore-de-Laprairie, Qu, Can. 185/N7
Saint-Ismier, Fr. 90/B2
Saint-Jacques, NB, Can. 184/C2
Saint-Jacques-de-la-Lande, Fr. 82/D4
Saint-Jacques-le-Mineur, Qu, Can. 185/P7
Saint-James, Fr. 82/D3
Saint-Jean (riv.), Qu, Can. 184/E1
Saint-Jean (lake), Qu, Can. 167/J4
Saint-Jean, FrG. 206/C1
Saint-Jean-Cap-Ferrat, Fr. 90/D5
Saint-Jean-d'Angély, Fr. 70/C4
Saint-Jean-de-Bboiseau, Fr. 82/D6
Saint-Jean-de-Bournay, Fr. 90/B2
Saint-Jean-de-Braye, Fr. 83/G5
Saint-Jean-de-Dieu, Qu, Can. 184/C1
Saint-Jean-de-la-Ruelle, Fr. 83/G5
Saint-Jean-de-Losne, Fr. 86/B3
Saint-Jean-de-Luz, Fr. 70/C5
Saint-Jean-de-Matha, Qu, Can. 187/K1
Saint-Jean-de-Muzols, Fr. 90/A2
Saint-Jean-en-Royans, Fr. 90/B2
Saint-Jean-Port-Joli, Qu, Can. 184/B2
Saint-Jean-sur-Richelieu, Qu, Can. 187/K2
Saint-Jeannet, Fr. 90/D5
Saint-Jeoire, Fr. 86/C5
Saint-Jérôme, Qu, Can. 185/N6
Saint-Joachim, Fr. 82/C6
Saint-Joseph, NB, Can. 184/E3
Saint-Joseph, Fr. 151/S15
Saint-Joseph-de-Beauce, Qu, Can. 184/B2
Saint-Joseph-de-Madawaska, NB, Can. 184/C2
Saint-Joseph-de-Mékinac, Qu, Can. 184/A2
Saint-Jovite, Qu, Can. 187/J1
Saint-Juéry, Fr. 70/E5
Saint-Julien, Fr. 86/B3
Saint-Julien-de-Vouvantes, Fr. 82/D5
Saint-Julien-en-Genevois, Fr. 86/C5
Saint-Julien-les-Villas, Fr. 70/F2
Saint-Julien-Mont-Denis, Fr. 90/C2
Saint-Junien, Fr. 70/D4
Saint-Just-en-Chaussée, Fr. 80/B4
Saint-Juste-de-Bretenières, Qu, Can. 184/B2
Saint-Lambert, Qu, Can. 185/P6
Saint-Laurent, Qu, Can. 185/N6
Saint-Laurent du Maroni (dist.), FrG. 206/C1
Saint-Laurent du Maroni, FrG. 206/C1
Saint-Laurent-Blangy, Fr. 80/B3
Saint-Laurent-de-Cerdans, Fr. 70/E5
Saint-Laurent-de-Mure, Fr. 90/B1
Saint-Laurent-des-Arbres, Fr. 90/A4
Saint-Laurent-du-Pont, Fr. 90/B2
Saint-Laurent-du-Var, Fr. 90/D5
Saint-Laurent-en-Grandvaux, Fr. 86/B4
Saint-Laurent-Nouan, Fr. 83/G5
Saint-Laurent-sur-Saône, Fr. 86/A5
Saint-Lazare, Qu, Can. 184/B2
Saint-Lazare, Qu, Can. 185/M7
Saint-Léger, Belg. 81/E4
Saint-Léger-en-Yvelines, Fr. 56/H5
Saint-Léger-lès-Domart, Fr. 80/B3
Saint-Léonard, Fr. 80/A2
Saint-Léonard, Qu, Can. 185/N6
Saint-Leu, Fr. 151/S15
Saint-Leu-D'Esserent, Fr. 80/B5
Saint-Leu-la-Forêt, Fr. 56/J4
Saint-Liboire, Qu, Can. 184/A3
Saint-Lô, Fr. 83/D2
Saint-Louis, Fr. 86/D2
Saint-Louis (pol. reg.), Sen. 140/B3
Saint-Louis, Sen. 140/A2
Saint-Louis, Fr. 151/S15
Saint-Louis du Nord, Haiti 201/H2
Saint-Louis-de-Gonzague, Qu, Can. 185/N7
Saint-Louis-de-Kent, NB, Can. 184/E2
Saint-Loup-sur-Semouse, Fr. 86/C2
Saint-Lubin-des-Joncherets, Fr. 83/G3
Saint-Luc, Qu, Can. 185/P7
Saint-Lucien, Fr. 56/G6
Saint-Lunaire, Fr. 82/C3
Saint-Magloire-de-Bellechasse, Qu, Can. 184/B2
Saint-Maixent l'École, Fr. 70/C3
Saint-Malachie, Qu, Can. 184/B2
Saint-Malo, Fr. 82/C3
Saint-Malo (gulf), UK 70/B2
Saint-Malo-de-Guersac, Fr. 82/C6
Saint-Mandrier-sur-Mer, Fr. 90/B6
Saint-Marc, Haiti 201/H2
Saint-Marc-des-Carrières, Qu, Can. 184/A2
Saint-Marc-sur-Richelieu, Qu, Can. 185/P6
Saint-Marcel, Fr. 83/G2
Saint-Marcel, Fr. 86/A4
Saint-Marcel (peak), FrG. 206/C2
Saint-Marcel-d'Ardèche, Fr. 90/A4
Saint-Marcel-lès-Valence, Fr. 90/A3
Saint-Marcellin, Fr. 90/B2
Saint-Marcouf (isls.), Fr. 83/D1
Saint-Mard, Fr. 56/L4
Saint-Mars-la-Brière, Fr. 83/F4
Saint-Mars-la-Jaille, Fr. 83/D5
Saint-Martin, Swi. 86/D5
Saint-Martin (isl.), Fr. 197/J4
Saint-Martin-Boulogne, Fr. 80/A2
Saint-Martin-d'Ablois, Fr. 80/C6
Saint-Martin-de-Belleville, Fr. 90/C2
Saint-Martin-de-Crau, Fr. 90/A5
Saint-Martin-des-Champs, Fr. 82/B3
Saint-Martin-d'Hères, Fr. 90/B2
Saint-Martin-du-Tertre, Fr. 56/K4
Saint-Martin-du-Var, Fr. 90/D5
Saint-Martin-la-Garenne, Fr. 56/H4
Saint-Martin-Vésubie, Fr. 90/D4
Saint-Mathieu (pt.), Fr. 82/A4
Saint-Mathieu-de-Beloeil, Qu, Can. 185/N7
Saint-Maur-des-Fossés, Fr. 56/K5
Saint-Maurice, Swi. 86/D5
Saint-Maurice (riv.), Qu, Can. 184/A2
Saint-Maurice (riv.), Qu, Can. 167/J4
Saint-Maurice-L'Exil, Fr. 90/A2
Saint-Max, Fr. 81/F6
Saint-Maxime-du-Mont-Louis, Qu, Can. 184/E1
Saint-Maximin-la-Sainte-Baume, Fr. 90/B6
Saint-Méen-le-Grand, Fr. 82/C4
Saint-Memmie, Fr. 81/D6
Saint-Méry, Fr. 56/L6
Saint-Michel, Fr. 81/D4
Saint-Michel (mtn.), Fr. 82/B4
Saint-Michel-Chef-Chef, Fr. 82/C6
Saint-Michel-de-Maurienne, Fr. 90/C2
Saint-Michel-des-Saints, Qu, Can. 187/K1
Saint-Michel-sur-Meurthe, Fr. 86/C1
Saint-Michel-sur-Orge, Fr. 56/J6
Saint-Mihiel, Fr. 81/E6
Saint-Mitre-les-Remparts, Fr. 90/B6
Saint-Montant, Fr. 90/A4
Saint-Nabord, Fr. 86/C1
Saint-Nazaire, Fr. 82/C6
Saint-Nazaire, FrG. 206/C1
Saint-Nicolas, Belg. 81/E2
Saint-Nicolas-d'Aliermont, Fr. 83/G1
Saint-Nicolas-du-Pélem, Fr. 82/B4
Saint-Nom-la-Bretèche, Fr. 56/J5
Saint-Omer, Fr. 80/B2
Saint-Omer-en-Chaussée, Fr. 80/A4
Saint-Ouen, Fr. 83/G5
Saint-Ouen, Fr. 80/B3
Saint-Ouen-en-Brie, Fr. 56/L6
Saint-Ouen-L'Aumône, Fr. 56/J4
Saint-Pabu, Fr. 82/A3
Saint-Pacôme, Qu, Can. 184/C2
Saint-Pair-sur-Mer, Fr. 82/D3
Saint-Pamphile, Qu, Can. 184/C2
Saint-Pascal, Qu, Can. 184/C2
Saint-Paterne, Fr. 83/F4
Saint-Pathus, Fr. 56/L4
Saint-Paul, Fr. 90/D5
Saint-Paul, Fr. 90/C3
Saint-Paul-du-Nord, Qu, Can. 184/C1
Saint-Paul-en-Jarez, Fr. 90/A2
Saint-Paul-lès-Dax, Fr. 70/C5
Saint-Paul-Trois-Châteaux, Fr. 90/A4
Saint-Pé-de-Bigorre, Fr. 70/C5
Saint-Péray, Fr. 90/A3
Saint-Père-en-Retz, Fr. 82/C6
Saint-Philippe-de-Laprairie, Qu, Can. 185/P7
Saint-Pierre (pt.), Qu, Can. 184/E1
Saint-Pierre, Nf, Fr. 185/J2
Saint-Pierre (lake), Qu, Can. 184/A2
Saint-Pierre, It. 90/D1
Saint-Pierre, Fr. 151/S15
Saint-Pierre, Fr. 197/N9
Saint-Pierre-d'Albigny, Fr. 90/C1
Saint-Pierre-d'Allevard, Fr. 90/C2
Saint-Pierre-de-Bœuf, Fr. 90/A2
Saint-Pierre-des-Corps, Fr. 83/F6
Saint-Pierre-des-Fleurs, Fr. 83/F2
Saint-Pierre-du-Mont, Fr. 70/C5
Saint-Pierre-du-Perray, Fr. 56/K6
Saint-Pierre-Église, Fr. 82/D1
Saint-Pierre-en-Faucigny, Fr. 86/C5
Saint-Pierre-en-Port, Fr. 83/F1
Saint-Pierre-la-Cour, Fr. 83/D4
Saint-Pierre-lès-Elbeuf, Fr. 83/G2
Saint-Pierre-Montlimart, Fr. 83/D6
Saint-Pierre-Quiberon, Fr. 82/B5
Saint-Pierre-sur-Dives, Fr. 83/E2
Saint-Point (lake), Fr. 86/C4
Saint-Pol-de-Léon, Fr. 82/B3
Saint-Pol-sur-Mer, Fr. 80/B1
Saint-Pol-sur-Ternoise, Fr. 80/B3
Saint-Pourçain-sur-Sioule, Fr. 70/E3
Saint-Prex, Swi. 86/C5
Saint-Priest, Fr. 90/A1
Saint-Prime, Qu, Can. 184/A1
Saint-Prix, Fr. 56/J4
Saint-Prosper, Qu, Can. 184/B2
Saint-Quay-Portrieux, Fr. 82/C3
Saint-Quentin, Fr. 80/C4
Saint-Quentin (pond), Fr. 56/H5
Saint-Quentin, Canal de (canal), Fr. 80/C4
Saint-Rambert-d'Albon, Fr. 90/A2
Saint-Rambert-en-Bugey, Fr. 86/B6
Saint-Raphaël, Qu, Can. 184/B2
Saint-Raphaël, Fr. 90/C6
Saint-Raymond, Qu, Can. 184/B2
Saint-Rémi, Qu, Can. 185/N7
Saint-Rémy-de-Provence, Fr. 90/A5
Saint-Rémy-lès-Chevreuse, Fr. 56/J5
Saint-Rémy-l'Honoré, Fr. 56/H5
Saint-Rémy-sur-Avre, Fr. 83/G3
Saint-Renan, Fr. 82/A4
Saint-René-de-Matane, Qu, Can. 184/D1
Saint-Roch-de-L'Achigan, Qu, Can. 185/N6
Saint-Romain-de-Colbosc, Fr. 83/F1
Saint-Romans, Fr. 90/B2
Saint-Saëns, Fr. 83/G1
Saint-Saturnin-lès-Apt, Fr. 90/B5
Saint-Saturnin-lès-Avignon, Fr. 90/A5
Saint-Saulve, Fr. 80/C3
Saint-Sauveur, Fr. 86/C2
Saint-Sauveur-des-Monts, Qu, Can. 185/M6
Saint-Sauveur-le-Vicomte, Fr. 82/D2
Saint-Sauveur-Lendelin, Fr. 82/D2
Saint-Savin, Fr. 90/B1
Saint-Sébastien, Qu, Can. 184/B3
Saint-Sébastien-sur-Loire, Fr. 82/D6
Saint-Sever, Fr. 70/C5
Saint-Sever-Calvados, Fr. 83/D3
Saint-Siméon-de-Bressieux, Fr. 90/B2
Saint-Soupplets, Fr. 56/L4
Saint-Sulpice, Fr. 70/D5
Saint-Sylvain-d'Anjou, Fr. 83/E5
Saint-Symphorien (arpt.), Fr. 83/F6
Saint-Symphorien-d'Ozon, Fr. 90/A1
Saint-Théodore-d'Acton, Qu, Can. 187/K2
Saint-Théophile, Qu, Can. 184/B3
Saint-Timothée, Qu, Can. 185/M7
Saint-Trivier-de-Courtes, Fr. 86/B5
Saint-Tropez (gulf), Fr. 90/C6
Saint-Tropez, Fr. 90/C6
Saint-Ubalde, Qu, Can. 184/A2
Saint-Urbain, Fr. 86/B1
Saint-Urbain, Qu, Can. 184/B2
Saint-Urbain-Premier, Qu, Can. 185/N7
Saint-Ursanne, Swi. 86/D3
Saint-Uze, Fr. 90/A2
Saint-Vaast-la-Hougue, Fr. 82/D1
Saint-Valery-en-Caux, Fr. 83/F1
Saint-Valery-sur-Somme, Fr. 80/A3
Saint-Vallier, Fr. 90/A2
Saint-Vallier, Fr. 70/F3
Saint-Vallier-de-Thiey, Fr. 90/C5
Saint-Vaury, Fr. 70/D3
Saint-Viâtre, Fr. 83/G5
Saint-Vigor-le-Grand, Fr. 83/E2
Saint-Vincent-de-Tyrosse, Fr. 70/C5
Saint-Vincent-des-Landes, Fr. 82/D5
Saint-Vit, Fr. 86/B3
Saint-Vith, Belg. 81/F3
Saint-Vrain, Fr. 56/K6
Saint-Wandrille-Rançon, Fr. 83/F1
Saint-Witz, Fr. 56/K4
Saint-Yrieix-la-Perche, Fr. 70/D4
Saint-Yvy, Fr. 82/B5
Saint-Zacharie, Fr. 90/B6
Saintala, India 121/D1
Sainte Agathe, Mb, Can. 182/F3
Sainte Amélie, Mb, Can. 182/E2
Sainte Anne, Mb, Can. 182/F3
Sainte Genevieve, Mo, US 188/B2
Sainte Rose du Lac, Mb, Can. 182/E2
Sainte-Adèle, Qu, Can. 187/J2
Sainte-Adresse, Fr. 83/F1
Sainte-Agathe-des-Monts, Qu, Can. 187/J1
Sainte-Anne-D'Auray, Fr. 82/C5
Sainte-Anne-de-Beaupré, Qu, Can. 184/B2
Sainte-Anne-de-Madawaska, NB, Can. 184/C2
Sainte-Anne-des-Monts, Qu, Can. 184/D1
Sainte-Anne-des-Plaines, Qu, Can. 185/N6
Sainte-Anne-du-Lac, Qu, Can. 187/J1
Sainte-Aulde, Fr. 56/M5
Sainte-Blandine, Qu, Can. 184/C1
Sainte-Cécile-les-Vignes, Fr. 90/A4
Sainte-Croix, Swi. 86/C4
Sainte-Croix, Qu, Can. 184/B2
Sainte-Croix-aux-Mines, Fr. 86/D1
Sainte-Florence, Qu, Can. 184/D1
Sainte-Foy, Qu, Can. 184/B2
Sainte-Foy-lès-Lyon, Fr. 90/A1
Sainte-Françoise, Qu, Can. 184/C1
Sainte-Gemmes-sur-Loire, Fr. 83/E6
Sainte-Geneviève-de-Batiscan, Qu, Can. 184/A2
Sainte-Geneviève-des-Bois, Fr. 56/K6
Sainte-Hénédine, Qu, Can. 184/B2
Sainte-Jamme-sur-Sarthe, Fr. 83/F4
Sainte-Julie, Qu, Can. 185/P6
Sainte-Julienne, Qu, Can. 187/K2
Sainte-Luce-sur-Loire, Fr. 82/D6
Sainte-Marie, Qu, Can. 184/B2
Sainte-Marie, Fr. 197/N9
Sainte-Marie-aux-Chênes, Fr. 81/F5
Sainte-Martine, Qu, Can. 185/N7
Sainte-Maxime, Fr. 90/C6
Sainte-Menehould, Fr. 81/D5
Sainte-Mère-Église, Fr. 82/D2
Sainte-Mesme, Fr. 56/H6
Sainte-Reine-de-Bretagne, Fr. 82/C6
Sainte-Rose-de-Watford, Qu, Can. 184/B2
Sainte-Rose-du-Nord, Qu, Can. 184/B1
Sainte-Sigolène, Fr. 70/F4
Sainte-Suzanne, Fr. 83/E4
Sainte-Thècle, Qu, Can. 184/A2
Sainte-Thérèse, Qu, Can. 185/N6
Sainte-Tulle, Fr. 90/B5
Sainte-Véronique, Qu, Can. 187/J1
Saintes, Fr. 70/C4
Saintfield, NI, UK 60/C3
Sainthia, India 123/F4
Saipan (isl.), NMar. 162/D3
Saipina, Bol. 212/C1
Sairakkala, Fin. 65/F4
Saiss (Fez) (int'l arpt.), Mor. 138/B3
Saitama (pref.), Japan 111/F2
Saito, Japan 110/B4
Saiwa Swamp NP, Kenya 145/A1
Sajama, Bol. 208/D5
Sajama (peak), Bol. 212/B1
Sajama NP, Bol. 212/B1
Sajānan, Tun. 138/L6
Sajószentpéter, Hun. 69/L4
Sak (riv.), SAfr. 150/C3
Sakado, Japan 109/C2
Sakae, Japan 109/E2
Sakahogi, Japan 109/L5
Sakai, Japan 111/F2
Sakai, Japan 110/E2
Sakai (riv.), Japan 109/C3
Sakai, Japan 109/C1
Sakaide, Japan 110/C3
Sakaigawa, Japan 109/B2
Sakaiminato, Japan 110/C3
Sakākah, SAr. 128/E4
Sakakawea (lake), ND, US 182/C4
Sakami (lake), Qu, Can. 167/J3
Sakania, D.R. Congo 149/F2
Sakar (isl.), PNG 155/G1
Sakaraha, Madg. 152/H8
Sakarya (riv.), Turk. 96/D4
Sakarya (prov.), Turk. 96/D4
Sakata, Japan 108/A4
Sakauchi, Japan 109/K4
Sakawa, Japan 110/C4
Sakay (riv.), Madg. 152/H7
Sakçagöze, Turk. 128/D2
Sakchu, NKor. 107/C2
Sakden, Bhu. 119/F2
Sake, D.R. Congo 147/G3
Sakeny (riv.), Madg. 152/H7
Saketa, Indo. 117/G4
Sakété, Ben. 141/F5
Sakhā, Egypt 139/B2
Sakhalin (isl.), Rus. 103/P4
Sakhalin (gulf), Rus. 101/Q4
Sakhalin Oblast, Rus. 101/Q4
Sakhnīn, Isr. 131/C3
Sakhnovshchyna, Ukr. 99/H3
Sakht Sar, Iran 129/G2
Şäki, Azer. 97/H4
Šakiai, Lith. 67/K4
Sākib, Jor. 131/D4
Sakishima (isl.), Japan 103/M7
Sakmara (riv.), Rus. 97/L1
Sakon Nakhon, Thai. 120/D2
Sakrand, Pak. 127/J3
Sakrivier, SAfr. 150/C3
Saksaul'skiy, Kaz. 100/G5
Sakti, India 122/D4
Saku, Japan 111/F2
Saku, Japan 109/A1
Sakura, Japan 109/E2
Sakura, Japan 109/E1
Sakuragawa, Japan 109/E2
Sakurai, Japan 109/J6
Saky, Ukr. 99/G5
Sakya Monastery, China 123/G1
Säkylä, Fin. 67/K1
Sal (riv.), Rus. 97/G3
Sal (pt.), Hon. 200/E3
Sal (isl.), CpV. 133/K10
Sal Rei, CpV. 133/K10
Sala, Swe. 66/G2
Sala, It. 92/D6
Šal'a, Slvk. 76/C1
Sala Baganza, It. 88/D4
Sala Consilina, It. 74/D2
Sala Mok, Laos 120/C1
Sala Pac Thu, Laos 120/C2
Salabangka, Indo. 116/D4
Salacgrīva, Lat. 67/L3
Salada (lake), Mex. 198/B1
Salada, Laguna (dry lake), Mex. 174/E4
Saladas, Arg. 212/E4
Saladilio (riv.), Arg. 215/J11
Saladillo, Arg. 214/F2
Saladillo (riv.), Arg. 212/C4
Salado (riv.), Cuba 201/G1
Salado (riv.), Arg. 203/C6
Salado (riv.), NM, US 175/J3
Salado, Tx, US 176/F2
Salado del Norte (riv.), Arg. 203/C5
Salaga, Gha. 141/E4
Salagle, Som. 145/C1
Şalah Ad Din (gov.), Iraq 129/E3
Sala'ilua, WSam. 163/R9
Salaise-sur-Sanne, Fr. 90/A2
Sălaj (co.), Rom. 69/M5
Sălaj (prov.), Rom. 77/F2
Salal, Chad 142/C2
Salala, Libr. 140/C5
Şalālah, Sudan 135/H4
Şalālah, Oman 126/F5
Salamá, Guat. 200/D3
Salamajärven NP, Fin. 94/E3
Salamanca, NY, US 187/G3
Salamanca, Sp. 72/C2
Salamanca, Chile 212/B4
Salamanca, Mex. 199/E4
Salamat (pref.), Chad 142/D3
Salamina, Col. 204/C2
Salamina, Col. 207/K7
Salamís, Gre. 75/H3
Salamís (isl.), Gre. 75/N9
Salamīyah, Syria 130/E2
Salāmūn, Egypt 139/C2
Salangen, Nor. 64/F1
Salantai, Lith. 67/J3
Salar de Arizaro, Arg. 212/B3
Salar de Ascotan, Bol. 212/B2
Salar de Atacama, Chile 212/B2
Salar de Coipasa, Bol. 212/B1
Salar de la Isla, Chile 212/B3
Salar de Pedernales, Chile 212/B3
Salar de Pipanaco, Arg. 212/C4
Salar de Punta Negra, Chile 212/B3
Salar de Uyuni, Bol. 212/B2
Salas, Sp. 72/B1
Salas, Peru 208/B2
Salas de los Infantes, Sp. 72/D1
Salat (riv.), Fr. 73/F1
Salatiga, Indo. 115/E3
Salavat, Rus. 97/K1
Salaverry, Peru 208/B3
Salayar (isl.), Indo. 162/B5
Salbris, Fr. 83/H6
Salcantay (peak), Peru 208/C4
Salcedo, Phil. 114/D3
Šalčininkai, Lith. 67/L4
Salcombe, Eng, UK 62/C6
Saldaña, Sp. 72/C1
Saldanhabaai (bay), Safr. 150/K10
Saldus, Lat. 67/K3
Sale, Austl. 159/C4
Sale, Eng, UK 61/F5
Sale, It. 88/B4
Salé (prov.), Mor. 138/A3
Salé, Mor. 138/A2
Sale (Rabat) (int'l arpt.), Mor. 138/A2
Sale City, Ga, US 191/F2
Sale Marasino, It. 88/D2
Salebabu (isl.), Indo. 117/G3
Salebhatta, India 121/D1
Salekhard, Rus. 100/G3
Salem, Ger. 87/F2
Salem, India 121/C4
Salem, Namb. 148/B4
Salem, Swe. 65/A1
Salem, Ar, US 179/J2
Salem, Il, US 188/C1
Salem, In, US 188/D1
Salem, Ma, US 187/L3
Salem, Mi, US 193/E7
Salem, Mo, US 179/J2
Salem, NH, US 187/L3
Salem, NJ, US 194/C4
Salem (co.), NJ, US 194/C4
Salem (cr.), NJ, US 194/C4
Salem, NM, US 175/J4
Salem, Oh, US 186/F4
Salem (cap.), Or, US 172/B1
Salem, SD, US 180/F2
Salem, WV, US 186/F5
Salem, Va, US 189/G2
Salemi, It. 74/C4
Salentina (pen.), It. 93/H3
Salernes, Fr. 90/C5
Salerno (prov.), It. 92/D6
Salerno, It. 92/D6
Salerno (gulf), It. 93/G2
Sales (pt.), Eng, UK 63/G3
Saleux, Fr. 80/B4
Salfīt, WBnk. 131/C4
Salford, Eng, UK 61/F5
Salgado Filho (int'l arpt.), Braz. 213/G4
Salgan, Rus. 95/K5
Salgar, Col. 204/C3
Salgesch, Swi. 86/D5
Salgótarján, Hun. 69/K4
Salgueiro, Braz. 207/G5
Salhus, Nor. 66/A1
Sali, Cro. 76/B4
Salida, Co, US 175/K1
Salies-de-Béarn, Fr. 70/C5
Salies-du-Salat, Fr. 70/D5
Şalīf, Yem. 144/B2
Salihli, Turk. 128/B2
Salima, Malw. 149/G2
Salīmah (oasis), Sudan 135/F4
Salims, Tanz. 145/B4
Salin, Myan. 112/B4
Salina (isl.), It. 93/G3
Salina (pt.), Bahm. 201/H1
Salina, Ks, US 179/F1
Salina, Ut, US 175/G1
Salina Cruz, Mex. 200/C2
Salina de Rincón, Chile 212/C2
Salinas, Ecu. 204/A5
Salinas (cape), Sp. 73/G3
Salinas, Ca, US 174/B2
Salinas (riv.), Ca, US 174/B2
Salinas de Ambargasta, Arg. 212/C4
Salinas de Garci Mendoza, Bol. 212/C1
Salinas de Hidalgo, Mex. 199/E4
Salinas Grande, Arg. 212/C2
Salinas Pueblo Missions Nat'l Mon., NM, US 175/J3
Salinas Victoria, Mex. 177/D5
Salinas Y Aguada Blanca, Res. Nacional, Peru 208/D4
Saline, La, US 179/H4
Saline, Sc, UK 59/C4
Saline (lake), La, US 190/B2
Saline, Mi, US 186/E3
Saline, It. 89/D7
Saline (riv.), Ks, US 181/"E4,
Saline Bayou (riv.), La, US 177/H1
Salinello (riv.), It. 92/C2
Salineno, Tx, US 177/E4
Salinópolis, Braz. 207/E3
Salins-les-Bains, Fr. 86/B4
Salins-les-Thermes, Fr. 90/C2
Salisbury (nbrhd.), Austl. 157/M8
Salisbury, NB, Can. 184/E2
Salisbury (isl.), Nun, Can. 167/J2
Salisbury, Eng, UK 63/E4
Salisbury (plain), Eng, UK 62/D4
Salisbury, Ct, US 187/K4
Salisbury, Md, US 189/K1
Salisbury, Mo, US 181/H4
Salisbury, NC, US 189/G3
Salisbury, NY, US 187/J3
Salisbury, NY, US 195/L9
Salisbury Downs, Austl. 158/B1
Salish (mts.), Mt, US 170/G3
Salitpa, Al, US 190/D2
Salitre, Ecu. 204/B5
Salitre (riv.), Braz. 211/E1
Salka, Slvk. 76/D2
Salkehatchie (riv.), SC, US 189/G4
Salla, Fin. 94/F2
Salladasburg, Pa, US 194/A1
Sallanches, Fr. 86/C6
Salland (phys. reg.), Neth. 78/D4
Sallatouk (pt.), Gui. 140/B4
Sallaumines, Fr. 80/B3
Sallent, Sp. 73/F2
Salles, Belg. 81/D3
Sallins, Ire. 58/D3
Salliqueló, Arg. 214/E3
Sallisaw, Ok, US 179/G3
Sallūm, Sudan 135/H5
Sally (pass), Ire. 60/B5
Salm (riv.), Ger. 81/F3
Salmān Pāk, Iraq 129/F3
Salmās, Iran 129/F2
Salme, Est. 67/K2
Salmo (riv.), BC, Can. 170/F3
Salmon (mts.), Ca, US 172/B3
Salmon (dam), Id, US 173/F2
Salmon, Id, US 173/G1
Salmon (riv.), Id, US 168/C2
Salmon (peak), Tx, US 177/D3
Salmon Arm, BC, Can. 170/E2
Salmon Cove, Nf, Can. 185/L2
Salmon Creek (res.), Id, US 173/F2
Salmon Creek, Wa, US 170/C5
Salmon Falls (cr.), Id, US 173/F2
Salmon Gums, Austl. 156/D5
Salmon River, NS, Can. 184/D3
Salmon River (mts.), Id, US 168/C2
Salmon Ruin, NM, US 175/H2
Salmon, Middle Fork (riv.), Id, US 173/F1
Salmon, South Fork (riv.), Id, US 172/F1
Salmtal, Ger. 81/F4
Salo, Fin. 67/K1
Salò, It. 88/D2
Salo, CAfr. 146/D2
Salole, Eth. 144/A4
Salome, Az, US 175/F4
Salon (riv.), Fr. 68/C5
Salon, India 122/C2
Salon-de-Provence, Fr. 90/B5
Salonga (riv.), D.R. Congo 147/E3
Salonga, PN de la, D.R. Congo 147/E3
Salonta, Rom. 76/E2
Salorno (Salurn), It. 87/H5
Salouël, Fr. 80/B4
Salpausselkä (mts.), Fin. 67/M1
Salpo, Peru 208/B3
Salses-le-Château, Fr. 70/E5
Sal'sk, Rus. 99/L4
Salso (riv.), It. 74/C4
Salsomaggiore Terme, It. 88/C4
Salt (range), Pak. 124/B3
Salt (riv.), SAfr. 150/C4
Salt, Sp. 73/G2
Salt (cr.), Mo, US 179/J1
Salt (lakes), Tx, US 177/B2
Salt (basin), Tx, US 178/B5
Salt (cr.), Il, US 181/K4
Salt Cay (isl.), UK 201/J1
Salt Draw (riv.), Tx, US 198/D2
Salt Fork (riv.), Ks,Ok, US 178/E2
Salt Lake City (cap.), Ut, US 173/H3
Salt Lake City (int'l arpt.), Ut, US 173/H3
Salt Meadow Nat'l Wild. Ref., Ct, US 195/F1
Salt Plains Nat'l Wildlife Res., Ok, US 179/E2
Salt, Middle Fork (riv.), Mo, US 181/H4
Salt, North (riv.), Mo, US 181/H4
Salta (int'l arpt.), Arg. 212/C3
Salta (prov.), Arg. 212/C3
Salta, Arg. 212/C3
Saltair, BC, Can. 170/C3
Saltaire, NY, US 195/E2
Saltash, Eng, UK 62/B6
Saltburn, Eng, UK 61/H2
Saltcoats, Sk, Can. 182/C2
Saltcoats, Sc, UK 59/B5
Saltdal, Nor. 64/E2
Saltee (isls.), Ire. 58/D5
Saltfjorden (inlet), Nor. 64/E2
Saltford, Eng, UK 62/D4
Saltholm (isl.), Den. 65/J7
Saltillo, Ms, US 188/C3
Saltillo, Tn, US 188/C3
Saltillo, Mex. 199/E3
Salto, Arg. 214/E2
Salto, Braz. 213/H2
Salto (lake), It. 92/C3
Salto (riv.), It. 92/B3
Salto (dept.), Uru. 213/E4
Salto, Uru. 212/E4
Salto da Divisa, Braz. 211/F3
Salto del Guairá, Par. 213/F3
Salto Grande (res.), Arg. 212/E4
Salto Santiago (res.), Braz. 213/F3
Salton Sea (lake), Ca, US 168/C5
Salton Sea Nat'l Wild. Ref., Ca, US 174/E4
Saltpond, Gha. 141/E5
Saltsjöbaden, Swe. 65/B1
Saltvik, Fin. 67/J1
Saltville, Va, US 189/G2
Saltykovka, Rus. 97/H1
Saluda (riv.), SC, US 189/G3
Saluda, SC, US 189/G3
Saluda, Va, US 189/J2
Salug, Phil. 114/C3
Saluggia, It. 88/B3
Salunga-Landisville, Pa, US 194/B3
Sālūr, India 121/D2
Salurn (Salorno), It. 87/H5
Salut (isls.), FrG. 206/C1
Saluta, Indo. 117/G3
Saluzzo, It. 90/D3
Salvación (bay), Chile 215/B6
Salvador (lake), La, US 190/C3
Salvador, Braz. 211/F2
Salvador, Sk, Can. 171/K1
Salvador Dali Museum, Fl, US 190/K8
Salvaleón de Higüey, DRep. 197/H4
Salvaterra, Braz. 206/D3
Salvaterra de Magos, Port. 72/A3
Salvatierra, Mex. 199/E4
Salvatierra de Miño, Sp. 72/A1
Salvisa, Ky, US 188/E2
Salween (riv.), Asia 103/J8
Salween (riv.), Myan.,Thai. 120/B2
Salween (Nu) (riv.), China 104/D5
Salyan, Azer. 129/G2
Salyān, Nepal 122/D1
Salyersville, Ky, US 189/F2
Salza (riv.), Aus. 69/H5
Salzach (riv.), Ger. 68/G5
Salzano, It. 89/F2
Salzbergen, Ger. 79/E4
Salzburg (prov.), Aus. 69/G5
Salzgitter, Ger. 79/H4
Salzhausen, Ger. 79/H2
Salzhemmendorf, Ger. 79/G4
Salzkotten, Ger. 79/F5
Salzwedel, Ger. 68/F2
Sam, Gabon 146/B2
Sam Houston Memorial Museum, Tx, US 177/G2
Sam Khok, Thai. 120/C3
Sam Ngao, Thai. 120/B2
Sam Rayburn (res.), Tx, US 177/G2
Sam Rayburn (dam), Tx, US 177/G2

293
Sam – Sand

Sam Rayburn (res.), Tx, US 196/C1
Sam Sao (mts.), Laos,Viet. 120/C1
Sam Son, Viet. 120/D2
Sama, Sp. 72/C1
Samādūn, Egypt 139/B4
Samagaltay, Rus. 125/G1
Samaipata, Bol. 212/D1
Samak (cape), Indo. 115/D3
Samalayuca, Mex. 177/A2
Samales Group (isls.), Phil. 114/C4
Samālkha, India 124/D5
Samālūt, Egypt 135/F2
Samāna, India 124/D4
Samaná (cape), DRep. 197/H4
Samana (isl.), Bahm. 201/H1
Samaná, Col. 207/K7
Samanco, Peru 208/B3
Samandağı, Turk. 130/D1
Samandira, Turk. 129/N7
Samani, Japan 108/C2
Samaniego, Col. 204/B4
Samannūd, Egypt 139/C3
Samar (isl.), Phil. 103/M8
Samar (sea), Phil. 114/D3
Samar, Jor. 131/D3
Samara (int'l arpt.), Rus. 97/J1
Samara, Rus. 97/J1
Samara (riv.), Rus. 97/K1
Samara Oblast, Rus. 97/J1
Samarai, PNG 162/E6
Samarate, It. 88/B2
Samarga (riv.), Rus. 105/M2
Samaria (reg.), Isr. 131/C4
Samariapo, Ven. 204/E3
Samarinda, Indo. 117/E4
Samarqand, Uzb. 100/G6
Sāmarrā', Iraq 129/E3
Samarskoye, Rus. 97/L1
Samarskoye, Rus. 99/K4
Samasata, Pak. 124/A5
Samāstipur, India 123/E3
Samate, Indo. 117/H4
Samatigila, C.d'Iv. 140/D4
Şamaxi, Azer. 97/J4
Sāmba, India 124/C3
Samba, D.R. Congo 147/E2
Samba, D.R. Congo 147/F4
Samba Lucala, Ang. 146/C5
Sambaíba, Braz. 207/E4
Sambaïlo, Gui. 140/B3
Sambao (riv.), Madg. 152/H7
Sambar (cape), Indo. 116/D4
Sambas, Indo. 116/C3
Sambava, Madg. 152/J6
Samberbaba, Indo. 117/J4
Sambhal, India 122/B1
Sambili, D.R. Congo 142/D4
Sambir, Ukr. 69/M4
Sambo, Ang. 148/C2
Sambo, Indo. 117/E4
Sambong-ni, NKor. 107/E2
Sambor Prei Kuk (ruin), Camb. 120/D3
Samborobón (riv.), Arg. 215/K11
Samborombón (bay), Arg. 215/F2
Sambre (riv.), Fr. 68/C3
Sambre à l'Oise, Canal de (canal), Fr. 80/C4
Sambriāl, Pak. 124/C3
Sambro, NS, Can. 184/F3
Sambu, Japan 109/E2
Sambuceto, It. 92/D3
Samburu, Kenya 145/B2
Samburu Nat'l Rsv., Kenya 145/B1
Samchi, Bhu. 123/G2
Samch'ŏk, SKor. 110/A2
Samch'ŏnp'o, SKor. 107/E5
Samdrup Jongkhar, Bhu. 123/H2
Same, Tanz. 145/B3
Same, Indo. 154/B2
Samedan, Swi. 87/F4
Samer, Fr. 80/A2
Samfya Mission, Zam. 149/F1
Sámi, Gre. 75/G3
Sami, Myan. 112/B4
Saminskiy Pogost, Rus. 94/H3
Samiria (riv.), Peru 208/C2
Samit (cape), Camb. 120/C4
Samjiyŏn, NKor. 107/E2
Samka, Myan. 120/B1
Şämkir, Azer. 97/H4
Samkos (peak), Camb. 120/C3
Sammamish (lake), Wa, US 193/C2
Sammatti, Fin. 65/D4
Sammeron, Fr. 56/M5
Samnangjin, SKor. 110/A3
Samnaun, Swi. 87/G4
Samnorwood, Tx, US 178/D3
Samnū, Libya 134/B3
Samo Alto, Chile 212/B4
Samobor, Cro. 76/B3
Samoëns, Fr. 86/C5
Samoggia (riv.), It. 89/E4
Samokov, Bul. 77/F4
Samora (riv.), Port. 73/Q10
Samora Correia, Port. 73/Q10
Sámos, Gre. 128/A2
Sámos (isl.), Gre. 128/A2
Samothráki, Gre. 75/J2
Samouay, Laos 120/D2
Samoylovka, Rus. 97/G2
Sampacho, Arg. 214/D2
Sampang, Indo. 115/F3
Samper de Calanda, Sp. 73/E2
Sampeyre, It. 90/D3
Sampit (riv.), Indo. 116/D4
Sampit, Indo. 116/D4
Sampwe, D.R. Congo 147/F5
Samrāla, India 124/D4
Samrē, Eth. 144/A2
Samrong Thap, Thai. 120/C3
Sams, Co, US 175/J1
Samsang, China 125/D5
Samsø (isl.), Den. 66/D4
Samsø Bælt (chan.), Den. 66/D4
Samson, Al, US 191/E2
Samson (mt.), Austl. 160/E6
Samson Ind. Res., Ab, Can. 171/H1
Samsonvale (lake), Austl. 160/E6
Samsu, NKor. 107/E2
Samsun, Turk. 96/F4
Samsun (prov.), Turk. 96/E4
Samthar, India 122/B3
Samuel (mt.), Austl. 154/D4
Samuels, Id, US 170/F3
Samugheo, It. 74/A3
Samui (isl.), Thai. 119/H6
Samukawa, Japan 109/C3
Samundri, Pak. 124/B4
Samur (riv.), Azer.,Rus. 100/E5
Samur (riv.), Rus. 97/H4
Samut Prakan, Thai. 120/C3
Samut Sakhon, Thai. 120/C3
Samut Songkhram, Thai. 120/B3
Samye Monastery, China 123/H1
San (riv.), Pol. 96/B2
San, Mali 140/D3
San (riv.), Camb. 120/D3
San (riv.), China 105/H5
San Acacia, NM, US 175/J3
San Adrián, Cabo de (cape), Sp. 72/A1
San Agustín, Col. 204/B4
San Agustin (cape), Phil. 114/D4
San Agustín, Bol. 212/C2
San Agustín, Bol. 209/F5
San Agustin de Guadalix, Sp. 73/N8
San Agustín, Parque Arqeológico, Col. 204/B4
San Agustin, Plains of (plains), NM, US 175/H4
Şān al Ḩajar al Qiblīyah, Egypt 139/C3
San Ambrosio (isl.), Chile 203/B5
San Andreas (lake), Ca, US 193/J11
San Andreas, Ca, US 172/C4
San Andrés, Bol. 209/E4
San Andrés, Col. 201/F3
San Andrés, Col. 204/C3
San Andrés, Col. 204/C3
San Andrés (lake), Mex. 200/B1
San Andres, Phil. 114/D2
San Andres (mts.), NM, US 175/J4
San Andrés Cuexcontitlán, Mex. 199/Q10
San Andrés de Giles, Arg. 215/J11
San Andrés de Machaca, Bol. 208/D5
San Andrés del Rabanedo, Sp. 72/C1
San Andres Nat'l Wild Ref., NM, US 175/J4
San Andrés Tuxtla, Mex. 200/C2
San Andrés, Isla de (isl.), Col. 196/E5
San Angelo, Tx, US 177/D2
San Anselmo, Ca, US 193/J11
San Antonio (cape), Arg. 215/F3
San Antonio, Arg. 214/D2
San Antonio, Bol. 209/E4
San Antonio, Chile 214/N8
San Antonio, Ecu. 204/B4
San Antonio, Mex. 198/C4
San Antonio, Peru 208/B4
San Antonio, Phil. 114/C2
San Antonio, Uru. 215/K11
San Antonio, Ven. 205/E2
San Antonio, Ven. 205/F2
San Antonio (bay), Tx, US 177/F3
San Antonio (riv.), Tx, US 196/B2
San Antonio (mt.), Ca, US 192/C2
San Antonio, Fl, US 190/L7
San Antonio (mtn.), NM, US 175/J2
San Antonio (res.), Ca, US 174/B3
San Antonio, NM, US 175/J4
San Antonio (int'l arpt.), Tx, US 177/E3
San Antonio, Tx, US 176/E3
San Antonio Abad, Sp. 73/F3
San Antonio de Areco, Arg. 215/J11
San Antonio de Caparo, Ven. 204/D3
San Antonio de Lípez, Bol. 212/C2
San Antonio de los Cobres, Arg. 212/C3
San Antonio de Tabasca, Ven. 205/F2
San Antonio de Tamanaco, Ven. 207/P8
San Antonio del Golfo, Ven. 205/F2
San Antonio del Táchira, Ven. 204/C3
San Antonio Oeste, Arg. 214/D4
San Antonio, Punta (pt.), Mex. 198/B2
San Ardo, Ca, US 174/B2
San Augustin (pass), NM, US 175/J4
San Augustine, Tx, US 177/G2
San Bartolo, Peru 208/B4
San Bartolomé de Tirajana, Sp. 136/B4
San Bartolome Tlaltelulco, Mex. 199/Q10
San Bartolomeo in Bosco, It. 89/E4
San Bartolomeo in Galdo, It. 92/E5
San Bautista, Uru. 215/L11
San Benedetto (range), It. 89/E5
San Benedetto dei Marsi, It. 92/C4
San Benedetto del Tronto, It. 92/C2
San Benedetto in Alpe, It. 89/E6
San Benedetto Po, It. 89/D3
San Benedicto (isl.), Mex. 198/C5
San Benito (mtn.), Ca, US 174/B2
San Benito (riv.), Ca, US 174/B2
San Benito, Tx, US 176/F4
San Bernard (riv.), Tx, US 177/F3
San Bernard NWR, Tx, US 177/G3
San Bernardino, Swi. 87/F5
San Bernardino (mts.), Ca, US 192/C2
San Bernardino (co.), Ca, US 192/C2
San Bernardino, Ca, US 192/C2
San Bernardino (str.), Phil. 114/D2
San Bernardino Nat'l Forest, Ca, US 192/C2
San Bernardino Nat'l Wild. Ref., Az, US 175/H5
San Bernardo, Arg. 212/D3
San Bernardo (pt.), Col. 204/C2
San Bernardo, Chile 214/N8
San Bernardo, Col. 207/L8
San Blas, Mex. 177/D4
San Blas (cape), Fl, US 191/F3
San Blas, Mex. 198/C3
San Blas, Mex. 198/D4
San Bonifacio, It. 89/E3
San Borja, Bol. 209/E4
San Bruno, Ca, US 193/K11
San Bruno, Mex. 198/B3
San Buenaventura, Mex. 177/D4
San Buenaventura (Ventura), Ca, US 192/A2
San Candido (Innichen), It. 71/K3
San Carlos, Arg. 212/C3
San Carlos, Bol. 212/D1
San Carlos, Chile 214/C3
San Carlos, Col. 207/L6
San Carlos, Mex. 199/F3
San Carlos, Mex. 177/D3
San Carlos, Nic. 201/E4
San Carlos, Pan. 204/B2
San Carlos, Par. 213/E2
San Carlos, Phil. 114/C2
San Carlos, Ven. 204/D2
San Carlos, Uru. 215/G2
San Carlos, Az, US 175/G4
San Carlos, Ca, US 193/K11
San Carlos (lake), Az, US 175/G4
San Carlos de Bariloche, Arg. 214/C4
San Carlos de Bariloche (int'l arpt.), Arg. 214/C4
San Carlos de Río Negro, Ven. 205/E4
San Carlos del Zulia, Ven. 204/D2
San Carlos Ind. Res., Az, US 175/G4
San Casciano in Val di Pesa, It. 89/E6
San Casimiro, Ven. 207/N7
San Cataldo, It. 75/F2
San Cayetano, Arg. 214/F3
San Cayetano, Col. 207/L7
San Cesario sul Panaro, It. 89/E4
San Cipriano d'Aversa, It. 92/D6
San Ciro de Acosta, Mex. 199/F4
San Clemente, Ca, US 192/C4
San Clemente, Sp. 72/D3
San Clemente, Chile 214/C2
San Clemente (isl.), Ca, US 174/C4
San Clemente del Tuyú, Arg. 215/F3
San Clemente in Casauria, It. 92/C3
San Colombano al Lambro, It. 88/C3
San Cristóbal, Arg. 212/D4
San Cristóbal, Bol. 212/C2
San Cristóbal, Bol. 209/F4
San Cristóbal, Cuba 201/F1
San Cristóbal (vol.), Nic. 200/E3
San Cristóbal, Ven. 204/C3
San Cristobal (isl.), Sol. 162/F6
San Cristóbal (isl.), Ecu. 208/K7
San Cristobal, NM, US 178/B2
San Cristóbal de las Casas, Mex. 200/C2
San Cristobal Wash (riv.), Az, US 198/B1
San Damiano d'Asti, It. 88/B4
San Damiano Macra, It. 90/D4
San Demetrio ne'Vestini, It. 92/C3
San Diego (cape), Arg. 215/D7
San Diego, Bol. 209/F5
San Diego, Bol. 212/C2
San Diego (co.), Ca, US 192/C4
San Diego (bay), Ca, US 192/C5
San Diego (aqueduct), Ca, US 192/C4
San Diego, Ca, US 192/C5
San Diego (riv.), Ca, US 174/D4
San Diego, Tx, US 177/E4
San Diego International-Lindbergh Field (int'l arpt.), Ca, US 192/C5
San Diego Naval Station Nav. Sta., Ca, US 192/C5
San Diego Wild Animal Park, Ca, US 192/C4
San Diego Zoo, Ca, US 192/C5
San Diequito (riv.), Ca, US 192/C5
San Dimas, Ca, US 192/C2
San Donà di Piave, It. 89/F2
San Donato Val di Comino, It. 92/C4
San Donnino, It. 89/E6
San Dorligo della Valle, It. 89/G2
San Elizario, Tx, US 177/A2
San Estanislao, Par. 213/E3
San Esteban de Gormaz, Sp. 72/D2
San Fabián de Alico, Chile 214/C3
San Felice a Cancello, It. 92/D6
San Felice Circeo, It. 92/C5
San Felice del Benaco, It. 88/D2
San Felice sul Panaro, It. 89/E4
San Felipe, Ven. 204/C2
San Felipe, Ven. 204/D2
San Felipe (cr.), Ca, US 174/D4
San Felipe, Chile 214/N8
San Felipe, Mex. 198/B2
San Felipe de Puerto Plata, DRep. 197/G4
San Felipe de Vichayal, Peru 208/A2
San Felipe Ind. Res., NM, US 175/J3
San Felipe Jalapa de Díaz, Mex. 199/F5
San Felipe Pueblo, NM, US 175/J3
San Felipe Torres Mochas, Mex. 199/E4
San Felix (isl.), Chile 203/A5
San Fernando, Arg. 215/J11
San Fernando, Arg. 212/C3
San Fernando, Chile 214/C2
San Fernando, Phil. 114/C2
San Fernando, Phil. 114/C1
San Fernando, Phil. 114/C2
San Fernando, Sp. 72/B4
San Fernando, Trin. 205/F2
San Fernando (valley), Ca, US 192/B2
San Fernando, Ca, US 192/F7
San Fernando de Apure, Ven. 205/E3
San Fernando de Atabapo, Ven. 204/E3
San Fernando de Henares, Sp. 73/N9
San Fernando de Presas, Mex. 199/F3
San Fidel, NM, US 175/J3
San Fior di Sopra, It. 89/F2
San Francesco al Campo, It. 88/A2
San Francisco (cr.), Tx, US 177/C3
San Francisco (co.), Ca, US 193/K11
San Francisco, Ven. 204/D2
San Francisco, ESal. 200/D3
San Francisco, Col. 204/B4
San Francisco (mts.), Az, US 175/G3
San Francisco (bay), Ca, US 174/A2
San Francisco (riv.), Az, US 175/H4
San Francisco (riv.), Arg. 212/C2
San Francisco, Arg. 212/D4
San Francisco, Bol. 209/E4
San Francisco, Bol. 212/E1
San Francisco, Col. 207/L8
San Francisco, Phil. 114/C2
San Francisco, Phil. 114/D3
San Francisco Acuautla, Mex. 199/R10
San Francisco Bay NWR, Ca, US 193/K11
San Francisco Chimalpa, Mex. 199/Q10
San Francisco de la Paz, Hon. 200/E3
San Francisco de Macorís, DRep. 197/G4
San Francisco de Mostazal, Chile 214/N8
San Francisco de Tiznados, Ven. 207/N8
San Francisco del Chañar, Arg. 212/D4
San Francisco del Mezquital, Mex. 198/D4
San Francisco del Monte de Oro, Arg. 214/D2
San Francisco del Oro, Mex. 198/D3
San Francisco del Rincón, Mex. 199/E4
San Francisco Telixtlahuaca, Mex. 196/B4
San Francisco, Cabo de (cape), Ecu. 204/A4
San Francisco, Paso de (pass), Arg.,Chile 212/B3
San Fratello, It. 74/D3
San Gabriel (riv.), Ca, US 192/C2
San Gabriel (res.), Ca, US 192/C2
San Gabriel, Ca, US 192/F7
San Gabriel, Ecu. 204/B4
San Gabriel (mts.), Ca, US 174/C3
San Gabriel, Chile 214/N8
San Gabriel, (pt.), Mex. 198/B2
San Gavino Monreale, It. 74/A3
San Gemini, It. 91/B2
San Genaro, Arg. 212/D5
San Germán, Cuba 201/G1
San Germano Vercellese, It. 88/B3
San Giacomo (Sankt Jakob), It. 87/H4
San Gil, Col. 204/C3
San Gimignano, It. 89/E7
San Ginesio, It. 92/C1
San Giorgio a Cremano, It. 92/D6
San Giorgio del Sannio, It. 92/D5
San Giorgio delle Pertiche, It. 89/E2
San Giorgio di Piano, It. 89/E4
San Giorgio Ionico, It. 75/E2
San Giorgio Piacentino, It. 88/C4
San Giovanni al Natisone, It. 89/G2
San Giovanni Bianco, It. 88/C2
San Giovanni Gemini, It. 74/C4
San Giovanni in Croce, It. 88/D3
San Giovanni in Fiore, It. 74/E3
San Giovanni in Marignano, It. 89/F6
San Giovanni in Persiceto, It. 89/E4
San Giovanni in Venere, It. 92/D3
San Giovanni Lupatoto, It. 89/E3
San Giovanni Rotondo, It. 74/D2
San Giovanni Valdarno, It. 89/E6
San Giuliano, It. 88/B4
San Giuliano Terme, It. 88/D6
San Giuseppe Vesuviano, It. 92/D6
San Giustino, It. 89/F6
San Giusto Canavese, It. 88/A2
San Gorgonio (mtn.), Ca, US 174/D3
San Gottardo, Passo del (pass), Swi. 87/E4
San Gregorio, Ca, US 193/K12
San Gregorio, Arg. 214/E2
San Gregorio, Uru. 215/L10
San Gregorio, Uru. 215/K10
San Guiliano Milanese, It. 88/C3
San Guillermo, Arg. 212/D4
San Hipólito Punta (pt.), Mex. 198/B3
San Ignacio, Belz. 200/D2
San Ignacio, Bol. 209/E4
San Ignacio, Bol. 209/F5
San Ignacio, Bol. 212/D1
San Ignacio, Chile 214/B3
San Ignacio, Par. 213/E3
San Ignacio, Peru 208/B2
San Ignacio (riv.), Mex. 198/B2
San Ignacio, Mex. 198/D4
San Ignacio, Mex. 198/B3
San Ildefonso, Sp. 72/D2
San Ildefonso (cape), Phil. 114/C1
San Isidro, Nic. 200/E3
San Isidro, CR 201/F4
San Isidro de Curuguaty, Par. 213/F3
San Jacinto, Col. 204/C2
San Jacinto, Nv, US 173/F3
San Jacinto, Ca, US 174/D4
San Jacinto, Phil. 114/C2
San Jacinto, Uru. 215/L11
San Jacinto (dam), Tx, US 177/M9
San Jacinto Battleground, Tx, US 177/M9
San Jaime, Arg. 212/E4
San Javier, Arg. 214/E4
San Javier, Arg. 212/E4
San Javier, Bol. 209/F5
San Javier, Bol. 209/E4
San Javier, Chile 214/C2
San Javier, Sp. 73/E4
San Javier, Uru. 215/J10
San Jerónimo, Col. 207/K6
San Jerónimo, Mex. 198/E3
San Joaquin (co.), Ca, US 193/L11
San Joaquin (hills), Ca, US 192/G8
San Joaquín, Col. 204/C3
San Joaquin, Ca, US 174/B2
San Joaquin (riv.), Ca, US 174/B2
San Joaquin (valley), Ca, US 174/B2
San Joaquín (peak), Ecu. 208/K7
San Joaquín (riv.), Bol. 209/F4
San Joaquín, Par. 213/E3
San Joaquín, Bol. 209/E4
San Joaquín, Ven. 207/N7
San Joaquin, South Fork (riv.), Ca, US 174/C2
San Jorge (gulf), Sp. 92/D2
San Jorge (riv.), Col. 201/H5
San Jorge (gulf), Arg. 203/C7
San Jorge (cape), Arg. 214/D5
San Jorge, Arg. 212/D4
San Jorge (bay), Mex. 198/B2
San José, Arg. 212/C4
San José (gulf), Arg. 214/D4
San José (cap.), CR 201/E4
San José, Col. 204/B4
San José (isl.), Mex. 198/C3
San José, Peru 208/B2
San José, Peru 208/D4
San José, Sp. 73/F3
San José (dept.), Uru. 215/K11
San José, Ven. 204/E3
San Jose, Phil. 114/C2
San Jose, Phil. 114/C3
San Jose (riv.), Uru. 215/K10
San Jose (hills), Ca, US 192/G7
San Jose, Il, US 181/K3
San Jose (riv.), NM, US 175/J3
San Jose (isl.), Tx, US 177/F4
San José de Amacuro, Ven. 205/F2
San José de Aura, Mex. 177/D4
San José de Chiquitos, Bol. 212/D1
San José de Feliciano, Arg. 212/E4
San José de Guanipa, Ven. 205/E2
San José de Guaribe, Ven. 205/E2
San José de Jáchal, Arg. 212/B4
San Jose de la Banda (int'l arpt.), Bol. 212/C1
San José de la Esquina, Arg. 214/E2
San Jose de Los Molinos, Peru 208/C4
San José de los Remates, Nic. 200/E3
San José de Maipo, Chile 214/N8
San José de Mayo, Uru. 215/K11
San José de Raíces, Mex. 199/E3
San José de Río Chico, Ven. 207/P7
San José de Seque, Ven. 204/D2
San José de Tiznados, Ven. 207/N8
San José del Cabo, Mex. 198/C4
San José del Guaviare, Col. 204/C4
San Jose del Monte, Phil. 114/F6
San José del Ocuné, Col. 204/D3
San José Iturbide, Mex. 199/E4
San José Viejo, Mex. 198/C4
San Juan (cape), Arg. 215/E7
San Juan (prov.), Arg. 212/B4
San Juan, Arg. 212/B4
San Juan (riv.), Bol. 212/C1
San Juan, Bol. 212/E1
San Juan (riv.), Col. 204/B3
San Juan (cape), EqG. 146/B2
San Juan (pt.), ESal. 200/D3
San Juan (riv.), Nic. 196/E5
San Juan, Peru 208/C4
San Juan, Peru 208/C4
San Juan, Phil. 114/C2
San Juan, Phil. 114/D3
San Juan, PR 197/M8
San Juan (cr.), Ca, US 192/C4
San Juan (mts.), Co, US 168/E4
San Juan (basin), NM, US 175/H2
San Juan, NM, US 175/J4
San Juan (isl.), Wa, US 170/C3
San Juan Abajo, Mex. 198/D4
San Juan Bautista, Ca, US 174/B2
San Juan Bautista, Par. 213/E3
San Juan Bautista Coixtlahuaca, Mex. 200/B2
San Juan Bautista de Ñeembucú, Par. 212/E3
San Juan Bautista Tuxtepec, Mex. 200/B2
San Juan Bautista Valle Nacional, Mex. 200/B2
San Juan Capistrano, Ca, US 192/C3
San Juan de Alicante, Sp. 73/E3
San Juan de Aznalfarache, Sp. 72/B4
San Juan de la Costa, Mex. 198/C3
San Juan de Lima, (pt.), Mex. 198/E5
San Juan de los Cayos, Ven. 204/D2
San Juan de los Lagos, Mex. 198/E4
San Juan de los Morros, Ven. 207/N8
San Juan de Manapiare, Ven. 205/E3
San Juan de Ríoseco, Col 207/L8
San Juan del Norte, Nic. 201/F4
San Juan del Piray, Bol 212/C2
San Juan del Potrero, Bol 212/C1
San Juan del Río, Mex. 199/F4
San Juan Guichicovi, Mex. 196/B4
San Juan Hot Springs, Ca, US 192/C3
San Juan Ixcaquixtla, Mex. 199/M8
San Juan Juquila Mixes, Mex. 200/C2
San Juan Nat'l Wild. Ref., Wa. US 170/C3
San Juan Nepomuceno, Col 204/C2
San Juan Nepomuceno, Par 213/F3
San Juan Pueblo, NM, US 175/J2
San Juanico, Mex. 198/B3
San Juanico Punta (pt.), Mex. 198/B3
San Juanito, Mex. 198/D2
San Justo, Arg. 212/D4
San Lázaro, Par. 212/E2
San Lázaro (cape), Mex. 198/B3
San Lazzaro, It. 89/E5
San Leandro (res.), Ca, US 193/K11
San Leandro, Ca, US 193/K11
San Leon, Tx, US 177/N9
San Leonardo in Passiria (Sankt Leonhard in Passeier), It. 87/H4
San Lorenzo, Bol. 209/E4
San Lorenzo, Bol. 209/E3
San Lorenzo, Bol. 212/C2
San Lorenzo (peak), Chile 215/B5
San Lorenzo (cape), It. 74/A3
San Lorenzo, Hon. 200/E3
San Lorenzo, Ecu. 204/B4
San Lorenzo, Nic. 200/E3
San Lorenzo, Peru 208/D3
San Lorenzo (riv.), Mex. 198/D3
San Lorenzo, Ca, US 193/K11
San Lorenzo, NM, US 175/J4
San Lorenzo al Mare, It. 88/A5
San Lorenzo de El Escorial, Sp. 73/M8
San Lorenzo in Campo, It. 89/F6
San Lucas, Nic. 200/E3
San Lucas, Bol. 212/C2
San Lucas, Cabo (cape), Mex. 198/C4
San Luis, Arg. 214/D2
San Luis (prov.), Arg. 212/C5
San Lucas, Ca, US 174/B2
San Luis (lake), Bol. 209/E4
San Luis, Bol. 212/E1
San Luis, Col. 207/K8
San Luís, Col. 207/L6
San Luis, Cuba 201/H1
San Luis, Guat. 200/D2
San Luis, Peru 208/B4
San Luis, Ven. 204/D2
San Luis, Az, US 174/E4
San Luis (dam), Ca, US 174/B2
San Luis (res.), Ca, US 174/B2
San Luis (cr.), Co, US 175/K1
San Luis, Co, US 178/B2
San Luis (valley), Co, US 175/J2
San Luis Acatlán, Mex. 200/B2
San Luis al Medio, Uru. 215/G2
San Luis Archaeological Site, Fl, US 191/F2
San Luis de la Paz, Mex. 199/E4
San Luis NWR, Ca, US 174/B2
San Luis Obispo, Ca, US 174/B3
San Luis Potosí (state), Mex. 196/A3
San Luis Potosí, Mex. 199/E4
San Luis Rey (riv.), Ca, US 192/C4
San Luis Rey, Ca, US 192/C4
San Manuel, Az, US 175/G4
San Manuel, Chile 212/B3
San Marcello Pistoiese, It. 89/D5
San Marco (peak), It. 92/D5
San Marco dei Cavoti, It. 92/D5
San Marco la Catola, It. 92/D4
San Marcos, Col. 204/C2
San Marcos, CR 201/E4
San Marcos, Guat. 200/D3
San Marcos, Mex. 196/B4
San Marcos, Peru 208/B2
San Marcos, Peru 208/B3
San Marcos, Ca, US 192/C4
San Marcos (riv.), Tx, US 177/F3
San Marcos, Tx, US 177/F3
San Maria di Porto Novo, It. 89/G6
San Mariano, Phil. 114/C1
San Marino (cap.), SMar. 89/F6
San Marino, Ca, US 192/F7
San Marino(ctry.) 55/F4
San Martín (lake), Arg. 203/B7
San Martín, Arg. 214/C2
San Martín (riv.), Bol. 209/F4
San Martín, Col. 204/C4
San Martín, Mex. 199/R9
San Martín, Peru 204/C5
San Martín (dept.), Peru 208/B2
San Martin (cape), Ca, US 174/B3
San Martin, Ca, US 174/B2
San Martin Cuautlalpan, Mex. 199/R10
San Martín de los Andes, Arg. 214/C4
San Martín de Valdeiglesias, Sp. 72/C2
San Martín Número Dos, Arg. 212/E3
San Martino al Cimino, It. 91/B3
San Martino Buon Albergo, It. 89/E3
San Martino di Lupari, It. 89/E2
San Martino di Venezze, It. 89/E3
San Martino in Passiria (Sankt Martin in Passieir), It. 87/H4
San Martino in Pensilis, It. 92/E4
San Martino in Rio, It. 89/D4
San Martino in Strada, It. 88/C3
San Martino Siccomario, It. 88/C3
San Martino-di-lota, Fr. 74/A1
San Mateo, Phil. 114/F6
San Mateo, Peru 208/B3
San Mateo, Sp. 73/F2
San Mateo, Ven. 207/N7
San Mateo, Fl, US 191/H3
San Mateo (cr.), Ca, US 192/C4
San Mateo (co.), Ca, US 193/K12
San Mateo, Ven. 205/E2
San Mateo, NM, US 175/J3
San Mateo (mts.), NM, US 175/J3
San Mateo Atarasquillo, Mex. 199/Q10
San Mateo Xoloc, Mex. 199/Q9
San Matías (gulf), Arg. 203/C7
San Matías, Bol. 209/G5
San Mauricio, Ven. 205/E2
San Maurizio d'Opaglio, It. 88/B2
San Mauro Pascoli, It. 89/F5
San Mauro Torinese, It. 88/A2
San Michele al Tagliamento, It. 89/F2
San Miguel, Arg. 212/E4
San Miguel, Bol. 209/E4
San Miguel, Bol. 209/F5
San Miguel (riv.), Bol. 212/D1
San Miguel (riv.), Bol. 209/F4
San Miguel (riv.), Col. 204/B4
San Miguel, ESal. 200/D3
San Miguel, Mex. 177/C3
San Miguel (gulf), Pan. 201/G4
San Miguel, Pan. 204/B2
San Miguel, Peru 208/C4
San Miguel, Peru 208/B2
San Miguel (bay), Phil. 114/C2
San Miguel (isl.), Ca, US 174/B3
San Miguel (riv.), Co, US 175/H1
San Miguel, NM, US 175/J4
San Miguel (cr.), Tx, US 177/E3
San Miguel Coatlincham, Mex. 199/R10
San Miguel de Allende, Mex. 199/E4
San Miguel de Huachi, Bol. 209/E4
San Miguel de los Bancos, Ecu. 204/B4
San Miguel de Tucumán, Arg. 212/C3
San Miguel del Monte, Arg. 215/J11
San Miguel Tlaixpan, Mex. 199/R9
San Miguel Totolapan, Mex. 196/A4
San Miguelito, Bol. 208/D3
San Miguelito, Bol. 209/F5
San Miniato, It. 89/D6
San Nicola la Strada, It. 92/D5
San Nicolas (isl.), Ca, US 174/C4
San Nicolás de los Arroyos, Arg. 214/E2
San Nicolás Hidalgo, Mex. 177/D5
San Nicolò, It. 88/C3
San Nicolò a Tordino, It. 92/C2
San Onofre, Col 204/C2
San Onofre, Ca, US 192/C4
San Onofre (mtn.), Ca, US 192/C4
San Pablo, Bol. 208/D5
San Pablo, Bol. 209/F4
San Pablo, Chile 214/B4
San Pablo, Col. 204/B4
San Pablo, Peru 208/B2
San Pablo, Phil. 114/C2
San Pablo (int'l arpt.), Sp. 72/C4
San Pablo, Ven. 205/E2
San Pablo (res.), Ca, US 193/K11
San Pablo, Ca, US 193/K11
San Pablo (bay), Ca, US 172/B4
San Pablo, Co, US 178/B2
San Pablo Bay NWR, Ca, US 193/K10
San Pablo de Borbur, Col. 207/L7
San Pablo de las Salinas, Mex. 199/Q9
San Pablo de Lípez, Bol. 212/C2
San Pablo Huixtepec, Mex. 200/B2
San Paolo, It. 88/D3
San Pascual, Phil. 114/C2
San Pawl il-Baħar, Malta 74/L7
San Pédro, C.d'Iv. 140/D5
San Pedro, Arg. 215/J10
San Pedro, Arg. 212/C3
San Pedro, Belz 200/E2
San Pedro, Bol. 212/C1
San Pedro, Bol. 209/E4
San Pedro, Bol. 209/E3
San Pedro, Bol. 209/F5
San Pedro, Bol. 208/E3
San Pedro, Chile 212/B2
San Pedro (pt.), Chile 212/B3
San Pedro, Chile 214/N8
San Pedro (vol.) Chile 212/B2
San Pedro, Col. 207/K6
San Pedro (riv.), Guat. 200/D2
San Pedro (riv.), Mex.,US 175/G4
San Pedro (dept.), Par. 210/A4
San Pedro, Par. 213/E3
San Pedro (mts.), Sp. 72/B3
San Pedro (riv.), Az, US 198/C1
San Pedro (nbrhd.), Ca, US 192/F8
San Pedro (chan.), Ca, US 174/C4
San Pedro Arriba, Mex. 199/Q10
San Pedro Carchá, Guat. 200/D3
San Pedro de Arimena, Col. 204/D3
San Pedro de Cajas, Peru 208/C3
San Pedro de Cururu, Bol. 209/F4
San Pedro de la Cueva, Mex. 198/C2
San Pedro de Las Bocas, Ven. 205/F3
San Pedro de las Colonias, Mex. 177/C5
San Pedro de Lloc, Peru 208/B2
San Pedro de Lóvago, Nic. 201/E3
San Pedro de Macorís, DRep. 197/H4
San Pedro del Paraná, Par. 213/E3
San Pedro del Pinatar, Sp. 73/E4
San Pedro Huamelula, Mex. 200/C2
San Pedro Pochutla, Mex. 200/B3
San Pedro Sula, Hon. 200/D3
San Pedro Tapanatepec, Mex. 200/C2
San Pedro Totoltepec, Mex. 199/Q10
San Pellegrino Terme, It. 88/C2
San Perlita, Tx, US 177/F4
San Piero a Sieve, It. 89/E6
San Piero in Bagno, It. 89/E6
San Pierre, In, US 186/C4
San Pietro (isl.), It. 92/E3
San Pietro in Casale, It. 89/E4
San Pietro in Gù, It. 89/E2
San Pietro in Vincoli, It. 89/F5
San Pietro in Volta, It. 89/F3
San Pitch (riv.), Ut, US 173/H4
San Polo d'Enza, It. 88/D4
San Polo di Piave, It. 89/F2
San Possidonio, It. 89/D4
San Prisco, It. 92/D5
San Quentin, Ca, US 193/K11
San Quintín, Mex. 198/B2
San Quintín, (cape), Mex. 198/B2
San Rafael, Arg. 214/C2
San Rafael, Bol. 208/D4
San Rafael, Bol. 209/F5
San Rafael, Chile 214/C2
San Rafael, Col. 207/K6
San Rafael, Mex. 199/N6
San Rafael, Peru 208/B3
San Rafael, Peru 208/B2
San Rafael (mts.), Ca, US 174/C3
San Rafael (hills), Ca, US 192/F7
San Rafael (riv.), Ut, US 173/H4
San Rafael, Ca, US 172/B5
San Rafael (des.), Ut, US 173/H4
San Rafael, NM, US 175/J3
San Rafael de Orituco, Ven. 207/P8
San Rafael del Moján, Ven. 204/D2
San Rafael Swell (upland), Ut, US 173/H4
San Ramón, Bol. 209/E4
San Ramón, Bol. 209/F4
San Ramón, CR 201/E4
San Ramón, Peru 208/C3
San Ramón, Uru. 215/L11
San Ramon, Ca, US 193/L11
San Ramón de la Nueva Orán, Arg. 212/C2
San Remo, It. 88/A5
San Rocco al Porto, It. 88/C3
San Romano, It. 89/D6
San Roque, Sp. 72/C4
San Roque, Col. 207/K6
San Rosendo, Chile 214/B3
San Saba (riv.), Tx, US 199/F2
San Saba, Tx, US 177/E2
San Salvador (cap.), ESal. 200/D3
San Salvador (riv.), Uru. 215/J10
San Salvador (isl.), Ecu. 208/J7
San Salvador, Arg. 212/E4
San Salvador (Watling) (isl.), Bahm. 197/G3
San Salvador de Jujuy, Arg. 212/C3
San Salvador el Seco, Mex. 199/M7
San Salvador, Isla (isl.), Bahm. 197/G3
San Salvatore Monferrato, It. 88/B4
San Salvo, It. 92/D3
San Sebastián, Sp. 70/C5
San Sebastián, Arg. 215/C7
San Sebastián, Ven. 207/N8
San Sebastián de los Reyes, Sp. 73/N8
San Sebastián de Yalí, Nic. 200/E3
San Sebastiano, It. 88/D2
San Secondo Parmense, It. 88/D4
San Severino Marche, It. 92/C1
San Severo, It. 74/D2
San Simeon, Ca, US 174/B3
San Simon (riv.), Az, US 175/H4
San Simón, Bol. 209/F4
San Simon Wash (riv.), Az, US 175/F4
San Telmo, (pt.), Mex. 198/E5
San Timoteo, Ven. 204/D2
San Tomé, Ven. 205/E2
San Valentín (peak), Chile 214/B5
San Valentino, It. 89/G2
San Vicente, Arg. 212/D4
San Vicente, Chile 214/C2
San Vicente, Chile 214/N9
San Vicente, ESal. 200/D3
San Vicente, Mex. 198/A2
San Vicente (res.) Ca, US 192/D5
San Vicente, Ven. 204/E3
San Vicente de Alcántara, Sp. 72/B3
San Vicente de Cañete, Peru 208/B4
San Vicente del Caguán, Col. 204/C4
San Vicente del Raspeig, Sp. 73/E3
San Vincenzo, It. 71/J5
San Vito (cape), It. 74/C3
San Vito, CR 201/F4
San Vito al Tagliamento, It. 89/F2
San Vito Chietino, It. 92/D3
San Vito Romano, It. 92/B4
San Xavier Ind. Res., Az, US 175/G4
San Ygnacio, Tx, US 177/E4
San Ysidro, Ca, US 192/C5
San Ysidro, NM, US 175/J3
Sana (riv.), Bosn. 76/C3
Sanā', Yem. 144/D1
Saña, Peru 208/B2
Şan'ā (Sanaa) (cap.), Yem. 144/C2
Sanaa (int'l arpt.), Yem. 144/C2
Sanaa (Şan'ā) (cap.), Yem. 144/C2
Sanae III, SAfr., Ant. 216/Z
Sanafā, Egypt 139/C3
Sanaga (riv.), Camr. 133/C4
Sanajärvi (lake), Fin. 65/F4
Sanām, SAr. 126/D4
Sanana (isl.), Indo. 117/G4
Sanandaj, Iran 129/F3
Sanandita, Bol. 212/D2
Sananduva, Braz. 213/G3
Sanankoroba, Mali 140/D3
Sanary-sur-Mer, Fr. 90/B6
Sanatorium, Ms, US 190/D2
Sanaur, India 124/D4
Sanāw, Yem. 126/F5
Sānāwad, India 118/C3
Sanborn, ND, US 182/E4
Sanborn, Mn, US 181/G1
Sanborn, NY, US 186/V9
Sanbu, China 104/E4
Sancha, China 113/F3
Sancha, China 104/E5
Sancha (riv.), China 112/E3
Sanchahe, China 107/B2
Sánchez Grande, Uru. 215/K10
Sanch'ŏng, SKor. 107/D5
Sanco, Tx, US 176/D1
Sancti Spíritu, Arg. 214/E2
Sancti Spíritus, Cuba 201/G1
Sand, Nor. 66/B2
Sand (hills), Ne, US 168/F3
Sand (cr.), SD, US 180/E1
Sand (pt.), Eng, UK 62/D4
Sand (riv.), SAfr. 150/D3
Sand am Main, Ger. 84/D3
Sand Arroyo (riv.), Ks,Co, US 178/D2
Sand Coulee, Mt, US 171/J4
Sand Draw (riv.), Ne,Co, US 180/D3
Sand Key (isl.), Fl, US 190/K8
Sand Lake, Tx, US 176/L7
Sand Lake NWR, SD, US 182/E5
Sand Lake NWR, SD, US 180/E1
Sand Patch (pt.), Austl. 159/D3

294

Sand – Sarar

Sand Springs, Mt, US 171/L4
Sanda (isl.), Sc, UK 60/C1
Sanda, Japan 109/H6
Sandakan, Malay. 114/B4
Sandan, Camb. 120/D3
Sandane, Nor. 64/C3
Sandanski, Bul. 75/H2
Sandaré, Mali 140/C3
Sandarne, Swe. 66/G1
Sanday (isl.), Sc, UK 57/V14
Sandbach, Eng, UK 61/F5
Sandberg, Ger. 84/C2
Sandborn, In, US 188/D1
Sande, Nor. 64/R9
Sande, Ger. 79/F1
Sandebukta (bay), Nor. 64/R9
Sandefjord, Nor. 66/D2
Sanderson, Tx, US 177/C2
Sandersville, Ms, US 190/D2
Sandersville, Ga, US 189/F4
Sandgate (nbrhd.), Austl. 160/F6
Sandhamn, Swe. 65/B1
Sandhead, Sc, UK 60/D2
Sandhill, On, Can. 186/T8
Sandhurst, Eng, UK 63/F4
Sandia, Peru 208/D4
Sandia Mil. Res., NM, US 175/J3
Sandia Park, NM, US 175/J3
Sandia Peak Tramway, NM, US 175/J3
Sandia Pueblo Ind. Res., NM, US 175/J3
Sandıklı, Turk. 128/B2
Sandīla, India 122/C2
Sandillon, Fr. 83/H5
Sanding (isl.), Indo. 115/C3
Sandino, Cuba 196/E3
Sandnes, Nor. 66/A2
Sandoa, D.R. Congo 147/E5
Sandomierz, Pol. 69/L3
Sandoná, Col. 204/B4
Sándorfalva, Hun. 76/E2
Sandougou (riv.), Sen. 140/B3
Sandoval, Il, US 188/C1
Sandover (riv.), Austl. 157/G2
Sandoway, Myan. 112/B5
Sandown, Eng, UK 63/E5
Sandpoint, Id, US 170/F3
Sandrakatsy, Madg. 152/J7
Sandrigo, It. 89/E2
Sandringham (nbrhd.), Austl. 158/G5
Sandrivier (riv.), SAfr. 149/F4
Sandrohy, Madg. 152/H8
Sands, Mi, US 183/L4
Sands (pt.), NY, US 195/L8
Sands Point, NY, US 195/L8
Sandstedt, Ger. 79/F2
Sandstone, Austl. 156/C3
Sandstone Nat'l Wild. Ref., Mn, US 183/H4
Sandu, China 113/G2
Sandu Shuizu Zizhixian, China 113/E3
Sandungen (lake), Nor. 64/S9
Sandusky, Mi, US 186/E3
Sandusky, Oh, US 186/E4
Sandusky (riv.), Oh, US 186/E4
Sandvika, Nor. 66/D2
Sandviken, Swe. 66/G1
Sandweiler, Lux. 81/F4
Sandwich, Ma, US 187/L4
Sandwich, NH, US 187/L3
Sandwich (cape), Austl. 160/B2
Sandwich, Il, US 181/K3
Sandwich, Eng, UK 63/H4
Sandwīp (isl.), Bang. 123/H4
Sandy (lake), Nf., Can. 185/J1
Sandy (cape), Austl. 160/D4
Sandy, Ut, US 173/H3
Sandy (lake), On, Can. 166/G3
Sandy, Eng, UK 63/F2
Sandy (pt.), SC, US 189/G4
Sandy (pt.), RI, US 195/G1
Sandy Creek, NY, US 187/H3
Sandy Hook(isl.) 195/J10
Sandy Hook, Ky, US 189/F1
Sandy Hook (bay), NJ, US 194/D3
Sandy Hook Lighthouse, NJ, US 195/J10
Sandy Lake, Mb, Can. 182/D2
Sandy Point, NS, Can. 184/E4
Sandy Springs, Ga, US 189/M7
Sandykachi, Trkm. 127/H1
Sandyville, WV, US 189/G1
Sanem, Lux. 81/E4
Sånfjällets NP, Swe. 64/E3
Sanford, Mb, Can. 182/F3
Sanford (mt.), Ak, US 168/Y12
Sanford, Co, US 175/K2
Sanford, Fl, US 191/H3
Sanford, Me, US 187/L3
Sanford, Ms, US 190/D2
Sanford, NC, US 189/H3
Sanfront, It. 90/D3
Sanga, D.R. Congo 147/G4
Sanga, Ang. 148/B1
Sangachaly, Azer. 129/G1
Sangamon (riv.), Il, US 181/J3
Sangān (mtn.), Afg. 127/H2
Sangano, It. 90/D2
Sangar, Rus. 101/N3
Sangar Sarāy, Afg. 124/A2
Sangardo, Gui. 140/C4
Sangareddi, India 121/C2
Sangaréya, Gui. 140/B4
Sangaria, India 124/C5
Sangatte, Fr. 80/A2
Sangay (vol.), Ecu. 204/B5
Sangbé, Camr. 142/B4
Sange, D.R. Congo 147/G3
Sangejing, China 104/F3
Sangenjo, Sp. 72/A1
Sanger, Tx, US 179/F4
Sanger, Ca, US 174/C2
Sanggan (riv.), China 106/C2
Sanggarmai, China 112/D1
Sanggau, Indo. 116/D3
Sanggou (bay), China 107/B4
Sangha (pol. ref), Congo 146/C2
Sangha (pref.), CAfr. 142/B5
Sangha (riv.), D.R. Congo 142/C5
Sangha (riv.), CAfr. 133/D4
Sanghar, Pak. 127/J3
Sangihe (isl.), Phil. 103/M9
Sangihe (isl.), Indo. 117/G3
Sangiyn Dalay (lake), Mong. 104/D2
Sangiyn Dalay, Mong. 104/E2
Sangju, SKor. 107/E4
Sangkha, Thai. 120/C3
Sangkhla, Thai. 120/B3
Sangkulirang, Indo. 117/E3
Sāngla, Pak. 124/B4
Sangley Point Nav. Air Sta., Phil. 114/E7
Sangmélima, Camr. 146/C2
Sangō, Japan 109/J6
Sangpang (mts.), Myan. 112/B3
Sangre de Cristo (mts.), Co, US 180/B4
Sangre Grande, Trin. 205/F2
Sangri, China 123/J1
Sangro (riv.), It. 74/D2
Sangrūr, India 124/C4
Sangsang, China 123/F1
Sangster (int'l arpt.), Jam. 201/G2
Sangue, Rio do (riv.), Braz. 209/G3
Sangüesa, Sp. 70/C5
Sanguie (prov.), Burk. 141/E4
Sanguinetto, It. 89/E3
Sangwŏn, NKor. 107/D3
Sanha (pref), Afr. 146/C2
Sanhe, China 106/H7
Sanhuang, China 113/F3
Sanhūr, Egypt 139/B6
Sani (pass), Les. 150/E3
Sāni Bheri (riv.), Nepal 122/D1
Sanibel (isl.), Fl, US 191/G4
San'in Kaigin NP, Japan 110/D3
Saniquellie, Libr. 140/C5
Sanito, Phil. 114/C4
Sanjahā, Egypt 139/C3
Sanje, Zam. 149/E2
Sanjia, China 113/F4
Sanjiang, China 113/E2
Sanjō, Japan 111/F2
Sankarbiriwa (peak), SLeo. 140/C4
Sankeyushu, China 107/C2
Sankh (riv.), India 123/E4
Sānko, India 124/C2
Sankoroni (riv.), Gui. 140/C4
Sankosh (riv.), India 123/G2
Sānkra, India 127/K3
Sankt Aegyd am Neuwalde, Aus. 71/L3
Sankt Agatha, Aus. 85/G6
Sankt Andrä-Wördern, Aus. 77/N7
Sankt Andreasberg, Ger. 79/H5
Sankt Anton am Arlberg, Aus. 87/G3
Sankt Augustin, Ger. 81/G2
Sankt Blasien, Ger. 86/E2
Sankt Florian am Inn, Aus. 85/G6
Sankt Gallen, Swi. 87/F3
Sankt Gallenkirch, Aus. 87/F3
Sankt Georgen bei Salzburg, Aus. 85/F7
Sankt Georgen im Attergau, Aus. 85/G7
Sankt Georgen im Schwarzwald, Ger. 87/E1
Sankt Goar, Ger. 81/G3
Sankt Goarshausen, Ger. 81/G3
Sankt Ingbert, Ger. 81/G5
Sankt Jakob (San Giacomo), It. 87/H4
Sankt Johann am Walde, Aus. 85/G6
Sankt Johann im Pongau, Aus. 71/K3
Sankt Johann in Tirol, Aus. 71/K3
Sankt Leonhard im Pitztal, Aus. 87/G3
Sankt Leonhard in Passeier (San Leonardo in Passiria), It. 87/H4
Sankt Marien, Aus. 85/H6
Sankt Martin im Mühlkreis, Aus. 85/H6
Sankt Martin in Passeier (San Martino in Passiria), It. 87/H4
Sankt Michael in Obersteiermark, Aus. 71/L3
Sankt Moritz, Swi. 87/F5
Sankt Moritz (Saint Moritz), Swi. 71/H3
Sankt Oswald bei Freistadt, Aus. 85/H5
Sankt Pantaleon, Aus. 85/F6
Sankt Pauli, Ger. 79/G1
Sankt Peter am Hart, Aus. 85/G6
Sankt Peter in der Au, Aus. 85/H6
Sankt Peter-Ording, Ger. 66/C4
Sankt Pölten, Aus. 69/H4
Sankt Stephan, Swi. 86/D4
Sankt Ulrich bei Steyr, Aus. 85/H6
Sankt Valentin, Aus. 85/H6
Sankt Veit, Aus. 76/B1
Sankt Veit an der Glan, Aus. 71/L3
Sankt Wendel, Ger. 81/G5
Sankt Wolfgang, Ger. 85/F6
Sankuru (riv.), D.R. Congo 147/E4
Sanlong, China 105/J5
Sanlúcar de Barrameda, Sp. 72/B4
Sanmatenga (prov.), Burk. 141/E3
Sanmenxia, China 106/B4
Sanming, China 113/H3
Sannan, Japan 109/H5
Sannār, Sudan 142/G2
Sannazzaro de'Burgondi, It. 88/B3
Sannicandro Garganico, It. 74/D2
Sannikova (str.), Rus. 101/P2
Sannio (mts.), It. 92/D5
San'nohe, Japan 108/B3
Sannois, Fr. 56/J5
Sannūr (wadi), Egypt 139/C6
Sano, Japan 111/F2
Sañogasta, Arg. 212/C4
Sanok, Pol. 69/M4
Sanostee, NM, US 175/H2
Sanpoil (riv.), Wa, US 170/E3
Sanqiao, China 106/K9
Sanquhar, Sc, UK 59/C6
Sanquianga, PN, Col. 204/B4
Sans Bois (mts.), Ok, US 179/G3
Sansalé, Gui. 140/B4
Sansepolcro, It. 89/F6
Sansha, China 113/J3
Sanshilipu, China 104/F4
Sansui, China 113/F3
Sant Adrià de Besòs, Sp. 73/L7
Sant 'Antioco (isl.), It. 92/E3
Sant Boi de Llobregat, Sp. 73/L7
Sant Carles de la Ràpita, Sp. 73/F2
Sant Celoni, Sp. 73/L6
Sant Cugat del Vallès, Sp. 73/L7
Sant Eufemia (gulf), It. 74/D3
Sant Feliu de Guíxols, Sp. 73/G2
Sant Feliu de Llobregat, Sp. 73/L7
Sant Julia, And. 70/D5
Sant Pere de Ribes, Sp. 73/K7
Sant Sadurní d'Anoia, Sp. 73/K7
Sant Vicenç de Castellet, Sp. 73/K6
Sant Vicenç dels Horts, Sp. 73/L7
Santa (riv.), Peru 208/B3
Santa, Peru 208/B3
Santa, Id, US 170/F4
Santa Ana, Bol. 212/E1
Santa Ana, Bol. 209/F5
Santa Ana, Bol. 209/E4
Santa Ana, Col. 204/D4
Santa Ana, Ecu. 204/A5
Santa Ana, ESal. 200/D3
Santa Ana (vol.), ESal. 200/D3
Santa Ana, Hon. 200/E3
Santa Ana, Mex. 198/C2
Santa Ana (riv.), Ca, US 192/C3
Santa Ana (riv.), Ca, US 192/C3
Santa Ana (mts.), Ca, US 192/C3
Santa Ana, Ca, US 192/G8
Santa Ana (mts.), Ca, US 174/D4
Santa Ana, Ven. 204/C3
Santa Ana, Ven. 204/D2
Santa Ana, Ven. 206/A1
Santa Ana del Alto Beni, Bol. 209/E4
Santa Ana Ind. Res., NM, US 178/A3
Santa Ana Ind. Res., NM, US 175/J3
Santa Ana Nat'l Wild. Ref., Tx, US 177/E4
Santa Anna, Tx, US 176/E2
Santa Bárbara, Braz. 211/E3
Santa Bárbara, Chile 214/B3
Santa Bárbara, Col. 207/K7
Santa Bárbara, Hon. 200/D3
Santa Bárbara, Mex. 198/D3
Santa Barbara, Phil. 114/C1
Santa Barbara, Ca, US 192/A2
Santa Barbara (chan.), Ca, US 174/B3
Santa Barbara (isl.), Ca, US 174/C4
Santa Barbara (co.), Ca, US 192/A1
Santa Bárbara, Ven. 205/E4
Santa Bárbara, Ven. 204/D2
Santa Bárbara, Ven. 204/D3
Santa Bárbara d'Oeste, Braz. 213/H2
Santa Barbara Mountains NRA, Ca, US 192/E7
Santa Catalina, Ven. 204/D3
Santa Catalina, Pan. 201/F4
Santa Catalina (isl.), CA, US 168/B5
Santa Catalina (gulf), Ca, US 174/D4
Santa Catalina, Phil. 114/C3
Santa Catarina (isl.), Braz. 213/G3
Santa Catarina (state), Braz. 213/G3
Santa Catarina, Mex. 199/E3
Santa Clara, Cuba 201/G1
Santa Clara, Mex. 198/E3
Santa Clara (res.), Port. 72/A4
Santa Clara (riv.), Ca, US 192/B2
Santa Clara, Ca, US 193/L12
Santa Clara (co.), Ca, US 193/L12
Santa Clara, Ca, US 174/B2
Santa Clara, Ut, US 175/F2
Santa Clara, Ven. 205/E2
Santa Clara de Olimar, Uru. 215/G2
Santa Clarita, Ca, US 192/B2
Santa Claus, In, US 188/D1
Santa Clotilde, Peru 204/C5
Santa Coloma de Farners, Sp. 73/G2
Santa Coloma de Gramanet, Sp. 73/L7
Santa Comba, Sp. 72/A1
Santa Croce (peak), It. 92/C5
Santa Croce di Magliano, It. 92/D4
Santa Croce sull'Arno, It. 89/D6
Santa Cruz (prov.), Arg. 214/C5
Santa Cruz (riv.), Arg. 203/B8
Santa Cruz (riv.), Bol. 209/F5
Santa Cruz, Braz. 207/G4
Santa Cruz, Chile 214/C2
Santa Cruz, CR 200/E4
Santa Cruz (isl.), Ecu. 208/J7
Santa Cruz (mts.), Guat. 200/D3
Santa Cruz, Mex. 175/G5
Santa Cruz (riv.), Mex., US 175/G5
Santa Cruz, Peru 208/C2
Santa Cruz, Phil. 114/D4
Santa Cruz, Phil. 114/B2
Santa Cruz, Phil. 114/C1
Santa Cruz, Phil. 114/C2
Santa Cruz, SaoT. 146/A2
Santa Cruz (isls.), Sol. 162/F6
Santa Cruz (isl.), Ca, US 174/C4
Santa Cruz da Graciosa, Azor., Port. 73/S12
Santa Cruz das Flores, Azor., Port. 73/R12
Santa Cruz de Bucaral, Ven. 204/D2
Santa Cruz de El Seibo, DRep. 197/H4
Santa Cruz de la Palma, Sp. 136/A3
Santa Cruz de la Sierra, Bol. 212/D1
Santa Cruz de la Zarza, Sp. 72/D3
Santa Cruz de Mudela, Sp. 72/D3
Santa Cruz de Orinoco, Ven. 205/E2
Santa Cruz de Tenerife, Sp. 136/A3
Santa Cruz del Quiché, Guat. 200/D3
Santa Cruz del Sur, Cuba 201/G1
Santa Cruz do Capibaribe, Braz. 207/G4
Santa Cruz do Cuando, Ang. 148/D3
Santa Cruz do Piauí, Braz. 207/F4
Santa Cruz do Rio Pardo, Braz. 213/G2
Santa Cruz do Sul, Braz. 213/F4
Santa Elena, Arg. 212/D4
Santa Elena, Arg. 212/E4
Santa Elena, Bol. 212/C2
Santa Elena, Hon. 200/E2
Santa Elena (bay), CR 200/E4
Santa Elena, Ecu. 204/A5
Santa Elena (cape), CR 200/E4
Santa Elena (peak), Arg. 214/D5
Santa Elena, Peru 208/C2
Santa Elena de Turuchipa, Bol. 212/C1
Santa Elena de Uairén, Ven. 205/F3
Santa Eugenia de Ribeira, Sp. 72/A1
Santa Eulalia del Río, Sp. 73/F3
Santa Fe, Arg. 212/D4
Santa Fe (prov.), Arg. 212/D4
Santa Fe, Bol. 209/E3
Santa Fe, Cuba 201/F1
Santa Fé, Sp. 72/D4
Santa Fe (riv.), Fl, US 191/G3
Santa Fe (lake), Fl, US 191/G3
Santa Fe (cap.), NM, US 175/K3
Santa Fe (mts.), NM, US 178/B3
Santa Fe, Tx, US 177/M9
Santa Fé do Sul, Braz. 213/B2
Santa Fe Springs, Ca, US 192/F8
Santa Felicia (dam), Ca, US 192/B2
Santa Filomena, Braz. 207/E4
Santa Giustina (lake), It. 87/H5
Santa Helena, Braz. 207/E3
Santa Helena, Braz. 213/F3
Santa Helena de Goiás, Braz. 210/C3
Santa Inés (isl.), Chile 215/B7
Santa Inês, Braz. 211/F2
Santa Inês, Braz. 207/E3
Santa Isabel, Arg. 214/E2
Santa Isabel, Arg. 214/D3
Santa Isabel, Braz. 211/K8
Santa Isabel, Braz. 212/C2
Santa Isabel, Col. 201/F3
Santa Isabel, Ecu. 208/B1
Santa Isabel (riv.), Guat. 200/D2
Santa Isabel (isl.), Sol. 162/E5
Santa Isabel, Ven. 205/E4
Santa Isabel de Sihuas, Peru 208/C5
Santa Isabel do Ivaí, Braz. 213/F2
Santa Isabel do Pará, Braz. 206/D3
Santa Isabel, Pico de (peak), EqG. 146/B2
Santa Juliana, Braz. 210/D3
Santa Lucía, Arg. 212/E4
Santa Lucía (riv.), Arg. 213/E4
Santa Lucía, Ecu. 204/B5
Santa Lucía, Peru 208/D4
Santa Lucía, Uru. 215/K11
Santa Lucía, Sp. 136/B4
Santa Lucía, Ven. 207/P7
Santa Lucia (range), Ca, US 174/B2
Santa Lucía, Ven. 204/D2
Santa Lucia di Piave, It. 89/F2
Santa Luz, Braz. 211/F1
Santa Luzia (isl.), CpV. 133/J10
Santa Luzia, Braz. 207/G4
Santa Luzia, Braz. 207/E3
Santa Magdalena, Arg. 214/E2
Santa Magdalena (isl.), Mex. 198/B3
Santa Margarita (isl.), Mex. 198/B3
Santa Margarita (riv.), Ca, US 192/C4
Santa Margarita (riv.), Ca, US 174/D4
Santa Margherita Ligure, It. 88/C5
Santa María, Arg. 212/C3
Santa María, Bol. 212/D1
Santa María, Bol. 209/F4
Santa María, Chile 214/N8
Santa María, Ecu. 208/J7
Santa María (isl.), Ecu. 208/J7
Santa María, Mex. 199/L7
Santa María (riv.), Mex. 198/D2
Santa María (bay), Mex. 198/C3
Santa Maria (cape), Port. 72/B4
Santa Maria, Ven. 205/E3
Santa Maria, Braz. 213/F4
Santa Maria (riv.), Braz. 213/F4
Santa Maria (isl.), Chile 214/B3
Santa Maria, CpV. 133/K10
Santa Maria, Phil. 114/D4
Santa Maria, Phil. 114/C1
Santa Maria, Phil. 114/E6
Santa Maria (isl.), Azor., Port. 73/T13
Santa Maria, Ca, US 174/B3
Santa Maria a Monte, It. 89/D6
Santa Maria a Vico, It. 92/D5
Santa Maria Capua Vetere, It. 92/D5
Santa Maria da Boa Vista, Braz. 207/G5
Santa Maria da Vitória, Braz. 210/D2
Santa María de Cayón, Sp. 72/D1
Santa Maria de Erebató, Ven. 205/E3
Santa María de Ipire, Ven. 205/E2
Santa María de Nanay, Peru 208/C1
Santa Maria degli Angeli, It. 91/B1
Santa María del Oro, Mex. 198/D3
Santa Maria della Versa, It. 88/C4
Santa Maria di Leuca (cape), It. 93/H3
Santa Maria di Leuca, Capo (cape), It. 75/F3
Santa Maria do Pará, Braz. 207/E3
Santa Maria do Suaçuí, Braz. 211/E3
Santa Maria la Carità, It. 92/D6
Santa Maria la Fossa, It. 92/D5
Santa Maria Maddalena, It. 89/E4
Santa Maria Maggiore, It. 87/E5
Santa Maria Nuova, It. 89/G7
Santa María Xadani, Mex. 196/B4
Santa Maria, Cabo de (cape), Moz. 151/F2
Santa Marta, Col. 204/C2
Santa Marta Grande, Cabo de (cape), Braz. 213/G4
Santa Marta, Sierra Nevada de (mts.), Col. 204/C2
Santa Monica (bay), Ca, US 192/B3
Santa Monica (mts.), Ca, US 192/B2
Santa Monica, Ca, US 192/F7
Santa Monica Mountains NRA, Ca, US 192/B2
Santa Olalla del Cala, Sp. 72/B4
Santa Paula (peak), Ca, US 192/A2
Santa Paula, Ca, US 192/A2
Santa Pola, Sp. 73/E3
Santa Pola, Cabo de (cape), Sp. 73/E3
Santa Quitéria, Braz. 207/F4
Santa Quitéria do Maranhão, Braz. 207/F3
Santa Rita, Braz. 207/H4
Santa Rita, Braz. 207/E3
Santa Rita, NM, US 175/H4
Santa Rita, Ven. 205/E2
Santa Rita, Ven. 204/D2
Santa Rita de Cássia, Braz. 210/D1
Santa Rita do Sapucaí, Braz. 211/L7
Santa Rosa, Arg. 212/C5
Santa Rosa, Arg. 212/C2
Santa Rosa, Arg. 214/D3
Santa Rosa, Braz. 213/F3
Santa Rosa, Bol. 209/E4
Santa Rosa, CR 200/E4
Santa Rosa, Uru. 215/K11
Santa Rosa, Bol. 209/E3
Santa Rosa, Bol. 212/C1
Santa Rosa, Braz. 206/C4
Santa Rosa, Par. 213/E3
Santa Rosa, Ecu. 208/B1
Santa Rosa, Peru 208/D4
Santa Rosa, Ca, US 172/B4
Santa Rosa (range), Nv, US 172/E3
Santa Rosa (isl.), Ca, US 174/C4
Santa Rosa, NM, US 178/B3
Santa Rosa(mts.), Nv, US168/C3
Santa Rosa, Ven. 204/D3
Santa Rosa, Ven. 204/D2
Santa Rosa, Ven. 204/E3
Santa Rosa de Aguán, Hon. 200/E3
Santa Rosa de Amanadona, Ven. 205/E4
Santa Rosa de Cabal, Col. 207/K8
Santa Rosa de Calamuchita, Arg. 212/C5
Santa Rosa de Copán, Hon. 200/D3
Santa Rosa de la Roca, Bol. 209/F5
Santa Rosa de Osos, Col. 204/C3
Santa Rosa de Viterbo, Braz. 213/H2
Santa Rosa del Palmar, Bol. 209/F5
Santa Rosa del Sara, Bol. 212/D1
Santa Rosa Wash (riv.), Az, US 175/F4
Santa Rosa, PN 196/C5
Santa Rosalía (pt.), Mex. 198/B2
Santa Rosalía, Mex. 198/B3
Santa Rosalía, Ven. 204/D2
Santa Rosalía, Ven. 205/E3
Santa Sofia, It. 89/E6
Santa Susana (mts.), Ca, US 192/B2
Santa Teresa, Austl. 157/G3
Santa Teresa, Braz. 211/E3
Santa Teresa (riv.), Braz. 210/C2
Santa Teresa, Braz. 210/C2
Santa Teresa, Ven. 207/P7
Santa Teresa Abor. Land, Austl. 157/G2
Santa Teresa, PN, Uru. 215/G2
Santa Teresinha, Braz. 210/C1
Santa Teresita, Arg. 215/F3
Santa Victoria, Arg. 212/D2
Santa Vitória, Braz. 210/C3
Santa Vitória do Palmar, Braz. 215/G2
Santa Ynez (mts.), Ca, US 192/A2
Santa Ynez (riv.), Ca, US 174/C3
Santa Ynez Ind. Res., Ca, US 174/B3
Santa Ysabel Ind. Res., Ca, US 174/D4
Santaella, Sp. 72/C4
Sant'Agata Bolognese, It. 89/E4
Sant'Agata di Militello, It. 74/D3
Sant'Agata Feltria, It. 89/F6
Sant'Agnello, It. 92/D6
Sant'Agostino, It. 89/E4
Sāntāhār, Bang. 123/G3
Sant'Alberto, It. 89/F4
Santana, Braz. 210/D2
Santana (isl.), Braz. 207/F3
Santana, Port. 136/A2
Santana, Port. 73/P11
Santana da Boa Vista, Braz. 213/F4
Santana do Acaraú, Braz. 207/F3
Santana do Cariri, Braz. 207/G4
Santana do Ipanema, Braz. 207/G5
Santana do Livramento, Braz. 213/F4
Sant'Anastasia, It. 92/D6
Santander (dept.), Col. 201/H5
Santander, Sp. 72/D1
Santander, Phil. 114/C3
Santander de Quilichao, Col. 204/B4
Santander Jiménez, Mex. 199/F3
Sant'Andrea del Pizzone, It. 92/D5
Sant'Angelo in Formis, It. 92/D5
Sant'Angelo in Vado, It. 89/F6
Sant'Angelo Lodigiano, It. 88/C3
Sant'Antioco, It. 92/F3
Sant'Antioco (isl.), It. 74/A3
Sant'Antonino di Susa, It. 90/D2
Sant'Antonio, It. 89/D3
Sant'Antonio Abate, It. 92/D6
Santañy, Sp. 73/G3
Sant'Apollinare in Classe, It. 89/F5
Santaquin, Ut, US 173/H4
Santarcángelo, It. 89/F5
Santarém (dist.), Port. 72/A3
Santarém, Port. 72/A3
Santarém, Braz. 206/C3
Santarém Novo, Braz. 207/E3
Sant'Arsenio, It. 74/D2
Santee, Ca, US 192/D5
Santee (pt.), SC, US 189/H4
Santee (dam), SC, US 189/G4
Santee (riv.), SC, US 189/H4
Santee Ind. Res., Ne, US 180/F2
Santee Nat'l Wild. Ref., SC, US 189/G4
Sant'Egidio alla Vibrata, It. 92/C2
Sant'Elia a Pianisi, It. 92/D4
Sant'Elia Fiumerapido, It. 92/C4
Sant'Elpidio a Mare, It. 92/C1
Santena, It. 88/A3
Santerno (riv.), It. 71/J4
Santeuil, Fr. 56/H4
Santhia, It. 88/B3
Santiago, Bol. 212/D1
Santiago, Braz. 213/F4
Santiago (cape), Chile 215/B6
Santiago (cap.), Chile 214/N8
Santiago (riv.), Ecu. 208/B1
Santiago (pt.), EqG. 146/B2
Santiago (mtn.), Pan. 201/F4
Santiago, Pan. 204/A2
Santiago, Par. 213/E3
Santiago (riv.), Peru 204/B5
Santiago, Peru 208/C4
Santiago, Phil. 114/C1
Santiago (int'l arpt.), Sp. 72/A1
Santiago (peak), Ca, US 192/C3
Santiago (res.), Ca, US 192/C3
Santiago (mts.), Tx, US 168/F5
Santiago (peak), Tx, US 177/C3
Santiago (Arturo Merino Benitez) (int'l arpt.), Chile 214/N8
Santiago Cuautlalpan, Mex. 199/Q9
Santiago Cuautlalpan, Mex. 199/R10
Santiago de Cao, Peru 208/B2
Santiago de Chocorvos, Peru 208/C4
Santiago de Chuco, Peru 208/B3
Santiago de Compostela, Sp. 72/A1
Santiago de Cuba, Cuba 201/H1
Santiago de los Caballeros, DRep. 197/G4
Santiago de Machaca, Bol. 208/D5
Santiago de Pacaguaras, Bol. 208/D4
Santiago del Estero (prov.), Arg. 212/D3
Santiago del Estero, Arg. 212/C3
Santiago do Cacém, Port. 72/A3
Santiago Ixcuintla, Mex. 198/D4
Santiago Jamiltepec, Mex. 200/B2
Santiago Juxtlahuaca, Mex. 200/B2
Santiago Miahuatlán, Mex. 199/M8
Santiago Papasquiaro, Mex. 198/D3
Santiago Pinotepa Nacional, Mex. 200/B2
Santiago Tilapa, Mex. 199/Q10
Santiago Tolman, Mex. 199/R9
Santiago Vázquez, Uru. 215/K11
Santiago Zacatepec, Mex. 200/C2
Santiam, North (riv.), Or, US 172/B1
Santiam, South (riv.), Or, US 172/B1
Santigi, Indo. 117/F3
Sant'Ilario d'Enza, It. 88/D4
Sāntipur, India 123/G4
Säntis (peak), Swi. 87/F3
Santisteban del Puerto, Sp. 72/D3
Santō, Japan 109/K5
Santō, Japan 109/G5
Santo, Tx, US 177/E1
Santo Amara (isl.), Braz. 211/K8
Santo Amaro (isl.), Braz. 211/K8
Santo Amaro, Braz. 211/F2
Santo Amaro das Brotas, Braz. 211/F1
Santo Anastácio, Braz. 213/G2
Santo André, Braz. 211/K8
Santo Ângelo, Braz. 213/F4
Santo Antão (isl.), CpV. 133/J9
Santo António, SaoT. 146/A2
Santo Antônio do Içá, Braz. 204/E5
Santo Antônio do Leverger, Braz. 210/A2
Santo Antônio do Sudoeste, Braz. 213/F3
Santo Antônio dos Lopes, Braz. 207/E4
Santo Augusto, Braz. 213/F3
Santo Corazón, Bol. 212/E1
Santo Domingo, Bol. 209/E3
Santo Domingo, Cuba 201/F1
Santo Domingo, Chile 214/N8
Santo Domingo (cap.), DRep. 197/H4
Santo Domingo (pt.), Mex. 198/B3
Santo Domingo, Mex. 199/E4
Santo Domingo de la Calzada, Sp. 70/B5
Santo Domingo de los Colorados, Ecu. 204/B5
Santo Domingo Petapa, Mex. 200/C2
Santo Domingo Pueblo, NM, US 175/J3
Santo Domingo Tehuantepec, Mex. 200/C2
Santo Domingo Zanatepec, Mex. 200/C2
Santo Stefano (isl.), It. 92/C6
Santo Stefano Belbo, It. 88/B4
Santo Stefano d'Aveto, It. 88/C4
Santo Stefano di Magra, It. 88/C5
Santo Stino di Livenza, It. 89/F2
Santo Tomás (vol.), Ecu. 208/J7
Santo Tomas (mt.), Phil. 114/C1
Santo Tomás, Peru 208/B2
Santo Tomás, Peru 208/C4
Santo Tomás, Mex. 198/A2
Santo Tomás, (pt.), Mex. 198/A2
Santo Tomé, Arg. 213/E4
Santo Tomé, Arg. 212/D4
Santoña, Sp. 70/B5
Sant'Onofrio, It. 91/G8
Sant'Oreste, It. 91/B3
Santorso, It. 89/E2
Santos, Braz. 211/K8
Santos Dumont (int'l arpt.), Braz. 211/N7
Santos Dumont, Braz. 211/N6
Santos Mercado, Bol. 209/E3
Santos Reyes Nopala, Mex. 200/B2
Santuario, Col. 207/K7
Santuario, Col. 207/K6
Santuario di Crea, It. 88/B3
Santuario di Monte Vergine, It. 92/D6
Santuario di Oropa, It. 88/A1
Santunying, China 106/J6
Şānūr, WBnk. 131/C4
Sanwa, Japan 109/D1
Sanxing, China 106/L8
Sanya, China 113/F5
Sanyang, China 113/H2
Sanyati (riv.), Zim. 149/F3
Sanyuanba, China 113/E1
Sanyuanpu, China 107/C1
Sanza Pombo, Ang. 146/C4
São Bartolomeu (riv.), Braz. 210/D3
São Benedito, Braz. 207/F4
São Benedito do Rio Prêto, Braz. 207/F3
São Bento, Braz. 207/G4
São Bento, Braz. 207/E3
São Bento do Sapucaí, Braz. 211/L7
São Bento do Sul, Braz. 213/G3
São Bento do Una, Braz. 207/G5
São Bernardo do Campo, Braz. 211/K8
São Borja, Braz. 213/F4
São Braz, Cabo de (cape), Ang. 146/C5
São Carlos, Braz. 213/H2
São Cristóvão, Braz. 211/F1
São Desidério, Braz. 210/D2
São Domingos, Braz. 210/D2
São Domingos (riv.), Braz. 210/D2
São Domingos, GBis. 140/A3
São Domingos do Capim, Braz. 206/E3
São Domingos do Maranhão, Braz. 207/E4
São Félix do Araguaia, Braz. 210/C1
São Félix do Piauí, Braz. 207/F4
São Félix do Xingu, Braz. 206/D4
São Fidélis, Braz. 211/E4
São Filipe, CpV. 133/J11
São Francisco (riv.), Braz. 203/F3
São Francisco (isl.), Braz. 213/G3
São Francisco, Braz. 210/D2
São Francisco do Sul, Braz. 213/G3
São Fransisco de Assis, Braz. 213/F4
São Fransisco de Paula, Braz. 213/G4
São Gabriel, Braz. 213/F4
São Gabriel da Palha, Braz. 211/E3
São Gonçalo, Braz. 211/N7
São Gonçalo do Sapuçaí, Braz. 211/L6
São Gotardo, Braz. 213/H1
Sao Hill, Tanz. 145/A4
São Joachim da Barra, Braz. 213/H2
São João Batista, Braz. 207/E3
São João Batista, Braz. 213/G3
São João da Aliança, Braz. 210/D2
São João da Boa Vista, Braz. 211/K6
São João da Madeira, Port. 72/A2
São João da Pesqueira, Port. 72/B2
São João da Ponte, Braz. 210/D2
São João das Lampas, Port. 73/P10
São João de Meriti, Braz. 211/N7
São João del Rei, Braz. 210/D4
São João do Araguaia, Braz. 206/D4
São João do Jaguaribe, Braz. 207/G4
São João do Paraíso, Braz. 211/E2
São João do Piauí, Braz. 207/F5
São João dos Patos, Braz. 207/F4
São João Evangelista, Braz. 211/E3
São João Nepomuceno, Braz. 211/N6
São João, Serra de (mts.), Braz. 209/F3
São Joaquim, Braz. 213/G4
São Joaquim, PN de, Braz. 213/G4
São Jorge (isl.), Azor., Port. 73/S12
São José, Braz. 213/G3
São José da Laje, Braz. 207/G5
São José de Mipibu, Braz. 207/H4
São José de Ribamar, Braz. 207/E3
São José do Belmonte, Braz. 207/G4
São José do Campestre, Braz. 207/H4
São José do Egito, Braz. 207/G4
São José do Gurupi, Braz. 207/E3
São José do Norte, Braz. 213/F5
São José do Peixe, Braz. 207/F4
São José do Rio Pardo, Braz. 211/K6
São José do Rio Prêto, Braz. 213/G2
São José dos Campos, Braz. 211/L8
São José dos Pinhais, Braz. 213/G3
São Julião, Braz. 207/F4
São Lourenço, Port. 73/P11
São Lourenço, Braz. 211/L7
São Lourenço (riv.), Braz. 209/G5
São Lourenço da Mata, Braz. 207/H5
São Lourenço do Sul, Braz. 213/G4
São Lourenço d'Oeste, Braz. 213/F3
São Lucas, Ang. 146/D5
São Luís, Braz. 207/E3
São Luís de Montes Belos, Braz. 210/C3
São Luís do Curu, Braz. 207/G3
São Luís do Quitunde, Braz. 207/H5
São Luís Gonzaga, Braz. 213/F4
São Mamede, Braz. 207/G4
São Marcos (bay), Braz. 203/E3
São Marcos (riv.), Braz. 210/D3
São Martinho do Porto, Port. 72/A3
São Mateus, Braz. 211/F3
São Mateus (riv.), Braz. 211/E3
São Mateus do Maranhão, Braz. 207/E4
São Mateus do Sul, Braz. 213/G3
São Miguel (isl.), Azor., Port. 73/T13
São Miguel, Braz. 207/G4
São Miguel do Araguaia, Braz. 210/C2
São Miguel do Guamá, Braz. 207/E3
São Miguel do Tapuio, Braz. 207/F4
São Miguel d'Oeste, Braz. 213/F3
São Miguel dos Campos, Braz. 211/F1
São Nicolau (isl.), CpV. 133/J10
São Paulo, Braz. 211/K8
São Paulo (state), Braz. 210/C4
São Paulo de Olivença, Braz. 208/D1
São Paulo do Potengi, Braz. 207/H4
São Pedro do Piauí, Braz. 207/F4
São Pedro do Sul, Port. 72/A2
São Pedro do Sul, Braz. 213/F4
São Rafael, Braz. 207/G4
São Raimundo das Mangabeiras, Braz. 207/E4
São Raimundo Nonato, Braz. 207/F5
São Romão, Braz. 210/D3
São Roque (cape), Braz. 207/H4
São Roque do Pico, Azor., Port. 73/S12
São Sebastião (pt.), Moz.149/G4
São Sebastião, Braz. 211/L8
São Sebastião (isl.), Braz. 210/D4
São Sebastião da Boa Vista, Braz. 206/D3
São Sebastião do Paraíso, Braz. 213/H2
São Sebastião do Tocantins, Braz. 206/D4
São Sebastião do Umbuzeiro, Braz. 207/G5
São Simão (riv.), Braz. 209/F4
São Simão (res.), Braz. 210/C3
São Simão, Braz. 210/C3
São Teotónio, Port. 72/A4
São Tiago (isl.), CpV. 133/K10
São Tomé (int'l arpt.), SaoT. 146/A2
São Tomé (isl.), SaoT. 146/A2
São Tomé (cap.), SaoT. 146/A2
São Tomé and Príncipe (ctry.) 133/C4
São Tomé, Cabo de (cape), Braz. 211/E4
São Vicente (cape), Port. 72/A4
São Vicente, Braz. 211/K8
São Vicente (isl.), CpV. 133/J10
São Vicente Ferrer, Braz. 207/E3
Saône (riv.), Fr. 92/E1
Saône-et-Loire (dept.), Fr. 86/B4
Saori, Japan 109/L5
Saouru, Oued (riv.), Alg. 137/E3
Sapāhār, Bang. 123/G3
Sápai, Gre. 75/J2
Sapallanga, Peru 208/C4
Sapanca, Turk. 77/K5
Saparua, Indo. 117/G4
Sapatgrām, India 123/H2
Sapawe, On, Can. 183/J3
Sapé, Braz. 207/H4
Sapele, Nga. 141/G5
Sapelo (isl.), Ga, US 191/H2
Şaphane, Turk. 96/D5
Sapiéndza (isl.), Gre. 75/G4
Sapkyo, SKor. 107/D4
Sapo (mts.), Pan. 201/G5
Sapo NP, Libr. 140/C5
Sapo-Sapo, D.R. Congo 147/E4
Saponé, Burk. 141/E3
Saposoa, Peru 208/B2
Sapozhok, Rus. 97/G1
Sappa (cr.), Ks, US 180/D4
Sappa, Middle Fork (cr.), Ks, US 178/D1
Sappa, South Fork (cr.), Ks, US 178/D1
Sappemeer, Neth. 78/D2
Sapphire, Austl. 160/B3
Sapporo, Japan 108/B2
Sapri, It. 74/D2
Sapsi (isl.), SKor. 107/D3
Sapt Kosi (riv.), Nepal 123/F2
Sapucaí (riv.), Braz. 211/L7
Sapucai (riv.), Braz. 213/H2
Sapucaia, Braz. 211/P6
Sapudi (isl.), Indo. 115/F3
Sapulpa, Ok, US 179/F3
Sapulut, Malay. 114/B4
Sāqiyat Sīdī Yūsuf, Tun. 138/L6
Saqqez, Iran 129/F2
Saquena, Peru 208/C2
Saquisilí, Ecu. 204/B5
Šar (mts.), Yugo 75/G1
Šar (mts.), Yugo. 76/E4
Sar Dasht, Iran 129/F2
Sara, Phil. 114/C3
Sara Buri, Thai. 120/C3
Sarāb, Iran 129/F2
Sarābiyūm, Egypt 139/D3
Saraceno (peak), It. 92/D5
Saraf Doungous, Chad 142/C2
Sarafjagān, Iran 129/G3
Saragosa, Tx, US 177/C2
Saragossa (Zaragoza), Sp. 73/E2
Saraguro, Ecu. 208/B1
Sarāi Alamgir, Pak. 124/B3
Sarāi Sidhu, Pak. 124/A4
Saraikela, India 123/E4
Sarāil, Bang. 123/H3
Saraipāli, India 121/D1
Sarajevo (cap.), Bosn. 76/D4
Saraktash, Rus. 97/L2
Saraland, Al, US 190/D2
Saramabila, D.R. Congo 147/F4
Saramacca (dist.), Sur. 205/H3
Saramati (peak), India 112/B3
Sarampiuni, Bol. 208/D4
Saran, Fr. 83/G5
Saran (peak), Indo. 116/D4
Saran', Kaz. 125/B2
Saranac Lake, NY, US 187/J2
Saranda, Tanz. 145/A3
Sarandapótamos (riv.), Gre. 75/N8
Sarandë, Alb. 75/G3
Sarandi, Braz. 213/F3
Sarandí de Navarro, Uru. 215/K10
Sarandí del Yi, Uru. 215/G2
Sarandí Grande, Uru. 215/K10
Sārangagada, India 121/E1
Sarangami (isls.), Phil. 117/G2
Sarangani (isls.), Phil. 114/D4
Sārangarh, India 121/D1
Sārangpur, India 118/C3
Saranley, Som. 145/C1
Saransk, Rus. 97/H1
Sarapul, Rus. 95/M4
Sarare (riv.), Ven. 204/D3

Sāraskheri, India 122/A3
Sarasota, Fl, US 191/G4
Sarata, Ukr. 77/J2
Saratoga, Ca, US 193/K12
Saratoga, Wy, US 173/K3
Saratoga Nat'l Hist. Park, NY, US 187/K3
Saratoga Springs, NY, US 187/K3
Saratok, Malay. 116/D3
Saratov (res.), Rus. 97/J1
Saratov, Rus. 97/H2
Saratov Oblast, Rus. 97/H2
Saravan, Laos 120/D3
Sarawaget (range), PNG 155/G1
Sarawak (reg.), Malay. 103/L9
Saray, Turk. 77/H5
Saraya, Sen. 140/C3
Sarayacu, Ecu. 204/B5
Sarāyan (riv.), India 122/C2
Sarayköy, Turk. 128/B2
Sarayönü, Turk. 128/C2
Sarbāz, Iran 127/H3
Sarbhāng, Bhu. 123/H2
Sárbogárd, Hun. 76/D2
Sarcari, Bol. 212/C2
Sarcelles, Fr. 56/K5
Sarco, Chile 212/B4
Sarcoxie, Mo, US 179/G2
Sārda (riv.), India 122/C1
Sārda (canal), India 122/C2
Sarda (riv.), India 118/D2
Sardara, It. 74/A3
Sardārpura, India 124/B5
Sardārshahar, India 124/C5
Sardegna (prov.), It. 74/A2
Sardhana, India 124/D5
Sardinata, Col. 204/C2
Sardinia (isl.), It. 74/A2
Sardinia, Oh, US 188/F1
Sardis (dam), Ms, US 188/C3
Sardis, Ms, US 188/C3
Sardis, Tx, US 176/L7
Sardis, Ga, US 189/G4
Sardis (lake), Ms, US 188/C3
Sareks NP, Swe. 64/F2
Sarektjåkko (peak), Swe 64/F2
Sarempaka (peak), Indo. 117/E4
Sārenga, India 123/F4
Sarentino, It. 87/H4
Sarepta, La, US 179/H4
Sarezzo, It. 88/D2
Sargans, Swi. 87/F3
Sargents, Co, US 175/J1
Sargodha, Pak. 124/B3
Sarh, Chad 142/C3
Sārī, Iran 129/H2
Sari (cape), Malay. 115/C2
Sari-Solenzara, Fr. 74/A2
Saria, India 124/C3
Saribi (cape), Indo. 117/J4
Sarigan (isl.), NMar. 162/D3
Sarigazi (arpt.), Turk. 129/N7
Sarıgöl, Turk. 128/B2
Sarıkamış, Turk. 128/E1
Sarikaya (prov.), Turk. 96/E5
Sarıkaya, Turk. 96/E5
Sarikei, Malay. 116/D3
Sarina, Austl. 160/C3
Sarine (riv.), Swi. 71/G3
Sariñena, Sp. 73/E2
Sarīr Kalanshiyū (des.), Libya 134/D3
Sarīr Kalanshiyū ar Ramlī al Kabīr (des.), Libya 134/D2
Sarīr Tibasti (des.), Libya 134/C4
Sarita, Tx, US 177/F4
Sariwŏn, NKor. 107/C3
Sarju (riv.), India 122/C1
Sark (isl.), Fr. 82/C2
Sark (isl.), Chl, UK 70/B2
Sarkad, Hun. 76/E2
Sarkant, Kaz. 100/H5
Särkijärvi (lake), Fin. 65/D4
Şarkîkaraağaç, Turk. 128/B2
Şarkışla, Turk. 128/D2
Şarköy, Turk. 77/H5
Sarlat-la-Canéda, Fr. 70/D4
Sarleinsbach, Aus. 85/G5
Sarmato, It. 88/C3
Sarmeola, It. 89/E3
Sarmi, Indo. 117/J4
Sarmiento, Arg. 214/C5
Sarmiento (peak), Chile 215/C7
Särna, Swe. 66/E1
Sarnano, It. 92/C1
Sarnen, Swi. 87/E4
Sarnia, On, Can. 186/E3
Sarnico, It. 88/C2
Sarno, It. 92/D6
Sarny, Ukr. 98/D2
Saroako, Indo. 117/F4
Sarolangun, Indo. 115/C3
Saroma (lake), Japan 108/C1
Saronic (gulf), Gre. 93/J3
Saronno, It. 88/C2
Saros (gulf), Turk. 96/C4
Sárospatak, Hun. 69/L4
Sarpsborg, Nor. 66/D2
Sarralbe, Fr. 81/G6
Sarras, Fr. 90/A2
Sarratt, Eng, UK 56/B1
Sarre (riv.), Fr. 80/F6
Sarre-Union, Fr. 81/G6
Sarrebourg, Fr. 81/G6
Sarreguemines, Fr. 81/G5
Sarria, Sp. 72/B1
Sarrians, Fr. 90/A4
Sarroch, It. 74/A3
Sarry, Fr. 81/D6
Sarsāwa, India 124/D4
Sarsina, It. 89/F6
Särsö (isl.), Swe. 65/B1
Sarstedt, Ger. 79/G4
Sarstsún (riv.), Guat. 200/D3
Sartang (riv.), Rus. 101/P3
Sarteano, It. 74/B1
Sartell, Mn, US 183/G5
Sartène, Fr. 74/A2
Sarthe (dept.), Fr. 83/F4
Sarthe (riv.), Fr. 70/C3
Sarthon (riv.), Fr. 83/E4
Sartilly, Fr. 82/D3
Sartrouville, Fr. 56/J5
Sarufutsu, Japan 108/C1
Saruhanlı, Turk. 96/C5
Şärur, Azer. 129/F2
Sárvár, Hun. 76/C2
Sarvestān, Iran 129/H4
Sárvíz (riv.), Hun. 76/D2
Sary Ishikotrau (des.), Kaz 125/C2
Saryagach, Kaz. 125/A3
Sarybasat, Kaz. 97/M3
Sarych (cape), Ukr. 99/G5
Saryg-Sep, Rus. 125/G1
Sarygamysh Köli (lake), Trkm. 97/L4
Saryshaghan, Kaz. 125/B2
Sarysu (riv.), Kaz. 100/G5
Sarzana, It. 88/C5
Sarzeau, Fr. 82/C5
Sas Van Gent, Neth. 80/C1
Sa'sa', Syria 131/E2
Sasabe, Az, US 175/G5
Sasaginnigack (lake), Mb, Can. 183/G2
Sasak, Indo. 115/B2
Sasarām, India 123/E3
Sasayama, Japan 109/H5
Sasayama (riv.), Japan 109/H5
Sásd, Hun. 76/D2
Sasebo, Japan 110/A4
Sashima, Japan 109/D1
Saskatchewan (riv.), Can. 165/G4
Saskatchewan (prov.), Can. 166/F3
Saskatoon, Sk, Can. 171/L1
Saslaya (mtn.), Nic. 200/E3
Saslaya, PN, Nic. 200/E3
Sāsni, India 122/B2
Sasolburg, SAfr. 150/D2
Sasoma, India 124/D2
Sasovo, Rus. 97/G1
Sassafras (peak), Tn, US 188/E3
Sassafras (mtn.), SC, US 189/F3
Sassafras, Md, US 194/C5
Sassafras (riv.), Md, US 194/B5
Sassandra, C.d'Iv. 140/D5
Sassandra (riv.), C.d'Iv. 140/D5
Sassari, It. 74/A2
Sasse (riv.), Fr. 90/C4
Sassello, It. 88/B5
Sassenage, Fr. 90/B2
Sassenberg, Ger. 79/F4
Sassenheim, Neth. 78/B4
Sasser, Ga, US 191/F2
Sassnitz, Ger. 66/E4
Sasso Marconi, It. 89/E5
Sassocorvaro, It. 89/F6
Sassoferrato, It. 89/F7
Sassoumbouroum, Niger 141/H3
Sasstown, Libr. 140/C5
Sassuolo, It. 89/D4
Sástago, Sp. 73/E2
Sastre, Arg. 212/D4
Sasykkol (lake), Kaz. 125/D2
Sata-misaki (cape), Japan 110/B5
Satadougou Tintiba, Mali 140/C3
Satara, SAfr. 149/F5
Satawan (isl.), Micr. 162/E4
Satellite Beach, Fl, US 191/H3
Satema, CAfr. 142/D4
Säter, Swe. 66/F1
Saticoy, Ca, US 192/A2
Satilla (riv.), Ga, US 191/G2
Satillieu, Fr. 90/A2
Satipo, Peru 208/C3
Satis, Rus. 95/J5
Sātkānia, Bang. 123/J4
Sātkhira, Bang. 123/G4
Satley, Eng, UK 61/G2
Satna, India 122/C3
Satolas (Lyon) (int'l arpt.), Fr. 86/B6
Sátoraljaújhely, Hun. 69/L4
Satpayev, Kaz. 125/A2
Satpura (range), India 118/C3
Sætre, Nor. 64/S8
Satsuma, Al, US 190/D2
Satsuma, Tx, US 177/M9
Sattahip, Thai. 120/C3
Satte, Japan 109/D1
Satteins, Aus. 87/F3
Satteldorf, Ger. 84/D4
Sattleberg, PNG 155/G1
Sättra, Swe. 65/A1
Satu Mare, Rom. 69/M5
Satu Mare (co.), Rom. 69/M5
Satuk, Thai. 120/C3
Satun, Thai. 120/C5
Satupaitea, WSam. 163/R9
Saturna, BC, Can. 170/C3
Sauce, Arg. 212/E4
Sauce, Peru 208/B2
Sauce de Luna, Arg 212/E4
Sauce Grande (riv.), Arg. 214/E3
Saucedo, Uru. 212/E4
Saucier, Ms, US 190/D2
Saucillo, Mex. 177/B3
Sauda, Nor. 66/B2
Saudhárkrókur, Ice. 64/N6
Saudi Arabia (ctry.) 103/B7
Sauer (riv.), Ger. 79/F5
Sauerlach, Ger. 87/H2
Sauerland (reg.), Ger. 68/D3
Sauêruiná (riv.), Braz. 209/G4
Saugatuck, Mi, US 186/C3
Saugatuck (riv.), Ct, US 195/E1
Saugeen (riv.), On, Can. 186/F2
Saugeen Ind. Res., On, Can. 186/F2
Saugerties, NY, US 187/K3
Sauiá, Braz. 206/B3
Saujon, Fr. 70/C4
Sauk (riv.), Mn, US 181/G1
Sauk Centre, Mn, US 183/G5
Sauk City, Wi, US 181/K2
Sauk Rapids, Mn, US 183/G5
Saukkola, Fin. 65/D4
Saül, FrG. 206/C2
Sauland, Nor. 66/C2
Saulce-sur-Rhône, Fr. 90/A3
Sauldre (riv.), Fr. 70/D3
Saulgau, Ger. 87/F1
Saulheim, Ger. 84/B3
Saulieu, Fr. 70/F3
Saulkrasti, Lat. 67/L3
Saulnierville, NS, Can. 184/D3
Sault, Fr. 90/B4
Sault aux Cochons (riv.), Qu, Can. 184/C1
Sault Sainte Marie, On, Can. 186/D1
Sault Sainte Marie, Mi, US 186/D1
Sault-lès-Rethel, Fr. 81/D5
Saulx, Fr. 86/C2
Saulx (riv.), Fr. 68/C4
Saulxures-sur-Moselotte, Fr. 86/C2
Saumlaki, Indo. 154/C1
Saumur, Fr. 83/E6
Saunders (cape), NZ 161/B4
Saunders (peak), Austl. 156/E3
Saundersfoot, Wal, UK 62/B3
Saura (riv.), India 123/F3
Saurimo, Ang. 147/E5
Sausalito, Ca, US 193/J11
Sausseron (riv.), Fr. 56/J4
Sausset-les-Pins, Fr. 90/B6
Sausu, Indo. 117/F4
Saut-Tigre, FrG. 206/C1
Sautatá, Col. 204/B3
Sautet (lake), Fr. 90/B3
Sauteurs, Gren. 205/F1
Sautron, Fr. 82/D6
Sauzon, Fr. 82/B6
Sava, It. 75/E2
Sava (riv.), Eur. 93/J1
Savá, Hon. 200/E3
Savage, Mt, US 182/B4
Savage (mtn.), Md, US 187/G5
Savage (dam), Ca, US 192/D5
Savage, Mn, US 183/P7
Savage River, Austl. 158/C4
Savai'i (isl.), WSam. 163/H6
Savalou, Ben. 141/F5
Savanna, Ok, US 179/G3
Savanna, Il, US 181/J2
Savanna-la-Mar, Jam. 201/G2
Savannah (riv.), US 165/J6
Savannah, Mo, US 181/G4
Savannah, Tn, US 188/C3
Savannah (brook), Austl. 156/L6
Savannah, Ga, US 189/G4
Savannah NWR, Ga, US 191/H1
Savannah River Plant, SC, US 189/G4
Savannakhet, Laos 120/D2
Savant (lake), On, Can. 183/J2
Savant Lake, On, Can. 183/J2
Sävar, Swe. 64/G3
Savaştepe, Turk. 96/C5
Savate, Ang. 148/C3
Savé, Ben. 141/F4
Save (riv.), Moz. 133/F7
Save (riv.), Zim. 149/G4
Sāveh, Iran 129/G3
Savena (riv.), It. 89/E4
Savenay, Fr. 82/D6
Săveni, Rom. 98/D4
Saverdun, Fr. 70/D5
Saverne, Fr. 81/G6
Savièse, Swi. 86/D5
Savigliano, It. 90/D3
Savignano sul Panaro, It. 89/E5
Savignano sul Rubicone, It. 89/F5
Savigné-L'Évêque, Fr. 83/F4
Savigny-le-Temple, Fr. 56/K6
Savigny-sur-Braye, Fr. 83/F5
Savigny-sur-Orge, Fr. 56/K5
Savines-le-Lac, Fr. 90/C3
Saviniemi, Fin. 65/E3
Sävja, Swe. 66/G2
Savognin, Swi. 87/F4
Savoie (dept.), Fr. 86/C6
Savona, It. 88/B5
Savona (prov.), It. 88/B4
Savona, BC, Can. 170/D2
Savonburg, Ks, US 179/G2
Savoy, Tx, US 179/F4
Savoy, Il, US 186/B4
Savoy (reg.), Fr. 92/E1
Savoy, SD, US 180/C1
Savoy, Mt, US 171/K3
Savoy Alps (mts.), Fr. 86/C6
Şavşat, Turk. 97/G4
Sävsjö, Swe. 66/F3
Savu (sea), Phil. 103/M10
Savusavu, Fiji 163/Z17
Sawahlunto, Indo. 115/C3
Sawākin, Sudan 135/H5
Sawang Daeh Din, Thai. 120/C2
Sawankhalok, Thai. 120/B2
Sawara, Japan 111/G3
Sawasaki-bana (pt.), Japan 111/F2
Sawatch (range), Co, US 180/A4
Sawbridgeworth, Eng, UK 63/G3
Sawdā', Jabal (peak), SAr. 126/D5
Sawdirī, Sudan 142/F2
Saweba (cape), Indo. 117/H4
Sawel (mtn.), NI, UK 60/A2
Sawena, Eth. 144/B4
Sāwi, India 119/F6
Sawkanah, Libya 134/B2
Sawmills, Zim. 149/F3
Sawpit, Co, US 175/H2
Sawston, Eng, UK 63/G2
Sawtell, Austl. 158/E1
Sawtooth (range), Id, US 173/F1
Sawtooth (mtn.), Mt, US 171/K3
Sawtooth Nat'l Rec. Area, Id, US 173/F1
Sawu, Indo. 154/A2
Sawu (isl.), Indo. 154/A2
Sawu (isls.), Indo. 117/F6
Sawyer, ND, US 182/D3
Sawyer, Ks, US 179/E2
Sawyers Bar, Ca, US 172/B3
Sax, Sp. 73/E3
Saxån (riv.), Swe. 65/K7
Saxarfjärden (sound), Swe. 65/B1
Saxilby, Eng, UK 61/H5
Saxis, Va, US 189/K2
Saxmundham, Eng, UK 63/H2
Saxon, Swi. 86/D5
Say, Niger 141/F3
Say-Utes, Kaz. 97/K3
Saya, Japan 109/L5
Saya, Bol. 212/C1
Sayabec, Qu, Can. 184/D1
Sayak, Kaz. 100/H5
Sayama, Japan 111/F3
Sayama, Japan 109/J6
Sayán, Peru 208/B3
Sayansk, Rus. 104/E1
Şaydā (Sidon), Leb. 131/C1
Şaydnāyā, Syria 131/E1
Sayḩūt, Yem. 144/D2
Sayil (ruin), Mex. 200/D1
Sayingpan, China 112/D3
Saykhin, Kaz. 97/H2
Saylah, Egypt 139/B6
Saynbach (riv.), Ger. 81/G2
Sayner, Wi, US 183/K5
Sayram (lake), China 125/D3
Sayre, Ok, US 178/E3
Sayre, Pa, US 187/H4
Sayreville, NJ, US 195/H10
Saysu, China 125/F3
Sayula, Mex. 198/E5
Sayville, NY, US 195/E2
Saywūn, Yem. 144/D2
Sazan (isl.), Alb. 75/F2
Sazan (isl.), Gre. 76/D5
Sazdy, Kaz. 97/J3
Sazīn, Pak. 124/B2
Sazli Dere (riv.), Turk. 129/M6
Sbaa, Alg. 137/E3
Scaër, Fr. 82/B4
Scafati, It. 92/D6
Scafell Pikes (peak), Eng, UK 61/E3
Scalasaig, Sc, UK 57/Q8
Scalby, Eng, UK 61/H3
Scald Law (peak), Sc, UK 59/C5
Scalea, It. 74/D3
Scalino (peak), It. 87/F5
Scalloway, Sc, UK 57/W13
Scandia, Ab, Can. 171/H2
Scandia, Ks, US 180/F4
Scandia, Mn, US 183/Q6
Scandia, Wa, US 193/B2
Scandiano, It. 89/D4
Scandicci, It. 89/E6
Scanlon, Mn, US 183/H4
Scanno, It. 92/C4
Scapa Flow (chan.), Sc, UK 57/V14
Scar Water (riv.), Sc, UK 60/E1
Scarborough, Eng, UK 61/H3
Scarborough, Trin. 205/F2
Scarborough (nbrhd.), Austl. 156/K6
Scarborough (co.), On, Can. 186/U8
Scarborough Shoal (isl.), Phil. 114/B2
Scardovari, It. 89/F4
Scarinish, Sc, UK 57/Q8
Scarpe (riv.), Fr. 68/B3
Scarperia, It. 89/E6
Scarriff, Ire. 58/B4
Scarsdale, NY, US 195/K7
Scatarie (isl.), Ns., Can. 185/H3
Scattery (isl.), Ire. 58/A4
Scauri, It. 92/C5
Sceaux, Fr. 56/J5
Scerni, It. 92/D3
Scey-sur-Saône-et-St-Albin, Fr. 86/B2
Schaefferstown, Pa, US 194/B3
Schaerbeek, Belg. 81/D2
Schaffer, Mi, US 183/L5
Schaffhausen, Swi. 87/E2
Schaffhausen (canton), Swi. 87/E2
Schäftlarn, Ger. 87/H2
Schagen, Neth. 78/B3
Schaijk, Neth. 78/C5
Schalchen, Aus. 85/G6
Schalkau, Ger. 84/E2
Schalksmühle, Ger. 79/E6
Schaller, Ia, US 181/G2
Schanck (cape), Austl. 159/B4
Schangnau, Swi. 86/D4
Scharans, Swi. 87/F4
Schardenberg, Aus. 85/G5
Schärding, Aus. 85/G6
Scharfreiter (peak), Aus. 87/H3
Scharhorn (isl.), Ger. 79/F1
Scharnebeck, Ger. 79/H2
Scharnhorst (pt.), PNG 155/G1
Scharnitz (pass), Ger. 87/H3
Scharnstein, Aus. 85/G7
Schashagen, Ger. 68/F1
Schattdorf, Swi. 87/E4
Schauenstein, Ger. 85/E2
Schaumburg, Il, US 193/P15
Scheemda, Neth. 78/D2
Scheer, Ger. 87/F1
Scheessel, Ger. 79/G2
Schefferville, Qu, Can. 167/K3
Scheibbs, Aus. 69/H4
Scheidegg, Ger. 87/F2
Scheinfeld, Ger. 84/D3
Schelde (riv.), Belg. 80/C2
Scheldt (riv.), Belg. 70/E1
Schelklingen, Ger. 84/C6
Schell City, Mo, US 179/G1
Schell Creek (range), Nv, US 173/F4
Schellerten, Ger. 79/H4
Schellville, Ca, US 193/K10
Schenectady, NY, US 187/K3
Schenefeld, Ger. 79/G1
Schererville, In, US 186/C4
Schermbeck, Ger. 78/D5
Scherpenzeel, Neth. 78/C3
Schertz, Tx, US 177/E3
Schesaplana (peak), Aus. 87/F3
Schesslitz, Ger. 84/E3
Scheveningen, Neth. 78/B4
Scheyern, Ger. 85/E5
Schiedam, Neth. 78/B5
Schieder-Schwalenberg, Ger. 79/G5
Schiehallon (peak), Sc, UK 59/B3
Schier Monnikoog (isl.), Neth. 68/D2
Schierling, Ger. 85/F5
Schiermonnikoog (isl.), Neth. 78/D1
Schiermonnikoog, Neth. 78/D2
Schiers, Swi. 87/F4
Schifferstadt, Ger. 84/B4
Schiffweiler, Ger. 81/G5
Schijndel, Neth. 78/C5
Schilde, Belg. 78/B6
Schildmeer (lake), Neth. 78/D2
Schillighörn (cape), Ger. 79/F1
Schillingfürst, Ger. 84/D4
Schiltach, Ger. 87/E1
Schiltigheim, Fr. 86/D1
Schinnen, Neth. 81/E2
Schinznach-Dorf, Swi. 86/E3
Schio, It. 89/E2
Schipbeek (riv.), Neth. 78/D4
Schiphol, Neth. 78/B4
Schipol (Amsterdam) (int'l arpt.), Neth. 78/B4
Schirmeck, Fr. 86/D1
Schkumbin (riv.), Alb. 75/G2
Schladen, Ger. 79/H4
Schladming, Aus. 71/K3
Schlanders (Silandro), It. 87/G4
Schlangen, Ger. 79/F5
Schlangenbad, Ger. 84/B2
Schlater, Ms, US 188/B4
Schleiden, Ger. 81/F2
Schleitheim, Swi. 87/E2
Schleiz, Ger. 85/E1
Schlema, Ger. 85/F1
Schleswig, Ger. 66/C4
Schleswig, Ia, US 181/G2
Schleswig-Holstein (state), Ger. 66/B4
Schleswig-Holsteinisches Wattenmeer NP, Ger. 66/C4
Schleuse (riv.), Ger. 84/D2
Schleusingen, Ger. 84/D1
Schliengen, Ger. 86/D2
Schlierbach, Aus. 85/H7
Schlieren, Swi. 87/E3
Schloss Herrenchiemsee, Ger. 85/F7
Schloss Holte-Stukenbrock, Ger. 79/F5
Schloss Sansoucci, Ger. 68/Q7
Schloss Wilhelmstein, Ger. 79/G4
Schlotheim, Ger. 79/H6
Schluchsee, Ger. 86/E2
Schlüchtern, Ger. 84/C2
Schluderns (Sluderno), It. 87/G4
Schlüsselfeld, Ger. 84/D3
Schlüsslberg, Aus. 85/G6
Schmallenberg, Ger. 79/F6
Schmeich (riv.), Ger. 84/C6
Schmelz, Ger. 81/F5
Schmiech (riv.), Ger. 87/F1
Schmitten, Swi. 86/D4
Schmitten, Ger. 84/B2
Schmutter (riv.), Ger. 84/D5
Schnaitsee, Ger. 85/F6
Schnaittach, Ger. 85/E3
Schnaittenbach, Ger. 85/F3
Schnarrtanne, Ger. 85/F1
Schnecksville, Pa, US 194/C2
Schneeberg (peak), Ger. 85/E2
Schneeberg, Ger. 85/F1
Schneeberg, Ger. 84/C3
Schneifel (upland), Ger. 68/D3
Schneverdingen, Ger. 79/G2
Schoenchen, Ks, US 178/E1
Schofield, Wi, US 181/K1
Schoharie, NY, US 187/J3
Scholle, NM, US 175/J3
Schollene, Ger. 68/G2
Schöllkrippen, Ger. 84/C2
Schömberg, Ger. 87/E1
Schömberg, Ger. 84/B5
Schönaich, Ger. 84/C5
Schönau im Schwarzwald, Ger. 86/D2
Schönberg, Ger. 66/D4
Schönberg, Ger. 85/G5
Schönbrunn, Ger. 84/D1
Schondorf am Ammersee, Ger. 87/H1
Schondra (riv.), Ger. 84/C2
Schönebeck, Ger. 68/F2
Schöneck, Ger. 84/B2
Schöneck, Ger. 85/F2
Schönecken, Ger. 81/F3
Schönefeld (int'l arpt.), Ger. 68/Q7
Schöneiche, Ger. 68/Q7
Schongau, Ger. 87/G2
Schöningen, Ger. 68/F2
Schönow, Ger. 68/Q6
Schönsee, Ger. 85/F3
Schonungen, Ger. 84/D2
Schönwald, Ger. 85/E2
Schoolcraft, Mi, US 186/D3
Schoonebeek, Neth. 78/D3
Schoonhoven, Neth. 78/B5
Schoorl, Neth. 78/B3
Schopfheim, Ger. 86/D2
Schopfheim, Ger. 81/G4
Schopfloch, Ger. 84/D4
Schöppenstedt, Ger. 79/H4
Schörfling, Aus. 85/G7
Schorndorf, Ger. 84/C5
Schortens, Ger. 79/E1
Schoten, Belg. 78/B6
Schotten, Ger. 84/C1
Schouten (isls.), Indo. 162/C5
Schouten (isl.), Austl. 158/D4
Schouwen (isl.), Neth. 78/A5
Schramberg, Ger. 87/E1
Schrankogel (peak), Aus. 87/H3
Schreckhorn (peak), Swi. 86/E4
Schreiber, On, Can. 183/L3
Schriesheim, Ger. 84/B4
Schriever, La, US 190/C3
Schrobenhausen, Ger. 84/E5
Schroeder, Mn, US 183/J4
Schroffenstein (peak), Namb. 150/B2
Schrozberg, Ger. 84/C4
Schruns, Aus. 87/F3
Schübelbach, Swi. 87/E3
Schuby, Ger. 66/C4
Schulenburg, Tx, US 177/F3
Schuler, Ab, Can. 171/J2
Schulter, Ok, US 179/G3
Schulzendorf, Ger. 68/Q7
Schunter (riv.), Ger. 79/H4
Schüpfheim, Swi. 86/E4
Schurz, Nv, US 172/D4
Schussen (riv.), Ger. 87/F2
Schussenried, Ger. 87/F1
Schutter (riv.), Ger. 84/A6
Schutterwald, Ger. 86/D1
Schüttorf, Ger. 79/E4
Schuyler, Ne, US 181/F3
Schuylkill (riv.), Pa, US 194/C3
Schuylkill (co.), Pa, US 194/B2
Schuylkill Haven, Pa US 194/B2
Schwabach, Ger. 84/D4
Schwabhausen bei Dachau, Ger. 85/E6
Schwäbisch Gmünd, Ger. 84/C5
Schwäbisch Hall, Ger. 84/C4
Schwäbische Alb (range), Ger. 68/E4
Schwabmünchen, Ger. 87/G1
Schwaig bei Nürnberg, Ger. 84/E4
Schwaigern, Ger. 84/C4
Schwalbach, Ger. 81/F5
Schwalbach am Taunus, Ger. 84/B2
Schwalm (riv.), Ger. 68/E3
Schwalmtal, Ger. 78/D6
Schwanden, Swi. 87/F4
Schwandorf im Bayern, Ger. 85/F4
Schwanebeck, Ger. 68/Q6
Schwanenstadt, Aus. 85/G6
Schwaner (mts.), Indo. 116/D4
Schwanewede, Ger. 79/F2
Schwanfeld, Ger. 84/D3
Schwangau, Ger. 87/G2
Schwarmstedt, Ger. 79/G3
Schwartz Elster (riv.), Ger. 69/G3
Schwartzerberg (peak), Namb. 150/B2
Schwarza (riv.), Ger. 84/E1
Schwarzach, Ger. 85/F5
Schwarzach (riv.), Ger. 85/E4
Schwarzach im Pongau, Aus. 71/K3
Schwarze Laber (riv.), Ger. 85/E4
Schwarzenbach am Wald, Ger. 85/E2
Schwarzenbek, Ger. 79/H1
Schwarzenberg, Ger. 85/F1
Schwarzenbruck, Ger. 84/E4
Schwarzenburg, Swi. 86/D4
Schwarzenfeld, Ger. 85/F4
Schwarzer Mann (peak), Ger. 81/F3
Schwarzhorn (peak), Aus. 87/H3
Schwarzrand (mts.), Namb. 148/C5
Schwarzwald (Black Forest) (for.), Ger. 84/B6
Schwaz, Aus. 71/J3
Schwebheim, Ger. 84/D3
Schwechat, Aus. 77/N7
Schwechat (int'l arpt.), Aus. 77/P7
Schwedt, Ger. 69/H2
Schwegenheim, Ger. 84/B4
Schweich, Ger. 81/F4
Schweighouse-sur-Moder, Fr. 81/G6
Schweinfurt, Ger. 84/D2
Schweitenkirchen, Ger. 85/E5
Schweizer-Reneke, SAfr. 150/D2
Schwelm, Ger. 79/E6
Schwendi, Ger. 87/F1
Schwenksville, Pa, US 194/C3
Schwerin, Ger. 66/D5
Schweriner (lake), Ger. 68/F2
Schwertberg, Aus. 85/H6
Schwerte, Ger. 79/E6
Schwetzingen, Ger. 84/B4
Schwinge (riv.), Ger. 79/G1
Schwörstadt, Ger. 86/D2
Schwülme (riv.), Ger. 79/G5
Schwülper, Ger. 79/H4
Schwyz (canton), Swi. 87/E3
Schwyz, Swi. 87/E3
Sciacca, It. 74/C4
Scicli, It. 74/D4
Science Hill, Ky, US 188/E2
Science Museum of Minnesota, Mn, US 183/P7
Scilly (isls.), Eng, UK 57/Q11
Ścinawa, Pol. 69/J3
Scio, Or, US 172/B1
Scionzier, Fr. 86/C5
Sciota, Pa, US 194/C2
Scioto (riv.), Oh, US 189/F1
Sclater, Mb, Can. 182/D2
Scobey, Mt, US 171/M3
Scofield (res.), Ut, US 173/H4
Scolt (pt.), Eng, UK 63/G1
Scone, Austl. 158/D2
Scooba, Ms, US 188/C4
Scopello, It. 88/B2
Scordia, It. 74/D4
Scorff (riv.), Fr. 82/B5
Scorzè, It. 89/F2
Scotch Corner, Eng, UK 61/G3
Scotch Creek, BC, Can. 170/E2
Scotch Plains, NJ, US 195/H9
Scotchman (peak), Id, US 170/F3
Scotia(sea) 216/W
Scotia, Ca, US 172/A3
Scotland, Tx, US 179/E4
Scotland, UK 60/D1
Scotland Neck, NC, US 189/J2
Scots Bay, NS, Can. 184/E3
Scotstown, Ire. 58/C1
Scott (cape), Austl. 154/C3
Scott (cape), BC, Can. 166/D3
Scott (cape), NW, Can. 167/R7
Scott (lake), NW, Can. 166/F2
Scott, Sk, Can. 171/K1
Scott, NZ, Ant. 216/M
Scott (riv.), Ca, US 172/B3
Scott (A.F.B.), Il, US 181/K4
Scott (co.), Mn, US 183/N7
Scott (mt.), Ok, US 179/E3
Scott City, Ks, US 178/D1
Scott City, Mo, US 188/C2
Scott NP, Austl. 156/B5
Scott Reef (reef), Austl. 154/A3
Scott Reef(reef) 153/B2
Scottburgh, SAfr. 151/E3
Scottdale, Pa, US 187/G4
Scottdale, Ga, US 189/M7
Scotts (cr.), Austl. 157/M9
Scotts Bluff Nat'l Mon., Ne, US 180/C3
Scotts Hill, Tn, US 188/C3
Scotts Peak (dam), Austl. 158/C4
Scottsbluff, Ne, US 180/C3
Scottsboro, Al, US 188/D3
Scottsburg, In, US 188/E1
Scottsdale, Austl. 158/C4
Scottsdale, Az, US 175/G4
Scottsmoor, Fl, US 191/H3
Scottsville, Ky, US 188/D2
Scottville, Mi, US 186/C3
Scotty's Castle, Ca, US 174/D2
Scoudouc, NB, Can. 184/E2
Scourie, Sc, UK 57/R7
Scranton, ND, US 182/C4
Scranton, Pa, US 187/J4
Scranton, SC, US 189/H4
Scraper, Ok, US 179/G2
Screven, Ga, US 191/G2
Scribner, Ne, US 181/F3
Scripps Aquarium/Museum, Ca, US 192/C5
Scrivia (riv.), It. 88/B3
Scunthorpe, Eng, UK 61/H4
Scuol, Swi. 87/G4
Scuppernong (riv.), Wi, US 193/N14
Scurdie Ness (pt.), Sc, UK 59/D3
Scurry, Tx, US 176/L7
Scutari (lake), Yugo. 75/F1
Scye (riv.), Fr. 82/D2
Sea (isls.), Ga, US 169/K5
Sea (isls.), Ga, SC, US 189/G5
Sea Cliff, Ca, US 192/A2
Sea Cliff, NY, US 195/L8
Sea Girt, NJ, US 194/D3
Sea Isle City, NJ, US 194/D5
Sea Lake, Austl. 158/B2
Sea Pines, SC, US 189/G4
Sea Ranch Lakes, Fl, US 190/P10
Sea World of Florida, Fl, US 190/N7
Sea-Tac, Wa, US 193/C3
Seabeck, Wa, US 193/B2
Seaboard, NC, US 189/J2
Seabold, Wa, US 193/B2
Seabra, Braz. 211/E2
Seabrook, NH, US 187/L3
Seabrook, NJ, US 194/C5
Seabrook, SC, US 189/G4
Seabrook, Tx, US 177/M9
Seadrift, Tx, US 176/F3
Seaford, Eng, UK 63/G5
Seaford, NY, US 195/M9
Seaford, De, US 189/K1
Seaforde, NI, UK 60/C3
Seaforth, On, Can. 186/F3
Seaforth, Austl. 160/C3
Seagoville, Tx, US 176/L7
Seagraves, Tx, US 178/C4
Seaham, Eng, UK 61/G2
Seahorse (pt.), Nun, Can. 167/J2
Seahurst, Wa, US 193/C3
Seal (isl.), Me, US 184/C4
Seal, Eng, UK 56/D3
Seal (riv.), MB, Can. 166/G3
Seal (pt.), Chile 214/B5
Seal (cape), SAfr. 150/C4
Seal Beach, Ca, US 192/F8
Seal Beach NWR, Ca, US 192/F8
Seal Cove, NS, Can. 184/D3
Seal Cove, Nf, Can. 185/J2
Seale, Eng, UK 56/A3
Seale, Al, US 188/E4
Sealy, Tx, US 176/F3
Seaman, Oh, US 188/F1
Seamer, Eng, UK 61/H3
Seano, It. 89/E6
Searchlight, Nv, US 174/E3
Searchmont, On, Can. 186/D1
Searcy, Ar, US 179/J3
Seascale, Eng, UK 60/E3
Seaside, Ca, US 174/B2
Seaside, Or, US 170/C5
Seaside Heights, NJ, US 194/D4
Seaside Park, NJ, US 194/D4
Seaton, Eng, UK 62/C5
Seaton (riv.), Eng, UK 62/B6
Seaton Carew, Eng, UK 61/G2
Seattle, Wa, US 170/C4
Seattle Art Museum, Wa, US 193/C2
Seattle Center, Wa, US 193/C2
Seattle-Tacoma (int'l arpt.), Wa, US 170/C4
Seatuck Nat'l Wild. Ref., NY, US 195/E2
Seba, Indo. 154/A2
Sébaco, Nic. 200/E3
Sebago (lake), Me, US 187/L3
Sebaou (riv.), Alg. 138/H4
Sebastian, Fl, US 191/H4
Sebastian, Tx, US 177/F4
Sebastián Vizcaíno (bay), Mex. 198/B2
Sebastopol, Austl. 159/A3
Sebastopol, Ca, US 172/B4
Sebastopol, Ms, US 188/C4
Sebastopol, Tx, US 177/G2
Sebatik (isl.), Malay. 114/B4
Sebayan (peak), Indo. 116/D4
Sebderat, Erit. 142/H2
Sebdou, Alg. 138/D2
Sébé (riv.), Gabon 146/C3
Sebec (lake), Me, US 184/C3
Sebeka, Mn, US 183/G4
Sébékoro, Mali 140/C3
Seben, Turk. 77/K5
Sebeş, Rom. 77/F3
Sebeta, Eth. 144/A3
Sebewaing, Mi, US 186/E3
Sebezh, Rus. 67/N3
Sebina, Bots. 149/E4
Şebinkarahisar, Turk. 128/D1
Sebiş, Rom. 76/F2
Sebkhet al Kalīyah (drylake), Alg. 138/M7
Seblat, Indo. 115/C3
Sebnitz, Ger. 69/H3
Seboruco, Ven. 204/C2
Seboto (pt.), Phil. 114/C4
Sebou (riv.), Mor. 138/B2
Sebou, Oued (riv.), Mor. 136/D2
Seboyeta, NM, US 175/J3
Sebree, Ky, US 188/D2
Sebring, Fl, US 191/H4
Sebuku (isl.), Indo. 117/E4
Sebuku (bay), Indo. 114/B5
Secaucus, NJ, US 195/J8
Secchia (riv.), It. 71/J4
Sechelt, BC, Can. 170/C3
Sechura, Peru 208/A2
Sechura (bay), Peru 208/A2
Sechura, Desierto de (des.), Peru 208/A2
Seclin, Fr. 80/C2
Seco (cr.), Tx, US 177/E3
Seco (riv.), Mex.,US 175/G5
Seco (riv.), Arg. 215/D6
Seco (riv.), Mex. 199/C2
Second Cataract (falls), Sudan 135/F4
Second Mesa, Az, US 175/G3
Second Mountain (mtn.), Pa, US 194/B3
Second San Diego Aqueduct (riv.), Ca, US 192/C4
Second Watchung (mtn.), NJ, US 195/H9
Section, Al, US 188/E3
Secunda, SAfr. 150/E2
Secure (riv.), Bol. 209/E4
Security-Widefield, Co, US 178/B1
Seda, Lith. 67/K3
Sedalia, Mo, US 179/H1
Sedalia, Ab, Can. 171/J2
Sedan, Ks, US 179/F2
Sedan, NM, US 178/C2
Sedan, Fr. 81/D4
Sedano, Sp. 72/D1
Sedaung (mtn.), Myan. 120/B3
Sedayu, Indo. 115/F3
Sedbergh, Eng, UK 61/F3
Seddenga Temple (ruin), Sudan 135/F4
Seddon, NZ 161/C3
Seddonville, NZ 161/B3
Seddülbahir, Turk. 75/K2
Sedeh, Iran 127/G2
Sederot, Isr. 131/B5
Sedgefield, Eng, UK 61/G2
Sedgewick, Ab, Can. 171/J1
Sedgwick, Ks, US 179/F2
Sedhiou, Sen. 140/B3
Sedlčany, Czh. 85/H3
Sedlo (peak), Czh. 85/H1
Sedona, Az, US 175/G3
Sedot Yam, Isr. 131/B4
Sedrata, Alg. 138/K6
Sedro-Woolley, Wa, US 170/C3
Šeduva, Lith. 67/K4
Sędziszów, Pol. 69/L3
Sędziszów Małopolski, Pol. 98/A2
Sée (riv.), Fr. 70/C2
Seeb (int'l arpt.), Oman 127/G4
Seebe, Ab, Can. 170/G2
Seeboden, Aus. 71/K3
Seedskadee NWR, Wy, US 173/J3
Seefeld in Tirol, Aus. 87/H3
Seefin (peak), Ire. 58/A6
Seefin (peak), Ire. 58/C5
Seeg, Ger. 87/G2
Seehausen, Ger. 68/F2
Seeheim, Namb. 150/B2
Seeheim-Jugenheim, Ger. 84/B3
Seeis, Namb. 148/C4
Seekirchen Markt, Aus. 85/G7
Seekooi (riv.), SAfr. 150/D3
Seeley, Ca, US 174/E4
Seeley Lake, Mt, US 171/H4
Seelow, Ger. 69/H2
Seeon-Seebruck, Ger. 85/F7
Seer Green, Eng, UK 56/B2
Sées, Fr. 83/F3
Seesen, Ger. 79/H5
Seeshaupt, Ger. 87/H2
Seeve (riv.), Ger. 79/G2
Seewalchen, Aus. 85/G7
Seewis im Prättigau, Swi. 87/F4
Séez, Fr. 90/C1
Şefaatlı, Turk. 128/C2
Seffner, Fl, US 190/L8
Sefhare, Bots. 149/E4
Sefīd Rūd (riv.), Iran 129/G2
Sefrou, Mor. 138/B3
Sefton (mt.), NZ 161/B3
Segag, Eth. 144/B4
Segama (riv.), Malay. 114/B4
Segamat, Malay. 115/C2
Segarcea, Rom. 77/F3
Ségbana, Ben. 141/F4
Ségélo-Koro, C.d'Iv. 140/D4
Segelstad Bru, Nor. 66/D1
Segen Wenz (riv.), Eth. 142/H4
Seget, Indo. 117/H4
Segezha, Rus. 94/G3
Segni, It. 92/C4
Segorbe, Sp. 73/E3
Ségou, Mali 140/D3
Ségou (pol. reg.), Mali 140/D3
Segovia, Col. 204/C3
Segovia, Sp. 72/C2
Segovia, Tx, US 177/E2
Segozero (lake), Rus. 94/G3
Segrate, It. 88/C3
Segré, Fr. 83/E5
Segre (riv.), Sp. 73/F2
Seguam (isl.), Ak, US 168/V13
Séguédine, Niger 134/B4
Séguéla, C.d'Iv. 140/D5
Séguénéga, Burk. 141/E3
Seguin, Tx, US 177/F3
Segundo (riv.), Arg. 212/D4
Segura (riv.), Sp. 92/C3
Segusino, It. 89/E2
Sehithwa, Bots 148/D4
Sehnde, Ger. 79/G4
Sehonghong, Les. 150/E3
Sehore, India 118/C3
Sehwān, Pak. 127/J3
Seibersbach, Ger. 81/G4
Seiche (riv.), Fr. 82/D5
Seiches-sur-le-Loir, Fr. 83/E5
Seiersberg, Aus. 76/B2
Seika, Japan 109/J6
Seiling, Ok, US 178/E2
Seille (riv.), Fr. 68/C5
Seinäjoki, Fin. 94/D3
Seine (riv.), On, Can. 183/J3
Seine (bay), Fr. 70/C2
Seine (riv.), On, Can. 166/G4
Seine (riv.), Fr. 55/E4
Seine-et-Marne (dept.), Fr. 80/B5
Seine-Maritime (dept.), Fr. 80/A4
Seine-st-Denis (dept.), Fr. 80/B6
Seitenstetten, Aus. 85/H6
Seiwa, Japan 109/K7
Seix, Fr. 70/D5
Seixal, Port. 73/P10
Seixas (pt.), Braz. 207/H4
Sejaka, Indo. 117/E4
Sejerø (isl.), Den. 66/D4
Sejerø (flat), Den. 65/H7
Sejny, Pol. 67/K4
Sekayu, Indo. 115/C3
Seke, Tanz. 145/A2
Seke-Banza, D.R. Congo 146/C4
Sekenke, Tanz. 145/A3
Seki (riv.), Turk. 130/A1
Seki, Japan 109/L5
Seki, Japan 109/K6
Sekigahara, Japan 109/K5
Sekijo, Japan 109/D1
Sekiyado, Japan 109/D1
Sekoma, Bots. 148/D5
Sekondi, Gha. 141/E5
Sek'ot'a, Eth. 144/A2
Sel, Nor. 64/D3
Selah, Wa, US 170/D4
Selama, Malay. 115/C1
Selangor (state), Malay. 115/C2
Selantan (cape), Indo. 115/F3
Selaön (isl.), Swe. 65/A1
Selaphum, Thai. 120/C2
Selargius, It. 74/A3
Selaru (isl.), Indo. 117/H5
Selatan (cape), Indo. 116/D4
Selawik (lake), Ak, US 168/W12
Selayar (isl.), Indo. 117/F5
Selb, Ger. 85/F2
Selbitz, Ger. 85/E2
Selbitz (riv.), Ger. 85/E2
Selbu, Nor. 64/D3
Selby, SD, US 182/D5
Selby, Eng, UK 61/G4
Selby-On-The-Bay, Md, US 194/B6
Selci, It. 89/F6
Selçuk, Turk. 128/A2
Selden, Ks, US 180/D4
Selden, NY, US 195/E2
Sele (riv.), It. 74/D2
Selebi-Phikwe, Bots. 149/E4
Seleka, Bots. 149/E4
Selela (pt.), Moz. 149/J2
Seleli (hill), Tanz. 147/H5
Selemdzha (riv.), Rus. 101/N4
Selenča, Yugo. 76/D3
Selenduma, Rus. 104/F1
Selenga (riv.), Rus. 104/F1
Selenge (prov.), Mong. 104/F2
Selenge (riv.), Mong. 104/F2
Selenginsk, Rus. 104/F1
Selenicë, Alb. 75/F2
Sélestat, Fr. 86/D1
Seletar (res.), Sing. 115/J6
Selety (riv.), Kaz. 125/B1
Seletyteniz (lake), Kaz. 125/B1
Seleznëvo, Rus. 67/N1
Selfoss, Ice. 64/N7
Selfridge, ND, US 182/D4
Sélia (well), Chad 142/C2
Sélibabi, Mrta. 140/B3
Seligenstadt, Ger. 84/B2
Seliger (lake), Rus. 94/G4
Seligman, Mo, US 179/H2
Seligman, Az, US 175/F3
Selim River, Malay. 115/C2
Selimbau, Indo. 116/D3
Selimiye, Turk. 128/A2
Selinsgrove, Pa, US 194/B2
Seljord, Nor. 66/C2
Selkan (tun.), Japan 108/B3
Selkirk, Sc, UK 59/D5
Selkirk, Mb, Can. 166/G3
Selkirk (mts.), BC, Can. 170/E2
Selleck, Wa, US 193/D3
Sellers, Al, US 191/E1
Sellersville, Pa, US 194/C3
Selles-sur-Cher, Fr. 83/G6
Sellières, Fr. 86/B4
Sells, Az, US 175/G5
Selly Oak, Eng, UK 62/E2
Sellye, Hun. 76/C3
Selm, Ger. 79/E5
Selma, Al, US 188/D4
Selma, Ar, US 179/J4
Selma, Ca, US 174/C2
Selma, NC, US 189/H3
Selman, Ok, US 178/E2
Selmer, Tn, US 188/C3
Selommes, Fr. 83/G5
Selongey, Fr. 86/B2
Selouma, Gui. 140/C4
Selous, Zim. 149/F3
Selous Game Reserve, Tanz 145/B4
Selsey, Eng, UK 63/F5
Selsey Bill (pt.), Eng, UK 63/F5
Selsingen, Ger. 79/G2
Sel'tso, Rus. 96/E1
Seltz, Fr. 84/B5
Selu (isl.), Indo. 154/C1
Sélune (riv.), Fr. 70/C2
Selvas (for.), Braz. 203/C3
Selvik, Nor. 64/R9
Selway (riv.), Id, US 173/F1
Selway (falls), Id, US 170/G4
Selwyn, Austl. 160/A3
Selwyn (range), Austl. 155/F5
Selydove, Ukr. 99/J3
Selz (riv.), Ger. 71/H2
Semara, WSah. 136/C4
Semarang, Indo. 115/E3
Semarsot, India 122/D4
Semau (isl.), Indo. 154/A2
Sembakung (riv.), Indo. 114/B4
Sembawang (nbrhd.), Sing. 115/J6
Sembé, Congo 146/C2
Sembehun, SLeo. 140/B5
Sembera (riv.), Czh. 85/H2
Semberong (riv.), Malay. 115/C2
Şemdinli, Turk. 129/F2
Séméac, Fr. 70/D5
Semelle (riv.), Fr. 83/F4

Semendua, D.R. Congo 146/D3
Semenivka, Ukr. 98/G1
Semenivka, Ukr. 99/G3
Semenov, Rus. 95/K4
Semeru (peak), Indo. 115/F3
Semey, Kaz. 125/D1
Semikarakorsk, Rus. 99/L4
Semilovo, Rus. 94/J5
Semiluki, Rus. 99/K2
Seminole, Fl, US 190/K8
Seminole (lake), Ga, US 191/F2
Seminole, Ok, US 179/F3
Seminole, Tx, US 177/C1
Seminoe (dam), Wy, US 173/K2
Seminoe (res.), Wy, US 173/K2
Seminole Draw (riv.), Tx, US 177/C1
Seminole Ind. Res., Fl, US 191/H4
Semipalatinsk (int'l arpt.), Kaz. 125/D1
Semirara (isl.), Phil. 114/C3
Semīrom, Iran 129/G4
Semitau, Indo. 116/D4
Semliki (riv.), D.R. Congo 147/G2
Semnān, Iran 129/H3
Semnān (gov.), Iran 129/H3
Semnon (riv.), Fr. 70/C3
Semois (riv.), Belg. 70/F2
Semouse (riv.), Fr. 86/C2
Semoy, Fr. 83/G5
Semoy (riv.), Fr. 81/D4
Sempach, Swi. 86/E3
Sempacher (lake), Swi. 86/D3
Semporna, Malay. 114/B4
Semprevisa (peak), It. 92/C4
Semsales, Swi. 86/C4
Semskefjellet (peak), Nor. 64/E2
Sen (riv.), Camb. 119/H5
Sen-san (peak), Japan 109/G7
Sena, Thai. 120/C3
Sena, Bol. 209/E3
Sena Madureira, Braz. 206/E5
Senador Pompeu, Braz. 207/G4
Senador Sá, Braz. 207/F3
Sen'afē, Erit. 144/A2
Senai, Malay. 115/C2
Senaja, Malay. 114/B4
Senaki, Geo. 97/G4
Senanga, Zam. 148/D3
Sénas, Fr. 90/B5
Senate, Sk, Can. 171/K3
Senath, Mo, US 188/B2
Senatobia, Ms, US 188/C3
Sence (riv.), Eng, UK 63/E1
Send, Eng, UK 56/B3
Sendafa, Eth. 144/A3
Sendai (riv.), Japan 110/D3
Sendai, Japan 111/G1
Sendai (int'l arpt.), Japan 111/G1
Sendai, Japan 110/B5
Sendai (bay), Japan 108/B4
Sendal (riv.), Japan 110/B5
Senden, Ger. 84/D6
Senden, Ger. 79/E5
Sendenhorst, Ger. 79/E5
Sendhwa, India 121/B1
Senebui, Indo. 115/C2
Senebui (cape), Indo. 115/C2
Senec, Slvk. 69/J4
Seneca, Mo, US 179/G2
Seneca (lake), NY, US 187/H3
Seneca, Or, US 172/D1
Seneca, SC, US 189/F3
Seneca, Ks, US 181/F4
Seneca Creek State Park, Md, US 194/A5
Seneca Falls, NY, US 187/H3
Seneca Rocks NRA, WV, US 189/H1
Senecaville (lake), Oh, US 186/F5
Seneffe, Belg. 81/D2
Sénégal (riv.), Afr. 140/B2
Senegal(ctry.) 133/A3
Sénégal (riv.), Sen. 133/A3
Senekal, SAfr. 150/D3
Seney, Mi, US 186/D1
Seney NWR, Mi, US 183/L4
Senezhskoye (lake), Rus. 94/W9
Senfi, Gha. 141/E5
Senftenberg, Ger. 69/H3
Senga Hill Mission, Zam. 147/G5
Sengenthal, Ger. 85/E4
Sênggê (riv.), China 125/D5
Sengilev, Rus. 97/J1
Sengor, Bhu. 123/H2
Senguer (riv.), Arg. 214/D3
Sengwe (riv.), Zim. 149/F3
Senhor do Bonfim, Braz. 211/E1
Senica, Slvk. 69/J4
Senirkent, Turk. 128/B2
Senise, It. 74/E2
Senj, Cro. 71/L4
Senja (isl.), Nor. 64/F1
Senkaku-shotō (isl.), Japan 111/G8
Şenkaya, Turk. 128/E1
Senkevychivka, Ukr. 98/C2
Şenköy, Turk. 130/E1
Senlac, Sk, Can. 171/K1
Senlis, Fr. 80/B5
Senmonoron, Camb. 120/D3
Sennan, Japan 109/H7
Sennar (dam), Sudan 142/G2
Senne (riv.), Belg. 81/D2
Sennecy-le-Grand, Fr. 86/A4
Sennfeld, Ger. 84/D2
Senno, Bela. 67/N4
Sennoy, Rus. 97/G2
Sennoy, Rus. 97/H1
Sennwald, Swi. 87/F3
Sennybridge, Wal, UK 62/C3
Séno (prov.), Burk. 141/F3
Senonches, Fr. 83/G3
Senones, Fr. 86/C1
Senorbì, It. 74/A3
Senou (Bamako) 140/D3
Senovo, Bul. 77/H4
Sens, Fr. 70/E2
Sens-de-Bretagne, Fr. 82/D4
Sensuntepeque, ESal. 200/D3
Senta, Yugo. 76/E3
Sentani, Indo. 117/K4
Sentery, D.R. Congo 147/F4
Sentinel, Ok, US 178/E3
Sentinel, Az, US 175/F4
Sentosa (isl.), Sing. 115/J6
Sentrum, SAfr. 149/E5
Senya Beraku, Gha. 141/E5
Senyavin (isls.), Micr. 162/E4
Senzig, Ger. 68/Q7
Seohārā, India 122/B1
Seon, Swi. 86/E3
Seondha, India 122/B2
Seoni, India 122/B4
Seonī Mālwā, India 122/A4
Seoul (Sŏul) (cap.), SKor. 105/K4
Seoul Grand Park, SKor. 107/G7
Seoul Jikhalsi (prov.), SKor. 107/D4
Sepang (pt.), Malay. 115/D2
Sepanjang (isl.), Indo. 115/F3
Separ, NM, US 175/H4
Separation (pt.), NZ 161/C3
Sepatini (riv.), Braz. 209/E3
Sepetiba (bay), Braz. 211/M8
Sepik (riv.), PNG 162/D5
Sepino, It. 92/D5
Sep'o, NKor. 107/D3
Sepo, Indo. 117/G3
Sępólno Krajeńskie, Pol. 69/J2
Sepopa, Bots. 148/D3
Sept-îles, Qu, Can. 167/K3
Septèmes-les-Vallons, Fr. 90/B6
Septemvri, Bul. 75/J1
Septeuil, Fr. 83/G3
Sepulveda (dam), Ca, US 192/F7
Sequeros, Sp. 72/B2
Sequim (bay), Wa, US 193/A1
Sequim, Wa, US 170/C3
Sequoia NP, Ca, US 174/C2
Sequoyah Nat'l Wildlife Res., Ok, US 179/G3
Sera (isl.), Indo. 154/C1
Serafimovich, Rus. 99/M3
Seraincourt, Fr. 56/H4
Seraing, Belg. 81/E2
Serambe, Sudan 142/E2
Serampore, India 123/G4
Sèran (riv.), Fr. 86/B6
Serang, Indo. 115/D3
Serangoon (nbrhd.), Sing. 115/J6
Serasan (str.), Indo.,Malay. 116/C3
Serasan, Indo. 116/C3
Seravezza, It. 88/D6
Serbeulangit (mts.), Indo. 115/B2
Serbia (reg.), Yugo. 93/J1
Serbia and Montenegro (see Yugoslavia) */*
Serbin, Tx, US 177/F2
Serchhīp, India 112/B4
Serchio (riv.), It. 88/D4
Serdang (cape), Indo. 115/D3
Serdo, Eth. 144/B3
Serdobsk, Rus. 97/H1
Serebryansk, Kaz. 100/J5
Serednikovo, Rus. 94/H5
Seredžius, Lith. 67/K4
Seregno, It. 88/C2
Serein (riv.), Fr. 68/D4
Serémange-Erzange, Fr. 81/F5
Seremban, Malay. 115/C2
Serengeti (plain), Tanz. 145/A2
Serengeti NP, Tanz. 145/A2
Serenje, Zam. 149/F2
Serere, Ugan. 145/A1
Sergach, Rus. 95/K5
Sergeantsville, NJ, US 194/D3
Sergen, Turk. 77/H5
Sergeya Kirova (isls.), Rus. 100/J2
Sergeyevka, Kaz. 95/Q5
Sergipe (state), Braz. 211/F1
Sergiyev Posad, Rus. 94/H4
Sergnano, It. 88/C3
Seria, Bru. 116/D3
Seriate, It. 88/C2
Sérifontaine, Fr. 80/A5
Sérifos, Gre. 75/J4
Sérifos (isl.), Gre. 75/J4
Sérignan, Fr. 70/E5
Serik, Turk. 128/B2
Serikbuya, China 125/C4
Seringa, Serra da (mts.), Braz. 206/D4
Serinyol, Turk. 130/E1
Serio (riv.), It. 88/C2
Serkout (peak), Alg. 137/G5
Sermaises, Fr. 83/H4
Sermaize-les-Bains, Fr. 81/D6
Sermata (isl.), Indo. 117/G5
Sermata (isls.), Indo. 154/C2
Sermide, It. 89/E4
Sermoneta, It. 92/B4
Sernaglia della Battaglia, It. 89/F2
Sernovodsk, Rus. 97/J1
Sernur, Rus. 95/L4
Serón, Sp. 72/D4
Serós, Sp. 73/F2
Serottini (peak), It. 87/G5
Serov, Rus. 100/G4
Serowe, Bots. 149/E4
Serpa, Port. 72/B4
Serpeddi (peak), It. 74/A3
Serpent Mound, Oh, US 189/F1
Serpent's Mouth (str.), Trin.,Ven. 205/F2
Serpentine (dam), Austl. 158/C4
Serpentine Lakes, Austl. 157/F4
Serpukhov, Rus. 94/H5
Serquigny, Fr. 83/F2
Serra (peak), It. 88/D6
Serra, Braz. 211/E4
Serra Branca, Braz. 207/G4
Serra da Bocaina, PN, Braz. 213/H2
Serra da Bocaína, PN da, Braz. 210/D4
Serra da Canastra, PN, Braz. 213/H2
Serra da Canastra, PN da, Braz. 210/D4
Serra da Capivara, PN da, Braz. 211/E1
Serra da Capivara, PN da, Braz. 207/F5
Serra da Chela (mts.), Ang. 148/B3
Serra da Estrela (peak), Port. 72/B2
Serra da Estrela (mts.), Port. 72/A3
Serra do Cipó, PN da, Braz. 211/E3
Serra do Congo (mts.), Ang. 146/C4
Serra do Navio, Braz. 206/C2
Serra dos Órgãos, PN da, Braz. 211/N7
Serra Negra do Norte, Braz. 207/G4
Serra San Bruno, It. 74/E3
Serra San Quirico, It. 89/G7
Serra Talhada, Braz. 207/G4
Sérrai, Gre. 75/H2
Serralta di San Vito (peak), It. 74/E3
Serramanna, It. 74/A3
Serramazzoni, It. 89/D5
Serrana Bank (isl.), Col. 197/F5
Serranía de la Cerbatana (mts.), Ven. 205/E3
Serranía de la Neblina, PN, Ven. 205/E4
Serranías del Burro (mts.), Mex. 198/E2
Serranilla Bank (isl.), Col. 197/F4
Serrano, Arg. 214/E2
Serranópolis, Braz. 210/B3
Serrat (cape), Tun. 74/A4
Serravalle, It. 89/F4
Serravalle, SMar. 89/F6
Serravalle di Chienti, It. 91/B1
Serravalle Scrivia, It. 88/B4
Serravalle Sesia, It. 88/B2
Serre (riv.), Fr. 68/B4
Serre Chevalier (peak), Fr. 90/C3
Serre-Ponçon (lake), Fr. 90/C3
Serrenti, It. 74/A3
Serres, Fr. 90/B4
Serrières, Fr. 90/A2
Serrinha, Braz. 211/F1
Serris, Fr. 56/L5
Serrita, Braz. 207/G4
Sêrro, Braz. 213/J1
Sersale, It. 74/E3
Sertã, Port. 72/A3
Sertânia, Braz. 207/G5
Sertãozinho, Braz. 213/H2
Sertavul (pass), Turk. 128/C2
Serteng (mts.), China 104/C4
Sēru, Eth. 144/B4
Serui, Indo. 117/J4
Serule, Bots. 149/E4
Serurumi (riv.), Bots. 148/E4
Seruwai, Indo. 115/B1
Seruyan (riv.), Indo. 116/D4
Servance, Fr. 86/C2
Servel (Lannion) (arpt.), Fr. 82/B3
Servi, Turk. 128/E2
Sérvia, Gre. 75/G2
Serviceton, Austl. 158/B3
Servigliano, It. 92/C1
Serwaru, Indo. 154/B2
Sesayap (riv.), Indo. 114/B5
Sese (isls.), Ugan. 147/G3
Sesebi (ruin), Sudan 135/F4
Sesepe, Indo. 117/G4
Sesfontein, Namb. 148/B3
Sesheke, Zam. 148/E3
Sesia (riv.), It. 71/H4
Sesimbra, Port. 72/A3
Sesimbra, Port. 73/P11
Seskar (isl.), Rus. 67/N1
Sespe, Ca, US 192/B2
Sespe (cr.), Ca, US 192/A1
Sespe Condor Sanctuary, Ca, US 174/C3
Sessa Aurunca, It. 92/C5
Sesser, Il, US 188/C1
Sesslach, Ger. 84/D2
Sesto Calende, It. 88/B2
Sesto Campano, It. 92/D5
Sesto Fiorentino, It. 89/E6
Sesto San Giovanni, It. 88/C2
Sesto Ulteriano, It. 88/C3
Sestola, It. 89/D5
Sestra (riv.), Rus. 94/W9
Sestri Levante, It. 88/C5
Sestroretsk, Rus. 94/S6
Sestroretskiy (lake), Rus. 94/T6
Sestu, It. 74/A3
Sesvenna (peak), It. 87/G4
Sesvete, Cro. 76/C3
Šeta, Lith. 67/L4
Setana, Japan 108/A2
Sète, Fr. 70/E5
Sete Cidades, PN de, Braz. 207/F4
Sete Lagoas, Braz. 210/D3
Seth, WV, US 189/G1
Sethārja, Pak. 127/J3
Seti (riv.), Nepal 122/C1
Seti (zone), Nepal 122/C1
Sétif, Alg. 138/H4
Sétif (wilaya), Alg. 138/H4
Seto, Japan 109/M5
Seto-Naikai NP, Japan 110/C4
Setouchi, Japan 111/K6
Settat, Mor. 136/D2
Setté-Cama, Gabon 146/B3
Settecamini, It. 91/B4
Settepani (peak), It. 88/B5
Settimo Torinese, It. 88/A2
Settimo Vittone, It. 88/A1
Settle, Eng, UK 61/F3
Settsu, Japan 109/J6
Setúbal (dist.), Port. 72/A3
Setúbal (bay), Port. 72/A3
Setúbal, Port. 73/Q10
Seubersdorf, Ger. 85/E4
Seudre (riv.), Fr. 70/C4
Seugne (riv.), Fr. 70/C4
Seuil-D'Argonne, Fr. 81/E6
Seul (lake), On, Can. 166/G3
Seulimeum, Indo. 115/A1
Seulles (riv.), Fr. 83/E2
Seurre, Fr. 86/B4
Seuzach, Swi. 87/E2
Sevan, Arm. 129/F1
Sevana (lake), Arm. 100/E5
Sevastopol', Ukr. 99/G5
Sevelen, Swi. 87/F3
Seven (riv.), Eng, UK 61/H3
Seven (cr.), Ab, Can. 171/J3
Seven Heads (pt.), Ire. 58/B6
Seven Oaks, Tx, US 177/G2
Seven Sisters Falls, Mb, Can. 182/F2
Seven Valleys, Pa, US 194/B4
Sevenmile (hill), Ne, US 180/D2
Sevenoaks, Eng, UK 56/D3
Sevenoaks Weald, Eng, UK 56/D3
Seventy Mile House, BC, Can. 170/D2
Séveraisse (riv.), Fr. 90/C3
Severn (riv.), Wal, UK 61/F6
Severn (riv.), On, Can. 166/G3
Severn (riv.), Md, US 194/B5
Severn, Md, US 194/B5
Severna Park, Md, US 194/B5
Severnaya Sos'va (riv.), Rus. 95/N3
Severnaya Zemlya (isls.), Rus. 103/K2
Severnaya Zemlya (isl.), Rus. 216/Z
Severnyy, Rus. 95/P2
Severo-Kuril'sk, Rus. 101/R4
Severo-Yeniseyskiy, Rus. 100/K3
Severobaykal'sk, Rus. 101/L4
Severočeský (pol. reg.), Czh. 71/L1
Severodvinsk, Rus. 94/H2
Severomoravsky (pol. reg.), Czh. 69/J4
Severomoravský (pol. reg.), Czh. 71/M1
Severomorsk, Rus. 94/G1
Severomuysk, Rus. 101/M4
Severoural'sk, Rus. 95/N3
Seversk, Ukr. 99/K3
Severskaya, Rus. 99/K5
Severukha, Rus. 95/P4
Severy, Ks, US 179/F2
Seveso, It. 88/C2
Sevier (lake), Ut, US 173/G4
Sevier (des.), Ut, US 173/G4
Sevier, Ut, US 175/F1
Sevier (riv.), Ut, US 168/D4
Sevier (plat.), Ut, US 175/F1
Sevier, East Fork (riv.), Ut, US 175/F2
Sevierville, Tn, US 189/F3
Sevilla, Col. 207/K8
Seville, Sp. 72/C4
Seville, Austl. 158/G5
Sevilleta Nat'l Wild. Ref., NM, US 175/J3
Sevlievo, Bul. 77/G4
Sevnica, Slov. 76/B2
Sevojno, Yugo. 76/D4
Sevran, Fr. 56/K5
Sevsk, Rus. 99/H1
Sewa (riv.), SLeo. 140/C5
Sewanee, Tn, US 188/E3
Seward (pen.), Ak, US 165/A3
Seward (pen.), Ak, US 168/W12
Seward, Ak, US 168/Y12
Seward, Ne, US 181/F3
Sewaren, NJ, US 195/J9
Sewell, Chile 214/N9
Sextons Creek, Ky, US 188/F2
Seyah Cheshmeh, Iran 129/F2
Seybaplaya, Mex. 200/D2
Seybouse, Oued (riv.), Alg. 138/K6
Seydhisfjördhur, Ice. 64/Q6
Seydişehir, Turk. 128/B2
Seyhan (dam), Turk. 128/C2
Seyhan (riv.), Turk. 130/D1
Seyitgazi, Turk. 128/B2
Seylac, Som. 144/B3
Seym (riv.), Rus. 96/E2
Seymour, Austl. 159/B3
Seymour, Ia, US 181/H3
Seymour, In, US 188/E1
Seymour, Mo, US 179/H2
Seymour, Tx, US 178/E4
Seymour, Wi, US 186/B2
Seymour Arm, BC, Can. 170/E2
Seymour Johnson (A.F.B.), NC, US 189/J3
Seyne, Fr. 90/C4
Seynod, Fr. 86/C6
Seyssel, Fr. 86/B6
Seyssinet-Pariset, Fr. 90/B2
Şeytan (riv.), Turk. 129/M6
Sežana, Slov. 71/K4
Sézanne, Fr. 80/C6
Sezimovo Ústí, Czh. 85/H4
Sezze, It. 92/C5
Sfîntu Gheorghe, Rom. 77/J3
Sfîntu Gheorghe, Rom. 77/G3
Sfîntu Gheorghe Branch (riv.), Rom. 77/J3
Sfizef, Alg. 138/E5
Sgurr a' Chaorachain (peak), Sc, UK 59/A2
Sgurr a' Choire Ghlais (peak), Sc, UK 59/B2
Sgurr a' Mhuilinn (peak), Sc, UK 59/B1
Sgurr Mór (peak), Sc, UK 59/A1
Sgurr na Ciche (peak), Sc, UK 59/A2
Sgurr na Lapaich (peak), Sc, UK 59/A2
Sha (riv.), China 106/C4
Sha Tau Kok, China 113/L6
Sha Tin, China 113/L7
Shaanxi (prov.), China 104/F5
Shab'ā, Leb. 131/D2
Shaba Nat'l Rsv., Kenya 145/B1
Shābah, Egypt 139/B2
Shabās al Milḩ, Egypt 139/B2
Shabās ash Shuhadā', Egypt 139/B2
Shabās 'Umayr, Egypt 139/B2
Shabashah, Sudan 142/G2
Shābāzpur (riv.), Bang. 123/H4
Shabla, Bul. 77/J4
Shabo, Ukr. 98/F4
Shabqadar, Pak. 124/A2
Shabunda, D.R. Congo 147/F3
Shabwah, Yem. 144/C2
Shache, China 125/C4
Shackan Ind. Res., BC, Can. 170/D2
Shackleford, Eng, UK 56/B3
Shadaogou, China 113/F2
Shade Mtn. (mtn.), Pa, US 194/A2
Shadehill (dam), SD, US 182/C5
Shadehill, SD, US 182/C5
Shadeland, In, US 186/C4
Shadrinsk, Rus. 95/P4
Shaduzup, Myan. 112/C3
Shady Cove, Or, US 172/B2
Shady Grove, Fl, US 191/G2
Shady Spring, WV, US 189/G2
Shadyside, Oh, US 186/F5
Shafer (lake), In, US 186/C4
Shafranovo, Rus. 95/M5
Shafter, Ca, US 174/C3
Shafter, Nv, US 173/F3
Shafter, Tx, US 177/B3
Shaftesbury, Eng, UK 62/D4
Shaftsbury, Vt, US 187/K3
Shag Harbour, NS, Can. 184/E4
Shagamu, Nga. 141/F5
Shagan (riv.), Kaz. 125/C2
Shagang, China 107/B2
Shagany (lake), Urk. 98/E5
Shagany (lake), Rom. 77/J3
Shagonar, Rus. 104/C1
Shah Alam, Malay. 115/C2
Shāh Kot, Pak. 124/B4
Shāhābād, India 124/D4
Shāhābād, India 122/B2
Shāhābād, India 122/B1
Shāhābād, India 122/A3
Shahbā', Syria 131/F3
Shāhbandar, Pak. 127/J4
Shahdād, Iran 127/G2
Shāhdādkot, Pak. 127/J3
Shāhdādpur, Pak. 127/J3
Shāhdara, Pak. 124/C4
Shāhdasht, Iran 129/F4
Shahdol, India 122/C4
Shahekan, China 104/F5
Shāhganj, India 122/D2
Shaḩḩāt, Libya 93/J4
Shāhjahānpur, India 122/B2
Shāhpur, Pak. 124/B3
Shāhpur, India 124/D3
Shāhpur, India 122/A4
Shāhpur Chākar, Pak. 118/A2
Shāhpura, India 122/C4
Shahr Sultān, Pak. 124/A5
Shahr-e Bābak, Iran 129/H4
Shahr-e Kord, Iran 129/G3
Shahr-e Monjān, Afg. 124/A1
Shahrak, Iran 129/G3
Shāhrūd, Iran 129/G3
Shahryār, Iran 129/G3
Shāhzādpur, India 124/D4
Shāhzādpur, Bang. 123/G3
Shā'ib al Banāt (peak), Egypt 135/G3
Shaikhpura, India 123/E3
Shāistāganj, Bang. 123/H3
Shājāpur, India 118/C3
Shaji, China 104/F4
Shajian, China 113/H3
Shajianzi, China 107/C2
Shakargarh, Pak. 124/C3
Shakaskraal, SAfr. 151/E3
Shakawe, Bots. 148/D3
Shakespeare (isl.), On, Can. 183/K3
Shakhbuz, Azer. 97/H5
Shakhtars'k, Ukr. 99/K3
Shakhtërsk, Rus. 105/N2
Shakhtinsk, Kaz. 100/H5
Shakhty, Rus. 99/L4
Shakhun'ya, Rus. 95/K4
Shaki, Nga. 141/F4
Shakīso, Eth. 144/A4
Shakopee, Mn, US 183/N7
Shakotan (pen.), Japan 108/B2
Shaksha, Rus. 95/N5
Shāl, Iran 129/G3
Shala (lake), Eth. 144/A4
Shalaanbood, Som. 145/D1
Shalbuzdag (peak), Rus. 97/H4
Shaldon, Eng, UK 62/C5
Shalford, Eng, UK 56/B3
Shali, Rus. 97/H4
Shaling, China 107/B2
Shallotte, NC, US 189/H4
Shallow Reach (inlet), Austl. 157/M8
Shallowater, Tx, US 178/D4
Shalqar, Kaz. 97/L3
Shal'skiy, Rus. 94/H3
Shaluli (mts.), China 104/D5
Shalyhyne, Ukr. 99/H2
Shama (riv.), Tanz. 145/A3
Shamary, Rus. 95/N4
Shamattawa (riv.), On, Can. 167/H3
Shambe, Sudan 142/F4
Shambu, Eth. 142/H3
Shambungu, D.R. Congo 146/D4
Shāmgarh, India 118/C3
Shamīl, Iran 129/J5
Shāmli, India 124/D5
Shammar, Jabal (mts.), SAr. 126/D3
Shamokin (cr.), Pa, US 194/B2
Shamokin, Pa, US 194/B2
Shamokin Dam, Pa, US 194/B2
Shāmpur, India 122/A2
Shamrock, Tx, US 178/D3
Shamsābād, India 122/A4
Shamsābād, India 122/B2
Shamva, Zim. 149/F3
Shan (state), Myan. 119/G3
Shan (plat.), Myan. 119/G3
Shan (pass), China 113/H3
Shan-Ngaw (range), Myan. 112/C3
Shanagolden, Ire. 58/A4
Shanchengzhen, China 107/C1
Shandī, Sudan 142/G1
Shandon, Ca, US 174/B3
Shandong (prov.), China 105/H4
Shandong (pen.), China 105/H4
Shandong (isl.), China 106/E3
Shangani, Zim. 149/F3
Shangani (riv.), Zim. 149/F3
Shangcai, China 106/C4
Shangcheng, China 106/C5
Shangchuan (isl.), China 113/G4
Shangdu, China 113/G3
Shangdu, China 104/G3
Shangfang, China 113/H2
Shanghai (prov.), China 105/J5
Shanghai, China 106/L8
Shanghe, China 106/D3
Shanghekou, China 107/C2
Shangjiahe, China 107/C2
Shangjiaodao, China 113/H2
Shangjing, China 113/H3
Shangliang, China 104/F5
Shanglin, China 119/J3
Shangolume, D.R. Congo 147/F5
Shangombo, Zam. 148/D3
Shangping, China 113/G3
Shangqiu, China 106/C4
Shangrao, China 113/H2
Shangshui, China 106/C4
Shangsi, China 120/D1
Shangyi, China 106/C2
Shangyou (riv.), China 113/G3
Shanhua, Tai. 113/J4
Shani, Nga. 142/B3
Shanklin, Eng, UK 63/E5
Shankou, China 113/F2
Shanks, WV, US 187/G5
Shanmatang (mtn.), China 113/F3
Shanmen, China 113/F3
Shannawona (peak), Ire. 58/A3
Shannon, Qu, Can. 184/B2
Shannon (int'l arpt.), Ire. 58/B4
Shannon (riv.), Ire. 58/B4
Shannon, NZ 161/C3
Shannon, Ga, US 188/E3
Shannon, Ms, US 188/C3
Shannon (lake), Wa, US 170/C3
Shannon Hills, Ar, US 179/H3
Shannonbridge, Ire. 58/B3
Shanshan, China 104/C3
Shanshūr, Egypt 139/C4
Shantangyi, China 113/F3
Shanṭānūf, Egypt 139/C4
Shantar (isl.), Rus. 103/N4
Shantar (isls.), Rus. 101/P4
Shantou, China 113/H4
Shanty Bay, On, Can. 187/G2
Shanwa, Tanz. 145/A2
Shanxi (prov.), China 104/G4
Shanyang, China 113/H3
Shanyao, China 113/H3
Shanyin, China 106/C3
Shaodong, China 113/F3
Shaoguan, China 113/G3
Shaoshan, China 113/G3
Shaoxing, China 113/J2
Shaoyang, China 113/F3
Shap, Eng, UK 61/F2
Shapa, China 113/F4
Shapki, Rus. 67/P2
Shapkina (riv.), Rus. 95/M2
Shaqiuhe, China 125/E2
Shaqlāwah, Iraq 129/F2
Shaqrā', SAr. 126/E3
Shaqrā', Yem. 144/C2
Sharafkhāneh, Iran 129/F2
Sharan, Rus. 95/M5
Sharanga, Rus. 95/K4
Sharbot Lake, On, Can. 187/H2
Sharga, Mong. 104/D2
Sharhorod, Ukr. 98/E3
Shari, Japan 108/D2
Sharïngol, Mong. 104/F2
Sharjah (int'l arpt.), UAE 127/G3
Shark (bay), Austl. 153/A3
Shark River (inlet), NJ, US 194/D3
Sharkovshchina, Bela. 67/M4
Sharlyk, Rus. 97/K1
Sharm ash Shaykh, Egypt 135/G3
Sharnbrook, Eng, UK 63/F2
Sharnūb, Egypt 139/B2
Sharon, Ct, US 187/K4
Sharon, Pa, US 186/F4
Sharon, Tn, US 188/C2
Sharon, Vt, US 187/K3
Sharon Springs, Ks, US 178/D1
Sharonville, Oh, US 186/D5
Sharovka, Ukr. 99/H2
Sharpe (lake), SD, US 180/E1
Sharpes, Fl, US 191/H3
Sharpsburg, Ky, US 188/F1
Sharqpur, Pak. 124/C4
Sharquī, Jazīrat ash (isl.), Tun. 93/F4
Shar'ya, Rus. 95/K4
Shasha, Eth. 142/G4
Shashe, Bots. 149/E4
Shashe (riv.), Bots. 149/F4
Shashemenē, Eth. 144/A4
Shashi, China 113/G2
Shasta (lake), Ca, US 172/B3
Shasta (mt.), Ca, US 172/B3
Shasta (dam), Ca, US 172/B3
Shatalovo, Rus. 94/G5
Shāṭi (wadi), Libya 134/B3
Shatsk, Rus. 97/G1
Shatsk, Bela. 67/M5
Shatskiy NP, Ukr. 69/M3
Shatt al Arab (riv.), Iraq 126/E2
Shattāy, Sudan 142/D2
Shattuck, Ok, US 178/E2
Shaughnessy, Ab, Can. 171/H3
Shaunavon, Sk, Can. 171/K3
Shavano Park, Tx, US 177/E3
Shave Ẕiyyon, Isr. 131/C3
Shaver Lake, Ca, US 174/C2
Shaw, La, US 190/C2
Shaw, Ms, US 188/B4
Shaw, Eng, UK 63/E4
Shaw (A.F.B.), SC, US 189/G4
Shawan, China 113/H3
Shawano, Wi, US 181/K1
Shawbury, Eng, UK 62/D1
Shawnee, Co, US 178/B1
Shawnee, Oh, US 186/E5
Shawnee, Ok, US 179/F3
Shawneetown, Il, US 188/C2
Shawnī, Egypt 139/B3
Shawville, Qu, Can. 187/H2
Shaxi, China 113/F3
Shay Gap, Austl. 156/D2
Shaykh Miskīn, Syria 131/E3
Shaykh Sa'd, Iraq 129/F3
Shaykh 'Uthmān, Yem. 144/C2
Shaykhān, Iraq 129/E2
Shaymak, Taj. 125/B4
Shazaoyuan, China 104/C4
Shazipo, China 113/F2
Shchara (riv.), Bela. 96/C1
Shchastya, Ukr. 99/K3
Shchedok, Rus. 97/G3
Shchekino, Rus. 96/F1
Shchelkovo, Rus. 94/W9
Shchel'yabozh, Rus. 95/N2
Shchel'yayur, Rus. 95/M2
Shcherbakty, Kaz. 100/H4
Shcherbinka, Rus. 94/W9
Shchigry, Rus. 99/J2
Shchors, Ukr. 98/F2
Shchuchin, Bela. 67/L5
Shchūchīnsk, Kaz. 125/B1
Shchuch'ye, Rus. 95/P5
She Xian, China 113/H2
Shea Stadium, NY, US 195/K9
Sheaville, Or, US 172/E2
Shebē, Eth. 142/H4
Shebekino, Rus. 99/J2
Sheberghān, Afg. 127/J1
Sheboygan, Wi, US 186/C3
Sheboygan Falls, Wi, US 186/C3
Shebunino, Rus. 105/N2
Shedd, Or, US 172/B1
Shediac, NB, Can. 184/E2
Shee (riv.), Sc, UK 59/C3
Sheelin (lake), Ire. 60/A4
Sheep (cr.), Id, US 172/F2
Sheep (mts.), Nv, US 174/E2
Sheep (riv.), Ab, Can. 170/G2
Sheep Mountain (peak), SD, US 180/C2
Sheepshead Bay (nbrhd.), NY, US 195/K9
Sheerness, Eng, UK 63/G4
Sheerness, Ab, Can. 171/J2
Sheet Harbour, NS, Can. 185/F3
Shefar'am, Isr. 131/C3
Shefayim, Isr. 131/B4
Sheffield, Eng, UK 61/G5
Sheffield, Ma, US 187/K3
Sheffield (isl.), Ct, US 195/M7
Sheffield, Austl. 158/C4
Sheffield, Ia, US 181/H2
Sheffield, Al, US 188/D3
Sheffield, Tx, US 177/D2
Shefford, Eng, UK 63/F2
Shegangshi, China 113/G2
Shegovary, Rus. 94/J3
Shēh Husēn, Eth. 144/B4
Shehēt, Eth. 144/A2
Shehuen (riv.), Arg. 215/C6
Shehy (mts.), Ire. 58/A6
Sheikh, Som. 144/C3
Sheila, NB, Can. 184/E2
Shejiaping, China 106/B3
Shek Uk (peak), China 113/M7
Shekhūpura, Pak. 124/B4
Shelagskiy (cape), Rus. 101/S2
Shelbina, Mo, US 181/H4
Shelburne (bay), Austl. 155/F2
Shelburne, NS, Can. 184/E4
Shelburne, On, Can. 186/F2
Shelburn, In, US 186/C5
Shelburne, Vt, US 187/K2
Shelby, Ia, US 181/G3
Shelby, Mi, US 186/C3
Shelby, Ms, US 188/B4
Shelby, Mt, US 171/J3
Shelby, NC, US 189/G3
Shelby, Ne, US 180/F3
Shelby, Oh, US 186/E4
Shelbyville, Il, US 181/K4
Shelbyville (lake), Il, US 181/K4
Shelbyville, In, US 186/D5
Shelbyville, Ky, US 188/E1
Shelbyville, Mo, US 181/H4
Shelbyville, Tn, US 188/D3
Shelbyville, Tx, US 177/G2
Sheldon, Ia, US 181/G2
Sheldon, Il, US 186/C4
Sheldon, Mo, US 179/G2
Sheldon, ND, US 182/F4
Sheldon, Tx, US 177/M9
Sheldon, Vt, US 187/K2
Sheldon, Wi, US 183/J5
Sheldon Antelope Range, Nv, US 172/D3
Shelekhov (gulf), Rus. 103/Q3
Shelekhov, Rus. 104/E1
Shelikof (str.), Ak, US 168/X13
Shell (cr.), Ne, US 180/F3
Shell (pt.), Eng, UK 63/G4
Shell Keys Nat'l Wild. Ref., La, US 177/J3
Shell Lake, Wi, US 183/J5
Shell Lake, Sk, Can. 171/L1
Shell Lake Nat'l Wild. Ref., ND, US 182/C3
Shell Rock, Ia, US 181/H2
Shell Rock (riv.), Ia, US 181/H2
Shellbrook, Sk, Can. 171/L1
Shelley, Id, US 173/G2
Shelley (isl.), Pa, US 194/B3
Shellharbour, Austl. 159/E2
Shellman, Ga, US 191/F2
Shelly, Mn, US 182/F4
Shelter (isl.), NY, US 195/F1
Shelter Island (sound), NY, US 195/F1
Shelton, Ct, US 195/E1
Shelton, Ne, US 180/E3
Shelton, Wa, US 170/C4
Shemgang, Bhu. 123/H2
Shen Xian, China 106/C3
Shenandoah, Ia, US 181/G3
Shenandoah (riv.), Va, US 189/H1
Shenandoah, Va, US 189/H1
Shenandoah, Pa, US 194/B2
Shenandoah NP, Va, US 189/H1
Shenandoah, South Fork (riv.), Va, US 188/C2
Shenchi, China 106/C3
Shendam, Nga. 141/H4
Shenge (pt.), SLeo. 140/B5
Shengena (peak), Tanz. 145/B3
Shengfang, China 106/H7
Shengjiaqiao, China 113/H2
Shëngjin, Alb. 75/F2
Shengjing (pass), China 112/E3
Shengli (pass), China 125/E3
Shengze, China 106/L9
Shenhu, China 113/H3
Shenkursk, Rus. 94/J3
Shennongjia, China 106/B5
Sheno, Eth. 144/A3
Shenqiu, China 106/C4
Shenstone, Eng, UK 63/E1
Shenyang, China 107/B2
Shenzao, China 105/J5
Shenzhen, China 113/G4
Sheoganj, India 118/B2
Sheopur, India 118/C2
Shepard, Ab, Can. 171/H2
Shepetivka, Ukr. 98/D2
Shepherd, Tx, US 177/G2
Shepherd (isls.), Van. 162/F6
Shepherdsville, Ky, US 188/E2
Sheppard (A.F.B.), Tx, US 179/E4
Shepparton, Austl. 159/B3
Sheppey, Isle of (isl.), Eng, UK 63/G4
Shepshed, Eng, UK 63/E1
Shepton Mallet, Eng, UK 62/D4
Sheqi, China 106/C4
Sherborne, Eng, UK 62/D5
Sherbro (isl.), SLeo. 140/B5
Sherbrooke, Qu, Can. 187/L2
Sherbrooke, NS, Can. 185/G3
Sherburn, Eng, UK 61/G2
Sherburne, NY, US 187/J3
Sherburne Nat'l Wild. Ref., Mn, US 181/H1
Shercock, Ire. 58/D2
Shere (hill), Nga. 141/H4
Shere, Eng, UK 56/B3
Sheremetyevo (int'l arpt.), Rus. 94/W9
Shergaon, India 123/J2
Sherghāti, India 123/E3
Sheridan, Ar, US 179/H3
Sheridan, Ca, US 172/C4
Sheridan, Il, US 181/K3
Sheridan, In, US 186/C4
Sheridan, Mt, US 173/G1
Sheridan, Or, US 172/B1
Sheridan, Wy, US 173/K1
Sheringham, Eng, UK 63/H1
Sherkin (isl.), Ire. 58/A7
Sherlovaya Gora, Rus. 104/H1
Sherman, Tx, US 179/F4
Sherman, Ms, US 188/C3
Sherman (dam), Ne, US 180/E3
Sherman (res.), Ne, US 180/E3
Sherman, NM, US 175/J4
Sherman, Il, US 181/K4
Sherman (cr.), Pa, US 194/A3
Sherman Oaks (nbrhd.), Ca, US 192/F7
Sherpur, Bang. 123/G3
Sherpur, Bang. 123/H3
Shertallai, India 121/C4
Sherwood, ND, US 182/D3
Sherwood, Ok, US 179/G3
Sherwood, PE, Can. 184/F2
Sherwood, Oh, US 186/D4
Sherwood, Tn, US 188/E3
Sherwood, Tx, US 177/D2
Sherwood (pt.), Ct, US 195/E1
Shetek (lake), Mn, US 181/G1
Shetianqiao, China 113/F3
Shetland (isls.), UK 216/G
Shetpe, Kaz. 97/K3
Sheung Shui-Fanling, China 113/L7
Shevchenko (int'l arpt.), Kaz. 97/J4
Shevchenkove, Ukr. 99/J3
Shewa (prov.), Eth. 142/H3
Shewa Gīmīra, Eth. 142/G4
Sheyang, China 106/E4
Sheyang (riv.), China 106/D4
Sheyenne, ND, US 182/E4
Sheyenne (riv.), ND, US 182/E4
Shhīm, Leb. 131/C1
Shi (riv.), China 106/C4
Shi San Ling, China 106/H6
Shiawassee (riv.), Mi, US 186/D3
Shiawassee Nat'l Wild. Ref., Mi, US 186/D3
Shibakawa, Japan 109/B3
Shibām, Yem. 144/D2
Shibantan, China 113/F2
Shibata, Japan 111/F2
Shibayama, Japan 109/E2
Shibecha, Japan 108/D2
Shibetsu, Japan 108/C1
Shibetsu, Japan 108/D2
Shibganj, Bang. 123/G3
Shibīn (canal), Egypt 139/C3
Shibīn al Kaum, Egypt 139/C3
Shibīn al Qanāṭir, Egypt 139/C4
Shiblanjah, Egypt 139/C4
Shibotsu (isl.), Rus. 108/E2
Shibushi (bay), Japan 110/B5
Shicheng (isl.), China 107/B3
Shicheng, China 107/C2
Shicheng, China 113/H3
Shicheng, China 113/H3
Shickshinny, Pa, US 194/B1
Shidao, China 107/B4
Shiderty (riv.), Kaz. 125/B1
Shidixi, China 113/F2
Shidler, Ok, US 179/F2
Shido, Japan 110/D3
Shield (cape), Austl. 155/E3
Shields, Mi, US 186/D3
Shields, ND, US 182/D4
Shi'erdaogou, China 107/D2
Shifnal, Eng, UK 62/D1
Shiga, Japan 109/J5
Shigaraki, Japan 109/K6
Shigony, Rus. 97/J1
Shihe, China 107/A3
Shihezi, China 125/E3
Shijak, Alb. 75/F2
Shijiaqiao, China 106/L9
Shijiazhuang, China 106/C3
Shijing, China 113/H3
Shijingshan, China 106/H7
Shijiu (lake), China 113/H2
Shijōnawate, Japan 109/J6
Shika, Nga. 141/G4
Shikabe, Japan 108/B2
Shikārpur, India 122/B1
Shikārpur, Pak. 127/J3
Shikata, Japan 109/G6
Shikatsu, Japan 109/L5
Shikishima, Japan 109/B2
Shikohābād, India 122/B2
Shikoku (isl.), Japan 103/N6
Shikoku (mts.), Japan 110/C4
Shikotan (isl.), Rus. 105/P3
Shikotsu (lake), Japan 108/B2
Shikotsu-Tōya NP, Japan 108/B2
Shikou, China 113/G3
Shilabo, Eth. 144/C4
Shilbottle, Eng, UK 59/E6
Shildon, Eng, UK 61/G2
Shilipu, China 113/G2
Shilka (riv.), Rus. 103/L4
Shilka, Rus. 104/H1
Shillelagh, Ire. 58/D4
Shillington, Pa, US 194/C3
Shillong, India 119/F2
Shiloango (riv.), Congo 146/C4
Shiloh, NJ, US 194/C5
Shiloh Nat'l Mil. Park, Tn, US 188/C3
Shilou, China 106/B3
Shilovo, Rus. 97/G1
Shimabara, Japan 110/B4
Shimagahara, Japan 109/K6
Shimamoto, Japan 109/J6
Shimane (pref.), Japan 110/C3
Shimanovsk, Rus. 105/K1
Shimasahi, Japan 109/K5
Shimba Hills Nat'l Rsvs., Kenya 145/B3
Shimbara (bay), Japan 110/B4
Shimber Berris (peak), Som. 144/C3
Shimen, China 106/H6
Shimenqiao, China 113/F2
Shimizu, Japan 111/F3
Shimizu, Japan 108/C2
Shimizu, Japan 109/B3
Shimo-koshiki (isl.), Japan 110/A5
Shimobe, Japan 109/A3
Shimoda, Japan 111/F3
Shimodate, Japan 111/F2
Shimofusa, Japan 109/E2
Shimoichi, Japan 109/J7
Shimokita (pen.), Japan 108/B3
Shimonita, Japan 109/B1
Shimonoseki, Japan 110/B4
Shimotsuma, Japan 109/D1
Shimoyama, Japan 109/M5
Shimsk, Rus. 67/P2
Shimukappu, Japan 108/C2
Shin (lake), Sc, UK 57/R7
Shin, Japan 109/C1
Shinan, China 120/E1
Shinano (riv.), Japan 105/M4
Shināş, Oman 127/G4
Shinch'ŏrwon, SKor. 107/D3
Shindo, SKor. 107/F6
Shiner, Tx, US 177/F3
Shingbwiyang, Myan. 112/C3
Shingleton, Mi, US 186/C1
Shingū, Japan 110/D4
Shingwidzi, SAfr. 149/F4
Shinhyŏn, SKor. 110/A3
Shinji (lake), Japan 110/C3
Shinjō, Japan 108/B4
Shinjō, Japan 109/J7
Shinkawa, Japan 109/L5
Shinminato, Japan 111/E2
Shinnecock (bay), NY, US 195/F2
Shinnecock Ind. Res., NY, US 195/F2
Shinnston, WV, US 186/F5
Shinrone, Ire. 58/C4
Shinsei, Japan 109/L5
Shintoku, Japan 108/C2
Shintone, Japan 109/E2
Shinyanga, Tanz. 145/A2
Shinyanga (prov.), Tanz. 145/A2
Shio-no-misaki (cape), Japan 110/D4
Shiogama, Japan 111/G1
Shioya-saki (pt.), Japan 111/G2
Ship (isl.), Ms, US 190/D2
Ship Bottom, NJ, US 194/D4
Shipai, China 113/H3
Shipbourne, Eng, UK 56/D3
Shiping, China 113/F3
Shipka, Bul. 77/G4
Shipley, Eng, UK 61/G4
Shipman, Va, US 189/H2
Shippan (pt.), Ct, US 195/L7
Shippegan, NB, Can. 184/E2
Shippegan (isl.), NB, Can. 184/E2
Shippensburg, Pa, US 187/H4
Shippo, Japan 109/L5
Shiprock, NM, US 175/H2
Shipston on Stour, Eng, UK 63/E2
Shipuqi (pass), China 125/C5
Shiqiao, China 113/H3
Shiqiao, China 113/E2
Shiqijie, China 105/K3
Shīr (mtn.), Iran 129/H4
Shirakami-misaki (cape), Japan 108/B3
Shirakawa, Japan 111/G2
Shirakawa, Japan 109/M4
Shirakawa-tōge (pass), Japan 110/E3
Shirako, Japan 109/E3
Shirane, Japan 109/A2
Shirane-san (peak), Japan 111/F2
Shirane-san (peak), Japan 111/F3
Shiranuka, Japan 108/D2
Shiraoi, Japan 108/B2
Shiraoka, Japan 109/D1
Shirati, Tanz. 145/A2
Shiraz (int'l arpt.), Iran 129/H4
Shīrāz, Iran 129/H4
Shirbīn, Egypt 139/C2
Shire (riv.), Malw. 149/G3
Shireet, Mong. 104/G2
Shiremoor, Eng, UK 61/G1
Shiren, China 107/D2
Shiretoko NP, Japan 108/D1
Shiretoko-misaki (cape), Japan 108/D1
Shiriya-zaki (pt.), Japan 108/B3
Shirjiu (lake), China 106/D5
Shirley, Ar, US 179/H3
Shirley, NY, US 195/F2
Shiro, Tx, US 177/G2
Shiroi, Japan 109/E2
Shiroishi, Japan 111/G1
Shirone, Japan 111/F2
Shiroyama, Japan 109/C2
Shīrvān, Iran 129/J2

Shishaldin (vol.), Ak, US 168/W13
Shishan, China 113/H3
Shishang, China 113/H3
Shīshgarh, India 122/B1
Shishhid (riv.), Mong.,Rus. 104/D1
Shishou, China 113/G2
Shisht al An'ām, Egypt 139/B3
Shisui, Japan 109/E2
Shitang, China 113/J2
Shitang, China 113/G3
Shithātha, Iraq 129/E3
Shiting (riv.), China 112/E2
Shituan, China 112/E2
Shivachevo, Bul. 77/H4
Shivalaya, Bang. 123/G4
Shiven (riv.), Ire. 58/B3
Shivers, Ms, US 190/D2
Shivpurī, India 122/A3
Shivpuri NP, India 122/A3
Shivwits (plat.), Az, Nv, US 175/F2
Shixing, China 119/K3
Shiyan, China 106/B4
Shizigoukou, China 104/F5
Shizipu, China 113/H2
Shizong, China 112/D3
Shizugawa, Japan 108/B4
Shizuishan, China 104/F4
Shizukuishi, Japan 108/B4
Shizunai, Japan 108/C2
Shizuoka, Japan 111/F3
Shizuoka (pref.), Japan 111/E3
Shklov, Bela. 67/P4
Shkodër, Alb. 75/F1
Shkumbin (riv.), Alb. 76/E5
Shoal (cr.), Il, US 181/K4
Shoal (pt.), Austl. 156/B4
Shoal Harbour, Nf, Can. 185/L1
Shoal Lake, Mb, Can. 182/D2
Shoalhaven Heads, Austl. 159/E2
Shoals, In, US 188/D1
Shoalwater Ind. Res., Wa, US 170/B4
Shōbara, Japan 110/C3
Shōbu, Japan 109/D1
Shōdo (isl.), Japan 110/D3
Shoe (mtn.), Ok, US 179/G3
Shoeburyness, Eng, UK 63/G3
Shoemakersville, Pa, US 194/C3
Shokanbetsu-dake (peak), Japan 108/B2
Sholāpur, India 121/B2
Sholl (peak), Arg. 215/D6
Shomron (ruin), WBnk. 131/C4
Shon (canal), Fl, US 190/N7
Shōnan, Japan 109/E2
Shonto, Az, US 175/G2
Shoreacres, BC, Can. 170/F3
Shoreham, Mn, US 182/G4
Shoreham, Mi, US 186/C3
Shoreham, Vt, US 187/K3
Shoreham-by-Sea, Eng, UK 63/F5
Shoreview, Mn, US 183/P6
Shorewood, Il, US 193/P16
Shorewood, Wi, US 193/Q13
Shorkot, Pak. 124/B4
Shorkot Road, Pak. 124/B4
Shorncliffe (nbrhd.), Austl. 160/F6
Shorne, Eng, UK 56/E2
Short (mtn.), Tn, US 188/E3
Shorter, Al, US 188/E4
Shorterville, Al, US 191/F2
Shortland (isls.), Sol. 162/E5
Shorwell, Eng, UK 63/E5
Shoshone (lake), Wy, US 173/H1
Shoshone, Ca, US 174/D3
Shoshone (mts.), Nv, US 172/E4
Shoshone (riv.), Wy, US 173/J1
Shoshone, Id, US 173/F2
Shoshone (falls), Id, US 173/F2
Shoshong, Bots. 149/E4
Shoshoni, Wy, US 173/J2
Shostka, Ukr. 99/G2
Shotley, Eng, UK 63/H3
Shotton, Eng, UK 61/G2
Shotts, Sc, UK 59/C5
Shou Xian, China 106/D4
Shouguang, China 106/D3
Shouyang, China 106/C3
Shoval, Isr. 131/B6
Show Low, Az, US 175/G3
Shōwa, Japan 109/B2
Shōwa, Japan 109/D2
Shoyna, Rus. 95/K2
Shozhma, Rus. 94/J3
Shpakovskoye, Rus. 99/M5
Shpanberga (chan.), Rus. 108/E2
Shpola, Ukr. 98/F3
Shreve, Oh, US 186/E4
Shreveport, La, US 176/H1
Shrewsbury, Eng, UK 62/D1
Shrewsbury, Pa, US 194/B4
Shriner Mtn. (mtn.), Pa, US 194/A2
Shropshire (co.), Eng, UK 61/E6
Shropshire Union (canal), Eng, UK 61/F6
Shrule, Ire. 58/A2
Shū (riv.), Kaz. 101/H5
Shū, Kaz. 100/H5
Shu (riv.), China 106/D5
Shu`bah (wadi), Libya 134/D2
Shuangbai, China 112/D3
Shuangcheng, China 101/N5
Shuangfeng, China 106/L8
Shuanghechang, China 113/E2
Shuangliao, China 106/E2
Shuangpai, China 119/K2
Shuangpaishan, China 113/G3
Shuangxi, China 113/H3
Shuangyang, China 105/K3
Shuangyashan, China 105/L2
Shubarkuduk, Kaz. 97/L2
Shubarshi, Kaz. 97/K2
Shubenacadie, NS, Can. 184/F3
Shubert, Ne, US 181/G3
Shubrā al Khaymah, Egypt 139/C4
Shubrā Khīt, Egypt 139/B2
Shubuta, Ms, US 190/D2
Shucheng, China 106/D5
Shu'fāţ, WBnk. 131/C5
Shuganu, India 112/B3
Shugurovo, Rus. 95/M5
Shuibatang, China 113/E2
Shuibei, China 113/H3
Shuiche, China 113/H3
Shuiji, China 113/H3
Shuijiang, China 113/E2
Shuikou, China 113/H3
Shuikou, China 113/G4
Shuikou, China 113/G3
Shuikouguan, China 120/D1
Shuiluo (riv.), China 112/D2
Shuimenzi, China 107/B3
Shuinan, China 113/H3
Shuiping, China 104/F5
Shuiyang (riv.), China 106/D5
Shuizhan, China 104/C4
Shujāābād, Pak. 124/A5
Shuksan (mt.), Wa, US 170/D3
Shulan, China 105/K3
Shule (riv.), China 100/K6
Shulehe, China 104/D3
Shulerville, SC, US 189/H4
Shumagin (isls.), Ak, US 168/W13
Shumanay, Uzb. 97/L4
Shumen, Bul. 77/H4
Shumerlya, Rus. 95/K5
Shumikha, Rus. 95/P5
Shumilinskaya, Rus. 99/L3
Shums'k, Ukr. 98/D2
Shuna (isl.), Sc, UK 59/A3
Shūnah (wadi), Egypt 139/C5
Shunak (peak), Kaz. 125/B2
Shūnat Nimrīn, Jor. 131/D5
Shun'ga, Rus. 94/G3
Shunyi, China 106/H6
Shuo Xian, China 106/C3
Shuoliang, China 113/E4
Shuolong, China 120/D1
Shupīyan, India 124/C3
Shuqualak, Ms, US 188/C4
Shūr (riv.), Iran 127/G2
Shūr Āb, Iran 129/G3
Shurayk, Sudan 142/G2
Shurugwi, Zim. 149/F3
Shūsh, Iran 129/G3
Shushenskoye, Rus. 125/F1
Shūshtar, Iran 129/G3
Shuswap (lake), BC, Can. 170/E2
Shuswap (riv.), BC, Can. 170/E2
Shuwak, Sudan 142/G2
Shuwaykah, WBnk. 131/C4
Shuya, Rus. 94/J4
Shuyang, China 106/D4
Shuyeretskoye, Rus. 94/G2
Shwebandaw, Myan. 112/B5
Shwebo, Myan. 112/B4
Shwedaung, Myan. 112/B5
Shwegun, Myan. 112/C5
Shwegyin, Myan. 112/C5
Shweli (riv.), Myan. 112/C4
Shwemawdaw Pagoda, Myan. 112/C5
Shwethalyaung (Reclining Buddha), Myan. 112/C5
Shyghys Qazaqstan (oblast), Kaz. 100/J5
Shymkent, Kaz. 125/A3
Shyok (riv.), India 125/C5
Shyroke, Ukr. 99/G4
Shyshaky, Ukr. 99/H3
Si Chiang Mai, Thai. 120/C2
Si Chon, Thai. 120/B4
Si Khiu, Thai. 120/C3
Si Piso-Piso (falls), Indo. 115/B2
Si Racha, Thai. 120/C3
Si Satchanalai (ruin), Thai. 120/B2
Si Satchanalai, Thai. 120/B2
Si Xian, China 106/D4
Siagne (riv.), Fr. 90/C5
Siāh Kūh (mts.), Afg. 127/H2
Siak (riv.), Indo. 116/B3
Siaksriinderapura, Indo. 115/C2
Siālkot, Pak. 124/C3
Sialum, PNG 155/G1
Siana, India 118/B2
Siano, It. 92/D6
Sianów, Pol. 66/G4
Sianton (isl.), Indo. 115/D2
Siapa (riv.), Ven. 205/E4
Siargao (isl.), Phil. 114/D3
Siasconset, Ma, US 184/C5
Siasi, Phil. 114/C4
Siasikabole, Zam. 149/E3
Siassi, PNG 155/G1
Siaton, Phil. 114/C3
Siaton (pt.), Phil. 114/C3
Siau (isl.), Indo. 117/G3
Šiauliai, Lith. 67/K4
Siavonga, Zam. 149/F3
Sibalom, Phil. 114/C3
Sibanyati, Zam. 149/E3
Sibasa, SAfr. 149/F4
Sibay, Rus. 97/L1
Sibbhultån (riv.), Swe. 65/L6
Sibbo (Sipoo), Fin. 67/L1
Šibenik, Cro. 76/B4
Siberia (reg.), Rus. 103/H3
Siberut (isl.), Indo. 103/J10
Sibi, Pak. 127/J3
Sibidiri, PNG 155/F2
Sibigo, Indo. 115/A2
Sibiloi NP, Kenya 142/H4
Sibirtsevo, Rus. 105/L3
Sibiti, Congo 146/C3
Sibiu (prov.), Rom. 77/G2
Sibiu, Rom. 77/G3
Sible Hedingham, Eng, UK 63/G3
Sibley, Ms, US 190/C2
Sibley, Ia, US 181/G2
Sibolga, Indo. 115/B2
Siboluton, Indo. 117/F3
Sibong, India 112/B3
Siborongborong, Indo. 115/B2
Sibsāgar, India 112/B3
Sibsoo, Bhu. 123/G2
Sibu, Malay. 116/D3
Sibuatan (mtn.), Indo. 115/B2
Sibuco, Phil. 114/C4
Sibuguey (bay), Phil. 114/C4
Sibuhuan, Indo. 115/B2
Sibut, CAfr. 142/C4
Sibutu Passage (chan.), Malay,Phil. 114/B4
Sibuyan (sea), Phil. 117/F1
Sibuyan (isl.), Phil. 117/F1
Siby, Burk. 140/E4
Sicamous, BC, Can. 170/E2
Sicapoo (mt.), Phil. 114/C1
Sichifulo (riv.), Zam. 148/E3
Sichuan (prov.), China 104/E5
Sicié (cape), Fr. 90/B6
Sicilia (pol. reg.), It. 74/C4
Sicily (str.), It. 93/F3
Sicily (isl.), It. 55/F5
Sicily Island, La, US 190/C2
Sicily Island (mtn.), La, US 190/C2
Sico (riv.), Hon. 196/D4
Sicuani, Peru 208/D4
Šid, Yugo. 76/D3
Sīdamo (prov.), Eth. 142/H4
Sidaogou, China 107/D2
Sidcup (nbrhd.), Eng, UK 56/D2
Sidéradougou, Burk. 140/D4
Siderno Marina, It. 74/E3
Sidirópolis, Braz. 213/G4
Sidewinder (mtn.), Ca, US 192/C1
Sidhaulī, India 122/C2
Sidhi, India 122/C3
Sidhirókastron, Gre. 75/H2
Sidhpur, India 127/K4
Sidi Aïssa, Alg. 138/G5
Sidi Allal el Bahraoui, Mor. 138/A2
Sīdī Barrānī, Egypt 135/E2
Sidi Bel-Abbes, Alg. 138/E5
Sidi Bennour, Mor. 136/C2
Sīdī Bū Zayd (gov.), Tun. 74/A5
Sīdī Ghāzī, Egypt 139/C2
Sidi Ifni, Mor. 136/C3
Sidi Kacem, Mor. 138/B2
Sidi Kacem (prov.), Mor. 138/B2
Sīdī Nājī, Tun. 138/M6
Sīdī Şāliḩ (well), Libya 134/C2
Sīdī Sālim, Egypt 139/B2
Sidi Slimane, Mor. 138/B2
Sīdī 'Umar Bū Ḩajalah, Tun. 74/B5
Sidi Yahya du Rharb, Mor. 138/A2
Sidikalang, Indo. 115/B2
Sidlaw (hills), Sc, UK 59/C3
Sidmouth (cape), Austl. 155/F3
Sidmouth, Eng, UK 62/C5
Sīdmūkh, India 124/C5
Sidnaw, Mi, US 183/K4
Sidney, BC, Can. 170/C3
Sidney, Mb, Can. 182/E3
Sidney, Ar, US 179/J2
Sidney, Ia, US 181/G3
Sidney, Mt, US 182/B4
Sidney, Ne, US 180/C3
Sidney, NY, US 187/J3
Sidney, Oh, US 186/D4
Sidney Draw (riv.), Co, Ne, US 180/C3
Sidney Lanier (res.), Ga, US 188/E3
Sidoarjo, Indo. 115/F3
Sidon (Şaydā), Leb. 131/C1
Sidra (gulf), Libya 133/D1
Sidrolândia, Braz. 213/F2
Sidvokodvo, Swaz. 151/E2
Sieci, It. 89/E6
Siedlce, Pol. 69/M2
Siedlce (prov.), Pol. 69/L2
Sieg (riv.), Ger. 71/G1
Siegburg, Ger. 81/G2
Siegel (mtn.), Mt, US 170/G4
Siegen, Ger. 81/H2
Siegenburg, Ger. 85/E5
Siegendorf im Burgenland, Aus. 76/C2
Sielo, Libr. 140/C4
Siemianówka (lake), Pol. 69/M2
Siemiatycze, Pol. 69/M2
Siempang, Camb. 120/D3
Siemreab, Camb. 120/C3
Siena (prov.), It. 89/E6
Siena, It. 71/J5
Sienne (riv.), Fr. 70/C2
Sieradz (prov.), Pol. 69/K3
Sieradz, Pol. 69/K3
Sieraków, Pol. 69/J2
Sierning, Aus. 85/H6
Sierpc, Pol. 69/K2
Sierra (peak), Ca, US 192/C3
Sierra Army Depot, Ca, US 172/C3
Sierra Blanca, Tx, US 177/B2
Sierra Chilengue (mts.), Ang. 148/B2
Sierra City, Ca, US 172/C4
Sierra Colorada, Arg. 214/D4
Sierra de Amambay (mts.), Par.,Braz. 213/F2
Sierra de Calalaste (mts.), Arg. 212/C3
Sierra de Juarez (mts.), Mex. 174/E4
Sierra de Misiones (mts.), Arg. 213/F3
Sierra de Olte (hills), Arg 214/C4
Sierra de S. Luis (mts.), Arg. 214/D2
Sierra de San Jonquín (mts.), Par. 213/F3
Sierra de la Giganta (mts.), Mex. 198/C3
Sierra de la Macarena, PN, Col. 204/C4
Sierra de Perijá (mts.), Col. 197/G6
Sierra de San Pedro Mártir, Mex. 198/B2
Sierra de Serpe de Coba (peak), Sp. 72/B1
Sierra del Carmen, Mex. 177/C3
Sierra del Nevado (mts.), Arg. 214/C3
Sierra Gorda, Chile 212/B2
Sierra Grande, Arg. 214/D4
Sierra Leone (cape), SLeo. 140/B4
Sierra Leone (ctry.) 133/A4
Sierra Madre, Ca, US 192/F7
Sierra Madre (mts.), Phil. 114/C1
Sierra Madre (mts.), Ca., US 174/C3
Sierra Madre del Sur (mts.), Mex. 196/A4
Sierra Madre Occidental (mts.), Mex. 165/G7
Sierra Madre Oriental (mts.), Mex. 165/G7
Sierra Maestra (mts.), Cuba 201/G2
Sierra Nacimiento (mts.), NM, US 178/A2
Sierra Nevada (mts.), Sp. 72/D4
Sierra Nevada (mts.), US 165/E6
Sierra Nevada de Santa Marta, Col. 201/H4
Sierra Nevada de Santa Marta, PN, Col. 197/G5
Sierra Nevada, PN, Ven. 197/G6
Sierra San Pedro Martir (mts.), Mex. 198/B2
Sierra Vieja (mts.), Mex. 177/B2
Sierra Vista, Az, US 175/G5
Sierra Vizcaíno (mts.), Mex. 198/B3
Sierras Bayas, Arg. 214/E3
Sierras de Córdoba (mts.), Arg. 212/C4
Sierre, Swi. 86/D5
Siesta Key (isl.), Fl, US 191/G4
Siete Picos (peak), Sp. 73/M8
Siete Tazas, PN, Chile 214/C2
Sieve (riv.), It. 89/E5
Sif Fatima, Alg. 137/H3
Sīfenī, Eth. 144/B2
Siffray, Gui. 140/C4
Sifié, C.d'Iv. 140/D5
Sífnos (isl.), Gre. 75/J4
Sig, Alg. 138/E5
Siga (hills), Tanz. 145/A2
Sigean, Fr. 70/E5
Sigep, Indo. 115/B3
Sigep (cape), Indo. 115/B3
Siggerud, Nor. 64/S8
Siġġiewi, Malta 74/L7
Sighetu Marmaţiei, Rom. 98/B4
Sighişoara, Rom. 77/G2
Sighty Crag (hill), Eng, UK 61/F1
Sigillo, It. 89/F7
Sigli, Indo. 115/A1
Sigli (cape), Alg. 138/H4
Siglufjördhur, Ice. 64/N6
Sigmaringen, Ger. 87/F1
Sigmarszell, Ger. 87/F2
Signa, It. 89/E6
Signakhi, Geo. 97/H4
Signal (hill), SD, US 180/C2
Signal de la Mère Boitier (peak), Fr. 70/F3
Signal de Saint-Andre (peak), Fr. 90/A1
Signal de Toussaines (peak), Fr. 82/B4
Signal d'Écouves (peak), Fr. 83/F3
Signal Hill, Ca, US 192/F8
Signau, Swi. 86/D4
Signes, Fr. 90/B6
Signy-L'Abbaye, Fr. 81/D4
Signy-le-Petit, Fr. 81/D4
Signy-Signets, Fr. 56/M5
Sigourney, Ia, US 181/H3
Sigriswil, Swi. 86/D4
Sigtuna, Swe. 66/G2
Siguatepeque, Hon. 200/E3
Sigüe, Ecu. 204/B4
Sigüenza, Sp. 72/D2
Siguiri, Gui. 140/C4
Sigulda, Lat. 67/L3
Sigura Gura (falls), Indo. 115/B2
Sigurd, Ut, US 175/G1
Sihl (riv.), Swi. 87/E3
Sihlsee (lake), Swi. 87/E3
Sihochac, Mex. 200/D2
Sihong, China 106/D4
Sihorā, India 122/C4
Sihuas, Peru 208/B3
Siilinjärvi, Fin. 94/E3
Si'īr, WBnk. 131/C5
Siirt, Turk. 128/E2
Siirt (prov.), Turk. 128/E2
Sijung, NKor. 107/D2
Sikandarābād, India 122/A1
Sikandarpur, India 123/E2
Sikandra Rao, India 122/B2
Sikanni Chief (riv.), BC, Can. 166/D3
Sikasso, Mali 140/D4
Sikasso (pol. reg.), Mali 140/D4
Sikaw, Myan. 112/C4
Sikeston, Mo, US 188/C2
Sikhote-alin' (mts.), Rus. 101/P5
Síkinos, Gre. 75/J4
Síkinos (isl.), Gre. 75/J4
Sikinssa, C.d'Iv. 140/D5
Sikkim (state), India 118/E2
Siklós, Hun. 76/D3
Sikoúrion, Gre. 75/H3
Siktyakh, Rus. 101/N3
Sikuati, Malay. 114/B4
Sikwane, Bots. 148/E5
Silai (riv.), India 123/F4
Šilalė, Lith. 67/K4
Silandro (Schlanders), It. 87/G4
Silao, India 123/E3
Silao, Mex. 199/E4
Sīlat Az Ẓahr, WBnk. 131/C4
Silay, Phil. 114/C3
Silchar, India 112/B3
Sildā, India 123/F4
Şile, Turk. 77/J5
Silea, It. 89/F2
Sileby, Eng, UK 63/E1
Silel (riv.), Som. 144/B3
Silenen, Swi. 87/E4
Siler City, NC, US 189/H3
Silesia (reg.), Pol. 69/H3
Silet, Alg. 137/G5
Siletz (riv.), Or, US 172/B1
Siletz, Or, US 172/B1
Silgadhī, Nepal 122/C1
Silifke, Turk. 130/C1
Silīguri, India 123/G2
Siling (lake), China 125/E5
Silisili (mt.), WSam. 163/R9
Silistra, Bul. 77/H3
Silivri, Turk. 77/J5
Siljan (lake), Swe. 66/F1
Siljansnäs, Swe. 66/F1
Silkeborg, Den. 66/C3
Silksworth, Eng, UK 61/G2
Sill (riv.), Aus. 87/H3
Silla, Sp 73/E3
Silla Tombs, SKor. 110/A3
Sillajguay (peak), Chile 212/B1
Sillajhuay (peak), Bol. 212/B1
Sillamäe, Est. 67/M2
Sillānwāli, Pak. 124/B4
Sillaro (riv.), It. 89/E4
Sillé-le-Guillame, Fr. 83/E4
Silleda, Sp. 72/A1
Sillen (lake), Swe. 65/A2
Sillian, Aus. 71/K3
Sillil, Som. 144/B3
Silloth, Eng, UK 61/E2
Sillustani (ruin), Peru 208/D4
Silly-le-Long, Fr. 56/L4
Silo, Ok, US 179/F3
Siloam Springs, Ar, US 179/G2
Silopi, Turk. 128/E2
Silsbee, Tx, US 177/G2
Silsden, Eng, UK 61/G4
Silsersee (lake), Swi. 87/F5
Siltcoos (lake), Or, US 172/A2
Silton, Sk, Can. 182/B2
Siltou (well), Chad 142/B1
Siluas, Indo. 116/C3
Siluko, Nga. 141/G5
Šilutė, Lith. 67/J4
Silva, Mo, US 188/B2
Silvan (dam), Turk. 128/E2
Silvāni, India 122/B4
Silvania, Col. 207/L8
Silvânia, Braz. 210/C3
Silvaplana, Swi. 87/F5
Silver (mtn.), Ca, US 192/C1
Silver (cr.), Ia, US 181/G3
Silver (riv.), Il, US 181/K4
Silver (cr.), Or, US 172/D2
Silver (lake), Or, US 172/C2
Silver, Tx, US 176/D1
Silver Bay, Mn, US 183/J4
Silver Bell, Az, US 175/G4
Silver City, NM, US 175/H4
Silver City, SD, US 180/C1
Silver Cliff, Co, US 178/B1
Silver Creek, NY, US 187/G3
Silver Lake, Mn, US 181/G1
Silver Lake, Or, US 172/C2
Silver Lake, Wi, US 193/P14
Silver Lake NWR, ND, US 182/E3
Silver Lake-Fircrest, Wa, US 193/C2
Silver Meadow (lake), NJ, US 194/C5
Silver Run, Md, US 194/A4
Silver Spring, Md, US 194/A6
Silver Springs, Fl, US 191/G3
Silver Springs, Nv, US 172/D4
Silver Star, Mt, US 173/G1
Silver Water, On, Can. 186/E2
Silverado, Ca, US 192/C3
Silverdale, Eng, UK 61/F3
Silverdale, Wa, US 170/C4
Silverdale, Austl. 159/E1
Silverstone, Eng, UK 63/E2
Silverton, Austl. 158/B1
Silverton, Eng, UK 62/C5
Silverton, Co, US 175/J2
Silverton, NJ, US 194/D3
Silverton, Or, US 172/B1
Silverton, Tx, US 178/C3
Silverton, Wa, US 170/C3
Silverwood (lake), Ca, US 192/C2
Silves, Port. 72/A4
Silves, Braz. 206/B3
Silvi, It. 92/C2
Silvia, Col. 204/B4
Silvies (riv.), Or, US 172/C2
Silvio Pettirossi (Asunción) (int'l arpt.), Par. 212/E3
Silvretta (mts.), Aus. 87/G4
Silyānah (gov.), Tun. 74/A4
Silyānah, Tun. 138/L6
Silz, Aus. 87/G3
Sim (cape), Mor. 136/C3
Sima, Com. 152/H6
Sima, Congo 146/C3
Simao, China 112/C4
Simão Dias, Braz. 211/F1
Şimareh (riv.), Iran 129/F3
Simav, Turk. 128/E2
Simba, D.R. Congo 147/E2
Simbach am Inn, Ger. 85/G6
Simbai, PNG 155/G1
Simbo, Tanz. 147/G4
Simbruini (mts.), It. 91/E3
Simcoe (lake), On, Can. 187/G2
Simcoe, On, Can. 186/F3
Simcoe (lake), Qu, Can. 167/J4
Simdega, India 123/E4
Simen (mts.), Eth. 142/H2
Simen Mountains NP, Eth. 142/H2
Simeria, Rom. 76/F3
Simeto (riv.), It. 93/G3
Simeulue (isl.), Indo. 103/J9
Simeyiz, Ukr. 99/H5
Simferopol (int'l arpt.), Ukr. 99/G5
Simferopol', Ukr. 99/H5
Simga, India 121/D1
Sími, Gre. 128/A2
Simi (hills), Ca, US 192/B2
Simi Valley, Ca, US 192/B2
Simijaca, Col. 207/M7
Simikot, Nepal 125/D6
Similaun (peak), Aus., It. 87/G4
Similkameen (riv.), BC, Can. 170/D3
Simití, Col. 204/C3
Simitli, Bul. 75/H2
Simiyu (riv.), Tanz. 145/A2
Simla, India 124/D4
Şimleu Silvaniei, Rom. 77/F2
Simme (riv.), Swi. 71/G3
Simmelsdorf, Ger. 85/E3
Simmerath, Ger. 81/F2
Simmerbach (riv.), Ger. 81/G4
Simmern, Ger. 81/G4
Simmertal, Ger. 81/G4
Simmesport, La, US 190/C2
Simmons, Mo, US 179/H2
Simmszand (isl.), Neth. 78/D2
Simnas, Lith. 67/K4
Simni (isl.), NKor. 107/C3
Simo, Fin. 94/E2
Simões, Braz. 207/F4
Simões Filho, Braz. 211/F2
Simojovel de Allende, Mex. 200/C2
Simón Bolívar (int'l arpt.), Ecu. 204/B5
Simón Bolívar (int'l arpt.), Ven. 207/P7
Simoncello (peak), It. 89/F6
Simonds, NB, Can. 184/D2
Simonstown, SAfr. 150/L11
Simonton, Tx, US 177/G3
Simpang, Indo. 115/D3
Simpang Tiga (int'l arpt.), Indo. 115/C2
Simpang-kiri (riv.), Indo. 116/A3
Simpangulim, Indo. 115/B1
Simpelveld, Neth. 81/E2
Simplício Mendes, Braz. 207/F4
Simplon, Swi. 86/E5
Simplonpass (pass), Swi. 86/E5
Simpson (isl.), On, Can. 183/L3
Simpson, La, US 190/B2
Simpson (riv.), Nun, Can. 166/G2
Simpson (pen.), Nun, Can. 166/G2
Simpson, Sk, Can. 171/M2
Simpson, Mt, US 171/J3
Simpson (des.), Austl. 153/C3
Simpson Desert Consv. Park, Austl. 157/H3
Simpson Desert NP, Austl. 157/H3
Simpsons Gap NP, Austl. 157/G2
Simrishamn, Swe. 66/F4
Sims, Ar, US 179/H3
Sims Bayou (riv.), Tx, US 177/M9
Simunul, Phil. 114/B4
Simupu (isl.), Indo. 154/A1
Sin-le-Noble, Fr. 80/C3
Sinabang, Indo. 115/B2
Sinadhago, Som. 144/C4
Sinaia, Rom. 77/G3
Sinait, Phil. 114/C1
Sinaloa (state), Mex. 198/D3
Sinaloa de Leyva, Mex. 198/C3
Sinalunga, It. 71/J5
Sinarca (riv.), It. 92/D4
Sīnāwin, Libya 137/H3
Sinazongwe, Zam. 149/E3
Sincé, Col. 204/C2
Sincelejo, Col. 204/C2
Sinceny, Fr. 80/C4
Sinch'ang, NKor. 107/E2
Sinch'ŏn, NKor. 107/C3
Sinclair, Wy, US 173/K3
Sinclair (pt.), Austl. 157/G5
Sinclair (res.), Ga, US 189/F4
Sind (riv.), India 118/C2
Sindal, Den. 66/D3
Sindañgan, Phil. 114/C3
Sindangbarang, Indo. 115/D3
Sindelfingen, Ger. 84/C5
Sindh (prov.), Pak. 118/A2
Sindhulimādi, Nepal 123/E2
Sindi, Est. 67/L2
Sindī (wadi), Sudan 142/E2
Sındırgı, Turk. 96/D5
Sindou, Burk. 140/D4
Sinegorskiy, Rus. 99/L3
Sinekçi, Turk. 77/H5
Sinello (riv.), It. 92/D3
Sinendé, Ben. 141/F4
Sines (cape), Port. 72/A4
Sines, Port. 72/A4
Sinfra, C.d'Iv. 140/D5
Sing Buri, Thai. 120/C3
Singapore (ctry.) 103/K9
Singapore (str.), Indo., Sing. 115/H7
Singapore City (nbrhd.), Sing. 115/J6
Singar, India 118/B2
Singaraja, Indo. 115/F3
Singen, Ger. 87/E2
Sîngeorz-Băi, Rom. 98/C4
Singerei, Mol. 98/E4
Singida (prov.), Tanz. 145/A3
Singida, Tanz. 145/A3
Singim, China 125/E3
Singitic (gulf), Gre. 93/K2
Singkaling Hkamti, Myan. 112/B3
Singkang, Indo. 117/F4
Singkawang, Indo. 116/C3
Singkep (isl.), Indo. 116/B4
Singkil, Indo. 115/B2
Singkuang, Indo. 115/B2
Singleton (mt.), Austl. 157/F2
Singleton (mt.), Austl. 156/C4
Singleton, Austl. 159/E1
Singou, Rés. Tot. de Faune Du Burk. 141/F4
Singra, Bang. 123/G3
Singu, Myan. 112/C4
Singuédeze (riv.), Moz. 149/F4
Sin'gye, NKor. 107/D3
Singou, Res Tot. de Faune du, Burk. 141/F4
Sinhŭng, NKor. 107/D2
Sinincay, Ecu. 204/B5
Siniscola, It. 74/A2
Siniye Lipyagi, Rus. 99/K2
Sinjah, Sudan 142/G2
Sinjār, Iraq 128/E2
Sinjil, WBnk. 131/C4
Sinkāt, Sudan 135/H5
Sinking (riv.), Ire. 58/B2
Sinlumkaba, Myan. 119/G3
Sinmak, NKor. 107/D3
Sinn (riv.), Ger. 68/E3
Sinnam-dok-san (peak), NKor. 107/D2
Sinnamary, FrG. 206/C1
Sinnamary (riv.), FrG. 206/C1
Sinnar, India 118/B4
Sînnicolau Mare, Rom. 76/E2
Sinnūris, Egypt 139/B6
Sinnyŏng, SKor. 107/E4
Sino (co.), Libr. 140/C5
Sinoe (lake), Rom. 93/L1
Sinop, Braz. 210/B1
Sinop (prov.), Turk. 96/E4
Sinop (pt.), Turk. 96/E4
Sinop, Turk. 96/E4
Sinos, Rio dos (riv.), Braz. 213/G4
Sinp'a-ŭp, NKor. 107/D2
Sinp'o, NKor. 107/E2
Sinp'yŏng, NKor. 107/D3
Sinsheim, Ger. 84/B4
Sint Annaland, Neth. 78/B5
Sint Hubert, Neth. 78/C5
Sint Jacobiparochie, Neth. 78/C2
Sint Maartensdijk, Neth. 78/B5
Sint-Genesius-Rode, Belg 81/D2
Sint-Gillis-Waas, Belg. 78/B6
Sint-Katelijne-Waver, Belg. 81/D1
Sint-Laureins, Belg. 80/C1
Sint-Martens-Voeren, Belg. 81/E2
Sint-Michielsgestel, Neth. 78/C5
Sint-Niklaas, Belg. 78/B6
Sint-Oedenrode, Neth. 78/C5
Sint-Pieters-Leeuw, Belg. 81/D2
Sint-Truiden, Belg. 81/E2
Sint'ae-ri, NKor. 107/E2
Sint'aein, SKor. 107/D5
Sintang, Indo. 116/D3
Sinton, Tx, US 177/F3
Sintra (range), Port. 73/P10
Sintra, Port. 73/P10
Sinú (riv.), Col. 197/F6
Sinŭiju, NKor. 107/C2
Sinujif, Som. 144/D3
Sinwŏn, NKor. 107/C3
Sinyang, NKor. 107/D3
Sinyavino, Rus. 94/U7
Sinzheim, Ger. 84/B5
Sinzig, Ger. 81/G2
Sió (riv.), Hun. 76/D2
Sio, Kenya 145/A1
Siocon, Phil. 114/C4
Siófok, Hun. 76/D2
Sioma Ngwezi NP, Zam. 148/D3
Sion, Swi. 86/D5
Sion Mills, NI, UK 57/Q9
Sion-les-Mines, Fr. 82/D5
Sioule (riv.), Fr. 70/E4
Sioux Center, Ia, US 181/F2
Sioux City, Ia, US 181/F2
Sioux Falls, SD, US 181/F2
Sioux Lookout, On, Can. 183/J2
Sioux Narrows, On, Can. 183/G3
Sioux Rapids, Ia, US 181/G2
Sipalay, Phil. 114/C3
Sipaliwini (riv.), Sur. 205/G4
Sipaliwini (dist.), Sur. 205/H4
Siparia, Trin. 205/F2
Sipí, Col. 204/B3
Siping, China 106/F2
Sipitang, Malay. 114/A4
Sipiwesk (lake), Mb, Can. 166/G3
Siple (isl.), Ant. 216/R
Sipocot, Phil. 114/C2
Siponto (ruin), It. 74/D2
Sipoo (Sibbo), Fin. 67/L1
Sipoonselkä (bay), Fin. 65/F4
Sipsey (riv.), Al, US 188/D4
Sipura (isl.), Indo. 116/A4
Sipura (str.), Indo. 115/B3
Siqueira Campos, Braz. 213/G2
Siquia (riv.), Nic. 196/E5
Siquijar (isl.), Phil. 114/C3
Siquisique, Ven. 204/D2
Sir Edward Pellew Group (isls.), Austl. 155/E3
Sir James Macbrien (mt.), NW, Can. 166/D2
Sir James Mitchell NP, Austl. 156/C5
Sir John (cape), Austl. 159/C5
Sir Muttra, India 122/A2
Sir Sandford (mt.), BC. Can. 170/F2
Sir Seewoosagur Ramgoolam (int'l arpt.), Mrts. 151/T15
Sir Seretse Khama (Gaborone) (int'l arpt.), Bots. 148/E5
Sir Thomas (mt.), Austl. 157/F3
Sira (riv.), Nor. 64/C4
Sīra, India 121/C3
Sirac (peak), Fr. 90/C3
Siracusa (Syracuse), It. 74/D4
Sirājganj, Bang. 123/G3
Şiran, Turk. 128/D1
Sīrē, Eth. 144/A3
Siren, Wi, US 183/H5
Sirente (peak), It. 92/C3
Siret (riv.), Rom. 96/C3
Siret, Rom. 98/D4
Sirha, Nepal 123/F2
Sirhind, India 124/D4
Sīrīk, Iran 129/J5
Sirik (cape), Malay. 116/D3
Sirikit (res.), Thai. 112/D5
Sirinhaém, Braz. 207/H5
Sīrīs, WBnk. 131/C4
Sirit (res.), Thai. 119/H4
Sīrjān, Iran 129/H4
Sirmione, It. 88/D3
Sirnach, Swi. 87/F3
Şırnak, Turk. 128/E2
Sirohi, India 118/B3
Sirolo, It. 89/G6
Sirombu, Indo. 115/B2
Sironj, India 122/A3
Síros (isl.), Gre. 75/J4
Sirotinskaya, Rus. 99/M3
Siroua (peak), Mor. 136/D3
Sırpsındığı, Turk. 77/H5
Sirs al Layyānah, Egypt 139/B4
Sirsa, India 124/C5
Sirsāganj, India 122/B2
Sirsi, India 122/B1
Sirtica (reg.), Libya 134/C2
Siruma, Phil. 114/C2
Sīrvān (riv.), Iran 129/F3
Širvintos, Lith. 67/L4
Sisak, Cro. 76/C3
Sisaket, Thai. 120/D3
Sishen, SAfr. 150/C2
Sishui, China 106/D4
Sisian, Arm. 129/F2
Sisib (lake), Mb, Can. 182/E1
Sisikon, Swi. 87/E4
Siskiyou (mts.), Or, US 172/B2
Sisophon, Camb. 120/C3
Sissach, Swi. 86/D3
Sisséla, Gui. 140/C4
Sisseton, SD, US 182/F5
Sisseton-Wahpeton Ind. Res., SD, US 181/F1
Sissili (prov.), Burk. 141/E4
Sissonne, Fr. 80/C4
Sissonville, WV, US 189/G1
Sister Bay, Wi, US 186/C2
Sister Grove (cr.), Tx, US 176/L6
Sisteron, Fr. 90/B4
Sistersville, WV, US 186/F5
Sistina, It. 89/G2
Sistine Chapel, VatC. 91/G7
Sisto (riv.), It. 92/C5
Siswā Bāzār, India 122/D2
Sitacocha, Peru 208/B2
Sītākunda, Bang. 119/F3
Sitalike, Tanz. 147/G4
Sītāmarhi, India 123/E2
Sītāpur, India 122/C2
Sitārganj, India 122/B1
Siteki, Swaz. 151/E2
Sitges, Sp. 73/K7
Sithoniá (pen.), Gre. 96/C5
Sitía, Gre. 93/K4
Sitian, China 104/C3
Siting, China 113/E3
Sítio d'Badia, Braz. 210/D2
Sítio Novo do Grajaú, Braz. 207/E4
Sitka, Ak, US 168/Z13
Sitno (peak), Slvk. 76/D1
Sito Ganno, India 124/C4
Sitoti, Zam. 148/D3
Sittard, Neth. 81/E2
Sittensen, Ger. 79/G2
Sitter (riv.), Swi. 87/F3
Sittingbourne, Eng, UK 63/G4
Sitton (peak), Ca, US 192/C3
Sittwe (Akyab), Myan. 119/F3
Situbondo, Indo. 115/F3
Siuntio (Sjundeå), Fin. 65/E4
Siuslaw (riv.), Or, US 172/B2
Sivac, Yugo. 76/D3
Sivakāsi, India 121/C4
Sivaki, Rus. 105/K1
Sīvand, Iran 129/H4
Sivas, Turk. 128/D2
Sivas (prov.), Turk. 96/F5
Sivash (sound), Ukr. 99/H4
Sivé, Mrta. 140/B3
Siverek, Turk. 128/D2
Siverskiy, Rus. 67/P2
Siviriez, Swi. 86/C4
Sivomaskinskiy, Rus. 95/P2
Sivrihisar, Turk. 128/B2
Sivry-Courtry, Fr. 56/L6
Siwa, Indo. 117/F4
Siwa Oasis (oasis), Egypt 135/E2
Sīwah, Egypt 135/E2
Siwālik (range), India,Nepal 118/D2
Siwān, India 123/E2
Siwāni, India 124/C5
Six Flags Great Adventure, NJ, US 194/D3
Six Flags Great America, Il, US 193/Q15
Six Flags Magic Mountain, Ca, US 192/B2
Six Flags Over Georgia, Ga, US 189/L7
Six Flags Over Texas, Tx, US 176/K7
Six-Fours-la-Plage, Fr. 90/B6
Sixes, Or, US 172/A2
Sixmile (lake), La, US 190/C3
Sixmilebridge, Ire. 58/B4
Sixmilecross, NI, UK 60/A2
Sixth Cataract (falls), Sudan 142/G1
Siyabuswa, SAfr. 149/F5
Siyāna, India 122/B1
Siyang, China 106/D4
Siyäzän, Azer. 97/J4
Siyichang, China 112/E2
Siyitang, China 104/F3
Sizhoutou, China 113/J2
Siziano, It. 88/C3
Sizun, Fr. 82/A4
Sizyahsk, Rus. 95/M2
Sjælland (isl.), Den. 64/D5
Sjællands (pen.), Den. 65/H7
Sjenica, Yugo. 76/D4
Sjöberg, Swe. 65/A1
Sjöbo, Swe. 66/E4
Sjónfridh (peak), Ice. 64/M6
Sjösa, Swe. 65/A2
Sjundeå (Siuntio), Fin. 65/E4
Sjuntorp, Swe 66/E2
Skadovs'k, Ukr. 98/G4
Skaftafell NP, Ice. 64/P7
Skagen, Den. 66/D3
Skagens (The Skaw) (cape), Den. 66/D3
Skagern (lake), Swe. 66/F2
Skagerrak (str.), Nor.,Den. 55/E3
Skaget (peak), Nor. 66/C1
Skagit (riv.), Wa, US 170/D3
Skagway, Ak, US 168/Z13
Skaidi, Nor. 64/H1
Skaistkalne, Lat. 67/L3
Skála, Gre. 75/H4
Skälderviken (bay), Swe. 66/E3
Skálfandafljót (riv.), Ice. 64/P7
Skalica, Slvk. 69/J4
Skalice (riv.), Czh. 71/K2
Skalka (res.), Czh. 85/F2
Skælskør, Den. 66/D4
Skanderborg, Den. 66/C3
Skåne (reg.), Swe. 66/E4
Skaneateles, NY, US 187/H3
Skanes (int'l arpt.), Tun. 74/B5
Skånland, Nor. 64/F1
Skänninge, Swe. 66/F2
Skanör, Swe. 66/E4
Skantzoura (isl.), Gre. 75/J3
Skara, Swe. 66/E2
Skaraborg (co.), Swe. 64/E4
Skärblacka, Swe. 66/F2
Skārdu, Pak. 124/C2
Skåre, Swe. 66/E2
Skärholmen, Swe. 65/A1
Skarszewy, Pol. 66/H4
Skarven (lake), Swe. 65/A1
Skarżysko-Kamienna, Pol. 69/L3
Skateraw, Sc, UK 59/D5
Skattkärr, Swe. 66/E2
Skaudvilė, Lith. 67/K4
Skavaböle (Hyrylä), Fin. 65/F4
Skævinge, Den. 65/J7
Skaw, The (Skagens) (cape), Den. 66/D3
Skawina, Pol. 69/K4
Skederid, Swe. 65/B1
Skedviken (lake), Swe. 65/B1
Skeena (mts.), BC, Can. 166/D3
Skeena (riv.), BC, Can. 168/AA13
Skegemog (lake), Mi, US 186/D2
Skegness, Eng, UK 61/J5
Skeleton Coast Park, Namb. 148/B3
Skellefteå, Swe. 64/G2
Skellefteälven (riv.), Swe. 94/C2
Skelleftehamn, Swe. 64/G2
Skellytown, Tx, US 178/D3
Skelmanthorpe, Eng, UK 61/G4
Skelmersdale, Eng, UK 61/F4
Skelmorlie, Sc, UK 59/B5
Skelton, Eng, UK 61/H2
Skerne (riv.), Eng, UK 61/G2
Skerries, Ire. 60/B4
Skhimatárion, Gre. 75/H3
Skhirat, Mor. 138/A3
Skhirat Temara (prov.), Mor. 138/A3
Skhiza (isl.), Gre. 75/G4
Skhodnya (riv.), Rus. 94/W9
Ski, Nor. 66/D2
Skíathos, Gre. 75/H3
Skiatook, Ok, US 179/F2
Skibbereen, Ire. 58/A6
Skibby, Den. 65/H7
Skidaway Island, Ga, US 191/H2
Skidel', Bela. 67/L5
Skídhra, Gre. 75/H2
Skidmore, Mo, US 181/G3
Skidmore, Tx, US 176/F3
Skidway Lake, Mi, US 186/D2
Skien, Nor. 66/C2
Skierniewice (prov.), Pol. 69/K3
Skierniewice, Pol. 69/L3
Skiff, Ab, Can. 171/J3
Skikda, Alg. 138/K6
Skillet Fork (riv.), Il, US 188/C1
Skinári (cape), Gre. 75/G4
Skinnskatteberg, Swe. 66/F2
Skipness, Sc, UK 59/A5
Skipperville, Al, US 191/F2
Skipsea, Eng, UK 61/H4
Skipton, Eng, UK 61/F4
Skiptvet, Nor. 64/T9
Skirfare (riv.), Eng, UK 61/F3
Skíros, Gre. 75/J3
Skivarpsån (riv.), Swe. 65/K7
Skive, Den. 66/C3
Skjærhollen, Nor. 66/D2
Skjeberg, Nor. 66/D2
Skjelåtinden (peak), Nor. 64/E2
Skjern, Den. 66/C4
Skjern (riv.), Den. 66/C4
Škofja Loka, Slov. 71/L3
Skoger, Nor. 64/R8
Skoghall, Swe. 66/E2
Skogstorp, Swe. 66/G2
Skokholm (isl.), Wal, UK 62/A3
Skokie, Il, US 186/C3
Skokie (riv.), Il, US 193/Q15
Skokloster, Swe. 66/G2
Skokomish Ind. Res., Wa, US 170/C4
Sköldvik, Fin. 65/F4
Skole, Ukr. 98/B3
Sköllersta, Swe. 66/F2
Skolniki Park, Rus. 94/W9
Skomer (isl.), Wal, UK 62/A3
Skon, Camb. 120/D3
Skookumchuck, BC, Can. 170/G3
Skópelos, Gre. 75/H3
Skópelos (isl.), Gre. 75/H3
Skopin, Rus. 96/F1
Skopje (cap.), FYROM 75/G1
Skopje (int'l. arpt.), FYROM 93/J2
Skorodnoye, Bela. 98/E2
Skorodnoye, Rus. 99/J2
Skotterud, Nor. 66/E2
Skoútari, Gre. 75/H2
Skövde, Swe. 66/E2
Skovorodino, Rus. 105/J1
Skownan, Mb, Can. 182/E2
Skrīveri, Lat. 67/L3
Skrudaliena, Lat. 67/M4
Skrunda, Lat. 67/K3
Skukuza, SAfr. 149/F5
Skull, Ire. 58/A6
Skull (valley), Ut, US 173/G3
Skull Valley, Az, US 175/F3
Skull Valley Ind. Res., Ut, US 173/G3
Skultorp, Swe. 66/E2
Skultuna, Swe. 66/G2
Skunk (riv.), Ia, US 181/J3
Skuodas, Lith. 67/J3
Skurup, Swe. 69/G1
Skutskär, Swe. 66/G1
Skvyra, Ukr. 98/E3
Skwierzyna, Pol. 69/H2
Skye (isl.), Sc, UK 57/Q8
Skykomish (riv.), Wa, US 170/D4
Skykomish, Wa, US 170/D4
Skyring (sound), Chile 215/B7
Skytop, Pa, US 194/C1
Slade NWR, ND, US 182/E4
Sladkovskoye, Rus. 95/Q4
Sladt (pt.), Austl. 155/F2
Slagelse, Den. 66/D4
Slagle, La, US 190/B2
Slaidburn, Eng, UK 61/F4
Slakovský Les (for.), Czh. 85/F2
Slamannan, Sc, UK 59/C5

299
South – Sturg

Southwood NP, Austl. 160/C4
Southworth, Wa, US 193/C3
Soutpansberg (mts.), SAfr. 149/F4
Sovata, Rom. 77/G2
Soverato Marina, It. 74/E3
Sovere, It. 88/D2
Sovetsk, Rus. 95/L4
Sovetsk, Rus. 67/J4
Sovetskaya, Rus. 99/L5
Sovetskaya Gavan', Rus. 105/N2
Sovetskiy, Rus. 95/L4
Sovetskoye, Rus. 97/H3
Sovets'kyy, Ukr. 99/H5
Sōwa, Japan 109/D1
Sowa Pan (salt pan), Bots. 148/E4
Sowerby Bridge, Eng, UK 61/G4
Soweto, SAfr. 150/D2
Sōya-misaki (cape), Japan 108/B1
Soyana (riv.), Rus. 94/J2
Soyang (lake), SKor. 110/A2
Soyaux, Fr. 70/D4
Soyen, Ger. 85/F6
Soyhières, Swi. 86/D3
Soyo, Ang. 146/C4
Sozh (riv.), Bela. 96/D1
Sozopol, Bul. 77/H4
Spa, Belg. 81/E3
Spaceport USA, Fl, US 191/H3
Spada (lake), Wa, US 193/D2
Spaichingen, Ger. 87/E1
Spain(ctry.) 55/D4
Spakenburg, Neth. 78/C4
Spalding, Eng, UK 61/H6
Spalding, Mi, US 186/C2
Spalding, Austl. 157/H5
Spalding, Sk, Can. 171/M1
Spallumcheen, BC, Can. 170/E2
Spalt, Ger. 84/D4
Spanaway, Wa, US 170/C4
Spangenberg, Ger. 79/G6
Spangle, Wa, US 170/F4
Spangler, Pa, US 187/G4
Spanish (pt.), Ire. 58/A4
Spanish Fork, Ut, US 173/H3
Spanish Fort, Al, US 190/E2
Spanish River Ind. Res., On, Can. 186/E1
Spanish Town, Jam. 201/G2
Spannort (peak), Swi. 87/E4
Spar City, Co, US 175/J2
Sparanise, It. 92/D5
Sparkman, Ar, US 179/H4
Sparks, Ga, US 191/G2
Sparks, Nv, US 172/D4
Sparks, Tx, US 176/F2
Sparlingville, Mi, US 193/G6
Sparreholm, Swe. 66/G2
Sparta, Ga, US 189/F4
Sparta, Mo, US 179/H2
Sparta, Mi, US 186/D3
Sparta, NC, US 189/G2
Sparta, Tn, US 188/E3
Sparta, Il, US 188/C1
Sparta, Wi, US 181/J2
Sparta, NJ, US 194/D1
Sparta (Spárti), Gre. 75/H4
Spartanburg, SC, US 189/G3
Spartel (cape), Mor. 138/B2
Spárti (Sparta), Gre. 75/H4
Spartivento (cape), It. 74/E4
Spartivento (cape), It. 92/F3
Sparwood, BC, Can. 170/G3
Spas-Demensk, Rus. 94/G5
Spassk-Dal'niy, Rus. 105/L3
Spasskaya Guba, Rus. 94/G3
Spáta, Gre. 75/N9
Spátha (cape), Gre. 75/H5
Spavinaw, Ok, US 179/G2
Spay, Ger. 81/G3
Spean (riv.), Sc, UK 59/D3
Spean Bridge, Sc, UK 59/B3
Spearfish, SD, US 180/C1
Spearman, Tx, US 178/D2
Spearville, Ks, US 178/E2
Speculator, NY, US 187/J3
Speedway, In, US 186/C5
Speer (peak), Swi. 87/F3
Speers, Sk, Can. 171/L1
Speicher, Swi. 87/F3
Speicher, Ger. 81/F4
Speichersdorf, Ger. 85/E3
Speke, Eng, UK 61/F5
Speke (int'l arpt.), Eng, UK 61/F5
Speke (gulf), Tanz. 145/A2
Spelle, Ger. 79/E4
Spello, It. 91/B2
Spence Bay, Nun, Can. 166/G2
Spencer, In, US 186/C5
Spencer (cape), Austl. 157/H5
Spencer, Wi, US 181/J1
Spencer, Ia, US 181/G2
Spencer, Tn, US 188/E3
Spencer, WV, US 189/G1
Spencer (gulf), Austl. 153/C4
Spencer, NC, US 189/G3
Spencerville, Ok, US 179/G3
Spencerville, Oh, US 186/D4
Spences Bridge, BC, Can. 170/D2
Spenge, Ger. 79/F4
Spennymoor, Eng, UK 61/G2
Spentrup, Den. 66/D3
Sperkhiás, Gre. 75/H3
Sperkhios (riv.), Gre. 75/H3
Sperlonga, It. 92/C5
Sperrin(mts.) 60/A2
Spessart (range), Ger. 84/C3
Spétsai, Gre. 75/H4
Spey (bay), Sc, UK 59/C1
Spey (riv.), Sc, UK 59/B2
Speyer, Ger. 84/B4
Speyerbach (riv.), Ger. 84/B4
Speyside, On, Can 186/T8
Spezzano Albanese, It. 74/E3
Špičák (peak), Czh. 85/F2
Spicer (isls.), Nun, Can. 167/H2
Spicer, Mn, US 181/G1
Spicewood, Tx, US 176/E2
Spickard, Mo, US 181/H3
Spiddle, Ire. 58/A3
Spiekeroog (isl.), Ger. 79/E1
Spiez, Swi. 86/D4
Spigno Monferrato, It. 88/B4
Spijkenisse, Neth. 78/B5
Spilamberto, It. 89/E4
Spilion, Gre. 75/J5
Spillersboda, Swe. 65/B1
Spillimacheen (riv.), BC, Can. 170/F2
Spillimacheen, BC, Can. 170/F2
Spilsby, Eng, UK 61/J5
Spilve (int'l arpt.), Lat. 67/L3
Spina (peak), It. 74/A2
Spinea, It. 89/F3
Spinetta Marengo, It. 88/B4
Spino d'Adda, It. 88/C3
Spirano, It. 88/C2
Spirit, Wi, US 183/J5
Spirit (lake), Ia, US 181/G2
Spirit Lake, Ia, US 181/G2
Spirit Lake, Id, US 170/F4
Spirit, North (lake), On, Can. 183/H1
Spiritwood, Sk, Can. 171/L1
Spiro, Ok, US 179/G3
Spišská Nová Ves, Slvk. 69/L4
Spitak, Arm. 97/H4
Spiti (riv.), India 124/D3
Spitsbergen (isl.), Nor. 100/B2
Spitsbergen (isl.), Sval. 216/E
Spittal an der Drau, Aus. 71/K3
Spivey, Ks, US 179/E2
Spivey (lake), Ga, US 189/M7
Splendora, Tx, US 177/G2
Split, Cro. 76/C4
Split (int'l arpt.), Cro. 76/C4
Split (lake), Mb, Can. 166/G3
Split (mtn.), Ca, US 174/C2
Splitrock (res.), NJ, US 195/H8
Spluga, Passo dello (pass), Swi. 87/F5
Splügen, Swi. 87/F4
Špogi, Lat. 67/M3
Spokane, Mo, US 179/H2
Spokane, Wa, US 170/F4
Spokane Ind. Res., Wa, US 170/E4
Spokoynaya, Rus. 99/L5
Spöl (riv.), It. 87/G5
Spoleto, It. 91/B2
Spoltore, It. 92/D3
Spook Cave, Ia, US 181/J2
Spoon (riv.), Il, US 181/K3
Spooner, Wi, US 183/J5
Spotorno, It. 88/B5
Spotswood, NJ, US 195/H10
Spotsylvania Courthouse, Va, US 189/J1
Sprague, Mb, Can 183/G3
Sprague (riv.), Or, US 172/C2
Sprague, Wa, US 170/F4
Sprang, Neth. 78/C5
Spranger (mt.), BC, Can. 170/D1
Spratly(isls.) 116/D2
Spray, Or, US 172/D1
Spree (riv.), Ger. 69/H2
Sprendlingen, Ger. 81/G4
Spresiano, It. 89/F2
Sprimont, Belg. 81/E3
Spring (lake), Ca, US 174/D3
Spring (cr.), Nv, US 172/E3
Spring (cr.), Ne, US 180/D3
Spring (mts.), Nv, US 174/E2
Spring, Tx, US 177/M8
Spring (riv.), Ar, US 188/B2
Spring City, Ut, US 173/H4
Spring City, Tn, US 188/E3
Spring City, Pa, US 194/C3
Spring Grove, Il, US 193/P15
Spring Grove, Mn, US 181/J2
Spring Grove, Pa, US 194/B4
Spring Hill, Ar, US 179/H4
Spring Hill, Ks, US 179/G1
Spring Hill, Tn, US 188/D3
Spring Hill, Fl, US 190/K7
Spring Lake, Fl, US 190/L7
Spring Lake, NJ, US 194/D3
Spring Lake, NC, US 189/H3
Spring Valley, Ca, US 192/D5
Spring Valley, NY, US 195/J7
Spring Valley, Mn, US 181/H2
Spring Valley, Tx, US 177/M9
Springbok, SAfr. 150/B3
Springbokvlakte (valley), SAfr. 149/F5
Springboro, Oh, US 186/D5
Springdale, Ar, US 179/G2
Springdale, Ut, US 175/F2
Springdale, Wa, US 170/F3
Springdale, SC, US 189/G3
Springe, Ger. 79/G4
Springer, Ok, US 179/F3
Springer, NM, US 178/B2
Springerville, Az, US 175/H3
Springfield, Co, US 178/C2
Springfield, Fl, US 191/F2
Springfield, Ga, US 189/G4
Springfield, Ky, US 188/E2
Springfield, Ma, US 187/K3
Springfield, Mi, US 186/D3
Springfield, Mo, US 179/H2
Springfield, Oh, US 186/E5
Springfield, NJ, US 195/H9
Springfield, Or, US 172/B1
Springfield, SD, US 180/F2
Springfield (cap.), Il, US 181/K4
Springfield, Tn, US 188/D2
Springfield, Va, US 194/A6
Springfield, Vt, US 187/K3
Springfontein, SAfr. 150/D3
Springhill, La, US 179/H4
Springhill, NS, Can. 184/E3
Springs, SAfr. 150/E2
Springs, NY, US 195/F1
Springsure, Austl. 160/C4
Springvale, Me, US 187/L3
Springvale (nbrhd.), Austl. 158/G5
Springview, Ne, US 180/E2
Springville, NY, US 187/G3
Springville, Ut, US 173/H3
Springville, Al, US 188/D4
Springwater, Ia, US 181/J2
Springwater, NY, US 187/H3
Springwater Nat'l Wild. Ref., ND, US 182/D4
Sprockhövel, Ger. 79/G6
Sprowston, Eng, UK 63/H1
Spruce (mtn.), Nv, US 173/F3
Spruce (peak), WV, US 189/H1
Spruce Knob NRA, WV, US 189/H1
Spruce Lake, Sk, Can. 171/K1
Spruce Pine, NC, US 189/F3
Spruce Run (res.), NJ, US 194/C2
Sprucewoods, Mb, Can. 182/E3
Spui (riv.), Neth. 78/B5
Spur, Tx, US 178/D4
Spurn (pt.), Eng, UK 61/J4
Spuzzum, BC, Can. 170/D3
Spydeberg, Nor. 64/T9
Spydeberg (peak), Nor. 64/S9
Squa Pan (lake), Me, US 184/C2
Squamish (riv.), BC, Can. 170/C3
Squamish, BC, Can. 170/C3
Square Butte, Mt, US 171/J4
Squaw Creek Nat'l Wild. Ref., Mo, US 181/G3
Squaw Lake, Mn, US 183/G4
Squaw Valley, Ca, US 174/C2
Squaxin Island Ind. Res., Wa, US 193/A3
Squinzano, It. 75/F2
Squires, WV, US 189/G2
Squires, Mo, US 179/H2
Squires (mt.), Austl. 157/E3
Srbobran, Yugo. 76/D3
Sre Ambel, Camb. 120/C4
Sre Khtum, Camb. 120/D3
Sre Noy, Camb. 120/D3
Srebrenica, Bosn. 76/D3
Sredna (mts.), Bul. 75/J1
Srednebelaya, Rus. 105/K1
Srednekolymsk, Rus. 101/R3
Sredniy Ikorets, Rus. 99/K2
Srednogorie, Bul. 77/G4
Srednyaya Akhtuba, Rus. 97/H2
Śrem, Pol. 69/J2
Sremčica, Yugo. 76/E3
Sremska Mitrovica, Yugo. 76/D3
Sreng (riv.), Camb. 120/C3
Srepok (riv.), Camb. 120/D3
Sretensk, Rus. 105/H1
Sri Dungargarh, India 127/K3
Sri Gangānagar, India 124/B5
Sri Jayawardanapura (Kotte), SrL. 121/C5
Sri Ksketra (ruin), Myan. 112/B5
Sri Lanka(ctry.) 103/H9
Srikākulam, India 121/D2
Srimangal, Bang. 123/H3
Srīnagar, India 124/C2
Srīrampur, India 121/B2
Srīvardhan, India 121/B2
Środa Śląska, Pol. 69/J3
Środa Wielkopolska, Pol. 69/J2
St-Floris, PN de, CAfr. 142/D3
Staaten (riv.), Austl. 155/F4
Staaten River NP, Austl. 155/F4
Stabbursdalen NP, Nor. 64/H1
Staberhuk (pt.), Ger. 66/D4
Stabroek, Belg. 78/B6
Stacyville, Ia, US 181/H2
Stadbroke, North (isl.), Austl. 153/E3
Stade, Ger. 79/G1
Staden, Belg. 80/C2
Stadl-Paura, Aus. 85/G6
Stadskanaal, Neth. 78/D3
Stadtbergen, Ger. 84/D6
Stadthagen, Ger. 79/G4
Stadtlauringen, Ger. 84/D2
Stadtlohn, Ger. 78/D5
Stadtoldendorf, Ger. 79/G5
Stadtsteinach, Ger. 85/E2
Stäfa, Swi. 87/E3
Staffanstorp, Swe. 66/E4
Staffelberg (peak), Ger. 84/E2
Staffelegg (pass), Swi. 86/E3
Staffelsee (lake), Ger. 87/H2
Staffelstein, Ger. 84/D2
Staffhorst, Ger. 79/F3
Staffora (riv.), It. 88/C3
Stafford, Eng, UK 61/F6
Stafford, Ct, US 187/K4
Stafford, Tx, US 177/M9
Stafford, Va, US 189/J1
Stagno, It. 88/D6
Stagnone, Isole della (isl.), It. 74/B4
Stahnsdorf, Ger. 68/Q7
Staicele, Lat. 67/L3
Staindrop, Eng, UK 61/G2
Staines, Eng, UK 56/B2
Stains, Fr. 56/K5
Stäket, Swe. 65/A1
Stakhanov, Ukr. 99/K3
Stalbridge, Eng, UK 62/D5
Stalden, Swi. 86/D5
Stalham, Eng, UK 63/H1
Stallarholmen, Swe. 66/H5
Stallworthy (cape), Nun, Can. 167/S6
Stalowa Wola, Pol. 69/M3
Stalwart, Sk, Can. 171/M2
Stalybridge, Eng, UK 61/F5
Stambaugh, Mi, US 183/K4
Stamboliyski, Bul. 75/J1
Stamford, Tx, US 178/E4
Stamford (lake), Tx, US 177/E1
Stamford, NY, US 187/J3
Stamford, Ct, US 195/L7
Stamford, Austl. 160/A3
Stamford, Eng, UK 63/F1
Stamford Bridge, Eng, UK 61/H4
Stampa, Swi. 87/F5
Stampede (res.), Ca, US 172/C4
Stampriet, Namb. 148/C5
Stamps, Ar, US 179/H4
Stamullen, Ire. 60/B4
Stanardsville, Va, US 189/H1
Stanberry, Mo, US 181/G3
Stanchfield, Mn, US 183/H5
Standard, Ab, Can. 171/H2
Standerton, SAfr. 150/E2
Standing Indian (peak), NC, US 189/F3
Standing Rock, Al, US 188/E4
Standing Rock Ind. Res., SD, US 180/D1
Standish, Mi, US 186/E3
Standish, Me, US 187/L3
Standish-with-Langtree, Eng, UK 61/F4
Stanfield, Az, US 175/G4
Stanfield, Or, US 170/E5
Stanford, Ky, US 188/E2
Stanford, Mt, US 171/J4
Stanford Rivers, Eng, UK 56/D1
Stanford-le-Hope, Eng, UK 63/G3
Stange, Nor. 66/D1
Stangelville, Wi, US 186/C2
Stanger, SAfr. 151/E3
Stanghella, It. 89/E3
Stanhope, Eng, UK 61/F2
Stanhope, NJ, US 194/D2
Stanišić, Yugo. 76/D3
Stanislaus (co.), Ca, US 193/M12
Stanislaus (riv.), Ca, US 172/C4
Stanke Dimitrov, Bul. 75/H1
Stanley, NB, Can. 184/D2
Stanley, ND, US 182/C3
Stanley, Sc, UK 59/C4
Stanley, Eng, UK 61/G2
Stanley, Austl. 158/C4
Stanley, NM, US 175/K3
Stanley, Wi, US 181/J1
Stanley (mt.), Austl. 157/F2
Stanley (res.), India 118/C5
Stanley (cap.), Falk. 215/F6
Stanley, China 113/L8
Stanley (mt.), Austl. 159/B5
Stanleytown, Va, US 189/H2
Stanleyville, NC, US 189/G2
Stanovo, Yugo. 76/E4
Stanovoy (range), Rus. 103/M4
Stans, Swi. 87/E4
Stanstead Plain, Qu, Can. 187/K2
Stansted, Eng, UK 56/D3
Stansted (int'l arpt.), Eng, UK 63/G3
Stansted Mountfitchet, Eng, UK 63/G3
Stanthorpe, Austl. 160/C5
Stanton, ND, US 182/D4
Stanton, Mi, US 186/D3
Stanton, Ca, US 192/G8
Stanton, Al, US 188/D4
Stanton, Ia, US 181/G3
Stanton, Ky, US 188/F2
Stanton, Tn, US 188/C3
Stanton, Ne, US 181/F3
Stanton, Tx, US 177/D1
Stanton, De, US 194/C4
Stanton, NJ, US 194/D2
Stanwell, Eng, UK 56/B2
Stanwood, Wa, US 170/C3
Stanychno-Luhans'ke, Ukr. 99/K3
Staphorst, Neth. 78/D3
Stapleford, Eng, UK 63/E4
Stapleford Abbotts, Eng, UK 56/D2
Staplehurst, Ne, US 181/F3
Staplehurst, Eng, UK 63/G4
Staples, Mn, US 183/G4
Staples, On, Can. 193/G7
Stapleton, Al, US 190/E2
Stapleton, Ne, US 180/D3
Stapleton, Ga, US 189/F4
Stąporków, Pol. 69/L3
Star', Rus. 96/E1
Star, Tx, US 177/E2
Star City, Ar, US 179/J4
Star City, Sk, Can. 171/M1
Star Lake, NY, US 187/J2
Stara Pazova, Yugo. 76/E3
Stara Planina (mts.), Yugo. 76/F3
Stara Vyzhivka, Ukr. 98/C2
Stara Zagora, Bul. 77/G4
Starachowice, Pol. 69/L3
Staranzano, It. 89/G2
Staraya Racheyka, Rus. 97/J1
Staraya Russa, Rus. 67/P2
Starbuck, Mb, Can. 182/F3
Starbuck, Mn, US 183/G5
Starbuck (isl.), Kiri. 163/K5
Starcke NP, Austl. 160/B1
Stargard Szczeciński, Pol. 66/F5
Stari Grad, Cro. 76/C4
Starke, Ks, US 179/G2
Starke, Fl, US 191/G3
Starkey, Or, US 172/D1
Starkville, Ms, US 188/C4
Starkweather, ND, US 182/E3
Starnberg, Ger. 85/E6
Starnbergersee (lake), Ger. 87/H2
Starobil's'k, Ukr. 99/K3
Staroderevyankovskaya, Rus. 99/K4
Starodub, Rus. 96/E1
Starogard Gdański, Pol. 66/H5
Starokostyantyniv, Ukr. 98/D3
Starominskaya, Rus. 99/K4
Staronizhestebliyevskaya, Rus. 99/K5
Staroshcherbinovskaya, Rus. 99/K4
Starotitarovskaya, Rus. 99/J5
Starovelichkovskaya, Rus. 99/K5
Start, La, US 179/J4
Start (pt.), Sc, UK 57/V14
Start (bay), Eng, UK 62/C6
Start (pt.), Eng, UK 62/C6
Startup, Wa, US 193/D2
Staryy Kistruss, Rus. 94/J5
Staryy Krym, Ukr. 99/H5
Staryy Oskol', Rus. 99/J2
Staryy Studenets, Rus. 95/L5
Staryye Dorogi, Bela. 96/D1
Staszów, Pol. 69/L3
State College, Pa, US 187/H4
State Fair Park (Cotton Bowl), Tx, US 176/L7
State Fairgrounds, De, US 194/C6
State Line, Ms, US 190/D2
Staten (isl.), NY, US 194/D2
Statenville, Ga, US 191/G2
States (int'l arpt.), Chl, UK 82/C2
Statesboro, Ga, US 189/G4
Statesville, NC, US 189/G3
Statham, Ga, US 188/F4
Statts Mills, WV, US 189/G1
Statue of Liberty Nat'l Mon., NY, US 195/J9
Staufen im Breisgau, Ger. 86/D2
Staufenberg, Ger. 68/E3
Staunton, Il, US 181/K4
Staunton, Eng, UK 62/D3
Staunton, Va, US 189/H1
Staunton on Wye, Eng, UK 62/D2
Stavanger, Nor. 66/A2
Staveley, Eng, UK 61/F3
Staveley, Eng, UK 61/G5
Stavelot, Belg. 81/E3
Stavely, Ab, Can. 171/H2
Staveren, Neth. 78/C3
Stavern, Nor. 66/D2
Stavropol', Rus. 99/M5
Stavropol' Kray, Rus. 100/E5
Stavrós, Gre. 75/H2
Stavsnäs, Swe. 65/E1
Stavyshche, Ukr. 98/F3
Stawell, Austl. 158/E3
Stayner, On, Can. 186/F2
Stayton, Or, US 172/E1
Steamboat Slough (riv.), Ca, US 193/L10
Steamboat Springs, Co, US 173/K3
Stearns, Ky, US 188/E2
Stebnyk, Ukr. 98/E3
Steckborn, Swi. 87/E2
Stederau (riv.), Ger. 79/H3
Steeg, Aus. 87/G3
Steel (mtn.), Id, US 173/F2
Steele, ND, US 182/E4
Steele, Mo, US 188/C2
Steele (cr.), Austl. 158/F5
Steele's Knowe (hill), Sc, UK 59/C4
Steeleville, Il, US 188/C1
Steelpoortrivier (riv.), SAfr. 151/E2
Steelton, Pa, US 194/B3
Steelville, Mo, US 179/J2
Steenbergen, Neth. 78/B5
Steenkool, Indo. 117/H4
Steens Mtn. Recreation Lands, Or, US 172/D2
Steensby (inlet), Nun, Can. 167/J1
Steenvoorde, Fr. 80/B2
Steenwijk, Neth. 78/D3
Steep (pt.), Austl. 156/B3
Steep Holm (isl.), Eng, UK 62/C4
Steep Rock, Mb, Can. 182/E2
Steeping (riv.), Eng, UK 61/J5
Ştefăneşti, Rom. 98/D4
Stefansson (isl.), Nun, Can. 166/F1
Steffen (peak), Chile 214/C5
Steffisburg, Swi. 86/D4
Steg, Swi. 86/D5
Stege, Den. 66/E4
Steglitz, Ger. 68/Q7
Steiermark (prov.), Aus. 69/H5
Steigerwald (for.), Ger. 71/J2
Steilacoom, Wa, US 193/B3
Steilloopbrug, SAfr. 149/F4
Steimbke, Ger. 79/G3
Stein (riv.), BC, Can. 170/D2
Stein am Rhein, Swi. 87/E2
Stein bei Nünnberg, Ger. 84/E4
Steina (riv.), Ger. 87/E2
Steinach, Ger. 84/E2
Steinach (riv.), Ger. 84/E2
Steinach, Ger. 85/F5
Steinach am Brenner, Aus. 87/H3
Steinau an der Strasse, Ger. 84/C2
Steinbach, Mb, Can. 182/F3
Steinbach an der Steyr, Aus. 85/H7
Steinbourg, Fr. 81/G6
Steinen, Ger. 86/D2
Steinen (riv.), Braz. 209/H4
Steinerkirchen an der Traun, Aus. 85/G6
Steinfeld, Ger. 84/B4
Steinfeld, Ger. 84/C3
Steinfeld, Ger. 79/F3
Steinfort, Lux. 81/E4
Steingaden, Ger. 87/G2
Steinhagen, Ger. 79/F4
Steinhatchee, Fl, US 191/G3
Steinhausen, Swi. 87/E3
Steinhausen, Namb. 148/C4
Steinhausen an der Rottum, Ger. 87/F1
Steinheid, Ger. 84/D2
Steinheim, Ger. 79/G5
Steinheim am Albuch, Ger. 84/D5
Steinheim an der Murr, Ger. 84/C5
Steinhorst, Ger. 79/H3
Steinhuder (lake), Ger. 79/G4
Steinkjer, Nor. 64/D2
Steinsland, Nor. 66/A1
Steinstücken, Ger. 68/Q7
Steinweiler, Ger. 84/B4
Stekene, Belg. 78/B6
Steklyanka, Rus. 94/J4
Stella (peak), It. 87/F5
Stella, Ne, US 181/G3
Stella, SAfr. 150/D2
Stellarton, NS, Can. 185/F3
Stelle, Ger. 79/H2
Stellenbosch, SAfr. 150/L10
Stello (peak), Fr. 74/A1
Stelvio, Passo di (pass), It. 87/G4
Stelvio, PN dello (nat'l park), It. 71/J3
Stenay, Fr. 81/E5
Stendal, Ger. 68/F2
Stende, Lat. 67/K3
Steneto NP, Bul. 77/G4
Stenhamra, Swe. 65/A1
Stenhousemuir, Sc, UK 59/C4
Stenlille, Den. 65/H7
Stenløse, Den. 65/J7
Stensån (riv.), Swe. 65/K6
Stenungsund, Swe. 66/D2
Step'anavan, Arm. 97/H4
Stepaside, Ire. 60/B5
Stephan, SD, US 180/E1
Stephansposching, Ger. 85/F5
Stephens, Ar, US 179/H4
Stephens City, Va, US 189/H1
Stephens Creek, Austl. 158/B1
Stephensburg, Ky, US 188/D2
Stephenson, Mi, US 186/C2
Stephenville, Nf, Can. 185/H1
Stephenville, Tx, US 177/E1
Stephenville Crossing, Nf, Can. 185/H1
Stepnoy, Rus. 95/P5
Stepnoye, Rus. 97/H3
Stepnoye, Rus. 97/H2
Steptoe (valley), Nv, US 173/F4
Steptoe, Wa, US 170/F4
Sterkspruit, SAfr. 150/D3
Sterkstroom, SAfr. 150/D3
Sterling, Ks, US 179/E1
Sterling, Ga, US 191/H2
Sterling, Mi, US 186/D2
Sterling, Co, US 180/C3
Sterling, Il, US 181/K3
Sterling, Ak, US 168/X12
Sterling City, Tx, US 177/D2
Sterling Heights, Mi, US 186/E3
Sterlington, La, US 179/H4
Sterlitamak, Rus. 97/K1
Sternstein (peak), Aus. 85/H5
Sterzing (Vipiteno), It. 87/H4
Stęszew, Pol. 69/J2
Štěti, Czh. 85/H2
Stetsonville, Wi, US 181/J1
Stettler, Ab, Can. 171/H1
Steubenville, Oh, US 186/F4
Stevenage, Eng, UK 63/F3
Stevens Point, Wi, US 181/K1
Stevenson (cr.), Austl. 157/G3
Stevenson, Al, US 188/E3
Stevenson, Wa, US 170/D5
Stevenston, Sc, UK 59/B5
Stevensville, Mi, US 186/C3
Stevensville, Mt, US 171/G4
Stevensville, Md, US 194/B6
Stevinsluizen (dam), Neth 78/C3
Stewardson, Il, US 188/C1
Stewart (isl.), NZ 153/G7
Stewart (riv.), Yk, Can. 166/C2
Stewart, Al, US 188/D4
Stewart, Ms, US 188/C4
Stewart, BC, Can. 168/AA13
Stewart (mt.), Ab, Can. 170/F1
Stewart Lake Nat'l Wild. Ref., ND, US 182/C4
Stewart Valley, Sk, Can. 171/L2
Stewarton, Sc, UK 59/B5
Stewartstown, NI, UK 60/B2
Stewartstown, Pa, US 194/B4
Stewartville, Mn, US 181/H2
Stewiacke, NS, Can. 184/F3
Steyning, Eng, UK 63/F5
Steynrus, SAfr. 150/D2
Steynsburg, SAfr. 150/D3
Steyr (riv.), Aus. 69/H5
Steyr, Aus. 85/H6
Steyregg, Aus. 85/H6
Steytlerville, SAfr. 150/D4
Stia, It. 89/E6
Stiava, It. 88/D6
Stickney (mt.), Wa, US 193/D2
Stiens, Neth. 78/C2
Stigler, Ok, US 179/G3
Stigtomta, Swe. 66/G2
Stikine (riv.), BC, Can. 166/D3
Stilbaai, SAfr. 150/C4
Stiles, Wi, US 186/B2
Stiles, Tx, US 177/D2
Stilfontein, SAfr. 150/D2
Stilís, Gre. 75/H3
Still Creek (res.), Pa, US 194/C2
Still Pond, Md, US 194/B5
Stilling, Den. 66/D3
Stillmore, Ga, US 189/F4
Stillwater, Ok, US 179/F2
Stillwater (res.), NY, US 187/J3
Stillwater (riv.), Mt, US 173/J1
Stillwater (range), Nv, US 172/D4
Stillwater, Mn, US 183/Q6
Stillwater (lake), Pa, US 194/C1
Stillwater, Pa, US 194/B1
Stillwater NWR, Nv, US 172/D4
Stilo (cape), It. 74/E3
Stilwell, Ok, US 179/G3
Štimlje, Yugo. 76/E4
Stimpfach, Ger. 84/D4
Stimson (mt.), Mt, US 171/H3
Stinchar (riv.), Sc, UK 60/D1
Stinking Water (cr.), Ne, US 180/D3
Stinnett, Tx, US 178/D3
Štip, FYROM 75/H2
Stiring-Wendel, Fr. 81/F5
Stírka (peak), Czh. 85/G4
Stirling, Sc, UK 59/C4
Stirling, On, Can. 187/H2
Stirling, Austl. 157/G2
Stirling (mt.), Austl. 156/C4
Stirling (nbrhd.), Austl. 157/M9
Stirling (nbrhd.), Austl. 156/K6
Stirling, Ab, Can. 171/H3
Stirling Range NP, Austl. 156/C5
Stirone (riv.), It. 88/C3
Stites, Id, US 170/G4
Stjørdal, Nor. 64/D3
Stob a' Choin (peak), Sc, UK 59/B4
Stob Choire Claurigh (peak), Sc, UK 59/B3
Stochov, Czh. 85/G2
Stock (lake), Fr. 81/F6
Stock, Eng, UK 56/E2
Stockach, Ger. 87/F2
Stockbridge, Mi, US 186/D3
Stockbridge, Ma, US 187/K3
Stockbridge, Ga, US 189/M7
Stockbridge, Eng, UK 63/E4
Stockbridge Ind. Res., Wi, US 181/K1
Stockbury, Eng, UK 56/E3
Stockdale, Tx, US 177/F3
Stockerau, Aus. 77/N7
Stockertown, Pa, US 194/C2
Stockett, Mt, US 171/J4
Stockheim, Ger. 84/E2
Stockholm, Sk, Can. 182/C2
Stockholm (cap.), Swe. 65/A1
Stockholm (co.), Swe. 66/G2
Stockholm, SD, US 181/F1
Stockhorn (peak), Swi. 86/D4
Stockpoort, SAfr. 149/E4
Stockport, Eng, UK 61/F5
Stocks (res.), Eng, UK 61/F4
Stocksbridge, Eng, UK 61/G5
Stockstadt am Rhein, Ger. 84/B3
Stocksund, Swe. 65/B1
Stockton (lake), Mo, US 179/G2
Stockton, Mo, US 179/H2
Stockton, Ga, US 191/G2
Stockton, Al, US 190/E2
Stockton, Il, US 181/J2
Stockton, Ks, US 180/E4
Stockton (plat.), Tx, US 198/E2
Stockton, NJ, US 194/D3
Stockton-on-Tees, Eng, UK 61/G2
Stockville, Ne, US 180/D3
Stod, Czh. 85/G3
Stodolishche, Rus. 94/G5
Stoeng Treng, Camb. 120/D3
Stoffberg, SAfr. 149/F5
Stoke (pt.), Eng, UK 62/B6
Stoke Poges, Eng, UK 56/B2
Stoke-on-Trent, Eng, UK 61/F6
Stokenchurch, Eng, UK 56/A2
Stokes (mt.), NZ 161/C3
Stokes (range), Austl. 154/C4
Stokes (pt.), Austl. 159/A5
Stokes NP, Austl. 156/D5
Stolac, Bosn. 76/C4
Stolberg, Ger. 81/F2
Stolbovoy (isl.), Rus. 101/P2
Stolbtsy, Bela. 67/M5
Stolin, Bela. 98/D2
Stöllet, Swe. 66/E1
Stolzenau, Ger. 79/G3
Stompneuspunt (pt.), SAfr. 150/K10
Ston, Cro. 76/C4
Stone, Eng, UK 61/F6
Stone, Ky, US 189/F2
Stone Forest, China 112/D3
Stone Harbor, NJ, US 194/D5
Stone Ind. Res., BC, Can. 170/C2
Stone Lake, Wi, US 183/J5
Stone Mountain, Ga, US 189/M7
Stone Mountain Park, Ga, US 189/M7
Stonecliffe, On, Can. 187/H1
Stonefort, Il, US 188/C2
Stoneham, Tx, US 177/G2
Stonehaven, Sc, UK 59/D3
Stonehenge, Austl. 160/A4
Stonehenge, Eng, UK 63/E4
Stonehouse, Sc, UK 59/C5
Stonehouse, Eng, UK 62/D3
Stones River Nat'l Bfld., Tn, US 188/D3
Stoneville, SD, US 180/C1
Stoneville, NC, US 189/H2
Stonewall, Mb, Can. 182/F2
Stonewall, Ok, US 179/F3
Stonewall, La, US 176/H1
Stonewall, Ms, US 188/C4
Stonewall, Ga, US 189/L7
Stoney Creek, On, Can. 186/T9
Stoney Point, On, Can. 193/G7
Stoneyburn, Sc, UK 59/C5
Stonington, Co, US 178/C2
Stonington, Ct, US 195/G1
Stony (pt.), Mb, Can. 182/F1
Stony (pt.), NY, US 187/H3
Stony (cr.), Ca, US 172/B4
Stony (cr.), Pa, US 194/B3
Stony Beach, Sk, Can. 182/B2
Stony Brook, NY, US 195/E2
Stony Creek (lake), Mi, US 193/E7
Stony Ind. Res., Ab, Can. 170/G2
Stony Man (mtn.), Va, US 189/H1
Stony Mountain, Mb, Can. 182/F2
Stony Point, NY, US 194/E1
Stony Point, NC, US 189/G3
Stony Tunguska (riv.), Rus. 103/J3
Stonybrook-Wilshire, Pa, US 194/B4
Stonyford, Ca, US 172/B4
Stör (riv.), Ger. 79/G1
Stor (isl.), Nun, Can. 167/S7
Stor-Elvdal, Nor. 66/D1
Storå, Swe. 66/F2
Stora Le (lake), Swe. 66/D2
Stora Sjöfallets NP, Swe. 64/F2
Storavan (lake), Swe. 64/F2
Storby, Fin. 67/H1
Stord (isl.), Nor. 66/A2
Store Bælt (chan.), Den. 66/D4
Store-Heddinge, Den. 65/J7
Storebø, Nor. 66/A1
Støren, Nor. 64/D3
Storfors, Swe. 66/F2
Storlien, Swe. 64/E3
Storm (bay), Austl. 153/D5
Storm Lake, Ia, US 181/G2
Storm Lake Nat'l Wild. Ref., ND, US 182/F4
Stormberg (mtn.), SAfr. 150/D3
Stormont, NI, UK 60/C2
Stormy (mtn.), Wa, US 170/D4
Stornoway, Sc, UK 57/Q7
Storo, It. 88/D2
Storö (isl.), Swe. 65/B1
Storozhevsk, Rus. 95/M3
Storozhynets', Ukr. 98/C3
Storrington, Eng, UK 63/F5
Storrs, Ct, US 187/K4
Storsjön (lake), Swe. 64/E3
Storsteinsfjellet (peak), Nor. 64/F1
Storstrøm (co.), Den. 66/D4
Storthoaks, Sk, Can. 182/D3
Storvik, Swe. 66/G1
Storvreta, Swe. 66/G2
Story, Wy, US 173/K1
Story City, Ia, US 181/H2
Stosch (isl.), Chile 215/A6
Stotfold, Eng, UK 63/F2
Stötten am Auerberg, Ger. 87/G2
Stoughton, Sk, Can. 182/C3
Stoughton, Eng, UK 56/B3
Stoughton, Wi, US 181/K2
Stoumont, Belg. 81/E3
Stour (riv.), Eng, UK 62/D5
Stourbridge, Eng, UK 62/D2
Stourport-on-Severn, Eng, UK 62/D2
Stout, Tx, US 179/G4
Stout (lake), On, Can. 183/G1
Stoutland, Mo, US 179/H2
Stover, Mo, US 179/H1
Stovring, Den. 66/C3
Stow, Sc, UK 59/D5
Stow, Oh, US 186/F4
Stow (cr.), NJ, US 194/C5
Stow-on-the-Wold, Eng, UK 63/E3
Stowe, Vt, US 187/K2
Stowe, Pa, US 194/C3
Stowell, Tx, US 177/G3
Stowmarket, Eng, UK 63/G2
Stoy (peak), Ukr. 98/B3
Stoyba, Rus. 105/L1
Stra, It. 89/F3
Strabane, NI, UK 57/Q9
Strabane (dist.), NI 60/A2
Strachan, Sc, UK 59/D2
Strachur, Sc, UK 59/A4
Stradbally, Ire. 58/C5
Stradbally, Ire. 58/C3
Stradella, It. 88/C3
Straelen, Ger. 78/D6
Straffan, Ire. 58/D3
Strafford, Mo, US 179/H2
Strahan, Austl. 158/C4
Strakonice, Czh. 85/G4
Straldzha, Bul. 77/H4
Stralsund, Ger. 66/E4
Strambino, It. 88/A2
Strand, SAfr. 150/L11
Strandhill, Ire. 58/B1
Strangford, NI, UK 60/C3
Strangford (lake), NI, UK 60/C3
Strängnäs, Swe. 66/G2
Strangways (mt.), Austl. 157/G2
Stranocum, NI, UK 60/B1
Stranraer, Sc, UK 60/C2
Strasbourg, Fr. 86/D1
Strasbourg (Entzheim) (int'l arpt.), Fr. 86/D1
Strasburg, ND, US 182/D4
Strasburg, Oh, US 186/F4
Strasburg, Pa, US 194/B4
Strasburg, Va, US 189/H1
Straseni, Mol. 98/E4
Strassen, Lux. 81/F4
Strasshof an der Nordbahn, Aus. 77/P7
Strasswalchen, Aus. 85/G7
Stratford, Ok, US 179/F3
Stratford, Tx, US 178/C2
Stratford, NH, US 187/L2
Stratford, NY, US 187/J3
Stratford, On, Can 186/F3
Stratford (har.), Ct, US 195/L8
Stratford, NZ 161/C2
Stratford, Ca, US 174/C2
Stratford, Wi, US 181/J1
Stratford (pt.), Ct, US 195/E1
Stratford, NJ, US 194/C4
Stratford, Ct, US 195/E1
Stratford, Austl. 159/C3
Stratford and Worcester (canal), Eng, UK 62/D2
Stratford-upon-Avon, Eng, UK 63/E2
Strathalbyn, Austl. 157/H5
Strathaven, Sc, UK 59/B5
Strathbeg (bay), Sc, UK 59/E1
Strathblane, Sc, UK 59/B5
Strathclair, Mb, Can. 182/D2
Strathclyde (co.), Sc, UK 59/B5
Strathearn (valley), Sc, UK 59/C4
Strathgorden, Austl. 158/C4
Strathmore (valley), Sc, UK 59/C3
Strathmore, Ab, Can. 171/H2
Strathpeffer, Sc, UK 59/B1
Strathroy, On, Can. 186/F3
Strathspey (valley), Sc, UK 59/C2
Strathyre, Sc, UK 59/B4
Stratton, On, Can. 183/G3
Stratton (mtn.), Vt, US 187/K3
Stratton, Me, US 187/L2
Stratton, Co, US 180/C4
Stratton, Eng, UK 62/B5
Straubing, Ger. 85/F5
Straumnes Horn (pt.), Ice. 64/M6
Straumsjøen, Nor. 64/E1
Strausberg, Ger. 68/Q6
Strausstown, Pa, US 194/B3
Strawberry, Ar, US 179/J3
Strawberry (peak), Ca, US 192/B2
Strawberry (res.), Ut, US 173/H3
Strawberry (riv.), Ut, US 173/H3
Strawberry, Ca, US 172/C4
Strawberry (mtn.), Or, US 172/D1
Strawberry Point, Ia, US 181/J2
Strawn, Tx, US 177/E1
Strawn (New Strawn), Ks, US 179/G1
Strayhorn, Ms, US 188/B3
Strazhitsa, Bul. 77/G4
Streaky (bay), Austl. 153/C4
Streaky Bay, Austl. 157/G5
Streamwood, Il, US 193/P15
Streatham (nbrhd.), Eng, UK 56/C2
Streatley, Eng, UK 63/E3
Streator, Il, US 181/K3
Středočeská Žulová Vrchovina (mts.), Czh. 69/H4
Středočeský (pol. reg.), Czh. 69/G3
Středoslovenský (pol. reg.), Czh. 69/H3
Street, Eng, UK 62/D4
Street, Md, US 194/B4
Streeter, ND, US 182/E4
Streeter, Tx, US 177/E2
Streetman, Tx, US 177/F2
Streetsville, On, Can. 186/T8
Strehaia, Rom. 77/F3
Streich (peak), Austl. 156/D4
Strekov, Slvk. 76/D2
Střela (riv.), Czh. 69/G3
Strelcha, Bul. 77/G4
Strelley Abor. Land, Austl. 156/C2
Strel'na (riv.), Rus. 94/H2
Strel'na, Rus. 94/S7
Strenči, Lat. 67/L3
Strengberg, Aus. 85/H6
Strengelbach, Swi. 86/D3
Strengen, Aus. 87/G3
Stresa, It. 88/B2
Streshin, Bela. 96/D1
Stretford, Eng, UK 61/F5
Stretham, Eng, UK 63/G2
Strettoia, It. 88/D6
Streu (riv.), Ger. 84/D2
Strezhevoy, Rus. 100/H3
Striano, It. 92/D6
Strib, Den. 66/C4
Stříbro, Czh. 85/G3
Strichen, Sc, UK 59/D1
Strickland (riv.), PNG 155/F1
Strickler, Ar, US 179/G3
Strigno, It. 87/H5
Strijen, Neth. 78/B5
Strimón (gulf), Gre. 96/C4
Strimónas (riv.), Gre. 75/H2
Stringer, Ms, US 190/D2
Stringtown, Ok, US 179/F3
Striven (lake), Sc, UK 59/A5
Strizhament (peak), Rus. 99/M5
Strobel (lake), Arg. 215/C6
Strøby Egede, Den. 65/J7
Stroeder, Arg. 214/E4
Strofádhes (isl.), Gre. 93/J3
Strogino (nbrhd.), Rus. 94/W9
Stroitel', Rus. 99/J2
Strokestown, Ire. 58/B2
Strom Thurmond (dam), SC, US 189/F4
Strom Thurmond (res.), Ga, US 189/F4
Stromberg, Ger. 81/G4
Stromboli (isl.), It. 93/G3
Strome, Ab, Can. 171/H1
Stromeferry, Sc, UK 57/R8
Strømmen, Nor. 66/D2
Stromness, Sc, UK 57/V14
Stromsburg, Ne, US 180/F3
Strömstad, Swe. 66/D2
Strömsund, Swe. 64/E3
Strona (riv.), It. 87/E6
Stroncone, It. 91/B3
Strong, Ar, US 179/H4
Strong, Me, US 187/L2
Strong (riv.), Ms, US 188/C4
Strong City, Ks, US 179/F1
Stronghurst, Il, US 181/J3
Strongoli, It. 75/E3
Strongsville, Oh, US 186/F4
Stronie Śląskie, Pol. 69/J3
Stronsay (isl.), Sc, UK 57/V14
Stronsay Firth (inlet), Sc, UK 57/V14
Strood, Eng, UK 56/E2
Stropnice (riv.), Czh. 85/H5
Stroppiana, It. 88/B3
Stroud, Ok, US 179/F3
Stroud, Eng, UK 62/D3
Stroudsburg, Pa, US 194/C2
Struan, Sc, UK 57/Q8
Struer, Den. 66/C3
Struga, FYROM 75/G2
Strugi-Krasnyye, Rus. 67/N2
Struisbaai (bay), SAfr. 150/C4
Strule (riv.), NI, UK 60/A2
Strum, Wi, US 181/J1
Struma (riv.), Bul. 96/B4
Strumble (pt.), Wal, UK 62/A2
Strumica, FYROM 75/H2
Strydenburg, SAfr. 150/C3
Stryker, Mt, US 170/G3
Stryn, Nor. 64/C3
Stryy, Ukr. 98/B3
Strzegom, Pol. 69/J3
Strzelce Krajeńskie, Pol. 69/H2
Strzelce Opolskie, Pol. 96/A2
Strzelecki (cr.), Austl. 157/J4
Strzelecki (mt.), Austl. 157/G2
Strzelecki (mt.), Austl. 159/D5
Strzelecki NP, Austl. 159/D5
Strzelin, Pol. 69/J3
Strzelno, Pol. 69/K2
Strzyżów, Pol. 69/L4
Stuart, Ok, US 179/F3
Stuart, Fl, US 191/H4
Stuart, Ia, US 181/G3
Stuart, Va, US 189/G2
Stuart (mt.), Wa, US 170/D4
Stuart Island, BC, Can. 170/B2
Stuart Town, Austl. 159/D1
Stuartburn, Mb, Can. 182/F3
Stuarts Draft, Va, US 189/H1
Stubbekøbing, Den. 66/E4
Stubbenkammer (pt.), Ger. 66/E4
Stuckey, SC, US 189/H4
Studland, Eng, UK 63/E5
Studley, Eng, UK 63/E2
Stühlingen, Ger. 87/E2
Stump (lake), ND, US 182/E4
Stump Lake Nat'l Wild. Ref., ND, US 182/E4
Stumpy Point, NC, US 189/K3
Stupino, Rus. 94/H5
Stura di Ala (riv.), It. 90/D2
Stura di Demonte (riv.), Fr. 90/D4
Stura di Lanzo (riv.), It. 88/A2
Stura di Val Grande (riv.), It. 90/D2
Stura di Viù (riv.), It. 90/D2
Sturakeen (peak), Ire. 58/B5
Sturgeon (bay), Mb, Can. 182/E1
Sturgeon (lake), On, Can. 183/J2
Sturgeon (riv.), On, Can. 186/F1
Sturgeon, PE, Can. 185/F2
Sturgeon, Mo, US 181/H4
Sturgeon Bay, Wi, US 186/C2

Taiama, SLeo. 140/B4
Tai'an, China 107/B2
Tai'an, China 106/D3
Tai'angang, China 106/L8
Taiarapu (pen.), FrPol. 163/X15
Taiaret (well), Mor. 136/B5
Taibai (peak), China 104/F5
Taibus, China 104/H3
Taicang, China 106/L8
T'aichung, Tai. 113/J3
Taiei, Japan 109/E2
Taigu, China 106/C3
Taihang (mts.), China 106/C3
Taihape, NZ 161/C2
Taihe, China 106/C4
Taihsi, Tai. 113/J4
Taihu, China 113/H2
Taikang, China 106/C4
Taiki, Japan 108/C2
Tailai, China 105/J2
Taileleo, Indo. 115/B3
Tailem Bend, Austl. 157/H5
Tailfingen, Ger. 84/B5
Taima, Japan 109/J6
Tain, Sc, UK 59/B1
Tain-L'Hermitage, Fr. 90/A2
T'ainan, Tai. 113/J4
Taínaron (cape), Gre. 75/H4
Taingainony, Madg. 152/H8
Taino, It. 88/B2
Taió, Braz. 213/G3
Taiobeiras, Braz. 211/E2
Taiohae, FrPol. 163/L5
Taiping, China 120/D1
Taiping, Malay. 115/C1
Taiping, China 113/F4
Taiping, China 113/H2
Taiping, China 113/G1
Taiping (peak), China 105/J2
Taipinggou, China 105/L2
Taipingshao, China 107/C2
Taipu, Braz. 207/H4
Tais, Indo. 115/C4
Taisha, Japan 110/C3
Taishan, China 113/G4
Taishi, Japan 109/J6
Taishun, China 113/H3
Taiskirchen im Innkreis, Aus. 85/G6
Taissy, Fr. 81/D5
Taitao (pen.), Chile 203/B7
Taiti (peak), Kenya 145/A1
T'aitung, Tai. 113/J4
Taiwan(ctry.) 103/M7
Taiwan (str.), China,Tai 162/A2
Taixing, China 106/E4
Taíyetos (mts.), Gre. 75/H4
Taiyuan, China 106/C3
Taizhao, China 112/B2
Taizhou, China 106/D4
Taizi (riv.), China 106/F2
Ta'izz, Yem. 144/C2
Tāj Mahal, India 122/B2
Tajarhī, Libya 134/B3
Tajikistan(ctry.) 103/G6
Tajima, Japan 111/F2
Tajimi, Japan 109/M5
Tajique, NM, US 175/J3
Tajiri, Japan 109/H7
Tājirwīn, Tun. 138/L7
Tajo (Tagus) (riv.), Sp. 72/C3
Tājpur, India 122/B1
Tajrīsh, Iran 129/G3
Tajumulco (vol.), Guat. 200/D3
Tajuña (riv.), Sp. 72/D2
Tājūrā, Libya 93/G4
Tak, Thai. 120/B2
Takāb, Iran 129/F2
Takahagi, Japan 111/G2
Takahama, Japan 109/J5
Takahama, Japan 109/L6
Takahashi (riv.), Japan 110/C3
Takahashi, Japan 110/C3
Takahata, Japan 111/G1
Takaishi, Japan 109/H6
Takajärvi (lake), Fin. 65/E3
Takaka, NZ 161/C3
Takama, Guy. 206/B1
Takamatsu, Japan 110/D3
Takami-yama (peak), Japan 109/K7
Takanabe, Japan 110/B4
Takane, Japan 109/A2
Takanosu, Japan 108/B3
Takanosu-yama (peak), Japan 109/C2
Takaoka, Japan 111/E2
Takapau, NZ 161/D3
Takapuna, NZ 161/F6
Takarazuka, Japan 109/H6
Takaroa (isl.), FrPol. 163/L6
Takasaki, Japan 111/F2
Takashima, Japan 109/K5
Takatomi, Japan 109/L5
Takatori, Japan 109/J7
Takatsuki, Japan 109/K5
Takatsuki, Japan 109/J6
Takaungu, Kenya 145/B2
Takayama, Japan 111/E2
Takefu, Japan 110/E3
Takehara, Japan 110/C3
Tākestān, Iran 129/G2
Taketa, Japan 110/B4
Taketoyo, Japan 109/L6
Takev, Camb. 120/D4
Takh, India 124/D3
Takhatgarh, India 118/B2
Takhatpur, India 122/C4
Takhli, Thai. 120/C3
Takht-i-Bhāi, Pak. 124/A2
Takhta, Rus. 99/M5
Takhta-Bazar, Trkm. 100/G6
Takhtamygda, Rus. 105/J1
Taki, Japan 109/L7
Takiéta, Niger 141/H3
Takijuq (lake), Nun, Can. 166/E2
Takikawa, Japan 108/B2
Takingeun, Indo. 115/B1
Takino, Japan 109/G6
Takla Makan (des.), China 103/H6
Tāknis, Libya 93/J4
Tako, Japan 109/E2
Takoradi, Gha. 141/E5
Takouch (cape), Alg. 138/K6
Takoukout, Niger 141/H3
Taksimo, Rus. 101/M4
Taksony, Hun. 77/R10
Takum, Nga. 141/H5
Takundi, D.R. Congo 146/D4
Tala, Kenya 145/B2
Talā, Egypt 139/B3
Tala, Uru. 215/L11
Tala, Mex. 198/E4
Tala Mugongo, Ang. 146/D5
Talacasto, Arg. 212/B4
Talacre, Wal, UK 61/E5
Talagang, Pak. 124/B3
Talagante, Chile 214/N8
Tālah, Tun. 138/L7
Talaimannar, SrL. 121/C4
Talāja, India 127/K4
Talak (phys. reg.), Niger 141/G2
Talala, Ok, US 179/G2
Talalayivka, Ukr. 99/G2
Talamanca (mts.), CR 201/F4
Talamba, Pak. 124/B4
Talamona, It. 87/F5
Talang (peak), Indo. 115/C3
Talanga, Hon. 200/E3
Talangbatu, Indo. 115/D3
Talangbetutu, Indo 115/D3
Talange, Fr. 81/F5
Talant, Fr. 86/A3
Talara, Peru 208/A2
Talas, Turk. 128/C2
Talas (riv.), Kaz. 125/B3
Talas, Kyr. 125/B3
Talata Ampano, Madg. 152/H8
Talata Mafara, Nga. 141/G3
Talaud (isl.), Phil. 103/M9
Talavera de la Reina, Sp. 72/C3
Talawakele, SrL. 121/D5
Talawdī, Sudan 142/F3
Talawgyi, Myan. 112/C3
Talayuela, Sp. 72/C3
Talbingo (dam), Austl. 159/D2
Talbingo (res.), Austl. 159/D2
Talbingo, Austl. 159/D2
Talbot (mt.), Austl. 156/E3
Talbot, Ab, Can. 171/J1
Talbot (co.), Md, US 194/B6
Talbotton, Ga, US 188/E4
Talca, Chile 214/C2
Talcahuano, Chile 214/B3
Tālcher, India 121/E1
Talcho, Niger 141/F3
Talco, Tx, US 179/G4
Talcott, WV, US 189/G2
Taldan, Rus. 105/J1
Taldykuduk, Kaz. 97/J2
Taldyqorghan, Kaz 125/C3
Taleex, Som. 144/D3
Talence, Fr. 70/C4
Talent (riv.), Swi. 86/C4
Talent, Or, US 172/B2
Tālesh, Iran 129/G2
Talfer (Talvera) (riv.), It. 87/H4
Talgar, Kaz. 100/H5
Tali Post, Sudan 142/F4
Taliabu (isl.), Indo. 117/F4
Tālibwāla, Pak. 124/B4
Talihina, Ok, US 179/G3
T'alin, Arm. 129/E1
Talinay, PN, Chile 212/B4
Taliouine, Mor. 136/D3
Talipaw, Phil. 114/C4
Talisayan, Indo. 117/E3
Talisayan, Phil. 114/D3
Talitsa, Rus. 95/P4
Taliwang, Indo. 117/E5
Tal'ka, Bela. 67/N5
Talkeetna, Ak, US 168/X12
Ţalkhā, Egypt 139/C2
Tall 'Afar, Iraq 128/E2
Tall al Muqayyar (ruin), Iraq 126/E2
Tall ar Rub' (ruin), Egypt 139/C3
Tall 'Āsūr (peak), WBnk. 131/C5
Tall Kayf, Iraq 129/E2
Tall Kūjik, Syria 128/E2
Tall Rāk, Egypt 139/C3
Tall Timay (ruin), Egypt 139/C3
Talladega, Al, US 188/D4
Tallaght, Ire. 60/B5
Tallahala (cr.), Ms, US 190/D1
Tallahassee (cap.), Fl, US 191/F2
Tallahatchie (riv.), Ms, US 188/B3
Tallangatta, Austl. 159/C3
Tallanstown, Ire. 60/B4
Tallapoosa, Ga, US 188/E4
Tallapoosa (riv.), Al, US 188/E4
Tallard, Fr. 90/C4
Tallassee, Al, US 188/E4
Tallering (peak), Austl. 156/B4
Talleyville, De, US 194/C4
Tallgrass Prairie Nat'l Prsv., Ks, US 181/F4
Tallinn (cap.), Est. 67/L2
Tallmadge, Oh, US 186/F4
Tallman Mountain State Park, NY, US 195/K7
Talloires, Fr. 86/C6
Tallow, Ire. 58/B5
Tallowa (dam), Austl. 159/E2
Talmage, Ut, US 173/H3
Talmassons, It. 89/G2
Talmoon, Mn, US 183/H4
Tal'ne, Ukr. 98/F3
Talo (peak), Eth. 142/H3
Taloda, India 121/B1
Taloga, Ok, US 178/E2
Tāloqān, Afg. 127/J1
Talovaya, Rus. 99/L2
Talpa, Tx, US 176/E2
Talpa de Allende, Mex. 198/D4
Talshand, Mong. 104/D2
Talsi, Lat. 67/K3
Talsperre Pöhl (res.), Ger. 85/F1
Taltal, Chile 212/B3
Taltson (riv.), NW, Can. 166/E2
Talty, Tx, US 176/L7
Taluk, Indo. 115/C3
Talukbayur, Indo. 117/E3
Talumphuk (pt.), Thai. 120/C4
Talut (pt.), Fr. 82/B5
Talvera (Talfer) (riv.), It. 87/H4
Talwandi Bhāi, India 124/C4
Talwandi Sābo, India 124/C5
Talwāra, India 124/C4
Taly, Rus. 99/L3
Ţalyā, Egypt 139/C4
Tam Ky, Viet. 120/E3
Tam Le, Viet. 120/D2
Tam Quan, Viet. 120/E3
Tama (riv.), Japan 109/D2
Tama, Japan 109/C2
Tama Abu (range), Malay. 114/A5
Tamagawa, Japan 109/C2
Tamaha, Ok, US 179/G3
Tamaho, Japan 109/B2
Tamaki (str.), NZ 161/F6
Tamaki, Japan 109/L7
Tamalameque, Col. 204/C2
Ţamalāy, Egypt 139/B3
Tamale, Gha. 141/E4
Tamamura, Japan 109/C1
Taman', Rus. 99/J5
Taman (bay), Rus. 99/J5
Taman, Indo. 116/D5
Taman Negara NP, Malay. 115/C1
Taman-Rasset, Oued (riv.), Alg. 137/F5
Tamaná (peak), Col. 204/B3
Tamana (isl.), Kiri. 162/G5
Tamanaco (riv.), Ven. 207/P8
Tamanar, Mor. 136/C3
Tamanghasset (pol. reg.), Alg. 141/F1
Tamanghasset, Oued (riv.), Alg. 137/F5
Tamanhint, Libya 134/B3
Tamanrasset, Alg. 137/G5
Tamanrasset (wilaya), Alg. 137/F4
Tamanthi, Myan. 112/B3
Tamaqua, Pa, US 194/C2
Tamar (riv.), Eng, UK 62/B5
Tamara (isl.), Japan 111/H8
Tamarac, Fl, US 190/P10
Tamarack, Mn, US 183/H4
Tamarack NWR, Mn, US 183/G4
Tamari, Japan 109/E1
Tamarike, Indo. 155/F2
Tamarindo Nat'l Wild. Ref., CR 200/E4
Tamarite de Litera, Sp. 73/F2
Tamaro (peak), Swi. 87/E5
Tamási, Hun. 76/D2
Tamassoumît, Mrta. 140/B2
Tamatama, Ven. 205/E4
Tamatsukuri, Japan 109/E1
Tamaulipas (state), Mex. 196/B3
Tamazula de Gordiano, Mex. 198/E5
Tamazunchale, Mex. 200/B1
Tamba, Japan 109/H5
Tamba (uplands), Japan 109/H5
Tambach, Kenya 145/A1
Tambacounda (pol. reg.), Sen. 140/B3
Tambacounda, Sen. 140/B3
Tambakara, Mali 140/C3
Tambaoura, Falaise de (cliff), Mali 140/C3
Tambar Springs, Austl. 158/D1
Tambara, Moz. 149/G3
Tambawel, Nga. 141/G3
Tambea, Indo. 117/F4
Tambelan (isls.), Indo. 116/C3
Tambellup, Austl. 156/C5
Tambey, Rus. 100/H2
Tambisan, Malay. 114/B4
Tambo (peak), Swi. 87/F5
Tambo, Austl. 160/B4
Tambo (riv.), Peru 208/C3
Tambo (riv.), Austl. 159/C3
Tambo Colorado (ruin), Peru 208/C4
Tambo de Mora, Peru 208/B4
Tambo Grande, Peru 208/A2
Tambobamba, Peru 208/C4
Tambohorano, Madg. 152/G7
Tambopata (riv.), Peru 208/D4
Tambora (peak), Indo. 117/E5
Tambores, Uru. 213/E4
Tamboril, Braz. 207/F4
Tamboritha (mt.), Austl. 159/C3
Tambov, Rus. 97/G1
Tambov Oblast, Rus. 97/G1
Tambre (riv.), Sp. 72/A1
Tambu, Indo. 117/E4
Tambul, PNG 155/F1
Tambunan, Malay. 114/B4
Tambura, Sudan 142/E4
Tamchaket, Mrta. 140/C2
Tame, Col. 204/D3
Tame (riv.), Eng, UK 63/E1
Tâmega (riv.), Port. 72/B2
Tamel Aike, Arg. 215/C6
Tamentit, Alg. 137/E4
Támesis, Col. 207/K7
Tamgak (peak), Niger 141/H2
Tamghas, Nepal 122/D1
Tamiahua (lag.), Mex. 200/B1
Tamiahua, Mex. 200/B1
Tamiami (canal), Fl, US 191/H5
Tamiami, Fl, US 190/P11
Tamiang (pt.), Indo. 115/B1
Tamil Nādu (state), India 118/C5
Taminango, Col. 204/B4
Tamines, Belg. 81/D3
Ţāmiyah, Egypt 139/B6
Tamkuhi, India 123/E2
Tamlūk, India 123/F4
Tāmma, India 112/B3
Tammany (mt.), NJ, US 194/C2
Tammaro (riv.), It. 92/D5
Tammela, Fin. 67/K1
Tammisaari (Ekenäs), Fin. 67/K2
Ţammūn, WBnk. 131/C4
Tamo, Ar, US 179/J3
Tampa, Ks, US 179/F1
Tampa, Fl, US 190/L8
Tampa (bay), Fl, US 190/K8
Tampa (int'l arpt.), Fl, US 190/K8
Tampalakamam, SrL. 121/D4
Tampang, Indo. 115/D3
Tampere, Fin. 67/K1
Tampere-Pirkkala (int'l arpt.), Fin. 67/K1
Tampico, Mex. 200/B1
Tampin, Malay. 115/C2
Tampines (nbrhd.), Sing. 115/J6
Tampoc (riv.), FrG. 205/H4
Tampon Ambohitra (peak), Madg. 152/J6
Tampulonanjing (peak), Indo. 115/B2
Tamra, Isr. 131/C3
Tamrah, SAr. 126/E4
Tamsalu, Est. 67/M2
Tamshiyacu, Peru 208/C2
Tamuín, Mex. 200/B1
Tamuín (riv.), Mex. 200/B1
Tāmulpur, India 123/H2
Tamur (riv.), Nepal 123/F2
Tamworth, Austl. 158/D1
Tamworth, Eng, UK 63/E1
Tamyang, SKor. 107/D5
Tan (riv.), China 119/K3
Tan An, Viet. 120/D4
Tan-Tan, Mor. 136/C3
Tana (riv.), Fin. 100/C3
Tana (riv.), Nor. 64/H1
Tana, Nor. 64/J1
Tana (lake), Eth. 133/F3
Tana (riv.), Kenya 133/G5
Tana River Primate Nat'l Rsv., Kenya 145/C2
Tanabe, Japan 110/D4
Tanabe, Japan 109/J6
Tanabi, Braz. 213/G2
Tanafjorden (estu.), Nor. 64/J1
Tanaga (isl.), Ak, US 101/U4
Tanagura, Japan 111/G2
Tanahbala (isl.), Indo. 116/A4
Tanahmasa (isl.), Indo. 115/B3
Tanahmerah, Indo. 155/F1
Tanahputih, Indo. 115/C2
Tanakpur, India 122/C1
Tanambe, Madg. 152/J7
Tanami, Austl. 154/C4
Tanami (des.), Austl. 153/C2
Tanami Desert Wildlife Sanctuary, Austl. 154/C5
Tanana (riv.), Ak, US 166/B2
Tanana (riv.), Ak, US 165/C3
Tanandava, Madg. 152/G8
Tanangozi, Tanz. 145/A3
Tanaro (riv.), It. 71/G4
Tancacha, Arg. 212/D5
Tancarville, Fr. 83/F2
Tancheng, China 106/D4
Tanch'ŏn, NKor. 107/E2
Tancítaro, Pico de (peak), Mex. 198/E5
Tancítaro, PN de, Mex. 196/A4
Tandā, India 122/D2
Tanda, C.d'Iv. 140/E5
Tanda (lake), Mali 140/D3
Tānda, India 122/B1
Tandag, Phil. 114/D3
Tandaltī, Sudan 142/F2
Ţăndărei, Rom. 77/H3
Tāndi, India 124/D3
Tandian, China 107/C2
Tandil, Arg. 214/F3
Tandjilé (pref.), Chad 142/C3
Tandjoaré, Togo 141/F4
Tāndliānwāla, Pak. 124/B4
Tando Ādam, Pak. 127/J3
Tando Allāhyār, Pak. 127/J3
Tando Muhammad Khān, Pak. 127/J3
Tandou (lake), Austl. 153/D4
Tandragee, NI, UK 60/B3
Tandrano, Madg. 152/H8
Taneatua, NZ 161/D2
Tanega (isl.), Japan 105/L5
Tanem (range), Myan.,Thai. 119/G4
Taneytown, Md, US 187/H5
Taneyville, Mo, US 179/H2
Tanezrouft (des.), Alg. 133/B2
Tanezrouft-n-Ahenet (des), Alg. 137/F5
Tang (riv.), China 106/C4
Tanga (prov.), Tanz. 145/B3
Tanga, Tanz. 145/B3
Tangail, Bang. 123/G3
Tangail (pol. reg.), Bang. 123/G3
Tangalī, Iran 129/H2
Tangali, Gui. 140/C4
Tangang, China 113/G2
Tanganyika (lake), D.R. Congo 133/F5
Tangará da Serra, Braz. 209/G4
Tangdan, China 112/D3
Tanger (prov.), Mor. 138/A2
Tanger, Mor. 138/B2
Tangerang, Indo. 115/D3
Tangerhütte, Ger. 68/F2
Tangerine, Fl, US 190/M6
Tangermünde, Ger. 68/F2
Tangfang, China 106/J7
Tanggula (pass), China 125/F5
Tanggula (mts.), China 125/E5
Tanghe, China 106/C4
Tangi, Pak. 124/A2
Tangier, Va, US 189/K2
Tangier (sound), Md, US 189/J1
Tangier (Boukhalf) (int'l arpt.), Mor. 138/B2
Tangipahoa (riv.), Ms, US 190/C2
Tangipahoa, La, US 190/C2
Tangjin, SKor. 107/D4
Tangkak, Malay. 115/C2
Tanglewilde-Thompson Place, Wa, US 193/B3
Tangmai, China 112/B2
Tango, Ang. 146/C5
Tangqi, China 106/L9
Tangra (lake), China 125/E5
Tangshan, China 106/J7
Tangtou, China 113/F3
Tangub, Phil. 114/C3
Tanguiéta, Ben. 141/F4
Tangwan, China 113/F3
Tangxi, China 113/H2
Tangyan (riv.), China 113/F2
Tangyin, China 106/C4
Tangyuan, China 105/K2
Tanhaçu, Braz. 211/E2
Taniantaweng (mts.), China 112/C2
Tanigumi, Japan 109/L4
Tanimbar (isl.), Indo. 103/N10
Taninges, Fr. 86/C5
Tanintharyi (state), Myan. 119/G5
Tanis (ruin), Egypt 139/C3
Taniwel, Indo. 117/G4
Tanjay, Phil. 114/C3
Tanjiachang, China 113/F2
Tanjong Malim, Malay. 115/C2
Tanjung, Indo. 116/E4
Tanjung Sedano (pt.), Indo. 115/F3
Tanjungbalai, Indo. 115/B2
Tanjungbatu, Indo. 115/C2
Tanjungenim, Indo. 115/C3
Tanjungkarang-Telukbetung, Indo. 115/D3
Tanjungpandan, Indo. 116/C4
Tanjungpinang, Indo. 115/D2
Tanjungpura, Indo. 115/B2
Tanjunguban, Indo. 115/D2
Tānk, Pak. 124/A3
Tankersley, Tx, US 177/D2
Tankwa Karoo NP, SAfr. 150/B4
Tann, Ger. 85/F6
Tanna (isl.), Van. 162/F6
Tanna, Ger. 85/E1
Tannan, Japan 109/H5
Tannersville, Pa, US 194/C1
Tannheim, Aus. 87/G3
Tannu-Ola (mts.), Rus. 104/C1
Tano (riv.), Gha. 141/E5
Tânout, Niger 141/H3
Tanqiu, China 113/G3
Tanque Verde, Az, US 175/G4
Tanquián de Escobedo, Mex. 200/B1
Tansen, Nepal 122/D2
Tānsing, Nepal 122/D2
Ţanţā, Egypt 139/B3
Tantabin, Myan. 112/C5
Tantallon, Sk, Can. 182/D2
Tantallon, Md, US 194/A6
Tantangara (dam), Austl. 159/D2
Tantō, Japan 109/G5
Tantou, China 113/H2
Tantoyuca, Mex. 200/B1
Tantu, China 105/J2
Tanuku, India 121/D2
Tanumshede, Swe. 66/D2
Tanunda, Austl. 158/A2
Tanxu, China 120/E1
Tanyang, SKor. 107/E4
Tanza, Phil. 114/E7
Tanzania(ctry.) 133/F5
Tanzawa-yama (peak), Japan 109/C3
Tanzishan, China 113/G3
Tao (isl.), Myan. 120/B4
Tao (riv.), China 104/E5
Taochuan, China 113/F3
Tao'er (riv.), China 105/J2
Taolañaro, Madg. 152/H9
Taole, China 104/F4
Taolin, China 113/G3
Taonan, China 105/J2
Taormina, It. 74/C4
Tāoru, India 124/C5
Taos, NM, US 178/E2
Taos, Mo, US 179/H1
Taoudenni, Mali 136/E5
Taounate, Mor. 138/E2
Taounate (town), Mor. 138/E2
Taourirt, Alg. 137/F4
Taourirt, Mor. 138/C2
Taoxi, China 113/H2
Taoyuan, China 119/K2
T'aoyüan, Tai. 113/J3
Tap Mun Chau (isl.), China 113/M7
Tap O'Neth (hill), Sc, UK 59/D2
Tapa, Est. 67/L2
Tapacarí, Bol. 212/C1
Tapachula, Mex. 200/C3
Tapah, Malay. 115/C1
Tapajós (riv.), Braz. 203/D3
Tapajós (Amazônia), PN de, Braz. 209/G2
Tapaktuan, Indo. 115/B2
Tapan, Indo. 115/C3
Tapanahoni (riv.), Sur. 205/H4
Tapanti Nat'l Wild. Ref., CR 201/F4
Tapanui, NZ 161/B4
Tapará, Serra da (mts.), Braz. 206/C3
Tapauá (riv.), Braz. 209/E2
Tapauá, Braz. 209/E2
Tapaz, Phil. 114/C3
Tapenagá (riv.), Arg. 212/E3
Taperoá, Braz. 207/G4
Tapeta, Libr. 140/C5
Taphan Hin, Thai. 120/C2
Tapi Aike, Arg. 215/C6
Tapia de Casariego, Sp. 72/B1
Tapiche (riv.), Peru 208/C2
Tapili, D.R. Congo 147/F2
Tapilula, Mex. 200/C2
Taping (riv.), Myan. 112/C3
Tapini, PNG 155/G2
Tapis (peak), Malay. 115/C1
Tāplejun, Nepal 123/F2
Tapo, Peru 208/C3
Tapoa (prov.), Burk. 141/F3
Tapolca, Hun. 76/C2
Tappahannock, Va, US 189/J2
Tappan (lake), Oh, US 186/F4
Tappan, NY, US 195/K7
Tappan Zee (riv.), NY, US 195/K7
Tappan Zee (lake), NY, US 195/E1
Tappanahoni (riv.), Sur. 206/C2
Tappen, ND, US 182/E4
Tappi-zaki (pt.), Japan 108/B3
Tappino (riv.), It. 92/D4
Tapps (lake), Wa, US 193/C3
Tāpti (riv.), India 118/B3
Tapul Group (isls.), Phil. 114/C4
Tapun, India 112/C3
Taqab, Sudan 135/F5
Taqātu' Hayyā, Sudan 126/C5
Taqian, China 113/H2
Taquari, Braz. 213/G4
Taquari (riv.), Braz. 210/A3
Taquari (riv.), Braz. 213/F1
Taquaritinga, Braz. 213/G2
Taquarituba, Braz. 213/G2
Taquaruçu (res.), Braz. 210/B4
Taquil, Ecu. 208/B1
Tar (riv.), Ire. 58/B5
Tar (riv.), Kyr. 125/B3
Tar (riv.), NC, US 189/J3
Tara, Rus. 100/H4
Tara (riv.), Yugo. 76/D4
Tara, Zam. 149/E3
Tara, Austl. 160/C4
Taraba (state), Nga. 141/H5
Taraba (riv.), Nga. 141/H4
Tarabuco, Bol. 212/C1
Ţarābulus, Leb. 130/D2
Ţarābulus (Tripoli) (cap.), Libya 93/G4
Taraclia, Mol. 77/J3
Taradale, NZ 161/D2
Tarairí, Bol. 212/D2
Tarakan (int'l arpt.), Indo. 117/E3
Tarakan, Indo. 117/E3
Tarakit (peak), Kenya 145/A1
Taraklı, Turk. 77/K5
Tārākot, Nepal 122/D1
Taraku (isl.), Rus. 108/E2
Taralga, Austl. 159/D2
Taramana, Indo. 154/B2
Taranagar, India 124/C5
Tarancón, Sp. 72/D2
Tarangire NP, Tanz. 145/A2
Taranna, Austl. 158/C4
Taranto, It. 75/E2
Taranto (gulf), It. 93/H2
Tarapacá, Col. 204/D5
Tarapacá (pol. reg.), Chile 212/B1
Tarapoa, Ecu. 204/B5
Tarapoto, Peru 208/B2
Tarare, Fr. 70/F4
Tarariras, Uru. 215/K11
Tararua (range), NZ 161/J9
Tarascon, Fr. 90/A5
Tarascon-sur-Ariège, Fr. 70/D5
Tarashcha, Ukr. 98/F3
Tarata, Bol. 212/C1
Tarata, Peru 212/B1
Tarauacá, Braz. 208/D3
Tarauacá (riv.), Braz. 208/D2
Taravai (isl.), FrPol. 163/M7
Tarawa (isl.), Kiri. 162/G4
Tarawa (cap.), Kiri. 162/G4
Tarawera (vol.), NZ 161/D2
Tarazona, Sp. 72/E2
Tarazona, Sp. 72/E3
Tarbagatay (mts.), Kaz. 125/D2
Tarbaj, Kenya 145/C1
Tarbat Ness (pt.), Sc, UK 59/C1
Tarbela (res.), Pak. 124/B2
Tarbela (dam), Pak. 124/B2
Tarbela (res.), India 125/B5
Tarbert, Sc, UK 57/Q8
Tarbert, Ire. 58/A4
Tarbes, Fr. 70/D5
Tarbolton, Sc, UK 59/B5
Tarboro, Ga, US 191/H2
Tarboro, NC, US 189/J3
Tarbûl Abu Khashîrât (peak), Egypt 139/C6
Tarcento, It. 71/K3
Tarcoola, Austl. 157/G4
Tarcutta, Austl. 159/C2
Tardes (riv.), Fr. 70/E3
Tardienta, Sp. 73/E2
Tardoire (riv.), Fr. 70/D4
Tardoki-Jani (peak), Rus. 105/M2
Taree, Austl. 158/E1
Tarf Water (riv.), Sc, UK 60/D2
Ţarfā' (wadi), Egypt 128/B4
Ţarfā' (wadi), Egypt 135/F2
Tarfaya, Mor. 136/B4
Target Rock Nat'l Wild. Ref., NY, US 195/M8
Targuist, Mor. 138/B2
Tarhūnah, Libya 93/G4
Tari, PNG 155/F1
Tariana, Col. 204/D4
Tarīf, UAE 126/F4
Tarifa, Sp. 72/C4
Tarifa, Ecu. 208/B1
Tarija (dept.), Bol. 212/C2
Tarija (int'l arpt.), Bol. 212/C2
Tarija, Bol. 212/C2
Tariku (riv.), Indo. 117/J4
Tariku-Taritatu (plain), Indo. 117/J4
Tarim (riv.), China 100/J5
Tarim (basin), China 100/J6
Tarīm, Yem. 144/D1
Tarim Liuchang, China 125/E3
Tarime, Tanz. 145/A2
Tarin (riv.), Afg. 127/J2
Tarin (Torino), It. 71/G4
Taring, Indo. 115/B2
Taritatu (riv.), Indo. 117/J4
Tarkastad, SAfr. 150/D4
Tarkhankut (cape), Ukr. 99/G5
Tarkio, Mo, US 181/G3
Tarkio (cr.), Mo, Ia, US 181/G3
Tarko-Sale, Rus. 100/H3
Tarkwa, Gha. 141/E5
Tarlac, Phil. 114/C2
Tarland, Sc, UK 59/D2
Tarlton Downs, Austl. 157/H2
Tarma, Peru 208/C3
Tarmstedt, Ger. 79/G2
Tarn (riv.), Fr. 93/D2
Tarn Tāran, India 124/C4
Tarna (riv.), Mong. 104/E2
Tarnak (riv.), Afg. 127/J2
Tårnby, Den. 65/J7
Tarnobrzeg (prov.), Pol. 69/M3
Tarnobrzeg, Pol. 69/L3
Tarnogskiy Gorodok, Rus. 95/J3
Tarnów, Pol. 69/L3
Tärnsjö, Swe. 66/G1
Tärnskär (isl.), Swe. 65/B1
Taro (riv.), It. 71/J4
Taro (lake), China 125/D5
Tarō, Japan 108/B4
Taroko NP, Tai. 113/J3
Ţārom, Iran 129/H4
Taroms'ke, Ukr. 99/H3
Taroom, Austl. 160/C4
Tarouca, Port. 72/B2
Taroudannt, Mor. 136/C3
Tarp, Ger. 66/C4
Tarpa, Hun. 76/F1
Tarpon (lake), Fl, US 191/G3
Tarpon Springs, Fl, US 190/K7
Tarporley, Eng, UK 61/F5
Tarqui, Peru 204/C5
Tarquinia, It. 74/B1
Tarqūmiyah, WBnk. 131/C5
Tarrafal, CpV. 133/K10
Tarragona, Sp. 73/F2
Tarraleah, Austl. 158/C4
Tarrant, Al, US 188/D4
Tarrant (co.), Tx, US 176/K7
Tàrrega, Sp. 73/F2
Tarrenz, Aus. 87/G3
Tarryall (mts.), Co, US 178/B1
Tarrytown, Fl, US 190/L6
Tarrytown, NY, US 195/K7
Tarshīhā, Isr. 131/C2
Tarsus, Turk. 128/C2
Tarsus (riv.), Turk. 130/D1
Tartagal, Arg. 212/E4
Tartagal, Arg. 212/D2
Tärtär, Azer. 129/F1
Tartaro (riv.), It. 89/E2
Tartarstan Aut. Rep., Rus. 100/Q6
Tartas, Fr. 70/C5
Tartu, Est. 67/M2
Ţarţūs, Syria 130/D2
Ţarţus (dist.), Syria 128/C3
Tarui, Japan 109/L5
Tarumizu, Japan 110/B5
Tarusa, Rus. 94/H5
Ţārūţ, Egypt 139/C3
Tarutao NP, Thai. 120/B5
Tarutung, Indo. 115/B2
Tarutyne, Ukr. 77/J2
Tarvagatay (mts.), Mong. 104/D2
Tarvin, Eng, UK 61/F5
Tarzan, Tx, US 177/D1
Tarzana (nbrhd.), Ca, US 192/E7
Taşağıl, Turk. 130/B1
Tasawāh, Libya 134/B3
Täsch, Swi. 86/D5
Taşçı, Turk. 128/C2
Taseko (mtn.), BC, Can. 170/C2
Taseko (riv.), BC, Can. 170/C2
Tash-Kömür, Kyr. 125/B3
Tashanta, Rus. 125/E2
Tashi Gang, Bhu. 123/H2
Ţashk (lake), Iran 129/H4
Tashkent (cap.), Uzb. 125/A3
Tashkent (int'l arpt.), Uzb. 125/A3
Tashkepri, Trkm. 127/H1
Tashtagol, Rus. 125/E1
Tasikmalaya, Indo. 115/E3
Taşkent, Turk. 128/C2
Taşköprü, Turk. 96/E4
Taşlıçay, Turk. 129/E2
Tasman (bay), NZ 153/H7
Tasman (cape), Austl. 158/C4
Tasman(sea) 162/E8
Tasman (pt.), Austl. 155/E3
Tasman (pen.), Austl. 153/D5
Tasman NP, NZ 161/C3
Tasmania (state), Austl. 153/D5
Tăşnad, Rom. 76/F2
Taşova, Turk. 96/F4
Tasquillo, Mex. 199/K6
Tassara, Niger 141/G2
Tassili Oua-n Ahaggar (mts.), Alg. 137/G5
Tassili-n-Ajjer (mts.), Alg. 137/G4
Tastrup, Den. 65/J7
Tastuba, Rus. 95/N5
Taşucu, Turk. 130/C1
Tasudi, Myan. 120/B2
Tata, Mor. 136/D3
Tata, Hun. 76/D2
Tata, D.R. Congo 142/F5
Tata Mailau (peak), Indo. 154/B2
Tataba, Indo. 117/F4
Tatabánya, Hun. 76/D2
Tatakoto (isl.), FrPol. 163/L6
Tatalin (riv.), China 104/D4
Tatamy, Pa, US 194/C2
Tatar (str.), Rus. 103/P5
Tatarbunary, Ukr. 77/J3
Tatarlar, Turk. 77/H5
Tatarsk, Rus. 100/H4
Tatau, Malay. 116/D3
Tataurovo, Rus. 95/L4
Tatāwīn (gov.), Tun. 137/H2
Tatāwīn, Tun. 92/F4
Tate, Ga, US 188/E3
Tate-yama (peak), Japan 111/E2
Tatebayashi, Japan 109/D1
Tatéma, Gui. 140/B4
Tateshina, Japan 109/A1
Tateville, Ky, US 188/E2
Tateyama, Japan 111/F3
Tathlina (lake), NW, Can. 166/E2
Tathlīth, SAr. 126/D5
Tathra, Austl. 159/D3
Tatilt (well), Mrta. 140/B2
Tatkon, Myan. 120/B1
Tatlayoko Lake, BC, Can. 170/B2
Tatlikbulak, China 125/E4
Tatnam (cape), Mb, Can. 166/G3
Tatomi, Japan 109/B2
Tatranský NP, Slvk. 69/K4
Tatsfield, Eng, UK 56/D3
Tatsinskiy, Rus. 99/L3
Tatsuno, Japan 111/E3
Tatsuta, Japan 109/L5
Tattershall, Eng, UK 61/H5
Tatuí, Braz. 213/H2
Tatum, Tx, US 177/G1
Tatura, Austl. 159/B3
Tatvan, Turk. 128/E2
Tauá, Braz. 207/F4
Taubaté, Braz. 211/L8
Tauber (riv.), Ger. 68/E4
Tauberbischofsheim, Ger. 84/C3
Tauca, Peru 208/B3
Tauchik, Kaz. 97/J3
Taufkirchen, Ger. 85/F6
Taufkirchen an der Pram, Aus. 85/G6
Taufstein (peak), Ger. 84/C1
Tauherenikau (riv.), NZ 161/J9
Taulignan, Fr. 90/A4
Taulihawa, Nepal 122/D2
Taum Sauk (mtn.), Mo, US 188/B2
Taumarunui, NZ 161/C2
Taung, SAfr. 150/D2
Taungdwingyi, Myan. 112/B4
Taunggyi, Myan. 112/C4
Taungthonlon (peak), Myan. 112/B3
Taungup (pass), Myan. 112/B5
Taungup, Myan. 112/B5
Taungzun, Myan. 120/B3
Taunsa, Pak. 124/A4
Taunton, Ma, US 187/L4
Taunton, Eng, UK 62/C4
Taunton, On, Can. 186/V8
Taunus (range), Ger. 84/A2
Taunusstein, Ger. 84/B2
Taupo (lake), NZ 153/H6
Taupo, NZ 161/D2
Tauragė, Lith. 67/K4
Tauranga, NZ 161/D2
Taurion (riv.), Fr. 70/D3
Taurisano, It. 75/F3
Tauroa (pt.), NZ 161/C1
Taurus (mts.), Turk 128/C2
Tauste, Sp. 72/E2
Tauta, PNG 155/G1
Taute (riv.), Fr. 70/C2
Tautira, FrPol. 163/X15
Tauu (isls.), PNG 162/E5
Tavanbulag, Mong. 104/E2
Tavannes, Swi. 86/D3
Tavānti (lake), Fin. 65/F3
Tavares, Fl, US 190/M6
Tavarnelle, It. 89/E6
Tavarnuzze, It. 89/E6
Tavas, Turk. 128/B2
Tavaux, Fr. 86/B3
Tavazzano, It. 88/C3
Tavda (riv.), Rus. 100/G4
Tavda, Rus. 95/Q4
Tavel, Fr. 90/A4
Taverham, Eng, UK 63/H1
Tavernerio, It. 88/C2
Tavernes, Fr. 90/C5
Taverny, Fr. 56/J4
Taveta, Kenya 145/B2
Taveuni (isl.), Fiji 163/Y18
Taviano, It. 75/F3
Tavin, Mong. 104/F2
Tavira, Port. 72/B4
Tavistock, Eng, UK 62/B5
Tavo (riv.), It. 92/D3
Tavoy (pt.), Myan. 120/B3
Tavoy (Dawei), Myan. 120/B3
Tavrichanka, Rus. 105/L3
Tavşanlı, Turk. 128/B2
Tavy (riv.), Eng, UK 62/B6
Taw (riv.), Eng, UK 62/C5
Tawa, NZ 161/H9
Tawaeli, Indo. 117/E4
Tawakoni (lake), Tx, US 177/F1
Tawaramoto, Japan 109/J6
Tawas City, Mi, US 186/E2
Tawau, Malay. 114/B4
Tawau (int'l arpt.), Malay. 114/B4
Tawe (riv.), Wal, UK 62/C3
Tawern, Ger. 81/F4
Tāwi (riv.), India 124/C3
Tawi, Tanz. 145/B4
Tawi-tawi (isl.), Phil. 114/B4
Tawo, China 113/F2
Ţāwūq, Iraq 129/F3
Tāwurghā', Libya 93/G4
Tāwurghā, Sabkhat (swamp), Libya 93/G4
Tawzar (gov.), Tun. 137/G2
Tawzar, Tun. 92/F4
Taxco, Mex. 199/K8
Taxila, Pak. 124/B3
Taxila (ruin), Pak. 124/B3
Taxkorgan Tajik Zizhixian, China 125/C4
Tay (riv.), Sc, UK 59/C3
Tay (lake), Sc, UK 59/B3
Tay Ninh, Viet. 120/D4
Tayabamba, Peru 208/B3
Tayandu (isls.), Indo. 154/C1
Taybola, Rus. 94/G1
Tayeegle, Som. 144/C4
Taylor, Ar, US 179/H4
Taylor, Pa, US 187/J4
Taylor, Al, US 191/F2
Taylor, Mi, US 193/F7
Taylor (riv.), Co, US 173/K4
Taylor, Az, US 175/G3
Taylor (mt.), NM, US 175/J3
Taylor, Ne, US 180/E3
Taylor, Tx, US 177/F2
Taylor Town, Tx, US 179/G4
Taylors, SC, US 189/F3
Taylorsville, Ms, US 190/D2
Taylorsville, In, US 186/D5
Taylorsville, Ca, US 172/C3
Taylorsville, Ky, US 188/E1
Taylorsville, NC, US 189/G3
Taylorsville-Bennion, Ut, US 173/H3
Taylortown, La, US 179/H4
Taylorville, Il, US 181/K4
Taymā', SAr. 128/D5
Taymouth, NB, Can. 184/D2
Taymyr (pen.), Rus. 103/H2
Taymyr (isl.), Rus. 101/L2
Taymyr (riv.), Rus. 100/K2
Tayoltita, Mex. 198/D3
Tayport, Sc, UK 59/D4
Tayrona, PN, Col. 204/C2
Tayshet, Rus. 101/K4
Tayside (pol. reg.), Sc, UK 59/C3
Taytay, Phil. 114/B3
Taytay, Phil. 114/F6
Tayu, Indo. 115/E3
Taz (riv.), Rus. 103/H3
Taza (prov.), Mor. 138/C2
Taza, Mor. 138/B2
Tazawako, Japan 108/B4
Tazekka (peak), Mor. 138/B2
Tazenakht, Mor. 136/D3
Tazewell, Va, US 189/G2
Tazewell, Tn, US 189/F2
Tazicheng, China 105/J2
Tāzirbū (oasis), Libya 134/D3
Tazovskiy, Rus. 100/H3
Tazrouk, Alg. 137/G5
Tāzughrān, Tun. 74/B4
Tazumal (ruin), ESal. 200/D3
T'bilisi (cap.), Geo. 97/H4
Tbilisskaya, Rus. 99/L5
Tchamba, Camr. 142/B3
Tchamba, Togo 141/F4
Tchaourou, Ben. 141/F4
Tchetti, Ben. 141/F5
Tchibanga, Gabon 146/B3
Tchikala-Tcholohanga, Ang. 148/C2
Tchin Tabaradene, Niger 141/G3
Tchindjenje, Ang. 148/B2
Tcholliré, Camr. 142/B3
Tchula, Ms, US 188/B4
Tczew, Pol. 67/H4
Te Anau, NZ 161/A4
Te Anu (lake), NZ 161/A4
Te Araroa, NZ 161/D2
Te Aroha, NZ 161/C2
Te Awamutu, NZ 161/C2
Te Kao, NZ 161/C1
Te Karaka, NZ 161/D2
Te Kauwhata, NZ 161/C2
Te Kopuru, NZ 161/C2
Te Kuiti, NZ 161/C2
Te Teko, NZ 161/D2
Tea (riv.), Braz. 205/E5
Teacapán, Mex. 198/D4
Teague, Tx, US 177/F2
Tealby, Eng, UK 61/H5
Teaneck, NJ, US 195/J8
Teano, It. 92/D5
Teapa, Mex. 200/C2
Teapot Dome Nav. Petroleum Rsv., Wy, US 180/A2
Teapot Dome Naval Res., Wy, US 173/K2
Tearce, FYROM 75/G1
Teasdale, Ut, US 175/G1
Tebak (peak), Indo. 115/D3
Teberda, Rus. 97/G4
Tébessa (wilaya), Alg. 137/G2
Tebessa (mts.), Alg. 138/L7
Tébessa, Alg. 138/L7
Tebesselamane (well), Mali 141/F2
Tebicuary (riv.), Par. 212/E3
Tebingtinggi, Indo. 115/C3
Tebingtinggi, Indo. 115/B2
Tebingtinggi (isl.), Indo. 115/C2
Tebtunis (ruin), Egypt 139/B6
Tebulos-mta (peak), Rus. 97/H4
Tecalitlán, Mex. 198/E5
Tecamac, Mex. 199/R9
Tecamachalco, Mex. 199/M8
Tech (riv.), Fr. 73/G1
Techirghiol, Rom. 77/J3
Tecirli, Turk. 128/D2
Tecka, Arg. 214/C4
Tecka (riv.), Arg. 214/C4
Teckla, Wy, US 180/B2
Tecklenberg, Ger. 79/E4
Teckomatorp, Swe. 65/K7
Tecolutla, Mex. 199/M6
Tecomán, Mex. 198/E5
Tecopa, Ca, US 174/D3
Tecozautla, Mex. 199/K6
Tecpan de Galeana, Mex. 199/E5
Tecuala, Mex. 198/D4
Tecuci, Rom. 77/H3
Tecumseh, Ok, US 179/F3
Tecumseh, Mi, US 186/E3
Tecumseh, On, Can. 193/G7
Tecumseh, Ne, US 181/F3
Ted Ceidaar Dabole, Som. 144/B4
Tedjert (well), Alg. 137/H1
Tedodita Sakan, Myan. 112/C5
Tedzhen (riv.), Trkm. 100/G6
Tees (bay), Eng, Uk 61/G2
Tees (riv.), Eng, UK 61/G3
Teesside (int'l arpt.), Eng, UK 61/G3
Tefé (riv.), Braz. 209/E2
Tefé, Braz. 209/E1
Tefé (int'l arpt.), Braz. 209/E1
Tefé (lake), Braz. 209/E1
Teferič, Yugo. 76/E4
Tega (lake), Japan 109/E2
Tega Cay, SC, US 189/G3
Tegal, Indo. 115/E3
Tegel (int'l arpt.), Ger. 68/Q6
Tegelen, Neth. 78/D6
Tegeler (lake), Ger. 68/Q6
Tegheri (well), Libya 137/H4
Teghra, India 123/E3
Tegina, Nga. 141/G4
Tegineneng, Indo. 115/D3
Teglio, It. 87/G5
Tégouma (riv.), Niger 141/H3
Tegouma (riv.), Niger 142/A2
Tegsh, Mong. 104/D2
Tegualda, Chile 214/B4
Tegucigalpa (cap.), Hon. 200/E3
Tehachapi, Ca, US 174/C3
Tehachapi (mts.), Ca, US 174/C3
Tehamiyam, Sudan 126/C5
Tehek (lake), Nun, Can. 166/G2
Tehoru, Indo. 117/G4
Tehrān (cap.), Iran 129/G3
Tehrān (gov.), Iran 129/G2
Tehri, India 125/C5
Tehuacán, Mex. 199/M8
Tehuacana, Tx, US 177/F2
Tehuantepec (riv.), Mex. 200/C2
Tehuantepec (gulf), Mex. 165/H8
Tehuantepec (isth.), Mex. 199/G5
Teide, Pico de (peak), Sp. 136/A3
Teifi (riv.), Wal, UK 62/B2
Teifiside (valley), Wal, UK 62/B2
Teiga (plat.), Sudan 142/E2
Teign (riv.), Eng, UK 62/C5
Teignmouth, Eng, UK 62/C5
Teignousse (str.), Fr. 82/B6
Teisendorf, Ger. 85/F7
Teith (riv.), Sc, UK 59/B4
Teixeira Pinto, GBis. 140/A3
Tejakula, Indo. 115/F3
Tejen, Trkm. 127/H1
Tejn, Den. 66/F4
Tejupilco de Hidalgo, Mex. 199/E5
Tekamah, Ne, US 181/F3
Tékane, Mrta. 140/B2
Tekapo (lake), NZ 161/B3
Tekāri, India 123/E3
Tekax de Álvaro Obregón, Mex. 200/D1
Teke, Turk. 77/J5
Tekeli, Kaz. 125/C3

Tekes (riv.), China 100/J5
Tekezē Wenz (riv.), Eth. 126/C6
Tekiliktag (peak), China 125/D4
Tekirdağ (prov.), Turk. 77/H5
Tekirdağ, Turk. 77/H5
Tekit, Mex. 200/D1
Tekkali, India 121/E2
Tekke, Turk. 128/D1
Tekkeköy, Turk. 96/F4
Tekman, Turk. 128/E2
Tekoa, Wa, US 170/F4
Teksneslia, Nor. 64/S9
Teku, Indo. 117/F4
Tel 'Akko (ruin), Isr. 131/C3
Tel Aviv (dist.), Isr. 130/D3
Tel Aviv-Yafo, Isr. 131/B4
Tel Hazor NP, Isr. 131/D2
Tel Megiddo (ruin), Isr. 131/C3
Tela, Hon. 200/E3
Télagh, Alg. 138/D2
Télataï, Mali 141/F2
T'elavi, Geo. 97/H4
Telde, Sp. 136/B3
Télé (lake), Mali 140/D2
Telefomin, PNG 117/K5
Telegraph, Tx, US 177/E2
Telekhany, Bela. 96/C1
Telêmaco Borba, Braz. 213/G3
Telemark (co.), Nor. 64/D4
Telen (riv.), Indo. 117/E3
Teleorman (prov.), Rom. 77/G4
Telephone, Tx, US 179/F4
Telertheba (peak), Alg. 137/G4
Teles Pires (riv.), Braz. 203/D3
Telescope (peak), Ca, US 174/D2
Telese, It. 92/D5
Telford, Pa, US 194/C3
Telford Dawley, Eng, UK 62/D1
Telfs, Aus. 87/H3
Telgate, It. 88/C2
Telgruc-sur-Mer, Fr. 82/A4
Telgte, Ger. 79/E5
Telica, Nic. 200/E3
Télig (well), Mali 136/E5
Télimélé, Gui. 140/B4
Telipok, Malay. 114/B4
Teljo (peak), Sudan 142/E2
Tell, Tx, US 178/D3
Tell Atlas (mts.), Alg. 92/D3
Tell City, In, US 188/D2
Telli (lake), Mrta. 136/C4
Tellico (lake), Tn, US 188/E3
Tellico Plains, Tn, US 188/E3
Tellier, Arg. 215/D5
Tellin, Belg. 81/E3
Telluride, Co, US 175/J2
Telmen (lake), Mong. 104/D2
Telok Anson, Malay. 115/C1
Teloloapan, Mex. 199/F5
Telotskoye (lake), Rus. 125/E1
Telsen, Arg. 214/D4
Telšiai, Lith. 67/K4
Teltow (reg.), Ger. 69/G2
Teltow, Ger. 68/Q7
Teluk Punggur (pt.), Indo. 115/C3
Telukbayur, Indo. 115/C3
Telukdalem, Indo. 115/B2
Telukmelano, Indo. 116/C4
Telukmerbau, Indo. 115/C2
Tema, Gha. 141/E5
Temacine, Alg. 137/G2
Temagami (lake), On, Can. 186/F1
Temanggung, Indo. 115/E3
Temax, Mex. 200/D1
Tembagapura, Indo. 117/J4
Tembesi (riv.), Indo. 115/C3
Tembilahan, Indo. 115/C3
Tembisa, SAfr. 150/E2
Temblador, Ven. 205/F2
Tembo, D.R. Congo 146/D4
Tembo Aluma, Ang. 146/D4
Tembue, Moz. 149/G2
Teme (riv.), Eng, UK 62/C2
Temecula, Ca, US 192/C4
Temelkovo, Bul. 77/F4
Temerin, Yugo. 76/D3
Temerloh, Malay. 116/B3
Teminabuan, Indo. 117/H4
Temir, Kaz. 97/L2
Temirtaū, Kaz. 125/B1
Témiscaming, Qu, Can. 187/G1
Temma, Austl. 158/C4
Temnik (riv.), Rus. 104/E1
Temoaya, Mex. 199/Q10
Temoe (isl.), FrPol. 163/M7
Temora, Austl. 159/C2
Tempe, Az, US 175/G4
Tempe Downs, Austl. 157/G3
Tempelhof (arpt.), Ger. 68/Q7
Tempelhof, Ger. 68/Q7
Temperance, Mi, US 186/E4
Temperanceville, Va, US 189/K2
Tempio Pausania, It. 74/A2
Temple, Ok, US 179/E3
Temple, La, US 190/B2
Temple (bay), Austl. 155/F3
Temple (mt.), Ab., Can. 170/F2
Temple, Tx, US 176/F2
Temple, Pa, US 194/C3
Temple City, Ca, US 192/F7
Temple of Lady Chua Xu, Viet. 120/D4
Temple Terrace, Fl, US 190/L7
Templemore, Ire. 58/C4
Templepatrick, NI, UK 60/B2
Templestowe (nbrhd.), Austl. 158/G5
Templetouhy, Ire. 58/C4
Templeuve, Fr. 80/C2
Templeville, Md, US 194/C5
Templin, Ger. 69/G2
Templiner (lake), Ger. 68/Q7
Tempoal de Sánchez, Mex. 200/B1
Têmpung, China 104/D4
Temryuk, Rus. 99/J5
Temryuk (gulf), Rus. 99/J5
Temse, Belg. 81/D1
Temuco, Chile 214/B3
Temuka, NZ 161/B4
Temyasovo, Rus. 97/L1
Ten Boer, Neth. 78/D2
Ten Mile, Tn, US 188/E3
Ten Sleep, Wy, US 173/K1
Ten Thousand (isls.), Fl, US 191/H5
Tena, Ecu. 204/B5
Tenabo, Mex. 200/D1
Ténado, Burk. 141/E3
Tenafly, NJ, US 195/K8
Tenaha, Tx, US 177/G2
Tenāli, India 121/D2
Tenancingo, Mex. 199/K8
Tenango, Mex. 199/R10
Tenango de Arista, Mex. 199/Q10
Tenasserim (range), Myan. 120/B3
Tenasserim, Myan. 120/B3
Tenay, Fr. 86/B6
Tenbury, Eng, UK 62/D2
Tenby, Wal, UK 62/B3
Tencarola, It. 89/E3
Tendaho, Eth. 144/B3
Tende, Fr. 90/D4
Tenderovsk (bay), Ukr. 77/K2
Tenderovsk Spit (isl.), Mol. 77/K2
Tendō, Japan 108/B4
Tendoy, Id, US 173/G1
Tendrara, Mor. 137/E2
Tendre (peak), Swi. 86/C4
Ténenkou, Mali 140/D3
Tenente Portela, Braz. 213/F3
Ténéré (des.), Niger 141/H1
Ténéré du Tafassasset (des.), Niger 137/H5
Tenerife, Col. 204/C2
Tenerife (isl.), Sp. 133/A2
Tenes (riv.), Sp. 73/L6
Ténès, Alg. 138/F4
Teng (riv.), Myan. 119/G3
Teng Xian, China 106/D4
Teng'aopu, China 107/B2
Tengchong, China 112/C3
Tenggarong, Indo. 117/E4
Tengger (des.), China 104/E4
Tengiz (lake), Kaz. 100/G4
Tengqiao, China 120/E2
Tenguel, Ecu. 204/B5
Tenibre (peak), Fr. 90/C4
Tenibres (peak), It. 90/C4
Teniente Enciso, PN, Par. 212/D2
Tenigerbad, Swi. 87/E4
Teningen, Ger. 86/D1
Tenino, Wa, US 170/C4
Tenja, Cro. 76/D3
Tenjo, Col. 207/L8
Tenkāsi, India 121/C4
Tenke, D.R. Congo 147/F5
Tenkiller (lake), Ok, US 179/G3
Tenkodogo, Burk. 141/E4
Tenmile (cr.), Tx, US 176/L7
Tenmile Wash (riv.), Az, US 175/F4
Tenna (riv.), It. 92/C1
Tennant Creek, Austl. 154/D4
Tennessee (state), US 169/J4
Tennessee (riv.), US 169/J5
Tennessee Ridge, Tn, US 188/D2
Tennessee-Tombigbee Waterway (canal), Ms, US 188/C3
Tenneville, Belg. 81/E3
Tennille, Al, US 191/F2
Tennille, Ga, US 189/F4
Tennuaca (well), Mor. 136/B5
Teno, Chile 214/C2
Tenojoki (riv.), Fin. 64/H1
Tenom, Malay. 114/A4
Tenosique de Pino Suárez, Mex. 200/D2
Tenri, Japan 109/J6
Tenryū, Japan 111/E3
Tenryū (riv.), Japan 111/E3
Tensas (basin), La, US 177/J2
Tensas (riv.), La, US 179/J5
Tensas River NWR, La, US 177/J1
Tensift (pol. reg.), Mor. 136/C3
Tensift, Oued (riv.), Mor. 136/C3
Tenstrike, Mn, US 183/G4
Tenta, Eth. 144/A3
Tentena, Indo. 117/F4
Tenterden, Eng, UK 63/G4
Tenterfield, Austl. 158/E1
Tentolomatinan (peak), Indo. 117/F3
Tenus (peak), Kenya 145/A1
Teo, Sp. 72/A1
Teocaltiche, Mex. 196/A3
Teocelo, Mex. 199/N7
Teodelina, Arg. 214/E2
Teodoro Sampaio, Braz. 213/F2
Teófilo Otoni, Braz. 211/E3
Teopisca, Mex. 200/C2
Teotihuacán (ruin), Mex. 199/R9
Teotihuacán, Mex. 199/R9
Teotitlán del Camino, Mex. 200/B2
Tepa, Indo. 154/C1
Tepache, Mex. 198/C2
Tepalcatepec, Mex. 198/E5
Tepalcingo, Mex. 199/L8
Tepatitlán de Morelos, Mex. 196/A3
Tepatlaxco, Mex. 199/M7
Tepeapulco, Mex. 199/L7
Tepebaşı, Turk. 130/C1
Tepee (mtn.), Ok, US 178/E3
Tepehuaje, Mex. 199/F4
Tepehuanes, Mex. 198/D3
Tepeji del Río de Ocampo, Mex. 199/K7
Tepelenë, Alb. 75/G2
Tepelská Plošina (mts.), Czh. 85/F2
Tepetlaoxtoc, Mex. 199/R9
Tepexi, Mex. 199/M8
Tepexpan, Mex. 199/R9
Tēpī, Eth. 142/G4
Tepic, Mex. 198/D4
Teplá (riv.), Czh. 68/G3
Teplá Vltava (riv.), Czh. 85/G5
Teplice, Czh. 69/G3
Tepoca (cape), Mex. 198/B2
Tepoca, Cabo (cape), Mex. 198/B2
Tepoto (isl.), FrPol. 163/L6
Tepotzotlán, Mex. 199/Q9
Tepoztlán, Mex. 199/K8
Tequila, Mex. 198/E4
Tequisquiapan, Mex. 199/F4
Tequixquiac, Mex. 199/K7
Ter (riv.), Sp. 73/G1
Ter Aar, Neth. 78/B4
Ter Apel, Neth. 79/E3
Téra, Niger 141/F3
Tera (riv.), Sp. 72/B1
Teraina (Washington) (isl.), Kiri. 163/J4
Terakeka, Sudan 142/F4
Teramo, It. 92/C2
Teramo (prov.), It. 92/C2
Terang, Austl. 158/B3
Terborg, Neth. 78/D5
Terbuny, Rus. 96/F1
Tercan, Turk. 128/E2
Terceira (isl.), Azor., Port. 73/S12
Tercero (riv.), Arg. 212/D5
Terebovlya, Ukr. 98/C3
Terek (riv.), Rus. 97/H4
Terek, Rus. 97/H4
Terekhovka, Bela. 98/F1
Terekli-Mekteb, Rus. 97/H3
Terempa, Indo. 115/D2
Terengganu (riv.), Malay. 115/C1
Terengganu (state), Malay. 115/C1
Terenuthis (ruin), Egypt 139/B4
Terenzano, It. 89/G2
Terepaima, PN, Ven. 204/D2
Teresina, Braz. 207/F4
Teresópolis, Braz. 211/P7
Terespol, Pol. 69/M2
Terevinto, Bol. 212/D1
Tergnier, Fr. 80/C4
Tergun Daba (mts.), China 104/D4
Terhathum, Nepal 123/F2
Terheijden, Neth. 78/B5
Teriberka, Rus. 94/G1
Teriberskiy (pt.), Rus. 94/G1
Terkaplesterpoelen (lake), Neth. 78/C2
Terlan (Terlano), It. 87/H4
Terlano (Terlan), It. 87/H4
Terlingua, Tx, US 176/C3
Termas del Arapey, Uru. 212/E4
Termeno (Tramin), It. 87/H5
Termessos (Güllükdağı) NP, Turk. 128/B2
Termini Imerese, It. 74/C4
Terminiers, Fr. 83/G4
Terminillo (peak), It. 92/B3
Terminio (peak), It. 92/D6
Términos (lag.), Mex. 200/D2
Terminus (dam), Ca, US 174/C2
Termit-Kaoboul, Niger 142/A2
Termiz, Uzb. 127/J1
Termo, Ca, US 172/C3
Termoli, It. 92/D4
Termonfeckin, Ire. 60/B4
Termunten, Neth. 78/E2
Ternate, Indo. 117/G3
Ternay, Fr. 90/A1
Ternberg, Aus. 85/H7
Terneuzen, Neth. 78/A6
Terney, Rus. 105/M2
Terni (prov.), It. 91/B2
Terni, It. 91/B2
Ternin (riv.), Fr. 70/F3
Ternivka, Ukr. 99/J3
Ternoise (riv.), Fr. 80/B3
Ternopil', Ukr. 98/C3
Ternopil's'ka (prov.), Ukr. 96/C2
Ternovka, Rus. 99/L2
Terowie, Austl. 158/C2
Terpeniya (bay), Rus. 101/Q5
Terpeniya (cape), Rus. 105/N2
Terpní, Gre. 75/H2
Terra Ceia, Fl, US 190/K8
Terra Cotta, On, Can. 186/T8
Terra del Sole, It. 89/E5
Terra Nova, Braz. 207/G5
Terra Nova NP, Nf, Can. 185/K1
Terra Rica, Braz. 213/F2
Terrabonne (bay), La, US 190/C3
Terrace, BC, Can. 166/D3
Terrace Bay, On, Can. 183/L3
Terrace Heights, Wa, US 170/D4
Terracina, It. 92/C5
Terråk, Nor. 64/E2
Terral, Ok, US 179/F4
Terralba, It. 74/A3
Terranuova Bracciolini, It. 89/E6
Terrassa, Sp. 73/L6
Terrasson-la-Villedieu, Fr. 70/D4
Terre Haute, In, US 186/C5
Terre Hill, Pa, US 194/B3
Terrebonne (co.), Qu, Can. 185/N6
Terrebonne, Qu, Can. 185/N6
Terrell, Tx, US 177/F1
Terrenceville, Nf, Can. 185/K2
Terreton, Id, US 173/G2
Terrey Hills (nbrhd.), Austl. 160/H8
Terri (peak), Swi. 87/F4
Terrigal, Austl. 159/E1
Terrington Saint Clement, Eng, UK 63/G1
Terry, Mt, US 171/M4
Tersakan, Trkm. 129/H2
Tersakkan (riv.), Kaz. 125/A1
Terschelling (isl.), Neth. 78/C2
Tertenia, It. 74/A3
Teruel, Sp. 73/E2
Terutao (isl.), Thai. 119/G6
Tervakoski, Fin. 65/E4
Tervel, Bul. 77/H4
Terza Grande (peak), It. 71/K3
Terzo d'Aquileia, It. 89/G2
Tes-Khem (riv.), Rus. 104/C1
Tešanj, Bosn. 76/C3
Tescott, Ks, US 179/F1
Tescou (riv.), Fr. 70/D5
Teseney (Tessenie), Erit. 142/H2
Tesero, It. 87/H5
Teshi, Gha. 141/E5
Teshikaga, Japan 108/D2
Teshio, Japan 108/B1
Teshio (riv.), Japan 108/C1
Teshio-dake (peak), Japan 108/C2
Tesiyn (riv.), Mong. 104/D2
Teslić, Bosn. 76/C3
Teslin (riv.), Yk, Can. 166/C2
Teslin (lake), BC, Can. 166/C3
Teslin, Yk, Can. 166/C2
Tësovo-Netyl'skiy, Rus. 67/P2
Tessalit, Mali 141/F1
Tessaoua, Niger 141/G3
Tessé-la-Madeleine, Fr. 83/E3
Tessenderlo, Belg. 81/E1
Tessenie (Teseney), Erit. 142/H2
Tessy-sur-Vire, Fr. 83/D3
Test (riv.), Eng, UK 63/E4
Testa del Gargano (pt.), It. 74/E2
Testa del Rutor (peak), It. 90/D1
Tét, Hun. 76/C2
Têt (riv.), Fr. 73/G1
Tetas (pt.), Chile 212/B2
Tete, Moz. 149/G3
Tete (prov.), Moz. 149/G2
Tête d'Alpe (peak), Fr. 90/D5
Tête de Faux (peak), Fr. 86/D1
Tête de l'Enchastraye (peak), Fr. 90/C4
Tête de l'Estrop (peak), Fr. 90/C4
Tête de Moïse (peak), Fr. 90/C4
Tête de Siguret (peak), Fr. 90/C4
Tête de Soulaure (peak), Fr. 90/C3
Tête du Torraz (peak), Fr. 86/C6
Tête Jaune Cache, BC, Can. 170/E1
Tête Nord des Fours (peak), Fr. 90/C1
Tête Ronde (peak), Swi. 86/D5
Tetela, Mex. 199/M7
Teterow, Ger. 66/E5
Teteven, Bul. 77/G4
Tetford, Eng, UK 61/H5
Tetiaroa (isl.), FrPol. 163/L6
Tetiyiv, Ukr. 98/E3
Tëtkino, Rus. 99/H2
Teton (riv.), Id, US 173/H2
Teton (range), Wy, US 173/H2
Teton, Id, US 173/H2
Tetonia, Id, US 173/H2
Tétouan, Mor. 138/B2
Tétouan (prov.), Mor. 138/B2
Tetovo, FYROM 75/G1
T'et'ritsqaro, Geo. 97/H4
Tettnang, Ger. 87/F2
Tetulia, Bang. 123/G2
Tetulia (riv.), Bang. 123/H4
Teublitz, Ger. 85/F4
Teuchezhsk, Rus. 99/K5
Teuco (riv.), Arg. 212/D3
Teufen, Swi. 87/F3
Teúl de González Ortega, Mex. 198/E4
Teulada (cape), It. 74/A3
Teulon, Mb, Can. 182/F2
Teupasenti, Hon. 200/E3
Teuri (isl.), Japan 108/B1
Teuschnitz, Ger. 85/E2
Teutoburger Wald (for.), Ger. 79/F4
Teutopolis, Il, US 188/C1
Tevere (Tiber) (riv.), It. 71/K5
Teverya, Isr. 131/D3
Teviot (riv.), Sc, UK 59/D6
Teviotdale (valley), Sc, UK 59/D6
Tevli, Bela. 69/N2
Tewantin-Noosa, Austl. 160/D4
Tewaukon Nat'l Wild. Ref., ND, US 182/F5
Tewkesbury, Eng, UK 62/D3
Texada (isl.), BC, Can. 170/B3
Texana (lake), Tx, US 177/F3
Texarkana, Ar, US 179/G4
Texarkana, Tx, US 179/G4
Texas, Austl. 158/D1
Texas (state), US 168/F5
Texas City, Tx, US 177/N9
Texas Point NWR, La, US 177/H3
Texas Safari Wildlife Park, Tx, US 177/F2
Texas Stadium, Tx, US 176/L7
Texcoco, Mex. 199/R9
Texel (isl.), Neth. 68/C2
Texhoma, Ok, US 178/D2
Texmelucan, Mex. 199/L7
Texoma (lake), Ok, US 169/G5
Teyateyaneng, Les. 150/D3
Teykovo, Rus. 94/J4
Tezio (peak), It. 91/B1
Teziutlán, Mex. 199/M7
Tezonapa, Mex. 199/N8
Tezontepec, Mex. 199/L7
Tezontepec de Aldama, Mex. 199/K6
Tezoyuca, Mex. 199/R9
Tezpur, India 112/B3
Tezu, India 112/C3
Tezze, It. 89/E2
Tha (riv.), Laos 112/D4
Tha Chin (riv.), Thai. 120/B3
Tha Mai, Thai. 120/C3
Tha Rua, Thai. 120/C3
Tha Sala, Thai. 120/B4
Tha Tum, Thai. 120/C3
Tha Wang Pha, Thai. 120/C2
Tha-Anne (riv.), Nun, Can. 166/G2
Thaba Nchu, SAfr. 150/D3
Thabana-Ntlenyana (peak), Les. 150/E3
Thabankulu (peak), SAfr. 151/E2
Thabazimbi, SAfr. 149/E5
Thabor (peak), Fr. 90/C2
Thādiq, SAr. 126/E3
Thaen (pt.), Thai. 120/B4
Thagaya, Myan. 120/B2
Thai Binh, Viet. 113/E4
Thai Nguyen, Viet. 112/E4
Thailand(ctry.) 103/K8
Thailand (gulf), Asia 103/K8
Thākurdwāra, India 122/B1
Thākurgaon, Bang. 123/G2
Thākurmunda, India 121/E1
Thal, Pak. 124/A3
Thal (des.), Pak. 124/A4
Tha'l (mtn.), Sudan 142/E2
Thal (des.), India 125/B5
Thalang, Thai. 120/B4
Thaleban NP, Thai. 120/C5
Thaleischweiler-Fröschen, Ger. 81/G5
Thalerhof (int'l arpt.), Aus. 76/B2
Thalgau, Aus. 85/G7
Thalheim bei Wels, Aus. 85/H6
Thalmann, Ga, US 191/H2
Thalmässing, Ger. 84/E4
Thalwil, Swi. 87/E3
Thame (riv.), Eng, UK 63/F3
Thame, Eng, UK 63/F3
Thames (riv.), Eng., UK 63/G4
Thames (riv.), On, Can. 186/F3
Thames, NZ 161/C2
Thames Barrier, Eng, UK 56/D2
Thāna, India 121/B2
Thāna Bhawan, India 124/D5
Thāna Kasbā, India 122/A3
Thanatpin, Myan. 112/C5
Thanbyuzayat, Myan. 120/B3
Thānesar, India 124/D5
Thāneswar, Bang. 123/H3
Thang Duc, Viet. 120/D3
Thanggu, India 123/G2
Thangool, Austl. 160/C4
Thanh Hoa, Viet. 112/E5
Thanh Lang Xa, Viet. 119/J4
Thanh Phu, Viet. 120/D4
Thanh Tri, Viet. 120/D4
Thānkot, Nepal 123/E2
Thann, Fr. 86/D2
Thannhausen, Ger. 87/G1
Thanya Buri, Thai. 120/C3
Thaoge (riv.), Bots. 148/D3
Thaon-les-Vosges, Fr. 86/C1
Thap Put, Thai. 120/B4
Thap Sakae, Thai. 120/B4
Thar (riv.), Fr. 82/D3
Thar (des.), Pak. 124/A5
Tharād, India 127/K4
Thargomindah, Austl. 160/A5
Tharrawaddy, Myan. 112/B5
Thásos, Gre. 75/J2
Thásos (isl.), Gre. 96/C4
That Khe, Viet. 113/E4
That Phanom, Thai. 120/D2
Thatcham, Eng, UK 63/E4
Thatcher, Id, US 173/H2
Thatcher, Az, US 175/H4
Thaton, Myan. 120/B2
Thaungdut, Myan. 112/B3
Thaur, Aus. 87/H3
Thaxted, Eng, UK 63/G3
Thaxton, Ms, US 188/C3
Thaya (riv.), Aus. 69/H4
Thayer, Mo, US 179/J2
Thayer, Ks, US 179/G2
Thayetmyo, Myan. 112/B5
Thayngen, Swi. 87/E2
Thazi, Myan. 112/C4
The Alamo, Tx, US 177/E3
The Atomium, Belg. 81/D2
The Ballpark, Tx, US 176/K7
The Bourne (riv.), Eng, UK 56/B3
The Broads NP, Eng, UK 63/H1
The Buck (peak), Sc, UK 59/D2
The Burren (reg.), Ire. 58/A3
The Calf (peak), Eng, UK 61/F3
The Caprock (cliff), NM, US 178/C3
The Cheviot (peak), Eng, UK 59/D6
The Colony, Tx, US 176/L6
The Curragh, Ire. 58/D3
The Dalles (dam), Or, US 172/C1
The Dalles, Or, US 172/C1
The English Companys (isls.), Austl. 155/E2
The Entrance, Austl. 159/E1
The Everglades (swamp), Fl, US 191/H5
The Fens (phys. reg.), Eng, UK 61/H6
The Fens (phys. reg.), Eng, UK 63/G1
The Flat Tops (mts.), Co, US 173/K4
The Gap (pass), Ire. 58/C5
The Gap, Austl. 158/B1
The Grampians (range), Austl. 158/B3
The Granites (peak), Austl. 157/F2
The Hague ('s-Gravenhage) (cap.), Neth. 78/B4
The Hermitage, NZ 161/B3
The Key Ind. Res., Sk, Can. 182/C2
The Lakes NP, Austl. 159/C3
The Lizard (pen.), Eng, UK 62/A6
The Loup, NI, UK 60/B2
The Machars (pen.), Sc, UK 60/D2
The Malpais (lava flow), NM, US 175/H3
The Malpais (lava flow), NM, US 175/J4
The Naze (pt.), Eng, UK 63/H3
The Oaks, Ca, US 192/B1
The Oaks, Austl. 159/E2
The Paps (peak), Ire. 58/A5
The Pas, Mb, Can. 166/F3
The Peak (peak), NC, US 189/G2
The Pilot (mtn.), Austl. 159/D3
The Pine (hills), Mt, US 171/M4
The Pinnacles (peak), BC, Can. 170/E2
The Plains, Oh, US 186/E5
The Quantocks (hills), Eng, UK 62/C4
The Range, Zim. 149/F3
The Raven (pt.), Ire. 58/D5
The Rhinns (pt.), Sc, UK 60/C2
The Rock, Austl. 159/C2
The Royal NP, Austl. 160/H9
The Saddle (peak), Sc, UK 59/A2
The Seven Hogs (isl.), Ire. 56/N10
The Sisters (isl.), NZ 161/E3
The Solent (chan.), Eng, UK 63/E5
The Storr (peak), Sc, UK 57/Q8
The Swale (riv.), Eng, Ire. 63/G4
The Twins (peak), Ab, Can. 170/F1
The Valley (cap.), Angu. 197/N8
The Woodlands, Tx, US 177/G2
The Wrekin (hill), Eng, UK 62/D1
The Yellow (mtn.), Austl. 159/C1
Theale, Eng, UK 63/E4
Thebes (ruin), Egypt 135/G3
Thedaw, Myan. 120/B1
Thedford, Ne, US 180/D3
Theilheim, Ger. 84/D3
Thelepte, Tun. 92/F4
Thelon (riv.), NW,Nun, Can. 166/F2
Thelon (riv.), Can. 165/G3
Themar, Ger. 84/D1
Thémericourt, Fr. 56/H4
Theo (mt.), Austl. 157/F2
Theodore, Sk, Can. 182/C2
Theodore, Al, US 190/D2
Theodore, Austl. 160/C4
Theodore Roosevelt (dam), Az, US 175/G4
Theodore Roosevelt (lake), Az, US 175/G4
Theodore Roosevelt NP, ND, US 182/C4
Theodosia, Mo, US 179/H2
Théoule-sur-Mer, Fr. 90/C6
Thérain (riv.), Fr. 70/D2
Thermaic (gulf), Gre. 96/B4
Thermal, Ca, US 174/D4
Thermalito, Ca, US 172/C4
Thérmi, Gre. 75/H2
Thermopílai (Thermopylae) (pass), Gre. 75/H3
Thermopolis, Wy, US 173/J2
Thermopylae (Thermopílai) (pass), Gre. 75/H3
Thérouanne (riv.), Fr. 56/L4
Thésée, Fr. 83/G6
Thesprotikón, Gre. 75/G3
Thessalon, On, Can. 186/E1
Thessaloníki, Gre. 75/H2
Thessaly (reg.), Gre. 93/J3
Thet (riv.), Eng, UK 63/G2
Thetford, Eng, UK 63/G2
Thetford Mines, Qu, Can. 184/B2
Thetkala, Myan. 112/C5
Theunissen, SAfr. 150/D3
Theux, Belg. 81/E2
Thève (riv.), Fr. 56/K4
Theydon Bois, Eng, UK 56/D2
Thiais, Fr. 56/K5
Thíamis (riv.), Gre. 75/G3
Thiant, Fr. 80/C3
Thiaucourt-Regniéville, Fr. 81/E6
Thiberville, Fr. 83/F2
Thibodaux, La, US 190/C3
Thick (mtn.), Pa, US 187/H4
Thickwood (hills), Sk, Can. 171/L1
Thief River Falls, Mn, US 182/F3
Thielle (riv.), Swi. 86/C4
Thielsen (mt.), Or, US 172/B2
Thien Ngon, Viet. 120/D4
Thiene, It. 89/E2
Thiérache (reg.), Fr. 80/C4
Thierhaupten, Ger. 84/D5
Thiers, Fr. 70/E4
Thiers-sur-Thève, Fr. 56/K4
Thierville-sur-Meuse, Fr. 81/E5
Thiès, Sen. 140/A3
Thiès (pol. reg.), Sen. 140/A3
Thiet Tra, Viet. 112/E4
Thika, Kenya 145/B2
Thimād al Khuwaymah (well), Libya 134/C2
Thimphu (cap.), Bhu. 123/G2
Thingvellir NP, Ice. 64/N7
Thio, NCal. 163/V12
Thionville, Fr. 81/F5
Thiou, Burk. 141/E3
Thíra, Gre. 75/J4
Thíra (isl.), Gre. 93/K3
Third Cataract (falls), Sudan 135/F5
Third Lake, Il, US 193/Q15
Thirlmere (lake), Eng, UK 61/E2
Thirlmere, Austl. 159/E2
Thiron Gardais, Fr. 83/G4
Thironne (riv.), Fr. 83/G4
Thirsk, Eng, UK 61/G3
Thirsty (mt.), Austl. 156/D5
Thirtymile (pt.), NY, US 186/W9
Thise, Fr. 86/C3
Thisted, Den. 66/C3
Thistilfjördhur (estu.), Ice. 64/P6
Thistle (isl.), Austl. 157/H5
Thithia (isl.), Fiji 163/Y18
Thívai, Gre. 75/H3
Thiverval-Grignon, Fr. 56/H5
Thjósa (riv.), Ice. 64/N7
Thlanship, India 112/B3
Thlewiaza (riv.), Nun, Can. 166/G2
Thoen, Thai. 120/B2
Thoeng, Thai. 120/C2
Thohoyandou, SAfr. 149/F4
Thoi Binh, Viet. 120/D4
Thoiry, Fr. 56/H5
Tholen (isl.), Neth. 78/B5
Tholen, Neth. 78/B5
Tholey, Ger. 81/G5
Thomas, Ok, US 179/E3
Thomas, WV, US 189/H1
Thomasboro, Il, US 186/B4
Thomaston, Al, US 188/D4
Thomaston, Ga, US 188/E4
Thomastown, Ire. 58/C4
Thomastown, Ms, US 188/C4
Thomasville, Mo, US 179/J2
Thomasville, Al, US 190/E2
Thomasville, Ga, US 191/G2
Thomasville, NC, US 189/G3
Thomasville, Pa, US 194/B4
Thomes (cr.), Ca, US 172/B4
Thompson (peak), NM, US 178/B3
Thompson, ND, US 182/F4
Thompson, Mi, US 186/C2
Thompson, Ct, US 187/L4
Thompson, Ut, US 175/H1
Thompson, Mb, Can. 166/G3
Thompson (peak), Ca, US 172/B3
Thompson (riv.), Ia,Mo, US 181/G3
Thompson (lake), Austl. 156/K7
Thompson (riv.), BC, Can. 170/D2
Thompson Falls, Mt, US 170/G4
Thompsonville, Mi, US 186/D2
Thompsonville, Il, US 188/C2
Thomsen (riv.), NW, Can. 166/E1
Thomson, Ga, US 189/F4
Thomson, Il, US 181/J3
Thomson (riv.), Austl. 153/D3
Thon Lac Nghiep, Viet. 120/E4
Thon Song Pha, Viet. 120/E4
Thongwa, Myan. 120/B2
Thonnance-lès-Joinville, Fr. 86/B1
Thonon-les-Bains, Fr. 86/C5
Thonotosassa, Fl, US 190/L7
Thonotosassa (lake), Fl, US 190/L7
Thoreau, NM, US 175/H3
Thorens-Glières, Fr. 86/C6
Thorigny-sur-Marne, Fr. 56/L5
Thorlákshöfn, Ice. 64/N7
Thorn (cr.), Il, US 193/Q16
Thornaby-on-Tees, Eng, UK 61/G2
Thornbury, On, Can. 186/F2
Thornbury, Eng, UK 62/D3
Thorndale, Tx, US 177/F2
Thorndale, Pa, US 194/C4
Thorne, Eng, UK 61/H4
Thorne, On, Can. 187/G1
Thorne Bay, Ak, US 168/Z13
Thornfield, Mo, US 179/H2
Thornhill, Sc, UK 60/E1
Thornhill, Sc, UK 59/B4
Thornhurst, Pa, US 194/C1
Thornley, Eng, UK 61/G2
Thornthwaite, Eng, UK 61/G3
Thornton, Ar, US 179/H4
Thornton, Ca, US 193/M10
Thornton, Co, US 180/B4
Thornton, Tx, US 177/F2
Thornton Cleveleys, Eng, UK 61/E4
Thornton Dale, Eng, UK 61/H3
Thorntonville, Tx, US 177/C2
Thorntown, In, US 186/C4
Thornwood Common, Eng, UK 56/D1
Thorold, On, Can. 186/U9
Thorold South, On, Can. 186/U9
Thorp, Wi, US 181/J1
Thorp, Wa, US 170/D4
Thorpe, Eng, UK 56/B2
Thorpe Thewles, Eng, UK 61/G2
Thorpe-le-Soken, Eng, UK 63/H3
Thorsby, Al, US 188/D4
Thorsby, Ab, Can. 171/G1
Thórshöfn, Ice. 64/P6
Thouarcé, Fr. 83/E6
Thouaré-sur-Loire, Fr. 82/D6
Thoubāl, India 112/B3
Thouet (riv.), Fr. 70/C3
Thourotte, Fr. 80/B5
Thousand (isl.), On, Can. 187/H2
Thousand Oaks, Ca, US 192/B2
Thousand Springs (cr.), Nv, US 173/F3
Thowa (riv.), Kenya 145/B2
Thrace (reg.), Bul.,Gre. 93/K2
Thracian (sea), Gre. 96/C4
Thread (cr.), Mi, US 193/E6
Thredbo Village, Austl. 159/D3
Three Bridges, NJ, US 194/D2
Three Creek, Id, US 173/F2
Three Forks, Mt, US 171/J5
Three Hills, Ab, Can. 171/H2
Three Kings (isls.), NZ 162/G8
Three Lakes, Wi, US 183/K5
Three Mile (isl.), Pa, US 194/B3
Three Mile Plains, NS, Can. 184/E3
Three Notch, Al, US 191/F1
Three Oaks, Mi, US 186/C4
Three Pagodas (pass), Myan. 120/B3
Three Points (cape), Gha. 141/E5
Three Rivers, Mi, US 186/D4
Three Rivers, NM, US 175/J4
Three Rivers, Austl. 156/C3
Three Springs, Austl. 156/B4
Three Valley, BC, Can. 170/E2
Threehills (cr.), Ab, Can. 171/H2
Thrifty, Tx, US 176/E2
Throckmorton, Tx, US 178/E4
Throssel (lake), Austl. 153/B3
Thrums, BC, Can. 170/F3
Thrumster, Sc, UK 57/S7
Thrushel (riv.), Eng, UK 62/B5
Thu Dau Mot, Viet. 120/D4
Thu Duc, Viet. 120/D4
Thud (pt.), Austl. 155/F3
Thuin, Belg. 81/D3
Thuir, Fr. 70/E5
Thulba (riv.), Ger. 84/C2
Thule Air Base, Den. 167/X7
Thun, Swi. 86/D4
Thunder (mtn.), Wi, US 183/K5
Thunder (bay), On, Can. 183/K3
Thunder Bay, On, Can. 183/K3
Thunder Butte (cr.), SD, US 180/C1
Thundersley, Eng, UK 56/E2
Thuner (lake), Swi. 71/G3
Thung Chang, Thai. 120/C2
Thung Salaeng Luang NP, Thai. 120/C2
Thung Song, Thai. 120/B4
Thüngersheim, Ger. 84/C3
Thunkar, Bhu. 123/H2
Thur (riv.), Swi. 71/H3
Thurgau (canton), Swi. 87/E2
Thüringen, Aus. 87/F3
Thüringen (state), Ger. 71/J1
Thüringer Schiefergebirge (mts.), Ger. 84/E2
Thüringer Wald (for.), Ger. 68/F3
Thurlaston, Eng, UK 63/E2
Thurles, Ire. 58/C4
Thurloo Downs, Austl. 158/B1
Thurlow, Mt, US 171/L4
Thurmont, Md, US 187/H5
Thurnau, Ger. 85/E2
Thurø By, Den. 66/D4
Thursday Island, Austl. 155/F2
Thursley, Eng, UK 56/A3
Thurso, Qu, Can. 187/J2
Thurso, Sc, UK 57/V14
Thurston (co.), Wa, US 193/A3
Thurston (isl.), Ant. 216/T
Thury-en-Valois, Fr. 56/M4
Thury-Harcourt, Fr. 83/E3
Thusis, Swi. 87/F4
Thyez, Fr. 86/C5
Thyolo, Malw. 149/G3
Ti-m-Merhsoï (riv.), Niger 141/G2
Ti-n-Essako, Mali 141/F2
Ti-n-Jedane, Oued (riv.), Alg. 137/G4
Ti-n-Toumma (reg.), Niger 142/A1
Ti-n-Zaouâtene, Mali 141/F2
Ti-Tree Abor. Land, Austl. 157/G2
Tia, Austl. 158/D1
Tiahuanco (ruin), Bol. 212/B1
Tian Shan (mts.), China 103/H5
Tianbao, China 113/H3
Tiancang, China 104/D3
Tianchang, China 106/D4
Tiandeng, China 113/E4
Tian'e, China 119/J2
Tianguá, Braz. 207/F3
Tianguistenco, Mex. 199/Q10
Tianhua, China 113/G3
Tianjin (prov.), China 105/H4
Tianjin, China 106/H7
Tianlin, China 119/J3
Tianmen, China 113/G2
Tianmu (mts.), China 106/K9
Tianping, China 113/F3
Tianqiao, China 113/F2
Tianshifu, China 107/C2
Tianshui, China 104/F5
Tianshuihai, China 125/C4
Tianzhen, China 106/C2
Tianzhu, China 113/F3
Tianzhuangtai, China 107/B2
Tiaret, Alg. 138/F5
Tiassalé, C.d'Iv. 140/D5
Tiatucurá, Uru. 215/K10
Tiavea, WSam. 163/S9
Tibagi (riv.), Braz. 210/C4
Tibagi, Braz. 213/G3
Tibaná, Col. 204/C3
Tibati, Camr. 142/B4
Tibba, Pak. 124/A5
Tibbee (cr.), Ms, US 188/C4
Tibberton, Eng, UK 62/D1
Tibbie, Al, US 190/D2
Tibble, Swe. 65/A1
Tibé, Pic de (peak), Gui. 140/C4
Tiber (riv.), It. 93/G2
Tiber (dam), Mt, US 171/J3
Tiber (Tevere) (riv.), It. 71/K5
Tiberias (lake), Isr. 130/D3
Tiberias, Isr. 131/D3
Tibert (peak), It. 90/D4
Tibesti (mts.), Chad 133/D3
Tibet (reg.), China 103/H6
Tibet (Xizang) (aut. reg.), China 104/C5
Tibiri, Niger 141/G3
Tibnīn, Leb. 131/C2
Tibooburra, Austl. 157/J4
Tibro, Swe. 66/F2
Tibshelf, Eng, UK 61/G5
Tiburon (cape), Haiti 197/G4
Tiburon, Ca, US 193/K11
Tiburón, Isla (isl.), Mex. 198/B2
Ticaco, Peru 208/D5
Ticehurst, Eng, UK 63/G4
Tichigan (lake), Wi, US 193/P14
Tîchît, Mrta. 140/C2
Tichla, Mor. 136/B5
Tichnor, Ar, US 179/J3
T'īcho, Eth. 144/A4
Ticino (canton), Swi. 87/E5
Ticino (riv.), Swi. 87/E6
Tickfaw, La, US 190/C2
Ţicleni, Rom. 77/F3
Ticllos, Peru 208/B3
Ticonderoga, NY, US 187/K3
Ticul, Mex. 200/D1
Tīdah, Egypt 139/B2
Tidaholm, Swe. 66/E2
Tiddim, Myan. 112/B4
Tideswell, Eng, UK 61/G5
Tidikelt (plain), Alg. 137/F4
Tidioute, Pa, US 187/G4
Tidjikdja, Mrta. 140/C2
Tidone (riv.), It. 88/C3
Tidore (isl.), Indo. 117/G3
Tidsit (lake), WSah. 136/B5
Tie Plant, Ms, US 188/C4
Tiébélé Corabie, Burk. 141/E4
Tiébissou, C.d'Iv. 140/D5
Tiéboro, Chad 134/C4
Tiechang, China 107/D2
Tiede, PN del, Sp. 136/A3
Tiefencastel, Swi. 87/F4
Tiefensee, Ger. 68/Q6
Tiéfinzo, C.d'Iv. 140/D4
Tiège, Belg. 81/E2
Tiel, Neth. 78/C5
Tieli, China 105/K2
Tieling, China 106/E2
Tielt, Belg. 80/C2
Tielt-Winge, Belg. 81/D2
Tiemba (riv.), C.d'Iv. 140/D4
Tiemen (pass), China 125/E3
Tien Yen, Viet. 120/D1
Tien Yen, Viet. 120/D2
Tienen, Belg. 81/D2
Tiénigbe, C.d'Iv. 140/D4
Tieniu (pass), China 113/H3
Tiercé, Fr. 83/E5
Tieri, Austl. 160/C3
Tieroko (peak), Chad 134/C4
Tierp, Swe. 66/G1
Tierra Amarilla, NM, US 175/J2
Tierra Amarilla, Chile 212/B3
Tierra Blanca (cr.), Tx,NM, US 178/C3
Tierra Blanca, Mex. 199/N8
Tierra Colorada, Mex. 199/F5
Tierra del Fuego (isl.), Arg. 203/C8
Tierra del Fuego, Antártida e Islas del Atlántico Sur, Arg. 215/C7
Tierra del Fuego, PN, Chile 215/C7
Tierradentro, Col. 204/B4
Tierranueva, Mex. 199/E4
Tiétar (riv.), Sp. 72/C2
Tietê (riv.), Braz. 203/D5
Tieton, Wa, US 170/D4
Tieton (peak), Wa, US 170/D4
Tieyon, Austl. 157/G3
Tifariti, WSah. 136/C4
Tiffany, Co, US 175/J2
Tiffany (mtn.), Wa, US 170/E3
Tiffin (riv.), Oh, US 186/D4
Tiffin, Oh, US 186/E4
Tiflet, Mor. 138/A3
Tifton, Ga, US 191/G2
Tigapuluh (mts.), Indo. 115/C3
Tigeaux, Fr. 56/L5
Tiger (hills), Mb, Can. 182/D3
Tiger (lake), Fl, US 190/N8
Tigerton, Wi, US 181/K1
Tighina (Bendery), Mol. 98/E4
Tighvein (hill), Sc, UK 59/A6
Tigil', Rus. 101/R4
Tignall, Ga, US 189/F4
Tignère, Camr. 142/B4
Tignieu-Jameyzieu, Fr. 86/B6
Tignish, PE, Can. 184/E2
Tigray (prov.), Eth. 142/H2
Tigre (riv.), Ven. 197/J6
Tigre (riv.), Ven. 205/F2
Tigre, Arg. 215/J11
Tigres (bay), Ang. 148/A3
Tigris (riv.), Iraq 103/C6
Tiguent, Mrta. 140/A2
Tigui (well), Chad 134/C5
Tiguidit, Falaise de (cliff), Niger 141/G2
Tigy, Fr. 83/H5
Tigzirt, Alg. 138/H4
Tihamat al Yaman (valley), Yem. 144/B1
Tihosuco, Mex. 200/D1
Tihuatlán, Mex. 200/B1
Tiilikkajärven NP, Fin. 94/F3
Tijāra, India 122/A2
Tijger (falls), Sur. 206/B2
Tījī, Libya 134/A1
Tijuana, Mex. 192/C5
Tijuca, PN da, Braz. 211/N7
Tijucas, Braz. 213/G3
Tijuco (riv.), Braz. 210/C3
Tikal (ruin), Guat. 200/D2
Tikal, Guat. 199/H5
Tīkamgarh, India 122/B3
Tikanlik, China 125/E3
Tikarapāra, India 121/D1
Tikaré, Burk. 141/E3
Tikehau (isl.), FrPol. 163/L6
Tikhoretsk, Rus. 99/L5
Tikhvin, Rus. 94/G4
Tiko, Camr. 146/B1
Tikrīt, Iraq 129/E3
Tiksi, Rus. 101/N2
Tikveš (lake), FYROM 75/H2
Tila, Mex. 200/C2
Tiläänjärvi (lake), Fin. 65/F4
Tilburg, Neth. 78/C5
Tilbury, On, Can. 186/E3
Tilbury, Eng, UK 56/E2
Tilcha, Austl. 157/J4
Tilden, Il, US 188/C1
Tilden, Tx, US 177/E3
Tilford, Eng, UK 56/A3
Tilford, SD, US 180/C1
Tilghman, Md, US 194/B6
Tilghman (isl.), Md, US 194/B6
Tilhar, India 122/B2
Tilin, Myan. 112/B4
Tilisarao, Arg. 214/D2
Till (riv.), Eng, UK 59/D5
Tillabéry, Niger 141/F3
Tillamook (bay), Or, US 172/A1
Tillamook, Or, US 170/C5
Tillar, Ar, US 179/J4
Tille (riv.), Fr. 68/C5
Tillery (lake), NC, US 189/G3
Tilley, Sk, Can. 171/J2
Tillicoultry, Sc, UK 59/C4
Tillières-sur-Avre, Fr. 83/G3
Tillmans Corner, Al, US 190/D2
Tillsonburg, On, Can. 186/F3
Tilly-sur-Seulles, Fr. 83/E2
Tilomar, Indo. 154/B2
Tilomonte, Chile 212/B2
Tilopozo, Chile 212/B2
Tilpa, Austl. 158/C1
Tilst, Den. 66/D3
Tilston, Mb, Can. 182/D3
Tilt (riv.), Sc, UK 59/C3
Tiltagara, Austl. 158/C1
Tiltil, Chile 214/N8
Tilton, Il, US 186/C4
Tim, Den. 66/C3
Tim, Rus. 99/J2
Ţimā, Egypt 128/B5
Timan (ridge), Rus. 100/F3
Timaná, Col. 204/C4
Timane (riv.), Par. 212/D2
Timanfaya, PN de, Sp. 136/B3
Timaru, NZ 161/B4
Timashevo, Rus. 97/J1
Timashevsk, Rus. 99/K5
Timbákion, Gre. 75/J5
Timbalier (bay), La, US 190/C3
Timbaúba, Braz. 207/H4
Timbédra, Mrta. 140/C2
Timber (mtn.), Tx, US 177/C2
Timber Lake, SD, US 182/D5
Timberlake, Va, US 189/H2
Timberville, Va, US 189/H1
Timbiquí, Col. 204/B4
Timbiras, Braz. 207/F4
Timbo, Gui. 140/C4

303

Timbó – Treba

Timbó, Braz. 213/G3
Timboon, Austl. 158/B3
Timbué (pt.), Moz. 149/H3
Timbuni (riv.), Indo. 117/H4
Timehri (int'l arpt.), Guy. 205/G3
Timelkam, Aus. 85/G6
Timenocalin (well), Libya 134/A3
Timetrine, Mali 141/E2
Timetrout (peak), Mor. 92/B4
Timfristós (peak), Gre. 75/G3
Timgad (ruin), Alg. 92/E4
Tîmia, Niger 141/H2
Timimoun, Alg. 137/F3
Timiris (cape), Mrta. 140/A2
Timiş (riv.), Rom. 96/B3
Timiş (prov.), Rom. 76/E3
Timişoara (int'l arpt.), Rom. 76/E3
Timişoara, Rom. 76/E3
Timmins, On, Can. 167/H4
Timmonsville, SC, US 189/H3
Timms (hill), Wi, US 183/J5
Timoleague, Ire. 58/B6
Timon, Braz. 207/F4
Timonium, Md, US 194/B5
Timor (isl.), Indo. 103/M10
Timor (sea), Asia,Austl. 103/M11
Timor Timur (prov.), Indo. 154/A2
Timóteo, Braz. 211/E3
Timpas, Co, US 178/C2
Timpson, Tx, US 177/G2
Timpton (riv.), Rus. 101/N4
Tims Ford (dam), Tn, US 188/D3
Tims Ford (lake), Tn, US 188/D3
Timsāḩ (lake), Egypt 139/D3
Timsher, Rus. 95/M3
Timucuan Nat'l Prsv., Fl, US 191/H2
Timurnī, India 122/A4
Tin Can Bay, Austl. 160/D4
Tin Shui Wai, China 113/K7
Tina (riv.), SAfr. 150/B1
Tinaca (pt.), Phil. 114/D4
Tinaco, Ven. 204/D2
Tinahely, Ire. 58/D4
Tinca, Rom. 76/E2
Tinchebray, Fr. 83/E3
Tincup, Co, US 175/J1
Tinderry (mtn.), Austl. 159/D2
Tindivanam, India 121/C3
Tindouf (wilaya), Alg. 136/D3
Tindouf, Alg. 136/C4
Tiné, Oued (riv.), Chad 142/D2
Tinée (riv.), Fr. 90/C4
Tineo, Sp. 72/B1
Ting (riv.), China 113/H3
Tinga (peak), CAfr. 142/D3
Tingalpa (res.), Austl. 160/F7
Tingaringy NP, Austl. 158/D3
Tingha, Austl. 158/D1
Tingi (mts.), SLeo. 140/C4
Tingjegaon, Nepal 122/D1
Tinglin, China 106/L9
Tingo María, Peru 208/C3
Tingping, China 113/F3
Tingréla, C.d'Iv. 140/D4
Tingri, China 123/F1
Tingsryd, Swe. 66/F3
Tinguiririca (vol.), Chile 214/C2
Tinh Gia, Viet. 120/D2
Tinharé (isl.), Braz. 211/F2
Tinian (isl.), NMar. 162/D3
Tinicum Nat'l Consv. Area, Pa, US 194/C4
Tinker (A.F.B.), Ok, US 179/F3
Tinkisso (riv.), Gui. 140/C4
Tinley Park, Il, US 193/Q16
Tinogasta, Arg. 212/C4
Tínos, Gre. 75/J4
Tínos (isl.), Gre. 93/K3
Tinqueux, Fr. 80/C5
Tinrhir, Mor. 136/D3
Tinsman, Ar, US 179/H4
Tinsukia, India 112/B3
Tinta, Peru 208/D4
Tintagel (pt.), Eng, UK 62/B5
Tintagel, Eng, UK 62/B5
Tîntâne, Mrta. 140/C2
Tinténiac, Fr. 82/D4
Tintern Abbey, Eng, UK 62/D3
Tintigny, Belg. 81/E4
Tintina, Arg. 212/D3
Tintinara, Austl. 158/B2
Tinto (peak), Sc, UK 59/C5
Tinto (riv.), Sp. 72/B4
Tinton Falls (New Shrewsbury), NJ, US 194/D3
Tintwistle, Eng, UK 61/G5
Tinui, NZ 161/D3
Tinyahuarco, Peru 208/B3
T'i'o, Erit. 144/B2
Tioga, Tx, US 179/F4
Tioga, ND, US 182/C3
Tioga (peak), Ca, US 174/C2
Tioga, WV, US 189/G1
Tiom, Indo. 117/J4
Tioman (isl.), Malay. 116/B3
Tione di Trento, It. 87/G5
Tionesta, Pa, US 187/G4
Tip Top (mt.), On, Can. 183/L3
Tipac (hill), Braz. 206/D2
Tipasa, Alg. 138/G4
Tipasa (wilaya), Alg. 138/F4
Tipp City, Oh, US 186/D5
Tipperary, Ire. 58/B5
Tipperary (co.), Ire. 58/C4
Tippettville, Ga, US 191/G1
Tipton, Ok, US 178/E3
Tipton, Mo, US 179/H1
Tipton, Pa, US 187/G4
Tipton, In, US 186/C4
Tipton, Ks, US 180/E4
Tipton, Ia, US 181/J3
Tiptonville, Tn, US 188/C2
Tiptree, Eng, UK 63/G3
Tiptūr, India 121/C3
Tiputa, FrPol. 163/L6
Tir Rhiwiog (peak), Wal, UK 62/C1
Tira, Tx, US 179/G4
Tīra Sujānpur, India 124/D4
Tiracambu, Serra do (mts.), Braz. 207/E4
Tiran (isl.), SAr. 135/G3
Tiran (str.), Egypt,SAr. 135/G3
Tiran Sinafir (isl.), SAr. 128/C5
Tiranë (cap.), Alb. 75/F2
Tirano, It. 87/G5
Tiraque, Bol. 212/C1
T'irarē Shet' (riv.), Eth. 144/A2
Tirari (des.), Austl. 157/H4
Tiraspol, Mol. 98/E4
Tirat Karmel, Isr. 131/B3
Tirat Ẕevi, Isr. 131/D4
Tire, Turk. 128/A2
Tirebolu, Turk. 96/F4
Tiree (isl.), Sc, UK 57/Q8
Tirest (well), Mali 141/F1
Tirgol, Eth. 142/G4
Tîrgovişte, Rom. 77/G3
Tîrgu Bujor, Rom. 77/H3
Tîrgu Cărbuneşti, Rom. 77/F3
Tîrgu Frumos, Rom. 98/D4
Tîrgu Jiu, Rom. 77/F3
Tîrgu Lăpuş, Rom. 77/F2
Tîrgu Mureş, Rom. 77/G2
Tîrgu Neamţ, Rom. 98/D4
Tîrgu Ocna, Rom. 77/H2
Tîrgu Secuiesc, Rom. 77/H2
Tiris (reg.), WSah. 136/B5
Tiris Zemmour (pol. reg.), Mrta. 136/C4
Tiritiri Matangi (isl.), NZ 161/F6
Tirlyanskiy, Rus. 95/N5
Tîrnava Mare (riv.), Rom. 77/G2
Tîrnava Mică (riv.), Rom. 77/F2
Tîrnăveni, Rom. 77/G2
Tírnavos, Gre. 75/H3
Tiro, Gui. 140/C4
Tirol (prov.), Aus. 68/F5
Tirrenia, It. 88/D6
Tirschenreuth, Ger. 85/F3
Tirso (riv.), It. 92/F2
Tirstup (int'l arpt.), Den. 66/D3
Tirúa, Chile 214/B3
Tiruchendūr, India 121/C4
Tiruntán, Peru 208/C2
Tirupati (int'l arpt.), India 121/C3
Tirūr, India 121/B4
Tiruttani, India 118/C3
Tiruvalla, India 121/C4
Tiruvannāmalai, India 121/C3
Tisa (riv.), Yugo. 93/K1
Tisbury, Eng, UK 62/D4
Tisdale, Sk, Can. 171/M1
Tishkovo, Rus. 97/J3
Tishomingo, Ok, US 179/F3
Tishomingo, Ms, US 188/C3
Tishomingo Nat'l Wildlife Res., Ok, US 179/F3
Ţisīyah, Syria 131/E4
Tissa, Mor. 138/B2
Tissemsilt, Alg. 138/F5
Tissemsilt (wilaya), Alg. 138/F5
Tissø (lake), Den. 65/H7
Tista (riv.), Bang. 123/G2
Tisvilde, Den. 65/J6
Tisza (riv.), Hun. 96/B3
Tiszaföldvár, Hun. 76/E2
Tiszafüred, Hun. 76/E2
Tiszakécske, Hun. 76/E2
Tiszalök, Hun. 76/E1
Tiszavasvári, Hun. 69/L5
Tit, Alg. 137/F4
Titano (peak), SMar. 89/F6
Titao, Burk. 141/E3
Titay, Phil. 114/C4
Titel, Yugo. 76/E3
Titerno (riv.), It. 92/D5
Titi, Congo 146/C3
Titicaca (lake), Bol.,Peru 203/B4
Titistee-Neustadt, Ger. 86/E2
Titlagarh, India 121/D1
Titlis (peak), Swi. 87/E4
Tito, It. 74/D2
Titov Veles, FYROM 75/G2
Titov vrh (peak), FYROM 75/G2
Titsey, Eng, UK 56/D3
Titting, Ger. 84/E5
Tittmoning, Ger. 85/F6
Titu, Rom. 77/G3
Titule, D.R. Congo 147/F2
Titusville, Pa, US 187/G4
Titusville, Fl, US 191/H3
Titusville, NJ, US 194/D3
Tiuni, India 124/D4
Tiva (riv.), Kenya 145/B2
Tivaouane, Sen. 140/A3
Tivat, Yugo. 76/D4
Tiverton, On, Can. 186/F2
Tiverton, Eng, UK 62/C5
Tivoli, It. 91/B4
Tivoli, Tx, US 177/F3
Tiwanacu, Bol. 212/B1
Ţīwī, Oman 127/G4
Tixán, Ecu. 208/B1
Tixtla de Guerrero, Mex. 199/F5
Tizayuca, Mex. 199/L7
Tizi Ouzou (wilaya), Alg. 138/H4
Tizi Ouzou, Alg. 138/H4
Tizimín, Mex. 200/D1
Tizmant ash Sharqīyah, Egypt 139/C6
Tiznados (riv.), Ven. 207/N8
Tiznap (riv.), China 127/L1
Tiznit, Mor. 136/C3
Tjæreborg, Den. 66/C4
Tjeldstø, Nor. 66/A1
Tjeukemeer (lake), Neth. 78/C3
Tjøme, Nor. 66/D2
Tjorn (isl.), Den. 66/D3
Tkhab (peak), Rus. 99/K5
Tkibuli, Geo. 97/G4
Tlachichuca, Mex. 199/M7
Tlacolula de Matamoros, Mex. 200/B2
Tlacotalpan, Mex 199/P8
Tlacotepec, Mex. 199/F5
Tlalixcoyan, Mex 199/N8
Tlalmanalco, Mex. 199/Q10
Tlalnepantla, Mex. 199/Q9
Tláloc (vol.), Mex. 199/Q10
Tlalpan (nbrhd.), Mex. 199/Q10
Tlaltenango de Sánchez Román, Mex. 198/E4
Tlaltizapan, Mex. 199/K8
Tlapa de Comonfort, Mex. 200/B2
Tlapacoya (ruin), Mex. 199/Q10
Tlapacoyan, Mex 199/M7
Tlapehuala, Mex. 199/E5
Tlaquepaque, Mex. 198/E4
Tlaquiltenango, Mex. 199/K8
Tlatlauquitepec, Mex. 199/M7
Tlaxcala (state), Mex. 196/A5
Tlaxcala, Mex. 199/L7
Tlaxco, Mex. 199/L7
Tlaxcoapan, Mex. 199/K6
Tlemcen, Alg. 138/D2
Tlokweng, Bots. 148/E5
Tmassah, Libya 134/B3
To-grenda, Nor. 64/S8
Toa Payoh (nbrhd.), Sing. 115/J6
Toabré, Pan. 204/A2
Toaca (peak), Rom. 77/G2
Toachi (riv.), Ecu. 204/B4
Toadlena, NM, US 175/H2
Toamasina, Madg. 152/J7
Toamasina (prov.), Madg. 152/J7
Toandos (pen.), Wa, US 193/B2
Toasi, Gha. 141/E5
Toast, NC, US 189/G2
Toau (isl.), FrPol. 163/L6
Toay, Arg. 214/D3
Toba (lake), Indo. 116/A3
Toba, China 104/D5
Toba, Japan 109/L7
Toba (inlet), BC, Can. 170/B2
Toba (riv.), BC, Can. 170/B2
Toba Kākar (range), Pak. 127/J2
Toba Tek Singh, Pak. 124/B4
Tobago (isl.), Trin. 197/J5
Tobarra, Sp. 72/E3
Tobbio (peak), It. 88/B4
Tobeatic Game Sanct., NS, Can. 184/E3
Tobercurry, Ire. 58/B1
Tobermore, NI, UK 60/B2
Tobermorey, Austl. 157/H2
Tobermory, On, Can. 186/F2
Tōbetsu, Japan 108/B2
Tobias, Ang. 146/C5
Tobias Barreto, Braz. 211/F1
Tobin (lake), Austl. 153/B3
Tobique (riv.), NB, Can. 184/D2
Tobishima, Japan 109/L5
Toblol (riv.), Kaz.,Rus. 103/F4
Toboali, Indo. 115/D3
Tobol (riv.), Rus. 95/Q5
Tobol, Kaz. 97/M1
Tobruk (Ţubruq), Libya 93/J4
Tobseda, Rus. 95/M1
Tobu, Japan 109/A1
Toburdanovo, Rus. 95/K5
Tobyhanna (lake), Pa, US 194/C1
Tobyhanna (riv.), Pa, US 194/C1
Tobyhanna, Pa, US 194/C1
Tobyhanna St. Park, Pa, US 194/C1
Tobyl (riv.), Rus.,Kaz. 100/G4
Tobysh (riv.), Rus. 95/L2
Tocache, Peru 208/B3
Tocaima, Col. 207/L8
Tocantínia, Braz. 206/D5
Tocantinópolis, Braz. 207/E4
Tocantins (riv.), Braz. 203/E4
Tocantins (state), Braz. 206/D5
Tocco da Casauria, It. 92/C3
Toccoa, Ga, US 189/F3
Toccoa (riv.), Ga, US 188/E3
Toce (riv.), It. 71/H3
Tochigi (pref.), Japan 111/F2
Tochigi, Japan 111/F2
Tochimilco, Mex. 199/L8
Tochio, Japan 111/F2
Tocina, Sp. 72/C4
Töcksfors, Swe. 66/D2
Toco, Tx, US 179/G4
Toco, Trin. 205/F2
Tocomechi, Bol. 212/D1
Tocopilla, Chile 212/B2
Tocumen, Pan. 204/B2
Tocumwal, Austl. 159/B2
Tocuyito, Ven. 204/D2
Tocuyo (riv.), Ven. 197/H5
Toda, Japan 109/D2
Toda Bhīm, India 118/C2
Toddington, Eng, UK 63/F3
Todenyang, Kenya 142/G4
Tödi (peak), Swi. 87/E4
Todi, It. 91/B2
Todmorden, Eng, UK 61/F4
Todos os Santos (bay), Braz. 211/F2
Todos Santos, Bol. 212/B1
Todos Santos, Bol. 209/E4
Todos Santos, Bol. 212/C1
Todos Santos, Mex. 198/C4
Todt Hill (nbrhd.), NY, US 195/J9
Todtmoos, Ger. 86/E2
Todtnau, Ger. 86/D2
Toe (pt.), Ire. 58/A7
T'oejo, NKor. 107/D3
Toffal (hill), Mrta. 136/C5
Toffo, Ben. 141/F5
Tofield, Ab, Can. 171/H1
Tofte, Nor. 64/S9
Tofua (isl.), Tonga 163/H6
Tōgane, Japan 109/E2
Togatax, China 125/D4
Togba (well), Mrta. 140/C2
Toggenburg (valley), Swi. 87/F3
Togher, Ire. 60/B5
Töging am Inn, Ger. 85/F6
Togo, Sk, Can. 182/D2
Tōgō, Japan 109/M5
Togo(ctry.) 133/C4
Tögrög, Mong. 104/C2
Togtoh, China 106/B2
Tōgyu-san NP, SKor. 107/D5
Togyz, Kaz. 97/M3
Tohāna, India 124/C5
Tohatchi, NM, US 175/H3
Tohickon (cr.), Pa, US 194/C3
Tohivea (peak), FrPol. 163/X15
Tōhoku (prov.), Japan 111/F1
Tohom, China 104/F3
Tohopekaliga (lake), Fl, US 191/H3
Tohopekaliga, East (lake), Fl, US 190/N7
Tohor (cape), Malay. 115/C2
Tohoun, Togo 141/F5
Toi, Japan 111/F3
Toibalawe, India 119/F5
Toijala, Fin. 65/D3
Tōin, Japan 109/L5
Toiyabe (range), Nv, US 172/E4
Tojō, Japan 110/C3
Tōjō, Japan 109/H6
Tok, Ak, US 168/Y12
Tokachi (riv.), Japan 108/C2
Tōkai, Japan 109/L5
Tokaj, Hun. 69/L4
Tōkamachi, Japan 111/F2
Tokanui, NZ 161/B4
Tokar, Sudan 135/H5
Tokar Game Reserve, Sudan 135/H5
Tokar Nat'l Rsv., Sudan 135/F4
Tokara (isls.), Japan 162/B1
Tokarevka, Rus. 97/G2
Tokat, Turk. 128/D1
Tokat (prov.), Turk. 96/F4
Tŏkchŏk (arch.), NKor. 107/C4
Tŏkchŏk (isl.), NKor. 107/C4
Tŏkch'ŏn, NKor. 107/D3
Tokeland, Wa, US 170/C4
Tokelau (terr.), NZ 163/H5
Toki (riv.), Japan 109/M5
Toki, Japan 109/M5
Tokigawa, Japan 109/C2
Tokio, ND, US 182/E4
Tokkya Chaung, Myan. 120/B3
Tokmak, Ukr. 99/H4
Tokmok, Kyr. 100/H5
Tokomaru Bay, NZ 161/D2
Tokoname, Japan 109/L6
Tokonou, Gui. 140/C4
Tokoro, Japan 108/D1
Tokoro (riv.), Japan 108/C2
Tokoroa, NZ 161/C2
Tokorozawa, Japan 111/F3
Tŏksŏng, NKor. 105/K3
Toksovo, Rus. 94/T6
Toksun, China 125/E3
Toktogul (res.), Kyr. 125/B3
Toktogul, Kyr. 125/B3
Tokuno (isl.), Japan 111/K7
Tokunoshima, Japan 111/K7
Tokur, Rus. 105/L1
Tokushima, Japan 110/D3
Tokushima (pref.), Japan 110/C4
Tokuyama, Japan 110/B3
Tokwe (riv.), Zim. 149/F3
Tōkyō (pref.), Japan 111/F3
Tōkyō (cap.), Japan 111/F3
Tōkyō (bay), Japan 109/D2
Tōkyō Disneyland, Japan 109/D2
Tola, Nic. 200/E4
Tolaga Bay, NZ 161/D2
Tolar, Tx, US 177/F1
Tolar Grande, Arg. 212/C3
Tolbazy, Rus. 95/M5
Tolbo, Mong. 104/C2
Toledo, Oh, US 186/E4
Toledo, Col. 204/C3
Toledo, Sp. 72/C3
Toledo, Or, US 172/B1
Toledo, Il, US 188/C1
Toledo, Ia, US 181/H3
Toledo, Phil. 114/C3
Toledo, Uru. 215/K11
Toledo, Braz. 213/F3
Toledo, Bol. 212/C1
Toledo, Wa, US 170/C4
Toledo Bend (dam), Tx, US 190/B2
Toledo Bend (res.), Tx, US 196/C1
Toledo, Montes de (mts.), Sp. 72/C3
Tolentino, It. 92/C1
Tolfa, It. 91/A3
Tolfaccia (peak), It. 91/A3
Tolhuaca, PN, Chile 214/C3
Toli, China 125/D2
Toliara, Madg. 152/G8
Toliara (prov.), Madg. 152/G8
Tolima, Col. 204/C5
Tolima (dept.), Col. 204/C4
Tolitoli, Indo. 117/F3
Tolka (riv.), Ire. 60/B5
Tolkis (Tolkkinen), Fin. 65/F4
Tolkkinen (Tolkis), Fin. 65/F4
Tolland, Ab, Can. 171/J1
Tollarp, Swe. 65/K7
Tollette, Ar, US 179/H4
Tolley, ND, US 182/D3
Tollo, It. 92/D3
Tølløse, Den. 65/H7
Tolmezzo, It. 71/K3
Tolna, ND, US 182/E4
Tolna (prov.), Hun. 76/D2
Tolna, Hun. 76/D2
Tolo, D.R. Congo 146/D3
Tolo (gulf), Indo. 117/F4
Tolo (chan.), China 113/L7
Tolochin, Bela. 67/N4
Tolokiwa (isl.), PNG 155/G1
Tolongoina, Madg. 152/H8
Tolono, Il, US 186/B5
Tolosa, Sp. 70/B5
Tolsan (isl.), SKor. 107/D5
Tolstoy, SD, US 180/E1
Tolt (riv.), Wa, US 193/D2
Tolt (res.), Wa, US 193/D2
Tolt, North Fork (riv.), Wa, US 193/D2
Tolt, South Fork (riv.), Wa, US 193/D2
Toltén, Chile 214/B3
Toltén (riv.), Chile 214/B3
Tolú, Col. 204/C2
Toluca, Il, US 181/K3
Toluca, Mex. 199/Q10
Tolúviejo, Col. 204/C2
Tol'yatti, Rus. 97/J1
Tolybay, Kaz. 97/M2
Tom' (riv.), Rus. 100/J4
Tom, Ok, US 179/G4
Tom Price, Austl. 156/C2
Toma, Burk. 140/E3
Toma, PNG 155/G2
Tomah, Wi, US 181/J2
Tomahawk, Wi, US 183/K5
Tomahawk, Ab, Can. 170/G1
Tomakin, Austl. 159/E2
Tomakivka, Ukr. 99/H4
Tomakomai, Japan 108/B2
Tomamae, Japan 108/B1
Tomanao, Phil. 114/D4
Tomanivi (peak), Fiji 163/Y18
Tomar, Port. 72/A3
Tomari, Rus. 105/N2
Tómaros (peak), Gre. 75/G3
Tomarpaån (riv.), Swe. 65/L7
Tomarza, Turk. 128/C2
Tomás, Peru 208/C4
Tomás Barrón, Bol. 212/C1
Tomás de Berlanga, Ecu. 208/J7
Tomashëvka, Bela. 69/M3
Tomaszów Lubelski, Pol. 69/M3
Tomaszów Mazowiecki, Pol. 69/L3
Tomat, Sudan 142/E3
Tomatin, Sc, UK 59/C2
Tomatlán, Mex. 198/D5
Tomave, Bol. 212/C2
Tomb of Qinshihuang, China 106/B4
Tombador, Serra do (mts.), Braz. 209/G3
Tomball, Tx, US 177/M8
Tombe, Sudan 142/F4
Tombigbee (riv.), Al, Ms, US 169/J5
Tomboco, Ang. 146/C4
Tombolo, It. 89/E2
Tombouctou (pol. reg.), Mali 136/D5
Tombouctou, Mali 140/E2
Tombstone, Az, US 175/G5
Tombua, Ang. 148/A2
Tomé (isl.), Fr. 70/E2
Tomé, Chile 214/E3
Tome, NM, US 175/J3
Tomé-Açu, Braz. 206/C3
Tomea (isl.), Indo. 154/A1
Tomelilla, Swe. 66/E4
Tomelloso, Sp. 72/D3
Tomika, Japan 109/L5
Tomina, Bol. 212/C1
Tomingley, Austl. 159/D1
Tomini (gulf), Indo. 103/M10
Tominian, Mali 140/D3
Tomiño, Sp. 72/A2
Tomintoul, Sc, UK 59/C2
Tomioka, Japan 109/E1
Tomisato, Japan 109/E2
Tomiura, Japan 109/D3
Tomiyama, Japan 111/F3
Tomizawa, Japan 109/A3
Tommot, Rus. 101/N4
Tomo (riv.), Col. 204/D3
Tomorlog, China 125/F4
Tompa, Hun. 76/D2
Tompe, Indo. 117/E4
Tompkins, Sk, Can. 171/K2
Tompkinsville, Ky, US 188/E2
Tompo, Indo. 117/F3
Toms (riv.), NJ, US 194/D3
Toms River, NJ, US 194/D4
Tomsk, Rus. 100/J4
Tömük, Turk. 130/D1
Tonalá, Mex. 200/C2
Tonale, Passo del (pass), It. 87/G5
Tonalea, Az, US 175/G2
Tonasket, Wa, US 170/E3
Tonate, FrG. 206/C1
Tonawanda (cr.), NY, US 186/V9
Tonawanda (res.), NY, US 186/V9
Tonawanda, NY, US 186/V9
Tonbridge, Eng, UK 56/D3
Tonckens (falls), Sur. 206/B1
Toncontín (int'l arpt.), Hon. 200/E3
Tondabayashi, Japan 109/J7
Tondano, Indo. 117/F3
Tondi Kiwindi, Niger 141/F3
Tondo, D.R. Congo 146/D3
Tondon, Gui. 140/B4
Tondoro, Namb. 148/C3
Tondu (peak), Fr. 86/C6
Tone (riv.), Japan 111/G3
Tone, Japan 109/E2
Tone (riv.), Eng, UK 62/C5
Tonekābon, Iran 129/G2
Tonelagee (peak), Ire. 60/B5
Tong (riv.), China 104/F5
Tong Fuk, China 113/K8
Tong Xian, China 106/H7
Tonga, Sudan 142/F3
Tonga(ctry.) 163/H7
Tongaat, SAfr. 151/E3
Tongala, Austl. 159/B3
Tong'an, China 113/H3
Tongareva (Penrhyn) (isl.), CookIs. 163/J5
Tongariro (vol.), NZ 161/C2
Tongariro NP, NZ 161/C2
Tongatapu (isl.), Tonga 163/H7
Tongbai, China 106/C4
Tongbei, China 105/K2
Tongbu, SKor. 107/G6
Tongbu (nbrhd.), SKor. 107/G6
Tongch'ang, NKor. 107/C2
Tongcheng, China 106/D5
Tongcheng, China 113/G2
T'ongch'ŏn, NKor. 107/D3
Tongchuan, China 106/B4
Tongdaemun (nbrhd.), SKor. 107/G6
Tongdao Dongzu Zizhixian, China 113/F3
Tongduch'on, SKor. 107/G6
Tongeren, Belg. 81/E2
Tonggou, China 107/C2
Tonggu, China 119/K2
Tonggu (peak), China 113/H3
Tonghae, SKor. 107/E4
Tongham, Eng, UK 56/A3
Tonghua, China 107/C2
Tonghua, China 107/C2
Tongjiadian, China 105/J3
Tongliao, China 106/E2
Tongling, China 113/H2
Tongmu, China 113/G3
Tongnae, SKor. 107/E5
Tongnan, China 112/E2
Tongnim, NKor. 107/C3
Tongno (riv.), NKor. 107/D2
Tongo, Austl. 158/B1
Tongo (peak), Indo. 117/E5
Tongobory, Madg. 152/H8
Tongren, China 113/F3
Tongsa (riv.), Bhu. 123/H2
Tongsa Dzong, Bhu. 123/H2
Tongshan, China 113/G2
Tongsin, NKor. 107/D2
Tongtian (riv.), China 104/D5
Tongue, Sc, UK 57/R7
Tongue (riv.), Mt, US 168/E2
Tongxu, China 106/C4
Tongyu, China 105/J3
Tongyuan, China 113/H2
Tongyuanpu, China 107/B2
Tonino-Anivskiy (pen.), Rus. 108/C1
Tönisvorst, Ger. 78/D6
Tonj (riv.), Sudan 142/F4
Tonj, Sudan 142/F4
Tonk, India 118/C2
Tonkawa, Ok, US 179/F2
Tonkin (gulf), China,Viet. 103/K7
Tonkoui (peak), C.d'Iv. 140/D5
Tonle Sap (lake), Camb. 119/H5
Tonneins, Fr. 70/D4
Tonnerre, Fr. 70/E3
Tönning, Ger. 66/C4
Tōno, Japan 108/B4
Tonopah, Az, US 175/F4
Tonoshō, Japan 110/D3
Tonosí, Pan. 204/A3
Tonota, Bots. 149/E4
Tons (riv.), India 122/C3
Tønsberg, Nor. 66/D2
Tonstad, Nor. 66/B2
Tonto Nat'l Mon., Az, US 175/G4
Tontouta (Noumea) (int'l arpt.), NCal. 163/V13
Tonya, Turk. 96/F4
Toodyay, Austl. 156/C4
Tooele, Ut, US 173/G3
Tooele Army Dep., Ut, US 173/G3
Tooke (lake), Fl, US 190/K6
Tool, Tx, US 177/F1
Tooleybuc, Austl. 158/B2
Toomsboro, Ga, US 189/F4
Toomuc (cr.), Austl. 158/G6
Toomyvara, Ire. 58/B4
Tooradin, Austl. 158/C3
Tooraweenah, Austl. 158/D1
Tooromt, Mong. 104/C1
Toosey Ind. Res., BC, Can. 170/C2
Toot Hill, Eng, UK 56/D1
Tootsi, Est. 67/L2
Toowoomba, Austl. 160/C4
Top (mt.), Austl. 157/G2
Top of the World (peak), Wy, US 180/B2
Top Springs, Austl. 154/C4
Topaipí, Col. 207/L7
Topanaga State Park, Ca, US 192/B2
Topanga, Ca, US 192/B2
Topanga Beach, Ca, US 192/E7
Topawa, Az, US 175/G5
Tope de Coroa (mtn.), CpV. 133/J10
Topeka, In, US 186/D4
Topeka (cap.), Ks, US 181/G4
Topia, Mex. 198/D3
Topkapi Palace, Turk. 129/M6
Toplița, Rom. 98/C4
Topock, Az, US 174/E3
Topohoco, Bol. 208/D5
Topol'čany, Slvk. 69/K4
Topol'níky, Slvk. 76/C2
Topolobampo, Mex. 198/C3
Topoloveni, Rom. 77/G3
Topolovgrad, Bul. 77/H4
Topozero (lake), Rus. 64/J2
Toppenish, Wa, US 170/D4
Toppenish (cr.), Wa, US 170/D4
Toprakkale, Turk. 130/E1
Topsham, Eng, UK 62/C5
Topton, Pa, US 194/C3
Toquepala, Peru 208/D5
Toquerville, Ut, US 175/F2
Toquima (range), Nv, US 172/E4
Tor, Eth. 142/G4
Tor (bay), Eng, UK 62/C6
Tor Lupara, It. 91/B4
Tora, D.R. Congo 147/G2
Torahime, Japan 109/K5
Torata, Peru 208/D5
Torawitan (cape), Indo. 117/G3
Torbalı, Turk. 128/A2
Torbat-e Ḩeydarīyeh, Iran 127/G1
Torbay, Nf, Can. 185/L2
Torbeck, Haiti 201/H2
Torbeyevo, Rus. 97/G1
Torch (lake), Mi, US 186/D2
Torcy, Fr. 56/K5
Tordera (riv.), Sp. 73/L6
Tordesillas, Sp. 72/C2
Tordino (riv.), It. 92/C2
Töreboda, Swe. 66/F2
Torekov, Swe. 65/J6
Torelló, Sp. 73/G1
Torez, Ukr. 99/K3
Torgelow, Ger. 66/E5
Torghay, Kaz. 100/G4
Torghay, Kaz. 100/G5
Torhamnsudde (pt.), Swe. 66/F3
Torhout, Belg. 80/C1
Tori, India 123/E4
Tori-shima (isl.), Japan 162/D1
Toride, Japan 109/E2
Torigni-sur-Vire, Fr. 83/E2
Torii-tōge (pass), Japan 111/E3
Toriñana (cape), Sp. 72/A1
Torino (prov.), It. 90/D2
Torino (Tarin), It. 71/G4
Torino (Turin), It. 88/A2
Torino di Sangro, It. 92/D3
Torit, Sudan 142/G4
Torkestān (mts.), Afg. 127/H1
Tormes (riv.), Sp. 72/C2
Torndirrup NP, Austl. 156/C5
Torne (riv.), Eng, UK 61/H4
Torneälven (riv.), Swe. 94/D2
Tornesch, Ger. 79/G1
Tornik (peak), Yugo. 76/D4
Tornillo, Tx, US 177/A2
Tornio, Fin. 64/H2
Tornionjoki (riv.), Fin. 94/D2
Torö, Swe. 65/A2
Torö (isl.), Swe. 65/A2
Toro, Sp. 72/C2
Toro (peak), Ca, US 174/D4
Toro Nat'l Rsv., Ugan. 147/G2
Toro, Cerro del (peak), Arg.,Chile 212/B4
Toro, PN, Ven. 204/D2
Torodi, Niger 141/F3
Torok, Chad 142/B3
Törökbálint, Hun. 77/Q10
Törökszentmikló, Hun. 76/E2
Toromélun, Gui. 140/B4
Toronaic (gulf), Gre. 75/H2
Toronao (peak), Arg. 212/C2
Torondoy, Ven. 204/D2
Toronto (lake), Ks, US 179/G2
Toronto (isl.), On, Can. 186/U8
Toronto (city), On, Can. 186/U8
Toronto (cap.), On, Can. 186/U8
Toropets, Rus. 67/P3
Tororo, Ugan. 145/A1
Toroshino, Rus. 67/N3
Torote (riv.), Sp. 73/N8
Torotoro, Bol. 212/C1
Torp (int'l arpt.), Nor. 66/D2
Torpa, Swe. 66/E3
Torphins, Sc, UK 59/D2
Torpoint, Eng, UK 62/B6
Ţorqebeh, Iran 127/G1
Torquay, Sk, Can. 182/C3
Torquay, Eng, UK 62/C6
Torquay, Austl. 159/B4
Torquemada, Sp. 72/C1
Torr (pt.), NI, UK 60/B1
Torrance, Ca, US 192/F8
Torrazza Piemonte, It. 88/A2
Torre Annunziata, It. 92/D6
Torre de Moncorvo, Port. 72/B2
Torre dè Passeri, It. 92/C3
Torre del Campo, Sp. 72/D4
Torre del Greco, It. 92/D6
Torre del Lago Puccini, It. 88/D6
Torre Gaia, It. 91/B4
Torre Maggiore (peak), It. 91/B2
Torre Pellice, It. 90/D3
Torre-Pacheco, Sp. 73/E4
Torrebelvicino, It. 89/E2
Torreblanca, Sp. 73/F2
Torredonjimeno, Sp. 72/D4
Torregaveta, It. 92/D6
Torreglia, It. 89/E3
Torrejón de Ardoz, Sp. 73/N9
Torrejoncillo, Sp. 72/B3
Torrelaguna, Sp. 72/D2
Torrelavega, Sp. 72/C1
Torrelodones, Sp. 73/N8
Torremaggiore, It. 74/D2
Torremolinos, Sp. 72/C4
Torrens (cr.), Austl. 155/G5
Torrens (riv.), Austl. 157/M8
Torrens (isl.), Austl. 157/M8
Torrens (lake), Austl. 153/C4
Torrente, Sp. 73/E3
Torreon, NM, US 175/J3
Torreón, Mex. 198/E3
Torreperogil, Sp. 72/D3
Torres (str.), Austl.,PNG 162/D6
Torres (isls.), Van. 162/F6
Tôrres, Braz. 213/G4
Torres (str.), Austl. 153/D1
Torres del Paine, PN, Chile 215/B6
Torres Martinez Ind. Res., Ca, US 174/D4
Torres Novas, Port. 72/A3
Torres Straight Island Abor. Land, Austl. 155/F2
Torres Vedras, Port. 72/A3
Torrevieja, Sp. 73/E4
Torrey, Ut, US 175/G1
Torri di Quartesolo, It. 89/E2
Torricella Peligna, It. 92/D3
Torridge (riv.), Eng, UK 62/B5
Torrijos, Sp. 72/C3
Torrington, Ct, US 187/K4
Torrington, Wy, US 180/B2
Torrington, Ab, Can. 171/H2
Torrita di Siena, It. 71/J5
Torroella de Montgrí, Sp. 73/G1
Torrone Alto (peak), Swi. 87/F5
Torrowangee, Austl. 158/B1
Torrox, Sp. 72/D4
Tors Cove, Nf, Can. 185/L2
Torsa (riv.), Bhu. 123/G2
Torsåker, Swe. 65/A2
Torsås, Swe. 66/F3
Torsby, Swe. 66/E1
Tórshavn, Den. 216/G
Tortel, Chile 215/B5
Torteval, ChI, UK 82/C2
Tortilla Flat, Az, US 175/G4
Torto (riv.), It. 91/B4
Tortola (isl.), UK 197/J4
Tortolì, It. 74/A3
Tortona, It. 88/B4
Tortoreto Lido, It. 92/C2
Tortosa (cape), Sp. 73/F2
Tortosa, Sp. 73/F2
Tortuga (isl.), Haiti 197/H5
Tortuguero, PN, CR 201/F4
Tortum, Turk. 97/G4
Ţorūd, Iran 129/H3
Torugart (pass), Kyr. 125/C3
Torul, Turk. 128/D1
Toruń, Pol. 69/K2
Torup, Swe. 66/E3
Tõrva, Est. 67/L2
Torvaianica, It. 91/B4
Tory (isl.), Ire. 57/P9
Torysa (riv.), Slvk. 69/L4
Torzhok, Rus. 94/G4
Tosa, Japan 110/C4
Tosa (bay), Japan 105/L5
Tosagua, Ecu. 204/A5
Tosashimizu, Japan 110/C4
Toscana (reg.), It. 88/C4
Toscanella, It. 89/E5
Toscanini, Namb. 148/B4
Toscolano-Maderno, It. 88/D2
Toshi (isl.), Japan 109/L6
Toshibetsu (riv.), Japan 108/A2
Toshviska, Rus. 95/M2
Tosna (riv.), Rus. 94/T7
Tosno, Rus. 67/P2
Toson (lake), China 104/D4
Tosontsengel, Mong. 104/D2
Töss (riv.), Swi. 71/H3
Tosson (hill), Eng, UK 59/E6
Tostado, Arg. 212/D4
Tõstamaa, Est. 67/L2
Tostedt, Ger. 79/G2
Tosu, Japan 110/B4
Tosya, Turk. 96/E4
Totana, Sp. 72/E4
Toteng, Bots. 148/D4
Tôtes, Fr. 83/G1
Totland, Eng, UK 63/E5
Tot'ma, Rus. 94/J4
Totnes, Eng, UK 62/C6
Totness, Sur. 205/G3
Toto, Ang. 146/C4
Totoral, Uru. 215/K10
Totoral, Chile 212/B3
Totoras, Arg. 212/D5
Totota, Libr. 140/C5
Totowa, NJ, US 195/J8
Totskoye, Rus. 97/K1
Totten (inlet), Wa, US 193/A3
Tottenham (nbrhd.), Eng, UK 56/C2
Tottenham, Austl. 158/C2
Tottenville (nbrhd.), NY, US 195/H9
Tottington, Eng, UK 61/F4
Totton, Eng, UK 63/E5
Tottori (pref.), Japan 110/C3
Tottori, Japan 110/D3
Totutla, Mex. 199/N7
Touâjîl, Mrta. 136/B5
Touat (reg.), Alg. 137/E4
Touba, Sen. 140/B3
Touba, Gui. 140/B4
Touba, C.d'Iv. 140/D4
Toubkal (peak), Mor. 136/D3
Toubkal, PN du, Mor. 136/D3
Touboro, Camr. 142/B4
Touboutou, Chutes de (falls), CAfr. 142/B4
T'ouch'eng, Tai. 113/J3
Touchet, Wa, US 170/E4
Touchwood (hills), Sk, Can. 171/M2
Toucy, Fr. 70/E3
Toudao (riv.), China 107/D1
T'oufen, Tai. 113/J3
Tougaloo, Ms, US 188/B4
Tougan, Burk. 140/E3
Touggourt, Alg. 137/G2
Toughkenamon, Pa, US 194/C4
Tougué, Gui. 140/C4
Touiel (riv.), Alg. 138/G5
Touil, Mrta. 140/C3
Toukoto, Mali 140/C3
Toul, Fr. 81/E6
Toulépleu, C.d'Iv. 140/C5
Toulon, Fr. 90/B6
Toulon, Il, US 181/K3
Toulourenc (riv.), Fr. 90/B4
Toulouse, Fr. 70/D5
Toumo (well), Niger 134/B4
Toumodi, C.d'Iv. 140/D5
Tounan, Tai. 113/J4
Toungo, Nga. 142/B3
Toungoo, Myan. 112/C5
Tounyifili, Gui. 140/B4
Toupeng, China 106/L9
Touques (riv.), Fr. 83/F2
Touquin, Fr. 56/M5
Toura, Monts du (mts.), C.d'Iv. 140/D5
Tourakom, Laos 120/C2
Tourcoing, Fr. 80/C2
Tourelle, Qu, Can. 184/D1
Tourfourine (well), Mali 136/D4
Tourlaville, Fr. 82/D1
Tournai, Belg. 80/C2
Tournairet (peak), Fr. 90/D4
Tournan-en-Brie, Fr. 56/L5
Tournavista, Peru 208/C3
Tournon-sur-Rhône, Fr. 90/A2
Tournus, Fr. 86/A4
Touronsuon NP, Fin. 65/D4
Touros, Braz. 207/H4
Tours, Fr. 83/F6
Tourves, Fr. 90/B6
Tourville-la-Rivière, Fr. 83/G2
Toury, Fr. 83/G4
Tous (res.), Sp. 73/E3
Toussiana, Burk. 140/D4
Toussidé (peak), Chad 134/C4
Toussière (peak), Fr. 90/B3
Toussoro (peak), CAfr. 142/D3
Touws (riv.), SAfr. 150/C4
Touwsrivier, SAfr. 150/M10
Toužim, Czh. 85/G2
Töv (prov.), Mong. 104/F2
Tovar, Ven. 204/D2
Tovarkovskiy, Rus. 96/F1
Tove (riv.), Eng, UK 63/E2
Tovil, Eng, UK 56/E3
Tovste, Ukr. 98/C3
Tovuz, Azer. 97/H4
Tow Law, Eng, UK 61/G2
Towaco, NJ, US 195/H8
Towada, Japan 111/G2
Towada (lake), Japan 108/B3
Towada-Hachimantai NP, Japan 108/B3
Towamba (riv.), Austl. 159/D3
Towanda, Pa, US 187/H4
Towang, India 123/H2
Towaoc, Co, US 175/H2
Towcester, Eng, UK 63/F2
Tower, Ire. 58/B6
Tower (falls), Wy, US 173/H1
Tower City, ND, US 182/F4
Tower City, Pa, US 194/B2
Tower Hamlets (bor.), Eng, UK 56/A1
Tower Hill, Il, US 181/K4
Tower of London, Eng, UK 56/C2
Town Bluff (dam), Tx, US 177/G2
Town 'n' Country, Fl, US 190/K7
Towner, ND, US 182/D3
Townsend, Wi, US 183/K5
Townsend (mt.), Wa, US 193/A2
Townsend, Tn, US 188/F3
Townsend, Mt, US 171/J4
Townsend, De, US 194/C5
Townsend, Va, US 189/K2
Townsends (inlet), NJ, US 194/D5
Townshend (cape), Austl. 160/C3
Townsville, Austl. 160/B2
Towot, Sudan 142/G4
Towr Kham, Afg. 124/A2
Towson, Md, US 194/B5
Towuti (lake), Indo. 117/F4
Toxey, Al, US 190/D2
Toxkan (riv.), Kyr. 125/C3
Toya (lake), Japan 108/B2
Toyah, Tx, US 177/C2
Toyahvale, Tx, US 177/C2
Toyama (pref.), Japan 111/E2
Toyama, Japan 111/E2
Toyama (bay), Japan 105/M4
Toyang, SKor. 107/D5
Toyoake, Japan 109/M5
Toyohashi, Japan 111/E3
Toyokawa, Japan 111/E3
Toyonaka, Japan 109/H6
Toyono, Japan 109/H6
Toyo'oka, Japan 110/D3
Toyosato, Japan 109/K5
Toyosato, Japan 109/E1
Toyoshina, Japan 111/E2
Toyota, Japan 109/M5
Toyotomi, Japan 109/B2
Toyoyama, Japan 109/L5
Tozer (mt.), Austl. 155/F3
Tpig, Rus. 97/H4
Tqvarch'eli, Geo. 97/G4
Tra Bong, Viet. 120/E3
Tra Cu, Viet. 120/D4
Tra Linh, Viet. 113/E4
Tra Mi, Viet. 120/E3
Tra On, Viet. 120/D4
Tra Vinh, Viet. 120/D4
Traben-Trarbach, Ger. 81/G4
Trabuco Canyon, Ca, US 192/C3
Trabzon (prov.), Turk. 96/F4
Trabzon, Turk. 96/F4
Tracadie, NB, Can. 184/E2
Trachselwald, Swi. 86/D3
Tracy, NB, Can. 184/D3
Tracy, Qu, Can. 187/K1
Tracy, Mn, US 181/G1
Tracy City, Tn, US 188/E3
Tracyton, Wa, US 193/B2
Tradate, It. 88/B2
Tradesville, SC, US 189/G3
Tradewater (riv.), Ky, US 188/D2
Traer, Ia, US 181/H2
Trafalgar (cape), Sp. 72/B4
Trafalgar, Austl. 159/C4
Trafoi, It. 87/G4
Trāghin, Libya 134/B3
Tragwein, Aus. 85/H6
Traiguén, Chile 214/B3
Trail, Or, US 172/B2
Trail, BC, Can. 170/F3
Trainou, Fr. 83/H5
Traipu, Braz. 211/F1
Trairi, Braz. 207/G3
Traisen (riv.), Aus. 69/H5
Traiskirchen, Aus. 77/N7
Traismauer, Aus. 69/H4
Trakai, Lith. 67/L4
Trakai NP, Lith. 67/L4
Trakan Phut Phon, Thai. 120/D3
Traki, Lith. 67/L4
Tralee, Ire. 58/A5
Tramelan, Swi. 86/D3
Tramin (Termeno), It. 87/H5
Trammel, Va, US 189/F2
Tramore, Ire. 58/C5
Tramore (bay), Ire. 58/C5
Tramperos (cr.), NM,Tx, US 178/C2
Tramping Lake, Sk, Can. 171/K1
Tranås, Swe. 66/F2
Tranbjerg, Den. 66/D3
Tranby, Nor. 64/R8
Trancoso, Port. 72/B2
Tranebjerg, Den. 66/D4
Tranemo, Swe. 66/E3
Tranent, Sc, UK 59/D5
Tranet (peak), Fr. 81/D4
Trang, Thai. 120/B5
Trangan (isl.), Indo. 117/H5
Trangie, Austl. 158/C2
Trängsletsjön (lake), Swe. 66/E1
Trani, It. 74/E2
Tranoroa, Madg. 152/H9
Tranqueras, Uru. 213/F4
Tranquillity, Ca, US 174/B2
Trans-en-Provence, Fr. 90/C5
Transantarctic (mts.), Ant. 216/W
Transylvania (reg.), Rom. 93/J1
Transylvanian Alps (mts.), Rom. 96/B3
Trapani, It. 74/C3
Trapeang Veng, Camb. 120/D3
Trapper (peak), Mt, US 170/G5
Trappes, Fr. 56/J5
Traralgon, Austl. 159/C4
Trarza (pol. reg.), Mrta. 140/B2
Trasacco, It. 92/C4
Trasimeno (lake), It. 71/K5
Trask (mtn.), Or, US 172/B1
Traskwood, Ar, US 179/H3
Träslövsläge, Swe. 66/E3
Trat, Thai. 120/C3
Traun (riv.), Aus. 68/H4
Traun, Aus. 85/H6
Traunreut, Ger. 85/F7
Traunsee (lake), Aus. 71/K3
Traunstein, Ger. 85/F7
Trautmannsdorf an der Leitha, Aus. 77/P7
Travagliato, It. 88/D2
Trave (riv.), Ger. 68/F2
Travedona Monate, It. 88/B2
Travelers Rest, SC, US 189/F3
Travellers (lake), Austl. 153/D4
Travemunde, Ger. 68/F2
Traverse (bay), Mb, Can. 182/F2
Traverse (lake), Mn, SD, US 181/F1
Traverse City, Mi, US 186/D2
Traversetolo, It. 88/D4
Travis (lake), Tx, US 177/E2
Travis (A.F.B.), Ca, US 172/C4
Travis AFB, Ca, US 193/L10
Travnik, Bosn. 76/C3
Trawsalt (peak), Wal, UK 62/C2
Trawsfynydd, Wal, UK 60/E6
Trbovlje, Slov. 71/L3
Tré-la-Tête (peak), Fr. 86/C6
Treachery (mt.), Austl. 157/G2
Treasure Island, Fl, US 190/K8
Trebaseleghe, It. 89/F2

305

Ubay – Valler

Ubay, Phil. 114/D3
Ubaye (riv.), Fr. 71/G4
Ubbergen, Neth. 78/C5
Ube, Japan 110/B4
Úbeda, Sp. 72/D3
Uberaba, Braz. 213/H1
Uberaba (lake), Braz. 209/G5
Überherrn, Ger. 81/F5
Uberlândia, Braz. 210/C3
Überlingen, Ger. 87/F2
Überlingersee (lake), Ger. 87/E2
Ubia (peak), Indo. 117/J4
Ubiaja, Nga. 141/G5
Ubina, Bol. 212/C2
Ubinas, Peru 208/D5
Ubly, Mi, US 186/E3
Ubombo, SAfr. 151/F2
Ubon Ratchathani, Thai. 120/D3
Ubrique, Sp. 72/C4
Ubundu, D.R. Congo 147/F3
Ubute, D.R. Congo 147/F3
Ucar, Azer. 129/F1
Ucayali (riv.), Peru 203/B3
Ucayali (dept.), Peru 208/C3
Uccle, Belg. 81/D2
Uch, Pak. 124/A5
Uch-Adzhi, Trkm. 127/H1
Uch-Aral, Kaz. 100/J5
Ucha (riv.), Rus. 94/W9
Uchab, Namb. 148/C3
Uchaly, Rus. 95/N5
Uchāna, India 124/D5
Ucharonidge, Austl. 154/D4
Uchinskoye (res.), Rus. 94/W9
Uchiura (bay), Japan 105/N3
Uchiza, Peru 208/B3
Uchkeken, Rus. 99/M6
Uchquduq, Uzb. 100/G5
Uchte (riv.), Ger. 68/F2
Uchte, Ger. 79/F3
Uchumarca, Peru 208/B2
Uchumayo, Peru 208/D5
Uchur (riv.), Rus. 101/P4
Ücker (riv.), Ger. 66/E5
Uckermark (reg.), Ger. 69/G2
Uckfield, Eng, UK 63/G5
Ucluelet, BC, Can. 170/B3
Ucon, Id, US 173/H2
Üçpınar, Turk. 130/C1
Ucross, Wy, US 173/K1
Ucua, Ang. 146/C5
Ucumasi, Bol. 212/C1
Uda (riv.), Rus. 101/M4
Udaipur, India 118/B3
Udaipur Garhi, Nepal 123/F2
Udaipura, India 122/B4
Udamalpet, India 121/C4
Udara, Nga. 141/G4
Uddevalla, Swe. 66/D2
Uddingston, Sc, UK 59/B5
Uddjaure (lake), Swe. 64/F2
Üdem, Ger. 78/D5
Uden, Neth. 78/C5
Udenhout, Neth. 78/C5
Uder, Ger. 79/H6
Udgīr, India 121/C2
Udhampur, India 124/C3
Udi, Nga. 141/G5
Udimskiy, Rus. 95/K3
Udine (prov.), It. 89/G1
Udine, It. 71/K3
Udmurtia Antonomous Republic, Rus. 100/Q6
Udomlya, Rus. 94/G4
Udon (riv.), Fr. 83/E3
Udon Thani, Thai. 120/C2
Ueckermünde, Ger. 66/F5
Ueda, Japan 111/F2
Uele (riv.), D.R. Congo 133/E4
Uelen, Rus. 168/W12
Uelsen, Ger. 78/D3
Uelzen, Ger. 79/H3
Ueno, Japan 109/K6
Ueno, Japan 109/B1
Uenohara, Japan 111/F3
Uere (riv.), D.R. Congo 142/E4
Uetendorf, Swi. 86/D4
Uetersen, Ger. 79/G1
Uetze, Ger. 79/H4
Ufa, Rus. 95/M5
Ufa (riv.), Rus. 95/N5
Uffenheim, Ger. 84/D3
Uffing, Ger. 87/H2
Uffington, Eng, UK 63/E3
Ufra, Trkm. 129/H2
Ugab (riv.), Namb. 148/B4
Ugāle, Lat. 67/K3
Ugalla (riv.), Tanz. 147/G4
Ugalla, Tanz. 147/G4
Ugalla River Game Rsv., Tanz. 147/G4
Uganda(ctry.) 133/F4
Ugbobo Ani, Nga. 141/G5
Ugento, It. 75/F3
Ugep, Nga. 141/H5
Ughelli, Nga. 141/G5
Ugie (riv.), Sc, UK 59/E1
Ugine, Fr. 86/C6
Uglegorsk, Ukr. 99/K3
Uglegorsk, Rus. 105/N2
Ugleural'skiy, Rus. 95/N4
Uglich, Rus. 94/H4
Ugljan (isl.), Cro. 71/L4
Uglovoye, Rus. 105/L3
Ugod, Hun. 76/C2
Ugol'nyye Kopi, Rus. 101/T3
Ugra (riv.), Rus. 94/G5
Ugŭrchin, Bul. 77/G4
Ugweno, Tanz. 145/B2
Uherské Hradiště, Czh. 69/J4
Uhingen, Ger. 84/C5
Uhland, Tx, US 176/F3
Úhlava (riv.), Czh. 69/G4
Úhlavka (riv.), Czh. 85/F3
Uhrichsville, Oh, US 186/F4
Uia di Ciamarella (peak), It. 90/D2
Uiangombe, Ang. 146/C5
Uig, Sc, UK 57/Q7
Uig, Sc, UK 57/Q8
Uíge (prov.), Ang. 146/C4
Uíge, Ang. 146/C4
Ŭihŭng, SKor. 107/E4
Ŭijŏngbu, SKor. 107/G6
Ŭiju, NKor. 107/C2
Uil, Kaz. 97/K2
Uil (riv.), Kaz. 97/K2
Uilkraal (riv.), SAfr. 150/L11
Uilpata (Gora Peak), Rus. 97/G4
Uinta (basin), Ut, US 173/H3
Uinta (mts.), Ut, US 173/H3
Uinta and Ouray Ind. Res., Ut, US 173/H3
Uiraúna, Braz. 207/G4
Ŭiryŏng, SKor. 107/E5
Ŭisŏng, SKor. 110/A2
Uitenhage, SAfr. 150/D4
Uitgeest, Neth. 78/B3
Uithoorn, Neth. 78/B4
Uithuizen, Neth. 78/D2
Uiwang, SKor. 107/F7
Ujae (isl.), Mrsh. 162/F4
Ujelang (isl.), Mrsh. 162/F4
Újfehértó, Hun. 69/L5
Ujhāni, India 122/B1
Uji (riv.), Japan 110/D3
Uji, Japan 109/J6
Ujiji, Tanz. 147/G4
Ujitawara, Japan 109/J6
Ujjain, India 118/C3
Ujohbilang, Indo. 116/E3
Ujung Pandang, Indo. 117/E5
Ujunggading, Indo. 115/B2
Ujunggenteng, Indo. 115/D3
Ukara (isl.), Tanz. 145/A2
Ukata, Nga. 141/G4
Ukerewe (isl.), Tanz. 145/A2
Ukhiya, Bang. 119/F3
Ukhta, Rus. 95/M3
Ukiah, Ca, US 172/B4
Ukiah, Or, US 172/D1
Uklāna, India 124/C5
Ukmergė, Lith. 67/L4
Ukraine(ctry.) 55/G4
Ukwama, Tanz. 145/A4
Ukwatutu, D.R. Congo 142/E4
Ul Bend NWR, Mt, US 171/L4
Ula, Turk. 93/L3
Ulaan-Uul, Mong. 104/G3
Ulaanbaatar (cap.), Mong. 104/F2
Ulaanbaatar (int'l arpt.), Mong. 104/F2
Ulaandel, Mong. 104/G2
Ulaangom, Mong. 125/F2
Ulaanjirem, Mong. 104/F2
Ulan Erge, Rus. 97/H3
Ulan Ul (lake), China 125/F5
Ulan-Burgasy (mts.), Rus. 104/F1
Ulan-Kholl, Rus. 97/H3
Ulan-Ude, Rus. 104/F1
Ulangati, D.R. Congo 147/F3
Ulanhot, China 105/J2
Ulatis (cr.), Ca, US 193/L10
Ulaya, Tanz. 145/B3
Ulchin, SKor. 110/A2
Ulcinj, Yugo. 75/F2
Ulcumayo, Peru 208/C3
Uldz (riv.), Mong. 104/G2
Ulefoss, Nor. 66/C2
Ulemiste (int'l arpt.), Est. 67/L2
Ulen, Mn, US 182/F4
Ulgain (riv.), China 105/H2
Ulhāsnagar, India 121/B2
Uliastay, Mong. 104/D2
Ulindi (riv.), D.R. Congo 147/F3
Ulithi (isl.), Micr. 162/C3
Uljma, Yugo. 76/E3
Ulla, Bela. 67/N4
Ulla (riv.), Sp. 72/A1
Ulla Ulla, Bol. 208/D4
Ulla Ulla, Res. Nacional, Bol. 208/D4
Ulladulla, Austl. 159/E2
Ullāpāra, Bang. 123/G3
Ullapool, Sc, UK 57/R8
Ullared, Swe. 66/E3
Ulldecona, Sp. 73/F2
Ullensvang, Nor. 66/B1
Ullerslev, Den. 65/G7
Üllő, Hun. 77/R10
Ulloma, Bol. 212/B1
Ullsfjorden (estu.), Nor. 64/F1
Ullswater (lake), Eng, UK 61/F2
Ullŭng (isl.), SKor. 105/L4
Ŭllyul, NKor. 107/C3
Ulm, Ar, US 179/J3
Ulm, Ger. 84/C6
Ulman, Mo, US 179/H1
Ulmarra, Austl. 158/E1
Ulmen, Ger. 81/F3
Ulonguè, Moz. 149/G2
Ulricehamn, Swe. 66/E3
Ulrichen, Swi. 87/E5
Ulrichsberg, Aus. 85/G5
Ulrichstein, Ger. 84/C1
Ulrum, Neth. 78/D2
Ulsan, SKor. 110/A3
Ulstein, Nor. 64/C3
Ulster (reg.), Ire. 60/A3
Ulster, Pa, US 187/H4
Ulster (riv.), Ger. 84/C1
Ulster American Folk Park, NI, UK 60/A2
Ulu, Sudan 142/G3
Ulu, Indo. 117/G3
Ulúa (riv.), Hon. 196/D4
Ulua (riv.), Hon. 200/E3
Uluçınar, Turk. 130/D1
Uludağ (peak), Turk. 128/B1
Uludoruk (peak), Turk. 129/F2
Uluguru (mts.), Tanz. 145/B3
Ulukışla, Turk. 128/C2
Ulundi, SAfr. 151/E3
Ulungur (riv.), China 104/B2
Ulungur (lake), China 104/B2
Uluru (Ayers Rock) (peak), Austl. 157/F3
Uluru NP, Austl. 157/F3
Ulutau (peak), Kaz. 125/A2
Ulverston, Eng, UK 61/E3
Ulverstone, Austl. 158/C4
Ulvik, Nor. 66/B1
Ulvila, Fin. 67/J1
Ul'yanovka, Rus 67/P2
Ul'yanovka, Ukr. 98/F3
Ul'yanovo, Rus. 96/E1
Ul'yanovsk, Rus. 95/L5
Ul'yanovsk Oblast, Rus. 97/H1
Ulysses, Ks, US 178/D2
Ulysses, Pa, US 187/H4
Ulysses, Ne, US 181/F3
Um Dafuq, Sudan 142/D3
Umala, Bol. 212/C1
Uman', Ukr. 98/F3
Umán, Mex. 200/D1
Umanum (pt.), Phil. 114/D3
Umari, Braz. 207/G4
Umarizal, Braz. 207/G4
Umarkot, India 121/D2
Umāsi La (pass), India 124/D3
Umatilla, Fl, US 191/H3
Umatilla (riv.), Or, US 172/D1
Umatilla, Or, US 170/E5
Umatilla Ind. Res., Or, US 172/D1
Umatilla NWR, Or, US 172/D1
Umba, Rus. 94/G2
Umbakumba, Austl. 155/E3
Umbeara, Austl. 157/G3
Umberto I, Arg. 212/D4
Umbogintwini, SAfr. 151/E3
Umboi (isl.), PNG 162/D5
Umbrail (peak), Swi. 87/G4
Umbrailpass (pass), Swi. 87/G4
Umbria (pol. reg.), It. 89/F6
Umbria (prov.), It. 71/K5
Umbuluze (riv.), Afr. 149/F5
Ume (riv.), Swe. 100/B3
Ume (riv.), Zim. 149/F3
Umeå, Swe. 64/G3
Umeälven (riv.), Swe. 64/F2
Umedpur, Bang. 123/G4
Umët, Rus. 97/G1
Umfolozi (riv.), SAfr. 151/E3
Umfreville (lake), On, Can. 183/G2
Umfuli (riv.), Zim. 149/F3
Umgeni (riv.), SAfr. 151/E3
Umhausen, Aus. 87/G3
Umkirch, Ger. 86/D1
Umkomaas, SAfr. 151/E3
Umm al Abīd, Libya 134/B3
Umm al Arānib, Libya 134/B3
Umm al Birak, SAr. 126/C4
Umm al Ghirbāl (well), Libya 134/B2
Umm al Khashab, SAr. 126/D5
Umm al Qaywayn, UAE 127/G3
Umm Buru, Sudan 142/D2
Umm Dam, Sudan 142/F2
Umm Dhibbān, Sudan 142/G2
Umm Dhibbān, Sudan 142/F2
Umm Durmān (Omdurman), Sudan 142/G2
Umm el Faḥm, Isr. 131/C3
Umm Inderaba, Sudan 142/F2
Umm Jawzah, Jor. 131/D4
Umm Kaddādah, Sudan 142/E2
Umm Lajj, SAr. 135/H3
Umm Qaşr, Iraq 129/F4
Umm Qawzayn, Sudan 142/E2
Umm Qays (Gedara) (ruin), Jor. 131/D3
Umm Ruwābah, Sudan 142/F2
Umm Sayyālah, Sudan 142/F2
Ummendorf, Ger. 87/F1
Umnak (isl.), Ak, US 101/V4
Umniati, Zim. 149/F3
Umniati (riv.), Zim. 149/F3
Umphang, Thai. 120/B2
Umpqua (riv.), Or, US 168/B3
Umpqua, Or, US 172/B2
Umpulo, Ang. 148/C2
Umraniye, Turk. 128/B2
Umred, India 121/C1
Ŭmsŏng, SKor. 107/D4
Umtata, SAfr. 150/E3
Umu Duru, Nga. 141/G5
Umuahia, Nga. 141/G5
Umuarama, Braz. 213/F2
Umuda (isl.), PNG 155/F2
Umunede, Nga. 141/G5
Umurbey, Turk. 75/K2
Umzimvubu (riv.), SAfr. 150/E3
Umzingwani (riv.), Zim. 149/F4
Umzinto, SAfr. 151/E3
Una, India 124/D4
Una (riv.), Bosn.,Cro. 93/H1
Una (mt.), NZ 161/C3
Una (riv.), Cro.,Bosn. 71/L4
Una, Braz. 211/F2
Unadilla, NY, US 187/J3
Unadilla, Ga, US 188/F4
Unaí, Braz. 210/D3
Unaka (mts.), Tn, US 189/F2
Unalaska (isl.), Ak, US 101/V4
Unalaska, Ak, US 168/W13
Unas (isl.), Fin. 65/F4
'Unayzah, SAr. 126/D3
Uncastillo, Sp. 73/E1
Unchahra, India 122/C3
Uncompaghre (riv.), Co, US 173/K4
Uncompaghre (plat.), Co, US 173/J4
Uncompahgre (peak), Co, US 175/J1
Undaunda, Zam. 149/F2
Unden (lake), Swe. 66/F2
Undenheim, Ger. 84/B3
Underberg, SAfr. 150/E3
Underbool, Austl. 158/B2
Underwood, ND, US 182/D4
Underwood-Petersville, Al, US 188/D3
Undof Zone, Syria 131/D2
Undu (pt.), Fiji 163/Z17
Unduavi, Bol. 208/E5
Une, Col. 207/L8
Unecha, Rus. 96/E1
Ungama (bay), Kenya 145/C2
Ungarie, Austl. 159/C1
Ungava (pen.), Qu, Can. 167/J2
Ungava (pen.), Can. 165/K3
Ungava (bay), Can. 165/L4
Unggi, NKor. 105/L3
Ungheni, Mol. 98/D4
Ungwariba (pt.), Austl. 155/E3
Unhošt, Czh. 85/H2
Unhŭng, NKor. 107/E2
União, Braz. 207/F4
União da Vitória, Braz. 213/G3
União dos Palmares, Braz. 207/G5
Unimak (isl.), Ak, US 101/V4
Unini (riv.), Braz. 205/F5
Unini, Peru 208/C3
Union (canal), Sc, UK 59/C5
Union, Oh, US 186/D5
Union, NJ, US 195/H9
Union, Or, US 172/E1
Union (mt.), Az, US 175/F3
Unión, Arg. 214/D2
Union, Al, US 188/D4
Union, Ms, US 188/C4
Union, Mo, US 188/B1
Union, WV, US 189/G2
Unión, Par. 213/E3
Union, SC, US 189/G3
Union (lake), NJ, US 194/C5
Union Beach, NJ, US 195/J10
Union Bridge, Md, US 194/A4
Union Center, SD, US 180/C1
Union City, Ok, US 179/F3
Union City, In, US 186/D4
Union City, Pa, US 187/G4
Union City, Mi, US 186/D3
Union City, Ca, US 193/K11
Union City, NJ, US 195/J8
Union City, Tn, US 188/C2
Union City, Ga, US 189/L7
Union Creek, Or, US 172/B2
Unión de Reyes, Cuba 201/F1
Unión de Tula, Mex. 198/D5
Union Flat (cr.), Wa, US 170/F4
Union Grove, Wi, US 186/B3
Unión Hidalgo, Mex. 200/C2
Union Mills, Md, US 194/A4
Union Park, Fl, US 190/N6
Union Pier, Mi, US 186/C4
Union Point, Ga, US 189/F4
Union Springs, NY, US 187/H3
Union Springs, Al, US 188/E4
Uniondale, NY, US 195/L9
Uniondale, SAfr. 150/C4
Unionhall, Ire. 58/A6
Uniontown, Ar, US 179/G3
Uniontown, Pa, US 187/G5
Uniontown, Ky, US 188/D2
Uniontown, Al, US 188/D4
Uniontown, Md, US 194/A4
Unionville, Mi, US 186/E3
Unionville, In, US 186/C5
Unionville, Ga, US 191/G2
Unionville, Nv, US 172/D3
Unionville, Mo, US 181/H3
Unionville, On, Can. 186/U8
Unionville, Va, US 189/J1
Unita (riv.), Ut, US 173/J3
United Arab Emirates (ctry.) 103/C7
United Kingdom(ctry.) 55/D3
United Nations, NY, US 195/K9
United Nations Mem. Cemetery, SKor. 110/A3
United States(ctry.) 165/G5
United States (range), Nun, Can. 167/T6
United States Coast Guard Receiving Center, NJ, US 194/D6
United States Department of Energy, Md, US 194/A5
United States Naval Academy, Md, US 194/B6
United States Naval Reservation Mil. Res., PR 197/M8
Unitsa, Rus. 94/G3
Unity, Or, US 172/D1
Unity, Wi, US 181/J1
Unity, Sk, Can. 171/K1
Unity Pd. (pond), Me, US 184/C3
Universal City, Tx, US 176/E3
Universal Studios Florida, Fl, US 190/M7
University of Minnesota Landscape Arboretum, Mn, US 183/N7
University Park, NM, US 175/J4
University Park, Tx, US 176/L7
University Place, Wa, US 193/B3
Unjha, India 127/K4
Unjŏn, NKor. 107/C3
Unkel, Ger. 81/G2
Unkurda, Rus. 95/N5
Unley (nbrhd.), Austl. 157/M8
Unna, Ger. 79/E5
Unnão, India 122/C2
Ŭnp'a, NKor. 107/C3
Unsan, NKor. 107/C2
Ŭnsan-ŭp, NKor. 107/D3
Unshin (riv.), Ire. 58/B1
Unst (isl.), Sc, UK 57/W13
Unsu-Nodongjagu, NKor. 107/D2
Unter Pleichfeld, Ger. 84/D3
Unterägeri, Swi. 87/E3
Unterargen (riv.), Ger. 87/F2
Untergriesbach, Ger. 85/G5
Unterhaching, Ger. 85/E6
Unteriberg, Swi. 87/E3
Unterkulm, Swi. 86/E3
Unterlüss, Ger. 79/H3
Unterschleissheim, Ger. 85/E6
Untersee (lake), Swi. 87/E2
Unterseen, Swi. 86/D4
Untersiggenthal, Swi. 87/E3
Unterthingau, Ger. 87/G2
Untervaz, Swi. 87/F4
Unterweissenbach, Aus. 85/H6
Unuli Horog, China 125/F4
Unverre, Fr. 83/G4
Ünye, Turk. 96/F4
Unzen-Amakusa NP, Japan 110/A4
Unzen-dake (peak), Japan 110/B4
Unzha (riv.), Rus. 100/E4
Unzimkulu, SAfr. 151/E3
Uonquén, Ven. 205/F3
Uozu, Japan 111/E2
Upala, CR 201/E4
Upalco, Ut, US 173/H3
Upanema, Braz. 207/G4
Upata, Ven. 205/F2
Upemba (lake), D.R. Congo 147/F5
Upemba, PN de l', D.R. Congo 147/F5
Uphall, Sc, UK 59/C5
Upi, Phil. 114/D4
Upington, SAfr. 150/C3
Upinniemi (Obbnäs), Fin. 65/E4
Upiriwombe, Zam. 145/A4
Upland, In, US 186/D4
Upland, Pa, US 194/C4
Upleta, India 127/K4
Upminster (nbrhd.), Eng, UK 56/D2
Upolu (isl.), ASam. 163/S9
Upolu (isl.), WSam. 163/H6
Upolu (pt.), Hi, US 168/S9
Upper (falls), Wy, US 173/H1
Upper (pen.), Mi, US 169/J2
Upper (lake), Ca, US 172/C3
Upper (bay), NY, US 194/D2
Upper Arlington, Oh, US 186/E4
Upper Arrow (lake), BC, Can. 170/F2
Upper Blackville, NB, Can. 184/E2
Upper Darby, Pa, US 194/C4
Upper Demerara-Berbice (pol. reg.), Guy. 205/G3
Upper Dicker, Eng, UK 63/G5
Upper East (pol. reg.), Gha. 141/E4
Upper Engadine (valley), Swi. 87/F5
Upper Fairmount, Md, US 189/K1
Upper Falls, Md, US 194/B5
Upper Ganges (canal), India 122/A1
Upper Hale, Eng, UK 56/A3
Upper Hutt, NZ 161/J9
Upper Iowa (riv.), Ia, US 181/J2
Upper Klamath (lake), Or, US 172/B2
Upper Klamath NWR, Or, US 172/C2
Upper Lake, Ca, US 172/B4
Upper Lough Erne (lake), NI, UK 57/Q9
Upper Marlboro (Marlboro), Md, US 194/B6
Upper Mesa (falls), Id, US 173/H1
Upper Ouachita NWR, La, US 177/H1
Upper Peoria (lake), Il, US 181/K3
Upper Red (lake), Mn, US 183/G3
Upper Rouge (riv.), Mi, US 193/F7
Upper Saddle River, NJ, US 195/J7
Upper Sandusky, Oh, US 186/E4
Upper Sioux Ind. Res., Mn, US 181/G1
Upper Souris NWR, ND, US 182/D3
Upper Takutu-Upper Essequibo (pol. reg.), Guy. 205/G4
Upper Thames (valley), Eng, UK 63/E3
Upper Trajan's Wall (wall), Mol. 96/D3
Upper Vaughan, NS, Can. 184/E3
Upper West (pol. reg.), Gha. 141/E4
Upper Yarra (res.), Austl. 159/B3
Upperglade, WV, US 189/G1
Upperlands, NI, UK 60/B2
Uppingham, Eng, UK 63/F1
Upplands-Bro, Swe. 65/A1
Upplands-Väsby, Swe. 66/G2
Uppsala (co.), Swe. 64/F3
Uppsala, Swe. 66/G2
Upsala, On, Can. 183/J3
Upshi, India 124/D3
Upson, Wi, US 183/J4
Upstart (cape), Austl. 160/B2
Upstart (bay), Austl. 155/G4
Upton, Wy, US 180/B1
Upton, Ky, US 188/E2
Upton upon Severn, Eng, UK 62/D2
Urabá (gulf), Col. 201/G4
Uracoa, Ven. 205/F2
Urad Qianqi, China 106/B2
Uraga (chan.), Japan 109/D3
Urahoro, Japan 108/C2
Urajärvi (lake), Fin. 65/F3
Urakawa, Japan 108/C2
Ural (riv.), Kaz. 97/J2
Ural (mts.), Rus. 55/L2
Ural (Zhāyya) (riv.), Rus. 100/F5
Uralla, Austl. 158/D1
Ural'skiy, Rus. 97/J2
Ural'skoye, Rus. 97/L1
Urambo, Tanz. 147/H4
Urana (lake), Austl. 159/C2
Urana, Austl. 159/C2
Urangeline (cr.), Austl. 159/C2
Urania, La, US 190/B2
Uranium City, Sk, Can. 166/F3
Uranquinty, Austl. 159/C2
Urapunga, Austl. 154/D3
Uraras, Namb. 148/B4
Uraricoera (riv.), Braz. 205/F4
Uraricoera, Braz. 205/F4
Urasoe, Japan 111/J7
Uravan, Co, US 175/H1
Urawa, Japan 111/F3
Uray, Rus. 100/G3
Urayasu, Japan 109/D2
Urazovka, Rus. 95/K5
Urazovo, Rus. 99/K2
Urbach, Ger. 84/C5
Urbana, Mo, US 179/H2
Urbana, Il, US 185/B4
Urbana, Oh, US 186/E4
Urbana, Md, US 194/A5
Urbandale, Ia, US 181/H3
Urbania, It. 89/F6
Urbano Santos, Braz. 207/F3
Urbenville, Austl. 163/D5
Urbino, It. 89/F6
Urcos, Peru 208/D4
Urda, Kaz. 97/H2
Urda, Sp. 72/D3
Urdinarrain, Arg. 215/J10
Urdorf, Swi. 87/E3
Urdzhar, Kaz. 125/D2
Ure (riv.), Eng, UK 61/G3
Urein, Egypt 139/B3
Ureki, Geo. 97/G4
Urengoy, Rus. 100/H3
Ures, Mex. 198/C2
Ureshino, Japan 109/K6
Ureterp, Neth. 78/D2
Urewera NP, NZ 161/D2
Urfa, Turk. 128/D2
Urfa (prov.), Turk. 128/D2
Urft (lake), Ger. 81/F2
Urft (riv.), Ger. 79/G6
Urgal, Rus. 105/L1
Urganch, Uzb. 100/G5
Urgnano, It. 88/C2
Urho Kekkosen NP, Fin. 64/H1
Uri, India 124/C2
Uri-Rotstock (peak), Swi. 87/E4
Uriah, Al, US 190/E2
Uriangato, Mex. 199/E4
Uribante (riv.), Ven. 204/D3
Uribia, Col. 204/C2
Uricani, Rom. 98/B5
Urich, Mo, US 179/G1
Urie (riv.), Sc, UK 59/D2
Urim, Isr. 131/B6
Urimán, Ven. 205/F3
Uriménil, Fr. 86/C1
Uriondo, Bol. 212/C2
Urique (riv.), Mex. 198/D3
Uriranteriña, Ven. 205/F3
Uritskiy, Kaz. 100/G4
Urjala, Fin. 67/K1
Urk, Neth. 78/C3
Urla, Turk. 96/C5
Urlaţi, Rom. 77/H3
Urlingford, Ire. 58/C4
Urman, Rus. 95/N5
Urmar, India 124/C4
Urmi (riv.), Rus. 104/L2
Urmia (lake), Iran 129/F2
Urmitz, Ger. 81/G3
Urmston, Eng, UK 61/F5
Urnäsch, Swi. 87/F3
Urnersee (lake), Swi. 87/E4
Uroševac, Yugo. 76/E4
Urr Water (riv.), Sc, UK 60/E1
Urrin (riv.), Ire. 58/D4
Ursensollen, Ger. 85/E4
Ursulo Galván, Mex. 199/N7
Urtazym, Rus. 97/L1
Uru Uru (lake), Bol. 212/C1
Uruaçu, Braz. 210/C2
Uruapan, Mex. 174/D5
Uruapan, Mex. 198/E5
Urubamba, Peru 208/C4
Urubamba (riv.), Peru 208/C3
Urubichá, Bol. 209/F4
Urubu (riv.), Braz. 205/G5
Urubuquara (hill), Braz. 206/C3
Uruburetama, Braz. 207/G3
Urucará, Braz. 206/B3
Urucu (riv.), Braz. 209/E2
Uruçuí, Braz. 207/E4
Uruçuí Preto (riv.), Braz. 207/E5
Uruçuí, Serra do (mts.), Braz. 207/E5
Urucuia (riv.), Braz. 210/D3
Urucurituba, Braz. 206/B3
Uruguai (riv.), Braz. 213/F3
Uruguaiana, Braz. 213/E4
Uruguay(ctry.) 203/D6
Uruguay (riv.), SAm. 203/D5
Urumaco, Ven. 204/D2
Ürümqi (int'l arpt.), China 125/E3
Ürümqi, China 125/E3
Urunga, Austl. 158/E1
Uruoca, Braz. 207/F3
Urup (isl.), Rus. 103/Q5
Ururi, It. 92/E4
Urus-Martan, Rus. 97/H4
Urussanga, Braz. 213/G4
Urussu, Rus. 97/K1
Uruwira, Tanz. 147/G4
Uruyén, Ven. 205/F3
Uryumkan (riv.), Rus. 105/H1
Uryupinsk, Rus. 99/M2
Urzhum, Rus. 95/L4
Urziceni, Rom. 77/H3
Us, Fr. 56/H4
Us (riv.), Rus. 104/C1
Usa (riv.), Rus. 100/F3
Usa, Japan 110/B4
USAF Academy, Co, US 180/B4
USAF Res., Tn, US 188/D3
Usagara, Tanz. 145/A2
Uşak, Turk. 128/B2
Uşak (prov.), Turk. 128/B2
Usakos, Namb. 148/B4
Usborne (mt.), UK 215/F6
Uscio, It. 88/C5
Usedom (isl.), Ger. 66/E4
Usedom, Ger. 66/E5
Useldange, Lux. 81/E4
Useless Loop, Austl. 156/B3
Usevia, Tanz. 147/G4
'Usfān, SAr. 126/C4
Ushachi, Bela. 67/N4
Ushaki, Rus. 67/P2
Ushashi, Tanz. 145/A2
'Ushayrah, SAr. 126/D4
Ushetu, Tanz. 147/H4
Ushibori, Japan 109/F2
Ushibuka, Japan 110/B4
Ushiku, Japan 109/E2
Ushirombo, Tanz. 147/G3
Ushkovo, Rus. 94/S6
Ushtobe, Kaz. 125/C2
Ushuaia, Arg. 215/C7
Ushumun, Rus. 105/K1
Usi, NKor. 107/C2
Usicayos, Peru 208/D4
Usilampatti, India 118/C6
Usinge, Tanz. 147/G4
Usingen, Ger. 84/B2
Usino, PNG 155/G1
Usinsk, Rus. 100/E4
Üsküdar (nbrhd.), Turk. 129/N7
Üsküp, Turk. 77/H5
Uslar, Ger. 79/G5
Usman', Rus. 96/F1
Usoke, Tanz. 147/H4
Usol'ye-Sibirskoye, Rus. 104/E1
Uson, Phil. 114/C2
Uspallata, Arg. 214/C2
Uspallata, Paso de (pass), Chile 214/N8
Uspenka, Ukr. 99/K3
Usquil, Peru 208/B2
Ussel, Fr. 70/E4
Ussel (riv.), Ger. 84/D5
Usses (riv.), Fr. 86/C5
Ussoque, Ang. 148/B2
Ussure, Tanz. 145/A3
Ussuri (riv.), China,Rus. 101/P5
Ussuriysk, Rus. 105/L3
Ussy-sur-Marne, Fr. 56/M5
Ust'-Orda Aut. Okrug, Rus. 101/Q6
Ust'-Barguzin, Rus. 104/F1
Ust'-Ilimsk, Rus. 101/L4
Ust'-Ishim, Rus. 100/H4
Ust'-Kamchatsk, Rus. 101/S4
Ust'-Karsk, Rus. 105/H1
Ust'-Kulom, Rus. 95/M3
Ust'-Kut, Rus. 101/L4
Ust'-Kuyga, Rus. 101/P2
Ust'-Labinsk, Rus. 99/K5
Ust'-Luga, Rus. 67/N2
Ust'-Man'ya, Rus. 95/P3
Ust'-Maya, Rus. 101/P3
Ust'-Nera, Rus. 101/Q3
Ust'-Ocheya, Rus. 95/L3
Ust'-Olenëk, Rus. 101/M2
Ust'-Omchug, Rus. 101/Q3
Ust'-Ordynskiy, Rus. 104/E1
Ust'-Pinega, Rus. 94/J2
Ust'-Port, Rus. 100/J3
Ust'-Pozhva, Rus. 95/N4
Ust'-Tsil'ma, Rus. 95/M2
Ust'-Uda, Rus. 104/E1
Úštěk, Czh. 85/H1
Uster, Swi. 87/E3
Ustica, It. 74/C3
Ustica (isl.), It. 93/G3
Ustka, Pol. 66/G4
Ustrzyki Dolne, Pol. 69/M4
Ust'ya (riv.), Rus. 95/K3
Ustyurt (plat.), Kaz. 103/D5
Ustyuzhna, Rus. 94/H4
Usu, China 125/D3
Usuda, Japan 109/A1
Usuki, Japan 110/B4
Usulután, ESal. 200/D3
Usuma, D.R. Congo 142/E4
Usumacinta (riv.), Mex. 196/C4
Uta, Indo. 117/J4
Utah (lake), Ut, US 173/G3
Utah (state), US 168/D4
Utah Beach, Fr. 82/D2
Utah Test and Training Range, Ut, US 173/G3
Utale, Malw. 149/G2
Utangan (riv.), India 122/A2
Utano, Japan 109/J7
Utashinai, Japan 108/C2
'Utaybah (lake), Syria 131/F1
Ute (cr.), NM, US 178/C2
Ute Mountain Ind. Res., Co, US 175/H2
Utembo (riv.), Ang. 148/D3
Utena, Lith. 67/L4
Utengule, Tanz. 145/A4
Utero (peak), It. 92/C2
Uterský (riv.), Czh. 85/G3
Utete, Tanz. 145/B3
Uthai Thani, Thai. 120/C3
Utica, NY, US 187/J3
Utica, Oh, US 186/E4
Utica, Mi, US 193/F6
Utica, Mo, US 181/H4
Utica, Ne, US 181/F3
Utica, Ms, US 188/B4
Utiel, Sp. 72/E3
Utila (isl.), Hon. 200/E2
Utinga, Braz. 211/E2
Utirik (isl.), Mrsh. 162/G3
Utiroa, Kiri. 162/G5
Utlyukskiy Estuary (estu.), Ukr. 99/H4
Utmānzai, Pak. 124/A2
Utnūr, India 121/C2
Utö (isl.), Swe. 65/B2
Utö, Swe. 65/B2
Utopia, Austl. 157/G2
Utopia, Tx, US 177/E3
Utopia Abor. Land, Austl. 157/G2
Utorgosh, Rus. 67/P2
Utraulā, India 122/D2
Utrecht (prov.), Neth. 78/C4
Utrecht, Neth. 78/C4
Utrecht, SAfr. 151/E2
Utrera, Sp. 72/C4
Utsunomiya, Japan 111/F2
Utta, Rus. 97/H3
Uttar Patiata, Bang. 123/G3
Uttar Pradesh (state), India 125/C6
Uttaradit, Thai. 120/C2
Uttendorf, Aus. 85/G6
Uttenweiler, Ger. 87/F1
Uttoxeter, Eng, UK 61/G6
Utuado, PR 197/M8
Utupua (isl.), Sol. 162/F6
Uturoa, FrPol. 163/K6
Utzenstorf, Swi. 86/D3
Uulu, Est. 67/L2
Üür (riv.), Mong. 104/E1
Üüreg (lake), Mong. 104/C1
Uusikaupunki, Fin. 67/J1
Uusimaa (prov.), Fin. 64/H3
Uva (riv.), Col. 204/D4
Uva (prov.), SrL. 121/D5
Uvalda, Ga, US 191/G1
Uvalde, Tx, US 177/E3
Uvarovo, Rus. 97/G2
Uvel'skiy, Rus. 95/P5
Uverito, Ven. 205/E2
Uvinza, Tanz. 147/G4
Uvira, D.R. Congo 147/G3
Uvongo, SAfr. 151/E3
Uvs (lake), Mong. 104/C1
Uvs (prov.), Mong. 104/C2
Uvs Nuur (lake), Mong. 125/F1
Uwajima, Japan 110/C4
'Uwaybid (peak), Egypt 139/D4
Uwayl, Sudan 142/E3
Uwekuli, Indo. 117/F4
Uwimmerah (riv.), Indo. 117/K5
Uxbridge (nbrhd.), Eng, UK 56/B2
Uxin Qi, China 106/B3
Uxmal (ruin), Mex. 200/D1
Üydzin, Mong. 104/F3
Uyo, Nga. 141/G5
Üyönch, Mong. 104/C2
Uyu (riv.), Myan. 112/B3
Uyuni, Bol. 212/C2
Uzbekistan(ctry.) 103/E5
Uzcudún, Arg. 214/D5
Uzein (int'l arpt.), Fr. 70/C5
Uzel, Fr. 82/C4
Uzen', Kaz. 97/K4
Uzerche, Fr. 70/D4
Uzès, Fr. 70/F4
Uzhhorod, Ukr. 69/M4
Uzhok (pass), Ukr. 69/M4
Užice, Yugo. 76/D4
Uzlovaya, Rus. 96/F1
Uznach, Swi. 87/E3
Üzümlü, Turk. 128/D2
Uzunköprü, Turk. 77/H5
Užventis, Lith 67/K4
Uzwil, Swi. 87/F3
Uzyn, Ukr. 98/F3

V

V.C. Bird (int'l arpt.), Anti. 197/N8
V.P. Rosales, PN, Chile 214/B4
Vääksy, Fin. 65/F3
Vaal (riv.), SAfr. 133/E7
Vaala, Fin. 64/H2
Vaalbos NP, SAfr. 150/D3
Vaaldam (res.), SAfr. 150/D2
Vaals, Neth. 81/F2
Vaalserberg (hill), Neth. 81/E2
Vaalwater, SAfr. 149/F5
Vaas, Fr. 83/F5
Vaasa (int'l arpt.), Fin. 64/G3
Vaasa (prov.), Fin. 64/G3
Vaasa (Vasa), Fin. 64/G3
Vaassen, Neth. 78/C4
Vabalninkas, Lith. 67/L4
Vác, Hun. 76/D2
Vaca (mt.), Ca, US 193/K10
Vaca (mts.), Ca, US 193/K10
Vacacai (riv.), Braz. 213/F4
Vacaria, Braz. 213/G4
Vacaria (riv.), Braz. 210/B4
Vacaville, Ca, US 172/C4
Vaccares (swamp), Fr. 90/A6
Vachères (peak), Fr. 90/B3
Vachères (riv.), Fr. 90/C3
Vachi, Rus. 97/H4
Vachon (riv.), Qu, Can. 167/J2
Vacov, Czh. 85/G4
Vad, Rus. 95/K5
Vada, It. 88/D7
Vaden, Ar, US 179/H4
Vadheim, Nor. 66/A1
Vado, NM, US 176/A1
Vado Ligure, It. 88/B5
Vadodara (Baroda), India 118/B3
Vadret (peak), Swi. 87/F4
Vadsø, Nor. 64/J1
Vadstena, Swe. 66/F2
Vadul lui Voda, Mol. 98/E4
Vaduz (cap.), Lcht. 87/F3
Vaernes (int'l arpt.), Nor. 64/D3
Vaga (riv.), Rus. 94/J3
Vågå, Nor. 64/D3
Vågan, Nor. 64/E1
Vaganski Vrh (peak), Cro. 76/B3
Vagay (riv.), Rus. 95/R4
Vaggeryd, Swe. 66/F3
Vagney, Fr. 86/C1
Vagnhärad, Swe. 65/A2
Vagos, Port. 72/A2
Vågsøy, Nor. 64/C3
Vah (riv.), Slvk. 69/J4
Vahermanjärvi (lake), Fin. 65/E4
Vahitahi (isl.), FrPol. 163/M6
Vaiano, It. 89/E6
Vaiano Cremasco, It. 88/C3
Vaich (lake), Sc, UK 59/B1
Vaiden, Ms, US 188/C4
Vaige (riv.), Fr. 83/E5
Vaiges, Fr. 83/E4
Vaihingen an der Enz, Ger. 84/B5
Vaijāpur, India 127/K5
Väike-Maarja, Est. 67/M2
Vail, Az, US 175/G4
Vailate, It. 88/C3
Vailsburg (nbrhd.), NJ, US 195/J9
Vaiņode, Lat. 67/J3
Vair (riv.), Fr. 86/B1
Vairano Patenora, It. 92/D5
Vaire (riv.), Fr. 90/C4
Vaisali (riv.), India 122/B2
Vaison-la-Romaine, Fr. 90/B4
Vaitupu (isl.), Tuv. 162/G5
Vaivre-et-Montoille, Fr. 86/C2
Vakaga (pref.), CAfr. 142/D3
Vakfıkebir, Turk. 96/F4
Vakh (riv.), Rus. 100/J3
Vākhān (mts.), Afg. 127/K1
Vakhrushev, Rus. 105/N2
Vakhrushi, Rus. 95/L4
Vakhsh (riv.), Taj. 127/J1
Vakhtan, Rus. 95/K4
Vál, Hun. 76/D2
Val de Cans (int'l arpt.), Braz. 206/D3
Val Lagarina (valley), It. 89/D1
Val Marie, Sk, Can. 171/L3
Val Venosta (valley), It. 87/G4
Val Verde, Ca, US 192/B2
Val-Brillant, Qu, Can. 184/D1
Val-d'Oise (dept.), Fr. 83/G2
Val-David, Qu, Can. 187/J1
Val-de-Marne (dept.), Fr. 80/B6
Val-de-Reuil, Fr. 83/G2
Val-des-Monts, Qu, Can. 187/J2
Val-d'Isère, Fr. 90/C2
Val-d'Or, Qu, Can. 167/J4
Valais (canton), Swi. 86/D5
Valajärvi (lake), Fin. 65/E4
Valaská Belá, Slvk. 69/K4
Valbo, Swe. 66/G1
Valburg, Neth. 78/C5
Valcheta, Arg. 214/D4
Valcourt, Qu, Can. 187/K2
Valdagno, It. 89/E2
Valdahon, Fr. 86/C3
Valdai (hills), Rus. 94/G4
Valdarno (valley), It. 89/E5
Valday, Rus. 94/G4
Valdecañas (res.), Sp. 72/C3
Valdemarpils, Lat. 67/K3
Valdemarsvik, Swe. 66/G2
Valdemorillo, Sp. 73/M8
Valdense, Uru. 215/K11
Valdepeñas, Sp. 72/D3
Valderas, Sp. 72/C1
Valderrobres, Sp. 73/F2
Valdés (pen.), Arg. 203/C7
Valdeverdeja, Sp. 72/C3
Valdez, Ecu. 204/B4
Valdez, Ak, US 168/Y12
Valdivia, Col. 204/C3
Valdivia, Chile 214/B3
Valdobbiadene, It. 89/F2
Valdoie, Fr. 86/C2
Valdosta, Ga, US 191/G2
Valdoviño, Sp. 72/A1
Vale, Chl, UK 82/C2
Vale, Geo. 97/G4
Vale, Or, US 172/E2
Vale of Conwy (valley), Wal, UK 60/E5
Vale of Evesham (valley), Eng, UK 62/D2
Vale of Pickering (valley), Eng, UK 61/H3
Vale of Powys (valley), Wal, UK 62/C1
Vale of St. Albans (valley), Eng, UK 56/B1
Vale of Sussex (valley), Eng, UK 63/F4
Vale of York (valley), Eng, UK 61/G3
Valea lui Mihai, Rom. 69/M5
Valeggio sul Mincio, It. 89/D3
Valemount, BC, Can. 170/E1
Valença, Port. 72/A1
Valença, Braz. 211/N7
Valença, Braz. 211/F2
Valença do Piauí, Braz. 207/F4
Valence, Fr. 90/A3
Valence, Fr. 70/D4
Valence-sur-Baïse, Fr. 70/D5
Valencia (isl.), Ire. 56/P11
Valencia, Ecu. 204/B5
Valencia (state), Sp. 72/E2
Valencia (int'l arpt.), Sp. 73/E3
Valencia, Sp. 73/E3
Valencia, NM, US 175/J3
Valencia, Phil. 114/D4
Valencia, Phil. 114/D3
Valencia (lake), Ven. 207/N7
Valencia (int'l arpt.), Ven. 207/N7
Valencia, Ven. 207/M7
Valencia de Alcántara, Sp. 72/B3
Valencia de Don Juan, Sp. 72/C1
Valenciennes, Fr. 80/C3
Valendas, Swi. 87/F4
Vălenii de Munte, Rom. 77/H3
Valensole, Fr. 90/B5
Valentigney, Fr. 86/C3
Valentin, Rus. 105/L3
Valentine, Az, US 175/F3
Valentine, Ne, US 180/D2
Valentine, Tx, US 177/B2
Valentine Nat'l Wild. Ref., Ne, US 180/D2
Valentines, Uru. 215/G2
Valentines, Va, US 189/J2
Valenton, Fr. 56/K5
Valenza, It. 88/B3
Valenzuela, Phil. 114/E6
Våler, Nor. 66/D2
Våler, Nor. 66/D1
Valera, Ven. 204/D2
Valfabbrica, It. 91/B1
Valff, Fr. 86/D1
Valga, Est. 67/M3
Valhalla, NY, US 195/K7
Valier (peak), Fr. 73/F1
Valier, Il, US 188/C1
Valier, Mt, US 171/H3
Valinco (gulf), Fr. 74/A2
Valinhos, Braz. 211/J7
Valjevo, Yugo. 76/D3
Valka, Lat. 67/M3
Valkeakoski, Fin. 67/K1
Valkeala, Fin. 67/M1
Valkenburg, Neth. 81/E2
Valkenswaard, Neth. 78/C6
Valkininkai, Lith. 67/L4
Valky, Ukr. 99/H3
Vall de Uxó, Sp. 73/E3
Valladolid, Mex. 200/D1
Valladolid, Sp. 72/C2
Valladolid (int'l arpt.), Sp. 72/C2
Vallangoujard, Fr. 56/J4
Vallauris, Fr. 90/D5
Valle, Nor. 66/B2
Valle, Ecu. 204/B5
Valle d Aosta (pol.reg.), It. 71/G4
Valle D'Aosta (pol. reg.), It. 90/D1
Valle d'Aosta (valley), It. 90/D1
Valle de Bravo, Mex. 199/E5
Valle de Cauca (dept.), Col. 204/B4
Valle de Encantado, PN, Chile 212/B4
Valle de Guanape, Ven. 205/E2
Valle de La Pascua, Ven. 207/P8
Valle de Santiago, Mex. 199/E4
Valle Fértil (valley), Arg. 212/C4
Valle Hermoso, Mex. 199/F3
Valle Lomellina, It. 88/B3
Valle, Río del (riv.), Arg. 212/C4
Valle Mosso, It. 88/B2
Vallecas (nbrhd.), Sp. 73/N9
Vallecillo, Mex. 177/E4
Vallecitos, NM, US 175/J2
Vallecitos de Zaragoza, Mex. 199/E5
Vallecorsa, It. 92/C5
Vallecrosia, It. 90/D5
Valledupar, Col. 204/C2
Valleé de l'Azaouak (riv.), Mali 141/G2
Vallée du Ferlo (riv.), Sen. 140/B3
Valleé du Mboune (riv.), Sen. 140/B3
Valleé du Saloum (riv.), Sen. 140/B3
Valleé du Serpent (riv.), Mali 140/C3
Vallée-Jonction, Qu, Can. 184/B2
Vallegrande, Bol. 212/C1
Vallehermoso, Sp. 136/A3
Vallejo, Ca, US 172/B4
Vallenar, Chile 212/B4
Vallendar, Ger. 81/G3
Vallentuna, Swe. 65/B1
Vallerano, It. 91/B3
Valleroy, Fr. 81/E5

307
Villa – Walt

Villa Jaragua, DRep. 201/J2
Villa Juárez, Mex. 198/C3
Villa Juárez, Mex. 198/D3
Villa La Angostura, Arg. 214/C4
Villa Lázaro Cárdenas, Mex. 199/M6
Villa Literno, It. 92/D6
Villa López, Mex. 198/D3
Villa Mantero, Arg. 215/J10
Villa María, Arg. 212/D5
Villa María Grande, Arg. 212/E4
Villa Martín, Bol. 212/C2
Villa Mazán, Arg. 212/C4
Villa Minetti, Arg. 212/D4
Villa Minozzo, It. 88/D5
Villa Montes, Bol. 212/D2
Villa Nueva, Nic. 200/E3
Villa Nueva, Guat. 200/D3
Villa Nueva, Arg. 214/C2
Villa Ocampo, Arg. 212/E4
Villa Ojo de Agua, Arg. 212/D4
Villa Opicina, It. 89/G2
Villa Oropeza, Bol. 212/C1
Villa Park, Ca, US 192/G8
Villa Park, Il, US 193/Q16
Villa Regina, Arg. 214/D3
Villa Rica, Ga, US 188/E4
Villa Rica, Peru 208/C3
Villa Rosario, Col. 204/C3
Villa San José, Arg. 212/E5
Villa Sandino, Nic. 201/E3
Villa Santa Maria, It. 92/D4
Villa Sarmiento, Arg. 214/D2
Villa Serrano, Bol. 212/C1
Villa Talavera, Bol. 212/C1
Villa Tunari, Bol. 212/C1
Villa Unión, Mex. 177/D3
Villa Unión, Mex. 200/C2
Villa Unión, Arg. 212/B4
Villa Unión, Mex. 198/D4
Villa Valeria, Arg. 214/D2
Villa Verucchio, It. 89/F6
Villa Viscarra, Bol. 212/C1
Villaba, Sp. 70/C5
Villaba, Phil. 114/D3
Villablino, Sp. 72/B1
Villacañas, Sp. 72/D3
Villacarrillo, Sp. 72/D3
Villada, Sp. 72/C1
Villadiego, Sp. 72/C1
Villadose, It. 89/E3
Villadossola, It. 87/E5
Villafamés, Sp. 73/E2
Villafranca, Sp. 72/E1
Villafranca d'Asti, It. 88/B4
Villafranca de los Barros, Sp. 72/B3
Villafranca del Bierzo, Sp. 72/B1
Villafranca del Cid, Sp. 73/E2
Villafranca di Verona, It. 89/D3
Villafranca in Lunigiana, It. 88/C5
Villafranca Piemonte, It. 90/D3
Villagarcía, Sp. 72/A1
Village, Ar, US 179/H4
Village (cr.), Tx, US 176/K7
Village (cr.), Ar, US 188/B2
Village Mills, Tx, US 177/G2
Villagrán, Mex. 199/F3
Villaguay, Arg. 212/E4
Villahermosa, Mex. 200/C2
Villahermosa, Sp. 72/D3
Villahermosa, Col. 207/K8
Villaines-la-Juhel, Fr. 83/E4
Villajoyosa, Sp. 73/E3
Villalba, Sp. 72/B1
Villalcampo (res.), Sp. 72/B2
Villaldama, Mex. 177/D4
Villalón de Campos, Sp. 72/C1
Villalonga, Arg. 214/E3
Villalpando, Sp. 72/C2
Villamartín, Sp. 72/C4
Villandro (peak), It. 87/H4
Villanova, It. 89/F5
Villanova, It. 89/E5
Villanova d'Asti, It. 88/A3
Villanova Mondovì, It. 88/A4
Villanterio, It. 88/C3
Villanueva, Hon. 200/E3
Villanueva, Col. 204/C2
Villanueva, Mex. 198/E4
Villanueva de Arosa, Sp. 72/A1
Villanueva de Córdoba, Sp. 72/C3
Villanueva de la Serena, Sp. 72/C3
Villanueva de los Infantes, Sp. 72/D3
Villanueva de Oscos, Sp. 72/B1
Villanueva del Arzobispo, Sp. 72/D3
Villanuova sul Clisi, It. 88/D2
Villány, Hun. 76/D3
Villar, Bol. 212/C1
Villar del Arzobispo, Sp. 73/E3
Villar Perosa, It. 90/D3
Villar-Saint-Pancrace, Fr. 90/C3
Villarcayo, Sp. 70/B5
Villard, Mn, US 183/G5
Villard-Bonnot, Fr. 90/B2
Villard-de-Lans, Fr. 90/B2
Villardevós, Sp. 72/B2
Villaret (cape), Austl. 154/A4
Villarreal de los Infantes, Sp. 73/E3
Villarrica (lake), Chile 214/B3
Villarrica, Chile 214/B3
Villarrica (vol.), Chile 214/C3
Villarrica, Par. 213/E3
Villarrica, PN, Chile 214/C3
Villarrobledo, Sp. 72/D3
Villarrubia de los Ojos, Sp. 72/D3
Villars-les-Dombes, Fr. 86/B6
Villars-sur-Glâne, Swi. 86/D4
Villars-sur-Var, Fr. 90/D5
Villas, NJ, US 194/D5
Villasana de Mena, Sp. 70/B5
Villasanta, It. 88/C2
Villastellone, It. 88/A3
Villaverde (nbrhd.), Sp. 73/N9
Villaverde del Río, Sp. 72/C4
Villaverla, It. 89/E2
Villavicencio, Col. 204/C3
Villaviciosa, Sp. 72/C1
Villaviciosa de Odón, Sp. 73/N9
Villazón, Bol. 212/C2
Ville Platte, La, US 190/B2
Villebarou, Fr. 83/G5
Villecresnes, Fr. 56/K5
Villedieu-les-Poêles, Fr. 82/D3
Villefermoy (pond), Fr. 56/L6
Villefontaine, Fr. 90/B1
Villefranche-de-Rouergue, Fr. 70/E4
Villefranche-sur-Cher, Fr. 83/G6
Villefranche-sur-Mer, Fr. 90/D5
Villejuif, Fr. 56/K5
Villelaure, Fr. 90/B5
Villemur-sur-Tarn, Fr. 70/D5
Villena, Sp. 73/E3
Villeneuve, Swi. 86/C5
Villeneuve-D'Ascq, Fr. 80/C2
Villeneuve-le-Comte, Fr. 56/L5
Villeneuve-le-Roi, Fr. 56/K5
Villeneuve-lès-Avignon, Fr. 90/A5
Villeneuve-Loubet, Fr. 90/D5
Villeneuve-Saint-Denis, Fr. 56/L5
Villeneuve-Saint-Georges, Fr. 56/K5
Villeneuve-Saint-Germain, Fr. 80/C5
Villeneuve-sur-Lot, Fr. 70/D4
Villeneuve-sur-Yonne, Fr. 70/E2
Villeneuve-Tolosane, Fr. 70/D5
Villennes-sur-Seine, Fr. 56/H5
Villeparisis, Fr. 56/K5
Villepinte, Fr. 56/K5
Villepreux, Fr. 56/J5
Villeroy, Fr. 56/L4
Villers-Bocage, Fr. 83/E2
Villers-Bretonneux, Fr. 80/B4
Villers-Cotterêts, Fr. 80/C5
Villers-en-Arthies, Fr. 56/H4
Villers-le-Bouillet, Belg. 81/E2
Villers-le-Lac, Fr. 86/C3
Villers-lès-Nancy, Fr. 81/F6
Villers-Saint-Genest, Fr. 56/L4
Villers-Saint-Paul, Fr. 80/B5
Villers-Semeuse, Fr. 81/D4
Villers-sur-Mer, Fr. 83/E2
Villersexel, Fr. 86/C2
Villerupt, Fr. 81/E5
Villeta, Col. 207/L7
Villette, Fr. 56/H5
Villeurbanne, Fr. 86/A6
Villevaudé, Fr. 56/K5
Villiers, SAfr. 150/E2
Villiers-en-Lieu, Fr. 81/D6
Villiers-le-Bel, Fr. 56/K4
Villiers-Saint-Georges, Fr. 80/C6
Villiers-sur-Marne, Fr. 56/K5
Villiers-sur-Morin, Fr. 56/L5
Villiersdorp, SAfr. 150/L10
Villieu-Loyes-Mollon, Fr. 86/B6
Villingen-Schwenningen, Ger. 87/E1
Villisca, Ia, US 181/G3
Villmar, Ger. 84/B2
Villongo, It. 88/C2
Villorba, It. 89/F2
Villupuram, India 121/C4
Vilnius (int'l arpt.), Lith. 67/L4
Vilnius (cap.), Lith. 67/L4
Vilonia, Ar, US 179/H3
Vils, Aus. 87/G2
Vils (riv.), Ger. 68/F4
Vilsbiburg, Ger. 85/F6
Vilseck, Ger. 85/E3
Vil'shanka, Ukr. 98/F3
Vilshofen, Ger. 85/G5
Vilters, Swi. 87/F3
Vilvoorde, Belg. 81/D2
Vilyuy (riv.), Rus. 103/L3
Vilyuy (range), Rus. 101/M3
Vilyuysk, Rus. 101/N3
Vimercate, It. 88/C2
Vimeu (reg.), Fr. 80/A3
Vimioso, Port. 72/B2
Vimmerby, Swe. 66/F3
Vimodrone, It. 88/C3
Vimoutiers, Fr. 83/F3
Vimperk, Czh. 85/G4
Vina (riv.), Camr. 142/B4
Viña del Mar, Chile 214/N8
Vinadio, It. 90/D4
Vinaigre (peak), Fr. 90/C6
Vinanivao, Madg. 152/J6
Vinaroz, Sp. 73/F2
Vinay, Fr. 90/B2
Vincennes (lake), Fr. 56/L5
Vincennes, Fr. 56/K5
Vincennes (bay), Ant. 216/H
Vincennes, In, US 188/D1
Vincent, Ca, US 192/B1
Vincent, Al, US 188/D4
Vincent, Tx, US 177/D1
Vincentown, NJ, US 194/D4
Vinces, Ecu. 204/B5
Vincey, Fr. 86/C1
Vinchiaturo, It. 92/D5
Vinchina, Arg. 212/B4
Vinchina (riv.), Arg. 212/B4
Vinchos, Peru 208/C4
Vinci, It. 89/D6
Vindeby, Den. 66/D4
Vindeln, Swe. 64/F2
Vindhya (range), India 122/A4
Vine Grove, Ky, US 188/E2
Vineland, Mn, US 183/H4
Vineland, On, Can. 186/U9
Vineland, NJ, US 194/C5
Vineland Station, On, Can. 186/U9
Vineta, Namb. 148/B4
Vineuil, Fr. 83/G5
Vingåker, Swe. 66/F2
Vingerklip, Namb. 148/B4
Vinh, Viet. 120/D2
Vinh Long, Viet. 120/D4
Vinh Quoi, Viet. 120/D4
Vinh Thanh, Viet 120/E3
Vinh Yen, Viet. 120/D1
Vinhais, Port. 72/B2
Vinhedo, Braz. 211/K8
Vinica, FYROM 75/H2
Vinings, Ga, US 189/M7
Vinita, Ok, US 179/G2
Vînju Mare, Rom. 76/F3
Vinkeveen, Neth. 78/B4
Vinkovci, Cro. 76/D3
Vinningen, Ger. 81/G5
Vinnyts'ka (prov.), Ukr. 96/D2
Vinnyts'ka (prov.), Bul. 77/J1
Vinnytsya, Ukr. 98/E3
Vinon-sur-Verdon, Fr. 90/B5
Vinovo, It. 90/D3
Vinslöv, Swe. 65/K6
Vinson Massif (peak), Ant. 216/U
Vinsulla, BC, Can. 170/D2
Vintar, Phil. 114/C1
Vinton, Ia, US 181/H2
Viny, Rus. 67/Q2
Viola, Ar, US 179/J2
Viola, NY, US 195/J7
Viola, Il, US 181/J3
Viola, De, US 194/C5
Violet Grove, Ab, Can. 170/G1
Violet Town, Austl. 159/B3
Violet Valley Abor. Land, Austl. 154/B4
Viosne (riv.), Fr. 80/A5
Viotá, Col. 207/L8
Vipiteno (Sterzing), It. 87/H4
Virac, Phil. 114/D2
Viracopos (int'l arpt.), Braz. 213/H2
Viranşehir, Turk. 128/D2
Virār, India 121/B2
Virbalis, Lith. 67/K4
Virden, Mb, Can. 182/D3
Virden, NM, US 175/H4
Virden, Il, US 181/K4
Vire, Fr. 83/E3
Vire (riv.), Fr. 70/C2
Virei, Ang. 148/B2
Viren (lake), Swe. 66/F2
Vireux-Wallerand, Fr. 81/D3
Virgelle, Mt, US 171/J3
Virgil, On, Can. 186/U9
Virgin (isls.), UK,US 165/L8
Virgin (riv.), Az, Ut, US 175/F2
Virgin Gorda (isl.), UK 197/M8
Virgin Gourda (int'l arpt.), UK 197/M8
Virgin Islands NP, USVI 197/M8
Virginia, Mn, US 183/H4
Virginia, Ire. 58/C2
Virginia (state), US 169/L4
Virginia, Il, US 181/J4
Virginia, SAfr. 150/D3
Virginia Beach, Va, US 189/K2
Virginia City, Nv, US 172/D4
Virginia City, Mt, US 173/H1
Virginia Dale, Co, US 180/B3
Virginia Water, Eng, UK 56/B2
Virgolândia, Braz. 211/E3
Viriat, Fr. 86/B5
Virieu-le-Grand, Fr. 86/B6
Virkkala, Fin. 65/E4
Virochey, Camb. 120/D3
Viroflay, Fr. 56/J5
Viroin (riv.), Belg. 81/D3
Viroqua, Wi, US 181/J2
Virovitica, Cro. 76/C3
Virserum, Swe. 66/F3
Virton, Belg. 81/E4
Virtsu, Est. 67/K2
Virú, Peru 208/B3
Viru Viru (int'l arpt.), Bol. 212/D1
Viru-Jaagupi, Est. 67/M2
Virudunagar, India 121/C4
Virunga, D.R. Congo 147/G3
Virunga, PN des, D.R. Congo 147/G3
Viry-Châtillon, Fr. 56/K6
Vis (isl.), Cro. 93/H2
Vis, Cro. 76/C4
Visaginas, Lith. 67/M4
Visalia, Ca, US 174/C2
Visan, Fr. 90/A4
Visandre (riv.), Fr. 56/M5
Visayan (sea), Phil. 117/F1
Visbek, Ger. 79/F3
Visby, Swe. 66/H3
Visciano, It. 92/D6
Visconde do Rio Branco, Braz. 211/E4
Viscount Melville (sound), NW,Nun, Can. 167/R7
Visé, Belg. 81/E2
Višegrad, Bosn. 76/D4
Viseu, Port. 72/B2
Viseu (dist.), Port. 72/B2
Viseu, Braz. 207/E3
Vişeu de Sus, Rom. 98/C4
Vishera (riv.), Rus. 95/L3
Vishnëvoye, Ukr. 98/F2
Vishoek, SAfr. 150/L11
Visinesti, Mol. 98/E4
Viskafors, Swe. 66/E3
Vislanda, Swe. 66/F3
Visnagar, India 127/K4
Višnjevac, Cro. 76/D3
Viso (peak), It. 90/D3
Visoko, Bosn. 76/D4
Visp, Swi. 86/D5
Visperterminen, Swi. 86/D5
Visselhövede, Ger. 79/G3
Vissenbjerg, Den. 66/D4
Vissoie, Swi. 86/D5
Vista, Ca, US 192/C4
Vistonís (lake), Gre. 75/J2
Vistula (riv.), Pol. 55/H3
Visviri, Chile 208/D5
Vit (riv.), Bul. 75/J1
Vita, Mb, Can. 182/F3
Viterbo (prov.), It. 91/B3
Viterbo, It. 91/B3
Vitez, Bosn. 76/C3
Viti Levu (isl.), Fiji 162/G6
Vitiaz (str.), PNG 155/G1
Vitichi, Bol. 212/C2
Vitigudino, Sp. 72/B2
Vitim (plat.), Rus. 101/M4
Vitim (riv.), Rus. 103/L4
Vitim, Rus. 101/M4
Vitimskiy, Rus. 101/M4
Vitinia, It. 91/B4
Vítkuv Kamen (peak), Czh. 85/H5
Vitomirica, Yugo. 76/E4
Vitor, Peru 208/D5
Vitoria, Sp. 70/B5
Vitória, Braz. 211/E4
Vitoría, Braz. 206/C3
Vitória da Conquista, Braz. 211/E2
Vitória de Santo Antão, Braz. 207/H5
Vitória do Mearim, Braz. 207/E3
Vitorino Freire, Braz. 207/E4
Vitosha NP, Bul. 77/F4
Vitré, Fr. 82/D4
Vitrey-sur-Mance, Fr. 86/B2
Vitrolles, Fr. 90/B6
Vitry-en-Artois, Fr. 80/B3
Vitry-le-François, Fr. 81/D6
Vitry-sur-Seine, Fr. 56/K5
Vitshumbi, D.R. Congo 147/G3
Vitsyebsk, Bela. 67/P4
Vitsyebskaya (prov.), Bela. 94/E5
Vittangi, Swe. 64/G2
Vittel, Fr. 86/B1
Vittoria, It. 74/D4
Vittorio Veneto, It. 71/K4
Vitträsk (lake), Fin. 65/E4
Vittsjö, Swe. 65/K6
Vitulano, It. 92/D5
Vitulazio, It. 92/D5
Viu, It. 90/D2
Vivarais (mts.), Fr. 70/F4
Viveiro, Sp. 72/B1
Viverone (lake), It. 88/B2
Viverone, It. 88/B3
Vivian, La, US 179/H4
Viviers, Fr. 90/A4
Vivonne, Fr. 70/D3
Vizcachilla, Bol. 212/C2
Vizcaya Museum, Fl, US 190/P11
Vize, Turk. 77/H5
Vizhas (riv.), Rus. 95/K2
Vizhas, Rus. 95/K2
Vizianagaram, India 121/D2
Vizille, Fr. 90/B2
Vizinga, Rus. 95/L3
Viziru, Rom. 77/H3
Vlaardingen, Neth. 78/B5
Vlădeasa (peak), Rom. 77/F2
Vladikavkaz, Rus. 97/H4
Vladimir (oblast), Rus. 94/J5
Vladimir, Rus. 94/J4
Vladivostok, Rus. 105/L3
Vlagtwedde, Neth. 79/E2
Vlăhiţa, Rom. 77/G2
Vlajna (peak), Yugo. 76/E4
Vlasenica, Bosn. 76/D3
Vlasotince, Yugo. 76/F4
Vleuten, Neth. 78/C4
Vlieland (isl.), Neth. 68/C2
Vliestroom (chan.), Neth. 78/C2
Vlijmen, Neth. 78/C5
Vlissingen, Neth. 78/A6
Vlorë, Alb. 75/F2
Vlotho, Ger. 79/F4
Vltava (riv.), Czh. 69/H4
Vnukovo (int'l arpt.), Rus. 94/W9
Vobarno, It. 88/D2
Voca, Tx, US 177/E2
Vöcklabruck, Aus. 85/G6
Vöcklamarkt, Aus. 85/G6
Vodice, Cro. 71/L4
Vodlozero (lake), Rus. 94/H3
Vodňany, Czh. 85/H4
Vodskov, Den. 66/D3
Voerde, Ger. 78/D5
Vogan, Togo 141/F5
Vogar, Mb, Can. 182/E2
Vogelsberg (mts.), Ger. 71/H1
Voghera, It. 88/C4
Vogogna, It. 87/E6
Vogorno (lake), Swi. 87/E5
Vogtareuth, Ger. 85/F7
Vogtland (reg.), Ger. 68/F3
Voh, NCal. 163/U12
Vohburg an der Donau, Ger. 85/E5
Vohenstrauss, Ger. 85/F3
Vohilava, Madg. 152/J8
Vohilava, Madg. 152/H8
Vohimena (cape), Madg. 152/H9
Vohimena, Madg. 152/J7
Vohipeno, Madg. 152/H8
Vohiposa, Madg. 152/H8
Vohitrambo, Madg. 152/H8
Võhma, Est. 67/L2
Voi, Kenya 145/B2
Void-Vacon, Fr. 81/E6
Voight (cr.), Wa, US 193/C3
Voil (lake), Sc, UK 59/B4
Voinjama, Libr. 140/C4
Voinsles, Fr. 56/M5
Voiron, Fr. 90/B2
Voise (riv.), Fr. 70/D2
Voisey (bay), Nf, Can. 167/K3
Voiteur, Fr. 86/B4
Vojakkala, Fin. 65/E4
Vojosë (riv.), Alb. 76/D5
Vojvodina (prov.), Yugo. 76/D3
Voka, Congo 146/C4
Vokhma, Rus. 95/K4
Völklingen, Ger. 81/F5
Volano, It. 87/H6
Volary, Czh. 85/G5
Volborg, Mt, US 171/M5
Volcán Barú, PN, Pan. 201/F4
Volcán Poás, PN, CR 201/E4
Volcano (isls.), Japan 162/C2
Volcans, PN des, Rwa. 147/G3
Volchiy Nos (cape), Rus. 67/Q1
Volda, Nor. 64/C3
Volendam, Neth. 78/C3
Volga, SD, US 181/F1
Volga (riv.), Rus. 55/J3
Volga-Baltic Waterway (canal), Rus. 94/H3
Volgelsheim, Fr. 86/D1
Volgodonsk, Rus. 99/M4
Volgograd (res.), Rus. 97/H2
Volgograd, Rus. 97/H2
Volgograd (int'l arpt.), Rus. 97/H2
Volgograd Oblast, Rus. 97/G2
Volimbos, Gre. 93/K4
Volkach, Ger. 84/D3
Volkach (riv.), Ger. 84/D3
Volkeradam (dam), Neth. 78/B5
Völkermarkt, Aus. 71/L3
Volketswil, Swi. 87/E3
Volkhov (riv.), Rus. 94/F4
Volkhov, Rus. 67/Q2
Volkmarsen, Ger. 79/G6
Volksrust, SAfr. 151/E2
Vollenhove, Neth. 78/C3
Volnovakha, Ukr. 99/J4
Volochanka, Rus. 100/K2
Volochayevka, Rus. 105/L2
Volochys'k, Ukr. 98/D3
Volodars'ke, Ukr. 99/J4
Volodarsky (nbrhd.), Rus. 94/T7
Volodymyr-Volyns'kyy, Ukr. 98/C2
Vologda, Rus. 94/H4
Vologda (oblast), Rus. 94/J3
Vologne (riv.), Fr. 68/D4
Volokolamsk, Rus. 94/G4
Volokonovka, Rus. 99/J2
Volonne, Fr. 90/C4
Vólos, Gre. 75/H3
Volos (gulf), Gre. 75/H3
Volosovo, Rus. 67/N2
Volot, Rus. 67/P3
Volovets', Ukr. 69/M4
Volovo, Rus. 96/F1
Volozhin, Bela. 67/M4
Volpago del Montello, It. 89/F2
Volpiano, It. 88/A2
Völs, Aus. 87/H3
Vols, Fin. 65/E4
Vol'sk, Rus. 97/H1
Volta (pol. reg.), Gha. 141/F5
Volta (riv.), Gha. 141/F5
Volta (lake), Gha. 133/B4
Volta Mantovana, It. 88/D3
Volta Redonda, Braz. 211/M7
Voltaire (cape), Austl. 154/B3
Voltana, It. 89/E4
Volterra, It. 89/D7
Voltlage, Ger. 79/E4
Voltri, It. 88/B5
Volturara Irpina, It. 92/D6
Volturino (peak), It. 74/D2
Volturno (riv.), It. 74/D2
Volubilis (ruin), Mor. 138/B2
Volvera, It. 90/D3
Vólvi (lake), Gre. 75/H2
Vólvi (lake), Yugo. 77/F5
Volx, Fr. 90/B5
Volyně, Czh. 85/G4
Volyňka (riv.), Czh. 85/G4
Volyno-Podol'sk Upland (upland), Ukr. 98/D3
Volyns'ka (prov.), Ukr. 96/C2
Volzhsk, Rus. 95/L5
Volzhskiy, Rus. 97/H2
Vom, Nga. 141/H4
Vomano (riv.), It. 92/C2
Vombsjön (lake), Swe. 65/K7
Vonda, Sk, Can. 171/L1
Vondrozo, Madg. 152/H8
Vonêche, Belg. 81/D3
Vónitsa, Gre. 75/G3
Vonne (riv.), Fr. 70/D3
Võnnu, Est. 67/M2
Voorburg, Neth. 78/B4
Voorne (isl.), Neth. 78/B5
Voorschoten, Neth. 78/B4
Voorst, Neth. 78/D4
Vopnafjördhur, Ice. 64/P6
Vorab (peak), Swi. 87/F4
Vorarlberg (prov.), Aus. 68/E5
Vorbach (riv.), Ger. 84/C4
Vorchdorf, Aus. 85/G6
Vorden, Neth. 78/D4
Vorderrhein (riv.), Swi. 71/H3
Vorderweissenbach, Aus. 85/H5
Vordingborg, Den. 66/D4
Vorë, Alb. 75/F2
Voreppe, Fr. 90/B2
Vorkuta, Rus. 95/P2
Vorkuta (int'l arpt.), Rus. 95/Q2
Vormsi (isl.), Est. 67/K2
Vóroi, Gre. 75/J5
Vorokhta, Ukr. 98/C3
Vorona (riv.), Rus. 97/G1
Voronezh (riv.), Rus. 96/F1
Voronezh, Rus. 99/K2
Voronezh (int'l arpt.), Rus. 99/K2
Voronezh Oblast, Rus. 97/G2
Voronovo, Bela. 67/L4
Voronovytsya, Ukr. 98/E3
Vorontsovka, Rus. 99/L2
Voron'ya (riv.), Rus. 94/G1
Voropayevo, Bela. 67/M4
Vorozhba, Ukr. 99/H2
Vorskla (riv.), Ukr. 96/E2
Vorst, Belg. 81/E1
Vorstershoop, SAfr. 150/C2
Võrts (lake), Est. 94/E4
Võru, Est. 67/M3
Vorya (riv.), Rus. 94/X8
Vorzel', Ukr. 98/F2
Vosburg, SAfr. 150/C3
Vösendorf, Aus. 77/N7
Vosges (dept.), Fr. 86/C1
Vosges (mts.), Fr. 68/D5
Voskresenka, Rus. 97/H2
Voskresensk, Rus. 94/H5
Voskresenskoye, Rus. 95/K4
Voskresenskoye, Rus. 94/H4
Voss, Nor. 66/B1
Vossburg, Ms, US 190/D2
Vostochnyy, Rus. 105/L3
Vostok (cape), Ant. 216/V
Vostok, Rus., Ant. 216/H
Vostok (isl.), Kiri. 163/K6
Votice, Czh. 85/H3
Votkinsk (res.), Rus. 95/M4
Votkinsk, Rus. 95/M4
Votorantim, Braz. 213/H2
Votuporanga, Braz. 213/G2
Vouga (riv.), Port. 72/A2
Vougba, CAfr. 142/D4
Vouglans (lake), Fr. 86/B5
Voujeaucourt, Fr. 86/C3
Voúla, Gre. 75/N9
Voulangis, Fr. 56/L5
Voutinainen, Fin. 65/E4
Vouvray, Fr. 83/F6
Vouvry, Swi. 86/C5
Voúxa (cape), Gre. 75/H5
Vouziers, Fr. 81/D5
Vouzon, Fr. 83/H5
Vovchans'k, Ukr. 99/J2
Voves, Fr. 83/G4
Vovodo (riv.), CAfr. 142/E4
Voy-Vozh, Rus. 95/M3
Voyageurs NP, Mn, US 183/H3
Voyeykov Ice Shelf, Ant. 216/J
Voytolovka (riv.), Rus. 94/T7
Vozhe (lake), Rus. 94/H3
Vozhega, Rus. 94/J3
Vozherovo, Rus. 95/K4
Voznesens'k, Ukr. 98/F4
Vrå, Den. 66/C3
Vradiyivka, Ukr. 98/F4
Vraine (riv.), Fr. 86/B1
Vramsån (riv.), Swe. 65/K6
Vrancea (prov.), Rom. 77/H3
Vrangelya (isl.), Rus. 103/T2
Vranje, Yugo. 76/E4
Vranjska Banja, Yugo. 76/E4
Vranov nad Teplou, Slvk. 69/L4
Vrapčište, FYROM 75/G2
Vratsa, Bul. 77/F4
Vrbas (riv.), Bosn. 93/H1
Vrbas, Yugo. 76/D3
Vrchy (peak), Czh. 85/H4
Vrede, SAfr. 150/E2
Vredefort, SAfr. 150/D2
Vreden, Ger. 78/D4
Vredenburg-Saldanha, SAfr. 150/K10
Vredendal, SAfr. 150/B3
Vresse-sur-Semois, Belg. 81/D4
Vrhnika, Slov. 71/L4
Vriddhāchalam, India 121/C4
Vries, Neth. 78/D2
Vriezenveen, Neth. 78/D4
Vrigstad, Swe. 66/F3
Vrin (riv.), Fr. 68/B5
Vrindāban, India 122/A2
Vrnjačka Banja, Yugo. 76/E4
Vrondádhos, Gre. 75/K3
Vroomshoop, Neth. 78/D4
Vršac, Yugo. 76/E3
Vryburg, SAfr. 150/D2
Vryheid, SAfr. 151/E2
Vsetín, Czh. 69/K4
Vsevolozhsk, Rus. 94/T6
Vtáčnik (peak), Slvk. 69/K4
Vu Liet, Viet. 120/D2
Vuca, Eth. 142/G4
Vučitrn, Yugo. 76/E4
Vught, Neth. 78/C5
Vukovar, Cro. 76/D3
Vulcan, Ab, Can. 171/H2
Vulcan, Rom. 77/F3
Vulcan, Mo, US 179/J2
Vulcăneşti, Mol. 77/J3
Vulcano (isl.), It. 74/D3
Vŭlchedrŭm, Bul. 77/F4
Vŭlchi Dol, Bul. 77/H4
Vulci (ruin), It. 74/B1
Vung Tau, Viet. 120/D4
Vunisea, Fiji 162/G6
Vuntut NP, Yt., Can. 168/Y12
Vuoggatjålme, Swe. 64/F2
Vuohijärvi (lake), Fin. 67/M1
Vuollerim, Swe. 64/G2
Vuoska (lake), Rus. 67/N1
Vuotso, Fin. 94/E1
Vŭrbitsa, Bul. 77/H4
Vuria (peak), Kenya 145/B2
Vurnary, Rus. 95/K5
Vŭrshets, Bul. 77/F4
Vuruena, Res. Florestal do, Braz. 210/A1
Vuyyūru, India 121/D2
Vvedenka, Kaz. 95/P5
Vwawa, Tanz. 147/H5
Vyāra, India 118/B3
Vyatka (riv.), Rus. 100/E4
Vyatskiye Polyany, Rus. 95/L4
Vyatskoye, Rus. 94/J4
Vyazemskiy, Rus. 105/L2
Vyaz'ma, Rus. 94/G5
Vyazovaya, Rus. 95/N5
Vyborg (nbrhd.), Rus. 94/T7
Vyborg (bay), Rus. 67/N1
Vyborg, Rus. 67/N1
Vychegda (riv.), Rus. 100/F3
Východočeský (pol. reg.), Czh. 69/H3
Vychodoslovensky (pol. reg.), Slvk. 69/L4
Vygozero (lake), Rus. 94/G3
Vyhorlat (peak), Slvk. 69/M4
Vyksa, Rus. 94/J5
Vylkove, Ukr. 77/J3
Vym' (riv.), Rus. 95/L3
Vynnyky, Ukr. 98/C3
Vynohradiv, Ukr. 69/M4
Vypolzovo, Rus. 94/G4
Vyritsa, Rus. 67/P2
Vyrnwy (riv.), Wal, UK 62/C1
Vyselki, Rus. 99/K5
Vyshgorodok, Rus. 67/N3
Vyshhorod, Ukr. 98/F2
Vyshniy Volochek, Rus. 94/G4
Vyshnivets', Ukr. 98/C3
Vyškov, Czh. 69/J4
Vyškovce nad Ipl'om, Slvk. 76/D1
Vysokogornyy, Rus. 105/M1
Vysokopillya, Ukr. 99/G4
Vysokovsk, Rus. 94/H4
Vysokoye, Bela. 69/M2
Vysotsk, Rus. 67/N1
Vyšší Brod, Czh. 85/H5
Vytegra, Rus. 94/H3
Vyyezdnoye, Rus. 95/J5
Vyzhnytsya, Ukr. 98/C3
Vzmor'ye, Rus. 105/N2

W

W du Benin, PN du, Ben. 141/F4
W du Burkino Faso, PN du, Burk. 141/F4
W du Niger, PN du, Niger 141/F3
W.F. George (res.), Al,Ga, US 188/E5
Wa, Gha. 141/E4
Waadi Luud (wadi), Som. 144/D3
Waajid, Som. 144/B5
Waal, Ger. 87/G2
Waal (riv.), Neth. 68/C3
Waal (riv.), Neth. 78/C5
Waalre, Neth. 78/C6
Waalwijk, Neth. 78/C5
Waany-Garawa Aboriginal Land, Austl. 155/E4
Waarschoot, Belg. 80/C1
Waasis, NB, Can. 184/D3
Wabag, PNG 155/F1
Wabamun, Ab, Can. 170/G1
Wabamun (lake), Ab, Can. 170/G1
Wabana, Nf, Can. 185/L2
Wabasca (riv.), Ab, Can. 166/E3
Wabash, In, US 186/D4
Wabash (riv.), Il, In, US 169/J4
Wabasha, Mn, US 181/H1
Wabasso, Mn, US 181/G1
Wabē Gestro Wenz (riv.), Eth. 144/B4
Wabē Shebelē Wenz (riv.), Eth. 133/G4
Wabeno, Wi, US 183/K5
Wabern, Ger. 79/G6
Wabigoon (lake), On, Can. 183/H3
Wabigoon, On, Can. 183/H3
Wąbrzeźno, Pol. 69/K2
Wabu, SKor. 107/G6
Wabu (lake), China 106/D4
Wabuda (isl.), PNG 155/F2
Waccamau (riv.), SC, US 189/H4
Waccasassa (bay), Fl, US 191/G3
Wachenheim an der Weinstrasse, Ger. 84/B4
Wachi, Japan 109/H5
Wach'īlē, Eth. 144/A4
Wachtebeke, Belg. 80/C1
Wachtendonk, Ger. 78/D6
Wächtersbach, Ger. 84/C2
Wackernheim, Ger. 84/B3
Wackersdorf, Ger. 85/F4
Waco, Tx, US 177/F2
Waconda (lake), Ks, US 180/E4
Waconia, Mn, US 183/N7
Waconia (lake), Mn, US 183/N7
Wad al Ḩaddād, Sudan 142/G2
Wad an Nail, Sudan 142/G2
Wad Bandah, Sudan 142/E2
Wad Ḩāmid, Sudan 142/G1
Wad Medanī, Sudan 142/G2
Wada, Japan 109/E3
Wadayama, Japan 109/G5
Waddān, Libya 134/C2
Waddell (dam), Az, US 175/F4
Waddenzee (sound), Neth. 68/C2
Waddington, Eng, UK 61/H5
Waddington, Eng, UK 61/F4
Waddinxveen, Neth. 78/B4
Waddy (pt.), Austl. 160/D4
Wade, Ok, US 179/F4
Wadebridge, Eng, UK 62/B5
Wadena, Sk, Can. 182/C2
Wadena, Mn, US 183/G4
Wädenswil, Swi. 87/E3
Wadern, Ger. 81/F4
Wadersloh, Ger. 79/F5
Wadesboro, NC, US 189/G3
Wadgassen, Ger. 81/F5
Wadhurst, Eng, UK 63/G4
Wādī al Layl, Tun. 138/M6
Wādī an Natrūn, Egypt 139/B4
Wādī As Sīr, Jor. 131/D5
Wādī Az Zarqā', Tun. 138/L6
Wādī Ḩalfā', Sudan 135/F4
Wādī Mūsá, Jor. 130/D4
Wading (riv.), NJ, US 194/D4
Wading River, NY, US 195/F2
Wadley, Ga, US 189/F4
Wadowice, Pol. 69/K4
Wadsworth, Tx, US 177/G3
Wadsworth, Oh, US 186/F4
Wadsworth, Il, US 193/Q15
Waegwan, SKor. 107/E5
Waelder, Tx, US 177/F3
Wafangdian, China 107/A3
Wafangdian, China 113/F1
Wafania, D.R. Congo 146/E3
Waffenrod, Ger. 84/D2
Wāgah, Pak. 124/C4
Wagait Abor. Land, Austl. 154/C3
Wagaru, Myan. 120/B3
Wagat, Ouadi (riv.), Chad 142/D2
Wagener, SC, US 189/G4
Wagenfeld-Hasslingen, Ger. 79/F3
Wageningen, Sur. 206/B1
Wageningen, Neth. 78/C5
Wager (bay), Nun, Can. 166/G2
Wagga Wagga, Austl. 159/C2
Waggrakine, Austl. 156/B4
Waghäusel, Ger. 84/B4
Wagin, Austl. 156/C5
Waging am See, Ger. 85/F7
Waginger (lake), Ger. 85/F7
Wägitaler-see (lake), Swi. 87/E3
Wagna, Aus. 76/B2
Wagner, SD, US 180/E2
Wagoner, Ok, US 179/G3
Wagontire, Or, US 172/D2
Wągrowiec, Pol. 69/J2
Wāh, Pak. 124/B3
Wah Wah (mts.), Ut, US 173/G4
Wahai, Indo. 117/G4
Wāḩāt ad Dākhilah (oasis), Egypt 135/F3
Wāḩāt al Farāfirah (oasis), Libya,Egypt 135/E3
Wahkon, Mn, US 183/H4
Wahlern, Swi. 86/D4
Wahoo, Ne, US 181/F3
Wahpeton, ND, US 182/F4
Wahrenholz, Ger. 79/H3
Wai, India 121/B2
Waialua, Hi, US 168/S9
Waiau (riv.), NZ 161/C3
Waiau, NZ 161/C3
Waibamiao, China 106/D2
Waiblingen, Ger. 84/C5
Waibstadt, Ger. 84/B4
Waidhaus, Ger. 85/F3
Waidhofen an der Thaya, Aus. 71/L2
Waidhofen an der Ybbs, Aus. 85/H7
Waigeo (isl.), Indo. 162/C4
Waigolshausen, Ger. 84/D3
Waigoumen, China 104/H3
Waiheke (isl.), NZ 161/G6
Waihou (riv.), NZ 161/C2
Waika, D.R. Congo 147/F3
Waikabubak, Indo. 117/E5
Waikanae, NZ 161/C3
Waikari, NZ 161/C3
Waikato (riv.), NZ 153/H6
Waikerie, Austl. 157/H5
Waikouaiti, NZ 161/B4
Wailuo, China 113/F4
Waimangaroa, NZ 161/B3
Waimate, NZ 161/B4
Waimes, Belg. 81/F3
Wainfleet, On, Can. 186/U10
Wainfleet All Saints, Eng, UK 61/J5
Waingangā (riv.), India 118/C3
Waingapu, Indo. 117/F5
Waini (riv.), Guy. 205/G2
Wainuiomata, NZ 161/H9
Wainuiomata (riv.), NZ 161/H9
Wainwright, Ok, US 179/G3
Wainwright, Ab, Can. 171/J1
Waiohine (riv.), NZ 161/J8
Waipahu, Hi, US 168/S9
Waipapa (pt.), NZ 161/B4
Waipara, NZ 161/C3
Waipawa, NZ 161/D2
Waipio, Hi, US 168/S9
Waipiro, NZ 161/D2
Waipukurau, NZ 161/D2
Wairarapa (lake), NZ 161/J9
Wairau (riv.), NZ 161/C3
Wairoa (riv.), NZ 161/C1
Wairoa, NZ 161/D2
Waischenfeld, Ger. 85/E3
Waitakere, NZ 161/F6
Waitakere (range), NZ 161/F6
Waitaki (riv.), NZ 161/B4
Waitangi, NZ 161/E3
Waitara, NZ 161/C2
Waitemata (har.), NZ 161/F6
Waitotara, NZ 161/C2
Waitsburg, Wa, US 170/E4
Waiuku, NZ 161/C2
Waiyevu, Fiji 163/Z17
Waizenkirchen, Aus. 85/G6
Wajima, Japan 111/E2
Wajir, Kenya 145/C1
Waka, D.R. Congo 146/E2
Waka, Eth. 142/H4
Waka, D.R. Congo 146/E3
Waka (cape), Indo. 117/G4
Wakakusa, Japan 109/A2
Wakapitu (lake), NZ 161/B4
Wakarusa, In, US 186/C4
Wakasa, Japan 110/D3
Wakasa (bay), Japan 109/H4
Wakaw, Sk, Can. 171/M1
Wakayama, Japan 110/D3
Wakayama (pref.), Japan 110/D4
Wake (isl.), Pac., US 162/F3
Wakeeney, Ks, US 178/E1
Wakefield, Eng, UK 61/G4
Wakefield, Ks, US 181/F4
Wakefield, Mi, US 183/K4
Wakefield, Ne, US 181/F2
Wakefield, Oh, US 189/F1
Wakema, Myan. 112/B5
Waki, Japan 110/D3
Wakita, Ok, US 179/F2
Wakkanai, Japan 108/B1
Wakool, Austl. 159/B2
Wakpala, SD, US 182/D5
Waku Kungo, Ang. 148/B1
Wakulla, Fl, US 191/F2
Wakuya, Japan 108/B4
Wal (peak), Camr. 142/B4
Wal Athiang, Sudan 142/F4
Wala (riv.), Tanz. 145/A3
Walachia (reg.), Rom. 93/K1
Walagan, China 105/J1
Walagunya Abor. Land, Austl. 156/D2
Walamba, Zam. 149/F2
Walan, Austl. 159/B3
Wałbrzych, Pol. 69/J3
Wałbrzych (prov.), Pol. 69/J3
Walbury (hill), Eng, UK 63/E4
Walcha, Austl. 158/D1
Walcheren (isl.), Neth. 78/A5
Walcott, ND, US 182/F4
Walcott (lake), Id, US 173/G2
Walcott, Wy, US 173/K3
Walcourt, Belg. 81/D3
Wałcz, Pol. 69/J2
Wald, Swi. 87/E3
Wald, Ger. 85/F4
Waldbillig, Lux. 81/F4
Waldbreitbach, Ger. 81/G2
Waldbröl, Ger. 81/G2
Waldbronn, Ger. 84/B5
Waldbrunn, Ger. 84/C3
Waldburg, Ger. 87/F2
Waldeck, Sk, Can. 171/L2
Walden, On, Can. 186/F1
Waldenbuch, Ger. 84/C5
Waldenburg, Swi. 86/D3
Waldenburg, Ger. 84/C4
Waldershof, Ger. 85/F3
Walderslade, Eng, UK 56/E3
Waldesch, Ger. 81/G3
Waldfischbach-Burgalben, Ger. 81/G5
Waldheim, Sk, Can. 171/L1
Waldighofen, Fr. 86/D2
Walding, Aus. 85/H6
Waldkappel, Ger. 79/G6
Waldkirch, Ger. 86/D1
Waldkraiburg, Ger. 85/F6
Waldmohr, Ger. 81/G5
Waldmünchen, Ger. 85/F4
Waldnaab (riv.), Ger. 85/F3
Waldo, Ar, US 179/H4
Waldo, Fl, US 191/G3
Waldo (lake), Or, US 172/B2
Waldorf, Md, US 189/J1
Waldport, Or, US 172/A1
Waldrach, Ger. 81/F4
Waldron, Ar, US 179/G3
Waldron, In, US 186/D5
Waldsassen, Ger. 85/F3
Waldshut-Tiengen, Ger. 87/E2
Waldstetten, Ger. 84/C5
Waldviertel (reg.), Aus. 69/H4
Waldwick, NJ, US 195/J8
Walea (str.), Indo. 117/F4
Waleabahi (isl.), Indo. 117/F4
Walensee (lake), Swi. 87/F3
Walenstadt, Swi. 87/F3
Wales (isl.), Nun, Can. 167/H2
Wales, UK 62/B3
Wales, Ut, US 173/H4
Wales, Wi, US 193/P14
Walewale, Gha. 141/E4
Walferdange, Lux. 81/F4
Walgett, Austl. 158/D1
Walhalla, Ger. 85/F4
Walhalla, ND, US 182/F3
Walhalla, Mi, US 186/C3
Walhalla, SC, US 189/F3
Walhalla Historical Site, ND, US 182/F3
Walikale, D.R. Congo 147/G3
Walker (bay), SAfr. 150/L11
Walker, Mn, US 183/G4
Walker, Mo, US 179/G2
Walker, Mi, US 186/D3
Walker (lake), Nv, US 172/D4
Walker (riv.), Nv, US 172/D4
Walker Art Center, Mn, US 183/P7
Walker River Ind. Res., Nv, US 172/D4
Walker, West (riv.), Ca, Nv, US 172/D4
Walkerburn, Sc, UK 59/C5
Walkers Ferry, Malw. 149/G2
Walkerston, Austl. 160/C3
Walkersville, Md, US 187/H5
Walkerton, On, Can. 186/F2
Walkerton, In, US 186/C4
Walkertown, NC, US 189/G2
Walkill (riv.), NY, US 194/D1
Wall, SD, US 180/C2
Wall, Tx, US 177/D2
Wall Of Ghenghis Khan (wall), Mong. 104/G2
Walla Walla, Wa, US 170/E4
Walla Walla, Austl. 159/C2
Wallace, Ca, US 172/C4
Wallace, Id, US 170/G4
Wallace, Ks, US 178/D1
Wallace, Ne, US 180/D3
Wallace, NS, Can. 184/F3
Wallace Lake, Mb, Can. 183/G2
Wallaceburg, On, Can. 186/E3
Wallacia, Austl. 159/E1
Wallaga Lake NP, Austl. 159/E3
Wallal Downs, Austl. 156/D1
Wallaroo, Austl. 157/H5
Wallasey, Eng, UK 61/E5
Wallblake (int'l arpt.), UK 197/N8
Walldorf, Ger. 84/B4
Walldorf, Ger. 84/D1
Walldürn, Ger. 84/C3
Walled (lake), Mi, US 193/F6
Walled City Hist. Site, SKor. 107/G7
Walled Lake, Mi, US 193/F6
Wallendbeen, Austl. 159/D2
Wallenhorst, Ger. 79/F4
Wallenpaupack (lake), Pa, US 187/J4
Waller, Tx, US 177/G2
Wallerawang, Austl. 159/E1
Wallern im Burgenland, Aus. 76/C2
Wallers, Fr. 80/C3
Wallersdorf, Ger. 85/F5
Wallersee (lake), Aus. 85/G7
Wallerstein, Ger. 84/D5
Wallingford, Ct, US 187/K4
Wallingford, Eng, UK 63/E3
Wallington, NJ, US 195/J8
Wallis (isls.), Wall. 163/H6
Wallis and Futuna (dpcy.), Fr. 162/G6
Wallisellen, Swi. 87/E3
Wallisville, Tx, US 177/N9
Walloon Brabant (prov.), Belg. 81/D2
Wallowa (mts.), Or, US 172/E1
Wallowa (riv.), Or, US 172/E1
Walls, Sc, UK 57/W13
Wallsend, Eng, UK 61/G2
Wallula, Wa, US 170/E4
Wallumbilla, Austl. 160/C4
Walney, Isle of (isl.), Eng, UK 61/E3
Walnut (riv.), Ks, US 179/F2
Walnut, Ca, US 192/G7
Walnut (cr.), Ga, US 189/M8
Walnut, Il, US 181/K3
Walnut (cr.), Ks, US 181/E4
Walnut, Ms, US 188/C3
Walnut Canyon Nat'l Mon., Az, US 175/G3
Walnut Creek, Ca, US 193/K11
Walnut Grove, Al, US 188/D3
Walnut Grove, Ca, US 193/L10
Walnut Grove, Ga, US 188/F4
Walnut Grove, Mo, US 179/H2
Walnut Grove, Ms, US 188/C4
Walnut Park, Ca, US 192/F8
Walnut Ridge, Ar, US 188/B2
Walnut Springs, Tx, US 176/F1
Walnutport, Pa, US 194/C2
Walpole, NH, US 187/K3
Walpole, Austl. 156/C5
Walpole Island Ind. Res., On, Can. 186/E3
Walpole-Nornalup NP, Austl. 156/C5
Walsall, Eng, UK 62/E1
Walsenburg, Co, US 178/B2
Walsh, Co, US 178/C2
Walsh, Austl. 160/A2
Walsingham (cape), Nun, Can. 167/K2
Walsingham, Eng, UK 63/G1
Walsrode, Ger. 79/G3
Walt Disney World, Fl, US 191/H3
Waltenhofen, Ger. 87/G2
Walter F. George (res.), Ga, US 191/F2
Walterboro, SC, US 189/G4
Walters, Ok, US 179/E3
Walters, La, US 190/C2
Walter's Ash, Eng, UK 56/A2
Walterville, Or, US 172/B1
Walthall, Ms, US 188/C4

Waltham Abbey, Eng, UK 56/D1
Waltham Forest (bor.), Eng, UK 56/A1
Waltham Saint Lawrence, Eng, UK 56/A2
Walthill, Ne, US 181/F2
Walthourville, Ga, US 191/H2
Waltman, Wy, US 173/K2
Walton, In, US 186/C4
Walton, Ky, US 188/E1
Walton, NY, US 187/J3
Walton, WV, US 189/G1
Walton-le-Dale, Eng, UK 61/F4
Walton-on-Thames, Eng, UK 56/B2
Walton-on-the-Naze, Eng, UK 63/H3
Waltrop, Ger. 79/E5
Walungchung Gola, Nepal 123/F2
Walvis Bay, Namb. 148/B4
Walworth, Wi, US 193/N14
Walworth (co.), Wi, US 193/N14
Walyahmoning (peak), Austl. 156/C4
Walyunga NP, Austl. 156/L6
Walzenhausen, Swi. 87/F3
Wama, Ang. 148/B2
Wamac, Il, US 188/C1
Wamaza, D.R. Congo 147/F4
Wamba, Nga. 141/H4
Wamba, D.R. Congo 147/F2
Wamba, Kenya 145/B1
Wamberal, Austl. 159/E1
Wamego, Ks, US 181/F4
Wamel, Neth. 78/C5
Wamena, Indo. 117/J4
Wami (riv.), Tanz. 145/B3
Wamic, Or, US 172/C1
Wampool (riv.), Eng, UK 61/E2
Wampsville, NY, US 187/J3
Wamsutter, Wy, US 173/K3
Wān Hsa-la, Myan. 120/B1
Wān Hwè-ün, Myan. 112/C5
Wanaaring, Austl. 158/C1
Wanaka, NZ 161/B4
Wanaka (lake), NZ 161/B4
Wanamassa, NJ, US 194/D3
Wanamingo, Mn, US 181/H1
Wanapum (dam), Wa, US 170/E4
Wanaque, NJ, US 195/H7
Wanaque (res.), NJ, US 194/D1
Wanblee, SD, US 180/D2
Wanci, Indo. 154/A1
Wanda (mts.), China 105/L2
Wandering, Austl. 156/C5
Wandi, Ugan. 147/G2
Wanding, China 112/C3
Wandlitz, Ger. 68/Q6
Wando, SKor. 107/D5
Wandoan, Austl. 160/C4
Wandong, Austl. 159/B3
Wandsbek, Ger. 79/H1
Wandsworth (bor.), Eng, UK 56/C2
Wanette, Ok, US 179/F3
Wanfried, Ger. 79/H6
Wanfu, China 107/B2
Wang (riv.), Thai. 119/G4
Wang Hip (peak), Thai. 120/B4
Wang Noi, Thai. 120/C3
Wang Saphung, Thai. 120/C2
Wanganella, Austl. 159/B2
Wanganui, NZ 161/C2
Wangaratta, Austl. 159/C3
Wangasi Turu, Gha. 141/E4
Wangcun, China 113/F2
Wangdu, China 106/C3
Wangdü Phodrang, Bhu. 123/G2
Wangen, Ger. 87/F2
Wangen an der Aare, Swi. 86/D3
Wangen bei Olten, Swi. 86/D3
Wangerooge (isl.), Ger. 79/E1
Wangerooge (arpt.), Ger. 79/E1
Wanggamet (peak), Indo. 117/F6
Wanggao, China 113/F3
Wanghai Shan (peak), China 107/A2
Wängi, Swi. 87/E3
Wangiwangi (isl.), Indo. 154/A1
Wangjiang, China 113/H2
Wangjiapu, China 107/B2
Wangkui, China 105/K2
Wangling, China 113/G3
Wangmao, China 113/F4
Wangmo Bouyeizu Miaozu Zizhixian, China 112/E3
Wangolodougou, C.d'Iv. 140/D4
Wangou, China 107/D1
Wangpan (bay), China 106/E5
Wangpang (sea), China 113/J2
Wangqing, China 105/K3
Wangqingmen, China 107/C2
Wangtan, China 113/J2
Wangting, China 106/L8
Wani (peak), Indo. 117/F4
Wanica (dist.), Sur. 205/H3
Wanie-Rukula, D.R. Congo 147/F2
Wanilla, Austl. 157/G5
Wanipitie (lake), On, Can. 186/F1
Wanjiabu, China 113/G2
Wanjialing, China 107/B3
Wank (peak), Ger. 87/H2
Wankie (Hwange) NP, Zim. 149/E3
Wanle Weyne, Som. 145/D1
Wann, Ok, US 179/G2
Wannaska, Mn, US 183/G3
Wanni̇n (spr.), Libya 134/B2
Wanning, China 119/K4
Wanouchi, Japan 109/L5
Wanquan (lake), China 125/D5
Wanquan, China 106/C2
Wanquan (riv.), China 113/F5
Wanrong, China 106/B4
Wansbeck (riv.), Eng, UK 61/G1
Wanshengchang, China 113/E2
Wansra, Indo. 117/H4
Wanstead (nbrhd.), Eng, UK 56/D2
Wantage, Eng, UK 63/E3
Wantagh, NY, US 195/M9
Wantan, China 113/F2
Wanwei, China 120/E1
Wanxian, China 113/F2
Wanze, Belg. 81/E2
Wao, Phil. 114/D4
Wapakoneta, Oh, US 186/D4
Wapanocca NWR, Ar, US 188/B3
Wapanucka, Ok, US 179/F3
Wapato, Wa, US 170/D4
Wapella, Sk, Can. 182/D2
Wapello, Ia, US 181/J3
Wapenamanda, PNG 155/F1
Wapinda, D.R. Congo 147/E2
Wapiti, Wy, US 173/J1
Waples, Tx, US 176/K7
Wapoga (riv.), Indo. 117/J4
Wappapello (lake), Mo, US 188/B2
Wappingers Falls, NY, US 187/K4
Wapsipinicon (riv.), Ia, US 181/H2
Wapske, NB, Can. 184/D2
Wapwallopen (cr.), Pa, US 194/B1
Wapwallopen, Pa, US 194/B1
Wāqid, Egypt 139/B3
Waqqāş, Jor. 131/D3
War, WV, US 189/G2
War Horse Nat'l Wild. Ref., Mt, US 171/K4
Warabi, Japan 109/D2
Waranga (basin), Austl. 159/B3
Waratah, Austl. 158/C4
Waratah (bay), Austl. 159/C4
Warba, Mn, US 183/H4
Warboys, Eng, UK 63/F2
Warburg, Ger. 79/G6
Warburg, Ab, Can. 170/G1
Warburton, Pak. 124/B4
Warburton, Austl. 156/E3
Warburton (cr.), Austl. 153/C3
Warburton, Austl. 159/B3
Warburton (Central Australia) Abor. Rsv., Austl. 157/E3
Warburton Range Abor. Reserve, Austl. 156/E3
Warcha (riv.), Belg. 81/F3
Ward, NZ 161/C3
Ward Hunt (cape), PNG 155/H2
Warden (pt.), Eng, UK 63/G4
Warden, SAfr. 150/E2
Warden, Wa, US 170/E4
Wardenburg, Ger. 79/F2
Wardlow, Ab, Can. 171/J2
Wardo, Indo. 117/J4
Ward's Stone (peak), Eng, UK 61/F3
Wardsville, Mo, US 179/H1
Ware, Eng, UK 63/F3
Ware Shoals, SC, US 189/F3
Waregem, Belg. 80/C2
Wareham, Eng, UK 62/D5
Waremme, Belg. 81/E2
Waren, Ger. 66/E5
Waren, Indo. 117/J4
Warendorf, Ger. 79/E5
Waretown, NJ, US 194/D4
Warffum, Neth. 78/D2
Warfield, BC, Can. 170/F3
Wargrave, Eng, UK 63/F4
Warialda, Austl. 158/D1
Warin Chamrap, Thai. 120/D3
Waring, Tx, US 177/E3
Waringstown, NI, UK 60/B3
Wark, Eng, UK 61/F1
Warka, Pol. 69/L3
Warkworth, On, Can. 187/H2
Warkworth, NZ 161/C2
Warlingham, Eng, UK 56/C3
Warlmanpa Abor. Land, Austl. 157/G2
Warlmanpa Aboriginal Land, Austl. 154/D5
Warm Lake, Id, US 172/F1
Warm Springs, Or, US 172/C1
Warm Springs (res.), Or, US 172/D2
Warm Springs, Va, US 189/H1
Warm Springs Ind. Res., Or, US 172/C1
Warman, Sk, Can. 171/L1
Warmbad, SAfr. 149/F5
Warmbad, Namb. 150/B3
Warme Bode (riv.), Ger. 79/H5
Warmebach (riv.), Ger. 79/G6
Warmenhuizen, Neth. 78/B3
Warmerville, Fr. 81/D5
Warmia (reg.), Pol. 69/K1
Warminster, Eng, UK 62/D4
Warminster, Pa, US 194/C3
Warnemünde, Ger. 66/E4
Warner, SD, US 182/E5
Warner, Ok, US 179/G3
Warner (mts.), Ca, US 172/C3
Warner Robins, Ga, US 188/F4
Warnes, Bol. 212/D1
Warnow (riv.), Ger. 66/D5
Warnsveld, Neth. 78/D4
Waroona, Austl. 156/B5
Waropko, Indo. 155/F1
Warrabri, Austl. 157/G2
Warrabri Abor. Land, Austl. 154/D5
Warragamba, Austl. 159/B3
Warragamba, Austl. 159/E1
Warragul, Austl. 159/B4
Warrakunta (pt.), Austl. 155/D3
Warrandirinna (lake), Austl. 157/H3
Warrandyte (nbrhd.), Austl. 158/G5
Warrego (range), Austl. 153/D3
Warrego (riv.), Austl. 153/D3
Warren, Austl. 158/C1
Warren (riv.), Austl. 156/C5
Warren, Ar, US 179/H4
Warren, Id, US 172/F1
Warren, In, US 186/D4
Warren, Mi, US 186/E3
Warren, Mn, US 182/F3
Warren (peak), Mt, US 171/H5
Warren (co.), NJ, US 194/C2
Warren, NJ, US 194/D2
Warren, Oh, US 186/F4
Warren, Or, US 170/C5
Warren, Pa, US 187/G4
Warren, RI, US 187/L4
Warrenpoint, NI, UK 60/B3
Warrens, Wi, US 181/J1
Warrensburg, Mo, US 179/H1
Warrensburg, NY, US 187/K3
Warrenton, SAfr. 150/D3
Warrenton, Ga, US 189/F4
Warrenton, Mo, US 181/J4
Warrenton, NC, US 189/H2
Warrenton, Or, US 170/C4
Warrenton, Va, US 189/J1
Warrenville, Il, US 193/P16
Warri, Nga. 141/G5
Warrina, Austl. 157/G4
Warringah, Austl. 159/E1
Warrington, Eng, UK 61/F5
Warrington, Fl, US 190/E2
Warrior, Al, US 188/D4
Warrior Reefs (reef), Austl. 155/F2
Warrnambool, Austl. 158/B3
Warroad, Mn, US 183/G3
Warrumbungle NP, Austl. 158/D1
Warsaw (Warszawa) (cap.), Pol. 69/L2
Warsaw, In, US 186/D4
Warsaw, Mo, US 179/H1
Warsaw, NY, US 187/G3
Warsaw, Ky, US 188/E1
Warsaw, Va, US 189/J2
Warsaw, NC, US 189/H3
Warscheneck (peak), Aus. 76/B2
Warshiikh, Som. 144/C5
Warslow, Eng, UK 61/G5
Warsop, Eng, UK 61/G5
Warstein, Ger. 79/F6
Warszawa (prov.), Pol. 69/L2
Warszawa (Warsaw) (cap.), Pol. 69/L2
Warta (riv.), Pol. 96/A1
Wartberg an der Krems, Aus. 85/H7
Wartberg ob der Aist, Aus. 85/H6
Wartburg, Tn, US 188/E2
Warthen, Ga, US 189/F4
Wartrace, Tn, US 188/D3
Waru, Indo. 117/H4
Warwick, Austl. 160/D5
Warwick, Eng, UK 63/E2
Warwick, Ga, US 191/G2
Warwick, Md, US 194/C5
Warwick, NY, US 194/D1
Warwick, RI, US 187/L4
Warwickshire (co.), Eng, UK 63/E2
Wasa, BC, Can. 170/G3
Wasagu, Nga. 141/G4
Wasatch (range), Ut, US 168/D4
Wasāwewāla, Pak. 124/B4
Wasbank, SAfr. 151/E3
Wasburn (riv.), Eng, UK 61/G4
Wascana (riv.), Sk, Can. 171/M2
Wasco, Ca, US 174/C3
Wascott, Wi, US 183/J4
Waseca, Mn, US 181/H1
Wash, The (bay), Eng, UK 61/J6
Washaw (bay), Mb, Can. 182/F2
Washburn, Wi, US 183/J4
Washburn, ND, US 182/D4
Washburn (lake), Nun, Can. 166/F1
Washdyke, NZ 161/B4
Washimiya, Japan 109/D1
Washingborough, Eng, UK 61/H5
Washington, Eng, UK 61/G2
Washington (state), US 168/B2
Washington (cap.), US 194/A6
Washington (int'l arpt.), DC, US 194/A6
Washington, Il, US 188/B1
Washington Battlefield, Belg. 81/D2
Washington, Ga, US 189/F4
Washington, Ia, US 181/J3
Washington, Il, US 181/K3
Washington, In, US 188/D1
Washington, Ks, US 181/F4
Washington, Ky, US 188/F1
Washington, La, US 190/B2
Washington (isl.), Mi, US 186/C2
Washington (co.), Mn, US 183/Q6
Washington, Mo, US 181/J4
Washington, Ms, US 190/C2
Washington, NJ, US 194/D2
Washington, Tx, US 177/F2
Washington, Ut, US 175/F2
Washington, Va, US 189/H1
Washington (lake), Wa, US 193/C2
Washington (mt.), Wa, US 170/C4
Washington, NC, US 189/J3
Washington, Pa, US 186/F4
Washington (isl.), Wi, US 183/L5
Washington, WV, US 189/G1
Washington (Teraina) (isl.), Kiri. 163/J4
Washington (Washington Court House), Oh, US 186/E5
Washington Court House (Washington), Oh, US 186/E5
Washington Dulles (int'l arpt.), DC, US 189/J1
Washingtonville, Pa, US 194/B1
Washita (riv.), Ok, Tx, US 178/D3
Washita Battlefield Nat'l Hist. Site, Ok, US 178/E3
Washita Nat'l Wildlife Res., Ok, US 178/E3
Washtenaw (co.), Mi, US 193/E7
Washtucna, Wa, US 170/E4
Wasilków, Pol. 69/M2
Wasilla, Ak, US 166/B2
Wāsiṭ (gov.), Iraq 129/F3
Wasior, Indo. 117/H4
Wasiri, Indo. 154/B1
Wasjabo, Sur. 206/B1
Waskadah, Mb, Can. 182/D3
Waskaganish (Rupert House), Qu, Can. 167/J3
Waskaka (bay), Japan 110/D3
Waskesiu Lake, Sk, Can. 171/L1
Wasleton, Indo. 154/C1
Waspán, Nic. 201/F3
Wassau Nat'l Wild Ref., Ga, US 191/H2
Wasselonne, Fr. 81/G6
Wassen, Swi. 87/E4
Wassenaar, Neth. 78/B4
Wassenberg, Ger. 81/F1
Wasser, Namb. 150/B2
Wasserbillig, Lux. 81/F4
Wasserburg, Ger. 84/D6
Wasserburg am Inn, Ger. 85/F6
Wasserkuppe (peak), Ger. 84/C2
Wasserliesch, Ger. 81/F4
Wassertrüdingen, Ger. 84/D4
Wassou, Gui. 140/B4
Wassuk (range), Nv, US 168/C4
Wassy, Fr. 86/A1
Wast Water (lake), Eng, UK 61/E3
Wasu, PNG 155/G1
Wat Bot, Thai. 120/C2
Wat Mahathat, Thai. 112/C5
Wat Phra Si Ratana Mahathat, Thai. 112/D5
Wat Phu, Laos 120/D3
Wat Xieng Thong, Laos 112/D5
Wataga, Il, US 181/J3
Watampone, Indo. 117/F4
Watarai, Japan 109/L7
Watarase (riv.), Japan 111/F2
Watari, Japan 111/G1
Watauga, Tx, US 176/K7
Watauga (lake), Tn, US 189/G2
Watch Hill (pt.), RI, US 195/G1
Watchet, Eng, UK 62/C4
Watchfield, Eng, UK 63/E3
Watchung (mts.), NJ, US 195/H9
Watchung, NJ, US 195/H9
Water of Ae (riv.), Sc, UK 60/E1
Water of Girvan (riv.), Sc, UK 60/D1
Water of Girvan (riv.), Sc, UK 59/B6
Water of Ken (riv.), Sc, UK 60/D1
Water Valley, Ky, US 188/C2
Water Valley, Ms, US 188/C3
Water Valley, Ab, Can. 170/G2
Waterbeach, Eng, UK 63/G2
Waterberg, Namb. 148/C4
Waterberg Plateau Park, Namb. 148/C4
Waterberge (mts.), SAfr. 149/E5
Waterbury, Vt, US 187/K2
Waterbury, Ct, US 187/K4
Waterdown, On, Can. 186/T9
Wateree (lake), SC, US 189/G3
Waterfall, Austl. 159/E2
Waterflow, NM, US 175/H2
Waterford (arpt.), Ire. 58/C5
Waterford, Ire. 58/C5
Waterford (har.), Ire. 58/C5
Waterford (co.), Ire. 58/C5
Waterford, Mi, US 186/E3
Waterford, Wi, US 186/B3
Waterford, Ct, US 195/F1
Waterford Works, NJ, US 194/D4
Watergate (bay), Eng, UK 62/A6
Watergrasshill, Ire. 58/B5
Waterhen (lake), Mb, Can. 182/E1
Waterhouse (riv.), Austl. 154/D3
Wateringbury, Eng, UK 56/E3
Waterloo, Austl. 154/C4
Waterloo, Belg. 81/D2
Waterloo, On, Can. 186/F3
Waterloo, Qu, Can. 187/K2
Waterloo, NY, US 187/H3
Waterloo, Ia, US 181/H2
Waterloo, Il, US 188/B1
Waterloo Battlesite, Belg. 81/D2
Waterloo Village, NJ, US 194/D2
Waterlooville, Eng, UK 63/E5
Watermael-Boitsfort, Belg. 80/D2
Waterproof, La, US 190/C2
Watersmeet, Mi, US 183/K4
Waterton Lakes NP, Ab, Can. 171/G3
Waterton Lks. Nat'l Pk., Ab, Can. 166/E4
Waterton Park, Ab, Can. 171/H3
Waterton-Glacier International Peace Park, Can., US 171/H3
Watertown, NY, US 187/J3
Watertown, Fl, US 191/G2
Watertown, Wi, US 181/K2
Watertown, SD, US 181/F1
Watertown, Mn, US 183/N7
Waterval-Boven, SAfr. 149/F5
Waterville, Ire. 56/N11
Waterville, Ks, US 181/F4
Waterville, NY, US 187/J3
Waterville, Oh, US 186/E4
Waterville, Wa, US 170/D4
Watervliet, Belg. 80/C1
Watervliet, NY, US 187/K3
Watford, On, Can. 186/F3
Watford, Eng, UK 56/B1
Watford City, ND, US 182/C4
Wa'th, Sudan 142/G3
Wath-upon-Dearne, Eng, UK 61/G4
Watheroo, Austl. 156/C4
Watheroo NP, Austl. 156/B4
Wāṭī Kuliyāh (wadi), Egypt 139/D4
Watkins Glen, NY, US 187/H3
Watkinsville, Ga, US 189/F4
Watling (San Salvador) (isl.), Bahm. 197/G3
Watlington, Eng, UK 63/F3
Watmuri, Indo. 154/C1
Watonga, Ok, US 179/E3
Watonwan (riv.), Mn, US 181/G1
Watowato (peak), Indo. 117/G3
Watrous, NM, US 178/B3
Watrous, Sk, Can. 171/M2
Watsa, D.R. Congo 147/G2
Watseka, Il, US 186/C4
Watson, Ar, US 179/J4
Watson, Ok, US 179/G3
Watson, Il, US 188/C1
Watson, Sk, Can. 171/M1
Watson Lake, Yt, Can. 168/AA13
Watsontown, Pa, US 194/B1
Watsonville, Ca, US 174/B2
Watten, Fr. 80/B2
Wattenheim, Ger. 84/B3
Wattens, Aus. 87/H3
Wattignies, Fr. 80/C2
Watton, Eng, UK 63/G1
Wattrelos, Fr. 80/C2
Watts Bar (dam), Tn, US 188/E3
Watts Bar (lake), Tn, US 188/E3
Wattwil, Swi. 87/F3
Wau, PNG 155/G1
Waubay, SD, US 182/F5
Waubay (lake), SD, US 180/F1
Waubay NWR SD, US 181/F1
Waubun, Mn, US 182/G4
Wauchope, Austl. 158/E1
Wauchula, Fl, US 191/H4
Wauconda, Il, US 193/P15
Waugh (mt.), Id, US 173/F1
Waukarlycarly (lake), Austl. 153/B3
Waukegan, Il, US 186/C3
Waukesha, Wi, US 186/B3
Waukesha (co.), Wi, US 193/P14
Waukomis, Ok, US 179/F2
Waukon, Ia, US 181/J2
Waun Fâch (peak), Wal, UK 62/C3
Waun-Oer (peak), Wal, UK 62/C1
Wauna, Wa, US 193/B3
Wauneta, Ne, US 180/D3
Waupaca, Wi, US 181/K1
Waupun, Wi, US 181/K2
Waurika, Ok, US 179/F3
Waurika (lake), Ok, US 179/E3
Wausau, Wi, US 181/K1
Wausaukee, Wi, US 186/C2
Wauseon, Oh, US 186/D4
Wautoma, Wi, US 181/K1
Wauwatosa, Wi, US 186/B3
Wave Hill, Austl. 154/C4
Waveland, Ar, US 179/H3
Waveland, Ms, US 190/D2
Waveney (riv.), Eng, UK 63/H2
Waver (riv.), Eng, UK 61/E2
Waverley, Austl. 159/C4
Waverley, NS, Can. 184/F3
Waverley, NZ 161/C2
Waverley Downs, Austl. 158/B1
Waverly, Fl, US 190/M8
Waverly, Ga, US 191/H2
Waverly, Ia, US 181/H2
Waverly, Ks, US 179/G1
Waverly, La, US 179/J4
Waverly, Ne, US 181/F3
Waverly, NY, US 187/H3
Waverly, Oh, US 189/F1
Waverly, Tn, US 188/D2
Waverly (nbrhd.), Austl. 158/G5
Waverly Hall, Ga, US 188/E4
Wavre, Belg. 81/D2
Wavrin, Fr. 80/B2
Wāw, Sudan 142/E4
Wāw al Kabīr, Libya 134/C3
Wawa, On, Can. 167/H4
Wawa, Nga. 141/G4
Wawa (riv.), Nic. 201/E3
Wawanesa, Mb, Can. 182/E3
Wawasang (peak), Nic. 201/E3
Wawayanda St. Park, NJ, US 194/D1
Wawo, Indo. 117/F4
Wawoi (riv.), PNG 155/F1
Wawota, Sk, Can. 182/C3
Waxahachie, Tx, US 176/L7
Waxahachie (cr.), Tx, US 176/L7
Waxxari, China 125/E4
Wayakuba, Indo. 117/G4
Wayamli, Indo. 117/G3
Wayatinah, Austl. 154/C4
Waycross, Ga, US 191/G2
Waygay, Indo. 117/G4
Wayhaya, Indo. 117/F4
Wayland, NY, US 187/H3
Wayland, Mi, US 186/D3
Wayne, Il, US 193/P16
Wayne, Mi, US 193/F7
Wayne, Ne, US 181/F2
Wayne, NY, US 187/H3
Wayne, NJ, US 195/H8
Wayne, WV, US 189/F1
Wayne, Ok, US 179/F3
Wayne, Pa, US 194/C3
Wayne (co.), Pa, US 194/C1
Wayne City, Il, US 188/C1
Waynesboro, Ga, US 189/F4
Waynesboro, Tn, US 188/D3
Waynesboro, Va, US 189/H1
Waynesboro, Ms, US 190/D2
Waynesboro, Pa, US 187/H5
Waynesburg, Pa, US 186/F5
Waynesville, Mo, US 179/H2
Waynesville, NC, US 189/F3
Waynoka, Ok, US 179/E2
Wayside, Ms, US 188/B4
Wayuan, China 113/G3
Waza, Camr. 142/B3
Waza, PN de, Camr. 142/B3
Waziers, Fr. 80/C3
Wazīrābād, Pak. 124/C3
Wazuka, Japan 109/J6
Wda (riv.), Pol. 69/K2
Wé, NCal. 163/V12
We (isl.), Malay. 115/A1
Weald, The (grsld.), Eng, UK 63/F4
Weam, PNG 155/F2
Wear (riv.), Eng, UK 61/G2
Wear (riv.), Eng, UK 61/F2
Wear Head, Eng, UK 61/F2
Weare, NH, US 187/L3
Weatherford, Ok, US 179/E3
Weatherford (lake), Tx, US 176/K7
Weatherford, Tx, US 177/F1
Weatherly, Pa, US 194/C2
Weaubleau, Mo, US 179/H2
Weaver (lake), Mb, Can. 182/F1
Weaver (riv.), Eng, UK 61/F5
Weaverville, Ca, US 172/B3
Weaverville, NC, US 189/F3
Webb, Al, US 191/F2
Webb, Ms, US 188/B4
Webb, Sk, Can. 171/K2
Webb (A.F.B.), Tx, US 177/D1
Webb City, Mo, US 179/G2
Webber, Ks, US 180/E4
Webbers Falls, Ok, US 179/G3
Webberville, Mi, US 186/D3
Weber (mt.), Mn, US 183/J4
Weber (riv.), Ut, US 173/H3
Webi Jubba (riv.), Som. 133/G4
Webi Shabeelle (riv.), Som. 144/C4
Webster, Fl, US 190/L6
Webster, Mt, US 182/B4
Webster, Ma, US 187/L3
Webster, SD, US 182/F5
Webster, Tx, US 177/M9
Webster City, Ia, US 181/H2
Webster Groves, Mo, US 181/J4
Webster Springs (Addison), WV, US 189/G1
Webuye, Kenya 145/A1
Wedde-Warden, Ger. 79/F1
Weddell (sea) 216/X
Weddell (isl.), Mald. 215/E6
Wedderburn, Austl. 158/B3
Weddin Mountains NP, Austl. 159/C1
Weddington, NC, US 189/G3
Wedel, Ger. 79/G1
Wedemark, Ger. 79/G3
Wedge (mt.), BC, Can. 170/C2
Wedgeport, NS, Can. 184/E4
Wedmore, Eng, UK 62/D4
Wednesbury, Eng, UK 62/D1
Wednesfield, Eng, UK 62/D1
Wedowee, Al, US 188/E4
Weduar (cape), Indo. 154/D1
Wedweil, Sudan 142/E4
Wedza, Zim. 149/F3
Wee Waa, Austl. 158/D1
Weed, Ca, US 172/B3
Weedon Bec, Eng, UK 63/E2
Weedon-Centre, Qu, Can. 174/L2
Weedpatch (hill), In, US 186/C5
Weedville, Pa, US 187/G4
Weehawken, NJ, US 195/J8
Weekapaug, RI, US 195/G1
Weekes, Sk, Can. 182/C1
Weeki Wachee, Fl, US 190/K6
Weeki Wachee Springs, Fl, US 190/K6
Weeks, La, US 190/C3
Weeksbury, Ky, US 189/F2
Weeksville, NC, US 189/J2
Weenen, SAfr. 151/E3
Weeping Water, Ne, US 181/F3
Weerselo, Neth. 78/D4
Weert, Neth. 78/C6
Weesatche, Tx, US 177/F3
Weesen, Swi. 87/F3
Weesp, Neth. 78/C4
Weethalle, Austl. 159/C1
Weeze, Ger. 78/D5
Wegberg, Ger. 81/F1
Weggis, Swi. 87/E3
Węgorzewo, Pol. 67/J4
Węgrów, Pol. 69/M2
Wegscheid, Ger. 85/G5
Wehingen, Ger. 87/E1
Wehnī, Eth. 142/H2
Wehr, Ger. 86/D2
Wehra (riv.), Ger. 86/D2
Wehre (riv.), Ger. 79/G6
Wehrheim, Ger. 84/B2
Wei (riv.), China 105/H4
Wei Xian, China 106/C3
Wei Xian, China 106/C3
Weibersbrunn, Ger. 84/C3
Weichang, China 105/H3
Weiden, Ger. 85/F3
Weidenthal, Ger. 84/A4
Weidman, Mi, US 186/D3
Weifang, China 106/D3
Weihai, China 107/B4
Weihenzell, Ger. 84/D4
Weikersheim, Ger. 84/C4
Weil (riv.), Ger. 84/B2
Weil der Stadt, Ger. 84/B5
Weilburg, Ger. 84/B2
Weiler-Simmerberg, Ger. 87/F2
Weilerswist, Ger. 81/F2
Weilheim, Ger. 87/H2
Weilheim an der Teck, Ger. 84/C5
Weilmünster, Ger. 84/B2
Weimar, Ger. 68/F3
Weimar, Tx, US 177/F3
Weinan, China 106/B4
Weiner, Ar, US 188/B3
Weinfelden, Swi. 87/F3
Weingarten, Ger. 84/B4
Weingarten, Ger. 87/F2
Weinheim, Ger. 84/B3
Weinsberg, Ger. 84/C4
Weinstadt, Ger. 84/C5
Weinviertel (reg.), Aus. 71/M2
Weipa, Austl. 155/F3
Weipa Abor. Rsv., Austl. 155/F3
Weipa South, Austl. 155/F3
Weir, Ks, US 179/G2
Weir, Tx, US 177/F2
Weirsdale, Fl, US 191/H3
Weirton, WV, US 186/F4
Weischlitz, Ger. 85/F2
Weisendorf, Ger. 84/D3
Weisenheim am Berg, Ger. 84/B3
Weiser, Id, US 172/E1
Weiser (riv.), Id, US 172/E1
Weishan, China 106/D4
Weishan (lake), China 105/H5
Weishi, China 106/C4
Weiskirchen, Ger. 81/F4
Weismain, Ger. 84/E2
Weiss (dam), Al, US 188/E3
Weiss (lake), Al, US 188/E3
Weissach, Ger. 84/B5
Weisse Elster (riv.), Ger. 68/G3
Weisse Laber (riv.), Ger. 85/E4
Weissenbach am Lech, Aus. 87/G3
Weissenburg im Bayern, Ger. 84/D4
Weissenfels, Ger. 68/F3
Weissenhorn, Ger. 87/G1
Weissensee, Ger. 68/Q6
Weissenstadt, Ger. 85/E2
Weissenthurm, Ger. 81/G3
Weisser (peak), Ger. 81/F3
Weisser Main (riv.), Ger. 85/E2
Weisshorn (peak), Swi. 86/D5
Weissmies (peak), Swi. 86/D5
Weisswasser, Ger. 69/H3
Weistrach, Aus. 85/H6
Weitefeld, Ger. 81/G2
Weiterstadt, Ger. 84/B3
Weitian, China 113/H3
Weitra, Aus. 69/H4
Weixi, China 119/G2
Weiyuan, China 104/E4
Weiyuan (riv.), China 112/D4
Weizhou (isl.), China 119/J3
Weizhou (isl.), Viet. 113/F4
Weiziyu, China 107/C2
Wejherowo, Pol. 66/H4
Wekame, Myan. 120/B3
Wekiva (riv.), Fl, US 190/N6
Welatam, Myan. 119/G2
Welbekend, SAfr. 150/E2
Welch, Ok, US 179/G2
Welch, WV, US 189/G2
Welch (hill), Pa, US 194/A3
Welcome, MD, US 189/G3
Welda, Ks, US 179/G1
Welden, Ger. 84/D6
Weldiya, Eth. 144/A3
Weldon, Tx, US 177/G2
Weldon (nbrhd.), Eng, UK 56/D2
Weldon (riv.), Ia, Mo, US 181/H3
Weldon, Eng, UK 63/F2
Weleetka, Ok, US 179/F3
Welega (pol. reg.), Eth. 142/G3
Welel (peak), Eth. 142/G3
Welford, Austl. 160/A4
Welford, Eng, UK 63/E4
Welham Green, Eng, UK 56/C1
Welkenraedt, Belg. 81/E2
Welk'īt'ē, Eth. 142/H3
Welkom, SAfr. 150/D3
Welland (riv.), Eng, UK 61/H6
Welland (canal), On, US 186/U10
Welland, On, Can. 186/U10
Wellandport, On, Can. 186/U9
Wellborn, Fl, US 191/G2
Wellen, Belg. 81/E2
Wellesley (isls.), Austl. 155/E4
Wellesley(isls.), Austl. 153/C2
Wellford, SC, US 189/F3
Wellin, Belg. 81/E3
Wellingborough, Eng, UK 63/F2
Wellington, Austl. 159/D1
Wellington (lake), Austl. 158/C3
Wellington, On, Can. 187/H3
Wellington (isl.), Chile 203/B7
Wellington (chan.), Nun, Can. 167/S7
Wellington, SAfr. 150/L10
Wellington (int'l arpt.), NZ 161/H9
Wellington (cap.), NZ 161/H9
Wellington, Ks, US 179/F2
Wellington, Tx, US 178/D3
Wellington, Nv, US 172/D4
Wellington, Co, US 180/B3
Wellington, Eng, UK 62/C5
Wellington, Eng, UK 62/D2
Wellington (co.), On, Can. 186/S8
Wellman, Tx, US 178/C4
Wellman, Ia, US 181/J3
Wells (lake), Austl. 153/B3
Wells, Eng, UK 62/D4
Wells, Tx, US 176/G2
Wells, NY, US 187/J3
Wells, Me, US 187/L3
Wells, Nv, US 173/F3
Wells, Mn, US 181/H2
Wells-next-the-Sea, Eng, UK 63/G1
Wellsboro, Pa, US 187/H4
Wellsburg, WV, US 186/F4
Wellsford, NZ 161/C2
Wellston, Ok, US 179/F3
Wellston, Mi, US 186/D2
Wellston, Oh, US 189/F1
Wellsville, Ks, US 179/G1
Wellsville, NY, US 187/H3
Wellsville, Ut, US 173/H3
Wellsville, Mo, US 181/J4
Wellsville, Pa, US 194/B3
Wellwood, Mb, Can. 182/E2
Welo (prov.), Eth. 144/A3
Wels, Aus. 85/H6
Welschbillig, Ger. 81/F4
Welsh, La, US 190/B2
Welshnofen (Nova Levante), It. 87/H5
Welshpool, Wal, UK 62/C1
Welty, Ok, US 179/F3
Welver, Ger. 79/E5
Welwel, Eth. 144/C4
Welwyn, Sk, Can. 182/D2
Welzheim, Ger. 84/C5
Wem, Eng, UK 61/F6
Wembere (riv.), Tanz. 145/A3
Wembley Stadium, Eng, UK 56/C2
Wemding, Ger. 84/D5
Wemindji, Qu, Can. 167/J3
Wemmel, Belg. 81/D2
Wemyss Bay, Sc, UK 59/B5
Wen Xian, China 106/C4
Wenago, Eth. 144/A4
Wen'an, China 106/H7
Wenatchee, Wa, US 170/D4
Wenatchee (mts.), Wa, US 170/D4
Wenchang, China 113/F5
Wencheng, China 113/J3
Wenchi, Gha. 141/E5
Wendeburg, Ger. 79/H4
Wendell, Mn, US 182/F4
Wenden, Ger. 81/G2
Wenden, Az, US 175/F4
Wendeng, China 107/B4
Wendi, China 113/F4
Wendlingen am Neckar, Ger. 84/C5
Wendo, Eth. 144/A4
Wendou Borou, Gui. 140/B4
Wendover, Nv, US 173/F3
Wendover, Eng, UK 63/F3
Wendron, Eng, UK 62/A6
Wendte, SD, US 180/D1
Wengdong, China 113/F3
Wengjiang, China 113/G2
Wengshui, China 119/G2
Wengyang, China 113/J2
Wengyuan, China 119/K3
Wenlock Edge (ridge), Eng, UK 62/D2
Wenne (riv.), Ger. 79/F6
Wennigsen, Ger. 79/G4
Wennington, Eng, UK 61/F3
Wenona, Il, US 181/K3
Wenonah, NJ, US 194/C4
Wenquan, China 113/E2
Wenquan, China 112/D2
Wenquan, China 125/F5
Wenquanzhen, China 113/G3
Wenshan, China 119/H3
Wenshang, China 106/D4
Wenshui, China 106/C3
Wensleydale (valley), Eng, UK 61/F3
Went (riv.), Eng, UK 61/G4
Wentang, China 113/G2
Wentworth, Austl. 158/B2
Wentworth, NC, US 189/H2
Wenxi, China 106/B4
Wenzhou, China 113/J3
Weott, Ca, US 172/B3
Wepener, SAfr. 150/D3
Wépion, Belg. 81/D3
Wer, India 122/A2
Werda, Bots. 148/D5
Werder, Eth. 144/C4
Werder, Ger. 68/P7
Werdohl, Ger. 79/E6
Were Īlu, Eth. 144/A3
Werinama, Indo. 117/G4
Werkendam, Neth. 78/B5
Werl, Ger. 79/E5
Werlte, Ger. 79/E3
Wermelskirchen, Ger. 81/G1
Wern (r.v.), Ger. 84/C3
Wernau, Ger. 84/C5
Wernberg-Köblitz, Ger. 85/F3
Werne an der Lippe, Ger. 79/E5
Werneck, Ger. 84/D3
Wernigerode, Ger. 68/D3
Werneuchen, Ger. 68/Q6
Wernigerode, Ger. 79/H5
Werong (mt.), Austl. 159/D2
Werra (riv.), Ger. 68/E3
Werra (riv.), Ger. 79/G6
Werribee, Austl. 158/F5
Werrikimbe NP, Austl. 158/E1
Werrimull, Austl. 158/B2
Werrington, Eng, UK 61/F5
Werris Creek, Austl. 158/D1
Werse (riv.), Ger. 79/E5
Wertach (riv.), Ger. 84/D6
Wertheim, Ger. 84/C3
Werther, Ger. 79/F4
Werther, Ger. 79/H6
Wertingen, Ger. 84/D5
Wervershoof, Neth. 78/C3
Wervik, Belg. 80/C2
Weschnitz (riv.), Ger. 84/B3
Weselgebirge (mts.), Ger. 79/F4
Wesel, Ger. 78/D5
Wesel-Datteln (canal), Ger. 79/E5
Wesely E. Seale (dam), Tx, US 177/F3
Wesenberg, Ger. 68/G2
Weser (riv.), Ger. 68/E2
Weslaco, Tx, US 177/F4
Wesley, Ia, US 181/H2
Wesley Hills, NY, US 195/J7
Wessel (cape), Austl. 155/E2
Wessel (isls.), Austl. 153/C2
Wesselburen, Ger. 66/C4
Wesseling, Ger. 81/F2
Wesselsbron, SAfr. 150/D2
Wessex (reg.), Eng, UK 62/D4
Wessington, SD, US 180/E1
Wessington Springs, SD, US 180/E1
Wesson, Ar, US 179/H4
Wesson, Ms, US 190/C2
West (riv.), Ia, US 190/D3
West (bay), La, US 190/D3
West (pt.), Wa, US 193/C2
West (pt.), Austl. 158/C4
West (cape), NZ 161/A4
West (isl.), Austl. 155/E3
West, Tx, US 177/F2
West Abor. Land, Austl. 155/E3
West Allis, Wi, US 186/B3
West Arichat, NS, Can. 185/G3
West Augusta, Ga, US 189/F4
West Augusta, Va, US 189/H1
West Babylon, NY, US 195/E2
West Bank 131/C4
West Baraboo, Wi, US 181/K2
West Barns, Sc, UK 59/D5
West Bay, NS, Can. 185/G3
West Bend, Sk, Can. 182/C2
West Bend, Wi, US 186/B3
West Bend, Ia, US 181/G2
West Bengal (state), India 118/E3
West Bergholt, Eng, UK 63/G3
West Bijou (cr.), Co, US 178/B1
West Bijou (cr.), Co, US 180/B4
West Blocton, Al, US 188/D4
West Branch, Mi, US 186/D2
West Branch Devers (canal), Tx, US 177/N9
West Brattleboro, Vt, US 187/K3
West Bridgford, Eng, UK 61/G6
West Bromwich, Eng, UK 62/E1
West Bylleet, Eng, UK 56/B3
West Caicos (isl.), UK 201/H1
West Calder, Sc, UK 59/C5
West Caldwell, NJ, US 195/H8
West Cap Howe NP, Austl. 156/C5
West Carthage, NY, US 187/J3
West Chester, Pa, US 194/C4
West Chicago, Il, US 193/P16
West Chyulu Game Consv. Area, Kenya 145/B2
West Clandon, Eng, UK 56/B3
West Coast NP, SAfr. 150/L10
West Columbia, Tx, US 176/G3
West Columbia, SC, US 189/G4
West Cornforth, Eng, UK 61/G2
West Covina, Ca, US 192/G7
West Creek, NJ, US 194/D4
West Crossett, Ar, US 179/J4
West Des Moines, Ia, US 181/H3
West Dover, NS, Can. 184/F3
West Elk (mts.), Co, US 173/K4
West Elmira, NY, US 187/H3
West End, Eng, UK 56/B3
West Falkland (isl.), UK 215/E6
West Fargo, ND, US 182/F4
West Farleigh, Eng, UK 56/E3
West Fayu (isl.), Micr. 162/D4
West Flamborough, On, Can. 186/S9
West Fork, Ar, US 179/G3
West Frankfort, Il, US 188/C2
West Frisian (isls.), Neth. 68/C2
West Frostproof, Fl, US 190/M8
West Glamorgan (co.), Wal, UK 62/C3
West Glen (riv.), Eng, UK 61/H6
West Green, Ga, US 191/G2
West Grove, Pa, US 194/C4
West Ham (nbrhd.), Eng, UK 56/D2
West Hanningfield, Eng, UK 56/E2
West Haven, Ct, US 195/F1
West Haverstraw, NY, US 194/E1
West Hawk Lake, Mb, Can. 183/G3
West Helena, Ar, US 188/B3
West Hempstead, NY, US 195/L9
West Hills, NY, US 195/M8
West Hollywood, Ca, US 192/F7
West Horndon, Eng, UK 56/E2
West Horsley, Eng, UK 56/B3
West Ice Shelf, Ant. 216/F
West Indies (isls.), NAm. 165/L7
West Islet (isl.), Austl. 153/E3
West Islip, NY, US 195/E2
West Jefferson, NC, US 189/G2
West Jordan, Ut, US 173/H3
West Kennebago (mt.), Me, US 187/L2
West Kilbride, Sc, UK 59/B5
West Kingsdown, Eng, UK 56/D3
West Kirby, Eng, UK 61/E5
West Knock (peak), Sc, UK 59/D3
West Lafayette, Oh, US 186/F4
West Lafayette, In, US 186/C4
West Lake Hills, Tx, US 177/F2
West Lamma (chan.), China 113/L8
West Lebanon, In, US 186/C4
West Liberty, Oh, US 186/E4
West Liberty, Ky, US 189/F2
West Liberty, Ia, US 181/J3
West Linn, Or, US 172/B1
West Lorne, On, Can. 186/F3
West Lunga NP, Afr. 148/E2
West Malling, Eng, UK 56/E3
West Melbourne, Fl, US 191/H3
West Memphis, Ar, US 188/B3
West Mersea, Eng, UK 63/G3
West Miami, Fl, US 190/P11
West Midlands (co.), Eng, UK 63/E1
West Milford, NJ, US 195/H7
West Milford, WV, US 189/G1
West Milton, Pa, US 194/B1
West Monroe, La, US 179/H4
West Monroe, Mi, US 186/E4
West New Britain (prov.), PNG 155/H1
West New York, NJ, US 195/J8
West Nicholson, Zim. 149/F4
West Nishnabotna (riv.), Ia, US 181/G3
West Nodaway (riv.), Ia, US 181/G3
West Nueces (riv.), Tx, US 177/E3
West Nyack, NY, US 195/K7
West Olive, Mi, US 186/C3
West Orange, Tx, US 177/H2
West Orange, NJ, US 195/J8
West Palm Beach (canal), Fl, US 190/P9
West Palm Beach, Fl, US 190/P9
West Paterson, NJ, US 195/J8
West Pensacola, Fl, US 190/E2
West Plains, Mo, US 179/J2
West Plains (Plains), Ks, US 178/D2
West Point, Ca, US 172/C4
West Point, Il, US 181/J3
West Point, Ia, US 181/J3
West Point, Ga, US 188/E4
West Point (dam), Ga, US 188/E4
West Point, Ms, US 188/C4
West Point, Ne, US 181/F3
West Point (res.), Ga, US 188/E4
West Point Mil. Acad, NY, US 187/J4
West Poplar, Sk, Can. 171/L3
West Reading, Pa, US 194/C3
West Redding, Ct, US 195/E1
West Richland, Wa, US 170/E4
West Road (riv.), BC, Can. 170/B1
West Sacramento, Ca, US 193/L9
West Saint Paul, Mn, US 183/P7
West Salem, Il, US 188/C1
West Sayville, NY, US 195/E2
West Seneca, NY, US 186/V10
West Siberian (plain), Rus. 100/H3
West Sister Island Nat'l Wild. Ref., Oh, US 186/E4
West Sussex (co.), Eng, UK 63/F4
West Tawakoni, Tx, US 179/F4

310
Wolco – Yate

Wolcottsville, NY, US 186/V9
Wołczyn, Pol. 69/K3
Wold-Chamberlain (Minneapolis-St. Paul) (int'l arpt.), Mn, US 183/P7
Woldingham, Eng, UK 56/C3
Woleai (isl.), Micr. 162/D4
Woleu (riv.), Gabon 146/B2
Woleu-Ntem (prov.), Gabon 146/B2
Wolf, Ok, US 179/F3
Wolf (cr.), Ks, US 178/G1
Wolf (mtn.), Ok, US 179/G3
Wolf (riv.), Wi, US 186/B2
Wolf (lake), In, US 193/Q16
Wolf (riv.), Wi, US 181/K1
Wolf (isl.), Ecu. 208/J6
Wolf (vol.), Ecu. 208/J7
Wolf (cr.), Ab, Can. 170/F1
Wolf Bayou, Ar, US 179/J3
Wolf Creek (res.), Ks, US 179/G1
Wolf Creek, Or, US 172/B2
Wolf Creek (dam), Ky, US 188/E2
Wolf Creek, Mt, US 171/H4
Wolf Lake, Mi, US 186/C3
Wolf Point, Mt, US 171/M3
Wolfach, Ger. 87/E1
Wolfach (riv.), Ger. 84/B6
Wolfe City, Tx, US 179/F4
Wolfe Creek Crater NP, Austl. 154/B4
Wolfe Island, On, Can. 187/H2
Wolfegg, Ger. 87/F2
Wolfen, Ger. 68/G3
Wolfenbüttel, Ger. 79/H4
Wolfern, Aus. 85/H6
Wölfersheim, Ger. 84/B2
Wolfforth, Tx, US 178/C4
Wolfhagen, Ger. 79/G6
Wolframs-Eschenbach, Ger. 84/D4
Wolfsburg, Ger. 79/H4
Wolfsegg am Hausruck, Aus. 85/G6
Wolfstein, Ger. 81/G4
Wolfurt, Aus. 87/F3
Wolfville, NS, Can. 184/E3
Wolgast, Ger. 66/E4
Wolhusen, Swi. 86/E3
Wolin, Pol. 66/F5
Woliński PN, Pol. 66/F5
Wolkersdorf, Aus. 77/P7
Wollaston (pen.), NW,Nun, Can. 166/E2
Wollaston (lake), Sk, Can. 166/F3
Wollaston (isl.), Chile 215/D7
Wollaston, Eng, UK 63/F2
Wollerau, Swi. 87/E3
Wollogorang, Austl. 155/E4
Wollomombi, Austl. 158/E1
Wollondilly (riv.), Austl. 159/D2
Wollongong, Austl. 159/E2
Wöllstadt, Ger. 84/B2
Wöllstein, Ger. 81/G4
Wolmaransstad, SAfr. 150/D2
Wolnzach, Ger. 85/E5
Wołomin, Pol. 69/L2
Wołów, Pol. 69/J3
Wolowaru, Indo. 154/A2
Wolphaartsdijk, Neth. 78/A5
Wolseley, Sk, Can. 182/C2
Wolseley, SAfr. 150/L10
Wolsey, SD, US 180/E1
Wolsingham, Eng, UK 61/G2
Wolsztyn, Pol. 69/J2
Wolters Mil. Res., Tx, US 179/E4
Woltersdorf, Ger. 68/Q7
Woluwé-Saint-Lambert, Belg. 81/D2
Wolvega, Neth. 78/D3
Wolverhampton, Eng, UK 62/D1
Wolverine Lake, Mi, US 193/F6
Wolverton, Mn, US 182/F4
Wolziger (lake), Ger. 68/Q7
Womanagh (riv.), Ire. 58/B5
Womboota, Austl. 159/B2
Wombourne, Eng, UK 62/D1
Wombwell, Eng, UK 61/G4
Womelsdorf, Pa, US 194/B3
Women's Rights Nat'l Hist. Park, NY, US 187/H3
Wompou, Mrta. 140/B3
Wondai, Austl. 160/C4
Wondang, SKor. 107/F6
Wonder (lake), Il, US 193/P16
Wonder Gorge, Zam. 149/F2
Wŏndong-ni, NKor. 107/E2
Wondreb (riv.), Ger. 85/F3
Wonersh, Eng, UK 56/B3
Wonfurt, Ger. 84/D2
Wong Chu (riv.), Bhu. 123/G2
Wonga-Wongué, PN de, Gabon 146/B3
Wongan Hills, Austl. 156/C4
Wŏnju, SKor. 107/D4
Wonnangatta (riv.), Austl. 159/C3
Wonnangatta-Moroka NP, Austl. 158/C3
Wonogiri, Indo. 115/E3
Wonosari, Indo. 115/E3
Wonosobo, Indo. 115/E3
Wonreli, Indo. 154/B2
Wŏnsan, NKor. 107/D3
Wonthaggi, Austl. 159/B4
Wonyulgunna (peak), Austl. 156/C3
Wooburn Green, Eng, UK 56/A2
Wood (riv.), Ne, US 180/E3
Wood (riv.), Sk, Can. 171/L3
Wood (mtn.), Sk, Can. 171/L3
Wood Buffalo NP, NW,Ab, Can. 166/E2
Wood Dale, Il, US 193/P16
Wood Lake, Mn, US 181/G1
Wood Lake, Ne, US 180/D2
Wood River, Ne, US 180/E3
Wood-Ridge, NJ, US 195/J8
Woodbine, Ks, US 179/F1
Woodbine, Ga, US 191/H2
Woodbine, Ky, US 188/E2
Woodbine, Ia, US 181/G3
Woodbine, NJ, US 194/D5
Woodbine, Md, US 194/A5
Woodbridge, NJ, US 195/H9
Woodbridge, Ca, US 193/M10
Woodbridge, Eng, UK 63/H2
Woodbridge, On, Can. 186/T8
Woodbridge, Va, US 189/J1
Woodbridge, Ct, US 195/E1
Woodburn, NI, UK 60/C2
Woodburn, Austl. 158/E1
Woodburn, Or, US 172/B1
Woodburn, On, Can. 186/T9
Woodbury, Tn, US 188/D3
Woodbury, Ga, US 188/E4
Woodbury, NJ, US 194/C4
Woodcliff Lake, NJ, US 195/J7
Woodcock (hill), Ire. 58/B4
Woodcock (mt.), Austl. 154/D4
Woodenbong, Austl. 158/E1
Woodenbridge, Ire. 60/B6
Woodend, Austl. 159/B3
Woodfield, SC, US 189/G3
Woodfin, NC, US 189/F3
Woodford, Ire. 58/B3
Woodgate, Austl. 160/D4
Woodgate NP, Austl. 160/D4
Woodhall Spa, Eng, UK 61/H5
Woodham Ferrers, Eng, UK 56/E2
Woodhaven, Mi, US 186/E3
Woodhull, Il, US 181/J3
Woodinville, Wa, US 193/C2
Woodlake, Ca, US 174/C2
Woodland, Mn, US 183/H4
Woodland, Ca, US 172/C4
Woodland, Ms, US 188/C4
Woodland, Wa, US 170/C5
Woodland Beach, On, Can. 186/G2
Woodland Hills (nbrhd.), Ca, US 192/E7
Woodland Park, Co, US 178/B1
Woodlands, Mb, Can. 182/F2
Woodlands (nbrhd.), Sing. 115/J6
Woodlark (isl.), Sol. 162/E5
Woodlawn, Tn, US 188/D2
Woodlawn, Il, US 188/C1
Woodlawn, Md, US 194/B5
Woodlawn, Va, US 189/G2
Woodley, Eng, UK 63/F4
Woodmere, NY, US 195/L9
Woodmont, Ct, US 195/F1
Woodridge, Mb, Can. 182/F3
Woodridge, Il, US 193/P16
Woodroffe (mt.), Austl. 157/F3
Woodrow, Co, US 180/C4
Woodruff, Az, US 175/G3
Woodruff, Ut, US 173/H3
Woodruff, Ks, US 180/E4
Woodruff, SC, US 189/F3
Woods (cr.), Wa, US 193/D2
Woods (lake), On, Can. 166/G4
Woods (lake), Austl. 154/D4
Woods (res.), Tn, US 188/D3
Wood's Point, Austl. 159/C3
Woods, Lake of the (lake), Can.,US 183/G3
Woodsboro, Tx, US 177/F3
Woodsboro, Md, US 194/A4
Woodseaves, Eng, UK 61/F6
Woodsfield, Oh, US 186/F5
Woodside, Mb, Can. 182/E2
Woodside, Pa, US 187/G5
Woodside, Ca, US 193/K12
Woodside, Ut, US 173/H4
Woodside, Austl. 157/M8
Woodside, De, US 194/C5
Woodside-Drifton, Pa, US 194/C2
Woodson, Ar, US 179/H3
Woodson, Tx, US 178/E4
Woodstock, NB, Can. 184/D2
Woodstock, On, Can. 186/F3
Woodstock, Il, US 186/B3
Woodstock, Eng, UK 63/E3
Woodstock, Austl. 159/D1
Woodstock, Va, US 189/H1
Woodstock, Md, US 194/B5
Woodston, Ks, US 180/E4
Woodstown, NJ, US 194/C4
Woodsville, NH, US 187/K2
Woodview, On, Can. 187/G2
Woodville, Tx, US 177/G2
Woodville, Ms, US 190/C2
Woodville, Fl, US 191/F2
Woodville, NZ 161/C3
Woodville, Wi, US 181/H1
Woodward, Ok, US 178/E2
Woodward, Ia, US 181/H3
Woodway, Wa, US 193/C2
Woodway, Va, US 189/F2
Woodway, Tx, US 177/F2
Woodworth, ND, US 182/E4
Woodworth, La, US 190/B2
Woody, Ca, US 174/C3
Wool, Eng, UK 62/D5
Woolavington, Eng, UK 62/D4
Wooler, Eng, UK 59/E5
Woolgar, Austl. 160/A2
Woolgoolga, Austl. 158/E1
Wooli, Austl. 158/E1
Woolrich, Pa, US 194/A1
Woolsington, Eng, UK 61/G1
Wooltana, Austl. 157/H4
Woolwich (nbrhd.), Eng, UK 56/D2
Woomera, Austl. 157/H4
Woomera Prohibited Area, Austl. 157/G4
Woonaloo (brook), Austl. 156/L6
Woonsocket, RI, US 187/L3
Woonsocket, SD, US 180/E1
Woorabinda Abor. Community, Austl. 160/C4
Wooramel (riv.), Austl. 156/B3
Wooramel, Austl. 156/B3
Woore, Eng, UK 61/F6
Wooster, Oh, US 186/F4
Wootton Basset, Eng, UK 63/E3
Worb, Swi. 86/D4
Worbis, Ger. 79/H6
Worcester, Ma, US 187/L3
Worcester, NY, US 187/J3
Worcester, SAfr. 150/L10
Worcester, Eng, UK 62/D2
Worcester and Birmingham (canal), Eng, UK 62/D2
Worden, Mt, US 171/K5
Wörgl, Aus. 71/K3
Workai (riv.), Indo. 154/D1
Workai (isl.), Indo. 154/D1
Workington, Eng, UK 60/E2
Worksop, Eng, UK 61/G5
Workum, Neth. 78/C3
Worland, Wy, US 173/K1
World 52/*
World Trade Center, NY, US 195/J9
Wormer, Neth. 78/B3
Wormhoudt, Fr. 80/B2
Wormley, Eng, UK 56/C1
Worms, Ger. 84/B3
Worms (pt.), Wal, UK 62/B3
Wörnitz (riv.), Ger. 71/J2
Worpswede, Ger. 79/F2
Wörrstadt, Ger. 84/B3
Wörsbach (riv.), Ger. 84/B2
Worsbrough, Eng, UK 61/G4
Worth, Il, US 193/Q16
Wörth am Main, Ger. 84/C3
Wörth am Rhein, Ger. 84/B4
Wörth an der Donau, Ger. 85/F4
Wörth an der Isar, Ger. 85/F5
Wortham, Tx, US 177/F2
Worthing, Eng, UK 63/F5
Worthington, Oh, US 186/E4
Worthington, In, US 188/D1
Worthington, Mn, US 181/G2
Wörthsee, Ger. 87/H1
Wörthsee (lake), Ger. 84/E6
Worton, Md, US 194/B5
Wotho (isl.), Mrsh. 162/F3
Wotjalum Abor. Land, Indo. 154/A4
Wotje (isl.), Mrsh. 162/G4
Wottonville, Qu, Can. 187/L2
Wotu, Indo. 117/F4
Woudenberg, Neth. 78/C4
Woudrichem, Neth. 78/B5
Wounta (lake), Nic. 201/F3
Wour, Chad 134/B4
Wouri (riv.), Camr. 146/B1
Wouw, Neth. 78/B5
Wowoni (isl.), Indo. 117/F4
Wragby, Eng, UK 61/H5
Wrangel (isl.), Rus. 216/U
Wrangell (mts.), Ak, US 166/B2
Wrangell, Ak, US 168/Z13
Wrangell-St. Elias NP, Ak, US 168/Y12
Wrangle, Eng, UK 61/J5
Wrath (cape), Sc, UK 57/R7
Wray, Co, US 180/C3
Wraysbury (res.), Eng, UK 56/B2
Wraysbury, Eng, UK 56/B2
Wreck (pt.), SAfr. 150/B3
Wreck (isl.), Md, US 189/K2
Wreck(reef) 153/E3
Wreck (bay), Austl. 159/E2
Wremen, Ger. 79/E2
Wrenbury, Eng, UK 61/F5
Wrens, Ga, US 189/F4
Wrenshall, Mn, US 183/H4
Wrexham, Wal, UK 61/F5
Wright, Wy, US 180/B2
Wright (co.), Mn, US 183/N6
Wright Brothers Nat'l Mem., NC, US 189/K2
Wright City, Ok, US 179/G3
Wright Patman (lake), Tx, US 177/G1
Wright-Patterson (A.F.B.), Oh, US 186/D5
Wrightsboro, NC, US 189/J3
Wrightstown, NJ, US 194/D3
Wrightsville, Ar, US 179/H3
Wrightsville, Ga, US 189/F4
Wrightwood, Ca, US 192/C2
Wrigley, NW, Can. 166/D2
Writing Rock Historical Site, ND, US 182/C3
Writtle, Eng, UK 63/G3
Wrocław, Pol. 69/J3
Wrocław (prov.), Pol. 69/J3
Wrong (lake), Mb, Can. 182/F1
Wrotham, Eng, UK 56/D3
Wroxeter, Eng, UK 62/D1
Wroxham, Eng, UK 63/H1
Wroxton, Sk, Can. 182/D2
Września, Pol. 69/J2
Wschowa, Pol. 69/J3
Wu (riv.), China 119/J2
Wu'an, China 106/C3
Wubin, Austl. 156/C4
Wuchang, China 105/K3
Wuchang, China 113/G2
Wuchang (lake), China 106/D5
Wucheng, China 106/D3
Wuchiu (isl.), Tai. 113/H3
Wuchuan, China 106/B2
Wudalianchi, China 105/K2
Wudang (mts.), China 113/F1
Wudang (mtn.), China 106/B4
Wudao, China 107/A3
Wudaogou, China 107/C1
Wudi, China 106/D3
Wudil, Nga. 141/H4
Wuding (riv.), China 106/B3
Wudinna, Austl. 157/G5
Wufeng, China 113/F2
Wufuting, China 113/G3
Wuguzhang, China 104/F4
Wuhai, China 104/F4
Wuhan, China 113/G2
Wuhe, China 106/D4
Wuhle (riv.), Ger. 68/Q6
Wuhu, China 106/D5
Wuhu, China 106/D5
Wuhuanchi, China 105/J3
Wuilo, Libr. 140/C5
Wujal Wujal Abor. Comm., Austl. 160/B1
Wujia (riv.), China 104/F3
Wujiang, China 113/H2
Wujiang, China 106/L8
Wukari, Nga. 141/H5
Wular (lake), India 124/C2
Wülfrath, Ger. 78/E6
Wulften, Ger. 79/H5
Wulian, China 106/D4
Wulian, China 104/F5
Wulian (mts.), China 112/D3
Wuliang (mts.), China 112/D4
Wuliara (isl.), Indo. 154/C1
Wulin, China 113/F4
Wuling (mts.), China 113/F2
Wulong, China 119/J2
Wulongbei, China 107/C2
Wulur, Indo. 154/C1
Wum, Camr. 141/H5
Wumang (isl.), China 107/B3
Wumeng (mts.), China 112/D3
Wümme (riv.), Ger. 79/F2
Wun Rog, Sudan 142/F3
Wun Shwai, Sudan 142/F3
Wundanyi, Kenya 145/B2
Wungong (brook), Austl. 156/L7
Wungong (res.), Austl. 156/L7
Wünnenberg, Ger. 79/F5
Wünnewil, Swi. 86/D4
Wunsiedel, Ger. 85/F2
Wunstorf, Ger. 79/G4
Wuntho, Myan. 119/G3
Wupatki Nat'l Mon., Az, US 175/G3
Wuppertal, Ger. 79/E6
Wuqi, China 106/B3
Wuqia, China 125/C4
Wuqiang, China 106/C3
Wuqiao, China 106/D3
Wuqing, China 106/H7
Würm (riv.), Ger. 81/H6
Würm K. (canal), Ger. 87/H1
Wurno, Nga. 141/G3
Würselen, Ger. 81/F2
Wurtsboro, NY, US 187/J4
Wurzbach, Ger. 85/E2
Würzburg, Ger. 84/C3
Wusheng (pass), China 106/C5
Wusheng, China 113/H2
Wushi, China 125/C3
Wusong, China 106/L8
Wüstegarten (peak), Ger. 79/G6
Wüstenrot, Ger. 84/C4
Wusuli (riv.), Rus.,China 105/L2
Wutach (riv.), Ger. 87/E2
Wutai (peak), China 106/C3
Wutai, China 106/C3
Wuteve (mt.), Libr. 140/C4
Wutha-Farnroda, Ger. 84/D1
Wutonggou, China 125/E3
Wutöschingen, Ger. 87/E2
Wuustwezel, Belg. 78/B6
Wuwei, China 104/E4
Wuwei, China 106/D5
Wuxi (riv.), China 113/H2
Wuxi, China 106/L8
Wuxiang, China 106/C3
Wuxue, China 113/G2
Wuyang, China 106/C4
Wuyi (mts.), China 113/H3
Wuyi, China 106/C3
Wuying, China 105/K2
Wuyuan, China 104/F3
Wuyur (riv.), China 105/K2
Wuzhai, China 106/B3
Wuzhen, China 106/L9
Wuzhi (peak), China 113/F5
Wuzhi, China 106/C4
Wuzhi (peak), China 106/J6
Wuzhou, China 113/F4
Wyalkatchem, Austl. 156/C4
Wyandanch, NY, US 195/M8
Wyandotte, Ok, US 179/G2
Wyandotte, Mi, US 186/E3
Wyandotte NWR, Mi, US 193/F7
Wyandra, Austl. 160/B4
Wyangala (res.), Austl. 159/D1
Wyangala (dam), Austl. 159/D1
Wyarno, Wy, US 173/K1
Wycheproof, Austl. 158/B3
Wyckoff, NJ, US 195/J8
Wye (riv.), Eng, UK 62/C2
Wye, Eng, UK 63/G4
Wye Mills, Md, US 194/B6
Wyee, Austl. 159/E1
Wyk, Ger. 66/C4
Wylie, Tx, US 176/L6
Wylie (lake), SC, US 189/G3
Wyllie's (pass), SAfr. 149/F4
Wylliesburg, Va, US 189/H2
Wymark, Sk, Can. 171/L2
Wymeswold, Eng, UK 63/E1
Wymondham, Eng, UK 63/H1
Wymore, Ne, US 181/F3
Wynbring, Austl. 157/G4
Wyndham, Austl. 154/C3
Wyndmere, ND, US 182/F4
Wynigen, Swi. 86/D3
Wynndel, BC, Can. 170/F3
Wynne, Ar, US 188/B3
Wynnewood, Ok, US 179/F3
Wynnum (nbrhd.), Austl. 160/F6
Wynona, Ok, US 179/F2
Wynyard, Sk, Can. 182/B2
Wynyard, Austl. 158/C4
Wyola, Mt, US 173/K1
Wyoming, Mn, US 183/H5
Wyoming, Mi, US 186/D3
Wyoming, On, Can. 186/E3
Wyoming (peak), Wy, US 173/H2
Wyoming (state), US 168/E3
Wyoming, Il, US 181/K3
Wyoming, Pa, US 194/C1
Wyoming, De, US 194/C5
Wyomissing, Pa, US 194/C3
Wyong, Austl. 159/E1
Wyperfeld NP, Austl. 158/B2
Wyralinu (peak), Austl. 156/D5
Wyre (riv.), Eng, UK 61/F4
Wyrzysk, Pol. 69/J2
Wysokie Mazowieckie, Pol. 69/M2
Wysox, Pa, US 187/H4
Wyszków, Pol. 69/L2
Wytheville, Va, US 189/G2

X

X-Can, Mex. 200/E1
Xa Binh Long, Viet. 120/D4
Xa Song Luy, Viet. 120/E4
Xa Tho Thanh, Viet. 120/D3
Xa Vo Dat, Viet. 120/D4
Xá-Muteba, Ang. 146/D5
Xaafuun, Som. 144/D3
Xabyaisamba, China 112/C2
Xaçmaz, Azer. 97/J4
Xagħra, Malta 74/L6
Xagquka, China 112/B2
Xai-Xai, Moz. 149/G5
Xainza, China 125/E5
Xaitongmoin, China 123/G1
Xaiva, Moz. 149/G4
Xalin, Som. 144/D3
Xaltianguis, Mex. 199/F5
Xam (riv.), Laos 112/E4
Xambioá, Braz. 206/D4
Xan (riv.), Viet. 120/D3
Xandel, Ang. 146/D5
Xangdoring, China 125/D5
Xankändı, Azer. 129/F2
Xanlar, Azer. 97/H4
Xanten, Ger. 78/D5
Xánthi, Gre. 75/J2
Xanxerê, Braz. 213/F3
Xapuri, Braz. 208/D3
Xar Moron (riv.), China 101/M5
Xarag, China 104/D4
Xarardheere, Som. 144/C4
Xarba (pass), China 123/E1
Xar'oi, China 104/E5
Xassengue, Ang. 146/D5
Xaudum (riv.), Bots. 148/D3
Xavantes (res.), Braz. 210/C4
Xavantes, Serra dos (mts.), Braz. 210/C1
Xavantina, Braz. 213/F2
Xaxim, Braz. 213/F3
Xayar, China 125/D3
Xel-há (ruin), Mex. 200/E1
Xenia, Oh, US 186/E5
Xenia, Il, US 188/C1
Xeno, Laos 120/D2
Xerta, Sp. 73/F2
Xertigny, Fr. 86/C1
Xhumo, Bots. 148/E4
Xi (riv.), China 103/L7
Xi (lake), China 106/E2
Xia'ao, China 113/E3
Xiadian, China 106/H7
Xiadong, China 104/D3
Xiaguan, China 112/D3
Xiahuaqiao, China 113/F3
Xiahuayuan, China 106/G6
Xiajia, China 113/E3
Xiajiang, China 113/F3
Xiajiapu, China 107/C1
Xiajin, China 106/C3
Xialuhe, China 107/C2
Xiamen (int'l arpt.), China 113/H3
Xiamen, China 113/H3
Xi'an, China 106/B4
Xianfeng, China 113/F2
Xiang (riv.), China 113/G3
Xiang Khoang (plat.), Laos 112/D5
Xiang Ngeun, Laos 112/D5
Xiangcheng, China 112/C2
Xiangcheng, China 106/C4
Xiangcheng, China 106/C4
Xiangdong, China 113/G3
Xiangfan, China 106/C4
Xiangfen, China 106/B4
Xianghe, China 106/H7
Xianghua (mtn.), China 113/G3
Xiangkhoang, Laos 120/C2
Xiangkou, China 113/H2
Xianglinpu, China 113/F3
Xiangning, China 106/B4
Xiangshui, China 106/D4
Xiangshui, China 112/E3
Xiangshuiba, China 113/F3
Xiangtan, China 113/G3
Xiangyangqiao, China 113/G3
Xiangyuan, China 106/C3
Xiangyun, China 112/D3
Xianju, China 113/J2
Xianning, China 113/G2
Xiantao, China 113/G2
Xianxia, China 113/H2
Xianxia (mtn.), China 113/H2
Xianxizhen, China 113/F3
Xianyang, China 104/F5
Xianyuan, China 113/H2
Xianzijiao, China 113/F3
Xiao (riv.), China 119/K2
Xiao Hinggan (mts.), China 105/K2
Xiao Qaidam, China 104/D4
Xiao Xian, China 106/D4
Xiaobole (peak), China 105/J1
Xiaodongliang, China 104/D4
Xiaofangshen, China 107/A2
Xiaogan, China 113/G2
Xiaogushan, China 107/B3
Xiaohenglong, China 113/F3
Xiaojiagang, China 113/G2
Xiaojiang, China 113/G3
Xiaojiang, China 113/J3
Xiaojin (riv.), China 112/D2
Xiaoliangshan, China 107/B1
Xiaolindian, China 113/G1
Xiaomei, China 113/H3
Xiaomei (pass), China 113/G3
Xiaomianzhen, China 113/E2
Xiaonanchuan, China 104/C4
Xiaopingyang, China 113/F4
Xiaoqiao, China 113/H3
Xiaoqing (riv.), China 106/D3
Xiaoshan, China 106/L9
Xiaosong, China 113/H3
Xiaotazi, China 107/B1
Xiaowutai (peak), China 106/C3
Xiaoxiba, China 112/E2
Xiaoyangjie, China 119/H3
Xiaoyi, China 106/B3
Xiaoyuan, China 113/G3
Xiapilin, China 113/F3
Xiasi, China 113/E3
Xiatianping, China 107/E1
Xiayi, China 106/D4
Xiazichang, China 113/E3
Xibaxa (riv.), China 112/B2
Xichahe, China 104/F5
Xichang, China 112/D3
Xichou, China 119/H3
Xichuan, China 106/B4
Xico, Mex. 199/N7
Xicohténcatl, Mex. 199/F4
Xicotepec, Mex. 199/M6
Xicute, Col. 204/D4
Xide, China 112/D2
Xidian, China 113/J2
Xifei (riv.), China 106/C4
Xifeng, China 119/J2
Xifeng, China 106/F2
Xifeng, China 104/F4
Xifengkou, China 106/J6
Xigazê, China 123/G1
Xihan (riv.), China 104/E5
Xihaoping, China 113/F2
Xihekou, China 106/B3
Xihua, China 106/C4
Xiis, Som. 144/C3
Xijin, China 113/H3
Xijir, China 104/C5
Xijir Ulan (lake), China 125/F4
Xijishui, China 104/E4
Xikouxu, China 113/H3
Xiliao (riv.), China 105/J3
Xiliao (bay), China 106/E3
Xilin, China 119/J3
Xilinji, China 105/J1
Xilitla, Mex. 200/B1
Xilókastron, Gre. 75/H3
Ximeng Vazu Zizhixian, China 112/C4
Ximiao, China 104/E3
Ximucheng, China 107/B2
Xin (riv.), China 113/H2
Xin Barag Zuoqi, China 105/H2
Xin Bulag Dong, China 105/H2
Xin'anjiang (res.), China 106/D5
Xin'an (riv.), China 106/D5
Xinan, China 113/H3
Xin'an, China 113/H3
Xin'an, China 106/C4
Xin'anjiang, China 113/H2
Xinavane, Moz. 149/G5
Xinbao'an, China 106/G6
Xinbin, China 107/C2
Xinbin, China 113/F4
Xincai, China 106/C4
Xinchang, China 113/H2
Xinchang, China 113/J2
Xincheng, China 113/G3
Xincheng, China 106/G7
Xinchengzi, China 107/B1
Xindi, China 113/F4
Xindu, China 113/F4
Xinfeng, China 119/K3
Xinfengjiang (res.), China 113/G4
Xing'an, China 113/F3
Xingcheng, China 106/E2
Xinge, Ang. 146/D5
Xinghua, China 106/D4
Xingkāi (Khākā) (lake), Rus. 105/L3
Xinglong, China 113/F5
Xinglong, China 106/H6
Xingping, China 113/F3
Xingqêngoin, China 112/D2
Xingshan, China 106/B5
Xingshutun, China 107/B3
Xingtai, China 106/C3
Xingu (riv.), Braz. 203/D3
Xingu, PN do, Braz. 210/B1
Xingxingxia, China 104/D3
Xingyang, China 106/C4
Xingyi, China 112/E3
Xinhe, China 125/D3
Xinhe, China 106/C3
Xinhezhen, China 106/L8
Xinhuang Dongzu Zizhixian, China 113/F3
Xining, China 104/E4
Xinji, China 106/C3
Xinjian, China 113/H2
Xinjiang (reg.), China 103/H5
Xinjiang, China 106/B4
Xinjiang Uygur (aut. reg.), China 125/D3
Xinjie, China 120/E2
Xinjin, China 107/A3
Xinkaihe, China 107/B2
Xinle, China 106/C3
Xinlitun, China 107/B1
Xinlong, China 113/H3
Xinmiao, China 105/J2
Xinmin, China 107/B1
Xinping Xian, China 112/D3
Xinqiang, China 113/G2
Xinqiao, China 113/F4
Xinshao, China 113/F3
Xinshi, China 106/L9
Xinsi, China 104/E5
Xintai, China 106/D4
Xinxiang, China 106/C4
Xinxing, China 105/J3
Xinxu, China 119/J3
Xinyang, China 106/C4
Xinye, China 106/C4
Xinyi, China 119/K3
Xinyi, China 106/D4
Xinyu, China 113/G3
Xinyuan, China 125/D3
Xinzheng, China 106/C4
Xinzhou, China 113/F5
Xinzhou, China 113/G2
Xinzhou, China 113/F2
Xinzo de Limia, Sp. 72/B1
Xiong Xian, China 106/H7
Xiongyuecheng, China 107/B2
Xiping, China 106/C4
Xiqin, China 113/H3
Xiqing (mts.), China 104/E5
Xique-Xique, Braz. 211/E1
Xishan, China 113/G2
Xishui, China 119/J2
Xitang, China 106/L9
Xitianmu (peak), China 113/H2
Xitiao (riv.), China 106/K9
Xitole, GBis. 140/B4
Xiu (riv.), China 113/G2
Xiuning, China 113/H2
Xiuwen, China 119/J2
Xiuwu, China 106/C4
Xiuyan, China 107/B2
Xixabangma (peak), China 123/E1
Xixi (riv.), China 112/D2
Xixi, China 113/H3
Xixia, China 106/B4
Xiyang (riv.), China 119/J3
Xizang (Tibet) (aut. reg..), China 118/E2
Xize, China 113/J2
Xizhai, China 113/F2
Xochicalco (ruin), Mex. 199/K8
Xochimilco (nbrhd.), Mex. 199/Q10
Xoka, China 112/B2
Xonacatlán, Mex. 199/Q10
Xorkol, China 104/C4
Xpujil, Mex. 200/D2
Xu (riv.), China 113/H3
Xuan'en, China 113/F2
Xuanhua, China 106/G6
Xuanwei, China 112/E3
Xuchang, China 106/C4
Xudat, Azer. 97/J4
Xuddur (Oddur), Som. 144/B4
Xue (mts.), China 112/C3
Xugin Gol (riv.), China 104/D4
Xugou, China 106/L8
Xuguanzhen, China 106/L8
Xujiatun, China 107/B2
Xun (riv.), China 104/F5
Xun Xian, China 106/C4
Xungru, China 123/E1
Xunjiansi, China 113/F2
Xunke, China 105/K2
Xunyang, China 106/B4
Xupu, China 106/L8
Xur, China 104/D4
Xuru (lake), China 125/E6
Xushui, China 106/G7
Xuwen, China 113/F4
Xuyi, China 106/D4
Xuyong, China 112/E2
Xuzhou, China 106/D4

Y

Y Llethr (peak), Wal, UK 60/E6
Yaak (riv.), Mt, US 170/G3
Ya'an, China 112/D2
Yaapeet, Austl. 158/B2
Yaaq-Baraawe, Som. 145/C1
Ya'bad, WBnk. 131/C4
Yabassi, Camr. 146/B1
Yabēlo, Eth. 144/A4
Yabia, D.R. Congo 147/E2
Yablanitsa, Bul. 77/G4
Yablis, Nic. 201/F3
Yablonov, Ukr. 98/C3
Yablonovo, Rus. 104/G1
Yablonovskiy, Rus. 99/K5
Yablonovyy (range), Rus. 103/L4
Yabrīn, SAr. 126/E4
Yabrūd, WBnk. 131/C5
Yabrūd, Syria 131/F1
Yabucoa, PR 197/M8
Yabuki, Japan 111/G2
Yabuzukahon, Japan 109/C1
Yacaré Norte (riv.), Par. 212/E2
Yachats, Or, US 172/A1
Yacheng, China 120/E2
Yachi (riv.), China 113/E3
Yachiho, Japan 109/A1
Yachimata, Japan 109/E2
Yachiyo, Japan 109/G5
Yachiyo, Japan 109/E2
Yachiyo, Japan 109/D1
Yacimiento Río Turbio, Arg. 215/B6
Yaco, Bol. 212/C1
Yacolt, Wa, US 170/C5
Yacopí, Col. 207/L7
Yacuiba, Bol. 212/D2
Yacuma (riv.), Bol. 209/E4
Yacumbu, PN, Ven. 204/D2
Yad Mordekhay, Isr. 131/B5
Yad-Mordechai NP, Isr. 131/B5
Yadé (mass.), CAfr. 142/B4
Yadkin (riv.), NC, US 189/G2
Yadkinville, NC, US 189/G2
Yadong, China 123/G2
Yadrin, Rus. 95/K5
Yaeyama (isls.), Japan 111/G8
Yāfā, Isr. 131/C3
Yafren, Libya 93/G4
Yağcılar, Turk. 96/D5
Yagi, Japan 109/J5
Yagodnoye, Rus. 101/Q3
Yagorlytsk (gulf), Ukr. 77/K2
Yagoua, Camr. 142/B3
Yagradagzê (peak), China 104/D4
Yaguale (riv.), Hon. 200/E3
Yaguarón (riv.), Uru. 215/G2
Yaguarú, Bol. 209/F4
Yaguas (riv.), Peru 204/D5
Yague del Sur (riv.), DRep. 201/J2
Yagur, Isr. 131/C3
Yahagi (riv.), Japan 109/M6
Yahk, BC, Can. 170/F3
Yahongqiao, China 106/H7
Yahotyn, Ukr. 98/F2
Yahualica de Gonzalez Gallo, Mex. 198/E4
Yahyalı, Turk. 128/C2
Yáios (Paxoí), Gre. 75/G3
Yaita, Japan 111/F2
Yaizu, Japan 111/F3
Yajalón, Mex. 200/C2
Yakacık, Turk. 130/E1
Yakapınar, Turk. 130/D1
Yakeshi, China 105/J2
Yakima, Wa, US 170/D4
Yakima (riv.), Wa, US 170/D4
Yakima Firing Range, Wa, US 170/D4
Yakima Ind. Res., Wa, US 170/D4
Yakishiri (isl.), Japan 108/B1
Yako, Burk. 141/E3
Yakoma, D.R. Congo 147/E1
Yakoruda, Bul. 75/H1
Yakovlevo, Rus. 99/J2
Yaksu-nodongjagu, NKor. 107/D2
Yaku (isl.), Japan 105/L5
Yakumo, Japan 108/B2
Yakuno, Japan 109/G5
Yakutat (bay), Ak, US 166/B3
Yakutat, Ak, US 168/Z13
Yakutsk, Rus. 101/N3
Yakymivka, Ukr. 99/H4
Yala, Thai. 120/C5
Yala NP, SrL. 121/D5
Yalaha, Fl, US 190/M6
Yalahua (lag.), Mex. 200/E1
Yalakom (riv.), BC, Can. 170/C2
Yalama, Azer. 97/J4
Yalangoz, Turk. 130/E1
Yalata Abor. Land, Austl. 157/F4
Yalbac (hills), Belz. 200/D2
Yalding, Eng, UK 56/E3
Yale, Ok, US 179/F2
Yale, Mi, US 186/E3
Yale, BC, Can. 170/D3
Yalgoo, Austl. 156/C4
Yalgorup NP, Austl. 156/B5
Yalinga, CAfr. 142/D4
Yallock, Austl. 158/C2
Yalnızçam, Turk. 97/G4
Yalobusha (riv.), Ms, US 188/B4
Yaloké, CAfr. 142/C4
Yalong (riv.), China 103/K6
Yalova, Turk. 77/J5
Yalova, Turk. 77/H5
Yalpuh (lake), Gre. 77/J3
Yalta, Ukr. 96/E3
Yalu (riv.), China, NKor. 101/N5
Yaluwe, D.R. Congo 147/F3
Yalvaç, Turk. 128/B2
Yamachiche, Qu, Can. 187/K1
Yamada, Japan 108/B4
Yamaga, Japan 110/B4
Yamagata, Japan 101/P6
Yamagata, Japan 111/G1
Yamagata (pref.), Japan 108/A4
Yamaguchi (pref.), Japan 110/B3
Yamaguchi, Japan 110/B3
Yamakita, Japan 109/C3
Yamal (pen.), Rus. 103/F2
Yamanaka (lake), Japan 109/B3
Yamanashi, Japan 109/B2
Yamanie (falls), Austl. 160/B2
Yamanie Falls NP, Austl. 160/B2
Yamantau (peak), Rus. 95/N5
Yamaoka, Japan 109/M5
Yamarna Abor. Reserve, Austl. 156/D4
Yamashiro, Japan 109/J6
Yamaska (riv.), Qu, Can. 184/A3
Yamato, Japan 111/F2
Yamato (riv.), Japan 109/J6
Yamato, Japan 109/E1
Yamato, Japan 109/B2
Yamato, Japan 109/C3
Yamato-kōriyama, Japan 109/J6
Yamatotakada, Japan 109/J6
Yamazoe, Japan 109/K6
Yamba, Austl. 158/E1
Yambah, Austl. 157/G2
Yambata, D.R. Congo 147/E2
Yambéring, Gui. 140/B4
Yambio, Sudan 142/F4
Yambol, Bul. 77/H4
Yambrasbamba, Peru 208/B2
Yamdena (isl.), Indo. 117/H5
Yamethin, Myan. 112/C4
Yamin (peak), Indo. 117/K4
Yamm, Rus. 67/N2
Yamma Yamma (lake), Austl. 153/D3
Yamoto, Japan 108/B4
Yamoussoukro (cap.), C.d'Iv. 140/D5
Yampa (riv.), Co, US 173/K3
Yampil', Ukr. 98/D3
Yampil', Ukr. 98/E3
Yamuna (riv.), India 118/C2
Yamunānagar, India 124/D4
Yamzho Yumco (lake), China 119/F2
Yan, Nga. 142/B3
Yan (riv.), SrL. 118/D6
Yan (riv.), China 104/F4
Yan Yean (res.), Austl. 158/G5
Yana (riv.), Rus. 103/N3
Yanac, Austl. 158/B3
Yanagawa, Japan 110/B4
Yanahuanca, Peru 208/B3
Yanai, Japan 110/C4
Yanaizu, Japan 109/L5
Yanam, India 121/D2
Yan'an, China 106/B3
Yanaoca, Peru 208/D4
Yanaul, Rus. 95/M4
Yanbian, China 119/H2
Yanbu' al Baḩr, SAr. 135/H3
Yancannia, Austl. 158/B1
Yancey, Tx, US 177/E3
Yanceyville, NC, US 189/H2
Yancheng, China 106/C4
Yancheng, China 106/E4
Yanchep NP, Austl. 156/B4
Yanco (cr.), Austl. 159/B2
Yanco, Austl. 159/C2
Yandeearra Abor. Reserve, Austl. 156/C2
Yanderra, Austl. 159/E2
Yandev, Nga. 141/H5
Yandong, China 113/E3
Yandongi, D.R. Congo 147/E2
Yandoon, Myan. 112/B5
Yanfolila, Mali 140/C4
Yang Talat, Thai. 120/C2
Yangalia, CAfr. 142/D4
Yangambi, D.R. Congo 147/F2
Ya'ngamdo, China 112/B2
Yangamo, Camr. 142/B4
Yangbi (riv.), China 119/G2
Yangchangba, China 112/E3
Yangcheng, China 106/C4
Yangcheng (lake), China 106/L8
Yangcun, China 113/G4
Yangdang (mts.), China 113/H3
Yangdŏk, NKor. 107/D3
Yanggang-do (prov.), NKor. 107/D2
Yanggao, China 106/C2
Yanggok, SKor. 107/F6
Yanggu, SKor. 107/D3
Yanggu, China 106/C3
Yangjiang, China 113/F4
Yangjiawan, China 112/E3
Yangliuqing, China 106/H7
Yangloudong, China 113/G2
Yangma (isl.), China 107/A4
Yangmei, Tai. 113/J3
Yangming (peak), China 113/F3
Yangon (state), Myan. 119/G4
Yangon (Rangoon) (cap.), Myan. 112/C5
Yangon (Rangoon) (int'l arpt.), Myan. 112/C5
Yangp'yŏng, SKor. 107/D4
Yangqiaopan, China 104/F4
Yangqu, China 106/C3
Yangquan, China 106/C3
Yangsan, SKor. 107/E5
Yangshan, China 119/K3
Yangshuo, China 119/K3
Yangtouyan, China 112/D3
Yangtze (Chang) (riv.), China 106/D5
Yangudi Rassa NP, Eth. 144/B3
Yangxi, China 113/G3
Yangxin, China 113/G2
Yangxin, China 106/D3
Yangxu, China 113/E4
Yangyang, SKor. 107/E3
Yangyuan, China 106/C2
Yangzhong, China 106/D4
Yangzhou, China 106/D4
Yanja, D.R. Congo 146/D3
Yanji, China 105/K3
Yanji, China 105/K3
Yanjia, China 107/A2
Yanjin, China 106/C4
Yanjin, China 112/E2
Yanjing, China 112/C2
Yankara, Nga. 141/G4
Yankari NP, Nga. 142/A3
Yankee Stadium, NY, US 195/K8
Yankton, SD, US 180/F2
Yankton Ind. Res., SD, US 180/E2
Yanling, China 106/C4
Yanmen (pass), China 106/C3
Yanonge, D.R. Congo 147/F2
Yanqing, China 106/G6
Yanrey, Austl. 156/B2
Yanshan, China 119/H3
Yanshan, China 106/D3
Yanshi, China 106/C4
Yanshi, China 113/H3
Yanshiping, China 104/C5
Yanshou, China 105/K2
Yantaa (riv.), Fin. 65/E4
Yantabulla, Austl. 158/C1
Yantai, China 106/E3
Yantara, Austl. 158/B1
Yantarnyy, Rus. 67/H4
Yanting, China 112/E2
Yantis, Tx, US 179/G4
Yantley, Al, US 188/C4
Yantra (riv.), Bul. 93/K2
Yanush, Ok, US 179/G3
Yanwa, China 112/C3
Yanxi, China 113/H3
Yanyuan, China 112/D3
Yanzhou, China 106/D4
Yao, Chad 142/C2
Yao, Japan 109/J6
Yao'an, China 119/H2
Yaodian, China 106/B3
Yaogu, China 113/G4
Yaotsu, Japan 109/M5
Yaoundé (cap.), Camr. 146/B2
Yap (isls.), Micr. 162/C4
Yapacana, PN, Ven. 205/E4
Yapacani (riv.), Bol. 209/E5
Yapei, Gha. 141/E4
Yapen (isl.), Indo. 162/C5
Yapen (str.), Indo. 117/J4
Yapirga, Bol. 212/D1
Yapraklı, Turk. 96/E4
Yaqueling, China 113/F2
Yaqui (riv.), Mex. 165/G7
Yaquina (bay), Or, US 172/A1
Yara, Cuba 201/G1
Yaracuy (state), Ven. 204/D2
Yaraka, Austl. 160/B4
Yaralıgöz (peak), Turk. 96/E4
Yaransk, Rus. 95/K4
Yardımcı (pt.), Turk. 130/B1
Yardley, Pa, US 194/D3
Yardville-Groveville, NJ, US 194/D3
Yardymly, Azer. 129/G2
Yare (riv.), Eng, UK 63/H1
Yarega, Rus. 95/M3
Yaremcha, Ukr. 98/C3
Yarensk, Rus. 95/L3
Yarí (riv.), Col. 204/C4
Yari-ga-take (peak), Japan 111/E2
Yarīm, Yem. 144/C2
Yarımca, Turk. 77/J5
Yaritagua, Ven. 204/D2
Yarkant (riv.), China 100/H6
Yarkovo, Rus. 95/Q4
Yarloop, Austl. 156/B5
Yarlung Zangbo (Brahmaputra) (riv.), China 123/G1
Yarmolyntsi, Ukr. 98/D3
Yarmouth, NS, Can. 184/D4
Yarmuk (riv.), Syria,Jor. 131/D3
Yarnell, Az, US 175/F3
Yaroslavl' (oblast), Rus. 94/H4
Yaroslavl', Rus. 94/H4
Yaroslavskiy, Rus. 105/L3
Yarpuz, Turk. 130/E1
Yarra (riv.), Austl. 158/G5
Yarra Glen, Austl. 158/G5
Yarra Junction, Austl. 159/B3
Yarragon, Austl. 159/C4
Yarram, Austl. 159/C4
Yarraman, Austl. 160/D4
Yarrawonga, Austl. 159/C3
Yarrow Point, Wa, US 193/C2
Yartsevo, Rus. 94/G5
Yartsevo, Rus. 100/K3
Yarumal, Col. 204/C3
Yarzhong, China 112/C2
Yasa, D.R. Congo 147/E3
Yasato, Japan 109/E1
Yasawa Group (isls.), Fiji 162/G6
Yasel'da (riv.), Bela. 96/C1
Yasenskaya, Rus. 99/K4
Yashalta, Rus. 99/M4
Yashbum, Yem. 144/C2
Yashi, Nga. 141/G3
Yashikera, Nga. 141/F4
Yashima, Japan 108/B4
Yashio, Japan 109/D2
Yashiro, Japan 109/G6
Yashkino, Rus. 97/K1
Yashkul', Rus. 97/H3
Yasinya, Ukr. 98/C3
Yasnogorka, Ukr. 99/J3
Yasnyy, Rus. 97/L2
Yasothon, Thai. 120/D3
Yass, Austl. 159/D2
Yasu (riv.), Japan 109/K6
Yasu, Japan 109/K5
Yasugi, Japan 110/C3
Yāsūj, Iran 129/G4
Yasun Burnu (pt.), Turk. 96/F4
Yasuni, PN, Ecu. 204/B5
Yasynuvata, Ukr. 99/J3
Yat (well), Niger 134/B4
Yata (riv.), CAfr. 142/D3
Yata (riv.), Bol. 209/E4
Yata, Bol. 209/E4
Yata-Ngaya, Rsv. de Faune de la, CAfr. 142/D3
Yatabe, Japan 111/G2
Yatağan, Turk. 128/B2
Yataity, Par. 213/E3
Yate, Eng, UK 62/D3

311
Yatel – Zheng

Yateley, Eng, UK 63/F4
Yatenga (prov.), Burk. 141/E3
Yates Center, Ks, US 179/G2
Yathkyed (lake), Nun, Can. 166/G2
Yatina, Bol. 212/C2
Yatolema, D.R. Congo 147/F2
Yatomi, Japan 109/L5
Yatsu-ga-take (peak), Japan 109/A2
Yatsuo, Japan 111/E2
Yatsushiro, Japan 110/B4
Yatsushiro, Japan 109/B2
Yatta (plat.), Kenya 145/B2
Yaṭṭah, WBnk. 131/C6
Yatton, Eng, UK 62/D4
Yauca, Peru 208/C4
Yauca (riv.), Peru 208/C4
Yauco, PR 197/M8
Yauli, Peru 208/B3
Yaúna Moloca, Col. 204/D5
Yaupi, Ecu. 204/B5
Yaupon Beach, NC, US 189/H4
Yaután, Peru 208/B3
Yauyos, Peru 208/C4
Yauza (riv.), Rus. 94/W9
Yavapai Ind. Res., Az, US 175/F3
Yavarí (riv.), Braz.,Peru 203/B3
Yavarí Mirim (riv.), Peru 208/C2
Yavaros, Mex. 198/C3
Yavatmāl, India 121/C1
Yavay (pen.), Rus. 100/H2
Yavita, Ven. 205/E4
Yaviza, Pan. 204/B2
Yavne, Isr. 131/B5
Yavne'el, Isr. 131/D3
Yavoriv, Ukr. 69/M4
Yavuzeli, Turk. 128/D2
Yawahara, Japan 109/E2
Yawata, Japan 109/J6
Yawatahama, Japan 110/C4
Yaxchilán (ruin), Guat. 200/D2
Yaxing, China 120/E2
Yaxley, Eng, UK 63/F1
Yaygın, Turk. 128/E2
Yayladaği, Turk. 130/E2
Yayladere, Turk. 128/E2
Yaysan, Kaz. 97/L2
Yayuan, China 107/D2
Yazd, Iran 129/H4
Yazd (gov.), Iran 129/H3
Yazhma, Rus. 95/K2
Yazhou, China 113/E3
Yazmān, Pak. 124/A5
Yazoo (riv.), Ms, US 188/B4
Yazoo City, Ms, US 188/B4
Yazykovo, Rus. 97/H1
Ybbs (riv.), Aus. 69/H4
Ybbs an der Donau, Aus. 71/L2
Ybor City, Fl, US 190/L8
Ybycuí, Par. 213/E3
Yding Skovhøj (peak), Den. 66/C3
Ye, Myan. 120/B3
Ye Xian, China 104/G5
Ye Xian, China 106/D3
Ye-ngan, Myan. 112/C4
Yea, Austl. 159/B3
Yeaddiss, Ky, US 189/F2
Yeadon, Eng, UK 61/G4
Yean, SKor. 107/E4
Yeay Sen (cape), Camb. 120/C4
Yebbi-Bou, Chad 134/C4
Yecheng, China 125/C4
Yech'ŏn, SKor. 107/E4
Yecla, Sp. 73/E3
Yécora, Mex. 198/C2
Yecuatla, Mex. 199/N7
Yedashe, Myan. 120/B2
Yedigöller NP, Turk. 96/D4
Yedikule, Turk. 129/M6
Yeditepe, Turk. 130/E2
Yeed, Som. 144/B4
Yeeda River, Austl. 154/A4
Yeelirrie, Austl. 156/D3
Yefimovskiy, Rus. 94/G4
Yéfira, Gre. 75/H2
Yefremov, Rus. 96/F1
Yegorlak (riv.), Rus. 97/G3
Yegorlykskaya, Rus. 99/L4
Yegorova (cape), Rus. 105/M3
Yehi'am's Fortress NP, Isr. 131/C3
Yehualtepec, Mex. 199/M8
Yehud, Isr. 131/B4
Yei (riv.), Sudan 142/F4
Yei, Sudan 147/G1
Yejmiadzin, Arm. 129/F1
Yekaterinburg (Sverdlovsk), Rus. 95/P4
Yekaterinoslavka, Rus. 105/K1
Yekaterinovka, Rus. 97/H1
Yekateriny (chan.), Rus. 108/E1
Yekepa, Libr. 140/C5
Yekia Sahal (well), Chad 142/C1
Yelabuga, Rus. 95/M5
Yelan', Rus. 97/G2
Yelarbon, Austl. 160/C5
Yelets, Rus. 96/F1
Yelgu, Sudan 142/G3
Yélimané, Mali 140/C3
Yelizavetinka, Rus. 97/L2
Yelizavetino, Rus. 67/N2
Yelizavetopol'skoye, Rus. 97/M1
Yelizovo, Rus. 101/R4
Yelkhovka, Rus. 97/J1
Yell (isl.), Sc, UK 57/W13
Yellamanchili, India 121/D2
Yellandu, India 121/D2
Yellel, Alg. 138/F5
Yellow (sea), Asia 103/M6
Yellow (riv.), Wi, US 181/J1
Yellow (riv.), Ga, US 189/M7
Yellow (Huang) (riv.), China 104/G4
Yellow Creek, Sk, Can. 171/M1
Yellow Dog (pt.), Mi, US 183/L4
Yellow Grass, Sk, Can. 182/B3
Yellow House Draw (stream), Tx, US 178/C4
Yellow Jacket, Co, US 175/H2
Yellow Pine, Al, US 190/D2
Yellow Pine, Id, US 172/F1
Yellowknife (riv.), NW, Can. 166/E2
Yellowknife (cap.), NW, Can. 166/E2
Yellowstone (riv.), US 165/G5
Yellowstone NP, US 173/H1
Yellowtail (dam), Mt, US 173/K1
Yellville, Ar, US 179/H2
Yelm, Wa, US 170/C4
Yel'nya, Rus. 94/G5
Yelshanka, Rus. 97/H2
Yel'sk, Bela. 98/E2
Yelverton, Eng, UK 62/B6
Yelwa, Nga. 141/G4
Yelwa, Nga. 141/H4
Yema, D.R. Congo 146/C4
Yema (riv.), China 104/D4
Yemaotai, China 107/B1
Yemassee, SC, US 189/G4
Yemen(ctry.) 103/D8
Yemetsk, Rus. 94/J3
Yemil'chyne, Ukr. 98/D2
Yen Bai, Viet. 112/E4
Yen Minh, Viet. 112/E4
Yenagoa, Nga. 141/G5
Yenakiyeve, Ukr. 99/K3
Yenangyaung, Myan. 112/B4
Yenanma, Myan. 112/B5
Yenda, Austl. 159/C2
Yende, Congo 146/D2
Yende Millimou, Gui. 140/C4
Yendi, Gha. 141/E4
Yenge (riv.), D.R. Congo 147/E3
Yengisar, China 125/C4
Yengo, Congo 146/C2
Yengo NP, Austl. 159/E1
Yengué, Gabon 146/B3
Yeniçağa, Turk. 77/L5
Yenice (riv.), Turk. 96/E4
Yenice, Turk. 130/D1
Yenice, Turk. 77/L5
Yenice, Turk. 77/H6
Yeniceoba, Turk. 128/C2
Yeniköy, Turk. 77/H5
Yeniköy, Turk. 129/M6
Yenişehir, Turk. 77/J5
Yenisey (riv.), Rus. 103/H3
Yeniseysk, Rus. 100/K4
Yenne, Fr. 90/B1
Yeno, Gabon 146/B3
Yenshui, Tai. 113/J4
Yeo (lake), Austl. 156/E3
Yeo(lake) 153/B3
Yeo Lake Nature Reserve, Austl. 156/E3
Yeoval, Austl. 159/D1
Yeovil, Eng, UK 62/D5
Yeping, China 113/H3
Yeppoon, Austl. 160/C3
Yeraifia (well), WSah. 136/B4
Yerakhtur, Rus. 97/G1
Yerakovoúni (peak), Gre. 75/H3
Yeraliyev, Kaz. 97/J4
Yerbas Buenas, Chile 214/C2
Yères (riv.), Fr. 80/A4
Yerevan (cap.), Arm. 129/F1
Yerichaña, Ven. 205/E3
Yerington, Nv, US 172/D4
Yerköy, Turk. 128/C2
Yerlisu, Turk. 77/H5
Yermak, Kaz. 125/C1
Yermekeyevo, Rus. 95/M5
Yermish', Rus. 94/J5
Yermitsa, Rus. 95/M2
Yermo, Ca, US 174/D3
Yermolayevo, Rus. 97/K1
Yerofey Pavlovich, Rus. 105/J1
Yeroḥam, Isr. 130/D4
Yerolimín, Gre. 75/H4
Yerre (riv.), Fr. 70/D2
Yerres, Fr. 56/K5
Yerseke, Neth. 78/B5
Yershov, Rus. 97/J2
Yershovka, Kaz. 95/Q5
Yertoma, Rus. 95/K3
Yerupaja (peak), Peru 208/B3
Yerushalayim (Jerusalem) (cap.), Isr. 131/C5
Yerville, Fr. 83/F1
Yesa, Bol. 212/D1
Yesagyo, Myan. 112/B4
Yesan, SKor. 107/D4
Yeşildere, Turk. 130/C1
Yeşilhisar, Turk. 128/C2
Yeşilırmak (riv.), Turk. 96/F4
Yeşilkent, Turk. 128/D2
Yeşilova, Turk. 128/B2
Yesodot, Isr. 131/B5
Yesŏng (riv.), NKor. 107/D3
Yessentuki, Rus. 97/G3
Yessey, Rus. 101/L3
Yeste, Sp. 72/D3
Yesud Hama'ala, Isr. 131/D2
Yete I, D.R. Congo 146/E3
Yetholm, Sc, UK 59/D5
Yetminster, Eng, UK 62/D5
Yetti (reg.), Mrta. 136/D4
Yeu, Ile d' (isl.), Fr. 70/B3
Yevlax, Azer. 97/H4
Yevpatoriya, Ukr. 99/G5
Yèvre (riv.), Fr. 81/D5
Yèvres, Fr. 83/G4
Yevsuh, Ukr. 99/K3
Yeya (riv.), Rus. 96/G3
Yeysk, Rus. 99/K4
Yeysk (bay), Rus. 99/K4
Yffinac, Fr. 82/C4
Ygatimí, Par. 213/F3
Ygos-Saint-Saturnin, Fr. 70/C5
Yi (riv.), Uru. 215/F2
Yi Xian, China 107/A2
Yi Xian, China 106/G7
Yi'ong (riv.), China 112/B2
Yialousa, Cyp. 130/D2
Yiangkou, China 107/B2
Yiannitsá, Gre. 75/H2
Yiánnouli, Gre. 75/H3
Yíaros (isl.), Gre. 75/J4
Yibin, China 112/E2
Yichang, China 104/G5
Yichang, China 113/F2
Yicheng, China 106/C5
Yicheng, China 106/B4
Yichuan, China 106/C4
Yichun, China 105/K2
Yichun, China 113/G3
Yidun, China 112/C2
Yifeng, China 119/K2
Yiftah, Isr. 131/D2
Yığılca, Turk. 77/K5
Yihuang, China 113/H3
Yilan, China 105/K2
Yıldız (peak), Turk. 128/D1
Yildiz Park, Turk. 129/N6
Yıldızeli, Turk. 128/D2
Yilehuli (mts.), China 105/J1
Yiliang, China 112/E3
Yiliping, China 104/C4
Yima, China 106/B4
Yimen, China 112/D3
Yimin (riv.), China 105/J2
Yin (mts.), China 101/L5
Yinan, China 106/D4
Yinchuan, China 104/F4
Yindarlgooda (lake), Austl. 153/B4
Ying (riv.), China 104/G5
Yingcheng, China 113/G2
Ying'emen, China 107/C1
Yinggehai, China 120/E2
Yingkou, China 107/B2
Yingpanxu, China 113/G3
Yingqian, China 113/G3
Yingshan, China 106/C5
Yingshang, China 106/D4
Yingshouyingzi, China 106/H6
Yingtan, China 113/H2
Yingui, Camr. 146/B1
Yining, China 125/D3
Yinyang, China 106/L8
Yi'ong (riv.), China 104/C5
Yirga 'Alem, Eth. 144/A4
Yirga Ch'efē, Eth. 144/A4
Yirkā, Isr. 131/C3
Yirol, Sudan 142/F4
Yirrkala, Austl. 155/E3
Yirshi, China 105/H2
Yishan, China 113/F3
Yishui, China 106/D4
Yíthion, Gre. 75/H4
Yitong (riv.), SKor. 106/C5
Yiwanquan, China 104/C3
Yiwu, China 104/C3
Yixing, China 106/K8
Yiyang, China 106/C4
Yiyang, China 113/G2
Yiyuan, China 106/D3
Yizhang, China 119/K2
Yizheng, China 106/D4
Ylakiai, Lith. 67/J3
Ylöjärvi, Fin. 67/K1
Ymir (mtn.), BC, Can. 170/F3
Ymir, BC, Can. 170/F3
Yngaren (lake), Swe. 66/G2
Yngern (lake), Swe. 65/A1
Yoakum, Tx, US 177/F3
Yobe (state), Nga. 141/H3
Yoboki, Djib. 144/B3
Yocalla, Bol. 212/C1
Yŏch'ŏn, SKor. 107/D5
Yockanookany (riv.), Ms, US 188/C4
Yocona (riv.), Ms, US 188/C3
Yoder, Ks, US 179/F2
Yoder, Wy, US 180/B3
Yodo (riv.), Japan 109/J6
Yodŏk, NKor. 107/D3
Yoduma (riv.), Rus. 101/P4
Yoff (Dakar) (int'l arpt.), Sen. 140/A3
Yog (pt.), Phil. 114/D2
Yogo, Japan 109/K4
Yoğuntaş, Turk. 77/H5
Yogyakarta, Indo. 115/E3
Yogyakarta (prov.), Indo. 115/E3
Yoho NP, BC, Can. 170/F2
Yoichi, Japan 108/B2
Yojoa (lake), Hon. 200/D3
Yŏju, SKor. 107/D4
Yokadouma, Camr. 146/C2
Yōkaichi, Japan 109/K5
Yokana, D.R. Congo 147/E2
Yokawa, Japan 109/H6
Yokena, Ms, US 190/C1
Yokkaichi, Japan 109/L6
Yoko, Camr. 142/B4
Yokohama, Japan 111/F3
Yokolo, D.R. Congo 147/E3
Yokoshiba, Japan 109/E2
Yokosuka, Japan 111/F3
Yokote, Japan 108/B4
Yokoze, Japan 109/C2
Yola, Nga. 142/B3
Yolaina (mts.), Nic. 201/E4
Yolboyu, Turk. 128/D2
Yolo (co.), Ca, US 193/L9
Yolo, Ca, US 193/L9
Yolombo, D.R. Congo 147/E3
Yom (riv.), Thai. 119/H4
Yombi, Gabon 146/B3
Yŏmju, NKor. 107/C3
Yomou, Gui. 140/C5
Yon (riv.), Fr. 70/C3
Yon (riv.), China 113/F4
Yonago, Japan 110/C3
Yonaguni (isl.), Japan 111/G8
Yonaha-dake (peak), Japan 111/K7
Yŏnan, NKor. 107/D4
Yoncalla, Or, US 172/B2
Yoneshiro (riv.), Japan 108/B3
Yonezawa, Japan 111/G2
Yong Peng, Malay. 115/C2
Yŏng-yang, SKor. 110/A2
Yŏngam, SKor. 107/D5
Yongamp'o, NKor. 107/C3
Yong'an (pass), China 113/F3
Yong'an, China 113/E2
Yong'an, China 113/H3
Yŏngbyŏn, NKor. 107/C3
Yongchang, China 104/E4
Yongcheng, China 106/D4
Yŏngch'ŏn, SKor. 110/A3
Yongde, China 119/G3
Yongding (riv.), China 101/M6
Yŏngdŏk, SKor. 110/A2
Yŏngdong, SKor. 107/D4
Yongdungp'o (nbrhd.), SKor. 107/F6
Yongfeng, China 104/F5
Yongfu, China 119/J3
Yonggang, NKor. 107/C3
Yŏnggwang, SKor. 107/D5
Yŏnghae, SKor. 107/E4
Yonghe, China 106/B3
Yŏnghŭng (riv.), NKor. 107/D3
Yŏnghŭng, NKor. 107/D3
Yongji, China 106/B4
Yŏngjong (isl.), SKor. 107/F6
Yŏngju, SKor. 110/A2
Yongle, China 113/E4
Yongling, China 107/C2
Yongmun-san (peak), SKor. 107/D4
Yongnian, China 106/C3
Yongning, China 120/E1
Yongningjian, China 107/A3
Yongo, D.R. Congo 147/E3
Yongping, China 113/H3
Yongping, China 106/B3
Yongqiang, China 113/J3
Yongqing, China 106/H7
Yongren, China 119/H2
Yŏngsan (riv.), SKor. 107/D5
Yongshan, China 112/D2
Yongsheng, China 112/D3
Yongshun, China 119/J2
Yŏngwŏl, SKor. 110/A2
Yŏngwŏn, NKor. 107/D3
Yongxin, China 119/K2
Yongzhou, China 113/F3
Yonibana, SLeo. 140/B4
Yonkers, NY, US 195/K8
Yonne (riv.), Fr. 68/B5
Yono, Japan 109/D2
Yonsa, NKor. 107/E2
Yŏnsan, NKor. 107/D3
Yopal, Col. 204/C3
Yopurga, China 125/C4
Yoqne'am 'Illit, Isr. 131/C3
Yorba Linda, Ca, US 192/G8
Yorii, Japan 109/C1
York, Eng, UK 61/G4
York (riv.), Qu, Can. 184/E1
York, Al, US 188/C4
York, Ne, US 180/F3
York (cape), Austl. 155/F2
York (sound), Austl. 154/B3
York, Austl. 156/C4
York (co.), On, Can. 186/T8
York (riv.), Va, US 189/J2
York, Pa, US 194/B4
York (co.), Pa, US 194/B4
York, SC, US 189/G3
York Factory, Mb, Can. 166/G3
York Haven, Pa, US 194/B3
York Minster, Eng, UK 61/G4
York Sound(bay) 153/B2
York Springs, Pa, US 194/A4
Yorke (pen.), Austl. 153/C4
Yorketown, Austl. 157/H5
Yorkshire, NY, US 187/G3
Yorkshire Dales NP, Eng, UK 61/F3
Yorkshire Wolds (hills), Eng, UK 61/H3
Yorkton, Sk, Can. 182/C2
Yorktown, Ar, US 179/J3
Yorktown, In, US 186/D4
Yorktown, Tx, US 177/F3
Yorktown, Va, US 189/J2
Yorktown Heights, NY, US 195/E1
Yorkville, Il, US 186/B4
Yoro, Hon. 200/E3
Yorō, Japan 109/L5
Yōrō (riv.), Japan 109/E3
Yoroi-zaki (pt.), Japan 109/L7
Yoron (isl.), Japan 111/K7
Yorosso, Mali 140/D3
Yorton, Eng, UK 61/F6
Yos Sudarso (isl.), Indo. 117/J5
Yosemite (falls), Ca, US 174/C2
Yosemite NP, Ca, US 174/C2
Yoshida, Japan 110/C4
Yoshida, Japan 109/C1
Yoshii (riv.), Japan 110/D3
Yoshii, Japan 109/B1
Yoshikawa, Japan 109/D2
Yoshima (riv.), Japan 110/D3
Yoshimi, Japan 109/C1
Yoshino (riv.), Japan 110/C4
Yoshino, Japan 109/J7
Yoshino-Kumano NP, Japan 110/E3
Yoshkar-Ola, Rus. 95/L4
Yŏsu, SKor. 107/D5
Yotaú, Bol. 209/F5
Yōtei-san (peak), Japan 108/B2
Yotsukaidō, Japan 109/E2
You (riv.), China 112/E3
Youbou, BC, Can. 170/B3
Youdunzi, China 104/C4
Youghal, Ire. 58/C6
Youghal (bay), Ire. 58/C6
Youghiogheny (riv.), Pa, US 187/G5
Youhamba (riv.), CAfr. 142/D4
Young, Az, US 175/G3
Young, Uru. 215/K10
Young, Sk, Can. 171/M2
Young, Austl. 159/D2
Young America, Mn, US 183/N7
Young Nick's (pt.), NZ 161/D2
Youngs (lake), Wa, US 193/C3
Youngstown, Fl, US 191/F2
Youngstown, Oh, US 186/F4
Youngstown, In, US 186/C5
Youngstown, NY, US 186/U9
Youngstown, Ab, Can. 171/J2
Youngsville, La, US 190/C2
Youngsville, NM, US 175/J2
Yountville, Ca, US 193/K10
Youshui, China 113/G3
Youssoufia, Mor. 136/C2
Youxi, China 113/F3
Youxikou, China 113/H3
Youyang, China 119/J2
Youyi, China 105/L2
Yoví (peak), Ven. 205/E3
Yozgat, Turk. 128/C2
Ypané (riv.), Par. 210/A4
Ypé Jhú, Par. 213/F2
Ypsilanti, ND, US 182/E4
Ypsilanti, Mi, US 193/E7
Yr Eifl (peak), Wal, UK 60/D6
Yreka, Ca, US 172/B3
Yser (riv.), Fr. 68/B3
Ysieux (riv.), Fr. 56/K4
Ystad, Swe. 66/E4
Ystad, Swe. 65/K7
Ystalyfera, Wal, UK 62/C3
Ystrad Mynach, Wal, UK 62/C3
Ystwyth (riv.), Wal, UK 62/B2
Ysyk Köl (lake), Kyr. 100/H5
Ythan (riv.), Sc, UK 59/D2
Ytrac, Fr. 70/E4
Ytre Enebakk, Nor. 64/T8
Ytre Sula (isl.), Nor. 66/A1
Ytterby, Swe. 66/D3
Ytterbyn, Swe. 64/G2
Ytterjärna, Swe. 65/A1
Yu (riv.), China 119/J3
Yü (peak), Tai. 113/J4
Yu Xian, China 106/C3
Yu Xian, China 106/C4
Yuan (riv.), China 103/K7
Yuan (lake), China 106/C5
Yuan (Red) (riv.), China 112/D4
Yuan'an, China 106/B5
Yuanba, China 104/F5
Yuanbao (mtn.), China 113/F3
Yuanping, China 106/C3
Yuanqu, China 106/B4
Yuanshan, China 112/E2
Yuanshi, China 106/C3
Yuantan, China 113/H2
Yuantan, China 113/G4
Yuanyang, China 106/C4
Yuba, Ok, US 179/F4
Yuba (riv.), Ca, US 172/C4
Yuba City, Ca, US 172/C4
Yūbari, Japan 108/B2
Yūbetsu, Japan 108/C1
Yūbetsu (riv.), Japan 108/C2
Yucaipa, Ca, US 192/C2
Yucatán (state), Mex. 196/D3
Yucatan (pen.), Mex. 165/J7
Yucatan (chan.), NAm. 165/J7
Yucca, Az, US 175/E3
Yucca House Nat'l Mon., Co, US 175/H2
Yucca Valley, Ca, US 174/D3
Yucheng, China 106/D3
Yucheng, China 106/C4
Yuci, China 106/C3
Yudu, China 113/G3
Yuechi, China 113/E2
Yuehedian, China 113/G1
Yuelaichang, China 113/E2
Yuen Long, China 113/L7
Yuendumu, Austl. 157/F2
Yuendumu Abor. Land, Austl. 157/F2
Yueqing, China 113/J2
Yuexi, China 119/H2
Yuexi (riv.), China 112/D2
Yuexi, China 113/H2
Yueyang, China 113/G2
Yug (riv.), Rus. 100/E4
Yugawara, Japan 109/C3
Yugorskiy (pen.), Rus. 95/P1
Yuhang, China 106/L9
Yuhuan, China 113/J2
Yui, Japan 109/B3
Yujiaxi, China 113/F2
Yūki, Japan 111/F2
Yuki Kengundu, D.R. Congo 146/C3
Yukon, Mo, US 179/J2
Yukon (riv.), Can.,US 165/E3
Yukon Territory Can. 168/Z12
Yüksekova, Turk. 129/F2
Yukuhashi, Japan 110/E4
Yulamasi, China 107/A1
Yulara, Austl. 157/F3
Yuldybayevo, Rus. 97/L1
Yuleba, Austl. 160/C4
Yulee, Fl, US 191/H2
Yuli, Nga. 141/H4
Yuli, China 125/E3
Yulin, China 106/B3
Yulin, China 113/F5
Yulin, China 113/F4
Yuling (pass), China 113/H2
Yulongxue (peak), China 112/D3
Yuma (des.), Az, US 174/E4
Yuma, Az, US 180/C3
Yuma, Co, US 180/C3
Yuma Marine Air Sta., Az, US 168/D5
Yuma Proving Ground, Az, US 174/E4
Yumbarra Consv. Park, Austl. 157/G4
Yumbe, Ugan. 147/G2
Yumbel, Chile 214/B3
Yumbi, D.R. Congo 146/D2
Yumbi, D.R. Congo 147/F3
Yumbi, D.R. Congo 146/D3
Yumbo, Col. 204/B4
Yumen, China 104/D4
Yumenzhen, China 104/D3
Yumin, China 125/D2
Yumurtalık, Turk. 130/D1
Yun (riv.), China 106/C5
Yun Xian, China 112/D3
Yun Xian, China 106/B4
Yuna, Austl. 156/B4
Yunak, Turk. 128/B2
Yuncheng, China 106/C4
Yuncheng, China 106/B4
Yundum, Gam. 140/A3
Yundum (Banjul) (int'l arpt.), Gam. 140/A3
Yungang Caves, China 106/C2
Yungas (phys. reg.), Bol. 209/E4
Yungay, Chile 214/B3
Yunguyo, Peru 208/D5
Yunhe, China 113/H2
Yunjiang, China 113/F3
Yunkai (mts.), China 113/F4
Yunkanjini Abor. Land, Austl. 157/F2
Yunlong, China 119/G2
Yunnan (prov.), China 119/H3
Yunta, Austl. 157/H5
Yuntai (peak), China 106/D4
Yunxi, China 106/B4
Yunyan (riv.), China 106/D4
Yunyanzhen, China 106/B3
Yunzhong (mtn.), China 106/C3
Yuping, China 119/J2
Yupukarri, Guy. 205/G4
Yuqiao (res.), China 106/H7
Yura, Bol. 212/C2
Yuracyacu, Peru 208/B2
Yuratishki, Bela. 67/L4
Yurga, Rus. 100/J4
Yurgamysh, Rus. 95/Q5
Yuri (isl.), Rus. 103/E2
Yurimaguas, Peru 208/B2
Yuroma, Rus. 95/K2
Yuruari (riv.), Ven. 205/F3
Yürük, Turk. 77/H5
Yurungkax (riv.), China 125/C4
Yur'ya, Rus. 95/L4
Yur'yev-Pol'skiy, Rus. 94/H4
Yur'yevets, Rus. 94/J4
Yur'yevets, Rus. 94/J4
Yur'yivka, Ukr. 99/J3
Yuryuzan', Rus. 95/N5
Yuryuzan' (riv.), Rus. 95/N5
Yuscarán, Hon. 200/E3
Yushan NP, Tai. 113/J4
Yushe, China 106/C3
Yushu, China 107/C2
Yushu, China 105/K3
Yusŏng, SKor. 107/D4
Yusufeli, Turk. 97/G4
Yutai, China 106/D4
Yutian, China 125/D4
Yutian, China 106/H7
Yuto, Arg. 212/C2
Yuty, Par. 213/E3
Yutz, Fr. 81/F5
Yuxi, China 113/H3
Yuxikou, China 113/H2
Yuyao, China 113/J2
Yuza, Japan 108/A4
Yuzawa, Japan 108/B4
Yuzhno-Kuril'sk, Rus. 108/D2
Yuzhno-Sakhalinsk, Rus. 105/N2
Yuzhno-Sakhalinsk (int'l arpt.), Rus. 105/N2
Yuzhno-Sukhokumsk, Rus. 97/H3
Yuzhnoural'sk, Rus. 95/P5
Yuzhnyy, Rus. 99/L4
Yuzhnyy, Rus. 125/D1
Yvel (riv.), Fr. 82/C4
Yvelines (dept.), Fr. 83/G3
Yverdon, Swi. 86/C4
Yvetot, Fr. 83/F1
Yvette (riv.), Fr. 80/B6
Yvoir, Belg. 81/D3
Yvonand, Swi. 86/C4
Yvron (riv.), Fr. 56/L6
Ywathit, Myan. 120/B2
Yxlan (isl.), Swe. 65/B1
Yxlö (isl.), Swe. 65/B2
Yzeron (riv.), Fr. 90/A1
Yzeure, Fr. 70/E3

Z

Za (riv.), China 104/D5
Za (riv.), Mor. 138/C2
Zaachila, Mex. 200/B2
Zaandam, Neth. 68/C2
Zaandijk, Neth. 78/B4
Zaanstad, Neth. 78/B4
Zabaykal'sk, Rus. 105/H2
Żabbar, Malta 74/M7
Zaber (riv.), Ger. 84/C4
Zabīd, Yem. 144/B2
Zabīd (wadi), Yem. 144/B2
Ząbki, Pol. 69/L2
Ząbkowice Śląskie, Pol. 69/J3
Žabljak, Yugo. 76/D4
Zābolī, Iran 127/H3
Zabré, Burk. 141/E4
Zábřeh, Czh. 69/J4
Zabrze, Pol. 69/K3
Zaburun'ye, Kaz. 97/J3
Zabzuga, Gha. 141/F4
Zacapa, Guat. 200/D3
Zacapoaxtla, Mex. 199/M7
Zacapu, Mex. 199/E5
Zacatecas (state), Mex. 196/A3
Zacatecas, Mex. 198/E4
Zacatecoluca, ESal. 200/D3
Zacatelco, Mex. 199/L7
Zacatepec, Mex. 199/K8
Zacatlán, Mex. 199/M7
Zachary, La, US 190/C2
Zacoalco de Torres, Mex. 198/E4
Zacualtipán, Mex. 200/E1
Zadar, Cro. 76/E3
Zadetkyi (isl.), Myan. 116/A2
Zadi (riv.), Ang. 146/D5
Zadi, Myan. 120/B3
Zadoi, China 104/D5
Zadonsk, Rus. 96/F1
Ẓafar al Qadīmah, Egypt 139/C3
Zafarwāl, Pak. 124/C3
Zafra, Sp. 72/B3
Żagań, Pol. 69/H3
Žagarė, Lith. 67/K3
Zagarolo, It. 91/B4
Zāgheh-ye Pā'īn, Iran 129/G3
Zaghwān (gov.), Tun. 74/A4
Zaghwān, Tun. 138/M6
Zagorá, Gre. 75/H3
Zagora, Mor. 136/D3
Zagorje ob Savi, Slov. 71/L3
Zagreb (cap.), Cro. 76/B3
Zagros (mts.), Iran 100/F6
Za'gya (riv.), China 125/F5
Zāhedān, Iran 127/H3
Zahirābād, India 121/C2
Zaḥlah, Leb. 131/D1
Záhony, Hun. 69/M4
Zahrez Chergui (dry lake), Alg. 138/G5
Zahrez Rharbi (dry lake), Alg. 92/D4
Zai NP, Jor. 131/D4
Zaidín, Sp. 73/F2
Zaidpur, India 122/C2
Zaima, China 113/F3
Zaïo, Mor. 138/C2
Zaire (prov.), Ang. 146/C4
Zaire (Congo)(riv.) 133/D4
Zaire (see Democratic Republic of the Congo) */*
Zaječar, Yugo. 76/F4
Zaka, Zim. 149/F4
Zakamensk, Rus. 104/E1
Zakarpats'ka (prov.), Ukr. 96/B2
Zakháro, Gre. 75/G4
Zakhodnyaya Dzvina (riv.), Bela. 94/E5
Zākhū, Iraq 129/E2
Zaki Biam, Nga. 141/H5
Zákinthos, Gre. 75/G4
Zákinthos (isl.), Gre. 75/G4
Zakopane, Pol. 69/K4
Zakouma, Chad 142/C3
Zakouma, PN de, Chad 142/C3
Zala (prov.), Hun. 76/C2
Zala (riv.), Hun. 76/C2
Zala, Eth. 142/H4
Zala, Ang. 146/C4
Zalaapáti, Hun. 76/C2
Zalaegerszeg, Hun. 76/C2
Zalamea de la Serena, Sp. 72/C3
Zalamea la Real, Sp. 72/B4
Zalanga, Nga. 141/H4
Zalantun, China 105/J2
Zalari, Rus. 104/E1
Zalaszentgrót, Hun. 76/C2
Zalău, Rom. 77/F2
Žalec, Slov. 76/B2
Ẕalim, SAr. 126/D4
Zalingei, Sudan 142/D2
Zalishchyky, Ukr. 98/C3
Zalṭan (well), Libya 134/C2
Zalṭan, Libya 134/C2
Zalṭan, Libya 93/F4
Zaltbommel, Neth. 78/C5
Zalun, Myan. 112/B5
Zalut, Myan. 120/B3
Zama, Japan 109/C3
Zamālat As Sawāsī, Tun. 74/B5
Zamānia, India 122/D3
Zambezi, Zam. 148/D2
Zambezi (riv.), Ang. 147/E5
Zambezi (riv.), Afr. 149/G3
Zambezi (riv.), Moz. 133/E6
Zambezi Escarpment (cliff), Zam. 149/E3
Zambézia (prov.), Moz. 149/H3
Zambia(ctry.) 133/E6
Zamboanga, Phil. 114/C4
Zambrów, Pol. 69/M2
Zambujal de Cima, Port. 73/P11
Zamfora (riv.), Nga. 141/G3
Zami (riv.), Myan. 120/B3
Zamoi, D.R. Congo 147/F2
Zamoi, D.R. Congo 142/E4
Zamora, Sp. 72/C2
Zamora (riv.), Ecu. 208/B2
Zamora, Ecu. 208/B2
Zamora de Hidalgo, Mex. 198/E5
Zamora-Chinchipe (prov.), Ecu. 208/B2
Zamość, Pol. 69/M3
Zamość (prov.), Pol. 98/B2
Zams, Aus. 87/G3
Zāmūs (well), Libya 134/B3
Zam'yany, Rus. 97/H3
Zamzam (wadi), Libya 134/B2
Zanaga, Congo 146/C3
Záncara (riv.), Sp. 92/C3
Zanda, China 125/C5
Zanderij (int'l arpt.), Sur. 206/C1
Zanderij, Sur. 206/C1
Zandkreekdam (dam), Neth. 78/A5
Zandu-Kansabala, D.R. Congo 146/D4
Zandvliet, Belg. 78/B6
Zandvoort, Neth. 78/B4
Zanè, It. 89/E2
Zanesville, Oh, US 186/E5
Zango, Nga. 141/H3
Zanhuang, China 106/C3
Zanjān, Iran 129/G2
Zanjān (gov.), Iran 129/G2
Zánka, Hun. 76/C2
Zannone (isl.), It. 92/C6
Zanthus, Austl. 156/D4
Zanul'ye, Rus. 95/L3
Zanzibar, Tanz. 145/B3
Zanzibar (isl.), Tanz. 133/F5
Zanzibar (Kisauni) (int'l arpt.), Tanz. 145/B3
Zanzibar North (prov.), Tanz. 145/B3
Zanzibar South (prov.), Tanz. 145/B3
Zanzibar West (prov.), Tanz. 145/B3
Zanzuzi (hill), Tanz. 145/A2
Zaō-san (peak), Japan 111/G1
Zaoheshi, China 113/G3
Zaoqiang, China 106/C3
Zaouiet Kounta, Alg. 137/E4
Zaoyang, China 106/C4
Zaozhuang, China 106/D4
Zapadno-Sakhalin (mts.), Rus. 105/N2
Zapadocesky (pol. reg.), Czh. 68/G4
Západočeský (pol. reg.), Czh. 71/K2
Zapadoslovensky (pol. reg.), Slvk. 69/J4
Zapai, D.R. Congo 142/E4
Zapala, Arg. 214/C3
Zapaleri (peak), Chile 212/C2
Zapaleri (peak), Arg. 212/C2
Zapallar, Chile 214/C2
Zapata (pen.), Cuba 201/F1
Zapata, Tx, US 177/E4
Zapatoca, Col. 204/C3
Zapatosa (lake), Col. 204/C2
Zapatosa (swamp), Col. 201/H4
Záplatský Rybnik (lake), Czh. 85/H4
Zapolyarnyy, Rus. 94/F1
Zapopan, Mex. 198/E4
Zaporizhzhya, Ukr. 99/H4
Zaporizhzhya (int'l arpt.), Ukr. 99/H4
Zaporiz'ka (prov.), Ukr. 96/E3
Zapotal, Ecu. 204/B5
Zapotillo, Ecu. 208/A2
Zapponeta, It. 74/D2
Zaprešić, Cro. 76/B3
Zaqatala, Azer. 97/H4
Zaqên, China 104/C5
Zaqqūṭ (well), Libya 134/C2
Zara, Turk. 128/D2
Zarafshon, Uzb. 100/G5
Zaragoza, Mex. 177/D3
Zaragoza, Col. 204/C3
Zaragoza (int'l arpt.), Sp. 73/E2
Zaragoza, Mex. 199/M7
Zaragoza (Saragossa), Sp. 73/E2
Zarand, Iran 129/J4
Zaranda (hill), Nga. 141/H4
Zarasai, Lith. 67/M4
Zárate, Arg. 215/J11
Zarauz, Sp. 70/B5
Zaraza, Ven. 205/E2
Zārch, Iran 129/H3
Zard (mtn.), Iran 129/G3
Zārdab, Azer. 129/F1
Zarechensk, Rus. 94/F2
Zareh Sharan, Afg. 127/J2
Zargān, Iran 129/H4
Zaria, Nga. 141/G4
Zarichne, Ukr. 98/D2
Zarinsk, Rus. 125/D1
Zarmest (pass), Afg. 127/H2
Zărneşti, Rom. 77/G3
Zarós, Gre. 75/J5
Zarqā' (riv.), Jor. 131/D4
Zarrentin, Ger. 79/H1
Zarrīn Shahr, Iran 129/G3
Zarrīneh (riv.), Iran 129/F2
Záruby (peak), Slvk. 76/C1
Zaruma, Ecu. 208/B1
Zarumilla, Peru 208/A1
Żary, Pol. 69/H3
Zarza la Mayor, Sp. 72/B3
Zarzaïtine, Alg. 137/H3
Zarzal, Col. 204/B3
Zasa, Lat. 67/L3
Zāskār (riv.), India 124/D3
Zāskār (range), India 125/C5
Zaslavl', Bela. 67/M4
Zastron, SAfr. 150/D3
Zasul'ye, Rus. 95/K2
Žatec, Czh. 85/G2
Zatobol'sk, Kaz. 95/P5
Zatoka, Ukr. 98/F4
Zauche (reg.), Ger. 68/P7
Zavalla, Tx, US 176/G2
Zavalla, Arg. 214/E2
Zavāreh, Iran 129/H3
Zavdi'el, Isr. 131/B5
Zaventem, Belg. 81/D2
Zavet, Bul. 77/H4
Zavidovići, Bosn. 76/D3
Zavitinsk, Rus. 105/K1
Zavodoukovsk, Rus 95/Q4
Závora (pt.), Moz. 149/G5
Zawadzkie, Pol. 69/K3
Zawi, Zim. 149/F3
Zawiercie, Pol. 69/K3
Zawīlah, Libya 134/B3
Zāwiyat al Mukhaylá, Libya 93/J4
Zāwiyat Masūs, Libya 134/D2
Zāwiyat Razīn, Egypt 139/B4
Zāwiyat Sīdī Ghāzī, Egypt 139/B2
Zaysan (lake), Kaz. 103/H5
Zaysan, Kaz. 125/D2
Zayü, China 112/C2
Zayü (riv.), China 104/D6
Zaza (riv.), Cuba 201/G1
Zazafotsy, Madg. 152/H8
Zāzamt (wadi), Libya 134/B2
Zazárida, Ven. 204/D2
Zbarazh, Ukr. 98/C3
Zbąszyń, Pol. 69/H2
Zbiroh, Czh. 85/G3
Zboriv, Ukr. 98/C3
Zbůch, Czh. 85/G3
Žd'ár nad Sázavou, Czh. 69/H4
Zdice, Czh. 85/G3
Zdolbuniv, Ukr. 98/D2
Zduńska Wola, Pol. 69/K3
Zealand, NB, Can. 184/D2
Zealandia, Sk, Can. 171/L2
Zeballos (peak), Arg. 215/C5
Żebbuġ, Malta 74/L7
Zebediela, SAfr. 149/F5
Zebulon, Ga, US 188/E4
Zeddine (riv.), Alg. 138/F5
Zedelgem, Belg. 80/C1
Zeebrugge, Belg. 80/C1
Zeehan, Austl. 158/C4
Zeeland, Mi, US 186/C3
Zeeland (prov.), Neth. 78/A5
Zeeland, Neth. 78/C5
Ze'elim, Isr. 131/B6
Zeerust, SAfr. 148/E5
Zeesen, Ger. 68/Q7
Zeewolde, Neth. 78/C4
Zefat, Isr. 131/D3
Zegrzyńskie (res.), Pol. 69/L2
Zeguo, China 113/J2
Zehdenick, Ger. 69/G2
Zehlendorf, Ger. 68/Q7
Zehner, Sk, Can. 182/B2
Zeigler, Il, US 188/C2
Zeil, Ger. 84/D2
Zeil (mt.), Austl. 157/G2
Zeiselmauer, Aus. 77/N7
Zeist, Neth. 78/C4
Zeitz, Ger. 68/G3
Żejtun, Malta 74/M7
Zekharya, Isr. 131/B5
Zele, Belg. 80/D1
Zelenchukskaya, Rus. 97/G4
Zelenoborskiy, Rus. 94/G2
Zelenodol'sk, Rus. 95/L5
Zelenodol's'k, Ukr. 98/G4
Zelenogorsk, Rus. 94/S6
Zelenograd, Rus. 94/Y9
Zelenogradsk, Rus. 67/J4
Zelenokumsk, Rus. 97/G3
Zelhem, Neth. 78/D4
Zelienople, Pa, US 186/F4
Zelimai, Libr. 140/C5
Zell, Swi. 86/D3
Zell, Swi. 87/E3
Zell, Ger. 81/G3
Zell, SD, US 180/E1
Zell am Harmersbach, Ger. 86/E1
Zell am Main, Ger. 84/C3
Zell am Moos, Aus. 85/G7
Zell am See, Aus. 71/K3
Zell an der Pram, Aus. 85/G6
Zell in Wiesental, Ger. 86/D2
Zellersee (lake), Ger. 87/E2
Zellersee (lake), Aus. 84/G7
Zellingen, Ger. 84/C3
Zellwood, Fl, US 190/M6
Zelouane, Mor. 138/C2
Zelów, Pol. 69/K3
Zeltingen-Rachtig, Ger. 81/G4
Zeltweg, Aus. 71/L3
Želva, Lith. 67/L4
Zelzate, Belg. 80/C1
Žemaičiu Naumiestis, Lith. 67/J4
Zemaitija NP, Lith. 67/J3
Zembra (isls.), Tun. 74/B4
Zêmdasam, China 104/E5
Zemen, Bul. 76/F4
Zemetchino, Rus. 97/G1
Zemio, CAfr. 142/E4
Zemmer, Ger. 81/F4
Zemmora, Alg. 138/F5
Zémongo, Rsv. de Faune de, CAfr. 142/E4
Zempoala (peak), Mex. 199/Q10
Zempoala, Mex. 199/N7
Zempoaltepec, Cerro (peak), Mex. 200/C2
Zemst, Belg. 81/D2
Zenda, Ks, US 179/E2
Zênda, China 104/D5
Zendeh Jān, Afg. 127/H2
Zenia, Ca, US 172/B3
Zenica, Bosn. 76/C3
Zenith, Wa, US 193/C3
Zenn (riv.), Ger. 71/J2
Zenne (riv.), Belg. 81/D1
Zenon Park, Sk, Can. 171/N1
Zentsūji, Japan 110/C3
Zenza do Itombe, Ang. 146/C5
Zeona, SD, US 182/C5
Žepče, Bosn. 76/D3
Zepernick, Ger. 68/Q6
Zephyr, Tx, US 176/E2
Zephyr Cove, Nv, US 172/D4
Zephyrhills, Fl, US 190/L7
Zeralda, Alg. 138/G4
Zermatt, Swi. 86/D5
Zernez, Swi. 87/G4
Zernien, Ger. 79/H2
Zernograd, Rus. 99/L4
Zero Branco, It. 89/F2
Zerqan, Alb. 75/G2
Zestap'oni, Geo. 97/G4
Zeta (lake), Nun, Can. 166/F1
Zêtang, China 123/H1
Zetel, Ger. 79/E2
Zeuthen, Ger. 68/Q7
Zeven, Ger. 79/G2
Zevenaar, Neth. 78/D5
Zevenbergen, Neth. 78/B5
Zevgolatíon, Gre. 75/H4
Zevio, It. 89/E3
Zeya (riv.), Rus. 101/N4
Zeya (res.), Rus. 103/M4
Zeya, Rus. 105/K1
Zeya-Bureya (plain), Rus. 101/N4
Zeytindağ, Turk. 96/C5
Zêzere (riv.), Port. 72/A3
Zghartā, Leb. 130/D2
Zgierz, Pol. 69/K3
Zgorzelec, Pol. 69/H3
Zhabasak, Kaz. 97/M2
Zhabinka, Bela. 69/N2
Zhailma, Kaz. 97/M2
Zhajiang, China 113/G3
Zhakou, China 113/F4
Zhambyl, Kaz. 125/B3
Zhan (riv.), China 105/K2
Zhanang, China 123/H1
Zhanatas, Kaz. 100/G5
Zhang (riv.), China 113/F2
Zhangaözen, Kaz. 97/K4
Zhangaqazaly, Kaz. 100/G5
Zhangguangcai (mts.), China 105/K3
Zhanghei, China 106/C2
Zhangjiabu, China 107/B4
Zhangjiakou, China 106/C2
Zhangla, China 112/D1
Zhangmu, China 113/F3
Zhangqiu, China 106/D3
Zhangshu, China 113/G2
Zhangwei (riv.), China 106/D3
Zhangye, China 104/E4
Zhangzhou, China 113/H3
Zhangzi (isl.), China 107/B3
Zhangzi, China 106/C3
Zhanhua, China 106/D3
Zhanjiang, China 113/F4
Zhanterek, Kaz. 97/K3
Zhanyu, China 105/J3
Zhao Xian, China 106/C3
Zhaobeikou, China 106/H7
Zhaodong, China 105/K2
Zhaojiachang, China 113/E2
Zhaojue, China 119/H2
Zhaoping, China 119/K3
Zhaoqing, China 113/G4
Zhaotong, China 112/D3
Zhaoyuan, China 105/K2
Zhaoyuan, China 106/E3
Zhaozhou, China 105/K2
Zhapo, China 119/K3
Zhapu, China 106/L9
Zhari Namco (lake), China 125/E5
Zharkamys, Kaz. 97/L2
Zharkovskiy, Rus. 94/G5
Zharma, Kaz. 125/D2
Zharmysh, Kaz. 97/K3
Zhashkiv, Ukr. 98/F3
Zhatay, Rus. 101/N3
Zhaxilhünbo, China 123/G1
Zhāyya (Ural)(riv.) 100/F5
Zhayyq (riv.), Kaz. 103/E5
Zhdanovsk, Azer. 97/H5
Zhecheng, China 106/C4
Zhedou (pass), China 112/D2
Zhejiang (prov.), China 106/D5
Zhelang, China 113/G4
Zhelaniya (cape), Rus. 100/G2
Zheleznodorozhnyy, Rus. 95/L3
Zheleznodorozhnyy, Rus. 94/X9
Zheleznodorozhnyy, Rus. 67/J4
Zheleznogorsk, Rus. 96/E1
Zheleznogorsk-Ilimskiy, Rus. 101/L4
Zheleznovodsk, Rus. 97/G3
Zhelin, China 106/L9
Zhëltoye, Rus. 97/L2
Zhenchang, China 106/G7
Zhenfeng Bouyeizu Miaozu Zizhixian, China 112/E3
Zheng'anpu, China 107/A2
Zhengding, China 106/C3
Zhengguo, China 113/G4
Zhenglan, China 104/H3
Zhengning, China 106/B4
Zhengyang, China 106/C4
Zhengyi, China 106/L8
Zhengzhou, China 106/C4

Zhenjiang, China 106/D4
Zhenkang, China 119/G3
Zhenlai, China 105/J2
Zhenlong, China 113/F4
Zhenning Bouyeizu Miaozu Zizhixian, China 119/J2
Zhenping, China 104/F5
Zhenping, China 106/C4
Zhenqian, China 113/H3
Zhentou (riv.), China 106/C4
Zhenwu (mtn.), China 106/B3
Zhenxiong, China 119/H2
Zhenyuan, China 119/H3
Zhenze, China 106/L9
Zherdevka, Rus. 99/L2
Zhestyanka, Rus. 97/J2
Zhetiqara, Kaz. 97/M1
Zhetybay, Kaz. 97/K4
Zhewang, China 105/H4
Zhexiang, China 113/E3
Zhezqazghan, Kaz. 125/A2
Zhezqazghan, Kaz. 125/A2
Zhicheng, China 113/F2
Zhigalovo, Rus. 101/L4
Zhigansk, Rus. 101/N3
Zhigulevsk, Rus. 97/J1
Zhigung, China 123/H1
Zhijiang, China 113/F2
Zhijiang, China 113/F3
Zhijin, China 119/J2
Zhilinda, Rus. 101/M2
Zhilino, Rus. 67/J4
Zhiloy (isl.), Azer. 97/J4
Zhiren'kupa, Kaz. 97/K2
Zhirnovsk, Rus. 97/H2
Zhitkovo, Rus. 67/N1
Zhixia, China 113/G3
Zhixia, China 113/H2
Zhizdra, Rus. 96/E1
Zhlobin, Bela. 96/D1
Zhmerynka, Ukr. 98/E3
Zhob, Pak. 127/J2
Zhob (riv.), Pak. 127/J2
Zhodino, Bela. 67/N4
Zhokhov (isl.), Rus. 101/R2
Zholymbet, Kaz. 125/B1
Zhong Xian, China 113/F2
Zhongba, China 125/D6
Zhongdu, China 113/F3
Zhonghuang, China 113/F3
Zhongjiang, China 112/E2
Zhongmiao, China 113/H2
Zhongshan, China 113/G4
Zhongxiang, China 106/C5
Zhongxin, China 113/G3
Zhongxin, China 113/E2
Zhongyang, China 106/B3
Zhouhu, China 113/G3
Zhoukou, China 106/C4
Zhoulichang, China 112/E2
Zhoupu, China 106/L8
Zhoushan (isl.), China 113/J2
Zhoushan (isls.), China 105/J5
Zhoushan, China 106/E5
Zhouzhou, China 106/G7
Zhovkva, Ukr. 98/B2
Zhovti Vody, Ukr. 99/G3
Zhovtneve, Ukr. 99/H2
Zhovtneve, Ukr. 99/G4
Zhuanghe, China 107/B3
Zhucang, China 112/E3
Zhucheng, China 106/D4
Zhuhai, China 113/G4
Zhujia (isl.), China 113/J2
Zhujiajiao, China 106/L8
Zhujiang Kou (bay), China 113/K7
Zhukovka, Rus. 96/E1
Zhukovskiy, Rus. 94/X9
Zhumadian, China 106/C4
Zhuokeji, China 104/E5
Zhuolu, China 106/G6
Zhuozi, China 106/C2
Zhushan, China 106/B4
Zhutan, China 113/G2
Zhuxi, China 113/H2
Zhuxi, China 106/B4
Zhuyu, China 113/G2
Zhuyuanba, China 112/E1
Zhuzhou, China 119/K2
Zhuzhou, China 113/G3
Zhydachiv, Ukr. 98/C3
Zhytkavichy, Bela. 96/C1
Zhytomyr, Ukr. 98/E2
Zhytomyrs'ka (prov.), Ukr. 96/C2
Zi (riv.), China 104/D5
Zia (int'l arpt.), Bang. 123/H4
Zia Ind. Res., NM, US 175/J3
Zia Town, Libr. 140/D5
Zibo, China 106/D3
Zibyu (hills), Myan. 112/B4
Ziębice, Pol. 69/J3
Ziegenrück, Ger. 85/E1
Zielona Góra (prov.), Pol. 69/H2
Zielona Góra, Pol. 69/H3
Ziemetshausen, Ger. 87/G1
Zienzu, Libr. 140/C5
Zierenberg, Ger. 79/G6
Zierikzee, Neth. 78/A5
Ziftá, Egypt 139/C3
Zigey, Chad 142/B2
Zigon, Myan. 112/B5
Zigong, China 112/E2
Zigui, China 106/B5
Ziguinchor (int'l arpt.), Sen. 140/A3
Ziguinchor (pol. reg.), Sen. 140/A3
Ziguinchor, Sen. 140/A3
Zihuatanejo, Mex. 199/E5
Zijing (mtn.), China 106/B3
Zijingguan, China 113/F3
Zijingguan, China 106/G7
Zikhron Ya'aqov, Isr. 131/B3
Zilair, Rus. 97/L1
Zile, Turk. 128/C1
Žilina, Slvk. 69/K4
Zillah, Libya 134/C2
Zillah, Wa, US 170/D4
Ziller (riv.), Aus. 71/J3
Zillisheim, Fr. 86/D2
Zilupe, Lat. 67/N3
Zim, Mn, US 183/H4
Zima, Rus. 104/E1
Zimapán, Mex. 199/F4
Zimatlán de Álvarez, Mex. 200/B2
Zimba, Zam. 148/E3
Zimba, Tanz. 147/G4
Zimbabwe(ctry.) 133/E6
Zimla (well), Alg. 136/E4
Zimmerman, Mn, US 183/H5
Zimnicea, Rom. 77/G4
Zimnitsa, Bul. 77/H4
Zimnyatskiy, Rus. 99/M3
Zimovniki, Rus. 99/M4
Zinapécuaro de Figueroa, Mex. 199/E5
Zinave, PN de, Moz. 149/G4
Zinder (dept.), Niger 141/H3
Zinder, Niger 141/H3
Zinga, CAfr. 146/D2
Zingyaik, Myan. 120/B2
Ziniaré, Burk. 141/E3
Zinjibār, Yem. 144/C2
Zin'kiv, Ukr. 99/H2
Zinnowitz, Ger. 66/E4
Zion, Il, US 186/C3
Zion, Md, US 194/C4
Zion NP, Ut, US 174/F2
Zionville, NC, US 189/G2
Zionz (lake), On, Can. 183/J2
Zipaquirá, Col. 207/M7
Zippori, Isr. 131/C3
Zirc, Hun. 76/C2
Žirje (isl.), Cro. 71/L5
Zirl, Aus. 87/H3
Zirndorf, Ger. 84/D4
Ziro, India 112/B3
Zitácuaro, Mex. 199/E5
Žitava (riv.), Slvk. 69/K5
Zittau, Ger. 69/H3
Živinice, Bosn. 76/D3
Ziwa Magharibi (pol. reg.), Tanz. 147/G3
Ziway (lake), Eth. 144/A3
Ziway, Eth. 144/A4
Zixing, China 113/G3
Ziya (riv.), China 106/D3
Ziyang, China 113/F1
Ziyun Miaozu Bouyeizu Zizhixian, China 113/E3
Ziz, Oued (riv.), Mor. 136/D2
Zlatna, Rom. 77/F2
Zlatograd, Bul. 75/J2
Zlatorsko (lake), Yugo. 75/F1
Zlatoust, Rus. 95/N5
Zlatoustovsk, Rus. 105/L1
Zlin, Czh. 69/J4
Zlīţan, Libya 93/G4
Zliv, Czh. 85/H4
Złocieniec, Pol. 69/J2
Zlot, Yugo. 76/E3
Złotoryja, Pol. 69/H3
Złotów, Pol. 69/J2
Žlutice, Czh. 85/G2
Żmigród, Pol. 69/J3
Znamenka, Rus. 96/E1
Znamensk, Rus. 67/J4
Znam'yanka, Ukr. 98/G3
Znam'yanka Druha, Ukr. 98/G3
Żnin, Pol. 69/J2
Znojmo, Czh. 69/J4
Zobia, D.R. Congo 147/F2
Zocca, It. 89/D5
Zoersel, Belg. 78/B6
Zoétélé, Camr. 146/B2
Zoetermeer, Neth. 78/B4
Zoeterwoude, Neth. 78/B4
Zofingen, Swi. 86/D3
Zofu, D.R. Congo 147/F4
Zogang, China 119/G2
Zogno, It. 88/C2
Zogqên, China 112/C1
Zográfos, Gre. 75/N9
Zohreh (riv.), Iran 126/F2
Zoissa, Tanz. 145/B3
Zola, It. 89/E5
Zola (lake), Fr. 90/B5
Zolfo Springs, Fl, US 191/H4
Zollikon, Swi. 87/E3
Zolochiv, Ukr. 98/C3
Zolochiv, Ukr. 99/H2
Zolote, Ukr. 99/K3
Zolotonosha, Ukr. 98/G3
Zolotukhino, Rus. 99/J1
Zomba, Malw. 149/G2
Zone (pt.), Eng, UK 62/A6
Zongia, D.R. Congo 147/F2
Zongjiafangzi, China 104/D4
Zongo, D.R. Congo 142/C4
Zongo, Bol. 208/D5
Zongolica, Mex. 199/N8
Zonguldak, Turk. 96/D4
Zonguldak (prov.), Turk. 96/E4
Zonguldak(prov.) 77/K5
Zongyang, China 113/H2
Zonhoven, Belg. 81/E2
Zonnebeke, Belg. 80/B2
Zonza, Fr. 74/A2
Zoo Baba (well), Niger 134/B5
Zorārganj, Bang. 119/F3
Zorge (riv.), Ger. 79/H5
Zorgo, Burk. 141/E3
Zorn (riv.), Fr. 68/D4
Zorneding, Ger. 85/E6
Zornheim, Ger. 84/B3
Zorritos, Peru 208/A1
Zortman, Mt, US 171/K4
Zoryns'k, Ukr. 99/K3
Zorzor, Libr. 140/C5
Zossen, Ger. 68/Q7
Zottegem, Belg. 80/C2
Zou (prov.), Ben. 141/F5
Zou Xian, China 106/D4
Zouar, Chad 134/C4
Zouérat, Mrta. 136/B5
Zound-Wéogo (prov.), Burk. 141/E4
Zouping, China 106/D3
Zousfana, Oued (riv.), Alg. 137/E3
Zoutkamp, Neth. 78/D2
Zrenjanin, Yugo. 76/E3
Zschopau (riv.), Ger. 85/F1
Zschorlau, Ger. 85/F1
Zuata, Ven. 205/E2
Zubia, Sp. 72/D4
Zubova Polyana, Rus. 97/G1
Zubūbā, Isr. 131/C3
Zucchero (peak), Swi. 87/E5
Zuckerhütl (peak), Aus. 87/H4
Zuénola, C.d'Iv. 140/D5
Zufaytat Mashtūl, Egypt 139/C4
Zug, Swi. 87/E3
Zug, WSah. 136/B5
Zugdidi, Geo. 97/G4
Zugersee (lake), Swi. 71/H3
Zughrār (well), Libya 137/H3
Zugspitze (peak), Ger. 87/G3
Zuhres, Ukr. 99/K3
Zuid Holland (prov.), Neth. 78/A5
Zuid-Willemsvaart (canal), Belg. 78/C6
Zuid-Willemsvaart (canal), Neth. 78/C6
Zuidbeveland (isl.), Neth. 78/A6
Zuidelijk Flevoland (polder), Neth. 78/C4
Zuidhorn, Neth. 78/D2
Zuidlaardermeer (lake), Neth. 78/D2
Zuidlaren, Neth. 78/D2
Zuidwolde, Neth. 78/D3
Zuienkerke, Belg. 80/C1
Zújar (riv.), Sp. 92/B3
Zújar, Sp. 72/D4
Zújar (res.), Sp. 72/C3
Zula, Erit. 144/A2
Zulia (riv.), Ven. 197/G6
Zulia (state), Ven. 201/H4
Zülpich, Ger. 81/F2
Zulte, Belg. 80/C2
Zululand (reg.), SAfr. 151/E2
Zumárraga, Sp. 70/B5
Zumba, Ecu. 208/B2
Zumbo, Moz. 149/F2
Zumbrota, Mn, US 181/H1
Zumpango de Ocampo, Mex. 199/K7
Zumpango del Río, Mex. 199/F5
Zundert, Neth. 78/B6
Zungeru, Nga. 141/G4
Zunhua, China 106/H6
Zuni, NM, US 175/H3
Zuni (mts.), NM, US 175/H3
Zuni (riv.), Az, US 175/H3
Zuni Ind. Res., NM, US 175/H3
Zunyi, China 113/E3
Zuo (riv.), China 119/J3
Zuo Jiang (riv.), China 120/D1
Zuolonggou, China 104/F5
Zuoquan, China 106/C3
Zuoyun, China 106/C3
Zuoz, Swi. 87/F4
Županja, Cro. 76/D3
Žur, Yugo. 75/G1
Zurayghiţ, SAr. 126/D3
Zurbāţīyah, Iraq 129/F3
Zürich (canton), Swi. 87/E2
Zürich (int'l arpt.), Swi. 87/E3
Zürich, Swi. 87/E3
Zurichsee (lake), Swi. 71/H3
Żuromin, Pol. 69/K2
Żurrieq, Malta 74/L7
Zürs, Aus. 87/G3
Zuru, Nga. 141/G4
Zurzach, Swi. 87/E2
Zusam (riv.), Ger. 71/J2
Zushi, Japan 109/D3
Zusmarshausen, Ger. 84/D6
Zutphen, Neth. 78/D4
Zuurberg NP, SAfr. 150/D4
Zuwārah, Libya 93/G4
Zuwayzā, Jor. 131/D5
Zuyevka, Rus. 95/L4
Zvenigovo, Rus. 95/L5
Zvenyhorodka, Ukr. 98/F3
Zverevo, Rus. 99/L3
Zverinogolovskoye, Rus. 95/Q5
Zvijesda NP, Bosn. 76/D4
Zvishavane, Zim. 149/F4
Zvorničko (lake), Bosn. 76/D3
Zvornik, Bosn. 76/D3
Zwaagwesteinde, Neth. 78/D2
Zwarte Meer (lake), Neth. 78/C3
Zwartsluis, Neth. 78/D3
Zwedru, Libr. 140/C5
Zweibrücken, Ger. 81/G5
Zweisimmen, Swi. 86/D4
Zwesten, Ger. 79/G6
Zwevelgem, Belg. 80/C2
Zwickauer Mulde (riv.), Ger. 68/G3
Zwiesel, Ger. 85/G4
Zwijndrecht, Belg. 81/D1
Zwijndrecht, Neth. 78/B5
Zwischenahner Meer (lake), Ger. 79/F2
Zwischenwasser, Aus. 87/F3
Zwoleń, Pol. 69/L3
Zwolle, La, US 176/H2
Zwolle, Neth. 78/D3
Zwönitz, Ger. 85/F1
Zwota, Ger. 85/F2
Żychlin, Pol. 69/K2
Żyrardów, Pol. 69/L2
Zyryan, Kaz. 125/D2
Zyryanka, Rus. 101/R3
Zyudev (isl.), Rus. 97/J3
Żywiec, Pol. 69/K4

165° W	150° W	135° W	120° W	105° W	90° W	75° W	60° W	45° W	30° W	15° W	0°
1 A.M.	2 A.M.	3 A.M.	4 A.M.	5 A.M.	6 A.M.	7 A.M.	8 A.M.	9 A.M.	10 A.M.	11 A.M.	NOON

ARCTIC   OCEAN

GREENLAND

NOON

11 A.M.

ICELAND
Reykjavík

3 A.M.
ALASKA

Anchorage

Whitehorse

CANADA

Nuuk

NORWAY

Oslo

Edmonton

Winnipeg

Seattle

Montréal

NEWFOUNDLAND

IRELAND

UNITED
KINGDOM

London

NETH.

BE

GER

Boise

Chicago

Detroit

8:30 A.M.
ST. PIERRE
& MIQUELON

Paris

FRANCE

SWIT

IT

UNITED   STATES

Denver

Washington

New
York

Halifax

PORTUGAL

SPAIN
Madrid

Ro

San Francisco

Atlanta

AZORES

Algiers

Los Angeles

Phoenix

MOROCCO

ALGERIA

Houston

BERMUDA

ATLANTIC

CANARY IS.

Honolulu

MEXICO

Miami

BAHAMAS

W. SAHARA

HAWAII

Mexico

CUBA

MAURITANIA

MALI

N

PACIFIC

Guatemala

BELIZE
HONDURAS

HAITI

JAMAICA

DOM.
REP.

PUERTO
RICO

ANTIGUA & BARBUDA
DOMINICA

CAPE
VERDE

Dakar

SENEGAL

El Salvador

NICARAGUA

BARBADOS
GRENADA

GAMBIA

BURKINA
FASO

NIGE

Costa Rica

PANAMA

TRINIDAD & TOBAGO

GUINEA-BISSAU

GUINEA

CÔTE
D'IVOIRE

GHANA

BENIN

Lagos

COLOMBIA

VENEZUELA

GUYANA

SIERRA LEONE

São Tomé
&
Príncipe

EQ. A

INTL DATE LINE

KIRIBATI

Bogotá

SURI.

FR. GUIANA

LIBERIA

ECUADOR

Manaus

OCEAN

2:30 A.M.
MARQUESAS IS.

PERU

Lima

BRAZIL

Recife

ASCENSION

FRENCH   POLYNESIA

La Paz
BOLIVIA

PARAGUAY

Rio de
Janeiro

Pitcairn Is.

EASTER I.

CHILE

URUGUAY

Santiago

ARGENTINA

Buenos
Aires

TRISTAN DA CUNHA

FALKLAND
IS.

S. GEORGIA

TIME ZONES OF THE WORLD

STANDARD TIME ZONES	3 A.M.	4 A.M.	5 A.M.	6 A.M.
AREAS USING HALF HOUR DEVIATIONS		5:30 P.M.		

1 A.M.	2 A.M.	3 A.M.	4 A.M.	5 A.M.	6 A.M.	7 A.M.	8 A.M.	9 A.M.	10 A.M.	11 A.M.	NOON